ISBN 978-0-331-75435-3
PIBN 11058036

FB &c Ltd, Dalton House, 60 Windsor Avenue, London, SW19 2RR.
Company number 08720141. Registered in England and Wales.

For support please visit www.forgottenbooks.com

THE

PUBLISHERS' WEEKLY

AMERICAN BOOK-TRADE JOURNAL

WITH WHICH IS INCORPORATED THE

American Literary Gazette and Publishers' Circular

ESTABLISHED IN THE YEAR 1852

VOL. LXII

JULY—DECEMBER, 1902

NEW YORK
OFFICE OF THE PUBLISHERS' WEEKLY
1902

THE PUBLISHERS' WEEKLY.

VOL. LXII. JULY TO DECEMBER, 1902.

EDITORIAL DEPARTMENT.

INDEX TO EDITORIALS, COMMUNICATIONS, SPECIAL LISTS AND PROMINENT NOTES.

INDEX TO ADVERTISERS.

213.1

WITH WHICH IS INCORPORATED

The American Literary Gazette and Publishers' Circular.

[ESTABLISHED 1852.]

PUBLICATION OFFICE, 298 BROADWAY, NEW YORK.

Entered at the Post-Office at New York, N. Y., as second-class matter.

VOL. LXII., No. 1. NEW YORK, July 5, 1902. WHOLE No. 1588

APPLETONS' NOTABLE NOVELS

The Way of Escape

By GRAHAM TRAVERS (DR. MARGARET TODD), author of "Mona Maclean," "Windyhaugh." etc. 12mo. cloth, $1.50.

"A classic."—*Philadelphia Item.*

"Exceptionally good."—*New York Tribune.*

"Undeniably clever."—*London Literary World.*

"Strong in dramatic incident."—*Boston Budget.*

"A work of unusual power."—*Chicago Record-Herald.*

"Vera is a marvellous piece of womanhood."—*London Star.*

"Elevated, stimulating, and powerful."—*St. Louis Republic.*

"A powerful and most interesting story."—*Edinburgh Scotsman.*

"Vera Carruthers is a convincing creation."—*London Athenæum.*

"This novel is quite the crown of the author's art"—*Glasgow Herald.*

"Will lay a strong hold upon thinking readers."—*Rochester (N. Y.) Times.*

These Delightful Americans

By MRS. EVERARD COTES (Sara Jeannette Duncan). 12mo. Cloth, $1.50.

"The reader has full money's worth."—*Gloucester Times.*

"Delightfully witty and delightfully clever."—*Philadelphia Item.*

"Spontaneously and genuinely humorous."—*New York Mail and Express.*

"Brimming over with good spirits and vitality."—*Westminster Gazette.*

"Highly interesting and told in a good-natured way."—*Boston Times.*

"Bright, good-natured, and thoroughly enjoyable." —*Philadelphia Quaker Quality.*

"Full of clever, humorous, oftentimes subtle, insights into American character."—*Chicago Record-Herald.*

"As a laugh is of more value than a bottle of medicine, 'Those Delightful Americans' is a very good investment."—*Philadelphia Telegraph.*

Kate Bonnet

The Romance of a Pirate's Daughter. By FRANK R. STOCKTON. Illustrated by A. I. Keller and H. S. Potter. 12mo. Cloth, $1.50.

"A capital story."—*London Times.*

"A real devilish pirate story."—*Chicago Inter-Ocean.*

"Touched with quaint humor."—*Louisville (Ky.) Post.*

"Read it. It is funny. It is good."—*Philadelphia Item.*

"A most original and charming tale."—*Washington Times.*

The Credit of the County

By W. E. NORRIS, author of "Matrimony," "The Flower of the Flock," etc. No. 313 in Appletons' Town and Country Library. 12mo. Cloth, $1.00; paper, 50 cents.

Any one who can appreciate firm delineation of even subordinate characters, a fancy which is playful and never prurient, and a manly and easy style, will take an interest in this new "Town and Country" novel.

D. APPLETON & COMPANY, Publishers, - NEW YORK

Page's Most Important Work for Summer Reading

THIRD EDITION

THE KINDRED OF THE WILD

BY

CHARLES G. D. ROBERTS

Author of "The Heart of the Ancient Wood," "The Forge in the Forest," etc.

Illustrated by CHARLES LIVINGSTON BULL

Cloth, Large 12mo - - - - - $2.00

"... is certainly an admirable work. The author's knowledge of animal life is wonderful, and his manner of writing of them unique. He writes for both the old and young—a most rare faculty."—Gen. Lew Wallace.

"Put this book on your list, and make a note of it as one that young readers will surely want, and the reading of which will fill their cup of happiness to the brim. Young and old will find a fascination about the book that cannot be resisted."—*Buffalo Commercial.*

"... one might quote scores of such beautiful passages from this book, which shows them at every opened page. ... No more perfect achievement of its kind has come from the hand of man."—*Chicago Tribune.*

"The volume is a fine example of the work of author, artist and publisher."—*Chicago Inter-Ocean.*

"Thoroughly original in conception and delightful in treatment."—*Brooklyn Eagle.*

ORDER THROUGH YOUR JOBBER OR FROM THE PUBLISHERS

L. C. PAGE & COMPANY, Boston

The Most Discussed Book

Of the present period of the publishing season is **Mr. T. W. H. Crosland's**

THE

Unspeakable Scot

There is every indication of a large demand for this half-serious indictment of Scotchmen. The book is interesting and piquant in the extreme. (July 7).

LENOX and the BERKSHIRE HIGHLANDS

By R. DE WITT MALLARY. 8vo. Fully illustrated from specially prepared photographs, *net*, $1.75 (by mail, $1.90).

A beautiful, valuable, and interesting book. It will satisfy all readers who care for the Berkshires, whether their bent is for history, recreation, literature, or natural beauty.

LIFE AT WEST POINT

The Making of an American Army Officer : His Studies, Discipline and Amusements. By H. IRVING HANCOCK. With an Introduction by A. L. MILLS, Colonel U. S. A., and Superintendent of the U. S. Military Academy. 12mo. Fully illustrated, *net*, $1.40 (by mail, $1.50).

SPANISH LIFE IN TOWN AND COUNTRY

By L. HIGGIN. No. 6. in *Our European Neighbours Series.* 12mo. Fully illustrated, *net*, $1.20 (by mail, $1.30).

As each volume of this charming series has appeared, it has been hailed as the "best of the group." It is indeed a very interesting book, and well maintains the extraordinary merit of the series.

G. P. Putnam's Sons

NEW YORK **LONDON**

The Publishers' Weekly.

JULY 5, 1902.

PUBLICATION OFFICE, 298 BROADWAY, P. O. BOX 943, N.Y.

INDEX TO ADVERTISERS

NOTES IN SEASON.

LOTHROP PUBLISHING COMPANY have just ready a new juvenile by Miss M. E. Waller, entitled "The Little Citizen," which will be found entertaining by young people and an influence for good. It has four spirited illustrations by H. G. Burgess.

R. H. RUSSELL has just brought out "The Wind in the Tree," a volume of short stories by the Duchess of Sutherland, who is no less distinguished in England for her literary ability than for her beauty. The volume has a frontispiece by Walter Crane.

CHARLES SCRIBNER'S SONS have just ready Richard Harding Davis's new book "Ranson's Folly"; also, the first two volumes of the *Beacon Edition* of the collected works of F. Hopkinson Smith, which they are publishing by arrangement with Houghton, Mifflin & Co.

LONGMANS, GREEN & CO. will publish shortly "Principles of English Constitutional History," by Lucy Dale, who presupposes a certain knowledge of what are commonly called the facts of English history, and therefore deals rather with the principles by the light of which alone these facts can really become intelligible.

LITTLE, BROWN & CO. have again been obliged to postpone "The Pharaoh and the Priest," the historical novel of ancient Egypt, translated from the original Polish of Alexander Glovatski, by Jeremiah Curtin, which they expected to publish before this. The author gives a vivid picture of the conflict between the secular and the ecclesiastical powers of Egypt in the time of Rameses XIII, eleven centuries before Christ. The volume is now promised to be ready in September.

LAIRD & LEE announce besides Opie Read's "The Starbucks," a strong character study by Miles Sandys entitled "Michael Carmichael," illustrated with nine half tone plates; also, D'Annunzio's "The Dead City," the play in which Duse takes the leading part, rendered into English by Professor C. Mantellini, which will have a colored frontispiece and a number of illustrations in black and white. A full line of Laird & Lee's newest publications will be shown during the book fair, to be held next week, at the Palmer House. They will occupy Room 448, and will make representatives of the trade welcome.

J. B. LIPPINCOTT COMPANY have just ready "Delhi, 1857," by Sir Henry Norman, a direct and interesting account of the great mutiny in India, with an exact description of the siege, assault and capture of Delhi, with numerous illustrations; also "Numbers" and the "Earlier Pauline Epistles," two new volumes of the *Temple Bible*. They have in preparation a new novel by Jack London, dealing with life in the Klondike region, to be entitled "A Daughter of the Snows." The illustrations of this book are to be by Yohn, and will be in colors. Another volume under way is a romance by Cyrus Townsend Brady entitled "Woven with a Ship."

G. P. PUTNAM'S SONS will publish at once T. W. H. Crosland's book on "The Unspeakable Scot," in which the author will try to prove that "in politics, art, letters, journalism, and sundry other departments of activity the Scot has never accomplished anything that really matters, and a lot more that will be unpleasant reading for "Sandy." They have nearly ready a work entitled "The Papal Monarchy," by Dr. William Barry, who describes the rise and fall of the Papacy as a world power in the period from the reign of Gregory the Great to Boniface VII. Dr. Barry, a well-known Catholic, will deal only with facts, not with speculations. They have in preparation "The Strange Story of Dr. Fortescue," a detective story, by Elizabeth Kent. This is a pseudonym, the author being a woman of prominence in New York society, now in Europe.

WEEKLY RECORD OF NEW PUBLICATIONS.

☞ Beginning with the issue of July 5, 1902, the titles of *net* books published under the rules of the American Publishers' Association are preceded by a double asterisk **, and the word net follows the price. The titles of *fiction* (not net) published under the rules are preceded by a dagger †. *Net* books not covered by the rules, whether published by members of the American Publishers' Association or not, are preceded by a single asterisk, and the word net follows the price. ☜

The abbreviations are usually self-explanatory. c. after the date indicates that the book is copyrighted; if the copyright date differs from the imprint date, the year of copyright is added. Books of foreign origin of which the edition (annotated, illustrated, etc.) is entered as copyright, are marked c. ed.; translations, c. tr.; n. p., in place of price, indicates that the publisher makes no price, either net or retail, and quotes prices to the trade only upon application.

A colon after initial designates the most usual given name, as: A: Augustus; B: Benjamin; C: Charles; D: David; E: Edward; F: Frederic; G: George; H: Henry; I: Isaac; J: John; L: Louis; N: Nicholas; P: Peter; R: Richard; S: Samuel; T: Thomas; W: William.

Sizes are designated as follows: F. (folio: over 30 centimeters high); Q. (4to: under 30 cm.); O. (8vo: 25 cm.); D. (12mo: 20 cm.); S. (16mo: 17½ cm.); T. (24mo: 15 cm.); Tt. (32mo: 12½ cm.); Fe. 48mo: 10 cm.). Sq., obl., nar., designate square, oblong, narrow books of these heights.

Alabama, *Supreme ct.* Reports of cases, Nov. term, 1898, to Nov. term, 1900, by Phares Coleman, st. rep. v. 122-129. Montgomery, Brown Print. Co., st. prs., 1900-1902. c. O. shp., ea., $3.75.

American state reports; cont. the cases of general value and authority subsequent to those contained in the "Am. decisions" and the "Am. reports," decided in the courts of last resort of the several states; sel., rep. and annot. by A. C. Freeman. v. 84. San Francisco, Bancroft-Whitney Co., 1902. c. 1035 p. O. shp., $4.

Ames, L: Annin. Etiquette of yacht colors; a treatise on yacht flags and their use, also containing the yacht codes of the new international code signals, wig-wag, storm and weather signals, yacht routine, etc. N. Y., Annin & Co., [1902.] c. 3-83 p. il. sq. S. canvas, 25 c.

Austrian, Delia. Love songs. Chic., W. B. Conkey Co., [1902.] c. 91 p. D. cl., $1.

Beaumarchais, Pierre Augustin Caron de. Le barbier de Séville and Lettres; ed., with introd. and notes, by G: D. Fairfield. Chic., Scott, Foresman & Co., 1902. c. 167 p. por. 16°, (Lake French classics.) cl., 50 c.

Behrens, C. Blossom and fruit in decorative arrangement; photographed from nature. N. Y., Bruno Hessling, 1902. 36 tinted heliotyped pls. 8°, $12.

Bouton, Eugene. Spelling and word building: a primary vocabulary. N. Y., University Pub. Co., [1902.] c. 118 p. il. sq. D. cl., 29 c.

The lists of words are made from seventeen standard school readers. The author's methods are to teach the pupil the phonic force of letters.

****Boutwell**, G: Sewall. Reminiscences of sixty years in public affairs. N. Y., McClure, Phillips & Co., 1902. c. 2 v., 676 p. 8°, cl., $5 net.

Bradner, G: W. New practice in supplementary proceedings with all the statutes on the subject and new forms for every case. 2d ed. Alb., W. C. Little & Co., 1902. c. 40+396 p. O. buckram, $4.

Brinckley, W: J. Physiology by the laboratory method. Chic., Ainsworth & Co., 1902. 500 p. 8°, cl., $1.25.

****Brown**, W: Garrott. Golf. Bost., Houghton, Mifflin & Co., 1902. [Je.] c. 2+64 p. S. cl., 50 c. net.

Cady, Mary R., *and* Dewey, Julia M. The art reader, number one. N. Y., Richardson, Smith & Co., [1902.] c. 127 p. il. 16°, cl., 35 c.

California, *Supreme ct.* Reports of cases; C. P. Pomeroy, rep. v. 133-134. (1901.) San Francisco, Bancroft-Whitney Co., 1902. c. '01. 39+788 p. O. shp., ea., $3.

***Case**, E. C. Palæontological notes. Chic., University of Chicago Press, 1902. 8 p. pls. 8°, (Contributions from Walker Museum, v. 1, no. 3.) pap., 25 c. net.

Catherwood, *Mrs.* Mary Hartwell. Craque o' doom. [New issue.] N. Y., Street & Smith, [1902.] c. '81, '02. 238 p. il. D. cl., $1.50.

***Chancellor**, W: Estabrook. Elementary school mathematics by grades; fifth book (grade 6,) standard measurements. N. Y., Globe School Book Co., [1902.] c. 12+13-160 p. il. D. (Globe ser.) cl., 28 c. net.

***Chancellor**. W: Estabrook. Elementary school mathematics by grades; sixth book (grade 7,) commercial affairs. N. Y., Globe School Book Co., [1902.] c. 176 p. il. D. (Globe ser.) cl., 28 c. net.

****Clewell**, J: H: History of Wachovia in North Carolina; the Unitas fratrum or Moravian church in North Carolina during a century and a half, 1752-1902, from the original German and English manuscripts and records in the Wachovia archives, Salem, North Carolina. N. Y., Doubleday, Page & Co., 1902. c. 14+365 p. il. maps, pl. por. 8°, cl., $2. net.

Coffin, C: Emmet. The gist of whist; being a concise guide to the modern scientific game, embracing the improved method of American leads and a complete glossary of the common and technical terms; to which is added the laws of whist and duplicate whist as revised at the last American whist congress. 7th ed. (rev.) N. Y., Brentano's, [1902.] c. '93-1902. 12+118 p. S. cl., 75 c.

†**Corelli**, Marie. Barabbas: a dream of the world's tragedy. N. Y., American News Co., 1902. 12°, (People's lib., no. 13.) pap., 50 c.

Crayon, Jos. Percy. Rockaway records of Morris county, N. J., families: cemetery records, church history, military records, local history, genealogies of the old families, nearly 20,000 data. Rockaway, N. J., Rockaway Publishing Co., 1902. c. 300 p. por. 12°, cl., $3.

†**Davis**, W: Stearns. Belshazzar: a tale of the fall of Babylon; il. by Lee Woodward Zigler. N. Y., Doubleday, Page & Co., 1902. [Je.] c. 1901, 1902. 6+427 p. D. cl., $1.50.

***De Costa**, B: Franklin. Whither goest thou? or, some historical facts related to current events and present tendencies, addressed to Anglicans and their Anglo-American coreligionists, together with others who may sincerely wish to inquire for the old paths and return to Catholic unity. N. Y., Christian Press Association Publishing Co., [1902.] c. 145 p. 12°, cl., 50 c. net; pap., 25 c. net.

Doyle, Arthur Conan. The war in South Africa; its cause and conduct. N. Y., McClure, Phillips & Co., 1902. 140 p. 12°, cl., 10 c.

Fiedler, A. Studies from the nude human figure in motion. N. Y., Bruno Hessling, 1902. 53 heliotype pls. f° $12.

Fitch, Eugene, ["Ironquill," *pseud.*] Some of the rhymes of Ironquill: (a book of moods.) 11th ed. N. Y., Putnam, 1902. c. 1900-1902. 12+365 p. D. cl., $1.50.

Foreign trade requirements; published annually with quarterly supplements, 1902; cont. complete information concerning the commercial countries of the world, as to trade conditions, traveling salesmen, agencies and advertising, credit customs, commercial, trade-mark and patent laws, transportation facilities, principal cities, postal regulations, coins and currencies, weights and measures, and cable rates. N. Y., Lewis, Scribner & Co., [1902.] c. 532 p. Q. cl., $10.

Gage, Alfred Payson. Introduction to physical science. Rev. ed. Bost., Ginn, 1902. c. '87. 8+359 p. il. D. cl., $1.

Haggerty, J: How to treat the trusts and how to win in 1904. N. Y., Abbey Press, 1902. c. 3+81 p. D. cl., 25 c.

The book proposes a secretary of trusts to run the trusts as a receiver runs bankrupt railroads, etc. He would fix prices to consumers by allowing labor fair wages and reasonable hours and capital a fair interest on actual investments.

Hamersly, Lewis Randolph, *comp.* The records of living officers of the U. S. navy and marine corps; comp. from official sources. 7th ed., rev., with additions. N. Y., L. R. Hamersly Co., 1902. c. 511 p. por. 8°, cl., $10.

Handy, W: Mathews. Banking systems of the world: an impartial statement of the conditions of note issue by banks in all nations and the workings of the systems. 3d ed. rev. Chic., Jamieson-Higgins Co., 1902. c. '97. 167 p. D. cl., $1.50.

Hartmann, Arnold, *and* Needham, A. C. The commercial code for the transmission of telegrams and cablegrams with economy and secrecy. Bost., Commercial Code Co., 1902. c. [illegible], flex. leath., $3.

Hastings, H: Mistress Dorothy of Haddon Hall; being the true love story of Dorothy Vernon of Haddon Hall. N. Y., R. F. Fenno & Co., 1902. c. 296 p. D. cl., $1.

A novel founded on an incident of the Elizabethan era, namely the elopement of Dorothy Vernon and John Manners. This episode was likewise the theme of the latest novel by the author of "When knighthood was in flower."

Houston, Edwin Ja., *and* Kennelly, Arthur Edwin. The electric telephone. 2d ed. enl. N. Y., McGraw Publishing Co., [1902.] 6+453 p. sq. S. (Elementary electro-technical ser.) cl., $1.

Contains three additional chapters which treat of the recent changes in the developing of telephonic engineering.

Howard, Hamilton Gay. Howard's law points to know: a popular treatise, consisting of 8 lectures on elementary law; [with lists of law and lyceum literary lectures.]. Detroit, Mich., Hamilton G. Howard, 1902. c. 98 p. por. S. pap., $1.

Hoyt, Helen Brown. A child's story of the life of Christ. Bost., W. A. Wilde Co., [1902.] c. 6+233 p. il. 12°, cl., $1.25.

Hudson's dictionary of Minneapolis: a guide and handbook, 1902. Minneapolis, Minn., H. B. Hudson, 1902. 126 p. il. maps, S. pap., 25 c.

***Illinois**. The homestead exemption laws of the state, by Albert Martin Kales. Chic., Callaghan & Co., 1902. c. 28+281 p. O. buckram, $4 net.

***Indiana**. Annot. practice code forms for use in the circuit, superior, supreme and appellate courts, (with references to Thornton & Ballard's annotated practice code.) 2d and rev. ed. in 1 v. Cin., W. H. Anderson & Co., 1902. c. 1710 p. O. shp., $6 net.

Jewett, Freeborn G., *comp.* Jewett's manual for election officers and voters in the state of New York. 10th ed. Alb., Matthew Bender, 1902. c. 10+504 p. O. shp., $2; pap., $1.50.

Contains the general election law, town meeting law, provisions relating to school meetings and the primary law of 1899, complete with amendments to date; also provisions of the penal code, general laws and constitution of the state of N. Y. relating to elections and elective officers, with annots., forms and instructions.

Jewish Chautauqua Society. Papers presented at the fifth annual session of the summer assembly of the Jewish Chautauqua Society held at Atlantic City., N. J., July 7 to July 28, 1901. Phil., Jewish Pub. Soc. of America, 1902. c. 3-118 p. S. (Special ser., no. 7.) 30 c.

Jokai, Maurus. Told by the death's head: a romantic tale; tr. by S. E. Boggs. Akron O., Saalfield Pub. Co., 1902. 348 p. D. cl., $1.50.

Jokai says in his preface that in a volume of the Rhenish *Antiquarius* he came across the description of a skull which used to swing, according to the above authority, in an enclosed metal casket suspended from an iron bar in the foundry of Ehrenbreitstein fortress. The skull is supposed to be that of a man, who by his own confession committed twenty-one crimes, but who was finally convicted of a twenty-second, which he refuted. The novel is founded on what purports to be the skull's version of the hideous deeds of the self accused.

Keene, Roswell W. The blue diamond: [a novel.] N. Y., Abbey Press., 1902. c. 2-477 p. D. cl., $1.50.

***Kennan,** G:, *comp. and tr.* Folk tales of Napoleon; Napoleonder; from the Russian; [also] The Napoleon of the people; tr. from the French of Honoré de Balzac, with introd. by G: Kennan. N. Y., Outlook Co., 1902. c. 3-107 p. O. bds., $1 net.

****Lamb,** C: The king and queen of hearts: an 1805 book for children; il. by W: Mulready; now re-issued in facsimile with introd. by E. V. Lucas. N. Y., McClure, Phillips & Co., 1902. c. 15 p. 16°, cl., 50 c. net.

***Landolt,** Hans Heinrich, [*and others.*] The optical rotating power of organic substances and its practical applications. 2d ed. Authorized English tr. with additions by Dr. John H. Long. Easton, Pa., Chemical Publishing Co., 1902. c. 21+751 p. il. diagr. 8°, cl., $7.50 net.

Lodge, H: Cabot; Hoar, G: F., [*and others.*] The United States and the Philippine Islands. Brooklyn, N. Y., Office of the *Brooklyn Daily Eagle,* [1902.] 54 p. Q. (Brooklyn Eagle lib., v. 17, no. 9; serial no. 68.) pap., 10 c.

Louisiana reports, v. 106. Judicial year 1901-1902. St. Paul, West Pub. Co., 1902. c. 19+486 p. O. (National reporter system ed.) shp., $8.

Cases argued and determined in the supreme court of La. reported in the La. reports, v. 106, and the southern reporter, vs. 30 and 31. With cross-reference tables, tables of cases cited, tables of code sections, legislative acts, and articles of the constitution cited and construed.

†**McLaws,** Lafayette. Jezebel: a romance in the days when Ahab was King of Israel; il. by Corwin K. Linson. Bost., Lothrop Pub. Co., [1902.] [Je.] c. 4+490 p. D. cl., $1.50.

***Mach,** Ernst. The science of mechanics: a critical and historical account of its development; 2d enl. ed.; tr. by T: J. McCormack. Chic., Open Court Pub. Co., 1902. 20+605 p. 12°, cl., $2 net.

Mason, Ja. F:, *comp.* Favorite songs of love. Limited ed. N. Y., Dodge Pub. Co., [1902.] c. 114 p. 16°, cl., $1.50; ooze cf., $2; English cf., $2.25; Eng. cf. tooled, $5.

Minnesota. Civil procedure in the district and supreme courts of the state, with forms; by B: J. Shipman. In 2 v. v. 1. St. Paul, Keefe-Davidson Law Book Co., 1902. c. 22+689 p. O. shp. (for complete work,) $13.

Myers, Philip Van Ness. Mediæval and modern history. pt. 1, The middle ages. [New rev. ed.] Bost., Ginn, 1902. c. '85, 1902. 8+454 p. D. cl., $1.20.

A revision of the first half of "Mediæval and modern history," the earliest impression of which was published sixteen years ago.

Nebraska. The law of probate and administration for Nebraska, including guardianship and adoption of children; with forms; by Arthur K. Dame. St. Paul, Keefe-Davidson Law Book Co., 1902. c. 37+970 p. O. shp., $7.50.

Needell, *Mrs.* J: Hodder. Unstable as water. N. Y., F: Warne & Co., 1902. 3-318 p. D. cl., $1.25.

The hero, Will Lambert, becomes the owner of a fine estate, through the supposed death of his cousin Roger Ormskirke. The latter, after spending seven years a captive in a prison in the Soudan, makes his escape and notifies his London lawyer that he is still alive. This news the lawyer communicates to Lambert forty-eight hours before his proposed marriage to a beautiful woman of social position. Lambert pretends not to have received the communication and goes on with his marriage. His cousin Roger in a short time appears in the flesh. Lambert's falsehood and deceit lead to tragical episodes.

New York. Abbott's cyclopedic digest of all the decisions of all the courts, from the earliest time to the year 1900; being the work of the late Austin Abbott and B. Vaughan Abbott, rev. and imp., and cont. many new and valuable features; ed. and comp. by the publishers' editorial staff, DeWitt C. Blashfield, ed.-in-chief. v. 9, Limitation of actions to municipal corporations. N. Y., New York Law Book Co., 1902. c. 8+1143 p. O. shp., $7.50.

New York. Criminal reports; reports of cases decided in all courts in the state, together with leading cases from other jurisdictions, involving questions of law and practice. with notes and references, by C: H. Mills. v. 15. Alb., W. C. Little & Co., 1902. c. 11+624 p. O. shp., $5.50.

New York. The highway law of the state of New York, 1902. Bender ed. Alb., N. Y., Matthew. Bender, 1902. c. 137 p. O. pap., $1.

Contains The highway law; Good roads law; Grade crossing law; Side path laws; Automobile law; County supervision of highways; The new law of the road, etc.; with all amendments to date and complete index.

New York. The highway law of the state, by H. Noyes Greene. 2d ed., by L. L. Boyce. Alb., Matthew Bender, 1902. c. 38+471 p. O. shp., $4.

Contains all laws relating to highways, including the general highway law (laws of 1890, chap. 568), the good roads law, grade crossing law, side path law, and all general and miscellaneous statutes relating to the subject of highways, as amended to the close of the legislative session of 1902, with annots., forms and class references.

New York. Jewett's primary election law of the state of New York; complete with amendments to date, including the town enrollment act of 1902, with forms and complete index. Albany, N. Y., Matthew Bender, 1902. 185-240 p. O. pap., 50 c.

These pages are taken from "Jewett's manual of election officers and voters." The pamphlet is not a substitute for the above work, but is issued in this form for the convenience of primary election officers.

New York. The New York code of civil procedure, cont. all amendments to June 1, 1902; with notes of decisions to date, also the state constitution and municipal court act of N. Y. city; with a complete topical index, prepared by J: C. Thomson. 27th ed. N. Y., Baker, Voorhis & Co., 1902. c. 6+1432 p. S. (Parsons' complete annot. pocket code.) flex. skiver, $3.50.

New York. Penal code of the state: amendments made by the legislature of 1902; 16th ed. by C. D. Rust. Alb., Matthew Bender, 1902. c. 18+238 p. D. flex. im. alligator, $3.50.

New York supplement, v. 75. (New York state reporter, v. 109. Permanent ed., Apr. 3-May 15, 1902. St. Paul, West Pub. Co., 1902. c. 24+1204 p. O. (National reporter system, N. Y. supp. and state reporter.) shp., $4.
Contains the decisions of the supreme and lower courts of record of N. Y. state. With table of N. Y. supp. cases that have been passed upon by the court of appeals. Also, tables of N. Y. supp. cases in vs. 65-67, appellate division reports; 9, N. Y. annot. cases; 1, Power's reports. A table of statutes construed is given in the index.

New York. The village laws, cont. the new village law of 1897, the general municipal law, the statutory construction law, [etc.] [as amended to May 31, 1902;] with explanatory notes, cross-references, decisions and forms, by Rob. C. Cumming and Frank B. Gilbert. Alb., Matthew Bender, 1902. c. 12+358 p. O. shp., $3.

Nordhoff guild, Washington, D. C. The Nordhoff guild cook book; sold for the benefit of the National homœopathic hospital. Wash., Press of McGill & Wallace, [1902.] c. 69 p. 12°, pap., 25 c.

Northwestern reporter, v. 89. Permanent ed., Mar. 1-May 3. 1902. St. Paul, West Pub. Co., 1902. c. 14+1231 p. O. (National reporter system, state ser.) shp., $4.
Contains all the decisions of the supreme courts of Minn., Wis., Ia., Mich., Neb., No. Dak., So. Dak. With table of northwestern cases in which rehearings have been denied. With tables of northwestern cases published in vs. 126, Mich. reports; 83, Minn. reports; 14, So. Dak. reports; 111, Wis. reports. A table of statutes construed is given in the index.

Parks, Ella M. Mary of Bethany: a message to young women. Phil., Pepper Pub. Co., 1902. c. 64 p. 16°, cl., 25 c.; pap., 15 c.

Pennsylvania. A digest of the general acts of assembly, for the incorporation and government of cities of the 3d class, with notes of decisions; 2d ed. by L. Richards. Newark, N. J., Soney & Sage, 1902. c. 21+286 p. O. buckram, $3.

Pennsylvania. The health ordinance of the borough of Edgewood, and health laws of the state, relating to powers and duties of boards of health in boroughs; with digest index, by Magnus Pflaum. Pittsburgh, Nicholson & Co., 1902. c. 52 p. O. pap., $1.

Schiller, Johann Christoph Friedrich v. The maid of Orleans; The bride of Messina; Wilhelm Tell; Demetrius, by Friedrich Schiller; tr. by Sir Theodore Martin, Anna Swanwick, and A. Lodge; ed. by Nathan Haskell Dole. Edition de luxe. Bost., F. A. Niccolls & Co., [1902.] c. 413 p. pl. 12°, cl. (Apply to pubs. for price.)

Shakespeare, W: Works. New century ed. In 24 v. v. 21-24. Ed. de luxe. Bost., Dana Estes & Co., 1902. c. por. 8°, cl., ea., $3.50.
Contents: v. 21, Doubtful plays, History of the drama, Hudson; Critical essays, Hudson; v. 22, Life of Shakespeare, by Dr. W. J. Rolfe; v. 23, Dyce's glossary, v. 1; v. 24, Dyce's glossary, v. 2.

Sibley, Hiram L. The right to and the cause for action, both civil and criminal, at law, in equity, and admiralty, under the common law, and under the codes. Cin., W. H. Anderson & Co., 1902. c. 10+165 p. D. cl., $1.50.

Texas. *Ct. of criminal appeals.* Reports during part of the Austin term, 1899; the Tyler term, 1899; the Dallas term, 1900; and part of the Austin term, 1900; rep. by J: P. White. v. 41. Austin, Gammel Book Co., 1902. c. 18+762 p. O. shp., $4.50.

****Thomas,** Calvin. Life and works of Friedrich Schiller. Students' ed. N. Y., H: Holt & Co., 1902. c. 16+481 p. O. cl., $1.50 net.
See notice, "Weekly Record," P. W., Dec. 14, 1901, [1559,] of more expensive edition.

****Turner,** J. Turner. The giant fish of Florida. Phil., Lippincott, 1902. il. 8°, cl., $3.50 net.

United States. *Circuit cts. of appeals.* Reports with annots; with table of cases in the U. S. circuit courts of appeals which have been passed upon by the supreme court of the U. S., and table of cases in the U. S. circuit courts of appeals in which rehearings have been granted or denied. v. 50. Rochester, N. Y., Lawyers' Co-op. Pub. Co., 1902. c. 44+774 p. O. shp., $3.35.

Vail, I. E. Three years on the blockade: a naval experience. N. Y., Abbey Press, 1902. c. 2+171 p. D. cl., $1.25.
The experience of a young officer in the navy, during the greater part of the Civil War, who served in each of the three great squadrons which did sentinel duty on our coast during that period. He describes many of the great naval demonstrations, and the exciting pursuit of blockade-runners, etc.

Virginia. *Supreme ct. of appeals.* Reports; Jefferson-33 Gratton, 1730-1880; annot. under the supervision of T: Johnson Michie. v. 7 and 8 Grattan's repts. Charlottesville, Michie Co., 1902. c. 774 p. O. shp., ea., $7.50.

Visitor's (A) guide to Paris. 7th ed. Brooklyn, N. Y., Office of the *Brooklyn Daily Eagle,* [1902.] c. 63 p. S. (Eagle lib., v. 17, no. 7; serial no. 66.) pap., 10 c.

***Voltaire,** François Marie Arouët de. Voltaire's philosophical dictionary (in English); unabridged and unexpurgated, with a special introd. by W: F. Fleming. N. Y., George Clarke, 1902. c. tr. 10 v., il. 8°, buckram, per set, subs., $18 net; hf. mor., per set, subs., $24 net.

****Washington,** Booker Taliaferro. Character building; being addresses delivered on Sunday evenings to the students of Tuskegee Institute. N. Y., Doubleday, Page & Co., 1902. [Je.] c. 8+290 p. D. cl., $1.50 net.
Earnest, simply worded talks entitled: Two sides of life; Helping others; Some of the rocks ahead; The virtue of simplicity; Have you done your best?; Don't be discouraged; On getting a home; Calling things by their right names; European impressions; The value of system in home life; What will pay?; Education that educates; The gospel of service; Your part in the negro conference; What is to be our future?; Some little great things, etc.

Watkins, Rob. Lincoln, *M.D.* Diagnosis by means of the blood; il. by 154 photo-micrographs of specimens of blood, as observed in general practice, showing products that are found in definite diseases. N. Y., The Physicians Book Pub. Co., 1902. c. 388 p. por. O. cl., $5.

Dr. Watkins contends that an examination of the blood is the surest way of diagnosing disease, and gives the methods of procedure for fresh blood examination. He also treats of the features of the blood that are diagnostically significant, and of various diseases in relation to the subject, giving specific directions for the use of the microscope and other appurtenances. Bibliography (6 p.).

Welch, J. Herbert, *and* Taylor, H. E. Destruction of St. Pierre, Martinique. N. Y., R. F. Fenno & Co., [1902.] c. 2-240 p. D. cl., 50 c.

Describes St. Pierre, the inhabitants, native customs, etc., and discusses the scientific causes and effects of the recent volcanic eruptions on the Island of Martinique.

Wentworth, G: Albert. A college algebra. Rev. ed. Bost., Ginn, 1902. c. '88, 1902. 5+530 p. D. hf. mor., $1.65.

****Wright**, G: F: Asiatic Russia. N. Y., McClure, Phillips & Co., 1902. c. 2 v., 290; 290-637 p. il. maps, 8°, leath., $7.50 net.

Young, C: A: Manual of astronomy: a text-book. Bost., Ginn, 1902. c. 7+611 p. il. O. hf. leath., $2.45.

Prepared in response to a demand for a class-room text-book intermediate between the author's "General astronomy" and his "Elements of astronomy." The former is found to be too bulky for convenient use in the curriculum of many institutions, while the latter is too meagre, and does not sufficiently utilize the mathematical knowledge possessed by the pupils when they naturally take up astronomy. The manual is largely made up of material drawn from the earlier books, but rearranged, rewritten when necessary, and added to, in order to suit it to its purpose, and bring it thoroughly down to date.

†**Zayas** Enriquez, Rafael de. El teniente de los gavilanes; novela de carácter histórico ilustrada con láminas y grabados. N. Y., Appleton, 1902. c. 341 p. 12°, pap., 50 c.

ORDER LIST.

ABBEY PRESS, 114 Fifth Ave., New York.

Haggerty, How to treat the trusts.... 25
Keene, The blue diamond............ $1.50
Vail, Three years on the blockade.... 1.25

AINSWORTH & Co., 378-388 Wabash Ave., Chicago.

Brinckley, Psychology for the laboratory method 1.25

AMERICAN NEWS Co., 39 Chambers St., New York.

†Corelli, Barabbas 50

W. H. ANDERSON & Co., 515 Main St., Cincinnati.

*Indiana, Annotated practice code forms. 2d rev. ed. in 1 v.........net, 6.00
Sibley, The right to and the cause for action both civil and criminal under common law 1.50

ANNIN & Co., Cor. Fulton and William Sts., New York.

Ames, Etiquette of yacht colors...... 25

D. APPLETON & Co., 72 Fifth Ave., New York.

†Zayas, El teniente de los gairlanes.. 50

BAKER, VOORHIS & Co., 66 Nassau St., New York.

New York, Code of civil procedure, amendments to 1902, 27th ed. (Thomson) 3.50

BANCROFT-WHITNEY Co., 438 Montgomery St., San Francisco, Cal.

American state reports. v. 84. ...... 4.00
California, *Supreme ct.*, repts., v. 133-134 (Pomeroy) ....ea., 3.00

MATTHEW BENDER, 511-513 Broadway, Albany, N. Y.

Jewett, Manual for election officers and voters in New York. 10th ed...$1.50; 2.00
New York, Highway law, 1902. Bender ed.. 1.00
——, Highway law, 2d ed. (Boyce).... 4.00
——, Jewett's primary election law.... 50

MATTHEW BENDER.—*Continued.*

New York, Penal code, 1902. 16th ed.. $3.50
——, Village laws, amended to 1902, (Cumming.) 3.00

BRENTANO'S, 5-9 Union Sq., New York.

Coffin, Gist of whist. 7th rev. ed.... 75

OFFICE OF THE BROOKLYN DAILY EAGLE, Eagle Bldg., Brooklyn, N. Y.

Lodge, *and others,* The United States and the Philippine Islands 10
Visitor's guide to Paris............. 10

BROWN PRINT Co., Montgomery, Ala.

Alabama, *Supreme ct.*, Repts., v. 122-129 (Coleman) ....ea., 3.75

CALLAGHAN & Co., 114 Monroe St., Chicago.

*Illinois, The homestead exemption laws. (Kales) ....net, 4.00

CHEMICAL PUBLISHING Co., Easton, Pa.

*Landolt *and others,* Optical rotating power ....net, 7.50

CHRISTIAN PRESS ASSOCIATION PUBLISHING Co., 25 Barclay St., New York.

*De Costa, Whither goest thou? net, 25 c.; net, 50

GEORGE CLARKE, Decker Building, New York.

*Voltaire's philosophical dictionary. 10 v.................subs., net, $18; 24.00

COMMERCIAL CODE Co., Boston.

Hartmann, Commercial code for the transmission of telegrams and cablegrams 3.00

W. B. CONKEY Co., 351 Dearborn St., Chicago.

Austrian, Love songs 1.00

DODGE PUB. Co., 40 W. 13th St., New York.

Mason, Favorite songs of love. Limited ed. $1.50; $2.00; $2.25; 5.00

DOUBLEDAY, PAGE & Co., 34 Union Sq. E., New York.

**Clewell, History of Wachovia in N. Carolina. ....net, $2.00
†Davis, Belshazzar....... .... 1.50
**Washington, Character building..net, 1.50

DANA ESTES & Co., 208-218 Summer St., Boston.

Shakespeare, Works. New century ed. v. 23-24 ....ea., 3.50

R. F. FENNO & Co., 9-11 E. 16th St. New York.

Hastings, Mistress Dorothy of Haddon Hall 1.00
Welch *and* Taylor, Destruction of St. Pierre.......... 50

GAMMELL BOOK Co., Austin, Texas.

Texas, *Ct. of criminal appeals*, Repts.,...... v. 41 (White).................... 4.50

GINN & Co., 29 Beacon St., Boston.

Gage, Introduction to physical science. Rev. ed. 1.00
Myers, Mediæval and modern history, pt. 1 New rev. ed.................. 1.20
Wentworth, College algebra.......... 1.65
Young, Astronomy 2.45

GLOBE SCHOOL BOOK Co., 103 Fifth Ave., New York.

*Chancellor, Elementary school mathematics. 5th and 6th bks....ea., net, 28

L. R. HAMERSLEY Co., New York.

Hamersley, Records of living officers of U. S. navy 10.00

BRUNO HESSLING, 64 E. 12th St., New York.

Behrens, Blossom and fruit in decorative arrangement....... .... 12.00
Fiedler, Studies from the nude 12.00

HENRY HOLT & Co., 29 W. 23d St., New York.

**Thomas, Life and works of Friedrich Schiller. Students' ed. ....net, 1.50

HOUGHTON, MIFFLIN & Co., 4 Park St., Boston.

**Brown, Golf. ....net, 50

HAMILTON G. HOWARD, Detroit, Mich.

Howard, Law points to know........ 1.00

H. B. HUDSON, Minneapolis, Minn.

Hudson, Dictionary of Minneapolis, 1902 25

JAMIESON-HIGGINS Co., 324 Dearborn St., Chicago.

Handy, Banking systems of the world. 3d ed., rev. 1.50

JEWISH PUB. SOC. OF AMERICA, 1015 Arch St., Philadelphia.

Jewish Chautauqua Society, Papers .. 30

KEEFE-DAVIDSON LAW BOOK Co., St. Paul.

Minnesota, Civil procedure in district and supreme cts., 2v...............$13.00
Nebraska, Law of probate and administration........ .... 7.50

LAWYERS CO-OPERATIVE PUB. Co., Rochester, N. Y.

United States, *Circuit cts of appeals*, Reps., v. 50. .... 3.35

LEWIS, SCRIBNER & Co., 125 E. 23d St., New York.

Foreign trade requirements.......... 10.00

J. B. LIPPINCOTT Co., Washington Sq., Philadelphia.

**Turner, Giant fish of Florida....net, 3.50

W. C. LITTLE & Co., 525 Broadway, New York.

Bradner, New practice in supplementary proceedings. 2d ed............ 4.00
New York, Criminal reports. v. 15 (Mills) 5.50

LOTHROP PUB. Co., 1030 Atlantic Ave., Boston.

†McLaws, Jezebel 1.50

MCCLURE, PHILLIPS & Co., 141-155 E. 25th St., New York.

**Boutwell, Reminiscences of sixty years in public affairs. 2 v. ..net, 5.00
Doyle, The war in South Africa...... 10
**Lamb, King and queen of hearts..net, 50
**Wright, Asiatic Russia..........net, 7.50

PRESS OF MCGILL & WALLACE, Washington, D. C.

Nordhoff guild cook book........... 25

MCGRAW PUBLISHING Co., 120 Liberty St., New York.

Houston *and* Kennelly, The electric telephone, 2d ed., enl............... 1.00

MICHIE Co., Charlottesville, Va.

Virginia, *Supreme ct. of appeals*. Repts., 1730-1880 v. 7 and 8 (Grattan) ....ea., 7.50

NEW YORK LAW BOOK Co., 303 Broadway, New York.

New York, Abbott's cyclopedic digest. v. 9. .... 7.50

F. A. NICCOLLS & Co., 196 Summer St., Boston.

Schiller, Maid of Orleans, etc. (Apply to pubs for price.)

NICHOLSON Co., Pittsburgh, Pa.

Pennsylvania, Health ordinance of the borough of Edgewood............. 1.00

OPEN COURT PUB. Co., 324 Dearborn St., Chicago.

*Mach, Science of mechanics. 2d enl. ed. ....net, 2.00

OUTLOOK Co., 287 Fourth Ave., New York.

*Kennan, Folk tales of Napoleon...net, 1.00

PEPPER PUBLISHING CO., Philadelphia.

Parks, Mary of Bethany........15 c.; 25

PHYSICIANS' BOOK PUBLISHING CO., New York.

Watkins, Diagnosis by means of blood. $5.00

G. P. PUTNAM'S SONS, 29 W. 23d St., New York.

Fitch, Some of the rhymes of "Ironquill", 11th ed...................... 1.50

RICHARDSON, SMITH & CO., 135 Fifth Ave., New York.

Cady, *and* Dewey, Art reader, no. 1.. 35

ROCKAWAY PUBLISHING CO., Rockaway, N. J.

Crayon, Rockaway records of Morris County, N. J., families.............. 3.00

SAALFIELD PUB. CO., Akron, O.

Jokai, Told by the death's head....... 1.50

SCOTT, FORESMAN & CO., 307-309 Wabash Ave., Chicago.

Beaumarchais, Le Barbier de Séville.. 50

SONEY & SAGE, Newark, N. J.

Pennsylvania, Digest of general acts of assembly. 2d ed.................... $3.00

STREET & SMITH, 238 William St., New York.

Catherwood, Craque o' doom, new issue. 1.50

UNIVERSITY OF CHICAGO PRESS, Chicago.

*Case, Palæontological notes......net, 25

UNIVERSITY PUB. CO., 27-29 W. 23d St. New York.

Bouton, Spelling and word building... 29

F. WARNE & CO., 36 E. 22d St., New York.

Needell, Unstable as water............ 1.25

WEST PUB. CO., 52-58 W. 3d St., St. Paul, Minn.

Louisiana reports, v. 106.............. 8.00
New York supplement. v. 75 .... 4.00
Northwestern reporter. v. 89........ 4.00

W. A. WILDE CO., 110 Boylston St., Boston.

Hoyt, Child story of the life of Christ.. 1.25

RECENT ENGLISH BOOKS.

ALBEE, E. History of English Utilitarianism. Sonnenschein. Roy. 8°, 9¼ x 5¾, 444 p., 10s. 6d.

BAESSLER, A. Ancient Peruvian art: contributions to the archæology of the empire of the Incas. Trans. by A. H. Keane. Part 1. Asher. Folio, 20 x 15, 11 plates in portf., 30s., net.

BALDRY, A. L. Modern mural decoration. Many illus. in black and white and in colors. Newnes. Imp. 8°, 10⅛ x 7⅛, 200 p., 12s. 6d., net.

BATESON, W. Mendel's principles of heredity: a defence. Trans. of Mendel's original papers on Hybridisation. Frowde. Cr. 8°, 7¾ x 5, 228 p., 4s., net.

BENSON, Jane. Quaker pioneers in Russia. Headley. Cr. 8°, 7¾ x 5, 120 p., 2s. 6d.

BOULGER, D. C. History of Belgium. Part 1: Cæsar to Waterloo. Author. 8°, 8¾ x 5½, 486 p., 18s.

DALMAN, G. The words of Jesus. Considered in light of Post-Biblical Jewish writings and the Aramaic language. Auth. English version by D. M. Kay. T. & T. Clark. Roy. 8°, 9⅛ x 5⅝, 364 p., 7s. 6d., net.

DARWIN, C. His life told in an autobiographical chapter, and in a selected series of his published letters; ed. by his son, Francis Darwin. New and cheaper ed. N. Y., Scribner, [imported,] 1902. 6+348 p. 12°, cl., $1, net.

DIRECTORY of Americans resident in London and Great Britain, American firms and agencies. Compiled and ed. under the direction of W. B. Bancroft. Eden Fisher. 12°, 5s., net.

GOTT, S. Message of men: book of ethical scriptures gathered from many sources and arranged. New ed. Sonnenschein. 12°, 6 x 3¼, 352 p., 2s., net.

GREEN, E. Bibliotheca Somersetensis: catalogue of books, etc., connected with County of Somerset. Vol. 1: Gen. intro., Bath books, pp. 606; vol. 2: County books (Bath excl.), A to K, pp. 564; vol. 3. L to Z, and Gen. index, pp. 528. (Taunton) Barnicott & P. 4°, 63s., net.

HARPER, C. G. The Holyhead road; the mail-coach road to Dublin. Il. by the author, and from old time prints and pictures. V. 1, London to Birmingham; v. 2, Birmingham to Holyhead. N. Y., Scribner, [imported,] 1902. 2 v., 18+314; 12+333 p. 8°, cl., $12.80.

LEE, Rawdon B. A history and description, with reminiscences, of the fox terrier; il. by Arthur Wardle. New enl. ed. N. Y., Scribner, [imported,] 1902. 12+260 p. 8°, cl., $2, net.

LINESMAN. Mechanism of war. Blackwood & S. Cr. 8°, 7½ x 4⅞, 190 p., 3s. 6d.

MASON. Principles of chess: a theory in practice. New ed. (4th), rev. and enl. N. Y., Scribner, [imported,] 1902. 7+330 p. 12°, cl., $1.50, net.

MAYSON, Walter H. Violin making. N. Y., Scribner, [imported,] 1902. 102 p. il. 12°, ("Strad" lib., no. 9.) cl., $2.

RECENT FRENCH AND GERMAN BOOKS.

FRENCH.

BOURGET, P. L'Etape. *Plon, Nourrit et Cie.* 16°, $1.

DEMENY, G. Les Bases scientifiques de l'éducation physique. *Alcan.* 8°, $1.80.

FAURE, L.-F. Les Femmes dans l'Œuvre de Dante. *Perrin et Cie.* 16°, $1.

KARPPE, S. Essais de critique et d'histoire de la philosophie. *Alcan.* 8°, $1.10.

MAEL, P. Le Sous-marin vengeur. *Ollendorff.* 18°, $1.

OHNET, G. La Marche à l'amour. *Ollendorff.* 18°, $1.

PREVOST, M. L'Automne d'une femme. *Lemerre.* 18°, $1.

RENAN, E. Lettres du séminaire. *Calmann-Levy.* 8°, $1.25.

TAINE, H. Sa vie, sa correspondance. *Hachette et Cie.* 16°, $1.

GERMAN.

BLUTHGEN, Vikt. Die Spiritisten. Roman. Leipzig, *H. Seemann Nachf.* 8°, cl., $1.35.

BOECKLIN, Aug. Wanderleben in den Vereinigten Staaten. Nach den Erinnergn. e. ehemal. Offiziers. Leipzig, *J. Cotta Nachf.* 8°, $1.

HEYNACHER, *Prof. Dr.* Max. Wie spiegelt sich die menschliche Seele in Goethes Faust? Berlin, *Weidman.* 8°, 50 c.

HUPP, Otto. Gutenbergs erste Drucke. Ein weiterer Beitrag zur Geschichte der ältesten Druckwerke. Regensburg, *Verlagsanstalt vorm G. J. Manz.* il. 4°, $6.

KLUGE, *Dir. Dr.* Männliches u. weibliches Denken. Ein Beitrag zur Frauen- u. Erziehungsfrage. Halle, *C. Marhold.* 8°, 35 c.

KUNSTLER-MONOGRAPHIEN. Hrsg. v. H. Knackfuss. Vol. LIX. Montandon, Marcel: Gysis, m. e. Einleitg. von F. v. Lenbach. Bielefeld, *Velhagen & Klasing.* por. and il. 8°, bds., $1.35.

LAND u. Leute. Monographien zur Erdkunde. Hrsg. v. A. Scobel. Vol. XIII. Neumann, Prof. Dr. Ludw.: Der Schwarzwald. Bielefeld, *Velhagen & Klasing.* il. and maps, 8°, bds., $1.35.

OMPTEDA, Geo. Frhr. v. Das schönere Geschlecht. Novellen. Berlin, *F. Fontane & Co.* 8°, cl., $2.20.

RAABE, Wilh. Hastenbeck. Eine Erzählg. Berlin, *O. Janke.* 8°, $1.

SAMAROW, Greg. Ein Gespenst. Roman. Breslau, *Schles. Buchdruckerei.* 8°, cl., $1.35.

CORRECTION IN PRICE AND OTHER DATA.

CHALMERS, Ja. James Chalmers; his autobiography and letters. N. Y. and Chic., Revell, 1902. [Je.] 510 p. 8°, cl., $1.50, net.

The Publishers' Weekly.

FOUNDED BY F. LEYPOLDT.

JULY 5, 1902.

"I hold every man a debtor to his profession, from the which, as men do of course seek to receive countenance and profit, so ought they of duty to endeavor themselves by way of amends to be a help and an ornament thereunto."—LORD BACON.

DEMAND FOR ENGLISH LITERATURE ON THE CONTINENT.

THE British Consul at Leghorn in his recent annual report calls attention to a fact that we have before endeavored to impress upon the American publisher, namely, that the knowledge of the English language and English literature is steadily widening, and that books printed in English are increasingly saleable in Italy as well as in France and Germany.

The Consul points out that nearly every educated Tuscan or Roman reads English and takes an interest in English literature—as any one acquainted with our Italian immigrants might know. "Small, inexpensive, neatly bound and effectively printed editions of the English classics," he continues, "should be enjoying a far greater sale than they have at present. And the same may be said of illustrated works on art, historical memoirs, and books of travel. British publishers rely too much on the few energetic Italian booksellers who are in the habit of keeping a lookout for the latest things published in the United Kingdom. . . . British publishers should obtain lists of the principal booksellers in the principal Italian cities and advise them by circulars and advertisements in Italian or French of any publications which are likely to be suitable for sale in Italy. . . . I am of opinion that there are no less than thirty cities in Italy where a moderate sale in cheap and well-got-up British books might be looked for."

These remarks may be addressed with equal force to American publishers. Year by year the English language grows in importance as a world language, hence, the demand for books in the English language is bound to grow in other than English-speaking countries. This field is now being cultivated on a hand-to-mouth plan by foreign booksellers who are either insufficiently acquainted with the sources of supply, or who are not particularly desirous to develop their trade in English books. Judging, however, from the results of the efforts made by the few continental booksellers who take an intelligent interest in the matter, and from the successful canvass of the publishers of a recently-established American magazine, we are confident that in a short time it will become necessary for the publishing trade of the United States to consider the advisability of fostering and extending trade on the continent—pushing it even into Russia—or else to let the opportunity go and leave the field to English competitors exclusively.

THE STATUS OF THE SECOND-CLASS MAIL CONTEST.

THERE appears to be a misunderstanding generally concerning the exact status of the injunctions restraining the Postmaster-General from excluding a group of fourteen "mail-order periodicals from the second-class privilege."

The cases came originally before Justice Bradley of the District Supreme Court, who died leaving them unsettled. They then came up in due course before Justice Barnard, who was obliged to cut them short in order to keep a personal engagement of long standing, and so the whole batch went over to the fall term. This became the sole basis for the report that the Justice had not dissolved, but continued, the injunctions, and that the publishers had scored a victory over the Post-office Department. Technically, it is quite true that the injunctions were not dissolved, but were continued, as the Justice could do nothing else with unheard cases. Actually, both parties are precisely in the same situation as before the cases came up for argument, the rights of neither having been in any way prejudiced by the postponement.

According to the Washington correspondent of the New York *Evening Post*, "the Justice's theory in cutting the hearing short and leaving matters as they were was that, as the periodicals involved had been paying only second-class postage for several years, the

Government would not suffer appreciably by letting them continue doing the same thing a few months longer. As a matter of fact, however—assuming, as many competent lawyers do, that the injunctions will be finally dissolved—the Government will lose a good many thousand dollars by the continuance, but the publishers will lose ultimately more, because, if the decision had been made now against them, they would have been able to readjust their business to the new conditions in the dull part of the year, and when the autumn season opened their advertising and subscriptions would have been upon a basis acceptable to the Department, so that they could have got the full benefit of the revival of trade. As it is, if the decision of the court is adverse, they will have missed this opportunity, and will have to plunge into the whole process of readjustment at a time when other publishers have their affairs in shape to catch the advantage of whatever is coming their way.

"One thing which causes so much confidence among usually well-informed observers that the Government will ultimately win this fight, is the growing indisposition of the courts to supersede the Executive authority by the judicial in matters where discretion plays a large part, and where distinctions of fact have continually to be drawn between different members of apparently one class of things."

PRINTING AND PUBLISHING IN THE UNITED STATES.

The Census Bureau issued on the 1st inst. a report on printing and publishing—especially of newspapers and periodicals in the United States—which shows a capital of $292,517,072 invested in the 22,312 establishments reporting for the industry. The value of the products is returned at $347,055,050, to produce which involved an outlay of $36,090,719 for salaries of officials, clerks, etc.; $84,249,889 for wages; $55,897,529 for miscellaneous expenses and $86,856,290 for materials used.

The report says that when the two branches of the industry are separated—as far as separation of products so closely related is possible—the total value of all book and job printing products is about equal to the total value of all distinctive newspaper products; the former, including the printing and publishing of music, being $168,930,707, or 48.7 per cent. of the total, and the latter $175,789,610, or 50.7 per cent. of the total.

The capital invested in both branches of this industry showed a marked increase, while the value of products per establishment declined. The number of establishments in the newspaper and periodical branches, proportionately 83 to every 100 publications in 1890, remained nearly stationary in 1900, being 84 to every 100 publications.

Of all newspaper and periodical establishments, 63.3 per cent. were owned by individuals; 19.7 per cent. in partnership, and only 17 per cent. by corporations, indicating that combinations of any consequence are unlikely in this industry.

The total number of wage earners increased only 10 per cent., but the value of products earned by them increased 24 per cent.

Of the total value of products, advertising formed 43 per cent., subscriptions and sales 35.8 per cent., and book and job printing, including miscellaneous products, 21.2 per cent.

The proportion of subscriptions and sales steadily declined from 1880, while the proportion which advertising formed steadily increased until it was over half.

In 1890 the increase in the number of all publications was greater than the increase in population, but in 1900 the increase in number of publications and in population was about the same.

During the decade there was an increase in the proportion of daily, tri-weekly, semiweekly and monthly publications; a marked decline in the proportion of publications devoted to special topics and an advance only in the classes devoted to news topics and to general reading. The total circulation per issue of dailies was enough to supply one for every five inhabitants. The total circulation per issue of weeklies and monthlies was one to two inhabitants.

Publications printed in English formed 94.3 per cent. of all publications reporting for 1900; showing a considerable increase over the corresponding figures for the preceding decade.

One and one-quarter billion pounds of paper were used during the census year. Of this amount 77.6 per cent. was consumed for newspapers, 16.4 per cent. for books and periodicals, and 6 per cent. for job printing; but the proportionate cost was 58.7 per cent., 24.7 per cent. and 16.6 per cent respectively.

Daily evening newspapers increased more rapidly than daily morning papers. In 1890 there were two evening papers to every morning paper; in 1900 the proportion was about three to one.

Ten leading States supplied four-fifths of the circulation per issue of all publications.

Weekly publications were more numerous in proportion to inhabitants in the West and Northwest. New England ranked high in dailies but low in weeklies suggesting that in that densely settled region the daily had to some extent supplanted the weekly. New York, New Jersey and Pennsylvania show the most striking advance in the proportion of the total circulation reported.

There were fifteen different languages or combinations of languages represented in 1880, thirty in 1890 and twenty-five in 1900. The principal languages in which increases in the number of periodicals published were shown in 1900 were English, Bohemian, Hebrew, Italian, Polish, Scandinavian and Spanish.

Decreases were shown in the number of periodicals published in Dutch, French and German. The languages represented by publications in 1880 or 1890 but not in 1900 were Armenian, Catalan, Gaelic, Irish, "Volapuk" and Welsh.

New York City, with a population of 3,437,202, has 58 papers, 29 of which are morning and 29 evening, the aggregate circulation per issue being 2,732,089, and the number of inhabitants to each copy per issue being 1.26.

REV. LOUIS ROU'S CRITICAL REMARKS ON CHESS.

Willard Fiske, through the librarian of the Cornell University, Ithaca, N. Y., is asking for information in regard to the missing manuscript of a tract relating to chess, written in 1734 by Rev. Louis Rou, then pastor of the French Protestant Church of New York City, and entitled: "Critical Remarks upon the Letter to *The Craftsman* on the Game of Chess, occasioned by his Paper of the 15th of Sept., 733, and dated from Slaughter's Coffee-House, Sept. 21." This manuscript, of which a brief account is given in the pamphlet, was during 1858-9 in the possession of George Henry Moore, then librarian of the New York Historical Society, by whom it was lent for a short time to Mr. Fiske; but its present whereabouts are not known to the New York Historical Society nor to the Lenox Library, with which Mr. Moore subsequently became connected in 1872.

The circumstances of the preparation of the tract are interesting. In 1733 an "Essay on Chess" had appeared in *The Craftsman*, a Tory paper published in London, and edited by Lord Bolingbroke and other opponents of the house of Brunswick—in reality a bold political document in allegorical form. Lord Hervey replied for the Court in a pamphlet written in the same strain, entitled: "Letter to *The Craftsman* on the Game of Chess, occasioned by his Paper of the 15th of this month." It was dated from Slaughter's Coffee-House, Sept. 21, 1733. This letter was widely circulated by friends of the Government, and a copy reached Gov. William Cosby, of New York, who requested Rou to write out some critical remarks on the chess portion of the letter. Thus Rou prepared the manuscript in question (for some reason never printed,) in which he criticized with much display of learning and knowledge of chess the many errors regarding the game which he found in both the letters.

MARSHALL LEFFERTS'S AMERICANA SOLD.

The American portion of the library of Marshall G. Lefferts, sold June 9 and 10, at Sotheby's, London, realized $19,011.37 for the 337 lots offered for sale. The total realized for the English section sold in April last by Bangs & Co. is estimated to have been between $37,000 and $40,000, so that the lots sold at auction aggregated possibly $60,000. In addition, a number of books of extreme rarity were sold in a private manner by George H. Richmond, who bought the entire collection from Mr. Lefferts last fall. At the Sotheby sale many of the rarer books were sold to American collectors.

The following were among the more valuable sold in London:

Eliot's "Indian Bible," one of the twenty copies sent to England for presentation purposes, bound by Bedford, £370.

Budd's "Good Order Established in New Jersey," a little volume which bears the distinction of being the first book printed south of Massachusetts, by Bradford, (two leaves in facsimile,) £125.

Franklin's edition of "Cato Major," 1744, £80.

"Indian Wars in New England," a complete set of five rare folios published from 1675 to 1677, £125.

Letter from the King to Earl Southampton, Treasurer, and the Council of Virginia, commanding the setting up of silk works and the planting of vines in Virginia; also "A Treatise on the Art of Making Silk, with Instructions How to Plant and Dress Vines," dated 1622, £67.

"True Account of Buccaneers in America," by Exquemeling, printed by William Crooke, 1684-1685, £55.

Lederer's "Discoveries in Three Marches from Virginia to the West of Carolina," 1670, with the map and the rare leaf of license, £120.

"General Laws and Liberties of the Massachusetts Colony," Boston, 1672, original sheepskin, £105.

Capt. John Smith's "Map of Virginia," 1612, with the very rare folding map, a number of leaves mended, £120. This book rarely occurs with the map, which was the first issue of the map of Virginia, later used in the "Generall Historie."

Thomas's "New Jersey," 1698, with the folding map, title page mended, a few leaves repaired in lower inner corner, £109.

ENGLISH BOOK AUCTIONEERS.

The death of William Simpson, the surviving partner and head of the famous firm of book auctioneers, Puttick & Simpson, of Leicester Square, London, at the age of eighty-seven, removes from the trade of book auctioneers its most venerable figure. The house of Puttick & Simpson, according to the London *Bookseller*, "was established in or about the year 1780 by Mr. Stewart, who was succeeded by Mr. Wheatley, in conjunction with Mr. Adlard; they were in turn succeeded by Mr. Fletcher, who disposed of the business to Mr. Puttick. Their first house was situated in Piccadilly, No. 191; but in 1859 they removed to a more central position at 47 Leicester Square, a former mansion of Sir Joshua Reynolds, which up to that date had been occupied by the Western Literary Association. In 1870 Mr. Puttick left the firm to join Debenham, Storr & Sons, his interest in the business being purchased by Mr. Simpson, who thus became sole proprietor, though he continued it under the same style. Mr. Puttick died in 1873. The oldest firm in the trade is that of Sotheby, Wilkinson & Hodge, which was founded by Samuel Baker in 1744 at a house in York Street, Covent Garden; the first establishment of its kind in this country. In 1774 Baker took into partnership George Leigh, an auctioneer of King Street, Covent Garden, and the style of the firm for some years was S. Baker & G. Leigh. Later on Baker's nephew, John Sotheby, became a partner, and when Baker died in 1778 the firm was styled Leigh & Sotheby. It was again changed in 1800 to Leigh, Sotheby & Son, owing to the admittance of Sotheby's nephew, Samuel, into the partnership. In 1803 the business was moved to 145 Strand.

John Sotheby died in 1807, and Leigh in 1815, after which date Samuel continued it by himself, removing in 1817 to 3, Waterloo Street, Strand. In due course he took his son, Samuel Leigh Sotheby, into the firm, which then became Sotheby & Son, and the house was eventually removed to 13 Wellington Street. Samuel Sotheby died in 1842, aged 71, and his son was accidentally drowned in the River Dart in 1861. In 1863 Mr. John Wilkinson, F.S.A., who had for many years acted as principal accountant to the firm, and since 1843 had been a partner, obtained entire control of the business. The urbanity of his manners in the rostrum, and the thorough knowledge of books which he possessed, made his a *clarum et venerabile nomen* in the trade. He passed away in 1894 at the ripe old age of 91. Another house of some note during the early years of last century was that of King & Lochee, who, at 38 King Street, Covent Garden, transferred many costly libraries from one collector to another; though in later years their rooms were devoted to the sales of other than books. Robert Harding Evans, of 93 Pall Mall, became famous in 1812 by the sale of the Roxburghe library, and many other important collections passed under his hammer, notably that of the Duke of Sussex, and the Sykes, Spencer, Dent, Hoare, Broadley, and Hibbert libraries. The last-named collection was distributed in 1829, and Messrs. Sotheby sold the library of Colonel Hibbert, a close relation, on the 9th of April this year. Evan's catalogues were noted for their excellence of detail, and his catalogue of the Sykes collection extorted praise from the critical Dibdin. Evans retired from business in 1846. Mr. J. W. Southgate commenced business in 1824 at No. 22 Fleet Street, in conjunction with Mr. Grimston and Mr. Wells. In course of time Mr. Grimston seceded from the firm to establish a similar business of his own somewhere in Holborn; but he met with poor success. Mr Southgate was eventually succeeded by a son, who continued the traditions of the house, taking Mr. Barrett into partnership. Another Fleet Street auctioneer was L. A. Lewis, who began in a small way in 1825 at a house near the Bank of England. He moved first to the Poultry, and afterwards to No. 125, Fleet Street, relinquishing the business in 1874. Amongst the numerous libraries sold by Lewis was that of William Pickering, the famous publisher of Chancery Lane, in 1854. Last but by no means the least, we come to the famous house of Hodgson, of Chancery Lane. The birth of this firm was due to the initiation of Mr. Robert Saunders, who started the business in Old Compton Street, Soho, removing to Fleet Street in 1812, where he rapidly formed a trade connection. He was joined about 1824 by Mr. Edmund Hodgson, the son of a well-to-do and much-respected bookseller in Wimpole Street. After the partnership had existed for some years, Saunders abandoned the auctioneering business altogether to form the once flourishing law-publishing house of Saunders & Benning, of Fleet Street, who were the successors of Joshua Butterworth; and Mr. Hodgson became sole proprietor. He continued the business with marked success, his punctuality and promptness in settling accounts soon making his name widely known; and the sale rooms —at that time situated on the block at the corner of Chancery Lane and Fleet Street, where Messrs. Partridge & Cooper's well-known establishment now stands—were always well attended by influential buyers. On retiring from business he was succeeded by his son, Mr. Henry Hodgson, a few years later by Mr. Barnard, and subsequently by Mr. Henry Hill Hodgson, the present proprietor, who is one of the treasurers of the Booksellers' Provident Institution. Mr. Edmund Hodgson was one of the founders, and at one time president, of that deserving charity. He died in 1875, aged eighty-one."

COPYRIGHT MATTERS.

UNAUTHORIZED USE OF AUTHOR'S NAME PROHIBITED.

By the action of the Supreme Court, Justice Giegerich, sitting in Special Sessions, the publishers of *Frank Leslie's Popular Monthly* recently secured an injunction against John Brisben Walker to restrain him from publishing the July issue of the *Cosmopolitan Magazine.* The circumstances attending the case are unique in contemporary publishing. After the famous description of the ship "Roraima" at the eruption of Mt. Pelee, the first survivor to reach New York was Chief Officer Ellery S. Scott. His exclusive magazine story was at once secured by the editors of *Leslie's Monthly,* with the written understanding that a single New York daily paper had already succeeded in interviewing Mr. Scott, but that no periodical had any right whatever to make use of his name. The *Cosmopolitan* then approached Mr. Scott, but the latter, obeying the terms of his contract, absolutely refused his signature. Failing in this direction, the *Cosmopolitan* bought an account re-written from the original newspaper story, and published it over Scott's signature. *Frank Leslie's Popular Monthly* alleged that this was a breach of faith with the public, which unwarrantably interfered with the success of its own authentic story. Although no previous cases have been decided upon exactly similar facts, an injunction against the *Cosmopolitan* was obtained upon these grounds, and Mr. Walker, recognizing the priority of the claims of *Leslie's Monthly,* consented to have reprinted all the covers of his magazine under his control, which bore Scott's signature prominently displayed, and to make satisfactory arrangements with *Leslie's Monthly,* which, for its part, allowed the injunction to be withdrawn.

EDISON LOSES COPYRIGHT IN MOVING PICTURES.

Thomas A. Edison, the inventor, on June 25, was refused a preliminary injunction by Judge Dallas in the United States Circuit Court, Philadelphia, in the equity suit which he instituted against Sigmund Lubin, of Philadelphia, to have the latter enjoined from infringing on an alleged copyrighted life-moving picture film called "The Launching of Emperor Wilhelm's Yacht 'Meteor.'" Ex-

Judge Howard W. Hayes unsuccessfully contended on behalf of Mr. Edison that no matter how many separate pictures were on one positive film, the same could be copyrighted as a whole by one registration. Mr. Hayes will take an appeal.

OBITUARY NOTES.

The Right Rev. William Garden Cowie, Bishop of Aukland, died at Wellington, New Zealand, June 26. He was born in 1831 at Auchterless, Aberdeenshire, Scotland, and was graduated from Trinity Hall, Cambridge, in 1854. He was Chaplain to Lord Clyde's army at the capture of Lucknow, in 1858, and then was Chaplain to the Governor General of India, until 1863. He was consecrated Bishop of Auckland in 1869. He had been Primate of New Zealand since 1895. He was the author of "Notes on the Temple of Cashmere," "A Visit to Norfolk Island," and "Our Last Year in New Zealand."

Charles Sotheran, journalist, author and bibliographer, died June 27 at his home in New York City. He was born at Newington, Surrey, Eng., July 8, 1847. After leaving St. Marie's, Rugby, he became associated with book business in London. In 1874 he came to the United States and began reportorial work on the New York *World*. He afterward served as literary writer on a number of other publications, being at one time editor of the *New York Echo, The Bibliopolist*, etc. For a time he prepared the auction catalogues for George A. Leavitt & Co. He was the author of "Alessandro di Cagliostro, Impostor or Martyr?" "Percy Bysshe Shelley as a Philosopher and Reformer;" "Horace Greeley and Other Pioneers of Socialism;" "The Theatres of New York," and a number of separate bibliographies. He was associated with many societies and clubs, a prominent Mason and Sheikh of Kaaba.

NOTES ON AUTHORS.

Yvette Guilbert has written another story which she calls "Les Demi Veilles."

Justin McCarthy has projected another volume of his reminiscences to be entitled "Portraits of the Sixties," which he will finish as soon as his work on the "Reign of Queen Anne" is off his hands.

Sir Lo Feng Lah, of the Chinese Legation in London, has been appointed official biographer of Li Hung Chang. A small army of Chinese men of letters are at work collecting material for the biography, which is to be issued in thirty volumes. There is a possibility of an abridged edition in English.

It appears that the report that Jules Verne is doomed to total blindness is greatly exaggerated. He has for some time been troubled with a cataract growth, but is able to work. He has just completed his eighty-second book, "Jean Marie Cabidoulin," and has seventeen more written and nearly ready for publication. These will be published at the rate of two a year.

JOURNALISTIC NOTES.

The Dolphin is the title of an "Ecclesiastical Monthly for Educated Catholics," just begun in New York City.

Sports and Pastimes is the name of a new monthly edited and published by C. P. Hurditch, at 226 South Fourth Street, Philadelphia. Each number is accompanied by colored portraits of local sportsmen. The June number exhibits Barclay Warburton in coaching dress.

The New York Observer has passed into the hands of the Rev. Dr. John Bancroft Devins, who will edit the journal, and John A. Offord, who will continue the business management. The new owners have been connected with the paper for several years. The *Observer* was founded in 1823 by Sidney E. and Richard C. Morse. In 1858 it passed into the hands of Dr. S. I. Prime and Sidney E. Morse, jr., the latter being succeeded in 1873 by Dr. Charles A. Stoddard, a son-in-law of Dr. Prime. In 1885, when Dr. Prime died, Dr. Stoddard became editor, and has furnished an "Augustus" letter every week since that time, taking the place occupied by the "Irenæus" letters for more than forty years. Dr. Stoddard will continue his weekly letter and the paper will be conducted along the general lines that made it the leading Presbyterian paper in the country.

Harper's Weekly with its issue for July 5 appears in a new form and in a new dress marking a distinct advance in weekly pictorial journalism. The contributors include such men as W. D. Howells, Mark Twain, Anthony Hope, Richard Harding Davis, Robert W. Chambers, Gilbert Parker, Henry Loomis Nelson, Booth Tarkington, John Kendrick Bangs, Carl Snyder, E. S. Martin, Thomas A. Janvier, E. W. Townsend, Sydney Brooks, Hamblen Sears, James MacArthur, and many other specialists. The editorial section under the direction of Colonel Harvey has already attracted wide comment and is truly said to have "set the highwater mark for modern journalistic enterprise." The cover of the new *Weekly* is striking, its chief feature being the Bartholdi Statue in New York Harbor of "Liberty Enlightening the World." The first issue comprises 44 pages, including a double-page picture in colors.

BUSINESS NOTES.

Council Grove, Kan.—Captain J. S. Winans has bought the bookstore here and will enlarge and improve the stock.

Hartford, Conn.—G. W. Blanchfield, formerly of 47 High Street, Newark, has settled in this city at 58 Ann Street at the sign of the "Garrett Book Shoppe."

Lincoln, Neb.—S. Hall has succeeded Wilson & Hall, booksellers.

Montgomery, Pa.—A new bookstore has been opened in the Mirror Building.

Salem, W. Va.—H. B. Smith, of the *West Union Record*, will open up a bookstore and news stand in the Smith Building.

LITERARY AND TRADE NOTES.

E. P. Dutton & Co have just ready "The Home Aquarium," by Eugene Smith, giving a description of the various plants and animals that thrive in the aquarium, and practical suggestions for their care.

James Pott & Co. have in preparation a work entitled "The Builders of the Republic," by the author of "Famous Homes of New York," who describes twenty-four of the tremendous personalities who, from the chaos of royal, and colonial government and misgovernment, brought forth our republic.

Harper & Brothers followed up their very handsome attention to the delegates of the American Booksellers' Association, by sending each one present a fine photograph of the group taken on the occasion of their visit to Franklin Square on June 16. A reproduction of this photograph was printed through the courtesy of Harper & Brothers in our issue for June 28.

W. L. Washburn, (The Palmetto Press,) Aiken, S. C., will publish shortly a reprint of "An Elegie upon the Death of the Reverend Mr. Thomas Shepard," by Urian Oakes, following the form and spelling of the copy of the first edition in the Brown University Library. There will be two editions—125 copies on hand-made paper and 25 copies on Japanese paper.

J. F. Taylor & Co. have secured from F. Newell Gilbert and Leon Mead, of Binghamton, N. Y., their "Manual of Forensic Quotations," a collection of celebrated passages and eloquent sayings derived from jury arguments of celebrated lawyers. The book will contain over thirty rare photographs of distinguished lawyers—English and American—from the time of Lord Erskine to the present period.

D. Appleton & Co. have made arrangements to print the autobiography of a convict under the title of "As I Sailed." This is said to be the production of a man who was a sailor in a whaling vessel, then in a merchant ship, then in the British navy, then an ensign in the American navy, taking part in the attack of Fort Fisher. Then he "runs the whole yellow streak of worthlessness, which ended in a quarter of a century behind prison bars," and died in a Western penitentiary. The editor, Stanley Waterloo, speaks of the man's unconscious self-revelation in this autobiography, in which he regrets nothing and betrays no sense of shame or contrition. They will publish early in the fall the first volume of Mme. Adam's memoirs, "Romance of My Childhood and Youth"; a series of Charles Darwin's letters, edited by his son, Francis Darwin; also H. G. Wells's new novel, "The Sea Ready."

The executors of Walt Whitman's estate, Thomas B. Harned, Horace L. Traubel, and Professor Oscar L. Triggs, are preparing a final and definite edition of all the writings of the "good gray poet," to be entitled the *Camden Limited Edition*. G. P. Putnam's Sons will publish the edition in ten octavo volumes, limiting the issue to one thousand sets. The first 100 sets will be extra illustrated in water colors, and in them will be bound some of the poet's own manuscripts. These will be offered at $1,000 a set. Other issues, differing in the style of binding, and, of course, in the matter of autographic illustrations, will be offered at prices ranging down from $500 to $60 a set. Horace L. Traubel proposes to publish in facsimile Whitman's personal copy of "Leaves of Grass," the edition printed by Thayer & Eldridge, Boston, 1860-'61, in which he did much of the work of revision for the edition that followed five years later. This copy of "Leaves of Grass" is historic. It is the volume abstracted by Secretary Harlan from Whitman's desk in the Interior Department and made the basis for his discharge from that branch of service. An account of this incident, written by Whitman himself, will be photographically reproduced and included in the reprint. The edition will be limited to 500 copies, and the price fixed will be $10 for each copy. The text matter of the volume will be printed from the original plates, which still exist. The chirographical matter in Whitman's hand will be superimposed and printed in exact facsimile.

The University of Chicago Press announces for publication during the summer months a volume entitled "The Diary and Correspondence of Wilhelm Müller." The work will be edited by Dr. Philip S. Allen, of the Germanic Department of the University of Chicago, assisted by Dr. James Taft Hatfield, of the Germanic Department of the Northwestern University. In order to preserve as far as possible the original qualities of the work the book will be done in German type. Wilhelm Müller was the father of Dr. Max Müller of Oxford, and was one of the most pleasing lyricists of the nineteenth century. He was a conspicuous representative of the later romantic school of Germany. In view of the fact that the library and personal papers of Wilhelm Müller were all destroyed by fire many years ago it is improbable that any other intimate record of the poet's activities and strivings will ever be published. The University of Chicago Press also announces the completion and appearance in book form of Volume III. of the *Studies in Classical Philology*. These volumes are under the editorial direction of a committee of the faculty of the Classical Departments of the University and consist of contributions from representative teachers. The volume which is just appearing contains three contributions, the first, entitled "Papyri from Karanis," by Dr. Edgar J. Goodspeed; the second, "The Use of Repetition in Latin to Secure Emphasis, Intensity and Distinctness of Impression," by Dr. Frank F. Abbott; and the third, "Epideictic Literature," by Theodore C. Burgess. The papers are all technical in nature, the first being distinctly brief, the latter forming the bulk of the volume.

PICK UPS.

A new book by the author of the "Dolly Dialogues" suggests the fine distinction made by a New York woman who, when asked what Anthony Hope had written, promptly replied: "'The Dolly Dialogues' and 'The Prisoner of Zenda.' All the rest are by a man named Hawkins."

BOOKS WANTED.

☞ In answering, please state edition, condition, and price, including postage or express charges.

Houses that are willing to deal exclusively on a cash-on-delivery basis will find it to their advantage to put after their firm-name the word [Cash].

☞ Write your wants plainly and on one side of the sheet only. Illegibly-written "wants" will be considered as not having been received. The "Publishers' Weekly" does not hold itself responsible for errors.

It should be understood that the appearance of advertisements in this column, or elsewhere in the "Publishers' Weekly" does not furnish a guarantee of credit. While it is endeavored to safeguard these columns by withdrawing the privilege of their use from advertisers who are not "good pay," booksellers should take the usual precaution, as to advertisers not known to them, that they would take in making sales to any unknown parties.

Arthur M. Allen, 508 Fulton St., Troy, N. Y.

Lossing, Field Book of Revolution.
Wellington, Earthworks, 2 v. Appleton.
Anything on John Brown.
Hollick, Nerves and the Nervous.

The Alliance Pub. Co., 569 5th Ave., N. Y.

Esdaile's Natural and Mesmeric Clairvoyance.

Alwil Shop, Ridgewood, N. J. [*Cash.*].

Alphabets, by Edward F. Strange, Macmillan & Co.'s "Ex-Libris" Ser.

Amer. Bapt. Pub. Soc., 279 Elm St., Dallas, Tex.

Acts of the Apostles Explained, 2 v., by Alexander. Pub. by Randolph.

American Press Co., Baltimore, Md.

Hawthorne, Twice-Told Tales, 1st ser., Boston, 1837; Mosses from an Old Manse, 1846, both 1st eds.
Thoreau, Summer, Early Spring in Mass., and other 1st eds.

Antiquarian Book Store, Omaha, Neb.

Set of Cooper, with Darley plates.
Halleck, International Law.
Book of Concord.
Speeches of Phillips, Grattan and Emmet.

Wm. M. Baine, 1019 Market St., Phila., Pa.

Lady Charlotte Guest's Mabinogion, tr.
Thompson's trans. Geoffrey of Monmouth History (British.)
Ritson's King Arthur.
Stuart Glennie's Journey Through Arthurian Scotland.
Schultz, Albert, Arthur the National Hero.
Townsend's U. S. Lothrop Pub. Co.

The Baker & Taylor Co., 33 E. 17th St., N. Y.

Eustace Diamonds, by Trollope, cl.
Golden Lion of Grand Pre, Trollope, cl.
Friends in Counsel, by Helps, 4 v. ed.

Bartlett's Book Store, 33 E. 22d St., N. Y.

Dowden Transcripts and Studies.
Seignobos, Political History of Europe Since 1814.
Geikie, Ice Age.
Landor, Imaginary Conversations, 5 v. ed.

Bartlett's Book Store.—*Continued.*

Bagehot, Literary Studies.
De Vere, Essays Chiefly on Poetry.
Stephen, History of English Thought in 18th Century, must be cheap.
Knickerbocker. Grolier Club.
Life Benvenuto Cellini, Nimmo ed.
Matthew Arnold, fine ed.
Herbert Spencer, fine ed.

Belknap & Warfield, Hartford, Conn.

Maximilian and Carlotta, Taylor. Putnam.

Bigham & Smith, Agts. Dallas, Tex.

The Great West. Pub. about 1873.
The Character of St. Paul, by Howson.

Bigham & Smith, Agts., Nashville, Tenn.

British Eloquence, by Goodrich, leath. binding.
Century Dictionary, 10 v., hf. mor., latest ed.
Here and Beyond, by Hugh Smith Carpenter.

Bonnell, Silver & Co., 24 W. 22d St., N. Y.

Genealogy Merritt Family.
Genealogy Fowler Family.
Booth, William, Life.

The Boston Book Co., 83 Francis St., Boston, Mass

Baptist Review, Jan., 1881 (with title-page and index of v. 2); Jan., '89; Oct., '90; Jan., '91; Oct., '92.

J. W. Bouton, 10 W. 28th St., N. Y.

Heywood, 6 v., L. P. Pearson.
Hawthorne, Twice Told Tales. 1837.
Hawthorne, Mosses from an Old Manse. 1846.
Baring-Gould, Curiosities of Olden Time.
Baring-Gould, Curious Myths of Middle Ages.

Brentano's, Wabash Ave. and Adams St., Chicago, Ill

Professor Wahl's Book on Ensilage.
Applied Forms, Ebenezer Prout. Scribner.

Brentano's, Union Sq., N. Y.

Appleton, W. S., Crane Family of Chilton.
Barlow, Julian, Ghost Bereft, and Other Poems. Saxon & Co., London.
All nos. of the *Saturday Press* (pub. in N. Y. about 1858) containing a column on Chess.
A History of the Minturn House and Family.
McPherson, History of Reconstruction.
Cassier's Magazine, v. 1.
Boston Directories, 1796, 1803, 1806.
Books on Albany previous to 1800.
Artistic Japan, pt. 10.
Century Dict., 10 v., cheap, for rebinding.
Hough, Thousand Islands. Davis B. & Co.
Castle Builders. Appleton, 1854.
Wister, Lady with the Rubies, Lipp. Pop. Lib., 75 c.
Morgan, Poppy Garden. Belknap & Warfield, 50 c.
Hearn, Chinese Ghosts.
Chambers' Miscellany.
Meredith, Glenaveril.
Hardy, Spectre of the Real.
Walmsley, Electric Currents. Cassell.
Kipling, v. 12, Outward Bound ed. de luxe.
Book of Jade. Pub. by Doxey.

Brentano's, 1015 Pennsylvania Ave., Washington, D. C.

Gross, Index to Dates. 1859.
Palgrave, Hermann Agha.
Harte, Bret, Earlier Stories.
Dana, Characteristics of Volcanoes.

The Burrows Bros. Co., Cleveland, O.

Forster, Life of Swift, v. 2. Harper.
Wis. Hist. Coll., v. 1, 2, 5, 6.
Jarves, Parisian, v. 1.
Orton, Ohio Geol. Repts., after '88.
Eugene Field, 1st ed.
Budd, Good Order in Pa. Gowans reprint.
Miller, Description of New York. Gowans reprint.

J. W. Cadby, 131 Eagle St., Albany, N. Y.

American Archives, 9 v., by Force.
Poor's Railroad Manuals, 1869-'70, and v. 11-12.
Notes and Queries, 1st ser., v. 7, 8, 11, 12; also 1876-1900.
National Magazine, v. 11, 13.
McClure's Magazine, Sept., Oct., 1893; Jan., Feb., Mar., '94.
Cosmopolitan, Nov., Dec., 1888.
Godey's Lady's Book, 1845-'46.
Niles' Register, v. 60, 61.
Critic (N. Y.), 1884, '85, '93-'96, bound preferred.

William J. Campbell, Phila., Pa.

Chauncey Memorial.

BOOKS WANTED.—*Continued.*

Carnegie Library, Pittsburgh, Pa.

Minnesota Historical Society Collections, v. 4 (Williams' History of St. Paul); v. 6, pts. 1, 3; v. 7; v. 8, pts. 1, 3; v. 9.
New York Tribune Index for 1900.

Case Library, Cleveland, O.

Dial (Boston), nos. 14, 15.
New England Historical and Genealogical Register, v. 16, 19, 44.
Schoolcraft, Algic Researches, 1st ser., v. 1.
Schaff, Creeds of Christendom.

C. N. Caspar Co., 437 E. Water St., Milwaukee, Wis.

Burton, Anatomy of Melancholy.
Appleton's Annual Encycl., 1872.
Upham, View of the Absolute Religion.

Jno. J. Case, 70 Wall St., N. Y.

Gordon, Revolution, 1788, v. 2, perfect or imperfect.
Jefferson, Thos., Mem. and Corr., odd v. 1829.
Adams, J. Q., Lectures, Rhetoric, v. 1. 1810.

The Central Printing and Pub. House, 329 Market St., Harrisburg, Pa.

Pulpit Commentary, second-hand.
Wood, Natural History, 3 v., Selmar Hess ed., copyright 1885, either in pts. or bound.

The A. H. Clark Co., Garfield Bldg., Cleveland, O.

Knight, Amer. Mechanical Dict., v. 3, 4, or complete.
Kellogg, Life and Death in Rebel Prisons.
Maryland, any books or papers rel. to.
Webb, Altowan.

E. H. Clarke & Bro., 362 Main St., Memphis, Tenn.

Kipling's Jungle Book, 1st and 2d ser., Swastika ed., Green.

The Robert Clarke Co., 31 E. 4th St., Cincinnati, O.

Balch, An American Career and its Triumph, or, Life of Blaine and Logan.
Drake, Black Hawk War and Life of Black Hawk.
Kautz, Customs of the Service for Officers.
Kautz, Customs of the Non-Coms. and Men.
Lieb, Emperor William I. Founder of New German Empire. Belford, Clarke & Co.
Townsend, Honors of the Empire State in War of the Rebellion.
Jas. G. Birney and His Times.

W. B. Clarke Co., Park and Tremont Sts., Boston, Mass.

Book Prices Current, v. 1.
Zululu. Pub. by Putnam.

Henry T. Coates & Co., Phila., Pa.

Atherton, Hermia Suydam.
Borrow, Romany Rye, 3 v.
Norman, Real Japan.
Feutchanger, On Gems.

J. H. Cosgrove, care of Doubleday, Page & Co., 34 Union Sq., N. Y.

The Life and Inventions of Thos. A. Edison, by W. K. L. Dickson and Antonio Dickson, copyright 1892, '93, '94. Pub. by T. Y. Crowell & Co.

C. P. Cox, 257 W. 125th St., N. Y.

Statuvolence, by Fahnestock.

Cushing & Co., 34 W. Baltimore St., Baltimore, Md.

Wedgewood, Etymological Dictionary.

Damrell & Upham, 283 Washington St., Boston, Mass.

Boston Directories, 1806 and 1810.
Neale and Littledall, Commentary on the Psalms.
Cumberland, British Theatre.
French, Standard Drama.
Overland, G. W. De Forest.
Wanderers, Keary.
Farmer's Vacation, by Waring.

A. Deutschberger, 117 4th Ave., N. Y.

Hager, Handbuch der Pharmaceutische Praxis.
Kipling, v. 8, 13, 17, Outward Bound ed.

DeWolfe, Fiske & Co., 361 Washington St., Boston, Mass.

Operative Surgery, 2 v., Bryant.
Operative Gynecology, 2 v., Kelly.
Astrophel and Stella, Sir Philip Sidney.
Early Boston directories.
Blithedale Romance. Boston, 1865, this date only.
The Earth not a Sphere, by Parallax.
Reminiscences of Oxford, by Tuckwell.

Dodd, Mead & Co., 372 Fifth Ave., N. Y.

Cooper, Jack Tier; Pilot; Red Skins; Townsend ed., cl.
Franklin's Autobiography, L. P. ed. Pub. by Lipp.
Very Little Tales for Very Little Children. Am. Tract Society.
Harris, W. T., Spiritual Sense of Dante's Divine Comedy. Appleton.
Mitchell, Donald G., From Celt to Tudor, 1889; From Elizabeth to Anne, 1890, in English Lands, Letters and Kings Series.
The Lorgnette, 2 v., 1850.
Burnett, F. H., That Lass o' Lowrie's, 1st ed. 1877.
Cable, G. W., The Grandissimes, 1st ed. 1880.

Alex. Duncker (H. von Carnap), 178 Fulton St., N. Y.

Sets, volumes or numbers.
Am. Chem. Journal.
Am. Journal of Pharmacy.
Chemical News.
Bulletin de la Societe Chimique de Paris.
Wagner's Jahresberichte d. Chem. Technologie.
Liebig's Annalen.
Engineering News.
Journal of the Am. Chem. Society.
Journal of Analytical Chemistry.

E. P. Dutton & Co., 31 W. 23d St., N. Y.

American Country Life, June.
The Lenape Stone, or, the Indian and the Mammoth.
Whirl Asunder, cl.
Narratives of the Spirits of Sir Henry Morgan and His Daughter Annie, by Henry T. Child, M.D.

D. T. Eaton, Muscatine, Ia.

Judge Edmonds, Spiritualism, 2 v.
Niles' Register.
Science, 1st and 2d ser., complete or odd v.

Elder & Shepard, 238 Post St., San Francisco, Cal.

Strange, Edward F., Japanese Illustrations. London, Geo. Bell, 1897.

C. P. Everitt, 218 5th Ave., N. Y.

Scott, Waverley Novels, v. 1 of the 25 v. ed. of either Gebbie or Black.

H. W. Fisher & Co., 1535 Chestnut St., Phila., Pa.

Whitman, Leaves of Grass, 1st ed.
Fiske, Discovery of America, 1st ed.
Fiske, American Revolution, 1st ed.
Fiske, Critical Periods, 1st ed.
Fiske, Beginnings of New England, 1st ed.
Davis, Friend of Cæsar, 1st ed.
Baker, American Engravers and Their Work.
Shakespeare's Comedies, il. by Abbey.

Goldsmith Bros., 206 E. Baltimore St., Baltimore, Md.

Sandow's Books on Physical Culture.

Edwin S. Gorham, 4th Ave. and 22d St., N. Y.

The World and the Logos, Bp. Thompson.
Mozley, Essays, second-hand.
Heylin, Restaurata Ecclesia.
Maurice, F. D., On Ten Commandments.
Papal Claims, Pott, Young & Co.
Bruce, Training of the Twelve, etc., second-hand.

F. E. Grant, 23 W. 42d St., N. Y.

Pamphlet containing article on Hybridity, by Dr. J. C. Nott. Pub. 1842 (?)
Ancilla Domini.
Boys at Home. (English book pub. about 50 yrs. ago.)
Hammersley, Records of Living Officers in the U. S. Navy.
The Soft Porcelain of Sevres, by Garnier.
Queens of the House of Hanover, by Dr. Doran, English ed.
Study of Browning, by Symons.
Comedy of Masques, by Dawson.
Adrian Rouke, by Dawson.
Enemies of Books, by Blake.
Growth of Love, by Robt. Bridges. Daniel Press, 1890.
Anthropology, by John Bachman.
Man—Where, Whence and Whither, by David Page.
Anthropology, by D. G. Brinton, M.D.
Indian Sign Language, by Clark.
Physical Culture, by Sandow.
Party Leaders, by Jas. W. Baldwin.
John Randolph of Roanoke, Letters to a Young Relative.
Randolph's Speeches.
The Bryan MS.
Jenkins' Vest-Pocket Lexicon of Unfamiliar Words.

BOOKS WANTED.—Continued.

F. E. Grant.—*Continued.*

Geology and Physical Geography of Brazil, by Prof. Harte.
McPherson, Political History of the U. S. During Reconstruction.
Englishman's Concordance of the Hebrew Bible.

Hasting's Book Store, Troy, N. Y.

Nooks and Corners New England Coast.
The Spectator, v. 1, Scribner's, 8 v., annotated by G. Gregory Smith, with introd. by Austin Dobson.

J. K. Hester, Cozad, Neb.

Fisher, Geo. P., Church History.
Life of Eld. John Smith.
Gospel Restored, Eld. Walter Scott.
Christian Messenger, B. W. Stone.

Hinds & Noble, 31 W. 15th St., N. Y.

Pitman, Spanish Phonography.

Joseph Horner Book Co., Ltd., 524 Penn Ave., Pittsburgh, Pa.

Porter, Summer Driftwood for the Winter Fire. Randolph.

E. W. Johnson, 2 E. 42d St., N. Y.

Harper's Weekly, war vols.
Howard, Physiology of Artistic Singing.
Wilde, Oscar, Intentions.
Macknight, On Epistles, 6 v., Greek text.

H. R. Johnson, 315 Main St., Springfield, Mass.

Chautauquan, Oct., Nov., Dec., 1890.
Dick's Encyclo. of Receipts.
Geissler, Church History, v. 4, 5.

L. Jonas & Co., Astor House, N. Y.

Life of T. M. Post.
Rhyme and Reason, Dulcken.
Real Japan, Norman.
Four Years in the Saddle, Gilmor.

Wilbur B. Ketcham Pub. Co., 156 5th Ave., N. Y.

Bush, The Soul.
Hitchcock, True Ideal and Use of Church History.

Kimball Bros., 618 Broadway, Albany, N. Y.

Munsell's Annals of Albany, v. 5, 6.
Lewis and Clark Expedition, by Coues. N. Y., Francis Harper.

J. Kirkpatrick, 1016 Woodland Ave., Cleveland, O. [Cash.]

100 White's Complete Arith., 20th century ed.
100 White's First Book of Arith., 20th century ed.
50 Dubbs's Complete Mental Arith.

Geo. Kleinteich, 397 Bedford Ave., Brooklyn, N. Y. [Cash.]

Wilson's Dict. of Astrology.
Hittell, Evidences Against Christianity, v. 1, 2d ed.
Stetson, Why Not Cycle Abroad Yourself?
The Challenge, v. 1, 2, or single nos.

Chas. E. Lauriat Co., 301 Washington St., Boston, Mass.

Boys and Girls of Revolution, by Woodman.
2 copies Villa on the Rhine, v. 1, Auerbach, ed. 1869.
2 copies Peter and Polly, by Douglas. Osgood.
Boys' Workshop, by Behrens.
Brown's Manual of Commerce, 12°, cl., new copy.
Masters of German Music, in Series of Masters of Contemporary Music. Imported by Scribner.
Lindsay, On the Morgan Horse.
The Recent Past, from a Southern Standpoint, by Richard Wilmer.
Obermann, Letters to a Friend, H., M. & Co.'s Limited ed.

Little, Brown & Co., 254 Washington St., Boston, Mass.

Bonar's Hymns.

S. Lagin, 1336 3d Ave., N. Y.

Atlantic Monthly, v. 1, 7, 30-38, 40, 46, 47, 53, 55, 61, 63, and all vols. after v. 63.

W. H. Lowdermilk & Co., Washington, D. C.

Reid, Works, 2 v., ed. by Hamilton.
American Archives, 4th ser., v. 1, 2, 4.
Carll, Calculus of Variations.
Motherwell, Poems.
Epistle Sophia.

W. H. Lowdermilk & Co.—*Continued.*

Pollard, Lee and His Lieutenants.
De Peyster, Life of Kearney.
Jeffries, Richard, Works, any.

S. B. Luyster, Jr., 76 Nassau St., N. Y.

Andrews, W. L., Choice Collections of Books. 1885.
Andrews, W. L., Short Historical Sketch on Art of Bookbinding. 1895.
Andrews, W. L., Jean Grolier.

C. D. Lyon, 20 Monroe St., Grand Rapids, Mich.

Growoll, The Booksellers' Library.
Medical Review of Reviews, v. 2, no. 2.
Eastman, Kitty Kent's Troubles.
Roe, James Montjoy.
Wright, Wife Hard Won.

Nathaniel McCarthy, Minneapolis, Minn.

Daudet's Tartarin on the Alps, Routledge's pap. bound ed.
Les Miserables, 5 v., Routledge's ed., 8°, pap. label.
Barnes' Notes of the New Testament.
Lange's Commentaries.
Pulpit Commentary.

Joseph McDonough, 30 Columbia St., Albany, N. Y.

British Essayists, v. 38, Little, Brown ed., black cl. 1857.
Schoolcraft, Algic Researches.
Bancroft, United States, v. 9, 10.
Pierson, Schenectady Patent.

S. F. McLean & Co., 44 E. 23d St., N. Y.

Writings of Petroleum V. Nasby. 1865.
Child, Maria, Life of Isaac Hopper.
Emerson, Sarah Hopper, Life of Abbey H. Gibbons.

P. F. Madigan, Albany, N. Y. [Cash.]

Bret Harte's Works, 16 v., Autograph ed. H., M. & Co.
Autograph Letters of Francis Parkman.
William Loring Andrews' books, any.

M. N. Maisel, 194 E. Broadway, N. Y. [Cash.]

Buckle, History of Civilization.
Books translated from the Russian in any quantity, if cheap.
Catalogues of second-hand books.

H. Malkan, Hanover Sq., N. Y.

Set of Eugene Field, Sabine ed.
2 sets Rand-McNally's Indexed Atlas of the World. cl.
Mrs. Seymour's Pamphlet on The Pickwick Papers.

The Edw. Malley Co., New Haven, Conn.

Lessons Toward Faith, by Robertson.
Reliable Candy Teacher, by Will O. Rigby.
Metallurgy of Cast Iron, 5th ed., by T. D. West.

March Bros., Lebanon, O.

Review of Reviews, 1st 10 v.

B. & J. F. Meehan, Bath, Eng.

Dickens, anything on author or works.
North American Review, Oct., 1853.
New York Times Saturday Review of Books, Nov. 16, 30, 1901.

R. H. Merriam, Hanover Sq., N. Y.

Early Settlers of Kings Co., by T. G. Bergen.
History of Charles the Bold. Lippincott.
Set of Huxley and Tyndall in Appleton's Scientific Library.
Stoddard's Lectures.

Dewitt Miller, P. O. Drawer 1351, Phila., Pa. [Cash.]

Female Hunter of Eddy Run, by Lucy Ann Slater, alias the Rev. Joseph Lobdell.
Forest and Jungle, P. T. Barnum.

Fred Miller, 173 Water St., N. Y.

1st eds. of Andrew Lang, state price and condition.

Estate of Henry Miller, 1 Barclay St., N. Y.

History of the Buell Family, by Albert Welles.

F. M. Morris, 171 Madison St., Chicago, Ill.

Barlow, The Voices.
Nordau, How Women Love.
Nordau, Soap Bubbles.
Henderson, Stonewall Jackson.

Noah Farnham Morrison, 893 Broad St., Newark, N. J. [Cash.]

The Child and the Bishop.
Schoolcraft, Amer. Indian, v. 6. Phila.

BOOKS WANTED.—Continued.

Old Corner Book Store, Springfield, Mass. [Cash.]
Plymouth Colony Records, v. 12, large 4° ed.
Diary Amer. Revolution, v. 2, Moore.
Astoria, v. 1, Irving. Phila., 1836.

E. J. O'Malley, Hanover Sq., N. Y.
Sets of Huxley and Tyndall, in Appleton's Scientific Library.
Whittier, any 1st eds.
N. Y. Civil List, 1867.

C. C. Ostrander, Islip, N. Y.
Mackenzie's Strictures on Tarleton.
Holmes' Annals (1826 ed.)
Burgoyne's State of the Expedition.
Moultrie's Memoirs.
Anything on Hamilton-Burr Duel.

The Pafraets Book Co., Cannon Pl., Troy, N. Y.
Anglo-Saxon Review, v. 9.

Peter Paul & Co., Buffalo, N. Y.
Owen, Grammar of Ornament.

The Pease-Lewis Co., 102 Church St., New Haven, Conn. [Cash.]
Fitz Reuter, Sowing and Reaping.
Fitz Reuter, In Year 13.
Fitz Reuter, His Little Serene Highness.
Browne, Venice, Historical Sketch. G. P. Putnam.
Winsor, Narrative and Critical Hist. of U. S., second-hand.
Kirke-Allibone, last ed., second-hand.

Pierce & Zahn, 633 17th St., Denver, Colo.
Burke's Extinct Peerage.
Scott, System of Logarithms.
Kady.

C. S. Pratt, 161 6th Ave., N. Y. [Cash.]
A Week in a French Country House.
Balzac, Physiology of Marriage.
Father Southwell's Poems.
Spirit of St. Francis de Sales.
Hall's Manual.

Presb. Bd. of Pub. and S. S. Work, 192 Michigan Ave., Chicago, Ill.
Facts and Fancies in Modern Science. Pub. by Amer. Bapt.

Presb. Bd. of Pub. and S. S. Work, Witherspoon Bldg., Phila., Pa.
Bancroft, History U. S., v. 9, 10.
Life of Simon Girty.
Summer Driftwood for Winter Fires, by Rose Porter. Randolph.

Purdy's Book Store, 1009 Congress Ave., Houston, Tex.
Little and Scott's Latin Dictionary.

G. P. Putnam's Sons, 27 W. 23d St., N. Y.
Sage, The Restigouche.

Geo. H. Richmond, 32 W. 33d St., N. Y.
Daly's Peg Woffington, with illus.
Vale Press books, any.

Geo. H. Rigby, 1113 Arch St., Phila., Pa.
Duchenne, Mechanisme de la physiognomie humaine.

Chas. M. Roe, 177 Wabash Ave., Chicago, Ill.
Early extra volume of Historical Series, by Livermore. John Hopkins Press.

Philip Roeder, 616 Locust St., St. Louis, Mo.
Du Barry, Memoirs, 4 v.
Horry and Weems, Life of Gen. Francis Marion.
Moore's Poems, Brydges ed.
Nicolls, Story of American Coals.
Morley, Life of Voltaire.

Rohde & Haskins, 16 Cortlandt St., N. Y.
League of the Iroquois, Morgan.
Lives of Naval Heroes, James Fenimore Cooper.
Tsar's Window, Anon. No Name Ser. Little, B.

Wm. S. Ropes, Mt. Vernon, Skagit Co., Wash.
Collins, W. W., Yellow Mask, Seaside or Appleton's Handy Vol.
Spratter, [illegible], Sporting Scenes, 2 v., complete, Eng. or Amer. ed.

John E. Scopes, 29 Tweddle Bldg., Albany, N. Y.
American Ancestry, v. 9, 10.
Wilkinson, Memoirs, v. 2, and atlas. Phila., 1816.

Scrantom, Wetmore & Co., Rochester, N. Y.
Mantz, Short Hist. Tapestry, tr.
Bombaugh, Gleanings for the Curious.
Drummond, Habitant, 1st ed.

Charles Scribner's Sons, 153 5th Ave., N. Y.
Bancroft, Battle of Lake Erie.
Kennedy, Father Clement. Peterson.
Mathews, C., Enchanted Moccasins.
Howitt, M., Who Shall be Greatest? Harper.
Murray, Russia.
Dorr, Flower of England's Face.
Mabie, My Study Fire, 1st ed. 1890.
Mabie, Our New England, 1st ed. 1890.
Mabie, Essays in Lit. Interpretation, 1st ed. 1892.
Mabie, My Study Fire, 2d ser., 1st ed. 1894.
Mabie, Essays on Nature and Culture, 1st ed. 1896.
Mabie, Essays on Work and Culture, 1st ed. 1900.

Shepard Book Co., 272 S. State St., Salt Lake City, U.
Pike, Albert, Prose Sketches and Poems, ed. of 1834.

Jos. Silk, 147 6th Ave., N. Y.
Craft, History of Wyalusing or Bradford Co., Pa.

Wm. H. Smith, Jr., 515 W. 173d St., N. Y.
Argonaut Letters.
Master Mechanics' Association Proceedings, v. 6, 7, 20.
The Hessians in the Revolution, Lowell.
History of Kingsbridge, Edsall.

Smith Bros., 12th and Washington Sts., Oakland, Cal.
Dragon of Wantley, Owen Wister.

Smith & Butterfield, 202 Main St., Evansville, Ind.
Parson Brownlow's Life and Writings.

Speyer & Peters, Berlin, N. W. F., Germany.
Annales des Maladies Gen.-Urin.
Archiv für Augen- u. Ohrenheilkunde.
Archiv f. Experim. Pathol. u. Pharmakol.
Archives of Pediatrics.
Brun, Beitraege z. Klin. Chirurgie.
Graefe, Archiv. f. Ophthalmologie.
Journal de l'Anatomie p. Robin.
Journal of the Amer. Chem. Soc.
Transactions of the Amer. Orthop. Association, v. 7, 8, 11, 13, 14.
Please offer sets or single vols. and nos.

Frank Stanton, Wheeling, W. Va.
Remarkable Occurrences in the Life and Travels of Col. James Smith. Lexington, Ky., 1799.
The Subaltern, Gleig. Blackwood, London.

G. E. Stechert, 9 E. 16th St., N. Y.
Lloyd, Strike of Millionaires against Miners.
Dana, Handbook of Libraries.
Freeman, Norman Conquest, 6 v.
Agassiz, Lake Superior.
Harris, Insects injurious to Vegetation.

E. Steiger & Co., 25 Park Place, N. Y. [Cash.]
Salter, Ethical Religion.
Shearman, Taxation of Personal Property. 1895.
Wells, Local Taxation in the U. S. 1874.
Wells, Principles of Taxation. 1899.
Patten, Principles of Rational Taxation. 1890.
Patten, Economic Basis of Protection.
Army and Navy Journal, nos. 1819, 1832, 1836, 1866, 1922, 1924, 1925.
American Journal of Forestry, complete set.
The Forester, complete set.
Bulletin of the Torrey Botanical Club, complete set.

Strawbridge & Clothier, Market St., Phila., Pa.
Encyclopedia Britannica, 31 v.

V. P. Strelitz, 167 Dearborn St., Chicago, Ill.
Books on precious stones.

Thos. J. Taylor, Taunton, Mass.
Osterlein, Katalog Einer Richard Wagner Bibliothek.
Bayreuther Taschen-Kalendar, any year.
The Liberator (anti-slavery paper), any complete v.

John C. Tredway, 202 Atlantic Ave., Brooklyn, N. Y.
Puck, v. 1, nos. 5, 8; v. 4, no. 85.
Brooklyn Eagle Almanacs, 1886 to 1890, incl., and 1896 with the maps

Henry K. Van Siclen, 413 W. 22d St., N. Y.
Library of Humor, [illegible] S. L. [illegible], subn. 1888 or later. Pub. by Webster.

BOOKS WANTED.—Continued.

T. B. Ventres, 507 Fulton St., Brooklyn, N. Y.

Business Forms and Letters, in Spanish.

Vinson & Korner, 150 Euclid Ave., Cleveland, O.

Century Dictionary, 10 v. ed.

John D. Walker, De Graaf Bldg., Albany, N. Y.

Philistine, v. 1, nos. 5, 6; v. 2, no. 2. Will pay $1 each.
Epi Lark.
New York Times Review, all before 1898.

John Wanamaker, N. Y.

Cyclopedia of Best Thoughts of Chas. Dickens, ed. by De Fontaine. Pub. E. J. Hale.
Josephine, by Ober.

John Wanamaker, Phila., Pa.

Memorial Address on Garfield, by Blaine.

Geo. E. Warner, Minneapolis, Minn.

Cobb, N. B., Poetical Geography of N. C.
Reynolds, J. M., Poems.
Any county atlas.
Bowen, J. W. E., Congress on Africa.

Oscar Wegelin, Stamford, Conn.

Morris, The Earthly Paradise, pt. 3, cl. Bost., 1869.

H. Welter, 4 Rue Bernard-Palissy, Paris.

American Journal of Science, origin-1886.
Singuira, Hindu Logic.
Palfrey, Hist. of New England, 4 v.
Williams, Descript. Anatomy of Domest. Cat.
Low's English Catalogue, v. 1-5, and Index, v. 1-4.

Edgar A. Werner, 35 Chestnut St., Albany, N. Y.

N. Y. Bar Association Reports, 7, 9, 15, 16, 20.
Grant, Mrs., American Lady. Albany, 1876.
Simms, Trappers of New York.
3 copies Insurance Department. N. Y., 1882.

Woodward & Lothrop, Washington, D. C.

Early directories of Baltimore, Phila., and Wash.

BOOKS FOR SALE.

Dodge Stationery Co., 123 Grant Ave., San Francisco, Cal.

American Catalogue, 1884-1895, 4 v., bound in black cl. Complete, $35.00.

Samuel T. Hammersmark, Norwood Park, Chicago, Ill.

Set 10 v. of the Standard ed. of the Library of Historic Characters and Famous Events, ed. by A. R. Spofford, hf. mor. Price $12.50.

King Bros., 34th St., San Francisco, Cal.

Any volume of Bancroft's Histories of Pacific States, shp., $2.50; cl., $2 each.

Meehan, Expert Bookseller, 32 Gay St., Bath, Eng.

Review of Reviews, nos. 1 to 14 (Jan., 1890 to Feb., 1891), necessary nos. to complete the American Issue, *free* at 25 c. each only. Payment in American currency will do. Cash with order. A big stock of duplicates of these nos. In sets of 14 nos. only.

John Skinner, 44 N. Pearl St., Albany, N. Y.

New England Genealogical Register, from v. 1 to date.
New York State Forest, Fish and Game Reports, complete set, 5 v., beautiful colored plates.

HELP WANTED.

WANTED.—A man or two men to take charge of stationery and book department, in book and stationery store, in a large city; want men thoroughly equipped in each or both departments, more especially the literary. Address, giving experience, salary, reference, single or married, etc., BOOK DEPARTMENT, care of PUBLISHERS' WEEKLY.

SITUATIONS WANTED.

BOOKKEEPER, accountant and office manager. 20 years' experience, wholesale and manufacturing, desires position. Can adapt to any system or conditions. Excellent references. Salary no object so long as prospects are good. Address WILLSTAN, care of PUBLISHERS' WEEKLY.

BUSINESS FOR SALE.

FOR SALE.—A well-equipped and established bookshop, containing about 15,000 volumes of old, scarce, and standard books. Also stock of old magazines, prints, etc. Good catalogue trade. Situated in business center of Chicago. Rent reasonable. Unincumbered. On account of business interests outside of city, owner will sell cheap. Address BOOKSTORE, 43 E. Van Buren St., Chicago.

COPYRIGHT NOTICES.

LIBRARY OF CONGRESS,
OFFICE OF THE REGISTER OF COPYRIGHTS,
WASHINGTON, D. C.

Class A, XXc, No. 35053.—To wit: *Be it remembered*, That on the 10th day of June, 1902, Mattie G. Browne, of Boston, Mass., hath deposited in this office the title of a book, the title of which is in the following words, to wit: "Massachusetts Reports, 109. Cases argued and determined in the Supreme Judicial Court of Massachusetts, November, 1871-March, 1872. Albert G. Browne, Jr. Boston, Houghton, Mifflin & Company," the right whereof she claims as proprietor in conformity with the laws of the United States respecting copyrights.

(Signed) HERBERT PUTNAM, *Librarian of Congress*.
By THORVALD SOLBERG, *Register of Copyrights*.
In renewal for 14 years from June 12, 1902.

SPECIAL NOTICES.

Books for Summer Travellers.

D. APPLETON & COMPANY, New York.

APPLETONS' GUIDE BOOKS.

Appletons' General Guide to the United States and Canada. With numerous maps and illustrations. 12mo, flexible morocco, with tuck, $2.50. (Part I., separately, NEW ENGLAND AND MIDDLE STATES AND CANADA; cloth, 75 cents. Part II., SOUTHERN AND WESTERN STATES, cloth, 75 cents.)

Appletons' Guide-Book to Alaska. By Miss E. R. Scidmore. New edition, including an Account of the Klondike. With maps and illustrations. 12mo, flexible cloth, $1.00.

A Landmark History of New York. By Albert Ulmann. With many illustrations. 12mo, cloth, $1.50.

In this book the reader makes visits in sequence to the old Dutch Settlement, the early English colony, the city as it was before the Revolution, and so on down to the present time. Copies of rare prints and maps and many plates made from recent photographs illustrate the work.

Appletons' Dictionary of [Greater] New York and Vicinity. With maps of New York and vicinity. Square 12mo, paper, 25 cents net; postage, 6 cents additional.

Puerto Rico and Its Resources. A book for Travellers, Investors, and others, containing full accounts of Natural Features and Resources, Products, People, Opportunities for Business, etc. By Frederick A. Ober, author of "Camps in the Caribbees," "Crusoe's Island," etc. With maps and illustrations. 12mo, cloth, $1.50.

A. S. BARNES & CO., New York.

A World's Shrine. (Lake Como.) By Virginia W. Johnson. Illustrated. 12mo, cloth, $1.20 net. (new.)

A History of Art. For Tourists. By Wm. H. Goodyear. Fully illustrated. 8vo, cloth, $2.80 net.

Switzerland, Annals of. By Julia M. Colton. Illustrated. 12mo, cloth, $1.25.

The Rhine, Legends of. By H. A. Guerber. Illustrated. 12mo, cloth, gilt top, $1.50 net.

BRENTANO'S, New York.

My Ocean Trip. By E. S. Cadigan. Illustrated with signals and flags printed in colors, and with blank pages for memoranda. 12mo, cloth, $1.00.

A work appealing especially to tourists and travellers, arranged for the record to be kept of an Ocean Voyage. In addition there are many items of interest, such as a complete code of signals, series of games for shipboard, entertainments, pages for the autographs of fellow passengers.

POCKET DICTIONARIES. Printed at the press of Bernhard Tauchnitz of Leipzig, Germany, from the plates of the famous Tauchnitz series, and bound specially for Brentano's. Each, cloth, $1.00.

Dictionary of the English and German Languages. By J. E. Wessely.

Dictionary of the English and French Languages. By J. E. Wessely.

Dictionary of the English and Italian Languages. By J. E. Wessely.

Dictionary of the English and Spanish Languages. By J. E. Wessely and Girones.

HOUGHTON, MIFFLIN & CO., Boston.

Our National Parks. By John Muir. Illustrated. $1.75 net; postpaid, $1.87.

Footing it in Franconia. $1.10 net; postpaid, $1.19.

HOUGHTON, MIFFLIN & CO.—*Continued.*

Picturesque Alaska. By Abby J. Woodman. Illustrations and maps. 16mo, $1.00.

September Days on Nantucket. By William Root Bliss.

Cape Cod. By H. D. Thoreau. $1.50.

WILLIAM R. JENKINS, New York.

The Complete Pocket-Guide to Europe. Edited by E. C. and T. L. Stedman. One vol., full leather, $1.25. Revised yearly. The best of its kind.

LEMCKE & BUECHNER, New York.

Baedeker's Guides. German and French.

Monographs on Artists.

Dictionaries and Grammars for the study of Foreign Languages. *Send for lists.*

McCLURE, PHILLIPS & CO., New York.

The Hound of the Baskervilles. A Sherlock Holmes novel by A. Conan Doyle. Illustrated. $1.25.

The Blazed Trail. An American novel by Stewart Edward White. Illustrated. $1.50.

Red Saunders. A humorous account of his doings West and East. By Henry Wallace Phillips. Frontispiece. $1.25.

The Madness of Philip. Stories of child life for grown-ups by Josephine Dodge Daskam. Illustrated. $1.50.

A Prince of Good Fellows. Tales of James V., the "Merry Monarch of Scotland," by Robert Barr. Illustrated. $1.50.

The Making of a Statesman. A novelette, together with other stories of Georgia life, by Joel Chandler Harris. $1.25.

The Gentleman From Indiana. A romance by Booth Tarkington. $1.50.

An Island Cabin. A record of outdoor life by Arthur Henry. $1.50.

Forest Neighbors. Life stories of wild animals by W. D. Hulbert. $1.50 net; postpaid, $1.68.

Next to the Ground. A nature narrative by Martha McCulloch-Williams. $1.20 net; postpaid, $1.32.

JOHN P. MORTON & CO., Louisville, Ky.

Mammoth Cave of Kentucky (A Perfect Guide To). By Hovey & Call. Paper, 50 cents; cloth, $1.00.

E. STEIGER & CO., New York.

Baedeker's and Other Guide-Books, in German. The largest assortment of Books for the Study of Foreign Languages. *Send for catalogue.*

A. WESSELS COMPANY, 7-9 W. 18th St., N. Y.

Historical Guide-Books to Paris, Venice, Florence, Cities of Belgium, Cities of Northern Italy, the Umbrian Towns. One volume each. By Grant Allen. Pocket size, 250 pp., cloth, $1.25 net.

London and Londoners. By R. A. Pritchard. Pocket size, 400 pp., cloth, $1.25.

THE

WITH WHICH IS INCORPORATED

The American Literary Gazette and Publishers' Circular.

[ESTABLISHED 1852.]

PUBLICATION OFFICE, 298 BROADWAY, NEW YORK.

Entered at the Post-Office at New York, N. Y., as second-class matter.

VOL. LXII., No. 2. NEW YORK, July 12, 1902. WHOLE No. 1589

BOOKSELLERS!

DO you know how long your customers have waited for a new novel by AUGUSTA EVANS WILSON? It is just fifteen years since the issue of "**At the Mercy of Tiberius,**" her last great dramatic story, and thirty-six years since "**St. Elmo,**" which is now as popular as ever. Advance orders for her new novel,

A Speckled Bird,

amount to nearly **75,000** copies.

It is a novel which *stands in the highest rank of modern fiction.*

It will command the largest sale of any novel of the year.

We advise every dealer to order liberally, and not to be caught without the needed stock when we may be unable to supply all orders.

G. W. DILLINGHAM CO., Publishers, New York.

A LETTER

received by a prominent Boston Bookseller and Publisher

BOSTON, July 2, 1902

DEAR SIRS:

Kindly send me a copy of Bowen-Merrill's latest book. I am sure of a good story, for I've read about all of their recent publications, and have yet to find one that is not interesting.

Very truly yours,

——— ———

THE BEST SELLING BOOKS IN AMERICA

are the latest BOWEN-MERRILL creations viz:

THE MISSISSIPPI BUBBLE. By EMERSON HOUGH

HEARTS COURAGEOUS. By HALLIE ERMINIE RIVES

THE BOWEN-MERRILL COMPANY, PUBLISHERS

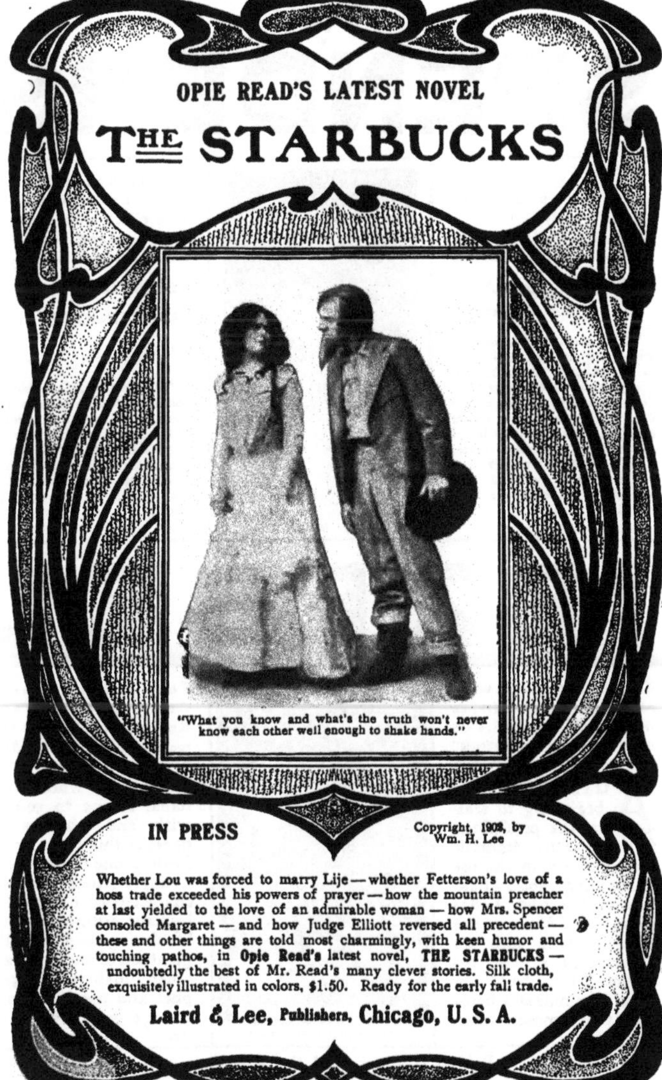
OPIE READ'S LATEST NOVEL
THE STARBUCKS
"What you know and what's the truth won't never know each other well enough to shake hands."
IN PRESS
Copyright, 1902, by Wm. H. Lee
Whether Lou was forced to marry Lije — whether Fetterson's love of a hoss trade exceeded his powers of prayer — how the mountain preacher at last yielded to the love of an admirable woman — how Mrs. Spencer consoled Margaret — and how Judge Elliott reversed all precedent — these and other things are told most charmingly, with keen humor and touching pathos, in Opie Read's latest novel, THE STARBUCKS — undoubtedly the best of Mr. Read's many clever stories. Silk cloth, exquisitely illustrated in colors, $1.50. Ready for the early fall trade.
Laird & Lee, Publishers, Chicago, U. S. A.

THE SPENDERS

A TALE OF THE THIRD GENERATION
By
HARRY LEON WILSON

BROOKLYN DAILY EAGLE says:

"It is racy, coruscating in wit, daring in love, and biting in its palpable caricature of many well-known persons in New York society; but it is so very much more than a clever society novel making the bid of audacity for ephemeral craze. This is the work not only of a bright society journalist and buoyant cynic, but of a born novelist."

AVICE MILBREY

Six Illustrations by O'NEILL LATHAM
Red silk cloth, gilt top, rough edges. Price, $1.50

LOUISVILLE COURIER-JOURNAL says:

"If there is such a thing as the American novel of a new method, this is one. Absolutely to be enjoyed is it from the first page to the last, founded on the elemental truth that 'the man is strongest who, Antaean-like, stands with his feet upon the earth.'"

JEZEBEL

A ROMANCE IN THE DAYS WHEN AHAB WAS KING OF ISRAEL
By LAFAYETTE McLAWS
Author of "When the Land was Young"

AUTHORS are just beginning to realize the possibilities for romantic, dramatic story-making in the use of the unexampled literature of the Old Testament. Miss McLaws has finely grasped such an opportunity in the romance "Jezebel," in which she makes a heroine of that famous woman

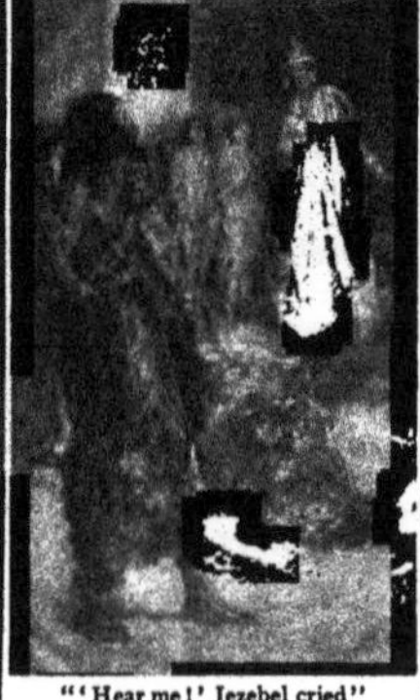

"'Hear me!' Jezebel cried"

Four Illustrations by CORWIN K. LINSON
Red silk cloth, gilt top, rough edges. Price, $1.50

and queen, whose very name is one to conjure with, and who, in the pages of this book, stands forth as one of the fascinatingly strong feminine characters of history, in a brilliant setting of court life during the days of the greatness of ancient Israel, when Elijah was its prophet and the worship of strange gods aroused his ire.

LOTHROP PUBLISHING COMPANY, BOSTON

The Publishers' Weekly.

JULY 12, 1902.

INDEX TO ADVERTISERS PAGE

NOTES IN SEASON.

McCLURE, PHILLIPS & Co. have in preparation a novel of the turf by W. A. Fraser, to be called "Thoroughbreds."

L. C. PAGE & Co. will publish next month, "Joe's Paradise," a sequel to "Beautiful Joe," by Marshall Saunders; also, "Old Love Stories Retold," by Richard Le Gallienne.

THE LOTHROP PUBLISHING COMPANY have just ready "Chanticleer," by Miss Violette Hall, a tale of married lovers who study birds and flowers. They have nearly ready "Stage Confidences," by Clara Morris, which will contain a large number of unpublished photographs in character.

D. APPLETON & Co. have in preparation a new series—the *Business Series*—the first volume of which will be "The Work of Wall Street," by Sereno S. Pratt. The book has twenty-three chapters, and deals with about everything in which the general reader may be supposed to have an interest, based on personal knowledge.

THE MACMILLAN COMPANY have just brought out in the *English Men of Letters*, a study of "William Hazlitt," by Augustine Birrell, who, while he brings out to the full the quality of his talent and personal charm, does not attempt to palliate the many things which made Hazlitt disagreeable and reprehensible. They will publish shortly, in the same series, Herbert Paul's monograph on "Matthew Arnold." Sir Alfred Lyall's "Tennyson" will be published in August, Frederic Harrison's "Ruskin," in September, and Gilbert Chesterton's "Browning," in October.

CHARLES SCRIBNER'S SONS have just ready a "Handbook of Best Readings," selected and edited by Professor S. H. Clark, of the University of Chicago. The book has grown slowly out of the editor's long and wide experience as a public reader. In his professional work he has, for several years, been testing hundreds of selections on the public platform and upon different audiences, with the ultimate preparation of this book in view. He has ascertained by the best possible test that every reading included will read. The volume covers a wide range of prose and poetry, dramatic, tragic, humorous, and pathetic. It will be a useful aid to the professional or amateur elocutionist and the general reader will find in it a wealth of good reading in attractive form. They have also just brought out a school edition of "Don Quixote," edited by Lucy Leffingwell Cable, daughter of George W. Cable, the novelist.

WILLIAM R. JENKINS has purchased from Dyrssen & Pfeiffer (F. W. Christern) the plates of and publishing rights in the standard educational works for teaching French and other languages, by Dr. L. Sauveur, and will hereafter supply the trade with these well-known text-books. They have just ready "Le Roi Apépi," by Victor Cherbuliez, in the *Romans Choisis* series, with preface and explanatory notes in English bv Professor Albert Schinz; also, "Les Malheurs de Sophie," by Mme. la Comtesse de Ségur, in the *Bibliothèque Choisie pour la Jeunesse*. In the department of veterinary literature they have just ready a hand book on "Tibio-peroneal Neurectcmy for the Relief of Spavin Lameness," by Prof. W. E. A. Wyman; the ninth edition of Dr. A. Liautard's work on "Animal Castration," revised and enlarged; the second edition of Professor K. Winslow's "Veterinary Materia Medica and Therapeutics"; also, "Operative Technique," the first volume of a new work on the practice of veterinary surgery, by Dr. John A. W. Dollar, which will be followed by a second volume on "General Surgery."

WEEKLY RECORD OF NEW PUBLICATIONS.

☞ Beginning with the issue of July 5, 1902, the titles of *net* books published under the rules of the American Publishers' Association are preceded by a double asterisk **, and the word net follows the price. The titles of *fiction* (not net) published under the rules are preceded by a dagger †. *Net* books not covered by the rules, whether published by members of the American Publishers' Association or not, are preceded by a single asterisk, and the word net follows the price. ☜

The abbreviations are usually self-explanatory. c. after the date indicates that the book is copyrighted; if the copyright date differs from the imprint date, the year of copyright is added. Books of foreign origin of which the edition (annotated, illustrated, etc.) is entered as copyright, are marked c. ed.; translations, c. tr.; n. p., in place of price, indicates that the publisher makes no price, either net or retail, and quotes prices to the trade only upon application.

A colon after initial designates the most usual given name, as: A: Augustus; B: Benjamin; C: Charles; D: David; E: Edward; F: Frederic; G: George; H: Henry; I: Isaac; J: John; L: Louis; N: Nicholas; P: Peter; R: Richard; S: Samuel; T: Thomas; W: William.

Sizes are designated as follows: F. (folio: over 30 centimeters high); Q. (4to: under 30 cm.); O. (8vo: 25 cm.); D. (12mo: 20 cm.); S. (16mo: 17½ cm.); T. (24mo: 15 cm.); Tt. (32mo: 12½ cm.); Fe. 48mo: 10 cm.). Sq., obl., nar., designate square, oblong, narrow books of these heights.

Adams, C: Francis. Shall Cromwell have a statue? Oration before the Phi Beta Kappa Society of the University of Chicago, Tuesday, June 17, 1902. Bost., C: E. Lauriat Co., 1902. 44 p. O. pap., 25 c.

***Alexander**, Hartley Burr. The problem of metaphysics and the meaning of metaphysical explanation: an essay in definitions. N. Y., Macmillan, 1902. 130 p. 8°, (Columbia University contributions to philosophy, psychology and education, v. 10, no. 1.) pap., 75 c. net.

Alger, Horatio, *jr.* Tom Turner's legacy and how he secured it; il. by J. Watson Davis. N. Y., A. L. Burt Co., 1902. c. '90 '02 316 p. 12°, (Alger ser.) cl., $1.

American digest; a complete digest of all reported American cases from the earliest times to 1896. Century ed. v. 33, Life estates-mantraps. St. Paul, West Pub. Co., 1902. c. 8 p. 2646 columns, shp., subs., $6.

Anderson, J: Jacob, *and* Flick, Alex. Clarence. A short history of the state of New York. N. Y., Maynard, Merrill & Co., [1901.] c. 8+407 p. il. maps, 12°, cl., $1.

Authorities, deductions and notes in commercial paper. Minneapolis, Minn., pr. by the University Press, 1902. c. 205 p., interleaved with ruled paper, O. shp., $2.25.

Babbitt, Frank Cole. A grammar of Attic and Ionic Greek. N. Y., Amer. Book Co., [1902.] [Jl1.] c. 448 p. D. cl., $1.50.

Bailey, Liberty Hyde. Nature portraits; studies with pen and camera of our wild birds, animals, fish and insects; text by the editor of "Country life in America," with fifteen large plates and many illustrations by the best nature photographers. N. Y., Doubleday, Page & Co., 1902. c. 8+40 p. il., 15 pl. (partly col.) in portfolio, 12 in. x 18 in. (Apply to pubs. for price.)

Bailey, Middlesex Alfred. High school algebra. N. Y., Amer. Book Co., [1902.] [Jl1.] c. 297 p. sq. S. hf. leath., 90 c.

Barnum, Francis. Grammatical fundamentals of the Innuit language as spoken by the Eskimo of the western coast of Alaska. Bost., Ginn, [1901.] c. 25+384 p. 8°, cl., $5.

Barret, Frederic Allen. Barret's medical hand book; what to do before the doctor comes: a book of practical information, giving full and simple instructions in case of sickness or accident. St. Louis, Mo., Barret Chemical Co., 1902. c. 66 p. por. 16°, cl., $1.

***Beach**, W: H. The First New York (Lincoln) cavalry from April 19, 1861, to July 7, 1865. Milwaukee, Wis., published by the Lincoln Cavalry Assoc., [for sale] by C. N. Caspar Co., 1902. 579 p. 8°, cl., $2.50 net.

Bible. The emphasized Bible: a new translation designed to set forth the exact meaning, the proper terminology and the graphic style of the sacred originals; arranged to show at a glance, narrative, speech, parallelism, and logical analysis; also to enable the student readily to distinguish the several divine names, and emphasized throughout after the idioms of the Hebrew and Greek tongues; with expository introd., select references and appendices of notes, by Jos. Bryant Rotherham. v. 1, Genesis-Ruth; v. 2, Samuel-Psalms. Wash., D. C., Woodward & Lothrop, 1902. 8°, cl., ea., $3.

This version has been adjusted in the Old Testament to the newly revised "Massoretico-critical" text (or assured emendations) of Dr. Ginsburg and in the New Testament to the critical text ("formed exclusively on documentary evidence") of Drs. Westcott and Hort.

†**Billy** Burgundy's letters. N. Y., J. F. Taylor & Co., 1902. [Je.] c. 5+74 p. il. S. cl., 75 c.

Humorous letters of phases of New York life.

****Birrell**, Augustine. William Hazlitt. N. Y., Macmillan, 1902. [Je24.] c. 8+244 p. 12°, (English men of letters.) cl., 75 c. net.

Bowhill, T: Manual of bacteriological technique and special bacteriology. 2d ed. N. Y., W: Wood & Co., 1902. 343 p. 8°, cl., $4.50.

Bowker, Alfred. The King Alfred millenary: a record of the proceedings of the national commemoration. N. Y., Macmillan, 1902. 16+212 p. il. 8°, cl., $3.

Brooks, E: The normal elementary algebra: part 1; containing the first principles of the science. Rev. ed. Phil.. Christopher Sower Co., [1901.] c. 12°, cl., 83 c.

Brown, W: Eugene. The divine key of the Revelation of Jesus Christ as given to John, the seer of Patmos. In 2 v. v. 2. Phil., Armstrong & Brown, 1902. c. il. map, diagr. 12°, cl., $1.50.

****Browne**, *Sir* T: Religio medici, Urn burial, Christian morals and other essays; ed. by C. J. Holmes: decorated by C. S. Ricketts. N. Y., J: Lane, 1902. 8°, (Vale Press ser.) cl., $12 net.

Browning, Rob. Sordello; ed. by H. Buxton Forman. N. Y., Macmillan, 1902. 209 p. 16°, (Temple classics.) cl., 50 c.; flex. leath., 75 c.

***Bunge,** G. Text-book of physiological and pathological chemistry. 2d English ed.; tr. from the 4th German ed., by Florence A. Starling and ed. by Ernest H. Starling, M.D. Phil., P. Blakiston's Son & Co., 1902. 470 p. 8°, cl., $3 net.

Bunzey, Rufus S. History of companies I and E, Sixth regt., Illinois volunteer infantry from Whiteside county; containing a detailed account of their experiences while serving as volunteers in the Porto Rican campaign during the Spanish-American war of 1898. Also a record of the two companies as state troops from the date of organization to April 30th, 1901. Morrison, Ill., Rufus Smith Bunzey, 1902. c. 364 p. por. il. 12°, cl., $2.

Carroll, C: Unpublished letters of Charles Carroll of Carrollton, and of his father, Charles Carroll of Doughoregan; comp. and ed., with a memoir, by T: Meagher Field. N. Y., United States Catholic Historical Society, 1902. c. 250 p. por., facsim. (The United States Catholic historical Society, Monograph ser., no. 1.) pap. (not for sale.)
The bulk of the correspondence contained in this volume is derived from the original letters of Charles Carroll of Carrollton, which belonged to his great-grandson, the late Charles Carroll Mactavish, Esq., of Baltimore, Md. They are published by permission of his widow, the present owner of the historic collection. The greater part, and the far more important of the documents are published now for the first time.

***Cathrein,** *Rev.* Victor. Socialism exposed and refuted: a chapter from the author's "Moral philosophy;" from the German by Rev. James Conway. 2d ed., with appendix containing the encyclicals of Pope Leo XIII. on the condition of labor and Christian democracy. N. Y., Benziger Brothers, 1902. c. 215 p. 12°, cl., $1.25 net.

Cherbuliez, C: V: Le Roi Apépi; with a preface and explanatory notes in English by Albert Schinz. N. Y., W: R. Jenkins, 1902. 12°, (Romans choisis, no. 25.) pap., 60 c.

Clark, W: L., *and* Marshall, W. L. Treatise on the law of private corporations. In 3 v. v. 3. St. Paul, Keefe-Davidson Law Book Co., 1901. c. 32+1717—3038 p. O. shp., $6.

***Clarke,** G: Kuhn. The descendants of Nathaniel Clarke and his wife Elizabeth Somerby of Newbury, Mass.: a history of ten generations, 1642-1902. Bost., privately printed, [T. R. Marvin & Son,] 1902. 468 p. il. por. 8°, buckram, $5 net. (130 copies.)

Collins, J: E. The truth about socialism; or. the socialization of industry the solution of the social question. Girard, Kan., J. A. Wayland, 1902. c. 6+111 p. 16°, pap., 25 c.

Cone, J: A. The man who pleases and the woman who fascinates: [short stories.] N. Y., F. T. Neely Co., [1901.] c. 131 p. 12°, cl., $1.

†**Cruger,** *Mrs.* Julia Storrow, [*Mrs.* Van Rensselaer Cruger; "Julien Gordon," *pseud.*] World's people. N. Y., J. F. Taylor & Co., 1902. [Je.] c. 3+352 p. D. cl., $1.50.
Thirteen short stores of the "world's people" entitled: Lady Star's apotheosis; Escapade; In palace gardens; Underbrush; At the villa; Moonlight; The black swan; Redemption; A lost line; Why I remained a bachelor; A Latin solution; A modern daughter; A modern mother.

Curle, J. H. The gold mines of the world. N. Y., Engineering and Mining Journal, 1902. 380 p. 4°, cl., $3.50.

Darby, Ja. Ezra, *D.D.* An analysis of the Acts and Epistles of the New Testament: a guide to the reading of these books, indicating the growth of Christianity and the development of doctrine from the historical point of view; with maps of Paul's missionary journeys. Waynesburg, Pa., Rev. Ja. Ezra Darby, 1902. c. 36 p. D. leatherette, 25 c.

Davey, J: The tree doctor: a book on tree culture; il. with photographs. Akron, O., published by the author, J: Davey, 1902. c. 87 p. O. cl., $1.

†**Davis,** R: Harding. Ranson's folly; il. by F: Remington, Walter Appleton Clark, and others. N. Y., Scribner, 1902. [Jl.] c. 8+345 p. D. cl., $1.50.
Contents: Ranson's folly; The bar sinister; A derelict; La lettre d'amour; In the fog. Five short stories.

***Dawes,** T. R. Bilingual teaching in Belgian schools; being the report on a visit to Belgian schools as Gilchrist travelling student presented to the court of the University of Wales. N. Y., Macmillan, 1902. 63 p. 12°, (Cambridge Univ. Press ser.) cl., 50 c. net.

De Clifford, Norman F: Egypt, the cradle of ancient masonry; comprising a history of Egypt, with a comprehensive and authentic account of the antiquity of masonry, resulting from many years of personal investigation and exhaustive research in India, Persia, Syria, and the valley of the Nile. Seattle, Wash., N. F: De Clifford, M.D., 1902. c. 644 p. pors. il. Q. cl., $10; russia, $12.

De Laurence, Lauron W: Practical lessons in hypnotism and magnetism, giving the only simple and practical course in hypnotism and vital magnetism which starts the student or practitioner out upon a plain, common sense basis; prepared especially for self-instruction. Chic., F: J. Drake & Co., [1902.] c. 261 p. por. pl. 12°, cl., $1; pap., 50 c.

***Del Mar,** Alex. History of money in Germany and other European states. N. Y., Cambridge Encyclopædia Co., 1902. c. 12°, cl., $2 net.

Dill, W: T. Changes and additions to Dill's constables' guide, made necessary by the act of 1901. Phil., T. & J. W. Johnson & Co., 1902. c. 32+20a, index, S. unbd. (Free to owners of the original edition.)

Dollar, J: A. W. Operative technique for veterinary surgeons. N. Y., W: R. Jenkins, 1902. 300 p. 8°, cl., $3.75.

Donnelly, Francis P. Imitation and analysis; English exercises based on Irving's sketch book, by Francis P. Donnelly. Bost., Allyn & Bacon, 1902. 194 p. S. cl., 60 c.

***Duggan**, Stephen Pierce Hayden. The eastern question: a study in diplomacy. N. Y., Macmillan, 1902. 152 p. 8°, (Columbia University studies in history, economics and public law, v. 14, no. 3.) pap., $1.50 net.

Emerson, Ralph Waldo. Nature: addresses and lectures. N. Y., A. L. Burt Co., 1902. 368 p. 12°, (Home lib.) cl., $1.

***Emerton**, Ja. H. The common spiders of the United States. Bost., Ginn, 1902. c. 18+225 p. il. sq. D. cl., $1.50 net.
Designed to make the reader acquainted with the common spiders most likely to be found over a large part of the United States as far south as Georgia and as far west as the Rocky Mountains.

****Ford**, Sheridan. The art of folly [poems.] Bost., Small, Maynard & Co., [1902.] c. 190 p. 8°, cl., $3 net.

***Fulda**, Ludwig. Unter vier Augen: lustspiel. [*Also*,] Der prozess: lustspiel v. Roderich Benedix; ed., with notes and vocabulary, by W: Addison Hervey. N. Y., H: Holt & Co., 1902. c. 8+135 p. S. cl., 35 c. net.

Haliburton, Marg. Winifred, *and* Norvell, F. T. Graded classics: Third reader. Richmond, Va., B. F. Johnson Pub. Co., [1902.] c. 224 p. il. sq. D. cl., 40 c.

Hatcher, W: E. The pastor and the Sunday-school: Sunday-school board seminary lecturers; course no. 1, delivered at Southern Baptist theological seminary, Louisville, Ky., Feb., 1902. Nashville, Tenn., Baptist Sunday-school board, Southern Baptist convention, [1902.] c. 180 p. por. il. 12°, cl., 75 c.

Heath, Herbert M. Comparative advantages of the corporation laws of all the states and territories. [Augusta, Me.,] Kennebec Journal Print, 1902. c. 80 p. O. pap., n. p.
This pamphlet, bound in cloth, sent free, on application, to counsel doing business with Heath and Andrews.

Henry, W. H. F. How to organize and conduct a meeting; especially arranged for the use of young men and women who may have to take an active part in organizing and successfully conducting a debating club, literary society, secret society, or who may be called upon to preside at a public meeting. 2d ed. N. Y., Hinds & Noble, [1902.] c. 5-130 p. 12°, cl., 75 c.

***Heredia**, José Maria de. Sonnets from the Trophies of José-Maria de Heredia, rendered into English by Edward Robeson Taylor. [3d ed.] San Francisco, P. Elder and Morgan Shepard, 1902. c. 15-176 p. 12°, bds., $1.25 net.

***Heusler**, F. The chemistry of the terpenes; authorized tr. by Frances J. Pond. Rev. enl. and corr. ed. Phil., P. Blakiston's Son & Co., 1902. 8°, cl., $4 net.

Hook, Alfred J. American negligence digest from the earliest time to 1902; a digest of all the decisions contained in the Am. negligence cases and the Am. negligence reports from the federal courts (supreme, circuit courts of appeals, circuit and district courts), the courts of last resort in the several states and territories, the intermediate courts, English cases and of all the notes and annots., 1902. N. Y., Remick, Schilling & Co., [1902.] c. 3+589 p. O. shp., $6.50.

Hooker, *Sir* Jos. Dalton. Nociones de botánica; Nueva ed. castellana, completamente reformada por el dr. Nicolás León. N. Y., Appleton, 1902. c. 136 p. il. 16°. (Nuevas cartillas cientificas.) cl., 40 c.

Horton, Walter F. Land buyer's, settler's and explorer's guide: a popular exposition of the theory and operation of homestead, timber and stone, and mineral laws; government, state, railroad and speculator's lands; manner of acquiring, terms of sale, location of, and how to reach them; surveying; land examining; timber estimating and scaling. Minneapolis, Minn., Press of Byron & Willard, [1902.] c. 136 p. maps, tab. 16°, pap., 25 c.

Howard, Eliza Berryman. Two waifs; or, the autobiography of Christmas and Ocean. N. Y., Abbey Press, [1902.] c. 121 p. D. cl., 50 c.
A story of two donkeys.

Hugo, Victor. John Brown: being a petition in behalf of the hero of Harper's Ferry; published in French in 1861. [Ridgewood, N. J.,] Alwil Shop, 1902. c. 35 p. facsim. sq. 12°, bds., $5, (150 copies;) hf. leath., $15, (15 copies.)

Hutchison, Jos. Chrisman. Lessons in physiology and hygiene. Second book for advanced grades. Rev. ed. N. Y., Maynard, Merrill & Co., 1902. c. '95. 371 p. il. col. pl. 12°, (Hutchison's physiological ser.) cl., 80 c.; bds., 40 c.

Illinois. A compilation of the laws of Illinois relating to township organization and management of county affairs with numerous forms, and notes of instruction, [etc.,] by Elijah M. Haines. 23d ed., rev., [etc.,] by Andre Matteson. Chic., Legal Adviser Pub. Co., [1902.] c. 24+33-622 p. O. shp., $3; hf. cl., $2.50.

Iowa. The citator: a compilation of citations of Iowa decisions, its constitution, code, session laws and court rules, etc. Lapeer, Mich., Reed Adams & Co., [1902.] c. 235 p. D. limp skiver, $3.
The citator is issued quarterly in Jan., Apr., July, and Oct. of each year.

***Jones**, Marcus Eugene. Utah. N. Y., Macmillan, 1902. c. 6+131 p. il. 12°, (Tarr and McMurry's geographies, supplementary volumes.) cl., 40 c. net.

Kaler, Ja. Otis, ["James Otis," *pseud.*] The cruise of the *Enterprise;* being a story of the struggle and defeat of the French privateering expeditions against the United States in 1779 [*i.e.* 1799;] il. by W: F.

Stecher. Bost., W. A. Wilde Co., [1902.] c. 359 p. il. 12°, cl., $1.50.

Kaler, Ja. Otis, ["James Otis," *pseud.*] The treasure of Cocos Island: a story of the Indian Ocean; il. by J. Watson Davis. N. Y., A. L. Burt Co., 1902. c. 352 p. 12°, (Alger ser.) cl., $1.

Keller, Sarah Kulp, ["*Mrs.* J. A. Keller."] The Pennsylvania German cook book. Rev. and enl.; containing 560 excellent recipes. Alliance, O., R. M. Scranton Print. Co., 1902. c. 71 p. O. pap., 50 c.

Kellogg, Elijah. A stout heart; or, the student from over the sea. Bost., Lee & Shepard, [1901.] c. 224 p. il. 12°, (The whispering pine ser.) cl., $1.25.

***Kenny**, Courtney Stanhope. Outlines of criminal law: based on lectures delivered in the University of Cambridge. N. Y., Macmillan, 1902. 22+528 p. 8°, (Cambridge Univ. Press ser.) cl., $2.50 net.

***Kersting**, Rudolph, *ed.* The white world; life and adventure within the Arctic circle portrayed by famous living explorers. N. Y., Lewis, Scribner & Co., 1902. 386 p. 12°, cl., $2 net.

***Kinosita**, Yetaro. The past and present of Japanese commerce. N. Y., Macmillan, 1902. 164 p. 8°, (Columbia University studies in history, economics, and public law, v. 16, no. 1.) pap., $1.50 net.

Kirk, May. The Baldwin primer. Tagalog ed. N. Y., Amer. Book Co., [1902.] [Jl1.] c. '99, 1902. 3-133 p. il. sq. D. cl., 35 c.

Knights of St. John. Souvenir of twenty-fourth annual convention Knights of St. John, Rochester, N. Y., June 23 to 27, 1902. Rochester, N. Y., E. Darrow & Co., 1902. 24 p. il. 8°, bds., 13 c.

Laird, Albert J. A complete manual of Laird's syllabic shorthand, an eclectic modernized system, stenographically adapted to the syllabic structure of English, securing extreme brevity through basic principles of contraction rather than by arbitrary abbreviation. Chic., H. Neil, [1902.] c. 4+312 p. il. 16°, cl., $2.

Lee, Margaret. Separation: [a novel.] N. Y., F. M. Buckles & Co., 1902. c. 271 p. D. cl., $1.25.

Liautard, A. Animal castration. 9th ed. rev. and enl. N. Y., W: R. Jenkins, 1902. il. 12°, cl., $2.

Lockwood, G: Browning. The New Harmony communities. Marion, Ind., The Chronicle Co., 1902. c. 6-281 p. il. pors. O. cl., $2.50.

New Harmony, originally named Harmonie, by the disciples of George Rapp, is fifty-one miles above the mouth of the Wabash River on the Indiana side. In 1815 eight hundred German peasants, who had protested, ten years previous to that date, against the religion of Germany, founded the Rappite colony, which paved the way for Robert Owens' social experiment in 1825. The present work is a study not only of these pioneer movements but it is likewise a history of the communistic life of New Harmony. Appendix.

Macdonald, G: A. How successful lawyers are educated: a work on the study of the law. N. Y., Temple Pub. Co., 1902. il. 8°, cl., $1.50.

McIntire, J: Jackson, ["Harvey Argyle," *pseud.*] As I saw it; stories illustrated. San Francisco, Cal., Home Pub. Co., [1902.] c. 263 p. il. facsim. D. cl., $1.25.

Contents: Incidents of the civil war in Missouri; The story of a blood-stained poem; A story of the mines; My first sweetheart and scenes of my childhood; The commercial traveler; A horse-race for a wife in the days of slavery.

***McMurry**, C: Alex., *ed.* Publications of the National Herbart Society. Chic., University of Chicago Press, 1902. 1040 p. 8°, cl., $5 net.

Marchmont, Arthur W. Miser Hoadley's secret: a detective story. N. Y., New Amsterdam Book Co., 1902. c. 5+305 p. il. D. cl., $1.25; pap., 50 c.

Marshall, T: W. Logarithmic tables of the measures of length, extending from 0 to 50 feet, at intervals of one-sixteenth of an inch. N. Y., D. Van Nostrand Co., 1902. 12°, cl., $2.

Martin, W: Elejius. Internal improvements in Alabama. Balt., Md., Johns Hopkins Press, 1902. c. 4-87 p. O. (Johns Hopkins Univ. studies in hist. and pol. science, 20th ser., no. 4.) pap., 30 c.

"This paper is an effort to trace the development of the public highways of Alabama and to point out their influence upon immigration and settlement. It indicates briefly what has been done within the state by the federal government in improving rivers and harbors and in aiding the construction of railroads; and discusses finally the policy of Alabama respecting public aid to such works."—*Preface.*

***Maynard**, *Mrs.* L. W. Birds of Washington and vicinity; including adjacent parts of Maryland and Virginia; with introd. by Florence Merriam Bailey. Wash., D. C., Woodward & Lothrop, 1902. c. '98, 1902. 3-210 p. D. cl., $1 net.

Meigs, H: B: Record of the descendants of Vincent Meigs, who came from Dorsetshire, England, to America about 1635. [Baltimore, Md., Henry B. Meigs, 1902.] c. 374 p. por. il. 8°, cl., $6; mor., $8.

Melvin, Ja. The journal of James Melvin, private soldier in Arnold's expedition against Quebec in 1775; with notes and introd. by Andrew A. Melvin. [Reprint.] Portland, Me., H. W. Bryant, 1902. 90 p. 12°, cl., $2. (250 copies.)

Meyer, J. G. A., *and* Peker, C: G. Easy lessons in mechanical drawing and machine designs. N. Y., Industrial Pub. Co., 1902. In 20 pts. subs., ea., 50 c.; or in 2 v., cl., v. 1, $6; v. 2, $4.

Morgan, D: B: Twentieth century horse book; method of handling and educating the horse; new and simple treatment of diseases by Morgan's twelve-remedy system; dentistry and castration; also a short treatise on cattle, swine, dogs and chickens, giving diseases and remedies. Fayetteville, Ark., D. B. Morgan, 1902. c. 121 p. il. por. 8°, pap., $1.50.

Musick, W: L. Combination shorthand dictionary and reader, adapted to the universal dictation course for Benn Pitman phonography. Springfield, Mo., W: L. Musick, [1902.] c. '97-'02. 46 p. 12°, cl., $1.50.

Neidlinger, Dan. H., *and* Bobbett, Walter. The squirrel and the crow. N. Y. and Chic., Rand, McNally & Co., 1902. c. 16°, hf., cl., 50 c.

****Nelson**, Aven. An analytical key to some of the common flowering plants of the Rocky mountain region. N. Y., Appleton, 1902. [Je.] c. 7+94 p. D. (Twentieth century text-books.) cl., 45 c. net.

****New England** History Teachers' Association; report to the New England History Teachers' Association, by a select committee, C: Downer Hazen, E. Gaylord Bourne, Sarah M. Dean and others. N. Y., Macmillan, 1902. [Je25.] c. 9+299 p. 12°, (Historical sources in schools ser.) cl., 60 c. net.

New York. The code of criminal procedure as amended, including 1893-1902, with notes of decisions, a table of sources, complete set of forms, and a full index. 21st rev. ed. Alb., Banks & Co., 1902. c. 25+551 p. D. canvas, $2.

New York. *Cts. of record.* Miscellaneous reports, other than the court of appeals and the appellate term of the supreme court, including the appellate term of the supreme court for the hearing of appeals from the city court of New York, for the boroughs of Manhattan and the Bronx, and the municipal courts of the city of New York for the boroughs of Manhattan and the Bronx; special terms and trial terms of the supreme court, city court of New York, the court of general sessions of the peace in and for the city and county of New York, county courts, and of the surrogates' courts, etc. Robert G. Scherer, rep. v. 36. Alb., Ja. B. Lyon, 1902. c. 41+929 p. O. shp., $2.

New York. Laws relating to general, religious and non-business corporations, taxations and exemption, Sunday observance, marriage and divorce, with revisers' notes, citations, decisions, civil and penal codes, cross-references, forms, etc., by Rob. C. Cumming and Frank B. Gilbert; comp. for the use of clergymen and trustees of religious corporations, by Rev. H. E. Waugh. 8th ed. Alb., Banks & Co., 1902. c. 10+321+140 p. O. canvas, $1.50; shp., $2.

New York. Membership and religious corporations, by Rob. C. Cumming and Frank B. Gilbert; rev. by Albert J. Danaher. Alb., Banks & Co., 1902. c. 13+511 p. O. buckram, $2.50; shp., $3.

Contains the new membership and church corporation laws, as revised by the statutory revision commission and enacted by the legislature of 1895, the former laws repealed thereby, and supplemental acts and code provisions relating to such corporations, thoroughly annot., with citations, [etc.], together with forms. [Also appended the tax law of 1896, amended to 1902, 138 p.]

New York. The penal code of the state; in force Dec. 1, 1882, as amended by laws of 1882-1902, with notes of decisions to date; a table of sources and a full index. 21st rev. ed. Alb., Banks & Co., 1902. c. 13+312 p. D. canvas, $2.

New York. Statutory revision of the laws affecting railroads, enacted 1892, and amended in 1893-1902, including the general railroad law, the general corporation law and stock corporation law, complete as amended, [etc.;] indexed; prepared by Andrew Hamilton. Alb., Banks & Co., 1902. c. 390 p. O. pap., $1.50; buckram, $2.

Tax law of 1896, amended to date by Andrew Hamilton, appended; title reads "Amended in 1893, '94, '95, '96, '97, '98, '99, 1900, 1901 and 1902."

Noble, Alfred, *and* Casgrain, W: T. Tables for obtaining horizontal distances and difference of level, from stadia readings; computed by Alfred Noble and Wm. T. Casgrain. N. Y., Engineering News Publishing Co., 1902. c. 48 p. diagrams, 12°, cl., $1.

North Carolina regimental histories: a complete history of the North Carolina troops, 1861-'65. ed. and written by participants in the war. Raleigh, N. C., M. O. Sherrell, State Librarian, 1902. 5 v. 12°, cl., $5; per v. $1.

Ohio. *Superior ct. of Cincinnati.* Reports of cases from 1854 to 1857; a reprint of v. 1 and 2, Handy's, and v. 1, Disney's reports, rev. and annot. to date. cited 12 dec. re. Norwalk, O., Laning Print. Co., [1902.] c. '02. 7+874 p. O. (O. decisions ser.) shp., $7.50.

†**Pain**, Barry. The one before; il. by Tom Browne. N. Y., Scribner, 1902. [Je.] c. 8+263 p. D. cl., $1.25.

The story of a magic ring having the property of endowing the actual wearer with the character of the last preceding wearer.

Parlin, Frank Edson. The Quincy word list, rev. and enl. with syllabication and primary accent; over seven thousand of the commonest English words carefully graded for elementary schools. [4th ed.] N. Y., Morse Co., 1902. c. 140 p. 12°, (New century ser.) cl., 24 c.

Pepper, G: Wharton, *and* Lewis, W. Draper. A digest of decisions and encyclopædia of Pennsylvania law, 1754-1898; being an encyclopædic summary, under appropriate titles, of the law of Pa.; supported by compendious statements of all the cases ever decided by courts of record in the commonwealth. v. 13, (Navigation and shipping to notaries public.) Phil., Rees Welsh & Co., 1902. c. 21401-23194 columns, O. buckram, $7.50.

Perley, Sidney. Practice in personal actions in the courts of Massachusetts. Bost., G: B. Reed, 1902. c. 49+728 p. O. shp., $6.50.

Peterkin, G: W: A history and record of the Protestant Episcopal church in the diocese of West Virginia, and, before the formation of the diocese in 1878, in the territory now known as the state of West Virginia. [Charleston, W. Va., The Tribune Co., printers,] 1902. c. 15+856-20 p. por. maps, 8°, cl., $2.50; hf. leath., $10.

Peterson, Reuben, *and* Lewis, H: F., *eds.* Obstetrics. Chic., Year Book publishers, 1902. 233 p. il. 12°, (Practical medicine ser. of year books, v. 5.) cl., $1.25.

Pictorial guide to Boston and the country around. Bost., The G. W. Armstrong Dining-Room & News Co., 1902. c. 203 p. il. map, S. pap., 25 c.

Plato. Euthyphro; with introd. and notes by W: Arthur Heidel. N. Y., Amer. Book Co., 1902. [Jl.] c. 115 p. D. (Greek ser. for colleges and schools.) cl., $1.

***Racine,** Jean Baptiste. Athalie: tragédie tirée de l' Ecriture Sainte; ed. with an introd. and notes, by F. C. de Sumichrast. N. Y., Macmillan, 1902. c. 52+198 p. 12°, (Macmillan's French classics.) cl., 60 c. net.

***Ramsay,** A. Maitland, *M.D.* Pharmacopœia of the Glasgow Royal Infirmary Ophthalmic Institution; based on the British Pharmacopœia of 1898; arr. with notes by A. Maitland Ramsay. N. Y., Macmillan, 1902. 8+104 p. 12°, cl., $1.25 net.

Rankin, Jeremiah Eames. Esther Burr's journal. 2d ed.; Jeremiah Eames Rankin, author and editor. Wash., D. C., Howard Univ. Print., [1902.] 4-100 p. por. sq. S. pap., 75 c.

A journal of a quiet, simple life beginning Feb. 13, 1741, at Esther's ninth birthday, and ending with her death in 1758. Esther Edwards Burr was the daughter of Jonathan Edwards, and the wife of President Burr of Princeton, and the mother of Aaron Burr.

Rénan, Ernest. The life of Jesus; with a biographical sketch by W: S. Hutchinson. N. Y., A. L. Burt Co., 1902. 393 p. 12°, (Home lib.) cl., $1.

†**Richards,** *Mrs.* Laura Eliz. Howe. Mrs. Tree. Handy volume ed. Bost., Dana Estes & Co., [1902.] [Je.] c. 6-282 p. il. S. cl., 75 c.

Mrs. Tree, an old lady of ninety, bright and witty, fond of gossip and full of reminiscences, is the chief character. She and her odd, elderly handmaiden are mixed up in all the various strange and romantic incidents of the story. The scene is the same New England village that formed a background to Geoffry Strong's story.

Rogers, Alice Ashmore. A waiting race: [a novel.] N. Y., Abbey Press, [1902.] c. 164 p. D. cl., 50 c.

Russell, W: Prescriptions and instructions for treating the diseases of the feet and legs of the horse; with a treatise on the teeth of the horse, by W. A. Lewis. Cin., Robert Clarke Co., 1902. c. 4-111 p. il. 8°, pap., $1.

***Seignobos,** C: History of the Roman people; translation ed. by W: Fairley. N. Y., H: Holt & Co., 1902. c. 528 p. il. D. cl., $1.25 net.

The aim of the American editor has been to fit the French work to American class-room use. Some slight additions have been made. The original work was carried only through the reign of Theodosius I. The period from that time to Charlemagne has been treated in four new chapters. Some omissions also have been made to bring the work into a certain compass. To each chapter has been appended a short list of sources in English. In appendix is a list of sources (5 p.) Index.

Sergeant, Adeline. The master of Beechwood: a novel. N. Y., A. L. Burt Co., [1902.] c. 434 p. 12°, (Manhattan lib. of new copyright fiction.) pap., 50 c.

Shakespeare, W: Works. Chiswick ed.; with introd. and notes by J: Dennis, and il. by Byam Shaw. v. 29. N. Y., Macmillan, 1902. 10+133 p. 16°, cl., 35 c.

Contents: All's well that ends well.

Sherman, G: Witherell *and* Andrew M., *eds.* Memorials of Lydia Whitney Sherman who passed away March 18, anno Domini, 1898. Lynbrook, N. J., George W. Sherman, 1902. c. 119 p. il. por. 12°, cl., $3.

Shofield, R. J., *comp.*, ["One of the craft," *pseud.*] Drummer's yarns and funny jokes; 9th crop original and selected American humor. N. Y., Excelsior Pub. Co., [1902.] c. 109 p. O. (Excelsior lib., no. 67.) pap., 25 c.

***Siborne,** W: The Waterloo campaign, 1815. 5th ed. N. Y., Dutton, 1902. 832 p. 8°, cl., $1.50 net.

Smith, Horace E. Studies in juridical law. Chic., T. H. Flood & Co., 1902. c. 26+359 p. O. shp., $3.50.

***Smith,** Sarah Saunders. The founders of the Massachusetts Bay Colony: a careful research of the earliest records of many of the foremost settlers of the New England Colony; compiled from the earliest church and state records. Wash., D. C., Woodward & Lothrop, 1902. il. 12°, cl., $5 net.

Spangenberg, Eugene. Spangenberg's practical arithmetic explained to the practical mechanic. St. Louis, G. A. Zeller, [1902.] c. 197 p. T. cl., 50 c.

***Tarr,** Ralph Stockman, *and* McMurry, Frank Morton. Complete geography. N. Y., Macmillan, 1902. c. 22+478+10 p. 12°, (Tarr and McMurry's geographies two book ser., Bk. 2.) hf. leath., $1 net.

***Tarver,** J. C. Tiberius the tyrant. N. Y., Dutton, 1902. 450 p. 8°, cl., $5 net.

Tennessee. *Supreme ct.* Reports of cases for the eastern, middle, and western divisions for 1886-1891; G. W. Pickle, rep. v. 1, 2, 3, 4, 5, 6. New ed., with annots., notes and references, by Rob. T. Shannon. [v. 85-90.] Louisville, Ky., Fetter Law Book Co., 1902. c. O. shp., ea., $3.

Texas. Notes on reports; a chronological ser. of annots. of the decisions of the supreme court and the various civil and criminal appellate courts of Texas, showing their present value as authority as disclosed by all the subsequent citations of those cases in later Texas cases, in the decision of sister states, and in all the federal reports, with parallel references to Am. decisions, Am. reports, Am. state reports, and the reporter system; by Walter Malins Rose. Book 2. San Francisco, Bancroft-Whitney Co., 1902. c. 6+1035 p. O. shp., $7.50.

Tileston, Merrill. Chiquita: an American novel; the romance of a Ute chief's daughter. Chic., Merrill Co., 1902. c. 2-306 p. D. cl., $1.50.

The story is of an Indian maiden who saves the life of a Boston boy from the renegade Utes who murdered Agent Meeker and ambushed Major Thornburg's command in 1879 on White River. By his aid "Chiquita" is educated in one of the great colleges on the Connecticut river, and devoted her life in studying the economics of civilization; finally throwing off her burdensome yoke, returning to the religion of her fathers.

***Ultzmann,** Rob. The neuroses of the genito-urinary system in the male with sterility and impotence. 2d ed., rev., with notes and a supplementary article on nervous impotence by the translator, Gardner W. Allen. Phil., F. A. Davis Co., 1902. c. 198 p. il. 12°, cl., $1 net.

Under sunny skies Bost., Ginn., 1902. c. 6+138 p. il. D. (Youth's companion ser., no. 3.) cl., 30 c.
Sketches from the writings of well-known authors descriptive of the outward aspects of life in Spain, Italy, Greece, Turkey, and Africa.

Van Arsdale, H: Twentieth century interest tables with up-to-date rates of two, two and one-half, three, three and one-half, four, four and one-half, five, five and one-half, six and seven per cent. per annum: showing the interest on any amount from $1 to $10,000 an accurate computation. Chic., Baker Vawter Co., 1902. c. 128 p. 8°, cl., $1.50.

Van Dyke, J: C: Italian painting. Bost. and N. Y., A. W. Elson & Co., 1902. c. 28 p. pl. 16°, bds., 50 c.
"This short monograph was written to accompany a series of fifty-nine large carbon photographs illustrating the progress of Italian painting, and is intended to be used as an introduction to the study of the pictures."—*Publishers' note.* Bibliography of Italian painting. (1 p.)

****Velvin,** Ellen. Rataplan, a rogue elephant, and other stories; il. by Gustave Verbeek. Phil., H: Altemus Co., [1902.] c. 13+15-328 p. col. pl. D. cl., $1.25 net.
Contents: Rataplan, rogue; Gean, the giraffe; Keesa, the kangaroo; Cara, the camel; Siccatee, the squirrel; Leo, the lion; Chaffer, the chamois; Jinks, the jackal; Pero, the porcupine; Tera, the tigress; Hippo, the hippopotamus; Cara, the ostrich; Seela, the seal; Brunie, the bear; Mona, the monkey; Bulon, the buffalo.

Wait, W: The law and practice in civil actions and proceedings in justices' courts, and in other courts not of record, and on appeals to the county courts of the state of N. Y., [etc.] In 3 v. v. 2. 7th ed., by Edwin Baylies. Alb., Matthew Bender, 1902. c. 60+959 p. O. shp., per v., $6.35; or per set, $19.

****Waller,** M. E. The little citizen; il. by H. G. Burgess. Bost., Lothrop Pub. Co., [1902.] [My.] c. 6-324 p. D. cl., $1 net.
The story of a little New York newsboy, who, crippled by a cable car, finds a home on a Vermont farm. An act of heroism wins for him the freedom of two villages and the title of the "little citizen."

Watrous, G: Ansel. First year English: syntax and composition. Bost., Sibley & Ducker, 1902. 349 p. 12°, cl., 75 c.

***Webb,** Jonathan E. A morphological study of the flower and embryo of spirala. Chic., University of Chicago Press, 1902. 10 p. 8°, (Contributions from the Hull botanical lib., no. 36.) pap., 25 c. net.

Whittelsey, C: Barney, *comp.* The Roosevelt genealogy, 1649-1902. Hartford, Ct., C. B. Whittelsey, 1902. c. 121 p. 12°, cl., $5.

Whitworth, Ernest. Practical cotton calculations; a treatise relating to cotton yarn, cloth structure, loom and miscellaneous cotton mill calculations. Fall River, Mass., R. Boardman, [1902.] c. 121 p. 16°, cl., $1.

***Winans,** G: M. Kansas. N. Y.. Macmillan, 1902. c. 9+47 p. il. 12°, (Tarr and McMurry's geographies supplementary volumes.) cl., 30 c. net.

Winslow, Kenelm, *M.D.* Veterinary materia medica and therapeutics. N. Y., W: R. Jenkins, 1902. 750 p. 8°, cl., $6.

Wyman, W. E. A. Tibio; peroneal neurectomy for the relief of spavin lameness. N. Y., W: R. Jenkins, 1902. 30 p. 8°, pap., 50 c.

Wyoming. *Supreme ct.* Reports from Dec. 19, 1899, to June 28, 1901; rep. by C: N. Potter. v. 9. Chic., Callaghan & Co., 1902. c. 14+574 p. O. shp., $5.

ORDER LIST.

ABBEY PRESS, 114 Fifth Ave., New York.

Howard, Two waifs 50
Rogers, A waiting race................ 50

REED ADAMS & Co., Lapeer, Mich.

Iowa, The citator $3.00

ALLYN & BACON, 172 Tremont St., Boston.

Donnelly, Imitation and analysis...... 60

H. ALTEMUS Co., 507-513 Cherry St., Philadelphia.

**Velvin, Rataplan ....net, 1.25

ALWIL SHOP, Ridgewood, N. J.

Hugo, John Brown. Limited ed.$5.00; 15.00

AMERICAN BOOK Co., 100 Washington Sq., E., New York.

Babbitt, Grammar of Attic and Ionic Greek.......... .... 1.50
Bailey, High school algebra.......... 90
Kirk, Baldwin primer, Tagalog ed... 35
Plato, Euthyphro........ .... 1.00

D. APPLETON & Co., 72 Fifth Ave., New York.

Hooker, Nociones de botanica, new Spanish ed.......... 40
**Nelson, Analytical key to some of the common flowering plants of the Rocky Mountains...... ....net, 45

G. W. ARMSTRONG DINING ROOM AND NEWS Co., Boston.

Pictorial guide to Boston............ 25

ARMSTRONG & BROWN, 411 Cherry St., Philadelphia.

Brown, Divine key of the Revelation of Jesus Christ, v. 2................. $1.50

BANCROFT-WHITNEY Co., 438 Montgomery St., San Francisco, Cal.

Texas, Notes on reports. (Rose).... 7.50

BANKS & Co.. Albany, N. Y.

New York, Code of criminal procedure, amended, 1893-1902. 21st rev. ed... 2.00

BANKS & Co.—*Continued.*

New York, Laws relating to general religious and non business corporations, etc. 8th ed............$1.50; $2.00

——, Membership and religious corporations. Rev. ed., 1902. (Danaher.) 3.00

——, Penal code amended, 1882-1902. 21st rev. ed...................... 2.00

——, Statutory revision of laws affecting railroads, 1892 amended 1893-1902. ....$1.50; 2.00

BAPTIST SUNDAY-SCHOOL BOARD, SOUTHERN BAPTIST CONVENTION, Nashville, Tenn.

Hatcher, The pastor and the Sunday-school.......... 75

BARRETT CHEMICAL Co., St. Louis, Mo.

Barrett, Medical handbook............ 1.00

MATTHEW BENDER, 511-513 Broadway, Albany.

Wait, Law and practice in civil actions. In 3 v. v. 2. 7th ed. per v., $6.35; per set (3 v.) 19.00

BENZIGER BROS., 36 Barclay St., New York.

*Cathrein, Socialism exposed and refuted ....net, 1.25

P. BLAKISTON'S SON & Co., 1012 Walnut St., Philadelphia.

*Bunge, Text-book of physiological chemistry, 2d English ed.........net, 3.00

*Heusler, Chemistry of the terpenes, net, 4.00

R. BOARDMAN, Fall River, Mass.

Whitworth, Practical cotton calculations........ .... 1.00

H. W. BRYANT, Portland, Me.

Melvin, Journal of James Melvin...... 2.00

F. M. BUCKLES & Co., 11 E. 16th St., New York.

Lee, Separation....... .... 1.25

RUFUS SMITH BUNZEY, Morrison, Ill.

Bunzey, History of companies I and E, Sixth Regiment, Illinois volunteer infantry 2.00

A. L. BURT Co., 52-58 Duane St., New York.

Alger, Tom Turner's legacy 1.00
Emerson, Nature 1.00
Kaler, Treasure of Cocos Island 1.00
Rénan, Life of Jesus 1.00
Sergeant, Master of Beechwood...... 50

PRESS OF BYRON & WILLARD, Minneapolis, Minn.

Horton, Land buyer's, settlers and explorer's guide.......... 25

CALLAGHAN & Co., 114 Monroe St., Chicago.

Wyoming, *Supreme ct.* Repts., v. 9 (Potter) 5.00

CAMBRIDGE ENCYCLOPAEDIA Co., P. O. Box 160, Madison Sq., New York.

*Del Mar, History of money in Germany and other European states.net, 2.00

C. N. CASPAR Co., 437 E. Water St., Milwaukee, Wis.

*Beach, First New York (Lincoln) Cavalry, 1861-1865..............net, $2.50

THE CHRONICLE Co., Marion, Ind.

Lockwood, The New Harmony community 2.50

ROBERT CLARKE Co., 31-35 E. 4th St., Cincinnati.

Russell, Prescriptions and instructions for treating the diseases of the feet and legs of the horse.............. 1.00

REV. JAMES EZRA DARBY, Waynesburg, Pa.

Darby, Analysis of the Acts and Epistles of the New Testament.,.... 25

E. DARROW & Co., Rochester, N. Y.

Knights of St. John souvenir........ 13

JOHN DAVEY, Akron, O.

Davey, The tree doctor............... 1.00

F. A. DAVIS' Co., 1914 Cherry St., Philadelphia.

*Ultzmann, Neuroses of the genito-urinary system ....net, 1.00

NORMAN F. DECLIFFORD, M.D., 1112 Fifth Ave., Seattle, Wash.

De Clifford, Egypt the cradle of ancient masonry....... ....$10; 12.00

DOUBLEDAY, PAGE & Co., 34 Union Sq. E., New York.

Bailey, Nature portraits (Apply to pubs. for price.)

F. J. DRAKE & Co., 352-356 Dearborn St., Chicago.

De Laurence, Practical lessons in hypnotism and magnetism 50; 1.00

E. P. DUTTON & Co., 31 W. 23d St., New York.

*Siborne, The Waterloo campaign, 5th ed....... ....net, 1.50

*Tarver, Tiberius the tyrant......net, 5.00

D. P. ELDER & MORGAN SHEPARD, 238 Post St., San Francisco, Cal.

*Heredia, Sonnets, 3d ed..........net, 1.25

A. W. ELSON & Co., Boston.

Van Dyke, Italian painting 50

ENGINEERING AND MINING JOURNAL, 253 Broadway, New York.

Curle, The gold mines of the world.... 3.50

ENGINEERING NEWS PUB. Co., 220 Broadway, New York.

Noble *and* Casgrain, Tables for obtaining horizontal distances............ 1.00

DANA ESTES & Co., 208-218 Summer St., Boston.

†Richards, Mrs. Tree................ 75

EXCELSIOR PUB. HOUSE, 8 Murray St., New York.

Schofield, Drummer's yarns, 9th crop.. 25

FETTER LAW BOOK CO., Louisville, Ky.

Tennessee, Supreme ct., Repts. 1886-91. v. 1-6. [85-90] Shannon........ea., $3.00

T. H. FLOOD & CO., 149 Monroe St., Chicago.

Smith, Studies in juridical law........ 3.50

GINN & CO., 29 Beacon St., Boston.

Barnum, Grammatical fundamentals of the Innuit language................. 5.00
*Emerton, Common spiders ......net, 1.50
Under sunny skies 30

HINDS & NOBLE, 31-35 W. 15th St., New York.

Henry, How to organize and conduct a meeting 75

HENRY HOLT & CO., 29 W. 23d St., New York.

*Fulda, Unter vier Augen........net, 35
*Seignobos, History of the Roman people........ ....net, 1.25

HOME PUB. CO., San Francisco, Cal.

McIntire, As I saw it................ 1.25

HOWARD UNIV. PRINT., Washington, D. C.

Rankin, Esther Burr's journal, 2d ed.. 75

INDUSTRIAL PUBLICATION CO., 16 Thomas St., New York.

Meyer, *and* Peker, Easy lessons in mechanical drawing. In 20 pts. subs. ea., 50 c.; or in 2 v., v. 1, $6; v. 2, 4.00

W. R. JENKINS, 851 Sixth Ave., New York.

Cherbuliez, Le Roi Apepi............ 60
Dollar, Operative technique for veterinary surgeons........ .... 3.75
Liautard, Animal castration, 9th rev. enl. ed.......... .... 2.00
Winslow, Veterinary materia medica.. 6.00
Wyman, Tibio........................ 50

JOHNS HOPKINS PRESS, Baltimore, Md.

Martin, Internal improvements in Alabama 30

B. F. JOHNSON PUB. CO., 901-905 E. Main St., Richmond, Va.

Haliburton *and* Norvell, Graded classics, Third reader................. 40

T. & J. W. JOHNSON & CO., 535 Chestnut St., Philadelphia.

Dill, Changes and additions to Dill's constables guide, (free to owners of original ed.)

KEEFE-DAVIDSON LAW BOOK CO., St. Paul, Minn.

Clark, *and* Marshall, On the law of private corporations 6.00

KENNEBEC JOURNAL PRINT., Augusta, Me.

Heath, Comparative advantages of the corporation laws of all the states and territories. n. p.

JOHN LANE, 67 Fifth Ave., New York.

**Browne, Religio medici........net, $12.00

LANNING PRINT CO., Norwalk, O.

Ohio, *Superior ct. of Cincinnati*, Repts., 1854-1857 reprint of v. 1 and 2 Handys and v. 1 Disney's repts. rev. and annot. to date................ 7.50

CHARLES E. LAURIAT CO., 301 Washington St., Boston.

Adams, Shall Cromwell have a statue. 25

LEE & SHEPARD, 202 Devonshire St., Boston.

Kellogg, A stout heart................ 1.25

LEGAL ADVISER PUB. CO., Chicago.

Illinois, Compilation of the laws of Illinois relating to township organization, etc....... ....$2.50; 3.00

LEWIS, SCRIBNER & CO., 125 E. 23d St., New York.

*Kersting. The white world......net, 2.00

LOTHROP PUB. CO., 530 Atlantic Ave., Boston.

**Waller, The little citizen........net, 1.00

JAMES B. LYON, 36 Beaver St., New York.

New York, *Cts. of record*, Miscellaneous repts. 1 v. 36 (Scherer)...... 2.00

MACMILLAN CO., 66 Fifth Ave., New York.

*Alexander, Problem of metaphysics, net, 75
**Birrell, William Hazlitt.........net, 75
Bowker, King Alfred millenary....... 3.00
Browning, Sordello............50 c.; 75
*Dawes, Bilingual teaching in Belgian schools....... ....net, 50
*Duggan, The eastern question...net, 1.50
*Jones, Utah.......... ....net, 40
*Kenny, Outlines of criminal law..net, 2.50
*Kinosita, Past and present of Japanese commerce...... ....net, 1.50
**New England History Teachers' Association Report...............net, 60
*Racine, Athalie....... ....net, 60
*Ramsay, Pharmacopœia of Glasgow Infirmary Ophthalmic Institution.net, 1.25
Shakespeare, Works, Chiswick ed., v 29....... 35
*Tarr *and* McMurry, Complete geography...... ....net, 1.00
*Winans, Kansas........ ....net, 30

T. R. MARVIN & SON, Boston.

*Clarke, Descendants of Nathaniel Clarke and his wife Elizabeth Somerby, 1642-1902........ ....net, 5.00

MAYNARD, MERRILL & CO., 29-33 E 19th St., New York.

Anderson *and* Flick, Short history of the state of New York............ 1.00
Hutchinson, Lessons in physiology and hygiene ....40 c.; 80

HENRY B. MEIGS, 205 Herald Building, Baltimore.

Meigs, Record of the descendants of Vincent Meigs...... ....$6; 8.00

MERRILL Co., 260 Kinzie St., Chicago.

Tileston, Chiquita $1.50

D. B. MORGAN, Fayetteville, Mo.

Morgan, Twentieth century horse book....... .... 1.50

MORSE Co., 96 Fifth Ave., New York.

Parlin, The Quincy word list, rev. and enl......... 24

W. L. MUSICK, Springfield, Mo.

Musick, Combination shorthand dictionary and reader................ 1.50

F. T. NEELY Co., 114 Fifth Ave., New York.

Cone, The man who pleases.......... 1.00

H. NEIL, Chicago, Ill.

Laird, Syllabic shorthand............. 2.00

NEW AMSTERDAM BOOK Co., 156 Fifth Ave., New York.

Marchmont, Miser Hoadley's secret, 50 c.; 1.25

RAND, MCNALLY & Co., 142 Fifth Ave., New York; 160-174 Adams St., Chicago.

Neidlinger, *and* Bobbett, The squirrel and the crow...................... 50

GEORGE B. REED, 4 Park St., Boston.

Perley, Practice in personal actions in the courts of Massachusetts........ 6.50

REMICK, SCHILLING & Co., 277 Broadway, New York.

Hook, American negligence digest, 1902 .... 6.50

R. M. SCRANTON PRINT. Co., Alliance, O.

Keller, Pennsylvania erman cook book, rev. enl. ed....G............ 50

CHARLES SCRIBNER'S SONS, 153-157 Fifth Ave., New York.

†Davis, Ranson's folly................ 1.50
†Pain, The one before................ 1.25

GEORGE W. SHERMAN, Lynbrook, N. Y.

Sherman, Memorials of Lydia Whitney Sherman 3.00

M. O. SHERRILL, Libn., State of North Carolina, Raleigh, N. C.

North Carolina regimental histories, 5 v................ ......$5; per v., 1.00

SIBLEY & DUCKER, 110 Boylston St., Boston.

Watrous, First year English.......... 75

SMALL, MAYNARD & Co., Pierce Bldg., Copley Sq., Boston.

**Ford, Art of folly..............net, 3.00

CHRISTOPHER SOWER Co., 614 Arch St., Philadelphia.

Brooks, Normal elementary algebra, pt. 1............ 83

J. F. TAYLOR Co., 5-7 E. 16th St., New York.

†Billy Burgundy's letters............. 75
†Cruger, World's people.............. 1.50

TEMPLE PUB. Co., 809 Eagle Ave., New York.

Macdonald, How successful lawyers are educated $1.50

THE TRIBUNE Co., Charleston, W. Va.

Peterkin, History and record of the Protestant Episcopal church in West Virginia....... ....$2.50; 10.00

UNITED STATES CATHOLIC HISTORICAL SOCIETY, New York

Carroll, Unpublished letters of Charles Carroll of Carrollton (not for sale.)

UNIVERSITY OF CHICAGO PRESS, Chicago.

*McMurry, Publications of the national Herbart Society. ....net, 5.00
*Webb, A morphological study of the flower and embryo of spirala....net, 25

UNIVERSITY PRESS, Minneapolis, Minn.

Authorities deductions and notes in commercial paper 2.25

D. VAN NOSTRAND Co., 23 Murray St., New York.

Marshall, Logarithmic tables.......... 2.00

BAKER VAWTER Co., Chicago.

Van Arsdale, Twentieth century interest tables. 1.25

C. B. WHITTELSEY, Hartford, Ct.

Whittelsey, The Roosevelt genealogy.. 5.00

WILLIAM WOOD & Co., 51 Fifth Ave., New York.

Bowhill, Bacteriological technique.... 4.50

WOODWARD & LOTHROP, 1013 F. St., Washington, D. C.

Bible, Emphasized Bible, new translation. v. 1 Genesis-Ruth; v. 2 Samuel-Psalms, 2 v..................ea., 3.00
*Maynard, Birds of Washington...net, 1.00
*Smith, Founders of the Massachusetts Bay Colony......... ....net, 5.00

J. A. WAYLAND, Girard, Kan.

Collins, The truth about socialism.... 25

REES WELSH & Co., 19 S. 19th St., Philadelphia.

Pepper, *and* Draper, Digest of decisions and encyclopædia of Pennsylvania law, 1754-1898. v. 13.............. 7.50

WEST PUB. Co., 52-58 W. 3d St., St. Paul.

American digest. v. 33. subs......... 6.00

W. A. WILDE Co., 110 Boylston St., Boston.

Kaler, Cruise of the *Enterprise*...... 1.50

YEAR BOOK PUBLISHERS, 40 Dearborn St., Chicago.

Peterson, *and* Lewis, Obstetrics....... 1.25

G. A. ZELLER, St. Louis. Mo.

Spangenberg, Practical arithmetic.... 50

The Publishers' Weekly.

FOUNDED BY F. LEYPOLDT.

JULY 12, 1902.

The editor does not hold himself responsible for the views expressed in contributed articles or communications

All matter, whether for the reading-matter columns or advertising pages, should reach this office not later than Wednesday noon, to insure insertion in the same week's issue.

Books for the "Weekly Record," as well as all information intended for that department, should reach this office by Tuesday morning of each week.

Publishers are requested to furnish title-page proofs and advance information of books forthcoming, both for entry in the lists and for descriptive mention. An early copy of each book published should be forwarded, as it is of the utmost importance that the entries of books be made as promptly and as perfectly as possible. In many cases booksellers depend on the PUBLISHERS' WEEKLY solely for their information. The Record of New Publications of the PUBLISHERS' WEEKLY is the material of the "American Catalogue" and so forms the basis of trade bibliography in the United States.

"I hold every man a debtor to his profession, from the which, as men do of course seek to receive countenance and profit, so ought they of duty to endeavor themselves by way of amends to be a help and an ornament thereunto."—LORD BACON.

THE WANE OF THE BOOK "BOOM."

THE impression that the "booming" of books is rapidly losing its force, if it has not already quite outlived itself, is steadily growing. The reported fate of one, if not two books, by authors whose former efforts were boosted into a sale of over 200,000 copies seems to confirm this impression. It is predicted by those who keep a close watch on the book market that while the quarter-of-a-million-in-a-year mark may be reached again, when it is reached it will mark an epoch in the annals of the booktrade, and not be an everyday event. "Booming," no doubt, was overdone and therefore was bound to react upon itself.

It is a question whether many will regret its passing, except the fortunate authors whose work was pushed, much of it, beyond its merits, and the newspaper press that reaped large tribute for its share in helping the "boom" along. From every other point of view the "booming" of books was demoralizing. The author was led to entertain an exaggerated opinion of the value of his work; the publisher was tempted to compete for the work of certain popular authors, in some cases, at rates that were hardly justified by the returns, especially when the expense of the heavy advertising necessary to nurse a "boom" was taken into consideration; the bookseller was at his wit's ends because what profit that accrued to him after competing with the price-cutter, was almost neutralized by the loss on the capital invested in the books that were not "boomed" and, hence, neglected by the majority of the public, which, for the time being, was so bewildered by the din of the "barkers" for this and that literary (?) curiosity, that they helplessly took the book most persistently pushed.

It was a great spree while it lasted, but it was inevitable that the imitation and multiplication of the devices that were employed to stimulate curiosity and to thrust new authors into general notice should lose their influence upon the reading public. If the tide now turns, as it promises to turn, in the direction of stimulating the sale of books generally, the booktrade will not regret to see the "boom" slide into oblivion.

BOOK LENDING, AS IT CONCERNS THE TRADE AND THE PUBLIC.

BY T. H. EWING.

A PROBLEM of rapidly growing seriousness is confronting the publishers and booksellers of America. The experience of several of the leading publishers, as well as of many of the retail dealers, during the past spring has indicated that this problem must be recognized and dealt with very soon, or publishers, dealers, and authors will suffer almost immeasurable loss.

The writer has talked with representatives of several prominent publishing houses, and with a number of the leading booksellers of New York, and they all say that the sale of books in the last few months has fallen very much below expectations, and much below the sale last year for the same period. Some of the books which were expected to have especially large popular sale have proven to be great disappointments in that respect.

One explanation is given everywhere for this state of affairs, and that is the sudden growth of a cheap and convenient system of book-lending which, as at present considered by thousands of people, makes the purchase of books unnecessary. Moreover, this popular system of book-lending is now only in the beginning of its proposed ascendency. The aim and the expectation of its promoters is that it shall spread over the entire country, and include among its constituents practically all of the book-reading public. The announced intention is to reach by its service at least half a million people. If the publishing and book-selling trade is already beginning to feel the injury which this system is working, what will the result be when the great aim of the managers of this circulating library is even in a considerable measure achieved?

A little consideration of the effect which this system is having and will have upon the trade, will startle those who have not thus far given it any special thought. An individual reader sees a certain book widely advertised and reviewed and hears it favorably spoken of by friends. He wonders if it is not just the book he would like to read, and he goes into a bookstore where the book is displayed and examines it. He decides that he would like to read the book, but instead of buying it, he leaves it on the counter, goes out of the store and around to some nickel-in-the-slot station, pays a few cents, and carries the book home with him. Then, after reading it, he returns it for a hundred and one other persons to borrow in the same way. A prominent bookseller on Fifth Avenue is complaining bitterly that his business is almost ruined by just such procedure.

Let us take another step. The managers of this circulating library purchase a book which is likely to be called for by its members. A new novel, we will say, which is not conspicuously before the public, and which the public at large knows very little of, will not be called for by this host of book borrowers, and consequently the buyer of the circulating library will not be at all likely to place an order for any considerable number of copies of this book. Before he can be induced to buy five hundred or a thousand copies, or even two hundred and fifty copies, he must be assured that it will be extensively advertised and in general demand. This means an expenditure of anywhere from three to ten thousand dollars for advertising by the publisher of the book. Then there will be a demand created which will justify the buyer afore mentioned in laying in a supply for the various library stations. As the number of stations increases, the number of copies he will need will increase; but five hundred copies, and even in the event of a greatly increased number of stations a thousand copies, will amply supply his requirements. In the meantime, the general sale of the book to the public at large is practically nil, because the readers will not spend $1.08 for a book which they can read for practically nothing. In other words, a sale of five hundred copies to the circulating library will take the place of a sale of ten to twenty thousand copies to the public at large, and the sale of one thousand copies to the circulating library may take the place of a sale of fifty thousand copies, more or less, to the public at large. But without the publicity given to the book, even this small sale to the circulating library would be unlikely.

Now, how long are the publishers going to be satisfied to spend several thousand dollars in advertising to create a demand for a book, which demand can be met by a sale of a thousand or less copies of the book to a circulating library?

I have put this feature of the situation somewhat strongly, but none too forcibly, if the experience of the spring and the present indications for the future are to be taken as a guide. The result is easy to see. The advertising expenditure being rendered unprofitable, will stop; the public sale of the book will stop; even the sale to the circulating library, which depends upon public demand, will stop; the publishers' profits will stop; the booksellers' profits will stop; the author's royalty will stop. Publishers, booksellers, authors, and even the circulating library itself will go to the everlasting bow-wows.

If anyone, putting the various causes and effects together, can figure out a different result, I should like to hear it. It is certainly time for publishers, booksellers and authors to interest themselves actively in this matter.

There is still another aspect of the case which concerns the public at large even more than it does the publishers and dealers. The indiscriminate interchange of books through the medium of local borrowing stations scattered over the country constitutes a danger which may well alarm anyone who gives it even the most casual consideration.

It is a well-known fact that no medium offers a more convenient or likely conveyance for the spreading of contagious disease germs than books. A statement appeared recently in the New York *Sun* to the effect that, "Experiments have shown that the bacillus of cholera will live in books 48 hours or more, that of diphtheria 28 days, that of tuberculosis 103 days. Small pox is eradicable only by the disinfecting of the most severe and careful kind." Thus a book may carry a supply of active disease germs enough to inoculate scores of persons in the course of its travels from hand to hand. The managers of public libraries have recognized this fact for a long time, and it has been brought to their attention daily by hundreds of people in every community who have discontinued drawing books, or have done so with hesitation, in spite of their better judgment, because of their fear that in taking them they run chances of bringing disease germs into their homes.

Prominent medical men have been studying this serious problem for a long time, and various plans have been tried experimentally for combating the danger which is so generally admitted. If such a danger exists in the case of an established institution, whose books are all cared for in one building, and taken from and returned to that building, and are under the constant care and supervision of the managers of the institution, how immeasurably more danger is there in the circulation of books through the medium of local exchange stations scattered over a wide territory, where a book may be taken from one station, and returned at another station, sometimes in entirely different localities.

Many books are read in sick rooms by persons who, because of their being shut in and laid aside from business or the ordinary occupations of life, have a period of enforced leisure, during which they are glad to beguile the weary hours with reading. According to the method of book borrowing and exchange referred to, there is absolutely no way of preventing these books from going directly from the sick room of one reader into the possession of another reader who is not sick, but who may quickly contract the disease brought to him within the covers of the book. The sickness of a person does not prevent him from borrowing as many books as he pleases, and is able to read. Any member of his family may return his book and get another in exchange for it, and in this way he may be persistently scattering germs of disease over a wide territory, entirely without the knowledge of the other book borrowers, or the managers of the system.

A gentleman told the writer recently that when his little girl was sick with scarlet fever her mother read story books to her while she lay in bed. Realizing the danger of allowing these books to be handled by others, every book was burned. This case is exceptional. Probably not one person in a thousand would take such precautions. It is manifestly unlikely where the books are borrowed from drop-a-nickel-in-the-slot machines, because the books do not belong to the readers and must be returned to go to others, disease germs and all. Moreover, travelers may carry books from one station to another, taking the disease germs from an infected district into a district where no disease exists. We hear continually of cases of contagious diseases breaking out in localities which seem not to have been subject to any infection, and we are often at a loss to account for the insidious spread of disease from family to family, and from locality to locality.

As the number of such local exchange stations and the number of users of them increase, the danger of spreading disease germs increases also, and careful people should avoid any participation in such work. The only safe way is for book lovers to purchase and keep their own books.

THE APPLETONS' NEW HOME.

D. Appleton & Co. expect to be settled in their new home, at 436 Fifth Avenue, New York, before the end of next week. Their new quarters are in a fine modern building of white stone, standing on the southwest corner of Thirty-ninth Street. Diagonally across the way is the Union League Club. One block to the north is the site of the dismantled old reservoir in Bryant Park, above which are rising the walls of the new Public Library building.

This change in the home office of D. Appleton & Co. makes interesting a reference to the various steps by which the house has advanced northward since it was founded by Daniel Appleton at No. 16 Exchange Place, seventy-seven years ago. Five years after the business was started Mr. Appleton removed to Clinton Hall, in Beekman Street, but in 1838 the rapid growth of his business compelled him to move again, and he went to No. 200 Broadway, which is between John and Fulton Streets. Here the business was conducted for a considerable time, and then the old Society Library Building, at Broadway and Leonard Street, was secured—a site now occupied by the great structure of the New York Life Insurance Company. Another removal was made about 1860 to Nos. 443 and 445 Broadway, and ten years later the office was transferred to Nos. 90-92-94 Grand Street. Two years afterward a change was made to Nos. 549 and 551 Broadway, which is near Spring Street. Here the firm remained for eight years, and then went to Nos. 1, 3 and 5 Bond Street, where it remained for fourteen. The removal next made was to No. 72 Fifth Avenue, a building from which the house now goes to the new one at the corner of Thirty-ninth Street.

In view of the removal of D. Appleton & Company, the accompanying facsimile of the title-page of "Crumbs from the Master's Table" will be interesting. This is the book with which the founder of the house began business as a publisher in 1831. How many copies were disposed of is no longer matter of record, but it is known that at least two editions were printed in the first year. It was also a sufficiently important enterprise to make stereotype plates. Very few copies of the little book are known to be in existence—not more than six. The copy of which the title-page is here shown is a perfect one, and has been bound in crushed blue levant by William Matthews, the book being provided also with a hinged morocco case.

CRUMBS

FROM

THE MASTER'S TABLE;

OR,

SELECT SENTENCES,

Doctrinal, Practical, and Experimental.

BY W. MASON

NEW-YORK:
D. APPLETON,
Clinton-Hall.
Stereotype Edition.
1831.

Mr. Derby, in his "Fifty Years among Authors, Books and Publishers," relates how, many years ago, when a copy of this book was wanted by the firm a paragraph was published as an advertisement stating that they would give in exchange the largest book published by the house. An old lady in Maryland saw the advertisement, and received for it a volume twenty times the size of "Crumbs." The next book published by Mr. Appleton was a volume similar in size to "Crumbs," and called "Gospel Seeds." In the following year he brought out "Refuge in Time of Plague and Pestilence" and "Thoughts in Affliction," the latter having a page about twice the size of "Crumbs." "Refuge in Time of Plague and Pestilence" appeared in the year when the Asiatic cholera spread terror throughout the whole country. It had an enormous sale, being often mistaken for a treatise on the cholera.

ROSTAND WILL NOT APPEAL.

The petition filed in Rostand's name on the 3d inst., in the U. S. Circuit Court at Chicago, by William Burry, attorney, by which leave was asked to reopen the Gross-Mansfield case, involving the authorship of "Cyrano de Bergerac," was withdrawn July 7, and thus the case, which has attracted so much attention in the local federal court for several years, was finally closed. Attorney Burry explained that he had withdrawn the petition under instructions from M. Rostand. He said the French playwright had no hand in the filing of the petition last week, but this was done at the request of a near relative through the French consul in Chicago.

E. & J. B. YOUNG & CO.'S CHRISTMAS NOVELTIES.

E. & J. B. Young & Co. have ready for the fall and holiday seasons a large line of novelties. Prominent among these are the "Autographic Christmas Cards," a series of artistic double and triplicate folding cards lithographed in color, gold and monotint, embossed and shaped, with landscapes, figure pieces, floral and combination designs. There are thirty-four numbers in boxes of eight and ten cards with envelopes. Of Castel Brothers' handsome cards and calendars they show an unusually large line of artistic beauty. Of the Christmas and New Year's cards they have twelve new numbers in boxes of from twenty to thirty assorted cards. Of the Castel calendars for 1903 they have twenty-seven new numbers, many of them in various designs. All these calendars are lithographed in full color and gold. The "turn-over" have shaped or embossed edges and are tied with silk ribbon. The "fancy shaped folding" are particularly artistic in design. In the line of Christmas booklets they have this year six new numbers to retail at five cents; six to retail at ten cents; four to retail at fifteen cents; two to retail at twenty cents; and five to retail at twenty-five cents. Each booklet contains a text and poetical quotation for every day in the month and is lithographed in full colors, the letter press in gold; the backs of the three higher priced booklets are tied with either silk ribbon or cord and tassells. They continue the sole agency in the United States of *The Empire* series of Christmas cards, dainty productions in photogravure, letter stamping, hand coloring, embracing upwards of 200 varieties, including religious cards and distinctively English, Scotch and Irish Christmas cards. They have made up a complete set of samples of this attractive series of cards which they will send to dealers prepaid at $12.50. They have also made extensive additions to their series of children's stationery, illustrated with charming decorative designs, reproduced in full color lithography from water-color drawings. Each box contains ten sheets of paper with the same number of envelopes to match.

THE SUIT AGAINST *THE THEATRE*.

Referring to the suit for an injunction brought by Manzi, Joyant & Co., of Paris, publishers of *Le Théatre* against Meyer Bros. & Co., publishers of *The Theatre*, Messrs. Meyer Bros. say: "It would be hard to conceive a more trivial and foundationless suit. Our counsel says that he has rarely seen such a flimsy action brought. Because Manzi, Joyant & Co. publish a magazine called *Le Théatre* in Paris, they seem to have an idea that no one else in the world may publish a magazine somewhat similar in character. As a matter of fact, the name *The Theatre*, and the character and purpose of the French magazine did not originate with Manzi, Joyant & Co. at all. There was a periodical entitled *The Theatre*, published regularly in London, as far back as 1877, and Clement Scott was one of its editors; and in New York, as we all know, there was also a monthly magazine entitled *The Theatre*, which appeared some years prior to 1898, when *Le Théatre* was first published in Paris. Both of these English periodicals contained pictures of the stage and portraits of actors and actresses. The idea of starting an American magazine dealing principally with American plays, illustrated with American portraits and containing original articles by American writers originated with Meyer Bros., who have duly protected themselves by copyright. The only reason for the present suit that we can see is, because we spell the word theater *Theatre*. Can anything be more ridiculous? The word "theatre" is a good English word, and is used in the majority of cases, the word "theater" being the exception both in the public prints and on buildings."

"As to the charge that we have wilfully represented our magazine *The Theatre* to be an American edition of the French *Le Théatre*, that is too absurd for any sane person to believe. As a matter of fact, it would hurt us considerably for people to think so, and we always impress upon everybody that our magazine is a distinctly original publication."

"MISSALE SPECIALE" AND "MISSALE ABBREVIATUM" ATTRIBUTED TO GUTENBERG'S PRESS.*

Since 1896 a controversy has been carried on, particularly in Germany, brought about by a "Missale Speciale," which a former owner, Otto Hupp, and the present owner, Ludwig Rosenthal, bookseller of Munich, claim to be one of the very earliest products of Gutenberg's press. The controversy raged strongest during 1898 and 1899, and was productive of quite a number of monographs and articles (Vide Publishers' Weekly, May 20, 1899, and March 31, 1900, for an examination and summary of this literature by the present writer). A new impetus has been given to the subject by the recent discovery of another and nearly identical "Missale speciale abbreviatum," in the Monastery of St. Paul in Lavantthale, Carinthia. They were both exhibited, side by side, at the Gutenberg Exhibition, held at Mentz in the summer of 1900. Dr. Adolf Schmidt, chief librarian of the Hofbibliothek of Darmstadt, informed me, in a letter written in July of that year, that the opponents of Hupp had been much strengthened in their adverse opinion of the "Missale speciale" by their comparison of both missals at this exhibition; among them were Dziatzko, Schwenke, Schorbach, Falk and Mademoiselle Pellechet. Prof. Dr. Velke, of the Gutenberg Museum of Mentz, wrote about the same time that "with the greatest probability Hupp's missal must be assigned to a late date, about 1470." With this view most of the best specialists agree. Yet, in spite of this fact, Rosenthal last year was asking 300,000 marks ($75,000) for this imperfect volume.

Hupp in his latest monograph contends that these early printed Missals stand isolated in

* Hupp (Otto.) Gutenbergs erste Drucke. Ein weiterer Beitrag zur Geschichte der ältesten Druckwerke. München-Regensburg: G. J. Manz, 1902. 4to, 98 p. il. pap., $6.

a class by themselves as well for their contents as for their typographical considerations. His nearly one hundred pages are tiresome reading, because he keeps repeating himself, as though he took especial delight in reiterating this or that point. He believes that the "Missale speciale" and "Missale abbreviatum" were both printed in the same office at the same time, and says there is evidence that certain leaves in both must have been pulled from the press in one and the same hour. Gutenberg he judges to have been the master-printer, but credits him with having printed comparatively few leaves himself—only the *Canon* and some of the rubricated or more difficult matter. The greater part of the Missals was printed by assistants, says Hupp, and he ascribes the beginning of the printing of them to the end of the year 1448, and their completion before the printing of the 42-line Bible.

The "Missale speciale" lacks sixteen leaves out of a total of 192 (there remain 345 *printed* pages). The "Missale abbreviatum" has no gaps, and consists of 72 leaves or 126 *printed* pages; the verso of the 69th leaf ends the printed text. Of these, 97 pages are exactly the same as in the "Missale speciale"; some others vary only in a minute degree; while 21 pages, although agreeing in contents, vary in composition (Satz). There is no colophon of any kind in the "Missale abbreviatum." From this Hupp concludes that the other Missal (imperfect at the end) also had none. But there is good reason to suppose that the "Missale speciale" originally had a colophon, dated sometime between 1470 and 1480.

In the "Missale abbreviatum" there is a full-page woodcut of the Crucifixion. It precedes the *Canon,* and has been colored and retouched by hand. Some experts in the art of early woodcuts place it as early as 1450; several say it may have been cut between 1450-1465, and not later than 1470. These are the admissions in Hupp's pamphlet, but they show a wide disagreement among the "doctors."

Finally there is little likelihood that Hupp's latest polemic will succeed in converting his opponents to his views, and we agree with Dr. Schmidt that "the two Missals will no doubt yet set many pens in motion."

VICTOR HUGO PALTSITS.

SIX BEST SELLING BOOKS, MAY-JUNE.

ACCORDING to *The Bookman* the six books that sold best in the order of demand from May 1 to June 1, are:

	POINTS.
1. Dorothy Vernon. Major. (*Macmillan.*)	263
2. The Mississippi Bubble. Hough. (*Bowen-Merrill Co.*)	196
3. The Hound of the Baskervilles. Doyle (*McClure, Phillips & Co.*)	180
4. The Lady Paramount. Harland. (*Lane.*)	111
5. Mrs. Wiggs of the Cabbage Patch. Hegan. (*Century Co.*)	110
6. The Leopard's Spots. Dixon. (*Doubleday, Page & Co.*)	80

NOTES ON AUTHORS.

JOHN MORLEY'S biography of Gladstone will not be ready for publication until next spring.

CONTRARY to the growing custom of illustrating popular novels, Augusta Evans Wilson's forthcoming book, "A Speckled Bird," will have no illustrations, the author objecting to artists' portrayal of her characters.

TOLSTOY is said to have entirely recovered, and is at work on his autobiography. The current issue of the *Open Court* contains an informing account of Tolstoy at close range by one who has been closely connected with him for many years.

OWING to a difference of opinion as to the exact date of birth, the centenary of the birth of Alexandre Dumas, the elder, will be celebrated on two separate days. One celebration was held in Paris on the 6th inst., the other will be held on July 26.

FREDERICK MACMONNIES, the sculptor, who is at present in New York City, is at work on a book on Paris, which he hopes will make life easier for the art student, especially the American student, for whom Europe and Paris are the final goal of ambition.

PAUL DU CHAILLU is writing a new book for young people about the wonders of the great African forest, to be entitled "King Mombo." The book will contain stories of many exciting experiences in hunting elephants, gorillas, crocodiles and other wild beasts.

CYRUS TOWNSEND BRADY has the distinction of being the most rapid worker among American writers—having written thirteen books and twenty-eight short stories in four years; and yet his working hours are from 9 A.M. to 3 P.M., six days a week, unless there's a football game somewhere around.

WALTER JERROLD, well known as the editor of Thackeray, Sterne, De Quincey and Emerson in the *Temple Classics,* is writing a volume on George Meredith for *The Writers of To-Day* series. Hamilton Fyfe, a prominent member of the staff of the London *Times,* is at work on a volume dealing with Arthur Pinero for the same series.

THOMAS HARDY, who on the 2d of June entered on his sixty-third year, began life as an architect, and practiced for five years with Sir A. Blomfield. His architectural knowledge is evidenced in more than one of his novels. He made his first notable success with "Far from the Madding Crowd" in 1874, but it is perhaps his later work—"Tess of the D'Urbervilles" and "Jude the Obscure" —that is considered most distinctive.

EDWARD F. JONES, of Binghamton, N. Y., former Lieutenant-Governor of New York, widely known as "Jones pays the freight," has just completed a novel entitled "Richard Baxter." For several years he has been nearly blind, being barely able to cross the street alone, but he has worked faithfully on his book, dictating to his stenographer. The scene of the novel is centred around Concord, N. H., and in many instances is said to recall "David Harum."

THE Duke d'Abruzzi's account of his Arctic expedition, in which he penetrated further north than Nansen, reaching latitude 86 degrees 33 minutes north, is completed, together with the translations of it made into the principal European languages. It will be simultaneously published in October in Italian, French, English, German, and the Scandinavian languages. Ulrico Hoepli, of Milan, Italy, who will publish the book in the original, is authorized to sell the copyright and make all the arrangements for an American edition.

DR. W. A. P. MARTIN will soon start for China to preside over the new University at Wu-Chang, negotiations having just been concluded by cable with Chang Chih Tung, the Viceroy of Hupeh and Hunan. Viceroy Chang, author of "China's Only Hope," is to-day the leader of the Reform Movement in China, and under him President Martin is to establish this center of education for the civil service of the Empire. Dr. Martin's two great books, "The Cycle of Cathay" and "The Lore of Cathay," have given him an international reputation.

THE COMTESSE DE ROCHAMBEAU, of the delegation of honor recently in this country, conferred upon Hallie Erminie Rives the honor of entertaining her *en famille*. She sent a special invitation to Miss Rives and received her in her own private suite at the Waldorf-Astoria. The story of Rochambeau's coming with his fleet to the aid of Washington and the part which French diplomacy and money played in the successful outcome of the American Revolution, forms the core and motive of Miss Rives's novel, "Hearts Courageous." The Comtesse carried with her a copy of the novel, autographed, for President Loubet, of France.

JOURNALISTIC NOTES.

Medical Book News is the title of a new bi-monthly publication devoted to the literature of medicine and the allied sciences published by P. Blakiston's Son & Co., Philadelphia. It will contain lists of new books, reviews taken from prominent periodicals, occasional criticisms, news items and advertisements. The first number is dated July 1.

The International Monthly will henceforth be issued every quarter from September on It will contain twice as many articles and be double the size of the monthly, and the type and margins will be enlarged proportionately. Two new departments will be added, one devoted to a criticism of the more important works of current literature, the other to the drama and fine arts. Frederick A. Richardson will continue as editor, and the political chronicle will be continued by Joseph B. Bishop. Among the contributors to *The International Quarterly* will be President Eliot of Harvard University, President Hadley of Yale, Capt. Alfred T. Mahan, Prof. Franklin H. Giddings of Columbia University, William Ostwald, Pasquale Villari, Ferdinand Brunetière, M. Coquelin, the French actor; John La Farge, Prof. Matthews of Columbia University, John W. Foster, Viscount de Vogüé, Andrew Lang, and the Right Hon. James Bryce.

OLD BOOK NOTES.

THE old book shops of Constantinople are interestingly described by Henry Otis Dwight in the June issue of *The Forum*.

AN EARLY POEM OF RUSKIN.—"A Cambridge bookseller, David Cadney, of 27 Regent Street, Cambridge," according to F. W. Bourdillon in the London *Athenæum*, "has discovered what appears pretty certainly to be the first published poem of Ruskin, in a volume dated 1834—that is, a year before the verses on Salzburg appeared in 'Friendship's Offering.' The full title of the book is 'The Bow in the Clouds, or, the Negro's Memorial, a Collection of Original Contributions in Prose and Verse, Illustrative of the Evils of Slavery, and Commemorative of its Abolition in the British Colonies.' It was published in London by Jackson & Walford. The editor's name is not given, but the preface is dated from Wincobank Hall (Yorkshire.) May 8, 1834; so it should be possible to discover it. How Ruskin became connected with the book is suggested by the fact that among the contributors is Thomas Pringle, to whom he had been introduced the year before (Collingwood, 'Biographical Data,' vol. i. p. 259 of 'Poems of John Ruskin.' 1891.) Ruskin's contribution, signed merely J. R., is entitled 'Repose for the Weary,' and consists of thirty-two lines of blank verse, beginning:

"'There is a spot within the Western isle
Where all is peace and freedom, and the Slave
In that small lone inclosure finds a home.'

"The seriousness and evident attempt at dignity of style, with a certain air of immaturity both of thought and expression, are very characteristic of Ruskin's early poetry, and, on both external and internal evidence, it seems probable that these lines are his."

In connection with the above item it may be remembered that Ruskin's earliest literary work came upon the market last year and was privately sold to Mr. Severn of Brantwood. This was "The Puppet Show, or, Amusing Characters for Children," an unpublished manuscript in printed characters on thirty leaves, with fifty-seven original drawings in color. It was written when Ruskin was nearly ten years of age.

THE Fountaine collection sold by Sotheby's, June 11-14, realized a total of £10,732. The highest price was paid by Quaritch for a fourteenth century manuscript of Gower's "Confessio Amantis." Two interesting books were secured for an American—report says for Marsden J. Perry, of Providence, R. I. The earliest of the two was "Polimanteia," 1595, by "W. C.," which contains the first-known printed reference to Shakespeare, a fine copy that fetched £131. The other was a fine copy of the first edition of "The Merry Devil of Edmonton," 1608, one of three known copies that sold for £300. Mr. Perry is also reported to have secured for £197 a copy of Shakespeare's "Henry the Fifth," 1617. The Fountaine library was chiefly collected by Sir Andrew Fountaine of Norfolk Hall, Norfolk, during the reigns of Queen Anne and King George I and II. The Perry library was recently removed to a historic old Colonial house in Providence, originally the Brown-Gammel mansion.

BUSINESS NOTES.

CINCINNATI, O.—J. R. Hawley, who has conducted a book, periodical and stationery store in Cincinnati for years, assigned on the 8th inst. The claims are mostly held by sporting goods dealers in New York and Chicago. Mr. Hawley recently removed to the Arcade, and the removal is said to have occasioned a pressure of creditors.

COLUMBIA, MO.—Sission & Vivion, booksellers, have made an assignment.

CRAWFORDSVILLE, IND.—Brower Brothers, booksellers, have filed a petition in bankruptcy.

DOVER, DEL.—The Investors' Development and Security Company, of New York, capital $2,500,000, was incorporated here on July 8. The company is to buy, sell and deal in patents, trademarks and copyrights. The corporators are W. J. Ball and Albert L. Conklin, Jr., of New York, and James Virdin, of Dover.

NASHVILLE, TENN.—Bigham and Smith were elected successors to Barbee & Smith at the General Conference at Dallas, Texas in May. The new agents took charge June 1. The business of this house will be conducted during the next four years under the name of Bigham & Smith, Agts.

NEW YORK CITY.—John R. Anderson has removed to 114 Fifth Avenue.

NEW YORK CITY.—Judge McCarthy of the City Court has appointed Eugene C. Gilroy receiver of the assets of the Columbia Publishing Company, of 141 East 25th Street, on the application of the Twelfth Ward Bank, which obtained two judgments against the company on July 1, 1901, for $2,041. The company was incorporated in August, 1894, under New Jersey laws, with a capital stock of $25,000, which was increased to $75,000 in November, 1897. It published *The Municipal and Railway Record.* Its plant, valued at $7,000, is in possession of another company at the same address under some kind of an agreement. The other assets consist of office furniture and shares of stock in several companies, value unknown.

LITERARY AND TRADE NOTES.

CHARLES F. DAVENPORT, formerly with the book department of Wanamaker's New York store, has taken charge of the book department of Gimbel Brothers, of Philadelphia.

W. H. WALKER, well known to the trade, has connected himself with the business of George D. Smith, dealer in rare books, at 50 New Street, New York.

WILLIAM DOXEY has, for the time being, at least, abandoned the Sign of the Lark, and may now be found in the fine book department of Dodd, Mead & Co.

THE action of the King's Reader of Plays in prohibiting the performance in London of Maeterlinck's new play, "Monna Vanna," has called forth a vigorous protest from a number of prominent English literary men.

ARCHIBALD CONSTABLE & CO., London, have in press a volume of "Reminiscences of *Punch* and its Contributors," by Arthur à Beckett, who has just retired from that journal after nearly thirty years' service.

CHARLES SCRIBNER'S SONS are fitting up an up-to-date printing plant in the Hallenbeck Building, at the corner of Pearl and Park Streets, New York, especially for the accommodation of *Scribner's Magazine.*

THE PHILOSOPHER PRESS, at the "Sign of the Green Pine Tree," Wausau, Wis., announces a reprint of William Wetmore Story's "A Roman Lawyer in Jerusalem," under the title of "In Defense of Judas."

S. F. HARRIMAN, Columbus, O., will publish in October the second volume of "The Hesperian Tree," to be edited also by the Hon. John James Piatt. The price of the first volume will be raised from $5 to $7.

WILLIAM GREEN whose name, through his father, has been connected with the printing business of New York for upwards of half a century, will, in connection with *Town Topics* and *Smart Set,* occupy an eleven-story building which is now being built at 310 to 324 West Thirty-eighth Street, New York.

HENRY ALTEMUS COMPANY will publish next month, "A Book of Toasts," by Mrs. Minna Thomas Antrim, ("Titan,") author of "Naked Truths and Veiled Allusions," now in its eighth edition; also, "For Prey and Spoils, or, the Boy Buccaneer," a story of pirates, by Frederick A. Ober.

R. H. RUSSELL has just brought out a pictorial souvenir of famous "Opera Singers," with biographic notices written by Gustav Kobbé, of Nordica, Calvé, Eames, the De Reszkes, Melba, Sembrich and Schuman-Heinck. There is also a chapter on "Opera Singers Off Duty," containing amusing anecdotes. The book is illustrated with half-tone reproductions of photographs of the different artists in costume and in ordinary dress.

THE CENTURY COMPANY will add to their popular *Thumb-Nail Series,* Tennyson's "In Memoriam," with an introduction by E. C. Stedman; Sheridan's "The Rivals," with an introduction by Joseph Jefferson; and "Thoughts of Pascal," newly translated from the French by Benjamin E. Smith. They will also publish John Bach McMaster's biography of Daniel Webster, some of which has already appeared in *The Century Magazine.*

DODD, MEAD & CO. have in preparation Sir Walter Besant's last novel, "No Other Way," which deals with the debtor side of English life many years ago, a glimpse of which is given in "The Vicar of Wakefield"; also, "A Song of a Single Note," by Amelia E. Barr, a story of New York in the early years of the Revolution while the British were in possession, which in point of time comes between the author's "The Bow of Orange Ribbon" and "Maid of Maiden Lane."

D. APPLETON & CO. have in press for early publication, "The Things That Are Cæsar's," a novel by Reginald Kauffman, author of "Jarvis of Harvard." They have in preparation for their *Library of Useful Stories*, "The Story of a Grain of Wheat"; for their *Story of the West* series, "The Story of the Trapper," by Miss A. C. Laut, author of the "Heralds of Empire"; also, "Up from Georgia," a new volume of poems by F. L. Stanton, author of "Up From the Soil."

Henry T. Coates & Co. will shortly issue in a limited edition, the four papers on "European Gardens," that appeared in *House and Garden*. The papers are "Italian Gardens," by Professor A. D. F. Hamlin, of Columbia University; "English Gardens," by R. Clipston Sturgis; "French Gardens," by John Galen Howard, and "Japanese Gardens," by K. Honda, of the Japanese Horticultural Society. The volume will have an attractive cover designed by Guernsey Moore.

Longmans, Green & Co. will publish immediately Section ix. of volume iii. of "The Norwegian North Pole Expedition, 1893-1896," which will treat of "the oceanography of the North Polar basin," and Section x. treating of hydrometer and the surface tension of liquids both by Fridtjof Nansen; also, the following from Edward Arnold's list: "Seven Roman Statesmen," a detailed study of the Gracchi, Cato, Marius, Sulla, Pompey and Cæsar, by Prof. Charles Oman of Oxford, and "A Primer of Physiology," by Leonard Hill.

The Frederick J. Quinby Company, Boston, propose to publish their translation of Paul de Kock's works, by Miss Mary Hanford Ford, in various luxurious styles, as for instance two separate sets of 100 volumes each for $200,000 and $150,000 respectively; an edition of twenty-five sets of fifty volumes at $5,000 the set; an edition of fifty sets of fifty volumes at $3,750 the set, and an edition of 100 sets of fifty volumes at $1,500 the set. Whether this is an advertising scheme to "boom" a long-delayed publication or a serious announcement we are unable to state.

Henry Holt & Co. will publish shortly a "History of the Roman People," by Professor Charles Seignobos, the translation of which is edited by Dr. William Fairley of the New York High Schools, who brings the history down from Theodosius I. to Charlemagne, and appends to each chapter a very full set of parallel readings and a list of sources available in English; the second volume of Professor J. P. Gordy's "Political Parties in the United States," continuing the history to 1829; a brief "Synopsis of Animal Classification," by Professor Wilder of Smith College; also, Malot's "Sans Famille," abridged by Hugo P. Thieme, of the University of Michigan.

John Lane will publish at once a volume entitled "With Napoleon at St. Helena," by Paul Frémeaux, from the memoirs of Dr. John Stokoe, naval surgeon, translated by Edith S. Stokoe. The purpose of the work appears to be to expose the methods Sir Hudson Lowe employed in treating his prisoner. Facsimiles of a number of letters, documents, etc., accompany the text. Mr. Lane will publish in this country an edition of Sir Thomas Browne's "Religio Medici," including also "Urn Burial," "Christian Morals" and other essays, edited by C. J. Holmes, and printed under the direction of C. S. Ricketts who has furnished the decorations.

M. O. Sherrill, State Librarian, Raleigh, N. C., is offering for sale a complete history of the North Carolina troops in the war of 1861-'65, in five large octavo volumes containing 4100 pages. The text was written and the work edited entirely by participants in the war, without charge for their services; and the engravings were furnished by friends. The State furinshed paper, printing and binding and owns the work, which it is selling at cost, viz., $1 a volume. There are over 1000 engravings of officers and private soldiers, including all of the 35 Generals from North Carolina; also, 13 full-page engravings of battles and 32 maps. The indexes embrace over 17,000 names. The edition is limited.

Little, Brown & Co. have postponed the publication of "The Queen of Quelparte," a romance of Korean politics, by Archer Butler Hulbert. They will publish in the fall, "The Speronare," by the elder Dumas, translated by Katherine Prescott Wormeley. In 1834 Dumas set forth upon a series of journeys which furnished material for some delightful sketches and stories. The pages of the guide-books of the present day are filled with the lore, historical and legendary, which Dumas gathered, and which is well known to travellers; but the great writer's tales and anecdotes are as fresh and entertaining as ever, and from this feast Miss Wormeley, the translator of Balzac, has gathered a series of volumes of which "The Speronare" will be the first. It describes a Mediterranean trip, taking the reader through Sicily.

Fleming H. Revell Company publish this week a new story by Mrs. Caroline Atwater Mason, entitled "The Little Green God," a pungent satire, witty, humorous and pathetic. It is a story of a returned missionary from India, who beholds to his amazement the heathenism of half-hearted Christianity. The book arouses sympathy for the horrified missionary, who ultimately turns his back on so-called Christian America, and seeks a refuge in heathen India. They will publish soon a popular handbook by the Rev. Dr. Howard A. Johnston, entitled "Bible Criticism and the Average Man," in which the subject is treated in plain words and in such a way as will tend to settle rather than disturb faith; also, "Soo Thah," the story of the Christianizing of the Karens of Burma, by Dr. Alonzo Bunker, who has been for thirty years a resident among the Karens.

The Macmillan Company will publish in August a work by George L. Bolen entitled "Plain Facts as to the Trusts and the Tariff, with chapters on the Railroad Problem and Municipal Monopolies;" also, "Development and Evolution," by Professor Baldwin, which forms the third volume in his series on genetic science of which the volumes on

"Mental Development" and "Social and Ethical Interpretations" are already so well known to educators as well as to psychologists and philosophers. They have also in preparation Sir Gilbert Parker's "History of Quebec," which will be brought out in two volumes, with upwards of a hundred illustrations from the author's large collection of old prints and new photographs of French Canada. They will publish in the fall Savage Landor's "Persia," which will have a large number of illustrations, mainly from the author's own photographs or drawings, and including artistic views. The ruined cities of Eastern Afghanistan and Baluchistan come within the range of this work, which will be expanded into two volumes.

G. P. PUTNAM'S SONS will publish shortly, "As Seen from the Ranks, a Boy in the Civil War," by Charles E. Benton, of the 150th N. Y. S. V., a private soldier's account of war, which is said to be of interest in studying the point of view of the private, and the problem of an army in the field as seen from the ranks. They also have in preparation "Old Paths and Legends of New England," by Katherine M. Abbott, with many illustrations of Massachusetts Bay, Old Colony, Rhode Island and Providence Plantations, and the Fresh river of the Connecticut valley; "The Hudson River from Ocean to Source—historical, legendary, picturesque," by Edgar Mayhew Bacon, with about one hundred illustrations; "Famous Families of New York," historic and biographic sketches of families which in successive generations have been identified with the development of the city by Margherita Arlina Hamm, in two volumes; "The Romance of the Colorado River," an account of the first discovery and of the explorations from 1540 to the present time, with particular reference to the two voyages of Powell through the line of the great canyons, by Frederick S. Dellenbaugh, a member of the U. S. Colorado River Expedition of 1871 and 1872, with an introduction by J. W. Powell, fully illustrated; "A Political History of Slavery," from the earliest agitations in the 18th century to the close of the Reconstruction period in America, by William Henry Smith, with an introduction by Whitelaw Reid; also, "Rhode Island; its Making and its Meaning," a survey of the annals of the Commonwealth from its settlement to the death of Roger Williams, 1636-1683, by Irving Berdine Richman, with an introduction by James Bryce. They have just ready in the *Story of the Nations* series: "Medieval Rome, from Hildebrand to Clement VIII., 1073-1600," by William Miller, and "Wales," by Owen M. Edwards.

OBITUARY NOTE.

HERVÉ AUGUSTE ETIENNE ALBANS FAYE, the celebrated French astronomer, died in Paris, July 4. He was the oldest member of the French Academy of Sciences, having been born at St. Benoit du Sault, October 5, 1814. In 1843 he discovered a new comet which bears his name. He wrote a number of astronomical works and translated a portion of Humboldt's "Cosmos."

BOOKS WANTED.

☞ In answering, please state edition, condition, and price, including postage or express charges.

Houses that are willing to deal exclusively on a cash-on-delivery basis will find it to their advantage to put after their firm-name the word [Cash].

☞ Write your wants plainly and on one side of the sheet only. Illegibly-written "wants" will be considered as not having been received. The "Publishers' Weekly" does not hold itself responsible for errors.

It should be understood that the appearance of advertisements in this column, or elsewhere in the "Publishers' Weekly" does not furnish a guarantee of credit. While it is endeavored to safeguard these columns by withdrawing the privilege of their use from advertisers who are not "good pay," booksellers should take the usual precaution, as to advertisers not known to them, that they would take in making sales to any unknown parties.

Arthur M. Allen, 508 Fulton St., Troy, N. Y.

Autobiography of James Nasmyth.
Voltaire, Philosophical Dictionary, in French.
Grove, Dictionary of Music, v. 4.

Almy, Bigelow & Washburn, Salem, Mass.

Any books on Illinois, historical, biographical, political, descriptive, or legal.
Any books on Indians of Illinois.
Grand Period of Growth in a Fruit of Cucurbita Pepo Determined by Weight, by Anderson.
Deviation in Development Due to the Use of Unripe Seeds, by J. C. Arthur.
Vegetable Cell Structure, etc., by Osburn.
New Onion Culture, by Greiner.
Classification of the Coleoptera of North America.
The Synopsis, Catalogue and Bibliography of the Neuropteroid Insects of Temperate North America, by Banks.
Anything on the science or art of library work, indexing, bookselling or bibliographing.

Abe C. Anderson, Henry, Bannock Co., Idaho.

Mormonism, the Bible and Polygamy, a discussion between Orson Pratt and Rev. Dr. J. P. Newman in S. L. C. U., any ed.
In the Toils, by Cornelia Paddock.
Life in Utah, by J. H. Beadle. 1870.

Antiquarian Book Store, Omaha, Neb.

Valentine Vox.
Hill, D. J., Genetic Philosophy.
Concordance to Browning.
Allibone's Dict. of Authors.
Hodges, Archibald, Popular Lectures.

The Baker & Taylor Co., 33 E. 17th St., N. Y.

Don Orsino, tan cl. ed. $1.00.

H. E. Barker, 419 Adams St., Springfield, Ill.

Herndon, Life of Lincoln, 3 v.
Boyd, Lincoln Bibliography.
Abbott, A. A., Life of Lincoln.
Send list of any Lincolniana with lowest cash price.

N. J. Bartlett & Co., 28 Cornhill, Boston, Mass.

Harvardiana, v. 3, 4, or any odd nos. of these vols.
Hutchinson, Massachusetts Bay.
Sargent, Andre.

BOOKS WANTED.—Continued.

Bigham & Smith, Agts., Nashville, Tenn.

The Union Pulpit.

Book Exchange, Toledo, O.

Copeland & Day's Christmas Booklet. 1894.
Gentle Art of Making Enemies.
Lehmann, In a Persian Garden.
Earthly Paradise, v. 2, 3. Boston, 1868.

Brentano's, 1015 Pennsylvania Ave., Washington, D. C.

Dr. Newton, Modern Bethesda.
Ida May (novel.)
Ridgway, Nomenclature of Colors.
Hearn, Chinese Ghosts.
Oldroyd, Lincoln's Campaign.
Macaulay's Essays, 1 v.

Bryant & Douglas Book and Stationery Co., 1002 Walnut St., Kansas City, Mo.

Redwood, Petroleum.
Sandys and Foster, The Violin.

Buffalo Book Exchange, 50 Seneca St., Buffalo, N. Y.

The Heathen Chinee, Plain Language from Truthful James, by Bret Harte. Illus. in card form, 9 or 10 cards, with poetry.

Burgersdijk & Niermans, Leyde, Holland.

American Journal of Science, 1818-73.

The Burrows Bros. Co., Cleveland, O.

Flaws, by a Lawyer.
Life and Speeches of H. W. Grady.
DeVere, Essays Literary and Ethical.
Schreiber, English Fans.
Loudon, Indian Narratives. 1808.
Ebers, Desert of Exodus.
Ebers, Through Goshen.
Ebers, Life of Fenelon.
Wilson and Bonaparte, Ornithology, original ed.
James, John Jones' Tales.

C. N. Caspar Co., 437 E. Water St., Milwaukee, Wis.

British and American English Grammars, before 1850.
Burton, Anatomy of Melancholy.
2 copies The Hollow Globe.

The Central Printing and Pub. House, 329 Market St., Harrisburg, Pa.

Geo. and Saul Duffield's English Hymns, Authors and History. Pub. by Funk & Wagnalls.

James J. Chapman, Washington, D. C. [*Cash.*]

Wet Days at Edgewood.

Chapman's Book Store, Montreal, Can. [*Cash.*]

Thoughts of a Soul, by J. Reid.

The A. H. Clark Co., Garfield Bldg., Cleveland, O.

Charlevoix's New France, ed. Shea, 6 v.
Club of Odd Volumes. Cat. Loan Exhibition Book Plates, 1898.
Hall Family Genealogy.
Memorial of the Morses. Boston, 1850.
Underwood Family Genealogy.
Whittlesey, C., War Memoranda.
Wright Family Genealogy.
Brackenridge, Voyage up the Missouri.

W. B. Clarke Co., Park and Tremont Sts., Boston, Mass.

History of the Art of Stenography, Upham.
Statesman's Year Book, 1901 (only in perfect condition.

Henry T. Coates & Co., Phila., Pa.

Jal, A., Dictionnaire Critique de Biographie et d'Histoire.
Lord Houghton, Poetical Works, 2 v. Murray.
Curzon, Persia, 2 v.
Bird, Nick of the Woods.

Frank W. Coburn, 47 Cornhill, Boston, Mass.

Vermont County Gazetteers, by Childs. Syracuse, N. Y.
Butler's Kentucky, imperfect copy.
Hudson's History of Lexington.

Irving S. Colwell, Auburn, N. Y.

Stoddard's Travel Lectures, 11 v.
Dict. Shakespeare Quotations, Claxton.
Everybody's Magazine, July, Aug., 1901.
Eugene Field's Works, Sabine ed.

J. H. Cosgrove, care of Doubleday, Page & Co., 33 Union Sq., N. Y.

The Life and Inventions of Thos. A. Edison, by W. K. L. Dickson and Antonio Dickson, copyright 1892, '93, '94. Pub. by T. Y. Crowell & Co.

Cunningham, Curtiss & Welch, 319 Sansome St., San Francisco, Cal.

Aubrey de Vere's Essays, Literary and Historical. Macmillan.

Cushing & Co., 34 W. Baltimore St., Baltimore, Md.

Hawes, S., Pastime of Pleasure.
Niles' Register, v. 50 to 65.
Palmer, Folk Songs.

Damrell & Upham, 283 Washington St., Boston, Mass.

Records of Old Town of Derby.

Davis' Book Store, 35 W. 42d St., N. Y.

Sphinx, *Ephemeris*, or any other astrological magazines.

F. M. DeWitt, 318 Post St., San Francisco, Cal.

Castelar, Old Rome and New Italy.
A Woman's Experience in Europe.
Thompson, Founding the Missions.

DeWolfe, Fiske & Co., 361 Washington St., Boston, Mass.

Ante-Nicene Fathers, v. 24, cl.
An Essay on Systematic Training of the Body, by C. H. Schaible. Trubner & Co.

Frederick Diehl, Louisville, Ky.

Tiele, History of the Egyptian Religion.
Upham, Salem Witchcraft in Outline.
James, Study of Primitive Christianity.
Supernatural Religion.
Mensinga, Was Christ a God?
Bettany, World's Religions.

Dodd, Mead & Co., 372 Fifth Ave., N. Y.

Weston, Historic Doubts as to the Execution of Marshal Ney. Whittaker.
Prime, Along New England Roads and Among Northern Hills.

The H. & W. B. Drew Co., Jacksonville, Fla.

System of Physical Training, by Sandow. Continental Pub. Co. ed.

E. P. Dutton & Co., 31 W. 23d St., N. Y.

Romance of Spain, by Chas. W. Wood.
Social and Domestic Religion, 2 v.
Ingram, Happiness in the Spiritual Life.
Fear-Nots of the Bible.
Cradle to School, by Bertha Meyer.
Little Grandpa, by M. A. C.

James R. Ewing, 169 4th St., Portland, Ore.

Simms, Poems.
From Eden to Eden.

Harry Falkenau, 167 Madison St., Chicago, Ill.

Catalogues of books on science, nat. history, etc.
Reconstruction, Gage.
Stevens, History of Georgia, v. 2.
Life and Speeches of H. Clay, v. 2.
Helps, Spanish Conquest in Am., v. 2.

S. B. Fisher, 5 E. Court St., Springfield, Mass.

Scribner, Index to Britannica, 9th ed.
Madam Guyon, v. 2, black cl. Harper, 1847.
Hunt, Talk on Art, pap. H., M. & Co.
La Barre, Pictorial History Civil War, v. 2.

W. R. Funk, Agt., Dayton, O.

Ridpath, History of the World, complete, cl., leath., or hf. mor.
Profit Sharing, by Taylor.

Funk & Wagnalls Co., 30 Lafayette Pl., N. Y.

Paper-Money Inflation in France, by Andrew D. White.
Mastery of Memory, by J. P. Downs.
Eye and Ear Memory.

Edwin S. Gorham, 4th Ave. and 22d St., N. Y.

Coleridge, Biographia Literaria, second-hand.
Peabody, Christian Belief.
Lever, Works, second-hand.
Scudamore, Notitia Eucharistica, 2d ed.
Bruce, Kingdom of God, and other works, second-hand.

BOOKS WANTED.—Continued.

L. Hammel & Co., Mobile, Ala.

Two Women and a Fool.
Told by Two.

W. S. Houghton, Lynn, Mass.

American Naturalist, vols. 18, 19, 20, 22.
Munsey and *Argosy* (weeklies), lot.
St. Nicholas and *Wide Awake*, lot.
Scribner's Monthly, 1870-1872, lot.

L. Indermark, 3211 Barrett St., St. Louis, Mo. [*Cash.*]

Amer. Chem. Jl., Balt., v. 1-7, whole, part or odd nos.; also years 1899 to date.
Science, N. Y. (old ser.), v. 15 to 18, indices, v. 13, 18, 21, 22; (new ser.), 1895, entire; 1896, no. 101; 1900, no. 276; and index v. 12.
Proc. Amer Assoc. Adv. Sci., 5, 15, and 21 meetings.

Wm. Jackson, 7 Ann St., N. Y.

The Pantheon of Heathen Gods, by John Horne Tooke.

George W. Jacobs & Co., 103 S. 15th St., Phila., Pa.

Keble's Hooker, 3 v., good condition.

U. P. James, 127 W. 7th St., Cincinnati, O.

Monist, v. 8, no. 1.
Quarterly Publication American Statistical Association, v. 1, no. 4.

E. T. Jett Book and News Co., 806 Olive St., St. Louis, Mo.

Altgeld, John, Speechmaking.
Songs and Stories from Tennessee, John T. Moore.

The E. P. Judd Co., New Haven, Conn. [*Cash.*]

Liberty and a Living, Hubert. Putnam.

King Bros., 3 4th St., San Francisco, Cal.

From Forecastle to Cabin, Samuel.
Le Conte, Elements of Geology.
25 Gayley, Classic Myths.
25 Beeman and Smith, New Plane Geometry.
25 Myers, Ancient History.
25 Tarr, First Book of Physical Geography.
25 Adams, European History.
25 Channing, Student's History.
25 Eggleston, First Book Amer. History.
10 Davies, Surveying, rev. by Van Amringe.

King's Old Book Store, 15 4th St., San Francisco, Cal.

Blue and Gold (University Year Book), any.
Bryant, What I Saw in California.
Vancouver's Voyages.
Robinson, Life in California.
Farnham, Oregon and California.

Geo. Kleinteich, 397 Bedford Ave., Brooklyn, N. Y. [*Cash.*]

Keys of the Creeds.
Effect of External Influence on Development. Oxford Press.

Chas. E. Lauriat Co., 301 Washington St., Boston, Mass.

Grey Hawk, Macaulay. Lippincott.
Tuckerman, Synopsis of No. Amer. Lichens, v. 1.
Household of Sir Thomas More. Scribner.
Peterkin Papers, 1st or early ed.
Character Sketches, Geo. Eliot, comp. by N. Shepard.

Leggat Bros., 81 Chambers St., N. Y.

Deal with the Devil.
Eastlake, Materials.
Any vols. about Virginia.
Gourgaud, Napoleon.
Burr, Atlas of State of N. Y.
Poe's Works, v. 1, 2, Amontillado ed.
Rufus King's Works, v. 1, 2. Putnam.
Washington's Works, v. 1 to 9. Putnam.
Hamilton's Works, v. 1 to 7. Putnam.
Jay's Works, v. 1. Putnam.
Jefferson's Works, v. 1 to 9. Putnam.

Paul Lemperly, Cleveland, O.

Life, Letters, and Literary Remains of Keats, 2 v. London, 1848.

Edw. E. Levi, Pittsburgh, Pa.

Philbrook, The Work of Electricity in Nature.
McHenry, The Wilderness.

Edw. E. Levi.—*Continued.*

Packard, Guide to the Study of Insects.
A good illustrated book on beetles.
Pasteur, Books on Distilling or Fermentation.

Library Co. of Phila., N. W. cor. Locust and Juniper Sts., Phila., Pa.

Brown, Edgar Huntley. Phila., 1857.

Geo. D. Luetscher, 240 Hopkinson House, U. of P. Dormitories, Phila., Pa.

Niles' Register.

Lyon, Kymer & Palmer Co., Grand Rapids, Mich.

3 Shakespeare and the Bible.

Nathaniel McCarthy, Minneapolis, Minn.

Yvernelle, by Norris.

McLaren's Old Book Shop, 81 4th Ave., N. Y.

Universal Guide Through the City of New York for Citizens and Strangers. Pub. by D. Longworth about 1818.
New York as It Is in 1837. Pub. by J. Disturnell.
Old guides, directories or prints of New York City prior to 1850.
Birch's Heads, folio. Pub. by Virtue.

John Jos. McVey, 39 N. 13th St., Phila., Pa.

Wellington, Pile and Pile Driving. Engineering News.
Atlas to Wilkes' U. S. Exploring Expedition. Phila., 1845.

H. Malkan, Hanover Sq., N. Y.

Whittier, large-pap. ed.
Mrs. Seymour's pamphlet on the Pickwick Papers.
Puritan Age and Rule, by Ellis.

R. H. Merriam, Hanover Sq., N. Y.

Set of Eugene Field, Sabine ed.
Will Phillips' Series, 4 v., by E. H. R. Lothrop.

Wm. H. Miner, 133 Euclid Ave., Cleveland, O.

Burns, illustrations.
Haggard, 1st eds.
Schoolcraft, Indians.

The Musson Book Co., Ltd., Toronto, Can.

A Master of Silence, by Irving Bacheller.

A. J. Ochs & Co., Boston Neck Book Store, 1781 Washington St., Boston, Mass.

Medico Botanico Coreoleo, Par de Renato de Grusourdi, 4 v., 4°. Pub. Paris.
Libraria de Francisco Brachet. 1864.
Adventures of Timothy Peacock, by Thompson. ? Pub. Knapp & Jewett, Middlebury, Vt., 1835.
Munn's Scientific Am. Receipt Book.

E. J. O'Malley, Hanover Sq., N. Y.

Venable's Syllabus.
Whitman, 1st eds.
History of Banking in all Nations, 4 v. Journal of Commerce.
Stoddard's Lectures.

Daniel O'Shea, 1584 Broadway, N. Y.

Chap Book (12mo form), v. 1, no. 7; v. 2, no. 9; v. 3, no. 4; v. 4, nos. 2, 5, 9, 11, 12; v. 5, nos. 1, 3, 6; v. 6, nos. 5, 6, 7, 8, 9, 10, 11, 12.

H. E. Peadry, Powers Bldg., Rochester, N. Y.

Standard Dictionary, Subscription ed.

Pierce & Zahn, 633 17th St., Denver, Colo.

20 copies *Everybody's Magazine*.
Essentials of Perspective, by L. W. Miller.
"U. S." Index of U. S. of A., by Townsend.

C. S. Pratt, 161 6th Ave., N. Y. [*Cash.*]

Kraft-Ebling, Psychopathia Sexualis.
Leland, Thos., History of Ireland.
Fitzpatrick, Secret Service Under Pitt.
Don Zalvo the Brave, novel.
The Black Aunt, novel.

Presb. Bd. of Pub. and S. S. Work, 156 5th Ave., N. Y.

Lectures on Landscape Gardening, Shephard Thomas. Sydney, 1839.

Preston & Rounds Co., Providence, R. I.

Waring, Village Improvement.
Glass, Mrs., Cook Book.
Geikie, Landmarks of Old Testament History.
Eiolart, Guide to Stereochemistry.

BOOKS WANTED.—*Continued.*

Fleming H. Revell Co., Chicago, Ill.

Elements of Religion, 2 v., by C. P. Tiele. Scribner.
Life of Jerry MacAuley.
Natural Religion, by Max Muller. Longmans.
Christian Science, its Truths and Errors, by Tenny. Burrows Bros.

Geo. H. Richmond, 32 W. 33d St., N. Y.

Brown, Portrait Gallery. Hartford, 1845.
Baker, Washington.
Indian books, any.

Robson & Adee, Saratoga Springs, N. Y.

Kipling, v. 16, Outward Bound ed.

Chas. M. Roe, 177 Wabash Ave., Chicago, Ill.

Life of Nathaniel Colver.
The Cause of God and Truth, by Dr. Gill.
Doctrine of the Trinity, by Dr. Gill.
Necessity of Good Works to Salvation, by Dr. Gill.
Truth Defined, by Dr. Gill.
Justification, by Dr. Gill.
Predestination, by Dr. Gill.

Rogers' Book Store, 39 Patton Ave., Asheville, N. C.

Conway, N. O., Barons of the Rappahannock.

Rohde & Haskins, 16 Cortlandt St., N. Y.

Samuel Rogers' Poems, il. by Turner.

Wm. B. Ropes, Mt. Vernon, Skagit Co., Wash.

Evans, A. J., St. Elmo, cl.
The Benefactress. Macmillan Co.
Pidgin, C. F., Blennerhassett.
Gray, Anatomy, col. plates, last ed.

E. G. Schermerhorn, 57 Chambers St., N. Y.

The following books by William Harrison Ainsworth, 12°, illustrated. Published by Geo. Routledge & Sons: The South Sea Bubble; Talbot Harland; Tower Hill; Merry England; The Goldsmith's Wife; Chetwynd Calverley; The Fall of Somerset; Beatrice Tyldesley.

John E. Scopes, 29 Tweddle Bldg., Albany, N. Y.

American Ancestry, v. 9, 10.
Wilkinson, Memoirs, v. 2, and atlas. Phila., 1816.

Scrantom, Wetmore & Co., Rochester, N. Y.

Austen, Jane, Sense and Sensibility, v. 1 or v. 1 and 2, Temple ed., leath.

Charles Scribner's Sons, 153 5th Ave., N. Y.

Her Picture, No Name Ser. Little, B. & Co.
Prentiss, Tanglethread.

Shepard Book Co., 272 S. State St., Salt Lake City, U.

The Utah Expedition by a Wagonmaster, etc. Cin., O., 1858.
Stenhouse, Tell it All.
Howe, Mormonism Unveiled.
Wife No. 19, by Young.
Brigham's Destroying Angel.
Mormonism, anything, cheap.

Sibley, Lindsay & Curr Co., Rochester, N. Y.

Wisdom of the Hindoos, Monier Williams.
India in Greece, E. Pococke. London, 1856.
Second-hand copies in good condition.

Frank Simmons, Springfield, Ill.

2 sets Debates of Constitutional Convention. Illinois, 1870.
Chicago Daily News Almanac, 1897, 1898, 1902, pap. or cloth.
Book Prices Current, any v.

John Skinner, 44 N. Pearl St., Albany, N. Y.

New England in Albany, by Tenny.
Memoirs of an American Lady, Munsell's ed. 1876.
Simms, Trappers of New York.
Simms, Frontiersmen of New York.

George D. Smith, 49 New St., N. Y.

Poe, 10 v. Stone & Kimball.
Behn, Mrs., 6 v., Pearson reprint.
Letters of Petroleum V. Nasby.
Stedman's Anthology, 2 v., large-pap.
Washington's Works, 10 v., ed. by Sparks.
Eager, History of Orange Co.
Stoddard's Lectures.
Biblia Innocentium. Kelmscott.
Earthly Paradise. Kelmscott.
Rossetti's Sonnets. Kelmscott.

Wm. T. Smith & Co., 145 Genesee St., Utica, N. Y.

Day, Art of Discourse.
Cronholm, Hist. of Sweden, 2 v.
Thompson, China and the Powers. Longmans.

A. H. Smythe, 43 S. High St., Columbus, O.

Vasari, Lives of the Painters, v. 3. Scribner.
Young, General Astronomy, rev. ed., new or shop-worn.
When Chickens Come Home to Roost, pap.

Speyer & Peters, Berlin, N. W. F., Germany.

Annales des Maladies Gen.-Urin.
Archiv für Augen- u. Ohrenheilkunde.
Archiv f. Experim. Pathol. u. Pharmakol.
Archives of Pediatrics.
Brun, Beitraege z. Klin. Chirurgie.
Graefe, Archiv. f. Ophthalmologie.
Journal de l'Anatomie p. Robin.
Journal of the Amer. Chem. Soc.
Transactions of the Amer. Orthop. Association, v. 7, 8, 11, 13, 14.
Please offer sets or single vols. and nos.

G. E. Stechert, 9 E. 16th St., N. Y.

Say, Treatise on Political Economy.
Riverside Natural History, 6 v.
Turkish Evening Entertainments. 1850.
Wolkonsky, Russian Life and Literature.
Hazlitt, Essays, 3 v.

E. Steiger & Co., 25 Park Place, N. Y. [*Cash.*]

Macoun, Catalogue of Canadian Plants, 2 v.
Gordon, Pinetum, the Coniferous Plants.
Sachs, Text-Book of Botany, Eng. tr.
Sachs, Plant Physiology, Eng. tr. by H. M. Ward.
Lindley, Vegetable Kingdom.
Ridgway, Nomenclature of Colors for Naturalists.
Lubbock, Buds and Stipules.
Hatfield, Transverse Strains.
Sargent, Woods of the United States.
Gray, Genera of the Plants of the United States, 2 v.
Torrey and Gray, Flora of North America.
Gray, Chapman and Watson, Botanical Contributions.
Nuttall, North American Silva, 2 v.
Michaux, North American Silva, 3 v.
Wundt, Outlines of Psychology. 1897.

The Stiefel Masonic Book Co., 106 E. 4th St., Cincinnati, O.

Hughan, Old Charges of British Freemasonry.
Moore, The Lost Tribes; or, the Saxons of the East and West.

Stout's Book Exchange, 612 5th St., San Diego, Cal.

Dr. Wm. Hammond's Novels, quote any.
Hist. 1st Council Nicæa.
Religion of Stars.
Mystic Test Book, Richmond.

Strawbridge & Clothier, Market St., Phila., Pa.

Thoughts from Edward Fitzgerald.

Wm. Thomson, 110 Fulton St., N. Y.

Proctor, Chance and Luck.
Tattersall's Rules of Betting.
The Doctrine of Chance.
Books on Turf Speculation.

H. H. Timby, Conneaut, O.

Bandelier, Delight Makers.
Wardlaw, Lectures on Magdalenism.
Convent Life of George Sand.
The Surveyor Boy.
Todd, Story of City of Washington.
Audubon's Birds.
Watkins, Hist. 1st Tenn. Regiment.

C. L. Traver, Trenton, N. J. [*Cash.*]

Voorhees Family Genealogy.
Nevins Family Genealogy.

John C. Tredway, 202 Atlantic Ave., Brooklyn, N. Y.

1842 map and 1853 map for N. Y. City Common Council Manuals of those dates.

United Presb. Bd. of Pub., Pittsburgh, Pa.

Hist. of Paraguay, Washburn. Lee & S.
Life in the Argentine Republic, Tarmiento.
Wanderings in Patagonia, Beerbohm.
The Land of Bolivar, J. M. Spence.
The Republic of Uruguay, Stanford.
Travels on the Amazon and Rio Negro, A. R. Wallace.
The Highlands of the Brazils, R. F. Burton.
Brazil and the Brazilians, Fletcher and Kidder. Little, B.

BOOKS WANTED.—Continued.

United Presb. Bd. of Pub.—Continued.

Dutch Guiana, W. Gifford Palgrave. Macmillan, '76.
Canoe and Camp Life in British Guiana, C. B. Browne.
Modern Russia, Eckhardt.
Rome of To-Day, Edmond About.
Tales of the Fells and Fjiords, Bjornson.
The Great Lone Land, W. F. Butler.
Indian Tribes of the U. S., F. S. Drake.
League of the Iroquois, L. H. Morgan.
Adventures in Apache Country, J. R. Browne.
Thirty Years with Indian Tribes, Schoolcraft.
Life of Schleiermacher.
Modern India, Monier Williams.
The Home of the Eddas, C. G. W. Lock.
Iceland, Hist. and Descriptive Account. Harper.
Iceland, its Scenes and Sagas, Baring-Gould.
Cuba, with Pen and Pencil, S. Hazard.
The Marquesas and South Sea Islanders, Herman Melville.
The Mutineers of the "Bounty" and Their Descendants, Lady Belcher.
The Heart of Africa, Schweinfurth.
Leopardi's Poems, Putnam.
Chinese Empire, Huc. Harper.
Old Rome and New Italy, Castelar. Harper.
Judas Maccabeus, R. C. Conder. Macmillan.
The Roof of the World, T. E. Gordon.
British Burmah and its People, C. J. Forbes.
Bush Life in Queensland, A. C. Grant.
Travels in Central America, E. G. Squiers.
South Africa, Anthony Trollope.
West Indies and the Spanish Main, Anthony Trollope.
Kingdom and people of Siam, Sir John Bowring.
The Land of the White Elephant, F. Vincent.
Travels of a Pioneer of Commerce, C. T. Cooper.

John Wanamaker, N. Y.

Maclay, History of the U. S. Navy, 2 v., original ed. Appleton.
Four Years at Yale.

John Wanamaker, Phila., Pa.

Book of Ruth, il. by W. B. McDougall. Pub. by Dodd, M. & Co.
Book of Job, il. by H. Granville Fell. Pub. by Dodd, M. & Co.

Montgomery Ward & Co., Chicago, Ill.

Wallace's Studies, Social and Scientific, v. 1 (only.) Pub. by Macmillan.

Geo. E. Warner, Minneapolis, Minn.

Lee, Franklyn W., Dreamy Hours.
Johnston, W. P., Pictures of the Patriarchs.
Any county atlas or biography.

Rees Welsh & Co., 901 Sansom St., Phila., Pa.

Wilkes, Spirit of the Times, for years 1864 and 1865, or odd nos.

Edgar A. Werner, 35 Chestnut St., Albany, N. Y.

Journal Almanacs, 1867.
Whig and *Tribune*, 1847, '51, '53, '69, '73, '90, '91, '92-'97, 1900.
Wilkinson, Annals of Binghamton. 1872.
Smith, History of Dutchess County.
Laws of N. Y., 1802. Will pay a high price.

Thomas Whittaker, 2 Bible House, N. Y.

New Testament, tr. into Italian by Dr. Achillis. New York, 1855 (?)
Thayer, Lexicon of New Testament Greek.

Wm. Wesley & Son, 28 Essex St., Strand, London.

Hartt's Physical Geography of Brazil.
American Naturalist, nos. 257, 265, 266, 270.
Annals of Obs. Harvard Coll., v. 6-8.
Botanical Gazette, Mar., 1897.

Mrs. H. Williams, 114 5th Ave., N. Y.

Chapters from Erie, by Chas. Francis Adams.
Rise and Progress of the Metropolitan City of America, by a New Yorker. N. Y., 1853.

Woodward & Lothrop, Washington, D. C.

The Morals and Maxims of the 17th Century, tr. by Stott. McClurg & Co.
Primitive Mind Cure, by W. F. Evans, cl. ed. Pub. by H. H. Carter.
Mental Medicine, by W. F. Evans, cl. ed. Pub. by H. H. Carter.

BOOKS FOR SALE.

Irving S. Colwell, Auburn, N. Y.

Century Dict., 10 v., hf. mor., new. $55.00.
Edward Irving's Collected Writings, 5 v.
Ellis, Hist. U. S., 8 v., cl., sub.
Smith, H. P., Hist. Buffalo and Erie Co., 2 v., hf. mor.

Dodge Stationery Co., 123 Grant Ave., San Francisco, Cal.

American Catalogue, 1884-1895, 4 v., bound in black cl. Complete, $35.00.

Hinds & Noble, 31 W. 15th St., N. Y.

3 Webster's International Dictionary, good second-hand, with patent index. Each, $4.25.

Leggat Bros., 81 Chambers St., N. Y.

10 Buffalo and Seneca's, 2 v. $1.00 set.
10 Recollections of a Busy Life. Each $1.00.
10 Smith's New Jersey. Each $1.50.
Encyclopedia Britannica, 15 v. $12.50.
Britannica, 25 v., cl. $22.50.
Britannica, 31 v., hf. mor. $35.00.
10 Sherratt's Elements of Handrailing. 50 cts.
10 Treatise on Wines, Liquors, etc. Pub. at $10.00; each 50 cts.

Meehan, Expert Bookseller, 32 Gay St., Bath, Eng.

Review of Reviews, nos. 1 to 14 (Jan., 1890 to Feb., 1891), necessary nos. to complete the American Issue, *free* at 25 c. each only. Payment in American currency will do. Cash with order. A big stock of duplicates of these nos. In sets of 14 nos. only.

Daniel O'Shea, 1584 Broadway, N. Y.

Back nos. of magazines, 5 cts. and upwards per no.

H. E. Pendry, Powers Bldg., Rochester, N. Y.

Scribner's Britannica, hf. mor.
Natural History New York, issue of State.

S. J. D., P. O. Box 943, N. Y.

Research Papers—Kent Chemical Laboratory. *Yale Bi-centennial Publications*. N. Y., Scribner, 1901. 2 v. $10.
Hopkins, E. W. The Great Epic of India. *Yale Bi-centennial Publications*. N. Y., Scribner, 1901. $2.
Supernatural Religion. 6th ed. 2 v. in 1. N. Y., Bennett, 1879. $1.75.
Doane, T. W. Bible Myths. 4th ed. N. Y., Truth Seeker Co., 1882. $1.
Ball, R. S. Story of the Heavens. N. Y., Cassell, 1900. $1.50.
Myer, Isaac. Qabbalah. Phila., 1888. (350 copies.) $8.
Wilder, A. Symbolical language of Ancient Art and Mythology. N. Y., Bouton, 1892. $1.50.
Wilder, A. Eleusinian and Bacchic Mysteries. N. Y., Bouton, 1891. $1.
Rae, John. Contemporary Socialism. N. Y., Scribner, 1884. $1.
Graham, W. Socialism New and Old. N. Y., Appleton, 1891. $1.
Will sell the lot *en bloc* for $25.

Wm. T. Smith & Co., 145 Genesee St., Utica, N. Y.

Surgeon-General's Report of the Civil War, 5 v., cl. Make offer.

SITUATIONS WANTED.

BOOKMAN, thoroughly posted, 8 years' experience, wants position where chance for advancement is open. Address BOOKWORM, care of PUBLISHERS' WEEKLY.

WANTED.—By young man, twenty years' experience in booktrade, position as manager or assistant with first-class house; would travel. First-class references. Address R. W. W., care of PUBLISHERS' WEEKLY.

BOOKKEEPER, accountant and office manager. 20 years' experience, wholesale and manufacturing, desires position. Can adapt to any system or conditions. Excellent references. Salary no object so long as prospects are good. Address WILLSTAN, care of PUBLISHERS' WEEKLY.

COPYRIGHT NOTICES.

LIBRARY OF CONGRESS,
OFFICE OF THE REGISTER OF COPYRIGHTS,
WASHINGTON, D. C.

Class A, XXc, No. 35053.—To wit: *Be it remembered*, That on the 10th day of June, 1902, Mattie G. Browne, of Boston, Mass., hath deposited in this office the title of a book, the title of which is in the following words, to wit: "Massachusetts Reports, 109. Cases argued and determined in the Supreme Judicial Court of Massachusetts, November, 1871-March, 1872. Albert G. Browne, Jr. Boston, Houghton, Mifflin & Company," the right whereof she claims as proprietor in conformity with the laws of the United States respecting copyrights.

(Signed) HERBERT PUTNAM, *Librarian of Congress.*
By THORVALD SOLBERG, *Register of Copyrights.*
In renewal for 14 years from June 12, 1902.

SPECIAL NOTICES.

Bibliographic Publications.

For all American books as they appear, take THE PUBLISHERS' WEEKLY; for an hour's glance each month at the important books and magazine papers, take LITERARY NEWS; for library matters take THE LIBRARY JOURNAL; for magazine articles in general, consult THE ANNUAL LITERARY INDEX; for books in print or issued of late years, see THE AMERICAN and ANNUAL CATALOGUES.

THE PUBLISHERS' WEEKLY. Established in 1872, with which was incorporated the *American Literary Gazette and Publishers' Circular* (established in 1852.) Recognized as the representative of the publishing and bookselling interests in the United States. Contains full weekly record of American publications, with monthly cumulative indexes, etc. Subscription, $3.00 a year, postpaid; to foreign countries, postpaid, $4.00 a year; single numbers, 10 cents, postpaid.

THE LIBRARY JOURNAL. Official Organ of the American Library Association. Chiefly devoted to library economy and bibliography. Established in 1876. Published monthly. Subscription, $5.00 a year, postpaid; single numbers, 50 cents. Price to Europe, or other countries in the Union, 20s a year; single numbers, 2s. (LITERARY NEWS *is sent free to subscribers of* THE LIBRARY JOURNAL.) Teachers may be interested in the "School Number" published in the spring of each year.

GENERAL INDEX TO THE LIBRARY JOURNAL, vols. 1–22, 1876–1897. Arranged to serve as an index to succeeding volumes or for other sources of professional information. 4°, in sheets, or paper binding, $2.50; A. L. A. half leather, $3.00.

LITERARY NEWS. A Monthly Journal of Current Literature. Contains the freshest news concerning books and authors; lists of new publications; reviews and critical comments; characteristic extracts; sketches and anecdotes of authors; bibliographical references; prominent topics of the magazines; portraits of authors, and illustrations from the newest books, etc., etc. Subscription, $1.00 a year, postpaid; single numbers, 10 cents.

THE AMERICAN CATALOGUE of books in print and for sale July 1, 1876, compiled under the direction of F. LEYPOLDT, and its supplements, 1876–84, 1884–90, 1890–95, and 1895–1900, compiled under the editorial direction of R. R. BOWKER, aims to present all the bibliographical features of the books in the American market, arranged in the first part alphabetically by both *authors* and *titles*, and in the second part alphabetically by *subjects*.

The Catalogue and its supplementary volumes form the only approximately complete guide in existence to the American books of the day, so arranged as to make reference easy from whatever direction the inquiry may come, whether from that of the author, or the title, or the subject. It not only furnishes the desired information about any particular book of which the consulter is in search, but shows what others there are by the same author or on the same subject in which he is interested. To the bookseller, therefore, it is valuable both in filling orders and in stimulating business; to the librarian, in supplying gaps and proportioning his collection; and to all who are practically concerned with books, in furnishing information which nowhere else is obtainable by so convenient a method, if obtainable at all.

The author-and-title volume of the 1876 volume is out of print. A limited number of the subject volume may be had in half leather binding at $15.

The volume covering the period 1876–84 is also out of print.

——, 1884–90, 4°, hf. mor., $25. (1 copy only remains.)
——, 1890–95, 4°, hf. mor., $15.
——, 1895–1900, 4°, hf. mor., $15.

THE ANNUAL AMERICAN CATALOGUE. Being the full titles, with descriptive notes, of all books recorded in THE PUBLISHERS' WEEKLY during the calendar year, with author, title, and subject index, publishers' annual lists and directory of publishers. Published annually since 1886. 8vo, sheets, *net*, $3.00; half morocco, $3.50.

THE PUBLISHERS' TRADE LIST ANNUAL. Contains: The latest catalogues of nearly 200 American publishers, contributed by themselves and arranged alphabetically by the firm-names and smaller lists at the end of the volume. These lists, all bound in one volume arranged alphabetically for ready reference, with marginal index, guiding the finger at once to the right letter, present in their combination so convenient and time-saving a working-tool as to make it indispensable to every one who has any interest in the purchase or sale of books. Large 8vo, with "Duplex Index," cloth, *net*, $2.00.

THE ANNUAL LITERARY INDEX, including Periodicals, American and English; Essays, Book-Chapters, etc., with Author-Index, Bibliographies, Necrology and Index to Dates of Principal Events. Edited, with the coöperation of members of the American Library Association and of *The Library Journal* staff, by W. I. FLETCHER and R. R. BOWKER. 8°, cloth, $3.50.

THE AMERICAN EDUCATIONAL CATALOGUE. Contains a price-list of all the text-books in use in the United States, arranged alphabetically by author's or editor's name, and a detailed subject-index, referring from each specific subject to authors of books on that subject. 8vo, leatherette, 50 cents.

THE ENGLISH CATALOGUE [Annual] giving full titles classified under author and subject in one strict alphabet, with particulars of the size, price, month of publication, and name of publisher of the books issued in Great Britain and Ireland, in the calendar year, being a continuation of the "London" and "British" Catalogues. [London: Sampson Low, Marston & Co.) 8vo, paper, *net*, $1.50. THE ENGLISH CATALOGUE and THE ANNUAL AMERICAN CATALOGUE bound in one volume, half leather, $5.00.

PUBLICATIONS OF SOCIETIES: a provisional list of the publications of American scientific, literary, and other societies from their organization. Compiled under the editorial direction of R. R. BOWKER. Schedules over 1100 societies issuing publications, and gives title-entries of all their publications, as far as data could be obtained from the societies and from libraries. 4°, paper, $2.50; cloth, $3.00.

STATE PUBLICATIONS: a provisional list of the official publications of the several States of the United States from their organization. Compiled under the editorial direction of R. R. BOWKER. Pt. 1: New England States—Maine, New Hampshire, Vermont, Massachusetts, Rhode Island, Connecticut. 4°, $2.00. (For complete work, $5.00.)

LIST OF AMERICAN PUBLISHERS, 1890–1895. The street address is given in nearly every case, and the abbreviation under which the firm's books are entered in the "American Catalogue," 1890–95. 4to, pap., $2.00.

UNITED STATES GOVERNMENT PUBLICATIONS. July 1, 1890 to June 30, 1895. Compiled, under the editorial direction of R. R. BOWKER, by J. H. HICKCOX. 60 pp., 4to, pap., $1.50.

THE SUNDAY-SCHOOL LIBRARY. By Rev. A. E. DUNNING. 16mo, cloth, 60 cents.

THE PROFESSION OF BOOKSELLING: a handbook of practical hints for the apprentice and bookseller. By A. GROWOLL, managing editor of THE PUBLISHERS' WEEKLY, and author of "A Bookseller's Library," "Book-trade Bibliography in the United States in the XIXth Century," etc. Pts. 1 and 2. 134 p. Large 8°, bds., each, $2.00. (*Concluding part in preparation.*)

Address the OFFICE OF THE PUBLISHERS' WEEKLY,

P. O. Box 943. **298 Broadway, New York.**

Books for Summer Travellers.

D. APPLETON & COMPANY, New York.

APPLETONS' GUIDE BOOKS.

Appletons' General Guide to the United States and Canada. With numerous maps and illustrations. 12mo, flexible morocco, with tuck, $2.50. (Part I., separately, NEW ENGLAND AND MIDDLE STATES AND CANADA; cloth, 75 cents. Part II., SOUTHERN AND WESTERN STATES, cloth, 75 cents.)

Appletons' Guide-Book to Alaska. By Miss E. R. Scidmore. New edition, including an Account of the Klondike. With maps and illustrations. 12mo, flexible cloth, $1.00.

A Landmark History of New York. By Albert Ulmann. With many illustrations. 12mo, cloth, $1.50.

In this book the reader makes visits in sequence to the old Dutch Settlement, the early English colony, the city as it was before the Revolution, and so on down to the present time. Copies of rare prints and maps and many plates made from recent photographs illustrate the work.

Appletons' Dictionary of [Greater] New York and Vicinity. With maps of New York and vicinity. Square 12mo, paper, 25 cents net; postage, 6 cents additional.

Puerto Rico and Its Resources. A book for Travellers, Investors, and others, containing full accounts of Natural Features and Resources, Products, People, Opportunities for Business, etc. By Frederick A. Ober, author of "Camps in the Caribbees," "Crusoe's Island," etc. With maps and illustrations. 12mo, cloth, $1.50.

A. S. BARNES & CO., New York.

A World's Shrine. (Lake Como.) By Virginia W. Johnson. Illustrated. 12mo, cloth, $1.20 net. (new.)

A History of Art. For Tourists. By Wm. H. Goodyear. Fully illustrated. 8vo, cloth, $2.80 net.

Switzerland, Annals of. By Julia M. Colton. Illustrated. 12mo, cloth, $1.25.

The Rhine, Legends of. By H. A. Guerber. Illustrated. 12mo, cloth, gilt top, $1.50 net.

BRENTANO'S, New York.

My Ocean Trip. By E. S. Cadigan. Illustrated with signals and flags printed in colors, and with blank pages for memoranda. 12mo, cloth, $1.00.

A work appealing especially to tourists and travellers, arranged for the record to be kept of an Ocean Voyage. In addition there are many items of interest, such as a complete code of signals, series of games for shipboard, entertainments, pages for the autographs of fellow passengers.

POCKET DICTIONARIES. Printed at the press of Bernhard Tauchnitz of Leipzig, Germany, from the plates of the famous Tauchnitz series, and bound specially for Brentano's. Each, cloth, $1.00.

Dictionary of the English and German Languages. By J. E. Wessely.

Dictionary of the English and French Languages. By J. E. Wessely.

Dictionary of the English and Italian Languages. By J. E. Wessely.

Dictionary of the English and Spanish Languages. By J. E. Wessely and Girones.

HOUGHTON, MIFFLIN & CO., Boston.

Our National Parks. By John Muir. Illustrated. $1.75 net; postpaid, $1.87.

Footing it in Franconia. $1.10 net; postpaid, $1.19.

HOUGHTON, MIFFLIN & CO.—*Continued.*

Picturesque Alaska. By Abby J. Woodman. Illustrations and maps. 16mo, $1.00.

September Days on Nantucket. By William Root Bliss.

Cape Cod. By H. D Thoreau. $1.50.

WILLIAM R. JENKINS, New York.

The Complete Pocket-Guide to Europe. Edited by E. C. and T. L. Stedman. One vol., full leather, $1.25. Revised yearly. The best of its kind.

LEMCKE & BUECHNER, New York.

Baedeker's Guides. German and French.

Monographs on Artists.

Dictionaries and Grammars for the study of Foreign Languages. *Send for lists.*

McCLURE, PHILLIPS & CO., New York.

The Hound of the Baskervilles. A Sherlock Holmes novel by A. Conan Doyle. Illustrated. $1.25.

The Blazed Trail. An American novel by Stewart Edward White. Illustrated. $1.50.

Red Saunders. A humorous account of his doings West and East. By Henry Wallace Phillips. Frontispiece. $1.25.

The Madness of Philip. Stories of child life for grown-ups by Josephine Dodge Daskam. Illustrated. $1.50.

A Prince of Good Fellows. Tales of James V., the "Merry Monarch of Scotland," by Robert Barr. Illustrated. $1.50.

The Making of a Statesman. A novelette, together with other stories of Georgia life, by Joel Chandler Harris. $1.25.

The Gentleman From Indiana. A romance by Booth Tarkington. $1.50.

An Island Cabin. A record of outdoor life by Arthur Henry. $1.50.

Forest Neighbors. Life stories of wild animals by W. D. Hulbert. $1.50 net; postpaid, $1.68.

Next to the Ground. A nature narrative by Martha McCulloch-Williams. $1.20 net; postpaid, $1.32.

JOHN P. MORTON & CO., Louisville, Ky.

Mammoth Cave of Kentucky (A Perfect Guide To). By Hovey & Call. Paper, 50 cents; cloth, $1.00.

E. STEIGER & CO., New York.

Baedeker's and Other Guide-Books, in German. The largest assortment of Books for the Study of Foreign Languages. *Send for catalogue.*

A. WESSELS COMPANY, 7-9 W. 18th St., N. Y.

Historical Guide-Books to Paris, Venice, Florence, Cities of Belgium, Cities of Northern Italy, the Umbrian Towns. One volume each. By Grant Allen. Pocket size, 250 pp., cloth, $1.25 net.

London and Londoners. By R. A. Pritchard. Pocket size, 400 pp., cloth, $1.25.

TWENTY-FIVE CENT EDITION

DOROTHY VERNON Or, THE BEAUTY OF HADDON HALL

THIS delightful, original romance was first published in England early in the present year, and must not be confounded with "DOROTHY VERNON OF HADDON HALL," by Mr. CHARLES MAJOR, a later and far inferior novel.

It is the very powerful, true narrative of the love of Dorothy, youngest daughter of Sir George Vernon, a great English noble. Dorothy is really a lovable little maid of sweet disposition, and all readers will become enthusiastic over the clever manner in which she and her lover, John Manners, outwit their persecutors.

It has never before been published in paper covered form, and will prove a source of profit and satisfaction to the dealer who is wise enough to order liberally. It is bound in very handsome multi-colored covers, is sewed, and is printed from clear, new type on fine wove paper. In short, it is the most attractive and notable 25c. book published in years.

Retail, 25c.; Trade, 15c. Fully Returnable

..................................1902

The..................................News Company.

Gentlemen: Kindly send me at once..................copies of Street & Smith's ***25c. Edition of "Dorothy Vernon; or, The Beauty of Haddon Hall,"*** *and oblige*

Name..................................

Street..................................

City.................................. *State..................................*

THE PUBLISHERS' WEEKLY

Reference List of New Publications

JANUARY–JUNE, 1902

MONTHLY CUMULATION, JULY, 1902

This Reference List enters the books recorded during the month under (1) author, in **Clarendon** *type; anonymous books having* **Clarendon** *type for the first word; (2) title in* Roman; *(3) subject-heading in* SMALL CAPS; *(4) name of series in Italics. The figures in parentheses are not the imprint date, but refer to the date of "The Publishers' Weekly" in which full title entry will be found and not to the day of publication, for which information should be sought in the full title entry thus indicated. Where not specified, the binding is cloth.*

A apple pie. Greenaway, K. 75 c. Warne.

A B C of banks and banking. Coffin, G: M. $1.25. S: A. Nelson.

A B C of electrical experiments. Clarke, W. J. $1. Excelsior.

A B C of the telephone. Homans, J. E. $1. Van Nostrand.

A B C of wireless telegraphy. Bubier, E: T. $1. Bubier.

A B C universal commercial electric telegraphic code. 5th ed., enl. '02(Je7) 8°, net, $7. Am. Code.

À la mode cookery. Salis, *Mrs.* H. A. de. $2. Longmans.

Aaron Crane. Tate, H: $1.50. Abbey Press.

Abbatt, W:, *ed.* *See* Heath, W:

ABBEYS.
See Cathedrals.

Abbott, Alex. C. Manual of bacteriology, 6th ed., rev. and enl. '02(My17) 12°, net, $2.75. Lea.

Abbott, J. H. M. Tommy Cornstalk: features of the So. African war from the point of view of the Australian ranks. '02(Je21) D. $2. Longmans.

Abbott, J: S. C. Christopher Carson, known as Kit Carson. '01. '02(Ap12) 12°, net, 87 c. Dodd.

Abbott, S: W., *ed.* *See* American yearbook of medicine.

Abbott's cyclopedic digest. *See* New York.

Abegg, R., *and* Herz, W. Practical chemistry; tr. by H. B. Calvert. '01. '02(Ja24) 12°, net, $1.50. Macmillan.

Abernethy, J. W. American literature. '02(Ap26) 12°, $1.10. Maynard, M. & Co.

Abner Daniel. Harben, W. N. $1.50. Harper.

Abroad with the Jimmies. Bell, L. $1.50. L. C. Page

ABSOLUTION.
See Confession.

ACCIDENTS.
Dickson. First aid in accidents. net, 50 c. Revell.
Doty. Prompt aid to the injured. $1.50. Appleton.

According to season. Parsons, *Mrs.* F. T. net, $1.75. Scribner.

ACCOUNTS.
See Arithmetic;—Bookkeeping.

Achenbach, H: Two-fold covenant. '02(Ap12) D. 50 c. Evangelical Press.

Achromatic spindle in spore mother-cells of osmunda regalis. Smith, R. W. net, 25 c. Univ. of Chic.

Acorn Club, Ct., pubs. 8°, pap. Case.
—Love. Thomas Short, first printer of Ct. $5. (6.) Case.

ACTIONS AT LAW.
Budd. Civil remedies under code system. $6. Palm.
Wait. Law and practice in civil actions and proceedings in justices' cts., [etc.] In 3 v. v. 1. $6.35; per set, $19. M. Bender.

ACTORS AND ACTRESSES.
Clapp. Reminiscences of a dramatic critic. net, $1.75. Houghton, M. & Co.
Hamm. Eminent actors and their homes. $1.25. Pott.
Whitton. Wags of the stage. $2.50. Rigby.

ACTS OF THE APOSTLES.
See Bible.

Adam, Ja. Texts to il. a course of elem. lectures on Greek philosophy after Aristotle. '02(Mr1) 8°. net, $1.25. Macmillan.

Adams, Braman B. Block system of signalling on Am. railroads. '01. '02(Mr22) 8°, $2. Railroad Gazette.

Adams, C: F. Lee at Appomattox, and other papers. '02(Je7) D. net, $1.50. Houghton, M. & Co.

ADAMS, Herb. B.
Vincent, *and others.* Herbert B. Adams: tribute of friends. n. p. Johns Hopkins.

Adams, W. T., ["Oliver Optic."] Money-maker. '01. '02(Je14) 12°, (Yacht club ser., v. 3.) $1.25. Lee & S.

Addams, Jane. Democracy and social ethics. '02(Je7) D. (Citizen's lib.) $1.25. Macmillan.

Addis, M. E. L. Cathedrals and abbeys of Presbyterian Scotland. '01. '02(F15) il. 12°, net, $2.50. Presb. Bd.

Addison, Jos. Essays; ed. by J: R: Green. '02(Mr29) il. 12°, (Home lib.) $1. Burt.

Adirondack stories. Deming, P. 75 c. Houghton, M. & Co.

Adler, G: J. German and Eng. dictionary. New ed., rev. by F. P. Foster and E: Althaus. '02(Ap26) 4°, $3.50. Appleton.

Adoration of the blessed sacrament. Tesnière, A. net, $1.25. Benziger.

Adventures of John McCue, socialist. '02(My17) D. (Socialist lib., v. 2, no. 1.) pap., 10 c. Socialistic Co-op.

Adventure ser. 12°, $1. Yewdale.
—Dee. James Griffin's adventures.

Adventures in Tibet. Carey, W: net, $1.50. Un. Soc. C. E.

Baldwin, Aaron D. Gospel of Judas Iscariot. '02(My24) D. $1.50. Jamison-H.
Baldwin, Ja. The book lover: guide to best reading. 13th rev. ed. '02(My3) nar. S. net, $1. McClurg.
Baldwin, Ja. F. The scutage and knight service in England. '02(Mr22) 8°, net, $1. Univ. of Chic.
Baldwin, Ja. M: Fragments in philosophy and science. '02(Ap19) O. net, $2.50. Scribner.
Baldwin, Ja. M: Social and ethical interpretations in mental development. 3d ed., rev. and enl. '02(Mr29) 8°, net, $2.60. Macmillan.
Baldwin, May. A popular girl. '01. '02 (F15) il. 12°, net, $1.20. Lippincott.
Baldwin, Myra. Nancy's Easter gift [poem.] '02(My24) il. D. 50 c. Abbey Press.
Baldwin, Willis. *See* Michigan. Law of personal injuries.
Bale marked circle X. Eggleston, G: C. net, $1.20. Lothrop.
Balfour, Arth. J. Foundations of belief. 8th ed., rev. '02(Je7) D. net, $2. Longmans.
Ball Estate Assoc. *See* Gans, E. W:
Ball, Fs. K. Elements of Greek. '02(My3) il. 12°, net, $1. Macmillan.
Ball, *Sir* Rob. S. Earth's beginning. '02 (My24) il. D. net, $1.80. Appleton.
BALL.
See Baseball.
BALLADS.
Book of romantic ballads. net, $1.25. Scribner.
Hale, *ed.* Ballads and ballad poetry. 40 c. Globe Sch. Bk.
Kinard, *ed.* Old English ballads. 40 c. Silver.
See also Songs.
Ballagh, Ja. C. Hist. of slavery in Virginia. '02(Ap26) O. (Johns Hopkins Univ. studies, extra v. 24.) $1.50. Johns Hopkins.
Ballance, C: A., *and* Stewart, P. Healing of nerves. '02(F1) 4°, net, $4.50. Macmillan.
Ballard, Eva C. She wanted to vote. '01. '02(Mr8) D. net, $1.40. Brower.
BALMANNO, Rob.
Clarke. Letters to an enthusiast. net, $2.50. McClurg.
Balzac, H. de. Best of Balzac; ed. by A. Jessup. '02(Ap26) 16°, (Best writings of great authors.) $1.25; ¾ lev. mor., $3. L. C. Page.
BANDAGING.
See Surgery.
Bang, *Mrs.* Marie. Livets alvor. '01. '02 (My17) D. pap., 65 c. M. Bang.
Bangs, J: K. Olympian nights. '02(Je21) D. $1.25. Harper.
Bangs, J: K. Uncle Sam, trustee. '02(My10) il. O. net, $1.75. Riggs.
BANKERS.
Sharp & Alleman's Co.'s lawyers' and bankers' directory, 1902. Jan. ed. $5. Sharp & A.
Banks, C: E., *and* Armstrong, L. Theodore Roosevelt, twenty-sixth President of the U. S. '02(Je28) 12°, $1.50; hf. rus., $2.25. Du Mont.
Banks, L: A. Great saints of the Bible. '01. '02(Ap12) 8°, $1.50. Eaton & M.
Banks, L: A. Windows for sermons. '02 (Ap12) D. net, $1.20. Funk.
Banks, L: A. *See also* Talmage, F. D.
Banks, Nancy H. Oldfield. '02(Je7) D. $1.50. Macmillan.
BANKS AND BANKING.
Barnett. State banking in the U. S. since passage of Nat. bank act. 50 c. Johns Hopkins.
Coffin. A B C of banks and banking. $1.25. S: A. Nelson.
Michie, *ed.* Banking cases, annot. v. 3. $5. Michie.
See also Savings-banks.
Bannister, H: M. *See* Brower, D. R.
Banquet book. Reynolds, C. net, $1.75. Putnam.
Banta, Thdr. M. Sayre family. '02(F15) il. 8°, hf. mor., $10. T. M. Banta.
BAPTISM.
Mahon. Token of the covenant; right use of baptism. 50 c. Pub. Ho. of M. E. Ch. So.
Wilson. Great cloud of witnesses. 50 c. Standard Pub.
BAPTIST CHURCH.
Merriam. Hist. of Am. Baptist missions. $1.25. Am. Bapt.
Newman, *ed.* Century of Baptist achievements, 1801-1900. net, $1.50. Am. Bapt.
Barbara. Culley, F. C. $1.25. F. C. Culley.
Barbarian invasions of Italy. Villari. P. 2 v. net, $7.50. Scribner.
Barber, Edn. A. Anglo-Am. pottery: old Eng. china; with Am. views. 2d ed., rev. and enl. '02(Ja18) il. 12°, net, $2. [Caspar] E. A. Barber.
Barber, Ed. A. Anglo-Am. pottery. 2d rev., enl. ed. '01. '02(Ap26) il. 8°, $2. Patterson & W.
Barber, F. M. Mechanical triumphs of ancient Egyptians. '01. '02(F22) 16°, net, $1.25. Dodd.
Bardeen, C: W. Manual of civics for N. Y. schools. '02(Ja25) D. net, $1. Bardeen.
Barclay, Wilbur F. *See* Methodist Epis. Church.
Barker, Wharton. The great issues: editorials fr. *The American*, 1897-1900. '02(Je21) 12°, $1; pap., 50 c. Ferris.
Barlow, C. A. Montague. *See* Avebury, *Lord*.
Barlow, Jane. At the back of beyond. '02 My10) D. $1.50. Dodd.
Barnard, C: Farming by inches. '01. '02 (F8) 12°, 40 c. Coates.
Barnard, C: My ten rod farm; or, how I became a florist. '01. '02(F8) 12°, 40 c. Coates.
Barnard, C: A simple flower garden for country homes. '01. '02(F8) 12°, 40 c. Coates.
Barnard, C: The strawberry garden, how planted, what it cost. '01. '02(F8) 12°, 40 c. Coates.
Barnard, C: Two thousand a year on fruits and flowers. '01. '02(F8) 12°, $1. Coates.
Barnes, C: W. Sorrow and solace of Esther, daughter of Ben-Amos. '02(Mr29) S. leatherette, net, 30 c. Jennings.
Barnes, Edn. N. C. Reconciliation of Randall Claymore. '02(Je28) D. $1. Earle.
Barnes, Louisa E., [*Mrs.* Arth. J. Barnes.] Shorthand lessons by the word method. '01. '02(Mr1) 12°, $1.25. A. J. Barnes.

Barnett, G: E. State banking in the U. S. since the passage of the Nat. bank act. '02(My17) O. (Johns Hopkins Univ. studies in hist. and pol. science ser. 20, nos. 2-3.) pap., 50 c. Johns Hopkins.

BARNUM, Phineas T.
Benton. Life of P. T. Barnum. $1. Donohue.

Barr, R., ["Luke Sharp."] Prince of good fellows. '02(Je7) il. D. $1.50. McClure, P.

Barrie, Ja. M. Little minister. '02(Ap5) 12°, (Home lib.) $1. Burt.

Barrie's antique gems from the Greek and Latin. il. 12°. (App. to pub. for price.) Barrie.
—Horace. Odæ, Epodæ, etc. (3.)
—Longus, Daphnis and Chloe. (4.)
—Lucian. Lucius, the ass. (5.)
—Ovid. Amorum libri tres. (6.)
—Theocritus. Idylls. (1.)

Barry, H: A. God the Holy Ghost. '02 (Ap12) 12°, $2. Angel Press.

Barry, J: W. American lumberman telecode. '02(Ap26) 8°, flex. leath., net, $5. Am. Lumberman.

Barry Lyndon. *See* Thackeray, W: M.

Bartholomew, J. G. Internat. student's atlas of modern geography. '02(Ap12) 4°, net, $2.25. Scribner.

Bartlett, Alb. L. A golden way: journey through Ireland, Scotland and England. '02(Mr1) il. D. $1.50. Abbey Press.

Bartlett, Emeline B. *See* Pearson, H: C.

Bartlett, Lillian L. Animals at home. '02 (My17) il. D. (Eclectic school readings.) 45 c. Am. Bk.

Barton, F:, *comp*. Pulpit power and eloquence. '01· '02(Mr8) 8°, $3.50. F. M. Barton.

Barton, G: A. Roots of Christian teaching as found in the O. T. '02(My24) D. $1.25. Winston.

Barton, G: A. Sketch of Semitic origins, social and religious. '02(F1) 8°, net, $3. Macmillan.

Barton, W: E. I go a fishing: study in progressive discipleship. '02(F8) 16°, 25 c. Revell.

BASEBALL.
Spalding's official baseball guide, 1902. 10 c. Am. Sports.

Basis of social relations. Brinton, D. G. net, $1.50. Putnam.

BASKETRY.
Firth. Cane basket work. 2 v. ea., 60 c. Scribner.

Bass, Edg. W. Elements of differential calculus. 2d ed., rev. '02(Ja11) il. 12°, net, $4. Wiley.

Bassett, Fk. J. *See* Campbell, H. A.

Bassett, Ma. E. S. Judith's garden. '02(Je7) O. $1.50. Lothrop.

Batt, Max. Treatment of nature in German literature from Günther to the appearance of Goethe's Werther. '02(F15) O. pap., net, $1. Univ. of Chic.

Battleground. Glasgow, E. $1.50. Doubleday, P.

Bauder, Emma P. Anarchy; its cause and cure told in story. '02(Ap12) il. D. $1; pap., 50 c. Occidental Pub.

Baur, T. P., *and* Herbert, H. F. Free thinkers' manual. '02(Je7) il. 8°, $4. Radical.

Bausman, B. Precept and practice. '02(Ap5) D. net, $1. Heidelberg.

BAVARIA.
See Ludwig II.

Baylies, Edn. *See* Wait, W:

Bayly, Ada E., ["Edna Lyall."] The hinderers. '02(Je7) D. $1. Longmans.

Beach, Harlan P. Geography and atlas of Protestant missions. v. 1, Geography. '01· '02(F15) 12°, $2.50; pap., per set, $1.75. Student Vol.

Beale, C: C. Book of legal dictation. 2d ed., rev. and enl. '01· '02(F1) D. 50 c. Beale Press.

Beard, Sidney H. Comprehensive guide book to natural, hygienic and humane diet. New ed. '02(Mr22) 16°, $1; pap., 50 c. Alliance.

Beard, Sidney H. Comprehensive guide-book to natural, hygienic and humane diet. [New issue.] '02(My17) D. net, $1. Crowell.

Bears of Blue River. Major, C: $1.50. Macmillan.

Beau's comedy. Dix, B. M. $1.50. Harper.

Beaton, Ja. A. Vest-pocket practical compend of electricity. '02(My17) il. nar. T. 50 c.; leath., 75 c. Laird.

BEAUTIFUL (The).
See Aesthetics.

Beck, Carl. Sonnenblicke aus der Amerikanischen praxis. '02(F15) O. pap., net, 30 c. Lemcke.

Becker, Fk. S. *See* New York civil and criminal justice.

Beddard, F. E. Mammalia. *See* Harmer, S. F:, *ed*.

Bedell, Edn. A., *rep*. *See* New York. *Ct. of appeals*. Digest.

Bedford, Jessie. *See* Godfrey, E.

Beecher, C: E. Studies in evolution. '01· '02(Mr15) 8°, (Yale bicentennial pub.) net, $5. Scribner.

Beeching, H. C. Inns of court sermons. '01· '02(Ja4) 12°, $1.25. Macmillan.

Beeman, Marion N. Analysis of the Eng. sentence; rev. and enl. '02(Je28) sq. D. (Progredior ser.) 50 c. Flanagan.

Beers, G: E. *See* Stephen, *Sir* J. F.

Behymer, Ida H. Seal of destiny. '01· '02 My10) 12°, $1.50. Neely.

Bek's first corner. Conklin, *Mrs*. J. M. D. $1. Burt.

Belinda. Egan, M. F. $1. Kilner.

Bell, *Mrs*. Arth. *See* Bell, *Mrs*. N. R. E. M.

Bell, Lilian, [*now Mrs*. Arth. Hoyt Bogue.] Abroad with the Jimmies. '02(My10) il. D. $1.50. L. C. Page.

Bell, Malcolm. Rembrandt Van Rijn. '01· '02(Ja4) il. 12°, (Great masters of painting and sculpture.) $1.75. Macmillan.

Bell, *Mrs*. Nancy R. E. M., ["N. D'Anvers."] Thomas Gainsborough. '02(Je28) il. 16°, (Bell's miniature ser. of painters.) leath., $1. Macmillan.

Bell, Roscoe R. *See* Veterinarian's call-book.

Belles, W: H: Cain's sin. '01· '02(F1) D. $1. W: H: Belles.

Belloc, Bessie R. In a walled garden. 5th ed. '02(Mr8) 8°, net, $1.25. Herder.

Belloc, Bessie R. Passing world. 2d ed. '02(Mr8) 8°, net, $1.25. Herder.

Belloc, Hilaire. The path to Rome. '02(Je21) il. O. net, $2. Longmans.

Belloc, Hilaire. Robespierre: a study. '01-'02(F1) O. net, $2. Scribner.
Bell's cathedral ser. 12°, 60 c. Macmillan.
—Hiatt. Westminster Abbey.
Bell's handbooks to continental churches. il. 12°, $1. Macmillan.
—Perkins. Amiens.
Bell's miniature ser. of painters. il. 16°, 50 c.; limp leath., $1. Macmillan.
—Anstruther. Hogarth.
—Bell. Gainsborough.
—Staley. Watteau.
—Williamson. Holman Hunt.
Beman, W. W., *and* Smith, D: E. Academic algebra. '02(My24) D. hf. leath., $1.25. Ginn.
Ben Hur. Wallace, L. $2.50. Harper.
Bender, Ida C., *ed. See* Judson, H. P.
Bender, Wilbur H. The teacher at work. '02 (Je28) D. 75 c. Flanagan.
Benedictine martyr in England. Camm, B. net, $1.25. Herder.
Benjamin, C: H: Notes on machine design. 2d ed. '02(My17) il. 16°, $2. C. H. Holmes.
Benjy in beastland. Ewing, *Mrs.* J. H. 50 c. Little, B. & Co.
Bennett, Arnold. T. Racksole and daughter. '02(My24) il. D. $1.50. New Amsterdam.
Bennie, the Pythian of Syracuse. Fretz, L. B. $1. Scroll Pub.
Benson, E: F. Scarlet and hyssop. '02 (Ap12) D. $1.50. Appleton.
Benson, E: W. Addresses on the Acts of the Apostles. '02(Mr29) il. 8°, net, $7. Macmillan.
Benton, Joel. Life of P. T. Barnum. '02 (My24) 12°, (Biographies of famous men.) $1. Donohue.
Bentzan, Therese. Constances. '02(Ap26) 12°, $1.50. Neely.
Bergholt, Ernest. *See* Leigh, L.
BERIN, *St.*
Field. Saint Berin, the apostle of Wessex. $1.50. E. & J. B. Young.
Berkeley, W: N. Lab'y work with mosquitoes. '02(My17) O. net, $1. Pediatrics Lab.
BERKELEY HILLS.
Lawson *and* Palache. The Berkeley Hills: coast range geology. 80 c. Univ. of Cal.
Berkleys (The). Wight, E. H. net, 40 c. Benziger.
BERKSHIRE, Mass.
See Lenox.
BERLIOZ, Hector.
Young. Mastersingers; with essay on Hector Berlioz. net, $1.50. Scribner.
Berlitz, M. D. Grammaire partique de la langue française. In 4 v. v. 3. '02(Ap26) 12°. 50 c. Berlitz.
Bernis, François J. de P., *Cardinal* de. Memoirs and letters; fr. orig. mss. by F. Masson. '02(F1) 2 v., il. 8°, (Versailles hist. ser.) subs., per v., $6; ¾ leath., per v. $9. Hardy, P. & Co.
Berry, G: R., *ed.* Letters of the Rm. 2 coll. in the British Museum. '02(F15) 8°, pap., net, 50 c. Univ. of Chic.
Besant, *Sir* W. Autobiography. '02(My10) O. net. $2.40. Dodd.
Best, Kenelm D. Victories of Rome and the temporal monarchy of the church. 4th ed., rev. '01-'02(Mr22) S. net, 45 c. Benziger.
Best, Noel R. College man in doubt. '02 (Je21) D. net, 50 c. Westminster.
Best nonsense verses. Daskam, J. D. 50 c. W: S. Lord.
Best writings of great authors. 16°, $1.25; $3. L. C. Page.
—Balzac. Best of Balzac.
Beyond the clouds. Patterson, C: B. $1. Alliance.
Beyond the vail. Nixon, J. H. $1.75. Hudson-K.
Bible. Greek Testament; ed. by E. Nestle; app. on irregular verbs by R. F. Weidner. '02(Ap5) 16°, net, $1; leath., net, $1.25. Revell.
Bible. Temple ed. In 24 v. v. 2-4. '01-'02(F1); vs. 5-12 (Je28) il. sq. T. ea., net, 40 c.; flex. leath., ea., net, 60 c. Lippincott.
Bible. O. T. Cambridge Bible. Psalms. (A. F. Kirkpatrick.) '02(Ap5) 12°, net, $2. Macmillan.
Bible. Old Testament. Cambridge Bible for schools; Psalms; introd. and notes by A. F. Kirkpatrick. v. 9. bks. 4 and 5. '02 (Ja18) 12°, net, 80 c. Macmillan.
Bible. Sunday-school scholars' Bible; ed. by A. F. Schauffler. '02(Je21) 12°, 55 c.; Fr. flex. mor., 75 c.; Fr. mor., $1. Nelson.
BIBLE.
Alexander. Demonic possession in the N. T. net, $1.50. Scribner.
Askwith. Introd. to the Thessalonian Epistles. net, $1.25. Macmillan.
Barton. Roots of Christian teaching as found in the O. T. $1.25. Winston.
Benson. Addresses on the Acts of the Apostles. net, $7. Macmillan.
Boteler. Side windows; or, lights on Scripture truths. 75 c. Standard Pub.
Brown, F., *and others, eds.* Hebrew and Eng. lexicon of the Old Testament. pt. 10. net, 50 c. Houghton, M. & Co.
Browne. Help to spiritual interpretation of the penitential Psalms. net, 40 c. Longmans.
Chase. Credibility of the Acts of the Apostles. $1.75. Macmillan.
Eadie. Biblical cyclopædia. net, $3.75. Lippincott.
Florer. Biblische geschichten. 40 c. Wahr.
Goodspeed. Newberry gospels. net, 25 c. Univ. of Chic.
Grethenbach. Secular view of the Bible. net, $2. Eckler.
Harper. Constructive studies in the priestly element in the O. T. $1. Univ. of Chic.
Hoare. Evolution of the Eng. Bible. net, $2.50. Dutton.
Knecht. Child's Bible hist. 25 c. Herder.
Lilley. Pastoral epistles. net, 75 c. Scribner.
McGarvey. Authorship of the Book of Deuteronomy. $2. Standard Pub.
Mackail. Biblia innocentium; for children. $1.75. Longmans.
Nash, *ed.* Practical explanation and application of Bible history. net, $1.50. Benziger.
Patterson. Broader Bible study: Pentateuch. net, 75 c. Jacobs.

BIBLE.—*Continued.*
Pattison. The Bible and the 20th century. 10 c. Am. Bapt.
Prime. Power of God's word. 3 c. Presb. Bd.
Rice. Our sixty-six sacred books. net, 50 c. Am. S. S.
Robertson. Lessons on the Gospel of St. Mark. net, 40 c. Revell.
Robertson. Studies in the Acts of the Apostles. 40 c. Revell.
Ruble. Wonders of the Revelation of Jesus Christ: expository treatment of [Revelation]. $1. Standard Pub.
Shepardson. Studies in the Epistles to the Hebrews. $1.50. Revell.
Wade. Old Testament history. $1.50. Dutton.
Wilberforce. Com. on the Epistle to the Ephesians. net, $1. Herder.
Williams. Shall we understand the Bible? net, 50 c. Macmillan.
Young people's Bible stories. 4 v. ea., $1.25. Saalfield.
See also Catechisms;—Christianity;—God;—Jesus Christ;—Religion and science;—Saints; — Sermon on the Mount;—Theology.

Bible character ser. 16°, 35 c. Pepper.
—Carradine. Gideon.

Bible class handbooks. 12°, net. Scribner.
—Lilley. Pastoral epistles. 75 c.

Bible class primers. 16°, pap., net. 20 c. Scribner.
—Murison. Babylonia and Assyria.

Bible lessons for little beginners. Haven, *Mrs.* M. J. C. net, 75 c. Revell.

Bible stories. *See* Children's.

Bible student's lib. 12°. E. & J. B. Young.
—Girdlestone. Grammar of prophecy. $2.50. (11.)

Biblia innocentium. Mackail, J: W: $1.75. Longmans.

BIBLIOGRAPHIES.
Andrews. Paul Revere and his engraving. $23.50; $40. Scribner.
Annual Am. catalogue, cumulated 1900-01. $2. Pub. Weekly.
Ballagh. Slavery in Va. $1.50. Johns Hopkins.
Batt. Treatment of nature in Germ. literature. net, $1. Univ. of Chic.
Bourne. Teaching of hist. and civics. $1.50. Longmans.
Brace, *ed.* Laws of radiation and absorption. net, $1. Am. Bk.
Deems, *comp.* Holy-days and holidays. $5. Funk.
De Quincey. Selections. $1.05. Ginn.
Dickinson. Music in the hist. of the estern church. net. $2.50. Scribner.
Dyer *and* Hassall. Hist. of modern Europe. v. 6. net, $2. Macmillan.
English catalogue of books for 1901. $1.50. Pub. Weekly.
Fish. Calisthenic dict. $1. Seminar.
Fitzgerald. Writings; incl. complete bibliog. 7 v. subs., ea., $6; $12.50; $35. Doubleday, P.
Fletcher *and* Bowker. Annual literary index, 1901. net, $3.50. Pub. Weekly.
Flint, *and others.* The trust. net, $1.25. Doubleday, P.

BIBLIOGRAPHIES.—*Continued.*
Ford, *ed.* Journals of Hugh Gaine, pr. net, $15; net, $25. Dodd.
Fowler. Hist. of ancient Greek literature. net, $1.40. Appleton.
Green. Facsimile reproductions rel. to Boston and neighborhood. net, $10. Littlefield.
Huddilston. Lessons from Gr. pottery, with bibliog. of Gr. ceramics. net, $1.25. Macmillan.
Kupfer. Greek foreshadowings of mod. metaphysical and epistemological thought. $1. J. S. Cushing.
Larned, *ed.* Literature of Am. history. net, $6; $7.50; $9. Houghton, M. & Co.
Legler. James Gates Percival. net, $1. Mequon Club.
Livingston. Bibliog. of the first ed. in book form of the works of Tennyson. $1. Dodd.
Livingston. Works of Rudyard Kipling: des. of first eds. net, $12; net, $20. Dodd.
Mackinnon. Growth and decline of French monarchy. $7.50. Longmans.
Marks. Outline of Eng. literature. $1. J. A. Marks.
Meyer. Nominating systems. net, $1.50. E. C. Meyer.
Miner. Daniel Boone. $1. Dibdin Club.
Nield. Guide to the best historical novels and tales. net, $1.75. Putnam.
Paulsen. Immanuel Kant. net, $2.50. Scribner.
Randall, *ed. and tr.* Expansion of gases by heat. $1. Am. Bk.
Richardson. War of 1812. subs., $3. Hist. Pub.
Schmidt. Solomon's temple. net, $1. Univ. of Chic.
Vanderpoel. Color problems. net, $5. Longmans.
Vincent, *and others.* H. B. Adams; with bibliog. of the dept. of history, politics and economics of Johns Hopkins Univ. free to subs. Johns Hopkins.
Webb, S. *and* B. P. Trade unionism. net, $2.60. Longmans.
Wilson. Bibliog. of child study. net, 25 c. Stechert.

Biblische geschichten. Florer, W. W. 40 c. Wahr.

Bicknell, P. C. Guide book of the Grand Canyon of Arizona. '02(Je28) sq. S. leath., 75 c.; pap., 50 c. Harvey.

Billings, Fk., *and* Stanton, S. C., *eds.* General medicine. '01- '02(Mr8) 8°, (Practical medicine ser. of year-books, no. 1.) $1.50. Year Bk.

Billings, Josh, *pseud.* *See* Shaw, H: W.

BIMETALLISM.
See Money.

Bingham, Grace A., *comp.* Two hundred bar examination questions. '02(Je7) S. pap., $1. Commercial.

Binkley, Christian. Sonnets and songs for a house of days. '02(Je21) D. bds., net, $1.25. A. M. Robertson.

Biographies of famous men. 12°, $1. Donohue.
—Benton. P. T. Barnum.
—Custis. George Washington.

BIOGRAPHY.
American ser. of popular biographies. Mass. ed. $17. Graves.
Gans. Pennsylvania pioneer. $6. Kuhl.
Good. Women of the Reformed church. $1. Heidelberg.
Graham. Scottish men of letters in 18th century. net, $4.50. Macmillan.
Lippincott's biog. dict. 2 v. subs., $15; $17.50; $20. Lippincott.
National cyclopædia of Am. biography. v. 11. subs., $10. J. T. White.
Who's who, 1902. $1.75. Macmillan.
See also Authors; — Autographs; — Booksellers; — Diaries; — Genealogy; — Heroes; — History; — Painters; — Popes; — Saints.

Birbeck, Chris. J., *ed.* Select recitations, orations and dramatic scenes. '02(Je7) il. D. $1. Wagner.

Bird play. Spangler, N. Y. 15 c. Kellogg.

BIRDS.
Fowler. More tales of the birds. $1. Macmillan.
Job. Among the water fowl. net, $1.35. Doubleday, P.
Jordan, *comp.* True tales of birds and beasts. 40 c. Heath.
Lord. First book upon birds of Oregon and Washington. 75 c. W: R. Lord.
Sandys *and* Van Dyke. Upland game birds. net, $2; net, $7.50. Macmillan.
Wheelock. Nestlings of forest and marsh. net, $1.40. McClurg.
See also Pigeons.

BIRTHDAY BOOKS.
Tennyson. Birthday book. 75 c.; $1; $1.25. Warne.

Birthright membership of believers' infants. Horton, F. A. 6 c. Presb. Bd.

Bishop, W: H: Queer people, incl. The brown stone boy. '02(My17) D. $1. Street.

Bishop, W: H: Tons of treasure. New and imp. ed. of The yellow snake. '02(Je7) D. $1. Street.

BISMARCK, *Prince* v.
Lieb. Prince Bismarck and the German people. $1.50; $2.25; $3.25. Dominion.

Bits of broken china. Fales, W: E. S. 75 c. Street.

Bivar, R. D. de. *See* Cid (The).

Bixby, Ja. T. The new world and the new thought. '02(Mr8) D. net, $1. Whittaker.

Bjorling, P. R. Pipes and tubes. '02(Je28) il. 12°, $1. Macmillan.

Black, J: S. *See* Cheyne, T: K.

BLACK, W:
Reid. William Black, novelist. net, $2.25. Harper.

Black cat club. Corrothers, J. D. net, $1. Funk.

Black Evan. Young, J. D. $1. Neely.

Blackie, J: S. On self-culture: (phonography.) '02(F15) S. pap., 35 c. Phonograph.

Blackwood's (*ed.*) philosophical classics. New ed. '01- '02(Mr1) 15 v., 12°, per v., net, 50 c. Lippincott.

Blain, Hugh M. Syntax of the verb in the Anglo-Saxon chronicle from 787 A.D. to 1001 A.D. '01- '02(Mr8) 12°, (University of Virginia monographs, school of Teutonic languages, no. 2.) pap., net, 50 c. Barnes.

Blaisdell, Alb. F. Life and health. '02(Je14) D. $1. Ginn.

Blaisdell, Etta A. *and* Ma. F. Child life fifth reader. '02(Mr29) il. 12°, net, 45 c. Macmillan.

Blake, G: H. Common sense ideas for dairymen. '01- '02(F8) 12°, $1. Coates.

Blake, Ja. V. Sonnets. '02(Ja25) sq. S. $1. J. H. West.

Blake, W: William Blake; ed. by T. S. Moore. '02(Ap26) Q. (Little engravings classical and contemporary, no. 2.) bds., net, $1.50. Longmans.

Blakiston's quiz compend ser. il. 12°, 80 c.; $1. Blakiston.
—Thayer. Compend of general pathology. (15.)

Blanchard, Amy E. Twenty little maidens. '01- '02(F15) il. 12°, $1.25. Lippincott.

Blashfield, De Witt C., *ed.* *See* New York. Abbott's digest.

Blauvelt, Ma. T. Development of cabinet government in England. '02(Mr22) 12°, net, $1.50. Macmillan.

Blazed trail. White, S. E: $1.50. McClure, P.

Bleininger, Alb., *ed.* *See* Seger, H. A:

Blighted rose. Wynne, J. F. $1.50. Angelus.

BLIND (Reading for).
Roosevelt. Message to the two houses of Congress. $1. N. Y. State Lib.

Blind spot. Watkinson, W: L. net, $1. Revell.

Bliss, W: R. September days on Nantucket. '02(Je28) D. net, $1. Houghton, M. & Co.

Blithedale romance. Hawthorne, N. $1. Burt.

BLOCK ISLAND.
Livermore. Block Island. 25 c. Ball.

Block system of signalling on Am. railroads. Adams, B. B. $2. Railroad Gazette.

Blomfield, Reginald. Formal garden in England. 3d ed. '02(F1) il. 12°, $3. Macmillan.

BLOOD.
Cabot. Clinical examination of the blood. net, $3.25. Wood.
Da Costa. Clinical hematology. net, $5. Blakiston.

Blood will tell. Davenport, B: R. $1.50. Caxton Bk.

Bloomfield, Will. Transplanting an old tree. '02(Mr22) D. $1. Blanchard.

Blouet, Paul, ["Max O'Rell."] English pharisees, French crocodiles. New issue. '01- '02(Ja4) D. $1.25. Abbey Press.

Blouët, Paul. 'Tween you an' I. pt. 1, Concerning men; pt. 2, Concerning women. '02(My24) D. $1.20. Lothrop.

BLOWPIPE.
Plattner. Qualitative and quantitative analysis with the blowpipe. net, $4. Van Nostrand.

Blum, A. R. Reduction tables for ascertaining with accuracy and rapidity freight charges for any quantity of grain on all standard bases, in Eng. money. '01- '02 (Je14) 4°, leath., net, $3. Am. Code.

Boardman, G: D. Our risen King's forty days. '02(Mr22) D. net, $1.25. Lippincott.

BOATING.
See Canoeing.

BOATS.
Martin. Album of designs for boats, launches and yachts. $1. F. W. Martin.
Mower. How to build a knockabout. $1. Rudder.
See also Yachts and yachting.

Bob o' Link. **Waggaman, M. T.** 40 c. Benziger.

Boccaccio, G., and Aretino, L. B. Earliest lives of Dante; fr. the Ital. by Ja. R. Smith. '01- '02(Mr15) O. (Yale studies in Eng., no. 10.) pap., 75 c. Holt.

Bodmer, G. R. Inspection of railway materials. '02(Je7) 12°, $1.50. Macmillan.

BODY AND MIND.
See **Mind and body.**

Body and soul. Wright, J. C. $1. J. C. Wright.

Body of Christ. Gore, C: $1.75. Scribner.

BOERS.
Davitt. Boer fight for freedom. net, $2. Funk.
Hiley *and* Hassell. Mobile Boer. $1.50. Grafton Press.
See also South Africa.

Boethius, A. M. S. Consolation of philosophy. '02(Mr22) 16°, (Temple classics.) 50 c.; leath., 75 c. Macmillan.

Bogue, *Mrs.* A. H. *See* Bell, L.

Bohn's standard lib. 12°, net, $1. Macmillan.
—Prescott. Conquest of Peru. 2 v.—Ferdinand and Isabella. 3 v.
—Swift. Prose works. v. 9.

Boiled-down booklets. Tt. 25 c. Success.
—Hungerford. Success club debater.

BOILERS.
Robertson. Water-tube boilers. $3. Van Nostrand.

Boisot, L: By-laws of private corporations. 2d ed. '02(F8) O. shp., $3. Keefe-D.

BOLINGBROKE, *Lord.*
Sichel. Bolingbroke and his times. pt. 2. $4. Longmans.

Bonesteel, Ma. Recruit Tommy Collins. '02 (Mr22) S. 45 c. Benziger.

Book, J. W. Mollie's mistake. '02(Mr8) 16°, pap., 15 c. Herder.

BOOK ILLUSTRATION.
Brothers Dalziel: record of work, 1840-90. net, $6.50. Dutton.

Book lover. Baldwin, J. net, $1. McClurg.

BOOK OF COMMON PRAYER.
Hall. Companion to the prayer book. net, 35 c. E. & J. B. Young.
See also **Protestant Epis. church.**

Book of forms to be used in connection with the study of criminal procedure in the Univ. of Mich. '02(My24) O. pap., 60 c. Bliss & A.

Book of golden deeds. Yonge, C. M. $1. Burt.

Book of romantic ballads. '02(Je21) il. 16°, (Caxton ser.) net, $1.25. Scribner.

Book of secrets. Dresser, H. W. net, $1. Putnam.

Book of the rifle. Fremantle, T. F. $5. Longmans.

Book of the vegetables. Wythes, G: net, $1. Lane.

BOOK-PLATES.
Stone. Women designers of book-plates. net, $1; net, $2. Beam.

BOOKBINDING.
Cockerell. Bookbinding and care of books. net, $1.20. Appleton.

BOOKKEEPING.
Goodyear. Theory of accounts. $1.50. Goodyear-M.
Ingerson. Normal method in double entry bookkeeping. 50 c. Interstate.

BOOKKEEPING.—*Continued.*
Snyder *and* Thurston. Universal system of prac. bookkeeping. $1.25. Am. Bk.

Booklover's lib.; ed. by H: B: Wheatley. S. Armstrong.
—Wheatley. How to make an index. $1.25; $2.50.

BOOKS AND READING.
Baldwin. Book lover: guide to best reading. net, $1. McClurg.
Hitchcock. Book-builder's handbook of types, scales, etc. net, 50 c. Grafton Press.
Right reading; choice and use of books. net, 80 c. McClurg.
See also **Bookbinding;—Fiction;—Literature.**

BOOKSELLERS.
Marston. Sketches of some booksellers of the time of Dr. Johnson. net, $2. Scribner.

BOONE, Dan.
Miner. Daniel Boone cont. toward a bibliog. $1. Dibdin Club.

Booth, H: M. Heavenly vision, and other sermons. Memorial ed. [New issue.] '02 (Mr22) D. net, $1. Beam.

Booth, Wa. S. *See* North Dakota. Township manual.

Boothby, Guy. Millionaire's love story. '01- '02(Mr29) D. $1.25. Buckles.

Border warfare in Pennsylvania. Shimmell, L. S. 50 c. R. L. Myers.

BORING.
Isler. Well boring for water, brine and oil. $4. Spon.

Borrow, G: The Zincali: acc. of gypsies of Spain. '01- '02(F22) il. D. $2. Putnam.

Bossard, F. Modern designs for surface decoration and coloring. '02(Mr1) f°, $8. Hessling.

Bossard, J: Decorative paintings: designs for col. surface decoration. '01. '02(Ja25) col. pls. f°, $8. Hessling.

BOSTON.
Green. Ten facsimile reproductions rel. to old Boston and neighborhood. net, $10. Littlefield.
Historic Boston: sightseeing towns around the Hub. net, 50 c.; net, 30 c. Pilgrim Press.

Boswell, J. Journal of a tour to the Hebrides. (H. B. Cotterill.) '02(My24) 12°, (Eng. classics.) net, 60 c. Macmillan.

Bosworth, Newton, ed. Hochelaga depicta; early hist. and present state of the city and island of Montreal. '01. '02(Mr8) il. D. (Facsimile repr. of early Canadian books, no. 1.) net, $3; Large-pap. ed., net, $4.50. Congdon.

BOTANY.
Bower *and* Vaughan. Practical botany for beginners. net, 90 c. Macmillan.
Caldwell. Lab'y manual of botany. 60 c.; 50 c. Appleton.
Campbell. University text-book of botany. net, $4. Macmillan.
Cowles. Ecological rel. of vegetation on the sand dunes of Lake Michigan. net, 75 c. Univ. of Chic.
Dickson. Linear groups. net, $4. Stechert.
Frye. Development of the pollen in some asclepiadaceæ. net, 25 c. Univ. of Chic.

BOTANY.—*Continued.*
Ganong. Lab'y course in plant physiology, as a basis for ecology. net, $1. Holt.
Leavitt. Outlines of botany. 2 v. $1; $1.80. Am. Bk.
Life. Tuber-like rootlets of cycas revoluta. net, 25 c. Univ. of Chic.
Lilley *and* Midgley. Studies in plant form. net, $2. Scribner.
Lyon. Study of the sporangia and gametophytes of selaginella apus and selaginella rupestris. net, 25 c. Univ. of Chic.
Macdougal. Elem. plant physiology. $1.20. Longmans.
Meier. Herbarium and plant description. 70 c. Ginn.
Overton. Parthenogenesis in thalictrum purpurascens. net, 25 c. Univ. of Chic.
Smith, R. W. Achromatic spindle in spore mother-cells of osmunda regalis. net, 25 c. Univ. of Chic.
Stevens. Gametrogenesis and fertilization in albugo. net, 25 c. Univ. of Chic.
See also Algæ;—Bacteria; — Evolution; — Forests and forestry;—Galls;—Trees.

Boteler, Mattie M. Side windows. '01- '02 (Ap12) D. 75 c. Standard Pub.

BOUDE FAMILY.
See Leach, J. G.

Bourget, P. Monica, and other stories. '02 (Ap12) D. $1.50. Scribner.

Bourne, E: G. Essays in hist. criticism. '01-'02(F15) 8°, (Yale bicentennial pub.) net, $2. Scribner.

Bourne, G. C: Introd. to the study of comparative anatomy of animals. v. 2. '02 (Ap12) il. 12°, net, $1.25. Macmillan.

Bourne, H: E. Teaching of history and civics in the elem. and secondary school. '02 (My10) O. (Am. teachers' ser.) $1.50. Longmans.

Bowdoin, W. G. James McNeill Whistler, the man and his work. '01- '02(F8) O. bds., net, $1.50. Beam.

Bowen, B. L. First scientific French reader. '02(Je14) D. (Modern lang. ser.) 90 c. Heath.

Bowen, W: A. Why two Episcopal Methodist churches in the U. S.? '01- '02(Mr15) S. 75 c Pub. Ho. M. E. Ch., So.

Bower, F. O., *and* Vaughan, D. T. G. Practical botany for beginners. '02(My24) 12°, net, 90 c. Macmillan.

Bowker, R: R. *See* Fletcher, W: I:

Boyden, H: P. Beginnings of the Cincinnati Southern railway, 1869-1878. '01- '02(F8) 8°, pap., 50 c. Clarke.

Boyle, *Sir* Courtenay. *See* Avebury, *Lord.*

Boyle, F: Woodland orchids. '02(Ja18) 4°, net, $7. Macmillan.

Boys' vacation ser. S. 75 c. Neely.
—Whittier. In the Michigan lumber camps.

Brace, D. B., *ed.* Laws of radiation and absorption. '01- '02(Ja11.) O. (Scientific memoirs, no. 15.) $1. Am. Bk.

Bradbury, Ht. B. The new philosophy of health. [New issue.] '02(Mr22) 16°, 75 c. Alliance.

Braddon, Ma. E. *See* Maxwell, *Mrs.* M. E. B.

Bradish, Sa. P. Stories of country life. '01-'02(Ja4) S. (Eclectic school readings.) 40 c. Am. Bk.

Bradley, C: *See* Bradley, J. P.

Bradley, Jos. P. Miscellaneous writings; with sketch of his life; ed. and comp. by C: Bradley. '02(Ap5) 8°, $3. Hardham.

Brady, Cyrus T. Hohenzollern. '02(Ap12) il. D. $1.50. Century Co.

Brady, Cyrus T. Quiberon touch. '01- '02 (F22) 12°, $1.50. Appleton.

Brain, Belle M. Fifty missionary programmes. '02(F1) S. 35 c. Un. Soc. C. E.

BRAIN.
Fuller. Architecture of the brain. net, $3.50. Fuller.
See also Insanity; — Mind and body; — Nervous system;—Phrenology.

Bramble brae. Bridges, R. net, $1.25. Scribner.

BRAMSHOTT, ENG.
See Hampshire.

Brand, N. F. Justices' code for the state of Washington. '02(F15) O. shp., $5. Bancroft-W.

Brandes, G: Main currents in nineteenth century literature. v. 2. '02(My17) 8°, net, $2.75. Macmillan.

Brassey, T: A., *Baron, ed.* Naval annual for 1902. '02(Je21) 8°, net, $7.50. Scribner.

Bread and wine. King, M. E. $1.25. Houghton, M. & Co.

Breaking and riding. Fillis, J. net, $5. Scribner.

BREATHING.
Semon. Principles of local treatment in diseases of the upper air passages. net, $1. Macmillan.

Breaux, Jos. A. *See* Louisiana. *Sup. ct.* Digest.

Brenton, Hilda. Uncle Jed's country letters. '02(Je7) il. D. 30 c. Dickerman.

Breviarium bothanum sive portiforium secundum usum ecclesiæ cujusdam in Scotia; 1900. '02(F8) 4°, $15. Longmans.

Brewer, D: J. American citizenship. '02 (Ap19) D. net, 75 c. Scribner.

Brewster, Lyman D. *See* Ames, J. B.

Bride's book. Cook, *Mrs.* E. T. net, $1.50. Dutton.

Bridge, Ja. H., *ed.* *See* Flint, C: R.

Bridge, Norman. Rewards of taste, and other essays. '02(Ap5) D. $1.50. H. S. Stone.

BRIDGE.
Dunn. New ideas on bridge. 50 c. Scribner.
Elwell. Bridge; its principles and rules of play. net, $1.25. Scribner.
Smith, C. Bridge condensed. 50 c. Scribner.
Steele. Simple rules for bridge. 50 c. Eichelberger.

Bridgeman, T: Flower gardening. '01. '02 (F8) il. 12°, 50 c. Coates.

Bridgeman, T: Fruit gardening. '01- '02 (F8) il. 12°, 50 c. Coates.

Bridgeman, T: Kitchen gardening. '01- '02 (F8) il. 12°, 50 c. Coates.

Bridges, Rob., ["Droch."] Bramble brae. '02(Mr22) D. net, $1.25. Scribner.

BRIDGES.
Merriman *and* Jacoby. Text-book on roofs and bridges. pt. 3, Bridge design. $2.50. Wiley.

Bridgman, L. J. Gulliver's bird book. '02 (Mr29) il. 4°, $1.50. L. C. Page.

Brigham, Alb. P. *See* Gilbert, G. K.

Bright days in merrie England. Honeyman, A. V. net, $1.50. Honeyman.

BRINGHURST FAMILY.
Leach. Hist. of the Bringhurst family. $5. Lippincott.

Brinkley, Fk. Japan; its history, arts and literature. 4 v. '02(Ap5); v. 5 (Je28) 8°, (Oriental ser.) per v., $50. Millet.

Brinton, Dan. G. Basis of social relations. '02(Mr22) 8°, (Science ser., v. 10.) net, $1.50. Putnam.

Brinton Eliot. Farmer, J. E. $1.50. Macmillan.

Britain and the British seas. Mackinder, H. J. $2. Appleton.

British-Am. guide to Carlsbad. Arany, S. A. 50 c. Abbey Press.

British vegetable galls. Connold, E: J. net, $4. Dutton.

Britton; Eng. tr. and notes by F. M. Nichols. '01· '02(Mr1) 12°, (Legal classic ser.) shp., $3. Byrne.

Broader Bible study. Patterson, A. net, 75 c. Jacobs.

Bronson, Wa. H., *ed.* *See* Ritchie, M. G.

Brooklyn *Daily Eagle* almanac, 1902. '02 (Ja11) 8°, (Eagle lib.) 50 c.; pap., 25 c. Brooklyn Eagle.

Brooklyn Eagle lib. 12°, pap. Brooklyn Eagle.
—New York City. Tenement house law. 10 c. (v. 17, 3.)

Brooks, H. J. Elements of mind. '02(Je7) O. $4. Longmans.

Brooks, H: *See* Dame, L. L.

Brooks, H: S. Progression to immortality. '02(Je7) D. net, 50 c. Wessels.

Brooks, Hildegard. Master of Caxton. '02 (Ap12) D. $1.50. Scribner.

Brooks, J: A., *rep.* *See* Michigan. *Sup. ct.* Repts.

Brooks, Phillips. Law of growth, and other sermons. '02(Mr29) 12°, net, $1.20. Dutton.

Brooks, S. J., *comp.* *See* Texas. Conflicting civil cases;—Repts.

BROOKS.
Miller. Brook book. net, $1.35. Doubleday, P.

Brothers Dalziel (The). Record of their work in connection with distinguished artists, 1840-1890. '02(Ap5) il. 4°, vellum, net, $6.50. Dutton.

Brounoff, Platon G. *See* Sharp, B. A.

Brower, Dan. R., *and* Bannister, H: M. Practical manual of insanity. '02(Mr29) 8°, $2. Saunders.

Brown, Abbie F. In the days of giants: Norse tales. '02My3) il. D. net, $1.15. Houghton, M. & Co.

Brown, C: F., *and* Croft, V. E. Outline study of U. S. hist. '01· '02(Je14) 16°, vellum, 50 c. Courier. Pr.

Brown, C: W. American star speaker and model elocutionist. '02(My17) il. 12°, $1.50. Donohue.

Brown, C: W. Ethan Allen. '02(My17) 12°, $1. Donohue.

Brown, C: W. John Paul Jones of naval fame. '02(Je28) D. (Am. patriot ser.) $1. Donohue.

Brown, C: W., *comp.* Comic recitations and readings. '02(My17) 12°, 50 c.; pap., 25 c. Donohue.

Brown, C: W., *comp.* Patriotic recitations and readings. '02(My17) 12°, 50 c.; pap., 25 c. Donohue.

Brown, Christian H:, *comp.* Optician's manual. v. 1 and 2. '02(Je28) il. 12°, ea., $2. Keystone.

Brown, D: W. Science and art of phrase-making; designed to teach stenographic phrasing by principle. '02(Ap5) 12°, $1.50. Shorthand Bu.

BROWN, Ford M.
Rossetti. Ford Madox Brown. net, 35 c. Beam.

Brown, Fs., Driver, S: R., *and* Briggs, C: A., *eds.* Hebrew and Eng. lexicon of the Old Testament. pt. 10. '02(Mr22) 8°, pap., net, 50 c. Houghton, M. & Co.

Brown, Grace M., ["Ione."] Studies in spiritual harmony. '02(Mr22) sq. S. $1. Reed.

Brown, J: Rab and his friends, and other dog stories; ed. by C: W. French. '02 (Je14) il. (Canterbury classics.) 25 c. Rand, McN. & Co.

Brown, P. H. History of Scotland. v. 2 '02(Ap26) 12°, (Cambridge hist. ser.) net, $1.50. Macmillan.

Brown, W: B. Gospel of the kingdom and the gospel of the church. '01(F8) D. $1. Whittaker.

Brown, W: G. The lower South in Am. history. '02(My24) 12°, net, $1.50. Macmillan.

Brown, W: G. Stephen Arnold Douglas. '02(Mr29) S. (Riverside biog. ser., no. 13.) net, 65 c.; School ed., net, 50 c. Houghton, M. & Co.

Brown, W: N., *ed.* Workshop wrinkles for decorators, painters and others. '01· '02 (My10) D. net, $1. Van Nostrand.

Browne, *Mrs.* A. B. B. Help to the spiritual interpretation of the penitential Psalms. '02 (Ap19) D. net, 40 c. Longmans.

Browne, D: McM. How to tell the time of night by the stars. '01· '02(Ap12) 8°, 50 c. Lee & S.

Browne, Fk. J. Graded mental arithmetic. '02(Je7) sq. 16°, net, 30 c. Whitaker & R.

Browne, Gordon. Proverbial sayings. '01· '02(F15) il. 4°, bds., net, $1. Stokes.

Browne, Wa. S. Rose of the wilderness. '01· '02(Mr1) il. D. $1.25. W. S. Browne.

Brownies (The) *See* Ewing, *Mrs.* J. H.

Bruce, W. S. Formation of Christian character. '02(My10) 12°, net, $1.75. Scribner.

Brugnot, Alice G. T. *See* Baillot, E. P.

Brühl, Gustav, *and* Politzer, A. Atlas epitome of otology. '02(Ap26) il. 12°, net, $3. Saunders.

Bruno. Dewey, B. S. 50 c. Little, B. & Co.

Brunton, *Sir* Lauder. On disorders of assimilation, digestion, etc. '01· '02(Ja4) il. 8°, net, $4; *Same,* (Ap12) hf. mor., net, $5. Macmillan.

Bryce, Alex. Ideal health and how to attain it. '01· '02(Mr1) 12°, pap., 50 c. Treat.

Bubbles. Newberry, F. E. $1. Burt.

Bubier, E: T. A B C of wireless telegraphy. '02(Je21) S. $1. Bubier.

Bubier, E: T. Experimental electricity. New rev. and enl. ed. '02(Je14) il. 16°, $1. Bubier.

Bubier, E: T. How to build dynamo-electric machinery. 2d ed. '02(Je14) il. 8°, $2.50. Bubier.
Buck, A. H. A reference handbook of the medical sciences. New ed., rev. and rewritten. v. 4. '02(Ap12) il. 8°, subs., $7; leath., $8; mor., $9. Wood.
Budd, J. L. *and* Hanson, N. E. Am. horticultural manual. '02(My17) 12°, $1.50. Wiley.
Budd, Jos. H. Civil remedies under the code system. '02(Ap12) O. shp., $6. Palm.
Buell Hampton. Emerson, W. G: $1.50. Forbes.
BUILDING.
See Architecture;—Engineering.
BULBS.
Arnott. Book of bulbs. net, $1. Lane.
Bulkley, L. D. *See* Duhring, L: A.
Bullen, Fk. T. Deep-sea plunderings. '02 (My19) il. D. $1.50. Appleton.
Bülow-Wendhausen, *Baroness v.* Life of the Baroness von Marenholtz Bülow. '01- '02 (Ja4) 2 v., O. net, $3.50. W: B. Harison.
BULOW, *Baroness* von Marenholtz.
Bulow-Wendhausen. Life of Baroness von Marenholtz Bülow. 2 v., net, $3.50. W: B. Harison.
BUNKER HILL.
Heath. Memoirs; [also] accounts of the Battle of Bunker Hill, by Gens. Dearborn, Lee and Wilkinson. net, $5. Abbatt.
Bunt and Bill. Mulholland, C. 45 c. Benziger.
Bunyan, J: The holy war. '01(Mr1) 16°, 50 c.; leath., 75 c. Macmillan.
Bunyan, J: Pilgrim's progress. '01- '02 (Ja11) 2 v., il. 16°, (Caxton ser.) flex. lambskin, net. $2.40. Scribner.
Burdens of local taxation. Purdy, L. 25 c. Public Policy.
Burdick, Alfr. S. Standard medical manual. '01- '02(Mr8) 8°. $4. Engelhard.
Burgert, Celia M. *See* Skinner, W. H.
Burgess, J: W. Reconstruction and the constitution, 1866-1876. '02(Mr22) D. (Am. hist. ser.) net, $1. Scribner.
Burghard, F. F. *See* Cheyne, W: W.
Buried temple. Maeterlinck, M. net, $1.40. Dodd.
Burke, Bridget E. McBride literature and art books. bks. 1-3. '01- '02(Mr22) il. 12°, bk. 1, 25 c.; bk. 2, 30 c.; bk. 3, 35 c. McBride.
Burke, Edm. Works. Beaconsfield ed. In 12 v., v. 1-4. '01- '02(F15) 8°, subs., per v., net, $3.50. Little, B. & Co.
Burke, Edm. Thoughts on the cause of the present discontents; ed. by F. G. Selby. '02(Je28) 12°, net, 60 c. Macmillan.
Burks, Martin P. *See* Virginia. *Sup. ct. of appeals.* Repts.
BURMA.
Smith. Ten years in Burma. net, $1. Eaton & M.; Jennings.
Burnett, *Mrs.* Fes. H. Methods of Lady Walderhurst. '02(F22) il. D. $1.25. Stokes.
Burnett, J. C. New cure for consumption by its own virus. 4th ed. 1900. '02(Ap5) 12°, $1. Boericke & T.
Burnham, Clara L. A great love. '02(Ap5) 16°, (Riverside pap. ser., no. 94.) pap., 50 c. Houghton, M. & Co.
Burns, Harrison. *See* Indiana. Statutes.
Burns, R. Complete poems and songs. (T: Carlyle.) '02(Mr8) 16°, (Caxton ser.) net, $1.20. Scribner.
Burns, R. Complete poetical works. Pocket ed. '02(My17) 12°, (New century lib.) $1.25; limp. leath., $1.75. Nelson.
Burns, R. Poems, epistles, songs, epigrams, and epitaphs; ed. by J. A. Manson. '02 (F1) 12°, net, $1; flex. leath., net, $1.50. Macmillan.
BURR, A.
Jenkinson. Aaron Burr, his rel. with Thos. Jefferson and Alex. Hamilton. $1.25. I: Jenkinson.
Todd. True Aaron Burr. net, 50 c. Barnes.
Burr, Enoch F. Aleph the Chaldean. [New issue.] '02(Ap12) 12°, $1.25. Whittaker.
Burrow, C: K. Patricia of the hills. '02 (Mr8) D. net, $1.20. Putnam.
Burt, Ma. E., *and* Howells, Mildred. Literary primer. '01- '02(Mr15) 16°, bds., net, 30 c. Scribner.
Burton, E. D., *and* Mathews, S. Constructive studies in the life of Christ. '02(F15) 8°, $1. Univ. of Chic.
Burton, R: Forces in fiction, and other essays. '02(Ap26) D. net, $1. Bowen-M.
Burton, Thdr. E. Financial crises and period of industrial and commercial depression. '02(Mr1) D. net, $1.40. Appleton.
Burt's fairy lib. il. 12°, $1. Burt.
—Valentine, *comp. and ed.* Old, old fairy tales.
—Yeats, *comp. and ed.* Irish fairy and folk tales.
Burt's fireside ser. il. 12°, $1. Burt.
—Armstrong. Very odd girl.
—Conklin. Bek's first corner.—Growing up. —Miss Prudence.—Tessa Wadsworth's discipline.
—Le Row. Duxbury doings.
—Newberry. Bubbles.—Joyce's investments. —Sara.
—Robbins. Miss Ashton's new pupil.
—Rouse. Annice Wynkoop, artist.—Deane girls.
—Smith. Daddy's girl.—Very naughty girl.
Burt's home lib. il. 12°, $1. Burt.
—Addison. Essays.
—Arnold. Essays in criticism.
—Barrie. Little minister.
—Chesterfield. Letters, sentences, and maxims.
—Elizabeth and her German garden.
—Emerson. Representative men.
—Harris. Rutledge.
—Hawthorne. Blithedale romance.—Marble faun.
—Headley. Napoleon and his marshals.—Washington and his generals.
—Holley. Samantha at Saratoga.
—Holmes. Cousin Maude and Rosamond.
—Ingraham. Throne of David.
—Johnson. Rasselas.
—Kingsley. Alton Locke.—Hereward the Wake.
—Le Sage. Gil Blas.
—Longfellow. Hyperion.
—Lubbock. Pleasures of life.
—Macaulay. Literary essays.
—Macdonald. David Elginbrod.

Burt's home lib.—Continued.
—Maggie Miller.
—More. Utopia.
—Parkman. Consniracy of Pontiac.
—Pater. Marius the epicurean.
—Plato. Republic.
—Poe. Murders in the Rue Morgue.
—Saint-Pierre. Paul and Virginia.
—Stowe. Minister's wooing.
—Taylor. Views afoot.
—Thoreau. Walden.
—Webster. Speeches.
—Yonge. Book of golden deeds.
Burt's little women ser. il. 12°, 75 c. Burt.
—Prentiss. Little Susy stories.
Burt's St. Nicholas ser. il. 12°, 75 c. Burt.
—Kaler. Wan Lun and Dandy.
—Molesworth. Grandmother dear.
—Newberry. Comrades.
—Prentiss. Six little princesses.
—Weber. Clock on the stairs.

Bury, J: B. Hist. of Greece to the death of Alex. the Great. '02(My17) 2 v., 8°, net, $8. Macmillan.

BUSINESS.
Avebury, *and others.* King's weigh-house: lectures to business men. 75 c. Macmillan.
Carnegie. Empire of business. subs., $3. Doubleday, P.
Perry. Legal adviser and business guide. $1.50. Pontiac.
Pitman, B. *and* Howard. Business letters. no. 1, 25 c. Phonograph.
Pitman, I: Business corr. in shorthand. no. 2, 30 c. Pitman.
See also Advertising;—Commerce;—Commercial law; — Finance; — Political economy; — Stock exchange.

BUSINESS EDUCATION.
Stevens. Business education. 15 c. Bardeen.
See also Bookkeeping.

"But Thy love and Thy grace." Finn, F. J. $1. Benziger.

Butler, C: H: Treaty-making power of the U. S. In 2 v. '02(Ap5) O. hf. shp., (complete work,) net, $12. Banks.

BUTLER FAMILY.
Rook. The Butler family. $3. Lakeside Press.

By the gray sea. '02(Mr8) 8°, net, 60 c. Herder.

Bylow Hill. Cable, G: W. $1.25. Scribner.

Byrd, W: Writings of "Col. William Byrd of Westover in Virginia, Esq."; ed. by J. S. Bassett. '02(Mr8) il. f°, net, $10. Doubleday, P.

Byron, G: G. N., *Lord.* Works. Ed. de luxe. v. 13-16. '02(Mr15) 8°. (App. to pubs. for price.) Niccolls.

Byron, G: G. N., *Lord.* Works. New rev., enl. ed. In 12 v. v. 11. '02(Ap12) 12°, $2. Scribner.

Bywater, B. Two thousand years in eternity. '01. '02(Je21) 8°, net, $2.15. Hudson-K.

C., *pseud. See* Cox, *Mrs.* J. F.

Caballero, Fernán. La familia de Alvareda. (P. B. Burnet.) '01. '02(Mr15) S. 75 c. Holt

Cable, G: W. Bylow Hill. '02(Je7) D. $1.25. Scribner.

Cabot, R: C. Guide to the clinical examination of the blood. 4th rev. ed. '01. '02 (F22) il. 8°, net, $3.25. Wood.

Cadigan, E. S. My ocean trip. '02(Je28) il. 12°, $1. Brentano's.

Cadiot, P. J. Clinical veterinary medicine and surgery. '01. '02(F22) il. 8°, $5.25. W: R. Jenkins.

Cadwallader, Starr. Story of home gardens. '02(Mr22) O. pap., 25 c. Home Gardening.

CAEDMON, *St.*
Gaskin. Caedmon, the first Eng. poet. 40 c. E. & J. B. Young.

Caesar. Commentaries on the Gallic war; vocab. by A. Harkness, assisted by C: H. Forbes. '02(F15) il. D. hf. leath., $1.25. Am. Bk.

CAESARS (The).
Van Santvoord. House of Cæsar and the imperial disease. net, $5.25. Pafraets.

Caffin, C: H. American masters of painting. '02(Ap5) D. net, $1.25. Doubleday, P.

Cain's sin. Belles, W: H: $1. W: H: Belles.

CAIRO.
Poole. Story of Cairo. $2; $2.50. Macmillan.

CALCULUS.
Bass. Elements of differential calculus. net, $4. Wiley.
Durège. Elements of the theory of functions of a complex variable. net, $2. Macmillan.
Smith. Elem. calculus. $1.25. Am. Bk.

Caldwell, Otis W: Laboratory manual of botany. '02(Je28) 12°, (Twentieth century text-books.) 60 c.; limp cl., 50 c. Appleton.

CALENDARS AND YEAR-BOOKS.
Daily praise. 15 c.; 20 c.; 25 c. Revell.
Epworth League yearbook, 1902. net, 10 c. Eaton & M.
See also Almanacs and annuals;—Devotional exercises and meditations.

Calhoun, W: P. The Caucasian and the negro in the U. S. '02(Je28) D. pap., 75 c. R. L. Bryan.

California. Code time table; by J. H. Kann. '02(Ap19) D. $1.50; interleaved, $2. Dempster.

California. Constitution; annot. by E: F. Treadwell. '02(F1) S. shp., $4. Bancroft-W.

California. *Superior ct.* Repts. (E. Tauszky.) '02(Ap12) 2 v., O. shp., ea., $5. Dempster.

CALIFORNIA.
Hershey. Quaternary of So. Cal. 20 c. Univ. of Cal.
Hufford. El camino real: orig. highway connecting the 21 missions. 35 c.; 75 c.; $1; $1.25. D: A. Hufford.
Stoddard. In the footprints of the padres. net, $1.50. A. M. Robertson.
See also Fresno Co.

CALISTHENICS.
See Gymnastics.

Callahan, C. E. Fogg's ferry. '02(Mr15) il. D. 75 c.; pap., 25 c. Laird.

Calmerton, Gail, *and* Wheeler, W: H: First reader. '02(Mr22) il. sq. 12°, (Graded readers.) 30 c. W: H: Wheeler.

CALVÉ, Emma.
Wisner. Emma Calvé. $1.50. Russell.

Calvin, Emily R. A Jewish carol and The insuperable barrier. '02(Je7) D. bds., 75 c. Westminster Pub.
Cambridge encyclopædia of esoteric subjects. Demorest, A. F. v. 3, net, $3. Cambridge.
Cambridge historical ser.; ed. by G: W. Prothero. 12°, net. Macmillan.
—Brown. Hist. of Scotland. v. 2. $1.50.
Cambridge natural history. *See* Harmer, S. F:, *ed.*
Cambridge Univ. Press ser. 12°, net. Macmillan.
—**Æschylus.** The choephori. $3.25.
—**Aristophanes.** The knights. net, $2.50.
—De Montmorency. State intervention in Eng. education. $1.50.
—Forsyth. Differential equations. v. 4. $3.75.
—Glover. Life and letters in the 4th century. net, $3.25.
—Laurie. Training of teachers. $1.50.
—Maitland, *and others.* Teaching of history. 75 c.
—Mayor. Chapters on Eng. metre. net, $2.25.
—Stokes. Mathematical and physical papers. v. 3. $3.75.
—Stokes *and* Strachan. Thesaurus palæohibernicus. v. 1. net, $8.
—Strutt. Scientific papers. v. 3. $5.
Cameron, J. H. Elements of French composition. '01· '02(Ja4) D. 75 c. Holt.
Cameron, V. L. Three sailor boys. '02(My17) 12°, 60 c. Nelson.
Camino (El) real. Hufford, D: A. 35 c.; 75 c.; $1; $1.25. D: A. Hufford.
Camm, Bede. A Benedictine martyr in England: life and times of Dom John Roberts. '02(Mr8) 8°, net, $1.25. Herder.
Campbell, Colin P. *See* Michigan. *Sup. ct.* Index digest.
Campbell, Douglas H. University text-book of botany. '02(My3) 8°, net, $4. Macmillan.
Campbell, Hardy W. Soil culture manual, 1902. '02(My17) il. D. pap., 40 c. H. W. Campbell.
Campbell, Hollis A., Sharpe, W: C., *and* Bassett, Fk. J. Seymour, past and present. '02(Je14) il. 8°, $3. W: C. Sharpe.
Campbell, J. G. D. Siam in the twentieth century. '02(Je7) il. O. net, $5. Longmans.
Campbell, W: C. A Colorado colonel, and other sketches. '01· '02(F8) il. D. $1.50. Crane.
Canada.
Henry. Travels in Canada, 1760-1776. $4. Little, B. & Co.
Jesuit relations. v. 72, 73. ea., $3.50. Burrows.
See also Indians;—Montreal.
Canadian books. *See* Bosworth, N.
Canals.
Johnson. Isthmian canal. 25 c. Am. Acad. Pol. Sci.
Pasco. Isthmian canal question. 25 c. Am. Acad. Pol. Sci.
Candy.
See Confectionery.
Cane basket work. *See* Firth, A.
Canfield, Ja. H. The college student and his problems. '02(F1) 12°, (Personal problem ser.) net, $1. Macmillan.
Canoeing.
Thwaites. Down historic waterways. net, $1.20. McClurg.
Canterbury classics. il., 25 c. Rand, McN. & Co.
—Brown. Rab and his friends.
Cape Cod ballads. Lincoln, J. C. net, $1.25. Brandt.
Capes, W. W. Scenes of rural life in Hampshire among the manors of Bramshott. '02(Ja18) 8°, net, $2.75. Macmillan.
Capital and Labor.
Kropotkin. Fields, factories and workshops. net, 90 c. Putnam.
Labor and capital. $1.50. Putnam.
Lafarque. Religion of capital. 10 c. Socialistic Co-op.
Marx. Wage-labor and capital. 50 c. N. Y. Labor News.
See also Labor and laboring classes;—Trusts.
Captain Fanny. Russell, W: C. $1.25; 50 c. New Amsterdam.
Captain Jinks, hero. Crosby, E. $1.50. Funk.
Captain Jinks of the Horse marines. Fitch, W: C. $1.25. Doubleday, P.
Captain of the Grayhorse troop. Garland, H. $1.50. Harper.
Card sewing. Maxwell, L. H. 50 c. M. Bradley
Cards.
Hart. Card language, 20 c. R. M. Hart.
Hart. Card language. 20 c. McEnally.
Roterberg. Card tricks. 25 c. Drake.
See also Bridge;—Fortune-telling;—Whist.
Careless Jane. Pyle, K. net, 75 c. Dutton.
Carey, W: Adventures in Tibet; incl. diary of Miss A. R. Taylor's journey from Ta-Chien Su through the forbidden land. '02 (Ja25) il. O. net, $1.50. Un. Soc. C. E.
Carey, Wymond. Monsieur Martin. '02 (Mr22) D. net, $1.20. Putnam.
Carhart, H: S., *and* Chute, H. N. Physics for high school students. '02(Ap26) il. 12°, $1.25. Allyn & B.
Carlsbad.
Arany. British-Am. guide to Carlsbad. 50 c. Abbey Press.
Carlyle, T: Past and present; ed. by O. Smeaton. '02(My24) 16°, (Temple classics.) 50 c.; flex. leath., 75 c. Macmillan.
Carman, Bliss. Ode on the coronation of King Edward. '02(Je14) 4°, net, $1. L. C. Page.
Carmichael, M. In Tuscany. New ed. '02 (Ap5) 12°, net, $2. Dutton.
Carmichael, M. Life of John William Walshe, T.S.A. [novel.] '02(Je14) 8°, net, $2. Dutton.
Carnegie, And. Empire of business. '02 (Ap19) O. subs., $3. Doubleday, P.
Caroline, *Queen of England.*
Wilkins. Caroline the illustrious Queen-Consort of George II. 2 v. $12. Longmans.
Carpenter, E:, *ed.* Ioläus: anthology of friendship. '02(Je14) sq. D. silk, net, $1.75. Goodspeed.
Carpenter, F. G. Europe. '02(Ap12) il. D. (Geographical readers.) 70 c. Am. Bk.
Carpenter, Stephen H. *See* Chaucer, G.
Carpenter prophet. Pearson, C: W. $1.50. H. S. Stone.

Carradine, Beverly. Gideon. '02(My24) 16°, (Bible character ser.) 35 c. Pepper.

Carroll, Stella W. Around the world; third book, home geography. '02(Mr22) il. 12°, (Geographical ser.) 60 c. Morse.

CARS.
Thompson. The motor car. $1. Warne.

CARSON, Kit.
Abbott. Christopher Carson, known as Kit. net, 87 c. Dodd.

Carson, W: H: The fool. '02(Je7) il. D. $1.50. G: W. Dillingham.

Carson, W: H: Hester Blair. '02(Mr1) il. D. $1.50. C. M. Clark.

Carter, Ernest. *See* Atkinson, R. W.

Carter, Eva N. Gleanings from nature. '02 (Ap26) il. D. $1. Abbey Press.

Carter, P: Peter Carter, 1825-1900. '01· '02 (F8) 8°, n. p. Privately pr.

CARVING.
See Ivory.

Cary, G: H. How to make and use the telephone. New rev. 2d ed. '02(Je14) il. 16°, $1. Bubier.

CASAS, Bartolomé de las.
Dutto. Life of Bartolomé de las Casas. net, $1.50. Herder.

Caskoden, Edwin, *pseud. See* Major, C:

Cassock of the pines. Daley, J. G. $1. W: H. Young.

Cast iron. Keep, W: J. $2.50. Wiley.

Castlemon, Harry, [*pseud.* for C: Austin Fosdick.] Floating treasure. '01. '02(Ja25) il. D. $1. Coates.

Castles in Spain. Stoner, W. S. $1. Abbey Press.

CAT.
Neel. Cats, how to care for them. 50 c. Boericke & T.
Hill. Diseases of the cat. $1.25. W: R. Jenkins.

CATALOGUING.
Hasse, *comp.* U. S. Government pubs.; handbk. for cataloguer. pt. 1. $1. Lib. Bu.

CATECHISMS.
Färber. Commentar zum (Catholic) katechismus. net, $1.50. Herder.
Macdonald, *ed.* Rev. catechism (Westminster Assembly's "shorter catechism.") $1.25. Macmillan.
Mangasarian. New catechism. 75 c. Open Court.
Nash, *ed.* Explanation and application of Bible history. [Questions and answers.] net, $1.50. Benziger.
Scadding. Direct answers to plain questions for Am. churchmen: expansion of the church catechism. net, 50 c. Whittaker
Staebler. Manual on the Book of books for juniors. 20 c. Mattill & L.

Cathcart, Ja. L. Tripoli; first war with the U. S.; letter book by J. L. Cathcart, first consul to Tripoli. '01. '02(Mr29) 12°, $4. J. B. C. Newkirk.

CATHEDRALS.
Addis. Cathedrals and abbeys of Presb. Scotland. net, $2.50. Presb. Bd.
See also Amiens;—Church architecture;—Westminster Abbey.

Catherine. *See* Thackeray, W: M.

Catherwood, *Mrs.* Ma. H. Craque o' Doom. '02(Je28) 12°, (People's lib., no. 30.) pap., 50 c. Am. News.

Catherwood, *Mrs.* Ma. H. Story of Tonty. 6th ed. enl. '01· '02(F1) il. D. $1.25. McClurg.

Catholic (The). '02(My10) 12°, $1.50. Lane.

Catholic church from within. '01· '02(Ja4) O. $2.50. Longmans.

Catholic church. Instructions and prayers for Catholic youth. '01· '02(Ja18) il. Tt. 60 c. Benziger.

Catholic Church. Litanei zum heiligsten Herzen Jesu. '02(Je28) 32°, pap., net, 3 c. Herder.

Catholic church. Priests' new ritual. [In Latin and Eng.;] by J: Murphy. '02(Ap19) 32°, leath., net, 75 c. Murphy.

CATHOLIC CHURCH.
Best. Victories of Rome and temporal monarchy of the church. net, 45 c. Benziger.
Catholic directory, almanac and clergy list quarterly. $1.25; $1.75. Wiltzius.
Galton. Our attitude toward Eng. Roman Catholics. net, $1. Dutton.
Lasance, *comp.* Short visits to the blessed sacrament. 25 c. Benziger.
Novene zu ehren des Heiligen Geistes. net, 3 c. Herder.
Poland. Find the church. net, 5 c. Herder.
Rainy. Ancient Catholic church, A.D. 98-451. net, $2.50. Scribner.
Raycroft. Sermons on the stations of the cross, the Our Father, Hail Mary, etc. net, $1.50. Pustet.
Rosen. The Catholic church and secret societies. net, $1. Caspar.
Tagzeiten zum heiligsten Herzen Jesu. 5 c. Herder.
Tesniere. Adoration of the blessed sacrament. net, $1.25. Benziger.
Vaughan. Holy sacrifice of the mass. 15 c. Herder.
See also Christianity;—Church history;—Church music;—Confession;—Convents;—Indulgences;—Jesus (society of);—Mary, *Virgin*;—Monasticism;—Popes;—Saints.

Catholic directory, almanac and clergy list—quarterly. '02(Ap26) D. pap., $1.25; leatherette, $1.75. Wiltzius.

Cat's paw. Croker, *Mrs.* B. M. $1; 50 c. Lippincott.

CATTLE.
McCallum & Hofer Cattle Co. Stockmen's calculator; cost of any amount from 5 to 32,000 lbs. $1.50. McCallum.
See also Veterinary medicine and surgery.

Caucasian and the negro in the U. S. Calhoun, W: P. 75 c. R. L. Bryan.

CAVALRY.
See Horse.

Caxton ser. 16°, net. Scribner.
—Bacon. Works. $1.25.
—Book of romantic ballads. $1.25.
—Bunyan. Pilgrim's progress. 2 v. $1.20.
—Cervantes Saavedra. Don Quixote. $1.25.
—Hood. Serious poems. $1.25.
—Irving. Sketch book. $1.25.
—La Motte Fouque. Undine [also] Aslauga's knight. $1.20.
—Milton. Complete poems. $1.20.
—Shakespeare. Plays and poems. 3 v. per set, $4.20. Scribner.

Caxton ser.—Continued.
—Shelley. Poetical works. $1.25.
—Tennyson. In memoriam. $1.20.
Celestial message. Gaffield, E. C. n. p. Lee & S.
CEMENT.
Lathbury *and* Spackman. Am. engineering practice in construction of rotary Portland cement plants. $2. G. M. S. Armstrong.
CENTRAL AMERICA.
Herbertson, *comp.* Desc. geographies; Central and South Am., with the West Indies. net, 70 c. Macmillan.
Century dictionary and cyclopedia. New ed. '01. '02(Ap5) 10 v., 4°, subs., $80 to $150. Century Co.
Century of Baptist achievements. Newman, R. H: net, $1.50. Am. Bapt.
CERAMICS.
Barber. Anglo-American pottery. net, $2. [Caspar] E. A. Barber.
Barber. Anglo-Am. pottery. $2. Patterson & W.
Huddilston. Lessons from Greek pottery. net, $1.25. Macmillan.
Monkhouse. Hist. and desc. of Chinese porcelain. net. $10. Wessels.
Seger. Collected writings; fr. records of the Royal porcelain factory at Berlin. v. 1. per set, $15. Chemical.
Cervantes Saavedra, M. de. Don Quixote. New ed. '01. '02(F22) 4 v., 12°, per set, $3; limp leath., $5. Dodd.
Cervantes Saavedra, M. de. Don Quixote de la Mancha; ed. by Ma. E. Burt and L. L. Cable. '02(Je7) il. D. (Ser. of school reading.) net, 60 c. Scribner.
Cervantes Saavedra, M. de. Life and achievements of Don Quixote de la Mancha. '02 (Ap12) 16°, (Caxton ser.) flex. lambskin, net, $1.25. Scribner.
Chadwick, H:, *ed.* *See* Spalding's official baseball guide.
Chalmers, Ja. James Chalmers; autobiog. and letters. '02(Je28) 8°, net, 75 c. Revell.
Chalmers, Rob. W: King in yellow. New issue. '02(Je21) il. D. $1.50. Harper.
Chamberlain, Leander T. Evolutionary philosophy. '02(My10) D. pap., 50 c. Baker & T.
Chamberlin, T: C. Attempt to frame a working hypothesis of the cause of glacial periods on an atmosphere basis. '01. '02 (Ja11) 8°, pap., net, 25 c. Univ. of Chic.
Chamberlin, T: C. Proposed genetic classification of pleistocence glacial formations. '01. '02(Ja11) 8°, net, 10 c. Univ. of Chic.
Chambers of the soul. Woelfkin, C. 35 c. Un. Soc. C. E.
Chambers's cyclopædia of Eng. literature; ed. by D: Patrick. New ed. 3 v. v. 1. '01. '02(Mr1) il. 8°, per v., net, $5. Lippincott.
Chambers's twentieth century dict. of Eng. language; ed. by T: Davidson. '01. '02 (Mr1) 8°, $1.50; hf. leath., $2. Lippincott.
CHAMPLAIN, S: de.
Sedgwick. Samuel de Champlain. net, 65 c.; net, 50 c. Houghton, M. & Co.
Champney, *Mrs.* Eliz. W. Witch Winnie ser. 9 v. New ed. '01. '02(F22) 12°, per set, $11.25. Dodd.
Chancellor, W: E. Children's arithmetic by grades. Second book. '02(Mr22) D. (Globe ser.) 20 c.; Third book (Mr22) 24 c.; Fourth book (Mr22) 24 c. Globe Sch. Bk.
Chancellor, W: E. Children's arithmetic by series. Primary. '02(Mr22) il. D. (Globe ser., in three books.) 28 c. Globe Sch. Bk.
Chandler, Bessie. Verses. '01. '02(Ap26) 16°, $1.25. Blue Sky Press.
Chanson de Geste. *See* Crabb, W. D.
Chaplain's experience ashore and afloat. Jones, H. W. $1.25. Sherwood.
Chapman, F: The foraminifera: introd. to study of the protozoa. '02(Ap26) il. O. $3.50. Longmans.
Chapman, G: T. Manual of the pathological treatment of lameness in the horse. '01. '02(F22) 8°, $2. W: R. Jenkins.
CHARACTER.
Bruce. Formation of Christian character. net, $1.75. Scribner.
Macdonald. Guarding the thoughts. 10 c. J. H. West.
Schofield. Springs of character. net, $1.30. Funk.
See also Christian life;—Conduct of life;—Ethics;—Phrenology;—Physiognomy.
CHARITIES.
Worcester. Works of charity. 25 c. Mass. New-Ch. Un.
Charles, Fes. In the country God forget. '02 (My3) D. $1.50. Little, B. & Co.
Charlotte. Walford, *Mrs.* L. B. $1.50. Longmans.
CHARTRES.
Headlam. Story of Chartres. $2; $2.50. Macmillan.
Chase, F: H: Credibility of the Book of the Acts of the Apostles. '02(Je14) 12°, (Hulsean lectures, 1900-01.) $1.75. Macmillan.
Chatfield-Taylor, Hobart C. *See* Taylor, H. C. Chatfield-.
Chats within the fold. Desmond, H. J. net, 75 c. Murphy.
Chaucer, G. English of the XIVth century; Prologue and Knightes tale. (S. H. Carpenter.) '01. '02(Ap26) 12°, 75 c. Ginn.
Chaucer, G. Nonne's preeste's tale of the cok and hen. '02(Je28) il. 8°, Japan vellum, $6.50; hand painted, $16.50. Grafton Press.
CHAUCER, Geoffrey.
Ten Brink. Language and metre of Chaucer. net, $1.50. Macmillan.
CHEMISTRY.
Abegg *and* Herz. Practical chemistry. net, $1.50. Macmillan.
Chittenden, *ed.* Studies in physiolog. chemistry. net, $4. Scribner.
Clarke *and* Dennis. Elem. chemistry. $1.10. Am. Bk.
Dennis *and* Clarke. Lab'y manual to accompany Elem. chemistry. 50 c. Am. Bk.
Dupre *and* Hake. Inorganic chemistry. $3. Lippincott.
Hessler *and* Smith. Essentials of chemistry. $1.20. Sanborn.
Holleman. Inorganic chemistry. pt. 2. $2.50. Wiley.
Jones. Elements of physical chemistry. net, $4. Macmillan.
Morgan. Elements of physical chemistry. $2. Wiley.

CHEMISTRY.—*Continued.*
Ostwald. Principles of inorganic chemistry. net, $6. Macmillan.
Perkin *and* Lean. Introd. to chemistry and physics. 2 v. ea., net, 50 c. Macmillan.
Prescott *and* Sullivan. Qualitative chemistry for studies of water solution and mass action. net, $1.50. Van Nostrand.
Remsen. Introd. to study of chemistry. $1.12. Holt.
Simon. Physiological chemistry. net, $3.25. Lea.
Thorpe. Essays in historical chemistry. net, $4. Macmillan.
Tilden. Introd. to the study of chemical philosophy: theoretical and systematic. $1.75. Longmans.
Watson. Elem. experimental chemistry, inorganic. net, $1.25. Barnes.
Wells, *ed.* Studies fr. the chemical lab'y of the Sheffield Scientific School. net, $7.50. Scribner.
Young. Elem. principles of chemistry. net, 95 c. Appleton.
See also Blowpipe;—Enzymes;—Fermentation;—Indicators.

Cheney, Fk. J. A life of unity, and other stories. '01· '02(F22) 12°, $1.50. Blade.

Cherished thoughts. Presset, A. L. $1.50; $1.75; $2.25. Skelton.

Chesterfield, *Earl of.* Letters, sentences and maxims. '02(Je14) 12°, (Home lib.) $1. Burt.

Chesterfield, *Earl of.* Letters to his son; ed. by C. Strachey. '01. '02(F22) 2 v., D. (Lib. of standard literature.) ea., $1.75. Putnam.

Cheyne, T: K., *and* Black, J: S., *eds.* Encyclopædia Biblica. v. 3, L-P. '02(My17) 8°, subs., net, $5; hf. mor., net, $7.50. Macmillan.

Cheyne, W: W., *and* Burghard, F. F. Manual of surgical treatment. In 7 v. v. 5. Treatment of the surgical affections of the head, face, jaws, etc., by H. L. Lack. '01. '02(Mr1) 8°, net, $5. Lea.

CHICAGO.
Clark. Public schools of Chicago. net, 50 c. Univ. of Chic.

Chiefs of Cambria. Jones, M. P. $1.25. Abbey Press.

Child for Christ. McKinney, A. H. net, 50 c. Revell.

Child stories from the masters. Menefee, M. 75 c. Rand, McN. & Co.

CHILD STUDY.
Wilson. Bibliog. of child study. net, 25 c. Stechert.

Childe, Cromwell, *comp.* Trolley exploring. '02(My17) S. pap., 10 c. Brooklyn Eagle.

CHILDREN.
Anthony. The children's covenant. $1. Jennings.
Compayré. Later infancy of the child. pt. 2. net, $1.20. Appleton.
Folks. Care of destitute, neglected, and delinquent children. net, $1. Macmillan.
McKinney. The child for Christ. net, 50 c. Revell.
Mundy. Eclectic practice in diseases of children. net, $2.50. Scudder.
Rotch. Pediatrics. subs., $6; $7. Lippincott.

CHILDREN.—*Continued.*
Worthington. The tocsin—our children in peril. 25 c. Cubery.
See also Education; — Girls; — Kindergarten; — Mothers.

Children of the palm lands. Allen, A. E. 50 c. Educ. Pub.

Children's Bible stories told in words of easy reading. '02(F1) 5 v., il. 4°, ea., 75 c. Saalfield.

Children's covenant. Anthony, C. V. $1. Jennings.

Children's friend ser. 16°, 50 c. Little, B. & Co.
—Alcott. Little button rose.
—Aulnoy *and* Perrault. Once upon a time.
—Dewey. Bruno.
—Ewing. Benjy in beastland.
—Gilman. Kingdom of coins.
—Moulton. Her baby brother.
—Perrault *and* Aulnoy. Fairy favorites.
—Phelps *and* Ward. Lost hero.
—Sullivan. Ivanhoe and Rob Roy, retold.
—Woolsey. Uncle and aunt.

Children's London. Thorpe, C. net, $4.50. Scribner.

Child's Bible hist. Knecht, F. J. 25 c. Herder.

Child's garden of verses. Stevenson, R. L: net, 60 c. Scribner.

Childs, E: E. Wonders of Mouseland. '01· '02(Ja11) D. $1.25. Abbey Press.

Chimmie Fadden and Mr. Paul. Townsend, E: W. $1.50. Century Co.

CHINA.
Allgood. China war, 1860. $5. Longmans.
Parker. John Chinaman, and a few others. $2.50. Dutton.
Thomson. China and the powers. $4. Longmans.
Van Bergen. Story of China. 60 c. Am. Bk.
See also Manchuria;—Paotingfu.

Chinese-English elem. reader and arithmetic. Gyim, P. L. $1.25. Taylor & M.

CHINESE EXCLUSION.
Quang Chang Ling. Why should the Chinese go? 25 c. Cambridge.

Chittenden, Hiram M. American fur trade of the far west. '02(Mr8) 3 v., il. O. net, $10. F. P. Harper.

Chittenden, Russell H., *ed.* Studies in physiolog. chemistry. '01· '02(Mr15) 8°, (Yale bicentennial pub.) net, $4. Scribner.

Choephori (The). Æschylus. net, $3.25. Macmillan.

Choir and chorus conducting. Wodell, F: W: $1.50. Presser.

Choralia. Powell, J. B. $1.50. Longmans.

Christ and his cross. Rutherford, S: $1. Longmans.

Christ our life. Moberly, R. C. net, $3. Longmans.

CHRISTENDOM.
See Christianity;—Church history;—History.

CHRISTIAN LIFE.
Babcock. Three whys and their answer. 35 c. Un. Soc. C. E.
Barton. I go a fishing: progressive discipleship. 25 c. Revell.
Bausman. Precept and practice. net, $1. Heidelberg.

CHRISTIAN LIFE.—*Continued.*
Fradenburgh. Twenty-five stepping stones toward Christ's kingdom. O. P. Fradenburgh.
Gladden. Christian way. 75 c. Dodd.
Keedy. Naturalness of Christian life. net, $1.25. Putnam.
Kyger, *ed.* Hand-book for soul-winners. 50 c. Kyger.
Mudge. Life of love. 25 c. Jennings.
Newell. Life worth living. $1. Abbey Press.
Sanders. How are we led? Who is it that leads us? $1.50. Donohue.
Sarles. Man's peerless destiny in Christ. net, 90 c. Funk.
Terry. The new and living way. net, 50 c. Eaton & M.
See also Conduct of life;—Devotional exercises and meditations;—Faith;—Prayer;—Revivals.
Christian ministry. Anderson, C: P. 20 c. Young Churchman.
CHRISTIAN SCIENCE.
Clark. Church of St. Bunco. $1. Abbey Press.
Cushman. The truth in Christian science. 60 c. J. H. West.
Gifford. Christian science against itself. $1. Jennings.
Seward. How to get acquainted with God: meaning of the Christian science movement. net, 50 c. Funk.
Whittaker. Christian science, is it safe? 10 c. Earle.
Christian study manuals; ed. by R. E. Welsh. S. 60 c. Armstrong.
—Gibson. Protestant principles.
—Margoliouth. Religion of Bible lands.
CHRISTIAN UNITY.
Henson. Godly union and concord. $2. Longmans.
Christian way. Gladden, W. 75 c. Dodd.
CHRISTIANITY.
Fairbairn. Philosophy of the Christian religion. net, $3.50. Macmillan.
Gilbert. Primer of the Christian religion. net, $1. Macmillan.
Grant, *ed.* Christendom Anno Domini 1901. 2 v. $2.50. W: D. Grant.
Islam and Christianity. $1. Am. Tr.
Mason. Christianity, what is it? 80 c. E. & J. B. Young.
Ovenden. To whom shall we go? $1. E. & J. B. Young.
Selden. Story of the Christian centuries. net, $1. Revell.
Christie, R: C. Selected essays and papers; ed., with memoir, by W: A. Shaw. '02 (Mr8) il. O. $5. Longmans.
Christmas rose. Macmillan, H. $1. Macmillan.
Christopher. Lockett, M. F. $1.25. Abbey Press.
Church, Arth. H. Chemistry of paints and painting. 3d ed., rev. and enl. '02(F15) 8°, $3. Macmillan.
Church, Irving P. Diagrams of mean velocity of uniform motion of water in open channels. '02(Je21) obl. 4°, pap., $1.50. Wiley.
CHURCH ARCHITECTURE.
Ayer. Rise and devel. of Chr. architecture. net, $1.50. Young Churchman.
Church Historical Soc. lectures. 16°. E. & J. B. Young.
—Mason. Christianity, what is it? 80 c.
CHURCH HISTORY.
Guggenberger. General hist. of the Christian era. In 3 v. ea., $1.50. Herder.
See also Huguenots;—*also* names of churches.
CHURCH MEMBERSHIP.
Clarke. Training the church of the future. net, 75 c. Funk.
Horton. Birthright membership of believers' infants in the N. T. church. 6 c. Presb. Bd.
See also Baptism.
CHURCH MUSIC.
Curwen. Studies in worship music, chiefly congregational singing. $1.75. Scribner.
Dickinson. Music in the hist. of the western church. net, $2.50. Scribner.
Powell. Choralia: for precentors and choir-masters. $1.50. Longmans.
Wodell. Choir and chorus conducting. $1.50. Presser.
Church of Christ. Green, E. T. $1.50. Macmillan.
CHURCH OF ENGLAND.
Creighton. The church and the nation. $2. Longmans.
Galton. Our attitude toward Eng. Roman Catholics. net, $1. Dutton.
Gee. Elizabethan prayer-book and ornaments. net, $1.25. Macmillan.
Grafton. Pusey and the church revival. net, 50 c. Young Churchman.
Green. Church of Christ. $1.50. Macmillan.
Henson. Cross-bench views of current church questions. $4. Longmans.
See also Confession;—Protestant Epis. church.
Church of St. Bunco. Clark, G. $1. Abbey Press.
CHURCHES.
See Syracuse First Presb. church.
Churchman's lib. 8°. Macmillan.
—Green. Church of Christ. $1.50.
—Mackay. Churchman's introd. to the O. T. $1.50.
Church's one foundation. Nicoll, W: R. $1.25. Armstrong.
Church's outlook for the twentieth century ser. 12°, net, $1. Dutton.
—Cobb. Theology, old and new.
Churton, W: R. William Ralph Churton: theolog. papers and sermons. '02(Ap26) 12°, $1.75. Macmillan.
Chute, H. N. *See* Carhart, H: S.
Cicero. Select orations and letters. Allen and Greenough's ed.; rev. by Greenough and Kittredge. '02(Je14) D. hf. leath., $1.45. Ginn.
Cid, R. D. de Bivar, *called the* Cid. Poem of the Cid; tr. by A. M. Huntington. v. 1, 2. '02(Je28) il. Q. vellum, ea., $25. Putnam.
Cid (Le). Corneille, P. net, 35 c. Holt.
CIDER.
See Apple.
CINCINNATI SOUTHERN RAILWAY.
Boyden. Beginnings of the Cincinnati Southern railway. 50 c. Clarke.
CIPHER.
See Codes.
CITIES.
See Municipal government.

Citizen's lib. of economics, politics and sociology; ed. by R: T. Ely. 12°, net, $1.25. Macmillan.
—Addams. Democracy and social ethics.
—Baker. Municipal engineering and sanitation.
—Reinsch. Colonial government.

CITIZENSHIP.
Brewer. American citizenship. net, 75 c. Scribner.

City of Angels. McGrady, T: 10 c. Standard.
City of the seven hills. Harding, C. H. 40 c. Scott, F. & Co.

CIVICS.
See Political science.

CIVIL ACTIONS.
See Actions at law.

CIVIL ENGINEERING.
See Engineering;—Surveying.

Civil government in U. S. Martin, G: H. 90 c. Am. Bk.

CIVIL LAW.
Justinianus. Pandects of Justinian. v. 1. $5. Cambridge.

CIVIL WAR.
See United States.

CIVILIZATION.
Colquhoun. Mastery of the Pacific. net, $4. Macmillan.
Kidd. Principles of western civilization. net, $2. Macmillan.
Stead. Americanization of the world. $1. Markley.
Wells. Anticipations of reaction of mechanical and scientific progress. net, $1.80. Harper.
See also History.

Clapp, H: A. Reminiscences of a dramatic critic. '02(Je7) O. net, $1.75. Houghton, M. & Co.
Clark, A. When bards sing out of tune. '02(My10) D. 50 c. Abbey Press.
Clark, C: An Antarctic queen. '01. '02 (My17) il. D. $1.75. Warne.
Clark, Ellery H. *See* Massachusetts. Street railway accident law.
Clark, Fs. E: Training the church of the future; lectures, with special ref. to the Young People's Soc. of Christian Endeavor. '02 (Ap12) il. D. net, 75 c. Funk.
Clark, Gordon. Church of St. Bunco. '01. '02(F15) D. $1. Abbey Press.
Clark, Hannah B. Public schools of Chicago. '02(Mr22) 8°, pap., net, 50 c. Univ. of Chic.
Clark, Salter S. The government, what it is, what it does. '02(My10) D. 75 c. Am. Bk.
Clark, W: *See* Lewis, M.
Clark, W: L., *and* Marshall, W: L. Treatise on the law of private corporations. In 3 v. v. 2. '01. '02(F1) O. shp., per v., $6. Keefe-D.
Clarke, F. W., *and* Dennis, L. M. Elementary chemistry. '02(Je21) D. $1.10. Am. Bk.
Clarke, Helen A. *See* Porter, C.
Clarke, *Mrs.* Ma. Cowden, [Mary Victoria Novello.] Letters to an enthusiast: add. to Rob. Balmanno; ed. by A. U. Nettleton. '02(My3) O. net, $2.50. McClurg.
Clarke, W. J. A B C of electrical experiments. '02(Ap5) il. D. $1. Excelsior.

CLARKSON FAMILY.
See Leach, J. G.

CLASSICAL PHILOLOGY.
See Dissertationes Americanæ.

CLASSIFICATION.
See Cataloguing.

Clay, *Mrs.* J: M. Frank Logan. '02(F22) il. D. $1. Abbey Press.
Claybornes (The). Sage, W: $1.50. Houghton, M. & Co.

CLAYTON-BULWER TREATY.
Travis. Hist. of the Clayton-Bulwer treaty. $1. Mich. Pol. Sci.

Clemens, G. C. *See* Kansas. Statutes conc. corporations.
Clemens, S: L., ["Mark Twain."] A double-barrelled detective story. '02(Ap19) il. D. $1.50. Harper.
Clement, G: A. Probate repts., annot. v. 6. '02(My24) O. shp., $5.50. Baker, V. & Co.
Clerical capitalist. McGrady, T: 10 c. Socialistic Co-op.

CLIFF DWELLERS.
Nordenskiold. The cliff dwellers of the Mesa Verde, southwestern Col. net, $20. Stechert.

Clifford, Chandler R. Period decoration. '01. '02(Ap12) il. 8°, $3. Clifford & L.
Clifford, *Mrs.* Lucy L. A long duel. '01. '02 (Mr22) 12°, pap., net, 25 c. Lane.
Clifford, *Mrs.* Lucy L. Margaret Vincent. '02(Ap26) D. $1.50. Harper.
Climates and baths of Great Britain. 8°, net. Macmillan.
—Ewart, *and others.* Climates of London, central and northern England, Wales and Ireland. $4. (2.)

CLINIC.
See Pathology.

Clinical psychiatry. Defendorf, A. R. net, $3.50. Macmillan.
Clinton, Major, *pseud.* *See* Culley, F. C.
Clock on the stairs. Weber, A. 75 c. Burt.
Clodd, E: Thomas Henry Huxley. '02 (Ap12) D. net, $1. Dodd.
Cloistering of Ursula. Scollard, C. $1.50. L. C. Page.
Clow, F: R. Comparative study of the administration of city finances in the U. S. '01. '02(Ja11) O. (Pub. of the Am. Economic Assoc., 3d ser., v. 2, no. 4.) pap., $1. Macmillan.
Clowes, W: L., *and others.* Royal navy. v. 5 and 6. '01. '02(Ja11) 8°, ea., net, $6.50. Little, B. & Co.

COAL.
Hughes. Text-book of coal mining. $7. Lippincott.

Coal oil Johnny. Steele, J: W. $1.50. J: A. Hill.
Coast of freedom. Shaw, A. M. $1.50. Doubleday, P.
Cobb, Sanford H. Rise of relig. liberty in America. '02(My17) 8°, net, $4. Macmillan.
Cobb, W. F. Theology, old and new. '02 (Ap5) 12°, (Church's outlook for the twentieth century ser., no. 1.) net, $1. Dutton.
Coburn, F: N. Prize designs for rural school buildings. '01. '02(Ja25) il. 12°, 25 c. Kellogg.
Cochrane, Rob. More animal stories. '01. '02(F15) il. 12°, net, $1. Lippincott.
Cockcroft, Ja., *ed.* Encyclopædia of forms and precedents for pleading and practice. (T: E. O'Brien.) v. 15. '02(My17) O. shp., $6. Cockcroft.

Cockerell, Douglas. Bookbinding and the care of books. '02(F8) il. D. (Artistic crafts ser. of technical handbooks, no. 1.) net, $1.20. Appleton.

CODES.
A B C universal commercial electric telegraphic code. net, $7. Am. Code.
Barry. Am. lumberman telecode. net, $5. Am. Lumberman.

Codman, J:, 2d. Arnold's expedition to Quebec. 2d ed. '02(Mr1) 8°, net, $2.25. Macmillan.

Cody, S. Selections from the world's greatest short stories. '02(My24) D. net, $1. McClurg.

Coffin, G: M. A B C of banks and banking. '01. '02(Ap5) il. S. (Wall street lib., v. 4.) $1.25. S: A. Nelson.

COHERER.
See Electricity.

Cohn, Alfr. I. Indicators and test-papers, their source, preparation, application, and tests for sensitiveness. 2d ed. '02(Je7) 12°, $2. Wiley.

Colburn, Bertha L. Graded physical exercises. '02(F22) D. $1. Werner.

Colby, Alb. L. Review and text of the Am. standard specifications for steel, adopt. Aug., 1901. 2d ed. '02(Ap5) 12°, net, $1.10. Chemical.

Colcock, Annie T. Margaret Tudor. '02 (Ap19) il. D. $1. Stokes.

Colden, Cadwallader. Hist. of the Five Indian nations of Canada. '02(My24) 2 v., 8°, (Commonwealth lib.) net, per v., $1. New Amsterdam.

Cole, Horace L. The flesh and the devil. '02(Ap26) 12°, $1.50. Neely.

Colemanite from So. California. Eakle, A. S. 15 c. Univ. of Cal.

Coleridge, S: T. Rime of the ancient mariner; ed. by N. H. Pitman. '01. '02(Ap19) S. (Ser. of Eng. classics.) keratol, 30 c.; flex. bds., 25 c. B. F. Johnson.

College chaps. Prune, N. 75 c. Mutual Bk.

College man in doubt. Best, N. R. net, 50 c. Westminster.

College student and his problems. Canfield, J. H. net, $1. Macmillan.

COLLEGES AND UNIVERSITIES.
See Oxford Univ.

Collingwood, W: G. Life of John Ruskin. [New rev., abb. ed.] '02(Mr29) O. net, $2. Houghton, M. & Co.

Colonel Harold de Lacey. Douglass, F. A. $1.25. Neely.

Colonial days. Welsh, L. D. 50 c. Educ. Pub.

COLONIAL GOVERNMENT.
Reinsch. Colonial government. net, $1.25. Macmillan.

Colonials (The). French, A. $1.50. Doubleday, P.

COLOR.
Vanderpoel. Color problems. net, $5. Longmans.
See also Dyeing;—Light;—Printing.

Color of the soul. Norris, Z. A. net, $1. Funk.

Colorado. Laws passed at an extra session of the 13th general assembly. '02(Je14) O. hf. shp., $2. Smith-B.

COLORADO.
Hatch. Civil government in Col. 60 c. Centennial.

COLORADO.—*Continued.*
Nordenskiold. Cliff dwellers of the Mesa Verde, southwestern Col. net, $20. Stechert.

Colorado colonel. Campbell, W: C. $1.50. Crane.

COLORADO RIVER.
James. In and around the Grand Canyon. net, $10. Little, B. & Co.

Colquhoun, Arch. R. Mastery of the Pacific. '02(Mr1) 8°, net, $4. Macmillan.

Colton, B. P. Elem. physiology and hygiene. '02(My24) il. D. 60 c. Heath.

Columbia Univ. Germanic studies. 8°, pap., net, $1. Macmillan.
—Remy. Influence of India and Persia on the poetry of Germany. (v. 1, 4.)

Columbia Univ. Indo-Iranian ser.; ed. by A. V. Williams Jackson. 8°, net. Macmillan.
—Avesta. Index verborum. $2.
—Gray. Indo-Iranian phonology. $3.

Columbia Univ. Oriental studies. 8°, net, $1.25. Macmillan.
—Gabirol. Improvement of moral qualities. (1.)

Columbia Univ. studies in comparative literature. 12°, net. Macmillan.
—Einstein. Italian Renaissance in England. $1.50.

Columbia Univ. studies in hist., economics and public law. 8°, net. Macmillan.
—Hall. Crime in its rel. to social progress. $3; $3.50. (15.)

Colville, W. J. Life and power from within. '02(Mr22) D. $1. Alliance.

Colyer, J. F. *See* Smale, M.

Commander, Lydia K. Marred in the making. '02(Ap12) O. limp chamois, satin-lined, $3; pap., 25 c. Eckler.

Comments of a Countess. '02(My10) 4°, net, $1.50. Lane.

COMMERCE.
Marchant. Commercial history. $1. Pitman.
Ware. Educational foundations of trade and industry. net, $1.20. Appleton.
See also Commercial law;—Political economy;—Railroads.

COMMERCIAL CORRESPONDENCE.
See Stenography.

COMMERCIAL LAW.
Hargis. Treatise on commercial law and business customs. 10 c. J. North.

Commonwealth lib. 8°, net, $1. New Amsterdam.
—Arnold. Literature and dogma.
—Colden. Hist. of the Five Indian nations of Canada. 2 v.
—Lewis *and* Clark. Expedition to the sources of the Missouri, etc.
—Mackenzie. Voyages fr. Montreal to the Pacific Ocean.

Commonwealth or empire. Smith, G. net, 60 c. Macmillan.

Commonwealth ser. 16°, $1.25. L. C. Page.
—Wheaton. The Russells in Chicago.

Compayré, Gabriel. Later infancy of the child; tr. by M. E. Wilson. '02(F22) 12°, (Internat. educ. ser., no. 53.) net, $1.20. Appleton.

Complete housebuilder. '02(My17) 12°, 50 c.; pap., 25 c. Donohue.

Complete pocket guide to Europe. Stedman, E. C. $1.25. W: R. Jenkins.

COMPOSERS.
See Musicians.

COMPOSITION.
See Rhetoric.

Comrades. Newberry, F. E. 75 c. Burt.

Condict, Alice B. Old glory and the gospel in the Philippines. '02(Ap19) 12°, net, 75 c. Revell.

CONDUCT OF LIFE.
Dresser. Book of secrets, studies in self-control. net, $1. Putnam.
Hillis. Master of science of right-living. net, 50 c. Revell.
Hind. Life's little things. $1.75. Macmillan.
Jordan. Kingship of self-control.—Majesty of calmness. ea., 50 c. Revell.
Mabie. Works and days. net, $1. Dodd.
Slicer. One world at a time. net, $1.35. Putnam.
See also Business;—Character;—Christian life;—Culture;—Ethics.

CONFECTIONERY.
Rigby. Reliable candy teacher and soda and ice cream formulas. $2. W. O. Rigby.

CONFESSION.
Fulham Palace Conference. Confession and absolution. net, $1. Longmans.

Confessions of a matchmaking mother. Davidson, L. C. $1.50 J. F. Taylor.

Confounding of Camelia. Sedgwick, A. D. $1.50. Century Co.

Conger, Arth. B. Religion for the time: six conferences on natural religion. '02(My3) D. net, $1. Jacobs.

CONJURING.
Roterberg. Card tricks; how to do them, and sleight of hand. 25 c. Drake.

Conklin, *Mrs.* Jennie M. D. Bek's first corner. '02(Mr29) il. 12°, (Fireside ser.) $1. Burt.

Conklin, *Mrs.* Jennie M. D. Growing up. '02(Mr29) il. 12°, (Fireside ser.) $1. Burt.

Conklin, *Mrs.* Jennie M. D. Miss Prudence. '02(Mr29) il. 12°, (Fireside ser.) $1. Burt.

Conklin, *Mrs.* Jennie M. D. Tessa Wadsworth's discipline. '02(Mr29) il. 12°, (Fireside ser.) $1. Burt.

Conley, J: W. Evolution and man. '02 (Ap19) 12°, net, 75 c. Revell.

Connelley, W: Elsey. *See* Root, F. A.

Connold, E: J. British vegetable galls. '02 (Mr22) f°, net, $4. Dutton.

Conqueror (The). Atherton, *Mrs.* G. F. $1.50. Macmillan.

Consolation of philosophy. Boethius, A. M. S. 50 c.; 75 c. Macmillan.

Conspiracy of Pontiac. Parkman, F. $1. Burt.

CONSTABLE, John.
Holmes. Constable. net, $1. Longmans.

CONSTABLES.
See Justices of the peace.

Constance Hamilton. Wyatt, L. M. L. 50 c. Abbey Press.

Constances. Bentzan, T. $1.50. Neely.

CONSTELLATIONS.
See Astronomy;—Stars.

CONSTITUTIONAL LAW.
See Roman empire.

Constructive Bible studies; ed. by W: R. Harper and E. D. Burton. O. $1. Univ. of Chic.
—Burton *and* Mathews. Life of Christ.

Constructiv Bible studies.—Continued.
—Harper. Constructive studies in the priestly element in the O. T.

CONSUMPTION.
Burnett. New cure for consumption by its own virus. $1. Boericke & T.

Contemporary science ser. *See* Scribner's.

CONTRACTS.
Lawson. Making of a contract. 25 c. Stephens.

CONUNDRUMS.
See Riddles.

CONVENTS.
Steele. Convents of Great Britain. net, $2. Herder.

CONVERSION.
Mason. Ministry of conversion. net, 90 c. Longmans.
See also Christian life;—Revivals.

CONVEYANCING.
Pennsylvania. Law of conveyancing. $6. T. & J. W. Johnson.

CONVICTS.
See Crime and criminals;—Prisons.

Conway, Kath. E. Lalor's Maples. 2d ed. '01. '02(Ja11) D. $1.25. Pilot.

Conway, Moncure D., *comp.* The sacred anthology (oriental.) 5th ed. '02(Mr29) 12°, $2. Holt.

Cook, *Mrs.* E. T. The bride's book. '02 (Ap5) 12°, net, $1.50. Dutton.

Cook, E: T. Rights and wrongs of the Transvaal war. New rev. ed. '02(Je7) D. $2. Longmans.

Cook, Ja. Three voyages around the world. '02(My17) 12°, (Home lib.) $1. Burt.

Cook, J: T. *See* New York. Code of criminal procedure and penal code.

Cooke, C. J. B. Some recent developments in locomotive practice. '02(Je7) il. 8°, $1. Macmillan.

COOKERY.
Curtis. Left-overs made palatable. $1. Judd.
Dainty dishes for slender incomes. net, 50 c. New Amsterdam.
Dennis. Cook book. $1.50. Mutual Pub. Co.
H. Grandmother's cook book. 50 c. New Amsterdam.
Palmer. Woman's exchange cook book. 70 c. Conkey.
Pierce. Hartley House cook book and household economist. 60 c. Lentilhon.
Rivas. Little French dinners. 50 c. New Amsterdam.
Salis. À la mode cookery. $2. Longmans.
Schaeffer. Metropolitan club cook-book. $1.75. Augsburg.
Seeley. Cook book: Fr. and Amer. cookery. net, $2; net, $3. Macmillan.
See also Diet;—Domestic economy;—Hygiene.

Coolidge, Susan, *pseud.* *See* Woolsey, S. C.

Cooper, E: H. A fool's year. '02(F15) D. (Town and country lib., no. 308.) $1; pap., 50 c. Appleton.

Coppée François. Morceau de pain et autres contes. '02(My3) sq. S. (Contes choisis, no. 22.) pap., 25 c. W: R. Jenkins.

COPPER.
Stevens, *comp.* Copper handbook. $2; $3. H. J. Stevens.

Corbin, J: An American at Oxford. '02 (My17) il. D. net, $1.50. Houghton, M. & Co.
Corinne's vow. Waggaman, M. T. $1.25. Benziger.
CORLISS ENGINE.
Lisk. Diagram of the Corliss engine, etc. 25 c. Spon.
Corn of heaven. Macmillan, H. $1.75. Macmillan.
Corneille, P. Le Cid; ed. by E: S. Joynes. New rev. enl. ed. '02(F1) D. (Students' ser. of classic Fr. plays, no. 1.) net, 35 c. Holt.
Cornell verse. Lyon, H: A. $1. Walton.
Cornwall, E: E. William Cornwall and his descendants. '01- '02(F1) 8°, $5. Tuttle, M. & T.
CORNWALL AND YORK, *Duke and Duchess of.*
Knight. With the royal tour. $2. Longmans.
Wallace. Web of empire: diary of the imperial tour. net, $6.50. Macmillan.
CORPORATIONS.
American and Eng. corporation cases. v. 15. $4.50. Michie.
Boisot. By-laws of private corporations. $3. Keefe-D.
Clark *and* Marshall. Law of private corporations. v. 2. $6. Keefe-D.
Kansas. Statutes conc. corporations and insurance companies. $1; $1.25. Crane.
Maine. Laws conc. business corporations, annot. gratis. Kennebec Journ.
New York. Statutory revision of laws affecting misc. corporations. $1.50. Banks & Co.
Smith. Cases on private corporations. net, $6. Harvard Law.
Walker. Taxation of corporations in the U. S. 25 c. Am. Acad. Pol. Sci.
White. On corporations. $5.50. Baker, V. & Co.
Wilgus. Law of private corporations. In 2 v. complete. $9; $10. Bowen-M.
See also Municipal corporations;—Securities.
CORRESPONDENCE.
See Letter-writing;—Letters;—Stenography.
Corrothers, Ja. D. Black cat club. '02(Mr22) D. net, $1. Funk.
Cosmos and the logos. Minton, H: C. net, $1.25. Westminster.
Cosy corner ser. il. 50 c. L. C. Page.
—Delano. Susanne.
—Fox. Little giant's neighbors.
Cotes, *Mrs.* Sara J. D. Those delightful Americans. '02(Je21) D. $1.50. Appleton.
Cotterell, E: The pocket Gray; or, anatomist's vade mecum. 5th rev. ed., ed. by C. H. Fagge. '02(F22) 16°, net, $1.25. Wood.
Couch, A. T: Quiller-. ["Q."] The Westcotes. '02(Ap12) il. D. (Griffin ser.) $1. Coates.
Coulevain, Pierre de. Eve triumphant. '02 (My10) 12°, net, $1.20. Putnam.
Country life lib. 8°, net, $3.75. Scribner.
—Jekyll, *comp.* Lilies for Eng. gardens.
COURAGE.
Wagner. Courage. $1.25. Dodd.
See also Heroes.
Courage of conviction. Sullivan, T. R. $1.50. Scribner.
Courier-Journal almanac for 1902. '02(Mr22) D. pap., 25 c. Courier-Journ.

Courtship of sweet Anne Page. Talbot, E. V. net, 40 c. Funk.
Cousin Maude and Rosamond. Holmes. *Mrs.* M. J. $1. Burt.
Cowles, H: C. Ecological rel. of the vegetation on the sand dunes of Lake Michigan. '01- '02(Ja11) 8°, (Hull botanical laboratory, no. 13.) pap., net, 75 c. Univ. of Chic.
Cox, *Mrs.* Ja. F., ["C."] Home thoughts. 2d ser. (Je7) D. net, $1.20. Barnes.
Crabb, Wilson D. Culture history in the Chanson de Geste-Aymeri de Narbonne. '02(Mr22) 8°, pap., net, $1.25. Univ. of Chic.
Crane, Wa. Bases of design. 2d ed. '02-(Ap26) il. 12°, $2.25. Macmillan.
Crane, Wa. Line and form. Cheaper ed. '02 (My3) il. 12°, $2.25. Macmillan.
Craque-o-Doom. Catherwood, *Mrs.* M. H. 50 c. Am. News.
Craufurd, H. J. Field training of a company of infantry. '02(Ap12) S. $1. Longmans.
Crawford, F. M. Works. New uniform ed. '02(F15) 3 v., 12°, ea., $1.50. Macmillan.
Crawford, F. M. In the palace of the king. Limited pap. ed. '02(Mr8) 12°, (People's lib., no. 27.) pap., 50 c. Am. News.
Crawford, J: J. Negotiable instruments law. 2d ed. '02(Ap12) O. $2.50. Baker, V. & Co.
Crawford,, T. D., *rep. See* Arkansas. *Sup. ct.* Repts.
Crawley, Ernest. The mystic rose: primitive marriage. '02(Mr22) 8°, net, $4. Macmillan.
Creamer, E: S. The Orphean tragedy. '02 (Mr29) D. $1. Abbey Press.
Creation, re-creation. *See* Lemcke, E. E:
CREEDS.
See Apostles' creed;—Catechisms.
Creighton, M. The church and the nation; ed. by L. Creighton. '01- '02(Ja11) D. $2. Longmans.
Creighton, M. Thoughts on education. '02(Je7) D. net, $1.60. Longmans.
Cresee, F. A. Practical pointers for patentees. '02(Ap12) 16°, $1. Munn.
Crew, H:, *and* Tatnall, Rob. R. Laboratory manual of physics. '02(F1) 12°, net, 90 c. Macmillan.
Crile, G: W. Research into certain problems rel. to surgical operations. '02(F15) il. 8°, net, $2.50. Lippincott.
CRIME AND CRIMINALS.
Hall. Crime in its relation to social progress. net, $3; $3.50. Macmillan.
See also Prisons.
CRIMINAL LAW.
Book of forms to be used with the study of criminal procedure in the Univ. of Mich. 60 c. Bliss & A.
Pattison. Instructions in criminal cases passed upon by the cts. of Mo. $5. Gilbert Bk.
See also Crime and criminals;—Evidence.
Crimson wing. Taylor, H. C. C. $1.50. H. S. Stone.
Cripps, Wilfred J. Old English plate: its makers and marks. New il. lib. ed. '01- '02(Ja11) facsimiles, 8°, net, $13.50. Scribner.
CRISES.
See Finance.

Crissey, Forrest. In Thompson's woods: [poems.] '01· '02(Mr1) 16°, bds., $1. Blue Sky Press

CRITICISM.
Arnold. Essays in criticism. $1. Burt.
Bourne. Essays in hist. criticism. net, $2. Scribner.
Margoliouth. Lines of defense of the biblical revelation. net, $1.50. Gorham.
See also Literature.

Crockett, S: R. The dark o' the moon. '02 (Mr29) il. D. $1.50. Harper.

Croft, Victor E. *See* Brown, C: F.

Croker, *Mrs.* Bertha M. The cat's paw. '02 (F1) D. (Select novels.) $1; pap., 50 c. Lippincott.

CROMWELL, Ol.
Payn. Cromwell on foreign affairs. net, $1.25. Macmillan.
Quayle. King Cromwell. net, 25 c. Jennings.

Cronholm, Neander N: Hist. of Sweden. '02 (Ap26) 2 v., il. 8°, $5. N. N: Cronholm.

Crosby, Ernest. Captain Jinks, hero. '02 (Mr8) D. $1.50. Funk.

Cross-bench views of current church questions. Henson, H. H. $4. Longmans.

Cross of Christ in Bolo-land. Dean, J: M. net, $1. Revell.

Crothers, T. D. Morphinism and narcomania from opium, cocain, etc. '02(Mr29) 12°, $2. Saunders.

Crowell, J. F. Present status and future prospects of Am. shipbuilding. '02(Mr22) 8°, (Pub. of the soc., no. 325.) pap., 15 c. Am. Acad. Pol. Sci.

Crowley, Ma. C. Heroine of the strait. '02 (Ap19) il. D. $1.50. Little, B. & Co.

Crowning of flora. Kellogg, A. M. 15 c. Kellogg.

Crozier, Hugh V. Temperance and the Anti-Saloon League. '01. '02(Mr29) 16°, 15 c. Barbee & S.

Cruickshank, J. W. *and* A. M. Umbrian towns. '02(Mr22) S. (Grant Allen's hist. guide books to the principal cities of Europe.) net, $1.25. Wessels.

CRYSTALS.
See Mineralogy.

Cub's career. Wheeler, H. $1. Abbey Press.

Cuentos selectos. S. pap., 35 c. W: R. Jenkins.
—Trueba. El molinerillo. (4.)

Cuffel, C: A. Durrell's Battery in the Civil War. '02(Mr22) il. O. subs., $2. C: A. Cuffel.

Cullen, C. L. More ex-tank tales. '02(Ap5) 12°, $1. Ogilvie.

Cullens, F: B. Where the magnolias bloom. '02(Mr1) D. 50 c. Abbey Press.

Culley, Fk. C., ["Major Clinton."] Barbara. '01. '02(Mr8) il. 12°, $1.25. F. C. Culley.

CULTURE.
Blackie. On self-culture. 35 c. Phonograph.

Culture history in the Chanson de Geste-Aymeri de Narbonne. Crabb, W. D. net, $1.25. Univ. of Chic.

CUMBERLAND PRESBYTERIAN CHURCH.
See Presbyterian church.

Cumming, A. N. Public house reform. '01· '02(Ja11) 12°, (Social sci. ser.) $1. Scribner.

Cummins, Harle O. Welsh rarebit tales. '02(Je7) il. D. $1.25. Mutual Bk.

Cuppy, H. A., *ed.* Pictorial natural history. '01. '02(Ap12) il. Q. (Farm and fireside lib., no. 199.) $1. Crowell & K.

Curschmann, H. *See* Osler, W:, *ed.*

Curtis, Is. G. Left-overs made palatable. '02 (F15) il. D. oilcloth, $1. Judd.

Curtiss, S: I. Primitive Semitic religion today. '02(Je7) il. 8°, net, $2. Revell.

Curwen, J: S. Studies in worship music, chiefly congregational singing. 1st ser. 3d ed., rev. and enl. '02(Mr8) 12°, $1.75. Scribner.

Cushing, Fk. H. Zuñi folk tales. '01· '02 (Ja25) O. net, $3.50. Putnam.

Cushman, Herb. E. Truth in Christian science. '02(My17) D. 60 c. J. H. West.

Cust, A. M. Ivory workers of the Middle Ages. '02(Mr8) il. 12°, (Handbooks of the great craftsmen.) $2. Macmillan.

Cust, Lionel. Desc. of the sketch-book by Sir Anthony Van Dyck. '02(Mr22) 4°, $17.50. Macmillan.

Cust, Lionel, *ed.* National portrait gallery. Ed. de luxe. In 2 v. v. 1. '02(Mr1) 4°, subs., complete work, net, $30. Cassell.

Custis, G: W. P. Life of George Washington. '02(Je28) 12°, (Biographies of famous men.) $1. Donohue.

Cutter, Sa. J., *comp.* Conundrums, riddles, puzzles and games. Rev., enl. ed. '02 (Ap5) S. 50 c.; pap., 25 c. Otis.

CYANIDE PROCESS.
James. Cyanide practice. $5. Engineering.
See also gold.

CYCLOPAEDIAS.
See Encyclopædias.

Cyr, Ellen M. Cyr readers. bks. 7 and 8. '01· '02(Mr8) il. 12°, ea., 45 c. Ginn.

Cyrano de Bergerac. Rostand, E. 50 c. W: R. Jenkins.

Da Costa, J: C., *jr.* Clinical hematology: guide to the examination of the blood. '01. '02(Ja11) il. col. pls. 8°, net, $5. Blakiston.

Daddy's girl. Smith, *Mrs.* E. T. $1. Burt.

Dadson, A. J. Evolution and its bearing on religion. '02(Ap5) net, $1.25. Dutton.

Dail, C. C. Sunlight and shadows. '02(Je21) il. 8°, $1.50. Hudson-K.

Daily praise: texts and hymns for every day. '02(F8) 32°, 15 c.; 20 c.; 25 c. Revell.

Dainty dishes for slender incomes. New ed. '02(My24) 12°, net, 50 c. New Amsterdam.

Dainty ser. 16°, pap., 50 c. Dutton.
—Smith. Lost Christmas.

DAIRY.
Blake. Common sense ideas for dairymen. $1. Coates.
Russell. Outlines of dairy bacteriology. $1. H. L. Russell.

Dalby, W: E. Balancing of engines. '02 (Mr22) O. $3.75. Longmans.

Daley, Jos. G. Cassock of the pines, and other stories. '02(Ap12) il. D. $1. W: H. Young.

Dallin, *Mrs.* Colonna M. Sketches of great painters for young people. '02(Je28) il. D. 90 c. Silver.

Dalton, Test. Role of the unconquered. '02 (F8) D. $1.50. G: W. Dillingham.

Daly, Ida M. Advanced rational speller. '02(Je7) S. 25 c. B: H. Sanborn.

DALZIEL BROTHERS.
Brothers Dalziel: record of work, 1840-1890. net, $6.50. Dutton.
DAMAGES.
Mechem. Case on the law of damages. net, $4. West Pub.
Dame, Lorin L., *and* Brooks, H: Handbook of the trees of New England. '02(F15) il. D. $1.35. Ginn.
Damsel (A) or two. Moore, F. F. $1.50. Appleton.
Dana, Fs. The decoy. '02(Mr8) 12°, $1.50. Lane.
Danaher, Alb. J. *See* New York. Amendments.
DANCING.
Quick. Guide to ball-room dancing. 50 c.; 25 c. Donohue.
Danger of youth. Jordans, J. 15 c. Herder.
Dangers of spiritualism, by a member of the Soc. of Psychical Research. '02(Je14) il. 8°, net, 75 c. Herder.
DANIEL.
Anderson. Daniel in the critics' den. net, $1.25. Revell.
Daniel Everton, volunteer-regular. Putnam, I. net, $1.20. Funk.
Dante Alighieri. Divine comedy: [prose tr.] by C: E. Norton. New rev. ed. '02(Mr22) O. $4.50; hf. cf. or hf. polished mor., $9.75. Houghton, M. & Co.
DANTE ALIGHIERI.
Boccaccio *and* Aretino. Earliest lives of Dante. 75 c. Holt.
Toynbee. Dante studies and researches. net, $3.50. Dutton.
Wright. Dante and the Divine comedy. net, $1. Lane.
D'Anvers, N., *pseud.* *See* Bell, *Mrs.* N. R. E. M.
Dark Continent. *See* Harding, W:
Dark o' the moon. Crockett, S: R. $1.50. Harper.
Darkie ways in Dixie. Richard, M. A. $1. Abbey Press.
Darkwood (The) tragedy. '02(Je14) 12°, $1.25. Neale.
Darley Dale, *pseud.* *See* Steele, F. M.
Darrow, Clarence S. A Persian pearl, and other essays. '02(My24) O. $1.50. Ricketts.
Daskam, Josephine D. Madness of Philip, and other tales of childhood. '02(Ap26) il. 12°, $1.50. McClure, P.
Daskam, Josephine D., *comp.* Best nonsense verses. '02(My10) 16°, bds., 50 c. W: S. Lord.
Datchet, C: Morchester: story of Am. society. '02(Ap26) D. net, $1.20. Putnam.
Daudet, A. Tartarin de Tarascon. (C. Fontaine.) '02(Mr8) il. D. 45 c. Am. Bk.
Daughters of the Revolution. Thayer, S. H: $1. Abbey Press.
Davenport, B: R. Blood will tell. '02(Je14) 12°, $1.50. Caxton Bk.
Davenport, Fs. H: Diseases of women. 4th ed., rev. and enl. '02(Mr22) il. 12°, net, $1.75. Lea.
Davenport, J: G. The fulfilment. '02(My17) D. net, 40 c. Dutton.
David Elginbrod. Macdonald, G: $1. Burt.
Davidson, *Mrs.* H. A. Study of Idylls of the king. '02(Mr8) S. pap., 50 c. Mrs. H. A. Davidson.
Davidson, Lillias C. Confessions of a match-making mother. '02(My17) D. $1.50. J. F. Taylor.
Davidson, Marie A. The two Renwicks. '02(Je7) D. $1.50. Neely.
Davis, Stanton K. As nature whispers. '02 (Mr29) 16°, 50 c. Alliance.
Davis, W: M. Elem. physical geography. '02(My24) D. $1.40. Ginn.
Davitt, Michael. Boer fight for freedom. '02(Je7) il. O. net, $2. Funk.
Day, Lewis E. Alphabets old and new. New ed. '02(Je21) 12°, $1.50. Scribner.
Days of the Son of man. Rhone, R. D. net, $1.20. Putnam.
Deal, Annie R. Life of Jennie O'Neill Potter. '02(Ap12) 12°, $1. Blanchard.
Dean, Howard. The iron hand. '02(Je14) D. $1. Abbey Press.
Dean, J: M. Cross of Christ in Bolo-land. '02(My17) il. 12°, net, $1. Revell.
Deane girls. Rouse, A. L. $1. Burt.
Death of Wallenstein. *See* Schiller, J. C. F. v.
DEBATES.
Hungerford. Success club debater. 25 c. Success.
Debates on federal constitution. Elliott, J. 5 v. net, $10; net, $12. Lippincott.
DECLAMATION.
See Orators and oratory.
DECORATION AND ORNAMENT.
Bossard, F. Modern designs for surface decoration and coloring. $8. Hessling.
Bossard, J: Decorative paintings. $8. Hessling.
Clifford. Period decoration. $3. Clifford & L.
Crane. Bases of design. $2.25. Macmillan.
See also Alphabets;—Lettering.
Decoy (The). Dana, F. $1.50. Lane.
Dee, Harry. James Griffin's adventures on land and sea. 1900. '02(F8) 12°, (Adventure ser.) $1. Yewdale.
Deeds of faith. Neale, J. M. 40 c. E. & J. B. Young.
Deel, G: A. Practical rapid calculator. '01. '02(Ja18) S. 50 c. G: A. Deel.
Deems, E: M., *comp.* Holy-days and holidays. '02(Ap12) O. $5. Funk.
Deep-sea plunderings. Bullen, F. T. $1.50. Appleton.
DEER.
Roosevelt, *and others.* The deer family. net, $2. Macmillan
Defendorf, A. Clinical psychiatry: adapted fr. the 6th Germ. ed. of Kraeplin's *Lehrbuch der psychiatrie.* '02(Je14) il. 8°, net, $3.50. Macmillan.
Definition of a gentleman. Newman, J: H: $1; 50 c. Kirgate Press.
De Forest, J. W. Poems; medley and Palestina. '02(Mr29) 12°, $1.25. Tuttle, M. & T.
Delano, Fes. J. Susanne. '02(Je7) il. D. (Cosy corner ser.) 50 c. L. C. Page.
DeLaurence, L. W: Hypnotism. 2d ed. '01. '02(Ap26) 12°, $1.50. Henneberry.

DELAWARE.
Sellers. Allied families of Del. $5. E. J. Sellers.

De Leon, Dan. Socialism *versus* anarchism. '01· '02(F15) D. pap., 10 c. N. Y. Labor News.

De Leon, T: C. Inauguration of President Watterson: Gormanius; Temple of trusts, and other travesties. '02(Mr1) il. D. pap., 25 c. Am. Writers'.

Del Mar, Alex. History of money in England and other states. '02(Je7) 8°, $2. Cambridge.

Del Mar, Alex. History of money in the Netherlands. '02(Je7) 8°, 50 c. Cambridge.

Del Mar, Alex. History of the precious metals. 2d ed. '02(Je7) 8°, net, $3. Cambridge.

DELSARTE SYSTEM.
Stebbins. Delsarte system of expression. $2. Werner.

Deming, Philander. Adirondack stories. New ed. '02(My17) 16°, 75 c. Houghton, M. & Co.

Democracy: Am. novel. [New ed.] '02 (Ap5) D. $1. Holt.

DEMOCRACY.
Addams. Democracy and social ethics. net, $1.25. Macmillan.
Lowell. Democracy. net, $2. Houghton, M. & Co.
See also Political science.

DEMONOLOGY.
Alexander. Demonic possession in the New Testament. net, $1.50. Scribner.
See also Devil.

De Montmorency, J. E. G. State intervention in Eng. education. '02(My24) 12°, (Cambridge Univ. Press ser.) net, $1.50. Macmillan.

Demorest, A. F., *ed.* Cambridge encyclopædia of esoteric subjects. v. 3. '02(Je7) 8°, net, $3. Cambridge.

Dendron, Bertram. Man in the moon. '02 (My10) il. T. 50 c. Bonnell.

Denning, Marg. Mosaics from India. '02 (Ap19) 12°, net, $1.50. Revell.

Dennis, Annie E. New Annie Dennis cook book. '01· '02(Ap12) 12°, $1.50. Mutual Pub. Co.

Dennis, Ja. S. Centennial survey of foreign missions: statistical supp. to Christian missions and social progress. '02(F15) il. obl. O. net, $4. Revell.

Dennis, L. M., *and* Clarke, F. W. Laboratory manual to accompany Elementary chemistry. '02(Je21) il. D. 50 c. Am. Bk.

DENTISTRY.
See Teeth.

DE PEYSTER FAMILY.
See Leach, J. G.

De Quincey, T: Selections; ed. by M. H. Turk. '02(Je21) D. (Athenæum Press ser.) $1.05. Ginn.

Desert and the sown. Foote, *Mrs.* M. H. $1.50. Houghton, M. & Co.

DESIGN.
See Decoration and ornament.

Desmond, H. J. Chats within the fold. '01. '02(Ja11) S. net, 75 c. Murphy.

De Solla, J. M. Fallacies of religion. New issue. '02(Mr29) 12°, pap., 25 c. Pierce & Z.

DETECTIVES.
Sullivan. Detective adviser. 60 c. Int. Detective.

DEUTERONOMY.
See Bible.

Deutsche gaben. Nies, K. 25 c. Witter.

Devereux, Ma. Lafitte of Louisiana. '02 (Je21) il. D. $1.50. Little, B. & Co.

Deveron, Hugh. Songs of the Sahkohnagas. '02(Ap26) D. $1.25. Abbey Press.

DEVOTIONAL EXERCISES AND MEDITATIONS.
Fourfold thoughts. $1. Revell.
Hall. Meditations and vows. $1.50. Dutton.
Matheson. Times of retirement. net, $1.25. Revell.
Quadrupani. Light and peace. net, 50 c. Herder.

DEVIL (The).
Townsend. Satan and demons. net, 25 c. Jennings.

Dewey, Byrd S. Bruno. New ed. '01. '02 (F15) 16°, (Children's friend ser.) bds., 50 c. Little, B. & Co.

DEWEY, G:
Halstead. Life and achievements of Admiral Dewey. $1.50; $2.25; $3.25. Dominion.

Dewey, J: Educational situation. '02(F1) D. (Cont. to educ., no. 3.) pap., net, 50 c. Univ. of Chic.

Dewey, J: Psychology and social practice. '01. '02(Ja11) S. (Univ. of Chic. cont. to educ., no. 2.) net, 25 c. Univ. of Chic.

Dewey, J: *See also* McLellan, J. A.

De Windt, Harry. Finland as it is. '02(Je7) 8°, net, $3. Dutton.

Dexter, Jos. S. Elem. practical exercises on sound, light, and heat. '01. '02(Mr8) il. D. (Practical elem. science ser.) 90 c. Longmans.

DIAGNOSIS.
Albert. Diagnosis of surgical diseases. $5; $5.50. Appleton.
Simon. Clinical diagnosis by microscopical and chemical methods. net, $3.75. Lea.

DIARIES.
Gower. Old diaries, 1881-1901. net, $4.50. Scribner.
Laird & Lee's diary and time saver, 1902. 25 c. Laird.

Diary of a goose girl. Wiggin, *Mrs.* K. D. $1. Houghton, M. & Co.

Dicey, E: Story of the Khedivate. '02(Je21) 8°, net, $4. Scribner.

Dickens, C: Holly Tree Inn, and Seven poor travellers. '01· '02(Mr1) 8°, net, $1.50. Lippincott.

Dickens, C: Story of Paul Dombey. '01. '02(Mr1) 12°, pap., 15 c. Lippincott.

Dickey Downy. Patteson, V. S. 25 c. A. J. Rowland.

Dickinson, E. Music in the hist. of the western church. '02(My10) O. net, $2.50. Scribner.

Dickson, C: R. First aid in accidents. '02 (Mr8) 18°, net, 50 c. Revell.

Dickson, Harris. Siege of Lady Resolute. '02(Mr1) D. $1.50. Harper.

Dickson, Leonard E. College algebra. '02 (F1) il. 8°, net, $1.50. Wiley.

Dickson, Leonard E. Linear groups; with exposition of the Galois Field theory. '02 (F15) 12°, net, $4. Stechert.

DICTIONARIES.
See Encyclopædias;—*also* names of languages and subjects.

DIET.
Beard. Guide book to natural, hygienic and humane diet. $1; 50 c. Alliance.
Beard. Guide-book to natural, hygienic and humane diet. net, $1. Crowell.
Jewett. Childbed nursing; notes on infant feeding. 80 c. Treat.
Richards *and* Williams. Dietary computer. net, $1.50. Wiley.
See also Hygiene;—Nurses and nursing.

DIGESTION.
Brunton. On disorders of assimilation, digestion, etc. net, $4; net, $5. Macmillan.

Dill, Ja. B. *See* New Jersey. General corp. act.—Laws rel. to corporations.

DINING.
See Cookery;—Toasts.

DIPHTHERIA.
Northrup, *ed.* Diphtheria, measles, etc. net, $5; $6. Saunders.

Direct answers to plain questions for Am churchmen. Scadding, C: net, 50 c. Whittaker.

DISEASE.
See Pathology.

DISSECTION.
Howes. Atlas of practical elem. zootomy. net, $3.50. Macmillan.
See also Anatomy;—Vivisection.

Dissertationes Americanæ; classical philology. O. pap. Scott, F. & Co.
—Hellems. Lex de imperio Vespasiani. 50 c. (1.)

Distinctive marks of the Episcopal church. McCormick, J: N. 25 c. Young Churchman.

District of Columbia. *Ct. of appeals.* Repts. (C: C. Tucker.) v. 18. '02(Mr1) O. shp., $5. Lowdermilk.

District of Columbia. Laws rel. to negotiable instruments. '02(Ap26) S. pap., 20 c. Lowdermilk.

Divine comedy. *See* Dante Alighieri;—*also* Wright, W. J. P.

Divine language of celestial correspondence. Turnbull, C. $2. Alliance.

Divine religion of humanity. Wilson, C. D. net, 20 c. Presb. Bd.

Dix, Beulah M., *and* Harper, Carrie A. The beau's comedy. '02(Mr29) il. D. $1.50. Harper.

Dix, Dorothy, *pseud.* *See* Gilmer, E. M.

Dixon, T:, *jr.* The leopard's spots. '02 (Mr22) il. D. $1.50. Doubleday, P.

Doane, W: C. Rhymes from time to time. '01. '02(Mr22) 12°, $1.50. Albany Diocesan Press.

Dobbins, Fk. Story of the world's worship. '02(Mr22) 12°, $2.25; hf. mor., $3.25. Dominion.

Dobson, Austin. Miscellanies. (2d ser.) '01. '02(Mr22) D. net, $1. Dodd.

DOCTRINES.
See Theology.

Dods, M. Parables of our Lord. New issue. '02(Ap12) 12°, $1.50. Whittaker.

Dog-day journal. Drum, B. 50 c. Abbey Press.

Dog of Flanders. La Rame, L. de. 15 c. Houghton, M. & Co.

DOGMA.
See Theology.

Dole, N. H., *ed.* *See* Schiller, J. C. F. v.

Dombey and son. *See* Dickens, C:

DOMESTIC ECONOMY.
Ellsworth. Queen of the household. $2.50. Ellsworth.
Lush. Domestic economy for scholarship and certificate students. net, 60 c. Macmillan.
Seeley. Cook book; with chap. on domestic servants, etc. net, $2; net, $3. Macmillan.
See also Cookery;—Gardening.

Don Carlos. *See* Schiller, J. C. F. v.

Don Quixote. *See* Cervantes Saavedra.

Dorothy South. Eggleston, G: C. $1.50. Lothrop.

Dorothy Vernon of Haddon Hall. Major, C: $1.50. Macmillan.

Doty, Alvah H. Prompt aid to the injured. 4th ed. rev. to date. '02(Ap26) 12°, $1.50. Appleton.

Double-barrelled detective story. Clemens, S: L. $1.50. Harper.

DOUBT.
See Faith;—Skepticism.

DOUGLAS, Stephen A.
Brown. Stephen Arnold Douglas. net, 65 c.; net, 50 c. Houghton, M. & Co.

Douglass, Fk. A. Colonel Harold de Lacey. '02(Je7) D. $1.25. Neely.

DOUW, G.
Martin. Gerard Douw. $1.75. Macmillan.

Down historic waterways. Thwaites, R. G. net, $1.20. McClurg.

Doyle, Arth. C. Hound of the Baskervilles. '02(Ap19) il. D. $1.25. McClure, P.

Doyle, Sherman. Presbyterian home missions. '02(Je21) il. D. net, $1. Presb. Bd.

Dragons of the air. Seeley, H. G. net, $1.40. Appleton.

DRAMA AND DRAMATISTS.
Schelling. The Eng. chronicle play. net, $2. Macmillan.
See also Actors and actresses.

DRAWING.
Augsburg. Drawing. 3 bks. ea., 75 c. Educ. Pub.
Crane. Line and form. $2.25. Macmillan.

DRAWINGS.
Underwood, *il.* Some pretty girls. $3; $5. Quail & W.

DREAMS.
See Fortune-tellers.

Dresser, Fk. F. Employers' liability, in N. Y., Mass., Ind., Ala., Colo., and Eng. '02 (My24) O. shp., $6. Keefe-D.

Dresser, Horatio W. Book of secrets, with studies in self-control. '02(Mr8) D. net, $1. Putnam.

Dresser, Julius A. True history of mental science; rev., with notes, by H. W. Dresser. [New issue.] '02(Mr22) D. 20 c. Alliance.

Dressler, Flo. Feminology. '02(F15) il. O. $3. Dressler.

Drewitt's dream. Alden, W: L. $1; 50 c. Appleton.

DRILLS (*fancy*).
Harper. Moral drill for the school-room. $1. Kellogg.
Hatch. Zobo patriotic drill. 15 c. Hints.

Droch, *pseud.* *See* Bridges, R.

Drude, Paul. Theory of optics; fr. the Germ. '02(My10) O. $4. Longmans.

Drum, Blossom, *pseud.* Dog-day journal. '02(F22) D. 50 c. Abbey Press.

Drummers' yarns. Schofield, R. J. 25 c. Excelsior.

Drummond, Hamilton. The Seigneur de Beaufoy. '02(My17) il. D. $1.50. L. C. Page.

DRUMMOND, H:
Simpson. Henry Drummond. 75 c. Scribner.

Drummond, Josiah H., *comp.* Maine masonic text-book. 5th ed. '02(Je7) 12°, $1.40; leath. tuck, $1.50. Berry.

DU BARRY, *Mme.*
Morehead. Madame Du Barry. 50 c. Donohue.

Du Bois, A: J. Mechanics of engineering. v. 1. '01. '02(Ja18) il. 4°, $7.50; v. 2. (Je21) $10. Wiley.

Du Bois, E. F., *comp.* Harvard Univ. songs. '02(Je28) 12°, $1.50. Ditson.

Duchess (The), *pseud.* *See* Hungerford, *Mrs.* M. H.

DUCK SHOOTING.
See Shooting.

Duckwitz, Louise C. What Thelma found in the attic. [New issue.] '01. '02(Mr22) il. O. $1. Alliance.

Dudeney, *Mrs.* H: Spindle and plough. '02 (Mr22) D. $1.50. Dodd.

Dudevant, *Mme.* A. L. A. *See* Sand, G:

Duff, Arch. Theology and ethics of the Hebrews. '02(My10) D. (Semitic ser.) net, $1.25. Scribner.

Duff, E: M., *and* Allen, T: G. Psychic research and gospel miracles. '02(Mr22) D. net, $1.50. Whittaker.

Duguid, C: Story of the Stock Exchange [London.] '02(Mr15) il. 12°, net, $2. Dutton.

Duhring, L: A., Lydston, G. F., *and others.* Syphilis. '02(Ap12) 12°, net, $1. Treat.

Dukesmith, Fk. H. The air brake, its use and abuse. '02(Je21) il. D. $1. F. H. Dukesmith.

Dull Miss Archinard. Sedgwick, A. D. $1.50. Century Co.

Dumas, Alex. Romances. Versailles ed. '02(Mr22) 40 v., il. 8°, subs., net, per v., $1.50. Little, B. & Co.

Dumas, Alex. The King's gallant; tr. by H: L. Williams. '02(Je7) il. D. $1. Street.

Dumas, Alex. Napoleon; adapt. and ed. by W. W. Vaughan. '02(Ap12) 12°, (Siepmann's elem. Fr. ser.) net, 50 c. Macmillan.

Dunbar, Paul L. Sport of the gods. '02(My10) D. $1.50. Dodd.

Dunn, Arch., *jr.* New ideas on bridge. '02 (Mr8) 16°, 50 c. Scribner.

Dunn, F. Veterinary medicines. New rev. ed. '01. '02(F22) 8°, $3.75. W: R. Jenkins.

Dunning, W: A. Hist. of political theories. '02(F22) 8°, net, $2.50. Macmillan.

Dupre, A., *and* Hake, H. W. Manual of inorganic chemistry. '01. '02(F15) 12°, $3. Lippincott.

Durand, W: F: Practical marine engineering. '02(Ap5) il. 8°, $5. Marine Engineering.

Durège, H. Elements of the theory of functions of a complex variable; ed. by G: E. Fisher and I: J. Schwatt. '01. '02(Ja4) 8°, net, $2. Macmillan.

Durrell's Battery. *See* Cuffel, C: A.

Dustin, Eddie. The make good book of parodies. '01. '02(Ja11) S. pap., 50 c. E. Dustin.

Dutiful child. Wetzel, F. X. 40 c. Herder.

Dutto, L. A. Life of Bartolomé de las Casas and first leaves of Am. ecclesiastical history. '02(Mr8) 8°, net, $1.50. Herder.

Duxbury doings. Le Row, C. B. $1. Burt.

Dwight, C: A. S. Railroading with Christ. '02(Je21) il. D. $1. Am. Tr.

DYEING.
Rawson, *and others.* Dictionary of dyes, mordants, and other compounds. net, $5. Lippincott.

Dyer, T: H:, *and* **Hassall, Arth.** History of modern Europe fr. fall of Constantinople. 3d ed., rev. v. 6; with bibliog. and index. '02(Mr8) 12°, net, $2. Macmillan.

Dynamic aspects of nutrition. Horridge, F. $1.50. Wood.

DYNAMOS AND MOTORS.
Arnold. Armature windings of direct current dynamos. $2. Van Nostrand
Bubier. How to build dynamo-electric machinery. $2.50. Bubier.
Harmsworth, *and others.* Motors and motor driving. $3.50; $5. Little, B. & Co.
Sheldon *and* Mason. Dynamo electric machinery. 2 v. ea., net, $2.50. Van Nostrand.
Wiener. Calculation of dynamo-electric machines. $3. Elec. World.
See also Cars.

Eadie, J: Biblical cyclopædia. New ed. '01. '02(Mr1) il. 8°, net, $3.75. Lippincott.

Eakle, Arth. S. Colemanite from So. California. '02(Je14) O. (Univ. of Cal.; bull. of dept. of geology, v. 3, no. 2.) pap., 15 c. Univ. of Cal.

EAR.
Brühl *and* Politzer. Atlas epitome of otology. net, $3. Saunders.
Gradle. Diseases of the nose, pharynx and ear. net, $3.50. Saunders.
Wood, *and others, eds.* Eye, ear, nose and throat. $1.50. Year Bk.

Earle, Stephen C. Rutland home of Maj. Gen. Rufus Putnam. '01. '02(Mr8) il. O. pap., 30 c., bds., 50 c. S. C. Earle.

Early Am. fiction. Wegelin, O. net, $2. O. Wegelin.

EARTH.
Ball. Earth's beginning. net, $1.80. Appleton.

East of the barrier. Graham, J. M. net, $1. Revell.

EASTER.
Swartz. Easter and the resurrection. net, 15 c. Revell.

Eastman, Eph. R: Poems. '02(Je7) S. $1. Hadley Pr.

Ebersole, E. C. *See* Iowa. Encyclopedia of law.

Eccles, W. M. Hernia. '02(My10) il. 8°, $2.50. Wood.

Ecclesiazusæ (The). *See* Aristophanes.

Eckley, W: T: *and* **Corinne B.** Regional anatomy of the head and neck. '02(Mr1) il. 8°, net, $2.50. Lea.

Eclectic manual. *See* Scudder's.

ECLECTIC MEDICINE.
Mundy. Eclectic practice in diseases of children. net, $2.50. Scudder.
Eclectic school readings. D. Am. Bk.
—Bartlett. Animals at home. 45 c.
—Bradish. Stories of country life. 40 c.
—McCullough. Little stories for little people. 25 c.
ECOLOGY.
See Botany.
Eddy, R:, *ed.* *See* Universalist register.
Edgerly, Webster. Natural reader. '02(Je28) 12°, $1.50. Ralston.
Edison, T: A. Telegraphy self-taught. '02 (Je21) il. D. $1. Drake.
Editorial echoes. Payne, W: M. net, $1. McClurg.
Edle blut (Das). Wildenbruch, E. A. v. 30 c. Am. Bk.
EDUCATION.
Creighton. Thoughts on education. net, $1.60. Longmans.
De Montmorency. State intervention in Eng. education. net, $1.50. Macmillan.
Dewey. Educational situation. net, 50 c. Univ. of Chic.
Fennell, *and others.* Notes of lessons on Herbartian methods. $1.10. Longmans.
Henderson. Education and the larger life. net, $1.30. Houghton, M. & Co.
Kemp. Hist. of education. net, $1.25. Lippincott.
Lang, *ed.* Educational creeds of the 19th century. 75 c. Kellogg.
Seeley. Foundations of education. $1. Hinds.
Taylor, *ed.* Practical school problems. v. 1, pt. 1. 30 c. [W: B. Harison] Soc. Sch. Problems.
Young. Some types of modern educ. theory. net, 25 c. Univ. of Chic.
See also Business education;—Children;—Examinations;—Home study;—Memory; — Psychology; —Schools;—Students;—Teachers and teaching.
Educational foundations of trade and industry. Ware, F. net, $1.20. Appleton.
EDWARD I., *King of England.*
Jenks. Edward Plantagenet, (Edward I.) net, $1.35; net, $1.60. Putnam.
EDWARD VII., *King of England.*
Carman. Ode on the coronation of King Edward. net, $1. L. C. Page.
Pascoe. Pageant and ceremony of the coronation of their majesties King Edward and Queen Alexandra. net, $1.50. Appleton.
Watson. Ode on day of the coronation of King Edward VII. net, $1; net, $3.50. Lane.
Efird, C. M., *rep.* *See* South Carolina. *Sup. ct.* Repts.
Effront, Jean. Enzymes and their applications; Eng. tr. by S: C. Prescott. v. 1. '02(F1) 8°, $3. Wiley.
Egan, Maurice F. Belinda. '02(F8) D. $1. Kilner.
Eggleston, G: C. American immortals; record of men whose names are inscribed in the Hall of Fame. '02(Mr22) 8°, $10. Putnam.
Eggleston, G: C. Bale marked circle X. '02 (My24) D. net, $1.20. Lothrop.
Eggleston, G: C. Dorothy South. '02(Mr29) D. $1.50. Lothrop.
EGYPT.
Babcock. Letters from Egypt and Palestine. net, $1. Scribner.
Baedeker, *ed.* Egypt. net, $4.50. Scribner.
Barber. Mechanical triumphs of ancient Egyptians. net, $1.25. Dodd.
Dicey. Story of the Khedivate. net, $4. Scribner.
Guide to Palestine and Egypt. net, $3.25. Macmillan.
See also Cairo.
Ehrlich, *Mrs.* Bertha. Light of our spirit. '02(Mr29) S. 25 c. B. Ehrlich.
Einstein, Lewis. Italian Renaissance in England: studies. '02(Ap12) il. 12°, (Columbia University studies in comparative literature.) net, $1.50. Macmillan.
Elbertus, *Fra, pseud.* *See* Hubbard, E.
Eldridge, J. L. What think ye of Christ, etc.: [poems.] '01. '02(Mr1) il. D. $1. Abbey Press.
ELECTRIC ENGINEERING.
Parr. Electrical engineering testing. net, $3.50. Van Nostrand.
ELECTRIC LIGHT.
Houston *and* Kennelly. Electric arc lighting.—Incandescent lighting. ea., $1. McGraw.
ELECTRIC MEASUREMENT.
Hobbs. Arithmetic of electrical measurements. 50 c. Van Nostrand.
See also Galvanometer.
ELECTRIC MOTORS.
See Dynamos and motors.
ELECTRICITY.
American electrical cases. v. 7. $6. M. Bender.
Atkinson. Electrical and magnetic calculations. net, $1.50. Van Nostrand.
Beaton. Vest-pocket compend of electricity. 75 c.; 50 c. Laird.
Bubier. Experimental electricity. $1. Bubier.
Clarke. A B C of electrical experiments. $1. Excelsior.
Hadley. Practical exercises in magnetism and electricity. net, 60 c. Macmillan.
Jackson. Elem. text-book on electricity and magnetism, and their applications. net, $1.40. Macmillan.
Munro. Nociones de electricidad. 40 c. Appleton.
Practical electricity. $2. Cleveland Armature.
Swoope. Lessons in practical electricity. net, $2. Van Nostrand.
Webber. Graduated coll. of problems in electricity. $3. Spon.
Wolcott. On the sensitiveness of the coherer. 20 c. Univ. of Wis.
Wordingham. Central electrical stations. $7.50. Lippincott.
See also Alternating currents;—Dynamos and motors;—Electric light;—Roentgen rays;—Telephone.
Elementary electro technical ser. sq. S. $1. McGraw.
—Houston *and* Kennelly. Alternating electric currents.—Electric arc lighting.—Electric incandescent lighting.
Elements and notation of music. McLaughlin, J. M. 55 c. Ginn.
ELIOT, George.
Stephen. George Eliot. net, 75 c. Macmillan.
Eliot, H: W., *jr.* *See* Hall, F: G.

Elisabeth, *Madame.* Memoir and letters of Madame Elisabeth, sister of Louis XVI. '02(Mr8) il. 8°, (Versailles hist. ser.) subs., per v., $6; ¾ leath., per v., $9. Hardy, P. & Co.
Elizabeth and her German garden. '02(My10) 12°, (Home lib.) $1. Burt.
Elizabethan prayer-book and ornaments. Gee, H: net, $1.25. Macmillan.
Ellacombe, H: N. In my vicarage garden. '02 (My24) 12°, net, $1.50. Lane.
Ellicott, J: M. Life of John Ancrum Winslow, Rear Admiral U. S. N. '02(Ja25) O. $2.50. Putnam.
Elliot, D. G. *See* Roosevelt, T.
Elliot lectures. *See* Orr, J.
Elliott, C: B. Law of insurance. '02(Ap19) O. shp., $4. Bowen-M.
Elliott, Jonathan. Debates on the federal constitution. '01. '02(Mr1) 5 v., 8°, net, $10; shp., net, $12. Lippincott.
Ellis, E: S. Life of William McKinley. '01. '02(F15) 12°, (Undine lib., no. 9.) pap., 25 c. Street.
Ellsworth, Tinnie, ["*Mrs.* M. W. Ellsworth."] Queen of the household. New century ed., rev. and enl. '02(Ja18) 12°, $2.50. Ellsworth.
Ellwood, C: A. Aristotle as a sociologist. '02(Mr22) 8°, (Pub. of the soc., no. 332.) pap., 15 c. Am. Acad. Pol. Sci.
ELMA, N. Y.
Jackman. Hist. of the town of Elma, Erie Co., N. Y., 1620-1901. $3. Hausauer.
Elmore, Ja. B. A lover in Cuba, and poems. '01. '02(Mr8) il. S. $1. J. B. Elmore.
ELOCUTION.
See Orators and oratory;—Preaching;—Readers and speakers;—Voice.
ELOQUENCE.
See Orators and oratory;—Preaching.
Elwell, J. B. Bridge; its principles and rules of play. '02(Ap19) S. net, $1.25. Scribner.
Ely, R. T. *See* Vincent, J: M.
EMBLEMS.
See Tombstones.
EMBRYOLOGY.
Keith. Human embryology and morphology. $4.50. Longmans.
Emerson, E: R. Story of the vine. '02 (Ap12) D. net, $1.25. Putnam.
Emerson, *Mrs.* Ellen R. Nature and human nature. '02(Mr15) D. net, $1.25. Houghton, M. & Co.
Emerson, R. W. [Essays.] '01. '02(Ap5) S. (Little masterpieces.) 50 c. Doubleday, P.
Emerson, R. W. Representative men. '02 (My17) 12°, (Home lib.) $1. Burt.
Emerson, Willis G: Buell Hampton. '02 (My10) D. $1.50. Forbes.
Emery, W: D'E. Handbook of bacteriolog. diagnosis, incl. instructions for clinical examination of the blood. '01. '02(F15) 12°, net, $1.50. Blakiston.
Empire of business. Carnegie, A. subs., $3. Doubleday, P.
Employers' liability. Dresser, F. F. $6. Keefe-D.
En son nom. Hale, E: E. $1. W: R. Jenkins.
ENCYCLOPAEDIAS.
Appleton's annual cyclopædia, 1901. subs., $5; $6; $7; $8. Appleton.

ENCYCLOPAEDIAS.—*Continued.*
Century dict. and cyclopedia. 10 v. subs., $80-$150. Century Co.
Cheyne *and* Black. Encyc. Biblica. v. 3. subs., net. $5; net, $7.50. Macmillan.
Eadie. Biblical cyclopædia. net, $3.75. Lippincott.
Holst, *ed.* Teachers' and pupils' cyclopædia. v. 1-3. $12.75. Holst.
Morris. 20th century encyclopædia. $3.50; $4.25; $5.50. Winston.
Sellow. Three thousand sample questions. 50 c. Bellows.
Spofford *and* Annandale, *eds.* XXth century cyclopædia and atlas. 8 v. $20; $26. Gebbie.
See also under special subjects.
Engels, F: Socialism; tr. by E: Aveling. '01. '02(F1) D. (Arm and hammer ser.) 50 c. N. Y. Labor News.
ENGINEERING.
Baker. Municipal engineering and sanitation. net, $1.25. Macmillan.
Du Bois. Mechanics of engineering. v. 1. $7.50; v. 2. $10. Wiley.
Harcourt. Civil engineering as app. in construction. $5. Longmans.
Hawkins. Aids to engineers' examinations. $2. Audel.
Hawkins. Handbook of calculations for engineers and firemen. $2. Audel.
Problems in the use and adjustment of engineering instruments. $1.25. Wiley.
See also Architecture;—Bridges;—Electrical engineering;—Hydraulic engineering;—Irrigation; — Marine engineering; — Railroads; — Sanitary engineering; — Steam engine; — Surveying; — Water-supply.
Engineering Magazine. Index, 1896-1900; ed. by H: H. Supplee. '02(Mr1) 8°, $7.50. Engineering Mag.
ENGINES.
Dalby. Balancing of engines. $3.75. Longmans.
See also Corliss engine;—Steam engines.
ENGLAND.
Baldwin. Scutage and knight service in England. net, $1. Univ. of Chic.
Blauvelt. Development of cabinet government in England. net, $1.50. Macmillan.
Blomfield. Formal garden in England. $3. Macmillan.
Einstein. Italian Renaissance in England. net, $1.50. Macmillan.
Honeyman. Bright days in merrie England. net, $1.50. Honeyman.
Jesse. Historical memoirs. 30 v. ea., $2.50; or set of 15 v., $37.40; $75. L. C. Page.
Lennox. Life and letters; also pol. sketch of the years 1760-1763. 2 v. net, $9. Scribner.
Lubbock. Scenery of England and the causes to which it is due. net, $2.50. Macmillan.
Macmillan's summary of Eng. history on the concentric plan; Senior. net, 15 c. Macmillan.
Maitland. Music in England in 19th century. net, $1.75. Dutton.
Medley. Student's manual of Eng. constitutional history. net, $3.50. Macmillan.
Mowry. First steps in the hist. of England. 70 c. Silver.

ENGLAND.—*Continued.*
Russell. Onlooker's note-book. net, $2.25. Harper.
Saussure. Foreign view of England in the reign of George I. and George II. net, $3. Dutton.
Traill *and* Mann, *eds.* Social England. v. I. net, $4.50. Putnam.
Wyckoff. Feudal rel. between the kings of England and Scotland under the early Plantagenets. net, $1. Univ. of Chic.
See also Caroline, *Queen of England*;—Clayton-Bulwer treaty;—Edward I., *King of England*;—Edward VII., *King of England*;—Hampshire;—Henry V., *King of England*;—Hertfordshire;—Jesus (Society of);—London; Malvern.
English catalogue of books, for 1901. '02 (Mr15) O. pap., $1.50. Pub. Weekly.
English chronicle play. Schelling, F. E. net, $2. Macmillan.
English classics, star ser. il. D. Globe Sch. Bk.
—Shakespeare. Julius Cæsar. 32 c.
English composition. Thornton, G. H. 75 c. Crowell.
English girl in Paris. '02(My24) 12°, $1.50. Lane.
ENGLISH LANGUAGE.
Adler. Germ. and Eng. dictionary. pt. I. $3.50. Appleton.
Aiton *and* Rankin. Exercises in syntax for summer schools, etc. 25 c. Hyde.
Beeman. Analysis of the Eng. sentence. 50 c. Flanagan.
Blain. Syntax of the verb in Anglo-Saxon chronicle, 787-1001. net, 50 c. Barnes.
Chambers's twentieth century dict. of Eng. language. $1.50; $2. Lippincott.
Krüger *and* Smith. Eng.-Germ. conversation book. 25 c. Heath.
Lewis. Applied Eng. grammar. net, 35 c. Macmillan.
Murray, *and others, eds.* New Eng. dictionary. v. 3, pts. 30-34; v. 4, pts. 35, 36. ea., 90 c. Oxford Univ.
Skinner *and* Burgert. Lessons in Eng. based upon principles of literary interpretation. 50 c. Silver.
Vories. Lab'y method of teaching Eng. and touch typewriting together. $1.25. Inland Pub.
English law reports, for 1900. '01. '02(F15) 6 v., 8°, shp., $28.50. Little, B. & Co.
ENGLISH LITERATURE.
Andrews. Topics and ref. for the study of Eng. literature. 15 c. Hyde.
Chambers's cyclopædia of Eng. literature. v. I. net, $5. Lippincott.
Chaucer. English of the XIVth century. 75 c. Ginn.
Marks. Brief hist. outline of Eng. literature. $1. J. A. Marks.
Moody. Hist. of Eng. literature. net, $1.25. Scribner.
Moulton, *and others, eds.* Lib. of literary criticism of Eng. and Am. authors. v. 3. $5; $6.50. Moulton Pub.
Phelps, *comp.* List of general reading, 1580-1902. net, 5 c. Pease-L.
English men of letters ser.; ed. by J: Morley. 12°, net, 75 c. Macmillan.
—Stephen. George Eliot.
English pharisees, French crocodiles. Blouët, P. $1.25. Abbey Press.
English tales in verse. Herford, C: H. $1.50. Scribner.
Englishwoman's year book and directory, 1902; ed. by E. Janes. '02(F1) 12°, $1.50. Macmillan.
Engraved gems. Sommerville, M. net, $1.50. Biddle.
ENGRAVERS AND ENGRAVING.
Altdorfer. Little engravings classical and contemporary. no. I. net, $1.50. Longmans.
Blake. Little engravings. no. 2. net, $1.50. Longmans.
Whitman. Print-collectors' handbook. net, $5. Macmillan.
Enoch Strone. Oppenheim, E. P. $1.50. G: W. Dillingham.
Enseñar á leer. Arnold, S. L. 40 c. Silver.
ENTERTAINMENTS.
Kellogg. Six musical entertainments. 15 c. Kellogg.
Nies. Deutsche gaben. 25 c.—Rosen im schnee. 50 c. Witter.
See also Drills.
ENTOMOLOGY.
See Insects.
ENZYMES.
Effront. Enzymes and their applications. $3. Wiley.
Eparchæan interval. Lawson, A. C. 10 c. Univ. of Cal.
EPHESIANS.
See Bible.
EPIGRAMS.
Antrim. Naked truths and veiled allusions. 50 c. Altemus.
EPISTLES (The).
See Bible.
Epstein, A. J. Tarquinius Superbus. '02 (My24) il. D. $1.25. Mutual Pub.
EPWORTH LEAGUE.
Nicholson *and* Woods. Notes on Epworth League prayer meeting topics. 15 c. Eaton & M.
Epworth League year-book for 1902. '02 (Ja25) S. pap., net, 10 c. Eaton & M.
EQUATIONS.
Forsyth. Theory of differential equations. v. 4. net, $3.75. Macmillan.
EQUITY.
Ames. Equity jurisdiction. pt. 2. 75 c. Harvard Law.
Erasmus, D. Select colloquies; ed. by M. Whitcomb. '02(Je7) D. (Sixteenth century classics.) $1. [Longmans;] Univ. of Penn.
Erdman, C: R. Ruling elder. '02(Je21) S. pap., 3 c. Presb. Bd.
Ernst, Harold C., *ed.* **Animal experimentation.** '02(Mr8) 8°, net, $1.50; pap., net, $1. Little, B. & Co.
Errand boy of Andrew Jackson. Stoddard, W: O. net, $1. Lothrop.
Ervin, Dayton. The hermitage and random verses. '02(Je7) S. $1. Grafton Press.
Esenwein, J. Berg. **How to attract and hold an audience.** '02(F1) D. $1. Hinds.
ESSAYS.
Miles. How to prepare essays, [etc.] net, $2. Dutton.
Estados Unidos. Constitucion: (Constitution of the U. S. in Spanish by C. Mexia.) '02 (Je7) 8°, $1. Cambridge.
Esther. Racine, J. 35 c. Holt.

ETHICS.
Gabirol. Improvement of moral qualities. net, $1.25. Macmillan.
Ladd. Philosophy of conduct. net, $3.50. Scribner.
Ritchie. Studies in political and social ethics. $1.50. Macmillan.
Schuyler. Systems of ethics. $1.50. Jennings.
See also Character;—Conduct of life;—Courage;—Crime and criminals;—Culture; — Fiction; — Law;—Utilitarianism.

Ethics in the school. Young, E. F. net, 25 c. Univ. of Chic.

ETHNOLOGY.
Hutchinson, *and others.* Living races of mankind. net, $5. Appleton.
See also Folk-lore;—Language.

EUGENE, *Prince.*
Sybel. Prinz Eugen von Savoyen. net, 60 c. Macmillan.

EUROPE.
Carpenter. Europe. 70 c. Am. Bk.
Dyer *and* Hassall. Hist. of modern Europe. v. 6. net, $2. Macmillan.
Helmolt, *and others, eds.* Hist. of the world. v. 4. The Mediterranean countries. $6. Dodd.
Northern Europe: Norway, Russia, the Netherlands, France, Germany and Switzerland. 30 c. Ginn.
Stedman. Complete pocket guide to Europe, 1902. $1.25. W: R. Jenkins.
See also names of countries.

Eustis, Edith. Marion Manning. '02(Je7) D. $1.50. Harper.

Eve of St. Agnes. *See* Keats, J:

Eve triumphant. Coulevain, P. de. net, $1.20. Putnam.

Evening Post. *See* New York Evening Post.

Evermann, B. W. *See* Jordan, D: S.

Eversley ser. 12°, $1.50. Macmillan.
—Jebb. Modern Greece.

Everybody's opportunity. Rowell, J. H. 10 c. Free Socialist.

EVIDENCE.
Ewbank. Indiana trial evidence. $6. Bowen-M.
Stephen. Digest of the law of evidence. $4. Dissell.
Trickett. Law of witnesses in Pa. $6. T. & J. W. Johnson.

EVOLUTION.
Beecher. Studies in evolution. net, $5. Scribner.
Conley. Evolution and man. net, 75 c. Revell.
Dadson. Evolution and its bearing on religion. net, $1.25. Dutton.
See also Embryology;—Religion and science.

Evolution of the Eng. Bible. Hoare, H. W. net, $2.50. Dutton.

Evolutionary philosophy. Chamberlain, L. T. 50 c. Baker & T.

Ewart, W:, Murrell, W:, *and others.* Climates of London, and of the central and no. portions of England with those of Wales and Ireland. '02(My17) 8°, (Climates and baths of Great Britain, v. 2.) net, $4. Macmillan.

Ewbank, L: B. Indiana trial evidence '02 (My24) O. shp., $6. Bowen-M.

Ewing, *Mrs.* Juliana H. Benjy in beastland. New ed. '01- '02(F15) 16°, (Children's friend ser.) bds., 50 c. Little, B. & Co.

Ewing, *Mrs.* Juliana H. Jackanapes; [also] The brownies; ed. by H: W. Boynton. '02 (My17) S. (Riverside literature ser., no. 151.) pap., net, 15 c. Houghton, M. & Co.

Exiled by the world. Imhaus, E. V. $1.50. Mutual Pub.

EXPANSION (political).
Halstead. Pictorial hist. of America's new possessions, the Isthmian canals, and national expansion. $2.50; $3.50; $4.50. Dominion.

Expansion of gases by heat. Randall, W. W. $1. Am. Bk.

EXPERIMENTS.
See Physics.

EXPRESSION.
See Voice.

EYE.
Brown, C. H., *comp.* Optician's manual. 2 v. ea., $2. Keystone.
Greeff. Microscopic examination of the eyes. net, $1.25. Blakiston.
Jennings. Ophthalmoscopy. net, $1.50. Blakiston.
Parsons. Elem. ophthalmic optics. net, $2. Blakiston.
Wood, *and others, eds.* Eye, ear, nose and throat. $1.50. Year Bk.

F., A. M. Tales of my father. '02(Ap19) D. $2. Longmans.

FABLES.
Kleckner. In the misty realm of fable. $1. Flanagan.

Fables of the elite. Gilmer, E. M. $1. Fenno.

Fabre, J. H. Insect life; fr. the Fr.; ed. by F. Merrifield. '02(Ja18) il. 12°, $1.75. Macmillan.

FACE.
See Physiognomy.

Faciology. Stevens, L. B. 25 c. Donohue.

Facsimile reprint of early Canadian books. il. D. net. Congdon.
—Bosworth, *ed.* Hochelaga depicta; Montreal. $3; $4.50.

Facts and comments. Spencer, H. net, $1.20. Appleton.

Fagge, C: H. Text-book of medicine. 4th ed. '02(Ap5) 2 v., 8°, net, $6. Blakiston.

Failure of success. Howard, *Lady* M. $1.50. Longmans.

Failures of vegetarianism. Miles, E. H. net, $1.50. Dutton.

Fairbairn, And. M. Philosophy of the Christian religion. '02(Je7) 8°, net, $3.50. Macmillan.

Fairbanks, Harold W. Home geography for primary grades. '02(My3) il. sq. O. 60 c. Educ. Pub.

Fairchild, Lee. The tippler's vow. '01- '02 (Mr8) il. f°, bds., $10. Croscup.

Fairie, Ja. Notes on lead ores. '01- '02 (My10) D. net, $1. Van Nostrand.

Fairview's mystery. Marquis, G: H. 75 c. Abbey Press.

Fairy favorites. Perrault, C: 50 c. Little, B. & Co.

FAIRY TALES.
Andersen. Selected stories. 15 c. Lippincott.
Brown. In the days of giants: Norse tales. net, $1.10. Houghton, M. & Co.

FAIRY TALES.—*Continued.*
O'Shea, *ed.* Old world wonder stories. 25 c. Heath.
Valentine, *comp. and ed.* Old, old fairy tales. $1. Burt.
Yeats, *comp.* Irish fairy and folk tales. $1. Burt.

FAITH.
Purves. Faith and life. net, $1.25. Presb. Bd.
Rainsford. Reasonableness of faith. net, $1.25. Doubleday, P.
See also Religion;—Theology.

Fales, W: E. S. Bits of broken china. '02 (My17) il. S. 75 c. Street.

Falkiner, C. L. Studies in Irish history and biog. mainly of the eighteenth century. '02(Mr8) O. $5. Longmans.

Fallon, Chris. *See* Pennsylvania. Conveyancing.

Fallows, S:, *ed.* Life of William McKinley; with short biog. of Lincoln and Garfield, and life of President Roosevelt. [Internat. memorial ed.] '01. '02(Ap12) 8°, $1.50; hf. mor., $2.25. Regan.

Familia de Alvareda. Caballero, F. 75 c. Holt.

FAMILIES.
See Genealogy.

Famous Scots ser. 12°, 75 c. Scribner.
—Simpson. Henry Drummond.

Fanning, J: T: Practical treatise on hydraulic and water-supply engineering. 15th rev., enl. ed. '02(Ap5) il. 8°, $5. Van Nostrand.

Färber, Wilhelm. Commentar zum katechismus. '02(Je28) 12°, net, $1.50. Herder.

Fargo, Kate M. Songs not set to music. '02 (Mr15) D. $1. Abbey Press.

Farley, Jos. P. West Point in the early sixties, with incidents of the war. '02(Je14) il. O. net, $2. Pafraets.

Farm and fireside lib. il. Q. $1. Crowell & K.
—Cuppy, *ed.* Pictorial natural history. (199.)

Farmer, Ja. E. Brinton Eliot. '02(Je7) 12°. $1.50. Macmillan.

Farmer's school and the visit. Kellogg, A. M. 15 c. Kellogg.

FARMS AND FARMING.
Barnard. Farming by inches.—My ten rod farm. ea., 40 c. Coates.
Shepard. Life on the farm. 50 c. Flanagan.
See also Irrigation.

Farquhar, A. B. Manufacturer's need of reciprocity. '02(Mr22) 8°, (Pub. of the soc., no. 330.) pap., 15 c. Am. Acad. Pol. Sci.

Farrington, Fk. Retail advertising for druggists and stationers. '01. '02(Ja11) D. net, $1. Baker & T.

Farson, C: T. *See* Illinois. Mechanics' lien law.

Fashions in literature. Warner, C: D. net, $1.20. Dodd.

FASTS AND FEASTS.
See Easter;—Holidays;—Lent;—Sunday.

Father Manners. Young, H. $1. Abbey Press.

FATHERS.
Swete. Patristic study. net, 90 c. Longmans.

Faust, C. A. Compendium of automatic pen lettering and designs. '01. '02(F1) obl. D. pap., complete bk., $1; alphabet pt., 75 c. Auto Pen.

Favor of princes. Luther, M. L. 50 c. Jamieson-H.

Feasey, H: J. Monasticism: what is it? '02 (Mr8) 8°, net, $1. Herder.

Federal citations. *See* Ash, M.

Federal reporter. *See* United States.

Feminology. Dressler, F. $3. Dressler.

FENELON, François.
St. Cyres. Life of François Fenelon. net, $2.50. Dutton.

Fennell, M., *and others.* Notes of lessons on the Herbartian methods. '02(Mr22) D. $1.10. Longmans.

FERDINAND, *King of Spain.*
Prescott. Ferdinand and Isabella, the Catholic. 3 v. net, $3. Macmillan.

FERMENTATION.
Matthews. Manual of alcoholic fermentation. net, $2.60. Longmans.
Oppenheimer *and* Mitchell. Ferments and their actions. net, $2.50. Lippincott.
See also Bacteria.

FERNS.
See Botany.

Fersen, *Count* Jean-Axel. Letters and papers; sel. pub. by his great-nephew, Baron R. M. Klinckowström. '02(Mr8) il. 8°, (Versailles hist. ser.) subs., per v., $6; ¾ leath., per v., $9. Hardy, P. & Co.

Feudal relations between the kings of England and Scotland. Wyckoff, C: T. net, $1. Univ. of Chic.

FEVER.
See Malarial fever;—Typhoid fever.

Fickett, M. G., *comp.* *See* Stone, G. L.

FICTION.
Burton. Forces in fiction. net, $1. Bowen-M.
Cody. Sel. from the world's greatest short stories. net, $1. McClurg.
Nield. Guide to best hist. novels and tales. net, $1.75. Putnam.
Wegelin. Early Am. fiction, 1774-1830. net, $2. O. Wegelin.

Fidler, T. C. Calculations in hydraulic engineering. pt. 2, Hydro-kinetics. '02(Ap26) O. (Civil engineering ser.) $3. Longmans.

Field, Eug. Nonsense for old and young. '01. '02(Mr29) il. D. 50 c. Dickerman.

Field, J: E: Saint Berin, the apostle of Wessex. '02(Je7) 12°, $1.50. E. & J. B. Young.

Field book of American wild flowers. Mathews, F. S. net, $1.75. Putnam.

FIELD FAMILY.
Pierce. Field genealogy. 2 v. $10. Conkey.

Field, forest and garden botany. *See* Leavitt, R. G.

Field training of a company of infantry. Craufurd, H. J. $1. Longmans.

Fielde, Adele M. Political primer of New York city and state. [New rev. ed.] '02 (Mr22) S. 75 c.; pap., 50 c. League for Pol. Educ.

Fields, factories, and workshops. Kropotkin, *Prince* P: A. net, 90 c. Putnam.

Fifth string. Sousa, J: P. $1.25. Bowen-M.

Fifty Puritan ancestors. Nash, E. T. $5. Tuttle, M. & T.

Fighting bishop. Hopkins, H. M. $1.50. Bowen-M.

Fillis, Ja. Breaking and riding; with military commentaries. '02(My10) il. 8°, net, $5. Scribner.

FINANCE.
Burton. Financial crises, and periods of industrial and commercial depression. net, $1.40. Appleton.
Norton. Statistical studies in N. Y. money-market. net, $1.50; net, $1. Macmillan.
See also Money.

Finck, H: T. Romantic love and personal beauty. New ed. '02(Mr1) 8°, net, $2. Macmillan.

Find the church. Poland, W: net, 5 c. Herder.

Findlay, J. J. Principles of class teaching. '02(Je28) 12°, (Manual for teachers.) net, $1.25. Macmillan.

FINE ARTS.
Cust. Desc. of the sketch-book by Sir Anthony Van Dyck. $17.50. Macmillan.
Cust, *ed.* National portrait gallery. v. 1. subs., for complete work, net, $30. Cassell.
Van der Kellen. Works of Michel Le Blond. net, $30; net, $35. Dodd.
See also Architecture; — Artists; — Book illustrations; — Ceramics; — Decoration and ornament; —Drawings;—Engravers and engraving;—Lace; —Music;—Photography;—Venus di Milo.

FINLAND.
De Windt. Finland as it is. net, $3. Dutton.
Frederiksen. Finland, its public and private economy. $2. Longmans.

Finn, Fs. J. "But Thy love and Thy grace."

FIREARMS.
See Rifle.

FIREMEN.
See Engineering.

Fireside ser. See Burt's.

Fireside university of modern invention, etc., for home circle study. McGovern, J: $2.50; $3.75. Union Pub.

Firey, M. J. Infant salvation. '02(F1) D. net, $1.20. Funk.

First aid in accidents. Dickson, C: R. net, 50 c. Revell.

First years of the life of the redeemed after death. Ulyat, W: C. $1.25. Abbey Press.

Firth, Annie. Cane basket work. 1st and 2d ser. '02(Je21) il. 12°, ea., 60 c. Scribner.

Fisguill, R: Mazel. '02(Ap26) D. $1.50. H. S. Stone.

Fish, A. L. Calisthenic dict.: terms used in Am. gymnasia. '02(My10) D. pap., $1. Seminar.

FISH AND FISHING.
Gregg *and* Gardner. Where, when, and how to catch fish on the east coast of Fla. $4. Matthews-N.
Jordan *and* Evermann. American food and game fishes. net, $4. Doubleday, P.
See also Salmon;—Trout.

Fisher, Amos T., *and* Patterson, M. J. Elements of physics. '02(My24) il. D. 60 c. Heath.

Fisher, Herb. How to build a model yacht. '02(Ap26) il. f°, ("How-to" ser.) $1. Rudder.

Fisher, J: I. Added interest tables. Rev. ed. '02(Mr29) 8°, $2.50. J: I. Fisher.

Fisher, J: I. 20th century interest tables. '02(Mr29) 12°, $2.50. J: I. Fisher.

Fisher, Ma. Gertrude Dorrance. '02(Ap12) D. $1.50. McClurg.

Fiske, G: B., *comp.* Prize gardening. '01. '02(Ja4) il. 12°, $1. Judd.

Fitch, W: C. Captain Jinks of the Horse marines. '02(Ap19) il. O. $1.25. Doubleday, P.

Fitchett, W: H: Tale of the great mutiny. '01. '02(Ja11) 12°, $1.50. Scribner.

Fitzgerald, E: Poetical and prose writings. '02(Mr15) 7 v., large 8°, subs., regular lim. ed., per v., $6; hand-made pap. ed., per v., $12.50; Jap. ed., per v., $35. Doubleday, P.

Fitzpatrick, T: King of Claddagh. '01. '02 (Ja11) 8°, net, $1.25. Herder.

Five little Peppers abroad. Lothrop, *Mrs.* H. M. net, $1.10. Lothrop.

Five Stuart princesses. Rait, R. S. net, $3.50. Dutton.

Flagg, I: Writer of Attic prose: models from Xenophon. '02(Ap19) D. $1. Am. Bk.

Flanagan's educational ser. S. Flanagan.
—Peterson. First steps in Eng. composition. 35 c.

Flanagan's home and school series for young folks. il. S. 50 c. Flanagan.
—Shepard. Life on the farm.

Flanagan's plan book ser. il. sq. D. pap., 15 c. Flanagan.
—Whitcomb. Little journey to Italy. (v. 5, 5.)—Scotland. (v. 5, 4.)

Fleming, G: Operative veterinary surgery. v. 2. '02(Ap26) 8°, net, $3.25. W: R. Jenkins.

Fleming, T: Around the "Pan" with Uncle Hank. '01. '02(Ja4) il. 12°, $2. Nutshell.

Fleming, W: H. Shakespeare's plots. '02 (Ja25) O. $1.80. Putnam.

Fleming, Wymble. Glimpses of South Africa in peace and in war. '02(Mr22) 12°, $3. Dominion.

Flesh and the devil. Cole, H. L. $1.50. Neely.

Fletcher, Banister. Hist. of architecture on the comparative method. 4th ed., rev. and enl. '01. '02(Ja11) il. 8°, net, $7.50. Scribner.

Fletcher, W: I., *and* Bowker, R: R., *eds.* Annual literary index, 1901. '02(Ap12) O. net, $3.50. Pub. Weekly.

Flight of the *Swallow.* Morgan, E. M. 50 c. Pott.

Flint, C: R., Hill, J. J., [*and others.*] The trust: its book; ed. by J. H. Bridge. '02 (Je7) D. net, $1.25. Doubleday, P.

Floating treasure. Castlemon, H. $1. Coates.

FLORENCE.
Ross. Florentine villas. $25. Dutton.

Florer, Warren W. Biblische geschichten und kapitel aus Weizsäcker's und Luther's Bibelübersetzungen. '01. '02(Mr8) S. 40 c. Wahr.

Florida. Index to the laws of a general nature, by T: P. Warlow. '02(Je14) O. pap., $1. W. F. Barnes.

Florilegium Latinum; ed. by F. St. John Thackeray and E. D. Stone. 12°. Lane.
—Pre-Victorian poets. $2.50. (1.)
—Victorian poets. net, $2. (2.)

Flower, Elliott. Policeman Flynn. '02(Mr1) il. D. $1.50. Century Co.

Flower and thorn. Whitby, B. $1.50. Dodd.

FLOWERS.
Bridgeman. Flower gardening. 50 c. Coates.
Mathews. Field book of Amer. wild flowers. net, $1.75. Putnam.

FLOWERS.—*Continued.*
Parsons. According to season. net, $1.75. Scribner.
Watson. Flowers and gardens. $1.50. Lane.
See also Botany;—Gardening;—Lilies;—Roses;—Window gardening.
Flowers of Parnassus; ed. by F. B. Money-Coutts. il. 16°, net, 50 c.; leath., net, 75 c. Lane.
—Way, *comp.* Reliques of Stratford-on-Avon. (16.)
Flynt, Josiah, *pseud. See* Willard, J. F.
Fogg's ferry. Callahan, C. E. 75 c.; 25 c. Laird.
FOLK-LORE.
Cushing. Zuñi folk tales. net, $3.50. Putnam.
See also Fairy tales.
Folks, Homer. Care of destitute, neglected, and delinquent children. '02(F15) 12°, (American philanthropy of the nineteenth century.) net, $1. Macmillan.
Folwell, A. P. Sewerage. 5th ed. '02(Ap19) 8°, $3. Wiley.
Folwell, A. P. Water-supply engineering. 2d ed. '02(F1) 8°, $4. Wiley.
FOOD.
Horridge. Dynamic aspects of nutrition. $1.50. Wood.
See also Cookery;—Diet;—Digestion;—Fruit;—Hygiene;—Meat;—Temperance.
Fool (The). Carson, W: H. $1.50. G: W. Dillingham.
Fool's errand. Tourgée, A. W. $1.50. Fords.
Fool's year. Cooper, E: H. $1; 50 c. Appleton.
Foote, *Mrs.* Ma. H. The desert and the sown. '02(Je7) D. $1.50. Houghton, M. & Co.
For a young queen's bright eyes. Savage, R: H. $1.25; 50 c. Home.
For the colours. Hayens, H. $2. Nelson.
Foraminifera (The). Chapman, F: $3.50. Longmans.
Forces in fiction. Burton, R: net, $1. Bowen-M.
Ford, P. L., *ed.* Journals of Hugh Gaine, printer. '02(My17) 2 v., il. 8°, net, $15; Jap. pap., net, $25. Dodd.
Foreign freemasonry. O'Connor, D. M. 5 c. Kilner.
FOREIGN MISSIONS.
See Missions.
Foreign view of England. Saussure, C. de. net, $3. Dutton.
Forest neighbors. Hulbert, W: D. net, $1.50. McClure, P.
FORESTS AND FORESTRY.
Gifford. Practical forestry. net, $1.20. Appleton.
See also Lumber;—Trees.
Forman, S. E. First lessons in civics. Penn. ed. '02(Je14) D. 60 c. Am. Bk.
Forney, E: J. Inductive lessons, adpt. to Isaac Pitman phonography. '01. '02(Mr8) obl. 24°, pap., 80 c. State Normal Sch.
FORREST, Nathan B.
Mathes. General Forrest. net, $1.50. Appleton.
Forsyth, And. R. Theory of differential equations. v. 4. '02(My17) 8°, (Cambridge Univ. Press ser.) net, $3.75. Macmillan.
FORTUNE-TELLERS.
Mystic fortune teller, dream book and policy player's guide. 50 c.; 25 c. Donohue.

FORTUNE-TELLERS.—*Continued.*
Zanciz. How to tell fortunes by cards. 25 c. Drake.
Fortune's wheel. Gray, M. $1. Abbey Press.
Fosdick, C: Austin. *See* Castlemon, H.
Fosdick, J. W. Honor of the Braxtons. '02 il. D. $1.50. J. F. Taylor.
Foster, Rob. V. The Lord's prayer. '02 (Mr22) S. pap., 10 c. Cumberland Press.
Foundations of belief. Balfour, A. J. net, $2. Longmans.
Foundations of education. Seeley, L. $1. Hinds.
Four old Greeks. Hall, J. 35 c. Rand, McN. & Co.
Fourcaut, A. *See* Silva, T.
Fourfold thoughts: four text books '02(F8) $1. Revell.
Fowler, Fk. H. Negatives of the Indo-European languages. '02(Mr22) 8°, pap., net, 50 c. Univ. of Chic.
Fowler, Harold N. Hist. of ancient Greek literature. '02(Mr29) il. D. (Twentieth century text-books.) net, $1.40. Appleton. '02(Ap12) 16°, $1. Benziger.
Fowler, W: W. More tales of the birds. '02 (Ap12) il. 12°, $1. Macmillan.
FOWLER FAMILY.
Arthur. Annals of the Fowler family. $3.50. Mrs. J. J. Arthur.
Fox, Emma A. Parliamentary usage for women's clubs. '02(My3) S. net, 65 c. Baker & T.
Fox, Fes. M. The little giant's neighbors. '02(Je28) il. D. (Cosy corner ser.) 50 c. L. C. Page.
Fradenburgh, O. P. Twenty-five stepping stones toward Christ's Kingdom. '02(F8) O. $1. O. P. Fradenburgh.
France, Anatole. Monsieur Bergeret. '02 (Ap19) 12°, (Ser. of modern lang. text-books.) $1. Silver.
FRANCE.
Cæsar. Gallic war. $1.25. Am. Bk.
Mackinnon. Growth and decline of the Fr. monarchy. $7.50. Longmans.
See also Chartres;—Huguenots;—Paris.
Francesca da Rimini. Morehead, G: 25 c. Ogilvie.
FRANCIS *of Assisi, St.*
Lady (The) Poverty: allegory conc. St. Francis of Assisi. net, $1.75. Tennant.
McIlvaine. St. Francis of Assisi. net, 85 c. Dodd.
Francis, *St.*, Third order of. *See* Kaercher, F. O.
Francis, *Mrs.* C. D. Weekly church teaching for the infants. '02(Je7) 32°, 25 c. E. & J. B. Young.
François, Victor E. Advanced Fr. prose composition. '02(My24) D. cl., 80 c. Am. Bk.
Frank Logan. Clay, *Mrs.* J: M. $1. Abbey Press.
FREDERICK *the Great.*
Macaulay. Frederick the Great. net, 40 c. Macmillan.
Schrader. Friedrich der Grosse und der Siebenjährige Krieg. net, 50 c. Macmillan.
Frederiksen, N. C. Finland, its public and private economy. '02(Ap19) O. $2. Longmans.
Frédérique. Prévost, M. $1.50. Crowell.

FREE THOUGHT.
Baur and Herbert. Free thinkers' manual. $4. Radical.

FREE TRADE.
See Tariff.

Free trade almanac, 1902. '02(Ja25) S. pap., 5 c. Am. Free Trade.

Freear, Rob. L: Shadow duellers. '02 (Mr22) D. net, 60 c. Blanchard.

Freeman, A. C. Law of void judicial sales. 4th ed., rev. and enl. '02(Ap12) O. shp., $4. Cen. Law Journ.

Freeman, Flora L. Religious and social work amongst girls. '02((Ap12) 12°, net, $1. Whittaker.

FREEMASONRY.
Drummond, *comp.* Maine masonic text-book. $1.40; $1.50. Berry.
McGee. Exposition and revelation of ancient free and accepted masonry. $1. J. B. McGee.
O'Connor. Foreign freemasonry. 5 c. Kilner.

Freer, Romeo H., *rep.* *See* West Virginia. *Sup. ct. of appeals.* Repts.

FREIGHT.
See Tables.

Fremantle, T. F. Book of the rifle. '01· '02 (Ja4) il. O. $5. Longmans.

Fremeaux, Paul. With Napoleon at St. Helena; tr. by E. S. Stokoe. '02(Je28) 12°, net, $1.50. Lane.

French, Allen. The colonials. '02(F8) D. $1.50. Doubleday, P.

French, Lillie H. Hezekiah's wives. '02 (Ap5) il. D. net, 85 c. Houghton, M. & Co.

French, N. S. Animal activities. '02(Ap19) il. D. $1.20. Longmans.

French, S: Gibbs. Two wars: autobiog. of Gen. Samuel G. French; Mexican war; war between the states. '01. '02(Ja18) il. 12°, $2. Confederate Veteran.

FRENCH LANGUAGE.
Alissas. Les histoires de tante. net, 40 c. Macmillan.
Baillot *and* Brugnot. French prose composition. 50 c. Scott, F. & Co
Berlitz. Grammaire partique de la langue française. v. 3. 50 c. Berlitz.
Bowen. First scientific Fr. reader. 90 c. Heath.
Cameron. Elements of Fr. composition. 75 c. Holt.
Coppée. Morceau de pain. 25 c. W: R. Jenkins.
Dumas. Napoleon. net, 50 c. Macmillan.
France. Monsieur Bergeret. $1. Silver.
François. Advanced Fr. prose composition. 80 c. Am. Bk.
Hale. En son nom. $1. W: R. Jenkins.
Ingres. Cours complet de langue Fr. v. 1. net, $1.50. Univ. of Chic.
La Brète. Mon oncle et mon curé. 50 c. Am. Bk.
Renan. Souvenirs d' enfance et de jeunesse. 75 c. Heath.
Ségur. Les malheurs de Sophie. 45 c. Heath.
Voltaire. Zaire and Epitres. 50 c. Scott, F. & Co.

FRENCH LITERATURE.
Crabb. Culture hist. in the Chanson de Geste-Aymeri de Narbonne. net, $1.25. Univ. of Chic.

FRENEAU, Philip.
Austin. Philip Freneau: life and times net, $2.50. Wessels.

FRESNO Co., Cal.
Hudson. California vineyards: scenes in Fresno Co. 35 c. H. B. Hudson.

Fretz, Lewis B. Bennie, the Pythian of Syracuse, and other titles. '01· '02(My24) S. $1. Scroll Pub.

Friedländer, L. Town life in ancient Italy; tr. by W: E. Waters. '02(Mr22) D. 75 c. B: H. Sanborn.

Frisbie, H: S: Prophet of the kingdom. '02(Ap12) 12°, $1.25. Neale.

Frogs (The). *See* Aristophanes.

Frost, T: G. Treatise on guaranty insurance. '02(Ap12) O. shp., $5. Little, B. & Co.

Frost, W: D. Laboratory guide in elem. bacteriology. 2d rev. ed. '02(My24) il. 8°, $1.60. W: D. Frost.

FRUIT.
Goff. Lessons in commercial fruit growing. $1. Univ. Co-op.
Bridgeman. Fruit gardening. 50 c. Coates.
See also Apple;—Gardening;—Strawberry.

Fruit from the tree of life. Kohaus, H. M. 30 c. Alliance.

Frye, Alexis E. Grammar school geography. [New ed.] '02(My3) il. f°. $1.45. Ginn.

Frye, T. C. Development of the pollen in some asclepiadaceæ. '02(F15) 8°, (Cont. from the Hull botanical laboratory, no. 32.) pap., net, 25 c. Univ. of Chic.

FUEL.
See Coal;—Gas and gas-fitting.

Fulda, Ludwig. Der talisman; ed. by C. W: Prettyman. '02(Ap5) S. (Modern lang. ser.) 35 c. Heath.

Fulfilment (The). Davenport, J: G. net, 40 c. Dutton.

Fulham Palace Conference. Confession and absolution; ed. by H: Wace. '02(Ap26) O. net, $1. Longmans.

Fuller, W: Architecture of the brain. '02 (Mr1) il. 8°, net, $3.50. Fuller.

FUMIGATION.
Johnson. Fumigation methods. $1. Judd.

Funk, I: K., *and* Moses, M. J., *eds.* Standard first reader. '02(My17) sq. O. (Standard reader ser.) 35 c. Funk.

Funk, I: K., *and* Moses, M. J., *eds.* Teachers' manual for first reader. '02(My17) T. (Standard reader ser.) 50 c. Funk.

FUR TRADE.
Chittenden. Am. fur trade of the far west. 3 v. net, $10. F. P. Harper.

Furneaux, W: S. Elem. practical hygiene, (sec. 1.) '01· '02(Mr8) D. (Practical elem. science ser.) 90 c. Longmans.

Fustel de Coulanges, N. D. The ancient city: study on the religion, laws, and institutions of Greece and Rome. (W. Small.) 10th ed. '01· '02(Je28) 12°, $2. Lee & S.

FUTURE LIFE.
Brooks. Progression to immortality. net, 50 c. Wessels.
Gregg. Dictum of reason on man's immortality. 50 c. Treat.
Hutton. The soul in the unseen world. net, $2. Dutton.

FUTURE LIFE.—*Continued.*
Momerie. Immortality. $1.50. Whittaker.
Ulyat. First years of the life of the redeemed after death. $1.25. Abbey Press.
See also Heaven;—Hell; — Resurrection; — Salvation;—Spiritualism.

Gabirol, S. I. Improvement of moral qualities; pr. from an unique Arabic ms. '02 (Ap12) 8°, (Columbia Univ. Oriental studies, v. 1.) net, $1.25. Macmillan.

Gabriel, C: H., *comp.* Joyful praise. '02 (Je7) O. 30 c. Jennings.

Gaffield, Erastus C. A celestial message. Private ed. '02(Ap5) 12°, n. p. Lee & S.

Gage, S. H: The microscope. 8th ed., rev. and enl. '01. '02(Mr22) il. O. $1.50. Comstock Pub.

GAINE, Hugh.
Ford, *ed.* Journals of Hugh Gaine, printer. net, $15; net, $25. Dodd.

GAINSBOROUGH, T:
Bell. Thomas Gainsborough. $1. Macmillan.

GALLS.
Connold. British vegetable galls. net, $4. Dutton.

GALLSTONE.
Keay. Medical treatment of gall stones. net, $1.25. Blakiston.

Gallup, *Mrs.* Eliz. W. Bi-literal cipher of Sir Francis Bacon. 3d ed. '01. '02(F15) O. $3.75. Howard.

Gallup, *Mrs.* Eliz. W. Tragedy of Anne Boleyn: drama in cipher found in works of Sir Fs. Bacon. '01 '02(F15) O. $1.50. Howard.

Gallus, A., *pseud. See* Wisner, A.

Galt, Sterling, *comp.* Lent, the holy season. '02(Ap26) 12°, silk, $1. Neale.

Galton, Arth. Our attitude toward Eng. Roman Catholics and the papal court. '02 (My10) 12°, net, $1. Dutton.

GALVANOMETER.
Nichols. The galvanometer. $1. Spon.

GALVESTON.
Halstead. Galveston. $1.50; $2.25. Dominion.

Game of love. Paterson, W: R. $1.50. Scribner.

GAMES.
See Baseball; — Bridge; — Golf; — Ping-pong; — Whist.

Gametrogenesis and fertilization in albugo. Stevens, F. L. net, 25 c. Univ. of Chic.

Ganong, W: F. Lab'y course in plant physiology, as a basis for ecology. '01. '02 (F1) il. O. net, $1. Holt.

Gans, E. W: A Pennsylvania pioneer: biog. sketch. '02(F15) 8°, hf. leath., $6. Kuhl.

GARDENING.
Bacon. Of gardens. net, 50 c. Lane.
Barnard. My ten rod farm.—Simple flower garden. ea., 40 c.—Two thousand a year on fruits and flowers. $1. Coates.
Blomfield. Formal garden in England. $3. Macmillan.
Bridgeman. Kitchen gardening. 50 c. Coates.
Budd *and* Hansen. Am. horticultural manual. $1.50. Wiley.
Cadwallader. Story of home gardens. 25 c. Home Gardening.
Ellacombe. In my vicarage garden. net, $1.50. Lane.
Fiske, *comp.* Prize gardening. $1. Judd.

GARDENING.—*Continued.*
Holme. Stray leaves from a border garden. net. $1.50. Lane.
In a Tuscan garden. net, $1.50. Lane.
Lowell, *ed.* American gardens. $7.50. Bates & G.
Sedding. Garden craft, old and new. net, $2.50. Lane.
Triggs. Formal gardens in England and Scotland. 3 pts. net, $25. Scribner.
Williams. Garden in the suburbs. net, $1.50. Lane.
See also Botany;—Flowers;—Fruit;—Window gardening.

Gardiner, Asa B. Discovery of the remains of Maj.-Gen. Nat. Greene; add. del. in Newport, July 4, 1901. '01. '02(Ap5) 8°, pap., n. p. [Blumenberg Press] Soc. R. I. Cincinnati.

Gardner, J: *See* Gregg, W: H.

Gardner, J: M., *ed.* American negligence repts. v. 10. '01. '02(Ja18) O. shp., $5.50. Remick.

Gardner, W. M. *See* Rawson, C.

GARFIELD, James A.
See Fallows, S:

Garland, Hamlin. Captain of the Grayhorse troop. '02(Mr29) D. $1.50. Harper.

GAS AND GAS-FITTING.
Gill. Gas and fuel analysis for engineers. $1.25. Wiley.
Hempel. Methods of gas analysis. net, $2.25. Macmillan.

GASES.
Randall, *ed. and tr.* Expansion of gases by heat. $1. Am. Bk.
Travers. Experimental study of gases. net, $3.25. Macmillan.

Gaskin, Rob. T. Caedmon, the first Eng. poet. '02(Je7) 12°, pap., 40 c. E. & J. B. Young.

Gate of the kiss. Harding, J: W. $1.50. Lothrop.

Gathered sunbeams. Pease, E. S. 75 c. Sun Pr. Co.

Gautier, T. Works. Limited ed. v. 13-16. '02(Je28) 8°, per v., $3.50; hf. mor., $6. Sproul.

Gaylord, Harvey R., *and* **Archoff**, Ludwig. Atlas of patholog. histology. '01. '02(Ja25) col. il. 4°, net, $7.50. Lea.

GEARS AND GEARING.
Grant. Treatise on gear wheels. net, $1. Caspar.

Gee, H: Elizabethan prayer-book and ornaments. '02(Mr22) 12°, net, $1.25. Macmillan.

GEMS.
See Precious stones.

GENEALOGY.
Nash. Fifty Puritan ancestors. $5. Tuttle, M. & T.
Sellers. Allied families of Delaware. $5. E. J. Sellers.
Van Meter. Genealogies and sketches of some old families. $2.25. Morton.
Watson. Royal lineage. $4.50. Whittet.
Wells. Hist. of Newburg, Vt.; with genealog. records. $2.25; $3; $3.50; $4. Caledonian.

General digest, Am. and Eng., annot. v. 12, '02(My10) O. shp., $6. Lawyers' Co-op.

Gentleman in literature. Quayle, W: A. net, 25 c. Jennings.

Geographical readers. il. D. Am. Bk.
—Carpenter. Europe. 70 c.

GEOGRAPHY.
Appleton's geografia superior ilustrada. (Spanish.) $1.50. Appleton.
Bartholomew. Internat. students' atlas of modern geography. net, $2.25. Scribner.
Carroll. Around the world. 60 c. Morse.
Fairbanks. Home geog. for primary grades. 60 c. Educ. Pub.
Frye. Grammar school geography. $1.45. Ginn.
Murché. Teacher's manual of object lessons in geography. net, 80 c. Macmillan.
Roddy. Complete geography. $1; Elem. geography. 50 c. Am. Bk.
Tarr *and* McMurry. 1st bk. Home geog. net, 60 c. Macmillan.
Wagner. New Pacific school geography. net, $1. Whitaker & R.
See also Physical geography;—Voyages and travels.

GEOLOGY.
Hershey. Quaternary of So. California. 20 c. Univ. of Cal.
Lawson. The eparchæan interval. 10 c. Univ. of Cal.
Zittel. Hist. of geology and paleontology to end of 19th century. $1.50. Scribner.
See also Berkeley Hills; — Evolution; — Glacial period.

GEOMETRY.
More. Trisection of a given angle geometrically solved. $1. Wickes.
See also Mathematics;—Perspective; — Trigonometry.

George, Marian M. *See* Whitcomb, C. E.

Georgia. Supp. to code. v. 4. (H. Van Epps.) '01- '02(Ap5) O. shp., $5. Marshall.

GEORGIA.
Mitchell. Georgia land and people. $1.25. F. L. Mitchell.

Georgian (The) period. In 3 v. v. 2, pt. 8; v. 3, pt. 9. '02(Mr15) il. portfolio, f°, ea., $4. Am. Architect.

Gerard, Fes. A. A Grand Duchess and her court. '02(Ap5) 2 v., 8°, net, $7.50. Dutton.

Gerard, Fes. A. Romance of King Ludwig II. of Bavaria. New ed. '01. '02(F22) 12°, net, $1.75. Dodd.

GERLACH, *St.*
Houck. Life of St. Gerlach. net, 55 c. Benziger

GERMAN LANGUAGE.
Adler. German and Eng. dictionary. pt. 1. $3.50. Appleton.
Florer. Biblische geschichten. 40 c. Wahr.
Fulda. Der talisman. 35 c. Heath.
Grillparzer. Traum ein leben. 60 c. Heath.
Heyse. Niels mit der offenen hand. 30 c. Heath.
Körner. Zriny ein trauerspiel in fünf aufzügen. 35 c. Heath.
Krüger *and* Smith. English-Germ. conversation book. 25 c. Heath.
Lange. 20th century system; key to the Germ. language. 50 c. Pamphlet.
Lessing. Minna von Barnhelm. 75 c. Heath.
Moser. Der bibliothekar. 45 c. Am. Bk.
Riehl. Das spielmannskind und stumme ratsherr. 35 c. Am. Bk.

GERMAN LANGUAGE.—*Continued.*
Stern. Geschichten von Deutschen städten. $1.25. Am. Bk.
Wesselhoeft. German composition. 45 c. Heath.

GERMAN LITERATURE.
Batt. Treatment of nature in Germ. literature from Günther to Goethe's Werther. net, $1. Univ. of Chic.
Brandes. Main currents in 19th century lit. v. 2, Romantic school in Germany. net, $2.75. Macmillan.

German opera texts. See Newson's.

GERMAN POETRY.
Remy. Influence of India and Persia on the poetry of Germany. net, $1. Macmillan.

GERMANY.
Baedeker, *ed.* Southern Germany. net, $1.80. Scribner.
Henderson. Short hist. of Germany. 2 v. net, $4. Macmillan.
Schiller. Hist. of the thirty years' war. (App. to pubs. for price.) Niccolls.
Veritas. German empire of to-day. $2.25. Longmans.

Gertrude Dorrance. Fisher, M. $1.50. McClurg.

Giants' gate. Pemberton, M. $1.50. Stokes.

Gibbes, Fes. G. Poems. '02(Ap19) 12°, $1. Neale.

Gibbons, W: F. Those black diamond men. '02(Je14) il. D. $1.50. Revell.

Gibbs, Josiah W. Elem. principles in statistical mechanics. '02(Je28) 8°, (Yale bicentennial pub.) $4. Scribner.

Gibbs, Josiah W. Vector analysis: text-book founded upon the lectures of J. Willard Gibbs by E. B. Wilson. '01. '02(F15) 8°, (Yale bicentennial pub.) net, $4. Scribner.

Gibbs, Mifflin W. Shadow and light: autobiog. '02(Mr29) D. $1.50. M. W. Gibbs.

Gibson, J. M. Protestant principles. '01. '02(F1) S. (Christian study manuals.) 60 c. Armstrong.

Gideon. Carradine, B. 35 c. Pepper.

Gifford, J: Practical forestry for beginners in forestry, agricultural students, and others. '02(My24) il. D. net, $1.20. Appleton.

Gifford, M. W. Christian science against itself. '02(Je14) D. $1. Jennings.

Gifford lectures. *See* James, W:

Gift of power. Tuttle, J: E. net, 25 c. Westminster.

Gil Blas. Le Sage, A. R. $1. Burt.

Gilbert, Fk. One thousand ways to make money. '02(My17) 12°, $1. Donohue.

Gilbert, G: H. Primer of the Christian religion. '02(F15) 12°, net, $1. Macmillan.

Gilbert, Grove K., *and* Brigham, A. P. Introd. to physical geography. '02(Je28) il. D. (Twentieth century text-books.) net, $1.25. Appleton.

Gildersleeve, B. L. Studies in honor of Basil L. Gildersleeve. '02(Je28) 8°, $6. Johns Hopkins.

Gill, A: H. Gas and fuel analysis for engineers. 3d rev., enl. ed. '02(Je7) 12°, $1.25. Wiley.

Gill, Joshua, Kirkpatrick, W: J., *and* Gilmour, H. L. Hymns of grace and glory. '02 (My10) D. bds., 30 c. Mattill & L.

Gilman, B. Kingdom of coins. New ed. '01· '02(F15) 16°, (Children's friend ser.) bds., 50 c. Little, B. & Co.
Gilman, Dan. Coit. *See* Vincent, J: M.
Gilmer, Eliz. M., ["Dorothy Dix."] Fables of the elite. '02(My3) il. S. net, $1. Fenno.
Gilmour, H. L. *See* Gill, J.
GIOTTO DI BONDONE.
Perkins. Giotto. $1.75. Macmillan.
Girdlestone, R. B. Grammar of prophecy. '01· '02(Ja11) 12°, (Bible students' lib., no. 11.) $2.50. E. & J. B. Young.
Girl from Mexico. Hyde, M. G. $1. Abbey Press.
Girl of Virginia. Thruston, L. M. $1.50. Little, B. & Co.
GIRLS.
Freeman. Religious and social work amongst girls. net, $1. Whittaker.
See also Children;—Education;—Woman;—Young women.
GLACIAL PERIOD.
Chamberlin. Proposed genetic classification of pleistocene glacial formations. net, 10 c. Univ. of Chic.
Chamberlin. Working hypothesis of cause of glacial periods on an atmosphere basis. net, 25 c. Univ. of Chic.
Gladden, W. Christian way. New ed. '01· '02(F22) 16°, 75 c. Dodd.
Gladden, W. Social salvation. '02(My3) D. net, $1. Houghton, M. & Co.
GLADSTONE, W: E.
Handford. William Ewart Gladstone. $1.50; $2.50. Dominion.
Locke. A 19th century crusader. net, 25 c. Jennings.
Glasgow, Ellen. The battleground. '02 (Mr29) il. D. $1.50. Doubleday, P.
Glasson, W: H. Nation's pension system as applied to the civil war and the war with Spain. '02(Mr22) 8°, (Pub. of the soc., no. 331.) pap., 25 c. Am. Acad. Pol. Sci.
Gleanings from nature. Carter, E. N. $1. Abbey Press.
Glenwood. Kensington, C. $1.25. Abbey Press.
Globe series. D. Globe Sch. Bk.
—Chancellor. Arithmetics. Primary. 28 c. —2d bk. 20 c.—3d bk. 24 c.—4th bk. 24 c.
Glover, Terrot R. Life and letters in the fourth century. '02(F15) 8°, (Cambridge Univ. Press ser.) net, $3.25. Macmillan.
GOD.
Leighton. Conceptions of God. net, $1.10. Longmans.
Reed. Idea of God in rel. to theology. net, 75 c. Univ. of Chic.
Thompson. The unknown God. 60 c. Warne.
See also Bible;—Holy Spirit;—Jesus Christ;—Religion;—Theology.
God of things. Whitehouse, F. B. $1.50. Little, B. & Co.
God the beautiful. B., E. P. net, 75 c. Beam.
Godfrey, Eliz., [*pseud*. for Jessie Bedford.] The winding road. '02(Mr22) D. $1.50. Holt.
Godly union and concord. Henson, H. H. $2. Longmans.
Goebel, F. Hermann der Cherusker und die schlacht im Teutoburger walde; ed. by J. Esser. Authorized ed. '02(F22) 12°, net, 50 c. Macmillan.
Goethe, J. W. v. Truth and fiction rel. to my life; ed. by N. H. Dole. Ed. de luxe. v. 1. '02(Je28) 12°, (app. to pubs. for price.) Niccolls.
Goethe, J. W. v. Wilhelm Meister's apprenticeship; ed. by N. H. Dole. Ed. de luxe. '02(Mr15) 2 v., 12°. (App. to pubs for price.) Niccolls.
Goethe, J. W. v. Wilhelm Meister's travels; and Recreations of the German emigrants; ed. by N. H. Dole. Ed. de luxe. '02 (Mr22) 8°. (App. to pubs. for price.) Niccolls.
Goff, E. S. Lessons in commercial fruit growing. '02(My10) il. 12°, (Vellum ser.) $1. Univ. Co-op.
GOLD.
Wilson. Cyanide processes. $1.50. Wiley.
See also Precious metals.
Golden Fluff. Morris, I. D. 50 c. Abbey Press.
Golden lily. Hinkson, *Mrs*. K. T. 40 c. Benziger.
Golden poppy. Smith, E. E. net, $1.50. E. E. Smith.
Golden way. Bartlett, A. L. $1.50. Abbey Press.
Goldsmith, O. Plays; ed. by A. Dobson. '02 (Mr22) 16°, (Temple classics.) 50 c.; leath., 75 c. Macmillan.
Goldsmith, O. Poems; ed. by A. Dobson. '02(Mr22) 16°, (Temple classics.) 50 c.; leath., 75 c. Macmillan.
Goldsmith, O. Selections. '01· '02(Ap5) S. (Little masterpieces.) 50 c. Doubleday, P.
Goldsmith, P: H. El idioma Inglés: Lib. primero. '02(Ap5) D. 40 c.; *Same*. Lib. segundo. 36 c. Globe Sch. Bk.
GOLF.
Harper's official golf guide, 1901. $1. Harper.
Travis. Practical golf. net, $2. Harper.
Good, Ja. I. Historical handbook of the Reformed church in the U. S. 2d ed., rev. '01. '02(Ap5) D. bds., 25 c. Heidelberg.
Good, Ja. I. Women of the Reformed church. '01. '02(Ap5) il. D. $1. Heidelberg.
Good and evil. *See* Lanier, J. J.
Good cheer nuggets. Pennington, J. G. 45 c.; $1. Fords.
Good gravy. Kendall, E. F. 25 c. Helman-T.
Goodell, T: D. Chapters on Greek metric. '01· '02(Mr15) 8°, (Yale bicentennial pub.) net, $2. Scribner.
Goodknight, Alva L. Modern association and railroading. '01· '02(Mr22) D. 50 c. Abbey Press.
Goodspeed, Edg. J. The Newberry gospels. '02(Ap5) il. O. (Hist. and linguistic studies in literature rel. to the N. T., v. 2, Greek texts, pt. 1.) pap., net, 25 c. Univ. of Chic.
Goodwin, J. J. The "sinker" stories of wit and humor. '02(Je28) D. $1. Ogilvie.
Goodyear, S: H. Theory of accounts. '02 (Ap19) Q. $1.50. Goodyear-M.
Gordon, Granville, *Lord*. Sporting reminiscences. '02(Je7) 8°, net, $4. Dutton.
Gordon, S: Strangers at the gate. '02(Je7) D. $1.50. Jewish Pub.
Gordy, Wilbur F. American leaders and heroes: U. S. history. '01· '02(Mr15) il. maps, 12°, net, 60 c. Scribner.

Gore, C: Body of Christ. 2d rev. enl. ed.; with reply to critics of the 1st ed. '01· '02 (Ja11) 12°, $1.75. Scribner.

Gore, Willard C. The imagination in Spinoza and Hume. '02(Je14) 8°, (Univ. of Chic. cont. to philosophy, v. 2, no. 4.) pap., net, 35 c. Univ. of Chic.

Gorky, Maxime, [*pseud.* for Alexei Maximovitch Pyeshkoff.] Tales from Gorky; with a biog. notice of author by R. N. Bain. 3d ed. '02(My3) D. net, $1.20. Funk.

Górky, Máxime. Twenty-six and one, and other stories; fr. the Russian. '02(Mr22) il. D. $1.25. J. F. Taylor.

Gormanius. *See* De Leon, T: C.

Gospel of Judas Iscariot. Baldwin, A. D. $1.50. Jamieson-H.

Gospel of the kingdom and the gospel of the church. Brown, W: B. $1. Whittaker.

Goss, W: F. M. Locomotive sparks. '02 (Ap19) il. 8°, $2. Wiley.

Gothenburg system. *See* National Temp. almanac.

Gould, G: M., *ed.* *See* American year-book of medicine.

Gould, W. R. Greater New York and state lawyer's diary for 1902. '02(Mr1) S. $1. W. R. Gould.

GOVERNMENT.
See **Political science.**

Government ownership of railroads. Knapp, M. A. 15 c. Am. Acad. Pol. Sci.

Gower, Ronald S., *Lord.* Old diaries, 1881-1901. '02(Ap12) il. 8°, net, $4.50. Scribner.

Gower, Ronald S., *Lord.* Sir David Wilkie. '02(Mr8) il. 12°, (Great masters in painting and sculpture.) $1.75. Macmillan.

Gower, Ronald S., *Lord.* Tower of London. v. 2. '02(Mr22) il. 8°, net, $6.50. Macmillan.

Grace of orders. Winston, N. B. $1. Abbey Press.

Gradle, H: Diseases of the nose, pharynx and ear. '02(Je28) il. 8°, net, $3.50. Saunders.

Grafton, C: C. Pusey and the church revival. '02(Ap12) il. D. net, 50 c. Young Churchman.

Graham, Alex. Roman Africa. '02(F8) O. $6. Longmans.

Graham, G: E: Schley and Santiago. '02 (F8) D. $1.50. Conkey.

Graham, H: G. Scottish men of letters in the eighteenth century. '02(F1) 8°. net, $4.50. Macmillan.

Graham, J. M. East of the barrier; or, Manchuria in miniature. '02(Je7) 12°, net, $1. Revell.

GRAND CANYON.
See **Arizona;—Colorado river.**

Grand Duchess and her court. Gerard, F. A. 2 v., net, $7.50. Dutton.

Grandmother dear. Molesworth, *Mrs.* M. L. 75 c. Burt.

Grandmother's cook book. H., A. P. 50 c. New Amsterdam.

Grant, *Mrs.* **Anne M. Memoirs of an Amer.** lady. New ed. '01· '02(F22) 8°, net, $7.50. Dodd.

Grant, G. B. Treatise on gear wheels. 8th ed. '02(Ap26) 8°, net, $1. Caspar.

Grant, W: D., *ed.* Christendom anno domini 1901. '02(Je7) 2 v., O. $2.50. W: D. Grant.

Gray, H: Anatomy. 15th ed. '01. '02(Ja25) il. 8°, net, $5.50; shp., net, $6.50; col. il. net, $6.25; shp., net, $7.25. Lea.

Gray, L: H. Indo-Iranian phonology. '02 (Je28) 8°, (Columbia Univ. and Indo-Iranian ser., v. 2.) net, $3. Macmillan.

Gray, Martha. Fortune's wheel. '02(My3) D. $1. Abbey Press.

Gray, W: C. Musings by camp-fire and wayside. '02(F1) O. net, $1.50. Revell.

Graystone. Nicolls, W: J. $1.50. Lippincott.

Great authors of all ages. Allibone, S: A. $2.50. Lippincott.

GREAT BRITAIN.

Bartlett. Golden way: notes on journey through Ireland, Scotland and England. $1.50. Abbey Press.

Mackinder. Britain and the British seas. $2. Appleton.

Great chancellor. High, J. L. net, $2.50; Callaghan.

Great cloud of witnesses. Wilson, L: A. 50 c. Standard Pub.

Great commanders' ser.; ed. by J. G. Wilson. D. net, $1.50. Appleton.
—Mathes. General Forrest.

Great issues. Barker, W. $1; 50 c. Ferris.

Great love. Burnham, C. L. 50 c. Houghton, M. & Co.

Great masters in painting and sculpture. See Macmillan's.

GREECE.

Bury. Hist. of Greece to death of Alexander. 2 v. net, $8. Macmillan.

Fustel de Coulanges. Ancient city: study on the rel., laws, and institutions of Greece and Rome. $2. Lee & S.

Jebb. Modern Greece. $1.75. Macmillan.

Greeff, R. Guide to the microscopic examination of the eyes; fr. the 2d Germ. ed., by H. Walker. '01. '02(Ja11) 12°, net. $1.25. Blakiston.

Greek foreshadowings of mod. metaphysical thought. Kupfer, L. $1. J. S. Cushing.

Greek hero stories. Niebuhr, B. G. $1. Dodd.

GREEK LANGUAGE.

Andrew. Greek prose composition. net, 90 c. Macmillan.

Ball. Elements of Greek. net, $1. Macmillan.

Pearson *and* Bartlett. Key to Pearson's Greek prose composition. 50 c. Am. Bk.

See also Attic prose.

GREEK LITERATURE.

Fowler. Hist. of ancient Gr. literature. net, $1.40. Appleton.

GREEK MANUSCRIPTS.

Goodspeed. Newberry gospels: Greek texts. net, 25 c. Univ. of Chic.

Greek myths in Eng. dress. Hale, E: E., *jr.* 40 c. Globe Sch. Bk.

GREEK POETRY.

Goodell Chapters on Greek metric. net, $2. Scribner.

Green, B: E. Shakespeare and Goethe on Gresham's law and the single gold standard. '01· '02(F8) D. pap., 25 c. MacGowan.

Green, E. T. Church of Christ. '02(Mr1) 12°, (Churchman's lib.) $1.50. Macmillan.

Green, S: A. Ten facsimile reproductions rel. to old Boston and neighborhood. '01- '02 (Ja11) F. net, $10. Littlefield.
Green fund book. D. net, 50 c. Am. S. S.
—Rice. Our sixty-six sacred books. (10.)
Greenaway, Kate. A apple pie. New ed. '01- '02(Ja25) obl. 8°, bds., 75 c. Warne.
Greene, Ja. G. *See* New York. Analy. decisions and citations.
GREENE, *Gen*. Nat.
Gardiner. Discovery of the remains of Maj.-Gen. Nathaniel Greene. n. p. [Blumenberg Press] Soc. R. I. Cincinnati.
Greenleaf, Sue. Liquid from the sun's rays. '02(Ap26) D. $1.50. Abbey Press.
Greenstone, Julius H. Religion of Israel. '02(Mr29) D. 50 c. Bloch.
Gregg, D: Dictum of reason on man's immortality. '02(Je21) D. 50 c. Treat.
Gregg, Hilda, ["Sydney C. Grier."] Prince of the captivity. '02(My17) D. $1.50. L. C. Page.
Gregg, W: H., *and* Gardner, J: Where, when, and how to catch fish on the east coast of Florida. '02(Je7) il. O. $4. Matthews-N.
Gregorovius, F. Hist. of Rome in the Middle Ages. '02(Ap5) 12°, net, $3. Macmillan.
Gregory, J. W. *See* Hutchinson, H. N.
Grenell, Z. The sandals: tale of Palestine. '02(Mr8) il. S. (Hour-glass stories, no. 2.) net, 40 c. Funk.
Grethenbach, Constantine. Secular view of the Bible. '02(Mr22) il. O. net, $2. Eckler.
Grier, Sydney C. *See* Gregg, H.
Griffin, Alb. Why the legal (or force) method of promoting temperance always has done—and always must do—more harm than good. '01- '02(Ja11) S. pap., 15 c. A. Griffin.
Griffin ser. il. D. $1. Coates.
—Couch. The Westcotes.
Grillparzer, Franz S. Traum ein leben; ed. by E: S. Meyer. '02(My3) D. (Modern lang. ser.) 60 c. Heath.
Grinnell, G: B. American duck shooting. '01- '02(F1) il. O. $3.50. Forest
Grove, *Lady* Agnes. Seventy-one days' camping in Morocco. '02(Ap19) il. O. net, $2.50. Longmans.
Growing up. Conklin, *Mrs*. J. M. D. $1. Burt.
Guarding the thoughts. Macdonald, L. B. 10 c. J. H. West
Guggenberger, A. General hist. of the Christian era. In 3 v. v. 2 and 3. '01- '02 (Mr8) 8°, ea., $1.50. Herder.
Guide to best hist. novels and tales. Nield, J. net, $1.75. Putnam.
Guide to Palestine and Egypt. '02(Ja18) 12°, (Macmillan's guides.) net, $3.25. Macmillan.
Guided and guarded. Malone, J. S. $1.25. Abbey Press.
Gulliver's bird book. Bridgman, L. J. $1.50. L. C. Page.
GUN.
See Rifle.
Gunter, A. C. Surprises of an empty hotel. '02(Ap5) il. D. $1; pap., 50 c. Home
Guthe, Karl E. *See* Reed, J: O.
Guthrie, Ben E., *rep*. *See* Missouri. *St. Louis and Kansas City cts. of appeals*. Cases.
Guyse, Eleanor. A movable quartette. '02 (My3) D. $1. Abbey Press.
Gwatkin, H: M. *See* Maitland, F: W:
Gyim, Paul L. Chinese-English elem. reader and arithmetic. '01- '02(Mr22) il. 16°, $1.25. Taylor & M.
GYMNASTICS AND PHYSICAL CULTURE.
Colburn. Graded physical exercises. $1. Werner.
Fish. Calisthenic dict. $1. Seminar.
See also Delsarte system.
GYNECOLOGY.
Davenport. Diseases of women: manual of gynecology. net, $1.75. Lea.
McKay. History of ancient gynæcology. net, $3. Wood.
GYPSIES.
See Zincali.
H., A. P. Grandmother's cook book. '02 (Ap26) sm. 4°, bds., 50 c. New Amsterdam.
Haddon Hall lib. il. 12°, $3. Macmillan.
—Shand. Shooting.
Hadley, H. E. Practical exercises in magnetism and electricity. '02(F22) 12°, net, 60 c. Macmillan.
Hadley, Wilfred J. Nursing—general, medical and surgical; with app. on sick-room cookery. '02(Mr22) 12°, net, $1.25. Blakiston.
Hahn, C: C. So fight I. '02(Ap12) 16°, pap., 10 c. Whittaker.
HAIR.
Stitson. Human hair. $1.25. Maple.
Hake, H. W. *See* Dupre, A.
Hale, E: E. En son nom, [In his name;] tr. par M. P. Sauveur. '01- '02(Ja4) D. $1. W: R. Jenkins.
Hale, E: E. Man without a country. Birthday ed. '02(Ap12) O. net, $1. Outlook.
Hale, E: E., *jr.*, *ed.* Ballads and ballad poetry. '02(Mr22) D. (Hawthorne classics, no. 2.) 40 c. Globe Sch. Bk.
Hale, E: E., *jr.*, *ed.* Greek myths in Eng. dress. '02(Mr22) D. (Hawthorne classics, no. 1.) 40 c. Globe Sch. Bk.
Hale, G: E. New star in Perseus. '01. '02 (Ja11) 8°, (Yerkes Observatory bulletin, no. 16.) pap., net, 10 c. Univ. of Chic.
HALE, Nathan.
Partridge. Nathan Hale, the ideal patriot. net, $1. Funk.
Hall, A. C. A. Companion to the prayer-book. '02(Mr8) S. net, 35 c. E. & J. B. Young.
Hall, A. C. A. Instruction and devotions on the holy communion. '02(F8) S. net, 25 c. Young Churchman.
Hall, Arth. C. Crime in its relation to social progress. '02(Ap12) 8°, (Columbia Univ. studies in history, economics and public law, v. 15.) net, $3; $3.50. Macmillan.
Hall, C: W., *ed.* Regiments and armories of Mass. v. 2. '01. '02(Ja4) il. 8°, per set, $12; hf. cf., $18; seal, $25. W. W. Potter.
Hall, E: H. Jamestown, [1607-1907.] '02 (Ap26) il. 16°, pap., 25 c. Am. Scenic.
Hall, F: G., Little, E: R., *and* Eliot, H: W., *jr.*, *eds.* Harvard celebrities. '02(F22) il. O. bds., $1.25. Univ. Press (Camb.)
Hall, Granville D. Rending of Virginia. '02 (Ap12) il. 8°, $2. Mayer.
Hall, H. S. Algebraical examples. '01. '02 (Ja4) 12°, net, 50 c. Macmillan.

Hall, Jennie. Four old Greeks. '02(Mr15) il. 12°, 35 c. Rand, McN. & Co.
HALL, John.
Hall. John Hall, pastor and preacher. net, $1.50. Revell.
Hall, Jos. Meditations and vows. '02(Mr8) 16°, $1.50. Dutton.
Hall, R. N., *and* Neal, W. G. Ancient ruins of Rhodesia. '02(My10) 8°, net. $6. Dutton.
Hall, T: C. John Hall, pastor and preacher. '01. '02(Ja11) 12°, net, $1.50. Revell.
HALL OF FAME.
Eggleston. American immortals; record of men whose names are inscribed in the Hall of Fame. $10. Putnam.
Halsey, Fs. W. Our literary deluge and some of its deeper waters. '02(Ap5) D. net, $1.25. Doubleday, P.
Halsey, Fs. W., *ed.* Authors of our day in their homes. '02(Mr15) 12°, $1.25. Pott.
Halstead, Murat. Full official hist. of the war with Spain. '02(Mr22) 12°, $3; mor., $4; cf., $6. Dominion.
Halstead, Murat. Galveston. '02(Mr22) 12°, $1.50; hf. mor., $2.25. Dominion.
Halstead, Murat. Life and achievements of Admiral Dewey. '02(Mr22) 12°, $1.50; hf. mor., $2.25; mor., $3.25. Dominion.
Halstead, Murat. Life of Theodore Roosevelt. '02(Je14) 8°, subs., $2.50; hf. mor., $3.75; ed. de luxe, $3.50; ¾ rus., $5. Saalfield.
Halstead, Murat. Pictorial hist. of America's new possessions. '02(Mr22) 12°, $2.50; hf. mor., $3.50; mor., $4.50. Dominion.
Halstead, Murat. Splendors of Paris and the glories of her Exposition. '02(Mr22) 12°, $1.50. Dominion.
Halstead, Murat. Story of the Philippines. '02(Mr22) 12°, $2; mor., $3. Dominion.
Halstead, Murat. Victorious republicanism. '02(Mr22) 12°, $1.50; hf. mor., $2.25. Dominion.
Halstead, Murat. William McKinley: (in Norwegian.) Oversat fra engelsk af P. O. Stromme. '01. '02(F15) il. O. $1.50; hf. mor., $2. J. Anderson Pub.
Halstead, Murat, *and* Munson, A. J. Life and reign of Queen Victoria. '02(Mr22) 12°, $1.50; hf. mor., $2.25. Dominion.
Halstead, Murat, *and* Munson, A. J. Life and services of William McKinley. '02 (Mr22) 12°, $1.50; hf. mor., $2.25. Dominion.
Hamill, H. M. The Sunday-school teacher. '02(Mr22) D. 50 c. Pub. Ho. M. E. Ch., So.
HAMILTON, Alexander.
See Atherton, *Mrs.* G. F.;—Burr, A.
Hamilton, And. *See* New York. Statutory revision of laws.
Hamilton, *Mrs.* E. J. Lee-. *See* Holdsworth, A. E.
Hamilton, Ja. H: Savings and savings institutions. '02(Je28) 12°, net, $2.25. Macmillan.
Hamm, Margherita A. Eminent actors and their homes. '02(Mr15) 12°, $1.25. Pott.
HAMPSHIRE, ENG.
Capes. Scenes of rural life in Hampshire. net, $2.75. Macmillan.
Hancock, H. I. Life at West Point. '02 (Je14) il. D. net, $1.40. Putnam.

Hand of God in Am. history. Thompson, R. E. net, $1. Crowell.
Handbooks for practical workers in church and philanthropy; ed. by S: M. Jackson. S. Lentilhon.
—Pierce. Hartley House cook book. 60 c.
Handbooks for the clergy; ed. by Arth. W. Robinson. D. net, 90 c. Longmans.
—Mason. Ministry of conversion.
—Montgomery. Foreign missions.
—Robinson. Personal life of the clergy.
—Swete. Patristic study.
Handbooks of practical gardening. il. 12°, net, $1. Lane.
—Arnott. Book of bulbs. (5.)
—Thomas. Book of the apple. (6.)
—Wythes. Book of the vegetables. (7.)
Handford, T: W. William Ewart Gladstone. '02(Mr22) 12°, $1.50; mor., $2.50. Dominion.
HANDWRITING.
See Autographs.
Handy information ser. S. net. Crowell.
—McSpadden. Shakesperian synopses. 45 c.
Hanford, B. Railroading in the U. S. '02 (Ap19) O. (Socialist lib., v. 1, no. 11.) pap., 5 c. Socialistic Co-op.
Hanna, C: A: The Scotch-Irish. '02(Mr29) 2 v., 8°. net, $10. Putnam.
Hannibal, P: M. Thrice a pioneer. '01. '02 (Mr1) 16°, 75 c.; pap., 40 c. Danish Luth.
HANOVER SQUARE.
Baillie. Oriental Club and Hanover Square. $9. Longmans.
Hansen, N. E. *See* Budd, J. L.
Har Lampkins. Patton, A. $1. Abbey Press.
Harben, Will N. Abner Daniel. '02(Je28) D. $1.50. Harper.
Harcourt, L. F. V. Civil engineering as applied in construction. '02(Mr8) il. O. (Civil engineering ser.) $5. Longmans.
Hardcastle, *Mrs.* M. A. Word signs made easy. '02(Mr29) sq. D. $1. M. A. Hardcastle.
Hardesty, Irving. Neurological technique. '01. '02(Ja11) O. net, $1.75. Univ. of Chic.
Hardie, T. Melville. *See* Wood, C. A., *ed.*
Harding, Caro. H. *and* S: B. City of the seven hills. '02(My24) il. S. (Lake history stories.) 40 c. Scott, F. & Co.
Harding, J: W. Gate of the kiss. '02(My17) il. D. $1.50. Lothrop.
Harding, S: B. *See* Harding, C. H.
Harding, W: War in South Africa and the Dark Continent from savagery to civilization. '02(Mr22) 12°, $2; hf. mor., $3; mor., $4. Dominion.
Hardwicke. Rood, H: E: $1.50. Harper.
Hargis, And. M. Treatise on commercial law and business customs. '01. '02(Je28) il. 12°, pap., 10 c. J. North.
Hargrave, W: L. Wallannah. '02(Mr8) il. D. $1.50. B. F. Johnson.
Harland, H:, ["Sidney Luska."] The lady paramount. '02(Ap19) D. $1.50. Lane.
Harmer, S. F:, *and* Shipley, A. E., *eds.* Cambridge natural history. v. 10, Mammalia, by F. E. Beddard. '02(Je28) il. 8°, net, $4. Macmillan.
Harmsworth, Alfr. C., Thompson, *Sir* H:, *and others.* Motors and motor driving. '02 (My17) 8°, (Badminton lib.) $3.50; hf. mor., $5. Little, B. & Co.

Harper, Carrie A. *See* Dix, B. M.
Harper, J: M. Moral drill for the schoolroom. '01· '02(Ja25) 12°, $1. Kellogg.
Harper, W: R. Constructive studies in the priestly element in the Old Testament. Rev. ed. '02(Ja18) O. (Constructive Bible studies.) $1. Univ. of Chic.
Harper's official golf guide for 1901. '01· '02(Mr1) 12°. $1. Harper.
Harriott, *Mrs.* Clara M. *See* Morris, C.
Harris, C: N. *See* Massachusetts digest.
Harris, Cicero W. Sectional struggle: troubles between the north and the south. '02(Mr29) 8°, net, $2.50. Lippincott.
Harris, H: E. King of Andorra. '01· '02 (F15) D. $1.25. Abbey Press.
Harris, Joel C., ["Uncle Remus."] Making of a statesman, and other stories. '02(My17) D. $1.25. McClure, P.
Harris, *Mrs.* Miriam C. Rutledge. '02(Je14) 12°, (Home lib.) $1. Burt.
Harris, W: C. *See* Sage, D.
Harrison, Walter. *See* Ritchie, M. J. G.
Harry, T. E. Infans amoris. '02(My3) D. $1.50. Abbey Press.
Hart, Rob. M. Card language. 3d rev., enl. ed. '02(Mr29) nar. O. pap., 20 c. R. M. McEnally.
Hart, Rob. M. Card language. [*also*] Play card cypher. 4th rev ed. '02(Je28) nar. O. pap., 20 c. R. M. Hart.
Harte, Fs. Bret. Openings in the old trail '02(My3) D. $1.25. Houghton, M. & Co.
Hartley House cook book. Pierce, E. A. 60 c. Lentilhon.
Harvard celebrities. Hall, F: G., *ed.* $1.25. Univ. Press (Camb.)
HARVARD UNIVERSITY.
Du Bois, *comp.* Harvard Univ. songs. $1.50. Ditson.
Harvey, L. D. Aids for the proper observance of Memorial day by the schools of Wis. '02(Ap26) O. pap., gratis. Democrat Pr.
Harvey, L. D. *See also* Arbor annual.
Hasse, Adelaide R., *comp.* United States Government pubs.: handbook for the cataloguer. pt. 1. '02(My10) O. $1. Lib. Bu.
Hassell, J: A. *See* Hiley, A. R. I.
Hatch, Adelaide W. Zobo patriotic drill. '01· '02(Ja11) S. (Hints ed. of novel and successful drills.) pap., 15 c. Hints.
Hatch, Dorus R. Civil government of Col. 7th ed. '01. '02(Ja18) il. 16°, 60 c. Centennial.
Haultmont, Marie. Marriage of Laurentia. '01. '02(Ja11) 8°, net, $1.60. Herder.
Haven, *Mrs.* Marg. J. C. Bible lessons for little beginners. '02(F8) 12°, net, 75 c. Revell.
Hawaiian almanac and annual for 1902. (T. G. Thrum.) '01· '02(Mr1) 12°, pap., 75 c. Thrum.
Hawkins, C: A. Legal counsellor and form book. '02(Je14) 8°, subs., $3: shp., $4. W. W. Wilson.
Hawkins, N. Aids to engineers' examinations. '01· '02(F8) il. 12°, leath., $2. Audel.
Hawkins, N. Handbook of calculations for engineers and firemen. '01. '02(F8) il. 12°. $2. Audel.
Hawley, Jos. R. New animal cellular therapy. '01. '02(Mr29) il. 12°, $1. Clinic.
Hawthorne, N. The Blithedale romance. '02 (Ap19) 12°, (Home lib.) $1. Burt.
Hawthorne, N. Main Street. '02(Mr1) sq. 12°, bds., $2. Kirgate Press.
Hawthorne, N. Marble faun. '02(Ap19) 12°, (Home lib.) $1. Burt.
Hawthorne classics. D. 40 c. Globe Sch. Bk.
—Hale, *ed.* Ballads and ballad poetry. (2.)
—Greek myths in Eng. dress. (1.)
Hay, J: William McKinley. '02(My17) D. (What is worth while ser.) leatherette, net, 28 c. Crowell.
Hayden, Ja. R. Pocket text-book of venereal diseases. 3d ed. '01· '02(Ja25) 12°, net, $1.75; net, $2.25. Lea.
Hayens, Herb. For the colours. '02(My17) il. 8°, $2. Nelson.
Hayes, H:, *pseud.* *See* Kirk, *Mrs.* E. O.
Haymond, *Mrs.* W. E. Agnes Cheswick. '01· '02(Mr22) D. net, 60 c. Blanchard.
Hazlitt, W: Carew. Shakespeare. '02(My10) 8°, net, $2.50. Scribner.
Hazell's annual for 1902; ed. by W. Palmer. '02(Mr8) 12°, net, $1.50. Scribner.
HEAD.
Eckley. Regional anatomy of head and neck. net, $2.50. Lea.
See also Hair;—Phrenology.
Headlam, Cecil. Peter Vischer. '02(My24) 12°, (Handbooks of the great craftsmen.) $2. Macmillan
Headlam, Cecil. Story of Chartres. '02(Je7) il. 12°, (Mediæval towns ser.) $2; leath., $2.50. Macmillan.
Headley, J. T. Napoleon and his marshals '02(My17) 12°, (Home lib.) $1. Burt.
Headley, J. T. Washington and his generals. '02(My17) 12°, (Home lib.) $1. Burt
Healing of nerves. Ballance, C: A. net, $4.50. Macmillan.
HEALTH.
See **Hygiene.**
HEART.
Mackenzie. Study of the pulse, and of the movements of the heart. net, $4.50. Macmillan
Hearth and home essays. Ruskay, E. J. 30 c. Jewish Pub.
Hearts courageous. Rives, H. E. $1.50. Bowen-M.
HEAT.
Dexter. Elem. exercises on sound, light and heat. 90 c. Longmans.
See also **Radiation.**
Heath, Harold. *See* Jordan, D: S.
Heath, W: Memoirs of Maj.-Gen. William Heath, by himself. New ed.; ed. by W: Abbatt; [also] acc. of the Battle of Bunker Hill. '01· '02(Ja11) O. net, $5. Abbatt.
Heath's home and school classics. il. D. 20 c.-60 c. Heath.
—Jordan, *comp.* True tales of birds and beasts.
—La Motte Fouqué. Undine. 30 c.
—Lamb. Tales from Shakespeare.
—Melville. Typee. 45 c.
—O'Shea, *ed.* Old world wonder stories.
—Perrault. Tales of Mother Goose.
Heath's modern language ser. S. Heath.
—Bowen. First scientific Fr. reader. 90 c.
—Fulda. Talisman. 35 c.
—Grillparzer. Traum ein leben. 60 c.

Heath's modern lang. ser.—Continued.
—Heyse. Niels mit der offenen hand. 30 c.
—Körner. Zriny ein trauerspiel in fünf aufzügen. 35 c.
—Krüger *and* Smith. Eng.-Germ. conversation book. 25 c.
—Lessing. Minna von Barnhelm. 75 c.
—Renan. Souvenirs d' enfance et de jeunesse. 75 c.
—Ségur. Les malheurs de Sophie. 45 c.
—Verne. Vingt mille lieues sous les mers. 40 c.
—Wesselhoeft. Germ. composition. 45 c.

HEATING.
Lawler. Modern plumbing, steam and hot water heating. $5. Popular.

HEAVEN.
Swedenborg. Heavenly arcana. v. 13. $1.25. Mass. New-Ch. Un.

Heavenly harmonies for earthly living. McLeod, M. J. net, 50 c. Revell.

Heavenly vision. Booth, H: M. net, $1. Beam.

HEBREWS (*Epistles*).
See Bible.

HEBRIDES.
Boswell. Journ. of a tour to the Hebrides. net, 60 c. Macmillan.

Hector, *Mrs.* Annie F., ["*Mrs.* Alexander."] The yellow fiend. '02(Mr22) D. $1.50. Dodd.

Heddle, Ethel F. Mystery of St. Rubes. '02 (Je21) 12°, $1.50. Scribner.

HELL.
Morton. Thoughts on hell. net, 50 c. Herder.

Hellems, Fred B. R. Lex de imperio Vespasiani. '02(My24) O. (Dissertationes Americanae. Classical philology, no. 1.) pap., 50 c. Scott, F. & Co

Helmolt, Hans F., *and others, eds.* Hist. of the world. In 8 v. v. 1. '02(F22); v. 4 (My24) il. O. ea., $6. Dodd.

Helps, *Sir* A. Spanish conquest in America. New ed. In 4 v. v. 2. '02(Je28) 12°, $1.50. Lane.

HEMATOLOGY.
See Blood.

Hemmeter, J: C. Diseases of the intestines. v. 2. '02(Mr22) il. 8°, net, $5; shp., net, $6. Blakiston.

Hempel, Walther. Methods of gas analysis; fr. 3d Germ. ed.; enl. by L. M. Dennis. '02(My3) 12°, net, $2.25. Macmillan.

Hemstreet, C: When old New York was young. '02(My10) il. O. net, $1.50. Scribner.

Henderson, C. H. Education and the larger life. '02(My3) D. net, $1.30. Houghton, M. & Co.

Henderson, Ernest F. Short hist. of Germany. In 2 v. '02(Mr29) 8°, net, $4. Macmillan.

HENRY V., *King of England.*
Kingsford. Henry v. the typical mediæval hero. net, $1.35; net, $1.60. Putnam.

Henry, Alex. Travels and adventures in Canada and the Indian Territories, between the years 1760 and 1776. New ed.; ed., with notes, by J. Bain. '01. '02(F8) il. 8°, net, $4. Little, B. & Co.

Henry, Arth. Island cabin. '02(My24) D. $1.50. McClure, P.

Henry, W: E., *comp.* State platforms of the two dominant political parties in Ind., 1850-1900. '02(My10) O. $1.50. W: E. Henry.

Henry Esmond. *See* Thackeray, W: M.

Hensman, H. Cecil Rhodes. '02(F8) il. O. leath., net, $5. Harper.

Henson, Herb. H. Cross-bench views of current church questions. '02(Ap26) O. $4. Longmans.

Henson, Herb. H. Godly union and concord. '02(Mr22) O. $2. Longmans.

Her baby brother. Moulton, *Mrs.* L. C. 50 c. Little, B. & Co.

Her Serene Highness. Phillips, D: G. $1.50. Harper.

Heralds of empire. Laut, A. C. $1.50. Appleton.

Herbarium and plant description. Meier, W. H. D. 70 c. Ginn.

Herbartian methods. *See* Fennell, M.

Herbert, H. F. *See* Baur, T. P.

Herbertson, F. D., *comp.* Descriptive geographies fr. original sources, Central and South America with the West Indies. '02 (Ap26) il. 12°, net, 70 c. Macmillan.

Herdman, Lee, *rep.* *See* Nebraska. *Sup. ct.* Repts.

Hereward the Wake. Kingsley, C: $1. Burt.

Herford, Brooke. Small end of great problems. '02(My10) D. net, $1.60. Longmans.

Herford, C: H., *ed.* English tales in verse. '02(My10) 12°, (Warwick lib. of Eng. literature.) $1.50. Scribner.

HERMANN *der Cherusker.*
Goebel. Hermann der Cherusker und die schlacht im Teutoburger walde. net, 50 c. Macmillan.

Hermitage. Ervin, D. $1. Grafton Press.

Hero ser. il. D. net, 25 c. Jennings.
—Locke. Nineteenth century crusade. (5.)
—Typical American. (2.)
—Quayle. The gentleman in literature. (4.)
—A hero, Jean Valjean. (1.)—King Cromwell. (6.)
—Smith. Abraham Lincoln. (3.)

HEROES.
Gordy. Am. leaders and heroes. net, 60 c. Scribner.
Muzzey. Spiritual heroes. net, $1.25. Doubleday, P.

Heroes of the nations ser.; ed. by E. Abbott. il. D. net, $1.35; net, $1.60. Putnam.
—Jenks. Edward Plantagenet. (35.)
—Kingsford. Henry v. (34.)

Heroine of the strait. Crowley, M. C. $1.50. Little, B. & Co.

Herron, W: Wright. *See* Texas. Supplements.

Hershey, O. H. Quaternary of Southern California. '02(My17) il. Q. (Univ. of Cal. pub., v. 3, no. 1.) pap., 20 c. Univ. of Cal.

Herter, C. A. Lectures on chemical pathology. '02(Ja25) 12°, net, $1.75. Lea.

HERTFORDSHIRE.
Tompkins. Highways and byways in Hertfordshire. $2. Macmillan.

Herz, W. *See* Abegg, R.

He's coming to-morrow. Stowe, H. B. net, 25 c. Revell.

Hesperian tree. Piatt, J: J. $2. J: Scott.

Hessler, J: C., *and* Smith, Alb. L. Essentials of chemistry for secondary schools. '02 (Je7) il. O. $1.20. B: H. Sanborn.

Hester Blair. Carson, W: H: $1.50. C. M. Clark.

Hettinger, Franz. Timothy; tr. and adapt. by V. Stepka. '02(Je14) 12°, net, $1.50. Herder.

Heyse, P. J. L. L'arrabbiata; tr. by W. W. Florer. '02(Je28) S. 35 c. Wahr.

Heyse, P. J. L. Niels mit der offenen hand. '02(F1) S. (Modern lang. ser.) 30 c. Heath.

Hezekiah's wives. French, L. H. net, 85 c. Houghton, M. & Co.

Hiatt, C: Westminster Abbey. '02(Ap12) 12°, (Bell's cathedral ser.) 60 c. Macmillan.

Hibbard, Augustine G: Genealogy of the Hibbard family desc. of Rob. Hibbard, of Salem, Mass. '01. '02(F1) 8°, $5. Case.

Hickox, W: E. Correspondent's manual: practical information on letter taking and letter writing. '02(Mr29) S. $1.50. Lee & S.

HICKS, Thos. H.
Radcliffe. Gov. Thomas H. Hicks of Md., and the civil war. 50 c. Johns Hopkins.

Higgin, L. Spanish life in town and country; with chaps. on Portuguese life by E. E. Street. '02(My24) il. D. (Our European neighbors.) net, $1.20. Putnam.

High, J. L. A great chancellor, and other papers; ed. by E. B. Smith. '01. '02(F15) 8°, net, $2.50. Callaghan.

High-caste Hindu woman. Ramabai Sarasvati. net, 75 c. Revell.

Highways and byways ser. 12°, $2. Macmillan.
—Tompkins. Highways and byways in Hertfordshire.

Hiley, Alan R. I., *and* Hassell, J: A. The mobile Boer. '02(Ap26) il. D. net, $1.50. Grafton Press.

Hill, F: T. The minority: (novel.) '02 (Ap19) D. $1. Stokes.

Hill, G. A. *See* Wentworth, G: A.

Hill, Grace L. An unwilling guest. '02(Je14) il. D. net, $1. Am. Bapt.

Hill, J. W. Diseases of the cat. '01. '02 (Ja4) il. D. $1.25. W: R. Jenkins.

Hill, Ja. J. *See* Flint, C: R.

Hillis, N. D. Master of the science of right living. '02(Ap12) 12°, bds., net, 50 c. Revell.

Hinchman, Lydia S. Early settlers of Nantucket. 2d rev. enl. ed. '02(F15) 8°, $5. Ferris.

Hind, C. L. Life's little things. '02(F1) 12°, $1.75. Macmillan.

Hinderers (The). Bayly, A. E. $1. Longmans.

Hinds, W: A. American communities; rev. ed., enl. '02(My3) il S. (Murby's sci. ser.) $1. Kerr.

HINDUS.
Ramabai Sarasvati. High-caste Hindu woman. net, 75 c. Revell.

Hinkson, H. A. Point of honour. '02(Mr22) il. D. $1.50. McClurg.

Hinkson, *Mrs.* Kath. T. Golden lily. '02 (Mr22) il. S. 40 c. Benziger.

Hinton, Ma. B. Other notes. '02(Ap12) 16°, $1. Neale.

Hints ed. of novel and successful drills. S. pap., 15 c. Hints.
—Hatch. Zobo patriotic drill.

Hints to small libraries. Plummer. M. W. net, 50 c. M. W. Plummer.

Histoires (Les) de tante. Alissas, R. d'. net, 40 c. Macmillan.

HISTOLOGY.
Gaylord *and* Archoff. Atlas of pathological histology. net, $7.50. Lea.
See also Microscope.

Historic Boston; sightseeing towns around the Hub. '01. '02(F15) 12°, net, 50 c.; pap., net, 30 c. Pilgrim Press.

Historical and linguistic studies in literature related to the New Testament. il. O. pap., net, 25 c. Univ. of Chic.
—Goodspeed. Newberry gospels. (v. 2, 1.)

HISTORY.
Bourne. Teaching of history and civics. $1.50. Longmans.
Helmolt, *and others, eds.* History of the world. v. 1, 4. ea., $6. Dodd.
Jesse. Historical memoirs. 30 v. ea., $2.50; complete set of 15 v., $37.40; $75. L. C. Page.
Kidd. Principles of western civilization. net, $2. Macmillan.
Larned, *ed.* Literature of Am. history. net, $6; $7.50; $9. Houghton, M. & Co.
Maitland, *and others.* Essays on the teaching of history. net, 75 c. Macmillan.
Tout *and* Tait, *eds.* Historical essays. $5. Longmans.
West. Ancient history to death of Charlemagne. $1.50. Allyn & B.

Hitchcock, F: H. Book-builder's handbook of types, scales, etc. [New issue.] '02 (Je28) S. leath., net, 50 c. Grafton Press.

Hoare, H. W. Evolution of the Eng. Bible. New cheap ed. '02(My10) 8°, net, $2.50. Dutton.

Hobbs, W. R. P. Arithmetic of electrical measurements; rev. by R: Wormell. 9th ed. '02(My3) S. 50 c. Van Nostrand.

Hobhouse, Leonard T. Mind in evolution. '02(F1) 8°, net, $3.25. Macmillan.

Hochelaga depicta. Bosworth, N. net, $3; net, $4.50. Congdon.

Hodder, Edn. Life of a century, 1800-1900. '01. '02(Ja11) 8°, net, $4. Scribner

Hodge, Clifton F. Nature study and life. '02 (Ap19) il. D. $1.65. Ginn.

Hodgman, F. Home's sweet harmonies: new part songs, quartets, etc. '02(F8) O. pap., 80 c. Home Pub.

Hodgson, Fred T. Estimating frame and brick houses. 2d rev., enl. ed. '02(Je7) il. 12°, $1. D: Williams.

Hoffman, F: L: Windstorm and tornado insurance. 3d ed. '02(Mr22) il. 16°, pap., 25 c. Spectator.

Hoffman, Harry C. Health and strength. '02 (F1) il. sq. D. pap., 25 c. H. C. Hoffman.

Hogarth, D: G: The nearer east. '02(Mr29) 8°, (World ser., no. 2.) $2. Appleton.

HOGARTH, W:
Anstruther. William Hogarth. $1. Macmillan.

Hohenzollern. Brady, C. T. $1.50. Century Co.

Holdsworth, Annie E., [*Mrs.* E. J. Lee-Hamilton.] Michael Ross, minister. '02(Mr22) D. $1.50. Dodd.

HOLIDAYS.
Deems, *comp.* Holy-days and holidays. $5. Funk.

Holiness of the church in the 19th century. Scheeben, M. J. 10 c. Benziger.

Holland, Clive. My Japanese wife. [New rev., enl. ed.] '02(Je7) il. D. $1.50. Stokes.

Holleman, A. F. Text-book of inorganic chemistry; fr. the Dutch by H. C. Cooper. pt. 2. '02(My3) 8°, $2.50. Wiley.

Holley, Marietta, ["Josiah Allen's wife."] Samantha at Saratoga. '02(Ap19) il. 12°, (Home lib.) $1. Burt.

Hollister, H. J., *and others.* Taxation in Mich. and elsewhere. '01. '02(F15) 8°, pap., 50 c. Mich. Pol. Sci. Assoc.

Holly Tree Inn. Dickens, C: net, $1.50. Lippincott.

Holme, Ma. P. M. Stray leaves from a border garden. '02(My10) il. 12°, net, $1.50. Lane.

Holmes, C. J. Constable. '01. '02(Ja11) il. O. (Artist's lib., no. 5.) net, $1. Longmans.

Holmes, *Mrs.* Ma. J. Cousin Maude and Rosamond. '02(Ap19) 12°, (Home lib.) $1. Burt.

Holst, Bernhart P., *ed.* Teachers' and pupils' cyclopædia. v. 1-3. '02(Ap26) 3 v., il. 8°, hf. mor., $12.75. Holst.

Holt's Am. science ser.; briefer course. D. $1.12. Holt.
—Remsen. Introd. to study of chemistry.

Holt's students' ser. of classic Fr. plays. D. net, 35 c. Holt.
—Corneille. Le Cid. (1.)
—Racine. Athalie. (2.)—Esther. (5.)

Holy-days and holidays. Deems, E: M. $5. Funk.

HOLY SPIRIT.
Barry. God the Holy Ghost. $2. Angel Press.
Tuttle. The gift of power. net, 25 c. Westminster.

Holy war. Bunyan, J: 50 c.; 75 c. Macmillan.

Homans, J. E. A B C of the telephone. '02 (F1) il. 12°, $1. Van Nostrand.

Home and school classics. See Heath's.

Home and school ser. See Flanagan's.

Home coming of autumn queen. Kellogg, A. M. 15 c. Kellogg.

Home lib. See Burt's.

HOME STUDY.
McGovern. Fireside university of modern invention, discovery, etc., for home circle study and entertainment. $2.50; $3.75. Union Pub.
Powell. 20th century home builder. 25 c. Pub. Ho. of M. E. Ch., So.

Home thoughts. Cox, *Mrs.* J. F. net, $1.20. Barnes.

Homeric society. Keller, A. G. $1.20. Longmans.

Home's sweet harmonies. Hodgman, F. 80 c. Home Pub.

Homing pigeon (The): treatise on training, breeding, [etc.] '02(Mr15) il. T. pap., 25 c. G: E. Howard.

Honeyman, A. Van D. Bright days in merrie England. '02(Ap12) il. 12°, net, $1.50. Honeyman.

Honor of the Braxtons. Fosdick, J. W. $1.50. J. F. Taylor.

Hood, T: Serious poems. '02(My10) il. 16°, (Caxton ser.) net, $1.25. Scribner.

Hood, Wharton P. Treatment of injuries by friction and movement. '02(Ap26) 12°, net, $1.25. Macmillan.

Hope, Laurence, *comp.* India's love lyrics. '02(Ap19) il. 4°, net, $1.50. Lane.

Hopkins, E: W. India old and new. '01. '02(F15) 8°, (Yale bicentennial pub.) net, $2.50. Scribner.

Hopkins, Herb. M. The fighting bishop. '02 (Mr15) D. $1.50. Bowen-M.

Horace. Odæ, Epodæ, Carmen sæculare, picturis illustratæ. '01. '02(Mr29) il. 12°, (Antique gems from the Greek and Latin, v. 3.) (App. to pubs. for price.) Barrie.

Horæ Latinæ. Ogilvie, R. $5. Longmans.

Hornbrook, A. R. Key to Primary arithmetic and Grammar school arithmetic. '02(Mr8) D. 65 c. Am. Bk.

Hornung, E. W: At large. '02(F15) D. $1.50. Scribner.

Horridge, Fk. Dynamic aspects of nutrition. '02(Je7) 12°, $1.50. Wood.

Horrocks, W. H. Introd. to the bacteriolog. examination of water. '01. '02(My10) 8°, net, $3.68. Blakiston.

HORSE.
Chapman. Pathological treatment of lameness in the horse. $2. W: R. Jenkins.
Fillis. Breaking and riding; with military commentary. net, $5. Scribner.
Mullen. How to break, educate and handle the horse. $1. W: Mullen.
See also Veterinary medicine and surgery.

HORTICULTURE.
See Flowers;—Fruit;—Gardening.

Horton, Fs. A. Birthright membership of believers' infants in the New Testament church. '02(Je7) S. pap., 6 c. Presb. Bd.

Hosmer, Ja. K. Hist. of the Louisiana purchase. '02(My10) il. D. net, $1.20. Appleton.

Hotchkiss, Chauncey C. Strength of the weak. '02(F1) D. $1.50. Appleton.

Houck, F: A. Life of St. Gerlach. 1900. '02(Mr22) D. net, 55 c. Benziger.

Hough, Emerson. Mississippi bubble. '02 (My3) il. D. $1.50. Bowen-M.

Hound of the Baskervilles. Doyle, A. C. $1.25. McClure, P.

Hour-glass stories. il. S. net, 40 c. Funk.
—Grenell. The sandals.
—Talbot. Courtship of sweet Anne Page.

Hours of the passion. King, H. E. H. net, $1.50. Dutton.

House of Cæsar. Van Santvoord, S. net, $5.25. Pafraets.

HOUSEKEEPING.
See Domestic economy.

Houston, Edn. J., *and* Kennelly, A. E. Alternating electric currents. 3d enl. ed. '02 (Je14) sq. S. (Elem. electro technical ser.) $1. McGraw.

Houston, Edn. J., *and* Kennelly, A. E. Electric arc lighting. 2d enl. ed. '02(Je14) sq. S. (Elem. electro technical ser.) $1. McGraw.

Houston, Edn. J., *and* Kennelly, A. E. Electric incandescent lighting. 2d enl. ed. '02 (Je14) sq. S. (Elem. electro technical ser.) $1. McGraw.

How are we led? Sanders, C: H. $1.50. Donohue.

How to attract an audience. Esenwein, J. B. $1. Hinds.

How to become a naturalized citizen. Pritchard, W: A. 10 c. Wehman.
How to break and handle the horse. Mullen, W: $1. W: Mullen.
How to build a knockabout. Mower, C. D. $1. Rudder.
How to build a model yacht. Fisher, H. $1. Rudder.
How to build a racing sloop. Mower, C. D. $1. Rudder.
How to build dynamo-electric machinery. Bubier, E: T. $2.50. Bubier.
How to get acquainted with God. Seward, T. F. net, 50 c. Funk.
How to make an index. Wheatley, H: B: $1.25; $2.50. Armstrong.
How to make the telephone. Cary, G: H. $1. Bubier.
How to prepare essays, lectures, [etc.] Miles, E. H. net, $2. Dutton.
How to teach about trees. Payne, F. O. 25 c. Kellogg.
How to teach aquatic life. Payne, F. O. 25 c. Kellogg.
How to teach composition writing. Kellogg, A. M. 25 c. Kellogg.
How to tell fortunes. Zancig, *Mme.* 25 c. Drake.
How to tell time by the stars. Browne, D: M. 50 c. Lee & S.
Howard, B: Prisoners of Russia: convict life in Sakhalin and Siberia. '02(Je21) D. net. $1.40. Appleton.
Howard, *Lady* Mabel. Failure of success. '01· '02(F8) D. $1.50. Longmans.
Howard, W: L. The perverts. '02(F15) D. $1.50. G: W. Dillingham.
Howe, Edn. D. *See* New York civil and criminal justice.
Howells, Mildred. *See* Burt, M. E.
Howells, W: D. The Kentons. '02(Ap26) D. $1.50. Harper.
Howes, G: B. Atlas of practical elem. zootomy. '02(Mr8) 4°, net, $3.50. Macmillan.
Hoyt, Eleanor. Misdemeanors of Nancy. '02 (Ap19) il. D. $1.50. Doubleday, P.
Hoyt, L: G. Practice in proceedings in the probate cts. of New Hampshire. '01· '02 (F8) O. shp., $2.50. Rumford Press.
Hoyt, T: A. Theology as a popular science. '02(Je21) S. pap., net, 10 c. Presb. Bd.
Hubbard, Elbert, ["Fra Elbertus."] Message to Garcia and thirteen other things. '01· '02(F15) 8°, limp leath., $2; $5; ¾ levant, $15. Roycrofters.
Hubbard, Elbert. Time and chance. '01· '02 (F15) D. $1.50. Putnam.
Huddilston, J: H. Lessons from Greek pottery, [with] bibliog. of Gr. ceramics. '02 (F1) 8°, net, $1.25. Macmillan.
Hudson, Horace B. California vineyards: scenes in Fresno Co. '02(Ap5) il. obl. D. pap., 35 c. H. B. Hudson.
Hufford, D: A. El camino real; highway connecting missions. '01. '02(F15) obl. Tt. pap., 35 c.; burnt yucca or redwood, 75 c.; burnt leath., $1; burnt orangewood, $1.25. D: A. Hufford.
Hufford, D: A. The real Ramona of Helen Hunt Jackson's famous novel. '02(F15) il. D. pap., 35 c.; burnt yucca or redwood, 75 c.; burnt leath., $1; burnt orangewood, $1.25. D: A. Hufford.
Hughes, Erlian. My island. '02(F15) 16°, $1.25. Dutton.
Hughes, H. W. Text-book of coal mining. New enl. ed. '01. '02(F15) il. 8°, $7. Lippincott.
Hughes, R. E. Schools at home and abroad. '02(Ap5) 12°, net, $1.50. Dutton.
Hugo, V. Notre-Dame de Paris; abr. and ed. by J: R. Wightman. '02(Ap5) S. 85 c. Ginn.

HUGUENOTS.
Baird. Hist. of Huguenot emigration to America. 2 v. net, $2.50. Dodd.
Stapleton. Memorials of the Huguenots in America. $1.50. Huguenot.

Hulbert, W: D. Forest neighbors. '02 (My24) il. O. net, $1.50. McClure, P.
Hull, Mattie E. Spirit echoes. '01· '02 (Ap12) 12°, net, 75 c. Sunflower.
Hull Botanical Laboratory contributions. O. pap., net. Univ. of Chic.
—Cowles. Ecological rel. of vegetation on the sand dunes of Lake Mich. 75 c. (13.)
—Life. Tuber-like rootlets of cycas revoluta. 25 c. (26.)
—Livingston. Stimulus which causes change in polymorphic green algae. 25 c. (22.)
—Lyon. Study of the sporangia and gametophytes of selaginella apus and selaginella rupestris. 25 c. (31.)
—Overton. Parthenogenesis in thalictrum purpurascens. 25 c. (35.)
—Smith, R. W. Achromatic spindle in spore mother-cells of osmunda regalis. 25 c. (23.)
—Stevens. Gametrogenesis and fertilization in albugo. 25 c. (29.)
Hulsean lectures. *See* Chase, F: H:
Humble heroine. Tiddeman, L. E. 15 c. Lippincott.

HUME, D:
Gore. Imagination in Spinoza and Hume. net, 35 c. Univ. of Chic.

Hume, Fergus W. Millionaire mystery. '01· '02(Ja4) D. $1.25. Buckles.
Hume, Fergus W. Pagan's cup. '02(F8) D. $1.25. G: W. Dillingham.
Humphreys, *Mrs.* Eliz. M. J. G., ["Rita."] Sin of Jasper Standish. '02(Mr22) D. $1.25. Fenno.
Hun, Marcus T. *See* New York. *Sup. ct.* Repts.
Huneker, Ja. Melomaniacs. '02(Mr1) D. $1.50. Scribner.
Hungerford, Herb. Success club debater. '01· '02(Mr1) Tt. (Boiled-down booklets.) 25 c. Success.
Hungerford, *Mrs.* Marg. H., ["The Duchess," *formerly Mrs.* Argles.] The three graces. '01. '02(Mr1) 12°, (Popular lib.) $1. Lippincott.

HUNT, Holman.
Williamson. Holman Hunt. 50 c. Macmillan.

Hunter, W: C. Twentieth century wonder book. '02(My17) 12°, 50 c.; pap., 25 c. Donohue.
Huntington, Annie O. Studies of trees in winter: des. of the deciduous trees of Northeastern America. '02(Ja18) il. O. net, $2.25. Knight.
Hurd, Harvey B., *comp. and ed.* *See* Illinois. *Gen. assembly.* Revised statutes.

Hurll, Estelle M., *ed.* Tuscan sculpture. Lib. ed. '02(Ap5) D. (Riverside art ser., no. 11.) net, 75 c.; School ed., net, 50 c.; pap., net, 35 c. Houghton, M. & Co.
Hurll, Estelle M., *ed.* Van Dyck. Lib. ed. '02(Je7) (Riverside art ser., no. 12.) net, 75 c.; School ed., net, 50 c.; pap., net, 35 c. Houghton, M. & Co.
Hurst, C: Hints on steam engine design and construction. '01· '02(F15) 16°, bds., 60 c. Lippincott.
Hurst, J: F. History of rationalism; emb. survey of present state of Protestant theology; rev. '01. '02(F15) 8°, $2.50. Eaton & M.
Hurst, J: F. The new hearthstone: bridal greeting. '02(Mr1) O. $1. Jennings.
Hurst, J: F. Upon the sunroad. '02(My17) 16°, 25 c. Revell.
Hutchinson, H. N., Gregory, J. W., *and* Lydekker, R. Living races of mankind. '02(Ap12) il. 8°, net, $5. Appleton.
Hutchinson, Ida W. Gospel story of Jesus Christ. '02(Mr29) 12°, $1.50. Dutton.
Hutton, R. E. The soul in the unseen world. '02(Ap5) 12°, net, $2. Dutton.
HUXLEY, T: H:
Clodd. Thomas Henry Huxley. net, $1. Dodd.
Hyde, Miles G. The girl from Mexico, and other stories and sketches. 3d ed. '02 (Ap26) D. $1. Abbey Press.
Hyde, W. H., *and* McManman, J. A. Telephone troubles. 8th ed. '01. '02(F15) 16°, pap., 25 c. Caspar.
HYDRAULIC ENGINEERING.
Church. Diagrams of mean velocity of uniform motion of water in open channels. $1.50. Wiley.
Fanning. Hydraulic and water-supply engineering. $5. Van Nostrand.
Fidler. Calculations in hydraulic engineering. pt. 2. $3. Longmans.
HYDRO-KINETICS.
See Hydraulic engineering.
HYDROTHERAPY.
Kellogg. Rational hydrotherapy. subs., $5; $6. Davis.
HYGIENE.
Balch. Manual for boards of health. $1.50. Banks & Co.
Bryce. Ideal health and how to attain it. 50 c. Treat.
Furneaux. Elem. practical hygiene. 90 c. Longmans.
Hoffman. Health and strength. 25 c. H. C. Hoffman.
Morris. Right living; or, how a woman can keep well. $1. Bardeen.
Sedgwick. Principles of sanitary science and public health. net, $3. Macmillan.
Smith. Anatomy, physiology and hygiene. $1. W: R. Jenkins.
Van Doren. Students' guide to health. $2. D. T. Van Doren.
Willoughby. Hygiene for students. $1.25. Macmillan.
See also Diet;—Mind and body; — Physiology; — Sanitary engineering.
HYMNS AND HYMN WRITERS.
Gabriel, *comp.* Joyful praise. 30 c. Jennings.
Gill, *and others.* Hymns of grace and glory. 30 c. Mattill & L.

Hypatia. *See* Kingsley, C:
Hyperion. Longfellow, H: W. $1. Burt.
HYPNOTISM.
Alpheus. Guide to hypnotism. 50 c.; 25 c. Donohue.
De Laurence. Hypnotism. $1.50. Henneberry.
HYSTERICS.
See Mind and body.
I go a fishing. Barton, W: E. 25 c. Revell.
I promessi sposi. Manzoni, A. $1.20. Silver.
ICE CREAM.
See Confectionery.
Idea of God. Reed, E. A. net, 75 c. Univ. of Chic.
Ideal health. Bryce, A. 50 c. Treat.
Ideal messages ser. net, 25 c. Revell.
—Stowe. He's coming to-morrow.
Ideal word book. Smith, E. E. 17 c. Flanagan.
Idole (L'). Michaud, H. 10 c. W: R. Jenkins.
Idylls. *See* Theocritus.
Idylls of the king. *See* Davidson, *Mrs.* H. A.
If I were king. McCarthy, J. H. $1.50. Russell.
Iliad and Odyssey. *See* Keller, A. G.
Illinois. *Appellate cts.* Repts. v. 97. '02 (Mr1); v. 98 (Mr29); v. 99 (My17) O. shp., ea., $3.75. Callaghan.
Illinois. Commentary on the mechanics' lien law, by C: T. Farson. '02(F1) O. net, $4. Callaghan.
Illinois. *General assembly.* Revised statutes, 1901. (H. B. Hurd.) '01· '02(Mr8) O. shp., net, $4. Chic. Leg. News.
Illinois. *Supreme ct.* Repts. v. 192. '02 (Mr29); v. 193 (My17) O. shp., ea., $2.25. Phillips.
ILLINOIS.
Arnold, *comp.* Manual of school laws. $1.75. Effingham Dem.
Illustrated family Christian almanac, 1902. '02(Mr1) sq. 12°, pap., 10 c. Am. Tr.
ILLUSTRATIONS (*religious*).
See Sermons.
ILLUSTRATORS.
See Book illustration.
Imagination in Spinoza and Hume. Gore, W. C. net, 35 c. Univ. of Chic.
Imhaus, Eliz. V. Exiled by the world. '02 (Mr8) il. D. $1.50. Mutual Pub.
Imitator (The): (novel.) '01· '02(Ap5) D. $1.25. W: M. Reedy.
IMMORTALITY.
See Future life.
Improprieties of Noah. Smedberg, H. V. 50 c. Abbey Press.
Improvement of moral qualities. Gabirol, S. I. net, $1.25. Macmillan.
In a Tuscan garden. '02(Je28) il. 12°, net, $1.50. Lane.
In a walled garden. Belloc, B. R. net, $1.25. Herder.
In and around the Grand Canyon. James, G: W. net, $10. Little, B. & Co.
In His name. *See* Hale, E: E.
In memoriam. Tennyson, A. *Lord.* net, $1.20. Scribner.
In my vicarage garden. Ellacombe, H: N. net, $1.50. Lane.
In Sicily. Sladen, D. 2 v. net, $20. Dutton.
In the country God forgot. Charles, F. $1.50. Little, B. & Co.

In the days of giants. Brown, A. F. net, $1.10. Houghton, M. & Co.
In the eagle's talon. Stevens, *Mrs.* S. $1.50. Little, B. & Co.
In the footprints of the padres. Stoddard, C: W. net, $1.50. A. M. Robertson.
In the Michigan lumber camps. Whittier, C: A. 75 c. Neely.
In the misty realm of fable. Kleckner, E. R. $1. Flanagan.
In the palace of the king. Crawford, F. M. 50 c. Am. News.
In Thompson's woods. Crissey, F. $1. Blue Sky Press.
In Tuscany. Carmichael, M. net, $2. Dutton.
In Viking land. Weborg, J. $1.25. J. C. Weborg.
In white and black. Pinson, W. W. $1.50. Saalfield.
Inauguration of President Watterson. De Leon, T: C. 25 c. Am. Writers.

INDEPENDENT CONG. CHURCH.
See Unitarian church.

INDEXING.
Engineering Magazine. Index, 1896-1900. $7.50. Engineering Mag.
Fletcher *and* Bowker. Annual literary index, 1901. net, $3.50. Pub. Weekly.
Wheatley. How to make an index. $1.25; $2.50. Armstrong.
See also Bibliographies;—Cataloguing.

INDIA.
Denning. Mosaics from India. net, $1.50. Revell.
Hopkins. India old and new. net, $2.50. Scribner.
Remy. Influence of India on the poetry of Germany. net, $1. Macmillan.
Russell. Village work in India. net, $1. Revell.

INDIAN MUTINY.
Fitchett. Tale of the great mutiny. $1.50. Scribner.

Indiana. General index of statutes cont. in annot. Ind. statutes; by H. Burns. '01. '02(My24) O. shp. (Sold only with the Ind. statutes.) Bowen-M.

INDIANA.
Ewbank. Ind. trial evidence. $6. Bowen-M.
Henry, *comp.* State platforms of the two dominant pol. parties in Ind. $1.50. W: E. Henry.
McDonald. Treatise on laws of Ind., pertaining to duties of justices of the peace, mayors, etc. net, $7.50. Clarke.
Works. Practice, pleading and forms adapt. to the new rev. code of Ind. v. 1-3. $18. Clarke.

Indiana girl. Lincoln, C: H: $1.50. Neale.
Indianapolis Sentinel year book and almanac, 1902. '01. '02(Ap26) 12°, pap., 25 c. Indianapolis Sentinel.

INDIANS.
Colden. Five Indian nations of Canada. 2 v. net, ea.. $1. New Amsterdam.
Parkman. Conspiracy of Pontiac. $1. Burt.
Trask, *ed.* Letters of Col. Thomas Westbrook and others rel. to Indian affairs in Maine, 1722-26. $5. Littlefield.
See also Zuñi Indians.

India's love lyrics. Hope, L. net, $1.50. Lane.

INDICATORS.
Cohn. Indicators and test-papers, their source and tests for sensitiveness. $2. Wiley.

INDO-IRANIAN LANGUAGE.
Gray. Indo-Iranian phonology. net, $3. Macmillan.

INDULGENCES.
Kaercher, *comp.* Summary of indulgences, granted to the secular branch of the Third order of St. Francis. 15 c. Herder.
Portiuncula. Indulgence of portiuncula. 5 c. Herder.

Industrial democracy. Webb, S. net, $4. Longmans.
Infans amoris. Harry, T. E. $1.50. Abbey Press.
Infant salvation. Firey, M. J. net, $1.20. Funk.

INFANTRY.
Craufurd. Field training of a company of infantry. $1. Longmans.

INFECTIOUS DISEASES.
See Hygiene;—Variola.

Ingersoll, Ernest. Wild life of orchard and field. '02(Mr29) il. D. net, $1.40. Harper.
Ingersoll, Rob. G. Works. In 12 v. v. 1-8. Dresden ed. [New rev., enl. ed.] '02 (My10); v. 9-12 (Je28) 8°, per v., $2.50. Dresden.
Ingerson, Carlos I. Normal method in double entry bookkeeping. '01. '02(Je28) 12°, 50 c. Interstate.
Ingraham, Jos. H. Throne of David. '02 (My10) 12°, (Home lib.) $1. Burt.
Ingram, Arth. F. M. Under the dome. '02 (Je7) 12°, $1.25. E. & J. B. Young.
Ingres, Maxime. Cours complet de langue Française; troiseme ed. v. 1. '01. '02 (Ja11) O. net, $1.50. Univ. of Chic.

INJURIES.
Hood. Treatment of injuries by friction and movement. net, $1.25. Macmillan.
Michigan. Law of personal injuries. net, $4. Callaghan.
See also Accidents.

Inns of court sermons. Beeching, H. C. $1.25. Macmillan.

INSANITY.
Brower *and* Bannister. Manual of insanity. $2. Saunders.
Defendorf. Clinical psychiatry. net, $3.50. Macmillan.
Mercier. Text-book of insanity. net, $1.75. Macmillan.
See also Brain;—Mind and body;—Nervous system.

INSCRIPTIONS.
Tolman. Guide to old Persian inscriptions. $1.50. Am. Bk.

INSECTS.
Fabre. Insect life. $1.75. Macmillan.
Sanderson. Insects injurious to staple crops. $1.50. Wiley.
See also Mosquitoes.

Insuperable barrier. *See* Calvin, E. R.

INSURANCE.
Elliott. Law of insurance $4. Bowen-M.
Frost. Treatise on guaranty insurance. $5. Little, B. & Co.
Hoffman. Windstorm and tornado insurance. 25 c. Spectator.
Kerr. Law of insurance. $6. Keefe-D.

INSURANCE.—*Continued.*
New York. Statutory revision of laws affecting insurance companies. $1.50. Banks & Co.
See also Corporations.
INTELLECT.
See Knowledge.
INTEREST.
Fisher. Added interest tables.—20th century interest tables. ea., $2.50. J: I. Fisher.
Interior decorations and furnishings of London Guild Halls. '02(Mr29) 40 pls., f°, portfolio, net, $12; bound, pls. guarded, net, $15. Helburn.
INTERMEDIATE STATE.
See Future life.
Intermere. Taylor, W: A. $1. XX Century.
International annual of Anthony's photographic bulletin and Am. process yearbook. v. 14 for 1902; ed. by W. I. Scandlin. '01-'02(Mr1) il. O. $1.25; pap., 75 c. Anthony.
International education ser. *See* Appleton's.
INTERNATIONAL LAW.
Taylor. Treatise on internat. public law. net, $6.50. Callaghan.
International medical annual, 1902. '02 (Ap12) il. 8°, net, $3. Treat.
International theol. lib.; ed. by S. D. F. Salmond and C: A. Briggs. O. net, $2.50. Scribner.
—Rainy. Ancient Catholic church, A.D 98-451.
International year book, 1901. '02(My24) Q. $4. Dodd.
Interviews with a monocle. Jordon, L. 50 c. Whitaker & R.
INTESTINES.
Hemmeter. Diseases of the intestines. v. 2. net, $5; net, $6. Blakiston.
Into the light. Taylor, E: R. net, 75 c. Elder.
INVENTIONS.
See Patents.
INVERTEBRATES.
Pratt. Course in invertebrate zoölogy. $1.35. Ginn.
INVESTMENTS.
See Railroads.
Ione, *pseud.* *See* Brown, G. M.
Iowa. Encyclopedia of Iowa law; cont. legal words and phrases, with comments by E. C. Ebersole. '02(Mr8) O. shp., $6. E. C. Ebersole.
IRAN.
See Persia.
IRELAND.
Falkiner. Studies in Irish hist. and biog. mainly of 18th century. $5. Longmans.
Martin. Traces of the elder faiths of Ireland. 2 v. $12. Longmans.
O'Byrne. Kings and vikings.—Land of heroes: stories fr. Irish history. ea., $1.25. Scribner.
O'Conor, *comp.* Irish com-all-ye's. 25 c. —Old time songs and ballads of Ireland. $2. Popular.
See also Patrick, *St.*
IRISH.
See Scots.
Irish fairy and folk tales. Yeats, W: B. $1. Burt.
IRISH LANGUAGE.
O'Growney. Revised simple lessons in Irish. pt. 1. 15 c. Gael.
IRISH LITERATURE.
Stokes *and* Strachan, *eds.* Thesaurus palæohibernicus: coll. of old Irish glosses, scholia, etc. net, $8. Macmillan.
Irish wit and humor. '02(Mr15) S. pap., 25 c. Drake.
IRON.
Keep. Cast iron: record of orig. research. $2.50. Wiley.
West. Metallurgy of cast iron. $3. Cleveland Pr.
Iron Age directory. '02(My24) 16°, flex. linen, 25 c. D: Williams.
Iron hand. Dean, H. $1. Abbey Press.
IRRIGATION.
Newell. Irrigation in the U. S. net, $2. Crowell.
Wilcox. Irrigation farming. $2. Judd.
Irving, W. Selections from Sketch-book. Regents ed.; ed. by C. T. Benjamin. '02 (F1) D. 50 c. Am. Bk.
Irving, W. Sketch book. '02(Je21) 2 v., il. 16°, (Caxton ser.) net, $1.25. Scribner.
Irving, W. Two selections: Legend of Sleepy Hollow and Rip Van Winkle from Sketch book; notes, etc., by J. W. Graham. '02 (Je7) 12°, leatherette, 25 c. Whitaker & R.
Irwin, Wallace. ["Omar Khayyám, jr."] Love sonnets of a hoodlum. '01. '02(Mr22) 16°, pap., 25 c.; Bandana ed., 50 c. Elder.
Irwin, Wallace. Rubáiyat of Omar Khayyám, jr. '02(My24) il. O. pap., net, 50 c. Elder.
Is the negro a beast? Schell, W: G. 60 c. Gospel Trumpet.
ISABELLA, *Queen of Castile.*
See Ferdinand, *King of Spain.*
Isabella. Keats, J: $1; 60 c. Macmillan.
Isham, F: S. The strollers. '02(Mr22) il. D. $1.50. Bowen-M.
Islam and Christianity. '01. '02(Mr1) 12°, $1. Am. Tr.
Island cabin. Henry. A. $1.50. McClure, P.
Isler, C. Well boring for water, brine and oil. '02(Ap5) il. 8°, $4. Spon.
Isolation in the school. Young, E. F. net, 50 c. Univ. of Chic.
Isthmian canal. Johnson, E. R. 25 c. Am. Acad. Pol. Sci.
Isthmian canal question. Pasco, S: 25 c. Am. Acad. Pol. Sci.
ITALIAN LANGUAGE.
Manzoni. I promessi sposi. $1.20. Silver.
Italian Renaissance in England. Einstein, L. net, $1.50. Macmillan.
ITALY.
Cruickshank. Umbrian towns. net, $1.25. Wessels.
Friedländer. Town life in ancient Italy. 75 c. B: H. Sanborn.
Villari. Barbarian invasions of Italy. 2 v. net, $7.50. Scribner.
Whitcomb. Little journey to Italy. 15 c. Flanagan.
See also Florence;—Medici;—Rome;—Sicily;—Tuscany.
It's up to you. McHugh, H. 75 c. G: W. Dillingham.
Ivanhoe and Rob Roy, retold for children. Sullivan, *Sir* E: 50 c. Little, B. & Co.
IVORY.
Cust. Ivory workers of the Middle Ages. $2. Macmillan.
J., C. J. Otis Grey, bachelor. '02(Je7) S. 75 c. Mutual Bk.

Jackanapes. Ewing, *Mrs.* J. H. net, 15 c. Houghton, M. & Co.
Jackman, Warren. Hist. of the town of Elma, Erie Co., N. Y. '02(My24) O. $3. Hausauer.
Jackson, Dugald C., *and* Jackson, J: P. Elem. text-book on electricity and magnetism. '02 (F22) il. 12°, hf. leath., net, $1.40. Macmillan.
Jackson, J: P. *See* Jackson, D. C.
Jacob, J: T: Christ the indweller. '02 (My3) 12°. $1.50. Macmillan.
Jacobs, W: W. At Sunwich port. '02(My10) il. D. $1.50. Scribner
Jacobson, W. H. A., *and* Steward, F. J Operations of surgery. '02(My17) 2 v., il. 8°, net, $10; shp., or hf. mor. $12. Blakiston.
Jacoby, Harold. Practical talks by an astronomer. '02(Ap12) il. D. net, $1. Scribner.
Jacoby, H: D. *See* Merriman, M.
James, Alfr. Cyanide practice. '01- '02 (Ja25) il. 4°, $5. Engineering.
James, Bushrod W. Political freshman. '02 (Ap19) D. $1.50. Bushrod Lib.
James, *Mrs.* Flor. A. P., ["Florence Warden."] The lovely Mrs. Pemberton. '02 (F8) D. $1.25. Buckles.
James, G: W. In and around the Grand Canyon. Pasadena ed. '01. '02(F22) il. 8°, hf. mor., net, $10. Little, B. & Co.
James, W: Varieties of religious experience. '02(Je21) O. (Gifford lectures, 3d ser.) net, $3.20. Longmans.
James Griffin's adventures on land and sea. Dee, H. $1. Yewdale.
JAMESTOWN, Va.
Hall. Jamestown, 1607-1907. 25 c. A'n. Scenic.
Janes, Emily, *ed.* *See* Englishwoman's year book.
Janes, L. G. Lewis G. Janes, philosopher, patriot, lover of man. '02(Ap19) il. D. $1. J. H. West.
Janet, Pierre. Mental state of hystericals; tr. by C. R. Corson. '02(Mr1) 12°, $3.50. Putnam.
JAPAN.
Brinkley. Japan. 5 v. ea., $50. Millet.
Menpes. Japan. net, $6. Macmillan.
Stead. Japan of to-day. net, $2. Dutton.
Jastrow, Morris, *jr.* Study of religion. '01. '02(Ja11) 12°, (Contemporary science ser.) $1.50. Scribner.
Jean Mitchell's school. Wray, A. W. $1.25. Public Sch. Pub.
Jean Valjean. *See* Quayle, W: A.
Jebb, *Sir* R: C. Modern Greece: two lectures del. before the philosophical institution of Edinburgh. 2d ed. '02(F1) 12°, (Eversley ser.) $1.75. Macmillan.
JEFFERSON, Thos.
See Burr, A.
Jegi, J: I. Syllabus of human physiology for schools and colleges. '01- '02(Mr8) il. 12°, $1. Gillan.
Jekyll, Gertrude, *comp.* Lilies for English gardens. '01- '02(Ja11) 8°, (Country life lib.) net, $3.75. Scribner.
Jellison, Edn. A: The wounded beast: [poem.] '01- '02(Mr29) D. pap., 25 c. E. A: Jellison.

Jenkins' contes choisis. sq. S. 40 c.; pap., 25 c. W: R. Jenkins.
—Coppée. Morceau de pain. (22.)
Jenkinson, I: Aaron Burr, his rel. with Thomas Jefferson and Alex. Hamilton. '02 (My3) D. $1.25. I: Jenkinson.
Jenks, E: Edward Plantagenet, (Edward I.): the Eng. Justinian. '02(Mr8) D. (Heroes of the nations ser., no. 35.) net, $1.35; hf. leath., net, $1.60. Putnam.
Jennings, J: E. Manual of ophthalmoscopy. '02(Mr1) il. 8°, net, $1.50. Blakiston.
Jesse, J: H. Historical memoirs. First ser. (15 v.) and second ser. (15 v.) '02(Ap5) 30 v., 8°, per v., $2.50; complete set of 15 v., (first or second ser.) $37.40; ¾ mor., $75. L. C. Page.
Jessup, Alex., *ed.* *See* Balzac, H. de.
Jesuit relations. (Thwaites.) In 73 v. v. 72, 73. Index to entire ser. '01- '02(Mr1) 8°, ea., net, $3.50. Burrows.
JESUITS.
See **Jesus (Society of).**
JESUS CHRIST.
Boardman. Our risen King's forty days. net, $1.25. Lippincott.
Burton *and* Mathews. Constructive studies in the life of Christ. $1. Univ. of Chic.
Hutchinson. Gospel story of Jesus Christ. $1.50. Dutton.
Jacob. Christ the indweller. $1.50. Macmillan.
Life and works of the Redeemer. net, $2. Dutton
McClelland. Verba crucis. 50 c. Crowell.
Moberly. Christ our life. net, $3. Longmans.
Nicoll. Church's one foundation, Christ. $1.25. Armstrong.
Pearson. Carpenter prophet. $1.50. H. S. Stone.
Rutherford. Christ and his cross. $1. Longmans.
Speer. Principles of Jesus app. to some questions of to-day. net, 80 c. Revell.
Stretton. New child's life of Christ. $1. Winston.
Taylor, *and others.* Studies in the life of Christ. 75 c. Jennings.
Vincent. What is it to believe on the Lord Jesus Christ? 5 c. Beam.
Wollpert. A man amongst men. 15 c. Eckler.
See also Bible; — Christianity; — Easter; — Lord's supper.
JESUS (Society of).
Jesuit relations v. 72, 73. ea., $3.50. Burrows.
Taunton. Hist of the Jesuits in England, 1580-1773. net, $3.75. Lippincott.
Jewett, C: Essentials of obstetrics. 2d ed. '01. '02(Ja25) 12° net, $2.25. Lea.
Jewett, C: Manual of childbed nursing. 5th ed., rev. and enl. '02(Ap5) D. 80 c. Treat.
Jewett, C:, *ed.* Practice of obstetrics, by Am. authors. 2d ed. '01- '02(Ja25) il. 8°, net, $5; shp., net, $6; hf. mor., net, $6.50. Lea.
Jewish carol. Calvin, E. R. 75 c. Westminster.
Jewish Pub. Soc. special ser. D. 30 c. Jewish Pub.
—Ruskay. Hearth and home essays. (6.)
JEWS.
Duff. Theology and ethics of the Hebrews. net, $1.25. Scribner.

JEWS.—*Continued.*
Greenstone. Religion of Israel. 50 c. Bloch.
Philipson. The Jew in Eng. fiction. net, $1. Clarke.
Peters. The Jew as a patriot. $1. Baker & T.
Robertson. Early religion of Israel. net, $1.60. Whittaker.
See also Semitic peoples.

Job, Herb. K. Among the waterfowl. '02 (Je7) il. sq. O. net, $1.35. Doubleday, P.

John Kenadie. Saunders, R. D. $1.50. Houghton, M. & Co.

Johns Hopkins Univ. studies. O. Johns Hopkins.
—Ballagh. Hist. of slavery in Va. $1.50. (extra v. 24.)

Johns Hopkins Univ. studies in hist. and pol. science. O. pap. Johns Hopkins.
—Barnett. State banking in U. S. 50 c. (ser. 20, 2, 3.)
—Radcliffe. Gov. Thomas H. Hicks of Md., and the civil war. 50 c. (ser. 19, 11, 12.)
—Steiner. Western Maryland in the Revolution. 30 c. (ser. 20, 1.)
—Vincent, *and others.* H. B. Adams; with bibliog. of the dept. of history, etc. (ser. 20, extra no.) free to subs.

JOHNSON, And.
Jones. Life of Andrew Johnson. $1.50. East Tenn.

Johnson, Emory R. Isthmian canal. '02 (Mr22) 8°, (Pub. of the soc., no. 323.) pap., 25 c. Am. Acad. Pol. Sci.

Johnson, J. B. Theory and practice of surveying. 16th ed., rev. and enl. '02(Ap5) il. 8°, $4. Wiley.

Johnson, R: B. Popular Eng. ballads. '01. '02(F15) 4 v., il. 12°, $3. Lippincott.

Johnson, Rob. U. Poems. '02(My24) D. net, $1.20. Century Co.

Johnson, S: Essays from The Rambler and The Idler. '01. '02(Ap5) S. (Little masterpieces.) 50 c. Doubleday, P.

Johnson, S: History of Rasselas, Prince of Abyssinia. '02(My10) 12°, (Home lib.) $1. Burt.

Johnson, Willis G. Fumigation methods. '02(Mr22) il. D. $1. Judd.

Johnson ser. of Eng. classics. 16°, 30 c.; 25 c. B. F. Johnson.
—Coleridge. Ancient mariner.

Johnston, Annie F. Asa Holmes. '02 (My17) S. $1. L. C. Page.

Johnston, J: W. Riddle of life. '02(F22) D. $1.50. Jennings.

Johnston, Ma. Audrey. '02(Mr1) il. D. $1.50. Houghton, M. & Co.

Joline, Adrian H. Meditations of an autograph collector. '02(My10) il. O. net, $3. Harper.

Jones, Harry C. Elements of physical chemistry. '02(F22) 8°, net, $4. Macmillan.

Jones Harry W. A chaplain's experience ashore and afloat; the *Texas* under fire. '01. '02(Ap12) 12°, $1.25. Sherwood.

Jones, Ja. S. Life of Andrew Johnson, seventeenth president of the U. S. '01. '02 (F8) il. 12°, $1.50. East Tenn.

JONES, J: Paul.
Brown. John Paul Jones. $1. Donohue.

Jones, Morgan P. Chiefs of Cambria. '02 (My3) il. D. $1.25. Abbey Press.

Jones, W: C. Illustrated hist. of the Univ. of California, 1868-1901. Rev. ed. '01. '02 (My24) il. F. $5. Berkeley.

Jordan, D: S., *comp.* True tales of birds and beasts. '02(Je14) il. D. (Home and school classics, young readers' ser.) 40 c. Heath.

Jordan, D: S., *and* Evermann, B. W. American food and game fishes. '02(Je14) Q. net, $4. Doubleday, P.

Jordan, D: S., *and* Heath, H. Animal forms: second book of zoology. '02(Je7) il. D. (Twentieth century text-books.) net, $1.10. Appleton.

Jordan, Eliz. G. Tales of destiny. '02(Je28) il. D. $1.50. Harper.

Jordan, Maggie O. Ways of the world. '02 (Ap26) 12°, $1.50. Neely.

Jordan, W: G: Kingship of self-control. '02 (F8) 12°, bds., 50 c. Revell.

Jordan, W: G: Majesty of calmness. '02 (F8) 12°, bds., 50 c. Revell.

Jordans, Jos. Danger of youth and a tried antidote; fr. the Germ. '02(Je28) 16°, 15 c. Herder.

Jordon, Leopold. Interviews with a monocle. '02(Ap12) 12°, pap., 50 c. Whitaker & R.

José. Valdés, A. P. $1.25. Brentano's.

JOSEPH.
Miller. Story of Joseph. net, 35 c. Revell.

Josephine Grahame. Wheeler, J. $1.50. Abbey Press.

Josh Billings' old farmers' allminax. Shaw, H: W. $1.50. G: W. Dillingham.

Josiah Allen's wife, *pseud.* *See* Holley, M.

Josselyn, C: True Napoleon. '02(Je7) O. net, $3.50. Russell.

Journal of a live woman. Van Anderson, H. $1. Alliance.

Journal to Stella. Swift, J. $1.75. Putnam.

Joy in service. Purves, G: T. 50 c. Am. Tr.

Joyce's investments. Newberry, F. E. $1. Burt.

Joyful praise. Gabriel, C: H. 30 c. Jennings.

Judah's lion. Tonna, *Mrs.* C. E. $1. Dodd.

Judd, D: H. That old kitchen stove: [poem.] '01. '02(Ap5) il. D. 50 c. Abbey Press.

Judith's garden. Bassett, M. E. S. $1.50. Lothrop.

Judson, Harry P., *and* Bender, Ida C., *eds.* Graded literature readers. bks. 6-8. '01. '02(Mr1) il. 12°, ea., 50 c. Maynard, M. & Co.

Julius Cæsar. *See* Shakespeare, W:

Jungfrau von Orleans. Schiller, J. C. F. v. net, 60 c. Holt.

JUSTICES OF THE PEACE.
Brand. Justices' code for Wash. $5. Bancroft-W.
Minnesota. Justice's manual. $1.50. Booth.

Justinianus, *Emperor.* Pandects of Justinian; tr. into Eng. by W: Maude. In 4 v., v. 1. '02(Je7) 8°, $5. Cambridge.

Kaercher, F. O., *comp.* Summary of indulgences, privileges and favors granted to the secular branch of the Third order of St. Francis. '02(Je14) 24°, pap., 15 c. Herder.

Kaler, J. O., ["James Otis."] Story of Pemaquid. '02(Mr8) il. D. (Pioneer towns of America, v. 2.) 50 c. Crowell.

Kaler, J. O. Wan Lun and Dandy. '02 (Je28) il. 12°, (St. Nicholas ser.) 75 c. Burt.

Kann, Jerome H., *ed.* *See* California. Code time table.

Kansas. *State board of educ.* County examination questions; with answers. No. 9. '02(Mr22) D. pap., 35 c. J. Macdonald.

Kansas. Statutes concerning domestic and foreign corporations for profit, and mutual and fraternal insurance companies; by G. C. Clemens. '02(Je28) O. pap., $1; hf. shp., $1.25. Crane.

Kant, Immanuel. Prolegomena to any future metaphysics; ed. in Eng., by P. Carus. '02 (Je28) 12°, net, 75 c.; *Same.* (Mr8) (Religion of sci. lib., no. 53.) pap., 50 c. Open Court.

KANT, Immanuel.
Paulsen. Immanuel Kant, his life and doctrine. net, $2.50. Scribner.

Kate Bonnet. Stockton, F. R: $1.50. Appleton.

Keane, A: H: South America. New rev. ed. '01. '02(F15) il. 8°, (Stanford's compendium of geog. and travel.) $4.50. Lippincott.

Keats, J: Isabella and the Eve of St. Agnes. '02(Ap12) il. 16°, 60 c.; leath., $1. Macmillan.

Keats, J: Odes. '02(Ap12) il. 16°, 60 c.; leath., $1. Macmillan.

Keay, J. H. Medical treatment of gall stones. '02(My17) 12°, net, $1.25. Blakiston.

Keedy, E: E. Naturalness of Christian life. '02(My3) il. D. 50 c. Abbey Press.

Keen, Ja. T. *See* Young, O. D.

Keep, W: J. Cast iron. '02(Ja18) il. 8°, $2.50. Wiley.

Keese, W: L. Siamese twins and other poems. '02(Je21) 12°, net, $1.25. E. W. Dayton.

Keith, Arth. Human embryology and morphology. '02(Mr8) O. $4.50. Longmans

Keith, Hannah E. Hist. sketch of internal improvements in Michigan, 1836-46. '02 (F15) 16°, pap., 50 c. Mich. Pol. Sci.

Keller, Alb. G. Homeric society: sociolog. study of the Iliad and Odyssey. '02(F8) D. $1.20. Longmans.

Keller, G. Legenden; ed. by M. Müller and C. Wenckebach. '02(Ap5) S. net, 35 c. Holt.

Kellogg, Amos M. Crowning of flora. '01. '02(Ja25) 12°, pap., 15 c. Kellogg.

Kellogg, Amos. M. Elements of algebra. '01. '02(Ja25) 12°, 25 c. Kellogg.

Kellogg, Amos M. Elements of civil government. '01. '02(Ja25) 12°, 25 c. Kellogg.

Kellogg, Amos M. Farmer's school and the visit. '01. '02(Ja25) 12°, pap., 15 c. Kellogg.

Kellogg, Amos M. Home coming of autumn queen. '01. '02(Ja25) 12°, pap., 15 c. Kellogg.

Kellogg, Amos M. How to teach composition writing. '01. '02(Ja25) 12°, 25 c. Kellogg.

Kellogg, Amos M. Our Lysander. '01. '02 (Ja25) 12°, pap., 15 c. Kellogg.

Kellogg, Amos M. Six musical entertainments. '01. '02(Ja25) 12°, pap., 15 c. Kellogg.

Kellogg, Amos M. Uncle Sam's examination. '01· '02(Ja25) 12°, pap., 15 c. Kellogg.

Kellogg, J. H. Rational hydrotherapy. '01· '02(Mr8) il. 8°, subs., $5; hf. rus., $6. Davis.

Kellor, Fes. A. Experimental sociology. '02 (F1) 8°, net, $2. Macmillan.

Kelsey, C: B. Surgery of the rectum. 6th ed. '02(Ap26) il. 8°, $3. Wood.

Kelsey, W. R. Physical determinations. '01· '02(Ja11) D. $1.50. Longmans.

Keltie, J: S., *ed.* *See* Statesmen's year-book.

Kemp, Ellwood L. Hist. of education. '02 (F1) 12°, (Educ. ser., v. 3.) net, $1.25. Lippincott.

Kendall, Ezra F. Good gravy: wit and humor. '01.' '02(Ja18) 12°, pap., 25 c. Helman-T.

Kenilworth. Scott, *Sir* W. net, 60 c. Macmillan.

Kennelly, Arth. E. *See* Houston, E. J.

Kensington, Cathmer. Glenwood. '02(Ap26) D. $1.25. Abbey Press.

Kentons (The). Howells, W: D. $1.50. Harper.

Kenyon, Orr. Amor victor. '02(Je7) il. D. $1.50. Stokes.

Kern, J: A. Way of the preacher. '02 (Mr22) D. $1.25. Pub. Ho. M. E. Ch., So.

Kern, Marg. Tale of a cat as told by herself. '02(My3) il. D. 50 c. Abbey Press.

Kerr, E. W. Power and power transmission. '02(Ja11) il. 8°, $2. Wiley.

Kerr, W: A. Law of insurance. '02(Ap19) O. shp., $6. Keefe-D.

Ketler, I: C. The tragedy of Paotingfu: authentic story of the missionaries who suffered martyrdom June 30 and July 1, 1900. '02(Je28) il. 8°, net, $2. Revell.

Kidd, B: Principles of western civilization. '02(F22) D. net, $2. Macmillan.

Kidder, Fk. E. Building construction and superintendence. pt. 2. 4th ed. '02(Je28) il. 8°, shp., $4. W: T. Comstock.

Kilbourne, E: W. Memory and its cultivation. '01· '02(Mr29) D. $1; leatherette, 50 c. Mullin.

Kilpatrick, Van Evrie. Language system of penmanship. In 9 nos. nos. 1-8. '02 (Ap5) il. sq. O. pap., per doz., 66 c. Globe Sch. Bk.

Kimber, Diana C., *comp.* Text-book of anatomy and physiology for nurses. New rev. ed. '02(Mr22) il. 8°, net, $2.50. Macmillan.

Kinard, Ja. P., *ed.* Old English ballads. '02 (Ap26) 12°, (Ser. of classics.) 40 c. Silver.

Kinder, Stephen. The sabertooth. '02(Ap12) il. D. 75 c.: pap., 25 c. Laird.

KINDERGARTEN.
Maxwell. Card sewing: for kindergartens. 50 c. M. Bradley.

Kindred of the wild. Roberts, C: G: D. $2. L. C. Page.

King, C: Way of the West. '02(Je7) il. S. 50 c. Rand, McN. & Co.

King, H. E. H. Hours of the passion. '02 (Ap5) 12°, net, $1.50. Dutton.

King, Maude E. Bread and wine. '02(My17) D. $1.25. Houghton, M. & Co.

King, T: A. Pearls from the Wonderbook. '01· '02(Ap12) 16°, 40 c. Swedenborg.

King, W. W., *comp.* *See* Texas. Conflicting civil cases;—Repts.
King for a summer. Pickering, E. net, $1. Lee & S.
King Henry VI. *See* Shakespeare, W:
King in yellow. Chalmers, R. W: $1.50. Harper.
King Lear. Shakespeare, W: $1.25. Bowen-M.
King of Andorra. Harris, H: E. $1.25. Abbey Press.
King of Claddagh. Fitzpatrick, T: net, $1.25. Herder.
King Richard III. Shakespeare, W: 15 c. Kellogg.
Kingdom of coins. Gilman, B. 50 c. Little, B. & Co.
KINGLAKE, Alex. W:
Tuckwell. A. W. Kinglake. $1.75. Macmillan.
King's gallant. Dumas, A. $1. Street.
King's weigh-house. Avebury, *Lord.* 75 c. Macmillan.
Kings and vikings. O'Byrne, W. L. $1.25. Scribner.
Kingsford, C: L. Henry V. the typical mediæval hero. '01. '02(Ja25) D. (Heroes of the nations ser., no. 34.) net, $1.35; hf. leath., net, $1.60. Putnam.
Kingship of self-control. Jordan, W: G: 50 c. Revell.
Kingsley, C: Life and works. Ed. de luxe. v. 4. '02(F15); v. 5 (Mr8); v. 6 (Ap26); v. 7 (My17); v. 8 (My24); v. 9 (Je28) 8°, net, ea., $3. Macmillan.
Kingsley, C: Alton Locke. '02(My17) 12°, (Home lib.) $1. Burt.
Kingsley, C: Hereward the Wake. '02 (My17) 12°, (Home lib.) $1. Burt.
Kingsley, C: Westward ho! '02(Je28) 2 v., 16°, (Temple classics.) ea., 50 c.; flex. leath., ea., 75 c. Macmillan.
Kingsley, *Mrs.* Flo. M. Prisoners of the sea. '02(Ap26) 12°, (Red letter ser.) $1.25; pap., 50 c. New Amsterdam.
Kinship of God and man. Lanier, J. J. $1. Whittaker.
Kinzie, *Mrs.* Juliette A. M. K. Wau-Bun, the "early day" of the Northwest. New ed., notes and index, by R. G. Thwaites. '01. '02(My3) il. O. ed. lim. to members. Caxton Club.
Kinzie, *Mrs.* Juliette A. M. K. Wau-Bun. New ed., introd. and note by E. K. Gordon. '01. '02(My3) il. D. $1.25. Rand, McN. & Co.
KIPLING, Rudyard.
Livingston. Works of Kipling: des. of first eds. net, $12; net, $20. Dodd.
Kirk, Eleanor, *pseud.* *See* Ames, *Mrs.* E. M. E.
Kirk, *Mrs.* Ellen O., ["Henry Hayes."] A remedy for love. '02(Je7) D. $1.25. Houghton, M. & Co.
Kirkman, M. M. Air brake: supp. to Science of railways. '02(Ap26) il. 8°, $2.50. World R'way.
Kirkpatrick, W: J. *See* Gill, J.
Kitchen gardening. Bridgeman, T: 50 c. Coates.
Kleckner, Emma R. In the misty realm of fable. 2d ed. '02(F15) il. 12°, $1. Flanagan.
Knapp, M. A. Government ownership of railroads. '02(Mr22) 8°, (Pub. of the soc., no. 326.) pap., 15 c. Am. Acad. Pol. Sci.
Knecht, F. J. Child's Bible history; tr. from the Germ. 8th Am. ed. '02(Mr8) il. 12°, 25 c. Herder.
Knight, E: F: With the royal tour: recent tour of the Duke and Duchess of Cornwall and York through Greater Britain. '02 (Mr8) il. D. $2. Longmans.
Knightes tale. *See* Chaucer, G.
Knights (The). Aristophanes. net, $2.50. Macmillan.
KNOWLEDGE.
Pierce. Studies in auditory and visual space perception. net, $2. Longmans.
Kohaus, Hannah M. Fruit from the tree of life. '02(Mr22) 16°, pap., 30 c. Alliance.
Kohaus, Hannah M. Remedies of the Great Physician. '02(Mr22) 32°, pap., 40 c. Alliance.
Kohaus, Hannah M. Soul fragrance. New issue. '02(Mr22) 16°, pap., 50 c. Alliance.
Komensky, J: A. Labyrinth of the world and the paradise of the heart. '02(Mr8) 12°, $1.50. Dutton.
Körner, Karl T. Zriny ein trauerspiel in fünf aufzügen; notes by F. Holzwarth. '02 (F1) S. (Modern lang. ser.) 35 c. Heath.
Kovalevsky, M. Russian political institutions. '02(F15) O. net, $1.50. Univ. of Chic.
Krag and Johnny Bear. Thompson, E. E. S. 60 c. Scribner.
Kropotkin, *Prince* P: A. Fields, factories and workshops. New popular ed. '01. '02 (F22) il. D. net, 90 c. Putnam.
Krüger, Gustav, *and* Smith, C. A. English-Germ. conversation book. '02(Je21) D. (Modern lang. ser.) 25 c. Heath.
Kuder, Emil. Medical prescription book for everybody. '01. '02(Ap26) $2. Journal Pr.
Kupfer, Lillian. Greek foreshadowings of modern metaphysical and epistemological thought. '01. '02(F15) 8°, $1. Cushing.
Kyger, J: C: F., *ed.* Hand-book for soul-winners. '02(My24) S. 50 c. Kyger.
Labor and capital: discussion of rel. of employer and employed; ed. by J: J. Peters. '02(My10) D. (Questions of the day, no. 98.) $1.50. Putnam.
LABOR AND LABORING CLASSES.
See Capital and labor;—Political economy;—Slavery;—Social science;—Woman.
La Brète, Jean de. Mon oncle et mon curé; ed. by E. M. White. '02(My3) D. 50 c. Am. Bk.
Labyrinth of the world and the paradise of the heart. Komensky, J: A. $1.50. Dutton.
LACE.
Palliser. Hist. of lace. net, $12. Scribner.
Lachmi Bai Rani of Jhansi. White, M. $1.50. J. F. Taylor.
Ladd, G: T. Philosophy of conduct. '02 (F22) 12°, net, $3.50. Scribner.
Lady of New Orleans. Thornton, M. E. $1.50. Abbey Press.
Lady paramount. Harland, H: $1.50. Lane.
Lady (The) Poverty: a XIIIth century allegory (Sacrum commercium Beati Francisci cum Domina Paupertate, A.D. 1227;) tr. and ed. by M. Carmichael. '02(Ap12) 6¼ x 4½ in., net, $1.75. Tennant.

Lafarque, Paul. Religion of capital. [also] Social effect of machinery by F. W. Cotton. '02(My17) O. (Socialist lib., v. 2, no. 2.) pap., 10 c. Socialistic Co-op.

Lafitte of Louisiana. Devereux, M. $1.50. Little, B. & Co.

Laird & Lee's diary and time saver, 1902. '02(Ja4) nar. T. leath., 25 c. Laird.

Lake, W: C: Memorials of William Charles Lake, Dean of Durham, 1869-1894. '01. '02(F8) O. $5.50. Longmans.

Lake French classics; ed. by E. P. Baillot. S. 50 c. Scott, F. & Co.

—Baillot *and* Brugnot. French prose composition.

—Moliere. Le misanthrope and L'avare.

—Voltaire. Zaïre and Epitres.

Lake history stories. S. il. Scott, F. & Co.

—Harding, C. H. *and* S: B. City of the seven hills.

Lalor's Maples. Conway, K. E. $1.25. Pilot.

Lamb, C: *and* Ma. Tales from Shakespeare. '01. '02(Mr1) il. D. (Home and school classics; young readers' ser.) 40 c. Heath.

Lamb, M. T. The Mormons and their Bible. '01. '02(F1) O. net, 25 c. Am. Bapt.

La Motte Fouque, F. H. K., *Freiherr* de. Undine. [also] Aslauga's knight. '01. '02 (Ja11) il. 16°, (Caxton ser.) flex. lambskin, net, $1.20. Scribner.

La Motte Fouqué. F. H. K., *Freiherr de.* Undine. '02(My17) il. D. (Home and school classics; young reader's ser.) 30 c. Heath.

LANCASTER, Pa.

Law. Lancaster—old and new. n. p. J. D. Law.

Land of heroes. O'Byrne, W. L. $1.25. Scribner.

Land of Nome. McKee, L. net, $1.25. Grafton Press.

Lane, Michael A. Level of social motion. '02(Mr29) 12°, net, $2. Macmillan.

Lang, Ossian H., *ed.* Educational creeds of the 19th century. '01. '02(Ja25) 12°, 75 c. Kellogg.

Langbein, G: Electro-deposition of metals; fr. the Germ.; add. by W: T. Brannt. 4th rev. enl. ed. '02(F15) il. 8°, $4. Baird.

Lange, L: Twentieth century system; key to the Germ. language. '02(Ap26) D. pap., 50 c. [San F. News] Pamphlet.

Lange, L: Twentieth century system Spanish course. '02(Ap26) D. pap., 25 c. [San F. News] Pamphlet.

LANGUAGE.

Fowler. Negatives of the Indo-European languages. net, 50 c. Univ. of Chic.

Oertel. Lectures on study of language. net, $3. Scribner.

See also Rhetoric;—*also* names of languages.

Lanier, J. J. Kinship of God and man. In 2 v. v. 1, Good and evil. '02(F8) D. $1. Whittaker.

La Ramé, Louise de, ["Ouida."] Dog of Flanders and The Nürnberg stove. '02 (Mr22) S. (Riverside lit. ser., no. 150.) pap., 15 c. Houghton, M. & Co.

Larned, J. N., *ed.* Literature of Amer. history: bibliog. guide. '02(Je21) O. net, $6; shp., $7.50; hf. mor., $9. Houghton, M. & Co.

Lasance, F. X. Little manual of St. Anthony of Padua. '02(Ap5) Tt. pap., 25 c. Benziger.

Lasance, F. X., *comp.* Short visits to the blessed sacrament. '01. '02(Ja18) Tt. 25 c. Benziger.

Last century maid. Wharton, A. H. $1.25. Lippincott.

Last fight of the 'Revenge" at sea. Raleigh, *Sir* W. net, $6. Houghton, M. & Co.

Late returning. Williams, M. $1.25. Macmillan.

Later infancy of the child. Compayré, G. pt. 2. net, $1.20. Appleton.

Lathbury, B. B., *and* Spackman, —. Am. engineering practice in the construction of rotary Portland cement plants. '02(My24) il. obl. O. $2. G. M. S. Armstrong.

Latimer, *Mrs.* Eliz. W. Prince Incognito. '02 (Ap12) D. $1.50. McClurg.

LATIN LANGUAGE.

Alford, *comp.* Latin passages for translation. net, 80 c. Macmillan.

Appleton's Latin dictionary. $1.50. Appleton.

Mellick. Latin composition. 40 c. Am. Bk.

Morris. On principles and methods in Latin syntax. net, $2. Scribner.

Ogilvie. Horæ Latinæ. $5. Longmans.

Reynolds. Rudiments of Latin. $1.25. A. B. Reynolds.

Smith, W: W. Course in first year Latin for Regents' examinations. $1. W: R. Jenkins.

West. Latin grammar. net, 90 c. Appleton.

LATTER-DAY SAINTS.

See Mormonism.

Laughlin, Ja. L. Elements of political economy. Rev. ed. '02(Mr22) D. $1.20. Am. Bk.

Laurel classics. 16°, 40 c. Birchard.

—Shakespeare. Merchant of Venice.

Laurie, H: Scottish philosophy in its national development. '02(My24) 12°, net, $1.75. Macmillan

Laurie, Simon S. Training of teachers and methods of instruction. '01. '02(Ja4) 12°, (Cambridge Univ. Press ser.) net, $1.50. Macmillan.

Laut, Agnes C. Heralds of empire. '02 (My10) D. $1.50. Appleton.

Law, Ja. D. Lancaster—old and new. Rev., enl. ed. '02(Ap26) 8°, pap., n. p. J. D. Law.

LAW.

American and Eng. encyclopædia of law. v. 20. ea., $7.50. E: Thompson.

American digest. v. 29. subs., ea., $6. West Pub.

American state repts. v. 82, 83. ea., $4. Bancroft-W.

Ash. Table of federal citations. 4 v. v. 1, 2. complete work, $30. Remick.

Bingham, *comp.* 200 bar examination questions. $1. Commercial.

Britton: Eng. tr. and notes. $3. Byrne.

English law rpts. 6 v. $28.50. Little, B. & Co.

General digest. v. 12. $6. Lawyers' Co-op.

Hawkins. Legal counselor and form book. subs., $3; $4. W. W. Wilson.

Lawyers' repts. annot. bks. 53, 54. ea., $5. Lawyers' Co-op.

LAW.—*Continued.*
McCall. Clerk's assistant; cont. legal forms and instruments. $6. Banks.
Mack *and* Nash, *eds.* Cyclopedia of law and procedure. v. 3. $6. Am. Law Bk.
Martindale. Am. law directory, 1902. 2 pts. net, $10. Martindale.
Pollock. Revised repts. v. 46-51. ea., net, $6. Little, B. & Co.
Russell *and* Winslow. Syllabus—digest of decisions of the sup. ct. v. 3. $6.50. Banks.
Seebohm. Tribal custom in Anglo-Saxon law. net, $5. Longmans.
Two centuries' growth of Am. law, 1701-1901. net, $4. Scribner.
Warvelle. Essays in legal ethics. $2.50. Callaghan.
See also Actions at law;—Attachment;—Commercial law; — Contracts; — Conveyancing; — Corporations; — Damages;—Equity;—Evidence; —Insurance;—International law;—Justices of the peace;—Lawyers;—Mines and mining;—Negligence; — Negotiable instruments; — Orphans;—Parliamentary law;—Patents;—Pleading and practice;—Prostitution;—Real property;—Saloons;—Star chamber:—Wills.

Law of growth. Brooks, P. net, $1.20. Dutton.
Lawler, Ja. J. Modern plumbing, steam and hot water heating. New ed. '02(F22) 12°, $5. Popular.
Lawrence, F. M. Practical medicine. '02 (Ap5) il. 8°, $3. Boericke & T.
Laws of radiation and absorption. Brace, D. B. $1. Am. Bk.
Lawson, And. C. Eparchæan interval. '02 (Je14) O. (Univ. of Cal. bull. of dept. of geology, v. 3, no. 3.) pap., 10 c. Univ. of Cal.
Lawson, And. C., *and* Palache, C: Berkeley Hills: coast range geology. '02(Ap5) il. O. (Univ. of Cal., bull. of the dept. of geology, v. 2, no. 12.) pap., 80 c. Univ. of Chic.
Lawson, J: D. Making of a contract. '01-'02(F8) O. pap., 25 c. Stephens.
Lawton, W: H: The singing voice and its practical cultivation. '01-'02(Mr15) il. 8°, $1.50. W: H: Lawton.

LAWYERS.
Gould. Greater New York and state lawyers' diary, 1902. $1. W. R. Gould.
Martindale. Am. law directory. net, $10. Martindale.
Perry. Legal adviser and business guide. $1.50. Pontiac.
Sharp & Alleman Co.'s lawyers' and bankers' directory, 1902. Jan. ed. $5. Sharp & A.

Lawyers' reports annot.; bks. 53, 54. '02 (Je28) O. shp., ea., $5. Lawyers' Co-op.
Laycock, W. F. *See* Rawson, C.
Leach, J. G. History of the Bringhurst family; with notes on the Clarkson, De Peyster and Boude families. '01-'02(Mr8) il. 4°, $5. Lippincott.

LEAD.
Fairie. Notes on lead ore. net, $1. Van Nostrand.

League of Am. Mothers. *See* Proudfoot, A. H.
Lean, Bevan. *See* Perkin, W: H:, *jr.*
Leaves from a life-book of to-day. Mills, J. D. 50 c. Swedenborg.
Leavitt, Rob. G. Outlines of botany. '01-'02(Ja4) O. $1. Am. Bk.
Leavitt, Rob. G. Outlines of botany. [also] Field, forest and garden botany. by A. Gray; rev. and enl. by L. H. Bailey. '01-'02(Ja4) il. O. $1.80. Am. Bk.

LE BLOND, Michel.
Van der Kellen. Works of Michel Le Blond: reprod. and accompanied by biog. notice, [etc.] net, $30; net, $35. Dodd.

Lee, Jennette. Son of a fiddler. '02(Ap5) D. $1.50. Houghton, M. & Co.
Lee, J: L. Message of to-morrow. '02(F8) 12°, net, $1.20. Revell.

LEE, Rob. E.
Adams. Lee at Appomattox. net, $1.50. Houghton, M. & Co.

Left-overs made palatable. Curtis, I. G. $1. Judd.
Legal classic ser. 12°. Byrne.
—Britton. $3.
Legal counselor and form book. Hawkins, C: A. subs., $3; $4. W. W. Wilson.
Legend of Sleepy Hollow. *See* Irving, W.
Legenden. Keller, G. net, 35 c. Holt.

LEGENDS.
Zitkala-sa. Old Indian legends. 50 c. Ginn.
See also Fairy tales;—Folk-lore.

Legler, H: E. James Gates Percival; sketch and bibliog. '01-'02(Mr22) S. bds., net, $1. Mequon Club.
Leibnitz, G. W. v. Discourses on metaphysics; Correspondence with Arnauld and Monodology. '02(Je28) 12°, net, 75 c.; *Same* (F22) D. (Religion of sci. lib., no. 52.) pap., 35 c. Open Court.
Leigh, Lennard, *and* Bergholt, Ernest. Principles and practice of whist. '02(Ap5) il. O. net, $1.50. Coates.
Leighton, Jos. A. Typical modern conceptions of God. '01-'02(F8) D. net, $1.10. Longmans.
Lemcke, E. E: Creation, re-creation: [poems.] '01-'02(F8) 16°, n. p. Privately pr.
Lennox. *Lady* Sa. Life and letters, 1745-1826: ed. by the Countess of Ilchester and Lord Stavordale. '01-'02(Ja11) 2 v., il. 8°, net, $9; *Same.* [1 v. ed.] '02(Je7) O. net, $4. Scribner.

LENOX, Mass.
Mallary. Lenox and the Berkshire Highlands. net, $1.75. Putnam.

LENT.
Galt, *comp.* Lent, the holy season. $1. Neale.

Leopard's spots. Dixon, T:, *jr.* $1.50. Doubleday, P.
Lepidus the centurion. Arnold, E. L. $1.50. Crowell.
Le Queux, W: Sign of the seven sins. '02 (Je28) D. (Select novels.) $1; pap., 50 c. Lippincott.
Le Row, Caro. B. Duxberry doings. '02 (Je14) 12°, (Fireside ser.) $1. Burt.
Leroy, W: A silken snare. '02(My3) D. 50 c. Abbey Press.
Le Sage, A. R. Adventures of Gil Blas of Santillane. New ed. '02(Ap19) 12°, (Home lib.) $1. Burt.
Lesley, Susan, *ed.* *See* Tiffany, N. M., *ed.*
Lespinasse, Julie J. E. de. Letters; with notes upon her life and character, and introd. by C. A. Sainte-Beuve. '02(F1) il. 8°, (Versailles hist. ser.) subs., per v., $6; ¾ leath., per v., $9. Hardy, P. & Co.

Lessing, G. E. Minna von Barnhelm; notes by S. Primer. Rev. ed. '02(F1) D. (Modern lang. ser.) 75 c. Heath.
Lessons from Gr. pottery. Huddilston, J: H. net, $1.25. Macmillan.
Lessons in English. il. D. 50 c. Silver.
—Skinner *and* Burgert. Lessons in Eng. based upon principles of literary interpretation.
Lethaby, W. R., *ed.* *See* Artistic crafts.
LETTER-WRITING.
Hickox. Correspondent's manual. $1.50. Lee & S.
North. Love letters and how to write them. 25 c.; 50 c. Donohue; Drake.
LETTERING.
Faust. Automatic pen lettering and designs. $1; alphabet pt., 75 c. Auto Pen.
LETTERS.
Berry, *ed.* Letters of the Rm. 2 coll. in the British Museum. net, 50 c. Univ. of Chic.
Glover. Life and letters in the 4th century. net, $3.25. Macmillan.
Letters of Mildred's mother to Mildred. Price, E. D. $1. Ogilvie.
Letters to an enthusiast. Clarke, *Mrs.* M. C. net, $2.50. McClurg.
Level of social motion. Lane, M. A. net, $2. Macmillan.
Lewis, Abram H. Sunday legislation. New rev. enl. ed. '02(F8) 12°, net, $1. Appleton.
Lewis, Alfr. H: Wolfville days. '02(F22) il. D. $1.50. Stokes.
Lewis, Alonzo F. Fryeburg Webster centennial. '02(Je28) il. 12°, pap., 50 c. A. F. Lewis.
Lewis, C: B., ["M. Quad."] Life and troubles of Mr. Bowser. '02(My24) il. 8°, $1. Jamieson-H.
Lewis, Edn. H. Text-book of applied Eng. grammar. '02(F15) il. 12°, net, 35 c. Macmillan.
Lewis, Merriwether, *and* Clarke, W: Hist. of the expedition to the sources of the Missouri: rep. of the ed. of 1814. '02(My24) 3 v., 8°, (Commonwealth lib.) net, per v., $1. New Amsterdam.
Lewis, W: D. *See* Pepper, G: W.
Lex de imperio Vespasiani. Hellems, F. B. R. 50 c. Scott, F. & Co.
LEXINGTON, Mass.
Piper. Lexington, the birthplace of Amer. liberty. 25 c. Lexington.
LIABILITY.
See Negligence.
LIBERTY.
See Democracy;—Religious liberty;—Slavery.
LIBRARIES.
New York Lib. Club. Libraries of Greater New York. net, 75 c.; net, 50 c. Stechert.
Plummer. Hints to small libraries. net, 50 c. M. W. Plummer.
Wisconsin. List of books for township libraries. 25 c. Wisconsin.
See also Books;—Cataloguing.
Library of literary criticism. *See* Moulton, C: W.
Library of Tribune extras. D. pap., 25 c. Tribune Assoc.
—Tribune almanac, 1902. (v. 14, 1.)

Liddell, Mark H. Introd. to the scientific study of Eng. poetry. '02(My10) D. net, $1.25. Doubleday, P.
Lieb, Hermann. Prince Bismarck and the German people. '02(Mr22) 12°, $1.50; hf. mor., $2.25; mor., $3.25. Dominion.
Life, And. C. Tuber-like rootlets of cycas revoluta. '02(F15) il. 8°, (Cont. to the Hull Botanical lab'y, no. 26.) pap., net, 25 c. Univ. of Chic.
Life and health. Blaisdell, R. F. $1. Ginn.
Life and letters in the 4th century. Glover, T. R. net, $3.25. Macmillan.
Life and power from within. Colville, W. J. $1. Alliance.
Life and troubles of Mr. Bowser. Lewis, C: B. $1. Jamieson-H.
Life and works of the Redeemer. '02(F15) 12°, net, $2. Dutton.
Life at West Point. Hancock, H. I. net, $1.40. Putnam.
Life histories. *See* Appleton's.
Life of a century. Hodder, E. net, $4. Scribner.
Life of John William Walshe, T.S.A. Carmichael, M. net, $2. Dutton.
Life of love. Mudge, J. 25 c. Jennings.
Life of unity. Cheney, F. J. $1.50. Blade.
Life on the farm. Shepard, H. M. 50 c. Flanagan.
Life worth living. Newell, W. C. $1. Abbey Press.
Life's little things. Hind, C. L. $1.75. Macmillan.
LIGHT.
Dexter. Elem. exercises on sound, light and heat. 90 c. Longmans.
Michelsen. Velocity of light. net, 25 c. Univ. of Chic.
See also Radiation;—Roentgen rays.
Light and peace. Quadrupani, R. P. net, 50 c. Herder.
Light of our spirit. Ehrlich, *Mrs.* B. 25 c. B. Ehrlich.
LILIES.
Jekyll, *comp.* Lilies for Eng. gardens. net, $3.75. Scribner.
Liljencrantz, Ottilie A. Thrall of Leif the lucky. '02(Mr29) O. $1.50. McClurg.
Lilley, A: E. V., *and* Midgley, W. Studies in plant form. New enl. ed. '02(Mr8) 8°, net, $2. Scribner.
Lilley, J. P. The pastoral epistles: new tr. with introd., commentary and app. '01. '02(Ja11) 12°, (Bible class handbooks.) net, 75 c. Scribner.
LINCOLN, Abr.
Smith, S. G. Abraham Lincoln. net, 25 c. Jennings.
See also Fallows, S:
Lincoln, Jos. C. Cape Cod ballads. '02(Ap19) il. D. net, $1.25. Brandt.
Lindsay, B. Story of animal life. '02(My24) il. S. (Lib. of useful stories.) net, 35 c. Appleton.
Line and form. Crane, W. $2.25. Macmillan.
Linear groups. Dickson, L. E. net, $4. Stechert.
Line-o'-type lyrics. Taylor, B. L. net, 50 c. W: S. Lord.
Lines of defense of the biblical revelation. Margoliouth, D. S. net, $1.50. Gorham.

Linn, Ja. W. The second generation: [novel.] '02(F1) 12°, $1.50. Macmillan.
Linn, W: A. Story of the Mormons. '02 (Je21) O. net, $4. Macmillan.
Lippincott's biog. dictionary. New ed. '01-'02(Mr1) 2 v., il. 8°, subs., $15; hf. rus., $17.50; hf. mor., $20. Lippincott.
Lippincott's educ. ser. 12°, net, $1.25. Lippincott.
—Kemp. Hist. of education. (3.)
Lippincott's elem. algebra. (Ja. M. Rawlins.) '01-'02(Mr1) 12°, 80 c. Lippincott.
Lippincott's elem. science readers. 3 pts. '01-'02(F15) pt. 1, 16°, bds., 25 c.; pt. 2, 30 c.; pt. 3, 35 c. Lippincott.
Lippincott's popular lib. 12°, $1.. Lippincott.
—Hungerford. Three graces.
Lippincott's practical arithmetic. '01. '02 (Mr1) 2 pts., 12°, ea., 40 c. Lippincott.
Lippincott's select novels. D. $1; pap., 50 c. Lippincott.
—Croker. Cat's paw.
—Le Queux. Sign of the seven sins.
—Neilson. Madame Bohemia.
Liquid from the sun's rays. Greenleaf, S. $1.50. Abbey Press.
Liquors.
See Fermentation.
Lisk, J. P. Diagram of the Corliss engine. '02(Je7) 8°, pap., 25 c. Spon.
Litanei zum heiligsten herzen Jesu. Catholic church. net, 3 c. Herder.
Literature.
Arnold. Literature and dogma. net, $1. New Amsterdam.
Brandes. Main currents in 19th century literature. v. 2. net $2.75. Macmillan.
Halsey. Our literary deluge. net, $1.25. Doubleday, P.
Payne. Editorial echoes.—Little leaders. ea., net, $1. McClurg.
See also Authors;—Bibliographies;—Books; — Fiction;—Letters; — Parody; — Quotations;—*also* names of nations and literatures.
Literature of Am. history. Larned, J. N. net, $6; $7.50; $9. Houghton, M. & Co.
Litsey, Edn. C. Love story of Abner Stone. '02(Je21) O. bds., net, $1.20. Barnes.
Little, E: R. *See* Hall, F: G.
Little books on devotion. sq. T. net, 25 c. Jennings.
—Mudge. Life of love.
Little books on doctrine. sq. T. 25 c. Jennings.
—Merrill *and* Warren. Discourses on miracles.
—Townsend. Satan and demons.
Little books on practice. T. net, 25 c. Jennings.
—Oliver. Our lay office-bearers.—Soul-winners' secrets.
Little brother. Willard, J. F. $1.50. Century Co.
Little button rose. Alcott, L. M. 50 c. Little, B. & Co.
Little engravings. Altdorfer, A. net, $1.50. Longmans.
Little French dinners. Rivas, E. de. 50 c. New Amsterdam.
Little giant's neighbors. Fox, F. M. 50 c. L. C. Page.
Little guides ser. S. net, 75 c. Dodd.
—Windle. Malvern country.
Little journeys. *See* Whitcomb, C. E.
Little leaders. Payne, W: M. net, $1. McClurg.
Little masterpieces; ed. by B. Perry. S. 50 c. Doubleday, P.
—Bacon. Essays.
—Emerson. Essays.
—Goldsmith. Selections.
—Johnson. Essays fr. Rambler and Idler.
—Milton. Selections.
—Swift. Selections.
Little memoirs of the 19th century. Paston, G: net, $3. Dutton.
Little minister. Barrie, J. M. $1. Burt.
Little stories for little people. McCullough, A. W. 25 c. Am. Bk.
Little Susy stories. Prentiss, *Mrs.* E. 75 c. Burt.
Littleton, W: S. Trumpeter's hand book and instructor. '02(Je21) 16°, leath., $1. Hudson-K.
Liturgies.
See Prayers.
Livermore, S: T. Block Island; ed. by C: E. Perry. '01-'02(Mr22) il. 16°, pap., 25 c. Ball.
Livets alvor. Bang, *Mrs.* M. 65 c. M. Bang.
Living races of mankind. Hutchinson, H. N. net, $5. Appleton.
Livingston, Burton E. On the nature of the stimulus which causes the change in form in polymorphic green algae. '02(F1) 8°, (Cont. from Hull botanical laboratory, no. 22.) pap., net, 25 c. Univ. of Chic.
Livingston, Luther S. Bibliog. of the first ed. in book form of the works of Alfred, Lord Tennyson. '01-'02(Ja11) 16°, pap., $1. Dodd.
Livingston, Luther S. Works of Rudyard Kipling: desc. of a set of the first eds. of his books. '01-'02(Ja11) facsimiles, 8°, 65 cop. on hand-made pap., bds., net, $12; 12 cop. on Jap. pap., net, $20. Dodd.
Locke, C: E: Nineteenth-century crusaders. [Gladstone.] '02(My24) D. (Hero ser., no. 5.) net, 25 c. Jennings.
Locke, C: E: Typical American. [Washington.] '02(My24) il. D. (Hero ser., no. 2.) net, 25 c. Jennings.
Lockett, Ma. F., ["The Princess."] Christopher. '02(My3) il. D. $1.25. Abbey Press.
Locomotives.
Baker. Economic locomotive management. $1.50. R'way Educ.
Cooke. Some recent developments in locomotive practice. $1. Macmillan.
Goss. Locomotive sparks. $2. Wiley.
See also Steam engines.
Logarithms.
Smith. Four-place logarithmic tables. net, 50 c. Holt.
See also Trigonometry.
Logic.
Aikins. Principles of logic. net, $1.50. Holt.
London.
Evart, *and others.* Climates of London. net, $4. Macmillan.
Thorpe. Children's London. net, $4.50. Scribner.
See also Oriental Club;—Stock Exchange.
London Guild Halls.
Interior decorations and furnishings of London Guild Halls. net, $12; net, $15. Helburn.

Long, J: L. Naughty Nan. '02(Mr1) il. D. $1.50. Century Co.
Long duel. Clifford, *Mrs.* L. L. net, $1.25. Lane.
Longfellow, H: W. Hyperion. '02(Ap19) 12°, (Home lib.) $1. Burt.
Longfellow, H: W. Poems; biog. sketch by N. H. Dole. '02(F15) 12°, $1.75. Crowell.
Longmans' Am. teachers' ser.; ed. by J. E. Russell. O. $1.50. Longmans.
—Bourne. Teaching of history and civics.
Longmans' artists' lib.; ed. by L. Binyon. il. sq. O. net, $1. Longmans.
—Holmes. Constable. (5.)
Longmans' civil engineering ser. il. O. Longmans.
—Fidler. Calculations in hydraulic engineering. $3.
—Harcourt. Civil engineering as app. to construction. $5.
Longmans' practical elem. science ser. D. 90 c. Longmans.
—Dexter. Sound, light and heat.
—Furneaux. Hygiene.
Longridge, G. Official and lay witness to the value of foreign missions. '02(Je21) 16°, 20 c. E. & J. B. Young.
Longus. Daphnis and Chloe. '02(Mr29) il. 12°, (Antique gems from the Greek and Latin, v. 4.) (App. to pubs. for price.) Barrie.
Lord, W: R. First book upon birds of Oregon and Washington. New rev., enl. ed. '02(Mr29) il. 12°, 75 c. W: R. Lord.
Lord Alingham, bankrupt. Manning, M. $1.50. Dodd.
LORD'S PRAYER.
Foster. The Lord's prayer. 10 c. Cumberland Press.
LORD'S SUPPER.
Gore. Body of Christ. $1.75. Scribner.
Hall. Instructions and devotions on the holy communion. net, 25 c. Young Churchman.
Paret. Reality in holy communion. 10 c. Whittaker.
Preparatio; preparation for holy communion. $2. Longmans.
See also Catholic church;—Token.
LOS ANGELES.
Willard. *Herald's* hist. of Los Angeles city. $1.50. Kingsley.
Lost Christmas. Smith, M. R. 50 c. Dutton.
Lost hero. Phelps, E. S. 50 c. Little, B. & Co.
Lost on the Orinoco. Stratemeyer, E: net, $1. Lee & S.
Lothrop, *Mrs.* H. M., ["Margaret Sidney."] Five little Peppers abroad. '02(Je7) il. D. net, $1.10. Lothrop.
Louisiana. *Supreme ct.* Digest; by J. A. Breaux. '01·'02(F8) O. shp., $20. Hansell.
LOUISIANA PURCHASE.
Hosmer. Hist. of the Louisiana purchase. net, $1.20. Appleton.
Louttit, G: W: Maid of the wildwood. '02(Je21) D. $1.50. Colonial.
Love, W: D. Thomas Short, the first printer of Conn. '01·'02(Ap26) 8°, (Acorn club, Ct., pub. no. 6.) pap., $5. Case.
LOVE.
Finck. Romantic love and personal beauty. net, $2. Macmillan.
Love in its tenderness. Aitken, J. R. $1; 50 c. Appleton.
Love letters and how to write them. *See* North, I.
Love never faileth. Simpson, C. $1.25. Revell.
Love poems. Suckling, *Sir* J: net. 50 c.; 75 c. Lane.
Love sonnets of a hoodlum. Irwin, W. 25 c.; 50 c. Elder.
Love-story masterpieces. Lyon, R. A. net, $1. W: S. Lord.
Love story of Abner Stone. Litsey, E. C. net, $1.20. Barnes.
Lovely Mrs. Pemberton. James, *Mrs.* F. A. P. $1.25. Buckles.
Lover, S: Works; introd. by J. J. Roche. Treasure trove ed. 10 v. '02(Mr22) il. 8°, subs., per v., net, $3.50; hf. mor., per v., net, $6.50; de luxe ed., ¾ lev., per v., net, $12. Little, B. & Co.
Lover in Cuba. Elmore, J. B. $1. J. B. Elmore.
Lover's lib. S. net, 50 c.; leath., net, 75 c. Lane.
—Shakespeare. Sonnets.
—Suckling. Love poems.
Lover's progress told by himself. Vizetelly, E. A. $1.50. Brentano's.
Love's itinerary. Snaith, J: C. $1; 50 c. Appleton.
Lovett, Rob. *See* Moody, W: V.
Lowell, Guy, *ed.* American gardens. '02(Je21) il. 4°, $7.50. Bates & G.
Lowell, Ja. R. Democracy. [Limited ed.] '02(Mr22) 16°, bds., net, $2. Houghton, M. & Co.
Lower South in Am. history. Brown, W: G. net, $1.50. Macmillan.
Lubbock, *Sir* J:, [*Lord* Avebury.] Pleasures of life. '02(My17) 12°, (Home lib.) $1. Burt.
Lubbock, *Sir* J: Scenery of England. '02(F22) il. 8°, net, $2.50. Macmillan.
Lucian. Lucius, the ass. '02(Je28) il. 12°, (Antique gems from the Gr. and Latin, v. 5.) (apply to pubs. for price.) Barrie.
Lucian. Translations, by A. M. C. Davidson. '02(Ap19) D. $2. Longmans.
Lucius, the ass. Lucian. (app. to pubs. for price.) Barrie.
LUDWIG II. *of Bavaria.*
Gerard. Romance of King Ludwig II. of Bavaria. net, $1.75. Dodd.
LUKE, *St.*
Selwyn. St. Luke the prophet. net, $2.75. Macmillan.
Luke Delmege. Sheehan, P. A. $1.50. Longmans.
LUMBER.
Rosenberger, *comp.* Law for lumbermen. $3.50. Am. Lumberman.
See also Forests and forestry.
Lunn, C: Philosophy of voice. [New rev., enl. ed.] '02(Ap26) il. O. net, $2. Schirmer.
Lupton, Arnold. Practical treatise on mine surveying. '02(Mr8) il. O. $5. Longmans.
Lush, Ethel R. Domestic economy for scholarship and certificate students. '01·'02(Ja4) 12°, net, 60 c. Macmillan.
Luska, Sidney, *pseud.* *See* Harland, H:
Luther, Mark L. Favor of princes: [novel.] '01·'02(Ja11) 12°, pap., 50 c. Jamieson-H.
Lyall, Edna, *pseud.* *See* Bayly, A. E.

Lydekker, R. *See* Hutchinson, H. N.
Lydston, G. F. *See* Duhring, L: A.
Lyman, A. J. Preaching in the new age: six lectures del. in Hartford Theol. Sem. upon the Carew foundation. '02(Je28) 12°, net, 75 c. Revell.
Lynch, Laurence L., *pseud. See* Van Deventer, E. M.
Lyon, Flo. M. Study of the sporangia and gametophytes of selaginella apus and selaginella rupestris. '02(F15) 8°, (Cont. from the Hull Botanical lab'y, no. 31.) pap., net, 25 c. Univ. of Chic.
Lyon, H: A., *comp.* Cornell verse. 2d ed. '02(Mr8) Tt. $1. Walton.
Lyon, Ralph A., *comp.* Love-story masterpieces. '02(Je21) D. bds., net, $1. W: S. Lord.
Lyrics to the queen. Noble, A. C: n. p. Blue Sky Press.
Mabel Thornley. Baily, R. C. $1.25. Abbey Press.
Mabie, Hamilton W. Parables of life. '02 (Mr29) O. net, $1. Outlook.
Mabie, Hamilton W. Works and days. '02 (My10) S. net, $1. Dodd.
Mabry, W. D. When love is king. '02(Ap26) D. $1.50. Fenno.
McArthur, N. J. *See* Texas. Citations.—Legislature.
Macaulay, T: B., *Lord.* Frederick the Great. '02(F1) 12°, (Eng. classics.) net, 40 c. Macmillan.
Macaulay, T: B., *Lord.* Literary essays. '02 (Ap5) 12°, (Home lib.) $1. Burt.
Macbeth. *See* Porter, C.—Shakespeare, W:
McBride literature and art books. *See* Burke, B. E.
McCall, H: S. The clerk's assistant; rev. and largely rewritten by H. B. Bradbury. 6th ed. '02(Mr.22) O. shp., $6. Banks.
McCall, S: W. Daniel Webster. '02(My17) D. net, 80 c. Houghton, M. & Co.
McCallum & Hofer Cattle Co. Stockmen's calculator. '02(F15) nar. 8°, $1.50. McCallum.
McCarthy, J. H. If I were king. '01. '02 (F8) il. D. $1.50. Russell.
McClelland, T. C. Verba crucis. '02(Mr8) D. 50 c. Crowell.
McClure, Ja. G. K. A mighty means of usefulness: plea for intercessory prayer. '02 (Ap19) 12°, net, 50 c. Revell.
McClure, Rob. American horse, cattle and sheep doctor. '01· '02(Je28) il. 12°, $1.50. Henneberry.
McCormick, J: N. Distinctive marks of the Episcopal church. '02(F22) S. 25 c. Young Churchman.
McCullough, Annie W. Little stories for little people. '02(Ap12) D. (Eclectic school readings.) 25 c. Am. Bk.
McCulloch, S: J. *See* Missouri statute annots.
McDaniel, *Mrs.* Helen P. War poems, 1861-1865. '02(Ap26) D. $1. Abbey Press.
McDonald, D: Treatise on the laws of Ind. pertaining to the powers and duties of and practice and procedure before justices of the peace. Rev. to date by B: F. Watson. '02 (My24) O. shp., net, $7.50. Clarke.
Macdonald, Duff, *ed.* Revised catechism. (Westminster Assembly's Shorter catechism.) '02(Je28) 12°, $1.25. Macmillan.
Macdonald, G: David Elginbrod. '02(My17) 12°, (Home lib.) $1. Burt.
Macdonald, Loren B. Guarding the thoughts. '02(Ja25) S. (Upward ser., no. 1.) pap., 10 c. J. H. West.
Macdonell, Arth. A. Sanskrit grammar for beginners. '01· '02(Ja11) D. $3. Longmans.
Macdonough, Rodney. Macdonough-Hackstaff ancestry. '01· '02(F1) il. sq. 8°, $7.50. R. Macdonough.
Macdougal, Dan. T. Elem. plant physiology. '02(Mr22) il. D. $1.20. Longmans.
MacDowell, Ja. N. Orthodontis: for students in dental colleges. '01· '02(Ja18) il. 8°, net, $4. Colegrove.
McElrath, Fes. The rustler. '02(My3) il. D. net. $1.20. Funk.
McElroy, Lucy C. Silent pioneer. '02(Mr8) il. D. $1.50. Crowell.
Macfadden, B. A. Power and beauty of superb womanhood. '01· '02(Ap12) il. 12°, $1. Physical Culture.
McGarvey, J. W. Authorship of the book of Deuteronomy. '02(Je7) O. $2. Standard.
McGee, Jos. B., *sr.* Complete exposition and revelation of ancient free and accepted masonry. '01· '02(My24) D. $1. J. B. McGee.
McGiffert, A. C. The Apostles' creed. '02 (F1) O. net, $1.25. Scribner.
McGovern, J: Fireside university of modern invention, discovery, industry and art for home circle study and entertainment. [Rev. 18th ed.] '02(My24) 8°. $2.50; mor., $3.75. Union Pub.
McGovern, J: Poems. '02(My24) D. net, $1. W: S. Lord.
McGrady, T: City of Angels. '01· '02 (My10) S. pap., 10 c. Standard.
McGrady, T: Clerical capitalist. '02(Ap19) O. (Socialist lib., v. 1, no. 10.) pap., 10 c. Socialistic Co-op.
McGrady, T: A voice from England. '02 (Ap5) S. (Standard lib.) pap., 10 c. Standard.
MACHINERY.
Benjamin. Notes on machine design. $2. C. H. Holmes.
Lafarque. Social effect of machinery. 10 c. Socialistic Co-op.
See also Electric engineering;—Locomotives.
McHugh, Hugh. It's up to you. '02(Je28) il. nar. S. 75 c. G: W. Dillingham.
McIlvaine, J. H. St. Francis of Assisi. '02 (Ap12) S. net, 85 c. Dodd.
Mack, W:, *and* Nash, H. P., *eds.* Cyclopedia of law and procedure. v. 3. '02(Ap5) O. shp., $6. Am. Law Bk.
Mackail, J: W: Biblia innocentium. pt. 2. '01· '02(Ja4) D. $1.75. Longmans.
Mackay, Angus M. Churchman's introduction to the Old Testament. '01· '02(Ja4) 12°. (Churchman's lib.) $1.50. Macmillan.
McKay, W. J. S. Hist. of ancient gynæcology. '01· '02(F22) 8°, net. $3. Wood.
McKee, Lanier. Land of Nome. '02(Je28) D. net, $1.25. Grafton Press.
Mackenzie, Alex. Voyages from Montreal through the Continent of North America to the Frozen and Pacific Oceans in 1789 and 1793. '02(My24) 2 v., 8°, (Commonwealth lib.) per v., net, $1. New Amsterdam.

Mackenzie, Ja. Study of the pulse, arterial, venous, and hepatic, and of the movements of the heart. '02(My17) il. 8°, net, $4.50. Macmillan.
Mackenzie, J: S. Outlines of metaphysics. '02(Ap26) 12°, net, $1.10. Macmillan.
Mackinder, H. J. Britain and the British seas. '02(F22) 8°, (World ser., no. 1.) $2. Appleton.
McKinley, W: Last speech of President McKinley. '02(Mr1) 12°, bds., $1.50; pap., $1. Kirgate Press.
McKINLEY, W:
Ellis. Life of William McKinley. 25 c. Street.
Fallows, *ed.* Life of William McKinley. $1.50; $2.25. Regan.
Halstead. William McKinley [in Norwegian.] $1.50; $2. J: Anderson.
Halstead *and* Munson. Life and services of William McKinley. $1.50; $2.25. Dominion.
Hay. William McKinley. net, 28 c. Crowell.
See also Wilson, J. G.
McKinney, A. H. The child for Christ. '02 (Je28) 16°, net, 50 c. Revell.
McKinney, W: M., *ed.* Encyclopædia of pleading and practice. v. 22, 23. '02(My24) O. shp., ea., $6. E: Thompson.
Mackinnon, Ja. Growth and decline of the French monarchy. '02(Je7) O. $7.50. Longmans.
McLaughlin, Ja. M. Elements and notation of music. '02(F1) D. 55 c. Ginn.
Maclay, E. S. Hist. of the U. S. Navy. New rev. ed. of v. 3. '02(Mr1) 3 v., il. 8°, per v., net, $3. Appleton.
McLellan, Ja. A., Dewey, J:, *and* Ames, A. F. Public school arithmetic for grammar grades. '02(F1) 12°, net, 60 c. Macmillan.
McLeod, Lorenzo C. A young man's problems. '02(Je7) D. 50 c. Flanagan.
McLeod, Malcolm J. Heavenly harmonies for earthly living. '02(F8) 12°, net, 50 c. Revell.
McManman, J. A. *See* Hyde, W. H.
McManus, L. The wager. '02(My17) D. $1.25. Buckles.
Macmillan, Hugh. Christmas rose and other thoughts in verse. '01· '02(Ja4) il. 12°, $1. Macmillan.
Macmillan, Hugh. Corn of Heaven. '02 (Ja18) 12°, $1.75. Macmillan.
Macmillan's classical ser. 12°, net. Macmillan.
—Sophocles. Antigone. 60 c.
Macmillan's Eng. classics. 12°, net, 60 c. Macmillan.
—Boswell. Journal of tour to the Hebrides.
—Scott. Kenilworth.—Quentin Durward.
Macmillan's Greek course. 12°. Macmillan.
—Andrew. Greek prose composition. net, 90 c.
Macmillan's guides. 12°. net. Macmillan.
—Guide to Palestine and Egypt. $3.25.
Macmillan's handbooks of great masters in painting and sculpture. il. 12°, $1.75. Macmillan.
—Bell. Rembrandt.
—Gower. Sir David Wilkie.
—Martin. Gerard Douw.
—Perkins. Giotto.
Macmillan's handbooks of the great craftsmen. il. 12°, $2. Macmillan.
—Cust. Ivory workers of the Middle Ages.
—Headlam. Peter Vischer.
Macmillan's handbooks to the great public schools. 12°, $1.50. Macmillan.
—Airy. Westminster.
Macmillan's manuals for teachers. 12°, net. Macmillan.
—Findlay. Principles of class teaching. $1.25.
Macmillan's mediæval towns ser. il. 12°. Macmillan.
—Headlam. Chartres. $2; $2.50.
—Poole. Cairo. $2; $2.50.
Macmillan's new geography readers: Africa and Australasia. '02(My24) 12°, net, 40 c. Macmillan.
Macmillan's new history readers; [bk. 3.] senior. '02(My24) il. 12°, net, 50 c. Macmillan.
Macmillan's personal problem ser. 12°, net, $1. Macmillan.
—Canfield. College student and his problems.
—Oppenheim. Mental growth and control.
Macmillan's Pitt Press ser. 12°, net. Macmillan.
—Sybel. Prinz Eugen von Savoyen. 60 c.
Macmillan's primary ser. of French and Germ. reading books. 12°, net. Macmillan.
—Alissas, d'. Les histoires de tante. 40 c.
Macmillan's summary of Eng. history on the concentric plan; senior. '02(My24) il. 12°, pap., net, 15 c. Macmillan.
Macmillan's Temple classics. 16°, 50 c.; flex. leath., 75 c. Macmillan.
—Arnold. Dramatic and early poems.
—Boethius. Consolation of philosophy.
—Carlyle. Past and present.
—Goldsmith. Plays.—Poems.
Macmillan's Temple classics for young people. 16°, net. 50 c.; flex. leath., 80 c. Macmillan.
—Perrault. Tales of passed times.
Macnab, Fes. Ride in Morocco among believers and fur traders. '02(Ap19) il. O. $5. Longmans.
McSpadden, J. W. Shakesperian synopses. '02(Ap5) S. (Handy information ser.) net, 45 c. Crowell.
Madame Bohemia. Neilson, F. $1; 50 c. Lippincott.
Mlle. Fouchette. Murray, C: T. $1.50. Lippincott.
Madness of Philip. Daskam, J. D. $1.50. McClure, P.
Maeterlinck, M. The buried temple; tr. by A. Sutro. '02(My10) D. net, $1.40. Dodd.
Maeterlinck, M. Sister Beatrice and Ardiane and Barbe Bleue: two plays; tr. by B. Miall. '02(Ap12) D. net, $1.20. Dodd.
Maggie Miller. '02(Ap19) 12°, (Home lib.) $1. Burt.
Magic key. Tucker, E. S. net, $1. Little, B. & Co.
Magic wheel. Stannard, *Mrs.* H. E. V. $1.25. Lippincott.
MAGNETISM.
See Electricity.
Mahon, R. H. Token of the covenant; or, right use of baptism. 4th ed. '02(My17) D. 50 c. Pub. Ho. M. E. Ch., So.
Mahoney million. Townsend, C: $1.25. New Amsterdam.

Maid of Bar Harbor. Rowe, H. G. $1.50. Little, B. & Co.
Maid of Montauk. Monroe, F. net, $1. W: R. Jenkins.
Maid of the wildwood. Louttit, G: W: $1.50. Colonial.
Main currents in 19th century literature. *See* Brandes, G:
Main street. Hawthorne, N. $2. Kirgate Press.
Maine. Laws concerning business corporations, (annot.) (H. M. Heath.) '02(Je7) O. pap., gratis. Kennebec Journ.
Maine. *Supreme judicial ct.* Repts., v. 95. (C: Hamlin.) '01- '02(Mr15) O. shp., $4. W: W. Roberts.
MAINE.
Drummond, *comp.* Maine masonic text-book. $1.40; $1.50. Berry.
Maitland, F: W:, Gwatkin; H: M., Poole, R. L., *and others.* Essays on the teaching of history. '01. '02(Ja4) 12°, (Cambridge Univ. Press ser.) net, 75 c. Macmillan.
Maitland, J: A. F. Music in England in the nineteenth century. '02(Ap5) 12°, net, $1.75. Dutton.
Majesty of calmness. Jordan, W: G: 50 c. Revell.
Major, C:, ["Edwin Caskoden."] Bears of Blue River. [New issue.] '02(Mr8) il. 12°, $1.50. Macmillan.
Major, C: Dorothy Vernon of Haddon Hall. '02(My3) il. D. $1.50. Macmillan.
Make good book of parodies. Dustin, E. 50 c. E. Dustin.
Making a country newspaper. Munson, A. J. $1. Dominion.
Making of a statesman. Harris, J. C. $1.25. McClure, P.
MALARIAL FEVER.
Ross. Malarial fever. net, 75 c. Longmans.
Malheurs de Sophie. Ségur, S. R., *Comtesse* de. 45 c. Heath.
Mallary, R. DeWitt. Lenox and the Berkshire Highlands. '02(Je21) il. O. net, $1.75. Putnam.
Malone, *Mrs.* Eva W. Out among the animals: [stories.] '02(Mr22) S. 75 c. Pub. Ho. M. E. Ch., So.
Malone, Jos. S. Guided and guarded. '02 (Ap26) D. $1.25. Abbey Press.
MALVERN, Eng.
Windle. Malvern country. net, 75 c. Dodd.
MAMMALIA.
Harmer *and* Shipley, *eds.* Cambridge natural history. v. 10, Mammalia, by F. E. Beddard. net, $4. Macmillan.
MAN.
See Anatomy;—Ethnology;—Evolution;—Physiology;—Sex.
Man amongst men. Wollpert, F: 15 c. Eckler.
Man in the moon. Dendron, B. 50 c. Bonnell.
Man of no account. Trelawney, D. 10 c. J. H. West.
Man without a country. Hale, E: E. net, $1. Outlook.
MANCHURIA.
Graham. East of the barrier; or, Manchuria in miniature. net, $1. Revell.
Mandeville, C. E. Minister's manual and pocket ritual. '02(F8) S. flex. leath., net, 60 c. Jennings.
Mangasarian, M. M. New catechism. 3d ed. '02(My10) D. pap., 75 c. Open Court.
Mann, Horace K. Lives of the Popes in the early Middle Ages. v. 1. pt. 1. '02(Je14) 8°, net, $3. Herder.
Manning, Marie. Lord Alingham, bankrupt. '02(Ap12) D. $1.50. Dodd.
Mannix, Ma. E. As true as gold. '02(Mr22) il. S. 45 c. Benziger.
Man's peerless destiny in Christ. Sarles, J: W. net, 90 c. Funk.
MANUAL TRAINING.
See Sloyd.
Manufacturers' need of reciprocity. Farquhar, A. B. 15 c. Am. Acad. Pol. Sci.
MANUSCRIPTS.
See Inscriptions;—Irish literature.
Many waters. Shackleton, R. $1.50. Appleton.
Manzoni, A. I promessi sposi; abr. and ed. by M. Levi. '01- '02(Ja25) D. (Silver ser. of modern lang. text-books.) $1.20. Silver.
Marble faun. Hawthorne, N. $1. Burt.
Marchant, J. R. V. Commercial history. '02 (Je7) il. D. (Commercial ser.) $1. Pitman.
Marchmont, Arth. W. Miser Hoadley's secret. '02(Ap26) 12°, (Red letter ser.) $1.25; pap., 50 c. New Amsterdam.
Marchmont, Arth. W. Sarita, the Carlist. '02 (My3) D. $1.50. Stokes.
Margaret Bowlby. Vincent, E. L. $1.50. Lothrop.
Margaret Tudor. Colcock, A. T. $1. Stokes.
Margaret Vincent. Clifford, *Mrs.* L. L. $1.50. Harper.
Margoliouth, D: S: Lines of defense of the biblical revelation. '02(Mr8) 12°, net, $1.50. Gorham.
Margoliouth, D: S: Religion of Bible lands. '02(My3) S. (Christian study manuals.) 60 c. Armstrong.
Maria Stuart. Schiller, J. C. F. v. net, 70 c. Holt.
MARINE ENGINEERING.
Durand. Practical marine engineering. $5. Marine Engineering.
MARINE ZOOLOGY.
See Aquatic life:—Protozoa.
Marion Manning. Eustis, E. $1.50. Harper.
Marius the epicurean. Pater, W. $1. Burt.
Marivaux, Pierre C. de C. de. Selection from comedies by E. W. Olmsted. '02 (Mr22) 12°, net, 90 c. Macmillan.
MARK, *St.*
See Bible.
Marks, Jeannette A. Brief hist. outline of Eng. literature. '02(Je28) D. $1. J. A. Marks.
Marlowe, Chris. Passionate shepherd to his love; and The nymph's reply to the shepherd, by Sir. W. Raleigh. '02(My10) sq. 8°, flex. vellum, net, $3.75.) Russell.
MARQUETTE, Jacques.
Thwaites. Father Marquette. net, $1. Appleton.
Marquis, G: H. Fairview's mystery. '01. '02(Mr1) D. 75 c. Abbey Press.
Marred in the making. Commander, L. K. $3; 25 c. Eckler.
MARRIAGE.
Cook. Bride's book. net, $1.50. Dutton.
Crawley. The mystic rose: study of primitive marriage. net, $4. Macmillan.

MARRIAGE.—*Continued.*
Hurst. New heartstone: bridal greeting. $1. Jennings.
Westermarck. Hist. of human marriage. net, $4.50. Macmillan.
Wood. Marriage. net, $1.25. Revell.
Marriage of Laurentia. Haultmont, M. net, $1.60. Herder.
Marsh, C: L. Not on the chart. '02(Je7) il. D. $1.50. Stokes.
Marsh, G: A singular will. '02(Je7) D. $1.50. Neely.
Marshall, Beatrice. Old Blackfriars. '02 (Ap5) il. 12°, $1.50. Dutton.
Marshall, J: S. Principles and practice of operative dentistry. '01. '02(F15) il. 8°, subs., $5; shp., $6. Lippincott.
Marshall, W: L. *See* Clark, W: L.
Marston, E: Sketches of some booksellers of the time of Dr. Samuel Johnson. '02 (My10) 16°, net, $2. Scribner.
Martin, Fred. W. Album of designs for boats, launches and yachts. [2d ed.] '02(My24) il. obl. T. pap., $1. F: W. Martin.
Martin, G: H. Civil government in the U. S. Rev. ed. '02(Ap26) D. 90 c. Am. Bk.
Martin, W. Gerard Douw; fr. the Dutch by Clara Bell. '02(My3) il. 12°, (Great masters in painting and sculpture.) $1.75. Macmillan.
Martin, W. G. W. Traces of the elder faiths of Ireland. '02(F8) 2 v., il. O. $12. Longmans.
Martindale, J. B. Am. law directory, Jan., 1902. '02(F1) O. shp., net, $10. Martindale.
Marvelous achievements of the 19th century. Morris, C: $2.50; $3.50. Winston.
Marx, Karl. Wage-labor and capital; also Free-trade. '02(Mr29) D. (Arm and hammer ser.) 50 c. N. Y. Labor News.
MARY, *Virgin.*
Palladino. Mary our mother. net, 15 c. Herder.
Mary Garvin. Pattee, F. L. $1.50. Crowell.
Mary Starkweather. Williamson, *Mrs.* C. C. $1.50. Abbey Press.
Mary Stuart. *See* Schiller, J. C. F. v.
Mary Tracy's fortune. Sadlier, A. T. 45 c. Benziger.
Maryland. *Ct. of appeals.* Repts. (Brantly.) v. 93. '02(My10) O. shp., $5. Baughman.
Maryland. *Ct. of appeals.* Repts. v. 59. '02(Mr1); v. 60 (My10); v. 61(Je21) O. shp., ea., $4. Curlander.
MARYLAND.
Steiner. Western Md. in the Revolution. 30 c. Johns Hopkins.
Mason, Arth. J. Christianity, what is it? '02(Je7) 16°, (Church Hist. Soc. lectures, no. 66.) 80 c. E. & J. B. Young.
Mason, Arth. J. Ministry of conversion. '02 (Mr8) D. (Handbooks for the clergy.) net, 90 c. Longmans.
Mason, Hobart. *See* Sheldon, S:
Mason, W: D. Water-supply (from a sanitary standpoint.) 3d ed., rewritten. '02 (My17) il. 8°, red. to $4. Wiley.
MASONRY.
See Bridges
MASS.
See Catholic church;—Lord's supper.

Massachusetts digest, supp. [v. 5,] by C: N. Harris. '02(Je28) Q. shp., net, $5. Little, B. & Co.
Massachusetts. *Supreme judicial ct.* Repts. v. 178. (H: W. Swift.) '02(Ap5) O. shp., $2. Little, B. & Co.
Massachusetts. Treatise on the street railway accident law; by E. H. Clark. '02 (Ap19) O. shp., $3.25. Lawyers' Bk.
MASSACHUSETTS.
American ser. of popular biographies. Mass. ed. $17. Graves.
Hall, *ed.* Regiments and armories of Mass. v. 2. per set, $12; $18; $25. W. W. Potter.
Tucker. Preparation of wills: Mass. law. $3.50. G: B. Reed.
See also Ancient and Hon. Artillery Co. of Mass.;—Boston;—Lexington.
MASSAGE.
See Injuries.
Master of Caxton. Brooks, H. $1.50. Scribner.
Master of science of right living. Hillis, N. D. net, 50 c. Revell.
Mastery of the Pacific. Colquhoun, A. R. net, $4. Macmillan.
MATABELELAND.
Hall *and* Neal. Ancient ruins of Rhodesia. net, $6. Dutton.
Mate of the good ship "York." Russell, W: C. $1.50. L. C. Page.
MATERIA MEDICA.
Murray. Rough notes on remedies. net, $1.25. Blakiston.
MATHEMATICS.
Deel. Practical rapid calculator. 50 c. G: A. Deel.
Gibbs. Vector analysis. net, $4. Scribner.
Stokes. Math. and physical papers. v. 3. net, $3.75. Macmillan.
See also Algebra;—Arithmetic;—Astronomy;—Calculus;—Interest;—Logarithms;—Surveying;—Trigonometry.
Mathes, J. H. General Forrest. '02(Ap26) D. (Great commanders' ser.) net, $1.50. Appleton.
Matheson, G: Spiritual development of St. Paul. '02(Ap12) 12°, net, 80 c. Whittaker.
Matheson, G: Times of retirement; with biog. sketch of the author by D. MacMillan. '01. '02(Ja11) 12°, net, $1.25. Revell.
Mathews, Ferd. S. Field book of Am. wild flowers. '02(Ap26) il. S. net, $1.75. Putnam.
Mathews, Shailer. *See* Burton, E. D.
Matthews, C: G. Manual of alcoholic fermentation and allied industries. '02(Ap19) D. net, $2.60. Longmans.
Matthews, Ja. B. Pen and ink: [essays.] 3d rev., enl. ed. '02(F15) D. net, $1.25. Scribner.
Maulde la Clavière, René de. Art of life; tr. by G: H. Ely. '01. '02(Ja25) D. net, $1.75. Putnam.
Mavor, W: English spelling book; il. by Kate Greenaway. '02(Je28) 16°, bds., 40 c. Warne.
Maxwell, Lucy H. Card sewing: for kindergartens. '02(My3) 16°, pap., 50 c. M. Bradley.
Maxwell, *Mrs.* Ma. E. B. El sacrificio de Elisa. (A. Elias y Pujol.) '01. '02(F22) 12°, pap., 50 c. Appleton.

Mayor, Jos. B. Chapters on Eng. metre. 2d ed., rev. and enl. '02(Ja18) 8°, (Cambridge Univ. Press ser.) net, $2.25. Macmillan.

Mazel. Fisguill, R: $1.50. H. S. Stone.

Mead, Spencer P. Hist. and genealogy of the Mead family of Fairfield Co., Conn. '01-'02(F8) il. O. $15. Knickerbocker.

Meade, L. T. *See* Smith, *Mrs.* E. T.

Meakin, Budgett. The Moors. '02(Mr29) il. 8°, net, $5. Macmillan.

Meakin, Nevill M. The Assassins. '02 (Mr22) D. $1.50. Holt.

MEAT.
Walley. Guide to meat inspection. $3. W: R. Jenkins.

Mechanical triumphs of ancient Egyptians. Barber, F. M. net, $1.25. Dodd.

MECHANICS.
Gibbs. Elem. principles in statistical mechanics, with especial ref. to the rational foundation of thermo-dynamics. $4. Scribner.
Reynolds. Papers on mechanical and physical subjects. v. 2. net, $6. Macmillan.
See also Engineering;—Power.

MECHANICS' LIENS.
Illinois. Commentary on mechanics' lien law. net, $4. Callaghan.

Mechanics of engineering. *See* Du Bois, A: J.

Mechem, Floyd R. Case on the law of damages. 3d ed. '02(Mr8) O. net, $4. West Pub.

Medical directory of the city of New York. '01. '02(F8) 12°, $1.50. Wynkoop.

Medical News pocket formulary for 1902; ed. by E. Q. Thornton. 4th ed. '02(F15) 18°, leath. tuck, net, $1.50. Lea.

Medical News visiting list, 1902. '01. '02 (F22) 16°, leath. tucks, $1.25; thumb-letter index, $1.50. Lea.

MEDICI (THE).
Smeaton. The Medici and the Italian Renaissance. $1.25. Scribner.

MEDICINE.
American year-book of medicine and surgery. 2 v. ea., net, $3; net, $3.75. Saunders.
Billings *and* Stanton, *eds.* General medicine. $1.50. Year Bk.
Buck. Reference handbook of the medical sciences. v. 4. subs., $7: $8; $9. Wood.
Burdick. Standard medical manual. $4. Engelhard.
Fagge. Text-book of medicine. 2 v. net, $6. Blakiston.
International medical annual, 1902. net, $3. Treat.
Lawrence. Practical medicine. $3. Boericke & T.
Medical News pocket formulary, 1902. net, $1.50. Lea.
Paget. Sel. essays and addresses. $5. Longmans.
Sajous, *ed.* Analytical encyclopædia of practical medicine. v. 1. subs., ea., $5; $6. Davis.
See also Accidents;—Chemistry;—Hygiene;—Mind and body;—Nervous system;—Pathology;—Pharmacy.

Meditations and vows. Hall, J. $1.50. Dutton.

Meditations of an autograph collector. Joline, A. H. net, $3. Harper.

Medley, Dudley J. Student's manual of Eng. constitutional history. 3d ed. '02(Je28) 8°, net, $3.50. Macmillan.

Meier, W. H. D. Herbarium and plant description. '01-'02(F1) Q. portfolio, 70 c. Ginn.

Melliar, A. F. Book of the rose. 2d ed. '02 (My24) 12°, $1.75. Macmillan.

Mellick, Anna C. Latin composition for classes reading Cæsar. '01-'02(Ja4) S. 40 c. Am. Bk.

Melomaniacs. Huneker, J. $1.50. Scribner.

Melville, Herman. Typee; ed. by W. P. Trent. '02(My17) il. D. (Home and school classics, young reader's ser.) 45 c. Heath.

Memoirs of an American lady. Grant, *Mrs.* A. M. net, $7.50. Dodd.

MEMORIAL DAY
Harvey. Aids for the proper observance of Memorial day by schools of Wis. gratis. Democrat Pr. Co.

MEMORY.
Kilbourne. Memory and its cultivation. $1; 50 c. Mullin.

MEN.
Blouët. 'Tween you an' I; pt. 1, Concerning men. $1.20. Lothrop.

Men and memories. Young, J: R. subs., $5; $3. Neely.

Menefee, Maud. Child stories from the masters. '02(My10) il. 16° 75 c. Rand, McN. & Co.

Menpes, Mortimer. Japan. '02(Ja18) il. 8°, net, $6. Macmillan.

MENTAL ARITHMETIC.
See Arithmetic.

Mental growth and control. Oppenheim, N. net, $1. Macmillan.

MENTAL SCIENCE.
Bradbury. New philosophy of health. 75 c. Alliance.
Dresser. True hist. of mental science. 20 c. Alliance.
Patterson. What the new thought stands for. 10 c. Alliance.
Patterson. The will to be well. $1. Alliance.
See also Christian science;—Mind and body.

Mental state of hystericals. Janet, P. $3.50. Putnam.

Merchant of Venice. *See* Shakespeare, W:

Mercier, C: A. Psychology, normal and morbid. '02(Mr1) 8°, net, $4. Macmillan.

Mercier, C: A. Text-book of insanity. '02 (My17) 12°, net, $1.75. Macmillan.

Merriam, Edm. F. Hist. of Am. Bapt. missions. '01-'02(F15) 12°, $1.25. Am. Bapt.

Merrill, S. M., *and* Warren, H: W. Discourses on miracles. '02(Mr22) sq. T. (Little books on doctrine.) net, 25 c. Jennings.

Merriman, Mansfield, *and* Jacoby, H: D. Text-book on roofs and bridges. Pt. 3. 4th ed., rewritten. '02(Ap19) 8°, $2.50. Wiley.

MESA VERDE.
See Colorado.

Message of to-morrow. Lee, J: L. net, $1.20. Revell.

Message to Garcia and thirteen other things. Hubbard, E. $2; $5; $15. Roycrofters.

METAL-WORK.
See Plate

Long, J: L. Naughty Nan. '02(Mr1) il. D. $1.50. Century Co.
Long duel. Clifford, *Mrs.* L. L. net, $1.25. Lane.
Longfellow, H: W. Hyperion. '02(Ap19) 12°, (Home lib.) $1. Burt.
Longfellow, H: W. Poems; biog. sketch by N. H. Dole. '02(F15) 12°, $1.75. Crowell.
Longmans' Am. teachers' ser.; ed. by J. E. Russell. O. $1.50. Longmans.
—Bourne. Teaching of history and civics.
Longmans' artists' lib.; ed. by L. Binyon. il. sq. O. net, $1. Longmans.
—Holmes. Constable. (5.)
Longmans' civil engineering ser. il. O. Longmans.
—Fidler. Calculations in hydraulic engineering. $3.
—Harcourt. Civil engineering as app. to construction. $5.
Longmans' practical elem. science ser. D. 90 c. Longmans.
—Dexter. Sound, light and heat.
—Furneaux. Hygiene.
Longridge, G. Official and lay witness to the value of foreign missions. '02(Je21) 16°, 20 c. E. & J. B. Young.
Longus. Daphnis and Chloe. '02(Mr29) il. 12°, (Antique gems from the Greek and Latin, v. 4.) (App. to pubs. for price.) Barrie.
Lord, W: R. First book upon birds of Oregon and Washington. New rev., enl. ed. '02(Mr29) il. 12°, 75 c. W: R. Lord.
Lord Alingham, bankrupt. Manning, M. $1.50. Dodd.
LORD'S PRAYER.
Foster. The Lord's prayer. 10 c. Cumberland Press.
LORD'S SUPPER.
Gore. Body of Christ. $1.75. Scribner.
Hall. Instructions and devotions on the holy communion. net, 25 c. Young Churchman.
Paret. Reality in holy communion. 10 c. Whittaker.
Preparatio; preparation for holy communion. $2. Longmans.
See also Catholic church;—Token.
LOS ANGELES.
Willard. *Herald's* hist. of Los Angeles city. $1.50. Kingsley.
Lost Christmas. Smith, M. R. 50 c. Dutton.
Lost hero. Phelps, E. S. 50 c. Little, B. & Co.
Lost on the Orinoco. Stratemeyer, E: net, $1. Lee & S.
Lothrop, *Mrs.* H. M., ["Margaret Sidney."] Five little Peppers abroad. '02(Je7) il. D. net, $1.10. Lothrop.
Louisiana. *Supreme ct.* Digest; by J. A. Breaux. '01- '02(F8) O. shp., $20. Hansell.
LOUISIANA PURCHASE.
Hosmer. Hist. of the Louisiana purchase. net, $1.20. Appleton.
Louttit, G: W: Maid of the wildwood. '02 (Je21) D. $1.50. Colonial.
Love, W: D. Thomas Short, the first printer of Conn. '01- '02(Ap26) 8°, (Acorn club, Ct., pub. no. 6.) pap., $5. Case.
LOVE.
Finck. Romantic love and personal beauty. net, $2. Macmillan.
Love in its tenderness. Aitken, J. R. $1; 50 c. Appleton.
Love letters and how to write them. *See* North, I.
Love never faileth. Simpson, C. $1.25. Revell.
Love poems. Suckling, *Sir* J: net. 50 c.; 75 c. Lane.
Love sonnets of a hoodlum. Irwin, W. 25 c.; 50 c. Elder.
Love-story masterpieces. Lyon, R. A. net, $1. W: S. Lord.
Love story of Abner Stone. Litsey, E. C. net, $1.20. Barnes.
Lovely Mrs. Pemberton. James, *Mrs.* F. A. P. $1.25. Buckles.
Lover, S: Works; introd. by J. J. Roche. Treasure trove ed. 10 v. '02(Mr22) il. 8°, subs., per v., net, $3.50; hf. mor., per v., net, $6.50; de luxe ed., ¾ lev., per v., net, $12. Little, B. & Co.
Lover in Cuba. Elmore, J. B. $1. J. B. Elmore.
Lover's lib. S. net, 50 c.; leath., net, 75 c. Lane.
—Shakespeare. Sonnets.
—Suckling. Love poems.
Lover's progress told by himself. Vizetelly, E. A. $1.50. Brentano's.
Love's itinerary. Snaith, J: C. $1; 50 c. Appleton.
Lovett, Rob. *See* Moody, W: V.
Lowell, Guy, *ed.* American gardens. '02 (Je21) il. 4°, $7.50. Bates & G.
Lowell, Ja. R. Democracy. [Limited ed.] '02 (Mr22) 16°, bds., net, $2. Houghton, M. & Co.
Lower South in Am. history. Brown, W: G. net, $1.50. Macmillan.
Lubbock, *Sir* J:, [*Lord* Avebury.] Pleasures of life. '02(My17) 12°, (Home lib.) $1. Burt.
Lubbock, *Sir* J: Scenery of England. '02 (F22) il. 8°, net, $2.50. Macmillan.
Lucian. Lucius, the ass. '02(Je28) il. 12°, (Antique gems from the Gr. and Latin, v. 5.) (apply to pubs. for price.) Barrie.
Lucian. Translations, by A. M. C. Davidson. '02(Ap19) D. $2. Longmans.
Lucius, the ass. Lucian. (app. to pubs. for price.) Barrie.
LUDWIG II. *of Bavaria.*
Gerard. Romance of King Ludwig II. of Bavaria. net, $1.75. Dodd.
LUKE, *St.*
Selwyn. St. Luke the prophet. net, $2.75. Macmillan.
Luke Delmege. Sheehan, P. A. $1.50. Longmans.
LUMBER.
Rosenberger, *comp.* Law for lumbermen. $3.50. Am. Lumberman.
See also Forests and forestry.
Lunn, C: Philosophy of voice. [New rev., enl. ed.] '02(Ap26) il. O. net, $2. Schirmer.
Lupton, Arnold. Practical treatise on mine surveying. '02(Mr8) il. O. $5. Longmans.
Lush, Ethel R. Domestic economy for scholarship and certificate students. '01- '02 (Ja4) 12°, net, 60 c. Macmillan.
Luska, Sidney, *pseud.* *See* Harland, H:
Luther, Mark L. Favor of princes: [novel.] '01- '02(Ja11) 12°, pap., 50 c. Jamieson-H.
Lyall, Edna, *pseud.* *See* Bayly, A. E.

MIND.—*Continued.*
Oppenheim. Mental growth and control. net, $1. Macmillan.
See also Intellect:—Mind and body;—Psychology.
MIND AND BODY.
Brown. Studies in spiritual harmony. $1. Reed Pub.
Janet. Mental state of hystericals. $3.50. Putnam.
Wright. Body and soul. $1. J. C. Wright.
See also Hypnotism;—Insanity;—Mental science;—Nervous system;—Psychology.
MIND READING.
See Telepathy.
Mind telegraph. Stay, J. B. 25 c. Alliance.
Miner, W: H. Daniel Boone: cont. toward a bibliog. '01- '02(F15) D. bds., $1. Dibdin Club.
MINERALOGY.
Eakle. Colemanite from So. California. 15 c. Univ. of Cal.
See also Assaying;—Blowpipe;—Geology;—Metals and metallurgy;—Mines and mining.
MINES AND MINING.
Oregon. Mining laws. 40 c. Or. Mining Journ.
Pratt. Supp. to Mining laws of Colorado. 35 c. Pratt Merc.
See also Copper;—Engineering; — Iron; — Metals and metallurgy.
Minister's wooing. Stowe, *Mrs.* H. B. $1. Burt.
MINISTERS (*of the Gospel*).
Anderson. Christian ministry. 20 c. Young Churchman.
Kern. Way of the preacher. $1.25. Pub. Ho. M. E. Ch., So.
Mandeville. Minister's manual and pocket ritual. net, 60 c. Jennings.
Robinson. Personal life of the clergy. net, 90 c. Longmans.
See also Missions and missionaries;—Ordination;—Preaching;—Priests.
Ministry of conversion. Mason, A. J. net, 90 c. Longmans.
Minneapolis Journal almanac and year book, 1902. '02(Ap26) 12°, pap., 25 c. Journal Pr. Co.
Minnesota. Justice's manual; by W. S. Booth. 12th ed. '01- '02(Ja18) D. pap., $1.50. Booth.
Minnesota. *Supreme ct.* Repts. v. 83. '02 (Ap5) O. shp., $2.75. Dufresne.
Minority (The). Hill, F: T. $1.50. Stokes.
Minton, H: C. The cosmos and the logos. '02(Mr22) O. net, $1.25. Westminster.
MIRACLES.
Merrill *and* Warren. Discourses on miracles. 25 c. Jennings.
See also Psychical research.
Misanthrope (Le). Moliere, J. B. P. de. 50 c. Scott, F. & Co.
Misdemeanors of Nancy. Hoyt, E. $1.50. Doubleday, P.
Miser Hoadley's secret. Marchmont, A. W. $1.25; 50 c. New Amsterdam.
Misérables (Les). *See* Quayle, W: A.
Miss Ashton's new pupil. Robbins, *Mrs.* S. S. $1. Burt.
Miss Petticoats. Tilton, D. $1.50. C. M. Clark.
Miss Prudence. Conklin, *Mrs.* J. M. D. $1. Burt.

MISSIONS AND MISSIONARIES.
Beach. Geography and atlas of Protestant missions. v. 1. $2.50; per set, $1.75. Student Vol.
Brain. Fifty missionary programmes. 35 c. Un. Soc. C. E.
Carey. Adventures in Tibet. net, $1.50. Un. Soc. C. E.
Dean. Cross of Christ in Bololand. net, $1. Revell.
Dennis. Centennial survey of foreign missions. net, $4. Revell.
Jesuit relations: travels and explorations of the Jesuit missionaries in New France, 1610-1791. 73 v. ea., net, $3.50. Burrows.
Ketler. Tragedy of Paotingfu, China. net, $2. Revell.
Longridge. Official and lay witness to the value of foreign missions. 20 c. E. & J. B. Young.
Montgomery. Foreign missions. net, 90 c. Longmans.
Smith, B. Uncle Boston's spicy breezes. net, $1. Am. Bapt.
Smith, J. Ten years in Burma. net, $1. Jennings.
Warneck. Outline of hist. of Protestant missions. net, $2. Revell.
See also Philippine Islands;—Protestantism;—*also* names of churches.
Mississippi. *Supreme ct.* Repts. v. 78. '01- '02(My10) O. shp., $4. Marshall.
Mississippi bubble. Hough, E. $1.50. Bowen-M.
Missouri. *St. Louis and the Kansas City cts. of appeals.* Cases. v. 89. '01. '02(Mr1) O. shp., $5. Stephens.
Missouri statute annots.; by S: J. McCulloch. 2d ed. '02(My24) O. hf. shp., $3. S: J. McCulloch.
Missouri. *Supreme ct.* Repts. (Rader.) v. 162, 163. '01- '02(Mr1); v. 164 (My10) O. shp., ea., $4. Stephens.
Mr. Whitman. Pullen, *Mrs.* E. $1.50. Lothrop.
Misunderstood. Montgomery, F. $1. Beam.
Mitchell, C. A. *See* Oppenheimer, C.
Mitchell, Fes. L. Georgia land and people. '02(Ap26) 12°, $1.25. F. L. Mitchell.
Mitton, G. E. The opportunist. '02(Mr8) 12°, $2. Macmillan.
Moberly, R. C. Christ our life. '02(Mr22) O. net, $3. Longmans.
Mobile Boer. Hiley, A. R. I. $1.50. Grafton Press.
Modern association and railroading. Goodknight, A. L. 50 c. Abbey Press.
Modern lang ser. See Heath's.
Molander, Anna. Scientific sloyd: for teachers and schools. '02(My3) S. 50 c. Bardeen.
Molesworth, *Mrs.* Ma. L. Grandmother dear. '02(Je28) il. 12°, (St. Nicholas ser.) 75 c. Burt.
Molesworth, *Mrs.* Ma. L. Robin Redbreast. '02(My3) il. 12°, (Fireside ser.) $1. Burt.
Molière, J. B. P. de. Le misanthrope and L'avare; ed. by W: F. Giese. '01. '02 (F15) S. (Lake French classics.) 50 c. Scott, F. & Co.
Molinerillo (El). Trueba, A. de. 35 c. W: R. Jenkins.
Mollie's mistake. Book, J. W. 15 c. Herder.
Momerie, A. W. Immortality, and other sermons. '02(Ap12) 12°, $1.50. Whittaker.

Mackenzie, Ja. Study of the pulse, arterial, venous, and hepatic, and of the movements of the heart. '02(My17) il. 8°, net, $4.50. Macmillan.

Mackenzie, J: S. Outlines of metaphysics. '02(Ap26) 12°, net, $1.10. Macmillan.

Mackinder, H. J. Britain and the British seas. '02(F22) 8°, (World ser., no. 1.) $2. Appleton.

McKinley, W: Last speech of President McKinley. '02(Mr1) 12°, bds., $1.50; pap., $1. Kirgate Press.

McKINLEY, W:
Ellis. Life of William McKinley. 25 c. Street.
Fallows, *ed.* Life of William McKinley. $1.50; $2.25. Regan.
Halstead. William McKinley [in Norwegian.] $1.50; $2. J: Anderson.
Halstead *and* Munson. Life and services of William McKinley. $1.50; $2.25. Dominion.
Hay. William McKinley. net, 28 c. Crowell.
See also Wilson, J. G.

McKinney, A. H. The child for Christ. '02 (Je28) 16°, net, 50 c. Revell.

McKinney, W: M., *ed.* Encyclopædia of pleading and practice. v. 22, 23. '02(My24) O. shp., ea., $6. E: Thompson.

Mackinnon, Ja. Growth and decline of the French monarchy. '02(Je7) O. $7.50. Longmans.

McLaughlin, Ja. M. Elements and notation of music. '02(F1) D. 55 c. Ginn.

Maclay, E. S. Hist. of the U. S. Navy. New rev. ed. of v. 3. '02(Mr1) 3 v., il. 8°, per v., net, $3. Appleton.

McLellan, Ja. A., Dewey, J:, *and* Ames, A. F. Public school arithmetic for grammar grades. '02(F1) 12°, net, 60 c. Macmillan.

McLeod, Lorenzo C. A young man's problems. '02(Je7) D. 50 c. Flanagan.

McLeod, Malcolm J. Heavenly harmonies for earthly living. '02(F8) 12°, net, 50 c. Revell.

McManman, J. A. *See* Hyde, W. H.

McManus, L. The wager. '02(My17) D. $1.25. Buckles.

Macmillan, Hugh. Christmas rose and other thoughts in verse. '01. '02(Ja4) il. 12°, $1. Macmillan.

Macmillan, Hugh. Corn of Heaven. '02 (Ja18) 12°, $1.75. Macmillan.

Macmillan's classical ser. 12°, net. Macmillan.
—Sophocles. Antigone. 60 c.

Macmillan's Eng. classics. 12°, net, 60 c. Macmillan.
—Boswell. Journal of tour to the Hebrides.
—Scott. Kenilworth.—Quentin Durward.

Macmillan's Greek course. 12°. Macmillan.
—Andrew. Greek prose composition. net, 90 c.

Macmillan's guides. 12°. net. Macmillan.
—Guide to Palestine and Egypt. $3.25.

Macmillan's handbooks of great masters in painting and sculpture. il. 12°, $1.75. Macmillan.
—Bell. Rembrandt.
—Gower. Sir David Wilkie.
—Martin. Gerard Douw.
—Perkins. Giotto.

Macmillan's handbooks of the great craftsmen. il. 12°, $2. Macmillan.
—Cust. Ivory workers of the Middle Ages.
—Headlam. Peter Vischer.

Macmillan's handbooks to the great public schools. 12°, $1.50. Macmillan.
—Airy. Westminster.

Macmillan's manuals for teachers. 12°, net. Macmillan.
—Findlay. Principles of class teaching. $1.25.

Macmillan's mediæval towns ser. il. 12°. Macmillan.
—Headlam. Chartres. $2; $2.50.
—Poole. Cairo. $2; $2.50.

Macmillan's new geography readers: Africa and Australasia. '02(My24) 12°, net, 40 c. Macmillan.

Macmillan's new history readers; [bk. 3.] senior. '02(My24) il. 12°, net, 50 c. Macmillan.

Macmillan's personal problem ser. 12°, net, $1. Macmillan.
—Canfield. College student and his problems.
—Oppenheim. Mental growth and control.

Macmillan's Pitt Press ser. 12°, net. Macmillan.
—Sybel. Prinz Eugen von Savoyen. 60 c.

Macmillan's primary ser. of French and Germ. reading books. 12°, net. Macmillan.
—Alissas, d'. Les histoires de tante. 40 c.

Macmillan's summary of Eng. history on the concentric plan; senior. '02(My24) il. 12°, pap., net, 15 c. Macmillan.

Macmillan's Temple classics. 16°, 50 c.; flex. leath., 75 c. Macmillan.
—Arnold. Dramatic and early poems.
—Boethius. Consolation of philosophy.
—Carlyle. Past and present.
—Goldsmith. Plays.—Poems.

Macmillan's Temple classics for young people. 16°, net. 50 c.; flex. leath., 80 c. Macmillan.
—Perrault. Tales of passed times.

Macnab, Fes. Ride in Morocco among believers and fur traders. '02(Ap19) il. O. $5. Longmans.

McSpadden, J. W. Shakesperian synopses. '02(Ap5) S. (Handy information ser.) net, 45 c. Crowell.

Madame Bohemia. Neilson, F. $1; 50 c. Lippincott.

Mlle. Fouchette. Murray, C: T. $1.50. Lippincott.

Madness of Philip. Daskam, J. D. $1.50. McClure, P.

Maeterlinck, M. The buried temple; tr. by A. Sutro. '02(My10) D. net, $1.40. Dodd.

Maeterlinck, M. Sister Beatrice and Ardiane and Barbe Bleue: two plays; tr. by B. Miall. '02(Ap12) D. net, $1.20. Dodd.

Maggie Miller. '02(Ap19) 12°, (Home lib.) $1. Burt.

Magic key. Tucker, E. S. net, $1. Little, B. & Co.

Magic wheel. Stannard, *Mrs.* H. E. V. $1.25. Lippincott.

MAGNETISM.
See Electricity.

Mahon, R. H. Token of the covenant; or, right use of baptism. 4th ed. '02(My17) D. 50 c. Pub. Ho. M. E. Ch., So.

Mahoney million. Townsend, C: $1.25. New Amsterdam.

Maid of Bar Harbor. Rowe, H. G. $1.50. Little, B. & Co.

Maid of Montauk. Monroe, F. net, $1. W: R. Jenkins.

Maid of the wildwood. Louttit, G: W: $1.50. Colonial.

Main currents in 19th century literature. *See* Brandes, G:

Main street. Hawthorne, N. $2. Kirgate Press.

Maine. Laws concerning business corporations, (annot.) (H. M. Heath.) '02(Je7) O. pap., gratis. Kennebec Journ.

Maine. *Supreme judicial ct.* Repts., v. 95. (C: Hamlin.) '01· '02(Mr15) O. shp., $4. W: W. Roberts.

MAINE.
Drummond, *comp.* Maine masonic text-book. $1.40; $1.50. Berry.

Maitland, F: W:, Gwatkin; H: M., Poole, R. L., *and others.* Essays on the teaching of history. '01· '02(Ja4) 12°, (Cambridge Univ. Press ser.) net, 75 c. Macmillan.

Maitland, J: A. F. Music in England in the nineteenth century. '02(Ap5) 12°, net, $1.75. Dutton.

Majesty of calmness. Jordan, W: G: 50 c. Revell.

Major, C:, ["Edwin Caskoden."] Bears of Blue River. [New issue.] '02(Mr8) il. 12°, $1.50. Macmillan.

Major, C: Dorothy Vernon of Haddon Hall. '02(My3) il. D. $1.50. Macmillan.

Make good book of parodies. Dustin, E. 50 c. E. Dustin.

Making a country newspaper. Munson, A. J. $1. Dominion.

Making of a statesman. Harris, J. C. $1.25. McClure, P.

MALARIAL FEVER.
Ross. Malarial fever. net, 75 c. Longmans.

Malheurs de Sophie. Ségur, S. R., *Comtesse* de. 45 c. Heath.

Mallary, R. DeWitt. Lenox and the Berkshire Highlands. '02(Je21) il. O. net, $1.75. Putnam.

Malone, *Mrs.* **Eva W.** Out among the animals: [stories.] '02(Mr22) S. 75 c. Pub. Ho. M. E. Ch., So.

Malone, Jos. S. Guided and guarded. '02 (Ap26) D. $1.25. Abbey Press.

MALVERN, Eng.
Windle. Malvern country. net, 75 c. Dodd.

MAMMALIA.
Harmer *and* Shipley, *eds.* Cambridge natural history. v. 10, Mammalia, by F. E. Beddard. net, $4. Macmillan.

MAN.
See Anatomy;—Ethnology; — Evolution; — Physiology;—Sex.

Man amongst men. Wollpert, F: 15 c. Eckler.

Man in the moon. Dendron, B. 50 c. Bonnell.

Man of no account. Trelawney, D. 10 c. J. H. West.

Man without a country. Hale, E: E. net, $1. Outlook.

MANCHURIA.
Graham. East of the barrier; or, Manchuria in miniature. net, $1. Revell.

Mandeville, C. E. Minister's manual and pocket ritual. '02(F8) S. flex. leath., net, 60 c. Jennings.

Mangasarian, M. M. New catechism. 3d ed. '02(My10) D. pap., 75 c. Open Court.

Mann, Horace K. Lives of the Popes in the early Middle Ages. v. 1, pt. 1. '02(Je14) 8°, net, $3. Herder.

Manning, Marie. Lord Alingham, bankrupt. '02(Ap12) D. $1.50. Dodd.

Mannix, Ma. E. As true as gold. '02(Mr22) il. S. 45 c. Benziger.

Man's peerless destiny in Christ. Sarles, J: W. net, 90 c. Funk.

MANUAL TRAINING.
See Sloyd.

Manufacturers' need of reciprocity. Farquhar, A. B. 15 c. Am. Acad. Pol. Sci.

MANUSCRIPTS.
See Inscriptions;—Irish literature.

Many waters. Shackleton, R. $1.50. Appleton.

Manzoni, A. I promessi sposi; abr. and ed. by M. Levi. '01· '02(Ja25) D. (Silver ser. of modern lang. text-books.) $1.20. Silver.

Marble faun. Hawthorne, N. $1. Burt.

Marchant, J. R. V. Commercial history. '02 (Je7) il. D. (Commercial ser.) $1. Pitman.

Marchmont, Arth. W. Miser Hoadley's secret. '02(Ap26) 12°, (Red letter ser.) $1.25; pap., 50 c. New Amsterdam.

Marchmont, Arth. W. Sarita, the Carlist. '02 (My3) D. $1.50. Stokes.

Margaret Bowlby. Vincent, E. L. $1.50. Lothrop.

Margaret Tudor. Colcock, A. T. $1. Stokes.

Margaret Vincent. Clifford, *Mrs.* L. L. $1.50. Harper.

Margoliouth, D: S: Lines of defense of the biblical revelation. '02(Mr8) 12°, net, $1.50. Gorham.

Margoliouth, D: S: Religion of Bible lands. '02(My3) S. (Christian study manuals.) 60 c. Armstrong.

Maria Stuart. Schiller, J. C. F. v. net, 70 c. Holt.

MARINE ENGINEERING.
Durand. Practical marine engineering. $5. Marine Engineering.

MARINE ZOOLOGY.
See Aquatic life:—Protozoa.

Marion Manning. Eustis, E. $1.50. Harper.

Marius the epicurean. Pater, W. $1. Burt.

Marivaux, Pierre C. de C. de. Selection from comedies by E. W. Olmsted. '02 (Mr22) 12°, net, 90 c. Macmillan.

MARK, *St.*
See Bible.

Marks, Jeannette A. Brief hist. outline of Eng. literature. '02(Je28) D. $1. J. A. Marks.

Marlowe, Chris. Passionate shepherd to his love; and The nymph's reply to the shepherd, by Sir. W. Raleigh. '02(My10) sq. 8°, flex. vellum, net, $3.75.) Russell.

MARQUETTE, Jacques.
Thwaites. Father Marquette. net, $1. Appleton.

Marquis, G: H. Fairview's mystery. '01· '02(Mr1) D. 75 c. Abbey Press.

Marred in the making. Commander, L. K. $3; 25 c. Eckler.

MARRIAGE.
Cook. Bride's book. net, $1.50. Dutton.
Crawley. The mystic rose: study of primitive marriage. net, $4. Macmillan.

MARRIAGE.—*Continued.*
Hurst. New heartstone: bridal greeting. $1. Jennings.
Westermarck. Hist. of human marriage. net, $4.50. Macmillan.
Wood. Marriage. net, $1.25. Revell.
Marriage of Laurentia. Haultmont, M. net, $1.60. Herder.
Marsh, C: L. Not on the chart. '02(Je7) il. D. $1.50. Stokes.
Marsh, G: A singular will. '02(Je7) D. $1.50. Neely.
Marshall, Beatrice. Old Blackfriars. '02 (Ap5) il. 12°, $1.50. Dutton.
Marshall, J: S. Principles and practice of operative dentistry. '01· '02(F15) il. 8°, subs., $5; shp., $6. Lippincott.
Marshall, W: L. *See* Clark, W: L.
Marston, E: Sketches of some booksellers of the time of Dr. Samuel Johnson. '02 (My10) 16°, net, $2. Scribner.
Martin, Fred. W. Album of designs for boats, launches and yachts. [2d ed.] '02(My24) il. obl. T. pap., $1. F: W. Martin.
Martin, G: H. Civil government in the U. S. Rev. ed. '02(Ap26) D. 90 c. Am. Bk.
Martin, W. Gerard Douw; fr. the Dutch by Clara Bell. '02(My3) il. 12°, (Great masters in painting and sculpture.) $1.75. Macmillan.
Martin, W. G. W. Traces of the elder faiths of Ireland. '02(F8) 2 v., il. O. $12. Longmans.
Martindale, J. B. Am. law directory, Jan., 1902. '02(F1) O. shp., net, $10. Martindale.
Marvelous achievements of the 19th century. Morris, C: $2.50; $3.50. Winston.
Marx, Karl. Wage-labor and capital; also Free-trade. '02(Mr29) D. (Arm and hammer ser.) 50 c. N. Y. Labor News.
MARY, *Virgin.*
Palladino. Mary our mother. net, 15 c. Herder.
Mary Garvin. Pattee, F. L. $1.50. Crowell.
Mary Starkweather. Williamson, *Mrs.* C. C. $1.50. Abbey Press.
Mary Stuart. *See* Schiller, J. C. F. v.
Mary Tracy's fortune. Sadlier, A. T. 45 c. Benziger.
Maryland. *Ct. of appeals.* Repts. (Brantly.) v. 93. '02(My10) O. shp., $5. Baughman.
Maryland. *Ct. of appeals.* Repts. v. 59. '02(Mr1); v. 60 (My10); v. 61(Je21) O. shp., ea., $4. Curlander.
MARYLAND.
Steiner. Western Md. in the Revolution. 30 c. Johns Hopkins.
Mason, Arth. J. Christianity, what is it? '02(Je7) 16°, (Church Hist. Soc. lectures, no. 66.) 80 c. E. & J. B. Young.
Mason, Arth. J. Ministry of conversion. '02 (Mr8) D. (Handbooks for the clergy.) net, 90 c. Longmans.
Mason, Hobart. *See* Sheldon, S:
Mason, W: D. Water-supply (from a sanitary standpoint.) 3d ed., rewritten. '02 (My17) il. 8°, red. to $4. Wiley.
MASONRY.
See **Bridges**
MASS.
See **Catholic church;—Lord's supper.**
Massachusetts digest, supp. [v. 5.] by C: N. Harris. '02(Je28) Q. shp., net, $5. Little, B. & Co.
Massachusetts. *Supreme judicial ct.* Repts. v. 178. (H: W. Swift.) '02(Ap5) O. shp., $2. Little, B. & Co.
Massachusetts. Treatise on the street railway accident law; by E. H. Clark. '02 (Ap19) O. shp., $3.25. Lawyers' Bk.
MASSACHUSETTS.
American ser. of popular biographies. Mass. ed. $17. Graves.
Hall, *ed.* **Regiments and armories of Mass. v. 2. per set, $12; $18; $25.** W. W. Potter.
Tucker. Preparation of wills: Mass. law. $3.50. G: B. Reed.
See also **Ancient and Hon. Artillery Co. of Mass.; —Boston;—Lexington.**
MASSAGE.
See **Injuries.**
Master of Caxton. Brooks, H. $1.50. Scribner.
Master of science of right living. Hillis, N. D. net, 50 c. Revell.
Mastery of the Pacific. Colquhoun, A. R. net, $4. Macmillan.
MATABELELAND.
Hall *and* Neal. Ancient ruins of Rhodesia. net, $6. Dutton.
Mate of the good ship "York." Russell, W: C. $1.50. L. C. Page.
MATERIA MEDICA.
Murray. Rough notes on remedies. net, $1.25. Blakiston.
MATHEMATICS.
Deel. Practical rapid calculator. 50 c. G: A. Deel.
Gibbs. Vector analysis. net, $4. Scribner.
Stokes. Math. and physical papers. v. 3. net, $3.75. Macmillan.
See also **Algebra; — Arithmetic; — Astronomy; — Calculus; — Interest; — Logarithms; — Surveying;—Trigonometry.**
Mathes, J. H. General Forrest. '02(Ap26) D. (Great commanders' ser.) net, $1.50. Appleton.
Matheson, G: Spiritual development of St. Paul. '02(Ap12) 12°, net, 80 c. Whittaker.
Matheson, G: Times of retirement; with biog. sketch of the author by D. MacMillan. '01· '02(Ja11) 12°, net, $1.25. Revell.
Mathews, Ferd. S. Field book of Am. wild flowers. '02(Ap26) il. S. net, $1.75. Putnam.
Mathews, Shailer. *See* Burton, E. D.
Matthews, C: G. Manual of alcoholic fermentation and allied industries. '02(Ap19) D. net, $2.60. Longmans.
Matthews, Ja. B. Pen and ink: [essays.] 3d rev., enl. ed. '02(F15) D. net, $1.25. Scribner.
Maulde la Clavière, René de. Art of life; tr. by G: H. Ely. '01· '02(Ja25) D. net, $1.75. Putnam.
Mavor, W: English spelling book; il. by Kate Greenaway. '02(Je28) 16°, bds., 40 c. Warne.
Maxwell, Lucy H. Card sewing: for kindergartens. '02(My3) 16°, pap., 50 c. M. Bradley.
Maxwell, *Mrs.* Ma. E. B. El sacrificio de Elisa. (A. Elias y Pujol.) '01. '02(F22) 12°, pap., 50 c. Appleton.

Mayor, Jos. B. Chapters on Eng. metre. 2d ed., rev. and enl. '02(Ja18) 8°, (Cambridge Univ. Press ser.) net, $2.25. Macmillan.

Mazel. Fisguill, R: $1.50. H. S. Stone.

Mead, Spencer P. Hist. and genealogy of the Mead family of Fairfield Co., Conn. '01-'02(F8) il. O. $15. Knickerbocker.

Meade, L. T. *See* Smith, *Mrs.* E. T.

Meakin, Budgett. The Moors. '02(Mr29) il. 8°, net, $5. Macmillan.

Meakin, Nevill M. The Assassins. '02 (Mr22) D. $1.50. Holt.

MEAT.

Walley. Guide to meat inspection. $3. W: R. Jenkins.

Mechanical triumphs of ancient Egyptians. Barber, F. M. net, $1.25. Dodd.

MECHANICS.

Gibbs. Elem. principles in statistical mechanics, with especial ref. to the rational foundation of thermo-dynamics. $4. Scribner.

Reynolds. Papers on mechanical and physical subjects. v. 2. net, $6. Macmillan.

See also Engineering;—Power.

MECHANICS' LIENS.

Illinois. Commentary on mechanics' lien law. net, $4. Callaghan.

Mechanics of engineering. *See* Du Bois, A: J.

Mechem, Floyd R. Case on the law of damages. 3d ed. '02(Mr8) O, net, $4. West Pub.

Medical directory of the city of New York. '01-'02(F8) 12°, $1.50. Wynkoop.

Medical News pocket formulary for 1902; ed. by E. Q. Thornton. 4th ed. '02(F15) 18°, leath. tuck, net, $1.50. Lea.

Medical News visiting list, 1902. '01-'02 (F22) 16°, leath. tucks, $1.25; thumb-letter index, $1.50. Lea.

MEDICI (The).

Smeaton. The Medici and the Italian Renaissance. $1.25. Scribner.

MEDICINE.

American year-book of medicine and surgery. 2 v. ea., net, $3; net, $3.75. Saunders.

Billings *and* Stanton, *eds.* General medicine. $1.50. Year Bk.

Buck. Reference handbook of the medical sciences. v. 4. subs., $7: $8: $9. Wood.

Burdick. Standard medical manual. $4. Engelhard.

Fagge. Text-book of medicine. 2 v. net, $6. Blakiston.

International medical annual, 1902. net, $3. Treat.

Lawrence. Practical medicine. $3. Boericke & T.

Medical News pocket formulary, 1902. net, $1.50. Lea.

Paget. Sel. essays and addresses. $5. Longmans.

Sajous, *ed.* Analytical encyclopædia of practical medicine. v. 1. subs., ea, $5; $6. Davis.

See also Accidents;—Chemistry;—Hygiene;—Mind and body;—Nervous system;—Pathology;—Pharmacy.

Meditations and vows. Hall, J. $1.50. Dutton.

Meditations of an autograph collector. Joline, A. H. net, $3. Harper.

Medley, Dudley J. Student's manual of Eng. constitutional history. 3d ed. '02(Je28) 8°, net, $3.50. Macmillan.

Meier, W. H. D. Herbarium and plant description. '01-'02(F1) Q. portfolio, 70 c. Ginn.

Melliar, A. F. Book of the rose. 2d ed. '02 (My24) 12°, $1.75. Macmillan.

Mellick, Anna C. Latin composition for classes reading Cæsar. '01. '02(Ja4) S. 40 c. Am. Bk.

Melomaniacs. Huneker, J. $1.50. Scribner.

Melville, Herman. Typee; ed. by W. P. Trent. '02(My17) il. D. (Home and school classics, young reader's ser.) 45 c. Heath.

Memoirs of an American lady. Grant, *Mrs.* A. M. net, $7.50. Dodd.

MEMORIAL DAY

Harvey. Aids for the proper observance of Memorial day by schools of Wis. gratis. Democrat Pr. Co.

MEMORY.

Kilbourne. Memory and its cultivation. $1; 50 c. Mullin.

MEN.

Blouët. 'Tween you an' I; pt. 1, Concerning men. $1.20. Lothrop.

Men and memories. Young, J: R. subs., $5; $3. Neely.

Menefee, Maud. Child stories from the masters. '02(My10) il. 16° 75 c. Rand, McN. & Co.

Menpes, Mortimer. Japan. '02(Ja18) il. 8°, net, $6. Macmillan.

MENTAL ARITHMETIC.

See Arithmetic.

Mental growth and control. Oppenheim, N. net, $1. Macmillan.

MENTAL SCIENCE.

Bradbury. New philosophy of health. 75 c. Alliance.

Dresser. True hist. of mental science. 20 c. Alliance.

Patterson. What the new thought stands for. 10 c. Alliance.

Patterson. The will to be well. $1. Alliance.

See also Christian science;—Mind and body.

Mental state of hystericals. Janet, P. $3.50. Putnam.

Merchant of Venice. *See* Shakespeare, W:

Mercier, C: A. Psychology, normal and morbid. '02(Mr1) 8°, net, $4. Macmillan.

Mercier, C: A. Text-book of insanity. '02 (My17) 12°, net, $1.75. Macmillan.

Merriam, Edm. F. Hist. of Am. Bapt. missions. '01. '02(F15) 12°, $1.25. Am. Bapt.

Merrill, S. M., *and* Warren, H: W. Discourses on miracles. '02(Mr22) sq. T. (Little books on doctrine.) net, 25 c. Jennings.

Merriman, Mansfield, *and* Jacoby, H: D. Text-book on roofs and bridges. Pt. 3. 4th ed., rewritten. '02(Ap19) 8°, $2.50. Wiley.

MESA VERDE.

See Colorado.

Message of to-morrow. Lee, J: L. net, $1.20. Revell.

Message to Garcia and thirteen other things. Hubbard, E. $2: $5: $15. Roycrofters.

METAL-WORK.

See Plate

METALS AND METALLURGY.
Langbein. Complete treatise on the electro-deposition of metals. $4. Baird.
Phillips, *ed.* Methods for analysis of ores, pig iron and steel. net, $1. Chemical.
See also Assaying;—Blowpipe;—Chemistry;—Copper;—Iron;—Precious metals;—Steel.

METAPHYSICS.
Kant. Prolegomena to any future metaphysics. 50 c. Open Court.
Leibnitz. Discourse on metaphysics. 35 c.; net, 75 c. Open Court.
Mackenzie. Outlines of metaphysics. net, $1.10. Macmillan.
See also Ontology.

METEOROLOGY.
See Weather.

Methodist Episcopal church. Constitution of churches in America, by W. F. Barclay. '02(My10) D. pap., 40 c. Pub. Ho. M. E. Ch., So.
Methodist Episcopal church, South. Minutes of the annual conferences for 1901. '01· '02 (My10) O. pap., net, 50 c. Pub. Ho. M. E. Ch., So.

METHODIST EPISCOPAL CHURCH.
Bowen. Why two Episcopal Methodist churches in the U. S.? 75 c. Pub. Ho. of M. E. Ch., So.
Oliver. Our lay office-bearers. net, 25 c. Jennings.
See also Epworth League.

Methods of keeping the public money of the U. S. Phillips, J: B. $1. Mich. Pol. Sci.
Methods of Lady Walderhurst. Burnett, *Mrs.* F. H. $1.25. Stokes.

METRE.
Mayor. Chapters on Eng. metre. net, $2.25. Macmillan.

Metropolitan club cook-book. Schaeffer, *Mrs.* J. $1.75. Augsburg.
Mets, J. A. Naval heroes of Holland. '02 (Je14) il. D. $1.50. Abbey Press.

MEXICO.
Wilkins. Glimpse of old Mexico. 75 c. Whitaker & R.

Meyer, B. H. Advisory councils in railway administration. '02(Mr22) 8°. (Pub. of the soc., no. 327.) pap., 15 c. Am. Acad. Pol. Sci.
Meyer, Ernest C. Nominating systems; with bibliog. and index '02(Ap5) 8°, net, $1.50. E. C. Meyer.
Meyers, R. C. V. Theodore Roosevelt, patriot and statesman. '02(F22) il. 12°. subs., $1.50; hf. mor., $2. W. W. Wilson.
Meyers, R. C. V. Theodore Roosevelt, patriot and statesman. '02(Mr15) il. 12°, $1.50; hf. rus., $2. Ziegler.
Michael Ferrier. Poynter, E. F. $1.50. Macmillan.
Michael Ross, minister. Holdsworth, A. E. $1.50. Dodd.
Michaud, Henri. L'idole. '02(My24) D. (Michaud's ser. of Fr. plays for schools, no. 9.) pap., 10 c. W: R. Jenkins.
Michelsen, Alb. A. Velocity of light. '02 (Ap19) O. pap., net, 25 c. Univ. of Chic.
Michie, T: J., *ed.* Banking cases annot. v. 3. '01. '02(Ja18) O. shp., $5. Michie.
Michie. T: J., *ed.* Municipal corporation cases annot. v. 6. '02(Mr1) O. shp., $5. Michie.
Michigan. Law of personal injuries, by W. Baldwin. '02(My24) O. shp., net, $4. Callaghan.
Michigan. *Supreme ct.* Index digest, July, 1898-Jan., 1902. (C. P. Campbell.) '02 (Mr22) O. shp., $3.50. Index Digest.
Michigan. *Supreme ct.* Repts. (J: A. Brooks.) v. 125. '01· '02(Ja18); v. 126 (My24) O. shp., ea., $3.50. Callaghan.

MICHIGAN.
Hollister, *and others.* Taxation in Mich. 50 c. Mich. Pol. Sci.
Keith. Historical sketch of internal improvements in Mich., 1836-1846. 50 c. Mich. Pol. Sci.

MICROSCOPE.
Gage. The microscope. $1.50. Comstock Pub.

MIDDLE AGES.
Cust. Ivory workers of the Middle Ages. $2. Macmillan.

MIDWIFERY.
Jewett. Essentials of obstetrics. net, $2.25. Lea.
Jewett. Practice of obstetrics. net, $5; $6; $6.50. Lea.

Mighty means of usefulness. McClure, J. G. K. net, 50 c. Revell.
Miles, Eustace H. Failures of vegetarianism. '02(Ap5) 12°, net, $1.50. Dutton.
Miles, Eustace H. How to prepare essays, lectures, [etc.] '02(F15) 12°, net, $2. Dutton.

MILITARY ART AND SCIENCE.
See Ancient and Hon. Artillery Co. of Mass.;—Infantry;—West Point.

Miller, Alf. S. Manual of assaying. 2d ed. '02(Je21) il. 16°, $1. Wiley.
Miller, And. J., *comp.* The toastmaster. '02 (Je7) sq. D. pap., n. p. W. M. Rogers.
Miller, Ja. R. Story of Joseph. '02(F8) 16°, net, 35 c. Revell.
Miller, *Mrs.* Ma. R. The brook book. '02 (My10) O. net, $1.35. Doubleday, P.
Miller, W: J. American church dict. and cyclopedia. '01. '02(Ja4) D. $1. Whittaker.
Millet's Oriental ser. 8°. Millet.
—Brinkley, Japan. 4 v. ea., $50.
Millionaire's love story. Boothby, G. $1.25. Buckles.
Millionaire mystery. Hume, F. W. $1.25. Buckles.
Mills, Harry E: Select sunflowers: [poems.] '01· '02(F8) 12°, $1. Sunflower Press.
Mills, Jane D., [*Mrs.* Ja. E. Mills.] Leaves from a life-book of to-day. '01. '02(Ja11) S. 50 c. Swedenborg.
Milne, W: J. Key to Academic algebra. '02 (Mr29) O. $1.50. Am. Bk.
Milne, W: J. Key to the Standard arithmetic and the Mental arithmetic. '01· '02 (Ja11) S. 75 c. Am. Bk.
Milton, J: Complete poems. '01· '02(Ja11) 16°. (Caxton ser.) flex. lambskin, net, $1.20. Scribner.
Milton, J: Selections. '01. '02(Ap5) S. (Little masterpieces.) 50 c. Doubleday, P.

MIND.
Brooks. Elements of mind. $4. Longmans.
Hobhouse. Mind in evolution. net, $3.25. Macmillan.

MIND.—*Continued.*
Oppenheim. Mental growth and control. net, $1. Macmillan.
See also Intellect:—Mind and body;—Psychology.

MIND AND BODY.
Brown. Studies in spiritual harmony. $1. Reed Pub.
Janet. Mental state of hystericals. $3.50. Putnam.
Wright. Body and soul. $1. J. C. Wright.
See also Hypnotism;—Insanity;—Mental science;—Nervous system;—Psychology.

MIND READING.
See Telepathy.

Mind telegraph. Stay, J. B. 25 c. Alliance.

Miner, W: H. Daniel Boone: cont. toward a bibliog. '01. '02(F15) D. bds., $1. Dibdin Club.

MINERALOGY.
Eakle. Colemanite from So. California. 15 c. Univ. of Cal.
See also Assaying;—Blowpipe;—Geology;—Metals and metallurgy;—Mines and mining.

MINES AND MINING.
Oregon. Mining laws. 40 c. Or. Mining Journ.
Pratt. Supp. to Mining laws of Colorado. 35 c. Pratt Merc.
See also Copper;—Engineering; — Iron; — Metals and metallurgy.

Minister's wooing. Stowe, *Mrs.* H. B. $1. Burt.

MINISTERS (*of the Gospel*).
Anderson. Christian ministry. 20 c. Young Churchman.
Kern. Way of the preacher. $1.25. Pub. Ho. M. E. Ch., So.
Mandeville. Minister's manual and pocket ritual. net, 60 c. Jennings.
Robinson. Personal life of the clergy. net, 90 c. Longmans.
See also Missions and missionaries;—Ordination;—Preaching;—Priests.

Ministry of conversion. Mason, A. J. net, 90 c. Longmans.

Minneapolis Journal almanac and year book, 1902. '02(Ap26) 12°, pap., 25 c. Journal Pr. Co.

Minnesota. Justice's manual; by W. S. Booth. 12th ed. '01. '02(Ja18) D. pap., $1.50. Booth.

Minnesota. *Supreme ct.* Repts. v. 83. '02 (Ap5) O. shp., $2.75. Dufresne.

Minority (The). Hill, F: T. $1.50. Stokes.

Minton, H: C. The cosmos and the logos. '02(Mr22) O. net, $1.25. Westminster.

MIRACLES.
Merrill *and* Warren. Discourses on miracles. 25 c. Jennings.
See also Psychical research.

Misanthrope (Le). Moliere, J. B. P. de. 50 c. Scott, F. & Co.

Misdemeanors of Nancy. Hoyt, E. $1.50. Doubleday, P.

Miser Hoadley's secret. Marchmont, A. W. $1.25; 50 c. New Amsterdam.

Misérables (Les). *See* Quayle, W: A.

Miss Ashton's new pupil. Robbins, *Mrs.* S. S. $1. Burt.

Miss Petticoats. Tilton, D. $1.50. C. M. Clark.

Miss Prudence. Conklin, *Mrs.* J. M. D. $1. Burt.

MISSIONS AND MISSIONARIES.
Beach. Geography and atlas of Protestant missions. v. 1. $2.50; per set, $1.75. Student Vol.
Brain. Fifty missionary programmes. 35 c. Un. Soc. C. E.
Carey. Adventures in Tibet. net, $1.50. Un. Soc. C. E.
Dean. Cross of Christ in Bololand. net, $1. Revell.
Dennis. Centennial survey of foreign missions. net, $4. Revell.
Jesuit relations: travels and explorations of the Jesuit missionaries in New France, 1610-1791. 73 v. ea.. net, $3.50. Burrows.
Ketler. Tragedy of Paotingfu, China. net, $2. Revell.
Longridge. Official and lay witness to the value of foreign missions. 20 c. E. & J. B. Young.
Montgomery. Foreign missions. net, 90 c. Longmans.
Smith, B. Uncle Boston's spicy breezes. net, $1. Am. Bapt.
Smith, J. Ten years in Burma. net, $1. Jennings.
Warneck. Outline of hist. of Protestant missions. net, $2. Revell.
See also Philippine Islands;—Protestantism;—*also* names of churches.

Mississippi. *Supreme ct.* Repts. v. 78. '01. '02(My10) O. shp., $4. Marshall.

Mississippi bubble. Hough, E. $1.50. Bowen-M.

Missouri. *St. Louis and the Kansas City cts. of appeals.* Cases. v. 89. '01. '02(Mr1) O. shp., $5. Stephens.

Missouri statute annots.; by S: J. McCulloch. 2d ed. '02(My24) O. hf. shp., $3. S: J. McCulloch.

Missouri. *Supreme ct.* Repts. (Rader.) v. 162, 163. '01. '02(Mr1); v. 164 (My10) O. shp., ea., $4. Stephens.

Mr. Whitman. Pullen, *Mrs.* E. $1.50. Lothrop.

Misunderstood. Montgomery, F. $1. Beam.

Mitchell, C. A. *See* Oppenheimer, C.

Mitchell, Fes. L. Georgia land and people. '02(Ap26) 12°, $1.25. F. L. Mitchell.

Mitton, G. E. The opportunist. '02(Mr8) 12°, $2. Macmillan.

Moberly, R. C. Christ our life. '02(Mr22) O. net, $3. Longmans.

Mobile Boer. Hiley, A. R. I. $1.50. Grafton Press.

Modern association and railroading. Goodknight, A. L. 50 c. Abbey Press.

Modern lang ser. *See* Heath's.

Molander, Anna. Scientific sloyd: for teachers and schools. '02(My3) S. 50 c. Bardeen.

Molesworth, *Mrs.* Ma. L. Grandmother dear. '02(Je28) il. 12°, (St. Nicholas ser.) 75 c. Burt.

Molesworth, *Mrs.* Ma. L. Robin Redbreast. '02(My3) il. 12°, (Fireside ser.) $1. Burt.

Molière, J. B. P. de. Le misanthrope and L'avare; ed. by W: F. Giese. '01. '02 (F15) S. (Lake French classics.) 50 c. Scott, F. & Co.

Molinerillo (El). Trueba, A. de. 35 c. W: R. Jenkins.

Mollie's mistake. Book, J. W. 15 c. Herder.

Momerie, A. W. Immortality, and other sermons. '02(Ap12) 12°, $1.50. Whittaker.

Mon oncle et mon curé. La Brète, J. de. 50 c. Am. Bk.
Monadology. *See* Leibnitz, *Baron* G. W. v.
Monaghan, Ja. *See* Pennsylvania. Digest.
MONASTICISM.
Feasey. Monasticism. net, $1. Herder.
Monell, S. H. System of instruction in X-ray methods. '02(My10) il. 8°, subs., hf. mor., $15. Pelton.
MONEY.
Del Mar. Hist. of money in England. $2.—Netherlands. 50 c. Cambridge.
Green. Shakespeare and Goethe on Gresham's law and the single gold standard. 25 c. MacGowan.
See also Finance.
Money-maker. Adams, W: T. $1.25. Lee & S.
Monica. Bourget, P. $1.50. Scribner.
Monkhouse, Cosmo. History and desc. of Chinese porcelain. '02(Mr15) il. 8°, net, $10. Wessels.
Monroe. Forest, [*pseud.* for Ferdinand G. Wiechmann.] Maid of Montauk. '02 (Ap26) il. D. net, $1. W: R. Jenkins.
Monroe, Ja. Writings. v. 5, 1807-16. '02 8°, hf. leath., subs., $5. Putnam.
Monroe, Lewis B., *ed.* Public and parlor readings. '01· '02(Mr1) 4 v., 12°, ea., $1. Lee & S.
Monroe Rebekah Lodge: semi-centennial of Monroe Rebekah Lodge, no. 1, I. O. O. F., Jan. 23, 1902. '02(Mr8) 8°, pap., 10 c. Darrow.
Monsell, J. R. The pink knight. '01· '02 (Ja18) il. 32°, bds., net, 40 c. Stokes.
Monsieur Bergeret. France, A. $1. Silver.
Monsieur Martin. Carey, W. net, $1.20. Putnam.
Montgomery, Flo. Misunderstood. [New issue.] '02(Ja4) D. $1. Beam.
Montgomery, H: H. Foreign missions. '02 (Ap26) D. (Handbooks for the clergy.) net, 90 c. Longmans.
MONTREAL.
Bosworth, *ed.* Hochelaga depicta; early hist. of city and island. net, $3; net, $4.50. Congdon.
MONUMENTS.
See Tombstones.
Moody, L:, *ed.* Corporation securities. '02 (Je28) O. $7.50; flex. leath., $10. Moody.
Moody, W: V., *and* Lovett, R. M. Hist. of Eng. literature. '02(My10) O. net, $1.25. Scribner.
Moore, Fk. F. A damsel or two. '02(Ap26) D. $1.50. Appleton.
Moore, *Sir* J: W:, *ed.* Variola, vaccination, cholera, erysipelas, etc. '02(Mr22) il. 8°, (Nothnagel's encyclopedia of practical medicine, v. 2.) net, $5; hf. mor., net, $6. Saunders.
Moore, T: E. My Lord Farquhar. '02(My3) D. $1.25. Abbey Press.
MOORS.
Meakin. The Moors. net, $5. Macmillan.
Moral drill. Harper, J: M. $1. Kellogg.
Morceau de pain. Coppée. F. 25 c. W: R. Jenkins.
Morchester. Datchet, C: net, $1.20. Putnam.
More, Egbert. Trisection of a given angle geometrically solved and illustrated. '01· '02(F1) il. O. pap., $1. Wickes.
More, *Sir* T: Utopia, and life of More, by W: Roper. '02(My10) 12°, (Home lib.) $1. Burt.
More animal stories. Cochrane, R. net, $1. Lippincott.
More ex-tank tales. Cullen, C. L: $1. Ogilvie.
More tales of the birds. Fowler, W: W. $1. Macmillan.
Morehead, G: Francesca Da Rimini. '02 (Mr22) il. D. (Sunnyside ser., no. 117.) pap., 25 c. Ogilvie.
Morehead, G: Madame Du Barry. '02(My17) 12°, pap., 50 c. Donohue.
Morehead, G: Nell Gwyn. '01· '02(F15) il. 12°, pap., 25 c. Ogilvie.
Morehead, G: Story of François Villon. '01. '02(F15) 12°, (Peerless ser., no. 124.) pap., 25 c. Ogilvie.
Morfill, W. R. Hist. of Russia from Peter the Great to Nicholas II. '02(Mr15) 12°, $1.75. Pott.
Morgan, Alex. Advanced physiography. '01. '02(F8) il. D. $1.50. Longmans.
Morgan, C: Herbert. *See* Taylor, T: E.
Morgan, Emily M. Flight of the *Swallow.* '02(Mr15) il. 12°, 50 c. Pott.
Morgan, J: L. R. Elements of physical chemistry. 2d ed., rev. and enl. '02(Mr8) 12°, $2. Wiley.
Morley, J:, *ed.* *See* English men of letters.
MORMONISM.
Lamb. The Mormons and their Bible. net, 25 c. Am. Bapt.
Linn. Story of the Mormons. net, $4. Macmillan.
MOROCCO.
Grove. Seventy-one days' camping in Morocco. net, $2.50. Longmans.
Macnab. Ride in Morocco. $5. Longmans.
MORPHINISM.
Crothers. Morphinism and narcomania from opium, etc. $2. Saunders.
MORPHOLOGY.
See Anatomy;—Embryology;—Histology.
Morrill, W: W. *See* Am. electrical cases.
Morris, C: Marvelous achievements of the 19th century. 16th ed. '02(Ap5) il. sq. 8°, $2.50; hf. mor., $3.50. Winston.
Morris, C: Twentieth century encyclopædia. '01. '02(Ap5) il. 12°, $3.50; hf. mor., $4.25; mor., $5.50 Winston.
Morris, Clara, [*Mrs.* Harriott.] A pasteboard crown. '02(Je7) il. D. $1.50. Scribner.
Morris, E: P. On principles and methods in Latin syntax. '01. '02(F15) 8°, (Yale bicentennial pubs.) net, $2. Scribner.
Morris, Ella G. Right living; or, how a woman can get well and keep well. '02 (My17) 8°, $1. Bardeen.
Morris, Ida D., [*Mrs.* Ja. E. Morris.] Golden Fluff. '01· '02(Ja18) il. 12°, 50 c. Abbey Press.
Morris, Mowbray. Tales of the Spanish Main. '01. '02(Ja18) il. D. $2. Macmillan.
Morris, W: Art and craft of printing. '02 (Mr15) 8°, bds., $5. Elston Press.
Morrow, Rob. G., *rep.* *See* Oregon. *Sup. ct.* Repts.
Morse's geographical ser. il. 16°. Morse.
—Carroll. Around the world. 60 c.
Morse's new century ser. 12°. Morse.
—Thompson. New century readers. 3d bk: 52 c.

Mortimer, Alfr. G. Catholic faith and practice. 2 pts. 2d ed., rev. '01· '02(Mr8) O. pt. 1, $2; pt. 2, $2.50. Longmans.
Morton, H: H. Genito-urinary disease and syphilis. '02(Mr29) il. 12°, net, $3. Davis.
Morton, Victor. Thoughts on hell. '02(Mr8) 8°, net, 50 c. Herder.
Mosaics from India. Denning, M. net, $1.50. Revell.
Moser, Gustav v. Der bibliothekar; ed. by W: A. Cooper. '02(Mr8) D. 45 c. Am. Bk.
Moses, Montrose J. *See* Funk, I: K.
Mosher's vest-pocket ser. nar. S. T: B. Mosher.
—Stevenson. Æs triplex, and other essays. 25 c.-$1.
MOSQUITOES.
Berkeley. Lab'y work with mosquitoes. net, $1. Pediatrics Lab'y.
Ross. Mosquito brigades and how to organize them. net, 90 c. Longmans.
Mother Margaret's bunch of flowers. Quinius, A. 5 c. J: G. Quinius.
MOTHER-PLAY.
Proudfoot. A year with the Mother-play. $1. Flanagan.
MOTORS.
See Cars;—Dynamos and motors.
Moule, H. C. G. Thoughts for the Sundays of the year. '02(Mr8) 12°, net, $1. Revell.
Moulton, C: W., *and others, eds.* Library of literary criticism of Eng. and Am. authors. v. 3. '02(Mr1) O. $5; hf. mor., $6.50. Moulton Pub.
Moulton, *Mrs.* Louise C. Her baby brother. New ed. '01. '02(F15) 16°, (Children's friend ser.) bds., 50 c. Little, B. & Co.
MOUNDS.
Peterson. The mound building age in N. A. 25 c. Clarke.
Mount of Olives. Saltus, F. S. $1; net, 25 c. Bk. Lover.
Mountaineers. Smith, J: W. $1; $1.50; $2; $2.50. Pub. Ho. of M. E. Ch., So.
Movable quartette. Guyse, E. $1. Abbey Press.
Mower, C: D. How to build a knockabout. '02(Ap26) il. f°, ("How-to" ser.) $1. Rudder.
Mower, C: D. How to build a racing sloop. '02(F15) Q. ("How-to" ser.) $1. Rudder.
Mowry, Arth. M. First steps in the history of England. '02(Je21) il. D. 70 c. Silver.
Moy, Eocha. One: a song of the ages. '02 (Ap26) 12°, $1.50. Neely.
Mudge, G. P. Text-book of zoology. '01· '02(Mr8) D. $2.50. Longmans.
Mudge, Ja. Life of love. '02(F15) sq. T. (Little books on devotion.) 25 c. Jennings.
Muench, Friedrich. Gesammelte lechriften. '02(Je28) 8°, $1.75; mor., $2.50. Witter.
Muirhead, J. H. Philosophy and life, and other essays. '02(My24) 12°, $1.50. Macmillan.
Muirhead, Ja. F. America, the land of contrasts. New ed. '02(F22) 12°, net, $1.20. Lane.
Mulholland, Clara. Bunt and Bill. '02(Mr8) il. S. 45 c. Benziger.
Mullen, W: How to break, educate and handle the horse for the uses of every-day life. '02(F1) il. D. $1. W: Mullen.
Muller, Ma. Wretched Flea; story of a Chinese boy. '01· '02(Ja11) il. S. 35 c. Flanagan.
Mundy, W: N. Eclectic practice in diseases of children. '02(Je21) D. (Eclectic manual, no. 5.) net, $2.50. Scudder.
MUNICIPAL CORPORATIONS.
Michie, *ed.* Municipal corporation cases. v. 6. $5. Michie.
Municipal engineering and sanitation. Baker, M. N. net, $1.25. Macmillan.
MUNICIPAL GOVERNMENT.
Clow. Comparative study of the administration of city finances in the U. S. $1. Macmillan.
Munn, C: C. Rockhaven. '02(Mr29) il. D. $1.50. Lee & S.
Munro, J: Nociones de electricidad. '01· '02 (F22) 18°, 40 c. Appleton.
Munson, A. J. Making a country newspaper. '02(Mr22) 16°, $1. Dominion.
Munson, A. J. *See also* Halstead, M.
Murché, V. T. Rural readers; for senior classes. '02(Ap12) il. 12°, net, 40 c. Macmillan.
Murché, V. T. Teacher's manual of object lessons for rural schools. '02(Ap12) il. 12°, net, 60 c. Macmillan.
Murché, V. T. Teacher's manual of object lessons in geography. '02(Je28) il. 12°, net, 80 c. Macmillan.
Murders in the Rue Morgue. Poe, E. A. $1. Burt.
Murison, Ross G. Babylonia and Assyria. '01· '02(Ja11) 16°, (Bible class primers.) net. 20 c. Scribner.
Murlin, Edg. L. Illustrated legislative manual; New York red book. '02(My17) 12°, $1. Lyon.
Murphy, J: B., *ed.* General surgery. '01· '02(Mr8) il. D. (Practical medicine ser. of year-books, v. 2.) $1.50. Year Bk.
Murray, C: T. Mlle. Fouchette. '02(Mr15) il. D. $1.50. Lippincott.
MURRAY, Ja.
Tiffany *and* Lesley, *eds.* Letters of James Murray, loyalist. net, $2.50. W: B. Clarke.
Murray, Ja. A: H:, *and others, eds.* New Eng. dictionary. v. 3. pts. 30-33. '01. '02 (Mr22); pt. 34 (Ap19); v. 4. pt. 35 (Je7); pt. 36 (Je21) f°, pap., ea., 90 c. Oxford Univ.
Murray, W: Rough notes on remedies. 4th ed. '02(F15) 12°, net, $1.25. Blakiston.
Murrell, W: *See* Ewart, W:
Murrin, F. D. Vocal exercises on the vocal factors of expression. '02(My3) S. bds., net, 50 c. A. M. Allen.
MUSIC.
McLaughlin. Elements and notation of music. 55 c. Ginn.
Maitland. Music in England in the 19th century. net, $1.75. Dutton.
Paderewski, *ed.* Century lib. of music. v. 17-20. subs., ea., $2; $4. Century Co.
Wead. Cont. to the history of musical scales. 50 c. Woodward & L.
See also Church music;—Musicians.
MUSICAL INSTRUMENTS.
See Trumpet.

MUSICIANS.
Thomas, *ed.* Famous composers and their music. 16 v. (App. to pubs. for price.) Millet.
Young. Mastersingers. net, $1.50. Scribner.
Musings by campfire and wayside. Gray, W: C. net, $1.50. Revell.
MUTINY.
See Indian mutiny.
Muzzey, D: S. Spiritual heroes. '02(My10) D. net, $1.25. Doubleday, P.
My captive. Altsheler, J. A. $1.25. Appleton.
My island. Hughes, E. $1.25. Dutton.
My Japanese wife. Holland, C. $1.50. Stokes.
My Lord Farquhar. Moore, T: E. $1.25. Abbey Press.
My ocean trip. Cadigan, E. S. $1. Brentano's.
My ten rod farm. Barnard, C: 40 c. Coates.
My trip to the Orient. Simmons, J. C. $1.50. Whitaker & R.
Myra of the Pines. Vielé, H. K. $1.50. McClure, P.
Mystery of St. Rubes. Heddle, E. F. $1.50. Scribner.
Mystery of the sea. Stoker, B. $1.50. Doubleday, P.
Mystic fortune teller, dream book, and policy player's guide. '02(My17) 12°, 50 c.: pap., 25 c. Donohue.
Mystic rose. Crawley, E. net, $4. Macmillan.
MYTHOLOGY.
Hale, *ed.* Greek myths in Eng. dress. 40 c. Globe Sch. Bk.
See also Fairy tales.
Naked truths and veiled allusions. Antrim, M. T. 50 c. Altemus.
Nameless hero. Anderson, J. B. net, $1. Wessels.
Nancy's Easter gift. Baldwin, M. 50 c. Abbey Press.
NANTUCKET ISLAND.
Bliss. September days on Nantucket. net, $1. Houghton, M. & Co.
Hinchman. Early settlers of Nantucket. $5. Ferris.
NAPOLEON I.
Fremeaux. With Napoleon at St. Helena. net, $1.50. Lane.
Headley. Napoleon and his marshals. $1. Burt.
Josselyn. The true Napoleon. net, $3.50. Russell.
Rose. Life of Napoleon I. 2 v. net, $4. Macmillan.
Sloane. Napoleon Bonaparte. 4 v. net, $18; net, $32. Century Co.
Watson. Napoleon. $2.25. Macmillan.
Napoleon. Dumas, A. net, 50 c. Macmillan.
Napoleon's letters to Josephine, 1796-1812; notes by H: F. Hall. '02(Mr1) 8°, net, $3. Dutton.
Nash, Eliz. T. Fifty Puritan ancestors, 1628-1660. '02(Ap26) 8°, $5. Tuttle, M. & T.
Nash, J: J., *ed.* Practical explanation and application of Bible history; [for catechism teachers.] '02(Ap19) D. net, $1.50. Benziger.
Nason, Fk. L. To the end of the trail. '02 (My17) D. $1.50. Houghton, M. & Co.
National cyclopædia of Am. biography. v. 11. '01-'02(Je28) il. 8°, subs., $10. White.
National (The) list. Directory of bonded attorneys. '02(My24) F.; *Same.* Abr. ed. S. (App. to pubs. for price.) Nat. Surety.
National portrait gallery. *See* Cust, L., *ed.*
National reporter system. O. shp. West Pub.
—Atlantic reporter. v. 50. $4.
—New York supplement, v. 72-74. ea., $4.
—Northeastern reporter. v. 61, 62. ea., $4.
—Northwestern reporter. v. 88. $4.
—Pacific reporter. v. 66, 67. ea., $4.
—Pacific reporter. Digest. net, $6.
—Southeastern reporter. v. 39, 40. ea., $4.
—Southern reporter. v. 30. $4.
—Southern reporter. Digest. net, $6.
—Southwestern reporter. v. 64-66. ea., $4.
—United States. Federal reporter. v. 110-113. ea., $3.50.
National Temperance almanac and teetotalers year-book, for 1902; also The Gothenburg system. '02(F1) S. pap., 10 c. Nat. Temp.
NATURAL HISTORY.
Cuppy, *ed.* Pictorial natural history. $1. Crowell & K.
Harmer *and* Shipley, *eds.* Cambridge natural history. v. 10. net, $4. Macmillan.
Pierson. Among the night people. net, $1. Dutton.
Roberts. Kindred of the wild. $2. L. C. Page.
See also Botany;—Chemistry;—Evolution;—Geology;—Microscope;—Nature;—Physical geography.
NATURAL RELIGION.
Conger. Religion for the time: six conferences on natural religion. net, $1. Jacobs.
James. Varieties of rel. experience; Gifford lectures on natural religion. net, $3.20. Longmans.
NATURALIZATION.
Pritchard, *comp.* How to become a naturalized citizen. 10 c. Wehman.
Naturalness of Christian life. Keedy, E: E. net, $1.25. Putnam.
NATURE.
Batt. Treatment of nature in Germ. literature. net, $1. Univ. of Chic.
Carter. Gleanings from nature. $1. Abbey Press.
Gray. Musings by camp-fire and wayside. net, $1.50. Revell.
Hodge. Nature study and life. $1.65. Ginn.
Miller. Brook book. net, $1.35. Doubleday, P.
Smith, C. W: Summer of Saturdays. 65 c. Gillan.
Talmage. Vacation with nature. net, $1. Funk.
Williams. Next to the ground. net, $1.20. McClure, P.
Nature and human nature. Emerson, *Mrs.* E. R. net, $1.25. Houghton, M. & Co.
Nature, myth and story. *See* Thompson, J: G.
Naughty Nan. Long, J: L. $1.50. Century Co.
Nauticus, *pseud.* The truth about the Schley case. '02(F22) D. pap., 25 c. Columbia.
NAVAL ART AND SCIENCE.
Brassey, *ed.* Naval annual, 1902. net, $7.50. Scribner.

NAVAL ART AND SCIENCE.—*Continued.*
Clowes, *and others.* Royal navy. v. 5, 6. ea., net, $6.50. Little, B. & Co.
Maclay. Hist. of U. S. Navy. 3 v. ea., net, $3. Appleton.
Mets. Naval heroes of Holland. $1.50. Abbey Press.

NAVIGATION.
See **Astronomy; — Canoeing; — Ship-building; — Voyages and travels.**

Neal, W. G. *See* Hall, R. N.

Neale, J. M. Deeds of faith: stories for children. '02(Je7) 12°, 40 c. E. & J. B. Young.

Nearer East. Hogarth, D: G: $2. Appleton.

Nebraska. Page's digest. vs. 1 to 60 of Neb. repts. In 2 v. v. 1. '02(My10); v. 2 (Je21) O. shp., (complete work,) $20. Bancroft-W.

Nebraska. *Supreme ct.* Repts. v. 61. (L. Herdman.) '02(My24) O. shp., $3. State Journ. Co.

NECK.
Eckley. Regional anatomy of head and neck. net, $2.50. Lea.

Neel, Edith K. Cats, how to care for them. '02(My10) 12°. 50 c. Boericke & T.

Neff, Ma. L. Prescription writing in Latin or Eng. '01. '02(Mr1) 12°, 75 c. Davis.

Negatives of the Indo-European languages. Fowler, F. H. net, 50 c. Univ. of Chic.

NEGLIGENCE.
Dresser. Employers' liability, acts and assumption of risks in N. Y., Mass., Ind., Ala., Col., and England. $6. Keefe-D.
Gardner, *ed.* Am. negligence repts. v. 10. $5.50. Remick.
Thompson. Commentaries on the law of negligence. v. 3. $6. Bowen-M.

NEGOTIABLE INSTRUMENTS.
Ames *and* Brewster. Negotiable instruments law. 30 c. Harvard Law.
Crawford. Negotiable instruments law. $2.50. Baker, V. & Co.
District of Columbia. Laws rel. to negotiable instruments. 20 c. Lowdermilk.
Pennsylvania. Negotiable instruments law. $2.50. Baker, V. & Co.
Selover. Law of negotiable instruments for N. Y., Mass., R. I., [etc.] $4. Keefe-D.

NEGROES.
Calhoun. The Caucasian and the negro in the U. S. 75 c. R. L. Bryan.
Schell. Is the negro a beast? 60 c. Gospel Trumpet.

Neill, Maidie. Tennessee Lee. '02(Ap26) 12°, $1. Neely.

Neilson, Fs. Madame Bohemia. '02(Mr8) D. (Select novels.) $1; pap., 50 c. Lippincott.

Nell Gwyn. Morehead, G: 25 c. Ogilvie.

Nelson's Wall St. lib. il. S. $1.25. S: A. Nelson.
—Coffin. A B C of banks and banking. (v. 4.)

NERVOUS SYSTEM.
Ballance *and* Stewart. Healing of nerves. net, $4.50. Macmillan.
Hardesty. Neurological technique. net, $1.75. Univ. of Chic.

Nestlings of forest and marsh. Wheelock, *Mrs.* I. G. net, $1.40. McClurg.

NETHERLANDS.
Schiller. Hist. of the revolt of the Netherlands. (App. to pubs. for price.) Niccolls.

Nettleship, R: L. Lectures on the Republic of Plato; ed. by G. R. Benson. '01. '02 (Ja4) 8°, net, $2.75. Macmillan.

NEURASTHENIA.
Savill. Clinical lectures on neurasthenia. $1.50. Wood.

Neurological technique. Hardesty, I. net, $1.75. Univ. of Chic.

New and living way. Terry, M. S. net, 50 c. Eaton & M.

New animal cellular therapy. Hawley, J. R. $1. Clinic.

New century lib. 12°, 1.25; $1.75. Nelson.
—Burns. Complete poetical works.

New child's life of Christ. Stretton, H. $1. Winston.

NEW ENGLAND.
Dame *and* Brooks. Trees of N. E. $1.35. Ginn.

New Hampshire. [*Supreme ct.*] Repts. (J. H. Riddell.) v. 70. '01. '02(My24) O. shp., $3.50. J: B. Clarke.

NEW HAMPSHIRE.
Hoyt. Practice in proceedings in probate cts. of N. H. $2.50. Rumford Press.

New hearthstone. Hurst, J: F. $1. Jennings.

New Jersey. General corporation act. Annots. and forms by J. B. Dill. 4th ed., with the amendments of 1902. '02(My17) O. pap., $1.50. New Jersey.

New Jersey. Laws rel. to corporations; with notes by Ja. B. Dill. '02(Je7) 8°, $3. Baker, V. & Co.

NEW JERSEY.
Parker, *comp.* New Jersey lawyers' diary, 1902. $1.50. Soney.

New Jersey orphans' court practice; with forms by C: F. Kocher. '02(Mr1) O. shp., $6. Soney.

New philosophy of health. Bradbury, H. B. 75 c. Alliance.

New songs for college glee clubs. '02(Mr15) 12°, pap., 50 c. Hinds.

NEW THOUGHT.
See **Mental science.**

New world and the new thought. Bixby, J. T. net, $1. Whittaker.

New York City standard guide. '01. '02 (Ja4) il. D. (Standard guide ser.) pap., 25 c. Foster & R.

New York City. Tenement house law and the building code. '02(Mr29) 12°, (Brooklyn Eagle lib., no. 62, v. 17, no. 3.) pap., 10 c. Brooklyn Eagle.

NEW YORK CITY.
Fielde. Political primer of New York city and state. 75 c.; 50 c. League Pol. Educ.
Hemstreet. When old New York was young. net, $1.50. Scribner.
Medical directory, 1901. $1.50. Wynkoop.
Norton. Statistical studies in N. Y. money-market. net, $1.50; net, $1. Macmillan.
Social evil, with special ref. to conditions existing in New York. net, $1.25. Putnam.
See also **Hall of fame;—Libraries.**

New York. [State.] Abbott's cyclopedic digest of decisions of all the courts fr. the earliest time to 1900. (Blashfield.) v. 5. '01. '02(Ja18); v. 6 (Mr1); v. 7 (Ap5); v. 8 (My10) O. shp., ea., $7.50. N. Y. Law.

New York. Amendments of the code of civil procedure, criminal procedure and penal code, 1902. '02(My24) O. pap., 50 c. Baker, V. & Co.

New York. Amendments of 1902. (A. J. Danaher.) '02(My24) O. pap., 50 c. Banks & Co.

New York. Analyzed decisions and citations, 1897-1901, by Ja. G. Greene. '02(Je28) O. shp., $8.50. Williamson Law Bk.

New York civil and criminal justice. 3d ed. by F. S. Becker and E. D. Howe. '02 (My24) O. shp., $6.50. Williamson Law Bk.

New York. Code of civil procedure, cont. amendments of 1902 by A. J. Parker, jr., rev. by A. J. Danaher. 2d ed. '02(My17) D. flex. skiver, $3.50. Banks & Co.

New York. Code of civil procedure, as amended, 1902. '02(Je21) D. (Chase's pocket code.) flex. skiver, net, $3.50. Banks.

New York. Code of criminal procedure. (L. R. Parker.) '02(Je7) D. flex. skiver, $1.50. Banks.

New York. Code of criminal procedure and penal code. (Cook.) '02(My17) O. shp., net, $5. H: B. Parsons.

New York. *Ct. of appeals.* Analyzed citations. v. 2; by Ja. G. Greene. '01. '02 (Je28) pr. on one side of leaf, O. $2.50. Williamson Law Bk.

New York. *Ct. of appeals.* Digest of opinions of J: C. Gray. v. 108-164. (E. A. Bedell.) '01. '02(Mr8) Q. limp roan, $5. Lyon.

New York. *Ct. of appeals.* Digest of opinions of [A.] Haight. v. 114-164. '02(Mr8) Q. limp roan, $5. Lyon.

New York. *Ct. of appeals.* Digest of opinions of [D.] O'Brien. v. 119-164. '01. '02 (Mr8) Q. limp roan, $5. Lyon.

New York. *Ct. of appeals.* Digest of opinions of [I. G.] Vann. v. 114-v. 164. '01. '02(Mr8) Q. limp roan, $5. Lyon.

New York. *Ct. of appeals.* Repts. (J: T. Cook.) bk. 33. '02(Mr15) O. shp., $5. H: B. Parsons.

New York. *Cts. of record.* Misc. repts. v. 35. '01. '02(Mr1) O. shp., $2. Lyon.

New York. Digest of statutes and repts. '02(Mr1) O. shp., $5. Baker, V. & Co.

New York. Digest of repts. and session laws. for 1901. '02(Mr1) O. shp., $4.50. Lyon.

New York. Penal code. (L. R. Parker.) '02(Je7) D. flex. skiver, $1.50. Banks.

New York. Statutory revision of the laws affecting banks, banking and trust companies 1892. (Hamilton.) '02(My24) O. pap., $1.50. Banks & Co.

New York. Statutory revision of the laws affecting insurance companies. (Hamilton.) '02(Je14) O. pap., $1.50. Banks & Co.

New York. Statutory revision of the laws affecting misc. corporations. (Hamilton.) '02(Je14) O. pap., $1.50. Banks & Co.

New York supplement, v. 72. '02(F1); v. 73 (Ap5); v. 74 (Je14) O. (Nat. reporter system.) shp., ea., $4. West Pub.

New York. *Supreme ct.* Repts. (Hun.) vs. 62, 63. Off. ed. '01. '02(Ja4); v. 65, 66 (Ap5); v. 67 (Ap19) O. shp., ea., net, $3. Lyon.

New York. *Surrogates' cts.* Repts.; with annots., by J: Power. '01. '02(F1) O. shp., $5.50. W. C. Little.

New York. Tax law of 1896, with index and amend. to date. (A. Hamilton.) '02(Je7) O. pap., 50 c. Banks & Co.

New York. Tax law, with amendments of 1897-1902. Bender ed. '02(Je28) O. pap., 50 c. M. Bender.

NEW YORK.
Murlin. Il. legislative manual; the N. Y. red book. $1. Lyon.
Purdy. Local option in taxation; with a draft of act to amend tax law. 10 c. N. Y. Tax Reform.
Redfield, *ed.* Repts. Surrogates' cts. v. 1. $6. Banks & Co.
Rumsey. Practice in civil actions in cts. of record in N. Y. v. 1. $6. Banks & Co.
Tarr. Physical geography of N. Y.; with chap. on climate. net, $3.50. Macmillan.
Wait. Law and practice in civil actions, [etc.] in N. Y. v. 1. $6.35; per set, $19. M. Bender.

New York Evening Post: hundredth anniversary number, Nov. 16, 1801-1901. '02 (My17) il. sq. O. $1. N. Y. Eve. Post.

New York Library Club. Libraries of Greater New York. '02(My17) D. net, 75 c.; pap., net. 50 c. Stechert.

Newberry, Fannie E. Bubbles. '02(Mr29) il. 12°, (Fireside ser.) $1. Burt.

Newberry, Fannie E. Comrades. '02(Mr29) il. 12°, (St. Nicholas ser.) 75 c. Burt.

Newberry, Fannie E. Joyce's investments. '02(Mr29) il. 12°, (Fireside ser.) $1. Burt.

Newberry, Fannie E. Sara: a princess. '02 (Mr29) il. 12°, (Fireside ser.) $1. Burt.

Newberry gospels. Goodspeed, E. J. net, 25 c. Univ. of Chic.

NEWBURG, Vt.
Wells. Hist. of Newburg. $2.25; $3; $3.50; $4. Caledonian.

Newcomb, Harry T. Concentration of railway control. '02(Mr22) 8°, (Pub. of the soc., no. 328.) pap., 15 c. Am. Acad. Pol. Sci.

Newcomes. *See* Thackeray, W: M.

Newell, F: H. Irrigation in the U. S. '02 (Mr8) D. net. $2. Crowell.

Newell, Grant. Elements of the law of real property. '02(Mr1) O. shp., $4. Flood.

Newell, Martin L., *rep. See* Illinois. *Appellate cts.* Repts.

Newell, Wilbur C. The life worth living. '02 (My3) il. D. $1. Abbey Press.

Newman, A. H:, *ed.* Century of Baptist achievements. '01. '02(F15) 12°, net, $1.50. Am. Bapt.

Newman, J: H: Definition of a gentleman; [repr.] '02(Mr1) sq. 12°. bds., $1; pap., 50 c. Kirgate Press.

Newman, J: H: Lives of the Eng. saints. '01. '02(Mr1) 6 v., il. 12°, net, $12. Lippincott.

NEWMAN, J: H:
Whyte. Newman. net, $1.10. Longmans.

Newson's Germ. opera texts. 16°. Newson.
—Wagner. Rheingold. 75 c. (1.)

NEWSPAPERS.
Munson. Making a country newspaper. $1. Dominion.

Next great awakening. Strong, J. 75 c. Baker & T.
Next to the ground. Williams, M. M. net, $1.20. McClure. P.
NICARAGUA.
Walker. Ocean to ocean: acc. of Nicaragua. net, $1.25. McClurg.
Nichols, E: L. The galvanometer. '02(Mr8) il. 8°, $1. Spon.
Nichols, Fs. M. *See* Britton.
Nicholson, T:, *and* Woods, C: C. Notes on Epworth League prayer meeting topics. 1st ser. '02(Ja25) S. pap., 15 c. Eaton & M.
Nicoll, W: R. The church's one foundation, Christ and recent criticism. '01· '02(F1) D. $1.25. Armstrong.
Nicolls, W: J. Graystone. '02(Mr15) il. D. $1.50. Lippincott.
Niebuhr, B. G. Greek hero stories. New ed. '01· '02(F22) 16°, $1. Dodd.
Nield, J. Guide to the best historical novels and tales. '02(Je21) O. net, $1.75. Putnam.
Nies, Konrad. Deutsche Gaben. '02(Je28) 8°, pap., 25 c. Witter.
Nies, Konrad. Rosen im Schnee. '02(Je28) 8°, pap., 50 c. Witter.
NINETEENTH CENTURY.
Hodder. Life of a century. net, $4. Scribner.
Morris. Marvelous achievements of the 19th century. $2.50; $3.50. Winston.
Nineteenth-century crusader. Locke, C: E: 25 c. Jennings.
Nitsche, G: E., *comp.* University of Penn.: proceedings at the dedication of the new building of the Dept. of Law, Feb. 21, 22, 1900. '01· '02(Ap26) il. O. $3; hf. mor., $3.50. Univ. of Penn.
Nixon, J. H. Beyond the vail; a comp. of narrations and il. of spirit experiences. '01· '02(Mr22) il. 8°, $1.75. Hudson-K.
Noble, Alden C: Lyrics to the queen. '02 (Je14) sq. S. pap., n. p. Blue Sky Press.
NOME.
McKee. Land of Nome. net, $1.25. Grafton Press.
Nominating systems. Meyer, E. C. net, $1.50. E. C. Meyer.
None but the brave. Sears, H. $1.50. Dodd.
Nonne's preeste's tale. Chaucer, G. $6.50; $16.50. Grafton Press.
Nonsense for old and young. Field, E. 50 c. Dickerman.
Nordenskiold, G. The cliff dwellers of the Mesa Verde, southwestern Colo. [also] Human remains from the cliff dwellings of the Mesa Verde, by G. Retzius. '01· '02 (Ja25) f°, net, $20. Stechert.
Norris, Zoe A. Color of the soul. '02(F1) nar. D. bds., net, $1. Funk.
North, Ingolsby. Love letters and how to write them. '02(My17) 12°, 50 c.; pap., 25 c. Donohue.
North, Ingoldsby. Love letters and how to write them. '02(Mr15) S. pap., 25 c. Drake.
North Dakota. Township manual; by W. S. Booth. 6th ed. '01· '02(F8) D. pap., 75 c. Booth.
Northcote, Stafford H: *See* St. Cyres, *Viscount.*
Northeastern reporter, v. 61. '02(Mr1); v. 62 (My10) O. (Nat. reporter system, state ser.) shp., ea., $4. West Pub.
Northern Europe. '02(Mr22) il. D. (Youth's Companion ser., no. 2.) 30 c. Ginn.
Northrup, A. J., *ed.* Early records of the First Presbyterian Church of Syracuse, N. Y. '02(Ap5) O. pap., 50 c. [Gill] Genealog. Soc.
Northrup, W: P., *ed.* Diphtheria [*also*] measles, scarlatina, German measles, by T. von Jurgensen. '02(Je28) il. 8°, (Nothnagel's encyc. of practical medicine, Am. ed., v. 3.) net, $5; shp. or hf. mor., $6. Saunders.
Northwestern reporter, v. 88. '02(Ap5) O. (Nat. reporter system, state ser.) shp., $4. West Pub.
Norton, J: P. Statistical studies in New York money-market. '02(My24) net, $1.50; pap., net, $1. Macmillan.
NORWAY.
Spender. Two winters in Norway. $4. Longmans.
Weborg. In Viking land. $1.25. J. C. Weborg.
NOSE.
Gradle. Diseases of the nose, pharynx and ear. net, $3.50. Saunders.
Turner. Accessory sinuses of the nose. $4. Longmans.
Wood, *and others, eds.* Eye, ear, nose and throat. $1.50. Year Bk.
Not on the chart. Marsh, C: L. $1.50. Stokes.
NOTARIES.
Smith. Texas notarial manual and form book. $4. Gammel.
Snyder. Notaries' and commissioners' manual. $1.50. Baker, V. & Co.
Nothnagel's encyclopedia of practical medicine. il. 8°, net, $5; hf. mor., $6. Saunders.
—Moore, *ed.* Variola, vaccination, etc. (2.)
—Northrup, *ed.* Diphtheria, measles, scarlatina, German measles. (3.)
—Osler, *ed.* Typhoid and typhus fevers. (1.)
Notre Dame de Paris. Hugo, V. 85 c. Ginn.
Novene zu Ehren des Heiligen Geistes. New ed. '02(Je28) 32°, pap., net. 3 c. Herder.
Noyes, C: J. Patriot and Tory. '02(Mr29) il. D. $1.50. Dickerman.
Nugent, Paul C. Plane surveying. '02(Ap5) il. 8°, $3.50. Wiley.
Nuggets ser. T. 45 c.; leath., $1. Fords.
—Pennington, *comp.* Good cheer nuggets
Nürnberg stove. *See* La Rame, L. de.
NURSES AND NURSING.
Hadley. Nursing; app. on sick-room cookery. net, $1.25. Blakiston.
Jewett. Childbed nursing. 80 c. Treat.
Nuverbis, [*pseud.* for Dillon Jordan Spotswood.] Out of the beaten track. '02(Mr22) D. $1. Abbey Press.
Nymph's reply to the shepherd. *See* Marlowe, C.
OBSTETRICS.
See Midwifery.
O'Byrne, W. L. Kings and vikings. '02 (Ap12) 12°, $1.25. Scribner.
O'Byrne, W. L. Land of heroes: Irish history. '02(Ap12) 12°, $1.25. Scribner.

OCCULTISM.
Demorest, *ed.* Cambridge encyclo. of esoteric subjects. v. 3. net, $3. Cambridge.
OCEAN.
See Seashore.
Ocean to ocean. Walker, J. W. G. net, $1.25. McClurg.
O'Connor, D. M. Foreign freemasonry. '02 (F1) S. pap., 5 c. Kilner.
O'Conor, M. Irish come-all-ye's and old-time songs and ballads of Ireland. '01· '02 (Ja4) 4°, pap., 25 c. Popular.
O'Conor, M., *comp.* Old-time songs and ballads of Ireland. '02(Ja25) O. $2. Popular.
ODD-FELLOWS.
Monroe Rebekah Lodge: semi-centennial, Jan. 23, 1902. 10 c. Darrow.
Odenheimer, Cordelia P. Phantom caravan. '01. '02(F15) D. $1. Abbey Press.
Oertel, Hanns. Lectures on the study of language. '01· '02(Mr15) 8°, (Yale bicentennial pub.) net, $3. Scribner.
Ogilvie, Rob. Horæ Latinæ: synonyms and syntax; ed. by A. Souter. '01· '02(F8) O. $5. Longmans.
O'Growney, Eug. Revised simple lessons in Irish. pt. 1. '02(Mr15) D. pap., 15 c. Gael.
Ohio. *Cts. of record.* Repts. v. 10, 11. '01· '02(My10) O. shp., ea., $2.50. Laning.
Ohio. *Supreme ct.* Repts. v. 64. '01. '02 (My10) O. shp., 2.50. Laning.
OHIO.
Wilson. Ohio. net, 30 c. Macmillan.
OHIO VALLEY.
Piatt. Hesperian tree. $2. J: Scott.
OLD AGE.
Ames. Prevention and cure of old age. 50 c. Kirk.
Old Blackfriars. Marshall, B. $1.50. Dutton.
Old diaries. Gower, R. S. net, $4.50. Scribner.
Old English ballads. Kinard, J. P. 40 c. Silver.
Old English plate. Cripps, W. J. net, $13.50. Scribner.
Old glory and the gospel in the Philippines. Condict, A. B. net, 75 c. Revell.
Old Indian legends. Zitkala-sa. 50 c. Ginn.
Old, old fairy tales. Valentine, *Mrs.* L. J. $1. Burt.
Old South leaflets. v. 5. nos. 101-125. '02 (My17) D. $1.50. Old South Work.
Old world wonder stories. O'Shea, M. V. 25 c. Heath.
Oldfield. Banks, N. H. $1.50. Macmillan.
Oliver, G. F. Our lay office-bearers. '01. '02(Ja4) sq. D. (Little books on practice.) net, 25 c. Jennings.
Oliver, G. F. Soul-winners' secrets: revival text-book. '02(F8) sq T. (Little books on practice.) 25 c. Jennings.
Olmsted, Everett W., *ed.* *See* Marivaux, P. C. de C. de.
Olympian nights. Bangs, J: K. $1.25. Harper
Omar Khayyâm. Rubaiyat. '02(F15) 12°, net, $1.50. Lane.
Omar Khayyâm. Rubaiyat. '02(My3) il. 16°, 60 c.; leath., $1. Macmillan.
Omar Khayyâm. Rubâiyât. (Fitzgerald.) privately pr. for N. H. Dole. '01· '02(Mr1) 8°, charcoal pap., $10; vellum, $25. Merrymount Press.
Omar Khayyam, *jr.*, *pseud.* *See* Irwin, W.
On the sensitiveness of the coherer. Wolcott, E. R. 20 c. Univ. of Wis.
Once upon a time. Aulnoy, M. C. J. de B. *Comtesse d'.* 50 c. Little, B. & Co.
One: a song of the ages. Moy, E. $1.50. Neely.
One of the craft, *pseud.* *See* Schofield, R. J.
One thousand ways to make money. Gilbert F. $1. Donohue.
One world at a time. Slicer, T: R. net, $1.35. Putnam.
Onlooker's note-book. Russell, G: W: E. $2.25. Harper.
ONTOLOGY.
Swedenborg. Ontology. 50 c. Mass. New-Ch. Un.
Openings in the old trail. Harte, F. B. $1.25. Houghton, M. & Co.
OPHTHALMOLOGY.
See Eye.
OPIUM.
See Morphinism.
Oppenheim, E. P. Enoch Strone. '02(Mr29) D. $1.50. G: W. Dillingham.
Oppenheim, N. Mental growth and control. '02(F15) 12°, (Personal problem ser.) net, $1. Macmillan.
Oppenheimer, C., *and* Mitchell, C. A. Ferments and their actions. '01. '02(F15) 12°, net, $2.50. Lippincott.
Opponents (The). Robertson, H. $1.50. Scribner.
Opportunist (The). Mitton, G. E. $2. Macmillan.
Optic, Oliver, *pseud.* *See* Adams, W: T.
OPTICS.
Drude. Theory of optics. $4. Longmans.
See also Eye;—Light.
ORATIONS.
See Rectitations.
ORATORS AND ORATORY.
Esenwein. How to attract and hold an audience. $1. Hinds.
See also Debates.
ORCHIDS.
Boyle. Woodland orchids. net, $7. Macmillan.
ORDINATION.
Stubbs. Ordination addresses. $2.25. Longmans.
Oregon. Mining laws. 2d ed. '01· '02(F1) D. pap., 40 c. Or. Mining Journ.
Oregon. *Supreme ct.* Repts. (R. G. Morrow.) v. 38. '01. '02(Ja4): v. 39 (Je7) O. shp., ea., $5. Leeds.
O'Rell, Max, *pseud.* *See* Blouët, P.
ORES.
See Metals and metallurgy;—Mines and mining.
ORIENT.
Simmons. My trip to the Orient. $1.50. Whitaker & R.
ORIENTAL CLUB.
Baillie. Oriental Club and Hanover Square. $9. Longmans.
ORIENTAL RELIGIONS.
Conway, *comp.* Sacred anthology (oriental). $2. Holt.
Oriental ser. *See* Millet's.
Ormsby, Fk. E., *ed.* *See* Planets and people.

ORPHANS.
New Jersey orphans' court practice; with forms. $6. Soney.
Orphean tragedy. Creamer, E: S. $1. Abbey Press.
Orr, Ja. Progress of dogma: Elliott lectures. '01 '02(F1) O. $1.75. Armstrong.
Orthodontia. MacDowell, J. N. net, $4. Colegrove.
O'Shea, M. V., *ed.* Old world wonder stories. '02(F8) il. D. (Home and school classics.) 25 c. Heath.
Osler, W:, *ed.* Typhoid and typhus fevers, by H. Curschmann. Am. ed. '02(Mr29) il. 8°, (Nothnagel's encyclopedia of practical medicine, no. 1.) net, $5; hf. mor., $6. Saunders.
Ostwald, Wilhelm. Principles of inorganic chemistry; tr. by A. Findlay. '02(Je7) 8°. net, $6. Macmillan.
Oswald, Felix. Vaccination a crime. '02 (My17) 8°, pap., 10 c. Physical Culture.
Other notes. Hinton, M. B. $1. Neale.
Otis, James, *pseud.* *See* Kaler, J. O.
Otis Grey, bachelor. J., C. J. 75 c. Mutual Bk.
OTOLOGY.
See Ear.
Oudin, Maurice A. Standard polyphase apparatus and systems. 3d ed., rev. '02(My3) il. O. $3. Van Nostrand.
Ouida, *pseud.* *See* La Rame, L. de.
Our attitude toward Eng. Roman Catholics. Galton, A. net, $1. Dutton.
Our country's story. Tappan, E. M. 65 c. Houghton, M. & Co.
Our European neighbors ser. il. D. net, $1.20. Putnam.
—Higgin. Spanish life in town and country. (6.)
—Story. Swiss life in town and country. (5.)
Our lay office-bearers. Oliver, G. F. net, 25 c. Jennings.
Our literary deluge. Halsey, F. W. net, $1.25. Doubleday, P.
Our Lysander. Kellogg, A. M. 15 c. Kellogg.
Our risen King's forty days. Boardman, G: D. net, $1.25. Lippincott.
Our sixty-six sacred books. Rice, E. W. net, 50 c. Am. S. S.
Out among the animals. Malone, *Mrs.* E. W. 75 c. Pub. Ho. M. E. Ch., So.
Out of the beaten track. Nuverbis, *pseud.* $1. Abbey Press.
Outlaws. Armstrong, L. $1.25. Appleton.
Ovenden, C. T. To whom shall we go? '02 (Je7) 16°, $1. E. & J. B. Young.
Overland stage to California. Root, F. A. $2.50; $3.50. Root & C.
Overton, Ja. B. Parthenogenesis in thalictrum purpurascens. '02(Je14) 8°, (Cont. from the Hull Botanical Laboratory, no. 35.) pap., net, 25 c. Univ. of Chic.
Ovid. Amorum libri tres. '02(Je28) il. 12°, (Antique gems from the Gr. and Latin, v. 6.) (Apply to pubs. for price.) Barrie.
Owens College. *See* Tout, T: F:
Oxenford, Ina, *and* Alpheus, A., *pseud.* Complete palmist. '02(My17) 12°, 50 c.; pap., 25 c. Donohue.
Oxford lib. of practical theology. D. $1.50. Longmans.
—Worlledge. Prayer.
OXFORD UNIVERSITY.
Corbin. An American at Oxford. net, $1.50. Houghton, M. & Co.
PACIFIC OCEAN.
Colquhoun. Mastery of the Pacific. net, $4. Macmillan.
Helmolt, *and others, eds.* Hist. of the world. v. 1, America and Pacific ocean. $6. Dodd.
Pacific reporter, v. 66. '02(Mr1); v. 67(Je7) O. (Nat. reporter system, state ser.) shp., ea., $4. West Pub.
Pacific reporter. Digest of decisions. '02 (Mr8) O. (Nat. reporter system digests, Pacific ser., v. 3.) shp., net, $6. West Pub.
Paderewski, I. J., *ed.* Century lib. of music. v. 17, 18. '02(Mr15); v. 19, 20 (Ap5) il., with music, f°, subs., per v., $2; hf. mor., $4. Century Co.
Pagan's cup. Hume, F. W. $1.25. G: W. Dillingham.
Page, Ernest Clifford. *See* Nebraska digest.
Page, Wa. H. Rebuilding of old commonwealths. '02(Je7) D. net, $1. Doubleday, P.
Paget, *Sir* Ja. Selected essays and addresses; ed. by S. Paget. '02(Ap19) O. $5. Longmans.
PAINT.
Church. Chemistry of paints and painting. $3. Macmillan.
PAINTERS.
Caffin. American masters of painting. net, $1.25. Doubleday, P.
Dallin. Sketches of great painters for young people. 90 c. Silver.
Roulet. St. Anthony in art, and other sketches. $2. Marlier.
See also Artists.
PAINTING.
See Painters.
Palache, C: *See* Lawson, A. C.
PALEONTOLOGY.
See Geology.
PALESTINE.
Babcock. Letters from Egypt and Palestine. net, $1. Scribner.
Guide to Palestine and Egypt. net, $3.25. Macmillan.
Palgrave, Ma. E. Mary Rich, Countess of Warwick, 1625-1678. '02(F15) 12°, net, $1.50. Dutton.
Palladino, L. B. Mary our mother. '02 (Je14) 12°, pap., net, 15 c. Herder.
Palliser, *Mrs.* Bury. History of lace. New ed., rev., rewritten and enl., by M. Jourdain and A. Dryden. '02(Mr8) 8°, net, $12. Scribner.
Palmer, B. M. Threefold fellowship and the threefold assurance. '02(Mr29) O. 75 c. Presb. Pub.
Palmer, *Mrs.* Minnie. Woman's exchange cook book. '01 '02(Ap26) il. 8°, 70 c. Conkey.
PALMISTRY.
Oxenford *and* Alpheus. Complete palmist. 50 c.; 25 c. Donohue.
Pan-American ser. il. D. net, $1. Lee & S.
—Stratemeyer. Lost on the Orinoco. (1.)

PANAMA CANAL.
Johnson. Isthmian canal. 25 c. Am. Acad. Pol. Sci.
Pasco. Isthmian canal question as affected by treaties and concessions. 25 c. Am. Acad. Pol. Sci.
Sonderegger. L' achèvement du canal de Panama. $2.50. Stechert.
Pangborn, Georgia W. Roman Biznet. '02 (My3) il. D. $1.50. Houghton, M. & Co.
Pansy, *pseud.* *See* Alden, *Mrs.* I. M.
Paolo and Francesca. Phillips, S. net, $1.25. Lane.
PAOTINGFU, China.
Ketler. Tragedy of Paotingfu. net, $2. Revell.
PARABLES.
Dods. Parables of our Lord. $1.50. Whittaker.
Parables of life. Mabie, H. W. net, $1. Outlook.
Paret, W: Reality in holy communion. '02 (Ap12) 16°, pap., 10 c. Whittaker.
PARIS.
Halstead. Splendors of Paris and glories of her exposition. $1.50. Dominion.
Walton. Paris from the earliest period to the present day. v. 6. $3. Barrie.
Parker, Amasa J., *jr.* *See* New York. Code of civil procedure.
Parker, Arnold. Ping-pong: [table tennis.] '02(Mr15) il. D. net, 75 c. Putnam.
Parker, Arnold. *See also* Ritchie, M. G.
Parker, C: W., *comp.* New Jersey lawyers' diary and bar directory, 1902. '02(Ja18) O. $1.50. Soney.
Parker, E. H. John Chinaman, and a few others. '02(Mr8) 12°, $2.50. Dutton.
Parker, Lewis R., *ed.* *See* New York. Codes.
Parkman, Fs. Writings. La Salle ed., incl. life of Parkman by C: H. Farnham. '02 (Mr22) 20 v., il. 8°, subs., per v., net, $5; ¾ lev. mor., per v., net, $10. Little, B. & Co.
Parkman, Fs. Conspiracy of Pontiac. '02 (Je14) 12°, (Home lib.) $1. Burt.
PARLIAMENTARY LAW.
Fox. Parliamentary usage for women's clubs. net, 65 c. Baker & T.
Sherman. Parliamentary law at a glance. 75 c. H: O. Shepard.
Stevens. Am. law of assemblies. net, $1. E: A. Stevens.
PARODY.
Dustin. The make good book of parodies. 50 c. E. Dustin.
Parr, G. D. A. Electrical engineering testing. '02(Ap19) il. 8°, net, $3.50. Van Nostrand.
Parson's handbook (The); cont. directions as to the management of the parish church and its services as set forth in the "Book of common prayer." 4th ed., rewritten and enl. '02(My10) 12°, net, $1.50. Young Churchman.
Parsons, *Mrs.* Fs. T. According to season. New enl. ed. '02(Mr22) il. D. net, $1.75. Scribner.
Parsons, J. H. Elementary ophthalmic optics. '01· '02(Ja11) 12°, net, $2. Blakiston.
Parthenogenesis in thalictrum purpurascens. Overton, J. B. net, 25 c. Univ. of Chic.
PARTIES (*political*).
See Indiana.

Partridge, W: O. Nathan Hale, the ideal patriot. '02(My17) D. net, $1. Funk.
Pasco, S: Isthmian canal question as affected by treaties and concessions. '02 (Mr22) 8°, (Pub. of the soc., no. 324.) pap., 25 c. Am. Acad. Pol. Sci.
Pascoe, C: E. Pageant and ceremony of the coronation of their majesties King Edward the seventh and Queen Alexandra. '02 (My3) il. D. net, $1.40. Appleton.
Passenger traffic of railways. Weyl, W. E. $1.50; $1. Ginn.
Passing world. Belloc, B. R. net, $1.25. Herder.
Passion flowers. Watson, *Mrs.* A. R. $1.60. Whittet.
Passionate shepherd to his love. Marlowe, C. net, $3.75. Russell.
Past and present. Carlyle, T: 50 c.; 75 c. Macmillan.
Pasteboard crown. Morris, C. $1.50. Scribner.
Paston, G:, [*pseud. for* E. M. Symonds.] Little memoirs of the nineteenth century. '02(Ap5) il. 8°, net, $3. Dutton.
Pastor Agnorum. Skrine, J: H. net, $1.60. Longmans.
Pastoral epistles. Lilley, J. P. net, 75 c. Scribner.
PATENTS.
Cresee. Pointers for patentees. $1. Munn.
Pater, Wa. H. Marius the epicurean. '02 (Je14) 12°, (Home lib.) $1. Burt.
Paterson, W: R., ["Benjamin Swift."] Game of love. '02(Ap12) D. $1.50. Scribner.
Path to Rome. Belloc, H. net, $2. Longmans.
PATHOLOGY.
Herter. Lectures on chemical pathology. net, $1.75. Lea.
Thayer. Compend of general pathology. 80 c.; $1. Blakiston.
Trudeau. Torture of the clinic. $1; 50 c. Bourguignon.
See also Diphtheria; — Ear;—Eye;—Gallstone;—Hair; — Histology;—Hygiene;—Insanity;—Malarial fever;—Nose;—Skin;—Throat;—Typhoid fever;—Urine and urinary organs;—Variola.
Paths to power. Wilson, F. B. $1. Fenno.
Patoma, Fk. The Venus di Milo. '02(Je7) 12°, 50 c. Cambridge.
Patricia of the hills. Burrow, C: K. net, $1.20. Putnam.
PATRICK, *St.*
Sanderson. Story of Saint Patrick: emb. sketch of Ireland. $1.50. Ketcham.
Patrick, J. N. Psychology for teachers. '02 (My3) D. hf. leath., $1. Educ. Pub.
Patriot and Tory. Noyes, C: J. $1.50. Dickerman.
Patristic study. Swete, H: B. net, 90 c. Longmans.
Pattee, F. L. Mary Garvin. '02(Ap5) il. D. $1.50. Crowell.
Pattee, W: S., *comp.* Authorities, reductions, and notes in real property. '02 (My24) O. shp., $2. Univ. Press.
Patten, S. N. Theory of prosperity. '02(F1) 12°, net, $1.25. Macmillan.
Patten, S. N. *See also* Seager, H: R.
Patterson, Alex. Broader Bible study. The Pentateuch. '02(Ap26) D. net, 75 c. Jacobs.

Patterson, C: B. Beyond the clouds. New issue. '02(Mr22) O. $1. Alliance.
Patterson, C: B. What the new thought stands for. '01. '02(Mr22) S. pap., 10 c. Alliance.
Patterson, C: B. The will to be well. '01. '02(Mr22) nar. O. $1. Alliance.
Patterson, Melvin J. *See* Fisher, A. T.
Patterson, Virginia S. Dickey Downy. Phœnix ed. '02(Ap5) S. 25 c. A. J. Rowland.
Pattison, Everett W. Instructions in criminal cases passed upon by the cts. of Missouri. '02(My24) O. shp., $5. Gilbert Bk.
Pattison, T. H. The Bible and the twentieth century. '02(Mr22) D. pap., 10 c. Am. Bapt.
Patton, Abel. "Har Lampkins." '02(Mr1) D. $1. Abbey Press.
PAUL, *St.*
Matheson. Spiritual development of St. Paul. net, 80 c. Whittaker.
Pratt. Life and Epistles of St. Paul. 75 c. Funk.
Wayland. Paul, the herald of the cross. 40 c. Brethren Pub. Ho.
Paul and Virginia. Saint-Pierre, J. H. B. de. $1. Burt.
Paulsen, Friedrich. Immanuel Kant, his life and doctrine; fr. rev. Germ. ed., by J. E. Creighton and A. Lefevre. '02(Mr1) O. net, $2.50. Scribner.
PAVEMENTS.
See Roads.
Payn, F. W. Cromwell on foreign affairs. '02(Mr8) 8°, net, $1.25. Macmillan.
Payne, Fk. O. How to teach about trees. '01. '02(Ja25) 12°, 25 c. Kellogg.
Payne, Fk. O. How to teach aquatic life. '01. '02(Ja25) 12°, 25 c. Kellogg.
Payne, W: M. Editorial echoes. '02(Ap12) D. net, $1. McClurg.
Payne, W: M. Little leaders. [New issue.] '02(Ap12) D. net, $1. McClurg.
Pearls from the Wonderbook. King, T: A. 40 c. Swedenborg.
Pease, Eunice S. Gathered sunbeams: poems. '02(Je7) S. bds., 75 c. Sun Pr. Co.
Pearson, C: W. The carpenter prophet. '02 (Ap26) D. $1.50. H. S. Stone.
Pearson, H: C., *and* Bartlett, Emeline B. Key to Pearson's Greek prose composition. '01. '02(F15) S. pap., 50 c. Am. Bk.
Peck, G: C. Ringing questions. '02(Mr22) D. $1. Eaton & M.
Peck, S: M. Alabama sketches. '02(Mr22) S. $1. McClurg.
PEDIATRICS.
See Children.
Peerless ser. D. pap., 25 c. Ogilvie.
—Morehead. Story of François Villon. (124.)
PEMAQUID, Me.
Kaler. Story of Pemaquid. 50 c. Crowell.
Pemberton, Max. The giant's gate. '02(F22) D. $1.50. Stokes.
Pemberton, T. E. Ellen Terry and her sisters. '02(Ap12) O. net, $3.50. Dodd.
Pen and ink. Matthews, J. B. net, $1.25. Scribner.
Pendel, T: F. Thirty-six years in the White House, Lincoln-Roosevelt. '02(Ap26) 12°, $1.50. Neale.
Pendennis. Thackeray, W: M. 3 v. $3. Macmillan.

Penitential Psalms. *See* Browne, *Mrs.* A. B. B.
PENMANSHIP.
Kilpatrick. Language system of penmanship. nos. 1-8. per doz., 66 c. Globe Sch. Bk.
Pennington, Jeanne G., *comp.* Good cheer nuggets. '02(Mr22) T. (Nuggets ser.) 45 c.: leath., $1. Fords.
Pennock, Arth. F. Twenty thousand miles by land and sea. '01. '02(My10) il. D. $1. Mason Pub.
Pennsylvania. *County cts.* Repts. v. 25. '02(Mr1) O. shp., $5. T. & J. W. Johnson.
Pennsylvania. *District ct.* Repts. v. 10. '01. '02(Ap5) O. shp., $5.25. H. W. Page.
Pennsylvania. Law of conveyancing, by C. Fallon. '02(F1) O. shp., $6. T. & J. W. Johnson.
Pennsylvania. Monaghan's cumulative annual digest. v. 3. '02(Ap19) O. $6. Soney.
Pennsylvania. Negotiable instruments law; annots. by J: J. Crawford. '02(Ap12) O. $2.50. Baker, V. & Co.
Pennsylvania. *Superior ct.* Repts., v. 17. (Schaffer and Weimer.) '02(Mr15); v. 18 (Je7) O. shp., ea., $2. Banks.
Pennsylvania. *Supreme ct.* Repts., v. 200. '02(Mr29) O. shp., $3.50. Banks.
PENNSYLVANIA.
Cuffel. Durrell's Battery in the Civil War. subs., $2. C: A. Cuffel.
Gans. A Pennsylvania pioneer. $6. Kuhl.
Sharpless. Quaker experiment in government. $1.50. Ferris.
Shimmell. Border warfare in Pa. during Revolution. 50 c. R. L. Myers.
Stapleton. Memorials of the Huguenots in America with special ref. to their emigration to Pa. $1.50. Huguenot.
Trickett. Law of witnesses in Pa. $6. T. & J. W. Johnson.
See also Lancaster.
Pennsylvania Society of New York; year book, 1902. '02(My3) O. $1. Penn. Soc. of N. Y.
PENSIONS.
Glasson. Nation's pension system. 25 c. Am. Acad. Pol. Sci.
PENTATEUCH.
See Bible.
People's lib. 12°, pap., 50 c. Am. News.
—Crawford. In the palace of the king. (27.)
Pepper, G: W., *and* Lewis, W: D. Digest of decisions. v. 12. '01. '02(Mr15) O. $7.50. Welsh.
Pepys, S: Diary and correspondence. New ed. '01. '02(F22) 10 v., 12°, $10; limp leath., $15. Dodd.
PERCEPTION.
See Knowledge.
PERCIVAL, Ja. G.
Legler. James Gates Percival. net, $1. Mequon Club.
Percival, Leila. Professor Archie. '02 (My17) 12°, 50 c. Nelson.
Perfect woman. Sainte-Foi, C: net, $1. Marlier.
Perkin, W: H:, *jr., and* Lean, Bevan. Introd. to chemistry and physics. New ed. '02(Mr1) 2 v., 12°, net, ea., 50 c. Macmillan.

Perkins, F. M. Giotto. '02(Ja14) il. 12°, (Great masters in painting and sculpture.) $1.75. Macmillan.
Perkins, G: R. Arithmética elemental. Neuva ed. '01· '02(F15) 12°, bds., 25 c. Appleton.
Perkins, T: Cathedral church of Amiens. '02(Mr29) 12°, (Bell's handbooks to continental churches.) $1. Macmillan.
Perrault, C: Tales of Mother Goose; new tr. '02(F8) il. D. (Home and school classics.) 25 c. Heath.
Perrault, C: Tales of passed times. '02 (Ja18) il. 16°, (Temple classics for young people.) net, 50 c.; flex. leath., 80 c. Macmillan.
Perrault, C:, *and* Aulnoy, Marie C. J. de B., *Comtesse d'*. Fairy favorites. New ed. '01· '02(F15) 16°, (Children's friend ser.) bds., 50 c. Little, B. & Co.
Perrault, C: *See also* Aulnoy, M. C. J. de B., *Comtesse d'*.
Perry, Stuart H. Legal adviser and business guide. '01· '02(Mr8) O. $1.50. Pontiac.

PERSIA.
Remy. Influence of Persia on the poetry of Germany. net, $1. Macmillan.
Sparroy. Persian children of the Royal family. net, $3.50. Lane.
Sykes. 10,000 miles in Persia. net, $6. Scribner.
See also Inscriptions.

Persian pearl. Darrow, C. S. $1.50. Ricketts.
Personal life of the clergy. Robinson, A. W. net, 90 c. Longmans.
Personal problem ser. *See* Macmillan's.

PERSPECTIVE.
Pratt. Perspective, incl. projection of shadows and reflections. 90 c. Longmans.

PERU.
Prescott. Conquest of Peru. 2 v. net, $2. Macmillan.

Perverts (The). Howard, W: L. $1.50. G: W. Dillingham.

PETER III.
Bain. Peter III., Emperor of Russia. net, $3.50. Dutton.

Peters, J: J. *See* Labor and capital.
Peters, Madison C. The Jew as a patriot. '02(F22) D. $1. Baker & T.
Peterson, C. A. Mound building age in North America. '02(My24) O. pap., 25 c. Clarke.
Peterson, Hans C. First steps in Eng. composition. '02(Mr29) S. (Educational ser.) 35 c. Flanagan.
Phantom caravan. Odenheimer, C. P. $1. Abbey Press.

PHARMACY.
Neff. Prescription writing in Latin or Eng. 75 c. Davis.

PHARYNX.
See Throat.

Phelps, Eliz. S., [*now Mrs.* H. D. Ward,] *and* Ward, H. D. A lost hero. New ed. '01· '02(F15) 16°, (Children's friend ser.) bds., 50 c. Little, B. & Co.
Phelps, W: L., *comp.* List of general reading in Eng. literature. '02(Ap26) 12°, pap., net, 5 c. Pease-L.
Philip Longstreth. Van Vorst, M. $1.50. Harper.

PHILIPPINE ISLANDS.
Condict. Old glory and the gospel in the Philippines. net, 75 c. Revell.

PHILIPPINE ISLANDS.—*Continued.*
Halstead. Story of the Philippines. $2; $3. Dominion.

Philipson, D: Jew in English fiction. New rev., enl. ed. '02(My17) D. net, $1. Clarke.
Phillipps, L. M. With Rimington. '01· '02 (Ja11) O. $2.50. Longmans.
Phillips, D: G. Her Serene Highness. '02 (My10) il. D. $1.50. Harper.
Phillips, Fs. C., *ed.* Methods for the analysis of ores, pig iron and steel in use at the laboratories about Pittsburg, Pa. 2d ed. '01· '02(F1) il. 8°, net, $1. Chemical Pub.
Phillips, H: W. Red Saunders. '02(My24) il. D. $1.25. McClure, P.
Phillips, J: B. Methods of keeping the public money of the U. S. '02(F15) 12°, pap., $1. Mich. Pol. Sci.
Phillips, Stephen. Paolo and Francesca. New ed. '02(Je28) 12°, net, $1.25. Lane.
Phillips, Stephen. Ulysses: a drama. '02 (F15) D. net, $1.25. Macmillan.

PHILOSOPHY.
Adam, *comp.* Texts to il. lectures on Greek philosophy. net, $1.25. Macmillan.
Baldwin. Fragments in philosophy and science. net, $2.50. Scribner.
Blackwood's philosophical classics. 15 v. ea., net, 50 c. Lippincott.
Boethius. Consolation of philosophy. 50 c.; 75 c. Macmillan.
Chamberlain. Evolutionary philosophy. 50 c. Baker & T.
Kupfer. Greek foreshadowings of modern metaphysical and epistemological thought. $1. J. S. Cushing.
Laurie. Scottish philosophy in its nat. development. net, $1.75. Macmillan.
Muirhead. Philosophy and life. $1.50. Macmillan.
Sidgwick. Philosophy. net, $2.25. Macmillan.
See also Ethics;—Mind and body;—Ontology;—Skepticism;—Utilitarianism;—*also* Kant, I.

Philosophy of conduct. Ladd, G: T. net, $3.50. Scribner.
Philosophy of the Christian religion. Fairbairn, A. M. net, $3.50. Macmillan.
Philosophy of voice. Lunn, C: net, $2. Schirmer.

PHONOGRAPHY.
See Stenography.

Photographic coloring. '02(Ap5) D. pap., 25 c. Acme Water Color.

PHOTOGRAPHY.
International annual of Anthony's photographic bulletin, 1902. $1.25; 75 c. Anthony.
Taylor. Why my photographs are bad. net, $1. Jacobs.

Phrase-making, Science of. *See* Brown, D: W.

PHRENOLOGY.
Windsor. Phrenology. 25 c. Donohue.
See also Physiognomy.

PHYSICAL CULTURE.
See Gymnastics and physical culture.

PHYSICAL GEOGRAPHY.
Davis. Elem. physical geography. $1.40. Ginn.
Gilbert *and* Brigham. Introd. to physical geography. net, $1.25. Appleton.

PHYSICAL GEOGRAPHY.—*Continued.*
Morgan. Advanced physiography. $1.50. Longmans.
See also Brooks;—Geography;—Geology;—Nature;—Seashore;—Water;—Weather.

PHYSICIANS.
Allen. Practitioner's manual. $6; $7. Wood.
Medical directory of the city of N. Y. $1.50. Wynkoop.

PHYSICS.
Ayres. Lab'y exercises in elem. physics. net, 50 c. Appleton.
Carhart *and* Chute. Physics for high school students. $1.25. Allyn & B.
Crew *and* Tatnall. Lab'y manual of physics. net, 90 c. Macmillan.
Fisher *and* Patterson. Elements of physics. 60 c. Heath.
Kelsey. Physical determinations. $1.50. Longmans.
Perkin *and* Lean. Introd. to chemistry and physics. 2 v., ea., net, 50 c. Macmillan.
Reed *and* Guthe. Manual of physical measurements. $1.50. Wahr.
Reynolds. Papers on mechanical and physical subjects. v. 2. net, $6. Macmillan.
Slate. Physics. net, $1.10. Macmillan.
Stewart. Nociones de fisica. 20 c. Appleton.
Wentworth *and* Hill. Lab'y exercises in elem. physics. 27 c. Ginn.
See also Chemistry;—Heat;—Light;—Mathematics;—Radiation;—Sound.

PHYSIOGNOMY.
Stevens. Faciology. 25 c. Donohue.

PHYSIOGRAPHY.
See Geology;—Physical geography.

PHYSIOLOGY.
Blaisdell. Life and health: text-book on physiology. $1. Ginn.
Colton. Elem. physiology and hygiene. 60 c. Heath.
Jegi. Syllabus of human physiology for schools. $1. Gillan.
Schäfer. Directions for class work in practical physiology. net, $1. Longmans.
Smith. Anatomy, physiology and hygiene. $1. W: R. Jenkins.
See also Anatomy;—Hygiene;—Mind and body;—Nervous system.

Piatt, J: J. The Hesperian tree. '02(F22) il. O. $2. J: Scott.
Piccolomini (The). Schiller, J. C. F. v. (App. to pubs. for price.) Niccolls.
Pickering, Edg. King for a summer. '02 (Ap26) il. D. net, $1. Lee & S.
Pickle, G: W., *rep.* *See* Tennessee. *Sup. ct.* Repts.
Pictorial natural history. Cuppy, H. A. $1. Crowell & K.
Pidgin, C: F. Stephen Holton. '02(My10) D. $1.50. L. C. Page.
Pierce, Arth. H. Studies in auditory and visual space perception. '01. '02(Ja11) D. net, $2. Longmans.
Pierce, Ella A. Hartley House cook book and household economist. '02(F8) S. (Handbooks for practical workers in church and philanthropy.) 60 c. Lentilhon.
Pierce, Ella M. Intermediate arithmetic. '02 (Mr22) il. 12°, (Pierce arithmetics.) 48 c. Silver.
Pierce, F: C. Field genealogy. '01. '02(F8) 2 v., il. 4°, $10. Conkey.
Pierce, Grace A. The silver cord and the golden bowl. '02(Mr1) O. $1. Abbey Press.
Pierson, Clara D. Among the night people. '02(My10) 12°, net, $1. Dutton.

PIGEONS.
Homing pigeon. 25 c. G: E. Howard.
Rice. Robinson method of breeding squabs. 50 c. Plymouth Rock.

Pilgrim's progress. *See* Bunyan, J:

PING-PONG.
Parker. Ping-pong: how to play it. net, 75 c. Putnam.
Ritchie *and* Harrison. Table tennis, and how to play it. 50 c. Lippincott.
Ritchie *and* Parker. Ping-pong. 50 c. Street.

Pink knight. Monsell, J. R. net, 40 c. Stokes.
Pinson, W. W. In white and black. '02 (Mr1) D. $1.50. Saalfield.
Pioneer towns of America. il. D. 50 c. Crowell.
—Kaler. Story of Pemaquid. (2.)
Piper, Fred. S. Lexington, the birthplace of Am. liberty. '02(Ap26) il. sq. S. pap., 25 c. Lexington.
Pipes and tubes. Bjorling, P. R. $1. Macmillan.
Pitman, Benn, *and* Howard, J. B. Business letters: no. 1. '02(My10) S. pap., 25 c. Phonograph.
Pitman, *Sir* I: Business corr. in shorthand: no. 2. Rev. ed. '02(My10) S. pap., 30 c. Pitman.
Pitman, *Sir* I: Phonographic teacher. Twentieth century ed. '02(My10) S. pap., 20 c. Pitman.
Pitman's commercial ser. il. D. Pitman.
—Marchand. Commercial history. $1.
Pitt Press Shakespeare. 12°, net, 40 c. Macmillan.
—Shakespeare. Macbeth.
Plane surveying. Nugent, P. C. $3.50. Wiley.
Planets and people; [1902,] annual. F. E. Ormsby, ed. '01. '02(Ja25) O. $1. F. E. Ormsby.

PLANTS.
See Botany;—Gardening.

PLATE.
Cripps. Old Eng. plate. net, $13.50. Scribner.

Plato. The republic. (J. L. Davies and D. J. Vaughan.) '02(Ap19) 12°, (Home lib.) $1. Burt.
Plato. The republic. bk. 2. '02(My10) D. pap., 15 c. Kerr.

PLATO.
Nettleship. Lectures on the Republic of Plato. net. $2.75. Macmillan.
Ritchie. Plato. $1.25. Scribner.

Plattner, K. F. Manual of qualitative and quantitative analysis with the blowpipe; tr. by H: B. Cornwall. 8th ed., rev. by F: Kolbeck. '02(My17) il. net, $4. Van Nostrand.

PLAYS.
See Drama and dramatists.

PLEADING AND PRACTICE.
Cockcroft, *ed.* Encyc. of forms for pleading and practice. v. 15. $6. Cockcroft
McKinney. Encyc. of pleading and practice. v. 22, 23. ea., $6. E: Thompson.

PLEADING AND PRACTICE.—*Continued.*
Young *and* Keen. Problems in practice and pleading at the common law. 50 c. Mudge.
See also Actions at law.

Pleasures of life. Lubbock, *Sir* J: $1. Burt.

Pleistocene glacial formations. *See* Chamberlin, T: C.

PLUMBING.
Bjorling. Pipes and tubes. $1. Macmillan.
Lawler. Modern plumbing. $5. Popular.

Plummer, Ma. W. Hints to small libraries. 3d ed., rev. and enl. '02(My17) sq. O. net, 50 c. M. W. Plummer.

Pocket Gray. Cotterell, E: net, $1.25. Wood.

Poe, Edg. A. Works. '02(Ap5) 4 v., 12°, hf. cf., $8. Burt.

Poe, Edg. A. Murders in the Rue Morgue, and other tales. '02(Mr29) il. 12°, (Home lib.) $1. Burt.

Poems of life and loving. Shelley, H. S. $1. Neely.

POETRY.
Liddell. Introd. to the scientific study of Eng. poetry. net, $1.25. Doubleday, P.
See Ballads;—Metre;—Quotations.

POETS.
Thackeray *and* Stone, *eds.* Pre-Victorian poets. $2.50.—Victorian poets. net, $2. Lane.

Point of honour. Hinkson, H. A. $1.50. McClurg.

Poland, W: Find the church. '02(Mr8) 8°, pap., net, 5 c. Herder.

Poland, W: Socialism; its economic aspect. '02(Je28) 8°, pap., net, 5 c. Herder.

Policeman Flynn. Flower, E. $1.50. Century Co.

POLICY.
See Fortune-tellers.

POLITICAL ECONOMY.
Gladden. Social salvation. net, $1. Houghton, M. & Co.
Laughlin. Elements of political economy. $1.20. Am. Bk.
Patten. Theory of prosperity. net, $1.25. Macmillan.
Phillips. Methods of keeping the public money of the U. S. $1. Mich. Pol. Sci.
Sidgwick. Principles of political economy. net, $4.50. Macmillan.
See also Finance;—Prosperity;—Trusts.

Political freshman. James, B. W. $1.50. Bushrod Lib.

Political primer. Fielde, A. M. 75 c.; 50 c. League Pol. Educ.

POLITICAL SCIENCE.
Ashley. American federal state. net, $2. Macmillan.
Bardeen. Manual of civics for N. Y. schools. net, $1. Bardeen.
Bourne. Teaching of history and civics. $1.50. Longmans.
Dunning. Hist. of political theories, ancient and mediæval. net, $2.50. Macmillan.
Forman. First lessons in civics. 60 c. Am. Bk.
Kellogg. Elements of civil government. 25 c. Kellogg.
Martin. Civil government in U. S. 90 c. Am. Bk.

POLITICAL SCIENCE.—*Continued.*
Meyer. Nominating systems; direct primaries vs. conventions in the U. S. net, $1.50. E. C. Meyer.
See also Citizenship; — Crime and criminals; — Democracy; — Municipal government; — Reciprocity;—*also* names of states and countries.

Politzer, A. *See* Brühl, G.

Pollock, *Sir* F: Revised reports. v. 46-51. '01. '02(F15) 8°, shp. or hf. cf., ea., net, $6. Little, B. & Co.

Polyphase apparatus. *See* Oudin, M. A.

PONTIAC'S WAR.
See Indians.

Poole, R. L. *See* Maitland, F: W:

Poole, Stanley Lane. Story of Cairo. '02 (My24) il. 12°, (Mediæval towns ser.) $2; leath., $2.50. Macmillan.

Poor's manual of the railroads of the U. S. 1901. '01· '02(F22) 8°, $10. Poor.

POPES.
Mann. Lives of the popes in early Middle Ages. v. 1, pt. 1. net, $3. Herder.

Popular girl. Baldwin, M. net, $1.20. Lippincott.

PORCELAIN.
See Ceramics.

Porter, Ctte., *and* Clarke, Helen A. Shakespeare studies: Macbeth. '01· '02(Ja4) S. 56 c. Am. Bk.

Portiuncula. Indulgence of portiuncula; fr. the German. New ed. '02(Je28) 48°, pap., 5 c. Herder.

PORTLAND CEMENT.
See Cement.

PORTRAITS.
Cust, *ed.* National portrait gallery. v. 1. subs., for complete work, net, $3. Cassell.

PORTUGAL.
Higgin. Spanish life; with chapters on Portuguese life by E. E. Street. net, $1.20. Putnam.

POTTER, Jennie O'Neil.
Deal. Life of Jennie O'Neil Potter. $1. Blanchard.

POTTERY.
See Ceramics.

Powell, Ja. B. Choralia: handy book for parochial precentors and choirmasters. '01. '02(F8) D. $1.50. Longmans.

Powell, Lewis. The twentieth century home builder. '02(Ap5) nar. D. pap., 25 c. Pub. Ho. M. E. Ch., So.

POWER.
Kerr. Power and power transmission. $2. Wiley.

Power of God's word. Prime, R. E. 3 c. Presb. Bd.

Powers, Harry H. Art of travel. '02(My17) D. pap., 25 c. Bu. Univ. Travel.

Poynter, E. F. Michael Ferrier. '02(Ap26) 12°, $1.50. Macmillan.

Practical electricity, with questions and answers. 3d ed. '01· '02(Mr29) il. 16°, leath., $2. Cleveland Armature.

Practical medicine ser. of year-books; ed. by G. P. Head. il. D. $1.50. Year Bk.
—Billings *and* Stanton, *eds.* General medicine. (1.)
—Murphy. General surgery. (2.)
—Wood, *and others, eds.* Eye, ear, nose and throat. (3.)

Pratt, H: S. Course in invertebrate zoölogy. '02(F15) il. O. $1.35. Ginn.

Pratt, Mara L. America's story for America's children. In 5 v. v. 5, Foundations of the Republic. '01. '02(Ja4) D. 40 c. Heath.

Pratt, Rob. Perspective, incl. the projection of shadows and reflections. '01. '02(Mr8) il. F. bds., 90 c. Longmans.

Pratt, S: W. Life and Epistles of St. Paul. '02(F1) map, S. 75 c. Funk.

Pratt, Stephen R. Supp. to Mining laws of Colo., etc. '02(Ap5) O. pap., 35 c. Pratt Merc.

PRAYER.
 Aitkin. Divine ordinance of prayer. $1.25. E. & J. B. Young.
 McClure. A mighty means of usefulness: intercessory prayer. net, 50 c. Revell.
 Worlledge. Prayer. $1.50. Longmans.
 See also Lord's prayer;—Prayers;—Worship.

PRAYER-BOOK.
 See Book of common prayer;—Church of England.

PRAYER-MEETINGS.
 See Epworth League.

PRAYERS.
 Breviarium bothanum sive portiforium secundum usum ecclesiæ cujusdam in Scotia. $15. Longmans.

Pre-Victorian poets. Thackeray, F. St. J: $2.50. Lane.

PREACHING.
 Barton, *comp.* Pulpit power and eloquence. $3.50. F. M. Barton.
 Lyman. Preaching in the new age. net, 75 c. Revell.
 See also Sermons.

Precept and practice. Bausman, B: net, $1. Heidelberg.

PRECIOUS METALS.
 Del Mar. Hist. of the precious metals. net, $3. Cambridge.
 See also Money.

PRECIOUS STONES.
 Sommerville. Engraved gems. net, $1.50. Biddle.

Prentiss, *Mrs.* Eliz. ["Aunt Susan."] Little Susy stories. '02(Mr29) il. 12°, (Little women ser.) 75 c. Burt.

Prentiss, *Mrs.* Eliz. Six little princesses and what they turned into. '02(Je28) il. 12°, (St. Nicholas ser.) 75 c. Burt.

Preparatio; or, notes of preparation for holy communion. '01. '02(Ja11) D. $2. Longmans.

Presbyterian church. General Assembly; twentieth century addresses. '02(Je7) D. net, $1. Presb. Bd.

PRESBYTERIAN CHURCH.
 Doyle. Presb. home missions. net, $1. Presb. Bd.
 Erdman. The ruling elder. 3 c. Presb. Bd.
 Stephens. Evolution of the confession of faith of the Cumberland Presb. church. 10 c. Cumberland.
 See also Syracuse, First Presb. church.

Prescott, Alb. B:, *and* Sullivan, Eug. C. First book of qualitative chemistry for studies of water solution and mass action. 11th ed., rewritten. '02(My17) O. net, $1.50. Van Nostrand.

Prescott, W: H. Hist. of the conquest of Peru; ed. by J: F. Kirk. '02(Ap12) 2 v., 12°, (Bohn's standard lib.) net, $2. Macmillan.

Prescott, W: H. Hist. of the reign of Ferdinand and Isabella the Catholic. '02 (Ap12) 3 v., 12°, (Bohn's standard lib.) net, $3. Macmillan.

PRESCRIPTIONS.
 Kuder. Medical prescription book. $2. Journal Pr.
 See also Pharmacy.

PRESIDENTS.
 See United States.

Presset, Anne L. Cherished thoughts in original poems and sketches. '01. '02 (My24) il. D. $1.50; im. mor., $1.75; full mor., $2.25. Skelton.

Prévost, Marcel. Frédérique; tr. by E. Marriage. '02(Mr8) D. $1.50. Crowell.

Price, E. D. Letters of Mildred's mother to Mildred. '01. '02(F15) 12°, $1. Ogilvie.

Price, Eleanor C. Angelot. '02(Ap5) il. D. $1.50. Crowell.

Price, Ja. A. Observations and exercises on the weather. '02(Ap26) O. pap., 30 c. Am. Bk.

Price inevitable. Sidner, A. L. $1. Popular.

PRIESTS.
 Harper. Constructive studies in the priestly element in the O. T. $1. Univ. of Chic.
 See also Catholic church.

Prime, Ralph E. Power of God's word. '02 (Je21) S. pap., 3 c. Presb. Bd.

PRIMERS.
 Alger. Primer of work and play. 30 c. Heath.
 Burt *and* Howells. Literary primer. net, 30 c. Scribner.

Prince Incognito. Latimer, *Mrs.* E. W. $1.50. McClurg.

Prince of good fellows. Barr, R. $1.50. McClure, P.

Prince of the captivity. Gregg, H. $1.50. L. C. Page.

Princess (The), *pseud.* *See* Lockett, M. F.

Princess. Tennyson, A. 25 c. Appleton.

Principles of western civilization. Kidd, B: net, $2. Macmillan.

Print-collector's handbook. Whitman, A. net, $5. Macmillan.

PRINTERS.
 See Short, T:

PRINTING.
 Morris. Art and craft of printing. $5. Elston Press.
 Sheldon. Practical colorist. $8. Owl Press.

Prisoners of the sea. Kingsley, *Mrs.* F. M. $1.25; 50 c. New Amsterdam.

PRISONS.
 Howard. Prisoners of Russia. net, $1.40. Appleton.
 Skinner. Prisons of the nation and their inmates. 10 c. Brooklyn Eagle.

Pritchard, W: A., *comp.* Wehman's how to become a naturalized citizen. '02(Mr8) S. pap., 10 c. Wehman.

Prize designs for rural school buildings. Coburn, F: N. 25 c. Kellogg.

Prize poetical speaker. '01. '02(Ja4) 12°, 75 c. Dickerman.

PROBATE.
 See Wills.

Problems in the use and adjustment of engineering instruments. 4th ed. rev. and enl. '02(Je21) 16°, $1.25. Wiley.

Professor Archie. Percival, L. 50 c. Nelson.

Progredior ser. sq. D. Flanagan.
—Beeman. Analysis of the Eng. sentence. 50 c.
Progress of dogma. Orr, J. $1.75. Armstrong.
Progression to immortality. Brooks, H: S. net, 50 c. Wessels.
PROJECTION.
See Perspective.
PROPERTY.
See Real property.
PROPHECY.
Girdlestone. Grammar of prophecy. $2.50. E. & J. B. Young.
Prophet of the kingdom. Frisbie, H: S: $1.25. Neale.
Prose quotations. Allibone, S: A. $2.50. Lippincott.
PROSPERITY.
Seager. Prof. Patten's theory of prosperity. 15 c. Am. Acad. Pol. Sci.
PROSTITUTION.
Social (The) evil. net, $1.25. Putnam.
PROTESTANT EPISCOPAL CHURCH.
Francis. Weekly church teaching for the infants. 25 c. E. & J. B. Young.
McCormick. Distinctive marks of the Episcopal church. 25 c. Young Churchman.
Miller. Amer. church dict. and cyclopedia. $1. Whittaker.
Parson's (The) handbook. net, $1.50. Young Churchman.
See also Catechisms;—Church of England;—Lent.
PROTESTANTISM.
Gibson. Protestant principles. 60 c. Armstrong.
PROTOZOA.
Chapman. The foraminifera: introd. to study of the protozoa. $3.50. Longmans.
Proudfoot, A. H. Year with the Mother-play; 2d year's study course of the League of Am. Mothers. '02(Je28) D. $1. Flanagan.
PROVERBS.
Browne. Proverbial sayings. net, $1. Stokes.
Providence Journal almanac for 1902. '02 (F8) 12°, pap., 10 c. Providence Journ.
Prune, Nat. College chaps. '02(Je14) S. 75 c. Mutual Bk.
PSALMS.
See Bible.
PSYCHIATRY.
See Insanity.
PSYCHICAL RESEARCH.
Duff *and* Allen. Psychic research and gospel miracles. net, $1.50. Whittaker.
PSYCHOLOGY.
Baldwin. Social and ethical interpretations in mental development. net, $2.60. Macmillan.
Brinton. Basis of social relations. net, $1.50. Putnam.
Dewey. Psychology and social practice. net, 25 c. Univ. of Chic.
Mercier. Psychology, normal and morbid. net, $4. Macmillan.
Patrick. Psychology for teachers. $1. Educ. Pub.
Vance. Rise of a soul. net, $1. Revell.
Witmer. Analytical psychology. $1.60. Ginn.
See also Character;—Hypnotism;—Mind and body;—Philosophy;—Phrenology;—Telepathy.
Public house reform. Cumming, A. N. $1. Scribner.
Public Ledger almanac, 1902; ed. by G: W. C. Drexel. '01. '02(Ja11) S. pap., gratis to subs. of *Public Ledger*. Drexel.
Puddicombe, *Mrs*. Beynon. *See* Raine, A.
Pullen, *Mrs*. Elisabeth. Mr. Whitman. '02 (My17) D. $1.50. Lothrop.
Pulpit power and eloquence. Barton, F: $3.50. F. M. Barton.
PULSE.
See Heart.
Purdy, L. Burdens of local taxation and who bears them. '01. '02(Ja11) D. 25 c. Public Policy.
Purdy, L. Local option in taxation. '02 (F15) D. pap., 10 c. Tax Reform.
Puron, Juan G. Lector moderno de Appleton, nos. 1-3. '01. '02(F22) 12°, bds., no. 1, 25 c.; no. 2, 35 c.; no. 3, 45 c. Appleton.
Purves, G: T. Faith and life: sermons. '02 (Je7) D. net, $1.25. Presb. Bd.
Purves, G: T. Joy in service. '01. '02(Ja4) D. 50 c. Am. Tr.
PUSEY, Edw. Bouverie.
Grafton. Pusey and the church revival. net, 50 c. Young Churchman.
Putnam, Israel. Daniel Everton, volunteer-regular. '02(My3) il. D. net, $1.20. Funk.
PUTNAM, Rufus.
Earle. Rutland home of Maj. Gen. Rufus Putnam. 30 c.; 50 c. S. C. Earle.
Putnam's lib. of standard literature. D. $1.75. Putnam.
—Chesterfield. Letters to his son.
—Swift. Journal to Stella.
Putnam's science ser. 8°, net. Putnam.
—Brinton. Basis of social relations. $1.50.
PUZZLES.
See Riddles.
Pyeshkoff, Alexêi M. *See* Górky, M.
Pyle, Howard. Some merry adventures of Robin Hood. '02(Je7) il. D. (Ser. of school reading.) net, 60 c. Scribner.
Pyle, Kath. Careless Jane, and other tales. '02(My10) 12°, net, 75 c. Dutton.
Q., *pseud.* *See* Couch, A. T: Quiller-.
Quad, M., *pseud.* *See* Lewis, C: B.
Quadrupani, R. P. Light and peace; from the Fr. 3d ed. '02(Mr8) 12°, net, 50 c. Herder.
Quaker experiment in government. Sharpless, I: $1.50. Ferris.
Quaku. Quinius, H. F. 3 c. J: G. Quinius.
Quang Chang Ling. Why should the Chinese go? '02(Je7) 8°, pap., 25 c. Cambridge.
Quayle, W: A. The gentleman in literature. '02(My24) por. D. (Hero ser., no. 4.) net, 25 c. Jennings.
Quayle, W: A. A hero—Jean Valjean. '02 (Ap26) D. (Hero ser., no. 1.) net, 25 c. Jennings.
Quayle, W: A. King Cromwell. '02(My24) il. D. (Hero ser., no. 6.) net, 25 c. Jennings.
Queen of the household. Ellsworth, T. $2.50. Ellsworth.
Queer people. Bishop, W: H: $1. Street.
Quentin Durward. Scott, *Sir* W. net, 60 c. Macmillan.
Questions of the day. D. Putnam.
—Labor and capital. $1.50. (98.)
Quiberon touch. Brady, C. T. $1.50. Appleton.

Quick, M. I. Complete guide to ball room dancing. '02(My17) 12°, 50 c.; pap., 25 c. Donohue.

Quinius, **Augusta**. **Mother Margaret's bunch** of flowers. '02(Mr1) T. pap., 5 c. J: G. Quinius.

Quinius, H. F. *and* Augusta. Quaku. '02 (Je28) T. pap., 3 c. J: G. Quinius.

QUOTATIONS.
  Allibone. Poetical quotations.—Prose quotations. ea., $2.50. Lippincott.

Rab and his friends. Brown, J: 25 c. Rand, McN. & Co.

Racine, Jean. Athalie; ed., with notes, by E: S. Joynes. New enl. ed. '02(F1) D. (Students' ser. of classic Fr. plays, no. 2.) net, 35 c. Holt.

Racine, Jean. Esther; ed. with notes by E: S. Joynes. [New ed.] '02(F8) D. (Students' ser. of classic Fr. plays, no. 5.) net, 35 c. Holt.

Radcliffe, G: L. P. Governor Thomas H. Hicks of Maryland and the Civil war. '01-'02(Mr8) O. (Johns Hopkins Univ. studies, 19th ser., nos. 11-12.) pap., 50 c. Johns Hopkins.

Rader, Perry S., *rep*. *See* Missouri. *Sup. ct.* Repts.

RADIATION.
  Brace, *ed*. Laws of radiation and absorption. $1. Am. Bk.
  See also Heat;—Light;—Sound.

Railroad repts. (v. 24, Am. and Eng. railroad cases;) ed. by T: J. Michie. v. 1. '02(Je7) O. shp., $5. Michie.

Railroading with Christ. Dwight, C: A. S. $1. Am. Tr.

RAILROADS.
  Adams. Block system of signalling. $2. Railroad Gazette.
  American and Eng. railroad cases. v. 23. ea., $5. Michie.
  American street railway investments. $5. Street R'way.
  Bodmer. Inspection of railway materials. $1.50. Macmillan.
  Goodknight. Modern association and railroading. 50 c. Abbey Press.
  Hanford. Railroading in the U. S. 5 c. Socialistic Co-op.
  Knapp. Government ownership of railroads. 15 c. Am. Acad. Pol. Sci.
  Meyer. Advisory councils in railway administration. 15 c. Am. Acad. Pol. Sci.
  Newcomb. Concentration of railway control. 15 c. Am. Acad. Pol. Sci.
  Poor's manual of railroads of the U. S., 1901. $10. Poor.
  Talbot. Railway transition spiral. $1.50. Van Nostrand.
  Weyl. Passenger traffic of railways. $1.50; $1. [Univ. of Penn.] Ginn.
  See also Air brake;—Cars;—Cincinnati Southern railway;—Locomotives;—Street-railroads.

Raine, Allen, [*pseud.* for *Mrs.* Beynon Puddicombe.] A Welsh witch. '02(Je7) D. (Town and country lib., no. 312.) $1; pap., 50 c. Appleton.

Rainsford, W: S. Reasonableness of faith. and other addresses. '02(My10) O. net. $1.25. Doubleday, P.

Rainy, Rob. Ancient Catholic church from accession of Trajan to the Fourth General Council, A.D. 98-451. '02(F1) O. (Internat. theol. lib.) net, $2.50. Scribner.

Rait, Rob. S. Five Stuart princesses. '02 (Mr29) il. 8°, net, $3.50. Dutton.

Raleigh, *Sir* Wa. The last fight of the "Revenge" at sea. '02(My10) 4°, net, $6. Houghton, M. & Co.

Ramabai Sarasvati, *Pundita*. High-caste Hindu woman. '02(Mr22) 12°, net, 75 c. Revell.

Ramal, Wa. Songs of childhood. '02(Ap19) il. S. net, $1.20. Longmans.

RAMONA.
  Hufford. The real Ramona of Helen Hunt Jackson's famous novel. 35 c.; 75 c.; $1; $1.25. D: A. Hufford.

Ramsey, M. M. Spanish grammar, with exercise. '02(My17) D. net, $1.50. Holt.

Randall, Wyatt W., *ed. and tr.* Expansion of gases by heat. '02(Ap19) O. (Scientific memoirs.) $1. Am. Bk.

Rankin, A. C. Saloon law nullification and its cure. '02(My17) 16°, 50 c. Advance.

Rankin, A. W. *See* Aiton, G:

Rasselas. *See* Johnson, S:

RATIONALISM.
  Hurst. Hist. of rationalism. $2.50. Eaton & M.

Rawlins, Ja. M. *See* Lippincott's elem. algebra.

Rawson, C., Gardner, W. M., *and* Laycock, W. F. Dict. of dyes, mordants, and other compounds. '01. '02(F15) 8°, net, $5. Lippincott.

Raycroft, B: J. Sermons on the stations of the cross, the Our Father, Hail Mary, etc. '02(Je7) 8°, net, $1.50. Pustet.

READERS AND SPEAKERS.
  Allen. Children of the palm lands. 50 c. Educ. Pub.
  American speaker. 50 c. Conkey.
  Blaisdell. Child life fifth reader. net, 45 c. Macmillan.
  Bradish. Stories of country life. 40 c. Am. Bk.
  Brown. Am. star speaker and model elocutionist. $1.50. Donohue.
  Burke. Literature and art books. Bks. 1-3. bk. 1, 25 c.; bk. 2, 30 c.; bk. 3, 35 c. McBride.
  Calmerton *and* Wheeler. First reader. 30 c. W: H: Wheeler.
  Carpenter. Europe. 70 c. Am. Bk.
  Cyr. Readers, bks. 7, 8. ea., 45 c. Ginn.
  Edgerly. Natural reader. $1.50. Ralston.
  Funk *and* Moses, *eds.* Standard first reader. 35 c. Funk.
  Gyim. Chinese-Eng. elem. reader and arithmetic. $1.25. Taylor & M.
  Judson *and* Bender, *eds.* Graded literature readers. bks. 6-8. ea., 50 c. Maynard, M. & Co.
  McCullough. Little stories for little people. 25 c. Am. Bk.
  Macmillan's new geog. readers: Africa and Australasia. net, 40 c. Macmillan.
  Macmillan's new hist. readers; Senior. net, 50 c. Macmillan.
  Murché. Rural readers. net, 40 c. Macmillan.
  Prize poetical speaker. 75 c. Dickerman.
  Shepard. Life on the farm: reading book. 50 c. Flanagan.
  Thompson. New century readers. 3d bk. 52 c. Morse.

READERS AND SPEAKERS.—*Continued.*
Virden. First science reader. 25 c.; 10 c. Flanagan.
Welsh. Colonial days. 50 c. Educ. Pub.
Whitcomb. Little journey to Italy.—Scotland. ea., 15 c. Flanagan.
Wide world. 30 c. Ginn.
See also Primers;—Recitations.

READING.
See Books and reading.

REAL PROPERTY.
Newell. Elements of law of real property. $4. Flood.
Pattee, *comp.* Authorities, deductions, and notes in real property. $2. Univ. Press.
Warvelle. American law of vendor and purchaser of real property. v. 1, 2. $12. Callaghan.
Washburn. Am. law of real property. 3 v. net, $18. Little, B. & Co.

Real Ramona. Hufford, D: A. 35 c.; 75 c.; $1; $1.25. D: A. Hufford.
Reasonableness of faith. Rainsford, W: S. net, $1.25. Doubleday, P.
Rebuilding of old commonwealths. Page, W. H. net, $1. Doubleday, P.

RECEIPTS.
See Cookery.

RECIPROCITY.
Farquhar. Manufacturers' needs of reciprocity. 15 c. Am. Acad. Pol. Sci.

RECITATIONS.
Birbeck, *ed.* Select recitations, orations, etc. $1. Wagner.
Brown, *comp.* Comic recitations.—Patriotic recitations. ea., 50 c.; 25 c. Donohue.
Monroe, *ed.* Public and parlor readings. 4 v. ea., $1. Lee & S.
See also Readers and speakers.

Reconciliation of Randall Claymore. Barnes, E. N. C. $1. Earle.
Reconstruction and the constitution. Burgess, J: W. net, $1. Scribner.
Recreations of the German emigrants. *See* Goethe, J. W. v.
Recruit Tommy Collins. Bonesteel, M. 45 c. Benziger.
Red anvil. Sherlock, C: R. $1.50. Stokes.
Red letter ser. il. 12°, $1.25; pap., 50 c. New Amsterdam.
—Kingsley. Prisoners of the sea.
—Marchmont. Miser Hoadley's secret.
—Russell. Captain Fanny.
Red Saunders. Phillips, H: W. $1.25. McClure, P.
Redfield, Amasa A., *ed.* Repts. of cases Surrogates' cts. of New York. In 5 v., v. 1. '01- '02(My17) 8°. shp., per v., $6. Banks & Co.
Reduction tables. Blum, A. R. net, $3. Am. Code.
Reed, Edn. Bacon and Shake-speare parallelisms. '02(Ap26) O. bds., net, $2.50. Goodspeed.
Reed, Edn. Francis Bacon, our Shakespeare. '02(Ap26) il. O. bds., net, $2. Goodspeed.
Reed, Eliphalet A. Idea of God in relation to theology. '02(F15) 8°, pap., net, 75 c. Univ. of Chic.
Reed, J: O., *and* Guthe, K. E. Manual of physical measurements. '02(Ap12) O. $1.50. Wahr.

REFORM.
See Temperance.

REFORMATION (The).
See Church history;—Huguenots.

REFORMED CHURCH.
Good. Historical handbk. of Ref. Ch. in U. S. 50 c.; 25 c. Heidelberg.
Good. Women of the Ref. Ch. $1. Heidelberg.

REGENERATION.
Sloan. Social regeneration the work of Christianity. net, 60 c. Westminster.
See also Salvation.

Regiments and armories of Mass. Hall, C: W. per set, $12; $18; $25. W. W. Potter.
Regional anatomy of head and neck. Eckley, W: T. net, $2.50. Lea.
Reid, *Sir* Wemyss. William Black, novelist. '02(Ap26) D. net, $2.25. Harper.
Reinsch, Paul S. Colonial government. '02 (Je21) D. (Citizen's lib. of economics, politics and sociology.) net, $1.25. Macmillan.

RELIGION.
De Solla. Fallacies of religion. 25 c. Pierce & Z.
Jastrow. Study of religion. $1.50. Scribner.
Spalding. Religion, agnosticism and education. net, 80 c. McClurg.
Tolstoi. What is religion? net, 60 c. Crowell.
See also Natural religion;—Revivals;—Skepticism.

RELIGION AND SCIENCE.
Bixby. The new world and the new thought. net, $1. Whittaker.
Smyth. Through science to faith. net, $1.50. Scribner.
See also Evolution;—Natural religion.

Religion for the time. Conger, A. B. net, $1. Jacobs.
Religion of Bible lands. Margoliouth, D: S: 60 c. Armstrong.
Religion of capital. Lafarque, P. 10 c. Socialistic Co-op.
Religion of Israel. Greenstone, J. H. 50 c. Bloch.
Religion of science lib. D. pap. Open Court.
—Kant. Prolegomena to any future metaphysics. 50 c. (53.) Open Court.
—Leibniz. Discourse on metaphysics. 35 c. (52.)

RELIGIONS.
Martin. Traces of the elder faiths of Ireland. 2 v. $12. Longmans.
See also Christianity;—Oriental religions.

Religious and social work amongst girls. Freeman, F. L. net, $1. Whittaker.

RELIGIOUS LIBERTY.
Cobb. Rise of rel. liberty in America. net, $4. Macmillan.

Religious life and influence of Queen Victoria. Walsh, W. net, $2.50. Dutton.
Reliques of Stratford-on-Avon. Way, A. E. net, 50 c.; net, 75 c. Lane.

REMBRANDT, H. van Rijn.
Bell. Rembrandt van Rijn. $1.75. Macmillan.

Remedies of the Great Physician. Kohaus, H. M. 40 c. Alliance.
Remedy for love. Kirk, *Mrs.* E. O. $1.25. Houghton, M. & Co.
Reminiscences of a dramatic critic. Clapp, H: A. net, $1.75. Houghton, M. & Co.
Remsen, Ira. Introd. to the study of chemistry. 6th rev., enl. ed. '01. '02(Mr15) D. (Am. sci. ser.; briefer course.) $1.12. Holt.

Remy, Arth. F. J. Influence of India and Persia on the poetry of Germany. '02(F1) 8°, (Columbia Univ. Germanic studies, v. 1, no. 4.) pap., net, $1. Macmillan.

RENAISSANCE.
Smeaton. The Medici and the Italian Renaissance. $1.25. Scribner.
See also names of countries.

Renan, Ernest. Souvenirs d' enfance et de jeunesse; ed. by I. Babbitt. '02(Mr8) D. (Modern lang. ser.) 75 c. Heath.

REPENTANCE.
See Confession.

Representative men. Emerson, R: W. $1. Burt.

REPTILES.
Seeley. Dragons of the air: extinct flying reptiles. net, $1.40. Appleton.

Republic of Plato. *See* Nettleship, R: L.—Plato.

REPUBLICAN PARTY.
Halstead. Victorious republicanism. $1.50; $2.25. Dominion.

Rescue (The). Sedgwick, A. D. $1.50. Century Co.

RESURRECTION.
Swartz. Easter and the resurrection. net, 15 c. Revell.
See also Future life;—Jesus Christ.

Retail advertising. Farrington, F. net, $1. Baker & T.

Retzius, G. *See* Nordenskiold, G.

REVERE, Paul.
Andrews. Paul Revere and his engraving. $23.50; $40. Scribner.

Revised repts. *See* Pollock, *Sir* F:

REVIVALS.
Oliver. Soul-winners' secrets: revival text-book. 25 c. Jennings.
Strong. The next great awakening. 75 c. Baker & T.

Rewards of taste. Bridge, N. $1.50. H. S. Stone.

Reynolds, Alphæus. Rudiments of Latin. '02 (Ap26) D. $1.25. A. B. Reynolds.

Reynolds, Cuyler. The banquet book. '02 (Ap12) il. D. net, $1.75. Putnam.

Reynolds, O. Papers on mechanical and physical subjects. v. 2, 1881-1900. '02 (Ap26) 8°, net, $6. Macmillan.

Rhead, E. L., *and* Sexton, A. H. Assaying and metallurgical analysis. '02(Ap19) il. O. $4.20. Longmans.

Rhead, L:, *ed.* Speckled brook trout, by various experts with rod and reel. '02 (Mr29) O. net, $3.50. Russell.

Rheingold. Wagner, R: 75 c. Newson.

RHETORIC.
Kellogg. How to teach composition writing. 25 c. Kellogg.
Peterson. First steps in Eng. composition. 35 c. Flanagan.
Scott. Composition literature. $1. Allyn & B.
Thornton. Eng. composition. 75 c. Crowell.

RHODE ISLAND.
Smith, J. J., *comp.* Civil and military list of R. I., 1800-1850. net, $7.50. Preston.
See also Block Island.

RHODES, Cecil.
Hensman. Cecil Rhodes. net, $5. Harper.

Rhodes, W. G. Elem. treatise on alternating currents. '02(Mr8) il. O. $2.60. Longmans.

RHODESIA.
See Matabeleland.

Rhone, Rosamond D. Days of the Son of man. '02(My24) D. net, $1.20. Putnam.

Rhymes from time to time. Doane, W: C. $1.50. Albany Diocesan Press.

Rice, Edn. W. Our sixty-six sacred books. 10th ed., enl., with analysis and questions. '02(F1) D. (Green fund book, no. 10.) net, 50 c. Am. S. S.

Rice, Elmer C. Robinson method of breeding squabs. '01- '02(Mr15); 2d ed., rev. with supp. (Je28) il. 12°, pap., ea., 50 c. Plymouth Rock.

Richard, Marg. A. Darkey ways in Dixie. '02(Ap26) il. D. $1. Abbey Press.

Richards, Ellen H., *and* Williams, Louise H. '02(Ap19) 8°, net, $1.50. Wiley.

Richardson, J: War of 1812; with notes and a life of author, by A. C. Casselman. '02 (Ap26) il. O. subs., $3. Hist. Pub.

Riddell, J: H., *rep.* *See* New Hampshire. *Sup. ct.* Repts.

Riddle of life. Johnston, J. W. $1.50. Jennings.

RIDDLES.
Cutter, *comp.* Conundrums, riddles, puzzles and games. 50 c.; 25 c. Otis.

Ride in Morocco. Macnab, F. $5. Longmans.

Rideal, S: Sewage and the bacterial purification of sewage. 2d ed. '02(Ap5) 8°, $3.50. Wiley.

Ridpath, J: C. Hist. of the U. S. '01- '02 (F15) 4 v. in 2 v., il. 12°, $6. Grosset.

Riehl, W. H. Das spielmannskind und stumme ratsherr; ed. by G: M. Priest. '02(F15) D. 35 c. Am. Bk.

RIFLE.
Fremantle. Book of the rifle. $5. Longmans.

Rigby, Will O. Reliable candy teacher and soda and ice cream formulas. [8th ed., rev. and enl.] '02(Ap12) D. pap., $2. W. O. Rigby.

Riggs, *Mrs.* G: C. *See* Wiggin, *Mrs.* K. D.

Right living. Morris, E. G. $1. Bardeen.

Right reading; counsel on the choice and use of books sel. fr. ten famous authors. '02 (Mr15) S. net, 80 c. McClurg.

Rights and wrongs of the Transvaal war. Cook, E: T. $2. Longmans.

Rime of the ancient mariner. Coleridge, S: T. 30 c.; 25 c. B. F. Johnson.

Ringing questions. Peck, G: C. $1. Eaton & M.

Rip Van Winkle. *See* Irving, W.

Rise and development of Chr. architecture. Ayer, J. C. net, $1.50. Young Churchman.

Rise of a soul. Vance, J. J. net, $1. Revell.

Rise of religious liberty in America. Cobb, S. H. net, $4. Macmillan.

Rita, *pseud.* *See* Humphreys, *Mrs.* E. M. J. G.

Ritchie, D: G. Plato. '02(Ap12) D. (World's epoch-makers.) $1.25. Scribner.

Ritchie, D: G. Studies in political and social ethics. '02(Mr29) 12°, $1.50. Macmillan.

Ritchie, M. J. G., *and* Harrison, W. Table tennis, and how to play it. '02(Je7) il. sq. S. 50 c. Lippincott.

Ritchie, M. J. G., *and* Parker, A. Ping-pong; ed. for Am. players by W. H. Bronson. '02 (My3) il. S. 50 c. Street.

RITUAL.
See **Ministers** (*of the Gospel*).

Rivas, Evelyn de. Little French dinners. '02 (My24) 12°, 50 c. New Amsterdam.

Riverside art ser. D. net, 75 c.; School ed., net, 50 c.; pap., net, 35 c. Houghton, M. & Co.
—Hurll, *ed.* Tuscan sculpture. (11.)—Van Dyck. (12.)

Riverside biog. ser. S. net, 65 c.; School ed., net, 50 c. Houghton, M. & Co.
—Brown. Stephen A. Douglas. (13.)
—Sedgwick. Samuel de Champlain. (14.)

Riverside literature ser. S. pap., net, 15 c. Houghton, M. & Co.
—Ewing. Jackanapes; [also] The brownies.
—La Rame. Dog of Flanders and Nürnberg stove. (150.)
—Shakespeare. Twelfth night. (149.)

Riverside pap. ser. 16°, pap., 50 c. Houghton, M. & Co.
—Burnham. A great love.

Rives, Hallie E. Hearts courageous. '02 (Je7) il. D. $1.50. Bowen-M.

ROADS.
Spalding. Text-book on roads and pavements. $2. Wiley.
See also Railroads;—Street-railroads.

Rob Roy. *See* Sullivan, *Sir* E:

Robbins, *Mrs.* S. S. Miss Ashton's new pupil. '02(Ap5) 12°, (Fireside ser.) $1. Burt

Roberts, C: G: D. Kindred of the wild. '02 (Je7) il. O. $2. L. C. Page.

Roberts. C: G: D. Poems. [New issue.] '02(My10) D. $1.50. L. C. Page.

ROBERTS, John.
Camm. Benedictine martyr in England: life and times of Dom John Roberts. net, $1.25. Herder.

Roberts, O. A. Hist. of the Military Company of the Mass., now called the Ancient and Honorable Artillery Co. of Mass., 1637-1888. In 4 v. v. 4. '01- '02(Mr22) 4°. [Sold only to members.] Mudge.

Robertson, A. I. Lessons on the Gospel of St. Mark. '02(Ap12) nar. 16°, net, 40 c. Revell.

Robertson, Harrison. The opponents. '02 (Ap19) D. $1.50. Scribner.

Robertson, Ja. Early religion of Israel. '02 (Ap12) 12°, net, $1.60. Whittaker.

Robertson, Leslie S. Water-tube boilers. '01-'02(Ja4) il. O. $3. Van Nostrand.

Robertson, W: Studies in the Acts of the Apostles. '02(F8) 16°, 40 c. Revell.

ROBESPIERRE, Max. M. I.
Belloc. Robespierre. net, $2. Scribner.

Robin Hood. *See* Pyle, H.

Robinson, Arth. W. Personal life of the clergy. '02(F8) D. (Handbooks for the clergy.) net, 90 c. Longmans.

Rockhaven. Munn, C: C. $1.50. Lee & S.

Roddy, H. J. Complete geography. '02 (Je28) il. F. $1. Am. Bk.

Roddy, H. J. Elem. geography. '02(My24) il. Q. 50 c. Am. Bk.

Roe, Alfr. S. Worcester Young Men's Christian Assoc. '01- '02(Mr22) O. $1. A. S. Roe.

ROENTGEN RAYS.
Monell. Instruction in X-ray methods and medical uses of light, hot air, vibration and high frequency currents. subs., $15. Pelton.
Walsh. Roentgen rays in medical work. net, $2.50. Wood.

Roget, M. *and* K. *See* **Alissas**, R. d'.

Role of the unconquered. Dalton, T. $1.50. G: W. Dillingham.

Rollins, Alice W. Story of Azron. '01- '02 (F22) 12°, $1. Holliswood.

Roman Africa. Graham, A. $6. Longmans.

Roman Biznet. Pangborn, G. W. $1.50. Houghton, M. & Co.

ROMAN EMPIRE.
Hellems. Lex de imperio Vespasiani. 50 c. Scott, F. & Co.

ROMAN LAW.
See Civil law.

Roman mystery. Bagot, R: $1.50. Lane.

Romance of a rogue. Sharts, J. W. $1.50. H. S. Stone.

ROMANISM.
See Catholic church.

Romantic love and personal beauty. Finck, H: T. net, $2. Macmillan.

ROME.
Belloc. Path to Rome. net, $2. Longmans.
Fustel de Coulanges. Ancient city: study on the rel., laws and institutions of Greece and Rome. $2. Lee & S.
Gregorovius. Rome in the Middle Ages. v. 8. net, $3. Macmillan.

Rood, H: E: Hardwicke. '02(My10) D. $1.50. Harper.

Rood, J: R. Treatise on the law of attachments, garnishments, judgments, and executions. '01. '02(Mr8) O. $3. Wahr.

ROOFS.
Merriman *and* Jacoby. Text-book on roofs and bridges. pt. 3. $2.50. Wiley.

Rook, Alb. W. The Butler family. '01- '02 (Ja11) $3. Lakeside Press.

Roosevelt, T. Message to the two houses at the beginning of the first session of the 57th Congress. '02(Mr29) sq. f°. $1. N. Y. State Lib.

Roosevelt, T. Rough Riders. New permanent lib. ed. '02(Mr1) il. 12°, $1.50. Scribner.

Roosevelt, T., Van Dyke, T. S., Elliot, D. G., *and* Stone, A. J. The deer family. '02 (My17) il. O. net, $2. Macmillan.

ROOSEVELT, T.
Banks *and* Armstrong. Theodore Roosevelt. $1.50; $2.25. Du Mont.
Halstead. Life of Theodore Roosevelt. subs., $2.50; $3.75; $3.50; $5. Saalfield.
Meyers. Theodore Roosevelt. subs., $1.50; $2. W. W. Wilson.
Meyers. Theodore Roosevelt. $1.50; $2. Ziegler.
See also Fallows, S.:—Wilson, J. G.

Root, Fk. A., *and* Connelley, W: E. Overland stage to California. '01- '02(Ap12) il. 12°, $2.50; hf. mor., $3.50. Root & C.

Roots of Christian teaching as found in the O. T. Barton, G: A. $1.25. Winston.

Roper, W: *See* More, *Sir* T:

Rose, J: H. Life of Napoleon I. '02(F22) 2 v., il. 8°, net, $4. Macmillan.

Rose, Wa. M. *See* Texas. Notes on repts.

Rose of the wilderness. Browne, W. S. $1.25. W. S. Browne.
Rosen, P: The Catholic church and secret societies. '02(My10) 12°, net, $1. Caspar.
Rosen im schnee. Nies, K. 50 c. Witter.
Rosenberger, J. L., *comp.* Law for lumbermen. '02(Je28) O. shp., $3.50. Am. Lumberman.
ROSES.
Melliar. Book of the rose. $1.75. Macmillan.
Ross, Janet. Florentine villas; with reproduction in photogravure from Zocchi's etchings. '02(Mr8) f°, $25. Dutton.
Ross, Ronald. Malarial fever. New 9th ed., rev. and enl. '02(Ap26) O. net, 75 c. Longmans.
Ross, Ronald. Mosquito brigades and how to organize them. '02(F8) O. net. 90 c. Longmans.
Rossetti, Helen M. M. Ford Madox Brown. '01. '02(F8) il. S. bds., net, 35 c. Beam.
Rostand, E. Cyrano de Bergerac; notes by Reed P. Clark. '02(Mr8) D. pap., 50 c. W: R. Jenkins.
Rostopchine, Sophie de. *See* Segur, S. R., *Comtesse* de.
Rotch, T: M. Pediatrics. New rev. ed. '01. '02(F15) 8°, subs., $6; shp., $7. Lippincott.
Roterberg, A. Card tricks. '02(Mr15) S. pap., 25 c. Drake.
Rough notes on remedies. Murray, W: net, $1.25. Blakiston.
ROUGH RIDERS.
Roosevelt. The Rough Riders. $1.50. Scribner.
Roulet, Ma. F. N. Saint Anthony in art, and other sketches. '01. '02(Ja11) il. D. $2. Marlier.
Rouse, Adelaide L. Annice Wynkoop, artist. '02(Mr29) il. 12°, (Fireside ser.) $1. Burt.
Rouse, Adelaide L. The Deane girls. '01. '02(Mr29) il. 12°, (Fireside lib.) $1. Burt.
Rouse, Adelaide L. Under my own roof. '02(Mr8) il. D. net, $1.20. Funk.
Rowe, Henrietta G. Maid of Bar Harbor. '02(Je21) il. D. $1.50. Little, B. & Co.
Rowell, J. H. Everybody's opportunity; or, quick socialism. '01. '02(Mr8) O. pap., 10 c. Free Socialist.
Rowell, J. H. Workingman's opportunity. 2d ed. '01. '02(Mr8) O. pap., 5 c. Free Socialist.
Royal lineage. Watson, *Mrs.* A. R. $4.50. Whittet.
Royal navy. Clowes, W: L. v. 5, 6. ea., net, $6.50. Little, B. & Co.
Rubáiyát. *See* Omar Khayyam.
Rubáiyat of Omar Khayyám, jr. Irwin, W. net, 50 c. Elder.
Ruble, W: Wonders of the Revelation of Jesus Christ. '01. '02(Mr22) D. $1. Standard Pub.
Rudder "how-to" ser. Q. $1. Rudder.
—Fisher. How to build a model yacht.
—Mower. How to build a knockabout.—How to build a racing sloop.
Ruggles, Jean. Exercises and problems in arithmetic. '01. '02(F22) 16°, pap., 25 c. W: R. Jenkins.
Ruling elder. Erdman, C: R. 3 c. Presb. Bd.
Rumsey, W: Practice in civil actions in courts of record of the state of N. Y., under the code of civil procedure. 2d ed. v. 1. '02(Je14) O. shp., $6. Banks & Co.
Ruskay, Esther J. Hearth and home essays. '02(Mr29) D. (Special ser., no. 6.) bds., 30 c. Jewish Pub.
Ruskin, J: Pen pictures. Pt. 2. '02(My17) T. $1. Longmans.
RUSKIN, John.
Collingwood. Life of John Ruskin. net, $2. Houghton, M. & Co.
Turner. Turner and Ruskin. 2 v. net, $50. Dodd.
Russell, C: E. Such stuff as dreams. '02 (Je28) 8°, net, $2. Bowen-M.
Russell, G: W: E. Onlooker's note-book. '02(Je7) O. net, $2.25. Harper.
Russell, Harry L. Outlines of dairy bacteriology. 5th ed., rev. '02(Mr29) il. 12°, $1. H. L. Russell.
Russell, Norman. Village work in India. '02 (My17) 12°, net, $1. Revell.
Russell, W: C. Captain Fanny. '02(Ap20) 12°, (Red letter ser.) $1.25; pap., 50 c. New Amsterdam.
Russell, W: C. Mate of the good ship "York." '02(Je7) D. $1.50. L. C. Page.
Russell, W: H., *and* Winslow, W: B. Syllabus-digest of decisions of the sup. ct. of the U. S. v. 3. '02(Ap5) O. shp., $6.50. Banks.
Russells (The) in Chicago. Wheaton, E. $1.25. L. C. Page.
RUSSIA.
Howard. Prisoners of Russia. net, $1.40. Appleton.
Kovalevsky. Russian political institutions. net, $1.50. Univ. of Chic.
Morfill. Hist. of Russia from Peter the Great to Nicholas II. $1.75. Pott.
See also Finland;—*also* Peter III.
RUSSIAN LITERATURE.
Wiener. Anthology of Russian literature. In 2 pts. pt. 1. net, $3. Putnam.
Rustler (The). McElrath, F. net, $1.20. Funk.
Rutherford, S: Christ and his cross. '02 (Mr8) S. $1. Longmans.
Ruthless rhymes. *See* Streamer, D.
Rutland home of Rufus Putnam. Earle, S. C. 30 c.: 50 c. S. C. Earle.
Rutledge. Harris, *Mrs.* M. C. $1. Burt.
Sabatini, R. Suitors of Yvonne. '02(Je7) D. net, $1.20. Putnam.
Sabertooth (The). Kinder, S. 75 c.; 25 c. Laird.
Sacred anthology. Conway, M. D. $2. Holt.
Sacred beetle. Ward, J: net, $3.50. Scribner.
Sacrificio (El) de Elisa. Maxwell, *Mrs.* M. E. B. 50 c. Appleton.
Sadlier, Anna T. Mary Tracy's fortune. '02 (Mr8) S. 45 c. Benziger.
Sage, Dean, Townsend, C. H., Smith, H. M., *and* Harris, W: C. Salmon and trout. '02 (Je28) il. 12°, (Am. sportsman's lib.) net, $2; large pap. ed., hf. mor., net, $7.50. Macmillan.
Sage, W: The Claybornes. '02(Ap26) il. D. $1.50. Houghton, M. & Co.
St. Cyres, *Viscount*, [Stafford Harry Northcote] Life of François Fenelon. '02(F15) 8°, net, $2.50. Dutton.

St. Nicholas ser. *See* Burt's.
Saint-Pierre, J. H. B. de. Paul and Virginia. '02(Ap19) il. D. (Home lib.) $1. Burt.
Sainte-Foi, C: The perfect woman; fr. the Fr., by Z. N. Brown. '01. '02(Ja11) S. net, $1. Marlier.
SAINTS.
Banks. Great saints of the Bible. $1.50. Eaton & M.
Newman. Lives of Eng. saints. 6 v. net, $12. Lippincott.
Scheeben. Holiness of the church in the 19th century. 10 c. Benziger.
See also Fathers.
Sajous, C: E. de M., *ed.* Analytical encyclopædia of practical medicine. Rev. ed. In 6 v. v. 1. '02(Ap26) il. 8°, subs., per v., $5; hf. rus., per v., $6. Davis.
SALE.
Freeman. Law of void judicial sales. $4. Cen. Law Journ.
Salis, *Mrs.* Ht. A. de. A la mode cookery up-to-date recipes. '02(Ap26) il. D. $2. Longmans.
SALMON.
Sage, *and others.* Salmon and trout. net, $2; net, $7.50. Macmillan.
SALOONS.
Rankin. Saloon law nullification and its cure. 50 c. Advance.
See also Temperance.
Saltus, F. S. Mount of Olives: [poem.] '02(Ap12) sq. S. bds., $1; pap., net, 25 c. Bk. Lover.
SALVATION.
Firey. Infant salvation. net, $1.20. Funk.
Gladden. Social salvation. net, $1. Houghton, M. & Co.
Samantha at Saratoga. Holley, M. $1. Burt.
Sand, George, [*pseud.* for A. L. A. Dudevant.] Masterpieces. v. 15. '02(Mr15); v. 16 (Ap5); v. 17, 18 (Je28) 8°. subs. (Apply to pubs. for price.) Barrie.
Sandals (The). Grenell, Z. net, 40 c. Funk.
Sanders, C: H. How are we led? and Who is it that leads us? '01· '02(Ja4) 8°, $1.50. Donohue.
Sanderson, E. D. Insects injurious to staple crops. '01· '02(Ja18) il. 12°, $1.50. Wiley.
Sanderson, Jos. Story of Saint Patrick. '02 (Je7) O. $1.50. Ketcham.
Sandys, Edwyn, *and* Van Dyke, T. S. Upland game birds. '02(Je7) il. 8°, (Am. sportsman's lib.) net, $2; large pap. ed., hf. mor., net, $7.50. Macmillan.
SANITARY ENGINEERING.
Baker. Municipal engineering and sanitation. net, $1.25. Macmillan.
See also Heating;—Plumbing;—Sewage and sewerage;—Water-supply.
SANITARY SCIENCE.
See Hygiene;—Sanitary engineering.
SANSKRIT LANGUAGE.
Macdonell. Sanskrit grammar for beginners. $3. Longmans.
SANTIAGO.
See Schley, W. S.
Sara. Newberry, F. E. $1. Burt.
Sarah the less. Swett, S. net, 75 c. Westminster.
Sarita, the Carlist. Marchmont, A. W. $1.50. Stokes.
Sarles, J: W. Man's peerless destiny in Christ. '01· '02(Mr1) 12°, net, 90 c. Funk.

Satan and demons. Townsend, L. T. net, 25 c. Jennings.
Satchel (A) guide for the vacation tourist in Europe. 1902. '02(Mr15) S. leath., net, $1.50. Houghton, M. & Co.
SATIRE.
See Parody;—Wit and humor.
Saunders, Ripley D. John Kenadie. '02 (My17) D. $1.50. Houghton, M. & Co.
Saussure, Cæsar de. Foreign view of England in the reign of George I. and George II. '02(Je7) 8°, net, $3. Dutton.
Savage, R: H. For a young queen's bright eyes. '02(My24) O. $1.25; pap., 50 c. Home.
Savill, T: D. Clinical lectures on neurasthenia. '02(Je28) 8°, $1.50. Wood.
SAVINGS-BANKS.
Hamilton. Savings and savings institutions. net, $2.25. Macmillan.
Savonarola, *Fra* Girolama. Triumph of the cross; ed. by Fa. J: Proctor. '02(Mr8) 8°, net, $1.35. Herder.
SAYRE FAMILY.
Banta. Sayre family. $10. T. M. Banta.
Scadding, C: Direct answers to plain questions for Am. churchmen: expansion of the church catechism. '01. '02(Ja4) D. (Grade A handbook.) bds., net, 50 c. Whittaker.
SCARABS.
Ward. Sacred beetle: treatise on Egyptian scarabs. net, $3.50. Scribner.
Scarlet and hyssop. Benson, E: F: $1.50. Appleton.
Scenery of England. Lubbock, *Sir* J: net, $2.50. Macmillan.
Scenes of rural life in Hampshire. Capes, W. W. net, $2.75. Macmillan.
Schaeffer, *Mrs.* Jennie. Metropolitan club cook-book, New York City. '02(Mr15) 16°, oil cl., $1.75. Augsburg.
Schäfer, E. A. Directions for class work in practical physiology. '01· '02(F8) il. O. net, $1. Longmans.
Schaffer, W: I., *rep.* *See* Penn. *Superior ct.* Repts.—*Supreme ct.* Repts.
Schauffler, A. F. *See* Bible. Sunday-school scholars' Bible.
Scheeben, M. J. Holiness of the church in the nineteenth century; fr. the Germ.; ed. by J: P. M. Schleuter. '02(My24) S. pap., 10 c. Benziger.
Schell, W: G. Is the negro a beast?: reply to Carroll's book entitled The negro a beast. '01. '02(F15) il. D. 60 c. Gospel Trumpet.
Schelling, Felix E. English chronicle play. '02(F1) 8°, net, $2. Macmillan.
Schiller, J. C. F. v. Don Carlos. Mary Stuart; ed. by N. H. Dole. Ed. de luxe. '02 (Je28) 12°. (App. to pubs. for price.) Niccolls.
Schiller, J. C. F. v. History of the revolt of the Netherlands; ed. by N. H. Dole. Ed. de luxe. '01· '02(Mr15) 8°. (App. to pubs. for price.) Niccolls.
Schiller, J. C. F. v. History of the thirty years' war in Germany; ed. by N. H. Dole. Ed. de luxe. '02(Mr15) 8°. (App. to pubs. for price.) Niccolls.
Schiller, J. C. F. v. Die jungfrau von Orleans; notes by A. B. Nichols and vocab. by W: A. Hervey. [New ed.] '01· '02 (F1) S. net, 60 c. Holt.

Schiller, J. C. F. v. **Maria Stuart**; ed. by E: S. Joynes; vocab. by W: A. Hervey. [New ed.] '02(F1) S. net, 70 c. Holt.
Schiller, J. C. F. v. **The Piccolomini; Death of Wallenstein; Wallenstein's camp**; ed. by N. H. Dole. Ed. de luxe. '02(Mr22) 8°. (App. to pubs. for price.) Niccolls.
Schiller, J. C. F. v. **Poems**; tr. into Eng. by E. P. Arnold-Foster. '02(My24) D. net, $1.60. Holt.
Schiller, J. C. F. v. **Wallenstein**; notes by W. H. Carruth. 2d ed., rev. '01- '02(F1) S. net, $1. Holt.
SCHLEY, Winfield Scott.
Graham. Schley and Santiago. $1.50. Conkey.
Nauticus, *pseud.* Truth about the Schley case. 25 c. Columbia.
Schmidt, Emanuel. Solomon's temple in the light of other oriental temples. '02(Je7) il. O. net, $1. Univ. of Chic.
Schofield, Alfr. T. Springs of character. '01-'02(Mr1) 8°, net, $1.30. Funk.
Schofield, R. J., ["One of the craft,"] *comp.* Drummers' yarns. 9th crop. '02(Je7) il. sq. 8°, pap., 25 c. Excelsior.
SCHOOL-HOUSES.
See Architecture.
SCHOOLS.
Clark. Public schools of Chicago. net, 50 c. Univ. of Chic.
Hughes. Schools at home and abroad. net, $1.50. Dutton.
Wray. Jean Mitchell's school. $1.25. Public Sch. Pub.
Young. Ethics in the school. net, 25 c.—Isolation in the school. net, 50 c. Univ. of Chic.
See also Education;—Illinois;—Kindergarten;—Sunday-school;—Westminster;—Wisconsin.
Schrader, Ferd. Friedrich der Grosse und der Siebenjährige Krieg; ed. by R. H. Allpress. Authorized ed. '02(My17) 12°, (Siepmann's elem. Germ. ser.) net, 50 c. Macmillan.
Schuyler, Aaron. Systems of ethics. '02 (My17) O. $1.50. Jennings.
Schuyler, M., *jr., comp. See* Avesta.
Schuyler, W: Ambassador of Christ: biog. of Rev. Montgomery Schuyler. '02(Mr8) 8°, $1.50. Gorham.
SCIENCE.
Lippincott's elem. science readers. 3 pts. pt. 1, 25 c.; pt. 2, 30 c.; pt. 3, 35 c. Lippincott.
Strutt. Scientific papers. v. 3, 1887-92. net, $5. Macmillan.
See also Chemistry;—Evolution;—Microscope;—Philosophy;—Religion and science.
Scientific memoirs; ed. by J. S. Ames. O. $1. Am. Bk.
—Brace, *ed.* Laws of radiation and absorption. (15.)
—Randall, *ed. and tr.* Expansion of gases by heat. (14.)
Scofield, Cora L. Study of the court of star chamber. '02(Mr22) 8°, pap., net, $1. Univ. of Chic.
Scollard, Clinton. Cloistering of Ursula. '02 (F15) il. D. $1.50. L. C. Page.
SCOTLAND.
Addis. Cathedrals and abbeys of Presb. Scotland. net, $2.50. Presb. Bd.
Brown. Hist. of Scotland. v. 2. net, $1.50. Macmillan.
SCOTLAND.—*Continued.*
Whitcomb. Little journey to Scotland. 15 c. Flanagan.
See also England;—Hebrides.
SCOTS.
Hanna. The Scotch-Irish. 2 v. net, $10. Putnam.
Scott, Fred N. Composition literature. '02 (Je28) 12°, $1. Allyn & B.
Scott, Temple, *ed. See* Swift, J.
Scott, *Sir* W. Kenilworth. '02(Mr22) 12°, (Eng. classics.) net, 60 c. Macmillan.
Scott, *Sir* W. Quentin Durward. '02(Mr8) 12°, (Eng. classics.) net, 60 c. Macmillan.
Scott, *Sir* W. Stories from Waverley for children. 5th ed. '02(My3) il. 12°, $1. Macmillan.
Scott, *Sir* W. Waverley; condensed and ed. for school reading by A. L. Bouton. '02 (My10) D. (Standard lit. ser., double no. 50.) 30 c.; pap., 20 c. University.
Scott, *Sir* W. *See also* Sullivan, *Sir* E:
Scottish men of letters in 18th century. Graham, H: G. net, $4.50. Macmillan.
Scottish philosophy in its national development. Laurie, H: net, $1.75. Macmillan.
Scribner's Am. hist. ser. D. net, $1. Scribner.
—Burgess. Reconstruction and the constitution, 1866-1876.
Scribner's contemporary sci. ser.; ed. by H. Ellis. 12°, $1.50. Scribner.
—Jastrow. Study of religion.
—Zittel. Hist. of geology and palæontology to end of 19th century.
Scribner's ser. of school reading. il. D. net, 60 c. Scribner.
—Cervantes Saavedra. Don Quixote.
—Pyle. Some merry adventures of Robin Hood.
—Thompson. Krag and Johnny Bear.
Scribner's social sci. ser. 12°, $1. Scribner.
—Cumming. Public house reform.
Scudder's eclectic manual. D. net, $2.50. Scudder.
—Mundy. Eclectic practice in diseases of children. (5.)
SCULPTURE.
Hurll, *ed.* Tuscan sculpture. net, 75 c.; net, 50 c.; net, 35 c. Houghton, M. & Co.
See also Ivory;—Tombstones.
Scutage and knight service in England. Baldwin, J. F. net, $1. Univ. of Chic.
Seager, H: R. Prof. Patten's theory of prosperity. '02(Mr22) 8°, (Pub. of the soc., no. 333.) pap., 15 c. Am. Acad. Pol. Sci.
Seal of destiny. Behymer, I. H. $1.50. Neely.
Searching for truth. '02(My24) O. $1.50. Eckler.
Sears, Hamblen. None but the brave. '02 (Ap12) il. D. $1.50. Dodd.
SEASHORE.
Wheeler. The sea coast. $4.50. Longmans.
SEAWEEDS.
See Algæ.
Second generation. Linn, J. W. $1.50. Macmillan.
SECRET SOCIETIES.
See Catholic church.
Sectional struggle. Harris, C. W. net, $2.50. Lippincott.
SECURITIES.
Moody, *ed.* Manual of corporation securities, 1902. $7.50; $10. Moody.

Sedding, J: D. Garden craft old and new. '02(Ap26) 8°, net, $2.50. Lane.
Sedgwick, Anne D. Confounding of Camelia. [New issue.] '02(My17) il. D. $1.50. Century Co.
Sedgwick, Anne D. Dull Miss Archinard. [New issue.] '02(My17) il. D. $1.50. Century Co.
Sedgwick, Anne D. The rescue. '02(My10) il. D. $1.50. Century Co.
Sedgwick, H: D., *jr.* Samuel de Champlain. '02(Ap5) S (Riverside biog. ser., no. 14.) net, 65 c.; School ed., net, 50 c. Houghton, M. & Co.
Sedgwick, W: T. Principles of sanitary science and the public health. '02(My17) 8°, net, $3. Macmillan.
Seebohm, F: **Tribal custom in Anglo-Saxon** law. '02(Mr8) O. net, $5. Longmans.
Seeley, H. G. Dragons of the air: extinct flying reptiles. '01. '02(F22) 12°, net, $1.40. Appleton.
Seeley, *Mrs.* L. **Cook book; with chapters** on domestic servants, and other details of household management. '02(Mr29) il. O. net, $2: hf. leath., net, $3. Macmillan.
Seeley, Levi. Foundations of education. '02 (F1) D. $1. Hinds.
Seger, Hermann A: Collected writings. In 2 v. v. 1. '02(Ap5) 8°, per set, $15. Chemical.
Segur, Sophie R., *Comtesse* de, [Sophie de Rostopchine.] Les malheurs de Sophie; ed. by E. White. '02(Je14) il. D. (Modern lang. ser.) 45 c. Heath.
Seigneur de Beaufoy. Drummond, H. $1.50. L. C. Page.
SELBORNE.
White. Natural history of Selborne. 2 v. net, $20. Lippincott.
Selden, E: G. Story of the Christian centuries. '02(My3) 12°, net, $1. Revell.
Select sunflowers. Mills, H. E: $1. Sunflower Press.
SELF-CULTURE.
See Culture.
Self-educator ser. D. 75 c. Crowell.
—Thornton. Eng. composition.
Sellers, Edn. J. Allied families of Delaware. '01. '02(Mr1) 8°, $5. E. J. Sellers.
Sellow, Grace E. Three thousand sample questions; [accompanying] Hill's Practical encyclopedia. '02(My10) il. D. pap., 50 c. Bellows.
Selover, A. W. Law of negotiable instruments for N. Y., Mass., Conn., R. I., [etc.] Iowa ed. '02(Je14) D. shp., $4. Keefe-D.
Selwyn, E: C. St. Luke the prophet. '01. '02(Ja4) 12°, net, $2.75. Macmillan.
Sema-Kanda. Turnbull, C. $1.25. Alliance.
SEMITIC LITERATURE.
Arnolt. Theolog. and Semitic literature for 1901. net, 50 c. Univ. of Chic.
SEMITIC PEOPLES.
Barton. Sketch of Semitic origins, social and religious. net, $3. Macmillan.
SEMITIC RELIGION.
Curtiss. Primitive Semitic religion to-day. net, $2. Revell.
Semitic ser. D. net, $1.25. Scribner.
—Duff. Theol. and ethics of the Hebrews. (2.)

Semon, *Sir* **Felix. Some thoughts on the** principles of local treatment in diseases of the upper air passages. '02(Mr22) 8°, net, $1. Macmillan.
September days on Nantucket. Bliss, W: R. net, $1. Houghton, M. & Co.
Series of school histories; ed by C: K. Adams. 12°, $1.50. Allyn & B.
—West. Ancient history to death of Charlemagne.
SERMON ON THE MOUNT.
Bacon. Sermon on the Mount. net, $1. Macmillan.
SERMONS.
Banks. Windows for sermons. net, $1.25. Funk.
SERVANTS.
See Domestic economy.
Service (The). Thoreau, H: D: net, $2.50; net, $10. Goodspeed.
Seton-Thompson, E. E. *See* Thompson, E. E. Seton-.
Seven poor travellers. *See* Dickens, C:
Seventy-one days' camping in Morocco. Grove, *Lady* A. net, $2.50. Longmans.
SEWAGE AND SEWERAGE.
Folwell. Sewerage. $3. Wiley.
Rideal. Sewage and the bacterial purification of sewage. $3.50. Wiley.
See also Sanitary engineering.
Seward, Thdr. F. **How to get acquainted with God: Christian Science movement.** '02(Mr29) nar. S. net, 50 c. Funk.
SEX.
Williams. Sex problems. net, $1. Revell.
Sexton, A. H. *See* Rhead, E. L.
SEYMOUR, Ct.
Campbell, *and others.* Seymour, past and present. $3. W: C. Sharpe.
Shackleton, Rob. Many waters. '02(Ap26) D. $1.50. Appleton.
Shadow and light. Gibbs, M. W. $1.50. M. W. Gibbs.
Shadow duellers. Freear, R. L: net, 60 c. Blanchard.
Shakespeare, W: Complete works. '02 (Ap5) il. 12°, $7; hf. mor., $10.50. Burt.
Shakespeare, W: Works. Dowden ed. (Craig [and] Dowden.) v. 3, King Lear. '02(Je28) 8°, $1.25. Bowen-M.
Shakespeare, W: Works. New century ed. (Is. Gollancz.) Ed. de luxe. In 24 v. v. 19-20. '02(Ap5) 8°, ea., $3.50. Estes.
Shakespeare, W: [Works.] Chiswick Shakespeare. v. 25, 26. '02(F22); v. 27, 28 (My3) 16°, ea., 35 c. Macmillan.
Shakespeare, W: **Complete plays and poems.** New pocket ed In 3 v. '02(Mr8) 16°, (Caxton ser.) per set, net, $4.20. Scribner.
Shakespeare, W: Sonnets. '02(My24) 16°, (Lover's lib., v. 11.) net, 50 c.; leath., net, 75 c. Lane.
Shakespeare, W: Julius Cæsar; ed. by A. H. Tolman. '02(Mr22) il. D. (Eng. classics, star ser.) 32 c. Globe Sch. Bk.
Shakespeare, W: King Richard III., adapt. for school use; by A. M. Kellogg. '01. '02 (F8) 16°, pap., 15 c. Kellogg.
Shakespeare, W: Macbeth; ed. by A. W. Verity. '02(Je7) 12°, (Pitt Press Shakespeare.) net, 40 c. Macmillan.
Shakespeare, W: Merchant of Venice; ed. by F: Manley. '02(Mr29) 16°, (Laurel classics.) 40 c. Birchard.

Shakespeare, W: Merchant of Venice; notes by E: E. Hale, jr. '01. '02(F8) 12°, (Standard lit. ser., no. 49.) pap. 20 c. University.

Shakespeare, W: Twelfth night; ed. by R: G. White. '02(Mr22) S. (Riverside lit. ser., no. 149.) pap., 15 c. Houghton, M. & Co.

Shakespeare, W: Twelfth night. '02(Ja11) 8°, (Vale Press Shakespeare, v. 22.) net, $8. Lane.

SHAKESPEARE, W:
Fleming. Shakespeare's plots. $1.80. Putnam.
Hazlitt. Shakespeare. net, $2.50. Scribner.
Lamb. Tales from Shakespeare. 40 c. Heath.
McSpadden. Shakesperian synopses. net, 45 c. Crowell.
Porter *and* Clarke. Shakespeare studies: Macbeth. 56 c. Am. Bk.
Sherman. What is Shakespeare? net, $1.50; net, $1. Macmillan.
Webb. Mystery of William Shakespeare. $4. Longmans.

SHAKESPEARE-BACON CONTROVERSY.
Gallup. Bi-literal cipher of Sir Francis Bacon. $3.75.—Tragedy of Anne Boleyn. $1.50. Howard.
Reed. Bacon and Shakes-peare parallel. net, $2.50.—Francis Bacon, our Shakespeare. net, $2. Goodspeed.

Shakespeare and Goethe on Gresham's law. *See* Green, B: E.

Shall we understand the Bible? Williams, T. R. net, 50 c. Macmillan.

Shand, Alex. I. Shooting. '02(F15) il. 12°, (Haddon Hall lib.) $3. Macmillan.

Shannon, Rob. T. *See* Tennessee. *Sup. ct.* Repts.

Sharp, B. A., [*pseud.* for Platon G. Brounoff.] Stolen correspondence from the "Dead letter" office between musical celebrities. '02 (Mr22) S. 50 c. Gervais.

Sharp, Luke, *pseud. See* Barr, R.

Sharp & Alleman Co.'s lawyers' and bankers' directory for 1902. Jan. ed. '02(Ja18) O. shp., $5. Sharp & A.

Sharpe, W: C. *See* Campbell, H. A.

Sharpless, I: Quaker experiment in government. 4th pop. ed. '02(F15) il. 12°, $1.50. Ferris.

Sharts, Jos. W. Romance of a rogue. '02 (Ap5) D. $1.50. H. S. Stone.

Shaw, Adèle M. Coast of freedom. '02 (Ap19) D. $1.50. Doubleday, P.

Shaw, H: W., ["Josh Billings."] Josh Billings' old farmer's allminax, 1870-79. '02 (Mr8) il. D. $1.50. G: W. Dillingham.

She wanted to vote. Ballard, E. C. net, $1.40. Brower.

Sheehan, P. A. Luke Delmege. '01. '02 (Ja4) D. $1.50. Longmans.

SHEEP.
See Veterinary medicine and surgery.

Sheldon, F: M. Practical colorist: for the artist printer. '02(F1) il. Q. $8. Owl Press.

Sheldon, S:, *and* Mason, H. Dynamo electric machinery. v. 1, Direct-current machines. 2d ed. '02(Je14); v. 2, Alternating current machines. '02(Je7) il. D. ea., net, $2.50. Van Nostrand.

Shelley, Ht. S. Poems of life and loving. '02(Ap26) 12°, $1. Neely.

Shelley, P. B. Poetical works. '02(Je21) 16°, (Caxton ser.) net, $1.25. Scribner.

Shepard, Hiram M. Life on the farm: reading book for grammar and high schools. '01. '02(Ja11) il. S. (Home and school ser. for young folks.) 50 c. Flanagan.

Shepardson, Dan. Studies in the Epistles to the Hebrews. '02(F8) 12°, $1.50. Revell.

Sheppard, J: S., *jr. See* Rumsey, W:

Sherer, Rob. G., *rep. See* New York. *Cts. of record.* Misc. repts.

Sheridan, Philip H: Personal memoirs. New enl. ed.; with acc. of life, by M. V. Sheridan. '02(Mr1) 2 v., il. 8°, net, $4. Appleton.

Sherlock, C: R. Red anvil. '02(Je7) il. D. $1.50. Stokes.

Sherman, L. A. What is Shakespeare? '02 (F1) 12°, net, $1.50; *Same.* School ed. (Mr29) 12°, net, $1. Macmillan.

Sherman, Ma. B. K. Parliamentary law at a glance. Rev. ed. '01. '02(F8) 16°, 75 c. H. O. Shepard.

Sherwood, Wa. J. Story of three. '01. '02 (Mr29) il. nar. Q. pap., 25 c. W: S. Lord.

Shiells, Rob. Story of the token as belonging to the sacrament of the Lord's supper. 2d ed. '02(Je21) D. net, $1. Presb. Bd.

Shimmell, Lewis S. Border warfare in Penn. during the Revolution. '01. '02(F22) 16°, pap., 50 c. R. L. Myers.

Ship of silence. Valentine, E: U. net, $1.20. Bowen-M.

Shipley, Arth. E., *ed. See* Harmer, S. F:, *ed.*

SHIPS AND SHIPBUILDING.
Crowell. Present status and future prospects of Am. shipbuilding. 15 c. Am. Acad. Pol. Sci.

SHOOTING.
Grinnell. Amer. duck shooting. $3.50. Forest.
Shand. Shooting. $3. Macmillan.
See also Rifle.

SHORE.
See Seashore.

SHORT, T:
Love. Thomas Short, first printer of Conn. $5. Case.

SHORTHAND.
See Stenography.

SIAM.
Campbell. Siam in the 20th century. net, $5. Longmans.

Siamese twins. Keese, W: L. net, $1.25. E. W. Dayton.

Sibyl's conquest. Stinchfield, M. I. $1.50. Neely.

Sichel, Wa. Bolingbroke and his times: the sequel. '02(Je7) O. $4. Longmans.

SICILY.
Sladen. In Sicily. 2 v. net, $20. Dutton.

Side windows. Boteler, M. M. 75 c. Standard Pub.

Sidgwick, H: Philosophy. '02(Je7) 8°, net, $2.25. Macmillan.

Sidgwick, H: Principles of political economy. 3d ed. '02(Je7) 8°, net, $4.50. Macmillan.

Sidner, Aurelia L. Price inevitable. '02 (My17) D. $1. Popular.

Sidney, Marg., *pseud. See* Lothrop, *Mrs.* H. M.

Siege of Lady Resolute. Dickson, H. $1.50. Harper.

Siepmann's elem. French ser. 12°, net, 50 c. Macmillan.
—Dumas. Napoleon.
Siepmann's elem. Germ. ser. 12°, net, 50 c. Macmillan.
—Schrader. Friedrich der Grosse.
—Zastrow. Wilhelm der Siegreiche.
Sign of the seven sins. Le Queux, W: $1; 50 c. Lippincott.
SIGNS.
See Stenography.
Silent pioneer. McElroy, L. C. $1.50. Crowell.
Silken snare. Leroy, W: 50 c. Abbey Press.
Silva, T., *and* Fourcaut, A. Lectura y conversación: new Spanish method. '01. '02 (Ja25) D. 60 c. Am. Bk.
SILVER.
See Precious metals.
Silver chord and the golden bowl. Pierce, G. A. $1. Abbey Press.
Silver ser. of classics. 12°. Silver.
—Kinard, *ed.* Old Eng. ballads. 40 c.
—Wordsworth. Selected poems. 30 c.
Silver ser. of modern lang. text-books; ed. by A. Cohn. D. Silver.
—France. Monsieur Bergeret. $1.
—Manzoni. I promessi sposi. $1.20.
Simmons, J. C. My trip to the Orient. '02 (Je7) il. 8°, $1.50. Whitaker & R.
Simon, C: E. Clinical diagnosis by microscopical and chemical methods. 4th ed. '02(F15) il. 8°, net, $3.75. Lea.
Simon, C: E. Text-book of physiolog. chemistry. '01. '02(Ja25) 8°, net, $3.25. Lea.
Simpson, C. Love never faileth. '02(Je7) D. $1.25. Revell.
Simpson, Ja. Y. Henry Drummond. '01. '02(Ja11) 12°, (Famous Scots.) 75 c. Scribner.
Sin of Jasper Standish. Humphreys, *Mrs.* E. M. J. G. $1.25. Fenno.
Sinclair, W. M. Unto you, young women. '01. '02(F15) 12°, net, $1. Lippincott.
SINGING.
See Church music;—Voice.
Singular will. Marsh, G: $1.50. Neely.
Sinker stories of wit and humor. Goodwin, J. J. $1. Ogilvie.
Sinnett, Brown. Widow Wiley and some other old folk. '02(F15) 12°, $1.50. Dutton.
Sister Beatrice. Maeterlinck, M. net, $1.20. Dodd.
Sister in name only. Wall, *Mrs.* D. H. $1. Neely.
Six little princesses. Prentiss, *Mrs.* E. 75 c. Burt.
Sixteenth century classics. D. $1. [Longmans] Univ. of Penn.
—Erasmus. Select colloquies.
SKEPTICISM.
Best. The college man in doubt. net, 50c. Westminster.
Searching for truth. $1.50. Eckler.
See also Agnosticism;—Free thought.
Sketch book. *See* Irving, W.
SKIN.
Allen. Diseases of the skin. $2. Boericke & T.
Skinner, C: M. Prisons of the nation and their inmates. '02(F8) Q. (Eagle lib., v. 17, no. 2.) pap., 10 c. Brooklyn Eagle.
Skinner, W. H., *and* Burgert, Celia M. Lessons in English based upon principles of literary interpretation. '02(Je21) il. D. (Lessons in English.) 50 c. Silver.
Skrine, J: H. Pastor Agnorum: a schoolmaster's afterthoughts. '02(Je7) D. net, $1.60. Longmans.
Sladen, Douglas. In Sicily. '02(F1) 2 v., il. 4°, net, $20. Dutton.
Slate, T: Physics: for secondary schools. '02(Je28) 12°, hf. leath., net, $1.10. Macmillan.
SLAVERY.
Ballagh. Hist. of slavery in Va. $1 50. Johns Hopkins.
SLEIGHT OF HAND.
See Conjuring.
Slicer, T: R. One world at a time. '02 (Mr22) O. net, $1.35. Putnam.
Sloan, W. N. Social regeneration the work of Christianity. '02(Je21) S. net, 60 c. Westminster.
Sloane, W: M. Napoleon Bonaparte. New lib. ed. '02(F22) 4 v., il. 4°, net, $18; hf. mor., net, $32. Century.
SLOYD.
Molander. Scientific sloyd. 50 c. Bardeen.
Smale, Morton, *and* Colyer, J. F. Diseases and injuries of the teeth. 2d ed. rev. and enl. '01. '02(F8) O. $7. Longmans.
Small, Albion W. The sociologists' point of view. '02(F1) 8°, pap., net, 10 c. Univ. of Chic.
Small end of great problems. Herford, B. net, $1.60. Longmans.
SMALLPOX.
See Variola.
Smeaton, O. The Medici and the Italian Renaissance. '01. '02(F1) D. (World's epochmakers.) $1.25. Scribner.
Smedberg, Harold V. Improprieties of Noah, and other stories. '01. '02(F15) D. 50 c. Abbey Press.
Smith, Alb. L. *See* Hessler, J: C.
Smith, Boston. Uncle Boston's spicy breezes. '02(Ja25) il. S. net, $1. Am. Bapt.
Smith, C. Alphonso. *See* Krüger, G.
Smith, C. P. Texas notarial manual and form book. '02(Je7) 8°, shp., $4. Gammel.
Smith, Chester W: A summer of Saturdays. '01. '02(Je7) il. 12°, 65 c. Gillan.
Smith, Colin. Bridge condensed. '02(Mr8) 16°, pap., 50 c. Scribner.
Smith, D: Eug. *See* Beman, W. W.
Smith, E. E. Ideal word book. '02(Je7) S. 17 c. Flanagan.
Smith, E. F. Text-book of anatomy, physiology and hygiene. 2d ed. rev. '01. '02 (F22) il. 12°, $1. W: R. Jenkins.
Smith, *Mrs.* Eliz. T., [*formerly* L. T. Meade.] Daddy's girl. '02(Je14) 12°, (Fireside ser.) $1. Burt.
Smith, *Mrs.* Eliz. T. Very naughty girl. '02(Ap19) il. 12°, (Fireside ser.) $1. Burt.
Smith, Emory E. The golden poppy. '02 (Mr22) il. O. net, $1.50. E. E. Smith.
Smith, G. C. Moore, *ed.* *See* Smith, *Sir* H.
Smith, Gipsy. His life and work by himself. '02(Ap19) 8°, net, $1.50. Revell.
Smith, Goldwin. Commonwealth or empire. '02(Ap12) 12°, net, 60 c. Macmillan.
Smith, H. M. *See* Sage, D.

Smith, *Sir* Harry. Autobiography; ed. with supp. chap., by G. C. Moore Smith. '02 (Mr29) 2 v., il. 8°, net, $8. Dutton.
Smith, Ja. M. *See* New York. Digest.
Smith, Jeremiah. Selection of cases on private corporations. 2d ed. '02(Je28) 2 v., O. net, $6. Harvard Law.
Smith, J: W., ["Jean Yelsew."] The mountaineers. '02(My24) D. $1; $1.50; hf. mor., $2; mor., $2.50. Pub. Ho. M. E. Ch. So.
Smith, Jos. J., *comp.* Civil and military list of Rhode Island, 1800-1850. '01- '02(Mr1) sq. 4°, net, $7.50. Preston.
Smith, Julius. Ten years in Burma. '02 (Je28) 12°, $1. Eaton & M.
Smith, Julius. Ten years in Burma '02 (Mr22) D. net, $1. Jennings.
Smith, M. R., *rep.* *See* Missouri. *St. Louis and Kansas City cts. of appeals.* Cases.
Smith, May R. The lost Christmas, and other poems. '01- '02(F15) 16°, (Dainty ser.) pap., 50 c. Dutton.
Smith, Percey F. Elementary calculus. '02 (Mr29) D. $1.25. Am. Bk.
Smith, Percey F. Four-place logarithmic tables. '02(Ap5) O. net, 50 c. Holt.
Smith, Roy W. Achromatic spindle in the spore mother-cells of osmunda regalis. '02 (F1) 8°, (Cont. from Hull botanical lab'y, no. 23.) pap., net, 25 c. Univ. of Chic.
Smith, S: G. Abraham Lincoln. '02(My24) D. (Hero ser., no. 3.) net, 25 c. Jennings.
Smith, *Mrs.* Toulmin. *See* Smith, *Mrs.* E. T.
Smith, W: W. Course in first year Latin for Regents' examinations. '02(F1) D. buckram, $1. W: R. Jenkins.

SMOKE.
See Fumigation.

Smyth, Newman. Through science to faith. '02(F15) O. net, $1.50. Scribner.
Smith, J: C. Love's itinerary. '02- '01 (Ja4) D. (Town and country lib., no. 307.) $1; pap., 50 c. Appleton.
Snyder, C., *and* Thurston, E. L. Universal system of practical bookkeeping. '02(Je7) Q. $1.25. Am. Bk.
Snyder, W: L. Notaries' and commissioners' manual. 7th rev., enl. ed. '02(Je14) O. $1.50. Baker, V. & Co.
So fight I. Hahn, C: C. 10 c. Whittaker.
Social and ethical interpretations in mental development. Baldwin, J. M: net, $2.60. Macmillan.
Social effect of machinery. *See* Lafarque, P.
Social England. Traill, H: D. v. 1. net, $4.50. Putnam.
Social (The) evil, with special ref. to conditions existing in the city of New York. '02(Mr22) 12°, net, $1.25. Putnam.
Social regeneration the work of Christianity. Sloan, W. N. net, 60 c. Westminster.
Social salvation. Gladden, W. net, $1. Houghton, M. & Co.

SOCIAL SCIENCE.
Kellor. Experimental sociology. net, $2. Macmillan.
Lane. Level of social motion. net, $2. Macmillan.
Small. The sociologist's point of view. net, 10 c. Univ. of Chic.
See also Civilization;—Crime and criminals;—Ethics;—Political economy;—Political science;—Socialism;—Temperance.

Social science ser. *See* Scribner's.

SOCIALISM.
De Leon. Socialism *vs.* anarchism. 10 c. N. Y. Labor News.
Engels. Socialism. 50 c. N. Y. Labor News.
McGrady. Voice from England. 10 c. Standard.
Poland. Socialism. net, 5 c. Herder.
Rowell. Everybody's opportunity; or, quick socialism. 10 c.—Workingman's opportunity. 5 c. Free Socialist.

Socialist lib. O. pap. Socialistic Co-op.
—Adventures of John McCue, socialist. 10 c. (v. 2, 1.)
—Hanford. Railroading in the U. S. 5 c. (v. 1, 11.)
—Lafarque. Religion of capital. 10 c. (v. 2, 2.)
—McGrady. Clerical capitalist. 10 c. (v. 1, 10.)

SOCIETIES.
Hinds. Am. communities. $1. Kerr.

SOCIOLOGY.
See Social science.

SODA WATER.
See Confectionery.

SOILS.
Campbell. Soil culture manual. 40 c. H. W. Campbell.

SOLOMON'S TEMPLE.
Schmidt. Solomon's Temple in the light of other oriental temples. net, $1. Univ. of Chic.

SOLUTION.
See Chemistry.

Some letters of Alfred Henry, the third—floorer. '02(Je28) T. 50 c. Informant.
Some merry adventures of Robin Hood. Pyle, H. net, 60 c. Scribner.
Some pretty girls. Underwood, C. F. $3; $5. Quail & W.
Some unpublished letters. Walpole, H. net, $1.50. Longmans.
Sommerville, Maxwell. Engraved gems. '01- '02(F22) O. net, $1.50. Biddle.
Son of a fiddler. Lee, J. $1.50. Houghton, M. & Co.
Sonderegger, C. L' achèvement du canal de Panama. '02(Mr8) O. pap., $2.50. Stechert.

SONG-BOOKS.
Army songster. 25 c. Bell Bk.
Tomlins, *ed.* Laurel song book. $1.50; $1. Birchard.
See also Hymns and hymn writers;—Songs.

SONGS.
Hodgman. Home's sweet harmonies. 80 c. Home Pub.
Johnson. Popular English ballads, ancient and modern. 4 v. $3. Lippincott.
New songs for college glee clubs. 50 c. Hinds.
O'Conor. Irish com-all-ye's. 25 c. Popular.
O'Conor, *comp.* Old time songs and ballads of Ireland. $2. Popular.
See also Ballads;—Church music.

Songs not set to music. Fargo, K. M. $1. Abbey Press.
Songs of childhood. Ramal, W. net, $1.20. Longmans.
Songs of the Eastern colleges. Atkinson, R. W. $1.25. Hinds.

Songs of the Sahkohnagos. Deveron, H. $1.25. Abbey Press.
Sonnenblicke aus der Amer. praxis. Beck, C. net, 30 c. Lemcke.
Sonnets and songs for a house of days. Binkley, C. net, $1.25. A. M. Robertson.
Sophocles. The Antigone; notes by M. A. Bayfield. '02(Mr22) 12°, (Classical ser.) net, 60 c. Macmillan.
Sorrow and solace of Esther. Barnes, C: W. net, 30 c. Jennings.
SOUL.
See Psychology.
Soul fragrance. Kohaus, H. M. 40 c. Alliance.
Soul in the unseen world. Hutton, R. E. net, $2. Dutton.
Soul-winners' secrets. Oliver, G. F. 25 c. Jennings.
SOUND.
Dexter. Elem. exercises on sound, light and heat. 90 c. Longmans.
Sousa, J: P. The fifth string. '02(F8) il. D. $1.25. Bowen-M.
SOUTH (The).
See United States;—*also* names of Southern states.
SOUTH AFRICA.
Abbott. Tommy Cornstalk. $2. Longmans.
Fleming. Glimpses of South Africa in peace and in war. $3. Dominion.
Harding. War in So. Africa and the Dark Continent from savagery to civilization. $2; $3; $4. Dominion.
Phillipps. With Rimington. $2.50. Longmans.
See also Boers;—Matabeleland.
SOUTH AMERICA.
Keane. South America. $4.50. Lippincott.
See also Central America;—Peru.
South Carolina. *Supreme ct.* Repts. v. 60. '01. '02(F1) O. shp., $5.75. Bryan.
South Dakota. *Supreme ct.* Repts. (Horner.) v. 14. '02(Ap5) O. shp., $3. State Pub.
Southeastern reporter, v. 39. Permanent ed. '01- '02(Ja18); v. 40(Je7) O. (Nat. reporter system, state ser.) shp., ea., $4. West Pub.
Southern reporter, v. 30. '02(Mr1) O. (Nat. reporter system, state ser.) shp., $4. West Pub.
Southern reporter. Digest of decisions. '02 (My24) O. (Nat. reporter system digests, Southern ser., v. 2.) shp., net, $6. West Pub.
Southwestern reporter, v. 64. Permanent ed. '01- '02(Ja18); v. 65 (Mr29); v. 66 (My17) O. (Nat. reporter system, state ser.) shp., ea., $4. West Pub.
Southworth, *Mrs.* Emma D. E. N. Hidden hand. '02(My3) 12°, (Home lib.) $1. Burt.
Spackman, —. *See* Lathbury, B. B.
SPAIN.
Helps. Spanish conquest of America. v. 2. $1.50. Lane.
Higgin. Spanish life in town and country. net, $1.20. Putnam.
See also Ferdinand, *King of Spain*;—Spanish-Am. war;—Zincali.
Spalding, F: P. Text-book on roads and pavements. 2d rev., enl. ed. '02(Mr22) il. 12°, $2. Wiley.
Spalding, J: L. Religion, agnosticism and education. '02(Je21) D. net, 80 c. McClurg.

Spalding's athletic lib. 16°, pap., 10 c. Am. Sports.
—Spalding's official athletic almanac. (v. 13, 145.)
—Spalding's official baseball guide. (v. 13, 150.)
Spalding's official athletic almanac; comp. by J. E. Sullivan, 1902. '02(Ap26) il. 16°, (Athletic lib., v. 13, no. 145.) pap., 10 c. Am. Sports.
Spalding's official baseball guide, 1902.; ed. by H: Chadwick. '02(My24) il. S. (Athletic lib., v. 13, no. 150.) pap., 10 c. Am. Sports.
Spangler, Nellie Y. Bird play. '01. '02 (Ja25) 12°, pap., 15 c. Kellogg.
SPANISH-AM. WAR.
Halstead. Full official hist. of the war with Spain. $3; $4; $6. Dominion.
Jones. Chaplain's experience; the "Texas" under fire. $1.25. Sherwood.
See also Rough Riders;—*also* Schley, W. S.
SPANISH LANGUAGE.
Appleton's geografia superior ilustrada. $1.50. Appleton.
Arnold. Enseñar á leer. 40 c. Silver.
Caballero. La familia de Alvareda. 75 c. Holt.
Estados Unidos. Constitucion. $1. Cambridge.
Goldsmith. Idioma Inglés. 1st bk., 40 c.; 2d bk., 36 c. Globe Sch. Bk.
Lange. 20th century system Spanish course. 25 c. [San F. News] Pamphlet.
Maxwell. El sacrificio de Elisa. 50 c. Appleton.
Munro. Nociones de electricidad. 40 c. Appleton.
Puron. El lector moderno de Appleton. nos. 1-3. no. 1, 25 c.; no. 2, 35 c.; no. 3, 45 c. Appleton.
Ramsey. Spanish grammar, with exercise. net, $1.50. Holt.
Silva *and* Fourcaut. Lectura y conversación. 60 c. Am. Bk.
Stewart. Nociones de fisica. 20 c. Appleton.
Velázquez de la Cadena, *comp.* Nuevo diccionario-Inglesa y Española. pt. 2. $3.50. Appleton.
Sparroy, Wilfrid. Persian children of the Royal family. '02(Je28) 8°, net, $3.50. Lane.
SPEAKERS.
See Readers and speakers.
Speer, Rob. E. Principles of Jesus applied to some questions of to-day. '02(My3) 16°, net, 80 c. Revell.
SPELLERS.
Daly. Advanced rational speller. 25 c. Sanborn.
Mavor. Eng. spelling book. 40 c. Warne.
Smith. Ideal word book. 17 c. Flanagan.
Wheeler's elem. speller. 25 c. W: H: Wheeler.
See also Primers.
Spencer, Herbert. Facts and comments. '02 (My24) O. net, $1.20. Appleton.
Spender, A. Edm. Two winters in Norway. '02(Mr8) il. O. $4. Longmans.
Spenders (The). Wilson, H. L. $1.50. Lothrop.
Spielmannskind (Das) und stumme ratsherr. Riehl, W. H. 35 c. Am. Bk.

Spindle and plough. **Dudeney,** *Mrs.* **H.** $1.50. Dodd.

SPINE.
See Nervous system.

SPINOZA, Benedict de.
Gore. Imagination in Spinoza and Hume. net, 35 c. Univ. of Chic.

Spirit echoes. Hull, M. E. net, 75 c. Sunflower.

Spiritual heroes. Muzzey, D: S. net, $1.25. Doubleday, P.

Spiritual pepper and salt. Stang, W: 30 c. Benziger.

SPIRITUALISM.
Dangers of spiritualism. net, 75 c. Herder.
Gaffield. Celestial message. n. p. Lee & S.
Nixon. Beyond the vail. $1.75. Hudson-K.

Spofford, A. R., *and* Annandale, C., *eds.* xxth century cyclopædia and atlas. '01·'02(Ap12) 8 v., il. 8°, art v., $20; hf. rus., $26. Gebbie.

Sport of the gods. Dunbar, P. L. $1.50. Dodd.

SPORTS AND SPORTSMEN.
Gordon. Sporting reminiscences. net, $4. Dutton.
See Baseball;—Canoeing;—Yachts and yachting.

Spotswood, Dillon J. *See* Nuverbis, *pseud.*

Springs of character. Schofield, A. T. net, $1.30. Funk.

SQUABS.
See Pigeons.

Staebler, C. Manual on the Book of books for juniors: first book in catechetical study. '02(My10) S. (Young people's alliance ser., no. 3.) pap., 20 c. Mattill & L.

Staley, Edgcumbe. Watteau, master painter of the Fêtes galantes. '01·'02(Ja4) il. 16°, (Bell's miniature ser. of painters.) 50 c. Macmillan.

Standard guide ser. il. D. pap., 25 c. Foster & R.
—New York City standard guide.

Standard lib. 16°, pap., 10 c. Standard.
—McGrady. Voice from England.

Standard literature ser. 12°, pap., 20 c. University.
—Scott. Waverley. (double no. 50.)
—Shakespeare. Merchant of Venice. (49.)

Standard reader ser. Funk.
—Funk *and* Moses, *eds.* Standard first reader. 35 c.—Teachers' manual for first reader. 50 c.

Stanford's compendium of geography and travel. il. 8°. Lippincott.
—Keane. South America. $4.50.

Stang, W: Spiritual pepper and salt for Catholics and non-Catholics. '02(Mr29) S. pap., 30 c. Benziger.

Stannard, *Mrs.* Henrietta E. V., ["John Strange Winter."] The magic wheel. '01. '02(Mr8) D. $1.25. Lippincott.

Stanton, S. C., *ed.* *See* Billings, F., *ed.*

Stapleton, Ammon. **Memorials of the Huguenots in America.** '01·'02(Mr22) il. O. $1.50. Huguenot.

STAR CHAMBER.
Scofield. Study of the court of Star Chamber. net, $1. Univ. of Chic.

STARS.
Browne. How to tell the time of night by the stars. 50 c. Lee & S.

STARS.—*Continued.*
Hale. New star in Perseus. net, 10 c. Univ. of Chic.
See also Astrology;—Astronomy.

State intervention in Eng. education. De Montmorency, J. E. G. net, $1.50. Macmillan.

Statesmen's (The) year book for 1902. (J. S. Keltie.) '02(Ap26) 12°, net, $3. Macmillan.

Stay, Jones B. Mind telegraph; tr. fr. the 6th Germ. ed. by Ivry. '01. '02(Mr8) 16°, pap., 25 c. Alliance.

Stead, Alfr. Japan of to-day. '02(My10) 12°, net, $2. Dutton.

Stead, W: T: Americanization of the world. '02(F22) 12°, $1. Markley.

STEAM ENGINE.
Hurst. Hints on steam engine design and construction. 60 c. Lippincott.
See also Locomotives;—Machinery.

Stebbins, Genevieve. Delsarte system of expression. 6th ed. rev. and enl. '02(F22) D. $2. Werner.

Stechhan, Otto. Unrequited love. '02(Mr1) D. $1. Abbey Press.

Stechhan, Otto. Whither are we drifting? '02(Mr8) D. $1. Abbey Press.

Stedman, E. C. *and* T: L., *eds.* Complete pocket guide to Europe. '02(Je14) T. leath., $1.25. W: R. Jenkins.

STEEL.
Colby. Review and text of the Am. standard specifications for steel. net, $1.10. Chemical.
See also Iron.

Steele, Francisca M., ["Darley Dale."] Convents of Great Britain. '02(Je28) il. 8°, net, $2. Herder.

Steele, J: W. Coal oil Johnny. '02(My17) 12°, $1.50. J: A. Hill.

Steele, K. N. Simple rules for bridge. '02 (Mr22) S. pap., 50 c. Eichelberger.

Steiner, Bernard C. Western Maryland in the Revolution. '02(Mr8) O. (Johns Hopkins Univ. studies, 20th ser., no. 1.) pap., 30 c. Johns Hopkins.

STENOGRAPHY.
Barnes. Shorthand lessons by the word method. $1.25. A. J. Barnes.
Beale. Book of legal dictation. 50 c. Beale Press.
Brown. Science and art of phrase-making. $1.50. Shorthand Bu.
Forney. Inductive lessons. 80 c. State Normal Sch.
Hardcastle. Word signs made easy. $1. M. A. Hardcastle.
Pitman, B. *and* Howard. Business letters: no. 1, Misc. corr. 25 c. Phonograph.
Pitman, I: Business corr. in shorthand. no. 2. 30 c.—Phonographic teacher, 20 c. Pitman.

Stephen, *Sir* Ja. F. Digest of the law of evidence; fr. the 5th ed. Am. notes by G: E. Beers. '01. '02(Mr22) D. shp., $4. Dissell.

Stephen, Leslie. George Eliot. '02(Je14) 12°, (English men of letters.) net, 75 c. Macmillan.

Stephen Holton. Pidgin, C: F. $1.50. L. C. Page.

Stephens, J: V. Evolution of the confession of faith of the Cumberland Presb. church. '02(My10) O. pap., 10 c. Cumberland.

Stern, Menco. Geschichten von Deutschen städten. '02(Ja25) D. $1.25. Am. Bk.
Sternberg, G: M. Text-book of bacteriology. 2d rev. ed. '01. '02(F22) il. 8°, net, $5; leath., net, $5.75. Wood.
Sterne, L. Sentimental journey through France and Italy. '02(My3) 12°. (Home lib.) $1. Burt.
Stevens, E: A. American law of assemblies applicable to lodges, conventions and public meetings. '01. '02(Mr29) S. net, $1. E: A. Stevens.
Stevens, E: L. Business education. '02 (My3) S. pap., 15 c. Bardeen.
Stevens, Fk. L. Gametrogenesis and fertilization in albugo. '02(F15) 8°, (Cont. from the Hull botanical lab'y, no. 29.) pap., net, 25 c. Univ. of Chic.
Stevens, Horace J., *comp.* Copper handbook; ed. of 1902. '02(Ap26) 8°, $2; full mor., $3. H. J. Stevens.
Stevens, L. B. Faciology. New ed. '02 (My17) 12°, pap., 25 c. Donohue.
Stevens, Sheppard. In the eagle's talon. '02 (Je14) il. D. $1.50. Little, B. & Co.
Stevenson, R. L: Æs triplex. '02(Mr22) nar. S. (Vest pocket ser.) pap., net, 25 c.; flex. cl., net, 40 c.; flex. leath., net, 75 c.; Jap. vellum ed., $1. T: B. Mosher.
Stevenson, R. L: Child's garden of verses. [New ed.] '01. '02(F1) il. D. net, 60 c. Scribner.
Steward, F. J. *See* Jacobson, W. H. A.
Stewart, Balfour. Nociones de fisica. Neuva ed. Castellana. '01. '02(F22) 18°, 20 c. Appleton.
Stewart, Purves. *See* Ballance, C: A.
Stiles, Ezra. Literary diary of Ezra Stiles, president of Yale College; ed. by F. B. Dexter. '01. '02(Mr15) 3 v., 8°, net, $7.50. Scribner.
STIMULANTS AND NARCOTICS.
See Morphinism.
Stinchfield, M. Ida. Sibyl's conquest. '02 (Ap26) 12°, $1.50. Neely.
Stitson, J. R. The human hair. '01. '02 (Ap12) 12°, $1.25. Maple.
STOCK BREEDING.
See Cattle.
STOCK EXCHANGE, London.
Duguid. Story of the Stock Exchange. net, $2. Dutton.
Stockett, J. Shaaf, *rep.* *See* Maryland. *Ct. of appeals.* Repts.
Stockmen's calculator. McCallum & Hefer Cattle Co. $1.50. McCallum.
Stockton, F. R: Kate Bonnet. '02(Mr1) D. $1.50. Appleton.
Stoddard, C: W. In the footprints of the padres. '02(F1) D. net, $1.50. Robertson.
Stoddard, W: O. Errand boy of Andrew Jackson. '02(My24) D. net, $1. Lothrop.
Stoker, Bram. Mystery of the sea. '02 (Mr29) D. $1.50. Doubleday, P.
Stokes, *Sir* G: G. Mathematical and physical papers: repr. with add. notes. v. 3. '01. '02(Ja4) 8°, (Cambridge Univ. Press ser.) net, $3.75. Macmillan.
Stokes, Whitley, *and* Strachan, J:, *eds.* Thesaurus palæohibernicus: coll. of old Irish glosses, scholia, prose and verse. v. 1. '02(Ja18) 8°, (Cambridge Univ. Press ser.) net, $8. Macmillan.

Stolen correspondence from the Dead Letter Office. Sharp, B. A. 50 c. Gervais.
STOMACH.
Thompson. Acute dilation of the stomach. 75 c. Wood.
See also Digestion.
Stone, A. J. *See* Roosevelt, T.
Stone, E. D. *See* Thackeray, F. St. J.
Stone, Gertrude L., *and* Fickett, M. G., *comps.* Trees in prose and poetry. '02 (Je21) il. sq. D. 50 c. Ginn.
Stone, Wilbur M. Women designers of bookplates. '02(Ap19) il. nar. D. bds., net, $1; Jap. vellum, net, $2. Beam.
Stoner, Winifred S. Castles in Spain, and other sketches in rhyme. '02(Mr1) D. $1. Abbey Press.
STORIES.
See Fairy tales;—Fiction;—Legends.
Stories from Waverley. Scott, *Sir* W. $1. Macmillan.
Stories of country life. Bradish, S. P. 40 c. Am. Bk.
Stories of the Tuscan artists. Wherry, A. net, $4. Dutton.
Story, Alf. T: Swiss life in town and country. '02(F1) il. D. (Our European neighbors ser., no. 5.) net, $1.20. Putnam.
Story of animal life. Lindsay, B. net, 35 c. Appleton.
Story of Azron. Rollins, A. W. $1. Holliswood.
Story of Cairo. Poole, S. L. $2; $2.50. Macmillan.
Story of China. Van Bergen, R. 60 c. Bardeen.
Story of Eden. Wyllarde, D. $1.50. Lane.
Story of François Villon. Morehead, G: 25 c. Ogilvie.
Story of home gardens. Cadwallader, S. 25 c. Home Gardening.
Story (The) of Mary Mac Lane, by herself. '02(Je14) il. D. $1.50. H. S. Stone.
Story of Paul Dombey. Dickens, C: 15 c. Lippincott.
Story of Pemaquid. Kaler, J. O. 50 c. Crowell.
Story of the Christian centuries. Selden, E: G. net, $1. Revell.
Story of the Khedivate. Dicey, E: net, $4. Scribner.
Story of the Mormons. Linn, W: A. net, $4. Macmillan.
Story of the Philippines. Halstead, M. $2; $3. Dominion.
Story of the token. Shiells, R. net, $1. Presb. Bd.
Story of the vine. Emerson, E: R. net, $1.25. Putnam.
Story of the world's worship. Dobbins, F. $2.25; $3.25. Dominion.
Story of three. Sherwood, W. J. 25 c. W: S. Lord.
Story of Tonty. Catherwood, *Mrs.* M. H. $1.25. McClurg.
Stowe, *Mrs.* Ht. E. B. He's coming to-morrow. '02(Ap12) 12°, (Ideal messages ser.) pap., net, 25 c. Revell.
Stowe, *Mrs.* Ht. E. B. Minister's wooing. '02(My17) 12°, (Home lib.) $1. Burt.
Stowe, *Mrs.* Ht. E. B. Uncle Tom's cabin. '02(Mr22) 12°, $2; hf. mor., $3; mor., $4. Dominion.
Strachan, J:, *ed.* *See* Stokes, W., *ed.*

Strangers at the gate. Gordon, S: $1.50. Jewish Pub.

Stratemeyer, E: Lost on the Orinoco. '02 (Ap26) il. D. (Pan-American ser., no. 1.) net, $1. Lee & S.

STRATFORD-ON-AVON.

Way, *comp.* Reliques of Stratford-on-Avon. 50 c.; 75 c. Lane.

STRAWBERRY.

Barnard. The strawberry garden, how it was planted, etc. 40 c. Coates.

Stray leaves from a border garden. Holme, M. P. M. net, $1.50. Lane.

Streamer, D. Ruthless rhymes for heartless homes. New ed. '01· '02(My3) il. sq. D. $1.25. Russell.

Street, Eug. E. *See* Higgin, L.

STREET-RAILROADS.

Andrews. Handbook for street railway engineers. $1.25. Wiley.

Street railway accident law. *See* Massachusetts.

Strength of the weak. Hotchkiss, C. C. $1.50. Appleton.

Stretton, Hesba. New child's life of Christ. '01. '02(Ap26) il. 12°, $1. Winston.

Strollers (The). Isham, F: S. $1.50. Bowen-M.

Strong, J. Next great awakening. '02 (Mr29) D. 75 c. Baker & T.

Strutt, J: W:, [*Baron* Rayleigh.] Scientific papers. v. 3, 1887-1892. '02(Mr8) 8°, (Cambridge Univ. Press ser.) net, $5. Macmillan.

STUARTS.

Rait. Five Stuart princesses. net, $3.50. Dutton.

Stubbs, W: Ordination addresses; ed. by E. E. Holmes. '01. '02(Ja11) D. $2.25. Longmans.

STUDENTS.

Canfield. College student and his problems. net, $1. Macmillan.

Students' guide to health. Van Doren, D. T. $2. D. T. Van Doren.

Studies in auditory and visual space perception. Pierce, A. H: net, $2. Longmans.

Studies in Irish hist. and biog. Falkiner, C. L. $5. Longmans.

Studies in spiritual harmony. Brown, G. M. $1. Reed Pub.

Studies of trees in winter. Huntington, A. O. net, $2.25. Knight.

STUDY.

See Home study.

Study of religion. Jastrow, M., *jr.* $1.50. Scribner.

Study of the court of Star Chamber. Scofield, C. L. net, $1. Univ. of Chic.

Styan, K. E. Short history of sepulchral cross slabs, with ref. to other emblems found thereon. '02(Je28) 8°, net, $3. E. & J. B. Young.

SUCCESS.

Gilbert. 1000 ways to make money. $1. Donohue.

See also Business.

Success club debater. Hungerford, H. 25 c. Success.

Such stuff as dreams. Russell, C: E. net, $2. Bowen-M.

Suckling, *Sir* J: Love poems. '02(Ja11) S. (Lover's lib., no. 8.) net, 50 c.; leath., 75 c. Lane.

Suitors of Yvonne. Sabatini, R. net, $1.20. Putnam.

Sullivan, *Sir* E: Ivanhoe and Rob Roy, retold for children. New ed. '01. '02(F15) 16°, (Children's friend ser.) bds., 50 c. Little, B. & Co.

Sullivan, Eug. C. *See* Prescott, A. B:

Sullivan, Fk. J: Detective adviser. '02 (My17) S. pap., 60 c. Int. Detective.

Sullivan, Ja. E., *comp.* *See* Spalding's official athletic almanac.

Sullivan, T. R. Courage of conviction. '02 (Je7) D. $1.50. Scribner.

Summer of Saturdays. Smith, C. W: 65 c. Gillan.

SUNDAY.

Lewis. Sunday legislation. net, $1. Appleton.

Moule. Thoughts for the Sundays of the year. net, $1. Revell.

SUNDAY-SCHOOL.

Arnold, *ed.* Internat. S. S. lessons, 1902. 50 c. Revell.

Bible. Sunday-school scholar's Bible. 75 c.; $1. Nelson.

Hamill. Sunday-school teacher. 50 c. Pub. Ho. M. E. Ch., So.

Sunlight and shadows. Dail, C. C. $1.50. Hudson-K.

Sunnyside ser. il. D. Ogilvie.

—Morehead. Francesca da Rimini. 25 c. (117.)

SUPERSTITION.

See Devil;—Spiritualism.

SURGERY.

American year-book of medicine and surgery. 2 v. ea., net, $3; net, $3.75. Saunders.

Cheyne *and* Burghard. Surgical treatment. v. 5. $5. Lea.

Crile. Research into problems rel. to surgical operations. net, $2.50. Lippincott.

Jacobson *and* Steward. Operations of surgery. 2 v. net, $10; $12. Blakiston.

Murphy, *ed.* General surgery. $1.50. Year Bk.

Wharton. Minor surgery and bandaging. net, $3. Lea.

Zuckerhandl. Atlas and epitome of operative surgery. net, $3.50. Saunders.

See also Accidents; — Anatomy; — Diagnosis; — Medicine;—Veterinary medicine and surgery.

Surprises of an empty hotel. Gunter, A. C. $1; 50 c. Home.

SURVEYING.

Johnson. Theory and practice of surveying. $4. Wiley.

Lupton. Mine surveying. $5. Longmans.

Nugent. Plane surveying. $3.50. Wiley.

See also Engineering;—Railroads;—Trigonometry.

Susanne. Delano, F. J. 50 c. L. C. Page.

Swartz, Joel. Easter and the resurrection. '02(Ap12) 12°, pap., net, 15 c. Revell.

Swartz, Joel. Poems. '01. '02(F15) 12°, $1; $1.25. Coates.

SWEDEN.

Cronholm. Hist. of Sweden. 2 v. $5. N. N: Cronholm.

Swedenborg, E. Heavenly arcana. Rotch ed. v. 13. '02(Mr15) D. $1.25. Mass. New-Ch. Un.

Swedenborg, E. Ontology; or, signification of philosoph. terms; tr. by A. Acton. '01. '02(F1) D. pap., 50 c. Mass. New-Ch. Un.

Sweet danger. Wilcox, *Mrs.* E. W. 50 c. Donohue.

Swete, H: B. Patristic study. '02(Mr22) D. (Handbooks for the clergy.) net, 90 c. Longmans.

Swett, Sophie. Sarah the less. '02(Je7) il. D. net, 75 c. Westminster.

Swift, B:, *pseud.* *See* Paterson, W: R.

Swift, H: Walton, *rep.* *See* Mass. *Sup. judicial ct.* Repts.

Swift, J. Journal to Stella; ed. by G: A. Aitken. '01. '02(F22) D. (Lib. of standard literature.) $1.75. Putnam.

Swift, J. Prose works; ed. by T. Scott. v. 9, Cont. to *The Tatler, Examiner*, etc. '02 (Je7) 12°, (Bohn's standard lib.) net, $1. Macmillan.

Swift, J. Selections. '01. '02(Ap5) S. (Little masterpieces.) 50 c. Doubleday, P.

SWITZERLAND.

Story. Swiss life in town and country. net, $1.20. Putnam.

Swoope, C. W. Lessons in practical electricity. '02(Je14) il. 8°, net, $2. Van Nostrand.

Sybel, H. v. Prinz Eugen von Savoyen; ed. by E. C. Quiggin. '02(Mr8) 12°, (Pitt Press ser.) net, 60 c. Macmillan.

Sykes, Percy M. Ten thousand miles in Persia; or, eight years in Iran. '02(Je21) il. 12°, net, $6. Scribner.

Symonds, E. M. *See* Paston, G:

Symons, Arth. Poems. '02(F15) 2 v., 8°, net, $3. Lane.

Syntax of the verb in the Anglo-Saxon chronicle. Blain, H. M. net, 50 c. Barnes.

SYPHILIS.

Duhring, *and others.* Syphilis. net, $1. Treat.

Morton. Genito-urinary disease and syphilis. net, $3. Davis.

SYRACUSE, FIRST PRESB. CHURCH.

Northrup, *ed.* Early records of First Presb. Church of Syracuse, N. Y. 50 c. [Gill] Genealog. Soc.

T. Racksole and daughter. Bennett, A. $1.50. New Amsterdam.

TABLE-TENNIS.

See Ping-pong.

TABLES.

Blum. Reduction tables for ascertaining freight charges, etc. net, $3. Am. Code.

TACTICS.

See Infantry.

Tagzeiten zum heiligsten Herzen Jesu. '02 (Je28) 24°, pap., 5 c. Herder.

Tait, Ja., *ed.* *See* Tout, T: F:

Talbot, A. N. Railway transition spiral. 3d ed., rev. '02(Ap19) 16°, flex. leath., $1.50. Van Nostrand.

Talbot, Ellen V. Courtship of sweet Anne Page. '02(Mr8) S. (Hour-glass stories.) net, 40 c. Funk.

Tale of a cat. Kern, M. 50 c. Abbey Press.

Tale of the great mutiny. Fitchett, W: H: $1.50. Scribner.

Tale of true love. Austin, A. net, $1.20. Harper.

Tales from Shakespeare. Lamb, C: 40 c. Heath.

Tales from *Town Topics*, no 43. '02(My10); no. 44 (Je7) 12°, pap., ea., 50 c. Town Topics.

Tales of destiny. Jordan, E. G. $1.50. Harper.

Tales of my father. F., A. M. $2. Longmans.

Tales of passed times. Perrault, C: net, 50 c.; 80 c. Macmillan.

Tales of the Spanish Main. Morris, M. $2. Macmillan.

Talisman. Fulda, L. 35 c. Heath.

Talmage, Fk. De W. A vacation with nature. '02(Je21) D. net, $1. Funk.

Talmage, Fk. De W., Banks, L: A., *and others.* Life and work of T. De Witt Talmage. '02(My10) 12°, subs., $2; hf. mor., $2.75; full mor., $3.75. Winston.

TALMAGE, T: De Witt.

Talmage, F. D., *and others.* Life and work of T. De Witt Talmage. subs., $2; $2.75; $3.75. Winston.

Tappan, Eva M. Our country's story: elem. hist. of the U. S. '02(My24) il. sq. D. 65 c. Houghton, M. & Co.

TARIFF.

Marx. Wage-labor and capital; [also] Free-trade. 50 c. N. Y. Labor News.

See also Taxation.

Tarquinius Superbus. Epstein, A. J. $1.25. Mutual Pub.

Tarr, R. S. Physical geography of New York state. '02(Je14) il. 8°, net, $3.50. Macmillan.

Tarr, R. S., *and* McMurry, F. M. First book: home geography. '02(Je28) il. 12°, (Geographies, two-book ser.) hf. leath., net, 60 c. Macmillan.

Tarr and McMurry's geographies. il. 12°, net, 30 c. Macmillan.

—Wilson. Ohio.

Tartarin de Tarascon. Daudet, A. 45 c. Am. Bk.

Tate, H: Aaron Crane. '02(Ap26) il. D. $1.50. Abbey Press.

Tatnall, Rob. R. *See* Crew, H:

Taunton, Ethelred L. Hist. of the Jesuits in England, 1580-1773. '01. '02(F15) il. 8°, net, $3.75. Lippincott.

Tauszky, Edm., *rep.* *See* California. *Superior ct.* Repts.

TAXATION.

Hollister, *and others.* Taxation in Michigan and elsewhere. 50 c. Mich. Pol. Sci.

Purdy. Burdens of local taxation and who bears them. 25 c. Public Policy.

Purdy. Local option in taxation. 10 c. N. Y. Tax Reform.

Walker. Taxation of corporations in the U. S. 25 c. Am. Acad. Pol. Sci.

See also Political economy;—Tariff.

Taylor, Bayard. Poetical works. Household ed. '02(Ap5) il. D. $1.50. Houghton, M. & Co.

Taylor, Bayard. Views afoot or Europe seen with knapsack and staff. '02(Ap19) 12°, (Home lib.) $1. Burt.

Taylor, Bret L. Line-o'-type lyrics. '02 (My24) S. bds., net, 50 c. W: S. Lord

Taylor, C: M., *jr.* Why my photographs are bad. '02(Je14) il. O. net, $1. Jacobs.

Taylor, E: R. Into the light. '02(Ap5) 12°, bds., net, 75 c. Elder.

Taylor, Hannis. Treatise on international public law. '01. '02(F8) O. shp., net, $6.50. Callaghan.

Taylor, Hobart C. C. Crimson wing. '02 (Ap5) D. $1.50. H. S. Stone.

Taylor, Jos. S., *ed.* Practical school problems. v. 1, pt. 1. '02(Ap5) O. pap., 30 c. [W: B. Harison] Practical Sch. Problems.

Taylor, S. Earl. *See* Taylor, T: E.

Taylor, T: E., Taylor, S. E., *and* Morgan, C: H. Studies in the life of Christ. '02 (Ap12) O. 75 c. Jennings.

Taylor, W: A. Intermere. '02(Ja11) D. $1. XX. Century.

T'bacca queen. Wilson, T. W. $1; 50 c. Appleton.

TEACHERS AND TEACHING.
Bender. The teacher at work. 75 c. Flanagan.
Findlay. Principles of class teaching. net, $1.25. Macmillan.
Funk *and* Moses, *eds.* Teachers' manual for first reader. 50 c. Funk.
Laurie. Training of teachers and methods of instruction. net, $1.50. Macmillan.
Murché. Teachers' manual of object lessons for rural schools. net, 60 c. Macmillan.
See also Education;—Memory;—Sunday-school.

TEETH.
MacDowell. Orthodontis. net, $4. Colegrove.
Marshall. Principles and practice of operative dentistry. subs., $5; $6. Lippincott.
Smale *and* Colyer. Diseases and injuries of the teeth. $7. Longmans.

Telegram almanac and cyclopedia, 1902. '02 (Mr15) 16°, pap., 20 c. Providence Telegram.

TELEGRAPHY.
Bubier. A B C of wireless telegraphy. $1. Bubier.
Edison. Telegraphy self-taught. $1. Drake.
See also Codes.

TELEPATHY.
Stay. Mind telegraph; telepathic influence of the human will. 25 c. Alliance.

TELEPHONE.
Cary. How to make and use the telephone. $1. Bubier.
Homans. A B C of the telephone. $1. Van Nostrand.
Hyde *and* McManman. Telephone troubles and how to find them on the magneto and common battery system. 25 c. Caspar.

TEMPERANCE.
Crozier. Temperance and the Anti-Saloon League. 15 c. Barbee & S.
Cumming. Public house reform. $1. Scribner.
Griffin. Why the legal (or force) method of promoting temperance does more harm than good. 15 c. A. Griffin.
National Temperance almanac, 1902. 10 c. Nat. Temp.
See also Wine.

Temple classics. See Macmillan's.

Temple of trusts. *See* De Leon, T: C.

TEMPLES.
See Solomon's temple.

Ten Brink, B. Language and metre of Chaucer. 2d ed., rev. by F. Kluge. '02(F15) 12°, net, $1.50. Macmillan.

Ten years in Burma. Smith, J. net, $1. Eaton & M.; Jennings.

Tennessee. *Supreme ct.* Repts. (G: W. Pickle.) New ed., with annots. by R. T. Shannon. v. 19-21 (103-105.) '02(Ap12) v. 7-18 (92-102.) (My24) O. shp., ea., $3. Fetter.

Tennessee. *Supreme ct.* Repts. (G: W. Pickle.) [v. 98-106.] '01- '02(Ap5) O. shp., ea., $3. Marshall.

Tennessee Lee. Neill, M. $1. Neely.

Tennyson, A., *Lord.* In memoriam. '01- '02 (Ja11) 16°, (Caxton ser.) flex. lambskin, net, $1.20. Scribner.

Tennyson, A., *Lord.* The princess ed., by F. T. Baker. '02(Je7) D. (Twentieth century text-books.) 25 c. Appleton.

Tennyson, A., *Lord.* Birthday book; quotations for each day; sel. and arr. by E. J. S. '02(F15) 24°, 75 c.; $1; mor., $1.25. Warne.

TENNYSON, A., *Lord.*
Livingston. Bibliog. of the first ed. in book form of the works of Tennyson. $1. Dodd.

Terrors of the law. Watt, F. net, $1.25. Lane.

TERRY, Ellen.
Pemberton. Ellen Terry and her sisters. net, $3.50. Dodd.

Terry, Milton S. New and living way. '02 (Je21) D. net, 50 c. Eaton & M.

Tesnière, A. Adoration of the blessed sacrament. '02(F1) D. net, $1.25. Benziger.

Tessa Wadsworth's discipline. Conklin, *Mrs.* J. M. D. $1. Burt.

Texas. Citations to amendments and changes of the revised statutes; ed. by N. J. McArthur. '02(Mr22) D. pap., 50 c. Gammel.

Texas. Conflicting civil cases in repts, from Dallam to v. 93, incl. v. 2, comp., arr. and annot. by W. W. King and S. J. Brooks. '02(Ap5) O. shp., $4. Gilbert Bk.

Texas court reporter. v. 3. '02(My24) O. shp., $3. B. C. Jones.

Texas. *Cts. of civil appeals.* Repts. v. 24. '02(Mr29) O. shp., $3. Texas.

Texas. Notes on repts; by W. M. Rose. Bk. 1. '02(Ap26) O. shp., $7.50. Bancroft-W.

Texas. Supp. to Sayles' civil statutes; incl. Texas repts., v. 93, and Southwestern reporter, v. 63. By W. W. Herron. '02 (My24) O. $1. Gilbert Bk.

Texas. Supp. to Willson's statutes; by W. W. Herron. '02(Mr22) O. 50 c. Gilbert Bk.

Texas. *Supreme ct.* Repts. (A. E. Wilkinson.) v. 94. '02(My17) O. shp., $5. Gammel.

Texas. 27th legislature and state administration. (M'Arthur and Wicks.) '01- '02 (F15) O. roan, $5. B. C. Jones.

TEXAS.
Smith. Texas notarial manual and form book. $4. Gammel.
See also Galveston.

Text-books of science. S. $1.75. Longmans.
—Tilden. Introd. to the study of chemical philosophy.

Texts to il. lectures on Greek philosophy. Adam, J. net, $1.25. Macmillan.

Thackeray, F. St. J., *and* Stone, E. D., *eds.* Pre-Victorian poets. '02(Je28) 12°, (Florilegium Latinum, v. 1.) $2.50. Lane.

Thackeray, F. St. J., *and* Stone, E. D. *eds.* Victorian poets. '02(Ap26) 12°, (Florilegium Latinum, v. 2.) net, $2. Lane.
Thackeray, W: M. Prose works. Barry Lyndon; ed. by W. Jerrold. '02(Mr22) il. 12°, $1. Macmillan.
Thackeray, W: M. Prose works: Henry Esmond; ed. by W. Jerrold. '02(Ap12) 2 v., il. 12°, $2. Macmillan.
Thackeray, W: M. Prose works. History of Henry Esmond, Esq. New uniform ed. '02(Mr29) 12°, $1. Macmillan.
Thackeray, W: M. Prose works. Memoirs of Barry Lyndon, Esq.; also Catherine. New uniform ed. '02(Je7) il. 12°, $1. Macmillan.
Thackeray, W: M. Prose works. The Newcomes. New uniform ed. '02(Ja18) 12°, $1. Macmillan.
Thackeray, W: M. Prose works. The Newcomes; ed. by W. Jerrold. New uniform ed. '02(Je14) 3 v., il. 12°, $3. Macmillan.
Thackeray, W: M. Prose works. Pendennis. New uniform ed. '02(F1) 3 v., il. 12°, $3. Macmillan.
Thackeray, W: M. Prose works. The Virginians. New uniform ed. '02(F22) il. 12°, $1. Macmillan.
That old kitchen stove. Judd, D: H. 50 c. Abbey Press.
Thayer, A. E. Compend of general pathology. '02(Mr22) il. 12°, (Quiz compend ser., no. 15.) 80 c.; interleaved, $1. Blakiston.
Thayer, Stephen H: Daughters of the Revolution. '01. '02(F8) D. $1. Abbey Press.
Theocritus. Idylls. '02(Mr15) il. 12°, (Antique gems from the Greek and Latin, v. 1.) (App. to pubs. for price.) Barrie.
Theological and Semitic literature. *See* Arnolt, W. M.
THEOLOGY.
Arnold. Literature and dogma. net, $1. New Amsterdam.
Balfour. Foundations of belief. net, $2. Longmans.
Cobb. Theology, old and new. net, $1. Dutton.
Hoyt. Theology as a popular science. net, 10 c. Presb. Bd.
Minton. The cosmos and the logos. net, $1.25. Westminster.
Mortimer. Catholic faith and practice. pt. 1, $2; pt. 2, $2.50. Longmans.
Orr. Progress of dogma. $1.75. Armstrong.
Reed. Idea of God in relation to theology. net, 75 c. Univ. of Chic.
See also Baptism;—Catechisms;—Christianity;—Devil;—Holy Spirit;—Natural religion;—Religion;—Skepticism.
Theology and ethics of the Hebrews. Duff, A. net, $1.25. Scribner.
Theory of accounts. Goodyear, S: H. $1.50. Goodyear-M.
Theory of prosperity. Patten, S. N. net, $1.25. Macmillan.
THERAPEUTICS.
Hawley. New animal cellular therapy. $1. Clinic.
See also Christian science;—Diet;—Hydrotherapy;—Medicine;—Nurses and nursing;—Pathology;—Roentgen rays.
THERMODYNAMICS.
See Mechanics.
Thesaurus palæohibernicus. Stokes, W. net, $8. Macmillan.
THESSALONIANS.
See Bible.
13th district. Whitlock, B. $1.50. Bowen-M.
Thirty-six years in the White House. Pendel, T: F. $1.50. Neale.
Thomas Aquinas, *St.* *See* Wilberforce, B. A.
Thomas, H. H. Book of the apple. '02 (Mr22) il. D. (Handbooks of practical gardening, no. 6.) net, $1. Lane.
Thomas, Thdr., *ed.* Famous composers and their music. Extra il. ed. '01. '02(Mr15) 16 v., il. col. pl. 8°. (App. to pubs. for price.) Millet.
Thompson, E. E. Seton-. Krag and Johnny Bear. '02(Ap26) il. D. (Ser. of school reading.) 60 c. Scribner.
Thompson, H. C. Acute dilation of the stomach. '02(Je7) 8°, 75 c. Wood.
Thompson, *Sir* H: Motor car. '02(My17) 12°, $1. Warne.
Thompson, *Sir* H: The unknown God. '02 (Je21) S. 60 c. Warne.
Thompson, *Sir* H: *See also* Harmsworth, A. C.
Thompson, J: G. *and* T: E. New century readers. 3d bk., Nature, myth and story. '02(My10) 12°, (New century ser.) 52 c. Morse.
Thompson, Rob. E. Hand of God in American history. '02(Mr8) D. net, $1. Crowell.
Thompson, Seymour D. Commentaries on the law of negligence. v. 3. '02(Mr29) O. shp., $6. Bowen-M.
Thomson, H. C. China and the powers. '02 (Ap19) il. O. $4. Longmans.
Thoreau, H: D: The service; ed. by F. B. Sanborn. '02(Je14) O. bds., neet, $2.50; 24 cop. on Japan, ea., net, $10. Goodspeed.
Thoreau, H: D: Walden. '02(Ap19) 12°, (Home lib.) $1. Burt.
Thornton, E. Quin, *ed.* *See* Medical News.
Thornton, G. H. Eng. composition. '02(Ap12) D. (Self-educator ser.) 75 c. Crowell.
Thornton, Marcellus E. Lady of New Orleans. '02(Mr29) D. $1.50. Abbey Press.
Thorpe, Ctte. The children's London. '01. '02(Ja11) il. 4°, net, $4.50. Scribner.
Thorpe, T: E: Essays in hist. chemistry. 2d ed. '02(Je14) 8°, net, $4. Macmillan.
Those black diamond men. Gibbons, W: F. $1.50. Revell.
Those delightful Americans. Cotes, *Mrs.* S. J. $1.50. Appleton.
Thoughts for the Sundays of the year. Moule, H. C. G. net, $1. Revell.
Thoughts on education. Creighton, M. net, $1.60. Longmans.
Thrall of Leif the lucky. Liljencrantz, O. A. $1.50. McClurg.
Three graces. Hungerford, *Mrs.* M. H. $1. Lippincott.
Three sailor boys. Cameron, V. L. 60 c. Nelson.
Three thousand sample questions. Sellow, G. E. 50 c. Bellows.
Three whys and their answer. Babcock, M. D. 35 c. Un. Soc. C. E.
Threefold fellowship. Palmer, B. M. 75 c. Presb. Pub.
Thrice a pioneer. Hannibal, P: M. 75 c.; 40 c. Danish Luth.

THROAT.
Gradle. Diseases of the nose, pharynx and ear. net, $3.50. Saunders.
Wood, *and others, eds.* Eye, ear, nose and throat. $1.50. Year Bk.
See also Breathing.
Throne of David. Ingraham, J. H. $1. Burt.
Through science to faith. Smyth, N. net, $1.50. Scribner.
Thrum, T: G., *ed.* *See* Hawaiian almanac.
Thruston, Lucy M. A girl of Virginia. '02 (Je14) il. D. $1.50. Little, B. & Co.
Thurber, Alwyn M. Zelma, the mystic. 3d ed. [New issue.] '02(Mr22) il. O. $1.25. Alliance.
Thurston, Ernest L. *See* Snyder, C.
Thwaites, R. G. Down historic waterways: canoeing upon Ill. and Wis. rivers. 2d ed., rev. '02(Mr15) il. D. net, $1.20. McClurg.
Thwaites, R. G. Father Marquette. '02 (Je21) D. (Life histories.) net, $1. Appleton.
Thwaites, R. G., *ed.* *See also* Jesuit relations.
TIBET.
Carey. Adventures in Tibet. net, $1.50. Un. Soc. C. E.
Tiddeman, Lizzie E. A humble heroine. '01. '02(F15) 12°, pap., 15 c. Lippincott.
Tiffany, Nina M., *and* Lesley, Susan, *eds.* Letters of James Murray, loyalist. '01. '02 (Ja25) 12°, net, $2.50. W: B. Clarke.
Tilden, W: A. Introd. to the study of chemical philosophy. 10th ed., rev. and enl. '01. '02(Ja11) S. (Text-books of science.) $1.75. Longmans.
Tilton, Dwight. Miss Petticoats. '02 (My24) il. D. $1.50. C. M. Clark.
TIME.
See Astronomy;—Stars.
Time and chance. Hubbard, E. $1.50. Putnam.
Times of retirement. Matheson, G: net, $1.25. Revell.
Timothy. Hettinger, F. net, $1.50. Herder.
Tippler's vow. Fairchild, L. $10. Croscup.
Titian, *pseud.* *See* Antrim, M. T.
To the end of the trail. Nason, F. L. $1.50. Houghton, M. & Co.
To whom shall we go? Ovenden, C. T. $1. E. & J. B. Young.
TOASTS.
Miller, *comp.* The toastmaster. n. p. W. M. Rogers.
Reynolds. Banquet book. net, $1.75. Putnam.
Tocsin (The). Worthington, E. S. 25 c. Cubery.
Todd, C: B. True Aaron Burr. '02(My3) sq. S. net, 50 c. Barnes.
Todd, Marg. G., ["Graham Travers."] Way of escape. '02(Je21) D. $1.50. Appleton.
Todhunter, I:, *and* Leathem, J. G. Spherical trigonometry; rev. by J. G. Leathem. '02 (Mr1) 12°, net, $1.75. Macmillan.
TOKEN.
Shiells. Story of the token as belonging to the sacrament of the Lord's supper. net, $1. Presb. Bd.
Token of the covenant. Mahon, R. H. 50 c. Pub. Ho. of M. E. Ch., So.
Tolman, Herb. C. Guide to old Persian inscriptions. '02(Mr15) il. 12°, $1.50. Am. Bk.
Tolstoï, *Count* L. N. What is religion? and other new articles and letters. '02(My17) D. net, 60 c. Crowell.
TOMBSTONES.
Styan. Hist. of sepulchral cross slabs, with ref. to other emblems found thereon. net, $3. E. & J. B. Young.
Tomlins, W: L., *ed.* Laurel song book. '02 (Mr29) 12°, $1.50; bds., $1. Birchard.
Tommy Cornstalk. Abbott, J. H. M. $2. Longmans.
Tompkins, Herb. W. Highways and byways in Hertfordshire. '02(Je14) il. 12°, (Highways and byways ser.) $2. Macmillan.
Tonna, *Mrs.* Ctte. E. Judah's lion. New ed. '01. '02(F22) 12°, $1. Dodd.
Tons of treasure. Bishop, W: H: $1. Street.
Torture of the clinic. Trudeau, L. $1; 50 c. Bourguignon.
Tourgée, A. W. A fool's errand. [New ed.] '02(Je7) il. D. $1.50. Fords.
Tout, T: F., *and* Tait, Ja., *eds.* Historical essays, by members of the Owens College, Manchester. '02(Ap19) O. $5. Longmans.
TOWER OF LONDON.
Gower. Tower of London. v. 2. net, $6.50. Macmillan.
Town and country lib. *See* Appleton's.
Town life in ancient Italy. Friedländer, L. 75 c. B: H. Sanborn.
Townesend, *Mrs.* Stephen. *See* Burnett, *Mrs.* F. H.
Townsend, C. H. *See* Sage, D.
Townsend, C: Mahoney million. '02(Ap26) 12°, $1.25. New Amsterdam.
Townsend, E: W. Chimmie Fadden and Mr. Paul. '02(My10) il. D. $1.50. Century Co.
Townsend, Luther T. Satan and demons. '02(My10) sq. T. (Little books on doctrine.) net, 25 c. Jennings.
Toynbee, Paget. Dante studies and researches. '02(Je7) 8°, net, $3.50. Dutton.
TRADE.
See Business;—Commerce;—Fur trade;—Tariff.
TRADE-MARKS.
See Plate.
TRADE-UNIONS.
Webb. Hist. of trade unionism. net, $2.60.—Industrial democracy. net, $4. Longmans.
Tragedy of Anne Boleyn. Gallup, *Mrs.* E. W. $1.50. Howard.
Traill, H: D., *and* Mann, J. S., *eds.* Social England. [New il. ed.] In 6 v. v. 1. '02 (F1) Q. net, $4.50. Putnam.
Training of teachers. Laurie, S. S. net, $1.50. Macmillan.
Training the church of the future. Clark, F. E: net, 75 c. Funk.
Transplanting an old tree. Bloomfield, W. $1. Blanchard.
TRANSPORTATION.
See Railroads.
TRANSVAAL.
Cook. Rights and wrongs of the Transvaal war. $2. Longmans.
See also Boers;—South Africa.
Trask, W. B., *ed.* Letters of Col. Thomas Westbrook and others rel. to Indian affairs in Maine, 1722-1726. '01. '02(Mr8) 8°, $5. Littlefield.
Traum ein leben. Grillparzer, F. S. 60 c. Heath.

TRAVEL.
Powers. Art of travel. 25 c.
See also Voyages and travels.

Travers, Graham, *pseud.* *See* Todd, M. G.

Travers, Morris W. Experimental study of gases; introd. pref. by W: Ramsay. '01-'02(Ja4) il. 8°, net, $3.25. Macmillan.

Travis, Ira D. Hist. of the Clayton-Bulwer treaty. '02(F15) 12°, pap., $1. Mich. Pol. Sci.

Travis, Wa. J. Practical golf. New rev. ed. '02(My10) il. 12°, net, $2. Harper.

TREATIES.
See United States.

TREES.
Dame *and* Brooks. Handbook of trees of New England. $1.35. Ginn.
Huntington. Studies of trees in winter. net, $2.25. Knight.
Payne. How to teach about trees. 25 c. Kellogg.
Stone *and* Fickett, *comps.* Trees in prose and poetry. 50 c. Ginn.
See also Botany;—Forests and forestry;—Fruit;—Lumber.

Trelawney, Dayrell. Man of no account. '02 (Ap19) sq. S. (Upward ser., no. 2.) pap., 10 c. J. H. West.

Treves, F: Surgical applied anatomy. New ed. '02(F15) il. 12°, net, $2. Lea.

Tribal custom in Anglo-Saxon law. Seebohm, F: net, $5. Longmans.

Tribune almanac and political register, 1902. '02(Ja11) D. (Lib. of *Tribune* extras, v. 14, no. 1.) pap., 25 c. Tribune Assoc.

Trickett, W: Law of witnesses in Penn. '02(Mr1) O. shp., $6. T. & J. W. Johnson.

Triggs, H. I. Formal gardens in England and Scotland. In 3 pts. pt. 1. '02(Mr8); pt. 2 (My10) f°, net, complete set, $25. Scribner.

TRIGONOMETRY.
Todhunter *and* Leathem. Spherical trigonometry. net, $1.75. Macmillan.
See also Geometry;—Logarithms;—Mathematics;—Navigation;—Surveying.

TRIPOLI.
Cathcart. Tripoli. $4. J. B. C. Newkirk.

Triumph of the cross. Savonarola, G. net, $1.35. Herder.

TROLLEY TRIPS.
Childe, *comp.* Trolley exploring. 10 c. Brooklyn Eagle.

Trollope, A. Writings. Collectors' ed. v. 8-16. '02(Mr15) il. 8°, crushed lev., subs. (App. to pubs. for price.) Gebbie.

TROUT.
Rhead. Speckled brook trout. net, $3.50. Russell.
Sage, *and others.* Salmon and trout. net, $2; net, $7.50. Macmillan.

Trudeau, L: Torture of the clinic. '01-'02 (Ja4) O. $1; pap., 50 c. Bourguignon.

True romance revealed by a bag of old letters. Anthony, H. G. $1. Abbey Press.

True tales of birds and beasts. Jordan, D: S. 40 c. Heath.

Trueba, Antonio de. El molinerillo y otros cuetos. (R. D. de la Cortina.) '02(My24) S. (Cuentos selectos, no. 4.) pap., 35 c. W: R. Jenkins.

Trueman, Anita. Anton's angels. '02(Mr22) 16°, 75 c. Alliance.

TRUMPET.
Littleton. Trumpeters' hand book and instructor. $1. Hudson-K.

TRUSTS.
Flint, *and others.* The trust. net, $1.25. Doubleday, P.
See also Capital and labor.

Truth about the Schley case. Nauticus, *pseud.* 25 c. Columbia.

Tuber-like rootlets of cycas revoluta. Life, A. C. net, 25 c. Univ. of Chic.

Tucker, C: Cowles, *rep.* *See* District of Columbia. *Ct. of appeals.* Repts.

Tucker, Eliz. S. Magic key. '01-'02(F15) 12°, net, $1. Little, B. & Co.

Tucker, G: F. Manual rel. to the preparation of wills: book of Mass. law. 2d ed. '02 (Mr29) D. shp., $3.50. G: B. Reed.

Tuckwell, W. A. W. Kinglake: biog. and literary study. '02(Ap12) il. 12°, $1.75. Macmillan.

Turnbull, Coulson. Divine language of celestial correspondence. '02(Mr22) 8°, $2. Alliance.

Turnbull, Coulson. Sema-Kanda. '02(Mr22) 12°, $1.25. Alliance.

Turner, A. L. Accessory sinuses of the nose. '02(F8) Q. $4. Longmans.

Turner, Jos. M. W: Turner and Ruskin. '01-'02(F22) 2 v., il. 4°, net, $50 Dodd.

Tuscan sculpture. Hurll, E. M. net, 75 c.; 50 c.; 35 c. Houghton, M. & Co.

TUSCANY.
Carmichael. In Tuscany. net, $2. Dutton.
See also Artists.

Tuttle, J: E. The gift of power: study of the Holy Spirit. '02(Je7) S. net, 25 c. Westminster.

Twain, Mark, *pseud.* *See* Clemens, S: L.

'Tween you an' I. Blouët, P. $1.20. Lothrop.

Twelfth night. *See* Shakespeare, W:

Twentieth century home builder. Powell, L. 25 c Pub. Ho. M. E. Ch., So.

Twentieth century text-books. il. D. net. Appleton.
—Caldwell. Lab'y manual of botany. 50 c.; 60 c.
—Fowler. Hist. of ancient Greek literature. $1.40.
—Gilbert *and* Brigham. Introd. to physical geography. $1.25.
—Jordan *and* Heath. Animal forms. $1.10.
—Tennyson. The princess. 25 c.
—West. Latin grammar. 90 c.

Twentieth century wonder book. Hunter, W: C. 50 c.; 25 c. Donohue.

Twenty-five steppingstones toward Christ's kingdom. Fradenburgh, O. P. $1. O. P. Fradenburgh.

Twenty little maidens. Blanchard, A. E. $1.25. Lippincott.

Twenty-six and one. Górky, M. $1.25. J. F. Taylor.

Twenty thousand miles by land and sea. Pennock, A. F. $1. Mason Pub.

Two centuries' growth of Am. law, 1701-1901. '01-'02(Mr15) 8°, (Yale bicentennial pub.) net, $4. Scribner.

Two-fold covenant. Achenbach, H: 50 c. Evangelical Press.

Two hundred bar exam. questions. Bingham, G. A. $1. Commercial.

Two of a trade, by the author of "Val." '02 (My17) 12°, 60 c. Nelson.
Two Renwicks. Davidson, M. A. $1.50. Neely.
Two thousand a year on fruits and flowers. Barnard, C: $1. Coates.
Two thousand years in eternity. Bywater, B. net, $2.15. Hudson-K.
Two wars. French, S: G. $2. Confederate Veteran.
Two winters in Norway. Spender, A. E. $4. Longmans.
Typee. Melville, H. 45 c. Heath.
TYPEWRITING.
Vories. Lab'y method of teaching Eng. and touch typewriting together. $1.25. Inland Pub.
TYPHOID FEVER.
Osler, *ed.* Typhoid and typhus fevers. net, $5; $6. Saunders.
Ulyat, W: C. The first years of the life of the redeemed after death. '01- '02(F15) D. $1.25. Abbey Press.
Ulysses. Phillips, S. net, $1.25. Macmillan.
Umbrian towns. Cruickshank, J. W. net, $1.25. Wessels.
Uncle and aunt. Woolsey, S. C. 50 c. Little, B. & Co.
Uncle Boston's spicy breezes. Smith, B. net, $1. Am. Bapt.
Uncle Jed's country letters. Brenton, H. 30 c. Dickerman.
Uncle Sam, trustee. Bangs, J: K. net, $1.75. Riggs.
Uncle Sam's examination. Kellogg, A. M. 15 c. Kellogg.
Uncle Tom's cabin. Stowe. H. B. $2: $3; $4. Dominion.
Under my own roof. Rouse, A. L. net, $1.20. Funk.
Under the dome. Ingram, A. F. M. $1.25. E. & J. B. Young.
Under the red cross. Wright, D: H: 35 c. Biddle.
Underwood, Clarence F., *il.* Some pretty girls. '01- '02(Mr1) 4°, regular ed., $3; de luxe ed., $5. Quail & W.
Undine. *See* La Motte Fouqué, F. H. K. *Freiherr* de.
Undine lib. 12°, pap., 25 c. Street.
—Ellis. Life of Wm. McKinley. (9.)
UNITARIAN CHURCH.
Wilbur. Hist. sketch of the Independent Cong. church, Meadville, Pa., 1825-1900. $1; 50 c. E. G. Huidekoper.
United States. *Circuit cts. of appeals.* **Repts.,** with annots. v. 47. '01- '02(Ja4); v. 48 (Mr1); v. 49 (Ap19) O. shp., ea., $3.35. Lawyers' Co-op.
United States. Federal reporter, v. 110. Permanent ed. '01- '02(Ja18); v. 111 (Mr1); v. 112 (My10); v. 113 (Je7) O. (Nat. reporter system, U. S. ser.) shp., ea., $3.50. West Pub.
United States. *Supreme ct.* Repts., v. 183. (J. C. B. Davis.) '02(Je7) O. shp., $2.30. Banks.
UNITED STATES.
Brown, C: F., *and* Croft. Outline study of U. S. history. 50 c. Courier Pr.
Brown, W: G. Lower South in Am. history. net, $1.50. Macmillan.

UNITED STATES.—*Continued.*
Burgess. Reconstruction and the constitution, 1866-1876. net, $1. Scribner.
Butler. Treaty-making power of the U. S. In 2 v. v. 1. complete work, net, $12. Banks.
Cathcart. Tripoli; first war with the U. S. $4. J. B. C. Newkirk.
Clark. The government, what it is, what it does. 75 c. Am. Bk.
Codman. Arnold's expedition to Quebec. net, $2.25. Macmillan.
Elliott. Debates of federal constitution. 5 v. net, $10; net, $12. Lippincott.
Farley. West Point in the early sixties, with incidents of the war. net, $2. Pafraets.
French. Two wars: Mexican war; war between the states. $2. Confederate Veteran.
Gordy. Am. leaders and heroes. net, 60 c. Scribner.
Halstead. Hist. of America's new possessions. $2.50; $3.50; $4.50. Dominion.
Harris. Sectional struggle: troubles between the North and South. net, $2.50. Lippincott.
McDaniel. War poems, 1861-1865. $1. Abbey Press.
Muirhead. America, the land of contrasts. net, $1.20. Lane.
Page. Rebuilding of old commonwealths. Southern states. net, $1. Doubleday, P.
Pendel. Thirty-six years in the White House. $1.50. Neale.
Phillips. Methods of keeping the public money of the U. S. $1. Mich. Pol. Sci.
Pratt. America's story. v. 5. 40 c. Heath.
Richardson. War of 1812. subs., $3. Historical.
Ridpath. Hist. of the U. S. from aboriginal times. $6. Grosset.
Root *and* Connelley. Overland stage to California. $2.50; $3.50. Root & C.
Tappan. Our country's story. 65 c. Houghton, M. & Co.
Thompson. Hand of God in Am. history. net, $1. Crowell.
Wagner. Current history. 25 c. Whitaker & R.
Westbrook. The West-brook drives. $1.25. Eckler.
Wilson, *ed.* Presidents of the U. S. $3.50; $6. Appleton.
See also Clayton-Bulwer treaty; — Lexington; — Louisiana purchase; — Pensions; — Political science;—*also* names of states.
United States Govt. publications. Hasse, A. R. pt. 1. $1. Lib. Bu.
Universalist register for 1902; ed. by R: Eddy. '02(F8) S. pap., 25 c. Universalist.
UNIVERSITY OF CALIFORNIA.
Jones. Il. hist. of the University of Cal., 1868-1901. $5. Berkeley.
University of Cal. bulletins. il. O. pap. Univ. of Cal.
—Eakle. Colemanite from So. California. 15 c. (v. 3, 2.)
—Hershey. Quaternary of So. Cal. 20 c. (v. 3, 1.)
—Lawson. The eparchæan interval. 10 c. (v. 3, 3.)
—Lawson *and* Palache. Berkeley Hills. 80 c. (v. 2, 12.)

University of Chicago constructive Bible studies; ed. by W: R. Harper and E. D. Burton. O. Univ. of Chic.
—Harper. Constructive studies in the priestly element in the O. T. $1.
University of Chicago cont. to education. S. pap., net. Univ. of Chic.
—Dewey. Educational situation. 50 c. (3.)
—Dewey. Psychology and social practice. 25 c. (2.)
—Young. Ethics in the school. 25 c. (4.)
—Young. Isolation in the school. 50 c. (1.)
—Young. Some types of modern educ. theory. 25 c. (6.)
Univ. of Chicago cont. to philosophy. 8°, pap., net, 35 c. Univ. of Chic.
—Gore. Imagination in Spinoza and Hume. (v. 2, 4.)
University of Chicago. Yerkes Observatory bulletin. 8°, net. Univ. of Chic.
—Hale. New star in Perseus. 10 c. (16.)
UNIVERSITY OF PENNSYLVANIA.
Nitzsche, *comp.* Proceedings at dedication of building of Dept. of law. $3; $3.50. Univ. of Penn.
University of Penn. pubs., ser. in pol. economy and public law. O. [Univ. of Penn.] Ginn.
—Weyl. Passenger traffic of railways. $1.50; $1. (16.)
University of Va. monographs, school of Teutonic languages. 12°, pap., net, 50 c. Barnes.
—Blain. Syntax of the verb in the Anglo-Saxon chronicle, 787 to 1001. (1.)
University of Wis. bulletins. O. pap. Univ. of Wis.
—Wolcott. On the sensitiveness of the coherer. 20 c. (51; science ser., v. 3, 1.)
Unknown God. Thompson, *Sir* H: 60 c. Warne.
Unrequited love. Stechhan, O. $1. Abbey Press.
Unto the end. Alden, *Mrs.* I. M. $1.50. Lothrop.
Unto you, young women. Sinclair, W. M. net, $1. Lippincott.
Unwilling guest. Hill, G. L. net, $1. Am. Bapt.
Upland game birds. Sandys, E. net, $2; net, $7.50. Macmillan.
Upward ser. sq. S. pap., 10 c. J. H. West.
—Macdonald. Guarding the thoughts. (1.)
—Trelawney. A man of no account. (2.)
Upon the sun-road. Hurst, J: F. 25 c. Revell.
URINE AND URINARY ORGANS.
Morton. Genito-urinary disease and syphilis. net, $3. Davis.
USEFUL ARTS.
Brown, *ed.* Workshop wrinkles. net, $1. Van Nostrand.
See also Bridges;—Commerce;—Dyeing;—Electric engineering;—Machinery;—Patents.
UTILITARIANISM.
Albee. Hist. of Eng. utilitarianism. net, $2.75. Macmillan.
Utopia. More, *Sir* T: $1. Burt.
Vacation with nature. Talmage, F. D. net, $1. Funk.
VACCINATION.
Oswald. Vaccination a crime. 10 c. Physical Culture.
See also Variola.

Valcourt-Vermont, Edg. de, ["*Comte* C. de Saint-Germain."] Practical astrology; with a hist. of astronomy. '02(Ap26) il. 12°, $1; pap., 50 c. Laird.
Valdés, A. P. José; tr. by Minna C. Smith. '01. '02(Mr8) D. $1.25. Brentano's.
Vale Press Shakespeare. 8°, net. Lane.
—Shakespeare. Twelfth night. $8. (22.)
Valentine, E: U. Ship of silence and other poems. '02(Je28) 12°. net, $1.20. Bowen-M.
Valentine, *Mrs.* Laura J., *comp. and ed.* Old, old fairy tales. '02(My10) il. 12°, (Fairy lib.) $1. Burt.
VALJEAN, Jean.
Quayle. A hero, Jean Valjean. 30 c. Jennings.
Valley of decision. Wharton, E. 2 v. $2. Scribner.
Van Anderson, Helen. Journal of a live woman. '02(Mr22) D. $1. Alliance.
Van Bergen, R. Story of China. '02(My3) il. D. 60 c. Am. Bk.
Vance, Ja. J. Rise of a soul. '02(My17) 12°, net, $1. Revell.
Van Der Kellen, M. J.-Ph. Works of Michel Le Blond. '02(Mr1) portfolio, net, $30; mor. portfolio, net, $35. Dodd.
Vanderpoel, Emily N. Color problems. '02 (My10) O. net, $5. Longmans.
Vandersloot, Lewis. History and genealogy of the Von der Sloot family. '01. '02 (Ap5) il. f°, $1. L. Vandersloot.
Van Deventer, E. M., ["Lawrence L. Lynch."] The woman who dared. '02(F22) D. 75 c.; pap., 25 c. Laird.
Van Doren, De W. T. Students' guide to health. '01. '02(F15) 12°, $2. T. Van Doren.
VAN DYCK, Ant.
Cust. Desc. of sketch-book used by Sir Anthony Van Dyck. $17.50. Macmillan.
Hurll, *ed.* Van Dyck. net, 75 c.; net, 50 c.; net, 35 c. Houghton, M. & Co.
Van Dyke, T. S. *See* Roosevelt, T.—Sandys, E.
Van Epps, Howard. *See* Georgia. Supp. to code.
Van Meter, B: F. Genealogies and sketches of some old families of Virginia and Kentucky especially. '01. '02(Ja18) 8°, $2.25. Morton.
Van Santvoord, S. House of Cæsar and the imperial disease. '02(F22) il. Q. net, $5.25. Pafraets.
Van Vorst, Marie. Philip Longstreth. '02 (Ap19) D. $1.50. Harper.
Van Zile, Philip T. Elements of the law of bailments and carriers. '02(My24) O. shp., $5. Callaghan.
Varieties of religious experience. James, W: net, $3.20. Longmans.
VARIOLA.
Moore, *ed.* Variola, vaccination, varicella, etc. net, $5; net, $6. Saunders.
Vaughan, D. T. G. *See* Bower, F. O.
Vaughan, Herbert. Holy sacrifice of the mass. 4th ed. '02(Je28) 16°, 15 c. Herder.
Vector analysis. Gibbs, J. W. net, $4. Scribner.
VEGETABLES.
Wythes. Book of vegetables. net, $1. Lane.
See also Gardening.

VEGETARIANS.
Miles. Failures of vegetarianism. net, $1.50. Dutton.
Velásquez de la Cadena, M. Nuevo diccionario de pronunciacion de las lenguas Inglesa y Espanola. pt. 2. '02(Je14) O. hf. leath., $3.50. Appleton.
Vellum ser. il. 12°, $1. Univ. Co-op.
—Goff. Lessons in commercial fruit growing.
Velocity of light. Michelsen, A. A. net, 25 c. Univ. of Chic.
VENEREAL DISEASES.
Hayden. Pocket text-book of venereal diseases. net, $2.25. Lea.
See also Syphilis.
VENUS DI MILO.
Patoma. Venus di Milo; its hist. and art. 50 c. Cambridge.
Verba crucis. McClelland, T. C. 50 c. Crowell.
Veritas, *pseud.* The German Empire of today. '02(Je7) D. $2.25. Longmans.
VERMONT.
Wilbur. Early hist. of Vt. v. 3. $1.50. L. F. Wilbur.
See also Newbury.
Verne, Jules. Vingt mille lieues sous les mers; abr. and ed. by C. Fontaine. '02 (Je14) S. (Modern lang. ser.) 40 c. Heath.
Versailles hist. ser.; ed. by K. P. Wormeley. il. 8°, subs., $6; leath., $9. Hardy. P. & Co.
—Bernis. Memoirs and letters. 2 v.
—Elisabeth, *Mme.* Memoir and letters.
—Fersen. Letters and papers.
—Lespinasse. Letters.
Very naughty girl. Smith, *Mrs.* E. T. $1. Burt.
Very odd girl. Armstrong, A. E. $1. Burt.
Veterinarian's call book for 1902. (R. R. Bell.) '01· '02(F22) 12°, leath., $1.25. W: R. Jenkins.
VETERINARY MEDICINE AND SURGERY.
Cadiot. Clinical veterinary medicine and surgery. $5.25. W: R. Jenkins.
Dunn. Veterinary medicines. $3.75. W: R. Jenkins.
Fleming. Operative veterinary surgery. v. 2. net, $3.25. W: R. Jenkins.
McClure. Amer. horse, cattle and sheep doctor. $1.50. Henneberry.
See also Horse.
VICTORIA, *Queen of England.*
Halstead *and* Munson. Life and reign of Queen Victoria. $1.50; $2.25. Dominion.
Walsh. Religious life and influence of Queen Victoria. net, $2.50. Dutton.
Victorian poets. Thackeray, F. St. J. net, $2. Lane.
Victories of Rome. Best, K. D. net, 45 c. Benziger.
Victorious republicanism. Halstead, M. $1.50; $2.25. Dominion.
Vielé, H. K. Myra of the Pines. '02(Je14) D. $1.50. McClure, P.
Viets, Fs. H. Genealogy of the Viets family. '02(Ap26) il. O. $3. Case.
Views afoot. Taylor, B. $1. Burt.
Village work in India. Russell, N. net, $1. Revell.
Villari, P. Barbarian invasions of Italy. '02 (My10) 2 v., il. 8°, net, $7.50. Scribner.

VILLAS.
See Architecture.
VILLON, François.
Morehead. Story of François Villon, the hero of the play "If I were king." 25 c. Ogilvie.
Vincent, Edg. L. Margaret Bowlby. '02 (My17) D. $1.50. Lothrop.
Vincent, J. M., Ely, R: T., Gilman, D. C., *and others.* Herbert B. Adams; with a bibliog. of the Dept. of history, politics and economics. '02(Ap26) O. (Johns Hopkins Univ. studies, v. 20, extra no.) pap. (free to subs.) Johns Hopkins.
Vincent, Marvin R. What is it to believe on the Lord Jesus Christ? '01· '02(F8) S. pap., 5 c. Beam.
VINEYARDS.
See Fresno Co., Cal.
Vingt mille lieues sous les mers. Verne, J. 40 c. Heath.
Virden, *Mrs.* Laura M. N. First science reader. New ed. '01· '02(Mr29) il. 16°, 25 c.; bds., 10 c. Flanagan.
Virgil. Æneid. bks. 1-6; tr. by H. H. Ballard. '02(Ap5) D. net, $1.50. Houghton, M. & Co.
Virginia-Carolina almanac, 1902. '02(Mr15) il. 16°, pap., gratis. Virginia-Carolina.
Virginia. Complete annot. digest. v. 8. '02 (Je7) O. shp., $6.50. Hurst & Co.
Virginia. *Supreme ct. of appeals.* Repts. Jefferson—33 Grattan, 1730-1880. (T: J. Michie.) v. 16-18. '01· '02(F8) Grattan's repts. v. 13-15 (Mr15); v. 11, 12 (My10); v. 9, 10 (My24) O. shp., ea., $7.50. Michie.
Virginia. *Supreme ct. of appeals.* Repts. (M. P. Burks.) v. 99. '02(My10) O. shp., $3.50. O'Bannon.
VIRGINIA.
Hall. Reading of Va. $2. Mayer.
See also Jamestown.
Virginian (The). Wister, O. $1.50. Macmillan.
Virginians. Thackeray, W: M. $1. Macmillan.
VISCHER, Peter.
Headlam. Peter Vischer. $2. Macmillan.
VIVISECTION.
Ernst. Animal experimentation. net, $1.50; net, $1. Little, B. & Co.
Vizetelly, Ernest A. Lover's progress told by himself. '01· '02(Mr8) D. $1.50. Brentano's.
VOICE.
Lawton. The singing voice and its practical cultivation. $1.50. W: H: Lawton.
Lunn. Philosophy of voice. net, $2. Schirmer.
Murrin. Vocal exercises on the vocal factors of expression. net, 50 c. A. M. Allen.
Voice from England. McGrady, T: 10 c. Standard.
Voltaire, F. M. A. de. Zaïre and Epîtres; ed. by C: A. Eggert. '02(Mr22) 16°, (Lake French classics.) 50 c. Scott, F. & Co.
VON DER SLOOT FAMILY.
See Vandersloot, L.
Vorce, C: M. Genealogical and hist. record of the Vorce family in America. '01· '02 (Ja18) 8°, $2. C: M. Vorce.

Vories, Hervey D. Laboratory method of teaching Eng. and touch typewriting together. '01· '02(Ja11) 8°, $1.25. Inland Pub.

VOYAGES AND TRAVELS.
Beck. Sonnenblicke aus der Amer. praxis net, 30 c. Lemcke.
Cadigan. My ocean trip. $1. Brentano's.
Gray. Musings by camp-fire and wayside. net, $1.50. Revell
Henry. Travels in Canada and the Indian territories, between 1760-1776. $4. Little, B. & Co.
Honeyman. Bright days in merrie England: four in hand journeys. net, $1.50. Honeyman.
Mackenzie. Voyages from Montreal through the Continent of N. A. to the frozen and Pacific Oceans. 2 v. net, $1. New Amsterdam.
Pennock. Twenty thousand miles by land and sea. $1. Mason Pub.
Satchel guide for vacation tourist in Europe. net, $1.50. Houghton, M. & Co.
Taylor. Views afoot, or, Europe seen with knapsack and staff. $1. Burt.
See also Geography;—Travel.

Wace, H:, *ed.* *See* Fulham Palace Conference.

Wade, G. W. Old Testament history. '02 (Mr8) 12°, $1.50. Dutton.

Wage-labor and capital. Marx, K. 50 c. N. Y. Labor News.

Wager (The). McManus, L. $1.25. Buckles.

Waggaman, Ma. T. Bob o' Link. '02(Mr22) il. D. 40 c. Benziger.

Waggaman, Ma. T. Corinne's vow. '02(F15) D. $1.25. Benziger.

Wagner, C: Courage. New ed. '01· '02 (F22) 12°, $1.25. Dodd.

Wagner, Harr. Current history: supp. to California state series history. Rev. ed. '02 (Je7) sq. D. leatherette, 25 c. Whitaker & R.

Wagner, Harr. New Pacific school geography. New ed. '02(Je7) Q. net, $1. Whitaker & R.

Wagner, R: Rheingold; ed. by R. A. von Minckwitz. '02(Je28) 16°, (German opera texts, v. 1.) 75 c. Newson.

Wags of the stage. Whitton, J. $2.50. Rigby.

Wait, W: Law and practice in civil actions and proceedings in justices' cts., and in other cts. not of record, and on appeals to county cts. of N. Y. In 3 v. v. 1. 7th ed., by E. Baylies. '02(Mr15) O. shp., per v., $6.35; or per set, $19. M. Bender.

Wakeman, Rob. P. Wakeman genealogy. '02(Ap5) il. 8°, $5; hf. mor., $7.50; full mor., $10. Journal Pub.

Walden. Thoreau, H: D: $1. Burt.

Walford, *Mrs.* Lucy B. Charlotte. '02 (Mr22) D. $1.50. Longmans.

Walker, Fs. A. Taxation of corporations in the U. S. '02(Mr22) 8°, (Pub. of the soc., no. 329.) pap., 25 c. Am. Acad. Pol. Sci.

Walker, J. G., *ed.* *See* Am. Bapt. year-book.

Walker, Ja. W. G. Ocean to ocean. '02 (Mr22) il. O. net, $1.25. McClurg.

Walkey, S. With redskins on the warpath. '01· '02(Ja11) il. D. $1.25. Cassell.

Wall, *Mrs.* D. H. Sister in name only. '02 (Ap26) 12°, $1. Neely.

Wall, W: What great men have said about great men. '02(Ap5) 12°, net, $2.50. Dutton.

Wallace, *Sir* Donald M. Web of empire: diary of the imperial tour of the Duke and Duchess of Cornwall and York, in 1901. '02(Je28) il. 8°, net, $6.50. Macmillan.

Wallace, Lew. Ben Hur. Players' ed. '01· '02(Mr1) il. 12°, $2.50. Harper.

Wallannah. Hargrave, W: L. $1.50. B. F. Johnson.

Wallenstein. Schiller, J. C. F. v. net, $1. Holt.

Wallenstein's camp. *See* Schiller, J. C. F. v.

Walley, T: Practical guide to meat inspection; rewritten and enl. '01· '02(Ja4) il 12°, $3. W: R. Jenkins.

Walpole, H. Some unpublished letters; ed. by Sir S. Walpole. '02(Ap26) O. net, $1.50. Longmans.

Walsh, D: Roentgen rays in medical work. 3d ed. '02(Mr29) 8°. net, $2.50. Wood.

Walsh, G: E. Allin Winfield. '02(F8) D. $1.50. Buckles.

Walsh, Wa. Religious life and influence of Queen Victoria. '02(Je14) 8°, net, $2.50. Dutton.

Walton, W: Paris from the earliest period to the present day. v. 6. Lib. ed. '02 (Mr15) il. 8°, per v., $3. Barrie.

Wan Lun and Dandy. Kaler, J. O. 75 c. Burt.

Wanklin, J. A. Arsenic. '01· '02(F15) 12°, $1. Lippincott.

WAR OF 1812.
See United States.

War poems, 1861-1865. McDaniel, *Mrs.* H. P. $1. Abbey Press.

Ward, Herb. D. *See* Phelps, E. S.

Ward, *Mrs.* Herb. D. *See* Phelps, E. S.

Ward, J: The sacred beetle: treatise on Egyptian scarabs in art and history. '02 (Mr8) il. 8°, net, $3.50. Scribner.

Warden, Florence, *pseud.* *See* James, *Mrs.* F. A. P.

Warden, W: A. Ancestors, kin and descendants of John Warden and Narcissa (Davis), his wife. '01· '02(F1) 8°, $5. W: A. Warden.

Ware, Fabian. Educational foundations of trade and industry. '02(F22) 12°, (Internat. educ. ser., no. 54.) net, $1.20. Appleton.

Warlow, T: P., *comp.* *See* Florida. Index to laws.

Warneck, Gustav. Outline of a history of Protestant missions. '02(F8) 8°, net, $2. Revell.

Warner, Beverley E. Young man in modern life. '02(Ap19) D. net, 85 c. Dodd.

Warner, C: D. Fashions in literature, and other essays. '02(My10) D. net, $1.20. Dodd.

Warren, H: W. *See* Merrill, S. M.

Warvelle, G: W. Essays in legal ethics. '02 (Mr29) D. $2.50. Callaghan.

Warvelle, G: W. Treatise on the Am. law of vendor and purchaser of real property. v. 1, 2. 2d ed. '02(Ja18) O. shp., $12. Callaghan.

WARWICK, *Countess of.*
Palgrave. Mary Rich, Countess of Warwick, 1625-1678. net, $1.50. Dutton.
Warwick lib. of Eng. literature. 12°, $1.50. Scribner.
—Herford, *ed.* Eng. tales in verse.
Washburn, Emory. Treatise on the Am. law of real property. 6th ed.; ed. by J: Wurts. '02(Mr29) 3 v., 8°, shp., net, $18. Little, B. & Co.
WASHINGTON, G:
Custis. George Washington. $1. Donohue.
Headley. Washington and his generals. $1. Burt.
Locke. Typical American. net, 25 c. Jennings
WASHINGTON.
Brand. Justices' code. $5. Bancroft-W.
WASHINGTON, D. C.
Winchester, *ed.* Aroung the throne. sketches of Wash. society . net, $1. Eichelberger.
WATER.
Horrocks. Introd. to bacteriolog. examination of water. net, $3.68. Blakiston.
See also Brooks;—Hydraulic engineering;—Physical geography,—Water-supply.
WATER-CURE.
See Hydrotherapy.
WATER-FOWL.
See Birds.
WATER-POWER.
See Hydraulic engineering.
WATER-SUPPLY.
Folwell. Water-supply engineering. $4. Wiley.
Mason. Water-supply (fr. a sanitary standpoint). red. to $4. Wiley.
See also Hydraulic engineering.
Water-tube boilers. Robertson, L. S. $3. Van Nostrand.
Waterhouse, Percy L. Story of the art of architecture in America. '01· '02(F8) il. S. (Lib. of useful stories.) net, 35 c. Appleton.
Watkinson, W: L. The blind spot, and other sermons. '02(Je7) 12°, net, $1. Revell.
Watrous, A. E. Young Howson's wife. '02 (Mr29) D. $1.50. Quail & W.
Watson, *Mrs.* Annah R. Passion flowers. '02(Ap12) 24°, $1.60. Whittet.
Watson, *Mrs.* Annah R. A royal lineage: Alfred the Great, 901-1901. '01· '02 (Ap12) 12°, $4.50. Whittet.
Watson, B: F. *See* McDonald, D:
Watson, Forbes. Flowers and gardens. '02 (My3) 12°, $1.50. Lane.
Watson, T: E. Napoleon. '02(Mr15) O. $2.25. Macmillan.
Watson, W: Ode on the day of the coronation of King Edward VII. '02(Je28) bds., net, $1; 250 cop. Jap. vellum, net, $3.50. Lane.
Watson, W: F. Elementary experimental chemistry, inorganic. '01· '02(F1) 12°, net, $1.25. Barnes.
Watt, Fs. Terrors of the law. '02(My24) 8°, net, $1.25. Lane.
WATTEAU, Jean Antoine.
Staley. Watteau, master painter of the "Fêtes galantes." 50 c. Macmillan.
Wau-Bun. *See* Kinzie, *Mrs.* J. A. M.
Waverley. *See* Scott, *Sir* W.

Way, A. E., *comp.* Reliques of Stratford-on-Avon. '02(Je14) 16°, (Flowers of Parnassus ser., v. 16.) net, 50 c.; leath., net, 75 c. Lane.
Way of escape. Todd, M. G. $1.50. Appleton.
Way of the preacher. Kern, J: A. $1.25. Pub. Ho. M. E. Ch., So.
Way of the West. King, C: 50 c. Rand, McN. & Co.
Wayland, J: W. Paul, the herald of the cross. '01. '02(Ja18) 16°, 40 c. Brethren Pub. Ho.
Ways of the world. Jordan, M. O. $1.50. Neely.
Wead, C: K. Cont. to the history of musical scales. '01· '02(Je14) O .pap., 50 c. Woodward & L.
WEATHER.
Price. Observations and exercises on the weather. 30 c. . Am. Bk.
Web of empire. Wallace, *Sir* D. M. net, $6.50. Macmillan.
Webb, Sidney *and* Beatrice. Hist. of trade unionism. New ed. '02(Ap19) O. net, $2.60. Longmans.
Webb, Sidney *and* Beatrice. Industrial democracy. New ed. 2 v. in 1. '02(Ap19) O. net, $4. Longmans.
Webb, T: E. Mystery of William Shakespeare. '02(Je7) O. $4. Longmans.
Webber, Rob. Graduated coll. of problems in electricity; fr. 3d Fr. ed., by E. A. O'Keeffe. '02(Je7) 12°, $3. Spon.
Weber, Alice. Clock on the stairs and other stories. '02(Je28) il. 12°, (St. Nicholas ser.) 75 c. Burt.
Weborg, Johanna. In Viking land. '02(Mr8) 12°, $1.25. J. C. Weborg.
Webster, Dan. Speeches; sel. by B. F. Tefft. '02(My3) 12°, (Home lib.) $1. Burt.
WEBSTER, Dan.
Lewis. Fryeburg Webster centennial. 50 c. A. F. Lewis.
McCall. Daniel Webster. net, 80 c. Houghton, M. & Co.
WEDDINGS.
See Marriage.
Weekly church teaching for the infants. Francis, *Mrs.* C. D. 25 c. E. & J. B. Young.
Wegelin, Oscar. Early American fiction, 1774-1830. '02(My17) 8°, net, $2. O. Wegelin.
Weimer, Alb. B., *rep.* *See* Pennsylvania. *Superior ct.* Repts.
Wells, F: P. Hist. of Newbury, Vt.; with genealog. records. '02(Ap26) il. 8°, $2.25; $3; hf. seal, $3.50; Lib. shp., $4. Caledonian.
Wells, Herb. G: Anticipations of the reaction of mechanical and scientific progress upon human life and thought. '02(Mr1) O. net, $1.80. Harper.
Wells, Horace L., *ed.* Studies from the chemical lab'y of the Sheffield Scientific School. '01· '02(Mr15) 2 v., 8°, (Yale bicentennial pub.) net, $7.50. Scribner.
WELLS.
See Boring.
Welsh, Lucie D. Colonial days. '02(My3) il. sq. O. 50 c. Educ. Pub.
Welsh rarebit tales. Cummins, H. O. $1.25. Mutual Bk.
Welsh witch. Raine, A. $1; 50 c. Appleton.

Wentworth, G: A., *and* **Hill**, G. A. Lab'y exercises in elem. physics. '01· '02(Mr1) 12°, pap., 27 c. Ginn.
Wesselhoeft, E. C. German composition. '02 (Je21) D. (Modern lang. ser.) 45 c. Heath.
West, And. F. Latin grammar. '02(Je7) D. (Twentieth century text-books.) net, 90 c. Appleton.
West, T. D. Metallurgy of cast iron. 4th ed. '02(Mr22) il. D. $3. Cleveland Pr.
West, Willis M. Ancient history to the death of Charlemagne. '02(Je28) 12°, (Ser. of school histories.) hf. leath., $1.50. Allyn & B.
West-brook drives. Westbrook, H. P. $1.25. Eckler.
WEST INDIES.
See Central America.
WEST POINT, N. Y.
Farley. West Point in the early sixties. net, $2. Pafraets
Hancock. Life at West Point. net, $1.40. Putnam.
West Virginia. *Supreme ct. of appeals.* Repts. (Freer.) v. 47. '01, '02(Je7) O. shp., $4.50. Tribune Co.
West Virginia. *Supreme ct. of appeals.* Repts.; by R. H. Freer. v. 48. '02(Mr15); v. 49 (My10) O. shp., ea., $4.50. Charleston Daily Mail.
Westbrook, Henrietta P. West-brook drives. '02(F22) il. D. $1.25. Eckler.
WESTBROOK, T:
Trask, *ed.* Letters of Col. Thomas Westbrook and others rel. to Indian affairs in Me., 1722-26. $5. Littlefield.
Westcotes. Ccuch, A. T: Q. $1. Coates.
Westcott, Brooke F. Words of faith and hope. '02(Ap26) 12°, $1.25. Macmillan.
Westermarck, E: History of human marriage. 3d ed. '02(Je28) 8°, net, $4.50. Macmillan.
WESTMINSTER ABBEY.
Hiatt. Westminster Abbey. 60 c. Macmillan.
WESTMINSTER ASSEMBLY.
See Catechisms.
WESTMINSTER SCHOOL.
Airy. Westminster. $1.50. Macmillan.
Westward ho! *See* Kingsley, C:
Wetzel, Fs. X. The dutiful child; fr. the Germ. 2d ed. '02(Mr8) 16°, 40 c. Herder.
Weyl, Wa. E. Passenger traffic of railways. '01. '02(Ja25) O. (Pub. of the Univ. of Pa., ser. in pol. economy and public law, no. 16.) $1.50; pap., $1. [Univ. of Penn.] Ginn.
Wharton, Anne H. Last century maid. '01. '02(F15) il. 12°, $1.25. Lippincott.
Wharton, Edith. Valley of decision. '02 (Mr1) 2 v., D. $2. Scribner.
Wharton, H: R. Minor surgery and bandaging. 5th ed. '02(Je14) il. 12°, net, $3. Lea.
What great men have said about great men. Wall. W: net, $2.50. Dutton.
What is it to believe on the Lord Jesus Christ? Vincent, M. R. 5 c. Beam.
What is religion? Tolstoï, *Count* L. N. net, 60 c. Crowell.
What is Shakespeare? Sherman, L. A. net, $1.50; net. $1. Macmillan.
What is worth while ser. D. leatherette. Crowell.
—Hay. William McKinley. net, 28 c.
What the new thought stands for. Patterson, C: B. 10 c. Alliance.
What Thelma found in the attic. Duckwitz, L. C. $1. Alliance.
What think ye of Christ. Eldridge, J. L. $1. Abbey Press.
What's what. Allen, F. S. net, 50 c. Bradley-W.
Wheatley, H: B: How to make an index. '02(Je14) S. (Booklover's lib.) $1.25; hf. mor., $2.50. Armstrong.
Wheaton, Emily. The Russells in Chicago. '02(Je14) il. 16°, (Commonwealth ser.) $1.25. L. C. Page.
Wheeler, Ht. Cub's career. '02(My3) il. D. $1. Abbey Press.
Wheeler, Jeannette. Josephine Grahame. '02 (Mr15) D. $1.50. Abbey Press.
Wheeler, W. H. The sea-coast. '02(Ap19) il. O. $4.50. Longmans.
Wheeler, W: H: *See* Calmerton, G.
Wheeler's elem. speller. '02(Mr22) il. O. 25 c. W: H: Wheeler.
Wheeler's graded readers. il. sq. D. W: H: Wheeler.
—Calmerton *and* Wheeler. First reader. 30 c.
Wheelock, *Mrs.* Irene G. Nestlings of forest and marsh. '02(Ap12) il. D. net, $1.40. McClurg.
WHEELS.
See Gears and gearing.
When bards sing out of tune. Clark, A. 50 c. Abbey Press.
When love is king. Mabry, W. D. $1.50. Fenno.
When old New York was young. Hemstreet, C: net, $1.50. Scribner.
Where the magnolias bloom. Cullens, F: B. 50 c. Abbey Press.
Where, when, and how to catch fish on east coast of Fla. Gregg, W: H. $4. Matthews-N.
Wherry, Abinia. Stories of the Tuscan artists. '02(F15) il. 8°, net, $4. Dutton.
WHIST.
Leigh *and* Bergholt. Principles of whist. net, $1.50. Coates.
See also Bridge.
WHISTLER, Ja. McN.
Bowdoin. James McNeill Whistler, the man and his work. net, $1.50. Beam.
Whitaker, Jos. and Sons, *comps.* Whitaker's almanac for 1902. '01. '02(Ja11) 12°, pap., net, 40 c.; *Same,* enl. ed., hf. roan, net, $1. Scribner.
Whitby, Beatrice. Flower and thorn '02 (Mr22) D. $1.50. Dodd.
Whitcomb, Clara E. Little journey to Italy; ed. by M. George. '02(Mr29) il. sq. D. (Plan book, v. 5. no. 5.) pap., 15 c. Flanagan.
Whitcomb, Clara E. Little journey to Scotland. '02(Mr29) il. 12°, (Plan book, v. 5, no. 4.) pap., 15 c. Flanagan.
White, C: J. Elements of theoretical and des. astronomy. 7th ed. rev. '01. '02(F8) il. 12°, $2.50. Wiley.
White, Emerson E. Grammar school algebra. New century ed. '02(Je21) S. 35 c. Am. Bk.
White, Fk. On corporations. 5th ed. '02 (My17) O. shp., $5.50. Baker, V. & Co.

White, Gilbert. Natural hist. and antiquities of Selborne. '01· '02(F15) 2 v., il. 8°, net, $20. Lippincott.

White, Michael. Lachmi Bai Rani of Jhansi, the Jeanne d'Arc of India. '02(Mr8) il. D. $1.50. J. F. Taylor.

White, Stewart E. Blazed trail. '02(My24) il. D. $1.50. McClure, P.

Whitehouse, Flo. B. God of things. '02 (My3) il. D. $1.50. Little, B. & Co.

Whither are we drifting? Stechhan, O. $1. Abbey Press.

Whitlock, Brand. The 13th district. '02 (Ap5) D. $1.50. Bowen-M.

Whitman, Alfr. Print-collector's handbook. 2d rev. ed. '02(My24) 8°, net, $5. Macmillan.

Whitney, Caspar, *ed.* *See* Amer. sportsman's lib.

Whittaker, N. T. Christian science, is it safe? '02(Ap5) 12°, pap., 10 c. Earle.

Whittaker's grade A handbook. D. net. Whittaker.

—Scadding. Answers to plain questions for Am. churchmen. 50 c.

Whittier, C: A. In the Michigan lumber camps. 4th ed. '02(Ap5) S. (Boys' vacation ser., first vacation.) 75 c. Neely.

Whitton, Jos. Wags of the stage. Ed. de luxe. '02(Je7) Q. $2.50. Rigby.

Who's who, 1902. '02(F1) 12°, $1.75. Macmillan.

Why my photographs are bad. Taylor, C: M., *Jr.* net, $1. Jacobs.

Why the legal method of promoting temperance always has done more harm than good. Griffin, A. 15 c. A. Griffin.

Whyte, Alex. Newman: an appreciation in two lectures. '02(Mr8) D. net, $1.10. Longmans.

Wicks, —. *See* Texas. 27th legislature.

Wide world (The). '02(Mr22) il. D. (Youth's (Youth's Companion ser., no. 1.) 30 c. Ginn.

Widow Wiley, and some other old folk. Sinnett, B. $1.50. Dutton.

Wiechmann, Ferdinand Gerhard. *See* Monroe, F.

Wiener, Alfr. E. Practical calculation of dynamo-electric machines. 2d ed, rev. and enl. '02(Ap5) il. 8°, $3. Elec. World.

Wiener, Leo. Anthology of Russian literature from the earliest period to the present time. In 2 pts. pt. 1. '02(Je21) O. net, $3. Putnam.

Wiggin, *Mrs.* Kate D. Diary of a goose girl. '02(My17) il. D. $1. Houghton, M. & Co.

Wight, Emma H. The Berkleys. '02(Mr29) il. S. net, 40 c. Benziger.

Wilberforce, Bertrand A. Devout commentary on the Epistle to the Ephesians; chiefly fr. St. Thomas Aquinas. '02(Je14) 8°, net, $1. Herder.

Wilbur, Earl M. Historical sketch of the Independent Cong. Church, [Unitarian,] Meadville, Pa. 1825-1900. '02(Je28) il. D. $1; pap., 50 c. E. G. Huidekoper.

Wilbur, La Fayette. Early history of Vermont. v. 3. '02(Ap26) 8°, $1.50. L. F. Wilbur.

Wilcox, *Mrs.* Ella W. Sweet danger. New ed. '02(My17) 12°, pap., 50 c. Donohue.

Wilcox, Lucius M. Irrigation farming. Rev. and enl. ed. '02(Je14) D. $2. Judd.

Wild life of orchard and field. Ingersoll, E. net, $1.40. Harper.

Wildenbruch, Ernst A. v. Das edle Blut; ed. by C: A. Eggert. '02(Je14) D. 30 c. Am. Bk.

Wilgus, Horace L. Cases on the general principles of the law of private corporations. In 2 v. v. 1. '02(Mr8); v. 2 (Ap5) O. (complete work,) $9; shp., $10. Bowen-M.

Wilhelm Meister's apprenticeship and travels. *See* Goethe, J. W. v.

WILKIE, *Sir* David.

Gower. Sir David Wilkie. $1.75. Macmillan.

Wilkins, Ja. H. Glimpse of old Mexico. '02 (Ap5) il. 16°, bds., 75 c. Whitaker & R.

Wilkinson, A. E., *rep.* *See* Texas. *Sup. ct.* Repts.

Wilkins, W: H: Caroline the illustrious Queen-Consort of George II. '01. '02(Ja4) 2 v., il. O. $12. Longmans.

Will to be well. Patterson, C: B. $1. Alliance.

Willard, C: D. *Herald's* history of Los Angeles City. '02(Ap5) il. D. $1.50. Kingsley.

Willard, Josiah F., ["Josiah Flynt."] The little brother: story of tramp life. '02 (Mr29) D. $1.50. Century Co.

WILLIAM I. *of Germany.*

Zastrow. Wilhelm der Siegreiche. net, 50 c. Macmillan.

Williams, *Mrs.* Leslie. A garden in the suburbs. '02(F15) 12°, net, $1.50. Lane.

Williams, Louise H. *See* Richards, E. H.

Williams, M. B. Sex problems. '02(Ap19) 12°, net, $1. Revell.

Williams, Margery. The late returning. '02 (Je7) 12°, $1.25. Macmillan.

Williams, Martha McC. Next to the ground. '02(My24) D. net, $1.20. McClure, P.

Williams, T. R. Shall we understand the Bible? Rev., enl. ed. '02(Ap26) 12°, pap., net, 50 c. Macmillan.

Williamson, *Mrs.* Corolin C. Mary Starkweather. '02(F22) D. $1.50. Abbey Press.

Williamson, G: C. Holman Hunt. '02(Mr8) il. 16°, (Miniature ser. of painters.) 50 c. Macmillan.

Willoughby, E: F. Hygiene for students. '01. '02(Ja4) 12°, $1.25. Macmillan.

WILLS.

Clement. Probate repts., annot. v. 6. $5.50. Baker, V. & Co.

Hoyt. Practice in probate cts. of New Hampshire. $2.50. Rumford Press.

Tucker. Preparation of wills. $3.50. G: B. Reed.

Wilson, Calvin D. Divine religion of humanity. '02(Je21) S. pap., net, 20 c. Presb. Bd.

Wilson, Edn. B. *See* Gibbs, J. W.

Wilson, Eug. B. Cyanide processes. 3d ed. rewritten. '02(Je21) 12°, $1.50. Wiley.

Wilson, Floyd B. Paths to power. '01· '02 (Ja4) D. $1. Fenno.

Wilson, Harry L. The spenders. '02(Je14) il. D. $1.50. Lothrop.

Wilson, Ja. G., *ed.* Presidents of the United States. New rev. ed., with life of W: McKinley and sketch of T. Roosevelt. '02 (Mr29) il. 8°, $3.50; hf. mor. or hf. cf., $6. Appleton.

Wilson, L: A. A great cloud of witnesses. '01- '02(Ap26) D. 50 c. Standard Pub.
Wilson, L: N. Bibliography of child study. '02(Mr8) O. pap., net, 25 c. Stechert.
Wilson, Stella S. Ohio. '02(Je7) il. 12°, (Tarr and McMurry's geographies, supp. v.) net, 30 c. Macmillan.
Wilson, Theodora W. T'bacca queen. '02 (My10) D. (Town and country lib., no. 311.) $1; pap., 50 c. Appleton.
Winchester, Paul, *ed.* Around the throne: sketches of Washington society. '02(Je14) 12°, net, $1. Eichelberger.
Winding road. Godfrey, E. $1.50. Holt.
Windle, Bertram C. A. The Malvern country. '01- '02(Ap12) il. S. (Little guides ser.) net, 75 c. Dodd.
WINDOW-GARDENING.
Allen, P. *and* G. Miniature and window gardening. net, 50 c. Pott.
Windows for sermons. Banks, L: A. net, $1.20. Funk.
Windsor, W: Phrenology. '02(My17) 12°, pap., 25 c. Donohue.
Windstorm and tornado insurance. Hoffman, F: L. 25 c. Spectator.
WINE.
Emerson. Story of the vine. net, $1.25. Putnam.
WINSLOW, J: A.
Ellicott. Life of John Ancrum Winslow, Rear Admiral U. S. N. $2.50. Putnam.
Winston, N. B. Grace of orders: [novel.] '02(F22) D. $1. Abbey Press.
Winter, John Strange, *pseud.* *See* Stannard, *Mrs.* H. E. V.
Wisconsin. List of books for township libraries. '02(My24) il. O. pap., 25 c. Wisconsin.
WISCONSIN.
Arbor and bird day annual for Wis. schools. gratis. Democrat Pr. Co.
Harvey. Aids for observance of Memorial day by schools of Wis. gratis. Democrat Pr. Co.
Wisner, Arth., ["A. Gallus."] Emma Calvé. '02(Je28) il. 4°, $1.50. Russell.
Wister, Owen. The Virginian. '02(Je21) il. D. $1.50. Macmillan.
Wistons. Amber, M. $1.50. Scribner.
WIT AND HUMOR.
Bangs. Olympian nights. $1.25. Harper.
Brenton. Uncle Jed's country letters. 30 c. Dickerman.
Bridgman. Gulliver's bird book. $1.50. L. C. Page.
Corrothers. Black cat club. net, $1. Funk.
Daskam, *comp.* Best nonsense verses. 50 c. W: S. Lord.
De Leon. Inauguration of President Watterson. 25 c. Am. Writers.
Field. Nonsense for old and young. 50 c. Dickerman.
Fleming. Around the Pan with Uncle Hank. $2. Nutshell.
Gilmer. Fables of the elite. $1. Fenno.
Goodwin. "Sinker" stories of wit and humor. $1. Ogilvie.
Irish wit and humor. 25 c. Drake.
Irwin. Rubáiyat of Omar Khayyám, jr. net, 50 c. Elder.
Kendall. Good gravy. 25 c. Helman-T.
Prune. College chaps. 75 c. Mutual Bk.

WIT AND HUMOR.—*Continued.*
Sharp. Stolen correspondence from dead letter office. 50 c. Gervais.
Shaw. Josh Billings' old farmer's allminax. $1.50. G: W. Dillingham.
See also Epigrams;—Parody.
Witch Winnie ser. Champney, *Mrs.* E. W. 9 v. $11.25. Dodd.
With Napoleon at St. Helena. Fremeaux, P. net, $1.50. Lane.
With redskins on the warpath. Walkey, S. $1.25. Cassell.
With Rimington. Phillipps, L. M. $2.50. Longmans.
With the royal tour. Knight, E: F: $2. Longmans.
Witmer, L. Analytical psychology. '02 (Ap5) O. $1.60. Ginn.
WITNESSES.
See Evidence.
Wodell, F: W: Choir and chorus conducting. '01- '02(F8) il. 12°. $1.50. Presser.
Woelfkin, Cornelius. Chambers of the soul. '02(Mr29) S. 35 c. Un. Soc. C. E.
Wolcott, Edson R. On the sensitiveness of the coherer. '02(My17) O. (Bull. of the Univ. of Wis., no. 51, science ser., v. 3. no. 1.) pap., 20 c. Univ. of Wis.
Wolfville days. Lewis, A. H: $1.50. Stokes.
Wollpert, F: A man amongst men. '02 (Ap5) sq. D. pap., 15 c. Eckler.
WOMAN.
Blouët. 'Tween you an' I. pt. 2, Concerning women. $1.20. Lothrop.
Dressler. Feminology. $3. Dressler.
Macfadden. Power and beauty of superb womanhood. $1. Physical Culture.
Maulde la Clavière. Art of life. net, $1.75. Putnam.
Sainte-Foi. The perfect woman. net, $1. Marlier.
Stone. Women designers of book-plates. net, $1; net, $2. Beam.
Women in the business world. $1.50; 50 c. Alliance.
See also Children; — Domestic economy; — Gynecology;—Home;—Nurses and nursing;—Sex.
Woman who dared. Van Deventer, E. M. 25 c. Laird.
Woman's exchange cook book. Palmer, *Mrs.* M. 70 c. Conkey.
Women in the business world. [New issue.] '02(Mr22) D. $1.50; pap., 50 c. Alliance.
Women of the Reformed church. Good, J. I. $1. Heidelberg.
Wonders of Mouseland. Childs, E: E. $1.25. Abbey Press.
Wonders of the Revelation of Jesus Christ. Ruble, W: $1. Standard Pub.
Wood, Casey A., Andrews, Alb. H., *and* Hardie, T. M., *eds.* Eye, ear, nose and throat. '02(Mr8) il. D. (Practical medicine ser. of year-books, v. 3.) $1.50. Year Bk.
Wood, *Mrs.* Ma. A. Marriage: its duties and privileges. '02(F8) 12°, net, $1.25. Revell.
WOOD-CARVING.
See Sloyd.
Woodland orchids. Boyle, F: net, $7. Macmillan.
Woods, C: Coke. *See* Nicholson, T:
WOODS.
See Forests and forestry.

Woodworth, Elijah B. Descendants of Walter Woodworth of Scituate, Mass.; Sketch of Samuel Woodworth and his descendants. '02(F22) 8°, $3. G. W. Humphrey.
Woolsey, Sa. C., ["Susan Coolidge."] Uncle and aunt. New ed '01. '02(F15) 16°, (Children's friend ser.) bds., 50 c. Little, B. & Co.
Worcester, J: Works of charity. '01. '02 (F1) sq. S. pap., 25 c. New-Ch. Un.
WORCESTER, Mass.
Roe. Worcester Young Men's Christian Assoc. $1. A. S. Roe.
Word signs made easy. Hardcastle, *Mrs.* M. A. $1. M. A. Hardcastle.
Wordingham, C: H. Central electrical stations. '01. '02(F15) il. 8°, $7.50. Lippincott.
Words of faith and hope. Westcott, B. F. $1.25. Macmillan.
Wordsworth, W: Selected poems; ed. by J. B. Seabury. '02(Ap26) 12°, (Ser. of classics.) 30 c. Silver.
Workingman's opportunity. Rowell, J. H. 5 c. Free Socialist.
Works, J: D. Practice pleading and forms adapt. to new rev. code of Indiana. 3d ed., rev. and enl. v. 1, 2, 3. '02(Je14) O. shp., $18. Clarke.
Works and days. Mabie, H. W. net, $1. Dodd.
Workshop wrinkles. Brown, W: N. net, $1. Van Nostrand.
World almanac and encyclopedia, 1902. '02 (Ja11) il. D. pap., 25 c. Press Pub.
World ser. *See* Appleton's.
World's epoch makers; ed. by O. Smeaton. D. $1.25. Scribner.
—Ritchie. Plato.
—Smeaton. The Medici and the Italian Renaissance.
Worlledge, Arth. J: Prayer. '02(Mr22) D. (Oxford lib. of practical theology.) $1.50. Longmans.
Wormell, R: *See* Hobbs, W. R. P.
WORSHIP.
Dobbins. Story of the world's worship. $2.25; $3.25. Dominion.
See also Church music;—Devotional exercises and meditations;—Prayer.
Worthington, Eliz. S. The tocsin—our children in peril. '01. '02(Mr22) 12°, pap., 25 c. Cubery.
Wounded beast. Jellison, E. A: 25 c. E. A: Jellison.
Wray, Angelina W. Jean Mitchell's school. '02(F15) il. D. $1.25. Public Sch. Pub.
Wretched Flea. Muller, M. 35 c. Flanagan.
Wright, D: H: Under the red cross: [poems.] '01. '02(F15) 12°, pap., 35 c. Biddle.
Wright, H: W., *comp.* Genealogy of the Wright family from 1639 to 1901. '01. '02 (Mr8) 8°, pap., 25 c. Pelham.
Wright, J. C. Body and soul: lectures del. in trance state. '02(My17) D. $1. J. C. Wright.
Wright, Ma. T. Aliens. '02(Mr22) D. net, $1.50. Scribner.
Wright, W. J. P. Dante and the Divine comedy. '02(My10) 8°, net, $1. Lane.
WRITING.
See Inscriptions;—Letter-writing;—Penmanship;—Typewriting.
Wurtzburg, Caro. A. *See* Ruskin, J:
Wyatt, Lucy M. L. Constance Hamilton. '02(Ap26) D. 50 c. Abbey Press.
Wyckoff, C: T. Feudal relations between the kings of Eng. and Scotland under the early Plantagenets. '02(Mr22) 8°, pap., net, $1. Univ. of Chic.
Wyllarde, Dolf. Story of Eden. '01. '02 (Mr1) 12°, $1.50. Lane.
Wynne, Jos. F. A blighted rose. '02(My24) D. $1.50. Angelus.
Wythes, G: Book of vegetables. '02(Je7) il. D. (Handbooks of practical gardening, v. 7.) $1. Lane.
X-RAYS.
See Roentgen rays.
XENOPHON.
See Attic prose.
YACHTS AND YACHTING.
Fisher. How to build a model yacht. $1. Rudder.
Mower. How to build a racing sloop. $1. Rudder.
Yacht club ser. 12°, $1.25 Lee & S.
—Adams. Money-maker. (3.)
Yale bicentennial pubs. 8°, net. Scribner.
—Beecher. Studies in evolution. $5.
—Bourne. Essays in hist. criticism. $2.
—Chittenden, *ed.* Studies in physiolog. chemistry. $4.
—Gibbs. Elem. principles in statistical mechanics.—Victor analysis. ea., $4.
—Goodell. Chapters on Greek metric. $2.
—Hopkins. India, old and new. $2.50.
—Morris. On principles and methods in Latin syntax. $2.
—Oertel. Study of language. $3.
—Two centuries' growth of Am. law. $4.
—Wells, *ed.* Studies from chemical lab'y of Sheffield Scientific School. 2 v. $7.50.
Yale lectures. *See* Brewer, D. J.
Yale studies in Eng.; ed. by A. S. Cook. O. pap. Holt.
—Boccaccio *and* Aretino. Earliest lives of Dante. 75 c. (10.)
YEAR BOOKS.
See Almanacs and annuals.
Year with the Mother-play. Proudfoot, A. H $1. Flanagan.
Yeats, W: B., *comp. and ed.* Irish fairy and folk tales. '02(My10) il. 12°, (Fairy lib.) $1. Burt.
Yellow fiend. Hector, *Mrs.* A. F. $1.50. Dodd.
Yelsew, Jean, *pseud.* *See* Smith, J: W.
Yerkes observatory bulletin. *See* Univ. of Chicago.
Yonge, Ctte. M., *comp.* Book of golden deeds of all times and all lands. '02(Ap12) 12°, (Home lib.) $1. Burt.
Young, Abram V. E. Elem. principles of chemistry. '01. '02(F22) 12°, net, 95 c. Appleton.
Young, Ella F. Ethics in the school. '02 (F22) D. (Cont. to educ., no. 4.) pap., net, 25 c. Univ. of Chic.
Young, Ella F. Isolation in the school. '01. '02(Ja11) S. (Univ. of Chic. cont. to education, no. 1.) pap., net, 50 c. Univ. of Chic.
Young, Ella F. Some types of modern educ. theory. '02(My24) D. (Univ. of Chic. cont. to education, no. 6.) pap., net, 25 c. Univ. of Chic.

Young, Filson. Mastersingers; with essay on Hector Berlioz. '02(Ap12) 12°, net, $1.50. Scribner.
Young, Hudson. Father Manners. '02(F22) D. $1. Abbey Press.
Young, J: R. Men and memories. Ed. de luxe. '02(Mr29) 2 v., subs., $5; in 1 v., 12°, subs., $3. Neely.
Young, Julia D. Black Evan. '02(Ap26) 12°, $1. Neely.
Young, Owen D., *and* Keen, Ja. T. Problems in practice and pleading at the common law. '02(Ap12) O. pap., 50 c. Mudge.
Young Howson's wife. Watrous, A. E. $1.50. Quail & W.
YOUNG MEN.
McLeod. Young man's problems. 50 c. Flanagan.
Warner. Young man in modern life. net, 85 c. Dodd.
See also Conduct of life;—Culture.
YOUNG PEOPLE.
Jordans. Danger of youth and a tried antidote. 15 c. Herder.
See also Children;—Girls;—Young men;—Young women.
Young People's Alliance ser. S. pap. Mattill & L.
—Staebler. Manual on the Book of books. 20 c.
Young people's Bible stories. '02(F1) 4 v., il. 4°, ea., $1.25. Saalfield.
YOUNG PEOPLE'S SOC. OF CHR. ENDEAVOR.
Clark. Training the church of the future; lectures, with special ref. to the Young People's Soc. of C. E. net, 75 c. Funk.
YOUNG WOMEN.
Sinclair. Unto you, young women. net, $1. Lippincott.
See also Conduct of life;—Culture;—Girls;—Young people;—Woman.
Youth's Companion ser. il. D. 30 c. Ginn.
—Northern Europe. (2.)
—Wide world. (1.)

Zaïre and Epitres. Voltaire, F. M. A. de. 50 c. Scott, F. & Co.
Zancis, *Mme.* —. How to tell fortunes by cards. '02(Mr15) S. pap., 25 c. Drake.
Zastrow, Karl. Wilhelm der Siegreiche; ed. by E. P. Ash. Authorized ed. '02(My24) 12°. (Siepmann's elem. Germ. ser.) net, 50 c. Macmillan.
Zelma, the mystic. Thurber, A. M. $1.25. Alliance.
ZINCALI.
Borrow. The Zincali. $2. Putnam.
Zitkala-sa. Old Indian legends. '01- '02 (Mr8) il. D. 50 c. Ginn.
Zittel, Karl A. v. Hist. of geology and palæontology to the end of the nineteenth century; tr. by M. M. Ogilvie-Gordon. '01-'02(Ap12) D. (Contemporary science ser.) $1.50. Scribner.
Zobo patriotic drill. Hatch, A. W. 15 c. Hints.
ZOOLOGY.
French. Animal activities. $1.20. Longmans.
Jordan *and* Heath. Animal forms. net, $1.10. Appleton.
Lindsay. Story of animal life. net, 35 c. Appleton.
Mudge. Text book of zoology. $2.50. Longmans.
See also Animals;—Evolution; — Invertebrates; — Protozoa.
ZOOTOMY.
See Dissection.
Zuckerkandl, Otto. Atlas and epitome of operative surgery; fr. 2d rev., enl. Germ. ed.; ed. by J. C. Da Costa. '02(Ap26) il. 12°, net, $3.50. Saunders.
ZUNI INDIANS.
Cushing. Zuñi folk tales. net, $3.50. Putnam.

RECORD OF SERIES.

ANTIGO PUBLISHING CO., Antigo, Wis.

No. *English Dialogues*, 12°, 10 c.

4. Stop that fiddle. Freund, E. J.
5. Schooling future housewives. Freund, E J.

A. L. BURT CO., 52 and 54 Duane St., New York.

Cornell Series of 12 mos., cl., 75 c.

Allan Quatermain. Haggard, H. R.
American girl in London. Duncan, S. J.
Biglow papers. Lowell, Ja. R.
Black Rock. Connor, R.
Blithedale romance. Hawthorne, N.
Book of golden deeds. Yonge, C. M.
Christmas stories. Dickens, C.
Cousin Maude. Holmes, M. J.
Don Quixote. Cervantes.
Education. Spencer, H.
Elizabeth and her German garden.
Gold bug, The. Poe, E. A.
Hidden hand, The. Southworth, E. D. E. N.
Hyperion. Longfellow, H. W.
Ishmael. Southworth, E. D. E. N.
Last confession, The. Caine, Hall.
Maggie Miller. Holmes, M. J.
Marble Faun. Hawthorne, N.
Merry Men. Stevenson, R. L.

W. B. CONKEY, CO., 351 Dearborn St., Chicago.

Homewood Series, 12°, cl., 36 c.

The marble faun. Hawthorne, N.
Beulah. Evans, A. J.
Moss Side. Harland, Marion.
Boy-path. Holland, John A.
Minister's Wooing. Stowe, Harriet Beecher.
Poe's tales. Poe, Edgar Allan.
Prisoners and captives. Merriam, Henry Seton.

Homewood Series.—Continued.

Tales from Tennyson. Allen, G. C.
In the Rockies. Kingston, W. H. G.
Tales from the Odyssey. Perry, W. C.
Pride and prejudice. Austen, J.
Cousin Maude. Holmes, M. J.
Homestead on hillside. Holmes, M. J.
English orphans. Holmes, M. J.
Rosmond. Holmes, M. J.
Lena Rivers. Holmes, M. J.
Tempest and sunshine. Holmes, M. J.
Meadow Brook. Holmes, M. J.
Macaria. Evans, A. J.
Inez. Evans, A. J.
Also in the Library Series, 12°, cl., 60 c.

G. W. DILLINGHAM CO., 119 W. 23d St., New York.

No. *Madison Sq. Library*, 12°, pap., 25 c.

165. Cris Rock. Reid, Mayne.
166. Invisible hands. Boggs, S. E.
167. The Meredith marriage. Payne, Harold.
168. Morris Julian's wife. Olmis, Eliz.
169. The Spanish treasure. Winter, E. C.
170. Wooing a widow. Koenig, Ewald A.
171. Mysterious Mr. Howard. Musick, John R.
172. Maud Morton. Calhoun, Alfred R.
173. The improvisatore. Andersen, Hans Christian.
174. Countess Obernau. Gordon, Julien.
175. Reunited.
176. The diamond seeker of Brazil. Lewis, Leon.

DODD, MEAD & CO., 372 Fifth Ave., New York.

Ajax Series of 12mos. Apply to pubs. for price.

110. Souls of passage. Barr, Amelia E.
111. The fanatics. Dunbar, Paul, L.
112. Pro patria. Pemberton, Max.

Phenix Series.

55. Miss Lou. Roe, E. P.
56. Charm and courtesy in letter-writing. Callaway, F. B.
57. Observations of Henry. Jerome, J. K.
58. Witch Winnie. Champney, E. W.
59. Master of his fate. Barr, A. E.
60. The rose of love. Teal, A.
61. An old-fashioned boy. Finley, M.
62. The love of Landry. Dunbar, P. L.
63. Ashes of roses. Wheatley, L. K.
64. Hilda Strafford. Harraden, B.

R. F. Fenno & Co., 9-11 East 16th St., New York.

Idle Hour Series, 12°, pap., 50 c.

Mistress Penwick. Payne, Dutton.
A missing hero. Alexander, Mrs.
Sin of Jasper Standish. "Rita."
The Castle Inn. Weyman, Stanley J.
In the name of a woman. Marchmont, A. W.
With ring of shield. Magee, Knox.
Tales of the ex-tanks. Cullen, Clarence Louis.
Colonel Carter of Cartersville. Smith, F. Hopkinson.
Forty modern fables. Ade, George.
Mr. Dooley's philosophy.

Laird & Lee, 263 Wabash Ave., Chicago.

No. *Pastime Series, 12°, pap., 25 c.*

250. Cousin Betty. Balzac, H. de.
251. The sabertooth. Kinder, S.

Lee & Shepard, 202 Devonshire St., Boston.

American Boys Series, 12°, cl., $1.

66. Facing the enemy: the life of Gen. Wm. Tecumseh Sherman. Headley, P. C.
67. Fight it out on this line: the life and deeds of Gen. U. S. Grant. Headley, P. C.
68. Fighting Phil: the life of Gen. Philip Henry Sheridan. Headley, P. C.
69. Old Salamander: the life of Admiral David G. Farragut. Headley, P. C.
70. Old Stars: the life of Gen. Ormsby M. Mitchell. Headley, P. C.
71. The miner boy and his monitor: the career of John Ericsson, engineer. Headley, P. C.
72. The young silver seekers. Cozzens, S. W.
73. Drake the sea king of Devon. Towle, G. M.
74. Magellan or, the first voyage around the world. Towle, G. M.
75. Marco Polo, his travels and adventures. Towle, G. M.
76. Pizarro, his adventures and conquests. Towle, G. M.
77. Raleigh, his voyages and adventures. Towle, G. Makepeace.
78. Vasco da Gama, his voyages and adventures. Towle, G. Makepeace.
79. The heroes and martyrs of invention. Towle, G. Makepeace.
80. Live boys, or Charlie and Nasho in Texas. Morecamp, A.
81. Live boys in the Black Hills, or, the young Texas gold hunters. Morecamp, A.
82. Down the west branch, or, camps and tramps around Katahdin. Farrar, C. A. J.
83. Eastward ho! or, adventures at Rangeley lakes. Farrar, C. A. J.
84. Up the North Branch, a summer's outing. Farrar, C. A. J.
85. Wild woods life, or, a trip to Parmachenee. Farrar, C. A. J.

American Girls Series, 12°, cl., $1.

31. 'Lisbeth Wilson. Blair, E. N.
32. Running to waste. Baker, G. M.
33. Barbara Thayer: her glorious career. Muller, A. J.
34. Katherine Earle. Trafton, A.
35. In the king's country. Douglas, A. M.

J. S. Ogilvie Publishing Co., 57 Rose St., New York.

New York Library, 12°, pap., 25 c.

1. The mystery of the Montauk Mills. Coolidge, E. L.
2. The mountain limited. Coolidge, E. L.
3. Gilt-edge Tom, conductor. Coolidge, E. L.
4. The Mossbank murder. Mills, Harry.
5. The woman stealer. Mills, Harry.
6. King Dan, the factory detective. Goode, G. W.
7. His downward path. Mills, Harry.
8. The overseer's daughter. Goode, G. W.
9. For the flag. Livingstone, W. C.
10. His mother's sin. Mellen, W. H.
11. The fortunes of a factory girl. Coolidge, E. L.
12. Fred Faithful, boy engineer. Coolidge, E. L.

No. *New York Library.—Continued.*

13. A fool and his money. Smythe, W. G.
14. Her fatal career. Mellen, W. H.
15. A Maine girl. Coolidge, E. L.
16. A daughter of Satan. Mills, Harry.
17. Ruled by fate. Smythe, W. G.
18. In folly's fetters. Stanley, F. R.
19. Storm Nest light. Mills, Harry.
20. The artist sisters. Mellen, W. H.
21. A confidential spy. Conrad, T. N.
22. Gaspar Desmond's passion. Grayson, P.
23. Mystery of a hansom cab. Hume, F. W.
24. The rector's secret. Abarbanell, J. R.
25. Her first adventure. Roe, E. G.
26. The captive bride. Cobb, Sylvanus, jr.
27. A bachelor in search of a wife. Swan, Annie S.
28. Inspector Henderson the Central Office detective. Hancock, Harrie I.
29. The double duel. Cobb, Sylvanus, jr.
30. The world's finger. Hanshew, T. W.

Peerless Series, 12°, pap., 25 c.

124. Francois Villon. Moorehead, George.
125. Count of Monte Cristo. Part 1. Dumas, Alex.
126. Count of Monte Cristo. Part 2. Dumas, Alex.

Sunset Series, 12°, pap., 25 c

164. John Ploughman's talks and pictures. Spurgeon, C. H.
165. Spurgeon's sermons. Spurgeon, C. H.
166. Five hundred merry laughs.
167. Some funny things said by clever people.
168. The umbrella mender. Harraden, Beatrice
169. Tour of the world in eighty days. Verne, Jules.
170. Life is worth living. Tolstoi, Leo.
171. As in a looking glass. Phillips, F. C.
172. Lady Valworth's diamonds. "The Duchess."
173. Tom Brown's school days. Hughes, T.
174. A house party. "Ouida."
175. Dark days. Conway, Hugh.
176. The merry men. Stevenson, R. L.
177. Mona's choice. Alexander, Mrs.
178. A mental struggle. "The Duchess."
179. Mrs. Rasher's curtain lectures.
180. Tin types taken in streets of New York. Quigg, Lemuel Ely.
181. Silas Snobden's office boy.
182. One thousand popular quotations. Ogilvie, J. S.
183. Reveries of an old maid.
184. Mahetible Hopkins on her travels. Hopkins, Mrs.
185. Ivan the fool. Tolstoi, Leo.
186. Inside the White House during war times.
187. The frozen pirate. Russell, W. Clark.
188. Mystery of a hansom cab. Hume, Fergus W
189. Called back. Conway, Hugh.
190. At bay. Alexander, Mrs.
191. A woman's temptation. Braeme, C. M.
192. Thrown on the world. Braeme, C. M.
193. Thorns and orange blossoms. Braeme, C. M.
194. Repented at leisure. Braeme, C. M.
195. Lord Lynne's choice. Braeme, C. M.
196. The false vow. Braeme, C. M.
197. Her second love. Braeme, C. M.
198. Her martyrdom. Braeme, C. M.
199. From out the gloom. Braeme, C. M.
200. The duke's secret. Braeme, C. M.
201. A broken wedding ring. Braeme, C. M.
202. Beyond pardon. Braeme, C. M.
203. At war with herself. Braeme, C. M.
204. The light that failed. Kipling, Rudyard.
205. Eureka recitations and readings, No. 1. Diehl, Anna B.
206. Eureka recitations and readings, No. 2. Diehl, Anna B.
207. Eureka recitations and readings, No. 3. Diehl, Anna B.
208. Eureka recitations and readings, No. 4. Diehl, Anna B.
209. Eureka recitations and readings, No. 5. Diehl, Anna B.
210. New Arabian nights. Stevenson, R. L.
211. Grimm's fairy tales. Brothers Grimm.
212. A change of air. Hope, Anthony.
213. Billy Bray, the king's son. Bourne, F. W.
214. Ten nights in a bar room. Arthur, T. S.
215. Maiwa's revenge. Haggard, H. Rider.
216. King Solomon's mines. Haggard, H. Rider.
217. She. Haggard, H. Rider.
218. Beaton's bargain. Alexander, Mrs.
219. Ralph Wilton's Weird. Alexander, Mrs.
220. By woman's wit. Alexander, Mrs.
221. Cousin Maude. Holmes, Mary J.
222. Rosamond. Holmes, Mary J.

Sunnyside Series, 12°, pap., 25 c.

No.
117. Francesca da Rimini. Moorhead, G.

Old Sleuth's Special Detective Series, 12°, pap., 25 c.

32. The giant detective; or, the feats of an athlete.
33. The cowboy detective.
34. The bicycle detective; or, Smart Jim.

Old Sleuth Special Detective Series.—Continued.

35. Dick, the boy detective; or, the streets of New York.
36. Aggravating Joe, the prince of mischief.
37. Jack the juggler's ordeal; or, tricks and triumphs.
38. Jack the juggler's trail. A story of magic.
39. A female ventriloquist; or, a girl's magic feats.
40. A desperate chance; or, Desmond Dare.
41. Detective Payne's "shadow"; or, a remarkable search.
42. Two wonderful detectives; or, Jack and Gil's Skill.
43. Saved by a detective; or, a beautiful fugitive.
44. The mystery man; or, fire-bomb Jack.
45. The fatal resemblance; or, a marvellous escape.
46. Nimble Ike, the detective; or, solving a mystery.
47. Bertie Bland the detective.
48. The West Point lieutenant; or, Arkie, the runaway.
49. From the streets to the footlights; or, Snap and Jenny.
50. The detective trio; or, the story of three country lads.

L. C. Page & Co., 200 Summer St., Boston.

Fleur-de-lis Library, 12°, pap., 50 c.

19. Captain Fracasse. Gautier, Theophile.
20. God—the king—my brother. Roulet, M. F. Nixon.
21. Omar Khayyám, a romance of Old Persia. Dole, Nathan Haskell.
22. Midst the wild Carpathians. Jokai, Maurus.
23. The Count of Nideck. Fiske, R. B.
24. Pretty Michal. Jokai, Maurus.

The Red Rose Library, 12°, pap., 50 c.

13. The gray house of the quarries. Norris, M. H.
14. The Guiana wilds. Rodway, Ja.
16. The archbishop's unguarded moment. Adams, Oscar Fay.
17. Winefred. Baring Gould, S.
18. The paths of the prudent. Fletcher, J. S.

G. P. Putnam's Sons, 27 and 29 W. 23d St., New York.

Hudson Library, 12°, pap., 50 c.

56. Uncle Jack's executors. Noble, A. L.
57. Eunice Lathrop, spinster. Noble, A. L.
58. Harvard stories. Post, Waldron K.
59. An artist in crime. Ottolengui, Rodrigues.
60. A conflict of evidence. Ottolengui, Rodrigues.
61. A modern wizard. Ottolengui, Rodrigues.
62. The story of Kennett. Taylor, Bayard.
63. A strange disappearance. Green, A. K.
64. Behind closed doors. Green, A. K.
65. Sword of Damocles. Green, A. K.
66. Cynthia Wakeham's money. Green, A. K.
67. The mill mystery. Green, A. K.
68. Dr. Izard. Green, A. K.
69. The old stone house. Green, A. K.
70. X. Y. Z. and 7 to 12. Green, A. K.
71. Patricia of the hills. Burrow, C. K.
72. One of the pilgrims. Fuller, Anna.
73. Love and honour. Carr, M. E.
74. Dwellers in the hills. Post, Melville D.
75. Smith Brunt, U. S. N. Post, Waldron K.
76. The final war. Tracy, Louis.

Street & Smith, 238 William St., New York.

Arrow Library, 12°, 10 c.

239. Nell Gwynn. Ainsworth, W. H.
240. Victor and vanquished. Hay, M. C.
241. Driven to bay. Marryat, F.
242. Dame Durden. "Rita."
243. Judith Shakespeare. Black, W.
244. Joseph Balsamo. Dumas, A.
245. Memoirs of a physician. Dumas, A.
246. Queen's necklace. Dumas, Alex.
247. Ange Pitou. Dumas, A.
248. Countess De Charny. Dumas, A.
249. The royal life guard.

Street & Smith's *Arrow Library.—Continued.*

No.
250. Andre De Taverny. Dumas, A.
251. The Chevalier de Maison Rouge. Dumas, A.
252. Cousin Maude. Holmes, M. J.
253. Rosamond Leyton. Holmes, M. J.

Bertha Clay Library, 12°, 10 c.

124. The hidden sin.
125. For a dream's sake.
126. The gambler's wife.
127. A great mistake.
128. Society's verdict.
129. Lady Gwendoline's dream.
130. The rival heiresses.
131. A bride from the sea.
132. A woman's trust.
133. A dream of love.
134. The sins of the father.
135. For love of her.
136. A loving maid.
137. A heart of gold.

Diamond Hand-Book Series, 12°, 10 c.

9. Art of boxing and self defense. Donovan

Eagle Library, 12°, 10 c.

246. True to herself. Walworth, J. H.
247. Within love's portals. Barrett, F.
248. Jeanne, Countess du Barry. Williams, H. L.
249. What love will do. Fleming, G.
250. A woman's soul. Garvice, C.
251. When love is true. Collins, M.
252. A handsome sinner. Delmar, D.
253. A fashionable marriage. Frazer, Mrs. A.
254. Little Miss Millions. Rathborne, St. G.
255. Little marplot. Sheldon, Mrs. G.
256. Thy name is woman. Howe, F. H.
257. A martyred love. Garvice, C.
258. An amazing marriage. Hayden, S.
259. By a golden cord. Delmar, D.
260. At a girl's mercy. Ludlum, J. K.

Eden Series, 12°, 10 c.

54. The doctor's wife. Braddon, M. E.
55. Birds of prey. Braddon, M. E.
56. The golden calf. Braddon, M. E.
57. Joshua Haggard's daughter. Braddon, M. E.
58. Barbara. Braddon, M. E.
59. Rupert Godwin. Braddon, M. E.
60. John Marchmont's legacy. Braddon, M. E.
61. The cloven foot. Braddon, M. E.
62. Nora's love test. Hay, M. C.
63. Lady Branksmere. "The Duchess."
64. With cupid's eyes. Marryat, F.
65. Nancy. Broughton, Rhoda.
66. Robert Ord's atonement. Carey, R. N.
67. The fair haired Alda. Marryat, F.
68. Mrs. Geoffrey. "The Duchess."

Magnet Detective Library, 12°, 10 c.

218. The man from London. Carter, N.
219. A hidden clew. Pierson, E. D.
220. The dumb witness. Carter, N.
221. Other people's money. Gaboriau, E.
222. A Prince of rogues. Carter, N.
223. Found dead. Strong, H.
224. Played to a finish. Carter, N.
225. Tracked by fate. Hume, Fergus.
226. A deal in diamonds. Carter, N.
227. From clew to climax. Harben, W. N.
228. A syndicate of rascals. Carter, N.
229. The Dexter bank robbery. Rockwood, H.
230. A race for ten thousand. Carter, N.
231. The crime of the golden gully. Rock, G.
232. The red signal. Carter, N.

Medal Library, 12°, 10 c.

136. From pole to pole. Stables, G.
137. The bush boys. Reid, M.
138. Striving for fortune. Alger, H.
139. Shore and ocean. Kingston, W. H. G.
140. The young buglers. Henty, G. A.
141. Ocean waifs. Reid, M.
142. The young explorer. Stables, G.
143. Hendricks the hunter. Kingston, W. H. G.
144. The boy tar. Reid, M.
145. Friends though divided. Henty, G. A.
146. Uncle Nat.
147. The cliff climbers. Reid, M.
148. The deerslayer. Cooper, J. F.
149. With Wolfe in Canada. Henty, G. A.
150. Frank Merriwell's school days. Standish, B. L.

DIRECTORY OF AMERICAN PUBLISHERS

January–June. 1902.

Abbatt.	Abbatt, William	281 Fourth Ave., New York.
Abbey Press.	Abbey Press	114 Fifth Ave., New York.
Acme Water Color.	Acme Water Color Co.	64 Wabash Ave., Chicago.
Advance.	Advance Pub. Co.	215 Madison St., Chicago.
Albany Diocesan Press.	Albany Diocesan Press	Albany, N. Y.
Allen, A. M.	Allen, Arthur M.	Troy, N. Y.
Allen, L. & S.	Allen, Lane & Scott	231 S. Fifth St., Philadelphia.
Alliance.	Alliance Publishing Co.	569 Fifth Ave., New York.
Allyn & B.	Allyn & Bacon	172 Tremont St., Boston.
Altemus.	Altemus, Henry, Co.	507–513 Cherry St., Philadelphia.
Am. Acad. Pol. Sci.	American Acad. of Pol. and Social Science	Station B, Philadelphia.
Am. Architect.	American Architect and Building News Co.	211 Tremont St., Boston.
Am. Bapt.	American Baptist Publication Soc.	1420 Chestnut St., Philadelphia.
Am. Bk.	American Book Co.	100 Washington Sq., E., New York.
Am. Code.	American Code Co.	83 Nassau St., New York.
	American Economic Assoc. *See* Macmillan.	
Am. Free Trade.	American Free Trade League	Boston.
Am. Law Bk.	American Law Book Co.	Cor. Liberty and William Sts., New York.
Am. Lumberman.	American Lumberman	315 Dearborn St., Chicago.
Am. News.	American News Co.	39 Chambers St., New York.
Am. Scenic.	American Scenic and Historic Preservation Society	Tribune Bldg., New York.
Am. Sports.	American Sports Pub. Co.	18 Park Pl., New York.
Am. S. S.	American Sunday School Union	1122 Chestnut St., Philadelphia.
Am. Tr.	American Tract Society	150 Nassau St., New York.
Am. Writers.	American Writers' Trust Co.	Box 102, Washington.
Anderson, J:	Anderson, John, Pub. Co.	183–187 N. Peoria St., Chicago.
Angel Press.	Angel Guardian Press	92 Ruggles St., Boston.
Angelus.	Angelus Pub. Co.	Detroit, Mich.
Anthony.	Anthony, E. & H. T., & Co.	122–124 Fifth Ave., New York.
Appleton.	Appleton, D., & Co.	72 Fifth Ave., New York.
Armstrong.	Armstrong, A. C., & Son	3–5 W. 18th St., New York.
Armstrong, G. M. S.	Armstrong, G. M. S.	Harrison Bldg., Philadelphia.
Arthur, Mrs. J. J.	Arthur, Mrs. J. J.	Austin, Tex.
Audel.	Audel, Theodore, & Co.	63 Fifth Ave., New York.
Augsburg.	Augsburg Pub. House	Minneapolis, Minn.
Auto Pen.	Auto Pen and Ink Mfg. Co.	Chicago.
Baird.	Baird, Henry Carey, & Co.	810 Walnut St., Philadelphia.
Baker & T.	Baker & Taylor Co.	33 E. 17th St., New York.
Baker, V. & Co.	Baker, Voorhis & Co.	66 Nassau St., New York.
Ball.	Ball, C. C.	Providence, R. I.
Bancroft-W.	Bancroft-Whitney Co.	438 Montgomery St., San Francisco.
Bang, M.	Bang, Mrs. Marie	Warren, Minn.
Banks.	Banks Law Pub. Co.	21 Murray St., New York.
Banks & Co.	Banks & Co.	Albany, N. Y.
Banta, T. M.	Banta, Theodore M.	New York.
Barbee & S.	Barbee & Smith, Agts. (now Bigham & Smith)	Nashville, Tenn.
Bardeen.	Bardeen, C. W.	406 S. Franklin St., Syracuse, N. Y.
Barnes.	Barnes, A. S., & Co.	156 Fifth Ave., New York.
Barnes, A. J.	Barnes, Arthur J.	St. Louis, Mo.
Barnes, W. F.	Barnes, W. F.	Spartanburg, S. C.
Barrie.	Barrie, George, & Son	1313 Walnut St., Philadelphia.
Barton, F. M.	Barton, Frank M.	617–625 Rose Bldg., Cleveland, O.
Bates & G.	Bates & Guild Co.	15 Exchange St., Boston.
Baughman.	Baughman Bros.	Frederick, Md.
Beale Press.	Beale Press	150 State St., Boston.
Beam.	Beam, Randolph R.	7 W. 18th St., New York.
Bell Bk.	Bell Book and Stationery Co.	Richmond, Va.
Belles, W: H:	Belles, William Henry	Potomac, Ill.
Bellows.	Bellows Bros. Co.	Chicago.
Bender, M.	Bender, Matthew	511–513 Broadway, Albany, N. Y.
Benziger.	Benziger Bros.	36 Barclay St., New York.
Berkeley.	Berkeley Bookstore	Berkeley, Cal.
Berlitz.	Berlitz & Co.	Madison Sq., New York.
Berry.	Berry, S.	Portland, Me.
Biddle.	Biddle, Drexel	228 S. 4th St., Philadelphia.
Birchard.	Birchard, C. C., & Co.	221 Columbus Ave., Boston.
Blade Pr.	Blade Printing and Paper Co.	Toledo, O.
Blakiston.	Blakiston's, P., Son & Co.	1012 Walnut St., Philadelphia.
Blanchard.	Blanchard, Isaac H., Co.	268 Canal St., New York.
Bliss & A.	Bliss & Amsden	340 S. State St., Ann Arbor, Mich.

Bloch.	Bloch Publishing Co.............................19 W. 22d St., New York.
Blue Sky Press.	Blue Sky Press.....................Woodlawn Ave. and 55th St., Chicago.
Blumenberg Press.	Blumenberg Press...............................218 William St., New York.
Boericke & T.	Boericke & Tafel...............................1011 Arch St., Philadelphia.
Bonnell.	Bonnell, Silver & Co...........................24 W. 22d St., New York.
Bk.-Lover.	Book-Lover Press ....53 W. 24th St., New York.
Booth.	Booth, Walter S., & Son...............................Minneapolis, Minn.
Bourguignon.	Bourguignon, L. H..Cohoes, N. Y.
Bowen-M.	Bowen-Merrill Co.................9 W. Washington St., Indianapolis, Ind.
Bradley, M.	Bradley, Milton, Co.......................49 Willow St., Springfield, Mass.
Bradley-W.	Bradley-White Co..............................220 Broadway, New York.
Brandt.	Brandt, Albert ....Trenton, N. J.
Brentano's.	Brentano's.....................................5-9 Union Sq., New York.
Brethren Pub. Ho.	Brethren Pub. House...Elgin Ill.
Brooklyn Eagle.	Brooklyn Daily Eagle.......................................Brooklyn, N. Y.
Brower.	Brower Bros..Crawfordsville, Ind.
Browne, W. S.	Browne, Walter S..Vineland, N. J.
Bryan, R. L.	Bryan, R. L., & Co..Columbia, S. C.
Bubier.	Bubier Pub. Co...Lynn, Mass.
Buckles.	Buckles, F. M., & Co..............................11 E. 16th St., New York.
Bu. Univ. Travel.	Bureau of University Travel.....................................Ithaca, N. Y.
Burrows.	Burrows Bros. Co...........................133 Euclid Ave., Cleveland, O.
Burt.	Burt, A. L., Co ....52-58 Duane St., New York.
Bushrod. Lib.	Bushrod Library..............................1717 Green St., Philadelphia.
Byrne.	Byrne, John, & Co..........................1322 F St., N. W., Washington.
Caledonian.	Caledonian Co...St. Johnsbury, Vt.
Callaghan.	Callaghan & Co....................................114 Monroe St., Chicago.
Cambridge.	Cambridge Encyclopædia Co........P. O. Box 160, Madison Sq., New York.
Campbell, H. W.	Campbell, Hardy W..Holdrege, Neb..
Case.	Case, Lockwood & Brainerd Co....................................Hartford, Ct.
Caspar.	Caspar, C. N., Co.........................437 E. Water St., Milwaukee, Wis.
Cassell.	Cassell & Co.......................................7-9 W. 18th St., New York
Caxton Bk.	Caxton Book Co..Cleveland, O.
Caxton Club.	Caxton Club...Chicago.
Centennial.	Centennial School Supply Co......................................Denver, Col.
Cen. Law Journ.	Central Law Journal Co..............................919 Olive St., St. Louis.
Century Co.	Century Co......................................33 E. 17th St., New York.
Charleston Daily Mail	Charleston Daily Mail Pub. Co..............................Charleston, W. Va.
Chemical.	Chemical Pub. Co...Easton, Pa.
Chic. Leg. News.	Chicago Legal News Co...................................87 Clark St., Chicago.
Clark, C. M.	Clark, C. M., Publishing Co..........................211 Tremont St., Boston.
Clarke.	Clarke, Robert, Co.................................31-35 E. 4th St., Cincinnati.
Clarke, J: B.	Clarke, John B., Co...Manchester, N. H.
Clarke, W: B.	Clarke, William B., Co......................Park and Tremont Sts., Boston.
Cleveland Armature.	Cleveland Armature Works...Cleveland, O.
Cleveland Pr.	Cleveland Printing and Pub. Co....................................Cleveland, O.
Clifford & L.	Clifford & Lawton...............................19 Union Sq., W. New York.
Clinic.	Clinic Publishing Co...Chicago.
Coates.	Coates, Henry T., & Co........................1222 Chestnut St., Philadelphia.
Cockcroft.	Cockcroft, James D...Northport, N. Y.
Colegrove.	Colegrove, E. H..................................94 Washington St., Chicago.
Colonial.	Colonial Press..Fort Wayne, Ind.
Columbia Press.	Columbia Press.................................Lock Box 278, Washington.
Commercial.	Commercial Press..Brighton, N. Y.
Comstock, W: T.	Comstock, William T...............................23 Warren St., New York.
Comstock Pub.	Comstock Pub. Co...Ithaca, N. Y.
Confederate Veteran.	Confederate Veteran..Nashville, Tenn.
Congdon,	Congdon & Britnell...Toronto, Can.
Conkey.	Conkey, W. B., Co...............................351 Dearborn St., Chicago.
Courier Journ.	Courier Journal Co., Office of..................................Louisville, Ky.
Courier Pr.	Courier Printing Co..Orrville, O.
Crane.	Crane & Co..Topeka, Kan.
Cronholm, N. N:	Cronholm, Neander Nicholas.........................91 Dearborn St., Chicago.
Croscup.	Croscup & Sterling Co...............................135 Fifth Ave., New York.
Crowell.	Crowell, Thomas Y., & Co.........................426 W. Broadway, New York.
Crowell & K.	Crowell & Kirkpatrick Co..Springfield, O.
Cubery.	Cubery & Co..San Francisco.
Cuffel, C: A.	Cuffel, Charles A..Doylestown, Pa.
Culley, F. C.	Culley, Frank Clinton..Kenosha, Wis.
Cumberland.	Cumberland Presbyterian Pub. House.........................Nashville, Tenn.
Cumberland Press.	Cumberland Press..Nashville, Tenn.
Curlander.	Curlander, M..........................208 N. Calvert St., Baltimore, Md.

Cushing, J. S.	Cushing, J. S., & Co....Norwood, Mass.
Danish Luth.	Danish Luth. Pub. House....Blair, Neb.
Darrow.	Darrow, Erastus, & Co....214 E. Main St., Rochester, N. Y.
Davidson, Mrs. H. A.	Davidson, Mrs. H. A....1 Sprague Pl., Albany, N. Y.
Davis.	Davis, F. A., Co.... 1914 Cherry St., Philadelphia.
Dayton, E. W.	Dayton, Edwin W....763 Fifth Ave., New York.
Deel, G: A.	Deel, George A....Poughkeepsie, N. Y.
Democrat Pr. Co.	Democrat Printing Co....Madison, Wis.
Dempster.	Dempster, L. R....35 Glen Park Ave., San Francisco.
Dibdin Club.	Dibdin Club (M. W. Greenhalgh, Sec.)....1135 Madison Ave., New York.
Dickerman.	Dickerman, Henry A., & Son....55 Franklin St., Boston.
Dillingham, G: W.	Dillingham, George W., Co....119 W. 23d St., New York.
Dissell.	Dissell Pub. Co....Hartford, Ct.
Ditson.	Ditson, Oliver, Co....457 Washington St., Boston.
Dodd.	Dodd, Mead & Co....372 Fifth Ave., New York.
Dole, N. H.	Dole, Nathan Haskell....Jamaica Plain, Mass.
Dominion.	Dominion Co....134 E. Van Buren St., Chicago.
Donohue.	Donohue, M. A., & Co....407-429 Dearborn St., Chicago.
Doubleday, P.	Doubleday, Page & Co....34 Union Sq., E., New York.
Drake.	Drake, Frederick J., & Co....352-356 Dearborn St., Chicago.
Dresden.	Dresden Pub. Co. (C. P. Farrell)....5-7 E. 16th St., New York.
Dressler.	Dressler & Co....2203 Gladys Ave., Chicago.
Drexel.	Drexel, George W. Childs....Ledger Bldg., Philadelphia.
Dufresne.	Dufresne, Frank P....85 E. 4th St., St. Paul, Minn.
Dukesmith, F. H.	Dukesmith, Frank H....Charlestown, Jefferson Co., W. Va.
Du Mont.	Du Mont, E. R....303 Dearborn St., Chicago.
Dustin, E.	Dustin, Eddie....1210 Olive, St., St. Louis.
Dutton.	Dutton, E. P., & Co....31 W. 23d St., New York.
Earle.	Earle, James H....178 Washington St., Boston.
Earle, S. C.	Earle, Stephen Carpenter....Worcester, Mass.
East Tenn.	East Tennessee Pub. Co....Greeneville, Tenn.
Eaton & M.	Eaton & Mains....150 Fifth Ave., New York.
Ebersole, E. C.	Ebersole, E. C....Toledo, Ia.
Eckler.	Eckler, Peter....35 Fulton St., New York.
Educ. Pub.	Educational Publishing Co.... 50 Bromfield St., Boston.
Effingham Dem.	Effingham Democrat....Effingham, Ill.
Ehrlich, B.	Ehrlich, Mrs. Bertha....Berlin, Wis.
Eichelberger.	Eichelberger, B. G....308 N. Charles St., Baltimore, Md.
Elder.	Elder, D. P., & Shepard, Morgan....238 Post St., San Francisco.
Elec. World.	Electrical World and Engineer....120 Liberty St., New York.
Ellsworth.	Ellsworth & Brey....Detroit, Mich.
Elmore, J. B.	Elmore, James B....Alamo, Ind.
Elston Press.	Elston Press....New Rochelle, N. Y.
Engelhard.	Engelhard, George P., & Co....358 Dearborn St., Chicago.
Engineering.	Engineering and Mining Journal....261 Broadway, New York.
Engineering Mag.	Engineering Magazine....220 Broadway, New York.
Estes.	Estes, Dana, & Co.... 208-218 Summer St., Boston.
Evangelical Press.	Evangelical Press....Harrisburg, Pa.
	Evening Post. *See* N. Y. Evening Post.
Excelsior.	Excelsior Publishing House....8 Murray St., New York.
Fenno.	Fenno, R. F., & Co.... 11 E. 16th St., New York.
Ferris.	Ferris & Leach....29 N. 7th St., Philadelphia.
Fetter.	Fetter Law Book Co....Louisville, Ky.
Fisher, J: I.	Fisher John I., Pub. Co....Cincinnati.
Flanagan.	Flanagan, A., Co....266-68 Wabash Ave., Chicago.
Flood.	Flood, T. H., & Co....149 Monroe St., Chicago.
Forbes.	Forbes & Co....P. O. Box 1478, Boston.
Fords.	Fords, Howard & Hulbert.... Bible House, New York.
Forest.	Forest and Stream Pub. Co....346 Broadway, New York.
Foster & R.	Foster & Reynolds.... 346 Broadway, New York.
Fradenburgh, O. P.	Fradenburgh, O. P....Liberty, N. Y.
Free Socialist.	Free Socialist Union....Chicago.
Frost, W: D.	Frost, William Dodge....Madison, Wis.
Fuller.	Fuller Anatomical Co....Grand Rapids, Mich.
Funk.	Funk & Wagnalls Co....30 Lafayette Pl., New York.
Gael.	Gael Pub. Co....150 Nassau St., New York.
Gammel.	Gammel Book Co....Austin, Tex.
Gebbie.	Gebbie & Co.... 1710 Market St., Philadelphia.
Genealog. Soc.	Genealogical Soc'y of Western New York....Syracuse, N. Y.
Gervais.	Gervais Pub. Co....10 E. 17th St., New York.
Gibbs, M. W.	Gibbs, Mifflin W....Washington.
Gilbert Bk.	Gilbert Book Co....205 N. 4th St., St. Louis.
Gill.	Gill, Watson....Syracuse, N. Y.

Gillan.	Gillan, S. Y., & Co	Milwaukee, Wis.
Ginn.	Ginn & Co.	29 Beacon St., Boston.
Globe Sch. Bk.	Globe School Book Co.	103 Fifth Ave., New York.
Goodspeed.	Goodspeed, Charles E.	5a Park St., Boston.
Goodyear-M.	Goodyear-Marshall Pub. Co.	Cedar Rapids, Ia.
Gorham.	Gorham, Edwin S.	285 Fourth Ave., New York.
Gospel Trumpet.	Gospel Trumpet Pub. Co.	Moundsville, West Va.
Gould, W. R.	Gould, W. Reid	139 Nassau St., New York.
Gov. Pr.	Government Printing Office	Washington.
Grafton Press.	Grafton Press	70 Fifth Ave., New York.
Grant, W: D.	Grant, William D.	27 Rose St., New York.
Graves.	Graves & Steinbarger	15 Court Sq., Boston.
Griffin, A.	Griffin, Albert	Topeka, Kan.
Grosset.	Grosset & Dunlap	11 E. 16th St., New York.
Hadley Pr.	Hadley Printing Co.	Toledo, O.
Hansell.	Hansell, F. F., & Bro.	714 Canal St., New Orleans, La.
Hardcastle, M. A.	Hardcastle, Mrs. M. A.	Mensing Bldg., Atlantic City, N. J.
Hardham.	Hardham, L. J.	243 Market St., Newark, N. J.
Hardy, P. & Co.	Hardy, Pratt & Co.	44 Federal St., Boston.
Harison, W: B.	Harison, William Beverley	65 E. 59th St., New York.
Harper.	Harper & Bros.	Franklin Sq., New York.
Harper, F. P.	Harper, Francis P.	14 W. 22d St., New York.
Hart, R. M.	Hart, Robert M., Ltd.	Honesdale, Pa.
Harvard Law.	Harvard Law Review Assoc.	Cambridge, Mass.
Harvey.	Harvey, Fred	Kansas City, Mo.
Hausauer.	Hausauer, G. M., & Son	Buffalo, N. Y.
Heath.	Heath, D. C., & Co.	120 Boylston St., Boston.
Heidelberg.	Heidelberg Press	1308 Arch St., Philadelphia.
Helburn.	Helburn, William	10 E. 16th St., New York.
Helman-T.	Helman-Taylor Co.	23–27 Euclid Ave, Cleveland, O.
Henneberry.	Henneberry Co.	409–429 Dearborn St., Chicago.
Henry, W: E.	Henry, William E.	State Lib'y, Indianapolis, Ind.
Herder.	Herder, B.	17 S. Broadway, St. Louis.
Hessling.	Hessling, Bruno	64 E. 12th St., New York.
Hill, J: A.	Hill, John A.	Franklin, Pa.
Hinds.	Hinds & Noble	31–35 W. 15th St., New York.
Hints.	Hints Pub. Co.	South Byron, N. Y.
Hist. Pub.	Historical Pub. Co.	36 St. James Ave., Toronto, Can.
Hoffman, H. C.	Hoffman, Harry C.	Harrisburg, Pa.
Holliswood.	Holliswood Press	Hollis, N. Y.
Holmes, C. H.	Holmes, C. H.	2303 Euclid Ave., Cleveland, O.
Holst.	Holst Pub. Co.	Boone, Ia.
Holt.	Holt, Henry, & Co.	29 W. 23d St., New York.
Home.	Home Pub. Co.	3 E. 14th St., New York.
Home Gardening.	Home Gardening Assoc.	Cleveland, O.
Home Pub.	Home Publishing Co.	Climax, Mich.
Honeyman.	Honeyman & Co.	Plainfield, N. J.
Houghton, M. & Co.	Houghton, Mifflin & Co.	4 Park St., Boston.
Howard.	Howard Pub. Co.	Detroit, Mich.
Howard, G: E.	Howard, George E., & Co.	Washington
Hudson, H. B.	Hudson, Horace B.	Bank of Commerce Bldg., Minneapolis, Minn.
Hudson-K.	Hudson-Kimberly Pub. Co.	1014 Wyandotte St., Kansas City, Mo.
Hufford, D: A.	Hufford, David A., & Co.	226 W. 6th St., Los Angeles, Cal.
Huguenot.	Huguenot Pub. Co.	Carlisle, Pa.
Huidekoper, E. G.	Huidekoper, Miss E. G.	504 Chestnut St., Meadville, Pa.
Humphrey, G: W.	Humphrey, George W.	26 Brattle St., Boston.
Hurst & Co.	Hurst & Co.	Luray, Va.
Hyde.	Hyde & Manuel	1401 14th Ave., S. E., Minneapolis, Minn.
Index Digest.	Index Digest Pub. Co.	Grand Rapids, Mich.
Indianapolis Sentinel.	Indianapolis Sentinel Co.	Indianapolis, Ind.
Informant.	Informant Co.	Cleveland, O.
Inland Pub.	Inland Publishing Co.	Terre Haute, Ind.
Int. Detective.	International Detective Agency	Milwaukee, Wis.
Interstate.	Interstate Book Co.	Chicago.
Jacobs.	Jacobs, George W., & Co.	103 S. 15th St., Philadelphia.
Jamieson-H.	Jamieson-Higgins Co.	324 Dearborn St., Chicago.
Jellison, E. A:	Jellison, Edwin Augustus	Santiago, Minn.
Jenkinson, I:	Jenkinson, Isaac	Richmond, Ind.
Jenkins, W: R.	Jenkins, Wm. R.	851 Sixth Ave., New York.
Jennings.	Jennings & Pye, Agts.	220 W. 4th St., Cincinnati, O.
Jewish Pub.	Jewish Pub. Soc. of America	1015 Arch St., Philadelphia.
Johns Hopkins.	Johns Hopkins Press	Baltimore, Md.
Johnson, B. F.	Johnson, B. F., Pub. Co.	901–905 E. Main St., Richmond, Va.

Johnson, T. & J. W.	Johnson, T. & J. W., Co.	535 Chestnut St., Philadelphia.
Jones, B. C.	Jones, B. C., & Co.	Austin, Tex.
Journal Pr.	Journal Printing Co.	Coffeyville, Kan.
Journal Pr. Co.	Journal Printing Co.	Minneapolis, Minn.
Journal Pub.	Journal Publishing Co.	Meriden, Ct.
Judd.	Judd, Orange, Co.	52 Lafayette Pl., New York.
Keefe-D.	Keefe-Davidson Law Book Co.	St. Paul, Minn.
Kellogg.	Kellogg, E. L., & Co.	61 E. 9th St., New York.
Kennebec Journ.	Kennebec Journal, Press of	Augusta, Me.
Kerr.	Kerr, Charles H., & Co.	56 Fifth Ave., Chicago.
Keystone.	Keystone (The)	19th and Brown Sts., Philadelphia.
Kilner.	Kilner, H. L., & Co.	824 Arch St., Philadelphia.
Kingsley-B.	Kingsley-Barnes & Neuner Co.	Los Angeles, Cal.
Kirgate Press.	Kirgate Press	Canton, Pa.
Kirk.	Kirk, Eleanor	696 Greene Ave., Brooklyn, N. Y.
KnickerbockerPress.	Knickerbocker Press	29 W. 23d St., New York.
Knight.	Knight & Millet	221 Columbus Ave., Boston.
Kuhl.	Kuhl, R. J.	Mansfield, O.
Kyger.	Kyger Music Co.	Waco, Tex.
Laird.	Laird & Lee	263 Wabash Ave., Chicago.
Lakeside Press.	Lakeside Press (R. R. Donnelley & Sons Co.)	Plymouth Place, Chicago.
Lane.	Lane, John	67 Fifth Ave., New York.
Laning.	Laning Printing Co.	Norwalk, O.
Law, J. D.	Law, James Duff	Lancaster, Pa.
Lawton, W: H:	Lawton, William Henry	108 W. 43d St., New York.
Lawyers' Bk.	Lawyers' Book Co.	Boston
Lawyers' Co-op.	Lawyers' Co-operative Pub. Co.	Rochester, N. Y.
Lea.	Lea Bros. & Co.	706 Sansom St., Philadelphia.
League Pol. Educ.	League of Political Education	23 W. 44th St., New York.
Lee & S.	Lee & Shepard	202 Devonshire St., Boston.
Leeds.	Leeds, W. H.	Salem, Ore.
Lemcke.	Lemcke & Buechner	812 Broadway, New York.
Lentilhon.	Lentilhon & Co.	150 Fifth Ave., New York.
Lewis, A. F.	Lewis, Alonzo F.	Fryeburg, Me.
Lexington.	Lexington, Pub. Co.	Lexington, Mass.
Lib. Bu.	Library Bureau	530 Atlantic Ave., Boston.
Lippincott.	Lippincott, J. B., Co.	Washington Sq., Philadelphia.
Little, W. C.	Little, W. C., & Co.	525 Broadway, Albany, N. Y.
Little, B. & Co.	Little, Brown & Co.	254 Washington St., Boston.
Littlefield.	Littlefield, G. E.	67 Cornhill, Boston.
Longmans.	Longmans, Green & Co.	91–93 Fifth Ave., New York.
Lord, W: R.	Lord, Wiliiam Rogers	Portland, Or.
Lord, W: S.	Lord, William S.	Evanston, Ill.
Lothrop.	Lothrop Pub. Co.	530 Atlantic Ave., Boston.
Lowdermilk.	Lowdermilk, W. H., & Co.	1424–26 F St., Washington.
Lyon.	Lyon, James B., Co.	36 Beaver St., Albany, N. Y.
McBride.	McBride, D. H., & Co.	31 Barclay St., New York.
McCallum.	McCallum & Hofer Cattle Co.	Wauneta, Neb.
McClure, P.	McClure, Phillips & Co.	141–155 E. 25th St., New York.
McClurg.	McClurg, A. C., & Co.	215–221 Wabash Ave., Chicago.
McCulloch, S: J.	McCulloch, Samuel J.	Thayer Bldg., Kansas City, Mo.
Macdonald, J.	Macdonald, J.	Topeka, Kan.
Macdonough, R.	Macdonough, Rodney	205 Washington St., Boston.
McEnally, R. M.	McEnally, Robert M.	Honesdale, Pa.
McGee, J. B.	McGee, Joseph B., Sr.	Leesville, La.
MacGowan.	Macgowan & Cooke Co.	Chattanooga, Tenn.
McGraw	McGraw Publishing Co.	120 Liberty St., New York.
Macmillan.	Macmillan Co.	66 Fifth Ave., New York.
Maple.	Maple Pub. Co.	156 Broadway, New York.
Marine Engineering.	Marine Engineering, Office of	309 Broadway, New York.
Markley.	Markley, Horace	6 Vestry St., New York.
Marks, J. A.	Marks, Jeannette A.	Mt. Holyoke College, South Hadley, Mass.
Marlier.	Marlier & Co.	173 Tremont St., Boston.
Marshall.	Marshall & Bruce	Nashville, Tenn.
Martin, F: W.	Martin, Fred W.	Waukegan, Ill.
Martindale.	Martindale, James B.	142 La Salle St., Chicago.
Mason Pub.	Mason Publishing and Printing Co.	Syracuse, N. Y.
Mass. New-Ch. Un.	Massachusetts New-Church Union	16 Arlington St., Boston.
Matthews-N.	Matthews-Northrup Works	179 Washington St., Buffalo, N. Y.
Mattill & L.	Mattill & Lamb	265-275 Woodland Ave., Cleveland, O.
Mayer.	Mayer & Miller	85 Fifth Ave., Chicago.
Maynard, M. & Co.	Maynard, Merrill & Co.	29–33 E. 19th St., New York.
Mequon Club.	Mequon Club	Milwaukee, Wis.

Meyer, E. C.	Meyer, Ernest C.......Madison, Wis.
Michie.	Michie Co.......Charlottesville, Va.
Mich. Pol. Sci.	Michigan Political Science Association.......Ann Arbor, Mich.
Millet.	Millet, J. B. Co.......221 Columbus Ave., Boston.
Mitchell, F. L.	Mitchell, Frances Letcher.......Atlanta, Ga.
Moody.	Moody, John, & Co.......35 Nassau St., New York.
Morse.	Morse Co.......96 Fifth Ave., New York.
Morton.	Morton, John P., & Co.......440–446 W. Main St., Louisville, Ky.
Mosher, T: B.	Mosher, Thomas B.......45 Exchange St., Portland, Me.
Moulton Pub.	Moulton Publishing Co.......Buffalo, N. Y.
Mudge.	Mudge, Alfred, & Son.......24 Franklin St., Boston.
Mullen, W:	Mullen, William.......Chicago.
Mullin.	Mullin, George H.......Cedar Rapids, Ia.
Munn.	Munn & Co.......361 Broadway, New York.
Murphy.	Murphy, John, & Co.......44 W. Baltimore St., Baltimore, Md.
Mutual Bk.	Mutual Book Co.......79 Franklin St., Boston.
Mutual Pub.	Mutual Pub. Co.......57 Warren St., New York.
Mutual Pub. Co.	Mutual Publishing Co.......67 E. Alabama St., Atlanta, Ga.
Myers, R. L.	Myers, R. L., & Co.......122 Market St., Harrisburg, Pa.
Nat. Surety.	National Surety Co.......Dept. of Bonded Attorneys, New York.
Nat. Temp	National Temperance Soc. and Pub'n House.......3 W. 18th St., New York.
Neale.	Neale Pub. Co.......431 Eleventh St., Washington.
Neely.	Neely, F. T., Co.......114 Fifth Ave., New York.
Nelson.	Nelson, Thomas, & Sons.......37–41 E. 18th St., New York.
Nelson, S: A.	Nelson, Samuel Armstrong.......16–18 Park Pl., New York.
New Amsterdam.	New Amsterdam Book Co.......156 Fifth Ave., New York.
New Jersey.	New Jersey, Department of State.......Trenton, N. J.
N. Y. Eve. Post.	New York Evening Post Pub. Co.......206 Broadway, New York.
N. Y. Labor News	New York Labor News Co.......2–6 New Reade St., New York.
N. Y. Law.	New York Law Book Co.......303 Broadway, New York.
N. Y. State Lib.	New York State Library.......Albany, N. Y.
N. Y. Tax Reform.	New York Tax Reform Assoc.......Room 30, 111 Broadway, New York.
	New York Tribune. *See* Tribune Ass'n.
	New York World. *See* Press Pub. Co.
Newkirk, J. B. C.	Newkirk, Mrs. J. B. C.......La Porte, Ind.
Newson.	Newson & Co.......15 E. 17th St., New York.
Niccolls.	Niccolls, Francis A., & Co.......212 Summer St., Boston.
North, J.	North, Jacob, & Co.......Lincoln, Neb.
Nutshell.	Nutshell, Pub. Co.......1057 Third Ave., New York.
O'Bannon.	O'Bannon, J. H.......Richmond, Va.
Occidental.	Occidental Pub. Co.......Oakland, Cal.
Ogilvie.	Ogilvie, J. S., Pub. Co.......57 Rose St., New York.
Old South Work.	Old South Work, Directors of.......Old South Meeting House, Boston.
Open Court.	Open Court Publishing Co.......324 Dearborn St., Chicago.
Or. Mining Journ.	Oregon Mining Journal.......Grants Pass, Or.
Ormsby, F. E.	Ormsby, Frank Earl & Co.......358 Dearborn St., Chicago.
Otis.	Otis, H. H., & Sons.......11 W. Swan St., Buffalo, N. Y.
Outlook.	Outlook Co.......287 Fourth Ave., New York
Owl Press.	Owl Press.......Burlington, Vt.
Oxford Univ.	Oxford University Press (Am. Branch).......91–93 Fifth Ave., New York.
Pafraets.	Pafraets Book Co.......Troy, N. Y.
Page, H. W.	Page, Howard W.......Philadelphia.
Page, L. C.	Page, L. C., & Co.......200 Summer St., Boston.
Palm.	Palm, Charles W., Co.......Los Angeles, Cal.
Pamphlet.	Pamphlet Pub. Co.......342-350 Geary St., Pacific Grove, Cal.
Parsons, H: B.	Parsons, Henry B.......105 Hudson Ave., Albany, N. Y.
Patterson & W.	Patterson & White Co.......518 Minor St., Philadelphia.
Pease-L.	Pease-Lewis Co.......102 Church St., New Haven, Ct.
Pediatrics Lab'y.	Pediatrics Laboratory.......254 W. 54th St., New York.
Pelham.	Pelham & King.......Middletown, Ct.
Pelton.	Pelton, Edward R.......19 E. 16th St., New York.
Penn. Soc. N. Y.	Pennsylvania Soc. of New York (Barr Ferree, Sec'y.). 7 Warren St., New York.
Pepper.	Pepper Pub. Co.......Philadelphia.
Phillips.	Phillips, Isaac Newton.......Springfield, Ill.
Phonograph.	Phonographic Institute Co.......222 W. 4th St., Cincinnati, O.
Physical Culture.	Physical Culture Pub. Co.. Townsend Bldg., 25th St. and B'way, New York.
Pierce & Z.	Pierce & Zahn.......633 17th St., Denver, Col.
Pilgrim Press.	Pilgrim Press.......14 Beacon St., Boston; 175 Wabash Ave., Chicago.
Pilot.	Pilot Pub. Co.......597 Washington St., Boston.
Pitman.	Pitman, Isaac, & Sons.......33 Union Sq., New York.
Plummer, M. W.	Plummer, Mary Wright.......Pratt Institute, Brooklyn, N. Y.
Plymouth Rock.	Plymouth Rock Squab Co.......Boston.
Pontiac.	Pontiac Pub. Co.......Pontiac, Mich.
Poor.	Poor, H. V., & H. W.......44 Broad St., New York.

Popular.	Popular Pub. Co. ....335 Broadway, New York.
Pott.	Pott, James, & Co. ....119 W. 23d St., New York.
Potter, W. W.	Potter, W. W., Co. ....91 Bedford St., Boston.
Pratt Merc.	Pratt Mercantile and Pub. Co. ....Denver, Col.
Presb. Bd.	Presbyterian Board of Publication....1319 Walnut St., Philadelphia.
Presb. Pub.	Presbyterian Com. of Publication....1001 Main St., Richmond, Va.
Press Pub.	Press Pub. Co. ....World Bldg., New York.
Presser.	Presser, Theodore....1708 Chestnut St., Philadelphia.
Preston.	Preston & Rounds Co. ....98 Westminster St., Providence, R. I.
Providence Journ.	Providence Journal, Office of....Providence, R. I.
Providence Telegram.	Providence Telegram Pub. Co. ....Providence, R. I.
Public Policy.	Public Policy Publishing Co. ....132 Market St., Chicago.
Public Sch. Pub.	Public School Pub. Co. ....Bloomington, Ill.
Pub. Weekly.	Publishers' Weekly (The), Office of....298 Broadway, New York.
Pub. Ho. of M. E. Ch., So.	Publishing House of the Meth. Epis. Church, South, (Bigham & Smith, Agts.), Nashville, Tenn.
Pustet.	Pustet, F., & Co. ....52 Barclay St., New York.
Putnam.	Putnam's, G. P., Sons....29 W. 23d St., New York.
Quail & W.	Quail & Warner....23 Park Row, New York.
Quinius, J: G.	Quinius, John G. ....4th and Main Sts., Dayton, O.
Radical.	Radical Publishing Co. .... 17 S. 16th St., Philadelphia.
Railroad Gazette.	Railroad Gazette....32 Park Pl., New York.
R'way Educ.	Railway Educational Assoc....227 Monroe St., New York.
Ralston.	Ralston Pub. Co. ....Washington.
Rand, McN. & Co.	Rand, McNally & Co. ....160-174 Adams St., Chic.; 142 Fifth Ave., New York.
Reed, G: B.	Reed, George B. ....4 Park St., Boston.
Reed Pub.	Reed Pub. Co. ....Denver, Col.
Reedy, W: M.	Reedy, William M. ....*The Mirror*, Ozark Bldg., St. Louis.
Regan.	Regan Printing House....Chicago.
Remick.	Remick, Schilling & Co. ....277 Broadway, New York.
Revell.	Revell, Fleming H., Co. ...156 5th Ave., New York; 63 Wash'n St., Chicago.
Reynolds, A. B.	Reynolds, Alphæus B. ....Battle Creek, Mich.
Ricketts.	Ricketts, C. L. ....First Nat. Bank Bldg., Chicago.
Rigby.	Rigby, George H. ....1113 Arch St., Philadelphia.
Rigby, W. O.	Rigby, Will O. ....Topeka, Kan.
Riggs.	Riggs Publishing Co. ....1123 Broadway, New York.
Roberts, W: W.	Roberts, William W. ....Portland, Me.
Robertson, A. M.	Robertson, A. M. ....126 Post St., San Francisco.
Roe, A. S.	Roe, Alfred S. ....Worcester, Mass.
Rogers, W. M.	Rogers, W. M., & Co. ....Montgomery, Ala.
Root & C.	Root, Frank A., and Connelley, William Elsey....Topeka, Kan.
Rowland, A. J.	Rowland, A. J. ....1420 Chestnut St. Philadelphia.
Roycrofters.	Roycrofters (The). ....East Aurora, N. Y.
Rudder.	Rudder Publishing Co. ....9 Murray St., New York.
Rumford Press.	Rumford Press....Concord, N. H.
Russell.	Russell, R. H. .... 3-7 W. 29th St., New York.
Russell, H. L.	Russell, Harry Luman....Madison, Wis.
Saalfield.	Saalfield Publishing Co. ....Akron, O.
Sanborn, B: H.	Sanborn, Benjamin H., & Co. ....120 Boylston St., Boston.
Saunders.	Saunders, W. B., & Co. ....925 Walnut St., Philadelphia.
Schirmer.	Schirmer, G. ....35 Union Sq., New York.
Scott, J:	Scott, John....Three Rivers Elm, North Bend, O.
Scott, F. & Co.	Scott, Foresman & Co. ....378-388 Wabash Ave., Chicago.
Scribner.	Scribner's, Charles, Sons....153-157 Fifth Ave., New York.
Scroll Pub.	Scroll Publishing Co. ....308 Dearborn St., Chicago.
Sellers, E. J.	Sellers, Edwin Jacquett....105 Betz Bldg., Philadelphia.
Seminar.	Seminar Pub. Co. ....Springfield, Mass.
Sharp & A.	Sharp & Alleman....37 S. 3d St., Philadelphia.
Sharpe, W: C.	Sharpe, William C. ....Seymour, Ct.
Shepard, H: O.	Shepard, Henry Olendorf....212 Monroe St., Chicago.
Sherwood.	Sherwood, A. G., & Co. ....47 Lafayette Pl., New York.
Shorthand Bu.	Shorthand Publication Bureau....Washington.
Silver.	Silver, Burdett & Co. ....29-33 E. 19th St., New York.
Skelton.	Skelton Pub. Co. ....Provo City, Utah.
Smith, E. E.	Smith, Emory Evans....Palo Alto, Cal.
Smith-B.	Smith-Brooks Printing Co. ....Denver, Col.
Socialistic Co.-op.	Socialistic Co-operative Assoc. ....184 William St., New York.
Soc. Practical Sch. Problems.	Society of Practical School Problems. *See* Harison, W: B.
Soc. R. I. Cincinnati.	Society of the Rhode Island Cincinnati....Newport, R. I.
Soney.	Soney & Sage....Newark, N. J.
Spectator.	Spectator Co. ....95 William St., New York.

Spon.	Spon & Chamberlain............................123 Liberty St., New York.
Sproul.	Sproul, George D............................150 Fifth Ave., New York.
Standard.	Standard Pub. Co....................................Terre Haute, Ind.
Standard Pub.	Standard Publishing Co........................16 E. 9th St., Cincinnati, O.
State Journ. Co.	State Journal Co..Lincoln, Neb.
State Normal Sch.	State Normal School and Industrial College.............Greensboro, N. C.
State Pub.	State Publishing Co.................................Pierre, South Dakota.
Stechert.	Stechert, G. E....................................9 E. 16th St., New York.
Stephens.	Stephens, E. W..Columbia, Mo.
Stevens, E. A.	Stevens, Edward A...Minneapolis, Minn.
Stevens, H. J.	Stevens, Horace J..Houghton, Mich.
Stokes.	Stokes, Frederick A., Co.........................5-7 E. 16th St., New York.
Stone, H. S.	Stone, Herbert S., & Co.......................... Eldridge Court, Chicago.
Street.	Street & Smith............................238 William St., New York.
Street R'way.	Street Railway Pub. Co..........................120 Liberty St., New York.
Student Vol.	Student Volunteer Movement for Foreign Missions..3 W. 29th St., New York.
Success.	Success Co..................University Bldg., Washington Sq., New York.
Sun Pr. Co.	Sun Printing Co..Pittsfield, Mass.
Sunflower.	Sunflower Pub. Co.. Lilly Dale, N. Y.
Sunflower Press.	Sunflower Press...Fort Scott, Kan.
Swedenborg.	Swedenborg Publishing Assoc. ....Germantown, Pa.
Taylor, J. F.	Taylor, J. F., & Co..............................5-7 E. 16th St., New York.
Taylor & M.	Taylor & Moriya................................111 Nassau St., New York.
Tennant.	Tennant & Ward..............................287 Fourth Ave., New York.
Texas.	Texas, State of ....Austin, Tex.
Thompson, E.	Thompson, Edward, Co..Northport, N. Y.
Thompson Litho.	Thompson Lithograph and Printing Co....................Little Rock, Ark.
Thrum.	Thrum, Thomas G..Honolulu, S. I.
Town Topics.	Town Topics Pub. Co.............................208 Fifth Ave., New York.
Treat.	Treat, E. B., & Co..............................241 W. 23d St., New York.
Tribune Assoc.	Tribune Association..............................Tribune Bldg., New York.
Tribune Co.	Tribune Co...Charleston, West Va.
Tuttle, M. & T.	Tuttle, Morehouse & Taylor Co...................................New Haven, Ct.
XX. Century.	XX. (The) Century Pub. Co..Columbus, O.
Union Pub.	Union Pub. House..Chicago.
Un. Soc. C. E.	United Society of Christian Endeavor.............Tremont Temple, Boston.
Universalist.	Universalist Publishing House........................30 West St., Boston.
University.	University Pub. Co..............................27-29 W. 23d St., New York.
Univ. Co-op.	University Co-operative Assoc.......................................Madison, Wis.
Univ. of Cal.	University of California...Berkeley, Cal.
Univ. of Chic.	University of Chicago Press...Chicago.
Univ. of Penn.	University of Pennsylvania...............34th and Chestnut Sts., Philadelphia.
Univ. of Wis.	University of Wisconsin..Madison, Wis.
Univ. Press.	University Press of Minn..........315 14th Ave., S. E., Minneapolis, Minn.
Vandersloot, L.	Vandersloot, Lewis...Harrisburg, Pa.
Van Doren, D. T.	Van Doren, De Witt Talmage.......................................Norwalk, Ct.
Van Nostrand.	Van Nostrand, D., Co...............................23 Murray St., New York.
Virginia-Carolina.	Virginia-Carolina Chemical Co ....Richmond, Va.
Vorce, C. M.	Vorce, Charles M..Cleveland, O.
Wagner.	Wagner, Joseph F...................................41 Union Sq., New York.
Wahr.	Wahr, George...Ann Arbor, Mich.
Walton.	Walton, L. B..................................211 Willow Ave., Ithaca, N. Y.
Warden, W. A.	Warden, William A...Worcester, Mass.
Warne.	Warne, Frederick, & Co...........................36 E. 22d St., New York.
Weborg, J. C.	Weborg, J. C...................................1720 Darrow Ave., Evanston, Ill.
Wegelin, O.	Wegelin, Oscar...Stamford, Ct.
Wehman.	Wehman, Henry J..................................108 Park Row, New York.
Welsh.	Welsh, Rees, & Co. ....19 S. 9th St., Philadelphia.
Werner.	Werner, E. S., Pub. and Supply Co...............43 E. 19th St., New York.
Wessels.	Wessels, A., Co.................................7-9 W. 18th St., New York.
West, J. H.	West, James H., Co.....................................79 Milk St., Boston.
West Pub.	West Pub. Co.................................52-58 W. 3d St., St. Paul, Minn.
Westminster.	Westminster Press ....1319 Walnut St., Philadelphia.
Westminster Pub.	Westminster Pub. Co...Chicago.
Wheeler, W. H.	Wheeler, William H., & Co.........................203 Michigan Ave., Chicago.
Whitaker & R.	Whitaker & Ray Co..............................723 Market St., San Francisco.
White, J. T.	White, James T., & Co...............................7 E. 16th St., New York.
Whittaker.	Whittaker, Thomas.....................................3 Bible House, New York.
Whittet.	Whittet & Shepperson..............................1001 Main St., Richmond, Va.
Wickes.	Wickes, Gregory, Pub. Co..Grand Rapids, Mich.
Wilbur, L. F.	Wilbur, La Fayette...Jericho, Vt.
Wiley.	Wiley, John, & Sons...................................43 E. 19th St., New York.
Williams, D.	Williams, David, Co...................................232-238 William St., New York.
Williamson Law Bk.	Williamson Law Book Co..............9-11 Exchange St., Rochester, N. Y.

Wilson, W. W.	Wilson, Western W..............................14 Thomas St., New York.
Wiltzius.	Wiltzius, M. H., Co..Milwaukee, Wis.
Winston.	Winston, John C., Co........................718–724 Arch St., Philadelphia.
Wisconsin.	Wisconsin, Dept. of Public Instruction, L. D. Harvey, State Supt. Madison, Wis.
Witter.	Witter, Conrad.......................................21 S. 4th St., St. Louis.
Wood.	Wood, William, & Co.............................51 Fifth Ave., New York.
Woodward & L.	Woodward & Lothrop................................1013 F St., Washington.
World R'way.	World Railway Pub. Co............................79 Dearborn St., Chicago.
Wright, J. C.	Wright, J. Clegg...Amelia, O.
Wynkoop.	Wynkoop, Hallenbeck, Crawford Co..............441 Pearl St., New York.
Year Bk.	Year Book Publishers.............................40 Dearborn St., Chicago.
Yewdale.	Yewdale, J. H., & Sons Co...Milwaukee, Wis.
Young, E. & J. B.	Young, E. & J. B., & Co..............................9 W. 18th St., New York.
Young, W. H.	Young, William H., & Co...........................27 Barclay St., New York.
Young Churchman.	Young Churchman Co.....................412 Milwaukee St., Milwaukee, Wis.
Ziegler.	Ziegler, P. W., & Co...........................720 Chestnut St., Philadelphia.

MEMBERS OF THE AMERICAN PUBLISHERS' ASSOCIATION.

Henry Altemus Company..Philadelphia.
American Baptist Publication Society..........................Philadelphia.
American News Company..New York.
D. Appleton & Company..New York.
Arnold & Company...Philadelphia.
A. S. Barnes & Co..New York.
Drexel Biddle..Philadelphia.
The Bowen-Merrill Company......................................Indianapolis, Ind.
Albert Brandt..Trenton, N. J.
Brentano's...New York.
The Century Company..New York.
C. M. Clark Publishing Company.................................Boston.
H. T. Coates & Co..Philadelphia.
The Robert Clarke Company......................................Cincinnati, O.
Thomas Y. Crowell & Co...New York.
G. W. Dillingham Co..New York.
Dodd, Mead & Company...New York.
Doubleday, Page & Company......................................New York.
E. P. Dutton & Co..New York.
Dana Estes & Co..Boston.
Funk & Wagnalls Company..New York.
Harper & Brothers..New York.
Henry Holt & Company...New York.
Houghton, Mifflin & Company....................................Boston.
Geo. W. Jacobs & Company.......................................Philadelphia.
John Lane..New York.
Lee & Shepard..Boston.
J. B. Lippincott Company.......................................Philadelphia.
Little, Brown & Company..Boston.
Longmans, Green & Company......................................New York.
The Lothrop Publishing Company.................................Boston.
The Macmillan Company..New York.
McClure, Phillips & Company....................................New York.
A. C. McClurg & Company..Chicago, Ill.
New Amsterdam Book Co..New York.
L. C. Page & Co..Boston.
Penn Publishing Co...Philadelphia.
James Pott & Company...New York.
G. P. Putnam's Sons..New York.
Fleming H. Revell Company......................................Chicago and New York.
R. H. Russell...New York.
Charles Scribner's Sons..New York.
Small, Maynard & Company.......................................Boston.
Frederick A. Stokes Company....................................New York.
H. S. Stone & Co...Chicago, Ill.
J. F. Taylor & Company...New York.
Vir Publishing Company...Philadelphia.
A. Wessels Co..New York.

For 1902
PUBLISHERS' TRADE LIST ANNUAL
(Thirtieth Year)

In response to the desires of the book trade we shall publish the forthcoming issue of THE PUBLISHERS' TRADE LIST ANNUAL, to be ready at the opening of the active Fall season, in August, 1902,

With a Complete Index

to the publishers' catalogues contained therein. The books will be indexed by author, title and, practically, by subject or class. The name of series, the price, and name of publisher will also be given, so that any book contained in the ANNUAL may be located at once by whatsoever clue the user may have. The Index will be printed in two columns to the page, in readable type, full face letters being used to make reference to authors' names more convenient.

The bulk of the volume, as heretofore, will consist of the latest CATALOGUES OF 250 FIRMS PUBLISHING BOOKS IN THE UNITED STATES, contributed by themselves and arranged alphabetically by the firm names, with the smaller lists and advertisements of single books at the end. The patent "Duplex Index," having the alphabet printed on the concave surface as well as on the margin of the page, enables instantaneous reference to the catalogues and the lists, whether the book is open or shut.

These lists, thus bound together, present in their combination so convenient and time-saving a working tool as to have made THE TRADE LIST ANNUAL for upwards of a quarter of a century indispensable to every one who has any interest in the purchase or sale of books published in the United States. With the reference index to the books listed in the publishers' catalogues its practical usefulness will be enhanced an hundred fold.

The work will be offered to the trade in two styles :

With the Index, in 2 Volumes, bound in cloth, $5 00
Without the Index, in 1 Volume, bound in cloth, 1 50

if ordered and paid for in advance of publication. After publication day the price of the work with the index will be raised to $7.00, and of the work without the index to $2.00. Orders, stating whether the volume is desired with or without the index, should be registered at

The Office of THE PUBLISHERS' WEEKLY
(P. O. Box 943) 298 Broadway, New York

WITH WHICH IS INCORPORATED

The American Literary Gazette and Publishers' Circular.

[ESTABLISHED 1852.]

PUBLICATION OFFICE, 298 BROADWAY, NEW YORK.

Entered at the Post-Office at New York, N. Y., as second-class matter.

VOL. LXII., No. 3. NEW YORK, July 19, 1902. WHOLE No. 1590

The Publishers' Weekly.

JULY 19, 1902.

INDEX TO ADVERTISERS

NOTES IN SEASON.

DODD, MEAD & Co. have in preparation "The Conquest of Charlotte," a new novel by David S. Meldrum, the scene of which is divided between Fife and London.

THE HOME PUBLISHING COMPANY, New York, will publish, on the 21st inst., a story of the "lower coast" of Louisiana, by Colonel Richard Henry Savage, entitled "Special Orders for Commander Leigh." Graphic pictures are given of the plotting of the agents of the Confederate Government in Europe, especially in Paris, and of the adventures and the destruction of the *Alabama*.

D. APPLETON & Co. have just ready an important book on "The Care of the Teeth," by Dr. S. A. Hopkins, Professor of Theory and Practice of Dentistry in Tuft's College Dental School. The book is addressed to dentists and physicians as well as to the general reader. They have also just ready "The Story of the Art of Music," by Frederick J. Crowest, a new volume in the *Library of Useful Stories;* and the fourth edition of Dr. Alvah H. Doty's handbook on "Prompt Aid to the Injured," revised to date.

THE BURROWS BROTHERS COMPANY have just ready an attractive reprint of Denton's "A Brief Description of New York, Formerly Called New Netherlands," with the title in facsimile. The text is reprinted from the original edition of 1670 in the Library of Congress, and is prefaced with the bibliographical introduction by Felix Neumann, printed in THE PUBLISHERS' WEEKLY a short time ago. The edition is limited to 250 copies on hand-made paper and 10 copies on Japan paper. This reprint will be followed by others of equal historic and bibliographic importance.

FUNK & WAGNALLS COMPANY have just ready the second volume of the truly colossal "Jewish Encyclopedia," covering the subject from "Apocrypha" to "Benash." It has been prepared under the direction of the same staff of editors and writers that made the first volume, and in every respect equals it in excellence and thoroughness. Considering that fully four-fifths of the material for this work had to be created, collected and digested for this special purpose, the work is not conventionally but truthfully a monument of research and information, and as such deserves a full measure of success. Typographically the work is all that can be desired. Especially is this true of the 147 illustrations that accompany this second volume.

F. WARNE & Co. announce a new novel by Mrs. J. H. Needell, author of "Julian Karslake's Secret," etc., entitled "Unstable as Water;" "The Presumption of Stanley Hay, M.P.," an interesting and exciting novel by Nowell Cay, a new writer; "Kitty's Victoria Cross," a pleasing romance of two Irish girls, by Robert Cromie; two new volumes in the *Library of Natural History Romance*—"Shell Life," by Edward Step, an entertaining as well as instructive book written with the idea of popularizing what has hitherto been considered an abstract subject, and "A Romance of Wild Flowers," also by Mr. Step, both volumes being very fully illustrated; "The Motor Car," an elementary handbook for all who contemplate motoring, by Sir Henry Thompson; also, an essay entitled "The Unknown God?" which is described as "an attempt to seek by careful deduction from available data some certain assurance respecting the influence which the infinite and eternal energy from which all things proceed "has exercised on man from the beginning."

WEEKLY RECORD OF NEW PUBLICATIONS.

☞ Beginning with the issue of July 5, 1902, the titles of *net* books published under the rules of the American Publishers' Association are preceded by a double asterisk **, and the word net follows the price. The titles of *fiction* (not net) published under the rules are preceded by a dagger †. *Net* books not covered by the rules, whether published by members of the American Publishers' Association or not, are preceded by a single asterisk, and the word net follows the price. ☜

The abbreviations are usually self-explanatory. c. after the date indicates that the book is copyrighted; if the copyright date differs from the imprint date, the year of copyright is added. Books of foreign origin of which the edition (annotated, illustrated, etc.) is entered as copyright, are marked c. ed.; translations, c. tr.; n. p., in place of price, indicates that the publisher makes no price, either net or retail, and quotes prices to the trade only upon application.

A colon after initial designates the most usual given name, as: A: Augustus; B: Benjamin; C: Charles; D: David; E: Edward; F: Frederic; G: George; H: Henry; I: Isaac; J: John; L: Louis; N: Nicholas; P: Peter; R: Richard; S: Samuel; T: Thomas; W: William.

Sizes are designated as follows: F. (folio: over 30 centimeters high); Q. (4to: under 30 cm.); O. (8vo: 25 cm.); D. (12mo: 20 cm.); S. (16mo: 17½ cm.); T. (24mo: 15 cm.); Tt. (32mo: 12½ cm.); Fe. 48mo: 10 cm.). Sq., obl., nar., designate square, oblong, narrow books of these heights.

Agricultural almanac, 1903; calculated for the meridian of Pennsylvania and the adjoin ing states. Lancaster, Pa., J. Baer's Sons, 1902. c. il. 4°, pap., 10 c.

Allen, May V. Battling with love and fate: [stories.] N. Y., Abbey Press, [1902.] c. 167 p. D. cl., $1.

****Allen,** Willis Boyd. Play away: a story of the Boston fire department; il. by L. J. Bridgman. Bost., Dana Estes & Co., [1902.] c. 171 p. 12°, cl., 75 c. net.

American corporation legal manual: a compilation of the essential features of the statutory law regulating general business corporations in America (North, Central and South,) and other countries of the world, with special digests of the U. S. street railway laws, building and loan association laws and trade-mark laws, [etc.] v. 10-1902, [to Jan. 1, 1902;] ed. by E: Q. Keasbey, A. V. D. Honeyman. Plainfield, N. J., Corporation Legal Manual Co., 1902. c. 1217+31 p. O. shp., $5.

Atlantic reporter, v. 51. Permanent ed., Feb. 12-June 4, 1902. St. Paul, West Pub. Co., 1902. c. 16+1204 p. O. (National reporter system, state ser.) shp., $4.

Contains all the reporter decisions of the supreme courts of Me., N. H., Vt., R. I., Conn., and Pa.; court of errors and appeals, court of chancery, and supreme and prerogative courts of N. J.; supreme court, court of chancery, superior court, court of general sessions, and court of oyer and terminer of Dela.; and court of appeals of Md. With tables of Atlantic cases published in vs. 95, Me. reports; 93, Md. reports; 70, N. H. reports; 65, N. J. law (36, Vroom) reports; 198, 199, Pa. reports; 73, Vt. reports. A table of statutes construed is given in the index.

***Bacon,** Gorham, *M.D.* A manual of otology. 3d ed. rev. and enl. Phil., Lea, Bros & Co., 1902. c. 430 p. il. 12°, cl., $2.25 net.

Balch, Edwin Swift. Antarctica. Phil., Press of Allen, Lane & Scott, 1902. c. 230 p. fold. maps, 8°, cl., (for private distribution.)

An enlargement of a paper published in vol CLI. and CLII. of the Journal of the Franklin Institute. *Contents:* The legendary "Terra Australis incognita" and voyages leading from a belief to a disbelief in it; Voyages up to and including the discovery of the continent of Antarctica; Voyages subsequent to the discovery of the continent of Antarctica.

Ballough, C: A: Sibylline leaves. De Land, Fla., E. O. Painter & Co., 1902. c. 71 p. por. sq. T. cl., $1.

A brief treatise on hypnotism; with formulas for hypnotizing.

Ballough, C: A: The power that heals and how to use it. De Land, Fla., E. O. Painter & Co., 1902. 3-65 p. por. S. cl., $1.

The author contends that harmony is the healing balm of the world. He endeavors to show the effect of mind upon the body in the effort to cure physical disease. He also strives to define the relationship of harmony and suggestion.

Barnett, Evelyn Snead. Jerry's reward; il. by Etheldred B. Barry. Bost., L. C. Page & Co., 1901, [1902.] [My.] c. 76 p. S. (Cosy corner ser.) cl., 50 c.

Barrett, Jos. H. Life of Abraham Lincoln. Chic., M. A. Donohue & Co., 1902. 842 p. 12°, (Biographies of famous men.) cl., $1.

Baskett, Ja. Newton, *and* Ditmars, Raymond L. The story of the amphibians and the reptiles. N. Y., Appleton, 1902. c. 23+217 p. D. (Appleton's home-reading books; ed. by W: T. Harris. Division 1, Natural history.) cl., 60 c.

Effort is made to familiarize the young reader with the anatomical structure and habits of many forms of amphibians and reptiles.

Bishop, Irving P. The red book of Niagara: a comprehensive guide to the scientific, historical, and scenic aspects of Niagara, for the use of travellers. Buffalo, N. Y., The Wenborne-Sumner Co., 1902. c. 3-117 p. il. map, S. pap., 25 c.

Bloch, I. S. The future of war, in its technical, economic and political relations; tr. by R. C. Long; [also] a conversation with the author, by W. T. Stead, and an introd. by Edwin D. Mead. [New issue.] Bost., Ginn, 1902. c. '99. 62+380 p. D. cl., 60 c.

***Bolza,** Oskar. Concerning the geodesic curvature and the isoperimetric problem on a given surface and proof of the sufficiency of Jacobi's condition for a permanent sign of the second variation in the co-called isoperimetric problems; printed from v. 9 of "The decennial publications." Chic., University of Chicago Press, 1902. c. 2+7 p. Q. (University of Chicago Decennial publications.) pap., 25 c. net.

Broome, I: The last days of the Ruskin Co-operative Association. Chic., C: H. Kerr & Co., 1902. c. 2-183 p. 16°, (Standard socialist ser.) cl., 50 c.

The Ruskin Co-operative Association was located west of Nashville in Tennessee. It was an attempt on the part of a group of people to escape from capitalism and to establish co-operation. The idea of founding the colony was originated by Wayland in 1893, shortly after he began the publication of *The*

Coming Nation. The author says his book is an expose of the facts, condition and characters that figured in a movement that was defective in organization and personnel.

California. *Supreme ct.* Reports of cases; C. P. Pomeroy, rep. v. 135, (1901-2.) San Francisco, Bancroft-Whitney Co., 1902. c. 36+768 p. O. shp., $3.

Chantepie de la Saussaye, Pierre Daniel. The religion of the Teutons; tr. from the Dutch by Bert J. Vos. Bost., Ginn, 1902. c. 7+504 p. maps, 12°, (Handbooks on the history of religions, v. 3.) cl., $2.50.

***Châteaubriand,** François René Auguste [*Vicomte de.*] Memoirs of François René Vicomte de Châteaubriand, sometime ambassador to England; being a translation by Alexander Teixera de Maltos of *Les mémoires d' Outre-Tombe;* il. from contemporary sources. N. Y., Putnam, 1902. 6 v., ea., $3.75 net.

***Cheyne,** W: Watson, *and* Burghard, F. F., *M.D.* Manual of surgical treatment. In 7 v. v. 6. Phil., Lea Bros. & Co., 1902. 8°, cl., $5 net.

Cohen, Alfred J., ["Alan Dale," *pseud.*] A girl who wrote. N. Y., Quail & Warner, [1902.] c. 3+375 p. il. D. cl., $1.50.
The scene is mostly laid in Newspaper Row, New York City. The novel offers a number of "composite" pictures of the managing editor, the reporters, men and women, and others connected with a sensational "daily." There is a love story, in which figures a bright, intelligent woman reporter.

Creswicke, L: South Africa and the Transvaal war. N. Y., Putnam, 1902. 6 v., il. col. pls. por. 8°, per v., $2.50.

****Crosland,** T. W. H. The unspeakable Scot. N. Y., Putnam, 1902. [Jl.] c. 3+215 p. D. cl., $1.25 net.
A half humorous, half serious, and wholly ironical indictment of the Scottish character and temperament. It shows that the vogue of the Scot in England and America is the outcome of Saxon indifference and not of Scottish capacity, that it is on the wane, and that it was achieved by the practice of cheap virtues. It aims to prove that in politics, arts, letters, journalism, and sundry other departments of activity, the Scot has never accomplished anything that really matters.

****Crowest,** F: J. The story of the art of music. N. Y., Appleton, 1902. [Jl1902.] c. 190 p. il. T. (Library of useful stories.) cl., 35 c. net.
A brief study of theoretical and instrumental progress in the development of music. Intended for general readers.

Davison, C: Stewart. Selling the bear's hide, and other tales. Richmond Hill, Long Island, N. Y., Nassau Press, [1902.] c. 131 p. il. S. cl., $1.
Contents: Selling the bear's hide; A slip on the Ortler; Up Clevedale and down again; How I sent my aunt to Baltimore; John O'Conor goes a-fishing; A winter wedding at Weldon.

****Day,** Holman F. Pine tree ballads; rhymed stories of unplaned human natur' up in Maine. Bost., Small, Maynard & Co., 1902. c. 12+256 p. il. D. cl., $1 net.

***Denton,** Dan. A brief description of New York, formerly called New Netherlands; reprinted from the original ed. of 1670; with a bibliographical introd. by Felix Neumann. Cleveland, Burrows Bros. Co., 1902. c. 63 p. O. bds., $1.50 net (250 copies); on Japan pap., $3 net (10 copies.)

***Dmitriev-Mámonóv,** A. I., *and* Zdziarski, A. F., *eds.* A guide to the great Siberian railway; English tr. by L. Kúkol-Yasnopólsky; rev. by J: Marshall. N. Y., Putnam, 1902. il. maps, plans, 8°, $3.50 net.

Doty, Alvah H., *M.D.* Manual of instruction in the principles of prompt aid to the injured; including a chapter on hygiene and the drill regulations for the hospital corps U. S. A.; designed for military and civil use. 4th ed. rev. and enl. N. Y., Appleton, 1902. c. '89. 16+302 p. il. D. cl., $1.50.

****Edwards,** Owen M. Wales. N. Y., Putnam, 1902. 18+421 p. il. D. (Story of the nations ser., no. 62.) cl., $1.35 net; hf. leath, $1.60 net.
In the first half of the work the author sketches the rise and fall of a princely caste; in the second the rise of a self-educated, self-governing peasantry. His chief authorities for the period of the Norman and English are Brut y Tywysogion, Ordericus Vitalis, the Monastic annalist, the Welsh laws and the Welsh poets of the Red book of Hergest.

****Fielding,** H: The journal of a voyage to Lisbon. Special ed. Bost., Houghton, Mifflin & Co., 1902. 8°, bds., $5 net, (limited to 300 copies.)

****Fiske,** J: Works. Ed. de luxe. Bost., Houghton, Mifflin & Co., 1902. c. 24 v., 8°, subs., buckram, ea., $5 net; ¾ levant, ea., $10 net, (limited to 1000 copies.)
Contents: 1st ser.: v. 1-3, The discovery of America; v. 4 and 5, Old Virginia and her neighbors; v. 6, The beginnings of New England; v. 7 and 8, The Dutch and Quaker colonies in America; v. 9, New France and New England; v. 10 and 11, The American Revolution; v. 12, The critical period of American history. Second ser.: v. 1-4, Outlines of cosmic philosophy; v. 5, The unseen world and other essays; v. 6, Darwinism and other essays; v. 7, Excursions of an evolutionist; v. 8, Myths and myth-makers; v. 9, A century of science and other essays; v. 10, The destiny of man; The idea of God; Through nature to God; Life everlasting; v. 11, The Mississippi valley in the Civil War; v. 12, Civil government in the United States.

Fowler, Gilbert J. Sewage works analyses. N. Y., J: Wiley & Sons, 1902. 7+135 p. 12°, cl., $2.

Gabelsberger Shorthand Society, *ed.* Reader to Henry Richter's graphic shorthand; (system F. X. Gabelsberger;) ed. by Gabelsberger Shorthand Society. N. Y., International News Co., 1902. 80 p. 16°, pap., 50 c.

Godbey, A. M. Life of Henry M. Stanley. Chic., M. A. Donohue & Co., 1902. 560 p. 12°, (Biographies of famous men.) cl., $1.

Hall, Rob. C. Pittsburg securities, a stock exchange handbook, 1902. [2d annual issue.] Pittsburg, R. C. Hall, [1902.] c. 89+4 p. D. pap., gratis.

Halstead, Murat. The world on fire. Chic., The Dominion Co., 1902. 450 p. il. 12°, cl., $1.50; $2.25; mor., $3.

Hamilton, W: R., *and* Bond, Paul Stanley, *comps.* The gunner's catechism: a series of questions and answers in untechnical language for the use of all artillerymen who desire to become either first or second class gunners. N. Y., J: Wiley & Sons, 1902. c. 10+163 p. 18°, cl., $1.

Hartfield, T. Walter. The exchange pocket cipher code for the use of bankers, brokers and investors. N. Y., T. W. Hartfield, 1902. c. 11+271 p. 16°, rus. leath., $2.

Hatfield, W: F: Geyserland and wonderland, a view and guide book of the Yellowstone national park. San Francisco, Hicks-Judd Co., 1902. c. 75 p. il. map, 24°, cl., 24 c.

Hawkins, Nehemiah. Self-help mechanical drawing: an educational treatise. N. Y., Theodore Audel & Co., 1902. c. 13-299 p. il. diagr. 8°, cl., $2.

Hedges, *Rev.* S: Statistics concerning education in the Philippine Islands; comp. from the report of the Commissioner of Education, 1899-1900. N. Y., Benziger Bros., 1902. c. 30 p. S. pap., 10 c.

Herrold, Maude McKinley. Woman: diseases and remedies; a collection of facts for woman; by approved authorities the statements contained in this book are proved. Kansas City, Mo., Woman's Publishing Co., 1902. c. 650 p. il. 8°, cl., $4; hf. mor., $5.

Holmes, Burton, [*pseud.* for Elias Burton.] The Burton Holmes lectures; with il. from photographs by the author. In 10 v. v. 1-6. Battle Creek, Mich., The Little-Preston Co., limited, 1901. c. il. pl. (partly col.) por. 8°, cl., subs, per set, $51; ¾ mor., $65.

****Hopkins,** S: A. The care of the teeth. N. Y., Appleton, 1902. [Jl.] c. 6+150 p. D. cl., 75 c. net.

A history of dentistry and an examination of the causes and effects of decay, with rules for the prevention of diseases of the mouth and for the preservation of the teeth. The author is professor of the theory and practice of dentistry in Tufts College Dental School.

****Hopkins,** W: Barton. The roller bandage. 5th ed., rev. Phil., Lippincott, 1902. c. 16+9-162 p. il. 12°, cl., $1.50 net.

Hunt, J. N., *and* Gourley, H. I. The modern pronouncing speller. Phil. and N. Y., Butler, Sheldon & Co., [1902.] c. 144 p. 12°, cl., 20 c.

Hutchinson, Jos. Primrose diplomacy; discords in the jingo symphony by an untuned lyre: [poetry.] N. Y., Abbey Press, [1902.] c. 182 p. 12°, cl., $1.25.

Illinois. *Appellate cts.* Reports of cases; with a directory of the judiciary department of the state, corrected to the 4th of June, 1902, and a table of cases reviewed by the supreme court to the date of the publication of this v. v. 100; ed. by Martin L. Newell. Chic., Callaghan & Co., 1902. c. 25+688 p. O. shp., $3.75.

International cable directory, *comp.* International cable directory of the world in conjunction with Western union telegraphic code system; comp. and pub. by International Cable Directory Company, New York and London. N. Y., International Cable Directory Co., 1902. c. 13+438+44 p. O. cl., $15.

Jeter, Jeremiah Bell. Baptist principles reset; consisting of articles on distinctive Baptist principles. New and enl. ed. Richmond, Va., Religious Herald Co., 1902. c. 319 p. por. 16°, cl., $1.

Johnson, Frank M., *M.D.* Forest, lake and river; The fishes of New England and eastern Canada. Bost., F. M. Johnson, M.D., 1902. c. col. il. pl. (partly col.) 2 v. and portfolio, 8°, edition de luxe, per set, $300; grand edition de luxe, per set, $500.

****Johnson,** Virginia W. A world's shrine. N. Y., A. S. Barnes & Co., 1902. [Je.] c. 5+287 p. il. D. cl., $1.20 net.

Describes the most beautiful of the Italian lakes, Lake Como, and the home of Pliny.

Johnson, W. Fletcher. Life of W. T. Sherman. Chic., M. A. Donohue & Co., 1902. 621 p. 12°, (Biographies of famous men.) cl., $1.

Judson, C: Francis, *and* Gittings, J. Claxton. The artificial feeding of infants, including a critical review of the recent literature of the subject, by C: F. Judson and J. Claxton Gittings. Phil., Lippincott, 1902. c. 368 p. diagr. 12°, cl., $2.

Judson, W. P. City roads and pavements suited to cities of moderate size. 2d ed. N. Y., Engineering News Co., 1902. il. 12°, cl., $2.

Kendall, Reese P., *M.D.* Pacific trail campfires: containing the Missouri column; The Applegate battalion, The "Pathfinder" detachment, The Barneburg contingent Chic., Scroll Pub. Co., [1902.] c. 4-437 p. D. cl., $1.50.

Knapp, Adeline. How to live; a manual of hygiene for use in the schools of the Philippine Islands. N. Y., Silver, Burdett & Co., [1902.] c. 90 p. il. 16°, cl., 36 c.

Kuttner, Bernhard. Kuttner's German conversation course; a graded series of object lessons, dialogues and grammar. (Sections 1 and 2.) N. Y., Abbey Press, [1902.] c. 122 p. D. cl., 50 c.

Langley, S: Pierpont. Experiments in aerodynamics. 2d ed. Wash., D. C. Smithsonian Inst., 1902. 3+115 p. F. (Smithsonian contributions to knowledge, no. 201.) cl., $1.

Leahy, *Rev.* Walter T: A child of the flood; or, a mother's prayer: a story for boys and girls. Phil., H. L. Kilner & Co., [1902.] c. 2-234 p. D. cl., $1.

Leroy, W: A silken snare: [a love story.] N. Y., Abbey Press, 1902. c. 3+113 p. il. D. cl., 50 c.

Lockwood, Sara Eliz. Husted. Teachers' manual to accompany Lockwood and Emerson's "Composition and rhetoric." Bost., Ginn, 1902. c. 14+66 p. 16°, pap., 30 c.

Longfellow, H: Wadsworth. Outre mer: a pilgrimage beyond the sea. N. Y., A. L. Burt Co., 1902. 324 p. 12°, (Home lib.) cl., $1.

McMaster, J. S. Commercial digest and business forms. N. Y., Commercial Book Co., 1900. [1902.] c. 1002 p. 8°, leath., $6.

McMaster, J. S. Irregular and regular commercial paper: a treatise on the law of notes, checks, drafts; clear, simple, complete. N. Y., McMaster Co., 1902. c. 262 p. size 12 x 4 ins. buckram, $2.

McMaster, J. S. McMaster's commercial cases. N. Y., Commercial Book Co., 1901, [1902.] c. 750 p. 8°, leath., $6.

These current cases are from the highest courts of the several states and the federal courts. The decisions numbered and printed in full are reversals in such courts.

Maloney, Ja. C. The 20th century guide for mixing fancy drinks. 3d ed. enl. Chic., James C. Maloney, 1902. c. 95 p. por. sq. S. pap., $1.

Malory, *Sir* T: King Arthur and his noble knights: stories from Sir T: Malory's "Morte D'Arthur," by Mary Macleod; with an introd. by J: W. Hales. N. Y., A. L Burt Co., 1902. 22+383 p. il. 12°, (Home lib.) cl., $1.

Maxwell, Hu. Jonathan Fish and his neighbors. Morgantown, W. Va., Acme Publishing Co., 1902. c. 3-110 p. O. cl., $1.

Contents: Jonathan Fish; The anarchist; The fiddler of Polebridge; The deserter's child; First impressions; Israel Thompson.

†**Merejkowski**, Dimitri. The romance of Leonardo da Vinci, the forerunner; exclusively authorized tr. from the Russian of "The resurrection of the gods," by Herbert Trench. N. Y., Putnam, 1902. 8+463 p. D. cl., $1.50.

The second volume of the author's trilogy, entitled "Christ and Anti-Christ," known in the original as "The resurrection of the gods." The first volume was called "The death of the gods," and dealt with the times of the Emperor Julian. The present story is of the Italian Renaissance.

****Merrill**, Catherine. The man Shakespeare, and other essays, with impressions and reminiscences of the author by Melville B. Anderson, and with some words of appreciation from John Muir. Indianapolis, Bowen-Merrill Co., [1902.] c. 210 p. por. 12°, cl., $1.25 net.

***Methodist** Episcopal church in America. The doctrines of the Methodist Episcopal church in America as contained in the disciplines of said church from 1788 to 1808 and so designated on their title-pages; comp. and ed. with an historical introd., by J: I. Tigert, D.D. Cin., O., Jennings & Pye, 1902. c. 2 v., 20+175; 14+152 p. sq. T. (Little books on doctrine.) cl., 50 c. net.

****Miller**, W: Mediæval Rome from Hilderbrand to Clement VIII., 1073-1600. N. Y., Putnam, 1902. 13+373 p. D. (Story of the nations ser., no. 63.) cl., $1.35 net; hf. leath., $1.60 net.

"I have endeavored," says the author, "to narrate the most striking incidents in the history of the city between the middle of the eleventh and the end of the sixteenth century, confining myself as far as possible to those events of which Rome was the theatre. I have accordingly based the story in the main on the latest German editions of Gregorovius," *Geschichte der stadt Rom im Mittelalter* (Stuttgart, 1886-96.)

Minnesota. *Supreme ct.* Reports; v. 84, June 21, 1901-Dec. 6, 1901; H: Burleigh Wenzell, rep. St. Paul, Frank P. Dufresne, [illegible] c. 21+578 p. O. shp., $2.75.

Morang's annual register of Canadian affairs, 1901; ed. and comp. by J. Castell Hopkins. Toronto, Can., G: N. Morang & Co., Ltd., 1902. c. 18+540 p. O. cl., $3; hf. mor., $4.

A record of the principal events connected with the history and development of the Dominion of Canada. The plan of the work, the publishers say, differs from the annual publications of other countries in the fact of the record being both statistical and historical in character. The editor has sought to be absolutely impartial in political matters.

****Morgan**, Lewis H: League of the Ho-de-no-sau-nee or Iroquois. New ed., with additional matter; ed. and annotated by Herbert M. Lloyd. N. Y., Dodd, Mead & Co., 1902. c. 2 v., il. col. pl. por. fold. maps, 8°, cl., on hand-made pap., $15 net (300 copies); Japan pap., $30 net (30 copies.)

Myers, Albert Cook. Quaker arrivals at Philadelphia, 1682-1750; being a list of certificates of removal received at Philadelphia monthly meeting of Friends. Phil., Ferris & Leach, 1902. c. 131 p. 16°, cl., $1.25.

New York. Amendments to Birdseye's revised statutes and general laws contained in the laws of 1902, together with all new general acts. N. Y., Baker, Voorhis & Co., 1902. c. 213 p. printed on one side of leaf, pap., $2.

New York. Supplement to the general laws and revised statutes of the state, cont. amendments to the general laws, the revised statutes and other general statutes, together with all independent general acts passed at the session of the legislature of 1902, [etc.;] comp. by E: L. Heydecker. Alb., Matthew Bender, 1902. c. 213 p. printed on one side of leaf, O. pap., $2.

†**Norris**, W: E: The credit of the county: a novel. N. Y., Appleton, 1902. [Je.] c. 323 p. D. (Appleton's town and country lib., no. 313.) cl., $1; pap., 50 c.

The efforts of a rich but uncultured husband and wife of Hebrew extraction to obtain an entrance into the best society of the hunting county of Trentshire, England, is the leading theme. When fair means fail them, they strike a blow at one of the families, by circulating a scandal, that has but slight basis of wrong. "The credit of the county," however, is in the end upheld, and Mr. and Mrs. Asher are obliged to move to another shire.

North Dakota. *Supreme ct.* Reports of cases, Nov., 1900, to Jan., 1902; also rules of practice of the supreme court; J: M. Cochrane, rep. v. 10. Grand Forks, Herald, state prs., 1902. c. 60+724 p. O. shp., $4.25.

***Oliver**, T., *M.D., ed.* Dangerous trades; the historical, social and legal aspects of industrial occupations as affecting public health by a number of experts; ed. by T. Oliver. N. Y., Dutton, 1902. 891 p. 8°, cl., $8 net.

Page, Kate Nelson. Tommy Atkins episode, and other stories. N. Y., Abbey Press, [1902.] c. 3+142 p. D. cl., $1.

Pennsylvania. *Supreme ct.* Reports, v. 201, at Jan. term, 1902; rep. by W: I. Schaffer, st. rep. N. Y., Banks Law Pub. Co., 1902. c. 28+724 p. O. shp., $3.50.

***Percy**, Hugh Earl (*Duke* of Northumberland.) Letters of Hugh Earl Percy, from

Boston and New York, 1774-1776; ed. by C. Knowles Bolton. Bost., C: E. Goodspeed, 1902. c. 88 p. por. sq. O. bds., $4 net.
Thirty-three letters addressed to Percy's father, the first Duke of Northumberland, the Rev. Thomas Percy, compiler of the "Reliques of Ancient English Poetry," General Harvey, Henry Reveley, and others. The peculiar position in English politics occupied by Percy is well known to students of American history, as is also his disaccord with the measures leading to the American war. The letters, which were first discovered in the library of Alnwick Castle, by the Rev. E: G. Porter, of Lexington, Mass., in 1878, contain comments upon men and events that add substantially to our stock of Revolutionary history. The letters have been carefully edited and supplied with an introduction and notes. The frontispiece has been specially etched by Sidney L. Smith.

Pinney, Aida Edmonds. Spanish and English conversation. First and second books. Bost., Ginn, 1902. c. 15+111; 13+107 p. D. cl., ea., 65 c.
The aim of these books is to teach the spoken language of the words and sentences in everyday use.

Poore, B: Perley, *and* Tiffany, O. H., *D.D.* Life of U. S. Grant. Chic., M. A. Donohue & Co., 1902. 594 p. 12°, (Biographies of famous men.) cl., $1.

Revelations from the eternal world given to one of the mystic brotherhood. No. 1, Ancient Hebrew writers, Angel of the covenant, Abraham, Moses, Joshua, Samuel, David, Elijah, Jeremiah, Daniel, Josephus. Springfield, Mass., Star Publishing Co., 1902. c. 2+64 p. sq. S. pap., 20 c.

***Rice**, Edwin Wilbur, *D.D.* A short history of the International lesson system, with a classified list of the International Sunday-school lessons for thirty-three years, 1872-1904, arranged according to their sequence in the Bible, with the date when each lesson was studied; prepared by Clarence Russell Williams. Phil., Amer. Sunday-School Union, 1902. c. 79 p. S. leath., 25 c. net.

Robb, Hunter, *M.D.* Aseptic surgical technique; with especial reference to gynæcological operations, together with notes on the technique employed in certain supplementary procedures. 2d ed., rev. Phil., Lippincott, 1902. c. 18+9-268 p. col. front, il. pl. (partly col.) 12°, cl., $2.

Rogers, C: Gordon. Government clerks: a book of ballads. East Orange, N. J., Jos St. Clair McQuilkin, 1902. c. 39 p. nar. O cl., $1; pap., 25 c.
Ballads entitled: Amelia; Monsieur L'Tweeleree; Diaphanous Day; Double Foolscap; Gubbins, etc.

Root, Edwin Alvin. Root's military topography and sketching, prepard for use in the United States infantry and cavalry school. Rev. and enl. by the department of engineering, Fort Leavenworth, Kansas, October, 1896. [3d ed. Rev. December, 1901.] Kansas City, Hudson-Kimberly Pub. Co., [1902.] 395 p. maps, il. pl. (partly fold.) diagr. 8°, cl., $2.50.

Ryan, M. B. Elocution and dramatic art, with selections from standard authors. Bost., Angel Guardian Press, 1902. c. 13-207 p. 16°, vellum cl., 75 c.

***Santanelli**, [*pseud.* for Ja. Hawthorne Loryea.] Is man a free agent? The law of suggestion including hypnosis, what and why it is, and how to induce it, the law of nature, mind, heredity. Lansing, Mich., Santanelli Publishing Co., 1902. c. 248 p. por. il. O. cl., $1 net.

***Schäfer**, E: Albert. Essentials in histology. 6th ed. Phil., Lea Bros. & Co., 1902. c. 428 p. il. 8°, cl., $3 net.

Sharp & Alleman Co.'s lawyers and bankers directory for 1902, July ed., cont. the names of over 7000 capable and trustworthy attorneys in all the cities and larger towns in the U. S. and Canada, [etc.] Phil., Sharp & Alleman, [1902.] c. 1459 p. O. shp., $5.

****Sill**, Edmund Rowland. Poems. Special ed. Bost., Houghton, Mifflin & Co., 1902. 8°, buckram and bds., $5 net, (limited to 500 copies.)

Simon, Pierre, [*Marquis* de La Place.] A philosophical essay on probabilities; from the 6th French ed., by F: Wilson Truscott and F: Lincoln Emory. N. Y., J: Wiley & Sons, 1902. c. tr. 4+196 p. 12°, cl., $2.

***Smart**, C:, *M.D.* A handbook for the hospital corps of the United States Army and state military forces. 3d ed. rev. and enl. N. Y., W: Wood & Co., 1902. 424 p. 12°, cl., $2.50 net.

Smiley, T: E. Lays and lyrics. N. Y., Abbey Press, [1902.] c. 169 p. por. D. cl., $1.25.

****Smith**, Eugene. The home aquarium and how to care for it: a guide to its fishes, other animals and plants. N. Y., Dutton, 1902. c. 210 p. 12°, cl., $1.20 net.

***Snowden**, W: H. Some old historic landmarks of Virginia and Maryland, described in a hand-book for the tourist over the Washington, Alexandria and Mount Vernon electric railway. 3d ed. Alexandria, Va., G. H. Ramey & Son, 1902. c. 122 p. il. 12°, pap., 25 c. net.

Southwestern reporter, v. 67. Permanent ed., Apr. 7-May 19, 1902. St. Paul, West Pub. Co., 1902. c. 40+1195 p. O. (National reporter system, state ser.) shp., $4.
Contains all the current decisions of the supreme and appellate courts of Ark., Ky., Mo., Tenn., Tex., and I. T. With table of southwestern cases in which rehearings have been denied. Also, table of writs of error denied by the supreme court of Texas in cases in the court of civil appeals. Also, tables of southwestern cases published in vs. 69, Ark. reports; 164, Mo. reports; 94, Texas reports. A table of statutes construed is given in the index.

****Stokes**, Anson Phelps. Cruising in the West Indies. N. Y., Dodd, Mead & Co., 1902. [Jl.] c. 3-126 p. O. cl., $1.25 net.
An address made by the author in the New York Yacht Club, May 15, 1902, giving an itinerary for a cruise to the West Indies next winter.

Story, W: Wetmore. In defense of Judas; being a reprint of "A Roman lawyer in Jerusalem." Wausau, Wis., The Philosopher Press, 1902. sq. 24°, bds., $1.

Thurston, Rob. H: Stationary steam engines, simple and compound; especially as adapted to light and power plants. 7th ed. rev. and enl. N. Y., J: Wiley & Sons, 1902. c. 341 p. il. pls., 8°, cl., $2.50.

***Tooker**, W: Wallace. Algonquian series; researches relating to the early Indians of New York and New England; their antiquities, language, etc. In 10 v. v. 9-10. N. Y., Francis P. Harper, 1902. ea., 12°, cl., $1.50 net.
Contents: No. 9. The names Chichahominy, Pamunkey and the Kuskarawaokes, 90 p.; no. 10, The significance of John Eliot's Natick and the name Merrimac, 56 p.

***Trask**, Rob. Dana. Human knowledge and human conduct. Haverhill, Mass., Robert Dana Trask, 1901, [1902.] c. '88. 8+200+20 p. O. cl., $2 net.
The author says that his purpose is to make a survey of the field of human knowledge; and that the prominent features of the present work are its outlines, tables, and chart. The book is arranged to convey information on history, philosophy, art, the mental and moral sciences, etc., and is intended as a guide to human conduct.

Twing, *Mrs.* Carolinn Edna Skinner. Henry Drummond in spirit life. Springfield, Mass., Star Publishing Co., 1902. c. 46 p. S. pap., 10 c.

Vancil, Frank M. The school congress; parliamentary rhetoricals for the use of public schools, societies, etc.; a concise and practical outline and treatise, adapted to literary assemblies, for the organizing and conducting of parliamentary debate, and the acquirement of parliamentary rules. N. Y., E. L. Kellogg & Co., [1902.] c. 48 p. 12°, limp cl., 25 c.

***Vaughan**, V. C., *M.D., and* Novey, F. G., *M.D.* Cellular toxins. 4th ed. Phil., Lea Bros. & Co., 1902. c. 480 p. 8°, cl., $3 net.

Waller, A. R., *and* Barrow, G. H. S. John Henry, Cardinal Newman. Bost., Small, Maynard & Co., 1901. c. 18+150 p. por. 24°, (Westminster biographies.) cl., 75 c.

Ware, W: Rotch, *ed.* Topical architecture: a library of classified architectural motives and details. Bost., American Architect and Building News Co., 1902. c. 2 v., pls. 4°, $7.50.

Warren, S: E: Warren's physical geography; rev. and brought up to the present time. Phil. and N. Y., Butler, Sheldon & Co., 1902. 144 p. il. maps, f°, bds., $1.25.

***White**, W. H. The book of orchids. N. Y., J: Lane, 1902. c. 15+118 p. il. D. (Handbooks of practical gardening, no. 8.) cl., $1 net.
The author was born in Exeter, Devonshire. He has for the past thirteen years filled the position of orchid grower to Sir Trevor Lawrence, president of the Royal Horticultural Society. He is a contributor to *The Orchid Review* and *The Gardiners' Chronicle*, and a member of the Royal Horticultural Society, to which he has sent many exhibits. Besides the information about orchid culture, there is a brief introduction on the history of the orchid.

Wynkoop, R: Schuremans, of New Jersey. 2d ed. N. Y., Richard Wynkoop, 1902. c. 142 p. por. 8°, cl., $3.

ORDER LIST.

ABBEY PRESS, 114 Fifth Ave., New York.

Allen, Battling with love $1.00
Hutchinson, Primrose diplomacy 1.25
Kuttner, German conversation course, Sections 1 and 2 50
Leroy, A silken snare 50
Page, Tommy Atkins episode 1.00
Smiley, Lays and lyrics 1.25

ACME PUBLISHING CO., Morgantown, W. Va.

Maxwell, Jonathan Fish and his neighbors. 1.00

ALLEN, LANE & SCOTT, 23 S. Fifth St., Philadelphia.

Balch, Antarctica (for private distribution)

AMERICAN ARCHITECT AND BUILDING NEWS CO., 211 Tremont St., Boston.

Ware, Topical architecture, 2 v....... 7.50

AMERICAN SUNDAY-SCHOOL UNION, 1122 Chestnut St., Philadelphia.

*Rice, Short history of the International lesson system............net, 25

ANGEL GUARDIAN PRESS, 92 Ruggles St., Boston.

Ryan, Elocution and dramatic art..... 75

D. APPLETON & CO., 72 Fifth Ave., New York.

Baskett *and* Ditmars, Story of the amphibians and reptiles.............. 60
**Crowest, Art of music........net, 35
Doty, Instruction in the principles of prompt aid to the injured, 4th rev. enl. ed. 1.50
**Hopkins, care of the teeth......net, 75

D. APPLETON & CO.—*Continued.*

†Norris, The credit of the country (A. T. C. L., 313)................50 c.; $1.00

THEODORE AUDEL & CO., 63 Fifth Ave., New York.

Hawkins, Self-help mechanical drawing. 2.00

J. BAER'S SONS, Lancaster, Pa.

Agricultural almanac, 1903........... 10

BAKER, VOORHIS & CO., 66 Nassau St., New York.

New York amendments to Birdseye's statutes and general laws........... 2.00

BANCROFT-WHITNEY CO., 438 Montgomery St., San Francisco, Cal.

California, *Supreme ct.*, Repts., v. 135 (Pomeroy) 3.00

BANKS LAW PUB. CO., 21 Murray St., New York.

Pennsylvania, *Supreme ct.*, Repts...... 3.50

A. S. BARNES & CO., 156 Fifth Ave., New York.

**Johnson, A world's shrine ......net, 1.00

MATTHEW BENDER, 511-513 Broadway, Albany, N. Y.

New York, Supplement to general laws and revised statutes of the state.... 2.00

BENZIGER BROS., 36 Barclay St., New York.

Hedges, Statistics concerning education in the Philippine Islands............ 10

BOWEN-MERRILL Co., 9-11 W. Washington St., Indianapolis.

**Merrill, The man Shakespeare...net, $1.25

BURROWS BROS. Co., 133 Euclid Ave., Cleveland, O.

*Denton, Brief description of New York. ....net, $1.50; net, 3.00

A. L. BURT Co., 52-58 Duane St., New York.

Longfellow, Outre mer 1.00
Malory, King Arthur and his noble knights 1.00

BUTLER, SHELDON & Co., 78 Fifth Ave., New York; 919 Walnut St., Philadelphia.

Hunt *and* Gourley, Modern pronouncing speller 20
Warren, Physical geography, rev. ed.. 1.25

CALLAGHAN & Co., 114 Monroe St., Chicago.

Illinois, *Appellate courts*, Repts., v. 100 (Newell) 3.75

COMMERCIAL BOOK Co., 69 Wall St., New York.

McMaster, Commercial digest and business forms. 6.00
——, Commercial cases 6.00

CORPORATION LEGAL MANUAL Co., Plainfield, N. J.

American Corporation Legal manual, v. 10, 1902 (Keasbey and Honeyman.) 5.00

DODD, MEAD & Co., 372 Fifth Ave., New York.

**Morgan, League of the Ho-de-no-sau-nee or Iroquois, limited ed., net, $15; net, 30.00
**Stokes, Cruising in the West Indies, net, 1.25

THE DOMINION Co., 134 E. Van Buren St., Chicago.

Halstead, The world on fire, $1.50; $2.25; 3.00

M. A. DONOHUE & C., 407-409 Dearborn St., Chicago.

Barrett, Life of Abraham Lincoln..... 1.00
Godbey, Life of Henry M. Stanley 1.00
Johnson, Life of W. T. Sherman...... 1.00
Poore *and* Tiffany, Life of U. S. Grant. 1.00

FRANK P. DUFRESNE, 85 E. 4th St., St. Paul, Minn.

Minnesota, *Supreme ct.*, Repts., v. 84 (Wenzell.) 2.75

E. P. DUTTON & Co., 31 W. 23d St., New York.

Oliver, Dangerous trades..........net, 8.00
**Smith, The home aquarium......net, 1.20

ENGINEERING NEWS Co., 220 Broadway, New York.

Judson, City roads and pavements, 2d ed. 2.00

DANA ESTES & Co., 208-218 Summer St., Boston.

**Allen, Play away................net, 75

FERRIS & LEACH, 20 N. 7th St., Philadelphia.

Myers, Quaker arrivals at Philadelphia, 1682-1750........ .... $1.25

GINN & Co., 29 Beacon St., Boston.

Bloch, The future of war, new issue.. 60
Chantepie, Religion of the Teutons.... 2.50
Lockwood, Teacher's manual to accompany Lockwood and Emerson's "Composition and rhetoric."........ 30
Pinney, Spanish and English composition, bks. 1 and 2................ea., 65

CHARLES E. GOODSPEED, 5A Park St., Boston.

*Percy, Letters of Hugh Earl Percy, net, 4.00

R. C. HALL, 345 Fourth Ave., Pittsburg, Pa.

Hall, Pittsburg securities............gratis

F. P. HARPER, 14 W. 22d St., New York.

*Tooker, Algonquian series, v. 9-10, ea., net, 1.50

T. W. HARTFIELD, 58 Broad St., New York.

Hartfield, Exchange pocket cipher code for bankers, etc.................... 2.00

HERALD STATE PRINTERS, Grand Forks, North Dakota.

North Dakota, *Supreme ct.*, Repts., v. 10 (Cochrane.) 4.25

HICKS-JUDD Co., San Francisco.

Hatfield, Geyserland and wonderland.. 24

HOUGHTON, MIFFLIN & Co., 4 Park St., Boston.

**Fielding, Journal of a journey to Lisbon limited. Special ed..........net, 5.00
**Fiske, Works, ed. de luxe, 24 v. subs., ea., net, $5; net, 10.00
**Sill, Poems, Special ed..........net, 5.00

HUDSON-KIMBERLY PUB. Co., 1014 Wyandotte St., Kansas City, Mo.

Root, Military topography, 3d rev. ed.. 2.50

INTERNATIONAL CABLE DIRECTORY Co., Chese-borough Bldg., 17 State St., New York.

International cable directory of the world 15.00

INTERNATIONAL NEWS Co., 83-85 Duane St., New York.

Gabelsberger Shorthand Society, Reader to Henry Richter's graphic shorthand 50

JENNINGS & PYE, 220 W. 4th St., Cincinnati, O.

*Methodist Episcopal church in America. 2 v........................net, 50

F. M. JOHNSON, M.D., 117 Beacon St., Boston.

Johnson, Forest, lake, and river; Fishes of New England and Canada, ed. de luxe, 2 v. and portfolio, per set, $300; 500.00

E. L. KELLOGG & Co., 61 E. 9th St., New York.

Vancil, The school congress parliamentary rhetoricals. 25

CHARLES H. KERR & Co., 56 Fifth Ave., Chicago.

Broome, Last days of the Ruskin Co-operative Association. 50

K. L. KILNER & Co., 824 Arch St., Philadelphia.

Leahy, A child of the flood............ $1.00

JOHN LANE, 67 Fifth Ave., New York.

Leahy, A child of the flood............ $1.00

LEA BROS. & Co., 706 Sansom St., Philadelphia.

*Bacon, Manual of otology, 3d rev. enl. ed. ....net, 2.25
*Cheyne *and* Burghard, Manual of surgical treatment, v. 6. ....net, 5.00
*Schafer, Essentials in histology.. net, 3.00
*Vaughan *and* Novey, Cellular toxins, 4th ed. ....net, 3.00

J. B. LIPPINCOTT Co., Washington Sq., Philadelphia.

**Hopkins, The roller bandage, 5th ed. rev. ....net, 1.50
Judson *and* Gittings, Artificial feeding of infants 2.00
Robb, Aseptic surgical technique 2.00

THE LITTLE-PRESTON Co., Battle Creek, Mich.

Holmes, The Burton Holmes lectures, 10 v., v. 1-6.....subs., per set, $51; 65.00

McMASTER Co., 69 Wall St., New York.

McMaster, Irregular and regular commercial paper 2.00

JOS. ST. CLAIR McQUILKIN, 63 Nooman St., East Orange, N. J.

Rogers, Government clerks ......25 c.; 1.00

JAMES C. MALONY, 236½ E. Madison St., Chicago.

Malony, 20th century guide for mixing fancy drinks 1.00

G. N. MORANG & Co., Ltd., Toronto, Can.

Morang's annual register of Canadian affairs, 1901. ....$3.00; 4.00

NASSAU PRESS, Richmond Hill, Long Island, N. Y.

Davison, Selling the bear's hide 1.00

L. C. PAGE & Co., 200 Summer St., Boston.

Barnett, Jerry's reward 50

E. O. PAINTER & Co., De Land, Fla.

Ballough, The power that heals. 1.00
Ballough, Sibylline leaves............ 1.00

THE PHILOSOPHER PRESS, Wausau, Wis.

Story, In defense of Judas 1.00

G. P. PUTNAM'S SONS, 29 W. 23d St., New York.

**Châteaubriand, Memoirs of François Rene *Vicomte* de Châteaubriand, 6 v., ea., net, 3.75
Creswicke, South Africa and the Transvaal war, 6 v. ....per v., 2.50
**Crosland, The unspeakable Scot, net, 1.25
**Dmitriev-Mamonóv *and* Zdziarski, Guide to the Great Siberian Railway,... net, 3.50

G. P. PUTNAM'S SONS.—*Continued.*

**Edwards, Wales ......net, $1.35; net, $1.60
†Merejkowski, Romance of Leonardo da Vinci 1.50
**Miller, Mediæval Rome.net, $1.35; net, 1.60

QUAIL & WARNER, 23 Park Row, New York.

Cohen, A girl who wrote............. 1.50

G. H. RAMEY & SON, Alexandria, Va.

*Snowden, Some old historic landmarks of Virginia and Maryland......net, 25

RELIGIOUS HERALD Co., Richmond, Va.

Jeter, Baptist principles reset.......... 1.00

SANTANELLI PUBLISHING Co., Lansing, Mich.

*Santanelli, Is man a free agent? ..net, 1.00

SCROLL PUB. Co., 308 Dearborn St., Chicago.

Kendall, Pacific trail campfires........ 1.50

SHARP & ALLEMAN, 37 S. 3d St., Philadelphia.

Sharp & Alleman Co.'s Lawyers and bankers' directory, 1902............. 5.00

SILVER, BURDETT & Co., 29-33 E. 19th St., New York.

Knapp, How to live 36

SMALL, MAYNARD & Co., Boston.

**Day, Pine tree ballads...........net, 1.00
Waller *and* Barrow, John Henry, Cardinal Newman 75

SMITHSONIAN INSTITUTE, Washington, D. C.

Langley, Experiments in aerodynamics. 1.00

STAR PUBLISHING Co., 91 Sherman St., Springfield, Mass.

Revelations from the eternal world... 20
Twing, Henry Drummond in spirit life. 10

ROBERT DANA TRASK, Haverhill, Mass.

*Trask, Human knowledge and human conduct ....net, 2.00

UNIVERSITY OF CHICAGO PRESS, Chicago.

*Bolza, Concerning the geodesic curvature. ....net, 25

THE WENBORNE-SUMMER Co., Buffalo, N. Y.

Bishop, The red book of Niagara 25

WEST PUB. Co., 52-58 W. 3d St., St. Paul, Minn.

Atlantic reporter, v. 51 .... 4.00
Southwestern reporter, v. 67 .... 4.00

JOHN WILEY & SONS, 41-45 E. 19th St., New York.

Fowler, Sewage works analyses...... 2.00
Hamilton *and* Bond, Gunner's catechism. 1.00
Simon, Philosophical essay 2.00

WOMAN'S PUBLISHING Co., Kansas City, Mo.

Herrold, Woman. $4; 5.00

WILLIAM WOOD & Co., 51 Fifth Ave., New York.

*Smart, Handbook for the hospital corps of the United States Army, 3d ed. rev. and enl.............net, 2.50

RICHARD WYNKOOP, New York.

Wynkoop, Schuremans of New Jersey, 2d ed. 3.00

BOWEN-ME

**Merrill,

BURROWS I

*Denton,
York. .

A. L. BUR
Longfellov
Malory, K
knights

BUTLER, S
York:

Hunt *and*
ing spel
Warren, I

CALLAGHA
Illinois,
(Newel

COMN

McMaste
ness fo
——, Co

CORPORAT

America
v. 10,
man.)

DODI

**Morga
sau-ne

**Stoke

THE D

Halstea

M. A. I

Barrett,
Godbey,
Johnson
Poore

FRANK

Minnel
(Wen

E. I

Oliver,
**Smi

Manufactures, Exported from the

The Publishers' Weekly.

FOUNDED BY F. LEYPOLDT.

JULY 19, 1902.

The editor does not hold himself responsible for the views expressed in contributed articles or communications

All matter, whether for the reading-matter columns or advertising pages, should reach this office not later than Wednesday noon, to insure insertion in the same week's issue.

Books for the "Weekly Record," as well as all information intended for that department, should reach this office by Tuesday morning of each week.

Publishers are requested to furnish title-page proofs and advance information of books forthcoming, both for entry in the lists and for descriptive mention. An early copy of each book published should be forwarded, as it is of the utmost importance that the entries of books be made as promptly and as perfectly as possible. In many cases booksellers depend on the PUBLISHERS' WEEKLY solely for their information. The Record of New Publications of the PUBLISHERS' WEEKLY is the material of the "American Catalogue" and so forms the basis of trade bibliography in the United States.

"I hold every man a debtor to his profession, from the which, as men do of course seek to receive countenance and profit, so ought they of duty to endeavor themselves by way of amends to be a help and an ornament thereunto."—LORD BACON.

A QUESTION OF MUSICAL COPYRIGHT.

A CASE now in the Circuit Court of the United States for the Southern District of New York is being anxiously watched by all interested in musical copyright. The case in question is one to determine whether the production of copyrighted music by means of perforated rolls used either in a mechanical piano or organ is an infringement under the Copyright law.

A similar case came before Judge Colt, of the United States District Court of Massachusetts, in 1888, whose opinion was adverse to the publishers. Judge Colt's opinion, in brief, was that—

"To the ordinary mind it is certainly a difficult thing to consider these strips of paper as sheet music. There is no clef, or bars, or lines, or spaces, or other marks which are found in common printed music, but only plain strips of paper, with rows of holes or perforations."

"Copyright is the exclusive right of the owner to multiply and to dispose of copies of an intellectual production. I cannot convince myself that these perforated slips of paper are copies of sheet music, within the meaning of the copyright law. They are not made to be addressed to the eye as sheet music, but they form part of a machine. They are not designed to be used for such purposes as sheet music, nor do they in any sense occupy the same field as sheet music. They are a mechanical invention made for the sole purpose of performing tunes mechanically upon a musical instrument."

Thus far there has been no successful appeal from Judge Colt's opinions, whence it seems to follow that the composer or publisher of a copyrighted piece of music has no protection against a new system of notation or method of performance. Copyright, according to Judge Colt, is not on the idea or the production of the brain, but only on printed notes instead of holes punched in strips of paper, and on the notes as a guide for reproduction by hands instead of by the feet. As *The Musical Age* points out, "Considering the great number of mechanical pianos now in existence, it is apparent that the publishers of music for them are highly privileged in this freedom to seize and issue any copyrighted composition they please and to sell the same in unlimited quantities without payment of royalty and in disregard of the equitable rights of the composers and the original publishers."

This is a perversion of the intention of the framers of the law, and there ought to be some way of stopping a form of piracy which up to the present time has not been successfully opposed.

TO PROTECT ORIGINALITY OF DESIGN AND TO REPEAL CUSTOMS DUTIES ON BOOKS.

THE INTERNATIONAL CONGRESS OF PUBLISHERS has sent a circular to the various national associations calling attention to the resolutions passed at the sessions of the Congress at Brussels and London regarding the protection of the "get-up" or form of a publication. At Brussels the following was passed:

"Starting with the consideration that the publisher should be protected, like every other manufacturer, in all things appertaining to the form or 'get up' of his productions, the Congress expresses a wish

"That the regulation for the protection of a new form or 'get up' of a publication should be inserted in the law concerning the protection of industrial property.

"The Congress advises the various Publishers' Associations in every country to aim at the realization of this desire, and later on to find out ways and means to make this question an international one, as also one of literary and artistic copyright."

In London the following resolution was passed:

"That the principle of material property in innovations with regard to form or model which are exemplified by a publication should be formally recognized by the legislatures of the different countries."

The "innovations in form" which it is desired should be better protected are set forth as follows:

"1. The outward appearance individualized by the cover, illustrated or not, the size and the letter-press of books forming a collection.

"2. The uniform character chosen by a publisher for all his works or for special publications.

"3. The arrangement, plan, idea, etc., of text-books, chrestomathies, methods, compilations, almanacs, etc."

Accompanying the circular is a table

questions addressed to the national associations designed to secure information for the Permanent Office in regard to the status of the movement in each country.

The Permanent Office also renews, in another circular, its request that the national associations keep it informed of any steps taken in their respective countries to secure the repeal of customs duties on books in accordance with resolutions passed by the Congress in 1896 and 1901.

NEWSPAPER NOT A MANUFACTURING ESTABLISHMENT.

JUDGE MILLER, according to the *Louisville Courier-Journal*, handed down an opinion in the case of the Columbia Finance and Trust Company against the *Dispatch* Publishing Company, in which he held that a newspaper is not a manufacturing establishment, like a rolling mill or a foundry, as specified by the statute. For this reason the lien claimed by the Manufacturers' Paper Company for $3,072.52 for paper furnished the defunct concern is denied.

The following is from the opinion: "It is true that a newspaper is sometimes spoken of as a manufacturer of public opinion, but in using this description it is not intended to convey the impression that a newspaper makes or manufactures public opinion for sale, in the sense that a rolling mill or foundry manufactures iron or iron implements for sale. The claim of the Manufacturers' Paper Company to a lien for material and supplies will have to be denied."

The opinion was upon exceptions to the Commissioner's report and in chief for final judgment.

MINNESOTA BACKS ITS AUTHORS AGAINST INDIANA'S.

"Indianapolis," says the *St. Paul Pioneer Press*, "is very much 'set up' about its literary standing, but the Twin Cities can boast of writers whose productions are doing the country more good than those of the whole crowd of novel writers. We refer to those connected with the Minnesota Agricultural School and Experiment Station. They are not only teaching American farmers how to make two blades of grass grow where only one grew before, but they are doubling the productivity of our wheats and other grains., increasing the weight of our cattle, multiplying our fruits, teaching us the food value of different products, and making life more 'worth living' than ever before. So long as St. Paul is the centre for the distribution of such beneficent literature as the class here referred to, we are quite willing that Indianapolis shall remain the centre for novels."

DATING WATER MARKS.

RICHARD GARNETT recently wrote to the London *Times:* "I should be glad to say a few words upon a subject of some importance to archivists and men of letters who may hereafter have to deal with the dates of documents, more especially private correspondence. I refer to the almost universal omission by paper-makers of the date of the manufacture of their paper, which used to be recorded by the water-mark.

"Everyone who has had occasion to determine the date of a letter left undated by the writer, and where the postmark was absent or illegible, must have felt under deep obligation to the paper-maker, by the aid of whose water-mark it could in most cases be approximately ascertained. It is to be feared that the inquirers of the future will frequently find themselves in difficulty; especially as in former days the postmark was impressed upon the letter itself, while it is now stamped upon an envelope which may easily be lost or thrown away.

"Nothing could be easier than to revert to the old practice, and such a step would earn for the manufacturers the gratitude of all concerned in historical or literary research.

"The great importance which a dated water-mark may possess in legal proceedings is strikingly illustrated by a passage in the interesting letters of Céar de Saussure on England in the time of the first Georges, recently published by Mr. Murray. A dishonest steward endeavored, by means of forged documents, to make his mistress, the Duchess of Buckingham, responsible for the repayment of large sums which had in fact never been advanced to her.

"A lengthy lawsuit followed, which came before the Court of King's Bench, and the Duchess, who had already been condemned to lose the lawsuit by the Judges of the Court below, was going to be condemned by those of the higher Court, when one of them had a sudden inspiration. Seizing a contested bill, the Judge held it up to the light, and, having examined it carefully, he discovered to a certainty that the bill was forged, the date and water-mark on the paper being several years posterior to the date of the writing."

COPYRIGHT MATTERS.

CANADIAN COPYRIGHT ASSOCIATION.

IN the Council Room of the Board of Trade at Toronto on July 7 a meeting of half a dozen of the publishing houses of Toronto was held and a Canadian Copyright Association was formed with the following officers: Honorary President, John Ross Robertson; President, W. J. Gage; First Vice-President, D. A. Rose; Second Vice-President, A. S. Hart; Secretary-Treasurer, A. Briggs; Executive Committee, W. P. Gundy, J. R. Barber, Atwell Flemming, A. E. Huestis, Thos. G. Wilson and J. A. Cooper. The object of the new association is to agitate for a satisfactory Canadian copyright law.

FALSE NOTICE OF COPYRIGHT.

JUDGE WALLACE, of the Federal Court, recently held that a defendant who imported from Germany and sold in the United States books bearing a false copyright notice which had been impressed on them by the publisher in Germany by defendant's authorization was not liable to the penalty, the statute having no extraterritorial effect.

OBITUARY NOTES.

Mrs. Annie French Hector, better known by her pseudonym, "Mrs. Alexander," died in London July 10. Mrs. Hector came of the well-known Irish family of French, of Roscommon, and was born in Dublin in 1825. She began to write at an early age, but her marriage with Alexander Hector, a Scotchman who was the companion of Layard in his exploration of Nineveh, interrupted achievements in this direction. After her husband's death she resumed her pen, and her first published work, "The Wooing O't," written in middle life, brought her at once a reputation with the public. But she herself recorded the fact that nearly every plot of her stories, which include "The Admiral's Ward," "Look Before You Leap," "A Crooked Path," "A Winning Hazard" and many more, was clearly formulated in her brain as long as five and twenty years previously, and, though she did not make any notes on the subjects, she remembered them all. Many of her novels were contributed in serial form to such magazines as *All the Year Round* and *Temple Bar*.

NOTES ON AUTHORS.

W. M. Ramsay, Professor of Humanity at Aberdeen, and author of a number of more or less popular books on the Scriptures, such as "Was Christ Born at Bethlehem?" etc., is at work on a life of St. Paul.

Mrs. Frances Hodgson Burnett Townsend has quite recovered her health and has taken a cottage at Easthampton, L. I., where she will spend the summer at work upon her next novel, "The Destiny of Bettina."

Wu Ting-Fang, the Chinese Minister, who will soon return to China, has made it known that he intends to write two books. One of these will record his impressions of America and will be for circulation in the United States. The other will consist of his world-wide observations outside of China, and is intended for sale in his own country to educate his people in Western civilization.

The order of knighthood has been conferred on F. C. Burnand, editor of *Punch;* Gilbert Parker, the well-known novelist; Dr. Conan Doyle, novelist and historian of the Boer war; William Laird Clowes, naval critic and historian, and William Allan, author of several volumes of poetry and other works of a practical order. Leslie Stephen, the first editor of "The Dictionary of National Biography," and author of "The Science of Ethics" and other philosophical works, is made K. C. B., and the same honor is conferred upon Professor William Ramsay, the well-known chemist. King Edward VII. has established a new Order of Merit, which, it is understood, does not carry with it any title or precedence, or the right to use any special letters after the names of its members. The order, however, is to be extremely limited in number, and suitable decorations and insignia are provided. A cross of red and blue enamel of eight points, bearing the words "For Merit" in gold letters, in a laurel wreath on a blue enamel centre, is to be the badge of the order. Members of the order will be permitted to affix a facsimile of the badge to their arms. The seal of the order will give a facsimile of the badge, with the Royal Arms on a white ground, inscribed "The Seal of the Order of Merit." Among the first members are the Right Hon. John Morley, the Right Hon. W. E. H. Lecky, Lord Kelvin and Lord Lister. Other honors conferred on men who are well known in literature are a Privy Councillorship for Sir Alfred Lyall, author of "Asiatic Studies" and other works, and a Companionship of the Bath upon Frank Marzials, of the War Office, who has written several biographies and edited, conjointly with Eric Robertson, the *Great Writers* series. Many of the other recipients of knighthoods and other honors have written books, especially the physicians and surgeons, who figure so liberally in this list as compared with previous occasions.

BIBLIOGRAPHIC NOTES.

Elliot Stock, London, will hereafter publish his "Book Prices Current" in quarterly parts as well as in the annual volume. The first part will be published shortly.

Alexander Denham & Co., London, who are represented in this country by E. A. Denham, 28 W. Thirty-third Street, New York, have published a very interesting catalogue of books, manuscripts, autographs and drawings, that is as handsome typographically as it is rich in contents. (195 titles + facsimiles. 2*s.* 6*d.*)

Dodd, Mead & Co. are now taking up subscriptions for the 1901-1902 volume of "American Book Prices Current," compiled, as heretofore, by Luther S. Livingston. As many intending subscribers were disappointed last season, and as the edition is limited to the number called for, with 116 copies to spare, all who desire a copy will do well to place their orders now. Thirty copies will be printed on large paper for those wishing to make annotations.

The Bulletin of Bibliography for July, published by the Boston Book Company, 83 Francis Street, Boston, contains an article on "Practical Bibliography," by J. I. Wyer, Jr., librarian of the Nebraska Library; the concluding portion of an annotated list of books and articles to aid in the study of King Alfred's life and times, by Mary Medlicott; a continuation of the "Errata in Poole's Index and Supplements," compiled by Frederika Wendté; also, Part viii of the second series of George Watson Cole's bibliography of "Bermuda in Periodical Literature."

Catalogues of New and Second-Hand Books.—*Joseph Baer & Co.*, Hochstr., 6, Frankfurt, A. M., Theoretische National Oekonomie, Social-wissenschaft, Arbeiter- u. Bodenfrage, Frauenfrage, Armenwesen, Utopien. (No. 457, 1656 titles;) also, Jurisprudenz, 2. Abth., Ausländisches Recht; 3. Abth., Strafrecht. (Nos. 458, 459, 1789, 3311 titles.)—*Breslauer & Meyer*, 136 Leipziger str., Berlin, the art library of the late Eduard Dobbert. (3319 titles.)—*Alexander Duncker*, 178 Fulton Street, New York, new and second-hand books on Chemistry, Pharmacy, Technology and the allied sciences. (No. 28 2428 titles.)—*Everett & Francis Co.*, 116 E. 23d Street, New York, Miscellaneous. (No. 4, 323 titles.)—*Harry Falkenau*, 167 Madison Street, Chicago, Ill., Americana, Metaphysics, Secret Societies, etc. (No. 19, 881 titles.)—*E. W. Johnson*, 2 E. 42d Street, New York, Americana, the drama, privately printed books, etc. (No. 24, 419 titles.)—*Karslake &Co.*, 61 Charing Cross, London, W. C., Rare books in fine modern, and a few in old historical bindings. (No. 95, 434 titles.)—*Maggs Bros.*, 109 Strand, London, W. C., Topographical, heraldic and miscellaneous. (No. 189, 1190 titles.)—*Bernard Quaritch*, 15 Piccadilly, London, Books on natural history, including selections from the libraries formed by the late Alphonse Milne Edwards, N. Burgess, William Matthews, Miss E. A. Ormerod, G. R. Ryder and John Young, also, important books from other sources. Pt. I. (No. 215, 727 titles *1s.*)—*M. Spirgatis*, 23 Marien str., Leipzig, Uralaltaische Völker u. Sprachen. (No. 89, 523 titles;) also, Ostasiatische, indochinesische u. malayo-polynesische Sprachen. (No. 90, 419 titles.)—*John E. Scopes*, 29 Tweddle Building, Albany, N. Y., America and American history. (No. 13, 122 titles.)—*Henry Stevens, Son & Stiles*, 39 Gt. Russell St., London, W. C., Americana. (No. 81, 236 titles.)

BUSINESS NOTES.

Boston, Mass.—The Sheriff is in possession of B. F. Larrabee's.

Boston, Mass.—Catharine G. McAdams has succeeded Charles W. McAdams, bookseller.

Cincinnati, O.—The American Book Company will erect a new building on the Anderson homestead property, 400x169 feet, at Third and Pike streets. The new building may not be begun before next year.

Corning, N. Y.—Harry J. Sternberg has purchased the old-established bookstore of Clute & Way, and extensive improvements in arrangement and equipment will follow. There will be an expansion of business all along the line.

Findlay, O.—D. C. Connell & Son, booksellers, are reported to have gone into involuntary bankruptcy.

Grand Island, Neb.—W. H. Platte, bookseller, is selling out and will retire from business.

Greensboro, N. C.—J. J. Stone & Co. have bought the bookstore formerly owned by E. P. Irwin.

Greenville, Miss.—G. F. Archer, bookseller, who has occupied the same store here for thirty-two years, is selling out his stock and will retire from business.

New York City.—The Metaphysical Publishing Company, of No. 114 West Thirty-second street, is in financial difficulties, and on July 14 Judge Fitzgerald, of the Supreme Court, appointed Vernon M. Davis temporary receiver of the assets, with a bond of $50,000, in proceedings for the voluntary dissolution of the corporation brought by Directors Leander E. Whipple, E. F. Stephenson and George A. M. Stevenson. The liabilities are $24,612 The nominal assets are $18,150, and actual assets $14,705.

South Bend, Ind.—Herr & Herr have bought out the Tribune Store, one of the largest book, stationery and fancy goods concerns in Northern Indiana and Southern Michigan, which for twenty-five years has been conducted by the Tribune Printing Company. It was founded in 1874, a few years after the organization of the Tribune Printing Company, in the store at what is now No. 127 West Washington street. When the Oliver Opera-House Block was completed the business was removed to North Main street. The new firm is composed of Charles C. Herr, of Goshen, the head of Herr & Co., one of the leading stationery stores in that city and of his uncle, Eugene M. Herr, the head of *The Tribune's* job department and one of the best-known men in South Bend. There will be no change in the *personnel* of the staff of the Tribune Store, Mr. Axtel Swanson and Miss Jessie Valentine both remaining in the positions that they have filled so ably for many years.

LITERARY AND TRADE NOTES.

E. P. Dutton & Co. have in preparation a translation of the Taine letters that were so favorably received in France.

Rees, Welsh & Co., of Philadelphia, have published a volume of poems by the late Daniel L. Dawson, entitled "The Seeker in the Marshes."

J. B. Lippincott Company will publish in the fall a life of Pinturicchio, the master of decoration and the friend of the youthful Raphael, by Corrado Ricci. The volume will be adequately illustrated.

E. R. F. Blogg has resigned his position with B. G. Eichelberger, of Baltimore, to become manager of the retail department of Wm. J. C. Dulany Company. He will be pleased to receive advance announcements, catalogues, etc.

The facsimile of the manuscript of Milton's minor poems, to which we referred in our issue for April 12, was actually made in 1899 for members of Trinity College, and it is the remaining copies of that facsimile that are now offered for sale by Deighton, Bell & Co. and Macmillan & Bowes, both of Cambridge, England.

The Century Company will publish a condensed edition of the Nicolay-Hay life of Lincoln, prepared by the late John G. Nicolay. It will contain all the essential facts of President Lincoln's life contained in the ten-volume edition. They will publish shortly a new story of Southern life by Mrs. Ruth McEnery Stuart, entitled "Napoleon Jackson."

Allan, Lane & Scott have published for Edwin Swift Balch a monograph entitled "Antarctica," an argument in favor of the claims of Lieutenant Wilkes in particular, and certain American sealers and traders in general, upholding the right of American names to appear and remain on the new continent, in which a greater interest is growing as our knowledge of it is increased.

A. Wessels Company have almost ready a volume of clever golf stories entitled "The Magic Mashie," by E. L. Sabin, a well-known contributor to *Outing, Golf* and other magazines devoted to out-door life; also, "The Conquest of the Air," by John Alexander, with chapters on the "Balloon in War," "Scientific Ballooning," "The Achievements of Santos-Dumont and Others," "The Air ship of Yesterday and To-day," with a preface by Sir Hiram Maxim. Both volumes will be illustrated.

A. H. Smythe, Columbus, O., has just ready an "Archæological History of Ohio—the Mound Builders and later Indians," by Gerard Fowke, published by the Ohio State Archæological and Historical Society. The work is not written for scientists or specialists, but is intended to lighten the labor of those interested in archæology who have not the time or opportunity to wade through the vast amount of literature that has accumulated on this subject in the past fifty years. The work is very fully illustrated.

Drexel Biddle, Philadelphia, is about to publish "A Wanderer's Legend," by Maxwell Sommerville, well known as a collector of engraved gems and a writer thereon, also as a writer of books on travel. The forthcoming book is the narrative of the Wandering Jew, who is supposed to have appeared at the Diet of Speyer and then to have related the history of his wanderings to the assembled ecclesiastics. The story embraces a variety of Talmudic and early Christian tradition, and some Moslem traditions also, and its general scope embraces a summary of the world's history, and particularly of the history of religion throughout the centuries during which Ahasuerus had been wandering. The book is illustrated with drawings by the author.

The Funk & Wagnalls Company have just published a little book by the Rev. Dr. Arthur T. Pierson, entitled "The Gordian Knot, or, The Problem Which Baffles Infidelity," which is the outcome of honest doubt seeking a true answer to great questions, and is addressed to candid enquirers after truth; also, four new abridged editions of their "Standard Dictionary," edited by James C. Fernald, viz.: *The Introductory Standard Dictionary*, which belongs to the Educational Series of the "Standard" editions, and *The Concise Standard, The Comprehensive Standard* and *The Comprehensive Standard* which belong to the commercial Series. They will publish on the 25th inst. a work of interest to Jews and Gentiles, entitled "Jesus the Jew and other Addresses," by Harris Weinstock, who opposes the isolation of the Jews and advocates the newer and more liberal views that are helping to break down the walls of prejudice that are keeping the Jew apart from the rest of mankind; also, "A Brief of Necroscopy and Its Medico-Legal Relation," by Dr. Gustav Schmitt, which is immediately and practically adapted to the needs of coroners and physicians who are called upon to make examinations of dead bodies, and is also of assistance to every lawyer and medical expert who is engaged in the detection of crime resulting from administrations of poisons or other means of producing sudden death.

Houghton, Mifflin & Co. expect to publish in September the following fiction: "The Diary of a Saint," by Arlo Bates, a novel, in the form of a diary, presenting an eventful year in the life of a New England girl; "The Right Princess," by Clara Louise Burnham, a pioneer book in the field of fiction, being a Christian science novel, with much episode and action; "A Downrenter's Son," by Ruth Hall, a story of love and adventure in New York during the strange attempt to abolish rents about sixty years ago; and a new and complete edition of Maria S. Cummins's "The Lamplighter," the ever-popular novel of which there are several unauthorized and garbled editions in the market. In the department of history, biography and letters they announce John Fiske's last work, "New France and New England," which treats of the victory of the English civilization over the French and completes his chain of histories of the early development of our country; "Where American Independence Began," by Daniel Monro Wilson, an anecdotal history of Quincy, Mass., and its great families, the Adamses, Quinceys, Hoars and others; Lockhart's "Life of Sir Walter Scott," in five volumes, with exhaustive notes by S. W. Francis; "Nathaniel Hawthorne," by Professor George E. Woodbury, in the *American Men of Letters;* also, volume v. of "Letters to Washington," edited by S. W. Hamilton.

Lee & Shepard have under way an *autograph edition* of Mrs. Elizabeth Akers's "Sunset Song, and Other Verses," a volume of poems hitherto unpublished, with a single exception, "Rock Me to Sleep, Mother," which is printed at the end of the volume with a note from the publisher, giving its history. The Philadelphia *Saturday Evening Post*, it appears, originally printed the poem, paying the author $5. A firm of music publishers issued it with a setting by Earnest Leslie and paid nothing, but offered the author $5 apiece for any more songs as good as the first. As their profits during the first six months amounted to many thousands, they could then afford this extravagance, but when Mrs. Akers actually sent them a song they refused it on the ground that they "could do nothing with it." A few years after the first appearance of the song Alexander T. W. Ball, of New Jersey, declared that it was his. Certain newspapers espoused his cause, and had he not published what Rossiter Johnson calls the most absurd pamphlet ever written the real author might have been deprived even of the crdit of originating her pseudonym of "Florence Percy." The pamphlet aroused some able defenders for her, and at last the late William Douglas O'Connor, writing in the *New York Times*, utterly refuted Mr. Ball's pretensions to be "Florence Percy" or anything but an imitator. In her new volume Mrs. Akers includes a grateful eulogy of her defender.

TERMS OF ADVERTISING.

Under the heading "Books Wanted" book-trade subscribers are given the privilege of a free advertisement for books out of print, of five nonpareil lines exclusive of address, in any issue except special numbers, to an extent not exceeding 100 lines a year. If more than five lines are sent, the excess is at 10 cents a line, and amount should be inclosed. Bids for current books and such as may be easily had from the publishers, and repeated matter, as well as all advertisements from non-subscribers, must be paid for at the rate of 10 cents a line.

Under the heading "Books for Sale," the charge to subscribers and non-subscribers is 10 cents a nonpareil line for each insertion. No deduction for repeated matter.

All other small, undisplayed, advertisements will be charged at the uniform rate of 10 cents a nonpareil line. Eight words may be reckoned to the line.

Parties with whom we have no accounts must pay in advance, otherwise no notice will be taken of their communications.

BOOKS WANTED.

☞ ***In answering, please state edition, condition, and price, including postage or express charges.***

Houses that are willing to deal exclusively on a cash-on-delivery basis will find it to their advantage to put after their firm-name the word [Cash].

☞ ***Write your wants plainly and on one side of the sheet only. Illegibly-written "wants" will be considered as not having been received. The "Publishers' Weekly" does not hold itself responsible for errors.***

It should be understood that the appearance of advertisements in this column, or elsewhere in the "Publishers' Weekly" does not furnish a guarantee of credit. While it is endeavored to safeguard these columns by withdrawing the privilege of their use from advertisers who are not "good pay," booksellers should take the usual precaution, as to advertisers not known to them, that they would take in making sales to any unknown parties.

Adam, Meldrum & Anderson Co., Buffalo, N. Y.

Salem Witchcraft, 2 v., by C. W. Upham. Boston, 1867.

Arthur M. Allen, 508 Fulton St., Troy, N. Y.

Hutton's Mathematical Tracts, v. 1.
Hutton's Course in Mathematics, 2 v.
Marshall, Emma, Under Salisbury Spire.

The American News Co., N. Y.

The Last Heir; or, the Prediction. Pub. by Harper.

American Tract Society, 150 Nassau St., N. Y.

The College Year Book and Athletic Record, by E. Emerson, Jr. Pub. by Stone & Kimball.

Americus Law Book Co., Americus, Ga.

Any early Mississippi item.
Life S. S. Prentiss, by Shields.
Southern Colonial historical items.
Campaigns of 1781, by Gen. Lee.
Leisure Labors, by J. B. Cobb.

John R. Anderson, 114 5th Ave., N. Y.

Standard Dictionary, v. 1, cl.
Knauff's Athletics for Physical Culture.
Recent catalogues from all others than publishers.

Antiquarian Book Store, Omaha, Neb.

Pulpit Commentary, complete.
Biblical Museum, complete.

Wm. Ballantyne & Sons, 428 7th St., Washington, D. C.

Scudder, Nomenclator Geologicus. Smithsonian Inst.

Bancroft-Whitney Co., 438 Montgomery St., San Francisco, Cal.

Aiken, Vermont Reports, 2 v.

Theo. M Barber, Box 144, Pittsburgh, Pa. [*Cash.*]

Graham's Magazine, v. 21, 22, 23, 25, 26, 27, 39, and following.
Graham Everitt's English Caricaturists.
Sakoontala, New York, 1885, on Japan.
Bing's Artistic Japan, complete.

G. H. Barbour, 6016 Stanton Ave., Pittsburgh, Pa.

Anything pertaining to the Roberts Family.

H. C. Barnhart, York, Pa. [*Cash.*]

Cambridge on the Cam, by Chas. Astor Bristed.
Seton-Thompson, Wild Animals I Have Known, 1st ed.
Southern Literary Messenger, v. 1, nos. 1, 2, 1835.

N. J. Bartlett & Co., 28 Cornhill, Boston, Mass.

Haldeman, Pennsylvania Dutch. 1872.
Songs of Ancient People, by Edna Dean Proctor.
Stedman and Hutchinson, Library of American Literature.
Dyer, Gods in Greece.
Pater's Works, 9 v., Ed. de luxe.
Discourses on Architecture, Viollet-le-Duc.
Gardiner, England, 1603-1623, 8°.

Bigham & Smith, Agts., Dallas, Tex.

Shakespeare in Germany, by Albert Cohn. 1865.
Cornhill Magazine, Oct., 1872.
Lyell, Geology.

The Boston Book Co., 83 Francis St., Boston, Mass.

Outlook, July 7; Aug. 11, 18, 25, 1894.

Brentano's, 1015 Pennsylvania Ave., Washington, D. C.

Brassey's Naval Annual, 1901.

S. E. Bridgman, 108 Main St., Northampton, Mass.

Story of Liberty, Coffin.
Village Reader.
Bunch of Cherries, Meade.
Kindling Thoughts, Peabody.
Psychological Basis of Christianity, Everett.
Bottom Plank of Mental Healing, Kirk.

The Brown, Eager & Hull Co., Toledo, O.

McElligott, American Debater.
Goodrich, British Eloquence.

Geo. Brumder, Milwaukee, Wis.

Walker, Money, Trade and Banking.

The Burrows Bros. Co., Cleveland, O.

Steiner, Hist. of Western Maryland.
Lippard, New York: Its Upper Ten.
Lippard, The Nazarene, The Entranced, Legends of Mex., and The Banker's Son.
Greenwood, Edward Edwards.
Nason, Recollections of Three Cities.
Reid, Beaconsfield.
Reid, Peel.
Taylor, The Young Islanders.
Burke, Armory.
Choate, Orations and Addresses. 1878.
Piozziana.
Williams, Firelands, or, Huron and Erie Co., O. Hist. of Cleveland. 1879.
Whitman, Imperial Germany.
Schurman, Generation of Cornell.
Prescott, Philip II., v. 2. Phillips, Sampson & Co., 1857.
Hergenrother, Catholic Church.

Carnegie Library, Pittsburgh, Pa.

Philippine Review, Nov., 1901.

Case Library, Cleveland, O.

Art Amateur, v. 32, no. 2.
Literary Era, Jan., 1895.
Literary World, v. 29, no. 16.
Magazine of Art, Jan., 1899; Feb., 1901.
Overland Monthly, June, 1894.

Casino Book Co., 1374 Broadway, N. Y. [*Cash.*]

Pope, Walter, Memoirs of Mons. Duval, or any other works on Claude Duval the highwayman.
Rockwood.
Casemate Forty, by Nannie Tunstall.
Crowe and Cavalcaselle, Italian Art, 5 v.

Jno. J. Cass, 70 Wall St., N. Y.

Gessner's Works, in English.
Poniatowsky's Gems Photographed, 2d ser.
Atlas to Wilkes' Exploring Expedition. 1845.

The A. H. Clark Co., Garfield Bldg., Cleveland, O.

Amer. Book Prices Current, 1895, 1900.
Archives of Ophthalmology, v. 19, 1890.
Audubon's Quadrupeds, text v. 3, 1854.
Brackenridge, Voyage Up Missouri River.
Billon, Annals of St. Louis, v. 1.
Browne, J. Ross, The Apache Country.
Burbank, Aztec Calendar.
Bronte, Life and Letters of Sisters, v. 5, 6, 7, Haworth ed. [illegible]
Brewer, World's Best Orations, v. 8, 9. [illegible]

BOOKS WANTED.—Continued.

The A. H. Clark Co.—*Continued.*

Calderon's Lays, tr. McCarthy.
Cutts, Conquest of Cal. and N. M.
Carleton, Condition of Indian Tribes.
Crook, Rept. on Condition of Indians in Ariz.
Campbell, Tryon Co., N. Y.
Du Bose, Life of W. L. Yancey.
Dawson and Skiff, The Ute War, pamph.
Dunlap Soc. Pubs., no. 1, 3, 5, 15.
Davis, Spanish Conquest of New Mex.
Eng. Book Prices Current, '90, '93, '97.
Engelhardt, Franciscans in Ariz.
Flint, Personal Narrative of Pattie.
Fitchett, How England Saved Europe, all v. but 1st.
Goldsmith, Hist. of Rome. Lond., 1796.
Galton, Human Faculty.
Galewood, Campaigning Against Victoria in 1879.
Gregg, Commerce of the Prairie.
Hamilton, Alex., Works, Putnam ed.
Hobbs, Wild Life in the Far West.
Holcombe, Hist. of Vernon Co., Mo.
Howard and Cooper Counties, Mo., Hist.
Margry, Pierre, Decouvertes et Etablissements des Francais dans l'Ouest et Sud d'Amerique.
Muir, Picturesque California.
Noted French Oratory.
N. Y. City Imprints, before 1800.
North, Hist. of Augusta, Me.
Palmer's Jour. of Travels Over Rocky Mts.
Rossel, L. N., Posthumous Papers.
Reade, Cloister and the Hearth, Ed. de luxe, l. p.
Robinson, Doniphan's Expedition.
Rept. of Commr. of Indian Affairs, 1868.
Sage, Rocky Mountain Life.
Schoolcraft, Indians.
Salpainte, Soldiers of the Cross.
U. S. Speller, about 1850.
Williams, Maids of Honor.
Walton's Angler, any eds. between 1834 and '66, also 1893.
Wislizenus, Ausflug nach d. Felsengebirge in 1836.
Wyeth, Journey from Atlantic to Pacific.
Webb, Altowan.

W. B. Clarke Co., Park and Tremont Sts., Boston, Mass.

Company F 44th Mass. Vols.
Hymns for Mothers and Children, 2d ser. Pub. by Nichols & Hall.
Romance of Colonization, v. 2, G. B. Smith.
Lodge's Speeches.
East and West.

Henry T. Coates & Co., Phila., Pa.

Philip Thaxter. Pub. by Rudd & Carleton, 1861.

Frank W. Coburn, 47 Cornhill, Boston, Mass.

History of Union, Me., by Sibley.
History of Industry, Me.
Vermont County atlases or gazetteers.

H. M. Connor, 232 Meridian St., E. Boston, Mass.

When the Dead Walk.
Boccaccio, Decameron.
Mills, System of Logic.
Mendeleeff, Principles of Chemistry.
Marvel, Dream Life, and Reveries, 1st ed.

David C. Cook Pub. Co., 146 5th Ave., N. Y.

Miss Majoribanks; Phœbe Junior; Chronicles of Carlingford, by Mrs. Oliphant.

J. H. Cosgrove, care of Doubleday, Page & Co., 34 Union Sq., N. Y.

The Life and Inventions of Thos. A. Edison, by W. K. L. Dickson and Antonio Dickson, copyright 1892, '93, '94. Pub. by T. Y. Crowell & Co.

W. S. Crowther & Co., 228 Union St., Ripon, Wis.

Story of Chicago, Kirkland.
Billon, Annals of St. Louis, v. 1, 2.
Coffin, Lincoln. Harper, 1893.
World's Best Orations, Brewer or Reid.
Douglass, F., Bondage, Freedom. N. Y., 1855.

Crusoe & Co., 81 Vermont St., Brooklyn, N. Y.

Coryat's Crudities, reprint.
De Morgan, A Budget of Paradoxes.

Cunningham, Curtiss & Welch, 319 Sansome St., San Francisco, Cal.

Cayley, Elementary Treatise on Elliptic Functions. Macmillan.

Cushing & Co., 34 W. Baltimore St., Baltimore, Md.

Fortnightly Review, Mar., 1902.

Damrell & Upham, 283 Washington St., Boston, Mass.

Cram, English Country Churches.
Along N. E. Roads, by Prime.
Owl Creek Letters, by Prime.

Dick & Fitzgerald, 18 Ann St., N. Y.

The Portfolio of Autograph Etchings. Pub. by Ticknor & Co., sometime in the seventies.

Dodd, Mead & Co., 372 Fifth Ave., N. Y.

Holland, J. G., Life of Lincoln. 1865.
Watson, Theoretical Astronomy. Philadelphia, 1868.
Gauss, Theoria Motus Corporum Coelestium, tr. by Davis. Boston, 1857.
Cooper, Precaution, Townsend ed., il. by Darley.
Nature, Mar. 12, 1885.

The H. & W. B. Drew Co., Jacksonville, Fla.

Artillery Drill Regulations.

Wm. J. C. Dulany Co., 8 Baltimore St., E., Baltimore, Md.

Essays, by Octavia Hill.
Ghosts, by Ibsen.
Catalogue of the Etched Works of Rembrandt, by Middleton.

Alex. Duncker (H. von Carnap), 174 Fulton St., N. Y.

American Gas Light Journal, 1895 to 1901, incl.
Journal of Gas Lighting, odd v.
Gas World, odd v.
Iron and Steel Institute, v. 1.
Iron and Steel Institute, v. 1.
Chemical News, v. 1 to 10, 32 to 36, 46 to 50, 56, 61 to 84.
Amer. Chemical Journal, set or odd v.
Amer. Journal of Science, set or odd v.
Amer. Journal of Pharmacy, v. 1 to 72.
Anything relating to Odd Fellows.
Dispensatory of the U. S., 16th ed., 1892.
Harris, Dental Dictionary.
Piersol, Histology.
Foster, Physiology.
Weisse, Practical Human Anatomy.
Amer. Text-Book of Physiology.
Gray, Anatomy (uncolored.)
Boehm-Davidoff (Huber.)
Ganot, Elem. Treat. on Physics, 16th ed.

D. T. Eaton, Muscatine, Ia.

The Carisbrooke Library, with the exception of 4, 13.

B. G. Eichelberger, 308 N. Charles St., Baltimore, Md.

Book Prices Current, any vols.
Any books on old prints, giving prices, etc.
Etched Works of Rembrandt, by Charles Henry Middleton. Pub. by John Murray, 1878.

Everitt & Francis Co., 116 E. 23d St., N. Y.

Duruy, History of Greece, v. 3, Sec. 1, Edition de Grand Luxe, Japan pap., hf. red mor. Estes & Lauriat, 1890.
Darwin, 15 v., hf. mor. Appleton.

Harry Falkenau, 167 Madison St., Chicago, Ill.

Book of Mormon.
Hearn, Sam'l, Journal of Travels.
Dobbs, Arthur, British Columbia.
Umphreville, Edw., Brit. Columbia.
Gems from the Talmud, R. I. Meyer.

S. B. Fisher, 5 E. Court St., Springfield, Mass.

Stoddard's Britannica, v. 25, shp.
St. Nicholas, Nov., 1874; Feb., '76; Apr., '81.

W. I. Fletcher, Amherst College Library, Amherst, Mass.

Cutter's Rules for Cataloging, several copies, send offers, good price will be paid.

I. Hammond, Charleston, S. C.

Voice from Carolina, Leland.
Our Women in the War. Charleston, 1885 (?)
Sketch of Marion, James.
The Revolution in S. C., Ramsey.
Memoirs of Am. Revolution, Moultrie.

F. F. Hansell & Bro., Ltd., 714 Canal St., New Orleans, La.

Collot, V., Journey in America. Circa 1829.
Dabroca, Americana.
Magruder, Allen B., Reflections on the Purchase of Louisiana. 1803.

BOOKS WANTED.—Continued.

Wm. Beverley Harison, 65 E. 59th St., N. Y.

The Art of Teaching and Studying Languages, by F. Gouin, tr. by Bétis and Swan.

Harvard Co-operative Soc., Cambridge, Mass.

Davis, R. H., Dr. Jameson's Raiders.

N. W. Henley & Co., 132 Nassau St., N. Y.

Rose's Modern Machine Shop Practice, state ed.

J. A. Hill & Co., 91 5th Ave., N. Y.

Journal of the Society of Chemical Industry, 1 set.

Hunter & Freeman, Belton, Tex.

Rise and Fall of the Confederate Government, by Jefferson Davis. Appleton.
Life and Literary Remains of Sam Houston, by William Cary Crane. Lippincott.

Hunter & Welburn, Nashville, Tenn.

25 copies Biddle, Materia Medica, 13th ed., new or second-hand.
U. S. Dispensatory, 16th ed., second-hand.

Hyland Bros., 229 Yamhill St., Portland, Ore.

Square of Seven, by Erasmus Stevenson.
Oregon Missions, De Smet.
Dr. Faulkner, Family Physician.
Grimshaw, Steam Engineering.
Ten Years in Oregon, Lee and Frost.

George W. Jacobs & Co., 103 S. 15th St., Phila., Pa.

100 Parrot Stories, cl. or pap., author unknown.

E. T. Jett Book and News Co., 806 Olive St., St. Louis, Mo.

Ole Mistis, John T. Moore.

H. L. Kilner & Co., 824 Arch St., Phila., Pa.

Ballerini, Commentary on the Psalms, in English.

Geo. Kleinteich, 397 Bedford Ave., Brooklyn, N. Y. [Cash.]

Moy O'Brien, an Irish story, pap. or cl.

J. Kuhlman, 117 N. 13th St., Phila., Pa. [Cash.]

Phila. Saturday Courier, 1847-1850, or complete set.
St. Nicholas, v. 1 to 4, or odd nos.
Potter's Amer. Monthly, nos. 106, 117, 119, 128.
Engineering Mag., v. 1, 2, or odd nos.
Cassier's Mag., v. 1, 2, or odd nos.
Mag. Am. History, v. 1, or odd nos.; also v. 9, no. 2.
Amer. Hist. Register for 1897.

Chas. E. Lauriat Co., 301 Washington St., Boston, Mass.

Index vol. to Encyclopedia Britannica, Scribner ed.
Memoirs of Baroness Riedesel.
Memoirs of Prince Metternich, v. 5, Scribner's 8° ed.
Mass. Year Book, 1901.
Whittaker's Peerage, 1902.
How to Catalogue a Library, by Wheatley.
Plea for Philosophic Doubt, by Balfour.
History of Rome, v. 3, by Niebuhr, tr. by J. C. Hare and Thirlwall. Phila., 1835.
Cousin from India, by Craik.
William Cook Taylor's History of Ireland, v. 1, Harper's Family Library.
Schumann, Purcell and Beethoven, in Great Musicians Series. Scribner.
Masters of German Music, in Contemporary Music Series. Scribner.
Report Concerning Last Sea Fight of the "Revenge," Sir W. Raleigh.
A Week in a French Country House.
Hell of a Cruise, by Murray.

Leggat Bros., 81 Chambers St., N. Y.

Thomas, Medical Dictionary.

Geo. E. Littlefield, 67 Cornhill, Boston, Mass.

Long, Stephen H., Account of His Expedition to the Rocky Mountains in 1819 and 1820, comp. by Edwin James. Phila., 1823.

W. H. Lowdermilk & Co., Washington, D. C.

Hertslet, Map of Europe by Treaty, 3 v.
Hall, Mexican Law.
Ridgway, Nomenclature of Colors.
Whiting Genealogy.
West, Life of W. H. Crawford.

Lyon, Kymer & Palmer Co., Grand Rapids, Mich.

Roberts, Western Avernus.
Gogol, Dead Souls.

Macauley Bros., 172 Woodward Ave., Detroit, Mich.

Ellis, Psychology of Sex.
Arkansas Bear. Pub. by R. H. Russell.
Paracelsus, by Franz Hartmann. Pub. by Geo. Redway, London.

T. J. McBride & Son, 71 Broadway, N. Y.

Paris Days and Evenings, by S. Henry.
Hours with Famous Parisians, by S. Henry.

Joseph McDonough, 39 Columbia St., Albany, N. Y.

London Graphic, v. 1-6, hf. mor. preferred.
Taylor, Songs of Yesterday.
N. Y. Historians, 1896 (Colonial Series, v. 1.)

S. F. McLean & Co., 44 E. 23d St., N. Y.

Lowrey, A Northern Light.
Rives, Life of Madison, v. 3. L., B. & Co.
Harper's Weekly, 1860.
Cleveland, John, Poems.
Kent's Commentaries, second-hand.
Dictionnaire Raisonne Du Mobilier Francais, by Viollet-Le-Duc, 6 v.

H. Malkan, Hanover Sq., N. Y.

Set 10 v., Section 5 of World's Great Classics, Ed. de luxe, cl., pap. label.
Forty Years Familiar Letters of James W. Hamilton, D.D.
Mount Vernon and Its Associations, B. J. Lossing.

Isaac Mendoza, 17 Ann St., N. Y.

Mitchell's or Kerl's Assaying.
Anything on tree or nut culture.

R. H. Merriam, Hanover Sq., N. Y.

Dawson, Westchester County.
Onderdonk, Revolutionary Incidents.
Bacon, Reminiscences of Thomas Jefferson.

H. A. Moos, 514 E. Houston St., San Antonio, Tex.

History of the United States, by Percy Gregg.
Twenty-five Years in a Wagon, by Anderson.
Life of Mrs. Siddons, by Thomas Campbell.
Prenticiana, by Geo. D. Prentice.

Chas. F. Nichols, Corner Book and Art Store, Concord, N. H.

Science and Health, 1st, 2d and 3d eds.
Talks to Pupil Nurses.

Daniel O'Shea, 1584 Broadway, N. Y.

Descent of Man, v. 2. Appleton.

E. T. Pardee, 146 Bowdoin St., Boston, Mass.

Chapters from Erie, by Charles Francis Adams.

C. C. Parker, 246 S. Broadway, Los Angeles, Cal. [Cash.]

Debt and Grace, as related to the doctrine of a future life, by Chas. Fred. Hudson.
British Eloquence, Goodrich.
There Is No Death, Marryat.

Pierce & Zahn, 633 17th St., Denver, Colo.

Any books on scene painting.
Intentions, by Wilde, second-hand.

The Pilgrim Press, 175 Wabash Ave., Chicago, Ill.

Govett, On the Sermon on the Mount; also any other books of Govett's.
Schaff-Herzog Cyclopedia, latest ed., cheap.
Stoddard's Lectures, cheap.

Pratt Institute Free Library, Ryerson St., Brooklyn, N. Y.

Chicago Banker, nos. Jan., 1899, and Oct., 1900.

Presb. Bd. of Pub. and S. S. Work, 156 5th Ave., N. Y.

2 copies Hopkins, Liturgy and Common Prayer. A. S. Barnes, 1883.

Presb. Bd. of Pub. and S. S. Work, Witherspoon Bldg., 1319 Walnut St., Phila., Pa.

Summer Driftwood for Winter's Fire, by Rose Porter.

Presb. Bd. of Pub. and S. S. Work, 1516 Locust St., St. Louis, Mo.

Jacox's Scripture Text, pt. 1 only.

Geo. H. Rigby, 1113 Arch St., Phila., Pa.

Southern Literary Messenger, nos. 1, 2 of v. 1.
King, Gas Manufacture.
Fresh Water Plants and Aquarium, anything on.
Morse, Sherburne, Hollister, Mass.

BOOKS WANTED.—Continued.

Robson & Adee, Schenectady, N. Y.

Fowler's Publicity.
Books on advertising.

Chas. M. Roe, 177 Wabash Ave., Chicago, Ill.

Life of John Fletcher of Madeley.
Eastern Side, or, Missionary Life in Siam, by Mrs. F. R. Feudge.

Chas. A. Rogers, 434 W. Jefferson St., Louisville, Ky.

Wm. G. Ward, Ideal of a Christian Church.
Tracts for the Times, 24th Tract, Newman.

E. H. Roller, 419 E. Water St., Milwaukee, Wis.

Lord, N. W., Metallurgical Notes.
Parkman, Conspiracy of Pontiac.
Gray, Bible Museum New Test., v. 4.

Wm. S. Ropes, Mt. Vernon, Skagit Co., Wash.

Fox, Regimental Losses in the Civil War.
Chap Book, Aug. 1, 15, 1894; Sept. 1, '95; Oct. 15, '96; Dec. 1, '96; v. 1, 2, 3, 4, 5, complete.

J. Francis Ruggles, Bronson, Mich.

Beautiful Thoughts. Bell & Co., Phila.
Leslie's Popular Monthly, Nov., 1880.
Paine, Common Sense, 1st ed. Pub. by Bell, 1776.
Sherwin, Life of Paine. London.

W. S. Rusk, 604 8th Ave., N. Y.

U. S. Dispensatory.
Sterne, Laurence, Works, in 1 v.
Lippincott's Gazetteer.
The Home Beyond, by Rev. S. Fellows, D.D.

St. Paul Book and Stationery Co., 5th and St. Peter Sts., St. Paul, Minn.

Pamela, by Richardson.
An International Marriage, by Princess De Bourg.

John E. Scopes, 29 Tweddle Bldg., Albany, N. Y.

American Ancestry, v. 9, 10.
Wilkinson, Memoirs, v. 2, and atlas. Phila., 1816.

Scrantom, Wetmore & Co., Rochester, N. Y.

Combe, Dr. Syntax.
Larned, History for Ready Reference.
Cranford, Hugh Thompson illus., 1st ed. Macmillan.

Charles Scribner's Sons, 153 5th Ave., N. Y.

Manning, Household of Sir Thomas More, with introduction by Hutton. N. Y., 1896.
McLean, Cape Cod Folks. Boston, 1881.
Mitford, M. R., Recollections of My Literary Life. Bentley, 1888.
L'Estrange, Life of Mitford, 5 v. Bentley, 1870-72.
Carroll, Rhyme and Reason.
Sage, Salmon Fishing on the Restigouche.
Whitman, Leaves of Grass, 1st ed.
Leland, Americans in Rome.
Century Atlas, 1899 ed. or later.
Freeman, Chief Periods of European History.

John Skinner, 44 N. Pearl St., Albany, N. Y.

Renan, Life of Jesus.
Autobiography of Capt. John Smith.

P. A. Smith, Lock Box 915, Fishkill Landing, N. Y.

History of Two Americas, by P. C. Headley.
Winter Evening Tales, by James Hogg.
Heart doctor books.
Dead Letter, by Seeley Regester.

Wm. H. Smith, Jr., 515 W. 173d St., N. Y.

Shelley, Prose Works, early English ed.
An Only Son. Pub. *Littell's Living Age.*
Persia and the Persians, Benjamin.
The Swiss Republic, Winchester.
The Alps from End to End, Conway.

Wm. T. Smith & Co., 145 Genesee St., Utica, N. Y.

Miller, In the Kitchen. Holt.
Margry, Pierre, Discoveries and Establishments of France in America, 1614-1754, 3 v. Paris, 1879.
Charlevoix, History of New France (in French), 3 v.
Lafiteau, Le R. P., Jean Francois, S. J., Mœurs des Sauvages Americains Comparées aux Mœurs des Premiers Temps, 2 v. Paris, 1724.
La Potherie, Claude, Charles Le Roy de, and Backqueville de la Potherie, Histoire de L'Amerique Septemtrionale, etc., 4 v. Paris, 1722.
Dollier de Casson, Francois, Histoire du Montreal, 1640-1672.

Wm. T. Smith & Co.—*Continued.*

Conseil Souverain, Jugements et deliberations du—de la Novelle France, 1663-1704 et du Conseil Supérieur, 1705-1716, 6 v. Québec, 1885.
American Archives, forming a documentary history of the North American Colonies, [comp.] by Peter Force, Ser. 4, v. 1-6; Ser. 5, v. 1-3, Washington, 1837-53, 9 v.
Edits et Ordonnances, 3 v. Pub. by Legislative Assembly of lower Canada, 1854.

The Smith Book Co., 143 E. 4th St., Cincinnati, O.

Appleton's Annuals, 1884 to 1897, hf. mor.
Appleton's Annuals, 1892 to 1900, shp.

Speyer & Peters, Berlin, N. W. F., Germany.

Annalės des Maladies Gen.-Urin.
Archiv für Augen- u. Ohrenheilkunde.
Archiv f. Experim. Pathol. u. Pharmakol.
Archives of Pediatrics.
Brun, Beitraege z. Klin. Chirurgie.
Graefe, Archiv. f. Ophthalmologie.
Journal de l'Anatomie p. Robin.
Journal of the Amer. Chem. Soc.
Transactions of the Amer. Orthop. Association, v. 7, 8, 11, 13, 14.
Please offer sets or single vols. and nos.

G. E. Stechert, 9 E. 16th St., N. Y.

Mackenzie, Commodore Perry.
Giles, Human Life in Shakespeare.
Jones, Handbook of Amer. Music and Musicians.
Gowan, Catalogue of Books on Freemasonry.
Bradley, Patronomatology. 1842.

E. Steiger & Co., 25 Park Place, N. Y. [*Cash.*]

Squier, Nicaragua.
Griffis, Japanese Fairy World.
Trask, Under King Constantine.
Trimble, The Tannins, 2 v.
Proceedings of the U. S. Naval Institute, v. 1 to 27, complete or odd v.

The Stiefel Masonic Book Co., 108 E. 4th St., Cincinnati, O.

O'Grady, The Elocution Class.
Anything on society gymnastics.
Hughan, Old Charges of British Freemasonry.

Stout's Book Exchange, 612 5th St., San Diego, Cal.

Wanderings of an F. R. G. S.
Lyra Anglicana, English ed.
Decameron, Unexpurgated English trans., good ed. wanted.

Syndicate Trading Co., 2 Walker St., N. Y.

Sonnets by Various Authors, Vinton.
Eugene Lee Hamilton, English Poet.
Mr. and Mrs. Hannibal Hawkins.
Vivian Bertram, by W. H. S. Reynolds.

H. H. Timby, Conneaut, O.

Any work on grinding sharp edged tools.
Abrams, Siege of Vicksburg.

W. H. Walker, 58 Moffatt St., Brooklyn, N. Y.

Riker's Harlem.
The Pioneer, any pts.
Privately printed books.
Gardiner's England, v. 1, 2.
Audubon's Quadrupeds, text, 1854.

John Wanamaker, N. Y.

Le Bon, Psychology of Peoples. Macmillan.
Select Organizations of the U. S. Knickerbocker Pub. Co.

John Wanamaker, Phila., Pa.

Capt. Brand of the "Centipede," by H. A. Wise.
Harry Gringo, H. A. Wise.
Our Wild Indians, by Richard Dodge.
Plains of the Great West, Richard Dodge.

Thomas Whittaker, 2 Bible House, N. Y.

Does the Bible Justify American Slavery?, by Goldwin Smith.
Maclay, History of the U. S. Navy, v. 3, 1st ed.
Hearts and Homes, Mrs. Ellis.
Secret of a Human Heart, Mrs. Ellis.
Wascart and Joubert's Electricity, 2 v.

H. Welter, 4 Rue Bernard-Palissy, Paris.

Publications of the Modern Language Society of America, v. 1-12.

H. W. Wilson, 315 14th Ave., S. E., Minneapolis, Minn.

Howes, Biological Atlas. Macmillan.

BOOKS WANTED.—Continued.

W. H. Wood & Co., 8 E. Main St., Springfield, O.

Peace and War, Tolstoi.
Scottish Version of the Psalms with Brown's Explanatory Remarks, Rousi's Version.
Life of Washington, by Weems.
Life of Marion, by Weems.

BOOKS FOR SALE.

John R. Anderson, 114 5th Ave., N. Y.

Reports N. Y. Chamber of Commerce, 1875 to 1900. $10.00.
Popular Science Monthly, v. 1 to 51, green cl. $20.
Wey's Rome. $2.50.
Year Book Sons Revolution, N. Y., 1899. $1.00.
Cabinet Cyclopedia, 8 v., cl. $3.00.
La Croix, Literature Middle Ages, shelf worn. $3.
La Croix, Military and Religious Life, full cf. $4.00.
Ancient Stone Implements. $1.50.
Ancient Bronze Implements. $1.50.
Chambers' Cyclopedia, Collier's ed., 6 v. $6.00.
Johnson's Cyclo., 8 v., latest ed., hf. mor. $20.00.
Benton's Debates, 16 v. $16.00.

Jno. J. Cass, 70 Wall St., N. Y.

Natural History of N. Y., v. 1 to 19. $40.00.

Dodge Stationery Co., 123 Grant Ave., San Francisco, Cal.

American Catalogue, 1884-1895, 4 v., bound in black cl. Complete, $35.00.

Alex. Duncker (H. von Carnap), 178 Fulton St., N. Y.

Engineering (London), v. 1 to 66.
The Engineer (London), v. 1 to 80.
Nature, v. 1 to 60.
Journal of the Amer. Chem. Soc., v. 1 to 23.
Dingler's Polytechnisches Journal, v. 1 to 314.
Berichte d. dtsch. chem. Ges., years 1 to 34.
Meyer, Konvers. Lexikon, 20 v., 5th (latest) ed.
Calvini Opera edd. Baum, Cunitz, Reuss, 59 v.
Transactions of the Am. Inst. of Mining Eng., v. 1 to 30.
Many earlier out of print and scarce vols. of the Geological Reports of the several States. List on demand.

Meehan, Expert Bookseller, 32 Gay St., Bath, Eng.

Review of Reviews, nos. 1 to 14 (Jan., 1890 to Feb., 1891), necessary nos. to complete the American Issue, *free* at 25 c. each only. Payment in American currency will do. Cash with order. A big stock of duplicates of these nos. In sets of 14 nos. only.

S. J. D., P. O. Box 943, N. Y.

Research Papers—Kent Chemical Laboratory. *Yale Bi-centennial Publications.* N. Y., Scribner, 1901. 2 v. $10.
Hopkins, E. W. The Great Epic of India. *Yale Bi-centennial Publications.* N. Y., Scribner, 1901. $2.
Supernatural Religion. 6th ed. 2 v. in 1. N. Y., Bennett, 1879. $1.75.
Doane, T. W. Bible Myths. 4th ed. N. Y., Truth Seeker Co., 1882. $1.
Ball, R. S. Story of the Heavens. N. Y., Cassell, 1900. $1.50.
Myer, Isaac. Qabbalah. Phila., 1888. (350 copies.) $8.
Wilder, A. Symbolical language of Ancient Art and Mythology. N. Y., Bouton, 1892. $1.50.
Wilder, A. Eleusinian and Bacchic Mysteries. N. Y., Bouton, 1891. $1.
Rae, John. Contemporary Socialism. N. Y., Scribner, 1884. $1.
Graham, W. Socialism New and Old. N. Y., Appleton, 1891. $1.
Will entertain a reasonable offer for the lot.

Scrantom, Wetmore & Co., Rochester, N. Y.

The China Hunters' Club.
Century Dictionary, 6 v., cl.
Century Dictionary, 10 v., hf. mor., latest ed.
Maria Edgeworth, Dent, l. p. ed., 12 v., cl.

SITUATIONS WANTED.

BOOKKEEPER, accountant and office manager. 20 years' experience, wholesale and manufacturing, desires position. Can adapt to any system or conditions. Excellent references. Salary no object so long as prospects are good. Address WILLIAMS, care of PUBLISHERS' WEEKLY.

WANTED.—A young man, at present manager of a book department, and with ten years' experience in the book business, wishes to identify himself with an established book and stationery house, in which a business interest may be acquired, if his services are found satisfactory. Address RETAIL BOOKSELLER, care of PUBLISHERS' WEEKLY.

BUSINESS FOR SALE.

FOR SALE.—One of the largest stocks of old and rare books, new books, stationery, etc., in the South. In city of 65,000, noted for its excellent climate. Constantly increasing business, very little competition. Good reasons for wishing to sell. Price $15,000. Address H. A. Moos, 514 E. Houston St., San Antonio, Texas.

COPYRIGHT NOTICES.

LIBRARY OF CONGRESS,
OFFICE OF THE REGISTER OF COPYRIGHTS,
WASHINGTON, D. C.

Class A, XXx, No. 33494.—To wit: *Be it remembered*, That on the 7th day of May, 1902, The Robert Clarke Company, of Cincinnati, O., hath deposited in this office the title of a book, the title of which is in the following words, to wit: "Manual of Universal Church History. By Rev. Dr. John Alzog. Translated by F. J. Pabisch and Rt. Rev. Thomas S. Byrne. Volume I. Cincinnati, The Robert Clarke Company," the right whereof they claim as proprietors in conformity with the laws of the United States respecting copyrights.

(Signed) HERBERT PUTNAM, *Librarian of Congress.*
By THORVALD SOLBERG, *Register of Copyrights.*
In renewal for 14 years from Sept. 12, 1902.

LIBRARY OF CONGRESS,
OFFICE OF THE REGISTER OF COPYRIGHTS,
WASHINGTON, D. C.

Class A, XXc, No. 35053.—To wit: *Be it remembered*, That on the 10th day of June, 1902, Mattie G. Browne, of Boston, Mass., hath deposited in this office the title of a book, the title of which is in the following words, to wit: "Massachusetts Reports, 109. Cases argued and determined in the Supreme Judicial Court of Massachusetts, November, 1871-March, 1872. Albert G. Browne, Jr. Boston, Houghton, Mifflin & Company," the right whereof she claims as proprietor in conformity with the laws of the United States respecting copyrights.

(Signed) HERBERT PUTNAM, *Librarian of Congress.*
By THORVALD SOLBERG, *Register of Copyrights.*
In renewal for 14 years from June 12, 1902.

SPECIAL NOTICES.

OP'S. English, Irish Books, Posters. PRATT, N. Y.

A. S. CLARK, 174 Fulton St. N. Y., will supply any magazine at market value.

BACK NUMBERS, volumes, and sets of magazines and reviews for sale at the AMERICAN AND FOREIGN MAGAZINE DEPOT, 47 Dey St., New York.

BOOKS.—All out-of-print books supplied, no matter on what subject. Write us. We can get you any book ever published. Please state wants. When in England call and see our 50,000 rare books. BAKER'S GREAT BOOKSHOP, 14-16 John Bright Street, Birmingham, England.

MAGGS BROS., 109 STRAND, W. C., LONDON, W., ENGLAND

Dealers in **Rare Books and Fine Library Editions of Standard Authors.**

Voyages and Travels, Early Printed Books, 1st Editions of 17th, 18th, and 19th Century Writers, Illustrated Works. Also *Rare Portraits, Line, Stipple, Mezzotints, and Color Engravings, and Autographs.*

Classified catalogues free on application.

Those visiting England should call and inspect our stock, which is both large and in [illegible]

Frederick Warne & Co.'s

TIMELY PUBLICATIONS

By the author of "Stephen Ellicott's Daughter," "Julian Karslake's Secret," etc.

UNSTABLE AS WATER

A New Novel. By MRS. J. H. NEEDELL. 12mo, cloth. $1.25.

BY A NEW WRITER

THE PRESUMPTION OF STANLEY HAY, M.P.

A Romance. By NOWELL CAY. 12mo, cloth. $1.25.

"Interesting to the point of excitement."—*Public Ledger*, Phila.

"Will be much read, and all read."—*The World*, N. Y.

By the author of "A Plunge Into Space," etc.

KITTY'S VICTORIA CROSS

By ROBERT CROMIE. 12mo, cloth. $1.25.

A pleasing romance of two Irish girls. *The New York Times Saturday Review* says: "Mr. Cromie's literary style is of the best, and his romance a most interesting one."

Library of Natural History Romance

SHELL LIFE

An Introduction to the British Mollusca. By EDWARD STEP, F.L.S. With 32 original plates photographed from the actual shells, and upwards of 600 woodcuts in the text. Crown 8vo, cloth gilt, gilt top. $2.00.

... This is not a dry-as-dust list of shells, but a really entertaining and instructive book written with the idea of popularizing what has hitherto been considered an abstruse subject.

ALSO, IN THE ABOVE SERIES

THE ROMANCE OF WILD FLOWERS

A Companion to the British Flora. By EDWARD STEP, F.L.S. With 200 illustrations, uniform with the above. $2.00.

From the preface: "Not intended for botanists, but for unscientific flower-lovers . . . To-day the naturalist is principally concerned in observing the habits of the plant, its attitude towards insects, and the relation of one species to another."

FOR ALL WHO CONTEMPLATE MOTORING

THE MOTOR CAR

An Elementary Handbook on Its Nature, Use and Management. By SIR HENRY THOMPSON, F.R.C.S. (London), &c. 12mo, cloth. $1.00.

... Sir Henry took to the motor car in his (youthful) old age, and in these few pages he describes his experiences in learning its mechanism and movement, its relation to the various living objects it encounters on the road, and naturally the writer touches on the hygienic advantages of this method of locomotion and the various forms of motive power.

Also by the same author a little *brochure* of timely interest

"THE UNKNOWN GOD"?

An Essay. In 18mo, cloth, gilt top, 60 cents; or, neat paper wrapper, 35 cents.

... An attempt to seek by careful deduction from available data, some certain assurance respecting the influence which the "Infinite and Eternal Energy from which all things proceed" has exercised on man from the beginning.

F. WARNE & CO.

~~36 East 22d Street~~, NEW YORK

The Genealogy of the Family of Morgan

tracing its pedigree to the year 1089 in the male line, and to the year 605 in the female line: **300 pages, 50 portraits**, by Dr. Appleton Morgan, which has been delivering to subscribers since 1891, is now completed. Of the 500 registered and hand numbered sets, thirty-seven remain in sheets, which can be sold for interleaved binding for individual Family Records, on receipt of **Ten Dollars per set.**

THE SHAKESPEARE PRESS

Westfield, New Jersey

PRINTING

of all kinds, plain and colored, also engraving and embossing, in any quantity, promptly attended to at the closest possible prices. We can refer to the largest banks, the largest manufacturing concerns, publishers and others in the United States. We shall take pleasure in having you call, or if it suits your convenience better, to call on you. Drop us a line.

ANDREW H. KELLOGG

409 Pearl St., ('Phone 3640 John,) New York

We have the **most extensive facilities** for **importing**

Foreign Books,

Periodicals, Maps, etc.

from all countries. We have **direct connections** with the publishers of Germany, Austria, Switzerland, England, France, etc., and besides import by mail through our **agents** at Bruxelles, Amsterdam, Madrid, Barcelona, Turin, Milan, Rome, Constantinople, Bucarest, Buda-Pesth, Warsaw, St. Petersburg, Helsingfors, Stockholm, Christiania, Copenhagen, Cairo, Calcutta, Batavia, Shanghai, Tokyo, Lima, Santiago, Buenos Aires, Rio, Havana, Mexico, Ottawa, Toronto, etc.

Second-hand Books

of all kinds imported. Prompt reply to all inquiries.

E. Steiger & Co., 25 Park Place, New York.

Accuracy. Promptness. Reliability.

KAY PRINTING HOUSE,

66-68 CENTRE STREET,

TELEPHONE 1558 FRANKLIN. **NEW YORK.**

Estimates Promptly Furnished.

~~Printers to THE PUBLISHERS' WEEKLY~~

Books for Summer Travellers.

D. APPLETON & COMPANY, New York.

APPLETONS' GUIDE BOOKS.

Appletons' General Guide to the United States and Canada. With numerous maps and illustrations. 12mo, flexible morocco, with tuck, $2.50. (Part I., separately, NEW ENGLAND AND MIDDLE STATES AND CANADA; cloth, 75 cents. Part II., SOUTHERN AND WESTERN STATES, cloth, 75 cents.)

Appletons' Guide-Book to Alaska. By Miss E. R. Scidmore. New edition, including an Account of the Klondike. With maps and illustrations. 12mo, flexible cloth, $1.00.

A Landmark History of New York. By Albert Ulmann. With many illustrations. 12mo, cloth, $1.50.

In this book the reader makes visits in sequence to the old Dutch Settlement, the early English colony, the city as it was before the Revolution, and so on down to the present time. Copies of rare prints and maps and many plates made from recent photographs illustrate the work.

Appletons' Dictionary of [Greater] New York and Vicinity. With maps of New York and vicinity. Square 12mo, paper, 25 cents net; postage, 6 cents additional.

Puerto Rico and Its Resources. A book for Travellers, Investors, and others, containing full accounts of Natural Features and Resources, Products, People, Opportunities for Business, etc. By Frederick A. Ober, author of "Camps in the Caribbees," "Crusoe's Island," etc. With maps and illustrations. 12mo, cloth, $1.50.

A. S. BARNES & CO., New York.

A World's Shrine. (Lake Como.) By Virginia W. Johnson. Illustrated. 12mo, cloth, $1.20 net. (new.)

A History of Art. For Tourists. By Wm. H. Goodyear. Fully illustrated. 8vo, cloth, $2.80 net.

Switzerland, Annals of. By Julia M. Colton. Illustrated. 12mo, cloth, $1.25.

The Rhine, Legends of. By H. A. Guerber. Illustrated. 12mo, cloth, gilt top, $1.50 net.

BRENTANO'S, New York.

My Ocean Trip. By E. S. Cadigan. Illustrated with signals and flags printed in colors, and with blank pages for memoranda. 12mo, cloth, $1.00.

A work appealing especially to tourists and travellers, arranged for the record to be kept of an Ocean Voyage. In addition there are many items of interest, such as a complete code of signals, series of games for shipboard, entertainments, pages for the autographs of fellow passengers.

POCKET DICTIONARIES. Printed at the press of Bernhard Tauchnitz of Leipzig, Germany, from the plates of the famous Tauchnitz series, and bound specially for Brentano's. Each, cloth, $1.00.

Dictionary of the English and German Languages. By J. E. Wessely.

Dictionary of the English and French Languages. By J. E. Wessely.

Dictionary of the English and Italian Languages. By J. E. Wessely.

Dictionary of the English and Spanish Languages. By J. E. Wessely and Girones.

HOUGHTON, MIFFLIN & CO., Boston.

Our National Parks. By John Muir. Illustrated. $1.75 net; postpaid, $1.87.

Footing it in Franconia. $1.10 net; postpaid, $1.19.

HOUGHTON, MIFFLIN & CO.—*Continued.*

Picturesque Alaska. By Abby J. Woodman. Illustrations and maps. 16mo, $1.00.

September Days on Nantucket. By William Root Bliss.

Cape Cod. By H. D. Thoreau. $1.50.

WILLIAM R. JENKINS, New York.

The Complete Pocket-Guide to Europe. Edited by E. C. and T. L. Stedman. One vol., full leather, $1.25. Revised yearly. The best of its kind.

LEMCKE & BUECHNER, New York.

Baedeker's Guides. German and French.

Monographs on Artists.

Dictionaries and Grammars for the study of Foreign Languages. *Send for lists.*

McCLURE, PHILLIPS & CO., New York.

The Hound of the Baskervilles. A Sherlock Holmes novel by A. Conan Doyle. Illustrated. $1.25.

The Blazed Trail. An American novel by Stewart Edward White. Illustrated. $1.50.

Red Saunders. A humorous account of his doings West and East. By Henry Wallace Phillips. Frontispiece. $1.25.

The Madness of Philip. Stories of child life for grown-ups by Josephine Dodge Daskam. Illustrated. $1.50.

A Prince of Good Fellows. Tales of James V., the "Merry Monarch of Scotland," by Robert Barr. Illustrated. $1.50.

The Making of a Statesman. A novelette, together with other stories of Georgia life, by Joel Chandler Harris. $1.25.

The Gentleman From Indiana. A romance by Booth Tarkington. $1.50.

An Island Cabin. A record of outdoor life by Arthur Henry. $1.50.

Forest Neighbors. Life stories of wild animals by W. D. Hulbert. $1.50 net; postpaid, $1.68.

Next to the Ground. A nature narrative by Martha McCulloch-Williams. $1.20 net; postpaid, $1.32.

JOHN P. MORTON & CO., Louisville, Ky.

Mammoth Cave of Kentucky (A Perfect Guide To). By Hovey & Call. Paper, 50 cents; cloth, $1.00.

E. STEIGER & CO., New York.

Baedeker's and Other Guide-Books, in German. The largest assortment of Books for the Study of Foreign Languages. *Send for catalogue.*

A. WESSELS COMPANY, 7-9 W. 18th St., N. Y.

Historical Guide-Books to Paris, Venice, Florence, Cities of Belgium, Cities of Northern Italy, the Umbrian Towns. One volume each. By Grant Allen. Pocket size, 250 pp., cloth, $1.25 net.

London and Londoners. By R. A. Pritchard. Pocket size, 400 pp., cloth, $1.25.

THE

Publishers' Weekly

THE AMERICAN

BOOK TRADE JOURNAL

WITH WHICH IS INCORPORATED

The American Literary Gazette and Publishers' Circular.

[ESTABLISHED 1852.]

PUBLICATION OFFICE, 298 BROADWAY, NEW YORK.

Entered at the Post-Office at New York, N. Y., as second-class matter.

VOL. LXII., No. 4. NEW YORK, July 26, 1902. WHOLE No. 15

Riverside Literature Series. Unabridged Masterpieces.

With Introductions, Historical and Biographical Sketches, and Notes. Many of the Books contain Portraits and Illustrations. Horace E. Scudder, late Supervising Editor. **Each regular single number, paper, 15 cents. All prices of the Riverside Literature Series are net.**

A descriptive circular, giving the table of contents of each number of the series, will be sent on application.

1. **Longfellow's Evangeline.** *Revised.**‡‡
2. **—— Courtship of Miles Standish; Elizabeth.***
3. **The Courtship of Miles Standish.** DRAMATIZED.
4. **Whittier's Snow-Bound, etc.***‡‡**
5. **—— Mabel Martin, etc.****
6. **Holmes's Grandmother's Story of Bunker Hill Battle, etc.*** **
7, 8, 9. **Hawthorne's Grandfather's Chair.** *Revised Edition.* In three parts.‡‡
10. **—— Biographical Stories.*** **
11. **Longfellow's Children's Hour, etc.****
12. **Studies in Longfellow, Whittier, Holmes and Lowell.**
13, 14. **Longfellow's Song of Hiawatha.**‡
15. **Lowell's Under the Old Elm, etc.****
16. **Bayard Taylor's Lars, etc.***
17, 18. **Hawthorne's Wonder-Book.**‡
19, 20. **Franklin's Autobiography.**‡
21. **—— Poor Richard's Almanac, etc.**
22, 23. **Hawthorne's Tanglewood Tales.**‡
24. **Washington's Rules of Conduct, Letters, and Addresses.***
25, 26. **Longfellow's Golden Legend.**‡
27. **Thoreau's Succession of Forest Trees, Wild Apples, and Sounds.** With a Biographical Sketch by R. W. EMERSON.‡‡
28. **John Burroughs's Birds and Bees.****‡‡
29. **Hawthorne's Little Daffydowndilly, etc.*** **
30. **Lowell's Vision of Sir Launfal, etc.***‡‡**
31. **Holmes's My Hunt After the Captain, etc.****
32. **Lincoln's Gettysburg Speech, etc.****
33, 34, 35. **Longfellow's Tales of a Wayside Inn.** In three parts.‡‡
36. **John Burroughs's Sharp Eyes, etc.****
37. **Warner's A-Hunting of the Deer, etc.***‡‡
38. **Longfellow's Building of the Ship, etc.**
39. **Lowell's Books and Libraries, etc.****
40. **Hawthorne's Tales of the White Hills, and Sketches.****
41. **Whittier's Tent on the Beach, etc.**
42. **Emerson's Fortune of the Republic, The American Scholar, etc.****
43. **Ulysses Among the Phæacians.** From W. C. BRYANT'S Translation of Homer's Odyssey.*
44. **Edgeworth's Waste Not, Want Not; and The Barring Out.**
45. **Macaulay's Lays of Ancient Rome.***
46. **Old Testament Stories in Scripture Language.**
47, 48. **Fables and Folk Stories.** In two parts.‡
49, 50. **Hans Andersen's Stories.** In two parts.‡
51, 52. **Washington Irving: Essays from the Sketch Book.** [51.] Rip Van Winkle, etc. [52.] The Voyage, etc.**
53. **Scott's Lady of the Lake.** ROLFE. *Double No., 30 cents.* (*Also, in Rolfe's Students' Series, cloth, to Teachers,* 53 *cents.*)
54. **Bryant's Sella, Thanatopsis, etc.***
55. **Shakespeare's Merchant of Venice.** THURBER.* **
56. **Webster's First Bunker Hill, and Adams and Jefferson.***
57. **Dickens's Christmas Carol.****
58. **—— The Cricket on the Hearth.****
59. **Verse and Prose for Beginners in Reading.***
60, 61. **The Sir Roger de Coverley Papers.**‡
62. **John Fiske's War of Independence.**§
63. **Longfellow's Paul Revere's Ride, etc.****
64, 65, 66. **Lambs' Tales from Shakespeare.**‡‡
67. **Shakespeare's Julius Cæsar.*** **
68. **Goldsmith's Deserted Village, etc.***
69. **Hawthorne's Old Manse, and a Few Mosses.****
70. **A Selection from Whittier's Child Life in Poetry.****
71. **—— From Whittier's Child Life in Prose.****
72. **Milton's L'Allegro, Il Penseroso, Comus, Lycidas, and Sonnets.*** **
73. **Tennyson's Enoch Arden, etc.***
74. **Gray's Elegy, etc.; Cowper's John Gilpin, etc.**
75. **Scudder's George Washington.**§
76. **Wordsworth's On the Intimations of Immortality, etc.**
77. **Burns's Cotter's Saturday Night, etc.***
78. **Goldsmith's Vicar of Wakefield.**§
79. **Lamb's Old China, and Other Essays of Elia.**
80. **Coleridge's Rime of the Ancient Mariner, etc.; Campbell's Lochiel's Warning, etc.***
81. **Holmes's Autocrat of the Breakfast-Table.**§§
82. **Hawthorne's Twice-Told Tales.**§§§
83. **George Eliot's Silas Marner.**§
84. **Dana's Two Years Before the Mast.**§§§
85. **Hughes's Tom Brown's School Days.**§§
86. **Scott's Ivanhoe.**§§§
87. **Defoe's Robinson Crusoe.**§§§
88. **Stowe's Uncle Tom's Cabin.**§§§
89. **Swift's Gulliver's Voyage to Lilliput.****
90. **—— Gulliver's Voyage to Brobdingnag.****
91. **Hawthorne's House of the Seven Gables.**§§§
92. **Burroughs's A Bunch of Herbs, etc.**
93. **Shakespeare's As You Like It.*** **
94. **Milton's Paradise Lost.** Books I.-III.**
95, 96, 97, 98. **Cooper's Last of the Mohicans.** In four parts. (*Also, bound in one vol. linen, 60 cents.*)
99. **Tennyson's Coming of Arthur, and Other Idylls of the King.**
100. **Burke's Conciliation with the Colonies.** Edited by ROBERT ANDERSEN, A.M.*
101. **Homer's Iliad.** Books I., VI., XXII., and XXIV. Translated by ALEXANDER POPE.*
102. **Macaulay's Johnson and Goldsmith.***
103. **—— Essay on Milton.*** **
104. **—— Life and Writings of Addison.*** **

Nos. 102, 103, 104 are edited by WILLIAM P. TRENT.

105. **Carlyle's Essay on Burns.** Edited by GEORGE R. NOYES.*
106. **Shakespeare's Macbeth.** Edited by HELEN GRAY CONE.* **
107, 108. **Grimms' German Household Tales.**‡
109. **Bunyan's Pilgrim's Progress.** Edited by WILLIAM VAUGHAN MOODY.§
110. **De Quincey's Flight of a Tartar Tribe.** Edited by MILTON HAIGHT TURK.*
111. **Tennyson's Princess.** ROLFE. *Double No., 30 cents.* (*Also in Rolfe's Students' Series, cloth, to Teachers,* 53 *cents.*)
112. **Virgil's Æneid.** Books I.-III. Translated by CHRISTOPHER PEARSE CRANCH.
113. **Poems from the Writings of Ralph Waldo Emerson.** Edited by GEORGE H. BROWNE.**
114. **Old Greek Folk Stories.** By JOSEPHINE PRESTON PEABODY.*
115. **Browning's Pied Piper of Hamelin, etc.**
116. **Shakespeare's Hamlet.** HELEN GRAY CONE.§
117, 118. **Stories from the Arabian Nights.**‡
119. **Poe's Raven, the Fall of the House of Usher, and Other Poems and Tales.****
120. **—— The Gold-Bug, The Purloined Letter, and Other Tales.**** (Nos. 119, 120 are edited by WILLIAM P. TRENT.)
121. **The Great Debate Between Hayne and Webster: Hayne's Speech.****
122. **—— Webster's Reply to Hayne.****

Nos. 121, 122 are edited by LINDSAY SWIFT.

123. **Lowell's Democracy, etc.****
124. **Aldrich's Baby Bell, The Little Violinist, and Other Verse and Prose.**
125. **Dryden's Palamon and Arcite.** Edited by ARTHUR GILMAN.*
126. **The King of the Golden River,** by JOHN RUSKIN; and Other Wonder Stories.*
127. **Keat's Ode on a Grecian Urn, The Eve of St. Agnes, etc.**
128. **Byron's Prisoner of Chillon, etc.**
129. **Plato's The Judgement of Socrates: being The Apology, Crito, and the closing scene of Phædo.** Translated by PAUL E. MORE.
130. **Emerson's The Superlative, etc.**
131. **—— Nature, and Compensation.** Edited by EDWARD W. EMERSON.

For explanation of signs see end of list.

☞ *CONTINUED ON THE NEXT PAGE.*

Books for Summer Travellers.

D. APPLETON & COMPANY, New York.

APPLETONS' GUIDE BOOKS.

Appletons' General Guide to the United States and Canada. With numerous maps and illustrations. 12mo, flexible morocco, with tuck, $2.50. (Part I., separately, NEW ENGLAND AND MIDDLE STATES AND CANADA; cloth, 75 cents. Part II., SOUTHERN AND WESTERN STATES, cloth, 75 cents.)

Appletons' Guide-Book to Alaska. By Miss E. R. Scidmore. New edition, including an Account of the Klondike. With maps and illustrations. 12mo, flexible cloth, $1.00.

A Landmark History of New York. By Albert Ulmann. With many illustrations. 12mo, cloth, $1.50.

In this book the reader makes visits in sequence to the old Dutch Settlement, the early English colony, the city as it was before the Revolution, and so on down to the present time. Copies of rare prints and maps and many plates made from recent photographs illustrate the work.

Appletons' Dictionary of [Greater] New York and Vicinity. With maps of New York and vicinity. Square 12mo, paper, 25 cents net; postage, 6 cents additional.

Puerto Rico and Its Resources. A book for Travellers, Investors, and others, containing full accounts of Natural Features and Resources, Products, People, Opportunities for Business, etc. By Frederick A. Ober, author of "Camps in the Caribbees," "Crusoe's Island," etc. With maps and illustrations. 12mo, cloth, $1.50.

A. S. BARNES & CO., New York.

A World's Shrine. (Lake Como.) By Virginia W. Johnson. Illustrated. 12mo, cloth, $1.20 net. (new.)

A History of Art. For Tourists. By Wm. H. Goodyear. Fully illustrated. 8vo, cloth, $2.80 net.

Switzerland, Annals of. By Julia M. Colton. Illustrated. 12mo, cloth, $1.25.

The Rhine, Legends of. By H. A. Guerber. Illustrated. 12mo, cloth, gilt top, $1.50 net.

BRENTANO'S, New York.

My Ocean Trip. By E. S. Cadigan. Illustrated with signals and flags printed in colors, and with blank pages for memoranda. 12mo, cloth, $1.00.

A work appealing especially to tourists and travellers, arranged for the record to be kept of an Ocean Voyage. In addition there are many items of interest, such as a complete code of signals, series of games for shipboard, entertainments, pages for the autographs of fellow passengers.

POCKET DICTIONARIES. Printed at the press of Bernhard Tauchnitz of Leipzig, Germany, from the plates of the famous Tauchnitz series, and bound specially for Brentano's. Each, cloth, $1.00.

Dictionary of the English and German Languages. By J. E. Wessely.

Dictionary of the English and French Languages. By J. E. Wessely.

Dictionary of the English and Italian Languages. By J. E. Wessely.

Dictionary of the English and Spanish Languages. By J. E. Wessely and Girones.

HOUGHTON, MIFFLIN & CO., Boston.

Our National Parks. By John Muir. Illustrated. $1.75 net; postpaid, $1.87.

Footing it in Franconia. $1.10 net; postpaid, $1.19.

HOUGHTON, MIFFLIN & CO.—*Continued.*

Picturesque Alaska. By Abby J. Woodman. Illustrations and maps. 16mo, $1.00.

September Days on Nantucket. By William Root Bliss.

Cape Cod. By H. D. Thoreau. $1.50.

WILLIAM R. JENKINS, New York.

The Complete Pocket-Guide to Europe. Edited by E. C. and T. L. Stedman. One vol., full leather, $1.25. Revised yearly. The best of its kind.

LEMCKE & BUECHNER, New York.

Baedeker's Guides. German and French.

Monographs on Artists.

Dictionaries and Grammars for the study of Foreign Languages. *Send for lists.*

McCLURE, PHILLIPS & CO., New York.

The Hound of the Baskervilles. A Sherlock Holmes novel by A. Conan Doyle. Illustrated. $1.25.

The Blazed Trail. An American novel by Stewart Edward White. Illustrated. $1.50.

Red Saunders. A humorous account of his doings West and East. By Henry Wallace Phillips. Frontispiece. $1.25.

The Madness of Philip. Stories of child life for grown-ups by Josephine Dodge Daskam. Illustrated. $1.50.

A Prince of Good Fellows. Tales of James V., the "Merry Monarch of Scotland," by Robert Barr. Illustrated. $1.50.

The Making of a Statesman. A novelette, together with other stories of Georgia life, by Joel Chandler Harris. $1.25.

The Gentleman From Indiana. A romance by Booth Tarkington. $1.50.

An Island Cabin. A record of outdoor life by Arthur Henry. $1.50.

Forest Neighbors. Life stories of wild animals by W. D. Hulbert. $1.50 net; postpaid, $1.68.

Next to the Ground. A nature narrative by Martha McCulloch-Williams. $1.20 net; postpaid, $1.32.

JOHN P. MORTON & CO., Louisville, Ky.

Mammoth Cave of Kentucky (A Perfect Guide To). By Hovey & Call. Paper, 50 cents; cloth, $1.00.

E. STEIGER & CO., New York.

Baedeker's and Other Guide-Books, in German. The largest assortment of Books for the Study of Foreign Languages. *Send for catalogue.*

A. WESSELS COMPANY, 7-9 W. 18th St., N. Y.

Historical Guide-Books to Paris, Venice, Florence, Cities of Belgium, Cities of Northern Italy, the Umbrian Towns. One volume each. By Grant Allen. Pocket size, 250 pp., cloth, $1.25 net.

London and Londoners. By R. A. Pritchard. Pocket size, 400 pp., cloth, $1.25.

LONGMANS, GREEN, & CO.'S

NEW EDUCATIONAL BOOKS

American Teachers Series.

A Series of Books for the Guidance and Assistance of Teachers in Elementary and Secondary Schools, and Students in Normal Schools and Teachers' Colleges.
Under the general editorship of JAMES E. RUSSELL, Ph.D., Dean of Teachers' College, Columbia University.

New Volume

The Teaching of History and Civics in the Elementary and the Secondary School. By HENRY E. BOURNE, B.A., B.D., Professor in the College for Women, Western Reserve University, Cleveland, O. Crown 8vo, 395 pages, $1.50.

Individuality and the Moral Aim in American Education.

Report presented to the Victoria University and the Gilchrist Trustees. February, 1901. By H. THISELTON MARK. Crown 8vo, 307 pages, $1.50, *net*. By mail, $1.60.

Mentioned in the *Educational Review* as one of the twelve best books on education published during the past year.

Longmans' English Grammar.

12mo. 343 pages. 65 cents. Mailing price, 70 cents.

CONTENTS: Part I—Parts of Speech. Part II—Classification and Inflection. Part III—Analysis of Sentences. Part IV—History and Derivation. Notes for Teachers. Index.

The Theory of Optics.

By PAUL DRUDE, Professor of Physics at the University of Giessen. Translated from the German by C. RIBORG MANN and ROBERT A. MILLIKAN, Assistant Professors of Physics at the University of Chicago. With 110 diagrams, 8vo, pp. xxvii.-546, $4.00.

Animal Activities.

A First Book in Zoölogy. By NATHANIEL S. FRENCH, Ph.D., Teacher of Zoölogy in the Roxbury High School. 12mo, 282 pages, with 205 illustrations, $1.20.

Directions for Class Work in Practical Physiology.

Elementary Physiology of Muscle and Nerve and of the Vascular and Nervous Systems. By E. A. SCHAFER, LL.D., F.R.S., Professor of Physiology in the University of Edinburgh; author of the "Essentials of History," etc. With 45 Diagrams, 8vo, $1.00.

Longmans' New School Atlas, Revised to 1901.

Consisting of 40 Colored Maps, with over 20 Insets and a very full Index. Imperial 8vo. $1.50.

The Theory of Equations.

Vol. II. With an introduction to the Theory of Binary Algebraic Forms. By W. S. BURNSIDE, M.A., D.Sc., and A. W. PANTON, M.A., D.Sc. Cloth 8vo, 304 pages, $2.75.

Elementary Plant Physiology.

By DANIEL TREMBLY MACDOUGALL, Ph.D., Director of the laboratories, New York Botanical Garden. Author of "Practical Text-book of Plant Physiology." 12 mo, 150 pages, with 108 illustrations, $1.20.

Plane and Solid Geometry.

By JAMES HOWARD GORE, Ph.D., Professor of Mathematics, Columbian University. Author of "Elements of Geodesy," "History of Geodesy," "Bibliography of Geodesy," etc., etc. Third Edition, thoroughly revised. With an Appendix of over 500 Additional Exercises. 12mo, 257 pages, $1.00.

An Introduction to the Practical Use of Logarithms, with Examples in Mensuration.

By F. GLANVILLE TAYLOR, M.A., B.Sc., Mathematical Lecturer of University College, Nottingham. 50 cents.

Longmans' Household Science Readers.

Lessons in Nature Study and Household Science. With many illustrations.

Book I. For the Third School Year. 133 pages and over 60 illustrations, 42 cents.

Pictorial Geographical Readers.

A new series of readings in Geography intended to arouse interest in the subject and to stimulate thought and to be placed in the hands of the pupils in Primary grades to supplement oral teaching.

Book I. With 7 Colored Plates and 75 Illustrations in black and white. 170 pages, 36 cents.

Deutsche Sagen.

A Reading-Book in German for Schools. By F. GEIBLER. With an Introduction by Dr. J. G. CROSWELL, Head Master of the Brearley School, New York. 12mo, 96 pages, 60 cents.

Homeric Society.

A Sociological Study of the Iliad and Odyssey. By ALBERT GALLOWAY KELLER, Ph D., Instructor in Social Science in Yale University. Crown 8vo, 341 pages, $1.20.

University of Pennsylvania.—Department of History Publications.

NOTE.—A descriptive circular containing information regarding these, and other books published by the Department of History of the University of Pennsylvania, and for sale by Longmans, Green, & Co., will be sent upon application.

LONGMANS, GREEN, & CO., 91-93 Fifth Avenue, New York

EDUCATIONAL NUMBER

Table of Contents.

EDUCATIONAL CATALOGUE

INDEX TO ADVERTISERS

LIST OF EDUCATIONAL PUBLISHERS.

With Key to Abbreviations used in the Educational Catalogue.

AL	Allyn & Bacon	Boston
AM	American Book Co	N. Y
AN	Ainsworth & Co	Chicago
AP	Appleton (D.) & Co	N. Y
AR	Armstrong (A. C.) & Son	N. Y
BA	Barnes (A. S.) & Co	N. Y
BB	Babcock, J. S	N. Y
BC	Bailey & Noyes	Portland, Me
BD	Baird (H. C.) & Co	Phila
BE	Benziger Bros	N. Y
BF	Baker & Taylor Co	N. Y
BG	Boname (L. C.)	Phila
BI	Bardeen, C. W	Syracuse, N. Y
BJ	Babyhood Publishing Co	N. Y
BL	Blakiston (P.) Son & Co	Phila
BM	Bloch Publishing Co	New York
BN	Boston School Supply Co	Boston
BO	Bradley (Milton) Co	Springfield, Mass
BP	Brumder, George	Milwaukee, Wis
BR	Belknap & Warfield	Hartford, Ct
BS	Barnes (C. M.) Company	Chicago
BT	Burke (J. W.) & Co	Macon, Ga
BU	Butler, Sheldon & Co	New York and Phila
BV	Burrows Bros. Co	Cleveland, O
BW	Ballantyne (W.) & Sons	Washington, D. C
BY	Bryant, J. C	Buffalo, N. Y
BX	Berlitz & Co	N. Y
CA	Cassell & Company, Ltd	N. Y
CB	Columbia Book Co	Phila
CE	Crane & Co	Topeka, Kan
CH	Christern, F. W. (Dyrsen & Pfeiffer, Succr's)	N. Y
CI	Christian Publishing Co	St. Louis, Mo
CL	Clarke (Robt.) Co	Cincinnati
CM	Comstock Publishing Co	Ithaca, N. Y
CN	Caspar Co., C. N	Milwaukee, Wis
CO	Collins, Chas. (Baker & T. Co.)	N. Y
CP	Chemical Publishing Co	Easton, Pa
CR	Church (John) Co	Cincinnati
CS	Central School Supply House	Chicago
CU	Cushing & Co	Baltimore, Md
DA	Darrow (E.) & Co	Rochester, N. Y
DH	Diehl, Frederick	Louisville, Ky
DI	Dick & Fitzgerald	N. Y
DR	Draper, Warren F	Andover, Mass
DS	Ditson (Oliver) & Co	Boston
DU	Duffie, W. J	Columbia, S. C
DW	De Wolfe, Fiske & Co	Boston
DY	Dulany (Wm. J. C.) Co	Baltimore, Md
EA	Eaton & Mains	N. Y
ED	Educational Publishing Co	Boston
EH	Ellsworth Company	N. Y
EL	Eldredge & Bro	Phila
EN	Engelhard (G. P.) & Co	Chicago
ET	Eaton & Company	Chicago
FL	Flanagan (A.) Co	Chicago
FO	Fortescue (W. S.) & Co	Phila
FU	Funk & Wagnalls Co	New York
FW	Fowler & Wells Co	N. Y
GI	Ginn & Co	Boston
GL	Globe School Book Co	N. Y
GM	Graham (Andrew J.) & Co	N. Y
HB	Hunter & Welburn	Nashville, Tenn
HD	Hardy, Charles G	Oakland, Cal
HE	Heath (D. C.) & Co	Boston
HM	Houghton, Mifflin & Co	Boston
HN	Hamilton (C. K.) & Co	Lebanon, O
HO	Holt (Henry) & Co	N. Y
HR	Herder, B	St. Louis, Mo
HS	Hinds & Noble	N. Y
HW	Harison, W. Beverley	N. Y
HY	Humphrey (J. N.)	Whitewater, Wis
ID	Indiana Publishing Co	Danville, Ind
IG	Ingerson Publishing Co	St. Louis, Mo
IN	Inland Publishing Co	Terre Haute, Ind
IR	Irish, F. V	Chicago
IT	International News Co	N. Y
JE	Jenkins, William R	N. Y
JH	Johnson (B. F.) Publishing Co	Richmond, Va
JN	Jones, G. W	Ithaca, N. Y
JO	Johnson (T. & J. W.) & Co	Phila
KC	Koehler (C. A.) & Co	Boston
KE	Kellogg (E. L.) & Co	N. Y
KH	Kroeh, C. F	Stevens Institute, Hoboken, N. J
KI	Kilner (H. L.) & Co	Phila
KL	Kelly, Thomas	N. Y
KN	Knofel, H	Louisville, Ky
KO	Kohler Publishing Co	Phila
KR	Krone Bros	N. Y
KT	Knight & Millet	Boston
KY	Kenedy, P. J	N. Y
LA	Lea Bros & Co	Phila
LB	Lemcke & Buechner (formerly B. Westermann & Co.)	N. Y
LE	Lee & Shepard	Boston
LI	Lippincott (J. B.) Co	Phila
LJ	Lane, John	N. Y
LN	Longmans, Green & Co	N. Y
LO	Lockwood, G. R. (Baker & T. Co., Agts.)	N. Y
LR	Lothrop Publishing Co	Boston
LT	Little, Brown & Co	Boston
LV	Lovell (A.) & Co	N. Y
MA	March Brothers	Lebanon, O
MB	Metric Bureau	Boston
MC	Macmillan (The) Co	N. Y
MD	McBride & Co. (D. H.)	N. Y
ME	Merriam (G. & C.) Co	Springfield, Mass
MG	McClurg (A. C.) & Co	Chicago
MI	Meisterschaft Publishing Co	Boston
MM	Mosher (T. B.)	Portland, Me
MO	Morton (John P.) & Co	Louisville, Ky
MP	Myers (R. L.) & Co	Harrisburg, Pa
MR	McKay, David	Phila
MS	Morse (The) Company	N. Y
MT	Mutual Book Co	N. Y
MU	Murphy (John) Company	Baltimore, Md
MY	Maynard, Merrill & Co	N. Y
NE	Nelson (Thos.) & Sons	N. Y
NN	Newson & Co	N. Y
NO	Normal Publishing House	Danville, Ind
OS	O'Shea, P	N. Y
PA	Page (L. C.) & Co	Boston
PB	Paul (Peter) Book Co	Buffalo, N. Y
PC	Pennybacker, Percy V	Palestine, Tex
PD	Pond (Wm. A.) & Co	N. Y
PE	Peck, H. H	New Haven, Ct
PH	Phonographic Institute Company	Cincinnati
PI	Pitman (Isaac) & Sons	N. Y
PL	Polock, M	Phila
PM	Potter & Putnam Co	N. Y
PO	Polyglot Book Co	Chicago
PP	Penn Publishing Co	Phila
PR	Prang Educational Co	Boston
PS	Public-School Publishing Co	Bloomington, Ill
PT	Pustet (Fr.) & Co	N. Y
PU	Putnam's (G. P.) Sons	N. Y
PW	Powers & Lyons	Chicago
PY	Practical Text-Book Company	Cleveland, O
RA	Rand, McNally & Co	Chicago
RB	Raub & Co	Phila
RD	Rutherford, Mildred	Athens, Ga
RE	Register Publishing Co	Ann Arbor, Mich
RI	Richmond & Backus Co	Detroit, Mich
RN	Richardson, Smith & Co	N. Y
RU	Routledge (George) & Sons, Limited	N. Y
SA	Sanborn (Benj. H.) & Co	Boston
SC	Scribner's (Chas.) Sons	N. Y
SB	Sever (C. W.) & Co	Cambridge, Mass
SI	Silver, Burdett & Co	N. Y
SK	Schwartz, Kirwin & Fauss	N. Y
SL	Sadler-Rowe Co	Baltimore, Md
SM	Schermerhorn (J. W.) & Co	N. Y
SN	Scrantom, Wetmore & Co	Rochester, N. Y
SO	Sower (Christopher) Co	Phila
SP	Spon & Chamberlain	N. Y
SR	Scott, Foresman & Co	Chicago
SS	Standard School-Book Co	St. Louis, Mo
ST	Steiger (E.) & Co	N. Y
SU	Southern Methodist Pub. House	Nashville, Tenn
SY	Sibley & Ducker	Boston
TH	Thompson, Brown & Co	Boston
TR	Tracy, Gibbs & Co	Madison, Wis
UC	University of Chicago Press	Chicago
UL	Ulbrich, Otto	Buffalo, N. Y
UN	University Publishing Co	N. Y
VN	Van Nostrand (D.) Co	N. Y
WA	Whitaker & Ray Co	San Francisco
WE	Werner, Edgar S	N. Y
WG	Wilde (A. E.) Co	Cincinnati
WH	Wheeler (W. H.) & Co	Chicago
WI	Wiley (John) & Sons	N. Y
WK	Whittaker, Thos	N. Y
WL	Wells, L. S	Columbus, O
WN	Warne (F.) & Co	N. Y
WO	Wood (Wm.) & Co	N. Y
WP	Western Publishing House	Chicago
WR	Werner School Book Co	Chicago
WT	Witter, Conrad	St. Louis, Mo
WY	Wycil & Co	N. Y
ZI	Zickel, S	N. Y

☞ *Be particular in ordering to specify editions, and to give the full name of the book, as quoted on this price-list. Old editions, superseded by new issues, are not included in this list; see previous catalogues.*

THE

AMERICAN EDUCATIONAL CATALOGUE FOR 1902.

[PUBLISHERS' PRICES.]

NOTICE.—In this Catalogue only prices made by publishers themselves are given—retail, if retail, in first column; "net" (wholesale), if "net," in second column; where a "mailing" percentage is specified by the publisher, the "mailing price" is given in the retail column marked with an asterisk (*), in addition to the wholesale price. When price-columns are left blank, the publisher failed, on application, to furnish price. A double asterisk (**) in price-columns designates books forthcoming. New books, issued since the publication of the Catalogue of 1901, *are designated by a single asterisk (*) before title.*

☞ *In comparing prices or ordering at retail, private buyers should bear in mind that a percentage must be added to prices quoted at wholesale, to cover freight, handling, delivering, etc. Discounts on quantities vary on different lines, according to the kind of prices adopted by the respective publishers.*

For subject classification (and for collective references to classic authors entered here under separate editors), see the second part of the Catalogue, following this main alphabet.

Title	Publ.	Retail	Net
Abbott's (E.) Paragraph U. S. History	LT	50	
Paragraph Hist. of America, Rev.	LT	50	
History of Greece, 2 pts. ea.	FU	2 25	
Abbott's (E. A.) How to Parse	LT	1 00	
How to Tell Parts of Speech	LT	75	
How to Write Clearly	LT	60	
Eng. Lessons for Eng. People	LT	1 50	
Abbott-Gaskell's Outlines for Study of Art	SI	*1 67	1 50
*Abegg & Herz's Practical Chemistry	MC	1 25	
Abeille (L') pour les Enfans	FO	35	30
Abercrombie's Intellectual Philosophy (Abbott)	CO	*80	72
Moral Philosophy (Abbott)	CO	*80	72
*Abernethy's American Literature	MY	*1 10	
Aborn's Mechanical Drawing	AM	*35	
Abram's (B. A.) Primer for Pupils of non-German Parentage	AM	*20	
Academy Series of English Classics [32 v., cl. and bds., various prices, 20c.-25c., 30c.-35c.-40c.]	AL		
Acme Declamation Book	HS	50	
—— pap.	HS	30	
Adams (C. K.) & Trent's (W. P.) History of the United States	AL	**	
Adams' (F. A.) Greek Prepositions	AM	*60	
Adams' (F. P.) Grammar Diagrams	NO	1 25	
Normal Parsing Book	NO	20	
Adams' (G. B.) Civilization During the Middle Ages	SC	2 50	
European History	MC	1 40	
Growth of the French Nation	MC	1 25	
Medieval and Modern History	MC	1 10	
Adams' (H. C.) Science of Finance	HO		3 50
Adams' (O. F.) Dict. of Am. Authors	HM	3 00	
Adams' Physical Laboratory Manual	WR	*75	
Addick's Elementary French	CO	*55	48
Adler's German Dictionary, 8°	AP	5 00	
—— abridged	AP	1 50	
Progressive German Reader	AM	*1 05	
Adriance's Laboratory Calculations	WI	1 25	
Æsop's Fables, with Vocabulary	HO		50
Agassiz's Methods in Natural History	HM	1 50	
Ahn's French Dialogues, No. 1	ST	40	
—— No. 1, bds	ST	30	
—— No. 2	ST	35	
—— " bds	ST	25	
—— No. 3	ST	40	
—— " bds	ST	30	
German School Dictionary	WT	60	
" Grammar	AM	*70	
French Method	AM	*52	
Italian Grammar	CH	1 40	
Spanish Method	AP	75	
Series of German Novels, pap., 18 v. ea.	ST	20	
Series of German Comedies, pap., 9 v., ea.	ST	25	
Ahn-Fischer's German Method	ST	1 00	
—— 1st Course	ST	50	
—— 2d "	ST	50	
—— Key to	ST		30
Ahn-Grauert's 1st German Reader	ST	50	
—— Key to	ST		30
Ahn-Grauert's 2d German Reader	ST	70	
—— Key to	ST		35
Ahn-Henn's French Series:			
French Primer	ST	25	
" Method	ST	1 00	
—— 1st Course	ST	40	
—— Key to	ST		25
—— 2d Course	ST	60	
—— Key to	ST		25
1st Reader, with notes, bds	ST	60	
—— with footnotes, bds	ST	60	
—— Key to	ST		30
2d Reader, with notes, bds	ST	80	
—— with footnotes, bds	ST	80	
—— Key to	ST		40
Ahn-Henn's German Series:			
1st German Book	ST	25	
2d " " bds	ST	45	
3d " " "	ST	45	
—— Key to	ST		25
4th German Book, bds	ST	60	
—— Key to	ST		25
Rudiments, 1st Course, bds	ST	65	
—— Key to	ST		25
Rudiments, 2d Course, bds	ST	1 00	
Complete Method	ST	1 75	
Synopsis of Ger. Grammar, bds	ST	80	
1st Reader, with notes, bds	ST	80	
—— with footnotes, bds	ST	60	
—— Key to	ST		30
2d Reader, with notes, bds	ST	1 00	
—— with footnotes, bds	ST	1 00	
—— Key to	ST		50
See also Henn-Ahn's.			
Ahn-Henn's Latin Series:			
Short Latin Course	ST	1 20	
—— Nos. 1 and 2, bds. ea.	ST	60	
—— Key to No. 1	ST		30
—— " " " 2	ST		40
New Latin Manual	ST	2 00	
—— 1st Course, bds	ST	60	
—— 2d and 3d Course, bds. ea.	ST	80	
1st Latin Book, bds	ST	60	
—— Key to	ST		40
2d and 3d Latin Bks., bds. ea.	ST	80	
—— Key to ea.	ST		40
Latin Method	ST	1 80	
" Grammar, bds	ST	80	
1st Latin Reader, bds	ST	70	
2d " " "	ST	80	
Latin Readers, complete	ST	1 50	
" Syntax, bds	ST	80	
Latin Prose Composition	ST	50	
" Vocab. for beginners, bds	ST	60	
Ahn-Oehlschläger's Pronouncing Ger. Method, bds	ST	1 15	
—— Key to	ST		[illegible]
—— 1st Course, bds	ST	80	
—— 2d " "	ST	40	
—— 1st Course, rev. ed	HR	50	34
—— 2d " " "	HR	50	34
—— 1st and 2d together, rev. ed	HR	90	60
French Method	AM	*52	

*Aikins' (H. A.) Manual of Logic, Deductive and Inductive	HO		1 50	
Ainsworth's Eng.-Latin and Latin-Eng. Dictionary, 8°	FO	3 50	3 00	
Airy's English History	LN	1 50		
*Alton's (G. B.) Descriptive Speller	GI	*30	22	
*Alarcon's El Capitan Veneno (Brownell)	AM	*50		
Alden's Intellectual Philosophy	AP	1 00		
First Principles of Pol. Economy	BI	75		
Citizen's Manual	BU	*36		
Science of Government	BU	*1 00		
Alderman's (E. A.) Brief Hist. of North Carolina	GI	*30	25	
Aldrich's (F. D) & Foster's (I. L.) Foundations of French	GI	*95	90	
Aldrich's (G. I.) & Forbes' (Alex.) Progressive Course in Reading:				
First Bk.	BU	*20		
Second "	BU	*30		
Third "	BU	*40		
Fourth "	BU	*50		
—— —— in 2 pts.	*ea.* BU	*35		
Fifth Bk	BU	*60		
—— —— in 2 pts.	*ea.* BU	*40		
Alexander's (A.) Moral Science	SC	1 50		
Alexander's (Mrs G. A.) Primer	CS		25	
Alexander's (W. D.) Hist. of the Hawaiian People	AM	*1 50		
*Alger's Primer of Work and Play	HE		30	
Allen's Mind Studies	KE	50		
Allen's Composition Blanks, 2 nos	*doz.* BU	*1 00		
Allen's (C. B. & M. A.) Man Wonderful in the House Beautiful	FW	1 50		
Allen's (C. R.) Laboratory Physics, Teachers' ed	HO		1 00	
—— Pupils' ed	HO		80	
Allen's (E. A.) School Grammar of English Language	HE	*60		
Allen's (F. D.) Euripides' Medea	GI	*1 10	1 00	
Wecklein's Æschylus' Prometheus	GI	*45	40	
—— with notes, cl.	GI	*1 50	1 40	
Allen's (F. J.) Topics in English History, bds.	HE	*30	25	
—— cl.	HE	*45	40	
Allen's (G. G.) Universal Phonography	LE	50		
Allen's (J G.) Topical Studies in Am. History	MC	40		
Allen's (J. H.) Latin Primer	GI	*1 00	90	
New Latin Method	GI	*1 00	90	
Allen's (O. D.) Fresenius' Quantitative Analysis	WI	6 00		
Allen's (W. F.) History Topics	HE	*30	25	
Introd. to Latin Composition	GI	*1 00	90	
Readers' Guide to Eng. Hist.	GI	*30	25	
Tacitus' Germania and Agricola	GI	*1 10	1 00	
Annals of Tacitus, Bks. 1-6	GI	*45	40	
—— with notes	GI	*1 65	1 50	
Short History of the Roman People	GI	*1 10	1 00	
Allen & Greenough's Latin Composition	GI	*1 25	1 12	
Latin Grammar, rev	GI	*1 30	1 20	
Shorter Latin Grammar	GI	*1 05	95	
New Cæsar	GI	*1 40	1 25	
" Cicero	GI	*1 55	1 40	
Cicero's de Senectute	GI	*55	50	
New Ovid, with Vocab	GI	*1 65	1 50	
Sallust, Rev	GI	*97	90	
Allinson's Greek Prose Composition	AL		1 00	
Allonge's (A.) Charcoal Drawing	HM	1 00		
Alliot's Auteurs Contemporains	HO		1 20	
Contes et Nouvelles	HO		1 00	
Alsop's First Lessons in Algebra	FO	60	50	
—— Key to	FO	60	50	
Treatise on Algebra	FO	1 25	1 00	
—— Key to	FO	75	60	
Treatise on Surveying	FO	2 25	1 75	
—— Key to	FO	1 25	1 00	
Altamira's Spanish Echo (Conversation)	KC	1 00		
Althaus' Synopsis of German Grammar	LN		60	
*American Citizen Series: Practical Sociology (Wright)	LN	1 50		
American History Leaflets, Hart & Channing	*ea.* LV	*10		
American History Series:				
Fisher's Colonial Era	SC		1 25	
Sloane's French War	SC		1 25	
Walker's Making of the Nation	SC		1 25	
Burgess' Middle Period	SC		1 75	
*—— Civil War and Reconstruction, 2 v.	*ea* SC		1 00	
*—— Reconstruction and the Constitution	SC		1 00	
American History told by Contemporaries; ed. by A. B. Hart. V. 1, Era of Colonization	MC	2 00		
—— V. 2, Building of the Republic	MC	2 00		
American History told by Contemporaries; ed. by A. B. Hart. V. 3, National Expansion	MC	2 00		
—— V. 4, Welding of the Nation, 1845-1900	MC	*2 19		
Complete sets, 4 v.	MC	8 00		
American Music System (Zuchtmann):				
American Music Reader, No. 1	RN	35		
" " " " 2	RN	45		
" " " " 3	RN	50		
" " " " 4	RN	75		
Zuchtmann's Teachers' Manual	RN	1 00		
American Song Book (Haaren & Mattfeld)	RN	50		
American Poems	HM	1 00		
Prose	HM	1 00		
American Primer (W. J. Davis)	MO	10		
American School Music Reader, Bk. 1	DS	35		
—— Bks. 2 and 3,	*ea.* DS	50		
—— Bks. 2 and 3 in 1 v.	DS	75		
American Science Series:				
Astronomy (Newcomb & Holden), Advanced	HO			2 00
—— Briefer Course	HO			1 12
Biology (Sedgwick & Wilson)	HO			1 75
Botany (Bessey), Advanced	HO			2 20
—— Briefer Course	HO			1 12
—— Introd. to Systematic Botany.	HO			**
Chemical Experiments (Remson & Randall)	HO			50
Chemistry, Inorganic (Remsen), Advanced	HO			2 80
—— Briefer Course	HO			1 12
—— Elementary Course	HO			80
—— Laboratory Manual	HO			40
Finance (Adams)	HO			3 50
Geology, Advanced Course (Chamberlin & S.)	HO			**
—Briefer Course (Chamberlin & S.)	HO			**
Human Body (Martin), Advanced	HO			2 50
—— Briefer Course (Rev. by Fitz)	HO			1 20
—— Elementary Course	HO			75
Physics (Barker)	HO			3 50
Political Economy (Walker), Advanced	HO			2 00
—— Briefer Course	HO			1 20
—— Elementary Course	HO			1 00
Psychology (James) 2 v., Advanced	HO			4 80
—— Briefer Course	HO			1 60
Zoölogy (Packard), Advanced	HO			2 40
—— Briefer Course	HO			1 12
—— Elementary Course	HO			80
American Spelling Blanks: Vertical Writing, Angular Hand	*doz.* AM		*48	
—— Round Hand	" AM		*48	
American Standard Penmanship, 6 nos.	*doz.* AM		*75	
American System of Vertical Writing, nos. 1 to 7	*doz.* AM		*96	
Vertical Writing Blanks, nos. 1, 2, and 3	*doz.* AM		*72	
Writing Speller, nos. 1 and 2	" AM		*45	
Ames's (A.) Elementary Hygiene for the Tropics	HE		**	
Ames's Theory of Physics	AM		1 60	
Ames & Bliss' Experiments in Physics	AM		1 80	
Analytical Copy-Bks., 11 nos	*doz.* SR		*1 04	90
Elementary ed., 5 nos	" SR		*75	65
Pen and Pencil ed., 3 nos	" SR		*47	40
Business forms, Bks. 1, 2	" SR		*1 80	1 60
—— Bk. 3	" SR		*2 47	2 20
—— Key to Nos. 1-3	SR		*17	15
Greek Lexicon	WI		2 50	
Anderegg & Roe's Trigonometry	GI		*80	75
Anderson's (J. H.) Public School Chemistry	CA		1 00	
Anderson's (J. J.) United States Histories:				
Junior Class	MY		*70	
New Grammar School	MY		*1 00	
Pictorial School	MY		*1 20	
Popular School	MY		*1 05	
New Manual of General History	MY		*1 70	
—— pt. 1, Ancient	MY		*1 05	
—— pt. 2, Mediæval and Modern	MY		*1 25	
School Hist. of England	MY		*1 20	
" " " France	MY		*1 25	
Leighton's Hist. of Rome	MY		*1 50	
United States Reader	MY		*1 10	
Historical Reader	MY		*1 35	
Short Hist. of England	MY		*95	
*Anderson (J. J.) and Flick's Short History of State of New York	MY		*1 00	
Anderson's (J. M.) Study of English Words	AM		*40	
Anderson's (W. G.) Light Gymnastics	MY		*1 50	
Anderson's Selections from Ovid	UN		1 15	1 00
Andre's Plan and Map Drawing	SP		3 75	
Andrews' (E. A.) First Latin Book	HM		70	
Viri Romæ	HM		1 00	

Andrews' (E. A.) Latin Lessons, Rev.....HM 70
Cæsar's Commentaries.............HM 1 05
Ovid.........................HM 1 00
Sallust.........................HM 1 10
Virgil.........................HM 1 20
Andrews & Stoddard's Latin Grammar, rev. by Preble.........HM 1 12
Andrews' (E. B.) History of the U. S., 2 v.SC 4 00
Institutes of Gen. History..........SI *2 25 2 00
" " Economics..........SI *1 30 1 10
Elementary Geology..........AM *1 00
Andrews' (G. A.) Composite Geometrical Figures..........GI *55 50
Andrews' (I. W.) Manual of Constitution.AM *1 00
Andrews' (J.) Seven Little Sisters.......GI *55 50
Stories Mother Nature Told..........GI *55 50
Geographical Plays..........GI *55 50
Each and all..........GI *55 50
Ten Boys..........GI *60 50
Stories of My Four Friends..........GI *85 75
Angell's (H.) Elementary Geometry......PU 75
Practical Plane Geometry, 2 v......PU 3 00
Angell's (J.) Animal Physiology.........PU 75
Animal Painting..........CA 1 50
Anthon's Abridged Eng.-Latin and Latin-Eng. Dictionary, 16°..........PO 1 50 1 25
Anthon's Cicero's Orations..........AM *1 10
Cicero's de Senectute, etc..........AM *1 10
" Tusculan Disputations....AM *1 10
Homer's Iliad..........AM *1 20
Horace..........AM *1 20
Juvenal and Persius..........AM *1 10
Livy..........AM *1 20
Sallust..........AM *1 10
Tacitus..........AM *1 10
Virgil's Æneid..........AM *1 20
Xenophon's Anabasis..........AM *1 10
" Memorabilia..........AM *1 10
Latin-Eng. and Eng.-Lat. Dictionary.AM *2 50
Smith's Dict. of Antiquities..........AM *4 25
Anthony & Brackett's Physics, Rev.....WI 3 00
Anthony's (G. C.) Mechanical Drawing..HE *1 65 1 50
Machine Drawing..........HE *1 65 1 50
Apgar's Geog. Drawing Book..........BU *42
Apgar's (E. A. and A. C.) New Plant Analysis..........AM *55
Appleton's (J. H.) Qualitative Analysis..SI *83 75
Quantitative " ....SI *1 40 1 25
Young Chemist..........SI *83 75
Chemical Philosophy..........SI *1 60 1 40
*Appletons' Latin Dictionary..........AP 1 ?0
Appletons' Standard Arithmetics:
First Lessons in Arithmetic..........AM *36
Numbers Applied..........AM *75
" " Key to..........AM *34
" " pts. 1 and 2, *ea*.....AM *50
" Illustrated..........AM *36
Appletons' Standard Elem. Geography..AM *55
Higher Geography..........AM *1 25
Physical " ....AM *1 60
Geography for Little Learners.........AM *81
Appletons' School History of the World (Quackenbos)..........AM *1 22
Appletons' Standard Writing Books:
Grammar Course, 10 nos.........*doz.* AM *96
Short " 7 " .... " AM *72
New Tracing " 4 " .... " AM *72
Business Course, 2 nos.......... " AM *1 20
—— No. 3.......... " AM *96
Manual of Penmanship..........AM *50
Appletons' 1st Reader..........AM *18
Appletons' 2d Reader..........AM *30
3d Reader..........AM *88
4th " ....AM *50
5th " ....AM *90
Introductory 4th Reader..........AM *50
Chart Primer..........AM *30
Word Manual (Leaflets) for 1st and 2d Reader..........AM *16
—— Complete..........AM *20
Select Spelling Lessons.........*doz.* AM *48
Appletons' Libro Primero de Lectura (English-Spanish First Reader), bds..........AM *30
—— cl..........AM *35
Appletons' School Physics..........AM *1 20
Arden Shakespeare, 16 vs..........*ea* HE 25
Arey's Elemen. Chemistry..........MC 90
Arithmetic in two books. *See* Colburn, W.; Wheeler, H. N..........HM
Arithmetical Table Cards..........*doz.* AM *55
Armstrong's (A. C.) Primer of U. S. History..........AR 50
Primer of Eng. History..........AR 50
Armstrong (J. E.) and Norton's (J. H.) Laboratory Manual of Chemistry.AM *50
*Arnold's (E. J.) Stories of Ancient Peoples.AM *50
Arnold's (H.) Practice in Parsing and Analysis..........LI *40
Arnold's (Hans) Ein Regentag auf dem Lande (Kern)..........AM *25
*Arnold's (S. L.) The Arnold Primer......SI 30
Arnold's (T.) English Literature..........GI *1 65 1 50
—— ....LN 2 00
Arnold's (T. K.) First and Second Latin Book, new ed. (Mulholland)......AM *1 00
Latin Prose Composition, new ed. (Mulholland)..........AM *1 00
Key to Arnold's New Latin Prose Composition..........AM *60
Greek Prose Composition..........AM *1 05
First Greek Book (Spencer)..........AM *87
Arrowsmith's (R.) and Knapp's Viri Romæ..........AM *75
—— Text ed..........AM *25
Arrowsmith & Whicher's First Latin Readings..........AM *1 25
Arthur, Barnes & Coulter's Plant Dissection..........HO 1 20
Ashton & Marsh's Plane and Spherical Trigonometry..........SC **
Athenæum Press Series..........GI
Atherton's Cæsar and Pompey in Greece.GI *50 45
Atkinson's (C. F.) Elementary Botany...HO 1 25
Lessons in Botany..........HO 1 12
Atkinson's (G. F.) First Studies of Plant Life..........GI *70 60
Atkinson. *See* Ganot.
Attfield's Chemistry, new rev. ed........LA 2 50
Atwater's Manual of Logic..........LI *1 00
Atwood's (G. E.) Complete Graded Arithmetic, pt. 1..........HE *35 30
" 2..........HE *75 65
pts. 3 to 8, 6 nos.........*ea.* HE 25
Exercises in Algebra..........MS *60
Standard School Algebra..........MS *1 20
Grammar School Algebra...?........MS *60
Higher Algebra..........MS *60
Aubert's Colloquial French Drill, pt. 1...HO 45
—— pt. 2..........HO 65
Littérature Française, 1st ser........HO 1 00
—— 2d ser..........HO 1 00
Aufrecht's Hebrew Primer..........BM 10
Augsburg's Easy Things to Draw........ED 30
Drawing Simplified..........ED 1 00 80
Drawing Cards..........*per set.* ED 30
Elemen. Drawing Simplified..........ED *75 60
Austen's Muck's Quantitative Analysis..........HE **
Austen's Pinner's Organic Chemistry....WI 1 50
Notes for Chemical Students..........WI 1 50
Autenrieth's Homeric Dictionary, new .AM *1 10
Authorized Physiology Series:
No. 1, Health for Little Folks.......AM *30
No. 2, Lessons in Hygiene (Johonnot & Bouton)..........AM *45
No. 3, Outlines of Anatomy, Physiology, and Hygiene (R. S. Tracy).AM *1 00
Avery's (A. S.) How to Draw, pt. 1.......UN *42 36
—— pt. 2..........UN *51 44
Avery's (E. M.) Elem. Natural Philosophy..........BU *1 15
First Principles of Nat. Philosophy..BU *96
Teachers' Handbook for Philosophy.BU *1 25
School Physics..........BU *1 25
—— Key to..........BU *75
Elemen. Physics..........BU *1 00
—— Key to..........BU *50
Elements of Chemistry..........BU *1 10
Complete Chemistry..........BU *1 40
Teachers' Handbk. for Chemistries..BU *75
Avery & Sinnott's First Lessons in Physical Science..........BU *60
Ayres' (A.) Orthoëpist..........AP 50
See also Cobbett.
*Ayres' (F. H.) Laboratory Manual of Exercises in Elementary Physics.AP 60
Babbitt's German at Sight..........HE *12 10
Babbittonian Copy-Bks., 8 nos........*doz.* SR *1 04 90
—— Primary.......... " SR *1 04 90
Babcock's Miscellaneous Words, rev. enl. ed..........BB 30 24
Bacheler's Reference Handbook of American History..........LE 50
Bacon's (A. M.) Manual of Gesture..........SI *1 25 1 12
Bacon's (E. F.) Neuer Leitfaden..........MY *1 25
New French Course..........AM *1 00
Bacon's (G. W.) Excelsior Elem. Atlas...SI 60
Bacon's (J. H.) English Composition.....PI 40 27
Bacon's (M. A.) Four Years in Number...GI *50 40
Number Primer..........GI *25 20
Badlam's (A. B.) Primer..........HE *30 25
1st Reader..........HE *35 30
Baer & Delitzsch's Hebrew Texts (Bible) (prices, *ea.*, 60c.; 75c.)..........LB
Bagot's Plane Surveying..........NO 1 00
Bailey's (F. H.) Elementary Inductive Physical Science..........HE *?5 50

Bailey's (L. H.) Lessons with Plants	MC	1 10	
First Lessons with Plants	MC	40	
Botany	MC	1 10	
Bailey's (M.) Essentials of Reading	BU	*50	
Introduction to Elocution	BU	*50	
Bailey's (M. A.) American Mental Arithmetic	AM	*35	
American Comprehensive Arithmetic	AM	*65	
American Elementary Arithmetic	AM	*35	
Bailey's (M. E.) Kindergarten System	BN		18
Bailey's (W. W.) Botanizing	HO		**
Bailey-Wiemer Arithmetics:			
First Book	AM	*20	
Second "	AM	*30	
Third "	AM	*35	
Bailey & Woods' Analytic Geometry	GI	*2 15	2 00
*Balliot & Twight-Brugnot's French Prose Composition	SR		50
Bain's (A.) Composition and Rhetoric, pt. 1	AM	*1 20	
—— Pt. 2	AM	*1 20	
Logic	AM	*1 40	
Mental Science	AM	*1 22	
Moral "	AM	*1 22	
Brief English Grammar	HO		40
—— Key to	HO		40
Composition Grammar	HO		1 10
Higher English Grammar	HO		80
Bain's (C. W.) First Latin Book	UN	*67	75
Homer's Odyssey, Bk. 6	GI	*40	35
—— Bk. 7	GI	*45	40
Baird's Classical Manual	BU	*64	
Baird's (R.) Greek-English Word-list	GI	*35	30
Baird's (S. W.) Graded Work in Arithmetic First and Second Years., bds. *ea.*	AM	*18	
—— cl.	" AM	*20	
Third and Fourth Years, bds.	" AM	*20	
—— cl.	" AM	*25	
*Fifth Year, bds.	" AM	*20	
*—— cl.	" AM	*25	
*Sixth Year, cl.	" AM	*25	
*Seventh " "	" AM	*25	
*Eighth " "	" AM	*25	
Practical Arithmetic for Grammar Grades	AM	*65	
Baker's (A. H.) Graphic Algebra	SN	*90	80
Baker's (A. L.) Elements of Solid Geom	GI	*90	80
Baker's (J. H.) Elem. Psychology	MY	*1 05	
Baker's (T. R.) Natural Philosophy	WR	*1 00	
Short Course in Chemistry	WR	*60	
Key to Philos. and Chemistry	WR	*60	
Baker's (W.) Geog. for Young Folks	ED	*30	24
Balderston's Laboratory Manual of Physics	LI	50	
Baldwin's (A.) Table Book	LO	15	12
Baldwin's (C. S.) Expository Paragraph and Sentence	LN	50	
Baldwin's (J.) English Lit., Poetry	CB		1 50
—— Prose	CB		1 50
Essentials of Eng. and Am. Lit.	CB	1 25	1 00
Industrial Arithmetic	GI	*55	45
Baldwin's (Ja.) Select English Classics, 4 v. *ea.*	SI	90	72
Baldwin's (Ja.) Readers: First Year	AM	*25	
Second Year	AM	*35	
Third "	AM	*40	
Fourth "	AM	*40	
Fifth "	AM	*40	
Sixth "	AM	*45	
Seventh "	AM	*45	
Eighth "	AM	*45	
Combined Fourth and Fifth Years	AM	*60	
" Sixth and Seventh "	AM	*65	
Baldwin Primer (May Kirk)	AM	*30	
Fairy Stories and Fables	AM	*35	
*Conquest of the Old Northwest	AM	*60	
Discovery of the Old Northwest	AM	*60	
Baldwin's (Ja.) Old Greek Stories	AM	*45	
Fifty Famous Stories Retold	AM	*35	
Old Stories of the East	AM	*45	
Baldwin's (J. M.) Psychology, v. 1	HO		1
—— v. 2	HO		2 80
Elements of Psychology	HO		1 50
Baldwin's (J. M.) Mental Development: v. 1, Methods and Processes	MC	1 75	
—— v. 2, Social and Ethical Interpretations	MC	2 60	
—— v. 3, Development and Evolution	MC	**	
Baldwin's (W. E.) Primary Physiology	WR	*35	
Advanced Physiology	WR	80	
Essential Lessons in Physiology	WR	*50	
Balgarnies' Xenophon's Anabasis, Bk. 4	HS	75	
*Ball's (F. K.) Elements of Greek	MC	1 00	
Ball's (R. S.) Applied Mechanics	CA	70	
Elements of Astronomy	MC	80	
Elements of Astronomy	LN	2 50	
Starland	GI	*1 10	1 00
Ballantine's Inductive Logic	GI	*90	80
Ballard's Handbook of Blunders	LE	50	
World of Matter	HE	1 00	
Ballard's (H. H.) Composition Writing Made Easy	HS	75	
Tr. Bks. 1-6 Virgil's Aeneid	HM	*1 68	
Ballou's (E. L.) Guide Right. Ethics for Young People	MA	**	
Bancroft's School Gymnastics:			
Free Hand Course	HE	1 50	
—— Light Apparatus Course	HE	1 75	
—— " " " In 3 pts. *ea.*	HE	75	
Bancroft's 1st Reader	WA	20	18
—— 2d Reader	WA	35	32
—— 3d "	WA	55	45
—— 4th "	WA	65	55
—— 5th "	WA	85	75
Bancroft's (T. W.) English Composition	GI	*55	50
Bangs' Outlines of Map Drawing	IN	*30	25
Banister's Music	HO		30
Bannan's Primer *doz.*	LI	*95	
Barbauld's Lessons in French	LO	50	40
Barbe's (W.) Going to College	HS	50	
Barbee's Geology, Rev. ed.	MO	1 00	
Barber's (G. E.) Plautus' Captivi	SA		30
Bardeen's Complete Rhetoric	AM	*1 50	
Shorter Course in Rhetoric	AM	*1 00	
Song Budget	BI	15	
" Budget Series, combined	BI	50	
" Century	BI	15	
" Patriot	BI	15	
Civics	BI	75	
Geography of the Empire State	BI	75	
Barker's College Chemistry, rev. ed.	MO	1 40	
Physics. *See* American Sci. Ser.			
Barlow's Tables of Squares, Cubes, etc.	SP	2 50	
Barnard's First Steps in Electricity	MY	*60	
Barnard's Civil Gov't of Missouri	WR	*1 00	
Barnes' (C. R.) Outlines of Plant Life	HO		1 00
Barnes' Picture Lessons in English	AM	*30	
Working Lessons in English	AM	*40	
Language Lessons (complete)	AM	*50	
Barnes' Elementary Geography	AM	*55	
Complete Geography	AM	*1 25	
Primary History of U. S.	AM	*60	
Brief Hist. of U. S.	AM	*1 00	
" " " France	AM	*1 00	
" " " Ancient Peoples	AM	*1 00	
" " " Modern Peoples	AM	*1 00	
" General History	AM	*1 60	
" History of Greece	AM	*75	
" " " Rome	AM	*1 00	
Barnes' National System of Penmanship:			
Larger Course, 6 nos. *doz.*	AM	*1 00	
Brief Course, 6 nos.	" AM	*75	
Tracing Course, Nos. 1, 2	" AM	*75	
Barnes' National Vertical Penmanship:			
Nos. 1 to 8 *doz.*	AM	*75	
Special Books, N-1 and N-2	" AM	*75	
Practice " Nos. 1 to 6, N-1 and N-2 *doz.*	AM	*50	
Pen and Pencil Ser. Bks. A, B, C and D *doz.*	AM	*60	
Barnes's Natural Slant Penmanship:			
Nos. 1 to 8	" AM	*75	
Practice Books. For Nos. 1-6	" AM	*50	
Pen and Pencil Ser. Bks. A, B, C and D *doz.*	AM	*60	
Barnes's Vertical Writing Speller	" AM	*48	
Barnes' New National 1st Reader	AM	*20	
" " 2d "	AM	*35	
" " 3d "	AM	*50	
" " 4th "	AM	*70	
" " 5th "	AM	*90	
Word Lists	AM	*10	
Sight Reading	AM	*10	
Barnes' (F. C.) Studies in Greek Accidence	AL		50
Barretti's Ital.-Eng. and Eng.-Ital. Dict., 2 v.	CH	8 40	
Barrow's (C. M.) Acts and Anecdotes of Authors	HW	*1 50	
Barry's (C. A.) Model and Object Drawing	LE		40
Primer of Design	LE		30
Bartholomew's (G. K.) Cæsar's Gallic War, with vocab.	AM	*90	
Bartholomew's (J.) Pocket Atlas	PU	1 25	
Pocket Gazetteer	PU	1 00	
*Barss' Writing Latin, Bk. 1	UN	*58	50
Bartholomew's (J.) Handy Reference Atlas	RU	3 00	
Bartholomew's (W. N.) New Drawing Ser.:			
Freehand Tracing Ser., 1-4 *doz.*	AM	*45	
Gram. School Course, 5-13	" AM	*96	
High School Course, 14-17	" AM	*1 44	
—— Linear Perspective, 18	" AM	*2 25	
Handbk. No. 2, Guide to 5-13	AM	*90	

Bartholowmew's (W. N.) Special Exercise Bks., A B C.... ....doz. AM *96
Bartlett's (A. L.) First Steps in English...SI 50 *38
Essentials of Language and Grammar, rev. ed.................. ....SI *62
Bartlett's (E. J.) Laboratory Exercises in Chemistry.............. . ...SY 50
*Bartlett's (L. L.) Animals at Home....AM *45
Bartlett's (W. H. C.) Acoustics and Optics ....BA *2 92 2 50
Analytical Mechanics.................BA *4 09 3 50
Spherical Astronomy.... .. ..BA *4 09 3 50
Bartley's Songs for the School...........AM *60
Bartol's (W. C.) Solid Geometry..........SA 75
Barton's (S. M.) Theory of Equations....HE 1 50
Bascom's Æsthetics......................
Ethics ....
Philosophy of Eng. Lit...............
" " Rhetoric 1 50
Science of Mind..................... ..PU 2 50
Baskett's (J. N.) Story of the Birds......AP 65
Baskett (J. N.) & Ditmars's (R. L.) Story of Amphibians and Reptiles.....AP **
Basis of Arithmetic.........................SM 18
Baskervill & Harrison's Anglo-Saxon Dictionary..............................BA 3 00 2 40
Anglo-Saxon Reader, new ed..........BA 1 20
Baskervill (W. M.) & Sewell's (J. W.) English Grammar..........................AM *90
Baskerville's (C.) School Chemistry......JH 60 48
—— Key to, cl..............................JH 50 40
Bass's Nature Reader, Plant Life..........HE *30 25
" " Animal " ....HE *40 35
Beginner's " ....HE 25
Basset's Latitude, Longitude, etc.........BI 25
Bastin's College Botany...................EN 2 50
Elements of Botany ....EN 1 25
Batchellor's Color Music for the Kindergarten ....BO 10
Dictionary of Mythology..............PP 50
Bates' (A.) Talks on the Study of English.......................................HM 1 50
Talks on Writing English: First Series.......................................HM 1 50
—— Second Series..... ....HM *1 45
Bates' (K. L. A.) American Literature...MO 1 00
Baumbach's (R.) Im Zwielicht, v. 1 (Bernhardt)...................................AM *65
—— v. 2 (Bernhardt)...................AM *65
Baumbach and Wildenbruch's Es war Einmal (Bernhardt)......... .... AM *65
Bayliss' In Brook and Bayou..............AP 60
*Beaman's (M. N.) English Sentence and Analysis ....FL 50
Beard's (J. R. & C.) Latin-English and English-Latin Dictionary ....CA 1 50
Beeton's (F.) English Grammar............LI *40
Beauvoisin's French Verbs at a Glance..JE 25
Bechtel's Handbook of Pronunciation..PP 50
Dictionary of Mythology ....PP 50
Becker's Spanish Idioms.................GI *2 00 1 80
Beckwith's Euripides' Bacchantes........GI *45 40
—— with notes..........................GI *1 35 1 25
Beddard's Elemen. Zoölogy...............LN 90
Beebe's First Steps among Figures......BI 45
—— Teacher's ed.......................BI 1 00
Beebe and Kingsley's First Year Nature Reader.......................................WR *35
Beers' (H. A.) English and American Literature..BA 1 00
From Chaucer to Tennyson..........MO 1 00
Initial Studies in Amer. Letters.........BA 1 00
Beers' (N. P.) Penmanship, 12 nos....doz. BA *1 05 90
Behrens' Microscope in Botany..........WD 5 00
Beiley's Der Practische Deutsche, rev ...JE 1 00
Beilstein's Qualitative Analysis.... ....VN 1 50
Beitzel's Primary Word Builder..........SO *25
Advanced Word Builder..............SO *31
Belfield's Graded Examples..............SR *18 15
—— with key..........................SR *28 25
Belfield's (H. H.) and Brooks's (S.) Rational Elemen. Arithmetic..........SR 45
Bell's (A. M.) English Line Writing....WE 60
Principles of Elocution.............WE 1 50
Bell's (D. C.) Standard Elocutionist......SO 1 50
Bellows' (C. F. R.) Elements of Geometry.CB 1 25 1 00
Trigonometry.... ....SH *1 12
Bellows' (J.) French Dictionary, roan....HO 2 55
—— larger type.... ....HO 1 00
Beman's & Smith's Plane and Solid Geometry.......................................GI *1 35 1 25
New Plane and Solid Geometry.......GI *1 35 1 25
New Plane Geometry ....GI *85 75
New Solid Geometry......... ....GI *80 75
Higher Arithmetic.....................GI *90 80
*Academic Algebra ....GI *1 25 1 12
Elements of Algebra....................GI *1 22 1 12
Problems of Geometry....................GI *55 50
Bemont's & Monod's Middle Ages in Europe.HO **

Benedict's Algebra..........................AR *1 64 1 40
Benedict's (M. G.) Primary Speller....... MP *20
Advanced Speller........................MP *25
*Benedix's Der Prozess and Wilhelm's Einer Muss Heiraten (Lambert)..AM 30
Benner's (A. R.) Homer's Iliad...........AP **
Bennett's (A. A.) Inorganic Chemistry, pts. 1 and 2................ ...ea SI *1 67 1 50
Bennett's (C. E.) Xenophon's Hellenica, Bks. 5-7..............................GI *45 40
—— with notes, cl.......................GI *1 50 1 40
Latin Grammar...........................AL 80
Latin Composition.......................AL 80
Latin Lessons........................... AL 70
*Odes and Epodes of Horace..........AL 1 40
Appendix to Latin Grammar ....AL 80
Complete edition (Grammar and Appendix)..............................AL 1 25
Tacitus' Dialogus de Oratoribus.......GI *80 75
Cato Maior de Senectute........... ....SA 80
Laelius de Amicitia.... ... .SA 60
The two above in 1 v ....SA 1 05
Foundations of Latin...................AL 90
Quantitative Reading of Latin Poetry.AL 25
Benson's Practical Speller: First Book..HE *25 18
Second Book..............................HE *25 18
Combined Book...........................HE *30 25
Benson & Glenn's Practical Speller and Definer. ....HE *40 30
Bent's Hints on Language...............LE 50
Bentley's Physiological Botany... .....AM *1 20
Benton's Laboratory Manual of General Chemistry............ ....HE *40 35
Benziger's Primary History of the United States ....BE 25
Beowulf; from the Old English, by C. B. Tinker .... NR 80
Berard's (A. B.) School Hist. of England.AM *1 20
History of the U. S...... ....BU *90
Bercy's (P.) La Langue Française, pt. 1..JE 1 25
—— pt. 2............ ....JE 1 25
Livre des Enfants....... ....JE 50
Le Second Livre des Enfants.........JE 75
Le Français Pratique ....JE 1 00
French Reader...........................JE 1 00
Lecture Faciles...........................JE 1 00
Child's First Steps in French..........JE 75
Selections for Translating English into French...............................JE 75
—— Key to ....JE 75
Conjugaison des Verbes Français avec Exercises.......................JE 50
Bercy's (P.) & Castegnier's (G.) Petite Grammaire Française..............JE **
Bercy. *See* Rippe.
Beren's Mythology.........................MY *95
Beresford-Webb's Beginners' German Tr. Book ....MY *50
German Historical Reader...........HO 90
Bergen's (F. D.) Glimpses at the Plant World...................................GI *55 50
Bergen's (J. Y.) Elements of Botany......GI *1 20 1 10
Foundations of Botany ....GI *1 70 1 50
Berkeley's Human Knowledge.............LI *2 16
Berlitz's French Methode, Premier Livre.BZ 75
—— Deuxième Livre.................BZ 1 00
—— Illustrated Method for Children.BZ 75
Litterature Française..................BZ 1 00
Observations Pratiques, pap..........BZ 25
Grammaire Pratique, 4 v...........ea BZ 50
Tableau du Verbe, pap ....BZ 10
" Muraux des Verbes ....BZ 1 25
Genre des Substantifs ....BZ 15
French With or Without a Master, v. 1.BZ 1 00
—— v. 2.................................BZ 1 25
—— Key to each v., pap............BZ 25
Berlitz's German Methode, Erstes Buch.BZ 75
—— Zweites Buch.....................BZ 1 00
—— Illustrated Method for Children........ ... .BZ 75
—— With or Without a Master, 2 v................................ea. BZ 1 00
—— Key to, 2 v., pap...... ......ea. BZ 25
German Verb and Idioms, pap ..... .BZ 25
Praktische Grammatik der Deutschen Sprache ....BZ 50
Das Geschlecht der Substantive, pap.BZ 25
Berlitz's Italian Metodo ....BZ 1 50
Berlitz's Spanish Metodo................ BZ 1 50
Spanish With or Without a Master...BZ 1 00
—— Key to, pap..................... BZ 25
Spanish Verbs, pap......................BZ 25
Pictures for the Object Lessons.......BZ 50
Selections for Idiomatic Translation into Foreign Languages......... BZ 80
—— Notes to, for Each Language. BZ 15
Bernard's (V. F.) L'Art d'interesser en Classe..................................JE 50
Le Français Idiomatique..............JE 50

Title	Price	Net
Bernard's (V. F.) Fautes de Langage.....JE	50	
Genre des Noms.....JE	25	
Traduction Orale et la Pronunciation Française.....JE	30	
Bernhardt's Novelletten Bibliothek, v. 1-2.....ea. HE	*75	60
Bernhardt's (W.) Deutsches Sprach- und Lesebuch, Pt. 1.....AM	*1 10	
—— Pt. 2.....AM	*1 10	
Deutsche Litteraturgeschichte.....AM	*75	
German-English Vocabulary.....AM	*75	
German Composition.....GI	*1 00	90
Berry & Michaelis' 135 Kindergarten Songs and Games.....BO	75	
Bert's First Steps in Scientific Knowledge.LI	*60	
Primer of Scientific Knowledge.....LI	*36	
Bessey's Botany. *See* American Science Series.		
Bétis and Swan's Class Room Conversations in French, Teacher's ed.....HW		80
—— Pupil's ed., 3 pts.....ea. HW		40
First Fact and Sentences in French, Teachers' ed.....HW		65
French ser., Facts of Life, Pt. 1.....HW		80
—— Pt. 2.....HW		80
German ser., Facts of Life, Pt 1.....HW		80
English ser., Facts of Life, Pt. 1.....HW		80
—— pt. 2.....HW		40
—— " 3.....HW		40
A First Lesson in French.....HW		80
Betz's (C.) Physical Culture for Schools:		
Bk. 1, Free Gymnastics.....FL		75
Bk. 2, Tactics.....FL		75
Bk. 3, Light Gymnastics.....FL		75
Bk. 4, Popular Gymnastics.....FL		60
Gems of School Song.....AM	*70	
Songs of Nature.....AM	*15	
" " the Season.....AM	*15	
" " Home and Pleasure.....AM	*15	
" for Morning, Evening, and Night.....AM	*15	
Bevier's French Grammar.....HO		1 00
Bevis' Inductive Geometry.....CB		60
Besiat de Bordes' Elements of French...SR	1 00	
Bibliothèque Choisie pour la Jeunesse, v. 1, cl.....JE	1 00	
—— pap.....JE	60	
—— v. 2, bds.....JE	75	
Biddulph's (E. L.) First Steps in Language.....HW		18
Bidgood's Practical Elementary Biology.LN	1 50	
Bierbower's Virtues and their Reasons...HS	1 00	
Bierwirth's (H. C.) Elements of German Grammar.....HO		1 25
Bigelow's Mistakes in Writing English....LE	50	
Handbook of Punctuation.....LE	50	
Billings' Standard Selections.....IN	*60	50
Bingham's Elem. Eng. Grammar.....BU	*25	
English Grammar.....BU	*60	
Latin Grammar.....BU	*1 08	
" Prose Composition.....BU	*72	
" Reader.....BU	*1 08	
Exercises for Translation.....BU	*18	
Cæsar.....BU	*1 08	
Vergil.....BU	*1 08	
See also McCabe.		
Bishop's (J. T.) Natural History Stories, Pts. 1-11, pap.....ea. HW		5
—— v. 1 and 2, bds....." HW		36
Black's and Carter's Natural History Lessons.....HO		*50
Blackley and Friedländer's German and English Dictionary.....LN	1 25	
Blackman's Graded Songs, No. 1.....CR	10	
—— No. 2.....CR	15	
—— No. 3.....CR	25	
—— No. 4.....CR	50	
—— No. 6.....CR	75	
Blackmar's (F. W.) Economics.....CS	1 00	
Blackwell's Ger. Prefixes and Suffixes...HO		60
Blaikie's (W.) Sound Bodies for Our Boys and Girls.....AM	*40	
Blair's (H.) Rhetoric (Mills) 12°.....LO	1 25	1 00
Rhetoric, Abr. ed.....WR	*45	
Blaisdell's (A. F.) Child's Book of Health.GI	*35	30
First Steps with Amer. and British Authors.....AM	90	
How to Keep Well.....GI	*55	45
Life and Health.....GI	**	
Our Bodies and How We Live.....GI	*75	65
Practical Physiology.....GI	*1 20	1 10
Stories from English History.....GI	*50	40
Story of American History.....GI	*75	60
Blaisdell's (E. A.) Child Life Readers:		
V. 1, Child Life. A First Reader.....MC	25	
V. 2, Child Life in Tale and Fable. A Second Reader.....MC	35	
V. 3, Child Life in Many Lands. A Third Reader.....MC	36	
Blaisdell's (E. A.) Child Life Readers:		
V. 4, Child Life in Literature. A Fourth Reader.....MC	40	
V. 5, The Child Life. A Fifth Reader.MC	45	
V. 6, " " " A Sixth Reader.MC	**	
Child Life Primer.....MC	25	
Speller, Bk. 1.....MC	16	
*Speller, " 2.....MC	20	
Speller Complete.....MC	25	
Blake's (R. W.) Xenophon's Hellenica....AL		1 20
Blakslee's Academic Trigonometry.....GI	*80	25
Blocher's (S. J.) Civil Gov't of Arkansas and U. S.....JH	80	64
Bloss' Ancient History. *See* Anderson.		
Bloxam's Chemistry.....LA	2 00	
—— 8th ed. rev. and enl.....BL		
Böcher's French Reader.....HO		1 10
See also College; Otto.		
Boise's Homer's Iliad, first 6 bks.....SR		1 50
—— first 3 bks.....SR		1 00
Exercises in Greek Syntax.....SR		1 25
Xenophon's Anabasis, with vocab....AM	*1 32	
Epistles of St. Paul, with notes.....AP	1 75	
Earlier Epistles of St. Paul.....AP	1 75	
Boise & Freeman's Greek Selections.....SR		1 50
Boise's & Pattengill's First Lessons in Greek, new ed.....SR		1 00
Boisen's Preparatory German Prose.....HE	*1 00	90
Bolmar's French Verbs.....BU	*80	
Bolton's Quantitative Analysis.....WI	1 50	
Boltwood's Grammar.....SR	*41	
Topical Outline of General History...SR	*50	
Inst., Gram., and High School Reader.SR	*40	35
Boltwood's (H. F.) Higher Speller.....SR		20
Boname's (L. C.) Study and Practice of French, v. 1.....BG	60	
—— v. 2.....BG	90	
—— v. 3.....BG	1 00	
Bond's Staff-ruled Writing Bks., Nos. 1, 2. doz. AM	*96	
—— No. 3....." AM	*50	
Bonnell's First Lessons in Composition..MO	58	
Manual of Composition.....MO	1 08	
Bonner's Greek Construction.....SR	**	1 00
Booth's Practical Grammar.....FL	75	
Borel's Grammaire Française.....HO		1 30
Bosworth's (M.) Graded Lessons in English.SR	*68	60
Botsford's (G. W.) History of Greece.....MO	1 10	
History of Rome for High Schools...MC	1 10	
*History of the Orient and Greece...MC	1 20	
History of the Orient. Paper.....MC	25	
Text Book of Ancient History.....MC	**	
Botta's Universal Literature.....HM	2 00	
*Bouton's Spelling and Word Building...UN	29	25
Boutwell's Constitution of the U. S.....HE	*3 00	2 50
Bouvet's Exercises in French Syntax and Composition.....HE		75
Bowen's (E. A.) Astronomy.....AM	*1 00	
*Bowen's (B. L.) First Scientific French Reader.....HE	1 00	90
Bowen's (F.) Logic.....AL		1 22
Hamilton's Metaphysics.....AL		1 50
Bowen's (J. A.) English Words.....GL	25	
——Stitched ed.....GL	20	
—— for Primary Grades.....GL	20	
—— —— Stitched ed.....GL	16	
Practical System of Vertical Writing, 6 nos.....doz. GL	66	
Bower's Public School Singing-Book.....FO	12	10
Bowne's (B. P.) Metaphysics, Rev.....AM	1 60	
Psychological Theory.....AM	1 75	
Principles of Ethics.....AM	1 75	
Philosophy of Theism.....AM	1 75	
Theory of Thought and Knowledge..AM	1 50	
Bowser's Academic Algebra.....HE	*1 25	1 12
College Algebra.....HE	*1 65	1 50
Plane and Solid Geometry.....HE	*1 40	1 25
Plane Geometry.....HE	*85	75
Trigonometry, Advanced.....HE	*1 60	1 50
Elementary Trigonometry.....HE	*95	90
Trigonometric Tables.....HE	*65	60
Analytical Geometry.....VN	1 75	1 40
Analytic Mechanics.....VN	3 00	
Calculus.....VN	2 25	1 80
Boyd's Annotated Poets, 5 v.....ea. BA	1 00	80
Milton.....BA	1 00	80
Bacon's Essays.....BA	1 00	80
Composition and Rhetoric.....AM	*90	
Kames' Criticism.....AM	*1 10	
Boyd's (C. E.) Civics for High Schools....MC	**	
Boyd's (J. H.) College Algebra.....SR	2 00	
Boyden's 1st and 2d Readers.....SR	*20	16
Boyden's (W. C.) First Book in Algebra..SI	66	60
Boyer's (E R.) Laboratory Manual in Elementary Biology.....HE	*90	80
Science Tablets.....CS	40	
Brace's Text-Book on Elocution.....SY		40
Brackett's Poetry for Home and School.FU	1 25	
Bradbury's Elementary Algebra.....TH		90

Bradbury's Elementary Algebra. Key of Answers	TH		20
— " " Solutions	TH		90
Emery's Academic Algebra	TH		1 08
" " Teacher's ed	TH		1 08
" " Key of Answers	TH		20
" Algebra for Beginners	TH		60
Algebra Examination papers	TH		50
Cogswell's Lessons in Numbers	TH		25
Academic Geometry, Plane	TH		75
" " " and Solid	TH		1 25
Elementary Geometry	TH		72
" Trigonometry	TH		72
" Geom. and Trig	TH		1 08
— Key to	TH		72
Elementary Geom. (Univ. ed.)	TH		1 08
Trigonometry and Surveying	TH		1 28
— Key to	TH		72
Logarithms of Numbers	TH		20
New Elementary Arithmetic	TH		25
Practical Arithmetic	TH		75
Bradbury's Sight Arithmetic	TH		30
Bradbury & Eaton's New Elementary Arithmetic	TH		45
— pt. 1	TH		18
— pt. 2	TH		25
Bradford's Problems in Percentage	BI	25	
Bradish's (S. P.) Old Norse Stories	AM	*45	
Bradley's (M.) Water Colors in the School-Room	BO	1	
Brambach's (W.) Latin Orthography	AM	*1	
Branch's National Prim. Speaker	BF		
" Junior "	BF	00	
" Advanced Speaker	BF	1 50	
Hamilton Speaker	DI	1 00	
Brand's Good Health for Children	SA		20
Health Lessons for Beginners	SA		30
Lessons on the Human Body	SA		50
Academic Physiology	SA		1 00
Brandt's German Grammar	AL		1 25
German Reader	AL		1 25
First German Book	AL		1 00
Brandt & Day's Reader in Scientific German	HO		85
Branson's Common School Speller, Bk. 1	JH	15	
— Bk. 2	JH	20	
Complete	JH	30	
Bregy's Smith's French Conversation	EL	*45	40
Bremiker's 6 pl. Logarithmic Tables	LB	1 85	
Brennan's (M. S) Astronomy New and Old	SK	1 00	60
Brensinger's Math. Note-Bk., No. 1	LV	*10	10
Brewer's Science of Familiar Things	AM	*90	
Brewster's 1st Bk. of Chemistry	AM	*66	
Brewster's & Thomas's Song Stories and Songs for Children	AM	*60	
Bridgman's Exercises on Lysias	AL		25
Briggs' Plane Analytic Geometry	WI	1 00	
Brigham's (A. P.) Text-Book of Geology	AP		1 40
Bright's (J. W.) Anglo-Saxon Reader	HO		1 50
Bright's (O. T.) Graded Instruction in English	AM	*36	
*Brinckley's (W. J.) Physiology	AN	1 20	
Briot's & Bouquet's Analytical Geometry. (Boyd)	WR	*2 00	
Bristol's Select Orations of Lysias	AL		1 00
*Brittain's (M. L.) Introd. to Cæsar	AM	*75	
*Britton's (N. L.) Flora of the Northern States and Canada	HO		2 25
Bronson's (C. P.) New Manual of Elocution	MO	1 35	
Bronson's (T. B.) Colloquial German	HO		65
— Key to	HO		65
Exercises in Every-day French	HO		60
— Key	HO		60
German Prose and Verse, with vocab.	HO		1 25
— pt. 1, Andersen & Grimm	HO		90
— " 2, Hauff's Karawane	HO		75
Bronson's (W. C.) Hist. of Amer. Lit.	HE	**	
Brooke's (S.) English Literature from the Beginning to the Norman Conquest	MC	1 50	
Brooke's (S.) & Carpenter's (G. R.) English Literature	MC	1 00	
Brooke's (S. A.) Primer of English Literature	AM	*35	
Brooks' (E.) New Primary Arithmetic	SO	*21	
New Mental Arithmetic	SO	*31	
— Key to	SO	*31	
Elementary Arithmetic	SO	*41	
— Key to	SO	*41	
New Written Arithmetic	SO	*80	
— Key to	SO	*80	
Higher Arithmetic	SO	*1 17	
— Key to	SO	*1 25	
Normal Rudiments of Arithmetic, with or without Ans	SO	*39	
Normal Standard Arithmetic, with or without Ans	SO	*72	
Normal Standard Arithmetic, with or without Ans. Key to	SO	*72	
Union Arithmetic, pt. 1	SO	*25	
— pt. 2 with or without Ans...*ea.*	SO	*44	
— " 3 " " " " "	SO	*44	
Union Arithmetic, pts. 2 & 3 in 1 v	SO	*88	
— pts. 2 & 3 in 1 v., without Ans	SO	*88	
— Key to	SO	*88	
Algebra, pt. 1	SO	*75	
Elementary Algebra	SO	*1	
— Key to	SO	*1	
Brooks' (E.) Elemen. Geometry	SO		
Elemen. Geometry and Trigonometry	SO	*1	
— Key to	SO	*1	
Plane Geometry, Complete	SO	*1	
" and Solid Geometry, Complete	SO	*1	
— Key to	SO	*1	
Plane and Spherical Trigonometry	SO	*1	
Manual of Elocution	EL		1 10
Brooks' (E.) Philosophy of Arithmetic	PP	*1 05	
Mental Science and Culture	PP	*[illegible]	
Brooks's (E. S.) Stories of the Old Bay State	AM	*60	
Brooks' (N.) How the Republic is Governed	SC		75
Brooks' (N. C.) Historia Sacra, with vocab. and 1st Latin Lessons, rev	HS	50	
Ovid, rev., with vocab	HS	1 50	
Virgil's Æneid, rev., with vocab.	HS	1 50	
First Lessons in Greek	HS	50	
Brown's (B. M.) Physiology for the Laboratory	GI	*85	75
Brown's (G.) Grammar of Grammars	WO	5 00	
Institutes of Grammar	WO	80	
First Lines of Grammar	WO	36	
Language Lessons	WO	40	
Brown's (I. H.) Universal Arithmetic papers, 5 pts...*ea.*	FL	15	
— Key	FL	60	
Algebra Problems, A, B...*ea.*	FL	15	
Popular Reading, Nos. 1, 2, 3... "	FL	25	
Brown's (J. H.) Short Course in German	IT	30	23
Brown's (K. L.) Plant Baby and Its Friends	SI	60	48
Brown's (M. T.) Synthetic Philosophy of Expression	HM	2 00	
Brown's (R. T.) Physiology and Hygiene	AM	*1 00	
Brown's (T. K.) Elementary Algebra	WR	*80	
Academic Algebra	WR	*1 10	
Brown's (W. G.) History of Alabama	UN	*1 15	1 00
Brown & De Garmo's Elements of English Grammar	WR	*60	
Browne & Haldeman's Clarendon Dict.	UN	*53	45
Browne & Scharf's Hist. of Maryland	DY	*1 20	1 00
Brownell's Inductive Lessons in Physics	BI	50	
Brubaker's Physiology	BL	*80	
Physiology, Interleaved	BL	*1 25	
Bruhns's 7 pl. Logarithmic Tables	LB	2 50	
Brumbaugh's Standard First Reader	SO	*22	
" " Second "	SO	*33	
" " Third "	SO	*45	
" " Fourth "	SO	*67	
" " Fifth "	SO	*83	
" Liberty Bell Leaflets, 1-6...*ea.*	SO	*5	
Brunner's French Reader	CL	60	
Bruns' Latin Grammar	MO	67	
" Reader	MO	67	
Brush's Determinative Mineralogy	WI	4 00	
Brusie's Geschichten aus der Tonne	GI	*65	60
Bryant's (J. C.) Practical and Progressive Bookkeeping:			
Countinghouse	BY	2 25	
— Blanks for, 15 bks...*set.*	BY	3 00	
Commercial	BY	1 65	
— Blanks for, 6 bks...*set.*	BY	1 50	
High School	BY	1 25	
— Blanks for, 6 bks...*set.*	BY	1 25	
Common School	BY	60	
— Blanks for, 4 bks...*set.*	BY	75	
Business Man's Commercial Law	BY	1 50	
*Shorthand Simplified (Davis)	BY	1 50	
*Shorthand Exercise Book	BY	30	
Bryant & Stratton Business Arithmetic	AB	1 50	1 50
Common School Bookkeeping	AM	*80	
— Key to	AM	*36	
— Blanks for *set* of 5	AM	*80	
New High School Bookkeeping	AM	*1 50	
— pt. 1	AM	*45	
— pt. 2	AM	*40	
— Blanks for *set* of 6	AM	*84	
New Countinghouse Bookkeeping	AM	*2 00	
Bryant's (W. C.) Tr. of Homer's Iliad, Student's ed	HM	1 00	
Tr. of Homer's Odyssey, Student's ed.	HM	1 00	
Bryant Leaflets	AP	40	
Bryce's (J.) Greece. *See* Freeman.			
— Social institution of the U. S.	KA	1 00	
American Commonwealth, Student's ed	MC	*1 75	

Title	Pub.	Price	Exch.
Buch's Elementary Class-Book of Physiology	BL		1 75
Buchanan's (L. A.) Algebraic Solution of Equations	WA	1 00	80
*Bücher's Industrial Evolution	HO		2 50
Buck's (M.) Elemen. of English Gram.	CB	50	40
Eng. Gram. and Analysis	CB	75	60
Buckbee's Primary Word Book	HE	*30	25
—— Spanish ed	HE	**	
Buckelew & Lewis' Human Body	LV	*30	
—— Teachers' ed	LV	*75	
A B C Reader	LV	*30	
Lessons on Plants	LV	*60	
Buckham's Analysis of Sentences	AM	*50	
Buckingham's (C. P.) Calculus	SI	*1 65	1 50
Buckingham's (L. H.) Eugene's Comparative French Grammar	HO		1 30
Elem. French Lessons	HO		60
Buckland's Story of Eng. Literature	CA	1 25	
Buckley's Fairy Land of Science	AP	1 50	
Life and Her Children	AP	1 50	
Buckwalter's Primary Speller	WR	*15	
Comprehensive Speller	WR	*20	
Buehler's (H. G.) Exercises in English	AM	50	
Exercises in Arithmetic	SO	*18	
—— without Answers	SO	*18	
*Modern English Lessons	NN		45
Buell's (C. S.) Essentials of Psychology	GI	*1 10	1 00
Bugbee's English Syntax	BI	35	
—— Key to	BI	35	
Bulfinch's Age of Fable, new rev. ed	ME	1 25	
Bullet's First Lessons in French	AM	*50	
Bullions' School Grammar	BU	*36	
Practical Eng. Grammar	BU	*72	
Cæsar	BU	*1 12	
Bullock's Introd. to Economics	SI	1 60	1 28
Bumpus' Laboratory Course in Invertebrate Zoölogy	HO		1 00
Burgess' Drill-Vocab. to Virgil	SI	*35	30
Burkinshaw's Landscape Draw. Studies	BN		1 44
Burnap & Wetmore's Polytechnic Collection	AM	*90	
Burnet's (M.) School Zoology	AM	*75	
Burns' (E. A.) English Grammar	PS	1 00	
Burritt's Celestial Atlas	BU	*94	
Geography of the Heavens	BU	*94	
Burroughs' (J.) Squirrels and Other Fur-Bearers	HM	60	
Burt's (M. E.) Literary Landmarks	HM	75	
Little Nature Studies	GI	*36	30
—— Rev. ed., 2 v	*ea.* GI	*30	25
Burton's (A. H.) Story of Our Country	WR	*60	
Story of the Indians of New England	MS	*67	
United States History	ET	1 00	
Bury's (J. B.) Roman Empire	AM	1 50	
History of Greece	MC	1 90	
Business Standard Copy-Books:			
Primary Course, 7 nos	*doz.* BU	*72	
Common School Course, 7 nos	" BU	*96	
Butler's 1st Reader	BU	*20	
2d Reader	BU	*30	
3d "	BU	*40	
4th "	BU	*50	
5th "	BU	*60	
Chart Primer	BU	*15	
Geographical Question-Book	BU	*36	
History of Maryland	BU	*60	
Butler's Complete Geography	BU	*1 20	
Elementary Geography	BU	*54	
Physical "	BU	*1 08	
One book course in Geography	BU	*1 10	
Tracing Maps, per 100	BU	*1 25	
Butler's Copybooks; Regular course, 6 nos	*doz.* BU	*96	
Tracing course, 2 nos	" BU	*96	
Vertical-Writing Speller	" BU	*50	
Butler's New Am. Arith., pt. 1	BU	*20	
—— pt. 2	BU	*30	
—— pt. 3	BU	*42	
—— Practical, pts. 2 and 3	BU	*60	
—— Key to	BU	*60	
New Am. Graded Problems	BU	*60	
—— Key to	BU	*60	
Butler's Pictorial History of U. S	BU	*1 00	
Butler's Elements of Chemistry	BU	*84	
Elements of Plane Geometry	BU	*54	
Butler's (F. R.) Elements of Literature	HE	**	
Butler's (G. P.) School English	AM	75	
Butler's (N.) First Book in Spelling	MO	12	
American Spelling-Book	MO	12	
Inductive Grammar	MO	53	
Introductory Grammar	MO	18	
Practical Grammar	MO	53	
New Practical Grammar, rev	MO	53	
Practical and Critical Grammar	MO	67	
Common School Speaker	MO	53	
New 1st School Reader	MO	12	
" 2d " "	MO	23	
" 3d " "	MO	33	
Butler's (N.) New 4th School Reader	MO	45	
" 5th " "	MO	67	
Butler-Goodrich's Com. School Primer	MO	10	
1st Reader	MO	12	
2d "	MO	23	
3d "	MO	33	
4th "	MO	45	
5th "	MO	73	
6th "	MO	1 00	
Butterfield's (C. W.) Punctuation	PA	25	
Buttmann's Greek Test. Grammar	DR	2 75	
*Byerly's (S.) Spelling-Book	PL		1 25
Byerly's (W. E.) Integral Calculus	GI	*2 15	2 00
Differential Calculus	GI	*2 15	2 00
Problems in Differential Calculus	GI	*80	75
Byrd's Laboratory Manual in Astronomy	GI	*1 35	1 25
*Caballero's La Familia de Alvereda	HO		75
Cady & Dewey's Art Reader, v. 1	RN		25
Caedmon's Exodus and Daniel, rev	GI	*65	60
Cairn's Quantitative Analysis	HO		2 00
Cairn's Introd. to Rhetoric	GI	*1 00	90
Cajori's History Elemen. Mathematics	MC	1 50	
History of Physics	MC	1 60	
Caldwell's (M.) Manual of Elocution	LI	*72	
Caldwell's (M. P.) Practical Arithmetic	BT	1 50	
*Caldwell's (O. W.) Laboratory Manual of Botany	AP	60	
Caldwell & Breneman's Chemical Practice	VN		1 50
*Calkins's Text-Book of Psychology	MC	2 00	
Callahan's (J. M.) Civil Gov't, Outlines	FL	15	
Physiology, Outlines	ED	40	32
U. S. History, Outlines	SR	*22	20
Cambridge Literature Series [various prices, 25c., 35c., 40c.]	SA		
Cameron's (A. G.) Selections from Edmond and Jules de Goncourt	AM	*1 25	
*Cameron's (J. H.) Elementary French Composition	HO		75
Campbell's (D. H.) Structural and Systematic Botany	GI	*1 25	1 12
Campbell's (L. J.) New Franklin Primer	BU	*12	
New Franklin 1st Reader	BU	*18	
" " Primer and 1st Reader combined	BU	*24	
" " 2d Reader	BU	*36	
" " 3d "	BU	*50	
" " 4th "	BU	*60	
" " 5th "	BU	*84	
" " Advanced 1st Reader	BU	*20	
" " " 2d "	BU	*36	
" " " 3d "	BU	*50	
" " " 4th "	BU	*60	
English Synonyms	LE	50	
Pronouncing Handbook of 3000 words, School ed	LE	50	[illegible]
Campbell's (W. A.) Series of Graded Readers, 12 v.	PM	**	
Campbell (W. A.) *See* Continental.			
Campbell's (W. T.) Observational Geometry	AM	*80	
Canfield's History and Government of Kansas	BU	*50	
Canfield's (A. G.) French Lyrics	HO		1 00
Canterbury Classics (K. L. Bates, ed)	RA		
Capel's (A. D.) Catch Questions in Arithmetic	HW	*25	
*Cappe's (E.) From Homer to Theocritus	SC		1 50
Carey's Social Science (McKean)	BD	2 00	
Carhart's Plane Surveying	GI	*2 00	1 80
Carhart's University Physics, pts. 1 and 2	*ea.* AL		1 50
Carhart's and Chute's Elements of Physics	AL		1 20
*Carhart (H. S.) & Chute's (H. N.) High School Physics	AL		1 25
Carpenter's (F. G.) Geographical Reader: Asia	AM	*60	
North America	AM	*60	
South America	AM	*60	
*Europe	AM	*70	
Carpenter's (G. R.) Exercises in Rhetoric	LE		60
Elements of Rhetoric and English Composition. First High School Course	MC	60	
Elements of Rhetoric and English —— —— Second High School Course	MC	50	
—— Advanced Course	MC	*1 00	
Rhetoric and Composition: First and Second High School Course in 1 v.	MC	1 00	
Elements of Grammar	MC	*75	
American Prose Selections	MC	1 00	
Carpenter's (S. H.) Anglo-Saxon Grammar and Reader	GI	*70	60
English of 14th Century	GI	*85	75
Carpenter's (T.) Speller	DU	25	20
——	KY	25	12

Title	Pub.	Price	Net
Carr's (E. McN.) Primary Arithmetic	JH	25	
Advanced Arithmetic	JH	45	
Beginners' Objective Arithmetic	JH	20	
Carrington's Patriotic Reader	LI	*1 20	
Carroll's (C. F.) Inductive Arithmetic, Bks. 2, 3, 4, 5, 6, 7, 8	ea. MS	25	
Elementary Arithmetic	MS	**	
Intermediate "	MS	40	
Advanced "	MS	**	
Carroll's (C. F. & S. W.) Geographical Ser.:			
Around the World, 1st Bk., Primary	MS	*40	
—— 2d Bk., 3d and 4th grades	MS	*50	
*—— 3d Bk., 5th and 6th "	MS	*60	
—— 4th Bk., 7th and 8th "	MS	**	
Carter's (J. P.) Elements of History	UN	*1 16	1 00
Latin Elegiac Poets	UN	*1 61	1 40
Carter (S. N.). *See* Putnam's Art.			
Cary's New Testament Greek	DR	75	
Casey's Conic Sections	LN	3 50	
Euclid's Elements	LN	1 40	
Sequel to Euclid	LN	1 10	
Cassell's Graduated Copy Bks., 18 bks.	ea. CA	10	
French-English Dictionary	CA	1 50	
Lessons in French, rev. ed	CA	1 25	
—— pts. 1 and 2	ea. CA	75	
—— Key to	CA	60	
Cassell's Lessons in Italian	CA	75	
German and English Dictionary	CA	1 50	
Public School French Reader	CA	1 00	
Latin-English Dictionary	CA	1 50	
English Dictionary	CA	1 50	
Cassell's New Standard Drawing Copies:			
Bks. A to F	ea. CA	8	
Bks. G, H, K, L, M, O	" CA	12	
Bks. N, P	" CA	15	
Casserly's Latin Prosody, Rev	HS	60	
Castarède's Conjugation of French Verbs	CH	60	
Castegnier's (G.) Greek and Roman Hist.	AM	*50	
Caswell & Ryan's Time and Tune, Bk. 1	GI	*75	65
—— Bk. 2	GI	*1 05	94
Catchpool's Text-Book of Sound	HS	1 00	
Catechism of Familiar Things	BE	1 00	60
Cathcart's Literary Reader	AM	*1 15	
Youth's Speaker	AM	*54	
Cattaneo's Italian Reader with vocab.	CH	95	
Cave's Learning to Draw and Teaching Colors	PU	1 25	
Cecilian Series of Study and Song (Tufts):			
Bk. 1	SI		48
" 2	SI		60
" 3	SI		84
" 4	SI		84
Common School Course, Complete	SI		60
—— Abridged	SI		48
Chamberlain's (C. J.) Methods in Plant Histology	UC		1 50
Chamber's 20 Less. in Bookkeeping	UN	*70	60
Chambers' (G. F.) Handbook Dictionary	PU	2 00	
Chambers' (W.) Zoölogy (Reese)	BA	*1 17	1 00
Introduction to Science	BA	*17	15
Vegetable and Animal Physiology	BA	*45	40
Champlin's (J. D.) Young Folks' Astronomy	HO	*53	48
Young Folks' Catechism	HO	*53	48
" " Cyclopædia of Common Things	HO		2 50
Young Folks' Cyclopædia of Persons and Places	HO		2 50
*Young Folks' Cyclopædia of Literature and Art	HO		2 50
Champlin's (J. T.) Selections from Tacitus	AL		1 10
Intellectual Philosophy, rev. ed	AM	*1 60	
Political Economy	AM	*90	
Æschines on the Crown	SE	1 25	
Demosthenes on the Crown	SE	1 25	
" Popular Orations	SE	1 25	
Chancellor's (W. E.) Arithmetics—By Grades:			
Bks. 1 and 2, Grade 2 and 3	ea. GL	20	
" 3 and 4, " 4 and 5	" GL	24	
" 5, 6 and 7, " 6, 7 and 8	" GL	28	
Chancellor's (W. E.) Arithmetics—By Series:			
*Primary Arithmetic	GL	30	
*Intermediate "	GL	36	
*Grammar School Arithmetic	GL	50	
Chancellor's (W. E.) Arithmetic	MS	1 00	
Chandler's (G.) Civil Gov't of Iowa and U. S.	FL	60	
Civil Government of Iowa	FL	50	
Practical Civics	FL	*60	
Channing's (E.) United States of America, 1765–1865	MC	*1 50	
Students' Hist. of U. S.	MC	1 40	
Short History of the U. S.	MC	90	
History of the U. S. for beginners	MC	**	
Channing & Hart's Guide to Study of Amer. Hist	GI	*2 15	2 00
Chapin's First Principles Pol. Economy	BU	*60	
Chapin's (H. E.) & Rettger's (A.) Zoölogy	EN	1 00	
*Chapman's (A. W.) Flora of the Southern U. S., rev	AM	*4 00	
Chapman's (C. H.) Elem. Course in Equations	WI	1 50	
Chapman's Am. Drawing-Book	BA	5 00	3 75
Elementary " "	BA	1 50	1 20
Chardenal's 1st French Course	AL & SE		60
2d French Course	AL & SE		60
French Exercises	AL & SE		90
Complete French Course	AL		1 00
French Primer	SE		30
First French Course	CH	60	
Chardenal's Second French Course	CH	80	
Exercise for Adv. Pupils	CH	1 25	
French Conversations	CH	60	
Charming Songs for Little Warblers	BN		20
Chase's (G. D.) Cornelius Nepos	AP	**	
Chase's (P. E.) Elem. of Meteorology, 2 pts	ea. WR	*75	
Macleane's Horace	AL		1 80
Chase & Stuart's First Year in Latin	EL	*95	85
Latin Grammar	EL	*1 10	1 00
" Reader	EL	*85	75
Cæsar's Commentaries, new ed	EL	*1 10	1 00
Virgil's Eclogues and Georgics, with Lex	EL	*1 05	95
" Æneid, First 6 Bks., with Lex.	EL	*1 05	95
Cicero's Sel. Orations, with Lex.	EL	*1 20	1 10
Chase & Stuart's Cicero's Tusculan Disputations	EL	*1 05	95
Cicero de Senectute, et de Amicitia	EL	*1 05	95
" " Officiis	EL	*1 20	1 10
" " Oratore, Bks. I, II, III.	EL	*1 20	1 10
" " " Bk. I	EL	*70	65
Cornelius Nepos, with Lex	EL	*1 05	95
Horace	EL	*1 20	1 10
" Selections from, with Lex.	EL	*1 10	1 00
Juvenal	EL	*1 05	95
Livy	EL	*1 20	1 10
Ovid, with Lex.	EL	*1 20	1 10
Sallust, with Lex	EL	*1 05	95
Tacitus	EL	*1 05	95
Terence	EL	*1 10	1 00
Cicero's Letters	EL	*1 10	1 00
Pliny's "	EL	*1 10	1 00
Chatty Readings in Elementary Science, v. 1 and 2	ea. LN	36	
—— v. 3	LN	45	
Chaucer for Schools (Haweis)	SO	1 00	
Chautauqua Lib. of Eng. Hist. and Lit.:			
From Earliest Times to Later Norman Period	EA	45	
Period of Early Plantagenets	EA	30	
War of the Roses	EA	30	
Chautauqua Text-Books, 49 v	ea. EA	10	
Chauvenet's Astronomy, 2 v.	LI	*6 00	
Geometry	LI	*1 40	
Geometry, Byerly's ed	LI	*1 20	
Plane Geometry, Byerly's ed	LI	*75	
Least Squares	LI	*1 28	
Trigonometry	LI	*1 98	
Cheney's Globe Manual	BI	25	
Chicago New Standard Ger. Ser., No. 1, new ed	BP	25	20
—— No. 2, new ed	BP	35	28
—— No. 3, new ed	BP	50	40
Child's First Book	doz. MO	35	
Child's Primer-Reader	RN	25	
Children's Musical Gift-Book	DS	30	
School Songs	DS	35	
Childs' Essentials of Bookkeeping	WA	90	75
Topical Anal. of U. S. Hist. and Constitution	WA	1 00	75
Chittenden's English Composition	SR		60
Choate's Elements of Eng. Speech	AP	1 00	
Chouquet's First Lessons in French	LO	60	48
Easy Conversations in French	LO	60	48
First Readings in French	LO	60	48
Christey's Spelling Blanks	doz. PB	60	36
Christian Brothers' 1st Reader	KY	18	7
2d Reader	KY	25	18
3d "	KY	63	28
4th "	KY	88	44
Primary Arithmetic	MD	30	24
Elementary Arithmetic	MD	45	36
Commercial Arithmetic	MD	45	
Complete Arithmetic	MD	80	64
—— Key to	MD	1 00	
Mensuration	SD	60	
Church's (A. E.) Analytical Geometry	AM	*1 75	
Calculus	AM	*1 75	
Descriptive Geometry, 2 v	AM	*2 50	
Churchill's (M. E.) and Sanford's (F. W.) Viri Romæ	SR		75

Title	Pub.	Price	Net
Chute's Physics	HE	1 25	1 12
Physical Laboratory Manual	HE	90	80
Cicero's Letters, Selections from, v. 1 and 2 ea.	HW		25
Orations and Letters (Minckwitz & Wilder)	MC	**	
Cincinnati Music Reader, No. 1	CR	15	
—— No. 2	CR	15	
—— Complete	CR	25	
Cincinnati Music Reader, No. 1, new ed	CR	20	15
—— No. 2, new ed	CR	20	15
—— " 3, "	CR	35	30
—— No. 1, rev. ed.	CR	20	
—— " 2, "	CR	20	
—— " 3, "	CR	20	
—— " 4, "	CR	30	
—— " 5, "	CR	35	
Cincinnati New German Speller	WG	25	
New 1st German Reader, with Transl. Exercises	WG	25	
New 2d German Reader, with Transl. Exercises	WG	35	
New 3d German Reader	WG	70	
Exercises and Transl., 5 bks ea.	WG	5	
Civil Service Question Book	BI	1 50	
Clapp's (E.) Homer's Iliad, Bks. 19, 24	GI	*1 90	) 75
Clarendon's Missouri (State and Local Government)	MY	*60	
Clark's Outlines of Civics	MC	75	
Clark's Manual of Trigonometry	UN	*1 15	1 00
Clark's (C. H.) Laboratory Manual in Practical Botany	AM	*96	
Clark's (H. F) Manual of English	HW		75
Clark's (J.) Elements of Drawing	BA	*88	75
Clark's (J. B.) Philosophy of Wealth	GI	*1 10	1 00
Clark's (J. S.) Practical Rhetoric	HO		1 00
—— Exercises, separately	HO		35
Briefer Practical Rhetoric	HO		90
Art of Reading Aloud	HO		60
Clark's (N. G.) Elem. of Eng. Language	SC	1 25	
*Clark's (S. S.) The Government	AM	*75	
Clark's (V. S.) Eutropius	SA		30
Clark's (W. A.) Physiol., Anat., and Hygiene	HN	75	
Arithmetic	HN	75	
Clarke's (C. C) French Subjunctive	HE		50
Clarke's (F. W.) Elem. of Chemistry	AM	*1 20	
Clarke's (G. S.) Practical Geometry	SP	4 00	
Perspective Explained	SP	1 25	
Clarke's (J. B.) Complete Algebra	WA	1 00	
Clarke's (J. F.) How to Find Stars	HE		15
Clarke's (M.) Story of Troy	AM	*60	
—— Ulysses	AM	*60	
—— Æneas	AM	*45	
—— Cæsar	AM	*45	
Classen's Quantitative Analysis	LA	2 00	
Classics for Children [58 v., var. prices, *40c.-$1.10, 30c.-85c. ea.]	GI		
Classic Series of Dictionaries:			
French-Eng. and Eng.-French	HS	2 00	
German-Eng. and Eng.-German	HS	2 00	
Latin-Eng. and Eng.-Lat	HS	2 00	
Greek-Eng. and Eng.-Greek	HS	2 00	
English-Greek	HS	1 00	
Classiques Français, 7 v ea.	JE	40	
—— pap "	JE	25	
Clauder's What Time is It?	HW	30	
Claxton's (P. P.) Tennessee History Stories	JH	**	
Clements' Civil Government	LV	*84	
Cleveland's (C. D.) Compendium of American Literature	AM	*1 75	
Compend. of Eng. Lit	AM	*1 75	
Eng. Lit. of 19th Century	AM	*1 75	
Cleveland's (F. A.) Constitutions, for Class Study ea.	SA		15
Cleveland's (H. M.) First Term's Work in Reading	SA		8
2d Primary Reader	SA		24
Beginners' Readers, 3 nos ea.	SA		10
" " in 1 v.	SA		25
Historical Reader, bk. 1	SA		25
Clifton & Grimaux's Fr.-Eng. and Eng.-Fr. Dict., 2 v	CH	9 60	
——	JE	9 60	
Clinger's (I. W.) Orthography and Orthœpy	HS	50	
Clowes' & Coleman's Elemen. Qualitative Analysis	BL	*1 00	
Coates' Am. Popular Speaker	WR	*85	
Comprehensive Speaker	WR	*1 00	
Young American Speaker	WR	*50	
Cobbett's Eng. Grammar (Ayres)	AP	1 00	
—— (Waters)	BA	75	60
Cocker's (W. J.) Punctuation	AM	*32	
Government of U. S	AM	*72	
Coe's First Studies in Drawing	WI	60	
Coe's (F. B.) Our American Neighbors	SI	*75	60
Coe's (F. B.) Modern Europe	SI	*75	60
Coffin's Conic Sections	CO	*1 20	1 08
Coffin's (V. C.) History of Germany	AL	**	
Cogswell, *see* Bradbury.			
Colt's Chemical Arithmetic	HE	*55	50
Colaw (J. M.) and Ellwood's (J. K.) Arithmetics:			
Primary	JH	35	
Advanced	JH	60	
Colbert's Fixed Stars	SR	*42	40
Mathematical Tables	SR	*32	30
Colburn's (W.) First Lessons, Intellect. Arith., rev†	HM	35	
—— Old ed	HM	30	
Colby's (F. M.) Outlines of General History	AM	*1 50	
Colby's Der Lehrer	CN	1 50	
Der Leitstern	CN	1 00	
Colby's Grammar	CN	1 00	
Cole's Institute Reader	AM	*80	
Choice Readings	BU	*60	
Coleman's (S. E.) Algebraic Arithmetic	MC	*60	
Coler's (C. S.) Character Building	HS	1 00	
Collar's (W. C.) Gradatim	GI	*45	40
New Gradatim	GI	*55	50
Practical Latin Composition	GI	*1 10	1 00
Gate to Cæsar	GI	*45	40
Cæsar's Gallic War, Bk. 2	GI	*40	35
Æneid, Bk. 7, with Vocab	GI	*50	45
—— with Translation	GI	*50	45
Via Latina	GI	*85	75
Collar's Eysenbach's German Lessons	GI	*1 30	1 20
Shorter Eysenbach	GI	1 10	1 00
English into German	GI	*30	25
Collar & Daniell's Beginner's Latin	GI	*1 10	1 00
First Latin Book	GI	*1 10	1 00
First Year Latin	GI	**	
Beginner's Greek Composition	GI	95	90
Latine Redenda	GI	20	
—— with vocab	GI	*33	30
Collard's Beginner's Reader, pt. 1	MY	*18	
—— pt. 2	MY	*18	
—— pt. 3	MY	*22	
*College Latin Series (various prices)	AL		
College Maid's 3 Minute Readings	HS	1 00	
College Men's 3 Minute Declamations	HS	1 00	
College Series of French Plays (Böcher), 2 v., cl ea.	HO		1 00
—— 9 v., pap "	HO		20
College Series of German Plays [8 v., var. prices, *27c.-*44c., 25c.-40c. ea.]	HO		
College Series of Greek Authors	GI		
College Series of Latin Authors	GI		
Collier's (W. F.) Hist. of Eng. Literature	NE	1 75	
Junior British History	NE	75	
Advanced British History	NE	1 75	
Senior British History	NE	1 25	
Hist. of British Empire	NE	1 00	
Great Events of History	NE	1 25	
—— Rev. ed	MU		90
History of Greece	NE	75	
" " Rome	NE	75	
Great Events of Hist. (Willis)	MY	90	
Collins' (J. V.) Text-Book of Algebra	SR		1 00
Collins' Advanced Mineralogy, 2 v	PU	2 00	
Elem. Mineralogy	PU	50	
Collot's Levizac's Fr. Anecdotes	JE	50	
Levizac's French Grammar	JE	50	
Progressive Pronouncing French Reader	JE	50	
—— Interlinear French Reader	JE	50	
—— French Dialogues	JE	50	
Colton's (B. P.) Practical Zoölogy	HE	*90	80
Physiology	HE		1 12
Physiology. Briefer Course	HE		90
Elemen. Physiology and Hygiene	HE		60
Colton's (C. W.) New Introd. Geography	BU	*60	
Common School Geography, with reference maps	BU	*1 25	
—— without reference maps	BU	*1 10	
Columbia Graded Spellers:			
Primary	EL	*23	20
Advanced	EL	*28	25
Columbia Vertical Penmanship:			
Tracing Course, Nos. 1 and 2 doz.	CB		72
Common School Course, Nos. 1-7. "	CB		72
Business and Social Forms, No. 8. "	CB		72
Slant Penmanship, 13 nos "	CB		72
Slant and Vertical Writing Spellers. doz.	CB		45
Columbian Primary Reader	WR	*20	
Second "	WR	*30	
Third "	WR	*40	
Fourth "	WR	*50	
Fifth "	WR	*60	
Columbus Series: First Reading Bk	SK	25	15

† *For* Second Lessons, *see* Wheeler, H. N.

Columbus Series: Second Reading Bk... SK 40 24
Third " " ..... SK 60 36
Fourth " " ..... SK 75 45
Columbus System of Vertical Writing. 6 nos.... *doz* SK 50
Coman & Kendall's English Hist. for High Schools.... MC 1 25
*Short Hist. of England.... MC 90
Comba's Lingua Italiana.... JE 1 50
Comba's (I. E.) Italian Pronunciation... LJ 60
Comegys' Primer of Ethics.... GI *50 40
Comfort's 1st Book in German.... AM *60
1st German Reader.... AM *50
German Course.... AM *1 00
German Conversation.... AM *84
Comly's Grammar.... LI *28
Reader.... LI *36
Spelling-Book (Bonsal's).... LI *15
Common Sense Arithmetic, pt. 1.... LV *30
—— pt. 2.... LV *40
—— In 5 nos.... *ea.* LV *10
Copy-Books, 10 nos.... *doz.* LV *72
Compayré's (G.) Elements of Psychology. LE 1 00
Composition Writing Made Easy, 5 pkts. *ea.* HS 20
Compton's (A. G.) First Lessons in Wood-Working.... AM *60
Logarithmic Computations.... WI 1 50
Comstock's (D. Y.) 1st Latin Book.... AL 1 00
Virgil's Æneid.... AL 1 40
Comstock's (G. C.) Astronomy.... AP 1 30
Comstock's (J. H.) Manual for Study of Insects.... CM 3 75
Comstock's (J. H.) & Kellogg's (V. L.) Elements of Insect Anatomy.... CM *1 00
Comstock's (J. H.) & Needham's (J. G.) Wings of Insects.... CM *1 00
Congdon's (E. A.) Qualitative Analysis... HO 60
Conington's Aeneid of Virgil.... AR 1 50
Conklin's (B. Y.) Grammar and Composition.... AM *60
Practical Lessons in Language.... AM *35
Connolly's English Reader.... BE 1 25 75
Conrad's Normal Methods of Teaching Arithmetic.... NO 50
Contanseau's Elem. French Course:
Accidence.... LN 20
Syntax.... LN 20
Conversation Book.... LN 20
1st Exercise Book.... LN 20
2d " ".... LN 20
Translation Book.... LN 20
Easy Delectus.... LN 20
1st Reader.... LN 20
2d ".... LN 20
Dialogues.... LN 20
Pocket French and Eng. Dictionary.. LN 60
Practical Fr. and Eng. Dict.... LN 1 25
French Dictionary, 12°.... LI *1 20
Contes Choisis, vs. 1-23.... *ea.* JE 40
—— pap.... " JE 25
Continental Copy-Books, 7 nos.... *doz.* HS 75
Continental 1st Reader.... MT 18
—— 2d Reader.... MT 36
—— 3d ".... MT 42
—— 4th ".... MT 54
—— 5th Reader.... MT 72
—— Reading Speller, 1st Bk.... MT 19
—— " " 2d Bk.... MT 28
Cook's Synthetic Arithmetic.... TR **
Cook's (A. S.) Beginner's Bk. in Old English.... GI 1 60 1 50
Siever's Old English Grammar.... GI *1 25 1 12
Exercises in Old English.... GI *40 35
Cook's (J. M.) Mental Arithmetic.... WS 50
Cook's (J. W.) Methods in Arithmetic... FL 50
Cook's (J. W.) and Cropsey's (N.) Elementary Arithmetic.... SI *56 50
Advanced.... SI *80 72
See Normal Course in Number.
Cooke's (J. E.) Stories of the Old Dominion.... AM *60
Cooke's Chemical Physics.... AL 4 50
Cooley's New Elem. Chem. for Beginners. AM *72
New Text-Book of Chemistry.... AM *90
Experiments in Physical Science.... AM *52
Elements of Natural Philosophy.... AM *72
New Text-Book of Physics.... AM *90
Laboratory Studies in Chemistry.... AM *50
Student's Manual of Physics.... AM *1 00
Coolidge's In the Storyland, pts. 1, 2, 3, *ea.* HW *20
—— Complete.... HW *50
Coombs' English Pronunciation.... NO 35
Ten Weeks' Course in Elocution.... HS 1 25
Coon's (H. C.) Civil Gov't of N. Y. State.. HS 75
Cooper, Lemmon & Estell's History of Our Country.... GI *1 15 1 00
Cooper's (S.) Animal Life.... AM *1 25
Coppée's Elements of Logic.... BU *90
Coppée's Elements of Rhetoric.... BU *1 15
Coppens's (C.) Logic and Mental Philosophy.... SK 1 25 75
Moral Philosophy.... SK 1 00 60
Oratorical Composition.... SK 1 25 75
Rhetoric.... SK 1 25 75
*Corneille's Le Cid, with vocab.... HO 35
Cornell's First Steps in Geography.... AM *31
Primary Geography, new ed.... AM *42
Intermediate Geography, new ed.... AM *86
Physical Geography, new ed.... AM *1 12
Cornish's (F. W.) Dict. of Greek and Roman Antiquities.... HO 4 00
Cornman & Gerson's Primer of Physiology.... EL **
Topical Survey of U. S. History.... HE 60
Corson's Browning.... HE 1 50
Anglo-Saxon and Early English.... HO 1 60
Chaucer's Canterbury Tales.... MC 90
Cortina's Spanish in Twenty Lessons.... CH 1 50
Corwin's (R. W.) Exercises to Whitney's German Grammar.... HO 25
Cotte's Contes Tires de Molière, 2 v. *ea.* JE 20
Coulanges' Ancient City.... LE 1 60
Coulter's (J. M.) Manual of the Botany of the Rocky Mountains.... AM *1 62
Plant Relations.... AP 1 10
Plant Structures.... AP 1 20
Plant Studies.... AP 1 25
Seed Plants.... AP 1 75
Plants.... AP 1 80
Coulter's Botany. *See* Gray
Courtenay's Calculus.... AM *2 00
Cowdery's Moral Lessons.... BU *60
Cowles's (W.) Adelphoe of Terence.... SA 80
Cox's (G. W.) Mythology.... HO 75
General Hist. of Greece.... AM *1 25
—— Abridged ed.... AM *60
Cox's (J.) Introd. to Physical Science.... SC **
Coy's (E. G.) Greek for Beginners.... AM *1 00
First Greek Reader.... AM *84
Coy's (E. W.) Latin Lessons.... AM *1 00
Crafts' Qualitative Chem. Analysis.... WI 1 50
Crafts & Fisk's Rhetoric Made Racy.... SR *61 55
Craig's (A. H.) New Common School Question Book, with answers.... HS 1 50
Pros and Cons (Complete Debates)... HS 1 50
Craig's (J. A.) Hebrew Word Manual.... CL 1 00
Craik's English of Shakespeare.... GI *1 00 90
Hist. of Eng. Lit., 2 v.... SC 5 00
Cranch's (C. P.) Tr. of Virgil's Ænied.... HM 1 00
Crane First Reader.... CE 20 16
Second ".... CE 30 24
Third ".... CE 40 32
Fourth ".... CE 50 40
Fifth ".... CE 60 48
Crane's Romantisme Français.... PU 1 50
Crane & Brun's Tableaux de la Revolution Française.... PU 1 50
Crawley's (E. S.) Elem. of Trigonometry. LI *1 00
Table of Logarithms.... LI 75
Trigonometry and Tables.... LI 1 25
Creery's (W. R.) Catechism of U. S. History.... DY *28 25
Primary School Speller.... AM *20
Grammar School Speller.... AM *35
Creighton's (J. E.) Logic, new ed.... MC 1 10
Creighton's (Mrs.) Hist. of England.... LN 50
Stories from Eng. Hist.... LN 1 25
Epochs of English History.... LN 1 50
First Hist. of England.... LN 80
First Hist. of France.... LN 1 25
Cremieux and Decourcelle's L'Abbe Constantin (François).... AM *35
Crew's Manual of French Verbs.... JE 35
Crew's Elements of Physics.... MC 1 10
*Créw's & Tatnall's Laboratory Manual of Physics.... MC 90
Critical Greek and English Testament.... WI 1 00
Crittenden's Bookkeeping:
New Counting-House.... FO 3 50 3 00
—— Key to.... FO 1 50 1 25
—— Blank-Bks. for, 56 in set.... FO 3 50 3 00
New High School.... FO 2 25 2 00
—— Key to.... FO 1 50 1 25
—— Blank-Bks. for, 37 in set.... FO 2 50 2 00
New Elementary.... FO 1 35 1 25
—— Key to.... FO 75 65
—— Blank-Bks. for, 17 in set.... FO 1 35 1 25
New Single Entry.... FO 75 65
—— Key to.... FO 75 65
—— Blank-Bks. for, 8 in set.... FO 75 65
Single Entry Explained.... FO 50 40
—— Key to.... FO 25 20
Commercial Arith., new ed.... EL *1 25 1 10
—— Key to.... EL *55 50
Crocker's (K. F.) History of England.... AP 60
Crockett's (C. W.) Elements of Plane and Spherical Trigonom., with Tables. AM *1 25

Crockett's (C. W.) Elem. of Plane and Spherical Trigonom., without Tables..AM *1 00
Logarithmic and Trig. Tables (Separate)..AM *1 00
Cromer's (F. G.) Historical Outline and Civil Government..MS *75
Cromwell's Easy Lettering for Primary Schools..SP 50
Crosby's (H.) Sophocles' Œdipus Tyrannus..AM *1 05
Crosby's (W. E.) Our Little Book for Little Folks..AM *30
Crosby's (W. H.) Quintus Curtius Rufus..AM *1 05
Crosby's (W. O.) Tables for Determination of Minerals..HE *1 35 1 25
Cross' (A. K.) National Drawing Course:
Drawing-Books..*doz.*GI 1 80
Free-Hand Drawing..GI *90 80
Mechanical " ..GI *1 10 1 00
Color Study..GI *65 60
Light and Shade..GI *1 10 1 00
National Drawing Models..GI 30
Outlines of Drawing Lessons, Primary Grades..GI *35 30
Outlines of Drawing Lessons, Grammar Grades..GI *35 30
Primary Drawing Copies..GI 10
Cross' (J. G.) Eclectic Shorthand, new ed. SR 1 50
Eclectic Shorthand Dict..SR 2 50
" " Lessons..SR 75
" " Phrase-Book.SR 1 50
Crowell's Sel. from Latin Poets..GI *1 55 1 40
Crowell & Richardson's Roman Literature..GI *1 10 1 00
Crozier's Botanical Dictionary..HO 2 40
Cruden's Calisthenics and Musical Drills.DI 50
Cruttwell's Roman Literature..SC 2 50
Cumming's (L.) Electricity..LN 1 50
Heat..LN 1 50
Cumnock's Choice Readings, new enl. ed. MG 1 50
School Speaker..MG 75
Curnow's English History..BN 90
Curtis's General Botany..LN 3 00
Curtiss' (C. C.) Manual of Bookkeeping..AM *81
—— Blanks, *set* of 10..AM *75
Vertical Copybooks, 6 nos..*doz.*AM *96
Semi-Vertical Copybooks, 6 nos.. " AM *96
Cutler's (C.) Beginnings of Ethics..AR 1 25 1 25
Cutler's (C. W.) Physics and Chemistry..PU 2 00
Cutler's (E. H.) Virgil's Æneid, Bk. 9..GI *50 45
Cutter's Beginner's Anatomy..LI *30
Intermediate Anatomy..LI *50
Comprehensive " ..LI *1 00
Cutting's Difficulties of Ger. Grammar..JE 30
Cyr's (E. M.) Children's Primer..GI *30 24
Children's First Reader..GI *35 28
" Second " ..GI *45 36
" Third " ..GI *60 50
" Fourth " ..GI *70 60
" Fifth " ..GI *80 70
See Interstate.
Cyr's (E. M.) Readers by Grades:
Book 1..GI *30 25
" 2..GI *35 30
" 3..GI *50 40
" 4..GI *50 40
" 5..GI *50 40
" 6..GI *55 45
" 7..GI *55 45
" 8..GI *55 45
Advanced First Reader..GI **
Cyr's Libro Primero de Lectura..GI *35 30
Libro Segundo de Lectura..GI *40 35
Dale's Outlines of Elocution..NO *1 50
Daly's (I. M.) Advanced Rational Speller.SA 25
Dalgleish's Grammatical Analysis..AM *48
Scott Reader..NE 75
Dalton's (J. C.) Physiology and Hygiene.AM *84
Dana's (J. D.) Geological Story, Rev. ed..AM *1 15
Manual of Geology, new ed..AM *5 00
New Text-Book of Geology, Rev..AM *1 40
Descriptive Mineralogy..WI 12 50
Manual of " ..WI 2 00
Text-Book of " ..WI 4 00
" " " Mechanics..WI 1 50
Dana's (W. S.) How to Know the Wild Flowers..SC 2 00
How to Know the Ferns..SC 1 50
Plants and Their Children..AM *65
—— Library ed..AM *1 20
Daniel's English Literature..BI 50
Daniell's (M. G.) Sentences for Writing Latin..AM *20
New Latin Composition..SA 1 00
—— Pt. 1..SA 60
—— Pts. 2 and 3..*ea.*SA 70
Latin Composition Blank..SA 15

*Daniels' (W. M.) Elements of Public Finance..HO 1 50
Darr's Verbes Francais demandant des Prepositions..JE 50
Spanish Words and Phrases..JE 25
D'Anvers' Elem. Hist. of Art, rev. ed., 1 v..SC 3 75
Science Ladders, 6 nos..*ea.*BN 18
—— in 3 v.. " BN 36
*Daudet's Selected Stories (Jenkins)..AM *50
L'Enfant Espion and other Stories (Goodell)..AM *45
Tartarin de Tarascon (Fontaine)..AM *45
Davenport's (C. B.) Introd. to Zoology..MC 1 10
Davenport's (H. J.) Elemen. Economics..MC 80
Davenport's & Emerson's Principles of Grammar..MC 65
David's (A. A.) Easy Stories and Exercises in German..LN 35
Davidson's (A. B.) Introd. Hebrew Gram.SC 2 25
Davidson's (B.) Anal. Hebrew Lexicon..WI 4 00
Davidson's (E. A.) Linear Drawing and Practical Geometry..CA 75
Linear Drawing and Projection..CA 1 25
Model Drawing..CA 1 00
Practical Perspective..CA 1 00
Davidson's (H. A.) Hist. of the U. S..GI *90 80
Davidson's (J. W.) School Hist. of South Carolina, rev..DU 60 50
Davidson's (W.) & Alcock's (G. C.) Intermediate English Grammar..SK 25 15
*Davidson's History of the United States..SR 80
Davies' (C.) Mathematics:
Arithmetic, First Book in..AM *40
" Complete..AM *70
" Primary..AM *15
" Intellectual..AM *25
" Elements of Written..AM *35
" School..AM *50
" —— Key to..AM *50
" Practical..AM *60
" —— Key to..AM *60
" University..AM *1 00
" —— Key to..AM *1 00
Algebra, New Elementary..AM *90
" —— Key to..AM *90
" University..AM *1 00
" —— Key to..AM *1 00
" Bourdon's..AM *1 60
" —— Key to..AM *1 60
Elem. Geometry and Trigonometry..AM *1 00
Legendre's Geometry and Trigonometry..AM *1 60
—— pt. 1 (Geometry only)..AM *1 25
—— Key to Exercises in Geometry.AM *1 60
—— pt. 2, Trigonometry, Mensuration, and Tables..AM *1 00
Elements of Surveying (Van Amringe)..AM *1 75
Differential and Integral Calculus..AM *1 40
Analytical Geometry..AM *1 40
" " and Calculus..AM *1 75
Descriptive Geometry..AM *2 00
Davies' Scientific French Reader..HE *45 40
Davies & Peck's Complete Arithmetic..AM *75
—— Key to..AM *75
Elementary Arithmetic..AM *50
First Lessons in Numbers..AM *30
Davis' (C. H.) Practical Questions U. S. History..PM *25
—— Answers..PM *25
Davis' (E. H.) Beginner's Reading-Book..UN *29 25
—— Teachers' ed..UN *29 25
Second Reading-Book..UN *46 40
Third " ..UN *64 56
Fourth " ..UN *92 80
Beginner's Reading Book (Scholar's edition), pt 1..UN *18 16
Beginner's Reading Book (Scholar's edition), pt. 2..UN *18 16
Second Reading Book, pt 1..UN *25 22
" " " " 2..UN *25 22
Third " " " 1..UN *35 30
" " " " 2..UN *35 30
Davis' (E. W.) Introd. to Logic of Algebra.WI 1 50
Davis' (N. K.) Elements of Psychology..SI *2 00 1 80
" " Deductive Logic..AM *90
" " Inductive " ..AM *1 00
Theory of Thought..AM *2 00
Elements of Ethics..SI 2 00 1 60
Elementary " ..SI 1 50 1 20
Davis' (W. J.) American Primer..MO 10
Davis' (W. M.) Elementary Meteorology..GI 2 70 2 50
*Physical Geography..GI *1 40 1 25
Dawes' How We Are Governed, Rev..GI *1 15 1 00
Day's (A.) Aid to Shorthand..BV 75
Shorthand Manual..BV *1 00
" " Copy Book..BV 25
New Amer. Shorthand..BV 1 50

Day's (A.) New Amer. Shorthand Copy Book........BV 25
Elements of Shorthand and Copy Book........BV 1 50
Vest Pocket Shorthand Dictionary. BV 1 00
Day's (H. N.) Elemen. of Logic, new ed. AM *1 00
Rhetorical Praxis........AM *1 00
Elements of Psychology........PU 1 50
Science of Æsthetics........PU 2 00
" " Ethics........PU 1 50
English Literature........SO 2 25
Day's (J.) Introduction to Algebra........PE 1 75
—— Key to........PE 1 50
Elements of Algebra (Thomson)........PE 85
—— Key to........PE 85
Dean's (P.) Intellectual Arithmetic........BU *84
Deane's (C. W.) Phonetic Reader........MS *40
—— First Bk........MS 28
—— Second Bk........MS 32
—— Third & Fourth Bks........MS **
Deane's (C. W.) & Davis's (M. R.) Elemen. Inductive Geography........PM *72
Inductive Geography........PM *1 00
De Fivas's (A.) Elementary French Reader........AM *52
Classic French Reader........AM *1 05
De Fivas's (V.) Grammar of French Grammars........AM *87
De Garmo's (C.) Tales of Troy........PS *35
—— bds........PS *30
Language Lessons, Bk. 1........WR *30
—— Bk. 2........WR *40
Complete Language Lessons (one Bk. course)........WR *50
De Garmo's Lindner's Psychology........HE *1 10 1 00
De Graff's Calisthenics, etc........BI 25
Pocket Pronunciation-Book........BI 15
Practical Phonics........BI 75
School-Room Chorus........BI 85
Degraff's (L.) Principles of Economics...FL *40
Delille's Condensed French........HO 40
Del Mar's Spanish Conversation........LO 75 60
De Lolme, Wallace & Bridgeman's French and English Dictionary........CA 1 50
Demarest's (A. J.) & Van Sickle's (W. M.) New Education Readers:
Bk. 1........AM *35
" 2........AM *35
" 3........AM *40
*" 4........AM *45
Denman's Bookkeeping........BF 50
—— Blanks for........BF 25
Dennis' A Study of Leaves........AP 50
De Peyrac's Comment on Parle à Paris..AM *1 05
De Rougemont's Litterature Française..JE 1 25
De Rougemot's La France........MY *75
Anecdotes Nouvelles........MY *30
Neue Aneckdoten........MY *40
Derry's United States History........BT *1 00
Descartes' Philosophy (Torrey)........HO 1 50
Deschanel's Natural Philosophy........AP 5 75
—— pts. 1-4........ea. AP 1 50
Dessar's German Grammar........WT 75
Small " "........WT 35
Elements of Hebrew Grammar........BM 15
DeThoma's (F.) Historia de Nuevo Mexico. AM *75
De Tornos' Spanish Method........AP 1 25
Dettmann's Phono-Stenography, pt. 1, pap........ST 60
—— cl........ST 75
—— pt. 2, pap........ST 60
—— cl........ST 75
Deutscher Hiawatha Primer........HM 50
Deutsch's German Reader........HE *1 00 90
Drillmaster in German........BF 1 50
——........JE 1 25
De Vere's Introduction to French........UN *60 52
French Grammar........UN *1 38 1 20
1st French Reader........UN *60 52
Spanish Grammar........AP 1 00
French Verb........JE 1 00
Devine's (E. T.) Elemen. Economics........MC 1 00
Dewey's (J.) Critical Theory of Ethics.. RE 1 50 1 20
Psychology........AM *1 25
Dewey's (J. M.) Lessons on Morals........HS 75
Lessons on Manners........HS 75
Dewey's & Tuft's Ethics........HO **
De Wolf's (D. F.) Instructive Speller........AM *17
*Diamond's (F. J.) Rational Speller........MC 24
Dickens' Child's Hist. of Eng........AM *60
——........HM 1 00
——........WR *67
——........RU 1 00
Dickinson's (W. J.) English Grammar Simplified........HW 1 00
Dictionary of English, French, German..ST 3 30
Diehl's Elocutionary Studies........WE 60
Practical Del Sarte Primer........BI 50
Dillard's Exercises in Arithmetic........CB 50 40

Dimitry's (J.) Hist. and Geog. of Louisiana........AM *60
Dinsmore's (T. H.) First Lessons in Physiology and Hygiene........AM *50
Dinsmore's (T. W.) Graded Spelling Blanks, 3 nos........doz. AM *84
Elem. Spelling Blanks........" AM *42
Model Script Writing Spell. Blanks " AM *45
Dippold's Scientific German Reader........GI *1 00 90
Dodds' (J. J.) Outline of Civil Government........NO 20 15
Dodge's Reader in Physical Geography..LN 70
Dodge's Elem. Practical Biology........AM *1 80
Dodge's (C. C.) & Tuttle's Latin Prose Composition........AM *75
Dodge's (L. S.) Der Führer (Ein Lesebuch)........CH 1 25
Dodge's (N. S.) Stories of Am. History....LE *35 30
Dodge's (T. A.) Student's Bird's-Eye View of Civil War........HM 1 00
Doederlein's Latin Synonyms........DR 1 25
Doerner's Treasury of General Knowledge, pt. 1........AM *50
—— pt. 2........AM *65
Dolbear's Natural Philosophy........GI *1 10 1 00
Dole's (C. F.) American Citizen........HE *1 00 90
The Young Citizen........HE 45
Donnegan's Greek Lexicon........BU *2 59
Donnelly's (F. P.) Imitation and Analysis: English Exercises based on Irving's Sketch Book........AL **
D'Ooge's (B. L.) Viri Romæ........GI *85 75
*Latin Composition........GI 45 40
*Cicero, Select Orations........SA 1 20
D'Ooge's (M. L.) Sophocles' Antigone........GI *45 40
—— with notes........GI *1 50 1 40
Demosthenes on the Crown........SR 1 25
Colloquia Latina........HE *45 40
Greek Composition Tablet........GI *25 20
Easy Latin for Sight Reading........GI *45 40
Doolittle's Practical Astronomy........WI 4 00
Doriot's Ill. Beginners' French Book......GI *90 80
—— pt. 2........GI *55 50
Beginners' Book in German........GI *90 80
Dorner's (H.) Elem. Science and Physiology........CN 50
*Douay's (G.) Elemen. French Reader....SI 1 00
Douglas' Civil Government of Conn........EL *55 50
Dowd's Physical Culture........FW 1 50
Dowden's Introd. to Shakespeare........SC 75
Downer's (C. A.) First Book in French...AP **
*Downey's (J. F.) Higher Algebra........AM *1 50
—— pt. 1........AM *90
Doyle's United States. *See* Freeman.
Drake's Fables of Phædrus........AL 30
Drake's (S. A.) Burgoyne's Invasion of 1777; Taking of Louisburg; Battle of Gettysburg; Campaign of Trenton, 4 v........ea. LE 40
Making of the Ohio Valley States; Virginia and the Middle Colonies; New England; The Great West; Border Wars of New England, 5 v. ea. SC 1 50
Draper's Anatomy, Physiology, and Hygiene........AM *2 50
Human Physiology........AM *3 50
Physics........LA 4 00
Drawing Made Easy Cards, 4 ser........ea. FL 25 20
Drechsel's Chemical Reactions........WI 1 25
Drew's Practical Bookkeeping........SR *1 19 1 10
—— Blanks for........SR *1 49 1 25
Dreyspring's Easy Lessons in French....AM *60
French Reader........AM *75
Easy Lessons in German........AM *60
First German Reader........AM *60
Dreyspring's German Method (Cumulative)........AM *1 20
German Verb Drill........AM *1 20
Constructive Process for Learning German........JE 1 25
Drisler's (F.) Conjugation of Latin Verbs, 50 sheets........JE 25
Dryer's Indiana Geography........IN 50
*Dryer's (E. R.) Physical Geography......AM *1 20
Dubbs' (E. L.) Arithmetical Problems, Teachers' ed........AM *1 00
—— Pupils' ed., 2 pts........ea. AM *25
Complete Mental Arithmetic........AM 35
*New Practical Arithmetic........AM *60
Du Bois' French Teacher........LE 1 00
*Du Bose's Sketches, Alabama History..EL *1 00 90
Du Croquet's (C.) French Grammar.....JE 1 25
Elementary French Grammar........JE 75
Conjugation of French Verbs, 50 sheets........JE 35
French Verbs in a Few Lessons........JE 35
French Conversation........JE 1 00
Le Français par la Conversation......JE 1 00

Title	Pub.	Price	Price
Du Croquet's (C.) La Conversation des Enfants	JE	75	
Du Cygne's Ars Rhetorica	MU		75
Duff's Bookkeeping (enlarged)	AM	*2 25	
Common School Bookkeeping	AM	*44	
—— Account Bks., for *set* of 4	AM	*50	
*Duff's Hebrew Grammar	MC	1 00	
Duffet's French Method, 2 pts. *ea.*	AM	*72	
Hennequin's New Fr. Method	AM	*1 20	
—— Key	AM	*60	
Dufour's (A.) French Grammar	GI	*70	60
French Reader, with vocab	GI	*1 10	1 00
Dulany's Standard Physiology	DY	*58	50
Martin's Elem. Human Body	DY	*84	75
Primer Physiology	DY	*35	30
School Hist. of Maryland	DY	*1 00	80
Primer and First Reader	DY	*28	25
Dumas' La Tulipe Noire (Brandon)	AM	*10	
Dunglison's Elem. Physiology	WR	*50	
School Physiology	WR	*1 00	
Dunton's (L.) Arithmetic in Primary Schools	SI		1 00
Dunton (L.) & Clark (C. G.) *See* Normal.			
Dunton & Kelley's Inductive Course in English:			
First Book	TH	40	
*Language Lessons	TH	50	
*English Grammar	TH	55	
Duntonian Copy-Books:			
Common School Ser., Nos. 1 to 8. *doz.*	TH	96	
Tracing Series, Nos. 0-1-2 "	TH	72	
Advanced Numbers, 9–10 "	TH	1 20	
Duplex, Nos. A to E "	TH	1 08	
Spelling Blank "	TH	45	
Vertical, Nos. 1–6 "	TH	96	
" Short Course, Nos. 1–5 "	TH	72	
Lettered Ser., with copies "	TH	72	
Duque & Phelan's Spanish in Spanish	WA	1 50	1 25
Durège's Theory of Functions	MC	2 00	
Durell's & Robbins's Grammar School Algebra	MP	*80	
School Algebra	MP	*1 00	
School Algebra Complete	MP	*1 25	
*First Lessons in Numbers	MP	*25	20
*Elementary Practical Arithmetic	MP	*40	32
*Advanced Practical Arithmetic	MP	*65	52
Durfee's (W. P.) Elements of Plane Trigonometry	GI	*80	75
Duruy's Middle Ages	HO		1 60
Modern Times	HO		1 60
Dutton's (S. T.) Historical Series:			
1st Bk., Indians and Pioneers	MS	*72	
2d " The Colonies	MS	*60	
3d " Revolutionary Days	MS	**	
4th " The Administrations	MS	**	
Duval's History of French Literature	HE	*1 10	1 00
Duval's (D.) Chardenal's Advanced exercises	AL		90
*Duval's (D.) *and* William's (H. J.) Le 17e Siecle en France	HO		35
Duvall's (J. J.) Civil Government Simplified	WA	25	
Dwight's Grecian and Roman Mythology	AM	*90	
—— 8°	BA	1 75	
Dyer's Plato's Apology and Crito, pap.	GI	*45	40
—— with notes	GI	*1 50	1 40
*Dymond's Moral Philosophy	CO	88	1 00
Eames' Phonography	BA	*1 40	1 20
*Earle's (M. S.) Sophocles' Oedipus Tyrannus	AM	*1 25	
Easy Primer	BN	30	24
Eaton's (A. J.) Latin Prose, Livy	GI	*40	36
Eaton's (S.) Easy Problems in Arithmetic	HW	*25	
New Arithmetic	HE	85	75
Exercises in Geography	HW	*25	
Practical Grammar	HW	*25	
Intellectual Arithmetic	TH	30	
Questions in "	TH	12	
Common School "	TH	68	
Business Forms, Customs and Accounts	AM	*1 00	
Exercise Manual of Business Forms	AM	*50	
—— Key to	AM	*50	
Easy Language Lessons	BE	50	30
Eben's Comp. German Primer	KO	15	9
Echol's (W. H.) Introd. to the Calculus	HO	**	
*Eckstorm's (F. H.) Bird Book	HE	60	
The Woodpeckers	HM	1 00	
Eclectic Bookkeeping (Ira Mayhew)	AM	*50	
—— Blanks for, 5 bks. *set.*	AM	*45	
—— Key to	AM	*50	
Eclectic Compos.-Bk., 32 pp. pap. *doz.*	AM	*1 00	
—— 48 pp., bds "	AM	*1 50	
Eclectic English Classics, 45 nos. [various prices, 20c.; 40c.; 50c.]	AM		
Eclectic German Primer	AM	*20	
German 1st Reader	AM	*25	
" 2d "	AM	*35	
Electic German 3d Reader	AM	*42	
" 4th "	AM	*60	
" 5th "	AM	*72	
Eclectic German Script Primer	AM	*20	
" 1st Book	AM	*20	
" Primer and 1st Reader	AM	*20	
" Advanced 4th Reader	AM	*60	
Eclectic German Vertical Penmanship, nos. 1–5. *doz.*	AM	*84	
Practical Bks., nos. 1–5 "	AM	*48	
Eclectic Indust. Drawing-Bks., rev., Nos. 1–3. *doz.*	AM	*1 20	
—— Nos. 4, 5 "	AM	*1 75	
—— " 6–8 "	AM	*2 00	
Mechanical Drawing	AM	*40	
Elements of Perspective	AM	*1 00	
Slate Exer. Draw. Cards, 12 nos. *doz.*	AM	*60	
High School Class Book of Drawing	AM	*50	
Normal Class Book of Drawing	AM	*50	
Eclectic Penmanship:			
Primary Copybook. *doz.*	AM	*72	
Elem. Tracing Course, 3 nos. "	AM	*72	
New Copybooks, 9 nos. "	AM	*96	
Exercise Copybook "	AM	*96	
New Handbook of Penmanship	AM	*50	
Writing Cards, 72 nos. manilla. *set.*	AM	*1 00	
German Copybooks, 5 nos. *doz.*	AM	*84	
Eclectic Elementary Geography	AM	*55	
Complete "	AM	*1 20	
Map-Blanks, 23 nos. *per* 100.	AM	*1 50	
Physical Geography (Hinman)	AM	*1 00	
Primary " No. 1	AM	*55	
Intermediate " " 2	AM	*1 10	
School " " 3	AM	*1 30	
Eclectic Primary U. S. Hist.	AM	*50	
New U. S. Hist. (Thalheimer)	AM	*1 00	
Writing Speller. *doz.*	AM	*50	
Language Lessons (Thalheimer)	AM	*35	
Physiology (Brown)	AM	*60	
School Geometry (Burns)	AM	*60	
Eclectic School Readings, 48 nos. [Var. prices, 25c.; 35c.; 40c.; 45c.; 50c.]	AM		
*Eclectic System of Modern Writing Books (Mrs. H. D. Abbott):			
*Short Course. Bks. A, B. *doz.*	NN		72
*Vertical Series. Bks. 1, 2, 3, 4, 5, 6. *doz.*	NN		84
*Slant Series. Bks. 1, 2, 3, 4, 5, 6. *doz.*	NN		84
Eclectic Temperance Physiologies:			
The House I Live in	AM	*30	
Youth's Temperance Manual	AM	*40	
Guide to Health	AM	*60	
Economical Writing Speller. *doz.*	AM	*42	
Edgarton's Western Orator	LI	*1 28	
Edgren's French Grammar	HE	*1 25	1 12
" " " Pt. 1	HE	*35	30
Spanish Grammar	HE	*90	80
Brief Italian Grammar	JE	90	
Edgren's (A. H.) Ital. and Eng. Dict.	HO	**	
*Edgren's (A. H.) & Burnet's (P. B.) French and English Dictionary	HO		2 50
Edgren & Fossler's Brief German Gram.	AM	*75	
Educational Music Course:			
First Reader	GI	*35	25
Second "	GI	*35	25
Third "	GI	*40	30
Fourth "	GI	*40	30
Fifth "	GI	*40	30
Sixth "	GI	*70	60
Educational System of Round-Hand, Rational Slant Writing:			
Nos. 1 and 2 (small size). *doz.*	SA		60
" 3–6 inclusive "	SA		75
" 7 Special Forms "	SA		75
Educational System of Roundhand Vertical Writing: Writing Primers, Nos. 1, 2, 3. *doz.*	SA		50
Tracing Course, Nos. A, B "	SA		75
Regular " " 1, 2, 3 "	SA		75
" " " 4, 5, 6, 7 "	SA		1 00
Business and Social Forms "	SA		1 25
Teachers' Manual "	SA		50
Educational System of Vertical Penmanship: Tracing Course, Nos. 1 and 2, *doz.*	SA		1 00
Regular Course, Nos. 1 to 8 "	SA		1 00
Course of Study in Vertical Writing. *doz.*	SA		**
Educational System of Penmanship (Slant Copies): Tracing Course, Nos. 1 and 2. *doz.*	SA		75
Progressive Course, Nos. 3, 4, 5 "	SA		75
Regular " " 1 to 7 "	SA		1 00
Edwards' (A. M.) Graded Lessons in Language, Nos. 1–6. *doz.*	BI	1 00	
500 Questions in Civics	BI	15	
Edwards' (G. C.) Elemen. of Geometry	MC	1 10	
Edwards' (J.) Differential Calculus for Beginners	MC	1 10	

Edward' (J.) Integral Calculus for Beginners... MC 1 10
Edwards' (J. F.) Catechism of Hygiene.. SK 40 24
Hygiene, Physiology ... SK 1 50 90
Edwards' (R.) Student's Readers:
1st Reader ... SR *20 16
—— in 3 pts ... doz. SR *63 54
2d Reader ... SR *30 25
—— in 5 pts ... doz. SR *63 54
3d Reader ... SR *48 .40
—— in 9 pts ... doz. SR *63 54
4th Reader ... SR *85 75
—— in 4 pts ... ea. *24 20
5th Reader ... *97 85
Student's Speller ... *24 20
Edwards' (S. A.) Handbk. of Mythology.. SR *1 05 95
Edwards & Warren's Analyt. Speller.... SR *21 18
Edwards & Webb's Analytical Ser.:
1st Reader ... SR *28 20
2d " ... SR *36 32
3d " ... SR *56 50
4th " ... SR *70 63
5th " ... SR *94 85
6th " ... SR *1 08 96
Egbert's (J. C.) Latin Inscriptions....... AM *3 50
Eggleston's Hist. of U. S ... AM *1 05
First Book in American History..... AM *60
Stories of American Life and Adventure... AM *50
Stories of Great Americans.......... AM *40
Eichberg. *See* National Music.
Ekeley's (J. B.) Elementary Experimental Chemistry... SI 90
Elementary History of the U. S.......... MU 25
Elementary Object Lessons in French.. NE 75
*Elementary Object Lessons in German.. NE 1 00
Eliot's American Authors... BU *60
Poetry for Children ... HM 30
Six Stories from Arabian Nights. ... HM 35
Eliot & Storer's Qualitative Chemical Analysis, rev. ed ... VN 1 50 1 25
Ellis's (E. S.) Primary Physiology........ BU *36
Young People's History of Our Country... SA 1 00
History of the United States..... ... WR *1 00
Common Errors in Writing and Speaking... HS 50
One Thousand Mythological Characters... HS 75
School History of New York State... BM 1 50
Ellsworth's Bookkeeping: Business Manual (Long Course)... EH 1 00 75
Bookkeeping, Pt. 1, Single Entry..... EH 75 45
" " 2, Double " ..... EH 75 45
" Blanks, Ledger and Journal... set (2). EH 30 20
Bookkeeping Blanks, DB, CB, SB, and BB... set (4). EH 60 40
Steps of Bookkeeping (Short Course). EH 50 40
" " " Blanks D, B, J and L ... set (3). EH 50 40
Ellsworth's Reversable Writing Books:
Large, 7 Nos. and 1 Tracing Bk.. doz. EH 1 1 08
Small, 8 " " 2 " " .. " EH . 75
Commercial, 5 Nos., Large....... " EH 1 96
" 5 " Small....... " EH 68
Manual of Penmanship or Key ..... EH 1 75
Lessons and Lectures on Penmanship. EH 2 1 50
Composition and Letter Writing ..... EH 20 60
Reversible Drawing Books, 6 nos. doz EH 2 25 1 80
Ellsworth's Primary and Kindergarten Series of Copybooks, 3 nos... doz. EH 96 75
Current Copybooks., Vertical, 6 nos., Nos 1, 2, 3... doz. EH 96 72
—— Nos. 4, 5, 6... " EH 1 08 96
Current Copybooks., New Slant, 6 nos., Nos 1, 2, 3... doz. EH 96 72
—— Nos. 4, 5, 6... " EH 1 08 96
Ellsworth's Reversible Copybooks:
Slanting Edition, 6 nos... doz. WR *96
Vertical " " ... " WR *96
Ellwood's (J. K.) Table Book and Test Problems... AM *1 00
Ely and Wicker's Elements of Political Economy ... MC **
Elmer's (H. C.) Phormio of Terence...... SA 1 00
Captivi of Plautus... AL 1 25
Elocutionist's Favorite... NO 1 00
Elson's Home and School Songs.......... LR *35 30
Elwall's German Dictionary... ST 2 00
—— ... LB 2 00
Ely's (R. T.) Introd. to Political Economy, new rev. ed ... EA 1 00
Outlines of Economics, new ed........ MC 1 25
Emerson's (A. W.) Composition and Criticism... BI 50
Emerson's (L.) Public School Hymnal.... DS 40
Morning Hour... GI *55 50
High School Hymnal... HE 50
Emerson's (I.) High School Hymnal, bds. ... 35
Emerson's (L. O.) Cheerful Voices....... DS 50
Golden Wreath... DS 50
Merry Chimes... DS 50
Royal Singer... DS 60
Song Bells ... DS 50
" Greeting ... DS 60
" Manual, Bk. 1... DS 30
" " Bk. 2... DS 40
" " Bk. 3... DS 50
United Voices ... DS 50
Emerson's (N. A.) Arithmetic, pt 1....... LI *12
—— pt. 2... LI *36
—— pt. 3... LI *68
—— Key to... LI *36
National Arithmetic, pt. 1........... AR *14 12
—— pt. 2... AR *47 40
Emerson's (O. F.) Brief History of English. MC 1 00
Middle English Reader... MC **
Emerson & Brown's Song Reader, Bk. 1.. DS 50
—— Bk 2... DS 60
Emerson & Swayne's Gems for Little Singers... DS 30
Emerson & Tilden's High School Choir.. DS 1 00
Hour of Singing... DS 1 00
Emerton's Introd. to Study of Middle Ages... GI *1 25 1 12
Mediæval Europe... GI *1 65 1 50
Emtage's (W. T. A.) Light... LN 1 50
English Classics. *See* Maynard. *Also* Student's Séries.
English Classics, Star series, 15 nos. .... GL [prices, 3?c.; 50c.]
English Composition, Exercises in........ NE 30
See also One Thousand Subjects for, Royal.
English Language, its History and Structure... NE 30
Composition, Paraphrasing, etc...... NE 50
English Readings for Students ... HO **
Englmann's Grammatical Series:
Latin Grammar ... BE 1 56 1 18
" Exercises in Etymology........ BE 1 31 94
" " " Syntax, Bks. 1 and 2... ea. BE 1 58 1 18
Eno's Compendium of Eng. Grammar .... SI *35 30
Ensign's U. S. Hist. Outlines... FL 25
Ancient History Outlines... FL 75
Entick's Latin Dictionary... CU 1 50 1 00
Episodes from Modern French Authors, 10 v... ea. LN 40
Episodes from Mod. German Authors, 4 v. LN [Various prices, 45c.; 50c., 60c.]
Epochs of American History. 3 v.... ea. LN 1 25
Epochs of Ancient History 11 v ...... " SC 1 00
—— 10 v... " LN 1 00
Epochs of English History, complete.... LN 1 50
Epochs of Modern History, 18 v....... ea. SC 1 00
—— 19 v... " LN 1 00
*Erckmann-Chatrian's Madame Thérèse (Fontaine)... AM *50
Erni's & Brown's Mineralogy Simplified.. BD 2 50
Erstes deutsches lesebuch... BP 28 25
Estill's Numerical Problems in Plane Geometry, with Tables. ... LN 90
Eugene. *See* Buckingham.
Evans' (E. P.) German Reader... HO 1 10
Evans' (G. W.) School Algebra... HO 1 12
Evans' (P. N.) Quantitative Chemical Analysis... GI *55 50
Evans' History of Georgia... UN *1 15 1 00
Everest's School Song-Book... DS 60
Everett's (C. C.) Science of Thought..... DW 1 50 1 20
Ethics for Young People... GI *55 50
Everett's (J. D.) Outlines of Natural Philosophy ... AM *84
Evers' Advanced Navigation... PU 1 00
Excelsior First Reader... CE 15 12
Second " ... CE 25 20
Third " ... CE 35 28
Fourth " ... CE 45 36
Fifth " ... CE 55 44
Excelsior Ser. *See* Sadlier, W. H.
Eysenbach's German Gram. with Vocab. CH 1 10
—— Key to... CH 50
Faber's (C.) New Script Primer ... PM *25
Fahsel's (A) Allerlei... AM *25
Fairbanks' (H. W.) School Songs:
Primary, 3 nos... ea. LR *10 8
" Nos. 1–3 in 1 v... LR *25 20
Intermediate, No. 1... LR *10 8
Grammar School, No. 1... LR *10 8
High School, No. 1... LR *10 8
Fairbanks' and Hebden's Elements of Algebra... TH 75
Fairchild's Moral Science ... BU *1 12
Fairclough's (H. R.) Andria of Terence... AL 1 75
Falckenberg's Modern Philosophy... ... HO 3 50

Title	Pub.		
Fall's (D.) Laboratory Manual in Chemistry	SY		60
Farley and Gunnison. *See* Normal Review Writing System.			
Fasnacht's (G. E.) French Grammar for schools	MC	*70	
Fasnacht. *See* Macmillan.			
Fasquelle's Introductory French Course	AM	*65	
Larger French Course	AM	*1 35	
Key to " "	AM	*90	
French Conversation	AM	*90	
Dumas' Napoleon	AM	*90	
Racine's Chefs d' Oeuvres	AM	*90	
Fenelon's Télémaque	AM	*90	
Faulhaber's One Year Course in German	HE	*65	60
Faunce's Descriptive Geometry	GI	*1 35	1 25
Fautes de Langage	JE	50	
Fay's (E. W.) Mostellaria of Plautus	AL	[illegible]	
Feller's Pocket Dictionaries:			
French, German, and English	RU	50	
German, English, and French	RU	50	
English and French	RU	50	
English and German	RU	50	
English and Italian	RU	50	
Italian and English	RU	50	
Spanish-English	KE	50	
English-Spanish	KE	50	
Fellows' First Steps in Grammar	BU	*18	
*Fellows' (G. E.) Recent European History, 1789-1900	SA		1 00
Felter's New Primary Arithmetic	AM	*30	
New Intermediate "	AM	*50	
Advanced Arithmetic	AM	*50	
Complete "	AM	*75	
—— Key to same	AM	*1 00	
First Lessons in Numbers	AM	*18	
Primary Arithmetic	AM	*22	
Intermediate "	AM	*54	
Practical "	AM	*72	
Felton's Æschylus' Agamemnon	SE	1 25	
Felton & Goodwin's Aristophanes' Birds	AL		1 10
Aristophanes' Clouds	AL		1 10
Isocrates' Panegyricus	AL		80
Fennell's Demosthenes Medias	HS	1 30	
Fenno's Elocution	HS	1 25	
Ferguson's (E. C.) An Aid to Greek at Sight	SI	*1 65	1 50
—— Abridged	SI	*85	80
Questions on Cæsar and Xenophon	GI	*1 25	1 12
Fernald's Selections from Greek Historians	AL		1 50
English Synonyms, Antonyms, and Prepositions	FU	1 50	
Classic Speller, pt. 1	PM	*15	
" " " 2	PM	*20	
Ferrell's Elementary Arithmetic	CE	30	24
Advanced Arithmetic	CE	60	48
*Ferris's (C. S.) Our First School Book	SI		30
Fewsmith's Elementary Grammar	SO	*38	
English Grammar	SO	*50	
Ficklen's (J. R.) Hist. and Civil Gov't of Louisiana	WR	*1 00	
Ficklin's (J.) Elementary Arithmetic, cl.	AM	*40	
—— bds	AM	*30	
Table-Book and Prim. Arith., cl.	AM	*28	
—— bds	AM	*18	
Practical Arithmetic	AM	*60	
—— Key to	AM	*60	
Advanced Arithmetic	AM	*80	
National Arithmetic	AM	*70	
—— Key to	AM	*70	
Elements of Algebra	AM	*75	
—— Key to	AM	*75	
Field's Gram. School Hist. of U. S	AM	*1 00	
Field's (M. L.) Outlines of Bookkeeping	CE	35	
Finch's Primer	GI	*35	30
First Reader	GI	*35	30
Finchi's Completely Parsed Cæsar	HS	1 50	
Fine's Number System in Algebra	HE		1 00
Finegan's & Stout's Civil Government for School Use	MC	[illegible]	
Finger's Civil Government	UN	*70	60
First German Reader	BP	28	25
First Steps in Reading	CS		25
Firth's Old Greece	HE	*35	30
Fischer's (A. A.) Practical Lessons in German	HO		75
Elementary Progressive German Reader	HO		70
Tables of German Grammar, rev. ed.	MR		65
Fischer's (W. H.) Essentials of German	SR		1 00
Fish's Arithmetic, No. 1	AM	*30	
—— No. 2	AM	*60	
—— Key to	AM	*60	
Fisher's (E. T.) Easy French Reading	HO		75
Fisher's (G. C.) Essentials of Geography	HW	*50	
Manual of Arithmetic for Primary Grades	HW	*40	
Fisher's (G. P.) Outlines of Universal History	AM	*2 40	

Title	Pub.		
Fisher's (G. P.) Outlines of Universal History, 3 v.	*ea.* AM	*1 00	
Brief History of the Nations	AM	*1 50	
Christian Evidences	SC	75	
Natural Theology	SC	75	
*Fisher & Patterson's Elements of Physics	HE		60
Fisher & Schwatt's Rudiments of Algebra	MC	60	
Secondary Algebra	MC	1 08	
Complete Secondary Algebra	MC	1 35	
Quadratics and Beyond	MC	90	
School Algebra	MC	1 00	
Elements of Algebra	MC	1 10	
Higher Algebra	MC	1 50	
Text Book of Algebra, pt. 1	MC	1 40	
Fisk's Greek Exercises	LH		65
Fiske's (J.) Civil Government	HM	1 00	
History of the U. S. for Schools	HM	1 00	
Fiske's Classical Literature	FO	4 50	4 00
—— Plates for	FO	1 50	1 25
—— Antiquities	FO	2 25	2 00
Fitch's Civil Gov't of U. S., new ed	AM	*85	
Fitz's Exercise Song-Book	DS	25	
Flagg's (I.) Anacreontics	GI	*40	35
Æschylus' Seven Against Thebes	GI	*1 10	1 00
Demosthenes' Hellenic Orations	GI	*1 10	1 00
Euripides' Iphigenia	GI	*45	40
—— with notes	GI	*1 50	1 40
Nepos, with vocab	SA		90
Nepos, without vocab	SA		75
Flanagan's Supplementary Reading Cards, 1st Reader	*set.* FL	10	
—— 2d Reader "	FL	12	
—— 3d " "	FL	15	
Number Cards	FL	15	
New Essentials of Grammar and Composition	FL	50	
New Lessons in English	FL	35	
Flanders' U. S. Constitution, rev	JO	1 25	
Fleming's (W.) Vocabulary of Philosophy	SC		3 00
Fleming & Tibbins' Fr.-Eng. and Eng.-Fr. Dictionary, 2 v	CH or JE	22 00	
Fletcher's (A. B.) Advanced Readings and Recitations	LE		1 20
Fletcher's (M.) Ethics	BA	*70	60
Fletcher & Carpenter's Theme Writing	AL		60
Fleury's Histoire de France	HO		1 10
Ancient Hist., French Notes	HO		70
Flickinger's (J. R.) Civil Government	HE		1 00
Outlines of General History	MP	*50	
Fluegel's German and English Dictionary, 3 v	LB	16 50	
—— School ed., 2 v	LB	5 20	4 50
—— German-Eng. part, separately	LB	3 00	2 60
Fluegel, Schmidt & Tanger's German and Eng. Dict., 2 v	CH	4 80	
Fobes' Elocution Simplified	LE	50	
—— pap	LE	30	
Five Minute Declamations, pt. 1	LE	50	
" " " " 2	LE	50	
" " Recitations	LE	50	
" " Readings	LE	50	
Fontaine's Livre de Lecture et de Conversation	HE	*1 00	90
Fontaine's (C.) Douze Contes Nouveaux	AM	*45	
Doce Cuentos Escogidos	JE	50	
Forbriger's Drawing Tablets 1-4	*doz.* AM	*2 00	
—— 5-8 "	AM	*3 00	
Ford's Spanish Composition	ZE		80
Ford's (N. W.) Nature's Byways (Natural Science for Primary)	ES	*40	
Foresti's Italian Reader	AM	*1 05	
Italian Grammar. *See* Ollendorff.			
Forman's (L. L.) A First Greek Book	AM	*1 20	
Forman's (S. E.) First Lessons in Civics	AM	*60	
Fortier's Histoire de la Littérature Française	HO		1 00
Foster's (L. C.) Syllabus of English Grammar	MC	60	
Foster's (M.) Physiology	MC	[illegible] 00	
Foster (M.) & Shore's Elemen. Physiology, new ed	MC	75	
Foster (M.) & Tracy's (R. S.) Physiology and Hygiene	AM	*35	
Foulché-Delbosc's French Echo Conversation	KC	90	
Fowler's (A. & J.) Arithmetic	DU	50	40
Fowler's (F.) Drawing in Charcoal	CA	[illegible] 50	
Fowler's (H. N.) Thucydides, Bk. 5	GI	*40	
—— with notes	GI	[illegible] 50	1 40
Quintus Curtius	GI	*35	30
—— Plautus' Menaechmi	SA		1 06
*History of Ancient Greek Literature	AP	[illegible] 40	
Fowne's Elementary Chemistry	LA	[illegible] 75	
Fox's Virginia Civil Government	RN	60	
Fox's (W.) & Thomas's (C. W.) Practical Course in Mechanical Drawing	VN	[illegible] 2[illegible]	

Title	Pub.	Price	Price
Francke's German Literature	HO		2 50
François (V. E.) Introductory French Prose Composition	AM	*25	
*Advanced French Prose Composition	AM	*80	
Frankland & Japp's Inorganic Chem.	LA	3 75	
Franklin Five-Cent Writing Speller..*doz.*	AM	*42	
Franklin Arithmetics	BU		
See Seaver & Walton.			
Franklin's Elemen. Algebra and Key	BU		
See Seaver & Walton.			
Franklin Readers	BU		
See Campbell (L. J.), and Hillard; Seaver & Walton.			
Franklin Speaker	BU	*84	
Franklin Sq. Song Collection, 8 nos...*ea.*	AM	*60	
Fraser's & Squair's French Grammar	HE		1 12
Elementary French Grammar	HE		90
Fredet's Ancient History	MU	1 50	
Modern History, new ed.	MU	1 50	
Freeland's (W.) Algebra for Schools and Colleges	LN	1 40	
Freeman's (E. A.) Historical Course:			
England (Thompson)	HO		88
France (Yonge)	HO		80
General Sketch of History	HO		1 10
Germany (Sime)	HO		80
Italy (Hunt)	HO		80
Scotland (Macarthur)	HO		80
United States (Doyle)	HO		1 00
Freer's (P. C.) General Chemistry	AL		3 00
Elementary Chemistry	AL		1 00
*French Literature Series, 6 v...*ea.*	SR		50
French Plays for Children, 4 v...*ea.*	HO		20
French Readings, 20 nos.	AM		
[Various prices, *35c. to $1.25.]			
French's (J. H.) First Lessons in Numbers	AM	*25	
Elementary Arithmetic	AM	*37	
—— Key to	AM	*67	
Mental Arithmetic	AM	*36	
Common School Arithmetic	AM	*70	
—— Key to	AM	*70	
French's (J. W.) Grammar	VN	1 50	
*Frenck's Animal Activities	LN	1 20	
Fresenius. *See* Allen (O. D.); Johnson (S. W.)			
Freytag's Die Journalisten (Johnson)	AM	*35	
Die Journalisten (Bronson)	AP	**	
—— (Manley)	AL	**	
—— (Joy)	HE		40
—— (Brown)	AP	30	
*Frieze's (H. S.) Aeneid. First Six Books, with notes and vocab., rev ed.	AM	*1 30	
*—— Complete with notes and vocab., rev. ed.	AM	*1 50	
*—— Text ed., rev.	AM	*50	
Quintilian, rev. ed.	AM	*1 20	
Vergil's Æneid, with Dictionary	AM	*1 30	
—— Text ed.	AM	*50	
Vergil's Æneid, 6 bks., Georgics and Bucolics	AM	*1 30	
—— Text ed.	AM	*25	
Vergil Complete, with Dictionary	AM	*1 60	
Frink's Rhetoric	SC		1 25
Frisbee's (I. F.) Beginners' Greek Bk.	HS		1 25
One Thousand Classical Characters	HS	75	
Frobisher's Voice and Action	AM	*90	
Froebel's Kindergarten System	BN	*18	
Mother Play	LE	1 50	
Elem. of Designing, 4 pts...*ea.*	ST	25	
Mother's Songs, Games, etc.	ST		2 00
Frost's (S. A.) How to Write a Composition	DI	50	
Frost's (W. G.) Greek Primer	AL		1 00
Frye's (A. E.) Primary Geography	GI	*75	08
Brooks and Brook Basins	GI	*70	02
The Child and Nature	GI	*1 00	89
Home and School Atlas	GI	1 00	
Complete Geography	GI	*1 55	1 25
Teacher's Manual	GI	*55	50
Elements of Geography	GI	*80	65
Geografía Elemental	GI	*90	75
*Grammar School Geography	GI	*1 50	1 25
Fuller's (J. E.) The Touch Writer	PH	50	
Fuller's (S.) Illus. Primer	HE	*30	25
—— Spanish ed.	HE	**	
Fulton & Eastman's Bookkeeping	PA	1 00	80
—— Blanks to	PA	75	60
Fulton & Trueblood's Choice Readings	GI	*1 65	1 50
Practical Elocution	GI	1 50	
Fundenberg's First Lessons in Reading	AM	*25	
—— Teachers' ed.	AM	*50	
Funk & Wagnall's Standard Dictionary:			
Sheep	FU	12 00	
" indexed	FU	12 75	
Students' Standard Dictionary:			
Cl., leath. back	FU	2 50	
Indexed	FU	3 00	
Full leath.	FU	4 00	
Funk & Wagnall's Students' Standard Dictionary:			
Full leath., indexed	FU	4 50	
Office Standard Dictionary:			
Cl. leath. back	FU	2 50	
Indexed	FU	3 00	
Full leath.	FU	4 00	
" " indexed	FU	4 50	
Grammar School Dictionary	FU	1 00	
Comprehensive Standard Dictionary	FU	1 00	
Introductory Standard Dictionary	FU	60	
Concise Standard Dictionary	FU	60	
Standard First Reader	FU	35	
Teachers' Manual	FU	50	
Furey's (F. T.) Constitution of U. S.	SK	50	30
Furneaux's Elementary Physiology	LN	80	
Furness's (H. H.) jr., Problems in Elemen. Physics	BU	*40	
Furst's (S. W.) Mensuration	MP	*50	
*Fusche's (O.) Handbook on Perspective	GI		
Fyffe's (C. A.) Modern Europe, 1 v.	HO		2 75
Gabriel's Rudiments of Hebrew Grammar	HR	1 00	65
Gage's (A. P.) Elements of Physics	GI	*1 25	1 12
—— Rev. ed.	GI	*1 20	1 12
Laboratory Manual	GI	*45	35
Introd. to Phys. Science	GI	*1 10	1 00
Principles of Physics	GI	*1 45	1 30
Physical Experiments	GI	*45	35
Galbraith & Houghton's Algebra	CA	2 75	
—— pt. 1	CA	1 00	
Euclid, Bks. 1-3	CA	1 00	
—— Bks. 4-6	CA	1 00	
Mathematical Tables	CA	1 25	
Mechanics	CA	1 25	
Galbraith's Composition in the School Room	PU	1 00	
Galer's Methods in Arithmetic	FL	60	
Gallandet's (E. M.) International Law	HO		1 80
*Ganong's Laboratory Course in Plant Physiology	HO		1 00
Ganot's Physics (Atkinson)	WO	5 00	
Popular Natural Philosophy	LN	2 50	
Gantvoort's (A. J.) Music Reader for Public and Private Schools	AM	*40	
Music Reader for Rural and Village Schools	AM	*40	
High School Ideal	AM	*60	
Gardenier's Pleasant Songs	NO	15	
Gardiner's (S. R.) Eng. Hist. for Schools	HO		80
Introd. to Eng. History	HO		80
Students' Hist. of England, in 1 v.	LN	3 00	
—— in 3 v...*ea.*	LN	1 20	
Atlas of English History	LN	1 50	
Gardner's (E. A.) Handbook to Greek Sculpture, in 1 v.	MC	2 50	
Gardner's (F.) Latin Lexicon	LI	1 80	
Garin's (P. A.) Industrial Drawing, pt. 1	HD	75	60
—— pt. 2	HD	75	60
Garner's (S.) Spanish Grammar	AM	*1 25	
Garnett's English Prose from Elizabeth to Victoria	GI	*1 65	1 50
Garrett & Harden's Organic Chemistry	LN	60	
Garrison's Civil Gov't of Texas	EL	*55	50
*Garrison's (C. L.) Manual and Diagram of Metcalf's Grammars	AM	*50	
Garvin's Qualitative Chemical Analysis	BE	**	
Gasc's Students' French Dictionary, 12°	HO		
—— 18°	HO		1 00
—— Translator, Eng. into French	HO		1 00
Gaspey-Otto-Sauer Method:			
Otto's French Conversation Grammar	WY	1 00	
—— Same, with Key	WY	1 25	
—— Key, separate	WY		85
Otto's German Conversation Grammar	WY	1 00	
—— Same, with Key	WY	1 25	
—— Key, separate	WY		85
Sauer's Spanish Conversation Grammar	WY	1 00	
—— Same, with Key	WY	1 25	
—— Key, separate	WY		85
Sauer's Italian Conversation Grammar	WY	1 00	
—— Same, with Key	WY	1 25	
—— Key, separate	WY		85
Otto's French Conversation Grammar	KC	1 00	
—— Key to	KC	40	
Otto's German Conversation Grammar	KC	1 00	
—— Key to	KC	40	
Sauer's Italian Conversation Grammar	KC	1 00	
—— Key to	KC	40	
Sauer's Spanish Conversation Grammar	KC	1 00	
—— Key to	KC	40	

Gastineau's Conversation Method, Fr...AM *1 25
Conversation Method, German.......AM *1 25
Gattermann's Practical Method of Organic Chemistry. 2d ed..........MC 1 60
Gautherot's Rational French Method, pt.1.JE 60
Gay's (G. E.) Business Bookkeeping, Single Entry ed ....GI *75 66
—— Double Entry ed....................GI *1 25 1 12
—— Complete ed......................GI *1 55 1 40
Drill-Book in English ....AL 45
Problems in Arith., Bks. 1 and 2, *ea*.....SA 25
Gaynor's (J.L.) Songs of the Child World..CR 1 00
Gazeau's (F.) Ancient History ....SK 40 24
Roman History..........................SK 50 30
History of Middle Ages.................SK 1 00 60
Modern History.........................SK 1 00 60
Ancient and Roman History.........SK 1 00 60
History of the World...................SK 1 50 90
Gee's Nature Knowledge ....MC 1 10
*Geibler's Deutsche Sagen................LN 60
Geikie's Physical Geography .... MC 1 10
Class Book of Geology..................MC 1 10
Gelbach's Das Erste Buch für Schule u. Haus..............................ST 50
—— Zweite ....ST 60
—— Dritte ....ST 70
—— Vierte ....ST 80
Gening's (J. F.) Working Principles of Rhetoric...............................GI *1 55 1 40
Genung's Elements of Rhetoric ....GI *1 40 1 25
Handbook of Rhetorical Analysis...GI *1 25 1 12
Outlines of Rhetoric..................GI *1 10 1 00
Gerfen's Die Deutsche Schule, Course 1..HN 60
—— Course 2.........................HN 60
—— Complete, with Vocab.........HN 1 00
German Readers for American Schools, ed. by I. H. Rosenstengel and E. Dapprich:
No. 1 (Primer)....................... BP 30
" 2..................................BP 40
" 3..................................BP 50
" 4..................................BP 1 00
German Readings, 36 nos. (various prices: 25c., 35c., 50c., 65c.)................AM
German Texts, with Vocab. and Foot notes:
Goethe's Hermann und Dorothea....HS 50
Lessing's Minna von Barnhelm.......HS 50
" Nathan der Weise......... HS 50
" Emilia Galotti.............HS 50
Schiller's Wilhelm Tell ....HS 50
" Der Neffe als Onkel.........HS 50
" Jungfrau von Orleans......HS 50
" Maria Stuart...............HS 50
German Writing-Books, 6 nos ....*ea*.WG 10
Germania Texts (Ed. by A. W. Spanhoofd), 12 v ....*ea*.AM *10
Germanus New Ser.: German Speller.... WG 25
1st German Reader......... ....WG 25
2d " " ....WG 40
Germanus New Series: 3d German Reader..................................WG 35
4th German Reader.................WG 75
Gesenius' Hebrew Lexicon. *See* Robinson; Tregelles.
Getman's Elements of Blowpipe Analysis ....MC 60
Ghegan's Copybooks, 11 nos..........*doz*.KY 80
Gibbens & Beach's Metric System ....PU 50
Gibbon's Rome...........................AM *1 25
Gibson's (J.) Chips from Earth's Crust ..NE 1 25
Monsters of the Sea ....NE 60
Gibson's (J. W.) History of the Civil War...............................FL 60
History of the United States...... ..FL 1 00
Gibson's (W. H.) Blossom Hosts and Insect Guests ....NN 80
*Gibson's Elemen. Treatise on the Calculus.................................MC 1 90
Gide's Political Economy..................HE 2 00
Gideon's Lessons in Language ....EL *40 36
Exercises in English..................EL *50 45
*Giddings's (F.H.) Elements of Sociology.MC 1 10
Inductive Sociology................ ..MC 2 00
Principles of Sociology..... ....MC 3 00
Giese's (W F.) First Book in Spanish ....AP **
Giffin's (W. M.) Civics for Young Americans ....LV *50
Grammar School Algebra............WR *50
Giffin's (W. S.) Supplementary Arithmetic, complete..........................FL 1 00
Gifford's Elementary Lessons in Physics.TH 60
Gilbert (G. K) & Brigham's (A. P.) Introd. to Physical Geography......AP **
Gilbert's (J. H.) Introductory Speller....SA 20
Graded Test Speller....................SA 20
School Studies in Words ....SA 25
Algebra Problems................*doz*.NE 1 44
Series of Number Lessons, 10 nos. " SY 75

Gilbert & Sullivan's Complete Algebra..RN *1 00
Practical Lessons in Algebra.........RN *60
Gilbert's Manual of Business Bookkeeping, School ed.........................SR 1 00
—— Blanks for. ....SR 75
Manual of Business Bookkeeping, Counting House ed.... ....CN 2 50
—— School ed..........................CN 1 00
Gildersleeve's New Latin Primer ....UN 87 75
Latin Grammar, new ed. (Lodge).....UN *1 38 1 20
" " School ed ....UN *92 80
" Reader...... ....UN 83 72
" Exercise-Book .... UN 83 72
Syntax of Classical Greek. Pt. 1....AM *1 50
Persius...................................AM *90
Gildersleeve's Pindar .. ..AM *1 50
Justin Martyr.......... ....AM *1 30
Gildersleeve-Lodge's Latin Composition..UN *87 75
—— Key to...... ....UN *69 60
Gillespie's Treatise on Surveying, New ed. (Staley), v. 1.............. ....AP 2 50
Gillet (J. A.) & Rolfe's (W. J.) Astronomy.AM *1 40
First Bk. in Astronomy, Short Course.AM *1 00
First Bk. in Natural Philosophy......AM *60
High School Natural Philosophy.....AM *1 40
Gillet's (J. A.) Euclidian Geometry......HO 1 25
Elementary Algebra..................HO 1 10
Elementary Algebra, with pt. 2.......HO 1 35
*Gilley's (F. M) Principles of Physics....AL 1 30
Gilman's (A.) First Steps in Eng. Lit....AM *60
First Steps in General History.. .....AM *75
Seven Historic Ages....................BA 1 00 80
Hist. of Am. People....................LR *1 15 1 00
Hist. Readers, No. 1, Discovery of America ....LR *40 36
—— No. 2, Colonization of Am......LR *55 48
—— No. 3, Making of Am. Nation..LR *70 60
Story of Rome...........................FC 1 50
Gilman's (N. P.) Laws of Daily Conduct. HM 1 00
Gilman's (N. P.) and Jackson's (E. P.) Conduct as a Fine Art............HM 1 50
Gilmore's (J. H.) Primary Speaker, pap...SN 25
Intermediate Speaker, pap ....SN 25
Academic Speaker.....................SN 1 00
Outline Studies in English and Amer. Literature........... ....SN 25
Gilmore's (J. T.) Outlines of Rhetoric....LH 90
Gilmore's (M. I.) Lessons in Industrial Drawing................................ED 50
Gilmour's New Catholic National Series:
Primer, pap ....BE 6 3
—— cl...................................BE 15 7½
1st Reader..............................BE 25 12½
2d " ....BE 40 20
3d " .... BE 60 30
4th " .... BE 75 37½
5th " .... BE 1 00 50
6th " .... BE 1 25 62½
Primary Speller........................BE 20 12
Speller and Word Book .... BE 25 15
Ginn's Addition Manual...................GI *10
Ginn's Vertical Writing Books, Large.*doz*.GI 75
—— Small........................ " GI 68
Ginn & Coady's Combined and Number Lang. Less., Teacher's ed.........GI *60 50
Seat Work for Pupils, 1-4 nos......*ea*.GI *10 8
Ginn & Co.'s Classical Atlas, cl. ....GI *2 30 2 00
—— bds..................................GI *1 40 1 25
Ginn's Copybooks:
Tracing Course....................*doz*.GI 60
Writing Books.................... " GI 75
Gist's Lessons in English............... . SR *67 60
Gitbauer's Cæsar's Commentaries, 2 v. *ea*.HR 50
Cornelius Nepos........................HR 40
Platonis Laches..... ....HR 25
Tacitus I............... .. .. HR 50
Glass's Speller..............................MY *20
Glazebrook's (R. T.) Physical Optics .....LN 2 00
Dynamics.... ....MC 1 10
Statics ....MC 90
Hydrostatics . .. .MC 90
Mechanics and Hydrostatics ....MC 2 50
Glazebrook & Shaw's Practical Physics.LN 2 50
Gleason's (C. W.) Gate to the Anabasis...GI *45 40
Gate to Vergil..........................GI *50 45
A Term of Ovid......... ....AM *75
Story of Cyrus..... ....AM *75
Xenophon's Cyropædia........ ....AM *1 25
Gleason (C. W.) and Atherton's (C. S.) First Greek Book...................AM *1 00
—— Key to............................AM *50
Glover's (N. L.) and Harris' (M. A.) Sunshine Melodies.........................LI *40 36
Godard's (H.) Outline Study U. S Hist....RI 50
Goebel's (L.) Deutsches Lesebuch I.......LB 30
—— II ....LB 60
—— new series. II ....DY *45 40
—— III ....DY *45 40

Title	Publisher	Price	Price
Goebel's (L.) Leitfaden für den Deutschen Sprachunterricht I	LB		20
Goethe's Egmont	HO		40
Egmont (Primer)	MC	60	
Faust, pt. 1	HO		48
Faust (Thomas), pt. 1	HE	1 25	1 12
—— Pt. 2	HE	1 65	1 50
Hermann u. Dorothea, vocab	HO		40
Hermann und Dorothea, with vocab.	BS	50	
Hermann and Dorothea (Hatfield)	MC	60	
Hermann and Dorothea (Hewett)	HE	85	75
Italienische Reise (Selected Letters)	MY	*50	
Iphigenie	HO		48
Iphigenie (Eggert)	MC	60	
Iphigenie (Rhoades)	HE	70	60
Götz von Berlichingen	HO		70
Poems (Learned)	MC	**	
Poems (German) Selected	HO		80
*Reineke Fuchs	HO		50
Goff's First Book in Arithmetic	BU	*25	
Elementary Arithmetic	BU	*40	
Complete Arithmetic	BU	*70	
—— Key to	BU	*80	
Arithmetical Problems	BU	*60	
Practical Arithmetic	BU	*60	
—— Key to	BU	*80	
Goho's (S. O.) Pennsylvania Reader	AM	*50	
Goldsmith's Natural History	PL	88	60
*Goldsmith's (P. H.) El Idioma Ingles:			
Libro Primero	GL	40	
" Segundo	GL	36	
" Tercero	GL	40	
Goodale's Botany. *See* Gray.			
Goodell's (T. D.) Greek in English	HO		60
A Greek Grammar	AP	**	
Greek Lessons	HO		1 25
Goodell (T. D.) & Morrison's (F. S.) First Greek Book	AP	**	
Goodeve's Elem. of Mechanics	LN	2 00	
Manual of Mechanics	LN	80	
Principles of Mechanics	LN	2 00	
Goodman's Bookkeeping	HB	1 00	
—— Blanks for	HB	60	
Goodman's Applied Mechanics	LN	**	
Goodrich's (C. A.) Child's U. S. History, bds	BU	*36	
—— cl	BU	*48	
Pictorial History of the World	BU	*1 25	
Goodrich's (S. G.) Am. Child's Pictorial Hist. of U. S	BU	*60	
Pictorial Hist. of England	BU	*1 25	
" " " France	BU	*1 25	
" " " Greece	BU	*1 25	
" " " Rome	BU	*1 25	
" " " U. S	BU	*1 25	
" Natural Hist	BU	*1 25	
Ancient History	MO	1 35	
Modern "	MO	1 35	
Goodwin's (W. W.) Greek Grammar, rev. ed	GI	*1 65	1 50
Greek Moods and Tenses, rev. ed	GI	*2 15	2 00
Greek Reader	GI	*1 65	1 50
Goodwin & White's Greek Selections	GI	*1 65	1 50
New Anabasis	GI	*1 65	1 50
Goodyear's Hist. of Art, illus	BA	3 50	2 80
Goodyear's Roman and Mediæval Art	MC	1 00	
Renaissance and Modern Art	MC	1 00	
Gordy's New Psychology	HS	1 25	
Gordy's (W. F.) Hist. of U. S	SC	1 00	
Gore's (J. H.) Elements of Geodesy	WI	2 50	
Geographical Manual	CS	*1 25	
German Science Reader	HE	*85	75
Gore's Plane and Solid Geometry	LN	1 00	
Gorham & Tower's Laboratory Guide for Dissection of the Cat	SC		1 00
Goss' Course of Bench-work in Wood	GI	*80	70
Gostwick & Harrison's German Literature	HO		2 00
Gouin's System, French Conversation and Grammar, First Bk	HW		60
—— Second Bk	HW		60
—— Complete	HW		1 00
French Facts of Life, pts. 1-3 *ea*	HW		80
Conversations, pts. 1-4 *ea.*	HW		40
——1 vol *ea*	HW		80
German Facts of Life, pt. 1	HW		80
English " " " 1	HW		80
—— pts. 2-3 *ea.*	HW		40
First Lessons	HW		80
Facts and Sentences	HW		65
Gould's (A. W.) Mother Nature's Children	GI	*70	60
Gourley & Hunt's Modern 1st Reader	BU	*30	
Modern 2d Reader	BU	*40	
" 3d "	BU	*50	
" Intermediate Reader	BU	*60	
" Gram. School "	BU	*80	
" Spelling-Book	BU	*20	
Gow's (A. M.) Morals and Manners	AM	*1 00	
Primer of Politeness	LI	*55	
Gowdy's English Grammar	AL	**	
Grabfield & Burn's Chem. Problems	HE	*30	25
Grace's Outlines of History	KY	50	
Graebner's Composition and Grammar	BP	50	38
Græca Minora	LI	*80	
Graff's Elem. German Grammar	ST	75	
—— hf. roan	ST	1 00	
Graham's (A. J.) Standard Phonographic Series:			
Little Teacher	GM	40	28
Synopsis	GM	50	35
Handbook, rev. ed	GM	2 00	1 20
1st Reader	GM	1 25	88
2d "	GM	1 25	88
Dictionary	GM	2 50	2 00
Amanuensis Practice	GM	1 25	88
Unvocalized Cor. Style	GM	50	35
Reporter's List	GM	2 50	2 00
Lady of the Lake, in shorthand	GM	1 50	1 00
Moral Culture, " "	GM	50	35
Brief Longhand	GM	60	45
Phonographic Numerals	GM	15	10
Business Letters (1st and 2d Series), in shorthand *ea.*	GM	50	35
Outlines of Astronomy, in shorthand	GM	35	25
Legend of Sleepy Hollow, in shorthand	GM	20	14
President on the War and the U. S. in 20th Century, in shorthand	GM	15	10
Handbook Writing Exercise Blanks	GM	10	7
Graham's (B.) Common School Arithmetic	GI	*60	50
Graham's (G. F.) English Synonyms	AM	*1 05	
Graham's (J. C.) Elemen. Text-book on the Calculus	SP	2 00	1 67
Graham's (J. W.) Primary Arithmetic	JH	*25	19
Elementary Arithmetic	JH	*35	26
Graham's (R.) Elemen. Algebra	LN	1 50	
Grandgent's Italian Grammar	HE	*85	80
Italian Composition	HE	*65	60
Materials for Fr. Compo., pts. 1-5 *ea.*	HE	*15	12
" " Italian Composition	HE	*65	60
German and English Sounds	GI	*55	50
French Grammar	HE	*65	60
" Lessons and Exercises, No. 1, High Schools	HE	*17	15
Essentials of French Grammar	HE		1 00
French Lessons and Exercises (College) no. 1	HE	*17	15
French Lessons and Exercises (Grammar School) no. 1	HE	*30	25
French Composition	HE		50
Granger's Metric Tables and Problems	BI	25	
Grant's Number Work for Children	LE	50	
Training of the Senses of Children	LE	50	
Graphic System of Object Drawing, Primary, 4 nos *doz.*	LV	*1 20	
—— nos 5, 6, 7 "	LV	*1 80	
—— Teacher's Manual	LV	*40	
Graphic System of Penmanship:			
Grammar Course, 9 nos *doz.*	LV	*96	
Shorter " 6 " "	LV	*72	
Tracing " 2 " "	LV	*72	
Practice Book "	LV	*36	
Blank Writing Book "	LV	*48	
Spelling Blanks "	LV	*48	
Graphic System of Vertical Penmanship:			
Short Course, 8 nos *doz*	LV	*72	
Tracing Course, No. 1 "	LV	*96	
Grammar Course, 7 nos "	LV	*96	
Spelling Blanks "	LV	*48	
Grauert's Zweites Deutsches Lesebuch	ST	65	
Drittes Deutsches Lesebuch	ST	75	
Viertes " "	ST	1 00	
See also Ahn-Grauert.			
Graves' New Graded Spelling Book	GI	*30	25
Graves' (F. P.) Sophocles' Philoctetes	SY		1 00
—— and Hawes' (E. S.) First Book in Greek	SY		1 00
Gray's (Asa) How Plants Behave	AM	*54	
How Plants Grow, with Flora	AM	*80	
Lessons in Botany, rev	AM	*94	
Field, Forest and Garden Botany	AM	*1 44	
School and Field-Book of "	AM	*1 80	
Manual of Botany, rev	AM	*1 62	
Lessons and Manual, 1 v., rev	AM	*2 16	
New Structural Botany	AM	*2 00	
New Physiol. Botany (Goodale)	AM	*2 00	
Gray & Coulter's Western Botany	AM	*2 16	
Greeley's Political Economy	WE	*1 00	
Green's (J. R.) Short History of English People	AM	*1 20	
——	MC	2 25	
Green's (S. G.) Handbook to Greek Testament Grammar		2 50	
Green's (W. H.) Elem. Hebrew Gram	WI	1 25	
Hebrew Grammar	WI	3 00	

Title	Pub.		
Greene's (C. H.) School Music Course, no. 1	WR	*30	
— no. 2	WR	*35	
— " 3	WR	*40	
Greene's (D.) Introd. to Spherical and Practical Astronomy	GI	*1 60	1 50
Greene's (F. B.) First Lessons in English	BU	*36	
Greene's (H. R.) English Language	HM	1 05	
Inductive Language Lessons	LV	*54	
Greene's (S. S.) Introd. to Eng. Grammar	BU	*40	
New Analysis of English Language	BU	*86	
English Grammar	BU	*75	
Greene's (W. H.) Chemistry	LI	*1 00	
Zoölogy	LI	*75	
Greenfield's Greek Test., with Lex.	MR	*75	
Greenleaf's First Less. in Numbers	SA		22
Brief Course in Arithmetic	SA		30
Complete Arithmetic	SA		65
New Primary Arithmetic	SA		18
" Elementary Arithmetic	SA		34
" Practical Arithmetic	SA		60
" Intellectual Arithmetic	SA		30
Manual of Intellectual Arithmetic	SA		30
Common School Arithmetic	SA		60
National Arithmetic	SA		1 00
New Elementary Algebra	SA		1 00
" Higher "	SA		1 34
" Elementary Geometry	SA		75
" Elements of "	SA		1 00
" " " Trigonometry	SA		68
" Geom. and Trigonometry	SA		1 34
Greenough's Satires and Epistles of Horace	GI	*45	40
— with notes	GI	*1 35	1 25
Livy, Bks. 1-2	GI	*45	40
— with notes	GI	*1 35	1 25
Progressive Pamphlets for Learning to Read Latin. No. 1, Eutropius	GI	*25	20
Greenough's & Daniell's Sallust's Catiline	GI	*97	90
Greenough, D'Ooge & Daniell's Cæsar's Gallic War	GI	*1 40	1 25
Second Year Latin Book	GI	*1 40	1 25
Greenough & Kittredge's Virgil, Æneid, I-VI., with vocab	GI	*1 65	1 50
Virgil, Æneid, I-VI., Bucolics, with vocab	GI	*1 75	1 60
Cicero's Orations and Letters	GI	**	
*Greenough & Kittredge's Words and their Ways in English Speech	MC	*1 27	
Greenough & Peck's Livy, Bks. 21-22	GI	*1 35	1 25
— I.-XI., with Bucolics	GI	*1 75	1 60
Greenough & Peck's Livy, Bks. 1, 21, 22	GI	*1 45	1 35
Livy, Bks. 1, 2, 21, 22	GI	*1 60	1 50
Greenwood's (J. M.) Elements of Language and Grammar	SI	*54	48
Studies in English Grammar	SI	*68	60
Gregory's (D. S.) Christian Ethics	EL	*1 25	1 10
Practical Logic	EL	*1 05	95
Gregory's (E. L.) Elements of Plant Anatomy	GI	*1 35	1 25
Gregory's (J. M.) New Political Economy	AM	*1 20	
Grieb's German Dictionary, 2 v.	KO	12 00	
— 2 v.	ST	7 00	
Griel's Glimpses of Nature for Little Folks	HE		30
Griffin's (I. L.) Topical Geography	BI	50	
Griffin's (L. R. F.) Natural Philosophy	SO	1 05	
Notes on Chemistry	SO	75	
Griffin's (W. M.) Gram. School Algebra	WR	*50	
Groesbeck's Bookkeeping, School ed.	EL	*85	75
— Blanks to	EL	*1 10	1 00
— Key to	EL	*80	75
Bookkeeping, College ed.	EL	*1 65	1 50
— Blanks to	EL	*3 00	2 80
Bookkeeping Blanks, Single Entry, 2 bks	EL	45	40
— Double Entry, 3 bks	EL	65	60
Grove's (J. H.) Latin Exercises, new ed.	WL		1 25
Grove's (S. J.) Greek Dictionary	LI	1 80	
Grube's German Stories, pts. 1, 2	ST	40	
Gudeman's (A.) Tacitus' Dialogues and Orations	GI	*3 00	2 75
Tacitus' Dialogues	AL		1 00
" Germania and Agricola	AL		1 40
Gudeman's Tacitus' Agricola	AL		1 00
Outlines of Classical Philology	GI	*1 05	1 00
Latin Literature of the Empire, v. 1, Prose	AM	*1 80	
— v. 2, Poetry	AM	*1 80	
Guerber's (H. A.) Märchen und Erzählungen, Pt. 1	HE	*65	60
— Pt. 2	HE	*70	65
Myths of Greece and Rome	AM	*1 50	
" " Northern Lands	AM	*1 50	
Legends of the Middle Ages	AM	*1 50	
Legends of the Rhine	BA	1 50	
Contes et Légendes, pt. 1	AM	*60	
— pt. 2	AM	*60	

Title	Pub.		
Guerber's H. A.) Story of the Great Republic	AM	*65	
— Thirteen Colonies	AM	*65	
— English	AM	*65	
— Chosen People	AM	*60	
— Greeks	AM	*60	
— Romans	AM	*60	
Guernsey's Skeleton Lessons on Physiology and Hygiene	LR	*15	18
Guides for Science Teaching:			
Agassiz' 1st Less. in Nat. Hist	HE	20	
Crosby's Minerals and Rocks	HE	40	
— cl.	HE	60	
Goodale's Few Common Plants	HE	20	
Hyatt's About Pebbles	HE	10	
" Corals, etc	HE	30	
" Mollusca	HE	30	
" Sponges	HE	20	
" Worms, etc	HE	30	
" Insects	HE	1 25	
Richards' First Lessons in Minerals	HE	10	
Bowditch's Physiology	HE	20	
Clapp's Minerals	HE	30	
Phenix's Lessons in Chemistry	HE	20	
Guilford's (A. B.) Primary Dict. Cards. *set.*	MA	10	
Easy Reading Leaflets	MA	15	
*Guilford's (A. B.) & Lovell's (A.) Guilford Speller	GI	*30	25
Guilford & Ortel's Graphic Reading Leaflets	LV	*20	20
Gulick's (C. B.) Life in Ancient Greece	AP	**	
Gummere's (F. B.) Handbook of Poetics	GI	*1 10	1 00
Surveying	WR	*1 50	
Gunnison (W. B.) and Harley's (W. S.) First Year of Latin	SI	**	
Gummere's (J.) Astronomy	FO	3 00	2 50
Gurney's Handbook of English History	GI	*85	75
Guttmann's Gymnastics of the Voice	WE	1 25	
Guyot Geographical Reader and Primer (Pratt)	AM	*6?	
New Intermediate Geography	AM	*1 00	
Physical Geography	AM	*1 60	
Earth and Man	SC	1 75	
Teachers' Manual of Geography	HW	25	
Haaren's Rhymes and Fables	UN	*14	12
Songs and Stories	UN	*17	15
Fairy Life	UN	*23	20
Ballads and Tales	UN	*29	25
Graded Speller	HE	**	
Habla Vd. Español	HO		40
Hadley's (A. T.) Economics	PU	2 50	
Hadley's (H.) Lessons in Lang., pt. 1	BU	*30	
— pt. 2	BU	*35	
Hadley's (J.) Greek Grammar (Allen)	AM	*1 50	
Brief Hist. of Eng. Language	ME	25	
Hafford's Drill-Book in Elocution	LI	*60	
Hagar's Primary Less. in Numbers	BU	*22	
Elementary Arithmetic	BU	*36	
Common School Arithmetic	BU	*72	
— Key to	BU	*72	
Elementary Algebra	BU	*90	
Hailes' (T. C.) Practical Drawing-Books, Introductory ser., No. 1, 2 ... *doz.*	MY	*1 00	
— Intermediate, 3-6 "	MY	*1 25	
— Advanced, 7, 8, 9 "	MY	*1 25	
— Manual of Drawing	MY	*50	
Haliburton & Norvell's Graded Classics:			
No. 1	JH	30	
" 2	JH	35	
Nos. 3 and 4	JH	**	
Hailmann's (E. L.) Songs, Games, and Rhymes	BO	1 75	
— bds.	BO	1 25	
Hailmann's (W. N.) Elementary German Reader	DH	50	
Literary German Reader	DH	1 00	
Kindergarten Manual, No. 1	BI	75	
" Culture	AM	*60	
Hale's (E. E.) Constructive Rhetoric	HO		1 00
Hale's (G. E.) Little Flower People	GI	*45	40
Hale's (W. G.) & Buck's (C. D.) A Latin Grammar	GI	**	
Hales' Longer English Poems	MC	1 10	
Hall's (A.) Composition Outlines	FL	15	
Hall's (A. G.) Botany	SR	*1 00	90
Common Sense Botany	FL	15	
Drawing Made Easy, 4 nos. ... *ea.*	FL	25	
Hall's (E. H.) and Bergen's (J. Y. jr.) Physics	HO		1 25
Lessons in Physics	HO		65
Hall's (F. H.) Arithmetic of the Farm	SR	*28	25
Helps in History	SR	*22	20
Arithmetic Reader for 2d Grade	SR	*23	20
" " " 3d "	SR	*30	25
Elementary Arithmetic	WR	*35	
Complete Arithmetic	WR	*60	
Hall's (G.) Common Sense of Commercial Arithmetic	MC	60	

Title	Pub.		
Hall & Knight's Algebra for Colleges and Schools New Amer. ed (Sevenoaks)	MC	1 10	
Algebra for Beginners, New Amer. ed. (Sevenoaks)	MC	60	
Hall & Knight's Elements of Algebra	MO	*90	
Higher Algebra	MC	1 90	
Elementary Trigonometry	MO	1 10	
Hall's (H. S.) & Stevens' (F. H.) Euclid's Elements, Bks. 1-6	MO	1 10	
Hall's (J. W.) New Century Primer of Hygiene	AM	*30	
Hall's (L.) Elements of Algebra	AM	*1 00	
—— Key to	AM	*1 00	
Hall's (M. L.) Our World Geog., No. 1	GI	*55	50
Our World Reader, No. 1	GI	*60	50
Hall's (W. D.) Primary Grammar and Composition	RA		35
Practical English Grammar	RA		55
Hall's (W. S.) Mensuration	GI	*55	50
Differential and Integral Calculus	VN		2 25
Hall's (W. S.) Elementary Anatomy, Physiology, and Hygiene	AM	*75	
Halls' (W. S. & J. W.) Intermediate Physiology and Hygiene	AM	*40	
Hallam's (Unabridged Student's):			
Constit. Hist. of Eng., 2 v	AR	2 50	1 66
Literature of Europe, 2 v	AR	2 50	1 66
Middle Ages, 2 v	AR	2 50	1 66
Constitutional Hist. of Eng., abridged	AM	*1 25	
Middle Ages, abridged	AM	*1 25	
Halleck's (R. P.) Psychology and Psychic Culture	AM	*1 25	
History of English Literature	AM	*1 25	
Hallock's Primary and Intermediate Lessons on the Human Body	KE	75	
Halsey's (C. S.) Etymology of Latin and Greek	GI	*1 25	1 12
Halsey's (W. M.) Beginner's Latin	JE	50	
Halsted's (G. B.) Elements of Geometry	WI	1 75	
Metrical Geometry	GI	*1 10	1 00
Synthetic "	WI	1 50	
Ham's (C. H.) Mind and Hand	AM	*1 25	
Hamann's German Echo (Conversation)	KO	90	
Hamer's (M.) Easy Steps in Latin	AM	*75	
Hamill's (S. S.) New Science of Elocution	EA	1 00	
Hamilton's (E. J.) The Perceptionalist (Mental Science)	HS	2 00	
Handbook for the Kindergarten	BO	1 00	
Handbook of Map Drawing	BU	*50	
Handbooks of American Government:			
Wisconsin, by R. G. Thwaites	MC	**	
Minnesota, by F. L. McVey	MC	75	
New York (W. C. Morey)	MC	**	
Handy Literal Translations, 89 vs.:			
Cæsar's Civil War	HS	50	
" Gallic War	HS	50	
Catullus	HS	50	
Cicero's Brutus	HS	50	
" Defence of Roscius	HS	50	
" De Officiis	HS	50	
" On Old Age and Friendship	HS	50	
" On Oratory	HS	50	
" On The Nature of the Gods	HS	50	
" Orations, enl. ed	HS	50	
" Select Letters	HS	50	
" Tusculan Disputations	HS	50	
Cornelius Nepos, complete	HS	50	
Eutropius	HS	50	
Horace, complete	HS	50	
Juvenal's Satires, complete	HS	50	
Livy, Bks. 1 and 2	HS	50	
" Bks. 21 and 22	HS	50	
Lucretius	HS	70	
Martial's Epigrams, pap	HS	50	
Ovid's Metamorphoses, 2 v ......*ea.*	HS	50	
Phaedrus' Fables	HS	50	
Plautus' Captivi, and Mostellaria	HS	50	
" Pseudolus & Miles Gloriosus	HS	50	
" Trinummus, and Menæchmi	HS	50	
Pliny's Select Letters, 2 v ......*ea.*	HS	50	
Quintilian, Bks. 10 and 12	HS	50	
Roman Life in Latin Prose and Verse	HS	50	
Sallust's Catiline, and The Jugurthine War	HS	50	
Seneca On Benefits	HS	50	
Tacitus' Annals, 1st 6 Bks	HS	50	
" On Oratory	HS	50	
" Germany and Agricola	HS	50	
Terence: Andria, Adelphi, Phormio	HS	50	
" Heautontimorumenos	HS	50	
Virgil's Æneid, 1st 6 Bks	HS	50	
" Eclogues and Georgics	HS	50	
Viri Romæ	HS	50	
Æschines' Against Ctesiphon	HS	50	
" Agamemnon	HS	50	
" Prometheus Bound; Seven Against Thebes	HS	50	
Handy Literal Translations, 89 vs.:			
Aristophanes' Clouds	HS	50	
" Birds, and Frogs	HS	50	
Demosthenes' On the Crown	HS	50	
Demosthenes' Olynthiacs and Philippics	HS	50	
Euripides' Alcestis, and Electra	HS	50	
" Bacchantes, and Hercules Furens	HS	50	
" Hecuba, and Andromache	HS	50	
" Iphigenia In Aulis, etc	HS	50	
" Medea	HS	50	
Herodotus, Bks. 6 and 7	HS	50	
" Bk. 8	HS	50	
Homer's Iliad, 1st 6 Bks	HS	50	
" Odyssey, 1st 12 Bks	HS	50	
Isocrates' Panegyric	HS	**	
Lucian's Select Dialogues, 2 v ......*ea.*	HS	50	
Lysias' Orations, complete	HS	50	
Plato's Apology, Crito, and Phaedo	HS	50	
" Gorgias	HS	50	
" Laches, pap	HS	50	
" Protagoras, and Euthyphron	HS	50	
" Republic	HS	**	
Sophocles' Œdipus Tyrannus, Electra, and Antigone	HS	50	
Sophocles' Œdipus Coloneus, pap	HS	50	
Thucydides, 2 v ......*ea*	HS	50	
Xenophon's Anabasis, 1st 4 Bks	HS	50	
" Cyropædia, 2 v ......*ea.*	HS	50	
" Hellenica, Symposium	HS	50	
" Memorabilia, complete	HS	50	
Freytag's Die Journalisten, pap	HS	50	
Goethe's Egmont	HS	50	
" Faust	HS	50	
" Hermann and Dorothea	HS	50	
" Iphigenia In Tauris	HS	50	
Lessing's Emilia Galotti	HS	50	
" Minna von Barnheim	HS	50	
" Nathan the Wise	HS	50	
Schiller's Ballads	HS	50	
" Der Neffe als Onkel	HS	50	
" Maid of Orleans	HS	50	
" Maria Stuart	HS	50	
" William Tell	HS	50	
" Wallenstein's Death	HS	50	
Corneille's Le Cid	HS	50	
Feuillet's Romance of a Poor Young Man	HS	50	
Racine's Athalie	HS	50	
See also McKay's.			
Handy Pieces to Speak, 8 pts ......*ea.*	HS	20	
Handy Series of Dictionaries:			
Spanish-Eng. and Eng.-Spanish	HS	1 00	
Italian-Eng. and Eng.-Italian	HS	1 00	
Hansell's Pract. Penmanship, 8 nos. ..*doz.*	UN	*1 10	96
Tracing Books, 3 nos. "	UN	*64	55
School Hist. of U. S	UN	*70	60
Higher Hist. of U. S	UN	*1 16	1 00
Primary Speller	UN	*15	13
Hanson's (S. C.) Merry Songs	FL	30	
Merry Melodies	FL	15	
New Century Songs	FL	30	
Gems of Song	FL	*30	
Golden Glees	FL	35	
Hanus' (P. H.) Determinants	GI	*1 90	1 80
Geometry	HE	25	
Harding's Greek Inflection	GI	*55	50
Hardter's Erstes Lesebuch	ST	18	
Zweites "	ST	30	
Hardy's (A. S.) Elem. of Quaternions	GI	*2 15	2 00
Analytic Geometry	GI	*1 60	1 50
Elements of the Calculus	GI	*1 60	1 50
Hardy's (I.) Eng. Composition Exercises	HO		80
Harison's Vertical Penmanship Pads. *doz.*	HW	*96	
Vertical Practice Blanks "	HW	*50	
Harkness' (A.) Complete Latin Grammar	AM	*1 25	
Short Latin Grammar	AM	*80	
Latin Grammar (Standard Edition)	AM	*1 12	
Easy Method for Beginners in Latin	AM	*1 20	
First Year in Latin, Complete Course	AM	*1 12	
Introduction to Latin Composition	AM	*1 05	
Introductory Latin Book	AM	*87	
New Latin Reader	AM	*87	
Latin Reader, with Exercises	AM	*1 05	
Arnold's First Latin Book	AM	*1 05	
Second Latin Book, and an Historical Latin Reader	AM	*87	
Cæsar's Commentaries, with Notes and Vocab	AM	*1 20	
Cicero's Orations, with Notes and Vocab	AM	*1 22	
Sallust's Catiline, with Notes and Vocab	AM	*90	
Course in Cæsar, Sallust, and Cicero	AM	*1 40	
First Greek Book, and a Greek Reader	AM	*1 05	

*Harkness (A.) & Forbes's (C. H.) Cæsar's Commentaries on the Gallic War.AM *1 25
Harley's Topical Outlines U. S. Hist......SO 25
Harlow's Introd. to Early Eng. Literature.BI 75
Harper's (W. R.) Elem. of Hebrew.......SC 2
Introd. Method and Manual..........SC 2
" Syntax........................SC 2
" Vocabularies, new ed.........SC 1 00
" New Test. Greek Method......SC 2 00
Harper's (W. R.) & Burgess' (I. B.) Inductive Latin Method...........AM *1 00
—— —— —— —— Primer..........AM *1 00
Inductive Studies in English.........AM *40
Elements of Latin....................AM *1 00
Harper's (W. R.) & Castle's (C. F.) Inductive Greek Primer............AM *1 25
Greek Prose Composition.............AM *75
Harper's (W. R.) & Gallup's (F. A.) Cicero's Select Orations..........AM *1 30
—— —— *Text ed..................AM *40
Harper's (W. R.) & Miller's (F. J.) Vergil's Æneid.......................AM *1 25
Vergil's Æneid and Bucolics.........AM *1 50
Harper's (W. R.) & Tolman's (H. C.) Cæsar's Gallic War..............AM *1 20
—— —— Text only..................AM *40
Harper's (W. R.) & Wallace's (Ja.) Xenophon's Anabasis...................AM *1 50
Harper's (W. R.) & Waters' (W. E.) Inductive Greek Method............AM *1 00
Harpers' 1st Book in Arithmetic.........AM *30
2d Book in Arithmetic...............AM *60
—— Key to........................AM *60
Advanced Arithmetic (French).......AM *60
—— Key to........................AM *60
Harpers' New Graded Copybooks:
Tracing Course, 2 nos...........doz.AM *72
Primary " 7 " .... " AM *72
Grammar " 8 " .... " AM 96
Harpers' Introductory Geography.......AM *48
School Geography....................AM *1 08
Harpers' New 1st Reader...............AM *24
2d Reader...........................AM *36
3d " ....AM *48
4th " ....AM *60
5th " ....AM *90
6th " ....AM *90
Harpers' Dictionary of Classical Literature and Antiquities, 1 v., cl......AM *6 00
—— hf. leath......................AM *8 00
—— 2 v., cl.......................AM *7 00
—— hf. leath......................AM *10 00
Harpers' Greek and Latin Texts, 19 v. ea.AM *50
Harpers' New Greek and Latin Literal Translations, 25 v.............ea.AM *75
Harpers' Latin Dictionary, shp.........AM *6 50
—— Russia.........................AM *10 00
Harpers' School Classics Series, 27 v..ea.AM *30
Harpers' School Speakers:
No. 1, Arbor Day and Memorial Day..AM *60
No. 2, Graded Selections............AM *60
No. 3, Miscellaneous Selections.......AM *60
Harrington's (C. L.) Grammar School Physics..........................AM *50
Harrington's (C. S.) Plautus............AM 90
Harrington's (H. F.) Graded Spelling-Book AM *20
—— pts. 1 and 2...............ea.AM *15
Harrington's (K. P.) Helps to Study of Latin...........................GI *40 35
Harrington's (K. P.) and Tolman's (H. C.) Greek and Roman Mythology, cl..SA 1 00
—— —— —— pap....................SA 40
Harris' (C.) German Composition........HE *60 50
German Lessons......................HE *70 60
" Reader.......................HO 1 00
Harris' (E. I.) Tr. of Two Tragedies of Seneca: Medea; The Daughters of Troy..........................HM 75
Harris's (J. C.) Stories of Georgia.......AM *60
Harrison's (J. A.) French Syntax........CB 2 00 1 50
Story of Greece......................PU 1 50
Harrison's (M.) English Language.......FO 1 50 1 25
Harrison's (W. J.) Science of Home Life, 3 v...........................ea.NE 40
—— Magnetism and Electricity, 3 v., ea.NE 30
—— 3 v. in 1 v.....................NE 75
Harrison & Blackwell's Easy Lessons in French............................CB 1 25 1 00
Harrison & Sharp's Beowolf.............GI *1 25 1 12
Harry's Hippolytus of Euripides.........GI *1 50 1 40
Hart's (A. B.) Formation of the Union..LN 1 25
Source Book Readers.................MC **
Hart's (E.) Chemistry for Beginners.....CP 1 50 1 25
Hart's (H. W.) School Manual of Classic Music..............................HE *1 20 1 00
Hart's (J. M.) Goethe's Faust, pt. 1......PU 1 00
Goethe's Hermann and Dorothea....PU 1 00
" Prose, Sel. from............PU 1 00
Hart's (J. M.) Lessing's Prose, Sel. (White)...........................PU 1 00
Schiller's Piccolomini................PU 1 00
" Ausgewählte Briefe (Buchheim)......................PU 1 00
English Composition..................EL *1 10 1 00
Hart's (J. S.) Essentials Prose Composition.............................EL **
Language Lessons for Beginners....EL *25 20
Elementary English Grammar, rev. ed..................................EL *40 35
English Grammar and Analysis, rev. ed..................................EL *75 65
First Lessons in Composition, cl.....EL *75 65
Composition and Rhetoric, old ed..EL *1 20 1 05
—— new rev. ed....................EL *1 15 1 00
Constitution of United States........EL *50 45
Punctuation..........................EL *55 50
Primary English Grammar...........JH 25 20
Advanced English Grammar.........JH 35 28
Hart's (S.) Persius.......................AL 75
Macleane's Juvenal...................AL 1 10
Cicero's Dream of Scipio.............AL 30
Hartigan's Anatomy and Physiology.....CB 1 25 1 00
Harvey's (A. F.) and Gorton's (E. S.) Atlas Outlines in Eng. Grammar..CS *40
Harvey's (A. N.) Introd. to Study of Zoology..................................AM *88
Harvey's (F. J.) Physical Exercises for Girls...............................LN 1 25
Harvey's (T. W.) Language Lessons (old).AM *20
New English Grammar for Schools..AM *60
Elementary Grammar and Comp., rev..................................AM *42
Practical English Grammar, rev.....AM *65
New Language Lessons..............AM *35
Elementary Grammar (old)..........AM *33
Graded School 1st Reader...........AM *18
" " 2d " ....AM *25
" " 3d " ....AM *36
" " 4th " ....AM *45
" " 5th " ....AM *70
" " Primary Speller.......AM *18
" " Speller................AM *18
Hassard's (J. R. G.) Introductory U. S. History..............................SK 40 24
United States History...............SK 1 50 90
—— Abridged.......................SK 1 00 60
Hastings & Beach's General Physics.....GI *2 95 2 75
Haswell's (C. H.) Mensuration and Practical Geometry...................AM *90
Hatfield's Physiology and Hygiene......EA 1 00
Hathaway's (B. A.) Thousand and One Questions and Answers: Arithmetic—Botany—English Grammar—General History—Geography—Natural Philosophy—Orthography and Reading—Physiology and Hygiene—U. S. History—Botany—Test Examples in Arithmetic, 11 v..............ea.HS 50
Hathaway's Bad English................HS 30
*Primer of Calculus..................MC 1 25
Primer of Quaternions...............MC 70
Haven's (E. O.) Rhetoric.................AM *90
Haven's (J.) Mental Philosophy..........BU *1 44
Moral Philosophy.....................BU *1 28
History of Philosophy................BU *1 44
Hawthorne Classics, 10 nos...........ea.GL 40
Hawthorne 1st Reader....................GL 24
2d Reader............................GL 36
3d " ....GL 48
4th " complete.....................GL 56
—— In 2 pts......................ea.GL 32
5th Reader, complete...................GL 60
—— In 2 pts......................ea.GL 40
Hawthorne & Lemmon's American Literature.................................HE *1 25 1 12
Hayes' (E.) Calculus, with applications...AL 1 20
Hayley's Verse of Terence...............GI *35 30
Alcestis of Euripides.................GI *1 60 1 50
Haynie's Syntax and Analysis...........SR *56 50
Hazen's Complete Speller................GI *30 25
—— pt. 1...........................GI 10
—— pts. 2 & 3......................GI 20
Grade Spellers: Book 1..............GI *20 15
—— Book 2........................GI *40 30
Hazen's Primer and First Reader........BU *20
Second Reader......................BU *35
Third " ....BU *45
Fourth " ....BU *65
Fifth " ....BU *90
First Year Book.....................BU *30
Hazen's Language Series: First Book...SI 40 32
Second Book.........................SI 75 60
Hazzard's (J. C.) Eutropius, with notes and vocab...........................AM *75
Heath's Complete Practical Arithmetic..HE 65
Primary Arithmetic....................HE 25

Heath's English Classics [various prices, from 20c. to 90c.].	HE		
Heath's Home and School Classics, 36 v. (cl., 20c.–35c.; pap., 10c.–15c.)	HE		
Heath's Modern Language Series [var. prices, from 15c. to $1.12].	HE		
Heath's New Ger.-Eng. and Eng.-Ger. Dict.	HE	*1 50	
—— New Fr.-Eng. and Eng.-Fr. Dict.	HE	*1 50	
Heath's Writing Books (Sloping Copies):			
Tracing Course (Haaren) nos. 1-2..*doz.*	HE	*90	72
Primary Tracing Course " 3-6.. "	HE	*90	72
Grammar " " " 7-10. "	HE	*1 12	96
Heatley's & Sloman's Gradatim	LN	50	
Hebel's German Primer	DH	15	
Hecht's History of the Jews	BM	50	
Hedge's (F. H.) German Prepositions	SE	25	
Hedge's (L.) Logic	AR	*60	60
Heerwart's Music for Kindergarten	ST	1 25	
Heffley's Pitman Phonography	AM	*1 25	
Heilprin's (A.) The Earth and Its Story	SI	1 25	1 00
Heilprin's (L.) Reformed Primer and First Reader	BJ	30	24
*Heinemann's (M.) Curso Completo de Arithmética	GI	*80	75
Heller's First Course in German	KO	40	24
Hempl's (G.) Old Eng. Gram. and Reader	HE	**	
Ger. Orthog. and Phonology	GI	*2 10	2 00
Easiest German Reading	GI	*45	40
Hempstead's School Hist. of Arkansas	UN	*1 06	90
Henderson's (C. H.) & Woodhull's Elements of Physics	AP		1 10
Physical Experiments, separately, with blank pages	AP		60
—— without	AP		45
—— with experiments	AP		1 25
Henderson's (J.) Elementary Physics	LN	75	
Henderson's (N. P.) Test Words	MY	*18	
Hendrick's Literature Questions	BI	35	
School History of New York State	BI	75	
Heness's Neue Leitfaden	HO		1 20
Sprechlehrer	HO		1 10
Kinder-Komödien, with notes	HO		48
Henkle's Test Speller	AM	*25	
Henn-Ahn's German Grammar	ST	1 75	
—— 1st Course	ST	65	
—— 2d "	ST	1 00	
—— No. 1	ST	25	
—— No. 2	ST	45	
—— No. 3	ST	45	
—— No. 4	ST	60	
Hennequin's French Verbs	AM	*65	
Idiomatic French	AM	*87	
French Model Auxiliaries	HE		50
See also Duffet.			
Henning's (J. R.) Geog. of Virginia	JH	25	20
Henry's Arithmetical Analysis	NO	1 00	
Henry's Normal U. S. History	HS	1 00	
Henry's (W. H. F.) High School Question Book	HS	1 50	
How to Organize and Conduct a Meeting	HS	75	
Henze's German Copy-Books, 9 nos. .*doz.*	ST	60	
Hepburn's Manual of Rhetoric	AM	*1 00	
Herbermann's Sallust's Jugurtha	AM	*1 12	
Sallust's Catiline, rev. ed	SA		1 00
—— with vocab	SA		90
—— without "	SA		75
Herder's German American Readers:			
First	HR	15	10
Second	HR	25	17
Third	HR	60	40
Fourth	HR	1 00	67
Herding's Petit à Petit	CH	95	
Herdler's Scientific French Reader	GI	*85	75
Herrick's (R.) & Damon's (L. T.) Composition and Rhetoric	SR		1 00
Herrick's (S. B.) Chapters on Plant Life	AM	*60	
The Earth in Past Ages	AM	*60	
Hertwig's (R.) General Principles of Zoölogy	HO		1 60
Text Book of Zoology	HO	**	
*Hessler's (J. C.) & Smith's (A. L.) Essentials of Chemistry, with Laboratory Manual	SA		1 20
Essentials of Chemistry, without Laboratory Manual	SA		1 00
Hewes's (H. F.) Anatomy, Physiology, and Hygiene	AM	*1 00	
Hewett's (E. C.) Psychology	AM	*65	
Hewett's (E. C.) Primary Arithmetic	RA		30
Practical Arithmetic	RA		60
Manual of Arithmetic	RA		50
Speller and Word Study Book	RA		25
Hewett's German Reader for Schools, vocab	MC	1 00	
Hewett's (W. T.) German Grammar for High Schools	MC	**	
Hey's Fabeln für Kinder	HO	*34	30
*Heydrick's (B. A.) How to Study Literature	HS	75	
Heyse's Das Madschen, etc. (Bernhardt)	AM	*30	
L'Arrabbiata (Lentz)	AM	*30	
Hiawatha Primer (Holbrook)	HM	40	
Hibben's Inductive Logic	SC	1 50	
Hickok. *See* Seelye.			
Hicks' Civil Government of Missouri	EL	*55	50
Hicks' (F. C.) History of France	AL		
Higby's (C. D.) Outline of Civil Government	LE	*35	30
Higginson's (T. W.) American Authors	LN		50
Young Folks' Book of Am. Explorers	LN		1 20
" " Hist. of U. S	LN		1 00
Higginson's & Channing's English History for Americans	LN		1 20
Higgs' Algebra Self-Taught	SP	60	45
Higley's (E. H.) Exercises in Gr. Composition	GI	*1 10	1 00
Hill's (A.) 24 Progressive Studies in Painting Flowers, etc	FO	1 00	80
—— Colored, for Teachers	FO	2 00	1 60
Hill's (A. S.) Foundations of Rhetoric	AM	1 00	
Principles of Rhetoric, rev. ed	AM	1 20	
Our English	AM	*80	
Punctuation	SE	25	
Hill's (D. J.) Elements of Rhetoric	BU	*1 00	
Science of Rhetoric	BU	*1 00	
Elements of Logic	BU	*1 00	
Elements of Psychology	BU	*1 28	
Hill's (G. A.) Geom. for Beginners	GI	*1 10	1 00
Lessons in Geometry	GI	*75	70
Hill's (H. B.) Qualitative Analysis	PU	75	
Hill's (W. H.) Ethics	MU	1 25	
Elements of Philosophy	MU	1 25	
Hillard & Campbell's Readers:			
Franklin Primer and 1st Reader	BU	*18	
" 1st Reader (Leigh)	BU	*21	
" 2d "	BU	*30	
" 2d " (Leigh)	BU	*36	
" 3d "	BU	*42	
" 4th "	BU	*54	
" 5th "	BU	*90	
" 6th "	BU	*1 00	
" Adv. Primer and 1st Reader	BU	*20	
" " " " 2d "	BU	*36	
" " " " 3d "	BU	*50	
" " " " 4th "	BU	*60	
Webster-Franklin Prim. and 1st Read.	BU	*18	
" " " " 2d "	BU	*30	
" " " " 3d "	BU	*42	
" " " " 4th "	BU	*54	
" " " " 5th "	BU	*90	
" " " " 6th "	BU	*1 00	
" " Advanced 1st Reader	BU	*20	
" " " 2d "	BU	*36	
" " " 3d "	BU	*50	
" " " 4th "	BU	*60	
Hillerns' (H. v.) Höher als die Kirche (Dauer)	AM	*25	
Höher als die Kirche (Jonas)	AL	50	
Hilliard's (C. E.) Lessons in Botany	JE	1 00	
Himes' (J. A.) Milton's Paradise Lost	AM	*1 20	
Hindman's 1001 Questions and Answers on Botany	BV	50	
Hinds & Noble's Bad English, pap	HS	30	
Bookkeeping Blanks *per set*	HS	30	
Handy Letter Writer	HS	75	
Handy Punctuation	HS	25	
Hebrew Grammar	HS	1 00	
Likes and Opposites (Eng. Synonyms and Antonyms)	HS	50	
New Dialogues and Plays	HS	1 50	
New Greek-Eng. New Testament Lexicon (Berry)	HS	1 00	
New Speller	HS	25	
Pieces for Prize Speaking Contests, vs. 1 and *2 *ea*	HS	1 25	
Recent Civil Service Exam. Ques. and Ans. ("How to Prepare")	HS	2 00	
Recent Entrance Examination Questions, pap	HS	30	
—— Answers to, pap	HS	50	
Two Hundred Lessons Outlined	HS	1 25	
U. S. Constitution, in Ger., Fr., Eng	HS	50	
Hinsdale's (B. A.) American Government, rev. ed	WR	*1 25	
Hist. and Civil Gov't of Ohio	WR	1 00	
Hist. and Civil Gov't of Penn	WR	1 00	
Historiæ Sacræ, Epitome	MU	*30	
Historia Sacræ	BU	*45	
Historical Classic Readings, 10 nos. *ea.*	MY	*12	
History Primers (Green's):			
Europe (Freeman)	AM	*35	
Egypt (Wendel)	AM	*35	

History of Primers (Green's):
France (Yonge)....AM *35
Geography (Grove)....AM *35
Greece (Fyffe)....AM *35
Mediæval Civilization (Adams)....AM *35
Old Greek Life (Mahaffy)....AM *35
Rome (Creighton)....AM *35
Roman Antiquities (Wilkins)....AM *35
" Constitution (Tighe)....AM *35
History of American Flag....HW 25
History of England for the Young....RU 75
Hitchcock's (E. E.) Anatomy, Physiology and Hygiene....AM *1 15
Hjelt's Organic Chemistry....LN 1 75
Hoadley's (G. A.) Brief Course in General Physics....AM *1 20
Hobbs' (C. A.) Academic Arithmetic....LV *1 00
Elements of Plane Geometry....LV 75
Elements of Plane and Solid Geometry....LV 1 25
Hoch's (J. C.) & Bert's (O. F. H.) A New Beginner's Latin Book....HS 1 00
Hodder's Civil Government of Kansas....EL *55 50
Hodgdon's Progressive Course in Vocal Music:
First Book, Pt. 1....SI 24
" " " 2....SI 24
Complete (2 pts. in 1 v.)....SI 36
Teacher's Manual....SI 40
*Hodge's (C. F.) Nature Study and Life....GI *1 65 1 50
Hodge's Linear Perspective....PU 75
Hodges' Scientific German....HE *85 75
Hodgkin's Studies in English Literature....HE *1 10 1 00
Hodskins' L ttle People's Reader....GI *30 24
Hoenshel's (E. J.) Elementary Grammar. CE 30 24
Complete Grammar....CE 50 40
Advanced "....CE 60 48
Key and Manual to Elemen. and Advanced Grammar....*ea.*CE 50 40
Hoff's (J. H. V't.) Chemical Dynamics....CP 2 50 2 00
Hogan's Popular Geology....LV *40
Hogue's (A.) Irregular Verbs of Attic Prose....GI *1 60 1 50
Hohman's Practical Music Course, pt. 2....DS 15
—— pt. 3....DS 15
—— pt. 4....DS 20
Hoitt's Excellent Quotations....LE 75
Holbrook's (A.) Training Lessons in Grammar....AM *40
New English Grammar....AM *65
Holbrook's (Irene) First Latin Lessons....AM *50
Holbrook's (N. M.) Arithmetic....BO 31 28
Holbrook's (R. H.) Gray's Elegy, Annotated....HN 50
—— pap....HN 30
Outlines U. S. Hist....HN 75
Holbrook-Rohrer Bookkeeping....HN 60
Condensed Countinghouse and School....HN 1 50
Complete Countinghouse....HN 3 00
Key to Bookkeeping....HN 1 50
Blanks, 2 v....HN 1 50
Holbrooke's Pliny's Letters....AL 1 00
Holden's (E. S.) The Earth and Sky....AP 28
The Family of the Sun....AP 50
Stories of Great Astronomers....AP 75
Elements of Astronomy....HO 1 20
Holden's Science Reader....MC **
Holder's Zoölogy....AM *1 20
Stories of Animal Life....AM *60
Holgate's (T. F.) Geometry for High Schools....MC **
Holman's (S. W.) Computation Rules and Logarithms....MC 1 00
Holmes' (A.) Demosthenes. *See* Tyler.
Holmes' (G. F.) Primer....UN *9 7
Elementary Spelling-Book....UN *15 13
New 1st Reader....UN *18 16
" 2d "....UN *29 25
" 3d "....UN *46 40
" 4th "....UN *58 50
" 5th "....UN *84 73
Academic, or Sixth Reader....UN *1 15 1 00
Larger First Reader....UN *23 20
English Grammar....UN *64 56
First Lessons in Eng. Gram....UN *42 36
New United States History....UN *1 15 1 00
Holmes' (M. H.) New Drawing-Books, 3 nos....*ea.* BS 25 20
New Drawing Cards, 10 nos....*set.* BS 10
Holmes' (O. W.) Leaflets, pamphlet....HM 30
*Holton Primer....RA 25
Holtzclaw's Wake-Robin Series of Biography: V. 1....PM *30
V. 2....PM *36
V. 3....PM *48
Honey's First Lessons in Linear Perspective....SC 50

Hooker's Child's Book of Nature....AM *1 00
—— pt. 1, Plants....AM *44
—— pt. 2, Animals....AM *44
—— pt. 3, Air, Water, etc....AM *44
Natural History....AM *90
First Book in Chemistry....AM *44
Second " " "....AM *90
Mineralogy and Geology....AM *90
Natural Philosophy....AM *90
Child's Bk. of Common Things....PE 80
New Physiology....BU *1 00
Hoose's Pestallozzian Arith., 1st Year....BI 35
Pestallozzian Teachers' Manual....BI 50
Second Year Arithmetic....BI 50
Hopkins' (A. G.) Tacitus' Germania and Agricola....SA 1 00
Hopkins' (B. J.) Astronomy for Every Day Readers....WE *40
Hopkins' (G. I.) Plane Geometry....HE *85 75
Hopkins' (L. P.) Handbook of the Earth....LE 40
Hopkins' (M.) Law of Love....SC 1 75
Outline Study of Man....SC 1 75
Moral Science....BU *1 12
Hopkins' (W. J.) Preparatory Physics....LN 1 25
Hornbrook's (A. R.) Concrete Geometry....AM *75
Primary Arithmetic....AM *35
Grammar School Arithmetic....AM *65
Primary and Grammar School Arithmetics, Key to....AM *65
Horne's Chemical Experiments....FL 25
Horton's Architecture....HM 1 50
Hosmer's Short History of German Literature....SC 2 00
Hossfeld's New Method:
English-Spanish Grammar....LJ 1 00
—— Key to....LJ 30
Spanish-English Grammar....LJ 1 00
—— Key to....LJ 30
Spanish Composition and Idioms....LJ 75
Conjugation of Spanish Verbs....LJ 15
Spanish Reader....LJ 60
" Dialogues....LJ 45
" Dictionary....LJ 60
English-French Grammar....LJ 1 00
—— Key to....LJ 30
French Reader....LJ 60
Elemen. French Grammar....LJ 30
French-English Dictionary....LJ 30
English-French "....LJ 30
The two dictionaries in 1 v....LJ 60
Advanced French Grammar....LJ 75
French Composition....LJ 75
French Conversations....LJ 45
Conjugation French Verbs....LJ 15
French Dialogues....LJ 45
French and Eng. Vocabulary....LJ 75
English-German Grammar....LJ 1 00
—— Key to....LJ 30
German Composition and Idioms....LJ 75
Conjugation German Verbs....LJ 15
Hossfeld's German Reader....LJ 60
English-German Dictionary....LJ 30
German-English "....LJ 30
The 2 Dictionaries in 1 v....LJ 60
German Dialogues....LJ 45
English-Italian Grammar....LJ 1 00
—— Key to....LJ 30
Italian Composition....LJ 75
Conjugation Italian Verbs....LJ 15
Scotti's Italian Reader....LJ 60
Melzi's Eng.-Italian and Italian.-Eng. Dict....LJ 2 00
Hossfeld's Italian Dictionary....LJ 60
Hotchkiss' (L. S.) Premier Livre de Français....HE 35
Hotchkiss' (V. P.) Lessons in Object Drawing....BI 50
Hotze's First Lessons in Physics....BS 75 60
Questions, etc., in Physics....BS 75 60
—— Answers to....BS 10 8
First Lessons in Physiology....BS 75 60
Houghton's French by Reading....HE *1 25 1 12
Houston's Physical Geography....EL *1 40 1 25
*—— Rev. 12° ed....EL 1 40 1 25
Easy Lessons in Natural Philosophy. EL *45 40
Intermediate " " Rev. EL *70 60
Elements of " " " EL *1 10 1 00
Elements of Chemistry....EL *1 25 1 10
Short Course in Chemistry....EL *90 80
How & Leigh's History of Rome....LN 2 00
How to Become Quick at Figures....HS 1 00
How to Draw Ser.:—Elementary Forms, etc....CA 25
How to Prepare for a Civil Service Examination....HS 2 00
—— abridged ed., pap....HS 50
Howard's (F. E.) Child-Voice in Singing....SI *1 00 75

Title	Pub.	Price	Net
Howard's (T. E.) Primary Grammar	SA		25
Howe's (H. A.) Elements of Descriptive Astronomy	SI	1 75	1 36
Howells's (W. D.) Stories of Ohio	AM	60	
Howells' (W. H.) Dissection of the Dog	HO		1 00
Howison's History of the United States	WY	1 50	
Howland's (G.) Homer's Iliad	MY	*25	
Homer's Odyssey	MY	*25	
Howland's (G. C.) Beginners Book in Italian	SI	**	
Howland's (R. B.) Conic Sections	BE		75
Howliston's Child's Song-Book	AM	*25	
*Hoxie's (C. De F.) Civics for New York State	AM	1 00	
Hoyle's Studies in German Literature: Lessing	SI	*60	48
Hubbard's Merry Songs and Games	ST		2 00
Huddilston's Essentials of New Testament Greek	MO	75	
Hudson's Classical Eng. Reader	GI	*1 10	1 00
Pamphlet Sections of Text-Books, 9 v. *ea.*	GI	*15	
Hudson's Shakespeare's Plays, enl. ed., 23 v. *ea.*	GI	*50	45
—— enl. ed., 23 v., pap. "	GI	*35	30
—— old ed., 15 v. "	GI	*15	
Three Vol. Shakespeare "	GI	*1 40	1 25
Text-Book of Poetry	GI	*1 40	1 25
" " Prose	GI	*1 40	1 25
Hugo's (V.) Ruy Blas, with Notes	HO	*48	40
Hull's Drawing-Book	FL	25	
Hull's Elemen. Arithmetic	BU	*35	
Complete "	BU	*65	
—— Key to	BU	*65	
Mental Arithmetic	BU	*30	
—— Key to	BU	*40	
Complete Algebra	BU	*1 00	
—— Teachers' ed	BU	*1 25	
Elements of Geometry	BU	*1 25	
Hume's History of Eng., abridged	AM	*1 50	
Philosophy (Aikins)	HO		1 00
Humphreys' (L. B.) Art of Reading Music, pt. 1	PD	40	
—— pt. 2	PD	50	
Humphreys' (M. W.) Aristophanes' Clouds	GI	*40	
—— with notes	GI	*1 50	1 40
Antigone of Sophocles	AM	1 50	
Humphreys' Willard's Quintus Curtius	GI	*55	50
Hunt's (E.) Concrete Geometry	HE	*35	30
Hunt's (E. M.) Hygiene	AM	*90	
Hunt's (J. N.) Primary Word Lessons	BU	*15	
Hunt's (L. B.) Light Gymnastics	LE	50	
Hunt's (T. W.) English Prose and Prose Writers	AR	1 20	1 20
Studies in Literature and Style	AR	1 00	1 00
Principles of Written Discourse	AR	1 00	1 00
Hunt's (W.) Italy. *See* Freeman.			
Hunt's (W. M.) Talks on Art. First and Second Series *ea.*	HM	1 00	
Hunter's History Helps	FL	40	
Hunter's (T.) Plane Geometry	AM	*60	
Readings in Hist. of U. S.	AM	*1 00	
Hunter's (S. J.) Elemen. Studies in Insect Life	CE	1 25	1 00
Huntington's (D.) Manual of Fine Arts	BA	1 60	1 20
Huntoon's American Speaker No. 1	NO	45	35
Hurst (J. F.) & Whiting's (H. C.) Seneca	AM	*1 30	
Huss' (H.) Oral German Instruction	HO		1 10
German Reader	HE	80	70
Hussak & Smith's Determination of Minerals	WI	2 00	
Hussey's (W. J.) Logarithmic Tables	AL		1 00
Huston's (W. H.) 100 Less. in Composition	HW	*25	
Hutchison's Laws of Health	MY	*68	
Physiology and Hygiene	MY	*1 10	
Physiology and Hygiene, rev. ed., 1902	MY	**	
First Lessons in Physiol. and Hygiene	MY	*30	
—— First Bk	MY	*40	
—— Second Bk	MY	*60	
Our Wonderful Bodies, First Bk	MY	*30	
" " " Second Bk	MY	*50	
Hutton's (A. J.) Wisconsin	MY	*40	
Hutton's (H. H.) Mensuration	BI	50	
Huxley & Youmans's Physiology	AM	*1 22	
Huxley's & Lee's Lessons in Elemen. Physiology	MC	1 40	
Hyde's Words as They Look and How to Spell Them	WR	*50	
Hyde's (E. W.) Directional Calculus	GI	*2 15	2 00
Hyde's (M. F.) Language Lessons, Bk. 1	HE	*40	35
—— Bk. 2 and Supp	HE	*70	60
—— Bk. 2, Plain	HE	*60	50
—— Supplement only	HE	*35	30
Word Analysis	HE	*12	10
Advanced Lessons in English	HE	*60	50
Lessons in English, Book 2 and Advanced Lessons	HE	*80	70
Hyde's (M. F.) Two Book Course in English, Bk. 1	HE		35
—— Bk. 2	HE		60
Hyde's (W. De W.) Practical Ethics	BO		80
Hydes' (W. D.) School Speaker and Reader	GI	*90	80
Hyslop's Elements of Logic	SC	2 00	1 34
" " " Ethics	SC	2 50	
Hyslop's (J. H.) Logic and Arguments	SC		75
Idioms of Cæsar (Mueller)	HS	25	
Ideal System of Vertical Writing. Juvenile Bks. A and B *doz.*	RN	*62	
Short Course, Nos. 1, 2, 3, 3½ "	RN	*72	
Grammar Course, Nos. 4, 5, 6, 7 "	RN	*90	
Business Forms, No. 8 "	RN	*90	
Ideophonic Text. William Tell	HS	1 00	
Indiana Speaker	NO	*1 00	1 60
Information Readers, 4 nos. *ea.*	BN	*60	50
Ingres' (M.) Cours Complet de Langue Française	UC		1 50
Interlinear Cæsar	MR	1 50	
Cicero	MR	1 50	
Cornelius Nepos	MR	1 50	
Homer's Iliad	MR	1 50	
Horace	MR	1 50	
Juvenal	MR	1 50	
Livy	MR	1 50	
Ovid	MR	1 50	
Sallust	MR	1 50	
Virgil	MR	1 50	
Xenophon's Anabasis	MR	1 50	
Interlinear Translations. New Classic Series:			
Cæsar	HS	1 50	
Cicero's Orations, rev. ed.	HS	1 50	
" On Old Age and Friendship.	HS	1 50	
Cornelius Nepos	HS	1 50	
Horace, complete	HS	1 50	
Juvenal	HS	**	
Livy, Bks. 21 and 22	HS	1 50	
Ovid's Metamorphoses, complete	HS	1 50	
Sallust	HS	1 50	
Virgil's Æneid, 1st 6 Bks, rev. ed	HS	1 50	
" " complete	HS	1 50	
" Eclogues, Georgics, and Last 6 Bks. Æneid	HS	1 50	
Xenophon's Anabasis	HS	1 50	
" Memorabilia	HS	1 50	
Homer's Iliad, 1st 6 Bks, rev. ed	HS	1 50	
Demosthenes' On the Crown	HS	1 50	
New Testament, without notes	HS	1 50	
Greek-English New Testament, with Lex. and Synonyms	HS	4 00	
Hebrew-English Old Testament: v. 1, Genesis and Exodus	HS	4 00	
International Modern Language Series [various prices, from 15 c. to $1.]	GI		
Interstate Primer and 1st Reader (Cyr).	LR	*30	24
2d Reader (Brown)	LR	*40	36
3d " (Lovejoy)	LR	*40	40
Primer Words	LR	*50	40
Little People (Brown)	LR	*10	8
Introduction to Study of Milton	BN		18
To Study of Shakespeare	BN		18
—— and Milton	BN		54
Ireland's Pocket Classical Dictionary	PU	50	
Irish's (C. W.) Qualitative Analysis	AM	*50	
Irish's (F. V.) Gram. and Anal. by Diagrams	AM	*1 25	
Orthography and Orthoepy	IR	50	
Irving's (C.) School Catechisms (Kerney): — Astronomy — Botany — Chemistry—Classical Biography—English History—Grecian Antiquities —Grecian History — Jewish Antiquities—Mythology—Roman Antiquities—Roman Hist., 11 v. *ea.*	MU	*15	12
See also Kerney.			
Ives's (J. W.) Orthoepy and Spelling, 4 pts. *ea*	WA	20	16
Ives's (M. L.) First Book Visible Speech Series	HW		30
Jackman's (W. S.) Nature Study	HO		1 20
Jackman's Nature Study for Grammar Grades	MC	1 00	
Jackson's Vertical Writing-Books, 10 nos *doz.*	HW	*96	
Theory and Practice of Writing	HW	1 00	
Teaching of Writing	HW	36	
*Jackson's (D. C. & J. P.) Elemen. Electricity and Magnetism	MC	1 40	
Jackson's (E. P.) Astronomical Geography	HE	40	
Character Building	HM	1 00	
Jacobs' Practical Speller	GI	*30	25
Jacobs & Piper's Practical Speller	GI	*25	20
Jacoby's (F. C.) Grammar Hand-Book	CE	35	

Jagemann's Materials for German Composition .... HO 90
German Syntax .... HO 80
Jago's Inorganic Chemistry .... LN 80
" " (Advanced) .. LN 1 50
James' (E. J.) and De Garmo's (C.) Students' Speller, rev .... SR 18
*James' (J A.) and Sanford's (A. H.) Government in State and Nation ..... SC 1 00
James' (W.) Psychology .... HO 4 80
—— Briefer Course .... HO 1 60
—— Talks to Teachers .... HO 1 50
German and English Dictionary ..... CH 2 05
James & Grassi's English and Ital. Dictionary .... CH 2 25
Janet's Elements of Morals (Corson) .... AM *1 00
Jannaris's Modern English Greek Dictionary .... AM *2 50
Janon's Recueil de Poésies .... HO 80
Javal's Physiology .... HW 25
Jarvis' (C. H.) Chiming Bells .... SO 38
—— pap .... SO 25
Jebb's Introduction to Homer .... GI *1 25 1 12
Jebbs' Sophocles' Electra .... LN 1 10
Jebb & Mather's Sophocles' Electra ...... AL 1 10
Jeffers' (E. T.) Shortest Road to Cæsar ... HS 75
Jenkins' (O. L.) English Literature ..... MU 1 25
Jenkins' Physiologies .... HE **
Jepson's (B.) Standard Music Reader,
No. 1 .... AM *30
" 2 .... AM *35
" 3 .... AM *50
" 4 .... AM *75
Progressive Music Readers, 3 nos., ea. AM *50
Jepson's (W. L.) Key to Flora of Pacific Slope .... AP **
Jervis' Student's Hist. of France .... AM *1 25
Jess' Arithmetic .... PL 38 25
—— Key to .... PL 75 50
Jevons' (F. B.) Hist. of Greek Literature. SC 2 50
Greek Antiquities .... SC 4 00
Jevons' (W. S.) Elementary Logic .... MC *40
Jewett. *See* Ollendorff.
Jocelyn's (L. P.) Academic Algebra ...... BU **
Johnson's (A. N.) True Juvenile Song-Book .... CR 35
True Singing-School Text-Book ...... CR 60
Johnson's (B. F.) Primer, pap .... JH 10
—— bds .... JH 15
First Reader, bds .... JH 16
—— cl .... JH 20
Second Reader, bds .... JH 25
—— cl .... JH 30
Third Reader .... JH 35
Fourth " .... JH 45
Fifth " .... JH 60
Vertical Writing-Books, 8 nos.:
Nos. 1 to 4 .... ea. JH 4
" 5 " 6 .... " JH 6
" 7 " 8 .... " JH 8
Physical Culture Primary Bk., rev ... JH 35 28
Series of English Classics (various prices, 24c. to 30c.) .... JH
Johnson's (C. F.) English Words .... AM *84
Elements of Literary Criticism ...... AM *80
Outline History of English and American Literature .... AM 1 25
Johnson's (H.) Schiller's Ballads .... HE *65 60
Johnson's (H. C.) Homer's Iliad, 3 bks., with vocab .... AM *1 32
Perseus' Satires .... BA *88 75
Tacitus' Germania and Agricola ..... BA *1 05 90
Johnson's (H. M.) Herodotus .... AM *1 05
Johnson's (J. B.) Surveying .... WI 4 00
Johnson's (S. W.) Fresenius' Qualitative Chemical Analysis .... WI 3 00
Johnson's (W. W.) Curve Tracing .... WI 1 00
Differential Equations .... WI 3 50
Integral Calculus .... WI 1 50
Least Squares .... WI *1 50
Johnson's and Humphrey's Work with Words .... HY 60
Johnston's Hist. up to date, School ed ... BA 1 00
Johnston's (A.) American Politics .... HO 80
U. S. History .... HO 1 00
—— Shorter Course .... HO 95
High School History of U. S .... HO
U. S. Hist. and Constitution .... SC 1 00
Johnston's (A. K.) Hist. Atlas .... SC 1 00
Physical Atlas .... SC 1 00
Political " .... SC 1 00
Quarto " .... SC 40
Six Penny " .... SC 20
Unrivalled " .... SC 2 00
—— bds .... SC 1 40
Unrivalled Classical Atlas .... SC 2 00
—— bds .... SC 1 40
Johnston's (H. W.) Cicero's Orations ..... SR 1 25
Johnston & Browne's Eng. Lit .... UN *1 15 1 00
Johonnot's Geographical Reader .... AM *1 00
Johonnot's Historical Readers:
Grandfather's Stories .... AM *27
Stories of Heroic Deeds .... AM *30
" " Our Country .... AM *40
" " Other Lands .... AM *40
" " the Olden Time .... AM *54
Ten Great Events in History .... AM *54
Johonnot's Natural History Readers:
Cats and Dogs .... AM *17
Friends in Feathers and Fur .... AM *30
Neighbors with Wings and Fins ...... AM *40
Some Curious Flyers, etc .... AM *40
Neighbors with Claws and Hoofs ..... AM *54
Animate World .... AM *1 00
Johonnot's Sentence and Word Book ... AM *24
Johonnot & Bouton's How We Live ...... AM *40
Jolly's Physical Education .... HW 25
Jones' (A. D.) Hebrew Grammar .... DR 1 50
Jones' (D. E.) Sound, Light and Heat .... MC 70
Jones' (E.) First Lessons in Latin, rev. ed .... SR 1 00
Greek Prose Composition, rev. ed .... SR 1 00
Latin " " .... SR 1 00
Jones' (F.) Junior Chemistry .... MC 70
Jones' (G. W.) Drill-Book in Algebra .... JN *1 00 75
Logarithmic Tables .... JN *1 00 75
Drill-Book in Trigonometry .... JN *1 00 75
Four-Place Tables .... JN *5 4
Five-Place Logarithms .... JN *60 45
Jones' (H. C.) Experimental Organic Chemistry .... VN 1 00 75
*Jones' (H. C.) Elements of Physical Chemistry .... MC 4 00
Jones' (H. P.) A German Reader .... AP 1 00
Jones' (J. W.) School Hist. of U. S .... UN *1 16 1 00
Jones' (L. E.) Hist. of U. S. for Young Ams. RU 75
Jordan's (D. S.) Factors in Organic Evolution .... GI *1 50 1 25
Manual of Vertebrates, new ed ...... MG 2 50
Jordan's (D. S.) & Heath's (H.) Animal Forms .... AP 1 20
Jordan's (D. S.) & Kellogg's (V. L.) Animal life .... AP 1 20
Jordan (D. S.), Kellogg & Heath's Animals. A text book of Zoölogy .... AP **
Jouanne's Gender of French Nouns ..... LO 50 40
Joy's Outline History of England .... EA 1 00
Grecian History .... EA 1 00
Joynes' German Reader .... HE *90 75
Minimum French Grammar .... HO 75
Joynes' Meissner's German Grammar ... HE *1 25 1 12
Shorter German Grammar .... HE *90 80
Joynes-Otto's 1st Book in French .... HO 30
Introductory French Lessons .... HO 1 00
" " Reader .... HO 80
1st Book in German .... HO 30
Introductory German Lessons .... HO 75
" " Reader .... HO 95
Translating English into German ... HO 80
—— Key to .... HO 80
Judd's (M. C.) Wigwam Stories .... GI *35
Judd's Classic Myths .... RA **
Judge's Supplementary Third Music Reader .... HE *32 25
Judson's (H. P.) Cæsar's Army .... GI *1 10 1 00
Latin in English, new ed .... HO 1 00
Young American (Civic Reader) ..... MY *60
Government of Illinois .... MY *75
Judson & Bender's Graded Literature Readers: 1st Bk .... MY *25
2d " .... MY *40
3d " .... MY *45
4th " .... MY *50
5th " .... MY *50
6th " .... MY *50
7th " .... MY *50
*8th " .... MY *50
5th and 6th Bks. Combined .... MY *70
7th and 8th Bks. Combined .... MY *70
Julland's Brief Views of U. S. Hist .... BI 35
Junkerman's (G. F.) Songs for Primary Schools, Nos. 1, 2 .... *ea.* CR 10
Kahn's (A.) Hours with Nature, v. 1 ..... PM *20
—— v. 2 .... PM *25
Kaiser's Erstes Lehrbuch .... HO 65
Kant's Philosophy (Watson) .... HO 1 75
Karn's Civil Government of Tennessee ... KL *55 50
Kase's Kleine Anfänge .... JE 75
Kastner's & Atkins' History of French Literature .... HO 1 25
Katzenberg's Phonetic Hebrew Primer BM 12
Keeler and Davis' English Composition .. AL 80
Keene's (H. G.) Literature of France ..... SC 1 00
Keep's (R. P.) Greek Lessons .... AM *1 20
Stories from Herodotus .... AM *90

Keep's (R. P.) Homer's Iliad, Books 1-6, with vocab	AL		1 60
—— Books 1-3, with vocab	AL		1 20
Moods in Greek and Latin, new ed	GI	*80	25
Keetels' Illust. First Book in French	MY	*75	
Elementary French Grammar	MY	*95	
Analytical and Practical French Grammar	MY	*1 50	
Collegiate French Course	MY	*1 50	
Analytical French Reader	MY	*1 25	
New French Method	BU	*1 28	
Oral French Course	BU	*1 28	
—— In 3 pts	ea. BU	*56	
Oral German Method	HO		1 30
Keightley's Mythology of Ancient Greece and Italy	AM	52	
Keigwin's Class-Book of Geometry	HO		1 00
Keiser's Laboratory Work in Chemistry	AM	*50	
Keith's Physics	SE	50	
Keller's Elemen. Perspective	CL	1 00	
Keller's (I.) Bilder aus der Deutschen Litteratur	AM	*75	
First Year in German	AM	*1 00	
Second Year in German	AM	*1 20	
Schreib und Lesefibel	ZI	30	
Kellerman's Elements of Botany	CB	1 25	1 00
Plant Analysis	CB	1 00	80
Elementary Botany	EL	*70	60
Elemen. Botany with Spring Flora	EL	*1 00	90
Practical Studies in Botany	EL	*30	25
Kellogg's First Lessons in Zoölogy	HO	**	
Kellogg's (A. M.) Song Treasures	KE	15	
Kellogg's (B.) English Literature	MY	*1 25	
Rhetoric	MY	*1 05	
—— Key to	MY	*75	
Shakespeare's Plays, 19 v	ea. MY	*30	
Kellogg's (B.) and Reed's (A.) The English Language	MY	*60	
Word-Building	MY	*39	
*Kellogg's (L. B.) and Taylor's (A. R.) Government of the State and Nation	HE		60
Kellogg's (E. M. C.) Australia and the Islands of the Sea	SI	*85	68
Kellogg's (J. H.) First Bk. in Physiology and Hygiene	AM	*40	
Second Bk. in Physiology and Hygiene	AM	*80	
Kellogg's (M.) Cicero's Brutus	GI	*45	40
—— with notes	GI	*1 35	1 25
Kellogg's Elemen. Psychology	KE		25
*Kellogg's Elementary Zoölogy	HO		1 20
Kelly's Short Stories of Our Shy Neighbors	AM	*50	
Kelly's Universal Primer	KL	13	
" 1st Reader	KL	15	
" 2d "	KL	24	
" 3d "	KL	36	
" 4th "	KL	45	
" 5th Reader	KL	60	
Kelly's Reading Speller, 1st Book	KL	18	
" " 2d "	KL	25	
Kelsey's Cæsar	AL		1 25
Cicero de Senectute and de Amicitia	AL		1 20
" " Amicitia	AL		70
" " Senectute	AL		70
Cicero's Orations	AL		1 25
Lucretius	AL		1 75
Greek and Roman Mythology	AL		20
Ovid	AL		1 25
Kelsey & Zenos' Xenophon's Anabasis	AL		1 60
Kendrick's (J. B.) Greek at Sight	GI	*15	
Kendrick & Ritter's Laudamus	DS	1 25	
—— bds	DS	1 00	
Kennedy's (J.) What Words Say, 2 pts	ea. AM	*45	
Stem Dictionary	AM	*1 00	
Kenyon's (W. C.) English Grammar	DA	85	72
Kerl's Language Lessons	AM	*32	
First Lessons in English Grammar	AM	*32	
Common School Grammar	AM	*72	
Comprehensive "	AM	*90	
Composition and Rhetoric	AM	*90	
Kern's (F.) How to Learn German	CN	40	
Kerney's Compendium of History	MU	1 25	
1st Class-Book " " new ed.	MU	75	
Abridgment of Murray's Grammar	MU	25	
Catechism of U. S. History	KI		15
See also Irving.			
Kerr's Bacchae of Euripides	GI	*1 05	1 00
Ketchum's Botany	LI	*1 00	
Kidd's New Elocution and Vocal Culture.	AM	*1 00	
Kiddle's (H.) Short Course in Astronomy	AM	*65	
New Elementary Astronomy	AM	*1 06	
Physics	WO	1 00	
Kilbon's Knife Work in the School-room	BO	1 00	
Elemen. Wood Work	LE	75	
Killick's Handbook to Mill's Logic	LN	1 00	
Kilpatrick's Semi Slant System of Writing, 8 nos	doz GL	66	
Kimball's (A. C.) Exercises in French Composition	HE		55
Materials for French Composition	HE	*15	12
Kimball's (L. G.) Structure of the English Sentence	AM	*75	
Kindergarten School Speaker (German)	WG	50	
King's (C. F.) Picturesque Geography Readers, 5 Books, Bk. 1	LE	*58	50
—— Bk. 2	LE	*83	72
—— Bks. 3, 4 and 5, The Land We Live In, pts. 1, 2 and 3	ea. LE	64	56
King's (D. B.) Latin Pronunciation	GI	*30	25
King's (J. A.) Civil Gov. of Michigan	EL	55	50
King's (W. J.) Normal Outlines, 9 nos.	ea. MA	10	
—— Complete	MA	75	
King & Ficklin's History of Louisiana	UN	*1 15	1 00
Kingsley's (J. S.) Zoölogy	HO		1 20
Vertebrate Zoölogy	HO		3 00
Kinkead's (E. S.) History of Kentucky	AM	*75	
Kirby's Public Speaking and Reading	LE		1 00
Kirk & Belfield's Model 1st Book in Arithmetic	SR	*46	
—— Answers to	SR	*12	10
Model 2d Book in Arithmetic	SR	*51	45
" 3d " " "	SR	*51	45
Revised Model Elem. Arithmetic	SR	*58	50
—— in 3 pts	ea. SR	*24	20
—— Answers to	SR	*12	10
New Model Arithmetic, Complete	SR	*75	65
Key to Model Arithmetics	SR	*70	65
Oral Course in "	SR	*17	15
Kirk's (A.) and Sabin's (A. R.) Oral Arithmetic, 2 pts	ea. AM	25	
Kirkland's (E. S.) 1000 Composition Subjects	HS	25	
Short History of France	MG	1 25	
" " " England	MG	1 25	
" " " English Literature	MG	1 50	
" " " Italy	MG	1 25	
Kirkland's (J. H.) Horace's Satires and Epistles	SA		1 20
Kirkpatrick's Inductive Psychology	KE		80
Kirtland's (J. C., Jr.) Correspondence of Cicero	AM	*50	
Kitchel's Plato's Apology, Crito and part of Phædo	AM	*1 25	
—— Text ed	AM	*30	
Kittredge's (G. L.) & Arnold's (S. L.) The Mother Tongue, Bk. 1	GI	*55	45
—— Bk. 2	GI	*70	60
—— Bk. 3	GI	**	
Klemm's Lese- und Sprachbücher, Kreis 1	HO		25
—— Kreis 2	HO		30
—— " 2, with Vocab	HO		35
—— " 3	HO		35
—— " 3, with Vocab.	HO		40
—— " 4	HO		40
—— " 5	HO		45
—— " 6	HO		50
—— " 7	HO		60
—— " 8 (Literature)	HO		1 20
Poesie für Haus und Schule	PU	1 25	
Klenze's Deutsche Gedichte	HO	*99	90
Kline's (M. A.) Step-ladder	BA	*60	
Kluge's & Lutz's English Etymology	HE	*70	60
Knapp's (C.) Stories from Aulus Gellius	AM	*30	
Knapp's (C.) Vergil's Aeneid	SR	1 50	
Knapp's (J. C.) 1st German Reader	DH	25	
Knapp's (W. I.) French Readings	GI	*90	80
Spanish Grammar	GI	*1 65	1 50
" Readings	GI	*1 65	1 50
Knight's (A. A.) Primer of Botany	GI	*35	30
Knight's (G. W.) Civil Gov. of Ohio	EL	*55	50
Knight's (N.) Quantitative Chemical Analysis	BA	98	80
Knight's (W.) Introd. to Philosophy	SC	**	
Knobel's (E.) Guides in Natural History Study, 8 nos	ea. WD	*50	40
Knoefel's German Primer	DH	15	
2d German Reader	DH	40	
3d " "	DH	60	
4th " "	DH	1 00	
Knoflach's German Simplified, cl	UN	*1 15	1 00
—— 12 nos., with Keys....*sets only*	UN	*1 38	1 20
Knoflach's Spanish Simplified, cl	UN	*1 15	1 00
—— 12 nos., with Keys....*sets only*	UN	*1 38	1 20
German Vertical Writing	IT	10	7
Knopp's Penmanship, 9 nos	doz. BE		70
—— German, 9 nos	" BE		70
Knowlton's Hints for Drawing, etc	HM	1 00	
Knowlton's (F. S.) Nature Songs for Children	BO	1 00	
Knox's (I. C.) Young Folks' History of England	CA	75	
Knox-Heath's Elementary Lessons in English, pt 1	GI	*45	40

Knox-Heath's Elementary Lessons in English, pt. 1, Teacher's ed..........GI *70 60
—— pt. 2..........GI *70 60
—— pt. 2, Teacher's ed..........GI *20 15
Köhler's (F.) Eng. and German Dict..........ST 2 60
Pocket German and Eng. Dict..........ST 55
Koehler & Witter's Pronouncing English Dictionary..........WT 1 00
Pronouncing German Dictionary..........WT 1 00
Kolbe's Inorganic Chemistry..........WI 1 50
Krackowizer's (A. M.) First Reader..........FL 25
Kraus-Boelte's Kindergarten Guide:
No. 1, 1st and 2d Gifts, pap..........ST 35
—— cl..........ST 65
No. 2, 3d to 6th Gifts, pap..........ST 70
—— cl..........ST 1 00
No. 3, 7th Gift, pap..........ST 50
—— cl..........ST 80
No. 4, 8th to 10th Gifts, pap..........ST 70
—— cl..........ST 1 00
No. 5, 11th to 13th Gifts, pap..........ST 70
—— cl..........ST 1 00
No. 6, 1st and 2d Occupation, pap..........ST 50
—— cl..........ST 80
No. 7, 3d and 4th Occupation, pap..........ST 1 00
—— cl..........ST 1 30
No. 8, 5th and 6th Occupation, pap..........ST 50
—— cl..........ST 80
No. 9, 7th and 8th Occupation, pap..........ST 60
—— cl..........ST 90
No. 10, 9th, 10th and 11th Occupation, pap..........ST 50
—— cl..........ST 80
First Volume (The Gifts), pap..........ST 2 00
—— cl..........ST 2 75
Second Volume (The Occupations), pap..........ST 2 25
—— cl..........ST 3 00
Krauskopf & Berkowitz's 1st Union Hebrew Reader..........BM 20
Krauskopf & Berkowitz's 2d Union Hebrew Reader..........BM 35
Krauss' First German Book..........TH 80
German Grammar..........TH 80
Kriege's Kindergarten Rhymes, etc..........ST 1 00
—— pap..........ST 50
Kroeh's (C. F.) Pronunciation of German.......... CH or KH 25
Pronunciation of French.......... CH or KH 35
" " Spanish.......... CH or KH 15
French Verb.......... CH or KH 50
How to Think in French.......... CH or KH 1 00
" " " " German.......... CH or KH 1 50
" " " " Spanish.......... CH or KH 1 50
Three-Year Preparatory Course in French, First Year..........MC 60
—— Teacher's ed..........MC 65
Second Year..........MC 80
Third Year..........MC 1 00
Krohn's Practical Less. in Psychology..........WR *1 25
Krone's Paragon System of Penmanship, Slanting:
" Regular Course, 15 nos. *doz.* KR 70
" Shorter " 4 " " KR 50
" Tracing " 3 " " KR 50
Paragon System of Penmanship, Vertical Ed.:
" Regular Course, 8 nos *doz.* KR 70
" Shorter " 5 " " KR 50
" Tracing " 2 " " KR 50
Modern System of Vertical Writing:
Regular Course, 6 nos. *doz.* KR 70
Paragon German Copy-Books, Slanting:
Regular Course, 10 nos. *doz.* KR 70
Paragon German Copy-Bks, Vertical Ed.:
" Regular Course, 6 nos. *doz.* KR 70
" Shorter " 3 " " KR 50
" Business Letters and Commercial Forms, 2 nos. *doz.* KR 1 20
" Spelling Blanks, 3 " " KR 45
Paragon Series of Drawing Books:
" Elementary Course, 7 nos. *doz.* KR 84
" Advanced Course, 12 nos. *doz.* KR 84
" High School " 8 nos. " KR 1 00
" Drawing Studies, 8 nos. *ea.* KR 40
" Series of Map Drawing Books: 6 books.... *doz.* KR 1 20
Series of Industrial Drawing: Free-hand Outline Drawing, 8 nos. *doz.* KR 1
Geometrical " 4 " " KR 1 00
Perspective " 3 " " KR 1 00
Krout's (M. H.) Alice's Visit to the Hawaiian Islands..........AM *45

Krüger & Smith's German Conversation Book..........HE *4
Krusi's Freehand and Indus. Drawing:
Synthetic Series, 1-4.......... " AM *12
Analytic Series, 5-8.......... " AM *16
Perspective Series, 9-12.......... " AM *21
Synthetic Manual..........AM *33
Analytic " ....AM *60
Perspective " ....AM *40
Drawing Tablets..........AM *12
Textile Designs, 5 nos.......... *ea.* AM *30
Outline and Relief, 5 nos.......... " AM *32
Mechanical Drawing, 5 nos.......... " AM *30
—— in 1 v..........AM *1 60
Architectural Drawing, 9 pts.......... *ea.* AM *36
—— in 1 v..........AM *3 24
Kuhns' (L. O.) French Reader for Beginners..........HO 70
Kuhn's (M. N.) Elements of Spoken French..........AM *20
Kulpe's Outlines of Psychology..........MC 2 60
Kummer's Epitome of English History..........BA *70 60
Kunst's American Dictionary of English and German..........KO 1 00 60
L. L. L.; or, Fifty Law Lessons (Clarke)..........AP 1 25
Labberton's New Historical Atlas and General History..........SI *2 25 2 00
Historical Atlas..........SI *1 40 1 25
*Labiche & Martin's Le Voyage de M. Perrichon (Castegnier)..........AM *35
*La Brète's (R.) Mon Oncle et Mon Curé (White)..........AM *50
Labriola's Italian Echo (Conversation)..........KC 1 00
Lachman's Chemistry..........MC 1 50
Lacombe's Growth of a People..........HO 80
Petite Histoire du Peuple Français..........HO 60
Ladd's Elements of Physiological Psychology..........SC 4 50
—— Outlines of..........SC 2 00
Introd. to Philosophy..........SC 3 00
Psychology, Descriptive and Explanatory..........SC 4 50
Primer of Psychology..........SC 1 00
Philosophy of Mind..........SC 3 00
Ladd's Lotze's Outlines of Æsthetics..........GI *1 00 80
Outlines of Logic..........GI *1 00 80
" " Metaphysics..........GI *1 00 80
" " Philos. of Religion..........GI *1 00 80
" " Pract. Philosophy..........GI *1 00 80
" " Psychology..........GI *1 00 80
" " Descriptive Psychology..........SC 1 50
Ladreyt's French Reader..........LE 1 00
—— in 4 pts.......... *ea.* LE 25
Lageman's German-English Translation, Bks. 1-5.......... *ea.* WG 15
Laidlaw's U. S. Constitution in German, French, and English..........HS 50
Laing's Life of a Bean..........HE 15
Lake English Classics (21 v., various prices, 25c. to 40c. each)..........SR
*Lake French Readings, 3 v.......... *ea.* SR 50
Lakeside Classics (37 v., various prices, 15c.-60c.)..........AN
Lakeside Literature Series:
Bk. 1, Fables and Rhymes, bds..........AM *25
—— cl..........AM *30
Bk. 2, Folk Story and Verse, cl..........AM *40
Bk. 3, Myths of Old Greece, cl..........AM *50
Lambert's Memory Gems..........GI *35 30
Lambert & Sardou's French Verbs..........AR *47 40
Idiomatic Key to French..........AR *1 40 1 20
Lambert's (P. A.) Analytic Geometry..........MC *1 50
Lamberton's Thucydides, Bks. VI., VII..........AM *1 50
La Moille's Favorite Primary Speaker..........FL 20 12
Favorite Intermediate Speaker..........FL 20 12
" Higher Speaker..........FL 25 17
Lamonts' (H.) English Compositions for High Schools..........SC **
Lancaster's English History, revised..........AM *1 00
Lane's Adjustments of Compass, Transit and Level..........GI *33 30
Lane's (G. M.) A Latin Grammar..........AM *1 50
Lane & Morgan's School Latin Grammar..........AM *1 00
Lane's (M. A. L.) Stories for Children..........AM *25
Oriole Stories..........GI *33 28
Lange's German Method for Beginners..........AL 1 00
Langley's Manual of Computation..........LN 1 00
Language Half Blanks, 2 nos.......... *ea.* LV 23 20
Languellier & Monsanto's French Course..........AM *1 45
—— Key to..........AM *90
Laplana's (M.) Latin Syntax, pts 1 and 2. *ea.* HR 70
—— Complete..........HR 1 40
Larned's (J. N.) History of England..........HM 1 25
Laughlin's Elem. of Polit. Economy, rev..........AM *1 20
Study of Political Economy..........AM *60
See also Mill.
Laughlin's New Ideal Copy Books..........MP
Lawrence's (P.) Model Speaker..........EL *1 25 1 10

Lawson's Geography of Coast Lines......BN 35
Geography of River Systems.........BN 35
Outlines of Geography. .. ..BN 90
—— pt. 1, British Isles...............BN 18
—— pt. 2, British Colonies..........BN 18
—— pt. 3, Europe......................BN 27
—— pt. 4, Asia, Africa, Amer.......BN 35
Lawton's (W. C.) Tr. of Three Dramas of Euripides: Alkestis, Medea, Hippolytos.......... ....HM 1 50
*American Literature.... ....GL 1 00
Leach's (O.) Civil Government of N. Y ..SY 35
Learned's (M. D), A German Grammar...AP **
*Leavitt's (R. G.) Outlines of Botany.....AM *1 00
—— with Gray's Field, Forest, etc..AM *1 80
Le Brun's Télémaque......................LI *1 20 1 00
Lochner's (A. R.) Easy Readings in German...............................MY *50
Le Conte's Compend of Geology, rev.....AM *1 20
Elements of Geology, new ed.........AP 4 00
Le Duc's Learning to Draw..............PU 2 00
Lee's (G. C.) Source Book of English History................ ....HO 2 00
Lee's (S. P.) Advanced School Hist. of U. S.................................JH 1 00 80
New School History of the U. S......JH 75 60
—— hf. mor........... ....JH 85 68
New Primary History of the U. S....JH 50 40
Lee & Hadley's English Grammar........BU *65
Lee & Shepard's Graded Lessons in English..... ....LE *40 36
Leete's Exercises in Geography..........LN 40
Lefevre's (A.) Number and Its Algebra..HE 1 25
Leffingwell's Reading-Book of English Classics..........................PU 1 25
Legendre. *See* Davies; Venable.
Legouve & Labiche's La Cigale (Farrer) AM *25
Leigh. *See* Edwards & Webb; Hillard; Monroe.
Leighton's New Greek Lessons...........GI *1 30 1 20
First Steps in Latin......................GI *1 25 1 12
Latin Lessons..........................GI *1 25 1 12
Rome. *See* Anderson.
Lemon's (C. M.) U. S. History Outlined..MA *15
—— cl...............................MA *20
Civil Government Outlined...........MA *10
Geography Outlined ....MA *10
—— cl...... .. ..MA *20
Lempriere's Classical Dictionary, 8°.....LI *2 60
—— ....RU 1 00
Le Row's Practical Reader...............MY *60
Le Row's (C. B.) Pieces for Every Occasion.................................HS 1 25
A Well-Planned Course in Reading...HS 1 00
Le Roy's (S.) French Conversation and Grammar, Pts. 1 and 2........*ea.*HW 60
—— Complete.................... .HW 1 00
Leslie's (E.) High School Book of Song...DS 75
Lesquereux & James' Mosses of North America..............................WD 4 00 3 20
Lessing's Minna v. Barnhelm (Lambert) .AM *50
Minna v. Barnhelm (Wilson) ....AP **
Minna von Barnhelm (Cutting).......MC 60
Emilia Galotti ....HO 80
Emilia Galotti (Winkler)....... .....HE 70 60
Minna v. Barnhelm (Whitney), vocab.HO 60
—— (Nichols), without vocab ......HO 60
Minna von Barnhelm (Primer) with vocab.................................HE 85 75
Nathan der Weise .. ..HO 60
Nathan der Weise (Cunne)............MC 60
Nathen der Weise (Primer) ....HE 1 00 90
Lessing's Minna v. Barnhelm, with vocab ....HS 50
Nathan der Weise, with vocab.......HS 50
Emilia Galotti, with vocab..... ......HS 50
*Lessons on Practical Subjects............HS 50
Lester-Barker's English-Spanish Phonography..................................AM *1 25
Letteris' Hebrew Bible............. .....WI 2 25
Leune's (A.) Difficult Modern French.....GI *85 75
Leusden's Greek and Latin Test..........LI *1 28
Leverett's Juvenal............. ....LI *90
Latin Lexicon.............................LI *2 80
Levermore's & Reddall's Academy Song-Book ....GI *1 10 94
—— abridged ....GI *85 75
Lewis' (C. M.) Beginnings of English Literature................................GI *95 90
Lewis' (C. T.) Latin Dictionary, cl........AM *4 50
—— hf. leath........... .... AM *5 00
—— Elementary . ...AM *2 00
Student's Hist. of Germany..........AM *1 50
Lewis' (E.) Plane and Spherical Trigonometry............ ....WR *1 20
Lewis' (E. H.) First Book in Writing English.............................MC 80
First Manual of Composition..........MC 60

Lewis' (E. H.) Second Manual of English Composition........................ MC 90
*Text Book of Applied English Grammar.................................MC 35
*—— complete.........................MC **
Lewis (L. R.) National School Library of Song, nos. 1 and 2 .... *ea.*GI *60 50
Lewis's Inductive Rhetoric...............HE
Lewis's History and Civil Gov't of Ohio..WR *1
Liddell's History of Rome..................AM *1
Liddell & Scott's Greek-Eng. Lexicon....GI*1 9 40
—— shp AM*1
—— Abridged ....GI 1 25
—— " ....AM
—— Intermediate, cl...............AM 0 [illegible]
—— Intermediate, hf. leath.........AM [illegible]
Lights to Literature by Grades: Eight Bk. Ser., Bk. 1................................RA
Bk. 2....................................RA
Bks. 3, 4, and 5........ ....*ea.*RA
Bk. 6.....................................RA 25
Bks. 7 and 8........... ....*ea.*RA 35
Lights to Literature: Five Book Series, Bk. 1....................... ....RA 25
—— Bk. 2..............................RA 36
—— Bk. 3..................... .RA 48
—— Bk. 4................... .....RA 60
—— Bk. 5.......................... .RA 90
Lilley's (G.) Elements of Algebra...........SI *1 25 1 12
Higher Algebra......... ....SI 1 28
Lincoln's (D. F.) Hygienic Physiology ...GI *90 80
Lincoln's (J. L.) Horace, with notes .....AM *1 22
Livy, with notes.........................AM *1 22
Ovid, with notes and vocab..........AM *1 22
Lind's Easy Experiments in Chemistry and Natural Philosophy..........NO 40
Normal Diacritical Speller... ....NO 20
Lessons in Physiology for Colleges ...ID *1 25 1 00
—— Beginners.......... . ...ID *60 50
Lindsay's (T. B.) Cornelius Nepos, Rev. ed. AM *1 10
—— Text ed...........................AM *40
Satires of Juvenal......................AM *1 00
Sight Slips in Latin, 4 nos ....*ea.*SA 5
Lindsay's & Rollins' Easy Latin Lessons..AL 1 00
Lingard's Hist. of England Abridged...MU 1 50
*Lippincott's Elem. Science Readers:
Pt. 1......................................LI 25
" 2...... ....LI 30
" 3.......................................LI 35
Practical Arithmetic, pt. 1............LI 40
" " " 2............LI 40
" Algebra.......................LI 80
Lippincott's Mental Arithmetic............LI 35
Elementary " ....LI 40
Practical " ....LI 65
Lippincott's Popular Reader, No. 1.......UN *24 20
Popular Reader, No. 2...................UN *40 33
" " " 3...................UN *52 44
" " " 4... ....UN *72 60
" " " 5...................UN *1 08 90
" " " 6 .. ..UN *1 15 1 00
Classic English Reader ....UN *1 15 1 00
Popular Spelling-Book..................UN 24 20
See Davis (E. H.).
Literal Translation: Andocides De Mysteriis ....HS 50
Literature Primers (Green):
American Literature (Watkins)......AM *35
Classical Geography (Tozer)..........AM *35
English Composition (Nichol).........AM *35
" Grammar (Morris)..........AM *35
" " Exercises (Morris & Bowen)...........................AM *35
English Literature (Brooke)..........AM *35
Greek Literature (Jebb)...............AM *35
Homer (Gladstone)......................AM *35
Philology (Peile)...... ....AM *35
Shakespeare (Dowden)..................AM *35
Studies in Bryant (Alden)............AM *35
Little's (G. E.) Illustrative Handbook of Drawing..............................AM *50
Little Folks' Model Arith. (Grube).........SR *23 20
Little Gems of Literature.................AM *36
Little Lessons in Plant Life ....JH 40 32
Little Teacher (Word Method)............AM *10
*Littlejohn's (E. G.) Texas History Stories.JH 50
Livre des Petits Enfants...... ....LO 65 52
Lloyd's Literature for Little Folks......SO *50
—— bds.............................SO *38
Lock and Miller's Trigonometry for Beginners, with tables ....MC 1 10
—— without tables... ....MC 90
Lock's (J. B.) and Scott's (C. A.) Arith....MC 70
Locke's Philosophy (Russell)..............HO 1 00
Lockwood's Angular Copybooks, 6 nos. *doz.*LO 1 50 1 20
Lockwood's (S.) Animal Memoirs, pt. 1, Mammals..........................AM *60
—— pt. 2, Birds.....................AM *60

Lockwood's (S. E. H.) Lessons in English .GI	*1 25	1 12	
*Lockwood (S. E. H.) & Emerson's (M. A.) Composition and Rhetoric.........GI	*1 15	*1 00	
Lockyer's Elementary Astronomy.......AM	*1 22		
Lodeman's Exercises for Translation into German ....AL		50	
Lodge's (A.) Mensuration... ....LN	1 50		
Lodge's (G.) Plato's Gorgias................GI	*1 75	1.65	
Lodge's (H. C.) Ballads and Lyrics..... HM	1 00		
Six Popular Tales, 1st and 2d Series ea.HM	16		
Lodge's (R.) Student's Hist. of Modern Europe ....AM	*1 50		
Loesberg's (J. P.) Gems of German Literature.......................... MS	*40	30	
Loesberg's (J. P.) and Kolbe's (C. F.) German Reader.......................MS	1 00		
Loiseaux's (L. A.) Elementary Spanish Grammar.............................SI			
Elemen. Spanish Reader...... ....SI			
Loiseaux's (L. A.) Spanish Composition...SI			
Loney's (S. L.) Plane Trignometry, pt. 1.MC	1		
— pt. 2.... .. ..MC	1		
— complete..........................MC	1		
Mechanics.......... ....MC	1 90		
Elements of Statics and Dynamics..MC	1 [illegible]		
" " Coördinate Geometry, new ed..................... ......MC	1 40		
Long's (C. C.) New Language Exercises, pt. 1..............................AM	*20		
— pt. 2.............................AM	*25		
Lessons in English ....AM	*35		
Language Exercises, pt. 1...... ......AM	*15		
— pt. 2.............................AM	*20		
— pt. 3.............................AM	*30		
Home Geography........................AM	*25		
Long's (G.) Classical Atlas................BU	*3 20		
Long's (G. V. Z.) Vertical Writing Slips..EL	**		
Model Vertical Series of Copy Books, nos. 1–7............................doz.EL	*80	75	
Long's (H. S.) First Less. in Grammar...LI	*18		
Long's (S. P.) Art: Its Laws, etc.........LE	2 00		
Long's (W. J.) Ways of Wood Folk ....GI	*50	60	
Wilderness Ways..........................GI	*45	50	
Secrets of the Woods ....GI	*60	50	
Longfellow Leaflets, pamphlet..........HM	30		
Longley's Eclectic Phonography.........CL	75		
— pap...... CL	65		
Longley's (I.) Smith Premier Typewriter Instructor ....PH	50		
Yost Typewriter Instructor..........PH	50		
National " " ....PH	50		
Longley's " " ....PH	50		
Longley's (M. V.) Caligraph Lessons.....PH	50		
Remington Typewriter Lessons.... PH	50		
Longmans' Classical Atlas..................LN	2 00		
Longmans' English Classics, 28 v..........LN			
*English Grammar.......... ....LN	65		
*Briefer " ....LN	35		
*Pictorial Geographical Reader......LN	36		
Longmans' French Composition (Bertenshaw & Janau)........................LN	1 00		
— Key to.............................LN	1 50		
Longmans' French Grammar (Bertenshaw), 2 pts. ....ea.LN	30		
— 2 pts. in 1 vol......................LN	60		
Key and Supp. to pts. 1 and 2......ea.LN		75	
— — — to complete in 1 v....LN		1 50	
School Geography.....................LN	1 25		
New School Atlas......................LN	1 50		
Longmans' German Composition, by Ransom.......................................LN	90		
— Key and Supplement to.........LN		1 50	
Longmans' German Dictionary.............LN	90		
Longmans' Ger. Grammar, pts. 1 and 2. ea.LN	50		
— Complete.........................LN	90		
Longmans' Illustrated First German Reading Book and Grammar (Beresford-Webb). ....LN		40	
Longmans' Ill. First Conversation French Reader ....LN	50		
Second French Reader................LN	50		
First Latin " ....LN	40		
" French " ....LN	35		
Longmans' Latin and Greek texts, with Vocab., 34 v., from 15 c. to 30 c..LN			
Longmans' McWilliams' Eng. Lit. 5 pts. ea.LN	30		
— In 1 v..............................LN	1 35		
Longmans' Music Course (Bertenshaw):			
— Pt. 1, Elements of Music.......LN	35		
— Pt. 2, Harmony and Counterpart..............................LN	1 00		
— Pt. 3, Rhythm, Analysis and Musical Form.......................LN	75		
Longmans' Music Course, complete......LN	1 75		
Longmans' New Political and Physical Atlas..............................LN	3 00		
Longmans' New Series of Drawing Bks.:			
Freehand, nos. 1–4...............ea.LN			5
" " 5-6-9-11.......... " LN			8
" Copies, 4 Bks.......... " LN			8
Geometry, Drawing to Scale, Bk. 7...LN			5
" Practical Plane, Bk. 8....LN			8
" " " Bk. 14...LN			10
" Solid, Bk. 10................LN			10
" " Bk. 15............... LN			15
Longmans' Object Lessons in Elementary Science (Woodhull)..........LN	1 10		
Longmans' Salmon's School Grammar...LN	75		
— — Primary " " ..LN	35		
— — School Composition.......LN	30		
— — Junior School Composition..............................LN	30		
Modern Copy-Books, 13 nos . .. doz.LN	60		
Longmans' School Mensuration.........LN	80		
Longmans' "Ship" Literary Readers:			
First Primer..........................LN	12		
Second " ....LN	12		
Infant Reader.........................LN	15		
Book 1................................LN	25		
" 2.............................LN	25		
" 3.............................LN	35		
" 4.............................LN	40		
" 5.............................LN	45		
" 6.............................LN	45		
Advanced Reader......................LN	60		
Longmans' Simple Stories from English History..............................LN	50		
Longwell's Outline of Eng. and Am. Literature..........................NO	35		
Loomis' (E.) Elements of Algebra........AM	*90		
— Key to.........................AM	*90		
Algebraic Problems....................AM	*90		
Treatise on Algebra...................AM	*1 00		
— Key to.........................AM	*1 00		
Trigonometry, Surveying, and Navigation..............................AM	*1 00		
Tables of Logarithms ....AM	*1 00		
Trigonometry and Tables... ....AM	*1 50		
Analytical Geometry..................AM	*1 00		
Calculus ....AM	*1 00		
Anal. Geom. and Calculus............AM	*1 75		
Elements of Astronomy...............AM	*1 00		
Practical " ....AM	*1 50		
Treatise on Meteorology ....AM	*1 50		
Loomis' (G. B.) Progressive Music Lessons, Bk. 1............................AM	*14		
— Bk. 2............................AM	*18		
— Bk. 3............................AM	*25		
— Bk. 4............................AM	*48		
— Bk. 5............................AM	*72		
Prog. Glee and Chorus Book.........AM	*84		
Lopes & Bensley's Span.-Eng. and Eng.-Span. Dict ....CH	7 00		
Lord's (F. E.) Roman Pronunciation of Latin..................................GI	*40	85	
Lord's (J.) Modern History...............MR	1 25		
Lord's (J. K.) Cicero's Laelius, Rev......AM	*70		
Livy, Bks. 21 and 22.....................SA		1 25	
— Text ed., pap......................SA		25	
— Bk. 1............ ....SA		30	
— Bks. 1, 21, 22:.....................SA		1 20	
*Lord's (J K) Atlas of the Geography and History of the Ancient World, cl......... .... SA		1 50	
pap...... .. ..SA		75	
Lossing's Outline U. S. Hist...............BU	*92		
Lossing's School U. S. Hist ....BU	*1 28		
Louage's Moral Philosophy...............KY		75	
Lounsbury's English Language..........HO		1 12	
— pt. 1...............................HO		90	
Lovejoy (M. I.). *See* Interstate.			
Low's Solid Geometry, pt. 1..............LN	60		
— pt. 2 ....LN	90		
Lowe's (C. M.) and Butler's (N.) Bellum Helveticum, rev ed.................SR		1 00	
Lowe's (C. M.) and Ewing's (J. T.) Cæsar's Gallic War.........................SR		1 25	
Lowe and Wyatt's Intermediate Eng. Lit., pt. 2 ....HS	1 00		
Lowell Leaflets, pamphlet................HM	30		
Lowry's Elem. of Civil Government......UN	*58	50	
Lowry & McCardle's Hist. of Miss.......UN	*1 15	1 00	
Lowson's Text-Book of Botany......... .HS	1 60		
Lubbock's (J.) Popular Natural Hist....WK	60	45	
Ludden's School Lyrics ....CR	75		
Lucian-Selections........................HW	35		
Lueken's German Primer................BP	25	20	
German Copy-Books, 6 nos. doz. ......BP	60	50	
" Grammar, pt. 1 ....WT	20		
" " pt. 2 ....WT	30		
Lupton's Concise English History. ....HO	1 50		
Lutz's (F.) Elemen. German Reader......SI	**		
Lyell's (C.) Elements of Geology, rev....AM	*2 25		
Lyman's (A. B) Comprehensive French-English Dictionary................JE	**		

Lyman's (E. A.) & Goddard's (E. C.) Computation Tables..............AL		50
Plane and Spherical Trigonometry and Computation Tables..........AL		1 12
Plane and Spherical Trigonometry...AL		90
Lyman's (F. A.) Normal Music Course in the Schoolroom............ .. ..SI		1 25
Lyman's Geometry Exercises. ......*doz.*HE		1 60
Lynd's New First Book in Etymology.... FO	60	50
Class-Book of Etymology.... ....FO	1 00	85
Lyon and Larpent's Primary French Translation Book. ....HE	*70	60
Lyons' American Elocutionist ....BU	*1 15	
Lyte's Bookkeeping...... ....SO	*75	
—— Blanks for, 2 sets............*ea.*SO	*60	
Elementary English ....AM	*35	
Elements of Grammar and Composition...............................AM	*50	
Advanced Grammar and Composition ....AM	*75	
English Grammar and Composition..AM	*65	
Macarthur's Scotland. *See* Freeman.		
Macbride's Elementary Botany ....AL		80
McBride's (J. M. J.) First School Reader.MD		15
First Reader.............................MD		18
Second " ....MD		17
Third " ....MD		20
Fourth " ....MD		25
Fifth " .... MD		40
Elementary Geography..............MD		**
Grammar School Geography.........MD		**
Macbride's Key to Plants................AL		25
MacCabe's (J.A.) Language and Grammar Lessons ....GI	*35	30
McCabe's (W. G.) Bingham's Cæsar......BU	*1 08	
Bingham's Latin Grammar...........BU	*1 08	
" " Reader ....BU	*1 08	
McCarthy's Outlines of Irish History...MU	50	
McCaskey's (J. P.) Lincoln Literary Collection.... ....AM	*1 00	
—— Favorite Songs and Hymns...AM	*80	
McCleary's Studies in Civics.............AM	*1 00	
Manual of Civics.......................AM	*1 00	
MacCord's (C. W.) Mechanical Drawing..WI	4 00	
McCormick's Practical Work in Geography...............................FL	75	
McCorvey's Civil Gov't of Alabama......EL	*55	50
McCosh's Logic. ....SC	1 50	
Psychology, 2 v.................. .*ea.*SC	1 50	
MacCoun's Hist. Geog. of U. S............SI	*1 00	90
McCurdy's (M.) Exercise-Bk. in Algebra ....HE		60
MacDonald's Plane Geometry......... . AL		80
Primary Algebra......... ....AL		30
Primary Algebra and Teacher's Guide...... ... .AL		75
*McDougall's (F C) Key to Common Plants of Eastern U. S............WP		2 50
—— with index to Genera, etc.. ..WP		30
*MacDougal's Elem. Plant Physiology..LN	1 90	
*Text-book of Plant Physiology... . LN	3 00	
McElroy's English Etymology ....CB		60
Structure of English Prose, rev. ed..AR	1 20	
McEwen's (J.) Latin Tests . ...NE	75	
Macfarlane's (A.) Elem Math. Tables....GI	*65	75
McGee's (G. R.) History of Tennessee....AM	*75	
McGranahan & Lafferty's Juvenile Class and Concert.........................CR	30	
McGuffey's Revised Eclectic Primer, pap...........................*doz.*AM	*1 00	
—— bds......................... " AM	*1 50	
Small Eclectic Primer..........*gross.*AM	*4 50	
Thin Eclectic Primer............*doz.*AM	*75	
Thick Eclectic Primer............*doz.*AM	*1 00	
Revised 1st Eclectic Reader..........AM	*17	
" 2d " " ....AM	*30	
" 3d " " ....AM	*42	
" 4th " " ....AM	*50	
" 5th " " ....AM	*72	
" 6th " " ....AM	*85	
Revised High School Reader..........AM	*85	
Revised First Eclectic Reader, Spanish-English ed......................AM	*32	
Word List ....AM	*10	
Revised Eclectic Spelling Book......AM	*17	
1st Eclectic Reader, old..............AM	*18	
2d " " " ....AM	*25	
3d " " " ....AM	*36	
4th " " " ....AM	*45	
5th " " " ....AM	*70	
Alternate Primer......................AM	*10	
" 1st Reader ....AM	*12	
" 2d " ....AM	*20	
" 3d " .... AM	*30	
" 4th " ....AM	*40	
" 5th " ....AM	*50	
" 6th " ....AM	*60	
" Spelling-Book..............AM	*12	
New Juvenile Speaker...............AM	*40	
McGuffey's New Eclectic Speaker........AM	*60	
New McGuffey Readers: First Reader.................................AM	*17	
Second Reader.........................AM	*30	
Third " ....AM	*40	
Fourth " ....AM	*50	
Fifth " ....AM	*60	
McGuffey's Natural History Readers:		
Familiar Animals...................AM	*50	
Living Creatures...................AM	*50	
MacGunn's (T.) Historical Geography of the U. S..........................SI	90	
McHenry & Davidson's Arithmetical Problems ....WR	*60	
McHenry's (O.) Practical Lessons and Exercises in Grammar...........AM	50	
McIlvaine's Elocution ....SC	1 75	
Mackail's Latin Literature ....SC		1 25
McKay's Handy Literal Translations:		
Cæsar's Commentaries, 6 Bks........MR	50	
Cicero's Defence of Roscius.......... MR	50	
" On Old Age and Friendship.MR	50	
" On Oratory...................MR	50	
" Select Orations..............MR	50	
" Select Letters...............MR	50	
Cornelius Nepos, complete...........MR	50	
Horace, complete......................MR	50	
Juvenal's Satires, complete..........MR	50	
Livy, Bks. 1 and 2.....................MR	50	
" " 21 and 22..................MR	50	
Ovid's Metamorphoses, Bks. 1-7......MR	50	
" " " 8-15.....MR	50	
Plautus' Captivi and Mostellaria......MR	50	
Sallust's Catiline and The Jugurthine War...................................MR	50	
Tacitus' Annals, first 6 Bks..........MR	50	
" Germany and Agricola......MR	50	
Virgil's Æneid, 6 Bks.................MR	50	
" Eclogues and Georgics.......MR	50	
Viri Romæ.............................MR	50	
Æschylus' Prometheus Bound and Seven Against Thebes............MR	50	
Aristophanes' Clouds, Birds, and Frogs, in 1 v. ....MR	50	
Demosthenes' On the Crown..........MR	50	
" Olynthiacs and Philippics ....MR	50	
Euripides' Alcestis and Electra......MR	50	
" Medea.....................MR	50	
Herodotus, Bks. 6 and 7...............MR	50	
Homer's Iliad, 9 Bks...................MR	50	
" Odyssey, 12 Bks..............MR	50	
Lysias' Select Orations................MR	50	
Plato's Apology, Crito and Phædo... MR	50	
" Gorgias ....MR	50	
Sophocles' Œdipus Tyrannus, Electra, and Antigone .... MR	50	
Xenophon's Anabasis, 5 Bks...........MR	50	
" Memorabilia, complete..MR	50	
Goethe's Egmont........ ....MR	50	
" Faust ....MR	50	
" Hermann and Dorothea....MR	50	
Lessing's Minna von Barnhelm ....MR	50	
" Nathan the Wise ....MR	50	
Schiller's Maid of Orleans............MR	50	
" Maria Stuart...............MR	50	
" William Tell...............MR	50	
See also Handy Literal Translations.		
McKay's 100 Experiments in Natural Science.. ....BI	15	
*Mackenzie's Outlines of Metaphysics...MC	1 10	
Mackenzie's (Ja.) History of Scotland ..NE	1 50	
Mackenzie's (J. S.) Manual of Ethics.....HS	1 50	
Mackenzie's (R.) America................NE	1 00	
Nineteenth Century..................NE	1 00	
Maclardy's (A. A.) Completely Scanned-Parsed Vergil's Æneid, Bk. 1.....HS	1 50	
Completely Parsed Cicero. Pts. 1 and 2............... ....*ea.*HS	1 50	
McLauchlin's (J. A.) Pensa Prima Latina JH	1 25	1 00
McLaughlin's (E. T.) Literary Criticism..HO		1 00
McLaughlin's Hist. of the American Nation.................... ....AP		1 40
McLaughlin & Veazie's. *See* National.		
McLaurin's Ladies' Angular Penmanship, 6 nos...........................*doz.*AM	*1 20	
MacLean's An Old and Middle English Reader. Based on Zupitza.......MC	2 00	
Macleane. *See* Chase; Hart.		
McLellan's Applied Psychology..........ED	1 25	
*McLellan & Ames' Public School Arithmetic, for Grammar Grades.. ..MC	60	
Primary Arithmetic....................MC	35	
——Teachers' ed.....................MC	50	
Mental Arithmetic ....MC	25	
MacLeod's Common Minerals............MA	25	
Composition Outlines.... ....MA	30	
Talks About Common Things.........FL	35	
Paper Folding and Cutting............MA	40	

Title	Publisher	Price	Price
MacLeod's Practical Drill Problems, 4 sets.........*per set.*	MA	15	
Macloskie's Elementary Botany..........	HO		1 30
McMahan's Hints on Letter-Writing....	BE	60	36
McMahon (J.) and Snyder's (V.) Differential Calculus..................	AM	*2 00	
McMaster's (J. B.) School Hist. of United States..........................	AM	*1 00	
Primary History of U. S...............	AM	**	
Macmillan's Classical Series, about 53 v., from 53 c. to $2.60	MC		
Macmillan's Elem. Classics, about 53 v., *ea.*, 40c.	MC		
Macmillan's Foreign School Classics, French and German (Fasnacht), 25 v., from 30 c. to $1.10..........	MC		
Macmillan's French Classics. (60 c. to 90 c.)..................................	MC		
Macmillan's German Classics.........*ea.*	MC	60	
——Double Nos	MC	1 00	
Macmillan's Latin Series:			
Barss's (J. E.) Cornelius Nepos	MC	90	
Macmillan's Pocket Series of English and American Classics ....*ea.*	MC	25	
Macmillan's Progressive French Composition:			
First Year	MC	60	
Second Year.........................	MC	1 10	
Macmillan's Progressive French Course (Fasnacht):			
1st Year..............................	MC	80	
——Teachers' Companion to.......	MC	1 10	
2d Year...............................	MC	55	
—— Teacher's Companion to.......	MC	1 10	
3d Year......................	MC	65	
—— Teacher's Companion to.......	MC	1 10	
Macmillan's Progressive French Reader (Fasnacht):			
1st Year...	MC	65	
2d "	MC	65	
Macmillan's Progressive German Course (Fasnacht):			
1st Year	MC	85	
—— Teacher's Companion to.......	MC	1 10	
2d Year..............................	MC	90	
—— Teacher's Companion to.......	MC	1 10	
*3d Year	MC	**	
Macmillan's Progressive German Reader (Fasnacht):			
1st Year	MC	65	
McMillan & Smith's Topographical Draw.	WI	2 50	
McMurrich's (J. P.) Invertebrate Morphology........................	HO	3 00	
McMurry's (C. A.) Special Method in History and Literature.	PS	*85	
—— —— —— Natural Science	PS	*50	
—— —— —— Geography	PS	*50	
General Method........................	PS	*75	
Pioneer History Stories...............	PS	*50	
—— bds............................		*40	
McMurry's (L. B.) Classic Stories, Teachers' ed..............................	PS	*40	
Pupils' ed..............................	PS	*35	
McNally's Geographies. *See* Monteith.			
System of Geography, new ed..... .	AM	*1 00	
McNeill's (I. C.) and Lynch's (S. A.) Introd. Lessons in English Literature................................	AM	*1 00	
Macnie's Algebraic equations............	BA		1 20
McPherson's Civil Gov't of Ga......	EL	*55	50
Macvane's Political Economy...........	MY	*1 65	
MacVicar's Elementary Arithmetic......	BU	*30	
Complete Arithmetic................	BU	*90	
—— Key to...........................	BU	*80	
McVicar's Am. Spelling Blanks......*doz.*	AM	*42	
McWilliams. *See* Longmans.			
Macy's Our Government, rev. ed.........	GI	*85	75
First Lessons in Civil Government...	GI	70	60
Macy's (M. L.) General Physiology for High Schools	AM	*1 10	
Maertz's Study of Eng. Literature.......	SI	*88	75
—— Key to...................... ..	SI	*50	
Magill's (E. H.) Reading French Grammar.	SO	60	48
Irregular French Verbs...............	SO	20	
Modern French Series, 4 nos.......*ea.*	SO	60	48
Magill's (W.) Inductive Less. in Science.	NE	30	
Magnenat's French Practical Course.....	MC	1 00	
—— Key..........	MC	25	
Magnus' Elementary Mechanics..........	LN	1 20	
Mahan's (A.) Mental Philosophy	SI	*1 12	1 00
Mahan's (D. H.) Industrial Drawing......	WI	3 50	
Maidment & Mill's Higher Latin Reader..	HS	50	
Maierstein's First Less. in German......	DH	30	
Maine's Scholars' Manual..............	MM		25
Mairet's La Tâche du Petit Pierre (Healy)	AM	*35	
L'Enfant de la Lune (Healy).........	AM	*35	
Manatt's Xenophon's Hellenica, Bks. 1–4.	GI	*45	40
—— with notes.......................	GI	*1 75	1 65
Manheimer's Hebrew Reader and Grammar....................	BM	1 50	
Manly's (L.) Southern Literature.........	JH	1 00	80
Mann's (E. C.) Rights and Duties of American Citizens	HW		75
Mann's (W.) Model Drawing.............	NE	1 50	
Manning's (E. W.) Spanish Grammar....	HO		1 00
Manning's (H. P.) Non-Euclidean Geometry	GI	*80	75
Mansfield's Political Manual.	BA	*1 05	90
Manson's Elem. Writing Speller. ..*doz.*	AM	*42	
Writing Speller, Nos. 1–3 .... "	AM	*48	
Model Spelling Blank............. "	AM	*65	
Economic Spelling Blank........ "	AM	*42	
Mantilla's Spanish Conversation...	LO	65	52
Spanish Reader, No. 1................	AM	*15	
—— No. 2..............................	AM	*54	
—— No. 3..............................	AM	*67	
Historia Universal.....................	AM	*90	
Manton's Handbook of Zoölogy..........	LE		40
Manus' Civil Government.................	HW	*75	60
March's (F. A.) Parser and Analyzer	AM	*85	
Anglo-Saxon Grammar................	AM	*1 80	
Anglo-Saxon Reader.................	AM	*1 10	
Latin Hymns........	AM	*1 30	
Tertullian..........................	AM	*1 30	
Eusebius	AM	*1 30	
Marion's (H.) Le Verbe en Quatre Tableaux Synoptiques...............	JB	25	
Maris' Normal Grammar.........	EL	50	
Markham's History of England..........	AM	*1 05	
Markwick's (W. F.) & Smith's (W. A.) The True Citizen	AM	*60	
Marlborough French Grammar...........	CA	1 00	
German Grammar....................	CA	1 25	
French Exercsies, Rev. ed............	CA	1 25	
Marsh's (A. J.) New Phonetic Short-Hand	WA	2 00	1 60
Marsh's (G. P.) Earth as Modified by Human Action........................	SC	3 50	
Lectures on Eng. Language..........	SC	3 50	
Origin and Hist. of Eng. Lang.........	SC	3 50	
Marsh & Ashton's Elementary Algebra..	SC	**	
Marshall & Hurst's Junior Course in Zoölogy	PU	3 50	
Martin's (G. H.) Civil Government, rev.	AM	*90	
Martin's (H. N.) Human Body, Special ed.................................	HO		1 20
See American Sci. Ser.; Dulany.			
Martindale's Anatomy, Physiology, and Hygiene	EL	*1 10	1 00
First Lessons in Nat. Philos	EL	*45	40
Martyn's (L. S.) Multiplication Chart and Gesture Drill.....................	UL	35	25
Mason's (H. L.) Students' Readings and Questions in English Literature..	MC	40	
Mason's (L.) Song Garden, Bk. 1.........	DS	50	
—— Bk. 2..............................	DS	80	
—— Bk. 3..............................	DS	1 00	
Mason's (L. W.) Music. *See* National.			
Mason's (L. W.) School Music Course, Bk. 1..............................	GI	*30	25
—— Bk. 2..............................	GI	*40	35
Mason's (L. W.) and Veazie's (G. A.) New Fourth Music Reader	GI	*1 05	90
Mason's (W. P.) Qualitative Analysis	CP	80	64
Mason's (S. W.) Gymnastic Exercises....	DW	40	
Mason & Lalor's Polit. Econ. Primer......	MG	60	
Masson's French Dictionary............	MC	1 00	
Masterpieces of American Literature....	HM	1 00	
—— of British Literature...........	HM	1 00	
—— of Greek Literature............	HM	1 00	**
—— of Latin Literature.............	HM	1 00	**
Mather's Æschylus' Prometheus........	AL		1 00
Herodotus and Thucydides...........	AL		90
Electra of Sophocles................	AL		1 10
Mather's (I. L.) Making of Illinois........	FL	*1 00	
—— Pupil's ed.........................	FL	*50	
Mather's (M. W.) & Wheeler's (A. L.) Passages for Latin Prose Writing..................................	AM	*1 00	
Key to Latin Prose Writings........	AM	*50	
Mathews' (H.) English Grammar	HE	*80	70
Mathews's (O. S. B.) Songs of All Lands..	AM	*50	
Matthews' (B.) Introd. to Am. Literature............	AM	*1 00	
Matzke's French Pronunciation..........	HO		25
First Spanish Readings	HE	*1 10	1 00
Maunoury's Anthology of Greek Roots..	HR	75	45
Maurice's Grammaire en Action.	EL	*85	80
Maury's (D. H.) History of Virginia.....	JH	75	50
Maury's (M. F.) Geographies:			
(New Series) Elementary	UN	*64	55
" " Revised Manual........	UN	*1 45	1 25
" " Rev. Physical.........	UN	*1 38	1 20
" " Map Drawing	UN	*18	15
Maxwell's (E.) Vertical Script Primer..	PM	*20	
Maxwell's (E. P.) Student's Standard Speller..............	PM	*25	

Maxwell's (W. H.) First Book in English..AM *40
Introductory Lessons in English Grammar ....AM *40
Advanced Lessons in Eng. Grammar..AM *60
Primary Lessons in Language and Composition..........AM *30
Maxwell's (W. H.) & Smith's (G. J.) Writing in English..........AM *75
Maxwell's Staff Ruled Writing Speller...FL 6
May's (C. H.) Anatomy, Physiology and Hygiene..........WO 75
Primary Physiology and Hygiene ...WO 50
Maycock's Educational Drawing-Books, 10 nos..........ea. UL 25 20
Mayer's (J.) German for Americans.....KO 1 00
— pap..........KO 60
— ....ST 1 00
— pap..........ST 60
Mayhew's Practical Bookkeeping ......BU *60
— Blanks for..........BU *60
— Key to..........BU *60
Standard Bookkeeping..........SI *2 00 1 80
— Blanks for..........SI *2 00 1 80
— Key to..........SI *2 00 1 80
University Bookkeeping..........SI *2 00 1 80
— Key to..........SI *2 00 1 80
Maynard's English Classics, 140 single nos., ea. MY *12
— 38 double nos..........ea. MY *24
— 4 triple " .... " MY *36
[11 addl. v., var. prices, *25c.-*30c., *35c.-*40c.-*50c. ea.]..........MY
Maynard's French Texts, 18 nos., [7 at *20c.-6 at *25c.]..........MY
Maynard's German Texts [18 nos., 8 at *25c.-10 at *40c.]..........MY
Mead's (I. M.) English Language and its Grammar..........SI *85 68
Mead's (S. P.) Elements of Chemistry.....SI *90 80
Elements of Physics..........SI *80 72
*Mead's (W. E.) Elemen. Composition and Rhetoric..........SY 90
Mead's (W. E.) & Gordy's (W. F.) Practical Composition and Rhetoric...SY 90
Meadowcroft's (W. H.) Simple A B C of Electricity..........HS 50
Meadows' French Pronouncing Dict......LO 1 25 1 00
Italian Dictionary..........AP *2 00
Meese's Facts in Literature ....MP *30
Meifuss' Graded Arithmetic Problems, Rev. ed. (Pupil's ed.), 6 pts....ea. HR 5
— pt. 7..........HR 10
— Teacher's ed., 7 pts..........ea. HR 10
Meiklejohn's English Grammar..........HE *90 80
English Literature..........HE *70 60
" Language..........HE *1 30 1 20
Meissner's German Conversation..........HE *75 65
German Method..........BI 1 25
German Grammar with exercises for translation..........CH 1 40
Meisterschaft System:—French..........MI 5 00
German ....MI 5 00
Italian ....MI 5 00
Spanish ....MI 5 00
Latin, pt. 1..........MI 50
Meleney & Giffin's Selected Words.......LV *20
*Mellick's (A. C.) Latin Prose Composition..........AM *40
Menard's Songs for Kindergarten and Primary Schools..........DS 80
Meras' Légendes Française, v. 1, Robert le Diable..........HO 20
V. 2, Le Bon Roi Dagobert..........HO 20
V. 3, Merlin l'enchanteur..........HO 30
Syntaxe Pratique de la Langue Française..........CH 1 25
—..........JE 1 25
—..........HO 1 00
Meras & Stern's Grammaire Française..........HO 1 25
Cinq Histoires..........HO 80
First Lessons in French..........HO 1 00
See Stern & Meras.
Merivale's Rome..........LN 2 00
General Hist. of Rome..........AM *1 25
— Abridged ed..........AM *75
Merriam's (A. C.) Herodotus, Bks. 6, 7...AM *1 50
Phæacians of Homer..........AM *1 50
Merriam's (F. A.) Birds of Village and Field..........HM 2 00
Merrill's New Copybooks, Intermediate Ser., 8 nos..........doz. MY *72
— with blotters.......... " MY *88
— Standard Ser., 6 nos.......... " MY *96
— Tracing Ser., 3 nos.......... " MY *72
— with blotters.......... " MY *88
Vertical Penmanship: Standard, 6 nos..........doz. MY *96
— Intermediate, 5 nos...... " . MY *72

Merrill's Vertical Penmanship: Supplemental ser., 2 nos..........doz. MY *96
Vertical Penmanship Chart, 3 nos..ea. MY *50
— Teacher's Manual..........MY *60
Modern Penmanship:
Chart, 2 nos..........ea. MY *50
Intermediate Ser., 4 nos......doz. MY *72
Standard Ser., 7 nos.......... " MY *80
Supplemental Numbers, 2 nos. " MY *80
Word and Sentence Book (Wilson)...MY *25
English History (Curry and Rolfe)...MY *80
Spelling Blank, Vertical Script..doz. MY *50
Merrill's (E. T.) Catullus..........GI 1 50 1 40
Fragments of Roman Satire..........AM *75
Merrill's Advanced 1st Reader.......... AM *19
" 2d " .... AM *25
" 3d " ....AM *38
Meservey's Single and Double Entry Bookkeeping..........TH 80
— Blanks for..........TH 88
— Key to..........TH 80
Single Entry Bookkeeping..........TH 60
— Blanks for..........TH 50
— Key to..........TH 60
Double Entry Bookkeeping..........TH 70
— Blanks to..........TH 60
Manual of Bookkeeping and Banking.TH 1 25
Political Economy..........TH 80
Metcalf's (R. C.) Spelling and Lang. Bk. AM *20
English Grammar..........AM *60
Elementary English..........AM *40
Metcalf's (R. C.) & Bright's Language Lessons, pt. 1..........AM *35
— pt. 2..........AM *55
Language Exercises.......... AM *42
Metcalf's & De Garmo's Dict. Work, New enl. ed..........MG 35
Methfessel's Arithmetical Primer.......LE 12
Metric Primer..........MB 40
*Mezes' (S. E.) Ethics..........MC 2 60
Michael's (G. W.) Penmanship, 7 nos. doz. AM *85
Michael's (O. S.) Algebra for Beginners...BI 75
Michaud's Conjugation des Verbes.......JE 25
Miles' (E. A.) Questions and Answers in Physiology..........NO 20 15
Mill's (H. R.) Realm of Nature..........SC *1 50 1 20
Mill's (J. S.) Logic..........LN 1 25
Political Economy..........LN 1 25
—..........RU 1 50
— (Laughlin)..........AP 3 50 2 80
See also Laughlin
Miller & Beeson's Second Latin Book....SR ** 1 25
Miller & Foerste's Elementary Physics...SC **
Miller's (E.) Plane and Spherical Trigonometery..........HE 1 15
Miller's (F. J.) Ovid, with vocab..........AM *1 40
— Text ed..........AM *50
Miller's (M. M.) and Raymond's (G. L.) Speaker..........SI *1 12 1 00
Miller's (O. T.) First Book of Birds.......HM 60
Second Book of Birds: Bird Families..........HM 1 00
Miller's (W.) Latin Composition..........SA 1 00
— in 2 pts..........ea. SA 60
Miller's (W. A.) Chemical Physics..........WI 2 00
Milley's (L. W.) Essentials of Perspective. SC 1 50
Millhouse's Italian Dictionary, 2 v..........AP *4 20
— 2 v..........LJ 4 00
Milligan's Civil Gov't of Illinois..........EL *55 50
Millikan's Mechanics, Molecular Physics and Heat..........SR ** 1 25
Mills' First Lessons in Physiology.......EL *65 60
Mills' Manual of Typewriting..........HW 1 50
Mills' Rhetoric. *See* Blair.
Milne's (J. M.) English Grammar..........SI 75
— Foundations of English Grammar..........SI **
Milne's (W. J.) Elements of Arithmetic..AM *30
Intermediate Arithmetic..........AM *30
Standard Arithmetic..........AM *65
Mental Arithmetic..........AM *35
Key to Standard and Mental Arithmetic..........AM *75
First Lessons in Arithmetic (Inductive Series)..........AM *22
Elementary Arithmetic (Inductive Series)..........AM *35
Practical Arithmetic (Inductive Ser.). AM *50
— Key to..........AM *50
Grammar School Algebra..........AM *50
Elements of Algebra..........AM *60
Key to Elements of Algebra and Grammar School Algebra..........AM *60
High School Algebra..........AM *1 00
— Key to..........AM *1 00
Inductive Algebra..........AM *80
— Key to..........AM *80
*Academic Algebra..........AM *1 25
— Key to..........AM *1 50

Milne's (W. J.) Plane and Solid Geometry..AM *1 25
Plane Geometry, Separate..........AM *75
Solid Geometry, Separate..........AM *75
Key to Geometry..........AM *1 25
Milwaukee 1st German Reader..........BP 25 20
2d German Reader..........BP 40 32
3d " " ....BP 60 48
Minckwitz's Sel. from Viri Romæ and Cornelius Nepos..........MY *60
Minifie's Geometrical Drawing..........VN 2 00
Mechanical Drawing..........VN 4 00
Minto's Characteristics of English Poets..GI *1 65 1 50
English Prose Literature..........GI *1 65 1 50
Logic..........SC 1 25
*Mirick's (G. A.) An Elementary Grammar..........MO 50
Mirick's (H. A.) Oral Lesson Book in Hygiene..........AM *1 00
Mitchell's (H. G.) Hebrew Lessons......HE *1 95 1 80
Mitchell's (S. A.) First Lessons in Geography..........BU *36
New Primary Geography, rev. ed.....BU *54
" Intermediate Geography, rev. ed..BU *1 20
" School Geography..........BU *72
" " Atlas..........BU *1 08
" Physical Geography..........BU *1 20
Ancient Geography..........BU *62
Ancient Atlas, sep..........BU *28
Mitchell's Essentials of Latin..........EL *1 10 1 00
*Mitchell's School and College Speaker..HO 1 00
Mixer's (A. H.) French Pronunciation...SN 35
Manual of French Poetry..........AM *1 00
Mixter's Chemistry..........WI 1 50
Model Algebra for Elementary Schools..EL **
Model Arithmetics (E. Gideon), new ed.:
Elementary, pt. 1..........EL *23 29
" " 2..........EL *36 33
Practical..........EL *65 60
Mental..........EL *35 30
Model Music Course Series:
Primer..........AM *25
Nos. 1, 2 and 3..........*ea.* AM *30
" 4, 5 " 6.......... " AM *40
Manual..........AM *50
Modern Classics, 34 v..........*ea.* HM 40
Modern French Comedies, 9 v....... " HO 20
Modern German Texts..........AM
[var. prices, *25c.; *30c., 65c.]
Modern Philosophers Series, v. 1-7.......HO
Modern Readers. *See* Gourley.
*Moliere's Athalie, with vocab..........HO 35
*Esther, with vocab..........HO 25
Mommsen's Rome, 5 v..........SC 10 60
Roman Republic..........SC 2 50
Monroe's (L. B.) 1st Reader..........BU *20
2d Reader..........BU *35
3d " ....BU *50
4th " ....BU *60
5th " ....BU *90
6th " ....BU *1 00
Chart Primer..........BU *12
Physical and Vocal Training..........BU *72
New Primer..........BU *15
" 1st Reader..........BU *20
" Spanish-English ed..........BU *30
" 2d " ....BU *30
" 3d " ....BU *42
" 4th " ....BU *66
" 5th " ....BU *84
First Steps in Spelling..........BU *18
Practical Speller..........BU *25
Complete Writing Speller........*doz.* BU *42
Word List..........BU *18
Monroe's (Mrs. L. B.) Story of Our Country..........LE 60
Monsanto & Languellier's Spanish Course AM *1 25
Montague's (A. P.) Letters of Cicero......EL 1 10 1 00
Letters of Pliny..........EL 1 10 1 00
Montagu's Elements of English Constitutional History..........LN 1 25
Monteith's (Jas.) First Lessons in Geography (National Series)..........AM *25
Introduction to Geography (National Series)..........AM *40
Manual of Geography (National Series)..........AM *75
Elementary Geography (Independent Series)..........AM *55
—— Special Edition for Pacific Coast..........AM *60
Comprehensive Geography (Independent Series)..........AM *1 10
(With Special State Editions.)
New Physical Geography..........AM *1 00
Boys and Girls' Atlas..........AM *40
Easy Lessons in Popular Science....AM *75
Popular Science Reader..........AM *75
Montieth's (J.) Natural History Readings, Bks. 1 and 2..........*ea.* RN 60

Montieth (John) Nociónes de Geografia Universal..........AM *60
Montonnier's Premiers Pas Dans François..........HO 75
Pour Appendre à Parler Français....HO 75
Montgomery's (D. H.) English History...GI *1 25 1 12
American History..........GI *1 15 1 00
French History..........GI *1 25 1 12
Beginner's American History..........GI *70 60
Student's American History..........GI *1 55 1 40
Rudimentos de la Historia de America..........GI *70 60
Montgomery's (J. L.) Modern Bookkeeping, Single Eutry..........MY *50
Single and Double Entry..........MY *80
—— Set of 6 Blank Books..........MY *60
*Moody's (W. V.) Hist. of English Literature..........SC 1 25
Mooney's (W. D.) Brief Latin Grammar..........AM *75
Moore's (A. O.) Science of Drawing in Art..........GI *90 80
Moore's (B. T.) Elemen. Physiology......LN 1 20
*Moore's (C. H.) Allen's Medea of Euripides..........GI *1 05 1 00
—— Text ed..........GI *45 40
Moore's Latin Prose Exercises..........UN *58 50
Moore's (C. H.) Examples in Delineation.HM 1 00
Moore's (E. H.) Grammar School Arithmetic..........AM *60
Moore's (J. W.) School History of N. C...AM *85
Moore's (N.) Kindergartner's Manual of Drawing..........BO 50
*Moore's (S. W.) English-Italian Language Book..........BE 80
Moran's Reporting Style of Shorthand, rev..........CI 1 50
—— Key to..........CI *2 00
Sign Book..........CI 25
Postal Manual..........CI 25
Moran's Mental Arithmetic..........CB *30
Moran's Shorthand Primer..........CI 10
More's Tr. of Æschylus' Prometheus Bound..........HM 75
Morey's (A.) Outline Work in Elementary English..........BI 50
Morey's (C.) Arithmetic..........DA 60 44
*Morey's (W. C.) Outlines of Roman History..........AM *1 00
Morgan's (A. H.) English and American Literature..........SY 1 00
Morgan's (A. P.) Plant Record..........AM *40
Morgan's (C. L.) Psychology..........SC 1 00
Morgan's Elemen. Physiography..........LN 90
Morgan's (M. H.) Eight Orations of Lysias..........GI *1 50 1 40
Morgan's (T. J.) Patriotic Citizenship...AM *1 00
Moritz's 1000 Questions..........HS 30
Answers..........HS 50
Morley's (H.) First Sketch of English Lit. CA 2 00
Morley's (M. W.) Bee People..........MG 1 25
The Honey Makers..........MG 1 50
Flowers and their Friends..........GI *60 50
A Few Familiar Flowers..........GI *70 60
Little Wanderers..........GI *35 30
Seed Babies..........GI *30 25
Morris' (C.) Manual of Classical Lit......SR *1 50
Elementary History of U. S..........LI *60
U. S. History..........LI 1 00
Primary Hist. of U. S..........LI 60
Young Students' History..........LI 75
Morris' (C. D.) Thucydides, Book 1........GI *45 40
—— with notes..........GI *1 75 1 65
Morris' (D.) History of England..........AM *1 00
Morris' (E. P.) Pseudolus of Plautus.....AL 1 20
Captives and Trinummus of Plautus..GI *1 35 1 25
—— Text ed..........GI *45 40
Morris' (R.) English Grammar..........AM *35
Morris's & Bowen's English Grammar Exercises..........AM *35
Morris' (W. H.) Elementa Latina..........LN 50
Greek Lessons..........LN 90
Morrison's (J.) Recitations, 2 nos.....*ea.* FL 20
Morrison's (T.) English Gram., Junior....NE 30
English Grammar, Senior..........NE 75
Morse Readers (Bulliet & Powers):
Bk. 1..........MS *28
" 2..........MS *40
" 3..........MS *50
Bks. 4 and 5..........*ea.* MS *67
Morse's (E. S.) First Book of Zoölogy....AM *67
Morse's (F. A.) Gymnastic Cards Song System..........*set.* HW *15
Morse's Speller (S. T. Dutton), complete..MS *30
—— bds..........MS *24
—— pt. 1..........MS *15
—— pt. 2..........MS *20
Mortimer's (E.) Practical Kindergarten Lessons..........NE 1 00

Title	Publ.	Price	Price
Morton's Civil Government, rev. ed.	MO	60	
*Morton's (E. H.) Elementary Geography.	BU	*55	
*Advanced Geography	BU	*1 20	
Morwitz's New Amer. Eng. and Ger. Dict	CN	1 50	
——	ST	1 50	
New Amer. Pocket Eng. and Ger. Dict	ST	1 00	
*Moser's Der Bibliothekar (Cooper)	AM	*45	
Moses's (E. P.) First Phonetic Reader	JE	25	20
Moss' (C. M.) 1st Greek Reader, new ed	AL		70
Motley's Leaflets	AM	*50	
Moulten's Preparatory Latin Composition, pt. 1	GI	*90	80
A Systematic Drill in Syntax, pt. 2	GI	*27	25
Complete ed. [Inc. 2 Preceding Bks.]	GI	*1 10	1 00
Mowry's (A. M.) First Steps in the History of England	SI	**	
Mowry's (W. A. & A. M.) Studies in Civil Government	SI	*1 05	96
Elements of Civil Government	SI	*80	72
History of the United States	SI	*1 80	1 00
Outline Map of U. S.	HE	35	30
First Steps in the History of Our Country	SI	75	60
Mowry's (W. A.) Territorial Growth of the United States	SI	**	
Mueller's Cæsar's Idioms	HS	25	
*Mueller's (W.) Deutsches Lese und Sprachbuch, Erst Stufe	SI		36
*Zweite Stufe	SI		42
Mueller & Blackman's School Songs:			
Book 1 (A) Primary	SR	*23	20
" 2 (A) Grammar	SR	*29	25
" 3 (A) " and High	SR	*29	25
" 4 (A) High	SR	*29	25
Popular Songs	SR	*65	60
Mugan's Advanced Graded Grammar	IG		50
—— Rev. Teacher's ed.	IG		30
—— " " " bds	IG		22
—— " Pupil's ed	IG		15
Muir's Practical Chemistry, pt. 1, Elementary	LN	1 50	
—— pt. 2	LN	**	
Muirhead's Elem. of Ethics	SC		1 00
*Muller's Graded System of Bookkeeping	DY	*82	75
Muller's (F. M.) Ger. Classics, 2 v	SC		6 00
Muller's (M.) & Wenckelbach's (C.) Schiller's Maria Stuart	GI	*1 00	90
Muller's (P. J.) Exercises for Tr. into Latin	PT	1 25	
Muller's (W.) Deutsches Lese-und Sprachbuch: Erste Stufe	SI	36	
—— Zweite Stufe	SI	42	
Political History of Recent Times	AM	*2 00	
Munro's (D. C.) History of the Middle Ages	AP	**	
Mulley's Songs and Games for Our Little Ones	MA	25	
Munson's Complete Phonographer	AM	*1 50	
Dictionary of Phonography	HM	3 00	
Art of Phonography	PU	2 00	
*Shorter Course	PU	1 25	
Murché's Object Lessons in Elemen. Science, v. 1	MC	*66	60
—— v. 2	MC	*83	75
—— v. 3	MC	*99	90
Object Lessons for Infants, vs. 1 and 2.	*ea.* MC		60
Science Readers, Nos. 1 and 2	*ea.* MC	28	25
—— Nos. 3 and 4	" MC	44	40
—— " 5 " 6	" MC	55	50
Murdoch's Analytic Elocution	AM	*1 00	
Plea for Spoken Language	AM	*1 00	
Muret-Sanders' Encyclopædic Eng. and Ger Dict. School ed., 2 v	IT	5 00	
Murphy's Illustrated Catholic Readers:			
Primer	MU		5
Infant Reader	MU		6
1st Reader	MU		9
2d "	MU		12
3d "	MU		18
4th "	MU		20
5th "	MU		25
6th "	MU		30
Murray's (A. S.) Mythology, new ed.	SC	1 75	
Manual of Mythology, rev. ed.	MR	1 25	
Murray's (D. A.) Differential Equations.	LN		1 90
Integral Calculus	AM	*2 00	
*Plane and Spherical Trigonometry	LN	1 25	
*Spherical Trigonometry	LN	60	
Plane Trigonometry	LN	90	
" " with Tables	LN	1 25	
Trigonometric Tables	LN	60	
*Murray's College Greek Prose	SR		1 25
Murray's (G.) History of Ancient Greek Literature	AP	1 50	
Murray (J. C.). *See* Hamilton (W.).			
Murray's (J. C.) Introd. to Ethics	DW	1 50	1 35
Handbook of Psychology	DW	1 75	1 58
Murray's (J. E.) Essential Lessons in English	CB		40
Advanced Lessons in English	CB		60
Murray's (J. O'K.) Lessons in Eng. Lit.	MU	75	
Murray's (L.) English Grammar	LI	*48	
English Grammar	MU	40	
—— abridged by Kerney	MU	25	
Murray & Pontius' International Day School Singer	CB	50	
Musick's (J. R.) Stories of Missouri	AM	*60	
Müter's's Practical Chemistry	BL	*1 25	
Muzzarelli's Antonymes de la Langue Française	JE	1 00	
—— Key to	JE	1 50	
Academic French Course, First Year.	AM	*1 00	
—— Key to	AM	*1 00	
French Course, Second Year	AM	*1 00	
—— Key to	AM	*1 00	
Brief French Course	AM	*1 25	
Myers' (P. V. N.) Mediæval and Modern History	GI	*1 65	1 50
General History	GI	*1 65	1 50
Eastern Nations and Greece	GI	*1 10	1 00
History of Greece	GI	*1 40	1 25
" Rome	GI	*1 10	1 00
Ancient History	GI	1 65	1 50
Myers' (P. V. N.) Rome, Its Rise and Fall	GI	*1 40	1 25
Myers' (P. V. N.) and Allen's (W. F.) Ancient History	GI	*1 65	1 50
Myers & Brooks' Rational Grammar School Arithmetic	SR	**	50
Nall's Elemen. Latin-English Dict	MC	1 00	
National Geographic Monographs ser., 10 nos	*ea.* AM	*20	
—— In 1 v	AM	*2 50	
Nash's (L.) Table-Book	BE	20	12
National Music Course:			
Introductory Music Reader	GI	*35	30
New 1st Music Reader	GI	*30	25
" 2d " "	GI	*45	40
" 3d " "	GI	*45	40
" 4th " "	GI	*1 05	90
" High School Music Reader	GI	*1 05	94
Girls' " " " "	GI	*1 40	1 25
Intermediate Music Reader	GI	*45	40
Independent Music Reader, abridged.	GI	*70	60
4th Music Reader	GI	*1 05	94
Abridged 4th Music Reader	GI	*85	75
Independent " "	GI	*80	70
National Music Teacher	GI	*45	40
Handbook (Tilden's) of Lessons for First Year Grade	GI	*12	10
National School Singer	AM	*30	
National Tablet Series:			
Algebra Tablets, 3 nos	*doz.* AM	*1 50	
—— Answers to	*ea.* AM	*5	
Language Tablets, 15 nos	*doz.* AM	*90	
—— Manual to	*ea.* AM	*25	
Language Spelling Tablets, nos. 1–3.	*doz.* AM	*1 00	
Number Tablets, Arith., nos. 1-12.	" AM	*90	
—— Answers to	*ea.* AM	*15	
Natural Elementary Geography (Redway & Hinman)	AM	*60	
Natural Advanced Geography	AM	*1 25	
Natural Brief Geography, One Book Course	AM	*80	
Natural History Hand Book	HW	75	
Natural History Stories 11 pts., pap.	*ea* HW	5	
—— 2 volumes, bds	" HW	36	
National Songs with Music	HW	10	
Natural Music Course (Ripley and Tapper):			
Primer	AM	*30	
Natural Music Reader, No. 1	AM	*30	
" " " " 2	AM	*35	
" " " " 3	AM	*35	
" " " " 4	AM	*35	
" " " " 5	AM	*50	
" " " Advanced	AM	*1 00	
Short Course in Music, Book 1	AM	*35	
—— Book 2	AM	*40	
Natural System of Vertical Writing (Newlands & Row), 6 Bks	*doz.* HE	*85	75
Business and Social Forms	HE	1 00	
Spelling Blank	HE	45	
Natural Speller and Word Book	AM	*20	
Needham's (J. G.) Elem. Zoölogy	AM	*90	
Outdoor Studies	AM	*40	
Neely's Speller	LI	*15	
Neidlinger's (W. H.) Earth, Sky, and Air in Song, Bk. 1	AM	*70	
—— Bk. 2	AM	*80	
Nelson's (A.) Key to Flora of Rocky Mountain Region	AP	**	
Nelson's Bookkeeping	MO	1 00	
Nelson's (E. T.) Herbarium	AL		75

Nelson's (M.) First Reader, bds.	FL	20	
" " cl.	FL	25	
Second " bds.	FL	25	
" " cl.	FL	30	
Nelson's (T.) Higher Grade English	NE	50	
Lower Grade English	NE	40	
Nelson's Colored Kindergarten Drawing-Book, Nos. 1, 2, 3, 4, 5, 6 ... *doz.*	NE	1 00	
Nelson's Colored Kindergarten Drawing-Cards, Set 1 ... *set.*	NE	1 00	
Nelson's Plain Kindergarten Drawing Books, Nos. 1, 2, 3, 4, 5, 6, 7, 8 *doz.*	NE	50	
Drawing Cards, 7 sets ... *ea.*	NE	50	
Nelson's Elements of Euclid, Bk. 1	NE	30	
—— Bks. 1 and 2	NE	50	
Nelson's First French Book	NE	30	
" Second " "	NE	50	
*Nelson's Supplementary Readers, 13 nos. ... *ea.*	NE	15	
Nesbitt's Grammarland	HO		1 00
Nesfield's English Grammar	MC	1 10	
Neuman & Baretti's Spanish Dict	LI	*1 08	
Neuville's French Plays for Girls	HO		85
New American Primary Speller	BU	*15	
Pronouncing Speller	BU	*20	
Advanced Speller	BU	*25	
1st Reader	BU	*15	
2d "	BU	*23	
3d "	BU	*33	
4th "	BU	*45	
5th "	BU	*63	
Etymological Reader	BU	*1 00	
See also Butler.			
New American Music Reader, no. 1	DY	*28	25
—— no. 2	DY	*43	40
—— " 3	DY	*85	75
New Arithmetic	HE	*75	65
New Century Busy Work, Primary, 6 sets ... *ea.*	MS	*15	
—— 3 sets ... "	MS	*20	
—— 3 " ... "	MS	*25	
New Century Copybooks, Intermedial System:			
Short Course, Primer and 4 Bks. ... *doz.*	MS	*72	
Regular Course, 8 Bks. ... "	MS	*96	
New Century Development Maps (Geography)	MS	*40	
New Century Readers (J. G. & T. E. Thompson) First Year, Childhood Days	MS	*28	
Second Year, Fairy Tale and Fable	MS	*40	
Third "	MS	*40	
Fairy Tale and Fable, Fourth Bk.	MS	**	
—— Fifth Bk.	MS	**	
New Century Readers by Grades, Bk. 1	RA	17	
—— Bks. 2, 3, and 4 ... *ea.*	RA	25	
—— " 5, 6, 7, and 8 ... "	RA	35	
New Century First Reader	RA	17	
Second Reader	RA	25	
Third "	RA	35	
Fourth "	RA	45	
Fifth "	RA	60	
New Century Series of Physiology	AM		
See Hewes, H. F.; Hall, W. S. & J. W.; and Mirick, H. A.			
New Education Readers	AM		
See Demarest & Van Sickle.			
New Era Readers (Black & Jones): First	ET	15	
Second	ET	25	
Third	ET	35	
Fourth	ET	45	
Fifth	ET	60	
New Era System of Vertical Writing (C. L. Ricketts): Nos. 1-7 ... *doz.*	ET	85	
New Franklin Arithmetics	BU		
See Seaver & Walton.			
New Franklin Readers	BU		
See Campbell, L. J.			
New Graded Readers: Am. Ed. Reader, No. 1	AM	*18	
—— No. 2	AM	*29	
—— No. 3	AM	*40	
—— No. 4	AM	*50	
—— No. 5	AM	*65	
New Ideal Vertical Copy Books, 6 nos., *doz.*	MP	*75	
New Inductive Arithmetics:			
First Lessons in Numbers	LH		22
Brief Course in Arithmetic	LH		38
Complete Arithmetic	LH		75
New Model Primary Arithmetic	EL	**	
" " Mental "	EL	**	
" " Elementary "	EL	**	
" " " " pt. 1	EL	**	
" " " " pt. 2	EL	**	
" " Practical "	EL	**	
New Normal First Reader	WR	*20	
Second Reader	WR	*35	
New Normal Third Reader	WR	*45	
Fourth Reader	WR	*60	
Fifth "	WR	*80	
Newcomb's College Algebra	HO		1 30
—— Key to	HO		1 30
School Algebra	HO		95
—— Key to	HO		95
Calculus	HO		1 50
Analytic Geometry	HO		1 20
Elements of "	HO		1 20
Plane Geometry and Trigonometry, with Tables	HO		1 10
Logarithmic, etc., Tables	HO		1 10
Essentials of Trigonometry	HO		1 00
Elements of Plane and Spher. Trigonometry	HO		1 20
—— with 5 Place Tables	HO		1 60
Newcomb's (S.) Elements of Astronomy	AM	*1 00	
Popular Astronomy	AM	*1 30	
Newcomb & Holden. *See* Amer. Science Series.			
Newcomer's (A. G.) Practical Course in English Composition	GI	90	80
Elements of Rhetoric	HO		1 00
*American Literature	SR	1 00	
Newell's (J. H.) Lessons in Botany, pt. 1, From Seed to Leaf	GI	*55	50
—— pt. 2, Flower and Fruit	GI	*90	80
Reader in Botany, pt. 1	GI	*70	60
—— pt. 2	GI	*70	60
Newell's Experimental Chemistry	HE	**	
Newell & Creary's Revised 1st Readers	DY	*18	15
" 2d "	DY	*30	25
" 3d "	DY	*42	36
" 4th "	DY	*51	45
" 5th "	DY	*84	75
" 6th "	DY	*1 00	90
Newhall's (B.) Plato's Charmides, Laches, and Lysis	AM	*1 25	
Newson's Modern Language Bks.:			
First French Book	NN	50	
Second " "	NN	50	
French Daily Life (Reader)	NN	75	
First German Book	NN	60	
German Reader	NN	75	
" Daily Life (Reader)	NN	75	
Newth's (G. S.) Inorganic Chemistry	LN		1 75
Chemical Analysis	LN		1 75
Elementary Inorganic Chemistry	LN		90
Nichols' (B. E.) Pract. Bookkeeping	RI	75	
—— with Commercial Law	RI	1 20	
Blanks, 3 mos. Course, 5 bks.	RI	30	
" 6 mos. " 5 "	RI	1 20	
" 1 yr. " 8 "	RI	1 75	
Teachers' Tablet	RI	15	
Nichols' (E. H.) Elementary Geometry	LN	75	
Nichols' (E. L.) Outlines of Physics	MC	1 40	
Nichols (E. L.) and Franklin's (W. S.) Elements of Physics, 3 v. V. 1	MC	1 50	
—— V. 2	MC	1 90	
—— V. 3	MC	1 50	
Nichols' (E. W.) Analytic Geometry	HE		1 25
Nichols' Differential and Integral Calculus	HE	**	
Nichols' (F. W.) Atlas Outlines in U. S. History	CS	*60	
—— Pts 1 and 2 ... *ea.*	CS	*40	
Nichols' (H.) Number and Space	GI	*1 10	1 00
Nichols' (W. F.) Topics in Geography	HE	65	
Graded Lessons in Arithmetic, Grades 2, 3, 4, 5, 6, 7, 8 ... *ea.*	TH	25	
*Arithmetical Problems	TH	30	
Nichols, Smith & Turton's Experimental Physics	GI	*1 00	90
Nicholson's Primary Arithmetic	UN	*21	18
Intermediate Arithmetic	UN	*40	35
Complete Arithmetic	UN	*75	65
—— Key to	UN	*75	65
Advanced Arithmetic	UN	*1 03	90
—— Key to	UN		90
Elementary Algebra	UN	*1 15	1 00
—— Key to	UN		1 00
Calculus	UN	*1 73	1 50
Nicholson's (H. A.) Introd. to the Study of Biology	AM	*52	
Zoölogy, new ed	AM	*1 33	
Nicholson's (H. H.) and Avery's (S.) Exercises in Chemistry	HO		60
Nicholson's (J. W.) Plane and Spherical Trigonometry, with tables	MC	1 10	
—— Without tables	MC	90	
Nicolson's (F. W.) Plutus of Aristophanes	GI	*90	80
Terence's Phormio	GI	*30	25
Niles's Elementary Geography	AM	*44	
Advanced Geography	AM	*1 00	
School History of the U. S	AM	*75	
Niles's Hist. and Civil Gov't of Minn.	WR	*1 00	
Nipher's (F. E.) Introd. to Graphic Alge.	HO		60
Noa's Plays for the Kindergarten	ST		30

Noble's Studies in Amer. Literature	MC	1 00	
Nodier's Le Chien de Brisquet (Syms)	AM	*35	
Noel & Chapsal's French Grammar	LO	1 50	1 20
—— Key to	LO	75	60
Abridgment of French Grammar	LO	1 25	1 00
Littérature Française	LO	1 50	1 20
Noetling's Elem. of Constructive Geom.	SI		36
Nordhoff's Politics for Young Americans	AM	*75	
Normal Course in Drawing (Shaylor):			
Bks. 1 to 3 inc. dos.	SI		96
" 4 to 9 " "	SI		1 80
Blank Drawing Book "	SI		72
Normal Course in Drawing (Shaylor):			
Handbook for Teachers	SI	*54	48
Normal Course in English (Welsh & Greenwood):			
Elements of Language and Grammar	SI	*54	48
Studies in English Grammar	SI	*68	60
Normal Music Course (Tufts, J. W.):			
1st Reader	SI	*35	32
2d "	SI	*65	60
—— pts. 1 and 2 ea.	SI	*40	36
3d Reader	SI	*65	60
—— for Female Voices	SI	*65	60
Introductory 3d Reader	SI	*45	40
High School Collection	SI	*1 00	90
Acedean Collection	SI	*1 12	1 00
Outline Study for	SI	*15	10
Euterpean, by J. W. Tufts	SI	*1 40	1 25
Quincy Course of Study, by Wade	SI	*45	40
Handbook of Vocal Music	SI		1 50
Normal Course in Number (Cook, J. W., Cropsey, N.):			
Elementary Arithmetic	SI	*56	50
New Advanced Arithmetic	SI	*80	72
Normal Course in Reading (Todd & Powell):			
Primer	SI	*20	18
Normal 1st Reader	SI	*28	24
2d "	SI	*40	36
3d "	SI	*54	48
4th "	SI	*66	60
5th "	SI	*1 00	84
Normal Alternate 1st Reader	SI	*28	24
" 2d "	SI	*40	36
" 3d "	SI	*54	48
Normal Course in Spelling (Dunton)	SI	*27	24
—— Primary Book	SI	*22	18
—— Advanced Book	SI	*24	20
Normal Spelling Blank, Slanting Script. dos.	SI	*47	42
—— Vertical Script	SI	*55	48
Normal Review System of Writing (Farley & Gunnison):			
Regular Course, Nos. 1-6 dos.	SI	*1 06	96
Short " Nos. 1, 4 "	SI	*80	72
Business Forms "	SI	*1 34	1 20
Tracing Course, nos. 1-2 "	SI	*80	72
Movement Course	SI	*1 34	1 20
Normal Review System of Writing, Vertical Copies:			
Regular Course, Nos. 1-10 dos.	SI		96
Short " " 1-6 "	SI		72
Tracing " " 1 and 2 "	SI		96
Movement " " " "	SI		1 20
First Steps, A, B "	SI		60
" " C, D "	SI		72
Standard Course, 6 nos. "	SI		96
Social and Business Forms, Nos. 1 and 2 dos.	SI		1 20
Normal Review Handbook of Vertical Writing	SI	*54	48
North Carolina Practical Spelling-Book	WS	20	
North Carolina Primer dos.	WS	60	
North Carolina Reader, No. 1	BA	*30	25
—— No. 2	BA	*53	45
—— " 3	BA	*82	70
North Carolina Writing-Books, 9 nos. dos.	WS	1 00	
Northam's Civil Government, N. Y., N. J., Mo. ea.	BI	75	
Fixing Facts of American History	BI	75	
Geography Conversational Lessons	BI	25	
Northend's Young Declaimer	AM	*50	
Norton's (C. E.) Heart of Oak Books:			
—— No. 1	HE	*30	25
—— " 2	HE	*40	35
—— " 3	HE	*50	45
—— " 4	HE	*60	50
—— " 5	HE	*65	55
—— " 6	HE	*70	60
Norton's (S. A.) Elements of Physics	AM	*80	
Natural Philosophy	AM	*1 10	
Elements of Chemistry	AM	*1 10	
Grammar. *See* Weld.			
Norton's (S. W.) Practical Studies in English Grammar	FL	*40	
Novelle Italiane, vs 1-*6 ea.	JE	35	
*Noyes's (A. A.) General Principles of Physical Science	HO		
Qualitative Chemical Analysis	MC	1 25	
Noyes's (W. A.) Organic Chemistry	HO	**	
Qualitative Analysis	HO		80
Nugent's French Dictionary	BU	*90	
—— (Brown & Martin)	BU	1 00	
—— Pronouncing (Brown & Martin)	WN	1 00	50
Number Lessons after Grube Method	BI	10	
*Nutting's (H. C.) A Supplementary Latin Composition	AL		
Nuttall's Standard Dictionary	WN	1 00	
——	BU	1 00	
Oakley's (I. G.) Nature Lessons	HW	*50	
Object Lessons in French	NE	75	
Object " " German	NE	1 00	
O'Brine's Guide in Chem. Analysis, rev.	WI	2 00	
O'Conor's (J. F. X.) Rhetoric and Oratory	HE		1 12
O'Grady's Select Recitations	BE		60
Ohio Reversible Writing Bks:			
Large Series, 6 nos. doz.	WL		1 08
Small " 3 " "	WL		75
*Olin's (W. H.) Commercial Geography	CE	1 00	
Oliver's (F. E.) Primary Script Reader	LE	*30	25
Ollendorff's German Method (Adler)	AM	*87	
—— Key to	AM	*70	
French Method (Jewett)	AM	*87	
—— Key to	AM	*70	
French Method (Value)	AM	*87	
—— Key to	AM	*70	
Italian Method (Foresti)	AM	*1 05	
—— Key to	AM	*70	
Spanish Grammar	AP	1 00	80
" Teacher (Vingut)	LO	1 50	1 20
—— Key to	LO	75	60
See also Kendrick; Sanders (G. J. H.).			
Olmsted's (D.) College Astronomy (Snell)	CO	*1 75	1 60
" Philosophy (Sheldon) new ed.	CO	*2 75	2 50
Olney's First Lessons in Arithmetic	BU	*24	
Practical Arithmetic	BU	*58	
—— pts. 1 and 2 ea.	BU	*40	
—— Key to	BU	*75	
Science of Arithmetic	BU	*96	
—— Key to	BU	*1 00	
First Principles of Algebra	BU	*72	
—— Key to	BU	*1 00	
Complete Algebra	BU	*1 10	
—— Key to	BU	*1 32	
University Algebra	BU	*1 44	
—— Key to	BU	*1 72	
Test Examples in Algebra	BU	*56	
Geometry, pts. 1 and 3 ea.	BU	*56	
Elements of Geometry	BU	*1 12	
New Elementary Geometry	BU	*1 25	
—— Key to	BU	*75	
University Geometry	BU	*1 44	
Elements of Trigonometry	BU	*1 12	
Tables of Logarithms	BU	*56	
General Geometry and Calculus	BU	*1 80	
Elements of Geometry and Trigonometry, School ed	BU	*1 80	
Geometry and Trigonometry, University ed., with Tables of Logarithms	BU	*2 10	
Geometry and Trigonometry, University ed., without Tables of Logarithms	BU	*1 90	
Teacher's Key to Geom. and Trig.	BU	*1 12	
Oman's England in the 19th Century	LN	1 25	
Oman's (C.) History of England	HO		1 50
History of Greece	LN	1 50	
Elemen. History of Greece	MC	65	
Onderdonk's History of Maryland	NU	75	
O'Neill's (K.), Graphic Dictation Blanks, Nos. 1-3 doz.	LV	*96	
Punctuation Practically Illustrated	LV	*40	
One Hundred Choice Selections, Nos. 1-37, cl ea.	PP	50	
—— pap. "	PP	30	
One Thousand Questions. *See* Moritz.			
One Thousand Subjects for Eng. Comp.	BU	*18	
One Thousand Words Writing Speller	BN	5	3
Orndorff. *See* Remsen.			
Orne's (M. R.) Manual of Analysis and Parsing	LE		30
Orton's Comparative Zoölogy, new rev. ed. (Dodge)	AM	*1 80	
Osborne's Examples of Differential Equations	GI	*60	50
Osborne's (G. A.) Calculus	HE		2 00
Osgood's American Primer	BU	*15	
American 1st Reader	BU	*20	
" 2d "	BU	*35	
" 3d "	BU	*45	
" 4th "	BU	*55	
" 5th "	BU	*60	
" 6th "	BU	*90	
Osgoodby's (W. W.) Phonetic Shorthand	WS	1 00	
O'Shea's Comprehensive Geog., No. 1	OS	50	30
—— No. 2	OS	1 00	60
—— " 3	OS	1 80	1 08

Title	Publisher	Price	Price
O'Shea's Graded Catholic 1st Reader	OS	25	15
Catholic 2d Reader	OS	40	24
" 3d "	OS	60	36
" 4th "	OS	80	48
" 5th "	OS	1 00	60
" Young Ladies' Reader	OS	1 25	75
O'Shea's Progressive Primer, bds.	OS	12	8
1st Reader	OS	25	15
2d "	OS	40	25
3d "	OS	65	39
4th "	OS	90	54
5th "	OS	1 20	72
6th "	OS	1 50	90
Young Ladies' Reader	OS	1 25	75
Spelling-Book	OS	25	15
O'Shea's Primary English Grammar	OS	30	18
Primary Spelling and Reading Book	OS	20	12
Oswald's Etymological Dictionary	PO	1 50	1 25
Otis' (C. P.) Elementary German	HO		80
Grimm's Märchen	HO		1 00
Introd. to Middle High German	HO		1 00
Ott's (C. v.) Graphic Statics	SP	1 50	
Ott's (E. A.) How to Use the Voice	HS	1 25	
How to Gesture	HS	75	
Otto's French Conversation Grammar	HO		1 20
—— Key to	HO		60
Bôcher's French Reader to	HO		1 10
German Conversation Grammar	HO		1 20
—— Key to	HO		60
Evans' German Reader to	HO		1 10
Easy German Course	DH	50	
Elementary German Grammar	HO	*69	80
See also Joynes-Otto and Gaspey-Otto-Sauer.			
Our New Possessions	AM	*10	
Our Song-Birds, 6 nos.	*ea.* CH	10	
Overton's (F.) Applied Physiology: Primary	AM	*30	
—— Intermediate	AM	*50	
—— Advanced	AM	*80	
Ovid, Selections from (Bain)	MC	**	
Owen's Homer's Iliad	AM	*1 40	
Homer's Odyssey	AM	*1 40	
Owen's (W. B.) Cicero's De Oratore	SA		1 00
Oxford Junior Speaker	BU	*56	
Senior Speaker	BU	*1 12	
Oxford Manuals: King and Parliament; Making of the English Nation; King and Baronage; Making of the British Empire; The Hundred Year War; England and the Reformation, 6 v.	*ea.* SC	50	
Packard's (A. S.) Comparative Embryology	HO		2 50
Entomology	HO		1 40
Guide to Study of Insects	HO		5 00
See also American Science Ser.			
Page's Flower Object Lessons	KT	75	68
Painter's (F. V. N.) Introd. to Eng. Lit.	SY	.	1 25
Introd. to Am. Lit., without sel	SY		1 00
" " " with annot.	SY		1 25
History of English Literature	SY		1 40
Palmer-Curtis Series of Sight-Reading Music Books:			
Manual	CR	1 00	
First Primary Reader	CR	50	
Second " "	CR	50	
First Intermediate Reader	CR	75	
Second " "	CR	75	
Advanced Reader	CR	75	
Palmer's (E.) New Parliamentary Manual	HS	75	
Palmer's (G. H.) Tr. of Homer's Odyssey	HM	1 00	
Tr. of Sophocles' Antigone	HM	75	
Palmer's (H. R.) Theory of Music	CR	1 00	
Music Class Teaching	CR	50	38
Palmer's (J. H.) Elements of Bookkeeping	BU	*72	
—— Key to	BU	*10	
—— Blanks for, 5 nos.	*ea.* BU	*10	
Pancoast's Introd. to English Literature	HO		1 25
Representative English Literature	HO		1 60
Introd. to American Literature	HO		1 00
Standard English Poems	HO		1 50
Standard English Prose	HO	**	
Panseron's A B C of Music, abridged	DS	1 00	
Paradise of Childhood, Quarter Century ed.	BO	2 00	
Park's (J. G.) English Grammar	AM	*65	
Language Lessons	AM	*35	
Parker's (F. W.) Quincy Course in Arith.	FL	15	
Language Lessons	FL	15	
Parker's (J. H.) Gothic Architecture: A B C of	SC	1 25	
Glossary of Terms	OR	3 00	
Introduction to Study of	LT	2 00	
*Parker & Parker's Elementary Course of Practical Zoology	MC	2 60	
Parker's (W. H.) Familiar Talks on Astron.	MG	1 00	
Parker & Haswell's Manual of Zoology	MC	*1 60	
Parker & Marvel's Suppl. Readers:			
1st Book	SA		30
2d "	SA		30
Parker & Watson's National Primer	AM	*12	
National 1st Reader	AM	*15	
" 2d "	AM	*25	
" 3d "	AM	*50	
" 4th "	AM	*60	
" Elementary Speller	AM	*18	
" Pronouncing "	AM	*25	
Parkes' Practical Hygiene, enl.	BL	4 50	
Parkman Leaflets	LT	50	
Parlate Italiano?	HO		40
Parley's Universal History	AM	*1 12	
See also Goodrich (S. G.).			
Parlez-Vous Français?	HO	*43	40
Parlin's (F. E.) Quincy Word List	MS	24	
Parmele's (M.) Short History of England	SC		60
" " " France	SC		60
" " " Germany	SC		60
" " " Spain	SC		60
*" " " Rome and Italy	SC		60
" " " Russia	SC		60
" " " United States	SC		60
Who? When? What?	HW	*60	
Parry's (C. H.) Fr. Passages for Unseen Translation, Elemen. Course	LN	80	
—— Higher Course	LN	1 00	
Parshall's Graded Exer. in Grammar	AM	*36	
Parsons' (F. T.) Calisthenic Songs	AM	*28	
Parsons' (J. C.) English Versification	SY		80
Parsons' (R.) Cebes' Tablet	GI	*85	75
Passano's History of Maryland	DY	*83	75
Pathfinder Physiologies, No. 1, Child's Health Primer	AM	*30	
—— No. 2, Young People's Physiol.	AM	*50	
—— No. 3, Hygienic Physiology (Steele)	AM	*1 00	
Patrick's (J. N.) Lessons in Language	LI	40	
Lessons in grammar	LI	50	
Pattee's (F. L.) Hist. of Amer. Lit.	SI	1 50	1 20
Reading Courses in " "	SI	*50	36
Patterson's Common School Speller	BU	*18	
Speller and Analyzer	BU	*32	
Centennial Spelling Blanks, 3 nos.	*ea.* BU	*7	
Elem. of Grammar and Composition	BU	*50	
Advanced Grammar and Rhetoric	BU	*94	
Geographical Drawing	*doz.* AM	*1 80	
American Word Book	AM	*25	
Patton's (J. H.) Political Economy	LV	*1 00	
Paulsen's Introduction to Philosophy	HO		3 00
System of Ethics	SC		3 00
Payne's (F. O.) Geographical Nature Studies	AM	*25	
Payson's (J. W.) Deutsches Schreibe System, 8 nos.	*doz.* AM	*84	
Deutsches System, Tracing Books	" AM	*84	
Payson (J. W.), Dunton & Scribner's Copy-Books, new ed., 6 nos.	*doz.* AM	*96	
Tracing Books, 2 nos.	" AM	*72	
Pencil Series, 7 nos.	*doz.* AM	*45	
Short Course, 7 nos.	" AM	*72	
New Handbook of Penmanship	AM	*25	
Peabody Primer and First Reader, New ed.	MU		25
2d Reader, New ed.	MU		30
3d " " "	MU		35
4th "	MU		40
5th "	MU		50
6th "	MU		60
Peabody's Moral Philosophy	AM	*90	
Peabody & Mann's After Kindergarten, What?	ST	45	
Peabody's (J. E.) Laboratory Exercises in Anatomy and Physiology	HO		60
Peabody (S. C.) Step by Step	GI	**	
Pearson's (H. C.) Gr. Prose Composition	AM	*90	
—— Key to	AM	*50	
English Composition	HE	*60	50
Pease's Singing-Book	GI	*80	70
Peaslee's Graded Selections for Memorizing	AM	*50	
Peavey's Manual of Geography	RI	75	
Peck's (H. T.) Suetonius' Cæsars	HO		1 20
Latin Pronunciation	HO		40
See Harper.			
Peck's (H. T.) and Arrowsmith's (R.) Roman Life in Latin Prose and Verse	AM	*1 50	
Peck's (W.) Constellations	SI	*1 25	
Peck's (W. G.) Manual of Algebra	AM	*1 00	
—— Key to	AM	*1 00	
Manual of Geometry	AM	*1 10	
Practical Calculus	AM	*1 25	
Analytical Geometry	AM	*1 25	
Ganot's Natural Philosophy, rev.	AM	*1 20	
Mechanics, with Calculus	AM	*1 60	

Title	Pub.	Price	Net
Peck's (W. G.) Analytical Mechanics....	AM	*1 40	
Determinants....	AM	*60	
Conic Sections....	AM	*40	
Peck's (W. M.) Graded Lessons in Numbers:			
Pt. 1, First Steps in Arithmetic....	LV	*30	
Pt. 2, Grammar School Arithmetic..	LV	*65	
Peck's (W. T.) Ovid's Metamorphoses, Bks. 1 and 2....	GI	*55	50
Peddie's (W.) Physics....	PU	2 50	
Peet's Course of Instruction, pt. 1....	BF	90	75
—— pt. 2....	BF	1 25	1 00
Language Lessons....	BF	1 25	1 00
U. S. History....	BF	1 50	1 50
Peiffer's French Drill Book, A....	JE	75	
" " " B....	JE	50	
French Pronunciation....	JE	50	
Peirce's (B. O.) Newtonian Potential Function....	GI	*1 60	1 50
Table of Integrals, rev....	GI	*1 05	1 00
Peirce's (J. M.) Elem. of Logarithms....	GI	*55	50
Mathematical Tables....	GI	*45	40
Pelham's (H. F.) Outlines of Roman Hist.	PU	1 75	
Penhallow's Vegetable Histology....	KT	1 00	
Pennell's Ancient Greece....	AL		60
Ancient Rome....	AL		60
Latin Subjunctive....	AL		25
Penniman's Common Words Difficult to Spell....	HE	*30	25
Prose Dictation Exercises....	HE	*30	25
School Poetry Book....	HE	*45	40
New Practical Speller....	HE	**	
Pennybacker's New Hist. of Texas, rev..	PC		75
Perdue's (H. A.) & Griswold's (S. E.) Language Through Nature....	RA	**	
Peres' Arithmetical Example Book....	SR	*10	8
Perkins' (C. A.) Electricity and Magnetism....	HO		1 10
Perkins' (H. S.) Song Echo....	DS	75	
Perkins' (W. O.) Golden Robin....	DS	50	
Laurel Wreath....	DS	1 00	
Mocking-Bird....	DS	50	
Vocal Echoes....	DS	1 00	
Whippoorwill....	DS	50	
Perkins' (W. O. & H. S.) Nightingale....	DS	50	
Perrin's (B.) Cæsar's Civil War, with vocabulary....	UN	*1 15	1 00
Homer's Odyssey, Bks. 1-4, text, pap....	GI	*40	
—— text and notes, cl....	GI	*1 50	1 40
—— Odyssey, Bks. 5-8....	GI	*1 50	1 40
Perrin (B.) & Seymour's (T. D.) Bks. 1-4, 9-12 of Homer's Odyssey....	GI	*1 65	1 50
—— Ed. of Four Bks....	GI	*1 35	1 25
Perrin's (M. L.) Algebra Problems....	LI	*60	
Perry's (B.) Study of Prose Fiction....	HM	**	
Perry's (A. L.) Introd. to Polit. Economy....	SC	1 50	
Principles of Political Economy....	SC	2 00	
Political Economy....	SC	2 50	
Perry's (J.) Applied Mechanics....	VN		2 50
Perry's (T. S.) Greek Literature....	HO		4 00
Perthes's Ancient Atlas....	LB		90
Peterman's Civil Government....	AM	*60	
Petermann's Neues Erstes Lesebuch....	ST	30	
—— Zweites....	ST	60	
—— Drittes....	ST	70	
Peters' (F. N.) Modern Chemistry....	MY	*1 10	
—— Laboratory Experiments....	MY	**	
Peterson's Familiar Science, 12°....	SO	*1 25	
—— 18°....	SO	*63	
Peterson's & Baldwin's Algebra Problems....	HE		30
*Peterson's (H. C.) First Steps in English Composition....	FL	35	
Pettee's Plane Geometry....	SI	*82	75
Phædri Augusti Liberti....	MU		30
Phelan's School History of Tennessee...	BU	*30	
Phelps' (E. C.) Crown of Song, No. 1....	BU	*40	
—— No. 2....	BU	*60	
Phelps & Lewis' Song Sheaf....	BU	*60	
Philbrick's American Union Speaker....	TH		1 25
Primary Union Speaker....	TH		48
" School Tablets.... *ea.*	TH		50
Phillips' Drawing-Books, 7 nos.... *doz.*	BN		1 08
Geographical Readers:			
First Steps, pt. 1....	BN	*32	27
—— pt. 2....	BN	*36	30
England....	BN	*43	36
British Isles, etc....	BN	*65	54
Europe....	BN	*75	63
The World....	BN	*86	72
Historical Readers:			
Stories from English History....	BN	*36	30
Early England....	BN	*42	35
Middle "....	BN	*62	52
Modern "....	BN	*62	52
1st Poetical Reading-Book....	BN		36
Poetical Reading-Book....	BN		90
Phillips' (M. G.) English Literature, 2 v..	AM	*4 00	
Phillips' (P.) Day School Singer....	AM	*30	
Song Life....	BI	50	
Phillips & Beebe's Graphic Algebra....	HO		1 60
Phillips-Fisher's Elements of Geometry..	AM	*1 75	
—— Key to....	AM	*1 50	
Elements of Geometry, Abridged....	AM	*1 25	
Plane Geometry....	AM	*80	
Geometry of Space....	AM	*1 25	
Logarithms of Numbers....	AM	*30	
Phillips-Strong's Elements of Trigonometry, Plane and Spherical....	AM	*90	
—— Key to....	AM	*1 25	
Logarithmic and Trigonometric Tables....	AM	1 00	
Trigonometry and Tables in 1 v....	AM	1 40	
Phyfe's How Should I Pronounce?....	PU	75	
The School Pronouncer....	PU	1 25	
Test Pronouncer....	PU	50	
Pickering's (E. C.) Physical Manipulations, v. 1....	HM	3 00	
—— v. 2....	HM	4 00	
Pickering's (J.) Greek Lexicon....	LI	*2 80	
Pierce's Problems in Element. Physics..	HO		60
Pierce's (E. M.) First Steps in Arithmetic....	SI	45	36
Elements of Arithmetic....	SI	45	36
*Intermediate Arithmetic....	SI		48
Pierson's (H. W.) One Syllable Histories:			
England....	RU	75	
France....	RU	75	
Germany....	RU	75	
Lives of the Presidents....	RU	75	
United States....	RU	75	
Pillsbury's (J. H.) Laboratory Guide in General Biology....	SI	*66	60
Pinneo's Primary Grammar....	AM	*30	
Analytical "....	AM	*45	
Guide to Composition....	AM	*60	
Pinney's Easy Lessons in French....	BU	*64	
First Book in French....	BU	*45	
*Pinney (A. E.) Spanish and English Conversation Bk. 1....	GI	65	60
Bk. 2....	GI	**	
Piper's (J.) Graded Seat Work in Arithmetic, Nos. 1-4.... *ea.*	AM	*8	
Pitman's (B.) Phrase-Book....	PH	1 00	
Pitman's (B.) & Howard's (J. B.) Reporter's Companion....	PH	1 00	
Reporter's 1st Reader....	PH	25	
Manual of Phonography....	PH	1 00	
Phonographic Copy-Book....	PH	7	
" Dictionary....	PH	2 50	
" Reader....	PH	25	
" 2d Reader....	PH	25	
*" Dictionary and Phrase-Book (in 1 v.)....	PH	3 00	
Business Letters, No. 1, in Shorthand.	PH	25	
Pitman's (I.) Shorthand Instructor....	PI	1 50	1 00
—— pt. 1....	PI	75	50
—— pt. 2....	PI	75	50
—— Key to, Complete....	PI	40	27
Pitman's (I.) Phonographic Teacher....	PI	20	14
—— Key to....	PI	20	14
Manual....	PI	50	34
—— Key to....	PI	20	14
Phonographic Reporter....	PI	60	40
Teacher and Manual in 1 v....	PI	90	60
Progressive Studies....	PI	40	27
Phonographic Reader....	PI	20	14
Phrase-Book....	PI	40	27
Phonographic Dictionary....	PI	1 50	1 00
Reporting Exercises....	PI	20	14
20th Century Dictation and Legal Forms....	PI	*75	50
Instruction in Legal Forms....	PI	25	17
Headline Shorthand Copy-Books, Books 1-3.... *ea.*	PI	10	7
Business Correspondence in Shorthand, Nos. 1 and 2.... *ea.*	PI	30	20
Selections from American Authors in Shorthand....	PI	40	27
Spanish Phonography....	PI	1 75	1 32
German "....	PI	50	38
French "....	PI	35	27
Abridged Shorthand Dictionary....	PI	85	57
Æsop's Fables....	PI	20	14
Evolutionary History of England (Oscar Browning)....	PI	60	40
Pitman's (I.) Rapid Series:			
Practical Spanish Grammar....	PI	40	27
" German "....	PI	40	27
Spanish, French and German Business Letters.... *ea.*	PI	20	14
Practical French Grammar....	PI	40	27
Plate's Lehr- u. Uebungsbuch, Bk. 1....	HR	35	25
" " " Bk. 2....	HR	45	30
Platner's Greek and Roman Versification.	AL		75
Platner's (S. B.) Pliny's Select Letters, pap....	SA		30

Platt's German Studies.....DH 1 35
Playfair's Euclid.....LI *1 28
Plays and Songs for Kindergarten.....ST 50
Ploetz's (C.) Epitome of History.....HM 3 00
Ploetz's French Grammar.....KC 80
Plummer's Supp. to Advanced Arith.....HE 25
Poitevin. *See* Maurice.
Poland's First Book for Pen or Pencil, pts. 1 and 2.....*doz.*AM *72
Poland's (W.) Fundamental Ethics.....SI 80 72
Polano's Hebrew Speller.....BM 12
Poll's Materials for German Prose Composition.....HO 90
Pollard's (J.) Battles of U. S. in One Syllable.....RU 75
Pollard's (R. S.) Synthetic Method of Teaching Reading:
Teachers' Manual.....AM *1 00
First Bk. for Little Folks.....AM *25
Primer.....AM *15
First Reader.....AM *24
Second ".....AM *35
Third ".....AM *45
Advanced Reader.....AM *85
Intermediate Reader.....AM *65
Speller.....AM *18
Advanced Speller.....AM *30
" " pt. 1.....AM *17
— pt. 2.....AM *18
Pollock's Cheerful Echoes.....DW 50
National Kindergarten Manual.....DW 75
" " Songs and Plays.....DW 50
Pomeroy's Introductory Reader.....UL 30 25
Introductory Speller.....UL 25 18
Pooler's Spelling Book.....AM *20
Popular Educator Arith., pts. 1 and 2. *ea.*ED 30
Popular System of Penmanship, nos. 1–5. *doz.*SO *83
Porter's (L. H.) Constitutional History of United States.....HO 1 20
Porter's (N.) Human Intellect.....SC 5 00
Intellectual Philosophy.....SC 3 00
Moral Science.....SC 3 00
Posse's Special Kinesiology of Educational Gymnastics.....LE *3 00
Handbook of School Gymnastics.....LE *55
— Interleaved ed.....LE *82 50
Post's (E.) Latin at Sight.....GI *90 80
Postgate's First Latin Primer.....CA 40
New Latin Primer.....CA 1 09
Potter's New Elementary Geography.....CB 60
— Teachers' ed.....CB 85
Advanced Geography.....CB 1 25
— Teachers' ed.....CB 1 50
Potter's Graded Review System of Penmanship.....*doz.*CB 1 00 80
Potter's (H. L. D.) Manual of Reading.....AM *1 00
Potter's (J. L.) Hebrew Lexicon. *See* Robinson (E.)
Potter & Putnam's Natural Drawing ser., 6 nos.....*doz.*PM *1 50
Potter & Putnam's System of Vertical Writing, 10 nos.....*doz.*PM *96
Economic System of Penmanship, 6 nos.....*doz.*PM *96
Poulson's Botanical Micro-Chemistry.....KT 1 00
*Poulsson's (E.) Holiday Songs.....BO 2 00
Powell's How to See.....BU *30
— Teachers' ed.....BU *42
How to Talk.....BU *42
" " Write.....BU *60
Powell's (F. Y.) & Tout's History of England, 3 v.....*ea.*LN 1 00
Powell's (W. B.) History of the United States for Beginners.....MC 65
Powell's (W. B.) & Connolly's (L.) Rational Grammar of the Eng. Language.....AM *60
Powers' (M. R.) Bookkeeping.....AM *80
— Blanks to.....AM *40
Powers' & Lyons' Complete Accountant:
Counting House ed.....PW 1 60
— Blanks for.....PW 2 00
— High School ed.....PW 1 00
— — Blanks for.....PW 80
First Lessons in Bookkeeping.....PW 75
— Blanks for.....PW 50
Single Entry Bookkeeping.....PW 35
New Business Arithmetic.....PW 1 05
Practical ".....PW 80
" Speller.....PW 20
Lessons in Munson's Phonography.....PW 1 50
" " Pitman's ".....PW 1 25
Manual of Business Writing.....PW 50
Twenty Lessons in Letter Writing.....PW 50
Shorthand Dictionary (Isaac Pitman System).....PW 1 00
Powers' & Lyons' Shorthand Dictionary (Munson System).....PW 1 00
Modern Business Speller.....PW 25
Modern Commercial Arithmetic PW **
Office Methods and practical Bookkeeping, pts. 1 and 2.....PW 2 75
— — Pt. 1.....PW 2 10
Poynter's Art Text-Books, 8 v.....*ea.*SC 2 00
Practical Anal. (Penmanship).....*doz.*SR *1 04 90
— Key.....SR *27 25
Practical Color Work for Primary and Ungraded Schools (Chace).....BO *25
Practical Copybooks:
Complete Course, 6 nos.....*doz.*WR *96
Shorter Course, 5 nos..... " WR *72
Practical Text-Books: Spelling.....PY 35 20
— Blanks.....PY 15 9
Commercial Arithmetic.....PY 1 25 75
High School Arithmetic.....PY 90 55
Shorthand.....PY 1 50 1 00
Progressive Bookkeeping.....PY 1 00 65
Mercantile ".....PY 1 50 90
Complete ".....PY 2 25 1 30
Bookkeeping Blanks, 1st set.....PY 50 35
" Intermediate.....PY 80 50
" Advanced.....PY 1 35 65
Letter Writing.....PY 75 50
Graded Letter Writing Lessons.....PY 30 18
Plain English.....PY 90 60
New Exercises in English.....PY 40 20
Typewriting Instructor.....PY 1 00 65
Prang's Drawing-Books and Manuals:
Primary Teachers' Manual, the Use of Models.....PR 50
— without Clay Modelling, 2 pts. *ea* PR 25
Primary Art Education, 1st Year.....PR 50
" " " 2d ".....PR 50
Prang's American Text-Book of Art Education:
Drawing-Books, 1–4, rev. ed.....*doz.*PR 1 00
" " 5–6, Clark Ed..... " PR 1 00
" " 7–10, " " " PR 2 00
Teachers' Manual for Bks. 1 to 9. *ea.*PR 50
Prang's Shorter Course in Form Study and Drawing:
Drawing-Books, 1–5.....*doz.*PR 1 80
Introductory Drawing-Book..... " PR 1 80
Teachers' Manual for Bks. 1–5.....*ea.*PR 50
Prang's Complete Course in Form Study and Drawing.
Drawing-Bks., 1–6, with patterns..*doz.*PR 1 20
" Bk. 7, " " " PR 2 40
" Bks. 8–10 (no patterns required).....*doz.*PR 2 40
Teachers' Manual for Bks. 1 to 6. *ea.*PR 50
" " " " 7 and 8. *ea.*PR 75
Prang's Drawing-Book of Geometric Problems.....*doz.*PR 3 00
Prang's Manual for Color Instruction.....PR 1 00
*Pratt (H. S.) A Course in Invertebrate Zoölogy.....GI *1 35 1 25
Pratt's (M. L.) New Calisthenics.....ED 1 25
Supplement to New Calisthenics.....ED 50
Practical Language Exercises.....ED 40
Fairyland of Flowers.....ED 1 00
American History Stories, 4 v.....*ea.*ED 36
Young Folks' Lib. of Am. Hist., 6 v..ED (30c.; 40c.; 60c.)
America's Story for American Children, 5 vs.; v. 1.....HE 30
— v. 3–5.....*ea.*HE 40
Pray's (M. L.) Motion Songs for Public Schools.....HE *48
Preble's (H.) Adelphoe of Terence.....GI *30
Preble (H.) and Hull's (L. C.) Latin Less..HO 1 40
Preble & Parker's Latin Writing.....GI *55 [illegible]
Preliminary French Drill.....JE 50
Prendergast's Mastery Series:
French.....AP 45
German.....AP 45
Spanish.....AP 45
Prentice's (W. A.) History of New York State.....BI 1 60
Preparatory Latin and Greek Texts.....HO 1 20
— Greek Part.....HO 60
— Latin ".....HO 80
Prescott's (A. B.) Qualitative Chemistry.....VN 1 50
Proximate Organic Analysis.....VN 1 75
Qualitative Chemical ".....VN 3 50
Prescott's (W. H.) Leaflets.....LI *36
Price's (E. D.) Students' Imperial Dictionary of the Eng. Language.....PU 1 50
Priest's Little Pieces for Little Speakers.LE 50

Title	Pub.	Price	Net
Prigg's Normal Speaker	HO	50	
Primary Drawing and Reading Cards	LB	*15	18
Prince's (J. T.) Arithmetic by Grades, Bks. 1-8 *ea.*	GI	*28	20
—— Manual for Teachers	GI	*90	80
Proctor's (M.) Astronomy:			
Stars and Constellations	HW		50
—— with map blanks	HW		75
Stories of Starland	PM	*50	
Proctor's (R. A.), Differential Calculus	LN	90	
Elementary Physical Geography	LN	60	
Easy Star Lessons	PU	2 50	
Half Hours with the Stars	PU	2 00	
Progressive Course in Reading	BU		
See Aldrich's and Forbes'.			
Pujol's & Van Norman's French Class-Book	AM	*1 60	
Putnam's Art Handbooks (Carter), 3 v. *ea.*	PU	1 25	
Pocket Atlas of the World, new ed	PU	1 25	
—— leather	PU	1 75	
Gem Pocket Dictionary, leath	PU	75	
Putnam's (D.) Elementary Psychology	AM	*90	
Text-Book of Psychology	AM	*1 00	
Putnam's (W. H.) Essentials of English Grammar	PM	*35	
Putzger's Historical School Atlas	LB	1 00	
Pyle's (K.) Prose and Verse for Children	AM	*40	
Pylodet's Beginning French	HO		45
Beginner's French Reader	HO		45
2d French Reader	HO		90
Littérature Française Classique	HO		1 20
" " Contemp	HO		1 16
Gouttes de Rosée	HO		50
Mère L'Oie	HO		40
German Conversation	HO		50
Pynchon's Chemical Physics	VN	3 00	
Quackenbos' (G. P.) Primary Arithmetic	AM	*18	
Elementary Arithmetic	AM	*31	
Mental "	AM	*28	
Practical " Pt. 1	AM	*35	
" " Pt. 2	AM	*35	
—— Key to	AM	*14	
Higher Arithmetic	AM	*67	
—— Key to	AM	*53	
First Book in Grammar	AM	*35	
English Grammar	AM	*63	
Illustr. Lessons in our Language	AM	*42	
First Lessons in Composition	AM	*63	
Composition and Rhetoric	AM	*1 05	
American History	AM	*1 03	
Primary History of U. S	AM	*63	
Elementary U. S. History, new ed	AM	*60	
School U. S. History	AM	*1 05	
Natural Philosophy	AM	*1 23	
Quackenbos' (J. D.) Hist. of Anc. Lit	AM	*1 20	
Practical Rhetoric	AM	*1 00	
Qualitative Chemical Analysis of Inorganic Substances	AM	*1 50	
Questions in Geography	TH		14
Quimby's Form of Parsing *doz.*	TH		36
Raby's Select Readings	HR	2 00	1 85
Racine's Iphigenie (Woodward)	AM	*60	
Racine's Athalie (Sumichrast)	MC	**	
Raddatz's Schiller's Der Neffe als Onkel	AL		50
Ragozin's (Z. A.) History of the World, Pt. 1, Earliest Peoples	HW	60	
" 2, Early Egypt	HW	60	
" 3, Greece	HW	**	
" 4, Rome	HW	**	
Siegfried	HW	60	
Beowulf	HW	60	
Frithjof	HW	60	
Rambeau & Passy's Chrestomathie Phonétique	HO		1 50
Ramsey's (M. M.) Modern Spanish	HO		1 80
Elementary Spanish Reader	HO		1 00
Spanish Grammar	HO		1 50
Ramsey's (M. M.) & Lewis' (A.) Exercises in Spanish Composition	HO		75
Rand's Practical Method of Singing	DS	1 00	
Rand, McNally & Co.'s Handy Atlas of the World	RA	1 60	
Indexed Handy Atlas of the World	RA	30 00	
" " " " " " 2 v.	RA	18 50	
Universal " " " " "	RA	4 50	
Pocket " " " " "	RA	25	
" Cyclopedia	RA	25	
Primary Geography	RA		55
Elementary "	RA		60
—— 1901 ed	RA	**	
Grammar School Geography	RA		1 25
—— 1901 ed	RA	**	
Rand-McNally U. S. History	RA	**	
Randall's (A. T) Reading and Elocution	AM	*1 00	
Randall (O. E.) Shades and Shadows and Perspective	GI	**	
Randolph's General Biology	HO		80

Title	Pub.	Price	Net
Rangabe's Practical Method Modern Greek Language	GI	*2 10	2 00
Ranke's Kaiserwahl Karl's V. (Schoenfeld)	AM	*35	
Rannie's Historical Outline of English Constitution	SC	1 00	
Ransome's (C.) Short History of England	LN	1 50	
Advanced History of England	MC	2 25	
Rapp's Test Words in Spelling	MP	31	**
Rasmussen's Physical Culture	SR	1 25	1 25
Rassweiler's (H. H.) Anatomy, Physiology, and Hygiene	CS	*75	60
Rational Method in Reading (Ward):			
Primer, Complete Book	SI		36
" pt. 1, Reading by the Word Method	SI		23
Primer, pt. 2, Sight and Phonetic Reading Combined	SI		24
First Reader, Complete Book	SI		36
" " pt. 1, Sight and Phonetic Reading	SI		23
First Reader, pt. 2, Sight and Phonetic Reading. Advance Work	SI		24
Second Reader, Complete Book	SI		44
" " pt. 1, Sight and Phonetic Reading. Advance Work	SI		24
Second Reader, pt. 2, Sight and Phonetic Reading. The Remaining Phonograms	SI		28
Manual of Instruction	SI		36
Phonetic Cards. First Set. To accompany Primer	SI		36
Phonetic Cards. Second Set. To accompany First Reader	SI		48
Phonetic Cards. Third Set. To accompany Second Reader	SI		36
Third Reader	SI	60	48
*Rational Slant System of Writing, 4 nos., *doz.*	EL		90
Rational Writing Books, Vertical *doz.*	WR	*72	
Rattan's California Flora and West Coast Botany	WA	1 50	1 25
Raub's Elementary Arithmetic	WR	*35	
Complete Arithmetic	WR	*60	
—— Key	WR	*60	
Lessons in English	WR	*35	
Practical English Grammar	WR	*60	
Normal Speller	SO	*28	
Primary Speller	SO	*21	
Raub's Literature for Beginners (Swineford)	RB	75	60
Studies in Eng. and Amer. Lit	RB	1 50	1 20
Tests in Spelling and Pronunciation	RB	40	32
Grammatical Analysis by Diagrams	RB	25	20
Practical Rhetoric	RB	1 20	96
Punctuation and Letter Writing	RB	40	32
Hints and Helps on English Gram	RB	1 00	80
Practical Language Work for Beginners	RB	40	32
Rawles' Civil Gov't of Indiana	EL	*55	50
Rawlinson's Story of Egypt	PU	1 50	
Manual of Ancient History	AM	*1 25	
Rawlinson's Origin of Nations	SC	1 00	
Ray's Mathematical Series:			
Arithmetic, New Test Examples	AM	*35	
" " —— with Ans	AM	*35	
" " Primary	AM	*15	
" " Intellectual	AM	*25	
" " Elementary	AM	*35	
" " Practical	AM	*50	
" " Key to Intellectual and Practical	AM	*50	
" " Higher	AM	*65	
" " —— Key to	AM	*75	
" " Rudiments of	AM	*35	
Test Example Tablets, 8 nos *doz.*	AM	*1 00	
Ans. to all Probs. in Tablets 4-8	AM	*10	
Algebra, New Elementary	AM	*60	
" " Higher	AM	*1 00	
" Key to Elem. and High	AM	*1 00	
" New Complete	AM	*1 00	
" —— Key to	AM	*1 00	
" Test Problems in	AM	*50	
" —— Answers and Solutions to	AM	*50	
Geometry, Plane and Solid	AM	*70	
" Analytic	AM	*1 75	
" Trigonom. and Tables	AM	*1 20	
Surveying and Navigation	AM	*1 20	
Elem. of the Infinites. Calculus	AM	*1 50	
New Elem. of Astronomy (Peabody)	AM	*1 20	
Raymond's (G. L.) Orator's Manual	SI	*1 25	1 12
Raymond's (G. L.) and Wheeler's (G. P.) Writer	SI	*90	
Raymond's (W. G.) Plane Surveying and Tables	AM	*3 00	
Reade's Business Reader	SR	*1 01	90
Reade's (A. A.) How to Write English	LI	*45	

Readings for Students (5 v., var. prices) .... HO
Redway's (J. W.) Elementary Physical Geography .... SC 1 25
Commercial Geography .... SC **
—— New Basis of Geography .... MC *1 10
Geography N. Y. State .... PM *50
Reed's (A.) Word Lessons .... MY *25
Introductory Language Work .... MY *40
Reed & Kellogg's Graded Lessons in English, 1901 ed. .... MY *40
Higher Lessons in English .... MY *63
Higher Lessons in English and Word Building .... MY *66
One-Book Course in English .... MY *63
*High School Grammar .... MY *80
Reese's Zoölogy. *See* Chambers'.
Reffelt's Earliest Lessons in Arithmetic .... ST 20
1st Book for School and House .... ST 30
2d " " " " " .... ST 50
Regal's Lessons for Little Readers .... HB 30
*Regent's Edition of Irving's Sketch Book (Benjamin) .... AM *50
Regent's Questions Complete .... BI 1 00
—— with Key .... BI 2 00
Arithmetic .... BI 25
—— Key to .... BI 25
Geography .... BI 25
—— Key to .... BI 25
Grammar .... BI 25
—— with Key .... BI 1 00
—— Key to .... BI 25
Spelling .... BI 25
Supplements, Nos. 1 to 2 .... *ea.* BI 25
" " 3 to 7 .... *ea.* BI 1 00
Algebra, Bookkeeping, Physics; American History; Civil Government and School Law; Drawing; Methods and School Economy; Physiology; 6 v. .... *ea.* BI 25
Poems for Memorizing (French and German) .... BI 25
—— .... HO 20
Reid's (L. H.) English Grammar Primer .... BR 30
Reid's Philosophy (Sneath) .... HO 1 50
*Reighard's & Jenning's Anatomy of the Cat .... HO 4 00
*Reiley's (K. C.) Practical Exercises on the Latin Verb .... AM *50
Relton's (W.) Graduated Writing Exercises in Phonography .... PH 30
Remsen's Organic Chemistry .... HB *1 30 1 20
Laboratory Manual (Orndorff) .... HB *40 35
Theoretical Chemistry, New ed. .... LA 2 00
*College Chemistry .... HO 2 00
See also American Sci. Ser.
Renton's Outlines of English Literature .... SC *1 00 80
Rettger's Advanced Physiology .... IN 2 00
Reynolds' (J. E.) Experimental Chemistry, pt. 1, Introduction .... LN 45
—— pt. 2, Non-metals .... LN 75
—— pt. 3, Metals .... LN 1 05
—— pt. 4, Organic .... LN 1 20
Reynolds' (J. L.) Reader and Speller. *doz.* WC 70
Primer .... " WC 45
1st Reader .... WC 13
—— Popular ed .... WC 7
2d Reader .... WC 20
—— Popular ed .... WC 12
3d Reader .... WC 30
—— Popular ed .... WC 21
4th Reader .... WC 40
—— Popular ed .... WC 25
5th Reader .... WC 60
Copy-Books, 6 nos. .... *doz.* WC 75
—— Tracing, 2 nos .... " WC 65
Rhoads' Primary Arithmetic .... SO 25
Rhoades's (L. I.) Story of Philadelphia .... AM *65
Rice's Rational Spelling Book, pt. 1, bds. .... AM *15
—— Pt. 1, cl. .... AM *17
—— Pt. 2, bds. .... AM *20
—— Pt. 2, cl. .... AM *22
Rice & Johnson's Differential Calculus .... WI 3 00
—— Abridged .... WI 1 50
Differential and Integral Calculus, Abridged .... WI 2 50
Rich's (A. W.) New Higher Arithmetic .... FL *75
New Practical Arithmetic .... FL *50
Richards' (E. L.) Plane and Spherical Trigonometry .... AM *1 20
Logarithmic Tables .... AM *60
*Navigation and Nautical Astronomy AM 75
Richards' (Z.) Natural Arithmetic .... LR *40 32
—— Teacher's ed .... LR *50 42
Richardson's Laboratory Manual and Principles of Chemistry .... MC 1 10
Richardson's (A. S.) Talks on English Literature, new ed. .... MG 1 50
Richardson's (C. F.) Am. Lit., pt. 1 .... PU 3 00
—— pt. 2 .... PU 3 00
Richardson's (C. F.) Am. Lit., New ed. in 1 v. .... PU 3 50
Primer of American Lit., rev. .... HM 35
Richardson's (R. B.) Æschines Against Ctesiphon .... GI *45 40
—— with notes .... GI *1 50 1 40
Richardson's (W. H.) Graded Language Exercises .... LR *25 20
—— in 3 pts. .... *ea.* LR *10 8
Richter's Inorganic Chemistry .... BL *1 75
Organic Chemistry, 3d ed., v. 1 .... BL 3 00
—— v. 2 .... BL 3 00
Richter's (H.) Graphic Shorthand (Gabelsberger), pt. 1, Corresponding Style .... IT 1 00 70
*Reader to .... IT 50
Richter's (J. P.) Selections (Collins) .... AM *60
Ricker's Elements of English .... LR *40 36
Rickett's Assaying .... WI 3 00
Rickoff's (R. D.) Suppl. First Reader .... AM *25
Ricks' Natural Hist. Object Lessons .... HB 1 50
Ridpath's U. S. Hist., Grammar School .. AM *60
U. S. History, Academic ed. .... AM *1 20
Riehl's (W. H.) Die Vierzehn Nothelfer and Trost um Trost (Sihler) .... AM *30
Der Fluch der Schönheit (Frost) .... AM *30
*Das Spielmanskind and Der Stumme Ratsherr (Priest) .... AM *35
Riggs' (J. D. S.) In Latinum (Cæsar), rev. ed. .... SR 50
In Latinum (Cicero), rev. ed. .... SR 50
Riggs' (S. M.) Studies in American Hist .... GI **
Rightmyer's Penmanship, 18 nos. .... *doz.* BB 70
Riley's New Phonic Primer .... PM *24
Riley's School Hist. of Mississippi .... JH 75 60
Rimmer's Elements of Design, new ed. .... LE 2 00
Ring's 3000 Exercises in Arithmetic .... FO 30 25
—— Key to .... FO 30 25
Riodu's Lucie, French and English Conversation .... HO 60
Ripley's Parsing and Analysis .... PB 40
Ripley (F. H.) and Tapper (T.). *See* Natural Music Course.
Rippe's Des Kindes Erstes Buch (Bercy) .... JE 40
Ritchie's (F.) First Steps in Greek .... LN 50
Latin Prose Composition .... LN 80
Easy Continuous Latin Prose .... LN 80
Easy Latin Passages .... LN 75
Ritter's (C.) Geographical Studies .... AM *1 00
Comparative Geography .... AM *1 00
Ritter's Musical History .... SO 75
Rivers' Mental Philosophy .... SU 1 00
Moral Philosophy .... SU 1 00
Riverside Art Series (E. M. Hurll):
1. Raphael, pap. .... HM 35
" cl. .... HM 50
2. Rembrandt, pap. .... HM 35
" cl. .... HM 50
3. Michelangelo, pap. .... HM 35
" cl. .... HM 50
4. J. F. Millet, pap. .... HM 35
" cl. .... HM 50
5. Sir Joshua Reynolds, pap. .... HM 35
" cl. .... HM 50
6. Murillo, pap .... HM 35
" cl. .... HM 50
7. Greek Sculpture, pap. .... HM 35
" cl. .... HM 50
8. Titian, pap. .... HM 35
" cl. .... HM 50
9. Landseer, pap. .... HM 35
" cl. .... HM 50
10. Correggio, pap. .... HM 35
" cl. .... HM 50
11. Tuscan Sculpture, pap. .... HM 35
" cl. .... HM 50
12. Van Dyck, pap. .... HM 35
" cl. .... HM 50
†Riverside Biographical Series, 15 v. .. *ea.* HM 50
Riverside Language and Reading Course:
Riverside Instruction Frame .... HM 10 00
" Manual for Teachers .... HM 15
" Primer and Reader, pap. .... HM 25
—— cl. .... HM 30
†Riverside Literature Ser., 141 nos. .... *ea.* HM 15
15 double nos., pap. .... " HM 30
2 triple no., pap. .... HM 45
6 quadruple nos., pap. .... *ea.* HM 50
1 quintuple no., pap. .... HM 60
1 special no., pap. .... HM 20
1 special no., pap. .... HM 25
36 nos., cl. .... *ea.* HM 25
42 double nos., cl. .... " HM 40
1 double no., bds. .... HM 40
7 triple nos., cl. .... *ea.* HM 50
7 quadruple nos., cl .... " HM 60

†For List see page 96.

†Riverside Literature Ser., 1 quintuple no., cl. ....HM 75
2 special nos., cl. ....HM 80
‡Riverside School Library, 50 v. ....HM
(prices, ea., 60c.; 70c.)
Riverside Song Book, pap. ....HM 30
—— bds. ....HM 40
Rix's Songs of School and flag ....RN 75
Roark's Psychology in Education ....AM *1 00
Robbins' Surveying and Navigation ....HS 50
Robbins' (E.) Primary Dictionary ....LO 35 21
Elements of Mythology ....EL *70 65
Robbins' (E. D.) Phonetics for Schools ..SA 20 15
Robbins' (R. D. C.) Xenophon's Memorabilia ....AM *1 40
Roberts' (A. W.) Nepos ....GI *85 75
Cæsar's Gallic War, Bk. 1 ....GI *50 45
Roberts' (J. P.) English and Italian Dictionary ....CH 2 75
Roberts' (R. D.) The Earth's History ....SC 1 50
Robertson's Bookkeeping ....BW *1 75 1 50
—— Blanks ....BW 45
Practice Blanks ....BW 35
Robertson's (G. C.) Elements of Psychology ....SC 1 00
General Philosophy ....SC 1 25
Robertson's (J. L.) English Literature ...AM *1 25
Robertson's (T.) Introductory French Course ....LO 1 20 96
Intermediate French Course ....LO 1 40 1 12
Whole French Course ....LO 1 60 1 28
—— Key to ....LO 50 40
New Spanish Course ....LO 1 50 1 20
Robinson's (E.) Greek Test. Lexicon ....HM 4 00
Gesenius' Hebrew-English Old Testament Lexicon ....HM 6 00
Potter's English-Hebrew Lexicon ....HM 2 00
Robinson's (E. G.) Principles and Practice of Morality ....SI *1 60 1 50
Christian Evidences ....SI 1 25
Robinson's (H. N.) New Primary Arithmetic ....AM *18
New Rudiments of Arithmetic ....AM *30
" Intellectual " ....AM *35
" Practical " ....AM *65
—— Key to ....AM *65
New Higher Arithmetic ....AM *1 00
—— Key to ....AM *1 00
Progressive Table-Book (Fish) ....AM *15
New Table-Book (Fish) ....AM *18
Progressive Primary Arithmetic (Fish) ....AM *18
First Lessons in Mental and Written Arithmetic ....AM *25
Progressive Intellectual Arithmetic (Fish) ....AM *29
Rudiments of Written Arithmetic (Fish) ....AM *32
Junior Class Arithmetic (Fish) ....AM *55
Elements of " ....AM *40
Progressive Practical Arithmetic (Fish) ....AM *66
—— Key to ....AM *65
Progressive Higher Arithmetic (Fish) ....AM *96
—— Key to ....AM *90
New Elementary Algebra ....AM *1 06
—— Key to ....AM *90
New University Algebra ....AM *1 58
—— Key to ....AM *1 50
New Geometry and Trigonometry ....AM *1 60
Surveying and Navigation (Root) ....AM *1 60
Conic Sections and Analytical Geometry (Quimby) ....AM *1 60
Geometry (separate) ....AM *90
Trigonometry (separate) ....AM *90
—— Key to Geometry and Trigonometry, etc ....AM *1 60
Differential and Integral Calculus (Quimby) ....AM *1 80
Robinson's (H. N.) Shorter Course:
First Book in Arithmetic (Fish) ....AM *30
Complete " " ....AM *75
—— pt. 1, with Answers ....AM *50
—— pt. 2, " " ....AM *50
—— Key to ....AM *72
Beginner's Book in Arithmetic ....AM *30
Graded School " ....AM *60
Arithmetical Problems, with Answers (Fish) ....AM *72
—— Key to ....AM *72
Complete Algebra (Ficklin) ....AM *1 44
—— Key to ....AM *90
Robinson's (W. S.) First History of Rome. LN 80
Roche's French Plays for Girls, 6 v. ...*ea.* MY *25
Rockliff's (J. A.) Exercises for translation into Latin ....PT 1 25

†For List see page 96. ‡For List see page 97

Rockwood's Cicero's Cato Major de Senectute ....AM *75
Rockwood's Cicero's De Officiis ....UN *1 04 90
*Roddy's (H. J.) Elementary Geography. AM *50
*Complete Geography ....AM *1 00
Rodger's Elements of Mensuration ....BU *42
—— Key to ....BU *42
Roehrich's Spanish Reader, with vocab. .CH 1 35
Roemer's Cours de Lecture, 3 v. ......*ea.* AP 1 25
Principles of Grammar ....AP 1 00
French Dict. of English Idioms ....LO 1 25 1 00
Rogers' Brief Introd. to Modern Philosophy ....MC 1 25
*Students' Hist. of Philosophy ....MC 2 00
Rogers' Social Economy ....PU 75
Rogers' (A. W.) Business Handwriting ....FI 35 21
Rogers' (L. C.) French Sight Reading ...AM *40
Rolfe's English Classics:
Shakespeare, 40 v ....*ea.* AM *56
Browning's Select Poems ....AM *56
Browning's Select Dramas ....AM *56
Goldsmith's Select Poems ....AM *56
Gray's Select Poems ....AM *56
Macaulay's Lays of Ancient Rome ...AM *56
Milton's Minor Poems ....AM *56
Wordsworth's Select Poems ....AM *56
Scott's Tales of Chivalry ....AM *50
Tales from English History ....AM *50
Fairy Tales ....AM *50
Tales from Scottish History ....AM *50
" " Shakespeare, Comedies ...AM *50
" " " Tragedies ...AM *50
Study of Elementary English ....AM *36
Rolfe's Students' Series:
Byron's Childe Harold ....HM 75
Morris' Atalanta's Race, etc ....HM 75
Scott's Lady of the Lake ....HM 75
" Lay of the Last Minstrel ....HM 75
" Marmion ....HM 75
Tennyson's Coming of Arthur, etc. ..HM 75
" Enoch Arden, etc ....HM 75
" In Memoriam ....HM 75
" Idylls of the King ....HM 1 00
" Lancelot and Elaine, etc. HM 75
" Princess ....HM 75
" Select Poems ....HM 75
Rolfe's Terence's Heauton Timorumenos ....GI *30 25
Rolfe's (J. C.) Viri Romæ ....AL 75
Cornelius Nepos ....AL 1 10
Livy, Bk. 1 ....AL 25
*Satires and Epistles of Horace ....AL 1 40
Rolfe & Dennison's Junior Latin Book ...AL 1 25
Rollins' Elementary French Reader ....AL 90
Romans Choisis, 24 v ....*ea.* JE 85
—— pap. ...." JE 60
Ronge's Kindergarten Guide ....ST 2 10
Root's (G. F.) Empire of Song ....CR 60
Forest Choir ....CR 40
First Years in Song Land ....CR 50
Normal Musical Handbook ....CR 3 00
—— Bks. 1-2 ....CR 1 00
—— Bk. 3 ....CR 1 00
—— Bks. 4-5 ....CR 1 00
Realm of Song ....CR 60
Silver Lute ....CR 35
Root & Case's Our Song World ....CR 60
Roscoe's Elementary Chemistry ....MC 1 10
—— Elementary Chemistry, rev. ed. MC **
Roscoe & Lunt's Inorganic Chemistry for Beginners ....MC 75
Rose's Mechanical Drawing ....BD 4 00
Rosenstengel's German Grammar ....WT 40
German Reader ....BS 75 60
High School and College Ger. Reader. PU 1 50
See German Readers for American Schools.
Rosenthal's Method of Practical Linguistry: French ....PO 5 00
German ....PO 5 00
Spanish ....PO 5 00
Rosenthal. *See* Meisterschaft.
Ross' (D. B.) Southern Speaker ....HS 1 00
Ross' (J. M.) Milton ....NE 1 25
Rossiter's Dict. of Scientific Terms ....PU 1 75
Roudebush Writing System, Rapid Vertical, 3 nos ....*doz.* CS *96
—— Tablets ...." CS *48
Business and Social Forms, A and B, *doz.* CS *1 20
Writing Speller ...." CS *45
Busy Work for Little Folks ....*ea.* CS *25 18
Drawing System, 5 Bks ....*doz.* CS *96
Rouillon's French Conversation ....LO 60
Round Rapid Writing Bks., 7 nos. ...*doz.* RA 48
Round Rapid Social and Business Forms, 2 nos ....*doz.* RA 72
Routledge's Fr.-Eng. and Eng.-Fr. Dict. . RU 1 00
Latin Dictionary ....RU 75

Title	Publ.	Price	
Roux's Oral French Method	SF	75	
Rowland (H. A.) and Ames' (J. S.) Elements of Physics	AM	*1 00	
Royal Copy-Books, 19 nos. *doz.*	NE	1 00	
Star Copy-Books, 10 nos. "	NE	1 00	
Upright Copy-Books, 9 nos. "	NE	1 00	
Royal Crown Primer, No. 1	NE	15	
—— No. 2	NE	20	
—— Infant's Reader, Nos. 1 and 2. *ea.*	NE	25	
Royal Crown Readers: No. 1, 30 c.; No. 2, 35 c.; No. 3, 50 c.; Nos. 4, 5, 6. *ea.*	NE	75	
Royal Drawing-Books, small, 12 nos. *doz.*	NE	50	
Freehand Drawing-Books, 6 nos. "	NE	1 00	
Model Drawing-Books, 6 nos. "	NE	1 00	
Brief History of England	NE	30	
History of England	NE	1 25	
Royal English Dictionary and Cyclopedia of Common Things	NE	1 50	
Royal English Dictionary and Word Treasury	NE	1 00	
Royal Reader (New) No. 1	NE	35	
" " " 2	NE	35	
" " " 3	NE	50	
" " " 4	NE	60	
" " " 5	NE	75	
" " " 6	NE	75	
See also English.			
Royal School Reader:			
Victoria the Great	NE	60	
Royal Science Reader, No. 1	NE	30	
—— No. 2	NE	35	
—— No. 3	NE	50	
Royal Stories from English History	NE	50	
Royce's Outlines of Psychology	MC	**	
Royce's (J.) Modern Philosophy	HM	2 50	
Royse's Manual of American Literature	BU	*1 00	
Manual of English Literature	BU	*1 50	
Runkle's (J. D.) Plane and Solid Analytic Geom	GI	*2 25	2 00
Rupert's (W. W.) Geographical Reader	SY		65
Hist. of U. S. Constitution	GI	*75	70
Rusk's Model Selections, 6 nos., pap. *ea.*	BV	15	
Russell's (L. W.) Native Trees	HW	*30	
Russell's (W.) Vocal Culture	HM	1 00	
Rutherford's (M.) English Authors	RD	1 60	1 20
American Authors	RD	1 60	1 20
Ryan's (C.) Systematic Drawing and Shading	CA	75	
Ryan's (J.) Vocalist for Schools	AM	*60	
Sabin's (H.) Making of Iowa	FL	*1 00	
—— Pupil's ed	FL	*60	
Sabin's (S. B.) and Lowry's (C. D.) Elem. Algebra	AM	*50	
—— Key to	AM	*50	
Sabine's Laboratory Course in Physical Measurements	GI	*1 35	1 25
Sachse's Deutsche Grammatik	HR		70
Sadler's (P.) Translating English into French	HO		1 00
Sadler-Rowe's Commercial Arithmetic, College ed	SL	1 00	80
—— School ed	SL	1 00	80
Counting-House Arithmetic	SL	1 25	1 10
Essentials of Arithmetic	SL	1 00	70
New Method Speller	SL	25	20
Banks' Touch Typewriting	SL	60	40
Business Bookkeeping and Practice	SL		1 00
Commercial and Industrial Bookkeeping	SL	1 60	
Sadlier's (A.) One Syllable Hist. of Ireland	RU	75	
Sadtler's Chemical Experimentation	MO	1 60	
St. Clair's Cæsar for Beginners	LN	1 20	
St. Pierre's Paul et Virginie, with Vocab	LO	90	72
Saintsbury's Hist. of 19th Century Lit.	MC		1 50
Short Hist. of English Literature	MC	1 50	
Sales-Josse's Spanish Grammar	LO	1 50	1 20
Sales' (S.) Spanish Hive	HO		1 00
Salmon's (G.) Conic Sections	LN	3 75	
Salmon (D.) *See* Longmans.			
Salvo's Spanish Method	BI	1 20	
Sanders' (A.) Plane Geometry	AM	*75	
Sanders' (C. W.) Primary School Primer, bds. *doz.*	AM	*64	
Union Pictorial Primer	AM	*15	
" Primary Speller	AM	*15	
" Speller	AM	*18	
" Reader No. 1	AM	*20	
" " " 2	AM	*36	
" " " 3	AM	*54	
" " " 4	AM	*90	
" " " 5	AM	*1 08	
New Speller, Definer, and Analyzer	AM	*18	
German and English Pict. Primer	AM	*20	
Pictorial Primer, green covers	AM	*14	
Sanders & McElligott's Analysis of English Words	AM	*55	
Sanders' (G. J. H.) French Student's 1st Book	FO	60	50
Ollendorff's French Course	FO	1 00	80
Sanderson's (E.) Epitome of the World's Hist., pt. 1, Ancient and Mediæval	BN	*1 20	1 00
—— pt. 2, Modern	BN	*1 20	1 00
Hist. of England, New abr. ed	WN	3 00	
Sandy's American Accountant, Pt. 1	UN	*1 15	1 00
—— complete	UN	*2 30	2 00
Sanford's Elements of Physics	BO	**	
Sanford's (E. C.) Physiological Psychology	HE	*1 00	90
Experimental Psychology	HE	*1 75	1 50
Sanford's (H. R.) Word Meth. in Number	BI	50	
Limited Speller	BI	25	
Sanford's (J. A.) Three Thousand Classic Greek Words	SI	*80	72
Sanford's (S. P.) Primary Arithmetic	UN	24	20
Intermediate Arithmetic	UN	*41	36
Common School "	UN	*74	64
—— Key to	UN		1 00
Higher School Arithmetic	UN	*1 15	1 00
Elementary Algebra	UN	*1 15	1 00
Sardou's (A.) French Language, with or without a teacher	JE	3 50	
Pt. 1, Pronounciation	JE	75	
" 2, Conversation, Anecdotes, Extracts, etc.	JE	1 25	
" 3, Grammar and Syntax	JE	1 25	
Chart of French Verbs	JE	35	
Pt. 3 and Chart together	JE	1 50	
Sargent's (E.) Pronouncing Speller	DY		25
School Etymology	BU	*68	
Sargent's (N. B.) Hour of Song	SY		85
Sauer's Italian Grammar	CH or ST	1 85	
—— Key to	CH or ST	60	
Spanish Grammar	CH or ST	1 85	
—— Key to	CH or ST	60	
See Gaspey-Otto-Sauer Method.			
Sauveur's Entretiens sur la Grammaire	JE	1 75	
Causeries avec mes Eleves	JE	1 50	
—— Key to	JE	25	
Petites Causeries	JE	1 25	
Causeries avec les Enfants	JE	1 25	
Fables de La Fontaine	JE	1 50	
Chansons de Béranger	JE	1 25	
Vade Mecum of the Latinist	JE	25	
Talks with Cæsar de Bello Gallico	JE	1 50	
—— Key to	JE	25	
Teaching Ancient Languages	JE	25	
" Living "	JE	25	
De L'Enseignement des Langues Vivantes	JE	25	
Contes Merveilleux	JE	1 50	
Petite Grammaire pour les Anglais	JE	1 25	
—— Key to	JE	50	
Grammaire des Enfants	JE	1 00	
Sauveur & Van Daell's La Parole Française	JE	1 00	
Sauveur and Lougee's Premières Leçons de Grammaire Française	JE	1 00	
—— Key to	JE	25	
Savay's (N. J.) Method in French	FL	60	
Sawyer's (H.) Words and Numbers	TH		25
Sawyer's (H. E.) Metric Manual	MB	40	
Sawyer's (W. C.) Practical German Grammar	SI		75
Complete German Manual	SI		1 00
Schanz's Der Assistent (Beinhorn)	AM	*35	
Schedler's Globe Manual, pap	ST	25	
Schenck & Gurber's Outline of Human Physiology	HO	1 75	
Scherer's History of German Lit., 2 v.	SC		3 50
Schiller's William Tell (Sachtleben)	HO		48
—— (Palmer)	HO		60
—— with vocab	HO		70
*Brant von Messina	HO		60
Jungfrau von Orleans	HO		60
Maria Stuart	HO		60
Wallenstein, complete	HO		1 00
Lied von der Glocke	HO		35
Neffe als Onkel, vocab	HO		40
Schiller's Jungfrau v. Orleans, with vocab	HS	50	
*Jungfrau von Orleans (Rhoades)	AP	60	
Jungfrau von Orleans (Wells), with vocab	HE	85	75
Jungfrau von Orleans (Humphreys)	MC	60	
Maria Stuart, with vocab	HS	50	
Maria Stuart (Rhoades), with vocab	HE	85	75
Maria Stuart (Schönfeld)	MC	60	
Neffe als Onkel, with vocab	HS	50	
Neffe als Onkel (Raddatz)	AL		50
Neffe als Onkel (Beresford, Webb), with vocab	HE	35	30
Wilhelm Tell (Carruth)	MC	50	
" " " with vocab	MC	60	
Wilhelm Tell, with vocab	HS	50	

Title		Net	Retail
Schiller's Wilhelm Tell (Deering), with vocab	HE	85	75
Wallenstein (Winkler)	MC	1 00	
Schiller's Gustav Adolf (Bernhardt)	AM	*45	
Schiller's Thirty Years' War (Palmer)	HO		80
Schilling's Spanish Grammar	CA	1 25	
Schlegel's (C. A.) French Grammar	ST	1 50	
Classical French Reader	ST	1 20	
German Grammar	ST	1 25	
First German Book	ST	1 00	
1st Classical German Reader	ST	1 00	
2d " " "	ST	1 50	
German and English Vocabulary	ST	40	
Skizzen zur Geschichte der Deutschen Literatur	ST	40	
Schlessing's Deutscher Wortschatz	CH	2 25	
Schmitz's (H. J.) Elements of the German Language, pts. 1 and 2...*ea.*	BU	*60	
—— pts. 1 and 2 in 1 v	BU	*1 00	
Schmitz's (J. A. & H. J.) German Grammar	LI	*80	
Schmitz's (W. & J.) Deutsche Grammatik	HR		70
Schmitz & Zumpt's Advanced Latin Exercises	LA	60	
—— hf. bd	LA	70	
Cæsar	LA	60	
—— hf. bd	LA	70	
Cornelius Nepos	LA	60	
—— hf. bd	LA	70	
Elementary Latin Exercises	LA	50	
Horace	LA	70	
—— hf. bd	LA	80	
Quintus Curtius	LA	80	
—— hf. bd	LA	90	
Sallust	LA	60	
—— hf. bd	LA	70	
Virgil	LA	85	
—— hf. bd	LA	1 00	
Schoenfeld's (H.) German Historical Prose	HO		80
Schofield's (A. T.) Physiology for Students, new ed	CA	2 00	
Scholar's Companion, revised	BU	*72	
Scholar's Gem Book	SY		10
Scholar's Spelling Blanks...*doz.*	SY		54
School Classics Series	GI		
School History of the United States	BE	75	45
Schrakamp's Berühmte Deutsche, notes and vocab	HO		85
Deutsches Buch	HO		65
Erzählungen aus der Deutschen Geschichte	HO		90
Deutsche Rechtschreibung	CH	31	
Sagen und Mythen, with vocab	HO		75
German Conversational Drill	HO		65
Exercises in Conversational Ger	HO		55
Supplementary Exercises to Das Deutsche Buch	HO		50
See also Wenckebach.			
Schultz's Latin Grammar	PT	1 25	
Latin Exercises	PT	1 25	
*Schultz's La Neuvaine de Colette (Lye)	AM	*45	
Schultze's & Sevenoak's Plane and Solid Geometry	MC	1 10	
Schulze's (V. H.) Praktische Lehrgang für den Deutschen Unterricht	JE	1 00	
Schurim's & Stevenson's Civil Government	LI	1 00	
Schuyler's (A.) Complete Algebra, Rev.	AM	*1 00	
—— Key to	AM	*1 00	
Elements of Geometry	AM	*1 00	
Trig., Mensuration and Logarithms	AM	*1 00	
Surveying and Navigation	AM	*1 20	
Principles of Logic	AM	*60	
Psychology	AM	*1 40	
Schwegler's History of Philosophy	PU	2 50	
Schwill's (F.) History of Modern Europe	SC		1 50
Science Primers:			
Astronomy (Lockyer)	AM	*35	
Botany (Hooker)	AM	*35	
Chemistry (Roscoe)	AM	*35	
Geology (Geikie)	AM	*35	
Introductory (Huxley)	AM	*35	
Inventional Geometry (Spencer)	AM	*35	
Logic (Jevons)	AM	*35	
Natural Resources (Patton)	AM	*35	
Philosophy (Hunter)	AM	*35	
Physical Geography (Geikie)	AM	*35	
Physics (Stewart)	AM	*35	
Physiology (Foster & Tracy)	AM	*35	
Political Economy (Jevons)	AM	*35	
Scomp's (H. A.) Modern Greek Pronunciation	AL		36
Scott's (C. E.) Nature Study and the Child	HE	**	
Scott's (D. B.) School History of U. S	AM	*80	
Small History of U. S	AM	*56	
Scott's (D. B., Jr.) Review Hist. of U. S	CO	*36	32

Title		Net	Retail
Scott (F. N.) and Denney's (J. V.) Elemen. Composition	AL	**	
Scott's Plane Analytical Geometry	MC	2 50	
Scott's (W. B.) Introd. to Geology	MC	1 90	
Scott & Denney's Paragraph-Writing	AL		1 00
Composition-Literature	AL		1 00
Composition-Rhetoric	AL		1 00
Scribner's Bookkeeping Exercises, Single Entry...*doz.*	AM	*3 36	
—— Double Entry...."	AM	*3 36	
Scribner's Ser. of School Reading, 17v.*ea.*	SC		60
Scripture's New Psychology	SC	1 50	
Scrivener's Greek Testament	HO		2 00
Scudder's (H. E.) Book of Fables	HM	40	
Book of Folk Stories	HM	60	
History of United States	BU	*1 00	
New History of United States	BU	*1 00	
Short History of United States	BU	*60	
Scudder's (J. W.) Gradatim	AL		50
First Latin Reader	AL		90
Sallust's Catiline	AL		1 00
Scudder's (M. T.) New York (State and Local Government)	MY	*40	
Scudder's (V. D.), English Literature	GL	1 20	
Scull's Greek Mythology Systematized	WR	*1 00	
Searing's Virgil's Æneid, Bucolics and Georgics, with vocab	AM	*1 60	
Virgil's Æneid, 6 books, with vocab	AM	*1 40	
Seaver's Trigonometric Formulas	BU	*6	
Elementary Trigonometry	BU	*96	
Seaver & Walton's Franklin Primary Arithmetic	BU	*20	
Franklin Elementary Arithmetic	BU	*35	
—— Key to	BU	*25	
Franklin Written Arithmetic	BU	*75	
—— Key to	BU	*75	
—— Written Arithmetic, pt. 1	BU	*28	
Franklin Elementary Algebra	BU	*90	
—— Key to	BU	*75	
Logarithmic and Trigon. Tables	BU	*60	
Metric System	BU	*15	
Mental Arithmetic	BU	*30	
New Franklin Arithmetic, 1st Bk	BU	*35	
" " " 2d "	BU	*65	
—— Key (to both)	BU	*90	
Seavy's (M.) Bookkeeping	HE	*1 50	1 40
Manual of Business Transactions	HE	*50	40
Bookkeeping blanks, 3 in sets, *per set.*	HE	*75	60
Sedgwick & Wilson. *See* Amer. Sci. Ser.			
Seelye's (J. H.) Hickok's Mental Science	GI	*1 25	1 12
Moral Science	GI	*1 25	1 12
Citizenship; Duty, 2 v...*ea.*	GI	*35	30
Seeley's (L.) Grube's Method of Arithmetic	KE	1 00	
Foundations of Education	HS	1 00	
Seeman's Classical Mythology	AM	*60	
Seerley's (H. H.) & Parish's (L. W.) Hist. and Civil Gov't of Iowa	WR	*1 00	
Seidel's Die Monate (Arrowsmith)	AM	*25	
Der Lindenbaum (Richard)	AM	*25	
Herr Omnia (Matthewman)	AM	*25	
Leberecht Hühnchen und andere Sonderlinge, with vocab. (Bernhardt)	AM	*50	
Selections for Little Folks	EL	40	
Sellers' (J. F.) Elementary Treatise on Qualitative Chemical Analysis	GI	*80	75
Sensenig's (D. M.) Elementary Algebra	AM	*1 16	
—— without Answers	AM	*1 08	
—— Answers to, separate	AM	*10	
—— Key to	AM	*1 00	
Advanced Algebra	AM	*1 40	
—— Pt. 1	AM	*1 20	
—— Pt. 2	AM	*1 08	
—— Key to	AM	*1 40	
Sensenig's (D. M.) and Anderson's (R. F.) New Complete Arithmetic	SI	1 12	90
*Essentials of Arithmetic	SI		60
Setchell's Laboratory Practice for Beginners in Botany	MC	90	
Sever's Speller	HE	*30	25
Sewall's (J. B.) Greek Conditional Sentences	AL		20
Sewall's Lucian's Timon	GI	*55	50
Sewell's (E.) First Hist. of Greece	AP	60	
First History of Rome	AP	60	
Sewell's (E. M.) Dictation Exercises	HO		45
Seymour's (G. E.) Elem. Arithmetic	BS	40	32
Practical Arithmetic	BS	60	48
New Mental "	BS	35	28
Seymour's (T. D.) Homer's Iliad, Bks. 1–3	GI	*45	40
—— with notes	GI	*1 50	1 40
—— Bks. 4–6	GI	*45	40
—— with notes	GI	*1 50	1 40
School Iliad with Vocab., Bks. 1–3, rev.	GI	*1 35	1 25
" " " " " 1–6, rev.	GI	*1 75	1 60
Vocab. to Homer's Iliad, Bks. 1–6	GI	*85	75
Language and Verse of Homer	GI	*80	75

Seymour's (T.D.) Language and Verse of Homer, pap. ....GI *65 60
Selected Odes of Pindar ....GI *1 55 1 40
Seymour & Wilson's Essentials of Physics ....FL 40
Shackelford's History of Middle Ages...HW 1 00
Shaffer's (V. C.) How to Remember History ....LI *1 00
Shaler's 1st Book of Geology........HE *70 60
Sharpless' Plane and Solid Geometry ...WR *80
Elements of Geometry........WR *60
Sharpless & Philips' Astronomy ....LI *1 00
Natural Philosophy........LI *1 00
—— Key to........LI *50
Shaw's (E. R.) English Composition .....HO 75
Physics by Experiment........MY *1 05
Big People and Little People of Other Lands........AM *30
Discoverers and Explorers... ....AM *35
*Shaw's (G. W.) Laboratory Exercises in Chemistry........AM *40
Shaw's (J. W.) Practice Book of Business Forms and Elementary Bookkeeping ....HE *60
Elemen. Bookkeeping........HE 60
Blanks for Elemen. Bookkeeping, sets of 4........HE 36
Blank forms for Elemen. Bookkeeping. HE 20
Shaw's (T. B.) New History of English Literature ....BU *1 25
Specimens of English Literature. ...BU *1 35
Shaw & Backus' Outlines of Literature, Eng. and Amer.... ....BU *1 25
Shaylor (H. W.) & Shattuck's (G. H.) Medial Writing Books, Nos. 1-8..*doz*.GI 60
Shea's Modern Europe........KY 1 25
Shearer's (J. W.) Combination Speller...JH *25 20
Shedd's (E. C.) First Latin Book........HW 1 00
Shedd's (G. T.), Theremin's Rhetoric.... DR 1 00
Sheldon's Elementary Arithmetic......BU *40
Complete Arithmetic........BU *67
—— Key to........ BU *75
Primary Graded Examples........ BU *30
Graded Exercises in Arithmetic, 1st Bk ....BU *30
—— Answers to 1st Bk........BU *20
—— 2d Bk........BU *35
" " Key to........BU *20
Sheldon's Elements of Algebra ....BU *1 08
—— Key to ....BU *1 50
Complete Algebra........BU *1 30
—— Key to........BU *1 50
Modern School 1st Reader........BU *20
" " 2d " .... BU *32
" " 3d " .... BU *44
" " 4th " .... BU *64
" " 5th " .... BU *90
Sheldon's Supplementary Reading, 3d Bk.BU *38
Word Studies .... BU *25
Language Lessons:
Primary, 1st Bk........BU *38
Advanced, 2d " ....BU *62
Vertical Writing, 10 nos.:
Elementary, 4 nos........*doz*.BU *72
Grammar, 6 " .... " BU *96
Vertical Writing Charts, 2 nos........BU *1 00
Sheldon's Standard Writing Books, 12 nos.:
Tracing, 1 no........ *doz*.BU *72
Elementary, 3 nos........ " BU *72
Grammar, 8 " .... " BU *96
Writing Manual........BU *75
—— Vertical........BU *75
Spelling and Language Blank....*doz* BU *48
Sheldon's (E. A.) Primer........ AM *14
Primary Speller........AM *18
Graded Speller........AM *25
1st Reader.... ....AM *15
2d " .... AM *30
3d " ....AM *42
4th " .... AM *50
5th " ....AM *72
Sheldon's (E. S.) Short German Gram....HE *65 60
Sheldon's (M. D.) Gr. and Roman Hist..HE *1 10 1 00
Studies in General History ....HE *1 75 1 60
—— Teachers' Manual to........HE 85
Studies in Amer. Hist........HE *1 25 1 12
—— Teachers' Manual to........HE 60
Sheldon's (S.) Chapters on Electricity, 2d ed........CO 1 10 1 00
Shelton's (C. E.) Practical Gymnastics..FL 40
Shepard's (E. M.) Mineralogy........BA *70 60
Shepard's (J. H.) Inorganic Chemistry...HE *1 25 1 12
Organic Chemistry........HE *30 25
Chemical Laboratory Note-Book....HE *40 35
Briefer Course in Chemistry........HE *90 80
Shepherd's Historical Readings ....AM *1 00
Sherrill's (J. E.) New Normal Question Bk.. ....HS 1 50

Sherwin's Mathematical Tables........TH 80
Common School Algebra. ....TH 80
Sherwood's Analytical Writing Speller and Definer........*doz*.SR *1 02 85
Five Cent Writing Speller........ " SR *55 45
—— with Blotters........ " SR *60 48
—— and Copy-Book........ " SR *60 48
Five Cent Spelling Blanks........ " SR *58 48
Nickel Writing Speller........ " SR *60 48
Six Col. " " .... " SR *1 00 85
—— with Blotters........ " SR *1 15 96
Speller and Pronouncer........ " SR *1 11 96
Spelling and Definition Blanks... " SR *1 00 85
Ten-Cent Spelling Blanks........ " SR *1 06 90
" Writ. Sp. & Copy-Book " SR *1 05 90
Writing Speller........ " SR *83 72
Primary Speaker........SR *28 25
Shewall Readers, 6 Bks........SA **
Shimmell's (L. S.) Pennsylvania History..MP *90
Shinn's (J. H.) Hist. of American People..AM *1 00
Shinn's Hist. of Arkansas.. .... JH 1 00 80
Shipley's (A. E.) & MacBride's (E. W.) Zoölogy........ .. MC **
Shoemaker's Practical Elocution........PP 1 25
Advanced Elocution........PP 1 25
Shorey's (P.) Horace's Odes and Epodes.SA 1 30
Shorey's (P.) & Kirkland's (J. H.) Horace's Odes and Epodes and Satires and Epistles, 1 vol........SA 1 75
Short Studies in Eng., Original ed., bds.AM *50
Shoup's (W. J.) Graded Speller........AM *19
Graded Didactics, v. 1........AM *50
" " v. 2........AM *60
Easy Words and How to Use Them..AM *15
Shove's (I.) Number Cards........GI *30 25
Showalter's Temple of Song........CR 60
Shryock's Golden Key........CR 25
Silver Clarion........CR 35
Shuckburgh's (E. S.) History of Rome to the Battle of Actium........MC 1 75
History of Rome for Beginners..... MC 90
Short History of the Greeks.... ....MC 1 10
Shumway's Latin Synonyms........GI *35 30
Sidgwick's (A.) Greek Prose Composition........GI *1 65 1 50
Siefert's (H. O. R.) Choice Songs, pts. 1 and 2........BU **
Siepmann's French and German Series, *ea.*, 50c.; 60c.; 75c.... ....MC
Siepmann's (O.) Public School German Primer ....MC 1 00
Sight Reader........BU *15
Siglar's English Grammar........HO 60
Sihler's (E. G.) Protagoras of Plato......AM *75
Sihler's Cicero's Second Philippic........UN *92 80
*Silva's (T.) & Fourcaut's (A.) Lectura y Conversacion........ ....AM *60
Silver Series of English Classics (various prices, *18c., *24c., *28c., *36c.)....SI
Silver's (H. J.) Primary Exercises in Arithmetic, Nos. 1 and 2 ......*ea.*AM *10
—— Nos. 3 and 4........ " AM *15
Silver Series of Modern Language Text-Books .... SI
(Various prices, 60c., 75c., $1, $1.20).
Simcox's Juvenal........ ....AL 1 20
Sime's Germany. *See* Freeman.
Simmons' Qualitative Analysis........SI *56 50
Simon's (W.) Manual of Chemistry ..... LA 3 35
Simonds's (W. E.) Students' Hist. of Eng Literature........HM **
Simonin's French Verb........AM *1 00
Simonson's German Ballad Book........HO 1 10
Simplified Penmanship Series:
Slant, 8 nos........*doz* UN *1 10 96
Vertical, 8 nos ....*doz.* UN *1 10 96
Simpson's (J.) Old Mother Earth........HW *36
999 Composition Subjects........MA *15
Primary Physical Geography........HW 36
Skeat's Etymological Dictionary... ....AM *1 25
Slate's (F.) Principles of Mechanics, pt. 1..MC 1 90
*Slate's Physics: A Text-book for Secondary Schools........MC 1 10
Slingo and Brooker's Problems in Electricity and Magnetism........LN 75
Sloane's Lessons in Fractions........HE *30 25
Fraction Cards, *per set* of six........HE 12 10
Small (A. W.) & Vincent's (G. E.) Sociology AM *1 80
Smart's School Gymnastics........AM *30
Smart (M. C.) A New Gradatim........SA 50
Smead's Demosthenes' Philippics........AM *1 05
Sophocles' Antigone........AM *1 22
Smiley (J. B.) & Storke's (H. L.) Beginner's Latin Book........AM *1 00
Smith's (A.) Wealth of Nations........NE 1 75
—— ....BU 1 00
Smith's (Alex.) Laboratory Manual of General Chemistry........UC 75

Title	Pub.	Retail	Introd.
Smith's (Asa) Illustrated Astronomy	HS	90	
Smith's (B. G.) Reading and Speaking	HE	*65	75
Smith's (C.) Elementary Conic Sections	MC	1 60	
Elementary Solid Geometry	MC	2 60	
Treatise on Algebra	MC	1 90	
Arithmetic, American ed. (Harrington)	MC	90	
Geometrical Conics	MC	1 60	
Smith's (C.) & Stringham's (I.) Elemen. Algebra, 2d complete ed	MC	1 20	
—— Briefer ed	MC	1 10	
Smith's (C. A.) Old English Grammar	AL		1 00
Smith's (C. F.) Thucydides, Bk. 7	GI	*1 50	1 40
—— Bk. 3	GI	*1 75	1 65
Valerius Maximus, Selections	SA		30
Smith's (C. L.) Odes and Epodes of Horace	GI	*1 60	1 50
Smith's (C. L.) & Greenough's (J. B.) Horace's Odes and Epodes, Satires and Epistles	GI	*2 15	2 00
Smith's (E.) Songs for Little Children, pt. 1	BO	1 25	
—— pap	BO	90	
Smith's (E.) Modern Music Series:			
Primer of Vocal Music	SI		25
First Book of Vocal Music	SI		30
Second " " " "	SI		40
Third " " " "	SI		50
School Songs by Grades, *per pt.*	SI		15
Smith's (E. B.) Syntax and Analysis	FL	50	
Smith's (E. E.) Ideal Combination Writing Speller	RA	10	
*Smith's (E. E.) Ideal Word Book	FL	16	
*Smith's (E. E.) 220 Lessons in Spelling and Construction	FL	12	
Smith's (E. F.) Electro-Chemical Analysis	BL	1 00	
Anatomy, Physiology, and Hygiene	JE	1 00	
Smith's (E. H.) Latin Selections	AL		1 50
Smith's (E. P.) Political Economy	BD	1 25	
Smith's (G. J.) Synopsis of English and American Literature	GI	*90	80
Smith's (G. M.) & Young's (C. M.) Hist. and Civil Gov't of South Dakota	WR	*1 00	
Smith's (H.) Elementary Algebra	LN	1 00	
Smith's (H. A.) One-Syllable History of Japan	BU	75	
One-Syllable History of Russia	BU	75	
Smith's (H. D.) Eng. Gram. Simplified	NE	40	
Smith's (H. P.) Intermedial Penmanship:			
Illustrated Writing Primer, *doz.*	RN	*72	
Short Course, nos. 1-4 "	RN	*72	
Regular Course, nos. 1-8 "	RN	*96	
Smith's (J. F.) School Geometry	RN	1 00	
Smith's (J. R.) Historical Readers:			
Columbus, Capt. Smith, Standish, Franklin, *pt.*	HW	36	
Washington	HW	35	
Smith's (L.) French Conv. *See* Bregy.			
Smith's (L. C.) Gramatica Practica de la Langua Castellana	GI	*70	60
Smith (L. W.) and Thomas (J. E.) A Modern Composition and Rhetoric (Brief Course)	SA		80
Smith's (L. W.) and Thomas's (J. E.) Composition and Rhetoric (Complete Course)	SA		1 10
Smith's (M. W.) English Literature	AM	*1 20	
Smith's (P.) Easy Experiments in Physics	MS	*60	
Smith's (P.) Ancient Hist. of the East	AM	*1 25	
History of the Christian Church, 2 v., *ea.*	AM	*1 50	
Smaller History of England	AM	*60	
*Smith's (P. F.) Elementary Calculus	AM	*1 25	
Smith's (R. B.) & Willard's (E. C.) Standard School Physiology, Hygiene, Anatomy	MS	*1 00	
Smith's (R. C.) Practical Arithmetic	LI	*40	
—— Key to	LI	*40	
New Arithmetic	LI	*68	
—— Key to	LI	*68	
English Grammar	BU	*40	
Smith's (R. M., jr.) Construction Work	FL	*75	
Smith's (T. B.) Studies in Nature and Language Lessons	HE	60	
Smith's (Walter) Drawing-Books:			
Am. Drawing-Cards, 2 ser., *ea.*	PR	15	
Primary Teachers' Manual	PR	1 00	
Intermediate, 3 nos., *ea.*	PR	15	
" Teachers' Manual	PR	1 25	
Freehand, 6 nos., *ea.*	PR	25	
Geometrical, 4 nos. "	PR	25	
Model and Object, 2 nos. "	PR	25	
Perspective, 3 nos. "	PR	25	
Smith's (Wm.) English-Latin Dictionary	AM	*4 00	
Smaller Classical Dictionary	AM	*1 25	
General History of Greece	AM	*1 25	
Smith's (Wm.) History of Greece, rev	AM	*1 00	
History of Rome, rev	AM	*1 00	
Old Testament History	AM	*1 25	
New " "	AM	*1 25	
Smaller Scripture "	AM	*60	
French Principia, pt. 1	AM	*50	
—— pt. 2	AM	*80	
—— pt. 3	AM	*1 00	
German Principia, pt. 1	AM	*50	
—— pt. 2	AM	*80	
Italian Principia, pt. 1	AM	*75	
—— pt. 2	AM	*90	
Latin Principia, pt. 1	AM	*55	
—— pt. 2	AM	*90	
Initia Graeca, pt. 1	AM	*60	
Smith's (W. A.) Topical Manual of Amer. Hist	PX	*60	
Smith's (W. B.) Co-ordinate Geometry	GI	*2 15	2 00
Smith's (W. L.) Practical Music Reader	AM	*30	
Smith's (W. T.) Elementary Physiology and Hygiene	AM	*50	
Primer of Physiology and Hygiene	AM	*30	
Smith's (W. W.) Condensed Etymology	AM	*50	
Handbook of Etymology	AM	*90	
Grammar School Speller	AM	*25	
Juvenile Definer	AM	*20	
Little Speller	AM	*14	
Definer's Manual	AM	*40	
*First Year Latin	JE	1 00	
Smith's Brief Compend of U. S. Hist	SY		25
*Smith's Four Place Logarithmic Tables	HO		50
Smith, Hamilton & Legros' French-English and English-French Dict	CH	6 50	
Smith & Young's Hist. and Civil Gov't of S. Dakota	WR	*1 00	
Smithdeal's Practical Grammar, Speller, and Letter-Writer	JH	75	60
Grammar	JH	25	20
Speller	JH	25	20
Letter-Writer	JH	25	20
First Book in Book-Keeping	JH	75	56
Second " "	JH	40	30
Slant Writing Bks, 6 nos., *ea.*	JH	5	4
Smithey's (R. B.) History of Virginia	AM	*75	
Civil Gov't of Virginia	AM	*60	
Smyth's (A. H.) American Literature	EL	*1 00	90
—— N. Y. Regent's ed	EL	*1 05	95
*Snyder's (C.) and Thurston's (E. L.) Practical Bookkeeping	AM	*7 25	
Snyder's (W. H.) & Palmer's (I. O.) One Thousand Problems in Physics	GI	*55	50
Snell's Astronomy, etc. *See* Olmsted.			
Soldan's (F. L.) Am. 2d German Reader	WT	1 25	
Grube's Method (Arithmetic)	LR	*30	25
Song Wave	AM	*65	
Songs of all the Colleges	HS	1 50	
Songs of the Eastern Colleges	HS	1 25	
" " " Western "	HS	1 25	
Sonnenburg-Schoelch, New Pract. German Grammar and Exercise Book	HR	1 00	66
Soper's Elocutionary Readings, 2 v., *ea.*	DN	1 00	67
Scrap-Book Recitations, 7 nos. "	DN	25	17
Sornberger's Normal Language Lessons	BI	50	
Soule & Campbell's Words Often Mispronounced	LE		30
Soule & Wheeler's First Less'n in Reading	LE		35
Pronunciation and Spelling	LE		1 20
Southwick's (A. P.) Quizzism and its Key	HS	1 00	
Southwick's (F. T.) Steps to Oratory	AM	*1 00	
Southwick's Dime Question-Bks., 23 nos., *ea.*	BI	10	
Short Studies in Literature	EL	*55	50
—— Key to	EL	*25	20
Southworth's Essentials of Arithmetic, Bk. 1	SA		40
—— Bk. 2	SA		60
Southworth's (G. V. D.) Story of the Empire State	AP	**	
*Southworth's New Composition and Grammar	SA		60
*New Language Lessons	SA		40
Southworth & Goddard's Our Language	SA		75
—— pt. 1	SA		36
—— pt. 2	SA		54
Composition and Grammar	SA		60
First Lessons in Language	SA		36
Spalding's (E. H.) Problem of Elementary Composition	HE	*45	40
Spalding's (V. M.) Introd. to Botany	HE	*90	80
Spalding & Moore's Language Speller, pt. 1	RN 20		
" 2	RN 30		
Spanhoofd's Deutsche Grammatik	HO		80
Spanhoofd's Lehrbuch der Deutschen Sprache	HE	1 00	
Spanish Serie Moderna: Nociones de Historia de los Estados Unidos	AM	*60	
Libro Primero (First Reader), bds	AM	*22	

Title	Pub.	Price	
Spanish Serie Moderna: Libro Primero (First Reader), cl.	AM	*28	
Libro Segundo (Second Reader), bds.	AM	*33	
" cl.	AM	*38	
Libro Tercero (Third Reader), bds.	AM	*50	
" cl.	AM	*55	
Lecciones de Lenguaje—Español-Inglés (Language Lessons—Spanish-English)	AM	*40	
Cuaderno de Aritmética (Arithmetic Tablets), nos. 1–10 *doz.*	AM	*1 00	
Nociones de Geografía Universal (Monteith)	AM	*60	
Spear's (M. A.) Leaves and Flowers	HE	*30	25
Preparing to Read	HW	*30	
Speer's (E.) Lectures on Constitution	BT	1 25	
Speer's (W. W.) Advanced Arithmetic	GI	*60	50
Primary Arithmetic	GI	*40	35
Elementary Arithmetic	GI	*55	45
Spencer's (C. P.) First Steps in North Carolina History	AM	*75	
Spencer's (J. A.) Greek New Testament	AM	*1 00	
—— *See* Arnold, T. K.			
Spencerian Copybooks:			
Tracing Series, 4 nos. *doz.*	AM	*72	
Shorter Course, 7 nos. "	AM	*72	
Common School Ser., 7 nos. "	AM	*96	
Business Ser., nos. 8–11 "	AM	*96	
New Compendium of Penmanship, 8 pts. *ea.*	AM	*50	
—— Text and Plates in 1 v.	AM	6 00	
Theory of Penmanship, pap.	AM	*18	
Key to Penmanship	AM	*1 08	
Spencerian Vertical Penmanship:			
Shorter Course, nos. 1 to 7 *doz.*	AM	*72	
Special Books, A and B "	AM	*72	
Common School Course, nos. 1 to 6 "	AM	*96	
Business Course, nos. 7 to 10 "	AM	*96	
Spencer Bros.' Copybooks, 12 nos. *doz.*	AM	*96	
Speyers' (C. E.) Physical Chemistry	VN		2 25
Spiers & Surenne's French Dict., 8°	AP	5 00	
—— Abridged, 12°	AP	1 50	
Spiess & Seiffert's Greek Grammar	PT	1 25	
Greek and English Exercises	PT	1 25	
Spinoza's Philosophy (Fullerton)	HO		1 50
Spooner's Practical Geometry	CA	1 00	
Sprague's (H. B.) Masterpieces in English Literature	LE	*1 65	1 50
Milton's Comus	LE	*25	20
Shakespeare's Hamlet	SI	*55	48
" Merchant of Venice	SI	*55	48
" Macbeth	SI	*55	48
" Julius Cæsar	SI	*55	48
" As You Like It	SI	*55	48
" The Tempest	SI	*55	48
" A Midsummer Night's Dream	SI	*55	48
Scott's Lady of the Lake	SI	*55	48
Vicar of Wakefield (Goldsmith)	SI	*55	48
Sel. from Milton, etc.	GI	*35	30
" " Irving's Sketch-Book	PU	50	
Sprague's (J. D.) Rapid Addition	GI	*12	10
*Sprague's (S. E.) Primer	RA	25	
Sprechen Sie Deutsch?	HO		40
Sprenkel's Ideal Music Course	MP		
Spyri's (J.) Rosenresli and Der Toni v. Kandergrund	AM	*25	
Stäger's Hints for German Conversation	CH	35	
Lehrfragen	CH	1 25	
Stahl's Versions, Erster Theil	ST	60	
—— Zweiter Theil	ST	60	
Stamm's First German Reader	WT	35	
Second " "	WT	50	
Stammer's Chemical Problems	BL	75	
Standard Elementary Arithmetic	SS		42
Complete Arithmetic	SS		60
Key to Standard Arithmetics	SS		75
1st Reader	SS		18
2d "	SS		30
3d "	SS		42
4th "	SS		48
5th "	SS		60
Standard Pronouncing Speller	SS		18
Standard English Classics: [Various prices, 22 nos., 20c.; 25c.; 30c.; 35c.; 40c.; 50c.]	GI		
†Standard Literature Series, 52 nos.: [Single nos., 12½c.; 20c.; double nos., 20c.; 30c.]	UN		
Standard Supplementary Readers:			
1st, Easy Steps for Little Feet	AM	*25	
2d, Golden Bk. of Choice Reading	AM	*30	
3d, Book of Tales	AM	*50	
4th, Readings in Nature's Book	AM	*65	
5th, Seven American Classics	AM	*50	
6th, " British Classics	AM	*50	

† For List see page 174.

Title	Pub.	Price	
Standard Vertical Writing, Nos. 1–6 *doz.*	SO	*83	
Stanley's (A. D.) Table of Logarithms	PE		2 50
Spherical Geometry and Trigonometry	PE		75
Stanwood's (E.) History of the Presidency	HM	2 50	
Starkweather's Aid to English Grammar	BI	50	
Statham's Architecture for General Readers	SC		2 00
Stebbins' Delsarte System	WE	2 00	
Society Gymnastics	WE	1 00	
Stedman's (T. L.) Modern Greek Mastery	AM	*1 50	
Steele's (G. H.) Political Economy	EA	60	
Steele's (G. M.) Rudimentary Psychology	SY		1 00
Rudimentary Economics	SY		90
Rudimentary Ethics	SY		1 00
Popular Astronomy, rev.	AM	*1 00	
Steele's (J. D.) Popular Astronomy, rev. by M. L. Todd	AM	*1 00	
Popular Physics	AM	*1 00	
Popular Zoölogy	AM	*1 20	
Popular Chemistry	AM	*1 00	
Hygienic Physiology	AM	*1 00	
—— abr.	AM	*50	
New Descriptive Astronomy	AM	*1 00	
14 Weeks in Botany	AM	*1 00	
14 Weeks in Chemistry	AM	*1 00	
14 Weeks in Geology	AM	*1 00	
14 Weeks in Physics	AM	*1 00	
14 Weeks in Physiology	AM	*1 00	
14 Weeks in Zoölogy	AM	*1 00	
New Key (Manual of Science)	AM	*1 00	
Steiger's Commercial German Reader	ST	50	
Steiger's Colloquial Ger. Method, No. 1	ST	*50	
" " " 2	ST	*45	
" " " 3	ST	*45	
" " " 4	ST	*50	
—— First Course (Nos. 1, 2.)	ST	*85	
—— Second Course (Nos. 3, 4)	ST	*85	
—— Complete (Nos. 1–4)	ST	*1 75	
—— Rudiments, pt. 1	ST	*35	
—— pt. 2	ST	*40	
First German Reader	ST	*40	
Steiger's Kindergarten Designs, 18 nos. *ea.*	ST	30	
Manual Kindergarten	ST	*1 25	
Tablet Laying	ST	60	
Painting	ST		75
Stein's German Exercises, Bks. 1 and 2 *ea.*	GI	*45	40
Stephens' School History of U. S., rev.	DU	1 50	1 12
Stepping Stones in Language (Analytical English Grammar)	IG	35	30
Stepping-Stones to Literature (Arnold, S. L., Gilbert, C. B.):			
First Reader	SI	40	30
Second "	SI	50	40
Third "	SI	65	50
Fourth "	SI	85	60
Fifth "	SI	90	75
Readers for Sixth, Seventh, and Higher Grades *ea.*	SI	85	60
Sterling's Southern Primer, pap. *doz.*	BT	90	
—— bds. "	BT	1 08	
Southern Pictorial Primer "	BT	2 40	
Elementary Spelling-Book "	BT	1 00	
1st Reader	BT	20	
2d "	BT	40	
3d "	BT	50	
4th "	BT	75	
5th "	BT	1 00	
Little Orator	BT	50	
Southern Orator	BT	1 50	
Copy-Books, 9 nos. *doz.*	BT	1 00	
Stern's Select German Comedies [7 v., var. prices, *35c.–*45c., 30c.–40c. *ea.*]	HO		
Studien und Plaudereien, 1st Ser.	HO		1 10
—— 2d Ser.	HO		1 20
First Lessons in German	HO		1 00
Stern & Meras' Etude Progressive	HO		1 20
First Lessons in French	HO		1 00
Stern's (M.) Geschichten vom Rhein	AM	*85	
Geschichten von Deutschen Städten	AM	*1 25	
Stern's (S. M.) Aus Deutschen Meisterwerken	HO		1 20
Sterne's Constitutional History of U. S.	PU	1 25	
Stetson's (W. W.) Hist. and Civil Gov't of Maine	WR	*1 00	
Stevens' Lysias' Select Orations	GR	*1 25	
Stewart's (B.) Elementary Physics	MC	1 10	
Stewart's (S. T.) Plane and Solid Geometry	AM	*1 12	
—— Key to	AM	*1 12	
Stewart & Gee's Elem. Physics, v. 1	MC	1 50	
—— v. 2	MC	2 25	
—— v. 3	MC	1 10	
Practical Physics, pt. 1, Electricity and Magnetism	MC	60	

Title	Pub.	Price	Price
Stickney's (A.) Cicero de Natura Deorum	GI	*1 55	1 40
Cicero de Officiis	AM	*1 50	
Stickney's (J. H.) Child's Book of Language, 4 nos.	*ea.* AM	*8	
—— Teacher's ed	AM	*80	
Primer	GI	*25	20
New 1st Reader	GI	*30	24
" 2d "	GI	*40	32
" 3d "	GI	*50	40
" 4th "	GI	*60	50
" 5th "	GI	*70	60
Alternate Fourth Reader	GI	*60	50
Word by Word, pt. 1, Primary	GI	*22	15
—— pt. 2, Advanced	GI	*28	20
—— Teacher's ed	GI	*40	30
Earth and Sky, no. 1	GI	*35	30
Pets (No 2) and Companions, no. 3	*ea.* GI	*40	30
Stickney's (J. H.) & Hoffmann's (R.) Bird World	GI	*70	60
Stifter's (A.) Das Heidedorf (Lentz)	AM	*25	
Stille's Mediæval History	LI	*1 44	
Stilwell's (L.) Exercises in Analysis and Parsing	KW	25	
Brief Lessons on the Human Body	MY	*45	
Practical Exercises in Analysis and Parsing	PM	*25	
Question Book	PM	*1 50	
Questions in Geography	PM	*25	
Answers " "	PM	*25	
Stockton's (F. R.) Stories of New Jersey	AM	*60	
Stoddard's (J. F.) Pictorial Primary Arithmetic	BU	*20	
Juvenile Mental Arithmetic	BU	*18	
New Intellectual Arithmetic	BU	*35	
—— Key to	BU	*50	
Rudiments of Arithmetic	BU	*32	
American Intellectual Arithmetic	BU	*29	
—— Key to	BU	*50	
Complete Arithmetic	BU	*96	
School Arithmetic	BU	*56	
Stoddard's (J. T.) Outlines of Qualitative Analysis	AM	*75	
*Stokes's (S.) Ten Common Trees	AM	*40	
Stone's Essentials of Arithmetic	WA	60	50
Stone's (A. P.) History of England	TH		85
Stone's (W. A.) Experimental Physics	GI	*1 10	1 00
Storer and Lindsay's Elemen. Chemistry	AM	*1 20	
Storm's (T.) Immensee (Dauer)	AM	*25	
—— (Whitenack)	AL		50
Storme's (G.) Select German Stories	CN	60	
Storr's French Syntax	HE	*35	30
Story's U. S. Constitution	AM	*90	
Stout's Manual of Psychology	HS	1 50	
Stowell's (C. H.) A Primer of Health	SI	*40	36
A Healthy Body	SI	*60	50
Essentials of Health	SI	*94	84
Simple Experiments in Physiology	SI	*40	36
High School Physiology	SI	**	
Stowell's (T. B.) Physiology	BI	1 00	
Strack's Hebrew Grammar, new ed	LS	1 80	
Strang's Exercises in English	HE	*50	45
Straw's (D. A.) Expression and Physical Drill	SR		60
Streatfeild's Organic Chemistry	SP	*1 25	
Strickland's Queens of England, abridged,	AM	*1 25	
Stronach's Simple Hist. Eng. Lit.	NE	75	
*Strong's (F.) & Schafer's (J.) Government of the American People	HM	85	
Stub-Pen Writing Bks., 2 nos.	*doz.* RA		84
Stuckenberg's Introd. to Study of Philos.	AR	1 50	1 50
Introd. to Study of Sociology	AR	1 50	1 50
Students' Classic French Plays, 3 v.	*ea.* HO		1 00
—— 9 v., pap	" HO		20
Students' Classic German Plays [10 v., var. prices, *35c.-*55c., 35c.-60c *ea.*]	HO		
Schiller's Wallenstein, complete	HO		1 00
Students' Series of English Classics, Library ed., [38 v., var. prices, 25c.-35c.-56c. *ea.*]	SY		
Students' Series of English Classics, Handy ed., 20 v.	*ea.* SY		25
Students' Series of Latin Classics, [40 v., var. prices.]	SA		
Sullivan's English Grammar	BE	25	15
Sully's Outlines of Psychology	AP	3 00	2 40
Teacher's Handbook of Psychology	AP	1 50	1 20
Sumner's Problems in Political Economy	HO		1 00
Super's (O. B.) Elementary German Reader	GI	*45	40
Preparatory French Reader	HE	*80	70
Readings from French History	AL		1 00
Histoire de France	HO		80
Supiée's Handbook of Civil Gov., new ed	EL	90	
Trench on Words, new rev. ed	AR	*1 00	
See also Trench.			
Sutherland's Primer of Geometry	LN		75
Sutton & Kimbrough's Pupils' Arithmetics:			
Primary Book	HE	*22	18
Intermediate Book	HE	*25	20
Lower Book	HE	*40	35
Higher Book	HE	*70	60
Swasey's Gymnastic Exercises	BO	15	
Sweeny's Natural Science Note-Book, No. 1, Mineralogy	LV	*25	
Sweet's (H.) Practical Study of Languages	HO		1 50
Swett's (J.) Normal Word Book	AM	*30	
School Elocution	AM	*1 00	
Swett's (S.) Stories of Maine	AM	*60	
Swift's Natural Philosophy, pt. 1	BR		40
—— pt. 2	BR		45
Swineford's Literature for Beginners	RB	75	60
Swinton's Introductory Geography	AM	*55	
Grammar-School "	AM	*1 25	
Primary Geography	AM	*54	
Elementary "	AM	*80	
Complete "	AM	*1 30	
Studies in English Literature	AM	*1 20	
1st Lessons in Our Country's History	AM	*48	
School History of United States	AM	*90	
Outlines of World's History	AM	*1 44	
Primer	AM	*12	
Primer and 1st Reader	AM	*25	
1st Reader	AM	*18	
2d "	AM	*35	
3d "	AM	*50	
4th "	AM	*65	
5th "	AM	*90	
6th or Classic English Reader	AM	*1 08	
Advanced 1st Reader	AM	*25	
" 2d "	AM	*35	
" 3d "	AM	*50	
" 4th "	AM	*65	
Institute Reader	AM	*25	
Word Primer	AM	*15	
Word Book or Speller	AM	*18	
Word Analysis	AM	*29	
New Word Analysis	AM	*35	
Language Primer	AM	*28	
" Lessons	AM	*38	
New English Grammar	AM	*56	
School Composition	AM	*82	
New English Grammar and Comp.	AM	*76	
Talking with the Pencil	AM	*30	
Swisher's Vertical Penmanship, nos. 1 to 5	*doz.* AM	*96	
Syle's From Milton to Tennyson	AL		1 00
Symes' Political Economy	LN	90	
Symonds' Elements of U. S. Hist.	BF	60	
Symonds' Elements of Arithmetic	HW	*80	
—— Algebra	HW	*80	
—— Arithmetic, Algebra, and Trigonometry, 1 v.	HW	80	
—— English Grammar	HW	*80	
—— U. S. History	HW	*80	
—— Geography	HW	*80	
Questions to each	HW	*50	
American Government	HW	50	
Syms's (L. C.) First Year in French	AM	*50	
Second Year in French	AM	*1 00	
Third Year in French	AM	*1 20	
Tacitus' Gudeman's Agricola	AL		1 00
Tafel's German-English Pocket Dict.	KO	90	54
Eng.-Ger. and Ger.-Eng. Dict.	ST	1 00	
Taine's English Literature Condensed (Fiske)	HO		1 40
Talbot's Quantitative Analysis	MC	1 50	
Tanner (G. H.) & Allen's (J.) Analytical Geometry	AM	*2 00	
*Tappan's (E. M.) England's Story	HM	85	
*—— Our Country's Story	HM	65	
Tappan's (W.) Pope's Tr. of Homer's Iliad, Bks. 1, 6, 22, 24	GI	*30	25
Tarbell's (H. S.) Complete Geography	WR	1 00	
Introductory Geography	WR	*50	
*Middle Atlantic ed	WR	1 10	
*W. Central States ed	WR	1 10	
*E. Central " "	WR	1 10	
Lessons in Language and Grammar, Bk. 1	GI	*45	35
—— Bk. 2	GI	*70	60
Tarbell's (H. S.) Lessons in Language, with Spanish Notes	GI	*35	30
Demosthenes' Philippics	GI	*1 10	1 00
Tarr's (R. S.) Elementary Physical Geography	MC	1 40	
Elementary Geology	MC	1 40	
First Book of Physical Geography	MC	1 10	
Tarr's (R. S.) & McMurray's (F. M.) Geographies:			
Bk. 1, Home Geography and the Earth as a Whole	MC	60	
" 2, North America	MC	75	
" 3, Other Continents	MC	75	

Todd and Powell. *See* Normal Reading Course.
Todhunter's Algebra for Beginners.....MO 75
Differential Calculus ....MC 2 60
Integral " ....MC 2 60
Euclid.................................MC 90
Plane Co-ordinate Geometry.........MC 1 80
Mechanics for Beginners.............MC 1 10
Plane Trigonometry...................MC 1 30
Trigonometry for Beginners..........MC 60
Todhunter & Hogg's Plane Trigonometry.MC 1 10
Todhunter's (I.) and Loney's (S. L.) Algebra for Beginners with Ans.......MC 1 10
—— Without Ans ....MC 1 00
Tolmie's Learner's Guide to Bookkeeping..PI 30 18
Tomlins' Children's Songs...............DS 30
Tomlins's (W.L.) Christmas Carols......AM *10
Tomlinson's Manual of Latin Grammar...GI *90
Latin for Sight Reading...............GI *1 10 1 00
Tomlinson's (E. T.) Stories of the American Revolution: First Series......SA 80
—— Second Series.....................SA 80
Stories of the War of 1812..............SA *4
Tooke's Pantheon of Heathen Gods......OU 1 25 84
Torrey's Milton's Paradise Lost.........HM 1 00
Torrey's (B.) Every-Day Birds............HM 1 00
Torrey's (J. J.) Elementary Studies in Chemistry ....HO 1 25
Tower & Tweed's Gram. of Composition..LE 40
Towle's (G. M.) Nation in a Nutshell, bds.LE 30
Young People's England, " .....LE 1 00
" " Ireland, " .....LE 1 00
Towle's (J. A.) Plato's Protagoras........GI *45 40
—— with notes..........................GI *1 35 1 25
Town's New Speller and Definer.........AR 20 20
Analysis.........................AR 48 48
Towne's Primary Arithmetic ....MO 20
Mental Arithmetic ....MO 27
Intermediate Arithmetic ....MO 38
Practical " ....MO 60
—— Key to....................MO 67
Algebra..............................MO 88
—— Key to............................MO 88
Townsend's (C.) Analysis of Civil Gov't..AM *1 08
Shorter Course in Civil Government.AM *72
Analysis of Letter-Writing ....AM *1 08
Commercial Law.......................AM *2 40
Townsend's (J. L.) Arith. Examples:
Primary...............................SN 15
Intermediate ....SN 20
Grammar School.......................SN 35
—— Answers to.......................SN 25
Questions in Geography...............SN 20
—— Answers to......................SN 25
Questions in Grammar.................SN 30
—— Answers to ....SN 25
Tracy's Introductory Course in Mechanical Drawing........................AM *1 80
Tracy's (R. S.) Anatomy and Physiology.AM *1 00
Trainer's How to Study History.........FL 1 00
Trask's (C. W.) Reference Handbook of Roman History......................LE 50
Grecian " ....LE 50
Traub's (P. E.) Spanish Verb.............AM *1 00
Treat's Home Studies in Nature.........AM *90
Tregelles' Gesenius' Hebrew Lexicon....WI 5 00
Tremain's (M.) Survey of English History.................................AN 75 65
Trimble's (E. J.) Handbook of Lit......EL *1 55 1 40
Short Course in Literature...........EL *1 25 1 10
Trobridge's Principles of Perspective....CA 1 25
—— pap...............................CA 75
Troeger's Science Book ....SR *55 50
Troeger's (J. W.) Harold's Discussions...AP **
Trotter's New Geography.................HE 1 00
Trowbridge's (O. R.) Civil Gov't of Ill....FL 75
Truan's Les Grands Écrivains Français..JE 1 50
True's Elements of Logic.................KA 40
True & Dickinson's Our Republic.........SY 85
Tuckerman's (A. L.) Short Hist. of Architecture............................SC 1 50
Tuell (H.) and Fowler's (H. N.) Beginner's Book in Latin ....SA 1 00
A First Book in Latin....................SA 1 00
Tuft's (J. W.) Questions on Geography...SE 25
Questions on Greece ....SE 25
" " Rome ....SE 25
Tuft's (John W.) Child Life in Song.......SI *65 60
Handbook of Vocal Music.............SI 1 50
Polyhymnia ....SI 1 50 1 12
See Cecilian Series of Study and Song.
Tufts & Holt. *See* Normal Music.
Tunstall's Cicero's Orations..............UN 1 38 1 20
Turner's Primer and 1st Reader..........GI *24 20
Stories for Young Children ....GI *24 20
Tweed's Grammar School Speller.........LE 20
Grammar for Common Schools ....LE 30
Graded Suppl. Reader, 12 pts.....*doz.*LE 60
—— 1st, 2d, and 3d Year, 3 pts..*ea.*LE 20

Tweed's (B. F.) Graded Lessons in Language.................................LE 30
Twentieth Century Classics (Davidson, W. M.), 18 nos., cl..............*ea.*CE 25
—— —— pap.........................." CE 10
Twentieth Century English Classics (prices 35c. to 50c., cl. and bds.)..AP
Twentieth Century Text-Books...........AP
(various prices, $1.20; 60c.; 45c.)
Tyler's (H. M.) Selections from Greek Lyric Poets...........................GI *1 10 1 00
Tyler's (M. C.) Literary History American Revolution, 2 v........... *ea.*PU 3 00
American Colonial Literature, 2 v. " PU 2 50
—— 2 v. in 1 v...................... " PU 3 00
Tyler's (W. S.) Demosthenes' On the Crown.................................AL 1 20
Demosthenes' Olynthiacs ....AL 70
—— and Philippics...................AL 1 20
Demosthenes' Philippics ....AL 80
Plato's Apology and Crito.............AM *1 05
Tacitus' Histories.......................AM *1 22
" Germania and Agricola.....AM *87
Homer's Iliad, Books 16-24.............AM *1 50
Tytler's Musical Composers..............LT 1 50
Modern Painters........................LT 1 50
Old Masters............................LT 1 50
Underhill's New Table-Book, pap.........CO *4 3
—— hf. bd...............................CO *6 6
Underwood's (F. H.) American Authors.LE 1 20
British Authors........................LE 1 20
Underwood's (L. M.) Systematic Plant Record ....MI 30
Our Native Ferns........................HO 1 00
Union Series, Physiology and Health:
No. 1, Primary.......................... BU *24
No. 2, Intermediate.....................BU *30
No. 3, Advanced........................BU *50
United States Primer..............*gross.*AR 9 00
" " 1st Reader ....AM *15
" " 2d " ....AM *24
" " 3d " ....AM *32
" " 4th " ....AM *48
" " 5th " ....AM *56
" " 6th " ....AM *60
Universal Spelling Book...................KI 10
University Series of Copy-Books. Slant:
Primary Course, nos. 1-4 and A B C. *doz.*UN *83 72
Grammar Course, nos. 5-7........ " UN *1 10 96
University Series of Copy-Books. Vertical:
Primary Course, nos. 1-6 and A Special........................*doz.*UN *83 72
Grammar Course, nos. 7-9........ " UN *1 10 96
Unwin's Exercises in Wood-Working ....LN 1 50
Upham's Mental Philosophy, abridged.. AM *1 00
Upright Rapid Writing Bks, 6 nos...*doz.*RA 84
Vaile's Vertical Writing Copy-Books:
School Course, Nos. 1 to 5........*doz.*BU *96
Business " " 6 and 7...... " BU *2 00
" " No 8, Single Entry Bookkeeping.......BU *2 00
—— Teachers' Manual..........*doz.*BU *96
Van Bergen's (R.) Story of Japan.........AM *65
*Story of China..........................AM *60
Van Daell's Leander's Märchen...........HE 45 40
Introd. to the French Language......GI 1 10 1 00
Preparatory German Reader..........GI *45 40
Introd to French Authors........... GI *90 80
Van der Smissen's Grimm's Märchen...HE *70 65
Hauff's Das Kalte Herz..............HE *70 65
Schiller's Der Taucher................HE *12 10
Van der Smissen & Fraser's Ger. Grammar.................................AM *1 25
Van Dyke's (J. C.) College Histories of Art:
1 History of Painting..................LN 1 50
2 " Architecture (Marquand & F.)...................LN 2 00
3 " Sculpture............ . LN 1 50
Van Laun's French Literature ....PU 3 50
Vannier's French Spelling and Pronun...LO 50 40
*Van Sant's (A. C.) Touch Typewriting Method...............................PS 50 34
Van Velzer & Slichter's School Algebra.TR *1 00 80
Logarithmic Tables, bds...............TR *75 65
" " book-form.......TR *30 24
University Algebra......................TR *2 00 1 60
Van Velzer & Shutts' Plane and Solid Geometry...........................TR *1 25 1 00
Plane Geometry........................TR *75 60
Solid " ....TR *75 60
Van Wie's Outlines and Questions in U. S. History ....BI 15
Varney's Brief History of Maine........MM 1 25 1 00
Veazie's Music Primer....................GI *5
Four-Part Song Reader ....GI *47 40
School Singer............................GI *60 50
Vega's 7 pl. Logarithmic Tables..........LB 2 50

Title	Pub.		
Velasquez's New Spanish Reader........	AP	1 25	
Spanish Dictionary, 8°..............	AP	5 00	
—— Abridged, 12°..................	AP	1 50	
See also Ollendorff.			
*Velazques & Simonné's Revised Ollendorff Method for Learning Spanish..............................	AP	1 00	
Venable's (C. S.) First Less. in Numbers.	UN	*21	18
Intermediate Arithmetic	UN	*42	36
Practical "	UN	*74	64
Mental "	UN	*33	28
Key to Arithmetics	UN	*69	60
New Elementary Arithmetic.........	UN	*46	40
New Practical "	UN	*76	65
—— Key to..........	UN		75
Easy Algebra.....................	UN	*69	60
High School Algebra...............	UN	*1 15	1 00
—— Key to	UN	*81	70
Legendre's Geometry.	UN	*1 72	1 50
Notes on "	UN	*1 15	1 00
Introduction to Modern Geometry ...	UN	35	30
Exercises in Plane Geometry	UN	*35	30
Venable's (F. P.) Short Hist. of Chemistry.	HE	*1 10	1 00
Qualitative Chemical Analysis......	UN	*69	60
"Veteran's" Initiatory French Readings...............	JE	75	
Preliminary French Drill............	JE	50	
Vibbert's Hebrew Text Reader	DR	1 00	
Vickroy's Circles in English Grammar..	BS	60	48
—— in 4 pts...................... *ea.*	BS	15	12
Elements of Grammar	WR	*30	
Complete Course in Grammar........	WR	*60	
Vietor's German Pronunciation..........	LB	80	
Viger's (G. E.) First Year's Latin Grammar...............................	MU	75	
Vincent's (F.) Plant World...............	AP		60
Vincent & Joy's Outline Hist. of Greece..	EA	50	
Outline History of Rome............	EA	70	
Vines' Elemen. Text-Book of Botany	MC	2 25	
Student's Text-Book of Botany......	MC	3 75	
Viri Romæ................................	BU	*50	
Vogdes' Mensuration and Geometry.....	FO	1 25	1 10
" pt. 1...	FO	60	50
" Key to	FO	75	60
United States Arithmetic	FO	70	60
—— Pt. 1..........................	FO	40	35
—— Key to.........................	FO	40	35
Volkmann-Leander's Träumereien (Hanstein)................................	AM	*35	
Voltaire's Charles XII., 18°....	LI	*45	
Voltaire's Selected Letters (Syms).......	AM	*75	
Von Klenze's Deutsche Gedichte.........	HO		90
Vos' (B. J.) Materials for German Conversation	HO		75
Vos' (B. J.) & Faust's (A. B.) Essentials of German Grammar.............	HO	**	
Vose's Geometrical Drawing.........	LE		5 00
Vuibert's Ancient History..........	MU	1 50	
Waddell's (J.) School Chemistry..........	MC	90	
Waddy's Elemen. Comp. and Rhetoric...	AM	*1 00	
Wagner's Plato's Phædo.................	AL		1 20
Plato's Apology and Crito............	AL		90
Wait's (H.) Grammatical Analysis.......	HW	50	
Wait's (W. H.) Orations of Lysias.......	AM	*1 25	
—— Text. ed........................	AM	*30	
Waites' Forgotten Meanings.............	LE	50	
Historical Student's Manual.........	LE	75	
Waldo's Descriptive Geometry..........	HE	*85	80
Waldo's (F.) Elementary Meteorology...	AM	*1 50	
Walker's (A.) Science of Wealth	LI	*1 08	
Walker (F. A.). *See* American Sci. Ser.			
Walker's (J.) Dictionary.................	KY	75	38
Walker's (Jerome) Anatomy, Physiology, and Hygiene......................	AL		1 20
Health Lessons......................	AM	*48	
Walker's (W.) Handbook of Drawing	SC	1 75	
Walker's Introd. to Physical Chemistry..	MC	3 00	
Walker & Jenks' Songs and Games for Little Ones.	DS	2 00	
*Wallbank's (N. E.) Outlines in Grammar.	FL	25	
Waller's Practical Physiology, pt. 1......	LN	35	
—— pt. 3	LN	90	
Walsh's Two-Book Series:			
Primary Arithmetic...................	HE	*35	30
Grammar School Arithmetic	HE	*75	65
Walsh's Mathemathics for Common Schools, pt. 1......................	HE	35	30
—— pt. 2..........	HE	40	35
—— pt. 3..........................	HE	75	65
Walter's (E. L.) Classic French Letters..	HO		75
Walter's (J. D.) Industrial Drawing:			
Bks. 1–10 Common Schools........ *ea.*	CE	10	
" 11–16 High " .... "	CE	15	
Walton (J. S.) & Brumbaugh's (M. G.) Stories of Pennsylvania..........	AM	*60	
Walton's New Arithmetical Table. *per* 100.	BU	*7 20	
—— Key to....	BU	*40	
Walton & Cogswell's Problems in Arith..	BU	*18	
—— With key (answers only)..	BU	*54	

Title	Pub.		
Ward's (E. G.) Grammar Blank, nos. 1, 2, *doz.*	AM	*90	
Letter Writing and Business Forms, nos. 1, 2....................... *ea.*	AM	*10	
—— nos. 3, 4 .... "	AM	*15	
—— Vertical ed., nos. 1 and 2.... *ea.*	AM	*10	
—— " " " 3 " 4.... "	AM	*15	
Graded Course in Penmanship, nos. 1 to 6 (small).................. *doz.*	AM	*72	
—— nos. 1 to 6 (large).......... "	AM	*96	
See Rational Method in Reading.			
Ward's (N.) New Amer. Stenography.....	KI		50
Ward's (R. H.) Plant Organization, bds..	GI	*85	75
Ward's (T. H.) English Poets, 4 v...... *ea.*	MC	1 00	
Warfel's (J. F.) Physiology Outlined:			
—— pap............................	MA	*10	
—— cl..............................	MA	*20	
Warman's Gestures and Attitudes......	LE	3 00	
Warne's Bacon's Essays...	WN	75	
Warren's (D. M.) Primary Geography....	BU	*50	
Common School "	BU	*1 12	
*New Physical Geography, rev. ed...	BU	*1 25	
Brief Course in "	BU	*1 00	
Warren's (Mrs. D. M.) Geographical Question Bk..........................	BU	*24	
Manual of Elocution..................	FO	60	50
Reading Selections..................	FO	1 00	80
Warren's (F. M.) French Literature.....	HE	*85	75
*Warren's (H. P.) Stories from English History...........................	HE		65
Warren's (H. W.) Recreations in Astronomy.............................	AM	*1 25	.
Warren's (M. A.) Class Word Speller.....	BU	*18	
Warren's (S. E.) Indus. Sci. Drawing:			
Free-hand Geometrical Drawing.....	WI	1 00	
Drafting Instruments................	WI	1 25	
Projection Drawing..................	WI	1 50	
Linear Perspective..................	WI	1 00	
Plane Problems in Elem. Geometry ..	WI	1 25	
Descriptive Geometry	WI	2 50	
Primary Geometry...................	WI	75	
Shades and Shadows................	WI	3 00	
Shadows and Perspective............	WI	3 50	
Problems in Linear Perspective......	WI	3 50	
Warren's Selections from Victor Hugo..	HO		70
Washburn's Early English Literature...	PU	1 50	
Watkin's (M. C.) American Literature...	AM	*85	
*Watrous's (G. A.) First Year English: Syntax and Composition..........	SY		75
*Second Year English: Composition and Rhetoric......................	SY		75
Watson's (J.) Phonograph Instructor....	PU	2 00	
Watson's (J. B.) German Sight-Reading..	HO		25
Watson's (J. M.) Independent Ser.:			
Primary Reader......................	AM	*18	
1st Reader..........................	AM	*18	
2d "	AM	*35	
3d "	AM	*50	
4th "	AM	*63	
—— cloth.........................	AM	*70	
5th Reader..........................	AM	*90	
6th "	AM	*1 00	
Complete Speller....................	AM	*20	
Elementary Spelling-Book...........	AM	*18	
Graphic Speller.....................	AM	*20	
Child's Speller in Script	AM	*18	
Youth's Speller in Script	AM	*35	
Callisthenics and Gymnastics........	ST	2 00	
Manual of Callisthenics..............	ST	1 20	
Watson's (W.) Elem. Practical Physics...	LN		90
*Watson's (W. M.) Experimental Chemistry..............................	BA	1 25	1 45
Watts' (J.) On the Mind (Fellows)	AM	*60	
Wavelet, The...........................	AM	*32	
Wayland's Intellectual Philosophy.......	BU	*1 28	
Moral Science.......................	BU	*1 28	
—— Abridged	BU	*48	
Chapin's Political Economy..........	BU	*1 28	
Weaver's Iowa (Constitution and Laws)..	MY	*40	
Webb's (A. C.) Model Definer, new ed.....	EL	*40	33
Model Etymology, new ed............	EL	*60	53
Manual of Etymology................	EL	*85	75
Webb's (J. R.) Model 1st Reader........	SR	*36	32
Model 2d Reader....................	SR	*42	37
" 3d "	SR	*65	56
" 4th and 5th Readers..........	SR	*1 08	96
New Model 1st Reader.........	SR	*35	32
New Word Method	AM	*24	
Webb's (J. R.) Word Method, new ed	UL	30	24
Webb, Ware & Zaner's Practical Drawing:			
Primary Grades, pts. 1, 2, 3, 4, card form .... *ea.*	HB	15	
—— Same, book form .... "	HB	15	
—— " " with 40 sheets of practice paper in envelope. *ea.*	HB	20	
Grammar Grades, book form, pts. 5, 6, 7, 8............ .... *ea.*	HB	20	
—— with 40 sheets of practice paper in envelope .... *ea.*	HB	25	

Title	Pub.	Price	Net
Weber's (A.) Hist. of Philosophy, new ed.	SC	2 50	
Webster's Primary Dictionary	AM	*48	
Common School "	AM	*72	
High " "	AM	*98	
Academic Dictionary, cl.	AM	*1 50	
—— indexed	AM	*1 80	
—— hf. cf.	AM	*2 75	
—— " indexed	AM	*3 00	
Countinghouse Dictionary, indexed	AM	*2 40	
Condensed " cl.	AM	*1 44	
—— indexed	AM	*1 75	
—— hf. cf.	AM	*2 75	
—— " indexed	AM	*3 00	
Handy Dictionary	AM	*15	
Pocket " cl.	AM	*57	
—— roan flex	AM	*69	
—— roan tucks	AM	*78	
—— mor., indexed	AM	*90	
American People's Dictionary and Manual	AM	*48	
Practical Dictionary	AM	*80	
Elementary Spelling-Book *doz.*	AM	*90	
Speller and Definer	MO	17	
Webster's Collegiate Dictionary, cl., indexed	ME	3 00	
—— shp., indexed	ME	4 00	
—— hf. mor., indexed	ME	5 00	
International Dictionary, new ed., shp.	ME	10 00	
—— 2 v., shp.	ME	12 00	
—— full rus.	ME	15 00	
Webster's (W. F.) English Composition and Literature	HM	90	
Weidenhamer's (E.) Mental Arithmetics	MP	*35	
Weil's Order of Words	GI	*1 25	
Weineck's (O.) German Conversation Grammar, rev. ed.	CH	1 10	
First German Reader	CH	40	
Second " "	CH	60	
Welch's (A. S.) Talks on Psychology	KE	*50	40
Welch's (E. A.) Intermediate Arithmetic Problems	BI	75	
—— Key to	BI	50	
Welch's Manual of Gymnastics	HW	*25	
Welch's & Duffield's Latin Sight Translation	MO	40	
Weld's Latin Lessons and Reader	BO	1 25	90
Revised Parsing-Book	BO	31	23
Weld & Quackenbos' English Grammar	BO	1 13	80
—— (Norton's)	BO	1 13	80
Wells's Text-Book of Biology, pts. 1 and 2, *ea.*	HS	1 00	
Wells' (B. W.) Schiller's Jungfrau von Orleans	HE	*65	60
Modern French Literature	LT	1 50	
" German "	LT	1 50	
Ca Ira Series of French Plays, 6 v. *ea.*	AL		36
Wells' (C. R.) Natural Movement Series of Writing, nos. 1-2 *doz.*	BI	84	
—— 3-5 "	BI	96	
Manual of the Movement Method	BI	25	
Wells' (D. A.) Natural Philosophy	AM	*1 15	
Principles of Chemistry	AM	*1 15	
Science of Common Things	AM	*85	
Wells' (W.) Plane Geometry	HE		75
Plane and Solid Geometry	HE		1 25
New Plane and Solid Geometry	HE		1 25
Essentials of Plane and Solid Geom.	HE		1 25
Solid Geometry	HE		75
Geometry and Trigonometry	HE		1 68
Academic Algebra	HE		1 08
University "	HE		1 50
Trigonometry	HE		1 15
—— with Tables	HE		1 25
Essentials of Trigonometry	HE		90
—— with Tables	HE		1 08
Plane Trigonometry	HE		75
Logarithms	HE		75
Logarithmic Tables, flex	HE		80
—— Pocket ed	HE		36
—— Four-Place Tables	HE		25
—— New Six-Place Tables	HE		60
College Algebra	HE		1 50
Higher Algebra	HE		1 32
New Higher Algebra	HE		1 32
Academic Arithmetic	HE		1 00
New Plane and Spherical Trigonometry	HE		1 25
Essentials of Algebra	HE		1 10
Complete Trigonometry	HE		90
—— with tables	HE		1 08
New Plane Trigonometry	HE		75
Wells' (W. H.) Shorter Course in Grammar and Composition	AM	*36	
Wells (W.) and Gerrish's Beginner's Algebra	HE	**	
Welsh's (A. H.) Complete Rhetoric	SI	*1 25	1 12
Essentials of English	SI	*1 00	90
English Masterpiece Course	SI	*83	75
Lessons in English Grammar	SI	*67	60
Welsh's (A. H.) First Lessons in English	SI	*54	48
English Literature, Univ. ed.	SR		2 25
Essentials of Geometry	SR		1 25
Trigonometry	SI	*1 12	1 00
English Composition	SI	*67	60
Welsh's (J. P.) English Grammar	SO	*60	
First Lessons in English Gram. and Comp.	SO	*40	
Wenckebach's Deutscher Anschauungs-Unterricht	HO		1 10
Deutsches Lesebuch	HO		80
Meisterwerke	HE		1 26
Schönsten Deutschen Lieder	HO		1 20
" Deutsche Literatur Geschichte, v. 1	HE	*60	50
—— v. 2 and 3	HE	**	
Deutsche Sprachlehre	HO		1 12
German Conversation based on Humorous Stories	HO		1 00
Wenckebach's Meissner's Aus Meiner Welt	HO		75
Wenckebach & Schrakamp's Deutsche Grammatik	HO		1 00
Wendell's English Composition	SC	1 50	
Wendell's (K.) Eng. Latin Vocabulary	JE	25	
Wenley's Outlines of Kant's Critique	HO	*80	75
Wentworth's (E.) Arith. Problems	AM	*32	
—— Teacher's ed.	AM	*36	
Wentworth's (G. A.) Mental Arithmetic	GI	*35	30
Primary Arithmetic	GI	*35	30
Elementary "	GI	*35	30
Practical "	GI	*75	65
Grammar School Arithmetic	GI	*75	65
Advanced Arithmetic	GI	*1 10	1 00
New School Algebra	GI	*1 25	1 12
First Steps in Algebra	GI	*70	60
School Algebra	GI	*1 25	1 12
Higher "	GI	*1 55	1 40
College "	GI	*1 65	1 50
Elements of Algebra	GI	*1 25	1 12
Shorter Course in Algebra	GI	*1 10	1 00
Complete Algebra	GI	*1 55	1 40
Plane Geometry	GI	*85	75
" and Solid Geometry	GI	*1 40	1 25
Plane Geometry, rev.	GI	*85	75
Solid " "	GI	*85	75
Plane and Solid Geometry, rev.	GI	*1 40	1 25
Syllabus of Geometry	GI	*27	25
Geometrical Exercises	GI	*12	10
Plane and Solid Geometry and Trigonometry	GI	*1 55	1 40
New Plane Trigonometry	GI	*45	40
—— and Tables	GI	*95	90
New Plane and Spherical Trigonometry	GI	*90	85
—— and Tables	GI	*1 30	1 20
—— Surveying and Navigation	GI	*1 30	1 20
New Plane Trigonometry, Surveying, and Tables	GI	*1 35	1 20
New Plane and Spherical Trigonometry, Surveying, with Tables	GI	*1 50	1 35
Analytic Geometry	GI	*1 35	1 25
Arithmética Elemental (all Spanish)	GI	*45	40
—— (Spanish-English)	GI	*55	45
Arithmética Practica	GI	*85	75
Wentworth & Hill's Exercises in Algebra	GI	*80	70
—— pt. 1, Exercise Manual	GI	*40	35
—— pt. 2, Examination Manual	GI	*40	35
Exercises in Arithmetic	GI	*90	80
—— pt. 1, Exercise Manual	GI	*55	50
—— pt. 2, Examination Manual	GI	*40	35
Exercise Manual in Geometry	GI	*80	70
First Steps in Geometry	GI	**	
High School Arithmetic	GI	*1 10	1 00
Log. and Trig. Tables (7 tables)	GI	*55	50
—— Complete ed.	GI	*1 10	1 00
A Text-Book of Physics	GI	*1 25	1 15
*Laboratory Exercises in Elementary Physics	GI	*27	25
Wentworth, McLellan & Glashan's Algebraic Analysis	GI	*1 60	1 50
Wentworth & Reed's First Steps in Numbers, Pupils' ed.	GI	*35	30
—— Teachers' ed.	GI	*1 00	90
—— " " pts. 1, 2 and 3, *ea.*	GI	*35	30
Werner's Introductory Geography (Tarbell)	WR	*55	
Grammar School Geography, pt. 1 (Tarbell)	WR	*60	
—— pt. 2 (Tarbell)	WR	*60	
Mental Arithmetic	WR	*30	
Primer	WR	*30	
Bookkeeping	WR	*80	
Journal Blanks and Ledger Blanks, *ea.*	WR	*30	
Werner Arithmetic, Bk. 1 (Hall)	WR	*40	
—— Bk. 2 (Hall)	WR	*40	
—— Bk. 3	WR	*50	
—— Teacher's Handbook (Hall)	WR	*25	

Werner's Modern Language Ser.:
  Martin's Inductive German Method, Bk. 1 ..... WR *30
  —— Bk. 2 ..... WR *30
  —— " 3 ..... WR *30
  —— " 4 ..... WR *30
  Martin's Compendium of German Grammar ..... WR **
Wernli & Hillmantel's German Copy-Books, 4 nos. ..... *doz.* BP 1 20 80
Wescott's (J. H.) Pliny's Letters ..... AL 1 25
*Wesselhoeft's German Composition ..... HE 45 40
Wessely's English and French Dict ..... } CH, LB, or ST 85
  English and German Dictionary 85
  " " Italian " 85
  " " Latin " 85
  " " Spanish " 85
Wessely's Dictionaries as above ..... *ea.* RU 60
West's English Grammar ..... MO 60
  English Grammar for Beginners ..... MO 30
  Terence ..... AM *1 50
*West's (A. F.) A Latin Grammar ..... AP 90
*West's (W. M.) Ancient History ..... AL 1 50
Westcott's (J. H.) Selections from Livy ..... AL 1 25
  Aulus Gellius ..... AL 30
  Martial ..... AL 30
  Cæsar's Commentaries ..... AP **
Westcott & Hort's Greek-English Test. ..... AM *3 50
  Student's Greek New Testament ..... AM *1 00
  Greek Testament, cl ..... MC 1 00
  —— With Lexicon, leath ..... MC 1 90
Westlake's Common School Literature ..... SO *50
  How to Write Letters ..... SO *34
  3000 Practice Words ..... EL *35 30
Whately's Bacon's Essays ..... LE 1 50
  English Synonyms ..... LE 50
  Logic, 12° ..... MO 65
  Rhetoric, 12° ..... MO 65
Wheatley's (W. A.) German Declensions ..... BI 15
Wheeler's (H. N.) Logarithms ..... SE 35
  Plane and Spherical Trigonometry ..... GI *1 10 1 00
  Second Lessons in Arithmetic ..... HM 60
  Answers to Second Lessons, pap. ..... HM 20
  For First Lessons, *see* Colburn, W.
Wheeler's Graded Studies in English ..... WH *40
  Graded Studies in Great Authors (a complete speller) ..... WH *40
  *Graded Readers. A Primer ..... WH *30
  —— —— *A First Reader ..... WH *30
  —— —— A Second Reader ..... WH **
  —— —— A Third Reader ..... WH **
  Elementary Speller ..... WH *25
  *Graded Studies in English: First Lessons in Gram. and Comp. ..... WH *40
  *Graded Studies on Great Authors: A Complete Speller ..... WH *40
Whelpley's Compend of History ..... CO *1 20 1 08
Whicher's (G. M.) Viri Romae ..... SA 50
Whitaker's (H. C.) Elements of Trigonometry ..... EL *1 10 1 00
Whitcomb's History Chart-Book ..... BA *1 64 1 40
Whitcomb's (M.) History of Modern Europe ..... AP **
White's (C. A.) Classic Literature ..... HO 1 60
  Students' Mythology ..... AR 1 25 94
White's (C. E.) Two Years with Numbers ..... HE *40 35
  Junior Arithmetic ..... HE *50 45
  Senior Arithmetic ..... HE 65
*White's (C. H.) Cicero's Pro Ligario, pap. ..... SA 30
White's (C. J.) Astronomy ..... WI 2 00
White's (E. E.) First Book of Arithmetic ..... AM *30
  New Elemen. Arithmetic ..... AM *50
  " Complete " ..... AM *65
  —— Key to ..... AM *30
  Primary Arithmetic, old ..... AM *22
  Intermediate Arithmetic, old ..... AM *35
  Complete Arithmetic, old ..... AM *65
  Manual and Key of Arithmetics, old ..... AM *75
  Oral Lessons in Number ..... AM *40
  School Algebra ..... AM *1 00
  —— Key to ..... AM *1 00
  Elements of Geometry (Macnie) ..... AM *1 25
  Plane Geometry (separate) ..... AM *75
  —— Key to Elements of Geometry ..... AM *1 00
White's Elementary Chemistry ..... GI *1 10 1 00
White's (F. H.) Outlines of U S. Hist. ..... AM *30
White's (G. G.) Indus. Drawing, rev., Nos. 1-8 ..... *doz.* PR 96
  —— Nos. 9-18 ..... " PR 1 80
  Practice Book. Small for Bks. 1-8 .. " PR 72
  " " Large " 9-18. " PR 96
  Theory of Design ..... PR 1 00
  Model and Object Drawing-Books, A and B ..... *ea.* PR 15
  Light and Shade and Landscape ..... PR 3 50
  New Course in Art Instruction:
    First Year Drawing-Book ..... *doz.* PR 1 00
    Second " " ..... " PR 1 00
White's (G. G.) New Courses in Art Instruction:
    Third Year Drawing-Book ..... *doz.* PR 1 00
    Fourth " " ..... " PR 1 80
    Fifth " " ..... " PR 1 80
    Sixth " " ..... " PR 1 80
    Seventh " " ..... " PR 1 80
    Eighth " " ..... " PR 1 80
    Ninth " " ..... " PR 1 80
  Manual for 1st, 2d and 3d Grades ..... PR 50
    Manuals for 4th to 9th Year Grades. *ea.* PR 50
White's (G. H.) and Waite's (G. W.) Straight Road to Cæsar ..... GI *1 25 1 13
White's (H. S.) German Composition ..... AL 90
White's (J. M.) Oral Arithmetic ..... AM *35
White's (J. T.) Junior Student's Lexicons:
  Latin-English ..... GI *1 15 1 00
  English-Latin ..... GI *1 65 1 50
  Latin-English and English-Latin ..... GI *2 55 2 25
  Grammar School Texts, Latin and Greek (various prices, from 25c.-55c.) ..... LN
White's (J. W.) First Lessons in Greek ..... GI *1 30 1 20
  First Greek Book ..... GI *1 35 1 25
  Sophocles' Œdipus Tyrannus ..... GI *1 25 1 13
  Passages for Translation at Sight, Greek, Pt. 4 ..... GI *90 80
  Beginner's Greek ..... GI *1 65 1 50
White's (L. B.) Outline of Chemical Theory ..... AM 25
White's (L. C.) Story of English Lit. ..... LE *90 75
White's (R. G.) Every Day English ..... HM 2 00
  Words and Their Uses ..... HM 1 00
White's (W. R.) Alphabet Made Easy ..... AM *5
White's (W. R.) and Morgan's Anabasis Dictionary ..... GI *1 35 1 25
*White's Qualitative Analysis ..... HO 80
Whiteley's (R. L.) Chemical Calculations LN 60
Whiting's (C. E.) Part Song and Chorus Bk. HE *1 10 96
  Public School Music Course, Bks. 1-5, *ea.* HE *30 25
  —— Book 6 ..... HE *60 54
  Complete Music Reader ..... HE *90 75
  Young People's Song-Book ..... HE *45 35
  Music Charts, Ser. 1 ..... HE *6 50 6 00
  " " " 2 ..... HE *3 50 3 00
  *School Song Book ..... HE 40
Whiting's (H.) Mathematical and Physical Tables ..... HE *60 50
  Physical Measurements, 4 pts. ..... *ea.* HE *1 35 1 20
  —— complete in 1 v. ..... HE *4 00 3 75
Whitney's (W. D.) French Grammar ..... HO 1 30
  —— Key to ..... HO 80
  Practical French ..... HO 90
  German Dictionary ..... HO *1 50
  " Grammar, rev ..... HO 1 30
  —— Key ..... HO 30
  Brief German Grammar ..... HO 60
  See also Corwin.
  German Reader ..... HO 1 50
  Brief French Grammar ..... HO 65
  Introductory French Reader ..... HO 70
  " German " ..... HO 1 00
  Essentials of English Grammar ..... GI *85 75
  Language and Study of Language ..... SC 2 50
Whitney's & Lockwood's English Gram. ..... GI *80 70
Whitney-Klemm's Elem. Ger. Reader ..... HO 80
  German by Practice ..... HO 90
Whiton's Latin Exercises ..... PE 45
  Latin Handbook ..... PE 1 00
  Auxilia Vergiliana ..... GI *20 15
  Six Weeks' Preparation for Reading Cæsar ..... GI *45 40
  Orations of Lysias ..... GI *1 10 1 00
Whittemore & Blackman's Graded Singers: No. 1 ..... CR 25
  —— No. 2 ..... CR 50
  —— No. 3 ..... CR 75
  —— No. 4 ..... CR 1 00
Whittier Leaflets, pamphlet ..... HM 30
Whybark's (J. N.) Child's Music Reader, nos. 1 and 2 ..... *ea.* FL 30
Wiebe's Paradise of Childhood ..... BO 2 00
  —— pap. ..... BO 1 50
Wiechmann's (F. G.) Chemistry ..... JE 1 00
Wiggin's Kindergarten Chimes ..... DS 1 50
  —— ..... ST 1 50
  —— bds. ..... DS 1 25
  —— " ..... ST 1 25
Wiggin's (K. D.) and Smith's (N. A.) Froebel's Gifts ..... HM 1 00
  " Occupations ..... HM 1 00
  Kindergarten Principles and Practice ..... HM 1 00
Wilbrandt's (A.) Der Meister v. Palmyra (Henckels) ..... AM *60
Wilby's How to Speak Latin ..... MU 75
Wilcox's Logic ..... WR *50

Wild and Stamm's Lesefibel ... HR 15 10
Wilder's Synopsis of Animal Classification ... HO **
Wildenbruch's (E. v.) Freudvoll und Leidvoll (Bernhardt) ... AM *65
Wilder's (M. E.) Study of English History. LE 40
Wilgus's Civil Gov't of Wisconsin ... EL *55 50
Wilkins' (E.) Map Drawing Book of the Continents ... BI 75
Map Drawing Book of U. S. ... BI 75
Wilkinson's (W. C.) Foreign Classics in English, 6 v. ... ea. FU 1 50
Will's Tables of Qual. Chem. Analysis ... BD 1 50
Willard's (Mrs.) Domestic Science Primers, Nos. 1-3 ... ea. SR *23 20
Willard's (E. C.) and Smith's (R. B.) Standard School Physiology, Hygiene, and Anatomy ... MS **
Williams' (A.) German Conversation and Composition ... HO 80
Williams' Reader for Beginners ... AM *15
Williams' (C. R.) Selections from Lucian. AL 1 40
Williams' (C. T.) Extracts from Greek Au. HO 1 00
Williams' (F.) German Dictionary ... WN 1 00 60
Williams' (F. S.) English into French ... BU *1 12
Williams' (G. E.) Outlines of Grammar... BD 30 24
Williams' (G. H.) Elements of Crystallography ... HO 1 25
Williams' (H. G.) Outlines of Psychology. BI 75
Williams' (H. S.) Geological Biology ... HO 2 80
Williams' (R. P.) Introduction to Chemical Science ... GI *90 80
Laboratory Manual ... GI *30 25
Chemical Experiments ... GI *60 50
Elements of Chemistry ... GI *1 20 1 10
Williams' (W.) Composition and Rhetoric. HE *1 00 90
Williams' (W. G.) Outlines of English Grammar ... WL 50
Williams' Choice Literature Series:
Bk. 1, Primary Grades ... BU *22
" 2, " " ... BU *25
" 1, Intermediate Grades ... BU *28
" 2, " " ... BU *35
" 1, Grammar Grades ... BU *40
" 2, " " ... BU *50
Williams' & Rogers' First Lessons in Bookkeeping ... AM *70
— Key to ... AM *50
New Introductive Bookkeeping ... AM *1 00
— Reference Book and Key to ... AM *50
New Complete Bookkeeping ... AM *1 60
— Reference Book for same ... AM *50
— Key to ... AM *50
Advanced Bookkeeping and Banking. AM *80
— Reference Book and Key to ... AM *50
Practice System of Business Training. First Course, Slant Script Edition, complete outfit ... AM *1 00
— Vertical Script Edition, complete outfit ... AM *1 00
— Guide to ... AM *50
Practice System of Business Training. Second Course, Slant Script Edition, complete outfit ... AM *1 00
— Guide to ... AM *50
Modern Illustrative Bookkeeping, Introductory Course ... AM *1 00
— Key to ... AM *50
Modern Illustrative Bookkeeping, Complete Course ... AM *1 50
— Key to ... AM *75
Office Routine and Bookkeeping. Introductory Course ... AM *1 00
— Key to ... AM *50
Office Routine and Bookkeeping. Complete Course ... AM *1 35
— Key to ... AM *75
Bookkeeping and Business Practice. Introductory Course ... AM *1 00
— Reference Book and Key to ... AM *50
Bookkeeping and Business Practice. Complete Course ... AM *1 60
— Reference Book for ... AM *50
— Key to ... AM *50
Mental Arithmetic ... AM *50
" Commercial Arithmetic ... AM *45
— Key to ... AM *25
Business Arithmetic ... AM *80
— Key to ... AM *50
Commercial Arithmetic ... AM *1 10
— Key to ... AM *50
Grammar School Algebra ... AM *75
— Key to ... AM *75
High School Algebra ... AM *1 10
Business Law ... AM *80
Pen-Written Slant Copies (Reproduced), complete ed ... AM *50
— Abridged ed ... AM *35
Pen-Written Vertical Copies (Reproduced) ... AM *25

Williams' & Rogers' Vertical Copy Books, 6 Bks ... doz. AM *72
New Practical Grammar ... AM *35
Correspondence ... AM *35
New Practical Grammar and Correspondence ... AM *60
English Punctuation ... AM *60
Studies for Letters ... AM *50
Hand in Hand with the Wise Men ... AM *40
Seventy Lessons in Spelling. Rev. ed. AM *20
— Blanks, No. 1 ... AM * 0
— Blanks, No. 2 ... AM *7
Test Lessons in Spelling ... AM *15
Pitmanic Shorthand Instructor ... AM *1 50
English-Spanish Phonography ... AM *1 25
New Civil Government ... AM *65
Descriptive Economics ... AM *65
Williams' & Tilford's Vertical Writing Books, with adjustable copy, 6 nos ... ea. JH 10 8
Williamson's Differential Calculus ... LN 3 50
Integral Calculus ... LN 3 50
Willis' (O. R.) Practical Flora ... AM *1 50
Willoughby's (W. W.) Rights and Duties of Amer. Citizenship ... AM *1 00
Wills. *See* Collier's Great Events.
Willson's (M.) Primer ... AM *15
1st Reader ... AM *24
2d " ... AM *32
3d " ... AM *48
4th " ... AM *60
5th " ... AM *90
Primary Speller ... AM *15
Larger " ... AM *24
New Speller and Analyzer ... AM *32
Wilson's (G.) Domestic Hygiene ... BL 1 00
Handbook of Hygiene ... BL 2 75
Wilson's (John) Punctuation ... AM *1 00
Wilson's (J. D.) Elementary English ... BI 35
English Grammar Made Practical ... BI 75
Wilson's (J. W.) Elementary Algebra ... EL *90 80
— Key to ... EL *90 80
Wilson's (L. L. W.) Nature Study in Elementary Schools: Manual ... MC 90
First Nature Reader ... MC 35
Second " " ... MC 35
History Reader ... MC 60
" Manual ... MC 30
Wilson's (W. D.) Political Economy ... BD 1 50
Wilson's (W.) The State ... HE 2 00
— Rev. ed ... HE 2 00
— U. S. Government ... HE *60 50
Wilson's Compendium of U. S. Hist. ... HE *45 40
Wilson's (W. N.) Geometrical Drawing ... LN 1 35
Wiltse's Kindergarten Stories ... GI *40 35
Wiltse's Morning Talks ... GI *85 75
Winans' Xenophon's Memorabilia ... AL 1 20
Xenophon's Symposium ... AL 50
Winchell's (A.) Geological Excursions ... SR 1 25
Geological Studies ... SR 2 50
Winchell's (S. R.) Primer Supplement ... LR *30 25
Orthography, Orthoepy and Punctuation ... FL *50
Winer's New Testament Grammar ... DR 4 00
Winslow's (H.) Elements of Moral Philosophy ... AM *1 05
*Winslow's (I. O.) Natural Arithmetic, Bk. 1 ... AM *30
— " 2 ... AM *40
— " 3 ... AM *50
Winsor's Readers' Handbook American Revolution ... HM 1 25
Winter's German Grammar ... DW 40
Wise's 100 Lessons in Drawing ... CS **
Compromise Slant Writing, 7 nos doz. CS *96
Wisely's Language for the Grades ... IN 40
New English Grammar ... IN 60
Witcomb & Bellenger's French Conversation ... HO 50
*Witmer's (L.) Analytical Psychology ... GI *1 60 1 50
Witt's Classic Mythology ... HO 1 00
Witter's German Primer ... WT 5
Revised New 1st Reader ... WT 35
" " 2d " ... WT 50
" " 3d " ... WT 75
" " 4th " ... WT 1 00
German Copy-Books, 6 nos ... ea. WT 10
Dictionaries. *See* Koehler.
Wohler's Organic Chemistry ... LA 3 00
Wood's (A.) Object Lessons in Botany ... AM *1 00
How to Study Plants ... AM *1 00
Lessons in Botany, rev ... AM *90
American Botanist and Florist ... AM *1 75
Descriptive Botany, Flora only ... AM *1 25
New Class-Book of Botany ... AM *2 50
Illustrated Plant Record ... AM *55
Plant Record, King's Tablets ... AM *55
Wood's (De V.) Analytical Mechanics ... WI 3 00
Elementary Mechanics ... WI 1 25
Co-ordinate Geometry ... WI 2 00

Wood's (De V.) Trigonometry ....WI	1 00	
Wood's (H. A.) Short Cuts in Arithmetic..BI	75	
Wood's (J. G.) Natural Hist., 1st Reader.BN	*25	20
Natural History, 2d Reader............BN	*36	30
" " 3d " ....BN	*50	42
" " 4th " ....BN	*65	54
" " 5th " ....BN	*65	54
" " 6th " ....BN	*65	54
Illustrated Natural History...........RU	75	
—— for Young People...............RU	1 00	
Popular Natural History..............RU	2 00	
—— ....WK	60	45
Wood's (M. J.) Companion 1st Reader....AM	*18	
Wood & Stahl's Elementary Mechanism..VN	2 00	
*Wood's (S. T) Primer of Political Economy..............................MO	50	
Woodbury's Easy Lessons in German....AM	*90	
Shorter German Course...............AM	*90	
—— Key to..........................AM	*72	
Woodhull's Easy Experiments in Science.KE	50	40
Woodhull's (J. F.) First Course in Science:		
1. Book of Experiments..............HO		50
2. Text-Book.........................HO		65
Woodhull & Van Arsdale's Chemical Experiments.....................HO		60
Woodhull & Van Arsdale's Physical Experiments.......................AP		60
Woodley's (O. I.) Foundation Lessons in English, Bk. 1...................MO	40	
*—— Bk. 2..........................MO	50	
Woodley & Carpenter's Foundation Lessons in English Grammar.........MO	**	
Woodruff's Greek Prose Composition.....SY		75
Woodward's (B. D.) Racine's Iphigénie ..AM	*60	
Woodward's (C. J.) A B C Logarithms....SP	1 60	
Five-Figure Logarithms ....SP	1 60	
Woodward's (G. H.) 1000 Test Problems in Arithmetic.....................NO	30	
Woodward's (L. J.) Number Stories.......GI	*45	40
Woodworth's Civil Gov't of N. Dakota...EL	*55	50
Woodworth's (J. B.) & Snyder's (W. H.) Elements of Geology.. ....SO	**	
Woody's Outlines of U. S. History.......NO	40	
Woolsey's International Law............SO	2 50	
Woolsey's Æschylus' Prometheus........BR		1 00
Euripides' Alcestis....................BR		1 00
Plato's Georgias......................BR		1 40
Sophocles' Antigone...................BR		1 00
" Electra ....BR		1 00
Wooster Arithmetic, Grade 1............CE	25	20
" " " 2............CE	30	21
" " " 3............CE	35	28
" Primer..........................CE	25	20
" Recitations for Grades 1 and 2..CE	25	20
Worcester & Campbell's Primary Spelling Book.........................BU	*17	
New Primary Spelling Book ....BU	*18	
Worcester & Campbell's New Pronouncing Spelling Book ....BU	*23	
Pronouncing Spelling Book...........BU	*23	
Comprehensive Spelling Book.........BU	*23	
Academic Dictionary..................LI	*1 50	
Comprehensive " LI	*1 40	
New School " LI	*80	
Pocket " cl.................LI	*30	
—— roan, flex.......................LI	*55	
—— tucks LI	*65	
Primary Dictionary...................LI	*48	
Quarto " LI	*10 00	
Elements of History..................TH		1 20
World and its People Series:		
Bk. 1, First Lessons.....................SI		36
" 2, Glimpses of the World..........SI		36
" 3, Our Own Country...............SI		50
" 4, Our American Neighbors.......SI		60
" 5, Modern Europe... ....SI		60
" 6, Life in Asia......................SI		60
" 7, Views in Africa..... ....SI		72
" 8, Australia and the Islands of the Sea.......................... ....SI		68
" 9, *South American Republics....SI		60
"World at Home" Geog. Reader No. 1..NE	25	
—— No. 2............................NE	30	
—— " 3...........................NE	50	
—— " 4...........................NE	75	
—— " 5...........................NE	75	
—— " 6...........................NE	75	
Worman's 1st French Book..............AM	*40	
2d French Book........................AM	*40	
French Echo (Conversation).........AM	*90	
Grammaire Française..................AM	*1 00	
1st Fr. Bk. & Le Questionnaire in 1 v..AM	*90	
Teacher's Handbook...................AM	*60	
1st German Book.......................AM	*30	
2d " " .... AM	*40	
1st and 2d German Bk. in 1 v ....AM	*75	
Elementary German Grammar.......AM	*1 00	
Complete " " .... ..AM	*1 40	
Elementary " Reader..........AM	*90	
Collegiate " " ....AM	*1 25	
Worman's German Echo (Conversation).AM	*90	
" Copy-Books, 3 nos.........*ea.*AM	*10	
1st Spanish Book......................AM	*40	
2d " " ....AM	*40	
Worthington's Phys. Laboratory Pract..AL		1 20
Wrage's (H. D.) Progressive German Reader, 1st Course.................ST	40	
Wright's Drillbook in English Gram .....SR	*23	20
Tabulated Forms for Parsing.........SR	*23	20
Wright's (A. D.) Orthography, rev.......AM	*18	
Wright's (D. S.) Exercises in Geometry...FL	40	
Wright's (G. F.) Christian Evidences....DR	1 50	
Wright's (H. C.) Children's Stories in American History.................SC	1 25	
Children's Stories of American Progress.................................SC	1 25	
Children's Stories in American Literature ....SC	60	
Wright's (H. P.) Satires of Juvenal.......GI	*1 35	1 25
—— Text ed................................GI	*45	40
Wright's (J. McN.) Nature Reader, No. 1.HE	*30	25
—— " " " 2.HE	*40	35
—— " " " 3.HE	*53	45
—— " " " 4.HE	*60	50
Botany.....................................PP	50	
Astronomy...............................PP	50	
Wright's (M. R.) Sound, Light, and Heat.LN	80	
Elementary Physics....................LN	80	
Wright's (T. W.) Mechanics, rev. ed.....VN	2 50	2 00
Wright's (W. V.) Mechanic's Arithmetic..HW	*25	
Wurtz's Chemistry.......................LI	*1 80	
Wurtete's Standard Measures............SP	50	
Wyman's Musical Text-Book............PD	50	
—— bds.................................PD	40	
Wythe's Easy Less. in Vegetable Biology.EA	30	
—— pap. ....EA	20	
Science of Life, Animal and Vegetable Biology......................EA	1 50	
Ybarra's Practical Spanish Method.....HE	1 00	80
Yeo's Physiology.............. ....BL	*2 50	
Yonge's (C. D.) English-Greek Lexicon.AM	*4 50	
—— ....LN	2 50	
Yonge's (C. M.) Ancient History..........HO		75
History of France.........................HO		80
Mediæval History........................HO		80
Modern History...........................HO		1 05
History of England............... } LR or EA	*90	
" " France...............	*90	
" " Germany.............	*90	
" " Greece	*90	
" " Rome..................	*90	
Cameos from English History, 9 v. *ea.* MO	*1 38	1 25
Youmans' (E. A.) Descriptive Botany....AM	*1 20	
First Book of Botany, rev...............AM	*64	
Youmans' (E. L.) New Chemistry.......AM	*1 22	
Young's (A. V. E.) Elementary Principles of Chemistry..........................AP		95
—— with experiments..................AP		1 10
Young's (A. W.) Government Class-Book....................................MY	*1 05	
Civil Government of N. Y............AM	*90	
Young's (C. A.) General Astronomy......GI	*3 00	2 75
Lessons in Astronomy...................GI	*1 30	1 20
Elements of " ....GI	*1 75	1 60
Manual of " ....GI	**	
Young's (H. A.) New Juvenile Speaker..DW	30	
—— pap................ ....DW	20	
Young's (J. S.) Civil Goverment of Colo..EL	55	50
Young's (J. W. A.) & Linebarger's (C. A.) Calculus...............................AP	2 20	
Young's (M. V.) Italian Grammar........HO	**	
Young Catholic Series:		
Illustrated Primer..........................SK	12	7½
" Speller..........................SK	18	10½
" 1st Reader.....................SK	18	10½
" 2d " ....SK	25	15
" 3d " ....SK	40	24
" 4th " ....SK	50	30
" 5th " ....SK	60	36
" 6th " ....SK	75	45
" Young Ladies' Reader....SK	60	36
Normal Reader...........................SK	75	45
Illustrated Table-Book..................SK	20	12
Grammar School Speller...............SK	60	36
*Youth's Companion Series:		
*Wide World.......................... GI	*30	25
*Northern Europe......................GI	*30	25
Zachos' New American Speaker..........CO	*1 50	1 25
Zahner's German and English Dict ......ST	75	
Zeller's Greek Philosophy................HO		1 40
Zimmermann's Classical German Reader.BP	1 20	1 00
Microscopical Botany.................HO		2 50
Zschokke's (H.) Der Zerbrochene Krug (Roelker).................................AM	25	
Zumpt. *See* Anthon ; Schmitz.		
Zundel (E. J.) and Ryan's (J. E.) School Harmonist—Vocal..................AM	*40	
—— Instrumental and vocal.......AM	*50	
Zur Brücke's Ger. without Gram., pt. 1..SI	*75	60
—— pt. 2............................. SI	*1 12	1 00

SUBJECT CLASSIFICATION

For the American Educational Catalogue for 1902.

Algebra.—Atwood, Alsop, Baker (A. H.), Beman & Smith, Benedict, Bowser, Boyd, Boyden, Bradbury, Briggs, Brooks (E.), Brown (I. H.), Brown (T. K.), Burton, Clarke (J. B.), Buchanan, Collin, Davies (C.), Davis, Day (J.), Downey, Durrell & R., Evans, Fairbanks & H., Ficklin, Fisher & Schwatt, Franklin, Freeland, Galbraith & H., Giffin, Gilbert, Gilbert & S., Gillett, Graham, Greenleaf, Griffin, Hagar, Hall, Hall & K., Higgs, Hull, Jocelyn, Johnson (W. W.), Jones (G. W.), Langley, Lefevre, Lilley, Macnie, McCurdy, McDonald, Marsh & Ashton, Michael, Milne, Model, Morey, Newcomb, Nicholson, Nipher, Olney, Peck (W. G.), Peirce (B.), Perrin (M. L.), Peterson & B., Phillips & B., Potts & S., Ray, Robinson (H. N.), Sabin & L., Sanford (S. P.), Schuyler, Seaver & W., Sensenig, Sheldon, Sherwin, Smith (C.), Smith (C.) & S., Smith (F. H.), Smith (H.), Symonds, Tablet Ser., Taylor, Thompson, Todhunter, Todhunter & L., Towne, Van Velzer & S., Venable (C. S.), Wells, Wells & Gerrish, Wentworth (G. A.), Wentworth & H., Wentworth, M. & G., Williams & R., Wilson (J. W.).

Anatomy.—Hartigan, May, Prang, Reighard & Jennings, Stilwell, Whitman.

Anatomy and Physiology.—American Science Series (Martin), Gorhar & Tower, Hewes, Hitchcock, House, Howell, Peabody.

Anatomy, Physiology, and Hygiene.—Allen (C. B. & A.), Brand, Clark (W. A.), Draper, Loomis (J. R.), Martindale, Smith (E. F.), Smith (R. B.) & W., Rasweiler, Walker (Jerome).

See also PHYSIOLOGY.

Anglo-Saxon.—Baskervill, Baskervill & H., Beowulf, Bright, Caedmon, Carpenter (S. H.), Cook, Corson, Harrison & S., Hempl, Johnson (H.), MacLean, March.

Antiquities.—Anthon, Cornish, Fiske, Harper's, History, Irving.

See also CLASSICAL.

Arithmetic.—*Business and Commercial.*—Baldwin, Bryant & S., Cook & Cropsey, Crittenden, Hall (F. H.), Hall (G.), How, Powers & Lyons, Sadler (W. H.), Taylor (F. M.), Thomson, Williams & Rogers.

Elementary, Practical and Higher.—Bailey, Basis, Belfield & Brooks, Beman & Smith, Bradbury, Bradford, Brooks, Buehrle, Caldwell (M. P.), Capel, Carr, Carroll, Chancellor, Christian Bros. Ser., Clark, Colaw & E., Coleman, Common Sense, Conrad, Cook, Cook (J. W.), Cook & Cropsey, Davies & Peck, Dean, Dillard, Dubbs, Durrell & R., Ferrell, Ficklin, Fine, Fowler, Franklin, Galer, Gay, Giffin, Goff, Graham, Hagar, Hall, Hathaway, Heath, Henry, Hewett, Hobbs, Hornbrook, Hull, Jess, King, Lippincott, McHenry & D., McLelland & A., MacLeod, MacVicar (M.), Martyn, Model, Moore, Moritz, Myers & Brooks, New American, New Arithmetic, New Franklin, New Inductive, New Model, Olney, Parker, Peck (W. M.), Peres, Pierce, Plummer, Popular, Powers & Lyons, Practical, Raub, Rich, Ring, Sadler-Rowe, Sandy, Sensenig & A., Seymour, Sheldon, Silver, Sloane, Smith (C.), Smith (C. & H.), Smith (R. C.), Southworth, Speer, Sprague (J. D.), Standard, Stoddard, Stone, Sutton & Kimbrough, Symonds, Tablet Ser., Vogdes, Walsh, Walton & Cogswell, Welch (E. A.), Wentworth (E.), Wentworth (G. A.), Wentworth & H., Werner, Wheeler (H. N.), White (C. E.), White (J. M.), Winslow, Woodward, Wooster, Wright.

First Lessons.—Bacon, Badlam, Barnes, Beebe, Belfield, Carr, Carroll, Christian Bros. Ser., Colburn, Dunton, Fisher, Franklin, Gilbert, Ginn, Goff, Grant, Hagar, Hazen, Holbrook (N. M.) Hoose, Hornbrook, Hull, Johnson (S. F.), Little Folks', Methfessel, New American, New Franklin, New Model, Number, Olney, Reffelt, Rhoads, Richards (Z.), Sadler-Rowe, Sanford (H. R.), Sawyer (H.), Seaver & W., Seeley, Sheldon, Shove, Soldan, Speer, Stoddard, Tablet Ser., Walsh, Wentworth & R., White (E. E.), Wood, Woodward (L. J.).

Graded Series.—Appletons', Atwood, Bacon, Bailey-Weimer, Baird (S. W.), Brooks (E.), Butler, Colburn, Davies (C.), Dubbs, Eaton, Emerson (N. A.), Felter, Ficklin, Fish, French, Goff, Greenleaf, Hagar, Hall, Harper's, Kirk & B., Kirk & S., MacVicar, Meifuss, Milne, New American, New Franklin, Nichols, Nicholson, Normal, Olney, Peck (W. G.), Piper, Prince, Quackenbos, Rand, McN., Ray, Robinson (H. N.), Sanford (S. P.), Seaver & Walton, Sheldon, Speer, Stoddard (J. F.), Thomson, Towne, Townsend (J. L.), Venable (C. S.), Walton, White (E. E.), Wooster.

Mental.—Bailey, Brooks, Cook, Cooke, Davies, Dubbs, French, Hull, Lippincott, McLellan & A., Milne, Moran, New Model, Quackenbos, Ray, Robinson, Stoddard, Weidenhamer, Werner; Williams & R.

Table-Books.—Baldwin, Brown, Ellwood, Ficklin, Flanagan, Gilbert, Nash (L.), Robinson (H. N.), Stepping Stone, Thomson, Ticknor, Underhill Walton, Young Catholic.

Art, Architecture, Painting, etc.—Abbott, Animal, Bascom, Beard, Cave, D'Anvers, Day, Frothingham, Gardner, Goodyear, Hill, Horton, Hunt, Huntington (D.), Ladd, Long (S. P.), Parker (J. H.), Poynter, Prang, Putnam, Randall, Riverside Art Ser., Steiger, Statham, Tuckerman (A. L.), Tytler, Van Dyke.

See also DRAWING.

Astronomy.—American Sci. Ser. (Newcomb & H.), Ball, Bartlett, Bowen, Brennan, Burritt, Byrd, Chauvenet, Coffin, Colbert, Comstock, Doolittle, Gillet & R., Greene, Gummere, Holden, Hopkins, Kiddle, Lockyer, Loomis, Moritz, Norton (W. A.), Olmsted, Parker, Peck (W.), Peck (W. G.), Proctor (M.), Proctor (R. A.), Ray, Sharpless & P., Smith (Asa), Steele (G. M.), Steele (J. D.), Todd, Todd (D. P.), Warren, White (C. J.), Wright (J. McN.), Young (C. A.).

First Lessons.—Champlin (J. D.), Clark (A.), Howe, Irving, Kiddle, Newcomb, Olmsted, Science, Young.

Biology.—American Science Series (Sedgwick & W.) Bidgood, Boyer, Dodge, Macginley, Nicholson Pillsbury, Randolph, Wells, Wythe.

Book-Keeping.—Bryant, Bryant & S., Chamber, Childs, Crittenden, Curtiss, Denman, Drew, Duff, Eclectic, Economical, Eaton, Ellsworth, Field, Fulton & E., Gay, Gilbert, Goodman, Groesbeck, Hansell, Hinds & Noble, Holbrook-Rohrer, Kinsley, Laing, Lyte, Mayhew, Meservey, Montgomery (J. L.), Muller, Nelson, Nichols (B. E.), Palmer, Powers & Lyons, Practical, Robertson, Sadler-Rowe, Scribner, Seavy, Shaw (J. W.), Snyder & T., Thomas (S. A.), Tolmie, Werner, Williams & Rogers.

Botany.—American Science Series (Bessey), Apgar, Arthur, Atkinson, Bailey, Barnes, Bass, Bastin, Behrens, Bentley, Bergen, Boyer, Britton, Caldwell, Campbell, Chapman, Clark, Coulter, Curtis, Dana, Dennis, Ford, Gibson, Gray, Gray & Coulter, Gregory, Griel, Hale (G. E.), Hall (A. G.), Hathaway, Herrick, Hilliard, Hindman, Jackman, Jepson, Kellerman, Ketchum, Knight, Knobel, Leavitt, Lesquereux Macloskie, McDougal, Morgan, Nelson, Newell, Oel, Page, Penhallow, Poulsen, Pratt, Rattan, Russell (L. W.), Spear, Steele, Stokes, Thomé, Thompson, Troeger, Underwood (L. M.), Vincent, Vines, Ward, Willis (O. R.), Wood (A.), Wright (J. McN.), Youmans (E. A.), Zimmermann.

First Lessons.—Aitken, Atkinson, Bailey, Buckelew & L., Gray, Hooker, Irving, Kellerman, Little, Macbride, Morley, Phelps (Mrs. L.), Science, Setchell, Spalding, Youmans (E. A.).

Dictionaries.—Crozier.

Business Correspondence. *See* LETTER-WRITING.

Calculus.—Bowser, Buckingham, Byerly, Church, Courtenay, Davies (C.), Echol, Edward (J.), Gibson, Hardy, Hathaway, Hayes, Hyde, Johnson (S. W.), Loomis, McMahon & S., Murray, Newcomb, Nicholson, Olney, Osborne, Peck (W. G.), Peirce, Proctor, Ray, Rice & J., Robinson (H. N.), Smith (P. F.), Taylor (J. M.), Todhunter, Williamson.

Calisthenics. *See* PHYSICAL EDUCATION; PHYSIOLOGY.

Chemistry.—American Science Series (Remsen), Anderson, Appleton, Arey, Armstrong & N., Attfield, Avery, Baker (T. R.), Barker, Bartlett, Baskerville, Benton, Bloxam, Boyer, Briggs, Butler, Caldwell & B., Clarke (F. W.), Colt, Cooley, Cutler, Drechsel, Ekeley, Eliot & S., Fall, Fowne, Freer, Greene (W. H.), Griffin (L. R. F.), Hart (E.), Hessler & Smith, Hoff, Hooker, Houston, King, Lind, Mixter, Newell, Nichols (E. L.), Norton, Peters, Remsen, Reynolds (J. E.), Rolfe & G., Shepard (J. H.), Simon, Steele, Stoddard (J. T.)-Tilden (W. A.) Wells (D. A.), Whiteley, Wiechmann, Williams (R. P.), Woodhull & Van A., Worthington, Würtz, Youmans, Young (A. V. E.).

First Lessons.—Appleton, Brewster, Hart, Hewitt & Pope, Henderson, Hooker, Irving, Jones (F.), Mead, Nichols (E. H.), Nicholson & Avery, Nicolson, Phelps, (Mrs. L.), Richardson, Science Primers, Roscoe, Storer & L., Tilden, Torrey, Venable, Waddell, White.

Inorganic.—Bennett (A. A.), Frankland & Japp, Jago, Kolbe, Newth, Qualitative, Remsen, Reynolds

(J. E.), Richter, Shepard (J. H.), Thorpe (J. E.), Wells.

Organic.—Austen, Garrett & H., Gattermann, Hjelt, Jones (H. C.), Jordan, Miller (W. A.), Noyes, Prescott (A. B.), Ramsen & R., Remsen, Reynolds (J. E.), Richter, Smith, Speyers, Streatfeild, Watts (W. M.), Williams (G. H.), Wohler.

Philosophy and Physics.—Cooke, Pynchon, Sadtler, Shaw, Walker.

Practical.—Abegg & Herz, Adriance, Bartlett, Muir, Muter, Tilden.

Problems.—Cooke, Grabfield, Stammer.

Qualitative Analysis. — Appleton, Beilstein, Cairn, Congdon, Crafts, Eliot & Storer, Garvin Getman, Hill (H. B.), Johnson (S W.), Keiser, Mason (W. P.), Newth, O'Brine, Prescott (A. B.), Rains, Sellers, Simmons, Smith, Stoddard (J. T.), Thorpe & Muir, Venable (F. P.), White, Will.

Quantitative Analysis.—Allen (O. D.), Appleton, Austen, Bolton, Classen, Clowes & C., Evans (P. N.), Irish (J. W.), Knight (N.), Muck, Smith, Talbot, Thorpe (T. E.), Venable (F. P.).

Christian Evidences.—Fisher, Robinson.

Civics.—*See* CONSTITUTION, GOVERNMENT AND LAW.

Civil Service Examinations.—Civil Service, Hinds & N., How to Prepare, etc.

Classical Dictionaries. — Ireland, Lemprière, Peck, Smith (Wm.).

Classical Handbooks.—Allen (T. P.), Baird, Hallburton & N., Irving, Jevons.

See also ANTIQUITIES; CLASSICAL DICTIONARIES.

Common Things.—*See* FAMILIAR SCIENCE.

Composition.—Abbott (E. A.), Allen, Bacon (J. H.), Black, Ballard, Bancroft (T. W.), Bardeen, Barnes, Beaman, Bigelow, Bonnell, Bright, Chittenden, Composition, Eclectic, Ellis, Ellsworth, Emerson, English, Flanagan, Fletcher & Carpenter, Franklin, Frost (S. A.), Galbraith, Hardy, Hart (J. M.), Hart (J. S.), Herrick & D., Hiley, Hinds & Noble, Hunt (T. W.), Huston, Keeler & Davis, Kimball, Kirkland, Kittredge & A., Kittredge & G., Lamont, Longman's Salmon's, Lyte, MacLeon, Maxwell (W. H.), Metcalf & De Garmo, Mead, Murray (J. E.), National, Newcomer, One Thousand Subjects, O'Neill, Patterson, Pearson, Pinneo, Powell, Quackenbos, Rand, McN., Reade (A. A.), Scott & D., Shaw (E. R.), Sheldon, Southworth & Goddard, Spalding, Tower & Tweed, Wheeler, Wells (W. H.), Welsh, Wendell, Young Catholic.

See also LETTER-WRITING.

First Lessons.—Ballard, Bonnell, Conklin. Ginn & Coady, Hall, Hart (J. M.), Harvey, Hyde, Jacob, Lewis, Literature, Longman's Salmon's, Maxwell, Peterson, Sadlier (W. H.), Simpson, Stickney (J. H.), Tarbell, Wilson (J. D.).

Composition and Rhetoric.—Arnold & K., Bain, Bardeen, Boyd, Carpenter, Flanagan, Gist, Greene (S. S.), Hart (J. M.), Hill (D. J.), Hunt, Kennedy, Kerl, Lockwood, Lockwood & Emerson, McElroy, Mead & G, Metcalf, Moulton, Quackenbos, Scott & Denney, Smith (L. W.), Smith (R. M., jr.), Tweed, Waddy, Watrous, Webster, Williams (W.).

See also RHETORIC.

Conic Sections.—*See* GEOMETRY, *Analytical.*

Constitution.—Alden, Andrews (I. W.), Boutwell, Cleveland, Flanders, Furey, Hart (J. M.), Hinds & N., Laidlaw, Rannie, Rupert, Story.

See also GOVERNMENT.

Copy-Books.—*See* PENMANSHIP.

Criticism.—Arnold (T.), Boyd, Johnson (C. F.), McLaughlin.

See also RHETORIC.

Dictionaries (English). — Browne & Haldeman, Cassell, Chambers, Feller, Nuttall, Price, Putnam, Rand, Robbins, Royal, Funk & Wagnalls ser. (includes Standard, Student's), Waites, Walker (J.), Webster, Worcester.

Etymological.—Nuttall, Oswald, Skeat.

Pronouncing.—Ayres, Bechtel, Campbell, Coombs, De Graff, Globe, Phyfe, Salisbury, Soule & Campbell, Tenney (L. M.), Webster, Worcester.

Synonyms. — Campbell, Fernald, Graham, Hinds & Noble, Popular, Synonyms, Whately.

Miscellaneous.—(Metaphysical Terms) Fleming (W.), (Science Terms) Rossiter, (Vulgarisms) Vulgarisms. *See also* under Special Topics.

For *Ancient and Foreign Languages see* FRENCH, GERMAN, GREEK, HEBREW, ITALIAN, LATIN, SPANISH.

Domestic Economy.—Harrison (W. J.), Huntington (E.), Willard (Mrs.).

Drawing. — *Geometrical.* — Andrews, Bartholomew (W. N.), Barry, Longmans, Minifie, Prang, Rimmer, Smith (Walter), Vose, Warren (S. E.), White (G. G.), Wilson (W. N.).

See also GEOMETRY, *Descriptive.*

Industrial and Mechanical.—Aborn, Anthony (G. C.), Barnes, Barry, Bartholomew (W. N.), Cassell, Cross (A. K.), Davidson (E. A.), Eclectic, Fox & Thomas, Garin, Gilmore, Goss, Halles, Krüsi, MacCord, McMillan & Smith, Mahan, Maycock, Minifie, Rimmer, Rose, Smith (Walter), Thompson, Tracy, Walters, Webb, Ware & Z., White (G. G.).

Kindergarten.—Nelson.

Linear and Perspective.—Barnes, Bartholomew (W. N.), Cassell, Clarke (G. S.), Davidson (E. A.), Eclectic, Fusche, Hall, Hodge, Honey, Hull, Keller, Krüsi, Miller (L. W.), Smith (Walter), Trobridge, Warren (S. E.), White (G. G.).

Map.—Andre, Apgar, Bangs, Handbook, Krone, Maury, Patterson, Sadlier (W. H.), Wilkins.

Primary and Elementary.—Allonge, Animal, Augsbury, Avery, Barnes, Barry, Bartholomew (W. N.), Burkinshaw, Cassell, Cavé, Chapman, Clark (J.), Coe, Cross (A. K.), Drawing, Easy, Eclectic, Forbriger, Fowler, Froebel, Holmes (M. H.), Hotchkiss, How, Jacobs & Brower, Knowlton, Krone, Krüsi, Le Duc, Little, Longmans, Mann, Moore (A. O.), Moore (C. H.), Moore (N.), Philips, Poland, Potter & P., Prang, Primary, Roudebusch, Royal, Sadlier (W. H.), Smith (Walter), Thompson (L. S.), Walker (W.), White (G. G.), Wise.

Shades and Shadows.—Ryan, Warren (S. E.), White (G. G.)

Electricity and Magnetism. — Hadley, Harrison (W. J.), Jackson (D. C. & J. P.), Meadowcroft, Perkins, Slingo & B., Thompson.

Elocution.—Bacon, Bailey, Bell (A. M.), Bell (D. C.), Brace, Bronson, Brooks (E.), Caldwell, Coombs, Dale, Diehl, Du Cygne, Fenno, Fobes, Frobisher, Guttmann, Hafford, Hamill, Kidd, Kirby, Lyons, McIlvaine, Monroe (L. B.), Murdoch, Ott, Randall, Ross (W. T.), Russell, Sadlier (W. H.), Salisbury, Shoemaker, Swett, Warman, Warren.

Debater.—Craig.

Dialogues.—Hinds & Noble.

First Lessons.—Badlam, Brace, Diehl, Hoitt Hoose, Lambert, Northend, Selections, Sherwood, Southwick, Sterling.

Oratory.—Brown (M. T.), Burrell, College Maids, College Men, Edgarton, Handy, Mitchell, Raymond (G. L.), Southwick, Stebbins, Sterling, Wiley.

Readings and Recitations. — Billings, Carrington, Commencement, Cumnock, Diehl, Elocutionist, English, Fenno, Fletcher, Fobes, Fulton & T., Hows, James, Jameson, Little Gems, McGuffey, Morrison, O'Grady, One Hundred, Peasley, Potter (H. L. D.), Raby, Randall, Rusk, Russell, Scholar's, Selections, Soper, Warman, Warren.

See also LITERATURE, *English*; READERS.

Speakers.—Acme, Branch, Brown (I. H.), Butler (N.), Cathcart, Coates, Cumnock, Denman, Edgarton & Russell, Franklin, Gilmore, Harpers', Hillard, Hinds & N., Huntoon, Indiana, Kindergarten, La Moille, Le Row, Lawrence (P.), McGuffey, Miller & R., Northend, Oxford, Philbrick, Priest, Prigg, Ross, Speaker's Garland, Swett, Town & Holbrook, Young (H. A.), Zachos.

English Language.—*Early English.*—Baldwin, Bartlett, Bates, Carpenter (S. H.), Cook, Corson, Kellogg, Normal Course, Pratt, Smith (C. A.), Sweet, Tarbell, Webster (W. F.), Woodley.

History, Philology, etc.—Angus, Ballard, Betis & S., Buehler, Clark, Craik, Dunton & K., Easy, Eclectic, English, Five Hundred, Garlands, Gay, Gideon, Gouin, Greene (H. R.), Greenough & K., Gudeman, Hadley (J.), Harper, Harrison (M.), Johnson, Kellner, Lewis (E. H.), Lounsbury, Mætzner, Marsh (G. P.), Meiklejohn, Morris (R.), Nelson, Parker (F. W.), Patrick, Shepherd, Short, Suplee, Tarbell, White (R. G.), Whitney (W. D.).

Shakespeare.—Abbott (E. A.), Arden, Craik.

Versification.—Parsons.

See also ANGLO-SAXON; COMPOSITION; DICTIONARIES; ETYMOLOGY; GRAMMAR; LITERATURE; PHILOLOGY; PRIMERS; READERS; RHETORIC; SPEAKERS.

Etymology.—Anderson (J. M.), Black, Johnson & Humphrey, Kluge & L., Lynd, McElroy, Sargent, Scholar's Companion, Smith (W. W.), Taylor (I.), Thomas (J.), Webb (A. C.).

Synonyms, Antonyms.—Fernald.

See also DICTIONARIES; LANGUAGE.

Euclid.—*See* GEOMETRY.

Familiar Science. — Bert, Brewer, Catechism, Champlin, Doerner, First, Guthrie, Harrison (W. J.), Hooker, Horne, Lessons, Macadam, Monteith, Moore (G.), Norton, Peterson, Wells (D. A.).

See also NATURAL PHILOSOPHY, *First Lessons.*

First Lessons.—*See* FAMILIAR SCIENCE; PRIMERS; SPELLERS, *etc.*

French.—*Composition.*—Bailiot & Twight, B., Bouvet, Cameron, Francois, Grandgent, Kimball, Lyon & De Larpent, Macmillan, Weekley, Williams (F. S.).

Conversation and Dialogues.—Ahn, Aubert, Bétis & Swan, Croquet, Brégy, Bronson, Chouquet, Collet,

Contanseau, De Peyrac, Du Croquet, Fautes de langage, Fasquelle, Fontaine, Foulché-Delbosc, Gastineau, Gouin, Hossfeld, Kuhn, Lambert & Sardou, Le Roy, Longmans, Lyman, Montonnier, Parlez, Perrin (J. B.), Pitman, Riodu, Rouillon, Sardou, Sauveur, Witcomb & B., Worman.

Dictionaries.—Bellows (J.), Chambers, Classic, Clifton, Collot, Contanseau, De La Voge, De Lolme, Dictionary, Edgren & Burnet, Feller, Fleming & Tibbins, Gasc, Heath, Hossfeld, Masson, Meadows, Muzzarelli, Nugent, Roemer, Routledge, Smith (H. & L.), Spiers, Spiers & S., Tauchnitz, Wessely.

First Books, Primers, etc.—Abeille, Ahn-Henn, Aldrich & Foster, Barbauld, Bercy, Berlitz, Bétis & Swan, Bezrat de Bordes, Buckingham, Bullet, Cassell, Chardenal, Chouquet, De Vere, Doriot, Downer, Dreyspring, Du Croquet, Elementary, Gautherot, Gouin, Hennequin, Herding, Hotchkiss, Joynes-Otto, Keetels, Kroeh, Livre, Meras & Stern, Montonnier, Nelson, Newson, Object, Otto, Pinney, Porney, Pylodet, Sanders (G. J. H.), Sauveur & Van Daell, Stern & M., Syms, Van Daell, Vannier, Worman.

Grammars, Exercises, etc.—Addick, Ahn, Ahn-Henn, Bacon, Bercy, Bercy & Castegnier, Berlitz, Bernard, Bevier & Logie, Boname Borel, Brégy, Breymann, Buckingham, Cassell, Chardenal, Clarke, Collet's Levizac's, DeFivas, Delille, De Vere, Du Bois, Du Croquet, Duffet, Dufour, Duval, Edgren, Fasnacht, Fraser & Squair, Fasquelle, Gaspey-Otto-Sauer, Gastineau, Gouin, Grandgent, Harrison (J. A.), Harrison & R. Hennequin, Hossfeld, Ingres, Joaynes, Jounne, Joynes-Otto, Keetels, Kroeh, Lambert & S., Languellier & M., Le Roy, Longmans, Macmillan, Macgill, Magnenat, Marlborough, Maurice, Meisterschaft, Meras, Meras & S., Monsanto, Muzzarelli, Newson, Noël & Chapsal, Ollendorff, Otto, Peiffer, Pitman, Ploetz, Preliminary, Prendergast, Pujol, Robertson, Rosenthal, Roux, Sanders (G. J. H.), Sardou, Sauveur, Sauveur & Lougee, Savay, Schlegel (C. A.), Smith (Wm.), Stern & M., Storr, Sym, Weekly & W., Whitney (W. D.), Worman.

Pronunciation.—Kroeh, Matzke, Mixer, Peiffer, Vannier.

Readers.—Ahn-Henn, Bercy, Berlitz, Bernard, Bowen, Brunner, Cassell, Chardenal, Chouquet, Contanseau, Davies, De Fivas, De Vere, Doriot, Douay, Dreyspring, Dufour, Fisher, Herdler, Houghton, Joynes-Otto, Keetels, Knapp, Kuhns, Lake, Leune, Longmans, Macmillan, Magill, Newson, Otto, Pylodet, Roemer, Rollins, Schlegel, Super, Walter.

Readings (General).—Æsop, Alliot, Böcher, Cameron, Canfield, Contes, Cotte, Cottin, Crane, Cremieux & D., Dumas, Episodes, Erckmann-Chatrian, Fasquelle, Fleury, Fontaine, Guerber, Handy, International, Lacombe, Ladreyt, Legouve & L., Marret, Maynard, Meras & Stern, Nodier, Perrin (J. B.), Racine, Raymond, Raymond & G., Rogers, Romans, Rougemont, St. Pierre, Sauveur, Silver, Stephens, Super, Timayenis, Veteran, Voltaire, Warren [Victor Hugo].

Literature.—Alliot, Aubert, Carter, Crane & Brun, Berlitz, Daudet, Duval & W., Fortier, French, Heath, La Rougemont, Macmillan's Classics, Mariet, Noël, Pylodet, Saintsbury, Siepmann, Truan, Wells (B. W.).

See also LITERATURE.

Plays.—Alarcon, College Series, Corneille, French Plays for Children, Gombert, Handy, International, Labiche & Martin, La Brete, Meras, Modern French, Moliere, Neuville, Racine, Ranke, Roche, Students' Classics, Théâtre, Wells.

Poetry.—Janon, Magill, Mixer, Pylodet.

Fénelon's Télémaque.—Bolmar, Fasquelle.

Translating English into French.—Bercy, Contanseau, Gasc, Handy, Sadler, Williams (F. S.).

Translating French into English.—Bernard, Literal, Parry.

Verbs.—Beauvoisin, Bercy, Berlitz, Bolmar, Boname, Castarède, Crew, Darr, De Vere, Du Croquet, Hennequin, Kroeh, Lambert & S., Magill, Marion, Michaud, Reynal, Simonin, Stone.

Geography.—*Ancient and Classical.*—Literature Primers, Long (G.), Mitchell, Perthes, Putnam.

See also, below, *Historical*

Astronomical.—Jackson (E. P.).

Atlases.—Bartholomew (J.), Frye, Ginn, Johnston (A. K.), Labberton, Long (G.), Longmans, Lord (J. K), Mitchell, Monteith, Public, Putnam, Rand.

Commercial.—Olin, Redway.

Elementary and Comprehensive.—Appletons', Baker, Barnes, Basset, Butler, Colton, Colton & Fitch, Cornell, Dryer, Eclectic, Fisher, Frye, Griffin, Guyot, Hall (M. L.), Harpers', Hopkins (L. P.), Johnson (B. F.), Johnston (A. K.), Lawson, Long, Longmans, McBride, McCormick, McMurray, Maury, Mitchell, Monteith, Monteith & McNally, Morton, Natural, Niles, Northam, O'Shea, Our, Peavey, Potter, Rand, McN., Redway, Roddy, Ritter, Swinton, Tarbell, Tarr & McM., Tilden, Trotters, Warren (D. M.), Werner.

First Lessons.—Cornell, Eclectic, Frye, Guyot, Hall (M. L.), Harpers', History, Johnson (B. F.), Lemon MacGunn, Maury, Mitchell, Monteith, Monteith & McNally, Rand, McN., Stepping Stone, Swinton, Warren (D. M.).

Globe Manuals.—Cheney, Schedler.

Historical.—Eclectic, Johnston (A. K.), Labberton, MacCoun, Putnam, Putzger, Worcester.

See also, above, *Ancient and Classical.*

Inductive.—Deane & Davis.

Physical.—Appletons', Butler, Boyer, Clauder, Cornell, Davis, Dryer, Eclectic, Frye, Geikie, Gilbert & Brigham, Gore, Guyot, Henning, Houston, Johnston (A. K.), Kellogg, Lawson, MacTurk, Marsh (G. P.), Maury, Mitchell, Monteith, Monteith & McNally, Morgan, National, Proctor, Redway, Science Primers, Simpson, Tarr, Warren (D. M.).

Questions.—Butler, Eaton, Hathaway, Leete, Mitchell, Montz, Nichols, Questions, Regents, Stillwell, Townsend (J. L.), Tufts, Warren.

See also READERS, *Geographical.*

Geology.—Amer. Sci. Ser., Andrews (E. B.), Barbee, Dana, Geikie, Heilprin (A.), Hogan, Hooker, Le Conte, Lyell, Nicholson (H. A.), Roberts, Science Primers, Shaler, Steele, Tarr, Tenney (S.), Wells (D. A.), Williams (H. S.), Winchell (A.), Woodworth & S.

Geometry.—Angel, Baker (A. L.), Bartol, Bellows, Beman & S., Bevis, Bowser, Brigham, Brooks, Bradbury, Brooks (E.), Burns (J. J.), Butler, Campbell, Carroll, Chapman, Chauvenet, Church, Clarke (G. S.), Davidson (E. A.), Davies (C.), Earl, Eclectic, Edwards, Estill, Galbraith & H., Gore Greenleaf, Halsted, Hanus, Haswell, Hill (G. A.), Hobbs, Holgate, Hopkins (G. I.), Hornbrook, Hull, Hunt, Hunter (T.), King, Loney, Loomis, Low, Lyman, MacDonald, Manning, Milne, Newcomb, Nichols, Olney, Peck (W. G.), Pettee, Phillips & Fisher, Pierce, Ray, Robinson (N. H.), Runkle, Sanders, Schuyler, Schultze & S., Science Primers, Scott, Sharpless, Smith (C.), Smith (J. F.), Smith (W. B.), Spooner, Stanley, Stewart (S. T.), Sutherland, Thompson, Van Velzer & S., Venable (C. S.), Vogdes, Warren (S. E.), Watson (H. W.), Wells, Welsh (A. H.), Wentworth (G. A.), Wentworth & H., White (E. E.), Wood (De V.), Wright, Young & L.

Analytical and Conic Sections.—Bailey & Woods, Bayma, Briot, Briot & Bouquet, Casey, Church, Coffin, Davies (C.), Hardy, Howland, Johnson (W. W.), Lambert, Loomis, Newcomb, Nichols, Noyes, Peck (W. G.), Ray, Robinson (H. N.), Salmon, Sestini, Smith (C.), Smith, Tanner & A., Todhunter, Wentworth.

Descriptive.—Baker, Church, Davies (C.), Faunce, Noetling, Smith (F. H.), Waldo, Warren (S. E.).

See also DRAWING, *Geometrical.*

Euclid.—Casey, Galbraith & H., Gillett, Hall & S., Lachman, Lock, Nelson, Playfair, Todhunter, Wallace.

German.—*Composition.*—Bernhardt, Harris, Higley, Longmans, Poll, Wesselhoeft.

Conversations and Dialogues.—Ahn-Grauert, Betis & Swan, Bronson, Comfort, Gastineau, Gouin, Harmann, Kruger-Smith, Kuphal, Meissner, Mueller, Pitman, Pylodet, Schlegel, Schrakamp, Sprechen, Stager, Stern, Vos, Wenckebach, Williams (A.), Worman.

Dictionaries.—Adler, Ahn, Bernhardt & B., Blackley-Chambers, Classic, Dictionary, Elwell, Feller, Fluegel, Fluegel, Schmidt & T., Grieb, Heath, Hossfeld, James, Koehler & W., Kohler, Kunst, Longman, Morwitz, Muret-Sanders, Oehlschläger, Schlessing, Tafel, Tauchnitz, Thieme, Wessely, Whitney (W. D.), Williams, Zahner

First Lessons, Primers, etc.—Abrams, Ahn-Henn, Babbitt, Berlitz, Bierwith, Brandt, Bronson, Brown (J. H.), Cincinnati, Comfort, Dessar, Deutsche Hiawatha Primer, Doriot, Dudge, Dreyspring, Eben, Eclectic, Elementary, Erlenkotter, Erstes, Faulhaber, Flügel, Gerfen, Germanus, Goebel, Hebel, Hempl, Hey, Huss, Joynes-Otto, Kaiser, Kase, Keller, Kern, Kleuze, Knoefel, Krauss, Kroeh, Lange, Lechner, Lueken, Lutz, Maierstein, Mugan, Muller (W.), Newson, Object, Otis, Plate, Reffelt, Rippe, Sanders, Schlegel (C. A.), Schmitz, Schrakamp, Schulzen, Siepmann, Spanhoofd, Stein, Stern, Super, Van der Smissen, Vietor, Wild & Stamm, Witter, Woodbury, Worman.

Grammars, Lessons, Methods, etc.—Ahn, Ahn-Fischer, Ahn-Henn, Ahn-Oehlschläger, Althaus, Bacon, Beiley, Berlitz, Blackwell, Brandt, Chicago, Collar, Colby, Comfort, Corwin, Cutting, Dessar,

Deutsch, Dreyspring, Edgren & Fowler, Eysenbach, Fischer, Gaspey-Otto-Sauer, Gerfen, Goebel, Graebner, Graff, Grauert, Harris, Hedge (Prepositions), Heller, Hempl, Heness, Henn-Ahn, Hewett, Hodges, Hossfeld, Jagemann, Joynes-Meissner, Joynes-Otto, Keetels, Keller, Knoflach, Krauss, Kroeh, Learned, Longmans, Lueken, Macmillan, Mayer, Marlborough, Meissner, Meisterschaft, Mengel, Naftel, Newson, Ollendorff, Otis, Otto, Plate, Prendergast, Rosenthal, Rosenstengel, Sachse, Sawyer, Schlegel (C. A.), Schmitz, Shulze, Sheldon (E. S.), Smith (Wm.), Sonnenburg & S., Spanhoofd, Stager, Steiger, Stern, Thomas (C.T.), Van der Smissen & F., Vos, Weineck, Wenckebach, Wenckebach & S., Werner, Wheatley, White, Whitney (W. D.), Winter, Woodbury, Worman, Zur Brücke.

Penmanship.—Eclectic, German, Henze, Knoflach, Knopp, Krone, Lueken, Payson, Wernli, Witter, Worman.

Pronunciation.—Berlitz, Grandgent, Kroeh, Victor.

Readers.—Adler, Ahn, Ahn-Grauert, Ahn-Henn, Berlitz, Boisen, Brandt, Brandt & Day, Cincinnati, Comfort, Deutsch, Dippold, Dodge, Dreyspring, Eclectic, Episodes, Evans, First, Fischer (A. A.), Gelbach, Germanus, German, Goebel, Gore, Grauert, Guerber, Hallmann, Hardter, Harris, Hewett, Herder, Hossfeld, Huss, Jones, Joynes, Joynes-Otto, Klemm, Knapp, Knoefel, Loesberg & K., Longmans, Macmillan, Maynard, Milwaukee, Monroe (L. B.), Naftel, Newson, Otto, Petermann, Pitman, Reffelt, Rosenstengel, Schrakamp, Schlegel, Soldan, Stamm, Thomas & H., Von Kleuze, Weineck, Wenckebach, Whitney (W. D.), Whitney-Klemm, Witter, Worman, Wrage, Zimmermann, Zschokke.

Readings (*General*).—Baumbach, Beresford-Webb, Bradish, Bronson, David (A. A.), De Rougement, Geibler, Goethe, Grube, Guerber, Handy, Hart (J. M.), Heyse, Hillern, International, Johnson (H.), Macmillan, Otis, Pitman, Raddatz, Richter (J.P.), Riehl, Schanz, Schiller, Schulitz, Schrakamp, Seidel, Silver, Spyri, Stern, Storm, Storme (G.), Van Dael, Van der Smissen, Volkmann-L., Watson, Wells (B. W.), Whitney, Wilbrandt, Wildenbruch, Zschokke.

Literature.—Adler, Bernhardt, Betis & Swan, Fahsel, Francke, Germania, Heath, Hosmer, Klemm, Loesberg, Modern, Rosenstengel, Schlegel, Schoenfeld, Siepmann, Wells (B. W.).

Plays.—Arnold, Benedix, College, Freytag, German Texts, Goethe, Handy, Heness, International, Lessing, McKay, Modern, Moser, Muller (M.), Riehl, Schiller, Stern, Students'.

Poetry.—Bronson, Klemm, Simonson, Wenckebach.

See also LITERATURE, *German.*

Translating Eng. into German.—Cincinnati, Collar, Handy, Joynes-O., Lagemann, Lodeman, Stahl.

Government and Law.—Alden, American, Bardeen, Biocher, Boyd, Brooks, Bryce, Bryant, Callahan, Chandler, Clarendon, Clark, Clark (S. S.), Cocker, Coon, Cromer, Douglas, Duvalle, Ficklin, Finegan, Finger, Fiske, Fitch, Flickinger, Forman, Fox, (S. E.), Garrison, Giffin, Handbooks, Hart, Haven (S.), Henry, Hicks, Higby, Hinsdale (B. A.), Hodder, Hoxie, International, James & Sanford, Johnston (A.), Judson, Karn, King (J. A.), Kellogg & Taylor, Knight, L. L. L., Laidlaw, Leach, Lewis, Lieber, Lowry, McCleary, McCorrey, McPherson, Macy, Maine, Mansfield, Manus, Markwick, Martin, Milligan, Montague, Morgan, Morton, Mowry, Niles, Nordhoff, Northam, Palmer, Peterman, Potter, Rawles, Schurim & S., Scudder, Seelye, Seerley, Smith & Y., Stetson, Stanwood, Strong & S., Suplee, Symonds, Taylor & K., Thornton, Thorpe (F. N.), Thorpe & G., Thorpe & R., Townsend (C.), Trowbridge, True & D., Weaver, Wilgus, Williams & Rogers, Wilson (W.), Woodworth, Woolsey, Young (A.W.), Young (J.S.).

See also CONSTITUTION.

Grammar (English).—*Analysis and Parsing.*—Abbott (E. A.), Adams (F. P.), Allen, Arnold, Beeton, Brown & De Garmo, Buck, Buckham, Buehler, Carpenter (S. H.), Clark, Conklin, Dalgleish, Davenport & E., Davidson, Dickinson, Eclectic, Flanagan, Foster, Gowdy, Greene (S. S.), Hart (J. M.), Harvey & G., Hoenshel, Irish, Johnson, King, Language, Lee & H., Lewis (E. H.), Longmans, March, Maris, Mathews (H.), Maxwell, Mead, Meiklejohn, Milne, Morris & B., Murray (J. E.), Nesfield, Norton, Orne, Park, Powell & C., Putnam (W. H.), Quimby, Reed & Kellogg, Ripley, Sanders & McE., Smith (E. B.), Smithdeal, Stilwell, Symonds, Tarbell, Town, Townsend, Wait, Welch, Weld, West, Wilson (J. D.), Wisely, Wright.

Elementary and Practical.—Bain, Barnes, Baskervill & Sewell, Bingham, Boltwood, Booth, Bosworth, Brown (G.), Buck, Buehrle, Bugbee, Bullions, Burns (E. A.), Butler (G. P.), Butler (N.), Carpenter (G. R.), Choate, Clark (N. G.), Clark (S. W.), Cobbett, Comly, Davidson & A., Eaton, Eno, Fewsmith, French (J. W.), Garrison, Gideon, Greene (H. R.), Greene (S. S.), Greenwood (J. M.), Greenwood (J. W.), Hadley, Hall (W. D.), Hart (J. M.), Harvey, Hathaway, Haynie, Holbrook (A.), Holmes, Hunter (J.), Jacoby, Kenyon, Kerney, Knox-Heath, Longmans, Lyte, MacCabe, McHenry, Meiklejohn, Metcalfe, Mirick, Morris (R.), Morrison (T.), Murison, Murray (J. E.), Murray (L.), O'Shea, Parshall, Patterson, Peet, Pinneo, Powell, Quackenbos, Raub, Reed & Kellogg, Regents, Reid, Richardson (W. H.), Roemer, Siglar, Smith (H. D.), Smith (M. W.), Smith (R. C.), Southworth & Stoddard, Starkweather, Stickney (J. H.), Strang, Sullivan, Swinton, Thring, Tweed, Weld & Quackenbos, Wells (W. H.), Welsh (A. H.), Welsh (J. P.), West, Wheeler, Whitney (W. D.), Whitney & Lockwood, Williams (G. E.), Williams (W. G.), Williams & Rogers, Wilson, Wright.

See also ENGLISH LANGUAGE; LANGUAGE.

First Lessons.—Ahn, Brown (G.), Butler (N.), Clark (S. W.), De Graff, Fellows, Gilmore, Greene (F. B.), Greene (S. S.), Hadley (H.), Hart (J. M.), Holmes, Howard (T. E.), Hyde (M. F.), Johonnot, Kerl, Lee & S., Literature Primers, Long (C. C.), Long (H. S.), Maxwell, Metcalf, Nesbitt, Powell, Primary, Quackenbos, Rand, McN., Reed & Kellogg, Ricker, Sheldon, Sornberger, Stepping Stone, Stickney (J. H.), Swinton, Tarbell, Thalheimer, Ward (E. G.), Wallbank, Welsh (A. H.), Woodley & Carpenter.

Punctuation.—Allardyce, Ayres, Bigelow, Butterfield, Cocker, Hart (J. M.), Hill (A. S)., Wilson (J.), Winchell.

Greek. — *Dictionaries.* — Autenreith, Baird, Blake, Classic, Donnegan, Grove (S. J.), Harding, Huddilston, Jannaris, Liddell & Scott, Pickering (J.), Sanford, Yonge (C. D.).

New Testament Dictionaries.—Analytical, Green (T. S.), Greenfield, Hinds & Noble, Robinson (E.), Scomp, Thayer.

First Lessons.—Arnold (T. K.), Ball, Boise, Brooks, Collar & Daniell, Coy, Forman (L. L.), Frisbee, Frost, Gildersleeve, Gleason & A., Goodell, Goodell & Morrison, Graves & Hawes, Harkness, Harper & C., Leighton, Morris (W. H.), Scarborough, White (J. W.).

Grammar and Exercises. — Adams (F. A.), Barnes, Boise, Bonner, Brooks (J.), Goodell, Goodwin (W. W.), Hadley (J.), Halsey (C. S.), Harper, Henry, Keep (R. P.), Maunoury, Rangabe, Spiess, Stedman, Weil, White (J. W.).

New Testament Grammars.—Buttmann, Cary, Green (S. G.), Harper (W. R.), Winer.

Prose Composition.—Allinson, Arnold (T. K.), D'Ooge, Jones (E.), Murray, Pearson, Sewall (J. B.), Sidgwick (A.), Woodruff.

Readers.—Bullions, Coy, Goodell, Goodwin (W. W.), Goodwin & White, Moss, Preparatory, Young.

Readings (*General*).—Boise & Freeman, College, Ferguson, Fernald, Flagg, Græca Minora, Longmans, Macmillan, March, Masterpieces, Parsons (R.), School Classics, Seymour, Tyler (H. M.), White (J. T.), Williams.

Translating English into Greek.—Handy, Harper, Interlinear, McKay, Sargent.

Translating Greek into English.—Cassell, Handy, Interlinear, Literal, McKay, Palmer, White.

Æschines.—Champlin (J. T.), Handy, Richardson, Simcox.

Æschylus.—Allen (F. D.), Felton, Flagg, Handy, McKay, Mather, More, Woolsey.

Æsop.—Timayenis.

Aristophanes.—Felton & Goodwin, Green (W. C.), Handy, Humphreys (M. W.), McKay, Nicolson.

Demosthenes.—Champlin (J. T.), D'Ooge, Fennell, Flagg, Handy, Interlinear, McKay, Smead, Tarbell, Tyler (W. S.).

Euripides.—Allen (F. D.), Anthon, Beckwith, Flagg & F., Handy, Harry, Kerr, Lawton, McKay, Moore, Woolsey.

Herodotus.—Johnson (H. M.), Handy, Keep (R. P.), McKay, Mather, Merriam.

Homer.—Anthon, Autenreith, Benner, Blake, Boise, Bryant, Clapp, Collar, Frieze, Handy, Hayes, Howland, Interlinear, Jebb, Johnson (H. C.), Keep (R. P.), McKay, Mason, Merriam, Owen, Palmer (G. H.), Perrin, Seymour (T. D.), Tappan, Tetlow, Thurber, Tyler (W. S.).

Isocrates.—Felton & Goodwin, Handy.

Lucian.—Handy, Lucian, Sewell, Williams (C. R.).

Lysias.—Bridgman, Bristol, Handy, McKay, Morgan, Stevens, Wait, Whiton.

New Testament.—Boise, Critical, Greenfield, Interlinear, Leusden, McKay, Owen, Scrivener, Spencer (J. A.), Tischendorf, Westcott & Hort.

Pindar.—Gildersleeve, Seymour (T. D.).

Plato.—Dyer, Gitbauer, Handy, Kitchel, Lodge, McKay, Newhall, Sihler, Towle, Tyler (W. S.), Wagner, Woolsey.

Plutarch.—Tyler (W. S.).

Sophocles.—Crosby, D'Ooge, Earle, Graves, Handy, Harpers', Haydon, Humphrey, Jebb, Jebb & Mather, McKay, Palmer, Smead, White (J. W.), Woolsey.

Thucydides.—Bigg, Fowler (H. N.), Handy, Lamberton, Mather, Morris (C. D.), Smith (C. F.), Stout & P.

Versification.—Platner.

Xenophon.—Anthon, Balgarnies, Bennett, Blake, Boise, Ferguson, Gleason, Goodwin & White, Handy, Harper & W., Interlinear, Kelsey, Kelsey & Zenos, McKay, Manatt, Robbins (R. D. C.), White, Winans, Young.

Gymnastics.—*See* PHYSICAL EDUCATION.

Heat.—Cummings, Nichols & Franklin, Stewart.
See MECHANICS.

Hebrew.—*Bible.*—Baer & D., Letteris, Theile.

First Lessons, Primers, etc.—Katzenberg, Polane.

Grammar and Reading Lessons.—Aufrecht, Davidson (A. B.), Dessar, Duff, Gabriel, Green (W. H.), Harper (W. R.), Hinds & N., Jones, Krauskopf & Berkowitz, Manheimer, Mitchell (H. G.), Strack, Vibbert.

Translation.—Interlinear.

Lexicon.—Craig, Davidson (B.), Gesenius, Hebrew, Robinson (E.), Tregelles.

History.—*Ancient.*—Anderson, Barnes, Botsford, Ensign, Epochs, Fleury, Fredet, Gazeau, Goodrich (S. G.), Myers, Ragozin, Rawlinson, Smith (P.), Thalheimer, West (W. M.), Yonge (C. M.)

England.—Airy, Allen (F. J.), Allen (W. F.), Anderson, Armstrong, Berard, Blaisdell, Chautauqua, Collier (W. F.), Coman & K., Creighton, Crocker, Curnow, Dickens, Emerson, Epochs, Freeman, Gardiner, Goodrich (S. G.), Green (J. R.), Gurney, Hallam, Higginson & Channing, History, Hume, Irving, Jones (L. E.), Joy, Kirkland, Knox, Kummer, Lancaster, Larned, Lee, Lingard, Lossing, Lupton, Markham, May, Montgomery (D. H.), Morris (D.), Mowry, Oman, Oxford Manuals, Parmele, Philips, Pierson (H. W.), Powell, Putnam's Manuals, Ransome, Royal, Sanderson, Smith (P.), Stone (A. P.), Stubbs, Tappan, Terry, Thalheimer, Thorpe Towle, Tremain, Wilder (M. E.), Yonge (C. M.).

China.—Van Bergen.

Colonial.—Thwaites.

European.—Adams (G. B.), Fellows, Lodge, Thatcher & Schwill.

France.—Adams (G. B.), Anderson, Barnes, Creighton, Fleury, Freeman, Goodrich (S. G.), Hicks (F. C.), History, Jervis, Kirkland, Lacombe, Montgomery (D. H.), Parmele, Pierson (H. W.), Putnam's Manuals, Super, Yonge.

General.—Alexander, Allen (W. F.), Anderson, Andrews (E. B.), Appleton, Balmes, Barnes, Boltwood, Carter, Champlin, Coe, Colby (F. M.), Cox, Ensign, Epochs, Fisher (G. P.), Flickinger, Freeman, Freman, Gazeau, Gilman, Goodrich (C. A.), Goodrich (S. G.), Grace, Great, Hall (F. H.), Hathaway, History, Hunter, Johnston, Kerney, King, Labberton, Lawrence (E. C.), Lemon, Lord, Mackenzie, McMurray, Markwich & S., Muller, Myers, Parley, Ploetz, Putnam's Manuals, Quackenbos (J. D.), Ransome, Robbins (R.), Sanderson, Schlegel (F.), Shaffer, Shea, Sheldon (M. D.), Smith (P.), Summary, Swinton, Taylor, Thalheimer, Trainer, Waites, Whelpley, Whitcomb, Willard (S.), Willson, Worcester.

Germany.—Coffin, Freeman, Lewis, Parmele, Pierson (H. W.), Putnam's, Schiller, Student's, Taylor (B.), Yonge (C. M.).

Greece.—Abbott (E.), Barnes, Bury, Botsford, Castegnier, Collier, Cox (G. W.), Firth, Goodrich (S. G.), Gulick, Harrison (J. A.), History, Irving, Joy, Myers, Osman, Pennell, Putnam's Manuals, Ragozin, Ritchie, Shuckburgh, Sewell (E.), Sheldon (M.D.), Smith (W.), Thalheimer, Trask, Tufts, Vincent, Yonge (C. M.).

Ireland.—McCarthy, Sadlier (A.), Towle.

Italy.—Freeman, Kirkland.

Japan.—Smith (H. A.), Van Bergin (R.)

Mediæval.—Adams, Anderson, Barnes, Bemont & Monod, Duruy, Emerton, Gazeau, Hallam, History, Munro, Myers, Shackelford, Smith, (W.), Stille, Thalheimer, Thatcher, Yonge (C. M.).

Modern.—Adams (G. B.), Anderson, Barnes, Coe, Duruy, Fredet, Fyffe, Gazeau, Goodrich (S. G.), Lord, Myers, Ransome, Schwill, Shea, Thalheimer, Whitcomb, Yonge (C. M.).

Rome.—Allen (W. F.), Anderson, Barnes, Botsford, Brownson, Bryce, Bury, Castegnier, Collier, Coulange, Gazeau, Gibbon, Gilman, Goodrich (S. G.), History, How & L., Irving, Kelsey, Liddell, Merivale, Mommsen, Morey, Pelham, Pennell, Putnam's Manuals, Ragozin, Robinson (W. S.), Sewell (E.), Sheldon (M. D.), Shuckburgh, Smith (W.), Thalheimer, Trask, Tufts, Vincent, Wilkins, Yonge (C. M.).

Russia.—Patrick, Smith (H. A.).

Scotland.—Freeman, Mackenzie, Royal.

Spain.—Parmele.

United States.—Abbott (E.), Adams & Trent, Allen (J. G.), American Contemporary Hist., American History Series, Anderson, Andrews, Armstrong, Barnes, Benziger, Berard, Blaisdell (A. F.), Brooks, Burgess, Burton, Butler, Campbell (L. J.), Channing, Channing & H., Childs, Claxton, Cornman & G., Cooke, Cooper, Creery, Davidson, Davis, Derry, Dodge, Drake, DuBose, Eclectic, Eggleston, Elementary, Eliot, Ellis, Epochs, Field, First Lessons, Fiske, Freeman, Gibson, Gilman, Godard, Goodrich (Chas. A.), Goodrich (S. G.), Gordy, Hansell, Harley, Harris, Hart & Channing, Hassard, Hathaway, Henry, Higginson, Holbrook, Holmes, Howells, Howison, Johnston (A.), Jones (L. E.), Julland, Kerney, Kimball, King & Ficklin, Kraut, Lee (S. P.), Lemmon & E., Lossing, Lowry & McCardley, Mackenzie, McLaughlin, McMaster, Monroe (Mrs. L. B.), Monteith, Montgomery, Morris, Mowry, Musick, Nichols, Niles, Northam, Parmele, Peet, Pierson (H. W.), Pollard, Porter (L. H.), Powell, Primary, Quackenbos, Rand, McN., Ridpath, Riggs, School, Scott, Scudder, Sheldon, Shinn, Smith, Smith (W. A.), Stephens, Sterne, Stockton, Swett, Swinton, Symonds, Tappan, Thomas (A. C.), Thousand Questions, Thompson, Thorpe, Thwaites, Tomlinson, Towle, Van Wie, Walton & B., White (F. H.), Wilson, Winsor, Woody.

State Histories.—*Alabama.*—Brown (W. G.).—*Arkansas.*—Hemstead, Shinn.—*Georgia.*—Evans.—*Iowa.*—Seerley & P., Sabin.—*Illinois.*—Mather.—*Kansas.*—Canfield.—*Kentucky.*—Kinkead.—*Louisiana.*—Dimitry; Ficklen, J. R.—*Maine.*—Varnye, Stetson.—*Maryland.*—Browne & Scharf, Butler, Dulany, Onderdonk, Passano.—*Minnesota.*—Niles.—*Mississippi.*—Riley.—*New York.*—Anderson & F., Ellis, Hendrick, Southworth. —*North Carolina.*—Alderman (E A.), Moore (J. W.), Spencer (C. P.).—*Pennsylsylvania.*—Shimmell.—*So. Carolina.*—Davidson (J. W.).—*So. Dakota.*—Smith & Y.—*Tennessee.*—McGee, Phelan.—*Texas*—Pennybacker, Thrall.—*Virginia.*—Maury (L. H.), Smithey (R. B.).—*Wisconsin.*—Hutton (A. J.).

City Histories.—*New York.*—Todd.—*Philadelphia.*—Rhoades.

See also READERS, *Historical; Miscellaneous.*

Hygiene.—Ames, Blaikie, Hunt (E. M.), Mirick, Parkes, Wilson (G.).
See also ANATOMY; PHYSIOLOGY.

Industrial Education.—Bucher, Compton, Goss, Ham, Kilbon Unwin, Whitaker.

Italian.—*Composition.*—Grandgent, Moore.

Conversation.—Labriola.

Dictionaries.—Barretti, Edgreen, Feller, Handy, Hossfeld, James & Grassi, Meadows, Millhouse, Roberts (J. P.), Tauchnitz, Wessely.

Grammars.—Ahn, Berlitz, Cassell, Comba, Edgren, Gaspey-Otto-Sauer, Grandgent, Hossfeld, Howland, Hugo, Meisterschaft, Ollendorff, Sauer, Smith (Wm.), Young.

Pronunciation.—Comba.

Readers.—Cattaneo, Foresti, Hossfeld's, Scotti.

Miscellaneous.—International, Novelle, Parlate.

Kindergarten.—Alger, Bailey (M. E.), Batchellor, Berry, Bradley, Froebel, Hallman, Hailmann (E. L.), Hailmann (W. N.), Ham, Handbook, Heerwart, Hubbard, Kilbon, Kindergarten, Knowlton, Kraus-Boelte, Kriege, MacLeod, Menard, Moore, Mortimer, Mulley, Nelson, New Century, Noa, Paradise, Peabody & Mann, Plays, Pollock, Practical, Prang, Ronge, Smith (E.), Steiger, Walker & Jenks, Wiebe, Wiggin, Wiggin & Smith, Wiltse.

Language.—*See* ENGLISH; FRENCH; GERMAN; GREEK; HEBREW; ITALIAN; LATIN; LITERATURE; PHILOLOGY; SPANISH.

Latin.—*Dictionaries.*—Ahn-Henn, Ainsworth, Anthon, Appleton, Beard (J. R. & C.), Bullions, Cassell, Classic, Entick, Gardner, Harpers', Leverett, Lewis, Nall, Routledge, Smith (Wm.), Wendell, Wessely, White (J. T.),

Etymology.—Andrews, Halsey (C. S.), Lapana.

First Lessons, Primers, etc.—Ahn-Henn, Andrews, Arnold (T. K.), Arrowsmith & Wicher, Bain, Bennett, Chase & Stuart, Collar, Collar & Daniell, Comstock (D. Y.), Coy, D'Ooge, Gildersleeve, Greenough, Greenough, Gunnison & H., D'Ooge & D., Harkness, Halsey (W. McD.), Hamer,

Harper & B., Heatley & S., Hoch & B., Holbrook (I.), Jones (E.), Leighton, Lindsay & Rollins, Longmans, McEwen, MacLauchlin, Morris (W. H.), Pantin, Postgate, Preble & Hull, Rolfe &D., Scudder, Smart, Shedd, Smiley & S., Smith (W. W.), Tetlow, Tuell & Fowler, Tuell & Snyder.

Grammar and Exercises.—Ahn-Henn, Allen & G., Andrews & S., Arnold (T. K.), Smith (W. W.), Bennett, Bingham, Bruns, Bares, Chase & S., Clark (D.), Drisler, Englmann, Gildersleeve, Grove, Hale & B., Harkness, Harper, Hayes & M., Hogue, Keep (R. P.), Lane, Leighton, McCabe, Meissner, Miller & Beeson, Mitchell, Mooney, Moore, Muller (P. J.), Pennell, Sauveur, Schmitz & Z., Schultz, Silber, Smith (Wm.), Tomlinson, Vigers, Weld, West, White & Waite, Whiton.

Parsing.—Goodrich (C. A.), MacLardy.

Pronunciation.—King, Lord, Peck, Wilby.

Prose Composition.—Ahn-Henn, Allen (W. F.), Allen & Greenough, Arnold (T. K.), Bennett, Bingham, Collar, Daniell, Dodge, D'Ooge (B. L.), Gildersleeve-Lodge, Harkness, Jones (E.), Judson, Mather & W., Mellick, Miller, Moulton, Nutting, Peck & A., Prebiel & Parker, Ritchie.

Prosody.—Casserley.

Readers.—Ahn-Henn, Allen (J. H.), Andrews, Bingham, Bruns, Chase & Stuart, Gildersleeve, Harkness, Harrington (K. P.), McCabe, Maidment & M., Preble & Hull, Preparatory, Smith (E. H.), Student's Series, Tomlinson.

Readings (*General*).—Andrews, Arrowsmith & Knapp, Brooks (N. C.), Buchanan & M., Churchell & Sanford Cicero, College, College Latin, Crowell, D'Ooge, Hanson, Historia, Leusden, L'Homond, Lindsay, Longmans, Macmillan, March, Masterpieces, School Classics, Viri Romæ, Whicher.

Verbs.—Reiley.

Cæsar.—Allen & G., Andrews, Ashmore, Atherton, Bartholomew, Bingham, Blackburn, Brittain, Brooks (N. C.), Bullions, Chase & S., Collar, D'Ooge & D., Ferguson, Gitbauer, Greenough's, Handy, Harkness, Harkness & Forbes, Harper, Idioms, Interlinear, Jeffers, Judson, Kelsey, Lowe & Ewing, McCabe, McKay, Mueller, Peck, Perrin (B.), Riggs, Roberts, Sauveur, Schmitz & Z., Westcott, Whiton, Wilkins.

Catullus.—Handy, Merrill (E. T.).

Cicero.—Allen & G., Anthon, Chase & Stuart, D'Ooge, Handy, Hanson, Harkness, Harper & G., Hart (S.), Haydon, Idioms, Interlinear, Kellogg (M.), Kelsey, Kirtland, Lord (J. K.), McKay, Montague, Moses & F., Owen, Riggs, Rockwood, St. Clair, Sihler, Stickney (A.), Tunstall, White, Wilkins, Young & M., Woodhouse

Cornelius Nepos.—Chase, Chase & Stuart, Flagg, Gardner, G. & B., Gitbauer, Handy, Interlinear, Lindsay, Rolfe, Schmitz & Zumpt.

Curtius Rufus (*Quintus*).—Crosby, Fowler, Humphrey, Schmitz & Zumpt.

Eutropius.—Clark, Greenough, Handy, Hazzard.

Horace.—Anthon, Bennett, Chase, Chase & S., Handy, Interlinear, Kirkland (J. H.), Lincoln, McKay, Rolfe, Schmitz & Z., Shorey, Shorey & Kirkland, Smith (E. L.), Smith & Greenough, Thompson.

Juvenal.—Anthon, Chase & Stuart, Handy, Hart (S.), Interlinear, Leverett, Lindsay, McKay, Simcox, Wright, (M. P.)

Livy.—Anthon, Chase & Stuart, Eaton, Greenough, Handy, Interlinear, Lincoln, Lord, Mason & A., McKay, Rolfe, Westcott, Woodhouse.

Lucretius.—Handy, Kelsey.

Martial.—Handy.

Ovid.—Allen & G., Anderson, Andrews, Brooks (N. C.), Chase & Stuart, Gleason, Handy, Haydon, Interlinear, Kelsey, Lincoln, McKay, Miller, Ovid, Peck (W. T.).

Persius.—Anthon, Gildersleeve, Hart (S.), Johnson.

Phædrus.—Drake, Handy, Phædri.

Plautus.—Barber, Elmer, Fowler, Fry, Handy, Harrington, Morris (E. P.), Proudfit.

Pliny.—Handy, Holbrooke, Montague, Platner, Wescott

Quintilian.—Frieze, Handy.

Sallust.—Allen & Greenough, Andrews, Anthon, Chase & Stuart, Handy, Harkness, Herbermann, Interlinear, McKay, Scudder, Schmitz & Zumpt.

Seneca.—Handy, Harris, Hurst & Whiting.

Tacitus.—Allen (W. F.), Anthon, Bennett, Champlin (J. T.), Chase & Stuart, Gitbauer, Gudeman, Handy, Hopkins (A. G.), Johnson (H. C.), McKay, Masom, Moses & F., Tyler (W. S.), Worthington (J. R.).

Terence.—Chase & Stuart, Cowles, Elmer, Fairclough, Handy, Nicolson, Preble, Rolfe, West.

Valerius Maximus.—Smith (C. F.).

Virgil.—Andrews, Anthon, Ballard, Bingham, Brooks (N. C.), Burgess, Comstock, Conington, Cranch, Cutler, Frieze, Gleason, Greenough & K., Handy, Harper & M., Interlinear, Knapp, McKay, Plaistowe & M., Schmitz & Z., Searing, Whiton.

Viri Romæ.—Arrowsmith, Handy, McKay.

Completely parsed Cæsar.—Finchi.

Synonyms.—Doederlein, Ramshorn, Shumway.

Translating English into Latin.—Handy, Harper, Interlinear, Literal, McKay, Rockliff.

Translating Latin into English.—D'Ooge, Egbert, Handy, Literal, McKay, Post, Welch & Duffield.

Versification.—Bennett, Platner.

Letter-Writing.—Ellsworth, Hinds & Noble, McMahan, Palmer, Powers & Lyons, Practical, Smithdeal, Townsend (C.), Ward (E. G.), Westlake, Williams & Rogers.

See also COMPOSITION.

Literature.—*American.*—Abernethy, Adams (O. F.), Baldwin (J.), Bates, Beers, Blaisdell, Bronson, Cambridge, Cleveland, Eliot, English, Gilmore, Hawthorne & Lemmon, Heath, Hendrick, Higginson, Johnson (C. F.), Lakeside, Lawton, Lockwood (S. E. H.), Lodge (H. C.), Longwell, Lowell, McCaskey, Macmillan, Manly, Matthew, Noble, Painter, Pancoast, Pattee, Readings, Regents, Richardson (C. F.), Riverside Biog. Ser., Royse, Rutherford, Shaw-Backus, Smyth, Tyler (M. C.), Underwood (F. H.), White, Wright.

Classical.—Bulfinch, Capps, Fiske, Heath, Morris (C.), Quackenbos (J. D.), Ragozin, Standard, Twentieth, White (C. A.), Wilkinson. *See also*, below, *Greek, Roman.*

English.—Academy, Adams (O. F.), Arnold (T.), Baldwin (J.), Bascom, Beers, Blaisdell, Brooke, Brooke & Carpenter, Buckland, Butler, Cambridge, Chaucer, Cleveland, Collier (W. F.), Corson, Craik, Daniels, Davies (J.), Day, Eclectic, English, Garnett, Gilman, Gilmore, Great, Hackett & Girvin, Hales, Halleck, Harlow, Heath, Hedrick, Hendrick, Hodgkins, Hudson, Hunt (T. W.), Jenkins (O. L.), Johnson (B. F.), Johnston & Browne, Kellogg, Lake, Lewis, Literature Primers, Lloyd, Longmans, Longmans & McWilliam, Longwell, McElroy, Macmillan, McNeill, Maertz, Meiklejohn, Minto, Moody, Morley, Murray (J. O'K.), Painter, Pancoast, Phillips (M. G.), Raub, Readings, Renton, Richardson (A. S.), Robertson, Royse, Rutherford, Saintsbury, Scudder, Shaw (T. B.), Shaw-Backus, Silver, Simonds, Smith (G. J.), Smith (M. W.), Spalding, Sprague (H. B.), Stronach, Students', Swinton, Syle, Taine, Underwood (F. H.), Washburne, Watkins, Welsh (A. H.), Westlake, Wheeler, Williams.

General.—Perry.

Miscellaneous Literary Selections.—American, Boyd, Bryant, Burt, Canterbury, Cathcart, Clark & M., Dalgleish, Holbrook, Holmes (O. W.), Irving, Leffingwell, Longfellow, McMurray; Masterpieces, Modern Classics, Motley, Northend, Parkman, Penniman, Prescott, Putnam, Pyle, Rival Collection, Riverside, Rolfe, Sprague (H. B.), Standard, Students' Ser., Thompson, Wheeler, Whiting, Whittier, Zell.

See also, above, *American; English;* ELOCUTION.

Poetry (*Selections*).—American, Baldwin (J.), Brackett, Eliot, Lodge, Pancros, Rolfe, Sargent, Ward (T. H.).

See also, above, *American; English; Miscellaneous.*

Bacon.—Warne, Whately.

Browning.—Rolfe.

Milton.—Hines, Introduction, Ross (J. M.), Sprague (H. B.), Torrey.

Shakespeare.—Arden, Corson, Dowden, Hows, Hudson, Introduction, Kellogg, Literature Primers, Rolfe, Sprague (H. B.).

French.—Duvall, Kastner & A., Keene, Saintsbury, Van Daell, Van Laun, Warren. *See also* FRENCH, *Literature.*

General.—Barrow, Bates, Botta, Burt, Champlin, Clarke, Gummere (F. B.) Hallam, Meese, Saintsbury, Southwick, Trimble.

German.—Gostwick & Harrison, Hoyle, Ideophonic, Muller (F. M.) Scherer, Taylor (M.), Tensler. *See also* GERMAN, *Literature.*

Greek.—Fowler, Jevons, Lawton, Literature, Murray (G.), Perry (T. S.) Wilkinson, Zeller.

Roman.—Crowell, Cruttwell, Gudeman, Knapp, Mackail, Schmitz (L.).

See also above, *Classical.*

Logarithms.—Barlow, Bowser, Bradbury, Bremiker, Bruhns, Compton (A. G.), Hussey, Jones, Loomis, Newcomb, Olney, Peirce (J. M.), Phillips-Strong, Schuyler, Seaver, Smith, Stanley, Vega, Wells, Wentworth & Hill, Wheeler, Woodward.

See also MATHEMATICS; TRIGONOMETRY.

Logic.—Aikins, Atwater, Bain, Ballantine, Bowen (F.), Coppée, Coppens, Creighton, Davis (N. K.), Day, Gilmore, Gregory, Hamilton (W.), Hedge (L.),

Hibben, Hill (D. J.), Holman, Hyslop, Jevons (W. S.), Killick, Ladd, McCosh, Mill, Minto, Schuyler, Science Primer, Thompson (W.), Tigert, True. Welton, Whately, Wilcox.

Map-Drawing.—*See* DRAWING.

Magnetism.—*See* ELECTRICITY.

Mathematics.—Barton, Brensinger, Cajari, Chauvenet, Clauder, Colbert, Davies (C.), Galbraith & H., Gore, Hanus, Hardy (A. S.), Harkness & M., Hastins, Hathaway, Lowey, Macfarlane, Merrifield. Osborne, Ott, Pierce (B. O.), Peirce (J. M.), Robinson (H. N.), Sherwin, Walsh, Weld, Whiting.
See also ALGEBRA; ARITHMETIC; ASTRONOMY; CALCULUS; DRAWING; GEOMETRY; LOGARITHMS; MECHANICS; MENSURATION; NATURAL PHILOSOPHY; NAVIGATION; SURVEYING; TRIGONOMETRY.

Mechanics.—Ball, Bartlett, Bowser, Dana, Durège Foster, Galbraith & H., Glazebrooke, Goodeve, Goodman, Harrison (W. J.), Magnus, Millikan, Peck (W G.), Perry (J.), Slate, Todhunter, Wood (De V.), Wood & S., Wright.

Mensuration.—Christian Brothers, Davies (C.), Furst, Hall, Halsted, Haswell, Hutton (H H.), Lodge, Longmans, Mecutchen, Murray (D. A.), Rodgers, Schuler, Vogdes.

Mental Philosophy.—Abercrombie, Alden, Allen, Bain, Bascom, Bascomb, Berkeley, Baldwin (J. M.), Brooks (E.), Champlin (J. T.), Coler, Coppens, Cowdery, Davis (N. K.), Descartes, Dewey. Everett, Falckenberg Hamilton, Haven, Hume, Kant, Knight, Ladd, Locke, Lowey Mahan, Mezes, Modern, Nichols, Paulsen, Rivers, Robertson, Rogers, Royce Science Primers, Seelye, Spinoza, Upham, Watts (J.), Wayland, Weber.
See also METAPHYSICS.

Metaphysics.—Bascom, Bowen (F.), Bowne, Day, Elmendorf, Fleming, Haven, Hill (W. H.), Hopkins (M.), Ladd, Mackenzie, Mayor, Porter (N.), Schwegler, Stewart (D.), Wilcox.
See also LOGIC; MENTAL PHILOSOPHY; MORAL PHILOSOPHY; PSYCHOLOGY.

Meteorology.—Chase, Davis, Loomis, Waldo.

Metric System.—Bibbens & B., Granger, Metric, Sawyer (H. E.), Seaver & W., Wurtete.
See WEIGHTS AND MEASURES.

Mineralogy.—Bodeman, Brush, Clapp, Collins, Crosby (W. O.), Dana, Erni & B., Hooker, Hussak, MacLeod, Mitchell (J.), Ricketts, Shepard (E. M.), Sweeny, Taylor, Williams.

Moral Philosophy and Ethics.—Abercrombie, Alexander, Bain, Ballou, Bierbower, Coler, Comegys, Coppens, Cowdery, Cutler (C.), Day, Dewey, Dewey & Tufts, Dymond, Everett, Fairchild, Falckenberg, Fisher, Fletcher (M.), Gilman (N. P.), Gilman & J., Gregory, Haven, Hill (W.H.), Hopkins (M.), Hume, Hyde, Hyslop, Jackson, Janet, Ladd, Louage, Mackenzie, Modern, Muirhead, Paulsen, Peabody (A. P.), Poland, Porter (N.), Reid, Rivers, Robinson (E. G.), Ryland, Seelye, Steele, Stuckenberg, Wayland, Winslow, Wright.

Music.—*Handbooks.*—Adam, Banister, Biographies, Caswell & Ryan, Davenport (F.), Helmholtz, Hohman, Levermore, National, Normal, Palmer, Panseron, Rand, Ritter, Root, Sargent (N. B.), Tilden, Tytler, Whiting (C. E.), Wyman.
Readers.—American, American System, Cincinnati, Educational, Eichberg, Gantvoort (A. J.), Humphreys (L. B.), Jepson, Judge, Loomis (G. B.), National, New American, Normal, Palmer-Curtis, Ryan (J.), Seward, Smith (W. L.), Veazie, Whiting (C. E.), Whybark,
School Singing.—Bardeen, Bartley, Betz, Blackman, Bower, Brewster & T., Burnap, Cecilian, Centennial, Charming, Children, Church, Elson, Emerson (I.), Emerson (L. O.), Emerson & Brown, Emerson & S., Emerson & T., Everest, Fairbanks, Fitz-Gardenier, Franklin Sq., Gaynor, Glover & H., Greene, Hanson, Hart, Hodgdon, Howliston, Howard (F. E.), International, Jarvis, Johnson, Junkerman, Kellogg (A. M.), Kendrick & R., Leslie (E.), Lewis (L. R.), Longmans, Ludden, Lyman, McCaskey, McGranahan, McLaughlin & Vierzie, Matthews, Menard, Model, Mueller & B., Murray & P., National, Natural, Normal, Our Song Birds, Parsons, Pease, Perkins (H. S.), Perkins (W. O.), Phelps (E. C.), Phelps & L., Phillips (P.), Poulson, Pray, Riverside Song Book, Root (G. F.), Root & Case, Rix, Showalter, Shryock, Siefert, Smith (E.), Song, Songs, Sprenkel, Tilden (W. S.), Tillinghast, Tomlins, Tufts (J. W.), Veazie, Wavelet, Whiting, Whitney, Whittemore & B., Zundel.

Mythology.—Bechtel, Beren, Cox (G. W.), Dwight, Edwards (S. A.), Ellis, Frisbee, Guerber, Harrington & Tolman, Irving, Judd, Keightley, Murray (A. S.), Robbins, Scull, Seeman, Tooke, White (C. A.), Witt.

Natural History.—Agassiz, Andrews, (J.), Bartlett, Bass, Baskett, Baskett & Ditman, Bayliss, Beebe & K., Bishop (J. T.), Black & C., Burroughs, Burt, Comstock, Cooper (S.), D'Anvers, Eckstoun, Frenck, Gibson, Goldsmith, Goodrich (S. G.), Gee, Gibson, Gould, Gregory, Guides, Hodge, Hooker, Hunter, Huxley, Jordan (D S. & H.), Jordan & K., Johonnot, Kahn, Knobel, Lockwood, Long, Lubbock, McMurrich, Marsh (G. P.), Merriam, Mill, Miller, Morley, Natural, Needham, Oakley, Packard, Payne, Peck, Perdue & G., Simpson, Stickney, Tenney (Sanb.), Thomson (T. A.), Torrey, Treat, Wilder, Wilson, Wood (J. G.).
See also BOTANY; GEOGRAPHY, *Physical*; GEOLOGY; MINERALOGY; READERS, *Miscellaneous*; ZOÖLOGY.

Natural Philosophy, Physics.—Adams, Allen (C. R.), American Science Series (Barker), Ames, Ames & Bliss, Anthony, Avery, Ayres, Baker (T. R.), Balderston, Boyer, Brodie, Cajori, Carhart, Carhart & C., Catchpool, Chute, Cooley, Cox, Crew & T., Cumming, Deschanel, Dolbear, Draper, Emtage, Everett (J. D.), Fisher & Paterson, Furness, Gage, Ganot, Gillet & Rolfe, Gilley, Glazebrook, Gordon, Griffin (L. R. F.), Hall, Hall & Bergen, Harrington, Hastings & B., Hathaway, Henderson & Woodhull, Hoadley, Hooker, Hopkins, Hotze, Houston, Jackman, Jones, Keith, Kiddle, Larden, Longmans, McKay, MacLeon, McMurray, Meade, Miller (W. A.), Murche, Neidlinger, Nichols (E. L.), Nichols, Norton (S. A.), Olmsted, Peddie, Pickering, Quackenbos, Remsen, Rolfe & Gillet, Rowland & A., Sanford, Sabine, Scott, Sharpless & Philips, Seymour & W., Shaw, Sheldon, Slate, Smith (O.), Smith (T. B.), Smith (T. F.), Snyder & P., Steele, Stewart (B.), Stewart & Gee, Stickney, Stone (W. A.), Swift, Thornton (J.), Thwing, Trowbridge, Watson, Wells, Wells (D. A.), Wentworth & Hill, Whitney, Woodhull, Woodhull & Van A., Wright (M. R.).
First Lessons.—Avery, Avery-Sinnott, Barnard, Brownell, Crew, Gillet & Rolfe, Gifford, Henderson, Hotze, Houston, Lind, Magill (W.), Martindale, Miller & Foerste, Moore (G.), Parker (R. G.), Phelps (Mrs. L.), Science, Thompson (S.), Woodhull.

Navigation.—Evers, Loomis, Maury, Ray, Richards, Robinson (H. N.), Schuyler, Wells & Robbins, Wentworth (G. A.).

Orthography.—*See* SPELLERS; *also* GRAMMAR.

Painting.—*See* ART.

Parsing.—*See* GRAMMAR, *Analysis and Parsing.*

Penmanship.—*Standard or Regular.*—American, Analytical, Appletons', Babbittonian, Barnes, Beers (N. P.), Bond, Business Standard, Butler, Cassell, Common Sense, Continental, Cromwell, Curtiss, Duntonian, Eclectic, Economical, Ellsworth, Ghegan, Ginn, Graphic, Harison, Harpers', Heath, Hill, Jackson, Knopp, Krone, Laughlin, Lockwood, Longmans, McLaurin, Merrill, Michael, New Century, Normal, North Carolina, Ohio, Payson D. & S., Pencil, Popular, Potter, Potter & P., Powers & Lyons, Practical, Rational, Raymond & W., Reynolds, Smith (H. P)., Rightmyer, Rogers, Shaylor & S., Sheldon, Sherwood, Simplified, Spencer, Spencerian, Sterling, Thompson (G. H.), University, Ward, Wells, Williams & Rogers.
Vertical.—American, Barnes, Bowen, Butler, Columbia, Columbus, Curtiss, Duntonian, Educational, Ellsworth, Ginn, Graphic, Heath, Hill, Ideal, Jackson, Johnson (B. F.), Krone, Long, Merrill, Natural, New Era, New Ideal, Normal, Potter & P., Rational, Roudebush, Sheldon, Simplified, Smith (H. P.), Spencerian, Standard, Swisher, University, Vaile, Williams & Rogers, Williams & Tilford.
Eclectic German Vertical.—Eclectic.
Natural Slant.—Barnes.
Rational Slant System.
Rapid Upright.—Rand, McN.
Round-Hand Rational Slant.—Educational.
Round-Hand, Vertical.—Educational, Hill.
Round Rapid.
Semi Slant.—Kilpatrick.
Slant.—Columbia, Educational, Wise.
Stub-Pen Writing.
Upright Rapid Writing.

Philology.—Edwards, Literature Primers, Smith-deal.
See also LANGUAGE.

Philosophy.—*See* MENTAL; MORAL; NATURAL.

Phonography.—Allen (G. G.), Baker (A. M.), Bryant, Cross (J. G.), Day (A.), Dettmann, Eames, Graham, Heffley, Lester-Barker, Longley, Marsh, Moran, Munson, Osgoodby, Pitman (B.), Pitman (I.), Pitman & Howard, Powers & Lyons, Practical, Relton, Richter, Watson (J.), Ward (N.), Williams & Rogers.

Physical Education.—Anderson, Bancroft, Betz, Cruden, De Graff, Dowd, Harvey (T. J.), Hunt (L. B.), Johnson (B. F.), Jolly, Mason, Morse, Parsons, Posse, Pratt, Rasmussen, Shelton, Smart, Stebbins, Straw, Swazey, Watson (J. M.), Welch.
See also PHYSIOLOGY.

Physics.—*See* NATURAL PHILOSOPHY; *also* CHEMISTRY.

Physiology.—Appleton, Baldwin, Blaisdell, Brinckley, Brown (E. F.), Brown, Brubaker, Buckelew & L. Dulany, Chambers, Colton, Dorner, Dulany, Dunglison. Eclectic, Foster, Ganong, Hooker, Huxley, Javal, Jenkin, Johnson, Lind, Macy, Noyes, Overton, Schenck, Schofield, Steele, Stout, Stowell, Tracy, Waller, Yeo.
Primary.—Baldwin, Bowditch, Buch, Callahan, Colton (B. P.), Cornman & G., Dulany Dunglison, Ellis (E. S.), Foster & Shore, Furneaux, Hall (J. W.), Hooker, Hotze, Hutchison, Huxley & L., Jarvis (E.), Johnson, Johonnot & Bouton, Lind, Miles, Mills, Moore, Putnam, Science Primers, Smith (W. T.), Stowell, Tidd, Warfel.
Physiology and Hygiene.—Baldwin, Blaisdell, Brand, Brown (R. T.), Dalton, Dinsmore, Eclectic, Edwards (Jos.), Guernsey, Hall (W. S. & J. W.), Hall (W. S.), Hallock. Hatfield, Hathaway, Hutchison, Huxley & Y., Kellogg (J. H.), Lincoln, May, Martin, Pathfinder, Smith (W. T.), Steele, Union Ser., Walker (Jerome), Willard & Smith.
See also ANATOMY; HYGIENE; ZOÖLOGY.

Political Economy.—Adams, Alden, American Science Series (Walker), Andrews, Blackmar (F. W.), Bryce, Carey, Champlin (J. T.), Chapin, Clark (J. B.), Clements, De Graff, Devine, Ely, Ely & Wicker, Giddings, Gide, Gore, Greeley, Gregory (J. M.), Hadley, Laughlin, Lemon, Macvane, Meservey, Mill, Patton, Perry, Rogers (J. E. T.), Small & V., Smith (A.), Smith (E. P.), Steele (G. H.), Steele (G. M.), Summer, Symes, Thompson (R. E.), Thurston, Walker (A.), Walker (F. A.), Wayland, Willoughby, Williams & Rogers, Wilson.
First Lessons.—Alden, Bullock, Daniels, Davenport, Dodd, Dole, Fawcett (H.), Mason & Labor, Science Primers, Wayland, Wood.

Primers.—Alexander (Mrs. G. A.), American, Appletons', Armstrong, Arnold, Badlam, Baldwin, Ballard, Bannan, Blaisdell (E. A.), Butler, Butler-Goodrich, Calkins, Child's, Cyr, Davis (W. J.), Deutscher, Dulany's, Faber, Ferris, Franklin, Fuller, Gilbert (J. H.), Gilmour, Hazen, Heilprin, Hiawatha, Hillard, Hillard & Campbell, Holmes, Holton, Johnson (B. F.), Johonnot, Kelly, Little Teacher, McGuffey, Macmillan, Maxwell (E.), Modern, Monroe, Morey, Murphy, New American, New Franklin, North Carolina, Osgood, Parker & Watson, Peabody, Peabody & Mann, Pollard, Progressive, Rand, McN., Reed (A.), Reynolds, Riverside, Royal, Sadlier (W. H.), Sanders, Sawyer (H.), Sheldon, Sprague, Sterling, Stickney (J. H.), Stickney & Peabody, Swinton, Turner, United States, Webb (J. R.), Webster-Franklin, White (W. R.), Willson, Winchell, Young Catholic.
Phonetic.—Douai, Hillard & Campbell, McGuffey, Parker & Watson, Riley, Sheldon (E. A.).

Pronunciation.—*See* DICTIONARIES; ELOCUTION.

Psychology.—Baker, Baldwin, Bowne, Buell, Calkins, Compayre, Day, Davis, De Garmo & Lindner, Dewey, Gordy, Halleck, Hewitt, Hill (D. J.), James, Kellogg, Kirkpatrick, Krohn, Kulpe, Ladd, McCosh, McLellan, Morgan, Murray, Putnam, Roark, Robertson, Royce, Sanford, Schuyler, Scripture, Steele, Sully, Titchener, Welch, Williams (H. G.), Witmer (L.).
See also MENTAL PHILOSOPHY.

Punctuation.—Cosker, Hinds & Noble, Nelson, Wilson.

Question Books, Examiners, etc.—Craig, Henry, Hinds & Noble, Moritz, Sherrill, Southwick.

Readers.—*Geographical.*—Carpenter, Carroll, Dodge, Guyot, Information, Johonnot, King, Longman's, Philips, Rupert's, World and its People, World at Home, Youth's Companion.
Graded Series.—Aldrich & Forbes, Appletons', Barnes, Baldwin, Bancroft, Boyden, Braumbaugh, Butler, Campbell (L. J.), Carroll, Christian Brothers, Columbus, Continental, Cyr, Davis, Demarest & Van Sickle, Edwards (R.), Excelsior, Finch, Franklin, Fundenberg, Gilmour, Goho, Harper, Harpers', Harvey, Hawthorne, Hazen, Hillard, Hillard & Campbell, Holmes, Interstate, Judson & B., Kelly, Kline, Krackowizer, Le Row, Lippincott, Lights of Lit., Lovejoy, McBride, McGuffey, Merrill, Modern, Monroe, Montieth, Murphy, Nelson, New American, New Century, New Education, New Era, New Franklin, New Graded, Newell & Creary, Normal, North Carolina, Norton, Osgood, O'Shea, Parker & Watson, Peabody, Pollard, Progressive, Rational, Reynolds, Riverside, Royal, Royal Crown, Royal School, Sanders, Scribner, Sheldon, Sheldon (E. A.), Shewall, Smith (B. G.), Standard, Stepping-Stones, Sterling, Stickney (J. H.), Swinton, Taylor, Town, Tweed, Warren, Watson (J. M.), Webb (J. R.), Webster-Franklin, Wheeler, Willson, Young Catholic.
Historical.—Anderson, Arnold (E. J.), Baldwin (Ja.), Ballou, Burton, Cleveland, Drake, Dutton, Guerber, Hart (A. H.), Historical, Hunter, Irving & Fiske, Johonnot, Judd, Littlejohn, Moore (N.), Philips, Pratt, Shepherd, Smith, (J. R.), Warren, Wilson (L. L. W.).
Miscellaneous and Supplementary.—Academy, American, Anderson, Andrews, Athenæum, Badlam, Baldwin, Blaisdell, Boltwood, Cady & Dewey, Cathcart, Chatty, Classics, Clarke, Cole, Connolly, De Garmo, Eclectic, Eggleston, Eliot, Emerson, Flanagan, Gleason, Good, Gow, Guerber, Hall, Harper, Holden, Holtzclaw, Hudson, Hyde, Johonnot, Lakeside, Lamb, Lights, Le Row, Lodge, Longmans, McGuffey, McMurray, Masterpieces, Modern Classics, Monteith, Morse, Nelson, Parker & Marvel, Philips, Pierson (H. W.), Ragozin, Reade, Rickoff, Riverside, Royal, Ruskin, Sadlier (Mrs.), Scudder, Sheldon, Sight Reader, Smith (H. A.), Standard, Stickney, Tenney (Mrs.), Tiffany, Troeger, Turner, Twentieth, Wiggin, Williams, Wilson (L. L. W.), Wood (J. G.), Wood (M. J.), Wright (J. McN.).
See also ELOCUTION; LITERATURE.
Phonetic.—Bell, Deane, DeGraff, Edwards & Webb, Fundenberg, Hillard, Ives, Leftwich (R. W.), McGuffey, Monroe, Moses, Pitman (I.), Rambeau & Passy, Rational, Robbins Watson (J. M.).
Primary and Elementary.—Badlam, Bass, Bent, Biddulph, Bishop (J. T.), Buckelew & Lewis, Child's, Cleveland, Collard, Coolidge, Columbia, Columbian, Comly, Crosby Cyr, Davis. Finch, First, Ford, Fundenberg, Gilford, Guilford & Ortel, Haaren, Hazen, Hodskin, Lane, Natural, Nelson (M.), Peabody, Pollard, Pomeroy, Potter, Primary, Regal, Royal, Sight Reader, Soule & Wheeler, Turner, Williams.

Rhetoric.—Bardeen, Bascom, Bates, Blair, Boyd, Cairns, Carpenter, Clark (J. S.), Coppée, Coppens, Crafts & Fisk, Day (H. N.), De Mille, Du Cygne, Frink, Gening, Genung, Gilmore, Hale, Hart (J. M.), Hart (J. S.), Haven, Hepburn, Hill (A. S.), Hill (D. J.), Kames, Kellogg, Lewis, McElroy, Mead, Newcomer, O'Conor, Patterson, Powell, Shedd, Welsh (A. H.), Whately, Wisely.
See also COMPOSITION AND RHETORIC.

Shorthand.—*See* PHONOGRAPHY.

Spanish.—*Arithmetics.*—Spanish Serie, Heinemann, Wentworth.
Composition.—Ford, Loiseaux, Ramsey.
Conversations.—Altimira, Darr, De Belem, Del Mar, Habla, Mantilla, Pinney, Silva.
Dictionaries.—Becker, Feller, Handy, Hossfeld, Lopes, Neuman, Vélasquez, Wessely.
Geography.—Frye, Monteith, Spanish Series.
Grammars and Methods.—Ahn, Berlitz, Buckbee Cortina, De Tornos, De Vere, Duque & Phelan, Edgren, Garner, Gaspey-Otto-Sauer, Giese. Goldsmith, Hossfeld, Knapp (W. I.), Knoflach, Kroeh, Loiseaux, Manning, Meisterschaft, Monsanto & Languellier, Ollendorff, Prendegast, Ramsey, Robertson, Rosenthal, Sales, Sales & Josse, Salvo, Sauer, Schilling, Smith (L. C.), Velasquez, & Simonne, Worman, Ybarra.
History.—De Thomas, Montgomery
Phonography.—Lester-Barker, Williams, Rogers.
Primers.—Fuller.
Pronunciation.—Kroeh.
Readers.—Appleton, Caballero, Cyr, Fontaine, Knapp, Loiseaux, Mantilla, Matzke, Monroe, Ramsey, Roehrich, Spanish Serie Moderne, Teatro, Tolon, Vélasquez.
Readings.—Tellez.
Verbs.—Traub.

Speakers.—*See* ELOCUTION.

Spellers.—Alton (G. B.), Appletons', Arithmetical, Babcock, Bales, Barnes, Beitzel, Benedict, Benson, Blaisdell (E. A.), Boltwood, Bouton, Bowen, Branson, Buckwalter, Butler (N.), Byerly, Campbell (W. A.), Carpenter (T.), Clinger, Columbia, Comly, Creery, Cyr, Daly, De Wolf, Diamond, Easy, Eclectic, Edwards & W., Fernald, Gilbert (J. H.), Gilmour, Glass, Gourley, Graves, Guilford & L., Haaren, Hansell, Harrington (H. F.), Harvey, Hazen, Hinds & N., Holmes, Hunt (J. N.), Hunt (N.), Irish, Jacobs, Jacobs & P., James & Deg., Kelly, Kline, Lippincott, McGuffey, Manson, Maxwell (E. P.), Meneley & G., Metcalf, Miscellaneous, Modern, Monroe, Morse, Natural, Neely, New American, Normal, North Carolina, Osgood, O'Shea, Parker & W., Patterson, Pollard, Pomeroy, Powers & Lyons, Practical, Primary, Progressive, Rand,

McN., Raub, Reed (A.), Regents, Reynolds, Rice, Rowe, Sanders, Sanford, Sargent, Sever, Shearer, Sheldon (E. A.), Sherwood, Sherwood (W.), Shoup, Smith, (E. E.), Smith (W. W.), Smithdeal, Soule & W., Spalding & Moore, Sterling, Swett, Swinton, Town, Tweed, Universal, Warren (M. A.), Watson (J. M.), Webster, Wheeler Williams & Rogers, Willson, Worcester, Word Lists, Young Catholic.

Analysers and Definers.—Ballard, Curd, Donnelly, Hazen, Hunt (J. N.), McElligott, Longmans, Metropolitan, Patterson, Sanders, Sherwood, Sherwood (W.), Smith (W. W.), Town, Webb (A. C.), Webster, Willson.

Dictation Exercises.—Guilford, Northend, O'Neill, Penniman, Sewell (E. M.).

Orthography. — Bowen, Clinger, Hathaway, Irish, Parlin, Penniman, Scholars', Winchell, Wright (A. D.).

Test Spellers. — Gilbert, Henderson, Henkle, Hyde, Patterson, Pooler, Rapp, Sanders, Westlake, Williams & R.

Writing Spellers.—American, Ballard, Barnes, Buckbee, Butler, Christey, Dinsmore, Eclectic, Franklin, Graphic, Lind, McVicar, Manson, Maxwell, Merrill (E. C.), Monroe, Oliver, One Thousand, Patterson, Philbrick, Roudebush, Scholar, Sheldon, Sherwood, Sherwood (W.), Smith (E. E.), Swinton, Ward.

Stenography.—*See* PHONOGRAPHY; SHORTHAND.

Surveying.—Alsop, Bagot, Bradbury, Carhart, Davies (C.), Gillespie, Gore, Gummere, Haupt, Johnson (J. B.), Lane, Loomis, McMillan & B., Merriman, Ray, Raymond (W. G.), Reed (H. A.), Robbins, Robinson (H. N.), Schuyler, Wells & Robbins, Wentworth (G. A.).

Trigonometry.— Anderegg & Roe, Ashton & Marsh, Bellows (C. F. R.), Blakslee, Bowser, Bradbury, Briggs', Brooks (E.), Chauvenet, Clark, Crawley, Crockett, Davies (C.), Durfee, Franklin, Galbraith & H., Greenleaf, Griffin (W. N.), Hall & Knight, Jones, Lewis (E.), Loney, Loomis, Miller (E.), Murray, Newcomb, Nicholson, Nixon, Olney, Phillips, Strong, Price, Ray, Richards (E. L.), Robinson (H. N.), Schuyler, Seaver, Seaver & W., Sharpless, Stanley, Todhunter, Wells, Welsh, Wentworth (G. A.), Wentworth & H., Wheeler, Whitaker, Wood.

Typewriting.—Fuller, Longley (I.), Longley (M. V.), Mills, Powers & L., Practical, Sadler & R., Van Sant.

Weights and Measures.—Davies (C.), Eaton, Gibbens & B., Granger, Metric, Sawyer (H. E.), Seaver & W., Wurtele.

Zoology.—American Science Series (Packard), Angell, Beddard, Bumpus, Burnett, Chambers (W.), Chapin & Rettger, Colton, Davenport (C. B.), Greene, Harvey (A. N.), Hertwig, Holden, Holder, Hooker, Jordon, Kellogg, Jordon, Kellogg & Heath, Kellogg, Kingsley, Lockwood, Manton, Marshall, Morse (E. S.), Needham, Nicholson (H. A.), Orton, Painter & H., Parker & Parker, Pratt (H. S.), Shipley & MacBride, Steele, Tenney (Sanb.), Wells & D.

See also NATURAL HISTORY.

For Students and Teachers.

Heroes of the Nations

35 volumes now ready.
Fully illustrated, 12mo, each, net, $1.35; by mail $1.50.

33. **Owen Glyndwr, the National Hero of Wales.** By A. G. BRADLEY.
34. **Henry V., the Typical Mediæval Hero.** By CHARLES L. KINGSFORD.
35. **Edward Plantagenet (Edward I.) the English Justinian.** By EDWARD JENKS.

Story of the Nations

Fully illustrated, 12mo, each, net, $1.35; by mail $1.50.

62. **Wales.** By O. M. EDWARDS.
63. **Mediæval Rome, 1073-1535.** By WILLIAM MILLER.
64. **The Papal Monarchy.** By WM. BARRY.

Andrew's Modern Europe. 2 vols in 1 . . . . *Net*	$2 75
Hadley's Economics . . . *Net*	2 50
Hadley's Railroad Transportation	1 50
Earle's English Grammar . . .	1 50
Compton's Errors of Speech . .	75
Phyfe's 5,000 Facts and Fancies *Net*	5 00
Phyfe's 7,000 Words Often Mis-Pronounced	1 00
Hamilton's The Federalist . . .	1 50
Richardson's American Literature	3 50
Dunbar's History of Banking . .	1 25
Noyes' 30 Years of Am. Finance	1 25
Taussig's Tariff History of U. S.	1 25
A Shorter Course in Munson Phonography . . . . . *Net*	1 25

G. P. PUTNAM'S SONS,
27 and 29 West 23d Street, **NEW YORK.**

SUPPLEMENTARY READING

THE CLASSICAL SERIES

Shakespeare's Stories Simply Told—Tragedies. By MARY SEYMOUR. 12mo, cloth, inked sides.	$1 25
Shakespeare's Stories Simply Told—Comedies. By MARY SEYMOUR. 12mo, cloth, inked sides.	1 25
Stories of the Days of King Arthur. By CHARLES HENRY HANSON. 12mo, cloth, inked sides	1 25
The Siege of Troy and the Wanderings of Ulysses. By CHARLES HENRY HANSON. 12mo, cloth.	1 25
Chaucer's Stories Simply Told. BY MARY SEYMOUR. 12mo, cloth, inked sides....................	1 25
Stories of Old Rome. By CHARLES HENRY HANSON. 12mo, cloth, inked sides....................	1 25

Beautifully illustrated by Howard, Scammell, Doré, Flaxman and others.

FAVORITE KIRBY BOOKS

Aunt Martha's Corner Cupboard; or, Stories about Tea, Coffee, Sugar, Rice, etc. By M. and E. KIRBY. With 36 engravings. 12mo, cloth....................	60
The World by the Fireside; or, Pictures and Scenes from Far-Off Lands. By MARY and ELIZABETH KIRBY. Small 4to, cloth extra. Profusely illustrated....................	1 75
The Sea and Its Wonders. A companion volume to "The World by the Fireside." By M. and E. KIRBY. Beautifully illustrated. Small 4to, cloth extra. *New and cheaper edition*....................	1 75

HISTORIES

Torch-Bearers of History. A connected Series of Historical Sketches. First and Second Series in one volume. From the Earliest Times to the Beginning of the French Revolution. By AMELIA HUTCHINSON STIRLING, M. A. Bound in Art Linen	1 50
History of the British Empire. By W. F. COLLIER, LL.D. 12mo, cloth....................	1 00
Great Events of History. By W. F. COLLIER, LL.D. With maps and illustrations. 416 pages.......	1 25
History of English Literature. By W. F. COLLIER, LL.D. In a Series of Biographical Sketches. *New and enlarged edition.* 12mo, cloth....................	1 75
The Nineteenth Century. A History. By R. MACKENZIE. 8vo, cloth....................	1 00
America. A History. By R. MACKENZIE. 8vo, cloth....................	1 00

Complete list of School-Books on Application.

THOMAS NELSON & SONS, PUBLISHERS AND IMPORTERS, **37 to 41 East 18th St., New York.**

Literal and Interlinear Translations.

LITERAL TRANSLATIONS OF THE CLASSICS.

These translations have been prepared with great care. They follow the original text literally, thus forming a valuable help to the student in his efforts to master the difficulties which beset him. Pleasing sketches of the authors appear in the form of an introduction to each of the volumes.

The books are in convenient form, being exceptionally handy for the pocket. They are printed from clear type, and are attractively and durably bound. Cloth binding, each 50 cents.

INTERLINEAR TRANSLATIONS. The Hamilton, Locke and Clark Series have long been the Standard and are now the *Best Translated* and *Most Complete* Series of Interlinears published.

12mo, well bound in half leather, each $1.50.

DAVID McKAY, Publisher,

1022 Market Street, - - - PHILADELPHIA.

THE MORSE CO.

96 Fifth Avenue, - - NEW YORK

	List Price.
Higher Algebra. ATWOOD	$0 80
Standard School Algebra. ATWOOD	1 20
Exercises in Algebra. ATWOOD	80
Grammar School Algebra. ATWOOD	60
Standard School Physiology	80
American History. Text Book. CHANCELLOR.	1 00
Indians and Pioneers; or, Earliest Days in America. DUTTON. Book I, 72c.; Colonies, Book II	80
Story of the Indians of New England. BURTON	67
Easy Experiments in Physics. SMITH	60
Revival of English Poetry in the Nineteenth Century. BUCKINGHAM	80
Sprache und Gesprach. LOESBERG-KOLBE	1 00
Gems of German Literature. LOESBERG	40
New Century Development Maps. Per Block 50	40
Nature Calendar. T. E. THOMPSON	36
Historical Outlines and Civil Government. CROMER	75
New Century Busy Work per box	15
Motor. Mental Education Boards. THOMPSON	50
Morse's Education System of Penmanship per dozen	60
The Morse Readers. BALLIET and POWERS. Book I, 28c.; Book II, 40c.; Book III, 50c.; Book IV, 67c.; Book V	67
New Century Readers. J. G. and T. E. THOMPSON. For Childhood Days, Book I, 28c.; Fairy Tale and Fable, Book II, 40c.; Nature, Myth and Story, Book III	52
Around the World. CARROLL. Book I, 40c.; Book II, 50c.; Book III	60
The Phonetic Reader. CHAS. W. DEANE	40
Morse Speller. S. T. DUTTON. Complete, 30c. In parts. Book I, 15c. Book II	20
Quincy Word List. F. E. PARLIN	24
Nature's Byways. N. W. FORD	40
Stories from the Poets. ATWATER	30
Far East and Far West Red Children.	28
Red Letter Days and Red Letter Facts.	60

BOOKS OF ALL PUBLISHERS

OUR stock of all the leading books, of all publishers, American and English, on **Medicine, Hygiene, Chemistry, Microscopy, Dentistry, Pharmacy, etc.**, is not only the largest, but the most complete in this country. It is classified by subjects, and we shall be pleased at any time to send you, free, complete details concerning any books on subjects allied to medicine you may be interested in. We are the only publishers of medical books in the country who render this sort of service, just as we are the only medical publishers who handle books other than our own publications.

P. Blakiston's Son & Co.

1012 Walnut Street, Philadelphia, Pa.

THE BAKER & TAYLOR CO.

SCHOOL BOOKS

AND ALL OTHER BOOKS

A perfectly developed system
A varied and complete stock
A record and an experience of eighty years
All make ours the best place at which to buy books

If CHEAPNESS, ACCURACY and DISPATCH count.

THE BAKER & TAYLOR CO., 33-37 E. 17th St., New York

Important Announcement

The following Standard Educational Works for Teaching French and other Languages, by

Dr. L. SAUVEUR

will hereafter be published by

WILLIAM R. JENKINS

851 and 853 Sixth Avenue, corner 48th Street, New York.

Publisher of the Bercy and other Series for teaching French and other Foreign Languages.

Introduction to the Teaching of Living Languages. 12mo, paper, 25 cents.
De l'Enseignement des Langues Vivantes. 12mo, paper, 25 cents.
Causeries avec les Enfants. 12mo, $1.00.
Petites Causeries. 12mo, $1.00.
La Parole Francaise. 12mo, $1.00.
Causeries avec mes Eleves. Illus., 12mo, $1.25.
Contes Merveilleux. 12mo, $1.50.
Fables de La Fontaine, avec notes. 12mo, $1.50.
Entretiens sur la Grammaire. 12mo, $1.50.
Petite Grammaire Francaise pour les Anglais. 12mo, $1.25.
Corrige des Exercises de la petite Grammaire Francaise. 12mo, paper, 50 cents.
Corrige des traductions des Causeries avec mes Eleves. 12mo, paper, 25 cents.
Corrige des Exercices et traductions des Petites Causeries. 12mo, paper, 15 cents.
Les Chansons de Beranger, avec notes et commentaires historiques. 12mo, $1.25.
Premieres Lecons de Grammaire Francaise By Marie-Louise Sauveur and Susan C. Lougee. 12mo, 75 cents.
Introduction to the Teaching of Ancient Languages. 12mo, paper, 25 cents.
The Vade Mecum of the Latinist. 12mo, p'r, 25c.
A Word for Word Rendering into English of C. Julius Cæsar Commentarii de Bello Gallico, Book I. 12mo, paper, 25 cents.
Talks with Cæsar de Bello Gallico. 12mo, $1.25

Complete Catalogue sent upon request.

Butler, Sheldon & Company

NEW YORK PHILADELPHIA CHICAGO BOSTON

PUBLISHERS OF

MORTON'S GEOGRAPHIES

THE PROGRESSIVE COURSE IN READING

WARREN'S NEW PHYSICAL GEOGRAPHY

REVISED EDITION

And of **many other text-books** of standard excellence

School officers and teachers should address the above-named firm before making changes in text-books. Correspondence is cordially invited.

STANDARD LITERATURE SERIES.

	Paper.	Cloth.
Alhambra (Irving), No. 4	$0.12½	$0.20
Black Beauty (Sewell), No. 31	20	30
Christmas Stories (Dickens), No. 5	12½	20
Courtship of Miles Standish, No. 47	20	30
David Copperfield's Childhood	20	30
Deerslayer (Cooper), No. 8	20	30
Dutchman's Fireside (Paulding), No. 44	12½	20
Enoch Arden, etc. (Tennyson), No. 6	12½	20
Evangeline (Longfellow), No. 21	12½	20
Fairy Tales (2d School Year), No. 30	12½	20
Five Great Authors, No. 42	20	30
Goldsmith, Gray, Burns and other Romantic Poets of the Eighteenth Century, No. 48	12½	20
Grandfather's Chair (Hawthorne)	20	30
Gulliver's Travels (Swift), No. 13	12½	20
Harold (Bulwer-Lytton), No. 12	20	30
Horseshoe Robinson (Kennedy), No. 10	20	30
Ivanhoe (Scott), No. 24	20	30
Julius Caesar (Shakespeare), No. 51	12½	20
Kenilworth (Scott), No. 7	20	30
Knickerbocker Stories (Irving), No. 23	12½	20
Lady of the Lake (Scott), No. 9	20	30
Last Days of Pompeii, No. 38	20	30
Last of the Mohicans (Cooper), No 29	20	30
Lay of the Last Minstrel (Scott), No. 40	12½	20
Little Nell (Dickens), No. 22	12½	20
Merchant of Venice (Shakespeare), No. 49	12½	20
Ninety-Three (Hugo), No. 18	20	30
Paul Dombey (Dickens), No. 14	12½	20
Peasant and the Prince, No. 41	20	30
Pilgrim's Progress (Bunyan), No. 30	12½	20
Pilot (Cooper), No. 2	20	30
Poems of Knightly Adventure, No. 26	20	30
Prisoner of Chillon, etc., No. 11	12½	20
Robinson Crusoe (Defoe), No. 25	12½	20
Rob Roy (Scott), No. 3	12½	20
Round the World in 80 Days, No. 34	20	30
Silas Marner (George Eliot), No. 43	20	30
Sketch-Book (Irving), No. 17	12½	20
Snow Image (Hawthorne), No. 20	12½	20
Song of Hiawatha (Longfellow), No. 37	20	30
Spy (Cooper), No. 1	12½	20
Swiss Family Robinson (Wyss), No. 35	12½	20
Tales of a Grandfather (Scott), No. 28	12½	20
Twice-Told Tales (Hawthorne), No. 15	12½	20
Two Years Before the Mast, No. 19	20	30
Vicar of Wakefield (Goldsmith), No. 45	20	30
Water-Witch (Cooper), No. 27	20	30
Waverly (Scott), No. 50	20	30
Westward-Ho! (Kingsley), No. 33	20	30
Wonder-Book (Hawthorne), No. 16	12½	20
Yemassee (Simms), No. 32	20	30

University Publishing Co.

27-29 W. 23d Street, NEW YORK.

STUDY AND PRACTICE OF FRENCH.

L. C. BONAME Author and Publisher,
258 South 16th Street, Philadelphia, Pa.

A carefully graded series for schools and colleges. Thorough drill in pronunciation and essentials of grammar. Practice in conversation and composition. *Part I.* (60 cents), *Part II.* (90 cents), for primary and intermediate grades. *Part III.* ($1.00), irregular verbs, idioms, composition, syntax, for advanced grades. *Part IV.* (35 cents), **Handbook of Pronunciation**, concise and comprehensive, for advanced grades.

A New and Enlarged Edition of

Webster's International Dictionary

of ENGLISH, Biography, Geography, Fiction, etc.

25,000 NEW WORDS, Etc.

Edited by W. T. HARRIS, Ph.D., LL.D.
United States Commissioner of Education.

New Plates throughout. Rich Bindings.
2364 Quarto Pages. 5000 Illustrations.

THE AUTHORITY IN ALL EDUCATIONAL WORK

Send for specimen pages, etc.

G. & C. Merriam Co., Springfield, Mass.

SCOTT, FORESMAN & CO.,

PUBLISHERS OF

High School and College Text-Books.

78-388 WABASH AVE., - Chicago, Ill.

Send for complete price-list.

¿Habla V. Español? Parlez-Vous Français? Sprechen Sie Deutsch? Parlate Italiano?

-IN TEN WEEKS-

You can at your own home, by the

MEISTERSCHAFT SYSTEM

Learn to speak fluently either **Spanish**, French, Italian, or German. Pupils taught as if actually in the presence of the teacher. Terms for membership, $5 00 for each language. All questions answered and all exercises corrected free of charge. Part I (3 **Lessons**), either language, sent on receipt of 25 cents.

MEISTERSCHAFT PUBLISHING CO., 212 Summer Street, Boston, Mass.

Books Published by CHARLES COLLINS,
AND FOR SALE BY
THE BAKER & TAYLOR CO.,
33 East 17th Street, - New York.

Abbott's Abercrombie's Intellectual Philosophy. Introduction price, 72c.; by mail, 80c.
Addick's Elementary French. 48c.; mail, 55c.
Coffin's Conic Sections. 6th edition. 8vo, $1.08; mail, $1 20.
Dymond's Moral Philosophy. 88c; mail, $1.00.
Olmsted's College Astronomy, Snell. $1 60; mail, $1.75.
Olmsted's College Philosophy, Sheldon. Fourth revised edition. $2.50; mail, $2.75.
Sheldon's Chapters on Electricity. Second edition. $1.00; mail, $1.20.
Underhill's New Table Book. Paper, dozen, 36c.; mail, 40c. Half board, dozen, 72c.; mail, 80c.
Whelpley's Compend of Universal History. $1.08; mail, $1.20.
Zachos' New American Speaker. $1.32; mail, $1.50.

The Berlitz Publications.

Methods, Grammars, etc., for Learning French, German, Spanish, Italian, Russian, etc.
Both for Schools and Self Instruction.
FRENCH COMEDIES AND NOVELS.
Send for complete catalogue and sample pages.
BERLITZ & CO, 1122 Broadway, New York

VAN EVEREN'S PAPER ADJUSTABLE BOOK COVERS. Simply made. Easy to apply. Cost little. No better made Samples on request. Order of your Jobber. P. F. VAN EVEREN, 60 Ann Street, New York.

Periodicals

from

England, Germany,

France and all other countries supplied by

E. Steiger & Co.,
25 Park Place, **New York.**

FOR THE LITERARY WORKER

The Annual Literary Index, 1901

Including Periodicals, American and English; Essays, Book-Chapters, etc.; with Author-Index Bibliographies, Necrology, and Index to Dates of Principal Events. Edited by W. I. FLETCHER and R. R. BOWKER, with the co-operation of members of the American Library Association and of the *Library Journal* staff.

THE ANNUAL LITERARY INDEX complements the "Annual American Catalogue" of books, published each year, by indexing (1) articles in periodicals published during the year of its issue; (2) essays and book-chapters in composite books; (3) authors of periodical articles and essays; (4) special bibliographies; (5) authors deceased; (6) dates of principal events during the year. The two volumes together make a comp ete record of the literary product of the year.

"Of great value to all who would keep advised of the topics and writers in the periodical literature of the day." —*Universalist Quarterly.*

"Good indexing could no further go."—*The Nation.*

One vol., cloth, $3.50, net.

ADDRESS THE **OFFICE OF THE PUBLISHERS' WEEKLY, (P. O. Box 943,) 298 Broadway, N. Y.**

BOOKS WANTED.

☞ ***In answering, please state edition, condition, and price, including postage or express charges.***

Houses that are willing to deal exclusively on a cash-on-delivery basis will find it to their advantage to put after their firm-name the word [Cash].

☞ ***Write your wants plainly and on one side of the sheet only. Illegibly-written "wants" will be considered as not having been received. The "Publishers' Weekly" does not hold itself responsible for errors.***

It should be understood that the appearance of advertisements in this column, or elsewhere in the "Publishers' Weekly" does not furnish a guarantee of credit. While it is endeavored to safeguard these columns by withdrawing the privilege of their use from advertisers who are not "good pay," booksellers should take the usual precaution, as to advertisers not known to them, that they would take in making sales to any unknown parties.

Arthur M. Allen, 508 Fulton St., Troy, N. Y.

Notes on Construction of Ordnance, v. 1, 2. Ordnance Dept. U. S. A.

Amee Bros., Cambridge, Mass. [*Cash.*]

Iliad, Way's trans.
Odyssey, Way's trans.

Amer. Bapt. Pub. Soc., 902 Olive St., St. Louis, Mo.

Broadus, Sermons and Addresses, state price and condition.

Americus Law Book Co., Americus, Ga.

Life of S. S. Prentiss, by Shields.
Cobb, Leisure Labors.
Early Mississippi items.

Antiquarian Book Concern, Omaha, Neb.

Bampton Lectures: The Personality and Office of the Comforter, by Heber; Prophecy a Preparation for Christ, by Smith; Atoning Work of Christ, by Thomson.

Bailey & Sackett, University Block, Syracuse, N. Y.

Greeley, American Conflict, 2 v.
Headley, History of the Rebellion.

The Baker & Taylor Co., 33 E. 17th St., N. Y.

Idylls of the King, Rhead illus., clean copy. Pub. by R. H. Russell.
Christian Experience and Ministerial Labor of Wm. Watters drawn up by himself. Pub. at Alexandria, 1806.

G. H. Barbour, 6016 Stanton Ave., Pittsburgh, Pa.

Anything pertaining to the Olmsted family.

N. J. Bartlett & Co., 28 Cornhill, Boston, Mass.

Jessup, The Women of the Arabs. Dodd, 1873.

Bigham & Smith, Agts., Dallas, Tex.

Dick, Theology, 1 v. ed.
Salvation by Faith Proven.

Bigham & Smith, Agts., Nashville, Tenn.

Defense of Human Liberty, by Jackson.

The Bowen-Merrill Co., Indianapolis, Ind.

Groesbeck, Incas: the Children of the Sun.
Taylor, Benj., Old Time Pictures and Sheaves of Rhyme.

Brentano's, Union Sq., N. Y.

Kipling, v. 12, Outward Bound, De Luxe ed., pub. at $10.00 per v.
Lectures on Real Presence. Pub. by O'Shea.
Yellow Wall Paper. Small, M. & Co.
Vale of Cedars. Pub. by Routledge.
Wood, Mildred Arkell.
Kidd, Control of Tropics. Macmillan.
Threads of Life, Rollins. Lamson, Wolfe.
A Burne-Jones Head, Rollins.
Her Picture. Roberts Bros.
Schussler's Therapeutics.
Confucian Analects.
Scharff, Creeds of Christendom, 3 v. Harper.
Robinson Crusoe, il. by Paget. Cassell & Co.
Bey, That Eurasian. Neely.
Leviticus, Joshua, and Ezekiel. Polychrome Bible, limp leather.
History of Colony of N. H., E. E. Atwater. New Haven, 1861.
Blessed Be Drudgery, Gannett. Pott.
Progress of S. Africa in the Century, Theal.
Ghost Bereft, etc., Barlow. Saxon & Co.
Hamlet, Romeo, Much Ado, and Henry VI., Temple ed., 1st eds.
McPherson, History of Reconstruction, 1865 to 1871.
Walcott Memorial.
Cassier's Magazine, v. 1.
Hardy, Spectre of the Real.
Boston Directories for 1796, 1803 and 1806.
Books on Albany previous to 1800.
Gogol, Taras Bulba, tr. by Curtin.
Major Jones' Courtship, Thompson, must be new. Appleton.
Mediæval London.
Morgan, Poppy Garden.
Popular American Dictionary. Belford, Clark & Co.
Hearn, Chinese Ghosts.
Livingston, Anecdotes of Alex. Hamilton.
Bing, Artistic Japan, pt. 10.
Dostoieffsky, Injury and Insult.
Kipling, Kim, Outward Bound ed.
Century Dict., 10 v., new ed., cheap, for rebinding.
Wilde, Oscar, Lady Windermere's Fan.
A good history of the Minturn House and Family.
Robin, Flight of Icarus, pap.
Hough, Thousand Islands. Davis, B. & Co., 1880.
Thebaud, Irish Race in the Past and Present. Sadlier, 1873.
Neilson, Economic Conditions of Manors of Ramsey Abbey.
Bernard Palissy, Works, 1880 ed.
Castle Builders. Appleton, 1854.
Creeds of All Nations.
Lacordaire, Easter Sermons.
History and Antiquities of Kilbourne Name and Family, Payne Kenyon Kilbourne. New Haven, Durrie & Peck, 1856.

Brentano's, 1015 Pennsylvania Ave., Washington, D. C.

Farr, W., Introd. to Analysis of Vital Statistics.
Howell, Conflicts Between Capital and Labor.
Gilbert's Plays, 3 v.
Sacred Books of the East, any or all.
Major in Washington, 2 v.
McPherson, Reconstruction.

S. E. Bridgman, 108 Main St., Northampton, Mass.

Jonathan Edwards' Works, v. 5 only, 1st American ed., 12°, leath. Worcester, 1808.
The Walkers of the Old Colony and Their Descendants.

The Brown, Eager & Hull Co., Toledo, O.

Letters of James Smeatham.

Buffalo Book Exchange, 50 Seneca St., Buffalo, N. Y.

Cliff Climbers of the Himalayas, an answer to The Plant Hunters of the Himalayas.

The Burrows Bros. Co., Cleveland, O.

James, The Cavalier.
Swiss Family Robinson, green cl., with map opposite p. 6.
Proceedings Grand Chapter R.A.M., O., 1862, 3 cop.
Proceedings Grand Chapter R.A.M., O., 1888, 1 copy.
Wheatley, How to Catalogue a Library.
Hollins, Hist. of the B. & O. R.R., 1853.
Scharf, Hist. of Delaware, 2 v.
Venn, Principles of Empirical Logic.
Berdoe, Browning's Message to His Own Times.

BOOKS WANTED.—Continued.

The Burrows Bros. Co.—*Continued.*

Berdoe, Essays on Poetry.
Tucker, Hist. of the U. S., 4 v.
Wisconsin Hist. Soc., v. 5.
Will the dealer who quoted the *Brooklyn Eagle* Daily Almanac, 1896, please reoffer.

Casino Book Co., 1374 Broadway, N. Y. [*Cash.*]

Booklover's Almanac. Duprat, 1896.
Wilde, Oscar, Woman of No Importance.
Wilde, Oscar, Lady Windermere's Fan.
American Book Prices Current, 1895, 1899.

Jno. J. Cass, 70 Wall St., N. Y.

Cooper, Darley plates, Precaution; Lionel Lincoln; Satanstoe; Miles Wallingford, hf. cf. or to bind.
Gamiani, any language.

A. H. Clapp, 32 Maiden Lane, Albany, N. Y.

Diana of the Crossways, Meredith, in original not revised ed. Roberts or Little, Brown.
Spencer's Essays and Comments.

The A. H. Clark Co., Garfield Bldg., Cleveland, O.

Brackenridge, Modern Chivalry.
Graydon's Memoirs.
Morton, New English Canaan.
Pitman, Mississippi, 1770.
Schoolcraft, Indians.

E. H. Clarke & Bro., 312 Main St., Memphis, Tenn.

1 copy each Kipling's First and Second Jungle Book, Swastika ed.

W. B. Clarke Co., Park and Tremont Sts., Boston, Mass.

Bailey, Cyclopedia of American Horticulture, v. 3.
English Life, T. C. Crawford. Frank E. Lovell & Co., 1888.
Cloister and the Hearth, 4 v., Dodd, Mead ed.
Forget-me-nots from Tennyson. Pub. by Dutton.

Henry T. Coates & Co., Phila., Pa.

Todhunter, Natural Philosophy for Beginners, in 2 pts.
Hoover, Enemies in the Rear.

Coe Bros., Springfield, Ill.

Statesman's Year Book, 1901.

Wm. G. Colesworthy, 66 Cornhill, Boston, Mass.

Townsend ed. of Cooper (Darley plates), Precaution; Last of the Mohicans; Home as Found; Mercedes of Castile; The Deerslayer; The Two Admirals; Afloat and Ashore; Miles Wallingford; Jack Tier; Oak Opening; The Ways of the Hour.

Irving S. Colwell, Auburn, N. Y.

Stoddard's Travel Lectures, 11 v.
Blackstone's Commentaries, cheap.

Cupples & Schoenhof, 128 Tremont St., Boston, Mass.

Lea, Inquisition of Spain, 3 v. Harper.
American Book Prices Current, v. 1-7.

Cushing & Co., 34 W. Baltimore St., Baltimore, Md.

Reynard the Fox, in English, any good ed. with il.

Damrell & Upham, 283 Washington St., Boston, Mass.

Anstey, On Narcotics.
American Architect, Sept., 1901.
Boston Directories, 1806 and 1810.
Two Hundred Years, A. Stevens.
Figaro, Feb., 1899.
Browning, v. 4, Smith-Elder ed.
Signers of Mayflower Compact, pt. 3.
New Illustrated Magazine, Sept., 1901; Jan., 1902.
Samuel, Birds of New England. Orange Judd Co.

E. Darrow & Co., Rochester, N. Y.

Autobiography of a Barrel of Bourbon.
Buckeye Plumbing Book.
Doolittle, Astronomy.

Chas. T. Dearing, 348 3d St., Louisville, Ky.

In God's Country, Higbee.

Edwin A. Denham, 28 W. 33d St., N. Y.

Lamb's Last Essays of Elia. Phila., 1828.
Elston Press, Notes on early woodcut books.

A. Deutschberger, 117 4th Ave., N. Y.

Kipling, v. 8, 13, 17, Outward Bound ed.

DeWolfe, Fiske & Co., 361 Washington St., Boston, Mass.

Operative Surgery, 2 v., J. D. Bryant.
American Family Physician, by John King. Indianapolis, 1864.
Astrophel and Stella, Sir P. Sidney.
White, Natural Hist. of Selborne.

Dives, Pomeroy & Stewart, Reading, Pa.

Brandes, G., Life of Beaconsfield. Scribner, $1.50.

Dodd, Mead & Co., 372 Fifth Ave., N. Y.

Parkman, Francis, Old Regime in Canada, 1874; Count Frontenac, 1877; Half Century of Conflict, 1892; Montcalm and Wolfe, 1884.
Whistler, The Gentle Art of Making Enemies, any ed.

Daniel Dunn, 677 Fulton St., Brooklyn, N. Y.

Prescott, Charles v. and Miscellanies, 8° ed.
Sci. Amer. Receipt Book, second-hand.
Hopkins, Experimental Science, second-hand.

E. P. Dutton & Co., 31 W. 23d St., N. Y.

Grapes of Wrath, by Norris.
Ruskin, v. 9. Wiley & Sons, 1885.
Pochelet, Engineering.

Peter Eckler, 35 Fulton St., N. Y.

Von Hartmann, Philosophy of the Unconscious, new.
Voltaire, Philosophical Dictionary.

C. P. Everitt, 219 5th Ave., N. Y.

Century Book of Names.
Century Atlas.
Symonds, Cellini, Nimmo ed.
Rochefoucauld's Works.
Superiority of the Anglo-Saxon Race.
Swigo Cornor's Health, printed in English.
Fitzgerald's Works, any good ed.

Harry Falkenau, 167 Madison St., Chicago, Ill.

Lossing's Field Book of the Revolution.
American Archives, set.
Hist. Sketches of Plymouth, Pa., by H. B. Wright.
Tucker, History of the U. S., v. 1.
Wood, Manual of Electricity, v. 2.

P. K. Foley, 36 Bromfield St., Boston, Mass.

Harte, Bret, 1st eds.
New York Clipper Annual, 1876-92, any year.
Poems of Places, 1876-79, any v.
Heraldic Journal, Bost., 1865-68, any nos.
Harbinger (Brook Farm Journal), any no.
Amer. Mag. of Useful Instruction, 1834-36, orig. wr.
The Collegian, Cambridge, 1830, nos. 1, 2, 3, or any.
Theatrical Censor, Phila., 1805-07, any nos.
The Present, N. Y., 1843-44, nos. 2, 7.
Boatswain's Whistle, Bost., 1864, any nos.
Spirit of the Fair, N. Y., 1864.
Boston Monthly Mag., 1825.
Young American's Mag., 1847, nos. 4, 5.
Harvardiana, Cambridge, 1835-38, any no.
Thespian Mirror, N. Y., 1805-06, any no.
The Club Room, Bost., 1820, any no.
Dramatic Mirror, Phila., 1841-2, any no.
Phalanx, N. Y., 1844-5, any no.
New England Review, Hartford, 1831, any no.
Thoreau, Early Spring. Bost., 1881, 1894.
Thoreau, Summer. Bost., 1884.
Thoreau, Winter. Bost., 1888.
Thoreau, Autumn. Bost., 1892.
Thoreau, Miscellanies; Letters; Excursions. 1894.

Garrett Books Shoppe (Garrett W. F. Blanchfield, Mgr.), 58 Ann St., Hartford, Conn.

Lyon, Colonial Furniture.
Trial of Mary Surratt.
Hayti, or, the Black Republic.
Platform Echoes, by John B. Gough.

J. F. Gepfert, 138 Superior St., Cleveland, O.

Columbiana Co., Ohio.
25 Avery, School Physics.
15 Channing, U. S. Hist.
25 Fiske, Civil Govt.
25 Gayley, Classic Myths.
10 Halleck, Literature, English.
15 each Kelsey, Cicero and Cæsar.
20 Fulton and Trueblood, Elocution.

Gotham Book Concern, 442 W. 50th St., N. Y.

The Californian, *Ballou Post*, *The Connoisseur* (Phila.), *The Philistine* (Cal.), *The Grasshopper* (Prov., R. I.), Atlantic Almanac.

The Grafton Press, 70 5th Ave., N. Y.

Atlantis Arisen. Pub. by J. B. Lippincott Co.

BOOKS WANTED.—Continued.

F. E. Grant, 23 W. 42d St., N. Y.

The Anglo-Saxon Race, by Sharon Turner.
O'Halloran's History of Ireland.
Aimwell Series (Juvenile books.)
Hammond, Jabez D., History of Political Parties in the State of New York.
Hazlitt, Life of Napoleon.
Inventions, Writings and Researches of Nicola Tesla, by Martin.
Hume, David, History of the Douglas and Angus Family. Printed about 1797.
Sandow, Physical Culture.
Modern English, by Fitz Edward Hall.
Kobbe, Gustav, New York.
Hymns for the Church on Earth.
Adventures on the Mosquito Coast.
Virgilius the Sorcerer, by David Nutt, 1893, frontispiece by A. Beardsley.
Lucian, True History, 4 or 5 drawings by Beardsley. Privately printed by Laurence & Bullen, 1894.
Earl Lavender, by John Davidson, frontispiece by Beardsley. Ward & Downey, 1895.
Pierrot's Library, cover by Beardsley. Lane, 1896.
An Evil Motherhood, by B. Ruding, frontispiece by Beardsley. Elkin, Mathews, 1896.
Lanier, Sidney, Tiger Lilies. Hurd & Houghton, 1857.
Lanier, Florida. J. B. Lippincott & Co., 1875.
Nystrom, Mechanics, by Wm. D. Marks, 19th, 20th or later ed.
Forty Years Familiar Letters of James W. Hamilton, D.D. Pub. 1860.
Mt. Vernon and Its Associations, by Benson J. Lossing.
Bacon, Reminiscences of Thos. Jefferson.
The Combatants.
The Revellers.
The Distant Hills.
The Dark River.
Englishman, Concordance of the Hebrew Testament, or Old Testament.
Adams Cable Codex, 9th ed., pap.
Complete Preacher, 3 v. Pub. by Funk & Wagnalls.

Martin I. J. Griffin, 2009 N. 12th St., Phila., Pa.

Lahontan's Voyages.
Margry, Decouvertes et Establissements.
Butterfield, Discovery of the Northwest by Jean Nicolet.
Blackbird, History of Ottawa Indians.
Works by John Gilmary Shea.

Wm. Beverley Harison, 65 E. 59th St., N. Y.

History of Ireland, unabridged, state condition, edition (date), and price.

Karl W. Hiersemann, Leipzig, Germany.

Fishback, American Law.
Walker, American Law, 10th ed.
Walker, Patent Laws.

Huston's Book Store, 386 Main St., Rockland, Me.

Cosmopolitan, Feb., Mar., Apr., 1892.

Iowa College Library, Grinnell, Ia.

Naumann, History of Music, original or trans.

Jennings & Pye, 57 Washington St., Chicago, Ill.

Clowes, Black America.
Justice and Jurisprudence. Pub. by Lippincott.
Mayo, A. D., Third Estate of the South. Pub. by Ellis, Boston.

E. T. Jett Book and News Co., 806 Olive St., St. Louis, Mo.

Senorita Marguerita.

E. W. Johnson, 2 E. 42d St., N. Y.

Edgar Poe and His Critics, Whitman.
Alpine Flowers, W. Robinson.
Inventions, etc., of Tesla, Martin.
Dowd, Memory Training.

F. H. Johnson, 15 Flatbush Ave., Brooklyn, N. Y.

Three Years in California, by Rev. Walter Colton. A. S. Barnes & Co., N. Y.

Jones' Book Store, 291 Alder St., Portland, Ore.

Olney, General Geometry, second-hand.
Cooper, Infidel Test Book.

Kimball Bros., 618 Broadway, Albany, N. Y.

Munsell's Annals of Albany, v. 5, 6.
Brodhead's Hist. of N. Y., v. 2.

Geo. Kleinteich, 397 Bedford Ave., Brooklyn, N. Y. [*Cash.*]

Works of Henry George, Memorial ed.
Ramsey's Poems.

Koelling & Klappenbach, 100 Randolph St., Chicago, Ill.

Ladies' Home Journal, 1900 to June, 1901, or 1900 and 1901 complete.

Chas. E. Lauriat Co., 301 Washington St., Boston, Mass.

Bancroft, History of the United States, 10 v. ed.
History of the Province of Mass. Bay, 3 v., by Hutchinson.

Leggat Bros., 81 Chambers St., N. Y.

Life and Public Services of Samuel J. Tilden, Cook. Appleton.

Henry E. Legler, Milwaukee, Wis. [*Cash.*]

Squibob Papers, by Phœnix.
Song of Milkanwatha, 3d ed. Albany, 1883.
Hee-haw-watha, a tale of the Oil Canadian Indians.

Lemcke & Buechner, 812 Broadway, N. Y.

Kenrick, Timothy, An Exposition of the Historical Writings of the New Test., 3 v. Boston, 1828.
Kendrick, Ariel, Sketches of the Life and Times of Elder Ariel Kendrick, 3d ed. Windsor, Vt., 1850.
Kenrick, John, Horrors of Slavery, 2 pts. Cambridge, Mass., 1817.
Kenrick, Wm., The New American Orchardist, 2d ed., Boston, 1835; or 3d ed., Boston, 1841.
Kenrick, Wm., Notes on Ogdensburg, etc. Boston, 1846.
Campbell, Practical Astronomy. Ann Arbor, 1892.

Edw. E. Levi, 820 Liberty St., Pittsburgh, Pa.

Kellner, Formulary.
Kossuth, Revolution Between Austria and Hungary.
Williams, The Harmony Society.
Penna. Archives, v. 1 of the 2d ser.
Bligh, Mutineers of the Bounty.

The Library of Congress, Washington, D. C.

Ede, G., Management of Steel. N. Y., Spon, 1901.
Lynch, James Daniel, The Bench and Bar of Miss. N. Y., E. J. Hale & Son, 1881.

The Literary Shop, 506 11th St, N. W., Washington, D. C.

Behind the Scenes, Elizabeth Keckly.
The Forum, v. 1.
Life and Times of Fred. Douglass, by himself.
History of Rebellion and Civil Wars in Ireland. Clarendon.

Little, Brown & Co., 254 Washington St., Boston, Mass.

Dole, Not Angels Quite. Lee & Shepard.
Macdonald, Marquis of Lossie. Lothrop.
Rollo's Journey to Cambridge, 1st ed., or any later ed.
Smith, Peace Pelican. Carleton.
4 copies The Tender Recollections of Irene MacGillicuddy. Harper.

C. D. Lyon, 20 Monroe St., Grand Rapids, Mich.

Deland, Florida Days.
Gibson, Heart of the White Mountains.
Crane, Claims of Decorative Art.

Lyon, Kymer & Palmer Co., Grand Rapids, Mich.

Greeley, The American Conflict.
Goodell, Slavery and Anti-Slavery.

Macauley Bros., 172 Woodward Ave., Detroit, Mich.

Art of Conversation, by Jas. G. Leland.
Proof Reading and Punctuation, Adelaide M. Smith.
Printing and Writing Materials, Adelaide M. Smith.
History of Peninsular War, 1807-1814, by W. F. P. Napier.

Estate of Henry Miller, 1 Barclay St., N. Y.

Salmon Fishing, Thaddeus. Pub. by W. H. Butler, 1865.

F. M. Morris, 171 E. Madison St., Chicago, Ill.

Gentleman's Magazine, Dec., 1877.

Frederick W. Morris, 114 5th Ave., N. Y.

Irving, Life of Washington. v. 1, G. Crayon ed., green cl.
Dunlap, History of the Arts of Design, v. 1. N. Y., 1834.
Bancroft, History of the U. S., v. 10, cl.
Stone, Life of Joseph Brant, v. 1. N. Y., 1838.

BOOKS WANTED.—Continued.

John Murphy, 243 Washington St., Brooklyn, N. Y.

Bankers' magazines, any or all before 1896 and some from '96 to present. Quote prices.

W. W. Nisbet, 12 S. Broadway, St. Louis, Mo.

Bird's-Eye View of Mississippi River, map.
Letters of Petronius.
Marriage and Divorce, Greeley and others.
Esmeralda.
Percy's Reliques.

H. H. Otis & Sons, 11 W. Swan St., Buffalo, N. Y.

Select Works of the British Poets, v. 1, 5, by Dr. Aiken, Philadelphia. Pub. in 1845 by Thomas Wardle, Phila., Pa.

C. C. Parker, 246 S. Broadway, Los Angeles, Cal. [*Cash.*]

Solitude of Nature and of Man, or, the Loneliness of Human Nature, Wm. Rounseville Alger.

E. R. Pelton, 19 E. 16th St., N. Y.

Virchow, Cellular Pathology, and any Virchow Monographs on same subject.

Pierce & Zahn, 633 17th St., Denver, Colo.

Chillingworth's Works, cheap.

The Pilgrim Press, 175 Wabash Ave., Chicago, Ill.

5 copies Ross, Church Kingdom. Cong. S. S. and Pub. Soc.
Dixon, Life of John Howard.

C. J. Price, 1004 Walnut St, Phila., Pa.

Comstock, Manual for the Study of Insects.
Denton, Butterflies and Moths of New England.
Fosbroke, British Monachism, 8°. London, 1825.
Barnard, 18 Character Sketches for Dickens, Photogravures. Gebbie & Co.
Darley plates to Dickens. Houghton, M. & Co.

Purdy's Book Store, 1009 Congress Ave., Houston, Tex.

Cooley's Blackstone, v. 1, 3d ed., shp. 1884.
Wendell's Blackstone, v. 1, 2, shp. 1854.

G. P. Putnam's Sons, 27 W. 23d St., N. Y.

Mason, Personal Traits of British Authors, 4 v.
Speeches of Curran, Grattan and Phillips.
Land of White Elephant, 3d or 4th ed.
Trollope's Autobiography.
Diplomat's Diary.
Vampires.
Essays in Anglo-Saxon.
Richmond During the War, by a Richmond Lady.
Howard, Fourteen Months in American Bastiles.
Abbott, Flatlands.
Peck Genealogy.

Geo. H. Richmond, 32 W. 33d St., N. Y.

Child of Pleasure.
Convention Episcopal Church. Phila., 1788-1789.
Grolier Club, Hawthorne.
Medallion.

Geo. H. Rigby, 1113 Arch St., Phila., Pa.

Wilson, Dict. of Astrology.
Pierce, On Astrology.

Robson & Adee, Schenectady, N. Y.

Warner Library.

Chas. M. Roe, 177 Wabash Ave., Chicago, Ill.

Social Spirit in America, by Henderson. Flood & V.

Philip Roeder, 616 Locust St., St. Louis, Mo.

Torrens, Transfer of Land.

Rohde & Haskins, 16 Cortlandt St., N. Y.

Seven Memorable Sieges of Rochefort, Viollet-le-Duc.
A Week in a French Country House, Fanny Kemble.
Hope Leslie.

E. H. Roller, 419 E. Water St., Milwaukee, Wis.

Pulpit Commentary New Testament.

Wm. B. Ropes, Mt. Vernon, Skagit Co., Wash.

Encyclopedia Britannica, with Amer. Ad., 1901 ed.
Hound of Baskervilles, Doyle.
Watson, Ind. 5th Reader, must contain story of Penn and Charles 2d. Barnes, 1881.

J. Francis Ruggles, Bronson, Mich.

Riley, Narrative of Loss of Brig "Commerce," and Sequel.
Thompson, The Doomed Chief and Gaut Gurley.
Beesley, Cataline, Clodius and Tiberius. Lond., 1878.
Any works in favor of atheism and against immortality.
Lewis, Algebra.

The St. Louis News Co., 1008 Locust St., St. Louis, Mo.

Lake Shore, by Emile Souvestre. Boston, 1855.

John E. Scopes, 29 Tweddle Bldg., Albany, N. Y.

American Ancestry, v. 9, 10.
Wilkinson, Memoirs, v. 2, and atlas. Phila., 1816.

Scrantom, Wetmore & Co., Rochester, N. Y.

Bibelot for May, June, Oct., Dec., 1901.
Miltiades, Peterkin Paul.
Delaborde, Engraving, Fine Art Lib.
Inman, Old Santa Fé Trail.
Hutson, Story of Language.
Tweedie, Mexico as I Saw It.

Charles Scribner's Sons, 153 5th Ave., N. Y.

Sandow, Physical Culture.
Whistler, Gentle Art of Making Enemies.
La Bruyere, Character, ed. by Van Laun. Nimmo, 1884.
Shorthouse, Sir Percival.

John V. Sheehan & Co. 160 Woodward Ave., Detroit, Mich.

Story of My Life, v. 1, 2, Augustus Hare.

J. C. Sickley, Poughkeepsie, N. Y.

Tyler, Baconian Philosophy.
Fischer, Bacon and His Times.
Radcliffe, Mystery of Udolpho.
Radcliffe, Romance of the Forest.
Wright, Domestic Manners in England.

Frank Simmons, Springfield, Ill.

2 copies Brackenridge, H. M., Recollections of Persons and Places in the West, 8vo. Phila., no date.

John Skinner, 44 N. Pearl St., Albany, N. Y.

Jones, History of N. Y. During the Revolution.

George D. Smith, 49 New St., N. Y.

Pitnam, Mississippi. 1770.
Pottery, by Beckworth.
Alex. Pushkin's Poems.
Charles Lamb's Letters, 2 v.
Dorland Genealogy.

Wm. T. Smith & Co., 145 Genesee St., Utica, N. Y.

Annals of Oneida County, N. Y.
Krehbiel, Notes on Choral Music.

A. H. Smythe, 43 S. High St., Columbus, O.

A Guide to the Knowledge of Life, by R. J. Mann. N. Y., 1859 or later.

Speyer & Peters, Berlin, N. W. 7, Germany.

Archiv für Mikroskop. Anatomie.
Archiv für Patholog. Anatomie. Virchow.
Archives of Laryngology.
Brain.
Engineering, v. 1.
Journal of Anatomy and Physiol., v. 1, 10, 32, 34.
Journal of Amer. Chem. Soc., 1889-1901.
Ophthalm. Soc. Transactions.
Transactions of Amer. Orthop. Association.
Please offer sets or single vols.
Annals of Surgery, sets.

E. Steiger & Co., 25 Park Place, N. Y. [*Cash.*]

Greely, American Weather. 1888.
Annunzio, Episcopo and Company. 1896.

The Stiefel Masonic Book Co., 106 E. 4th St., Cincinnati, O.

Findel, History of Freemasonry.
Dallaway, Historical Account of Master and Freemason.
Hope, Historical Essay on Architecture.

Thos. J. Taylor, Taunton, Mass.

Klein, Herman, Musical Notes (annual), 1887, 1888, 1889. London, Novello.

BOOKS WANTED.—Continued.

H. H. Timby, Conneaut, O.

Meredith, early eds.
Anything by or life of Lord John Somers, Sir Henry Wotton, John Thompson, Lord Haversham, Book Plates, or Portraits of.
English Dramatists, Pickering ed.
Wall Street, anything, fiction or history.

C. L. Traver, Trenton, N. J. [Cash.]

Brewer's Great Orations.
Chambers' Ency., v. 8, 9, 10, shp. Lippincott.
Mellick, Story of an Old Farm.

Otto Ulbrich, 386 Main St., Buffalo, N. Y.

Songs of Russian People, by Ralston.
Russian Folk Songs, by Ralston.
Music, Dec., 1898.
Plant Lore and Garden Craft of Shakespeare, by Canon Ellacombe. Pub. by Arnold.

Geo. E. Warner, Minneapolis, Minn.

History First Baptist Church. Chicago, 1889.
Cobb, N. B., Poetical Geography of North Carolina.
Any local history or biography.
Reynolds, J. Mason, Poems. 1882.

E. A. Werner, 35 Chestnut St., Albany, N. Y.

O'Callahan, Laws and Ordinances New Netherlands.
O'Callahan, History of New Netherlands, 2 v.
Railroad Investigation, 1879, 5 v.
Agassiz, Lake Superior.

Wesleyan University Library, Middletown, Conn.

Muther, History of Modern Painting, 3 v. Macmillan, 1896.
Modern Language Notes, v. 1-4, 6-8.
Publications of the Modern Language Association of America, v. 4.
Journal of Social Science, v. 29, 31.

Thomas Whittaker, 2 Bible House, N. Y.

Hubbard, On the Psalms.
Milman, Latin Christianity, v. 1. Boston, 1861.

Clarence E. Wolcott, Syracuse, N. Y.

Thomes, Life in the East Indies, cl. Lee & Shepard.
Wagner's Courage. Dodd, Mead & Co.

Woodward & Lothrop, Washington, D. C.

Seven Champions of Christendom. Pub. I. Blackwood, London, or any other.

BOOKS FOR SALE.

C. M. Barnes Co., Chicago, Ill.

The American Catalogue, 1876-84, subject index.
The American Catalogue, 1884-90.
The American Catalogue, 1890-95.
Submit offers. Good condition.

Hall N. Jackson, 36 W. 6th St., Cincinnati, O.

Century Dictionary, including Cyclopedia Names and Atlas, 8 v., royal 4°, hf. russia, fine copy. Cost $100.00 cash; will take $50.00.

SITUATIONS WANTED.

BOOKKEEPER, accountant and office manager. 20 years' experience, wholesale and manufacturing, desires position. Can adapt to any system or conditions. Excellent references. Salary no object so long as prospects are good. Address WILLSTAN, care of PUBLISHERS' WEEKLY.

WANTED.—A position as manager or assistant manager of a book publishing department. Understands the duties thoroughly; well acquainted with the book trade of U. S. An all round man. Salary according to worth. First-class references. Address KNOWLEDGE, care of PUBLISHERS' WEEKLY.

WANTED.—A young man, at present manager of a book department, and with ten years' experience in the book business, wishes to identify himself with an established book and stationery house, in which a business interest may be acquired, if his services are found satisfactory. Address RETAIL BOOKSELLER, care of PUBLISHERS' WEEKLY.

COPYRIGHT NOTICES.

LIBRARY OF CONGRESS.
OFFICE OF THE REGISTER OF COPYRIGHTS,
WASHINGTON, D. C.

Class A, XXc, No. 33494.—To wit: *Be it remembered*, That on the 7th day of May, 1902, The Robert Clarke Company, of Cincinnati, O., hath deposited in this office the title of a book, the title of which is in the following words, to wit: "Manual of Universal Church History. By Rev. Dr. John Alzog. Translated by F. J. Pabisch and Rt. Rev. Thomas S. Byrne. Volume I. Cincinnati, The Robert Clarke Company," the right whereof they claim as proprietors in conformity with the laws of the United States respecting copyrights.

(Signed) HERBERT PUTNAM, *Librarian of Congress*
By THORVALD SOLBERG, *Register of Copyrights.*
In renewal for 14 years from Sept. 12, 1902.

LIBRARY OF CONGRESS,
OFFICE OF THE REGISTER OF COPYRIGHTS,
WASHINGTON, D. C.

Class A, XXc, No. 35053.—To wit: *Be it remembered*, That on the 10th day of June, 1902, Mattie G. Browne, of Boston, Mass., hath deposited in this office the title of a book, the title of which is in the following words, to wit: "Massachusetts Reports, 109. Cases argued and determined in the Supreme Judicial Court of Massachusetts, November, 1871-March, 1872. Albert G. Browne, Jr. Boston, Houghton, Mifflin & Company," the right whereof she claims as proprietor in conformity with the laws of the United States respecting copyrights.

(Signed) HERBERT PUTNAM, *Librarian of Congress.*
By THORVALD SOLBERG, *Register of Copyrights.*
In renewal for 14 years from June 12, 1902.

SPECIAL NOTICES.

Bibliographic Publications.

For all American books as they appear, take THE PUBLISHERS' WEEKLY; for an hour's glance each month at the important books and magazine papers, take LITERARY NEWS; for library matters take THE LIBRARY JOURNAL; for magazine articles in general, consult THE ANNUAL LITERARY INDEX; for books in print or issued of late years, see THE AMERICAN and ANNUAL CATALOGUES.

THE PUBLISHERS' WEEKLY. Established in 1872, with which was incorporated the *American Literary Gazette and Publishers' Circular* (established in 1852.) Recognized as the representative of the publishing and bookselling interests in the United States. Contains full weekly record of American publications, with monthly cumulative indexes, etc. Subscription, $3.00 a year, postpaid; to foreign countries, postpaid, $4.00 a year; single numbers, 10 cents, postpaid.

THE LIBRARY JOURNAL. Official Organ of the American Library Association. Chiefly devoted to library economy and bibliography. Established in 1876. Published monthly. Subscription, $5.00 a year, postpaid; single numbers, 50 cents. Price to Europe, or other countries in the Union, 20s. a year; single numbers, 2s. (LITERARY NEWS *is sent free to subscribers of* THE LIBRARY JOURNAL.) Teachers may be interested in the "School Number" published in the spring of each year.

GENERAL INDEX TO THE LIBRARY JOURNAL, vols. 1–22, 1876–1897. Arranged to serve as an index to succeeding volumes or for other sources of professional information. 4°, in sheets, or paper binding, $2.50; A. L. A. half leather, $3.00.

LITERARY NEWS. A Monthly Journal of Current Literature. Contains the freshest news concerning books and authors; lists of new publications; reviews and critical comments; characteristic extracts; sketches and anecdotes of authors; bibliographical references; prominent topics of the magazines; portraits of authors, and illustrations from the newest books, etc., etc. Subscription, $1.00 a year, postpaid; single numbers, 10 cents.

THE AMERICAN CATALOGUE of books in print and for sale July 1, 1876, compiled under the direction of F. LEYPOLDT, and its supplements, 1876–84, 1884–90, 1890–95, and 1895–1900, compiled under the editorial direction of R. R. BOWKER, aims to present all the bibliographical features of the books in the American market, arranged in the first part alphabetically by both *authors* and *titles*, and in the second part alphabetically by *subjects*.

The Catalogue and its supplementary volumes form the only approximately complete guide in existence to the American books of the day, so arranged as to make reference easy from whatever direction the inquiry may come, whether from that of the author, or the title, or the subject. It not only furnishes the desired information about any particular book of which the consulter is in search, but shows what others there are by the same author or on the same subject in which he is interested. To the bookseller, therefore, it is valuable both in filling orders and in stimulating business; to the librarian, in supplying gaps and proportioning his collection; and to all who are practically concerned with books, in furnishing information which nowhere else is obtainable by so convenient a method, if obtainable at all.

The author-and-title volume of the 1876 volume is out of print. A limited number of the subject volume may be had in half leather binding at $15.

The volume covering the period 1876–84 is also out of print.

——, 1884–90, 4°, hf. mor., $25. (1 copy only remains.)
——, 1890–95, 4°, hf. mor., $15.
——, 1895–1900, 4°, hf. mor., $15.

THE ANNUAL AMERICAN CATALOGUE. Being the full titles, with descriptive notes, of all books recorded in THE PUBLISHERS' WEEKLY during the calendar year, with author, title, and subject index, publishers' annual lists and directory of publishers. Published annually since 1886. 8vo, sheets, *net*, $3.00; half morocco, $3.50.

THE PUBLISHERS' TRADE LIST ANNUAL. Contains: The latest catalogues of nearly 200 American publishers, contributed by themselves and arranged alphabetically by the firm-names and smaller lists at the end of the volume. These lists, all bound in one volume arranged alphabetically for ready reference, with marginal index, guiding the finger at once to the right letter, present in their combination so convenient and time-saving a working-tool as to make it indispensable to every one who has any interest in the purchase or sale of books. Large 8vo, with "Duplex Index," cloth, *net*, $2.00.

THE ANNUAL LITERARY INDEX, including Periodicals, American and English; Essays, Book-Chapters, etc., with Author-Index. Bibliographies, Necrology and Index to Dates of Principal Events, Edited, with the coöperation of members of the American Library Association and of *The Library Journal* staff, by W. I. FLETCHER and R. R. BOWKER. 8°, cloth, $3.50.

THE AMERICAN EDUCATIONAL CATALOGUE. Contains a price-list of all the text-books in use in the United States, arranged alphabetically by author's or editor's name, and a detailed subject-index, referring from each specific subject to authors of books on that subject. 8vo, leatherette, 50 cents.

THE ENGLISH CATALOGUE [Annual] giving full titles classified under author and subject in one strict alphabet, with particulars of the size, price, month of publication, and name of publisher of the books issued in Great Britain and Ireland, in the calendar year, being a continuation of the "London" and "British" Catalogues. [London: Sampson Low, Marston & Co.] 8vo, paper, *net*, $1.50. THE ENGLISH CATALOGUE and THE ANNUAL AMERICAN CATALOGUE bound in one volume, half leather, $5.00.

PUBLICATIONS OF SOCIETIES: a provisional list of the publications of American scientific, literary, and other societies from their organization. Compiled under the editorial direction of R. R. BOWKER. Schedules over 1100 societies issuing publications, and gives title-entries of all their publications, as far as data could be obtained from the societies and from libraries. 4°, paper, $2.50; cloth, $3.00.

STATE PUBLICATIONS: a provisional list of the official publications of the several States of the United States from their organization. Compiled under the editorial direction of R. R. BOWKER. Pt. 1: New England States—Maine, New Hampshire, Vermont, Massachusetts, Rhode Island, Connecticut. 4°, $2.00. (For complete work, $5.00.)

LIST OF AMERICAN PUBLISHERS, 1890–1895. The street address is given in nearly every case, and the abbreviation under which the firm's books are entered in the "American Catalogue," 1890–95. 4to, pap., $2.00.

UNITED STATES GOVERNMENT PUBLICATIONS. July 1, 1890 to June 30, 1895. Compiled, under the editorial direction of R. R. BOWKER, by J. H. HICKCOX. 60 pp., 4to, pap., $1.50.

THE SUNDAY-SCHOOL LIBRARY. By Rev. A. E. DUNNING. 16mo, cloth, 60 cents.

THE PROFESSION OF BOOKSELLING: a handbook of practical hints for the apprentice and bookseller. By A. GROWOLL, managing editor of THE PUBLISHERS' WEEKLY, and author of "A Bookseller's Library," "Book-trade Bibliography in the United States in the XIXth Century," etc. Pts. 1 and 2. 134 p. Large 8°, bds., each, $2.00. (*Concluding part in preparation.*)

Address the OFFICE OF THE PUBLISHERS' WEEKLY,

P. O. Box 943. **298 Broadway, New York.**

For 1902

PUBLISHERS' TRADE LIST ANNUAL

(Thirtieth Year)

In response to the desires of the book trade we shall publish the forthcoming issue of THE PUBLISHERS' TRADE LIST ANNUAL, to be ready at the opening of the active Fall season, in August, 1902,

With a Complete Index

to the publishers' catalogues contained therein. The books will be indexed by author, title and, practically, by subject or class. The name of series, the price, and name of publisher will also be given, so that any book contained in the ANNUAL may be located at once by whatsoever clue the user may have. The Index will be printed in two columns to the page, in readable type, full face letters being used to make reference to authors' names more convenient.

The bulk of the volume, as heretofore, will consist of the latest CATALOGUES OF 250 FIRMS PUBLISHING BOOKS IN THE UNITED STATES, contributed by themselves and arranged alphabetically by the firm names, with the smaller lists and advertisements of single books at the end. The patent "Duplex Index," having the alphabet printed on the concave surface as well as on the margin of the page, enables instantaneous reference to the catalogues and the lists, whether the book is open or shut.

These lists, thus bound together, present in their combination so convenient and time-saving a working tool as to have made THE TRADE LIST ANNUAL for upwards of a quarter of a century indispensable to every one who has any interest in the purchase or sale of books published in the United States. With the reference index to the books listed in the publishers' catalogues its practical usefulness will be enhanced an hundred fold.

The work will be offered to the trade in two styles :

With the Index, in 2 Volumes, bound in cloth, $5 00
Without the Index, in 1 Volume, bound in cloth, 1 50

if ordered and paid for in advance of publication. After publication day the price of the work with the index will be raised to $7.00, and of the work without the index to $2.00. Orders, stating whether the volume is desired with or without the index, should be registered at

The Office of THE PUBLISHERS' WEEKLY
(P. O. Box 943) 298 Broadway, New York

THE

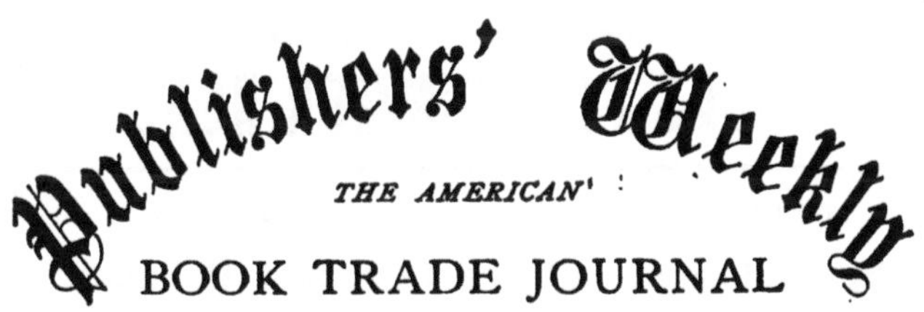

WITH WHICH IS INCORPORATED

The American Literary Gazette and Publishers' Circular.

[ESTABLISHED 1852.]

PUBLICATION OFFICE, 298 BROADWAY, NEW YORK.

Entered at the Post-Office at New York, N. Y., as second-class matter.

VOL. LXII., No. 5. NEW YORK, August 2, 1902. WHOLE No. 1592

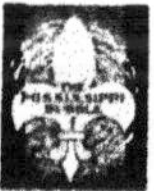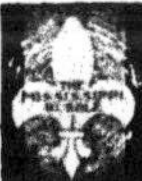

How
The Star of
Good Fortune
Rose and Set and
Rose Again, by a
Woman's Grace,
for one John Law
of Lauriston . . . .
THE
MISSISSIPPI
BUBBLE
A NOVEL
BY
EMERSON
HOUGH

A DOCUMENT IN EVIDENCE

TORONTO, July 19th, 1902.

THE BOWEN-MERRILL COMPANY, Indianapolis.

GENTLEMEN:—

Rush shipment two thousand more "MISSISSIPPI BUBBLE," and advise by wire when same will be shipped.

We have had a greater demand for this book up to the present date than any issue in Canada, considering the time since publication.

Very truly yours,

McLEOD & ALLEN.

The Most Popular Book in America and Canada

THE BOWEN-MERRILL COMPANY, Publishers

Ready in September

The Pharaoh and the Priest
An Historical Novel of Ancient Egypt
from the original Polish of Alexander Glovatski,
by Jeremiah Curtin, Translator of Quo Vadis, etc.

No novel of such interest and power as "The Pharaoh and the Priest" has been written about Egypt thus far.
In this book the Egyptian state stands before us as a mighty living organism.

ILLUSTRATED · 12MO · $1.50
LITTLE·BROWN·&·CO· Publishers Boston

Ready in September

THE QUEEN OF QUELPARTE

By ARCHER BUTLER HULBERT

A novel plot, striking incidents and stirring action make this romance of the Far East a remarkable story.

The scene is laid in Quelparte, Korea, shortly after the war between Japan and China. Russian intrigue, Chinese ingenuity and a love story in which a young American is the hero combine to make this

ONE OF THE POPULAR FALL NOVELS

12mo. Illustrated. $1.50

New and Popular Fiction—12mo, $1.50 each.

LAFITTE OF LOUISIANA

By MARY DEVEREUX, author of "From Kingdom to Colony" and "Up and Down the Sands of Gold," etc. Illustrated. *Second edition.*

THE HEROINE OF THE STRAIT

A Romance of Detroit in the Time of Pontiac. By MARY CATHERINE CROWLEY; author of "A Daughter of New France." Illustrated. *Ninth thousand.*

IN THE COUNTRY GOD FORGOT

A Story of To-Day. By FRANCES CHARLES. *Second edition.*

IN THE EAGLE'S TALON

A Romance of the Louisiana Purchase. By SHEPPARD STEVENS. Illustrated. *Second edition.*

THE GOD OF THINGS

A Novel of Modern Egypt. By FLORENCE BROOKS WHITEHOUSE. Illustrated. *Second edition.*

A GIRL OF VIRGINIA

A Love Story of the University. By LUCY MEACHAM THRUSTON, author of "Mistress Brent." Illustrated. *Second edition.*

A MAID OF BAR HARBOR

By HENRIETTA G. ROWE. Illustrated. *Second edition.*

THE ABOVE BOOKS ARE PUBLISHED BY

Little, Brown & Company, Boston

The Publishers' Weekly.

AUGUST 2, 1902.

INDEX TO ADVERTISERS

NOTES IN SEASON.

D. APPLETON & Co. will publish shortly "A Lady's Honor," a romantic historical novel of England in the seventeenth century, by a lady who hides her identity under the pseudonym of "Bass Blake."

LONGMANS, GREEN & Co. announce a new volume entitled "Historical Essays," by the late Bishop Stubbs, which comprises his introductions to the historical papers in the *Rolls Series*. They have also in preparation a work on Charles II.'s famous profligate courtier, entitled "Rochester and His Contemporaries," by the author of "The Life of Kenelm Digby.

THOMAS Y. CROWELL & Co. will publish shortly a volume by Mrs. Annie Russell Marble, entitled "Thoreau, His Home, Friends and Books," which will contain extracts from unpublished letters and journals of the Thoreau family and intimate friends, all of which will help to dispel the oft-repeated unsupported charges against the pioneer interpreter of nature-lore, of selfishness and inconsistency. The volume will contain a number of illustrations.

THE LOTHROP PUBLISHING COMPANY have just brought out a useful book entitled "Training for Citizenship," an elementary treatise on the rights and duties of citizens, "based on the relations which exist between organized society and its individual members, and between the individual members of organized society," by Joseph Warren Smith, formerly superintendent of schools of Bay City, Mich. They announce a new work by James Creelman, a patriotic love story, entitled "Eagle Blood." The illustrations are by Rose Cecil O'Neil, who was recently married to Mr. Wilson, the author of "The Spenders," and one time editor of *Puck*.

DODD, MEAD & Co. will publish shortly the authorized "Biography of Bret Harte," by T. Edgar Pemberton, who knew Bret Harte intimately for over twenty years and who has been in close touch with him for the last eleven years, collaborating in a work which it is believed Mr. Pemberton will complete. Mr. Harte's family have cordially offered to place all material at Mr. Pemberton's disposal; and, in fact, it was their desire that Mr. Pemberton should write his life. The biographer has also the same assurance from Bret Harte's intimate friends. Dodd, Mead & Co. will publish on August 28 Miss Marie Corelli's new novel, which she has named "Temporal Power: a study in supremacy." This is the first story Miss Corelli has written since "The Master Christian" was published, and promises to be as widely discussed a book as that novel.

J. B. LIPPINCOTT COMPANY have just ready "The Night Side of London," by Robert Machray, an interesting account of what takes place in London streets, theatres, clubs, dance halls and places of fashionable and Bohemian resort during gaslight hours, with illustrations by Tom Browne; "Mother and Child," a plain book of common-sense advice for the wife and mother, by Dr. Edward P. Davis, a well-known specialist, with twenty-one full-page illustrations; "Delhi" (1857), a story of the siege and of life in the city made famous by the Indian mutiny, drawn from the diary, letters and telegrams of Colonel Keith Young, edited by Sir Henry Norman, illustrated with photographs, colored plates and collotypes; also, "Trades Waste," an exhaustive and up-to-date consideration of the utilization of mill refuse and the prevention of river pollution, designed for manufacturers, engineers, analysts and inspectors, and elaborately illustrated with folding diagrams, full-page plates, etc.

WEEKLY RECORD OF NEW PUBLICATIONS.

☞ Beginning with the issue of July 5, 1902, the titles of *net* books published under the rules of the American Publishers' Association are preceded by a double asterisk **, and the word net follows the price. The titles of *fiction* (not net) published under the rules are preceded by a dagger †. *Net* books not covered by the rules, whether published by members of the American Publishers' Association or not, are preceded by a single asterisk, and the word net follows the price. ☜

The abbreviations are usually self-explanatory. c. after the date indicates that the book is copyrighted; if the copyright date differs from the imprint date, the year of copyright is added. Books of foreign origin of which the edition (annotated, illustrated, etc.) is entered as copyright, are marked c. ed.; translations, c. tr.; n. p., in place of price, indicates that the publisher makes no price, either net or retail, and quotes prices to the trade only upon application.

A colon after initial designates the most usual given name, as: A: Augustus; B: Benjamin; C: Charles: D: David; E: Edward; F: Frederic; G: George; H: Henry; I: Isaac; J: John; L: Louis; N: Nicholas; P: Peter; R: Richard; S: Samuel; T: Thomas; W: William.

Sizes are designated as follows: F. (folio: over 30 centimeters high); Q. (4to: under 30 cm.); O. (8vo: 25 cm.); D. (12mo: 20 cm.); S. (16mo: 17½ cm.); T. (24mo: 15 cm.); Tt. (32mo: 12½ cm.); Fe. 48mo: 10 cm.). Sq., obl., nar., designate square, oblong, narrow books of these heights.

Achilles Tatius. Leucippe and Clitophon; il. by M. Méaulle. Phil., printed for subscribers only by G. Barrie & Son, [1902.] c. 16+844 p. 8°, (Antique gems from the Greek and Latin, v. 7.) cl. (Apply to pubs. for price.)
Greek and English on opposite pages. "Bibliographical note," p. 839-943.

Adams, C: Francis. The life and sermons of Rev. T. De Witt Talmage. Chic., M. A. Donohue & Co., [1902.] c. 500 p. il. 12°, cl., $1.25.

Allen, J: Harden. Judah's sceptre and Joseph's birthright; or, the royal family and the many nations of Israel. Portland, Ore., J: Harden Allen, [1902.] c. 377 p. map, il. 12°, cl., $1.50.

American and English encyclopædia of law; ed. by D: S. Garland and Lucius P. McGehee, under the supervision of Ja. Cockcroft. 2d ed. v. 21, (Municipal courts to Partition.) Northport, N.Y., E: Thompson Co., 1902. c. 8+1291 p. O. shp., $7.50.

Anacreon. Odes; translations by Bourne, Fawkes, Moore, and others; with il. by P. Avril. Phil., printed for subscribers only by G. Barrie & Son, [1902.] c. 18+201 p. 8°, (Antique gems from the Greek and Latin, v. 8.) cl. (Apply to pubs for price.)
Greek and English on opposite pages. "Bibliographical note," p. 181-199.

****Atwater,** Emily Paret. How Sammy went to coral-land. Phil., G: W. Jacobs & Co., [1902.] [Jl.] c. 7-112 p. il. D. cl., 40 c. net.
"Sammy" is the diminutive for a handsome salmon, whose adventures are told by a grandmother, who wishes to convey some lessons in natural history to her grandchildren while they are summering at the seaside.

Baldwin, Ja. Mark. Development and evolution; including psychophysical evolution, evolution by orthoplasy, and the theory of genetic modes. N. Y., Macmillan, 1902. [Jl.] c. 16+395 p. 8°, cl., $2.60 net.

Banks, C: Eugene, *and* Cook, G: C. Authorized and authentic life and works of T. De Witt Talmage, assisted by Marshall Everett. Chic., The Bible House, 1902. c. 479 p. il. por. 12°, cl., $1.75.

****Bartholomew's** physical atlas. v. 1, Meteorology, by Alex. Buchan. Phil., Lippincott, 1902. maps, f°, hf. mor., $17.50 net.

Berrier, Leroy. The new life. Davenport, Ia., Leroy Berrier, [1902.] c. 2+126 p. D. cl., $1.
According to an explanatory note printed on the title-page: "This book deals with the principles and laws which open unto man the floodgates of infinite creative power and put him into conscious possession of his birthright—the mastery over all things."

Bible. The Holy Bible containing the Old and New Testaments; tr. out of the original tongues: being the version set forth A.D. 1611; compared with the most ancient authorities and revised A.D. 1881-1885; newly ed. by the American Revision Committee. Standard ed. N. Y., T: Nelson & Sons, [1902.] c. maps, O. leath., $1-$7.
A smaller edition of the American Standard Edition of the Revised Bible, set in bourgeois type.

Blackwood, Alexander Leslie. Diseases of the lungs. Chic., Halsey Bros. Co., 1902. c. 9+338 p. il. 12°, cl., $2.

***Blanden,** C: G. A drift of song: [poems.] Evanston, Ill., W: S. Lord, 1902. [Je.] c. 6-60 p. sq. S. bds., 50 c. net.

Blashfield, De Witt C. A treatise on instructions to juries in civil and criminal cases, including province of court on jury. St. Paul, Keefe-Davidson Co., 1902. c. 27+1068 p. O. shp., $6.

Blatchford, Rob., ["Nunquam," *pseud.*] Britain for the British. Chic., C: H. Kerr & Co., [1902.] c. 5+177 p. D. cl., 50 c.; pap., 25 c.
"The purpose of this book," says the author, "is to convert the reader to socialism; to convince him that the present system—political, industrial and social—is bad; to explain to him why it is bad, and to prove to him that socialism is the only true remedy." The author is the editor of *The Clarion* published in London.

***Brink,** B: Myer. The early history of Saugerties; inscribed to the Saugerties Chapter, Daughters of American Revolution. Kingston, N. Y., R. W. Anderson & Son, 1902. c. 365+12 p. il. 12°, cl., $1.50 net.

****Brontë,** Charlotte, [*Mrs.* Nicholls; "Currer Bell," *pseud.*] Jane Eyre; to which is added "The Moores," an unpublished fragment, by Charlotte Brontë; with an introd. by W. Robertson Nicoll. N. Y., Dodd, Mead & Co., 1902. 12°, cl., $1.60 net.

Brown, Allan L. True marriage guide; or, talks on nature. Chic., Westminster Publishing Co., 1901 [1902.] c. 154 p. il. 12°, cl., 55 c.; pap., 35 c.

Brown, C: Carroll, *ed.* Directory of American cement industries and handbook for cement users. 2d ed., rev. and enl. Indianapolis, Ind., and N. Y., Municipal Engineering Co., 1902. c. cl., $5.

Brown, Grace M., ["Ione," *pseud.*] Food studies. Denver, Reed Publishing Co., 1902. c. 101 p. sq. T. pap., 50 c.

Burne, C. With the Naval Brigade in Natal, 1899-1900: journal of active service kept during the Relief of Ladysmith and subsequent operations in Northern Natal and the Transvaal under General Sir Redvers Buller. [N. Y., Longmans, Green & Co.,] 1902. 9+156 p. il. map, O. cl., $2.50.

Case, Nelson. European constitutional history; or, the origin and development of the governments of modern Europe, from the fall of the western Roman Empire to the close of the nineteenth century. Cin., O., Jennings & Pye, [1902.] c. 8+421 p. O. cl., $1.50.

Chambers's concise gazetteer; topographical, statistical and historical. New ed. Phil., Lippincott, 1902. 8°, hf. leath., $2.

Childe, Cromwell. Water exploring: a guide to pleasant steamboat trips everywhere: journeys of a morning or an afternoon; tours of a day to a week, Sound, Hudson, seacoast and inland rivers, north, south, east, and west. Brooklyn, N. Y., Office of the *Brooklyn Daily Eagle*, 1902. c. 112 p. S. (Eagle lib., v. 17, no. 69.) pap., 10 c.

****Clark,** Solomon H:, *ed.* Handbook of best readings; selected and ed. by S. H: Clark. N. Y., Scribner, 1902. c. 27+561 p. D. cl., $1.50 net.
Prose and poetical selections intended for public reading. Only selections which have a fair claim to literary merit and those that are adapted for reading aloud have been included.

Clark, W: L., *jr.* Hand-book of criminal law. 2d ed., by Francis B. Tiffany. St. Paul, West Pub. Co., 1902. c. 12+517 p. O. (The Hornbook ser., no. 2.) shp., $3.75.

Clough, Emma Rauschenbusch. John E. Clough, missionary to the Telugus of South India: a sketch. Bost., American Baptist Missionary Union, 1902. c. 28 p. por. S. (Biographical ser.) pap., 10 c.

Culp, H: Travis. Reuben Green's experience in a large city. Conneaut, O., H: T. Culp, [1902.] c. 80 p. il. por. 16°, pap., 25 c.

****Davis,** E: P., *M.D.* Mother and child. Phil., Lippincott, 1902. il. 12°, cl., $1.50 net.

Dawes, *Mrs.* S. E. Stories of our country. v. 1 and 2. Bost., Educational Publishing Co., [1902.] c. 1901. 190; 208 p. sq. S. cl., ea., 40 c.
Contents: v. 1, Story of the Norsemen; The story of Pocahontas; Story of the pilgrims; The Boston tea party; The liberty bell; Lexington and Concord. v. 2, The Revolution; Stories of our country; Battle of Long Island; Saratoga and Valley Forge; Closing battles of the Revolution; How the United States became a nation; Story of the blue jackets.

Dawson, J: Ja. The voice of the boy: a new conception of its nature and needs in development and use, and of its relation to the adult male voice. N. Y., E. L. Kellogg & Co., [1902.] c. 44 p. 12°, pap., 25 c.

Defoe, Dan. Robinson Crusoe; with notes; for the use of schools; il. by Gordon Browne. Bost., Educational Pub. Co., [1902.] 3-192 p. il. map, D. cl., 60 c.; bds., 40 c.
Extracts from the text of the original edition of 1719, with biographic sketch of Defoe and a glossary of the more difficult words.

De Witt, F: M. De Witt's guide to central California; an illustrated and descriptive hand-book for tourists and strangers. San Francisco, F. M. De Witt, [1902.] c. 180 p. 16°, map, plans, bds., 50 c.

***Early** English printed books in the University Library, Cambridge, (1475-1640.) v. 2, E. Mattes to R. Mariot and English provincial presses. N. Y., Macmillan, 1902. 18+633-1312 p. 8°, (Cambridge Univ. Press ser.) cl., $5 net.

Fernald, Ja. C., *ed.* The concise standard dictionary of the English language; designed to give the orthography, pronunciation and meaning of about 28,000 words and phrases in the speech and literature of the English-speaking peoples; abridged from "Funk & Wagnalls' standard dictionary of the English language." N. Y., Funk & Wagnalls Co., 1902. c. 4+478 p. S. cl., 60 c.
The Appendix contains simple Rules for Spelling; a pronouncing list of Proper Names, historical, geographical, etc.; Foreign Words and Phrases current in literature with their meanings in English; tables of Weights and Measures (including the Metric System); tables of Current Coinage; Symbolic Flowers and Gems with characteristic sentiments; a list of Abbreviations commonly used, etc.

***Ferry,** I. I. Fonografia española; systema el más simple, más fácil y más moderno para adquirir la más grande velocidad, conservando al mismo tiempo toda claridad al escribir las palabras de viva voz. Revisado por el Don Luis Duque. San Francisco, Whitaker & Ray Co., 1902. c. '98. 66 p. 16°, cl., $1 net.

Fields, Elizabeth. Freedom in marriage. N. Y., Abbey Press, [1902.] c. 56 p. D. cl., 50 c.
The author treats the subject under the following heads: Origin of the marriage custom; Marriage today; Causes for inadequacy of marriage; The remedy which the author thinks lies in greater freedom in the divorce laws.

Fiske, G. B. Poultry appliances. N. Y., Orange Judd Co., 1902. [Agr.] c. 125 p. 12°, cl., 50 c.

Fiske, G. B. Poultry architecture. N. Y., Orange Judd Co., 1902. [Agr.] c. 125 p. 12°, cl., 50 c.

Fowke, Gerard. Archæological history of Ohio: the mound builders and later Indians. Columbus, O., published by the Ohio State Archæological and Historical Society, [for sale by A. H. Smythe,] 1902. c. 16+760 p. il. O. cl., $5.
Written for those desiring to increase their knowledge of archæology, but who have not time for ex-

tensive study. The explorations recorded were made by Mr. Fowke at the instance of the Ohio Archæological and Historical Society. Mr. Fowke has conducted explorations for the National Bureau of Ethnology and for the American Museum of Natural History and is a well-known contributor to ethnological magazines.

Fox, G: H:, *M.D.* A practical treatise on smallpox. Phil., Lippincott, 1902. col. pls., 8°, cl., $3.

Gardner, J: M. American negligence reports, current ser. [cited Am. neg. rep.;] all the current negligence cases decided in the federal courts of the U. S., the courts of last resort of all the states and territories and selections from the intermediate courts, together with notes of Eng. cases and annotations. v. 11. N. Y., Remick & Schilling, 1902. c. 36+739 p. O. shp., $5.50.

***Gauss.** Karl Friedrich. General investigations of curved surfaces of 1827 and 1825; tr. with notes and a bibliography by James Caddall Morehead and Adam Miller Hiltebeitel. [Princeton,] N. J., Princeton University Library, 1902. c. 6+126 p. Q. cl., $1.75 net.
Bibliography (10 p.). This is limited to books, memoirs, etc., which use Gauss's method and which treat, more or less generally, one or more of the following subjects: curvilinear coordinates, geodesic and isometric lines, curvature of surfaces, deformation of surfaces, orthogonal systems, and the general theory of surfaces.

Georgia. *Supreme ct.* Reports of cases at the Oct. term, 1901, and Mar. term, 1902. v. 114. Stevens and Graham, reps. Atlanta, Georgia State Library, 1902. c. 32+1108 p. O. shp., $5.

****Gordy,** J. P. Political history of the United States; with special reference to the growth of political parties. In 4 v. v. 2. 2d ed., rev. N. Y., H: Holt & Co., 1902. c. 8+581 p. D. cl., $1.75 net.
"In working over this volume the author has arrived at two important conclusions: that unwise financial legislation was primarily responsible for the dangerous position of the country at the close of the War of 1812, and that the public opinion of the North with reference to the negro prior to 1830 differed but little from that of the South; the greater readiness to free him in the former section having been due to the fact that if freed he would live at the South. To give the facts that led to these conclusions their proper setting necessitated a recasting of the entire book."—*Preface.*

Gospel primer (The). 45th ed. Nashville, Tenn., Southern Publishing House, 1901. c. '95. 128 p. D. bds., 25 c.

Gottsberger, Francis. Accountant's guide for executors, administrators, assignees, receivers and trustees. N. Y., G: G. Peck, [1902.] c. 196 p. Q. cl., $5.

Gwinn, D. Howard. Gold of Ophir: [a novel.] N. Y., Abbey Press, [1902.] c. 5+335 p. 12°, cl., $1.

Haines, G: Ancestry of the Haines, Sharp, Collins, Wills, Gardiner, Prickitt, Eves, Evans, Moore, Troth, Borton and Engle families; comp. from notes of the late G: Haines, M.D.; with some additions by the comp., R: Haines. Medford, N. J., Richard Haines, 1902. c. 456 p. pl. por. facsimile, 8°, cl., $3.

***Hammond,** Eleanor Prescott. On the text of Chaucer's Parlement of Foules. Chic., University of Chicago Press, 1902. [Ap10.] c. 25 p. Q. (Decennial publications, reprints.) pap., 50 c. net.
Reprinted from v. 7 "Decennial publications."

Handy book of synonyms. New ed. Phil., Lippincott, 1902. 8°, limp cl., 50 c.

Hannan, W. I. The textile fibres of commerce: handbook on the preparation and use of the animal, vegetable and mineral fibres used in cotton, woollen, paper, silk, brush and hat manufactures. Phil., Lippincott, 1902. 8°, cl., $3.

Harris, W. H. Law governing the issuing, transfer and collection of municipal bonds. Cin., W. H. Anderson Co., 1902. c. 20+357 p. O. shp., $4.

***Hart,** Albert Bushnell, *and* Hazard, Blanche E. Source readers in American history. no. 1, Colonial children; selected and annotated by Albert Bushnell Hart; with the collaboration of Blanche E. Hazard. N. Y., Macmillan, 1902. c. 17+233 p. 12°, cl., 40 c. net.

Hatton, Jos. A vision of beauty: a novel. N. Y., A. L. Burt Co., [1902.] c. 312 p. 1 il. 12°, (The Manhattan library of new copyright fiction.) pap., 50 c.

Hawkins, *Mrs.* May Anderson. A wee lassie; or, a unique republic. Richmond, Va., Presbyterian Committee of Publication, [1902.] c. 2-277 p. il. D. cl., $1.
Many incidents in the story, according to the preface, are based on real experiences. The story is written, principally, to interest the reader in Christian work among the convicts.

†**Hector,** *Mrs.* Annie French, ["*Mrs.* Alexander," *pseud.*] Stronger than love. N. Y., Brentano's, 1902. c. 3+364 p. D. cl., $1.50.
London is the scene of the story. Monica Deering, who was adopted by Katharine Leigh, a kinswoman, meets and loves a man who reciprocates her feelings; but her consideration for the kinswoman to whom she owes so much leads her to sacrifice her own happiness.

Herbert, G: B. Herbert's illustrated history of the civil war in America; a complete narrative of events, military, naval, political and congressional, that occurred during the war for the Union, with full information as to the causes which brought on the rebellion. Springfield, O., Crowell & Kirkpatrick Co., [1901.] c. 20+413 p. il. 12° (Farm and fireside lib., no. 197.) pap., 25 c.

****Hewitt,** Emma Churchman. The three little Denvers: [a story for young people.] Phil., G: W. Jacobs & Co., [1902.] c. 2-106 p. 1 il. D. cl., 40 c. net.

High, Edwin W. History of the Sixty-eighth Regiment, Indiana Volunteer Infantry, 1862-1865, with a sketch of E. A. King's brigade, Reynolds' division, Thomas' corps, in the battle of Chickamauga; published by request of the Sixty-eighth Indiana Infantry Association, 1902. [Metamora, Ind.,] Edwin W. High, 1902. 520 p. il. por. 8°, cl., $2.25; hf. mor., $3.50.

Hill, Leonard Erskine. Physiology for beginners. [N. Y., Longmans, Green & Co., 1902.] 8+124 p. D. cl., 35 c.

***Hiorns**, Arthur H. Metallography: an introduction to the study of the structure of metals, chiefly by the aid of the microscope. N. Y., Macmillan, 1902. 14+158 p. il. 12°, cl., $1.40 net.

Hogan, J: Caryl. Our new heraldry. Seattle, Wash., Lowman & Hanford, [1902.] c. 208 p. 12°, cl., $1.

Holmes, Oliver Wendell. The professor at the breakfast table. N. Y., A. L. Burt Co., 1902. 356 p. 12°, (Home lib.) cl., $1.

Holmes, T: Pictures and problems from London police courts. Popular ed. [N. Y., Longmans, Green & Co., 1902. 8+224 p. D. cl., $1.25.

Hood, G. Durant. Dr. Hood's plain talks about the human system—the habits of men and women—the causes and prevention of disease—our sexual relations and social natures—embracing "Common sense medical adviser." Chic., Hood Medical Book Co., [1902.] c. 1080 p. il. col. pl. 8°, cl., $5.

Hood, G. Durant. Practical family physician: a complete treatise on the human system; embracing "Common sense medical adviser." Chic., Hood Medical Book Co., [1901.] c. 1072 p. il. 8°, cl., $2.50.
Also issued under title "Dr. Hood's plain talks about the human system. *See* above.

Howard, Hamilton Gay. Howard's law points to know: a popular treatise, consisting of eight lectures on elementary law. Detroit, Mich., Howard Hamilton Gay, 1902. c. 98 p. por. 16°, leatherette, $1.

***Hutchinson**, Horace G. A friend of Nelson. N. Y., Longmans, Green & Co., 1902. 3+299 p. D. cl., $1.50 net.

Illinois. An index-digest of the reports, including all the supreme court reports to v. 190, inclusive, and all of the appellate court reports to v. 95, inclusive. In 2 v. v. 1. Chic., T. H. Flood & Co., 1902. c. 1076 p. O. shp., $18.

Illinois. *Supreme ct.* Reports of cases. v. 194. cont. cases in which opinions were filed in Dec., 1901, and Feb., 1902, and cases in which rehearings were denied at the Feb. term, 1902; I: Newton Phillips, rep. Springfield, I: Newton Phillips, 1902. c. 703 p. O. shp., $2.25.

Ingelow, Jean. Wonder-box tales; il. by Diantha W. Horne. Bost., D. Estes & Co., [1902.] c. 97 p. 1 il. 12°, (The young of heart ser., no. 35.) cl., 35 c.

Jarvis, Lucy Cushing, *ed.* Sketches of church life in colonial Connecticut: being the story of the transplanting of the Church of England into forty-two parishes of Connecticut, with the assistance of the Society for the Propagation of the Gospel; written by members of the parishes in celebration of the 200th anniversary of the society. New Haven, Ct., The Tuttle, Morehouse & Taylor Co., 1902. 188 p. por. 12°, cl., $1.

Jenkins, C: Francis. The guide book to historic Germantown; prepared for the Site and Relic Society. Germantown, Pa., Site and Relic Society, 1902. 170 p. il. map, 12°, cl., 50 c.
Contains a bibliography.

Jenkins's vest-pocket lexicon. New ed. Phil., Lippincott, 1902. 16°, limp leath., 60 c.; limp leath., with tuck, 75 c.

†**Johnston**, Annie Fellows. Cicely and other stories; il. by Sears Gallagher and others. Bost., L. C. Page & Co., 1903, [1902.] [My.] c. 137 p. D. (Cosy corner ser.) cl., 50 c.
Contents: Cicely; Alida's homeliness; The hand of Douglas; Elsie's "palmistry evening"; Their ancestral latch-string.

Jones, S: I: Mathematical puzzles: a collection of the most amusing properties of numbers, and many of the most difficult mathematical problems with their answers. Denton, Tex., News Print, [1902.] c. 76 p. il. diagrams, 16°, pap., 25 c.

Kansas. *Supreme ct.* Reports of cases; rep., T: Emmet Dewey. v. 62, June 9, 1900-Apr. 6, 1901. Topeka, W. Y. Morgan, st. pr., 1901. c. 1902. 26+972 p. O. shp., $3.50.

Karr, H: Seton-. The call to arms, 1900-1901; or, a review of the imperial yeomanry movement and some subjects connected therewith. N. Y., Longmans, Green & Co., 1902. 18+329 p. il. D. cl., $2.

Keary, C: F. The brothers: a fairy masque. N. Y., Longmans, Green & Co., 1902. 9+147 p. D. cl., $1.50.
A fantasy. The two brothers who figure therein were originally characters in a sort of fairy opera, which the author began in collaboration with F. Delius. Nothing of that slight original sketch, according to the author, is included excepting the names of the brothers, Niels and Irmelin.

†**Kennard**, *Mrs.* Mary E., [*Mrs.* E: Kennard.] The golf lunatic and his cycling wife. N. Y., Brentano's, 1902. 8+341 p. D. cl., $1.50.
An English wife who is extremely fond of cycling, discovers that her husband has developed as strong a liking for golf. The cycling wife describes some amusing incidents in both their lives which were brought about through an over-indulgence in their favorite sports and by the "golf lunatic's" susceptibility to the fair sex.

King C: A conquering corps badge, and other stories of the Philippines; il. by Alida Goodwin, B. Martin Justice, and Stuart Travis. Milwaukee, Wis., L. A. Rhodes & Co., 1902. c. 1901. 6+309 p. D. cl., $1.25.
Contents: A conquering corps badge; Jack Royal; Dovecote days; A rival ally; The senator's plight; The luck of the horseshoe; A camera capture; The fate of Guadalupe; The manila wire; Betrayed by a button; Biography of General C. King, by Forrest Crissey from *Ainslee's Magazine.*

***Kingsley**, C: Life and works of Charles Kingsley. Ed. de luxe. In 19 v. v. 10, Hypatia; or, new foes with an old face. In 2 v. v. 2. N. Y., Macmillan, 1902. 6+243 p. 8°, cl., $3 net.

Laache, Nils Jacob. Book of family prayer; Bible lessons with meditations for each day, arranged after the church year; tr. from the Norwegian by Peer O. Stromme. Decorah, Ia., Lutheran Publishing House, 1902. c. 622 p. 8°, hf. leath., $1.65; mor., $2.25.

***Lamb**, C: Essays of Elia; with introd. and notes by Alfred Ainger. In 12 v. v. 1, 2. Troy, N. Y., Pafraets Book Co., 1902. 8°, cl., ea., $3 net.

Lathbury, Clarence. The code of joy: the ten requisites of perfect manhood: [sermons on the Beatitudes;] with prefatory verses by Mary A. Lathbury. Germantown, Pa., Swedenborg Publishing Assoc., 1902. c. 219 p. 12°, cl., 50 c.

Lehfeldt, R. A. A text-book of physics; with sections on the application of physics to physiology and medicine. [N. Y., Longmans, Green & Co., 1902.] 8+304 p. il. D. cl., $2.

Lessing, Gotthold Ephraim. Nathan der Weise; with introd., notes, and an appendix of parallel passages by Tobias J. C. Dickhoff. N. Y., Amer. Book Co., [1902.] c. 2-368 p. D. cl., 80 c.

Lewis, Julius A. Sir Walter of Kent: a truthful history of three centuries ago; printed with the consent of Sir Walter's few living descendants; ed. by Julius A. Lewis. N. Y., Bonnell, Silver & Co., 1902. c. 343 p. D. cl., $1.50; pap., 50 c.
A novel of the Elizabethan era. The story of Walter Wynnington, of Kent, as supposed to be told by himself, begins in 1633. The scene is Merton Hall, the ancestral home of Sir Walter. In the character caste are Miguel De Cervantes, William Shakespeare, and Henry of Navarre. Among the episodes of an adventurous life is a love story in which Constance Leigh, ward of Count de Brecy, figures.

Lingelbach, W. E. The merchant adventurers of England, their laws and ordinances, with other documents. Phil., Department of History of the University of Pennsylvania; N. Y., Longmans, Green & Co., [1902.] 39+260 p. D. (Translations and reprints from the original sources of European history (established 1894); 2d ser., v. 2.) cl., $1.25.

Lippincott's pocket medical dictionary, including the pronunciation and definition of 20,000 of the principal terms used in medicines and the allied sciences; with many tables; ed. by Ryland W. Greene. New ed. Phil., Lippincott, 1902. 16°, flex. cl., 50 c.

Livermore, Virgil B., *and* Williams, Ja. How to become a competent motorman: a practical treatise on the proper method of operating a street railway motor car, also giving details how to overcome certain defects. Brooklyn, N. Y., W: S. Livermore, 1902. 232 p. il. 12°, diagrams, cl., $1.

Lowell, Ja. Russell. The Biglow papers. N. Y., A. L. Burt Co., 1902. 18+279 p. 12°, (Cornell lib.) 75 c.

****Machray**, Rob. The night side of London; il. by Tom Browne. Phil., Lippincott, 1902. c. 12+300 p. il. 8°, cl., $2.50 net.
"A record of things seen in London by night in the first two years of the twentieth century. The artist and the author worked together, visiting the places described and seeing the scenes herein set forth. The volume is therefore the result of what may be called their common observation."—*Preface.*

"**Man** (The) in the street" stories from the *New York Times;* containing over six hundred humorous after-dinner stories about prominent persons; with an introd. by Chauncey M. Depew. N. Y., J. S. Ogilvie Pub. Co., [1902.] 3-310 p. por. D. cl., $1.
A collection of the stories printed in the Sunday edition of the *New York Times* under the department of "The Man in the Street."

†**Mason**, Caroline Atwater. The little green god. N. Y. and Chic., Revell, 1902. 146 p. 12°, cl., 75 c.

Men of Buffalo: a collection of portraits of men who deserve to rank as typical representatives of the best citizenship, foremost activities and highest aspirations of the city of Buffalo. Chic., A. N. Marquis & Co., 1902. c. 416 p. por. 8°, mor., $15.

Miller, Ja. Martin, *and* Durham, J: Stevens. The Martinique horror and St. Vincent calamity; containing a full and complete account of the most appalling disaster of modern times. Phil., National Pub. Co., [1902.] c. 600 p. il. por. maps, 12°, cl., $1.50; texoderm, $2.

****Moncrief**, J: Wildman. A short history of the Christian church for students and general readers. N. Y. and Chic., Revell Company, 1902. [Ap.] c. 456 p. 12°, cl., $1.50.
Contains a bibliography.

***Moore**, Addison Webster. The functional versus the representational theories of knowledge in Locke's essay. Chic., University of Chicago Press, 1902. c. 67 p. 8°, (University of Chicago contributions to philosophy, v. 3, no. 1.) pap., 35 c. net.

Moulton, C: Wells, *and others, eds.* The library of literary criticism of English and American authors. v. 4, 1785-1824; ed. by C: W. Moulton; assisted by a corps of able contributors. Buffalo, N. Y., Moulton Publishing Co., 1902. c. 768 p. O. cl., $5; hf. mor., $6.50.
See notice of work under first volume, Moulton, C. W., in "Weekly Record," P. W., April 13, 1901, [1524.]

****Murfree**, Mary Noailles, ["Charles Egbert Craddock," *pseud.*] The champion. Bost., Houghton, Mifflin & Co., 1902. c. 257 p. 1 il. 12°, cl., $1.20 net.

Myrtle, Frank, [*pseud.* for C. A: Haviland.] A lawyer's idle hours: sentiment, satire, humor, life, death, glory; a half century. Brooklyn, N. Y., C. A: Haviland, 1902. c. 178 p. 12°, cl., $1; pap., 50 c.

Nellis, Andrew J. Law of street surface railroads, as compiled from statutes and decisions in the various states and territories, showing the manner of organizing corporations to construct and operate street surface railroads, the acquisition of their franchises and property, their regulation, etc., by statute and municipal ordinance, their rights and liabilities both as to other users of the streets and highways and as to passengers and employees. Alb., Matthew Bender, 1902. c. 102+682 p. O. shp., $6.

New York. The code of civil procedure of the state, with all amendments thereto, down to and including those enacted in 1902, fully and exhaustively annot., by R. M. Stover. 6th ed., by Amasa J. Parker, jr. v. 1, cont. chapters 1 to 10; v. 2, cont. chapters 11 to 17, inc. N. Y., Banks Law Pub. Co., 1902. c. 8+1260+36; 6+1261-2354+35 p. O. shp., $7.50.

**Norman, *Sir* H: Delhi (1857): an account of the great mutiny in India. Phil., Lippincott, 1902. il. 8°, cl., $8 net.

Ostrom, Kurre Wilhelm. Massage and the original Swedish movements; their application to various diseases of the body. 5th ed., rev. and enl. Phil., P. Blakiston's Son & Co., 1902. c. tr. 8+9-181 p. il. 12°, cl., $1.

Paget, Francis, (*Bp.*) Christ the way; four addresses given at Haileybury, January 11 and 12, 1902. N. Y., Longmans, Green & Co., 1902. 2+54 p. S. cl., 75 c.

Parsons' [W. F.] hand-book of forms: a compendium of business and social rules and a complete work of reference and self-instruction. 12th ed., rev. and enl. Nashville, Tenn., Southern Publishing Assoc., 1902. c. 672 p.; 32 p. [unp. of poetical selections] il. O. cl., $3; shp., $4.

Phillips, Walter S., *comp.* Indian fairy tales: folk-lore legends and myths as told by the Indians around their camp fires by their tribal story tellers; gathered in the Pacific Northwest by W. S. Phillips. Chic., Star Publishing Co., 1902. 326 p. il. 12°, cl., $1.50.

***Plautus**, Titus Maccius. Mostellaria; with introd. and notes by Edwin W. Fay. Bost., Allyn & Bacon, 1902. [Ag1.] c. 205 p. 12°, (Allyn & Bacon's college Latin ser.) cl., $1 net.

Poe, Edgar Allan. The gold bug; ed. by Theda Gildemeister; il. by G. C. Widney. Chic., Rand, McNally & Co., [1902.] c. 111 p. il. 16°, (The Canterbury classics.) cl., 25 c.

Poore, G: Vivian. The earth in relation to the preservation and destruction of contagia: being the Milroy lectures delivered at the Royal College of Physicians in 1899; with other papers on sanitation. N. Y., Longmans, Green & Co., 1902. 10+257 p. D. cl., $1.75.

Rapp, J: Michael. Geographical outline manual of North America, considering the physical features of the continent in regard to their influence upon some historic movements and industrial developments; designed for the use of students and teachers. Neola, Ia., published by the author, J: M. Rapp, 1902. c. 58 p. 8°, pap., 35 c.

Rawnsley, *Rev.* Hardwicke Drummond. A rambler's note-book at the English lakes. N. Y., Macmillan, 1902. 8+258 p. il. 12°, cl., $2.

Read, Opie P., ["Arkansaw traveller," *pseud.*] The Starbucks: a novel; with character il., [reproduced in colors from photographs.] Chic., Laird & Lee, [1902.] c. 4-322 p. D. cl., $1.50.

A novel founded on the drama of the same name, produced at the Dearborn Theatre, Chicago. The scene is East Tennessee.

***Rhodes**, Ja. Ford. History of the United States from the compromise of 1850. N. Y., Macmillan, 1902. 4 v., 12°, price changed, ea., $2.50 net.

Robinson, C: H: Human nature: a revelation of the divine: a sequel to "Studies in the character of Christ." N. Y., Longmans, Green & Co., 1902. 19+364 p. D. cl., $2.

"The first part consists of further 'studies' in the character of Christ. In these I have tried to develop the former thesis and, at the same time, to discuss some of the objections which this line of argument called forth. The second part is an attempt to show that the argument for the inspiration of the Old Testament rests upon internal rather than external evidence. Part three contains "Studies in worship.'"—*Preface.*

Robinson, Morgan Poitiaux. The evolution of the Mason and Dixon line; published by special request. Richmond, Va., Oracle Publishing Co., 1902. c. 15 p. il. facsimile, 8°, pap., 25 c.

Sadler, Cora G. Skoot: a story of unconventional goodness. Cin., O., Jennings & Pye, [1902.] c. 141 p. D. cl., 50 c.

"Skoot" was the sobriquet of a bootblack who lived in a slum called Pinch Alley. Another child of the tenements figures in the story, a little blind girl called Pansy. Through the ministry of this child several of the characters are awakened to a realizing sense of their moral obligations, and one young woman is influenced to become a deaconess.

Saley, Met Lawson. Realm of the retailer; the retail lumber trade, its difficulties and successes, its humor and philosophy, its theory and practice, with practical yard ideas; comp. from "The realm of the retailer" as published in the *American Lumberman*. Chic., The American Lumberman, 1902. c. 386 p. por. il. 12°, cl., $1.50.

Sandys, Miles. Michael Carmichael: a story of love and mystery. Chic., Laird & Lee, [1902.] c. 4-317 p. D. cl., $1.25.

Michael Carmichael is supposed to tell his own story, which is substantially that of a man of dual personality. While dominated by his evil nature, and influenced by a man who acquires a mysterious power over him, Michael Carmichael commits murder, and figures in the sensational incidents described.

Sanford, Fernando. Elements of physics. N. Y., H: Holt & Co., 1902. c. 31+426 p. D. cl., $1.20.

"This book is a result of the attempt of the writer to apply the scientific method in all its steps to the teaching of physics. It does not contain as many laboratory experiments as are recommended in some books, but most of those it does contain are vital to the successful teaching of the book. . . It is not prepared with the idea that it will need supplementing by a lecture course; neither is it intended to dispense with the services of a teacher. In fact, it has been prepared especially for the teacher who has had adequate training in the physical laboratory, and it is not likely to succeed with any other teacher."—*Preface.*

Sayler, G: W. Skid and I; or, the devil in chains. Elwood, Ind., Sayler Publishing Co., 1902. 19+427 p. por. D. cl., $2.50.

In "Skid and I" the author gives his experiences religious and otherwise, in blank verse. Twenty-seven verses on as many different subjects make up the book.

Schwatka, Frederick. The children of the cold. New ed. Bost., Educational Publishing Co., [1902.] c. '99. 212 p. il. 12°, $1.25.

****Seligman,** E: Rob. Anderson. The economic interpretation of history. N. Y., Macmillan, 1902. [Jl2.] c. 9+166 p. 12°, cl., $1.50 net.

Singer, Isidore, *and others, eds.* Jewish encyclopædia: a descriptive record of the history, religion, literature and customs of the Jewish people from the earliest times to the present day; prepared by more than four hundred scholars and specialists under the direction of Cyrus Adler, I: K. Funk, D.D., Frank H. Vizetelly and others. In 12 v. v. 2, Apocrypha-Benash. N. Y.: Funk & Wagnalls Co., 1902. c. 22+686 p. il. Q. cl., subs., per v., $7; hf. mor., $9.

See notice, "Weekly Record," P. W., July 6, 1901, [1536] for plan of this exhaustive encyclopædia. One deviation has been made from this plan. The delimitations of the various departments having proved extremely difficult, it has been found more practical to print the initials of the department editors on the left side and the initials of the contributors on the right. A list of these initials and the names they stand for opens the volume. The pictures included are of a high order of merit. The names of the experts interested and the testimony of the two volumes now issued give assurance of an epoch-making addition to the great works of reference.

****Smith,** Jos. Warren. Training for citizenship: an elementary treatise on the rights and duties of citizens; based on the relations which exist between organized society and its individual members, and between the individual members of organized society. Bost., Lothrop Pub. Co., [1902.] c. 345 p. D. cl., 90 c. net.

Sons of the American Revolution: a national register of the society Sons of the American Revolution; comp. and published under the auspices of the National Publication Committee by L: H. Cornish; register list collated and ed. by A. Howard Clark. N. Y., L: H. Cornish, 1902. c. 1035 p. il. 8°, hf. mor., $5.

Southern reporter, v. 31. Permanent ed., Jan. 22-May 28, 1902. St. Paul, West Pub. Co., 1902. c. 12+1130 p. O. (National reporter system, state ser.) shp., $4.

Contains all the decisions of the supreme courts of Ala., La., Fla., Miss. With table of southern cases in which rehearings have been denied. Also tables of southern cases published in vs. 127, 128, Ala. reports; 106, La. reports. A table of statutes construed is given in the index.

Southworth, *Mrs.* Emma Dorothy Eliza Nevitte. Ishmael; or, in the depths. N. Y., A. L. Burt Co., 1902. 549 p. 12°, (Home lib.) cl., $1.

Southworth, *Mrs.* Emma Dorothy Eliza Nevitte. Ishmael; or, in the depths. N. Y., Y., A. L. Burt Co., 1902. 499 p. 12°, (Home lib.) cl., $1.

***Stelwagon,** H: W., *M.D.* Treatise on disease of the skin, for the use of advanced students. Phil., W: B. Saunders & Co., 1902. 1125 p. il. 8°, cl., $6 net; shp., $7 net.

Stevenson, Ja. H: Assyrian and Babylonian contracts, with Aramaic reference notes. N. Y., Amer. Book Co., [1902.] c. 206 p. D. (Vanderbilt Oriental ser.; ed. by Herbert Cushing Tolman and Ja. H: Stevenson.) cl., $1.

The tablets presented are selected from the different collections of the British Museum because they constitute a group in which appear the so-called "Aramaic dockets." The author has endeavored to reproduce as accurately as he might the Aramaic on each tablet, and at the same time to make the cuneiform trustworthy.

***Sultan,** G: Atlas and epitome of abdominal hernia; ed., with additions, by W: B. Coley, M.D. Phil., W. B. Saunders & Co., 1902. 227 p. il. 8°, (Saunders' medical hand atlases.) cl., $3 net.

United States Army. Company commanders' manual of army regulations; by W: H. Waldron. Kansas City, Mo., Hudson-Kimberly Pub. Co., 1902. 272 p. 12°, cl., $1.

Vanderlip, Frank A. The American "commercial invasion" of Europe; republished from *Scribner's Magazine,* 1902. [N. Y., National City Bank of New York, 1902.] c. 3+97 p. il. O. pap., n. p.

A comparison of American and European commercial conditions, made for the purpose of showing the effects of American competition in the industrial field, upon the finances and trade of the Continental countries. The author is vice-president of the National City Bank of New York, and was formerly Assistant Secretary U. S. Treasury.

Virgil, [*Lat.* Virgilius] Maro, Publius. Æneid. bks. 1-6; with introd., notes and vocabulary by H: S. Frieze; rev. by Walter Dennison. N. Y., Amer. Book Co., [1902.] c. 180+198+221 p. il. D. hf. leath., $1.30.

Watson, Archibald Robinson. Law of the clearing house. N. Y., Banks Law Pub. Co., 1902. c. 14+107 p. D. buckram, $1.75.

Weltmer, S. A. Telepathy and thought transference. Kansas City, Mo., Hudson-Kimberly Pub. Co., 1902. c. 200 p. 12°, cl., $1.

West Virginia. *Supreme ct. of appeals.* Reports of cases, from Nov. 9, 1901, to Mar. 1, 1902, by Romeo H. Freer, ex-off. rep. v. 50. Charleston, Charleston Daily Mail Pub. Co., 1902. c. 31+692+45 p. O. shp., $4.50.

White, Ja. Edson. Best stories from the best book: an illustrated Bible companion for the home; with an introductory department of easy lessons for children, by Ella King Sanders. Nashville, Tenn., Southern Publishing Assoc., [1902.] c. 3-194 p. sq. O. bds., 50 c.

The first part of the book is intended for very young children. The second part is for both young and old.

White, Ja. Edson. The coming King. Nashville, Tenn., Southern Publishing Assoc., 1902. c. '98. 5-305 p. il. D. cl., $1.

Williams, J: H: The painter's guide book; containing practical information for mixing colors and paint and hints on how to use them. Selma, Ala., J: H: Williams, [1902.] c. 100 p. 12°, cl., $1.50.

Wilson, *Mrs.* Augusta Jane Evans. Inez: a tale of the Alamo. N. Y., A. L. Burt Co., 1902. 320 p. 12°, (Cornell ser.) cl., 75 c.

ORDER LIST.

ABBEY PRESS, 114 Fifth Ave., New York.

Fields, Freedom in marriage.......... $0.50
Gwinn, Gold of Ophir.............. 1.00

JOHN H. ALLEN, Portland, Ore.

Allen, Judah's sceptre................ 1.50

ALLYN & BACON, 172 Tremont St., Boston.

*Plautus, Mostellaria...... ....net, 1.00

AMERICAN BAPTIST MISSIONARY UNION, Boston.

Clough, John E. Clough, missionary to the Telugus....... 10

AMERICAN BOOK CO., 100 Washington Sq., E., New York.

Lessing, Nathan der Weise........... 80
Stevenson, Assyrian and Babylonian contracts.... .... 1.00
Virgil, Æneid, bks. 1-6............... 1.30

AMERICAN LUMBERMAN, 315 Dearborn St., Chicago.

Saley, Realm of the retailer........... 1.50

R. W. ANDERSON & SON, Kingston, N. Y.

*Brink, Early history of Saugerties.net, 1.50

W. H. ANDERSON & CO., 515 Main St., Cincinnati.

Harris, Law governing the issuing, transfer and collection of municipal bonds..... .... 4.00

BANKS LAW PUB. CO., 21 Murray St., New York.

New York, Code of civil procedure, amendments to 1902............... 7.50
Watson, Law of the clearing house... 1.75

GEORGE BARRIE & SON, 1313 Walnut St., Philadelphia.

Achilles, Leucippe and Clitophon. (Apply to pubs. for price.)
Anacreon, Odes..(Apply to pubs. for price.)

MATTHEW BENDER, 511-513 Broadway, Albany, N. Y.

Nellis, Law of street surface railroads. 6.00

LEROY BERRIER, Davenport, Ia.

Berrier, The new life............... 1.00

THE BIBLE HOUSE, Chicago.

Banks *and* Cook, Authentic life and works of T. De Witt Talmage...... 1.75

P. BLAKISTON'S SON & CO., 1012 Walnut St., Philadelphia.

Ostrom, Massage and the original Swedish movement, 5th ed., rev. and enl...... .... 1.00

BONNELL, SILVER & CO., 24 W. 22d St., New York.

Lewis, Sir Walter of Kent.......50 c.; 1.50

BRENTANO'S, 5-9 Union Sq., New York.

†Hector, Stronger than love........... 1.50
†Kennard, The golf lunatic........... 1.50

OFFICE OF THE BROOKLYN DAILY EAGLE, Eagle Bldg., Brooklyn, N. Y.

Childe, Water exploring............. 10

A. L. BURT CO., 52-58 Duane St., New York.

Hatton, A vision of beauty........... $0.50
Holmes, The professor at the breakfast table....... .... 1.00
Lowell, The Biglow papers........... 75
Southworth, Ishmael..... .... 1.00
——, Self-raised...... .... 1.00
Wilson, Inez........ 75

LOUIS H. CORNISH, New York.

Sons of the American Revolution, National register.......................... 5.00

CROWELL & KIRKPATRICK CO., Springfield, O.

Herbert, Herbert's illustrated history of the Civil War....... 25

O. H. T CULP, Conneaut, O.

Culp, Reuben Green's experience in a large city.......................... 25

CHARLESTON DAILY MAIL PUB. CO., Charleston, W. Va.

West Virginia, *Supreme ct. of appeals*, Repts., v. 50 (Freer)............... 4.50

F. M. DE WITT. San Francisco, Cal.

De Witt's guide to Central California.. 50

DODD, MEAD & CO., 372 Fifth Ave., New York.

**Brontë, Jane Eyre...............net. 1.60

M. A. DONOHUE & CO., 407-429 Dearborn St., Chicago.

Adams, Life and sermons of T. De Witt Talmage........... .... 1.25

EDUCATIONAL PUBLISHING CO., 63 Fifth Ave., New York; 50 Bromfield St., Boston.

Dawes, Stories of our country, v. 1 and 2..... ....ea., 40
Defoe, Robinson Crusoe........40 c.; 60
Schwatka, Children of the cold....... 1.25

DANA ESTES & CO., 208-218 Summer St., Boston.

Ingelow, Wonder-box tales............ 35

T. H. FLOOD & CO., 149 Monroe St., Chicago.

Illinois, Index-digest of reports to v. 190, supreme ct., and v. 95, appellate ct., repts., in 2 v., v. 1............. 18.00

FUNK & WAGNALLS CO., 30 Lafayette Pl., New York.

Fernald, Concise standard dictionary.. 60
Singer, *and others*, Jewish encyclopædia, in 12 v., v. 2.......subs., per v., $7; 9.00

GEORGIA STATE LIBRARY, Atlanta.

Georgia, *Supreme ct.*, Repts., v. 114 (Stevens and Graham).............. 5.00

RICHARD HAINES, Medford, N. J.

Haines, Ancestry of the Haines family. 3.00

HALSEY BROS., Chicago.

Blackwood, Diseases of the lungs..... 2.00

C. A. HAVILAND, 982 Fulton St., Brooklyn, N. Y.

Myrtle, A lawyer's idle hours....50 c.; 1.00

EDWIN W. HIGH, Metamora, Ind.

High, History of the Sixty-eighth Regiment, Indiana Volunteers, 1862-65. $2.25; 3.50

HENRY HOLT & Co., 29 W. 23d St., New York.

**Gordy, Political history of the United States...... ....net, $1.75
Sanford, Elements of physics.......... 1.20

HOOD MEDICAL BOOK Co., Chicago.

Hood, Dr. Hood's plain talks about the human system....... .... 5.00
——, Practical family physician....... 2.50

HOUGHTON, MIFFLIN & Co., 4 Park St., Boston.

**Murfree, The champion.........net, 1.20

HAMILTON GAY HOWARD, Detroit, Mich.

Howard's law points................. 1.00

HUDSON-KIMBERLY PUB. Co., 1014 Wyandotte Ave., Kansas City, Mo.

United States Army, Company commanders' manual....... .... 1.00
Weltmer, Telepathy and thought transference....... .... 1.00

GEORGE W. JACOBS & Co., 103 S. Fifth St., Philadelphia.

**Atwater, How Sammy went to coral land.... ....net, 40
**Hewitt, Three little Denvers....net, 40

JENNINGS & PYE, 220 W. 4th St., Cincinnati.

Case, European constitutional history.. 1.50
Sadler, Skoot...... 50

KEEFE-DAVIDSON LAW BOOK Co., St. Paul, Minn.

Blashfield, Instructions to juries...... 6.00

E. L. KELLOGG & Co., 61 E. 9th St., New York.

Dawson, The voice of the boy........ 25

CHARLES H. KERR & Co., 56 Fifth Ave., Chicago.

Blatchford, Britain for the British.25 c.; 50

LAIRD & LEE, 263 Wabash Ave., Chicago.

Read, The Starbucks................. 1.50
Sandys, Michael Carmichael.......... 1.25

J. B. LIPPINCOTT Co., Washington Sq., Philadelphia.

**Bartholomew's physical atlas, v. 1.net, 17.50
Chambers's concise gazetteer, new ed.. 2.00
**Davis, Mother and child.........net, 1.50
Fox, On smallpox................... 3.00
Handy book of synonyms, new ed..... 50
Hannan, Textile fabrics of commerce.. 3.00
Jenkins, Vest pocket lexicon, new ed.. 75
Lippincott's pocket medical dictionary, new ed..... 50
**Machray, The night side of London. net, 2.50
**Norman, Delhi (1857).........net, 8.00

W. S. LIVERMORE, Brooklyn, N. Y.

Livermore *and* Williams, How to become a competent motorman........ 1.00

LONGMANS, GREEN & Co., 91-93 Fifth Ave., New York.

Burne, With the naval brigade in Natal, 1899-1900.... .... 2.50
Hill, Physiology for beginners......... 35
Holmes, Pictures and problems from London police courts.............. 1.25

LONGMANS, GREEN & Co.—*Continued.*

*Hutchinson, A friend of Nelson...net, $1.50
Karr, The call to arms, 1900-1901..... 2.00
Keary, The brothers.................. 1.50
Lehfeldt, Text-book of physics........ 2.00
Lingelbach, The Merchant Adventurers. 1.25
Paget, Christ the way................ 75
Poore, The earth in relation to the preservation and destruction of contagia....... .... 1.75
Robinson, Human nature............. 2.00

W. S. LORD, Evanston, Ill.

*Blander, A drift of song..........net, 50

LOTHROP PUB. Co., 530 Atlantic Ave., Boston.

**Smith, Training for citizenship..net, 90

LOWMAN & HANFORD, Seattle, Wash.

Hogan, Our new heraldry............ 1.00

LUTHERAN PUBLISHING HOUSE, Decorah, Ia.

Laache, Book of family prayer..$1.65; 2.25

MACMILLAN Co., 66 Fifth Ave., New York.

**Baldwin, Development and evolution, net, 2.60
*Early English printed books in the University Library, Cambridge...net, 5.00
*Hart *and* Hazard, Source readers in American history, no. 1........net, 40
*Hiorns, Metallography..... ......net, 1.40
*Kingsley, Life and works, v. 10, Hypatia, v. 2..................net, 3.00
Rawnsley, A rambler's note book..... 2.00
*Rhodes, History of the United States from the compromise of 1850, 4 v., ea., net, 2.50
**Seligman, Economic interpretation of history.... ....net, 1.50

A. N. MARQUIS & Co., 352 Dearborn St., Chicago.

Men of Buffalo...................... 15.00

W. Y. MORGAN, Topeka, Kan.

Kansas, *Supreme ct.*, Repts., v. 62 (Dewey).... .... 3.50

MOULTON PUB. Co., 37 Court St., Buffalo, N. Y.

Moulton, Library of literary criticism. 6.50

MUNICIPAL ENGINEERING Co., Indianapolis, Ind., and 1 Broadway, N. Y.

Brown, Directory of American cement industries..... .... 5.00

NATIONAL CITY BANK OF NEW YORK, New York.

Vanderlip, American commercial invasion of Europe.................... n. p.

NATIONAL PUBLISHING Co., Philadelphia.

Miller *and* Durham, The Martinique horror.... ....$1.50; 2.00

THOMAS NELSON & SONS, 37-41 E. 18th St., New York.

Bible, Standard ed.................$1.00-7.00

NEWS PRINT, Denton, Tex.

Jones, Mathematical puzzles.......... 25

J. S. OGILVIE PUB. Co., 57 Rose St., New York.

"Man in the street".................. 1.00

ORACLE PUBLISHING CO., Richmond, Va.

Robinson, Evolution of the Mason and Dixon line...... .... $0.25

ORANGE JUDD CO., 52 Lafayette Pl., New York.

Fiske, Poultry appliances............ 50
—— Poultry architecture..... 50

PAFRAETS BOOK CO., Troy, N. Y.

*Lamb, Essays of Elia, in 12 v., v. 1, 2, ea., net, 3.00

L. C. PAGE & CO., Summer St., Boston.

†Johnston, Cicely.......... 50

GEORGE G. PECK, 117 Chambers St., New York.

Gottsberger, Accountant's guide....... 5.00

I. NEWTON PHILLIPS, Springfield, Ill.

Illinois, *Supreme ct.*, Repts., v. 194 (Phillips)...... .... 2.25

PRESBYTERIAN COMMITTEE OF PUBLICATION, Richmond, Va.

Hawkins, A wee lassie............... 1.00

PRINCETON UNIVERSITY LIBRARY, Princeton, N. J.

*Gauss, General investigations of curved surfaces...... ....net, 1.75

RAND, MCNALLY & CO., 142 Fifth Ave., New York; 160-174 Adams St., Chicago.

Poe, The gold bag.................. 25

JOHN M. RAPP, Neola, Ia.

Rapp, Geographical outline manual of North America..... 35

REED PUBLISHING CO., Denver, Col.

Brown, Food studies................ 50

REMICK & SCHILLING, 277 Broadway, New York.

Gardner, American negligence reports. 5.50

FLEMING H. REVELL CO., 156 Fifth Ave., New York. 63 Washington St., Chicago.

Mason, The little green god.......... 75
**Moncrief, Short history of the Christian church.......... ....net, 1.50

L. A. RHODES, 112 Wisconsin St., Milwaukee, Wis.

King, A conquering corps.............. 1.25

W. B. SAUNDERS & CO., 925 Walnut St., Philadelphia.

*Stelwagon, On disease of the skin..$6; 7.00
*Sultan, Atlas and epitome of abdominal hernia...... ....net, 3.00

SAYLER PUBLISHING CO., Elwood, Ind.

Sayler, Skid and I.................... $2.50

CHARLES SCRIBNER'S SONS, 153-157 Fifth Ave., New York.

**Clark, Handbook of best readings, net, 1.50

SITE AND RELIC SOCIETY, Germantown, Pa.

Jenkins, Guide book to historic Germantown..... 50

A. H. SMYTHE, 41 S. High St., Columbus, O.

Fowke, Archæological history of Ohio. 5.00

SOUTHERN PUBLISHING ASSOC., Nashville, Tenn.

Gospel primer, 45th ed............:.. 25
Parsons, Hand-book of forms.....$3; 4.00
White, Best stories from the best book. 50
—— The coming King................ 1.00

STAR PUBLISHING CO., 211-213 Madison St., Chicago.

Phillips, Indian fairy tales............. 1.50

SWEDENBORG PUBLISHING ASSOC., Germantown, Pa.

Lathbury, Code of joy............... 50

E. THOMPSON CO., Northport, N. Y.

American and English encyclopædia of law, 2d ed., v. 21.................. 7.50

TUTTLE, MOREHOUSE & TAYLOR CO., New Haven, Ct.

Jarvis, Church life in Colonial Connecticut..... .... 1.00

UNIVERSITY OF CHICAGO PRESS, Chicago.

*Hammond, On the text of Chaucer's parlement of Foules............net, 50
*Moore, Functional versus representational theories of knowledge.....net, 35

WEST PUB. CO., 52-58 W. 3d St., St. Paul, Minn.

Clark, Criminal law, 2d ed............ 3.75
Southern reporter, v. 31.............. 4.00

WESTMINSTER PUBLISHING CO., Chicago.

Brown, True marriage guide....35 c.; 55

WHITAKER & RAY CO., 723 Market St., San Francisco, Cal.

*Ferry, Fonografía española.......net, 1.00

J. H. WILLIAMS, Selma, Ala.

Williams, Painter's guide book........ 1.50

RECENT ENGLISH BOOKS

ADDERLEY, J. G., *and* Marson, C. L. Third orders: a transl. of an ancient rule of the Tertiaries, together with an account of some modern Third Orders, two sermons on St. Francis, and an article on the religious life. Mowbray. 12°, 6⅝ x 4⅛, 94 p., 1s., net.

ALBERT, E. Diagnosis of surgical diseases. Hirschfeld. 8°, 18s., net.

ALL the world's fighting ships. Part 1: Navies of the world. Part 2: Articles on naval progress. Founded and ed. by Fred. T. Jane. Publ. for the Naval Syndicate. 5th year of issue. Low. Obl. imp. 8°, 7½ x 12, 394 p., 15s., net.

ANNESLEY, C. Standard opera glass: detailed plots of 134 celebrated operas. 20th thou. Rev. ed. Low. 12°, 6¼ x 4¼, 458 p., 3s. 6d.

BIBLE in modern English. Vol. 2: History of the people of Israel by Isaiah-Ben-Amoz, the Prophet, from the conquests of Joshua to the death of King Hezekiah. Trans. direct from Hebrew into English, with critical intro. and notes, by Ferrar Fenton. Partridge. Cr. 8°, 2s. 6d., net.

BIBLE, The Century. Revelation. Introd., auth. version, rev. version, notes, index, map. Ed. by C. Anderson Scott, Jack. 12°, 6½ x 4⅛, 312 p., 2s., net; lthr., 3s., net.

CHARPENTIER, P. Timber: comprehensive study of wood in all its aspects. commercial and botanical, showing different applications and uses of timber in various trades, etc. Trans. from the French by J. Kennell. Scott & G. Imp. 8°, 10⅝ x 6⅝, 454 p., 12s. 6d., net.

DIRECTORY of Americans in London and Great Britain, May, 1902. Eden, Fisher. Cr. 8°, 5s.

DRY, W. Wagner's Tristan and Isolde. De la More Press. Cr. 8°, swd., 1s. 6d., net.

FURNESS, *Sir* C. The American invasion. Simpkin. Illus. cr. 8°, 7½ x 4⅞, 102 p., 1s., net.

FYFE, H. C. Submarine warfare, past, present, and future. Introd. by Hon. Sir Edmund Robert Fremantle. Chapter on Probable future of submarine boat construction by Sir Edward J. Reed. 50 illus. Richards. 8°, 8¾ x 5⅝, 360 p., 7s. 6d., net.

GALVANE, S. War horses, present and future; or, remount life in South Africa. Everett. Cr. 8°, 7½ x 4⅞, 202 p., 2s. 6d., net.

JOHNSTON, *Sir* H. The Uganda Protectorate: attempt to give some description of physical geography, botany, zoology, anthropology, languages, and history of territories under British protection in East Central Africa, between Congo Free State and Rift Valley, and between First Degree of South Latitude and Fifth Degree of North Latitude. 2 vols. Hutchinson. Imp. 8°, 10¼ x 7¼, 490, 562 p., 42s., net.

KERR, G. L. Elementary coal mining. Designed to meet requirements of students attending classes on coal mining, and of miners and others engaged in practical work. 200 illus. Griffin. Cr. 8°, 7¼ x 4¾, 230 p., 3s. 6d.

KNOPF, S. A. Tuberculosis as a disease, and how to combat it. Rebman. 8°, swd., 1s., net.

LEHNER, S. Ink manufacture. Incl. writing, copying, lithographic, marking, stamping, and laundry inks. Scott & G. Cr. 8°, 7½ x 4⅞, 174 p., 5s., net.

LINDSAY, M. Prophet Peter: study in delusions. Frontispiece by F. H. Townsend. Ward & L. Cr. 8°, 8¼ x 5⅜, 352 p., 6s.

LISTS and indexes—manuscripts and other objects in the Museum of the Public Record Office. Catalogue, with brief descriptive and historical notes by Sir H. C. Maxwell Lyte, K.C.B. Eyre & S. 6d.

MILNE, JA. The epistles of Atkins. N. Y., Scribner, [imported,] 1902. 7+227 p. il. 12°, cl., $2.25.

MITCHELL, W. Reminiscences of a professional billiard player; ed. by F. M. Hotine. Treherne. Cr. 8°, 7¼ x 4¾, 140 p., swd., 1s.

NAYLOR, W. Trades waste: its treatment and utilization; with special reference to prevention of rivers pollution. Handbook for Borough engineers, surveyors, architects, and analysts. Griffin. Roy. 8°, 9⅞ x 6¼, 284 p., 21s., net.

PFUNGST, A. A German Buddhist: a biographical sketch. Luzac. Cr. 8°, 2s., net.

PRINCE and Princess of Wales; by the author of "His Most Gracious Majesty King Edward VII." N. Y., Scribner, [imported,] 1902. 12+390 p. il. 12°, cl., $2.50, net.

PROUDHOUN, P. J. What is property: an inquiry into the principle of right and of government. W. Reeves. Cr. 8°, 3s. 6d.

REPORT on collections of natural history in Antarctic regions during voyage of "Southern Cross." Dulau. 53 plates. British Museum (Nat. hist. publication.) 40s.

TEA and coffee, 1900—statements showing imports of, into principal countries of Europe, United States, and certain British Colonies, with statistical tables for recent years. Eyre & S. 6d.

THWAITE, B. H. The American invasion; or, England's commercial danger and triumphal progress of United States, with remedies proposed to enable England to preserve her industrial position. Sonnenschein. 8°, 42 p., swd., 3d.

RECENT FRENCH AND GERMAN BOOKS.

FRENCH.

AUBRY, J.-H. Alexandra, reine d'Angleterre. *Juven.* 16°, $1.

BEAUCHAMP, *Comte* de. Louis XIII. *Laurens.* 8°, $7.50.

CROSS, C.-F. *et* Bevan, E.-J. Manuel de la fabrication du papier. *Béranger.* 8°, $4.50.

DESCHAMPS, P. La Reine Victoria et le roi Edouard VII. *Lemerre.* 18°, $1.50.

GIRAUD, V. Taine. *Picard et fils.* 8°, $1.50.

GORKY, M. Les Petits bourgeois. *Mercure de France.* 18°, $1.

HASLAN, H. Légendes et vérités de la guerre franco-allemande. *Ollendorff.* 18°, $1.

LE BON, *Dr.* G. Psychologie de l'éducation. *Flammarion.* 18°, $1.

PREVOST, M. Le Pas relevé. *Lemerre.* 18°, $1.

TAVERNIER, E. Du Journalisme, son histoire. *H. Oudin.* 12°, $1.

GERMAN.

ASENIJEFF, Elsa. Max Klingers Beethoven. Eine kunst-techn. Studie. Leipzig, *H. Seemann Nachf.* il. 4°, cl., $6.60.

BAUMANN, Fel. Im dunkelsten Amerika. Sittenschilderungen aus den Vereinigten Staaten. Dresden, *E. Beutelspacher & Co.* 8°, 85 c.

ESCHRICHT, E. Pfarrer Streccius. Roman. Berlin, *A. Schall.* 8°, cl., $1.35.

GRAESEL, Arnim. Handbuch der Bibliothekslehre. 2d ed. Leipzig, *J. J. Weber.* il. 8°, pap., $5; hf. leath., $6.

KUNSTLER-MONOGRAPHIEN. Hrsg. v. H. Knackfuss. LX. Heilmeyer, Alex.: Adolf Hildebrand. Bielefeld, *Velhagen & Klasing.* il. 8°, $1.

MYSING, Osk. (O. Mora.) Das neue Geschlecht. Roman. Leipzig, *H. Seemann Nachf.* 8°, $1.

OMPTEDA, Geo. Frhr. v. Traum im Süden. Berlin, *F. Fontane & Co.* 8°, cl., $1.

PERFALL, Karl v. Loras Sommerfrische. Roman. Berlin, *F. Fontane & Co.* 8°, $1.35.

RHEUDE, Lor. M. Bibliothekszeichen. 32 Exlibris; with preface by L. Gerster. Zürich, *F. Amberger.* with 14 pl. 8°, in portfolio, $1.50.

SCHACHJAHRBUCH f. 1901. Zusammengestellt u. m. eingeh. Erläutergn. versehen v. Ludw. Bachmann. Ansbach, *C. Brügel & Sohn.* with diagrams, 12°, cl., 70 c.

BIBLIOGRAPHIC NOTES.

THE LITERARY COLLECTOR COMPANY, 33 W. Forty-second Street, New York, has just published a price list, with the buyers' names, of the first edition collected by W. H. Arnold and sold at Bangs's May 7, 1902; also, a price list of the Marshall C. Lefferts's collection of English literature sold by Bangs & Co., April 21-24, 1902.

LAWRENCE J. BURPEE, 351 Stewart Street, Ottawa, Canada, announces that he has in preparation for the Royal Scotch Society of Canada a bibliography of Canadian publications issued during 1901. He will be glad to receive information, giving place of publication, publisher, and other full technical data, of books, pamphlets, magazines, articles, or papers in society transactions, by Canadians, published in 1901.

CATALOGUES OF NEW AND SECOND-HAND BOOKS.—*H. W. Bryant,* 223 Middle St., Portland, Me., Americana. (No. 20, 179 titles.)—*Casino Book Company,* 1374 Broadway, New York, American first editions, etc. (No. 4, 1478 titles.)—*Francis Edwards,* 83 High St., Marylebone, London, W., Miscellaneous. (No. 257, 809 titles.)—*Joseph McDonough,* 39 Columbia St., Albany, N. Y., Americana, first editions, travel, French, etc. (No. 176, 662 titles.)—*A. Maurice & Co.,* 23 Bedford St., London, Books on Africa, America, etc. (No. 115, 345 titles.)—*D. Sutherland,* 288 Yonge St., Toronto, Americana, theology, first editions. (No. 17, 661 titles.)

The Publishers' Weekly.

FOUNDED BY F. LEYPOLDT.

AUGUST 2, 1902.

The editor does not hold himself responsible for the views expressed in contributed articles or communications

All matter, whether for the reading-matter columns or advertising pages, should reach this office not later than Wednesday noon, to insure insertion in the same week's issue.

Books for the "Weekly Record," as well as all information intended for that department, should reach this office by Tuesday morning of each week.

Publishers are requested to furnish title-page proofs and advance information of books forthcoming, both for entry in the lists and for descriptive mention. An early copy of each book published should be forwarded, as it is of the utmost importance that the entries of books be made as promptly and as perfectly as possible. In many cases booksellers depend on the PUBLISHERS' WEEKLY solely for their information. The Record of New Publications of the PUBLISHERS' WEEKLY is the material of the "American Catalogue" and so forms the basis of trade bibliography in the United States.

"I hold every man a debtor to his profession, from the which, as men do of course seek to receive countenance and profit, so ought they of duty to endeavor themselves by way of amends to be a help and an ornament thereunto."—LORD BACON.

TO DESIGNATE SIZES OF BOOKS BY THE METRIC SYSTEM.

THE Permanent Office of the International Congress of Publishers at Berne is making a canvass to discover what progress has been made in the adoption by the publishing trade of the metric system for the determining of the sizes and forms of volumes. This is in pursuance of resolutions passed by the Congress at its sessions in Paris and Brussels desiring that in all book catalogues or advertisements the size of the book should be indicated by its dimensions in centimeters, the first number indicating the height and the second the width of the uncut volume. No other specification as to size of paper is to be added to this. By this method the size of a quarto volume, for example, would be indicated in centimeters thus: 32-25, and an 8°: 25-16. The American Library Association's standard, adopted by THE PUBLISHERS' WEEKLY, it will be noticed, varies considerably from this, the measurement of a quarto being from 25 up to 30 centimeters outside height, and that of an octavo 20 up to 25 centimeters outside height. As yet the reform has nowhere been put into practice by publishers, especially not in England or in the United States, owing to the present uncertain status of the metric system; but it is believed that it will eventually be adopted in all the principal book-producing countries.

The Permanent Office also submits to the auxiliary associations various resolutions in the shape of simple recommendations to publishers with a view to their own interests. The first of these calls for the adoption of a definite custom in regard to "overs" in printing. Another advises publishers, especially when issuing *editions de luxe,* to provide for extra sheets, illustrations, etc., which may be substituted, if necessary, for those soiled or missing. Publishers of newspapers and periodicals are urged to use stronger wrappers for mailing to foreign countries.

The most important suggestion, perhaps, is the recommendation that, to prevent the confusion arising from the use of the ambiguous term "edition," this word should be used hereafter only for works which have undergone a partial or material revision of text, while some specific term should apply to simple repeated printings of the same text. The word "impression" (*tirage*) is proposed for the latter case; but as this is already employed to denote specifically the printing of a single sheet, a new application of it would only add to the present confusion. If a satisfactory word can be found, it would be in the interest of publishers to adopt it because of the natural distrust with which the public at present regards the advertisement of "new editions."

Circular No. 4, just issued by the Permanent Office to the auxiliary associations, is accompanied by the following long list of other resolutions of the Congress relative to copyright, book-postage, etc., to be presented to the various governments:

REFORMS IN THE NATIONAL AND INTERNATIONAL REGULATIONS CONCERNING COPYRIGHT AND PUBLISHERS' RIGHT.

On duty copies.
Translations' right.
On the publication of extracts.
The reproduction of a literary work by means of public reading.
On the rights of the publisher with regard to the publication of letters.
The reproduction of newspaper articles.
Improvement of the laws on copyright and publishers' right with regard to works of art and photographs.
International uniformity of copyright and publishers' right.
The alienation of works of art and of the right of reproduction.
The law of copyright as regards photographs.
Photographs ordered by a publisher for the illustration of a work.
On exclusive right in characteristic titles of books.
On the protection of new forms.
The need for more complete protection of copyright in educational works.
On localized editions (literature and music).
The suppression of the warrant "*Judicatum solvi.*"
Protection of the copyright owner against reproduction of musical compositions by mechanical instruments.
Legal measures against the sale of conterfeited music in the streets.
Suppression of the liability of duty on intellectual products.

IMPROVEMENTS IN POSTAL SERVICE:

On the postage of book parcels and printed matters. Introduction of parcel postal rates of 5 kilos in those countries where only packages of 3 kilos are accepted. The extension of the system of parcels post to those countries where it does not yet exist. Increase of the weight to 3 kilos (instead of 2 kilos) for printed matter which is circulated in the countries belonging to the Universal Postal Union.

On the registration of printed matters, (Tariff improvements.)

On the sending of parcels of printed matter. (Extension of this service in the Universal Postal Union and Tariff improvements.)

AMERICAN BOOK COMPANY WINS IN KANSAS.

The Supreme Court on July 21 enjoined the American Book Company from transacting business in Kansas until it shall have complied with the Corporation law and paid into the treasury $2,000 to cover charter fees for three years, or since the present Corporation law was enacted.

In May the American Book Company secured five-year contracts from the State Text Book Commission for about 50 per cent. of the common school books used in the State, amounting to $250,000. Suit was then brought by Crane & Co., which was defeated by the American Book Company. On July 22 the American Book Company paid into the treasury the $2,000, as directed by the Court, and proceeded with the fulfilment of the contracts with the State Commission.

BOOK TRADE ASSOCIATIONS.

THE BOOKSELLERS OF THE CITY OF NEW YORK.

The organization of The Booksellers of New York City was completed at a meeting held at Brentano's on the evening of July 18. The constitution was read, approved and adopted and the following officers were elected:

Simon Brentano, President.
F. E. Grant, Vice-President.
E. S. Gorham, Secretary.
Henry C. Holtin, Treasurer.

The following gentlemen were added to the Standing Committee: Robert H. Dodd, Charles S. Pratt and A. Mackel.

After the election of officers the members present entered into a general discussion of trade matters.

The following is a list of the members: American Baptist Publication Society, American Tract Society, Ammon & Mackel, (Leggat Brothers,) Brentano's, E. W. Dayton, Bonnell, Silver & Co., Coryell & Co., R. W. Crothers, E. P. Dutton & Co., Dodd, Mead & Co., Eaton & Mains, (Methodist Book Concern,) Charles P. Everitt, John Francis, F. E. Grant, Edwin S. Gorham, Henry C. Holtin, J. A. Jenkins, William R. Jenkins, L. Jonas & Co., Henry Malkan, T. J. McBride & Son, S. F. McLean & Co., G. P. Putnam's Sons, Charles S. Pratt, Fleming H. Revell Co., Rohde & Haskins, D. Van Nostrand Co., T. B. Ventres, Miss M. J. Whaley, and Thomas A. Whittaker.

OBITUARY NOTES.

William H. Williams, general manager of the Union News Company, New York, died July 17 from heart disease at his home in Orange, N. J. He was born in New York State sixty-two years ago and came to New York City when a boy. He started as a newsboy, and a few years later obtained employment with the American News Company, with which he remained until 1873, when he organized the Union News Company and became its general manager. The company gradually increased its business until it controlled the news business of all the railroad lines through the country. Before the introduction of fast trains on the railroads Mr. Williams induced the companies to run special newspaper trains for the purpose of carrying the news to distant points early in the morning.

Professor Van Buren Denslow, journalist and author, died in New York City, July 17. He was born in Yonkers, N. Y., in 1833. From 1863 to 1868 he was editor-in-chief of the Chicago *Tribune* and of the Chicago *Republic*, and a member of the staff of the New York *Tribune*. In 1869 he returned to Chicago to resume his position on the *Tribune* of that city. Until 1880 he was the head of the Union College of Law, attached to the Northwestern University and the University of Chicago. In 1880 he renewed his connection with the press as one of the staff of the Chicago *Inter Ocean*. He wrote a work on "Fremont and McClellan: their political and military careers reviewed," "Modern Thinkers: principally upon social science;" also, "Principles of the Economic Philosophy of Society, Government and Industry."

John Southward, whose name has been a household word in connection with English typography for many years, died suddenly on July 9, at Streatham, London, Eng. He was born in Liverpool, April 27, 1840. When seventeen he became the editor of a local literary magazine, and later on took charge of the *Liverpool Observer*, the first penny weekly in the town, which was printed and published by his father. In 1865 he went to London intending to apply for an opening at Hansard's, but being misdirected, found himself at Cox & Wyman's, obtained a post as reader, and thus commenced his lengthy connection with that firm. Four years later he became editor of the *Printer's Register*, and from this time devoted himself almost entirely to typographical literature. In 1891 Mr. Southward became the proprietor of *Paper and Printing Trades Journal*, which he purchased from its founder, Andrew Tuer, but he shortly after disposed of his interest to devote himself to writing. The following are among his best-known works: "A Dictionary of Typography," "Practical Printing," "Principles and Practice of Printing Machinery," "Modern Printing," and "Historical Printing," the latter being unfortunately interrupted by the author's death. He contributed the articles on printing and kindred subjects to the "Encyclopædia Britannica," "Chambers's Encyclopædia," and "Cassell's

Storehouse of General Information." No man endeavored more to raise the status of the practical side of letterpress printing than Southward, while on the history of the invention and progress of the art he was a reliable authority.

PROFESSOR CHARLES KENDALL ADAMS, President of the University of Wisconsin, died at Redlands, Cal., July 26. Professor Adams was born at Derby, Vt., January 24, 1835, was graduated from the University of Michigan in 1861, from 1862 to 1865 was instructor in history and Latin at that college, and later became professor of history. For two years he studied at German and French universities, and returning to this country in 1869 he founded a historical seminary at Ann Arbor. When the school of political science was organized at the University of Michigan he was made dean. In 1881 he became non-resident professor of history at Cornell, and four years later, upon the resignation of Andrew D. White, was elected president. Under him the number of students more than doubled, the egineering schools were extended, the Sage school of philosophy and the President White school of history and political science were created and the law school was organized. There was friction between Professor Adams and the faculty, however, and in 1892 he resigned on account of grave and seemingly irreconcilable differences of opinion in regard to matters of administrative importance. He then became president of the University of Wisconsin, which post he held until 1901, when he retired on account of ill health. Since then Professor Adams lived in Southern California, but the university declined to accept his resignation, and he was still president when he died. Professor Adams was the author of a number of works on historical and educational subjects, including "Monarchy and Democracy in France," "A Manual of Historical Literature," "British Orations," and "Christopher Columbus, his life and work." He married the widow of A. S. Barnes, the founder of the publishing house of A. S. Barnes & Co.

CHARLES KEGAN PAUL, the senior member of the firm of Kegan Paul, Trench, Trübner & Co., of London, died July 20. Mr. Paul was born March 8, 1828, at White Lackington, near Ilminster, Somerset, of which village his father was curate in sole charge. He was educated at Eton and at Exeter College, Oxford, where he resided during the feverish days of the Tractarian movement. In 1851 he became curate of Tew, in the diocese of Oxford, and in the same year was ordained deacon. A year later he took sole charge of Bloxham, a large village near Banbury, where he was ordained priest. In 1853 he became tutor to two boys, with whom he travelled for a year through France, Switzerland and Germany, after which he received a conductship, or chaplaincy, at Eton. He remained at Eton until 1862, when he became vicar of Sturminster Marshall. In 1874 he resigned his living and went to London, where he was offered a position in the publishing house of Henry S. King, in Cornhill, by whom Mr. Paul had been for some time engaged as reader. A few years later Mr. King, desiring to devote himself exclusively to his Indian department, sold his publishing business to Mr. Paul and a partner, who commenced business as C. Kegan Paul & Co. at Paternoster Square. In 1881 Mr. Paul was joined by Mr. Trench. In 1886 the firms of C. Kegan Paul & Co., George Redway and Trübner & Co. amalgamated under the firm name of Kegan, Paul, Trench, Trübner & Co., which it has remained to this day. Mr. Paul, in his "Memoirs," published in 1899, recalled the fact with pride that his firm, for good or evil, always preferred to be literary and scholarly, though he was ready to admit that a literary man is not, as a rule, a good publisher, because he is on the one hand tempted to accept books unlikely to succeed because they fall in with his own literary tastes, and, on the other, to reject those which may have considerable sale at the time because they are in no true sense literature. Thomas Hardy, George Meredith, Tennyson, Archbishop Trench, Sir Richard and Lady Burton, and Coventry Patmore are only a few of the distinguished writers with whom Mr. Paul had business relations, and he always referred with pride to the fact that his firm was associated with Andrew Lang and Robert Louis Stevenson before either of them had attained the fame which he was afterward to enjoy. Mr. Paul himself was an author of some note. He wrote a life of Godwin and edited the letters of Mary Wollstonecraft; "Biographical Sketches;" "Faith and Unfaith, and Other Essays;" "On the Wayside;" "Memories," and a translation of "Faust" and a translation of "Thoughts of Blaise Pascal." Though he remained in the Church of England until 1872, his religious convictions steadily forced him to lose sympathy with the Anglican church and finally led him, after many years of Positivism, to join the Roman church. Politically he was, as he himself put it, "an extreme Radical, a Republican, a Socialist, so far as these things can be carried on without breach of public order."

JOURNALISTIC NOTES.

DOUBLEDAY, PAGE & CO. have made arrangements with William Heinemann, of London, to publish an English edition of *The World's Work*, which will be edited by Henry Norman, M.P., well known as an author and journalist.

The Essene is the title of a new monthly published at 1756 Champa Street, Denver, Colo., at $1 a year. It is the mouthpiece of the Essenes, "a people of real spiritual vision, who practice brotherhood in their lives." It is edited by James Arthur Edgerton and Grace M. Brown.

THE "midsummer number" of *The Book Lover* is as full of meat as it is handsome in appearance. The principal feature of this issue is a facsimile reproduction, in five colors and gold, of the first page of the Mazarin Bible printed on Japan paper. An article of interest to booksellers is an essay on "Rare Books," by Charles E. Goodspeed, the bookseller and publisher of Boston, Mass., giving a list of valuable books recently sold; a Bret Harte bibliography, and an article on book-binding with many illustrations of notable bindings.

The Philadelphia Public Ledger was sold on the 20th inst. to Adolph S. Ochs, who is the principal owner of *The New York Times, The Philadelphia Times* and *The Chattanooga Times. The Philadelphia Public Ledger* is one of the oldest and most prosperous newspapers in this country. It was established in 1836; from 1864 to 1894 it was conducted by George W. Childs, after whose death it passed to the ownership of the A. J. Drexel estate. The price paid was not made public, but it is said that more than $2,225,000 is involved in the transaction.

NOTES ON AUTHORS.

MRS. CRAIGIE, ("John Oliver Hobbes,") calls her new novel "Love and the Soul Hunters."

"THE LETTERS OF HER MOTHER TO ELIZABETH" was written by W. R. H. Trowbridge, author of "A Girl of the Multitude," a novel of the French Revolution.

ZOLA'S new novel, "Truth," will be published in an English version during the fall by Chatto & Windus. This is the third in the *Four Evangelists Series*, the first two being "Fruitfulness" and "Labor." The last will be "Justice."

OLD BOOK NOTES.

ANDREW CARNEGIE recently purchased at private sale the library formed by the late Lord Acton, professor of history at Cambridge, and presented it to John Morley, who has practically abandoned politics for literature. Lord Acton, according to the London *Times*, left behind a library of secular and ecclesiastical history which is equalled by few public institutions and surpassed by no private collection in the world. For many years he had been gathering the material for a general history of civil and religious liberty in Europe, and the richness of this portion of his library can hardly be overestimated.

W. M. VOYNICH, of London, recently discovered in an old book which he wanted rebound a fragment of a manuscript map of the world and an equidistant polar projection of the sixteenth century, which, if the theories of authorities are correct takes precedence over Gerardus Mercator's projection. F. G. Ravenstein, one of the authorities on maps quoted by the London *Times*, declares the map discovered by Mr. Voynich, which includes only parts of Europe, East Asia and North Africa, to be an authentic work by some Spaniard, while he says that the empty space between the two hemispheres, which is filled by a rough sketch of Magellan Straits, with the outline of a ship and a flag, indicates that it was drawn after the arrival of one of Magellan's ships in 1522. The polar hemispheres of this map, which Mr. Ravenstein believes was drawn in Spain immediately after the arrival of Magellan's ship *Vittoria*, must be the earliest employment of the equidistant polar projection, hitherto believed to have been employed first by Mercator in his chart of 1569. The natural assumption, says Mr. Ravenstein, is that the map was drawn to illustrate a never-published work on Magellan's expedition.

BUSINESS NOTES.

ATLANTA, GA.—J. F. Lester, for many years in the book business at 60 Peachtree and 57 North Broad Streets, has sold out to a corporation, which will continue the business as the Lester Book and Stationery Co. John Aldridge and Ormond Jarnigan, long connected with the firm, will be the managers of the new concern. They have many friends, and bring large experience and energy to the new management. James C. Sturges, for the past twelve years with Lester's and for eighteen years before that connected with R. H. Richards & Co. and Williams, Sturges & Co., at Knoxville, Tenn., remains with the new concern.

BOELUS, NEB.—M. J. Morrow has succeeded Samuel F. Woodward, bookseller.

CHICAGO, ILL.—Sidney C. Eastman, referee in the matter of George M. Hill Company, bankrupt, gives notice to the creditors of that concern that he will declare and direct the payment of the first dividend on claims against the Hill Company which have been proved and allowed. The payments are to be made within ten days from August 5 at the office of Robert O. Law, 518 First National Bank Building.

CUBA, ILL.—James Welch has opened a bookstore in the Cline Building.

DALLAS, TEX.—The Dallas Book Company has been succeeded by the Texas Drug Company.

LOCKPORT, N. Y.—I. Wilbur, for forty-five years in the book and drug business, has sold out his drug business and will hereafter devote himself entirely to the book and stationery business.

NEW HAVEN, CONN.—Butler & Alger have been discharged from bankruptcy.

NORWICH, CONN.—Noyes & Davis have dissolved partnership, Charles D. Noyes retiring. The business was originally established by Sherman B. Bishop, Charles D. Noyes and George A. Davis succeeding Bishop in 1874. The business has grown steadily and developed in many directions, so that at present besides books and stationery this firm has also a large stock of silverware and novelties as well as sporting goods which they job as well as retail. The business will be continued by Mr. Davis under the old firm name.

PIQUA, O.—C. S. Zimmer & Co., booksellers, have assigned. No schedules have as yet been made public.

SAN JACINTO, CAL.—Edwin Minor, bookseller, has removed to more commodious quarters.

SHELTON, NEB.—The Paxton Drug Co., booksellers, have been succeeed by Sutherland & Co.

TEXARKANA, ARK.—Van Dyne Brothers, formerly of Pine Bluff, Ark., have opened up a bookstore here.

WEST PLAINS, MO.—J. L. Van Wormer, bookseller, has sold out.

LITERARY AND TRADE NOTES.

E. P. DUTTON & CO. announce a work on "Submarine Warfare, Past, Present and Future," by Henry C. Fyfe.

A. C. MCCLURG & CO. have in preparation a fairy story for young people by Mrs. Harrison, the wife of the Mayor of Chicago.

MCCLURE, PHILLIPS & CO. will publish next month Arthur Morrison's new story of low life in London, entitled "A Hole in the Wall."

HENRY T. COATES & CO. have in press a romance of Thibet and China, entitled "The Tu-tze's Tower," by Louise Betts Edwards.

DOUBLEDAY, PAGE & CO. will publish in October Kipling's latest book of Indian stories for young people, entitled "Just-so Stories," which will be illustrated by the author's own drawings.

HARPER & BROTHERS announce a new edition of their successful *Thistle edition* of the Waverley novels. There will be forty-eight new half-tone frontispieces of pictures of scenes in Scotland.

GRANT RICHARDS, London, announces a work entitled "The Unspeakable Englishman," which in particular will bowl over "The Unspeakable Scot," and in general add to the gayety of nations.

THE OUTLOOK COMPANY will soon publish a collection of "The Spectator" essays, that for twenty years or so have occupied much the same place in *The Outlook* that the "Easy Chair" essays hold in *Harper's*.

"CAPE COD BALLADS AND OTHER VERSE," by Joe Lincoln, with pictures by Kemble, published recently by Albert Brandt, Trenton, N. J., has acquired a steady sale all over the country, and is now selling in its second edition.

THOMAS WHITTAKER, New York, will add to his series of anatomical models a complete popular "Mannikin," which, like the ones on the eye, the head and the body, will comprise a series of superimposed plates, together with a complete reference index.

AXTEL S. SWANSON, manager of the South Bend, Ind., Tribune Store, read a paper on "The Psychology of King Lear," before the American branch of the Anglo-American Shakesperian Society, at Chicago, on July 21. The paper attracted considerable attention and received warm praise.

PAFRAETS BOOK COMPANY, of Troy, N. Y., announce a reprint of Canon Ainger's edition of "The Essays of Elia," in twelve octavo volumes, limited to 1,000 sets. The work is being printed at the Merrymount Press. The first two volumes are now ready, and the balance will follow at intervals of about one month.

THE first edition of 75,000 copies of "A Speckled Bird," Augusta Evans Wilson's new novel, was sold three weeks in advance of publication, and another edition of 25,000 is in press to fill further demands. It will be issued simultaneously in England and Canada on August 12. The Dillingham Company expect to sell over 200,000 copies of the book before the end of the year.

JOHN MURRAY, London, has in press a "History of the Royal Yacht Squadron," by Montague Guest, honorary librarian of the squadron, and William B. Boulton. The volume will also contain a complete list of members and their yachts, from the foundation of the club to the present time, together with an inquiry into the history of yachting and its development in the Solent.

WILLIAM CRAMP & SON, Philadelphia, have published for private circulation a monograph entitled "Cramp's Shipyard, 1830-1902," which contains portraits of William Cramp and Charles H. Cramp, and pictures of all the ships built by the Cramps, from the clipper ship *Manitou* down to the latest floating derrick. The text contains exhaustive data concerning all the ships turned out by the Cramps.

THE FLEMING H. REVELL COMPANY announces for early publication a new volume by Howard Agnew Johnston, D.D., which gives to Bible readers and students in plain words information regarding present-day biblical discussion, free from technicality, yet which will enable them to distinguish the constructive and the useful from the destructive and valueless in the discussion of the authority and inspiration of the Bible.

THE CENTURY COMPANY have in preparation "The Story of Athens," by Howard Crosby Butler, lecturer on architecture at Princeton, which will describe life and art in Athens from the beginning, with numerous illustrations; also, "Barnaby Lee," a story for young people of New Amsterdam during the sway of Peter Stuyvesant, by John Bennett, author of "Master Skylark." They will publish shortly, in book form, J. H. Stoddard's "Recollections of a Player," with an introduction by William Winter.

JOHN C. RICHARD, the manager of the stationery department of the American News Company, rounds out his thirtieth year with that house this month. Mr. Richard is known to the American trade for close upon half a century. In 1869 he joined his friend Leopoldt Illfelder in forming the firm of Illfelder, Richard & Co., importers of stationery. Three years afterward he joined the forces of the American News Company, where his judgment and experience have always been of great value. We offer our hearty congratulations to Mr. Richard.

THE NEW AMSTERDAM BOOK COMPANY have made arrangements with McClure, Phillips & Co. to publish in their red paper book series Anthony Hope's "Tristram of Blent." They will bring out in the same series: "Joan of the Sword Hand," by S. R. Crockett, and "Three Men on Wheels," by Jerome K. Jerome. They have in preparation a reprint of Lady Charlotte Guest's English version of the mediæval Welsh tales, commonly known as the "Mabinogian," edited by Alfred Nutt; also, a prose translation, by Miss Jessie L. Weston, from the mediæval Dutch version of "Lancelot," entitled "Morien."

BURROWS BROTHERS COMPANY, Cleveland, will follow their reprint of Denton's "Brief Description of New York" with reprints of Wooley's "Journal During Two Years' Residence in New York," edited by Professor E. G. Bourne, of Yale; Miller's "Description of New York," Budd's "Good Order in Pennsylvania," and Alsop's "A Character of the Province of Maryland," described in Sabin's "Bibliotheca Americana" as "one of the rarest of books." Thev have also in preparation an edition of Ferdinand Columbus's life of his father, Christopher Columbus, prepared by Professor E. G. Bourne.

THE AMERICAN BOOK COMPANY announce "Plato's Euthyphro," edited with introduction by William Arthur Heidel, professor in Iowa College. This is the first of a new Greek series for colleges and schools to appear under the general editorial supervision of Professor Herbert Weir Smyth, of Harvard. The introduction to this volume considers the lives of Plato and Socrates, the contents and import of the Euthyphro, and its place in the economy of Plato's works. The notes explain all allusions. An appendix gives a bibliography, as well as critical notes on the text, while a Greek and an English index follow.

LITTLE, BROWN & CO. have put up thirty of their more popular books for young people, in uniform cloth bindings, as *The Boys' and Girls' Bookshelf.* The following are among the authors represented: Louisa M. Alcott, Susan Coolidge, Mrs. Ewing, Laura Richards, Mary P. Wells Smith, Louise Chandler Moulton, Robert Louis Stevenson, Lily F. Weselhoeft, A. G. Plympton, Harriet Prescott Spofford, and Jean Ingelow. They have also just added to their *Children's Friend Series* "Pansies and Water-Lilies," by Louisa M. Alcott; "The Doll's Journey," by Louisa M. Alcott; "A Very Ill-Tempered Family," bv Juliana H. Ewing; "Snap Dragons," by Juliana H. Ewing; also, "The Little Women Play" and "The Little Men Play," adapted from Miss Alcott's stories by Elizabeth L. Gould.

C. N. CASPAR CO., Milwaukee, have brought out a baker's dozen of souvenir postal cards with views of Milwaukee. These are in two sizes, ten different views on cards of the regulation postal card size and three giant cards with a quadruple folder, two containing eight and eleven views respectively, and the third giving a fine panoramic view of Milwaukee, 4x14 inches. These larger cards are closed with an ornamental wafer. They retail for 10 cents each, or three for 25 cents. The small card contains one large or two small views, printed in different tints, and retails at two for 5 cents, or ten for 25 cents. The custom of using these cards is growing in favor with the public in this country, and these additions will no doubt find a ready sale. We may add that the process by which these cards have been printed gives them an artistic and graceful appearance.

CHARLES SCRIBNER'S SONS will publish as one of the *Yale Bicentennial Publications* "Elements of Experimental Phonetics," by Dr. Edward W. Scripture, assistant professor of experimental psychology. The first part of the book is devoted to speech curves, the methods of obtaining them by talking machine, the methods of analysis, and the deductions concerning vocal sounds that have been made from them. The second part discusses the organ of hearing, the psychology of speech perception, the association of speech ideas and experimental results that bear upon the teaching of languages. The physiology of the vocal organs is considered in a third part, the phenomenon of breathing, the action of the larynx, and so forth. The nature of vowels and diphthongs, melody of speech, rhythmic action and verse rhythm are also touched upon. They also announce a work on "Madame de Pompadour," by H. Noel Williams, illustrated with sixteen photogravures reproduced from famous paintings.

THOMAS Y. CROWELL & CO. have in preparation for fall a work entitled "Mind Power and Privileges," a scientific study of mesmerism, hypnotism, Christian Science, etc., by Albert B. Olston; "Word Coinage," a study of slang and provincialisms, by Leon Mead; "Economics of Forestry," a study of forestry from the standpoint of political economy, by B. E. Fernow, and "Messages of the Masters," a series of discussions of the spiritual interpretations of great paintings, by Amory H. Bradford. New editions of standard authors announced by the same firm include the *Virginia Edition* of Edgar Allan Poe's works in seventeen volumes, edited by Professor James A. Harrison, of the University of Virginia; the *Lenox Edition* of Nathaniel Hawthorne's Romances, in fourteen volumes, edited by Professor Katharine Lee Bates, of Wellesley College, and the *Farringford Edition* of Tennyson's works, in ten volumes, edited by Professor Eugene Parsons. The latest catalogue of Messrs. Crowell & Co. show that they have added 738 new volumes to their list during the year—this total including new editions and new styles of binding as well as new titles.

DODD, MEAD & CO. have in preparation "A History of the Nineteenth Century Year by Year," by Edwin Emerson, Jr., which groups in moderate compass the central facts of each country's development during the past century in such a way as to make them easily accessible to the inquirer; "The Weather and Practical Methods of Forecasting," by "Farmer" Dunn, a well-known government "weather shark"; "The Uganda Protectorate," by Sir Harry Johnston, an important contribution to the history of East Central Africa, that contains within an area of some 150,000 square miles nearly all the wonders and some of the horrors of the Dark Continent; "Cruising in the West Indies," by Anson Phelps Stokes, that should prove interesting to yachtsmen who may plan to visit the West Indies; "The Lady of the Barge," a delightfully humorous book by W. W.

Jacobs; "Paul Kelver," the first long novel by Jerome K. Jerome; also, an entertaining book by Walter Russell, famous as a painter of children's portraits, treating of the training of children from the child's point of view, in which the child's mind will be shown not only in the text, but also in a series of beautiful pictures drawn by the author.

THE MACMILLAN COMPANY contradict in the Chicago *Record-Herald* certain statements recently made in regard to Charles Major's "Dorothy Vernon of Haddon Hall." There has been a good dead of curiosity to know what inducements the Macmillans offered Mr. Major to change his publishers after the Bowen-Merrill Company had made his reputation by the wide advertising of "When Knighthood Was in Flower." Among others, a statement was made that Mr. Major had been guaranteed a royalty on 100,000 copies, adding in regard to the size of the royalty, "the gossips put it all the way from 12½ to 25 per cent., but Mr. Major's friends say he was guaranteed $5,000." The Macmillans say not one of these statements is correct. They also deny that the book is not selling as well as expected, or that they are in any danger of losing money on the book. The Macmillans have made arrangements to publish the lectures delivered by the late Lord Acton as Regius Professor of Modern History at Cambridge, on "The French Revolution" and on "General Modern History.' These lectures will be published in two volumes, together with a reprint of Lord Acton's inaugural lecture. It is hoped also later on to publish one or more volumes of essays. The present Lord Acton has entrusted the work of editing and seeing the lectures through the press to R. Vere Laurence, Fellow of Trinity College, Cambridge.

J. B. LIPPINCOTT COMPANY announce a work on "Elementary Coal Mining," a new field and practical book by George L. Kerr, the author of "Practical Coal Mining," intended for those beginning the study of mining, with over two hundred illustrations; "Breachly-Black Sheep," the newest novel by the writer of vivid and adventurous stories of life in the South Sea Islands, Louis Becke, who is considered to be to that part of the world what Robert Louis Stevenson was to Samoa and Rudyard Kipling is to English India; "Arms and Armour-English Heraldry," two volumes, by Charles Boutell, which deal authoritatively with the subjects indicated by their titles, elaborately illustrated with drawings and reproductions from photographs; "The Opera," a sketch of its development from the earliest times, with a full description of every work of importance in the modern repertory, by R. A. Streatfield; a special edition, limited to 356 copies, of "The Thousand and One Nights," from Edward W. Lane's version of the original Arabic, in six volumes, elaborately illustrated; also, a sumptuous edition of "The Essays of Elia," introduced by a biographical note, and an appreciation of Lamb by E. B. Lucas, with drawings in broad line by A. Garth Jones. They will publish shortly "Gentleman Garnet," a romantic tale of a Tasmanian Robin Hood and his band, by Harry B. Vogel; also, "Sign of the Seven Sins," a new story by Le Queux.

SMALL, MAYNARD & CO. whose address is now 10 Arrow Street, Cambridge, Mass., will add to their *Beacon Biographies* a life of Audubon, by John Burroughs, whose fitness to write such a sketch will be recognized by all. They announce that the first edition of 2000 copies of Holman Day's new poems, entitled "Pine Tree Ballads," was exhausted within a week after publication, and that this book bids fair to exceed the remarkable success of Mr. Day's first book, "Up in Maine," of which nearly 10,000 copies have been sold. They announce that the authors of the stories which appeared anonymously in "A House Party" are as follows: "The Angel of the Lord," George W. Cable; "Artemisia's Mirror," Bertha Runkle; "Aunt Nancy's Annuity," Frank R. Stockton; "The Broken Story," Ruth McEnery Stuart; "Dawson's Dilemma," John Kendrick Bangs; "The Fairy Godmother," Mrs. Burton Harrison; "A Family Tradition," Paul Leicester Ford; "The Green Bowl," Sarah Orne Jewett; "The Messenger," Octave Thanet; "Mother," Owen Wister; "The Red Oxen of Bonval," Charles G. D. Roberts; "A Surrender," Robert Grant. In the original competition no correct guess was received, the nearest being that of Mrs. Horace Silsbee, of Seneca Falls, N. Y., who guessed correctly the authorship of eleven out of twelve stories. In the second contest, in which the names of the authors were given and the question was which author wrote each story, twenty-four correct answers were received.

G. P. PUTNAM'S SONS will bring out here "The Poet and Penelope," by L. Parry Truscott, a novel that has attracted some attention in England. The poetic temperament is set upon a pedestal and at the same time tied to her apron strings by the spirit of common sense and practicality. A man and a maid find mutual attraction in their incapacity for complete understanding of one another, and serve the novelist with no little store of misunderstanding full of dynamic possibility for plot. With his assistance they finally make out what they are severally about, and end by liking one another all the better for their temporary misconceptions. They have in preparation an authorized English version, by L. G. Meyer, of "The Youth of La Grande Mademoiselle (1627-1652,") by Arvède Barine; "William Morris, poet, craftsman and socialist," by Elizabeth Luther Cary, also, library editions of Miss Cary's "Browning, poet and man," "Tennyson, his homes, his friends and his work," and "The Rossettis;" "St. Augustine and His Age," by Joseph McCabe, author of "Peter Abelard;" "The Romance of Leonardi da Vinci, the forerunner," an authorized translation of Dmitri Mérejkowski's "The Resurrection of the Gods," edited by Professor Herbert French; "Lavender and Old Lace," by Myrtle Reed, author of "The Spinster Book;" "The Earth and the Fulness Thereof," by Peter Rosegger, translated by Francis E. Skinner; "The Lost Art of Reading," by Gerald Stanley Lee; also, "A Guide to the Best Historical Novels and Tales," by Jonathan Nield.

TERMS OF ADVERTISING.

Under the heading "Books Wanted" ***book-trade subscribers are given the privilege of a free advertisement for books out of print, of five nonpareil lines exclusive of address, in any issue except special numbers, to an extent not exceeding 100 lines a year. If more than five lines are sent, the excess is at 10 cents a line, and amount should be inclosed.*** *Bids for current books and such as may be easily had from the publishers, and repeated matter, as well as all advertisements from non-subscribers, must be paid for at the rate of 10 cents a line.*

Under the heading "Books for Sale," the charge to subscribers and non-subscribers is 10 cents a nonpareil line for each insertion. No deduction for repeated matter.

All other small, undisplayed, advertisements will be charged at the uniform rate of 10 cents a nonpareil line. Eight words may be reckoned to the line.

Parties with whom we have no accounts must pay in advance, otherwise no notice will be taken of their communications.

BOOKS WANTED.

☞ ***In answering, please state edition, condition, and price, including postage or express charges.***

Houses that are willing to deal exclusively on a cash-on-delivery basis will find it to their advantage to put after their firm-name the word [Cash].

☞ ***Write your wants plainly and on one side of the sheet only. Illegibly-written "wants" will be considered as not having been received. The "Publishers' Weekly" does not hold itself responsible for errors.***

It should be understood that the appearance of advertisements in this column, or elsewhere in the "Publishers' Weekly" does not furnish a guarantee of credit. While it is endeavored to safeguard these columns by withdrawing the privilege of their use from advertisers who are not "good pay," booksellers should take the usual precaution, as to advertisers not known to them, that they would take in making sales to any unknown parties.

Arthur M. Allen, 508 Fulton St., Troy, N. Y.

Montalembert. Monks of the West.
Allies Formation of Christendom.
Rosenthal, German Method, 10 pts.
Books on ordnance and gunnery.

Amer. Bapt. Pub. Soc., 177 Wabash Ave., Chicago.

Fairbairn, Typology.
Robt. South's Sermons.
Rev. John Gill's Sermons, 2 v.
Calmet, Dict. of the Bible, 5 v., cl.
Paley, Natural Theology, etc.
Alford, Dean, Gr. Test. with revised text.
Life of Moody, by Goss.
2 copies of The Prize S. S. Song Book, by Geo. F. Root. Pub. by John Church & Co.
A. J. Gordon on F. W. Robertson's Baptismal Regeneration.
Alexander Carson and His Times.
John Bunyan and His Biographers.
A. C. Kendrick on Dale's Classic Baptism.
Memoir of Dr. Stanford.

Amer. Bapt. Pub. Soc., 279 Elm St, Dallas, Tex.

Carson, On Baptism. American Baptist Pub. Soc.

Amer. Bapt. Pub. Soc., 902 Olive St., St. Louis, Mo.

Infant Baptism Examined, by J. Torrey Smith. Amer. Bapt. Pub. Soc., 1850.

Antiquarian Book Concern, Omaha, Neb.

Report of Missionary Conference, London, 1888.
Murphy, On the Pentateuch.
Monthelon and Gourgaud's Memoirs of Napoleon.

Astor Book Shop, 4 Barclay St., N. Y.

Silliman's Journal, 2d and 3d ser.
Lives of Lord Chancellors and Chief Justices.
Mademoiselle De Maupin.
Vasari, Lives of the Painters.

The Baker & Taylor Co., 33 E. 17th St., N. Y.

Anstey, The Talking Horse, pap. or cl. U. S. Book Co.
Dumas, Napoleon. Putnam.
Eaton, Civil Service of Great Britain, new or second-hand. Harper.

G. H. Barbour, 6016 Stanton Ave., Pittsburgh, Pa.

Anything pertaining to the Biddle Family.

Bartlett's Book Store, 33 E. 22d St., N. Y.

Poe's Poems, good binding.
Knickerbocker's New York. Grolier Club.
Matthew Arnold, good binding.
Darley plates of Dickens.
Mechanism of Wall Street.

W. L. Beekman, 55 E. 5th St., St. Paul, Minn.

Red Cloud, by Butler.
Any history of physics.
The War in Nicaragua, by Walker.
Walker's Filibusters.
An Anarchist on Anarchy.
Physical Basis of Life, by Alexander.
History of Court Fools, by Doran.
Photo. Times, Jan., Feb., '01.
Gallery of Players, no. 11.

The Bell Book and Stationery Co., Richmond, Va.

Comedy of Noctes Ambrosianae.

B. D. Berry, 378 Wabash Ave., Chicago, Ill. [*Cash.*]

Beall, Alexander, English Grammar, 12°. 1841.
Burr, Jonathan, English Grammar, 18°. 1818.
Chapin, Joel, English Grammar, 12°. 1842.
Cooper, J. G., English Grammar, 12°. 1831.

The Boston Book Co., 83 Francis St., Boston, Mass.

Amer. Naturalist, Dec., 1876; June, July, Aug., Oct., '78.
Botanical Gazette, v. 1-18.
Torrey, Botanical Club Bulletin, v. 1-20.
Harper's Weekly, Aug. 24, 1878.

J. W. Bouton, 10 W. 28th St., N. Y.

Clark, Organ Construction.
Nicholson, Organ Tuning.
Bartlett's Illustrated Works, 8 v.
Sand, George, Letters of, 3 v. 1885.
Cooper, History of the Rod.
Stone, Life of Brant.
Stone, Life of Red Jacket.
Ripley, History of the Mexican War.
Riker, Annals of Newtown.
1st eds. of Roosevelt's Works, cl.

The Bowen-Merrill Co., Indianapolis, Ind.

Muther, Modern Painters, v. 3.
Brakespeare, by Geo. A. Lawrence.

Brentano's, 218 Wabash Ave., Chicago, Ill.

Historical Sketches of Plymouth and of the Wyoming Valley, Luzerne Co., Penn., by H. B. Wright. Pub. about 1876 by Peterson, Philadelphia.
Stewart Pearce of Wilkesbarre, Penn., Annals of Luzerne Co., a record of interesting events, traditions and anecdotes from the first settlement of Wyoming to 1860.
National Calendar and Annals of U. S. for 1833, 12°, 336 pages, Washington, 1833, by Peter Force.
Miss Traumerei, by Bagby.
Our Church and Our Village, by Birch.
Songs of Toil and Triumph, by McCreery.
Brenners, by Eugene Sue.
Earth's Enigmas, by Roberts.

Brentano's, Union Sq., N. Y.

Myers, Remains of Lost Empires. Harper.
Corbin, English School Boy Life. Harper.
Adams, C. F., Chapter of Evil, etc.
Cæsar's Column, pap. or cl.
Baby's Biography, white and gold, new. Brentano's.
Wister, Lady with Rubies, cl. Lippincott.
Trollope, T. Adolphus, Works, 4 v., English book.
McHenry, Geo., The Cotton Trade. 1863.
Olmstead, F. L., Cotton Kingdom, 2 v. 1862.
Williams, S. W., Chinese Immigration. Scribner, 1879.
Nordhoff, C., Cotton States. Appleton.
Nieboer, Slavery as an Industrial System. 1900.
Dick, Apology for Life of James Fennell. Phila., 1874.
Reed, J. W., Hist. of Reed Family in Europe and America, 1861. Privately printed.
Amer. Catalogue, 1895-1900, second-hand.
Matter of Honor. Whittaker.
Dewey, Beauty in Dress. Harper.
Appleton, W. S., Crane Family of Chilton. 1868.
Alcock, Capital of the Tycoon. 1863.
Beecher, Norwood. F., H. & H.

BOOKS WANTED.—Continued.

Brentano's, 1015 Pennsylvania Ave., Washington, D. C.

The Newsboy, Ida Norman.
Frye, Military Reminiscences. Brentano's, 1889.

The Brown, Eager & Hull Co., Toledo, O.

New Century Dictionary, 10 v.

The Burnham Antique Book Store, Milk St., Boston, Mass. [*Cash.*]

F. L. Olmstead's works: Walks and Talks of Amer. Farmer; Journey to a Back Country; Texas Journey; Seaboard Slave States; Cotton Kingdom; and Books on landscape gardening, by same author.

The Burrows Bros. Co., Cleveland, O.

Symonds, Doge's Farm.
Anything by Jacob Boehme.
2 copies McDonnell, Love Songs of Three Centuries.
Troilius, Iron and Steel Analysis.
Rowley (Chatterton), Poems. 1777.
Lord, Notes on Metallurgy.

C. N. Caspar Co., 437 E. Water St., Milwaukee, Wis.

St. Nicholas, Jan. to Nov., 1875, incl.; Jan., June, July, Aug., Oct., Nov., '76.
Richmond, Religion of the Stars.
Old English and American grammars.
Lyon, Hollow Globe.
Upham, View of the Absolute Religion.
McAlpine, Treasures from the Prose World.

A. H. Clapp, 32 Maiden Lane, Albany, N. Y.

Diana of the Crossways, Meredith, in original, not revised ed.

The A. H. Clark Co., Garfield Bldg., Cleveland, O.

Toland, Conn., any hist. of.
W. Springfield, Mass., any hist. of.

W. B. Clarke Co., Park and Tremont Sts., Boston, Mass.

Oliver, Life of Edgeworth.
Anything of Walter Crane, in colors, before 1890.

Henry T. Coates & Co., Phila., Pa.

Stowe, Uncle Tom's Cabin, 2 v., limited ed.
Wilde, Oscar, The Happy Prince.
Sanborn, Homes and Haunts of Emerson.

Cohin & Peyran, 405 N Oregon St., El Paso, Tex.

Why We Laugh, by S. S. Cox, second-hand or new.
Prescott, Conquest of Mexico, v. 1, by Kirk, second-hand. Lippincott.
Rupert of Hentzau, Hope, pap. or second-hand.
Spanish Fiction, second-hand or pap.

Geo. H. Colby & Co., 22 Main St., Lancaster, N. H.

Du Bose, W. L. Yancey. 1894.
Tinman's Manual, by I. R. Butts.

H. M. Connor, 232 Meridian St., E. Boston, Mass.

Cord and Crease.
Voltaire, Philosophy.
Knock Magon.
Collier's Chambers' Ency., v. 7.
Second-hand book catalogues.

Cornell Co-operative Society, Ithaca, N Y.

Jenks, Const. Experiments of the Commonwealth.
Du Bose, Life and Times of Yancey.
Pike, First Blows of the Civil War.
Harrell, The Brooks and Baxter War.
Capers, Life of Memminger.

R. W. Crothers, 246 4th Ave., N. Y.

Bible of Saint Mark's.

Crusoe & Co., 81 Vermont St., Brooklyn, N. Y.

Weber's ed. of Beaumont and Fletcher, v. 6.
Bullen's ed. of Middleton, v. 8.
Armstrong's ed. of Pope.
How to Make Money Out of Patents.

Cushing & Co., 34 W. Baltimore St., Baltimore, Md.

Hawke, Ecclesiastical History P. E. Church, Virginia, v. 1.

D. & Co., care of The Publishers' Weekly, N. Y.

Mémoires sur l'Egypt Publiés Pendant les Campagnes de Bonaparte.
Physiology of Marriage, Balzac.

Damrell & Upham, 283 Washington St., Boston, Mass.

Larned, History, v. 6, shp.
Sheahan's Life of Douglas.
Letters from High Latitudes, Lady Dufferin.

Henry Delatush, 562 Newark Ave., Jersey City, N. J. [*Cash.*]

Knickerbocker Magazine, v. 32, 1848.
New England History, v. 2 only, Elliott. Scribner, 1857.
Works of President Edwards, v. 1, perfect or imperfect. Baines, Leeds, 1807.

A. W. Dellquest & Co., 206 Mesa Ave., El Paso, Tex. [*Cash.*]

Howe, History of Virginia.
Mustang Gray.
Mier Prisonero, or, Prisoners of Perote.
Simon Suggs.
Red Stick, a Georgia story.
Tiger Lilies, by Sidney Lanier.
Spofford, Land Survey.
Anything about the Huguenots in America.
Anything about missions in New Mexico.
Lost Atlantis, by Donnelly.

Edwin A. Denham, 28 W. 33d St., N. Y.

Wilson, Francis, Recollections of a Player. 1897.
Elston Press, Art and Crafts of Printing.

DeWolfe, Fiske & Co., 361 Washington St., Boston, Mass.

Burton's Arabian Nights.
Dict. of Everyday Wants, Youman.

Dick & Fitzgerald, 18 Ann St., N. Y.

The Portfolio of Autograph Etchings. Pub. by Ticknor & Co.

Dodd, Mead & Co., 372 Fifth Ave., N. Y.

Quintin Matsys, by Pierce Egan.
Archie Lovell, by Edwards.
The World's Orators, v. 1, L. P. Putnam.
The Book-Lover, nos. 1, 2.
Spence's Observations, Anecdotes and Characters, ed. by Malone. 1820.
Des Cars, Pruning Forest and Ornamental Trees. Cupples.
A Book of Wise Sayings of Great Men.
Long Island Sports.
Nature, Mar. 12, 1885.
Whistler, The Gentle Art of Making Enemies, any ed.
Parkman, Old Regime in Canada, 1874; Count Frontenac, 1877; Half Century of Conflict, 1892; Montcalm and Wolfe, 1884.

Wm. J. C. Dulany Co., 8 Baltimore St., East, Baltimore, Md.

Catalogue of the Etchings of Jas. McN. Whistler, by Fred. Wedmore.

Daniel Dunn, 677 Fulton St., Brooklyn, N. Y.

Huxley and Tyndall, sets, hf. mor. Appleton.
Pocket ed. of Dickens, set.
Battles and Leaders, pt. 10, quote odd nos.

E. P. Dutton & Co., 31 W. 23d St., N. Y.

Howlett, On Driving.
Memorials of Quiet Life, Hare.
Chaplain of the Fleet, Besant.
Stevenson's Works, 26 v., Thistle ed.

G. Engelke, 225 N. Clark St., Chicago, Ill. [*Cash.*]

Dutch Republic, v. 3, Motley.
Hist. of New Netherlands, v. 3, Motley.
Brownson, Am. Republic.
Hill, Rev. Walter, Elem. of Philosophy.

C. P. Everitt, 219 5th Ave., N. Y.

Fitzgerald's Works, any good ed.

Harry Falkenau, 167 Madison St., Chicago, Ill.

Saxe, Physiology of Plants.

The W. Y Foote Co., University Block, Syracuse, N. Y

Therapeutic Magazine, May, 1893.
Mushrooms of America, Edible and Poisonous, ed. by Palmer. Pub. by Prang & Co., 1885.

Funk & Wagnalls Co., 30 Lafayette Pl., N. Y.

Customs of the Ancients, by Thomas Hope, 2d or later ed.
Prospectus of Monograph on Flavoring Extracts, by Joseph Harrop.

Goodspeed's Book Shop, 5a Park St., Boston, Mass. [*Cash.*]

Lowell, Favorite Poems. Boston, 1877.
Thoreau, Excursion. Boston, 1863.

BOOKS WANTED.—*Continued.*

Gotham Book Concern, 442 W. 56th St., N. Y.

Overland Monthly, June, 1870; Jan., '83.
English Illus. Mag., copies in v. 10.
Idler, copies in 1893-94.
Longmans' Mag., copies in v. 2, 3, 4, 6.
Strand, Eng. ed., copies in 1891, '95, '96.
Macmillan's Mag., copies in v. 58, 59, 64, 65.
Galaxy, copies in v. 5.
Comic Monthly, 1870.

F. E. Grant, 23 W. 42d St., N. Y.

History of St. Lawrence County, Hough.
Modern English, Fitz Edward Hall.
Ruthless Hymns for Heartless Homes, Sumner.
Sources of the Constitution, Stevens.
Memoirs of the Baroness Riedesel.
George Carsterberry's Will.
For Better or Worse, an English story.
Books dealing with the Texas War of Independence.
Old Families of Munster, Miss Cusack.
The Female Volunteer, etc., Eliza Allen, 8°, 68 pp. 1851.
Dreadful Sufferings of Emigrant to Cal., Geo. Adam. St. Louis, 1850.
The Gold Seekers, Geo. Aimard. Phila.
Scenes in Hawaiian Islands and Cal., Mary Anderson. Boston, 1865.
From the Atlantic to the Pacific Overland, Demas Barnes. N. Y., 1865.
Lady of the West, J. Ballou. Cin., 1895.
Address which he was prevented from giving at Sac., Geo. Bates. S. F., 1850.
Early California, W. Bausman. S. F., 1864.
In Memory of Thomas Starr King, H. W. Bellows. S. F., 1864.
The Undeveloped West, J. H. Beadle. Phila., 1873.
Notes on Stratigraphy of Cal., G. F. Becker. Wash., 1855.
Plea for the Indian, Jno. Berson. N. Y., 1852.
Journey to Cal., Jno. Bidwell.
Homes for Educated Englishmen, D. A. Binney. 1875.
Hist. of Bowers Map Bill, A. B. Bowers. S. F., 1869.
The Pacific R. R., Sam. Bowles. Boston, 1869.
From the Orient to the Occident, Lanson Boyer. N. Y., 1876.
Sadalpha, or, a Voyage of Life, Col. J. Bradford. San Jose, 1880.
Chinese in Cal., C. W. Brooks. S. F., 1877.
J. Ross Browne, Letter in Relation to Proposed Townsite of Berkeley. S. F., 1870.
Movement for Univ. of Cal., Horace Bushnell. S. F., 1857.
Vasquez, P. Biers. N. Y., 1875.
Gold of Cal., G. Berry. London, 1849.
Hist. Journ. of Exped. by Sea and Land to North of Cal., 1769 to the following, from the Spanish Manuscripts, W. Beverly, 4°. London, 1790.
Captive in Patagonia, B. F. Bourne. Bost., 1853.

Simon Hart, Newport, R. I.

Roderick Hudson, Henry James.
Cook Book for Lent. Benziger.

W. W. Haygood, 17 Dexter Ave., Montgomery, Ala.

Cicero and the Fall of the Roman Republic, S. Davidson.
Life of Julius Cæsar, Froude.
Napoleon and the Fair Sex, Masson.
Napoleon Bonaparte, Masson.
Japanese Girls and Women, A. M. Bacon.

Herr & Co., 122 S. Main St., Goshen, Ind.

Carey, H., Sally in Our Alley, with music and ils., list $1.25. White & A.
Nelly was a Lady, illus. poem.

Hyland Bros., 229 Yamhill St., Portland, Ore.

Early Recollections of Washington City, Christian Hines.
Young, Chronicles of the Pilgrims.
Bradford Letter Book Plymouth Church Records.
"Mayflower" and Her Log.
Wigwam and War Path, Meacham.
Heroes of the Plains, Buell.
Encyclopedia of Etiquette, Emily Holt.

E. T. Jett Book and News Co., 806 Olive St., St. Louis, Mo.

How I Won My Spurs, J. G. Edgar.

E. W. Johnson, 2 E. 42d St., N. Y.

In the Valley, Harold Frederic.
Physiology of Love, Mantegazzi.

H. R. Johnson, 313 Main St., Springfield, Mass.

Prince, Chronological History New England, all of v. 2 published.

L. Jonas & Co., Astor House, N. Y.

The Astonishing History of a Troy Town, by "Q."

Kimball Bros., 618 Broadway, Albany, N. Y. [*Cash.*]

German Allies in the Am. Revolution.
N. Y. S. Muster Rolls, v. 7, 8, will pay good price.
Munsell, Annals of Albany, v. 5, 6, will pay good price.

King's Old Book Store, 15 4th St., San Francisco, Cal.

Bartlett, Personal Narrative, v. 1.
Blue and Gold (California State University Year Book), any.
Mountains of California, Muir.
Wright, History of Ireland, v. 1.
Rose, Machine Shop Practice, pt. 16.
Stephens, Central America, v. 1.
Squiers, Nicaragua, v. 1.
Belcher, Voyage Round the World, v. 1.
Cox, Columbia River, v. 1.

Geo. Kleinteich, 387 Bedford Ave., Brooklyn, N. Y. [*Cash.*]

Armageddon, by Baldwin.

Koelling & Klappenbach 100 Randolph St., Chicago, Ill.

Ladies' Home Journal, 1900 to June, 1901, or 1900 and 1901 complete.

Chas. E. Lauriat Co., 301 Washington St., Boston, Mass.

Edgar Allan Poe, Holland pap. library ed., either a set or odd v. Pub. by Barrie, Phila.
The Buccaneers, by R. Jones.
History of a Thug, by Col. Meadows Taylor.
Taras Bulba, Gogol.
New Guide to Health, or, Botanic Family Physician, by Samuel Thompson, 3d ed. 1827.
Philosophy of Shakespeare's Plays Unfolded, by Delia Bacon, either Eng. or Am. ed.

Leary's Book Store, 9 S. 9th St., Phila., Pa.

Evans, Mental Cure.
Evans, Primitive Mind Cure.

Leggat Bros., 81 Chambers St., N. Y.

Songs and ballads of American Revolution, Frank Moore.

Henry E. Legler, Milwaukee, Wis. [*Cash.*]

Magazine of American History, Feb., 1883.
Hamilton's Parodies, v. 1.
Catalogues John Carter-Brown Library, 4 v.

Lemcke & Buechner, 812 Broadway, N. Y.

Allibone, Dictionary of English Literature, 3 v., latest ed.
Kirk's Supplement to the same in 2 v.

Edw. E. Levi, 820 Liberty St., Pittsburgh, Pa.

Harris, T. W., Insects Injurious to Vegetation, Flint ed.

Library Clearing House, 140 Wells St., Chicago, Ill.

Senior, Treatise on Political Economy.
Gems of the Talmud.
Luther, On Galatians.
Calvin, On Romans.
Englishman's Greek Concordance.

Little, Brown & Co., 254 Washington St., Boston, Mass.

Headless Horseman, by Reed, cl.
Tarbox, Life of Gen. Israel Putnam. Pub. by Lothrop.

W. H. Lowdermilk & Co., Washington, D. C.

Gallatin, Albert, Writings, ed. by Adams.
Chapman, History of Wyoming (Penn.)
Gayarre, History of Louisiana, 4 v. 1885.

T. J. McBride & Son, 71 Broadway, N. Y.

Spanish-American War. Pub. by Quinlan.

Nathaniel McCarthy, Minneapolis, Minn.

Heavenly Vision, by Dr. Booth.
Kabbalah Unveiled, by S. L. McGregor Mather, second-hand. Pub. by George Redway.

BOOKS WANTED.—Continued.

McLaren's Old Book Shop, 81 4th Ave., N. Y.

Old guides, directory, or prints of New York City.
Birch's Heads, folio. Pub. by Virtue.
New York Mirror, 1827 to 1834.
Old English prints (colored), pub. before 1840, state size, subject, condition.

S. F. McLean & Co., 44 E. 23d St., N. Y.

Benjamin, Art in America.
Hitchcock, Etching in America.
Hazard, Freedom of Mind in Willing.
McPherson, Political History of U. S. During Reconstruction.
Very Little Tales for Very Little Children.
Read, Reed, and Reid Families.
Savage, The Falcon Family.
Savage, My Uncle the Curate.

John Jos. McVey, 39 N. 13th St., Phila., Pa.

The Mind, v. 1, 4. 1st ser. Pub. by Williams & Norgate.
Rhode Island Historical Tracts, pt. 2, no. 19; 2d ser., pt. 4.

M. N. Maisel, 194 E. Broadway, N. Y. [*Cash.*]

Noyes, American Socialism.
Lange, History of Materialism.
Marx and Ruge, Deutsch-Französische Jahrbücher.
Files of any Socialist periodicals, German, French, or English.

H. Malkan, Hanover Sq., N. Y.

Ellis, Puritan Age and Rule. L., B. & Co.
Century Dictionary, 24 pts.
My Lady's Face.
Bootle's Baby, good cl. ed.
Helps' Essays, good ed.

R. H. Merriam, Hanover Sq., N. Y.

Bacon's Reminiscences of T. Jefferson.
Forty Years Familiar Letters of J. W. Hamilton.

H. A. Moos, 514 E. Houston St., San Antonio, Tex.

Recollections of Fifty Years, by Sparks.

F. M. Morris, 171 Madison St., Chicago, Ill.

Jordan and Evermann's Fishes of North and Middle America.

H. H. Morse, 20 Monroe St., Grand Rapids, Mich.

Nicoll, Letters on Life.
Wiley, Yosemite, Alaska and the Yellowstone.
Kirkland Genealogy.
Stephens, Constit. View of Late War Bet. States.

A. J. Ochs & Co., 1781 Washington St., Boston, Mass.

Negro or Beast, by Wise. Am. Bible and Book Co., St. Louis.
Hour and the Man, by Harriet Martineau.
Tuckett's Monthly Insurance Journal, Phila., 1850 to 1861, any v. or nos.
N. Y. Insurance Journal, v. 39 to 52.

E. J. O'Malley, Hanover Sq., N. Y.

Genealogy of the Bergen Family. 1876.
Mrs. Seymour's Pamphlet on the Pickwick Papers.
Mount Vernon and its Associations, B. J. Lossing.

W. Millard Palmer, 20 Monroe St., Grand Rapids, Mich.

Henderson, The Rainbow's End.
Collingwood, Art Teaching of John Ruskin.
Thwaites, Afloat on the Ohio.
Smythe, Conquest of Arid America.

C. C. Parker, 246 S. Broadway, Los Angeles, Cal. [*Cash.*]

Beautiful Gems, H. D. Northup.

The Perkins Book Co., 296 Broadway, N. Y.

Williams' Life of Alexander.

Phila. Magazine Depot, 117 N. 13th St., Phila., Pa. [*Cash.*]

St. Nicholas, v. 1; also job lot, 1890 to date.
Potter's Am. Monthly, nos. 80, 103, 106, 109 to 112, 116, 117, 120, 128.
Engineering Mag., v. 1, 2, or odd nos.
Cassier's Mag., v. 1, 2, or odd nos.
Am. Hist. Register, Phila., 1897, nos.
Am. Cath. Hist. Researches, 1885-87, or odd nos.
Cath. Quar. Rev., Jan., 1879; Jan., Apr., '80; Jan., July, '81; July, Oct., '82; Jan., July, Oct., '83; Jan., July, '86.

Phila. Magazine Depot.—*Continued.*

The Esoteric, pub. in Boston and Applegate, Cal., v. 2, 3, 4, 6, and all after v. 8.

Pierce & Zahn, 633 17th St., Denver, Colo.

Intentions, by Wilde.
Marius the Epicurean, by Pater.

The Pilgrim Press, 175 Wabash Ave., Chicago, Ill.

Foundation Truths of the Gospel, by John Ritchie.
Funk & Wagnalls, Columbian Novels, 13 v., cheap.

C. S. Pratt, 161 6th Ave., N. Y. [*Cash.*]

The Confessions of Connaught.
La Fontaine, Tales not Fables.
Claudius Ptolemy, Tetrabiblos, Astrology.
Any books by Lady Morgan and Madam Adam.
De Mille, The Cryptogram.

Preston & Rounds Co., Providence, R. I.

Story of Ida, by Francesca.
Modern Horsemanship, Anderson.

Public Library, Cincinnati, O.

Orcutt, History of Stratford, Conn.
Inland Printer, v. 24, 26.

Purdy's Book Store, 1009 Congress St., Houston, Tex

Haswell, Engineer's and Mechanic's Pocket-Book.

G. P. Putnam's Sons, 27 W. 23d St., N. Y.

Badeau, Aristocracy. Harper.
Cook, Patch of Pansies.
Milton, Prose Works, 2-v. ed. Griswold, 1847.
Flint, Early Long Island. Putnam.
Irving, Van Gelder Papers.
Bayles, Suffolk Co., etc. 1874.
Child's Own Book of Fairy Tales, Miller.

Fleming H. Revell Co., Chicago, Ill.

Mahan, Asa, Baptism of the Holy Spirit. Palmer.

Geo. H. Rigby, 1113 Arch St., Phila., Pa.

DeVinne, The Practice of Typography, Correct Composition, etc. Century Co., 1901.
American in Paris.
Luce, Writing for the Press.

Rogers' Book Store, 39 Patton Ave., Asheville, N. C.

Barons of the Rappahannock and the Potomac, by Moncure D. Conway.

J. Francis Ruggles, Bronson, Mich.

Three Stations in Life, by M. E. Dowling.
Hertell, Judge, Cause of Intemperate Drinking.
Murray, Dialects of So. Scotland. 1873.
Any dict. of Lowland Scotch.

The St. Louis News Co., 1008 Locust St., St. Louis, Mo.

Legends of the Sioux, by Mrs. Eastman.

John E. Scopes, 29 Tweddle Bldg., Albany, N. Y.

American Ancestry, v. 9, 10.
Wilkinson, Memoirs, v. 2, and atlas. Phila., 1816.

Scrantom, Wetmore & Co., Rochester, N. Y.

Lord's Beacon Lights, odd v., quote subjects and price.
Butler's Autobiography.
Lark, nos. 18, 19, 21, 22, 23, 24, 25.

Charles Scribner's Sons, 153 5th Ave., N. Y.

Townsend, Malcolm, United States. Lothrop.
Norman, Real Japan.

John V. Sheehan & Co., 160 Woodward Ave., Detroit, Mich.

Cathcart, Literary Reader.

John Skinner, 44 N. Pearl St., Albany, N. Y.

Gazetteer State New York, 1813, 1824, 1836.
Annals of Tryon Co.
Broadhead's New York.
Irving's Conquest of Spain, Sunnyside ed., cl. or hf. mor.

George D. Smith, 49 New St., N. Y.

View of Park Fountain. 1848, Valentine Manual.
Sketches of Yale College. New York, 1843.
Trollope, Paul the Pope and Paul the Prior.
Robinson, Life of Father Paul Sarpi.
Hymns of Hildebert, tr. by Erastus Benedict.
Christ in Song, by Dr. Schaff.
Christian Life and Song, by Mrs. Charles.
Diary, or, Life of Chief Justice Chase.
Life and Speeches of Thomas Corwin.

Wm. T. Smith & Co., 145 Genesee St., Utica, N. Y.

Uttermost Rim and Beyond.

BOOKS WANTED.—Continued.

Smith & McCance, 38 Bromfield St., Boston, Mass.

Irwin, History of the 19th Army Corps.
Dunlop, History of the Art of Design.
Christian Science Journal, v. 2 and after.
Science and Health, 1881.

Speyer & Peters, Berlin, N. W. 7, Germany.

Archiv für Mikroskop. Anatomie.
Archiv für Patholog. Anatomie. Virchow.
Archives of Laryngology.
Brain.
Engineering, v. 1.
Journal of Anatomy and Physiol., v. 1, 10, 32, 34.
Journal of Amer. Chem. Soc., 1889-1901.
Ophthalm. Soc. Transactions.
Transactions of Amer. Orthop. Association.
Please offer sets or single vols.
Annals of Surgery, sets.

Frank Stanton, Wheeling, W. Va.

Destruction and Reconstruction, Gen'l Rich. Taylor.

G. E. Stechert, 9 E. 16th St., N. Y.

Tredwell, Apollonius of Tyana. 1886.
Styx, Hermetic Philosophy, 3 v.
Butler, Movable Feasts, etc. N. Y., 1836.
Hodges, Edward Hodges.
Am. Chemical Journal, any odd v.

E. Steiger & Co., 25 Park Place, N. Y. [*Cash.*]

Edmunds, Patents for Inventions. 1883.
Gibbons, Banks of New York. 1870.
Journal of the Amer. Geographical Society, v. 1, 2.
Richardson, Messages and Papers of the Presidents. 1899.
American Agriculturist, v. 59 to 68, complete or odd v.

The Stiefel Masonic Book Co., 106 E. 4th St., Cincinnati, O.

Transactions, also Official Bulletin issued by the Sup. Council, A. A. S. R. Southern Jur.
Universal Masonic Library, v. 11, 17, 18, 22, 23, 25, 27, 29, 30.

Stout's Book Exchange, 612 5th St., San Diego, Cal.

Personal Sketches, Barrington.
Auto. Ed. Wortley Montagu.
Ismailia, Sir Samuel Baker.
Phœnixiana, 1st ed.

Strawbridge & Clothier, Market St., Phila., Pa.

Aucassin and Nicolette, Lang, Stone ed.
Ticknor, History of Spanish Literature, v. 1 only.

Thos. J. Taylor, Taunton, Mass.

Catalogue of Richard Wagner's Works. Pub. by P. Pabst, Leipzig, 1896.
Pamphlets and books on Richard Wagner in any language.

H. H. Timby, Conneaut, O.

Life of Marie Bashkirtseff.
5 copies Altgeld, Oratory.
Stevenson, Thistle ed.

W. H. Walker, 58 Moffatt St., Brooklyn, N. Y.

The Federalist, v. 1, 1788.
Records of New Amsterdam, 7 v.
Irving, Sketch Book, il.

John Wanamaker, Phila., Pa.

Lyell, Principles of Geology.
Lyell, Geological Antiquity of Man.
Geikie, Prehistoric Europe.

Geo. E. Warner, Minneapolis, Minn.

Memoirs of Johnson and Matheson, by Patterson.
Johnson, Seventeen Seventy-six, and Other Poems.
Atlas of any county.
Life of Sam. Houston, by Lester.

Thomas Whittaker, 2 Bible House, N. Y.

The Criterion, A. C. Coxe.
Rays of Sunlight for Dark Days, Vaughan.

T. Williams, 916 Pine St., Phila., Pa.

Amherst College catalogues before 1850.

W. H. Wood & Co., 8 E. Main St., Springfield, O.

Plantation Melodies and Jubilee Songs.
Martensen, Dogmatics.

W. H. Wood & Co.—Continued.

Royal Path of Life.
McCoy, Shorthand of Masonry.
Mackey, Jurisprudence of Masonry.

BOOKS FOR SALE.

Bargain, 49 Columbus Ave., N. Y.

Being overcrowded we will sell 1000 novels for $10.

King Bros., 3 4th St., San Francisco, Cal.

Any volume of Bancroft's Histories of Pacific States, shp., $2.50; cl., $2 each.

Daniel O'Shea, 1584 Broadway, N. Y.

Back nos. of magazines from 5 c. upwards.

Phila. Mag. Depot, 117 N. 13th St., Phila., Pa [*Cash.*]

Libraries please take notice:
Engineering Mag., set, v. 1-23, no. 2.
Am. Mag. of History, set 9 v., ¾ mor., bal. in nos.
Hist. Mag. and *Notes and Queries*, by N. Dawson, complete set in nos., uncut, with all extra nos.
Atlantic Monthly, set, about half bound.
Pop. Science Monthly, set, about half bound.
Rev. of Reviews, set, a few v. bound.
Bookman, set, in nos.
Scribner's Mag., set, about half bound.
Century Mag., set, 1881-1902, about half bound.
Arena, v. 1-21, nos.
Putnam's Mag., v. 1-10, hf. mor.; n. s., v. 1-6, publ. cl.
International Rev., set; v. 1, cl.; v. 2, nos.; bal. hf. leath.
Galaxy, set, publisher's cl.
Lippincott's Mag., set, v. 1-51, bound, bal. in nos.
N. J. Archives, 1st ser., 20 v., cl.
Pa. Archives and Col. Records, 78 v.
Benton's Debates, 16 v., bound.
Proc. of Am. Assoc. for Adv. of Science, v. 1-43.
Records of Am. Cath. Hist. Soc., set, Phila., Pa.
McClure's Mag., set, in nos.
American Rev., 1845-52, set, mostly bound.
English Illus. Mag., v. 1-6, hf. leath.
Self Culture, 1895-1902, set, in nos.
New York Review, set.
Land We Love, set.
Harper's Family Library, set 150 v., 12°, cl.
Harper's Mag., v. 1-103, hf. mor.
Also many other complete and incomplete sets of magazines. Send list of wants.

HELP WANTED.

WANTED.—Young man for responsible position in mail order house. Must be a good buyer, active, and with a knowledge of printing. Address confidentially, with full particulars, R. WAKEFIELD, P. O. Box 489, N. Y. City.

BOOKKEEPER.—A young man with some experience of publishing accounts and books—accuracy and good penmanship indispensable. Apply in the first place by letter, with references, to N. Y. PUBLISHER, care of PUBLISHERS' WEEKLY.

SITUATIONS WANTED.

WANTED.—A position as manager or assistant manager of a book publishing department. Understands the duties thoroughly; well acquainted with the book trade of U. S. An all round man. Salary according to worth. First-class references. Address KNOWLEDGE, care of PUBLISHERS' WEEKLY.

WANTED.—A young man, at present manager of a book department, and with ten years' experience in the book business, wishes to identify himself with an established book and stationery house, in which a business interest may be acquired, if his services are found satisfactory. Address RETAIL BOOKSELLER, care of PUBLISHERS' WEEKLY.

WANTED.—By a young man (a thorough bibliographer), at present manager of a large book and stationery house, and with 12 years of experience in the book business—8 years as buyer—a position with an Eastern house, where knowledge of the business will be recognized. Address EXPERIENCED BOOKMAN, care of PUBLISHERS' WEEKLY.

COPYRIGHT NOTICES.

LIBRARY OF CONGRESS.
OFFICE OF THE REGISTER OF COPYRIGHTS,
WASHINGTON, D. C.

Class A, XXc, No. 33494.—To wit: *Be it remembered*, That on the 7th day of May, 1902, The Robert Clarke Company, of Cincinnati, O., hath deposited in this office the title of a book, the title of which is in the following words, to wit: "Manual of Universal Church History. By Rev. Dr. John Alzog. Translated by F. J. Pabisch and Rt. Rev. Thomas S. Byrne. Volume I. Cincinnati, The Robert Clarke Company," the right whereof they claim as proprietors in conformity with the laws of the United States respecting copyrights.

(Signed) HERBERT PUTNAM, *Librarian of Congress*.
By THORVALD SOLBERG, *Register of Copyrights*.
In renewal for 14 years from Sept. 12, 1902.

SPECIAL NOTICES.

THE

WITH WHICH IS INCORPORATED

The American Literary Gazette and Publishers' Circular.

[ESTABLISHED 1852.]

PUBLICATION OFFICE, 298 BROADWAY, NEW YORK.

Entered at the Post-Office at New York, N. Y., as second-class matter.

VOL. LXII., No. 6. NEW YORK, August 9, 1902. WHOLE No. 1593

The Publishers' Weekly.

AUGUST 9, 1902.

RATES OF ADVERTISING.

One page	$20 00
Half page	12 00
Quarter page	6 00
Eighth page	4 00
One-sixteenth page	2 00

Copyright Notices, Special Notices, and other undisplayed advertisements, 10 cents a line of nonpareil type.

The above prices do not include insertions in the "Annual Summary Number," the "Summer Number," the "Educational Number," or the "Christmas Bookshelf," for which higher rates are charged.

Special positions $5 a page extra. Applications for special pages will be honored in the order of their receipt.

Special rates for yearly or other contracts.

All matter for advertising pages should reach this office not later than Wednesday noon, to insure insertion in the same week's issue.

RATES OF SUBSCRIPTION.

One year, postage prepaid in the United States	$3 00
One year, postage prepaid to foreign countries	4 00

Single copies, 8 cents; postpaid, 10 cents. Special numbers: Educational Number, in leatherette, 50 cents; Christmas Number, 25 cents; the numbers containing the three, six and nine months' Cumulated Lists, 25 cents each. Extra copies of the Annual Summary Number, *to subscribers only*, 50 cents each.

PUBLICATION OFFICE, 298 BROADWAY, P. O. BOX 943, N.Y.

INDEX TO ADVERTISERS

NOTES IN SEASON.

JAMES POTT & CO. have in preparation a new book by John Goldworth Alger, entitled "Paris, 1789-1794." Nearly twenty years' study, not merely of the latest publications on the subject, but of a mass of manuscripts mostly uncalendared in the national archives, enables the author to throw new light on the French Revolution.

LONGMANS, GREEN & CO. will publish a new book of historical research by Andrew Lang, entitled "James VI. and the Gowrie Conspiracy." The Gowrie Conspiracy took place in 1600, and its sequel is the affair of Logan of Restalrig in 1608-9. Mr. Lang has studied contemporary manuscripts hitherto unpublished, and he believes that one point is at any rate demonstrated—the innocence of James VI. Among the illustrations of the book are facsimile reproductions of the disputed letters of the plot.

L. C. PAGE & CO. have just ready "The Best of Stevenson," selections from Robert Louis Stevenson's "Will of the Mill," "Virginibus Puerisque," etc., with a bibliography of Stevenson's writings edited by Alexander Jessup; also, a third series of that excellent collection of college verse—"Cap and Gown," by L. L. Paget. They will publish shortly a novel by Alice MacGowan, entitled "The Last Word," which gives a picture of some of the phases of New York as seen through the fresh, keen eyes of a young girl from the broad prairies of the southwest.

DOUBLEDAY, PAGE & CO. will publish on the 27th inst. a volume of poems by Ellen Glasgow, author of "The Battleground," a number of which will be familiar to readers of the *Atlantic Monthly* and other periodicals. In October they will bring out an illustrated edition of Miss Glasgow's "Voice of the People." They have in preparation a book on "Weddings," in which Mrs. Burton Kingsland will digest and codify the unwritten laws on the subject. The book will be illustrated with photographs of large weddings of recent date to give an exact idea of how the thing must be done.

THE CENTURY COMPANY have in preparation another volume of engravings by Timothy Cole, to be entitled "Old English Masters," which will have text from Mr. Cole's own notes and by Professor John C. Van Dyke. The volume will contain Mr. Cole's engravings of the work of the English school, including Hogarth, Reynolds, Gainsborough, Turner and Landseer. For eighteen years Mr. Cole has been engaged in reproducing upon wood, for *The Century Magazine* and his books, the work of the great masters of the world. He has already covered the art of Italy, Holland, Flanders and England, and is now working upon the Spanish school.

THE MACMILLAN COMPANY have in preparation two volumes of essays by the late John Fiske, that were left completed and ready for the press before the author's death. The contents of the volumes will be Thomas Hutchinson, last Royal Governor of Massachusetts; Charles Lee, the soldier of fortune; Alexander Hamilton; Thomas Jefferson, the conservative reformer; James Madison, the constructive statesman; Andrew Jackson, frontiersman and soldier; Andrew Jackson, and American Democracy sixty years ago; "Tippecanoe and Tyler Too;" Daniel Webster; "Old and New Ways of Treating History;" "The Boston Tea Party;" "Evolution and the Present Age;" John Milton; John Tyndall; "Koschei the Deathless;" "The Story of a New England Town;" "Reminiscences of Huxley."

WEEKLY RECORD OF NEW PUBLICATIONS.

☞ **Beginning with the issue of July 5, 1902, the titles of *net* books published under the rules of the American Publishers' Association are preceded by a double asterisk **, and the word net follows the price. The titles of *fiction* (not net) published under the rules are preceded by a dagger †. *Net* books not covered by the rules, whether published by members of the American Publishers' Association or not, are preceded by a single asterisk, and the word net follows the price.** ☜

The abbreviations are usually self-explanatory. c. after the date indicates that the book is copyrighted; if the copyright date differs from the imprint date, the year of copyright is added. Books of foreign origin of which the edition (annotated, illustrated, etc.) is entered as copyright, are marked c. ed.; translations, c. tr.; n. p., in place of price, indicates that the publisher makes no price, either net or retail, and quotes prices to the trade only upon application.

A colon after initial designates the most usual given name, as: A: Augustus; B: Benjamin; C: Charles; D: David; E: Edward; F: Frederic; G: George; H: Henry; I: Isaac; J: John; L: Louis; N: Nicholas; P: Peter; R: Richard; S: Samuel; T: Thomas; W: William.

Sizes are designated as follows: F. (folio: over 30 centimeters high); Q. (4to: under 30 cm.); O. (8vo: 25 cm.); D. (12mo: 20 cm.); S. (16mo: 17½ cm.); T. (24mo: 15 cm.); Tt. (32mo: 12½ cm.); Fe. 48mo: 10 cm.). Sq., obl., nar., designate square, oblong, narrow books of these heights.

American newspaper annual, [1902.] Phil., N. W. Ayer & Son, 1902. 8°, cl., $5.

American newspaper directory. 34th year. N. Y., G. P. Rowell & Co., 1902. 12°, cl., $5.

Annunzio, Gabriele d'. The dead city: a tragdy; rendered into English by G. Mantellini; il. from the stage productions of Eleonora Duse. Chic., Laird & Lee, [1902.] c. 282 p. il. D. cl., $1.25.
The first English version of a play that was written for Eleonora Duse, and produced by her in Europe.

Barnett, J. M. Mother Goose paint book. Akron, O., Saalfield Pub. Co., 1902. [Jl15.] c. 105 p. il. obl. 8°, bds., $1.25.

Beall, St. Clair. The winning of Sarenne; il. by L: F. Grant. N. Y., Federal Book Co., 1902. c. 343 p. il. 12°, cl., 50 c.; pap., 25 c.

****Blanchard,** Amy Ella. Little Miss Oddity; il. by Ida Waugh. Phil., G: W. Jacobs & Co., [1902.] [Jl.] c. 225 p. il. D. cl., 80 c. net.
Cassy Law was a strange little girl, who loved spiders and bugs, and other wonders of natural history; on this account she was called by her schoolmates, "Miss Oddity." Her story is odd like the name conferred on her.

Bonehill, Ralph. The boy land boomer. Akron, O., Saalfield Pub. Co., 1902. [Ag1.] c. 233 p. il. 12°, cl., $1.

Bonsall, C: Money: its nature and its functions: a logical, historic and economic treatise. [Salem, O., M. S. Schwartz & Co., 1902.] c. 103 p. 12°, cl., 50 c.; pap., 25 c.

Braden, Ja. A. Far past the frontier. Akron, O., Saalfield Pub. Co., 1902. [Ag1.] c. 347 p. il. 12°, cl., $1.

Brown, W: Perry. Ralph Granger's fortunes. Akron, O., Saalfield Pub. Co., 1902. [Ag1.] c. 305 p. il. 12°, cl., $1.

Cameron, *Mrs.* Emily Sharp Lovett. A woman's no. N. Y., F. M. Buckles Co., 1902. c. 2-294 p. D. cl., $1.25.
An English Lord, who was betrothed to one girl, falls in love with a second, and is inveigled into eloping with a third. Repenting of his folly, he strives to atone to the woman he loves, who proves the truth of the old adage, that a woman's negative is equivalent to her affirmative.

Castlemon, Harry, [*pseud.* for C: A. Fosdick.] A struggle for a fortune. Akron, O., Saalfield Pub. Co., 1902. [Ag1.] c. 297 p. il. 12°, cl., $1.

Chipman, C: B. Last cruise of the *Electra.* Akron, O., Saalfield Pub. Co., 1902. [Ag1.] c. 268 p. il. 12°, cl., $1.

Collins, Cornelius F. The municipal court practice act, annot.: a complete codification of the laws relating to the practice and procedure of the municipal court, [etc.;] with rules of practice, sections of the code of civil procedure, relating to summary proceedings; forms and extensive index. N. Y., Banks Law Pub. Co., 1902. c. 25+381 p. O. shp., $5.

Coronation stone (The) of Great Britain and Israel: Jacob's pillar; God's house; Bethel David's throne forever. New Haven, Ct., Our Race Pub. Co., 1902. c. 64 p. 12°, (Our Race news leaflet, no. 93.) pap., 50 c.

***Cresee,** F. A. Practical pointers for patentees; containing valuable information and advice on the sale of patents: an elucidation of the best methods employed by the most successful inventors in handling their inventions. N. Y., Munn & Co., 1902. 144 p. 16°, cl., $1 net.

Crumrine, Boyd. The courts of justice, bench and bar of Washington county, Pennsylvania; with sketches of the early courthouses, the judicial system, the law judges, and the roll of attorneys of that county; and a history of the erection and dedication of the court-house of 1900, under the auspices of the Washington Bar Assoc., Washington, Pa. Washington, Pa., Washington Bar Assoc., 1902. c. 366 p. il. por. facsimiles, map, 8°, cl., $4; mor., $6.

Deharbe, Jos. Abridged catechism of Christian doctrine. New ed. specially adapted for use in the parochial schools of the United States. N. Y., F: Pustet & Co., 1902. c. 1901. 74 p. 18°, cl., 15 c.

Deharbe, Jos. Catechism of Christian doctrine. New ed. specially adapted for use in the parochial schools of the United States, by a father of the Society of Jesus. N. Y., F: Pustet & Co., 1902. c. 1901. 147 p. 8°, cl., 25 c.

Denison, Mary A. The yellow violin. Akron, O., Saalfield Pub. Co., [1902.] [Ag1.] c. 311 p. il. 12°, cl., $1.

Doty, Douglas Zabriskie. Pictures of paintbox town. N. Y., Dutton, [1902.] c. 39 p. il. oblong 16°, bds., $1.

Felt, Orson B. Parliamentary procedure for deliberative assemblies; with proper forms for disposing of parliamentary inquiries, points of order, appeals, etc. Chic., G: K. Hazlitt & Co., 1902. c. 196+11 p. 12°, flex. leath., 75 c.; pap., 35 c.

Finegan, T: E. Text-book on New York school law, including the consolidated school act, the university law, the decisions of the courts, and the rulings and decisions of state superintendents. Alb., H: B. Parsons, 1902. 8+384 p. D. buckram, $1.
Prepared for the use of normal schools, training classes, teachers and school officers.

Ford, Ja. Tooker. The dying lamp, the glorious dawn: a tale of the fall of Jerusalem. Freeport, Ill., Brown & Dollmeyer, [1902.] c. 260 p. 12°, cl., 75 c.

Fuller, Phœbe W. Shadows cast before: a novel. N. Y., Abbey Press, [1902.] c. 240 p. 12°, cl., $1.50.

***Furneaux**, W. S., *ed.* [Thomas] Whittaker's popular mannikin. [The human body.] N. Y., T: Whittaker, '1902.] 4 p.+superimposed plate, obl. F. bds., $1 net.
A model of the human body, with explanatory text, showing in five superimposed plates the organs of the chest and abdomen; the anterior muscles of the body; the heart and blood vessels; the nervous system; the skeleton and the internal organs.

Gore, James Howard. Dutch art as seen by a layman. N. Y., Holland-American Line, [1902.] c. 44 p. il. nar. Q. pap., n. p.

Griffiths, D: Pugh. The last of the quills: a story of Welsh life. Binghamton, N. Y., D: P. Griffiths, 1902. 423 p. por. 12°, cl., $1.50.

Haliburton, Marg. Winifred, *and* Norvell, F. T. Graded classics. Second reader. Richmond, Va., B. F. Johnson Pub. Co., 1902. c. il. sq. D. cl., 35 c.

Hunt, A. M. United Mercantile Agency credit ratings for the marble, granite and stone dealers of the United States and Canada, 1902. [12th year.] Bost. United Mercantile Agency, [A. M. Hunt & Co.,] [1902.] c. 291 p. 8°, subs., cl., $25.

Hunt, Mary A. Scientific Bible. Reason—revelation—rapture. Twentieth century testimony. Nature and "me"—one. Knowable, human, natural, personal God. Self-eternal substance. Natural law. [Poem.] Chic., F. E. Ormsby & Co., [1902.] c. 1901. 80 p. 12°, cl., $1.

Illinois. An index-digest of the reports, including all the supreme court reports to v. 190, inclusive, and all of the appellate court reports to v. 95, inclusive; by Ira M. Moore. In 2 v. v. 2. (L to Z.) Chic., T. H. Flood & Co., 1902. c. 1077-2183 p. O. shp., $9.

Ireland, Mary E. Timothy and his friend. Akron, O., Saalfield Pub. Co., 1902. [Ag1.] c. 317 p. il. 12°, cl., $1.

Jack, C: B. Outline of mining law for miners: a concise statement of law upon questions of most interest to miners, with directions for locating mineral ground. [Salt Lake City, Utah,] A. R. Derge & Co., 1902. c. 121 p. S. cl., $1; pap., 50 c.

Johnson, W: Franklin. Poco a poco. Akron, O., Saalfield Pub. Co., 1902. [Ag1.] c. 307 p. il. 12°, cl., $1.50.

Kentucky. Practice act in force June 16, 1902; with notes on its construction and effect and the practice thereunder, embracing directions to clerks; by Lucius P. Little. Louisville, J: P. Morton & Co., 1902. c. 24 p. O. flex. cl., 65 c.

Lewis, Enrique H. Phil and Dick. Akron, O., Saalfield Pub. Co., 1902. [Ag1.] c. 291 p. il. 12°, cl., $1.

***Lloyd**, J. W: The natural man: a romance of the golden age. Newark, N. J., Benedict Prieth, [1902.] c. 140 p. S. cl., $1 net.
The hero of this "Arcadian romance," excepting for the companionship of his mare and his dogs, lives alone in a wood. He is a poet, a sculptor, and a scholar who loves nature, and has the courage to set aside conventionalities and live the untrammelled life of a "natural man."

***Loeb**, Jacques. On the production and suppression of muscular twitching and hypersensitiveness of the skn by electrolytes. Chic., University of Chicago Press, [1902.] 13 p. 8°, (University of Chicago decennial publications, v. 10, reprints.) pap., net, 25 c.

***McKay**, Henry Jay. Poetical works. Wausau, Wis., Eugene B. Thayer, [1902.] c. 175 p. por. 12°, cl., $1 net.

Merrill, J. M. His mother's letter. Akron, O., Saalfield Pub. Co., 1902. [Ag1.] c. 303 p. il. 12°, cl., $1.

Michie, T: Johnson, *ed.* Municipal corporation cases annot.: a coll. of all cases affecting municipal corporations decided by the courts of last resort in the U. S. v. 7. Charlottesville, Va., The Michie Co., 1902. c. 14+1014 p. O. shp., $5.

Milburn, B. A. Curious cases: a coll. of American and English decisions, selected for their readability. Charlottesville, Va., The Michie Co., 1902. c. 16+441 p. O. shp., $3.

***Morozzo**, Carlo Giuseppe. A treatise of spiritual life; from the Latin by Rev. D. A. Donovan. 2d rev. ed. N. Y., F: Pustet & Co., 1902. c. 1901. 513 p. cl., net, $1.

New York. Supplement to the general laws and other general statutes of the state, cont. the amendatory and other general statutes enacted by the legislature of 1902, together with decisions of the courts construing the statute law, rendered since the publication of the above work; with index and tables of laws; comp. and annot. by Rob. C. Cumming and Frank B. Gilbert. N. Y., The Banks Law Pub. Co., 1902. c. 391 p. O. shp., $3.50.

Pacific reporter, v. 68. Permanent ed., Apr. 10-June 12, 1902. St. Paul, West Pub. Co., 1902. c. 16+1221 p. O. (National reporter system, state ser.) shp., $4.
Contains all the decisions of the supreme courts of Cala., Kan., Ore., Wash., Colo., Mont., Ariz., Id., Wyo., Utah, N. M., Okl., and court of appeals of Colo. With table of Pacific cases in which rehearings have been granted or denied. With tables of Pacific cases published in vs. 134, Cala. reports; 39, Ore. reports; 25, Wash. reports. A table of statutes construed is given in the index.

Perin, Carl Louis. Perin's science of palmistry: a complete and authentic treatise, logically arranged and profusely illustrated, on the science of palmistry, based upon the principles of astrology, the works of ancient and modern palmists and the experiences of the author; with a reproduction of famous hands and others peculiarly interesting. Chic., Star Publishing Co., [1902.] c. 229 p. il. 12°, cl., $1.50.

Poe, Edgar Allan. Poems and tales; selected and ed. by Alphonso G. Newcomer. Chic., Scott, Foresman & Co., 1902. c. 6-323 p. S. (Lake English classics.) cl., 30 c.

Pollak, Gustav, *ed.* Our success in child-training: practical experiences of many mothers. N. Y., Contemporary Publishing Co., [1902.] c. 21+210 p. 12°, cl., $1.

Protestant Episcopal Church. Liber precum publicarum Ecclesiæ Anglicanæ, A. Gulielmo Bright, et Petro Goldsmith Medd, Latine redditus; editio quarta, (1890,) cum appendice denuo recognita. N. Y., Longmans, Green & Co., 1902. 42+434 p. S. cl., $2.

Rand, McNally & Co.'s pictorial guide to Washington and environs; including complete descriptions of the Capitol, Library of Congress, White House, the departments, Mount Vernon, Arlington, and all other points of interest. N. Y. and Chic., Rand, McNally & Co., 1902. c. 204 p. il. maps, plans, 16°, pap., 25 c.

Riggs, Sara M. Studies in United States history: a guide for the use of students and teachers. Bost., Ginn, 1902. c. 13+173 p. D. cl., 65 c.
The aim of the author has been primarily that of turnishing a guide for the use of students of American history in high schools, academies or normal schools. The book will be found useful also to teachers who wish a thorough preparation in American history, or helpful suggestions in methods of teaching the subject. The "library" and "source" methods have been combined, and complete references given in connection with each topic. The book contains topical outlines together with research questions leading to close analysis and original investigation and thought. The aim has been to present the subject in such a way as to cultivate the judgment and not merely the memory. Full directions as to notebook and map work have been given.

Roberts, Frank H. H. The nation and the state: civil government of Ohio; introd. by Grace Raymond Hebard. Syracuse, N. Y., C. W. Bardeen, 1902. c. 229 p. 1 il. por. maps, 16°, (Nation and the state ser., no. 2.) cl., $1.

†**Roberts**, Morley. The way of a man: a romance. N. Y., Appleton, 1902. [Jl.] c. 311 p. D. (Appleton's town and country lib., no. 314.) cl., $1; pap., 50 c.
A novel founded on incidents in the life of an English girl, who is supposed to have been associated with General Fonseca, Guttierrez and other noted figures in the South American revolt.

****Robins**, E: Chasing an iron horse; or, a boy's adventures in the Civil War. Phil., G: W. Jacobs & Co., [1902.] [Ag.] c. 2+293 p. il. O. cl., $1 net.
The locomotive chase in Georgia which forms what may be called the background of this story, was an actual occurrence of the Civil War.

Rowell, J. Herbert. Pure economy; the rich how, the poor why: productive labor, unproductive labor and destructive labor. Austin, Ill., Free Socialist Union, 1902. 54 p. 1 il. O. pap., 10 c.

Sappho. Odes, bridal songs, epigrams; translations by Arnold, Moore, Palgrave, Tennyson and others; il. by P. Avril. Phil., printed for subscribers only by G: Barrie & Son, [1902.] c. 18+63 p. (Antique gems from the Greek and Latin, v. 8.) (Apply to pubs. for price.)

***Sawyer**, Timothy T. Old Charlestown: historical, biographical, reminiscent. Bost., Ja. H. West Co., 1902. c. 2-527 p. por. O. cl., $2 net.
Papers based on authentic historical records and on personal observation. They were originally printed in *The Charlestown (Mass.) Enterprise.*

****Schmitt**, Gustav, *M.D.*, *ed.* A brief of necroscopy and its medico-legal relation; arr. by Gustav Schmitt. N. Y., Funk & Wagnalls Co., 1902. [Jl.] c. 3-186 p. nar. S. cl., $1 net.
The author supplies in condensed form, but with sufficient detail, the practical facts connected with the study, diagnosis, technique and medico-legal aspect of a post-mortem examination.

Sedgwick, J: Correspondence of John Sedgwick, Major-General; ed. by Carl Stoeckel. v. 1. Norfolk, Ct., [privately printed for C. and E. B. Stockel,] 1902. c. 188 p. 12°, cl. 300 copies for presentation.

Sherman, *Rev.* Andrew M. Life of Captain Jeremiah O'Brien of Machias, Me., commander of the first American flying squadron of the Revolution; introd. by J: D. Long. Lynbrook, N. Y., G: W. Sherman, 1902. 300 p. il. 12°, cl., $2.

Shipp, E. R: Questions and answers on contracts; prepared with reference to Anson, Bishop, Clark, Lawson, Parsons, Smith, and selected cases on contracts. Wash., D. C., J: Byrne & Co., 1902. c. 80 p. S. (J: Byrne Co.'s quiz books.) pap., 50 c.

Simonds, W: Edgar. American date book: a handbook of reference relating to the United States of America. Hartford, Ct., Kama Co., [1902.] {Je.] c. 7+211 p. 12°, cl., $1.

Smiley, Ja. Bethuel, *ed.* Household cook book: a complete and comprehensive collection of new, choice and thoroughly tested recipes, including every department of domestic cookery, especially adapted for household use. New century ed. Chic., F: J. Drake & Co., [1902.] [Je10.] c. 656 p. il. 12°, oilcl., $1.50.

***Smith**, Adèle Millicent. Proof-reading and punctuation. Overbrook, Pa., Adèle Millicent Smith, 1902. c. 9+181 p. 16°, cl., 90 c. net.

South Carolina. Code of laws, 1902. In 2 v. v. 1, The civil code. Columbia, The State Co., 1902. c. 21+1385+3 p. O. shp., $5.

Southworth, *Mrs.* Emma Dorothy Eliza Nevitte. Self-raised; or, from the depths. N. Y., A. L. Burt Co., 1902. 499 p. 12°, (Home lib.) cl., $1.

Talling, *Rev.* Marshall P. Communion with God: extempore prayer, public and private; its principles, preparation and practice.

N. Y. and Chic., Revell, [1902.] c. 202 p. 12°, cl., $1.25.

**Taylor, J. H. Taylor on golf: impressions, comments, and hints; with 48 il. almost entirely from photographs. N. Y., Appleton, 1902. 8+328 p. D. cl., $1.60 net.
The author is an English professional. He was open champion, 1894, 1895, and 1900.

Tcherkesoff, W. Pages of socialist history: teachings and acts of Social Democracy. N. Y., C. B. Cooper, 1902. 4-106 p. O. pap., 25 c.
"The chapters of this book were not written altogether consecutively. Most of them appeared serially in the *London Freedom* and in *Les Temps Nouveaux*, Paris. When it was resolved to collect them in the present volume, the author made certain additions and emendations."—*Prefatory note.*

Texas. Notes on reports: a chronological ser. of annots. of the decisions of the supreme court, and the various civil and criminal appellate courts of Texas, showing their present value as authority as disclosed by all the subsequent citations of those cases in later Texas cases, in the decisions of sister states, and in all the federal reports; with parallel references to Am. decisions, Am. reports, Am. state reports, and the reporter system; by Walter Malins Rose. book 3. San Francisco, Bancroft-Whitney Co., 1902. c. 6+1154 p. O. shp., $7.50.

United States. Federal reporter, v. 114. Permanent ed., May-June, 1902. St. Paul, West Pub. Co., 1902. c. 32+1074 p. O. (National reporter system, U. S. ser.) shp., $3.50.
Cases argued and determined in the circuit courts of appeals and circuit and district courts of the U. S. A table of statutes construed is given in the index.

Viaud, L: Marie Julien, ["Pierre Loti," *pseud.*] Lives of two cats; from the French by M. B. Richards; il. by C. E. Allen. Bost., D. Estes & Co., [1902.] c. 1900. 96 p. il. 12°, (The young of heart ser., no. 35.) cl., 50 c.

Vose, G: L. A graphic method for solving certain questions in arithmetic or algebra. 2d ed. N. Y., D. Van Nostrand Co., 1902. c. '75, 1902. 3-62 p. 1 il. T. (Van Nostrand's science ser., no. 16.) bds., 50 c.

Welch, *Rev.* A. C. Character photography: chapters on the developing process in the better life. Cin., O., Jennings & Pye, [1902.] c. 260 p. D. cl., $1.
Contents: Composite pictures; Time-exposures; Look pleasant; In groups; Down by the old home; Nature studies; Battle scenes; Historic views; On crowded streets; In quiet nooks; In the dark room, The developing lamp; Lights and shadows; Blue prints; Defective negatives; Finishing touches.

West, T: Dyson. Metallurgy of cast iron: a complete exposition of the processes involved in its treatment, chemically and physically, from the blast furnace through the foundry to the testing machine: a practical compilation of original research. 5th ed. Cleveland, O., Cleveland Printing and Publishing Co., 1902. c. 20+627 p. il. diagrams, 8°, cl., $3.

Winfield, Arthur. Larry Barlow's ambition. Akron, O., Saalfield Pub. Co., 1902. [Ag1.] c. 206 p. il. 12°, cl., $1.

ORDER LIST.

ABBEY PRESS, 114 Fifth Ave., New York.
Fuller, Shadows cast before........... $1.50

D. APPLETON & Co., 72 Fifth Ave., New York.
†Roberts, The way of a man (A. T. C. L., 314)..................50 c.; 1.00
**Taylor, On golf.................net, 1.60

N. W. AYER & SON, Philadelphia.
American newspaper annual, [1902].... 5.00

BANCROFT-WHITNEY Co., 438 Montgomery St., San Francisco.
Texas, Notes on reports, bk. 3 (Rose). 7.50

BANKS LAW PUB. Co., 21 Murray St., New York.
Collins, Municipal court practice act annot......... 5.00
New York Supplement to general laws. 3.50

C. W. BARDEEN, 406 S. Franklin St., Syracuse, N. Y.
Roberts, The nation and the state...... 1.00

GEORGE BARRIE & SON, 1313 Walnut St., Philadelphia.
Sappho, Odes, etc..subs., (Apply to pubs for price.)

BROWN & DOLLMEYER, Freeport, Ill.
Ford, The dying lamp................ 75

F. M. BUCKLES & Co., 11 E. 16th St., New York.
Cameron, A woman's no............. 1.25

J. BYRNE & Co., 1322 F St., Washington, D. C.
Shipp, Questions and answers on contracts..... 50

CLEVELAND PRINTING Co., Cleveland, O.
West, Metallurgy of cast iron, 5th ed.. $3.00

CONTEMPORARY PUBLISHING Co., 138 Nassau St., New York.
Pollak, Our success in child training.. 1.00

C. B. COOPER, 114 Fourth Ave., New York.
Tcherkesoff, Pages of social history... 25

A. R. DERGE & Co., Salt Lake City, Utah.
Jack, Outline of mining law.....50 c.; 1.00

F. J. DRAKE & Co., 352-356 Dearborn St., Chicago.
Smiley, Household cook book......... 1.50

E. P. DUTTON & Co., 31 W. 23d St., New York.
Doty, Pictures of paint-box town....... 1.00

DANA ESTES & Co., 208-218 Summer St., Boston.
Viaud, Lives of two cats............ 50

THE FEDERAL BOOK Co., 52-58 Duane St., New York.
Beall, Winning of Sarenne......25 c.; 50

T. H. FLOOD & Co., 149 Monroe St., Chicago.
Illinois, Index digest, including all the supreme ct, repts. to v. 190, supreme ct. and v. 95 appellate ct. repts., v. 2. 9.00

FREE SOCIALIST UNION, Austin, Ills.
Rowell, Pure economy............... 10

FUNK & WAGNALLS CO., 30 Lafayette Pl., New York.
**Schmitt, Brief of necroscopy.....net, $1.00

GINN & CO., 29 Beacon St., Boston.
Riggs, Studies in United States history. 65

D. P. GRIFFITHS, Binghamton, N. Y.
Griffiths, Last of the quills............. 1.50

GEORGE K. HAZLITT & CO., 273 Dearborn St., Chicago.
Felt, Parliamentary procedure for deliberative assemblies...........35 c.; 75

HOLLAND-AMERICAN LINE, New York.
Gore, Dutch art as seen by a layman..,n. p.

GEORGE W. JACOBS & CO., 103 S. 15th St., Philadelphia.
**Blanchard, Little Miss Oddity..net, 80
**Robins, Chasing an iron horse...net, 1.00

JENNINGS & PYE, 220 W. 4th St., Cincinnati.
Welch, Character photography........ 1.00

B. F. JOHNSON PUB. CO., 901-905 E. 9th st., Richmond, Va.
Haliburton *and* Norvell, Graded classics: Second reader................ 35

KAMA CO., Hartford, Ct.
Simonds, American date book......... 1.00

LAIRD & LEE, 263 Wabash Ave., Chicago.
Annunzio, The dead city.............. 1.25

LONGMANS, GREEN & CO., 91-95 Fifth Ave., New York.
Protestant Episcopal Church, Liber precum publicarum Ecclesiæ Anglicanæ........................... 2.00

MICHIE CO., Charlottesville, Va.
Michie, Municipal corporation cases, annot., v. 7......................... 5.00
Milburn, Curious cases............... 3.00

J. P. MORTON & CO., Louisville, Ky.
Kentucky, Practice act, June 16, 1902.. 65

MUNN & CO., 361 Broadway, New York.
*Cresee, Practical pointers for patentees, net, 1.00

F. E. ORMSBY & CO., Chicago.
Hunt, Scientific Bible................. 1.00

OUR RACE PUB. CO., 673 Chapel St., New Haven, Ct.
Coronation stone (The).............. 50

H. B. PARSONS, 105 Hudson Ave., Albany.
Finegan, Text-book on New York school law........ .... 1.00

BENEDICT PRIETH, Newark, N. J.
*Lloyd, The natural man..........net, 1.00

F. PUSTET & CO., 52 Barclay St., New York.
Deharbe, Abridged catchism of Christian doctrine, new ed............... 15
——, Catechism of Christian doctrine, new ed..... 25
*Morozzo, Spiritual life............net, 1.00

RAND, MCNALLY & CO., 142 Fifth Ave., New York; 160-174 Adams St., Chicago.
Rand, McNally & Co.'s pictorial guide to Washington....... 25

FLEMING H. REVELL CO., 156 Fifth Ave., New York, 63 Washington St., Chicago.
Talling, Communion with God........ $1.25

GEORGE P. ROWELL & CO., 10 Spruce St., New York.
American newspaper directory, 34th year........ .... 5.00

SAALFIELD PUB. CO., Akron, O.
Barnett, Mother Goose paint book..... 1.25
Bonehill, The boy land boomer........ 1.00
Braden, Far past the frontier.......... 1.00
Brown, Ralph Granger's fortune....... 1.00
Castlemon, A struggle for a fortune... 1.00
Chipman, Last cruise of the *Electra*.... 1.00
Denison, The yellow violin........... 1.00
Ireland, Timothy and his friend....... 1.00
Johnson, Poco a poco................ 1.50
Lewis, Phil and Dick................. 1.00
Merrill, His mother's letter........... 1.00
Winfield, Leroy Barlow's ambition..... 1.00

M. S. SCHWARTZ & CO., Salem, O.
Bonsall, Money.................25 c.; 50

SCOTT, FORESMAN & CO., 378-388 Wabash Ave., Chicago.
Poe, Poems and tales................ 30

GEORGE W. SHERMAN, Lynbrook, N. Y.
Sherman, Life of Captain Jeremiah O'Brien...... .... 2.00

ADELE MILLICENT SMITH, Overbrook, Pa.
*Smith, Proof-reading...... ......net, 90

STAR PUBLISHING CO.. Chicago.
Perrin, Science of palmistry.......... 1.50

THE STATE CO., Columbia, S. C.
South Carolina, Code, 1902, in 2 v., v. 1. 5.00

C. & E. B. STOECKEL, Norfolk, Ct.
Sedgwick, Correspondence of John Sedgwick.......300 copies for presentation

EUGENE B. THAYER, Wausau, Wis.
*McKay, Poetical works...........net, 1.00

UNITED MERCANTILE AGENCY, Boston.
Hunt, United Mercantile Agency credit ratings..... ....subs., 25.00

UNIVERSITY OF CHICAGO PRESS, Chicago, Ill.
*Loeb, On production and suppression of muscular twitching...........net, 25

D. VAN NOSTRAND CO., 23 Murray St., New York.
Vose, Graphic method of solving certain questions in arithmetic......... 50

WASHINGTON BAR ASSOCIATION, Washington, Pa.
Crumrine, Courts of justice, bench and bar of Washington Co...........$4; 6.00

JAMES H. WEST CO., 79 Milk St., Boston.
*Sawyer, Old Charlestown........net, 2.00

WEST PUB. CO., 52-58 W. 3d St., St. Paul.
Pacific reporter, v. 68................. 4.00
United States Federal reporter, v. 114. 3.50

THOMAS WHITTAKER, 3 Bible House, New York.
*Furneaux, Whittaker's popular manniken...... ....net, 1.00

The Publishers' Weekly.

FOUNDED BY F. LEYPOLDT.

AUGUST 9, 1902.

The editor does not hold himself responsible for the views expressed in contributed articles or communications

All matter, whether for the reading-matter columns or advertising pages, should reach this office not later than Wednesday noon, to insure insertion in the same week's issue.

Publishers are requested to furnish title-page proofs and advance information of books forthcoming, both for entry in the lists and for descriptive mention. An early copy of each book published should be forwarded, as it is of the utmost importance that the entries of books be made as promptly and as perfectly as possible. In many cases booksellers depend on the PUBLISHERS' WEEKLY solely for their information. The Record of New Publications of the PUBLISHERS' WEEKLY is the material of the "American Catalogue" and so forms the basis of trade bibliography in the United States.

"I hold every man a debtor to his profession, from the which, as men do of course seek to receive countenance and profit, so ought they of duty to endeavor themselves by way of amends to be a help and an ornament thereunto."—LORD BACON.

SHORTER HOURS AND HOLIDAYS.

EARLY closing and vacations are growing in favor among all classes of merchants, and the booktrade, we are gratified to note, is not backward in the movement. Even those who a few years ago protested that a Saturday half holiday meant the jeopardizing of the profits of the year, are enthusiastic over early closing all the year around excepting, of course, in the holiday season.

There is no doubt as to the benefit of closing early in the evening to both the merchant and his assistants. Especially during these dog days it is most desirable to remove the strain as early as possible, and to enable the clerks to get out into the open air, and to obtain that change and recreation that will make them better workmen in the morning. The same rule applies with equal force to the employer. Nothing is more dangerous than trying to work all the time. The very intensity of a man's ambition to get on may keep him back. A bow that is bent constantly loses its elasticity; hence, every one should put a layer of pleasure, of genuine recreation, into his life at certain periods of the year.

And no time of the year offers such an opportunity for rest and recreation to the bookseller as the summer. The bulk of his business must be done during the winter, and long hours are required to care for the trade. With the advent of summer, publishing lags, retail business quiets down, and less strenuous efforts are required to keep up with the trade that remains or may be worked up. Many employers have recognized this, and while there has been no canvass of the matter, so far as we are aware, in many of the larger cities—and our remarks apply chiefly to these—the trade almost with one accord has closed its stores at five o'clock every evening during the summer, and at one o'clock on Saturday afternoons. Vacations of a week or longer have also become commoner this year than ever before, both with the employer and his clerks, to the decided benefit and improvement of all concerned.

In all this we note an encouraging sign. While there is a sound business reason for shorter hours and more frequent holidays, it is undoubtedly true that as the world grows older employers have more regard for the happiness and welfare of those who serve them.

PAPER FROM OAT HULLS.

AN important test in the manufacture of strawboard and paper has just been concluded at the Gas City plant of the Western Strawboard Company, at Richmond, Ind. The process, according to the *New York Times,* which will mean much in the future manufacture of strawboard, is the converting of oat hulls into paper. This is something that has long been considered by the manufacturers of paper, but the man who has been conducting the tests is the first to hit upon a successful process.

Oat hulls are very similar in organic composition to the straw used in the manufacture of paper, but some slight difference in the two has made the use of the hulls hitherto impossible. The new process overcomes the difficulty and by it paper and board can be made equal in quality to that made from straw and old paper.

The above report moves a contemporary to think that *tenui musam meditamur avena* of the Eclogue—Sydney Smith's "we cultivate literature on a little oatmeal"—may have a new meaning for the innumerable new verse smiths of this age; and that "we write poetry on this oat-hull paper" may be the proper translation of the Virgilian phrase.

SIX BEST-SELLING BOOKS JUNE-JULY.

THE six books that have sold best in the order of demand, from June 1 to July 1, according to *The Bookman*, are:

	POINTS.
1. The Mississippi Bubble. Hough. *Bowen-Merrill Co.*	245
2. Dorothy Vernon. Major. *Macmillan Co.*	225
3. Mrs. Wiggs of the Cabbage Patch. Hegan. *Century Co.*	155
4. The Virginian. Wister. *Macmillan Co.*	112
5. The Leopard's Spots. Dixon. *Doubleday, Page & Co.*	95
6. The Hound of the Baskervilles. Doyle. *McClure, Phillips & Co.*	

FROGS' SKINS FOR BOOKBINDINGS.

In the Philadelphia Terminal market recently, according to the *Philadelphia Record*, a dealer in all kinds of game said that the skins of frogs, if carefully removed and cured, have some slight value. They are used, it seems, in bookbinding; not in general bookbinding, but in the fantastic, "precious" sort—used, in a word, as chicken skin was used in fan making in the time of Carlo Van Loo. Frogskin makes a very fine and soft leather, and in dyeing it will take the most delicate colors. Hence it is inlaid, in circles and stars for centrepieces, into the calf or the crushed levant of sumptuous book covers, and it makes a very striking and beautiful decoration. A noted English binder has achieved some of his best effects by the judicious employment of frogskin as a decorative agent.

A WESTERN LIBRARY MEETING.

A meeting of librarians, trustees, and all others of the west and middle west interested in library work, will be held at the State Historical Library Building, at Madison, Wis., on August 28, 29 and 30, 1902. "Public Documents," "The Relation of the Publisher to the Public," "The Bookseller and the Librarian," "The Book Review—Its Worth and Worthlessness," "The Relation of the City Government to Boards of Library Trustees," "The Local, Untrained Applicant vs. Trained Service," "Principles of Book Selection by Book Committees," "The Establishment of Branches, Stations and the Extension of Library Privileges to Rural Communities," are some of the topics to be discussed. "Library Architecture" will be the subject of the morning session on August 30, and an exhibit of library plans by prominent architects will be made.

BOOKTRADE ASSOCIATIONS.

VIRGINIA BOOKSELLERS' ASSOCIATION.

A belated report of the annual meeting of the Virginia Booksellers' Association, held in Richmond, Va., June 26 and 27, has just reached us. From this report we gather that since the organization of the association there has probably been no better meeting or more enthusiastic and earnest attendance than was manifested this year. The position in regard to the handling of school books that the booksellers of Virginia will be forced to take, unless an organized effort is made to prevent it, made each member realize the importance of co-operation; hence the trade of Norfolk, Portsmouth, Danville, Richmond, Charlottesville, Staunton, Roanoke, Newport News and Petersburg was fully represented, and cheering letters were received from the absentees, as well as from the American Publishers' Association and from the American Booksellers' Association.

The Association has made a contract with a number of publishers, with the approval of the Superintendent of Education, to provide for the prompt supply of school books for the schools of every county of Virginia.

Resolutions in memory of the late Montgomery West, one of the organizers of the Association, were passed.

The following new members were elected: Anderson Brothers, of University of Virginia; A. W. Morton and James E. Abbe, of Newport News; Moose Brothers Company, of Lynchburg; and Caldwell-Sites Co., of Bristol.

The following officers were elected for the ensuing year: T. S. Beckwith, president; C. R. Cadwell, vice-president; and J. O. Boatwright, secretary and treasurer. The Executive Committee consists of the officers and R. J. Alfriend, C. W. Hunter and A. C. Brechin.

The next annual meeting is to be held at Charlottesville unless two-thirds of the members express a desire for some other place. The question in regard to the new adoption to take place next May, after much discussion was left in the hands of the Executive Committee with power to act.

OBITUARY NOTES.

Friedrich Pustet, senior member of the firm of Fr. Pustet & Co., of New York and Cincinnati, publishers of Catholic books and dealers in church goods, died at Ratisbon, or Regensburg, Bavaria, August 4, aged seventy. The present house of Fr. Pustet & Co. was founded at Regensburg by the father of Mr. Pustet in 1826 under the firm name of Friedrich Pustet. The first American branch was established in New York in 1865, and another, in Cincinnati, in 1867, and an Italian branch was established in Rome in 1899. Mr. Pustet was a Knight of the Order of St. Gregory the Great, and was printer to the Holy See and to the Sacred Congregation of Rites.

Mrs. Elizabeth Drew Barston Stoddard, the wife of Richard Henry Stoddard, died August 1, at her home, 329 East Fifteenth Street, New York. Mrs. Stoddard was born at Mattapoisett, Mass., on Buzzard's Bay, May 6, 1823, and was married to Mr. Stoddard in 1852 in New York, which had since been her home. She herself was a poet and novelist of repute. Her verses were for the most part contributed to periodicals, although in 1883 a collection of them was published by the Scribners. During the Civil War Mrs. Stoddard wrote three novels—"The Morgesons" (1862.) "Two Men" (1865,) and "Temple House" (1867.) All are studies of New England life and character. She also wrote a book for young people entitled "Dolly Dink's Doings." Lately a new edition of her works was published by Henry T. Coates & Co., of Philadelphia, with an introduction by Edmund Clarence Stedman, her friend, and her husband's. Mr. Stoddard, who survives his wife, is also advanced in age and infirm. The illness of his wife has been a severe strain upon him, but it is hoped that he will not break down under his bereavement. Lorimer Stoddard, the son of the couple, died last year, and since then Mrs. Stoddard's decline in health has been steady.

Lynds Eugene Jones, who, under the direction of Mr. F. Leypoldt, compiled "The American Catalogue" for 1876, died at his home, 47 Brevoort Place, Brooklyn, N. Y., August 3. Mr. Jones was born in Brooklyn, in 1853. After passing through the public schools he entered the New York Free Academy, now the College of the City of New York, from which he was graduated in 1873, when he received an appointment in the New York evening schools. From 1874 to 1875 he was connected with the editorial staff of the *New York Evening Mail,* and in 1875 he became associated with Mr. Leypoldt in the work upon "The American Catalogue." In 1883 he became Curator of the New York Art Students' League, which position he held until 1887. In 1887 he took an editorial position in the New York house of George Routledge & Sons, which he resigned in 1891 to become librarian of the Century Association. For two years, from 1893 to 1895, he was business manager of *The Art Amateur,* and from 1896 to 1897 he was connected with the publishing house of Selmar Hess. In 1897 he became senior member of the Board of Examiners of the Civil Service Commission of New York. In this important position he earned the respect and confidence of all acquainted with his work, which was of a peculiarly delicate and important nature. His alert intelligence, sound judgment, entire fairness and constant fidelity made his service of the highest value in the establishment and application of the merit system. In private life he was singularly simple and loyal, and his death will be sincerely mourned by a large circle of friends. Besides his work on "The American Catalogue" Mr. Jones was joint editor of "Books of All Time," published by Mr. Leypoldt in 1881; "The Best Reading," published by G. P. Putnam's Sons in 1883, 1888 and 1892; "History of United States for Young People," published by George Routledge & Sons, in 1889; "Tabular Views of History," and "Outdoor Sports for Boys and Girls," both published by George Routledge & Son, in 1890; and American editor of "Men and Women of the Time," since 1884. He was also the author of the articles on Booktrade, Bibliography and Libraries in the American supplement to the "Encyclopædia Britannica."

JOURNALISTIC NOTES.

The Evangelist, one of the oldest Presbyterian weeklies in the United States, has been absorbed by *Christian Work,* and will hereafter be published under the title of *Christian Work of the Evangelist.* The Rev. Dr. Joseph Newton Hallock, the proprietor, will act as editor-in-chief.

WITH the July number *The Edinburgh Review* concludes the 100th year of its publication. Sydney Smith, Francis Jeffrey, Lord Brougham and Francis Horner were the chief writers at the start, Jeffrey editing it for twenty-six years. Among the best-known of its contributors were Carlyle, Napier, John Stuart Mill, Thackeray, Macaulay, Bulwer-Lytton and George Henry Lewes. The October issue will contain an article dealing with the whole history of the *Review,* together with some portraits.

THE first number of the first Japanese newspaper printed from movable type east of San Francisco made its appearance in New York City on the 2d inst. It is entitled *New York Shu Ho,* or, New York Japanese weekly. Goroku Ikeda is the editor and proprietor. This is not strictly the first journal in which the two thousand Japanese in and about New York have been able to read the news in their own language, but it is the first to be printed from type. Hajime Hoshi's paper, the *Nichi-Bai,* or, *Japanese-American Weekly,* is written out with a brush on lithographic stones, and printed off by hand.

LITERARY AND TRADE NOTES.

METHUEN & Co., London, have in preparation a new humorous story by Anstey Guthrie, entitled "A Bayard from Bengal."

LOUIS BOTHA, with the help of Generals De Wet and De La Rey, will write the history of the Boer War from the Boer point of view.

THE BLUE SKY PRESS, Chicago, will publish shortly Browning's "In a Balcony," with an introduction by Laura McAdoo Triggs, and designs by W. A. Dwiggins and F. W. Goudy.

HARPER & BROTHERS will publish shortly a book entitled "Lady Beatrix and the Forbidden Man: a Girl's Diary." It is a satire on contemporaneous British society. Some of the material has already appeared in *Vanity Fair.*

JOHN S. BROOKS & Co., 120 Boylston Street, Boston, Mass., will publish shortly a novel entitled "Stillman Gott, Farmer and Fisherman," by Edwin Day Sibley, a story of real life along the coast and in the woods of Maine.

THOMAS WHITTAKER, New York, will publish a second and concluding volume of the Rev. J. J. Lanier's work on the "Kingship of God and Man," under the title of "The Master Key." This and the author's previous volume form a comprehensive study of biological theology on fresh and very suggestive lines.

BENEDICT PRIETH, 75 Market Street, Newark, N. J., has just published an Arcadian romance, entitled "The Natural Man: a romance of the Golden Age," by J. William Lloyd, author of "Dawn Thought and Wind Harp Songs." The book has been printed under the direction of Frank B. Rae, Jr., at the Alwil Shop, Ridgewood, N. J.

E. P. DUTTON & Co. have just ready "An Anthology of Victorian Poetry," by Sir Mountstuart E. Grant Duff. They will publish shortly a new edition of the Rev. Alexander Dyce's "Glossary to the Works of William Shakespeare," with new notes by Harold Littledale, professor of English of the University College of South Wales and Monmouthshire.

AT Puttick & Simpson's, London, there was sold to an American collector, on July 16, a copy of Tennyson's "Poems by Two Brothers," uncut and in the original boards, for £39: also, a copy of that rare Lamb item,

"Prince Dorus, or, Flattery Put Out of Countenance," 1811, in the original covers, uncolored plates, that was secured by an American for the record price of £62.

THE BOWEN-MERRILL COMPANY will bring out in September a new and revised edition of "One Thousand Fungi," by Charles McIlvaine. Though this edition will be published at a popular price, it will contain all the color plates, engravings and etchings of the expensive *Author's edition*, and will be supplemented with the more recent investigations of the author.

THE NUSBAUM BOOK AND ART CO., at the corner of Granby Street and Brook Avenue, Norfolk, Va., have made up an attractive window display of "Mrs. Wiggs of the Cabbage Patch" that is attracting a great deal of attention. The window shows Mrs. Wiggs, as natural almost as life, in the centre of a real cabbage patch, and distributed among the cabbages are copies of the book.

HENRY S. ALLEN, well known to the trade through his connection with the firms of Leavitt & Allen, Allen Brothers and George W Carleton, who retired from business some time ago, is tiring of play and desires to get back into a position where his knowledge of the book business in all its branches may be utilized. Any one desiring to commuincate with Mr. Allen may address him at Stamford, N. Y., his summer home.

DREXEL BIDDLE, Philadelphia, announces a religious romance entitled "On the Cross—a romance of the Passion Play at Oberammergau," by Wilhelmine von Hillern and Mary J. Safford; also, "Her Lord and Master," by Martha Morton, a book full of smart dialogue and interesting characters that contrasts the freedom and lack of restraint in our American ways with the severe, tight-laced customs of the aristocratic English.

GEORGE W. SHERMAN, Lynbrook, N. Y., has just published "The Life of Captain Jeremiah O'Brien, of Machias, Me.," by the Rev. A. M. Sherman. It is a well written account of an interesting and prominent character in the Revolutionary War, and throws much light on the methods and manners of that interesting period in our national history. A feature of the work is the introduction written by former secretary of the navy, John D. Long, who is thoroughly conversant with the subject treated by Mr. Sherman.

JAMIESON-HIGGINS COMPANY, Chicago, have in preparation "Tales from Longfellow," by Molly K. Bellew, with illustrations by Ike Morgan; "Dickens's Christmas Stories for Children," by Molly K. Bellew, with illustrations by H. S. Campbell; also, "A Round Robin," a collection of stories, poems, anecdotes, etc., for children, by Mary Hartwell Catherwood, Margaret Sangster, Peter Dunne, Alfred Henry Lewis, etc., edited by Laura Dayton Fessenden, and illustrated by Ike Morgan.

A LONDON publisher, according to the New York *Times*, recently made the following remark in a conversation, and is said to have repeated what is to be heard in all London literary circles: "Five out of every six novels published barely pay; three out of every six are absolute failures. The finding of new authors is a gamble, and a very risky gamble, and half the known writers have a dwindling and inconsiderable public. It is becoming more and more common for the sums paid on account of royalties when a book is bought never to be earned."

WILLIAM ABBATT, of New York, will have ready early in November a new and enlarged edition of Winthrop Sargent's "Life and Career of Major John André." The volume will contain twenty illustrations, including portraits of Honora Sulyd, Anna Seward, General Grey, Colonel Musgrave, two of André, and Mr. Sargent himself. There will also be facsimiles of two very interesting letters—one by André, hitherto unpublished, and one by Edward Shippen, the father of Mrs. Arnold. The edition will be limited to 500 copies at $8 and 75 copies on large paper at $15.

GINN & CO. are publishing M. de Bloch's "The Future of War," with W. T. Stead's "free rendering" of conversations which he had with the author, and an introduction by Edwin D. Mead, telling of his meeting with M. de Bloch in London last year. Mr. Ginn's purpose in issuing this book is not mercantile. It was issued nearly three years ago, and is already familiar to those who would naturally read it. It is his hope that the work in this form will direct public opinion toward peace. The book is sold at a price precluding much profit and is really Mr. Ginn's contribution to the cause of peace.

WILLIAM J. BELL, the business manager of the OFFICE OF THE PUBLISHERS' WEEKLY, met with a serious accident on his way home on Saturday evening, August 2. In crossing one of the temporary bridges over the subway excavations near the City Hall he stepped on a plank that gave way and precipitated him into the pit thirty feet below. When taken to the Hudson street branch of the New York Hospital it was found that he had broken one and dislocated another of the lumbar vertebræ. As we go to press Mr. Bell is still alive and conscious, but his condition is declared by the doctors to be most critical, and we can only hope that in some way his life may be saved.

CHAPMAN & HALL, London, will commence in September the publication of their new *Biographical edition* of the "Works of Charles Dickens," which is intended to be a library edition at a popular price. It will be complete in eighteen volumes, containing all the original illustrations, which have been specially reproduced for this edition from the original plates. The biographical introductions are founded upon material in the hands of Chapman & Hall, (who are the owners of Dickens's copyrights,) and will aim at giving the story of each book, and its place in its author's life, briefly and sympathetically. All bibliographical *ana* will be avoided, the object being to provide an interesting narrative, unencumbered by machinery. The volumes will appear two a month, in their chronological order. The binding is to be a special feature, with a full gold back designed by W. B. Macdougall, and delicate end-papers to match.

DODD, MEAD & Co. have in preparation the second volume of Professor George Saintsbury's "History of Criticism," which has been extended so that it will require a third volume to complete the work. The first volume presented an account of the higher rhetoric and poetry, the theory and practice of literary criticism and taste, during ancient and mediæval times; the second volume deals with the matter from the Renaissance to the death of eighteenth century classicism, and the third volume will be on modern criticism. They also announce a new book by Ian Maclaren, entitled "The Homely Virtues," in which Dr. Watson treats practical subjects in a very pointed and practical way; "The American Idea as Expounded by American Statesmen," a collection of typical documents, such as the Declaration of Independence, Washington's Inaugural Address, etc., made by Joseph B. Gilder, with an introduction by Andrew Carnegie; "The Autobiography of a 'Newspaper Girl,'" by Elizabeth L. Banks, author of "Campaigns of Curiosity," whose experience in newspaper work is said to be varied and interesting; also, "Red-Head," a new novel by John Uri Lloyd, who, in drawing the picture of a Kentucky feud, introduces one of the characters from his "Stringtown on the Pike." Mr. Lloyd's story will be illustrated as a Christmas book by Reginald Birch, every page being decorated in color.

HENRY HOLT & Co. evidently do not believe in the decline of the demand for books in series, or for historical fiction, as is evidenced in their announcement of a scheme which they have long had under consideration, of a uniform series of reprints of standard historical novels. They expect the co-operation of an English house famous for its success with several series of books selected and made with extraordinary taste and discretion. *The Standard Historical Novels Series* will naturally include the old stand-bys, such as Bulwer's "Last Days of Pompeii," Kingsley's "Hypatia," Bulwer's "Harold," Scott's "Ivanhoe," George Eliot's "Romola," Scott's "Quentin Durward," Reade's "The Cloister and the Hearth," Mrs. Charles's "Schönberg-Cotta Family," Hawthorne's "Scarlet Letter," Thackeray's "Henry Esmond," Cooper's "Spy," Dickens's "Tale of Two Cities," and if encouragement is received probably, with others, most of the following: Ebers's "Egyptian Princess" and "Uarda," Flaubert's "Salammbo," Lockhart's "Valerius," Newman's "Callista," Fouqué's "Thiodolf the Icelander," Scheffel's "Ekkehard," Kingsley's "Hereward the Wake," Scott's "Talisman," Jane Porter's "Scottish Chiefs," Bulwer's "Rienzi," Kingsley's "Westward Ho," DeVigny's "Cinq Mars," Thackeray's "Virginians," Victor Hugo's "93." So far as practicable, the series will present a somewhat systematic general view of history. Enough editorial matter will be given to afford a notion of the author and of the historical relations of the work.

HOUGHTON, MIFFLIN & Co. will publish next month a *Riverside edition* of the complete works of Bret Harte in sixteen volumes; an edition of the complete works of Clara Louise Burnham, in fifteen volumes; a new *Wayside edition* of Hawthorne's complete works in twelve volumes; a *Riverside edition* of Tennyson's poetical works in seven volumes; a re-issue of William Vaughn Moody's dramatic poem, "The Masque of Judgment;" a holiday edition of "Japanese Girls and Women," by Alice M. Bacon, with twelve exquisite colored illustrations and numerous outline drawings, by a distinguished Japanese artist; the first volume of "The Argive Heraeum," an archæological work of great importance and value, giving the results of the latest excavations in Argolis, edited by Professor Charles Waldstein, adequately illustrated; "Eternalism: a Theory of Infinite Justice," by Orlando J. Smith, a stimulating argument for the pre-existence of the soul; "American Navigation," a review of the rise and decline of the American marine, by William W. Bates; the thirteenth and fourteenth volumes, completing the work, of Professor Sargent's monumental work on "The Silva of North America;" a new handy-volume edition of Dr. Oliver Wendell Holmes's "Breakfast Tables Series," in four volumes; "A Book of Nature Myths," by Florence Holbrook, stories for children explaining everyday facts of life which will recall Kipling's "Just-So Stories;" "A History of English Literature," a text-book for high schools, by Professor William E. Simonds, of Knox College; "Masterpieces of Greek Literature," edited by Professor T. D. Seymour; "Masterpieces of Latin Literature," edited by Dr. G. J. Laing; Longfellow's "Hiawatha," dramatized by Florence Holbrook, in the *Riverside Literature Series;* also, the following books for young people: "The Flag on the Hilltop," a boy's story of war times in southern Illinois when "copperhead" plots were rife, by Mary Tracy Earle; and "Lois Mallet's "Dangerous Gift," the tale of a Quaker girl whose beauty cost her dear, by Mary Catherine Lee.

BUSINESS NOTES.

BOSTON, MASS.—John S. Brooks & Co. is the name of a new firm of publishers who have established themselves in the Walker Building, at 120 Boylston Street, for the purpose of publishing a general line of books. They write us that it is their intention to make all books bearing their imprint as good as skilled labor can make them. "We are starting out on the principle that it is a poor book that requires a good cover to make it sell, but that it is a poorer publisher who, given a good book, does not put it in a good binding and print it on good paper in clear, legible type."

LITTLE ROCK, ARK.—Dr. J. P. Webb, well known to the western stationery trade, committed suicide by shooting himself in Springdale, Ark., on July 24. Dr. Webb was formerly the head of the firm of Wilson & Webb, stationers, of this city.

TERMS OF ADVERTISING.

Under the heading "Books Wanted" **book-trade subscribers are given the privilege of a free advertisement for books out of print, of five nonpareil lines exclusive of address, in any issue except special numbers, to an extent not exceeding 100 lines a year. If more than five lines are sent, the excess is at 10 cents a line, and amount should be inclosed.** *Bids for current books and such as may be easily had from the publishers, and repeated matter, as well as all advertisements from non-subscribers, must be paid for at the rate of 10 cents a line.*

Under the heading "Books for Sale," the charge to subscribers and non-subscribers is 10 cents a nonpareil line for each insertion. No deduction for repeated matter.

All other small, undisplayed, advertisements will be charged at the uniform rate of 10 cents a nonpareil line. Eight words may be reckoned to the line.

Parties with whom we have no accounts must pay in advance, otherwise no notice will be taken of their communications.

BOOKS WANTED.

☞ In answering, please state edition, condition, and price, including postage or express charges.

Houses that are willing to deal exclusively on a cash-on-delivery basis will find it to their advantage to put after their firm-name the word (Cash).

☞ Write your wants plainly and on one side of the sheet only. Illegibly-written "wants" will be considered as not having been received. The "Publishers' Weekly" does not hold itself responsible for errors.

It should be understood that the appearance of advertisements in this column, or elsewhere in the "Publishers' Weekly" does not furnish a guarantee of credit. While it is endeavored to safeguard these columns by withdrawing the privilege of their use from advertisers who are not "good pay," booksellers should take the usual precaution, as to advertisers not known to them, that they would take in making sales to any unknown parties.

The Albany News Co., Albany, N. Y.

Vas-Verhaltlichen- und Waldbanne, Gegens Sicht und Schetten, by Gustave Heyer. Pub. by Steiger.

Arthur M. Allen, 508 Fulton St., Troy, N. Y.

Century Cook Book.
Presbyterian Looking for the Church.
Weston, Historic Doubts as to the Execution of Marshal Ney.
Set Jane Austen.

The Alliance Pub. Co., 569 5th Ave., N. Y.

Unknown Life of Christ, by N. Notovitch.

Almy, Bigelow & Washburn, Salem, Mass.

Walks and Talks of an American Farmer in England, by Olmsted.

Amer. Bapt. Pub. Soc., 69 Whitehall St., Atlanta, Ga.

Duplicate Whist, by Street. Originally pub. by Brentano's.

Amer. Bapt. Pub. Soc., 177 Wabash Ave., Chicago.

Encyclopædia of Religious Knowledge, by J. Newton Brown, rev. by George P. Tyler. Amer. Bapt. Pub. Soc.
Niles' Register, set.
William Watson's Collected Poems, 1st ed. 1898.

Amer. Bapt. Pub. Soc., 279 Elm St., Dallas, Tex.

Carson, On Baptism. Pub. by Amer. Bapt. Pub. Soc.

Antiquarian Book Concern, Omaha, Neb.

Latham, Baldwin, Civil Engineering.
Schellendorf, The Duties of the General Staff.

Americus Law Book Co., Americus, Ga.

Anything on Revolutionary War South.
Graves, I. R., Great Iron Wheel.
The Campaigns in 1781 in S. C., by Lee.
O'Neal, Bench and Bar of So. Car.
Proceedings Natl. Political Conventions.

Wm. M. Bains, 1019 Market St., Phila., Pa.

Adventures of Sol Smith, Theatrical Apprentice. Peterson, Phila.
Moore, F., Modern Juan, or, Mike Fletcher.

The Baker & Taylor Co., 33 E. 17th St., N. Y.

Lingard, John, History of England, v. 9, 10, black cl. J. C. Nimmo & Bain, London.

Wm. Ballantyne & Sons, 428 7th St., Washington.

Davies, Logic and Utility of Mathematics.

G. H. Barbour, 6016 Stanton Ave., Pittsburgh, Pa.

Anything pertaining to the Meekins family.

Bigham & Smith, Agts., Dallas, Tex.

Ruth Hall, by Fannie Fern. Pub. about 1860.
Art and Science of Embalming. Barnes & Co.
The Broken Home, by Palmer.

G. Blatchford, Pittsfield, Mass.

Habitation of Man, Viollet-le-Duc.

Book Exchange, Toledo, O.

Morris, Æneids; Jason; Well at the World's End; Earthly Paradise, 4 v. ed.
The Lark, nos. 3, 18, 19, unopened.
Volumes in Folio; Retrospective Reviews.

The Boston Book Co., 83 Francis St., Boston, Mass.

Baptist Quarterly Review, Jan., July, 1889; Oct., '90; Oct., '92; title-page and index v. 2, '80.
Conservative Review, any nos.

The Bowen-Merrill Co., Indianapolis, Ind.

Clarke, Samuel, Life of Drake. London, 1671.
Anna Besant's Autobiography.
Hutchison, Barkeep Stories.

Brentano's, 218 Wabash Ave., Chicago, Ill.

Circle of Science.
Daughter of Music, by Mrs. Dunn Colmore., D. Appleton & Co.
Burmah Treasure.
Crumbs from a Master's Table, by Mason, 1st ed. Pub. by D. Appleton & Co., 1831.

Brentano's, 1015 Pennsylvania Ave., Washington, D. C.

Rodway, In the Guiana Forest.
Wallace, Travels on the Amazons.
Belt, Naturalists in Nicaragua.
Forbes, A Naturalist's Wanderings in the Eastern Archipelago.
Huber, Nat. Hist. of Bee.
Conrad, Children of the Sea.
Saintsbury, Specimens of English Prose.

S. E. Bridgman & Co., 108 Main St., Northampton, Mass

Rumford Leaflets, Plain Words About Food.
England and Spain, by C. M. Young.
Spanish Vistas, by G. P. Lothrop.
Feuf's Stamp Catalogue.
History of the Clapp Family, by Ebenezer Clapp.
Southwick Genealogy.
White Genealogy.
Facts for Farmers, 2 v.
Recent Developments in Massage, Douglas Graham.
Roman Sculpture, Reinsch.
History of the Boer War, Dulles, pap. ed.
Wood Engraving, Fuller.

The Brooklyn Library, Montague St., Brooklyn, N. Y

The Pictures of 1899, 1900, and 1901. Pub. by the *Art Journal*, London.
Year's Art, 1896 to date, incl.

The Burrows Bros. Co., Cleveland, O.

Bartram, J., Travels, Kalm's ed. London, 1751.
Life of Louis Wetzel.
Lewes, Aristotle.
N. Y. Medical Journal, Oct. 19, 1901.
Appleton's European Guide.
Almost a Nun.
Almost a Priest.
Priest and Nun.

John Byrne & Co., Washington, D C.

Electrical World and Engineer, v. 37, no. 6.
Todd, Parliamentary Government.
Guthrie, The Fourteenth Amendment.

William J. Campbell, Phila., Pa.

Delaware Laws, v. 7.

Jno. J. Cass, 70 Wall St., N. Y.

U. S. Army Register, 1861 to '65.
Cruise of the "Dolphin."
Thirty Years at Sea.
Any mining books South or Central America.
Darley, Cooper, 2d ed.: Precaution; Satanstoe; Wallingford.

H. B. Claflin Co., N. Y. City.

Longstreet, From Manassas to Appomattox, $4 00 ed.

BOOKS WANTED.—Continued.

A. H. Clapp, 32 Maiden Lane, Albany, N. Y.

Kitwyk Tales. C. Co.
Septic Conditions of the Infantile Alimentary Canal, F. W. Forbes Ross.
The Feet of Love, Aldrich.
Rose of Flame, Aldrich.

A. S. Clark, 174 Fulton St., N. Y.

Beatson, Robert, Naval and Military Memoirs of Great Britain, from 1727 to 1783. London, 1838.

The A. H. Clark Co., Garfield Bldg., Cleveland, O.

Griffin, Bibliography of Amer. Hist. Socs.
Hunt's Merchants Mag., 63 v., complete.
McKenney, Tour of the Lakes.
N. Y. Freeman's Jour., any v.

The Robert Clarke Co., 31 E. 4th St., Cincinnati, O.

The Broad Aisle, by Mrs. C. S. Daggett.

W. B. Clarke Co., Park and Tremont Sts., Boston, Mass.

Under Lock and Key, Speight. Lippincott.
Adventures of Captain Kettle.
Ridpath, Library of Universal Literature, 25 v.

Wm. G. Colesworthy, 66 Cornhill, Boston, Mass.

Cooper, Townsend ed., Darley plates: Precaution; Deerslayer; The Ways of the Hour; Jack Tier; Miles Wallingford; Afloat and Ashore.

Irving S. Colwell, Auburn, N. Y.

Stoddard's Travel Lectures, 11 v.

Cong. S. S. and Pub. Soc., 175 Wabash Ave., Chicago, Ill.

Set Jane Austen, Temple ed., leath.
Set Jane Austen, Temple ed., cl., cheap.

H. M. Connor, 232 Meridian St., E. Boston, Mass.

Cord and Crease.
Harvey, Hist. of Newfoundland.
Haswell, Engineer's Pocket-Book.
Brave Iconoclast.
Voltaire's Philosophy.

David C. Cook Pub. Co., 146 5th Ave., N. Y.

Chronicles of Carlingford, by Mrs. Oliphant.

Cossitt Library, Memphis, Tenn.

Kernan, Flaming Meteor.

A. J. Crawford, 10th and Pine Sts., St. Louis, Mo.

St. Nicholas Magazine, Aug., Dec., 1897; Sept., '98.

Crusoe & Co., 81 Vermont St., Brooklyn, N. Y.

Sweet, History of English Sounds.
Gospel of St. Mark in Mœso-Gothic.
Works on free-hand pen-and-ink drawing.

Damrell & Upham, 283 Washington St., Boston, Mass.

Crew of "Sam Weller."

E. Darrow & Co., Rochester, N. Y.

Deaver's Surgical Anatomy, v. 2.

Davis' Book Store, 35 W. 42d St, N. Y.

Bancroft's History of U. S., v. 10 only. Little, Brown & Co.
Rabelais, Works, Bohn's extra v., v. 2 only.

A. W. Dellquest & Co., El Paso, Tex.

Shemseddin Mohamed Hafez, tr. by John Payne.
Erin's Vow.
Map of U. S. West of Miss. River. Pub. previous to the Civil War.
Mustang Grav.
Geological reports.

Edwin A. Denham, 28 W. 33d St., N. Y.

Parkman, Francis, A. L. s.
Webster, Daniel, A. L. s.

F. M. DeWitt, 318 Post St., San Francisco, Cal.

Maspero, G., Dawn of Civilization.
Maspero, Struggle of the Nations.
Harte, Bret, 1st eds.

DeWolfe, Fiske & Co., 361 Washington St., Boston, Mass.

Ladies' Book Plates, by Madame Labouchere.

Dodd, Mead & Co., 372 Fifth Ave., N. Y.

Darby, John, Man and His World, or, Two Thousand Years Ago. Lippincott.
Wilde, Lady Windermere's Fan.

G. Dunn & Co., St. Paul, Minn.

The Green Hand, by Cupples.
Divine Union, by Prof. Upham.
International Studio, Nov., Dec., 1889.
Argosy, v. 1, 2.

E. P. Dutton & Co., 31 W. 23d St., N. Y.

McLennan, Essays on Ancient History, 1st ser.
Sèrum Missal.
Christian Church, by Ernest Renan.
Happiness in the Spiritual Life.
Social and Domestic Religion, 2 v.
The Mother of Angels, Mrs. Trask.

Peter Eckler, 35 Fulton St., N. Y.

Ingersoll's 44 Lectures.

Kenneth B. Elliman, 419 W. 118th St., N. Y.

Poe's Works, odd v., Stone & Kimball ed.
Dowden, Shakspere: His Mind and Art, second-hand.
Spencer, J. A., History of U. S., v. 1. Johnson, Fry & Co.

G. Engelke, 225 N. Clark St., Chicago, Ill. [*Cash*

Houston, Electrical Dict. 1898.
Standard Dict., v. 2, mor., index.
Standard Dict., v. 1, cl., index.
Great and Eccentric Characters of the World.

C. P. Everitt, 219 5th Ave., N. Y.

English Lands, Letters and Kings, Mitchell.
Queen of the Adriatic, C. E. Clement.
Venetian Days, Howells.
Golden Book of Venice, Turnbull.
Century Atlas.

James R. Ewing, 169 4th St., Portland, Ore.

Table Altar, Vincent.

Harry Falkenau, 167 Madison St., Chicago, Ill.

Speeches of Thos. F. Marshall. Cincinnati, 1858.
Trial of H. W. Beecher, 3 v. 1875.
Ency. Brit., Index v., Scribner ed., cl.

A. F. Farnell & Son, 46 Court St., Brooklyn, N. Y.

Newton's Principia.
Unseen Universe, by Tait.
Flowers for Children, by Lucy Childs.

H. W. Fisher & Co., 1535 Chestnut St., Phila., Pa.

Lewis and Clark's Expedition, 4 v., large pap. Francis Harper.
Rob. Browning's Poems, v. 9. Smith, Elder & Co.
Audubon's Birds and Quadrupeds, 8vo ed.
Birds of Manitoba, by Seton-Thompson.
Schoolcraft's Indians, v. 6.
Palgrave's Golden Treasury, large pap.
Horn's Classes of Coleoptera.
Song of Solomon, il. by Bida, 4to.

Gay & Bird, 22 Bedford St., Strand, London, Eng.

The New Brazil, Its Resources, etc., by Mrs. Marie Robinson Wright, second-hand copy. Pub. at $10 by Messrs. G. Barrie & Son, Phila.
Griffin and Little, Chemistry of Paper Making.
Optical Journal, Jan., Feb., 1902.
Keystone (Jeweller's trade), Jan., Feb., Mar., 1902.

J. A. Hill & Co., 91 5th Ave., N. Y.

Appleton's American Cyclopædia, 1898, cl. or hf. mor.

George W. Jacobs & Co., 103 S. 15th St., Phila., Pa.

Ridpath, History of the World, v. 1, 4, 11, 14, 17. (17 v. ed.), hf. leath.
Wreck of the "Medusa," clear copy, cl.

U. P. James, 127 W. 7th St., Cincinnati, O.

Statesman's Year Book, 1896, '97, '98, clean copies.

E. T. Jett Book and News Co., 806 Olive St., St. Louis, Mo.

In the Heart of the Bitter Root Mountains, E. L. A. Himmelwright.
Confessions of Rousseau, pap.

E. W. Johnson, 2 E. 42d St., N. Y.

Poor's R.R. Manuals, 1890-'98.
Index to Brinley's Catalogue.

F. H. Johnson, 15 Flatbush Ave., Brooklyn, N. Y.

Prime, History of Long Island. Carter.

W. H. Kuhl, 73 Jager-Str., Berlin W., Germany.

The Engineer (Cleveland), 1902, nos. 1-6.
Notes on Naval Progress, Apr., 1898.
Kent, Comment. on Amer. Law. '96.
Glass, Marine Intern. Law. '85.
De Toussard, Amer. Artillerist's Comp. 1811.
Bourne, Rules of Navigation. 1567.
Transact. of Soc. of Naval Archit. and Marine Eng. 1899.

BOOKS WANTED.—Continued.

Chas. E. Lauriat Co., 301 Washington St., Boston, Mass.

Count de Segur's Memoirs.
The Three Spaniards.
Devil of a Trip, by Knox, pap.
Wallock's American Trotting Register, v. 1, 2, 2 copies each.
Allen's Book Plates.
Abbeys, Castles, etc., of England, v. 3, by Timbs.
Gladstone Parliament, by Lucy. Cassell & Co.
Hawaiian Islands, by Cole.
Hawaii First, by Goodhue.

Leggat Bros., 81 Chambers St., N. Y.

Supplement to Watt's Dictionary of Chemistry.
Samuels, From Forecastle to Cabin.

Lemcke & Buechner, 812 Broadway, N. Y.

Campbell, A History of Virginia.
Semple, Rise and Progress of Va. Baptists.
Taylor, Virginia Baptist Ministers.
Foote, Sketches of North Carolina.
Moore, History of North Carolina, 2 v. 1880.
Hawks, History of North Carolina. 1858.
Benedict, History of the Baptists of Virginia.
Taylor, Lives of Baptist Ministers of Virginia.
Williamson, History of North Carolina.
Winsor, Narrative and Critical History of America, 8 v., 8vo. 1889.
Histories of Hanover Co., Va., King William Co., Va., Brunswick Co., Va., also of York, Isle of Wight and Surrey.

Library Clearing House, 140 Wells St., Chicago, Ill.

Ballads of Ireland.
Oliphant, Scientific Religion.
Cynnicus, Cartoons and Satires.
John Gay's Plays.

The Library of Congress, Washington, D. C.

Electrical Engineering (Chicago), v. 10, no. 60.
Engineering Magazine (N. Y.), v. 1, nos. 1, 3, 4.
New England Bibliopolist, v. 10, nos. 5, 6; v. 11, no. 6.
Praeco Latinus (Phila.), v. 1 to 3.
Talent (N. Y.), v. 2, no. 7, Jan., 1892.

Walter Scott Lieber, Roslyn P. O, Montg. Co., Pa.

From Hearts Content, by Clara Doty Bates.

Little, Brown & Co., 254 Washington St., Boston, Mass.

The Day Book of Bertha Hardacre.

J. S. Lockwood, 530 Atlantic Ave., Boston, Mass.

Anderson, R. B., America not Discovered by Columbus. 1883.
Anderson, T. M., Political Conspiracies preceding the Rebellion.
Burk, John, History of Virginia, 4 v. Petersburg, Va., 1804-5.
Butterfield, C. W. Correspondence of George Washington and Wm. Crawford Concerning Western Lands.
Campbell, Jas. F., Outlines of the Political History of Michigan.
Elliott, Chas. W., The New England History. N. Y., 1857.
Lowell, E. J., Hessians and Other German Auxiliaries of Great Britain in Revolution.
O'Callaghan, E. B., History of New Netherlands, 2 v., 2d ed. N. Y., 1855.
O'Neill, E. D., Virginia Vetusta. Albany, 1885.
Ripley, R. S., The War with Mexico, 2 v.
Thornton, J. W., Peter Oliver's Puritan Commonwealth reviewed.
Amory, Life John Sullivan.
Hillard, Geo. S., Memoir and Correspondence of Jeremiah Mason.
Kapp, F., Life of John Kalb. N. Y., 1870.
Muhlenberg, H. A., Life of Peter Muhlenberg. Phila., 1849.
Sargent, W., Life and Career of Maj. John André. Boston, 1861.
Vallandigham, J. L., Life of Clement L. Vallandigham. Baltimore, 1872.
Schoolcraft, Myth of Hiawatha.
Trumbull, J. H., True Blue Laws of Connecticut and New Haven. N. Y., 1870.
Tucker, G., Hist. of U. S., 4 v. Phila., 1860.
Bates, Mary, Private Life of J. C. Calhoun. Charleston, 1852.
Callender, E. B., Thaddeus Stevens.
Colton, E. R., Life of Nathaniel Macon. Balt., 1840.
Conkling, A. R., Life and Letters of Roscoe Conkling.

J. S. Lockwood.—*Continued.*

Campbell, W. W., Life and Writings of DeWitt Clinton. N. Y., 1849.
Cone, Mary, Life of Rufus Putnam. Cleveland, 1886.
Ellis, G. E., Life of Mrs. Anne Hutchinson. Boston, 1845.
Grimke, A. H., Wm. Lloyd Garrison. N. Y., 1891.
Hall, Henry, Ethan Allen. N. Y., 1892.

I. M. Low, Colorado Springs, Colo. [*Cash.*]

Nick of the Woods, Bird. Pub. by Routledge.

S. F. McLean & Co., 44 E. 23d St., N. Y.

Robinson, Biblical Researches.
Murray, Guide to Holy Land, old ed.
Murray, Guide to Spain, old ed.
Milkanwatha.
Eastlake, Materials.
Quad, Odds.
Stoddard, Lectures, 11 v.
Densmon, How Nature Cures.

H. Malkan, Hanover Sq., N. Y.

Kidd, Control of Tropics.
Any N. Y. daily paper of March 18, 1899.
Records of New Amsterdam, v. 3, shp.

The Edw. Malley Co., New Haven, Conn.

The Unpublished Letters of Charles Carroll of Carrollton. Pub. by the U. S. Catholic Historical Soc.

Masonic Book Co., P. O. Box 7, N. Y.

United States Investor, any v. or nos. previous to 1901.

Isaac Mendoza, 17 Ann St., N. Y.

Life and Adventures of Peter Still.
Tales of Grandfather, 3 v., Cadell ed.

R. H. Merriam, Hanover Sq., N. Y.

Century Dictionary, in 24 pts.
My Lady's Face.
Essays by Sir Arthur Helps.
Bootle's Baby, J. S. Winter.

Miss Millard, Teddington, Middlesex, Eng.

Dixson, Subject Index to Prose Fiction.
Fuller, Art of Memory.
Renov, Monograms and Cyphers.
Manuel Fresco Manual: 300 Designs.
Galton, Meteorographica, Mapping the Weather.

F. M. Morris, 171 Madison St., Chicago, Ill

Recollections of a Private Soldier, by Wilkinson.

Frederick W. Morris, 114 5th Ave., N. Y.

Percy Manuscripts of Old English Ballads, pt. 1 of v. 1, and v. 2, pt. 1, pap.
Hamilton, History of Republic, v. 7.
Nare, Glossary, particularly Shakespeare, v. 1. 1888.

H. H. Morse, 20 Monroe St., Grand Rapids, Mich.

Prime, Alhambra and Kremlin.
Murray, Russians of To-Day.
Stoddard, Red Letter Days Abroad.
Kalakaua, King of Hawaii, The Legends and Myths of Hawaii.

New Amsterdam Book Co, 156 5th Ave., N. Y.

Catechism of Palmistry. London, Geo. Redway.

New England Methodist Book Depository, 38 Bromfield St., Boston, Mass.

Pilgrim's Wallet, by Bishop Golbert Haven

W. W. Nisbet, 12 S. Broadway, St. Louis, Mo.

Pictorial St. Louis, 1875, or any ed.
Thackeray's Complete Works.
Rose-Finkner Inorganische Chemie.
Brewer's World's Best Orations.
Texas Fever or Southern Cattle Fever, 1892. U. S. Report.

Old Corner Book Store, Springfield, Mass. [*Cash.*]

History Brooklyn, N. Y., v. 3, by H. R. Stiles.
Lossing's Field Book Rev. War, v. 1, hf. cf.
History Mass., 3d Period, by Barry.

E. J. O'Malley, Hanover Sq., N. Y.

Genealogy of the Bergen Family. 1876.
Anything on the history of Jersey City or New Jersey.
Puritan Age and Rule, Ellis.

Martin F. Onnen, 114 5th Ave., N. Y.

Le Médecin, Organe de l'Ecole Medical Belge, Bruxelles, v. 1, nos. 2, 3; v. 4, no. 18; v. 6, nos. 1, 2, 3, 5, 46, 47, 48, 50; v. 7, nos. 3, 6, 9, 36; v. 10, no. 5; v. 11, nos. 1, 11.

BOOKS WANTED.—Continued.

Daniel O'Shea, 1584 Broadway, N. Y.

Prophecies of Kilumcull.
Any books on Logic by De Morgan with the exception of Formal Logic.
People's Medical Lighthouse, by Root.
Lover's Marriage Lighthouse, by Root.
Pamela, by Richardson.
Descent of Man, v. 2, by Darwin.

H. H. Otis & Sons, 11 W. Swan St., Buffalo, N. Y.

Lectures on the Religion of the Semites, by W. Robertson Smith.

W. M. Palmer, 20 Monroe St, Grand Rapids, Mich.

Pool, In a Dyke Shanty.
Ludlow, My Saint John.
Swineford, Alaska.
Curtis, Land of the Nihilist.
De Colange, Picturesque Russia and Greece.

Patterson & McTaggart, Port Huron, Mich.

Set Stoddard's Lectures, 11 v., new ed., hf. mor.

W. L. Paxson, 22 7th St., San Francisco, Cal.

Bryan, Dictionary of Engravers and Painters.
Philistine, v. 8.

Geo. B. Peck Dry Goods Co., Book Dpt., Kansas City, Mo.

China Hunter's Club, 1st ed.
A Purple Week.
Zurbruken, Mountain Climbing.
Anything in well illustrated, and good limited and no. ed. Cat. of second-hand dealers.

H. E. Peadry, Powers Bldg., Rochester, N. Y.

Stoddard's Lectures.
Lists of second-hand text-books for sale.

M. Pfister, 948 8th Ave., N. Y.

History France, v. 2, 3, by M. Guizot. N. Y., Am. Pub. Corporation.

Pierce & Zahn, 633 17th St., Denver, Colo.

Review of Reviews, v. 1, 2.
Life of Bishop Jolly, by Walker.
Crested Butte Anthracite Folio (Geological.)
Tiger Lilies, by Sidney Lanier.

The Pilgrim Press, 175 Wabash Ave., Chicago, Ill.

Scott, Minstrelsy of the Scottish Border, good copy.

T. Pillot, 409 Main St., Houston, Tex.

Alte und Neue Welt, a monthly, pub. by Benziger Bros., New York, years 1871, '72, '73.
Any books on early Texas history.
Clifford Troupe, by Westmoreland.
New Library of Poetry and Song, ed. by Wm. C. Bryant.

E. W. Porter, St. Paul, Minn.

Whistler, Gentle Art of Making Enemies.
Portraits of Ruskin and Wm. Morris, 8vo.
McCarthy, Four Georges and William IV., large type, English ed.
King James Army List.
Athenian Society Publications, v. 6, 7.
Phantasmagoria, by Lewis Carroll.
Vizetelly & Co.'s eds. of Temple of Gnidus.
Beauty's Day.
Bohemian of the Latin Quarter.
Renee Mauperin.
The Emotions of Polydore Marasquin.

Presb. Bd. of Pub. and S. S. Work, 156 5th Ave., N. Y.

At Hand. United Brethren Pub. Co.

Presb. Bd. of Pub. and S. S. Work, 1319 Walnut St., Phila., Pa.

Way of the Cross, a Pictorial Pilgrimage from Bethlehem to Calvary. Pub. A. J. Holman, Phila.

Presbyterian Book Store, Pittsburgh Pa.

Spiritual Development of St. Paul, Mathewson.
Renan, Life St. Paul.

Preston & Rounds Co., Providence, R. I.

The Dance of Death, by William Herman. 1877.

G. P. Putnam's Sons, 27 W. 23d St., N. Y.

Lyman Beecher Autobiog., 2 v. Harper.
Letters from John Chinaman. Mansfield.
Commons, Distribution of Wealth. Macmillan.
House and Garden, July, Aug., Sept., Oct. nos., v. 1.
Taine, Ancient Regime.

Fleming H. Revell Co., Chicago, Ill.

Out of the Deep, Kingsley.
Interior Life, Upham.
Restitution of all Things, Jukes.

J. D. Rice, Trenton, N. J. [*Cash.*]

Memoirs of Madam Vestris.
Yarker's Freemasonry.
Psychopathia Sexualis, tr. Chaddock. Phila., 1893.
The Monk, by M. G. Lewis, early ed.
Elegies of Propertius, Bohn ed.

Geo. H. Richmond, 32 W. 33d St., N. Y.

Baber, Memoirs of Zehir-eddin, Emperor of Hindustan, 4to. London, 1826.
Stoddard, Lectures.
Sloane, Napoleon.

Geo. H. Rigby, 1113 Arch St., Phila., Pa.

Kane, Illian, or, Curse of Old South Church.

A. M. Robertson, 126 Post St., San Francisco, Cal.

Poems, Father Tabb.
Lyrics, Father Tabb.
Napoleon Bibliography. Pub. by *The Bulletin*, Providence, R. I.
Why Priests Should Wed.

Philip Roeder, 616 Locust St., St. Louis, Mo.

Sand, Indiana.

Wm. B. Ropes, Mt. Vernon, Skagit Co., Wash.

Blackwood's Mag., Oct., 1868.
Philistine, v. 1, 2, 3, 4, 5, 6, 7, 8, 9.
Heart of Old Hickory. Arena or Estes.
Booth's Prompt Book: Hamlet; Richelieu; Macbeth; Merchant of Venice; Fool's Revenge.

J. Francis Ruggles, Bronson, Mich.

Anderson, A Voice from Harper's Ferry.
Redpath, Echoes of Harper's Ferry. 1860.
Ante-Nicene Fathers.
Emblems and Allegories.

St. Paul Book and Stationery Co., 5th and St. Peter Sts., St. Paul, Minn.

Familiar Quotations in French and Italian, Ramage.

John E. Scopes, 29 Tweddle Bldg., Albany, N. Y.

American Ancestry, v. 9, 10.
Wilkinson, Memoirs, v. 2, and atlas. Phila., 1816.

Scrantom, Wetmore & Co., Rochester, N. Y.

Leslie, Old Sea Wings and Ways.

Charles Scribner's Sons, 153 5th Ave., N. Y.

Beecher, Lyman, Autobiography, 2 v.
Douglas, Picture Poems for Young Folks. Osgood, 1872.
Hymns for Mothers and Children, compiled by the author of the Violet, Daisy, etc. Walker & Fuller, Boston, 1866.
Cupples, Green Hand.
Clapp, Reminiscences of a Dramatic Critic. $2.00 ed.
Norton, C. E., Historical Studies of Church Building in the Middle Ages.

The Shorthand Institute, 8 Beacon St., Boston, Mass.

Day's Shorthand. China (Maine), 1836.
Bailey's Stenography. 1819, '20, '21, '31.
Rees' Stenography. Phila., 1819.
Hewett's Stenography. Phila., 1823.
Old shorthand books of all kinds.

Jos. Silk, 147 6th Ave., N. Y.

Craft, History of Wyalusing or Bradford Co., Pa.
Brooks, Guide to Popular Terms Science and Art.

George D. Smith, 50 New St., N. Y.

Gorland Genealogy.
Dusseldorf Gallery.
Philistine, v. 1-9.
Mexican War, the Other Side, Ramsey. N. Y., 1850.
La Fontaine's Tales, 2 v., Eisen plates.

Wm. H. Smith, Jr., 515 W. 173d St., N. Y.

Arthur's Antiquarian, v. 2.
Aristophanes, v. 1, Bohn, old ser.
Bovee, Intuition and Summaries of Thought.
Edsall, History of Kingsbridge.
Hazlitt, Table Talk, 1st ser.

A. H. Smythe, 43 S. High St., Columbus, O.

Tecumseh, or, the West Thirty Years Ago, a poem, by Geo. H. Colton. N. Y., Wiley, 1842.
Forest Rangers, a poetic tale of the Western Wilderness in 1794, Andrew Coffinberry. Columbus, 1842.

Southern Book Exchange, Atlanta, Ga. [*Cash.*]

500 school books, all kinds used anywhere in U. S.
Medical text-books, law books, all kinds, send lists.

BOOKS WANTED.—*Continued.*

Southern Book Exchange.—*Continued.*

Stephens, War Between the States, 2 v.
McCall, History of Georgia, 2 v.
Century Dictionary, 10 or 6 v. set.
Modern Eloquence (Sub.), 10 v.
Burton, Anatomy of Melancholy.

Speyer & Peters, Berlin, N. W. 7, Germany.

Archiv für Mikroskop. Anatomie.
Archiv für Patholog. Anatomie. Virchow.
Archives of Laryngology.
Brain.
Engineering, v. 1.
Journal of Anatomy and Physiol., v. 1, 10, 32, 34.
Journal of Amer. Chem. Soc., 1889-1901.
Ophthalm. Soc. Transactions.
Transactions of Amer. Orthop. Association.
Please offer sets or single vols.
Annals of Surgery, sets.
Centralblatt für Chirurgie, sets.
Deutsche Chirurgie, all out.
Transactions of Amer. Orthop. Association, v. 7-14.
Zeitschrift für Biologie, v. 1-11.
Zeitschrift für Chirurgie, sets.
Annales de l'Institut Pasteur.
Journal de l'Anatomie (Robin.)

G. E. Stechert, 9 E. 16th St., N. Y.

Amer. Philos. Soc. Proceedings, any nos.
Harper's Pictorial Hist. War of Rebellion.
Bliss, W. R., Paradise in the Pacific.
Nordhoff, Northern California. 1874.
Ballou, Hist. of Cuba. 1854.

E. Steiger & Co., 25 Park Place, N. Y. [*Cash.*]

Transactions of the American Society of Civil Engineers, v. 5, 1876.
Stephens, Incidents of Travel in Yucatan. N. Y., 1843.
Dana, Characteristics of Volcanoes.
Ely, Adam Smith, 1723-1790.
Ely, J. St. Mill, 1806-1873.
Annals of Amer. Academy of Political and Social Science, 1896 to 1900, complete or odd v.
Political Science Quarterly, 1896 to 1900, complete or odd v.

The Stiefel Masonic Book Co., 106 E. 4th St., Cincinnati, O.

Hughan, Old Charges of British Freemasons.
Groetz, History of the Jews.
5000 copies of Masonic Proceedings.

Stout's Book Exchange, 612 5th St., San Diego, Cal.

Tyndall's Belfast Address.

Strawbridge & Clothier, Market St., Phila., Pa.

Stories of Naples and the Camorra, by Chas. Grant.
How Nature Cures, E. Densmore. Tillman & Co.

Syndicate Trading Co., 2 Walker St., N. Y.

Adventures of a Chinaman. Lee & S, $1.50.

Henry K. Van Siclen, 413 W. 22d St., N. Y.

Davies, Cp., The "Swan" and Her Crew. Pub. in 1877, $2.50, Scribner.

T. B. Ventres, 597 Fulton St., Brooklyn, N. Y.

Shadow of John Wallace.
Right to the Point, Cuyler.
2 copies Old Streams, Abbott. Pub. by Lothrop.

W. H. Walker, 58 Moffatt St., Brooklyn, N. Y.

Zola's Novels, Vizetelly eds.
Rousseau's Confessions, good ed.
Semmes, Service Afloat.
Taylor, Construction and Reconstruction.
Life of Godwin, by C. Kegan Paul.
Biographical Sketches, by C. Kegan Paul.
Memories, by C. Kegan Paul.
Books by Edgar Saltus.

John Wanamaker, N. Y.

Josephine, by Ober.
The Private Stable, by Jorrocks.
Debit and Credit, Freytag. Pub. by Harper.
Memoirs of the Confederate War for Independence, 2 v., by Heros von Borcke. Wm. Blackwood & Sons.
Autobiography and Correspond. of Lyman Beecher. Harper & Bros.

John Wanamaker, Phila., Pa.

Major in Washington.

Montgomery Ward & Co., Chicago, Ill.

Duplais' Treatise on the Manufacture and Distillation of Alcoholic Liquors, tr. from the French.

Geo. E. Warner, Minneapolis, Minn.

Salmon, C. A., The Burlington Strike.
Boyd, J. P., Life of J. G. Blaine.
Any county history or atlas.
Burnet, Jacob, Northwest Territory.

The Washington Book Shop, 509 7th St., N. W., Washington, D. C.

Household ed., green cl., Gregory imprint: Our Mutual Friend; Master Humphrey's Clock; Mystery of Edwin Drood.

E. A. Werner, 35 Chestnut St., Albany, N. Y.

Whig and *Tribune* Almanacs, 1847, '51, '53, '69, '90, '91, '92, '93, '94, '95, '96, '97, 1900.
O'Callaghan, History of New Netherlands, 2 v.
Campbell, Annals of Tryon County.

Thomas Whittaker, 2 Bible House, N. Y.

Maurice's Village Sermons.
The Hundred Greatest Men of History, by Wallace Wood.
Bouton, Bible Myths Compared.

Williams' Book Exchange, 519 10th St., N. W., Washington, D. C. [*Cash.*]

Chap Book, v. 1, 2, or odd nos.
Savoy, London, original binding, 3 v., or pts.
Philistine, v. 1, 2.
Ch. Aubert. Péchés Roses, 10 pts. Paris, 1884.

H. W. Wilson, 315 14th Ave., S. E. Minneapolis, Minn.

Lippincott's Biographical Dictionary.
Century Dictionary of Names.
Shakespeare, Abbey ed.

C. Witter, 19 S. Broadway, St. Louis, Mo.

Heimburg, Her Only Brother, tr. from the German.

Woodward & Lothrop, Washington, D. C.

The World's Best Books, ed. by Frank Parsons and others Pub. by Little, Brown & Co.
Chambers' Encyclopædia, quote price.
Locke, On Human Understanding. Routledge.

BOOKS FOR SALE.

N. J. Bartlett & Co., 28 Cornhill, Boston, Mass.

100 theological books, cl. binding, good condition, almost no duplicates, 12° and 8° in size. $5.00.

Leggat Bros., 81 Chambers St., N. Y.

100 Sword of the Pyramids. Pub. 25 cts.; 5 cts.
500 Selections from Boccaccio's Decameron. 5 cts.
300 Kennedy's Treatise on the Horse. 5 cts.
350 Dr. B. C. Callaway's Remedies for the Horse. 5 cts.
500 Cruise of the "Cachalot," cl. 10 cts.
25 Anderson's Manufacture of Gunpowder. $1.00.
100 A Few Short Stories, George Gorden. 5 cts.
15 Wild White Cattle of Great Britain. 60 cts.
5 Carlyle's Frederick the Great, 8 v. Set, $3 20.
25 Recollections of Henry Watkins Allen. 40 cts.
25 Carolina Tribute to Calhoun. 35 cts.
25 Genius and Character of Robert Burns. 40 cts.
50 Fernald's Republic. 10 cts.
50 Wilks' Solo Whist. 10 cts.
25 Froude's Carlyle. 40 cts.
100 Archibald the Cat. 5 cts.
Studer's American Ornithology, full mor. $15.00.
Family Histories and Genealogies, 5 v., by Salisbury. $50.00.
2 Appleton's Universal Encyc., hf. leath. $50.00.
Scribner Britannica, 25 v., hf. mor. $60.00.
Werner Britannica, 31 v., hf. mor. $31.50.

H. E. Pendry, Powers Bldg., Rochester, N. Y.

Century Dictionary, 10 v., full mor., as new.
Secret Court Memoirs.
Natural History N. Y. State.

James P. Taylor, 52 High St., Haverhill, Mass.

Plutarch Morals, by W. W. Goodwin, introd. by R. W. Emerson, 5 v. Boston, 1871. $8.00.
Invertebrata of Mass., Gould Binney. Boston, 1870. $5.00.
Tom and Jerry, il. by J. R. and G. Cruikshank. London, n. d. $3.00.
Key to American Birds, Coues. Salem, 1872. $4.00.
Leaves of Grass, by W. W. Boston, J. Osgood & Co., 1881-2.
Recent and Fossil Shells, by Woodward. London, 1868. $2.00.

HELP WANTED.

WANTED.—Sept. 1st or sooner, experienced book and stationery clerk at Tampa, Fla. Give age, reference, married or single and salary expected. Address G., care of PUBLISHERS' WEEKLY.

BOOKKEEPER.—A young man with some experience of publishing accounts and books—accuracy and good penmanship indispensable. Apply in the first place by letter, with references, to N. Y. PUBLISHER, care of PUBLISHERS' WEEKLY.

SITUATIONS WANTED.

WANTED.—Young man, 32 years of age, thoroughly posted in book business, desires position where knowledge and efficiency would be appreciated. Address R. W., care of PUBLISHERS' WEEKLY.

BOOKKEEPER, accountant and office manager. 20 years' experience, wholesale and manufacturing, desires position. Can adapt to any system or conditions. Excellent references. Salary no object so long as prospects are good. Address WILLSTAN, care of PUBLISHERS' WEEKLY.

BUSINESS FOR SALE.

FOR SALE.—Book and Stationery business in Fla. town of 25,000; net profit over 50 %; last year's sales, $17,812.00. Good reason for selling. Address W. E. C., 176 Court St., Kankakee, Ill.

COPYRIGHT NOTICES.

LIBRARY OF CONGRESS,
OFFICE OF THE REGISTER OF COPYRIGHTS,
WASHINGTON, D. C.

Class A, XXc, No. 33494.—To wit: *Be it remembered*, That on the 7th day of May, 1902, The Robert Clarke Company, of Cincinnati, O., hath deposited in this office the title of a book, the title of which is in the following words, to wit: "Manual of Universal Church History. By Rev. Dr. John Alzog. Translated by F. J. Pabisch and Rt. Rev. Thomas S. Byrne. Volume I. Cincinnati, The Robert Clarke Company," the right whereof they claim as proprietors in conformity with the laws of the United States respecting copyrights.

(Signed) HERBERT PUTNAM, *Librarian of Congress*.
By THORVALD SOLBERG, *Register of Copyrights*.
In renewal for 14 years from Sept. 12, 1902.

LIBRARY OF CONGRESS,
OFFICE OF THE REGISTER OF COPYRIGHTS,
WASHINGTON, D. C.

To wit: *Be it remembered*, That on the 2d day of July, 1902, D. B. Ivison, of United States, hath deposited in this office the title of a book, the title of which is in the following words, to wit: "Robinson's Mathematical Series. The Junior Class Arithmetic. Oral and Written. Designed for Graded Schools. By Daniel W. Fish, A.M. New York, Cincinnati, Chicago, American Book Company," the right whereof he claims as proprietor in conformity with the laws of the United States respecting copyrights.

(Signed) HERBERT PUTNAM, *Librarian of Congress*.
By THORVALD SOLBERG, *Register of Copyrights*.
In renewal for 14 years from December 7, 1902.

LIBRARY OF CONGRESS,
OFFICE OF THE REGISTER OF COPYRIGHTS,
WASHINGTON, D. C.

To wit: *Be it remembered*, That on the 2d day of July, 1902, D. B. Ivison, of United States, hath deposited in this office the title of a book, the title of which is in the following words, to wit: "Robinson's Shorter Course. Complete Arithmetic. Oral and Written. First Part. By Daniel W. Fish, A.M. New York, Cincinnati, Chicago, American Book Company," the right whereof he claims as proprietor in conformity with the laws of the United States respecting copyrights.

(Signed) HERBERT PUTNAM, *Librarian of Congress*.
By THORVALD SOLBERG, *Register of Copyrights*.
In renewal for 14 years from December 7, 1902.

LIBRARY OF CONGRESS,
OFFICE OF THE REGISTER OF COPYRIGHTS,
WASHINGTON, D. C.

To wit: *Be it remembered*, That on the 2d day of July, 1902, D. B. Ivison, of United States, hath deposited in this office the title of a book, the title of which is in the following words, to wit: "Robinson's Shorter Course. The Complete Arithmetic. Oral and Written. Second Part. By Daniel W. Fish, A.M. New York, Cincinnati, Chicago, American Book Company," the right whereof he claims as proprietor in conformity with the laws of the United States respecting copyrights.

(Signed) HERBERT PUTNAM, *Librarian of Congress*.
By THORVALD SOLBERG, *Register of Copyrights*.
In renewal for 14 years from December 7, 1902.

LIBRARY OF CONGRESS,
OFFICE OF THE REGISTER OF COPYRIGHTS,
WASHINGTON, D. C.

To wit: *Be it remembered*, That on the 2d day of July, 1902, D. B. Ivison, of United States, hath deposited in this office the title of a book, the title of which is in the following words, to wit: "Robinson's Shorter Course. Key to the Complete Arithmetic. For Teachers and Private Learners. New York, Cincinnati, Chicago, American Book Company," the right whereof he claims as proprietor in conformity with the laws of the United States respecting copyrights.

(Signed) HERBERT PUTNAM, *Librarian of Congress*.
By THORVALD SOLBERG, *Register of Copyrights*.
In renewal for 14 years from December 7, 1902.

LIBRARY OF CONGRESS,
OFFICE OF THE REGISTER OF COPYRIGHTS,
WASHINGTON, D. C.

To wit: *Be it remembered*, That on the 2d day of July, 1902, Emma H. Watson, of United States, hath deposited in this office the title of a book, the title of which is in the following words, to wit: "Independent Youth's Speller. Printed in imitation of Writing with original classification of words, formations of columns, dictation exercises, orthographical and orthoepical treatise, appendix, etc. By J. Madison Watson. New York, Cincinnati, Chicago, American Book Company," the right whereof she claims as proprietor in conformity with the laws of the United States respecting copyrights.

(Signed) HERBERT PUTNAM, *Librarian of Congress*.
By THORVALD SOLBERG, *Register of Copyrights*.
In renewal for 14 years from October 17, 1902.

LIBRARY OF CONGRESS,
OFFICE OF THE REGISTER OF COPYRIGHTS,
WASHINGTON, D. C.

To wit: *Be it remembered*, That on the 3d day of July, 1902, Guy D. Peck, of Gallia, N. J., hath deposited in this office the title of a book, the title of which is in the following words, to wit: "First Lessons in Numbers. By William G. Peck, Ph.D., LL.D. New York, Cincinnati, Chicago, American Book Company," the right whereof he claims as proprietor in conformity with the laws of the United States respecting copyrights.

(Signed) HERBERT PUTNAM, *Librarian of Congress*.
By THORVALD SOLBERG, *Register of Copyrights*.
In renewal for 14 years from December 29, 1902.

LIBRARY OF CONGRESS,
OFFICE OF THE REGISTER OF COPYRIGHTS,
WASHINGTON, D. C.

To wit: *Be it remembered*, That on the 2d day of July, 1902, Lyman P. Spencer, of United States, hath deposited in this office the title of a book, the title of which is in the following words, to wit: "Theory of Spencerian Penmanship. For schools and private learners, developed by questions and answers, with practical illustrations. Designed to be studied by pupils in connection with the use of the Spencerian Copy-Books. By The 'Spencerian Authors.' New York, Cincinnati, Chicago, American Book Company," the right whereof he claims as author and proprietor in conformity with the laws of the United States respecting copyrights.

(Signed) HERBERT PUTNAM, *Librarian of Congress*.
By THORVALD SOLBERG, *Register of Copyrights*.
In renewal for 14 years from December 29, 1902.

LIBRARY OF CONGRESS,
OFFICE OF THE REGISTER OF COPYRIGHTS,
WASHINGTON, D. C.

Class A, XXc, No. 35699.—To wit: *Be it remembered*, That on the 18th day of June, 1902, John Foster Kirk, of Philadelphia, Pa., hath deposited in this office the title of a book, the title of which is in the following words, to wit: "The History of the Reign of the Emperor Charles the Fifth. By William Robertson, D.D. With an Account of the Emperor's Life after His Abdication. By William H. Prescott. New Edition. Volume I. Philadelphia, J. B. Lippincott Company," the right whereof he

COPYRIGHT NOTICES.—*Continued.*

claims as proprietor in conformity with the laws of the United States respecting copyrights.
(Signed) HERBERT PUTNAM, *Librarian of Congress.*
By THORVALD SOLBERG, *Register of Copyrights.*
In renewal for 14 years from December 11, 1902.

LIBRARY OF CONGRESS,
OFFICE OF THE REGISTER OF COPYRIGHTS,
WASHINGTON, D. C.

Class A, XXc, No. 35700.—To wit: *Be it remembered,* That on the 18th day of June, 1902, John Foster Kirk, of Philadelphia, Pa., hath deposited in this office the title of a book, the title of which is in the following words, to wit: "The History of the Reign of the Emperor Charles the Fifth. By William Robertson, D.D. With an Account of the Emperor's Life after His Abdication. By William H. Prescott. New Edition. Volume II. Philadelphia, J. B. Lippincott Company," the right whereof he claims as proprietor in conformity with the laws of the United States respecting copyrights.
(Signed) HERBERT PUTNAM, *Librarian of Congress.*
By THORVALD SOLBERG, *Register of Copyrights.*
In renewal for 14 years from December 11, 1902.

LIBRARY OF CONGRESS,
OFFICE OF THE REGISTER OF COPYRIGHTS,
WASHINGTON, D. C.

Class A, XXc, No. 35701.—To wit: *Be it remembered,* That on the 18th day of June, 1902, John Foster Kirk, of Philadelphia, Pa., hath deposited in this office the title of a book, the title of which is in the following words, to wit: "The History of the Reign of the Emperor Charles the Fifth. By William Robertson, D.D. With an Account of the Emperor's Life after His Abdication. By William H. Prescott. New Edition. Volume III. Philadelphia, J. B. Lippincott Company," the right whereof he claims as proprietor in conformity with the laws of the United States respecting copyrights.
(Signed) HERBERT PUTNAM, *Librarian of Congress.*
By THORVALD SOLBERG, *Register of Copyrights.*
In renewal for 14 years from December 11, 1902.

SPECIAL NOTICES.

OP'S. English, Irish Books, Posters. PRATT, N. Y.

A. S. CLARK, 174 Fulton St. N. Y., will supply any magazine at market value.

GAME LANDS OF MAINE. Van Dyke. 10 cts. Trade price, cts. NASSAU PRESS, Richmond Hill, L. I., N. Y. 5

BACK NUMBERS, volumes, and sets of magazines and reviews for sale at the AMERICAN AND FOREIGN MAGAZINE DEPOT, 47 Dey St., New York.

BOOKS.—All out-of-print books supplied, no matter on what subject. Write us. We can get you any book ever published. Please state wants. When in England call and see our 50,000 rare books. BAKER'S GREAT BOOKSHOP, 14-16 John Bright Street, Birmingham, England.

Books of All Publishers on
MEDICINE, DENTISTRY,
PHARMACY AND ALLIED SCIENCES.
We have the largest miscellaneous stock in the country of American and English Books on these subjects.
Trade and Library Orders Solicited.
P. BLAKISTON'S SON & CO.
1012 Walnut Street, Philadelphia.

(ESTABLISHED 1868)
C. D. CAZENOVE & SON
Solicit Agency Business from American Publishers and Booksellers
Miscellaneous orders for Books and Periodicals handled economically and promptly. Shipping and forwarding attended to.
26 Henrietta St., Covent Garden, London, England
CABLES: EIKON. LONDON

THE BEST ILLUSTRATIONS
By half-tone or other photo-engraving processes are made by
COOPER ENGRAVING COMPANY
320 Pearl Street, New York
TELEPHONE "97 JOHN"
Successors to New York Engraving and Printing Co.

FOWLER & WELLS CO.,
Phrenologists and Publishers.
WORKS ON
PHRENOLOGY, PHYSIOGNOMY, MENTAL SCIENCE, AND HYGIENE.
Write for Catalogue.
24 East 22d Street, New York.

MAGGS BROS., 109 STRAND, W. C., LONDON, W., ENGLAND
Dealers in **Rare Books and Fine Library Editions of Standard Authors,**
Voyages and Travels, Early Printed Books, 1st Editions of 17th, 18th, and 19th Century Writers, Illustrated Works. Also *Rare Portraits, Line, Stipple, Mezzotints, and Color Engravings, and Autographs.*
Classified catalogues free on application.
Those visiting England should call and inspect our stock, which is both large and in choice condition

JOHN J. MURPHY
DEALER IN
Fine Book, Coated and Cover Papers
47 John and 5 Dutch Streets, N. Y.
Refers to "The Publishers' Weekly"

MEDICAL BOOKS.
(THE TRADE SUPPLIED.)
A full-priced Catalogue of all Medical and Surgical Books Sent on Application.
E. R. PELTON,
19 East 16th St. (bet. Broadway and 5th Ave.), **New York**

SHORTHAND—ISAAC PITMAN'S
☞ Exclusively adopted in the Commercial Course of New York High Schools.

SHORTHAND INSTRUCTOR (Complete System),	$1.50
ISAAC PITMAN'S MANUAL,	.50
" " TEACHER,	.20
" " SHORTHAND DICTIONARY,	1.50

Liberal Discount to Dealers
ISAAC PITMAN & SONS, 33 Union Sq., N. Y.

VAN EVEREN'S PAPER ADJUSTABLE BOOK COVERS. Simply made. Easy to apply. Cost little. No better made. Samples on request. Order of your Jobber. P. F. VAN EVEREN, 60 Ann Street, New York.

The Best FOR SELF-INSTRUCTION FOR CLASS USE

Sauer's Spanish Grammar, with Key,	$1 25
Sauer's Italian Grammar, " "	1 25
Otto's French Grammar, " "	1 25
Otto's German Grammar, " "	1 25

All these methods may be obtained for School and College use without the keys at $1.00 each retail.
Liberal Discount to Dealers.
WYCIL & CO., 83 Nassau Street, NEW YORK.

A MIDSUMMER EVENT

By special arrangement with McClure, Phillips & Co., the New Amsterdam Book Company have just added to their popular Red Letter Series of Paper Books

TRISTRAM OF BLENT

By ANTHONY HOPE

Author of "The Prisoner of Zenda"

FIFTY CENTS

Now that the rainy season is past, people will turn to thoughts of country and seaside, and that means a sale of paper covered novels. Dealers should have stock on hand of this great novel by Anthony Hope if they want to do good business. The book is ready for shipment.

HERE ARE A FEW RECENT RED PAPER BOOKS

CAPTAIN FANNY. By W. Clark Russell

WITH SWORD AND CRUCIFIX. By Edward S. Van Zile

THE SHADOW OF HILTON FERNBROOK. By Atha Westbury

MISER HOADLEY'S SECRET. By Arthur W. Marchmont

10,000 sold in three weeks

THE INDIAN MYSTERY. By Grant Allen

PRISONERS OF THE SEA. By Florence Morse Kingsley

All of them illustrated except "Tristram of Blent"

NEW AMSTERDAM BOOK COMPANY

156 Fifth Avenue, New York

ADVANCE NOTES—A. C. McCLURG & CO.

FOR the information of the trade, we take pleasure in giving herewith some advance data about our Fall books of 1902, which we believe will be of interest. Our list will include seventeen titles, and in matter and make-up it will be the most generally attractive line we have ever put out.

Our most noteworthy undertaking is the new trade edition of **"The Expedition of Lewis and Clark."** In two square octavo volumes of over 500 pages each, printed from new type of a large clear face, on fine laid paper, with new photogravure portraits and fac-simile maps, and with an introduction by Dr. James K. Hosmer and a copious index, this will undoubtedly take its place as the standard popular edition of Lewis and Clark. (In box, $5.00 net.)

Probably the most beautifully embellished book we have ever issued will be **"The Birds of the Rockies."** The text is by Leander S. Keyser, the well-known author of "In Bird Land," and the pictorial features include eight full-page plates, four of which are in color, by the eminent nature painter, Louis Agassiz Fuertes, thirty-three charming text illustrations by Bruce Horsfall, and eight full-page scenic plates from photographs. The binding and printing of the book are strikingly attractive. (In box, $3.00 net.)

In response to repeated requests from the trade, we have prepared an elegant illustrated edition of Max Müller's **"Memories"**—a classic which has now reached a sale with us of nearly 40,000 copies. The book will be a handsome square octavo, and is printed from entirely new plates, with eight beautiful charcoal drawings and other pictorial embellishments by Blanche Ostertag. The cover, also designed by Miss Ostertag, is unique. (In box, $2.00 net.)

Our fiction will include a volume of clever stories of Chicago business life by Will Payne, called **"On Fortune's Road,"** with illustrations by Thomas Fogarty ($1.50); a spirited and exciting historical novel, **"The Holland Wolves,"** illustrated in a highly dramatic manner by the Kinneys (illustrators of "The Thrall of Leif the Lucky") ($1.50); an illustrated edition of the popular romance of Indian Oregon, **"The Bridge of the Gods,"** with eight strong pictures by the well-known western artist, L. Maynard Dixon ($1.50), and **"A Captive of the Roman Eagles,"** a historical romance by Felix Dahn, translated from the German by Mary J. Safford ($1.50).

A unique volume in typography, binding, and illustrations is **"In Argolis,"** by Mr. George Horton, a delightful personal account of family life in Greece ($1.75 net). Another admirable gift book, especially for music lovers, is Mr. George P. Upton's **"Musical Pastels,"** a series of essays on quaint and curious musical subjects, illustrated from rare wood engravings (In box, $2.00 net).

Mr. Upton has also added to his well-known series of musical handbooks a new volume on **"The Standard Light Operas,"** which will be widely popular ($1.20 net). Mr. William Morton Payne has followed his "Little Leaders" and "Editorial Echoes" with **"Various Views"** ($1.00 net), and the popular "Helpful Thoughts Series" will have a new volume, **"Catch Words of Cheer,"** by Sara A. Hubbard (80 cts. net).

In regard to our juveniles we have no hesitation in saying that the trade has seldom been offered so attractive a line in matter and make-up. A notable feature of several volumes will be illustrations in color, and the cover designs are novel, artistic, and striking. The titles include a most engaging book of nonsense by Carolyn Wells, **"The Pete and Polly Stories,"** with irresistable pictures by Fanny Young Cory ($1.50 net); **"Little Mistress Good Hope,"** a volume of fairy stories by Mary Imlay Taylor, with notable colored drawings by Jessie Willcox Smith ($1.50 net); **"Mayken,"** a historical story of Holland, illustrated by the Kinneys ($1.20 net); two volumes of delightful fairy stories with charming illustrations in color by Lucy Fitch Perkins: **"Coquo and the King's Children,"** by Cornelia Baker ($1.50 net), and **"Prince Silver Wings,"** by Edith Ogden Harrison ($1.75 net). Mrs. Harrison is the wife of Mayor Carter H. Harrison of Chicago, and in this volume she makes a graceful literary debut.

THE PUBLISHERS' WEEKLY

Reference List of New Publications

JANUARY-JULY, 1902

MONTHLY CUMULATION, AUGUST, 1902

This Reference List enters the books recorded during the month under (1) author, in **Clarendon** *type, anonymous books having* **Clarendon** *type for the first word; (2) title in* Roman; *(3) subject-heading in* SMALL CAPS; *(4) name of series in Italics. The figures in parentheses are not the imprint date, but refer to the date of "The Publishers' Weekly" in which full title entry will be found and not to the day of publication, for which information should be sought in the full title entry thus indicated. Where not specified, the binding is cloth.*

A apple pie. Greenaway, K. 75 c. Warne.
A B C of banks and banking. Coffin, G: M. $1.25. S: A. Nelson.
A B C of electrical experiments. Clarke, W. J. $1. Excelsior.
A B C of the telephone. Homans, J. E. $1. Van Nostrand.
A B C of wireless telegraphy. Bubier, E: T. $1. Bubier.
A B C universal commercial electric telegraphic code. 5th ed., enl. '02(Je7) 8°, net, $7. Am. Code.
A la mode cookery. Salis, *Mrs.* H. A. de. $2. Longmans.
Aaron Crane. Tate, H: $1.50. Abbey Press.
Abbatt, W:, *ed. See* Heath, W:
ABBEYS.
See Cathedrals.
Abbott, Alex. C. Manual of bacteriology, 6th ed., rev. and enl. '02(My17) 12°, net, $2.75. Lea.
Abbott, J. H. M. Tommy Cornstalk: features of the So. African war from the point of view of the Australian ranks. '02(Je21) D. $2. Longmans.
Abbott, J: S. C. Christopher Carson, known as Kit Carson. '01. '02(Ap12) 12°, net, 87 c. Dodd.
Abbott, S: W., *ed. See* American yearbook of medicine.
Abbott's cyclopedic digest. *See* New York.
Abegg, R., *and* Herz, W. Practical chemistry; tr. by H. B. Calvert. '01. '02(Ja24) 12°, net, $1.50. Macmillan.
Abernethy, J. W. American literature. '02 (Ap26) 12°, $1.10. Maynard, M. & Co.
Abner Daniel. Harben, W. N. $1.50. Harper.
Abroad with the Jimmies. Bell, L. $1.50. L. C. Page

ABSOLUTION.
See Confession.
ACCIDENTS.
Dickson. First aid in accidents. net, 50 c. Revell.
Doty. Prompt aid to the injured. $1.50. Appleton.
According to season. Parsons, *Mrs.* F. T. net, $1.75. Scribner.
ACCOUNTS.
See Arithmetic;—Bookkeeping.
Achenbach, H: Two-fold covenant. '02 (Ap12) D. 50 c. Evangelical Press.
Achromatic spindle in spore mother-cells of osmunda regalis. Smith, R. W. net, 25 c. Univ. of Chic.
Acorn Club, Ct., pubs. 8°, pap. Case.
—Love. Thomas Short, first printer of Ct. $5. (6.) Case.
ACTIONS AT LAW.
Bradner. New practice in supplementary proceedings. $4. W. C. Little.
Budd. Civil remedies under code system. $6. Palm.
Perley. Practice in personal actions in cts. of Mass. $6.50. G: B. Reed.
Sibley. Right to and cause for action, both civil and criminal. $1.50. W. H. Anderson & Co.
Wait. Law and practice in civil actions and proceedings in justices' cts., [etc.] In 3 v. v. 1, 2. ea., $6.35; per set, $19. M. Bender.
ACTORS AND ACTRESSES.
Clapp. Reminiscences of a dramatic critic. net, $1.75. Houghton, M. & Co.
Hamm. Eminent actors and their homes. $1.25. Pott.
Whitton. Wags of the stage. $2.50. Rigby.
ACTS OF THE APOSTLES.
See Bible.
Adam, Ja. **Texts to il. a course of elem.** lectures on Greek philosophy after Aristotle. '02(Mr1) 8°, net, $1.25. Macmillan.
Adams, Braman B. **Block system of signalling** on Am. railroads. '01. '02(Mr22) 8°, $2. Railroad Gazette.
Adams, C: F. Lee at Appomattox, and other papers. '02(Je7) D. net, $1.50. Houghton, M. & Co.
Adams, C: F. Shall Cromwell have a statue? '02(Jl12) O. pap., 25 c. Lauriat.
ADAMS, Herb. B.
Vincent, *and others.* Herbert B. Adams: tribute of friends. n. p. Johns Hopkins.
Adams, W. T., ["Oliver Optic."] Moneymaker. '01. '02(Je14) 12°, (Yacht club ser., v. 3.) $1.25. Lee & S.
Addams, Jane. Democracy and social ethics. '02(Je7) D. (Citizen's lib.) $1.25. Macmillan.
Addis, M. E. L. Cathedrals and abbeys of Presbyterian Scotland. '01. '02(F15) il. 12°, net, $2.50. Presb. Bd.
Addison, Jos. Essays; ed. by J: R: Green. '02(Mr29) il. 12°, (Home lib.) $1. Burt.
Adirondack stories. Deming, P. 75 c. Houghton, M. & Co.
Adler, G: J. German and Eng. dictionary. New ed., rev. by F. P. Foster and E: Althaus. '02(Ap26) 4°, $3.50. Appleton.

Adoration of the blessed sacrament, Tesnière, A. net, $1.25. Benziger.
Adventures of John McCue, socialist. '02 (My17) D. (Socialist lib., v. 2, no. 1.) pap., 10 c. Socialistic Co-op.
Adventure ser. 12°, $1. Yewdale.
—Dee. James Griffin's adventures.
Adventures in Tibet. Carey, W: net, $1.50. Un. Soc. C. E.

ADVERTISING.
Farrington. Retail advertising. net, $1. Baker & T

Æneid. *See* Virgil.
AERODYNAMICS.
Langley. Experiments in aerodynamics. $1. Smith. Inst.
Æs triplex. Stevenson, R. L: net, 25 c.-$1. T: B. Mosher
Aeschylus. The choephori; with crit. notes, etc. '02(Ja18) 8°, (Cambridge Univ. Press ser.) net, $3.25. Macmillan
AESTHETICS.
B., E. P. God the beautiful. net, 75 c. Beam
AFRICA.
Graham. Roman Africa. $6. Longmans.
See also Egypt; — Morocco; — South Africa: — Tripoli.
Agnes Cheswick. Haymond, *Mrs.* W. E. net, 60 c. Blanchard.
AGNOSTICISM.
Sloan. Religion, agnosticism and education. net, 80 c. McClurg.
Agricultural almanac, 1903. '02(Jl19) il. 4°, pap., 10 c. Baer.
AGRICULTURE.
See Dairy;—Domestic economy;—Farms and farming; — Forestry; — Fruit; — Gardening; — Insects;—Irrigation;—Land;—Soils;—Vegetables.
Aikins, Herb. A. Principles of logic. '02 '02(My17) D. net, $1.50. Holt.
AIR BRAKES.
Dukesmith. Air brake, its use and abuse. $1. F. H. Dukesmith.
Kirkman. Air brake. $2.50. World R'way.
AIR PASSAGES.
See Breathing.
Airy, Reginald. Westminster. '02(Mr22) 12°, (Handbooks to the great public schools.) $1.50. Macmillan.
Aitken, J. R. Love in its tenderness: idylls. '02(Mr22) D. (Town and country lib., no. 309.) $1; pap., 50 c. Appleton.
Aitkin, W. H. Divine ordinance of prayer. '02(Je7) 12°, $1.25. E. & J. B. Young.
Alton, G: B., *and* Rankin, A. W. Exercises in syntax for summer schools, etc. '01 '02 (Ap26) 12°, pap., 25 c. Hyde.
Alabama. *Supreme ct.* Repts. v. 122-129. 1900. '02(Jl5) O. shp., ea., $3.75. Brown Pr. Co.
ALABAMA.
Martin. Internal improvement in Ala. 30 c. Johns Hopkins.
Alabama sketches. Peck, S: M. $1. McClurg.
ALASKA.
Balch. Alasko-Canadian frontier. $1. Allen, L. & S.
Albee, Ernest. History of Eng. utilitarianism. '02(Je28) 8°, net, $2.75. Macmillan.
Albert, Eduard. Diagnosis of surgical diseases; fr. the 8th enl. and rev ed. by R. T. Frank. '02(Je7) il. 8°, $5; $5.50. Appleton.

Alcott, Louisa M. Little button rose. New ed. '01 '02(F15) 16°, (Children's friend ser.) bds., 50 c. Little, B. & Co.
Alden, *Mrs.* Is. M., ["Pansy."] Unto the end. '02(Je7) D. $1.50. Lothrop.
Alden, W: L. Drewitt's dream. '02(Ap12) D. (Town and country lib., no. 310.) $1; pap., 50 c. Appleton.
Aleph the Chaldean. Burr, E. F. $1.25. Whittaker.
Alexander, *Mrs. See* Hector, *Mrs.* A. F.
Alexander, Hartley B. Problem of metaphysics and meaning of metaphysical explanation. '02(Jl12) 8°, (Columbia University cont. to philosophy, psychology and education, v. 10, no. 1.) pap., *75 c. net. Macmillan.
Alexander, W: M. Demonic possession in the New Testament. '02(Ap12) 8°, net, $1.50. Scribner.
ALEXANDRA, *Queen of England.*
See Edward VII., *King of England.*
Alford, M., *comp.* Latin passages for translation. '02(Ap12) 12°, net, 80 c. Macmillan.
ALFRED *the Great.*
Bowker. King Alfred millenary. $3. Macmillan.
ALGAE.
Livingston. Nature of the stimulus which causes change in form in polymorphic green algae. net, 25 c. Univ. of Chic.
ALGEBRA.
Bailey. High school algebra. 90 c. Am. Bk.
Beman *and* Smith. Academic algebra. $1.25. Ginn.
Brooks. Normal elem. algebra. pt. 1. 83 c. Sower.
Dickson. College algebra. net, $1.50 Wiley.
Hall. Algebraical examples. net. 50 c. Macmillan.
Kellogg. Elements of algebra. 25 c. Kellogg.
Lippincott's elem. algebra. 80 c. Lippincott.
Milne. Key to Academic algebra. $1.50 Am. Bk
Wentworth. College algebra. $1.65. Ginn.
White. Grammar school algebra. 35 c. Am. Bk.
See also Mathematics.
Alger, Edith G. Primer of work and play. '02(Mr15) il. sq. D. 30 c. Heath.
Alger, H., *jr.* Tom Turner's legacy and how he secured it. '02(Jl12) il. 12°, (Alger ser.) $1. Burt.
Alger ser. il. 12°, $1. Burt.
—Alger. Tom Turner's legacy.
—Kaler. Treasure of Cocos Island.
Algonkian. *See* Lawson, A. C.
Algonquian series. *See* Tooker, W: W.
Aliens. Wright, M. T. $1.50. Scribner.
Alissas, R. d', [M. *and* K. Roget.] Les histoires de tante. '02(Mr1) 12°, (Primary ser. of Fr. and Germ. reading books.) net, 40 c. Macmillan.
Allen, Alice E. Children of the palm lands. '02(My3) D. 50 c. Educ Pub.
Allen, C: W. Practitioner's manual. '02 (Je7) 8°, $6; mor., $7. Wood.
ALLEN, Ethan.
Brown. Ethan Allen. $1. Donohue.
Allen, F. S. What's what? at home and abroad. '02(Je7) S. net, 50 c. Bradley-W.

Allen, Godfrey. *See* Allen, Phœbe.
Allen, J. H: Diseases and therapeutics of the skin. '02(My24) 12°, $2. Boericke & T.
Allen, May V. Battling with love and fate. '02(Jl19) D. $1. Abbey Press.
Allen, Phœbe *and* Godfrey. Miniature and window gardening. '02(Ap19) D. net, 50 c. Pott.
Allen, T: G. *See* **Duff, E: M.**
Allen, Willis B. Play away: story of the Boston fire department. '02(Jl19) il. 12°, **75 c. net. Estes.
Allen's (Grant) hist. guide books to the principal cities of Europe. S. net, $1.25. Wessels.
—Cruickshank. The Umbrian towns.
Allgood, G: **China war, 1860: letters and** journal. '01· '02(F8) il. obl. O. $5. Longmans.
Allibone, S: A. Great authors of all ages. New ed. '01. '02(Mr1) 8°, $2.50. Lippincott.
Allibone, S: A. Poetical quotations. New ed. '01· '02(Mr1) 8°, $2.50. Lippincott.
Allibone, S: A. Prose quotations. New ed. '01· '02(Mr1) 8°, $2 50. Lippincott.
Allin Winfield. Walsh, G: E. $1.50. Buckles.
ALMANACS AND ANNUALS.
Agricultural almanac, 1903. 10 c. Baer.
American Baptist year-book, 1902. 25 c. Am. Bapt
Annual Am. catalogue, cumulated 1900. 1901. $2. Pub. Weekly.
Arbor and bird day annual for Wis. schools. gratis. Democrat Pr. Co.
Brassey. Naval annual, 1902. net, $7.50. Scribner.
Brooklyn *Daily Eagle* almanac, 1902. 50 c.: 25 c. Brooklyn Eagle.
Courier-Journal almanac, 1902. 25 c. Courier-Journ.
Englishwoman's year-book and directory, 1902. $1.50. Macmillan.
Free trade almanac, 1902. 5 c. Am. Free Trade
Hawaiian almanac and annual, 1902. 75 c. Thrum.
Hazell's annual for 1902. net, $1.50. Scribner.
Illustrated family Christian almanac, 1902. 10 c. Am. Tr.
Indianapolis *Sentinel* year-book and almanac, 1902. 25 c. Indianapolis Sentinel.
International annual of Anthony's photographic bulletin, 1902. $1.25; 75 c. Anthony.
International year-book, 1901. $4. Dodd.
Minneapolis *Journal* almanac and yearbook, 1902. 25 c Journal Pr. Co.
National Temperance almanac and teetotalers year-book, 1902. 10 c. Nat. Temp.
Planets and people: annual yearbook of the heavens. $1. F. E. Ormsby.
Providence *Journal* almanac, 1902. 10 c. Providence Journ.
Public *Ledger* almanac, 1902. gratis. Drexel
Spalding's official athletic almanac. 10 c. Am. Sports
Statesmen's year-book, 1902. net, $3. Macmillan
Telegram almanac and cyclopedia. 1902. 20 c. Providence Telegram.

ALMANACS AND ANNUALS.—*Continued.*
Tribune almanac and pol. register, 1902. 25 c. Tribune Assoc.
Virginia-Carolina almanac for 1902. gratis. Virginia-Carolina.
Whitaker, *comp.* Almanac for 1902. net, 40 c.; net, $1. Scribner.
World almanac and encyclopedia, 1902. 25 c. Press Pub.
See also under special subjects.
ALPHABETS.
Day. Alphabets old and new. $1.50. Scribner.
ALPHABETS (*ornamental*).
See Lettering.
Alpheus, A., *pseud.* Complete guide to hypnotism. '02(My17) 12°, 50 c.; pap., 25 c. Donohue.
Alpheus, A., *pseud. See also* Oxenford, I.
Altdorfer, Albrecht. Albrecht Altdorfer: 71 woodcuts. '02(Ap26) il. O. (Little engravings classical and contemporary, no. 1.) bds., net, $1.50. Longmans.
ALTERNATING CURRENTS.
Houston *and* Kennelly. Alternating electric currents. $1. McGraw.
Oudin. Standard polyphase apparatus and systems. $3. Van Nostrand.
Rhodes. Elem. treatise on alternating currents. $2.60. Longmans.
Sheldon *and* Mason. Dynamo electric machinery. v. 2, Alternating-current machines. net, $2.50. Van Nostrand.
Alton Locke. *See* Kingsley, C:
Altsheler, Jos. A. My captive. '02(Je7) D. $1.25. Appleton.
Ambassador of Christ. Schuyler, W: $1.50. Gorham.
Amber, Miles. Wistons. '02(F15) D. $1.50. Scribner.
AMERICA.
Helmolt, *and others, eds.* Hist. of the world. v. 1, Prehistoric America. $6. Dodd.
See also Huguenots.
American Acad. of Pol. and Soc. Science pubs. 8°, pap. Am. Acad. Pol. Sci.
—Crowell. Status and prospects of Am. shipbuilding. 15 c. (325.)
—Elwood. Aristotle as a sociologist. 15 c. (332.)
—Farquhar. Manufacturers' need of reciprocity. 15 c. (330.)
—Glasson. Nation's pension system. 25 c. (331.)
—Johnson. Isthmian canal. 25 c. (323.)
—Knapp. Government ownership of railroads. 15 c. (326.)
—Meyer. Advisory councils in railway administration. 15 c. (327.)
—Newcomb. Concentration of railway control. 15 c. (328.)
—Pasco. Isthmian canal question. 25 c. (324.)
—Seager. Patten's theory of prosperity. 15 c. (333.)
—Walker. Taxation of corporations in the U. S. 25 c. (329.)
American and Eng. corporation cases. (T: J. Michie.) v. 15. '02(Je7) O. shp., $4.50. Michie.
American and Eng. encyclopædia of law. (Garland and McGehee.) 2d ed. v. 20. '02(Mr15) O. shp., $7.50. E: Thompson

American and Eng. railroad cases. v. 23. '02(Mr15) O. shp., $5. Michie.
American and Eng. railroad cases. *See also* Railroad repts.
American at Oxford. Corbin, J: net, $1.50. Houghton, M. & Co.
American, Bapt. year-book, 1902; ed. by J. G. Walker. '02(Ap12) O. pap., 25 c. Am. Bapt.
American church dictionary. Miller, W: J. $1. Whittaker.
American communities. Hinds, W: A. $1. Kerr.
American corp. legal manual. v. 10. '02 (Jl19) O. shp., $5. Corp. Leg. Co.
American digest, annot.; 1901 B. '02(My10) O. (Am. digest system, 1901.) shp., $6. West Pub.
American digest. Century ed. v. 29. '01-'02(Ja4); v. 30 (Mr15); v. 31 (Ap5); v. 32 (Je14); v. 33 (Jl12) O. shp., subs., ea., $6. West Pub.
American digest. v. 33. '02(Jl12)
American digest system. O. shp., $6. West Pub.
—Am. digest, annot.
American duck shooting. Grinnell, G: B. $3.50. Forest.
American Economic Assoc.: papers and proceedings of the fourteenth annual meeting. '02(My3) 8°, (Am. Econ. Assoc. pubs., v. 3, no. 1.) pap., net, $1.50. Macmillan.
American Economic Assoc. pubs. 8°, pap., net. Macmillan.
—Amer. Economic Assoc. 14th annual meeting. $1.50. (v. 3, 1.)
—Clow. Comparative study of administration of city finances in U. S. $1. (3d ser., v. 2, 4.)
American electrical cases; ed. by W: W. Morrill. v. 7. '02(My3) O. shp., $6. M. Bender.
American engineering practice in construction of cement plants. Lathbury, B. B. $2. G. M. S. Armstrong.
American federal state. Ashley, R. L. net, $2. Macmillan.
American food and game fishes. Jordan, D: S. net, $4. Doubleday, P.
American fur trade of the far west. Chittenden, H. M. 3 v. net, $10. F. P. Harper.
American gardens. Lowell, G. $7.50. Bates & G.
American horse, cattle and sheep doctor. McClure, R. $1.50. Henneberry.
American immortals. Eggleston, G: C. $10. Putnam.
American law of assemblies. Stevens, E: A. net, $1. E: A. Stevens.
American leaders and heroes. Gordy, W. F. net, 60 c. Scribner.
AMERICAN LITERATURE.
  Abernethy. Am. literature. $1.10. Maynard, M. & Co.
  Moulton, *and others, eds.* Lib. of literary criticism of Eng. and Am. authors. v. 3. $5; $6.50. Moulton Pub.
  Warner. Fashions in literature. net, $1.20. Dodd.
  See also **Bibliographies.**
American lumberman telecode. Barry, J. W. net, $5. Am. Lumberman.
American masters of painting. Caffin, C: H. net, $1.25. Doubleday, P.
American negligence digest. Hook, A. J. $6.50. Remick.
American negligence repts. *See* Gardner, J: M.
American patriot ser. D. $1. Donohue.
—Brown. John Paul Jones.
American philanthropy of the 19th century. 12°, net. Macmillan.
—Folks. Care of destitute children.
AMERICAN REVOLUTION.
  See United States.
American series of popular biographies. Massachusetts ed. '01-'02(Mr1) il. 4°, $17. Graves.
American speaker; for colleges, public and private entertainments. '02(Ap12) il. 4°, pap., 50 c. Conkey.
American sportsman's lib.; ed. by C. Whitney. net, $2; large pap. ed., hf. mor., net, $7.50. Macmillan.
—Sage, *and others.* Salmon and trout.
—Sandys *and* Van Dyke. Upland game birds.
American state repts. (A. C. Freeman.) v. 82. '02(My10); v. 83 (My17); v. 84 (Jl5) O. shp., ea., $4. Bancroft-W.
American street railway investments. [annual.] '02(Je7) F. $5. Street R'way.
American year-book of medicine and surgery; ed. by S: W. Abbott and others. '02 (Mr1) 2 v., il. 8°, ea., net, $3; shp. or hf. mor., ea., net, $3.75. Saunders.
Americanization of the world. Stead, W: T: $1. Markley.
America's story for America's children. Pratt, M. L. v. 5, 40 c. Heath
Ames, A. F. *See* McLellan, J. A.
Ames, *Mrs.* Eleanor M. E., ["Eleanor Kirk."] Prevention and cure of old age. '02(Mr8) D. pap., 50 c. Kirk.
Ames, Ja. B. Selection of cases in equity jurisdiction. pt. 2. '01-'02(Ap12) 12°. 75 c. Harvard Law.
Ames, Ja. B., *and* Brewster, L. D. Negotiable instruments law. '02(Ap12) O. 30 c. Harvard Law.
Ames, L: A. Etiquette of yacht colors; cont. yacht codes, storm and weather signals, etc. '02(Jl5) il. sq. S. canvas, 25 c. Annin.
AMIENS CATHEDRAL.
  Perkins. Cathedral church of Amiens. $1. Macmillan.
Among the night people. Pierson, C: D. net, $1. Dutton.
Among the water fowl. Job, H. K. net, $1.35. Doubleday, P.
Amor victor. Kenyon, O. $1.50. Stokes.
AMPHIBIA.
  Baskett *and* Ditmars. Story of the amphibians and the reptiles. 60 c. Appleton.
AMUSEMENTS.
  See Cards;—Dancing;—Drills; — Entertainments; —Riddles.
ANALYSIS.
  See **Assaying;—Blowpipe;—Chemistry.**
ANARCHY.
  See **Socialism.**
Anarchy. Bauder, E. P. $1; 50 c. Occidental.
ANATOMY.
  Cotterell. Pocket Gray; or, **Anatomist's** vade mecum. net, $1.25. Wood.
  Gray. Anatomy, descriptive and surgical. net, $5.50-$7.25. Lea.
  Kimber, *comp.* Anatomy and physiology. net, $2.50. Macmillan.
  Smith. Anatomy, physiology and hygiene. $1. W: R. Jenkins.

ANATOMY.—*Continued.*
Treves. Surgical applied anatomy. net, $2. Lea.
See also Animals;—Brain; — Dissection;—Eye; — Head;—Intestines;—Neck;—Nervous system;—Nose;—Physiology; — Surgery;—Teeth;—Vivisection.
ANATOMY FOR ARTISTS.
Fiedler. Studies from the nude human figure in motion. $12. Hessling.
ANCESTRY.
See Genealogy.
ANCIENT AND HON. ARTILLERY CO. OF MASS.
Roberts. Hist. of the Military Co. now called the Ancient and Hon. Artillery Co. of Mass. v. 4. [Sold only to members.] Mudge.
Ancient city. Fustel de Coulanges, N. D. $2. Lee & S.
ANCIENT HISTORY.
See History.
Ancient ruins of Rhodesia. Hall, R. N. net, $6. Dutton.
Andersen, Hans C. Selected stories. '01· '02 (Mr1) 12°, pap., 15 c. Lippincott.
Anderson, C: P. The Christian ministry. '02(F22) O. pap., 20 c. Young Churchman.
Anderson, Ja. B. The nameless hero, and other poems. '02(Mr1) D. net, $1. Wessels.
Anderson, J: J., *and* Flick, Alex. C. Short hist. of the state of New York. '01· '02 (Jl12) il. 12°, $1. Maynard, M. & Co.
Anderson, *Sir* Rob. Daniel in the critics' den. '02(Je28) 12°, net, $1.25. Revell.
Andrew, S. O. Greek prose composition. '02 (Je14) 12°, (Greek course.) net, 90 c. Macmillan.
Andrews, Alb. H. *See* Wood, C. A.
Andrews, Alice E. Topics and ref. for the study of Eng. literature. '01. '02(Ap5) D. bds., 15 c. Hyde.
Andrews, H. B. Handbook for street railway engineers. '02(Je21) il. 16°, mor., $1.25. Wiley.
Andrews, W: L. **Paul Revere and his engraving.** '01· '02(Mr22) $23.50; Japan ed., $40. Scribner.
Angelot. Price, E. C. $1.50. Crowell.
ANGLICAN CHURCH.
See Church of England.
Anglo-Am. pottery. *See* Barber, E. A.
Animal activities. French, N. S. $1.20. Longmans.
Animal castration. Liautard, A. $2. W: R. Jenkins.
Animal experimentation. Ernst, H. C. net, $1.50; net, $1. Little, B. & Co.
Animal forms. Jordan, D: S. net, $1.10. Appleton.
ANIMAL MAGNETISM.
See Hypnotism.
ANIMALS.
Bourne. Comparative anatomy of animals. v. 2. net, $1.25. Macmillan.
Hulbert. Forest neighbors. net, $1.50. McClure, P.
Ingersoll. Wild life of orchard and field. net, $1.40. Harper.
See also Zoölogy.
Animals at home. Bartlett, L. L. 45 c. Am. Bk.
Annandale, C., *ed. See* Spofford, A. R.
Annice Wynkoop, artist. Rouse, A. L. $1. Burt.
Annual Am. catalogue. cumulated 1900-1901; with directory of publishers. '02(Ap5) Q. $2. Pub. Weekly.
ANNUALS.
See Almanacs and annuals;—Calendars and yearbooks.
Anstruther, G. E. William Hogarth. '02 (Je28) il. 16°, (Bell's miniature ser. of painters.) leath., $1. Macmillan.
Antarctic queen. Clark, C: $1.75. Warne.
ANTARCTIC REGIONS.
Balch. Antarctica. n. p. Allen, L. & S.
ANTHOLOGIES.
See Oriental religions;—*also* names of literatures.
ANTHONY, *St.*
Lasance. Little manual of St. Anthony of Padua. 25 c. Benziger.
Roulet. Saint Anthony in art. $2. Marlier.
Anthony, C. V. Children's covenant. '02 (F1) D. $1. Jennings.
Anthony, Harold G., *ed.* True romance revealed by a bag of old letters. '02(Je14) D. $1. Abbey Press.
ANTHROPOLOGY.
See Civilization;—Ethnology;—Language;—Woman.
Anticipations. Wells, H. G: net, $1.80. Harper.
Antigone. Sophocles. net, 60 c. Macmillan.
Antique gems from the Gr. and Latin. See Barrie's.
Antoninus, Marcus Aurelius. Helpful thoughts fr. "Meditations." (W. L. Brown.) '02 (Ap12) S. net, 80 c. McClurg.
Anton's angels. Trueman, A. 75 c. Alliance.
Antrim, Minna T., ["Titian."] Naked truths and veiled allusions. '02(F22) S. 50 c. Altemus.
ANUS AND RECTUM.
Kelsey. Surgery of the rectum. $3. Wood.
APOSTLES' CREED.
McGiffert. Apostles' creed. net, $1.25. Scribner.
APPLE.
Thomas. Book of the apple; and Preparation of cider. net, $1. Lane.
Appleton's Annual cyclopædia for 1901. '02 (Mr1) 8°, subs., $5; shp., $6; hf. mor., $7; hf. rus., $8. Appleton.
Appleton's Geografia superior ilustrada. '01· '02(F22) 4°, bds., $1.50. Appleton.
Appleton's home-reading books; ed. by W: T. Harris. D. Appleton.
—Baskett *and* Ditmars. Story of the amphibians and the reptiles. 60 c. (Div. 1, natural history.)
Appleton's international educ. ser. 12°, net. Appleton.
—Compayré. Later infancy of the child. pt. 2. $1.20. (53.)
—Ware. Educational foundations of trade and industry. $1.20. (54.)
Appleton's Latin dictionary; rev. by J. R. V. Marchant and J. F. Charles. '01· '02 (F22) 8°, $1.50. Appleton.
Appleton's lib. of useful stories. il. T. **35 c. net. Appleton.
—Crowest. Story of the art of music.
—Lindsay. Story of animal life.
—Waterhouse. Art of building.
Appleton's life histories. D. net, $1. Appleton.
—Thwaites. Father Marquette.

Appleton's nuevas cartillas cientificas. il. 16°, 40 c. Appleton.
—Hooker. Nociones de botanica.
Appleton's town and country lib. D. $1; pap., 50 c. Appleton.
—Aitken. Love in its tenderness. (309.)
—Alden. Drewitt's dream. (310.)
—Cooper. A fool's year. (308.)
—Norris. Credit of the country. (313.)
—Raine. Welsh witch. (312.)
—Snaith. Love's itinerary. (307.)
—Wilson. T'bacca queen. (311.)
Appleton's world ser.; ed. by H. J. Mackinder. 8°, $2. Appleton.
—Hogarth. The nearer East. (2.)
—Mackinder. Britain and the British seas. (1.)
AQUARIUM.
Smith. Home aquarium and how to care for it. **$1.20 net. Dutton.
AQUATIC LIFE.
Payne. How to teach aquatic life. 25 c. Kellogg.
Arany, S. A. British-American guide to Carlsbad. 3d Am. ed. '02(Mr8) il. D. pap., 50 c. Abbey Press.
Arbor and bird day annual for Wis. schools. (L. D. Harvey.) '02(Ap26) Q. pap., gratis. Democrat Pr. Co.
ARCHAEOLOGY.
See Architecture; — Bible; — Civilization; — Cliff-dwellers;— Ethnology;— Folk-lore;—History;— Marriage;—Middle Ages;—Mounds.
ARCHITECTURE.
Coburn. Prize designs for rural school buildings. 25 c. Kellogg.
Complete housebuilder. 50 c.; 25 c. Donohue.
Fletcher. Hist. of architecture. net, $7.50. Scribner.
Georgian period. In 3 v. pt. 8, 9. ea. pt., $4. Am. Architect.
Hodgson. Estimating frame and brick houses. $1. D: Williams.
Kidder. Building construction and superintendence. pt. 2. $4. W: T. Comstock.
Ross. Florentine villas. $25. Dutton.
Ware, *ed.* Topical architecture. 2 v. $7.50. Am. Architect.
Waterhouse. Story of the art of building. net, 35 c. Appleton.
See also Bridges;—Cathedrals;—Church architecture;—Decorations and ornament;—Fine arts; —Roofs;—Sanitary engineering.
Architecture of the brain. Fuller, W: net, $3.50. Fuller.
Archoff, Ludwig. *See* Gaylord, H. R.
ARCTIC REGIONS.
Kersting, *ed.* White world. *$2 net. Lewis.
Ardiane and Barbe Bleue. *See* Maeterlinck, M.
Aretino, Lionardo Bruni. *See* Boccaccio, G.
Argyle, Harvey, *pseud.* *See* McIntire, J: J.
Aristophanes. Comedies; ed. by B: B. Rogers. In 6 v. v. 5. '02(Ap12) 8°, $6. Macmillan.
Aristophanes. The knights; ed. by R. A. Neil. '02(Ja18) 8°, (Cambridge Univ. Press ser.) net, $2.50. Macmillan.
ARISTOTLE.
Ellwood. Aristotle as a sociologist. 15 c. Am. Acad. Pol. Sci.
ARITHMETIC.
Atwood. Complete graded arithmetic. 4 v. ea., 25 c. Heath.

ARITHMETIC.—*Continued.*
Baird. Graded work in arithmetic. 25 c. Am. Bk.
Browne. Graded mental arithmetic. net, 30 c. Whitaker & R.
Chancellor. Children's arithmetics: Primary, 28 c.—2d bk., 20 c.—3d bk., 24 c.—4th bk., 24 c. Globe School Bk.
Gyim. Chinese-Eng. elem. reader and arithmetic. $1.25. Taylor & M.
Hornbrook. Key to Primary arithmetic and Grammar school arithmetic. 65 c. Am. Bk.
Lippincott's practical arithmetic. 2 v. ea., 40 c. Lippincott.
McLellan, *and others.* Public school arithmetic for grammar grades. net, 60 c. Macmillan.
Milne. Key to Standard arithmetic and Mental arithmetic. 75 c. Am. Bk.
Perkins. Arithmética elemental. 25 c. Appleton.
Pierce. Intermediate arithmetic. 48 c. Silver.
Ruggles. Exercises and problems in arithmetic. 25 c. W: R. Jenkins.
Spangenberg. Practical arith. explained to practical mechanic. 50 c. Zeller.
See also Bookkeeping;—Interest.
Arithmetic of electrical measurements. Hobbs, W. R. P. 50 c. Van Nostrand.
ARIZONA.
Bicknell. Guide book of the Grand Canyon of Arizona. 75 c.; 50 c. Harvey.
James. In and around the Grand Canyon. net, $10. Little, B. & Co.
Arkansas. *Supreme ct.* Repts. v. 69. '02 (Ap19) O. shp., $3.50. Thompson Litho.
Arm and hammer ser.; ed. by Lucien Sanial. D. 50 c. N. Y. Labor News.
—Engels. Socialism.
—Marx. Wage-labor and capital; [also] Free trade.
Armature windings of direct current dynamos. Arnold, E. $2. Van Nostrand.
ARMINIUS.
See Hermann der Cherusker.
Armstrong, Annie E. **Very odd girl.** '02 (Mr29) il. 12°, (Fireside ser.) $1. Burt.
Armstrong. Le Roy. The outlaws. '02(Ap26) D. $1.25. Appleton.
Armstrong, Le Roy. *See also* Banks, C: E.
Army songster (The): [repr. of 1864.] '02 (Je21) S pap., 25 c. Bell Bk.
ARNOLD, Benedict.
Codman. Arnold's expedition to Quebec. net, $2.25. Macmillan.
Melvin. Journal of soldier in Arnold's expedition. $2. H. W. Bryant.
Arnold, E. Armature windings of direct current dynamos: fr. orig. Germ. by F. B. De Gress. '02(My3) il. O. $2. Van Nostrand.
Arnold, Edn. L. Lepidus the centurion. '02 (Mr8) D. $1.50. Crowell.
Arnold. Jonathan A., *comp. and ed.* Manual of school laws of Illinois. '01- '02(Mr1) 8°, $1.75. Effingham Democrat.
Arnold, Matt. Dramatic and early poems; ed. by H. B. Forman. '02(My17) 16°, (Temple classics.) 50 c.; flex. leath., 75 c. Macmillan.
Arnold, Matt. Essays in criticism. 1st and 2d ser. '02(Ap19) 12°, (Home lib.) $1. Burt.

Arnold, Matt. Literature and dogma. '02 (My24) 8°, (Commonwealth lib.) net, $1. New Amsterdam.
Arnold, Sa. L. Ensełiar & leer. '01· '02 (Mr8) il. 12°, 40 c. Silver.
Arnold, *Mrs.* T. B., *ed.* Sabbath school commentary on Internat. lessons, 1902. '02 (Ap12) 8°, 50 c. Revell.
Arnolt, W. M. Theolog. and Semitic literature for 1901. '02(My3) 8°, pap., net, 50 c. Univ. of Chic.
Arnott, S. Books of bulbs. '02(F15) 12°, (Handbooks of practical gardening; ed. by H. Roberts, v. 5.) net, $1. Lane.
Around the "Pan" with Uncle Hank. Fleming, T: $2. Nutshell.
Around the throne. Winchester, P. net, $1. Eichelberger.
Around the world. Carroll, S. W. 60 c. Morse.
Arrabbiata (L'). *See* Heyse, P. J. L.
ARSENIC.
Wanklin. Arsenic. $1. Lippincott.
Art and craft of printing. Morris, W: $5. Elston Press.
Art of folly. Ford, S. **$3 net. Small.
Art of life. Maulde la Clavière, R. de. net. $1.75. Putnam
Art reader. Cady, M. R. 35 c. Richardson, S.
ARTHUR, *King of Britain.*
Malory. King Arthur and his noble knights. $1. Burt.
Arthur, *Mrs.* J. J. Annals of the Fowler family. '02(F22) il. 8°, $3.50. Mrs. J. J. Arthur.
Artificial feeding of infants. Judson, C: F. $2. Lippincott.
ARTILLERY.
See Gunnery.
Artistic crafts ser. of technical handbooks; ed. by W. R. Lethaby. il. D. net. Appleton.
—Cockerell. Bookbinding and the care of books. $1.20. (1.)
ARTISTS.
Wherry. Stories of the Tuscan artists. net, $4. Dutton.
See also Painters.
Artists' lib. *See* Longmans'.
As I saw it. McIntire, J: J. $1.25. Home Pub. Co.
As nature whispers. Davis, S. K. 50 c. Alliance.
As true as gold. Mannix, M. E. 45 c. Benziger.
Asa Holmes. Johnston, A. F. $1. L. C. Page.
Ash, Mark *and* W: Table of federal citations. v. 1. '01. '02(F8); v. 2 (My24) O. shp., (for complete work.) $30. Remick.
Ashley, Roscoe L. American Federal state. '02(Mr1) 12°, net. $2. Macmillan.
ASIA.
See Assyria;—China;—India;—Japan;—Persia;—Siam.
Asiatic Russia. Wright, G: F: 2 v. **$7.50 net. McClure, P.
Askwith, E. H. Introd. to the Thessalonian Epistles. '02(Ap12) 12°, net, $1.25. Macmillan.
Aslauga's knight. *See* La Motte Foque, F. H. K. *Freiherr* de.
Assassins. Meakin, N. M. $1.50. Holt.
ASSAYING.
Miller. Manual of assaying. $1. Wiley.
Rhead *and* Sexton. Assaying and metallurgical analysis. $4.20. Longmans.
See also Blowpipe;—Metals and metallurgy.
ASSYRIA.
Murison. Babylonia and Assyria. net, 20 c. Scribner.
ASTROLOGY.
Turnbull. Divine language of celestial correspondence. $2. Alliance.
Valcourt-Vermont. Practical astrology. $1; 50 c. Lee & S.
ASTRONOMY.
Jacoby. Practical talks by an astronomer. net, $1. Scribner.
White. Elements of theoretical and des. astronomy. $2.50. Wiley.
Young. Manual of astronomy. $2.45. Ginn.
See also Almanacs and annuals; — Astrology; — Stars.
At large. Hornung, E. W: $1.50. Scribner.
At Sunwich port. Jacobs, W. W. $1.50. Scribner.
At the back of beyond. Barlow, J. $1.50. Dodd.
Athalie. *See* Racine, J.
Athenæum Press ser. D. Ginn.
—De Quincey. Selections. $1.05.
Atherton, *Mrs.* Gertrude F. The conqueror. '02(Mr29) D. $1.50. Macmillan.
Athletic lib. *See* Spalding's.
Atkinson, A. A. Electrical and magnetic calculations. '02(Je7) D. net, $1.50. Van Nostrand.
Atkinson, Rob. W., *and* Carter, E. Songs of the Eastern colleges. '02(F1) O. $1.25. Hinds.
Atlantic reporter, v. 50. '02(Mr29); v. 51 (Jl19) O. (Nat. reporter system, state ser.) shp., ea., $4. West Pub.
ATLASES.
See Encyclopædias;—Geography.
ATTACHMENT.
Rood. On attachments, garnishments, judgments, and executions. $3. Wahr.
ATTIC PROSE.
Flagg. Writer of attic prose: models fr. Xenophon. $1. Am. Bk.
ATTORNEYS.
National list. Directory of bonded attorneys. (App. to pubs. for price.) Nat. Surety.
Atwater, Fs., *comp.* Atwater history and genealogy. '01. '02(F8) il. 8°, $5; hf. mor., $7.50; full mor., $10. Journal Pub.
Atwood, G: E. Complete graded arithmetic. Grades 3-6. '01· '02(Je7) 4 v., D. ea., 25 c. Heath.
Audrey. Johnston, M. $1.50. Houghton, M. & Co.
Augsburg, D. R. Drawing. In 3 bks. '02 (My3) sq. O. ea., 75 c. Educ. Pub.
Aulnoy, Marie C. J. de B., *Comtesse* d', *and* Perrault, C: Once upon a time. New ed. '01. '02(F15) 16°, (Children's friend ser.) bds., 50 c. Little, B. & Co.
Aulnoy, Marie C. J. de B. *Comtesse* de. *See also* Perrault, C:
Aunt Susan, *pseud.* *See* Prentiss, *Mrs.* E.
Austin, A. Tale of true love, and other poems. '02(Ap26) D. net, $1.20. Harper.
Austin, Ma. S. Philip Freneau; the poet of the Revolution. '01· '02(F1) O. net, $2.50. Wessels.

Austrian, Delia. Love songs. '02(Jl5) D. $1. Conkey.
Authorities, deductions and notes in commercial paper. '02(Jl12) interleaved, O. shp., $2.25. Univ. Press.
Author's (The) yearbook for 1902. '02 (Mr29) D. bds., $1. Book-Lover.
AUTHORS.
Allibone. Great authors of all ages. $2.50. Lippincott.
Halsey, *ed.* Authors of our day in their homes. $1.25. Pott.
See also Bibliographies;—Literature;—Musicians.
AUTOGRAPHS.
Joline. Meditations of an autograph collector. net, $3. Harper.
Automatic pen lettering and designs. *See* Faust, C. A.
AUTOMOBILES.
Thompson. The motor-car. $1. Warne.
Avare (L'). Molière, J. B. P. de. 50 c. Scott, F. & Co.
Avebury, *Lord*, Barlow, C. A. Montague, Boyle, *Sir* C., *and others*. The King's weigh-house: lectures to business men. '01·'02(Ja4) 12°, 75 c. Macmillan.
Avebury, *Lord*. *See also* Lubbock, *Sir* J:
Avesta. Index verborum, by M. Schuyler, jr. '02(Je14) 8°, (Columbia Univ. Indo-Iranian ser.) net, $2. Macmillan.
Ayer, Jos. C. Rise and development of Christian architecture. '02(My17) il. F. net, $1.50. Young Churchman.
Ayres, Franklin H. Laboratory exercises in elem. physics. '01· '02(F15) il. 12°, net, 50 c. Appleton.
B., E. P. God the beautiful. '02(Ap12) nar. D. net, 75 c. Beam.
Babbitt, Fk. C. Grammar of Attic and Ionic Greek. '02(Jl12) D. $1.50. Am. Bk.
Babcock, M. D. Letters from Egypt and Palestine. '02(Mr22) il. D. net, $1. Scribner.
Babcock, M. D. Three whys and their answer. '01· '02(F15) S. 35 c. Un. Soc. C. E.
BABYLONIA.
Murison. Babylonia and Assyria. net. 20 c. Scribner
Bacon, B: W. Sermon on the Mount. '02 (My3) 12°, net, $1. Macmillan.
Bacon, Fs., *Lord*. Works. '02(Je21) 12°, (Caxton ser.) net, $1.25. Scribner.
Bacon, Fs., *Lord*. Essays. '01· '02(Ap5) S. (Little masterpieces.) 50 c. Doubleday, P.
Bacon, Fs., *Lord*. Of gardens. '02(Mr29) 16°, net, 50 c. Lane.
BACON, Fs., *Lord*.
Gallup. Bi-literal cipher of Sir Francis Bacon. $3.75. Howard.
See also Shakespeare-Bacon controversy.
Bacon, Gorham. Manual of otology. 3d ed., rev. and enl. '02(Jl19) il. 12°, *$2.25 net. Lea.
BACTERIA.
Abbott. Manual of bacteriology. net, $2.75. Lea.
Bowhill. Manual of bacteriological technique and spec. bacteriology. $4.50. Wood.
Emery. Bacteriological diagnosis. net. $1.50. Blakiston
BACTERIA.—*Continued.*
Frost. Lab'y guide in elem. bacteriology. $1.60. W: D. Frost.
Sternberg. Text-book of bacteriology. net, $5: net, $5.75. Wood.
See also Fermentation.
Badminton lib. 8°. Little, B. & Co.
—Harmsworth, *and others*. Motors and motor driving. $3.50; $5.
Baedeker, K., *ed.* Egypt. 5th rev. ed. '02 (Mr8) il. 12°, (Baedeker's guides.) net, $4.50. Scribner.
Baedeker, K., *ed.* Southern Germany. 9th rev. ed. '02(Mr8) 12°, (Baedeker's guides.) net, $1.80. Scribner.
Bagot, R: Roman mystery. '02(Ap5) 12°, $1.50. Lane.
Bailey, L. H. Nature portraits; studies with pen and camera of our wild birds, animals, fish and insects. '02(Jl12) il. portfolio, 12 x 18 in. App. to pubs. for price. Doubleday, P.
Bailey, Middlesex A. High school algebra. '02(Jl12) sq. S. hf. leath., 90 c. Am. Bk.
Baillie, Alex. F. The Oriental Club and Hanover Square. '01· '02(Ja4) il. 4°, $9. Longmans
Baillot, Edouard P., *and* **Brugnot**, Alice G. T. French prose composition. '01· '02(Ja4) S. (Lake French ser.) 50 c. Scott, F. & Co.
BAILMENTS.
Van Zile. Elements of the law and bailments. $5. Callaghan.
Bally, R. C. Mabel Thornley. '02(Mr29) D. $1.25. Abbey Press.
Bain, Ja. *See* Henry, Alex.
Bain, Rob. N. Peter III., Emperor of Russia. '02(Mr29) il. 8°, net, $3.50. Dutton.
Baird, C: W. Hist. of Huguenot emigration to America. New ed. '01· '02(F22) 2 v., 8°, net, $2.50. Dodd.
Baird, S. W. Graded work in arithmetic. 8th year. '02(Ap19) D. 25 c. Am. Bk.
Baker, G: H. Economic locomotive management. 2d lib. ed. '02(Je7) il. D. $1.50. R'way Educ.
Baker, Moses N. Municipal engineering and sanitation. '02(F1) 12°, (Citizen's lib.) hf. leath., net, $1.25. Macmillan.
Balch, Edn. S. Antarctica. '02(Jl19) 8°. (for private distribution.) Allen, L. & S.
Balch, Lewis. Manual for boards of health and health officers. '02(Je14) D. $1.50. Banks & Co.
Balch, T: W. Alasko-Canadian frontier. '02(Ap19) 8°, $1. Allen L. & S.
Baldwin, Aaron D. Gospel of Judas Iscariot. '02(My24) D. $1.50. Jamison-H.
Baldwin, Ja. The book lover: guide to best reading. 13th rev. ed. '02(My3) nar. S. net, $1. McClurg.
Baldwin, Ja. F. The scutage and knight service in England. '02(Mr22) 8°, net, $1. Univ. of Chic.
Baldwin, Ja. M: Fragments in philosophy and science. '02(Ap19) O. net, $2.50. Scribner.
Baldwin, Ja. M: Social and ethical interpretations in mental development. 3d ed., rev. and enl. '02(Mr29) 8°, net, $2.60. Macmillan.
Baldwin, May. A popular girl. '01. '02 (F15) il. 12°, net, $1.20. Lippincott.

Baldwin, Myra. Nancy's Easter gift [poem.] '02(My24) il. D. 50 c. Abbey Press.
Baldwin, Willis. *See* Michigan. Law of personal injuries.
Baldwin primer. Kirk, M. 35 c. Am. Bk.
Bale marked circle X. Eggleston, G: C. net, $1.20. Lothrop.
Balfour, Arth. J. Foundations of belief. 8th ed., rev. '02(Je7) D. net, $2. Longmans.
Ball Estate Assoc. *See* Gans, E. W:
Ball, Fs. K. Elements of Greek. '02(My3) il. 12°, net, $1. Macmillan.
Ball, *Sir* Rob. S. Earth's beginning. '02 (My24) il. D. net, $1.80. Appleton.
BALL.
See Baseball.
BALLADS.
Book of romantic ballads. net, $1.25. Scribner.
Hale, *ed.* Ballads and ballad poetry. 40 c. Globe Sch. Bk.
Kinard, *ed.* Old English ballads. 40 c. Silver.
See also Songs.
Ballagh, Ja. C. Hist. of slavery in Virginia. '02(Ap26) O. (Johns Hopkins Univ. studies, extra v. 24.) $1.50. Johns Hopkins.
Ballance, C: A., *and* Stewart, P. Healing of nerves. '02(F1) 4°, net. $4.50. Macmillan.
Ballard, Eva C. She wanted to vote. '01-'02(Mr8) D. net, $1.40. Brower.
Ballough, C: A. Power that heals and how to use it. '02(Jl19) S. $1. Painter.
Ballough, C: A. Sibylline leaves. '02(Jl19) sq. T. $1. Painter.
BALMANNO, Rob.
Clarke. Letters to an enthusiast. net, $2.50. McClurg.
Balzac, H. de. Best of Balzac; ed. by A. Jessup. '02(Ap26) 16°, (Best writings of great authors.) $1.25; ¾ lev. mor., $3. L. C. Page.
BANDAGES.
Hopkins. Roller bandage. **$1.50 net. Lippincott.
See also Surgery.
Bang, *Mrs.* Marie. Livets alvor. '01-'02 (My17) D. pap., 65 c. M. Bang.
Bangs, J: K. Olympian nights. '02(Je21) D. $1.25. Harper.
Bangs, J: K. Uncle Sam, trustee. '02(My10) il. O. net, $1.75. Riggs.
BANKERS.
Sharp & Alleman's Co.'s lawyers' and bankers' directory, 1902. Jan. ed. $5. Sharp & A.
Banks, C: E., *and* Armstrong, L. Theodore Roosevelt, twenty-sixth President of the U. S. '02(Je28) 12°, $1.50; hf. rus., $2.25. Du Mont.
Banks, L: A. Great saints of the Bible. '01-'02(Ap12) 8°, $1.50. Eaton & M.
Banks, L: A. Windows for sermons. '02 (Ap12) D. net, $1.20. Funk.
Banks, L: A. *See also* Talmage, F. D.
Banks, Nancy H. Oldfield. '02(Je7) D. $1.50. Macmillan.
BANKS AND BANKING.
Barnett. State banking in the U. S. since passage of Nat. bank act. 50 c. Johns Hopkins.

BANKS AND BANKING.—*Continued.*
Coffin. A B C of banks and banking. $1.25. S: A. Nelson.
Handy. Banking systems of the world. $1.50. Jamieson-H.
Michie, *ed.* Banking cases, annot. v. 3. $5. Michie.
See also Savings-banks.
Bannister, H: M. *See* Brower, D. R.
Banquet book. Reynolds, C. net, $1.75. Putnam.
Banta, Thdr. M. Sayre family. '02(F15) il. 8°, hf. mor., $10. T. M. Banta.
BAPTISM.
Mahon. Token of the covenant; right use of baptism. 50 c. Pub. Ho. of M. E. Ch. So.
Wilson. Great cloud of witnesses. 50 c. Standard Pub.
BAPTIST CHURCH.
Jeter. Baptist principles reset. $1. Rel. Herald.
Merriam. Hist. of Am. Baptist missions. $1.25. Am. Bapt.
Newman, *ed.* Century of Baptist achievements, 1801-1900. net, $1.50. Am. Bapt.
Barbara. Culley, F. C. $1.25. F. C. Culley.
Barbarian invasions of Italy. Villari, P. 2 v. net, $7.50. Scribner.
Barber, Edn. A. Anglo-Am. pottery: old Eng. china; with Am. views. 2d ed., rev. and enl. '02(Ja18) il. 12°, net, $2. [Caspar] E. A. Barber.
Barber, Ed. A. Anglo-Am. pottery. 2d rev., enl. ed. '01-'02(Ap26) il. 8°, $2. Patterson & W.
Barber, F. M. Mechanical triumphs of ancient Egyptians. '01. '02(F22) 16°, net, $1.25. Dodd.
Barbier de Séville. Beaumarchais, P. A. C. de. 50 c. Scott, F. & Co.
Bardeen, C: W. Manual of civics for N. Y. schools. '02(Ja25) D. net, $1. Bardeen.
Barclay, Wilbur F. *See* Methodist Epis. Church.
Barker, Wharton. The great issues: editorials fr. *The American*, 1897-1900. '02(Je21) 12°, $1; pap., 50 c. Ferris.
Barlow, C. A. Montague. *See* Avebury, *Lord.*
Barlow, Jane. At the back of beyond. '02 My10) D. $1.50. Dodd.
Barnard, C: Farming by inches. '01-'02 (F8) 12°, 40 c. Coates.
Barnard, C: My ten rod farm; or, how I became a florist. '01-'02(F8) 12°, 40 c. Coates.
Barnard, C: A simple flower garden for country homes. '01-'02(F8) 12°, 40 c. Coates.
Barnard, C: The strawberry garden, how planted, what it cost. '01-'02(F8) 12°, 40 c. Coates.
Barnard, C: Two thousand a year on fruits and flowers. '01-'02(F8) 12°, $1. Coates.
Barnes, C: W. Sorrow and solace of Esther, daughter of Ben-Amos. '02(Mr29) S. leatherette, net, 30 c. Jennings.
Barnes, Edn. N. C. Reconciliation of Randall Claymore. '02(Je28) D. $1. Earle.
Barnes, Louisa E., [*Mrs.* Arth. J. Barnes.] Shorthand lessons by the word method. '01-'02(Mr1) 12°, $1.25. A. J. Barnes.

ADVANCE NOTES—A. C. McCLURG & CO.

FOR the information of the trade, we take pleasure in giving herewith some advance data about our Fall books of 1902, which we believe will be of interest. Our list will include seventeen titles, and in matter and make-up it will be the most generally attractive line we have ever put out.

Our most noteworthy undertaking is the new trade edition of "**The Expedition of Lewis and Clark.**" In two square octavo volumes of over 500 pages each, printed from new type of a large clear face, on fine laid paper, with new photogravure portraits and fac-simile maps, and with an introduction by Dr. James K. Hosmer and a copious index, this will undoubtedly take its place as the standard popular edition of Lewis and Clark. (In box, $5.00 net.)

Probably the most beautifully embellished book we have ever issued will be "**The Birds of the Rockies.**" The text is by Leander S. Keyser, the well-known author of "In Bird Land," and the pictorial features include eight full-page plates, four of which are in color, by the eminent nature painter, Louis Agassiz Fuertes, thirty-three charming text illustrations by Bruce Horsfall, and eight full-page scenic plates from photographs. The binding and printing of the book are strikingly attractive. (In box, $3.00 net.)

In response to repeated requests from the trade, we have prepared an elegant illustrated edition of Max Müller's "**Memories**"—a classic which has now reached a sale with us of nearly 40,000 copies. The book will be a handsome square octavo, and is printed from entirely new plates, with eight beautiful charcoal drawings and other pictorial embellishments by Blanche Ostertag. The cover, also designed by Miss Ostertag, is unique. (In box, $2.00 net.)

Our fiction will include a volume of clever stories of Chicago business life by Will Payne, called "**On Fortune's Road,**" with illustrations by Thomas Fogarty ($1.50); a spirited and exciting historical novel, "**The Holland Wolves,**" illustrated in a highly dramatic manner by the Kinneys (illustrators of "The Thrall of Leif the Lucky") ($1.50); an illustrated edition of the popular romance of Indian Oregon, "**The Bridge of the Gods,**" with eight strong pictures by the well-known western artist, L. Maynard Dixon ($1.50), and "**A Captive of the Roman Eagles,**" a historical romance by Felix Dahn, translated from the German by Mary J. Safford ($1.50).

A unique volume in typography, binding, and illustrations is "**In Argolis,**" by Mr. George Horton, a delightful personal account of family life in Greece ($1.75 net). Another admirable gift book, especially for music lovers, is Mr. George P. Upton's "**Musical Pastels,**" a series of essays on quaint and curious musical subjects, illustrated from rare wood engravings (In box, $2.00 net).

Mr. Upton has also added to his well-known series of musical handbooks a new volume on "**The Standard Light Operas,**" which will be widely popular ($1.20 net). Mr. William Morton Payne has followed his "Little Leaders" and "Editorial Echoes" with "**Various Views**" ($1.00 net), and the popular "Helpful Thoughts Series" will have a new volume, "**Catch Words of Cheer,**" by Sara A. Hubbard (80 cts. net).

In regard to our Juveniles we have no hesitation in saying that the trade has seldom been offered so attractive a line in matter and make-up. A notable feature of several volumes will be illustrations in color, and the cover designs are novel, artistic, and striking. The titles include a most engaging book of nonsense by Carolyn Wells, "**The Pete and Polly Stories,**" with irresistable pictures by Fanny Young Cory ($1.50 net); "**Little Mistress Good Hope,**" a volume of fairy stories by Mary Imlay Taylor, with notable colored drawings by Jessie Willcox Smith ($1.50 net); "**Mayken,**" a historical story of Holland, illustrated by the Kinneys ($1.20 net); two volumes of delightful fairy stories with charming illustrations in color by Lucy Fitch Perkins: "**Coquo and the King's Children,**" by Cornelia Baker ($1.50 net), and "**Prince Silver Wings,**" by Edith Ogden Harrison ($1.75 net). Mrs. Harrison is the wife of Mayor Carter H. Harrison of Chicago, and in this volume she makes a graceful literary debut.

THE PUBLISHERS' WEEKLY

Reference List of New Publications

JANUARY–JULY, 1902

MONTHLY CUMULATION, AUGUST, 1902

This Reference List enters the books recorded during the month under (1) author, in **Clarendon** *type. anonymous books having* **Clarendon** *type for the first word; (2) title in* Roman; *(3) subject-heading in* SMALL CAPS; *(4) name of series in Italics. The figures in parentheses are not the imprint date, but refer to the date of "The Publishers' Weekly" in which full title entry will be found and not to the day of publication, for which information should be sought in the full title entry thus indicated. Where not specified, the binding is cloth.*

A apple pie. Greenaway, K. 75 c. Warne.
A B C of banks and banking. Coffin, G: M. $1.25. S: A. Nelson.
A B C of electrical experiments. Clarke, W. J. $1. Excelsior.
A B C of the telephone. Homans, J. E. $1. Van Nostrand.
A B C of wireless telegraphy. Bubier, E: T. $1. Bubier.
A B C universal commercial electric telegraphic code. 5th ed., enl. '02(Je7) 8°, net, $7. Am. Code.
A la mode cookery. Salis, *Mrs.* H. A. de. $2. Longmans.
Aaron Crane. Tate, H: $1.50. Abbey Press.
Abbatt, W:, *ed. See* Heath, W:
ABBEYS.
See Cathedrals.
Abbott, Alex. C. Manual of bacteriology, 6th ed., rev. and enl. '02(My17) 12°, net, $2.75. Lea.
Abbott, J. H. M. Tommy Cornstalk: features of the So. African war from the point of view of the Australian ranks. '02(Je21) D. $2. Longmans.
Abbott, J: S. C. Christopher Carson, known as Kit Carson. '01. '02(Ap12) 12°, net, 87 c. Dodd.
Abbott, S: W., *ed. See* American yearbook of medicine.
Abbott's cyclopedic digest. *See* New York.
Abegg, R., *and* Herz, W. Practical chemistry; tr. by H. B. Calvert. '01· '02(Ja24) 12°, net, $1.50. Macmillan.
Abernethy, J. W. American literature. '02 (Ap26) 12°, $1.10. Maynard, M. & Co.
Abner Daniel. Harben, W. N. $1.50. Harper.
Abroad with the Jimmies. Bell, L. $1.50. L. C. Page
ABSOLUTION.
See Confession.
ACCIDENTS.
Dickson. First aid in accidents. net, 50 c. Revell.
Doty. Prompt aid to the injured. $1.50. Appleton.
According to season. Parsons, *Mrs.* F. T. net, $1.75. Scribner.
ACCOUNTS.
See Arithmetic;—Bookkeeping.
Achenbach, H: Two-fold covenant. '02 (Ap12) D. 50 c. Evangelical Press.
Achromatic spindle in spore mother-cells of osmunda regalis. Smith, R. W. net, 25 c. Univ. of Chic.

Acorn Club, Ct., pubs. 8°, pap. Case.
—Love. Thomas Short, first printer of Ct. $5. (6.) Case.
ACTIONS AT LAW.
Bradner. New practice in supplementary proceedings. $4. W. C. Little.
Budd. Civil remedies under code system. $6. Palm.
Perley. Practice in personal actions in cts. of Mass. $6.50. G: B. Reed.
Sibley. Right to and cause for action, both civil and criminal. $1.50. W. H. Anderson & Co.
Wait. Law and practice in civil actions and proceedings in justices' cts., [etc.] In 3 v. v. 1, 2. ea., $6.35; per set, $19. M. Bender.
ACTORS AND ACTRESSES.
Clapp. Reminiscences of a dramatic critic. net, $1.75. Houghton, M. & Co.
Hamm. Eminent actors and their homes. $1.25. Pott.
Whitton. Wags of the stage. $2.50. Rigby.
ACTS OF THE APOSTLES.
See Bible.
Adam, Ja. Texts to il. a course of elem. lectures on Greek philosophy after Aristotle. '02(Mr1) 8°, net, $1.25. Macmillan.
Adams, Braman B. Block system of signaling on Am. railroads. '01· '02(Mr22) 8°, $2. Railroad Gazette.
Adams, C: F. Lee at Appomattox, and other papers. '02(Je7) D. net, $1.50. Houghton, M. & Co.
Adams, C: F. Shall Cromwell have a statue? '02(Jl12) O. pap., 25 c. Lauriat.
ADAMS, Herb. B.
Vincent, *and others.* Herbert B. Adams: tribute of friends. n. p. Johns Hopkins.
Adams, W. T., ["Oliver Optic."] Moneymaker. '01· '02(Je14) 12°, (Yacht club ser., v. 3.) $1.25. Lee & S.
Addams, Jane. Democracy and social ethics. '02(Je7) D. (Citizen's lib.) $1.25. Macmillan.
Addis, M. E. L. Cathedrals and abbeys of Presbyterian Scotland. '01. '02(F15) il. 12°, net, $2.50. Presb. Bd.
Addison, Jos. Essays; ed. by J: R: Green. '02(Mr29) il. 12°, (Home lib.) $1. Burt.
Adirondack stories. Deming, P. 75 c. Houghton, M. & Co.
Adler, G: J. German and Eng. dictionary. New ed., rev. by F. P. Foster and E: Althaus. '02(Ap26) 4°, $3.50. Appleton.

Adoration of the blessed sacrament. Tesnière, A. net, $1.25. Benziger.
Adventures of John McCue, socialist. '02 (My17) D. (Socialist lib., v. 2, no. 1.) pap., 10 c. Socialistic Co-op.
Adventure ser. 12°, $1. Yewdale.
—Dee. James Griffin's adventures.
Adventures in Tibet. Carey, W: net, $1.50. Un. Soc. C. E.

ADVERTISING.
Farrington. Retail advertising. net, $1. Baker & T

Æneid. *See* Virgil.
AERODYNAMICS.
Langley. Experiments in aerodynamics. $1. Smith. Inst.
Æs triplex. Stevenson, R. L: net, 25 c.-$1. T: B. Mosher.
Aeschylus. The choephori; with crit. notes, etc. '02(Ja18) 8°. (Cambridge Univ. Press ser.) net, $3.25. Macmillan
AESTHETICS.
B., E. P. God the beautiful. net, 75 c. Beam

AFRICA.
Graham. Roman Africa. $6. Longmans.
See also Egypt; — Morocco; — South Africa: — Tripoli.
Agnes Cheswick. Haymond, *Mrs.* W. E. net, 60 c. Blanchard.
AGNOSTICISM.
Sloan. Religion, agnosticism and education. net, 80 c. McClurg.
Agricultural almanac, 1903. '02(Jl19) il. 4°, pap., 10 c. Baer.
AGRICULTURE.
See Dairy;—Domestic economy;—Farms and farming: — Forestry: — Fruit; — Gardening; — Insects;—Irrigation;—Land;—Soils;—Vegetables.
Aikins, Herb. A. Principles of logic. '02 '02(My17) D. net, $1.50. Holt.
AIR BRAKES.
Dukesmith. Air brake, its use and abuse. $1. F. H. Dukesmith.
Kirkman. Air brake. $2.50. World R'way.
AIR PASSAGES.
See Breathing.
Airy, Reginald. Westminster. '02(Mr22) 12°. (Handbooks to the great public schools.) $1.50. Macmillan.
Aitken, J. R. Love in its tenderness: idylls. '02(Mr22) D. (Town and country lib., no. 309.) $1; pap., 50 c. Appleton.
Aitkin, W. H. Divine ordinance of prayer. '02(Je7) 12°, $1.25. E. & J. B. Young.
Aiton, G: B., *and* Rankin, A. W. Exercises in syntax for summer schools, etc. '01 '02 (Ap26) 12°, pap., 25 c. Hyde.
Alabama. *Supreme ct.* Repts. v. 122-129. 1900. '02(Jl5) O. shp., ea., $3.75. Brown Pr. Co.
ALABAMA.
Martin. Internal improvement in Ala. 30 c. Johns Hopkins.
Alabama sketches. Peck, S: M. $1. McClurg.
ALASKA.
Balch. Alasko-Canadian frontier. $1. Allen, L. & S.
Albee, Ernest. History of Eng. utilitarianism. '02(Je28) 8°, net, $2.75. Macmillan.
Albert, Eduard. Diagnosis of surgical diseases; fr. the 8th enl. and rev. ed. by R. T. Frank. '02(Je7) il. 8°. $5: $5.50. Appleton.
Alcott, Louisa M. Little button rose. New ed. '01. '02(F15) 16°, (Children's friend ser.) bds., 50 c. Little, B. & Co.
Alden, *Mrs.* Is. M., ["Pansy."] Unto the end. '02(Je7) D. $1.50. Lothrop.
Alden, W: L. Drewitt's dream. '02(Ap12) D. (Town and country lib., no. 310.) $1; pap., 50 c. Appleton.
Aleph the Chaldean. Burr, E. F. $1.25. Whittaker.
Alexander, *Mrs. See* Hector, *Mrs.* A. F.
Alexander, Hartley B. Problem of metaphysics and meaning of metaphysical explanation. '02(Jl12) 8°, (Columbia University cont. to philosophy, psychology and education, v. 10, no. 1.) pap., *75 c. net. Macmillan.
Alexander, W: M. Demonic possession in the New Testament. '02(Ap12) 8°, net, $1.50. Scribner.
ALEXANDRA, *Queen of England.*
See Edward VII., *King of England.*
Alford, M., *comp.* Latin passages for translation. '02(Ap12) 12°, net, 80 c. Macmillan.
ALFRED *the Great.*
Bowker. King Alfred millenary. $3. Macmillan.
ALGAE.
Livingston. Nature of the stimulus which causes change in form in polymorphic green algae. net, 25 c. Univ. of Chic.
ALGEBRA.
Bailey. High school algebra. 90 c. Am. Bk.
Beman *and* Smith. Academic algebra. $1.25. Ginn.
Brooks. Normal elem. algebra. pt. 1. 83 c. Sower.
Dickson. College algebra. net, $1.50. Wiley.
Hall. Algebraical examples. net. 50 c. Macmillan.
Kellogg. Elements of algebra. 25 c. Kellogg.
Lippincott's elem. algebra. 80 c. Lippincott.
Milne. Key to Academic algebra. $1.50 Am. Bk
Wentworth. College algebra. $1.65. Ginn.
White. Grammar school algebra. 35 c. Am. Bk.
See also Mathematics.
Alger, Edith G. Primer of work and play. '02(Mr15) il. sq. D. 30 c. Heath.
Alger, H., *jr.* Tom Turner's legacy and how he secured it. '02(Jl12) il. 12°, (Alger ser.) $1. Burt.
Alger ser. il. 12°, $1. Burt.
—Alger. Tom Turner's legacy.
—Kaler. Treasure of Cocos Island.
Algonkian. *See* Lawson, A. C.
Algonquian series. *See* Tooker, W: W.
Aliens. Wright, M. T. $1.50. Scribner.
Alissas, R. d', [M. *and* K. Roget.] Les histoires de tante. '02(Mr1) 12°, (Primary ser. of Fr. and Germ. reading books.) net, 40 c. Macmillan.
Allen, Alice E. Children of the palm lands. '02(My3) D. 50 c. Educ Pub.
Allen, C: W. Practitioner's manual. '02 (Je7) 8°, $6; mor., $7. Wood.
ALLEN, Ethan.
Brown Ethan Allen. $1. Donohue.
Allen, F. S. What's what? at home and abroad. '02(Je7) S. net, 50 c. Bradley-W.

Allen, Godfrey. *See* Allen, Phœbe.
Allen, J. H: Diseases and therapeutics of the skin. '02(My24) 12°, $2. Boericke & T.
Allen, May V. Battling with love and fate. '02(Jl19) D. $1. Abbey Press.
Allen, Phœbe *and* Godfrey. Miniature and window gardening. '02(Ap19) D. net, 50 c. Pott.
Allen, T: G. *See* **Duff, E: M.**
Allen, Willis B. Play away: story of the Boston fire department. '02(Jl19) il. 12°, **75 c. net. Estes.
Allen's (Grant) hist. guide books to the principal cities of Europe. S. net, $1.25. Wessels.
—Cruickshank. The Umbrian towns.
Allgood, G: **China war, 1860: letters and** journal. '01· '02(F8) il. obl. O. $5. Longmans.
Allibone, S: A. **Great authors of all ages.** New ed. '01· '02(Mr1) 8°, $2.50. Lippincott.
Allibone, S: A. **Poetical quotations.** New ed. '01· '02(Mr1) 8°, $2.50. Lippincott.
Allibone, S: A. **Prose quotations. New ed.** '01· '02(Mr1) 8°, $2 50. Lippincott.
Allin Winfield. Walsh, G: E. $1.50. Buckles.
ALMANACS AND ANNUALS.
Agricultural almanac, 1903. 10 c. Baer.
American Baptist year-book, 1902. 25 c. Am. Bapt
Annual Am. catalogue, cumulated 1900. 1901. $2. Pub. Weekly.
Arbor and bird day annual for Wis. schools. gratis. Democrat Pr. Co.
Brassey. Naval annual, 1902. net, $7.50. Scribner.
Brooklyn *Daily Eagle* almanac, 1902. 50 c.: 25 c. Brooklyn Eagle.
Courier-Journal almanac, 1902. 25 c. Courier-Journ.
Englishwoman's year-book and directory, 1902. $1.50. Macmillan.
Free trade almanac, 1902. 5 c. Am. Free Trade
Hawaiian almanac and annual, 1902. 75 c. Thrum.
Hazell's annual for 1902. net, $1.50. Scribner.
Illustrated family Christian almanac, 1902. 10 c. Am. Tr.
Indianapolis *Sentinel* year-book and almanac, 1902. 25 c. Indianapolis Sentinel.
International annual of Anthony's photographic bulletin, 1902. $1.25; 75 c. Anthony.
International year-book, 1901. $4. Dodd.
Minneapolis *Journal* almanac and yearbook, 1902. 25 c Journal Pr. Co.
National Temperance almanac and teetotalers year-book, 1902. 10 c. Nat. Temp.
Planets and people: annual yearbook of the heavens. $1. F. E. Ormsby.
Providence *Journal* almanac, 1902. 10 c. Providence Journ.
Public *Ledger* almanac, 1902. gratis. Drexel
Spalding's official athletic almanac. 10 c. Am. Sports
Statesmen's year-book, 1902. net, $3. Macmillan
Telegram almanac and cyclopedia. 1902. 20 c. Providence Telegram.

ALMANACS AND ANNUALS.—*Continued.*
Tribune almanac and pol. register, 1902. 25 c. Tribune Assoc.
Virginia-Carolina almanac for 1902. gratis. Virginia-Carolina.
Whitaker, *comp.* Almanac for 1902. net, 40 c.; net, $1. Scribner.
World almanac and encyclopedia, 1902. 25 c. Press Pub.
See also **under special subjects.**
ALPHABETS.
Day. Alphabets old and new. $1.50. Scribner.
ALPHABETS (*ornamental*).
See **Lettering.**
Alpheus, A., *pseud.* Complete guide to hypnotism. '02(My17) 12°, 50 c.; pap., 25 c. Donohue.
Alpheus, A., *pseud. See also* Oxenford, I.
Altdorfer, Albrecht. Albrecht Altdorfer: 71 woodcuts. '02(Ap26) il. O. (Little engravings classical and contemporary, no. 1.) bds., net, $1.50. Longmans.
ALTERNATING CURRENTS.
Houston *and* Kennelly. Alternating electric currents. $1. McGraw.
Oudin. Standard polyphase apparatus and systems. $3. Van Nostrand.
Rhodes. Elem. treatise on alternating currents. $2.60. Longmans.
Sheldon *and* Mason. Dynamo electric machinery. v. 2, Alternating-current machines. net, $2.50. Van Nostrand.
Alton Locke. *See* Kingsley, C:
Altsheler, Jos. A. My captive. '02(Je7) D. $1.25. Appleton.
Ambassador of Christ. Schuyler, W: $1.50. Gorham.
Amber, Miles. Wistons. '02(F15) D. $1.50. Scribner.
AMERICA.
Helmolt, *and others, eds.* Hist. of the world. v. 1, Prehistoric America. $6. Dodd.
See also **Huguenots.**
American Acad. of Pol. and Soc. Science pubs. 8°, pap. Am. Acad. Pol. Sci.
—Crowell. Status and prospects of Am. shipbuilding. 15 c. (325.)
—Elwood. Aristotle as a sociologist. 15 c. (332.)
—Farquhar. Manufacturers' need of reciprocity. 15 c. (330.)
—Glasson. Nation's pension system. 25 c. (331.)
—Johnson. Isthmian canal. 25 c. (323.)
—Knapp. Government ownership of railroads. 15 c. (326.)
—Meyer. Advisory councils in railway administration. 15 c. (327.)
—Newcomb. Concentration of railway control. 15 c. (328.)
—Pasco. Isthmian canal question. 25 c. (324.)
—Seager. Patten's theory of prosperity. 15 c. (333.)
—Walker. Taxation of corporations in the U. S. 25 c. (329.)
American and Eng. corporation cases. (T: J. Michie.) v. 15. '02(Je7) O. shp., $4.50. Michie.
American and Eng. **encyclopædia** of law. (Garland and McGehee.) 2d ed. v. 20. '02(Mr15) O. shp., $7.50. E: Thompson

American and Eng. railroad cases. v. 23. '02(Mr15) O. shp., $5. Michie.
American and Eng. railroad cases. *See also* Railroad repts.
American at Oxford. Corbin, J: net, $1.50. Houghton, M. & Co.
American, Bapt. year-book, 1902; ed. by J. G. Walker. '02(Ap12) O. pap., 25 c. Am. Bapt.
American church dictionary. Miller, W: J. $1. Whittaker.
American communities. Hinds, W: A. $1. Kerr.
American corp. legal manual. v. 10. '02 (Jl19) O. shp., $5. Corp. Leg. Co.
American digest, annot.; 1901 B. '02(My10) O. (Am. digest system, 1901.) shp., $6. West Pub.
American digest. Century ed. v. 29. '01·'02(Ja4); v. 30 (Mr15); v. 31 (Ap5); v. 32 (Je14); v. 33 (Jl12) O. shp., subs., ea., $6. West Pub.
American digest. v. 33. '02(Jl12)
American digest system. O. shp., $6. West Pub.
—Am. digest, annot.
American duck shooting. Grinnell, G: B. $3.50. Forest.
American Economic Assoc.: papers and proceedings of the fourteenth annual meeting. '02(My3) 8°, (Am. Econ. Assoc. pubs., v. 3, no. 1.) pap., net, $1.50. Macmillan.
American Economic Assoc. pubs. 8°, pap., net. Macmillan.
—Amer. Economic Assoc. 14th annual meeting. $1.50. (v. 3, 1.)
—Clow. Comparative study of administration of city finances in U. S. $1. (3d ser., v. 2, 4.)
American electrical cases; ed. by W: W. Morrill. v. 7. '02(My3) O. shp., $6. M. Bender.
American engineering practice in construction of cement plants. Lathbury, B. B. $2. G. M. S. Armstrong.
American federal state. Ashley, R. L. net, $2. Macmillan.
American food and game fishes. Jordan, D: S. net, $4. Doubleday, P.
American fur trade of the far west. Chittenden, H. M. 3 v. net, $10. F. P. Harper.
American gardens. Lowell, G. $7.50. Bates & G.
American horse, cattle and sheep doctor. McClure, R. $1.50. Henneberry.
American immortals. Eggleston, G: C. $10. Putnam.
American law of assemblies. Stevens, E: A. net, $1. E: A. Stevens.
American leaders and heroes. Gordy, W. F. net, 60 c. Scribner.
AMERICAN LITERATURE.
Abernethy. Am. literature. $1.10. Maynard, M. & Co.
Moulton, *and others, eds.* Lib. of literary criticism of Eng. and Am. authors. v. 3. $5; $6.50. Moulton Pub.
Warner. Fashions in literature. net, $1.20. Dodd.
See also Bibliographies.
American lumberman telecode. Barry, J. W. net, $5. Am. Lumberman.
American masters of painting. Caffin, C: H. net, $1.25. Doubleday, P.
American negligence digest. Hook, A. J. $6.50. Remick.
American negligence repts. *See* Gardner, J: M.
American patriot ser. D. $1. Donohue.
—Brown. John Paul Jones.
American philanthropy of the 19th century. 12°, net. Macmillan.
—Folks. Care of destitute children.
AMERICAN REVOLUTION.
See United States.
American series of popular biographies. Massachusetts ed. '01·'02(Mr1) il. 4°, $17. Graves.
American speaker; for colleges, public and private entertainments. '02(Ap12) il. 4°, pap., 50 c. Conkey.
American sportsman's lib.; ed. by C. Whitney. net, $2; large pap. ed., hf. mor., net, $7.50. Macmillan.
—Sage, *and others.* Salmon and trout.
—Sandys *and* Van Dyke. Upland game birds.
American state repts. (A. C. Freeman.) v. 82. '02(My10); v. 83 (My17); v. 84 (Jl5) O. shp., ea., $4. Bancroft-W.
American street railway investments. [annual.] '02(Je7) F. $5. Street R'way.
American year-book of medicine and surgery; ed. by S: W. Abbott and others. '02 (Mr1) 2 v., il. 8°, ea., net, $3; shp. or hf. mor., ea., net, $3.75. Saunders.
Americanization of the world. Stead, W: T: $1. Markley.
America's story for America's children. Pratt, M. L. v. 5, 40 c. Heath
Ames, A. F. *See* McLellan, J. A.
Ames, *Mrs.* Eleanor M. E., ["Eleanor Kirk."] Prevention and cure of old age. '02(Mr8) D. pap., 50 c. Kirk.
Ames, Ja. B. Selection of cases in equity jurisdiction. pt. 2. '01·'02(Ap12) 12°. 75 c. Harvard Law.
Ames, Ja. B., *and* Brewster, L. D. Negotiable instruments law. '02(Ap12) O. 30 c. Harvard Law.
Ames, L: A. Etiquette of yacht colors; cont. yacht codes, storm and weather signals, etc. '02(Jl5) il. sq. S. canvas, 25 c. Annin.
AMIENS CATHEDRAL.
Perkins. Cathedral church of Amiens. $1. Macmillan.
Among the night people. Pierson, C: D. net, $1. Dutton.
Among the water fowl. Job, H. K. net, $1.35. Doubleday, P.
Amor victor. Kenyon, O. $1.50. Stokes.
AMPHIBIA.
Baskett *and* Ditmars. Story of the amphibians and the reptiles. 60 c. Appleton.
AMUSEMENTS.
See Cards;—Dancing;—Drills;—Entertainments;—Riddles.
ANALYSIS.
See Assaying;—Blowpipe;—Chemistry.
ANARCHY.
See Socialism.
Anarchy. Bauder, E. P. $1; 50 c. Occidental.
ANATOMY.
Cotterell. Pocket Gray; or, Anatomist's vade mecum. net, $1.25. Wood.
Gray. Anatomy, descriptive and surgical. net, $5.50-$7.25. Lea.
Kimber, *comp.* Anatomy and physiology. net, $2.50. Macmillan.
Smith. Anatomy, physiology and hygiene. $1. W: R. Jenkins.

ANATOMY.—*Continued.*
Treves. Surgical applied anatomy. net, $2. Lea.
See also Animals;—Brain; — Dissection;—Eye; — Head;—Intestines;—Neck;—Nervous system;—Nose;—Physiology; — Surgery;—Teeth;—Vivisection.

ANATOMY FOR ARTISTS.
Fiedler. Studies from the nude human figure in motion. $12. Hessling.

ANCESTRY.
See Genealogy.

ANCIENT AND HON. ARTILLERY CO. OF MASS.
Roberts. Hist. of the Military Co. now called the Ancient and Hon. Artillery Co. of Mass. v. 4. [Sold only to members.] Mudge.

Ancient city. Fustel de Coulanges, N. D. $2. Lee & S.

ANCIENT HISTORY.
See History.

Ancient ruins of Rhodesia. Hall, R. N. net, $6. Dutton.

Andersen, Hans C. Selected stories. '01- '02 (Mr1) 12°, pap., 15 c. Lippincott.

Anderson, C: P. The Christian ministry. '02(F22) O. pap., 20 c. Young Churchman.

Anderson, Ja. B. The nameless hero, and other poems. '02(Mr1) D. net, $1. Wessels.

Anderson, J: J., *and* Flick, Alex. C. Short hist. of the state of New York. '01- '02 (Jl12) il. 12°, $1. Maynard, M. & Co.

Anderson, *Sir* Rob. Daniel in the critics' den. '02(Je28) 12°. net, $1.25. Revell.

Andrew, S. O. Greek prose composition. '02 (Je14) 12°, (Greek course.) net, 90 c. Macmillan.

Andrews, Alb. H. *See* Wood, C. A.

Andrews, Alice E. Topics and ref. for the study of Eng. literature. '01- '02(Ap5) D. bds., 15 c. Hyde.

Andrews, H. B. Handbook for street railway engineers. '02(Je21) il. 16°, mor., $1.25. Wiley.

Andrews, W: L. Paul Revere and his engraving. '01- '02(Mr22) $23.50; Japan ed., $40. Scribner.

Angelot. Price, E. C. $1.50. Crowell.

ANGLICAN CHURCH.
See Church of England.

Anglo-Am. pottery. *See* Barber, E. A.

Animal activities. French, N. S. $1.20. Longmans.

Animal castration. Liautard, A. $2. W: R. Jenkins.

Animal experimentation. Ernst, H. C. net, $1.50; net, $1. Little, B. & Co.

Animal forms. Jordan, D: S. net, $1.10. Appleton.

ANIMAL MAGNETISM.
See Hypnotism.

ANIMALS.
Bourne. Comparative anatomy of animals. v. 2. net, $1.25. Macmillan.
Hulbert. Forest neighbors. net, $1.50. McClure, P.
Ingersoll. Wild life of orchard and field. net, $1.40. Harper.
See also Zoölogy.

Animals at home. Bartlett, L. L. 45 c. Am. Bk.

Annandale, C., *ed.* *See* Spofford, A. R.

Annice Wynkoop, artist. Rouse, A. L. $1. Burt.

Annual Am. catalogue. cumulated 1900-1901; with directory of publishers. '02(Ap5) Q. $2. Pub. Weekly.

ANNUALS.
See Almanacs and annuals;—Calendars and year-books.

Anstruther, G. E. William Hogarth. '02 (Je28) il. 16°, (Bell's miniature ser. of painters.) leath., $1. Macmillan.

Antarctic queen. Clark, C: $1.75. Warne.

ANTARCTIC REGIONS.
Balch. Antarctica. n. p. Allen, L. & S.

ANTHOLOGIES.
See Oriental religions;—*also* names of literatures.

ANTHONY, *St.*
Lasance. Little manual of St. Anthony of Padua. 25 c. Benziger.
Roulet. Saint Anthony in art. $2. Marlier.

Anthony, C. V. Children's covenant. '02 (F1) D. $1. Jennings.

Anthony, Harold G., *ed.* True romance revealed by a bag of old letters. '02(Je14) D. $1. Abbey Press.

ANTHROPOLOGY.
See Civilization;—Ethnology;—Language;—Woman.

Anticipations. Wells, H. G: net, $1.80. Harper.

Antigone. Sophocles. net, 60 c. Macmillan.

Antique gems from the Gr. and Latin. See Barrie's.

Antoninus, Marcus Aurelius. Helpful thoughts fr. "Meditations." (W. L. Brown.) '02 (Ap12) S. net, 80 c. McClurg.

Anton's angels. Trueman, A. 75 c. Alliance.

Antrim, Minna T., ["Titian."] Naked truths and veiled allusions. '02(F22) S. 50 c. Altemus.

ANUS AND RECTUM.
Kelsey. Surgery of the rectum. $3. Wood.

APOSTLES' CREED.
McGiffert. Apostles' creed. net, $1.25. Scribner.

APPLE.
Thomas. Book of the apple; and Preparation of cider. net, $1. Lane.

Appleton's Annual cyclopædia for 1901. '02 (Mr1) 8°, subs., $5; shp., $6; hf. mor., $7; hf. rus., $8. Appleton.

Appleton's Geografía superior ilustrada. '01- '02(F22) 4°, bds., $1.50. Appleton.

Appleton's home-reading books; ed. by W: T. Harris. D. Appleton.
—Baskett *and* Ditmars. Story of the amphibians and the reptiles. 60 c. (Div. 1, natural history.)

Appleton's international educ. ser. 12°, net. Appleton.
—Compayré. Later infancy of the child. pt. 2. $1.20. (53.)
—Ware. Educational foundations of trade and industry. $1.20. (54.)

Appleton's Latin dictionary; rev. by J. R. V. Marchant and J. F. Charles. '01- '02 (F22) 8°. $1.50. Appleton.

Appleton's lib. of useful stories. il. T. **35 c. net. Appleton.
—Crowest. Story of the art of music.
—Lindsay. Story of animal life.
—Waterhouse. Art of building.

Appleton's life histories. D. net, $1. Appleton.
—Thwaites. Father Marquette.

Appleton's nuevas cartillas cientificas. il. 16°, 40 c. Appleton.
—Hooker. Nociones de botanica.
Appleton's town and country lib. D. $1; pap., 50 c. Appleton.
—Aitken. Love in its tenderness. (309.)
—Alden. Drewitt's dream. (310.)
—Cooper. A fool's year. (308.)
—Norris. Credit of the country. (313.)
—Raine. Welsh witch. (312.)
—Snaith. Love's itinerary. (307.)
—Wilson. T'baccá queen. (311.)
Appleton's world ser.; ed. by H. J. Mackinder. 8°, $2. Appleton.
—Hogarth. The nearer East. (2.)
—Mackinder. Britain and the British seas. (1.)
AQUARIUM.
Smith. Home aquarium and how to care for it. **$1.20 net. Dutton.
AQUATIC LIFE.
Payne. How to teach aquatic life. 25 c. Kellogg.
Arany, S. A. British-American guide to Carlsbad. 3d Am. ed. '02(Mr8) il. D. pap., 50 c. Abbey Press.
Arbor and bird day annual for Wis. schools. (L. D. Harvey.) '02(Ap26) Q. pap., gratis. Democrat Pr. Co.
ARCHAEOLOGY.
See Architecture; — Bible; — Civilization; — Cliff-dwellers;— Ethnology;— Folk-lore;—History;—Marriage;—Middle Ages;—Mounds.
ARCHITECTURE.
Coburn. Prize designs for rural school buildings. 25 c. Kellogg.
Complete housebuilder. 50 c.; 25 c. Donohue.
Fletcher. Hist. of architecture. net, $7.50. Scribner.
Georgian period. In 3 v. pt. 8, 9. ea. pt., $4. Am. Architect.
Hodgson. Estimating frame and brick houses. $1. D: Williams.
Kidder. Building construction and superintendence. pt. 2. $4. W: T. Comstock.
Ross. Florentine villas. $25. Dutton.
Ware, *ed.* Topical architecture. 2 v. $7.50. Am. Architect.
Waterhouse. Story of the art of building. net, 35 c. Appleton.
See also Bridges;—Cathedrals;—Church architecture;—Decorations and ornament;—Fine arts;—Roofs;—Sanitary engineering.
Architecture of the brain. Fuller, W: net, $3.50. Fuller.
Archoff, Ludwig. *See* Gaylord, H. R.
ARCTIC REGIONS.
Kersting, *ed.* White world. *$2 net. Lewis.
Ardiane and Barbe Bleue. *See* Maeterlinck, M.
Aretino, Lionardo Bruni. *See* Boccaccio, G.
Argyle, Harvey, *pseud. See* McIntire, J: J.
Aristophanes. Comedies; ed. by B: B. Rogers. In 6 v. v. 5. '02(Ap12) 8°, $6. Macmillan.
Aristophanes. The knights; ed. by R. A. Neil. '02(Ja18) 8°, (Cambridge Univ. Press ser.) net, $2.50. Macmillan.
ARISTOTLE.
Ellwood. Aristotle as a sociologist. 15 c. Am. Acad. Pol. Sci.
ARITHMETIC.
Atwood. Complete graded arithmetic. 4 v. ea., 25 c. Heath.

ARITHMETIC.—*Continued.*
Baird. Graded work in arithmetic. 25 c. Am. Bk.
Browne. Graded mental arithmetic. net, 30 c. Whitaker & R.
Chancellor. Children's arithmetics: Primary, 28 c.—2d bk., 20 c.—3d bk., 24 c.—4th bk., 24 c. Globe School Bk.
Gyim. Chinese-Eng. elem. reader and arithmetic. $1.25. Taylor & M.
Hornbrook. Key to Primary arithmetic and Grammar school arithmetic. 65 c. Am. Bk.
Lippincott's practical arithmetic. 2 v. ea., 40 c. Lippincott.
McLellan, *and others.* Public school arithmetic for grammar grades. net, 60 c. Macmillan.
Milne. Key to Standard arithmetic and Mental arithmetic. 75 c. Am. Bk.
Perkins. Arithmética elemental. 25 c. Appleton.
Pierce. Intermediate arithmetic. 48 c. Silver.
Ruggles. Exercises and problems in arithmetic. 25 c. W: R. Jenkins.
Spangenberg. Practical arith. explained to practical mechanic. 50 c. Zeller.
See also Bookkeeping;—Interest.
Arithmetic of electrical measurements. Hobbs, W. R. P. 50 c. Van Nostrand.
ARIZONA.
Bicknell. Guide book of the Grand Canyon of Arizona. 75 c.; 50 c. Harvey.
James. In and around the Grand Canyon. net, $10. Little, B. & Co.
Arkansas. *Supreme ct.* Repts. v. 69. '02 (Ap19) O. shp., $3.50. Thompson Litho.
Arm and hammer ser.; ed. by Lucien Sanial. D. 50 c. N. Y. Labor News.
—Engels. Socialism.
—Marx. Wage-labor and capital; [also] Free trade.
Armature windings of direct current dynamos. Arnold, E. $2. Van Nostrand.
ARMINIUS.
See Hermann der Cherusker.
Armstrong, Annie E. Very odd girl. '02 (Mr29) il. 12°, (Fireside ser.) $1. Burt.
Armstrong, Le Roy. The outlaws. '02(Ap26) D. $1.25. Appleton.
Armstrong, Le Roy. *See also* Banks, C: E.
Army songster (The): [repr. of 1864.] '02 (Je21) S pap., 25 c. Bell Bk.
ARNOLD, Benedict.
Codman. Arnold's expedition to Quebec. net, $2.25. Macmillan.
Melvin. Journal of soldier in Arnold's expedition. $2. H. W. Bryant.
Arnold, E. Armature windings of direct current dynamos: fr. orig. Germ. by F. B. De Gress. '02(My3) il. O. $2. Van Nostrand.
Arnold, Edn. L. **Lepidus the centurion.** '02 (Mr8) D. $1.50. Crowell.
Arnold, Jonathan A., *comp. and ed.* Manual of school laws of Illinois. '01- '02(Mr1) 8°, $1.75. Effingham Democrat.
Arnold, Matt. Dramatic and early poems; ed. by H. B. Forman. '02(My17) 16°, (Temple classics.) 50 c.; flex. leath., 75 c. Macmillan.
Arnold, Matt. Essays in criticism. 1st and 2d ser. '02(Ap19) 12°, (Home lib.) $1. Burt.

Arnold, Matt. Literature and dogma. '02 (My24) 8°, (Commonwealth lib.) net, $1. New Amsterdam.
Arnold, Sa. L. **Ensefiar á leer.** '01· '02 (Mr8) il. 12°, 40 c. Silver.
Arnold, *Mrs.* T. B., *ed.* Sabbath school commentary on Internat. lessons, 1902. '02 (Ap12) 8°, 50 c. Revell.
Arnolt, W. M. Theolog. and Semitic literature for 1901. '02(My3) 8°, pap., net, 50 c. Univ. of Chic.
Arnott, S. Books of bulbs. '02(F15) 12°, (Handbooks of practical gardening; ed. by H. Roberts, v. 5.) net, $1. Lane.
Around the "Pan" with Uncle Hank. Fleming, T: $2. Nutshell.
Around the throne. Winchester, P. net, $1. Eichelberger.
Around the world. Carroll, S. W. 60 c. Morse.
Arrabbiata (L'). *See* Heyse, P. J. L.
ARSENIC.
Wanklin. Arsenic. $1. Lippincott.
Art and craft of printing. Morris, W: $5. Elston Press.
Art of folly. Ford, S. **$3 net. Small.
Art of life. Maulde la Clavière, R. de. net, $1.75. Putnam
Art reader. Cady, M. R. 35 c. Richardson, S.
ARTHUR, *King of Britain.*
Malory. King Arthur and his noble knights. $1. Burt.
Arthur, *Mrs.* J. J. Annals of the Fowler family. '02(F22) il. 8°, $3.50. Mrs. J. J. Arthur.
Artificial feeding of infants. Judson, C: F. $2. Lippincott.
ARTILLERY.
See Gunnery.
Artistic crafts ser. of technical handbooks; ed. by W. R. Lethaby. il. D. net. Appleton.
—Cockerell. Bookbinding and the care of books. $1.20. (1.)
ARTISTS.
Wherry. Stories of the Tuscan artists. net, $4. Dutton.
See also Painters.
Artists' lib. *See* Longmans'.
As I saw it. McIntire, J: J. $1.25. Home Pub. Co.
As nature whispers. Davis, S. K. 50 c. Alliance.
As true as gold. Mannix, M. E. 45 c. Benziger.
Asa Holmes. Johnston, A. F. $1. L. C. Page.
Ash, Mark *and* W: Table of federal citations. v. 1. '01· '02(F8); v. 2 (My24) O. shp., (for complete work.) $30. Remick.
Ashley, Roscoe L. American Federal state. '02(Mr1) 12°, net, $2. Macmillan.
ASIA.
See Assyria;—China;—India;—Japan;—Persia;—Siam.
Asiatic Russia. Wright, G: F: 2 v. **$7.50 net. McClure, P.
Askwith, E. H. Introd. to the Thessalonian Epistles. '02(Ap12) 12°, net, $1.25. Macmillan.
Aslauga's knight. *See* La Motte Foque, F. H. K. *Freiherr* de.
Assassins. Meakin, N. M. $1.50. Holt.
ASSAYING.
Miller. Manual of assaying. $1. Wiley.
Rhead *and* Sexton. Assaying and metallurgical analysis. $4.20. Longmans.
See also Blowpipe;—Metals and metallurgy.
ASSYRIA.
Murison. Babylonia and Assyria. net, 20 c. Scribner.
ASTROLOGY.
Turnbull. Divine language of celestial correspondence. $2. Alliance.
Valcourt-Vermont. Practical astrology. $1; 50 c. Lee & S.
ASTRONOMY.
Jacoby. Practical talks by an astronomer. net, $1. Scribner.
White. Elements of theoretical and des. astronomy. $2.50. Wiley.
Young. Manual of astronomy. $2.45. Ginn.
See also Almanacs and annuals;—Astrology;—Stars.
At large. Hornung, E. W: $1.50. Scribner.
At Sunwich port. Jacobs, W. W. $1.50. Scribner.
At the back of beyond. Barlow, J. $1.50. Dodd.
Athalie. *See* Racine, J.
Athenæum Press ser. D. Ginn.
—De Quincey. Selections. $1.05.
Atherton, *Mrs.* Gertrude F. The conqueror. '02(Mr29) D. $1.50. Macmillan.
Athletic lib. *See* Spalding's.
Atkinson, A. A. Electrical and magnetic calculations. '02(Je7) D. net, $1.50. Van Nostrand.
Atkinson, Rob. W., *and* Carter, E. Songs of the Eastern colleges. '02(F1) O. $1.25. Hinds.
Atlantic reporter, v. 50. '02(Mr29); v. 51 (Jl19) O. (Nat. reporter system, state ser.) shp., ea., $4. West Pub.
ATLASES.
See Encyclopædias;—Geography.
ATTACHMENT.
Rood. On attachments, garnishments, judgments, and executions. $3. Wahr.
ATTIC PROSE.
Flagg. Writer of attic prose: models fr. Xenophon. $1. Am. Bk.
ATTORNEYS.
National list. Directory of bonded attorneys. (App. to pubs. for price.) Nat. Surety.
Atwater, Fs., *comp.* Atwater history and genealogy. '01· '02(F8) il. 8°, $5; hf. mor., $7.50; full mor., $10. Journal Pub.
Atwood, G: E. Complete graded arithmetic. Grades 3-6. '01· '02(Je7) 4 v., D. ea., 25 c. Heath.
Audrey. Johnston, M. $1.50. Houghton, M. & Co.
Augsburg, D. R. Drawing. In 3 bks. '02 (My3) sq. O. ea., 75 c. Educ. Pub.
Aulnoy, Marie C. J. de B., *Comtesse* d', *and* Perrault, C: Once upon a time. New ed. '01· '02(F15) 16°, (Children's friend ser.) bds., 50 c. Little, B. & Co.
Aulnoy, Marie C. J. de B. *Comtesse* de. *See also* Perrault, C:
Aunt Susan, *pseud.* *See* Prentiss, *Mrs.* E.
Austin, A. Tale of true love, and other poems. '02(Ap26) D. net, $1.20. Harper.
Austin, Ma. S. Philip Freneau; the poet of the Revolution. '01· '02(F1) O. net, $2.50. Wessels.

Austrian, Delia. Love songs. '02(Jl5) D. $1. Conkey.
Authorities, deductions and notes in commercial paper. '02(Jl12) interleaved, O. shp., $2.25. Univ. Press.
Author's (The) yearbook for 1902. '02 (Mr29) D. bds., $1. Book-Lover.
AUTHORS.
Allibone. Great authors of all ages. $2.50. Lippincott.
Halsey, *ed.* Authors of our day in their homes. $1.25. Pott.
See also Bibliographies;—Literature;—Musicians.
AUTOGRAPHS.
Joline. Meditations of an autograph collector. net, $3. Harper.
Automatic pen lettering and designs. *See* Faust, C. A.
AUTOMOBILES.
Thompson. The motor-car. $1. Warne.
Avare (L'). Molière, J. B. P. de. 50 c. Scott, F. & Co.
Avebury, *Lord*, Barlow, C. A. Montague, Boyle, *Sir* C., *and others.* The King's weigh-house: lectures to business men. '01- '02(Ja4) 12°, 75 c. Macmillan.
Avebury, *Lord.* *See also* Lubbock, *Sir* J:
Avesta. Index verborum, by M. Schuyler, jr. '02(Je14) 8°, (Columbia Univ. Indo-Iranian ser.) net, $2. Macmillan.
Ayer, Jos. C. Rise and development of Christian architecture. '02(My17) il. F. net, $1.50. Young Churchman.
Ayres, Franklin H. Laboratory exercises in elem. physics. '01- '02(F15) il. 12°, net, 50 c. Appleton.
B., E. P. God the beautiful. '02(Ap12) nar. D. net, 75 c. Beam.
Babbitt, Fk. C. Grammar of Attic and Ionic Greek. '02(Jl12) D. $1.50. Am. Bk.
Babcock, M. D. Letters from Egypt and Palestine. '02(Mr22) il. D. net, $1. Scribner.
Babcock, M. D. Three whys and their answer. '01- '02(F15) S. 35 c. Un. Soc. C. E.
BABYLONIA.
Murison. Babylonia and Assyria. net. 20 c. Scribner
Bacon, B: W. Sermon on the Mount. '02 (My3) 12°, net, $1. Macmillan.
Bacon, Fs., *Lord.* Works. '02(Je21) 12°, (Caxton ser.) net, $1.25. Scribner.
Bacon, Fs., *Lord.* Essays. '01- '02(Ap5) S. (Little masterpieces.) 50 c. Doubleday, P.
Bacon, Fs., *Lord.* Of gardens. '02(Mr29) 16°, net, 50 c. Lane.
BACON, Fs., *Lord.*
Gallup. Bi-literal cipher of Sir Francis Bacon. $3.75. Howard.
See also Shakespeare-Bacon controversy.
Bacon, Gorham. Manual of otology. 3d ed., rev. and enl. '02(Jl19) il. 12°, *$2.25 net. Lea.
BACTERIA.
Abbott. Manual of bacteriology. net, $2.75. Lea.
Bowhill. Manual of bacteriological technique and spec. bacteriology. $4.50. Wood.
Emery. Bacteriological diagnosis. net. $1.50. Blakiston
BACTERIA.—*Continued.*
Frost. Lab'y guide in elem. bacteriology. $1.60. W: D. Frost.
Sternberg. Text-book of bacteriology. net, $5; net, $5.75. Wood.
See also Fermentation.
Badminton lib. 8°. Little, B. & Co.
—Harmsworth, *and others.* Motors and motor driving. $3.50; $5.
Baedeker, K., *ed.* Egypt. 5th rev. ed. '02 (Mr8) il. 12°, (Baedeker's guides.) net, $4.50. Scribner.
Baedeker, K., *ed.* Southern Germany. 9th rev. ed. '02(Mr8) 12°, (Baedeker's guides.) net, $1.80. Scribner.
Bagot, R: Roman mystery. '02(Ap5) 12°, $1.50. Lane.
Bailey, L. H. Nature portraits; studies with pen and camera of our wild birds, animals, fish and insects. '02(Jl12) il. portfolio, 12 x 18 in. App. to pubs. for price. Doubleday, P.
Bailey, Middlesex A. High school algebra. '02(Jl12) sq. S. hf. leath., 90 c. Am. Bk.
Baillie, Alex. F. The Oriental Club and Hanover Square. '01. '02(Ja4) il. 4°, $9. Longmans
Baillot, Edouard P., *and* Brugnot, Alice G. T. French prose composition. '01- '02(Ja4) S. (Lake French ser.) 50 c. Scott, F. & Co.
BAILMENTS.
Van Zile. Elements of the law and bailments. $5. Callaghan.
Baily, R. C. Mabel Thornley. '02(Mr29) D. $1.25. Abbey Press.
Bain, Ja. *See* Henry, Alex.
Bain, Rob. N. Peter III., Emperor of Russia. '02(Mr29) il. 8°, net, $3.50. Dutton.
Baird, C: W. Hist. of Huguenot emigration to America. New ed. '01- '02(F22) 2 v., 8°, net, $2.50. Dodd.
Baird, S. W. Graded work in arithmetic. 8th year. '02(Ap19) D. 25 c. Am. Bk.
Baker, G: H. Economic locomotive management. 2d lib. ed. '02(Je7) il. D. $1.50. R'way Educ.
Baker, Moses N. Municipal engineering and sanitation. '02(F1) 12°, (Citizen's lib.) hf. leath., net, $1.25. Macmillan.
Balch, Edn. S. Antarctica. '02(Jl19) 8°. (for private distribution.) Allen, L. & S.
Balch, Lewis. Manual for boards of health and health officers. '02(Je14) D. $1.50. Banks & Co.
Balch, T: W. Alasko-Canadian frontier. '02(Ap19) 8°, $1. Allen L. & S.
Baldwin, Aaron D. Gospel of Judas Iscariot. '02(My24) D. $1.50. Jamison-H.
Baldwin, Ja. The book lover: guide to best reading. 13th rev. ed. '02(My3) nar. S. net, $1. McClurg.
Baldwin, Ja. F. The scutage and knight service in England. '02(Mr22) 8°, net, $1. Univ. of Chic.
Baldwin, Ja. M: Fragments in philosophy and science. '02(Ap19) O. net, $2.50. Scribner.
Baldwin, Ja. M: Social and ethical interpretations in mental development. 3d ed., rev. and enl. '02(Mr29) 8°, net, $2.60. Macmillan.
Baldwin, May. A popular girl. '01- '02 (F15) il. 12°, net, $1.20. Lippincott.

Baldwin, Myra. Nancy's Easter gift [poem.] '02(My24) il. D. 50 c. Abbey Press.
Baldwin, Willis. *See* Michigan. Law of personal injuries.
Baldwin primer. Kirk, M. 35 c. Am. Bk.
Bale marked circle X. Eggleston, G: C. net, $1.20 Lothrop.
Balfour, Arth. J. Foundations of belief. 8th ed., rev. '02(Je7) D. net, $2. Longmans.
Ball Estate Assoc. *See* Gans, E. W:
Ball, Fs. K. Elements of Greek. '02(My3) il. 12°, net, $1. Macmillan.
Ball, *Sir* Rob. S. Earth's beginning. '02 (My24) il. D. net, $1.80. Appleton.
BALL.
See **Baseball.**
BALLADS.
Book of romantic **ballads**. net, $1.25. Scribner.
Hale, *ed.* Ballads and ballad poetry. 40 c. Globe Sch. Bk.
Kinard, *ed.* Old English ballads. 40 c. Silver.
See also **Songs.**
Ballagh, Ja. C. Hist. of slavery in Virginia. '02(Ap26) O. (Johns Hopkins Univ. studies, extra v. 24.) $1.50. Johns Hopkins.
Ballance, C: A., *and* Stewart, P. Healing of nerves. '02(F1) 4°, net, $4.50. Macmillan.
Ballard, Eva C. She wanted to vote. '01-'02(Mr8) D. net, $1.40. Brower.
Ballough, C: A. Power that heals and how to use it. '02(Jl19) S. $1. Painter.
Ballough, C: A. Sibylline leaves. '02(Jl19) sq. T. $1. Painter.
BALMANNO, Rob.
Clarke. Letters to an enthusiast. net, $2.50. McClurg.
Balzac, H. de. Best of Balzac; ed. by A. Jessup. '02(Ap26) 16°, (Best writings of great authors.) $1.25; ¾ lev. mor., $3. L. C. Page.
BANDAGES.
Hopkins. Roller bandage. **$1.50 net. Lippincott.
See also **Surgery.**
Bang, *Mrs.* Marie. Livets alvor. '01-'02 (My17) D. pap., 65 c. M. Bang.
Bangs, J: K. Olympian nights. '02(Je21) D. $1.25. Harper.
Bangs, J: K. Uncle Sam, trustee. '02(My10) il. O. net, $1.75. Riggs.
BANKERS.
Sharp & Alleman's Co.'s lawyers' and bankers' directory, 1902. Jan. ed. $5. Sharp & A.
Banks, C: E., *and* Armstrong, L. Theodore Roosevelt, twenty-sixth President of the U. S. '02(Je28) 12°, $1.50; hf. rus., $2.25. Du Mont.
Banks, L: A. Great saints of the Bible. '01. '02(Ap12) 8°, $1.50. Eaton & M.
Banks, L: A. Windows for sermons. '02 (Ap12) D. net, $1.20. Funk.
Banks, L: A. *See also* Talmage, F. D.
Banks, Nancy H. Oldfield. '02(Je7) D. $1.50. Macmillan.
BANKS AND BANKING.
Barnett. State banking in the U. S. since passage of Nat. bank act. 50 c. Johns Hopkins.

BANKS AND BANKING.—*Continued.*
Coffin. A B C of banks and banking. $1.25. S: A. Nelson.
Handy. Banking systems of the world. $1.50. Jamieson-H.
Michie, *ed.* Banking cases, annot. v. 3. $5. Michie.
See also **Savings-banks.**
Bannister, H: M. *See* **Brower, D. R.**
Banquet book. Reynolds, C. net, $1.75. Putnam.
Banta, Thdr. M. Sayre family. '02(F15) il. 8°, hf. mor., $10. T. M. Banta.
BAPTISM.
Mahon. Token of the covenant; right use of baptism. 50 c. Pub. Ho. of M. E. Ch. So
Wilson. Great cloud of witnesses. 50 c. Standard Pub.
BAPTIST CHURCH.
Jeter. Baptist principles reset. $1. Rel. Herald.
Merriam. Hist. of Am. Baptist missions. $1.25. Am. Bapt.
Newman, *ed.* Century of Baptist achievements, 1801-1900. net, $1.50. Am. Bapt.
Barbara. Culley, F. C. $1.25. F. C. Culley.
Barbarian invasions of Italy. Villari, P. 2 v. net, $7.50. Scribner.
Barber, Edn. A. Anglo-Am. pottery: old Eng. china; with Am. views. 2d ed., rev. and enl. '02(Ja18) il. 12°, net, $2. [Caspar] E. A. Barber
Barber, Ed. A. Anglo-Am. pottery. 2d rev., enl. ed. '01. '02(Ap26) il. 8°, $2. Patterson & W.
Barber, F. M. Mechanical triumphs of ancient Egyptians. '01. '02(F22) 16°, net. $1.25. Dodd.
Barbier de Séville. Beaumarchais, P. A. C. de. 50 c. Scott, F. & Co.
Bardeen, C: W. Manual of civics for N. Y. schools. '02(Ja25) D. net, $1. Bardeen.
Barclay, Wilbur F. *See* Methodist Epis. Church.
Barker, Wharton. The great issues: editorials fr. *The American*, 1897-1900. '02(Je21) 12°, $1; pap., 50 c. Ferris.
Barlow, C. A. Montague. *See* **Avebury**, *Lord.*
Barlow, Jane. At the back of beyond. '02 (My10) D. $1.50. Dodd.
Barnard, C: Farming by inches. '01-'02 (F8) 12°, 40 c. Coates.
Barnard, C: My ten rod farm; or, how I became a florist. '01. '02(F8) 12°, 40 c. Coates.
Barnard, C: A simple flower garden for country homes. '01-'02(F8) 12°, 40 c. Coates.
Barnard, C: The strawberry garden, how planted, what it cost. '01-'02(F8) 12°, 40 c. Coates.
Barnard, C: Two thousand a year on fruits and flowers. '01. '02(F8) 12°, $1. Coates
Barnes, C: W. Sorrow and solace of Esther, daughter of Ben-Amos. '02(Mr29) S. leatherette, net, 30 c. Jennings.
Barnes, Edn. N. C. Reconciliation of Randall Claymore. '02(Je28) D. $1. Earle.
Barnes, Louisa E., [*Mrs.* Arth. J. Barnes.] Shorthand lessons by the word method. '01-'02(Mr1) 12°, $1.25. A. J. Barnes.

Barnett, Evelyn S. Jerry's reward. '01· '02 (Jl19) il. S. (Cosy corner ser.) 50 c. L. C. Page.

Barnett, G: E. State banking in the U. S. since the passage of the Nat. bank act. '02(My17) O. (Johns Hopkins Univ. studies in hist. and pol. science ser. 20, nos. 2-3.) pap., 50 c. Johns Hopkins.

Barnum, Fs. Grammatical fundamentals of the Innuit language as spoken by the Eskimo of the western coast of Alaska. '01. '02(Jl12) 8°, $5. Ginn.

BARNUM, Phineas T.
Benton. Life of P. T. Barnum. $1. Donohue.

Barr, R., ["Luke Sharp."] Prince of good fellows. '02(Je7) il. D. $1.50. McClure, P.

Barret, F. A. Medical hand book. '02 (Jl12) 16°, $1. Barret Chemical.

Barrett, Jos. H. Life of Abraham Lincoln. '02(Jl19) 12°, (Biographies of famous men.) $1. Donohue.

Barrie, Ja. M. Little minister. '02(Ap5) 12°, (Home lib.) $1. Burt.

Barrie's antique gems from the Greek and Latin. il. 12°. (App. to pub. for price.) Barrie.
—Horace. Odæ, Epodæ, etc. (3.)
—Longus, Daphnis and Chloe. (4.)
—Lucian. Lucius, the ass. (5.)
—Ovid. Amorum libri tres. (6.)
—Theocritus. Idylls. (1.)

Barrow, G. H. S. *See* Waller, A. R.

Barry, H: A. God the Holy Ghost. '02 (Ap12) 12°, $2. Angel Press.

Barry, J: W. American lumberman telecode. '02(Ap26) 8°, flex. leath., net, $5. Am. Lumberman.

Barry Lyndon. *See* Thackeray, W: M.

Bartholomew, J. G. Internat. student's atlas of modern geography. '02(Ap12) 4°, net, $2.25. Scribner.

Bartlett, Alb. L. **A golden way: journey through Ireland, Scotland and England.** '02(Mr1) il. D. $1.50 Abbey Press.

Bartlett, Emeline B. *See* Pearson, H: C.

Bartlett, Lillian L. Animals at home. '02 (My17) il. D. (Eclectic school readings.) 45 c. Am. Bk.

Barton, F:, *comp.* **Pulpit power and eloquence.** '01· '02(Mr8) 8°, $3.50. F. M. Barton.

Barton, G: A. Roots of Christian teaching as found in the O. T. '02(My24) D. $1.25. Winston.

Barton, G: A. Sketch of Semitic origins, social and religious. '02(F1) 8°, net, $3. Macmillan.

Barton, W: E. I go a fishing: study in progressive discipleship. '02(F8) 16°, 25 c. Revell.

BASEBALL.
Spalding's official baseball guide 1902. 10 c. Am. Sports.

Basis of social relations. Brinton, D. G. net. $1.50. Putnam.

BASKETRY.
Firth. Cane basket work. 2 v. ea., 60 c. Scribner.

Baskett, Ja. N., *and* Ditmars, R. L. Story of the amphibians and the reptiles. '02(Jl19) D. (Home-reading books: Div. 1, Nat. history.) 60 c. Appleton.

Bass, Edg. W. **Elements of differential calculus.** 2d ed., rev. '02(Ja11) il. 12°. net, $4. Wiley.

Bassett, Fk. J. *See* Campbell, H. A.

Bassett, Ma. E. S. Judith's garden. '02(Je7) O. $1.50. Lothrop.

Batt, Max. Treatment of nature in German literature from Günther to the appearance of Goethe's Werther. '02(F15) O. pap., net, $1. Univ. of Chic.

Battleground. Glasgow, E. $1.50. Doubleday, P.

Battling with love and fate. Allen, M. V. $1. Abbey Press.

Bauder, Emma P. Anarchy; its cause and cure told in story. '02(Ap12) il. D. $1: pap., 50 c. Occidental Pub.

Baur, T. P., *and* Herbert, H. F. Free thinkers' manual. '02(Je7) il. 8°, $4. Radical.

Bausman, B. Precept and practice. '02(Ap5) D. net, $1. Heidelberg.

BAVARIA.
See Ludwig II.

Baylies, Edn. *See* Wait, W:

Bayly, Ada E., ["Edna Lyall."] The hinderers. '02(Je7) D. $1. Longmans.

Beach, Harlan P. Geography and atlas of Protestant missions. v. 1, Geography. '01· '02(F15) 12°, $2.50; pap., per set, $1.75. Student Vol

Beach, W: H. First New York (Lincoln) cavalry. '02(Jl12) 8°, *$2.50 net. [Caspar] Lincoln Cavalry.

Beale, C: C. Book of legal dictation. 2d ed., rev. and enl. '01· '02(F1) D. 50 c. Beale Press.

Beard, Sidney H. **Comprehensive guide book** to natural, hygienic and humane diet. New ed. '02(Mr22) 16°, $1; pap., 50 c. Alliance.

Beard, Sidney H. Comprehensive guide-book to natural, hygienic and humane diet. [New issue.] '02(My17) D. net, $1. Crowell.

Bears of Blue River. Major, C: $1.50. Macmillan.

Beaumarchais, Pierre A. C. de. Barbier de Seville and Lettres; ed. by G: D. Fairfield. '02(Jl5) 16°, (Lake French classics.) 50 c. Scott, F. & Co.

Beau's comedy. Dix, B. M. $1.50. Harper.

Beaton, Ja. A. Vest-pocket practical compend of electricity. '02(My17) il. nar. T. 50 c.; leath., 75 c. Laird.

BEAUTIFUL (The).
See Aesthetics.

Beck, Carl. **Sonnenblicke aus der Amerikanischen praxis.** '02(F15) O. pap., net, 30 c. Lemcke.

Becker, Fk. S. *See* New York civil and criminal justice.

Beddard, F. E. Mammalia. *See* Harmer, S F:, *ed.*

Bedell, Edn. A., *rep.* *See* New York. *Ct. of appeals.* Digest.

Bedford, Jessie. *See* Godfrey, E.

Beecher, C: E. Studies in evolution. '01· '02(Mr15) 8°. (Yale bicentennial pub.) net, $5. Scribner.

Beeching, H. C. Inns of court sermons. '01· '02(Ja4) 12°, $1.25. Macmillan.

Beeman, Marion N. Analysis of the Eng. sentence; rev. and enl. '02(Je28) sq. D. (Progredior ser.) 50 c. Flanagan.

Beers, G: E. *See* Stephen, *Sir* J. F.

Behrens, C. Blossom and fruit in decorative arrangement. '02(Jl5) pls. 8°, $12. Hessling.
Behymer, Ida H. Seal of destiny. '01· '02 My10) 12°, $1.50. Neely.
Bek's first corner. Conklin, *Mrs.* J. M. D. $1. Burt.
Belinda. Egan, M. F. $1. Kilner.
Bell, *Mrs.* Arth. *See* Bell, *Mrs.* N. R. E. M.
Bell, Lilian, [*now Mrs.* Arth. Hoyt Bogue.] Abroad with the Jimmies. '02(My10) il. D. $1.50. L. C. Page.
Bell, Malcolm. Rembrandt Van Rijn. '01. '02(Ja4) il. 12°, (Great masters of painting and sculpture.) $1.75. Macmillan.
Bell, *Mrs.* Nancy R. E. M., ["N. D'Anvers."] Thomas Gainsborough. '02(Je28) il 16°, (Bell's miniature ser. of painters.) leath., $1. Macmillan.
Bell, Roscoe R. *See* Veterinarian's call-book.
Belles, W: H: Cain's sin. '01. '02(F1) D. $1 W: H: Belles.
Belloc, Bessie R. In a walled garden. 5th ed. '02(Mr8) 8°, net, $1.25. Herder.
Belloc, Bessie R. Passing world. 2d ed. '02(Mr8) 8°, net, $1.25. Herder.
Belloc, Hilaire. The path to Rome. '02(Je21) il. O. net, $2. Longmans.
Belloc, Hilaire. Robespierre: a study. '01. '02(F1) O. net, $2. Scribner.
Bell's cathedral ser. 12°, 60 c. Macmillan.
—Hiatt. Westminster Abbey.
Bell's handbooks to continental churches. il. 12°, $1. Macmillan.
—Perkins. Amiens.
Bell's miniature ser. of painters. il. 16°, 50 c.; limp leath., $1. Macmillan.
—Anstruther. Hogarth.
—Bell. Gainsborough.
—Staley. Watteau.
—Williamson. Holman Hunt.
Belshazzar. Davis, W: S. †$1.50. Doubleday, P.
Beman, W. W., *and* Smith, D: E. Academic algebra. '02(My24) D. hf. leath., $1.25. Ginn.
Ben Hur. Wallace, L. $2.50. Harper.
Bender, Ida C., *ed.* *See* Judson, H. P.
Bender, Wilbur H. The teacher at work. '02 (Je28) D. 75 c. Flanagan.
Benedictine martyr in England. Camm, B. net, $1.25. Herder.
Benedix, R. J. Der prozess. *See* Fulda, L.
Benjamin, C: H: Notes on machine design. 2d ed. '02(My17) il. 16°, $2. C. H. Holmes.
Benjy in beastland. Ewing, *Mrs.* J. H. 50 c. Little, B. & Co.
Bennett, Arnold. T. Racksole and daughter. '02(My24) il. D. $1.50. New Amsterdam.
Bennie, the Pythian of Syracuse. Fretz, L. B. $1. Scroll Pub.
Benson, E: F. Scarlet and hyssop. '02 (Ap12) D. $1.50. Appleton.
Benson, E: W. Addresses on the Acts of the Apostles. '02(Mr29) il. 8°, net, $7 Macmillan.
Benton, Joel. Life of P. T. Barnum. '02 (My24) 12°, (Biographies of famous men.) $1. Donohue.
Bentzan, Therese. Constances. '02(Ap26) 12°, $1.50. Neely.
Bergholt, Ernest. *See* Leigh, L.
BERIN, *St.*
Field. Saint Berin, the apostle of Wessex. $1.50. E. & J. B. Young.
Berkeley, W: N. Lab'y work with mosquitoes. '02(My17) O. net, $1. Pediatrics Lab.
BERKELEY HILLS.
Lawson *and* Palache. The Berkeley Hills: coast range geology. 80 c. Univ. of Cal.
Berkleys (The). Wight, E. H. net, 40 c. Benziger.
BERKSHIRE, Mass.
See Lenox.
BERLIOZ, Hector.
Young. Mastersingers; with essay on Hector Berlioz. net, $1.50. Scribner.
Berlitz, M. D. Grammaire partique de la langue française. In 4 v. v. 3. '02(Ap26) 12°, 50 c. Berlitz.
Bernis, François J. de P., *Cardinal* de. Memoirs and letters; fr. orig. mss. by F. Masson. '02(F1) 2 v., il. 8°, (Versailles hist. ser.) subs., per v., $6; ¾ leath., per v. $9. Hardy, P. & Co.
Berry, G: R., *ed.* Letters of the Rm. 2 coll. in the British Museum. '02(F15) 8°, pap., net, 50 c. Univ. of Chic.
Besant, *Sir* W. Autobiography. '02(My10) O. net, $2.40. Dodd.
Best, Kenelm D. Victories of Rome and the temporal monarchy of the church. 4th ed., rev. '01· '02(Mr22) S. net, 45 c. Benziger.
Best, Noel R. College man in doubt. '02 (Je21) D. net, 50 c. Westminster.
Best nonsense verses. Daskam, J. D. 50 c. W: S. Lord.
Best writings of great authors. 16°, $1.25; $3. L. C. Page.
—Balzac. Best of Balzac.
BEVERAGES.
Maloney. 20th century guide for mixing fancy drinks. $1. J. C. Maloney.
Beyond the clouds. Patterson, C: B. $1. Alliance.
Beyond the vail. Nixon, J. H. $1.75. Hudson-K.
Bible. The emphasized Bible: new tr. designed to set forth the exact meaning, etc.; expository introd., ref. and app., by Jos. B. Rotherham. v. 1, Genesis-Ruth; v. 2, Samuel-Psalms. '02(Jl12) 8°, ea., $3. Woodward & L.
Bible. Greek Testament; ed. by E. Nestle; app. on irregular verbs by R. F. Weidner. '02(Ap5) 16°, net, $1; leath., net, $1.25. Revell.
Bible. Temple ed. In 24 v. v. 2-4. '01. '02(F1); vs. 5-12 (Je28) il. sq. T. ea., net, 40 c.: flex. leath., ea., net, 60 c. Lippincott.
Bible. O. T. Cambridge Bible. Psalms. (A. F. Kirkpatrick.) '02(Ap5) 12°, net, $2. Macmillan.
Bible. Old Testament. Cambridge Bible for schools; Psalms; introd. and notes by A. F. Kirkpatrick. v. 9. bks. 4 and 5. '02 (Ja18) 12°, net, 80 c. Macmillan.
Bible Sunday-school scholars' Bible: ed. by A. F. Schauffler. '02(Je21) 12°, 55 c.; Fr. flex. mor., 75 c.; Fr. mor., $1. Nelson.
BIBLE.
Alexander. Demonic possession in the N. T. net, $1.50. Scribner.

BIBLE.—*Continued.*

Askwith. Introd. to the Thessalonian Epistles. net, $1.25. Macmillan.
Barton. Roots of Christian teaching as found in the O. T. $1.25. Winston.
Benson. Addresses on the Acts of the Apostles. net, $7. Macmillan.
Boteler. Side windows; or, lights on Scripture truths. 75 c. Standard Pub.
Brown, F., *and others, eds.* Hebrew and Eng. lexicon of the Old Testament. pt. 10. net, 50 c. Houghton, M. & Co.
Brown, W: E. Divine key of the Revelation of Jesus Christ. v. 2. $1.50. Armstrong & B.
Browne. Help to spiritual interpretation of the penitential Psalms. net, 40 c. Longmans.
Chase. Credibility of the Acts of the Apostles. $1.75. Macmillan.
Darby. Analysis of the Acts and Epistles of the N. T. 25 c. J. E. Darby.
Eadie. Biblical cyclopædia. net, $3.75. Lippincott
Florer. Biblische geschichten. 40 c. Wahr.
Goodspeed. Newberry gospels. net, 25 c. Univ. of Chic.
Grethenbach. Secular view of the Bible. net, $2. Eckler.
Harper. Constructive studies in the priestly element in the O. T. $1. Univ. of Chic.
Hoare. Evolution of the Eng. Bible. net, $2.50. Dutton.
Knecht. Child's Bible hist. 25 c. Herder.
Lilley. Pastoral epistles. net, 75 c. Scribner.
McGarvey. Authorship of the Book of Deuteronomy. $2. Standard Pub.
Mackail. Biblia innocentium; for children. $1.75. Longmans.
Nash, *ed.* Practical explanation and application of Bible history. net, $1.50. Benziger.
Patterson. Broader Bible study: Pentateuch. net, 75 c. Jacobs.
Pattison. The Bible and the 20th century. 10 c. Am. Bapt.
Prime. Power of God's word. 3 c. Presb. Bd.
Rice. Our sixty-six sacred books. net, 50 c. Am. S. S.
Robertson. Lessons on the Gospel of St. Mark. net. 40 c. Revell.
Robertson. Studies in the Acts of the Apostles. 40 c. Revell.
Ruble. Wonders of the Revelation of Jesus Christ: expository treatment of [Revelation]. $1. Standard Pub.
Shepardson. Studies in the Epistles to the Hebrews. $1.50. Revell.
Wade. Old Testament history. $1.50. Dutton.
Wilberforce. Com. on the Epistle to the Ephesians. net, $1. Herder.
Williams. Shall we understand the Bible? net, 50 c. Macmillan.
Young people's Bible stories. 4 v. ea., $1.25. Saalfield.

See also Catechisms;—Christianity;—God;—Jesus Christ;—Religion and science;—Saints;—Sermon on the Mount;—Theology.

Bible character ser. 16°, 35 c. Pepper.
—Carradine. Gideon.
Bible class handbooks. 12°, net. Scribner.
—Lilley. Pastoral epistles. 75 c.
Bible class primers. 16°, pap., net. 20 c. Scribner.
—Murison. Babylonia and Assyria.
Bible lessons for little beginners. Haven, *Mrs.* M. J. C. net, 75 c. Revell.
Bible stories. *See* Children's.
Bible student's lib. 12°. E. & J. B. Young.
—Girdlestone. Grammar of prophecy. $2.50. (11.)
Biblia innocentium. Mackail, J: W: $1.75. Longmans.

BIBLIOGRAPHIES.

Andrews. Paul Revere and his engraving. $23.50; $40. Scribner.
Annual Am. catalogue, cumulated 1900-01. $2. Pub. Weekly.
Ballagh. Slavery in Va. $1.50. Johns Hopkins.
Batt. Treatment of nature in Germ. literature. net, $1. Univ. of Chic.
Bourne. Teaching of hist. and civics. $1.50. Longmans.
Brace, *ed.* Laws of radiation and absorption. net, $1. Am. Bk.
Deems, *comp.* Holy-days and holidays. $5. Funk.
De Quincey. Selections. $1.05. Ginn.
Dickinson. Music in the hist. of the estern church. net. $2.50. Scribner.
Dyer *and* Hassall. Hist. of modern Europe. v. 6. net, $2. Macmillan
English catalogue of books for 1901. $1.50. Pub. Weekly.
Fish. Calisthenic dict. $1. Seminar.
Fitzgerald. Writings; incl. complete bibliog. 7 v. subs., ea., $6; $12.50; $35. Doubleday, P.
Fletcher *and* Bowker. Annual literary index, 1901. net, $3.50. Pub. Weekly.
Flint, *and others.* The trust. net, $1.25. Doubleday, P.
Ford, *ed.* Journals of Hugh Gaine, pr. net, $15; net, $25. Dodd.
Fowler. Hist. of ancient Greek literature. net, $1.40. Appleton.
Green. Facsimile reproductions rel. to Boston and neighborhood. net, $10. Littlefield.
Huddilston. Lessons from Gr. pottery, with bibliog. of Gr. ceramics. net, $1.25. Macmillan.
Kupfer. Greek foreshadowings of mod. metaphysical and epistemological thought. $1. J. S. Cushing.
Larned, *ed.* Literature of Am. history. net, $6; $7.50; $9. Houghton, M. & Co.
Legler. James Gates Percival. net, $1. Mequon Club.
Livingston. Bibliog. of the first ed. in book form of the works of Tennyson. $1. Dodd.
Livingston. Works of Rudyard Kipling: des. of first eds. net. $12; net, $20. Dodd.
Mackinnon. Growth and decline of French monarchy. $7.50. Longmans.
Marks. Outline of Eng. literature. $1. J. A. Marks.
Meyer. Nominating systems. net. $1.50. E. C. Meyer.

BIBLIOGRAPHIES.—*Continued.*
Miner. Daniel Boone. $1. Dibdin Club.
Nield. Guide to the best historical novels and tales. net, $1.75. Putnam.
Paulsen. Immanuel Kant. net, $2.50. Scribner.
Randall, *ed. and tr.* Expansion of gases by heat. $1. Am. Bk.
Richardson. War of 1812. subs., $3. Hist. Pub.
Schmidt. Solomon's temple. net, $1. Univ. of Chic.
Seignobos. Hist. of the Roman people. *$1.25 net. Holt.
Vanderpoel. Color problems. net, $5. Longmans.
Van Dyke. Italian painting. 50 c. Elson.
Vincent, *and others.* H. B. Adams; with bibliog. of the dept. of history, politics and economics of Johns Hopkins Univ. free to subs. Johns Hopkins.
Watkins. Diagnosis by means of the blood. $5. Physicians.
Webb, S. *and* B. P. Trade unionism. net, $2.60. Longmans.
Wilson. Bibliog. of child study. net, 25 c. Stechert.

Biblische geschichten. Florer, W. W. 40 c. Wahr.

Bicknell, P. C. Guide book of the Grand Canyon of Arizona. '02(Je28) sq. S. leath., 75 c.; pap., 50 c. Harvey.

Bilingual teaching in Belgian schools. Dawes, T. R. *50 c. net. Macmillan.

Billings, Fk., *and* Stanton, S. C., *eds.* General medicine. '01- '02(Mr8) 8°, (Practical medicine ser. of year-books, no. 1.) $1.50. Year Bk.

Billings, Josh, *pseud. See* Shaw, H: W.

Billy Burgundy's letters. '02(Jl12) il. S. †75 c. J. F. Taylor.

BIMETALLISM.
See Money.

Bingham, Grace A., *comp.* Two hundred bar examination questions '02(Je7) S. pap., $1. Commercial Press.

Binkley, Christian. Sonnets and songs for a house of days. '02(Je21) D. bds., net, $1.25. A. M. Robertson.

Biographies of famous men. 12°, $1. Donohue.
—Barrett. Abraham Lincoln.
—Benton. P. T. Barnum.
—Custis. George Washington.
—Godbey. Henry M. Stanley.
—Johnson. W. T. Sherman.
—Poore *and* Tiffany. U. S. Grant.

BIOGRAPHY.
American ser. of popular biographies. Mass. ed. $17. Graves.
Gans. Pennsylvania pioneer. $6. Kuhl.
Good. Women of the Reformed church. $1. Heidelberg.
Graham. Scottish men of letters in 18th century. net, $4.50. Macmillan.
Lippincott's biog. dict. 2 v. subs., $15; $17.50; $20. Lippincott.
National cyclopædia of Am. biography. v. 11. subs., $10. J. T. White.
Who's who, 1902. $1.75. Macmillan.
See also Authors; — Autographs; — Booksellers; — Diaries; — Genealogy; — Heroes; — History; — Painters; — Popes; — Saints.

Birbeck, Chris. J., *ed.* Select recitations, orations and dramatic scenes. '02(Je7) il. D. $1. Wagner.

Bird play. Spangler, N. Y. 15 c. Kellogg.

BIRDS.
Fowler. More tales of the birds. $1. Macmillan.
Job. Among the water fowl. net, $1.35. Doubleday, P.
Jordan, *comp.* True tales of birds and beasts. 40 c. Heath.
Lord. First book upon birds of Oregon and Washington. 75 c. W: R. Lord.
Maynard. Birds of Washington and vicinity. *$1 net. Woodward & L.
Sandys *and* Van Dyke. Upland game birds. net, $2; net, $7.50. Macmillan.
Wheelock. Nestlings of forest and marsh. net, $1.40. McClurg.
See also Pigeons.

Birrell, A. William Hazlitt. '02(Jl12) 12°, (Eng. men of letters.) **75 c. net. Macmillan.

BIRTHDAY BOOKS.
Tennyson. Birthday book. 75 c.; $1; $1.25. Warne.

Birthright membership of believers' infants. Horton, F. A. 6 c. Presb. Bd.

Bishop, Irving P. Red book of Niagara. '02 (Jl19) il. S. pap., 25 c. Wenborne-S.

Bishop, W: H: Queer people, incl. The brown stone boy. '02(My17) D. $1. Street.

Bishop, W: H: Tons of treasure. New and imp. ed. of The yellow snake. '02(Je7) D. $1. Street.

BISMARCK, *Prince* v.
Lieb. Prince Bismarck and the German people. $1.50; $2.25; $3.25. Dominion.

Bits of broken china. Fales, W: E. S. 75 c. Street.

Bivar, R. D. de. *See* Cid (The).

Bixby, Ja. T. The new world and the new thought. '02(Mr8) D. net, $1. Whittaker.

Bjorling, P. R. Pipes and tubes. '02(Je28) il. 12°, $1. Macmillan.

Black, J: S. *See* Cheyne, T: K.

BLACK, W:
Reid. William Black, novelist. net, $2.25. Harper.

Black cat club. Corrothers, J. D. net, $1. Funk.

Black Evan. Young, J. D. $1. Neely.

Blackie, J: S. On self-culture: (phonography.) '02(F15) S. pap., 35 c. Phonograph.

Blackwood's (*ed.*) philosophical classics. New ed. '01- '02(Mr1) 15 v., 12°, per v., net, 50 c. Lippincott.

Blain, Hugh M. Syntax of the verb in the Anglo-Saxon chronicle from 787 A.D. to 1001 A.D. '01- '02(Mr8) 12°, (University of Virginia monographs, school of Teutonic languages, no. 2.) pap., net, 50 c. Barnes.

Blaisdell, Alb. F. Life and health. '02(Je14) D. $1. Ginn.

Blaisdell, Etta A. *and* Ma. F. Child life fifth reader. '02(Mr29) il. 12°. net, 45 c. Macmillan.

Blake, G: H. Common sense ideas for dairymen. '01. '02(F8) 12°, $1. Coates.

Blake, Ja. V. Sonnets. '02(Ja25) sq. S. $1. J. H. West.

Blake, W: William Blake; ed. by T. S. Moore. '02(Ap26) Q. (Little engravings classical and contemporary, no. 2.) bds., net, $1.50. Longmans.

Blakiston's quiz compend ser. il. 12°, 80 c.; $1. Blakiston.
—Thayer. Compend of general pathology. (15.)

Blanchard, Amy E. Twenty little maidens. '01· '02(F15) il. 12°, $1.25. Lippincott.

Blashfield, De Witt C., *ed.* *See* New York. Abbott's digest.

Blauvelt, Ma. T. Development of cabinet government in England. '02(Mr22) 12°, net, $1.50. Macmillan.

Blazed trail. White, S. E: $1.50. McClure, P.

Bleininger, Alb., *ed.* *See* Seger, H. A:

Blighted rose. Wynne, J. F. $1.50. Angelus.

BLIND (Reading for).
Roosevelt. Message to the two houses of Congress. $1. N. Y. State Lib.

Blind spot. Watkinson, W: L. net, $1. Revell.

Bliss, W: R. September days on Nantucket. '02(Je28) D. net, $1. Houghton, M. & Co.

Blithedale romance. Hawthorne, N. $1. Burt.

Bloch, I. S. Future of war, in its technical, economic and pol. relations. [New issue.] '02(Jl19) D. 60 c. Ginn.

BLOCK ISLAND.
Livermore. Block Island. 25 c. Ball.

Block system of signalling on Am. railroads. Adams, B. B. $2. Railroad Gazette.

Blomfield, Reginald. Formal garden in England. 3d ed. '02(F1) il. 12°, $3. Macmillan.

BLOOD.
Cabot. Clinical examination of the blood. net, $3.25. Wood.
Da Costa. Clinical hematology. net, $5. Blakiston.

Blood will tell. Davenport, B: R. $1.50. Caxton Bk.

Bloomfield, Will. Transplanting an old tree. '02(Mr22) D. $1. Blanchard.

Blossom and fruit in decorative arrangement. Behrens, C. $12. Hessling.

Blouet, Paul, ["Max O'Rell."] English pharisees, French crocodiles. New issue. '01 '02(Ja4) D. $1.25. Abbey Press.

Blouët, Paul. 'Tween you an' I. pt. 1. Concerning men; pt. 2, Concerning women. '02(My24) D. $1.20. Lothrop.

BLOWPIPE.
Plattner. Qualitative and quantitative analysis with the blowpipe. net, $4. Van Nostrand.

Blue diamond. Keene. R. W. $1.50. Abbey Press.

Blum, A. R. Reduction tables for ascertaining with accuracy and rapidity freight charges for any quantity of grain on all standard bases, in Eng. money. '01· '02 (Je14) 4°, leath., net, $3. Am. Code.

Boardman, G: D. Our risen King's forty days. '02(Mr22) D. net, $1.25. Lippincott.

BOATING.
See Canoeing.

BOATS.
Martin. Album of designs for boats, launches and yachts. $1. F. W. Martin.
Mower. How to build a knockabout. $1. Rudder.
See also Yachts and yachting.

Bob o' Link. Waggaman, M. T. 40 c. Benziger

Bobbett, Wa. *See* Neidlinger, D. H.

Boccaccio, G., *and* **Aretino**, L. B. Earliest lives of Dante; fr. the Ital. by Ja. R. Smith. '01· '02(Mr15) O. (Yale studies in Eng., no. 10.) pap., 75 c. Holt.

Bodmer, G. R. Inspection of railway materials. '02(Je7) 12°, $1.50. Macmillan.

BODY AND MIND.
See Mind and body.

Body and soul. Wright, J. C. $1. J. C. Wright.

Body of Christ. Gore, C: $1.75. Scribner.

BOERS.
Davitt. Boer fight for freedom. net, $2. Funk.
Hiley *and* Hassell. Mobile Boer. $1.50. Grafton Press.
See also South Africa.

Boethius, A. M. S. Consolation of philosophy. '02(Mr22) 16°, (Temple classics.) 50 c.; leath., 75 c. Macmillan.

Bogue, *Mrs.* A. H. *See* Bell, L.

Bohn's standard lib. 12°, net, $1. Macmillan.
—Prescott. Conquest of Peru. 2 v.—Ferdinand and Isabella. 3 v.
—Swift. Prose works. v. 9.

Boiled-down booklets. Tt. 25 c. Success.
—Hungerford. Success club debater.

BOILERS.
Robertson. Water-tube boilers. $3. Van Nostrand

Boisot, L: By-laws of private corporations. 2d ed. '02(F8) O. shp., $3. Keefe-D.

BOLINGBROKE, *Lord.*
Sichel. Bolingbroke and his times. pt. 2. $4. Longmans.

Bolza, O. Concerning the geodesic curvature and the isoperimetric problem on a given surface. '02(Jl19) Q. (Univ. of Chic. decennial pub.) pap., *25 c. net. Univ. of Chic.

Bond, Paul S. *See* Hamilton, W: R.

Bonesteel, Ma. Recruit Tommy Collins. '02 (Mr22) S. 45 c. Benziger.

Book, J. W. Mollie's mistake. '02(Mr8) 16°, pap., 15 c. Herder.

BOOK ILLUSTRATION.
Brothers Dalziel: record of work, 1840-90. net, $6.50. Dutton.

Book lover. Baldwin, J. net, $1. McClurg.

BOOK OF COMMON PRAYER.
Hall. Companion to the prayer book. net, 35 c. E. & J. B. Young.
See also Protestant Epis. church.

Book of forms to be used in connection with the study of criminal procedure in the Univ. of Mich. '02(My24) O. pap., 60 c. Bliss & A.

Book of golden deeds. Yonge, C. M. $1. Burt.

Book of romantic ballads. '02(Je21) il. 16°, (Caxton ser.) net, $1.25. Scribner.

Book of secrets. Dresser, H. W. net, $1. Putnam.

Book of the rifle. Fremantle, T. F. $5. Longmans.

Book of vegetables. Wythes, G: net, $1. Lane.

BOOK-PLATES.
Stone. Women designers of book-plates. net, $1; net, $2. Beam.

BOOKBINDING.
Cockerell. Bookbinding and care of books. net, $1.20. Appleton.

BOOKKEEPING.
Goodyear. Theory of accounts. $1.50. Goodyear-M.
Ingerson. Normal method in double entry bookkeeping. 50 c. Interstate.
Snyder *and* Thurston. Universal system of prac. bookkeeping. $1.25. Am. Bk.

Booklover's lib.; ed. by H: B: Wheatley. S. Armstrong.
—Wheatley. How to make an index. $1.25; $2.50.

BOOKS AND READING.
Baldwin. Book lover: guide to best reading. net, $1. McClurg.
Hitchcock. Book-builder's handbook of types, scales, etc. net, 50 c. Grafton Press.
Right reading; choice and use of books. net, 80 c. McClurg.
See also Bookbinding;—Fiction;—Literature.

BOOKSELLERS.
Marston. Sketches of some booksellers of the time of Dr. Johnson. net, $2. Scribner.

BOONE, Dan.
Miner. Daniel Boone cont. toward a bibliog. $1. Dibdin Club.

Booth, H: M. Heavenly vision, and other sermons. Memorial ed. [New issue.] '02 (Mr22) D. net, $1. Beam.

Booth, Wa. S. *See* North Dakota. Township manual.

Boothby, Guy. Millionaire's love story. '01-'02(Mr29) D. $1.25. Buckles.

Border warfare in Pennsylvania. Shimmell, L. S. 50 c. R. L. Myers.

BORING.
Isler. Well boring for water, brine and oil. $4. Spon.

Borrow, G: The Zincali: acc. of gypsies of Spain. '01-'02(F22) il. D. $2. Putnam.

Bossard, J: Decorative paintings: designs for col. surface decoration. '01-'02(Ja25) col. pls. f°, $8. Hessling.

BOSTON.
Green. Ten facsimile reproductions rel. to old Boston and neighborhood. net, $10. Littlefield.
Historic Boston: sightseeing towns around the Hub. net, 50 c.; net, 30 c. Pilgrim Press.
Pictorial guide to Boston and the country around. 25 c. G. W. Armstrong.

Boswell, J. Journal of a tour to the Hebrides. (H. B. Cotterill.) '02(My24) 12°, (Eng. classics.) net, 60 c. Macmillan.

Bosworth, Newton, *ed.* Hochelaga depicta; early hist. and present state of the city and island of Montreal. '01-'02(Mr8) il. D. (Facsimile repr. of early Canadian books, no. 1.) net, $3; Large-pap. ed., net, $4.50. Congdon.

BOTANY.
Bower *and* Vaughan. Practical botany for beginners. net, 90 c. Macmillan.
Caldwell. Lab'y manual of botany. 60 c.; 50 c. Appleton.
Campbell. University text-book of botany. net, $4. Macmillan.

BOTANY.—*Continued.*
Cowles. Ecological rel. of vegetation on the sand dunes of Lake Michigan. net, 75 c. Univ. of Chic.
Dickson. Linear groups. net, $4. Stechert.
Frye. Development of the pollen in some asclepiadaceæ. net, 25 c. Univ. of Chic.
Ganong. Lab'y course in plant physiology, as a basis for ecology. net, $1. Holt.
Hooker. Nociones de botánica. 40 c. Appleton.
Leavitt. Outlines of botany. 2 v. $1; $1.80. Am. Bk.
Life. Tuber-like rootlets of cycas revoluta. net, 25 c. Univ. of Chic.
Lilley *and* Midgley. Studies in plant form. net, $2. Scribner.
Lyon. Study of the sporangia and gametophytes of selaginella apus and selaginella rupestris. net, 25 c. Univ. of Chic.
Macdougal. Elem. plant physiology $1.20. Longmans.
Meier. Herbarium and plant description. 70 c. Ginn.
Nelson. Analytical key to some of the common flowering plants of the Rocky Mt. region. **45 c. net. Appleton.
Overton. Parthenogenesis in thalictrum purpurascens. net, 25 c. Univ. of Chic.
Smith, R. W. Achromatic spindle in spore mother-cells of osmunda regalis. net, 25 c. Univ. of Chic.
Stevens. Gametrogenesis and fertilization in albugo. net, 25 c. Univ. of Chic.
Webb. Morphological study of the flower and embryo of spirala. *25 c. net. Univ. of Chic.
See also Algæ;—Bacteria;—Evolution;—Forests and forestry;—Galls;—Trees.

Boteler, Mattie M. Side windows. '01-'02 (Ap12) D. 75 c. Standard Pub.

BOUDE FAMILY.
See **Leach, J. G.**

Bourget, P. Monica, and other stories. '02 (Ap12) D. $1.50. Scribner.

Bourne, E: G. Essays in hist. criticism. '01-'02(F15) 8°, (Yale bicentennial pub.) net, $2. Scribner.

Bourne, E. G. *See* New Eng. Hist. Teachers' Assoc.

Bourne, G. C: Introd. to the study of comparative anatomy of animals. v. 2. '02 (Ap12) il. 12°, net, $1.25. Macmillan.

Bourne, H: E. Teaching of history and civics in the elem. and secondary school. '02 (My10) O. (Am. teachers' ser.) $1.50. Longmans.

Bouton, Eug. Spelling and word building. '02(Jl5) il. sq. D. 29 c. University.

Boutwell, G: S. Reminiscences of sixty years in public affairs. '02(Jl5) 2 v., 8°, **$5 net. McClure, P.

Bowdoin, W. G. James McNeill Whistler, the man and his work. '01-'02(F8) O. bds., net, $1.50. Beam.

Bowen, B. L. First scientific French reader. '02(Je14) D. (Modern lang. ser.) 90 c. Heath.

Bowen, W: A. Why two Episcopal Methodist churches in the U. S.? '01-'02(Mr15) S. 75 c Pub. Ho. M. E. Ch., So.

Bower, F. O., *and* Vaughan, D. T. G. Practical botany for beginners. '02(My24) 12°, net, 90 c. Macmillan.

Bowhill, T: Manual of bacteriological technique and special bacteriology. 2d ed. '02 (Jl12) 8°, $4.50. Wood.
Bowker, Alfr. King Alfred millenary. '02 (Jl12) il. 8°, $3. Macmillan.
Bowker, R: R. *See* Fletcher, W: I:
Boyden, H: P. Beginnings of the Cincinnati Southern railway, 1869-1878. '01. '02(F8) 8°, pap., 50 c. Clarke.
Boyle, *Sir* Courtenay. *See* Avebury, *Lord.*
Boyle, F: Woodland orchids. '02(Ja18) 4°, net, $7. Macmillan.
Boys' vacation ser. S. 75 c. Neely.
—Whittier. In the Michigan lumber camps.
Brace, D. B., *ed.* Laws of radiation and absorption. '01. '02(Ja11.) O. (Scientific memoirs, no. 15.) $1. Am. Bk.
Bradbury, Ht. B. The new philosophy of health. [New issue.] '02(Mr22) 16°, 75 c. Alliance.
Braddon, Ma. E. *See* Maxwell, *Mrs.* M. E. B.
Bradish, Sa. P. Stories of country life. '01. '02(Ja4) S. (Eclectic school readings.) 40 c. Am. Bk.
Bradley, C: *See* Bradley, J. P.
Bradley, Jos. P. Miscellaneous writings; with sketch of his life; ed. and comp. by C: Bradley. '02(Ap5) 8°, $3. Hardham.
Bradner, G: W. New practice in supplementary proceedings. 2d ed. '02(Jl5) O. $4. W. C. Little.
Brady, Cyrus T. Hohenzollern. '02(Ap12) il. D. $1.50. Century Co
Brady, Cyrus T. Quiberon touch. '01. '02 (F22) 12°, $1.50. Appleton
Brain, Belle M. Fifty missionary programmes. '02(F1) S. 35 c. Un. Soc. C. E.
BRAIN.
Fuller. Architecture of the brain. net, $3.50. Fuller
See also Insanity; — Mind and body; — Nervous system;—Phrenology.
Bramble brae. Bridges, R. net, $1.25. Scribner
BRAMSHOTT, ENG.
See Hampshire.
Brand, N. F. Justices' code for the state of Washington. '02(F15) O. shp., $5. Bancroft-W
Brandes, G: Main currents in nineteenth century literature. v. 2. '02(My17) 8°, net. $2.75. Macmillan.
Brassey, T: A., *Baron, ed.* Naval annual for 1902. '02(Je21) 8°, net, $7.50. Scribner.
Bread and wine. King, M. E. $1.25. Houghton, M. & Co.
Breaking and riding. Fillis, J. net, $5. Scribner.
BREATHING.
Semon. Principles of local treatment in diseases of the upper air passages. net, $1. Macmillan.
Breaux, Jos. A. *See* Louisiana. *Sup. ct.* Digest.
Brenton, Hilda. Uncle Jed's country letters. '02(Je7) il. D. 30 c. Dickerman.
Breviarium bothanum sive portiforium secundum usum ecclesiæ cujusdam in Scotia; 1900. '02(F8) 4°, $15. Longmans.
Brewer, D: J. American citizenship. '02 (Ap19) D. net, 75 c. Scribner.
Brewster, Lyman D. *See* Ames, J. B.
Bride of Messina. *See* Schiller, J. C. F. v.
Bride's book. Cook, *Mrs.* E. T. net, $1.50. Dutton.
Bridge, Ja. H., *ed.* *See* Flint, C: R.
Bridge, Norman. Rewards of taste, and other essays. '02(Ap5) D. $1.50. H. S. Stone.
BRIDGE.
Dunn. New ideas on bridge. 50 c. Scribner.
Elwell. Bridge; its principles and rules of play. net, $1.25. Scribner.
Smith, C. Bridge condensed. 50 c. Scribner.
Steele. Simple rules for bridge. 50 c. Eichelberger.
Bridgeman, T: Flower gardening. '01. '02 (F8) il. 12°, 50 c. Coates.
Bridgeman, T: Fruit gardening. '01. '02 (F8) il. 12°, 50 c. Coates.
Bridgeman, T: Kitchen gardening. '01. '02 (F8) il. 12°, 50 c. Coates.
Bridges, Rob., ["Droch."] Bramble brae. '02(Mr22) D. net, $1.25. Scribner.
BRIDGES.
Merriman *and* Jacoby. Text-book on roofs and bridges. pt. 3, Bridge design. $2.50. Wiley.
Bridgman, L. J. Gulliver's bird book. '02 (Mr29) il. 4°, $1.50. L. C. Page.
Brigham, Alb. P. *See* Gilbert, G. K.
Bright days in merrie England. Honeyman, A. V. net, $1.50. Honeyman.
Brinckley, W: J. Physiology by the laboratory method. '02(Jl5) 8°, $.25. Ainsworth.
BRINGHURST FAMILY.
Leach. Hist. of the Bringhurst family. $5. Lippincott.
Brinkley, Fk. Japan; its history, arts and literature. 4 v. '02(Ap5); v. 5 (Je28) 8°, (Oriental ser.) per v., $50. Millet.
Brinton, Dan. G. Basis of social relations. '02(Mr22) 8°, (Science ser., v. 10.) net, $1.50. Putnam.
Brinton Eliot. Farmer, J. E. $1.50. Macmillan.
Britain and the British seas. Mackinder, H. J. $2. Appleton.
British-Am. guide to Carlsbad. Arany, S. A. 50 c. Abbey Press.
British vegetable galls. Connold, E: J. net, $4. Dutton.
Britton; Eng. tr. and notes by F. M. Nichols. '01. '02(Mr1) 12°, (Legal classic ser.) shp., $3. Byrne.
Broader Bible study. Patterson, A. net, 75 c. Jacobs.
Bronson, Wa. H., *ed.* *See* Ritchie, M. G.
Brooklyn *Daily Eagle* almanac, 1902. '02 (Ja11) 8°, (Eagle lib.) 50 c.; pap., 25 c. Brooklyn Eagle.
Brooklyn Eagle lib. Q. pap. Brooklyn Eagle.
—Lodge, *and others.* The U. S. and the Philippine Islands. 10 c. (v. 17, 9.)
—New York City. Tenement house law. 10 c. (v. 17, 3.)
Brooks, E: Normal elem. algebra: pt. 1. Rev. ed. '01. '02(Jl12) 12°. 83 c. Sower.
Brooks, H. J. Elements of mind. '02(Je7) O. $4. Longmans.
Brooks, H: *See* Dame, L. L.
Brooks, H: S. Progression to immortality. '02(Je7) D. net, 50 c. Wessels.
Brooks, Hildegard. Master of Caxton. '02 (Ap12) D. $1.50. Scribner.

Brooks, J: A., *rep.* *See* Michigan. *Sup. ct.* Repts.

Brooks, Phillips. Law of growth, and other sermons. '02(Mr29) 12°, net, $1.20. Dutton.

Brooks, S. J., *comp.* *See* Texas. Conflicting civil cases;—Repts.

BROOKS.
Miller. Brook book. net, $1.35. Doubleday, P.

Broome, I: Last days of the Ruskin Cooperative Association. '02(Jl19) 16°, (Standard socialist ser.) 50 c. Kerr.

Brothers Dalziel (The). Record of their work in connection with distinguished artists, 1840-1890. '02(Ap5) il. 4°, vellum, net, $6.50. Dutton.

Brounoff, Platon G. *See* Sharp, B. A.

Brower, Dan. R., *and* Bannister, H: M. Practical manual of insanity. '02(Mr29) 8°, $2. Saunders.

Brown, Abbie F. In the days of giants: Norse tales. '02My3) il. D. net, $1.15. Houghton, M. & Co.

Brown, C: F., *and* Croft, V. E. Outline study of U. S. hist. '01· '02(Je14) 16°, vellum, 50 c. Courier. Pr.

Brown, C: W. American star speaker and model elocutionist. '02(My17) il. 12°, $1.50. Donohue.

Brown, C: W. Ethan Allen. '02(My17) 12°, $1. Donohue.

Brown, C: W. John Paul Jones of naval fame. '02(Je28) D. (Am. patriot ser.) $1. Donohue.

Brown, C: W., *comp.* Comic recitations and readings. '02(My17) 12°, 50 c.; pap., 25 c. Donohue.

Brown, C: W., *comp.* Patriotic recitations and readings. '02(My17) 12°, 50 c.; pap., 25 c. Donohue.

Brown, Christian H:, *comp.* Optician's manual. v. 1 and 2. '02(Je28) il. 12°, ea., $2. Keystone.

Brown, D: W. Science and art of phrasemaking; designed to teach stenographic phrasing by principle. '02(Ap5) 12°, $1.50. Shorthand Bu.

BROWN, Ford M.
Rossetti. Ford Madox Brown. net, 35 c. Beam.

Brown, Fs., Driver, S: R., *and* Briggs, C: A., *eds.* Hebrew and Eng. lexicon of the Old Testament. pt. 10. '02(Mr22) 8°, pap., net, 50 c. Houghton, M. & Co.

Brown, Grace M., ["Ione."] Studies in spiritual harmony. '02(Mr22) sq. S. $1. Reed.

Brown, J: Rab and his friends, and other dog stories; ed. by C: W. French. '02 (Je14) il. (Canterbury classics.) 25 c. Rand, McN. & Co.

BROWN, J:
Hugo. John Brown: a petition in behalf of the hero of Harper's Ferry. $5; $15. Alwil Shop.

Brown, P. H. History of Scotland. v. 2 '02(Ap26) 12°, (Cambridge hist. ser.) net, $1.50. Macmillan.

Brown, W: B. Gospel of the kingdom and the gospel of the church. '01(F8) D. $1. Whittaker.

Brown, W: E. Divine key of the Revelation of Jesus Christ. In 2 v. v. 2. '02(Jl12) il. 12°, $1.50. Armstrong & B.

Brown, W: G. Golf. '02(Jl5) S. **50 c. net. Houghton, M. & Co.

Brown, W: G. The lower South in Am. history. '02(My24) 12°, net, $1.50. Macmillan.

Brown, W: G. Stephen Arnold Douglas. '02(Mr29) S. (Riverside biog. ser., no. 13.) net, 65 c.; School ed., net, 50 c. Houghton, M. & Co.

Brown, W: N., *ed.* Workshop wrinkles for decorators, painters and others. '01. '02 (My10) D. net, $1. Van Nostrand.

Browne, *Mrs.* A. B. B. Help to the spiritual interpretation of the penitential Psalms. '02 (Ap19) D. net, 40 c. Longmans.

Browne, D: McM. How to tell the time of night by the stars. '01· '02(Ap12) 8°, 50 c. Lee & S.

Browne, Fk. J. Graded mental arithmetic. '02(Je7) sq. 16°, net, 30 c. Whitaker & R.

Browne, Gordon. Proverbial sayings. '01· '02(F15) il. 4°, bds., net, $1. Stokes.

Browne, Wa. S. Rose of the wilderness. '01· '02(Mr1) il. D. $1.25. W. S. Browne.

Browne, *Sir* T: Religio medici, Urn burial, Christian morals and other essays; ed. by C. J. Holmes. '02(Jl12) 8°, (Vale Press ser.) **$12 net. Lane.

Brownies (The) *See* Ewing, *Mrs.* J. H.

Browning, Rob. Sordello; ed. by H. B. Forman. '02(Jl12) 16°, (Temple classics.) 50 c.; flex. leath., 75 c. Macmillan.

Bruce, W. S. Formation of Christian character. '02(My10) 12°, net, $1.75. Scribner.

Brugnot, Alice G. T. *See* Baillot, E. P.

Brühl, Gustav, *and* Politzer, A. Atlas epitome of otology. '02(Ap26) il. 12°, net, $3. Saunders.

Bruno. Dewey, B. S. 50 c. Little, B. & Co.

Brunton, *Sir* Lauder. On disorders of assimilation, digestion, etc. '01· '02(Ja4) il. 8°, net, $4; *Same*, (Ap12) hf. mor., net, $5. Macmillan.

Bryce, Alex. Ideal health and how to attain it. '01· '02(Mr1) 12°, pap., 50 c. Treat.

Bubbles. Newberry, F. E. $1. Burt.

Bubier, E: T. A B C of wireless telegraphy. '02(Je21) S. $1. Bubier.

Bubier, E: T. Experimental electricity. New rev. and enl. ed. '02(Je14) il. 16°, $1. Bubier.

Bubier, E: T. How to build dynamo-electric machinery. 2d ed. '02(Je14) il. 8°, $2.50. Bubier.

Buck, A. H. A reference handbook of the medical sciences. New ed., rev. and rewritten. v. 4. '02(Ap12) il. 8°, subs., $7; leath., $8; mor., $9. Wood.

Budd, J. L. *and* Hanson, N. E. Am. horticultural manual. '02(My17) 12°, $1.50. Wiley.

Budd, Jos. H. Civil remedies under the code system. '02(Ap12) O. shp., $6. Palm.

Buell Hampton. Emerson, W. G: $1.50. Forbes.

BUILDING.
See **Architecture;—Engineering.**

BULBS.
Arnott. Book of bulbs. net, $1. Lane.

Bulkley, L. D. *See* Duhring, L: A.

Bullen, Fk. T. Deep-sea plunderings. '02 (My19) il. D. $1.50. Appleton.

Bülow-Wendhausen, *Baroness v.* Life of the Baroness von Marenholtz Bülow. '01. '02 (Ja4) 2 v., O. net, $3.50. W: B. Harison.

BULOW, *Baroness* von Marenholtz.
Bulow-Wendhausen. Life of Baroness von Marenholtz Bülow. 2 v., net, $3.50. W: B. Harison.

Bunge, G. Text-book of physiolog. and patholog. chemistry. 2d Eng. ed.; ed. by E. H. Starling. '02(Jl12) 8°, *$3 net. Blakiston.

BUNKER HILL.
Heath. Memoirs; [also] accounts of the Battle of Bunker Hill, by Gens. Dearborn, Lee and Wilkinson. net, $5. Abbatt.

Bunt and Bill. Mulholland, C. 45 c. Benziger.

Bunyan, J: The holy war. '01(Mr1) 16°, 50 c.; leath., 75 c. Macmillan.

Bunyan, J: Pilgrim's progress. '01· '02 (Ja11) 2 v., il. 16°, (Caxton ser.) flex. lambskin, net, $2.40. Scribner.

Bunzey, Rufus S. Hist. of companies I and E, Sixth regt., Ill. vol. infantry from Whiteside co. '02(Jl12) il. 12°, $2. R. S. Bunzey.

Burdens of local taxation. Purdy, L. 25 c. Public Policy

Burdick, Alfr. S. Standard medical manual. '01. '02(Mr8) 8°, $4. Engelhard.

Burgert, Celia M. *See* Skinner, W. H.

Burgess, J: W. Reconstruction and the constitution, 1866-1876. '02(Mr22) D. (Am. hist. ser.) net, $1. Scribner.

Burghard, F. F. *See* Cheyne, W: W.

Buried temple. Maeterlinck. M. net, $1.40. Dodd.

Burke, Bridget E. McBride literature and art books. bks. 1-3. '01. '02(Mr22) il. 12°, bk. 1, 25 c.; bk. 2, 30 c.; bk. 3, 35 c. McBride.

Burke, Edm. Works. Beaconsfield ed. In 12 v., v. 1-4. '01· '02(F15) 8°, subs., per v., net, $3.50. Little, B. & Co.

Burke, Edm. Thoughts on the cause of the present discontents; ed. by F. G. Selby. '02(Je28) 12°, net, 60 c. Macmillan.

Burks, Martin P. *See* Virginia. *Sup. ct. of appeals.* Repts.

BURMA.
Smith. Ten years in Burma. net, $1. Eaton & M.; Jennings.

Burnett, *Mrs.* Fes. H. Methods of Lady Walderhurst. '02(F22) il. D. $1.25. Stokes.

Burnett, J. C. New cure for consumption by its own virus. 4th ed. 1900. '02(Ap5) 12°, $1. Boericke & T.

Burnham, Clara L. A great love. '02(Ap5) 16°, (Riverside pap. ser., no. 94.) pap., 50 c. Houghton, M. & Co.

Burns, Harrison. *See* Indiana. Statutes.

Burns, R. Complete poems and songs. (T: Carlyle.) '02(Mr8) 16°, (Caxton ser.) net, $1.20. Scribner.

Burns, R. Complete poetical works. Pocket ed. '02(My17) 12°, (New century lib.) $1.25; limp. leath., $1.75. Nelson.

Burns, R. Poems, epistles, songs, epigrams, and epitaphs; ed. by J. A. Manson. '02 (F1) 12°, net, $1; flex. leath., net, $1.50. Macmillan.

BURR, A.
Jenkinson. Aaron Burr, his rel. with Thos. Jefferson and Alex. Hamilton. $1.25. I: Jenkinson.
Todd. True Aaron Burr. net, 50 c. Barnes.

Burr, Enoch F. Aleph the Chaldean. [New issue.] '02(Ap12) 12°, $1.25. Whittaker.

BURR, Esther.
Rankin. Esther Burr's journal. 75 c. Howard Univ.

Burrow, C: K. Patricia of the hills. '02 (Mr8) D. net, $1.20. Putnam.

Burt, Ma. E., *and* Howells, Mildred. Literary primer. '01· '02(Mr15) 16°, bds., net, 30 c. Scribner.

Burton, E. D., *and* Mathews, S. Constructive studies in the life of Christ. '02(F15) 8°, $1. Univ. of Chic.

Burton, Elias. *See* Holmes, B.

Burton, R: Forces in fiction, and other essays. '02(Ap26) D. net, $1. Bowen-M.

Burton, Thdr. E. Financial crises and period of industrial and commercial depression. '02(Mr1) D. net, $1.40. Appleton.

Burton Holmes lectures. *See* Holmes, B.

Burt's fairy lib. il. 12°, $1. Burt.
—Valentine, *comp. and ed.* Old, old fairy tales.
—Yeats, *comp. and ed.* Irish fairy and folk tales.

Burt's fireside ser. il. 12°, $1. Burt.
—Armstrong. Very odd girl.
—Conklin. Bek's first corner.—Growing up.—Miss Prudence.—Tessa Wadsworth's discipline.
—Le Row. Duxbury doings.
—Newberry. Bubbles.—Joyce's investments.—Sara.
—Robbins. Miss Ashton's new pupil.
—Rouse. Annice Wynkoop, artist.—Deane girls.
—Smith. Daddy's girl.—Very naughty girl.

Burt's home lib. il. 12°, $1. Burt.
—Addison. Essays.
—Arnold. Essays in criticism.
—Barrie. Little minister.
—Chesterfield. Letters, sentences, and maxims.
—Elizabeth and her German garden.
—Emerson. Nature.
—Emerson. Representative men.
—Harris. Rutledge.
—Hawthorne. Blithedale romance.—Marble faun.
—Headley. Napoleon and his marshals.—Washington and his generals.
—Holley. Samantha at Saratoga.
—Holmes. Cousin Maude and Rosamond.
—Ingraham. Throne of David.
—Johnson. Rasselas.
—Kingsley. Alton Locke.—Hereward the Wake.
—Le Sage. Gil Blas.
—Longfellow. Hyperion.—Outre mer.
—Lubbock. Pleasures of life.
—Macaulay. Literary essays.
—Macdonald. David Elginbrod.
—Maggie Miller.
—Malory. King Arthur.
—More. Utopia.
—Parkman. Conspiracy of Pontiac.
—Pater. Marius the epicurean.

Burt's home lib.—Continued.
—Plato. Republic.
—Poe. Murders in the Rue Morgue.
—Rénan. Life of Jesus.
—Saint-Pierre. Paul and Virginia.
—Stowe. Minister's wooing.
—Taylor. Views afoot.
—Thoreau. Walden.
—Webster. Speeches.
—Yonge. Book of golden deeds.
Burt's little women ser. il. 12°, 75 c. Burt.
—Prentiss. Little Susy stories.
Burt's Manhattan lib. of new copyright fiction. 12°, pap., 50 c. Burt.
—Sergeant. Master of Beechwood.
Burt's St. Nicholas ser. il. 12°, 75 c. Burt.
—Kaler. Wan Lun and Dandy.
—Molesworth. Grandmother dear.
—Newberry. Comrades.
—Prentiss. Six little princesses.
—Weber. Clock on the stairs.
Bury, J: B. Hist. of Greece to the death of Alex. the Great. '02(My17) 2 v., 8°, net, $8. Macmillan.
BUSINESS.
Avebury, *and others*. King's weigh-house: lectures to business men. 75 c. Macmillan.
Carnegie. Empire of business. subs., $3. Doubleday, P.
McMaster. Commercial digest and business forms. $6. Commercial Bk.
Perry. Legal adviser and business guide. $1.50. Pontiac.
Pitman, B. *and* Howard. Business letters. no. 1, 25 c. Phonograph.
Pitman, I: Business corr. in shorthand. no. 2, 30 c. Pitman.
See also Advertising;—Commerce;—Commercial law; — Finance; — Political economy; — Stock exchange.
BUSINESS EDUCATION.
Stevens. Business education. 15 c. Bardeen.
See also Bookkeeping.
"But Thy love and Thy grace." Finn, F. J. $1. Benziger.
Butler, C: H: Treaty-making power of the U. S. In 2 v. '02(Ap5) O. hf. shp., (complete work,) net, $12. Banks.
BUTLER FAMILY.
Rook. The Butler family. $3. Lakeside Press.
By the gray sea. '02(Mr8) 8°, net, 60 c. Herder.
Bylow Hill. Cable, G: W. $1.25. Scribner.
Byrd, W: Writings of "Col. William Byrd of Westover in Virginia, Esq."; ed. by J. S. Bassett. '02(Mr8) il. f°, net, $10. Doubleday, P.
Byron, G: G. N., *Lord*. Works. Ed. de luxe. v. 13-16. '02(Mr15) 8°. (App. to pubs. for price.) Niccolls.
Byron, G: G. N., *Lord*. Works. New rev., enl. ed. In 12 v. v. 11. '02(Ap12) 12°, $2. Scribner.
Bywater, B. Two thousand years in eternity. '01. '02(Je21) 8°, net, $2.15. Hudson-K.
C., *pseud.* *See* Cox, *Mrs.* J. F.
Caballero, Fernán. La familia de Alvareda. (P. B. Burnet.) '01. '02(Mr15) S. 75 c. Holt
Cable, G: W. Bylow Hill. '02(Je7) D. $1.25 Scribner.
Cabot, R: C. Guide to the clinical examination of the blood. 4th rev. ed. '01. '02 (F22) il. 8°, net, $3.25. Wood.
Cadigan, E. S. My ocean trip. '02(Je28) il. 12°, $1. Brentano's.
Cadiot, P. J. Clinical veterinary medicine and surgery. '01. '02(F22) il. 8°, $5.25. W: R. Jenkins.
Cadwallader, Starr. Story of home gardens. '02(Mr22) O. pap., 25 c. Home Gardening.
Cady, Ma. R., *and* Dewey, Julia M. Art reader no. 1. '02(Jl5) il. 16°, 35 c. Richardson, S.
CAEDMON, *St.*
Gaskin. Caedmon, the first Eng. poet. 40 c. E. & J. B. Young.
Caesar. Commentaries on the Gallic war; vocab. by A. Harkness, assisted by C: H. Forbes. '02(F15) il. D. hf. leath., $1.25. Am. Bk.
CAESARS (The).
Van Santvoord. House of Cæsar and the imperial disease. net, $5.25. Pafraets.
Caffin, C: H. American masters of painting. '02(Ap5) D. net, $1.25. Doubleday, P.
Cain's sin. Belles, W: H: $1. W: H: Belles.
CAIRO.
Poole. Story of Cairo. $2; $2.50. Macmillan.
CALCULUS.
Bass. Elements of differential calculus. net, $4. Wiley.
Durège. Elements of the theory of functions of a complex variable. net, $2. Macmillan.
Smith. Elem. calculus. $1.25. Am. Bk.
Caldwell, Otis W: Laboratory manual of botany. '02(Je28) 12°, (Twentieth century text-books.) 60 c.; limp cl., 50 c. Appleton.
CALENDARS AND YEAR-BOOKS.
Daily praise. 15 c.; 20 c.; 25 c. Revell.
Epworth League yearbook, 1902. net, 10 c. Eaton & M.
See also Almanacs and annuals;—Devotional exercises and meditations.
Calhoun, W: P. The Caucasian and the negro in the U. S. '02(Je28) D. pap., 75 c. R. L. Bryan.
California. Code time table; by J. H. Kann. '02(Ap19) D. $1.50; interleaved, $2. Dempster.
California. Constitution; annot. by E: F. Treadwell. '02(F1) S. shp., $4. Bancroft-W.
California. *Superior ct.* Repts. (E. Tauszky.) '02(Ap12) 2 v., O. shp., ea., $5. Dempster
California. *Supreme ct.* Repts. v. 133, 134: '02(Jl5); v. 135 (Jl19) O. shp., ea., $3. Bancroft-W.
CALIFORNIA.
Hershey. Quaternary of So. Cal. 20 c. Univ. of Cal.
Hufford. El camino real: orig. highway connecting the 21 missions. 35 c.; 75 c.; $1; $1.25. D: A. Hufford.
Stoddard. In the footprints of the padres. net, $1.50. A. M. Robertson.
See also Fresno Co.
CALISTHENICS.
See Gymnastics.
Callahan, C. E. **Fogg's ferry.** '02(Mr15) il. D. 75 c.; pap., 25 c. Laird.

Calmerton, Gail, *and* **Wheeler,** W: H: First reader. '02(Mr22) il. sq. 12°, (Graded readers.) 30 c. W: H: Wheeler.

CALVÉ, Emma.
Wisner. Emma Calvé. $1.50. Russell.

Calvin, Emily R. A Jewish carol and The insuperable barrier. '02(Je7) D. bds., 75 c. Westminster Pub.

Cambridge encyclopædia of esoteric subjects. Demorest, A. F. v. 3. net, $3. Cambridge.

Cambridge historical ser.; ed. by G: W. Prothero. 12°, net. Macmillan.
—Brown. Hist. of Scotland. v. 2. $1.50.

Cambridge natural history. *See* Harmer, S. F:, *ed.*

Cambridge Univ. Press ser. 12°. Macmillan.
—Æschylus. The choephori. $3.25.
—Aristophanes. The knights. net, $2.50.
—Dawes. Bilingual teaching in Belgian schools. *50 c. net.
—De Montmorency. State intervention in Eng. education. $1.50.
—Forsyth. Differential equations. v. 4. $3.75.
—Glover. Life and letters in the 4th century. net, $3.25.
—Kenny. Outlines of criminal law. *$2.50 net.
—Laurie. Training of teachers. $1.50.
—Maitland, *and others.* Teaching of history. 75 c.
—Mayor. Chapters on Eng. metre. net, $2.25.
—Stokes. Mathematical and physical papers. v. 3. $3.75.
—Stokes *and* Strachan. Thesaurus palæo hibernicus. v. 1. net, $8.
—Strutt. Scientific papers. v. 3. $5.

Cameron, J. H. Elements of French composition. '01- '02(Ja4) D. 75 c. Holt.

Cameron, V. L. Three sailor boys. '02(My17) 12°, 60 c. Nelson.

Camino (El) real. Hufford, D: A. 35 c.; 75 c.; $1; $1.25. D: A. Hufford.

Camm, Bede. A Benedictine martyr in England: life and times of Dom John Roberts. '02(Mr8) 8°, net, $1.25. Herder.

Campbell, Colin P. *See* Michigan. *Sup. ct.* Index digest.

Campbell, Douglas H. University text-book of botany. '02(My3) 8°, net, $4. Macmillan.

Campbell, Hardy W. Soil culture manual, 1902. '02(My17) il. D. pap., 40 c. H. W. Campbell.

Campbell, Hollis A., Sharpe, W: C., *and* Bassett, Fk. J. Seymour, past and present. '02(Je14) il. 8°, $3. W: C. Sharpe.

Campbell, J. G. D. Siam in the twentieth century. '02(Je7) il. O. net, $5. Longmans.

Campbell, W: C. A Colorado colonel, and other sketches. '01- '02(F8) il. D. $1.50. Crane.

CANADA.
Henry. Travels in Canada, 1760-1776. $4. Little, B. & Co.
Jesuit relations. v. 72, 73. ea., $3.50. Burrows.
Morang's annual register of Canadian affairs, 1901. $3; $4. Morang.
See also Indians;—Montreal.

Canadian books. *See* Bosworth, N.

CANALS.
Johnson. Isthmian canal. 25 c. Am. Acad. Pol. Sci.
Pasco. Isthmian canal question. 25 c. Am. Acad. Pol. Sci.

CANDY.
See Confectionery.

Cane basket work. *See* Firth, A.

Canfield, Ja. H. The college student and his problems. '02(F1) 12°, (Personal problem ser.) net, $1. Macmillan.

CANOEING.
Thwaites. Down historic waterways. net, $1.20. McClurg.

Canterbury classics. il., 25 c. Rand, McN. & Co.
—Brown. Rab and his friends.

Cape Cod ballads. Lincoln, J. C. net, $1.25. Brandt.

Capes, W. W. Scenes of rural life in Hampshire among the manors of Bramshott. '02(Ja18) 8°, net, $2.75. Macmillan.

CAPITAL AND LABOR.
Kropotkin. Fields, factories and workshops. net, 90 c. Putnam.
Labor and capital. $1.50. Putnam.
Lafarque. Religion of capital. 10 c. Socialistic Co-op.
Marx. Wage-labor and capital. 50 c. N. Y. Labor News.
See also Labor and laboring classes;—Trusts.

Captain Fanny. Russell, W: C. $1.25; 50 c. New Amsterdam.

Captain Jinks, hero. Crosby, E. $1.50. Funk.

Captain Jinks of the Horse marines. Fitch, W: C. $1.25. Doubleday, P.

Captain of the Grayhorse troop. Garland, H. $1.50. Harper.

Card sewing. Maxwell, L. H. 50 c. M. Bradley

CARDS.
Hart. Card language, 20 c. R. M. Hart.
Hart. Card language. 20 c. McEnally.
Roterberg. Card tricks. 25 c. Drake.
See also Bridge;—Fortune-telling;—Whist.

Careless Jane. Pyle, K. net, 75 c.. Dutton.

Carey, W: Adventures in Tibet; incl. diary of Miss A. R. Taylor's journey from Ta-Chien Su through the forbidden land. '02 (Ja25) il. O. net, $1.50. Un. Soc. C. E.

Carey, Wymond. Monsieur Martin. '02 (Mr22) D. net, $1.20. Putnam.

Carhart, H: S., *and* Chute, H. N. Physics for high school students. '02(Ap26) il. 12°, $1.25. Allyn & B.

CARLSBAD.
Arany. British-Am. guide to Carlsbad. 50 c. Abbey Press.

Carlyle, T: Past and present; ed. by O. Smeaton. '02(My24) 16°, (Temple classics.) 50 c.; flex. leath., 75 c. Macmillan.

Carman, Bliss. Ode on the coronation of King Edward. '02(Je14) 4°, net, $1. L. C. Page.

Carmichael, M. In Tuscany. New ed. '02 (Ap5) 12°. net, $2. Dutton.

Carmichael, M. Life of John William Walshe, T.S.A. [novel.] '02(Je14) 8°, net, $2. Dutton.

Carnegie, And. Empire of business. '02 (Ap19) O. subs., $3. Doubleday, P.

CAROLINE, *Queen of England.*
Wilkins. Caroline the illustrious Queen-Consort of George II. 2 v. $12. Longmans.
Carpenter, E:, *ed.* Iolāus: anthology of friendship. '02(Je14) sq. D. silk, net, $1.75. Goodspeed.
Carpenter, F. G. Europe. '02(Ap12) il. D. (Geographical readers.) 70 c. Am. Bk.
Carpenter, Stephen H. *See* Chaucer, G.
Carpenter prophet. Pearson, C: W. $1.50. H. S. Stone.
Carradine, Beverly. Gideon. '02(My24) 16°, (Bible character ser.) 35 c. Pepper.
Carroll, C: Unpublished letters of Charles Carroll of Carrollton, and of his father, Charles Carroll of Doughoregan; comp. and ed. by T: M. Field. '02(Jl12) O. (United States Cath. Hist. Soc., monograph ser. no. 1.) pap. (not for sale.) U. S. Cath.
Carroll, Stella W. Around the world; third book, home geography. '02(Mr22) il. 12°, (Geographical ser.) 60 c. Morse.
CARS.
Thompson. The motor car. $1. Warne.
CARSON, Kit.
Abbott. Christopher Carson, known as Kit. net, 87 c. Dodd.
Carson, W: H: The fool. '02(Je7) il. D. $1.50. G: W. Dillingham.
Carson, W: H: Hester Blair. '02(Mr1) il. D. $1.50. C. M. Clark.
Carter, Ernest. *See* Atkinson, R. W.
Carter, Eva N. Gleanings from nature. '02 (Ap26) il. D. $1. Abbey Press.
Carter, P: Peter Carter, 1825-1900. '01· '02 (F8) 8°, n. p. Privately pr.
CARVING.
See Ivory.
Cary, G: H. How to make and use the telephone. New rev. 2d ed. '02(Je14) il. 16°, $1. Bubier.
CASAS, Bartolomé de las.
Dutto. Life of Bartolomé de las Casas. net, $1.50. Herder.
Case, E. C. Palæontological notes. '02(Jl5) 8°, (Cont. from Walker Museum, v. 1, no. 3.) pap., *25 c. net. Univ. of Chic.
Casgrain, W: T. *See* Noble, A.
Caskoden, Edwin, *pseud.* *See* Major, C:
Cassock of the pines. Daley, J. G. $1. W: H. Young.
Cast iron. Keep, W: J. $2.50. Wiley.
Castlemon, Harry, [*pseud.* for C: Austin Fosdick.] Floating treasure. '01. '02(Ja25) il. D. $1. Coates.
Castles in Spain. Stoner, W. S. $1. Abbey Press.
CAT.
Neel. Cats, how to care for them. 50 c. Boericke & T.
Hill. Diseases of the cat. $1.25. W: R. Jenkins.
CATALOGUING.
Hasse, *comp.* U. S. Government pubs.; handbk. for cataloguer. pt. 1. $1. Lib. Bu.
CATECHISMS.
Färber. Commentar zum (Catholic) katechismus. net, $1.50. Herder.
Macdonald, *ed.* Rev. catechism (Westminster Assembly's "shorter catechism.") $1.25. Macmillan.

CATECHISMS.—*Continued.*
Mangasarian. New catechism. 75 c. Open Court.
Nash, *ed.* Explanation and application of Bible history. [Questions and answers.] net, $1.50. Benziger.
Scadding. Direct answers to plain questions for Am. churchmen: expansion of the church catechism. net, 50 c. Whittaker
Staebler. Manual on the Book of books for juniors. 20 c. Mattill & L.
Cathcart, Ja. L. Tripoli; first war with the U. S.; letter book by J. L. Cathcart, first consul to Tripoli. '01· '02(Mr29) 12°, $4. J. B. C. Newkirk.
CATHEDRALS.
Addis. Cathedrals and abbeys of Presb. Scotland. net, $2.50. Presb. Bd.
See also Amiens;—Church architecture;—Westminster Abbey.
Catherine. *See* Thackeray, W: M.
Catherwood, *Mrs.* Ma. H. Craque o' Doom. '02(Je28) 12°, (People's lib., no. 30.) pap., 50 c. Am. News.
Catherwood, *Mrs.* Ma. H. Craque o' Doom. [New issue.] '02(Jl5) il. D. $1.50. Street.
Catherwood, *Mrs.* Ma. H. Story of Tonty. 6th ed. enl. '01· '02(F1) il. D. $1.25. McClurg.
Catholic (The). '02(My10) 12°, $1.50. Lane.
Catholic church from within. '01· '02(Ja4) O. $2.50. Longmans.
Catholic church. Instructions and prayers for Catholic youth. '01· '02(Ja18) il. Tt. 60 c. Benziger.
Catholic Church. Litanei zum heiligsten Herzen Jesu. '02(Je28) 32°, pap., net, 3 c. Herder.
Catholic Church. Priests' new ritual. [In Latin and Eng.;] by J: Murphy. '02(Ap19) 32°, leath., net, 75 c. Murphy.
CATHOLIC CHURCH.
Best. Victories of Rome and temporal monarchy of the church. net, 45 c. Benziger.
Catholic directory, almanac and clergy list quarterly. $1.25; $1.75. Wiltzius.
De Costa. Whither goest thou? *50 c. net; 25 c. net. Chr. Press.
Galton. Our attitude toward Eng. Roman Catholics. net, $1. Dutton.
Lasance, *comp.* Short visits to the blessed sacrament. 25 c. Benziger.
Novene zu ehren des Heiligen Geistes. net, 3 c. Herder.
Poland. Find the church. net, 5 c. Herder.
Rainy. Ancient Catholic church, A.D. 98-451. net, $2.50. Scribner.
Raycroft. Sermons on the stations of the cross, the Our Father, Hail Mary, etc. net, $1.50. Pustet.
Rosen. The Catholic church and secret societies. net, $1. Caspar.
Tagzeiten zum heiligsten Herzen Jesu. 5 c. Herder.
Tesniere. Adoration of the blessed sacrament. net, $1.25. Benziger.
Vaughan. Holy sacrifice of the mass. 15 c. Herder.
See also Christianity;—Church history;—Church music;—Confession;—Convents;—Indulgences;—Jesus (society of);—Mary, *Virgin*;—Monasticism;—Popes;—Saints.

Catholic directory, almanac and clergy list—quarterly. '02(Ap26) D. pap., $1.25; leatherette, $1.75. Wiltzius.
Cathrein, Victor. Socialism exposed and refuted; fr. the Germ. by J. Conway. 2d ed. '02(Jl12) 12°, *$1.25 net. Benziger.
Cat's paw. Croker, *Mrs.* B. M. $1; 50 c. Lippincott.
CATTLE.
McCallum & Hofer Cattle Co. Stockmen's calculator; cost of any amount from 5 to 32,000 lbs. $1.50. McCallum.
See also Veterinary medicine and surgery.
Caucasian and the negro in the U. S. Calhoun, W: P. 75 c. R. L. Bryan.
CAVALRY.
See Horse.
Caxton ser. 16°, net. Scribner.
—Bacon. Works. $1.25.
—Book of romantic ballads. $1.25.
—Bunyan. Pilgrim's progress. 2 v. $1.20.
—Cervantes Saavedra. Don Quixote. $1.25.
—Hood. Serious poems. $1.25.
—Irving. Sketch book. $1.25.
—La Motte Fouque. Undine [also] Aslauga's knight. $1.20.
—Milton. Complete poems. $1.20.
—Shakespeare. Plays and poems. 3 v. per set, $4.20. Scribner
—Shelley. Poetical works. $1.25.
—Tennyson. In memoriam. $1.20.
Celestial message. Gaffield, E. C. n. p. Lee & S.
Cellular toxins. Vaughan, V. C. *$3 net. Lea.
CEMENT.
Lathbury *and* Spackman. Am. engineering practice in construction of rotary Portland cement plants. $2. G. M. S. Armstrong.
CENTRAL AMERICA.
Herbertson. *comp.* Desc. geographies: Central and South Am., with the West Indies. net, 70 c. Macmillan.
Century dictionary and cyclopedia. New ed. '01- '02(Ap5) 10 v., 4°, subs., $80 to $150. Century Co.
Century of Baptist achievements. Newman, R. H: net, $1.50. Am. Bapt.
CERAMICS.
Barber. Anglo-American pottery. net, $2 [Caspar] E. A. Barber.
Barber. Anglo-Am. pottery. $2. Patterson & W.
Huddilston. Lessons from Greek pottery. net, $1.25. Macmillan.
Monkhouse. Hist. and desc. of Chinese porcelain. net. $10. Wessels
Seger Collected writings: fr. records of the Royal porcelain factory at Berlin. v. 1. per set, $15. Chemical.
Cervantes Saavedra, M. de. Don Quixote. New ed. '01- '02(F22) 4 v., 12°, per set, $3; limp leath., $5. Dodd
Cervantes Saavedra, M. de. Don Quixote de la Mancha; ed. by Ma. E. Burt and L. L. Cable. '02(Je7) il. D. (Ser. of school reading.) net, 60 c. Scribner.
Cervantes Saavedra, M. de. Life and achievements of Don Quixote de la Mancha. '02 (Ap12) 16°, (Caxton ser.) flex. lambskin. net. $1.25. Scribner
Chadwick, H: *ed.* *See* Spalding's official baseball guide.

Chalmers, Ja. James Chalmers; autobiog. and letters. '02(Je28) 8°, net, 75 c. Revell.
Chalmers, Rob. W: King in yellow. New issue. '02(Je21) il. D. $1.50. Harper.
Chamberlain, Leander T. Evolutionary philosophy. '02(My10) D. pap., 50 c. Baker & T.
Chamberlin, T: C. **Attempt to frame a working hypothesis of the cause of glacial periods on an atmosphere basis.** '01. '02 (Ja11) 8°, pap., net, 25 c. Univ. of Chic.
Chamberlin, T: C. **Proposed genetic classification of pleistocene glacial formations.** '01- '02(Ja11) 8°, net, 10 c. Univ. of Chic.
Chambers of the soul. Woelfkin, C. 35 c. Un. Soc. C. E.
Chambers's cyclopædia of Eng. literature; ed. by D: Patrick. New ed. 3 v. v. 1. '01- '02(Mr1) il. 8°, per v., net, $5. Lippincott.
Chambers's twentieth century dict. of Eng. language: ed. by T: Davidson. '01. '02 (Mr1) 8°, $1.50; hf. leath., $2. Lippincott.
CHAMPLAIN, S: de.
Sedgwick. Samuel de Champlain. net, 65 c.: net, 50 c. Houghton, M & Co.
Champney, *Mrs.* Eliz. W. Witch Winnie ser. 9 v. New ed. '01. '02(F22) 12°, per set, $11.25. Dodd.
Chancellor, W: E. Children's arithmetic by grades. Second book. '02(Mr22) D. (Globe ser.) 20 c.; Third book (Mr22) 24 c.; Fourth book (Mr22) 24 c. Globe Sch. Bk.
Chancellor, W: E. Children's arithmetic by series. Primary. '02(Mr22) il. D. (Globe ser., in three books.) 28 c. Globe Sch. Bk.
Chancellor, W: E. Elementary school mathematics by grades: fifth bk., (grade 6.) standard measurements: sixth bk., (grade 7.) commercial affairs. '02(Jl5) il. D. (Globe ser.) ea., *28 c. net. Globe Sch. Bk.
Chandler, Bessie. Verses. '01- '02(Ap26) 16°, $1.25. Blue Sky Press.
Chantepie de la Saussaye, P. D. Religion of the Teutons: fr. the Dutch by B. J. Vos. '02(Jl19) 12°, (Handbooks on the history of religions, v. 3.) $2.50. Ginn.
Chanson de Geste. *See* Crabb, W. D.
Chaplain's experience ashore and afloat. Jones, H. W. $1.25. Sherwood.
Chapman, F: The foraminifera: introd. to study of the protozoa. '02(Ap26) il. O. $3.50 Longmans.
Chapman, G: T. Manual of the pathological treatment of lameness in the horse. '01. '02(F22) 8°, $2. W: R. Jenkins.
CHARACTER.
Bruce. Formation of Christian character. net $1.75. Scribner.
Macdonald. Guarding the thoughts. 10 c. J. H. West.
Schofield. Springs of character. net, $1.30. Funk.
Washington. Character building. **$1.50 net. Doubleday, P.
See also Christian life;—Conduct of life;—Ethics;—Phrenology;—Physiognomy.
CHARITIES.
Worcester. Works of charity. 25 c. Mass. New-Ch. Un.
Charles, Fes. In the country God forgot. '02 (My3) D. $1.50. Little, B. & Co.
Charlotte. Walford, *Mrs.* L. B. $1.50. Longmans.

CHARTRES.
Headlam. Story of Chartres. $2; $2.50. Macmillan.

Chase, F: H: Credibility of the Book of the Acts of the Apostles. '02(Je14) 12°, (Hulsean lectures, 1900-01.) $1.75. Macmillan.

Chase, G: *See* New York. Code of civil procedure.

Châteaubriand, F. R. A. *Vicomte de.* Memoirs; tr. by A. Teixera de Maltos. '02(Jl19) 6 v., ea., *$3.75 net. Putnam.

Chatfield-Taylor, Hobart C. *See* Taylor, H. C. Chatfield-.

Chats within the fold. Desmond, H. J. net, 75 c. Murphy.

Chaucer, G. English of the XIVth century; Prologue and Knightes tale. (S. H. Carpenter.) '01· '02(Ap26) 12°, 75 c. Ginn.

Chaucer, G. Nonne's preeste's tale of the cok and hen. '02(Je28) il. 8°, Japan vellum, $6.50; hand painted, $16.50. Grafton Press.

CHAUCER, Geoffrey.
Ten Brink. Language and metre of Chaucer. net, $1.50. Macmillan.

CHEMISTRY.
Abegg *and* Herz. Practical chemistry. net, $1.50. Macmillan.
Bunge. Text-book of physiological and patholog. chemistry. *$3 net. Blakiston.
Chittenden, *ed.* Studies in physiolog. chemistry. net, $4. Scribner.
Clarke *and* Dennis. Elem. chemistry. $1.10. Am. Bk.
Dennis *and* Clarke. Lab'y manual to accompany Elem. chemistry. 50 c. Am. Bk.
Dupre *and* Hake. Inorganic chemistry. $3. Lippincott.
Hessler *and* Smith. Essentials of chemistry. $1.20. Sanborn.
Holleman. Inorganic chemistry. pt. 2. $2.50. Wiley.
Jones. Elements of physical chemistry. net, $4. Macmillan.
Landolt. Optical rotating power of organic substances. *$7.50 net. Chemical.
Morgan. Elements of physical chemistry. $2. Wiley.
Ostwald. Principles of inorganic chemistry. net, $6. Macmillan.
Perkin *and* Lean. Introd. to chemistry and physics. 2 v. ea., net, 50 c. Macmillan.
Prescott *and* Sullivan. Qualitative chemistry for studies of water solution and mass action. net, $1.50. Van Nostrand.
Remsen. Introd. to study of chemistry. $1.12. Holt.
Simon. Physiological chemistry. net, $3.25. Lea.
Thorpe. Essays in historical chemistry. net, $4. Macmillan.
Tilden. Introd. to the study of chemical philosophy: theoretical and systematic. $1.75. Longmans.
Watson. Elem. experimental chemistry, inorganic. net, $1.25. Barnes.
Wells, *ed.* Studies fr. the chemical lab'y of the Sheffield Scientific School. net, $7.50. Scribner.
Young. Elem. principles of chemistry. net, 95 c. Appleton.
See also Blowpipe;—Enzymes;—Fermentation;—Indicators.

Chemistry of the terpenes. Heusler, F. *$4 net. Blakiston.

Cheney, Fk. J. A life of unity, and other stories. '01· '02(F22) 12°, $1.50. Blade.

Cherbuliez, C: V: Le Roi Apépi; notes in Eng. by A. Schinz. '02(Jl12) 12°, (Romans choisis, no. 25.) pap., 60 c. W: R. Jenkins.

Cherished thoughts. Presset, A. L. $1.50; $1.75; $2.25. Skelton.

Chesterfield, *Earl of.* Letters, sentences and maxims. '02(Je14) 12°, (Home lib.) $1. Burt.

Chesterfield, *Earl of.* Letters to his son; ed. by C. Strachey. '01· '02(F22) 2 v., D. (Lib. of standard literature.) ea., $1.75. Putnam.

Cheyne, T: K., *and* Black, J: S., *eds.* Encyclopædia Biblica. v. 3, L-P. '02(My17) 8°, subs., net, $5; hf. mor., net, $7.50. Macmillan.

Cheyne, W: W., *and* Burghard, F. F. Manual of surgical treatment. In 7 v. v. 5, '01· '02(Mr1); v. 6 (Jl19) 8°, ea., *$5 net. Lea.

CHICAGO.
Clark. Public schools of Chicago. net, 50 c. Univ. of Chic.

Chiefs of Cambria. Jones, M. P. $1.25. Abbey Press.

Child for Christ. McKinney, A. H. net, 50 c. Revell.

Child of the flood. Leahy, W. T: $1. Kilner.

Child stories from the masters. Menefee, M. 75 c. Rand, McN. & Co.

CHILD STUDY.
Wilson. Bibliog. of child study. net, 25 c. Stechert.

Childe, Cromwell, *comp.* Trolley exploring. '02(My17) S. pap., 10 c. Brooklyn Eagle.

CHILDREN.
Anthony. The children's covenant. $1. Jennings.
Compayré. Later infancy of the child. pt. 2. net, $1.20. Appleton.
Folks. Care of destitute, neglected, and delinquent children. net, $1. Macmillan.
McKinney. The child for Christ. net, 50 c. Revell.
Mundy. Eclectic practice in diseases of children. net, $2.50. Scudder.
Rotch. Pediatrics. subs., $6; $7. Lippincott.
Worthington. The tocsin—our children in peril. 25 c. Cubery.
See also Education;—Girls;—Kindergarten;—Mothers.

Children of the palm lands. Allen, A. E. 50 c. Educ. Pub.

Children's Bible stories told in words of easy reading. '02(F1) 5 v., il. 4°, ea., 75 c. Saalfield.

Children's covenant. Anthony, C. V. $1. Jennings.

Children's friend ser. 16°, 50 c. Little, B. & Co.
—Alcott. Little button rose.
—Aulnoy *and* Perrault. Once upon a time.
—Dewey. Bruno.
—Ewing. Benjy in beastland.
—Gilman. Kingdom of coins.
—Moulton. Her baby brother.
—Perrault *and* Aulnoy. Fairy favorites.
—Phelps *and* Ward. Lost hero.

Children's friend ser.—Continued.
—Sullivan. Ivanhoe and Rob Roy, retold.
—Woolsey. Uncle and aunt.
Children's London. Thorpe, C. net, $4.50. Scribner
Child's Bible hist. Knecht, F. J. 25 c. Herder.
Child's garden of verses. Stevenson, R. L: net, 60 c. Scribner.
Child's story of the life of Christ. Hoyt, H. B. $1.25. W. A. Wilde.
Childs, E: E. Wonders of Mouseland. '01-'02(Ja11) D. $1.25. Abbey Press.
Chimmie Fadden and Mr. Paul. Townsend, E: W. $1.50. Century Co.
CHINA.
Allgood. China war, 1860. $5. Longmans.
Parker. John Chinaman, and a few others. $2.50. Dutton.
Thomson. China and the powers. $4. Longmans.
Van Bergen. Story of China. 60 c. Am. Bk.
See also Manchuria;—Paotingfu.
Chinese-English elem. reader and arithmetic. Gyim, P. L. $1.25. Taylor & M.
CHINESE EXCLUSION.
Quang Chang Ling. Why should the Chinese go? 25 c. Cambridge.
Chiquita. Tileston, M. $1.50. Merrill.
Chittenden, Hiram M. American fur trade of the far west. '02(Mr8) 3 v., il. O. net, $10. F. P. Harper.
Chittenden, Russell H., *ed.* Studies in physiolog. chemistry. '01-'02(Mr15) 8°, (Yale bicentennial pub.) net, $4. Scribner.
Choephori (The). Æschylus. net, $3.25. Macmillan.
Choir and chorus conducting. Wodell, F: W: $1.50. Presser.
Choralia. Powell, J. B. $1.50. Longmans.
Christ and his cross. Rutherford, S: $1. Longmans.
Christ our life. Moberly, R. C. net, $3. Longmans.
CHRISTENDOM.
See Christianity;—Church history;—History.
CHRISTIAN LIFE.
Babcock. Three whys and their answer. 35 c. Un. Soc. C. E.
Barton. I go a fishing: progressive discipleship. 25 c. Revell.
Bausman. Precept and practice. net, $1. Heidelberg.
Fradenburgh. Twenty-five stepping stones toward Christ's kingdom. O. P. Fradenburgh.
Gladden. Christian way. 75 c. Dodd.
Keedy. Naturalness of Christian life. net, $1.25. Putnam.
Kyger, *ed.* Hand-book for soul-winners. 50 c. Kyger.
Mudge. Life of love. 25 c. Jennings.
Newell. Life worth living. $1. Abbey Press.
Sanders. How are we led? Who is it that leads us? $1.50. Donohue.
Sarles. Man's peerless destiny in Christ. net, 90 c. Funk.
Terry. The new and living way. net, 50 c. Eaton & M.
See also Conduct of life;—Devotional exercises and meditations;—Faith;—Prayer;—Revivals.
Christian ministry. Anderson, C: P. 20 c. Young Churchman.
CHRISTIAN SCIENCE.
Clark. Church of St. Bunco. $1. Abbey Press.
Cushman. The truth in Christian science. 60 c. J. H. West.
Gifford. Christian science against itself. $1. Jennings.
Seward. How to get acquainted with God: meaning of the Christian science movement. net, 50 c. Funk.
Whittaker. Christian science, is it safe? 10 c. Earle.
Christian study manuals; ed. by R. E. Welsh. S. 60 c. Armstrong.
—Gibson. Protestant principles.
—Margoliouth. Religion of Bible lands.
CHRISTIAN UNITY.
Henson. Godly union and concord. $2. Longmans.
Christian way. Gladden, W. 75 c. Dodd.
CHRISTIANITY.
Fairbairn. Philosophy of the Christian religion. net, $3.50. Macmillan.
Gilbert. Primer of the Christian religion. net, $1. Macmillan.
Grant, *ed.* Christendom Anno Domini 1901. 2 v. $2.50. W: D. Grant.
Islam and Christianity. $1. Am. Tr.
Mason. Christianity, what is it? 80 c. E. & J. B. Young.
Ovenden. To whom shall we go? $1. E. & J. B. Young.
Selden. Story of the Christian centuries. net, $1. Revell.
Christie, R: C. Selected essays and papers; ed., with memoir, by W: A. Shaw. '02 (Mr8) il. O. $5. Longmans.
Christmas rose. Macmillan, H. $1. Macmillan.
Christopher. Lockett, M. F. $1.25. Abbey Press.
Church, Arth. H. Chemistry of paints and painting. 3d ed., rev. and enl. '02(F15) 8°. $3. Macmillan.
Church, Irving P. Diagrams of mean velocity of uniform motion of water in open channels. '02(Je21) obl. 4°, pap., $1.50. Wiley
CHURCH ARCHITECTURE.
Ayer. Rise and devel. of Chr. architecture. net, $1.50. Young Churchman.
Church Historical Soc. lectures. 16°. E. & J. B. Young.
—Mason. Christianity, what is it? 80 c.
CHURCH HISTORY.
Guggenberger. General hist. of the Christian era. In 3 v. ea., $1.50. Herder.
See also Huguenots;—*also* names of churches.
CHURCH MEMBERSHIP.
Clarke. Training the church of the future. net, 75 c. Funk.
Horton. Birthright membership of believers' infants in the N. T. church. 6 c. Presb. Bd.
See also Baptism.
CHURCH MUSIC.
Curwen. Studies in worship music, chiefly congregational singing. $1.75. Scribner.
Dickinson. Music in the hist. of the western church. net, $2.50. Scribner.

Church music.—Continued.
Powell. **Choralia: for precentors and choir-masters.** $1.50. Longmans.
Wodell. Choir and chorus conducting. $1.50. Presser.
Church of Christ. Green, E. T. $1.50. Macmillan.
CHURCH OF ENGLAND.
Creighton. The church and the nation. $2. Longmans.
Galton. Our attitude toward Eng. Roman Catholics. net, $1. Dutton.
Gee. Elizabethan prayer-book and ornaments. net, $1.25. Macmillan.
Grafton. Pusey and the church revival. net, 50 c. Young Churchman.
Green. Church of Christ. $1.50. Macmillan.
Henson. Cross-bench views of current church questions. $4. Longmans.
See also Confession;—Protestant Epis. church.
Church of St. Bunco. Clark, G. $1. Abbey Press.
CHURCHES.
See Syracuse First Presb. church.
Churchman's lib. 8°. Macmillan.
—Green. Church of Christ. $1.50.
—Mackay. Churchman's introd. to the O. T. $1.50.
Church's one foundation. Nicoll, W: R. $1.25. Armstrong.
Church's outlook for the twentieth century ser. 12°, net, $1. Dutton.
—Cobb. Theology, old and new.
Churton, W: R. William Ralph Churton: theolog. papers and sermons. '02(Ap26) 12°, $1.75. Macmillan.
Chute, H. N. *See* Carhart, H: S.
Cicero. Select orations and letters. Allen and Greenough's ed.; rev. by Greenough and Kittredge. '02(Je14) D. hf. leath., $1.45. Ginn.
Cid. R. D. de Bivar, *called the* Cid. Poem of the Cid; tr. by A. M. Huntington. v. 1, 2. '02(Je28) il. Q. vellum, ea., $25. Putnam.
Cid (Le). Corneille, P. net, 35 c. Holt.
CIDER.
See Apple.
CINCINNATI SOUTHERN RAILWAY.
Boyden. Beginnings of the Cincinnati Southern railway. 50 c. Clarke.
CIPHER.
See Codes.
Citator (The). Iowa. $3. R. Adams.
CITIES.
See Municipal government.
Citizen's lib. of economics, politics and sociology; ed. by R: T. Ely. 12°, net, $1.25. Macmillan.
—Addams. Democracy and social ethics.
—Baker. Municipal engineering and sanitation.
—Reinsch. Colonial government.
CITIZENSHIP.
Brewer. American citizenship. net, 75 c. Scribner.
City of Angels. McGrady, T: 10 c. Standard.
City of the seven hills. Harding, C. H. 40 c. Scott, F. & Co.
CIVICS.
See Political science.
CIVIL ACTIONS.
See Actions at law.
CIVIL ENGINEERING.
See Engineering;—Surveying.
Civil government in U. S. Martin, G: H. 90 c. Am. Bk.
CIVIL LAW.
Justinianus. Pandects of Justinian. v. 1. $5. Cambridge.
CIVIL WAR.
See United States.
CIVILIZATION.
Colquhoun. Mastery of the Pacific. net, $4. Macmillan.
Kidd. Principles of western civilization. net, $2. Macmillan.
Stead. Americanization of the world. $1. Markley.
Wells. Anticipations of reaction of mechanical and scientific progress. net, $1.80. Harper.
See also History.
Clapp, H: A. Reminiscences of a dramatic critic. '02(Je7) O. net, $1.75. Houghton, M. & Co.
Clark, A. When bards sing out of tune. '02(My10) D. 50 c. Abbey Press.
Clark, C: An Antarctic queen. '01- '02 (My17) il. D. $1.75. Warne.
Clark, Ellery H. *See* Massachusetts. Street railway accident law.
Clark, Fs. E: Training the church of the future; lectures, with special ref. to the Young People's Soc. of Christian Endeavor. '02 (Ap12) il. D. net, 75 c. Funk.
Clark, Gordon. Church of St. Bunco. '01. '02(F15) D. $1. Abbey Press.
Clark, Hannah B. Public schools of Chicago. '02(Mr22) 8°, pap., net, 50 c. Univ. of Chic.
Clark, Salter S. The government, what it is, what it does. '02(My10) D. 75 c. Am. Bk.
Clark, W: *See* Lewis, M.
Clark, W: L., *and* Marshall, W: L. Treatise on the law of private corporations. In 3 v. v. 2. '01- '02(F1); v. 3 (Jl12) O. shp., per v. $6. Keefe-D.
Clarke, F. W., *and* Dennis, L. M. Elementary chemistry. '02(Je21) D. $1.10. Am. Bk.
Clarke, G: K. Descendants of Nathaniel Clarke and his wife Elizabeth Somerby of Newbury, Mass. '02(Jl12) il. 8°, *$5 net. Marvin.
Clarke, Helen A. *See* Porter, C.
Clarke, *Mrs.* Ma. Cowden, [Mary Victoria Novello.] Letters to an enthusiast: add. to Rob. Balmanno; ed. by A. U. Nettleton. '02(My3) O. net, $2.50. McClurg.
Clarke, W. J. A B C of electrical experiments. '02(Ap5) il. D. $1. Excelsior.
CLAKE FAMILY.
Clarke. Descendants of Nathaniel Clarke and Eliz. Somerby. *$5 net. Marvin.
CLARKSON FAMILY.
See Leach, J. G.
CLASSICAL PHILOLOGY.
See Dissertationes Americanæ.
CLASSIFICATION.
See Cataloguing.
Clay, *Mrs.* J: M. Frank Logan. '02(F22) il. D. $1. Abbey Press.
Claybornes (The). Sage, W: $1.50. Houghton, M. & Co.
CLAYTON-BULWER TREATY.
Travis. Hist. of the Clayton-Bulwer treaty. $1. Mich. Pol. Sci.
Clemens, G. C. *See* Kansas. Statutes conc. corporations.

Clemens, S: L., ["Mark Twain."] A double-barrelled detective story. '02(Ap19) il. D. $1.50. Harper.
Clement, G: A. Probate repts., annot. v. 6. '02(My24) O. shp., $5.50. Baker, V. & Co.
Clerical capitalist. McGrady, T: 10 c. Socialistic Co-op.
Clewell, J: H: Hist. of Wachovia in N. C.; the Unitas fratrum or Moravian church, 1752-1902. '02(Jl5) il. 8°, **$2 net. Doubleday, P.
CLIFF DWELLERS.
Nordenskiold. The cliff dwellers of the Mesa Verde, southwestern Col. net, $20. Stechert.
Clifford, Chandler R. Period decoration. '01-'02(Ap12) il. 8°, $3. Clifford & L.
Clifford, *Mrs.* Lucy L. A long duel. '01-'02 (Mr22) 12°, pap., net, 25 c. Lane.
Clifford, *Mrs.* Lucy L. Margaret Vincent. '02(Ap26) D. $1.50. Harper.
Climates and baths of Great Britain. 8°, net. Macmillan.
—Ewart, *and others.* Climates of London, central and northen England, Wales and Ireland. $4. (2.)
CLINIC.
See Pathology.
Clinical psychiatry. Defendorf, A. R. net, $3.50. Macmillan.
Clinton, Major, *pseud.* *See* Culley, F. C.
Clock on the stairs. Weber, A. 75 c. Burt.
Clodd, E: Thomas Henry Huxley. '02 (Ap12) D. net, $1. Dodd.
Cloistering of Ursula. Scollard, C. $1.50. L. C. Page.
Clow, F: R. Comparative study of the administration of city finances in the U. S. '01-'02(Ja11) O. (Pub. of the Am. Economic Assoc., 3d ser., v. 2, no. 4.) pap., $1. Macmillan.
Clowes, W: L., *and others.* Royal navy. v. 5 and 6. '01-'02(Ja11) 8°, ea., net, $6.50. Little, B. & Co.
COAL.
Hughes. Text-book of coal mining. $7. Lippincott.
Coal oil Johnny. Steele, J: W. $1.50. J: A. Hill.
Coast of freedom. Shaw, A. M. $1.50. Doubleday, P.
Cobb, Sanford H. Rise of relig. liberty in America. '02(My17) 8°, net, $4. Macmillan.
Cobb, W. F. Theology, old and new. '02 (Ap5) 12°, (Church's outlook for the twentieth century ser., no. 1.) net, $1. Dutton.
Coburn, F: N. Prize designs for rural school buildings. '01-'02(Ja25) il. 12°, 25 c. Kellogg.
Cochrane, J: M., *rep.* *See* North Dakota. *Sup. ct.* Repts.
Cochrane, Rob. More animal stories. '01-'02(F15) il. 12°, net, $1. Lippincott.
Cockcroft, Ja., *ed.* Encyclopædia of forms and precedents for pleading and practice. (T: E. O'Brien.) v. 15. '02(My17) O. shp., $6. Cockcroft.
Cockerell, Douglas. Bookbinding and the care of books. '02(F8) il. D. (Artistic crafts ser. of technical handbooks, no. 1.) net, $1.20. Appleton.
CODES.
A B C universal commercial electric telegraphic code. net, $7. Am. Code.
CODES.—*Continued.*
Barry. Am. lumberman telecode. net, $5. Am. Lumberman.
Hartfield. Exchange pocket cipher code. $2. T. W. Hartfield.
Hartmann *and* Needham. Commercial code for the transmission of telegrams and cablegrams. $3. Commercial Code.
International Cable Directory Co., *comp.* Internat. cable directory of the world in conjunction with Western Union telegraphic code system. $15. Int. Cable.
Codman, J:, *2d.* Arnold's expedition to Quebec. 2d ed. '02(Mr1) 8°, net, $2.25. Macmillan.
Cody, S. Selections from the world's greatest short stories. '02(My24) D. net, $1. McClurg.
Coffin, C: E. Gist of whist. 7th ed., rev. '02(Jl5) S. 75 c. Brentano's.
Coffin, G: M. A B C of banks and banking. '01. '02(Ap5) il. S. (Wall street lib., v. 4.) $1.25. S: A. Nelson.
Cohen, Alfr. J., ["Alan Dale."] Girl who wrote. '02(Jl19) il. D. $1.50. Quail & W.
COHERER.
See Electricity.
Cohn, Alfr. I. Indicators and test-papers, their source, preparation, application, and tests for sensitiveness. 2d ed. '02(Je7) 12°, $2. Wiley.
Colburn, Bertha L. Graded physical exercises. '02(F22) D. $1. Werner.
Colby, Alb. L. Review and text of the Am. standard specifications for steel, adopt. Aug., 1901. 2d ed. '02(Ap5) 12°, net, $1.10. Chemical.
Colcock, Annie T. Margaret Tudor. '02 (Ap19) il. D. $1. Stokes.
Colden, Cadwallader. Hist. of the Five Indian nations of Canada. '02(My24) 2 v., 8°, (Commonwealth lib.) net, per v., $1. New Amsterdam.
Cole, Horace L. The flesh and the devil. '02(Ap26) 12°, $1.50. Neely.
Coleman, Phares, *rep.* *See* Alabama. *Sup. ct.* Repts.
Colemanite from So. California. Eakle, A. S. 15 c. Univ. of Cal.
Coleridge, S: T. Rime of the ancient mariner; ed. by N. H. Pitman. '01. '02(Ap19) S. (Ser. of Eng. classics.) keratol, 30 c.; flex. bds., 25 c. B. F. Johnson.
College chaps. Prune, N. 75 c. Mutual Bk.
College man in doubt. Best, N. R. net, 50 c. Westminster.
College student and his problems. Canfield, J. H. net, $1. Macmillan.
COLLEGES AND UNIVERSITIES.
See Oxford Univ.
Collingwood, W: G. Life of John Ruskin. [New rev., abb. ed.] '02(Mr29) O. net, $2. Houghton, M. & Co.
Collins, J: E. Truth about socialism. '02 (Jl12) 16°, pap., 25 c. J. A. Wayland.
Colonel Harold de Lacey. Douglass, F. A. $1.25. Neely.
Colonial days. Welsh, L. D. 50 c. Educ. Pub.
COLONIAL GOVERNMENT.
Reinsch. Colonial government. net, $1.25. Macmillan.
Colonials (The). French, A. $1.50. Doubleday, P.

COLOR.
Vanderpoel. Color problems. net, $5. Longmans.
See also Dyeing;—Light;—Printing.

Color of the soul. Norris, Z. A. net, $1. Funk.

Colorado. Laws passed at an extra session of the 13th general assembly. '02(Je14) O. hf. shp., $2. Smith-B.

COLORADO.
Hatch. Civil government in Col. 60 c. Centennial.
Nordenskiold. Cliff dwellers of the Mesa Verde, southwestern Col. net, $20. Stechert.

Colorado colonel. Campbell, W: C. $1.50. Crane.

COLORADO RIVER.
James. In and around the Grand Canyon. net, $10. Little, B. & Co.

Colquhoun, Arch. R. Mastery of the Pacific. '02(Mr1) 8°, net, $4. Macmillan.

Colton, B. P. Elem. physiology and hygiene. '02(My24) il. D. 60 c. Heath.

Columbia Univ. cont. to philosophy, psychology and education. 8°, pap. Macmillan.
—Alexander. Problem of metaphysics. *75 c. net. (v. 10, 1.)

Columbia Univ. Germanic studies. 8°, pap., net, $1. Macmillan
—Remy. Influence of India and Persia on the poetry of Germany. (v. 1, 4.)

Columbia Univ. Indo-Iranian ser.; ed. by A. V. Williams Jackson. 8°, net. Macmillan.
—Avesta. Index verborum. $2.
—Gray. Indo-Iranian phonology. $3.

Columbia Univ. Oriental studies. 8°, net, $1.25. Macmillan.
—Gabirol. Improvement of moral qualities. (1.)

Columbia Univ. studies in comparative literature. 12°, net. Macmillan.
—Einstein. Italian Renaissance in England. $1.50.

Columbia Univ. studies in hist., economics and public law. 8°. Macmillan.
—Duggan. Eastern question. *$1.50 net. (v. 14, 3.)
—Hall. Crime in its rel. to social progress. $3 net: $3.50 net. (v. 15.)
—Kinosita. Past and present of Japanese commerce. *$1.50 net. (v. 16, 1.)

Colville, W. J. Life and power from within. '02(Mr22) D. $1. Alliance.

Colyer, J. F. *See* Smale, M.

Commander, Lydia K. Marred in the making. '02(Ap12) O. limp chamois, satin-lined, $3; pap., 25 c. Eckler.

Comments of a Countess. '02(My10) 4°, net, $1.50. Lane.

COMMERCE.
Foreign trade requirements (annual). $10. Lewis.
Kinosita. Past and present of Japanese commerce. *$1.50 net. Macmillan.
Marchant. Commercial history. $1. Pitman.
Ware. Educational foundations of trade and industry. net, $1.20. Appleton.
See also Commercial law;—Political economy;—Railroads.

COMMERCIAL CORRESPONDENCE.
See Stenography.

Commercial digest and business forms. McMaster, J. S. $6. Commercial Bk.

COMMERCIAL LAW.
Authorities, deductions and notes in commercial paper. $2.25. Univ. Press.
Hargis. Treatise on commercial law and business customs. 10 c. J. North.
McMaster. Irregular and regular commercial paper. $2.—Commercial cases. $6. Commercial Bk.
See also Attachment;—Contracts;—Conveyancing;—Corporations;—Negotiable instruments;—Sale;—Trusts.

Commonwealth lib. 8°, net, $1. New Amsterdam.
—Arnold. Literature and dogma.
—Colden. Hist. of the Five Indian nations of Canada. 2 v.
—Lewis *and* Clark. Expedition to the sources of the Missouri, etc.
—Mackenzie. Voyages fr. Montreal to the Pacific Ocean.

Commonwealth or empire. Smith, G. net. 60 c. Macmillan.

Commonwealth ser. 16°, $1.25. L. C. Page.
—Wheaton. The Russells in Chicago

COMMUNISM.
Lockwood. New Harmony communities. $2.50. Chronicle.

Compayré, Gabriel. Later infancy of the child; tr. by M. E. Wilson. '02(F22) 12°, (Internat. educ. ser., no. 53.) net, $1.20. Appleton.

Complete housebuilder. '02(My17) 12°, 50 c.; pap., 25 c. Donohue

Complete pocket guide to Europe. Stedman, E. C. $1.25. W: R. Jenkins.

COMPOSERS.
See Musicians.

COMPOSITION.
See Rhetoric.

Comrades. Newberry, F. E. 75 c. Burt.

Condict, Alice B. Old glory and the gospel in the Philippines. '02(Ap19) 12°, net, 75 c. Revell.

CONDUCT OF LIFE.
Dresser. Book of secrets, studies in self-control. net, $1. Putnam.
Hillis. Master of science of right-living. net, 50 c. Revell.
Hind. Life's little things. $1.75. Macmillan.
Jordan. Kingship of self-control.—Majesty of calmness. ea., 50 c. Revell.
Mabie. Works and days. net, $1. Dodd.
Slicer. One world at a time. net, $1.35. Putnam.
See also Business;—Character;—Christian life;—Culture;—Ethics;—Knowledge.

Cone, J: A. Man who pleases and the woman who fascinates. '01- '02(Jl12) 12°, $1. Neely.

CONFECTIONERY.
Rigby. Reliable candy teacher and soda and ice cream formulas. $2. W. O. Rigby.

CONFESSION.
Fulham Palace Conference. Confession and absolution. net, $1. Longmans.

Confessions of a matchmaking mother. Davidson, L. C. $1.50 J. F. Taylor.

Confounding of Camelia. Sedgwick, A. D. $1.50. Century Co.

Conger, Arth. B. Religion for the time: six conferences on natural religion. '02(My3) D. net. $1. Jacobs.

CONJURING.
Roterberg. Card tricks; how to do them, and sleight of hand. 25 c. Drake.
Conklin, *Mrs.* Jennie M. D. Bek's first corner. '02(Mr29) il. 12°, (Fireside ser.) $1. Burt.
Conklin, *Mrs.* Jennie M. D. Growing up. '02(Mr29) il. 12°, (Fireside ser.) $1. Burt.
Conklin, *Mrs.* Jennie M. D. Miss Prudence. '02(Mr29) il. 12°, (Fireside ser.) $1. Burt.
Conklin, *Mrs.* Jennie M. D. Tessa Wadsworth's discipline. '02(Mr29) il. 12°, (Fireside ser.) $1. Burt.
Conley, J: W. Evolution and man. '02 (Ap19) 12°, net, 75 c. Revell.
Connelley. W: Elsey. *See* Root, F. A.
Connold, E: J. British vegetable galls. '02 (Mr22) f°, net, $4. Dutton.
Conqueror (The). Atherton, *Mrs.* G. F. $1.50. Macmillan.
Consolation of philosophy. Boethius, A. M. S. 50 c.; 75 c. Macmillan.
Conspiracy of Pontiac. Parkman, F. $1. Burt.
CONSTABLE, John.
Holmes. Constable. net, $1. Longmans.
CONSTABLES.
Dill. Changes and add. to constables' guide. T. & J. W. Johnson.
See also Justices of the peace.
Constance Hamilton. Wyatt, L. M. L. 50 c. Abbey Press.
Constances. Bentzan, T. $1.50. Neely.
CONSTELLATIONS.
See Astronomy;—Stars.
CONSTITUTIONAL LAW.
See Roman empire.
Constructive Bible studies; ed. by W: R. Harper and E. D. Burton. O. $1. Univ. of Chic.
—Burton *and* Mathews. Life of Christ.
—Harper. Constructive studies in the priestly element in the O. T.
CONSUMPTION.
Burnett. New cure for consumption by its own virus. $1. Boericke & T.
Contemporary science ser. See Scribner's.
CONTRACTS.
Lawson. Making of a contract. 25 c. Stephens.
CONUNDRUMS.
See Riddles.
CONVENTS.
Steele. Convents of Great Britain. net, $2. Herder.
CONVERSION.
Mason. Ministry of conversion. net, 90 c. Longmans.
See also Christian life;—Revivals.
CONVEYANCING.
Pennsylvania. Law of conveyancing. $6. T. & J. W. Johnson.
CONVICTS.
See Crime and criminals;—Prisons.
Conway, Kath. E. Lalor's Maples. 2d ed. '01. '02(Ja11) D. $1.25. Pilot.
Conway, Moncure D., *comp.* The sacred anthology (oriental.) 5th ed. '02(Mr29) 12°, $2. Holt.
Cook, *Mrs.* E. T. The bride's book. '02 (Ap5) 12°, net, $1.50. Dutton.
Cook, E: T. Rights and wrongs of the Transvaal war. New rev. ed. '02(Je7) D. $2. Longmans.
Cook, Ja. Three voyages around the world. '02(My17) 12°, (Home lib.) $1. Burt.
Cook, J: T. *See* New York. Code of criminal procedure and penal code.
Cooke, C. J. B. Some recent developments in locomotive practice. '02(Je7) il. 8°, $1. Macmillan.
COOKERY.
Curtis. Left-overs made palatable. $1. Judd.
Dainty dishes for slender incomes. net, 50 c. New Amsterdam.
Dennis. Cook book. $1.50. Mutual Pub. Co.
H. Grandmother's cook book. 50 c. New Amsterdam.
Keller. Pennsylvania German cook book. 50 c. R. M. Scranton.
Nordhoff guild cook book. 25 c. McGill.
Palmer. Woman's exchange cook book. 70 c. Conkey.
Pierce. Hartley House cook book and household economist. 60 c. Lentilhon.
Rivas. Little French dinners. 50 c. New Amsterdam.
Salis. A la mode cookery. $2. Longmans.
Schaeffer. Metropolitan club cook-book. $1.75. Augsburg.
Seeley. Cook book: Fr. and Amer. cookery. net, $2; net, $3. Macmillan.
See also Diet;—Domestic economy;—Hygiene.
Coolidge, Susan, *pseud. See* Woolsey, S. C.
Cooper, E: H. A fool's year. '02(F15) D. (Town and country lib., no. 308.) $1; pap., 50 c. Appleton.
CO-OPERATION.
See Ruskin Co-operative Assoc.; — Socialism; — Trade-unions.
Coppée François. Morceau de pain et autres contes. '02(My3) sq. S. (Contes choises, no. 22.) pap., 25 c. W: R. Jenkins.
COPPER.
Stevens, *comp.* Copper handbook. $2; $3. H. J. Stevens.
Corbin, J: An American at Oxford. '02 (My17) il. D. net, $1.50. Houghton, M. & Co.
Corinne's vow. Waggaman, M. T. $1.25. Benziger.
CORLISS ENGINE.
Lisk. Diagram of the Corliss engine, etc. 25 c. Spon.
Corn of heaven. Macmillan, H. $1.75. Macmillan.
Corneille, P. Le Cid; ed. by E: S. Joynes. New rev. enl. ed. '02(F1) D. (Students' ser. of classic Fr. plays, no. 1.) net, 35 c. Holt.
Cornell verse. Lyon, H: A. $1. Walton.
Cornwall, E: E. William Cornwall and his descendants. '01· '02(F1) 8°, $5. Tuttle, M. & T.
CORNWALL AND YORK, *Duke and Duchess of.*
Knight. With the royal tour. $2. Longmans.
Wallace. Web of empire: diary of the imperial tour. net, $6.50. Macmillan.
CORPORATIONS.
American and Eng. corporation cases. v. 15. $4.50. Michie.
American corp. legal manual, 1902. $5. Corp. Leg. Co.
Boisot. By-laws of private corporations. $3. Keefe-D.

CORPORATIONS.—*Continued.*

Clark *and* Marshall. Law of private corporations. v. 2. $6. Keefe-D.

Heath. Comparative advantages of the corp. laws of all the states and territories. n. p. Kennebec Journ.

Kansas. Statutes conc. corporations and insurance companies. $1; $1.25. Crane.

Maine. Laws conc. business corporations, annot. gratis. Kennebec Journ.

New York. Laws rel. to general, religious and non-business corporations. $1.50. $2. Banks & Co.

New York. Membership and religious corporations. $2.50; $3. Banks & Co.

New York. Statutory revision of laws affecting misc. corporations. $1.50. Banks & Co.

Smith. Cases on private corporations. net, $6. Harvard Law.

Walker. Taxation of corporations in the U. S. 25 c. Am. Acad. Pol. Sci.

White. On corporations. $5.50. Baker, V. & Co.

Wilgus. Law of private corporations. In 2 v. complete, $9; $10. Bowen-M.

See also Municipal corporations;—Securities.

CORRESPONDENCE.

See Letter-writing;—Letters;—Stenography.

Corrothers, Ja. D. Black cat club. '02(Mr22) D. net, $1. Funk.

Cosmos and the logos. Minton, H: C. net, $1.25. Westminster.

Cosy corner ser. il. 50 c. L. C. Page.
—Barnett. Jerry's reward.
—Delano. Susanne.
—Fox. Little giant's neighbors.

Cotes, *Mrs.* Sara J. D. Those delightful Americans. '02(Je21) D. $1.50. Appleton.

Cotterell, E: The pocket Gray; or, anatomist's vade mecum. 5th rev. ed., ed. by C. H. Fagge. '02(F22) 16°, net, $1.25. Wood.

COTTON.

Whitworth. Cotton calculations. $1. Boardman.

Couch, A. T: Quiller-, ["Q."] The Westcotes. '02(Ap12) il. D. (Griffin ser.) $1. Coates.

Coulevain, Pierre de. Eve triumphant. '02 (My10) 12°, net, $1.20. Putnam.

Country life lib. 8°, net, $3.75. Scribner.
—Jekyll, *comp.* Lilies for Eng. gardens.

COURAGE.

Wagner. Courage. $1.25. Dodd.

See also Heroes.

Courage of conviction. Sullivan, T. R. $1.50. Scribner.

Courier-Journal almanac for 1902. '02(Mr22) D. pap., 25 c. Courier-Journ.

Courtship of sweet Anne Page. Talbot, E. V. net, 40 c. Funk.

Cousin Maude and Rosamond. Holmes. *Mrs.* M. J. $1. Burt.

Cowles, H: C. Ecological rel. of the vegetation on the sand dunes of Lake Michigan. '01. '02(Ja11) 8°, (Hull botanical laboratory. no. 13.) pap., net, 75 c. Univ. of Chic.

Cox, *Mrs.* Ja. F., ["C."] Home thoughts. 2d ser. (Je7) D. net, $1.20. Barnes.

Crabb, Wilson D. Culture history in the Chanson de Geste-Aymeri de Narbonne. '02(Mr22) 8°, pap., net, $1.25. Univ. of Chic.

Crane, Wa. Bases of design. 2d ed. '02 (Ap26) il. 12°, $2.25. Macmillan.

Crane, Wa. Line and form. Cheaper ed. '02 (My3) il. 12°, $2.25. Macmillan.

Craque o' Doom. *See* Catherwood, *Mrs.* M. H.

Craufurd, H. J. Field training of a company of infantry. '02(Ap12) S. $1. Longmans.

Crawford, F. M. Works. New uniform ed. '02(F15) 3 v., 12°, ea., $1.50. Macmillan.

Crawford, F. M. In the palace of the king. Limited pap. ed. '02(Mr8) 12°, (People's lib., no. 27.) pap., 50 c. Am. News.

Crawford, J: J. Negotiable instruments law. 2d ed. '02(Ap12) O. $2.50. Baker, V. & Co.

Crawford,, T. D., *rep.* *See* Arkansas. *Sup. ct.* Repts.

Crawley, Ernest. The mystic rose: primitive marriage. '02(Mr22) 8°, net, $4. Macmillan.

Crayon, Jos. P. Rockaway records of Morris county, N. J., families. '02(Jl5) 12°, $3. Rockaway.

Creamer, E: S. The Orphean tragedy. '02 (Mr29) D. $1. Abbey Press.

Creation, re-creation. *See* Lemcke, E. E:

Credit of the county. Norris, W: E: †$1; 50 c. Appleton

CREEDS.

See Apostles' creed;—Catechisms.

Creighton, M. The church and the nation; ed. by L. Creighton. '01. '02(Ja11) D. $2. Longmans.

Creighton, M. Thoughts on education. '02(Je7) D. net, $1.60. Longmans.

Cresee, F. A. Practical pointers for patentees. '02(Ap12) 16°, $1. Munn.

Crew, H:, *and* Tatnall, Rob. R. Laboratory manual of physics. '02(F1) 12°, net, 90 c. Macmillan.

Crile, G: W. Research into certain problems rel. to surgical operations. '02(F15) il. 8°, net, $2.50. Lippincott.

CRIME AND CRIMINALS.

Hall. Crime in its relation to social progress. net, $3; $3.50. Macmillan.

See also Prisons.

CRIMINAL LAW.

Book of forms to be used with the study of criminal procedure in the Univ. of Mich. 60 c. Bliss & A.

Kenny. Outlines of criminal law. *$2.50. Macmillan.

Pattison. Instructions in criminal cases passed upon by the cts. of Mo. $5. Gilbert Bk.

See also Crime and criminals;—Evidence;—*also* names of states.

Crimson wing. Taylor, H. C. C. $1.50. H. S. Stone.

Cripps, Wilfred J. Old English plate: its makers and marks. New il. lib. ed. '01. '02(Ja11) facsimiles, 8°, net, $13.50. Scribner.

CRISES.

See Finance.

Crissey, Forrest. In Thompson's woods: [poems.] '01. '02(Mr1) 16°, bds., $1. Blue Sky Press

CRITICISM.

Arnold. Essays in criticism. $1. Burt.

Bourne. Essays in hist. criticism. net, $2. Scribner.

Margoliouth. Lines of defense of the biblical revelation. net, $1.50. Gorham.

See also Literature.

Crockett, S: R. The dark o' the moon. '02 (Mr29) il. D. $1.50. Harper.
Croft, Victor E. *See* Brown, C: F.
Croker, *Mrs.* Bertha M. The cat's paw. '02 (F1) D. (Select novels.) $1; pap., 50 c. Lippincott.

CROMWELL, Ol.
Adams. Shall Cromwell have a statue? 25 c. Lauriat.
Payn. Cromwell on foreign affairs. net, $1.25. Macmillan.
Quayle. King Cromwell. net, 25 c. Jennings.

Cronholm, Neander N: Hist. of Sweden. '02 (Ap26) 2 v., il. 8°, $5. N. N: Cronholm.
Crosby, Ernest. Captain Jinks, hero. '02 (Mr8) D. $1.50. Funk.
Crosland, T. W. H. The unspeakable Scot. '02(Jl19) D. **$1.25 net. Putnam.
Cross-bench views of current church questions. Henson, H. H. $4. Longmans.
Cross of Christ in Bolo-land. Dean, J: M. net. $1. Revell.
Crothers, T. D. Morphinism and narcomania from opium, cocain, etc. '02(Mr29) 12°, $2. Saunders.
Crowell, J. F. Present status and future prospects of Am. shipbuilding. '02(Mr22) 8°, (Pub. of the soc., no. 325.) pap., 15 c. Am. Acad. Pol. Sci.
Crowest, F: J. Story of the art of music. '02 (Jl19) il. T. (Lib. of useful stories.) **35 c. net. Appleton.
Crowley, Ma. C. Heroine of the strait. '02 (Ap19) il. D. $1.50. Little, B. & Co.
Crowning of flora. Kellogg, A. M. 15 c. Kellogg.
Crozier, Hugh V. Temperance and the Anti-Saloon League. '01. '02(Mr29) 16°, 15 c. Barbee & S.
Cruger, *Mrs.* Julia S., ["Julien Gordon."] World's people. '02(Jl12) D. †$1.50. J. F. Taylor.
Cruger, *Mrs.* Van Rensselaer. *See* Cruger, *Mrs.* J. S.
Cruickshank, J. W. *and* A. M. Umbrian towns. '02(Mr22) S. (Grant Allen's hist. guide books to the principal cities of Europe.) net, $1.25. Wessels.
Cruise of the "Enterprise." Kaler, J. O. $1.50. W. A. Wilde.
Cruising in the West Indies. Stokes, A. P. **$1.25 net. Dodd.

CRYSTALS.
See Mineralogy.

Cub's career. Wheeler, H. $1. Abbey Press.
Cuentos selectos. S. pap., 35 c. W: R. Jenkins.
—Trueba. El molinerillo. (4.)
Cuffel, C: A. Durrell's Battery in the Civil War. '02(Mr22) il. O. subs., $2. C: A. Cuffel.
Cullen, C. L. More ex-tank tales. '02(Ap5) 12°, $1. Ogilvie
Cullens, F: B. Where the magnolias bloom. '02(Mr1) D. 50 c. Abbey Press.
Culley, Fk. C., ["Major Clinton."] Barbara. '01- '02(Mr8) il. 12°, $1.25. F. C. Culley.

CULTURE.
Blackie. On self-culture. 35 c. Phonograph.

Culture history in the Chanson de Geste-Aymeri de Narbonne. Crabb, W. D. net. $1.25. Univ. of Chic.

CUMBERLAND PRESBYTERIAN CHURCH.
See Presbyterian church.

Cumming, A. N. Public house reform. '01- '02(Ja11) 12°, (Social sci. ser.) $1. Scribner.
Cumming, R. C. *See* New York Laws; Membership and relig. corps.
Cummins, Harle O. Welsh rarebit tales. '02(Je7) il. D. $1.25. Mutual Bk.
Cuppy, H. A., *ed.* Pictorial natural history. '01. '02(Ap12) il. Q. (Farm and fireside lib., no. 199.) $1. Crowell & K.
Curle, J. H. Gold mines of the world. '02 (Jl12) 4°, $3.50. Engineering.
Curschmann, H. *See* Osler, W:, *ed.*
Curtis, Is. G. Left-overs made palatable. '02 (F15) il. D. oilcloth, $1. Judd.
Curtiss, S: I. Primitive Semitic religion today. '02(Je7) il. 8°, net, $2. Revell.
Curwen, : S. Studies in worship music, chiefly Jcongregational singing. 1st ser. 3d ed., rev. and enl. '02(Mr8) 12°, $1.75. Scribner.
Cushing, Fk. H. Zuñi folk tales. '01. '02 (Ja25) O. net. $3.50. Putnam.
Cushman, Herb. E. Truth in Christian science. '02(My17) D. 60 c. J. H. West.
Cust, A. M. Ivory workers of the Middle Ages. '02(Mr8) il. 12°, (Handbooks of the great craftsmen.) $2. Macmillan.
Cust, Lionel. Desc. of the sketch-book by Sir Anthony Van Dyck. '02(Mr22) 4°, $17.50. Macmillan.
Cust, Lionel, *ed.* National portrait gallery. Ed. de luxe. In 2 v. v. 1. '02(Mr1) 4°, subs., complete work, net. $30. Cassell.
Custis, G: W. P. Life of George Washington. '02(Je28) 12°, (Biographies of famous men.) $1. Donohue.
Cutter, Sa. J., *comp.* Conundrums, riddles, puzzles and games. Rev., enl. ed. '02 (Ap5) S. 50 c.; pap., 25 c. Otis.

CYANIDE PROCESS.
James. Cyanide practice. $5. Engineering.
See also Gold.

CYCLOPAEDIAS.
See Encyclopædias.

Cyr, Ellen M. Cyr readers. bks. 7 and 8. '01- '02(Mr8) il. 12°, ea., 45 c. Ginn.
Cyrano de Bergerac. Rostand, E. 50 c. W: R. Jenkins.

Da Costa, J: C., *jr.* Clinical hematology: guide to the examination of the blood. '01- '02(Ja11) il. col. pls. 8°, net, $5. Blakiston.
Daddy's girl. Smith, *Mrs.* E. T. $1. Burt.
Dadson, A. J. Evolution and its bearing on religion. '02(Ap5) net, $1.25. Dutton.
Dail, C. C. Sunlight and shadows. '02(Je21) il. 8°, $1.50. Hudson-K.
Daily praise: texts and hymns for every day. '02(F8) 32°, 15 c.: 20 c.; 25 c. Revell.
Dainty dishes for slender incomes. New ed. '02(My24) 12°, net. 50 c. New Amsterdam.
Dainty ser. 16°, pap., 50 c. Dutton.
—Smith. Lost Christmas.

DAIRY.
Blake. Common sense ideas for dairymen. $1. Coates.
Russell. Outlines of dairy bacteriology. $1. H. L. Russell.

Dalby, W: E. Balancing of engines. '02 (Mr22) O. $3.75. Longmans.
Dale, Alan, *pseud.* *See* Cohen, A. J.

Daley, Jos. G. Cassock of the pines, and other stories. '02(Ap12) il. D. $1. W: H. Young.
Dallin, *Mrs.* Colonna M. Sketches of great painters for young people. '02(Je28) il. D. 90 c. Silver.
Dalton, Test. Role of the unconquered. '02 (F8) D. $1.50. G: W. Dillingham.
Daly, Ida M. Advanced rational speller '02(Je7) S. 25 c. B: H. Sanborn.
DALZIEL BROTHERS.
Brothers Dalziel: record of work, 1840-1890. net, $6.50. Dutton.
DAMAGES.
Mechem. Case on the law of damages. net, $4. West Pub.
Dame, Arthur K. *See* Nebraska. Law of probate.
Dame, Lorin L., *and* Brooks, H: Handbook of the trees of New England. '02(F15) il. D. $1.35. Ginn.
Damsel (A) or two. Moore, F. F. $1.50. Appleton.
Dana, Fs. The decoy. '02(Mr8) 12°, $1.50. Lane.
Danaher, Alb. J. *See* New York. Amendments.
DANCING.
Quick. Guide to ball-room dancing. 50 c.; 25 c. Donohue.
Danger of youth. Jordans, J. 15 c. Herder.
Dangerous trades. Oliver, T. *$8 net. Dutton.
Dangers of spiritualism, by a member of the Soc. of Psychical Research. '02(Je14) il. 8°, net, 75 c. Herder.
DANIEL.
Anderson. Daniel in the critics' den. net, $1 25. Revell.
Daniel Everton, volunteer-regular. Putnam, I. net, $1.20. Funk.
Dante Alighieri. Divine comedy: [prose tr.] by C: E. Norton. New rev. ed. '02(Mr22) O. $4.50; hf. cf. or hf. polished mor., $9.75. Houghton, M. & Co.
DANTE ALIGHIERI.
Boccaccio *and* Aretino. Earliest lives of Dante. 75 c. Holt.
Toynbee. Dante studies and researches. net, $3.50. Dutton.
Wright. Dante and the Divine comedy. net, $1. Lane.
D'Anvers, N., *pseud.* *See* Bell, *Mrs.* N. R. E. M.
Darby, Ja. E. Analysis of the Acts and Epistles of the New Testament. '02(Jl12) D. leatherette, 25 c. J. E. Darby.
Dark Continent. *See* Harding, W:
Dark o' the moon. Crockett, S: R. $1.50. Harper.
Darkie ways in Dixie. Richard, M. A. $1. Abbey Press.
Darkwood (The) tragedy. '02(Je14) 12°, $1.25. Neale.
Darley Dale, *pseud.* *See* Steele, F. M.
Darrow, Clarence S. A Persian pearl, and other essays. '02(My24) O. $1.50. Ricketts.
Daskam, Josephine D. Madness of Philip, and other tales of childhood. '02(Ap26) il. 12°, $1.50. McClure, P.
Daskam, Josephine D., *comp.* Best nonsense verses. '02(My10) 16°, bds., 50 c. W: S. Lord.

Datchet, C: Morchester: story of Am. society. '02(Ap26) D. net, $1.20. Putnam.
Daudet, A. Tartarin de Tarascon. (C. Fontaine.) '02(Mr8) il. D. 45 c. Am. Bk.
Daughters of the Revolution. Thayer, S. H: $1. Abbey Press.
Davenport, B: R. Blood will tell. '02(Je14) 12°, $1.50. Caxton Bk.
Davenport, Fs. H: Diseases of women. 4th ed., rev. and enl. '02(Mr22) il. 12°, net, $1.75. Lea.
Davenport, J: G. The fulfilment. '02(My17) D. net, 40 c. Dutton.
Davey, J: The tree doctor. '02(Jl12) il. O. $1. J: Davey.
David Elginbrod. Macdonald, G: $1. Burt.
Davidson, *Mrs.* H. A. Study of Idylls of the king. '02(Mr8) S. pap., 50 c. Mrs. H. A. Davidson.
Davidson, Lillias C. Confessions of a match-making mother. '02(My17) D. $1.50. J. F. Taylor.
Davidson, Marie A. The two Renwicks. '02(Je7) D. $1.50. Neely.
Davis, R: H. Ranson's folly. '02(Jl12) il. D. †$1.50. Scribner.
Davis, Stanton K. As nature whispers. '02 (Mr29) 16°, 50 c. Alliance.
Davis, W: M. Elem. physical geography. '02(My24) D. $1.40. Ginn.
Davis, W: S. Belshazzar. '02(Jl5) il. D. †$1.50. Doubleday, P.
Davison, C: S. Selling the bear's hide, and other tales. '02(Jl19) il. S. $1. Nassau Press.
Davitt, Michael. Boer fight for freedom. '02(Je7) il. O. net, $2. Funk.
Dawes, T. R. Bilingual teaching in Belgian schools. '02(Jl12) 12°. (Cambridge Univ. Press ser.) *50 c. net. Macmillan.
Day, Holman F. Pine tree ballads. '02 (Jl19) il. D. **$1 net. Small.
Day, Lewis E. Alphabets old and new. New ed. '02(Je21) 12°, $1.50. Scribner.
Days of the Son of man. Rhone, R. D. net, $1.20. Putnam.
Deal, Annie R. Life of Jennie O'Neill Potter. '02(Ap12) 12°, $1. Blanchard.
Dean, Howard. The iron hand. '02(Je14) D. $1. Abbey Press.
Dean, J: M. Cross of Christ in Bolo-land. '02(My17) il. 12°, net, $1. Revell.
Deane girls. Rouse, A. L. $1. Burt.
Death of Wallenstein. *See* Schiller, J. C. F. v.
DEBATES.
Hungerford. Success club debater. 25 c. Success.
Debates on federal constitution. Elliott, J. 5 v. net, $10; net, $12. Lippincott.
DECLAMATION.
See Orators and oratory.
De Clifford, Norman F: Egypt, the cradle of ancient masonry. '02(Jl12) il. Q. $10; russia, $12. N. F: De Clifford.
DECORATION AND ORNAMENT.
Behrens. Blossom and fruit in decorative arrangement. $12. Hessling.
Bossard. Decorative paintings. $8. Hessling.
Clifford. Period decoration. $3. Clifford & L.
Crane. Bases of design. $2.25. Macmillan.
See also Alphabets;—Lettering.

De Costa, B: F. Whither goest thou? '02 (Jl5) 12°, *50 c. net; pap., 25 c. net. Chr. Press.

Decoy (The). Dana, F. $1.50. Lane.

Dee, Harry. James Griffin's adventures on land and sea. 1900. '02(F8) 12°, (Adventure ser.) $1. Yewdale.

Deeds of faith. Neale, J. M. 40 c. E. & J. B. Young.

Deel, G: A. Practical rapid calculator. '01. '02(Ja18) S. 50 c. G: A. Deel.

Deems, E: M., *comp.* Holy-days and holidays. '02(Ap12) O. $5. Funk.

Deep-sea plunderings. Bullen, F. T. $1.50. Appleton.

DEER.
Roosevelt, *and others.* The deer family. net, $2. Macmillan

Defendorf, A. Clinical psychiatry: adapted fr. the 6th Germ. ed. of Kraeplin's *Lehrbuch der psychiatrie.* '02(Je14) il. 8°, net, $3.50. Macmillan.

Definition of a gentleman. Newman, J: H: $1; 50 c. Kirgate Press.

De Forest, J. W. Poems; medley and Palestina. '02(Mr29) 12°, $1.25. Tuttle, M. & T.

Delano, Fes. J. Susanne. '02(Je7) il. D. (Cosy corner ser.) 50 c. L. C. Page.

DeLaurence, L. W: Hypnotism. 2d ed. '01. '02(Ap26) 12°, $1.50. Henneberry.

De Laurence, L. W: Practical lessons in hypnotism and magnetism. '02(Jl12) 12°, $1; pap., 50 c. Drake.

DELAWARE.
Sellers. Allied families of Del. $5. E. J. Sellers.

De Leon, Dan. Socialism *versus* anarchism. '01. '02(F15) D. pap., 10 c. N. Y. Labor News.

De Leon, T: C. Inauguration of President Watterson: Gormanius; Temple of trusts, and other travesties. '02(Mr1) il. D. pap., 25 c. Am. Writers'.

Del Mar, Alex. History of money in England and other states. '02(Je7) 8°, $2. Cambridge.

Del Mar, Alex. History of money in Germany and other European states. '02(Jl12) 12°. *$2 net. Cambridge.

Del Mar, Alex. History of money in the Netherlands. '02(Je7) 8°, 50 c. Cambridge.

Del Mar, Alex. History of the precious metals. 2d ed. '02(Je7) 8°, net, $3. Cambridge.

DELSARTE SYSTEM.
Stebbins. Delsarte system of expression. $2. Werner.

Demetrius. *See* Schiller, J. C. F. v.

Deming, Philander. Adirondack stories. New ed. '02(My17) 16°, 75 c. Houghton, M. & Co.

Democracy: Am novel. [New ed.] '02 (Ap5) D. $1. Holt.

DEMOCRACY.
Addams. Democracy and social ethics. net, $1.25. Macmillan.
Lowell. Democracy. net, $2. Houghton, M. & Co.
See also Political science.

DEMONOLOGY.
Alexander. Demonic possession in the New Testament. net, $1.50. Scribner.
See also Devil.

De Montmorency, J. E. G. State intervention in Eng. education. '02(My24) 12°, (Cambridge Univ. Press ser.) net, $1.50. Macmillan.

Demorest, A. F., *ed.* Cambridge encyclopædia of esoteric subjects. v. 3. '02(Je7) 8°, net, $3. Cambridge.

Dendron, Bertram. Man in the moon. '02 (My10) il. T. 50 c. Bonnell.

Denning, Marg. Mosaics from India. '02 (Ap19) 12°, net, $1.50. Revell.

Dennis, Annie E. New Annie Dennis cook book. '01. '02(Ap12) 12°, $1.50. Mutual Pub. Co.

Dennis, Ja. S. Centennial survey of foreign missions: statistical supp. to Christian missions and social progress. '02(F15) il. obl. O. net, $4. Revell.

Dennis, L. M., *and* Clarke, F. W. Laboratory manual to accompany Elementary chemistry. '02(Je21) il. D. 50 c. Am. Bk.

DENTISTRY.
See Teeth.

Denton, Dan. Brief description of New York; repr. from orig. ed. of 1670. '02(Jl19) O. bds., *$1.50 net; Jap. pap., $3 net. Burrows.

DE PEYSTER FAMILY.
See Leach, J. G.

De Quincey, T: Selections; ed. by M. H. Turk. '02(Je21) D. (Athenæum Press ser.) $1.05. Ginn.

Desert and the sown. Foote, *Mrs.* M. H. $1.50. Houghton, M. & Co.

DESIGN.
See Decoration and ornament.

Desmond, H. J. Chats within the fold. '01. '02(Ja11) S. net, 75 c. Murphy.

De Solla, J. M. Fallacies of religion. New issue. '02(Mr29) 12°, pap., 25 c. Pierce & Z.

DETECTIVES.
Sullivan. Detective adviser. 60 c. Int. Detective.

DEUTERONOMY.
See Bible.

Deutsche gaben. Nies, K. 25 c. Witter.

Devereux, Ma. Lafitte of Louisiana. '02 (Je21) il. D. $1.50. Little, B. & Co.

Deveron, Hugh. Songs of the Sahkohnagas. '02(Ap26) D. $1.25. Abbey Press.

DEVOTIONAL EXERCISES AND MEDITATIONS.
Fourfold thoughts. $1. Revell.
Hall. Meditations and vows. $1.50. Dutton.
Matheson. Times of retirement. net, $1.25. Revell.
Quadrupani. Light and peace. net, 50 c. Herder.

DEVIL (The).
Townsend. Satan and demons. net, 25 c. Jennings.

Dewey, Byrd S. Bruno. New ed. '01. '02 (F15) 16°, (Children's friend ser.) bds., 50 c. Little, B. & Co.

DEWEY, G:
Halstead. Life and achievements of Admiral Dewey. $1.50; $2.25; $3.25. Dominion.

Dewey, J: Educational situation. '02(F1) D. (Cont. to educ., no. 3.) pap., net, 50 c. Univ. of Chic.
Dewey, J: Psychology and social practice. '01· '02(Ja11) S. (Univ. of Chic. cont. to educ., no. 2.) net, 25 c. Univ. of Chic.
Dewey, J: *See also* McLellan, J. A.
Dewey, Julia M. *See* Cady, M. R.
De Windt, Harry. Finland as it is. '02(Je7) 8°, net, $3. Dutton.
Dexter, Jos. S. Elem. practical exercises on sound, light, and heat. '01· '02(Mr8) il. D. (Practical elem. science ser.) 90 c. Longmans.

DIAGNOSIS.
Albert. Diagnosis of surgical diseases. $5; $5.50. Appleton.
Simon. Clinical diagnosis by microscopical and chemical methods. net, $3.75. Lea.
Watkins. Diagnosis by means of the blood. $5. Physicians'.

DIARIES.
Gower. Old diaries, 1881-1901. net, $4.50. Scribner.
Laird & Lee's diary and time saver, 1902. 25 c. Laird.

Diary of a goose girl. Wiggin, *Mrs.* K. D. $1. Houghton, M. & Co.
Dicey, E: Story of the Khedivate. '02(Je21) 8°, net, $4. Scribner.
Dickens, C: Holly Tree Inn, and Seven poor travellers. '01· '02(Mr1) 8°, net, $1.50. Lippincott.
Dickens, C: Story of Paul Dombey. '01· '02(Mr1) 12°, pap., 15 c. Lippincott.
Dickey Downy. Patteson, V. S. 25 c. A. J. Rowland.
Dickinson, E. Music in the hist. of the western church. '02(My10) O. net, $2.50. Scribner.
Dickson, C: R. First aid in accidents. '02 (Mr8) 18°, net, 50 c. Revell.
Dickson, Harris. Siege of Lady Resolute. '02(Mr1) D. $1.50. Harper.
Dickson, Leonard E. College algebra. '02 (F1) il. 8°, net, $1.50. Wiley.
Dickson, Leonard E. Linear groups; with exposition of the Galois Field theory. '02 (F15) 12°, net, $4. Stechert.

DICTIONARIES.
See Encyclopædias;—*also* names of languages and subjects.

DIET.
Beard. Guide book to natural, hygienic and humane diet. $1; 50 c. Alliance.
Beard. Guide-book to natural, hygienic and humane diet. net, $1. Crowell.
Jewett. Childbed nursing; notes on infant feeding. 80 c. Treat.
Judson *and* Gittings. Artificial feeding of infants. $2. Lippincott.
Richards *and* Williams. Dietary computer. net, $1.50. Wiley.
See also Hygiene;—Nurses and nursing.

DIGESTION.
Brunton. On disorders of assimilation, digestion, etc. net, $4; net, $5. Macmillan.

Dill, Ja. B. *See* New Jersey. General corp. act.—Laws rel. to corporations.
Dill, W: T. Changes and adds. to Dill's constables' guide, made necessary by the act of 1901. '02(Jl12) index, S. (Free to owners of the orig. ed.) T. & J. W. Johnson.

DINING.
See Cookery;—Toasts.

DIPHTHERIA.
Northrup, *ed.* Diphtheria, measles, etc. net, $5; $6. Saunders.

DIPLOMACY.
See Eastern question.

Direct answers to plain questions for Am churchmen. Scadding, C: net, 50 c. Whittaker.

DISEASE.
See Pathology.

DISSECTION.
Howes. Atlas of practical elem. zootomy. net, $3.50. Macmillan.
See also Anatomy;—Vivisection.

Dissertationes Americanæ; classical philology. O. pap. Scott, F. & Co.
—Hellems. Lex de imperio Vespasiani. 50 c. (1.)
Distinctive marks of the Episcopal church. McCormick, J: N. 25 c. Young Churchman.
District of Columbia. *Ct. of appeals.* Repts. (C: C. Tucker.) v. 18. '02(Mr1) O. shp., $5. Lowdermilk.
District of Columbia. Laws rel. to negotiable instruments. '02(Ap26) S. pap., 20 c. Lowdermilk.
Ditmars, Raymond L. *See* Baskett, J. N.
Divine comedy. *See* Dante Alighieri;—*also* Wright, W. J. P.
Divine key of the Revelation. Brown, W: E. v. 2. $1.50. Armstrong & B.
Divine language of celestial correspondence. Turnbull, C. $2. Alliance.
Divine religion of humanity. Wilson, C. D. net, 20 c. Presb. Bd.
Dix, Beulah M., *and* **Harper**, Carrie A. The beau's comedy. '02(Mr29) il. D. $1.50. Harper.
Dix, Dorothy, *pseud.* *See* Gilmer, E. M.
Dixon, T:, *jr.* The leopard's spots. '02 (Mr22) il. D. $1.50. Doubleday, P.
Dmitriev-Mámonóv, A. I., *and* Zdziarski, A. F., *eds.* Guide to the great Siberian railway: Eng. tr. by L. Kúkol-Yasnopólsky. '02(Jl19) il. 8°, *$3.50 net. Putnam.
Doane, W: C. Rhymes from time to time. '01· '02(Mr22) 12°, $1.50. Albany Diocesan Press.
Dobbins, Fk. Story of the world's worship. '02(Mr22) 12°, $2.25; hf. mor., $3.25. Dominion.
Dobson, Austin. Miscellanies. (2d ser.) '01· '02(Mr22) D. net, $1. Dodd.

DOCTRINES.
See Theology.

Dods, M. Parables of our Lord. New issue. '02(Ap12) 12°, $1.50. Whittaker.
Dog-day journal. Drum, B. 50 c. Abbey Press.
Dog of Flanders. La Rame, L. de. 15 c. Houghton, M. & Co.

DOGMA.
See Theology.

Dole, N. H., *ed.* *See* Schiller, J. C. F. v.
Dollar, J: A. W. Operative technique for veterinary surgeons. '02(Jl12) 8°, $3.75. W: R. Jenkins.
Dombey and son. *See* Dickens, C:

DOMESTIC ECONOMY.
Ellsworth. Queen of the household. $2.50. Ellsworth.

DOMESTIC ECONOMY.—*Continued.*
Lush. Domestic economy for scholarship and certificate students. net, 60 c. Macmillan.
Seeley. Cook book; with chap. on domestic servants, etc. net, $2; net, $3. Macmillan.
See also Cookery;—Gardening.
Don Carlos. *See* Schiller, J. C. F. v.
Don Quixote. *See* Cervantes Saavedra.
Donnelly, Fs. P. Imitation and analysis; Eng. exercises. '02(Jl12) S. 60 c. Allyn & B.
Dorothy South. Eggleston, G: C. $1.50. Lothrop.
Dorothy Vernon of Haddon Hall. Major, C: $1.50. Macmillan.
Doty, Alvah H. Manual of instruction in the principles of prompt aid to the injured. 4th ed., rev. and enl. '02(Jl19) il. D. $1.50. Appleton
Double-barrelled detective story. Clemens, S: L. $1.50. Harper.
DOUBT.
See Faith;—Skepticism.
DOUGLAS, Stephen A.
Brown. Stephen Arnold Douglas. net, 65 c.; net, 50 c. Houghton, M. & Co.
Douglass, Fk. A. Colonel Harold de Lacey. '02(Je7) D. $1.25. Neely.
DOUW, G.
Martin. Gerard Douw. $1.75. Macmillan.
Down historic waterways. Thwaites, R. G. net, $1.20. McClurg.
Doyle, A. C. Hound of the Baskervilles. '02(Ap19) il. D. $1.25. McClure, P.
Doyle, A. C. War in South Africa. '02 (Jl5) 12°, 10 c. McClure, P.
Doyle, Sherman. Presbyterian home missions. '02(Je21) il. D. net, $1. Presb. Bd.
Dragons of the air. Seeley, H. G. net, $1.40. Appleton.
DRAMA AND DRAMATISTS.
Schelling. The Eng. chronicle play. net, $2. Macmillan.
See also Actors and actresses.
DRAWING.
Augsburg. Drawing. 3 bks. ea., 75 c. Educ. Pub.
Crane. Line and form $2.25. Macmillan.
See also Anatomy for artists;—Decoration and ornament;—Mechanical drawing;—Perspective;—Topographical drawing.
DRAWINGS.
Underwood, *il.* Some pretty girls. $3; $5. Quail & W.
DREAMS.
See Fortune-tellers.
Dresser, Fk. F. Employers' liability, in N. Y., Mass., Ind., Ala., Colo., and Eng. '02 (My24) O. shp., $6. Keefe-D.
Dresser, Horatio W. Book of secrets, with studies in self-control. '02(Mr8) D. net, $1. Putnam.
Dresser, Julius A. True history of mental science; rev., with notes, by H. W. Dresser. [New issue.] '02(Mr22) D. 20 c. Alliance.
Dressler, Flo. Feminology. '02(F15) il. O. $3. Dressler.
Drewitt's dream. Alden, W: L. $1; 50 c. Appleton.
DRILLS (*fancy*).
Harper. Moral drill for the school-room. $1. Kellogg.
Hatch. Zobo patriotic drill. 15 c. Hints
DRINKS.
See Beverages.
Droch, *pseud.* *See* Bridges, R.
Drude, Paul. Theory of optics; fr. the Germ. '02(My10) O. $4. Longmans.
Drum, Blossom, *pseud.* Dog-day journal. '02(F22) D. 50 c. Abbey Press.
Drummers' yarns. Schofield, R. J. 25 c. Excelsior.
Drummond, Hamilton. The Seigneur de Beaufoy. '02(My17) il. D. $1.50. L. C. Page.
DRUMMOND, H:
Simpson. Henry Drummond. 75 c. Scribner.
Twing. Henry Drummond in spirit life. 10 c. Star
Drummond, Josiah H., *comp.* Maine masonic text-book. 5th ed. '02(Je7) 12°, $1.40; leath. tuck, $1.50. Berry.
DU BARRY, *Mme.*
Morehead. Madame Du Barry. 50 c. Donohue.
Du Bois, A: J. Mechanics of engineering. v. 1. '01. '02(Ja18) il. 4°, $7.50; v. 2. (Je21) $10. Wiley.
Du Bois, E. F., *comp.* Harvard Univ. songs. '02(Je28) 12°, $1.50. Ditson.
Duchess (The), *pseud.* *See* Hungerford, *Mrs.* M. H.
DUCK SHOOTING.
See Shooting.
Duckwitz, Louise C. What Thelma found in the attic. [New issue.] '01. '02(Mr22) il. O. $1. Alliance.
Dudeney, *Mrs.* H: Spindle and plough. '02 (Mr22) D. $1.50. Dodd.
Dudevant, *Mme.* A. L. A. *See* Sand, G:
Duff, Arch. Theology and ethics of the Hebrews. '02(My10) D. (Semitic ser.) net, $1.25. Scribner.
Duff, E: M., *and* Allen, T: G. Psychic research and gospel miracles. '02(Mr22) D. net, $1.50. Whittaker.
Duggan, S. P. H. Eastern question. '02 (Jl12) 8°, (Columbia Univ. studies in history, economics and public law, v. 14, no. 3.) pap., *$1.50 net. Macmillan.
Duguid, C: Story of the Stock Exchange [London.] '02(Mr15) il. 12°, net, $2. Dutton.
Duhring, L: A., Lydston, G. F., *and others.* Syphilis. '02(Ap12) 12°, net, $1. Treat.
Dukesmith, Fk. H. The air brake, its use and abuse. '02(Je21) il. D. $1. F. H. Dukesmith.
Dull Miss Archinard. Sedgwick, A. D. $1.50. Century Co.
Dumas, Alex. Romances. Versailles ed. '02(Mr22) 40 v., il. 8°, subs., net, per v., $1.50. Little, B. & Co.
Dumas, Alex. The King's gallant; tr. by H: L. Williams. '02(Je7) il. D. $1. Street.
Dumas, Alex. Napoleon; adapt. and ed. by W. W. Vaughan. '02(Ap12) 12°, (Siepmann's elem. Fr. ser.) net, 50 c. Macmillan.
Dunbar, Paul L. Sport of the gods. '02(My10) D. $1.50. Dodd.
Dunn, Arch., *jr.* New ideas on bridge. '02 (Mr8) 16°, 50 c. Scribner.

Dunn, F. Veterinary medicines. New rev. ed. '01- '02(F22) 8°, $3.75. W: R. Jenkins.
Dunning, W: A. Hist. of political theories. '02(F22) 8°, net, $2.50. Macmillan.
Dupre, A., *and* Hake, H. W. Manual of inorganic chemistry. '01- '02(F15) 12°, $3. Lippincott.
Durand, W: F: Practical marine engineering. '02(Ap5) il. 8°, $5. Marine Engineering.
Durège, H. Elements of the theory of functions of a complex variable; ed. by G: E. Fisher and I: J. Schwatt. '01- '02(Ja4) 8°, net, $2. Macmillan.
Durrell's Battery. *See* Cuffel, C: A.
Dustin, Eddie. The make good book of parodies. '01- '02(Ja11) S. pap., 50 c. E. Dustin.
Dutiful child. Wetzel, F. X. 40 c. Herder.
Dutto, L. A. Life of Bartolomé de las Casas and first leaves of Am. ecclesiastical history. '02(Mr8) 8°, net, $1.50. Herder.
Duxbury doings. Le Row, C. B. $1. Burt.
Dwight, C: A. S. Railroading with Christ. '02(Je21) il. D. $1. Am. Tr.
DYEING.
Rawson, *and others.* Dictionary of dyes, mordants, and other compounds. net, $5. Lippincott.
Dyer, T: H:, *and* Hassall, Arth. History of modern Europe fr. fall of Constantinople. 3d ed., rev. v. 6; with bibliog. and index. '02(Mr8) 12°, net, $2. Macmillan.
Dynamic aspects of nutrition. Horridge, F. $1.50. Wood.
DYNAMICS.
See Aerodynamics; — Electricity; — Mechanics; — Physics.
DYNAMOS AND MOTORS.
Arnold. Armature windings of direct current dynamos. $2. Van Nostrand
Bubier. How to build dynamo-electric machinery. $2.50. Bubier.
Harmsworth, *and others.* Motors and motor driving. $3.50; $5. Little, B. & Co.
Sheldon *and* Mason. Dynamo electric machinery. 2 v. ea., net, $2.50. Van Nostrand.
Wiener. Calculation of dynamo-electric machines. $3. Elec. World.
See also Cars.
Eadie, J: Biblical cyclopædia. New ed. '01- '02(Mr1) il. 8°, net, $3.75. Lippincott.
Eagle lib. S. pap. Brooklyn Eagle.
—Visitor's guide to Paris. 10 c. (v. 17, 7.)
See also Brooklyn Eagle library.
Eakle, Arth. S. Colemanite from So. California. '02(Je14) O. (Univ. of Cal.; bull. of dept. of geology, v. 3, no. 2.) pap., 15 c. Univ. of Cal.
EAR.
Bacon. Manual of otology. *$2.25 net. Lea.
Brühl *and* Politzer. Atlas epitome of otology. net, $3. Saunders.
Gradle. Diseases of the nose, pharynx and ear. net, $3.50. Saunders.
Wood, *and others, eds.* Eye, ear, nose and throat. $1.50. Year Bk.
Earle, Stephen C. Rutland home of Maj. Gen. Rufus Putnam. '01- '02(Mr8) il. O. pap., 30 c., bds., 50 c. S. C. Earle.
Early Am. fiction. Wegelin, O. net, $2. O. Wegelin.

EARTH.
Ball. Earth's beginning. net, $1.80. Appleton.
See also Geodesy.
East of the barrier. Graham, J. M. net, $1. Revell.
EASTER.
Swartz. Easter and the resurrection. net, 15 c. Revell.
EASTERN QUESTION.
Duggan. Eastern question. *$1.50 net. Macmillan.
Eastman, Eph. R: Poems. '02(Je7) S. $1. Hadley Pr.
Easy lessons in mechanical drawing. *See* Meyer, J. G. A.
Ebersole, E. C. *See* Iowa. Encyclopedia of law.
Eccles, W. M. Hernia. '02(My10) il. 8°, $2.50. Wood.
Ecclesiazusæ (The). *See* Aristophanes.
Eckley, W: T: *and* Corinne B. Regional anatomy of the head and neck. '02(Mr1) il. 8°, net, $2.50. Lea.
Eclectic manual. See Scudder's.
ECLECTIC MEDICINE.
Mundy. Eclectic practice in diseases of children. net, $2.50. Scudder.
Eclectic school readings. D. Am. Bk.
—Bartlett. Animals at home. 45 c.
—Bradish. Stories of country life. 40 c.
—McCullough. Little stories for little people. 25 c.
ECOLOGY.
See Botany.
Eddy, R:, *ed. See* Universalist register.
Edgerly, Webster. Natural reader. '02(Je28) 12°, $1.50. Ralston.
EDGEWOOD, Pa.
Pennsylvania. Health ordinance of the borough of Edgewood. $1. Nicholson.
Edison, T: A. Telegraphy self-taught. '02 (Je21) il. D. $1. Drake.
Editorial echoes. Payne, W: M. net, $1. McClurg.
Edle blut (Das). Wildenbruch, E. A. v. 30 c. Am. Bk.
EDUCATION.
Creighton. Thoughts on education. net, $1.60. Longmans.
De Montmorency. State intervention in Eng. education. net, $1.50. Macmillan.
Dewey. Educational situation. net, 50 c. Univ. of Chic.
Fennell, *and others.* Notes of lessons on Herbartian methods. $1.10. Longmans.
Henderson. Education and the larger life. net, $1.30. Houghton, M. & Co.
Kemp. Hist. of education. net, $1.25. Lippincott.
Lang, *ed.* Educational creeds of the 19th century. 75 c. Kellogg.
Seeley. Foundations of education. $1. Hinds.
Taylor, *ed.* Practical school problems. v. 1, pt. 1. 30 c. [W: B. Harison] Soc. Sch. Problems.
Young. Some types of modern educ. theory. net, 25 c. Univ. of Chic.
See also Business education; — Children; — Examinations; — Home study; — Knowledge; — Memory; — Psychology; — Schools; — Students; — Teachers and teaching; — *also* National Herbart Soc.
Educational foundations of trade and industry. Ware, F. net, $1.20. Appleton.

EDWARD I., *King of England.*
Jenks. Edward Plantagenet, (Edward I.) net, $1.35; net, $1.60. Putnam.

EDWARD VII., *King of England.*
Carman. Ode on the coronation of King Edward. net, $1. L. C. Page.
Pascoe. Pageant and ceremony of the coronation of their majesties King Edward and Queen Alexandra. net, $1.50. Appleton.
Watson. Ode on day of the coronation of King Edward VII. net, $1; net, $3.50. Lane.

Edwards, Owen M. Wales. '02(Jl19) il. D. (Story of the nations ser., no. 62.) **$1.35 net; hf. leath., $1.60 net. Putnam.

Efird, C. M., *rep.* *See* South Carolina. *Sup. ct.* Repts.

Effront, Jean. Enzymes and their applications; Eng. tr. by S: C. Prescott. v. I. '02(F1) 8°, $3. Wiley.

Egan, Maurice F. Belinda. '02(F8) D. $1. Kilner.

Eggleston, G: C. American immortals; record of men whose names are inscribed in the Hall of Fame. '02(Mr22) 8°, $10. Putnam.

Eggleston, G: C. Bale marked circle X. '02 (My24) D. net, $1.20. Lothrop.

Eggleston, G: C. Dorothy South. '02(Mr29) D. $1.50. Lothrop.

EGYPT.
Babcock. Letters from Egypt and Palestine. net, $1. Scribner
Baedeker, *ed.* Egypt. net, $4.50. Scribner.
Barber. Mechanical triumphs of ancient Egyptians. net, $1.25. Dodd.
De Clifford. Egypt, the cradle of ancient masonry. $10; $12. N. F: De Clifford.
Dicey. Story of the Khedivate. net, $4. Scribner.
Guide to Palestine and Egypt. net, $3.25. Macmillan.
See also Cairo.

Ehrlich, *Mrs.* Bertha. Light of our spirit. '02(Mr29) S. 25 c. B. Ehrlich

Einstein, Lewis. Italian Renaissance in England: studies. '02(Ap12) il. 12°, (Columbia University studies in comparative literature.) net, $1.50. Macmillan.

Elbertus, *Fra, pseud.* *See* Hubbard, E.

Eldridge, J. L. What think ye of Christ, etc.: [poems.] '01· '02(Mr1) il. D. $1. Abbey Press.

ELECTIONS.
Jewett, *comp.* Manual for election officers and voters. $2; $1.50. M. Bender.
New York. Jewett's primary election law. 50 c. M. Bender.

ELECTRIC ENGINEERING.
Parr. Electrical engineering testing. net, $3.50. Van Nostrand.

ELECTRIC LIGHT.
Houston *and* Kennelly. Electric arc lighting.—Incandescent lighting. ea., $1. McGraw.

ELECTRIC MEASUREMENT.
Hobbs. Arithmetic of electrical measurements. 50 c. Van Nostrand.
See also Galvanometer.

ELECTRIC MOTORS.
See Dynamos and motors;—Cars.

ELECTRICITY.
American electrical cases. v. 7. $6. M. Bender.
Atkinson. Electrical and magnetic calculations. net, $1.50. Van Nostrand.
Beaton. Vest-pocket compend of electricity. 75 c.; 50 c. Laird.
Bubier. Experimental electricity. $1. Bubier.
Clarke. A B C of electrical experiments. $1. Excelsior.
Hadley. Practical exercises in magnetism and electricity. net, 60 c. Macmillan.
Jackson. Elem. text-book on electricity and magnetism, and their applications. net, $1.40. Macmillan.
Munro. Nociones de electricidad. 40 c.' Appleton.
Practical electricity. $2. Cleveland Armature.
Swoope. Lessons in practical electricity. net, $2. Van Nostrand.
Webber. Graduated coll. of problems in electricity. $3. Spon.
Wolcott. On the sensitiveness of the coherer. 20 c. Univ. of Wis.
Wordingham. Central electrical stations $7.50. Lippincott.
See also Alternating currents;—Dynamos and motors;—Electric light;—Roentgen rays;—Telephone.

Elementary electro technical ser. sq. S. $1. McGraw.
—Houston *and* Kennelly. Alternating electric currents.—Electric arc lighting.—Electric incandescent lighting.—Electric telephone.

Elements and notation of music. McLaughlin, J. M. 55 c. Ginn

ELIOT, George.
Stephen. George Eliot. net, 75 c. Macmillan.

Eliot, H: W., *jr.* *See* Hall, F: G.

Elisabeth, *Madame.* Memoir and letters of Madame Elisabeth, sister of Louis XVI. '02(Mr8) il. 8°, (Versailles hist. ser.) subs., per v., $6; ¾ leath., per v., $9. Hardy, P. & Co.

Elizabeth and her German garden. '02(My10) 12°, (Home lib.) $1. Burt.

Elizabethan prayer-book and ornaments. Gee, H: net, $1.25. Macmillan.

Ellacombe, H: N. In my vicarage garden. '02 (My24) 12°, net, $1.50. Lane.

Ellicott, J: M. Life of John Ancrum Winslow, Rear Admiral U. S. N. '02(Ja25) O. $2.50. Putnam.

Elliot, D. G. *See* Roosevelt, T.

Elliot lectures. *See* Orr, J.

Elliott, C: B. Law of insurance. '02(Ap19) O. shp., $4. Bowen-M.

Elliott, Jonathan. Debates on the federal constitution. '01. '02(Mr1) 5 v., 8°, net, $10; shp., net, $12. Lippincott.

Ellis, E: S. Life of William McKinley. '01. '02(F15) 12°, (Undine lib., no. 9.) pap., 25 c. Street.

Ellsworth, Tinnie, ["*Mrs.* M. W. Ellsworth."] Queen of the household. New century ed., rev. and enl. '02(Ja18) 12°, $2.50. Ellsworth.

Ellwood, C: A. Aristotle as a sociologist. '02(Mr22) 8°, (Pub. of the soc., no. 332.) pap., 15 c. Am. Acad. Pol. Sci.

ELMA, N. Y.
Jackman. Hist. of the town of Elma, Erie Co., N. Y., 1620-1901. $3. Hausauer.
Elmore, Ja. B. A lover in Cuba, and poems. '01· '02(Mr8) il. S. $1. J. B. Elmore.
ELOCUTION.
Ryan. Elocution and dramatic art. 75 c. Angel Press.
See also Orators and oratory;—Preaching;—Readers and speakers;—Voice.
ELOQUENCE.
See Orators and oratory;—Preaching.
Elwell, J. B. Bridge; its principles and rules of play. '02(Ap19) S. net, $1.25. Scribner.
Ely, R. T. *See* Vincent, J: M.
EMBLEMS.
See Tombstones.
EMBRYOLOGY.
Keith. Human embryology and morphology. $4.50. Longmans.
Emerson, E: R. Story of the vine. '02 (Ap12) D. net, $1.25. Putnam.
Emerson, *Mrs.* Ellen R. Nature and human nature. '02(Mr15) D. net, $1.25. Houghton, M. & Co.
Emerson, R. W. [Essays.] '01· '02(Ap5) S. (Little masterpieces.) 50 c. Doubleday, P.
Emerson, R. W. Nature. '02(Jl12) 12°, (Home lib.) $1. Burt.
Emerson, R. W. Representative men. '02 (My17) 12°, (Home lib.) $1. Burt.
Emerson, Willis G: Buell Hampton. '02 (My10) D. $1.50. Forbes.
Emerton, Ja. H. Common spiders of the U. S. '02(Jl12) il. sq. D. *$1.50 net. Ginn.
Emery, W: D'E. Handbook of bacteriolog. diagnosis, incl. instructions for clinical examination of the blood. '01· '02(F15) 12°, net, $1.50. Blakiston.
Empire of business. Carnegie, A. subs., $3. Doubleday, P.
Employers' liability. Dresser, F. F. $6. Keefe-D.
En son nom. Hale, E: E. $1. W: R. Jenkins.
ENCYCLOPAEDIAS.
Appleton's annual cyclopædia, 1901. subs., $5; $6; $7; $8. Appleton.
Century dict. and cyclopedia. 10 v. subs., $80-$150. Century Co.
Cheyne *and* Black. Encyc. Biblica. v. 3. subs., net. $5; net, $7.50. Macmillan.
Eadie. Biblical cyclopædia. net, $3.75. Lippincott.
Holst, *ed.* Teachers' and pupils' cyclopædia. v. 1-3. $12.75. Holst.
Morris. 20th century encyclopædia. $3.50; $4.25; $5.50. Winston.
Sellow. Three thousand sample questions. 50 c. Bellows.
Spofford *and* Annandale, *eds.* xxth century cyclopædia and atlas. 8 v. $20; $26. Gebbie.
See also under special subjects.
Engels, F: Socialism; tr. by E: Aveling. '01· '02(F1) D. (Arm and hammer ser.) 50 c. N. Y. Labor News.
ENGINEERING.
Baker. Municipal engineering and sanitation. net, $1.25. Macmillan.
Du Bois. Mechanics of engineering. v. 1. $7.50; v. 2. $10. Wiley.
Harcourt. Civil engineering as app. in construction. $5. Longmans.

ENGINEERING.—*Continued.*
Hawkins. Aids to engineers' examinations. $2. Audel.
Hawkins. Handbook of calculations for engineers and firemen. $2. Audel.
Problems in the use and adjustment of engineering instruments. $1.25. Wiley.
See also Architecture;—Bridges;—Electrical engineering;—Hydraulic engineering;—Irrigation;—Marine engineering;—Railroads;—Sanitary engineering;—Steam engine;—Surveying;—Water-supply.
Engineering Magazine. Index, 1896-1900; ed. by H: H. Supplee. '02(Mr1) 8°, $7.50. Engineering Mag.
ENGINES.
Dalby. Balancing of engines. $3.75. Longmans.
See also Corliss engine;—Steam engines.
ENGLAND.
Baldwin. Scutage and knight service in England. net, $1. Univ. of Chic.
Blauvelt. Development of cabinet government in England. net, $1.50. Macmillan.
Blomfield. Formal garden in England. $3. Macmillan.
Einstein. Italian Renaissance in England. net, $1.50. Macmillan.
Honeyman. Bright days in merrie England. net, $1.50. Honeyman.
Jesse. Historical memoirs. 30 v. ea., $2.50; or set of 15 v., $37.40; $75. L. C. Page.
Lennox. Life and letters; also pol. sketch of the years 1760-1763. 2 v. net, $9. Scribner.
Lubbock. Scenery of England and the causes to which it is due. net, $2.50. Macmillan.
Macmillan's summary of Eng. history on the concentric plan; Senior. net, 15 c. Macmillan.
Maitland. Music in England in 19th century. net, $1.75. Dutton.
Medley. Student's manual of Eng. constitutional history. net, $3.50. Macmillan.
Mowry. First steps in the hist. of England. 70 c. Silver.
Russell. Onlooker's note-book. net, $2.25. Harper.
Saussure. Foreign view of England in the reign of George I. and George II. net, $3. Dutton.
Traill *and* Mann, *eds.* Social England. v. 1. net, $4.50. Putnam.
Wyckoff. Feudal rel. between the kings of England and Scotland under the early Plantagenets. net, $1. Univ. of Chic.
See also Caroline, *Queen of England*;—Clayton-Bulwer treaty;—Edward I., *King of England*;—Edward VII., *King of England*;—Hampshire;—Henry V., *King of England*;—Hertfordshire;—Jesus (Society of);—London;—H. Malvern;—Waterloo.
English catalogue of books, for 1901. '02 (Mr15) O. pap., $1.50. Pub. Weekly.
English chronicle play. Schelling, F. E. net, $2. Macmillan.
English classics, star ser. il. D. Globe Sch. Bk.
—Shakespeare. Julius Cæsar. 32 c.
English composition. Thornton, G. H. 75 c. Crowell.
English girl in Paris. '02(My24) 12°, $1.50. Lane.

ENGLISH LANGUAGE.
Adler. Germ. and Eng. dictionary. pt. 1. $3.50. Appleton.
Aiton *and* Rankin. Exercises in syntax for summer schools, etc. 25 c. Hyde.
Beeman. Analysis of the Eng. sentence. 50 c. Flanagan.
Blain. Syntax of the verb in Anglo-Saxon chronicle, 787-1001. net, 50 c. Barnes.
Chambers's twentieth century dict. of Eng. language. $1.50; $2. Lippincott.
Donnelly. Imitation and analysis: exercises based on Irving's sketch book. 60 c. Allyn & B.
Krüger *and* Smith. Eng.-Germ. conversation book. 25 c. Heath.
Lewis. Applied Eng. grammar. net, 35 c. Macmillan.
Murray, *and others, eds.* New Eng. dictionary. v. 3, pts. 30-34; v. 4, pts. 35, 36. ea., 90 c. Oxford Univ.
Pinney. Spanish and English conversation. 1st, 2d bks. ea., 65 c. Ginn.
Skinner *and* Burgert. Lessons in Eng. based upon principles of literary interpre tation. 50 c. Silver.
Vories. Lab'y method of teaching Eng. and touch typewriting together. $1.25. Inland Pub.
Watrous. First year English. 75 c. Sibley & D.

English law reports, for 1900. '01- '02(F15) 6 v., 8°, shp., $28.50. Little, B. & Co.

ENGLISH LITERATURE.
Andrews. Topics and ref. for the study of Eng. literature. 15 c. Hyde.
Chambers's cyclopædia of Eng. literature. v. 1. net, $5. Lippincott.
Chaucer. English of the XIVth century. 75 c. Ginn.
Marks. Brief hist. outline of Eng. literature. $1. J. A. Marks.
Moody. Hist. of Eng. literature. net, $1.25. Scribner.
Moulton, *and others, eds.* Lib. of literary criticism of Eng. and Am. authors. v. 3. $5; $6.50. Moulton Pub.
Phelps, *comp.* List of general reading, 1580-1902. net, 5 c. Pease-L.

English men of letters ser.; ed. by J: Morley. 12°, **75 c. net. Macmillan.
—Birrell. William Hazlitt.
—Stephen. George Eliot.

English pharisees, French crocodiles. Blouët, P. $1.25. Abbey Press.

English tales in verse. Herford, C: H. $1.50. Scribner.

Englishwoman's year book and directory, 1902; ed. by E. Janes. '02(F1) 12°, $1.50. Macmillan.

Engraved gems. Sommerville, M. net, $1.50. Biddle.

ENGRAVERS AND ENGRAVING.
Altdorfer. Little engravings classical and contemporary. no. 1. net, $1.50. Longmans.
Blake. Little engravings. no. 2. net, $1.50. Longmans.
Whitman. Print-collectors' handbook. net, $5. Macmillan.

Enoch Strone. Oppenheim, E. P. $1.50. G: W. Dillingham.

Enseñar á leer. Arnold, S. L. 40 c. Silver.

ENTERTAINMENTS.
Kellogg. Six musical entertainments. 15 c. Kellogg.
Nies. Deutsche gaben. 25 c.—Rosen im schnee. 50 c. Witter.
See also Drills.

ENTOMOLOGY.
See Insects.

ENZYMES.
Effront. Enzymes and their applications. $3. Wiley.

Eparchæan interval. Lawson, A. C. 10 c. Univ. of Cal.

EPHESIANS.
See Bible.

EPIGRAMS.
Antrim. Naked truths and veiled allusions. 50 c. Altemus.

EPISTLES (The).
See Bible.

Epstein, A. J. Tarquinius Superbus. '02 (My24) il. D. $1.25. Mutual Pub.

EPWORTH LEAGUE.
Nicholson *and* Woods. Notes on Epworth League prayer meeting topics. 15 c. Eaton & M.

Epworth League year-book for 1902. '02 (Ja25) S. pap., net, 10 c. Eaton & M.

EQUATIONS.
Forsyth. Theory of differential equations. v. 4. net, $3.75. Macmillan.

EQUITY.
Ames. Equity jurisdiction. pt. 2. 75 c. Harvard Law.
See also Actions at law.

Erasmus, D. Select colloquies; ed. by M. Whitcomb. '02(Je7) D. (Sixteenth century classics.) $1. [Longmans;] Univ. of Penn.

Erdman, C: R. Ruling elder. '02(Je21) S. pap., 3 c. Presb. Bd.

Ernst, Harold C., *ed.* Animal experimentation. '02(Mr8) 8°, net, $1.50; pap., net, $1. Little, B. & Co

Errand boy of Andrew Jackson. Stoddard, W: O. net, $1. Lothrop.

Ervin, Dayton. The hermitage and random verses. '02(Je7) S. $1. Grafton Press.

Esenwein, J. Berg. How to attract and hold an audience. '02(F1) D. $1. Hinds.

ESKIMOS.
See Innuit language.

ESSAYS.
Miles. How to prepare essays, [etc.] net, $2. Dutton.

Estados Unidos. Constitucion: (Constitution of the U. S. in Spanish by C. Mexia.) '02 (Je7) 8°. $1. Cambridge.

Esther. Racine, J. 35 c. Holt.

ETHICS.
Gabirol. Improvement of moral qualities. net, $1.25. Macmillan.
Ladd. Philosophy of conduct. net, $3.50. Scribner.
Ritchie. Studies in political and social ethics. $1.50. Macmillan.
Schuyler. Systems of ethics. $1.50. Jennings.
See also Character;—Conduct of life;—Courage;—Crime and criminals;—Culture;—Fiction;—Law;—Utilitarianism.

Ethics in the school. Young, E. F. net, 25 c. Univ. of Chic.

ETHNOLOGY.
Hutchinson, *and others.* Living races of mankind. net, $5. Appleton.
See also Folk-lore;—Language.

EUGENE, *Prince.*
Sybel. Prinz Eugen von Savoyen. net, 60 c. Macmillan.

EUROPE.
Carpenter. Europe. 70 c. Am. Bk.
Dyer *and* Hassall. Hist. of modern Europe. v. 6. net, $2. Macmillan.
Helmolt, *and others, eds.* Hist. of the world. v. 4, The Mediterranean countries. $6. Dodd.
Northern Europe: Norway, Russia, the Netherlands, France, Germany and Switzerland. 30 c. Ginn.
Stedman. Complete pocket guide to Europe, 1902. $1.25. W: R. Jenkins.
See also names of countries.

Eustis, Edith. Marion Manning. '02(Je7) D. $1.50. Harper.
Euthyphro. Plato. $1. Am. Bk.
Eve of St. Agnes. *See* Keats, J:
Eve triumphant. Coulevain, P. de. net, $1.20. Putnam.
Evening Post. *See* New York Evening Post.
Evermann, B. W. *See* Jordan, D: S.
Eversley ser. 12°, $1.50. Macmillan.
—Jebb. Modern Greece.
Everybody's opportunity. Rowell, J. H. 10 c. Free Socialist.

EVIDENCE.
Ewbank. Indiana trial evidence. $6. Bowen-M.
Stephen. Digest of the law of evidence. $4. Dissell.
Trickett. Law of witnesses in Pa. $6. T. & J. W. Johnson.

EVOLUTION.
Beecher. Studies in evolution. net, $5. Scribner.
Conley. Evolution and man. net, 75 c. Revell.
Dadson. Evolution and its bearing on religion. net, $1.25. Dutton.
See also Embryology;—Religion and science.

Evolution of the Eng. Bible. Hoare, H. W. net, $2.50. Dutton.
Evolutionary philosophy. Chamberlain, L. T. 50 c. Baker & T.
Ewart, W:, Murrell, W:, *and others.* Climates of London, and of the central and no. portions of England with those of Wales and Ireland. '02(My17) 8°, (Climates and baths of Great Britain, v. 2.) net, $4. Macmillan.
Ewbank, L: B. Indiana trial evidence '02 (My24) O. shp., $6. Bowen-M.
Ewing, *Mrs.* Juliana H. Benjy in beastland. New ed. '01- '02(F15) 16°, (Children's friend ser.) bds., 50 c. Little, B. & Co.
Ewing, *Mrs.* Juliana H. Jackanapes; [also] The brownies; ed. by H: W. Boynton. '02 (My17) S. (Riverside literature ser., no. 151.) pap., net, 15 c. Houghton, M. & Co.
Excelsior lib. O. pap., 25 c. Excelsior.
—Schofield, *comp.* Drummer's yarns and funny jokes. (67.)
Exiled by the world. Imhaus, E. V. $1.50. Mutual Pub.

EXPANSION (political).
Halstead. Pictorial hist. of America's new possessions, the Isthmian canals, and national expansion. $2.50; $3.50; $4.50. Dominion.

Expansion of gases by heat. Randall, W. W. $1. Am. Bk.

EXPERIMENTS.
See Physics.

EXPRESSION.
See Voice.

EYE.
Brown, C. H., *comp.* Optician's manual. 2 v. ea., $2. Keystone.
Greeff. Microscopic examination of the eyes. net, $1.25. Blakiston.
Jennings. Ophthalmoscopy. net, $1.50. Blakiston.
Parsons. Elem. ophthalmic optics. net, $2. Blakiston.
Wood, *and others, eds.* Eye, ear, nose and throat. $1.50. Year Bk.

F., A. M. Tales of my father. '02(Ap19) D. $2. Longmans.

FABLES.
Kleckner. In the misty realm of fable. $1. Flanagan.

Fables of the elite. Gilmer, E. M. $1. Fenno.
Fabre, J. H. Insect life; fr. the Fr.; ed. by F. Merrifield. '02(Ja18) il. 12°, $1.75. Macmillan.

FACE.
See Physiognomy.

Faciology. Stevens, L. B. 25 c. Donohue.
Facsimile reprint of early Canadian books. il. D. net. Congdon.
—Bosworth, *ed.* Hochelaga depicta; Montreal. $3; $4.50.
Facts and comments. Spencer, H. net, $1.20. Appleton.
Fagge, C: H. Text-book of medicine. 4th ed. '02(Ap5) 2 v., 8°, net, $6. Blakiston.
Failure of success. Howard, *Lady* M. $1.50. Longmans.
Failures of vegetarianism. Miles, E. H. net, $1.50. Dutton.
Fairbairn, And. M. Philosophy of the Christian religion. '02(Je7) 8°, net, $3.50. Macmillan.
Fairbanks, Harold W. Home geography for primary grades. '02(My3) il. sq. O. 60 c. Educ. Pub.
Fairchild, Lee. The tippler's vow. '01- '02 (Mr8) il. f°, bds., $10. Croscup.
Fairie, Ja. Notes on lead ores. '01- '02 (My10) D. net, $1. Van Nostrand.
Fairview's mystery. Marquis, G: H. 75 c. Abbey Press.
Fairy favorites. Perrault, C: 50 c. Little, B. & Co.

FAIRY TALES.
Andersen. Selected stories. 15 c. Lippincott.
Brown. In the days of giants: Norse tales. net, $1.10. Houghton, M. & Co.
O'Shea, *ed.* Old world wonder stories. 25 c. Heath.
Valentine, *comp. and ed.* Old, old fairy tales. $1. Burt.
Yeats, *comp.* Irish fairy and folk tales. $1. Burt.

FAITH.
Purves. Faith and life. net, $1.25. Presb. Bd.

FAITH.—*Continued.*
Rainsford. Reasonableness of faith. net, $1.25. Doubleday, P.
See also Religion;—Theology.
Fales, W: E. S. Bits of broken china. '02 (My17) il. S. 75 c. Street.
Falkiner, C. L. Studies in Irish history and biog. mainly of the eighteenth century. '02(Mr8) O. $5. Longmans.
Fallon, Chris. *See* Pennsylvania. Conveyancing.
Fallows, S:, *ed.* Life of William McKinley; with short biog. of Lincoln and Garfield, and life of President Roosevelt. [Internat. memorial ed.] '01- '02(Ap12) 8°, $1.50; hf. mor., $2.25. Regan.
Familia de Alvareda. Caballero, F. 75 c. Holt.
FAMILIES.
See Genealogy.
Famous Scots ser. 12°, 75 c. Scribner.
—Simpson. Henry Drummond.
Fanning, J: T: Practical treatise on hydraulic and water-supply engineering. 15th rev., enl. ed. '02(Ap5) il. 8°, $5. Van Nostrand.
Färber, Wilhelm. Commentar zum katechismus. '02(Je28) 12°, net, $1.50. Herder.
Fargo, Kate M. Songs not set to music. '02 (Mr15) D. $1. Abbey Press.
Farley, Jos. P. West Point in the early sixties, with incidents of the war. '02(Je14) il. O. net, $2. Pafraets.
Farm and fireside lib. il. Q. $1. Crowell & K.
—Cuppy, *ed.* Pictorial natural history. (199.)
Farmer, Ja. E. Brinton Eliot. '02(Je7) 12°. $1.50. Macmillan.
Farmer's school and the visit. Kellogg, A. M. 15 c. Kellogg
FARMS AND FARMING.
Barnard. Farming by inches.—My ten rod farm. ea., 40 c. Coates.
Shepard. Life on the farm. 50 c. Flanagan.
See also Irrigation.
Farquhar, A. B. Manufacturer's need of reciprocity. '02(Mr22) 8°. (Pub. of the soc., no. 330.) pap., 15 c. Am. Acad. Pol. Sci.
Farrington, Fk. Retail advertising for druggists and stationers. '01. '02(Ja11) D net, $1. Baker & T.
Farson, C: T. *See* Illinois. Mechanics' lien law.
Fashions in literature. Warner, C: D. net. $1.20. Dodd.
FASTS AND FEASTS.
See Easter;—Holidays;—Lent;—Sunday.
Father Manners. Young, H. $1. Abbey Press.
FATHERS.
Swete. Patristic study. net, 90 c. Longmans.
Faust, C. A. Compendium of automatic pen lettering and designs. '01- '02(F1) obl. D. pap., complete bk., $1; alphabet pt., 75 c. Auto Pen.
Favor of princes. Luther, M. L. 50 c. Jamieson-H.
Favorite songs of love. Mason, J. F. $1.50-$5. Dodge.
Feasey, H: J. Monasticism: what is it? '02 (Mr8) 8°, net, $1. Herder.
Federal citations. *See* Ash, M.
Federal reporter. *See* United States.
Feminology. Dressler, F. $3. Dressler
FENELON, François.
St. Cyres. Life of François Fenelon. net, $2.50. Dutton.

Fennell, M., *and others.* Notes of lessons on the Herbartian methods. '02(Mr22) D. $1.10. Longmans.
FERDINAND, *King of Spain.*
Prescott. Ferdinand and Isabella, the Catholic. 3 v. net, $3. Macmillan.
FERMENTATION.
Matthews. Manual of alcoholic fermentation. net, $2.60. Longmans.
Oppenheimer *and* Mitchell. Ferments and their actions. net, $2.50. Lippincott.
See also Bacteria.
FERNS.
See Botany.
Fersen, *Count* Jean-Axel. Letters and papers; sel. pub. by his great-nephew, Baron R. M. Klinckowström. '02(Mr8) il. 8°. (Versailles hist. ser.) subs., per v., $6; ¼ leath., per v., $9. Hardy, P. & Co.
Feudal relations between the kings of England and Scotland. Wyckoff, C: T. net, $1. Univ. of Chic.
FEVER.
See Malarial fever;—Typhoid fever.
Fickett, M. G., *comp.* *See* Stone, G. L.
FICTION.
Burton. Forces in fiction. net, $1. Bowen-M.
Cody. Sel. from the world's greatest short stories. net, $1. McClurg.
Nield. Guide to best hist. novels and tales. net, $1.75. Putnam.
Wegelin. Early Am. fiction, 1774-1830. net, $2. O. Wegelin.
Fidler, T. C. Calculations in hydraulic engineering. pt. 2, Hydro-kinetics. '02(Ap26) O. (Civil engineering ser.) $3. Longmans.
Fiedler, A. Studies from the nude human figure in motion. '02(Jl5) pls. f°, $12. Hessling.
Field, Eug. Nonsense for old and young. '01- '02(Mr29) il. D. 50 c. Dickerman.
Field, J: E: Saint Berin, the apostle of Wessex. '02(Je7) 12°, $1.50. E. & J. B. Young.
Field book of American wild flowers. Mathews, F. S. net, $1.75. Putnam.
FIELD FAMILY.
Pierce. Field genealogy. 2 v. $10. Conkey.
Field, forest and garden botany. *See* Leavitt, R. G.
Field training of a company of infantry. Craufurd, H. J. $1. Longmans.
Fielde, Adele M. Political primer of New York city and state. [New rev. ed.] '02 (Mr22) S. 75 c.; pap., 50 c. League for Pol. Educ.
Fielding, H: Journal of a voyage to Lisbon. Special ed. '02(Jl19) 8°, bds., **$5 net. Houghton, M. & Co.
Fields, factories, and workshops. Kropotkin, *Prince* P: A. net, 90 c. Putnam.
Fifth string. Sousa, J: P. $1.25. Bowen-M.
Fifty Puritan ancestors. Nash, E. T. $5. Tuttle, M. & T.
Fighting bishop. Hopkins, H. M. $1.50. Bowen-M.
Fillis, Ja. Breaking and riding; with military commentaries. '02(My10) il. 8°, net, $5. Scribner.
FINANCE.
Burton. Financial crises, and periods of industrial and commercial depression. net, $1.40. Appleton.

FINANCE.—*Continued.*
Norton. Statistical studies in N. Y. money-market. net, $1.50; net, $1. Macmillan.
See also Money.
Finck, H: T. Romantic love and personal beauty. New ed. '02(Mr1) 8°, net, $2. Macmillan.
Find the church. Poland, W: net. 5 c. Herder.
Findlay, J. J. Principles of class teaching. '02(Je28) 12°, (Manual for teachers.) net, $1.25. Macmillan.
FINE ARTS.
Cust. Desc. of the sketch-book by Sir Anthony Van Dyck. $17.50. Macmillan.
Cust, *ed.* National portrait gallery. v. 1. subs., for complete work, net, $30. Cassell.
Van der Kellen. Works of Michel Le Blond. net, $30; net, $35. Dodd.
See also Anatomy for artists;—Architecture;—Artists;—Book illustrations;—Ceramics;—Decoration and ornament;—Drawings;—Engravers and engraving;—Lace;—Music;—Painting;—Photography;—Venus di Milo.
FINLAND.
De Windt. Finland as it is. net, $3. Dutton.
Frederiksen. Finland, its public and private economy. $2. Longmans.
Finn, Fs. J. "But Thy love and Thy grace."
FIREARMS.
See Rifle.
FIREMEN.
See Engineering.
Fireside ser. *See* Burt's.
Fireside university of modern invention, etc., for home circle study. McGovern, J: $2.50; $3.75. Union Pub.
Firey, M. J. Infant salvation. '02(F1) D. net, $1.20. Funk.
First aid in accidents. Dickson, C: R. net, 50 c. Revell.
First years of the life of the redeemed after death. Ulyat, W: C. $1.25. Abbey Press.
Firth, Annie. Cane basket work. 1st and 2d ser. '02(Je21) il. 12°, ea., 60 c. Scribner.
Fisguill, R: Mazel. '02(Ap26) D. $1.50. H. S. Stone.
Fish, A. L. Calisthenic dict.: terms used in Am. gymnasia. '02(My10) D. pap., $1. Seminar.
FISH AND FISHING.
Gregg *and* Gardner. Where, when, and how to catch fish on the east coast of Fla. $4. Matthews-N.
Johnson. Forest, lake and river: fishes of N. E. and eastern Canada. 2 v. per set, $300; $500. F. M. Johnson.
Jordan *and* Evermann. American food and game fishes. net, $4. Doubleday, P.
Turner. Giant fish of Fla. **$3.50 net. Lippincott.
See also Salmon;—Trout.
Fisher, Amos T., *and* Patterson, M. J. Elements of physics. '02(My24) il. D. 60 c. Heath.
Fisher, Herb. How to build a model yacht. '02(Ap26) il. f°, ("How-to" ser.) $1. Rudder.
Fisher, J: I. Added interest tables. Rev. ed. '02(Mr29) 8°, $2.50. J: I. Fisher.
Fisher, J: I. 20th century interest tables. '02(Mr29) 12°, $2.50. J: I. Fisher.
Fisher, Ma. Gertrude Dorrance. '02(Ap12) D. $1.50. McClurg.
Fiske, G: B., *comp.* Prize gardening. '01. '02(Ja4) il. 12°, $1. Judd.
Fiske, J: Works. Ed. de luxe. '02(Jl19) 24 v., 8°, subs., ea., **$5 net; ¾ levant, ea., $10 net. Houghton, M. & Co.
Fitch, Eug., ["Ironquill."] Some of the rhymes of Ironquill. 11th ed. '02(Jl5) D. $1.50. Putnam.
Fitch, W: C. Captain Jinks of the Horse marines. '02(Ap19) il. O. $1.25. Doubleday, P.
Fitchett, W: H: Tale of the great mutiny. '01. '02(Ja11) 12°, $1.50. Scribner.
Fitzgerald, E: Poetical and prose writings. '02(Mr15) 7 v., large 8°, subs., regular lim. ed., per v., $6; hand-made pap. ed., per v., $12.50; Jap. ed., per v., $35. Doubleday, P.
Fitzpatrick, T: King of Claddagh. '01. '02 (Ja11) 8°, net, $1.25. Herder.
Five little Peppers abroad. Lothrop, *Mrs.* H. M. net, $1.10. Lothrop.
Five Stuart princesses. Rait, R. S. net, $3.50. Dutton.
Flagg, I: Writer of Attic prose: models from Xenophon. '02(Ap19) D. $1. Am. Bk.
FLAGS.
Ames. Etiquette of yacht colors; yacht flags and their use. 25 c. Annin.
Flanagan's educational ser. S. Flanagan.
—Peterson. First steps in Eng. composition. 35 c.
Flanagan's home and school series for young folks. il. S. 50 c. Flanagan.
—Shepard. Life on the farm.
Flanagan's plan book ser. il. sq. D. pap., 15 c. Flanagan.
—Whitcomb. Little journey to Italy. (v. 5. 5.)—Scotland. (v. 5, 4.)
Fleming, G: Operative veterinary surgery. v. 2. '02(Ap26) 8°, net, $3.25. W: R. Jenkins.
Fleming, T: Around the "Pan" with Uncle Hank. '01. '02(Ja4) il. 12°, $2. Nutshell.
Fleming, W: F. *See* Voltaire.
Fleming, W: H. Shakespeare's plots. '02 (Ja25) O. $1.80. Putnam.
Fleming, Wymble. Glimpses of South Africa in peace and in war. '02(Mr22) 12°, $3. Dominion.
Flesh and the devil. Cole, H. L. $1.50. Neely.
Fletcher, Banister. Hist. of architecture on the comparative method. 4th ed., rev. and enl. '01. '02(Ja11) il. 8°, net, $7.50. Scribner.
Fletcher, W: I., *and* Bowker, R: R., *eds.* Annual literary index, 1901. '02(Ap12) Q. net, $3.50. Pub. Weekly.
Flick, Alex. C. *See* Anderson, J: J.
Flight of the *Swallow.* Morgan, E. M. 50 c. Pott.
Flint, C: R., Hill, J. J., [*and others.*] The trust: its book; ed. by J. H. Bridge. '02 (Je7) D. net, $1.25. Doubleday, P.
Floating treasure. Castlemon, H. $1. Coates.
FLORENCE.
Ross. Florentine villas. $25. Dutton.
Florer, Warren W. Biblische geschichten und kapitel aus Weizsäcker's und Luther's Bibelübersetzungen. '01. '02(Mr8) S. 40 c. Wahr.
Florida. Index to the laws of a general nature, by T: P. Warlow. '02(Je14) O. pap., $1. W. F. Barnes.

Florilegium Latinum; ed. by F. St. John Thackeray and E. D. Stone. 12°. Lane.
—Pre-Victorian poets. $2.50. (1.)
—Victorian poets. net, $2. (2.)
Flower, Elliott. Policeman Flynn. '02(Mr1) il. D. $1.50. Century Co.
Flower and thorn. Whitby, B. $1.50. Dodd.
FLOWERS.
Bridgeman. Flower gardening. 50 c. Coates.
Mathews. Field book of Amer. wild flowers. net, $1.75. Putnam.
Parsons. According to season. net, $1.75. Scribner.
Watson. Flowers and gardens. $1.50. Lane.
See also Botany;—Gardening;—Lilies;—Roses;—Window gardening.
Flowers of Parnassus; ed. by F. B. Money-Coutts. il. 16°, net, 50 c.; leath., net, 75 c. Lane.
—Way, *comp.* Reliques of Stratford-on-Avon. (16.)
Flynt, Josiah, *pseud. See* Willard, J. F.
Fogg's ferry. Callahan, C. E. 75 c.; 25 c. Laird.
FOLK-LORE.
Cushing. Zuñi folk tales. net, $3.50. Putnam.
See also Fairy tales.
Folk tales of Napoleon. Kennan, G: *$1 net. Outlook.
Folks, Homer. Care of destitute, neglected, and delinquent children. '02(F15) 12°, (American philanthropy of the nineteenth century.) net, $1. Macmillan.
Folwell, A. P. Sewerage. 5th ed. '02(Ap19) 8°, $3. Wiley.
Folwell, A. P. Water-supply engineering. 2d ed. '02(F1) 8°, $4. Wiley.
FOOD.
Horridge. Dynamic aspects of nutrition. $1.50. Wood.
See also Cookery;—Diet;—Digestion;—Fruit;—Hygiene;—Meat;—Temperance.
Fool (The). Carson, W: H. $1.50. G: W. Dillingham.
Fool's errand. Tourgée, A. W. $1.50. Fords.
Fool's year. Cooper, E: H. $1; 50 c. Appleton.
Foote, *Mrs.* Ma. H. The desert and the sown. '02(Je7) D. $1.50. Houghton, M. & Co.
For a young queen's bright eyes. Savage, R: H. $1.25; 50 c. Home.
For the colours. Hayens, H. $2. Nelson.
Foraminifera (The). Chapman, F: $3.50. Longmans.
FORCE.
See Aerodynamics.
Forces in fiction. Burton, R: net, $1. Bowen-M.
Ford, P. L., *ed.* Journals of Hugh Gaine, printer. '02(My17) 2 v., il. 8°, net, $15; Jap. pap., net, $25. Dodd.
Ford, Sheridan. Art of folly: [poems.] '02 (Jl12) 8°, **$3 net. Small.
Foreign freemasonry. O'Connor, D. M. 5 c. Kilner.
FOREIGN MISSIONS.
See Missions.
Foreign trade requirements; pub. annually with quarterly supp. '02(Jl5) Q. $10. Lewis.
Foreign view of England. Saussure, C. de. net, $3. Dutton.
Forest, lake and river. Johnson, F. M. $300; $500. F. M. Johnson.
Forest neighbors. Hulbert, W: D. net, $1.50. McClure, P.
FORESTS AND FORESTRY.
Gifford. Practical forestry. net, $1.20. Appleton.
See also Lumber;—Trees.
Forman, S. E. First lessons in civics. Penn. ed. '02(Je14) D. 60 c. Am. Bk.
Forney, E: J. Inductive lessons, adpt. to Isaac Pitman phonography. '01. '02(Mr8) obl. 24°, pap., 80 c. State Normal Sch.
FORREST, Nathan B.
Mathes. General Forrest. net, $1.50. Appleton.
Forsyth, And. R. Theory of differential equations. v. 4. '02(My17) 8°, (Cambridge Univ. Press ser.) net, $3.75. Macmillan.
FORTUNE-TELLERS.
Mystic fortune teller, dream book and policy player's guide. 50 c.; 25 c. Donohue.
Zanciz. How to tell fortunes by cards. 25 c. Drake.
Fortune's wheel. Gray, M. $1. Abbey Press.
Fosdick, C: Austin. *See* Castlemon, H.
Fosdick, J. W. Honor of the Braxtons. '02 il. D. $1.50. J. F. Taylor.
Foster, Rob. V. The Lord's prayer. '02 (Mr22) S. pap., 10 c. Cumberland Press.
Foundations of belief. Balfour, A. J. net, $2. Longmans.
Foundations of education. Seeley, L. $1. Hinds.
Founders of the Mass. Bay Colony. Smith, S. S. *$5 net. Woodward & L.
Four old Greeks. Hall, J. 35 c. Rand, McN. & Co.
Fourcaut, A. *See* Silva, T.
Fourfold thoughts: four text books '02(F8) $1. Revell.
Fowler, Fk. H. Negatives of the Indo-European languages. '02(Mr22) 8°, pap., net, 50 c. Univ. of Chic.
Fowler, Gilbert J. Sewage works analyses. '02(Jl19) 12°, $2. Wiley.
Fowler, Harold N. Hist. of ancient Greek literature. '02(Mr29) il. D. (Twentieth century text-books.) net, $1.40. Appleton. '02(Ap12) 16°, $1. Benziger.
Fowler, W: W. More tales of the birds. '02 (Ap12) il. 12°, $1. Macmillan.
FOWLER FAMILY.
Arthur. Annals of the Fowler family. $3.50. Mrs. J. J. Arthur.
Fox, Emma A. Parliamentary usage for women's clubs. '02(My3) S. net, 65 c. Baker & T.
Fox, Fes. M. The little giant's neighbors. '02(Je28) il. D. (Cosy corner ser.) 50 c. L. C. Page.
Fradenburgh, O. P. Twenty-five stepping stones toward Christ's Kingdom. '02(F8) O. $1. O. P. Fradenburgh.
France, Anatole. Monsieur Bergeret. '02 (Ap19) 12°. (Ser. of modern lang. text-books.) $1. Silver.
FRANCE.
Cæsar. Gallic war. $1.25. Am. Bk.
Mackinnon. Growth and decline of the Fr. monarchy. $7.50. Longmans.
See also Chartres;—Huguenots;—Paris;—Waterloo.

Francesca da Rimini. Morehead, G: 25 c. Ogilvie.

Francis *of Assisi, St.*
Lady (The) Poverty: allegory conc. St. Francis of Assisi. net, $1.75. Tennant.
McIlvaine. St. Francis of Assisi. net, 85 c. Dodd.

Francis, *St.*, Third order of. *See* Kaercher, F. O.

Francis, *Mrs.* C. D. Weekly church teaching for the infants. '02(Je7) 32°, 25 c. E. & J. B. Young.

François, Victor E. Advanced Fr. prose composition. '02(My24) D. cl., 80 c. Am. Bk.

Frank Logan. Clay, *Mrs.* J: M. $1. Abbey Press.

FREDERICK *the Great.*
Macaulay. Frederick the Great. net, 40 c. Macmillan.
Schrader. Friedrich der Grosse und der Siebenjährige Krieg. net, 50 c. Macmillan.

Frederiksen, N. C. Finland, its public and private economy. '02(Ap19) O. $2. Longmans.

Frédérique. Prévost, M. $1.50. Crowell.

FREE THOUGHT.
Baur *and* Herbert. Free thinkers' manual. $4. Radical.

FREE TRADE.
See Tariff.

Free trade almanac, 1902. '02(Ja25) S. pap., 5 c. Am. Free Trade.

Freear, Rob. L: Shadow duellers. '02 (Mr22) D. net, 60 c. Blanchard.

Freeman, A. C. Law of void judicial sales. 4th ed., rev. and enl. '02(Ap12) O. shp., $4. Cen. Law Journ.

Freeman, A. C., *rep.* *See also* American state repts.

Freeman, Flora L. Religious and social work amongst girls. '02((Ap12) 12°, net, $1. Whittaker.

FREEMASONRY.
De Clifford. Egypt, the cradle of ancient masonry; with acct. of the antiquity of masonry. $10; $12. N. F: De Clifford.
Drummond, *comp.* Maine masonic textbook. $1.40; $1.50. Berry.
McGee. Exposition and revelation of ancient free and accepted masonry. $1. J. B. McGee.
O'Connor. Foreign freemasonry. 5 c. Kilner.

Freer, Romeo H., *rep.* *See* West Virginia. *Sup. ct. of appeals.* Repts.

FREIGHT.
See Tables.

Fremantle, T. F. Book of the rifle. '01· '02 (Ja4) il. O. $5. Longmans.

Fremeaux, Paul. With Napoleon at St. Helena; tr. by E. S. Stokoe. '02(Je28) 12°, net, $1.50. Lane.

French, Allen. The colonials. '02(F8) D. $1.50. Doubleday, P.

French, Lillie H. Hezekiah's wives. '02 (Ap5) il. D. net, 85 c. Houghton, M. & Co.

French, N. S. Animal activities. '02(Ap19) il. D. $1.20. Longmans.

French, S: Gibbs. Two wars: autobiog. of Gen. Samuel G. French; Mexican war; war between the states. '01· '02(Ja18) il. 12°, $2. Confederate Veteran.

French classics. *See* Macmillan's.

FRENCH LANGUAGE.
Alissas. Les histoires de tante. net, 40 c. Macmillan.
Baillot *and* Brugnot. French prose composition. 50 c. Scott, F. & Co
Beaumarchais. Barbier de Séville and Lettres. 50 c. Scott, F. & Co.
Berlitz. Grammaire partique de la langue française. v. 3. 50 c. Berlitz.
Bowen. First scientific Fr. reader. 90 c. Heath.
Cameron. Elements of Fr. composition. 75 c. Holt.
Coppée. Morceau de pain. 25 c. W: R. Jenkins.
Dumas. Napoleon. net, 50 c. Macmillan.
France. Monsieur Bergeret. $1. Silver.
François. Advanced Fr. prose composition. 80 c. Am. Bk.
Hale. En son nom. $1. W: R. Jenkins.
Ingres. Cours complet de langue Fr. v. 1. net, $1.50. Univ. of Chic.
La Brète. Mon oncle et mon curé. 50 c. Am. Bk.
Renan. Souvenirs d' enfance et de jeunesse. 75 c. Heath.
Ségur. Les malheurs de Sophie. 45 c. Heath.
Voltaire. Zaïre and Epîtres. 50 c. Scott, F. & Co.

FRENCH LITERATURE.
Crabb. Culture hist. in the Chanson de Geste-Aymeri de Narbonne. net, $1.25. Univ. of Chic.

FRENEAU, Philip.
Austin. Philip Freneau: life and times. net, $2.50. Wessels.

FRESNO Co., Cal.
Hudson. California vineyards: scenes in Fresno Co. 35 c. H. B. Hudson.

Fretz, Lewis B. Bennie, the Pythian of Syracuse, and other titles. '01. '02(My24) S. $1. Scroll Pub.

Friedländer, L. Town life in ancient Italy; tr. by W: E. Waters. '02(Mr22) D. 75 c. B: H. Sanborn.

FRIENDS (Society of).
Myers. Quaker arrivals at Philadelphia, 1682-1750. $1.25. Ferris.

FRIENDSHIP.
Carpenter, *ed.* Ioläus; anthology of friendship. net, $1.75. Goodspeed.

Frisbie, H: S: Prophet of the kingdom. '02(Ap12) 12°, $1.25. Neale.

Frogs (The). *See* Aristophanes.

Frost, T: G. Treatise on guaranty insurance. '02(Ap12) O. shp., $5. Little, B. & Co.

Frost, W: D. Laboratory guide in elem. bacteriology. 2d rev. ed. '02(My24) il. 8°, $1.60. W: D. Frost.

FRUIT.
Goff. Lessons in commercial fruit growing. $1. Univ. Co-op.
Bridgeman. Fruit gardening. 50 c. Coates.
See also Apple;—Gardening;—Strawberry.

Fruit from the tree of life. Kohaus, H. M. 30 c. Alliance.

Frye, Alexis E. Grammar school geography. [New ed.] '02(My3) il. f°. $1.45. Ginn.

Frye, T. C. Development of the pollen in some asclepiadaceæ. '02(F15) 8°, (Cont. from the Hull botanical laboratory, no. 32.) pap., net, 25 c. Univ. of Chic.

FUEL.
See Coal;—Gas and gas-fitting.
Fulda, Ludwig. Der talisman; ed. by C. W: Prettyman. '02(Ap5) S. (Modern lang. ser.) 35 c. Heath.
Fulda, Ludwig. Unter vier Augen; [also,] Der prozess; ed. by W: A. Hervey. '02 (Jl12) S. *35 c. net. Holt.
Fulfilment (The). Davenport, J: G. net, 40 c. Dutton.
Fulham Palace Conference. Confession and absolution; ed. by H: Wace. '02(Ap26) O. net, $1. Longmans.
Fuller, W: Architecture of the brain. '02 (Mr1) il. 8°, net, $3.50. Fuller.
FUMIGATION.
Johnson. Fumigation methods. $1. Judd.
Funk, I: K., *and* Moses, M. J., *eds.* Standard first reader. '02(My17) sq. O. (Standard reader ser.) 35 c. Funk.
Funk, I: K., *and* Moses, M. J., *eds.* Teachers' manual for first reader. '02(My17) T. (Standard reader ser.) 50 c. Funk.
FUR TRADE.
Chittenden. Am. fur trade of the far west. 3 v. net, $10. F. P. Harper.
Furneaux, W: S. Elem. practical hygiene, (sec. 1.) '01' '02(Mr8) D. (Practical elem. science ser.) 90 c. Longmans.
Fustel de Coulanges, N. D. The ancient city: study on the religion, laws, and institutions of Greece and Rome. (W. Small.) 10th ed. '01. '02(Je28) 12°, $2. Lee & S.
FUTURE LIFE.
Brooks. Progression to immortality. net, 50 c. Wessels.
Gregg. Dictum of reason on man's immortality. 50 c. Treat.
Hutton. The soul in the unseen world. net, $2. Dutton.
Momerie. Immortality. $1.50. Whittaker.
Ulyat. First years of the life of the redeemed after death. $1.25. Abbey Press.
See also Heaven;—Hell; — Resurrection; — Salvation;—Spiritualism.
Future of war. Bloch, I. S. 60 c. Ginn.
Gabelsberger Shorthand Society, *ed.* Reader to Henry Richter's graphic shorthand. '02 (Jl19) 16°, pap., 50 c. Int. News.
Gabirol, S. I. Improvement of moral qualities: pr. from an unique Arabic ms. '02 (Ap12) 8°, (Columbia Univ. Oriental studies, v. 1.) net, $1.25. Macmillan.
Gabriel, C: H., *comp.* Joyful praise. '02 (Je7) O. 30 c. Jennings.
Gaffield, Erastus C. A celestial message. Private ed. '02(Ap5) 12°, n. p. Lee & S.
Gage, Alfr. P. Introd. to physical science. Rev. ed. '02(Jl5) il. D. $1. Ginn.
Gage, S. H: The microscope. 8th ed., rev. and enl. '01' '02(Mr22) il. O. $1.50. Comstock Pub.
GAINE, Hugh.
Ford, *ed.* Journals of Hugh Gaine, printer. net, $15; net, $25. Dodd.
GAINSBOROUGH, T:
Bell. Thomas Gainsborough. $1. Macmillan.
GALLS.
Connold. British vegetable galls. net, $4. Dutton.
GALLSTONE.
Keay. Medical treatment of gall stones. net, $1.25. Blakiston.

Gallup, *Mrs.* Eliz. W. Bi-literal cipher of Sir Francis Bacon. 3d ed. '01' '02(F15) O. $3.75. Howard.
Gallup, *Mrs.* Eliz. W. Tragedy of Anne Boleyn: drama in cipher found in works of Sir Fs. Bacon. '01 '02(F15) O. $1.50. Howard.
Gallus, A., *pseud.* *See* Wisner, A.
Galt, Sterling, *comp.* Lent, the holy season. '02(Ap26) 12°, silk, $1. Neale.
Galton, Arth. Our attitude toward Eng. Roman Catholics and the papal court. '02 (My10) 12°, net, $1. Dutton.
GALVANOMETER.
Nichols. The galvanometer. $1. Spon.
GALVESTON.
Halstead. Galveston. $1.50; $2.25. Dominion.
Game of love. Paterson, W: R. $1.50. Scribner.
GAMES.
See Baseball; — Bridge; — Golf; — Ping-pong; — Whist.
Gametrogenesis and fertilization in albugo. Stevens, F. L. net, 25 c. Univ. of Chic.
Ganong, W: F. Lab'y course in plant physiology, as a basis for ecology. '01' '02 (F1) il. O. net, $1. Holt.
Gans, E. W: A Pennsylvania pioneer: biog. sketch. '02(F15) 8°, hf. leath., $6. Kuhl.
GARDENING.
Bacon. Of gardens. net, 50 c. Lane.
Barnard. My ten rod farm.—Simple flower garden. ea., 40 c.—Two thousand a year on fruits and flowers. $1. Coates.
Blomfield. Formal garden in England. $3. Macmillan.
Bridgeman. Kitchen gardening. 50 c. Coates.
Budd *and* Hansen. Am. horticultural manual. $1.50. Wiley.
Cadwallader. Story of home gardens. 25 c. Home Gardening.
Ellacombe. In my vicarage garden. net, $1.50. Lane.
Fiske, *comp.* Prize gardening. $1. Judd.
Holme. Stray leaves from a border garden. net. $1.50 Lane.
In a Tuscan garden. net, $1.50. Lane.
Lowell, *ed.* American gardens. $7.50. Bates & G.
Sedding. Garden craft, old and new. net, $2.50. Lane.
Triggs. Formal gardens in England and Scotland. 3 pts. net, $25. Scribner.
Williams. Garden in the suburbs. net, $1.50. Lane.
See also Botany:—Flowers;—Fruit;—Window gardening.
Gardiner, Asa B. Discovery of the remains of Maj.-Gen. Nat. Greene; add. del. in Newport, July 4, 1901. '01' '02(Ap5) 8°, pap., n. p. [Blumenberg Press] Soc. R. I. Cincinnati.
Gardner, J: *See* Gregg, W: H.
Gardner, J: M., *ed.* American negligence repts. v. 10. '01. '02(Ja18) O. shp., $5.50 Remick.
Gardner, W. M. *See* Rawson, C.
GARFIELD, James A.
See Fallows, S:
Garland, Hamlin. Captain of the Grayhorse troop. '02(Mr29) D. $1.50. Harper.

GAS AND GAS-FITTING.
Gill. Gas and fuel analysis for engineers. $1.25. Wiley.
Hempel. Methods of gas analysis. net, $2.25. Macmillan.
GASES.
Randall, *ed. and tr.* Expansion of gases by heat. $1. Am. Bk.
Travers. Experimental study of gases. net, $3.25. Macmillan.
Gaskin, Rob. T. Caedmon, the first Eng. poet. '02(Je7) 12°, pap., 40 c. E. & J. B. Young.
Gate of the kiss. Harding, J: W. $1.50. Lothrop.
Gathered sunbeams. Pease, E. S. 75 c. Sun Pr. Co.
Gautier, T. Works. Limited ed. v. 13-16. '02(Je28) 8°, per v., $3.50; hf. mor., $6. Sproul.
Gaylord. Harvey R., *and* Archoff, Ludwig. Atlas of patholog. histology. '01- '02(Ja25) col. il. 4°, net, $7.50. Lea.
GEARS AND GEARING.
Grant. Treatise on gear wheels. net, $1. Caspar.
Gee, H: Elizabethan prayer-book and ornaments. '02(Mr22) 12°, net, $1.25. Macmillan.
GEMS.
See **Precious stones.**
GENEALOGY.
Crayon. Rockaway records of Morris Co., N. J., families. $3. Rockaway.
Nash. Fifty Puritan ancestors. $5. Tuttle, M. & T.
Sellers. Allied families of Delaware. $5. E. J. Sellers.
Van Meter. Genealogies and sketches of some old families. $2.25. Morton.
Watson. Royal lineage. $4.50. Whittet.
Wells. Hist. of Newburg, Vt.; with genealog. records. $2.25; $3; $3.50; $4. Caledonian.
See also **Biography.**
General digest, Am. and Eng., annot. v. 12, '02(My10) O. shp., $6. Lawyers' Co-op.
GENERATIVE ORGANS.
Ultzmann. Neuroses of the genito-urinary system in the male with sterility and impotence. *$1 net. Davis.
See also **Syphilis;—Urine and urinary organs.**
Gentleman in literature. Quayle, W: A. net, 25 c. Jennings.
GEODESY.
Bolza. Concerning the geodesic curvature and the isoperimetric problem on a given surface. *25 c. net. Univ. of Chic.
See also **Earth;—Surveying.**
Geographical readers. il. D. Am. Bk.
—Carpenter. Europe. 70 c.
GEOGRAPHY.
Appleton's geografia superior ilustrada. (Spanish.) $1.50. Appleton.
Bartholomew. Internat. students' atlas of modern geography. net, $2.25. Scribner.
Carroll. Around the world. 60 c. Morse.
Fairbanks. Home geog. for primary grades. 60 c. Educ. Pub.
Frye. Grammar school geography. $1.45. Ginn.
Murché. Teacher's manual of object lessons in geography. net, 80 c. Macmillan.

GEOGRAPHY.—*Continued.*
Roddy. Complete geography. $1; Elem. geography. 50 c. Am. Bk.
Tarr *and* McMurry. 1st bk. Home geog. net, 60 c. 2d bk. Complete geog. *$1 net. Macmillan.
Wagner. New Pacific school geography. net, $1. Whitaker & R.
See also **Physical geography;—Voyages and travels.**
GEOLOGY.
Hershey. Quaternary of So. California. 20 c. Univ. of Cal.
Lawson. The eparchæan interval. 10 c. Univ. of Cal.
Zittel. Hist. of geology and paleontology to end of 19th century. $1.50. Scribner.
See also **Berkeley Hills; — Earth; — Evolution; — Glacial period;—Mineralogy;—Paleontology.**
GEOMETRY.
More. Trisection of a given angle geometrically solved. $1. Wickes.
See also **Mathematics;—Perspective; — Trigonometry.**
George, Marian M. *See* Whitcomb, C. E.
Georgia. Supp. to code. v. 4. (H. Van Epps.) '01- '02(Ap5) O. shp., $5. Marshall.
GEORGIA.
Mitchell. Georgia land and people. $1.25. F. L. Mitchell.
Georgian (The) period. In 3 v. v. 2, pt. 8; v. 3, pt. 9. '02(Mr15) il. portfolio, f°, ea., $4. Am. Architect.
Gerard, Fes. A. A Grand Duchess and her court. '02(Ap5) 2 v., 8°, net, $7.50. Dutton.
Gerard, Fes. A. Romance of King Ludwig II. of Bavaria. New ed. '01- '02(F22) 12°, net, $1.75. Dodd.
GERLACH, *St.*
Houck. Life of St. Gerlach. net, 55 c. Benziger.
GERMAN LANGUAGE.
Adler. German and Eng. dictionary. pt. 1. $3.50. Appleton.
Florer. Biblische geschichten. 40 c. Wahr.
Fulda. Der talisman. 35 c. Heath.
Fulda. Unter vier Augen. *35 c. net. Holt.
Grillparzer. Traum ein leben. 60 c. Heath.
Heyse. Niels mit der offenen hand. 30 c. Heath.
Körner. Zriny ein trauerspiel in fünf aufzügen. 35 c. Heath.
Krüger *and* Smith. English-Germ. conversation book. 25 c. Heath.
Kuttner. German conversation course. 50 c. Abbey Press.
Lange. 20th century system; key to the Germ. language. 50 c. Pamphlet.
Lessing. Minna von Barnhelm. 75 c. Heath.
Moser. Der bibliothekar. 45 c. Am. Bk.
Riehl. Das spielmannskind und stumme ratsherr. 35 c. Am. Bk.
Stern. Geschichten von Deutschen städten. $1.25. Am. Bk.
Wesselhoeft. German composition. 45 c. Heath.
GERMAN LITERATURE.
Batt. Treatment of nature in Germ. literature from Günther to Goethe's Werther. net, $1. Univ. of Chic.
Brandes. Main currents in 19th century lit. v. 2, Romantic school in Germany. net, $2.75. Macmillan.

German opera texts. See Newson's.
GERMAN POETRY.
Remy. Influence of India and Persia on the poetry of Germany. net, $1. Macmillan.
GERMANY.
Baedeker, *ed.* Southern Germany. net, $1.80. Scribner.
Henderson. Short hist. of Germany. 2 v. net, $4. Macmillan.
Schiller. Hist. of the thirty years' war. (App. to pubs. for price.) Niccolls.
Veritas. German empire of to-day. $2.25. Longmans.
Gertrude Dorrance. Fisher, M. $1.50. McClurg.
Geyserland and wonderland. Hatfield, W: F: 24 c. Hicks-J.
Giant fish of Florida. Turner, J. T. **$3.50 net. Lippincott.
Giants' gate. Pemberton, M. $1.50. Stokes.
Gibbes, Fes. G. Poems. '02(Ap19) 12°, $1. Neale.
Gibbons, W: F. Those black diamond men. '02(Je14) il. D. $1.50. Revell.
Gibbs, Josiah W. Elem. principles in statistical mechanics. '02(Je28) 8°, (Yale bicentennial pub.) $4. Scribner.
Gibbs, Josiah W. Vector analysis: text-book founded upon the lectures of J. Willard Gibbs by E. B. Wilson. '01. '02(F15) 8°. (Yale bicentennial pub.) net, $4. Scribner.
Gibbs, Mifflin W. Shadow and light: autobiog. '02(Mr29) D. $1.50. M. W. Gibbs.
Gibson, J. M. Protestant principles. '01. '02(F1) S. (Christian study manuals.) 60 c. Armstrong.
Gideon. Carradine, B. 35 c. Pepper.
Gifford, J: Practical forestry for beginners in forestry, agricultural students, and others. '02(My24) il. D. net, $1.20. Appleton.
Gifford, M. W. Christian science against itself. '02(Je14) D. $1. Jennings.
Gifford lectures. *See* James, W:
Gift of power. Tuttle, J: E. net, 25 c. Westminster.
Gil Blas. Le Sage, A. R. $1. Burt.
Gilbert, Fk. One thousand ways to make money. '02(My17) 12°, $1. Donohue.
Gilbert, Fk. B. *See* New York. Laws; Membership and relig. corps.
Gilbert, G: H. Primer of the Christian religion. '02(F15) 12°, net, $1. Macmillan.
Gilbert, Grove K., *and* Brigham, A. P. Introd. to physical geography. '02(Je28) il. D. (Twentieth century text-books.) net, $1.25. Appleton.
Gildersleeve, B. L. Studies in honor of Basil L. Gildersleeve. '02(Je28) 8°, $6. Johns Hopkins.
Gill, A: H. Gas and fuel analysis for engineers. 3d rev., enl. ed. '02(Je7) 12°, $1.25. Wiley.
Gill, Joshua, Kirkpatrick, W: J., *and* Gilmour. H. L. Hymns of grace and glory. '02 (My10) D. bds., 30 c. Mattill & L.
Gilman, B. Kingdom of coins. New ed. '01. '02(F15) 16°, (Children's friend ser.) bds., 50 c. Little, B. & Co.
Gilman, Dan. Coit. *See* Vincent, J: M.
Gilmer, Eliz. M., ["Dorothy Dix."] Fables of the elite. '02(My3) il. S. net, $1. Fenno.
Gilmour, H. L. *See* Gill, J.
Ginn's handbooks on the history of religions. 12°, $2.50. Ginn.
—Chantepie de la Saussaye. Religion of the Teutons. (3.)
GIOTTO DI BONDONE.
Perkins. Giotto. $1.75. Macmillan.
Girdlestone, R. B. Grammar of prophecy. '01. '02(Ja11) 12°, (Bible students' lib., no. 11.) $2.50. E. & J. B. Young.
Girl from Mexico. Hyde, M. G. $1. Abbey Press.
Girl of Virginia. Thruston, L. M. $1.50. Little, B. & Co.
Girl who wrote. Cohen, A. J. $1.50. Quail & W.
GIRLS.
Freeman. Religious and social work amongst girls. net, $1. Whittaker.
See also Children;—Education;—Woman;—Young women.
Gittings, J. C. *See* Judson, C: F.
GLACIAL PERIOD.
Chamberlin. Proposed genetic classification of pleistocene glacial formations. net, 10 c. Univ. of Chic.
Chamberlin. Working hypothesis of cause of glacial periods on an atmosphere basis. net, 25 c. Univ. of Chic.
Gladden, W. Christian way. New ed. '01. '02(F22) 16°, 75 c. Dodd.
Gladden, W. Social salvation. '02(My3) D. net, $1. Houghton, M. & Co.
GLADSTONE, W: E.
Handford. William Ewart Gladstone. $1.50; $2.50. Dominion.
Locke. A 19th century crusader. net, 25 c. Jennings.
Glasgow, Ellen. The battleground. '02 (Mr29) il. D. $1.50. Doubleday, P.
Glasson, W: H. Nation's pension system as applied to the civil war and the war with Spain. '02(Mr22) 8°, (Pub. of the soc., no. 331.) pap., 25 c. Am. Acad. Pol. Sci.
Gleanings from nature. Carter, E. N. $1. Abbey Press.
Glenwood. Kensington, C. $1.25. Abbey Press.
Globe series. D. Globe Sch. Bk.
—Chancellor. Arithmetics. Primary. 28 c. —2d bk. 20 c.—3d bk. 24 c.—4th bk. 24 c.
—Chancellor. Mathematics by grades. bks. 5, 6. ea., *28 c. net.
Glover, Terrot R. Life and letters in the fourth century. '02(F15) 8°, (Cambridge Univ. Press ser.) net, $3.25. Macmillan.
GOD.
Leighton. Conceptions of God. net, $1.10. Longmans.
Reed. Idea of God in rel. to theology. net, 75 c. Univ. of Chic.
Thompson. The unknown God. 60 c. Warne.
See also Bible:—Holy Spirit;—Jesus Christ;—Religion;—Theology.
God of things. Whitehouse, F. B. $1.50. Little, B. & Co.
God the beautiful. B., E. P net, 75 c. Beam.
Godbey, A. M. Life of Henry M. Stanley. '02(Jl19) 12°, (Biographies of famous men.) $1. Donohue.
Godfrey, Eliz., [*pseud.* for Jessie Bedford.] The winding road. '02(Mr22) D. $1.50. Holt.

Godly union and concord. Henson, H. H. $2. Longmans.
Goebel, F. Hermann der Cherusker und die schlacht im Teutoburger walde; ed. by J. Esser. Authorized ed. '02(F22) 12°, net, 50 c. Macmillan.
Goethe, J. W. v. Truth and fiction rel. to my life; ed. by N. H. Dole. Ed. de luxe. v. 1. '02(Je28) 12°, (app. to pubs. for price.) Niccolls.
Goethe, J. W. v. Wilhelm Meister's apprenticeship; ed. by N. H. Dole. Ed. de luxe. '02(Mr15) 2 v., 12°. (App. to pubs for price.) Niccolls.
Goethe, J. W. v. Wilhelm Meister's travels; and Recreations of the German emigrants; ed. by N. H. Dole. Ed. de luxe. '02 (Mr22) 8°. (App. to pubs. for price.) Niccolls.
Goff, E. S. Lessons in commercial fruit growing. '02(My10) il. 12°, (Vellum ser.) $1. Univ. Co-op.
GOLD.
Curle. Gold mines of the world. $3.50. Engineering.
Wilson. Cyanide processes. $1.50. Wiley.
See also Precious metals.
Golden Fluff. Morris, I. D. 50 c. Abbey Press
Golden lily. Hinkson, *Mrs.* K. T. 40 c. Benziger.
Golden poppy. Smith, E. E. net, $1.50. E. E. Smith.
Golden way. Bartlett, A. L. $1.50. Abbey Press.
Goldsmith, O. Plays; ed. by A. Dobson. '02 (Mr22) 16°, (Temple classics.) 50 c.; leath., 75 c. Macmillan.
Goldsmith, O. Poems; ed. by A. Dobson. '02(Mr22) 16°, (Temple classics.) 50 c.; leath., 75 c. Macmillan.
Goldsmith, O. Selections. '01. '02(Ap5) S. (Little masterpieces.) 50 c. Doubleday, P.
Goldsmith, P: H. El idioma Inglés: Lib. primero. '02(Ap5) D. 40 c.; *Same*. Lib. segundo. 36 c. Globe Sch. Bk.
GOLF.
Brown. Golf. **50 c. net. Houghton, M. & Co.
Harper's official golf guide, 1901. $1. Harper.
Travis. Practical golf. net, $2. Harper.
Good, Ja. I. Historical handbook of the Reformed church in the U. S. 2d ed., rev. '01. '02(Ap5) D. bds., 25 c. Heidelberg.
Good, Ja. I. Women of the Reformed church. '01· '02(Ap5) il. D. $1. Heidelberg.
Good and evil. *See* Lanier, J. J.
Good cheer nuggets. Pennington, J. G. 45 c.; $1. Fords.
Good gravy. Kendall, E. F. 25 c. Helman-T.
Goodell, T: D. Chapters on Greek metric. '01. '02(Mr15) 8°, (Yale bicentennial pub.) net, $2. Scribner.
Goodknight, Alva L. Modern association and railroading. '01. '02(Mr22) D. 50 c. Abbey Press.
Goodspeed, Edg. J. The Newberry gospels. '02(Ap5) il. O. (Hist. and linguistic studies in literature rel. to the N. T., v. 2, Greek texts, pt. 1.) pap., net, 25 c. Univ. of Chic.
Goodwin, J. J. The "sinker" stories of wit and humor. '02(Je28) D. $1. Ogilvie.
Goodyear, S: H. Theory of accounts. '02 (Ap19) Q. $1.50. Goodyear-M.
Gordon, Granville, *Lord*. Sporting reminiscences. '02(Je7) 8°, net, $4. Dutton.
Gordon, Julien, *pseud*. *See* Cruger, *Mrs*. J. S.
Gordon, S: Strangers at the gate. '02(Je7) D. $1.50. Jewish Pub.
Gordy, Wilbur F. American leaders and heroes: U. S. history. '01· '02(Mr15) il. maps, 12°, net, 60 c. Scribner.
Gore, C: Body of Christ. 2d rev. enl. ed.; with reply to critics of the 1st ed. '01. '02 (Ja11) 12°, $1.75. Scribner.
Gore, Willard C. The imagination in Spinoza and Hume. '02(Je14) 8°, (Univ. of Chic. cont. to philosophy, v. 2, no. 4.) pap., net, 35 c. Univ. of Chic.
Gorky, Maxime, [*pseud*. for Alexei Maximovitch Pyeshkoff.] Tales from Gorky; with a biog. notice of author by R. N. Bain. 3d ed. '02(My3) D. net, $1.20. Funk.
Górky, Máxime. Twenty-six and one, and other stories; fr. the Russian. '02(Mr22) il. D. $1.25. J. F. Taylor.
Gormanius. *See* De Leon, T: C.
Gospel of Judas Iscariot. Baldwin, A. D. $1.50. Jamieson-H.
Gospel of the kingdom and the gospel of the church. Brown, W: B. $1. Whittaker.
Goss, W: F. M. Locomotive sparks. '02 (Ap19) il. 8°, $2. Wiley.
Gothenburg system. *See* National Temp. almanac.
Gould, G: M., *ed*. *See* American year-book of medicine.
Gould, W. R. Greater New York and state lawyer's diary for 1902. '02(Mr1) S. $1. W. R. Gould.
GOVERNMENT.
See Political science.
Government clerks. Rogers, C: G. $1; 25 c. McQuilkin
Government ownership of railroads. Knapp, M. A. 15 c. Am. Acad. Pol. Sci.
Gower, Ronald S., *Lord*. Old diaries, 1881-1901. '02(Ap12) il. 8°. net, $4.50. Scribner.
Gower, Ronald S., *Lord*. Sir David Wilkie. '02(Mr8) il. 12°, (Great masters in painting and sculpture.) $1.75. Macmillan.
Gower, Ronald S., *Lord*. Tower of London. v. 2. '02(Mr22) il. 8°, net, $6.50. Macmillan.
Grace of orders. Winston, N. B. $1. Abbey Press.
Graded classics. *See* Haliburton, M. W.
Gradle, H: Diseases of the nose, pharynx and ear. '02(Je28) il. 8°, net, $3.50. Saunders.
Grafton, C: C. Pusey and the church revival. '02(Ap12) il. D. net, 50 c. Young Churchman.
Graham, Alex. Roman Africa. '02(F8) O. $6. Longmans.
Graham, G: E: Schley and Santiago. '02 (F8) D. $1.50. Conkey.
Graham, H: G. Scottish men of letters in the eighteenth century. '02(F1) 8°. net. $4.50. Macmillan.
Graham, J. M. East of the barrier; or, Manchuria in miniature. '02(Je7) 12°, net, $1. Revell.
GRAND CANYON.
See Arizona;—Colorado river.

Grand Duchess and her court. Gerard, F. A. 2 v., net, $7.50. Dutton.
Grandmother dear. Molesworth, *Mrs.* M. L. 75 c. Burt.
Grandmother's cook book. H., A. P. 50 c. New Amsterdam.
Grant, *Mrs.* **Anne M.** Memoirs of an Amer. lady. New ed. '01. '02(F22) 8°, net, $7.50. Dodd.
Grant, G. B. Treatise on gear wheels. 8th ed. '02(Ap26) 8°, net, $1. Caspar.
GRANT, Ulysses S.
Poore *and* Tiffany. U. S. Grant. $1. Donohue.
Grant, W: D., *ed.* Christendom anno domini 1901. '02(Je7) 2 v., O. $2.50. W: D. Grant.
Gray, H: Anatomy. 15th ed. '01- '02(Ja25) il. 8°, net, $5.50; shp., net, $6.50; col. il. net, $6.25; shp., net, $7.25. Lea.
Gray, L: H. Indo-Iranian phonology. '02 (Je28) 8°, (Columbia Univ. and Indo-Iranian ser., v. 2.) net, $3. Macmillan.
Gray, Martha. Fortune's wheel. '02(My3) D. $1. Abbey Press.
Gray, W: C. Musings by camp-fire and wayside. '02(F1) O. net, $1.50. Revell.
Graystone. Nicolls, W: J. $1.50. Lippincott.
Great authors of all ages. Allibone, S: A. $2.50. Lippincott.
GREAT BRITAIN.
Bartlett. Golden way: notes on journey through Ireland, Scotland and England. $1.50. Abbey Press.
Mackinder. Britain and the British seas. $2. Appleton.
Great chancellor. High, J. L. net, $2.50; Callaghan.
Great cloud of witnesses. Wilson, L: A. 50 c. Standard Pub
Great commanders' ser.; ed. by J. G. Wilson. D. net, $1.50. Appleton.
—Mathes. General Forrest.
Great issues. Barker, W. $1; 50 c. Ferris.
Great love. Burnham, C. L. 50 c. Houghton, M. & Co.
Great masters in painting and sculpture. See Macmillan's.
GREECE.
Bury. Hist. of Greece to death of Alexander. 2 v. net, $8. Macmillan.
Fustel de Coulanges. Ancient city: study on the rel., laws, and institutions of Greece and Rome. $2. Lee & S.
Jebb. Modern Greece. $1.75. Macmillan.
Greeff, R. Guide to the microscopic examination of the eyes; fr. the 2d Germ. ed., by H. Walker. '01- '02(Ja11) 12°, net. $1.25. Blakiston.
Greek foreshadowings of mod. metaphysical thought. Kupfer, L. $1. J. S. Cushing.
Greek hero stories. Niebuhr, B. G. $1. Dodd.
GREEK LANGUAGE.
Andrew. Greek prose composition. net, 90 c. Macmillan.
Babbitt. Grammar of Attic and Ionic Greek. $1.50. Am. Bk.
Ball. Elements of Greek. net, $1. Macmillan.
Pearson *and* Bartlett. Key to Pearson's Greek prose composition. 50 c. Am. Bk.
See also Attic prose.
GREEK LITERATURE.
Fowler. Hist. of ancient Gr. literature. net, $1.40. Appleton.
GREEK MANUSCRIPTS.
Goodspeed. Newberry gospels: Greek texts. net, 25 c. Univ. of Chic.
Greek myths in Eng. dress. Hale, E: E., *jr.* 40 c. Globe Sch. Bk.
GREEK POETRY.
Goodell Chapters on Greek metric. net, $2. Scribner.
Greek ser. for colleges and schools. D. $1. Am. Bk.
—Plato. Euthyphro.
Green, B: E. Shakespeare and Goethe on Gresham's law and the single gold standard. '01- '02(F8) D. pap., 25 c. MacGowan.
Green, E. T. Church of Christ. '02(Mr1) 12°, (Churchman's lib.) $1.50. Macmillan.
Green, S: A. Ten facsimile reproductions rel. to old Boston and neighborhood. '01- '02 (Ja11) F. net, $10. Littlefield.
Green fund book. D. net, 50 c. Am. S. S.
—Rice. Our sixty-six sacred books. (10.)
Greenaway, Kate. A apple pie. New ed. '01- '02(Ja25) obl. 8°, bds., 75 c. Warne.
Greene, Ja. G. *See* New York. Analy. decisions and citations.
GREENE, *Gen.* Nat.
Gardiner. Discovery of the remains of Maj.-Gen. Nathaniel Greene. n. p. [Blumenberg Press] Soc. R. I. Cincinnati.
Greenleaf, Sue. Liquid from the sun's rays. '02(Ap26) D. $1.50 Abbey Press.
Greenstone, Julius H. Religion of Israel. '02(Mr29) D. 50 c. Bloch.
Gregg, D: Dictum of reason on man's immortality. '02(Je21) D. 50 c. Treat.
Gregg, Hilda, ["Sydney C. Grier."] Prince of the captivity. '02(My17) D. $1.50. L. C. Page.
Gregg, W: H., *and* **Gardner, J:** Where, when, and how to catch fish on the east coast of Florida. '02(Je7) il. O. $4. Matthews-N.
Gregorovius, F. Hist. of Rome in the Middle Ages. '02(Ap5) 12°, net, $3. Macmillan.
Gregory, J. W. *See* Hutchinson, H. N.
Grenell, Z. The sandals: tale of Palestine. '02(Mr8) il. S. (Hour-glass stories, no. 2.) net, 40 c. Funk.
Grethenbach, Constantine. Secular view of the Bible. '02(Mr22) il. O. net, $2. Eckler.
Grier, Sydney C. *See* Gregg, H.
Griffin, Alb. Why the legal (or force) method of promoting temperance always has done—and always must do—more harm than good. '01- '02(Ja11) S. pap., 15 c. A. Griffin.
Griffin ser. il. D. $1. Coates.
—Couch. The Westcotes.
Grillparzer, Franz S. Traum ein leben; ed. by E: S. Meyer. '02(My3) D. (Modern lang. ser.) 60 c. Heath.
Grinnell, G: B. American duck shooting. '01- '02(F1) il. O. $3.50. Forest
Grove, *Lady* **Agnes.** Seventy-one days' camping in Morocco. '02(Ap19) il. O. net, $2.50. Longmans.
Growing up. Conklin, *Mrs.* J. M. D. $1. Burt.
Guarding the thoughts. Macdonald, L. B. 10 c. J. H. West

Guggenberger, A. General hist. of the Christian era. In 3 v. v. 2 and 3. '01· '02 (Mr8) 8°, ea., $1.50. Herder.

Guide to best hist. novels and tales. Nield, J. net, $1.75. Putnam.

Guide to Palestine and Egypt. '02(Ja18) 12°, (Macmillan's guides.) net, $3.25. Macmillan.

Guided and guarded. Malone, J. S. $1.25. Abbey Press.

Gulliver's bird book. Bridgman, L. J. $1.50. L. C. Page.

GUN.
See **Rifle.**

GUNNERY.
Hamilton *and* Bond. Gunner's catechism. $1. Wiley.

Gunter, A. C. Surprises of an empty hotel. '02(Ap5) il. D. $1; pap., 50 c. Home

Guthe, Karl E. *See* Reed, J: O.

Guthrie, Ben E., *rep.* *See* Missouri. *St. Louis and Kansas City cts. of appeals.* Cases.

Guyse, Eleanor. A movable quartette. '02 (My3) D. $1. Abbey Press.

Gwatkin, H: M. *See* Maitland, F: W:

Gyim, Paul L. Chinese-English elem. reader and arithmetic. '01· '02(Mr22) il. 16°, $1.25. Taylor & M.

GYMNASTICS AND PHYSICAL CULTURE.
Colburn. Graded physical exercises. $1. Werner.
Fish. Calisthenic dict. $1. Seminar.
See also **Delsarte system.**

GYNECOLOGY.
Davenport. Diseases of women: manual of gynecology. net, $1.75. Lea.
Herrold. Woman: diseases and remedies. $4; $5. Woman's Pub.
McKay. History of ancient gynæcology. net, $3. Wood.

GYPSIES.
See **Zincali.**

H., A. P. Grandmother's cook book. '02 (Ap26) sm. 4°, bds., 50 c. New Amsterdam.

Haddon Hall lib. il. 12°, $3. Macmillan.
—Shand. Shooting.

Hadley, H. E. Practical exercises in magnetism and electricity. '02(F22) 12°, net, 60 c. Macmillan.

Hadley, Wilfred J. Nursing—general, medical and surgical; with app. on sick-room cookery. '02(Mr22) 12°, net, $1.25. Blakiston.

Haggerty, J: How to treat the trusts and how to win in 1904. '02(Jl5) D. 25 c. Abbey Press.

Hahn, C: C. So fight I. '02(Ap12) 16°, pap., 10 c. Whittaker.

Haines, E. M. *See* Illinois. Laws.

HAIR.
Stitson. Human hair. $1.25. Maple.

Hake, H. W. *See* Dupre, A.

Hale, E: E. En son nom, [In his name;] tr. par M. P. Sauveur. '01· '02(Ja4) D. $1. W: R. Jenkins.

Hale, E: E. Man without a country. Birthday ed. '02(Ap12) O. net, $1. Outlook.

Hale, E: E., *jr.*, *ed.* Ballads and ballad poetry. '02(Mr22) D. (Hawthorne classics, no. 2.) 40 c. Globe Sch. Bk

Hale, E: E., *jr.*, *ed.* Greek myths in Eng. dress. '02(Mr22) D. (Hawthorne classics, no. 1.) 40 c. Globe Sch. Bk.

Hale, G: E. New star in Perseus. '01· '02 (Ja11) 8°, (Yerkes Observatory bulletin, no. 16.) pap., net, 10 c. Univ. of Chic.

HALE, Nathan.
Partridge. Nathan Hale, the ideal patriot. net, $1. Funk.

Haliburton, Marg. W., *and* Norvell, F. T. Graded classics: Third reader. '02(Jl12) il. sq. D. 40 c. B. F. Johnson.

Hall, A. C. A. Companion to the prayer-book. '02(Mr8) S. net, 35 c. E. & J. B. Young.

Hall, A. C. A. Instruction and devotions on the holy communion. '02(F8) S. net, 25 c. Young Churchman.

Hall, Arth. C. Crime in its relation to social progress. '02(Ap12) 8°, (Columbia Univ. studies in history, economics and public law, v. 15.) net, $3; $3.50. Macmillan.

Hall, C: W., *ed.* Regiments and armories of Mass. v. 2. '01· '02(Ja4) il. 8°, per set, $12; hf. cf., $18; seal, $25. W. W. Potter.

Hall, E: H. Jamestown, [1607-1907.] '02 (Ap26) il. 16°, pap., 25 c. Am. Scenic.

Hall, F: G., Little, E: R., *and* Eliot, H: W., *jr.*, *eds.* Harvard celebrities. '02(F22) il. O. bds., $1.25. Univ. Press (Camb.)

Hall, Granville D. Rending of Virginia. '02 (Ap12) il. 8°, $2. Mayer.

Hall, H. S. Algebraical examples. '01· '02 (Ja4) 12°, net, 50 c. Macmillan.

Hall, Jennie. Four old Greeks. '02(Mr15) il. 12°, 35 c. Rand, McN. & Co.

HALL, John.
Hall. John Hall, pastor and preacher. net, $1.50. Revell.

Hall, Jos. Meditations and vows. '02(Mr8) 16°, $1.50. Dutton.

Hall, R. N., *and* Neal, W. G. Ancient ruins of Rhodesia. '02(My10) 8°, net, $6. Dutton.

Hall, Rob. C. Pittsburg securities, a stock exchange handbook, 1902. '02(Jl19) D. pap., gratis. R. C. Hall.

Hall, T: C. John Hall, pastor and preacher. '01· '02(Ja11) 12°, net, $1.50. Revell.

HALL OF FAME.
Eggleston. American immortals; record of men whose names are inscribed in the Hall of Fame. $10. Putnam.

Halsey, Fs. W. Our literary deluge and some of its deeper waters. '02(Ap5) D. net, $1.25. Doubleday, P.

Halsey, Fs. W., *ed.* Authors of our day in their homes. '02(Mr15) 12°, $1.25. Pott.

Halstead, Murat. Full official hist. of the war with Spain. '02(Mr22) 12°, $3; mor., $4; cf., $6. Dominion.

Halstead, Murat. Galveston. '02(Mr22) 12°, $1.50; hf. mor., $2.25. Dominion.

Halstead, Murat. Life and achievements of Admiral Dewey. '02(Mr22) 12°, $1.50; hf. mor., $2.25; mor., $3.25. Dominion.

Halstead, Murat. Life of Theodore Roosevelt. '02(Je14) 8°, subs., $2.50; hf. mor., $3.75; ed. de luxe, $3.50; ¾ rus., $5. Saalfield.

Halstead, Murat. Pictorial hist. of America's new possessions. '02(Mr22) 12°, $2.50; hf. mor., $3.50; mor., $4.50. Dominion.

Halstead, Murat. Splendors of Paris and the glories of her Exposition. '02(Mr22) 12°, $1.50. Dominion.

Halstead, Murat. Story of the Philippines. '02(Mr22) 12°, $2; mor., $3. Dominion.
Halstead, Murat. Victorious republicanism. '02(Mr22) 12°, $1.50; hf. mor., $2.25. Dominion.
Halstead, Murat. William McKinley: (in Norwegian.) Oversat fra engelsk af P. O. Stromme. '01. '02(F15) il. O. $1.50; hf. mor., $2. J. Anderson Pub.
Halstead, Murat. World on fire. '02(Jl19) il. 12°. $1.50; $2.25; mor., $3. Dominion.
Halstead, Murat, *and* Munson, A. J. Life and reign of Queen Victoria. '02(Mr22) 12°, $1.50; hf. mor., $2.25. Dominion.
Halstead, Murat, *and* Munson, A. J. Life and services of William McKinley. '02 (Mr22) 12°, $1.50; hf. mor., $2.25. Dominion.
Hamersly, Lewis R., *comp.* Records of living officers of the U. S. navy and marine corps. 7th ed., rev., with add. '02(Jl5) 8°. $10. Hamersly.
Hamill, H. M. The Sunday-school teacher. '02(Mr22) D. 50 c. Pub. Ho. M. E. Ch., So.
HAMILTON, Alexander.
See Atherton, *Mrs.* G. F.;—Burr, A.
Hamilton, And. *See* New York. Statutory revision of laws.
Hamilton, *Mrs.* E. J. Lee-. *See* Holdsworth, A. E.
Hamilton, Ja. H: Savings and savings institutions. '02(Je28) 12°, net, $2.25. Macmillan.
Hamilton, W: R., *and* Bond, P. S., *comps.* The gunner's catechism: for artillerymen. '02(Jl19) 18°, $1. Wiley.
Hamm, Margherita A. Eminent actors and their homes. '02(Mr15) 12°, $1.25. Pott.
HAMPSHIRE, ENG.
Capes. Scenes of rural life in Hampshire. net, $2.75. Macmillan.
Hancock, H. I. Life at West Point. '02 (Je14) il. D. net, $1.40. Putnam.
Hand of God in Am. history. Thompson, R. E. net. $1. Crowell.
Handbooks for practical workers in church and philanthropy; ed. by S: M. Jackson. S. Lentilhon.
—Pierce. Hartley House cook book. 60 c.
Handbooks for the clergy; ed. by Arth. W. Robinson. D. net, 90 c. Longmans.
—Mason. Ministry of conversion.
—Montgomery. Foreign missions.
—Robinson. Personal life of the clergy.
—Swete. Patristic study.
Handbooks of practical gardening. il. 12°, net, $1. Lane.
—Arnott. Book of bulbs. (5.)
—Thomas. Book of the apple. (6.)
—White. Book of orchids.* (8.)
—Wythes. Book of vegetables. (7.)
Handbooks on the history of religions. See Ginn's.
Handford, T: W. William Ewart Gladstone. '02(Mr22) 12°, $1.50; mor., $2.50. Dominion.
HANDWRITING.
See Autographs.
Handy, W: M. Banking systems of the world. 3d ed. rev. '02(Jl5) D. $1.50. Jamieson-H.
Handy information ser. S. net. Crowell.
—McSpadden. Shakesperian synopses. 45 c.
Hanford, B. Railroading in the U. S. '02 (Ap19) O. (Socialist lib., v. 1, no. 11.) pap., 5 c. Socialistic Co-op.
Hanna, C: A: The Scotch-Irish. '02(Mr29) 2 v., 8°, net, $10. Putnam.
Hannibal, P: M. Thrice a pioneer. '01. '02 (Mr1) 16°, 75 c.; pap., 40 c. Danish Luth.
HANOVER SQUARE.
Baillie. Oriental Club and Hanover Square. $9. Longmans.
Hansen, N. E. *See* Budd, J. L.
Har Lampkins. Patton, A. $1. Abbey Press.
Harben, Will N. Abner Daniel. '02(Je28) D. $1.50. Harper.
Harcourt, L. F. V. Civil engineering as applied in construction. '02(Mr8) il. O. (Civil engineering ser.) $5. Longmans.
Hardcastle, *Mrs.* M. A. Word signs made easy. '02(Mr29) sq. D. $1. M. A. Hardcastle.
Hardesty, Irving. Neurological technique. '01. '02(Ja11) O. net, $1.75. Univ. of Chic.
Hardie, T. Melville. *See* Wood, C. A., *ed.*
Harding, Caro. H. *and* S: B. City of the seven hills. '02(My24) il. S. (Lake history stories.) 40 c. Scott, F. & Co.
Harding, J: W. Gate of the kiss. '02(My17) il. D. $1.50. Lothrop.
Harding, S: B. *See* Harding, C. H.
Harding, W: War in South Africa and the Dark Continent from savagery to civilization. '02(Mr22) 12°, $2; hf. mor., $3; mor., $4. Dominion.
Hardwicke. Rood, H: E: $1.50. Harper.
Hargis, And. M. Treatise on commercial law and business customs. '01. '02(Je28) il. 12°, pap., 10 c. J. North.
Hargrave, W: L. Wallannah. '02(Mr8) il. D. $1.50. B. F. Johnson.
Harland, H:, ["Sidney Luska."] The lady paramount. '02(Ap19) D. $1.50. Lane.
Harmer, S. F:, *and* Shipley, A. E., *eds.* Cambridge natural history. v. 10, Mammalia, by F. E. Beddard. '02(Je28) il. 8°, net, $4. Macmillan.
Harmsworth, Alfr. C., Thompson, *Sir* H:, *and others.* Motors and motor driving. '02 (My17) 8°, (Badminton lib.) $3.50; hf. mor., $5. Little, B. & Co.
Harper, Carrie A. *See* Dix, B. M.
Harper, J: M. Moral drill for the schoolroom. '01. '02(Ja25) 12°, $1. Kellogg.
Harper, W: R. Constructive studies in the priestly element in the Old Testament. Rev. ed. '02(Ja18) O. (Constructive Bible studies.) $1. Univ. of Chic.
Harper's official golf guide for 1901. '01. '02(Mr1) 12°. $1. Harper.
Harriott, *Mrs.* Clara M. *See* Morris, C.
Harris, C: N. *See* Massachusetts digest.
Harris, Cicero W. Sectional struggle: troubles between the north and the south. '02(Mr29) 8°, net, $2.50. Lippincott.
Harris, H: E. King of Andorra. '01. '02 (F15) D. $1.25. Abbey Press.
Harris, Joel C., ["Uncle Remus."] Making of a statesman, and other stories. '02(My17) D. $1.25. McClure, P.
Harris, *Mrs.* Miriam C. Rutledge. '02(Je14) 12°, (Home lib.) $1. Burt.
Harris, W: C. *See* Sage, D.
Harrison, Walter. *See* Ritchie, M. J. G.

Harry, T. E. Infans amoris. '02(My3) D. $1.50. Abbey Press.

Hart, Rob. M. Card language. 3d rev., enl. ed. '02(Mr29) nar. O. pap., 20 c. R. M. McEnally.

Hart, Rob. M. Card language. [*also*] Play card cypher. 4th rev. ed. '02(Je28) nar. O. pap., 20 c. R. M. Hart.

Harte, Fs. Bret. Openings in the old trail '02(My3) D. $1.25. Houghton, M. & Co.

Hartfield, T. W. Exchange pocket cipher code. '02(Jl19) 16°, rus. leath., $2. T. W. Hartfield.

Hartley House cook book. Pierce, E. A. 60 c. Lentilhon.

Hartmann, A., *and* Needham, A. C. Commercial code for the transmission of telegrams and cablegrams. '02(Jl5) 12°, flex. leath., $3. Commercial Code.

Harvard celebrities. Hall, F: G., *ed.* $1.25. Univ. Press (Camb.)

HARVARD UNIVERSITY.
Du Bois, *comp.* Harvard Univ. songs. $1.50. Ditson.

Harvey, L. D. Aids for the proper observance of Memorial day by the schools of Wis. '02(Ap26) O. pap., gratis. Democrat Pr.

Harvey, L. D. *See also* Arbor annual.

Hasse, Adelaide R., *comp.* United States Government pubs.: handbook for the cataloguer. pt. 1. '02(My10) O. $1. Lib. Bu.

Hassell, J: A. *See* Hiley, A. R. I.

Hastings, H: Mistress Dorothy of Haddon Hall. '02(Jl5) D. $1. Fenno.

Hatch, Adelaide W. Zobo patriotic drill. '01-'02(Ja11) S. (Hints ed. of novel and successful drills.) pap., 15 c. Hints.

Hatch, Dorus R. Civil government of Col. 7th ed. '01-'02(Ja18) il. 16°, 60 c. Centennial.

Hatcher, W: E. Pastor and the Sunday-school. '02(Jl12) il. 12°, 75 c. Bapt. S. S. Bd.

Hatfield, W: F: Geyserland and wonderland, (Yellowstone national park.) '02(Jl19) il. 24°, 24 c. Hicks-J.

Haultmont, Marie. Marriage of Laurentia. '01-'02(Ja11) 8°, net, $1.60. Herder.

Haven, *Mrs.* Marg. J. C. Bible lessons for little beginners. '02(F8) 12°, net, 75 c. Revell.

Hawaiian almanac and annual for 1902. (T. G. Thrum.) '01. '02(Mr1) 12°, pap., 75 c. Thrum.

Hawkins, C: A. Legal counsellor and form book. '02(Je14) 8°, subs., $3; shp., $4. W. W. Wilson.

Hawkins, N. Aids to engineers' examinations. '01-'02(F8) il. 12°, leath., $2. Audel.

Hawkins, N. Handbook of calculations for engineers and firemen. '01-'02(F8) il. 12°. $2. Audel.

Hawkins, N. Self-help mechanical drawing. '02(Jl19) il. 8°, $2. Audel.

Hawley, Jos. R. New animal cellular therapy. '01. '02(Mr29) il. 12°, $1. Clinic.

Hawthorne, N. The Blithedale romance. '02(Ap19) 12°, (Home lib.) $1. Burt.

Hawthorne, N. Main Street. '02(Mr1) sq. 12°, bds., $2. Kirgate Press.

Hawthorne, N. Marble faun. '02(Ap19) 12°, (Home lib.) $1. Burt.

Hawthorne classics. D. 40 c. Globe Sch. Bk.
—Hale, *ed.* Ballads and ballad poetry. (2.)
—Greek myths in Eng. dress. (1.)

Hay, J: William McKinley. '02(My17) D. (What is worth while ser.) leatherette, net, 28 c. Crowell.

Hayden, Ja. R. Pocket text-book of venereal diseases. 3d ed. '01-'02(Ja25) 12°, net, $1.75; net, $2.25. Lea.

Hayens, Herb. For the colours. '02(My17) il. 8°, $2. Nelson.

Hayes, H:, *pseud.* *See* Kirk, *Mrs.* E. O.

Haymond, *Mrs.* W. E. Agnes Cheswick. '01-'02(Mr22) D. net, 60 c. Blanchard.

Hazell's annual for 1902; ed. by W. Palmer. '02(Mr8) 12°, net, $1.50. Scribner.

Hazen, C: D. *See* New Eng. Hist. Teachers' Assoc.

HAZLITT, W:
Birrell. William Hazlitt. **75 c. net. Macmillan.

Hazlitt, W: Carew. Shakespeare. '02(My10) 8°, net, $2.50. Scribner.

HEAD.
Eckley. Regional anatomy of head and neck. net, $2.50. Lea.
See also Hair;—Phrenology.

Headlam, Cecil. Peter Vischer. '02(My24) 12°, (Handbooks of the great craftsmen.) $2. Macmillan.

Headlam, Cecil. Story of Chartres. '02(Je7) il. 12°, (Mediæval towns ser.) $2; leath., $2.50. Macmillan.

Headley, J. T. Napoleon and his marshals. '02(My17) 12°, (Home lib.) $1. Burt.

Headley, J. T. Washington and his generals. '02(My17) 12°, (Home lib.) $1. Burt.

Healing of nerves. Ballance, C: A. net, $4.50. Macmillan.

HEALTH.
See Hygiene.

HEART.
Mackenzie. Study of the pulse, and of the movements of the heart. net, $4.50. Macmillan.

Hearth and home essays. Ruskay, E. J. 30 c. Jewish Pub.

Hearts courageous. Rives, H. E. $1.50. Bowen-M.

HEAT.
Dexter. Elem. exercises on sound, light and heat. 90 c. Longmans.
See also Radiation.

Heath, Harold. *See* Jordan, D: S.

Heath, Herb. M. Comparative advantages of the corporation laws of all the states and territories. '02(Jl12) O. pap., n. p. Kennebec Journ.

Heath, W: Memoirs of Maj.-Gen. William Heath, by himself. New ed.; ed. by W: Abbatt; [also] acc. of the Battle of Bunker Hill. '01-'02(Ja11) O. net, $5. Abbatt.

Heath's home and school classics. il. D. 20 c.-60 c. Heath.
—Jordan, *comp.* True tales of birds and beasts.
—La Motte Fouqué. Undine. 30 c.
—Lamb. Tales from Shakespeare.
—Melville. Typee. 45 c.
—O'Shea, *ed.* Old world wonder stories.
—Perrault. Tales of Mother Goose.

Heath's modern language ser. S. Heath.
—Bowen. First scientific Fr. reader. 90 c.
—Fulda. Talisman. 35 c.
—Grillparzer. Traum ein leben. 60 c.
—Heyse. Niels mit der offenen hand. 30 c.
—Körner. Zriny ein trauerspiel in fünf aufzügen. 35 c.
—Krüger *and* Smith. Eng.-Germ. conversation book. 25 c.
—Lessing. Minna von Barnhelm. 75 c.
—Renan. Souvenirs d' enfance et de jeunesse. 75 c.
—Ségur. Les malheurs de Sophie. 45 c.
—Verne. Vingt mille lieues sous les mers. 40 c.
—Wesselhoeft. Germ. composition. 45 c.

HEATING.
Lawler. Modern plumbing, steam and hot water heating. $5. Popular.

HEAVEN.
Swedenborg. Heavenly arcana. v. 13. $1.25. Mass. New-Ch. Un.

Heavenly harmonies for earthly living. McLeod, M. J. net, 50 c. Revell.

Heavenly vision. Booth, H: M. net, $1. Beam.

HEBREWS (*Epistles*).
See Bible.

HEBRIDES.
Boswell. Journ. of a tour to the Hebrides. net, 60 c. Macmillan.

Hector, *Mrs.* **Annie F.,** ["*Mrs.* Alexander."] The yellow fiend. '02(Mr22) D. $1.50. Dodd.

Heddle, Ethel F. Mystery of St. Rubes. '02 (Je21) 12°, $1.50. Scribner.

Hedges, S: Statistics concerning education in the Philippine Islands. '02(Jl19) S. pap., 10 c. Benziger.

HELL.
Morton. Thoughts on hell. net, 50 c. Herder.

Hellems, Fred B. R. Lex de imperio. Vespasiani. '02(My24) O. (Dissertationes Americanae. Classical philology, no. 1.) pap., 50 c. Scott, F. & Co

Helmolt, Hans F., *and others, eds.* Hist. of the world. In 8 v. v. 1. '02(F22); v. 4 (My24) il. O. ea., $6. Dodd.

Helps, *Sir* A. Spanish conquest in America. New ed. In 4 v. v. 2. '02(Je28) 12°, $1.50. Lane.

HEMATOLOGY.
See Blood.

Hemmeter, J: C. Diseases of the intestines. v. 2. '02(Mr22) il. 8°, net, $5; shp., net, $6. Blakiston.

Hempel, Walther. Methods of gas analysis; fr. 3d Germ. ed.; enl. by L. M. Dennis. '02(My3) 12°, net, $2.25. Macmillan.

Hemstreet, C: When old New York was young. '02(My10) il. O. net, $1.50. Scribner.

Henderson, C. H. Education and the larger life. '02(My3) D. net, $1.30. Houghton, M. & Co.

Henderson, Ernest F. Short hist. of Germany. In 2 v. '02(Mr29) 8°, net, $4. Macmillan.

HENRY V., *King of England.*
Kingsford. Henry v. the typical mediæval hero. net, $1.35; net, $1.60. Putnam.

Henry, Alex. Travels and adventures in Canada and the Indian Territories, between the years 1760 and 1776. New ed.; ed., with notes, by J. Bain. '01· '02(F8) il. 8°, net, $4. Little, B. & Co.

Henry, Arth. Island cabin. '02(My24) D. $1.50. McClure, P.

Henry, W. H. F. How to organize and conduct a meeting. 2d ed. '02(Jl12) 12°, 75 c. Hinds.

Henry, W: E., *comp.* State platforms of the two dominant political parties in Ind., 1850-1900. '02(My10) O. $1.50. W: E. Henry.

Henry Esmond. *See* Thackeray, W: M.

Hensman, H. Cecil Rhodes. '02(F8) il. O. leath., net, $5. Harper.

Henson, Herb. H. Cross-bench views of current church questions. '02(Ap26) O. $4. Longmans.

Henson, Herb. H. Godly union and concord. '02(Mr22) O. $2. Longmans.

Her baby brother. Moulton, *Mrs.* L. C. 50 c. Little, B. & Co.

Her Serene Highness. Phillips, D: G. $1.50. Harper.

Heralds of empire. Laut, A. C. $1.50. Appleton.

Herbarium and plant description. Meier, W. H. D. 70 c. Ginn.

Herbartian methods. *See* Fennell, M.

Herbert, H. F. *See* Baur, T. P.

Herbertson, F. D., *comp.* Descriptive geographies fr. original sources, Central and South America with the West Indies. '02 (Ap26) il. 12°, net, 70 c. Macmillan.

Herdman, Lee, *rep.* *See* Nebraska. *Sup. ct.* Repts.

Heredia, J. M. de. Sonnets from Trophies; rendered into Eng. by E. R. Taylor. [3d ed.] '02(Jl12) 12°, bds., *$1.25 net. Elder.

Hereward the Wake. Kingsley, C: $1. Burt.

Herford, Brooke. Small end of great problems. '02(My10) D. net, $1.60. Longmans.

Herford, C: H., *ed.* English tales in verse. '02(My10) 12°, (Warwick lib. of Eng. literature.) $1.50. Scribner.

HERMANN *der Cherusker.*
Goebel. Hermann der Cherusker und die schlacht im Teutoburger walde. net, 50 c. Macmillan.

Hermitage. Ervin, D. $1. Grafton Press.

Hero ser. il. D. net, 25 c. Jennings.
—Locke. Nineteenth century crusade. (5.)
—Typical American. (2.)
—Quayle. The gentleman in literature. (4.)
—A hero. Jean Valjean. (1.)—King Cromwell. (6.)
—Smith. Abraham Lincoln. (3.)

HEROES.
Gordy. Am. leaders and heroes. net, 60 c. Scribner
Muzzey. Spiritual heroes. net, $1.25. Doubleday, P.

Heroes of the nations ser.; ed. by E. Abbott. il. D. net, $1.35; net, $1.60. Putnam.
—Jenks. Edward Plantagenet. (35.)
—Kingsford. Henry v. (34.)

Heroine of the strait. Crowley, M. C. $1.50. Little, B. & Co.

Herrold, Maude M. Woman: diseases and remedies. '02(Jl19) il. 8°, $4; hf. mor., $5. Woman's Pub.

Herron, W: Wright. *See* Texas. Supplements.

Hershey, O. H. Quaternary of Southern California. '02(My17) il. Q. (Univ. of Cal. pub., v. 3, no. 1.) pap., 20 c. Univ. of Cal.

Herter, C. A. Lectures on chemical pathology. '02(Ja25) 12°, net, $1.75. Lea.

HERTFORDSHIRE.
Tompkins. Highways and byways in Hertfordshire. $2. Macmillan.

Herz, W. *See* Abegg, R.

He's coming to-morrow. Stowe, H. B. net, 25 c. Revell.

Hesperian tree. Piatt, J: J. $2. J: Scott.

Hessler, J: C., *and* Smith, Alb. L. Essentials of chemistry for secondary schools. '02 (Je7) il. O. $1.20. B: H. Sanborn.

Hester Blair. Carson, W: H: $1.50. C. M. Clark.

Hettinger, Franz. Timothy; tr. and adapt. by V. Stepka. '02(Je14) 12°, net, $1.50. Herder.

Heusler, F. Chemistry of the terpenes; tr. by F. J. Pond. Rev., enl. and corr. ed. '02 (Jl12) 8°, *$4 net. Blakiston.

Heydecker, E: L., *comp. See* New York. Supp. to general laws.

Heyse, P. J. L. L'arrabbiata; tr. by W. W. Florer. '02(Je28) S. 35 c. Wahr.

Heyse, P. J. L. Niels mit der offenen hand. '02(F1) S. (Modern lang. ser.) 30 c. Heath.

Hezekiah's wives. French, L. H. net, 85 c. Houghton, M. & Co.

Hiatt, C: Westminster Abbey. '02(Ap12) 12°, (Bell's cathedral ser.) 60 c. Macmillan.

Hibbard, Augustine G: Genealogy of the Hibbard family desc. of Rob. Hibbard, of Salem, Mass. '01- '02(F1) 8°, $5. Case.

Hickox, W: E. Correspondent's manual: practical information on letter taking and letter writing. '02(Mr29) S. $1.50. Lee & S.

HICKS, Thos. H.
Radcliffe. Gov. Thomas H. Hicks of Md., and the civil war. 50 c. Johns Hopkins.

Higgin, L. Spanish life in town and country; with chaps. on Portuguese life by E. E. Street. '02(My24) il. D. (Our European neighbors.) net. $1.20. Putnam.

High, J. L. A great chancellor, and other papers; ed. by E. B. Smith. '01- '02(F15) 8°, net, $2.50. Callaghan.

High-caste Hindu woman. Ramabai Sarasvati. net, 75 c. Revell.

Highways and byways ser. 12°, $2. Macmillan.
—Tompkins. Highways and byways in Hertfordshire.

Hiley, Alan R. I., *and* Hassell, J: A. The mobile Boer. '02(Ap26) il. D. net, $1.50. Grafton Press.

Hill, F: T. The minority: (novel.) '02 (Ap19) D. $1. Stokes.

Hill, G. A. *See* Wentworth, G: A.

Hill, Grace L. An unwilling guest. '02(Je14) il. D. net, $1. Am. Bapt.

Hill, J. W. Diseases of the cat. '01- '02 (Ja4) il. D. $1.25. W: R. Jenkins.

Hill, Ja. J. *See* Flint, C: R.

Hillis, N. D. Master of the science of right living. '02(Ap12) 12°, bds., net, 50 c. Revell.

Hinchman, Lydia S. Early settlers of Nantucket. 2d rev. enl. ed. '02(F15) 8°, $5. Ferris.

Hind, C. L. Life's little things. '02(F1) 12°, $1.75. Macmillan.

Hinderers (The). Bayly, A. E. $1. Longmans.

Hinds, W: A. American communities; rev. ed., enl. '02(My3) il S. (Murby's sci. ser.) $1. Kerr.

HINDUS.
Ramabai Sarasvati. High-caste Hindu woman. net, 75 c. Revell.

Hinkson, H. A. Point of honour. '02(Mr22) il. D. $1.50. McClurg.

Hinkson, *Mrs.* Kath. T. Golden lily. '02 (Mr22) il. S. 40 c. Benziger.

Hinton, Ma. B. Other notes. '02(Ap12) 16°, $1. Neale.

Hints ed. of novel and successful drills. S. pap., 15 c. Hints.
—Hatch. Zobo patriotic drill.

Hints to small libraries. Plummer, M. W. net, 50 c. M. W. Plummer.

Histoires (Les) de tante. Alissas, R. d'. net, 40 c. Macmillan.

HISTOLOGY.
Gaylord *and* Archoff. Atlas of pathological histology. net, $7.50. Lea.
Schäfer. Essentials in histology. *$3 net. Lea.
See also Microscope.

Historic Boston; sightseeing towns around the Hub. '01- '02(F15) 12°, net, 50 c.; pap., net, 30 c. Pilgrim Press.

Historical and linguistic studies in literature related to the New Testament. il. O. pap., net, 25 c. Univ. of Chic.
—Goodspeed. Newberry gospels. (v. 2, 1.)

Historical sources in schools ser. See Macmillan's.

HISTORY.
Bourne. Teaching of history and civics. $1.50. Longmans.
Helmolt, *and others, eds.* History of the world. v. 1, 4. ea., $6. Dodd.
Jesse. Historical memoirs. 30 v. ea., $2.50; complete set of 15 v., $37.40; $75. L. C. Page.
Kidd. Principles of western civilization. net, $2. Macmillan.
Larned, *ed.* Literature of Am. history. net, $6; $7.50; $9. Houghton, M. & Co.
Maitland, *and others.* Essays on the teaching of history. net, 75 c. Macmillan.
New England History Teachers' Assoc.; rept. **60 c. net. Macmillan.
Tout *and* Tait, *eds.* Historical essays. $5. Longmans.
West. Ancient history to death of Charlemagne. $1.50. Allyn & B.
See also Biography;—Church history;—Civilization;—Eastern question;—Ethnology;—Finance;—Middle ages;—Political science;—Slavery;—Social science.

Hitchcock, F: H. Book-builder's handbook of types, scales, etc. [New issue.] '02 (Je28) S. leath., net, 50 c. Grafton Press.

Hoar, G: F. *See* Lodge, H: C.

Hoare, H. W. Evolution of the Eng. Bible. New cheap ed. '02(My10) 8°, net, $2.50. Dutton.

Hobart, G: V. *See* McHugh, H.
Hobbs, W. R. P. Arithmetic of electrical measurements; rev. by R: Wormell. 9th ed. '02(My3) S. 50 c. Van Nostrand.
Hobhouse, Leonard T. Mind in evolution. '02(F1) 8°, net, $3.25. Macmillan.
Hochelaga depicta. Bosworth, N. net, $3; net, $4.50. Congdon.
Hodder, Edn. Life of a century, 1800-1900. '01· '02(Ja11) 8°, net, $4. Scribner
Hodge, Clifton F. Nature study and life. '02 (Ap19) il. D. $1.65. Ginn.
Hodgman, F. Home's sweet harmonies: new part songs, quartets, etc. '02(F8) O. pap., 80 c. Home Pub.
Hodgson, Fred T. Estimating frame and brick houses. 2d rev., enl. ed. '02(Je7) il. 12°, $1. D: Williams.
Hoffman, F: L: Windstorm and tornado insurance. 3d ed. '02(Mr22) il. 16°, pap., 25 c. Spectator.
Hoffman, Harry C. Health and strength. '02 (F1) il. sq. D. pap., 25 c. H. C. Hoffman.
Hogarth, D: G: The nearer east. '02(Mr29) 8°, (World ser., no. 2.) $2. Appleton.
HOGARTH, W:
Anstruther. William Hogarth. $1. Macmillan.
Hohenzollern. Brady, C. T. $1.50. Century Co.
Holdsworth, Annie E., [*Mrs.* E. J. Lee-Hamilton.] Michael Ross, minister. '02(Mr22) D. $1.50. Dodd.
HOLIDAYS.
Deems, *comp.* Holy-days and holidays. $5. Funk.
Holiness of the church in the 19th century. Scheeben, M. J. 10 c. Benziger.
Holland, Clive. My Japanese wife. [New rev., enl. ed.] '02(Je7) il. D. $1.50. Stokes.
Holleman, A. F. Text-book of inorganic chemistry; fr. the Dutch by H. C. Cooper. pt. 2. '02(My3) 8°, $2.50. Wiley.
Holley, Marietta, ["Josiah Allen's wife."] Samantha at Saratoga. '02(Ap19) il. 12°, (Home lib.) $1. Burt.
Hollister, H. J., *and others.* Taxation in Mich. and elsewhere. '01· '02(F15) 8°, pap., 50 c. Mich. Pol. Sci. Assoc.
Holly Tree Inn. Dickens, C: net, $1.50. Lippincott.
Holme, Ma. P. M. Stray leaves from a border garden. '02(My10) il. 12°, net, $1.50. Lane.
Holmes, Burton, [*pseud.* for Elias Burton.] Burton Holmes lectures. In 10 v. v. 1-6. '01· '02(Jl19) il. 8°, subs., per set, $51; ¾ mor., $65. Little-P.
Holmes, C. J. Constable. '01· '02(Ja11) il. O. (Artist's lib., no. 5.) net, $1. Longmans.
Holmes, *Mrs.* Ma. J. Cousin Maude and Rosamond. '02(Ap19) 12°, (Home lib.) $1. Burt.
Holst, Bernhart P., *ed.* Teachers' and pupils' cyclopædia. v. 1-3. '02(Ap26) 3 v., il. 8°, hf. mor., $12.75. Holst.
Holt's Am. science ser.; briefer course. D. $1.12. Holt.
—Remsen. Introd. to study of chemistry.
Holt's students' ser. of classic Fr. plays. D. net, 35 c. Holt.
—Corneille. Le Cid. (1.)
—Racine. Athalie. (2.)—Esther. (5.)

Holy-days and holidays. Deems, E: M. $5. Funk.
HOLY SPIRIT.
Barry. God the Holy Ghost. $2. Angel Press.
Tuttle. The gift of power. net, 25 c. Westminster.
Holy war. Bunyan, J: 50 c.; 75 c. Macmillan.
Homans, J. E. A B C of the telephone. '02 (F1) il. 12°, $1. Van Nostrand.
Home and school classics. See Heath's.
Home and school ser. See Flanagan's.
Home coming of autumn queen. Kellogg, A. M. 15 c. Kellogg.
Home lib. See Burt's.
HOME STUDY.
McGovern. Fireside university of modern invention, discovery, etc., for home circle study and entertainment. $2.50; $3.75. Union Pub.
Powell. 20th century home builder. 25 c. Pub. Ho. of M. E. Ch., So.
Home thoughts. Cox, *Mrs.* J. F. net, $1.20. Barnes.
Homeric society. Keller, A. G. $1.20. Longmans.
Home's sweet harmonies. Hodgman, F. 80 c. Home Pub.
Homing pigeon (The): treatise on training, breeding, [etc.] '02(Mr15) il. T. pap., 25 c. G: E. Howard.
Honeyman, A. Van D. Bright days in merrie England. '02(Ap12) il. 12°, net, $1.50. Honeyman.
Honor of the Braxtons. Fosdick, J. W. $1.50. J. F. Taylor.
Hood, T: Serious poems. '02(My10) il. 16°, (Caxton ser.) net, $1.25. Scribner.
Hood, Wharton P. Treatment of injuries by friction and movement. '02(Ap26) 12°, net, $1.25. Macmillan.
Hook, Alfr. J. American negligence digest fr. earliest time to 1902. '02(Jl12) O. shp., $6.50. Remick.
Hooker, *Sir* Jos. D. Nociones de botánica. Nueva ed. (N. León.) '02(Jl12) il. 16°, (Nuevas cartillas cientificas.) 40 c. Appleton.
Hope, Laurence, *comp.* India's love lyrics. '02(Ap19) il. 4°, net, $1.50. Lane.
Hopkins, E: W. India old and new. '01· '02(F15) 8°, (Yale bicentennial pub.) net, $2.50. Scribner.
Hopkins, Herb. M. The fighting bishop. '02 (Mr15) D. $1.50. Bowen-M.
Hopkins, S: A. Care of the teeth. '02(Jl19) D. **75 c. net. Appleton.
Hopkins, W: B. Roller bandage. 5th ed., rev. '02(Jl19) il. 12°, **$1.50 net. Lippincott.
Horace. Odæ, Epodæ, Carmen sæculare, picturis illustratæ. '01· '02(Mr29) il. 12°, (Antique gems from the Greek and Latin, v. 3.) (App. to pubs. for price.) Barrie.
Horæ Latinæ. Ogilvie, R. $5. Longmans.
Hornbrook, A. R. Key to Primary arithmetic and Grammar school arithmetic. '02(Mr8) D. 65 c. Am. Bk.
Hornung, E. W: At large. '02(F15) D. $1.50. Scribner.
Horridge, Fk. Dynamic aspects of nutrition. '02(Je7) 12°, $1.50. Wood.

Horrocks, W. H. Introd. to the bacteriolog. examination of water. '01· '02(My10) 8°, net, $3.68. Blakiston.

HORSE.

Chapman. Pathological treatment of lameness in the horse. $2. W: R. Jenkins.

Fillis. Breaking and riding; with military commentary. net, $5. Scribner.

Morgan. Twentieth century horse book. $1.50. D: B: Morgan.

Mullen. How to break, educate and handle the horse. $1. W: Mullen.

Russell. Prescriptions and instructions for treating diseases of feet and legs of the horse. $1. Clarke.

See also **Veterinary medicine and surgery.**

HORTICULTURE.

See **Flowers;—Fruit;—Gardening.**

Horton, Fs. A. Birthright membership of believers' infants in the New Testament church. '02(Je7) S. pap., 6 c. Presb. Bd.

Horton, Wa. F. Land buyer's, settler's and explorer's guide. '02(Jl12) 16°, pap., 25 c. Byron.

Hosmer, Ja. K. Hist. of the Louisiana purchase. '02(My10) il. D. net, $1.20. Appleton.

HOSPITALS.

Smart. Hdbk. for the hospital corps of the U. S. army and state military forces. *$2.50 net. Wood

Hotchkiss, Chauncey C. Strength of the weak. '02(F1) D. $1.50. Appleton.

Houck, F: A. Life of St. Gerlach. 1900. '02(Mr22) D. net, 55 c. Benziger.

Hough, Emerson. Mississippi bubble. '02 (My3) il. D. $1.50. Bowen-M.

Hound of the Baskervilles. Doyle, A. C. $1.25. McClure, P.

Hour-glass stories. il. S. net, 40 c. Funk.

—Grenell. The sandals.

—Talbot. Courtship of sweet Anne Page.

Hours of the passion. King, H. E. H. net, $1.50. Dutton.

House of Cæsar. Van Santvoord, S. net, $5.25. Pafraets.

HOUSEKEEPING.

See **Domestic economy.**

Houston, Edn. J., *and* Kennelly, A. E. Alternating electric currents. 3d enl. ed. '02 (Je14) sq. S. (Elem. electro technical ser.) $1. McGraw.

Houston, Edn. J., *and* Kennelly, A. E. Electric arc lighting. 2d enl. ed. '02(Je14) sq. S. (Elem. electro technical ser.) $1. McGraw.

Houston, Edn. J., *and* Kennelly, A. E. Electric incandescent lighting. 2d enl. ed. '02 (Je14) sq. S. (Elem. electro technical ser.) $1. McGraw.

Houston, Edn. J., *and* Kennelly, A. E. Electric telephone. 2d ed., enl. '02(Jl5) sq. S. (Elem. electro-technical ser.) $1. McGraw.

How are we led? Sanders, C: H. $1.50. Donohue.

How successful lawyers are educated. Macdonald, G: A. $1.50. Temple Pub.

How to attract an audience. Esenwein, J. B. $1. Hinds.

How to become a naturalized citizen. Pritchard, W: A. 10 c. Wehman.

How to break and handle the horse. Mullen, W: $1. W: Mullen.

How to build a knockabout. Mower, C. D. $1. Rudder.

How to build a model yacht. Fisher, H. $1. Rudder.

How to build a racing sloop. Mower, C. D. $1. Rudder.

How to build dynamo-electric machinery. Bubier, E: T. $2.50. Bubier.

How to get acquainted with God. Seward, T. F. net, 50 c. Funk.

How to live. Knapp, A. 36 c. Silver.

How to make an index. Wheatley, H: B: $1.25; $2.50. Armstrong.

How to make the telephone. Cary, G: H. $1. Bubier.

How to organize and conduct a meeting. Henry, W. H. F. 75 c. Hinds.

How to prepare essays, lectures, [etc.] Miles, E. H. net, $2. Dutton.

How to teach about trees. Payne, F. O. 25 c. Kellogg.

How to teach aquatic life. Payne, F. O. 25 c. Kellogg.

How to teach composition writing. Kellogg, A. M. 25 c. Kellogg.

How to tell fortunes. Zancig, *Mme.* 25 c. Drake.

How to tell time by the stars. Browne, D: M. 50 c. Lee & S.

How to treat the trusts. Haggerty, J: 25 c. Abbey Press.

Howard, B: Prisoners of Russia: convict life in Sakhalin and Siberia. '02(Je21) D. net, $1.40. Appleton.

Howard, Eliza B. Two waifs. '02(Jl12) D. 50 c. Abbey Press.

Howard, Hamilton G. Law points to know: treatise, consisting of 8 lectures on elem. law. '02(Jl5) S. pap., $1. H. G. Howard.

Howard, *Lady* Mabel. Failure of success. '01· '02(F8) D. $1.50. Longmans.

Howard, W: L. The perverts. '02(F15) D. $1.50. G: W. Dillingham.

Howe, Edn. D. *See* New York civil and criminal justice.

Howells, Mildred. *See* Burt, M. E.

Howells, W: D. The Kentons. '02(Ap26) D. $1.50. Harper.

Howes, G: B. Atlas of practical elem. zootomy. '02(Mr8) 4°, net, $3.50. Macmillan.

Hoyt, Eleanor. Misdemeanors of Nancy. '02 (Ap19) il. D. $1.50. Doubleday, P.

Hoyt, Helen B. Child's story of the life of Christ. '02(Jl5) il. 12°, $1.25. W. A. Wilde.

Hoyt, L: G. Practice in proceedings in the probate cts. of New Hampshire. '01· '02 (F8) O. shp., $2.50. Rumford Press.

Hoyt, T: A. Theology as a popular science. '02(Je21) S. pap., net, 10 c. Presb. Bd.

Hubbard, Elbert, ["Fra Elbertus."] Message to Garcia and thirteen other things. '01· '02(F15) 8°, limp leath., $2; $5; ¾ levant, $15. Roycrofters.

Hubbard, Elbert. Time and chance. '01· '02 (F15) D. $1.50. Putnam.

Huddilston, J: H. Lessons from Greek pottery, [with] bibliog. of Gr. ceramics. '02 (F1) 8°, net, $1.25. Macmillan.

Hudson, Horace B. California vineyards: scenes in Fresno Co. '02(Ap5) il. obl. D. pap., 35 c. H. B. Hudson.

Hudson, H. B. Dict. of Minneapolis, 1902. '02(Jl5) il. S. pap., 25 c. H. B. Hudson.
Hufford, D: A. El camino real; highway connecting missions. '01· '02(F15) obl. Tt. pap., 35 c.; burnt yucca or redwood, 75 c.; burnt leath., $1; burnt orangewood, $1.25. D: A. Hufford.
Hufford, D: A. The real Ramona of Helen Hunt Jackson's famous novel. '02(F15) il. D. pap., 35 c.; burnt yucca or redwood, 75 c.; burnt leath., $1; burnt orangewood, $1.25. D: A. Hufford.
Hughes, Erlian. My island. '02(F15) 16°, $1.25. Dutton.
Hughes, H. W. Text-book of coal mining. New enl. ed. '01· '02(F15) il. 8°, $7. Lippincott.
Hughes, R. E. Schools at home and abroad. '02(Ap5) 12°, net, $1.50. Dutton.
Hugo, V. John Brown. '02(Jl12) sq. 12°, bds., $5; hf. leath., $15. Alwil Shop.
Hugo, V. Notre-Dame de Paris; abr. and ed. by J: R. Wightman. '02(Ap5) S. 85 c. Ginn.
HUGUENOTS.
Baird. Hist. of Huguenot emigration to America. 2 v. net, $2.50. Dodd.
Stapleton. Memorials of the Huguenots in America. $1.50. Huguenot.
Hulbert, W: D. Forest neighbors. '02 (My24) il. O. net, $1.50. McClure, P.
Hull, Mattie E. Spirit echoes. '01· '02 (Ap12) 12°, net, 75 c. Sunflower.
Hull Botanical Laboratory contributions. O. pap., net. Univ. of Chic.
—Cowles. Ecological rel. of vegetation on the sand dunes of Lake Mich. 75 c. (13.)
—Life. Tuber-like rootlets of cycas revoluta. 25 c. (26.)
—Livingston. Stimulus which causes change in polymorphic green algae. 25 c. (22.)
—Lyon. Study of the sporangia and gametophytes of selaginella apus and selaginella rupestris. 25 c. (31.)
—Overton. Parthenogenesis in thalictrum purpurascens. 25 c. (35.)
—Smith, R. W. Achromatic spindle in spore mother-cells of osmunda regalis. 25 c. (23.)
—Stevens. Gametrogenesis and fertilization in albugo. 25 c. (29.)
—Webb. Morpholog. study of the flower and embryo of spirala. *25 c. (36.)
Hulsean lectures. *See* Chase, F: H:
HUMAN FIGURE.
See Anatomy for artists.
Human knowledge. Trask, R. D. *$2 net. R. D. Trask.
Humble heroine. Tiddeman, L. E. 15 c. Lippincott.
HUME, D:
Gore. Imagination in Spinoza and Hume. net, 35 c. Univ. of Chic.
Hume, Fergus W. Millionaire mystery. '01· '02(Ja4) D. $1.25. Buckles
Hume, Fergus W. Pagan's cup. '02(F8) D. $1.25. G: W. Dillingham.
Humphreys, *Mrs.* Eliz. M. J. G., ["Rita."] Sin of Jasper Standish. '02(Mr22) D. $1.25. Fenno.
Hun, Marcus T. *See* New York. *Sup. ct.* Repts.
Huneker, Ja. Melomaniacs. '02(Mr1) D. $1.50. Scribner.
Hungerford, Herb. Success club debater. '01· '02(Mr1) Tt. (Boiled-down booklets.) 25 c. Success.
Hungerford, *Mrs.* Marg. H., ["The Duchess," *formerly Mrs.* Argles.] The three graces. '01· '02(Mr1) 12°, (Popular lib.) $1. Lippincott.
HUNT, Holman.
Williamson. Holman Hunt. 50 c. Macmillan.
Hunt, J. N., *and* Gourley, H. I. Modern pronouncing speller. '02(Jl19) 12°, 20 c. Butler.
Hunter, W: C. Twentieth century wonder book. '02(My17) 12°, 50 c.; pap., 25 c. Donohue.
Huntington, Annie O. Studies of trees in winter: des. of the deciduous trees of Northeastern America. '02(Ja18) il. O. net, $2.25. Knight.
Hurd, Harvey B., *comp. and ed.* *See* Illinois. *Gen. assembly.* Revised statutes.
Hurll, Estelle M., *ed.* Tuscan sculpture. Lib. ed. '02(Ap5) D. (Riverside art ser., no. 11.) net, 75 c.; School ed., net, 50 c.; pap., net, 35 c. Houghton, M. & Co.
Hurll, Estelle M., *ed.* Van Dyck. Lib. ed. '02(Je7) (Riverside art ser., no. 12.) net, 75 c.; School ed., net, 50 c.: pap., net, 35 c. Houghton, M. & Co.
Hurst, C: Hints on steam engine design and construction. '01· '02(F15) 16°, bds., 60 c. Lippincott.
Hurst, J: F. History of rationalism; emb. survey of present state of Protestant theology; rev. '01· '02(F15) 8°, $2.50. Eaton & M.
Hurst, J: F. The new hearthstone: bridal greeting. '02(Mr1) O. $1. Jennings.
Hurst, J: F. Upon the sunroad. '02(My17) 16°, 25 c. Revell.
Hutchinson, H. N., Gregory, J. W., *and* Lydekker, R. Living races of mankind. '02(Ap12) il. 8°, net, $5. Appleton.
Hutchinson, Ida W. Gospel story of Jesus Christ. '02(Mr29) 12°. $1.50. Dutton.
Hutchinson, Jos. Primrose diplomacy: [poetry.] '02(Jl19) 12°, $1.25. Abbey Press.
Hutchison, Jos. C. Lessons in physiology and hygiene. 2d bk. for advanced grades. Rev. ed. '02(Jl12) il. 12°, (Hutchison's physiological ser.) 80 c.; bds., 40 c. Maynard, M. & Co.
Hutton, R. E. The soul in the unseen world. '02(Ap5) 12°, net, $2. Dutton.
HUXLEY, T: H:
Clodd. Thomas Henry Huxley. net, $1. Dodd.
Hyde, Miles G. The girl from Mexico, and other stories and sketches. 3d ed. '02 (Ap26) D. $1. Abbey Press.
Hyde, W. H., *and* McManman, J. A. Telephone troubles. 8th ed. '01· '02(F15) 16°, pap., 25 c. Caspar.
HYDRAULIC ENGINEERING.
Church. Diagrams of mean velocity of uniform motion of water in open channels. $1.50. Wiley.
Fanning. Hydraulic and water-supply engineering. $5. Van Nostrand.
Fidler. Calculations in hydraulic engineering. pt. 2. $3. Longmans.
HYDRO-KINETICS.
See Hydraulic engineering.

HYDROTHERAPY.
Kellogg. Rational hydrotherapy. subs., $5; $6. Davis.
HYGIENE.
Balch. Manual for boards of health. $1.50. Banks & Co.
Bryce. Ideal health and how to attain it. 50 c. Treat.
Furneaux. Elem. practical hygiene. 90 c. Longmans.
Hoffman. Health and strength. 25 c. H. C. Hoffman.
Knapp. How to live. 36 c. Silver.
Morris. Right living; or, how a woman can keep well. $1. Bardeen.
Sedgwick. Principles of sanitary science and public health. net, $3. Macmillan.
Smith. Anatomy, physiology and hygiene. $1. W: R. Jenkins.
Van Doren. Students' guide to health. $2. D. T. Van Doren.
Willoughby. Hygiene for students. $1.25. Macmillan.
See also Diet;—Mind and body; — Physiology; — Sanitary engineering.
HYMNS AND HYMN WRITERS.
Gabriel, *comp.* Joyful praise. 30 c. Jennings.
Gill, *and others.* Hymns of grace and glory. 30 c. Mattill & L.
Hypatia. *See* Kingsley, C:
Hyperion. Longfellow, H: W. $1. Burt.
HYPNOTISM.
Alpheus. Guide to hypnotism. 50 c.; 25 c. Donohue.
Ballough. Sibylline leaves. $1. Painter.
De Laurence. Hypnotism and magnetism. $1; 50 c. Drake.
De Laurence. Hypnotism. $1.50. Henneberry.
Santanelli. Is man a free agent? Law of suggestion, [etc.] *$1 net. Santanelli.
HYSTERICS.
See Mind and body.
I go a fishing. Barton, W: E. 25 c. Revell.
I promessi sposi. Manzoni. A. $1.20. Silver.
ICE CREAM.
See Confectionery.
Idea of God. Reed, E. A. net, 75 c. Univ. of Chic.
Ideal health. Bryce, A. 50 c. Treat.
Ideal messages ser. net, 25 c. Revell.
—Stowe. He's coming to-morrow.
Ideal word book. Smith, E. E. 17 c. Flanagan.
Idole (L'). Michaud, H. 10 c. W: R. Jenkins.
Idylls. *See* Theocritus.
Idylls of the king. *See* Davidson, *Mrs.* H. A.
If I were king. McCarthy, J. H. $1.50. Russell.
Iliad and Odyssey. *See* Keller, A. G.
Illinois. *Appellate cts.* **Repts. v. 97.** '02 (Mr1); v. 98 (Mr29); v. 99 (My17); v. 100 (Jl19) O. shp., ea., $3.75. Callaghan.
Illinois. Commentary on the mechanics' lien law, by C: T. Farson. '02(F1) O. net, $4. Callaghan.
Illinois. Compilation of laws rel. to township organization and county affairs, by F. M. Haines. 23d ed., rev., by A. Matteson. '02(Jl12) O. shp., $3; hf. cl., $2.50. Legal Adv
Illinois. *General assembly.* Revised statutes, 1901. (H. B. Hurd.) '01- '02(Mr8) O. shp., net, $4. Chic. Leg. News.
Illinois. Homestead exemption laws, by A. M. Kales. '02(Jl5) O. *$4 net. Callaghan.
Illinois. *Supreme ct.* **Repts. v. 192.** '02 (Mr29); v. 193 (My17) O. shp., ea., $2.25. Phillips.
ILLINOIS.
Arnold, *comp.* Manual of school laws. $1.75. Effingham Dem.
Bunzey. Hist. of companies I and E, 6th Regt. Ill. Vol. Inf. $2. R. S. Bunzey.
Illustrated family Christian almanac, 1902. '02(Mr1) sq. 12°, pap., 10 c. Am. Tr.
ILLUSTRATIONS (*religious*).
See Sermons.
ILLUSTRATORS.
See Book illustration.
Imagination in Spinoza and Hume. Gore, W. C. net, 35 c. Univ. of Chic.
Imhaus, Eliz. V. **Exiled by the world.** '02 (Mr8) il. D. $1.50. Mutual Pub.
Imitation and analysis. Donnelly, F. P. 60 c. Allyn & B.
Imitator (The): (novel.) '01- '02(Ap5) D. $1.25. W: M. Reedy.
IMMORTALITY.
See Future life.
Improprieties of Noah. Smedberg, H. V. 50 c. Abbey Press.
Improvement of moral qualities. Gabirol, S. I. net, $1.25. Macmillan.
In a Tuscan garden. '02(Je28) il. 12°, net, $1.50. Lane.
In a walled garden. Belloc, B. R. net, $1.25. Herder.
In and around the Grand Canyon. James, G: W. net, $10. Little, B. & Co.
In defense of Judas. Story, W: W. $1. Philosopher Press.
In His name. *See* Hale, E: E.
In memoriam. Tennyson, A. *Lord.* net, $1.20. Scribner.
In my vicarage garden. Ellacombe, H: N. net, $1.50. Lane.
In Sicily. Sladen, D. 2 v. net, $20. Dutton.
In the country God forgot. Charles, F. $1.50. Little, B. & Co.
In the days of giants. Brown, A. F. net, $1.10. Houghton, M. & Co.
In the eagle's talon. Stevens, *Mrs.* S. $1.50. Little, B. & Co.
In the footprints of the padres. Stoddard, C: W. net, $1.50. A. M. Robertson.
In the Michigan lumber camps. Whittier, C: A. 75 c. Neely.
In the misty realm of fable. Kleckner, E. R. $1. Flanagan.
In the palace of the king. Crawford, F. M. 50 c. Am. News.
In Thompson's woods. Crissey, F. $1. Blue Sky Press.
In Tuscany. Carmichael. M. net, $2. Dutton.
In Viking land. Weborg, J. $1.25. J. C. Weborg.
In white and black. Pinson, W: W. $1.50. Saalfield.
Inauguration of President Watterson. De Leon, T: C. 25 c. Am. Writers.
INDEPENDENT CONG. CHURCH.
See Unitarian church.

INTERMEDIATE STATE.
See Future life.
Intermere. Taylor, W: A. $1. XX Century.
Internal improvements in Alabama. Martin, W: E. 30 c. Johns Hopkins.
International annual of Anthony's photographic bulletin and Am. process yearbook. v. 14 for 1902; ed. by W. I. Scandlin. '01-'02(Mr1) il. O. $1.25; pap., 75 c. Anthony.
International Cable Directory Co., *comp.* Internat. cable directory of the world in conjunction with Western Union telegraphic code system. '02(Jl19) O. $15. Int. Cable.
International education ser. See Appleton's.
INTERNATIONAL LAW.
Taylor. Treatise on internat. public law. net, $6.50. Callaghan.
International medical annual, 1902. '02 (Ap12) il. 8°, net, $3. Treat.
International theol. lib.; ed. by S. D. F. Salmond and C: A. Briggs. O. net, $2.50. Scribner.
—Rainy. Ancient Catholic church, A.D 98-451.
International year book, 1901. '02(My24) Q. $4. Dodd.
Interviews with a monocle. Jordon, L. 50 c. Whitaker & R.
INTESTINES.
Hemmeter. Diseases of the intestines. v. 2. net, $5; net, $6. Blakiston.
Into the light. Taylor, E: R. net, 75 c. Elder.
INVENTIONS.
See Patents.
INVERTEBRATES.
Pratt. Course in invertebrate zoölogy. $1.35. Ginn.
INVESTMENTS.
See Railroads.
Ioläus. Carpenter, E: net, $1.75. Goodspeed.
Ione, *pseud. See* Brown, G. M.
Iowa. The citator. '02(Jl12) D. limp skiver, $3. R. Adams.
Iowa. Encyclopedia of Iowa law; cont. legal words and phrases, with comments by E. C. Ebersole. '02(Mr8) O. shp., $6. E. C. Ebersole.
IRAN.
See Persia.
IRELAND.
Falkiner. Studies in Irish hist. and biog. mainly of 18th century. $5. Longmans.
Martin. Traces of the elder faiths of Ireland. 2 v. $12. Longmans.
O'Byrne. Kings and vikings.—Land of heroes: stories fr. Irish history. ea., $1.25. Scribner.
O'Conor, *comp.* Irish com-all-ye's. 25 c. —Old time songs and ballads of Ireland. $2. Popular.
See also Patrick, *St.*
IRISH.
See Scots.
Irish fairy and folk tales. Yeats, W: B. $1. Burt.
IRISH LANGUAGE.
O'Growney. Revised simple lessons in Irish. pt. 1. 15 c. Gael.
IRISH LITERATURE.
Stokes *and* Strachan, *eds.* Thesaurus palæohibernicus: coll. of old Irish glosses, scholia, etc. net, $8. Macmillan.
Irish wit and humor. '02(Mr15) S. pap., 25 c. Drake.

IRON.
Keep. Cast iron: record of orig. research. $2.50. Wiley.
West. Metallurgy of cast iron. $3. Cleveland Pr.
Iron Age directory. '02(My24) 16°, flex. linen, 25 c. D: Williams.
Iron hand. Dean, H. $1. Abbey Press.
Ironquill, *pseud. See* Fitch, E.
IROQUOIS.
Morgan. League of the Ho-de-no-sau-nee or Iroquois. 2 v. **$15 net; $30 net. Dodd.
Irregular and regular commercial paper. McMaster, J. S. $2. McMaster.
IRRIGATION.
Newell. Irrigation in the U. S. net, $2. Crowell.
Wilcox. Irrigation farming. $2. Judd.
Irving, W. Selections from Sketch-book. Regents ed.; ed. by C. T. Benjamin. '02 (F1) D. 50 c. Am. Bk.
Irving, W. Sketch book. '02(Je21) 2 v., il. 16°, (Caxton ser.) net, $1.25. Scribner.
Irving, W. Two selections: Legend of Sleepy Hollow and Rip Van Winkle from Sketch book; notes, etc., by J. W. Graham. '02 (Je7) 12°, leatherette, 25 c. Whitaker & R.
Irwin, Wallace. ["Omar Khayyâm, jr."] Love sonnets of a hoodlum. '01. '02(Mr22) 16°, pap., 25 c.; Bandana ed., 50 c. Elder.
Irwin, Wallace. Rubâiyat of Omar Khayyâm, jr. '02(My24) il. O. pap., net, 50 c. Elder.
Is man a free agent? Santanelli. *$1 net. Santanelli.
Is the negro a beast? Schell, W: G. 60 c. Gospel Trumpet.
ISABELLA, *Queen of Castile.*
See Ferdinand, *King of Spain.*
Isabella. Keats, J: $1; 60 c. Macmillan.
Isham, F: S. The strollers. '02(Mr22) il. D. $1.50. Bowen-M.
Islam and Christianity. '01. '02(Mr1) 12°, $1. Am. Tr.
Island cabin. Henry, A. $1.50. McClure, P.
Isler, C. Well boring for water, brine and oil. '02(Ap5) il. 8°, $4. Spon.
Isolation in the school. Young, E. F. net, 50 c. Univ. of Chic.
Isthmian canal. Johnson, E. R. 25 c. Am. Acad. Pol. Sci.
Isthmian canal question. Pasco, S: 25 c. Am. Acad. Pol. Sci.
ITALIAN LANGUAGE.
Manzoni. I promessi sposi. $1.20. Silver.
Italian painting. Van Dyke, J: C: 50 c. Elson.
Italian Renaissance in England. Einstein, L. net, $1.50. Macmillan.
ITALY.
Cruickshank. Umbrian towns. net, $1.25. Wessels.
Friedländer. Town life in ancient Italy. 75 c. B: H. Sanborn.
Villari. Barbarian invasions of Italy. 2 v. net, $7.50. Scribner.
Whitcomb. Little journey to Italy. 15 c. Flanagan.
See also Florence;—Medici; — Rome;—Sicily; —Tuscany.
It's up to you. McHugh, H. 75 c. G: W. Dillingham.
Ivanhoe and Rob Roy, retold for children. Sullivan, *Sir* E: 50 c. Little, B. & Co.

IVORY.
Cust. Ivory workers of the Middle Ages. $2. Macmillan.
J., C. J. Otis Grey, bachelor. '02(Je7) S. 75 c. Mutual Bk.
Jackanapes. Ewing, *Mrs.* J. H. net, 15 c. Houghton, M. & Co.
Jackman, Warren. Hist. of the town of Elma, Erie Co., N. Y. '02(My24) O. $3. Hausauer.
Jackson, Dugald C., *and* Jackson, J: P. Elem. text-book on electricity and magnetism. '02 (F22) il. 12°, hf. leath., net, $1.40. Macmillan.
Jackson, J: P. *See* Jackson, D. C.
Jacob, J: T: Christ the indweller. '02 (My3) 12°. $1.50. Macmillan.
Jacobs, W: W. At Sunwich port. '02(My10) il. D. $1.50. Scribner
Jacobson, W. H. A., *and* Steward, F. J. Operations of surgery. '02(My17) 2 v., il. 8°, net, $10; shp., or hf. mor. $12. Blakiston.
Jacoby, Harold. Practical talks by an astronomer. '02(Ap12) il. D. net, $1. Scribner.
Jacoby, H: D. *See* Merriman, M.
James, Alfr. Cyanide practice. '01. '02 (Ja25) il. 4°, $5. Engineering.
James, Bushrod W. Political freshman. '02 (Ap19) D. $1.50. Bushrod Lib.
James, *Mrs.* Flor. A. P., ["Florence Warden."] The lovely Mrs. Pemberton. '02 (F8) D. $1.25. Buckles.
James, G: W. In and around the Grand Canyon. Pasadena ed. '01. '02(F22) il. 8°, hf. mor., net, $10. Little, B. & Co.
James, W: Varieties of religious experience. '02(Je21) O. (Gifford lectures, 3d ser.) net, $3.20. Longmans.
James Griffin's adventures on land and sea. Dee, H. $1. Yewdale.
JAMESTOWN, Va.
Hall. Jamestown, 1607-1907. 25 c. Am. Scenic.
Janes, Emily, *ed.* *See* Englishwoman's year book.
Janes, L. G. Lewis G. Janes, philosopher, patriot, lover of man. '02(Ap19) il. D. $1. J. H. West.
Janet, Pierre. Mental state of hystericals; tr. by C. R. Corson. '02(Mr1) 12°, $3.50. Putnam.
JAPAN.
Brinkley. Japan. 5 v. ea., $50. Millet.
Kinosita. Past and present of Japanese commerce. *$1.50 net. Macmillan.
Menpes. Japan. net, $6. Macmillan.
Stead. Japan of to-day. net, $2. Dutton.
Jastrow, Morris, *jr.* Study of religion. '01. '02(Ja11) 12°, (Contemporary science ser.) $1.50. Scribner.
Jean Mitchell's school. Wray, A. W. $1.25. Public Sch. Pub.
Jean Valjean. *See* Quayle, W: A.
Jebb, *Sir* R: C. Modern Greece: two lectures del. before the philosophical institution of Edinburgh. 2d ed. '02(F1) 12°, (Eversley ser.) $1.75. Macmillan.
JEFFERSON, Thos.
See Burr, A.
Jegi, J: I. Syllabus of human physiology for schools and colleges. '01. '02(Mr8) il. 12°. $1. Gillan.

Jekyll, Gertrude, *comp.* Lilies for English gardens. '01. '02(Ja11) 8°, (Country life lib.) net, $3.75. Scribner.
Jellison, Edn. A: The wounded beast: [poem.] '01. '02(Mr29) D. pap., 25 c. E. A: Jellison.
Jenkins' contes choisis. sq. S. 40 c.; pap., 25 c. W: R. Jenkins.
—Coppée. Morceau de pain. (22.)
Jenkinson, I: Aaron Burr, his rel. with Thomas Jefferson and Alex. Hamilton. '02 (My3) D. $1.25. I: Jenkinson.
Jenks, E: Edward Plantagenet, (Edward I.): the Eng. Justinian. '02(Mr8) D. (Heroes of the nations ser., no. 35.) net, $1.35; hf. leath., net, $1.60. Putnam.
Jennings, J: E. Manual of ophthalmoscopy. '02(Mr1) il. 8°. net, $1.50. Blakiston.
Jerry's reward. Barnett, E. S. 50 c. L. C. Page.
Jesse, J: H. Historical memoirs. First ser. (15 v.) and second ser. (15 v.) '02(Ap5) 30 v., 8°, per v., $2.50; complete set of 15 v., (first or second ser.) $37.40; ¾ mor., $75. L. C. Page.
Jessup, Alex., *ed.* *See* Balzac, H. de.
Jesuit relations. (Thwaites.) In 73 v. v. 72, 73. Index to entire ser. '01. '02(Mr1) 8°, ea., net, $3.50. Burrows.
JESUITS.
See Jesus (Society of).
JESUS CHRIST.
Boardman. Our risen King's forty days. net, $1.25. Lippincott.
Burton *and* Mathews. Constructive studies in the life of Christ. $1. Univ. of Chic.
Hoyt. Child's story of the life of Christ. $1.25. W. A. Wilde.
Hutchinson. Gospel story of Jesus Christ. $1.50. Dutton.
Jacob. Christ the indweller. $1.50. Macmillan.
Life and works of the Redeemer. net, $2. Dutton.
McClelland. Verba crucis. 50 c. Crowell.
Moberly. Christ our life. net, $3. Longmans.
Nicoll. Church's one foundation, Christ. $1.25. Armstrong.
Pearson. Carpenter prophet. $1.50. H. S. Stone.
Rénan. Life of Jesus. $1. Burt.
Rutherford. Christ and his cross. $1. Longmans.
Speer. Principles of Jesus app. to some questions of to-day. net, 80 c. Revell
Stretton. New child's life of Christ. $1. Winston.
Taylor, *and others.* Studies in the life of Christ. 75 c. Jennings.
Vincent. What is it to believe on the Lord Jesus Christ? 5 c. Beam.
Wollpert. A man amongst men. 15 c. Eckler.
See also Bible; — Christianity; — Easter; — Lord's supper.
JESUS (Society of).
Jesuit relations v. 72, 73. ea., $3.50. Burrows.
Taunton. Hist of the Jesuits in England. 1580-1773. net, $3.75. Lippincott.
Jeter, J. B. Baptist principles reset. New and enl. ed. '02(Jl19) 16°..$1. Rel. Herald.
Jewett, C: Essentials of obstetrics. 2d ed. '01. '02(Ja25) 12° net. $2.25. Lea.

Jewett, C: Manual of childbed nursing. 5th ed., rev. and enl. '02(Ap5) D. 80 c. Treat.

Jewett, C:, *ed.* Practice of obstetrics, by Am. authors. 2d ed. '01- '02(Ja25) il. 8°, net, $5; shp., net, $6; hf. mor., net, $6.50. Lea.

Jewett, F. G., *comp.* Manual for election officers and voters in N. Y. 10th ed. '02(Jl5) O. shp., $2; pap., $1.50. M. Bender.

Jewett, F. G., *comp. See also* New York. Primary election law.

Jewish carol. Calvin, E. R. 75 c. Westminster.

Jewish Chautauqua Society. Papers presented at the fifth annual session of the summer assembly, July 7-28, 1901. '02(Jl5) S. (Special ser., no. 7.) 30 c. Jewish Pub.

Jewish Pub. Soc. special ser. D. 30 c. Jewish Pub.
—Jewish Chautauqua Soc. Papers. (7.)
—Ruskay. Hearth and home essays. (6.)

JEWS.
Duff. Theology and ethics of the Hebrews. net, $1.25. Scribner.
Greenstone. Religion of Israel. 50 c. Bloch.
Philipson. The Jew in Eng. fiction. net, $1. Clarke.
Peters. The Jew as a patriot. $1. Baker & T.
Robertson. Early religion of Israel. net, $1.60. Whittaker.
See also Semitic peoples.

Jezebel. McLaws, L. †$1.50. Lothrop.

Job, Herb. K. Among the waterfowl. '02 (Je7) il. sq. O. net, $1.35. Doubleday, P.

John Kenadie. Saunders, R. D. $1.50. Houghton, M. & Co.

Johns Hopkins Univ. studies. O. Johns Hopkins.
—Ballagh. Hist. of slavery in Va. $1.50. (extra v. 24.)

Johns Hopkins Univ. studies in hist. and pol. science. O. pap. Johns Hopkins.
—Barnett. State banking in U. S. 50 c. (ser. 20, 2, 3.)
—Martin. Internal improvements in Alabama. 30 c. (ser. 20, 1.)
—Radcliffe. Gov. Thomas H. Hicks of Md., and the civil war. 50 c. (ser. 19, 11, 12.)
—Steiner. Western Maryland in the Revolution. 30 c. (ser. 20, 1.)
—Vincent, *and others.* H. B. Adams; with bibliog. of the dept. of history, etc. (ser. 20, extra no.) free to subs.

JOHNSON, And.
Jones. Life of Andrew Johnson. $1.50. East Tenn.

Johnson, Emory R. Isthmian canal. '02 (Mr22) 8°, (Pub. of the soc., no. 323.) pap., 25 c. Am. Acad. Pol. Sci.

Johnson, Fk. M. Forest, lake and river; fishes of New England and eastern Canada. '02(Jl19) col. il. 2 v. and portfolio. 8°, ed. de luxe, per set, $300; grand ed. de luxe, per set, $500. F. M. Johnson.

Johnson, J. B. Theory and practice of surveying. 16th ed., rev. and enl. '02(Ap5) il. 8°, $4. Wiley.

Johnson, R: B. Popular Eng. ballads. '01- '02(F15) 4 v., il. 12°, $3. Lippincott.

Johnson, Rob. U. Poems. '02(My24) D. net, $1.20. Century Co.

Johnson, S: Essays from The Rambler and The Idler. '01. '02(Ap5) S. (Little masterpieces.) 50 c. Doubleday, P.

Johnson, S: History of Rasselas, Prince of Abyssinia. '02(My10) 12°, (Home lib.) $1. Burt.

Johnson, Virginia W. A world's shrine. '02 (Jl19) il. D. **$1.20 net. Barnes.

Johnson, W. F. Life of W. T. Sherman. '02 (Jl19) 12°, (Biographies of famous men.) $1. Donohue.

Johnson, Willis G. Fumigation methods. '02(Mr22) il. D. $1. Judd.

Johnson ser. of Eng. classics. 16°, 30 c.; 25 c. B. F. Johnson.
—Coleridge. Ancient mariner.

Johnston, Annie F. Asa Holmes. '02 (My17) S. $1. L. C. Page.

Johnston, J: W. Riddle of life. '02(F22) D. $1.50. Jennings.

Johnston, Ma. Audrey. '02(Mr1) il. D. $1.50. Houghton, M. & Co.

Jokai, Maurus. Told by the death's head. '02(Jl5) D. $1.50. Saalfield.

Joline, Adrian H. Meditations of an autograph collector. '02(My10) il. O. net, $3. Harper.

Jonathan Fish and his neighbors. Maxwell, H. $1. Acme.

Jones, Harry C. Elements of physical chemistry. '02(F22) 8°, net, $4. Macmillan.

Jones Harry W. A chaplain's experience ashore and afloat; the *Texas* under fire. '01- '02(Ap12) 12°, $1.25. Sherwood.

Jones, Ja. S. Life of Andrew Johnson, seventeenth president of the U. S. '01- '02 (F8) il. 12°, $1.50. East Tenn.

JONES, J: Paul.
Brown. John Paul Jones. $1. Donohue.

Jones, Marcus E. Utah. '02(Jl12) il. 12°, (Tarr and McMurry's geographies, supp. volumes.) *40 c. net. Macmillan.

Jones, Morgan P. Chiefs of Cambria. '02 (My3) il. D. $1.25. Abbey Press.

Jones, W: C. Illustrated hist. of the Univ. of California, 1868-1901. Rev. ed. '01- '02 (My24) il. F. $5. Berkeley.

Jordan, D: S., *comp.* True tales of birds and beasts. '02(Je14) il. D. (Home and school classics, young readers' ser.) 40 c. Heath.

Jordan, D: S., *and* Evermann, B. W. American food and game fishes. '02(Je14) Q. net, $4. Doubleday, P.

Jordan, D: S., *and* Heath, H. Animal forms: second book of zoology. '02(Je7) il. D. (Twentieth century text-books.) net, $1.10. Appleton.

Jordan, Eliz. G. Tales of destiny. '02(Je28) il. D. $1.50. Harper.

Jordan, Maggie O. Ways of the world. '02 (Ap26) 12°, $1.50. Neely.

Jordan, W: G: Kingship of self-control. '02 (F8) 12°, bds., 50 c. Revell.

Jordan, W: G: Majesty of calmness. '02 (F8) 12°, bds., 50 c. Revell.

Jordans, Jos. Danger of youth and a tried antidote; fr. the Germ. '02(Je28) 16°, 15 c. Herder.

Jordon. Leopold. Interviews with a monocle. '02(Ap12) 12°, pap., 50 c. Whitaker & R.

José. Valdés, A. P. $1.25. Brentano's.

JOSEPH.
Miller. Story of Joseph. net, 35 c. Revell.
Josephine Grahame. Wheeler, J. $1.50. Abbey Press.
Josh Billings' old farmers' allminax. Shaw, H: W. $1.50. G: W. Dillingham.
Josiah Allen's wife, *pseud.* *See* Holley, M.
Josselyn, C: True Napoleon. '02(Je7) O. net, $3.50. Russell.
Journal of a live woman. Van Anderson, H. $1. Alliance.
Journal to Stella. Swift, J. $1.75. Putnam.
Joy in service. Purves, G: T. 50 c. Am. Tr.
Joyce's investments. Newberry, F. E. $1. Burt.
Joyful praise. Gabriel, C: H. 30 c. Jennings.
Judah's lion. Tonna, *Mrs.* C. E. $1. Dodd.
Judd, D: H. That old kitchen stove: [poem.] '01. '02(Ap5) il. D. 50 c. Abbey Press.
Judith's garden. Bassett, M. E. S. $1.50. Lothrop.
Judson, C: F., *and* Gittings, J. C. Artificial feeding of infants. '02(Jl19) 12°, $2. Lippincott.
Judson, Harry P., *and* Bender, Ida C., *eds.* Graded literature readers. bks. 6-8. '01' '02(Mr1) il. 12°, ea., 50 c. Maynard, M. & Co.
Judson. W. P. City roads and pavements suited to cities of moderate size. 2d ed. '02(Jl19) il. 12°, $2. Engineering News.
Julius Cæsar. *See* Shakespeare, W:
Jungfrau von Orleans. Schiller, J. C. F. v. net, 60 c. Holt.
JUSTICES OF THE PEACE.
Brand. Justices' code for Wash. $5. Bancroft-W.
Minnesota. Justice's manual. $1.50. Booth.
Justinianus, *Emperor.* Pandects of Justinian; tr. into Eng. by W: Maude. In 4 v., v. 1. 02(Je7) 8°, $5. Cambridge.
Kaercher, F. O., *comp.* Summary of indulgences, privileges and favors granted to the secular branch of the Third order of St. Francis. '02(Je14) 24°, pap., 15 c. Herder.
Kaler, J. O., ["James Otis."] Cruise of the "Enterprise." '02(Jl12) il. 12°, $1.50. W. A. Wilde.
Kaler, J. O. Story of Pemaquid. '02(Mr8) il. D. (Pioneer towns of America, v. 2.) 50 c. Crowell.
Kaler, J. O. Treasure of Cocos Island. '02 (Jl12) 12°, (Alger ser.) $1. Burt.
Kaler, J. O. Wan Lun and Dandy. '02 (Je28) il. 12°, (St. Nicholas ser.) 75 c. Burt.
Kales, Albert Martin. *See* Illinois. Homestead exemption laws.
Kann, Jerome H., *ed.* *See* California. Code time table.
Kansas. *State board of educ.* County examination questions; with answers. No. 9. '02(Mr22) D. pap., 35 c. J. Macdonald.
Kansas. Statutes concerning domestic and foreign corporations for profit. and mutual and fraternal insurance companies; by G. C. Clemens. '02(Je28) O. pap., $1; hf. shp., $1.25. Crane.

KANSAS.
Winans. Kansas. *30 c. net. Macmillan.
Kant, Immanuel. Prolegomena to any future metaphysics; ed. in Eng., by P. Carus. '02 (Je28) 12°, net, 75 c.; *Same.* (Mr8) (Religion of sci. lib., no. 53.) pap., 50 c. Open Court.
KANT, Immanuel.
Paulsen. Immanuel Kant, his life and doctrine. net, $2.50. Scribner.
Kate Bonnet. Stockton, F. R: $1.50. Appleton.
Keane, A: H: South America. New rev. ed. '01' '02(F15) il. 8°, (Stanford's compendium of geog. and travel.) $4.50. Lippincott.
Keats, J: Isabella and the Eve of St. Agnes. '02(Ap12) il. 16°, 60 c.; leath., $1. Macmillan.
Keats, J: Odes. '02(Ap12) il. 16°, 60 c.; leath., $1. Macmillan.
Keay, J. H. Medical treatment of gall stones. '02(My17) 12°, net, $1.25. Blakiston.
Keedy, E: E. Naturalness of Christian life. '02(My3) il. D. 50 c. Abbey Press.
Keen, Ja. T. *See* Young, O. D.
Keene, Roswell W. The blue diamond. '02 (Jl5) D. $1.50. Abbey Press.
Keep, W: J. Cast iron. '02(Ja18) il. 8°, $2.50. Wiley.
Keese, W: L. Siamese twins and other poems. '02(Je21) 12°, net, $1.25. E. W. Dayton.
Keith, Arth. Human embryology and morphology. '02(Mr8) O. $4.50. Longmans.
Keith, Hannah E. Hist. sketch of internal improvements in Michigan, 1836-46. '02 (F15) 16°, pap., 50 c. Mich. Pol. Sci.
Keller, Alb. G. Homeric society: sociolog. study of the Iliad and Odyssey. '02(F8) D. $1.20. Longmans.
Keller, G. Legenden; ed. by M. Müller and C. Wenckebach. '02(Ap5) S. net, 35 c. Holt.
Keller, Sa. K. Pennsylvania German cook book. Rev. and enl. 02(Jl12) O. pap., 50 c. R. M. Scranton.
Kellogg, Amos M. Crowning of flora. '01' '02(Ja25) 12°, pap., 15 c. Kellogg.
Kellogg, Amos. M. Elements of algebra. '01. '02(Ja25) 12°, 25 c. Kellogg.
Kellogg, Amos M. Elements of civil government. '01' '02(Ja25) 12°, 25 c. Kellogg.
Kellogg, Amos M. Farmer's school and the visit. '01' '02(Ja25) 12°, pap., 15 c. Kellogg.
Kellogg, Amos M. Home coming of autumn queen. '01' '02(Ja25) 12°, pap., 15 c. Kellogg.
Kellogg, Amos M. How to teach composition writing. '01' '02(Ja25) 12°, 25 c. Kellogg.
Kellogg, Amos M. Our Lysander. '01' '02 (Ja25) 12°, pap., 15 c. Kellogg.
Kellogg, Amos M. Six musical entertainments. '01' '02(Ja25) 12°, pap., 15 c. Kellogg.
Kellogg, Amos M. Uncle Sam's examination. '01' '02(Ja25) 12°, pap., 15 c. Kellogg.
Kellogg, Elijah. A stout heart. '01' '02 (Jl12) il. 12°, (Whispering pine ser.) $1.25. Lee & S.

Kellogg, J. H. Rational hydrotherapy. '01. '02(Mr8) il. 8°, subs., $5; hf. rus., $6. Davis.
Kellor, Fes. A. Experimental sociology. '02 (F1) 8°, net, $2. Macmillan.
Kelsey, C: B. Surgery of the rectum. 6th ed. '02(Ap26) il. 8°, $3. Wood.
Kelsey, W. R. Physical determinations. '01-'02(Ja11) D. $1.50. Longmans.
Keltie, J: S., *ed.* *See* Statesmen's year-book.
Kemp, Ellwood L. Hist. of education. '02 (F1) 12°, (Educ. ser., v. 3.) net, $1.25. Lippincott.
Kendall, Ezra F. Good gravy: wit and humor. '01. '02(Ja18) 12°, pap., 25 c. Helman-T.
Kendall, Reese P. Pacific trail campfires. c2(Jl19) D. $1.50. Scroll Pub.
Kenilworth. Scott, *Sir* W. net, 60 c. Macmillan.
Kennan, G:, *comp and tr.* Folk tales of Napoleon; Napoleonder; fr. the Russian; [also] The Napoleon of the people: fr. the Fr. of Balzac. '02(Jl5) O. bds., *$1 net. Outlook.
Kennelly, Arth. E. *See* Houston, E. J.
Kenny, C. S. Outlines of criminal law. '02 (Jl12) 8°, (Cambridge Univ. Press ser.) *$2.50 net. Macmillan.
Kensington, Cathmer. Glenwood. '02(Ap26) D. $1.25. Abbey Press.
Kentons (The). Howells, W: D. $1.50. Harper.
Kenyon, Orr. Amor victor. '02(Je7) il. D. $1.50. Stokes.
Kern, J: A. Way of the preacher. '02 (Mr22) D. $1.25. Pub. Ho. M. E. Ch., So.
Kern, Marg. Tale of a cat as told by herself. '02(My3) il. D. 50 c. Abbey Press.
Kerr, E. W. Power and power transmission. '02(Ja11) il. 8°, $2. Wiley.
Kerr, W: A. Law of insurance. '02(Ap19) O. shp., $6. Keefe-D.
Kersting, Rudolph, *ed.* The white world; life and adventure within the Arctic circle. '02(Jl12) 12°, *$2 net. Lewis.
Ketler, I: C. The tragedy of Paotingfu: authentic story of the missionaries who suffered martyrdom June 30 and July 1, 1900. '02(Je28) il. 8°, net, $2. Revell.
Kidd, B: Principles of western civilization. '02(F22) D. net, $2. Macmillan.
Kidder, Fk. E. Building construction and superintendence. pt. 2. 4th ed. '02(Je28) il. 8°, shp., $4. W: T. Comstock.
Kilbourne, E: W. Memory and its cultivation. '01-'02(Mr29) D. $1; leatherette, 50 c. Mullin.
Kilpatrick, Van Evrie. Language system of penmanship. In 9 nos. nos. 1-8. '02 (Ap5) il. sq. O. pap., per doz., 66 c. Globe Sch. Bk.
Kimber, Diana C., *comp.* Text-book of anatomy and physiology for nurses. New rev. ed. '02(Mr22) il. 8°, net, $2.50. Macmillan.
Kinard, Ja. P., *ed.* Old English ballads. '02 (Ap26) 12°, (Ser. of classics.) 40 c. Silver.
Kinder, Stephen. The sabertooth. '02(Ap12) il. D. 75 c.; pap., 25 c. Laird.
KINDERGARTEN.
Maxwell. Card sewing: for kindergartens. 50 c. M. Bradley.

Kindred of the wild. Roberts, C: G: D. $2. L. C. Page.
King, C: Way of the West. '02(Je7) il. S. 50 c. Rand, McN. & Co.
King, H. E. H. Hours of the passion. '02 (Ap5) 12°, net, $1.50. Dutton.
King, Maude E. Bread and wine. '02(My17) D. $1.25. Houghton, M. & Co.
King, T: A. Pearls from the Wonderbook. '01. '02(Ap12) 16°, 40 c. Swedenborg.
King, W. W., *comp.* *See* Texas. Conflicting civil cases;—Repts.
King Alfred millenary. Bowker, A. $3. Macmillan.
King and queen of hearts. Lamb, C: **50 c. net. McClure, P.
King Arthur and his noble knights. Malory, *Sir* T: $1. Burt.
King for a summer. Pickering, E. net, $1. Lee & S.
King Henry VI. *See* **Shakespeare, W:**
King in yellow. Chalmers, R. W: $1.50. Harper.
King Lear. Shakespeare, W: $1.25. Bowen-M.
King of Andorra. Harris, H: E. $1.25. Abbey Press.
King of Claddagh. Fitzpatrick, T: net, $1.25. Herder.
King Richard III. Shakespeare, W: 15 c. Kellogg.
Kingdom of coins. Gilman, B. 50 c. Little, B. & Co.
KINGLAKE, Alex. W:
Tuckwell. A. W. Kinglake. $1.75. Macmillan.
King's gallant. Dumas, A. $1. Street.
King's weigh-house. Avebury, *Lord.* 75 c. Macmillan.
Kings and vikings. O'Byrne, W. L. $1.25. Scribner.
Kingsford, C: L. Henry V. the typical mediæval hero. '01. '02(Ja25) D. (Heroes of the nations ser., no. 34.) net, $1.35; hf. leath., net, $1.60. Putnam.
Kingship of self-control. Jordan, W: G: 50 c. Revell.
Kingsley, C: Life and works. Ed. de luxe. v. 4. '02(F15); v. 5 (Mr8); v. 6 (Ap26); v. 7 (My17); v. 8 (My24); v. 9 (Je28) 8°, net, ea., $3. Macmillan.
Kingsley, C: Alton Locke. '02(My17) 12°, (Home lib.) $1. Burt.
Kingsley, C: Hereward the Wake. '02 (My17) 12°, (Home lib.) $1. Burt.
Kingsley, C: Westward ho! '02(Je28) 2 v., 16°, (Temple classics.) ea., 50 c.; flex. leath., ea., 75 c. Macmillan.
Kingsley, *Mrs.* Flo. M. Prisoners of the sea. '02(Ap26) 12°, (Red letter ser.) $1.25; pap., 50 c. New Amsterdam.
Kinosita, Yetaro. Past and present of Japanese commerce. '02(Jl12) 8°, (Columbia Univ. studies in history, economics, and public law, v. 16, no. 1.) pap., *$1.50 net. Macmillan.
Kinship of God and man. Lanier, J. J. $1. Whittaker.
Kinzie, *Mrs.* Juliette A. M. K. Wau-Bun, the "early day" of the Northwest. New ed., notes and index, by R. G. Thwaites. '01-'02(My3) il. O. ed. lim. to members. Caxton Club.

Kinzie, *Mrs.* Juliette A. M. K. Wau-Bun. New ed., introd. and note by E. K. Gordon. '01. '02(My3) il. D. $1.25. Rand, McN. & Co.

Kipling, Rudyard.
Livingston. Works of Kipling: des. of first eds. net, $12; net, $20. Dodd.

Kirk, Eleanor, *pseud.* *See* Ames, *Mrs.* E. M. E.

Kirk, *Mrs.* Ellen O., ["Henry Hayes."] A remedy for love. '02(Je7) D. $1.25. Houghton, M. & Co.

Kirk, May. Baldwin primer. Tagalog ed. '02(Jl12) il. sq. D. 35 c. Am. Bk.

Kirkman, M. M. Air brake: supp. to Science of railways. '02(Ap26) il. 8°, $2.50. World R'way.

Kirkpatrick, W: J. *See* Gill, J.

Kitchen gardening. Bridgeman, T: 50 c. Coates.

Kleckner, Emma R. In the misty realm of fable. 2d ed. '02(F15) il. 12°, $1. Flanagan.

Knapp, Adeline. How to live: a manual of hygiene for schools of the Philippine Islands. '02(Jl19) il. 16°, 36 c. Silver.

Knapp, M. A. Government ownership of railroads. '02(Mr22) 8°, (Pub. of the soc., no. 326.) pap., 15 c. Am. Acad. Pol. Sci.

Knecht, F. J. Child's Bible history; tr. from the Germ. 8th Am. ed. '02(Mr8) il. 12°, 25 c. Herder.

Knight, E: F: With the royal tour: recent tour of the Duke and Duchess of Cornwall and York through Greater Britain. '02 (Mr8) il. D. $2. Longmans.

Knightes tale. *See* Chaucer, G.

Knights (The). Aristophanes. net, $2.50. Macmillan.

Knights of St. John. Souvenir of 24th annual convention. '02(Jl12) il. 8°, bds., 13 c. Darrow.

Knowledge.
Pierce. Studies in auditory and visual space perception. net, $2. Longmans.
Trask. Human knowledge and human conduct. *$2 net. R. D. Trask.
See also Education;—Philosophy;—Science.

Kohaus, Hannah M. Fruit from the tree of life. '02(Mr22) 16°, pap., 30 c. Alliance.

Kohaus, Hannah M. Remedies of the Great Physician. '02(Mr22) 32°, pap., 40 c. Alliance.

Kohaus, Hannah M. Soul fragrance. New issue. '02(Mr22) 16°, pap., 50 c. Alliance.

Komensky, J: A. Labyrinth of the world and the paradise of the heart. '02(Mr8) 12°, $1.50. Dutton.

Körner, Karl T. Zriny ein trauerspiel in fünf aufzügen; notes by F. Holzwarth. '02 (F1) S. (Modern lang. ser.) 35 c. Heath.

Kovalevsky, M. Russian political institutions. '02(F15) O. net, $1.50. Univ. of Chic.

Krag and Johnny Bear. Thompson, E. E. S. 60 c. Scribner.

Kropotkin, *Prince* P: A. Fields, factories and workshops. New popular ed. '01· '02 (F22) il. D. net, 90 c. Putnam.

Krüger, Gustav, *and* Smith, C. A. English-Germ. conversation book. '02(Je21) D. (Modern lang. ser.) 25 c. Heath.

Kuder, Emil. Medical prescription book for everybody. '01· '02(Ap26) $2. Journal Pr.

Kupfer, Lillian. Greek foreshadowings of modern metaphysical and epistemological thought. '01. '02(F15) 8°, $1. Cushing.

Kuttner, B. German conversation course. (Sec. 1 and 2.) '02(Jl19) D. 50 c. Abbey Press.

Kyger, J: C: F., *ed.* Hand-book for soul-winners. '02(My24) S. 50 c. Kyger.

Labor and capital: discussion of rel. of employer and employed; ed. by J: J. Peters. '02(My10) D. (Questions of the day, no. 98.) $1.50. Putnam.

Labor and laboring classes.
See Capital and labor;—Political economy;—Slavery;—Social science;—Woman.

La Brète, Jean de. Mon oncle et mon curé; ed. by E. M. White. '02(My3) D. 50 c. Am. Bk.

Labyrinth of the world and the paradise of the heart. Komensky, J: A. $1.50. Dutton.

Lace.
Palliser. Hist. of lace. net, $12. Scribner.

Lachmi Bai Rani of Jhansi. White, M. $1.50. J. F. Taylor.

Ladd, G: T. Philosophy of conduct. '02 (F22) 12°, net, $3.50. Scribner.

Lady of New Orleans. Thornton, M. E $1.50. Abbey Press

Lady paramount. Harland, H: $1.50. Lane.

Lady (The) Poverty: a XIIIth century allegory (Sacrum commercium Beati Francisci cum Domina Paupertate, A.D. 1227;) tr. and ed. by M. Carmichael. '02(Ap12) 6¼ x 4½ in., net, $1.75. Tennant.

Lafarque, Paul. Religion of capital. [also] Social effect of machinery by F. W. Cotton. '02(My17) O. (Socialist lib., v. 2, no. 2.) pap., 10 c. Socialistic Co-op.

Lafitte of Louisiana. Devereux, M. $1.50. Little, B. & Co.

Laird, Alb. J. Complete manual of syllabic shorthand. '02(Jl12) il. 16°, $2. Neil.

Laird & Lee's diary and time saver, 1902. '02(Ja4) nar. T. leath., 25 c. Laird.

Lake, W: C: Memorials of William Charles Lake, Dean of Durham, 1869-1894. '01· '02(F8) O. $5.50. Longmans.

Lake French classics; ed. by E. P. Baillot. S. 50 c. Scott, F. & Co.
—Baillot *and* Brugnot. French prose composition.
—Beaumarchais. Barbier de Séville and Lettres.
—Moliere. Le misanthrope and L'avare.
—Voltaire. Zaïre and Epitres.

Lake history stories. S. il. Scott, F. & Co.
—Harding, C. H. *and* S: B. City of the seven hills.

Lalor's Maples. Conway, K. E. $1.25. Pilot.

Lamb, C: The king and queen of hearts: an 1805 book for children; re-issued in facsim. '02(Jl5) il. 16°, **50 c. net. McClure, P.

Lamb, C: *and* Ma. Tales from Shakespeare. '01· '02(Mr1) il. D. (Home and school classics; young readers' ser.) 40 c. Heath.

Lamb, M. T. The Mormons and their Bible. '01. '02(F1) O. net, 25 c. Am. Bapt.

La Motte Fouque, F. H. K., *Freiherr* de. Undine. [also] Aslauga's knight. '01. '02 (Ja11) il. 16°, (Caxton ser.) flex. lambskin, net, $1.20. Scribner.

La Motte Fouqué. F. H. K., *Freiherr de.* Undine. '02(My17) il. D. (Home and school classics; young reader's ser.) 30 c. Heath.

LANCASTER, Pa.
Law. Lancaster—old and new. n. p. J. D. Law.

LAND.
Horton. Land buyer's, settler's and explorer's guide. 25 c. Byron.
Illinois. Homestead exemption laws. *$4 net. Callaghan.

Land of heroes. O'Byrne, W. L. $1.25. Scribner.

Land of Nome. McKee, L. net, $1.25. Grafton Press.

Landolt, H. H., *and others.* Optical rotating power of organic substances. 2d ed. Authorized Eng. tr. with add. by Dr. J. H. Long. '02(Jl5) il. 8°, *$7.50 net. Chemical.

Lane, Michael A. Level of social motion. '02(Mr29) 12°, net, $2. Macmillan.

Lang, Ossian H., *ed.* Educational creeds of the 19th century. '01. '02(Ja25) 12°, 75 c. Kellogg.

Langbein, G: Electro-deposition of metals; fr. the Germ.; add. by W: T. Brannt. 4th rev. enl. ed. '02(F15) il. 8°, $4. Baird.

Lange, L: Twentieth century system; key to the Germ. language. '02(Ap26) D. pap., 50 c. [San F. News] Pamphlet.

Lange, L: Twentieth century system Spanish course. '02(Ap26) D. pap., 25 c. [San F. News] Pamphlet.

Langley, S: P. Experiments in aerodynamics. 2d ed. '02(Jl19) F. (Smithsonian cont. to knowledge, no. 201.) $1. Smith. Inst.

LANGUAGE.
Fowler. Negatives of the Indo-European languages. net, 50 c. Univ. of Chic.
Oertel. Lectures on study of language. net, $3. Scribner.
See also Rhetoric;—*also* names of languages.

Lanier, J. J. Kinship of God and man. In 2 v. v. 1, Good and evil. '02(F8) D. $1. Whittaker.

La Ramé, Louise de, ["Ouida."] Dog of Flanders and The Nürnberg stove. '02 (Mr22) S. (Riverside lit. ser., no. 150.) pap., 15 c. Houghton, M. & Co.

Larned, J. N., *ed.* Literature of Amer. history: bibliog. guide. '02(Je21) O. net, $6; shp., $7.50; hf. mor., $9. Houghton, M. & Co.

Lasance, F. X. Little manual of St. Anthony of Padua. '02(Ap5) Tt. pap., 25 c. Benziger.

Lasance, F. X., *comp.* Short visits to the blessed sacrament. '01. '02(Ja18) Tt. 25 c. Benziger.

Last century maid. Wharton, A. H. $1.25. Lippincott.

Last fight of the 'Revenge" at sea. Raleigh, *Sir* W. net, $6. Houghton, M. & Co.

Late returning. Williams, M. $1.25. Macmillan.

Later infancy of the child. Compayré, G. pt. 2. net, $1.20. Appleton.

Lathbury, B. B., *and* Spackman, —. Am. engineering practice in the construction of rotary Portland cement plants. '02(My24) il. obl. O. $2. G. M. S. Armstrong.

Latimer, *Mrs.* Eliz. W. Prince Incognito. '02 (Ap12) D. $1.50. McClurg.

LATIN LANGUAGE.
Alford, *comp.* Latin passages for translation. net, 80 c. Macmillan.
Appleton's Latin dictionary. $1.50. Appleton.
Mellick. Latin composition. 40 c. Am. Bk.
Morris. On principles and methods in Latin syntax. net, $2. Scribner.
Ogilvie. Horæ Latinæ. $5. Longmans.
Reynolds. Rudiments of Latin. $1.25. A. B. Reynolds.
Smith, W: W. Course in first year Latin for Regents' examinations. $1. W: R. Jenkins.
West. Latin grammar. net, 90 c. Appleton.

LATTER-DAY SAINTS.
See Mormonism.

Laughlin, Ja. L. Elements of political economy. Rev. ed. '02(Mr22) D. $1.20. Am. Bk.

Laurel classics. 16°, 40 c. Birchard.
—Shakespeare. Merchant of Venice.

Laurie, H: Scottish philosophy in its national development. '02(My24) 12°, net, $1.75. Macmillan

Laurie, Simon S. Training of teachers and methods of instruction. '01. '02(Ja4) 12°, (Cambridge Univ. Press ser.) net, $1.50. Macmillan.

Laut, Agnes C. Heralds of empire. '02 (My10) D. $1.50. Appleton.

Law, Ja. D. Lancaster—old and new. Rev., enl. ed. '02(Ap26) 8°, pap., n. p. J. D. Law.

LAW.
American and Eng. encyclopædia of law. v. 20, 21. ea., $7.50. E: Thompson.
American digest. v. 29. subs., ea., $6. West Pub.
American state repts. v. 82, 83. ea., $4. Bancroft-W.
Ash. Table of federal citations. 4 v. v. 1, 2. complete work, $30. Remick.
Bingham, *comp.* 200 bar examination questions. $1. Commercial Press.
Britton: Eng. tr. and notes. $3. Byrne.
English law rpts. 6 v. $28.50. Little, B. & Co.
General digest. v. 12. $6. Lawyers' Co-op.
Hawkins. Legal counselor and form book. subs., $3; $4. W. W. Wilson.
Howard. Law points to know. $1. H. G. Howard.
Lawyers' repts. annot. bks. 53, 54. ea., $5. Lawyers' Co-op.
McCall. Clerk's assistant; cont. legal forms and instruments. $6. Banks.
Mack *and* Nash, *eds.* Cyclopedia of law and procedure. v. 3. $6. Am. Law Bk.
Martindale. Am. law directory, 1902. 2 pts. net, $10. Martindale.
Pollock. Revised repts. v. 46-51. ea., net, $6. Little, B. & Co.
Russell *and* Winslow. Syllabus—digest of decisions of the sup. ct. v. 3. $6.50. Banks.
Seebohm. Tribal custom in Anglo-Saxon law. net, $5. Longmans.
Smith. Studies in juridical law. $3.50. Flood.

LAW.—*Continued.*
Two centuries' growth of Am. law, 1701-1901. net, $4. Scribner.
Warvelle. Essays in legal ethics. $2.50. Callaghan.
See also Actions at law;—Attachment;—Commercial law;—Contracts;—Conveyancing;—Corporations;—Damages;—Equity;—Evidence;—Insurance;—International law;—Justices of the peace;—Land;—Lawyers;—Mines and mining;—Negligence;—Negotiable instruments;—Orphans;—Parliamentary law;—Patents;—Pleading and practice;—Prostitution;—Real property;—Saloons;—Star chamber;—Wills.

Law of growth. Brooks, P. net, $1.20. Dutton.

Lawler, Ja. J. Modern plumbing, steam and hot water heating. New ed. '02(F22) 12°, $5. Popular.

Lawrence, F. M. Practical medicine. '02 (Ap5) il. 8°, $3. Boericke & T.

Laws of radiation and absorption. Brace, D. B. $1. Am. Bk.

Lawson, And. C. Eparchæan interval. '02 (Je14) O. (Univ. of Cal. bull. of dept. of geology, v. 3, no. 3.) pap., 10 c. Univ. of Cal.

Lawson, And. C., *and* Palache, C: Berkeley Hills: coast range geology. '02(Ap5) il. O. (Univ. of Cal., bull. of the dept. of geology, v. 2, no. 12.) pap., 80 c. Univ. of Chic.

Lawson, J: D. Making of a contract. '01-'02(F8) O. pap., 25 c. Stephens.

Lawton, W: H: The singing voice and its practical cultivation. '01. '02(Mr15) il. 8°, $1.50. W: H: Lawton.

LAWYERS.
Gould. Greater New York and state lawyers' diary, 1902. $1. W. R. Gould.
Macdonald. How successful lawyers are educated. $1.50. Temple Pub.
Martindale. Am. law directory. net, $10. Martindale.
Perry. Legal adviser and business guide. $1.50. Pontiac.
Sharp & Alleman Co.'s lawyers' and bankers' directory, 1902. 2 v. ea., $5. Sharp & A.

Lawyers' reports annot.; bks. 53, 54. '02 (Je28) O. shp., ea., $5. Lawyers' Co-op.

Laycock, W. F. *See* Rawson, C.

Lays and lyrics. Smiley, T: E. $1.25. Abbey Press.

Leach, J. G. History of the Bringhurst family; with notes on the Clarkson, De Peyster and Boude families. '01-'02(Mr8) il. 4°, $5. Lippincott.

LEAD.
Fairie. Notes on lead ore. net, $1. Van Nostrand.

League of Am. Mothers. *See* Proudfoot, A. H.

Leahy, Wa. T: Child of the flood. '02 (Jl19) D. $1. Kilner.

Lean, Bevan. *See* Perkin, W: H:, *jr.*

LEARNING.
See Education;—Knowledge.

Leaves from a life-book of to-day. Mills, J. D. 50 c. Swedenborg.

Leavitt, Rob. G. Outlines of botany. '01-'02(Ja4) O. $1. Am. Bk.

Leavitt, Rob. G. Outlines of botany. [also] Field, forest and garden botany. by A. Gray; rev. and enl. by L. H. Bailey. '01-'02(Ja4) il. O. $1.80. Am. Bk.

LE BLOND, Michel.
Van der Kellen. Works of Michel Le Blond: reprod. and accompanied by biog. notice, [etc.] net, $30; net, $35. Dodd.

Lee, Jennette. Son of a fiddler. '02(Ap5) D. $1.50. Houghton, M. & Co.

Lee, J: L. Message of to-morrow. '02(F8) 12°, net, $1.20. Revell.

Lee, Marg. Separation. '02(Jl12) D. $1.25. Buckles.

LEE, Rob. E.
Adams. Lee at Appomattox. net, $1.50. Houghton, M. & Co.

Left-overs made palatable. Curtis, I. G. $1. Judd.

Legal classic ser. 12°. Byrne.
—Britton. $3.

Legal counselor and form book. Hawkins, C: A. subs., $3; $4. W. W. Wilson.

Legend of Sleepy Hollow. *See* Irving, W.

Legenden. Keller, G. net, 35 c. Holt.

LEGENDS.
Zitkala-sa. Old Indian legends. 50 c. Ginn.
See also Fairy tales;—Folk-lore.

Legler, H: E. James Gates Percival; sketch and bibliog. '01-'02(Mr22) S. bds., net, $1. Mequon Club.

Leibnitz, G. W. v. Discourses on metaphysics; Correspondence with Arnauld and Monodology. '02(Je28) 12°, net, 75 c.; *Same* (F22) D. (Religion of sci. lib., no. 52.) pap., 35 c. Open Court.

Leigh, Lennard, *and* Bergholt, Ernest. Principles and practice of whist. '02(Ap5) il. O. net, $1.50. Coates.

Leighton, Jos. A. Typical modern conceptions of God. '01-'02(F8) D. net, $1.10. Longmans.

Lemcke, E. E: Creation, re-creation: [poems.] '01-'02(F8) 16°, n. p. Privately pr.

Lennox, *Lady* Sa. Life and letters, 1745-1826: ed. by the Countess of Ilchester and Lord Stavordale. '01-'02(Ja11) 2 v., il. 8°, net, $9; *Same.* [1 v. ed.] '02(Je7) O. net, $4. Scribner.

LENOX, Mass.
Mallary. Lenox and the Berkshire Highlands. net, $1.75. Putnam.

LENT.
Galt, *comp.* Lent, the holy season. $1. Neale.

Leopard's spots. Dixon, T:, *jr.* $1.50. Doubleday, P.

Lepidus the centurion. Arnold, E. L. $1.50. Crowell.

Le Queux, W: Sign of the seven sins. '02 (Je28) D. (Select novels.) $1; pap., 50 c. Lippincott.

Le Row, Caro. B. Duxberry doings. '02 (Je14) 12°, (Fireside ser.) $1. Burt.

Leroy, W: A silken snare. '02(My3) D. 50 c. Abbey Press.

Le Sage, A. R. Adventures of Gil Blas of Santillane. New ed. '02(Ap19) 12°, (Home lib.) $1. Burt.

Lesley, Susan, *ed.* *See* Tiffany, N. M., *ed.*

Lespinasse, Julie J. E. de. Letters; with notes upon her life and character, and introd. by C. A. Sainte-Beuve. '02(F1) il. 8°, (Versailles hist. ser.) subs., per v., $6; ¾ leath., per v., $9. Hardy, P. & Co.

Lessing, G. E. Minna von Barnhelm; notes by S. Primer. Rev. ed. '02(F1) D. (Modern lang. ser.) 75 c. Heath.
Lessons from Gr. pottery. Huddilston, J: H. net, $1.25. Macmillan.
Lessons in English. il. D. 50 c. Silver.
—Skinner *and* Burgert. Lessons in Eng. based upon principles of literary interpretation.
Lethaby, W. R., *ed.* *See* Artistic crafts.
LETTER-WRITING.
Hickox. Correspondent's manual. $1.50. Lee & S.
North. Love letters and how to write them. 25 c.; 50 c. Donohue; Drake.
LETTERING.
Faust. Automatic pen lettering and designs. $1; alphabet pt., 75 c. Auto Pen.
LETTERS.
Berry, *ed.* Letters of the Rm. 2 coll. in the British Museum. net, 50 c. Univ. of Chic.
Glover. Life and letters in the 4th century. net, $3.25. Macmillan.
Letters of Mildred's mother to Mildred. Price, E. D. $1. Ogilvie.
Letters to an enthusiast. Clarke, *Mrs.* M. C. net, $2.50. McClurg.
Level of social motion. Lane, M. A. net, $2. Macmillan.
Lewis, Abram H. Sunday legislation. New rev. enl. ed. '02(F8) 12°, net, $1. Appleton.
Lewis, Alfr. H: Wolfville days. '02(F22) il. D. $1.50. Stokes.
Lewis, Alonzo F. Fryeburg Webster centennial. '02(Je28) il. 12°, pap., 50 c. A. F. Lewis.
Lewis, C: B., ["M. Quad."] Life and troubles of Mr. Bowser. '02(My24) il. 8°, $1. Jamieson-H.
Lewis, Edn. H. Text-book of applied Eng. grammar. '02(F15) il. 12°, net, 35 c. Macmillan.
Lewis, H: F., *ed.* *See* Peterson, R.
Lewis, Merriwether, *and* Clarke, W: Hist. of the expedition to the sources of the Missouri: rep. of the ed. of 1814. '02(My24) 3 v., 8°, (Commonwealth lib.) net, per v., $1. New Amsterdam.
Lewis, W. D. *See* Pepper, G: W.
Lex de imperio Vespasiani. Hellems, F. B. R. 50 c. Scott, F. & Co.
LEXINGTON, Mass.
Piper. Lexington, the birthplace of Amer. liberty. 25 c. Lexington.
LIABILITY.
See Negligence.
Liautard, A. Animal castration. 9th ed., rev. and enl. '02(Jl12) il. 12°, $2. W: R. Jenkins.
LIBERTY.
See Democracy;—Religious liberty;—Slavery.
LIBRARIES.
New York Lib. Club. Libraries of Greater New York. net, 75 c.; net, 50 c. Stechert.
Plummer. Hints to small libraries. net, 50 c. M. W. Plummer.
Wisconsin. List of books for township libraries. 25 c. Wisconsin.
See also Books and reading;—Cataloguing.
Library of literary criticism. *See* Moulton, C: W.
Library of Tribune extras. D. pap., 25 c. Tribune Assoc.
—Tribune almanac, 1902. (v. 14, 1.)
Library of useful stories. *See* Appleton's.
Liddell, Mark H. Introd. to the scientific study of Eng. poetry. '02(My10) D. net, $1.25. Doubleday, P.
Lieb, Hermann. Prince Bismarck and the German people. '02(Mr22) 12°, $1.50; hf. mor., $2.25; mor., $3.25. Dominion.
Life, And. C. Tuber-like rootlets of cycas revoluta. '02(F15) il. 8°, (Cont. to the Hull Botanical lab'y, no. 26.) pap., net, 25 c. Univ. of Chic.
Life and health. Blaisdell, R. F. $1. Ginn.
Life and letters in the 4th century. Glover, T. R. net, $3.25. Macmillan.
Life and power from within. Colville, W. J. $1. Alliance.
Life and troubles of Mr. Bowser. Lewis, C: B. $1. Jamieson-H.
Life and works of the Redeemer. '02(F15) 12°, net, $2. Dutton.
Life at West Point. Hancock, H. I. net, $1.40. Putnam.
Life histories. *See* Appleton's.
Life of a century. Hodder, E. net, $4. Scribner.
Life of John William Walshe, T.S.A. Carmichael, M. net, $2. Dutton.
Life of love. Mudge, J. 25 c. Jennings.
Life of unity. Cheney, F. J. $1.50. Blade.
Life on the farm. Shepard, H. M. 50 c. Flanagan.
Life worth living. Newell, W. C. $1. Abbey Press.
Life's little things. Hind, C. L. $1.75. Macmillan.
LIGHT.
Dexter. Elem. exercises on sound, light and heat. 90 c. Longmans.
Michelsen. Velocity of light. net, 25 c. Univ. of Chic.
See also Radiation;—Roentgen rays.
Light and peace. Quadrupani, R. P. net, 50 c. Herder.
Light of our spirit. Ehrlich, *Mrs.* B. 25 c. B. Ehrlich.
LILIES.
Jekyll, *comp.* Lilies for Eng. gardens. net, $3.75. Scribner.
Liljencrantz, Ottilie A. Thrall of Leif the lucky. '02(Mr29) O. $1.50. McClurg.
Lilley, A: E. V., *and* Midgley, W. Studies in plant form. New enl. ed. '02(Mr8) 8°, net, $2. Scribner.
Lilley, J. P. The pastoral epistles: new tr. with introd., commentary and app. '01. '02(Ja11) 12°, (Bible class handbooks.) net, 75 c. Scribner.
LINCOLN, Abr.
Barrett. Abraham Lincoln. $1. Donohue.
Smith, S. G. Abraham Lincoln. net, 25 c. Jennings.
See also Fallows, S:
Lincoln, Jos. C. Cape Cod ballads. '02(Ap19) il. D. net, $1.25. Brandt.
Lindsay, B. Story of animal life. '02(My24) il. S. (Lib. of useful stories.) net, 35 c. Appleton.
Line and form. Crane, W. $2.25. Macmillan.
Linear groups. Dickson, L. E. net, $4. Stechert.

Line-o'-type lyrics. Taylor, B. L. net, 50 c. W: S. Lord.

Lines of defense of the biblical revelation. Margoliouth, D. S. net, $1.50. Gorham.

Linn, Ja. W. The second generation: [novel.] '02(F1) 12°, $1.50. Macmillan.

Linn, W: A. Story of the Mormons. '02 (Je21) O. net, $4. Macmillan.

Lippincott's biog. dictionary. New ed. '01. '02(Mr1) 2 v., il. 8°, subs., $15; hf. rus., $17.50; hf. mor., $20. Lippincott.

Lippincott's educ. ser. 12°, net, $1.25. Lippincott.

—Kemp. Hist. of education. (3.)

Lippincott's elem. algebra. (Ja. M. Rawlins.) '01. '02(Mr1) 12°, 80 c. Lippincott.

Lippincott's elem. science readers. 3 pts. '01-'02(F15) pt. 1, 16°, bds., 25 c.; pt. 2, 30 c.; pt. 3, 35 c. Lippincott.

Lippincott's popular lib. 12°, $1.. Lippincott.

—Hungerford. Three graces.

Lippincott's practical arithmetic. '01- '02 (Mr1) 2 pts., 12°, ea., 40 c. Lippincott.

Lippincott's select novels. D. $1; pap., 50 c. Lippincott.

—Croker. Cat's paw.

—Le Queux. Sign of the seven sins.

—Neilson. Madame Bohemia.

Liquid from the sun's rays. Greenleaf, S. $1.50. Abbey Press.

LIQUORS.
See Fermentation.

Lisk, J. P. Diagram of the Corliss engine. '02(Je7) 8°, pap., 25 c. Spon.

Litanei zum heiligsten herzen Jesu. Catholic church. net, 3 c. Herder.

LITERATURE.

Arnold. Literature and dogma.* net, $1. New Amsterdam.

Brandes. Main currents in 19th century literature. v. 2. net $2.75. Macmillan.

Halsey. Our literary deluge. net, $1.25. Doubleday, P.

Payne. Editorial echoes.—Little leaders. ea., net, $1. McClurg.

See also Authors;—Bibliographies;—Books; — Fiction;—Letters; — Parody; — Quotations;—*also* names of nations and literatures.

Literature of Am. history. Larned, J. N. net, $6; $7.50; $9. Houghton, M. & Co.

Litsey, Edn. C. Love story of Abner Stone. '02(Je21) O. bds., net, $1.20. Barnes.

Little, E: R. *See* Hall, F: G.

Little books on devotion. sq. T. net, 25 c. Jennings.

—Mudge. Life of love.

Little books on doctrine. sq. T. 25 c. Jennings.

—Merrill *and* Warren. Discourses on miracles.

—Methodist Epis. church in America. Doctrines.

—Townsend. Satan and demons.

Little books on practice. T. net, 25 c. Jennings.

—Oliver. Our lay office-bearers.—Soul-winners' secrets.

Little brother. Willard, J. F. $1.50. Century Co.

Little button rose. Alcott, L. M. 50 c. Little, B. & Co.

Little citizen. Waller, M. E. **$1 net. Lothrop.

Little engravings. Altdorfer, A. net, $1.50. Longmans.

Little French dinners. Rivas, E. de. 50 c. New Amsterdam.

Little giant's neighbors. Fox, F. M. 50 c. L. C. Page.

Little guides ser. S. net, 75 c. Dodd.

—Windle. Malvern country.

Little journeys. *See* Whitcomb, C. E.

Little leaders. Payne, W: M. net, $1. McClurg.

Little masterpieces; ed. by B. Perry. S. 50 c. Doubleday, P.

—Bacon. Essays.

—Emerson. Essays.

—Goldsmith. Selections.

—Johnson. Essays fr. Rambler and Idler.

—Milton. Selections.

—Swift. Selections.

Little memoirs of the 19th century. Paston, G: net, $3. Dutton.

Little minister. Barrie, J. M. $1. Burt.

Little stories for little people. McCullough, A. W. 25 c. Am. Bk.

Little Susy stories. Prentiss, *Mrs.* E. 75 c. Burt.

Littleton, W: S. Trumpeter's hand book and instructor. '02(Je21) 16°, leath., $1. Hudson-K.

LITURGIES.
See Prayers.

Livermore, S: T. Block Island; ed. by C: E. Perry. '01- '02(Mr22) il. 16°, pap., 25 c. Ball.

Livets alvor. Bang, *Mrs.* M. 65 c. M. Bang.

Living races of mankind. Hutchinson, H. N. net, $5. Appleton.

Livingston, Burton E. On the nature of the stimulus which causes the change in form in polymorphic green algae. '02(F1) 8°, (Cont. from Hull botanical laboratory, no. 22.) pap., net, 25 c. Univ. of Chic.

Livingston, Luther S. Bibliog. of the first ed. in book form of the works of Alfred, Lord Tennyson. '01- '02(Ja11) 16°, pap., $1. Dodd.

Livingston, Luther S. Works of Rudyard Kipling: desc. of a set of the first eds. of his books. '01- '02(Ja11) facsimiles, 8°, 65 cop. on hand-made pap., bds., net, $12; 12 cop. on Jap. pap., net, $20. Dodd.

Locke, C: E: Nineteenth-century crusaders. [Gladstone.] '02(My24) D. (Hero ser., no. 5.) net, 25 c. Jennings.

Locke, C: E: Typical American. [Washington.] '02(My24) il. D. (Hero ser., no. 2.) net, 25 c. Jennings.

Lockett, Ma. F., ["The Princess."] Christopher. '02(My3) il. D. $1.25. Abbey Press.

Lockwood, G: B. New Harmony communities. '02(Jl12) il. O. $2.50. Chronicle.

Lockwood, Sara E. H. Teachers' manual to accompany Composition and rhetoric. '02 (Jl19) 16°, pap., 30 c. Ginn.

LOCOMOTIVES.

Baker. Economic locomotive management. $1.50. R'way Educ.

Cooke. Some recent developments in locomotive practice. $1. Macmillan.

Goss. Locomotive sparks. $2. Wiley.

See also Steam engines.

Lodge, H: C.; Hoar, G: F., *and others.* The United States and the Philippine Islands. '02(Jl5) Q. (Brooklyn Eagle lib., v. 17, no. 9; serial no. 68.) pap., 10 c. Brooklyn Eagle.
LOGARITHMS.
Marshall. Logarithmic tables of measures of length. $2. Van Nostrand.
Smith. Four-place logarithmic tables. net, 50 c. Holt.
See also Trigonometry.
LOGIC.
Aikins. Principles of logic. net, $1.50. Holt.
LONDON.
Evart, *and others.* Climates of London. net, $4. Macmillan.
Thorpe. Children's London. net, $4.50. Scribner.
See also Oriental Club;—Stock Exchange.
LONDON GUILD HALLS.
Interior decorations and furnishings of London Guild Halls. net, $12; net, $15. Helburn.
Long, J: L. Naughty Nan. '02(Mr1) il. D. $1.50. Century Co.
Long duel. Clifford, *Mrs.* L. L. net, $1.25. Lane.
Longfellow, H: W. Hyperion. '02(Ap19) 12°, (Home lib.) $1. Burt.
Longfellow, H: W. Outre mer. '02(Jl19) 12°, (Home lib.) $1. Burt.
Longfellow, H: W. Poems; biog. sketch by N. H. Dole. '02(F15) 12°, $1.75. Crowell.
Longmans' Am. teachers' ser.; ed. by J. E. Russell. O. $1.50. Longmans.
—Bourne. Teaching of history and civics.
Longmans' artists' lib.; ed. by L. Binyon. il. sq. O. net, $1. Longmans.
—Holmes. Constable. (5.)
Longmans' civil engineering ser. il. O. Longmans.
—Fidler. Calculations in hydraulic engineering. $3.
—Harcourt. Civil engineering as app. to construction. $5.
Longmans' practical elem. science ser. D. 90 c. Longmans
—Dexter. Sound, light and heat.
—Furneaux. Hygiene.
Longridge, G. Official and lay witness to the value of foreign missions. '02(Je21) 16°, 20 c. E. & J. B. Young.
Longus. Daphnis and Chloe. '02(Mr29) il. 12°, (Antique gems from the Greek and Latin, v. 4.) (App. to pubs. for price.) Barrie.
Lord, W: R. First book upon birds of Oregon and Washington. New rev., enl. ed. '02(Mr29) il. 12°, 75 c. W: R. Lord.
Lord Alingham, bankrupt. Manning, M. $1.50. Dodd.
LORD'S PRAYER.
Foster. The Lord's prayer. 10 c. Cumberland Press.
LORD'S SUPPER.
Gore. Body of Christ. $1.75. Scribner.
Hall. Instructions and devotions on the holy communion. net, 25 c. Young Churchman.
Paret. Reality in holy communion. 10 c. Whittaker.
Preparatio; preparation for holy communion. $2. Longmans.
See also Catholic church;—Token.
Loryea, Ja. Hawthorne. *See* Santanelli.
LOS ANGELES.
Willard. *Herald's* hist. of Los Angeles city. $1.50. Kingsley.
Lost Christmas. Smith, M. R. 50 c. Dutton.
Lost hero. Phelps, E. S. 50 c. Little, B. & Co.
Lost on the Orinoco. Stratemeyer, E: net, $1. Lee & S.
Lothrop, *Mrs.* H. M., ["Margaret Sidney."] Five little Peppers abroad. '02(Je7) il. D. net, $1.10. Lothrop.
LOUISIANA PURCHASE.
Hosmer. Hist. of the Louisiana purchase. net, $1.20. Appleton.
Louisiana repts., v. 106. '02(Jl5) O. (Nat. reporter system ed.) shp., $8. West Pub.
Louisiana. *Supreme ct.* Digest; by J. A. Breaux. '01. '02(F8) O. shp., $20. Hansell.
Louttit, G: W: Maid of the wildwood. '02(Je21) D. $1.50. Colonial.
Love, W: D. Thomas Short, the first printer of Conn. '01. '02(Ap26) 8°, (Acorn club, Ct., pub. no. 6.) pap., $5. Case.
LOVE.
Finck. Romantic love and personal beauty. net, $2. Macmillan.
Love in its tenderness. Aitken, J. R. $1; 50 c. Appleton.
Love letters and how to write them. *See* North, I.
Love never faileth. Simpson, C. $1.25. Revell.
Love poems. Suckling, *Sir* J: net. 50 c.; 75 c. Lane.
Love songs. Austrian, D. $1. Conkey.
Love sonnets of a hoodlum. Irwin, W. 25 c.; 50 c. Elder.
Love-story masterpieces. Lyon, R. A. net, $1. W: S. Lord.
Love story of Abner Stone. Litsey, E. C. net, $1.20. Barnes.
Lovely Mrs. Pemberton. James, *Mrs.* F. A. P. $1.25. Buckles.
Lover, S: Works; introd. by J. J. Roche. Treasure trove ed. 10 v. '02(Mr22) il. 8°, subs., per v., net, $3.50; hf. mor., per v., net, $6.50; de luxe ed., ¾ lev., per v., net, $12. Little, B. & Co.
Lover in Cuba. Elmore, J. B. $1. J. B. Elmore.
Lover's lib. S. net, 50 c.; leath., net, 75 c. Lane.
—Shakespeare. Sonnets.
—Suckling. Love poems.
Lover's progress told by himself. Vizetelly, E. A. $1.50. Brentano's.
Love's itinerary. Snaith, J: C. $1; 50 c. Appleton.
Lovett, Rob. *See* Moody, W: V.
Lowell, Guy, *ed.* American gardens. '02(Je21) il. 4°, $7.50. Bates & G.
Lowell, Ja. R. Democracy. [Limited ed.] '02(Mr22) 16°, bds., net, $2. Houghton, M. & Co.
Lower South in Am. history. Brown, W: G. net, $1.50. Macmillan.
Lubbock, *Sir* J:, [*Lord* Avebury.] Pleasures of life. '02(My17) 12°, (Home lib.) $1. Burt.
Lubbock, *Sir* J: Scenery of England. '02(F22) il. 8°, net, $2.50. Macmillan.

Lucian. Lucius, the ass. '02(Je28) il. 12°, (Antique gems from the Gr. and Latin, v. 5.) (apply to pubs. for price.) Barrie.
Lucian. Translations, by A. M. C. Davidson. '02(Ap19) D. $2. Longmans.
Lucius, the ass. Lucian. (app. to pubs. for price.) Barrie.
LUDWIG II. *of Bavaria.*
Gerard. Romance of King Ludwig II. of Bavaria. net, $1.75. Dodd.
LUKE, *St.*
Selwyn. St. Luke the prophet. net, $2.75. Macmillan.
Luke Delmege. Sheehan, P. A. $1.50. Longmans.
LUMBER.
Rosenberger, *comp.* Law for lumbermen. $3.50. Am. Lumberman.
See also Forests and forestry.
Lunn, C: Philosophy of voice. [New rev., enl. ed.] '02(Ap26) il. O. net, $2. Schirmer.
Lupton, Arnold. Practical treatise on mine surveying. '02(Mr8) il. O. $5. Longmans.
Lush, Ethel R. Domestic economy for scholarship and certificate students. '01. '02 (Ja4) 12°, net, 60 c. Macmillan.
Luska, Sidney, *pseud. See* Harland, H:
Luther, Mark L. Favor of princes: [novel.] '01. '02(Ja11) 12°, pap., 50 c. Jamieson-H.
Lyall, Edna, *pseud. See* Bayly, A. E.
Lydekker, R. *See* Hutchinson, H. N.
Lydston, G. F. *See* Duhring, L: A.
Lyman, A. J. Preaching in the new age: six lectures del. in Hartford Theol. Sem. upon the Carew foundation. '02(Je28) 12°, net, 75 c. Revell.
Lynch, Laurence L., *pseud. See* Van Deventer, E. M.
Lyon, Flo. M. Study of the sporangia and gametophytes of selaginella apus and selaginella rupestris. '02(F15) 8°, (Cont. from the Hull Botanical lab'y, no. 31.) pap., net, 25 c. Univ. of Chic.
Lyon, H: A., *comp.* Cornell verse. 2d ed. '02(Mr8) Tt. $1. Walton.
Lyon, Ralph A., *comp.* Love-story masterpieces. '02(Je21) D. bds., net, $1. W: S. Lord.
Lyrics to the queen. Noble, A. C: n. p. Blue Sky Press.
Mabel Thornley. Baily, R. C. $1.25. Abbey Press.
Mabie, Hamilton W. Parables of life. '02 (Mr29) O. net, $1. Outlook.
Mabie, Hamilton W. Works and days. '02 (My10) S. net, $1. Dodd.
Mabry, W. D. When love is king. '02(Ap26) D. $1.50. Fenno.
McArthur, N. J. *See* Texas. Citations.—Legislature.
Macaulay, T: B., *Lord.* Frederick the Great. '02(F1) 12°, (Eng. classics.) net, 40 c. Macmillan.
Macaulay, T: B., *Lord.* Literary essays. '02 (Ap5) 12°, (Home lib.) $1. Burt.
Macbeth. *See* Porter, C.—Shakespeare, W:
McBride literature and art books. *See* Burke, B. E.
McCall, H: S. The clerk's assistant; rev. and largely rewritten by H. B. Bradbury. 6th ed. '02(Mr.22) O. shp., $6. Banks.
McCall, S: W. Daniel Webster. '02(My17) D. net, 80 c. Houghton, M. & Co.
McCallum & Hofer Cattle Co. Stockmen's calculator. '02(F15) nar. 8°, $1.50. McCallum.
McCarthy, J. H. If I were king. '01. '02 (F8) il. D. $1.50. Russell.
McClelland, T. C. Verba crucis. '02(Mr8) D. 50 c. Crowell.
McClure, Ja. G. K. A mighty means of usefulness: plea for intercessory prayer. '02 (Ap19) 12°, net, 50 c. Revell.
McClure, Rob. American horse, cattle and sheep doctor. '01. '02(Je28) il. 12°, $1.50. Henneberry.
McCormick, J: N. Distinctive marks of the Episcopal church. '02(F22) S. 25 c. Young Churchman.
McCullough, Annie W. Little stories for little people. '02(Ap12) D. (Eclectic school readings.) 25 c. Am. Bk.
McCulloch, S: J. *See* Missouri statute annots.
McDaniel, *Mrs.* Helen P. War poems, 1861-1865. '02(Ap26) D. $1. Abbey Press.
McDonald, D: Treatise on the laws of Ind. pertaining to the powers and duties of and practice and procedure before justices of the peace. Rev. to date by B: F. Watson. '02 (My24) O. shp., net, $7.50. Clarke.
Macdonald, Duff, *ed.* Revised catechism. (Westminster Assembly's Shorter catechism.) '02(Je28) 12°, $1.25. Macmillan.
Macdonald, G: David Elginbrod. '02(My17) 12°, (Home lib.) $1. Burt.
Macdonald, G: A. How successful lawyers are educated. '02(Jl12) il. 8°, $1.50. Temple Pub
Macdonald, Loren B. Guarding the thoughts. '02(Ja25) S. (Upward ser., no. 1.) pap., 10 c. J. H. West.
Macdonell, Arth. A. Sanskrit grammar for beginners. '01. '02(Ja11) D. $3. Longmans.
Macdonough, Rodney. Macdonough-Hackstaff ancestry. '01. '02(F1) il. sq. 8°, $7.50. R. Macdonough.
Macdougal, Dan. T. Elem. plant physiology. '02(Mr22) il. D. $1.20. Longmans.
MacDowell, Ja. N. Orthodontis: for students in dental colleges. '01. '02(Ja18) il. 8°, net, $4. Colegrove.
McElrath, Fes. The rustler. '02(My3) il. D. net. $1.20. Funk.
McElroy, Lucy C. Silent pioneer. '02(Mr8) il. D. $1.50. Crowell.
Macfadden, B. A. Power and beauty of superb womanhood. '01. '02(Ap12) il. 12°, $1. Physical Culture.
McGarvey, J. W. Authorship of the book of Deuteronomy. '02(Je7) O. $2. Standard.
McGee, Jos. B., *sr.* Complete exposition and revelation of ancient free and accepted masonry. '01. '02(My24) D. $1. J. B. McGee.
McGiffert, A. C. The Apostles' creed. '02 (F1) O. net, $1.25. Scribner.
McGovern, J: Fireside university of modern invention, discovery, industry and art for home circle study and entertainment. [Rev. 18th ed.] '02(My24) 8°. $2.50; mor., $3.75. Union Pub.
McGovern, J: Poems. '02(My24) D. net, $1. W: S. Lord.
McGrady, T: City of Angels. '01. '02 (My10) S. pap., 10 c. Standard.

McGrady, T: Clerical capitalist. '02(Ap19) O. (Socialist lib., v. 1, no. 10.) pap., 10 c. Socialistic Co-op.

McGrady, T: A voice from England. '02 (Ap5) S. (Standard lib.) pap., 10 c. Standard.

Mach, Ernst. Science of mechanics. 2d enl. ed.; tr. by T: J. McCormack. '02(Jl5) 12°, *$2 net. Open Court.

MACHINERY.
Benjamin. Notes on machine design. $2. C. H. Holmes.
Lafarque. Social effect of machinery. 10 c. Socialistic Co-op.
Meyer *and* Peker. Easy lessons in mechanical drawing and machine designs. In 20 pts. subs., ea., 50 c.; or in 2 v., v. 1, $6; v. 2, $4. Indust.
See also Electric engineering;—Locomotives.

McHugh, Hugh., [*pseud.* for G: V. Hobart.] It's up to you. '02(Je28) il. nar. S. 75 c. G: W. Dillingham.

McIlvaine, J. H. St. Francis of Assisi. '02 (Ap12) S. net, 85 c. Dodd.

McIntire, J: J., ["Harvey Argyle."] As I saw it. '02(Jl12) il. D. $1.25. Home Pub.

Mack, W:, *and* Nash, H. P., *eds.* Cyclopedia of law and procedure. v. 3. '02(Ap5) O. shp., $6. Am. Law Bk.

Mackail, J: W: Biblia innocentium. pt. 2. '01· '02(Ja4) D. $1.75. Longmans.

Mackay, Angus M. Churchman's introduction to the Old Testament. '01· '02(Ja4) 12°. (Churchman's lib.) $1.50. Macmillan.

McKay, W. J. S. Hist. of ancient gynæcology. '01· '02(F22) 8°, net, $3. Wood.

McKee, Lanier. Land of Nome. '02(Je28) D. net, $1.25. Grafton Press.

Mackenzie, Alex. Voyages from Montreal through the Continent of North America to the Frozen and Pacific Oceans in 1789 and 1793. '02(My24) 2 v., 8°, (Commonwealth lib.) per v., net, $1. New Amsterdam.

Mackenzie, Ja. Study of the pulse, arterial, venous, and hepatic, and of the movements of the heart. '02(My17) il. 8°, net, $4.50. Macmillan.

Mackenzie, J: S. Outlines of metaphysics. '02(Ap26) 12°, net, $1.10. Macmillan.

Mackinder, H. J. Britain and the British seas. '02(F22) 8°, (World ser., no. 1.) $2. Appleton.

McKinley, W: Last speech of President McKinley. '02(Mr1) 12°, bds., $1.50; pap., $1. Kirgate Press.

MCKINLEY, W:
Ellis. Life of William McKinley. 25 c. Street.
Fallows, *ed.* Life of William McKinley. $1.50; $2.25. Regan.
Halstead. William McKinley [in Norwegian.] $1.50; $2. J: Anderson.
Halstead *and* Munson. Life and services of William McKinley. $1.50; $2.25. Dominion.
Hay. William McKinley. net, 28 c. Crowell.
See also Wilson, J. G.

McKinney, A. H. The child for Christ. '02 (Je28) 16°, net, 50 c. Revell.

McKinney, W: M., *ed.* Encyclopædia of pleading and practice. v. 22, 23. '02(My24) O. shp., ea., $6. E: Thompson.

Mackinnon, Ja. Growth and decline of the French monarchy. '02(Je7) O. $7.50. Longmans.

Maclane, Ma. *See* Story of.

McLaughlin, Ja. M. Elements and notation of music. '02(F1) D. 55 c. Ginn.

McLaws, Lafayette. Jezebel. '02(Jl5) il. D. †$1.50. Lothrop.

Maclay, E. S. Hist. of the U. S. Navy. New rev. ed. of v. 3. '02(Mr1) 3 v., il. 8°, per v., net, $3. Appleton.

McLellan, Ja. A., Dewey, J:, *and* Ames, A. F. Public school arithmetic for grammar grades. '02(F1) 12°, net, 60 c. Macmillan.

McLeod, Lorenzo C. A young man's problems. '02(Je7) D. 50 c. Flanagan.

McLeod, Malcolm J. Heavenly harmonies for earthly living. '02(F8) 12°, net, 50 c. Revell.

Macleod, Ma. *See* Malory, *Sir* T:

McManman, J. A. *See* Hyde, W. H.

McManus, L. The wager. '02(My17) D. $1.25. Buckles.

McMaster, J. S. Commercial cases. '01· '02 (Jl19) 8°, leath., $6. Commercial Bk.

McMaster, J. S. Commercial digest and business forms. 1900. '02(Jl19) 8°, leath., $6. Commercial Bk.

McMaster, J. S. Irregular and regular commercial paper. '02(Jl19) 12 x 4 in. $2. McMaster.

Macmillan, Hugh. Christmas rose and other thoughts in verse. '01· '02(Ja4) il. 12°, $1. Macmillan.

Macmillan, Hugh. Corn of Heaven. '02 (Ja18) 12°, $1.75. Macmillan.

Macmillan's classical ser. 12°, net. Macmillan.
—Sophocles. Antigone. 60 c.

Macmillan's Eng. classics. 12°, net, 60 c. Macmillan.
—Boswell. Journal of tour to the Hebrides.
—Scott. Kenilworth.—Quentin Durward.

Macmillan's French classics. 12°, *60 c. net. Macmillan.
—Racine. Athalie.

Macmillan's Greek course. 12°. Macmillan.
—Andrew. Greek prose composition. net, 90 c.

Macmillan's guides. 12°, net. Macmillan.
—Guide to Palestine and Egypt. $3.25.

Macmillan's handbooks of great masters in painting and sculpture. il. 12°, $1.75. Macmillan.
—Bell. Rembrandt.
—Gower. Sir David Wilkie.
—Martin. Gerard Douw.
—Perkins. Giotto.

Macmillan's handbooks of the great craftsmen. il. 12°, $2. Macmillan.
—Cust. Ivory workers of the Middle Ages.
—Headlam. Peter Vischer.

Macmillan's handbooks to the great public schools. 12°, $1.50. Macmillan.
—Airy. Westminster.

Macmillan's historical sources in school ser. 12°. **60 c. net. Macmillan.
—New England History Teachers' Assoc. Report.

Macmillan's manuals for teachers. 12°, net. Macmillan.
—Findlay. Principles of class teaching. $1.25.

Macmillan's mediæval towns ser. il. 12°. Macmillan.
—Headlam. Chartres. $2; $2.50.
—Poole. Cairo. $2; $2.50.
Macmillan's new geography readers: Africa and Australasia. '02(My24) 12°, net, 40 c. Macmillan.
Macmillan's new history readers; [bk. 3,] senior. '02(My24) il. 12°, net, 50 c. Macmillan.
Macmillan's personal problem ser. 12°, net, $1. Macmillan.
—Canfield. College student and his problems.
—Oppenheim. Mental growth and control.
Macmillan's Pitt Press ser. 12°, net. Macmillan.
—Sybel. Prinz Eugen von Savoyen. 60 c.
Macmillan's primary ser. of French and Germ. reading books. 12°, net. Macmillan.
—Alissas, d'. Les histoires de tante. 40 c.
Macmillan's summary of Eng. history on the concentric plan; senior. '02(My24) il. 12°, pap., net, 15 c. Macmillan.
Macmillan's Temple classics. 16°, 50 c.; flex. leath., 75 c. Macmillan.
—Arnold. Dramatic and early poems.
—Boethius. Consolation of philosophy.
—Browning. Sordello.
—Carlyle. Past and present.
—Goldsmith. Plays.—Poems.
Macmillan's Temple classics for young people. 16°, net. 50 c.; flex. leath., 80 c. Macmillan.
—Perrault. Tales of passed times.
McMurry, C: A., *ed.* Pubs of the National Herbart Society. '02(Jl12) 8°, *$5 net. Univ. of Chic.
Macnab, Fes. Ride in Morocco among believers and fur traders. '02(Ap19) il. O. $5. Longmans.
McSpadden, J. W. Shakesperian synopses. '02(Ap5) S. (Handy information ser.) net, 45 c. Crowell.
Madame Bohemia. Neilson, F. $1; 50 c. Lippincott.
Mlle. Fouchette. Murray, C: T. $1.50. Lippincott.
Madness of Philip. Daskam, J. D. $1.50. McClure, P.
Maeterlinck, M. The buried temple; tr. by A. Sutro. '02(My10) D. net, $1.40. Dodd.
Maeterlinck, M. Sister Beatrice and Ardiane and Barbe Bleue: two plays; tr. by B. Miall. '02(Ap12) D. net, $1.20. Dodd.
Maggie Miller. '02(Ap19) 12°, (Home lib.) $1. Burt.
Magic key. Tucker, E. S. net, $1. Little, B. & Co.
Magic wheel. Stannard, *Mrs.* H. E. V. $1.25. Lippincott.

MAGNETISM.
See Electricity.

Mahon, R. H. Token of the covenant; or, right use of baptism. 4th ed. '02(My17) D. 50 c. Pub. Ho. M. E. Ch., So.
Mahoney million. Townsend, C: $1.25 New Amsterdam.
Maid of Bar Harbor. Rowe, H. G. $1.50. Little, B. & Co.
Maid of Montauk. Monroe, F. net, $1. W: R. Jenkins.
Maid of Orleans. *See* Schiller, J. C. F. v.
Maid of the wildwood. Louttit, G: W: $1.50. Colonial.
Main currents in 19th century literature. *See* Brandes, G:
Main street. Hawthorne, N. $2. Kirgate Press.
Maine. Laws concerning business corporations, (annot.) (H. M. Heath.) '02(Je7) O. pap., gratis. Kennebec Journ.
Maine. *Supreme judicial ct.* **Repts.,** v. 95. (C: Hamlin.) '01. '02(Mr15) O. shp., $4. W: W. Roberts.

MAINE.
Drummond, *comp.* Maine masonic textbook. $1.40; $1.50. Berry.

Maitland, F: W:, Gwatkin, H: M., Poole, R. L., *and others.* Essays on the teaching of history. '01. '02(Ja4) 12°, (Cambridge Univ. Press ser.) net, 75 c. Macmillan.
Maitland, J: A. F. Music in England in the nineteenth century. '02(Ap5) 12°, net, $1.75. Dutton.
Majesty of calmness. Jordan, W: G: 50 c. Revell.
Major, C:, ["Edwin Caskoden."] Bears of Blue River. [New issue.] '02(Mr8) il. 12°, $1.50. Macmillan.
Major, C: Dorothy Vernon of Haddon Hall. '02(My3) il. D. $1.50. Macmillan.
Make good book of parodies. Dustin, E. 50 c. E. Dustin.
Making a country newspaper. Munson, A. J. $1. Dominion.
Making of a statesman. Harris, J. C. $1.25. McClure, P.

MALARIAL FEVER.
Ross. Malarial fever. net, 75 c. Longmans.

Malheurs de Sophie. Ségur, S. R., *Comtesse* de. 45 c. Heath.
Mallary, R. DeWitt. Lenox and the Berkshire Highlands. '02(Je21) il. O. net, $1.75. Putnam.
Malone, *Mrs.* Eva W. Out among the animals: [stories.] '02(Mr22) S. 75 c. Pub. Ho. M. E. Ch., So.
Malone, Jos. S. Guided and guarded. '02 (Ap26) D. $1.25. Abbey Press.
Maloney, Ja. C. 20th century guide for mixing fancy drinks. 3d ed. enl. '02(Jl19) sq. S. pap., $1. J. C. Maloney.
Malory, *Sir* T: King Arthur and his noble knights: stories from Morte D'Arthur, by M. Macleod. '02(Jl19) il. 12°, (Home lib.) $1. Burt.

MALVERN, Eng.
Windle. Malvern country. net, 75 c. Dodd.

MAMMALIA.
Harmer *and* Shipley, *eds.* Cambridge natural history. v. 10, Mammalia, by F. E. Beddard. net, $4. Macmillan.

MAN.
See Anatomy;—Ethnology; — Evolution; — Physiology;—Sex.

Man amongst men. Wollpert, F: 15 c. Eckler.
Man in the moon. Dendron, B. 50 c. Bonnell.
Man of no account. Trelawney, D. 10 c. J. H. West.
Man without a country. Hale, E: E. net, $1. Outlook.
Man who pleases and the woman who fascinates. Cone, J: A. $1. Neely.

MANCHURIA.
Graham. East of the barrier; or, Manchuria in miniature. net, $1. Revell.

Mandeville, C. E. Minister's manual and pocket ritual. '02(F8) S. flex. leath., net, 60 c. Jennings.
Mangasarian, M. M. New catechism. 3d ed. '02(My10) D. pap., 75 c. Open Court.
Manhattan lib. of new copyright fiction. See Burt's.
Mann, Horace K. Lives of the Popes in the early Middle Ages. v. 1. pt. 1. '02(Je14) 8°, net, $3. Herder.
Manning, Marie. Lord Alingham, bankrupt. '02(Ap12) D. $1.50. Dodd.
Mannix, Ma. E. As true as gold. '02(Mr22) il. S. 45 c. Benziger.
Man's peerless destiny in Christ. Sarles, J: W. net, 90 c. Funk.
MANUAL TRAINING.
See Sloyd.
Manufacturers' need of reciprocity. Farquhar, A. B. 15 c. Am. Acad. Pol. Sci.
MANUSCRIPTS.
See Inscriptions;—Irish literature.
Many waters. Shackleton, R. $1.50. Appleton.
Manzoni, A. I promessi sposi; abr. and ed. by M. Levi. '01. '02(Ja25) D. (Silver ser. of modern lang. text-books.) $1.20. Silver.
Marble faun. Hawthorne, N. $1. Burt.
Marchant, J. R. V. Commercial history. '02 (Je7) il. D. (Commercial ser.) $1. Pitman.
Marchmont, Arth. W. Miser Hoadley's secret. '02(Jl12) il. D. (Red letter ser.) $1.25; pap., 50 c. New Amsterdam.
Marchmont, Arth. W. Sarita, the Carlist. '02 (My3) D. $1.50. Stokes.
Margaret Bowlby. Vincent, E. L. $1.50. Lothrop.
Margaret Tudor. Colcock, A. T. $1. Stokes.
Margaret Vincent. Clifford, *Mrs.* L. L. $1.50. Harper.
Margoliouth, D: S: Lines of defense of the biblical revelation. '02(Mr8) 12°, net, $1.50. Gorham.
Margoliouth, D: S: Religion of Bible lands. '02(My3) S. (Christian study manuals.) 60 c. Armstrong.
Maria Stuart. Schiller, J. C. F. v. net, 70 c. Holt.
MARINE ENGINEERING.
Durand. Practical marine engineering. $5. Marine Engineering.
MARINE ZOOLOGY.
See Aquatic life:—Protozoa.
Marion Manning. Eustis, E. $1.50. Harper.
Marius the epicurean. Pater, W. $1. Burt.
Marivaux, Pierre C. de C. de. Selection from comedies by E. W. Olmsted. '02 (Mr22) 12°, net, 90 c. Macmillan.
MARK, *St.*
See Bible.
Marks, Jeannette A. Brief hist. outline of Eng. literature. '02(Je28) D. $1. J. A. Marks.
Marlowe, Chris. Passionate shepherd to his love; and The nymph's reply to the shepherd, by Sir. W. Raleigh. '02(My10) sq. 8°, flex. vellum, net, $3.75.) Russell.
MARQUETTE, Jacques.
Thwaites. Father Marquette. net, $1. Appleton.
Marquis, G: H. Fairview's mystery. '01. '02(Mr1) D. 75 c. Abbey Press.
Marred in the making. Commander, L. K. $3; 25 c. Eckler.

MARRIAGE.
Cook. Bride's book. net, $1.50. Dutton.
Crawley. The mystic rose: study of primitive marriage. net, $4. Macmillan.
Hurst. New heartstone: bridal greeting. $1. Jennings.
Westermarck. Hist. of human marriage. net, $4.50. Macmillan.
Wood. Marriage. net, $1.25. Revell.
Marriage of Laurentia. Haultmont, M. net, $1.60. Herder.
Marsh, C: L. Not on the chart. '02(Je7) il. D. $1.50. Stokes.
Marsh, G: A singular will. '02(Je7) D. $1.50. Neely.
Marshall, Beatrice. Old Blackfriars. '02 (Ap5) il. 12°, $1.50. Dutton.
Marshall, J: S. Principles and practice of operative dentistry. '01. '02(F15) il. 8°, subs., $5; shp., $6. Lippincott.
Marshall, T: W. Logarithmic tables of the measures of length. '02(Jl12) 12°, $2. Van Nostrand.
Marshall, W: L. *See* Clark, W: L.
Marston, E: Sketches of some booksellers of the time of Dr. Samuel Johnson. '02 (My10) 16°, net, $2. Scribner.
Martin, Fred. W. Album of designs for boats, launches and yachts. [2d ed.] '02(My24) il. obl. T. pap., $1. F: W. Martin.
Martin, G: H. Civil government in the U. S. Rev. ed. '02(Ap26) D. 90 c. Am. Bk.
Martin, W. Gerard Douw; fr. the Dutch by Clara Bell. '02(My3) il. 12°, (Great masters in painting and sculpture.) $1.75. Macmillan.
Martin, W. G. W. Traces of the elder faiths of Ireland. '02(F8) 2 v., il. O. $12. Longmans.
Martin, W: E. Internal improvements in Alabama. '02(Jl12) O. (Johns Hopkins Univ. studies in hist. and pol. science, 20th ser., no. 4.) pap., 30 c. Johns Hopkins.
Martindale, J. B. Am. law directory, Jan., 1902. '02(F1) O. shp., net, $10. Martindale.
MARTINIQUE.
See St. Pierre.
Marvelous achievements of the 19th century. Morris, C: $2.50; $3.50. Winston.
Marx, Karl. Wage-labor and capital; also Free-trade. '02(Mr29) D. (Arm and hammer ser.) 50 c. N. Y. Labor News.
MARY, *Virgin.*
Palladino. Mary our mother. net, 15 c. Herder.
Mary Garvin. Pattee, F. L. $1.50. Crowell.
Mary of Bethany. Parks, E. M. 25 c.; 15 c. Pepper.
Mary Starkweather. Williamson, *Mrs.* C. C. $1.50. Abbey Press.
Mary Stuart. *See* Schiller, J. C. F. v.
Mary Tracy's fortune. Sadlier, A. T. 45 c. Benziger.
Maryland. *Ct. of appeals.* Repts. (Brantly.) v. 93. '02(My10) O. shp., $5. Baughman.
Maryland. *Ct. of appeals.* Repts. v. 59. '02(Mr1); v. 60 (My10); v. 61(Je21) O. shp., ea., $4. Curlander.
MARYLAND.
Snowden. Some old historic landmarks of Va. and Md. *25 c. net. Ramey.
Steiner. Western Md. in the Revolution. 30 c. Johns Hopkins.

Mason, Arth. J. Christianity, what is it? '02(Je7) 16°, (Church Hist. Soc. lectures, no. 66.) 80 c. E. & J. B. Young.
Mason, Arth. J. Ministry of conversion. '02 (Mr8) D. (Handbooks for the clergy.) net, 90 c. Longmans.
Mason, Hobart. *See* Sheldon, S:
Mason, Ja. F:, *comp.* Favorite songs of love. Limited ed. '02(Jl5) 16°, $1.50; ooze cf., $2; Eng. cf., $2.25; Eng. cf. tooled, $5. Dodge.
Mason, W: D. Water-supply (from a sanitary standpoint.) 3d ed., rewritten. '02 (My17) il. 8°, red. to $4. Wiley.
MASONRY.
See Bridges
MASS.
See Catholic church;—Lord's supper.
Massachusetts digest, supp. [v. 5,] by C: N. Harris. '02(Je28) Q. shp., net, $5. Little, B. & Co.
Massachusetts. *Supreme judicial ct.* Repts. v. 178. (H: W. Swift.) '02(Ap5) O. shp., $2. Little, B. & Co.
Massachusetts. Treatise on the street railway accident law; by E. H. Clark. '02 (Ap19) O. shp., $3.25. Lawyers' Bk.
MASSACHUSETTS.
American ser. of popular biographies, Mass. ed. $17. Graves.
Hall, *ed.* Regiments and armories of Mass. v. 2. per set, $12; $18; $25. W. W. Potter.
Perley. Practice in personal actions in cts. of Mass. $6.50. G: B. Reed.
Smith. Founders of the Mass. Bay Colony. *$5 net. Woodward & L.
Tucker. Preparation of wills: Mass. law. $3.50. G: B. Reed.
See also Ancient and Hon. Artillery Co. of Mass.;—Boston;—Lenox;—Lexington;—Nantucket Island.
MASSAGE.
See Injuries.
Master of Beechwood. Sergeant, A. 50 c. Burt.
Master of Caxton. Brooks, H. $1.50. Scribner.
Master of science of right living. Hillis, N. D. net, 50 c. Revell.
Mastery of the Pacific. Colquhoun, A. R. net, $4. Macmillan.
MATABELELAND.
Hall *and* Neal. Ancient ruins of Rhodesia. net, $6. Dutton
Mate of the good ship "York." Russell, W: C. $1.50. L. C. Page.
MATERIA MEDICA.
Murray. Rough notes on remedies. net, $1.25. Blakiston.
See also Pharmacy;—Therapeutics.
MATHEMATICS.
Chancellor. Elem. school mathematics by grades. bks. 5, 6. ea., *28 c. net. Globe Sch. Bk.
Deel. Practical rapid calculator. 50 c. G: A. Deel.
Gibbs. Vector analysis. net, $4. Scribner.
Stokes. Math. and physical papers. v. 3. net, $3.75. Macmillan.
See also Algebra;—Arithmetic;—Astronomy;—Calculus;—Geodesy;—Interest;—Logarithms;—Probabilities;—Surveying;—Trigonometry.
Mathes, J. H. General Forrest. '02(Ap26) D. (Great commanders' ser.) net, $1.50. Appleton.
Matheson, G: Spiritual development of St. Paul. '02(Ap12) 12°, net, 80 c. Whittaker.
Matheson, G: Times of retirement; with biog. sketch of the author by D. MacMillan. '01. '02(Ja11) 12°, net, $1.25. Revell.
Mathews, Ferd. S. Field book of Am. wild flowers. '02(Ap26) il. S. net, $1.75. Putnam.
Mathews, Shailer. *See* Burton, E. D.
Matteson, A., *ed.* *See* Illinois. Laws rel. to township organization.
Matthews, C: G. Manual of alcoholic fermentation and allied industries. '02(Ap19) D. net, $2.60. Longmans.
Matthews, Ja. B. Pen and ink: [essays.] 3d rev., enl. ed. '02(F15) D. net, $1.25. Scribner.
Maulde la Clavière, René de. Art of life; tr. by G: H. Ely. '01. '02(Ja25) D. net, $1.75. Putnam.
Mavor, W: English spelling book; il. by Kate Greenaway. '02(Je28) 16°, bds., 40 c. Warne.
Maxwell, Hu. Jonathan Fish and his neighbors. '02(Jl19) O. $1. Acme.
Maxwell, Lucy H. Card sewing: for kindergartens. '02(My3) 16°, pap., 50 c. M. Bradley.
Maxwell, *Mrs.* Ma. E. B. El sacrificio de Elisa. (A. Elias y Pujol.) '01. '02(F22) 12°, pap., 50 c. Appleton.
Maynard, *Mrs.* L. W. Birds of Washington and vicinity. '02(Jl12) D. *$1 net. Woodward & L.
Mayor, Jos. B. Chapters on Eng. metre. 2d ed., rev. and enl. '02(Ja18) 8°, (Cambridge Univ. Press ser.) net, $2.25. Macmillan.
Mazel. Fisguill, R: $1.50. H. S. Stone.
Mead, Spencer P. Hist. and genealogy of the Mead family of Fairfield Co., Conn. '01. '02(F8) il. O. $15. Knickerbocker.
Meade, L. T. *See* Smith, *Mrs.* E. T.
Meakin, Budgett. The Moors. '02(Mr29) il. 8°, net, $5. Macmillan.
Meakin, Nevill M. The Assassins. '02 (Mr22) D. $1.50. Holt.
MEAT.
Walley. Guide to meat inspection. $3. W: R. Jenkins.
MECHANICAL DRAWING.
Hawkins. Self-help mechanical drawing. $2. Audel.
Meyer *and* Peker. Easy lessons in mechanical drawing and machine designs. In 20 pts. subs., ea., 50 c.: or in 2 v., v. 1. $6; v. 2, $4. Indust.
Mechanical triumphs of ancient Egyptians. Barber, F. M. net, $1.25. Dodd.
MECHANICS.
Gibbs. Elem. principles in statistical mechanics, with especial ref. to the rational foundation of thermo-dynamics. $4. Scribner.
Mach. Science of mechanics. *$2 net. Open Court.
Reynolds. Papers on mechanical and physical subjects. v. 2. net, $6. Macmillan.
See also Engineering;—Power.
MECHANICS' LIENS.
Illinois. Commentary on mechanics' lien law. net, $4. Callaghan.
Mechanics of engineering. *See* Du Bois, A: J.

Mechem, Floyd R. Case on the law of damages. 3d ed. '02(Mr8) O. net, $4. West Pub.

MEDIAEVAL HISTORY.
See Middle Ages.

Mediæval Rome. Miller, W: **$1.35 net; $1.60 net. Putnam.

Medical directory of the city of New York. '01- '02(F8) 12°, $1.50. Wynkoop.

Medical News pocket formulary for 1902; ed. by E. Q. Thornton. 4th ed. '02(F15) 18°, leath. tuck, net, $1.50. Lea.

Medical News visiting list, 1902. '01- '02 (F22) 16°, leath. tucks, $1.25; thumb-letter index, $1.50. Lea.

MEDICI (The).
Smeaton. The Medici and the Italian Renaissance. $1.25. Scribner.

MEDICINE.
American year-book of medicine and surgery. 2 v. ea., net, $3; net, $3.75. Saunders.
Barret. Medical handbook. $1. Barret Chemical.
Billings *and* Stanton, *eds.* General medicine. $1.50. Year Bk.
Buck. Reference handbook of the medical sciences. v. 4. subs., $7; $8; $9. Wood.
Burdick. Standard medical manual. $4. Engelhard.
Fagge. Text-book of medicine. 2 v. net, $6. Blakiston.
International medical annual, 1902. net, $3. Treat.
Lawrence. Practical medicine. $3. Boericke & T.
Medical News pocket formulary, 1902. net, $1.50. Lea.
Paget. Sel. essays and addresses. $5. Longmans.
Sajous, *ed.* Analytical encyclopædia of practical medicine. v. 1. subs., ea., $5; $6. Davis.
See also Accidents;—Chemistry;—Hygiene;—Mind and body;—Nervous system;—Pathology;—Pharmacy;—Veterinary medicine and surgery.

Meditations and vows. Hall, J. $1.50. Dutton.

Meditations of an autograph collector. Joline, A. H. net, $3. Harper.

Medley, Dudley J. Student's manual of Eng. constitutional history. 3d ed. '02(Je28) 8°, net, $3.50. Macmillan.

Meier, W. H. D. Herbarium and plant description. '01- '02(F1) Q. portfolio, 70 c. Ginn.

Meigs, H: B: Record of the descendants of Vincent Meigs. '02(Jl12) il. 8°, $6; mor., $8. H: B: Meigs.

Mellier, A. F. Book of the rose. 2d ed. '02 (My24) 12°, $1.75. Macmillan.

Mellick, Anna C. Latin composition for classes reading Cæsar. '01- '02(Ja4) S. 40 c. Am. Bk.

Melomaniacs. Huneker, J. $1.50. Scribner.

Melville, Herman. Typee; ed. by W. P. Trent. '02(My17) il. D. (Home and school classics, young reader's ser.) 45 c. Heath.

Melvin, Ja. Journal. [Repr.] '02(Jl12) 12°, $2. H. W. Bryant.

Memoirs of an American lady. Grant, *Mrs.* A. M. net, $7.50. Dodd.

MEMORIAL DAY
Harvey. Aids for the proper observance of Memorial day by schools of Wis. gratis. Democrat Pr. Co.

MEMORY.
Kilbourne. Memory and its cultivation. $1; 50 c. Mullin.

MEN.
Blouët. 'Tween you an' I; pt. 1, Concerning men. $1.20. Lothrop.

Men and memories. Young, J: R. subs., $5; $3. Neely.

Menefee, Maud. Child stories from the masters. '02(My10) il. 16°, 75 c. Rand, McN. & Co.

Menpes, Mortimer. Japan. '02(Ja18) il. 8°, net, $6. Macmillan.

MENTAL ARITHMETIC.
See Arithmetic.

Mental growth and control. Oppenheim, N. net, $1. Macmillan.

MENTAL SCIENCE.
Ballough. Power that heals and how to use it. $1. Painter.
Bradbury. New philosophy of health. 75 c. Alliance.
Dresser. True hist. of mental science. 20 c. Alliance.
Patterson. What the new thought stands for. 10 c. Alliance.
Patterson. The will to be well. $1. Alliance.
See also Christian science;—Mind and body.

Mental state of hystericals. Janet, P. $3.50. Putnam.

Merchant of Venice. *See* Shakespeare, W:

Mercier, C: A. Psychology, normal and morbid. '02(Mr1) 8°, net, $4. Macmillan.

Mercier, C: A. Text-book of insanity. '02 (My17) 12°, net, $1.75. Macmillan.

Merejkowski, Dimitri. Romance of Leonardo da Vinci, the forerunner; authorized tr. of The resurrection of the gods, by H. Trench. '02(Jl19) D. †$1.50. Putnam.

Merriam, Edm. F. Hist. of Am. Bapt. missions. '01- '02(F15) 12°, $1.25. Am. Bapt.

Merrill, Cath. The man Shakespeare, and other essays. '02(Jl19) 12°, **$1.25 net. Bowen-M.

Merrill, S. M., *and* Warren, H: W. Discourses on miracles. '02(Mr22) sq. T. (Little books on doctrine.) net, 25 c. Jennings.

Merriman, Mansfield, *and* Jacoby, H: D. Text-book on roofs and bridges. Pt. 3. 4th ed., rewritten. '02(Ap19) 8°, $2.50. Wiley.

MESA VERDE.
See Colorado.

Message of to-morrow. Lee, J: L. net, $1.20. Revell.

Message to Garcia and thirteen other things. Hubbard, E. $2; $5; $15. Roycrofters.

METAL-WORK.
See Plate.

METALS AND METALLURGY.
Langbein. Complete treatise on the electro-deposition of metals. $4. Baird.
Phillips, *ed.* Methods for analysis of ores, pig iron and steel. net, $1. Chemical.
See also Assaying;—Blowpipe;—Chemistry;—Copper;—Iron;—Precious metals;—Steel.

METAPHYSICS.
Alexander. Problem of metaphysics and the meaning of metaphysical explanation. *75 c. net. Macmillan.
Kant. Prolegomena to any future metaphysics. 50 c. Open Court.
Leibnitz. Discourse on metaphysics. 35 c.; net, 75 c. Open Court.
Mackenzie. Outlines of metaphysics. net, $1.10. Macmillan.
See also Ontology.
METEOROLOGY.
See Weather.
Methodist Episcopal church. Constitution of churches in America, by W. F. Barclay. '02(My10) D. pap., 40 c. Pub. Ho. M. E. Ch., So.
Methodist Episcopal church in America. Doctrines; comp. and ed. by J: I. Tigert. '02 (Jl19) 2 v., sq. T. (Little books on doctrine.) *50 c. net. Jennings.
Methodist Episcopal church, South. Minutes of the annual conferences for 1901. '01- '02 (My10) O. pap., net, 50 c. Pub. Ho. M. E. Ch., So.
METHODIST EPISCOPAL CHURCH.
Bowen. Why two Episcopal Methodist churches in the U. S.? 75 c. Pub. Ho. of M. E. Ch., So.
Oliver. Our lay office-bearers. net, 25 c. Jennings.
See also Epworth League.
Methods of keeping the public money of the U. S. Phillips, J: B. $1. Mich. Pol. Sci.
Methods of Lady Walderhurst. Burnett, *Mrs.* F. H. $1.25. Stokes.
METRE.
Mayor. Chapters on Eng. metre. net, $2.25. Macmillan.
Metropolitan club cook-book. Schaeffer, *Mrs.* J. $1.75. Augsburg.
Mets, J. A. Naval heroes of Holland. '02 (Je14) il. D. $1.50. Abbey Press.
MEXICO.
Wilkins. Glimpse of old Mexico. 75 c. Whitaker & R.
Meyer, B. H. Advisory councils in railway administration. '02(Mr22) 8°, (Pub. of the soc., no. 327.) pap., 15 c. Am. Acad. Pol. Sci.
Meyer, Ernest C. Nominating systems; with bibliog. and index '02(Ap5) 8°, net, $1.50. E. C. Meyer.
Meyer, J. G. A., *and* Peker, C: G. Easy lessons in mechanical drawing and machine designs. '02(Jl12) in 20 pts., subs., ea., 50 c.; or in 2 v., v. 1, $6; v. 2, $4. Indust.
Meyers, R. C. V. Theodore Roosevelt, patriot and statesman. '02(F22) il. 12°. subs., $1.50; hf. mor., $2. W. W. Wilson.
Meyers, R. C. V. Theodore Roosevelt, patriot and statesman. '02(Mr15) il. 12°, $1.50; hf. rus., $2. Ziegler.
Michael Ferrier. Poynter, E. F. $1.50. Macmillan.
Michael Ross, minister. Holdsworth, A. E. $1.50. Dodd.
Michaud, Henri. L'idole. '02(My24) D. (Michaud's ser. of Fr. plays for schools, no. 9.) pap., 10 c. W: R. Jenkins.
Michelsen, Alb. A. Velocity of light. '02 (Ap19) O. pap., net, 25 c. Univ. of Chic.
Michie, T: J., *ed.* Banking cases annot. v. 3. '01- '02(Ja18) O. shp., $5. Michie.
Michie, T: J., *ed.* Municipal corporation cases annot. v. 6. '02(Mr1) O. shp., $5. Michie.
Michigan. Law of personal injuries, by W. Baldwin. '02(My24) O. shp., net, $4. Callaghan.
Michigan. *Supreme ct.* Index digest, July, 1898-Jan., 1902. (C. P. Campbell.) '02 (Mr22) O. shp., $3.50. Index Digest.
Michigan. *Supreme ct.* Repts. (J: A. Brooks.) v. 125. '01- '02(Ja18); v. 126 (My24) O. shp., ea., $3.50. Callaghan.
MICHIGAN.
Hollister, *and others.* Taxation in Mich. 50 c. Mich. Pol. Sci.
Keith. Historical sketch of internal improvements in Mich., 1836-1846. 50 c. Mich. Pol. Sci.
MICROSCOPE.
Gage. The microscope. $1.50. Comstock Pub.
MIDDLE AGES.
Cust. Ivory workers of the Middle Ages. $2. Macmillan.
Myers. Mediæval and modern history. pt. 1, Middle Ages. $1.20. Ginn.
See also Monasticism;—Renaissance.
MIDWIFERY.
Jewett. Essentials of obstetrics. net, $2.25. Lea.
Jewett. Practice of obstetrics. net, $5; $6; $6.50. Lea.
Peterson *and* Lewis, *eds.* Obstetrics. $1.25. Year Bk.
Mighty means of usefulness. McClure, J. G. K. net, 50 c. Revell.
Miles, Eustace H. Failures of vegetarianism. '02(Ap5) 12°, net, $1.50. Dutton.
Miles, Eustace H. How to prepare essays, lectures, [etc.] '02(F15) 12°, net, $2. Dutton.
MILITARY ART AND SCIENCE.
See Ancient and Hon. Artillery Co. of Mass.;—Gunnery;—Hospitals;—Infantry;—West Point.
Military topography and sketching. Root, E. A. $2.50. Hudson-K.
Miller, Alf. S. Manual of assaying. 2d ed. '02(Je21) il. 16°, $1. Wiley.
Miller, And. J., *comp.* The toastmaster. '02 (Je7) sq. D. pap., n. p. W. M. Rogers.
Miller, Ja. R. Story of Joseph. '02(F8) 16°, net, 35 c. Revell.
Miller, *Mrs.* Ma. R. The brook book. '02 (My10) O. net, $1.35. Doubleday, P.
Miller, W: Mediæval Rome from Hilderbrand to Clement VIII., 1073-1600. '02(Jl19) D. (Story of the nations ser., no. 63.) **$1.35 net; hf. leath., $1.60 net. Putnam.
Miller, W: J. American church dict. and cyclopedia. '01- '02(Ja4) D. $1. Whittaker.
Millet's Oriental ser. 8°. Millet.
—Brinkley. Japan. 4 v. ea., $50.
Millionaire's love story. Boothby, G. $1.25. Buckles.
Millionaire mystery. Hume, F. W. $1.25. Buckles.
Mills, C: H. *See* New York. Criminal repts.
Mills, Harry E: Select sunflowers: [poems.] '01- '02(F8) 12°, $1. Sunflower Press.
Mills, Jane D., [*Mrs.* Ja. E. Mills.] Leaves from a life-book of to-day. '01- '02(Ja11) S. 50 c. Swedenborg.

Milne, W: J. Key to Academic algebra. '02 (Mr29) O. $1.50. Am. Bk.
Milne, W: J. Key to the Standard arithmetic and the Mental arithmetic. '01- '02 (Ja11) S. 75 c. Am. Bk.
Milton, J: Complete poems. '01- '02(Ja11) 16°, (Caxton ser.) flex. lambskin, net, $1.20. Scribner.
Milton, J: Selections. '01. '02(Ap5) S. (Little masterpieces.) 50 c. Doubleday, P.
MIND.
Brooks. Elements of mind. $4. Longmans.
Hobhouse. Mind in evolution. net, $3.25. Macmillan.
Oppenheim. Mental growth and control. net, $1. Macmillan.
See also Intellect:—Mind and body;—Psychology.
MIND AND BODY.
Brown. Studies in spiritual harmony. $1. Reed Pub.
Janet. Mental state of hystericals. $3.50. Putnam.
Wright. Body and soul. $1. J. C. Wright.
See also Hypnotism;—Insanity;—Mental science; —Nervous system;—Psychology.
MIND READING.
See Telepathy.
Mind telegraph. Stay, J. B. 25 c. Alliance
Miner, W: H. Daniel Boone: cont. toward a bibliog. '01- '02(F15) D. bds., $1. Dibdin Club.
MINERALOGY.
Eakle. Colemanite from So. California. 15 c. Univ. of Cal.
See also Assaying;—Blowpipe;—Geology;—Metals and metallurgy;—Mines and mining.
MINES AND MINING.
Oregon. Mining laws. 40 c. Or. Mining Journ.
Pratt. Supp. to Mining laws of Colorado. 35 c. Pratt Merc.
See also Cooper;—Engineering;—Gold;—Iron;—Metals and metallurgy.
Minister's wooing. Stowe, *Mrs.* H. B. $1. Burt.
MINISTERS (*of the Gospel*).
Anderson. Christian ministry. 20 c. Young Churchman.
Kern. Way of the preacher. $1.25. Pub. Ho. M. E. Ch., So.
Mandeville. Minister's manual and pocket ritual. net, 60 c. Jennings.
Robinson. Personal life of the clergy. net, 90 c. Longmans.
See also Missions and missionaries;—Ordination; —Preaching;—Priests.
Ministry of conversion. Mason, A. J. net, 90 c. Longmans.
MINNEAPOLIS.
Hudson. Dict. of Minneapolis. 25 c. H. B. Hudson.
Minneapolis Journal almanac and year book, 1902. '02(Ap26) 12°, pap., 25 c. Journal Pr. Co.
Minnesota. Civil procedure in the district and sup. cts. (B: J. Shipman.) In 2 v. v. 1. '02(Jl5) O. shp., (complete work,) $13. Keefe-D.
Minnesota. Justice's manual; by W. S. Booth. 12th ed. '01- '02(Ja18) D. pap., $1.50. Booth.
Minnesota. *Supreme ct.* Repts. v. 83. '02 (Ap5); v. 84 (Jl19) O. shp., ea., $2.75. Dufresne.

Minority (The). Hill, F: T. $1.50. Stokes.
Minton, H: C. The cosmos and the logos. '02(Mr22) O. net, $1.25. Westminster.
MIRACLES.
Merrill *and* Warren. Discourses on miracles. 25 c. Jennings.
See also Psychical research.
Misanthrope (Le). Moliere, J. B. P. de. 50 c. Scott, F. & Co.
Misdemeanors of Nancy. Hoyt, E. $1.50. Doubleday, P.
Miser Hoadley's secret. Marchmont, A. W. $1.25; 50 c. New Amsterdam.
Misérables (Les). *See* Quayle, W: A.
Miss Ashton's new pupil. Robbins, *Mrs.* S. S. $1. Burt.
Miss Petticoats. Tilton, D. $1.50. C. M. Clark.
Miss Prudence. Conklin, *Mrs.* J. M. D. $1. Burt.
MISSIONS AND MISSIONARIES.
Beach. Geography and atlas of Protestant missions. v. 1. $2.50; per set, $1.75. Student Vol.
Brain. Fifty missionary programmes. 35 c. Un. Soc. C. E.
Carey. Adventures in Tibet. net, $1.50. Un. Soc. C. E.
Dean. Cross of Christ in Bololand. net, $1. Revell.
Dennis. Centennial survey of foreign missions. net, $4. Revell.
Jesuit relations: travels and explorations of the Jesuit missionaries in New France, 1610-1791. 73 v. ea.. net, $3.50. Burrows.
Ketler. Tragedy of Paotingfu, China. net, $2. Revell.
Longridge. Official and lay witness to the value of foreign missions. 20 c. E. & J. B. Young.
Montgomery. Foreign missions. net, 90 c. Longmans.
Smith, B. Uncle Boston's spicy breezes. net, $1. Am. Bapt.
Smith, J. Ten years in Burma. net, $1. Jennings.
Warneck. Outline of hist. of Protestant missions. net, $2. Revell.
See also Philippine Islands;—Protestantism;—*also* names of churches.
Mississippi. *Supreme ct.* Repts. v. 78. '01- '02(My10) O. shp., $4. Marshall.
Mississippi bubble. Hough, E. $1.50. Bowen-M.
Missouri. *St. Louis and the Kansas City cts. of appeals.* Cases. v. 89. '01- '02(Mr1) O. shp., $5. Stephens.
Missouri statute annots.; by S: J. McCulloch. 2d ed. '02(My24) O. hf. shp., $3. S: J. McCulloch.
Missouri. *Supreme ct.* Repts. (Rader.) v. 162, 163. '01- '02(Mr1); v. 164 (My10) O. shp., ea., $4. Stephens.
Mr. Whitman. Pullen, *Mrs.* E. $1.50. Lothrop.
Mistress Dorothy of Haddon Hall. Hastings, H: $1. Fenno.
Mrs. Tree. Richards, *Mrs.* L. E. H. †75 c. Estes.
Misunderstood. Montgomery, F. $1. Beam.
Mitchell, C. A. *See* Oppenheimer, C.
Mitchell, Fes. L. Georgia land and people. '02(Ap26) 12°, $1.25. F. L. Mitchell.

Mitton, G. E. The opportunist. '02(Mr8) 12°, $2. Macmillan.
Moberly, R. C. Christ our life. '02(Mr22) O. net, $3. Longmans.
Mobile Boer. Hiley, A. R. I. $1.50. Grafton Press.
Modern association and railroading. Goodknight, A. L. 50 c. Abbey Press.
Modern lang ser. *See* Heath's.
Molander, Anna. Scientific sloyd: for teachers and schools. '02(My3) S. 50 c. Bardeen.
Molesworth, *Mrs.* Ma. L. Grandmother dear. '02(Je28) il. 12°, (St. Nicholas ser.) 75 c. Burt.
Molesworth, *Mrs.* Ma. L. Robin Redbreast. '02(My3) il. 12°, (Fireside ser.) $1. Burt.
Molière, J. B. P. de. Le misanthrope and L'avare; ed. by W: F. Giése. '01- '02 (F15) S. (Lake French classics.) 50 c. Scott, F. & Co.
Molinerillo (El). Trueba, A. de. 35 c. W: R. Jenkins.
Mollie's mistake. Book, J. W. 15 c. Herder.
Momerie, A. W. Immortality, and other sermons. '02(Ap12) 12°, $1.50. Whittaker.
Mon oncle et mon curé. La Brète, J. de. 50 c. Am. Bk.
Monadology. *See* Leibnitz, *Baron* G. W. v.
Monaghan, Ja. *See* Pennsylvania. Digest.
MONASTICISM.
Feasey. Monasticism. net, $1. Herder.
Monell, S. H. System of instruction in X-ray methods. '02(My10) il. 8°, subs., hf. mor., $15. Pelton.
MONEY.
Del Mar. Hist. of money in England. $2.—Netherlands. 50 c.—Germany and other European states. *$2 net. Cambridge.
Green. Shakespeare and Goethe on Gresham's law and the single gold standard. 25 c. MacGowan.
See also Finance.
Money-maker. Adams, W: T. $1.25. Lee & S.
Monica. Bourget, P. $1.50. Scribner.
Monkhouse, Cosmo. History and desc. of Chinese porcelain. '02(Mr15) il. 8°, net. $10. Wessels.
Monroe. Forest, [*pseud.* for Ferdinand G. Wiechmann.] Maid of Montauk. '02 (Ap26) il. D. net, $1. W: R. Jenkins.
Monroe, Ja. Writings. v. 5, 1807-16. '02 8°, hf. leath., subs., $5. Putnam.
Monroe, Lewis B., *ed.* Public and parlor readings. '01. '02(Mr1) 4 v., 12°, ea., $1. Lee & S.
Monroe Rebekah Lodge: semi-centennial of Monroe Rebekah Lodge, no. 1, I. O. O. F., Jan. 23, 1902. '02(Mr8) 8°, pap., 10 c. Darrow.
Monsell, J. R. The pink knight. '01- '02 (Ja18) il. 32°, bds., net, 40 c. Stokes.
Monsieur Bergeret. France, A. $1. Silver.
Monsieur Martin. Carey, W. net, $1.20. Putnam.
Montgomery, Flo. Misunderstood. [New issue.] '02(Ja4) D. $1. Beam.
Montgomery, H: H. Foreign missions. '02 (Ap26) D. (Handbooks for the clergy.) net, 90 c. Longmans.
MONTREAL.
Bosworth, *ed.* Hochelaga depicta; early hist. of city and island. net, $3; net, $4.50. Congdon.
MONUMENTS.
See Tombstones.
Moody, J:, *ed.* Corporation securities. '02 (Je28) O. $7.50; flex. leath., $10. Moody.
Moody, W: V., *and* Lovett, R. M. Hist. of Eng. literature. '02(My10) O. net, $1.25. Scribner.
Moore, Fk. F. A damsel or two. '02(Ap26) D. $1.50. Appleton.
Moore, *Sir* J: W:, *ed.* Variola, vaccination, cholera, erysipelas, etc. '02(Mr22) il. 8°, (Nothnagel's encyclopedia of practical medicine, v. 2.) net, $5; hf. mor., net, $6. Saunders.
Moore, T: E. My Lord Farquhar. '02(My3) D. $1.25. Abbey Press.
MOORS.
Meakin. The Moors. net, $5. Macmillan.
Moral drill. Harper, J: M. $1. Kellogg.
Morang's annual register of Canadian affairs, 1901; ed. and comp. by J. C. Hopkins. '02 (Jl19) O. $3; hf. mor., $4. Morang.
MORAVIAN CHURCH.
Clewell. Hist. of Wachovia, N. C.; Unitas fratum or Moravian church, 1752-1902. **$2 net. Doubleday, P.
Morceau de pain. Coppée, F. 25 c. W: R. Jenkins.
Morchester. Datchet, C: net, $1.20. Putnam.
More, Egbert. Trisection of a given angle geometrically solved and illustrated. '01- '02(F1) il. O. pap., $1. Wickes.
More, *Sir* T: Utopia, and life of More, by W: Roper. '02(My10) 12°, (Home lib.) $1. Burt.
More animal stories. Cochrane, R. net, $1. Lippincott.
More ex-tank tales. Cullen, C. L: $1. Ogilvie.
More tales of the birds. Fowler, W: W. $1. Macmillan.
Morehead, G: Francesca Da Rimini. '02 (Mr22) il. D. (Sunnyside ser., no. 117.) pap., 25 c. Ogilvie.
Morehead, G: Madame Du Barry. '02(My17) 12°, pap., 50 c. Donohue.
Morehead, G: Nell Gwyn. '01. '02(F15) il. 12°, pap., 25 c. Ogilvie.
Morehead, G: Story of François Villon. '01. '02(F15) 12°, (Peerless ser., no. 124.) pap., 25 c. Ogilvie.
Morfill, W. R. Hist. of Russia from Peter the Great to Nicholas II. '02(Mr15) 12°, $1.75. Pott.
Morgan, Alex. Advanced physiography. '01- '02(F8) il. D. $1.50. Longmans.
Morgan, C: Herbert. *See* Taylor, T: E.
Morgan, D: B: Twentieth century horse book; also a short treatise on cattle, swine, dogs and chickens. '02(Jl12) il. 8°, pap., $1.50. D: B: Morgan.
Morgan, Emily M. Flight of the *Swallow*. '02(Mr15) il. 12°, 50 c. Pott.
Morgan, J: L. R. Elements of physical chemistry. 2d ed., rev. and enl. '02(Mr8) 12°, $2. Wiley.
Morley, J:, *ed.* *See* English men of letters.
Morgan, Lewis H: League of the Ho-de-no-sau-nee or Iroquois. New ed.; ed. and annot. by H. M. Lloyd. '02(Jl19) 2 v., il. 8°, hand-made pap., **$15 net; Japan pap., $30 net. Dodd.
MORMONISM.
Lamb. The Mormons and their Bible. net, 25 c. Am. Bapt.

MORMONISM.—*Continued.*
Linn. Story of the Mormons. net, $4. Macmillan.

MOROCCO.
Grove. Seventy-one days' camping in Morocco. net, $2.50. Longmans.
Macnab. Ride in Morocco. $5. Longmans.

MORPHINISM.
Crothers. Morphinism and narcomania from opium, etc. $2. Saunders.

MORPHOLOGY.
See **Anatomy;—Embryology;—Histology.**

Morrill, W: W. *See* Am. electrical cases.

Morris, C: Marvelous achievements of the 19th century. 16th ed. '02(Ap5) il. sq. 8°, $2.50; hf. mor., $3.50. Winston.

Morris, C: Twentieth century encyclopædia. '01· '02(Ap5) il. 12°, $3.50; hf. mor., $4.25; mor., $5.50. Winston.

Morris, Clara, [*Mrs.* Harriott.] A pasteboard crown. '02(Je7) il. D. $1.50. Scribner.

Morris, E: P. On principles and methods in Latin syntax. '01. '02(F15) 8°, (Yale bicentennial pubs.) net, $2. Scribner.

Morris, Ella G. Right living; or, how a woman can get well and keep well. '02 (My17) 8°. $1. Bardeen.

Morris, Ida D., [*Mrs.* Ja. E. Morris.] Golden Fluff. '01· '02(Ja18) il. 12°, 50 c. Abbey Press.

Morris, Mowbray. Tales of the Spanish Main. '01. '02(Ja18) il. D. $2. Macmillan.

Morris, W: Art and craft of printing. '02 (Mr15) 8°, bds., $5. Elston Press.

Morrow, Rob. G., *rep. See* Oregon. *Sup. ct.* Repts.

Morse's geographical ser. il. 16°. Morse.
—Carroll. Around the world. 60 c.

Morse's new century ser. 12°. Morse.
—Thompson. New century readers. 3d bk: 52 c.

Mortimer, Alfr. G. Catholic faith and practice. 2 pts. 2d ed., rev. '01· '02(Mr8) O. pt. 1, $2; pt. 2, $2.50. Longmans.

Morton, H: H. Genito-urinary disease and syphilis. '02(Mr29) il. 12°, net, $3. Davis.

Morton, Victor. Thoughts on hell. '02(Mr8) 8°, net, 50 c. Herder.

Mosaics from India. Denning, M. net, $1.50. Revell.

Moser, Gustav v. Der bibliothekar; ed. by W: A. Cooper. '02(Mr8) D. 45 c. Am. Bk.

Moses, Montrose J. *See* Funk, I: K.

Mosher's vest-pocket ser. nar. S. T: B. Mosher.
—Stevenson. Æs triplex, and other essays. 25 c.-$1.

MOSQUITOES.
Berkeley. Lab'y work with mosquitoes. net, $1. Pediatrics Lab'y.
Ross. Mosquito brigades and how to organize them. net, 90 c. Longmans.

Mother Margaret's bunch of flowers. Quinius, A. 5 c. J: G. Quinius.

MOTHER-PLAY.
Proudfoot. A year with the Mother-play. $1. Flanagan.

MOTORS.
See **Cars;—Dynamos and motors.**

Moule, H. C. G. Thoughts for the Sundays of the year. '02(Mr8) 12°, net, $1. Revell.

Moulton, C: W., *and others, eds.* Library of literary criticism of Eng. and Am. authors. v. 3. '02(Mr1) O. $5; hf. mor., $6.50. Moulton Pub.

Moulton, *Mrs.* Louise C. Her baby brother. New ed. '01. '02(F15) 16°, (Children's friend ser.) bds., 50 c. Little, B. & Co.

MOUNDS.
Peterson. The mound building age in N. A. 25 c. Clarke.

Mount of Olives. Saltus, F. S. $1; net, 25 c. Bk. Lover.

Mountaineers. Smith, J: W. $1; $1.50; $2; $2.50. Pub. Ho. of M. E. Ch., So.

Movable quartette. Guyse, E. $1. Abbey Press.

Mower, C: D. How to build a knockabout. '02(Ap26) il. f°, ("How-to" ser.) $1. Rudder.

Mower, C: D. How to build a racing sloop. '02(F15) Q. ("How-to" ser.) $1. Rudder.

Mowry, Arth. M. First steps in the history of England. '02(Je21) il. D. 70 c. Silver.

Moy, Eocha. One: a song of the ages. '02 (Ap26) 12°, $1.50. Neely.

Mudge, G. P. Text-book of zoology. '01. '02(Mr8) D. $2.50. Longmans.

Mudge, Ja. Life of love. '02(F15) sq. T. (Little books on devotion.) 25 c. Jennings.

Muench, Friedrich. Gesammelte lechriften. '02(Je28) 8°, $1.75; mor., $2.50. Witter.

Muirhead, J. H. Philosophy and life, and other essays. '02(My24) 12°, $1.50. Macmillan.

Muirhead, Ja. F. America, the land of contrasts. New ed. '02(F22) 12°, net, $1.20. Lane.

Mulholland, Clara. Bunt and Bill. '02(Mr8) il. S. 45 c. Benziger.

Mullen, W: How to break, educate and handle the horse for the uses of every-day life. '02(F1) il. D. $1. W: Mullen.

Muller, Ma. Wretched Flea; story of a Chinese boy. '01· '02(Ja11) il. S. 35 c. Flanagan.

Mundy, W: N. Eclectic practice in diseases of children. '02(Je21) D. (Eclectic manual, no. 5.) net, $2.50. Scudder.

MUNICIPAL CORPORATIONS.
Michie, *ed.* Municipal corporation cases. v. 6. $5. Michie.

Municipal engineering and sanitation. Baker, M. N. net, $1.25. Macmillan.

MUNICIPAL GOVERNMENT.
Clow. Comparative study of the administration of city finances in the U. S. $1. Macmillan.

Munn, C: C. Rockhaven. '02(Mr29) il. D. $1.50. Lee & S.

Munro, J: Nociones de electricidad. '01· '02 (F22) 18°. 40 c. Appleton.

Munson, A. J. Making a country newspaper. '02(Mr22) 16°, $1. Dominion.

Munson, A: J. *See also* Halstead, M.

Murché, V. T. Rural readers; for senior classes. '02(Ap12) il. 12°, net, 40 c. Macmillan.

Murché, V. T. Teacher's manual of object lessons for rural schools. '02(Ap12) il. 12°, net, 60 c. Macmillan.

Murché, V. T. Teacher's manual of object lessons in geography. '02(Je28) il. 12°, net. 80 c. Macmillan.

Murders in the Rue Morgue. Poe, E. A. $1. Burt.
Murison, Ross G. Babylonia and Assyria. '01- '02(Ja11) 16°, (Bible class primers.) net. 20 c. Scribner.
Murlin, Edg. L. Illustrated legislative manual; New York red book. '02(My17) 12°, $1. Lyon.
Murphy, J: B., *ed.* General surgery. '01- '02(Mr8) il. D. (Practical medicine ser. of year-books, v. 2.) $1.50. Year Bk.
Murray, C: T. Mlle. Fouchette. '02(Mr15) il. D. $1.50. Lippincott.
MURRAY, Ja.
Tiffany *and* Lesley, *eds.* Letters of James Murray, loyalist. net, $2.50. W: B. Clarke.
Murray, Ja. A: H:, *and others, eds.* New Eng. dictionary. v. 3. pts. 30-33. '01- '02 (Mr22); pt. 34 (Ap19); v. 4. pt. 35 (Je7); pt. 36 (Je21) f°, pap., ea., 90 c. Oxford Univ.
Murray, W: Rough notes on remedies. 4th ed. '02(F15) 12°, net, $1.25. Blakiston.
Murrell, W: *See* Ewart, W:
Murrin, F. D. Vocal exercises on the vocal factors of expression. '02(My3) S. bds., net, 50 c. A. M. Allen.
MUSIC.
Crowest. Story of the art of music. **35 c. net. Appleton.
McLaughlin. Elements and notation of music. 55 c. Ginn.
Maitland. Music in England in the 19th century. net, $1.75. Dutton.
Paderewski, *ed.* Century lib. of music. v. 17-20. subs., ea., $2; $4. Century Co.
Wead. Cont. to the history of musical scales. 50 c. Woodward & L.
See also **Church music;—Musicians.**
MUSICAL INSTRUMENTS.
See **Trumpet.**
MUSICIANS.
Thomas, *ed.* Famous composers and their music. 16 v. (App. to pubs. for price.) Millet.
Young. Mastersingers. net, $1.50. Scribner.
Musick, W: L. Combination shorthand dictionary and reader. '02(Jl12) 12°, $1.50. W: L. Musick.
Musings by campfire and wayside. Gray, W: C. net, $1.50. Revell.
MUTINY.
See **Indian mutiny.**
Muzzey, D: S. Spiritual heroes. '02(My10) D. net, $1.25. Doubleday, P.
My captive. Altsheler, J. A. $1.25. Appleton.
My island. Hughes, E. $1.25. Dutton.
My Japanese wife. Holland, C. $1.50. Stokes.
My Lord Farquhar. Moore, T: E. $1.25. Abbey Press.
My ocean trip. Cadigan, E. S. $1. Brentano's.
My ten rod farm. Barnard, C: 40 c. Coates.
My trip to the Orient. Simmons, J. C. $1.50. Whitaker & R.
Myers, Alb. C. Quaker arrivals at Philadelphia, 1682-1750. '02(Jl19) 16°, $1.25. Ferris.
Myers, P. V. Mediæval and modern history. pt. 1, Middle Ages. [New rev. ed.] '02 (Jl5) D. $1.20. Ginn.

Myra of the Pines. Vielé, H. K. $1.50. McClure, P.
Mystery of St. Rubes. Heddle, E. F. $1.50. Scribner.
Mystery of the sea. Stoker, B. $1.50. Doubleday, P.
Mystic fortune teller, dream book, and policy player's guide. '02(My17) 12°, 50 c.: pap., 25 c. Donohue.
Mystic rose. Crawley, E. net, $4. Macmillan.
MYTHOLOGY.
Hale, *ed.* Greek myths in Eng. dress. 40 c. Globe Sch. Bk.
See also **Fairy tales.**
Naked truths and veiled allusions. Antrim, M. T. 50 c. Altemus.
Nameless hero. Anderson, J. B. net, $1. Wessels.
Nancy's Easter gift. Baldwin, M. 50 c. Abbey Press.
NANTUCKET ISLAND.
Bliss. September days on Nantucket. net, $1. Houghton, M. & Co.
Hinchman. Early settlers of Nantucket. $5. Ferris.
NAPOLEON I.
Fremeaux. With Napoleon at St. Helena. net, $1.50. Lane.
Headley. Napoleon and his marshals. $1. Burt.
Josselyn. The true Napoleon. net, $3.50. Russell.
Kennan, *comp. and tr.* Folk tales of Napoleon. *$1 net. Outlook.
Rose. Life of Napoleon I. 2 v. net, $4. Macmillan.
Sloane. Napoleon Bonaparte. 4 v. net, $18; net, $32. Century Co.
Watson. Napoleon. $2.25. Macmillan.
See also **Waterloo.**
Napoleon. Dumas, A. net, 50 c. Macmillan.
Napoleon's letters to Josephine, 1796-1812; notes by H: F. Hall. '02(Mr1) 8°, net, $3. Dutton.
Nash, Eliz. T. Fifty Puritan ancestors, 1628-1660. '02(Ap26) 8°, $5. Tuttle, M. & T.
Nash, J: J., *ed.* Practical explanation and application of Bible history; [for catechism teachers.] '02(Ap19) D. net, $1.50. Benziger.
Nason, Fk. L. To the end of the trail. '02 (My17) D. $1.50. Houghton, M. & Co.
National cyclopædia of Am. biography. v. 11. '01-'02(Je28) il. 8°, subs., $10. White.
NATIONAL HERBART SOC.
McMurry, *ed.* Pubs. of National Herbart Soc. *$5 net. Univ. of Chic.
National (The) list. Directory of bonded attorneys. '02(My24) F.; *Same.* Abr. ed. S. (App. to pubs. for price.) Nat. Surety.
National portrait gallery. *See* Cust, L., *ed.*
National reporter system. O. shp. West Pub.
—Atlantic reporter. v. 50, 51. ea., $4.
—Louisiana repts. v. 106. $8.
—New York supplement, v. 72-74. ea., $4.
—Northeastern reporter. v. 61, 62. ea., $4.
—Northwestern reporter. v. 88. $4.
—Pacific reporter. v. 66, 67. ea., $4.
—Pacific reporter. Digest. net, $6.
—Southeastern reporter. v 39, 40. ea., $4.
—Southern reporter. v. 30. $4.
—Southern reporter. Digest. net, $6.
—Southwestern reporter. v. 64-67. ea., $4.

National reporter system.—Continued.
—United States. Federal reporter. v. 110-113. ea., $3.50.
National Temperance almanac and teetotalers year-book, for 1902; also The Gothenburg system. '02(F1) S. pap., 10 c. Nat. Temp.
NATURAL HISTORY.
Cuppy, *ed.* Pictorial natural history. $1. Crowell & K.
Harmer *and* Shipley, *eds.* Cambridge natural history. v. 10. net, $4. Macmillan.
Pierson. Among the night people. net, $1. Dutton.
Roberts. Kindred of the wild. $2. L. C. Page.
See also Aquarium;—Botany;—Chemistry;—Evolution;—Geology; — Microscope; — Nature; — Paleontology;—Physical geography;—Science.
NATURAL RELIGION.
Conger. Religion for the time: six conferences on natural religion. net, $1. Jacobs.
James. Varieties of rel. experience; Gifford lectures on natural religion. net, $3.20. Longmans.
NATURALIZATION.
Pritchard, *comp.* How to become a naturalized citizen. 10 c. Wehman.
Naturalness of Christian life. Keedy, E: E. net, $1.25. Putnam.
NATURE.
Bailey. Nature portraits. (App. to pubs. for price.) Doubleday, P.
Batt. Treatment of nature in Germ. literature. net, $1. Univ. of Chic.
Carter. Gleanings from nature. $1. Abbey Press.
Emerson. Nature. $1. Burt.
Gray. Musings by camp-fire and wayside. net, $1.50. Revell.
Hodge. Nature study and life. $1.65. Ginn.
Miller. Brook book. net, $1.35. Doubleday, P.
Smith, C. W: Summer of Saturdays. 65 c. Gillan.
Talmage. Vacation with nature. net, $1. Funk.
Williams. Next to the ground. net, $1.20. McClure, P.
Nature and human nature. Emerson, *Mrs.* E. R. net, $1.25. Houghton, M. & Co.
Nature, myth and story. *See* Thompson, J: G.
Naughty Nan. Long, J: L. $1.50. Century Co.
Nauticus, *pseud.* The truth about the Schley case. '02(F22) D. pap., 25 c. Columbia.
NAVAL ART AND SCIENCE.
Brassey, *ed.* Naval annual, 1902. net, $7.50. Scribner.
Clowes, *and others.* Royal navy. v. 5, 6. ea., net, $6.50. Little, B. & Co.
Hamersly, *comp.* Records of living officers of the U. S. navy and marine corps. $10. Hamersly.
Maclay. Hist. of U. S. Navy. 3 v. ea., net, $3. Appleton.
Mets. Naval heroes of Holland. $1.50. Abbey Press.
NAVIGATION.
See Astronomy; — Canoeing; — Ship-building; — Voyages and travels.
Neal, W. G. *See* Hall, R. N.
Neale, J. M. Deeds of faith: stories for children. '02(Je7) 12°, 40 c. E. & J. B. Young.

Nearer East. Hogarth, D: G: $2. Appleton.
Nebraska. Law of probate and administration. (A. K. Dame.) '02(Jl5) O. shp., $7.50. Keefe-D.
Nebraska. Page's digest. vs. 1 to 60 of Neb. repts. In 2 v. v. 1. '02(My10); v. 2 (Je21) O. shp., (complete work,) $20. Bancroft-W.
Nebraska. *Supreme ct.* Repts. v. 61. (L. Herdman.) '02(My24) O. shp., $3. State Journ. Co.
NECK.
Eckley. Regional anatomy of head and neck. net, $2.50. Lea.
Needell, *Mrs.* Ma. A., [*Mrs.* J: H. Needell.] Unstable as water. '02(Jl5) D. $1.25. Warne.
Needham, A. C. *See* Hartmann, A.
Neel, Edith K. Cats, how to care for them. '02(My10) 12°, 50 c. Boericke & T.
Neff, Ma. L. Prescription writing in Latin or Eng. '01. '02(Mr1) 12°, 75 c. Davis.
Negatives of the Indo-European languages. Fowler, F. H. net, 50 c. Univ. of Chic.
NEGLIGENCE.
Dresser. Employers' liability, acts and assumption of risks in N. Y., Mass., Ind., Ala., Col., and England. $6. Keefe-D.
Gardner, *ed.* Am. negligence repts. v. 10. $5.50. Remick.
Hook. Am. neg. digest. $6.50. Remick.
Thompson. Commentaries on the law of negligence. v. 3. $6. Bowen-M.
NEGOTIABLE INSTRUMENTS.
Ames *and* Brewster. Negotiable instruments law. 30 c. Harvard Law.
Crawford. Negotiable instruments law. $2.50. Baker, V. & Co.
District of Columbia. Laws rel. to negotiable instruments. 20 c. Lowdermilk.
Pennsylvania. Negotiable instruments law. $2.50. Baker, V. & Co.
Selover. Law of negotiable instruments for N. Y., Mass., R. I., [etc.] $4. Keefe-D.
See also Commercial law;—Interest.
NEGROES.
Calhoun. The Caucasian and the negro in the U. S. 75 c. R. L. Bryan.
Schell. Is the negro a beast? 60 c. Gospel Trumpet.
Neidlinger, Dan. H., *and* Bobbett, Wa. The squirrel and the crow. '02(Jl12) 16°, hf. cl., 50 c. Rand, McN. & Co.
Neill, Maidie. Tennessee Lee. '02(Ap26) 12°, $1. Neely.
Neilson, Fs. Madame Bohemia. '02(Mr8) D. (Select novels.) $1; pap., 50 c. Lippincott.
Nell Gwyn. Morehead, G: 25 c. Ogilvie.
Nelson, Aven. Analytical key to some of the common flowering plants of the Rocky mountain region. '02(Jl12) D. (Twentieth century text-books.) **45 c. net. Appleton.
Nelson's Wall St. lib. il. S. $1.25. S: A. Nelson.
—Coffin. A B C of banks and banking. (v. 4.)
NERVOUS SYSTEM.
Ballance *and* Stewart. Healing of nerves. net, $4.50. Macmillan.
Hardesty. Neurological technique. net, $1.75. Univ. of Chic.
Nestlings of forest and marsh. Wheelock, *Mrs.* I. G. net, $1.40. McClurg.

NETHERLANDS.
Schiller. Hist. of the revolt of the Netherlands. (App. to pubs. for price.) Niccolls.
Nettleship, R: L. Lectures on the Republic of Plato; ed. by G. R. Benson. '01. '02 (Ja4) 8°, net, $2.75. Macmillan.
NEURASTHENIA.
Savill. Clinical lectures on neurasthenia. $1.50. Wood.
Neurological technique. Hardesty, I. net, $1.75. Univ. of Chic.
Neuroses of the genito-urinary system. Ultzmann, R. *$1 net. Davis.
New and living way. Terry, M. S. net, 50 c. Eaton & M.
New animal cellular therapy. Hawley, J. R. $1. Clinic.
New century lib. 12°, 1.25; $1.75. Nelson.
—Burns. Complete poetical works.
New century ser. 12°, 24 c. Morse.
—Parlin. Quincy word list.
New child's life of Christ. Stretton, H. $1. Winston.
NEW ENGLAND.
Dame *and* Brooks. Trees of N. E. $1.35. Ginn.
New England History Teachers' Assoc.; rept. by C: D. Hazen, E. G. Bourne and others. '02(Jl12) 12°, (Historical sources in schools ser.) **60 c. net. Macmillan.
New Hampshire. [*Supreme ct.*] Repts. (J. H. Riddell.) v. 70. '01. '02(My24) O. shp., $3.50. J: B. Clarke.
NEW HAMPSHIRE.
Hoyt. Practice in proceedings in probate cts. of N. H. $2.50. Rumford Press.
NEW HARMONY, Ind.
Lockwood. New Harmony communities. $2.50. Chronicle.
New hearthstone. Hurst, J: F. $1. Jennings.
New Jersey. General corporation act. Annots. and forms by J. B. Dill. 4th ed., with the amendments of 1902. '02(My17) O. pap., $1.50. New Jersey.
New Jersey. Laws rel. to corporations; with notes by Ja. B. Dill. '02(Je7) 8°, $3. Baker, V. & Co.
NEW JERSEY.
Parker, *comp.* New Jersey lawyers' diary, 1902. $1.50. Soney.
New Jersey orphans' court practice; with forms by C: F. Kocher. '02(Mr1) O. shp., $6. Soney.
New philosophy of health. Bradbury, H. B. 75 c. Alliance.
New songs for college glee clubs. '02(Mr15) 12°, pap., 50 c. Hinds.
NEW TESTAMENT.
See Bible.
NEW THOUGHT.
See Mental science.
New world and the new thought. Bixby, J. T. net, $1. Whittaker.
New York City standard guide. '01. '02 (Ja4) il. D. (Standard guide ser.) pap., 25 c. Foster & R.
New York City. Tenement house law and the building code. '02(Mr29) 12°, (Brooklyn Eagle lib., no. 62, v. 17, no. 3.) pap., 10 c. Brooklyn Eagle.
NEW YORK CITY.
Denton. Brief desc. of New York. *$1.50 net; $3 net. Burrows.

NEW YORK CITY.—*Continued.*
Fielde. Political primer of New York city and state. 75 c.; 50 c. League Pol. Educ.
Hemstreet. When old New York was young. net, $1.50. Scribner.
Medical directory, 1901. $1.50. Wynkoop.
Norton. Statistical studies in N. Y. money-market. net, $1.50; net, $1. Macmillan.
Social evil, with special ref. to conditions existing in New York. net, $1.25. Putnam.
See also Hall of fame;—Libraries.
New York. [State.] Abbott's cyclopedic digest of decisions of all the courts fr. the earliest time to 1900. (Blashfield.) v. 5. '01. '02(Ja18); v. 6 (Mr1); v. 7 (Ap5); v. 8 (My10); v. 9 (Jl5) O. shp., ea., $7.50. N. Y. Law.
New York. Amendments of the code of civil procedure, criminal procedure and penal code, 1902. '02(My24) O. pap., 50 c. Baker, V. & Co.
New York. Amendments of 1902. (A. J. Danaher.) '02(My24) O. pap., 50 c. Banks & Co.
New York. Amendments to Birdseye's revised statutes and general laws. '02(Jl19) pap., $2. Baker, V. & Co.
New York. Analyzed decisions and citations, 1897-1901, by Ja. G. Greene. '02(Je28) O. shp., $8.50. Williamson Law Bk.
New York civil and criminal justice. 3d ed. by F. S. Becker and E. D. Howe. '02 (My24) O. shp., $6.50. Williamson Law Bk.
New York. Code of civil procedure, as amended, 1902. '02(Je21) D. (Chase's pocket code.) flex. skiver, net, $3.50. Banks.
New York. Code of civil procedure, cont. amendments of 1902 by A. J. Parker, jr., rev. by A. J. Danaher. 2d ed. '02(My17) D. flex. skiver, $3.50. Banks & Co.
New York. Code of civil procedure; topical index. (J: C. Thomson.) 27th ed. '02 (Jl5) S. (Complete annot. pocket code.) flex. skiver, $3.50. H: B. Parsons.
New York. Code of criminal procedure. (L. R. Parker.) '02(Je7) D. flex. skiver, $1.50. Banks.
New York. Code of criminal procedure. 21st rev. ed. '02(Jl12) D. canvas, $2. Banks & Co.
New York. Code of criminal procedure and penal code. (Cook.) '02(My17) O. shp., net, $5. H: B. Parsons.
New York. *Ct. of appeals.* Analyzed citations, v. 2; by Ja. G. Greene. '01. '02 (Je28) pr. on one side of leaf, O. $2.50. Williamson Law Bk.
New York. *Ct. of appeals.* Digest of opinions of J: C. Gray. v. 108-164. (E. A. Bedell.) '01. '02(Mr8) Q. limp roan, $5. Lyon.
New York. *Ct. of appeals.* Digest of opinions of [A.] Haight. v. 114-164. '02(Mr8) Q. limp roan, $5. Lyon.
New York. *Ct. of appeals.* Digest of opinions of [D.] O'Brien. v. 119-164. '01. '02 (Mr8) Q. limp roan, $5. Lyon.
New York. *Ct. of appeals.* Digest of opinions of [I. G.] Vann. v. 114-v. 164. '01. '02(Mr8) Q. limp roan, $5. Lyon.

New York. *Ct. of appeals.* Repts. (J: T. Cook.) bk. 33. '02(Mr15) O. shp., $5. H: B. Parsons.
New York. *Cts. of record.* Misc. repts. v. 35. '01- '02(Mr1); v. 36 (Jl12) O. shp., ea., $2. Lyon.
New York. Criminal repts. (C: H. Mills.) v. 15. '02(Jl5) O. shp., $5.50. W. C. Little.
New York. Digest of statutes and repts. '02(Mr1) O. shp., $5. Baker, V. & Co.
New York. Digest of repts. and session laws. for 1901. '02(Mr1) O. shp., $4.50. Lyon.
New York. Highway law. 2d ed., by L. L. Boyce. '02(Jl5) O. shp., $4; Bender ed., pap., $1. M. Bender.
New York. Jewett's primary election law; with forms and complete index. '02(Jl5) O. pap., 50 c. M. Bender.
New York. Laws rel. to general, religious and non-business corporations, etc. 8th ed. '02(Jl12) O. canvas, $1.50; shp., $2. Banks & Co.
New York. Membership and religious corporations. '02(Jl12) O. $2.50; shp., $3. Banks & Co.
New York. Penal code. (L. R. Parker.) '02(Je7) D. flex. skiver, $1.50. Banks.
New York. Penal code. 21st rev. ed. '02 (Jl12) D. canvas, $2. Banks & Co.
New York. Penal code. 16th ed. (C. D. Rust.) '02(Jl5) D. flex. im. alligator, $3.50. M. Bender.
New York. Statutory revision of the laws affecting banks, banking and trust companies 1892. (Hamilton.) '02(My24) O. pap., $1.50. Banks & Co.
New York. Statutory revision of the laws affecting insurance companies. (Hamilton.) '02(Je14) O. pap., $1.50. Banks & Co.
New York. Statutory revision of the laws affecting misc. corporations. (Hamilton.) '02(Je14) O. pap., $1.50. Banks & Co.
New York. Statutory revision of the laws affecting railroads. (Hamilton.) '02(Jl12) O. $2; pap., $1.50. Banks & Co.
New York supplement, v. 72. '02(F1); v. 73 (Ap5); v. 74 (Je14); v. 75 (Jl5) O. (Nat. reporter system.) shp., ea., $4. West Pub.
New York. Supp. to the general laws and revised statutes; comp. by E: L. Heydecker. '02(Jl19) O. pap., $2. M. Bender.
New York. *Supreme ct.* Repts. (Hun.) vs. 62, 63. Off. ed. '01. '02(Ja4); v. 65, 66 (Ap5); v. 67 (Ap19) O. shp., ea., net, $3. Lyon.
New York. *Surrogates' cts.* Repts.; with annots., by J: Power. '01- '02(F1) O. shp., $5.50. W. C. Little.
New York. Tax law of 1896, with index and amend. to date. (A. Hamilton.) '02(Je7) O. pap., 50 c. Banks & Co.
New York. Tax law, with amendments of 1897-1902. Bender ed. '02(Je28) O. pap., 50 c. M. Bender.
New York. Village laws, 1902. (Cumming and Gilbert.) '02(Jl5) O. shp., $3. M. Bender.

NEW YORK.
Anderson *and* Flick. Short hist. of state of N. Y. $1. Maynard, M. & Co.
Beach. First N. Y. (Lincoln) cavalry, Ap. 19, 1861-July 7, 1865. *$2.50 net. [Caspar] Lincoln Cavalry.

NEW YORK.—*Continued.*
Jewett, *comp.* Manual for election officers and voters. $2; $1.50. M. Bender.
Murlin. Il. legislative manual; the N. Y. red book. $1. Lyon.
Purdy. Local option in taxation; with a draft of act to amend tax law. 10 c. N. Y. Tax Reform.
Redfield, *ed.* Repts. Surrogates' cts. v. 1. $6. Banks & Co.
Rumsey. Practice in civil actions in cts. of record in N. Y. v. 1. $6. Banks & Co.
Tarr. Physical geography of N. Y.; with chap. on climate. net, $3.50. Macmillan.
Wait. Law and practice in civil actions, [etc.] in N. Y. v. 1. $6.35; per set, $19. M. Bender.

New York Evening Post: hundredth anniversary number, Nov. 16, 1801-1901. '02 (My17) il. sq. O. $1. N. Y. Eve. Post.
New York Library Club. Libraries of Greater New York. '02(My17) D. net, 75 c.; pap., net, 50 c. Stechert.
Newberry, Fannie E. Bubbles. '02(Mr29) il. 12°, (Fireside ser.) $1. Burt.
Newberry, Fannie E. Comrades. '02(Mr29) il. 12°, (St. Nicholas ser.) 75 c. Burt.
Newberry, Fannie E. Joyce's investments. '02(Mr29) il. 12°, (Fireside ser.) $1. Burt.
Newberry, Fannie E. Sara: a princess. '02 (Mr29) il. 12°, (Fireside ser.) $1. Burt.
Newberry gospels. Goodspeed, E. J. net, 25 c. Univ. of Chic.

NEWBURG, Vt.
Wells. Hist. of Newburg. $2.25; $3; $3.50; $4. Caledonian.

Newcomb, Harry T. Concentration of railway control. '02(Mr22) 8°, (Pub. of the soc., no. 328.) pap., 15 c. Am. Acad. Pol. Sci.
Newcomes. *See* Thackeray, W: M.
Newell, F: H. Irrigation in the U. S. '02 (Mr8) D. net, $2. Crowell.
Newell, Grant. Elements of the law of real property. '02(Mr1) O. shp., $4. Flood.
Newell, Martin L., *rep.* *See* Illinois. *Appellate cts.* Repts.
Newell, Wilbur C. The life worth living. '02 (My3) il. D. $1. Abbey Press.
Newman, A. H:, *ed.* Century of Baptist achievements. '01- '02(F15) 12°, net, $1.50. Am. Bapt.
Newman, J: H: Definition of a gentleman; [repr.] '02(Mr1) sq. 12°, bds., $1; pap., 50 c. Kirgate Press.
Newman, J: H: Lives of the Eng. saints. '01- '02(Mr1) 6 v., il. 12°, net, $12. Lippincott.

NEWMAN, J: H:
Waller *and* Barrow. John Henry, Cardinal Newman. 75 c. Small.
Whyte. Newman. net, $1.10. Longmans.

Newson's Germ. opera texts. 16°. Newson.
—Wagner. Rheingold. 75 c. (1.)

NEWSPAPERS.
Munson. Making a country newspaper. $1. Dominion.

Next great awakening. Strong, J. 75 c. Baker & T.
Next to the ground. Williams, M. M. net, $1.20. McClure, P.

NIAGARA FALLS.
Bishop. Red book of Niagara. 25 c. Wenborne-S.

NICARAGUA.
Walker. Ocean to ocean: acc. of Nicaragua. net, $1.25. McClurg.

Nichols, E: L. The galvanometer. '02(Mr8) il. 8°, $1. Spon.

Nichols, Fs. M. *See* Britton.

Nicholson, T:, *and* Woods, C: C. Notes on Epworth League prayer meeting topics. 1st ser. '02(Ja25) S. pap., 15 c. Eaton & M.

Nicoll, W: R. The church's one foundation, Christ and recent criticism. '01· '02(F1) D. $1.25. Armstrong.

Nicolls, W: J. Graystone. '02(Mr15) il. D. $1.50. Lippincott.

Niebuhr, B. G. Greek hero stories. New ed. '01· '02(F22) 16°, $1. Dodd.

Nield, J. Guide to the best historical novels and tales. '02(Je21) O. net, $1.75. Putnam.

Nies, Konrad. Deutsche Gaben. '02(Je28) 8°, pap., 25 c. Witter.

Nies, Konrad. Rosen im Schnee. '02(Je28) 8°, pap., 50 c. Witter.

NINETEENTH CENTURY.
Hodder. Life of a century. net, $4. Scribner.
Morris. Marvelous achievements of the 19th century. $2.50; $3.50. Winston.

Nineteenth-century crusader. Locke, C: E: 25 c. Jennings.

Nitzsche, G: E., *comp.* University of Penn.: proceedings at the dedication of the new building of the Dept. of Law, Feb. 21, 22, 1900. '01· '02(Ap26) il. O. $3; hf. mor., $3.50. Univ. of Penn.

Nixon, J. H. Beyond the vail: a comp. of narrations and il. of spirit experiences. '01· '02(Mr22) il. 8°, $1.75. Hudson-K.

Noble, Alden C: Lyrics to the queen. '02 (Je14) sq. S. pap., n. p. Blue Sky Press.

Noble, Alfr., *and* Casgrain, W: T. Tables for obtaining horizontal distances and difference of level, from stadia readings. '02 (Jl12) 12°, $1. Engineering News.

Nociones de botánica. Hooker, *Sir* J. D. 40 c. Appleton.

NOME.
McKee. Land of Nome. net, $1.25. Grafton Press.

Nominating systems. Meyer, E. C. net, $1.50. E. C. Meyer.

None but the brave. Sears, H. $1.50. Dodd.

Nonne's preeste's tale. Chaucer, G. $6.50; $16.50. Grafton Press.

Nonsense for old and young. Field, E. 50 c. Dickerman.

Nordenskiold, G. The cliff dwellers of the Mesa Verde, southwestern Colo. [also] Human remains from the cliff dwellings of the Mesa Verde, by G. Retzius. '01· '02 (Ja25) f°. net, $20. Stechert.

Nordhoff guild, Washington, D. C. Cook book. '02(Jl5) 12°, pap., 25 c. McGill.

Norris, W: E: Credit of the county. '02 (Jl19) D. (Town and country lib., no. 313.) †$1: pap., 50 c. Appleton.

Norris, Zoe A. Color of the soul. '02(F1) nar. D. bds., net, $1. Funk.

North, Ingolsby. Love letters and how to write them. '02(My17) 12°, 50 c.; pap., 25 c. Donohue.

North, Ingoldsby. Love letters and how to write them. '02(Mr15) S. pap., 25 c. Drake.

North Carolina regimental histories, 1861-'65; ed. and written by participants in the war. '02(Jl12) 5 v., 12°, $5; per v., $1. M. O. Sherrell.

North Dakota. *Supreme ct.* Repts. (J: M. Cochrane.) v. 10. '02(Jl19) O. shp., $4.25. Grand Forks Herald.

North Dakota. Township manual; by W. S. Booth. 6th ed. '01. '02(F8) D. pap., 75 c. Booth.

Northcote, Stafford H: *See* St. Cyres, *Viscount.*

Northeastern reporter, v. 61. '02(Mr1); v. 62 (My10) O. (Nat. reporter system, state ser.) shp., ea., $4. West Pub.

Northern Europe. '02(Mr22) il. D. (Youth's Companion ser., no. 2.) 30 c. Ginn.

Northrup, A. J., *ed.* Early records of the First Presbyterian Church of Syracuse, N. Y. '02(Ap5) O. pap., 50 c. [Gill] Genealog. Soc.

Northrup, W: P., *ed.* Diphtheria [*also*] measles, scarlatina, German measles, by T. von Jurgensen. '02(Je28) il. 8°, (Nothnagel's encyc. of practical medicine, Am. ed., v. 3.) net, $5; shp. or hf. mor., $6. Saunders.

Northwestern reporter, v. 88. '02(Ap5); v. 89 (Jl5) O. (Nat. reporter system, state ser.) shp., ea., $4. West Pub.

Norton, J: P. Statistical studies in New York money-market. '02(My24) net, $1.50; pap., net, $1. Macmillan.

NORWAY.
Spender. Two winters in Norway. $4. Longmans.
Weborg. In Viking land. $1.25. J. C. Weborg.

NOSE.
Gradle. Diseases of the nose, pharynx and ear. net, $3.50. Saunders.
Turner. Accessory sinuses of the nose. $4. Longmans.
Wood, *and others, eds.* Eye, ear, nose and throat. $1.50. Year Bk.

Not on the chart. Marsh, C: L. $1.50. Stokes.

NOTARIES.
Smith. Texas notarial manual and form book. $4. Gammel.
Snyder. Notaries' and commissioners' manual. $1.50. Baker, V. & Co.

Nothnagel's encyclopedia of practical medicine. il. 8°, net, $5; hf. mor., $6. Saunders.
—Moore, *ed.* Variola, vaccination, etc. (2.)
—Northrup, *ed.* Diphtheria, measles, scarlatina, German measles. (3.)
—Osler, *ed.* Typhoid and typhus fevers. (1.)

Notre Dame de Paris. Hugo, V. 85 c. Ginn.

Novene zu Ehren des Heiligen Geistes. New ed. '02(Je28) 32°, pap., net, 3 c. Herder.

Novey, F. G. *See* Vaughan, V. C.

Noyes, C: J. Patriot and Tory. '02(Mr29) il. D. $1.50. Dickerman.

Nugent, Paul C. Plane surveying. '02(Ap5) il. 8°, $3.50. Wiley.

Nuggets ser. T. 45 c.; leath., $1. Fords.
—Pennington, *comp.* Good cheer nuggets

Nürnberg stove. *See* La Rame, L. de.

NURSES AND NURSING.
Hadley. Nursing; app. on sick-room cookery. net, $1.25. Blakiston.
Jewett. Childbed nursing. 80 c. Treat.
See also Accidents;—Diet;—Hospitals.
Nuverbis, [*pseud.* for Dillon Jordan Spotswood.] Out of the beaten track. '02(Mr22) D. $1. Abbey Press.
Nymph's reply to the shepherd. *See* Marlowe, C.

OBSTETRICS.
See Midwifery.
O'Byrne, W. L. Kings and vikings. '02 (Ap12) 12°, $1.25. Scribner.
O'Byrne, W. L. Land of heroes: Irish history. '02(Ap12) 12°, $1.25. Scribner.

OCCULTISM.
Demorest, *ed.* Cambridge encyclo. of esoteric subjects. v. 3. net, $3. Cambridge.

OCEAN.
See Seashore.
Ocean to ocean. Walker, J. W. G. net, $1.25. McClurg.
O'Connor, D. M. Foreign freemasonry. '02 (F1) S. pap., 5 c. Kilner.
O'Conor, M. Irish come-all-ye's and old-time songs and ballads of Ireland. '01. '02 (Ja4) 4°, pap., 25 c. Popular.
O'Conor, M., *comp.* Old-time songs and ballads of Ireland. '02(Ja25) O. $2. Popular.

ODD-FELLOWS.
Monroe Rebekah Lodge: semi-centennial, Jan. 23, 1902. 10 c. Darrow.
Odenheimer, Cordelia P. Phantom caravan. '01. '02(F15) D. $1. Abbey Press.
Oertel, Hanns. Lectures on the study of language. '01. '02(Mr15) 8°, (Yale bicentennial pub.) net, $3. Scribner.
Ogilvie, Rob. Horæ Latinæ: synonyms and syntax; ed. by A. Souter. '01. '02(F8) O. $5. Longmans.
O'Growney, Eug. Revised simple lessons in Irish. pt. 1. '02(Mr15) D. pap., 15 c. Gael.
Ohio. *Cts. of record.* Repts. v. 10, 11. '01. '02(My10) O. shp., ea., $2.50. Laning.
Ohio. *Superior ct. of Cincinnati.* Repts. fr. 1854 to 1857; repr. '02(Jl12) O. (O. decisions ser.) shp., $7.50. Laning.
Ohio. *Supreme ct.* Repts. v. 64. '01. '02 (My10) O. shp., 2.50. Laning.

OHIO.
Wilson. Ohio. net, 30 c. Macmillan.

OHIO VALLEY.
Piatt. Hesperian tree. $2. J: Scott.

OLD AGE.
Ames. Prevention and cure of old age. 50 c. Kirk.
Old Blackfriars. Marshall, B. $1.50. Dutton.
Old diaries. Gower, R. S. net, $4.50. Scribner.
Old English ballads. Kinard, J. P. 40 c. Silver.
Old English plate. Cripps, W. J. net, $13.50. Scribner.
Old glory and the gospel in the Philippines. Condict, A. B. net, 75 c. Revell.
Old Indian legends. Zitkala-sa. 50 c. Ginn.
Old, old fairy tales. Valentine, *Mrs.* L. J. $1. Burt.
Old South leaflets. v. 5. nos. 101-125. '02 (My17) D. $1.50. Old South Work.
Old world wonder stories. O'Shea, M. V. 25 c. Heath.
Oldfield. Banks, N. H. $1.50. Macmillan.
Oliver, G. F. Our lay office-bearers. '01. '02(Ja4) sq. D. (Little books on practice.) net, 25 c. Jennings.
Oliver, G. F. Soul-winners' secrets: revival text-book. '02(F8) sq T. (Little books on practice.) 25 c. Jennings.
Oliver, T., *ed.* Dangerous trades; aspects of industrial occupations as affecting public health. '02(Jl19) 8°, *$8 net. Duton.
Olmsted, Everett W., *ed.* *See* Marivaux, P. C. de C. de.
Olympian nights. Bangs, J: K. $1.25. Harper
Omar Khayyám. Rubaiyat. '02(F15) 12°, net, $1.50. Lane.
Omar Khayyám. Rubaiyat. '02(My3) il. 16°, 60 c.; leath., $1. Macmillan.
Omar Khayyám. Rubáiyát. (Fitzgerald.) privately pr. for N. H. Dole. '01. '02(Mr1) 8°, charcoal pap., $10; vellum, $25. Merrymount Press.
Omar Khayyam, *jr., pseud.* *See* Irwin, W.
On the sensitiveness of the coherer. Wolcott, E. R. 20 c. Univ. of Wis.
Once upon a time. Aulnoy, M. C. J. de B. *Comtesse d'.* 50 c. Little, B. & Co.
One: a song of the ages. Moy, E. $1.50. Neely.
One before (The). Pain, B. †$1.25. Scribner.
One of the craft, *pseud.* *See* Schofield, R. J.
One thousand ways to make money. Gilbert F. $1. Donohue.
One world at a time. Slicer, T: R. net, $1.35. Putnam.
Onlooker's note-book. Russell, G: W: E. $2.25. Harper.

ONTOLOGY.
Swedenborg. Ontology. 50 c. Mass. New-Ch. Un.
Openings in the old trail. Harte, F. B. $1.25. Houghton, M. & Co.

OPHTHALMOLOGY.
See Eye.

OPIUM.
See Morphinism.
Oppenheim, E. P. Enoch Strone. '02(Mr29) D. $1.50. G: W. Dillingham.
Oppenheim, N. Mental growth and control. '02(F15) 12°, (Personal problem ser.) net, $1. Macmillan.
Oppenheimer, C., *and* Mitchell, C. A. Ferments and their actions. '01. '02(F15) 12°, net, $2.50. Lippincott.
Opponents (The). Robertson, H. $1.50. Scribner.
Opportunist (The). Mitton, G. E. $2. Macmillan.
Optic, Oliver, *pseud.* *See* Adams, W: T.
Optical rotating power of organic substances. Landolt, H. H. *$7.50 net. Chemical.

OPTICS.
Drude. Theory of optics. $4. Longmans.
See also Eye;—Light.

ORATIONS.
See Recitations.

ORATORS AND ORATORY.
Esenwein. How to attract and hold an audience. $1. Hinds.
See also Debates.

ORCHIDS.
Boyle. Woodland orchids. net, $7. Macmillan.
White. Book of orchids. *$1 net. Lane.
ORDINATION.
Stubbs. Ordination addresses. $2.25. Longmans.
Oregon. Mining laws. 2d ed. '01. '02(F1) D. pap., 40 c. Or. Mining Journ.
Oregon. *Supreme ct.* Repts. (R. G. Morrow.) v. 38. '01. '02(Ja4): v. 39 (Je7) O. shp., ea., $5. Leeds.
O'Rell, Max, *pseud.* *See* Blouët, P.
ORES.
See Metals and metallurgy;—Mines and mining.
ORIENT.
Simmons. My trip to the Orient. $1.50. Whitaker & R.
ORIENTAL CLUB.
Baillie. Oriental Club and Hanover Square. $9. Longmans.
ORIENTAL RELIGIONS.
Conway, *comp.* Sacred anthology (oriental). $2. Holt.
Oriental ser. *See* Millet's.
Ormsby, Fk. E., *ed.* *See* Planets and people.
ORPHANS.
New Jersey orphans' court practice; with forms. $6. Soney.
Orphean tragedy. Creamer, E: S. $1. Abbey Press.
Orr, Ja. Progress of dogma: Elliott lectures. '01. '02(F1) O. $1.75. Armstrong.
Orthodontis. MacDowell, J. N. net, $4. Colegrove.
O'Shea, M. V., *ed.* Old world wonder stories. '02(F8) il. D. (Home and school classics.) 25 c. Heath.
Osler, W:, *ed.* Typhoid and typhus fevers, by H. Curschmann. Am. ed. '02(Mr29) il. 8°, (Nothnagel's encyclopedia of practical medicine, no. 1.) net, $5; hf. mor., $6. Saunders.
Ostwald, Wilhelm. Principles of inorganic chemistry; tr. by A. Findlay. '02(Je7) 8°. net, $6. Macmillan.
Oswald, Felix. Vaccination a crime. '02 (My17) 8°, pap., 10 c. Physical Culture.
Other notes. Hinton, M. B. $1. Neale.
Otis, James, *pseud.* *See* Kaler, J. O.
Otis Grey, bachelor. J., C. J. 75 c. Mutual Bk.
OTOLOGY.
See Ear.
Oudin, Maurice A. Standard polyphase apparatus and systems. 3d ed., rev. '02(My3) il. O. $3. Van Nostrand.
Ouida, *pseud.* *See* La Rame, L. de.
Our attitude toward Eng. Roman Catholics. Galton, A. net, $1. Dutton.
Our country's story. Tappan, E. M. 65 c. Houghton, M. & Co.
Our European neighbors ser. il. D. net, $1.20. Putnam.
—Higgin. Spanish life in town and country. (6.)
—Story. Swiss life in town and country. (5.)
Our lay office-bearers. Oliver, G. F. net, 25 c. Jennings.
Our literary deluge. Halsey, F. W. net, $1.25. Doubleday, P.
Our Lysander. Kellogg, A. M. 15 c. Kellogg.
Our risen King's forty days. Boardman, G: D. net, $1.25. Lippincott.
Our sixty-six sacred books. Rice, E. W. net, 50 c. Am. S. S.
Out among the animals. Malone, *Mrs.* E. W. 75 c. Pub. Ho. M. E. Ch., So.
Out of the beaten track. Nuverbis, *pseud.* $1. Abbey Press.
Outlaws. Armstrong, L. $1.25. Appleton.
Outre mer. Longfellow, H: W. $1. Burt.
Ovenden, C. T. To whom shall we go? '02 (Je7) 16°, $1. E. & J. B. Young.
Overland stage to California. Root, F. A. $2.50; $3.50. Root & C.
Overton, Ja. B. Parthenogenesis in thalictrum purpurascens. '02(Je14) 8°, (Cont. from the Hull Botanical Laboratory, no. 35.) pap., net, 25 c. Univ. of Chic.
Ovid. Amorum libri tres. '02(Je28) il. 12°, (Antique gems from the Gr. and Latin, v. 6.) (Apply to pubs. for price.) Barrie.
Owens College. *See* Tout, T: F:
Oxenford, Ina, *and* Alpheus, A., *pseud.* Complete palmist. '02(My17) 12°, 50 c.; pap., 25 c. Donohue.
Oxford lib. of practical theology. D. $1.50. Longmans.
—Worlledge. Prayer.
OXFORD UNIVERSITY.
Corbin. An American at Oxford. net, $1.50. Houghton, M. & Co.
PACIFIC OCEAN.
Colquhoun. Mastery of the Pacific. net, $4. Macmillan.
Helmolt, *and others, eds.* Hist. of the world. v. 1, America and Pacific ocean. $6. Dodd.
Pacific reporter, v. 66. '02(Mr1); v. 67(Je7) O. (Nat. reporter system, state ser.) shp., ea., $4. West Pub.
Pacific reporter. Digest of decisions. '02 (Mr8) O. (Nat. reporter system digests, Pacific ser., v. 3.) shp., net, $6. West Pub.
Pacific trail campfires. Kendall, R. P. $1.50. Scroll Pub.
Paderewski, I. J., *ed.* Century lib. of music. v. 17, 18. '02(Mr15); v. 19, 20 (Ap5) il., with music, f°, subs., per v., $2; hf. mor., $4. Century Co.
Pagan's cup. Hume, F. W. $1.25. G: W. Dillingham.
Page, Ernest Clifford. *See* Nebraska digest.
Page, Kate N. Tommy Atkins episode, and other stories. '02(Jl19) D. $1. Abbey Press.
Page, Wa. H. Rebuilding of old commonwealths. '02(Je7) D. net, $1. Doubleday, P.
Paget, *Sir* Ja. Selected essays and addresses; ed. by S. Paget. '02(Ap19) O. $5. Longmans.
Pain, Barry. The one before. '02(Jl12) il. D. †$1.25. Scribner.
PAINT.
Church. Chemistry of paints and painting. $3. Macmillan.
PAINTERS.
Caffin. American masters of painting. net, $1.25. Doubleday, P.
Dallin. Sketches of great painters for young people. 90 c. Silver.
Roulet. St. Anthony in art, and other sketches. $2. Marlier.
See also Artists.

PAINTING.
Van Dyke. Italian painting. 50 c. Elson.
See also Painters.
Palache, C: *See* Lawson, A. C.
PALEONTOLOGY.
Case. Palæontological notes. *25 c. net. Univ. of Chic.
See also Geology.
PALESTINE.
Babcock. Letters from Egypt and Palestine. net, $1. Scribner.
Guide to Palestine and Egypt. net, $3.25. Macmillan.
Palgrave, Ma. E. Mary Rich, Countess of Warwick, 1625-1678. '02(F15) 12°, net, $1.50. Dutton.
Palladino, L. B. Mary our mother. '02 (Je14) 12°, pap., net, 15 c. Herder.
Palliser, *Mrs.* Bury. History of lace. New ed., rev., rewritten and enl., by M. Jourdain and A. Dryden. '02(Mr8) 8°, net, $12. Scribner.
Palmer, B. M. Threefold fellowship and the threefold assurance. '02(Mr29) O. 75 c. Presb. Pub.
Palmer, *Mrs.* Minnie. Woman's exchange cook book. '01· '02(Ap26) il. 8°, 70 c. Conkey.
PALMISTRY.
Oxenford *and* Alpheus. Complete palmist. 50 c.; 25 c. Donohue.
Pan-American ser. il. D. net, $1. Lee & S.
—Stratemeyer. Lost on the Orinoco. (1.)
PANAMA CANAL.
Johnson. Isthmian canal. 25 c. Am. Acad. Pol. Sci.
Pasco. Isthmian canal question as affected by treaties and concessions. 25 c. Am. Acad. Pol. Sci.
Sonderegger. L' achèvement du canal de Panama. $2.50. Stechert.
Pangborn, Georgia W. Roman Biznet. '02 (My3) il. D. $1.50. Houghton, M. & Co.
Pansy, *pseud.* *See* Alden, *Mrs.* I. M.
Paolo and Francesca. Phillips, S. net, $1.25. Lane.
PAOTINGFU, China.
Ketler. Tragedy of Paotingfu. net, $2. Revell.
PARABLES.
Dods. Parables of our Lord. $1.50. Whittaker.
Parables of life. Mabie, H. W. net, $1. Outlook.
Paret, W: Reality in holy communion. '02 (Ap12) 16°, pap., 10 c. Whittaker.
PARIS.
Halstead. Splendors of Paris and glories of her exposition. $1.50. Dominion.
Visitors' guide to Paris. 10 c. Brooklyn Eagle.
Walton. Paris from the earliest period to the present day. v. 6. $3. Barrie.
Parker, Amasa J., *jr.* *See* New York. Code of civil procedure.
Parker, Arnold. Ping-pong: [table tennis.] '02(Mr15) il. D. net, 75 c. Putnam.
Parker, Arnold. *See also* Ritchie, M. G.
Parker, C: W., *comp.* New Jersey lawyers' diary and bar directory, 1902. '02(Ja18) O. $1.50. Soney.
Parker, E. H. John Chinaman, and a few others. '02(Mr8) 12°, $2.50. Dutton.
Parker, Lewis R., *ed.* *See* New York. Codes.

Parkman, Fs. Writings. La Salle ed., incl. life of Parkman by C: H. Farnham. '02 (Mr22) 20 v., il. 8°, subs., per v., net, $5; ¾ lev. mor., per v., net, $10. Little, B. & Co.
Parkman, Fs. Conspiracy of Pontiac. '02 (Je14) 12°, (Home lib.) $1. Burt.
Parks, Ella M. Mary of Bethany. '02(Jl5) 16°, 25 c.; pap., 15 c. Pepper.
PARLIAMENTARY LAW.
Fox. Parliamentary usage for women's clubs. net, 65 c. Baker & T.
Henry. How to organize and conduct a meeting. 75 c. Hinds.
Sherman. Parliamentary law at a glance. 75 c. H: O. Shepard.
Stevens. Am. law of assemblies. net, $1. E: A. Stevens.
Vancil. School congress. 25 c. Kellogg.
Parlin, Fk. E. Quincy word list, rev. and enl. [4th ed.] '02(Jl12) 12°, (New century ser.) 24 c. Morse.
PARODY.
Dustin. The make good book of parodies. 50 c. E. Dustin.
Parr, G. D. A. Electrical engineering testing. '02(Ap19) il. 8°, net, $3.50. Van Nostrand.
Parson's handbook (The); cont. directions as to the management of the parish church and its services as set forth in the "Book of common prayer." 4th ed., rewritten and enl. '02(My10) 12°, net, $1.50. Young Churchman.
Parsons, *Mrs.* Fs. T. According to season. New enl. ed. '02(Mr22) il. D. net, $1.75. Scribner.
Parsons, J. H. Elementary ophthalmic optics. '01. '02(Ja11) 12°, net, $2. Blakiston.
Parthenogenesis in thalictrum purpurascens. Overton, J. B. net, 25 c. Univ. of Chic.
PARTIES (*political*).
See Indiana.
Partridge, W: O. Nathan Hale, the ideal patriot. '02(My17) D. net, $1. Funk.
Pasco, S: Isthmian canal question as affected by treaties and concessions. '02 (Mr22) 8°, (Pub. of the soc., no. 324.) pap., 25 c. Am. Acad. Pol. Sci.
Pascoe, C: E. Pageant and ceremony of the coronation of their majesties King Edward the seventh and Queen Alexandra. '02 (My3) il. D. net, $1.40. Appleton.
Passenger traffic of railways. Weyl, W. E. $1.50; $1. Ginn.
Passing world. Belloc, B. R. net, $1.25. Herder.
Passion flowers. Watson, *Mrs.* A. R. $1.60. Whittet.
Passionate shepherd to his love. Marlowe, C. net, $3.75. Russell.
Past and present. Carlyle, T: 50 c.; 75 c. Macmillan.
Past and present of Japanese commerce. Kinosita, Y. *$1.50 net. Macmillan.
Pasteboard crown. Morris, C. $1.50. Scribner.
Paston, G:, [*pseud. for* E. M. Symonds.] Little memoirs of the nineteenth century. '02(Ap5) il. 8°, net, $3. Dutton.
Pastor Agnorum. Skrine, J: H. net, $1.60. Longmans.
Pastor and the Sunday-school. Hatcher, W: E. 75 c. Bapt. S. S. Bd.

Pastoral epistles. Lilley, J. P. net, 75 c. Scribner.

PATENTS.
Cresee. Pointers for patentees. $1. Munn.

Pater, Wa. H. Marius the epicurean. '02 (Je14) 12°, (Home lib.) $1. Burt.

Paterson, W: R., ["Benjamin Swift."] Game of love. '02(Ap12) D. $1.50. Scribner.

Path to Rome. Belloc, H. net, $2. Longmans.

PATHOLOGY.
Herter. Lectures on chemical pathology. net, $1.75. Lea.
Thayer. Compend of general pathology. 80 c.; $1. Blakiston.
Trudeau. Torture of the clinic. $1; 50 c. Bourguignon.
See also Diphtheria;—Ear;—Eye;—Gallstone;—Hair;—Histology;—Hygiene;—Insanity;—Malarial fever;—Nose;—Skin;—Throat;—Typhoid fever;—Urine and urinary organs;—Variola.

Paths to power. Wilson, F. B. $1. Fenno.

Patoma, Fk. The Venus di Milo. '02(Je7) 12°, 50 c. Cambridge.

Patricia of the hills. Burrow, C: K. net, $1.20. Putnam.

PATRICK, *St.*
Sanderson. Story of Saint Patrick; emb. sketch of Ireland. $1.50. Ketcham.

Patrick, J. N. Psychology for teachers. '02 (My3) D. hf. leath., $1. Educ. Pub.

Patriot and Tory. Noyes, C: J. $1.50. Dickerman.

Patristic study. Swete, H: B. net, 90 c. Longmans.

Pattee, F. L. Mary Garvin. '02(Ap5) il. D. $1.50. Crowell.

Pattee, W: S., *comp.* Authorities, reductions, and notes in real property. '02 (My24) O. shp., $2. Univ. Press.

Patten, S. N. Theory of prosperity. '02(F1) 12°, net, $1.25. Macmillan.

Patten, S. N. *See also* Seager, H: R.

Patterson, Alex. Broader Bible study. The Pentateuch. '02(Ap26) D. net, 75 c. Jacobs.

Patterson, C: B. Beyond the clouds. New issue. '02(Mr22) O. $1. Alliance.

Patterson, C: B. What the new thought stands for. '01. '02(Mr22) S. pap., 10 c. Alliance.

Patterson, C: B. The will to be well. '01. '02(Mr22) nar. O. $1. Alliance.

Patterson, Melvin J. *See* Fisher, A. T.

Patterson, Virginia S. Dickey Downy. Phœnix ed. '02(Ap5) S. 25 c. A. J. Rowland.

Pattison, Everett W. Instructions in criminal cases passed upon by the cts. of Missouri. '02(My24) O shp., $5. Gilbert Bk.

Pattison, T. H. The Bible and the twentieth century. '02(Mr22) D. pap., 10 c. Am. Bapt.

Patton, Abel. "Har Lampkins." '02(Mr1) D. $1. Abbey Press.

PAUL, *St.*
Matheson. Spiritual development of St. Paul. net, 80 c. Whittaker.
Pratt. Life and Epistles of St. Paul. 75 c. Funk.
Wayland. Paul, the herald of the cross. 40 c. Brethren Pub. Ho.

Paul and Virginia. Saint-Pierre, J. H. B. de. $1. Burt.

Paulsen, Friedrich. Immanuel Kant, his life and doctrine; fr. rev. Germ. ed., by J. E. Creighton and A. Lefevre. '02(Mr1) O. net, $2.50. Scribner.

PAVEMENTS.
See Roads.

Payn, F. W. Cromwell on foreign affairs. '02(Mr8) 8°, net, $1.25. Macmillan.

Payne, Fk. O. How to teach about trees. '01. '02(Ja25) 12°, 25 c. Kellogg.

Payne, Fk. O. How to teach aquatic life. '01. '02(Ja25) 12°, 25 c. Kellogg.

Payne, W: M. Editorial echoes. '02(Ap12) D. net, $1. McClurg.

Payne, W: M. Little leaders. [New issue.] '02(Ap12) D. net, $1. McClurg.

Pearls from the Wonderbook. King, T: A. 40 c. Swedenborg.

Pease, Eunice S. Gathered sunbeams: poems. '02(Je7) S. bds., 75 c. Sun Pr. Co.

Pearson, C: W. The carpenter prophet. '02 (Ap26) D. $1.50. H. S. Stone.

Pearson, H: C., *and* **Bartlett, Emeline B.** Key to Pearson's Greek prose composition. '01. '02(F15) S. pap., 50 c. Am. Bk.

Peck, G: C. Ringing questions. '02(Mr22) D. $1. Eaton & M.

Peck, S: M. Alabama sketches. '02(Mr22) S. $1. McClurg.

PEDIATRICS.
See Children.

Peerless ser. D. pap., 25 c. Ogilvie.
—Morehead. Story of François Villon. (124.)

Peker, C: G. *See* Meyer, J. G. A.

PEMAQUID, Me.
Kaler. Story of Pemaquid. 50 c. Crowell.

Pemberton, Max. The giant's gate. '02(F22) D. $1.50. Stokes.

Pemberton, T. E. Ellen Terry and her sisters. '02(Ap12) O. net, $3.50. Dodd.

Pen and ink. Matthews, J. B. net, $1.25. Scribner.

Pendel, T: F. Thirty-six years in the White House, Lincoln-Roosevelt. '02(Ap26) 12°, $1.50. Neale.

Pendennis. Thackeray, W: M. 3 v. $3. Macmillan.

Penitential Psalms. *See* Browne, *Mrs.* A. B. B.

PENMANSHIP.
Kilpatrick. Language system of penmanship. nos. 1-8. per doz., 66 c. Globe Sch. Bk.

Pennington, Jeanne G., *comp.* Good cheer nuggets. '02(Mr22) T. (Nuggets ser.) 45 c.; leath., $1. Fords.

Pennock, Arth. F. Twenty thousand miles by land and sea. '01. '02(My10) il. D. $1. Mason Pub.

Pennsylvania. *County cts.* Repts. v. 25. '02(Mr1) O. shp., $5. T. & J. W. Johnson.

Pennsylvania. Digest of the general acts of assembly, for the incorporation and government of cities of the 3d class. 2d ed., by L. Richards. '02(Jl5) O. $3. Soney.

Pennsylvania. *District ct.* Repts. v. 10. '01. '02(Ap5) O. shp., $5.25. H. W. Page.

Pennsylvania. Health ordinance of the borough of Edgewood, and health laws of the state; digest index, by M. Pflaum. '02 (Jl5) O. pap., $1. Nicholson.

Pennsylvania. Law of conveyancing, by C. Fallon. '02(F1) O. shp., $6. T. & J. W. Johnson.
Pennsylvania. Monaghan's cumulative annual digest. v. 3. '02(Ap19) O. $6. Soney.
Pennsylvania. Negotiable instruments law; annots. by J: J. Crawford. '02(Ap12) O. $2.50. Baker, V. & Co.
Pennsylvania. *Superior ct.* Repts., v. 17. (Schaffer and Weimer.) '02(Mr15); v. 18 (Je7) O. shp., ea., $2. Banks.
Pennsylvania. *Supreme ct.* Repts., v. 200. '02(Mr29); v. 201 (Jl19) O. shp., ea., $3.50. Banks.

PENNSYLVANIA.
Cuffel. Durrell's Battery in the Civil War. subs., $2. C: A. Cuffel.
Gans. A Pennsylvania pioneer. $6. Kuhl.
Pepper *and* Lewis. Encyclopædia of Pa. law, 1754-1898. v. 13. $7.50. Welsh.
Sharpless. Quaker experiment in government. $1.50. Ferris.
Shimmell. Border warfare in Pa. during Revolution. 50 c. R. L. Myers.
Stapleton. Memorials of the Huguenots in America with special ref. to their emigration to Pa. $1.50. Huguenot.
Trickett. Law of witnesses in Pa. $6. T. & J. W. Johnson.
See also Edgewood;—Lancaster;—Philadelphia.

Pennsylvania German cook book. Keller, S. K. 50 c. R. M. Scranton.
Pennsylvania Society of New York; year book, 1902. '02(My3) O. $1. Penn. Soc. of N. Y.

PENSIONS.
Glasson. Nation's pension system. 25 c. Am. Acad. Pol. Sci.

PENTATEUCH.
See Bible.

People's lib. 12°, pap., 50 c. Am. News.
—Crawford. In the palace of the king. (27.)
Pepper, G: W., *and* Lewis, W: D. Digest of decisions. v. 12. '01· '02(Mr15) O. of decisions. v. 12. '01· '02(Mr15); v. 13 (Jl12) O. ea., $7.50. Welsh.
Pepys, S: Diary and correspondence. New ed. '01. '02(F22) 10 v., 12°, $10; limp leath., $15. Dodd.

PERCEPTION.
See Knowledge.

PERCIVAL, Ja. G.
Legler. James Gates Percival. net, $1. Mequon Club.

Percival, Leila. Professor Archie. '02 (My17) 12°, 50 c. Nelson.
Percy, Hugh E. Letters of Hugh Earl Percy, from Boston and New York, 1774-1776; ed. by C. K. Bolton. '02(Jl19) sq. O. bds., *$4 net. Goodspeed.
Perfect woman. Sainte-Foi, C: net, $1. Marlier.
Perkin, W: H:, *jr., and* Lean, Bevan. Introd. to chemistry and physics. New ed. '02(Mr1) 2 v., 12°, net, ea., 50 c. Macmillan.
Perkins, F. M. Giotto. '02(Ja14) il. 12°, (Great masters in painting and sculpture.) $1.75. Macmillan.
Perkins, G: R. Arithmética elemental. Neuva ed. '01. '02(F15) 12°, bds., 25 c. Appleton.
Perkins, T: Cathedral church of Amiens. '02(Mr29) 12°, (Bell's handbooks to continental churches.) $1. Macmillan.

Perley, Sidney. Practice in personal actions in the cts. of Mass. '02(Jl12) O. shp., $6.50. G: B. Reed.
Perrault, C: **Tales of Mother Goose; new tr.** '02(F8) il. D. (Home and school classics.) 25 c. Heath.
Perrault, C: **Tales of passed times.** '02 (Ja18) il. 16°, (Temple classics for young people.) net, 50 c.; flex. leath., 80 c. Macmillan.
Perrault, C:, *and* **Aulnoy, Marie C. J. de B.,** *Comtesse d'.* Fairy favorites. New ed. '01· '02(F15) 16°, (Children's friend ser.) bds., 50 c. Little, B. & Co.
Perrault, C: *See also* **Aulnoy, M. C. J. de B.,** *Comtesse d'.*
Perry, Stuart H. **Legal adviser and business guide.** '01· '02(Mr8) O. $1.50. Pontiac.

PERSIA.
Remy. Influence of Persia on the poetry of Germany. net, $1. Macmillan.
Sparroy. Persian children of the Royal family. net, $3.50. Lane.
Sykes. 10,000 miles in Persia. net, $6. Scribner.
See also Inscriptions.

Persian pearl. Darrow, C. S. $1.50. Ricketts.
Personal life of the clergy. Robinson, A. W. net, 90 c. Longmans.
Personal problem ser. See Macmillan's.

PERSPECTIVE.
Pratt. Perspective, incl. projection of shadows and reflections. 90 c. Longmans.

PERU.
Prescott. Conquest of Peru. 2 v. net, $2. Macmillan.

Perverts (The). Howard, W: L. $1.50. G: W. Dillingham.

PETER III.
Bain. Peter III., Emperor of Russia. net, $3.50. Dutton.

Peterkin, G: W: Hist. and record of the Protestant Episcopal church in the diocese of West Va. '02(Jl12) 8°, $2.50; hf. leath., $10. Tribune Co.
Peters, J: J. *See* Labor and capital.
Peters, Madison C. The Jew as a patriot. '02(F22) D. $1. Baker & T.
Peterson, C. A. Mound building age in North America. '02(My24) O. pap., 25 c. Clarke.
Peterson, Hans C. First steps in Eng. composition. '02(Mr29) S. (Educational ser.) 35 c. Flanagan.
Peterson, Reuben, *and* Lewis, H: F., *eds.* Obstetrics. '02(Jl12) il. 12°, (Practical medicine ser. of year books, v. 5.) $1.25. Year Bk.
Pflaum, Magnus. *See* Pennsylvania. Health ordinance.
Phantom caravan. Odenheimer, C. P. $1. Abbey Press.
Pharmacopœia of Glasgow Roy. Infirm. Ophthalmic Inst. Ramsay, A. M. *$1.25 net. Macmillan.

PHARMACY.
Neff. Prescription writing in Latin or Eng. 75 c. Davis.
Ramsay. Pharmacopœia of the Glasgow Royal Infirmary Ophthalmic Institution. *$1.25 net. Macmillan.

PHARYNX.
See Throat.

Phelps, Eliz. S., [*now Mrs.* H. D. Ward,] *and* Ward, H. D. A lost hero. New ed. '01- '02(F15) 16°, (Children's friend ser.) bds., 50 c. Little, B. & Co.
Phelps, W: L., *comp.* List of general reading in Eng. literature. '02(Ap26) 12°, pap., net, 5 c. Pease-L.
Philip Longstreth. Van Vorst, M. $1.50. Harper.
PHILADELPHIA.
Myers. Quaker arrivals at Philadelphia, 1682-1750. $1.25. Ferris.
PHILIPPINE ISLANDS.
Condict. Old glory and the gospel in the Philippines. net, 75 c. Revell.
Halstead. Story of the Philippines. $2; $3. Dominion.
Hedges. Statistics conc. education in the Philippine Islands. 10 c. Benziger.
Lodge, *and others.* The U. S. and the Philippine Islands. 10 c. Brooklyn Eagle.
Philipson, D: Jew in English fiction. New rev., enl. ed. '02(My17) D. net, $1. Clarke.
Phillipps, L. M. With Rimington. '01- '02 (Ja11) O. $2.50. Longmans.
Phillips, D: G. Her Serene Highness. '02 (My10) il. D. $1.50. Harper.
Phillips, Fs. C., *ed.* Methods for the analysis of ores, pig iron and steel in use at the laboratories about Pittsburg, Pa. 2d ed. '01- '02(F1) il. 8°, net, $1. Chemical Pub.
Phillips, H: W. Red Saunders. '02(My24) il. D. $1.25. McClure, P.
Phillips, J: B. **Methods of keeping the public money of the U. S.** '02(F15) 12°, pap., $1. Mich. Pol. Sci.
Phillips, Stephen. Paolo and Francesca. New ed. '02(Je28) 12°, net, $1.25. Lane.
Phillips, Stephen. **Ulysses: a drama.** '02 (F15) D. net, $1.25. Macmillan.
Philosophical dict. Voltaire, F. M. A. de. 10 v. per set, subs., *$18 net; $24 net. G: Clarke.
PHILOSOPHY.
Adam, *comp.* Texts to il. lectures on Greek philosophy. net, $1.25. Macmillan.
Baldwin. Fragments in philosophy and science. net, $2.50. Scribner.
Blackwood's philosophical classics. 15 v. ea., net, 50 c. Lippincott.
Boethius. Consolation of philosophy. 50 c.; 75 c. Macmillan.
Chamberlain. Evolutionary philosophy. 50 c. Baker & T.
Kupfer. Greek foreshadowings of modern metaphysical and epistemological thought. $1. J. S. Cushing.
Laurie. Scottish philosophy in its nat. development. net, $1.75. Macmillan.
Muirhead. Philosophy and life. $1.50. Macmillan.
Sidgwick. Philosophy. net, $2.25. Macmillan.
See also Ethics;—Mind and body;—Ontology;—Skepticism;—Utilitarianism;—*also* Kant, I.
Philosophy of conduct. Ladd, G: T. net, $3.50. Scribner.
Philosophy of the Christian religion. Fairbairn, A. M. net, $3.50. Macmillan.
Philosophy of voice. Lunn, C: net, $2. Schirmer.
PHONOGRAPHY.
See Stenography.

Photographic coloring. '02(Ap5) D. pap., 25 c. Acme Water Color.
PHOTOGRAPHY.
International annual of Anthony's photographic bulletin, 1902. $1.25; 75 c. Anthony.
Taylor. Why my photographs are bad. net, $1. Jacobs.
Phrase-making, Science of. *See* Brown, D: W.
PHRENOLOGY.
Windsor. Phrenology. 25 c. Donohue.
See also Physiognomy.
PHYSICAL CULTURE.
See Gymnastics and physical culture.
PHYSICAL GEOGRAPHY.
Davis. Elem. physical geography. $1.40. Ginn.
Gilbert *and* Brigham. Introd. to physical geography. net, $1.25. Appleton.
Morgan. Advanced physiography. $1.50. Longmans.
Warren. Physical geography. $1.25. Butler.
See also Brooks;—Geography;—Geology;—Nature;—Seashore;—Water;—Weather.
PHYSICAL SCIENCE.
See Science.
PHYSICIANS.
Allen. Practitioner's manual. $6; $7. Wood.
Medical directory of the city of N. Y. $1.50. Wynkoop.
PHYSICS.
Ayres. Lab'y exercises in elem. physics. net, 50 c. Appleton.
Carhart *and* Chute. Physics for high school students. $1.25. Allyn & B.
Crew *and* Tatnall. Lab'y manual of physics. net, 90 c. Macmillan.
Fisher *and* Patterson. Elements of physics. 60 c. Heath.
Kelsey. Physical determinations. $1.50. Longmans.
Perkin *and* Lean. Introd. to chemistry and physics. 2 v., ea., net, 50 c. Macmillan.
Reed *and* Guthe. Manual of physical measurements. $1.50. Wahr.
Reynolds. Papers on mechanical and physical subjects. v. 2. net, $6. Macmillan.
Slate. Physics. net, $1.10. Macmillan.
Stewart. Nociones de fisica. 20 c. Appleton.
Wentworth *and* Hill. Lab'y exercises in elem. physics. 27 c. Ginn.
See also Chemistry;—Heat;—Light;—Mathematics;—Radiation;—Sound.
PHYSIOGNOMY.
Stevens. Faciology. 25 c. Donohue.
PHYSIOGRAPHY.
See Geology;—Physical geography.
PHYSIOLOGY.
Blaisdell. Life and health: text-book on physiology. $1. Ginn.
Brinckley. Physiology by the lab'y method. $1.25. Ainsworth.
Colton. Elem. physiology and hygiene. 60 c. Heath.
Hutchison. Lessons in physiology and hygiene. 2d bk. 80 c.; 40 c. Maynard, M. & Co.
Jegi. Syllabus of human physiology for schools. $1. Gillan.
Schäfer. Directions for class work in practical physiology. net, $1. Longmans.

PHYSIOLOGY.—*Continued.*
Smith. Anatomy, physiology and hygiene. $1. W: R. Jenkins.
See also **Anatomy;—Hygiene;—Mind and body;—Nervous system.**

Piatt, J: J. The Hesperian tree. '02(F22) il. O. $2. J: Scott.

Piccolomini (The). Schiller, J. C. F. v. (App. to pubs. for price.) Niccolls.

Pickering, Edg. King for a summer. '02 (Ap26) il. D. net, $1. Lee & S.

Pickle, G: W., *rep.* *See* Tennessee. *Sup. ct. Repts.*

Pictorial guide to Boston and the country around. '02(Jl12) il. S. pap., 25 c. G. W. Armstrong.

Pictorial natural history. Cuppy, H. A. $1. Crowell & K.

Pidgin, C: F. Stephen Holton. '02(My10) D. $1.50. L. C. Page.

Pierce, Arth. H. Studies in auditory and visual space perception. '01. '02(Ja11) D. net, $2. Longmans.

Pierce, Ella A. Hartley House cook book and household economist. '02(F8) S. (Handbooks for practical workers in church and philanthropy.) 60 c. Lentilhon.

Pierce, Ella M. Intermediate arithmetic. '02 (Mr22) il. 12°, (Pierce arithmetics.) 48 c. Silver.

Pierce, F: C. Field genealogy. '01. '02(F8) 2 v., il. 4°. $10. Conkey.

Pierce, Grace A. The silver cord and the golden bowl. '02(Mr1) O. $1. Abbey Press.

Pierson, Clara D. Among the night people. '02(My10) 12°, net, $1. Dutton.

PIGEONS.
Homing pigeon. 25 c. G: E. Howard.
Rice. Robinson method of breeding squabs. 50 c. Plymouth Rock.

Pilgrim's progress. *See* Bunyan, J:

Pine tree ballads. Day, H. F. **$1 net. Small.

PING-PONG.
Parker. Ping-pong: how to play it. net, 75 c. Putnam.
Ritchie *and* Harrison. Table tennis, and how to play it. 50 c. Lippincott.
Ritchie *and* Parker. Ping-pong. 50 c. Street.

Pink knight. Monsell, J. R. net, 40 c. Stokes.

Pinney, Aida E. Spanish and Eng. conversation. First and second books. '02(Jl19) D. ea., 65 c. Ginn.

Pinson, W. W. In white and black. '02 (Mr1) D. $1.50. Saalfield.

Pioneer towns of America. il. D. 50 c. Crowell.
—Kaler. Story of Pemaquid. (2.)

Piper, Fred. S. Lexington, the birthplace of Am. liberty. '02(Ap26) il. sq. S. pap., 25 c. Lexington.

Pipes and tubes. Bjorling, P. R. $1. Macmillan.

Pitman, Benn, *and* Howard, J. B. Business letters: no. 1. '02(My10) S. pap., 25 c. Phonograph.

Pitman, *Sir* I: Business corr. in shorthand: no. 2. Rev. ed. '02(My10) S. pap., 30 c. Pitman.

Pitman, *Sir* I: Phonographic teacher. Twentieth century ed. '02(My10) S. pap., 20 c. Pitman.

Pitman's commercial ser. il. D. Pitman.
—Marchand. Commercial history. $1.

Pitt Press Shakespeare. 12°, net, 40 c. Macmillan.
—Shakespeare. Macbeth.

Plane surveying. Nugent, P. C. $3.50. Wiley.

Planets and people; [1902,] annual. F. E. Ormsby, ed. '01. '02(Ja25) O. $1. F. E. Ormsby.

PLANTS.
See **Botany;—Gardening.**

PLATE.
Cripps. Old Eng. plate. net, $13.50. Scribner.

Plato, Euthyphro; notes by W: A. Heidel. '02(Jl12) D. (Greek ser. for coll. and schools.) $1. Am. Bk.

Plato. The republic. (J. L. Davies and D. J. Vaughan.) '02(Ap19) 12°, (Home lib.) $1. Burt.

Plato. The republic. bk. 2. '02(My10) D. pap., 15 c. Kerr.

PLATO.
Nettleship. Lectures on the Republic of Plato. net, $2.75. Macmillan.
Ritchie. Plato. $1.25. Scribner.

Plattner, K. F. Manual of qualitative and quantitative analysis with the blowpipe; tr. by H: B. Cornwall. 8th ed., rev. by F: Kolbeck. '02(My17) il. net, $4. Van Nostrand.

Play away. Allen, W. B. **75 c. net. Estes.

PLAYS.
See **Drama and dramatists.**

PLEADING AND PRACTICE.
Cockcroft, *ed.* Encyc. of forms for pleading and practice. v. 15. $6. Cockcroft
McKinney. Encyc. of pleading and practice. v. 22, 23. ea., $6. E: Thompson.
Young *and* Keen. Problems in practice and pleading at the common law. 50 c. Mudge.
See also **Actions at law.**

Pleasures of life. Lubbock, *Sir* J: $1. Burt.

Pleistocene **glacial** formations. *See* Chamberlin, T: C.

PLUMBING.
Bjorling. Pipes and tubes. $1. Macmillan.
Lawler. Modern plumbing. $5. Popular.

Plummer, Ma. W. Hints to small libraries. 3d ed., rev. and enl. '02(My17) sq. O. net, 50 c. M. W. Plummer.

Pocket Gray. Cotterell, E: net, $1.25. Wood.

Poe, Edg. A. Works. '02(Ap5) 4 v., 12°, hf. cf., $8. Burt.

Poe, Edg. A. Murders in the Rue Morgue, and other tales. '02(Mr29) il. 12°, (Home lib.) $1. Burt.

Poems of life and loving. Shelley, H. S. $1. Neely.

POETRY.
Liddell. Introd. to the scientific study of Eng. poetry. net, $1.25. Doubleday, P.
See **Ballads;—Metre;—Quotations.**

POETS.
Thackeray *and* Stone, *eds.* Pre-Victorian poets. $2.50.—Victorian poets. net, $2. Lane.

Point of honour. **Hinkson, H. A.** $1.50. McClurg.

POISONS.
Vaughan *and* Novey. Cellular toxins. *$3 net. Lea.

Poland, W: Find the church. '02(Mr8) 8°, pap., net, 5 c. Herder.

Poland, W: Socialism; its economic aspect. '02(Je28) 8°, pap., net, 5 c. Herder.

Policeman Flynn. Flower, E. $1.50. Century Co.

POLICY.
See Fortune-tellers.

POLITICAL ECONOMY.
Gladden. Social salvation. net, $1. Houghton, M. & Co.
Laughlin. Elements of political economy. $1.20. Am. Bk.
Patten. Theory of prosperity. net, $1.25. Macmillan.
Phillips. Methods of keeping the public money of the U. S. $1. Mich. Pol. Sci.
Sidgwick. Principles of political economy. net, $4.50. Macmillan.
See also Finance;—Prosperity;—Trusts.

Political freshman. James, B. W. $1.50. Bushrod Lib.

Political primer. Fielde, A. M. 75 c.; 50 c. League Pol. Educ.

POLITICAL SCIENCE.
Ashley. American federal state. net, $2. Macmillan.
Bardeen. Manual of civics for N. Y. schools. net, $1. Bardeen.
Bourne. Teaching of history and civics. $1.50. Longmans.
Dunning. Hist. of political theories, ancient and mediæval. net, $2.50. Macmillan.
Forman. First lessons in civics. 60 c. Am. Bk.
Kellogg. Elements of civil government. 25 c. Kellogg.
Martin. Civil government in U. S. 90 c. Am. Bk.
Meyer. Nominating systems; direct primaries vs. conventions in the U. S. net, $1.50. E. C. Meyer.
See also Citizenship; — Crime and criminals; — Democracy; — Municipal government; — Reciprocity;—*also* names of states and countries.

Politzer, A. *See* Brühl, G.

Pollock, *Sir* F: Revised reports. v. 46-51. '01- '02(F15) 8°, shp. or hf. cf., ea., net, $6. Little, B. & Co.

Polyphase apparatus. *See* Oudin, M. A.

Pomeroy, C. P., *rep.* *See* California. *Sup. ct.* Repts.

PONTIAC'S WAR.
See Indians.

Poole, R. L. *See* Maitland, F: W:

Poole, Stanley Lane. Story of Cairo. '02 (My24) il. 12°, (Mediæval towns ser.) $2; leath., $2.50. Macmillan.

Poore, B: P., *and* Tiffany, O. H. Life of U. S. Grant. '02(Jl19) 12°, (Biog. of famous men.) $1. Donohue.

Poor's manual of the railroads of the U. S. 1901. '01- '02(F22) 8°, $10. Poor.

POPES.
Mann. Lives of the popes in early Middle Ages. v. 1, pt. 1. net, $3. Herder.

Popular girl. Baldwin, M. net, $1.20. Lippincott.

PORCELAIN.
See Ceramics.

Porter, Ctte., *and* **Clarke**, **Helen A.** Shakespeare studies: Macbeth. '01- '02(Ja4) S. 56 c. Am. Bk.

Portiuncula. Indulgence of portiuncula; fr the German. New ed. '02(Je28) 48°, pap., 5 c. Herder.

PORTLAND CEMENT.
See Cement.

PORTRAITS.
Cust, *ed.* National portrait gallery. v. 1. subs., for complete work, net, $3. Cassell.

PORTUGAL.
Higgin. Spanish life; with chapters on Portuguese life by E. E. Street. net, $1.20. Putnam.

POTTER, Jennie O'Neil.
Deal. Life of Jennie O'Neil Potter. $1. Blanchard.

POTTERY.
See Ceramics.

Powell, **Ja. B.** Choralia: handy book for parochial precentors and choirmasters. '01- '02(F8) D. $1.50. Longmans.

Powell, Lewis. The twentieth century home builder. '02(Ap5) nar. D. pap., 25 c. Pub. Ho. M. E. Ch., So.

POWER.
Kerr. Power and power transmission. $2. Wiley.

Power of God's word. Prime, R. E. 3 c. Presb. Bd.

Power that heals. Ballough, C: A. $1. Painter.

Powers, Harry H. Art of travel. '02(My17) D. pap., 25 c. Bu. Univ. Travel.

Poynter, E. F. Michael Ferrier. '02(Ap26) 12°, $1.50. Macmillan.

Practical electricity, with questions and answers. 3d ed. '01- '02(Mr29) il. 16°, leath., $2. Cleveland Armature.

Practical medicine ser. of year-books; ed. by G. P. Head. il. D. $1.50. Year Bk.
—Billings *and* Stanton, *eds.* General medicine. (1.)
—Murphy. General surgery. (2.)
—Peterson *and* Lewis, *eds.* Obstetrics. (5.)
—Wood, *and others, eds.* Eye, ear, nose and throat. (3.)

Pratt, H: S. Course in invertebrate zoölogy. '02(F15) il. O. $1.35. Ginn.

Pratt, Mara L. America's story for America's children. In 5 v. v. 5, Foundations of the Republic. '01- '02(Ja4) D. 40 c. Heath.

Pratt, Rob. Perspective, incl. the projection of shadows and reflections. '01- '02(Mr8) il. F. bds., 90 c. Longmans.

Pratt, S: W. Life and Epistles of St. Paul. '02(F1) map, S. 75 c. Funk.

Pratt, Stephen R. Supp. to Mining laws of Colo., etc. '02(Ap5) O. pap., 35 c. Pratt Merc.

PRAYER.
Aitkin. Divine ordinance of prayer. $1.25. E. & J. B. Young.
McClure. A mighty means of usefulness: intercessory prayer. net, 50 c. Revell.
Worlledge. Prayer. $1.50. Longmans.
See also Lord's prayer;—Prayers;—Worship.

PRAYER-BOOK.
See Book of common prayer;—Church of England.

PRAYER-MEETINGS.
See Epworth League.

PRAYERS.
Breviarium bothanum sive portiforium secundum usum ecclesiæ cujusdam in Scotia. $15. Longmans.
Pre-Victorian poets. Thackeray, F. St. J: $2.50. Lane.
PREACHING.
Barton, *comp.* Pulpit power and eloquence. $3.50. F. M. Barton.
Lyman. Preaching in the new age. net, 75 c. Revell.
See also Sermons.
Precept and practice. Bausman, B: net, $1. Heidelberg.
PRECIOUS METALS.
Del Mar. Hist. of the precious metals. net, $3. Cambridge.
See also Money.
PRECIOUS STONES.
Sommerville. Engraved gems. net, $1.50. Biddle.
Prentiss, *Mrs.* Eliz. ["Aunt Susan."] Little Susy stories. '02(Mr29) il. 12°, (Little women ser.) 75 c. Burt.
Prentiss, *Mrs.* Eliz. Six little princesses and what they turned into. '02(Je28) il. 12°, (St. Nicholas ser.) 75 c. Burt.
Preparatio; or, notes of preparation for holy communion. '01. '02(Ja11) D. $2. Longmans.
Presbyterian church. General Assembly; twentieth century addresses. '02(Je7) D. net, $1. Presb. Bd.
PRESBYTERIAN CHURCH.
Doyle. Presb. home missions. net, $1. Presb. Bd.
Erdman. The ruling elder. 3 c. Presb. Bd.
Stephens. Evolution of the confession of faith of the Cumberland Presb. church. 10 c. Cumberland.
See also Syracuse, First Presb. church.
Prescott, Alb. B:, *and* Sullivan, Eug. C. First book of qualitative chemistry for studies of water solution and mass action. 11th ed., rewritten. '02(My17) O. net, $1.50. Van Nostrand.
Prescott, W: H. Hist. of the conquest of Peru; ed. by J: F. Kirk. '02(Ap12) 2 v., 12°, (Bohn's standard lib.) net, $2. Macmillan.
Prescott, W: H. Hist. of the reign of Ferdinand and Isabella the Catholic. '02 (Ap12) 3 v., 12°, (Bohn's standard lib.) net, $3. Macmillan.
PRESCRIPTIONS.
Kuder. Medical prescription book. $2. Journal Pr.
See also Pharmacy.
Prescriptions and instructions. Russell, W: $1. Clarke.
PRESIDENTS.
See United States.
Presset, Anne L. Cherished thoughts in original poems and sketches. '01. '02 (My24) il. D. $1.50; im. mor., $1.75; full mor., $2.25. Skelton.
Prévost, Marcel. Frédérique; tr. by E. Marriage. '02(Mr8) D. $1.50. Crowell.
Price, E. D. Letters of Mildred's mother to Mildred. '01. '02(F15) 12°, $1. Ogilvie.
Price, Eleanor C. Angelot. '02(Ap5) il. D. $1.50. Crowell.
Price, Ja. A. Observations and exercises on the weather. '02(Ap26) O. pap., 30 c. Am. Bk.
Price inevitable. Sidner, A. L. $1. Popular.
PRIESTS.
Harper. Constructive studies in the priestly element in the O. T. $1. Univ. of Chic.
See also Catholic church.
Prime, Ralph E. Power of God's word. '02 (Je21) S. pap., 3 c. Presb. Bd.
PRIMERS.
Alger. Primer of work and play. 30 c. Heath.
Burt *and* Howells. Literary primer. net, 30 c. Scribner.
Kirk. Baldwin primer. 35 c. Am. Bk.
Primrose diplomacy. Hutchinson, J. $1.25. Abbey Press.
Prince Incognito. Latimer, *Mrs.* E. W. $1.50. McClurg.
Prince of good fellows. Barr, R. $1.50. McClure, P.
Prince of the captivity. Gregg, H. $1.50. L. C. Page.
Princess (The), *pseud.* *See* Lockett, M. F.
Princess. Tennyson, A. 25 c. Appleton.
Principles of western civilization. Kidd, B: net, $2. Macmillan.
Print-collector's handbook. Whitman, A. net, $5. Macmillan.
PRINTERS.
See Short, T:
PRINTING.
Morris. Art and craft of printing. $5. Elston Press.
Sheldon. Practical colorist. $8. Owl Press.
Prisoners of the sea. Kingsley, *Mrs.* F. M. $1.25; 50 c. New Amsterdam.
PRISONS.
Howard. Prisoners of Russia. net, $1.40. Appleton.
Skinner. Prisons of the nation and their inmates. 10 c. Brooklyn Eagle.
Pritchard, W: A., *comp.* Wehman's how to become a naturalized citizen. '02(Mr8) S. pap., 10 c. Wehman.
Prize designs for rural school buildings. Coburn, F: N. 25 c. Kellogg.
Prize poetical speaker. '01. '02(Ja4) 12°, 75 c. Dickerman.
PROBATE.
See Wills.
PROBABILITIES.
Simon. Philosoph. essay on probabilities. $2. Wiley.
Problems in the use and adjustment of engineering instruments. 4th ed. rev. and enl. '02(Je21) 16°, $1.25. Wiley.
Professor Archie. Percival, L. 50 c. Nelson.
Progredior ser. sq. D. Flanagan.
—Beeman. Analysis of the Eng. sentence. 50 c.
Progress of dogma. Orr, J. $1.75. Armstrong.
Progression to immortality. Brooks, H: S. net, 50 c. Wessels.
PROJECTION.
See Perspective.
PROPERTY.
See Real property.
PROPHECY.
Girdlestone. Grammar of prophecy. $2.50. E. & J. B. Young.
Prophet of the kingdom. Frisbie, H: S: $1.25. Neale.

Prose quotations. Allibone, S: A. $2.50. Lippincott.

PROSPERITY.
Seager. Prof. Patten's theory of prosperity. 15 c. Am. Acad. Pol. Sci.

PROSTITUTION.
Social (The) evil. net, $1.25. Putnam.

PROTESTANT EPISCOPAL CHURCH.
Francis. Weekly church teaching for the infants. 25 c. E. & J. B. Young.
McCormick. Distinctive marks of the Episcopal church. 25 c. Young Churchman.
Miller. Amer. church dict. and cyclopedia. $1. Whittaker.
Parson's (The) handbook. net, $1.50. Young Churchman.
Peterkin. Hist. and record of Prot. Episc. Ch. in W. Va. $2.50; $10. Tribune Co.
See also Catechisms;—Church of England;—Lent.

PROTESTANTISM.
Gibson. Protestant principles. 60 c. Armstrong.

PROTOZOA.
Chapman. The foraminifera: introd. to study of the protozoa. $3.50. Longmans.

Proudfoot, A. H. Year with the Mother-play; 2d year's study course of the League of Am. Mothers. '02(Je28) D. $1. Flanagan.

PROVERBS.
Browne. Proverbial sayings. net, $1. Stokes.

Providence Journal almanac for 1902. '02 (F8) 12°, pap., 10 c. Providence Journ.

Prozess (Der). *See* Fulda, L.

Prune, Nat. College chaps. '02(Je14) S. 75 c. Mutual Bk.

PSALMS.
See Bible.

PSYCHIATRY.
See Insanity.

PSYCHICAL RESEARCH.
Duff *and* Allen. Psychic research and gospel miracles. net, $1.50. Whittaker.

PSYCHOLOGY.
Baldwin. Social and ethical interpretations in mental development. net, $2.60. Macmillan.
Brinton. Basis of social relations. net, $1.50. Putnam.
Dewey. Psychology and social practice. net, 25 c. Univ. of Chic.
Mercier. Psychology, normal and morbid. net, $4. Macmillan.
Patrick. Psychology for teachers. $1. Educ. Pub.
Vance. Rise of a soul. net, $1. Revell.
Witmer. Analytical psychology. $1.60. Ginn.
See also Character;—Hypnotism;—Mind and body;—Philosophy;—Phrenology;—Telepathy.

Public house reform. Cumming, A. N. $1. Scribner.

Public Ledger almanac, 1902; ed. by G: W. C. Drexel. '01. '02(Ja11) S. pap., gratis to subs. of *Public Ledger.* Drexel.

Puddicombe, *Mrs.* Beynon. *See* Raine, A.

Pullen, *Mrs.* Elisabeth. Mr. Whitman. '02 (My17) D. $1.50. Lothrop.

Pulpit power and eloquence. Barton, F: $3.50. F. M. Barton.

PULSE.
See Heart.

Purdy, L. Burdens of local taxation and who bears them. '01. '02(Ja11) D. 25 c. Public Policy.

Purdy, L. Local option in taxation. '02 (F15) D. pap., 10 c. Tax Reform.

Puron, Juan G. Lector moderno de Appleton, nos. 1-3. '01. '02(F22) 12°, bds., no. 1, 25 c.; no. 2, 35 c.; no. 3, 45 c. Appleton.

Purves, G: T. Faith and life: sermons. '02 (Je7) D. net, $1.25. Presb. Bd.

Purves, G: T. Joy in service. '01. '02(Ja4) D. 50 c. Am. Tr.

PUSEY, Edw. Bouverie.
Grafton. Pusey and the church revival. net, 50 c. Young Churchman.

Putnam, Israel. Daniel Everton, volunteer-regular. '02(My3) il. D. net, $1.20. Funk.

PUTNAM, Rufus.
Earle. Rutland home of Maj. Gen. Rufus Putnam. 30 c.; 50 c. S. C. Earle.

Putnam's lib. of standard literature. D. $1.75. Putnam.
—Chesterfield. Letters to his son.
—Swift. Journal to Stella.

Putnam's science ser. 8°, net. Putnam.
—Brinton. Basis of social relations. $1.50.

PUZZLES.
See Riddles.

Pyeshkoff, Alexéi M. *See* Górky, M.

Pyle, Howard. Some merry adventures of Robin Hood. '02(Je7) il. D. (Ser. of school reading.) net, 60 c. Scribner.

Pyle, Kath. Careless Jane, and other tales. '02(My10) 12°, net, 75 c. Dutton.

Q., *pseud.* *See* Couch, A. T: Quiller-.

Quad, M., *pseud.* *See* Lewis, C: B.

Quadrupani, R. P. Light and peace; from the Fr. 3d ed. '02(Mr8) 12°, net, 50 c. Herder.

Quaker experiment in government. Sharpless, I: $1.50. Ferris.

QUAKERS.
See Friends (Society of).

Quaku. Quinius, H. F. 3 c. J: G. Quinius.

Quang Chang Ling. Why should the Chinese go? '02(Je7) 8°, pap., 25 c. Cambridge.

Quayle, W: A. The gentleman in literature. '02(My24) por. D. (Hero ser., no. 4.) net, 25 c. Jennings.

Quayle, W: A. A hero—Jean Valjean. '02 (Ap26) D. (Hero ser., no. 1.) net, 25 c. Jennings.

Quayle, W: A. King Cromwell. '02(My24) il. D. (Hero ser., no. 6.) net, 25 c. Jennings.

Queen of the household. Ellsworth, T. $2.50. Ellsworth.

Queer people. Bishop, W: H: $1. Street.

Quentin Durward. Scott, *Sir* W. net, 60 c. Macmillan.

Questions of the day. D. Putnam.
—Labor and capital. $1.50. (98.)

Quiberon touch. Brady, C. T. $1.50. Appleton.

Quick, M. I. Complete guide to ball room dancing. '02(My17) 12°, 50 c.; pap., 25 c. Donohue.

Quincy word list. Parlin, F. E. 24 c. Morse.

Quinius, Augusta. Mother Margaret's bunch of flowers. '02(Mr1) T. pap., 5 c. J: G. Quinius.

Quinius, H. F. *and* Augusta. Quaku. '02 (Je28) T. pap., 3 c. J: G. Quinius.

QUOTATIONS.
Allibone. Poetical quotations.—Prose quotations. ea., $2.50. Lippincott.

Rab and his friends. Brown, J: 25 c. Rand, McN. & Co.

Racine, Jean B. Athalie; ed., with notes, by E: S. Joynes. New enl. ed. '02(F1) D. (Students' ser. of classic Fr. plays, no. 2.) net, 35 c. Holt.

Racine, Jean B. Athalie; ed. by F. C. de Sumichrast. '02(Jl12) 12°, (French classics.) *60 c. net. Macmillan.

Racine, Jean B. Esther; ed., with notes, by E: S. Joynes. [New ed.] '02(F8) D. (Students' ser. of classic Fr. plays, no. 5.) net, 35 c. Holt.

Radcliffe, G: L. P. Governor Thomas H. Hicks of Maryland and the Civil war. '01-'02(Mr8) O. (Johns Hopkins Univ. studies, 19th ser., nos. 11-12.) pap., 50 c. Johns Hopkins.

Rader, Perry S., *rep.* *See* Missouri. *Sup. ct.* Repts.

RADIATION.

Brace, *ed.* Laws of radiation and absorption. $1. Am. Bk.

See also Heat;—Light;—Sound.

Railroad repts. (v. 24, Am. and Eng. railroad cases;) ed. by T: J. Michie. v. 1. '02(Je7) O. shp., $5. Michie.

Railroading with Christ. Dwight, C: A. S. $1. Am. Tr.

RAILROADS.

Adams. Block system of signalling. $2. Railroad Gazette.

American and Eng. railroad cases. v. 23. ea., $5. Michie.

American street railway investments. $5. Street R'way.

Bodmer. Inspection of railway materials. $1.50. Macmillan.

Goodknight. Modern association and railroading. 50 c. Abbey Press.

Hanford. Railroading in the U. S. 5 c. Socialistic Co-op.

Knapp. Government ownership of railroads. 15 c. Am. Acad. Pol. Sci.

Meyer. Advisory councils in railway administration. 15 c. Am. Acad. Pol. Sci.

New York. Statutory revision of the laws affecting railroads. $1.50; $2. Banks & Co.

Newcomb. Concentration of railway control. 15 c. Am. Acad. Pol. Sci.

Poor's manual of railroads of the U. S., 1901. $10. Poor.

Talbot. Railway transition spiral. $1.50. Van Nostrand.

Weyl. Passenger traffic of railways. $1.50; $1. [Univ. of Penn.] Ginn.

See also Air brake;—Cars;—Locomotives;—Street railroads;—*also* Cincinnati Southern railway;—Siberian railway.

Raine, Allen, [*pseud.* for *Mrs.* Beynon Puddicombe.] A Welsh witch. '02(Je7) D. (Town and country lib., no. 312.) $1; pap., 50 c. Appleton.

Rainsford, W: S. Reasonableness of faith, and other addresses. '02(My10) O. net, $1.25. Doubleday, P.

Rainy, Rob. Ancient Catholic church from accession of Trajan to the Fourth General Council, A.D. 98-451. '02(F1) O. (Internat. theol. lib.) net, $2.50. Scribner.

Rait, Rob. S. Five Stuart princesses. '02(Mr29) il. 8°, net, $3.50. Dutton.

Raleigh, *Sir* Wa. The last fight of the "Revenge" at sea. '02(My10) 4°, net, $6. Houghton, M. & Co.

Ramabai Sarasvati, *Pundita.* High-caste Hindu woman. '02(Mr22) 12°, net, 75 c. Revell.

Ramal, Wa. Songs of childhood. '02(Ap19) il. S. net, $1.20. Longmans.

RAMONA.

Hufford. The real Ramona of Helen Hunt Jackson's famous novel. 35 c.; 75 c.; $1; $1.25. D: A. Hufford.

Ramsay, A. M. Pharmacopœia of the Glasgow Royal Infirmary Ophthalmic Inst. '02 12°, *$1.25 net. Macmillan.

Ramsey, M. M. Spanish grammar, with exercise. '02(My17) D. net, $1.50. Holt.

Randall, Wyatt W., *ed. and tr.* Expansion of gases by heat. '02(Ap19) O. (Scientific memoirs.) $1. Am. Bk.

Rankin, A. C. Saloon law nullification and its cure. '02(My17) 16°, 50 c. Advance.

Rankin, A. W. *See* Aiton, G:

Rankin, J. E. Esther Burr's journal. 2d ed. '02(Jl12) sq. S. pap., 75 c. Howard Univ.

Ranson's folly. Davis, R: H. †$1.50. Scribner.

Rasselas. *See* Johnson, S:

Rataplan, a rogue elephant. Velvin, E. **$1.25 net. Altemus.

RATIONALISM.

Hurst. Hist. of rationalism. $2.50. Eaton & M.

Rawlins, Ja. M. *See* Lippincott's elem. algebra.

Rawson, C., Gardner, W. M., *and* Laycock, W. F. Dict. of dyes, mordants, and other compounds. '01-'02(F15) 8°, net, $5. Lippincott.

Raycroft, B: J. Sermons on the stations of the cross, the Our Father, Hail Mary, etc. '02(Je7) 8°, net, $1.50. Pustet.

READERS AND SPEAKERS.

Allen. Children of the palm lands. 50 c. Educ. Pub.

American speaker. 50 c. Conkey.

Blaisdell. Child life fifth reader. net, 45 c. Macmillan.

Bradish. Stories of country life. 40 c. Am. Bk.

Brown. Am. star speaker and model elocutionist. $1.50. Donohue.

Burke. Literature and art books. Bks. 1-3. bk. 1, 25 c.; bk. 2, 30 c.; bk. 3, 35 c. McBride.

Cady *and* Dewey. Art reader, no. 1. 35 c. Richardson, S.

Calmerton *and* Wheeler. First reader. 30 c. W: H: Wheeler.

Carpenter. Europe. 70 c. Am. Bk.

Cyr. Readers, bks. 7, 8. ea., 45 c. Ginn.

Edgerly. Natural reader. $1.50. Ralston.

Funk *and* Moses, *eds.* Standard first reader. 35 c. Funk.

Gyim. Chinese-Eng. elem. reader and arithmetic. $1.25. Taylor & M.

Haliburton *and* Norvell. Graded classics: 3d reader. 40 c. B. F. Johnson.

Judson *and* Bender, *eds.* Graded literature readers. bks. 6-8. ea., 50 c. Maynard, M. & Co.

McCullough. Little stories for little people. 25 c. Am. Bk.

READERS AND SPEAKERS.—*Continued.*
Macmillan's new geog. readers: Africa and Australasia. net, 40 c. Macmillan.
Macmillan's new hist. readers; Senior. net, 50 c. Macmillan.
Marché. Rural readers. net, 40 c. Macmillan.
Prize poetical speaker. 75 c. Dickerman.
Shepard. Life on the farm: reading book. 50 c. Flanagan.
Thompson. New century readers. 3d bk. 52 c. Morse.
Virden. First science reader. 25 c.; 10 c. Flanagan.
Welsh. Colonial days. 50 c. Educ. Pub.
Whitcomb. Little journey to Italy.—Scotland. ea., 15 c. Flanagan.
Wide world. 30 c. Ginn.
See also Primers;—Recitations.
READING.
See Books and reading.
REAL PROPERTY.
Newell. Elements of law of real property. $4. Flood.
Pattee, *comp.* Authorities, deductions, and notes in real property. $2. Univ. Press.
Warvelle. American law of vendor and purchaser of real property. v. 1, 2. $12. Callaghan.
Washburn. Am. law of real property. 3 v. net, $18. Little, B. & Co.
See also Conveyancing;—Land;—Sale;—Taxation.
Real Ramona. Hufford, D: A. 35 c.; 75 c.; $1; $1.25. D: A. Hufford.
Reasonableness of faith. Rainsford, W: S. net, $1.25. Doubleday, P.
Rebuilding of old commonwealths. Page, W. H. net, $1. Doubleday, P.
RECEIPTS.
See Cookery.
RECIPROCITY.
Farquhar. Manufacturers' needs of reciprocity. 15 c. Am. Acad. Pol. Sci.
RECITATIONS.
Birbeck, *ed.* Select recitations, orations, etc. $1. Wagner.
Brown, *comp.* Comic recitations.—Patriotic recitations. ea., 50 c.; 25 c. Donohue.
Monroe, *ed.* Public and parlor readings. 4 v. ea., $1. Lee & S.
See also Readers and speakers.
Reconciliation of Randall Claymore. Barnes, E. N. C. $1. Earle.
Reconstruction and the constitution. Burgess, J: W. net, $1. Scribner.
Recreations of the German emigrants. *See* Goethe, J. W. v.
Recruit Tommy Collins. Bonesteel, M. 45 c. Benziger.
Red anvil. Sherlock, C: R. $1.50. Stokes.
Red letter ser. il. 12°, $1.25; pap., 50 c. New Amsterdam.
—Kingsley. Prisoners of the sea.
—Marchmont. Miser Hoadley's secret.
—Russell. Captain Fanny.
Red Saunders. Phillips, H: W. $1.25. McClure, P.
Redfield, Amasa A., *ed.* Repts. of cases Surrogates' cts. of New York. In 5 v., v. 1. '01- '02(My17) 8°, shp., per v., $6. Banks & Co.
Reduction tables. Blum, A. R. net, $3. Am. Code.

Reed, Edn. Bacon and Shake-speare parallelisms. '02(Ap26) O. bds., net, $2.50. Goodspeed.
Reed, Edn. Francis Bacon, our Shakespeare. '02(Ap26) il. O. bds., net, $2. Goodspeed.
Reed, Eliphalet A. Idea of God in relation to theology. '02(F15) 8°, pap., net, 75 c. Univ. of Chic.
Reed, J: O., *and* Guthe, K. E. Manual of physical measurements. '02(Ap12) O. $1.50. Wahr.
REFORM.
See Temperance.
REFORMATION (The).
See Church history;—Huguenots.
REFORMED CHURCH.
Good. Historical handbk. of Ref. Ch. in U. S. 50 c.; 25 c. Heidelberg.
Good. Women of the Ref. Ch. $1. Heidelberg.
REGENERATION.
Sloan. Social regeneration the work of Christianity. net, 60 c. Westminster.
See also Salvation.
Regiments and armories of Mass. Hall, C: W. per set, $12; $18; $25. W. W. Potter.
Regional anatomy of head and neck. Eckley, W: T. net, $2.50. Lea.
Reid, *Sir* Wemyss. William Black, novelist. '02(Ap26) D. net, $2.25. Harper.
Reinsch, Paul S. Colonial government. '02 (Je21) D. (Citizen's lib. of economics, politics and sociology.) net, $1.25. Macmillan.
Religio medici. Browne, *Sir* T: **$12 net. Lane.
RELIGION.
De Solla. Fallacies of religion. 25 c. Pierce & Z.
Jastrow. Study of religion. $1.50. Scribner.
Spalding. Religion, agnosticism and education. net, 80 c. McClurg.
Tolstoi. What is religion? net, 60 c. Crowell.
See also Natural religion;—Revivals;—Skepticism.
RELIGION AND SCIENCE.
Bixby. The new world and the new thought. net, $1. Whittaker.
Smyth. Through science to faith. net, $1.50. Scribner.
See also Evolution;—Natural religion.
Religion for the time. Conger, A. B. net, $1. Jacobs.
Religion of Bible lands. Margoliouth, D: S: 60 c. Armstrong.
Religion of capital. Lafarque, P. 10 c. Socialistic Co-op.
Religion of Israel. Greenstone, J. H. 50 c. Bloch.
Religion of science lib. D. pap. Open Court.
—Kant. Prolegomena to any future metaphysics. 50 c. (53.) Open Court.
—Leibniz. Discourse on metaphysics. 35 c. (52.)
RELIGIONS.
Chantepie de la Saussaye. Religion of the Teutons. $2.50. Ginn.
Martin. Traces of the elder faiths of Ireland. 2 v. $12. Longmans.
See also Christianity;—Oriental religions.
Religious and social work amongst girls. Freeman, F. L. net, $1. Whittaker.
RELIGIOUS LIBERTY.
Cobb. Rise of rel. liberty in America. net, $4. Macmillan.

Religious life and influence of Queen Victoria. Walsh, W. net, $2.50. Dutton.
Reliques of Stratford-on-Avon. Way, A. E. net, 50 c.; net, 75 c. Lane.
REMBRANDT, H. van Rijn.
Bell. Rembrandt van Rijn. $1.75. Macmillan.
Remedies of the Great Physician. Kohaus, H. M. 40 c. Alliance.
Remedy for love. Kirk, *Mrs.* E. O. $1.25. Houghton, M. & Co.
Reminiscences of a dramatic critic. Clapp, H: A. net, $1.75. Houghton, M. & Co.
Remsen, Ira. Introd. to the study of chemistry. 6th rev., enl. ed. '01· '02(Mr15) D. (Am. sci. ser.; briefer course.) $1.12. Holt.
Remy, Arth. F. J. Influence of India and Persia on the poetry of Germany. '02(F1) 8°, (Columbia Univ. Germanic studies, v. 1, no. 4.) pap., net, $1. Macmillan.
RENAISSANCE.
Smeaton. The Medici and the Italian Renaissance. $1.25. Scribner.
See also names of countries.
Rénan, J. Ernest. Life of Jesus. '02(Jl12) 12°, (Home lib.) $1. Burt.
Renan, J. Ernest. Souvenirs d' enfance et de jeunesse; ed. by I. Babbitt. '02(Mr8) D. (Modern lang. ser.) 75 c. Heath.
REPENTANCE.
See Confession.
Representative men. Emerson, R: W. $1. Burt.
REPTILES.
Seeley. Dragons of the air: extinct flying reptiles. net, $1.40. Appleton.
See also Amphibia.
Republic of Plato. *See* Nettleship, R: L.—Plato.
REPUBLICAN PARTY.
Halstead. Victorious republicanism. $1.50; $2.25. Dominion.
Rescue (The). Sedgwick, A. D. $1.50. Century Co.
RESURRECTION.
Swartz. Easter and the resurrection. net, 15 c. Revell.
See also Future life;—Jesus Christ.
Retail advertising. Farrington, F. net, $1. Baker & T.
Retzius, G. *See* Nordenskiold, G.
REVELATION (Book of).
See Bible.
Revelations from the eternal world given to one of the mystic brotherhood. no. 1. '02 (Jl19) sq. S. pap., 20 c. Star.
REVERE, Paul.
Andrews. Paul Revere and his engraving. $23.50; $40. Scribner.
Revised repts. *See* Pollock, *Sir* F:
REVIVALS.
Oliver. Soul-winners' secrets: revival textbook. 25 c. Jennings.
Strong. The next great awakening. 75 c. Baker & T.
Rewards of taste. Bridge, N. $1.50. H. S. Stone.
Reynolds, Alphæus. Rudiments of Latin. '02 (Ap26) D. $1.25. A. B. Reynolds.
Reynolds, Cuyler. The banquet book. '02 (Ap12) il. D. net, $1.75. Putnam.
Reynolds, O. Papers on mechanical and physical subjects. v. 2, 1881-1900. '02 (Ap26) 8°, net, $6. Macmillan.
Rhead, E. L., *and* Sexton, A. H. Assaying and metallurgical analysis. '02(Ap19) il. O. $4.20. Longmans.
Rhead, L:, *ed.* Speckled brook trout, by various experts with rod and reel. '02 (Mr29) O. net, $3.50. Russell.
Rheingold. Wagner, R: 75 c. Newson.
RHETORIC.
Kellogg. How to teach composition writing. 25 c. Kellogg.
Lockwood. Teachers' manual to accompany Composition and rhetoric. 30 c. Ginn.
Peterson. First steps in Eng. composition. 35 c. Flanagan.
Scott. Composition literature. $1. Allyn & B.
Thornton. Eng. composition. 75 c. Crowell.
RHODE ISLAND.
Smith, J. J., *comp.* Civil and military list of R. I., 1800-1850. net, $7.50. Preston.
See also Block Island.
RHODES, Cecil.
Hensman. Cecil Rhodes. net, $5. Harper.
Rhodes, W. G. Elem. treatise on alternating currents. '02(Mr8) il. O. $2.60. Longmans.
RHODESIA.
See Matabeleland.
Rhone, Rosamond D. Days of the Son of man. '02(My24) D. net, $1.20. Putnam.
Rhymes from time to time. Doane, W: C. $1.50. Albany Diocesan Press.
Rice, Edn. W. Our sixty-six sacred books. 10th ed., enl., with analysis and questions. '02(F1) D. (Green fund book, no. 10.) net, 50 c. Am. S. S.
Rice, Edn. W. Short hist. of the Internat. lesson system, with classified list of lessons for thirty-three years; prep. by C. R. Williams. '02(Jl19) S. leath., *25 c. net. Amer. S. S.
Rice, Elmer C. Robinson method of breeding squabs. '01· '02(Mr15); 2d ed., rev. with supp. (Je28) il. 12°, pap., ea., 50 c. Plymouth Rock.
Richard, Marg. A. Darkey ways in Dixie. '02(Ap26) il. D. $1. Abbey Press.
Richards, Ellen H., *and* Williams, Louise H. '02(Ap19) 8°, net, $1.50. Wiley.
Richards, *Mrs.* Laura E. H. Mrs. Tree. Handy vol. ed. '02(Jl12) il. S. †75 c. Estes.
Richardson, J: War of 1812; with notes and a life of author, by A. C. Casselman. '02 (Ap26) il. O. subs., $3. Hist. Pub.
Riddell, J: H., *rep.* *See* New Hampshire. *Sup. ct.* Repts.
Riddle of life. Johnston, J. W. $1.50. Jennings.
RIDDLES.
Cutter, *comp.* Conundrums, riddles, puzzles and games. 50 c.; 25 c. Otis.
Ride in Morocco. Macnab, F. $5. Longmans.
Rideal, S: Sewage and the bacterial purification of sewage. 2d ed. '02(Ap5) 8°, $3.50. Wiley.
Ridpath, J: C. Hist. of the U. S. '01, '02 (F15) 4 v. in 2 v., il. 12°, $6. Grosset.
Riehl, W. H. Das spielmannskind und stumme ratsherr; ed. by G: M. Priest. '02(F15) D. 35 c. Am. Bk.

RIFLE.
Fremantle. Book of the rifle. $5. Longmans.

Rigby, Will O. Reliable candy teacher and soda and ice cream formulas. [8th ed., rev. and enl.] '02(Ap12) D. pap., $2. W. O. Rigby.

Riggs, *Mrs.* G: C. *See* Wiggin, *Mrs.* K. D.

Right living. Morris, E. G. $1. Bardeen.

Right reading; counsel on the choice and use of books sel. fr. ten famous authors. '02 (Mr15) S. net, 80 c. McClurg.

Rights and wrongs of the Transvaal war. Cook, E: T. $2. Longmans.

Rime of the ancient mariner. Coleridge, S: T. 30 c.; 25 c. B. F. Johnson.

Ringing questions. Peck, G: C. $1. Eaton & M.

Rip Van Winkle. *See* Irving, W.

Rise and development of Chr. architecture. Ayer, J. C. net, $1.50. Young Churchman.

Rise of a soul. Vance, J. J. net, $1. Revell.

Rise of religious liberty in America. Cobb, S. H. net, $4. Macmillan.

Rita, *pseud.* *See* Humphreys, *Mrs.* E. M. J. G.

Ritchie, D: G. Plato. '02(Ap12) D. (World's epoch-makers.) $1.25. Scribner.

Ritchie, D: G. Studies in political and social ethics. '02(Mr29) 12°, $1.50. Macmillan.

Ritchie, M. J. G., *and* Harrison, W. Table tennis, and how to play it. '02(Je7) il. sq. S. 50 c. Lippincott.

Ritchie, M. J. G., *and* Parker, A. Ping-pong; ed. for Am. players by W. H. Bronson. '02 (My3) il. S. 50 c. Street.

RITUAL.
See **Ministers** (*of the Gospel*).

Rivas, Evelyn de. Little French dinners. '02 (My24) 12°, 50 c. New Amsterdam.

Riverside art ser. D. net, 75 c.; School ed., net, 50 c.; pap., net, 35 c. Houghton, M. & Co.
—Hurll, *ed.* Tuscan sculpture. (11.)—Van Dyck. (12.)

Riverside biog. ser. S. net, 65 c.; School ed., net, 50 c. Houghton, M. & Co.
—Brown. Stephen A. Douglas. (13.)
—Sedgwick. Samuel de Champlain. (14.)

Riverside literature ser. S. pap., net, 15 c. Houghton, M. & Co.
—Ewing. Jackanapes; [also] The brownies.
—La Rame. Dog of Flanders and Nürnberg stove. (150.)
—Shakespeare. Twelfth night. (149.)

Riverside pap. ser. 16°, pap., 50 c. Houghton, M. & Co.
—Burnham. A great love.

Rives, Hallie E. Hearts courageous. '02 (Je7) il. D. $1.50. Bowen-M.

ROADS.
Judson. City roads and pavements. $2. Engineering News.
Spalding. Text-book on roads and pavements. $2. Wiley.
See also Railroads;—Street-railroads.

Rob Roy. *See* Sullivan, *Sir* E:

Robb, Hunter. Aseptic surgical technique. 2d ed., rev. '02(Jl19) il. 12°, $2. Lippincott.

Robbins, *Mrs.* S. S. Miss Ashton's new pupil. '02(Ap5) 12°, (Fireside ser.) $1. Burt.

Roberts, C: G: D. Kindred of the wild. '02 (Je7) il. O. $2. L. C. Page.

Roberts, C: G: D. Poems. [New issue.] '02(My10) D. $1.50. L. C. Page.

ROBERTS, John.
Camm. Benedictine martyr in England: life and times of Dom John Roberts. net, $1.25. Herder.

Roberts, O. A. Hist. of the Military Company of the Mass., now called the Ancient and Honorable Artillery Co. of Mass., 1637-1888. In 4 v. v. 4. '01. '02(Mr22) 4°. [Sold only to members.] Mudge.

Robertson, A. I. Lessons on the Gospel of St. Mark. '02(Ap12) nar. 16°, net, 40 c. Revell.

Robertson, Harrison. The opponents. '02 (Ap19) D. $1.50. Scribner.

Robertson, Ja. Early religion of Israel. '02 (Ap12) 12°, net, $1.60. Whittaker.

Robertson, Leslie S. Water-tube boilers. '01-'02(Ja4) il. O. $3. Van Nostrand.

Robertson, W: Studies in the Acts of the Apostles. '02(F8) 16°, 40 c. Revell.

ROBESPIERRE, Max. M. I.
Belloc. Robespierre. net, $2. Scribner.

Robin Hood. *See* Pyle, H.

Robinson, Arth. W. Personal life of the clergy. '02(F8) D. (Handbooks for the clergy.) net, 90 c. Longmans.

ROCKAWAY, N. J.
Crayon. Rockaway records of Morris Co., N. J., families. $3. Rockaway.

Rockhaven. Munn, C: C. $1.50. Lee & S.

ROCKY MOUNTAINS.
Nelson. Analytical key to some of the common flowering plants of the Rocky Mt. region. **45 c. net. Appleton.

Roddy, H. J. Complete geography. '02 (Je28) il. F. $1. Am. Bk.

Roddy, H. J. Elem. geography. '02(My24) il. Q. 50 c. Am. Bk.

Roe, Alfr. S. Worcester Young Men's Christian Assoc. '01- '02(Mr22) O. $1. A. S. Roe.

ROENTGEN RAYS.
Monell. Instruction in X-ray methods and medical uses of light, hot air, vibration and high frequency currents. subs., $15. Pelton.
Walsh. Roentgen rays in medical work. net, $2.50. Wood.

Rogers, Alice A. A waiting race. '02(Jl12) D. 50 c. Abbey Press.

Rogers, C: G. Government clerks: (ballads.) '02(Jl19) nar. O. $1; pap., 25 c. McQuilkin.

Roget, M. *and* K. *See* Alissas, R. d'.

Roi Apépi (Le). Cherbuliez, C: V: 60 c. W: R. Jenkins.

Role of the unconquered. Dalton, T. $1.50. G: W. Dillingham.

Rollins, Alice W. Story of Azron. '01. '02 (F22) 12°, $1. Holliswood.

Roman Africa. Graham, A. $6. Longmans.

Roman Biznet. Pangborn, G. W. $1.50. Houghton, M. & Co.

ROMAN EMPIRE.
Hellems. Lex de imperio Vespasiani. 50 c. Scott, F. & Co.

ROMAN LAW.
See **Civil law**.

Roman mystery. Bagot, R: $1.50. Lane.

Romance of a rogue. Sharts, J. W. $1.50. H. S. Stone.

Romance of Leonardo da Vinci, the forerunner. Merejkowski, D. †$1.50. Putnam.
ROMANISM.
See Catholic church.
Romans choisis. 12°, pap. W: R. Jenkins.
—Cherbuliez. Le roi Apépi. 60 c. (25.)
Romantic love and personal beauty. Finck, H: T. net, $2. Macmillan.
ROME.
Fustel de Coulanges. Ancient city: study on the rel., laws and institutions of Greece and Rome. $2. Lee & S.
Gregorovius. Rome in the Middle Ages. v. 8. net, $3. Macmillan.
Miller. Mediæval Rome from Hilderbrand to Clement VIII. **$1.35 net; $1.60 net. Putnam.
Seignobos. Hist. of the Roman people. *$1.25 net. Holt.
See also Tiberius.
Rood, H: E: Hardwicke. '02(My10) D. $1.50. Harper.
Rood, J: R. Treatise on the law of attachments, garnishments, judgments, and executions. '01. '02(Mr8) O. $3. Wahr.
ROOFS.
Merriman *and* Jacoby. Text-book on roofs and bridges. pt. 3. $2.50. Wiley.
Rook, Alb. W. The Butler family. '01. '02 (Ja11) $3. Lakeside Press.
Roosevelt, T. Message to the two houses at the beginning of the first session of the 57th Congress. '02(Mr29) sq. f°, $1. N. Y. State Lib.
Roosevelt, T. Rough Riders. New permanent lib. ed. '02(Mr1) il. 12°, $1.50. Scribner.
Roosevelt, T., Van Dyke, T. S., Elliot, D. G., *and* Stone, A. J. The deer family. '02 (My17) il. O. net, $2. Macmillan.
ROOSEVELT, T.
Banks *and* Armstrong. Theodore Roosevelt. $1.50; $2.25. Du Mont.
Halstead. Life of Theodore Roosevelt. subs., $2.50; $3.75: $3.50; $5. Saalfield.
Meyers. Theodore Roosevelt. subs., $1.50; $2. W. W. Wilson.
Meyers. Theodore Roosevelt. $1.50; $2. Ziegler.
See also Fallows, S.;—Wilson, J. G.
ROOSEVELT FAMILY.
Whittelsey, *comp.* Roosevelt genealogy, 1649-1902. $5. C: B. Whittelsey.
Root, Edn. A. Military topography and sketching. Rev. and enl. [3d] ed. '02 (Jl19) il. 8°, $2.50. Hudson-K.
Root, Fk. A., *and* Connelley, W: E. Overland stage to California. '01. '02(Ap12) il. 12°, $2.50; hf. mor., $3.50. Root & C.
Roots of Christian teaching as found in the O. T. Barton, G: A. $1.25. Winston.
Roper, W: *See* More, *Sir* T:
Rose, J: H. Life of Napoleon I. '02(F22) 2 v., il. 8°, net, $4. Macmillan.
Rose, Wa. M. *See* Texas. Notes on repts.
Rose of the wilderness. Browne, W. S. $1.25. W. S. Browne.
Rosen, P: The Catholic church and secret societies. '02(My10) 12°, net, $1. Caspar.
Rosen im schnee. Nies, K. 50 c. Witter.
Rosenberger, J. L., *comp.* Law for lumbermen. '02(Je28) O. shp., $3.50. Am. Lumberman.

ROSES.
Melliar. Book of the rose. $1.75. Macmillan.
Ross, Janet. Florentine villas; with reproduction in photogravure from Zocchi's etchings. '02(Mr8) f°, $25. Dutton.
Ross, Ronald. Malarial fever. New 9th ed., rev. and enl. '02(Ap26) O. net, 75 c. Longmans.
Ross, Ronald. Mosquito brigades and how to organize them. '02(F8) O. net, 90 c. Longmans.
Rossetti, Helen M. M. Ford Madox Brown. '01· '02(F8) il. S. bds., net, 35 c. Beam.
Rostand, E. Cyrano de Bergerac; notes by Reed P. Clark. '02(Mr8) D. pap., 50 c. W: R. Jenkins.
Rostopchine, Sophie de. *See* Segur, S. R., *Comtesse* de.
Rotch, T: M. Pediatrics. New rev. ed. '01· '02(F15) 8°, subs., $6; shp., $7. Lippincott.
Roterberg, A. Card tricks. '02(Mr15) S. pap., 25 c. Drake.
Rough notes on remedies. Murray, W: net, $1.25. Blakiston.
ROUGH RIDERS.
Roosevelt. The Rough Riders. $1.50. Scribner.
Roulet, Ma. F. N. Saint Anthony in art, and other sketches. '01. '02(Ja11) il. D. $2. Marlier.
Rouse, Adelaide L. Annice Wynkoop, artist. '02(Mr29) il. 12°, (Fireside ser.) $1. Burt.
Rouse, Adelaide L. The Deane girls. '01. '02(Mr29) il. 12°, (Fireside lib.) $1. Burt.
Rouse, Adelaide L. Under my own roof. '02(Mr8) il. D. net, $1.20. Funk.
Rowe, Henrietta G. Maid of Bar Harbor. '02(Je21) il. D. $1.50. Little, B. & Co.
Rowell, J. H. Everybody's opportunity; or, quick socialism. '01. '02(Mr8) O. pap., 10 c. Free Socialist.
Rowell, J. H. Workingman's opportunity. 2d ed. '01. '02(Mr8) O. pap., 5 c. Free Socialist.
Royal lineage. Watson, *Mrs.* A. R. $4.50. Whittet.
Royal navy. Clowes, W: L. v. 5, 6. ea., net, $6.50. Little, B. & Co.
Rubáiyát. *See* Omar Khayyam.
Rubáiyat of Omar Khayyám, jr. Irwin, W. net, 50 c. Elder.
Ruble, W: Wonders of the Revelation of Jesus Christ. '01· '02(Mr22) D. $1. Standard Pub.
Rudder "how-to" ser. Q. $1. Rudder.
—Fisher. How to build a model yacht.
—Mower. How to build a knockabout.—How to build a racing sloop.
Ruggles, Jean. Exercises and problems in arithmetic. '01. '02(F22) 16°, pap., 25 c. W: R. Jenkins.
Ruling elder. Erdman, C: R. 3 c. Presb. Bd.
Rumsey, W: Practice in civil actions in courts of record of the state of N. Y., under the code of civil procedure. 2d ed. v. 1. '02(Je14) O. shp., $6. Banks & Co.
Ruskay, Esther J. Hearth and home essays. '02(Mr29) D. (Special ser., no. 6.) bds., 30 c. Jewish Pub.
Ruskin, J: Pen pictures. Pt. 2. '02(My17) T. $1. Longmans.

RUSKIN, John.
Collingwood. Life of John Ruskin. net, $2. Houghton, M. & Co.
Turner. Turner and Ruskin. 2 v. net, $50. Dodd.
RUSKIN CO-OPERATIVE ASSOC.
Broome. Last days of the Ruskin Co-operative Assoc. 50 c. Kerr.
Russell, C: E. Such stuff as dreams. '02 (Je28) 8°, net, $2. Bowen-M.
Russell, G: W: E. Onlooker's note-book. '02(Je7) O. net, $2.25. Harper.
Russell, Harry L. Outlines of dairy bacteriology. 5th ed., rev. '02(Mr29) il. 12°, $1. H. L. Russell.
Russell, Norman. Village work in India. '02 (My17) 12°, net, $1. Revell.
Russell, W: Prescriptions and instructions for treating the diseases of the feet and legs of the horse. '02(Jl12) il. 8°, pap., $1. Clarke.
Russell, W: C. Captain Fanny. '02(Ap20) 12°, (Red letter ser.) $1.25; pap., 50 c. New Amsterdam.
Russell, W: C. Mate of the good ship "York." '02(Je7) D. $1.50. L. C. Page.
Russell, W: H., *and* Winslow, W: B. Syllabus-digest of decisions of the sup. ct. of the U. S. v. 3. '02(Ap5) O. shp., $6.50. Banks.
Russells (The) in Chicago. Wheaton, E. $1.25. L. C. Page.
RUSSIA.
Howard. Prisoners of Russia. net, $1.40. Appleton.
Kovalevsky. Russian political institutions. net, $1.50. Univ. of Chic.
Morfill. Hist. of Russia from Peter the Great to Nicholas II. $1.75. Pott.
Wright. Asiatic Russia. 2 v. **$7.50 net. McClure, P.
See also Finland;—*also* Peter III.
RUSSIAN LITERATURE.
Wiener. Anthology of Russian literature. In 2 pts. pt. 1. net, $3. Putnam.
Rust, C. D. *See* New York. Penal code.
Rustler (The). McElrath, F. net, $1.20. Funk.
Rutherford, S: Christ and his cross. '02 (Mr8) S. $1. Longmans.
Ruthless rhymes. *See* Streamer, D.
Rutland home of Rufus Putnam. Earle, S. C. 30 c.; 50 c. S. C. Earle.
Rutledge. Harris, *Mrs.* M. C. $1. Burt.
Ryan, M. B. Elocution and dramatic art. '02(Jl19) 16°, 75 c. Angel Press.
Sabatini, R. Suitors of Yvonne. '02(Je7) D. net, $1.20. Putnam.
Sabertooth (The). Kinder, S. 75 c.; 25 c. Laird.
Sacred anthology. Conway, M. D. $2. Holt.
Sacred beetle. Ward, J: net, $3.50. Scribner.
Sacrificio (El) de Elisa. Maxwell, *Mrs.* M. E. B. 50 c. Appleton.
Sadlier, Anna T. Mary Tracy's fortune. '02 (Mr8) S. 45 c. Benziger.
Sage, Dean, Townsend, C. H., Smith, H. M., *and* Harris, W: C. Salmon and trout. '02 (Je28) il. 12°, (Am. sportsman's lib.) net, $2; large pap. ed., hf. mor., net, $7.50. Macmillan.
Sage, W: The Claybornes. '02(Ap26) il. D. $1.50. Houghton, M. & Co.
St. Cyres, *Viscount*, [Stafford Harry Northcote.] Life of François Fenelon. '02(F15) 8°, net, $2.50. Dutton.
St. Nicholas ser. See Burt's.
Saint-Pierre, J. H. B. de. Paul and Virginia. '02(Ap19) il. D. (Home lib.) $1. Burt.
ST. PIERRE.
Welch *and* Taylor. Destruction of St. Pierre, Martinique. 50 c. Fenno.
Sainte-Foi, C: The perfect woman; fr. the Fr., by Z. N. Brown. '01. '02(Ja11) S. net, $1. Marlier.
SAINTS.
Banks. Great saints of the Bible. $1.50. Eaton & M.
Newman. Lives of Eng. saints. 6 v. net, $12. Lippincott.
Scheeben. Holiness of the church in the 19th century. 10 c. Benziger.
See also Fathers.
Sajous, C: E. de M., *ed.* Analytical encyclopædia of practical medicine. Rev. ed. In 6 v. v. 1. '02(Ap26) il. 8°, subs., per v., $5; hf. rus., per v., $6. Davis.
SALE.
Freeman. Law of void judicial sales. $4. Cen. Law Journ.
Salis, *Mrs.* Ht. A. de. A la mode cookery up-to-date recipes. '02(Ap26) il. D. $2. Longmans.
SALMON.
Sage, *and others*. Salmon and trout. net, $2; net, $7.50. Macmillan.
SALOONS.
Rankin. Saloon law nullification and its cure. 50 c. Advance.
See also Temperance.
Saltus, F. S. Mount of Olives: [poem.] '02(Ap12) sq. S. bds., $1; pap., net, 25 c. Bk. Lover.
SALVATION.
Firey. Infant salvation. net, $1.20. Funk.
Gladden. Social salvation. net, $1. Houghton, M. & Co.
Samantha at Saratoga. Holley, M. $1. Burt.
Sand, George, [*pseud.* for A. L. A. Dudevant.] Masterpieces. v. 15. '02(Mr15); v. 16 (Ap5); v. 17, 18 (Je28) 8°, subs. (Apply to pubs. for price.) Barrie.
Sandals (The). Grenell, Z. net, 40 c. Funk.
Sanders, C: H. How are we led? and Who is it that leads us? '01. '02(Ja4) 8°, $1.50. Donohue.
Sanderson, E. D. Insects injurious to staple crops. '01. '02(Ja18) il. 12°, $1.50. Wiley.
Sanderson, Jos. Story of Saint Patrick. '02 (Je7) O. $1.50. Ketcham.
Sandys, Edwyn, *and* Van Dyke, T. S. Upland game birds. '02(Je7) il. 8°, (Am. sportsman's lib.) net, $2; large pap. ed., hf. mor., net, $7.50. Macmillan.
SANITARY ENGINEERING.
Baker. Municipal engineering and sanitation. net, $1.25. Macmillan.
See also Heating;—Plumbing;—Sewage and sewerage;—Water-supply.
SANITARY SCIENCE.
See Hygiene;—Sanitary engineering.
SANSKRIT LANGUAGE.
Macdonell. Sanskrit grammar for beginners. $3. Longmans.
Santanelli, [*pseud.* for Ja. Hawthorne Loryea.] Is man a free agent? The law of suggestion. '02(Jl19) il. O. *$1 net. Santanelli.

SANTIAGO.
See **Schley, W. S.**
Sara. Newberry, F. E. $1. Burt.
Sarah the less. Swett, S. net, 75 c. Westminster.
Sarita, the Carlist. Marchmont, A. W. $1.50. Stokes.
Sarles, J: W. **Man's peerless destiny in** Christ. '01. '02(Mr1) 12°, net, 90 c. Funk.
Satan and demons. Townsend, L. T. net, 25 c. Jennings.
Satchel (A) guide for the vacation tourist in Europe. 1902. '02(Mr15) S. leath., net, $1.50. Houghton, M. & Co.
SATIRE.
See **Parody;—Wit and humor.**
Saunders, Ripley D. John Kenadie. '02 (My17) D. $1.50. Houghton, M. & Co.
Saussure, Cæsar de. Foreign view of England in the reign of George I. and George II. '02(Je7) 8°, net, $3. Dutton.
Savage, R: H. For a young queen's bright eyes. '02(My24) O. $1.25; pap., 50 c. Home.
Savill, T: D. Clinical lectures on neurasthenia. '02(Je28) 8°, $1.50. Wood.
SAVINGS-BANKS.
Hamilton. Savings and savings institutions. net, $2.25. Macmillan.
Savonarola, *Fra* Girolama. Triumph of the cross; ed. by Fa. J: Proctor. '02(Mr8) 8°, net, $1.35. Herder.
SAYRE FAMILY.
Banta. Sayre family. $10. T. M. Banta.
Scadding, C: Direct answers to plain questions for Am. churchmen: expansion of the church catechism. '01. '02(Ja4) D. (Grade A handbook.) bds., net, 50 c. Whittaker.
SCARABS.
Ward. Sacred beetle: treatise on Egyptian scarabs. net, $3.50. Scribner.
Scarlet and hyssop. Benson, E: F: $1.50. Appleton.
Scenery of England. Lubbock, *Sir* J: net, $2.50. Macmillan.
Scenes of rural life in Hampshire. Capes, W. W. net, $2.75. Macmillan.
Schaeffer, *Mrs.* Jennie. **Metropolitan club cook-book, New York City.** '02(Mr15) 16°, oil cl., $1.75. Augsburg.
Schäfer, E. A. Directions for class work in practical physiology. '01. '02(F8) il. O. net, $1. Longmans.
Schäfer, E: A. Essentials in histology. 6th ed. '02(Jl19) il. 8°, *$3 net. Lea.
Schaffer, W: I., *rep. See* Penn. *Superior ct.* Repts.—*Supreme ct.* Repts.
Schauffler, A. F. *See* Bible. Sunday-school scholars' Bible.
Scheeben, M. J. Holiness of the church in the nineteenth century; fr. the Germ.; ed. by J: P. M. Schleuter. '02(My24) S. pap., 10 c. Benziger.
Schell, W: G. **Is the negro a beast?: reply** to Carroll's book entitled The negro a beast. '01. '02(F15) il. D. 60 c. Gospel Trumpet.
Schelling, Felix E. **English chronicle play.** '02(F1) 8°, net, $2. Macmillan.
Scherer, Rob. G., *rep. See* New York. *Cts. of record.* Misc. repts.
Schiller, J. C. F. v. Don Carlos, Mary Stuart; ed. by N. H. Dole. Ed. de luxe. '02 (Je28) 12°. (App. to pubs. for price.) Niccolls.
Schiller, J. C. F. v. **History of the revolt of** the Netherlands; ed. by N. H. Dole. Ed. de luxe. '01. '02(Mr15) 8°. (App. to pubs. for price.) Niccolls.
Schiller, J. C. F. v. **History of the thirty** years' war in Germany; ed. by N. H. Dole. Ed. de luxe. '02(Mr15) 8°. (App. to pubs. for price.) Niccolls.
Schiller, J. C. F. v. **Die jungfrau von Orleans;** notes by A. B. Nichols and vocab. by W: A. Hervey. [New ed.] '01. '02 (F1) S. net, 60 c. Holt.
Schiller, J. C. F. v. Maid of Orleans; Bride of Messina; Wilhelm Tell; Demetrius. Ed. de luxe. '02(Jl5) 12°. (App. to pubs. for price.) Niccolls.
Schiller, J. C. F. v. **Maria Stuart; ed. by E:** S. Joynes; vocab. by W: A. Hervey. [New ed.] '02(F1) S. net, 70 c. Holt.
Schiller, J. C. F. v. **The Piccolomini; Death** of Wallenstein; Wallenstein's camp; ed. by N. H. Dole. Ed. de luxe. '02(Mr22) 8°. (App. to pubs. for price.) Niccolls.
Schiller, J. C. F. v. Poems; tr. into Eng. by E. P. Arnold-Foster. '02(My24) D. net, $1.60. Holt.
Schiller, J. C. F. v. **Wallenstein; notes by** W. H. Carruth. 2d ed., rev. '01. '02(F1) S. net, $1. Holt.
SCHILLER, J. C. F. v.
Thomas. Life and works of Schiller. **$1.50 net. Holt.
SCHLEY, Winfield Scott.
Graham. Schley and Santiago. $1.50. Conkey.
Nauticus, *pseud.* Truth about the Schley case. 25 c. Columbia.
Schmidt, Emanuel. Solomon's temple in the light of other oriental temples. '02(Je7) il. O. net, $1. Univ. of Chic.
Schofield, Alfr. T. **Springs of character.** '01. '02(Mr1) 8°, net, $1.30. Funk.
Schofield, R. J., *comp.*, ["One of the craft."] Drummer's yarns and funny jokes; 9th crop. '02(Jl12) O. (Excelsior lib., no. 67.) pap., 25 c. Excelsior.
School congress. Vancil, F. M. 25 c. Kellogg.
SCHOOL-HOUSES.
See **Architecture.**
SCHOOLS.
Clark. Public schools of Chicago. net, 50 c. Univ. of Chic.
Hughes. Schools at home and abroad. net, $1.50. Dutton.
Wray. Jean Mitchell's school. $1.25. Public Sch. Pub.
Young. Ethics in the school. net, 25 c.—Isolation in the school. net, 50 c. Univ. of Chic.
See also **Education;—Illinois;—Kindergarten;—Sunday-school;—Westminster;—Wisconsin.**
Schrader, Ferd. Friedrich der Grosse und der Siebenjährige Krieg; ed. by R. H. Allpress. Authorized ed. '02(My17) 12°, (Siepmann's elem. Germ. ser.) net, 50 c. Macmillan.
SCHUREMAN FAMILY.
Wynkoop. Schuremans of N. J. $3. R: Wynkoop.

Schuyler, Aaron. Systems of ethics. '02 (My17) O. $1.50. Jennings.
Schuyler, M., *jr., comp. See* Avesta.
Schuyler, W: Ambassador of Christ: biog. of Rev. Montgomery Schuyler. '02(Mr8) 8°, $1.50. Gorham.
SCIENCE.
Gage. Introd. to physical science. $1. Ginn.
Lippincott's elem. science readers. 3 pts. pt. 1, 25 c.; pt. 2, 30 c.; pt. 3, 35 c. Lippincott.
Strutt. Scientific papers. v. 3, 1887-92. net, $5. Macmillan.
See also Chemistry;—Evolution; — Microscope; — Philosophy;—Religion and science.
Scientific memoirs; ed. by J. S. Ames. O. $1. Am. Bk.
—Brace, *ed.* Laws of radiation and absorption. (15.)
—Randall, *ed. and tr.* Expansion of gases by heat. (14.)
Scofield, Cora L. Study of the court of star chamber. '02(Mr22) 8°, pap., net, $1. Univ. of Chic.
Scollard, Clinton. Cloistering of Ursula. '02 (F15) il. D. $1.50. L. C. Page.
SCOTLAND.
Addis. Cathedrals and abbeys of Presb. Scotland. net, $2.50. Presb. Bd.
Brown. Hist. of Scotland. v. 2. net, $1.50. Macmillan.
Whitcomb. Little journey to Scotland. 15 c. Flanagan.
See also England;—Hebrides.
SCOTS.
Crosland. The unspeakable Scot. **$1.25 net. Putnam.
Hanna. The Scotch-Irish. 2 v. net, $10. Putnam.
Scott, Fred N. Composition literature. '02 (Je28) 12°, $1. Allyn & B.
Scott, Temple, *ed. See* Swift, J.
Scott, *Sir* W. Kenilworth. '02(Mr22) 12°, (Eng. classics.) net, 60 c. Macmillan.
Scott, *Sir* W. Quentin Durward. '02(Mr8) 12°, (Eng. classics.) net, 60 c. Macmillan.
Scott, *Sir* W. Stories from Waverley for children. 5th ed. '02(My3) il. 12°, $1. Macmillan.
Scott, *Sir* W. Waverley; condensed and ed. for school reading by A. L. Bouton. '02 (My10) D. (Standard lit. ser., double no. 50.) 30 c.; pap., 20 c. University.
Scott, *Sir* W. *See also* Sullivan, *Sir* E:
Scottish men of letters in 18th century. Graham, H: G. net, $4.50. Macmillan.
Scottish philosophy in its national development. Laurie, H: net, $1.75. Macmillan.
Scribner's Am. hist. ser. D. net, $1. Scribner.
—Burgess. Reconstruction and the constitution, 1866-1876.
Scribner's contemporary sci. ser.; ed. by H. Ellis. 12°, $1.50. Scribner.
—Jastrow. Study of religion.
—Zittel. Hist. of geology and palæontology to end of 19th century.
Scribner's ser. of school reading. il. D. net, 60 c. Scribner.
—Cervantes Saavedra. Don Quixote.
—Pyle. Some merry adventures of Robin Hood.
—Thompson. Krag and Johnny Bear.
Scribner's social sci. ser. 12°, $1. Scribner.
—Cumming. Public house reform.
Scudder's eclectic manual. D. net, $2.50. Scudder.
—Mundy. Eclectic practice in diseases of children. (5.)
SCULPTURE.
Hurll, *ed.* Tuscan sculpture. net, 75 c.; net, 50 c.; net, 35 c. Houghton, M. & Co.
See also Ivory;—Tombstones.
Scutage and knight service in England. Baldwin, J. F. net, $1. Univ. of Chic.
Seager, H: R. Prof. Patten's theory of prosperity. '02(Mr22) 8°, (Pub. of the soc., no. 333.) pap., 15 c. Am. Acad. Pol. Sci.
Seal of destiny. Behymer, I. H. $1.50. Neely.
Searching for truth. '02(My24) O. $1.50. Eckler.
Sears, Hamblen. None but the brave. '02 (Ap12) il. D. $1.50. Dodd.
SEASHORE.
Wheeler. The sea coast. $4.50. Longmans.
SEAWEEDS.
See Algæ.
Second generation. Linn, J. W. $1.50. Macmillan.
SECRET SOCIETIES.
See Catholic church.
Sectional struggle. Harris, C. W. net, $2.50. Lippincott.
SECURITIES.
Hall. Pittsburg securities, 1902. gratis. R. C. Hall.
Moody, *ed.* Manual of corporation securities, 1902. $7.50; $10. Moody.
Sedding, J: D. Garden craft old and new. '02(Ap26) 8°, net, $2.50. Lane.
Sedgwick, Anne D. Confounding of Camelia. [New issue.] '02(My17) il. D. $1.50. Century Co.
Sedgwick, Anne D. Dull Miss Archinard. [New issue.] '02(My17) il. D. $1.50. Century Co.
Sedgwick, Anne D. The rescue. '02(My10) il. D. $1.50. Century Co.
Sedgwick, H: D., *jr.* Samuel de Champlain. '02(Ap5) S (Riverside biog. ser., no. 14.) net, 65 c.; School ed., net, 50 c. Houghton, M. & Co.
Sedgwick, W: T. Principles of sanitary science and the public health. '02(My17) 8°, net, $3. Macmillan.
Seebohm, F: Tribal custom in Anglo-Saxon law. '02(Mr8) O. net, $5. Longmans.
Seeley, H. G. Dragons of the air: extinct flying reptiles. '01· '02(F22) 12°, net, $1.40. Appleton.
Seeley, *Mrs.* L. Cook book; with chapters on domestic servants, and other details of household management. '02(Mr29) il. O. net, $2; hf. leath., net, $3. Macmillan.
Seeley, Levi. Foundations of education. '02 (F1) D. $1. Hinds.
Seger, Hermann A: Collected writings. In 2 v. v. 1. '02(Ap5) 8°, per set, $15. Chemical.
Segur, Sophie R., *Comtesse* de, [Sophie de Rostopchine.] Les malheurs de Sophie; ed. by E. White. '02(Je14) il. D. (Modern lang. ser.) 45 c. Heath.
Seigneur de Beaufoy. Drummond, H. $1.50. L. C. Page.

Seignobos, C: Hist. of the Roman people; ed. by W: Fairley. '02(Jl12) il. D. *$1.25 net. Holt.

SELBORNE.
White. Natural history of Selborne. 2 v. net, $20. Lippincott.

Selden, E: G. Story of the Christian centuries. '02(My3) 12°, net, $1. Revell.

Select sunflowers. Mills, H. E: $1. Sunflower Press.

SELF-CULTURE.
See Culture.

Self-educator ser. D. 75 c. Crowell.
—Thornton. Eng. composition.

Sellers, Edn. J. Allied families of Delaware. '01· '02(Mr1) 8°, $5. E. J. Sellers.

Selling the bear's hide. Davison, C: S. $1. Nassau Press.

Sellow, Grace E. Three thousand sample questions; [accompanying] Hill's Practical encyclopedia. '02(My10) il. D. pap., 50 c. Bellows.

Selover, A. W. Law of negotiable instruments for N. Y., Mass., Conn., R. I., [etc.] Iowa ed. '02(Je14) D. shp., $4. Keefe-D.

Selwyn, E: C. St. Luke the prophet. '01· '02(Ja4) 12°, net, $2.75. Macmillan.

Sema-Kanda. Turnbull, C. $1.25. Alliance.

SEMITIC LITERATURE.
Arnolt. Theolog. and Semitic literature for 1901. net, 50 c. Univ. of Chic.

SEMITIC PEOPLES.
Barton. Sketch of Semitic origins, social and religious. net, $3. Macmillan.

SEMITIC RELIGION.
Curtiss. Primitive Semitic religion to-day. net, $2. Revell.

Semitic ser. D. net, $1.25. Scribner.
—Duff. Theol. and ethics of the Hebrews. (2.)

Semon, *Sir* Felix. Some thoughts on the principles of local treatment in diseases of the upper air passages. '02(Mr22) 8°, net, $1. Macmillan.

Separation. Lee, M. $1.25. Buckles.

September days on Nantucket. Bliss, W: R. net, $1. Houghton, M. & Co.

Sergeant, Adeline. Master of Beechwood. '02(Jl12) 12°, (Manhattan lib. of new copyright fiction.) pap., 50 c. Burt.

Series of school histories; ed by C: K. Adams. 12°, $1.50. Allyn & B.
—West. Ancient history to death of Charlemagne.

SERMON ON THE MOUNT.
Bacon. Sermon on the Mount. net, $1. Macmillan.

SERMONS.
Banks. Windows for sermons. net, $1.25. Funk.

SERVANTS.
See Domestic economy.

Service (The). Thoreau, H: D: net, $2.50; net, $10. Goodspeed.

Seton-Thompson, E. E. *See* Thompson, E. E. Seton-.

Seven poor travellers. *See* Dickens, C:

Seventy-one days' camping in Morocco. Grove, *Lady* A. net, $2.50. Longmans.

SEWAGE AND SEWERAGE.
Folwell. Sewerage. $3. Wiley.
Fowler. Sewage works analyses. $2. Wiley.

SEWAGE AND SEWERAGE.—*Continued.*
Rideal. Sewage and the bacterial purification of sewage. $3.50. Wiley.
See also Sanitary engineering.

Seward, Thdr. F. How to get acquainted with God: Christian Science movement. '02(Mr29) nar. S. net, 50 c. Funk.

SEX.
Williams. Sex problems. net, $1. Revell.

Sexton, A. H. *See* Rhead, E. L.

SEYMOUR, Ct.
Campbell, *and others.* Seymour, past and present. $3. W: C. Sharpe.

Shackleton, Rob. Many waters. '02(Ap26) D. $1.50. Appleton.

Shadow and light. Gibbs, M. W. $1.50. M. W. Gibbs.

Shadow duellers. Freear, R. L: net, 60 c. Blanchard.

Shakespeare, W: Works. Dowden ed. (Craig [and] Dowden.) v. 3, King Lear. '02(Je28) 8°, $1.25. Bowen-M.

Shakespeare, W: Complete works. '02 (Ap5) il. 12°, $7; hf. mor., $10.50. Burt.

Shakespeare, W: Works. New century ed. (Is. Gollancz.) Ed. de luxe. In 24 v. v. 19-20. '02(Ap5); v. 21-24 (Jl5) 8°, ea., $3.50. Estes.

Shakespeare, W: [Works.] Chiswick Shakespeare. v. 25, 26. '02(F22); v. 27, 28 (My3); v. 29 (Jl12) 16°, ea., 35 c. Macmillan.

Shakespeare, W: Complete plays and poems. New pocket ed. In 3 v. '02(Mr8) 16°, (Caxton ser.) per set, net, $4.20. Scribner.

Shakespeare, W: Sonnets. '02(My24) 16°, (Lover's lib., v. 11.) net, 50 c.; leath., net, 75 c. Lane.

Shakespeare, W: Julius Cæsar; ed. by A. H. Tolman. '02(Mr22) il. D. (Eng. classics, star ser.) 32 c. Globe Sch. Bk.

Shakespeare, W: King Richard III., adapt. for school use; by A. M. Kellogg. '01. '02 (F8) 16°, pap., 15 c. Kellogg.

Shakespeare, W: Macbeth; ed. by A. W. Verity. '02(Je7) 12°, (Pitt Press Shakespeare.) net, 40 c. Macmillan.

Shakespeare, W: Merchant of Venice; ed. by F: Manley. '02(Mr29) 16°, (Laurel classics.) 40 c. Birchard.

Shakespeare, W: Merchant of Venice; notes by E: E. Hale, jr. '01. '02(F8) 12°, (Standard lit. ser., no. 49.) pap. 20 c. University.

Shakespeare, W: Twelfth night; ed. by R: G. White. '02(Mr22) S. (Riverside lit. ser., no. 149.) pap., 15 c. Houghton, M. & Co.

Shakespeare, W: Twelfth night. '02(Ja11) 8°, (Vale Press Shakespeare, v. 22.) net, $8. Lane.

SHAKESPEARE, W:
Fleming. Shakespeare's plots. $1.80. Putnam.
Hazlitt. Shakespeare. net, $2.50. Scribner.
Lamb. Tales from Shakespeare. 40 c. Heath.
McSpadden. Shakesperian synopses. net, 45 c. Crowell.
Merrill. The man Shakespeare. **$1.25 net. Bowen-M.
Porter *and* Clarke. Shakespeare studies: Macbeth. 56 c. Am. Bk.

SHAKESPEARE.—*Continued.*
Sherman. What is Shakespeare? net, $1.50; net, $1. Macmillan.
Webb. Mystery of William Shakespeare. $4. Longmans.

SHAKESPEARE-BACON CONTROVERSY.
Gallup. Bi-literal cipher of Sir Francis Bacon. $3.75.—Tragedy of Anne Boleyn. $1.50. Howard.
Reed. Bacon and Shakes-peare parallel. net, $2.50.—Francis Bacon, our Shakespeare. net, $2. Goodspeed.

Shakespeare and Goethe on Gresham's law. *See* Green, B: E.

Shall Cromwell have a statue? Adams, C: F. 25 c. Lauriat.

Shall we understand the Bible? Williams, T. R net, 50 c. Macmillan.

Shand, Alex. I. Shooting. '02(F15) il. 12°, (Haddon Hall lib.) $3. Macmillan.

Shannon, Rob. T. *See* Tennessee. *Sup. ct.* Repts.

Sharp, B. A., [*pseud.* for Platon G. Brounoff.] Stolen correspondence from the "Dead letter" office between musical celebrities. '02 (Mr22) S. 50 c. Gervais.

Sharp, Luke, *pseud. See* Barr, R.

Sharp & Alleman Co.'s lawyers' and bankers' directory for 1902. Jan. ed. '02(Ja18); July ed. (Jl19) O. shp., ea., $5. Sharp & A.

Sharpe, W: C. *See* Campbell, H. A.

Sharpless, I: Quaker experiment in government. 4th pop. ed. '02(F15) il. 12°, $1.50. Ferris.

Sharts, Jos. W. Romance of a rogue. '02 (Ap5) D. $1.50. H. S. Stone.

Shaw, Adèle M. Coast of freedom. '02 (Ap19) D. $1.50. Doubleday, P.

Shaw, H: W., ["Josh Billings."] Josh Billings' old farmer's allminax, 1870-79. '02 (Mr8) il. D. $1.50. G: W. Dillingham.

She wanted to vote. Ballard, E. C. net, $1.40. Brower.

Sheehan, P. A. Luke Delmege. '01· '02 (Ja4) D. $1.50. Longmans.

SHEEP.
See Veterinary medicine and surgery.

Sheldon, F: M. Practical colorist: for the artist printer. '02(F1) il. Q. $8. Owl Press.

Sheldon, S:, *and* Mason, H. Dynamo electric machinery. v. 1, Direct-current machines. 2d ed. '02(Je14); v. 2, Alternating current machines. '02(Je7) il. D. ea., net, $2.50. Van Nostrand.

Shelley, Ht. S. Poems of life and loving. '02(Ap26) 12°, $1. Neely.

Shelley, P. B. Poetical works. '02(Je21) 16°, (Caxton ser.) net, $1.25. Scribner.

Shepard, Hiram M. Life on the farm: reading book for grammar and high schools. '01· '02(Ja11) il. S. (Home and school ser. for young folks.) 50 c. Flanagan.

Shepardson, Dan. Studies in the Epistles to the Hebrews. '02(F8) 12°, $1.50. Revell.

Sheppard, J: S., *jr. See* Rumsey, W:

Sherer, Rob. G., *rep. See* New York. *Cts. of record.* Misc. repts.

Sheridan, Philip H: Personal memoirs. New enl. ed.; with acc. of life, by M. V. Sheridan. '02(Mr1) 2 v., il. 8°, net, $4. Appleton

Sherlock, C: R. Red anvil. '02(Je7) il. D. $1.50. Stokes.

Sherman, G: W., *and* And. M., *eds.* Memorials of Lydia Whitney Sherman. '02 (Jl12) il. 12°, $3. G: W. Sherman.

Sherman, L. A. What is Shakespeare? '02 (F1) 12°, net, $1.50; *Same.* School ed. (Mr29) 12°, net, $1. Macmillan.

SHERMAN, Lydia W.
Sherman, *eds.* Memorials of Lydia Whitney Sherman. $3. G: W. Sherman.

Sherman, Ma. B. K. Parliamentary law at a glance. Rev. ed. '01· '02(F8) 16°, 75 c. H. O. Shepard.

SHERMAN, William T.
Johnson. W: T. Sherman. $1. Donohue.

Sherwood, Wa. J. Story of three. '01· '02 (Mr29) il. nar. Q. pap., 25 c. W: S. Lord.

Shiells, Rob. Story of the token as belonging to the sacrament of the Lord's supper. 2d ed. '02(Je21) D. net, $1. Presb. Bd.

Shimmell, Lewis S. Border warfare in Penn. during the Revolution. '01· '02(F22) 16°, pap., 50 c. R. L. Myers.

Ship of silence. Valentine, E: U. net, $1.20. Bowen-M.

Shipley, Arth. E., *ed. See* Harmer, S. F:, *ed.*

Shipman, B: J. *See* Minnesota. Civil procedure.

SHIPS AND SHIPBUILDING.
Crowell. Present status and future prospects of Am. shipbuilding. 15 c. Am. Acad. Pol. Sci.

SHOOTING.
Grinnell. Amer. duck shooting. $3.50. Forest.
Shand. Shooting. $3. Macmillan.
See also Rifle.

SHORE.
See Seashore.

SHORT, T:
Love. Thomas Short, first printer of Conn. $5. Case.

SHORTHAND.
See Stenography.

SIAM.
Campbell. Siam in the 20th century. net, $5. Longmans.

Siamese twins. Keese, W: L. net, $1.25. E. W. Dayton.

SIBERIAN RAILWAY.
Dmitriev-Mámonóv *and* Zdziarski, *eds.* Guide to the great Siberian railway. *$3.50 net. Putnam.

Sibley, Hiram L. Right to and the cause for action, both civil and criminal. '02(Jl5) D. $1.50. W. H. Anderson & Co.

Siborne. W: Waterloo campaign, 1815. 5th ed. '02(Jl12) 8°, *$1.50 net. Dutton.

Sibylline leaves. Ballough, C: A. $1. Painter.

Sibyl's conquest. Stinchfield, M. I. $1.50. Neely.

Sichel, Wa. Bolingbroke and his times: the sequel. '02(Je7) O. $4. Longmans.

SICILY.
Sladen. In Sicily. 2 v. net, $20. Dutton.

Side windows. Boteler, M. M. 75 c. Standard Pub.

Sidgwick, H: Philosophy. '02(Je7) 8°. net, $2.25. Macmillan.

Sidgwick, H: Principles of political economy. 3d ed. '02(Je7) 8°, net, $4.50. Macmillan.

Sidner, Aurelia L. Price inevitable. '02 (My17) D. $1. Popular.

Sidney, Marg., *pseud.* *See* Lothrop, *Mrs.* H. M.
Siege of Lady Resolute. Dickson, H. $1.50. Harper.
Siepmann's elem. French ser. 12°, net, 50 c. Macmillan.
—Dumas. Napoleon.
Siepmann's elem. Germ. ser. 12°, net, 50 c. Macmillan.
—Schrader. Friedrich der Grosse.
—Zastrow. Wilhelm der Siegreiche.
Sign of the seven sins. Le Queux, W: $1; 50 c. Lippincott.
SIGNALS.
See Flags.
SIGNS.
See Stenography.
Silent pioneer. McElroy, L. C. $1.50. Crowell.
Silken snare. Leroy, W: 50 c. Abbey Press.
Sill, E: Rowland. Poems. Special ed. '02 (Jl19) 8°, buckram and bds., **$5 net. Houghton, M. & Co.
Silva, T., *and* Fourcaut, A. Lectura y conversación: new Spanish method. '01. '02 (Ja25) D. 60 c. Am. Bk.
SILVER.
See Precious metals.
Silver chord and the golden bowl. Pierce, G. A. $1. Abbey Press.
Silver ser. of classics. 12°. Silver.
—Kinard, *ed.* Old Eng. ballads. 40 c.
—Wordsworth. Selected poems. 30 c.
Silver ser. of modern lang. text-books; ed. by A. Cohn. D. Silver.
—France. Monsieur Bergeret. $1.
—Manzoni. I promessi sposi. $1.20.
Simmons, J. C. My trip to the Orient. '02 (Je7) il. 8°, $1.50. Whitaker & R.
Simon, C: E. Clinical diagnosis by microscopical and chemical methods. 4th ed. '02(F15) il. 8°, net, $3.75. Lea.
Simon, C: E. Text-book of physiolog. chemistry. '01. '02(Ja25) 8°, net, $3.25. Lea.
Simon, Pierre, *Marquis* de La Place. Philosophical essay on probabilities; fr. 6th Fr. ed., by F: W. Truscott and F: L. Emory. '02(Jl19) 12°, $2. Wiley.
Simpson, C. Love never faileth. '02(Je7) D. $1.25. Revell.
Simpson, Ja. Y. Henry Drummond. '01. '02(Ja11) 12°, (Famous Scots.) 75 c. Scribner.
Sin of Jasper Standish. Humphreys, *Mrs.* E. M. J. G. $1.25. Fenno.
Sinclair, W. M. Unto you, young women. '01. '02(F15) 12°, net, $1. Lippincott.
SINGING.
See Church music;—Voice.
Singular will. Marsh, G: $1.50. Neely.
Sinker stories of wit and humor. Goodwin, J. J. $1. Ogilvie.
Sinnett, Brown. Widow Wiley and some other old folk. '02(F15) 12°, $1.50. Dutton.
Sister Beatrice. Maeterlinck, M. net, $1.20. Dodd.
Sister in name only. Wall, *Mrs.* D. H. $1. Neely.
Six little princesses. Prentiss, *Mrs.* E. 75 c. Burt.
Sixteenth century classics. D. $1. [Longmans] Univ. of Penn.
—Erasmus. Select colloquies.

SKEPTICISM.
Best. The college man in doubt. net, 50c. Westminster.
Searching for truth. $1.50. Eckler.
See also Agnosticism;—Free thought.
Sketch book. *See* Irving, W.
SKIN.
Allen. Diseases of the skin. $2. Boericke & T.
Skinner, C: M. Prisons of the nation and their inmates. '02(F8) Q. (Eagle lib., v. 17, no. 2.) pap., 10 c. Brooklyn Eagle.
Skinner, W. H., *and* Burgert, Celia M. Lessons in English based upon principles of literary interpretation. '02(Je21) il. D. (Lessons in English.) 50 c. Silver.
Skrine, J: H. Pastor Agnorum: a schoolmaster's afterthoughts. '02(Je7) D. net, $1.60. Longmans.
Sladen, Douglas. In Sicily. '02(F1) 2 v., il. 4°. net, $20. Dutton.
Slate, T: Physics: for secondary schools. '02(Je28) 12°, hf. leath., net, $1.10. Macmillan.
SLAVERY.
Ballagh. Hist. of slavery in Va. $1.50. Johns Hopkins.
SLEIGHT OF HAND.
See Conjuring.
Slicer, T: R. One world at a time. '02 (Mr22) O. net, $1.35. Putnam.
Sloan, W. N. Social regeneration the work of Christianity. '02(Je21) S. net, 60 c. Westminster.
Sloane, W: M. Napoleon Bonaparte. New lib. ed. '02(F22) 4 v., il. 4°, net, $18; hf. mor., net, $32. Century.
SLOYD.
Molander. Scientific sloyd. 50 c. Bardeen.
Smale, Morton, *and* Colyer, J. F. Diseases and injuries of the teeth. 2d ed. rev. and enl. '01. '02(F8) O. $7. Longmans.
Small, Albion W. The sociologists' point of view. '02(F1) 8°, pap., net, 10 c. Univ. of Chic.
Small end of great problems. Herford, B. net, $1.60. Longmans.
SMALLPOX.
See Variola.
Smart, C: Handbook for the hospital corps of the U. S. army and state military forces. 3d ed. rev. and enl. '02(Jl19) 12°, *$2.50 net. Wood.
Smeaton, O. The Medici and the Italian Renaissance. '01. '02(F1) D. (World's epochmakers.) $1.25. Scribner.
Smedberg, Harold V. Improprieties of Noah, and other stories. '01. '02(F15) D. 50 c. Abbey Press.
Smiley, T: E. Lays and lyrics. '02(Jl19) D. $1.25. Abbey Press.
Smith, Alb. L. *See* Hessler, J: C.
Smith, Boston. Uncle Boston's spicy breezes. '02(Ja25) il. S. net, $1. Am. Bapt.
Smith, C. Alphonso. *See* Krüger, G.
Smith, C. P. Texas notarial manual and form book. '02(Je7) 8°, shp., $4. Gammel.
Smith, Chester W: A summer of Saturdays. '01. '02(Je7) il. 12°, 65 c. Gillan.
Smith, Colin. Bridge condensed. '02(Mr8) 16°, pap., 50 c. Scribner.
Smith, D: Eug. *See* Beman, W. W.

Smith, E. E. Ideal word book. '02(Je7) S. 17 c. Flanagan.
Smith, E. F. Text-book of anatomy, physiology and hygiene. 2d ed. rev. '01· '02 (F22) il. 12°, $1. W: R. Jenkins.
Smith, *Mrs.* Eliz. T., [*formerly* L. T. Meade.] Daddy's girl. '02(Je14) 12°, (Fireside ser.) $1. Burt.
Smith, *Mrs.* Eliz. T. Very naughty girl. '02(Ap19) il. 12°, (Fireside ser.) $1. Burt.
Smith, Emory E. The golden poppy. '02 (Mr22) il. O. net, $1.50. E. E. Smith.
Smith, Eug. Home aquarium and how to care for it. '02(Jl19) 12°, **$1.20 net. Dutton.
Smith, G. C. Moore, *ed.* *See* Smith, *Sir* H.
Smith, Gipsy. His life and work by himself. '02(Ap19) 8°, net, $1.50. Revell.
Smith, Goldwin. Commonwealth or empire. '02(Ap12) 12°, net, 60 c. Macmillan.
Smith, H. M. *See* Sage, D.
Smith, *Sir* Harry. Autobiography; ed. with supp. chap., by G. C. Moore Smith. '02 (Mr29) 2 v., il. 8°, net, $8. Dutton.
Smith, Horace E. Studies in juridical law. '02(Jl12) O. shp., $3.50. Flood.
Smith, Ja. M. *See* New York. Digest.
Smith, Jeremiah. Selection of cases on private corporations. 2d ed. '02(Je28) 2 v., O. net, $6. Harvard Law.
Smith, J: W., ["Jean Yelsew."] The mountaineers. '02(My24) D. $1; $1.50; hf. mor., $2; mor., $2.50. Pub. Ho. M. E. Ch. So.
Smith, Jos. J., *comp.* Civil and military list of Rhode Island, 1800-1850. '01· '02(Mr1) sq. 4°, net, $7.50. Preston.
Smith, Julius. Ten years in Burma. '02 (Je28) 12°, $1. Eaton & M.
Smith, Julius. Ten years in Burma '02 (Mr22) D. net, $1. Jennings.
Smith, M. R., *rep.* *See* Missouri. *St. Louis and Kansas City cts. of appeals.* Cases.
Smith, May R. The lost Christmas, and other poems. '01· '02(F15) 16°, (Dainty ser.) pap., 50 c. Dutton.
Smith, Percey F. Elementary calculus. '02 (Mr29) D. $1.25. Am. Bk.
Smith, Percey F. Four-place logarithmic tables. '02(Ap5) O. net, 50 c. Holt.
Smith, Roy W. Achromatic spindle in the spore mother-cells of osmunda regalis. '02 (F1) 8°, (Cont. from Hull botanical lab'y, no. 23.) pap., net, 25 c. Univ. of Chic.
Smith, S: G. Abraham Lincoln. '02(My24) D. (Hero ser., no. 3.) net, 25 c. Jennings.
Smith, Sa. S. Founders of the Mass. Bay Colony. '02(Jl12) il. 12°, *$5 net. Woodward & L.
Smith, *Mrs.* Toulmin. *See* Smith, *Mrs.* E. T.
Smith, W: W. Course in first year Latin for Regents' examinations. '02(F1) D. buckram, $1. W: R. Jenkins.
Smithsonian cont. to knowledge. Smith. Inst.
—Langley. Experiments in aerodynamics. $1.
SMOKE.
See Fumigation.
Smyth, Newman. Through science to faith. '02(F15) O. net, $1.50. Scribner.
Smaith, J: C. Love's itinerary. '02· '01 (Ja4) D. (Town and country lib., no. 307.) $1; pap., 50 c. Appleton.
Snowden, W: H. Some old historic landmarks of Virginia and Maryland for the tourist over the Washington. Alexandria and Mount Vernon electric railway. 3d ed. '02(Jl19) il. 12°, pap., *25 c. net. Ramey.
Snyder, C., *and* Thurston, E. L. Universal system of practical bookkeeping. '02(Je7) Q. $1.25. Am. Bk.
Snyder, W: L. Notaries' and commissioners' manual. 7th rev., enl. ed. '02(Je14) O. $1.50. Baker, V. & Co.
So fight I. Hahn, C: C. 10 c. Whittaker.
Social and ethical interpretations in mental development. Baldwin, J. M: net, $2.60. Macmillan.
Social effect of machinery. *See* Lafarque, P.
Social England. Traill, H: D. v. 1. net, $4.50. Putnam.
Social (The) evil, with special ref. to conditions existing in the city of New York. '02(Mr22) 12°, net, $1.25. Putnam.
Social regeneration the work of Christianity. Sloan, W. N. net, 60 c. Westminster.
Social salvation. Gladden, W. net, $1. Houghton, M. & Co.
SOCIAL SCIENCE.
Kellor. **Experimental sociology.** net, $2. Macmillan.
Lane. **Level of social motion.** net, $2. Macmillan.
Small. **The sociologist's point of view.** net, 10 c. Univ. of Chic.
See also Civilization; — Crime and criminals; — Ethics; — Political economy; — Political science; — Socialism; — Temperance.
Social science ser. *See* Scribner's.
SOCIALISM.
Cathrein. Socialism exposed and refuted. *$1.25 net. Benziger.
Collins. Truth about socialism. 25 c. J. A. Wayland.
De Leon. **Socialism vs. anarchism.** 10 c. N. Y. Labor News.
Engels. Socialism. 50 c. N. Y. Labor News.
McGrady. Voice from England. 10 c. Standard.
Poland. Socialism. net, 5 c. Herder.
Rowell. **Everybody's opportunity; or, quick socialism.** 10 c.—**Workingman's opportunity.** 5 c. Free Socialist.
See also Communism.
Socialist lib. O. pap. Socialistic Co-op.
—Adventures of John McCue, socialist. 10 c. (v. 2, 1.)
—Hanford. Railroading in the U. S. 5 c. (v. 1, 11.)
—Lafarque. Religion of capital. 10 c. (v. 2, 2.)
—McGrady. Clerical capitalist. 10 c. (v. 1, 10.)
SOCIETIES.
Hinds. Am. communities. $1. Kerr.
SOCIOLOGY.
See Social science.
SODA WATER.
See Confectionery.
SOILS.
Campbell. Soil culture manual. 40 c. H. W. Campbell.
SOLOMON'S TEMPLE.
Schmidt. Solomon's Temple in the light of other oriental temples. net, $1. Univ. of Chic.

SOLUTION.
See Chemistry.
Some letters of Alfred Henry, the third-floorer. '02(Je28) T. 50 c. Informant.
Some merry adventures of Robin Hood. Pyle, H. net, 60 c. Scribner.
Some pretty girls. Underwood, C. F. $3; $5. Quail & W.
Some unpublished letters. Walpole, H. net, $1.50. Longmans.
Sommerville, Maxwell. Engraved gems. '01. '02(F22) O. net, $1.50. Biddle.
Son of a fiddler. Lee, J. $1.50. Houghton, M. & Co.
Sonderegger, C. L' achèvement du canal de Panama. '02(Mr8) O. pap., $2.50. Stechert.
SONG-BOOKS.
Army songster. 25 c. Bell Bk.
Tomlins, *ed.* Laurel song book. $1.50; $1. Birchard.
See also Hymns and hymn writers;—Songs.
SONGS.
Hodgman. Home's sweet harmonies. 80 c. Home Pub.
Johnson. Popular English ballads, ancient and modern. 4 v. $3. Lippincott.
New songs for college glee clubs. 50 c. Hinds.
O'Conor. Irish com-all-ye's. 25 c. Popular.
O'Conor, *comp.* Old time songs and ballads of Ireland. $2. Popular.
See also Ballads;—Church music.
Songs not set to music. Fargo, K. M. $1. Abbey Press.
Songs of childhood. Ramal, W. net, $1.20. Longmans.
Songs of the Eastern colleges. Atkinson, R. W. $1.25. Hinds.
Songs of the Sahkohnagos. Deveron, H. $1.25. Abbey Press.
Sonnenblicke aus der Amer. praxis. Beck, C. net, 30 c. Lemcke.
Sonnets and songs for a house of days. Binkley, C. net, $1.25. A. M. Robertson.
Sonnets from the Trophies. Heredia, J. M. de. *$1.25 net. Elder.
Sophocles. The Antigone; notes by M. A. Bayfield. '02(Mr22) 12°, (Classical ser.) net, 60 c. Macmillan.
Sordello. Browning, R. 75 c. Macmillan.
Sorrow and solace of Esther. Barnes, C: W. net, 30 c. Jennings.
SOUL.
See Psychology.
Soul fragrance. Kohaus, H. M. 40 c. Alliance.
Soul in the unseen world. Hutton, R. E. net, $2. Dutton.
Soul-winners' secrets. Oliver, G. F. 25 c. Jennings.
SOUND.
Dexter. Elem. exercises on sound, light and heat. 90 c. Longmans.
Sousa, J: P. The fifth string. '02(F8) il. D. $1.25. Bowen-M.
SOUTH (The).
See United States;—*also* names of Southern states.
SOUTH AFRICA.
Abbott. Tommy Cornstalk. $2. Longmans.
Doyle. War in South Africa. 10 c. McClure, P.

SOUTH AFRICA.—*Continued.*
Fleming. Glimpses of South Africa in peace and in war. $3. Dominion.
Harding. War in So. Africa and the Dark Continent from savagery to civilization. $2; $3; $4. Dominion.
Phillipps. With Rimington. $2.50. Longmans.
See also Boers;—Matabeleland.
SOUTH AMERICA.
Keane. South America. $4.50. Lippincott.
See also Central America;—Peru.
South Carolina. *Supreme ct.* Repts. v. 60. '01. '02(F1) O. shp., $5.75. Bryan.
South Dakota. *Supreme ct.* Repts. (Horner.) v. 14. '02(Ap5) O. shp., $3. State Pub.
Southeastern reporter, v. 39. Permanent ed. '01. '02(Ja18); v. 40(Je7) O. (Nat. reporter system, state ser.) shp., ea., $4. West Pub.
Southern reporter, v. 30. '02(Mr1) O. (Nat. reporter system, state ser.) shp., $4. West Pub.
Southern reporter. Digest of decisions. '02(My24) O. (Nat. reporter system digests, Southern ser., v. 2.) shp., net, $6. West Pub.
Southwestern reporter, v. 64. Permanent ed. '01. '02(Ja18); v. 65 (Mr29); v. 66 (My17); v. 67 (Jl19) O. (Nat. reporter system, stat ser.) shp., ea., $4. West Pub.
Southworth, *Mrs.* Emma D. E. N. Hidden hand. '02(My3) 12°, (Home lib.) $1. Burt.
Spackman, —. *See* Lathbury, B. B.
SPAIN.
Helps. Spanish conquest of America. v. 2. $1.50. Lane.
Higgin. Spanish life in town and country. net, $1.20. Putnam.
See also Ferdinand, *King of Spain*;—Spanish-Am. war;—Zincali.
Spalding, F: P. Text-book on roads and pavements. 2d rev., enl. ed. '02(Mr22) il. 12°, $2. Wiley.
Spalding, J: L. Religion, agnosticism and education. '02(Je21) D. net. 80 c. McClurg.
Spalding's athletic lib. 16°, pap., 10 c. Am. Sports.
—Spalding's official athletic almanac. (v. 13, 145.)
—Spalding's official baseball guide. (v. 13, 150.)
Spalding's official athletic almanac; comp. by J. E. Sullivan, 1902. '02(Ap26) il. 16°, (Athletic lib., v. 13, no. 145.) pap., 10 c. Am. Sports.
Spalding's official baseball guide, 1902.; ed. by H: Chadwick. '02(My24) il. S. (Athletic lib., v. 13, no. 150.) pap., 10 c. Am. Sports.
Spangenberg, Eug. Practical arithmetic explained to the practical mechanic. '02(Jl12) T. 50 c. Zeller.
Spangler, Nellie Y. Bird play. '01. '02 (Ja25) 12°, pap., 15 c. Kellogg.
SPANISH-AM. WAR.
Halstead. Full official hist. of the war with Spain. $3; $4; $6. Dominion.
Jones. Chaplain's experience; the "Texas" under fire. $1.25. Sherwood.
See also Rough Riders;—*also* Schley, W. S.
SPANISH LANGUAGE.
Appleton's geografia superior ilustrada. $1.50. Appleton.

SPANISH LANGUAGE.—*Continued.*
Arnold. Enseñar á leer. 40 c. Silver.
Caballero. La familia de Alvareda. 75 c. Holt.
Estados Unidos. Constitucion. $1. Cambridge.
Goldsmith. Idioma Inglés. 1st bk., 40 c.; 2d bk., 36 c. Globe Sch. Bk.
Lange. 20th century system Spanish course. 25 c. [San F. News] Pamphlet.
Maxwell. El sacrificio de Elisa. 50 c. Appleton.
Munro. Nociones de electricidad. 40 c. Appleton.
Pinney. Spanish and Eng. conversation. 1st and 2d bks. ea., 65 c. Ginn.
Puron. El lector moderno de Appleton. nos. 1-3. no. 1, 25 c.; no. 2, 35 c.; no. 3, 45 c. Appleton.
Ramsey. Spanish grammar, with exercise. net, $1.50. Holt.
Silva *and* Fourcaut. Lectura y conversación. 60 c. Am. Bk.
Stewart. Nociones de fisica. 20 c. Appleton.
Velázquez de la Cadena, *comp.* Nuevo diccionario-Inglesa y Española. pt. 2. $3.50. Appleton.
Sparroy, Wilfrid. Persian children of the Royal family. '02(Je28) 8°, net, $3.50. Lane.
SPEAKERS.
See Readers and speakers.
Speer, Rob. E. Principles of Jesus applied to some questions of to-day. '02(My3) 16°, net, 80 c. Revell.
SPELLERS.
Bouton. Spelling and word building. 29 c. University.
Daly. Advanced rational speller. 25 c. Sanborn.
Hunt *and* Gourley. Modern pronouncing speller. 20 c. Butler.
Mavor. Eng. spelling book. 40 c. Warne.
Parlin. Quincy word list. 7000 Eng. words. 24 c. Morse.
Smith. Ideal word book. 17 c. Flanagan.
Wheeler's elem. speller. 25 c. W: H: Wheeler.
See also Primers.
Spencer, Herbert. Facts and comments. '02 (My24) O. net, $1.20. Appleton.
Spender, A. Edm. Two winters in Norway. '02(Mr8) il. O. $4. Longmans.
Spenders (The). Wilson, H. L. $1.50. Lothrop
SPIDERS.
Emerton. Common spiders of the U. S. *$1.50 net. Ginn.
Spielmannskind (Das) und stumme ratsherr. Riehl, W. H. 35 c. Am. Bk.
Spindle and plough. Dudeney, *Mrs.* H. $1.50. Dodd.
SPINE.
See Nervous system.
SPINOZA, Benedict de.
Gore. Imagination in Spinoza and Hume. net, 35 c. Univ. of Chic.
Spirit echoes. Hull, M. E. net, 75 c. Sunflower.
Spiritual heroes. Muzzey, D: S. net, $1.25. Doubleday, P.
Spiritual pepper and salt. Stang, W: 30 c. Benziger.
SPIRITUALISM.
Dangers of spiritualism. net, 75 c. Herder.
Gaffield. Celestial message. n. p. Lee & S.
Nixon. Beyond the vail. $1.75. Hudson-K.
Revelations from the eternal world. 20 c. Star.
Twing. Henry Drummond in spirit life. 10 c. Star.
Spofford, A. R., *and* Annandale, C., *eds.* xxth century cyclopædia and atlas. '01. '02(Ap12) 8 v., il. 8°, art v., $20; hf. rus., $26. Gebbie.
Sport of the gods. Dunbar, P. L. $1.50. Dodd.
SPORTS AND SPORTSMEN.
Gordon. Sporting reminiscences. net, $4. Dutton.
See also Baseball;—Canoeing;—Yachts and yachting.
Spotswood, Dillon J. *See* Nuverbis, *pseud.*
Springs of character. Schofield, A. T. net, $1.30. Funk.
SQUABS.
See Pigeons.
Squirrel and the crow. Neidlinger, D. H. 50 c. Rand, McN. & Co.
Staebler, C. Manual on the Book of books for juniors: first book in catechetical study. '02(My10) S. (Young people's alliance ser., no. 3.) pap., 20 c. Mattill & L.
Staley, Edgcumbe. Watteau, master painter of the Fêtes galantes. '01. '02(Ja4) il. 16°, (Bell's miniature ser. of painters.) 50 c. Macmillan.
Standard guide ser. il. D. pap., 25 c. Foster & R.
—New York City standard guide.
Standard lib. 16°, pap., 10 c. Standard.
—McGrady. Voice from England.
Standard literature ser. 12°, pap., 20 c. University.
—Scott. Waverley. (double no. 50.)
—Shakespeare. Merchant of Venice. (49.)
Standard reader ser. Funk.
—Funk *and* Moses, *eds.* Standard first reader. 35 c.—Teachers' manual for first reader. 50 c.
Standard socialist ser. 16°. Kerr.
—Broome. Last days of the Ruskin Co-operative Assoc. 50 c.
Stanford's compendium of geography and travel. il. 8°. Lippincott.
—Keane. South America. $4.50.
Stang, W: Spiritual pepper and salt for Catholics and non-Catholics. '02(Mr29) S. pap., 30 c. Benziger.
STANLEY, H: M.
Godbey. Henry M. Stanley. $1. Donohue.
Stannard, *Mrs.* Henrietta E. V., ["John Strange Winter."] The magic wheel. '01. '02(Mr8) D. $1.25. Lippincott.
Stanton, S. C., *ed.* *See* Billings, F., *ed.*
Stapleton, Ammon. Memorials of the Huguenots in America. '01. '02(Mr22) il. O. $1.50. Huguenot.
STAR CHAMBER.
Scofield. Study of the court of Star Chamber. net, $1. Univ. of Chic.
STARS.
Browne. How to tell the time of night by the stars. 50 c. Lee & S.

STARS.—*Continued.*
Hale. New star in Perseus. net, 10 c. Univ. of Chic.
See also Astrology;—Astronomy.

State intervention in Eng. education. De Montmorency, J. E. G. net, $1.50. Macmillan.

Statesmen's (The) year book for 1902. (J. S. Keltie.) '02(Ap26) 12°, net, $3. Macmillan.

Stay, Jones B. Mind telegraph; tr. fr. the 6th Germ. ed. by Ivry. '01. '02(Mr8) 16°, pap., 25 c. Alliance.

Stead, Alfr. Japan of to-day. '02(My10) 12°, net, $2. Dutton.

Stead, W: T: Americanization of the world. '02(F22) 12°, $1. Markley.

STEAM ENGINE.
Hurst. Hints on steam engine design and construction. 60 c. Lippincott.
Thurston. Stationary steam engines, simple and compound. $2.50. Wiley.
See also Locomotives;—Machinery.

Stebbins, Genevieve. Delsarte system of expression. 6th ed. rev. and enl. '02(F22) D. $2. Werner.

Stechhan, Otto. Unrequited love. '02(Mr1) D. $1. Abbey Press.

Stechhan, Otto. Whither are we drifting? '02(Mr8) D. $1. Abbey Press.

Stedman, E. C. *and* T: L., *eds.* Complete pocket guide to Europe. '02(Je14) T. leath., $1.25. W: R. Jenkins.

STEEL.
Colby. Review and text of the Am. standard specifications for steel. net, $1.10. Chemical.
See also Iron.

Steele, Francisca M., ["Darley Dale."] Convents of Great Britain. '02(Je28) il. 8°, net, $2. Herder.

Steele, J: W. Coal oil Johnny. '02(My17) 12°, $1.50. J: A. Hill.

Steele, K. N. Simple rules for bridge. '02 (Mr22) S. pap., 50 c. Eichelberger.

Steiner, Bernard C. Western Maryland in the Revolution. '02(Mr8) O. (Johns Hopkins Univ. studies, 20th ser., no. 1.) pap., 30 c. Johns Hopkins.

STENOGRAPHY.
Barnes. Shorthand lessons by the word method. $1.25. A. J. Barnes.
Beale. Book of legal dictation. 50 c. Beale Press.
Brown. Science and art of phrase-making. $1.50. Shorthand Bu.
Forney. Inductive lessons. 80 c. State Normal Sch.
Gabelsberger Shorthand Soc., *ed.* Reader to Richter's graphic shorthand. 50 c. Int. News.
Hardcastle. Word signs made easy. $1. M. A. Hardcastle.
Laird. Manual of syllabic shorthand. $2. Neil.
Musick. Combination shorthand dict. and reader: Benn Pitman phonography. $1.50. W: L. Musick.
Pitman, B. *and* Howard. Business letters: no. 1, Misc. corr. 25 c. Phonograph.
Pitman, I: Business corr. in shorthand. no. 2. 30 c.—Phonographic teacher, 20 c. Pitman.

Stephen, *Sir* Ja. F. Digest of the law of evidence; fr. the 5th ed. Am. notes by G: E. Beers. '01. '02(Mr22) D. shp., $4. Dissell.

Stephen, Leslie. George Eliot. '02(Je14) 12°, (English men of letters.) net, 75 c. Macmillan.

Stephen Holton. Pidgin, C: F. $1.50. L. C. Page.

Stephens, J: V. Evolution of the confession of faith of the Cumberland Presb. church. '02(My10) O. pap., 10 c. Cumberland.

Stern, Menco. Geschichten von Deutschen städten. '02(Ja25) D. $1.25. Am. Bk.

Sternberg, G: M. Text-book of bacteriology. 2d rev. ed. '01. '02(F22) il. 8°, net, $5; leath., net, $5.75. Wood.

Sterne, L. Sentimental journey through France and Italy. '02(My3) 12°. (Home lib.) $1. Burt.

Stevens, E: A. American law of assemblies applicable to lodges, conventions and public meetings. '01. '02(Mr29) S. net, $1. E: A. Stevens.

Stevens, E: L. Business education. '02 (My3) S. pap., 15 c. Bardeen.

Stevens, Fk. L. Gametrogenesis and fertilization in albugo. '02(F15) 8°, (Cont. from the Hull botanical lab'y, no. 29.) pap., net, 25 c. Univ. of Chic.

Stevens, Horace J., *comp.* Copper handbook; ed. of 1902. '02(Ap26) 8°, $2; full mor., $3. H. J. Stevens.

Stevens, L. B. Faciology. New ed. '02 (My17) 12°, pap., 25 c. Donohue.

Stevens, Sheppard. In the eagle's talon. '02 (Je14) il. D. $1.50. Little, B. & Co.

Stevenson, R. L: Æs triplex. '02(Mr22) nar. S. (Vest pocket ser.) pap., net, 25 c.; flex. cl., net, 40 c.; flex. leath., net, 75 c.; Jap. vellum ed., $1. T: B. Mosher.

Stevenson, R. L: Child's garden of verses. [New ed.] '01. '02(F1) il. D. net, 60 c. Scribner.

Steward, F. J. *See* Jacobson, W. H. A.

Stewart, Balfour. Nociones de fisica. Neuva ed. Castellana. '01. '02(F22) 18°, 20 c. Appleton.

Stewart, Purves. *See* Ballance, C: A.

Stiles, Ezra. Literary diary of Ezra Stiles, president of Yale College; ed. by F. B. Dexter. '01. '02(Mr15) 3 v., 8°, net, $7.50. Scribner.

STIMULANTS AND NARCOTICS.
See Morphinism.

Stinchfield, M. Ida. Sibyl's conquest. '02 (Ap26) 12°, $1.50. Neely.

Stitson, J. R. The human hair. '01. '02 (Ap12) 12°, $1.25. Maple.

STOCK BREEDING.
See Cattle.

STOCK EXCHANGE, London.
Duguid. Story of the Stock Exchange. net, $2. Dutton.

Stockett, J. Shaaf, *rep.* *See* Maryland. *Ct. of appeals.* Repts.

Stockmen's calculator. McCallum & Hofer Cattle Co. $1.50. McCallum.

Stockton, F. R: Kate Bonnet. '02(Mr1) D. $1.50. Appleton.

Stoddard, C: W. In the footprints of the padres. '02(F1) D. net, $1.50. Robertson.

Stoddard, W: O. Errand boy of Andrew Jackson. '02(My24) D. net, $1. Lothrop.

Stoker, Bram. Mystery of the sea. '02 (Mr29) D. $1.50. Doubleday, P.
Stokes, Anson P. Cruising in the West Indies. '02(Jl19) O. **$1.25 net. Dodd.
Stokes, *Sir* G: G. Mathematical and physical papers: repr. with add. notes. v. 3. '01- '02(Ja4) 8°, (Cambridge Univ. Press ser.) net, $3.75. Macmillan.
Stokes, Whitley, *and* Strachan, J:, *eds.* Thesaurus palæohibernicus: coll. of old Irish glosses, scholia, prose and verse. v. 1. '02(Ja18) 8°, (Cambridge Univ. Press ser.) net, $8. Macmillan.
Stolen correspondence from the Dead Letter Office. Sharp, B. A. 50 c. Gervais.

STOMACH.
Thompson. Acute dilation of the stomach. 75 c. Wood.
See also Digestion.

Stone, A. J. *See* Roosevelt, T.
Stone, E. D. *See* Thackeray, F. St. J.
Stone, Gertrude L., *and* Fickett, M. G., *comps.* Trees in prose and poetry. '02 (Je21) il. sq. D. 50 c. Ginn.
Stone, Wilbur M. Women designers of bookplates. '02(Ap19) il. nar. D. bds., net, $1; Jap. vellum, net, $2. Beam.
Stoner, Winifred S. Castles in Spain, and other sketches in rhyme. '02(Mr1) D. $1. Abbey Press.

STORIES.
See Fairy tales;—Fiction;—Legends.

Stories from Waverley. Scott, *Sir* W.. $1. Macmillan.
Stories of country life. Bradish, S. P. 40 c. Am. Bk.
Stories of the Tuscan artists. Wherry, A. net, $4. Dutton.
Story, Alf. T: Swiss life in town and country. '02(F1) il. D. (Our European neighbors ser., no. 5.) net, $1.20. Putnam.
Story, W: W. In defense of Judas; repr. of A Roman lawyer in Jerusalem. '02(Jl19) sq. 24°, bds., $1. Philosopher Press.
Story of animal life. Lindsay, B. net, 35 c. Appleton.
Story of Azron. Rollins, A. W. $1. Holliswood.
Story of Cairo. Poole, S. L. $2; $2.50. Macmillan.
Story of China. Van Bergen, R. 60 c. Bardeen.
Story of Eden. Wyllarde, D. $1.50. Lane.
Story of François Villon. Morehead, G: 25 c. Ogilvie.
Story of home gardens. Cadwallader, S. 25 c. Home Gardening.
Story (The) of Mary Maclane, by herself. '02(Je14) il. D. $1.50. H. S. Stone.
Story of Paul Dombey. Dickens, C: 15 c. Lippincott.
Story of Pemaquid. Kaler, J. O. 50 c. Crowell.
Story of the amphibians. Baskett, J. N. 60 c. Appleton.
Story of the art of music. Crowest, F: J. **35 c. net. Appleton.
Story of the Christian centuries. Selden, E: G. net, $1. Revell.
Story of the Khedivate. Dicey, E: net, $4. Scribner.
Story of the Mormons. Linn, W: A. net, $4. Macmillan.
Story of the nations ser. il. D. **$1.35 net; hf. leath., $1.60 net. Putnam.
—Edwards. Wales. (62.)
—Miller. Mediæval Rome. (63.)
Story of the Philippines. Halstead, M. $2; $3. Dominion.
Story of the token. Shiells, R. net, $1. Presb. Bd.
Story of the vine. Emerson, E: R. net, $1.25. Putnam.
Story of the world's worship. Dobbins, F. $2.25; $3.25. Dominion.
Story of three. Sherwood, W. J. 25 c. W: S. Lord.
Story of Tonty. Catherwood, *Mrs.* M. H. $1.25. McClurg.
Stout heart. Kellogg, E. $1.25. Lee & S.
Stowe, *Mrs.* Ht. E. B. He's coming to-morrow. '02(Ap12) 12°, (Ideal messages ser.) pap., net, 25 c. Revell.
Stowe, *Mrs.* Ht. E. B. Minister's wooing. '02(My17) 12°, (Home lib.) $1. Burt.
Stowe, *Mrs.* Ht. E. B. Uncle Tom's cabin. '02(Mr22) 12°, $2; hf. mor., $3; mor., $4. Dominion.
Strachan, J:, *ed.* *See* Stokes, W., *ed.*
Strangers at the gate. Gordon, S: $1.50. Jewish Pub.
Stratemeyer, E: Lost on the Orinoco. '02 (Ap26) il. D. (Pan-American ser., no. 1.) net, $1. Lee & S.

STRATFORD-ON-AVON.
Way, *comp.* Reliques of Stratford-on-Avon. 50 c.; 75 c. Lane.

STRAWBERRY.
Barnard. The strawberry garden, how it was planted, etc. 40 c. Coates.

Stray leaves from a border garden. Holme, M. P. M. net, $1.50. Lane.
Streamer, D. Ruthless rhymes for heartless homes. New ed. '01- '02(My3) il. sq. D. $1.25. Russell.
Street, Eug. E. *See* Higgin, L.

STREET-RAILROADS.
Andrews. Handbook for street railway engineers. $1.25. Wiley.

Street railway accident law. *See* Massachusetts.
Strength of the weak. Hotchkiss, C. C. $1.50. Appleton.
Stretton, Hesba. New child's life of Christ. '01- '02(Ap26) il. 12°, $1. Winston.
Strollers (The). Isham, F: S. $1.50. Bowen-M.
Strong, J. Next great awakening. '02 (Mr29) D. 75 c. Baker & T.
Strutt, J: W:, [*Baron* Rayleigh.] Scientific papers. v. 3, 1887-1892. '02(Mr8) 8°, (Cambridge Univ. Press ser.) net, $5. Macmillan.

STUARTS.
Rait. Five Stuart princesses. net, $3.50. Dutton.

Stubbs, W: Ordination addresses; ed. by E. E. Holmes. '01- '02(Ja11) D. $2.25. Longmans.

STUDENTS.
Canfield. College student and his problems. net, $1. Macmillan.

Students' guide to health. Van Doren, D. T. $2. D. T. Van Doren.
Studies from the nude human figure in motion. Fiedler, A. $12. Hessling.

Studies in auditory and visual space perception. Pierce, A. H: net, $2. Longmans.
Studies in Irish hist. and biog. Falkiner, C. L. $5. Longmans.
Studies in spiritual harmony. Brown, G. M. $1. Reed Pub.
Studies of trees in winter. Huntington, A. O. net, $2.25. Knight.
STUDY.
See Home study.
Study of religion. Jastrow, M., *jr.* $1.50. Scribner.
Study of the court of Star Chamber. Scofield, C. L. net, $1. Univ. of Chic.
Styan, K. E. Short history of sepulchral cross slabs, with ref. to other emblems found thereon. '02(Je28) 8°, net, $3. E. & J. B. Young.
SUCCESS.
Gilbert. 1000 ways to make money. $1. Donohue.
See also Business.
Success club debater. Hungerford, H. 25 c. Success.
Such stuff as dreams. Russell, C: E. net, $2. Bowen-M.
Suckling, *Sir* J: Love poems. '02(Ja11) S. (Lover's lib., no. 8.) net, 50 c.; leath., 75 c. Lane.
SUGGESTION (Mental).
See Hypnotism.
Suitors of Yvonne. Sabatini, R. net, $1.20. Putnam.
Sullivan, *Sir* E: Ivanhoe and Rob Roy, retold for children. New ed. '01- '02(F15) 16°, (Children's friend ser.) bds., 50 c. Little, B. & Co.
Sullivan, Eug. C. *See* Prescott, A. B:
Sullivan, Fk. J: Detective adviser. '02 (My17) S. pap., 60 c. Int. Detective.
Sullivan, Ja. E., *comp.* *See* Spalding's official athletic almanac.
Sullivan, T. R. Courage of conviction. '02 (Je7) D. $1.50. Scribner.
Summer of Saturdays. Smith, C. W: 65 c. Gillan.
SUNDAY.
Lewis. Sunday legislation. net, $1. Appleton.
Moule. Thoughts for the Sundays of the year. net, $1. Revell.
SUNDAY-SCHOOL.
Arnold, *ed.* Internat. S. S. lessons, 1902. 50 c. Revell.
Bible. Sunday-school scholar's Bible. 75 c.; $1. Nelson.
Hamill. Sunday-school teacher. 50 c. Pub. Ho. M. E. Ch., So.
Hatcher. Pastor and the Sunday-school. course no. 1. 75 c. Bapt. S. S. Bd.
Rice. Short hist. of the Internat. lesson system. *25 c. net. Am. S. S.
Sunlight and shadows. Dail, C. C. $1.50. Hudson-K.
Sunnyside ser. il. D. Ogilvie.
—Morehead. Francesca da Rimini. 25 c. (117.)
SUPERSTITION.
See Devil;—Spiritualism.
SURGERY.
American year-book of medicine and surgery. 2 v. ea., net, $3; net, $3.75. Saunders.

SURGERY.—*Continued.*
Cheyne *and* Burghard. Surgical treatment. v. 5, 6. ea., *$5. Lea.
Crile. Research into problems rel. to surgical operations. net, $2.50. Lippincott.
Jacobson *and* Steward. Operations of surgery. 2 v. net, $10; $12. Blakiston.
Murphy, *ed.* General surgery. $1.50. Year Bk.
Robb. Aseptic surgical technique. $2. Lippincott.
Wharton. Minor surgery and bandaging. net, $3. Lea.
Zuckerhandl. Atlas and epitome of operative surgery. net, $3.50. Saunders.
See also Accidents; — Anatomy; — Diagnosis; — Medicine;—Veterinary medicine and surgery.
Surprises of an empty hotel. Gunter, A. C. $1; 50 c. Home.
SURVEYING.
Johnson. Theory and practice of surveying. $4. Wiley.
Lupton. Mine surveying. $5. Longmans.
Noble *and* Casgrain. Tables for obtaining horizontal distances and difference of level, from stadia readings. $1. Engineering News.
Nugent. Plane surveying. $3.50. Wiley.
See also Engineering;—Railroads;—Topographical drawing;—Trigonometry.
Susanne. Delano, F. J. 50 c. L. C. Page.
Swartz, Joel. Easter and the resurrection. '02(Ap12) 12°, pap., net, 15 c. Revell.
Swartz, Joel. Poems. '01- '02(F15) 12°, $1; $1.25. Coates.
SWEDEN.
Cronholm. Hist. of Sweden. 2 v. $5. N. N: Cronholm.
Swedenborg, E. Heavenly arcana. Rotch ed. v. 13. '02(Mr15) D. $1.25. Mass. New-Ch. Un.
Swedenborg, E. Ontology; or, signification of philosoph. terms; tr. by A. Acton. '01- '02(F1) D. pap., 50 c. Mass. New-Ch. Un.
Sweet danger. Wilcox, *Mrs.* E. W. 50 c. Donohue.
Swete, H: B. Patristic study. '02(Mr22) D. (Handbooks for the clergy.) net, 90 c. Longmans.
Swett, Sophie. Sarah the less. '02(Je7) il. D. net, 75 c. Westminster.
Swift, B:, *pseud.* *See* Paterson, W: R.
Swift, H: Walton, *rep.* *See* Mass. *Sup. judicial ct.* Repts.
Swift, J. Journal to Stella; ed. by G: A. Aitken. '01- '02(F22) D. (Lib. of standard literature.) $1.75. Putnam.
Swift, J. Prose works; ed. by T. Scott. v. 9, Cont. to *The Tatler, Examiner*, etc. '02 (Je7) 12°, (Bohn's standard lib.) net, $1. Macmillan.
Swift, J. Selections. '01. '02(Ap5) S. (Little masterpieces.) 50 c. Doubleday, P.
SWITZERLAND.
Story. Swiss life in town and country. net, $1.20. Putnam.
Swoope, C. W. Lessons in practical electricity. '02(Je14) il. 8°, net, $2. Van Nostrand.
Sybel, H. v. Prinz Eugen von Savoyen; ed. by E. C. Quiggin. '02(Mr8) 12°, (Pitt Press ser.) net, 60 c. Macmillan.
Sykes, Percy M. Ten thousand miles in Persia; or, eight years in Iran. '02(Je21) il. 12°, net, $6. Scribner.

Symonds, E. M. *See* Paston, G:
Symons, Arth. Poems. '02(F15) 2 v., 8°, net, $3. Lane.
Syntax of the verb in the Anglo-Saxon chronicle. Blain, H. M. net, 50 c. Barnes.
SYPHILIS.
Duhring, *and others*. Syphilis. net, $1. Treat.
Morton. Genito-urinary disease and syphilis. net, $3. Davis.
SYRACUSE, FIRST PRESB. CHURCH.
Northrup, *ed.* Early records of First Presb. Church of Syracuse, N. Y. 50 c. [Gill] Genealog. Soc.
T. Racksole and daughter. Bennett, A. $1.50. New Amsterdam.
TABLE-TENNIS.
See Ping-pong.
TABLES.
Blum. Reduction tables for ascertaining freight charges, etc. net, $3. Am. Code.
TACTICS.
See Infantry.
Tagzeiten zum heiligsten Herzen Jesu. '02 (Je28) 24°, pap., 5 c. Herder.
Tait, Ja., *ed.* *See* Tout, T: F:
Talbot, A. N. Railway transition spiral. 3d ed., rev. '02(Ap19) 16°, flex. leath., $1.50. Van Nostrand.
Talbot, Ellen V. Courtship of sweet Anne Page. '02(Mr8) S. (Hour-glass stories.) net, 40 c. Funk.
Tale of a cat. Kern, M. 50 c. Abbey Press.
Tale of the great mutiny. Fitchett, W: H: $1.50. Scribner.
Tale of true love. Austin, A. net, $1.20. Harper.
Tales from Shakespeare. Lamb, C: 40 c. Heath.
Tales from *Town Topics*, no 43. '02(My10); no. 44 (Je7) 12°, pap., ea., 50 c. Town Topics.
Tales of destiny. Jordan, E. G. $1.50. Harper.
Tales of my father. F., A. M. $2. Longmans.
Tales of passed times. Perrault, C: net, 50 c.; 80 c. Macmillan.
Tales of the Spanish Main. Morris, M. $2. Macmillan.
Talisman. Fulda, L. 35 c. Heath.
Talmage, Fk. De W. A vacation with nature. '02(Je21) D. net, $1. Funk.
Talmage, Fk. De W., Banks, L: A., *and others*. Life and work of T. De Witt Talmage. '02(My10) 12°, subs., $2; hf. mor., $2.75; full mor., $3.75. Winston.
TALMAGE, T: De Witt.
Talmage, F. D., *and others*. Life and work of T. De Witt Talmage. subs., $2; $2.75; $3.75. Winston.
Tappan, Eva M. Our country's story: elem. hist. of the U. S. '02(My24) il. sq. D. 65 c. Houghton, M. & Co.
TARIFF.
Marx. Wage-labor and capital; [also] Free-trade. 50 c. N. Y. Labor News.
See also Taxation.
Tarquinius Superbus. Epstein, A. J. $1.25. Mutual Pub.
Tarr, R. S. Physical geography of New York state. '02(Je14) il. 8°, net, $3.50. Macmillan.
Tarr, R. S., *and* McMurry, Fk. M. Complete geography. '02(Jl12) 12°, (Geographies, two book ser., bk. 2.) hf. leath., *$1 net. Macmillan.
Tarr, R. S., *and* McMurry, F. M. First book: home geography. '02(Je28) il. 12°, (Geographies, two-book ser.) hf. leath., net, 60 c. Macmillan.
Tarr and McMurry's geographies. il. 12°, net. Macmillan.
—Jones. Utah. *40 c.
—Wilson. Ohio. 30 c.
—Winans. Kansas. 30 c.
Tartarin de Tarascon. Daudet, A. 45 c. Am. Bk.
Tarver, J. C. Tiberius the tyrant. '02(Jl12) 8°, *$5 net. Dutton.
Tate, H: Aaron Crane. '02(Ap26) il. D. $1.50. Abbey Press.
Tatnall, Rob. R. *See* Crew, H:
Taunton, Ethelred L. Hist. of the Jesuits in England, 1580-1773. '01. '02(F15) il. 8°, net, $3.75. Lippincott.
Tausky, Edm., *rep.* *See* California. *Superior ct.* Repts.
TAXATION.
Hollister, *and others*. Taxation in Michigan and elsewhere. 50 c. Mich. Pol. Sci.
Purdy. Burdens of local taxation and who bears them. 25 c. Public Policy.
Purdy. Local option in taxation. 10 c. N. Y. Tax Reform.
Walker. Taxation of corporations in the U. S. 25 c. Am. Acad. Pol. Sci.
See also Political economy;—Tariff.
Taylor, Bayard. Poetical works. Household ed. '02(Ap5) il. D. $1.50. Houghton, M. & Co.
Taylor, Bayard. Views afoot or Europe seen with knapsack and staff. '02(Ap19) 12°. (Home lib.) $1. Burt.
Taylor, Bret L. Line-o'-type lyrics. '02 (My24) S. bds., net, 50 c. W: S. Lord.
Taylor, C: M., *jr.* Why my photographs are bad. '02(Je14) il. O. net, $1. Jacobs.
Taylor, E: R. Into the light. '02(Ap5) 12°, bds.. net, 75 c. Elder.
Taylor, H. E. *See* Welch, J. H.
Taylor, Hannis. Treatise on international public law. '01. '02(F8) O. shp., net, $6.50. Callaghan.
Taylor, Hobart C. C. Crimson wing. '02 (Ap5) D. $1.50. H. S. Stone.
Taylor, Jos. S., *ed.* Practical school problems. v. 1, pt. 1. '02(Ap5) O. pap., 30 c. [W: B. Harison] Practical Sch. Problems.
Taylor, S. Earl. *See* Taylor, T: E.
Taylor, T: E., Taylor, S. E., *and* Morgan, C: H. Studies in the life of Christ. '02 (Ap12) O. 75 c. Jennings.
Taylor, W: A. Intermere. '02(Ja11) D. $1. XX. Century.
T'bacca queen. Wilson, T. W. $1; 50 c. Appleton.
TEACHERS AND TEACHING.
Bender. The teacher at work. 75 c. Flanagan.
Dawes. Bilingual teaching in Belgian schools. *50 c. net. Macmillan.
Findlay. Principles of class teaching. net, $1.25. Macmillan.
Funk *and* Moses, *eds.* Teachers' manual for first reader. 50 c. Funk.

TEACHERS AND TEACHING.—*Continued.*
Laurie. Training of teachers and methods of instruction. net, $1.50. Macmillan.
Murché. Teachers' manual of object lessons for rural schools. net, 60 c. Macmillan.
See also Education;—Memory;—Sunday-school.
TEETH.
Hopkins. Care of the teeth. **75 c. net. Appleton.
MacDowell. Orthodontis. net, $4. Colegrove.
Marshall. Principles and practice of operative dentistry. subs., $5; $6. Lippincott.
Smale *and* Colyer. Diseases and injuries of the teeth. $7. Longmans.
Telegram almanac and cyclopedia, 1902. '02 (Mr15) 16°, pap., 20 c. Providence Telegram.
TELEGRAPHY.
Bubier. A B C of wireless telegraphy. $1. Bubier.
Edison. Telegraphy self-taught. $1. Drake.
See also Codes.
TELEPATHY.
Stay. Mind telegraph; telepathic influence of the human will. 25 c. Alliance.
TELEPHONE.
Cary. How to make and use the telephone. $1. Bubier.
Homans. A B C of the telephone. $1. Van Nostrand.
Houston *and* Kennelly. Electric telephone. $1. McGraw.
Hyde *and* McManman. Telephone troubles and how to find them on the magneto and common battery system. 25 c. Caspar.
TEMPERANCE.
Crozier. Temperance and the Anti-Saloon League. 15 c. Barbee & S.
Cumming. Public house reform. $1. Scribner.
Griffin. Why the legal (or force) method of promoting temperance does more harm than good. 15 c. A. Griffin.
National Temperance almanac, 1902. 10 c. Nat. Temp.
See also Wine.
Temple classics. See Macmillan's.
Temple of trusts. *See* De Leon, T: C.
TEMPLES.
See Solomon's temple.
Ten Brink, B. Language and metre of Chaucer. 2d ed., rev. by F. Kluge. '02(F15) 12°, net, $1.50. Macmillan.
Ten years in Burma. Smith, J. net, $1. Eaton & M.; Jennings.
Teniente de los gavilanes. Zayas Enriquez, R. de. †50 c. Appleton.
Tennessee. *Supreme ct.* Repts. (G: W. Pickle.) New ed., with annots. by R. T. Shannon. v. 19-21 (103-105.) '02(Ap12) v. 7-18 (92-102.); v. 1-6 (85-90) (Jl12) O. shp., ea., $3. Fetter.
Tennessee. *Supreme ct.* Repts. (G: W. Pickle.) [v. 98-106.] '01- '02(Ap5) O. shp., ea., $3. Marshall.
Tennessee Lee. Neill, M. $1. Neely.
Tennyson, A., *Lord.* In memoriam. '01- '02 (Ja11) 16°, (Caxton ser.) flex. lambskin, net, $1.20. Scribner.
Tennyson, A., *Lord.* The princess ed., by F. T. Baker. '02(Je7) D. (Twentieth century text-books.) 25 c. Appleton.
Tennyson, A., *Lord.* Birthday book; quotations for each day; sel. and arr. by E. J. S. '02(F15) 24°, 75 c.; $1; mor., $1.25. Warne.
TENNYSON, A., *Lord.*
Livingston. Bibliog. of the first ed. in book form of the works of Tennyson. $1. Dodd.
TERPENES.
Heusler. Chemistry of the terpenes. *4 net. Blakiston.
Terrors of the law. Watt, F. net, $1.25. Lane.
TERRY, Ellen.
Pemberton. Ellen Terry and her sisters. net, $3.50. Dodd.
Terry, Milton S. New and living way. '02 (Je21) D. net, 50 c. Eaton & M.
Tesnière, A. Adoration of the blessed sacrament. '02(F1) D. net, $1.25. Benziger.
Tessa Wadsworth's discipline. Conklin, *Mrs.* J. M. D. $1. Burt.
TEUTONS.
Chantepie de la Saussaye. Religion of the Teutons. $2.50. Ginn.
Texas. Citations to amendments and changes of the revised statutes; ed. by N. J. McArthur. '02(Mr22) D. pap., 50 c. Gammel.
Texas. Conflicting civil cases in repts, from Dallam to v. 93, incl. v. 2, comp., arr. and annot. by W. W. King and S. J. Brooks. '02(Ap5) O. shp., $4. Gilbert Bk.
Texas. *Ct. of criminal appeals.* Repts. (J: P. White.) v. 41. '02(Jl5) O. shp., $4.50. Gammel.
Texas court reporter. v. 3. '02(My24) O. shp., $3. B. C. Jones.
Texas. *Cts. of civil appeals.* Repts. v. 24. '02(Mr29) O. shp., $3. Texas.
Texas. Notes on repts; by W. M. Rose. Bk. 1. '02(Ap26); bk. 2 (Jl12) O. shp., ea., $7.50. Bancroft-W.
Texas. Supp. to Sayles' civil statutes; incl. Texas repts., v. 93, and Southwestern reporter, v. 63. By W. W. Herron. '02 (My24) O. $1. Gilbert Bk.
Texas. Supp. to Willson's statutes; by W. W. Herron. '02(Mr22) O. 50 c. Gilbert Bk.
Texas. *Supreme ct.* Repts. (A. E. Wilkinson.) v. 94. '02(My17) O. shp., $5. Gammel.
Texas. 27th legislature and state administration. (M'Arthur and Wicks.) '01. '02 (F15) O. roan, $5. B. C. Jones.
TEXAS.
Smith. Texas notarial manual and form book. $4. Gammel.
See also Galveston.
Text-books of science. S. $1.75. Longmans.
—Tilden. Introd. to the study of chemical philosophy.
Texts to il. lectures on Greek philosophy. Adam, J. net, $1.25. Macmillan.
Thackeray, F. St. J., *and* Stone, E. D., *eds.* Pre-Victorian poets. '02(Je28) 12°, (Florilegium Latinum, v. 1.) $2.50. Lane.
Thackeray, F. St. J., *and* Stone, E. D. *eds.* Victorian poets. '02(Ap26) 12°, (Florilegium Latinum, v. 2.) net, $2. Lane.

Thackeray, W: M. Prose works. Barry Lyndon; ed. by W. Jerrold. '02(Mr22) il. 12°, $1. Macmillan.
Thackeray, W: M. Prose works: Henry Esmond; ed. by W. Jerrold. '02(Ap12) 2 v., il. 12°, $2. Macmillan.
Thackeray, W: M. Prose works. History of Henry Esmond, Esq. New uniform ed. '02(Mr29) 12°, $1. Macmillan.
Thackeray, W: M. Prose works. Memoirs of Barry Lyndon, Esq.; also Catherine. New uniform ed. '02(Je7) il. 12°, $1. Macmillan.
Thackeray, W: M. Prose works. The Newcomes. New uniform ed. '02(Ja18) 12°, $1. Macmillan.
Thackeray, W: M. Prose works. The Newcomes; ed. by W. Jerrold. New uniform ed. '02(Je14) 3 v., il. 12°, $3. Macmillan.
Thackeray, W: M. Prose works. Pendennis. New uniform ed. '02(F1) 3 v., il. 12°, $3. Macmillan.
Thackeray, W: M. Prose works. The Virginians. New uniform ed. '02(F22) il. 12°, $1. Macmillan.
That old kitchen stove. Judd, D: H. 50 c. Abbey Press.
Thayer, A. E. Compend of general pathology. '02(Mr22) il. 12°, (Quiz compend ser., no. 15.) 80 c.; interleaved, $1. Blakiston.
Thayer, Stephen H: Daughters of the Revolution. '01- '02(F8) D. $1. Abbey Press.
Theocritus. Idylls. '02(Mr15) il. 12°, (Antique gems from the Greek and Latin, v. 1.) (App. to pubs. for price.) Barrie.
Theological and Semitic literature. *See* Arnolt, W. M.
THEOLOGY.
Arnold. Literature and dogma. net, $1. New Amsterdam.
Balfour. Foundations of belief. net, $2. Longmans.
Cobb. Theology, old and new. net, $1. Dutton.
Hoyt. Theology as a popular science. net, 10 c. Presb. Bd.
Minton. The cosmos and the logos. net, $1.25. Westminster.
Mortimer. Catholic faith and practice. pt. 1, $2; pt. 2, $2.50. Longmans.
Orr. Progress of dogma. $1.75. Armstrong.
Reed. Idea of God in relation to theology. net, 75 c. Univ. of Chic.
See also Baptism;—Catechisms;—Christianity;—Devil;—Holy Spirit;—Natural religion;—Religion;—Skepticism.
Theology and ethics of the Hebrews. Duff, A. net, $1.25. Scribner.
Theory of accounts. Goodyear, S: H. $1.50. Goodyear-M.
Theory of prosperity. Patten, S. N. net, $1.25. Macmillan.
THERAPEUTICS.
Hawley. New animal cellular therapy. $1. Clinic.
See also Christian science;—Diet;—Hydrotherapy;—Medicine;—Nurses and nursing;—Pathology;—Roentgen rays.
THERMODYNAMICS.
See Mechanics.
Thesaurus palæohibernicus. Stokes, W. net, $8. Macmillan.
THESSALONIANS.
See Bible.

13th district. Whitlock, B. $1.50. Bowen-M.
Thirty-six years in the White House. Pendel, T: F. $1.50. Neale.
Thomas Aquinas, *St. See* Wilberforce, B. A.
Thomas, Calvin. Life and works of Friedrich Schiller. Students' ed. '02(Jl5) O. **$1.50 net. Holt.
Thomas, H. H. Book of the apple. '02 (Mr22) il. D. (Handbooks of practical gardening, no. 6.) net, $1. Lane.
Thomas, Thdr., *ed.* Famous composers and their music. Extra il. ed. '01- '02(Mr15) 16 v., il. col. pl. 8°. (App. to pubs. for price.) Millet.
Thompson, E. E. Seton-. Krag and Johnny Bear. '02(Ap26) il. D. (Ser. of school reading.) 60 c. Scribner.
Thompson, H. C. Acute dilation of the stomach. '02(Je7) 8°, 75 c. Wood.
Thompson, *Sir* H: Motor car. '02(My17) 12°, $1. Warne.
Thompson, *Sir* H: The unknown God. '02 (Je21) S. 60 c. Warne.
Thompson, *Sir* H: *See also* Harmsworth, A. C.
Thompson, J: G. *and* T: E. New century readers. 3d bk., Nature, myth and story. '02(My10) 12°, (New century ser.) 52 c. Morse.
Thompson, Rob. E. Hand of God in American history. '02(Mr8) D. net, $1. Crowell.
Thompson, Seymour D. Commentaries on the law of negligence. v. 3. '02(Mr29) O. shp., $6. Bowen-M.
Thomson, H. C. China and the powers. '02 (Ap19) il. O. $4. Longmans.
Thoreau, H: D: The service; ed. by F. B. Sanborn. '02(Je14) O. bds., neet, $2.50; 22 cop. on Japan, ea., net, $10. Goodspeed.
Thoreau, H: D: Walden. '02(Ap19) 12°, (Home lib.) $1. Burt.
Thornton, E. Quin, *ed. See* Medical News.
Thornton, G. H. Eng. composition. '02(Ap12) D. (Self-educator ser.) 75 c. Crowell.
Thornton, Marcellus E. Lady of New Orleans. '02(Mr29) D. $1.50. Abbey Press.
Thorpe, Ctte. The children's London. '01- '02(Ja11) il. 4°, net, $4.50. Scribner.
Thorpe, T: E: Essays in hist. chemistry. 2d ed. '02(Je14) 8°, net, $4. Macmillan.
Those black diamond men. Gibbons, W: F. $1.50. Revell.
Those delightful Americans. Cotes, *Mrs.* S. J. $1.50. Appleton.
Thoughts for the Sundays of the year. Moule, H. C. G. net, $1. Revell.
Thoughts on education. Creighton, M. net, $1.60. Longmans.
Thrall of Leif the lucky. Liljencrantz, O. A. $1.50. McClurg.
Three graces. Hungerford, *Mrs.* M. H. $1. Lippincott.
Three sailor boys. Cameron, V. L. 60 c. Nelson.
Three thousand sample questions. Sellow, G. E. 50 c. Bellows.
Three whys and their answer. Babcock, M. D. 35 c. Un. Soc. C. E.
Three years on the blockade. Vail, I. E. $1.25. Abbey Press.
Threefold fellowship. Palmer, B. M. 75 c. Presb. Pub.

Thrice a pioneer. Hannibal, P: M. 75 c.; 40 c. Danish Luth.

THROAT.

Gradle. Diseases of the nose, pharynx and ear. net, $3.50. Saunders.

Wood, *and others, eds.* Eye, ear, nose and throat. $1.50. Year Bk.

See also Breathing.

Throne of David. Ingraham, J. H. $1. Burt.

Through science to faith. Smyth, N. net, $1.50. Scribner.

Thrum, T: G., *ed.* *See* Hawaiian almanac.

Thruston, Lucy M. A girl of Virginia. '02 (Je14) il. D. $1.50. Little, B. & Co.

Thurber, Alwyn M. Zelma, the mystic. 3d ed. [New issue.] '02(Mr22) il. O. $1.25. Alliance.

Thurston, Ernest L. *See* Snyder, C.

Thurston, Rob. H: Stationary steam engines, simple and compound. 7th ed., rev. and enl. '02(Jl19) il. 8°, $2.50. Wiley.

Thwaites, R. G. Down historic waterways: canoeing upon Ill. and Wis. rivers. 2d ed., rev. '02(Mr15) il. D. net, $1.20. McClurg.

Thwaites, R. G. Father Marquette. '02 (Je21) D. (Life histories.) net, $1. Appleton.

Thwaites, R. G., *ed.* *See also* Jesuit relations.

TIBERIUS, *Emperor of Rome.*

Tarver. Tiberius the tyrant. *$5 net. Dutton.

TIBET.

Carey. Adventures in Tibet. net, $1.50. Un. Soc. C. E.

Tibio. Wyman, W. E. A. 50 c. W: R. Jenkins.

Tiddeman, Lizzie E. A humble heroine. '01-'02(F15) 12°, pap., 15 c. Lippincott.

Tiffany, Nina M., *and* Lesley, Susan, *eds.* Letters of James Murray, loyalist. '01. '02 (Ja25) 12°, net, $2.50. W: B. Clarke.

Tiffany, O. H. *See* Poore, B: P.

Tigert, J: I., *comp. and ed.* *See* Methodist Epis. Ch. in America.

Tilden, W: A. Introd. to the study of chemical philosophy. 10th ed., rev. and enl. '01. '02(Ja11) S. (Text-books of science.) $1.75. Longmans.

Tileston, Merrill. Chiquita. '02(Jl12) D. $1.50. Merrill.

Tilton, Dwight. Miss Petticoats. '02 (My24) il. D. $1.50. C. M. Clark.

TIME.

See Astronomy;—Stars.

Time and chance. Hubbard, E. $1.50. Putnam.

Times of retirement. Matheson, G: net, $1.25. Revell.

Timothy. Hettinger, F. net, $1.50. Herder.

Tippler's vow. Fairchild, L. $10. Croscup.

Titian, *pseud.* *See* Antrim, M. T.

To the end of the trail. Nason, F. L. $1.50. Houghton, M. & Co.

To whom shall we go? Ovenden, C. T. $1. E. & J. B. Young.

TOASTS.

Miller, *comp.* The toastmaster. n. p. W. M. Rogers.

Reynolds. Banquet book. net, $1.75. Putnam.

Tocsin (The). Worthington, E. S. 25 c. Cubery.

Todd, C: B. True Aaron Burr. '02(My3) sq. S. net, 50 c. Barnes.

Todd, Marg. G., ["Graham Travers."] Way of escape. '02(Je21) D. $1.50. Appleton.

Todhunter, I:, *and* Leathem, J. G. Spherical trigonometry; rev. by J. G. Leathem. '02 (Mr1) 12°, net, $1.75. Macmillan.

TOKEN.

Shiells. Story of the token as belonging to the sacrament of the Lord's supper. net, $1. Presb. Bd.

Token of the covenant. Mahon, R. H. 50 c. Pub. Ho. of M. E. Ch., So.

Told by the death's head. Jokai, M. $1.50. Saalfield.

Tolman, Herb. C. Guide to old Persian inscriptions. '02(Mr15) il. 12°, $1.50. Am. Bk.

Tolstoï, *Count* L. N. What is religion? and other new articles and letters. '02(My17) D. net, 60 c. Crowell.

Tom Turner's legacy. Alger, H. $1. Burt.

TOMBSTONES.

Styan. Hist. of sepulchral cross slabs, with ref. to other emblems found thereon. net, $3. E. & J. B. Young.

Tomlins, W: L., *ed.* Laurel song book. '02 (Mr29) 12°, $1.50; bds., $1. Birchard.

Tommy Atkins episode. Page, K. N. $1. Abbey Press.

Tommy Cornstalk. Abbott, J. H. M. $2. Longmans.

Tompkins, Herb. W. Highways and byways in Hertfordshire. '02(Je14) il. 12°, (Highways and byways ser.) $2. Macmillan.

Tonna, *Mrs.* Ctte. E. Judah's lion. New ed. '01- '02(F22) 12°, $1. Dodd.

Tons of treasure. Bishop, W: H: $1. Street.

Tooker, W: W. Algonquian series. In 10 v. v. 9, 10. '02(Jl19) 12°, ea., *$1.50 net. F. P. Harper.

Topical architecture. Ware, W: R. 2 v. $7.50. Am. Architect.

TOPOGRAPHICAL DRAWING.

Root. Military topography and sketching. $2.50. Hudson-K.

Torture of the clinic. Trudeau, L. $1; 50 c. Bourguignon.

Tourgée, A. W. A fool's errand. [New ed.] '02(Je7) il. D. $1.50. Fords.

Tout, T: F., *and* Tait, Ja., *eds.* Historical essays, by members of the Owens College, Manchester. '02(Ap19) O. $5. Longmans.

TOWER OF LONDON.

Gower. Tower of London. v. 2. net, $6.50. Macmillan.

Town and country lib. *See* Appleton's.

Town life in ancient Italy. Friedländer, L. 75 c. B: H. Sanborn.

Townesend, *Mrs.* Stephen. *See* Burnett, *Mrs.* F. H.

TOWNS.

Illinois. Laws of Ill. rel. to township organization. $2.50; $3. Legal Adv.

Townsend, C. H. *See* Sage, D.

Townsend, C: Mahoney million. '02(Ap26) 12°, $1.25. New Amsterdam.

Townsend, E: W. Chimmie Fadden and Mr. Paul. '02(My10) il. D. $1.50. Century Co.

Townsend, Luther T. Satan and demons. '02(My10) sq. T. (Little books on doctrine.) net, 25 c. Jennings.

TOXINS.
See Poisons.
Toynbee, Paget. Dante studies and researches. '02(Je7) 8°, net, $3.50. Dutton.
TRADE.
See Business;—Commerce;—Fur trade;—Tariff.
TRADE-MARKS.
See Plate.
TRADE-UNIONS.
Webb. Hist. of trade unionism. net, $2.60.—Industrial democracy. net, $4. Longmans.
TRADES.
See Useful arts.
Tragedy of Anne Boleyn. Gallup, *Mrs.* E. W. $1.50. Howard.
Traill, H: D., *and* Mann, J. S., *eds.* Social England. [New il. ed.] In 6 v. v. 1. '02 (F1) Q. net, $4.50. Putnam.
Training of teachers. Laurie, S. S. net, $1.50. Macmillan.
Training the church of the future. Clark, F. E: net, 75 c. Funk.
Transplanting an old tree. Bloomfield, W. $1. Blanchard.
TRANSPORTATION.
See Railroads.
TRANSVAAL.
Cook. Rights and wrongs of the Transvaal war. $2. Longmans.
See also Boers;—South Africa.
Trask, Rob. D. Human knowledge and human conduct. '01- '02(Jl19) O. *$2 net. R. D. Trask.
Trask, W. B., *ed.* Letters of Col. Thomas Westbrook and others rel. to Indian affairs in Maine, 1722-1726. '01- '02(Mr8) 8°, $5. Littlefield.
Traum ein leben. Grillparzer, F. S. 60 c. Heath.
TRAVEL.
Powers. Art of travel. 25 c.
See also Voyages and travels.
Travers, Graham, *pseud.* *See* Todd, M. G.
Travers, Morris W. Experimental study of gases; introd. pref. by W: Ramsay. '01- '02(Ja4) il. 8°, net, $3.25. Macmillan.
Travis, Ira D. Hist. of the Clayton-Bulwer treaty. '02(F15) 12°, pap., $1. Mich. Pol. Sci.
Travis, Wa. J. Practical golf. New rev. ed. '02(My10) il. 12°, net, $2. Harper.
Treasure of Cocos Island. Kaler, J. O. $1. Burt.
TREATIES.
See United States.
TREES.
Dame *and* Brooks. Handbook of trees of New England. $1.35. Ginn.
Davey. The tree doctor. $1. J: Davey.
Huntington. Studies of trees in winter. net, $2.25. Knight.
Payne. How to teach about trees. 25 c. Kellogg.
Stone *and* Fickett, *comps.* Trees in prose and poetry. 50 c. Ginn.
See also Botany;—Forests and forestry;—Fruit;—Lumber.
Trelawney, Davrell. Man of no account. '02 (Ap19) sq. S. (Upward ser., no. 2.) pap., 10 c. J. H. West.
Treves, F: Surgical applied anatomy. New ed. '02(F15) il. 12°, net, $2. Lea.
Tribal custom in Anglo-Saxon law. Seebohm, F: net, $5. Longmans.
Tribune almanac and political register, 1902. '02(Ja11) D. (Lib. of *Tribune* extras, v. 14, no. 1.) pap., 25 c. Tribune Assoc.
Trickett, W: Law of witnesses in Penn. '02(Mr1) O. shp., $6. T. & J. W. Johnson.
Triggs, H. I. Formal gardens in England and Scotland. In 3 pts. pt. 1. '02(Mr8); pt. 2 (My10) f°, net, complete set, $25. Scribner.
TRIGONOMETRY.
Todhunter *and* Leathem. Spherical trigonometry. net, $1.75. Macmillan.
See also Geodesy; — Geometry; — Logarithms; — Mathematics;—Navigation;—Surveying.
TRIPOLI.
Cathcart. Tripoli. $4. J. B. C. Newkirk.
Triumph of the cross. Savonarola, G. net, $1.35. Herder.
TROLLEY TRIPS.
Childe, *comp.* Trolley exploring. 10 c. Brooklyn Eagle.
Trollope, A. Writings. Collectors' ed. v. 8-16. '02(Mr15) il. 8°, crushed lev., subs. (App. to pubs. for price.) Gebbie.
TROUT.
Rhead. Speckled brook trout. net, $3.50. Russell.
Sage, *and others.* Salmon and trout. net, $2; net, $7.50. Macmillan.
Trudeau, L: Torture of the clinic. '01- '02 (Ja4) O. $1; pap., 50 c. Bourguignon.
True romance revealed by a bag of old letters. Anthony, H. G. $1. Abbey Press.
True tales of birds and beasts. Jordan, D: S. 40 c. Heath.
Trueba, Antonio de. El molinerillo y otros cuetos. (R. D. de la Cortina.) '02(My24) S. (Cuentos selectos, no. 4.) pap., 35 c. W: R. Jenkins.
Trueman, Anita. Anton's angels. '02(Mr22) 16°, 75 c. Alliance.
TRUMPET.
Littleton. Trumpeters' hand book and instructor. $1. Hudson-K.
TRUSTS.
Flint, *and others.* The trust. net, $1.25. Doubleday, P.
Haggerty. How to treat the trusts. 25 c. Abbey Press.
See also Capital and labor.
Truth about socialism. Collins, J: E. 25 c. J. A. Wayland.
Truth about the Schley case. Nauticus, *pseud.* 25 c. Columbia.
Tuber-like rootlets of cycas revoluta. Life, A. C. net, 25 c. Univ. of Chic.
Tucker, C: Cowles, *rep.* *See* District of Columbia. *Ct. of appeals.* Repts.
Tucker, Eliz. S. Magic key. '01- '02(F15) 12°, net, $1. Little, B. & Co.
Tucker, G: F. Manual rel. to the preparation of wills: book of Mass. law. 2d ed. '02 (Mr29) D. shp., $3.50. G: B. Reed.
Tuckwell, W. A. W. Kinglake: biog. and literary study. '02(Ap12) il. 12°, $1.75. Macmillan.
Turnbull, Coulson. Divine language of celestial correspondence. '02(Mr22) 8°, $2. Alliance.
Turnbull, Coulson. Sema-Kanda. '02(Mr22) 12°, $1.25. Alliance.
Turner, A. L. Accessory sinuses of the nose. '02(F8) Q. $4. Longmans.

Turner, J. T. Giant fish of Florida. '02 (Jl5) il. 8°, **$3.50 net. Lippincott.
Turner, Jos. M. W: Turner and Ruskin. '01-'02(F22) 2 v., il. 4°. net, $50 Dodd.
Tuscan sculpture. Hurll, E. M. net, 75 c.; 50 c.; 35 c. Houghton, M. & Co.
TUSCANY.
Carmichael. In Tuscany. net, $2. Dutton.
See also Artists.
Tuttle, J: E. The gift of power: study of the Holy Spirit. '02(Je7) S. net, 25 c. Westminster.
Twain, Mark, *pseud. See* Clemens, S: L.
'Tween you an' I. Blouët, P. $1.20. Lothrop.
Twelfth night. *See* Shakespeare, W:
Twentieth century home builder. Powell, L. 25 c Pub. Ho. M. E. Ch., So.
Twentieth century horse book. Morgan, D: B: $1.50. D: B: Morgan.
Twentieth century text-books. il. D. net. Appleton.
—Caldwell. Lab'y manual of botany. 50 c.; 60 c.
—Fowler. Hist. of ancient Greek literature. $1.40.
—Gilbert *and* Brigham. Introd. to physical geography. $1.25.
—Jordan *and* Heath. Animal forms. $1.10.
—Nelson. Analyt. key to some of the common flowering plants of Rocky Mt. region. **45 c.
—Tennyson. The princess. 25 c.
—West. Latin grammar. 90 c.
Twentieth century wonder book. Hunter, W: C. 50 c.; 25 c. Donohue.
Twenty-five steppingstones toward Christ's kingdom. Fradenburgh, O. P. $1. O. P. Fradenburgh.
Twenty little maidens. Blanchard, A. E. $1.25. Lippincott.
Twenty-six and one. Gôrky, M. $1.25. J. F. Taylor.
Twenty thousand miles by land and sea. Pennock, A. F. $1. Mason Pub.
Twing, *Mrs.* Caro. E. S. Henry Drummond in spirit life. '02(Jl19) S. pap., 10 c. Star.
Two centuries' growth of Am. law, 1701-1901. '01. '02(Mr15) 8°, (Yale bicentennial pub.) net, $4. Scribner.
Two-fold covenant. Achenbach, H: 50 c. Evangelical Press.
Two hundred bar exam. questions. Bingham, G. A. $1. Commercial Press.
Two of a trade, by the author of "Val." '02 (My17) 12°, 60 c. Nelson.
Two Renwicks. Davidson, M. A. $1.50. Neely.
Two thousand a year on fruits and flowers. Barnard, C: $1. Coates.
Two thousand years in eternity. Bywater, B. net, $2.15. Hudson-K.
Two waifs. Howard, E. B. 50 c. Abbey Press.
Two wars. French, S: G. $2. Confederate Veteran.
Two winters in Norway. Spender, A. E. $4. Longmans.
Typee. Melville, H. 45 c. Heath.
TYPEWRITING.
Vories. Lab'y method of teaching Eng. and touch typewriting together. $1.25. Inland Pub.

TYPHOID FEVER.
Osler, *ed.* Typhoid and typhus fevers. net, $5; $6. Saunders.
Ultzmann, Rob. Neuroses of the genito-urinary system in the male with sterility and impotence. 2d ed., rev. with notes by the tr., G. W. Allen. '02(Jl12) il. 12°, *$1 net. Davis.
Ulyat, W: C. The first years of the life of the redeemed after death. '01-'02(F15) D. $1.25. Abbey Press.
Ulysses. Phillips, S. net, $1.25. Macmillan.
Umbrian towns. Cruickshank, J. W. net, $1.25. Wessels.
Uncle and aunt. Woolsey, S. C. 50 c. Little, B. & Co.
Uncle Boston's spicy breezes. Smith, B. net, $1. Am. Bapt.
Uncle Jed's country letters. Brenton, H. 30 c. Dickerman.
Uncle Sam, trustee. Bangs, J: K. net, $1.75. Riggs.
Uncle Sam's examination. Kellogg, A. M. 15 c. Kellogg.
Uncle Tom's cabin. Stowe, H. B. $2: $3; $4. Dominion.
Under my own roof. Rouse, A. L. net, $1.20. Funk.
Under sunny skies. '02(Jl12) il. D. (Youth's companion ser., no. 3.) 30 c. Ginn.
Under the dome. Ingram, A. F. M. $1.25. E. & J. B. Young.
Under the red cross. Wright, D: H: 35 c. Biddle.
Underwood, Clarence F., *il.* Some pretty girls. '01-'02(Mr1) 4°, regular ed., $3; de luxe ed., $5. Quail & W.
Undine. *See* La Motte Fouqué, F. H. K. *Freiherr* de.
Undine lib. 12°, pap., 25 c. Street.
—Ellis. Life of Wm. McKinley. (9.)
UNITARIAN CHURCH.
Wilbur. Hist. sketch of the Independent Cong. church, Meadville, Pa., 1825-1900. $1; 50 c. E. G. Huidekoper.
United States. *Circuit cts. of appeals.* **Repts.**, with annots. v. 47. '01-'02(Ja4); v. 48 (Mr1); v. 49 (Ap19); v. 50 (Jl5) O. shp., ea., $3.35. Lawyers' Co-op.
United States. **Federal reporter, v. 110.** Permanent ed. '01. '02(Ja18); v. 111 (Mr1); v. 112 (My10); v. 113 (Je7) O. (Nat. reporter system, U. S. ser.) shp., ea., $3.50. West Pub.
United States. *Supreme ct.* Repts., v. 183. (J. C. B. Davis.) '02(Je7) O. shp., $2.30. Banks.
UNITED STATES.
Brown, C: F., *and* Croft. Outline study of U. S. history. 50 c. Courier Pr.
Brown, W: G. Lower South in Am. history. net, $1.50. Macmillan.
Burgess. Reconstruction and the constitution, 1866-1876. net, $1. Scribner.
Butler. Treaty-making power of the U. S. In 2 v. v. 1. complete work. net, $12. Banks.
Cathcart. Tripoli; first war with the U. S. $4. J. B. C. Newkirk.
Clark. The government, what it is, what it does. 75 c. Am. Bk.
Codman. Arnold's expedition to Quebec. net, $2.25. Macmillan.

UNITED STATES.—*Continued.*
Elliott. Debates of federal constitution. 5 v. net, $10; net, $12. Lippincott.
Farley. West Point in the early sixties, with incidents of the war. net, $2. Pafraets.
French. Two wars: Mexican war; war between the states. $2. Confederate Veteran.
Gordy. Am. leaders and heroes. net, 60 c. Scribner.
Halstead. Hist. of America's new possessions. $2.50; $3.50; $4.50. Dominion.
Harris. Sectional struggle: troubles between the North and South. net, $2.50. Lippincott.
Lodge, *and others*. The United States and the Philippine Islands. 10 c. Brooklyn Eagle.
McDaniel. War poems, 1861-1865. $1. Abbey Press.
Melvin. Journal, in Arnold's expedition against Quebec. $2. H. W. Bryant.
Muirhead. America, the land of contrasts. net, $1.20. Lane.
Page. Rebuilding of old commonwealths. Southern states. net, $1. Doubleday, P.
Pendel. Thirty-six years in the White House. $1.50 Neale.
Phillips. Methods of keeping the public money of the U. S. $1. Mich. Pol. Sci.
Pratt. America's story. v. 5. 40 c. Heath.
Richardson. War of 1812. subs., $3. Historical.
Ridpath. Hist. of the U. S. from aboriginal times. $6. Grosset.
Root *and* Connelley. Overland stage to California. $2.50: $3.50. Root & C.
Tappan. Our country's story. 65 c. Houghton, M. & Co.
Thompson. Hand of God in Am. history. net, $1. Crowell.
Wagner. Current history. 25 c. Whitaker & R.
Westbrook. The West-brook drives. $1.25. Eckler.
Wilson, *ed.* Presidents of the U. S. $3.50; $6. Appleton.
See also Clayton-Bulwer treaty; — Lexington; — Louisiana purchase; — Pensions; — Political science;—*also* names of states.

United States Catholic historical soc., monograph ser. pap. (not for sale.) U. S. Cath.
—Carroll. Unpublished letters. (1.)

United States Govt. publications. Hasse, A. R. pt. 1. $1. Lib. Bu.

Universalist register for 1902; ed. by R: Eddy. '02(F8) S. pap., 25 c. Universalist.

UNIVERSITY OF CALIFORNIA.
Jones. Il. hist. of the University of Cal., 1868-1901. $5. Berkeley.

University of Cal. bulletins. il. O. pap. Univ. of Cal.
—Eakle. Colemanite from So. California. 15 c. (v. 3, 2.)
—Hershey. Quaternary of So. Cal. 20 c. (v. 3, 1.)
—Lawson. The eparchæan interval. 10 c. (v. 3, 3.)
—Lawson *and* Palache. Berkeley Hills. 80 c. (v. 2, 12.)

University of Chicago constructive Bible studies; ed. by W: R. Harper and E. D. Burton. O. Univ. of Chic.
—Harper. Constructive studies in the priestly element in the O. T. $1.

University of Chicago cont. to education. pap., net. Univ. of Chic
—Dewey. Educational situation. 50 c. (3.
—Dewey. Psychology and social practice. 25 c. (2.)
—Young. Ethics in the school. 25 c. (4.)
—Young. Isolation in the school. 50 c. (1.)
—Young. Some types of modern educ. theory. 25 c. (6.)

Univ. of Chicago cont. to philosophy. 8° pap., net, 35 c. Univ. of Chic.
—Gore. Imagination in Spinoza and Hume. (v. 2, 4.)

University of Chicago decennial pubs. Q. pap., *25 c. net. Univ. of Chic.
—Bolza. Concerning the geodesic curvature.

University of Chicago, Walker museum conts. 8°, net. Univ. of Chic.
—Case. Palæontological notes. 25 c. (v. 1, 3.)

University of Chicago. Yerkes Observatory bulletin. 8°, net. Univ. of Chic.
—Hale. New star in Perseus. 10 c. (16.)

UNIVERSITY OF PENNSYLVANIA.
Nitzsche, *comp.* Proceedings at dedication of building of Dept. of law. $3; $3.50. Univ. of Penn.

University of Penn. pubs., ser. in pol. economy and public law. O. [Univ. of Penn.] Ginn.
—Weyl. Passenger traffic of railways. $1.50; $1. (16.)

University of Va. monographs, school of Teutonic languages. 12°, pap., net, 50 c. Barnes.
—Blain. Syntax of the verb in the Anglo-Saxon chronicle, 787 to 1001. (1.)

University of Wis. bulletins. O. pap. Univ. of Wis.
—Wolcott. On the sensitiveness of the coherer. 20 c. (51; science ser., v. 3, 1.)

Unknown God. Thompson, *Sir* H: 60 c. Warne.

Unrequited love. Stechhan, O. $1. Abbey Press.

Unstable as water. Needell, *Mrs.* M. A. $1.25. Warne.

Unter vier augen. Fulda, L. *35 c. net. Holt.

Unto the end. Alden, *Mrs.* I. M. $1.50. Lothrop.

Unto you, young women. Sinclair, W. M. net, $1. Lippincott.

Unwilling guest. Hill, G. L. net, $1. Am. Bapt.

Upland game birds. Sandys, E. net, $2; net, $7.50. Macmillan.

Upward ser. sq. S. pap., 10 c. J. H. West.
—Macdonald. Guarding the thoughts. (1.)
—Trelawney. A man of no account. (2.)

Upon the sun-road. Hurst, J: F. 25 c. Revell.

URINE AND URINARY ORGANS.
Morton. Genito-urinary disease and syphilis. net, $3. Davis.
See also Generative organs.

Urn burial. *See* Brown, *Sir* T:

USEFUL ARTS.
Brown, *ed.* Workshop wrinkles. net, $1. Van Nostrand.
Oliver. Dangerous trades. *$8 net. Dutton.
See also Bridges;—Commerce; — Dyeing; — Electric engineering;—Machinery;—Patents.

UTAH.
Jones. Utah. *40 c. net. Macmillan.

UTILITARIANISM.
Albee. Hist. of Eng. utilitarianism. net, $2.75. Macmillan.

Utopia. More, *Sir* T: $1. Burt.

Vacation with nature. Talmage, F. D. net, $1. Funk.

VACCINATION.
Oswald. Vaccination a crime. 10 c. Physical Culture.
See also Smallpox.

Vail, I. E. Three years on the blockade. '02 (Jl5) D. $1.25. Abbey Press.

Valcourt-Vermont, Edg. de, ["*Comte* C. de Saint-Germain."] Practical astrology; with a hist. of astronomy. '02(Ap26) il. 12°, $1; pap., 50 c. Laird.

Valdés, A. P. José; tr. by Minna C. Smith. '01· '02(Mr8) D. $1.25. Brentano's.

Vale Press ser. 8°. Lane.
—Browne. Religio medici, and other essays. **$12 net.

Vale Press Shakespeare. 8°, net. Lane.
—Shakespeare. Twelfth night. $8. (22.)

Valentine, E: U. Ship of silence and other poems. '02(Je28) 12°, net, $1.20. Bowen-M.

Valentine, *Mrs.* Laura J., *comp. and ed.* Old, old fairy tales. '02(My10) il. 12°, (Fairy lib.) $1. Burt.

VALJEAN, Jean.
Quayle. A hero, Jean Valjean. 30 c. Jennings.

Valley of decision. Wharton, E. 2 v. $2. Scribner.

Van Anderson, Helen. Journal of a live woman. '02(Mr22) D. $1. Alliance.

Van Arsdale, H. Twentieth century interest tables. '02(Jl12) 8°, $1.50. Vawter.

Van Bergen, R. Story of China. '02(My3) il. D. 60 c. Am. Bk.

Vance, Ja. J. Rise of a soul. '02(My17) 12°, net, $1. Revell.

Vancil, Fk. M. The school congress. '02 (Jl19) 12°, 25 c. Kellogg.

Van Der Kellen, M. J.-Ph. Works of Michel Le Blond. '02(Mr1) portfolio, net, $30; mor. portfolio, net, $35. Dodd.

Vanderpoel, Emily N. Color problems. '02 (My10) O. net, $5. Longmans.

Vandersloot, Lewis. History and genealogy of the Von der Sloot family. '01· '02 (Ap5) il. f°, $1. L. Vandersloot.

Van Deventer, E. M., ["Lawrence L. Lynch."] The woman who dared. '02(F22) D. 75 c.; pap., 25 c. Laird.

Van Doren, De W. T. Students' guide to health. '01. '02(F15) 12°, $2. T. Van Doren.

VAN DYCK, Ant.
Cust. Desc. of sketch-book used by Sir Anthony Van Dyck. $17.50. Macmillan.
Hurll, *ed.* Van Dyck. net, 75 c.; net, 50 c.; net, 35 c. Houghton, M. & Co.

Van Dyke, J: C: Italian painting. '02(Jl12) 16°, bds., 50 c. Elson.

Van Dyke, T. S. *See* Roosevelt, T.—Sandys, E.

Van Epps, Howard. *See* Georgia. Supp. to code.

Van Meter, B: F. Genealogies and sketches of some old families of Virginia and Kentucky especially. '01· '02(Ja18) 8°, $2.25. Morton.

Van Santvoord, S. House of Cæsar and the imperial disease. '02(F22) il. Q. net, $5.25. Pafraets.

Van Vorst, Marie. Philip Longstreth. '02 (Ap19) D. $1.50. Harper.

Van Zile, Philip T. Elements of the law of bailments and carriers. '02(My24) O. shp., $5. Callaghan.

Varieties of religious experience. James, W: net, $3.20. Longmans.

VARIOLA.
Moore, *ed.* Variola, vaccination, varicella, etc. net, $5; net, $6. Saunders.

Vaughan, D. T. G. *See* Bower, F. O.

Vaughan, Herbert. Holy sacrifice of the mass. 4th ed. '02(Je28) 16°, 15 c. Herder.

Vaughan, V. C., *and* Novey, F. G. Cellular toxins. 4th ed. '02(Jl19) 8°, *$3 net. Lea.

Vector analysis. Gibbs, J. W. net, $4. Scribner.

VEGETABLES.
Wythes. Book of vegetables. net, $1. Lane.
See also Gardening.

VEGETARIANS.
Miles. Failures of vegetarianism. net, $1.50. Dutton.

Velázquez de la Cadena, M. Nuevo diccionario de pronunciacion de las lenguas Inglesa y Espanola. pt. 2. '02(Je14) O. hf. leath., $3.50. Appleton.

Vellum ser. il. 12°, $1. Univ. Co-op.
—Goff. Lessons in commercial fruit growing.

Velocity of light. Michelsen, A. A. net, 25 c. Univ. of Chic.

Velvin, Ellen. Rataplan, a rogue elephant, and other stories. '02(Jl12) il. D. **$1.25 net. Altemus.

VENEREAL DISEASES.
Hayden. Pocket text-book of venereal diseases. net, $2.25. Lea.
See also Syphilis.

VENUS DI MILO.
Patoma. Venus di Milo; its hist. and art. 50 c. Cambridge.

Verba crucis. McClelland, T. C. 50 c. Crowell.

Veritas, *pseud.* The German Empire of today. '02(Je7) D. $2.25. Longmans.

VERMONT.
Wilbur. Early hist. of Vt. v. 3. $1.50. L. F. Wilbur.
See also Newbury.

Verne, Jules. Vingt mille lieues sous les mers; abr. and ed. by C. Fontaine. '02 (Je14) S. (Modern lang. ser.) 40 c. Heath.

Versailles hist. ser.: ed. by K. P. Wormeley. il. 8°, subs., $6; leath., $9. Hardy, P. & Co.
—Bernis. Memoirs and letters. 2 v.
—Elisabeth, *Mme.* Memoir and letters.
—Fersen. Letters and papers.
—Lespinasse. Letters.

Very naughty girl. Smith, *Mrs.* E. T. $1. Burt.

Very odd girl. Armstrong, A. E. $1. Burt.

Veterinarian's call book for 1902. (R. R. Bell.) '01· '02(F22) 12°, leath., $1.25. W: R. Jenkins.

VETERINARY MEDICINE AND SURGERY.
Cadiot. Clinical veterinary medicine and surgery. $5.25. W: R. Jenkins.
Dollar. Operative technique for veterinary surgeons. $3.75. W: R. Jenkins.
Dunn. Veterinary medicines. $3.75. W: R. Jenkins.
Fleming. Operative veterinary surgery. v. 2. net, $3.25. W: R. Jenkins.
Liautard. Animal castration. $2. W: R. Jenkins.
McClure. Amer. horse, cattle and sheep doctor. $1.50. Henneberry.
Morgan. Twentieth century horse book; also treatise on cattle, [etc.,] giving diseases and remedies. $1.50. D: B: Morgan.
Wyman. Tibio; neurectomy for relief of spavin. 50 c. W: R. Jenkins.
See also Horse.

VICTORIA, *Queen of England.*
Halstead *and* Munson. Life and reign of Queen Victoria. $1.50; $2.25. Dominion.
Walsh. Religious life and influence of Queen Victoria. net, $2.50. Dutton.

Victorian poets. Thackeray, F. St. J. net, $2. Lane.

Victories of Rome. Best, K. D. net, 45 c. Benziger.

Victorious republicanism. Halstead, M. $1.50; $2.25. Dominion.

Vielé, H. K. Myra of the Pines. '02(Je14) D. $1.50. McClure, P.

Viets, Fs. H. Genealogy of the Viets family. '02(Ap26) il. O. $3. Case.

Views afoot. Taylor, B. $1. Burt.

Village work in India. Russell, N. net, $1. Revell.

Villari, P. Barbarian invasions of Italy. '02 (My10) 2 v., il. 8°, net, $7.50. Scribner.

VILLAS.
See Architecture.

VILLON, François.
Morehead. Story of François Villon, the hero of the play "If I were king." 25 c. Ogilvie.

Vincent, Edg. L. Margaret Bowlby. '02 (My17) D. $1.50. Lothrop.

Vincent, J. M., Ely, R: T., Gilman, D. C., *and others.* Herbert B. Adams; with a bibliog. of the Dept. of history, politics and economics. '02(Ap26) O. (Johns Hopkins Univ. studies, v. 20, extra no.) pap. (free to subs.) Johns Hopkins.

Vincent, Marvin R. What is it to believe on the Lord Jesus Christ? '01· '02(F8) S. pap., 5 c. Beam.

VINEYARDS.
See Fresno Co., Cal.

Vingt mille lieues sous les mers. Verne, J. 40 c. Heath.

Virden, *Mrs.* Laura M. N. First science reader. New ed. '01· '02(Mr29) il. 16°, 25 c.; bds., 10 c. Flanagan.

Virgil. Æneid. bks. 1-6; tr. by H. H. Ballard. '02(Ap5) D. net, $1.50. Houghton, M. & Co.

Virginia-Carolina almanac, 1902. '02(Mr15) il. 16°, pap., gratis. Virginia-Carolina.

Virginia. Complete annot. digest. v. 8. '02 (Je7) O. shp., $6.50. Hurst & Co.

Virginia. *Supreme ct. of appeals.* Repts. Jefferson—33 Grattan, 1730-1880. (T: J. Michie.) v. 16-18. '01· '02(F8) Grattan's repts. v. 13-15 (Mr15); v. 11, 12 (My10); v. 9, 10 (My24); v. 7, 8 (Jl5) O. shp., ea., $7.50. Michie.

Virginia. *Supreme ct. of appeals.* Repts. (M. P. Burks.) v. 99. '02(My10) O. shp., $3.50. O'Bannon.

VIRGINIA.
Hall. Rending of Va. $2. Mayer.
Snowden. Some old historic landmarks of Va. and Md. *25 c. net. Ramey.
See also Jamestown.

Virginian (The). Wister, O. $1.50. Macmillan.

Virginians. Thackeray, W: M. $1. Macmillan.

VISCHER, Peter.
Headlam. Peter Vischer. $2. Macmillan.

Visitor's (A) guide to Paris. 7th ed. '02 (Jl5) S. (Eagle lib., v. 17, no. 7; ser. no. 66.) pap., 10 c. Brooklyn Eagle.

VIVISECTION.
Ernst. Animal experimentation. net, $1.50; net, $1. Little, B. & Co.

Vizetelly, Ernest A. Lover's progress told by himself. '01· '02(Mr8) D. $1.50. Brentano's.

VOICE.
Lawton. The singing voice and its practical cultivation. $1.50. W: H: Lawton.
Lunn. Philosophy of voice. net, $2. Schirmer.
Murrin. Vocal exercises on the vocal factors of expression. net, 50 c. A. M. Allen.

Voice from England. McGrady, T: 10 c. Standard.

Voltaire, F. M. A. de. Philosophical dictionary (in Eng.); introd. by W: F. Fleming. '02(Jl5) 10 v., il. 8°. per set, subs., *$18 net; hf. mor., $24 net. G: Clarke.

Voltaire, F. M. A. de. Zaïre and Epîtres; ed. by C: A. Eggert. '02(Mr22) 16°, (Lake French classics.) 50 c. Scott, F. & Co.

VON DER SLOOT FAMILY.
See Vandersloot, L.

Vorce, C: M. Genealogical and hist. record of the Vorce family in America. '01· '02 (Ja18) 8°, $2. C: M. Vorce.

Vories, Hervey D. Laboratory method of teaching Eng. and touch typewriting together. '01· '02(Ja11) 8°, $1.25. Inland Pub.

VOYAGES AND TRAVELS.
Beck. Sonnenblicke aus der Amer. praxis net, 30 c. Lemcke.
Belloc. Path to Rome. net, $2. Longmans.
Cadigan. My ocean trip. $1. Brentano's.
Fielding. Journal of a voyage to Lisbon. **$5 net. Houghton, M. & Co.
Gray. Musings by camp-fire and wayside. net, $1.50. Revell.
Henry. Travels in Canada and the Indian territories, between 1760-1776. $4. Little, B. & Co.
Honeyman. Bright days in merrie England: four in hand journeys. net, $1.50. Honeyman.
Mackenzie. Voyages from Montreal through the Continent of N. A. to the frozen and Pacific Oceans. 2 v. net, $1. New Amsterdam.
Pennock. Twenty thousand miles by land and sea. $1. Mason Pub.

VOYAGES AND TRAVELS.—*Continued.*
Satchel guide for vacation tourist in Europe. net, $1.50. Houghton, M. & Co.
Taylor. Views afoot, or, Europe seen with knapsack and staff. $1. Burt.
See also **Geography;—Travel.**

Wace, H:, *ed. See* Fulham Palace Conference.

WACHOVIA.
Clewell. Hist. of Wachovia, N. C. **$2 net. Doubleday, P.

Wade, G. W. Old Testament history. '02 (Mr8) 12°, $1.50. Dutton.

Wage-labor and capital. Marx, K. 50 c. N. Y. Labor News.

Wager (The). McManus, L. $1.25. Buckles.

Waggaman, Ma. T. Bob o' Link. '02(Mr22) il. D. 40 c. Benziger.

Waggaman, Ma. T. Corinne's vow. '02(F15) D. $1.25. Benziger.

Wagner, C: Courage. New ed. '01. '02 (F22) 12°, $1.25. Dodd.

Wagner, Harr. Current history: supp. to California state series history. Rev. ed. '02 (Je7) sq. D. leatherette, 25 c. Whitaker & R.

Wagner, Harr. New Pacific school geography. New ed. '02(Je7) Q. net, $1. Whitaker & R.

Wagner, R: Rheingold; ed. by R. A. von Minckwitz. '02(Je28) 16°, (German opera texts, v. 1.) 75 c. Newson.

Wags of the stage. Whitton, J. $2.50. Rigby.

Wait, W: Law and practice in civil actions and proceedings in justices' cts., and in other cts. not of record, and on appeals to county cts. of N. Y. In 3 v. v. 1. 7th ed., by E. Baylies. '02(Mr15); v. 2 (Jl12) O. shp., per v., $6.35; or per set, $19. M. Bender.

Waiting race. Rogers, A. A. 50 c. Abbey Press.

Wakeman, Rob. P. Wakeman genealogy. '02(Ap5) il. 8°, $5; hf. mor., $7.50; full mor., $10. Journal Pub.

Walden. Thoreau, H: D: $1. Burt.

WALES.
Edwards. Wales. **$1.35 net; $1.60 net. Putnam.

Walford, *Mrs.* Lucy B. Charlotte. '02 (Mr22) D. $1.50. Longmans.

Walker, Fs. A. Taxation of corporations in the U. S. '02(Mr22) 8°, (Pub. of the soc., no. 329.) pap., 25 c. Am. Acad. Pol. Sci.

Walker, J. G., *ed. See* Am. Bapt. year-book.

Walker, Ja. W. G. Ocean to ocean. '02 (Mr22) il. O. net, $1.25. McClurg.

Walkey, S. With redskins on the warpath. '01. '02(Ja11) il. D. $1.25. Cassell.

Wall, *Mrs.* D. H. Sister in name only. '02 (Ap26) 12°, $1. Neely.

Wall, W: What great men have said about great men. '02(Ap5) 12°, net, $2.50. Dutton.

Wallace, *Sir* Donald M. Web of empire: diary of the imperial tour of the Duke and Duchess of Cornwall and York, in 1901. '02(Je28) il. 8°, net, $6.50. Macmillan.

Wallace, Lew. Ben Hur. Players' ed. '01. '02(Mr1) il. 12°, $2.50. Harper.

Wallannah. Hargrave, W: L. $1.50. B. F. Johnson.

Wallenstein. Schiller, J. C. F. v. net, $1. Holt.

Wallenstein's camp. *See* Schiller, J. C. F. v.

Waller, A. R., *and* Barrow, G. H. S. John Henry, Cardinal Newman. '01. '02(Jl19) 24°, (Westminster biographies.) 75 c. Small.

Waller, M. E. The little citizen. '02(Jl12) il. D. **$1 net. Lothrop.

Walley, T: Practical guide to meat inspection; rewritten and enl. '01. '02(Ja4) il 12°, $3. W: R. Jenkins

Walpole, H. Some unpublished letters; ed. by Sir S. Walpole. '02(Ap26) O. net, $1.50. Longmans.

Walsh, D: Roentgen rays in medical work. 3d ed. '02(Mr29) 8°, net, $2.50. Wood.

Walsh, G: E. Allin Winfield. '02(F8) D. $1.50. Buckles.

Walsh, Wa. Religious life and influence of Queen Victoria. '02(Je14) 8°, net, $2.50. Dutton.

Walton, W: Paris from the earliest period to the present day. v. 6. Lib. ed. '02 (Mr15) il. 8°, per v., $3. Barrie.

Wan Lun and Dandy. Kaler, J. O. 75 c. Burt.

Wanklin, J. A. Arsenic. '01. '02(F15) 12°, $1. Lippincott.

WAR.
Bloch. Future of war. 60 c. Ginn.

WAR OF 1812.
See **United States.**

War poems, 1861-1865. McDaniel, *Mrs.* H. P. $1. Abbey Press.

Ward, Herb. D. *See* **Phelps, E. S.**

Ward, *Mrs.* Herb. D. *See* Phelps, E. S.

Ward, J: The sacred beetle: treatise on Egyptian scarabs in art and history. '02 (Mr8) il. 8°, net, $3.50. Scribner.

Warden, Florence, *pseud. See* **James,** *Mrs.* **F. A. P.**

Warden, W: A. Ancestors, kin and descendants of John Warden and Narcissa (Davis), his wife. '01. '02(F1) 8°, $5. W: A. Warden.

Ware, Fabian. Educational foundations of trade and industry. '02(F22) 12°, (Internat. educ. ser., no. 54.) net, $1.20. Appleton.

Ware, W: R., *ed.* Topical architecture. '02 (Jl19) 2 v., pls. 4°, $7.50. Am. Architect.

Warlow, T: P., *comp. See* **Florida.** Index to laws.

Warneck, Gustav. Outline of a history of Protestant missions. '02(F8) 8°, net, $2. Revell.

Warner, Beverley E. Young man in modern life. '02(Ap19) D. net, 85 c. Dodd.

Warner, C: D. Fashions in literature, and other essays. '02(My10) D. net, $1.20. Dodd.

Warren, H: W. *See* Merrill, S. M.

Warren, S: E: Physical geography; rev. '02 (Jl19) il. f°, bds., $1.25. Butler.

Warvelle, G: W. Essays in legal ethics. '02 (Mr29) D. $2.50. Callaghan.

Warvelle, G: W. Treatise on the Am. law of vendor and purchaser of real property. v. 1, 2. 2d ed. '02(Ja18) O. shp., $12. Callaghan.

WARWICK, *Countess of.*
Palgrave. Mary Rich, Countess of Warwick, 1625-1678. net, $1.50. Dutton.

Warwick lib. of Eng. literature. 12°, $1.50. Scribner.
—Herford, *ed.* Eng. tales in verse.
Washburn, Emory. Treatise on the Am. law of real property. 6th ed.; ed. by J: Wurts. '02(Mr29) 3 v., 8°, shp., net, $18. Little, B. & Co.
Washington, Booker T. Character building. '02(Jl5) D. **$1.50 net. Doubleday, P.
WASHINGTON, G:
Custis. George Washington. $1. Donohue.
Headley. Washington and his generals. $1. Burt.
Locke. Typical American. net, 25 c. Jennings
WASHINGTON.
Brand. Justices' code. $5. Bancroft-W.
WASHINGTON, D. C.
Maynard. Birds of Washington and vicinity. *$1 net. Woodward & L.
Winchester, *ed.* Aroung the throne. sketches of Wash. society . net, $1. Eichelberger.
WATER.
Horrocks. Introd. to bacteriolog. examination of water. net, $3.68. Blakiston.
See also Brooks;—Hydraulic engineering;—Physical geography,—Water-supply.
WATER-CURE.
See Hydrotherapy.
WATER-FOWL.
See Birds.
WATER-POWER.
See Hydraulic engineering.
WATER-SUPPLY.
Folwell. Water-supply engineering. $4. Wiley.
Mason. Water-supply (fr. a sanitary standpoint). red. to $4. Wiley.
See also Hydraulic engineering.
Water-tube boilers. Robertson, L. S. $3. Van Nostrand.
Waterhouse, Percy L. Story of the art of architecture in America. '01· '02(F8) il. S. (Lib. of useful stories.) net, 35 c. Appleton.
WATERLOO.
Siborne. Waterloo campaign, 1815. *$1.50 net. Dutton.
Watkins, Rob. L. Diagnosis by means of the blood. '02(Jl5) il. O. $5. Physicians.
Watkinson, W: L. The blind spot, and other sermons. '02(Je7) 12°, net, $1. Revell.
Watrous, A. E. Young Howson's wife. '02 (Mr29) D. $1.50. Quail & W.
Watrous, G: A. First year English: syntax and composition. '02(Jl12) 12°, 75 c. Sibley & D.
Watson, *Mrs.* Annah R. Passion flowers. '02(Ap12) 24°, $1.60. Whittet.
Watson, *Mrs.* Annah R. A royal lineage: Alfred the Great, 901-1901. '01· '02 (Ap12) 12°, $4.50. Whittet.
Watson, B: F. *See* McDonald, D:
Watson, Forbes. Flowers and gardens. '02 (My3) 12°, $1.50. Lane.
Watson, T: E. Napoleon. '02(Mr15) O. $2.25. Macmillan.
Watson, W: Ode on the day of the coronation of King Edward VII. '02(Je28) bds., net, $1; 250 cop. Jap. vellum, net, $3.50. Lane.
Watson, W: F. Elementary experimental chemistry, inorganic. '01. '02(F1) 12°, net, $1.25. Barnes.
Watt, Fs. Terrors of the law. '02(My24) 8°, net, $1.25. Lane.
WATTEAU, Jean Antoine.
Staley. Watteau, master painter of the "Fêtes galantes." 50 c. Macmillan.
Wau-Bun. *See* Kinzie, *Mrs.* J. A. M.
Waugh, H. E., *comp.* *See* New York. Laws.
Waverley. *See* Scott, *Sir* W.
Way, A. E., *comp.* Reliques of Stratford-on-Avon. '02(Je14) 16°, (Flowers of Parnassus ser., v. 16.) net, 50 c.; leath., net, 75 c. Lane.
Way of escape. Todd, M. G. $1.50. Appleton.
Way of the preacher. Kern, J: A. $1.25. Pub. Ho. M. E. Ch., So.
Way of the West. King, C: 50 c. Rand, McN. & Co.
Wayland, J: W. Paul, the herald of the cross. '01· '02(Ja18) 16°, 40 c. Brethren Pub. Ho.
Ways of the world. Jordan, M. O. $1.50. Neely.
Wead, C: K. Cont. to the history of musical scales. '01· '02(Je14) O .pap., 50 c. Woodward & L.
WEATHER.
Price. Observations and exercises on the weather. 30 c. Am. Bk.
Web of empire. Wallace, *Sir* D. M. net, $6.50. Macmillan.
Webb, Jonathan E. Morphological study of the flower and embryo of spirala. '02(Jl12) 8°, (Cont. from the Hull botanical lib., no. 36.) pap., *25 c. net. Univ. of Chic.
Webb, Sidney *and* Beatrice. Hist. of trade unionism. New ed. '02(Ap19) O. net, $2.60. Longmans.
Webb, Sidney *and* Beatrice. Industrial democracy. New ed. 2 v. in 1. '02(Ap19) O.* net, $4. Longmans.
Webb, T: E. Mystery of William Shakespeare. '02(Je7) O. $4. Longmans.
Webber, Rob. Graduated coll. of problems in electricity; fr. 3d Fr. ed., by E. A. O'Keeffe. '02(Je7) 12°, $3. Spon.
Weber, Alice. Clock on the stairs and other stories. '02(Je28) il. 12°, (St. Nicholas ser.) 75 c. Burt.
Weborg, Johanna. In Viking land. '02(Mr8) 12°, $1.25. J. C. Weborg.
Webster, Dan. Speeches; sel. by B. F. Tefft. '02(My3) 12°, (Home lib.) $1. Burt.
WEBSTER, Dan.
Lewis. Fryeburg Webster centennial. 50 c. A. F. Lewis.
McCall. Daniel Webster. net, 80 c. Houghton, M. & Co.
WEDDINGS.
See Marriage.
Weekly church teaching for the infants. Francis, *Mrs.* C. D. 25 c. E. & J. B. Young.
Wegelin, Oscar. Early American fiction, 1774-1830. '02(My17) 8°, net, $2. O. Wegelin.
Weimer, Alb. B., *rep.* *See* **Pennsylvania.** *Superior ct.* Repts.
Welch, J. H., *and* Taylor, H. E. Destruction of St. Pierre, Martinique. '02(Jl5) D. 50 c. Fenno.
Wells, F: P. Hist. of Newbury, Vt.: with genealog. records. '02(Ap26) il. 8°. $2.25; $3; hf. seal, $3.50; Lib. shp., $4. Caledonian.

Wells, Herb. G: **Anticipations of the reaction of mechanical and scientific progress upon human life and thought.** '02(Mr1) O. net, $1.80. Harper.
Wells, Horace L., *ed.* **Studies from the chemical lab'y of the Sheffield Scientific School.** '01· '02(Mr15) 2 v., 8°, (Yale bicentennial pub.) net, $7.50. Scribner.
WELLS.
See Boring.
Welsh, Lucie D. Colonial days. '02(My3) il. sq. O. 50 c. Educ. Pub.
Welsh rarebit tales. Cummins, H. O. $1.25. Mutual Bk.
Welsh witch. Raine, A. $1; 50 c. Appleton.
Wentworth, G: A. College algebra. Rev. ed. '02(Jl5) D. hf. mor., $1.65. Ginn.
Wentworth, G: A., *and* Hill, G. A. Lab'y exercises in elem. physics. '01· '02(Mr1) 12°, pap., 27 c. Ginn.
Wesselhoeft, E. C. German composition. '02 (Je21) D. (Modern lang. ser.) 45 c. Heath.
West, And. F. Latin grammar. '02(Je7) D. (Twentieth century text-books.) net, 90 c. Appleton.
West, T. D. **Metallurgy of cast iron.** 4th ed. '02(Mr22) il. D. $3. Cleveland Pr.
West, Willis M. Ancient history to the death of Charlemagne. '02(Je28) 12°. (Ser. of school histories.) hf. leath., $1.50. Allyn & B.
West-brook drives. Westbrook, H. P. $1.25. Eckler.
WEST INDIES.
Stokes. Cruising in the West Indies. **$1.25 net. Dodd.
See also Central America.
WEST POINT, N. Y.
Farley. West Point in the early sixties. net, $2. Pafraets
Hancock. Life at West Point. net, $1.40. Putnam.
West Virginia. *Supreme ct. of appeals.* Repts. (Freer.) v. 47. '01· '02(Je7); v. 48 (Mr15); v. 49 (My10) O. shp., ea., $4.50. Charleston Daily Mail; Tribune Co.
WEST VIRGINIA.
Peterkin. Hist. and record of Prot. Episc. ch. in W. Va. $2.50; $10. Tribune Co.
Westbrook, Henrietta P. West-brook drives. '02(F22) il. D. $1.25. Eckler.
WESTBROOK, T:
Trask, *ed.* Letters of Col. Thomas Westbrook and others rel. to Indian affairs in Me., 1722-26. $5. Littlefield.
Westcotes. Ccuch, A. T: Q. $1. Coates.
Westcott, Brooke F. Words of faith and hope. '02(Ap26) 12°, $1.25. Macmillan.
Westermarck, E: History of human marriage. 3d ed. '02(Je28) 8°, net, $4.50. Macmillan.
WESTMINSTER ABBEY.
Hiatt. Westminster Abbey. 60 c. Macmillan.
WESTMINSTER ASSEMBLY.
See Catechisms.
Westminster biographies. T. 75 c. Small.
—Waller *and* Barrow. John Henry Newman.
WESTMINSTER SCHOOL.
Airy. Westminster. $1.50. Macmillan.
Westward ho! *See* Kingsley, C:
Wetzel, Fs. X. The dutiful child; fr. the Germ. 2d ed. '02(Mr8) 16°, 40 c. Herder.
Weyl, Wa. E. **Passenger traffic of railways.** '01. '02(Ja25) O. (Pub. of the Univ. of Pa., ser. in pol. economy and public law, no. 16.) $1.50; pap., $1. [Univ. of Penn.] Ginn.
Wharton, Anne H. Last century maid. '01· '02(F15) il. 12°, $1.25. Lippincott.
Wharton, Edith. Valley of decision. '02 (Mr1) 2 v., D. $2. Scribner.
Wharton, H: R. Minor surgery and bandaging. 5th ed. '02(Je14) il. 12°, net, $3. Lea
What great men have said about great men. Wall, W: net, $2.50. Dutton.
What is it to believe on the Lord Jesus Christ? Vincent, M. R. 5 c. Beam.
What is religion? Tolstoï, *Count* L. N. net, 60 c. Crowell.
What is Shakespeare? Sherman, L. A. net, $1.50; net. $1. Macmillan.
What is worth while ser. D. leatherette. Crowell.
—Hay. William McKinley. net, 28 c.
What the new thought stands for. Patterson, C: B. 10 c. Alliance.
What Thelma found in the attic. Duckwitz, L. C. $1. Alliance.
What think ye of Christ. Eldridge, J. L. $1. Abbey Press.
What's what. Allen, F. S. net, 50 c. Bradley-W.
Wheatley, H: B: How to make an index. '02(Je14) S. (Booklover's lib.) $1.25; hf. mor., $2.50. Armstrong.
Wheaton, Emily. The Russells in Chicago. '02(Je14) il. 16°, (Commonwealth ser.) $1.25. L. C. Page.
Wheeler, Ht. Cub's career. '02(My3) il. D. $1. Abbey Press.
Wheeler, Jeannette. Josephine Grahame. '02 (Mr15) D. $1.50. Abbey Press.
Wheeler, W. H. The sea-coast. '02(Ap19) il. O. $4.50. Longmans.
Wheeler, W: H: *See* Calmerton, G.
Wheeler's elem. speller. '02(Mr22) il. O. 25 c. W: H: Wheeler.
Wheeler's graded readers. il. sq. D. W: H: Wheeler.
—Calmerton *and* Wheeler. First reader. 30 c.
Wheelock, *Mrs.* Irene G. Nestlings of forest and marsh. '02(Ap12) il. D. net, $1.40. McClurg.
WHEELS.
See Gears and gearing.
When bards sing out of tune. Clark, A. 50 c. Abbey Press.
When love is king. Mabry, W. D. $1.50. Fenno.
When old New York was young. Hemstreet, C: net, $1.50. Scribner.
Where the magnolias bloom. Cullens, F: B. 50 c. Abbey Press.
Where, when, and how to catch fish on east coast of Fla. Gregg, W: H. $4. Matthews-N.
Wherry, Abinia. Stories of the Tuscan artists. '02(F15) il. 8°. net, $4. Dutton.
Whispering pine ser. il. 12°, $1.25. Lee & S.
—Kellogg. Stout heart.
WHIST.
Coffin. Gist of whist. 75 c. Brentano's.
Leigh *and* Bergholt. Principles of whist. net, $1.50. Coates.
See also Bridge.

WHISTLER, Ja. McN.
Bowdoin. James McNeill Whistler, the man and his work. net, $1.50. Beam.
Whitaker, Jos. and Sons, *comps.* Whitaker's almanac for 1902. '01· '02(Ja11) 12°, pap., net, 40 c.; *Same*, enl. ed., hf. roan, net, $1. Scribner.
Whitby, Beatrice. Flower and thorn '02 (Mr22) D. $1.50. Dodd.
Whitcomb, Clara E. Little journey to Italy; ed. by M. George. '02(Mr29) il. sq. D. (Plan book, v. 5, no. 5.) pap., 15 c. Flanagan.
Whitcomb, Clara E. Little journey to Scotland. '02(Mr29) il. 12°, (Plan book, v. 5, no. 4.) pap., 15 c. Flanagan.
White, C: J. Elements of theoretical and des. astronomy. 7th ed. rev. '01· '02(F8) il. 12°, $2.50. Wiley.
White, Emerson E. Grammar school algebra. New century ed. '02(Je21) S. 35 c. Am. Bk.
White, Fk. On corporations. 5th ed. '02 (My17) O. shp., $5.50. Baker, V. & Co.
White, Gilbert. Natural hist. and antiquities of Selborne. '01· '02(F15) 2 v., il. 8°, net, $20. Lippincott.
White, J: P., *rep.* *See* Texas. *Ct. of criminal appeals.* Repts.
White, Michael. Lachmi Bai Rani of Jhansi, the Jeanne d'Arc of India. '02(Mr8) il. D. $1.50. J. F. Taylor.
White, Stewart E. Blazed trail. '02(My24) il. D. $1.50. McClure, P.
White, W. H. Book of orchids. '02(Jl19) il. D. (Handbooks of practical gardening, no. 8.) *$1 net. Lane.
White world. Kersting, R., *ed.* *$2 net. Lewis.
Whitehouse, Flo. B. God of things. '02 (My3) il. D. $1.50. Little, B. & Co.
Whither are we drifting? Stechhan, O. $1. Abbey Press.
Whither goest thou? De Costa, B: F. *50 c. net; 25 c. net. Chr. Press.
Whitlock, Brand. The 13th district. '02 (Ap5) D. $1.50. Bowen-M.
Whitman, Alfr. Print-collector's handbook. 2d rev. ed. '02(My24) 8°, net, $5. Macmillan.
Whitney, Caspar, *ed.* *See* Amer. sportsman's lib.
Whittaker, N. T. Christian science, is it safe? '02(Ap5) 12°, pap., 10 c. Earle.
Whittaker's grade A handbook. D. net. Whittaker.
—Scadding. Answers to plain questions for Am. churchmen. 50 c.
Whittelsey, C: B., *comp.* Roosevelt genealogy, 1649-1902. '02(Jl12) 12°. $5. C: B. Whittelsey.
Whittier. C: A. In the Michigan lumber camps. 4th ed. '02(Ap5) S. (Boys' vacation ser., first vacation.) 75 c. Neely.
Whitton, Jos. Wags of the stage. Ed. de luxe. '02(Je7) Q. $2.50. Rigby.
Whitworth, Ernest. Practical cotton calculations. '02(Jl12) 16°, $1. Boardman.
Who's who, 1902. '02(F1) 12°, $1.75. Macmillan.
Why my photographs are bad. Taylor, C: M., *Jr.* net, $1. Jacobs.
Why the legal method of promoting temperance always has done more harm than good Griffin, A. 15 c. A. Griffin.
Whyte, Alex. Newman: an appreciation in two lectures. '02(Mr8) D. net, $1.10. Longmans.
Wicks, —. *See* Texas. 27th legislature.
Wide world (The). '02(Mr22) il. D. (Youth's (Youth's Companion ser., no. 1.) 30 c. Ginn
Widow Wiley, and some other old folk. Sinnett, B. $1.50. Dutton.
Wiechmann, Ferdinand Gerhard. *See* Monroe, F.
Wiener, Alfr. E. Practical calculation of dynamo-electric machines. 2d ed., rev. and enl. '02(Ap5) il. 8°, $3. Elec. World
Wiener, Leo. Anthology of Russian literature from the earliest period to the present time. In 2 pts. pt. 1. '02(Je21) O. net, $3. Putnam.
Wiggin, *Mrs.* Kate D. Diary of a goose girl. '02(My17) il. D. $1. Houghton, M. & Co.
Wight, Emma H. The Berkleys. '02(Mr29) il. S. net, 40 c. Benziger.
Wilberforce, Bertrand A. Devout commentary on the Epistle to the Ephesians; chiefly fr. St. Thomas Aquinas. '02(Je14) 8°. net, $1. Herder.
Wilbur, Earl M. Historical sketch of the Independent Cong. Church, [Unitarian,] Meadville, Pa. 1825-1900. '02(Je28) il. D. $1; pap., 50 c. E. G. Huidekoper.
Wilbur, La Fayette. Early history of Vermont. v. 3. '02(Ap26) 8°, $1.50. L. F. Wilbur.
Wilcox, *Mrs.* Ella W. Sweet danger. New ed. '02(My17) 12°, pap., 50 c. Donohue.
Wilcox, Lucius M. Irrigation farming. Rev. and enl. ed. '02(Je14) D. $2. Judd.
Wild life of orchard and field. Ingersoll, E. net, $1.40. Harper.
Wildenbruch, Ernst A. v. Das edle Blut; ed. by C: A. Eggert. '02(Je14) D. 30 c. Am. Bk.
Wilgus, Horace L. Cases on the general principles of the law of private corporations. In 2 v. v. 1. '02(Mr8); v. 2 (Ap5) O. (complete work,) $9; shp., $10. Bowen-M.
Wilhelm Meister's apprenticeship and travels. *See* Goethe, J. W. v.
Wilhelm Tell. *See* Schiller, J. C. F. v.
WILKIE, *Sir* David.
Gower. Sir David Wilkie. $1.75. Macmillan.
Wilkins, Ja. H. Glimpse of old Mexico. '02 (Ap5) il. 16°. bds., 75 c. Whitaker & R.
Wilkinson, A. E., *rep.* *See* Texas. *Sup. ct.* Repts.
Wilkins, W: H: Caroline the illustrious Queen-Consort of George II. '01. '02(Ja4) 2 v., il. O. $12. Longmans.
Will to be well. Patterson, C: B. $1. Alliance.
Willard, C: D. *Herald's* history of Los Angeles City. '02(Ap5) il. D. $1.50. Kingsley.
Willard, Josiah F., ["Josiah Flynt."] The little brother: story of tramp life. '02 (Mr29) D. $1.50. Century Co.
WILLIAM I. *of Germany.*
Zastrow. Wilhelm der Siegreiche. net. 50 c. Macmillan.
Williams, *Mrs.* Leslie. A garden in the suburbs. '02(F15) 12°, net, $1.50. Lane
Williams, Louise H. *See* Richards, E. H.
Williams, M. B. Sex problems. '02(Ap19) 12°, net. $1. Revell.

Williams, Margery. The late returning. '02 (Je7) 12°, $1.25. Macmillan.
Williams, Martha McC. Next to the ground. '02(My24) D. net, $1.20. McClure, P.
Williams, T. R. Shall we understand the Bible? Rev., enl. ed. '02(Ap26) 12°, pap., net. 50 c. Macmillan.
Williamson, *Mrs.* Corolin C. Mary Starkweather. '02(F22) D. $1.50. Abbey Press.
Williamson, G: C. Holman Hunt. '02(Mr8) il. 16°, (Miniature ser. of painters.) 50 c. Macmillan
Willoughby, E: F. Hygiene for students. '01. '02(Ja4) 12°, $1.25. Macmillan.
WILLS.
Clement. Probate repts., annot. v. 6. $5.50. Baker, V. & Co.
Hoyt. Practice in probate cts. of New Hampshire. $2.50. Rumford Press.
Tucker. Preparation of wills. $3.50. G: B. Reed.
Wilson, Calvin D. Divine religion of humanity. '02(Je21) S. pap., net, 20 c. Presb. Bd.
Wilson, Edn. B. *See* Gibbs, J. W.
Wilson, Eug. B. Cyanide processes. 3d ed. rewritten. '02(Je21) 12°, $1.50. Wiley.
Wilson, Floyd B. Paths to power. '01. '02 (Ja4) D. $1. Fenno.
Wilson, Harry L. The spenders. '02(Je14) il. D. $1.50. Lothrop.
Wilson, Ja. G., *ed.* Presidents of the United States. New rev. ed., with life of W: McKinley and sketch of T. Roosevelt. '02 (Mr29) il. 8°, $3.50; hf. mor. or hf. cf., $6. Appleton.
Wilson, L: A. A great cloud of witnesses. '01. '02(Ap26) D. 50 c. Standard Pub.
Wilson, L: N. Bibliography of child study. '02(Mr8) O. pap., net, 25 c. Stechert.
Wilson, Stella S. Ohio. '02(Je7) il. 12°, (Tarr and McMurry's geographies, supp. v.) net, 30 c. Macmillan.
Wilson, Theodora W. T'bacca queen. '02 (My10) D. (Town and country lib., no. 311.) $1; pap., 50 c. Appleton.
Winans, G: M. Kansas. '02(Jl12) il. 12°, (Tarr and McMurry's geographies, supp. v.) *30 c. net. Macmillan.
Winchester, Paul, *ed.* Around the throne: sketches of Washington society. '02(Je14) 12°, net, $1. Eichelberger.
Winding road. Godfrey, E. $1.50. Holt.
Windle, Bertram C. A. The Malvern country. '01. '02(Ap12) il. S. (Little guides ser.) net, 75 c. Dodd.
WINDOW-GARDENING.
Allen, P. *and* G. Miniature and window gardening. net, 50 c. Pott.
Windows for sermons. Banks, L: A. net, $1.20. Funk.
Windsor, W: Phrenology. '02(My17) 12°, pap., 25 c. Donohue.
Windstorm and tornado insurance. Hoffman, F: L. 25 c. Spectator.
WINE.
Emerson. Story of the vine. net, $1.25. Putnam.
WINSLOW, J: A.
Ellicott. Life of John Ancrum Winslow, Rear Admiral U. S. N. $2.50. Putnam.
Winston, N. B. Grace of orders: [novel.] '02(F22) D. $1. Abbey Press.
Winter, John Strange, *pseud.* *See* Stannard, *Mrs.* H. E. V.
Wisconsin. List of books for township libraries. '02(My24) il. O. pap., 25 c. Wisconsin.
WISCONSIN.
Arbor and bird day annual for Wis. schools. gratis. Democrat Pr. Co.
Harvey. Aids for observance of Memorial day by schools of Wis. gratis. Democrat Pr. Co.
Wisner, Arth., ["A. Gallus."] Emma Calvé. '02(Je28) il. 4°, $1.50. Russell.
Wister, Owen. The Virginian. '02(Je21) il. D. $1.50. Macmillan.
Wistons. Amber, M. $1.50. Scribner.
WIT AND HUMOR.
Bangs. Olympian nights. $1.25. Harper.
Brenton. Unce Jed's country letters. 30 c. Dickerman.
Bridgman. Gulliver's bird book. $1.50. L. C. Page.
Corrothers. Black cat club. net, $1. Funk.
Daskam, *comp.* Best nonsense verses. 50 c. W: S. Lord.
De Leon. Inauguration of President Watterson. 25 c. Am. Writers.
Field. Nonsense for old and young. 50 c. Dickerman.
Fleming. Around the Pan with Uncle Hank. $2. Nutshell.
Gilmer. Fables of the elite. $1. Fenno.
Goodwin. "Sinker" stories of wit and humor. $1. Ogilvie.
Irish wit and humor. 25 c. Drake.
Irwin. Rubâiyat of Omar Khayyâm, jr. net, 50 c. Elder.
Kendall. Good gravy. 25 c. Helman-T.
Prune. College chaps. 75 c. Mutual Bk.
Sharp. Stolen correspondence from dead letter office. 50 c. Gervais.
Shaw. Josh Billings' old farmer's allminax. $1.50. G: W. Dillingham.
See also **Epigrams;—Parody.**
Witch Winnie ser. Champney, *Mrs.* E. W. 9 v. $11.25. Dodd.
With Napoleon at St. Helena. Fremeaux, P. net, $1.50. Lane.
With redskins on the warpath. Walkey, S. $1.25. Cassell.
With Rimington. Phillipps, L. M. $2.50. Longmans.
With the royal tour. Knight, E: F: $2. Longmans.
Witmer, L. Analytical psychology. '02 (Ap5) O. $1.60. Ginn.
WITNESSES.
See **Evidence.**
Wodell, F: W: Choir and chorus conducting. '01. '02(F8) il. 12°. $1.50. Presser.
Woelfkin, Cornelius. Chambers of the soul. '02(Mr29) S. 35 c. Un. Soc. C. E.
Wolcott, Edson R. On the sensitiveness of the coherer. '02(My17) O. (Bull. of the Univ. of Wis., no. 51, science ser., v. 3. no. 1.) pap., 20 c. Univ. of Wis.
Wolfville days. Lewis, A. H: $1.50. Stokes.
Wollpert, F: A man amongst men. '02 (Ap5) sq. D. pap., 15 c. Eckler.
WOMAN.
Blouët. 'Tween you an' I. pt. 2, Concerning women. $1.20. Lothrop.
Dressler. Feminology. $3. Dressler.

WOMAN.—*Continued.*
Macfadden. Power and beauty of superb womanhood. $1. Physical Culture.
Maulde la Clavière. Art of life. net, $1.75. Putnam.
Sainte-Foi. The perfect woman. net, $1. Marlier.
Stone. Women designers of book-plates. net, $1; net, $2. Beam.
Women in the business world. $1.50; 50 c. Alliance.
See also Children;—Domestic economy;—Gynecology;—Home;—Nurses and nursing;—Sex;—Young women.
Woman who dared. Van Deventer, E. M. 25 c. Laird.
Woman's exchange cook book. Palmer, *Mrs.* M. 70 c. Conkey.
Women in the business world. [New issue.] '02(Mr22) D. $1.50; pap., 50 c. Alliance.
Women of the Reformed church. Good, J. I. $1. Heidelberg.
Wonders of Mouseland. Childs, E: E. $1.25. Abbey Press.
Wonders of the Revelation of Jesus Christ. Ruble, W: $1. Standard Pub.
Wood, Casey A., Andrews, Alb. H., *and* Hardie, T. M., *eds.* Eye, ear, nose and throat. '02(Mr8) il. D. (Practical medicine ser. of year-books, v. 3.) $1.50. Year Bk.
Wood, *Mrs.* Ma. A. Marriage: its duties and privileges. '02(F8) 12°, net, $1.25. Revell
WOOD-CARVING.
See Sloyd.
Woodland orchids. Boyle, F: net, $7. Macmillan.
Woods, C: Coke. *See* Nicholson, T:
WOODS.
See Forests and forestry.
Woodworth, Elijah B. Descendants of Walter Woodworth of Scituate, Mass.; Sketch of Samuel Woodworth and his descendants. '02(F22) 8°. $3. G: W. Humphrey.
Woolsey, Sa. C., ["Susan Coolidge."] Uncle and aunt. New ed '01. '02(F15) 16°, (Children's friend ser.) bds., 50 c. Little, B. & Co.
Worcester, J: Works of charity. '01. '02 (F1) sq. S. pap., 25 c. New-Ch. Un.
WORCESTER, Mass.
Roe. Worcester Young Men's Christian Assoc. $1. A. S. Roe.
Word signs made easy. Hardcastle, *Mrs.* M. A. $1. M. A. Hardcastle.
Wordingham, C: H. Central electrical stations. '01. '02(F15) il. 8°, $7.50. Lippincott.
Words of faith and hope. Westcott, B. F. $1.25. Macmillan.
Wordsworth, W: Selected poems; ed. by J. B. Seabury. '02(Ap26) 12°, (Ser. of classics.) 30 c. Silver.
Workingman's opportunity. Rowell, J. H. 5 c. Free Socialist.
Works, J: D. Practice pleading and forms adapt. to new rev. code of Indiana. 3d ed., rev. and enl. v. 1, 2, 3. '02(Je14) O. shp., $18. Clarke.
Works and days. Mabie, H. W. net, $1. Dodd.
Workshop wrinkles. Brown, W: N. net, $1. Van Nostrand.
World almanac and encyclopedia, 1902. '02 (Ja11) il. D. pap., 25 c. Press Pub.
World on fire. Halstead, M. $1.50; $2.25; $3. Dominion.
World ser. See Appleton's.
World's epoch makers; ed. by O. Smeaton. D. $1.25. Scribner.
—Ritchie. Plato.
—Smeaton. The Medici and the Italian Renaissance.
World's people. Cruger, *Mrs.* J. S. †$1.50. J. F. Taylor.
World's shrine. Johnson, V. W. **$1.20 net. Barnes.
Worlledge, Arth. J: Prayer. '02(Mr22) D. (Oxford lib. of practical theology.) $1.50. Longmans.
Wormell, R: *See* Hobbs, W. R. P.
WORSHIP.
Dobbins. Story of the world's worship. $2.25; $3.25. Dominion.
See also Church music;—Devotional exercises and meditations;—Prayer.
Worthington, Eliz. S. The tocsin—our children in peril. '01. '02(Mr22) 12°, pap., 25 c. Cubery
Wounded beast. Jellison, E. A: 25 c. E. A: Jellison.
Wray, Angelina W. Jean Mitchell's school. '02(F15) il. D. $1.25. Public Sch. Pub.
Wretched Flea. Muller, M. 35 c. Flanagan.
Wright, D: H: Under the red cross: [poems.] '01. '02(F15) 12°, pap., 35 c. Biddle.
Wright, G: F: Asiatic Russia. '02(Jl5) 2 v., il. 8°, leath., **$7.50 net. McClure, P.
Wright, H: W., *comp.* Genealogy of the Wright family from 1639 to 1901. '01. '02 (Mr8) 8°, pap., 25 c. Pelham.
Wright, J. C. Body and soul: lectures del. in trance state. '02(My17) D. $1. J. C. Wright.
Wright, Ma. T. Aliens. '02(Mr22) D. net, $1.50. Scribner.
Wright, W. J. P. Dante and the Divine comedy. '02(My10) 8°, net, $1. Lane.
WRITING.
See Inscriptions;—Letter-writing;—Penmanship;—Typewriting.
Wurtzburg, Caro. A. *See* Ruskin, J:
Wyatt, Lucy M. L. Constance Hamilton. '02(Ap26) D. 50 c. Abbey Press
Wyckoff, C: T. Feudal relations between the kings of Eng. and Scotland under the early Plantagenets. '02(Mr22) 8°, pap., net, $1. Univ. of Chic.
Wyllarde, Dolf. Story of Eden. '01. '02 (Mr1) 12°, $1.50. Lane.
Wyman, W. E. A. Tibio; peroneal neurectomy for the relief of spavin lameness. '02 (Jl12) 8°, pap., 50 c. W: R. Jenkins
Wynkoop, R: Schuremans, of New Jersey. 2d ed. '02(Jl19) 8°, $3. R: Wynkoop.
Wynne, Jos. F. A blighted rose. '02(My24) D. $1.50. Angelus.
Wyoming. *Supreme ct.* Repts. (Potter.) v. 9. '02(Jl12) O. shp., $5. Callaghan.
Wythes, G: Book of vegetables. '02(Je7) il. D. (Handbooks of practical gardening, v. 7.) $1. Lane.
X-RAYS.
See Roentgen rays.
XENOPHON.
See Attic prose.
YACHTS AND YACHTING.
Ames. Etiquette of yacht colors. 25 c. Annin.

YACHTS AND YACHTING.—*Continued.*
Fisher. How to build a model yacht. $1. Rudder.
Mower. How to build a racing sloop. $1. Rudder.
Yacht club ser. 12°, $1.25 Lee & S.
—Adams. Money-maker. (3.)
Yale bicentennial pubs. 8°, net. Scribner.
—Beecher. Studies in evolution. $5.
—Bourne. Essays in hist. criticism. $2.
—Chittenden, *ed.* Studies in physiolog. chemistry. $4.
—Gibbs. Elem. principles in statistical mechanics.—Victor analysis. ea., $4.
—Goodell. Chapters on Greek metric. $2.
—Hopkins. India, old and new. $2.50.
—Morris. On principles and methods in Latin syntax. $2.
—Oertel. Study of language. $3.
—Two centuries' growth of Am. law. $4.
—Wells, *ed.* Studies from chemical lab'y of Sheffield Scientific School. 2 v. $7.50.
Yale lectures. *See* Brewer, D. J.
Yale studies in Eng.; ed. by A. S. Cook. O. pap. Holt.
—Boccaccio *and* Aretino. Earliest lives of Dante. 75 c. (10.)
YEAR BOOKS.
See Almanacs and annuals.
Year with the Mother-play. Proudfoot, A. H $1. Flanagan.
Yeats, W: B., *comp. and ed.* Irish fairy and folk tales. '02(My10) il. 12°, (Fairy lib.) $1. Burt.
Yellow fiend. Hector, *Mrs.* A. F. $1.50. Dodd.
YELLOWSTONE PARK.
Hatfield. Geyserland and wonderland. 24 c. Hicks-J.
Yelsew, Jean, *pseud.* *See* Smith, J: W.
Yerkes observatory bulletin. *See* Univ. of Chicago.
Yonge, Ctte. M., *comp.* Book of golden deeds of all times and all lands. '02(Ap12) 12°. (Home lib.) $1. Burt.
Young, Abram V. E. Elem. principles of chemistry. '01· '02(F22) 12°, net, 95 c. Appleton.
Young, C: A: Manual of astronomy. '02 (Jl5) il. O. hf. leath., $2.45. Ginn.
Young, Ella F. Ethics in the school. '02 (F22) D. (Cont. to educ., no. 4.) pap., net, 25 c. Univ. of Chic.
Young, Ella F. Isolation in the school. '01· '02(Ja11) S. (Univ. of Chic. cont. to education, no. 1.) pap., net, 50 c. Univ. of Chic.
Young, Ella F. Some types of modern educ. theory. '02(My24) D. (Univ. of Chic. cont. to education, no. 6.) pap., net, 25 c. Univ. of Chic.
Young, Filson. Mastersingers; with essay on Hector Berlioz. '02(Ap12) 12°, net, $1.50. Scribner.
Young, Hudson. Father Manners. '02(F22) D. $1. Abbey Press.
Young, J: R. Men and memories. Ed. de luxe. '02(Mr29) 2 v., subs., $5; in 1 v., 12°, subs., $3. Neely.
Young, Julia D. Black Evan. '02(Ap26) 12°, $1. Neely.
Young, Owen D., *and* Keen, Ja. T. Problems in practice and pleading at the common law. '02(Ap12) O. pap., 50 c. Mudge.
Young Howson's wife. Watrous, A. E. $1.50. Quail & W.
YOUNG MEN.
McLeod. Young man's problems. 50 c. Flanagan.
Warner. Young man in modern life. net, 85 c. Dodd.
See also Conduct of life;—Culture.
YOUNG PEOPLE.
Jordans. Danger of youth and a tried antidote. 15 c. Herder.
See also Children;—Girls;—Young men;—Young women.
Young People's Alliance ser. S. pap. Mattill & L.
—Staebler. Manual on the Book of books. 20 c.
Young people's Bible stories. '02(F1) 4 v., il. 4°, ea., $1.25. Saalfield.
YOUNG PEOPLE'S SOC. OF CHR. ENDEAVOR.
Clark. Training the church of the future; lectures, with special ref. to the Young People's Soc. of C. E. net, 75 c. Funk.
YOUNG WOMEN.
Sinclair. Unto you, young women. net, $1. Lippincott.
See also Conduct of life;—Culture;—Girls;—Young people;—Woman.
Youth's companion ser. il. D. 30 c. Ginn.
—Northern Europe. (2.)
—Under sunny skies. (3.)
—Wide world. (1.)
Zaïre and Epîtres. Voltaire, F. M. A. de. 50 c. Scott, F. & Co.
Zancig, *Mme.* —. How to tell fortunes by cards. '02(Mr15) S. pap., 25 c. Drake.
Zastrow, Karl. Wilhelm der Siegreiche; ed. by E. P. Ash. Authorized ed. '02(My24) 12°. (Siepmann's elem. Germ. ser.) net, 50 c. Macmillan.
Zayas Enríquez, R. de. El teniente de los gavilanes. '02(Jl5) 12°, pap., †50 c. Appleton.
Zdziarski, A. F., *ed.* *See* Dmitriev-Mámonóv, A. I., *ed.*
Zelma, the mystic. Thurber, A. M. $1.25. Alliance.
ZINCALI.
Borrow. The Zincali. $2. Putnam.
Zitkala-sa. Old Indian legends. '01· '02 (Mr8) il. D. 50 c. Ginn.
Zittel, Karl A. v. Hist. of geology and palæontology to the end of the nineteenth century; tr. by M. M. Ogilvie-Gordon. '01· '02(Ap12) D. (Contemporary science ser.) $1.50. Scribner.
Zobo patriotic drill. Hatch, A. W. 15 c. Hints.
ZOOLOGY.
French. Animal activities. $1.20. Longmans.
Jordan *and* Heath. Animal forms. net, $1.10. Appleton.
Lindsay. Story of animal life. net, 35 c. Appleton.
Mudge. Text book of zoology. $2.50. Longmans.
See also Amphibia;—Animals;—Evolution;—Invertebrates;—Protozoa.
ZOOTOMY.
See Dissection.
Zuckerhandl, Otto. Atlas and epitome of operative surgery: fr. 2d rev., enl. Germ. ed.; ed. by J. C. Da Costa. '02(Ap26) il. 12°, net, $3.50. Saunders.
ZUNI INDIANS.
Cushing. Zuñi folk tales. net, $3.50. Putnam.

RECORD OF SERIES.

STREET & SMITH, 238 William St., New York.

Arrow Library, 12°, 10 c.

No.
254. The way of the world. Murray, D. C.
255. Pure gold. Cameron, H. L.
256. Annan Water. Buchanan, R.
257. What's bred in the bone. Allen, G.
258. Dolores. Forrester, Mrs.
259. Doctor Cupid. Broughton, R.
260. I say no. Collins, W.
261. The canon's ward. Payn, J.
262. The wooing o't. Alexander, M.
263. Roy and Viola. Forrester, Mrs.
264. Borderland. Fothergill, J.
265. Love's harvest. Farjeon, B. L.
266. Robin. Parr, L.
267. Monte Cristo and wife. Dumas, A.

Bertha Clay Library, 12°, 10 c.

138. The price of a bride. Clay, B. M.
139. Love in a mask. Clay, B. M.
140. A woman's witchery. Clay, B. M.
141. The burden of a secret. Clay, B. M.
142. One woman's sin. Clay, B. M.
143. How will it end? Clay, B. M.
144. The hand without a wedding ring. Clay, B. M.
145. A sinful secret. Clay, B. M.
146. Lady Marchmont's widowhood. Clay, B. M.
147. The broken trust. Clay, B. M.
148. Lady Ethel's whim. Clay, B. M.
149. A wife's peril. Clay, B. M.
150. Tragedy of Lime Hall. Clay, B. M.
151. Lady Ona's sin. Clay, B. M.

Diamond Hand-Book Series, 12°, 10 c.

10. Key to hypnotism. Ellsworth, R. G., M.D.

Eagle Library, 12°, 10 c.

261. A siren's heart. Rowlands, E. A.
262. A woman's faith. Wallace, H.
263. An American nabob. Rathborne, S. G.
264. For gold or soul. Sheldon, L. W.
265. First love is best. Hocking, S. K.
266. The Welfleet mystery. Sheldon, G.
267. Jeanne. Garvice, C.
268. Olivia. Garvice, C.
269. Brunette and blonde. Miller, A. McV.
270. Had she foreseen. Delmar, D.
271. With love's laurel crowned. Stiles, W. C.
272. So fair, so false. Garvice, C.
273. At sword's points. Rathborne, S. G.

STREET & SMITH.—*Continued.*

Eden Series, 12°, 10 c.

69. The dove in the eagle's nest. Yonge, C.
70. Hostages of fortune. Braddon, M. E.
71. Girls of Feversham. Marryat, F.
72. The Arundel motto. Hay, M. C.
73. Wooed and married. Carey, R. N.
74. Chantry House. Yonge, C. M.
75. Written in fire. Marryat, M.
76. Strangers and pilgrims. Braddon, M. E.
77. Old Myddleton's money. Hay, M. C.
78. Under the lilies and roses. Marryat, F.
79. Portia. "The Duchess."
80. My young Alcides. Yonge, C. M.
81. The artist's love. Southworth, E. D. E.
82. Dorothy's venture. Hay, M. C.

Magnet Library, 12°, 10 c.

233. The secret of the missing checks. Rock H.
234. The tell-tale photograph. Carter, N.
235. True detective tales. Moser, M.
236. A move in the dark. Carter, N.
237. A kidnapped millionaire. Wainwright, R.
238. The claws of the tiger. Carter, N.
239. The man from the south. Taylor, J. R.
240. Weaving the web. Carter, N.
241. From thief to detective. Hume, F.
242. Run to earth. Carter, N.
243. The man and the crime. Rockwood, H.
244. A trusted rogue. Carter, N.
245. A victim of villainy. Broughton, F. L.
246. Nick Carter's death warrant. Carter, N.

Medal Library, 12°, 10 c.

150. Frank Merriwell's school days. Standish, B. L.
151. The flag of distress. Reid, M.
152. The last of the Mohicans. Cooper, J. F.
153. Bonnie Prince Charlie. Henty, G. A.
154. Paul the peddler. Alger, H., jr.
155. The young voyagers. Reid, M.
156. The pathfinder. Cooper, J. F.
157. Randy the pilot. Lounsberry, L.
158. With Lee in Virginia. Henty, G. A.
159. Phil the fiddler. Alger, H., jr.
160. Little by little. Optic, Oliver.
161. Reuben Green's adventures at Yale. Otis, J.
162. The pioneers. Cooper, J. F.
163. Slow and sure. Alger, H., jr.
164. The coronet of horse. Henty, G. A.

D 13.1

WITH WHICH IS INCORPORATED

The American Literary Gazette and Publishers' Circular.

[ESTABLISHED 1852.]

PUBLICATION OFFICE, 298 BROADWAY, NEW YORK.

Entered at the Post-Office at New York, N. Y., as second-class matter.

VOL. LXII., No. 7. NEW YORK, August 16, 1902. WHOLE No. 1594

WOMAN.—*Continued.*
Macfadden. Power and beauty of superb womanhood. $1. Physical Culture.
Maulde la Clavière. Art of life. net, $1.75. Putnam.
Sainte-Foi. The perfect woman. net, $1. Marlier.
Stone. Women designers of book-plates. net, $1; net, $2. Beam.
Women in the business world. $1.50; 50 c. Alliance.
See also Children; — Domestic economy; — Gynecology;—Home;—Nurses and nursing;—Sex;—Young women.
Woman who dared. Van Deventer, E. M. 25 c. Laird.
Woman's exchange cook book. Palmer, *Mrs.* M. 70 c. Conkey.
Women in the business world. [New issue.] '02(Mr22) D. $1.50; pap., 50 c. Alliance.
Women of the Reformed church. Good, J. I. $1. Heidelberg.
Wonders of Mouseland. Childs, E: E. $1.25. Abbey Press.
Wonders of the Revelation of Jesus Christ. Ruble, W: $1. Standard Pub.
Wood, Casey A., **Andrews**, Alb. H., *and* Hardie, T. M., *eds.* Eye, ear, nose and throat. '02(Mr8) il. D. (Practical medicine ser. of year-books, v. 3.) $1.50. Year Bk.
Wood, *Mrs.* **Ma.** A. Marriage: its duties and privileges. '02(F8) 12°, net, $1.25. Revell
WOOD-CARVING.
See Sloyd.
Woodland orchids. Boyle, F: net, $7. Macmillan.
Woods, C: Coke. *See* Nicholson, T:
WOODS.
See Forests and forestry.
Woodworth, Elijah B. Descendants of Walter Woodworth of Scituate, Mass.; Sketch of Samuel Woodworth and his descendants. '02(F22) 8°, $3. G: W. Humphrey.
Woolsey, Sa. C., ["Susan Coolidge."] Uncle and aunt. New ed '01· '02(F15) 16°, (Children's friend ser.) bds., 50 c. Little, B. & Co.
Worcester, J: Works of charity. '01· '02 (F1) sq. S. pap., 25 c. New-Ch. Un.
WORCESTER, Mass.
Roe. Worcester Young Men's Christian Assoc. $1. A. S. Roe.
Word signs made easy. Hardcastle, *Mrs.* M. A. $1. M. A. Hardcastle.
Wordingham, C: H. Central electrical stations. '01· '02(F15) il. 8°, $7.50. Lippincott.
Words of faith and hope. Westcott, B. F. $1.25. Macmillan.
Wordsworth, W: Selected poems; ed. by J. B. Seabury. '02(Ap26) 12°, (Ser. of classics.) 30 c. Silver.
Workingman's opportunity. Rowell, J. H. 5 c. Free Socialist.
Works, J: D. Practice pleading and forms adapt. to new rev. code of Indiana. 3d ed., rev. and enl. v. 1, 2, 3. '02(Je14) O. shp., $18. Clarke.
Works and days. Mabie, H. W. net, $1. Dodd.
Workshop wrinkles. Brown, W: N. net, $1. Van Nostrand.
World almanac and encyclopedia, 1902. '02 (Ja11) il. D. pap., 25 c. Press Pub.
World on fire. Halstead, M. $1.50; $2.25; $3. Dominion.
World ser. See Appleton's.
World's epoch makers; ed. by O. Smeaton. D. $1.25. Scribner.
—Ritchie. Plato.
—Smeaton. The Medici and the Italian Renaissance.
World's people. Cruger, *Mrs.* J. S. †$1.50. J. F. Taylor.
World's shrine. Johnson, V. W. **$1.20 net. Barnes.
Worlledge, Arth. J: Prayer. '02(Mr22) D. (Oxford lib. of practical theology.) $1.50. Longmans.
Wormell, R: *See* Hobbs, W. R. P.
WORSHIP.
Dobbins. Story of the world's worship. $2.25; $3.25. Dominion.
See also Church music;—Devotional exercises and meditations;—Prayer.
Worthington, Eliz. S. The tocsin—our children in peril. '01· '02(Mr22) 12°, pap., 25 c. Cubery.
Wounded beast. Jellison, E. A: 25 c. E. A: Jellison.
Wray, Angelina W. Jean Mitchell's school. '02(F15) il. D. $1.25. Public Sch. Pub.
Wretched Flea. Muller, M. 35 c. Flanagan.
Wright, D: H: Under the red cross: [poems.] '01· '02(F15) 12°, pap., 35 c. Biddle.
Wright, G: F: Asiatic Russia. '02(Jl5) 2 v., il. 8°, leath., **$7.50 net. McClure, P.
Wright, H: W., *comp.* Genealogy of the Wright family from 1639 to 1901. '01· '02 (Mr8) 8°, pap., 25 c. Pelham.
Wright, J. C. Body and soul: lectures del. in trance state. '02(My17) D. $1. J. C. Wright.
Wright, Ma. T. Aliens. '02(Mr22) D. net. $1.50. Scribner.
Wright, W. J. P. Dante and the Divine comedy. '02(My10) 8°, net, $1. Lane.
WRITING.
See Inscriptions;—Letter-writing;—Penmanship;—Typewriting.
Wurtzburg, Caro. A. *See* Ruskin, J:
Wyatt, Lucy M. L. Constance Hamilton. '02(Ap26) D. 50 c. Abbey Press.
Wyckoff, C: T. Feudal relations between the kings of Eng. and Scotland under the early Plantagenets. '02(Mr22) 8°, pap., net, $1. Univ. of Chic.
Wyllarde, Dolf. Story of Eden. '01· '02 (Mr1) 12°, $1.50. Lane.
Wyman, W. E. A. Tibio; peroneal neurectomy for the relief of spavin lameness. '02 (Jl12) 8°, pap., 50 c. W: R. Jenkins.
Wynkoop, R: Schuremans, of New Jersey. 2d ed. '02(Jl19) 8°, $3. R: Wynkoop.
Wynne, Jos. F. A blighted rose. '02(My24) D. $1.50. Angelus.
Wyoming. *Supreme ct.* Repts. (Potter.) v. 9. '02(Jl12) O. shp., $5. Callaghan.
Wythes, G: Book of vegetables. '02(Je7) il. D. (Handbooks of practical gardening, v. 7.) $1. Lane.
X-RAYS.
See Roentgen rays.
XENOPHON.
See Attic prose.
YACHTS AND YACHTING.
Ames. Etiquette of yacht colors. 25 c. Annin.

YACHTS AND YACHTING.—*Continued.*
Fisher. How to build a model yacht. $1. Rudder.
Mower. How to build a racing sloop. $1. Rudder.
Yacht club ser. 12°, $1.25 Lee & S.
—Adams. Money-maker. (3.)
Yale bicentennial pubs. 8°, net. Scribner.
—Beecher. Studies in evolution. $5.
—Bourne. Essays in hist. criticism. $2.
—Chittenden, *ed.* Studies in physiolog. chemistry. $4.
—Gibbs. Elem. principles in statistical mechanics.—Victor analysis. ea., $4.
—Goodell. Chapters on Greek metric. $2.
—Hopkins. India, old and new. $2.50.
—Morris. On principles and methods in Latin syntax. $2.
—Oertel. Study of language. $3.
—Two centuries' growth of Am. law. $4.
—Wells, *ed.* Studies from chemical lab'y of Sheffield Scientific School. 2 v. $7.50.
Yale lectures. *See* Brewer, D. J.
Yale studies in Eng.; ed. by A. S. Cook. O. pap. Holt.
—Boccaccio *and* Aretino. Earliest lives of Dante. 75 c. (10.)
YEAR BOOKS.
See Almanacs and annuals.
Year with the Mother-play. Proudfoot, A. H $1. Flanagan.
Yeats, W: B., *comp. and ed.* Irish fairy and folk tales. '02(My10) il. 12°, (Fairy lib.) $1. Burt.
Yellow fiend. Hector, *Mrs.* A. F. $1.50. Dodd.
YELLOWSTONE PARK.
Hatfield. Geyserland and wonderland. 24 c. Hicks-J.
Yelsew, Jean, *pseud.* *See* Smith, J: W.
Yerkes observatory bulletin. *See* Univ. of Chicago.
Yonge, Ctte. M., *comp.* Book of golden deeds of all times and all lands. '02(Ap12) 12°. (Home lib.) $1. Burt.
Young, Abram V. E. Elem. principles of chemistry. '01. '02(F22) 12°, net, 95 c. Appleton.
Young, C: A: Manual of astronomy. '02 (Jl5) il. O. hf. leath., $2.45. Ginn.
Young, Ella F. Ethics in the school. '02 (F22) D. (Cont. to educ., no. 4.) pap., net, 25 c. Univ. of Chic.
Young, Ella F. Isolation in the school. '01. '02(Ja11) S. (Univ. of Chic. cont. to education, no. 1.) pap., net, 50 c. Univ. of Chic.
Young, Ella F. Some types of modern educ. theory. '02(My24) D. (Univ. of Chic. cont. to education, no. 6.) pap., net, 25 c. Univ. of Chic.
Young, Filson. Mastersingers; with essay on Hector Berlioz. '02(Ap12) 12°, net, $1.50. Scribner.
Young, Hudson. Father Manners. '02(F22) D. $1. Abbey Press.
Young, J: R. Men and memories. Ed. de luxe. '02(Mr29) 2 v., subs., $5; in 1 v., 12°, subs., $3. Neely.
Young, Julia D. Black Evan. '02(Ap26) 12°, $1. Neely.
Young, Owen D., *and* Keen, Ja. T. Problems in practice and pleading at the common law. '02(Ap12) O. pap., 50 c. Mudge.
Young Howson's wife. Watrous, A. E. $1.50. Quail & W.

YOUNG MEN.
McLeod. Young man's problems. 50 c. Flanagan.
Warner. Young man in modern life. net, 85 c. Dodd.
See also Conduct of life;—Culture.
YOUNG PEOPLE.
Jordans. Danger of youth and a tried antidote. 15 c. Herder.
See also Children;—Girls;—Young men;—Young women.
Young People's Alliance ser. S. pap. Mattill & L.
—Staebler. Manual on the Book of books. 20 c.
Young people's Bible stories. '02(F1) 4 v., il. 4°, ea., $1.25. Saalfield.
YOUNG PEOPLE'S SOC. OF CHR. ENDEAVOR.
Clark. Training the church of the future; lectures, with special ref. to the Young People's Soc. of C. E. net, 75 c. Funk.
YOUNG WOMEN.
Sinclair. Unto you, young women. net, $1. Lippincott.
See also Conduct of life;—Culture;—Girls;—Young people;—Woman.
Youth's companion ser. il. D. 30 c. Ginn.
—Northern Europe. (2.)
—Under sunny skies. (3.)
—Wide world. (1.)
Zaïre and Epitres. Voltaire, F. M. A. de. 50 c. Scott, F. & Co.
Zancig, *Mme.* —. How to tell fortunes by cards. '02(Mr15) S. pap., 25 c. Drake.
Zastrow, Karl. Wilhelm der Siegreiche; ed. by E. P. Ash. Authorized ed. '02(My24) 12°. (Siepmann's elem. Germ. ser.) net, 50 c. Macmillan.
Zayas Enriquez, R. de. El teniente de los gavilanes. '02(Jl5) 12°, pap., †50 c. Appleton.
Zdziarski, A. F., *ed.* *See* Dmitriev-Mámonóv, A. I., *ed.*
Zelma, the mystic. Thurber, A. M. $1.25. Alliance.
ZINCALI.
Borrow. The Zincali. $2. Putnam.
Zitkala-sa. Old Indian legends. '01. '02 (Mr8) il. D. 50 c. Ginn.
Zittel, Karl A. v. Hist. of geology and palæontology to the end of the nineteenth century; tr. by M. M. Ogilvie-Gordon. '01. '02(Ap12) D. (Contemporary science ser.) $1.50. Scribner.
Zobo patriotic drill. Hatch, A. W. 15 c. Hints.
ZOOLOGY.
French. Animal activities. $1.20. Longmans.
Jordan *and* Heath. Animal forms. net, $1.10. Appleton.
Lindsay. Story of animal life. net, 35 c. Appleton.
Mudge. Text book of zoology. $2.50. Longmans.
See also Amphibia; — Animals;—Evolution;—Invertebrates;—Protozoa.
ZOOTOMY.
See Dissection.
Zuckerhandl, Otto. Atlas and epitome of operative surgery; fr. 2d rev., enl. Germ. ed.; ed. by J. C. Da Costa. '02(Ap26) il. 12°, net, $3.50. Saunders.
ZUNI INDIANS.
Cushing. Zuñi folk tales. net, $3.50. Putnam.

WEEKLY RECORD OF NEW PUBLICATIONS.

☞ Beginning with the issue of July 5, 1902, the titles of *net* books published under the rules of the American Publishers' Association are preceded by a double asterisk **, and the word net follows the price. The titles of *fiction* (not net) published under the rules are preceded by a dagger †. *Net* books not covered by the rules, whether published by members of the American Publishers' Association or not, are preceded by a single asterisk, and the word net follows the price. ☜

The abbreviations are usually self-explanatory. c. after the date indicates that the book is copyrighted; if the copyright date differs from the imprint date, the year of copyright is added. Books of foreign origin of which the edition (annotated, illustrated, etc.) is entered as copyright, are marked c. ed.; translations, c. tr.; n. p., in place of price, indicates that the publisher makes no price, either net or retail, and quotes prices to the trade only upon application.

A colon after initial designates the most usual given name, as: A: Augustus; B: Benjamin; C: Charles; D: David; E: Edward; F: Frederic; G: George; H: Henry; I: Isaac; J: John; L: Louis; N: Nicholas; P: Peter; R: Richard; S: Samuel; T: Thomas; W: William.

Sizes are designated as follows: F. (folio: over 30 centimeters high); Q. (4to: under 30 cm.); O. (8vo: 25 cm.); D. (12mo: 20 cm.); S. (16mo: 17½ cm.); T. (24mo: 15 cm.); Tt. (32mo: 12½ cm.); Fe. 48mo: 10 cm.). Sq., obl., nar., designate square, oblong, narrow books of these heights.

Andersen, Hans Christian. Fairy tales from Hans Christian Andersen; tr. by E. Lucas; il. by T. H., C., and W. H. Robinson. N. Y., Macmillan, 1902. 8+312 p. 16°, (Temple classics for young people.) cl., 50 c., leath., 80 c.

Atherton, E:, *ed.* The adventures of Marco Polo, the great traveller. N. Y., Appleton, 1902. [Jl.] c. 24+163 p. il. por. map, D. (Appleton's home reading books; ed. by W: T. Harris, division 3, history.) cl., 65 c.

A supplementary reader in history intended principally for young people.

†Balch, F. H. The bridge of the gods: a romance of Indian Oregon. 7th ed.; il. by L. Maynard Dixon. Chic., A. C. McClurg & Co., 1902. [Ag.] c. '90, 1902. 12+280 p. D. cl., $1.50.

See note, "Weekly Record," P. W., December 20, 1890 [986.] From the legends of the Columbia River and the mystical "bridge of the gods," the author has derived a realistic picture of the powerful tribes that inhabited the Oregon country two centuries ago. The tragic fate of the young minister who came from New England to convert the Indians is the climax of a story in which savage superstitions and Christian courage struggle for mastery.

***Bateson,** W. Mendel's principles of heredity: a defence; with a translation of Mendel's original papers on "Hybridization." N. Y., Macmillan, 1902. 14+212 p. 12°, (Cambridge University Press ser.) $1.30 net.

Besant, *Sir* Walter, *ed.* The fascination of London. [*Also*] Chelsea, by G. E. Mitton. N. Y., Macmillan, 1902. 9+99 p. 16°, cl., 80 c.

Birbeck, C. J. Elocution self-taught; select recitations, orations and dramatic scenes, with action and emphasis. N. Y., Jos. F. Wagner, 1902. il. 12°, cl., $1.

Browder, Jonathan Bayley. The time elements of the Orestean trilogy: a thesis submitted for the degree of Doctor of philosophy, University of Wisconsin, 1897. Madison, Wis., University of Wisconsin, 1902. [Jl.] 76 p. O. (Bulletin of the University of Wisconsin, no. 62; Philology and literature ser., v. 2, no. 1.) pap., 35 c.

An inquiry into the length of time spanned by the action of the Oresteia. The author argues that Orestes did not proceed directly to Athens, but that he first wandered far and wide on what appears to have been a prolonged pilgrimage of self-purification and atonement.

Burdick, Francis Marion. The essentials of business law. N. Y., Appleton, 1902. [Ag.] c. 20+285 p. por. D. (Twentieth century text-books.) cl., $1.25.

For boys and girls in our secondary schools. The purpose is to show how the rules of law, governing ordinary business transactions, have been developed, and to tell what they are. Technical law terms have been discarded as far as possible. When they have been used, care has been taken to explain and illustrate their meaning, so as to render them easily intelligible to the young student.

***Campbell,** T: Selections from Campbell; ed., with introd. and notes, by W. T. Webb. N. Y., Macmillan, 1902. 40+133 p. 12°, cl., 50 c. net.

Coit, Stanton, *comp.* The message of man: a book of ethical scriptures; gathered from many sources and arr. by Stanton Coit. N. Y., Macmillan, 1902. 12+340 p. 16°, cl., 75 c.; leath., $1.

***Cunningham,** Dan J:, *M.D., ed.* Text-book of anatomy. N. Y., Macmillan, 1902. 29+1309 p. 1 col. il. 8°, cl., $9 net; shp., $10 net; hf. mor., $11 net.

***Davies,** Gerald S. Franz Hals. N. Y., Macmillan, 1902. 18+157 p. il. 8°, cl., $14 net.

***Douglas,** Langton. Fra Angelico. 2d rev., enl. ed. N. Y., Macmillan, 1902. 19+185 p. il. 8°, cl., $6 net.

Durand, W: F: Practical marine engineering for marine engineers and students; with aids for applicants for marine engineers' licensees. N. Y., Marine Engineering, 1901. c. 14+706 p. il. 12°, cl., $5.

Epworth League reading course, 1902-1903. N. Y., Eaton & Mains, [1902.] c. 3 v., S. cl., $1.

Contents: Nature's miracles, familiar talks on science. v. 2, Energy and vibration, energy, sound, heat, light, explosives. 2d ser., by Elisha Gray, 6+255 p.; Youth of famous Americans, by L: Albert Banks, D.D., 2-302 p.; Our church: what Methodists believe, and how they work, by Jesse Lyman Hurlbut, D.D., 247 p.

***First** yearbook of the National Society for the scientific study of education. pts. 1 and 2. Chic., University of Chicago Press, 1902. c. 76; 3-58 p. O. pap., ea., 50 c. net.

Contents: Pt. 1, Some principles in the teaching of history, by Lucy M. Salmon: a paper prepared for discussion at the general meeting of the society in conjunction with the meeting of the Department of superintendence at Chicago, Thursday, February 27, 1902. Pt. 2, The progress of geography in the schools, by W. M. Davis: a paper prepared for discussion at the general meeting of the Society at Minneapolis at the time of the National Educational Association, July 9, 1902.

Grand Rapids, Mich. Tax list. Grand Rapids, Commercial Credit Co., Ltd., [1902.] c. 437 p. O. cl., $10.
This book contains a list of the property owners, both real estate and personal, together with the assessed valuation of same as shown by the records on file at Grand Rapids, Mich., July 1, 1902.

Heath, Christopher, *M.D.* Clinical lectures on surgical subjects. 2d ser. Phil., P. Blakiston's Son & Co., 1902. 16°, cl., $2.

Hubbard, Elbert. Botticelli. East Aurora. N. Y., The Roycrofters, 1902. sq. 12°, (Little journeys to the homes of eminent artists, v. 10, no. 3.) pap., 25 c.

Hubbard, Elbert. Gainsborough. East Aurora, N. Y. The Roycrofters, 1902. 3+113-134 p. por. sq. D. (Little journeys to the homes of eminent artists, v. 10, no. 5.) pap., 25 c.

Hubbard, Elbert. Leonardo. East Aurora, N. Y., The Roycrofters, 1902. sq. 12°, (Little journeys to the homes of eminent artists, v. 10, no. 2.) pap., 25 c.

Hubbard, Elbert. Raphael. East Aurora, N. Y., The Roycrofters, 1902. sq. 12°, (Little journeys to the homes of eminent artists. v. 10, no. 1.) pap., 25 c.

Hubbard, Elbert. Thorwaldsen. East Aurora, N. Y., The Roycrofters, 1902. sq. 12°, (Little journeys to the homes of eminent artists, v. 10, no. 4.) pap., 25 c.

Hubbard, Elbert. Velasquez. East Aurora, N. Y., The Roycrofters, 1902. sq. 12°, (Little journeys to the homes of eminent artists, v. 10, no. 6.) pap., 25 c.

Kaufman, Matthias S., *D.D., and* Nye, *Rev.* C: Lyman. Notes on the Epworth League prayer meeting topics. 2d ser., 1902. N. Y., Eaton & Mains, 1902. c. 72 p. S. pap., 15 c.

Kentucky decisions as reported by E. W. Hines, in the southwestern reporter, vs. 63, 64, 65 and 66, May, 1901, to Mar., 1902; to be cited by v. and p. of the southwestern reporter. St. Paul, West Pub. Co., 1902. c. O. shp., $4.

Kenyon, Ja. B: Remembered days. N. Y., Eaton & Mains, 1902. c. 239 p. D. cl., $1.
Sketches of out-door life, entitled: The trout brook; An Island camp; Three days; A shore dinner; Wild ducks; The monarch of the stream, etc.

***Kingsley**, C: Life and works of Charles Kingsley. Ed. de luxe. In 19 v. v. 11 and 12, Hereward the wake, last of the English. 2 v. N. Y., Macmillan, 1902. 9+270; 7+262 p. 8°, cl., ea., $3 net.

†**Knowles**, F: Lawrence, ["R. L. Paget," *pseud.,*] *ed.* Cap and gown. 3d ser.; selected by R. L. Paget. Bost., L. C. Page & Co., 1903, [1902.] c. 14+331 p. 1 il. S. cl., $1.25.
The editor as a rule has confined himself to verse printed in the college publications of the last four years, although in several instances he has gone back further. None of the poems in this volume was included in the previous volumes of the series.

La Seer, Elmer J. The hand and its lines: a short treatise on palmistry. Grand Rapids, Mich., Dean & Hicks, 1902. c. 20 p. nar. O., pap., gratis.

***Laughlin**, J. Laurence. Credit. Chic., University of Chicago Press, 1902. [Ag4.] c. 28 p. Q. (Decennial publications, from v. 4.) pap., 50 c. net.
A treatise on credit, by the professor and head of the department of political economy in University of Chicago.

Lessing, O. E. Schiller's einfluss auf Grillparzer: eine litterarhistorische studie: a thesis submitted for the decree of Doctor of philosophy, University of Michigan, 1901. Madison, University of Wisconsin, 1902. [Ag.] 77-204 p. O. (Bulletin of the University of Wisconsin, no. 54; Philology and literature ser., v. 2, no. 2.) pap., 50 c.
The author finds by comparing Grillparzer's "Blanka von Kastilien" with Schiller's "Don Karlos," and his "Ahnfrau" with "Die Räuber," that Grillparzer decidedly worked under the spell of Schiller's influence.

***Lewis**, Edwin Herbert. Text-book of applied English grammar; complete. N. Y., Macmillan, 1902. 12°, cl., 50 c. net.

***Lewis**, Edwin Herbert. Text-book of applied English grammar. pt. 2. N. Y., Macmillan, 1902. c. 14+167-363 p. 12°, cl., 35 c. net.

Lützow, *Count* Francis. The story of Prague; il. by Nelly Erichsen. N. Y., Macmillan, 1902. 19+211 p. 12°, (Mediæval towns ser.) cl., $1.50; leath., $2.

May, Eliz. Animal life in rhymes and jingles. Akron, O., Saalfield Pub. Co., 1902. [Ag15.] il. 4°, bds., $1.25.

Merriam, J: C. Triassic ichthyopterygia from California and Nevada. Berkeley, Cal., University of California, 1902. 63-108 p. Q. (University of California publications, bulletin of the Department of geology, v. 3, no. 4.) pap., 50 c.

Montgomery, Frances T. Billy Whiskers; or, the autobiography of a goat. Akron, O., Saalfield Pub. Co., 1902. [Ag15.] c. il. 4°, bds., $1.

***Millard**, Bailey. Songs of the press, and other adventures in verse. San Francisco, Cal., Elder & Shepard, 1902. c. 2-113 p. D. bds., 75 c. net.

Neesen, Victor, *M.D.* Rusted spokes; dedicated to all lovers of sport. N. Y., New Amsterdam Book Co., 1902. 16°, pap., 50 c.

New York [state.] Abbott's cyclopedic digest of the decisions of all the courts from the earliest time to the year 1900: being the work of the late Austin Abbott and B. Vaughan Abbott, rev. and imp. and cont. many new and valuable features; ed. and comp. by the publishers' editorial staff, De-Witt C. Blashfield, ed.-in-chief. v. 10, (municipal courts-pleas.) N. Y., N. Y. Law Book Co., 1902. c. 8+1120 p. O. shp., $7.50.

***Oesterley,** *Rev.* W. O. E. Studies in the Greek and Latin versions of the Book of Amos. N. Y., Macmillan, 1902. 7+112 p. 8°, (Cambridge University Press ser.) cl., $1.30 net.

***Pallen,** Condé Benoist. The death of Sir Launcelot, and other poems. Bost., Small, Maynard & Co., 1902. c. 8+124 p. D. cl., $1 net.

Parsons, Mary Eliz. The wild flowers of California; their names, haunts and habits. 4th ed., rev. and corr.; il. by Marg. Warriner Buck. San Francisco, Cal., Payat, Upham & Co., 1902. c. '97, 1902. 48+411 p. O. cl., $2.

***Rouse,** W: H: Denham. Greek votive offerings: an essay in the history of the Greek religion. N. Y., Macmillan, 1902. 15+463 p. 8°, (Cambridge Univ. Press ser.) cl., $4.50 net.

****Segall,** J. B. Corneille and the Spanish drama. N. Y., Macmillan, 1902. [Jl2.] c. 9+147 p. 12°, (Columbia Univ. studies in romance, philology and literature.) cl., $1.50 net.

Seignobos, C: The feudal régime; tr. ed. by Earle W. Dow. N. Y., H: Holt & Co., 1902. c. 6+70 p. O. pap., 50 c.

"This account of the feudal régime forms the first chapter in the second volume of the 'Histoire générale du IV. Siecle à nos Jours,' edited by M. M. Lavisse and Rambaud. It is now done into English in the hope that it may be useful as a short description of the social organization prevailing in Europe, especially from the tenth to the thirteenth century. It seems particularly fitted for collateral reading in high school and college classes in history, and at the same time it may prove of interest outside the schools."—*Preface.*

†**Stevenson,** Rob. L: The best of Stevenson; ed. by Alex. Jessup. Bost., L. C. Page & Co., 1902. c. 4+390 p. por. D. cl., $1.25.

Contents: A brief critical analysis of the life and works of Robert Louis Stevenson; Will o' the mill; Virginibus Puerisque; The flight in the heather; The strange case of Dr. Jekyll and Mr. Hyde; The voice among the trees; Markheim; Æs triplex; Poems. Bibliography (15 p.) based on the lists prepared by E. D. North for *The Bookbuyer,* Sept., 1896, and the list appended to Balfour's "Life" of Stevenson.

****Stowe,** *Mrs.* Harriet Eliz. Beecher. The story of little Eva from "Uncle Tom's Cabin." Bost., Dana Estes & Co., [1902.] c. 10+165 p. 16°, (Famous children of literature ser.) cl., 75 c. net.

***Sturt,** H:, *ed.* Personal idealism: philosophical essays, by eight members of the University of Oxford. N. Y., Macmillan, 1902. 9+393 p. 8°, cl., $3.25 net.

†**Sutherland,** Millicent. The wind in the tree: seven love stories; with a frontispiece by Walter Crane. N. Y., R. H. Russell, 1902. c. 6+226 p. il. 16°, cl., $1.50.

Taylor, Frances Lilian. The Taylor school readers. Second reader. Chic., Werner School Book Co., [1902.] c. 160 p. il. D. cl., 35 c.

***Tennant,** F. R. The origin and propagation of sin: being the Hulsean lectures delivered before the University of Cambridge in 1901-2. N. Y., Macmillan, 1902. 15+231 p. 12°, (Cambridge Univ. Press ser.) cl., $1.10 net.

Thayer, Alfred E:. *M.D.* Compend of special pathology. Phil., P. Blakiston's Son & Co., 1902. 322 p. il. 12°, cl., 80 c.; interleaved, $1.

***Thorne,** W. Bezly, *M.D.* The Schott methods of the treatment of diseases of the heart; with an account of the Nauheim baths and of the therapeutic exercises. 4th ed. Phil., P. Blakiston's Son & Co., 1902. il. 8°, cl., $2 net.

Timby, Theodore Ruggles. Lighted lore for gentle folk. N. Y., Morningside Publishing Co., 1902. c. 5+305 p. por. D. cl., $2.

Expresses briefly, in prose, verse and epigram, the author's thoughts on the mental and moral forces, the illusions of mankind, current events, scientific discoveries, and other timely subjects.

***United States** naval examination papers, 1899-1902; comp. and arr. by M. C. Dugan. Balt., Md., Cushing & Co., 1902. c. 100 p. D. cl., $1 net.

Contains besides the examination papers, introductory notes, general and special remarks to candidates.

***Vivekananda,** *Swami.* The song of the Sannyasin. N. Y., H: J. Van Haagen, 1902. unp. obl. F°, leatherette, 15 c. net.

A poem illustrating the ideals of the Indian monks, showing that much of the so-called "new thought" is very old.

****Weinstock,** Harris. Jesus the Jew, and other addresses. N. Y., Funk & Wagnalls Co., 1902. [Jl.] c. 229 p. D. cl., $1 net.

"What is the modern Jewish idea of Jesus? Do the Jews look forward to the coming of a Messiah? Do the Jews continue to look upon themselves as God's chosen people? Does the modern Jew believe in intermarriage? These and similar questions have been asked of the author by non-Jews who were seeking enlightenment on these subjects. In the following chapters the author has endeavored to answer these and kindred queries as a Jewish liberal."—*Introduction.*

Wisser, J: P. The tactics of coast defense. Kansas City, Mo., Hudson-Kimberly Publishing Co., [1902.] c. 232 p. O. cl., $2.

The present work is the outcome of lectures delivered by Major Wisser at the Naval War College and at Cornell University, Ithaca, and of five years of study on the tactics of coast defense, supplementary to nearly twenty years of study of tactics in general. The chapters treat of principles of strategy and tactics involved in coast defense, armament, sites for batteries and forts, coast artillery material, organization of coast artillery, instruction and training, battle tactics of coast defense, etc. List of books and articles consulted (2 p.).

***Whitaker,** Jos. & Sons, *comps.* The reference catalogue of current literature; containing the full titles of books now in print and on sale; with the prices at which they may be obtained of all booksellers and an index containing nearly one hundred and forty thousand references, 1902. N. Y., Office of The Publishers' Weekly, [1902.] 2 v., no regular paging, index 798 p.+publishers' catalogues, O. hf. leath., $5 net.

The present issue of the [English] Reference Catalogue of Current Literature is even bulkier than its immediate forerunner, and contains the complete or abridged lists of one hundred and seventy-nine publishers. A notable fact is the increase in colonial and foreign houses who have inserted their catalogues, thus further enhancing the utility of the publication. The Index now extends to seven hundred and ninety-eight pages, containing an aggregate of one hundred and thirty-five thousand entries, an increase on that of the last edition of two hundred and twenty-two pages, and comprising nearly thirty-eight thousand additional references. Every book contained in the "Reference Catalogue" will be found in the Index, under title, subject and author.

White, Emma Siggins. Genealogy of the descendants of John Walker, of Wigton, Scotland, with records of a few allied families; also, war records and some fragmentary notes pertaining to the history of Va., 1600-1902. Custer, S. Dak., Mrs. E. S. White, 1902. c. 30+722 p. pors. il. O. cl., $6.

Wilson, *Mrs.* Augusta Jane Evans. A speckled bird. N. Y., G: W. Dillingham Co., [1902.] [Ag.] c. 5-526 p. D. cl., $1.50.

About reconstruction times a scheming New England judge eloped with a high bred Southern girl. The hatred which the Southern people thereafter felt for the judge, is reflected later in their attitude to his daughter, who is, according to the parable quoted in the story, "As a speckled bird, the birds round about are against her."

***Woodley,** Oscar Israel, *and* Carpenter, G. R. M. Sand foundation; lessons in English language and grammar. N. Y., Macmillan, 1902. c. 15+269+9+166 p. 12°, cl., 65 c. net.

ORDER LIST.

D. Appleton & Co., 72 Fifth Ave., New York.

Atherton, Adventures of Marco Polo.. 65
Burdick, Essentials of business law.... $1.25

P. Blakiston's Son & Co., 1012 Walnut St., Philadelphia.

Heath, Clinical lectures on surgical subjects, 2d ser.................... 2.00
Thayer, Compend of special pathology, 80 c.; 1.00
*Thorne, Schott methods of treating diseases of the heart.............net, 2.00

Commercial Credit Co., Ltd., Grand Rapids, Mich.

Grand Rapids, (Mich.,) Tax list...... 10.00

Cushing & Co., 34 W. Baltimore St., Baltimore, Md.

*United States examination papers.net, 1.00

Dean & Hicks, Grand Rapids, Mich.

La Seer, The hand and its lines...... gratis.

G. W. Dillingham Co., 119 W. 23d St., New York.

†Wilson, A speckled bird............. 1.50

Eaton & Mains, 150 Fifth Ave., New York.

Epworth League reading course, 1902-1903, 3 v....................per set, 1.00
Kaufman *and* Nye, Notes on the Epworth League prayer meeting topics, 2d ser.......... 15
Kenyon, Remembered days............ 1.00

D. P Elder & Morgan Shepard, 238 Post St., San Francisco.

*Millard, Songs of the press.......net, 75

Dana Estes & Co., 200-208 Summer St., Boston.

**Stowe, Story of little Eva.......net, 75

Funk & Wagnalls Co., 30 Lafayette Pl., New York.

**Weinstock, Jesus the Jew.......net, 1.00

Henry Holt & Co., 29 West 23d St., New York.

Seignobos, Feudal régime............ 50

Hudson-Kimberly Publishing Company, 1014 Wyandotte St., Kansas City, Mo.

Wisser, Tactics of coast defense....... 2.00

A. C. McClurg & Co., 215-221 Wabash Ave., Chicago.

†Balch, Bridge of the gods............ 1.50

Macmillan Co., 66 Fifth Ave., New York.

Andersen, Fairy tales...........50 c.; 80
*Bateson, Mendel's principles of heredity....... ....net, $1.30
Besant, The fascination of London.... 80
*Campbell, Selections......... ....net, 50
Coit, The message of man.......75c.; 1.00
*Cunningham, Text-book of anatomy, net, $9; net, $10; net, 11.00
*Davies, Franz Hals..............net, 14.00
*Douglas, Fra Angelico, 2d rev., enl. ed..... ....net, 6.00
*Kingsley, Life and works, v. 11 and 12, Hereward the wake.........ea., net, 3.00
*Lewis, Text-book of applied English grammar, complete..... ....net, 50
*——, Text-book of applied English grammar, pt. 2.................net, 35
Lützow, Story of Prague........$1.50; 2.00
*Oesterley, Studies in Greek and Latin versions of the Book of Amos...net, 1.30
*Rouse, Greek votive offerings....net, 4.50
**Segall, Corneille and Spanish drama, net, 1.50
*Sturt, Personal idealism..........net, 3.25
*Tennant, Origin and propagation of sin...... ....net, 1.10
*Woodley *and* Carpenter, Foundation lessons in English language and grammar..... ....net, 65

Marine Engineering, 309 Broadway, New York.

Durand, Practical marine engineering. 5.00

Morningside Publishing Co., New York.

Timby, Lighted lore................. 2.00

New Amsterdam Book Co., 156 Fifth Ave., New York.

Neesen, Rusted spokes................ 50

New York Law Book Co., 303 Broadway, New York.

New York, Abbott's cyclopedic digest, v. 10...... .... 7.50

L. C. Page & Co., 200 Summer St., Boston.

†Knowles, Cap and gown, 3d ser....... 1.25
†Stevenson, The best of Stevenson.... 1.25

R. H. Russell, 3-7 W. 29th St., New York.

†Sutherland, The wind in the tree..... 1.50

Payat, Upham & Co., 204 Pine St., San Francisco, Cal.

Parsons, Wild flowers of California, 4th ed., rev. and corr.............. 2.00

OFFICE OF THE PUBLISHERS' WEEKLY, 298 Broadway, New York.

*Whitaker, Reference catalogue, 1902, 2 v.........net, $5.00

THE ROYCROFTERS, East Aurora, N. Y.

Hubbard, Botticelli...... 25
——, Gainsborough...... 25
——, Leonardo...... 25
——, Raphael...... 25
——, Thorwaldsen...... 25
——, Velasquez...... 25

SAALFIELD PUBLISHING CO., Akron, O.

May, Animal life in rhymes........... 1.25
Montgomery, Billy Whiskers.......... 1.00

SMALL, MAYNARD & CO., 10 Arrow St., Cambridge.

*Pallen, Death of Sir Launcelot...net, 1.00

UNIVERSITY OF CALIFORNIA, Berkeley, Cal.

Merriam, Triassic ichthyopterygia from California and Nevada.............. 50

UNIVERSITY OF CHICAGO PRESS, Chicago.

*First yearbook of the National Society for the scientific study of education, pts, 1, 2...................ea., net, 50
*Laughlin, Credit................net, 50

UNIVERSITY OF WISCONSIN, Madison, Wis.

Browder, The time elements of the Orestean trilogy....... 35

UNIVERSITY OF WISCONSIN.—*Continued.*

Lessing, Schiller's einfluss auf Grillparzer....... 50

HENRY J. VAN HAAGEN, 1267 Broadway, New York.

*Vivekananda, Song of Sannyasin..net, 15

JOS. F. WAGNER, 103 Fifth Ave., New York.

Birbeck, Elocution self-taught......... $1.00

WERNER SCHOOL BOOK CO., 378-388 Wabash Ave., Chicago.

Taylor school readers: Second reader. 35

WEST PUB. CO., 52-58 W. 3d St., St. Paul, Minn.

Kentucky decisions (Hines)........... 4.00

MRS. E. S. WHITE, Custer, S. Dak.

White, Genealogy of the descendants of J. Walker, of Wigton........... 6.00

CORRECTION IN PRICE AND OTHER DATA

FURNEAUX, W. S., *ed.* [Thomas] Whittaker's popular mannikin. [The human body.] N. Y., T: Whittaker, [1902.] 4 p+superimposed plate, obl. F. bds., $1.50. *Corr. price.*

WALLACE, Alfred Russell. Contributions to the theory of natural selection, etc. N. Y., Macmillan, 1902. 12°, cl., *price changed to* $2.

WALLACE, Alfred Russell. Island life. N. Y., Macmillan, 1902. 12°, cl., *price changed to* $2.

WALLACE, Alfred Russell. The Malay Archipelago. N. Y., Macmillan, 1902. 12°, cl., *price changed to* $2.

BIBLIOGRAPHIC NOTES.

THE GOVERNMENT PRINTING OFFICE, Washington, D. C., has just published for the Library of Congress, (Division of Bibliography.) a "List of References on Reciprocity [in] Books, Articles in Periodicals and Congressional Documents," compiled by A. P. C. Griffin, Chief of Division of Bibliography. No effort has been made to cover the entire literature of the subject, but to present a suggestive list of authorities. The references are largely to discussions of the subject. (38 p. 8°, cl.)

THE SUPERINTENDENT OF DOCUMENTS, Government Printing Office, Washington, D. C., has just issued a "Catalogue of the Public Documents of the Fifty-fifth Congress and of other departments of the Government of the United States for the period from July 1, 1897, to June 30, 1899." This is the fourth volume of the "Comprehensive Index," and contains in addition to the documents and reports submitted to Congress during the period named all publications of the executive departments, bureaus and offices of the government issued during the two fiscal years 1897-1899. The compilation was begun under the supervision of Miss Mary A. Hartwell and finished under that of Miss Alice C. Fichtenkam. (1070 p. 4°, cl.)

BULLETIN 26 of the Bureau of American Ethnology, which is about ready, is the first issued of a new series recently authorized by Congress. The initial number of the new series is 25, "Natick-English and English-Natick Dictionary," by James Hammond Trumbull, which will be ready for distribution within a few weeks. Number 27, "Tsimshian Texts," recorded and translated by Franz Boas, is in press; several others are in preparation, including a new edition of the "Introduction to the Study of Indian Languages," by J. W. Powell, and the "Diccionario de Motul," an extended dictionary of the Maya language, revised by the late Dr. Berendt and afterward by the late Dr. Brinton, and now undergoing final revision by Señor Andomaro Molina, of Merida, Yucatan. The "Cyclopedia of Indian Tribes" is well advanced. It has been arranged to send one or more volumes to press for publication in Bulletin form during the current year. The Nineteenth Annual Report for 1897-1898, in two parts, is now in the bindery and will be published shortly.

CATALOGUES OF NEW AND SECOND-HAND BOOKS.—*A. M. Kühl*, 73 Jägerstr., Berlin, W., Aëronautische Bibliographie, II., 1895-1902, Bücher u. Abhandl. über theoretische und praktische Luftschiffahrt, Militär- und Marine-Aëronautik, Flugtechnik, Vogelflug, dynamische u. aëronautische Luftschiffe, sowie über die damit zusammenhängenden Wissenschaften u. Gewerbe: Gastechnik, Motorbau, Seilerei, Korbwaren- und Firnisfabrikation, Meteorologie, Photographie, etc. (22 p. 16°, 50 pfg.)—*Otto Schulze & Co.*, 20 S. Frederick St., Edinburgh, Choice books, many in fine bindings. (No. 18, 2043-3330 titles.)—*Arthur Reader*, 1 Orange St., London, W.C., Drama, witches, early printing, etc. (No. 315, 373 titles.)—*Walter T. Spencer*, 27 New Oxford St., London, Miscellaneous. (No. 111, 1192 titles.)—*Franz Teubner*, 16 Oststr., Düsseldorf, Germany, Studentica, Universitets-wesen, Gelehrtengeschichte. (No. 143, 3427-3724 titles.)

The Publishers' Weekly.

FOUNDED BY F. LEYPOLDT.

AUGUST 16, 1902.

The editor does not hold himself responsible for the views expressed in contributed articles or communications. All matter, whether for the reading-matter columns or advertising pages, should reach this office not later than Wednesday noon, to insure insertion in the same week's issue.

Books for the "Weekly Record," as well as all information intended for that department, should reach this office by Tuesday morning of each week.

"I hold every man a debtor to his profession, from the which, as men do of course seek to receive countenance and profit, so ought they of duty to endeavor themselves by way of amends to be a help and an ornament thereunto."—Lord Bacon.

AS TO "BOOK TRUSTS."

Ever since the formation of the two trade associations and the carrying into effect of their rules that are intended to recover for the book trade what it has been in danger of losing altogether—its honorable position as a commercial and educational element in the community—there has been much unconsidered and silly talk about the danger of the "book trust." Especially has this cry been raised lately by a Western daily and an Eastern trade paper over the enforcement by the American Booksellers' Association of Reform Resolution No. 1, which calls for the exclusion of the books of a publishing house that refuses to co-operate in maintaining prices. In this cry the standpoint of the American Publishers' Association and the standpoint of the American Booksellers' Association are confused, and the action of the Booksellers' Association is treated from a point of view that is, to say the least, based upon a misconception. As all who are interested and informed on the subject know, the objective point of both associations is the same; but the individual action of each must be judged by itself. The publishers may elect to obtain results by one course and the booksellers decide to gain their point by another; yet each would resist most emphatically were the action of one association judged by the action of the other.

As to the charge of "combination" or "trust," in the sense of a consolidation of certain large interests to exterminate competition, nothing could be more absurd than to apply the term to the present movement for reform in the book trade. It is certainly no "combination" to publish books at prices that can be trusted; it is no "combination" to make such retail prices as allow a living profit to those who earn it by their calling; it is no "combination" to deny the privilege of discount to one who abuses it to the detriment of that calling; it is no "combination" to abolish a system of inflated prices, calculated to inveigle weak-minded persons with imaginary deductions and bargains; it is no "combination" to decline being a party to the baiting game as practised by the underseller; it is no "combination" to decline giving the underseller free advertising in the bargain, for it is the very advertising of the publisher that forms the freshest bait; it is no "combination" to refuse to discredit one's legitimate agents by underselling them over their heads; it is no "combination" to protest against being discredited one's self by having one's own prices given the lie; it is no "combination" to put a stop to pernicious practices that have dragged down the book trade to the lowest level of cheap-John fakirs; it is, in brief, no "combination" to adhere to principles which alone can restore the confidence of the trade and public.

Let us for once have our say on this misapplied word "trust" ever flung at us when it is simply a question of fair dealing; let us say that this clamor against the so-called "book trust" is nothing but the baldest jingoism, intended to deceive people and to excuse crooked business. If simple adherence to sane business principles is a "trust" or "combination," then, on the same theory, the common practice invariably resorted to by ignorance or recklessness is a "trust," but a "combination" as corrupt and disreputable as the action of the book trade associations to reform its business methods is sound and honorable. For the "liberal art" of underselling—the lowest and cheapest trick of the trade—is as easy as sucking eggs; it needs no professional training, no tried business experience, no solid investment, no hard work and application, no devotion to a calling, no respect for the usages of the trade, no regard for the rights of others, no conscience, no pride, no principle. On the contrary; for the possession of any one positive quality would disqualify for successful underselling. The art of underselling, in short, is the art of living on the industry and enterprise of others. It was to correct these evils and to limit the depredations on honest trading, and not for restraint of trade in any sense of the word, that the book trade combined. To obfuscate its intentions by libelling this movement as a "trust" is not only malicious but silly.

THE AMERICAN NEWSPAPER.

William S. Rossiter, expert special agent of the Census Bureau, according to the Washington correspondent of the *New York Tribune*, has prepared a report of unusual interest on printing and publishing in the United States in the last decade. The statistics he has gathered show that there has been no radical change in the gathering of news or in the management and scope of daily newspapers. One characteristic of the decade, however, was the great increase in the quantity of news published. "Partly because of the ambitious and progressive spirit of the period," says Mr. Rossiter, "and partly because of the lavish expenditures of capital made by reorganized or newly-established publications in order to break into the patronage of prosperous competitors and secure a foothold, the dailies of the great cities became the purveyors of the news of the world to an extent never before attempted. In many cases—especially in New York City—it was freely admitted that this expediture was carried beyond the boundaries of business prudence."

On the subject of the principal sources of newspaper income and expenditures Mr. Rossiter says:

"By 1900 it had become customary for large advertisers to form combinations; it is said that the patronage of fewer than twenty advertisers forms more than half the total quantity of advertising appearing in the daily newspapers of New York City. The only new source of income in the field of advertising was found in newcomers—principally tobaccos, whiskeys, cereals and books. Of these interests the publisher, formerly the most conservative advertiser, became the most daring. The professional advertising agent might be termed another cause of loss to the daily papers to the amount of commissions exacted. Between the opposing perplexities of competition and combinations of the advertisers there has been a decline in the advertising earning power of leading newspapers.

"After passing 300,000 circulation the value of advertising becomes a race between the receipts from that source and the cost of white paper. The advertising in one of the New York evening papers, with circulation much exceeding 300,000, was recently declared to entail a cost of 21 cents per line for white paper. Evidently the publisher who secures a circulation of huge proportions confronts the necessity of securing from his advertising patrons a return of the cost of the paper space which they occupy, with a margin of profit. For reasons already noted, the profit is in many cases uncertain, and, as the decade drew to a close, for certain newspapers in the great cities a new problem arose. The population had become so vast, and means of communication with surrounding territory so easy, that systematic search for circulation had been rewarded by enormous sales, the penalty for which was reduction or complete wiping out of profits on advertising. The circulation ball, once in motion, is not easy to stop, and the serious nature of this problem appeared when the cost of white paper threatened to exceed the return from the advertiser. At the close of the decade such a possibility confronted several American daily newspapers. Overcirculation necessitated also an increase in capital invested in plant, with the added burden of interest which it represented.

"It may be said, therefore, that at the close of the decade from 1890 to 1900 the daily newspaper was more of a public institution than ever before, because it sacrificed an increased share of its revenue for the public benefit, obtaining no compensating financial return from either purchaser or advertiser. This was a condition very much to the advantage of the public, but one which tended to periods of reduced dividends in those establishments appearing to be most prosperous. Daily publications suffered from the rage for enlarged business and narrow profits so characteristic of all industries during the decade, but the relief which other callings found in combinations was not open to the publishers of daily newspapers, because the inequalities of circulation forever make combinations of newspapers impossible. Prosperity for the daily newspaper clearly lies in a middle course, if conditions permit, with respect to both news and circulation. The changes which occurred in weekly publications during the last decade were not such as to merit more than passing consideration."

SCOTTISH HISTORICAL PRINTING.

The Edinburgh Bibliographical Society is at present engaged upon a work of importance to all interested in the history of printing. Six years ago, says a writer in the *Glasgow Herald*, the society resolved to begin the compilation of a bibliographical catalogue of books, etc., published in Scotland before 1700. The direction of the work was undertaken by H. G. Aldis, now of the University Library, Cambridge, in whose hands the material has accumulated to such an extent that the title-slips now number about 3500. In order to facilitate further progress, and to enable contributors to know what titles are still unrecorded or defective, it has been decided to issue a preliminary hand-list of one-line titles, which it is hoped will soon be in the hands of the printer. This hand-list will consist of about 150 quarto pages, and will contain the titles arranged in chronological order, followed by a list of the printers and booksellers and an index of authors, etc. The main object in printing the list is that copies may be distributed to bibliographers and others who have opportunities of furthering the completion of the bibliography, and who may be willing to send in additional information.

But beyond the particular purpose it is intended to serve, the list will form a useful record of Scottish printing of the period dealt with. At present there is no formal history of printing in Scotland during the seventeenth century. Dickson's and Edmond's admirable "Annals of Scotland Printing" comes down only to 1600, and a knowledge of what was being done by Scottish printers during the next hundred years can only be picked up, slowly and laboriously, from such books as Watson's preface or Mr. Edmond's volume on the Aberdeen printers, or a recondite work with the unpromising title of Lee's "Memorial for the Bible Societies of Scotland." Despite a few works printed at Stirling and St. Andrews, and possibly by John Scot, at Dundee, in the sixteenth century, it was only in the next century that printing was generally practiced outside Edinburgh.

COMMUNICATIONS.

TO DESIGNATE SIZES OF BOOKS BY THE METRIC SYSTEM.

To the Editor of the Publishers' Weekly.

SIR: Your editorial of August 2 calling attention to the strong recommendation of the international congress of publishers that the size of books be given in cm. leads me to remind American publishers that in 1876 a strong committee of librarians was appointed to investigate this matter thoroughly. Their report was that the best method of giving size was to "give the size" in cm. Every few years from that time to this some committee or body has taken up the subject afresh, the last one being the special committee of the American Library Association in revising the rules in connection with the Library of Congress for the printed catalogue cards. It is significant that thorough investigation each time reaches exactly the same result. Is it not the part of wisdom to get rid of the present lack of system and adopt at once what is bound to be the international method? The other reports have sometimes given height without width and one proposition was to give the nearest half cm., a refinement quite unnecessary except for bibliographic rarities. It is enough to give the nearest height in cm. of the uncut page or of the squares of the bound book followed by the width if greater accuracy is desired, and always if the book is square or oblong, the height and width being separated preferably by x instead of by a dash as in your editorial. As I have served on several of these committees I know that the variation you comment on is not a real one. If we give exact measurements there can be no discrepancy in systems. The scheme made by our committee 25 years ago which THE PUBLISHERS' WEEKLY has used was based on actual measurement of hundreds of volumes, but in drawing the dividing line between sizes some arbitrary point had to be chosen which would seem large for the smaller size and small for the larger. With the adoption of the cm. system, however, the whole world would be in harmony, there could be no mistake and it would be much easier for laymen to undertsand the kind of book they were getting to see the height in cm. than to see the conventional 8°, 12°, etc.

I take exception to your statement also that "the march of reform is delayed by the present unsettled status of the metric system." This was never so firmly established as now, and Congress recently passed a bill making it obligatory in this country and then reconsidered it, not from doubt as to the wisdom, but in order to give a little more time for consideration. Those most familiar with the subject have no doubt that this action will soon be taken. Nearly all the civilized world has long been using the metric system as its only measure, and the people who declaim against it have been silent many years. Even those who for some fanciful reason do not like it admit that it is inevitably to be universal. The book trade should co-operate with librarians in dropping one and forever the size letters O, D, S, etc., and the old fold symbols 8°, 12°, 16°, etc., and hereafter record size by giving size in the international measures.

MELVIL DEWEY.

POSTAL MATTERS.

THE REDEMPTION OF UNCANCELLED POSTAL CARDS.

THE postoffice department has called a halt and revoked the recent order which was to go in effect August 1, providing for the redemption of uncancelled postal cards, pending the decision of the attorney-general as to the legality of such a course. The order is held up because some one called the attention of the postmaster-general to that clause in the law which reads: "No postmaster shall sell or dispose of stamps in any manner except for cash, under penalty of a fine or imprisonment."

OBITUARY NOTES.

JAMES JOSEPH JACQUES TISSOT, the artist, and illustrator of "The Life of Christ," brought out in this country by the S. S. McClure Company and McClure, Phillips & Co., the originals of which are in the Brooklyn Institute of Arts and Sciences, died in Paris, August 9. He was born at Nantes, France, on October 15, 1836.

DR. MARTIN LUTHER HOLBROOK, an old friend in the book trade, died at his home, No. 46 East Twenty-first Street, New York, August 12, after a lingering illness. Dr. Holbrook was born in Mantua, Portage Co., Ohio, February 3, 1831, of a New England family whose ancestors were among the first to settle in the Western Reserve. Brought up as a farmer, he studied in the Ohio Agricultural College, and was for three years editor of *The Ohio Farmer.* He began to take an interest in hygiene and medicine, and late in the fifties became a practicing physician. In 1861-'63 he was associated with Dr. Dio Lewis in Boston in his propaganda of physical culture and hygiene and the introduction of the Lewis system into the schools of various cities. In 1864 Dr. Holbrook came to New York City and became a member of the firm of Miller, Wood & Holbrook, publishers of medical books and *The Herald of Health,* of which paper Dr. Holbrook remained editor until 1898. During the war he had much to do with army sanitation. About that time, too, his firm established the first Turkish bath in New York City, in Laight Street, close to their place of business. The place was headquarters for writers and physicians interested in advocating what were then regarded as mere theories as to hygiene, but to-day are accepted and applied by most practitioners. He was one of the earliest advocates in the United States of the kindergarten system. As a writer of many medical treatises and as editor for twenty-four years Dr. Holbrook gained pre-eminence as a teacher of ways and means to prevent and protect against disease rather than merely to cure it. His published works include "Hygiene of the Brain and Cure of Nervousness," "Eating for Strength," "Parturition Without Pain," "Liver Complaint," "Mental Dyspepsia and Headache," "Chastity," "Marriage and Parentage," "Hygienic Treatment of Consumptives," "Stirpiculture," etc. Dr. Holbrook's wife, Lucy Lee Holbrook, an artist and conspicuous member of Sorosis, died several years ago.

JOURNALISTIC NOTES.

The New York Times has acquired the triangle bounded by Broadway, West Forty-second Street and Seventh Avenue, in New York City, and will at once begin the erection thereon of a large modern steel construction building primarily for its own use. It is expected that the building will be ready for occupancy early in 1904. In the nearly fifty-one years of its existence the *New York Times* has thus far occupied four different buildings on three sites. The first of these, in 1851, was at 113 Nassau Street. The second was at the northeast corner of Nassau and Beekman Streets. The third was the one whereon the newspaper is now published. Two buildings in succession have been erected on the present site, the first in 1857 and the second in 1888.

BUSINESS NOTES.

Beeville, Tex.—Miss Bobbitt Barclay has opened a book and news stand here.

Binghamton, N. Y.—Walter R. Miller & Co. have rented the block at 170 Washington Street, and will change their quarters from 82 and 84 State Street to the new store early in October.

Boston, Mass.—The Federal Book Company has been incorporated, under the laws of New Jersey, to acquire the publishing business of the James H. Lamb Company, at 372 Boylston Street. The concern is capitalized at $100,000. The incorporators are Ernest H. Johnson, A. Moriarty, and Clarence B. Benedict.

Columbia, S. C.—H. J. Shoemaker, a well-known insurance man, has bought the Palmetto Bookstore, which has been conducted by J. H. Carlisle, Jr., and J. W. Bishop. The store will be continued at the old location by Mr. Shoemaker.

Nashville, Tenn.—C. B. Huggins, bookseller, has sold out.

Valdosta, Ga.—C. S. Bondurant will open a bookstore here.

LITERARY AND TRADE NOTES.

Henry A. Dickerman & Son, Boston, will publish a parody of "The Story of Mary MacLane," under the title of "The Story of Lizzie McGuire."

Doubleday, Page & Co. have in preparation a volume of verse taken from the pages of *Life*, to be entitled "Rhymes and Roundelays." The book will be liberally illustrated.

Clarke Conwell, (The Elston Press,) Pelham Road, New Rochelle, N. Y., has in preparation a special edition of Pope's "The Rape of the Lock," limited to 160 copies. The other eleven issues of this press are quite out of print.

D. C. Heath & Co. will publish shortly Goldoni's "Il Vero Amico," one of the most entertaining easy Italian comedies, arranged with notes and vocabulary by Professor Geddes and Professor Josselyn, of Boston University.

The Macmillan Company have in preparation a prose work by Alfred Austin, the poet laureate, entitled "Haunts of Ancient Peace," in which the author describes several places of that "restful charm" which he has depicted in his poems.

Herbert S. Stone & Co. have just published "Castle Craneycrow," a new story by George Barr McCutcheon, the author of "Graustark." The first edition of 50,000 was exhausted on the day of publication and another edition is being made ready.

Coryell & Co., 61 Chambers Street, New York, call attention to their large line of standards, neatly printed on good paper, and attractively bound in cloth, half leather and half calf. There are upwards of forty-one different sets that may be offered as illustrated, library or popular editions.

The Oxford University Press will publish shortly, in three small volumes for school use, "Graduated Lessons on the Old Testament," by the Rev. U. Z. Rule. The work has been edited by the Rev. L. J. M. Bebb, principal of St. David's College, Lampeter. Mr. Rule has followed the text of the Revised Version, and has called special attention to the moral and religious lessons which may be drawn from the history.

Dodd, Mead & Co. will publish next month "The Life of James Martineau," who was probably the most conspicuous metaphysician of his day, prepared by the Rev. James Drummond and Dr. Charles B. Upton, the former of whom succeeded Dr. Martineau as principal of Manchester New College. They will also publish next month "The Blood-Tax," a military romance of to-day, by Dorothea Gerard, author of "One Year." The scene is laid in Germany.

Fleming H. Revell Company will publish shortly what they call an "unfictitious novel," entitled "A Chinese Quaker," by Nellie Blessing Eyster. It is really the story of a Chinaman who as a boy was brought up by a young Quaker woman and became a consistent Friend. He is now a high mandarin at the head of large enterprises in China and a

Quaker still. Incidentally the story makes appalling revelations of woman slavery on our Pacific Coast.

JOHN LANE announces a new book by Constance Maud, author of "Wagner's Heroines," etc., entitled "Heroines of Poetry;" "New Letters and Memorials of Jane Welch Carlyle," with illustrations, portraits and facsimiles; and an edition of Kenneth Grahame's "Dream Days," with ten full-page illustrations by Maxfield Parrish. Mr. Lane will bring out early in September a novel entitled "Love with Honor," by Charles Marriott, author of "The Column."

THE CENTURY COMPANY has in preparation a new nature book entitled "Caterpillars and Their Moths," by Ida Mitchell and Caroline Gray Soule, which represents the result of more than twenty years spent in studying and rearing moths. The illustrations are made from photographs and show the actual size. They have in preparation a new "Topsy and Turvy" book, made up of selections from Peter Newell's two previous books, published in 1893 and 1894, both of which are out of print.

THOMAS W. LAWSON, of Boston, the builder of *Independence*, a rejected aspirant to defend the *America's* cup, has published for private circulation a work entitled "The Lawson History of the America's Cup," which is characterized as "a preliminary to a long and expensive legal struggle to assert his right to defend the *America's* cup should other challenges come from foreign yachtsmen." In preparing this book Mr. Lawson was assisted by Winfield M. Thompson, who has written the history of the cup. The edition consists of 3000 copies, printed in sumptuous style.

LITTLE, BROWN & Co. have in press a volume of essays by Captain A. T. Mahan, entitled "Retrospect and Prospect," which will contain articles on "The Development of Political Feeling and Outlook in the United States During the Last Decade," "Effect of the War in South Africa on the Prestige of the British Empire," "Motives to Imperial Federation," "Conditions Influencing the Distribution of Navies," "The Relation of the Persian Gulf to World Politics," and "The Military Rule of Obedience."

D. APPLETON & Co. have in preparation an important book of travel in Hesketh Pritchard's "Through Patagonia." It presents the results of an exhaustive tour of this still uncharted antarctic land, which Mr. Pritchard was led to make by his curiosity concerning an animal that was said to be extinct. He found its bones and its skin, but no living specimen. He did, however, discover many facts of scientific and popular interest about the country. The volume will be extensively illustrated in color by John G. Millais.

J. B. LIPPINCOTT COMPANY have in preparation a new book by Cyrus Townsend Brady, entitled "Woven with the Ship," with illustrations by Christy, Leyendecker, Glackens, Parkhurst and Crawford; a work on the "Home Life of the Borneo Head-Hunters," by Dr. W. H. Furness, 3d, who lived for a while among the Borneoese, which will be illustrated by almost 100 heliotypes reproduced from photographs; a work on the volcanic disturbances at Mt. Pelee, by Professor Angelo Heilprin, who descended the burning mountain soon after its outburst; also, a revised edition of the *Variorum edition* of "Macbeth," first published nearly thirty years ago.

THE BURROWS BROTHERS COMPANY, Cleveland, Ohio, will publish shortly a reprint of "Wolley's Journal: a two-years' Journal in New York and part of its territories in America." This is a reprint of the 1701 edition, originally issued in reprint as No. 2 of Gowan's "Bibliotheca Americana" during 1860. Wolley's has long been considered one of the rarest books in the English language which in any way relate to New York, and in this particular even surpasses Denton's "Brief Description," just published by this house as No. 1 of their *"B. B." Reprints*. Professor Edward Gaylord Bourne, of Yale, has written for this issue a delightfully lucid and valuable historical introduction.

E. P. DUTTON & Co. will publish at once a critical study by Henry Vignaud, first secretary of the United States Embassy at Paris, of the letter and chart of Toscanelli on the route to the Indies by way of the West, sent in 1474 to the Portuguese, Furnham Martins, and later to Christopher Columbus. To many readers the subject of this book will suggest sensationalism, but to students the revelations made will help to solve the problem of how Columbus, who, according to the best information obtainable, was a man of no scientific learning, could possibly have conceived the ideas that eventually led to the discovery of America. Toscanelli was a learned Florentine, and Mr. Vignaud lays the facts in regard to Toscanelli before the student, who can draw his own conclusions.

HOUGHTON, MIFFLIN & Co. will publish early in October "Our Lady of the Beeches," by Baroness von Hutten, a story of a romance growing out of a group of letters; "The Strongest Master," by Helen Choate Prince, the story of a young college man who falls a victim to socialistic heresies, but finally learns the folly of his ways; "Tracts Relating to the Currency of the Massachusetts Bay, 1682-1721," eighteen rare pamphlets bearing on the money question as it arose two hundred years ago, edited by Andrew McFarland Davis; "Daniel Ricketson and His Friends," a memorial of a citizen Quaker of New Bedford, a friend of Thoreau and other famous men; "Captain Craig," a book of verse, by Edwin A. Robinson; "Under Colonial Colors," a book for boys, by Everett T. Tomlinson; also, "Jesus's Way," by William De Witt Hyde, who presents the gist of Christ's teachings.

CHARLES E. GOODSPEED, Boston, Mass., will publish in October a reprint, in enlarged form, of W. E. Channing's life of "Thoreau, the Poet-Naturalist," the original edition of which was published by Roberts Brothers in 1873. Since Mr. Channing's death, his literary executor, F. B. Sanborn, has been desirous of bringing out a new and enlarged edition of the book, for which material was left by Mr. Channing. The forthcoming publication will contain about eighty pages of new material, including an introduction by Mr. Sanborn, notes, and a full index. There will be two editions—the ordinary edition, with a new etched portrait of the author, and a limited edition of 275 copies, 250 of which will be on toned French hand-made paper, with the etchings in two states. Besides the portrait of Mr. Channing, there will be five full-page etchings by Sidney L. Smith, namely, a portrait of Thoreau, after the crayon drawing by S. W. Rowse, a view of Thoreau's birthplace before the alterations, interior of Barrett's grist mill, Conantum pool, and dead leaves in the forest.

The Office of The Publishers' Weekly will publish August 16 the "Catalogues" volume of "The Publishers' Trade List Annual" for 1902. The "Index" volume will follow early in September. The index includes about 140,000 entries, greatly exceeding our original estimate and slightly delaying publication. Inasmuch as the index covers every book listed by the 250 publishers represented in the main volume, including the announcements sent up to August 1, we may claim that its publication a month after the volume to which it belongs will be among the rare instances of an index being published so close upon the conclusion of the final editorial work. We have just received the copies allotted for the American market of Whitaker's "Reference List of English Literature," the English counterpart of the "Publishers' Trade List Annual." Whitaker's this year contains the trade lists of 179 publishers and an index of about 800 pages, giving 135,000 references by author, title and subject. Intending subscribers are reminded that the number of copies is limited, and that after the supply is exhausted no more copies can be had.

George W. Jacobs & Co., Philadelphia, have in preparation a volume of travel by Jeremiah Zimmerman, entitled Spain and Her People;" "Ann Arbor Tales," by Karl Edwin Harriman, to be brought out uniform with the Pennsylvania and Bryn Mawr stories already published; "The Revenge of Adnah: a Tale of the Christ;" also, "Some Early Printers and their Colophons," by Joseph Spencer Kennard, which will be gotten up in sumptuous style for book collectors. They also announce a work dealing with early Colonial social life, by Edward Robins, entitled "Romances of Early America," to which we have already made reference. There will be chapters giving an account of the famous Meschianza, given in Philadelphia in the days of the British occupancy of the city, and of the love affairs of Mistress Sally Wister. Other sketches included in the volume have for their heroines Dolly Madison, Agnes Surriage, of Masachusetts; Mary Vining, the Revolutionary belle of Delaware, and Flora MacDonald, the ardent North Carolina Tory. Mr. Robins has also something to say of the men who made history in those earlier days, telling of the love affairs of Washington and Thomas Jefferson, and adding a chapter which strikes a later note in "Edwin Forrest's First Love."

TERMS OF ADVERTISING.

Under the heading "Books Wanted" ***book-trade subscribers are given the privilege of a free advertisement for books out of print, of five nonpareil lines exclusive of address, in any issue except special numbers, to an extent not exceeding 100 lines a year. If more than five lines are sent, the excess is at 10 cents a line, and amount should be inclosed.*** *Bids for current books and such as may be easily had from the publishers, and repeated matter, as well as all advertisements from non-subscribers, must be paid for at the rate of 10 cents a line.*

Under the heading "Books for Sale," the charge to subscribers and non-subscribers is 10 cents a nonpareil line for each insertion. No deduction for repeated matter.

All other small, undisplayed, advertisements will be charged at the uniform rate of 10 cents a nonpareil line. Eight words may be reckoned to the line.

Parties with whom we have no accounts must pay in advance, otherwise no notice will be taken of their communications.

BOOKS WANTED.

☞ ***In answering, please state edition, condition, and price, including postage or express charges.***

Houses that are willing to deal exclusively on a cash-on-delivery basis will find it to their advantage to put after their firm-name the word [Cash].

☞ ***Write your wants plainly and on one side of the sheet only. Illegibly-written "wants" will be considered as not having been received. The "Publishers' Weekly" does not hold itself responsible for errors.***

It should be understood that the appearance of advertisements in this column, or elsewhere in the "Publishers' Weekly" does not furnish a guarantee of credit. While it is endeavored to safeguard these columns by withdrawing the privilege of their use from advertisers who are not "good pay," booksellers should take the usual precaution, as to advertisers not known to them, that they would take in making sales to any unknown parties.

Arthur M. Allen, 508 Fulton St., Troy, N. Y.

Lossing's Field Book Civil War.
Lossing's Field Book War of 1812.
Winsor's Narrative and Critical History of America.

The Alliance Pub. Co., 569 5th Ave., N. Y.

Book of Israel, by Sidartha.

Almy, Bigelow & Washburn, Salem, Mass.

Books on Japan, state very fully all particulars.

Alwil Shop, Ridgewood, N. J. [*Cash.*]

Unsought Shrine, by Thos. Wood Stevens, hand-made pap. ed. Pub. by Alwil Shop.

Amer. Bapt. Pub. Soc., 69 Whitehall St., Atlanta, Ga.

Great Iron Wheel.

Amer. Bapt. Pub. Soc., 177 Wabash Ave., Chicago.

Dr. Chalmers' Works, 12 v.
Robert South's Sermons, 2 v.

Amer. Bapt. Pub. Soc., 132 E. 23d St., N. Y.

Monday Club Sermons on Int. Lessons, v. 11, 18.

Amer. Bapt. Pub. Soc., 902 Olive St., St. Louis, Mo.

A Summer on the Hebrew Mountains, by J. R. Macduff, 50 c. ed. Pub. by Herrick.

Amer. Bapt. Pub. Soc., 279 Elm St., Dallas, Tex.

Carson, On Baptism. Pub. by Amer. Bapt. Pub. Soc.

American Tract Soc., 150 Nassau St., N. Y.

Sketches of Huguenots. Pub. by Disosway.
Guide to New Rochelle. Pub. in 1842.
Any book about New Rochelle.

Antiquarian Book Concern, Omaha, Neb.

Phillipps, Grattan and Emmet's Speeches.
Luther's Church Postil.
Book of Concord.
De Smet's Travels.
Esoteric Christianity, by Annie Besant.

G. H. Barbour, 6016 Stanton Ave., Pittsburgh, Pa.

Anything pertaining to the Loomis Family.

BOOKS WANTED.—Continued.

N. J. Bartlett & Co., 28 Cornhill, Boston, Mass.

The Broken Shaft.

Bartlett's Book Store, 33 E. 22d St., N. Y.

Gayarré, History of Louisiana.
Symonds' Life Cellini, Nimmo ed.
Matthew Arnold, good binding.
Poor's Manuals.
Financial Chronicle, bound.

Beecher & Kymer, Kalamazoo, Mich.

Marcella, 2 v.

B. D. Berry, 378 Wabash Ave., Chicago, Ill. [*Cash.*]

Cornell, William M., English Grammar. Bost., 1841.
Crane, George, English Grammar. London, 1843.
Davenport, B., English Grammar. Wilmington, 1830.

Bonnell, Silver & Co., 24 W. 22d St., N. Y.

Reliquary new ser.

The Boston Book Co., 86 Francis St., Boston, Mass.

American Artisan, v. 40.
American Contractor, v. 21.
Amer. Gas Light Jour., v. 73.
Amer. Iron and Steel Assoc. Bulletin, v. 34.
Amer. Jour. of Photography, v. 20.
Electrical World, v. 36.
Forum, v. 1-4, odd nos. or complete file.
Geological Soc. of America Bulletin, v 11.
House Furnishing Review, v. 17-18.
Irrigation Age, v. 14, nos. 4-12.
Metal Worker, v. 54.

The Bowen-Merrill Co., Indianapolis, Ind.

Campbell's Lives of the Chief Justices.
Life and Letters of Sydney Smith.

Brentano's, 218 Wabash Ave., Chicago, Ill.

Curtiss, Protection and Prosperity. Pub. by the Pan-American Pub. Co., New York.
Dingley Tariff Bill as passed July, 1897. Pub. by Pitt & Scott, N. Y.
Frederic, National Party Platforms of the U. S. Pub. by Frederic, Akron, O.
Patton, Political Parties of U. S. New Amsterdam.
West, Inheritance Tax. Seligman.
Brann's Iconoclast, v. 1, 2, original vols.

Brentano's, Union Sq., N. Y.

Wages of Sin, Racowitza. G. W. Dillingham Co.
Basket of Flowers. Warne & Co.
Brown Book, 2 v. Pub. by Iconoclast.
Jonathan Slick.
Dick, Christian Beneficence.
O'Shaughnessy, An Epic of Woman. Chatto & Windus.
Captain's Romance. Neely.
Howlett, On Driving.
Adams, Chas. F., Chapters of Erie, and Other Essays.
Ouida, Ariadne.
Black, Jeremiah S., Essays and Speeches. Appleton.
Eastlake, Art Methods.
Burton, Literary Likings. S., M & Co.
Kohl, J. G., Intercourse and Settlements of Human Race as they Depend on Conformation of Earth's Surface. Dresden and Leipzig, 1843.
Any books by J. G. Kohl.
Any geographical books by K. Ritter.
Any geographical books by Cotta.
Vaughan, R., Age of Great Cities. 1843.

Brentano's, 1015 Pennsylvania Ave., Washington, D. C.

Lockwood's Harmony Communities.
Edwards' Coals and Cokes of West Virginia.
Guy Ormsby. Dillingham.

The Brown, Eager & Hull Co., Toledo, O.

Belton's Foreign Quotations.

The Burrows Bros. Co., Cleveland, O.

Morford, Spur of Monmouth.
Saltus, What Dreams May Come.
Williams, Our Iron Trade, 1882.
Taylor, Young Islanders.
Cole, Voyage of Life, engravings.
Trollope, Orley Farm.
Uzanne, French Woman of the Century.
Schreiber, English and Foreign Fans.
Wilson, Life of Chatterton.
Books on Vermont, Ira Allen.
Way, Homer's Iliad, 2 v.

Callaghan & Co., Chicago, Ill.

Am. Law Register, odd v.
Am. Law Review, odd v.
Emory S. Storrs' Life.

Carnegie Library, Pittsburgh, Pa.

Herringshaw, T. W., Poets of America.

Case Library, Cleveland, O.

Poushkin's Poems from the Russian.
Green, Lives of Princesses of England.
Early American eds. of Dickens.

C. N. Caspar Co., 437 E. Water St., Milwaukee, Wis

Munsey's Sept.-Dec., 1892; Jan., Feb., May-Sept., '93.
Abbott, History of Civil War, v. 2.
Atlas to Du Bois Graphic Statistics, or complete work.
Bangs, Our Familiar Songs. Harper.
St. Nicholas, v. 1, nos. 1, 2.
Michaud, History of the Crusades, pts. 14, 18. Barrie.

W. B. Clarke Co., Park and Tremont Sts., Boston, Mass.

Bridge Up to Date, 1st ed., pap.
King of Cuba, or book with principal character so-called.
Sonnets, by George Santayana.
Oregon, by John B. Wyett.
French Humorists from the 12th to the 19th Century, Walter Besant.

Henry T. Coates & Co., Phila., Pa.

My Reminiscences, by Gorver.

Frank W. Coburn, 47 Cornhill, Boston, Mass.

History of Denham, Mass.
History of Alfred, Maine.
History of Shapleigh, Maine.
Hutchinson's Diary, 2 v.
Atlas of Orange Co., Vt.
Selections from Writings of Wm. Crafts.

G. H. Colby & Co., 22 Main St., Lancaster, N. H.

Coon Stories, by Ed. Mathews.
Old Settler Stories, by Ed. Mathews.

The Columbian Book Co., Atlanta, Ga.

O'Hara's Irish Pedigrees.
Gilmore's Georgians.
A Treatise on Beverages, by Chas. H. Suls.

Cong. S. S. and Pub. Soc., 14a Beacon St., Boston.

10 copies Pine Cones, by Willis Boyd Allen, copies to be in good condition.

P. T. Cunningham, 151 Centre St., N. Y.

Buckley's Introd. to Cryptogamic Botany, latest ed.
Work of Isaac Adriance entitled, Conveyances on Record in the Register's Office, by Dudley Selden, from Jan. 1, 1835 to Jan. 1, 1838. Printed by A. S. Gould, 144 Nassau St., N. Y., 1838.

Cushing & Co., 34 W. Baltimore St., Baltimore, Md

Harland, Loitering in Pleasant Paths.
Zeigler, It Was Marlowe.
Forwood, Historical and Descriptive Narrative of the Mammoth Cave, Ky.
Gentle Art of Making Enemies.
Foley, American Authors.

Damrell & Upham, 283 Washington St., Boston, Mass.

Doolittle's Hist. of Belchertown, Mass.
Judd's Hist. of Hadley, Mass.
Barber's Hist. Collections of Mass.

Davis' Book Store, 35 W. 42d St., N. Y.

Froude's History of England, v. 10, 11 only, brown cl. N. Y., Scribner, 1867.
History of Ireland, v. 2, any ed.

DeWolfe, Fiske & Co., 361 Washington St., Boston, Mass.

Life and Works Alexander Hamilton.
Ante-Nicene Fathers, v. 24.

E. F. Dillingham, Bangor, Me.

Hutchinson's History of Mass. Bay Colony, 3 v. Boston, 1764, '67, '69.
Minot's Continuation History Mass. Bay Colony, v. 1. Boston, 1798.
Caleb Snow's History of Boston.
Trial of British Soldiers for Murder of Crispus Attricks, etc., 1770. Boston, 1824.
Peter Edes Diary. Bangor, 1837.
Sullivan's History District of Maine.
Lays of Calderon, tr. by McCarthy.
Bernard Shaw's Irrational Knot.
Bernard Shaw's Socialism.
Anything by Bernard Shaw.
Thomas Hardy's Spectre of the Real.
Atlas to go with Greenleaf's Survey of Maine. 1829.

Dives, Pomeroy & Stewart, Reading, Pa.

Lang, Andrew, Life of J. G. Lockhart.

BOOKS WANTED.—Continued.

Dodd, Mead & Co., 372 Fifth Ave., N. Y.

Lowe, R. W., Bibliographical Account of English Theatrical Literature. Bouton.
American Book Prices Current, 1901, large pap. D., M. & Co.
Paulding, Dutchman's Fireside, any ed.
Des Cars, Pruning Forest and Ornamental Trees. Cupples.
The Book Lover, no. 2.
Cooper, James Fenimore, Precaution, a novel, 2 v., 12mo, Townsend ed., Darley plates. N. Y.
Hardy's Printer's Marks, S. P. & L. P. eds.

Doubleday, Page & Co., 219 5th Ave., N. Y.

Brann, W. C., Writings of (editor of the *Iconoclast*, Waco, Tex.)
Jefferson, v. 5. Washington, 1853.

The H. & W. B. Drew Co., Jacksonville, Fla.

From My Corner.
Hell Up To Date.

Alex. Duncker (H. von Carnap), 178 Fulton St., N. Y [*Cash.*]

Faraday's Chemical Manipulation, 3d ed. 1842.
Journal of Am. Chem. Soc., v. 1 to 12, 20.
Transactions of Am. Soc. of Civ. Engineers, v. 36 to 47.
Zeitschrift f. Angewandte Chemie, any v.
Chemische Berichte, any v.
Iron and Steel Institute, set or early v.
Watt's Dict. of Chemistry, 4 v., Rev. ed., 1894 to '99.
Chemical News, set or earlier v.
Engineering News, 1899 and 1900.
Engineering Record, v. 41.
Journal of the Soc. of Chemical Industry (London), set or odd v.
Silliman's Elements of Chemistry, 2 v., 1831, or v. 1 separate.
Regnault's Elements of Chemistry, 3d ed. 1853.
Any work on Ichtyology.
Any history of Odd Fellows.

Eaton & Mains, 21 Adams Ave. E., Detroit, Mich.

The Atonement in Modern Religious Thought.

Emery, Bird, Thayer Co., Kansas City, Mo.

Life of Victoria, by Oliphant.

G. Engelke, 225 N. Clark St., Chicago, Ill. [*Cash.*]

Harkaway Series.
Household ed. Scott. Ticknor & Fields.
Monastery, v. 2, buckram.
Quentin Durward, 2 v.
Two Drovers, The Laird's Jock, 2 v.

S. B. Fisher, 5 E. Court St., Springfield, Mass. [*Cash.*]

White, Warfare Between Science and Theology.
Supernatural Religion.
Stephens, Travels in Yucatan, v. 2. Harper, 1848.

Free Public Library, Jersey City, N. J.

Smithsonian Miscellaneous Collections, nos, 594, 664, 665, 708, 969, 971, 972.

Funk & Wagnalls Co., 30 Lafayette Pl., N. Y.

Spiritual Guide, by Dr. M. de Molinos.

J. F. Gapfert, 138 Superior St., Cleveland, O.

Sparks from the Anvil, Burritt.
Voice from the Forge, Burritt.
On Uses and Trusts, Sanders.
The Lost Prince, Henson.

Edwin S. Gorham, 4th Ave. and 22d St., N. Y.

Maskell's Ancient Liturgy of Church of England.
Maurice, On the Ten Commandments.
Shuckford's Sacred and Profane History.
Bishop Coxe's Pamphlet in Reply to Pope Pius on the Vatican Council.
Papal Claims. Pott, Young & Co.
All second-hand.

F. E. Grant, 23 W. 42d St., N. Y.

Literature and Philosophy, by Caird (?)
Readiania, Seaside ed., containing letters by Charles Reade on the Violin.
Chess for Beginners and Beginnings of Chess, by R. B. Swinton.
Les Memories de Monsieur d'Artagnan Capitaine Lieutenant de la Premiere Compagnie des Mousquetaries du Roi, by Courtils de Sandraz, tr. by Ralph Nevil. Pub. by H. S. Nichols, Soho Sq., London.

F. E. Grant.—*Continued.*

Charles Wesley Seen in Finer and Less Familiar Poems, by F. M. Bird.
Life of John Wesley, by Tyermann.
Letters of a Parsee Merchant to Horace Greeley. Pub. about 1867.
Introduction to the Study of Browning, by Arthur Symonds.
Sonnets from the Portuguese, by Mrs. Browning.
The Philobiblon, by R. DeBury.
Reynold's Works: Lord Saxondale, Count Christobal, Kenneth the Earl of Glengyle, The Necromancer, Isabella Vincent, Vivian Bertram, Countess of Lascelles, Duke of Marchmont, Child of Waterloo, Massacre of Glencoe, Mary Stewart, Robert Bruce, Life in Paris.
Scouts, Spies and Heroes of the Great Civil War, by Joseph P. Hazelton. Jersey City, 1892.
Secrets of the Late Rebellion, by Dr. Freese. Phila., 1882.
Our Own Arithmetic (Confederate), by S. Lieander. Greensboro, 1863.
Jeremy Taylor's Sermons.
The Art Journal (Virtue), for 1857 and other years.

H. Gregory, Providence, R. I. [*Cash.*]

Hugo's Les Miserables, 5 v., royal 8vo, cl., pap. labels. George Routledge & Sons.
Treasures Old and New, by Alice L. Williams. Belford, Clark & Co.

Walter M. Hill, 31 Washington St., Chicago, Ill.

Life of Marat, by Bax.

Henry C. Heitle, Christopher St. Ferry, N. Y.

Wallace's Monthly, a complete set, single vols. or in single nos.

Humphrey's Book Store, 26 Brattle St., Boston, Mass.

Prenticeana.

L. Indermark, 3211 Barrett St., St. Louis, Mo. [*Cash.*]

Wiley's Agricultural Analysis, v. 3, pts. 2, 3, 4, 6, 7, 12, or entire.
Amer. Jl. of Science (3d ser.), v. 1-36, 1892, '94, '95, '99.
Die Chemische Industrie, 1893, '97, 1901.
Astrophysical Journal, v. 1, 2, 9, 10.

U. P. James, 127 W. 7th St., Cincinnati, O.

Seybert, Report on Spiritualism. Lippincott.

Jennings & Pye, 57 Washington St., Chicago, Ill.

Life of John Wesley, John Whitehead, M.D.
Memoirs of John Wesley, John Hampson.
Wedgewood, Wesley and the Evangelical Reaction of the 18th Century.
Wesley the Man, His Teaching and His Work.

E. T. Jett Book and News Co., 806 Olive St., St. Louis, Mo.

Sunset on the Hebrew Mountains, Macduff.
Wedded by Fate, Georgia Sheldon, cl. ed.

E. W. Johnson, 2 E. 42d St., N. Y.

St. Simon's Memoirs.
Jeffrey's Essays, Eng. ed.
Wyeth's Life Gen. De Forest.

H. R. Johnson, 313 Main St., Springfield, Mass.

Family Prayer Book. Pub. 1842.
Unto the Uttermost, Campbell.

J. Kirkpatrick, 1014 Woodward Ave., Cleveland, O. [*Cash.*]

La Inolente Virginia.
Un Joven Misterioso.
Las Majereres el Vino y el Juego.
Un Marido Infiel.
Translated from French to Spanish by Paul De Kock.

Geo. Kleinteich, 397 Bedford Ave., Brooklyn, N. Y. [*Cash.*]

Reid, A., Present Evolution of Man.
Halpine, Private Miles O'Reilly.
Jukes, Andrew, The Church's Teachings.
Jukes, Andrew, New Man and Eternal Life.

C. W. Kroeck, 911 Pine St., St. Louis, Mo.

The Judaid, by Pierson. St. Louis, 1844.
The Rose, by Henry Shaw.
Secrets of St. Louis, Boernstein.
Tribute to the Memory of Ruth C. Gray.
Poems, by Albert Pike.

BOOKS WANTED.—Continued.

Chas. E. Lauriat Co., 301 Washington St., Boston, Mass.

Audubon's Ornithological Biography, 5 v. 8vo.
Streeter's Pearls and Pearling Life.

Lemcke & Buechner, 812 Broadway, N. Y.

Cicero, Philippic Orations, with notes by King, 2d larges ed.

Library Clearing House, 140 Wells St., Chicago, Ill.

Fishes of Pennsylvania.
Lot cheap cl. or pap. Spanish, Italian, and German fiction.
Dipper's Saturomastix.
Tempelogue ed. Lever, 2d ser. only.

Robert M Lindsay, 1028 Walnut St., Phila., Pa.

Ros Rosarum. Pub. about 1850.
Baker, American Engravers, large-pap. copy, roy. 8vo.
Baker, Engraved Portraits of Washington.
Portraits (framing size) of Edm. Burke, Wm. Shippen, Jr., James Woodhouse, John Redman Coxe, Jas. B. Rogers.

W. H. Lowdermilk & Co., Washington, D. C.

Pennell, Pen Drawing and Pen Draftsmen.
Thompson, Byways and Birdnotes.
Tyson, Queens of the Kitchen.
Boys in Blue.

C. D. Lyon, 20 Monroe St., Grand Rapids, Mich.

Parsons, On Contracts, 3 v.
Modern Eloquence, 10 v.
Flint, Mexico Under Maximilian.

S. F. McLean & Co., 44 E. 23d St., N. Y.

Hansard, Geo. A., The Book of Archery. Lond., 1840. and later.
Outlook, v. 59.
Havard, Hy. (Henri), On Delft.

H. Malkan, Hanover Sq., N. Y.

Century Dictionary, 24 pts.
Bootle's Baby, Winter.
Genealogy of Bergen Family. 1876.
Puritan Age and Rule, Ellis.
Records of New Amsterdam, v. 3, shp.

Isaac Mendoza, 17 Ann St., N. Y.

Thudicum and Dupre, On Wines, etc.
Vizetelly, On Wines, etc.
Viticultural Soc'y (Cal.) pubs.
Standard works relating to Cal. wines.
Bickley's History of Tazewell, Va.
Fleshly School of Poetry, Buchanan.

R. H. Merriam, Hanover Sq., N. Y.

Macaulay's Herodotus, 2 v. Macmillan.
Toyar's Confectionery Receipts.
The Virginian, O. Wister, 1st ed.

Edw. Mills, 807 Chestnut St., St. Louis, Mo.

Private Journal of Aaron Burr, v. 1.
Benton's Thirty Years, v. 2.
Patriotism of Illinois, v. 2.
Lewis and Clark's Travels, v. 2, Harper ed.

F. M. Morris, 171 Madison St., Chicago, Ill.

Forty Lies and Other Liars.

A. J. Ochs & Co., 1781 Washington St., Boston, Mass.

Shepherd, H. E., History of the English Language. Pub. Hale, N. Y., 1874, or later.
Dyer's Life of Jackson. Bonner.

E. J. O'Malley, Hanover Sq., N. Y.

Any N. Y. daily of March 18, 1899.
Life of Samuel J. Tilden.
Macaulay's Speeches.
Auctioneer's Guide, J. P. Johnston.
Index volume to the World's Great Classics.

Martin F. Onnen, 114 5th Ave., N. Y.

Clark, H., An Introduction to Heraldry. Lond., 1829.
Featherman, Social History of the Races of Mankind, 5 v. London, 1883.

Daniel O'Shea, 1584 Broadway, N. Y.

Sleight of Hand, by Edwin Sacks.

The Pafraets Book Co., Cannon Pl., Troy, N. Y.

6 copies Gladden, Practice of Immortality. McClelland & Co., Columbus, O.

The Pilgrim Press, 175 Wabash Ave., Chicago, Ill.

The volume of Bret Harte containing:
"She lunched and lunched until she came to Oregon
And then she crossed the world's backbone and travelled a little farther on
Until she came to Oregon."

Presb. Bd. of Pub. and S. S. Work, 192 Michigan Ave., Chicago, Ill.

Wines, Introductory Essay to Laws of Ancient Hebrews. Presbyterian Board.

Preston & Rounds Co., Providence, R. I.

Guide of Drawing the Acanthus and every Description of Ornamental Foliage, by I. Page. Atchley & Co., London.

C. J. Price, 1004 Walnut St, Phila., Pa.

Taine's Venice and Florence, 8vo, cl. Holt, 1871.
Good Words for 1863, cl. or nos.
Coleridge's Biographia Literaria, 2 v., 12mo, cl., Pickering's ed.

Peter Reilly, 133 N. 13th St., Phila., Pa.

Von Hartman's Philosophy of the Unconscious.
Chinese dictionaries.
Christian Science journals.
Burton's Song of the Sword. 1750.

A. M. Robertson, 126 Post St., San Francisco, Cal.

Pioneer Reminiscences of California, Burnett.

Robson & Adee, Schenectady, N. Y.

Essay on Friendship, Thoreau, Limited ed. Houghton, M. & Co.

Rohde & Haskins, 16 Cortlandt St., N. Y.

Virgil's Æneid, trans. by Dryden. Pub. by Harper.

J. Francis Ruggles, Bronson, Mich.

Wilson's Noctes Ambrosianæ.
Parson Brownlow's Book.
Beal's Bioplasm.

The St. Louis News Co., 1008 Locust St., St. Louis, Mo.

Rufus King, v. 1.

John E. Scopes, 29 Tweddle Bldg., Albany, N. Y.

American Ancestry, v. 9, 10.
Wilkinson, Memoirs, v. 2, and atlas. Phila., 1816.

Scrantom, Wetmore & Co., Rochester, N. Y.

Fiske, Myths and Myth Makers. 1872.
Fiske, Destiny of Man. 1884.
Fiske, Am. Political Ideas. 1885.
Fiske, Crit. Period Am. History. 1888.
Fiske, American Revolution. 1891.
Fiske, Discovery of America. 1892.
Fiske, History U. S. Schools. 1894.
Fiske, Century of Science. 1899.
Fiske, Dutch Colonies (and Quaker.) 1899.

The Shorthand Institute, 8 Beacon St., Boston, Mass.

Trials, Debates, etc., Reported by Thomas Lloyd.
Franklin Institute Journal, v. 104.
Philosophical Trans. (Royal Soc.) for 1748.
Chalmers' British Poets, v. 15. 1810.
Any old work on shorthand.

Frank Simmons, Springfield, Ill.

2 sets Appleton's Universal Encyclopædia, hf. mor.

Wm. H. Smith, Jr., 515 W. 173d St., N. Y.

Habitations of Man, Viollet-le-Duc, trans.
Viollet-le-Duc, various, trans. or not.
Autobiography Robert Owen. London, 1857.

Smith Bros., 12th and Washington Sts., Oakland, Cal.

I Swear, Frank Powers.

Southern Methodist Book Depository, Staunton, Va.

Statesman's Year-Book, 1901.
Appleton's Annual Cyclopædia, 1875, shp., good condition.
Proceedings Society of Psychical Research, 1890.

Frank Stanton, Wheeling, W. Va.

Ohio Valley genealogies. Chas. A. Hanna. Privately printed.
Our Western Border. McKnight, Phila.
Life of Lewis Witzel, Myers. Phila.

G. E. Stechert, 9 E. 16th St., N. Y.

Hunt, Past and Present Sandwich Islands. '53.
Whitney, Hawaiian Guide Book. 1875.
Hardy, W., Cuban Expedition. Cinn., 1850.
Jarvis, Scenes, etc., in the Sandwich Islands.
Madeira, Annals of Music in Phila.

BOOKS WANTED.—*Continued.*

E. Steiger & Co., 25 Park Place, N. Y. [*Cash.*]

Crosswell, Collection of Patent Cases.
Whitham, Constructive Steam Engineering.

The Stiefel Masonic Book Co., 106 E. 4th St., Cincinnati, O.

Findel, History of Freemasonry.
Gould's Military Lodges.
Catalogues from second-hand booksellers.

Stout's Book Exchange, 812 5th St., San Diego, Cal.

Life of Lewis Wetzel.
Life of Grizzly Adams.
Geological Survey California.

Strawbridge & Clothier, Market St., Phila., Pa.

Warner's Library, v. 10, red cl.

H. H. Timby, Conneaut, O.

Reade, Martyrdom of Man.
Oswald, The Secret of the East.
Why Priests Should Wed.

United Presb. Bd. of Pub., Pittsburgh, Pa.

Wilson's Dictionary of the Ojibway Language.
Wilson's Ojibway Grammar.
Moore's Life of Sheridan.

John Wanamaker, N. Y.

Decorative Illustration, by Walter Crane. Macmillan.

Geo. E. Warner, Minneapolis, Minn.

Cobb, N. B., Poetical Geography of North Carolina.
Elijah Coffin, Life of, by Son.
Any county atlas or biography.

BOOKS FOR SALE.

S. B. Fisher, 4 E. Court St., Springfield, Mass.

Complete sets magazines: *Bay State*, 6 v.; *Bookman* 14 v.; *Century*, 41 v.; *Galaxy*, 24 v.; *Good Housekeeping*, 33 v.; *Harper's*, 103 v.; *New England*, 25 v.; *Review of Reviews*, 24 v.; *Scribner's Monthly*, 22 v.; *Scribner's Mag.*, mostly in nos.; *St. Nicholas*, 28 v. Make offer.

Nillis Johnson & Co., 289 W. 14th St., Chicago, Ill.

100 Avery's School Physics. New, 30 % off; second-hand, 60 % off.
100 Shaw's Outlines of Literature. New, 30 % off; second-hand, 60 % off.
100 Hill's Foundation of Rhetoric. New, 30 % off; second-hand, two-thirds off.
50 Harkness' First Year in Latin. New, 30 % off; second-hand, two-thirds off.
50 Appleton's School Physics. Two-thirds off.
50 each Sanford's Arithmetics. Two-thirds off.
25 Fisher and Schwatt, Text-Book of Algebra, pt. 1. Two-thirds off.
25 Kellogg's Rhetoric, New ed., fresh. 50 % off.
50 Harper's Sixth Readers. Two-thirds off.
50 Tarbell's Less. in Language, pt. 1. Two-thirds off.
500 Rand, McNally's Gram. School Geog. 30 cts. each.
500 Rand, McNally's Primary Geog. 15 cts. each.

Wm. H. Smith, Jr., 515 W. 173d St., N. Y.

English Catalogue, 1835-1862.
Roorbach's Bibliotheca Americana, 1820-1858.
Am. Book Prices Current, complete set.
Warne's Library, 45 v., Ed. de luxe.
Poor's Manuals, odd v.

HELP WANTED.

WANTED.—Sept. 1st or sooner, experienced book and stationery clerk at Tampa, Fla. Give age, reference, married or single and salary expected. Address G., care of PUBLISHERS' WEEKLY.

SITUATIONS WANTED.

BOOKKEEPER, accountant and office manager. 20 years' experience, wholesale and manufacturing, desires position. Can adapt to any system or conditions. Excellent references. Salary no object so long as prospects are good. Address WILLSTAN, care of PUBLISHERS' WEEKLY.

BUSINESS FOR SALE.

FOR SALE.—Book and Stationery business in Fla. town of 25,000; net profit over 50 %; last year's sales, $17,812.00. Good reason for selling. Address W. E. C., 176 Court St., Kankakee, Ill.

COPYRIGHT NOTICES.

LIBRARY OF CONGRESS,
OFFICE OF THE REGISTER OF COPYRIGHTS,
WASHINGTON, D. C.

To wit: *Be it remembered*, That on the 2d day of July, 1902, D. B. Ivison, of United States, hath deposited in this office the title of a book, the title of which is in the following words, to wit: "Robinson's Mathematical Series. The Junior Class Arithmetic. Oral and Written. Designed for Graded Schools. By Daniel W. Fish, A.M. New York, Cincinnati, Chicago, American Book Company," the right whereof he claims as proprietor in conformity with the laws of the United States respecting copyrights.

(Signed) HERBERT PUTNAM, *Librarian of Congress.*
By THORVALD SOLBERG, *Register of Copyrights.*
In renewal for 14 years from December 7, 1902.

LIBRARY OF CONGRESS,
OFFICE OF THE REGISTER OF COPYRIGHTS,
WASHINGTON, D. C.

To wit: *Be it remembered*, That on the 2d day of July, 1902, D. B. Ivison, of United States, hath deposited in this office the title of a book, the title of which is in the following words, to wit: "Robinson's Shorter Course. Complete Arithmetic. Oral and Written. First Part. By Daniel W. Fish, A.M. New York, Cincinnati, Chicago, American Book Company," the right whereof he claims as proprietor in conformity with the laws of the United States respecting copyrights.

(Signed) HERBERT PUTNAM, *Librarian of Congress.*
By THORVALD SOLBERG, *Register of Copyrights.*
In renewal for 14 years from December 7, 1902.

LIBRARY OF CONGRESS,
OFFICE OF THE REGISTER OF COPYRIGHTS,
WASHINGTON, D. C.

To wit: *Be it remembered*, That on the 2d day of July, 1902, D. B. Ivison, of United States, hath deposited in this office the title of a book, the title of which is in the following words, to wit: "Robinson's Shorter Course. The Complete Arithmetic. Oral and Written. Second Part. By Daniel W. Fish, A.M. New York, Cincinnati, Chicago, American Book Company," the right whereof he claims as proprietor in conformity with the laws of the United States respecting copyrights.

(Signed) HERBERT PUTNAM, *Librarian of Congress.*
By THORVALD SOLBERG, *Register of Copyrights.*
In renewal for 14 years from December 7, 1902.

LIBRARY OF CONGRESS,
OFFICE OF THE REGISTER OF COPYRIGHTS,
WASHINGTON, D. C.

To wit: *Be it remembered*, That on the 2d day of July, 1902, D. B. Ivison, of United States, hath deposited in this office the title of a book, the title of which is in the following words, to wit: "Robinson's Shorter Course. Key to the Complete Arithmetic. For Teachers and Private Learners. New York, Cincinnati, Chicago, American Book Company," the right whereof he claims as proprietor in conformity with the laws of the United States respecting copyrights.

(Signed) HERBERT PUTNAM, *Librarian of Congress.*
By THORVALD SOLBERG, *Register of Copyrights.*
In renewal for 14 years from December 7, 1902.

LIBRARY OF CONGRESS,
OFFICE OF THE REGISTER OF COPYRIGHTS,
WASHINGTON, D. C.

To wit: *Be it remembered*, That on the 2d day of July, 1902, Emma H. Watson, of United States, hath deposited in this office the title of a book, the title of which is in the following words, to wit: "Independent Youth's Speller. Printed in imitation of Writing with original classification of words, formations of columns, dictation exercises, orthographical and orthoepical treatise, appendix, etc. By J. Madison Watson. New York, Cincinnati, Chicago, American Book Company," the right whereof she claims as proprietor in conformity with the laws of the United States respecting copyrights.

(Signed) HERBERT PUTNAM, *Librarian of Congress.*
By THORVALD SOLBERG, *Register of Copyrights.*
In renewal for 14 years from October 17, 1902.

LIBRARY OF CONGRESS,
OFFICE OF THE REGISTER OF COPYRIGHTS,
WASHINGTON, D. C.

To wit: *Be it remembered*, That on the 3d day of July, 1902, Guy D. Peck, of Gallia, N. J., hath deposited in this office the title of a book, the title of which is in the following words, to wit: "First

COPYRIGHT NOTICES.—Continued.

Lessons in Numbers. By William G. Peck, Ph.D., LL.D. New York, Cincinnati, Chicago, American Book Company," the right whereof he claims as proprietor in conformity with the laws of the United States respecting copyrights.
(Signed) HERBERT PUTNAM, *Librarian of Congress.*
By THORVALD SOLBERG, *Register of Copyrights.*
In renewal for 14 years from December 29, 1902.

LIBRARY OF CONGRESS,
OFFICE OF THE REGISTER OF COPYRIGHTS,
WASHINGTON, D. C.

To wit: *Be it remembered,* That on the 2d day of July, 1902, Lyman P. Spencer, of United States, hath deposited in this office the title of a book, the title of which is in the following words, to wit: "Theory of Spencerian Penmanship. For schools and private learners, developed by questions and answers, with practical illustrations. Designed to be studied by pupils in connection with the use of the Spencerian Copy-Books. By The 'Spencerian Authors.' New York, Cincinnati, Chicago, American Book Company," the right whereof he claims as author and proprietor in conformity with the laws of the United States respecting copyrights.
(Signed) HERBERT PUTNAM, *Librarian of Congress.*
By THORVALD SOLBERG, *Register of Copyrights.*
In renewal for 14 years from December 29, 1902.

LIBRARY OF CONGRESS,
OFFICE OF THE REGISTER OF COPYRIGHTS,
WASHINGTON, D. C.

Class A, XXc, No. 35699.—To wit: *Be it remembered,* That on the 18th day of June, 1902, John Foster Kirk, of Philadelphia, Pa., hath deposited in this office the title of a book, the title of which is in the following words, to wit: "The History of the Reign of the Emperor Charles the Fifth. By William Robertson, D.D. With an Account of the Emperor's Life after His Abdication. By William H. Prescott. New Edition. Volume I. Philadelphia, J. B. Lippincott Company," the right whereof he claims as proprietor in conformity with the laws of the United States respecting copyrights.
(Signed) HERBERT PUTNAM, *Librarian of Congress.*
By THORVALD SOLBERG, *Register of Copyrights.*
In renewal for 14 years from December 11, 1902.

LIBRARY OF CONGRESS,
OFFICE OF THE REGISTER OF COPYRIGHTS,
WASHINGTON, D. C.

Class A, XXc, No. 35700.—To wit: *Be it remembered,* That on the 18th day of June, 1902, John Foster Kirk, of Philadelphia, Pa., hath deposited in this office the title of a book, the title of which is in the following words, to wit: "The History of the Reign of the Emperor Charles the Fifth. By William Robertson, D.D. With an Account of the Emperor's Life after His Abdication. By William H. Prescott. New Edition. Volume II. Philadelphia, J. B. Lippincott Company," the right whereof he claims as proprietor in conformity with the laws of the United States respecting copyrights.
(Signed) HERBERT PUTNAM, *Librarian of Congress.*
By THORVALD SOLBERG, *Register of Copyrights.*
In renewal for 14 years from December 11, 1902.

LIBRARY OF CONGRESS,
OFFICE OF THE REGISTER OF COPYRIGHTS,
WASHINGTON, D. C.

Class A, XXc, No. 35701.—To wit: *Be it remembered,* That on the 18th day of June, 1902, John Foster Kirk, of Philadelphia, Pa., hath deposited in this office the title of a book, the title of which is in the following words, to wit: "The History of the Reign of the Emperor Charles the Fifth. By William Robertson, D.D. With an Account of the Emperor's Life after His Abdication. By William H. Prescott. New Edition. Volume III. Philadelphia, J. B. Lippincott Company," the right whereof he claims as proprietor in conformity with the laws of the United States respecting copyrights.
(Signed) HERBERT PUTNAM, *Librarian of Congress.*
By THORVALD SOLBERG, *Register of Copyrights.*
In renewal for 14 years from December 11, 1902.

LIBRARY OF CONGRESS,
OFFICE OF THE REGISTER OF COPYRIGHTS,
WASHINGTON, D. C.

Class A, XXc, No. 31662.—To wit: *Be it remembered,* That on the 26th day of April, 1902, Laura Abbott Buck, of New York, N. Y., hath deposited in this office the title of a book, the title of which is in the following words, to wit: "Captain William Kidd and others of the Buccaneers. By John S. C. Abbott. New York, Dodd, Mead & Company," the right whereof she claims as proprietor in conformity with the laws of the United States respecting copyrights.
(Signed) HERBERT PUTNAM, *Librarian of Congress.*
By THORVALD SOLBERG, *Register of Copyrights.*
In renewal for 14 years from October 8, 1902.

SPECIAL NOTICES.

NOW READY

The Smaller Size of the

American Standard Edition of the

REVISED BIBLE

with carefully selected references and topical headings prepared by the American Revision Committee, whose attestation appears on the back of the title page.

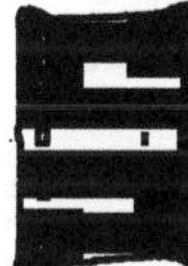

The Biblical World says:

"The American Standard Edition of the Revised Bible is by far and in every respect the best English translation of the Bible in existence, both for scholars and for people."

Bourgeois 8vo. Prices from $1.00 Upward

THOMAS NELSON & SONS, Publishers, 37-41 East 18th St., New York

---

Subscribers to the

Publishers' Trade List Annual for 1902

may be interested to know that the Catalogues volume will be ready about August 18. This volume contains the lists of 250 publishers, approximating 7000 pages. The price of this volume with an Index, in cloth binding, is $5, and without the Index $1.50, if subscribed and paid for before date of publication. After that the prices will be raised to $7 for the indexed volume, and $2 for the unindexed Catalogues volume.

The Index volume is expected to be ready about September 15. It will contain upwards of 140,000 references to books in print, by author, title, and subject catch-word.

The edition is printed from type and is limited to 1750 copies.

Address

THE OFFICE OF THE PUBLISHERS' WEEKLY,

298 BROADWAY, NEW YORK.

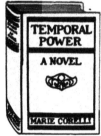

THE

Publishers' Weekly

THE AMERICAN

BOOK TRADE JOURNAL

WITH WHICH IS INCORPORATED

The American Literary Gazette and Publishers' Circular.

[ESTABLISHED 1852.]

PUBLICATION OFFICE, 298 BROADWAY, NEW YORK.

Entered at the Post-Office at New York, N. Y., as second-class matter.

VOL. LXII., No. 8. NEW YORK, August 23, 1902. WHOLE No. 1595

PAGE'S IMPORTANT FALL PUBLICATIONS

FOUR NOTABLE NOVELS

Ready August 25th

THE LAST WORD

By ALICE MacGOWAN

$1.50

An intense love story—the story of a woman's heart—and such a story of the heart as has not made its appearance since the days of "Jane Eyre." The sort of book which one friend hands to another with the recommendation, "You never read anything like it—because there never was anything like it before."

COUNCILS of CROESUS

By MARY KNIGHT POTTER

Author of "Love in Art," etc.

$1.25

The latest number in the "Commonwealth Series" vivaciously pictures life in wealthy and fashionable New York society. The author is already favorably known for her clever magazine work, and the readers of the amusing "Boston Experiences" and the entertaining "Russells in Chicago" will follow with interest the fortunes of the charming heroine of "The Councils of Croesus."

Ready September 15th

BARBARA LADD

By CHARLES G. D. ROBERTS

Author of "The Kindred of the Wild," "The Heart of the Ancient Wood," etc.

Illustrated in tints by FRANK VER BECK

$1.50

A story of the Revolution and the days that ushered it; yet the war theme is subordinate to the love story and the wayward, winsome heroine, fair Mistress Barbara, whose passion for nature recalls to the mind the enchanting Miranda in "The Heart of the Ancient Wood."

HOPE LORING

By LILIAN BELL

Author of "Abroad with the Jimmies," "The Expatriates," etc.

Illustrated by FRANK T. MERRILL

$1.50

Hope Loring—wilful, unconventional, lovable—is perhaps the most charming character ever drawn by Miss Bell. The love theme is beautifully developed, and the minor characters and episodes are drawn with convincing ability.

THE LEADING JUVENILE OF THE YEAR

Ready August 25th

BEAUTIFUL JOE'S PARADISE or, The Island of Brotherly Love

A Sequel to "Beautiful Joe"

By MARSHALL SAUNDERS, author of "Beautiful Joe," "'Tilda Jane," etc.

Illustrated by CHARLES LIVINGSTON BULL

$1.20 net. Postage extra

One of the most original books for children of all growths that has appeared for years; bubbling over with spirits and the gayest, most fantastic humor, appealing to every lover of animals, it is a tale so genuine, so touching in its quality, that tears are almost ready to follow in the wake of laughter as one reads.

ORDER THROUGH YOUR JOBBER OR FROM THE PUBLISHERS

L. C. PAGE & COMPANY, Boston

THE SPENDERS

15TH THOUSAND

By HARRY LEON WILSON. Six Illustrations by O'NEILL LATHAM. Price, $1.50

LOUISVILLE COURIER-JOURNAL SAYS:

"If there is such a thing as the American novel of a new method, this is one. Absolutely to be enjoyed is it from the first page to the last, founded on the elemental truth that 'the man is strongest who, Antæan-like, stands with his feet upon the earth.' It is a good, stirring novel."

DOROTHY SOUTH

27TH THOUSAND

By GEORGE CARY EGGLESTON, Author of "A CAROLINA CAVALIER." Six Illustrations by C. D. WILLIAMS. Price, $1.50

BOOK NEWS FOR MAY SAYS:

"In 'Dorothy South' Mr. Eggleston has created a simple and beautiful romance, full of nobility and of all the finer emotions, wholesome, joyous, graceful, with just a slight scattering of sage but smiling philosophy intercepted by touches here and there of sparkling wit. None such woman character as Dorothy has appeared in fiction for many a long day."

JEZEBEL

A ROMANCE IN THE DAYS WHEN AHAB WAS KING. *By* LAFAYETTE McLAWS, author of "When the Land was Young." Illustrated by CORWIN K. LINSON. Price, $1.50

LOUISVILLE COURIER-JOURNAL SAYS:

"Jezebel is a woman of steel, true to her faith, brave as a lioness, vulnerable in only one place, her surpassing love for her husband. To give him the vineyards he desires, she has stoned to death the old Jew, Naboth, and his two sons. This makes one of the most interesting and pathetic pictures in the book."

JUDITH'S GARDEN

By MARY E. STONE BASSETT. Illustrations in Four Colors by GEORGE WRIGHT. Price, $1.50

BROOKLYN DAILY EAGLE SAYS:

"It is a beautiful, idyllic story, this romance of 'Judith's Garden,' fascinating to one who loves the smell of earth, and who finds Mother Nature and her children the most satisfying of friends."

CHANTICLEER

By VIOLETTE HALL. Eight Three-color Illustrations. Three *by* W. GRANVILLE SMITH. Price, $1.50

This is an idyll of modern life. Roger and Mary, happily mated, lose by fire their house with its belongings. They create a simple but adequate camping-place in the rural solitude. A love story of charming sweetness develops. The book will appeal to lovers of nature, and also to all men and women who like a good romance.

THIS should prove the popular novel of the season

The Author's Longest Completest and Most Ambitious Novel

Beautifully Illustrated by WALTER APPLETON CLARK

HE chief part of the novel deals with the career of an artist in New York, and so gives Mr. Smith the opportunity to picture the artistic and literary life of New York during the last thirty-five years, with the atmosphere and environment of which he has been so thoroughly familiar. To the telling of the story he brings the powers of humor and pathos that he has shown in his other well-known novels.

$1.50

CHARLES SCRIBNER'S SONS, New York

The Publishers' Weekly.

AUGUST 23, 1902.

INDEX TO ADVERTISERS

NOTES IN SEASON.

D. APPLETON & Co. have just ready "An Elementary Commercial Geography," by Cyrus K. Adams, giving particular emphasis to improved transportation, the application of steam power, and the progress in chemical science as the main factors in the present development of progress and industry.

CHARLES SCRIBNER'S SONS are bringing out F. Hopkinson Smith's "The Fortunes of Oliver Horn," which has had such great success in its serial career. The chief part of the book deals with the career of an artist in New York, and this gives the artist-author the opportunity to picture the artistic and literary side of New York which he knows so well. Humor, pathos and a great knowledge of human nature are Mr. Smith's well-known gifts. The book is illustrated by Walter Appleton Clark.

LOTHROP PUBLISHING CO. announce two striking new novels in "Richard Gordon," a story of New York social and political life, by Alexander Black; and "Eagle Blood," by James Creelman, the veteran journalist, who tells the story of a young Englishman who becomes a journalist in the United States and later a war correspondent in the Philippines, and is involved in a chain of stirring adventures. It is stated that H. L. Wilson's novel, "The Spenders," published by this house in June, is now in its twentieth thousand.

L. C. PAGE & CO. will publish on August 25 "The Last Word," by Alice McGowan, the story of a woman's heart which challenges comparison with "Jane Eyre;" "Councils of Croesus," by Mary Knight Potter, a novel of fashionable New York society; "Barbara Ladd," by Charles G. D. Roberts, a story of the days of the Revolution; and "Hope Loring," by Lilian Bell, the story of a wilful, unconventional, lovable heroine. On the same day they will issue their leading juvenile for the coming holiday season, the sequel of "Beautiful Joe," by Marshall Saunders, which is entitled "Beautiful Joe's Paradise," and is said to bubble over with gay spirits and fantastic humor that will appeal especially to all lovers of animals. Dickens's "Child's Dream of a Star" takes its place in the *Cosy Corner Series;* and *The Little Cousin Series* for 1902 will instruct young minds about the Filipinos, the Cubans, the Eskimos, the Porto Ricans and African young people.

THE SAALFIELD PUBLISHING COMPANY have entered the autumn field with a captivating array of new juveniles. These include "Billy Whiskers," by Frances T. Montgomery, telling the amusing adventures of a pet goat; "A Redman of Quality," a stirring tale of Indian adventure, by Edward Everett Billings; "Animal Life in Rhyme and Jingles," by Elizabeth May; "The Mother Goose Paint Book," a novel painting book, with ready-to-use paint box attached; "The Little Woman in the Spout," by Mary Agnes Byrne, who writes of school-girl days; and "In a Car of Gold," an Alice-in-Wonderland tale of a trip to Mars. Other new juveniles include a variety of titles, by Harry Castlemon, Charles P. Chipman, Mary E. Ireland, Mary Denison and others. This house has a number of striking books for grown readers. There is Murat Halstead's "Life of Theodore Roosevelt," fully illustrated and brought closely up to date; and recent novels include Maurus Jokai's volume of weird tales; "Told by the Death's Head;" "Poco a Poco," William Franklin Johnson's novel of American Life; "In the Days of St. Clair," a romance of pioneer Ohio, by Dr. James Ball Naylor; and "The Invisibles," a romance by E. Earl Christopher. "Seeds of April's Sowing" is a little volume of verse by Adah Louise Sutton.

WEEKLY RECORD OF NEW PUBLICATIONS.

☞ Beginning with the issue of July 5, 1902, the titles of *net* books published under the rules of the American Publishers' Association are preceded by a double asterisk **, and the word net follows the price. The titles of *fiction* (not net) published under the rules are preceded by a dagger †. *Net* books not covered by the rules, whether published by members of the American Publishers' Association or not, are preceded by a single asterisk, and the word net follows the price. ☜

The abbreviations are usually self-explanatory. c. after the date indicates that the book is copyrighted; if the copyright date differs from the imprint date, the year of copyright is added. Books of foreign origin of which the edition (annotated, illustrated, etc.) is entered as copyright, are marked c. ed.; translations, c. tr.; n. p., in place of price, indicates that the publisher makes no price, either net or retail, and quotes prices to the trade only upon application.

A colon after initial designates the most usual given name, as: A: Augustus; B: Benjamin; C: Charles; D: David; E: Edward; F: Frederic; G: George; H: Henry; I: Isaac; J: John; L: Louis; N: Nicholas; P: Peter; R: Richard; S: Samuel; T: Thomas; W: William.

Sizes are designated as follows: F. (folio: over 30 centimeters high); Q. (4to: under 30 cm.); O. (8vo: 25 cm.); D. (12mo: 20 cm.); S. (16mo: 17½ cm.); T. (24mo: 15 cm.); Tt. (32mo: 12½ cm.); Fe. 48mo: 10 cm.). Sq., obl., nar., designate square, oblong, narrow books of these heights.

Adams, Cyrus Cornelius, *ed.* An elementary commercial geography. N. Y., Appleton, 1902. [Jl.] c. 12+351 p. il. maps, D. cl., $1.10.
The approval given to the author's "Text-book of commercial geography" has encouraged the preparation of this smaller book, which, it is hoped, will meet the needs of a large number of students who complete their school drill in the grammar grades. The author has attempted to give, simply and broadly, a view of the world in its relation to man as a producer and a trader. The natural laws of trade are made easily understandable.

American educational catalogue for 1902. N. Y., Office of The Publishers' Weekly, 1902. O. leatherette, 50 c.

Ames, Azel. Elementary hygiene for the tropics. Bost., Heath, 1902. c. 180 p. il. 16°, cl., 60 c.

Atkinson, E: The cost of war and warfare from 1898 to 1902, inclusive; seven hundred million dollars, [$700,000,000;] statement compiled, computed and proved from the official reports of the Government. Bost., E: Atkinson, 1902. 19 p. Q. pap., 6 c.

***Baedeker**, Karl. London and its environs: a handbook. New 13th rev. ed. N. Y., Scribner, [imported,] 1902. 454+44 p. 12°, cl., $1.80 net.

Banister, H: C. Musical analysis: a handbook for students; with musical examples. N. Y., Scribner, [imported,] 1902. 81 p. 12°, cl., 75 c.

Bible. New Testament. The self-pronouncing New Testament of our Lord and Saviour Jesus Christ; tr. out of the original Greek, and with the former translations diligently compared and revised. [Holman ed.] Phil., A. J. Holman & Co., [1902.] c. 1+261 p. 32°, mor., 50 c.

†**Boothby**, Guy. A cabinet secret. Phil., Lippincott, 1902. c. 1900. 5-329 p. D. (Lippincott's select novels.) cl., $1; pap., 50 c.
See note, "Weekly Record," March 9, 1901, [1915.]

Budge, Ernest Alfred Wallis. History of Egypt from the end of the Neolithic period to the death of Cleopatra, VII. B.C., 30. v. 1, Egypt in the Neolithic and archaic periods. [N. Y., Oxford Univ. Press,] (Amer. Branch,) 1902. 24+222 p. D. (Books on Egypt and Chaldea.) cl., $1.25.
The present volume is the first of a group of volumes dealing with the history of Egypt, which will be published at frequent intervals in the series of "Books on Egypt and Chaldea." The narrative begins with an account of Egypt and her people in the latter part of the Neolithic period, and ends with the description of her conquest by the Romans under Cæsar Octavinus B.C. 30.

***Cadness**, H: Decorative brush-work and elementary design: a manual for the use of teachers and students in elementary, secondary and technical schools. N. Y., Scribner, [imported,] 1902. 9+174 p. il. pls. 12°, cl., $1.40 net.

Carleton, R. W. Will-o'-the-wisp: a romance of the Mississippi. Chic., Scroll Publishing Co., 1901. c. 206 p. il. 16°, cl., $1.25.

Carter, W: Harding. Horses, saddles and bridles. 2d ed. Balt., Md., Lord Baltimore Press, 1902. c. 10+422 p. il. pl. 12°, cl., $2.75.

Catholic yearbook of New England for 1902; ed. and comp. by John Francis Marrin. [7th year.] Bost., J. K. Waters Co., 1902. c. O. pap., 25 c.

***Chamberlain**, Basil Hall. Things Japanese: being notes on various subjects connected with Japan for the use of travellers and others. New rev., enl. 4th ed. N. Y., Scribner, [imported,] 1902. 6+545 p. 8°, cl., $4 net.

****Clark**, H. H. The admiral's aid: a story of life in the new navy; il. by I. B. Hazelton. Bost., Lothrop Pub. Co., [1902.] [Jl.] c. 4-412 p. D. cl., $1 net.
Chaplain Clark's previous stories "Boy life in the United States navy" and "Naval cadet Bentley" dealt with the old navy. The present story is devoted to an account of the progress and development of the new navy. This is done through the career of a youth, David Stockton, from his entrance to the naval academy till he becomes an officer in active service.

***Dalman**, Gustav. The words of Jesus, considered in the light of post-Biblical Jewish writings and the Aramaic language: authorized English version, by D. M. Kay. N. Y., Scribner, [imported,] 1902. 14+344 p. 8°, cl., $2.50 net.

Davis, *Rev.* H: Turner. Coals from the altar. Cin., [Mrs. M. W. Knapp.] Office of "God's Revivalist," 1902. c. 179 p. D. cl., 75 c.; pap., 20 c.

***Delitzsch**, Friedrich. Babel and the Bible: a lecture on the significance of Assyriological research for religion, delivered before the German emperor; from the German by T: J. McCormack. Chic., Open Court Pub. Co., 1902. c. 2+66 p. il. O. bds., 50 c. net.

†**Dickens**, C: A child's dream of a star and the child's story. Bost., L. C. Page & Co., 1903, [1902.] c. 8-51 p. D. (Cosy corner ser.) cl., 50 c.

****Dickens**, C: The story of little Nell from "The old curiosity shop" of C: Dickens; il. by Etheldred B. Barry. Bost., Dana Estes & Co., [1902.] c. 5+160 p. 12°, (Famous children of literature ser.) cl., 75 c. net.

****Eliot**, C: W: Charles Eliot, landscape architect, a lover of nature and of his kind, who trained himself for a new profession, practiced it happily and through it wrought much good. Bost., Houghton, Mifflin & Co., 1902. c. 24+770 p. il. pl. por. maps, (partly fold.,) plans, facsim., 8°, cl., $3.50 net.

Grenell, Judson. Economic tangles; industrial problems explained through lessons drawn from passing events. Chic., Purdy Pub. Co., [1902.] c. 220 p. D. cl., $1.
Contents: Struggle the law of progress; Improvement in industrial conditions; The world's tribute to monopoly; Increasing the length of the work day a bad economic move; Trusts and labor organizations; The modern way of conducting a strike; Guilds of the Middle Ages; Arbitration and the industrial situation; Immigration; The regulator of wages; Half a loaf vs. no bread; The woman reporter and the dinner pail brigade; Progress of socialism; Who pays the taxes?; Newspapers, the public and the single tax.

Hagen, Hugo von. Reading character from handwriting: a hand-book of graphology for experts, students and laymen. N. Y., [Graphology Pub. Co.,] [1902.] c. 3+189 p. por. O. cl., $1.
Explains the theory of reading character from handwriting; the explanations are fully illustrated by facsimiles of handwriting, etc.

Hale, E: Everett, *jr.*, *ed.* English essays. N. Y. and Chic., Globe School Book Co., [1902.] c. 14+240 p. 16°, (Hawthorne classics.) cl., 40 c.

***Hall**, Hubert. Society in the Elizabethan age. 3d ed. N. Y., Dutton, 1902. 805 p. 8°, cl., $2.50 net.

Hall, J: Lesslie, (*tr.*) Judith, Phœnix, and other Anglo-Saxon poems; tr. from the Grein-Wülker text. N. Y., Silver, Burdett & Co, [1902.] 9+119 p. 12°, cl., 75 c.

†**Hall**, Violette. Chanticleer: a pastoral romance; il. by W. Granville Smith. Bost., Lothrop Pub. Co., [1902.] [Jl.] c. 4-304 p. D. cl., $1.50.
An idyll of modern life. Roger and Mary, happily mated, lose by fire their house with its belongings. They are artists by temperament, though Roger's ostensible vocation is literature; and they determine to get away from their accustomed life, with its exactions and its cares, and go back to nature. They create a simple but adequate abode in the rural solitude. Embraces fine descriptions of nature.

***Hamilton**, *Count* Anthony. Memoirs of Count Grammont; ed., with notes, by Sir Walter Scott; eleven etchings by L. Boisson after original designs by C. Delort. New cheaper ed. N. Y., Scribner, [imported,] 1902. 36+396 p. 8°, cl., $3 net.

†**Harrison**, *Mrs.* Ma. Kingsley, ["Lucas Malet," *pseud.*] A counsel of perfection. New ed. N. Y., Appleton, 1902. 12°, cl., $1.

Henley, Micajah. Divine healing. Cin., O., Mrs. M. W. Knapp, Office of "God's Revivalist," [1902.] 3-118 p. D. (Pentecostal holiness lib., v. 5, no. 8.) pap., 10 c.; cl., 75 c.
A biblical exegesis of the subject.

Higginson, H: Lee. Four addresses: The soldier's field; The Harvard union I.; The Harvard union II.; Robert Gould Shaw. Bost., D. B. Updike, [Merrymount Press,] 1902. c. 3+106+2 p. por. D. bds., 75 c.; Japan ed., $5.

Hoadley, G: A. Teachers' manual to accompany "A brief course in physics." N. Y., Amer. Book Co., 1902. [Ag8.] c. 32 p. D. pap., 25 c.

Hocking, Silas Kitto. The awakening of Anthony Weir; il. by Harold Copping. Phil., Union Press, 1902. 5+431 p. D. cl., $1.50.
Anthony Weir was the popular pastor of a wealthy city church. He was ambitious of social success, and schemed to marry a rich girl. His schemes are met with counter schemes, culminating in a mysterious and dastardly plot that nearly proved his undoing. His tribulations awaken him to the true meaning of life and its opportunities.

***Holborn**, Alfred. The Pentateuch in the light of to-day: being a simple introduction to the Pentateuch on the lines of the higher criticism. N. Y., Scribner, [imported,] 1902. 8+113 p. 12°, cl., 75 c. net.

****Hopkins**, W: J. The sandman: his farm stories; il. by Ada Clendenin Williamson. Bost., L. C. Page & Co., 1903, [1902.] [Ag.] c. 4-217 p. il. O. cl., $1.20 net.
Simple and instructive stories, told at bed time to a little boy of six years, about a farm and its many attractive features.

Hutchison, Jos. Chrisman. A treatise on physiology and hygiene, for educational institutions and general readers. New ed. N. Y., Maynard, Merrill & Co., 1902. c. 388 p. il. col. pl. 12°, cl., $1.

***Hutton**, R. E: Studies in the lives of the saints. N. Y., Dutton, 1902. 157 p. 12°, cl., $1.25 net.

***Jekyll**, Gertrude, *and* Mawley, E:, *comps.* Roses for English gardens. N. Y., Scribner, [imported,] 1902. 16+166 p. 8°, cl., $3.75 net.

Keats, J: The eve of St. Agnes, and other poems; ed., with introd. and notes, by Katharine Lee Bates. N. Y., Silver, Burdett & Co., [1902.] c. 157 p. por. 16°, (Silver ser. of classics.) cl., 40 c.

***Keeling**, Elsa d' Esterre. Sir Joshua Reynolds, P.R.A. N. Y., Scribner, [imported,] 1902. 12+232 p. por. sq. 8°, (Makers of British art; ed. by Ja. Manson.) cl., $1.25 net.

***Lanier**, *Rev.* J. J. Kinship of God and man. In 2 v. v. 2, The master key. N. Y., T. Whittaker, 1902. c. 8+284 p. D. cl., $1 net.

Leo XIII., [Gioacchino Pecci,] *Pope.* Poems, charades, inscriptions of Pope Leo XIII., including the revised compositions of his early life in chronological order; with English tr. and notes by H. T. Henry. N. Y.

and Phil., American Ecclesiastical Review, 1902. c. 2+5-321 p. D. bds., $1.50.
Latin and English on opposite pages. The Ludicra and carmen "A Monsignor Orfei" are in Italian.

McCutcheon, G: Barr. Castle Craneycrow. Chic., H. S. Stone & Co., 1902. [Ag15.] c. 2+391 p. D. cl., $1.50.
The author of "Graustark" presents another novel of adventure, with the scene in Europe. The efforts of a rich, handsome American to prove that a fascinating Italian nobleman, engaged to the playmate of his youth, is a criminal and altogether unworthy of her, is the story. Many exciting episodes and original detective work make up the narrative.

***McKernan**, Ja. Forty-five sermons written to meet objections of the present day. N. Y., F. Pustet & Co., [1902.] c. 3-291 p. D. cl., $1 net.

***Manson**, Ja. A. Sir Edwin Landseer. N. Y., Scribner, [imported,] 1902. 16+219 p. sq. 8°, (Makers of British art.) cl., $1.25 net.

****Marden**, Orison Swett, assisted by Abner Bayley. Stepping stones; essays for every-day living. Bost., Lothrop Pub. Co., [1902.] [Jl.] c. 3-323 p. por. D. cl., $1 net.
Contains talks to young people of both sexes full of practical value, happy sketches of great characters, salient suggestions on deportment and conduct, and shrewd advice of all kinds touching every-day living.

Marsh, Lucius Bolles, *and* Parker, *Mrs.* Harriet F., *comps.* Bronsdon and Box families. Pt. 1, Robert Bronsdon, merchant, and his descendants. Pt. 2, John Box, ropemaker, and his descendants. (Published by Mrs. Parker.) Lynn, Mass., The Nichols Press, 1902. c. 19+311 p. pl. por. facsim., 8°, cl., $4.

Merriman, Roger Bigelow. Life and letters of Thomas Cromwell. In 2 v. v. 1, Life, letters to 1535; v. 2, Letters from 1536, notes, index. [N. Y., Oxford Univ. Press,] (Amer. Branch,) 1902. 8+442; 4+356 p. pors. facsimile, O. cl., $6.
"This book is an attempt to present the life of Thomas Cromwell as a statesman, and to estimate his work without religious bias. Though it would certainly be difficult to overrate his importance in the history of the Church of England, I, [the author] maintain that the motives that inspired his actions were invariably political, and that the many ecclesiastical changes carried through under his guidance were but incidents of his administration, not ends in themselves."—*Preface.*

***Miller**, E. D. Modern polo; ed. by M. H. Hayes. 2d ed., rev. and enl. N. Y., Scribner, [imported,] 1902. 16+540 p. 8°, cl., $5 net.

Modern American tanning: a practical treatise on the manufacture of leather compiled from original articles describing modern methods printed in "Hide and Leather" and written by well-known tannery foremen, superintendents and chemists. Chic., Jacobsen Publishing Co., 1902. c. 292 p. 8°, cl., $5.

Moulthrop, S: P. Iroquois; il. and arr. by Sadie Pierpont Barnard. Rochester, N. Y., Ernest Hart, 1901. c. 5+155 p. sq. O. cl., 75 c.; pap., 50 c.
Facts from many sources regarding the origin, habits and traditions of the Iroquois (or tobacco people.) Intended as a supplementary reader.

Murray, Ja. A: H:, [*and others,*] *eds.* A new English dictionary on historical principles, founded mainly on the materials collected by the Philological Society. [Reissue in monthly parts.] v. 3. pts. 37, 38, Doubtable-Effective. N. Y., Oxford Univ. Press, (Amer. Branch,) 1902. 617-740+48 p.+ title-page and prefatory notes to v. 3, D, ed. by J. A. H. Murray; E, ed. by H: Bradley, f°, pap., ea., 90 c.

Myer, Edmund J. The Renaissance of the vocal art: a practical study of vitality, vitalized energy, of the physical, mental and emotional powers of the singer, through flexible, elastic bodily movements. Bost., Boston Music Co., [G. Schirmer, jr.,] 1902. c. 136 p. D. cl., $1.

Norton, Alice J. [History of Lake] Compounce, 1846-1902. New Haven, Ct., Tuttle, Morehouse & Taylor Co., 1902. c. 37 p. il. facsim., 12°, cl., 75 c.

Norton, C: Eliot, *ed.* The heart of oak books. First book. Rhymes, jingles and fables. Rev. ed. Bost., Heath., 1902. c. 13+113 p. il. 16°, cl., 25 c.

***Nott**, C: Cooper, *ed.* The seven great hymns of the mediæval church; annotated. 2d rev., enl. ed. N. Y., E. S. Gorham, 1902. c. 23+154 p. 12°, cl., $1 net.

***Nyrop**, Christopher, *M.D.* The kiss and its history; tr. by W: F: Harvey. N. Y., Dutton, 1902. 12°, cl., $2 net.

Oman, C: A history of the Peninsular war. v. 1, 1807-1809; from the treaty of Fontainebleau to the battle of Corunna. N. Y., [Oxford Univ. Press,] (Amer. Branch,) 1902. 15+656 p. pors., maps, plans, O. cl., $4.75.
Since Napier's "Peninsular war" was published some sixty years ago, an enormous bulk of valuable material has been accumulating in English, French, and Spanish, which has practically remained unutilized. Chiefly does the writer consider himself indebted to the papers of the diplomatist Sir Charles Vaughan. New matter and a new interpretation of many events are the principal qualities of this exhaustive work.

***Phin**, J: The Shakespeare cyclopædia and new glossary; with an introd. by E: Dowden. N. Y., Industrial Publication Co., 1902. c. 28+428 p. O. cl., $1.50 net.
"Giving the meaning of the old and unusual words found in Shakespeare's works and of the ordinary words used in unusual senses and in unusual forms of construction—explanations of idiomatic phrases and of mythological, biographical and antiquarian reference—notes on folk lore, local traditions, legends, allusions, proverbs, old English customs, etc., with the most important variorum readings; intended as a supplement to all the ordinary editions of Shakespeare's works."

Price, Lillian L. Wandering heroes. N. Y., Silver, Burdett & Co., [1902.] c. 15+192 p. 8°, (Stories of heroes.) cl., 50 c.

***Publishers'** trade list annual, 1902. 30th year: catalogues as supplied by publishers of books in print, 1902. N. Y., Office of The Publishers' Weekly, 1902. [Ag.] no paging, Q. cl., net, $1.50; in 2 v., with index, net, $5.
The catalogues of 250 publishers, approximating 7000 pages, are contained in this the first part of the

1902 "Publishers' Trade List." We are now delivering this volume. The second volume, containing an index which embraces under author, title and subject every book that appears in the catalogues part of the work, will be ready for delivery the first week in September.

Ridgeway, (*Major,*) [*pseud.* for W: Ross Hartpence.] Early recollections of James Whitcomb Riley. Harrison, Hamilton Co., O., W: Ross Hartpence, 1902. 2+89 p. por. sq. S. pap., 50 c.
An "appreciation" of the character and literary ability of "the hoosier poet." The author was associated with him in the office of *The Greenfield News.* He is also familiar with the "Old swimmin hole," "Kingry's mills," and other favorite haunts of Mr. Riley's. Contains an autograph letter written by James Whitcomb Riley.

Ross, P: A history of Long Island, from its earliest settlement to the present time. N. Y. and Chic., Lewis Publishing Co., 1902. c. 3 v. 1500 p. il. pl. por. sq. 8°, ½ leath., $18.

Sand, George, [*pseud.* for *Mme.* A. L. A. Dudevant.] The rosy cloud; il. by Diantha W. Horne. Bost., Dana Estes & Co., [1902.] c. 4+11-68 p. 12°, (Young of heart ser., no. 33.) cl., 50 c.

***Sapte,** W., *jr.* By the way ballads: being some trivial tales in varied verse; il. by Frank Reynolds and J: Hassell. N. Y., Dutton, 1902. 153 p. 12°, cl., $1.50 net.

***Sherren,** Wilkinson. The Wessex of romance. New cheaper il. ed. N. Y., Scribner, [imported,] 1902. 10+312 p. 12°, cl., $1.50 net.

***Sidis,** Boris. Psychopathological researches: studies in mental dissociation; published under the auspices of the trustees of the Psychopathic hospital, department of the New York Infirmary for women and children. N. Y., G. E. Stechert, 1902. c. 22+329 p. il. pls. Q. cl., $3 net.
Consists of a series of experimental studies in the domain of abnormal mental life followed along the lines of pathological individual psychology. The facts of mental dissociation and degeneration are closely studied in interesting individual cases with important, theoretical, and practical results. The field of research is new and important in the domain of psychic life, normal or abnormal. The subject is of interest, not only to the psychiatrist and neurologist, but also to the psychologist and to the general reader who takes an interest in the phenomena of abnormal mental life.

***Spence,** H: Donald Maurice, (*Dean.*) Early Christianity and Paganism, A.D. 64 to the peace of the church in the fourth century: a narrative mainly based upon contemporary records and remains. N. Y., Dutton, 1902. 14+550 p. 8°, cl., $4 net.

Stephen, *Sir* Ja. Fitzjames. A digest of the law of evidence; from the 5th ed. (1899) of Sir Herbert Stephen and Harry Lushington Stephen; with both general Am. notes and notes especially adapted to the state of Ohio by G: E. Beers, assisted by C: P. Sherman. Hartford, Ct., Dissell Pub. Co., 1902. c. 35+579 p. D. shp., $4.

***Stephens,** W: R. Wood, *D.D., and* Hunt, W., *eds.* History of the English church. In 7 v. v. 3, The 14th and 15th centuries, by W. W. Capes; v. 4, The 16th century, from the accession of Henry VIII. to the death of Mary, by Ja. Gairdner. N. Y., Macmillan, 1902. 12°, cl., ea., $2 net.

***Stevenson,** Rob. L: The pocket R. L. S.: being favorite passages from the works of Stevenson. N. Y., Scribner, [imported,] 1902. 217 p. 32°, cl., $1 net.

***Strachan,** *Rev.* Ja. Hebrew ideals from the story of the patriarchs: a study of Old Testament faith and life. pt. 1, Genesis. N. Y., Scribner, [imported,] 1902. 204 p. 12°, (Bible class handbooks.) cl., 60 c. net.

Thompson, Winfield M., *and* Lawson, T: W. The Lawson history of the *America's* cup. Bost., Winfield M. Thompson, 1902. c. 402 p. por. maps, il. 8°, canvas. (for private distribution.)

***Tolman,** Herbert Cushing. Urbs beata: a vision of the perfect life; with a commendatory by the Bishop of Milwaukee. Milwaukee, Wis., Young Churchman Co., 1902. c. 4-87 p. D. cl., 75 c. net.

***Turton,** W. H., *comp.* The truth of Christianity: being an examination of the more important arguments for and against believing in that religion; comp. from various sources. Milwaukee, Wis., Young Churchman Co., 1902. 13+538 p. D. cl., $1.25 net.

Van Cleve, C: Liggett. The history of the Phi Kappa Psi Fraternity, from its foundation in 1852 to its fiftieth anniversary Phil., Franklin Printing Co., 1902. c. 325 p. pl. por. facsim., 8°, cl., $2; levant, $4.

†**Vogel,** Harry B. Gentleman Garnet: a tale of old Tasmania. Phil., Lippincott, 1902. 3+351 p. D. (Lippincott's select novels.) cl., $1; pap., 50 c.
The English penal colony of Tasmania in the year 1838, is the scene of a romantic novel of adventure. The heroes are bushrangers led by "Gentleman Garnet." They are gentlemanly robbers, not without some admirable qualities. The story aims to show that the cruel prison system of the colony was responsible for the bushrangers.

****Wade,** Mary Hazelton. Little cousin series. Bost., L. C. Page & Co., 1902. [Je.] c. 6 v. 98; 106; 2-110; 2-102; 3-99; 106 p. il. D. cl., ea., 50 c. net.
Contents: Our little African cousin; Our little Cuban cousin; Our little Eskimo cousin; Our little Philippine cousin; Our little Hawaiian cousin; Our little Porto Rican cousin.

Warde, Ja. Cook. Jimmy Warde's experiences as a lunatic: a true story; a full account of what I thought, saw, heard, did and experienced just before and during my confinement of one hundred and eighty-one days as a lunatic in the Arkansas lunatic asylum. Little Rock, Ark., Ja. Cook Warde, [1902.] c. 300 p. 16°, cl., $1.

***Westcott,** *Rev.* Frank N. Catholic principles as illustrated in the doctrine, history, and organization of the American Catholic church in the United States commonly called the Protestant Episcopal church. Milwaukee, Wis., Young Churchman Co., [1902.] c. 4-410 p. D. cl., $1.25 net.

Wilson, H. W. Directory of booksellers, stationers, librarians and publishers in the United States and Canada. Minneapolis, Minn., H. W. Wilson, 1902. c. 175 p. 8°, pap., $10.

****Winslow,** Helen Maria. Literary Boston of to-day. Bost., L. C. Page & Co., [1902.] [Ag.] c. 2+444 p. pors. D. (Little pilgrimages ser.) cl., $1.20 net.
Sketches of literary life and works, with in many instances photographs of T: Bailey Aldrich, T: W. Higginson, E: E. Hale, Julia Ward Howe, Mrs. Ja. T. Fields, Sarah Orne Jewett, Alice Brown, Margaret Deland, Elizabeth Stuart Phelps, Herbert D. Ward, Harriet Prescott Spofford, Arlo Bates, Bradford Torrey, Nathan Haskell Dole, C: Follen Adams, and many other Boston literary celebrities.

Yersin, Marie *and* Jeanne. The Yersin phonorhythmic method of French pronunciation, accent and diction; French and English. Phil., Lippincott, 1902. c. 245 p. por. il. fold. tab., 12°, cl., $1.25.
French part has title: Methode Yersin phono-rhythmique pour la prononciation et la diction françaises à l'usage des étrangers, en français et en anglais.

ORDER LIST.

AMERICAN BOOK CO., 100 Washington Sq., E., New York.
Hoadley, Teacher's manual to accompany "A brief course in physics"... 25

AMERICAN ECCLESIASTICAL REVIEW, New York and Philadelphia.
Leo XIII (Pope), Poems, charades, etc. $1.50

D. APPLETON & CO., 72 Fifth Ave., New York.
Adams, Elementary commercial geography........ 1.10
†Harrison, A counsel of perfection, New ed........ 1.00

EDWARD ATKINSON, Box 112, Boston.
Atkinson, Cost of war, 1898-1902...... 6

BOSTON MUSIC CO., [G. SCHIRMER, Jr.,] Boston.
Meyer, Renaissance of the vocal art... 1.00

DISSELL PUB. CO., Hartford, Ct.
Stephen, Digest of the law of evidence especially adapted to the state of Ohio. 4.00

E. P. DUTTON & CO., 31 W. 23d St., New York.
*Hall, Society in the Elizabethan age, 3d ed........net, 2.50
*Hutton, Studies in the lives of the saints........net, 1.25
*Nyrop, The kiss and its history..net, 2.00
*Sapte, By the way ballads........net, 1.50
*Spence, Early Christianity and Paganism........net, 4.00

DANA ESTES & CO., 200-208 Summer St., Boston.
**Dickens, Story of little Nell......net, 75
Sand, The rosy cloud........ 50

FRANKLIN PRINTING CO., Philadelphia.
Van Cleve, History of the Phi Kappa Psi Fraternity........$2; 4.00

GLOBE SCHOOL BOOK CO., 103 Fifth Ave., New York.
Hale, English essays........ 40

EDWIN S. GORHAM, 285 Fourth Ave., New York.
*Nott, Seven great hymns of the mediæval church, rev., enl. ed......net, 1.00

GRAPHOLOGY PUB. CO., 503 Fifth Ave., New York.
Hagen, Reading character from handwriting........ 1.00

ERNEST HART, Rochester, N. Y.
Moulthrop, Iroquois........50 c.; 75

W. ROSS HARTPENCE, Harrison, O.
Ridgeway, Early recollections of James Whitcomb Riley........ 50

D. C. HEATH & CO., 110 Boylston St., Boston.
Ames, Elementary hygiene for the tropics........ 60
Norton, Heart of oak books. First book, rev. ed........ 25

A. J. HOLMAN & CO., 1224 Arch St., Philadelphia.
Bible, Self-pronouncing New Testament, Holman ed........ 50

HOUGHTON, MIFFLIN & CO., 4 Park St., Boston.
**Eliot, Charles Eliot, landscape artist, net, $3.50

INDUSTRIAL PUBLICATION CO., 16 Thomas St., New York.
*Phin, Shakespeare cyclopædia....net, 1.50

JACOBSEN PUBLISHING CO., Chicago.
Modern American tanning........ 5.00

MRS. M. W. KNAPP, Office of God's Revivalist, Cincinnati, O.
Davis, Coals from the altar.....20 c.; 75
Henley, Divine healing........10c.; 75

LEWIS PUBLISHING CO., New York and Chicago.
Ross, History of Long Island, 3 v..... 18.00

J. B. LIPPINCOTT CO., Washington Sq., Philadelphia.
†Boothby, A cabinet secret......50 c.; 1.00
†Vogel, Gentleman Garnet.......50 c.; 1.00
Yersin's phonorhythmic method of French pronunciation........ 1.25

THE LORD BALTIMORE PRESS, Baltimore, Md.
Carter, Horses, saddles and bridles, 2d ed........ 2.75

LOTHROP PUB. CO., 530 Atlantic Ave., Boston.
**Clark, The admiral's aid........net, 1.00
†Hall, Chanticleer........ 1.50
**Marden, Stepping stones........net, 1.00

MACMILLAN CO., 66 Fifth Ave., New York.
*Stephens *and* Hunt, *eds.*, History of the English church, v. 3 and 4, ea., net, 2.00

MAYNARD, MERRILL & CO., 29-33 E. 19th St., New York.
Hutchinson, On physiology and hygiene, new ed........ 1.00

NICHOLS PRESS, Lynn, Mass.
Marsh *and* Parker, Bronsdon and Box families........ 4.00

OPEN COURT PUB. CO., 324 Dearborn St., Chicago.

*Delitzsch, Babel and the Bible...net, 50

OXFORD UNIVERSITY PRESS, (AMER. BRANCH,) 91-93 Fifth Ave., New York.

Budge, History of Egypt, v. 1......... $1.25
Merriman, Life and letters of Thomas Cromwell, 2 v...................... 6.00
Murray, *and others*, New English dictionary, v. 3, pts. 37, 38.........ea., 90
Oman, History of the Peninsular war, v. 1...... .... 4.75

L. C. PAGE & CO., 200 Summer St., Boston.

†Dickens, Child's dream of a star..... 50
**Hopkins, The sandman..........net, 1.20
**Wade, Little cousin series, 6 v., ea., net, 50
**Winslow, Literary Boston of to-day, net, 1.20

OFFICE OF THE PUBLISHERS' WEEKLY, 298 Broadway, New York.

American educational catalogue, 1902. 50
*Publishers' trade list annual, 1902, net, $1.50; in 2 v., with index, net, 5.00

PURDY PUB. CO., 74 Madison St., Chicago.

Grenell, Economic tangles............ 1.00

F. PUSTET & CO., 52 Barclay St., New York.

*McKernan, Forty-five sermons....net, 1.00

CHARLES SCRIBNER'S SONS, Importations, 153-157 Fifth Ave., New York.

*Baedeker, London and its environs, new 13th rev. ed................net, 1.80
Banister, Musical analysis............ 75
*Cadness, Decorative brush-work..net, 1.40
*Chamberlain, Things Japanese, new rev., enl. 4th ed.................net, 4.00
*Dalman, Words of Jesus.........net, 2.50
*Hamilton, Memoirs of Count Grammont, new cheaper ed..........net, 3.00
*Holborn, The Pentateuch........net, 75
*Jekyll *and* Mawley, Roses for English gardens........ ....net, 3.75
*Keeling, Sir Joshua Reynolds, P.R.A., net, 1.25
*Manson, Sir Edwin Landseer....net, 1.25
*Miller, Modern polo.............net, 5.00
*Sherren, The Wessex of romance, new cheaper il. ed.............net, 1.50
*Stevenson, The pocket R. L. S...net, 1.00
*Strachan, Hebrew ideals from the study of the patriarchs, pt. 1, Genesis, net, 60

SCROLL PUBLISHING CO., 308 Dearborn St., Chicago.

Carleton, Will-o'-the-wisp....... ..... $1.25

SILVER, BURDETT & CO., 29-33 E. 19th St., New York.

Hall, Judith, etc...................... 75
Keats, Eve of St. Agnes.............. 40
Price, Wandering heroes............ 50

G. E. STECHERT, 9 E. 16th St., New York.

*Sidis, Psychopathological researches, net, 3.00

H. S. STONE & CO., Eldridge Court, Chicago.

McCutcheon, Castle Craneycrow...... 1.50

WINFIELD M. THOMPSON, Boston.

Thompson *and* Lawson, History of the *America's* cup...(for private distribution)

TUTTLE, MOREHOUSE & TAYLOR CO., New Haven, Ct.

Norton, Hist. of Lake Compounce, 1846-1902..... 75

UNION PRESS, 1122 Chstnut St., Philadelphia.

Hocking, Awakening of Anthony Weir. 1.50

D. B. UPDIKE CO., [MERRYMOUNT PRESS,] 104 Chestnut St., Boston.

Higginson, Four addresses, 75 c.; Japan ed., 5.00

JAMES COOK WARDE, Room 16, Adams Bldg., Little Rock, Ark.

Warde, Jimmy Warde's experiences as a lunatic....... .... 1.00

J. K. WATERS CO., Boston.

Catholic year book of New England, 1902...... 25

THOMAS WHITTAKER, 3 Bible House, New York.

*Lanier, Kinship of God and man, v. 2, The master key............net, 1.00

H. W. WILSON, 315 14th Ave., Minneapolis, Minn.

Wilson, Directory of booksellers, librarians and publishers................ 10.00

YOUNG CHURCHMAN CO., 412 Milwaukee St., Milwaukee, Wis.

*Tolman, Urbs beata.............net, 75
*Turton, Truth of Christianity....net, 1.25
*Westcott, Catholic principles as illustrated in the doctrine, history and organization of the American Catholic church...... ....net, 1.25

RECENT ENGLISH BOOKS

BADDELEY, M. J. B. Ireland. Part 1: Northern Counties, incl. Dublin and Neighbourhood. 20 maps and plans by Bartholomew. 5th ed. rev. Dulau. 12°, 6½ x 4¼, 228 p., 4s., net.

BULLOCK, T. L. Progressive exercises in the Chinese written language. Low. 10 x 6, 264 p., 10s. 6d., net.

FERRYMAN, A. F. M. Annals of Sandhurst: chronicles of the Royal Military College from its foundation to present day, with sketch of history of Staff College. Heinemann. Illus. roy. 8°, 9⅛ x 5¾, 328 p., 5s.

HEWLETT, R. T. Manual of bacteriology, clinical and applied. Appendix on bacterial remedies, etc. 2d ed. Churchill. 8°, 8¼ x 5¼, 546 p., 12s.

IRELAND—industrial and agricultural. Simpkin. 8°, 10 x 6¾, 544 p., 5s., net.

MASSEE, G. European fungus flora: agaricaceæ. Duckworth. Cr. 8°, 7½ x 4⅞, 280 p., 6s., net.

PEDDER, H. C. Right Hon. Joseph Chamberlain: study of his character as a statesman. Stock. Cr. 8°, 7⅝ x 5, 108 p., 2s. 6d., net.

WRIGHT, A., *and* Smith, P. Parliament, past and present: popular and picturesque account of a thousand years in the Palace of Westminster, the Home of the Mother of Parliaments Vol. 1. 337 illus., including photogravure and 9 coloured. Hutchinson. Imp. 8°, 11⅛ x 8⅝, 300 p., 7s. 6d. net.

The Publishers' Weekly.

FOUNDED BY F. LEYPOLDT.

AUGUST 23, 1902.

The editor does not hold himself responsible for the views expressed in contributed articles or communications. All matter, whether for the reading-matter columns or advertising pages, should reach this office not later than Wednesday noon, to insure insertion in the same week's issue.

Books for the "Weekly Record," as well as all information intended for that department, should reach this office by Tuesday morning of each week.

"I hold every man a debtor to his profession, from the which, as men do of course seek to receive countenance and profit, so ought they of duty to endeavor themselves by way of amends to be a help and an ornament thereunto."—LORD BACON.

CHANGING TRAVELLERS.

CHANGING travellers from season to season is a mistake, and so is transferring them to different sections after acquaintance has once been formed. It is a great mistake also—often made by the man himself—to change houses as frequently as some do, often for some trivial cause, more frequently for no other reason than to make a change. There are a few things to be learned sooner or later by every bumptious young man who considers himself just a shade better qualified to judge of business affairs and what is to the interest of the business than his employer, even if he has had the extended experience of a first trip. One of these things is that few men are discharged without some just cause. If he is discharged he may be able to persuade the friends that he has made to accept his side of the story; when he makes a second change his friends may begin to suspect that some of the fault may lie with him; while the third time, even if this time he may be entirely without blame, he is apt to be left out in the cold. Here the rule applies: Be sincere. Don't try to fool your constituents, because they will not be fooled—at least not all the time. An average collection of men can usually tell the difference between an honest man and a pretender. The test of a man in business is whether he is honest or not—conscientiously, broadly honest, we mean, not alone honest in the legal sense of the word. No dishonest man can pass through the world for any length of time undetected, nor will the honest man be long mistaken for a fakir.

Besides being honest a traveller must aim to be cheerful and optimistic. He has many hardships to put up with, many trials to undergo, many unpleasant duties to perform—all who have had experience on the road know that and are ready to admit it—but that is no reason why he should add to his misery and to the discomfort of his employers, his customers and his friends, by complaining and making himself disagreeable. Nor will it help him any to change his berth, if his relations with his employers are agreeable, because the conditions against which he has to contend remain unchanged no matter under which flag he elects to fight.

BOOKTRADE ASSOCIATIONS.

AMERICAN PUBLISHERS' ASSOCIATION.

156 FIFTH AVE., NEW YORK, August 12, 1902.

To the Trade:

IN entering upon the second fall season since the establishment of protected prices we beg leave to call attention to the fact that with few exceptions prices are well maintained throughout the United States. The general satisfaction attending the working of the new system has been marked, and dealers everywhere are looking forward so hopefully to a business season under conditions which afford them reasonable return for their capital and labor, that little thought is given to the fact that there are still a few undersellers.

The only danger in this situation is that in some instances vigilance may be so far relaxed as to permit the chief underseller to secure stock where he has hitherto failed, and it is to prevent this that we are addressing the trade at this time. The fact should not be lost sight of that the underseller referred to is still active, and although it may appear that less importance attaches to his attitude as time passes, it is still necessary to prevent him so far as possible from securing stock.

While he has managed to secure many of the new books his general stock is practically nothing, and it is only by a stretch of the imagination that he can be called a dealer in books. His efforts to secure stock in bulk have been so frequently baffled that at present he is picking up books in lots of five and ten copies each of small dealers, and for this purpose has enlisted the services of one or two commission men who are well known in the book business.

These agents have appeared in the West as well as in New England and the Middle States, but dealers should have no difficulty in recognizing them, and if this Association is given proper support few books will be procured in this way. Should such an agent try to arrange for the purchase of books kindly send us his name and we will undertake to see that his future usefulness is seriously interfered with. In this we shall have the hearty support of the dealers of the country, as they will hardly be willing to purchase of a salesman, no matter what his line is, who is so regardless of their interest as to give assistance to the underseller.

It is possible also that during the fall the

underseller may try to buy in quantity through "dummy" dealers as he has done before with more or less success, but we believe that the publishers and jobbers in the light of the experience of the past year and a half can be relied on to frustrate these attempts, and if the smaller dealer will do his part well the underseller's prospect for a fall stock is not considered bright.

With hearty congratulations on the success of the undertaking, we are

Yours very truly,
AMERICAN PUBLISHERS' ASSOCIATION,
GEORGE S. EMORY, *Manager.*

OBITUARY NOTES.

ORRIN S. COOK, who for fifteen years has held a responsible position with Silver, Burdett & Co., died at his home in Chicago on July 30. The publishers send us this word, and write very appreciatively of Mr. Cook's work for education and his personal characteristics, which had earned him many friends throughout the trade.

GEORGE DALZIEL, the founder of the firm of engravers known throughout the world as the "Dalziel Brothers," died in England, on Monday, August 4, at the advanced age of eighty-seven. George Dalziel, the son of Alexander Dalziel, an artist of Wooler, Northumberland, was born on December 1, 1815. For over half a century the Dalziel Brothers were in the first rank of London engravers, but the popular introduction of the various processes of reproducing illustrations by photographic means almost banished wood engraving, and in 1893 George Dalziel and his brother retired from the concern which by their skill and enterprise they had successfully created and maintained. Mr. George Dalziel possessed considerable literary gifts, and several volumes of poems and short stories by him have been published from time to time.

DR. LEOPOLD SCHENK, author of the epoch-making book "Determination of Sex," died at Vienna, on August 18. Dr. Schenk was born at Ilemeny, Hungary, on August 23, 1840. He was for many years regarded as an authority in physiology and embryology, and for twenty-three years was director of the Embryological Institute in Vienna. In 1898 Dr. Schenk astonished the scientific world by announcing that he had discovered the secret of sex, and that it could be regulated by diet on the part of the mother. He was much opposed and finally forced to resign his position. He claimed to the last that his theory was proved by many cases trusted to his surveillance. Dr. Schenk was the author of "Handbook of Histology," "Handbook of Comparative Embryology of Vertebrate Animals," "A Contribution to the Theory of Artificial Trout Culture," "The Influence of Color on the Development of the Life of Animals," "On Micro-organism," and a two-volume work, "History of Evolution." Besides these Professor Schenk wrote a great number of scientific treatises on physiology and embryology.

NOTES ON AUTHORS.

HENRY DEMAREST LLOYD, well known as a champion of socialistic doctrines, has spent most of the summer in Europe, arranging for the translations into French, Italian and German of his books "Wealth against Commonwealth," "Newest England," and "A Country without Strikes."

EDMUND GOSSE is now engaged in writing a history of English literature, and in connection with that fact there is revived the story of Mr. Gosse's application for the place of Clark lectures, at Trinity College, Cambridge. There were many candidates and each handed in a host of testimonials from more or less famous men of letters. Gosse presented only three testimonials, but those three were written by Matthew Arnold, Alfred Tennyson and Robert Browning. He was appointed.

JOURNALISTIC NOTES.

J. F. TAYLOR & Co. have just ready a new volume of stories of Jewish life, by Herman Bernstein, entitled "In the Gates of Israel," and a novel of American life, called "The Heart of Woman," by Harry W. Desmond.

Collier's Weekly will make its issue of September 6 a "Labor Day number," of 28 pages, devoted mainly to a "Labor Review," covering the various fields of industry, and prepared by leading representatives of the great national labor bodies. It will have a striking special cover, designed by Leyendecker.

John Bull is a new English comic weekly, intended in a measure as a rival to *Punch*, which, however, has little cause to fear competition in its own historic field. Arthur a' Beckett, son of the comic historian of England, and for nearly thirty years on the staff of *Punch*, is the editor. The title *John Bull* has been used before in this connection, notably by Theodore Hook, who founded a paper of that name in 1820.

LITERARY AND TRADE NOTES.

HENRY HOLT & Co. will issue this month a lower-priced and more compact edition of Lavignac's "Music and Musicians," edited by H. E. Krehbril, which they have already printed three times in their large-paper edition.

GRAPHOLOGY PUBLISHING Co., 503 Fifth Avenue, Manhattan, call attention to Dr. Von Hagen's book, "Reading Character from Handwriting," which offers proof for the claim that handwriting is a reliable index to the most complex points of character.

GINN & Co. have added to their list of textbooks two new volumes—"The Advanced First Reader," by Ellen M. Cyr, and "Towards the Rising Sun," the fourth volume in the *Youth's Companion Series* of geographical readers. A special feature of the new Cyr reader is the series of excellent reproductions of famous paintings, engraved on wood by Henry Wolf.

L. C. PAGE & Co. have added to the popular series *Little Pilgrimages* "Literary Boston of To-day," by Helen M. Winslow, whose book "Concerning Cats" was received with marked favor; and "The Sandman: His Farm Stories," by William J. Hopkins, who puts before childish minds much valuable information on food products and all the endless detail that fills a farmer's life.

ELDER & SHEPARD, San Francisco, have in press an essay by Dr. David Storr Jordan on "The Philosophy of Despair." Dr. Jordan takes for his text certain quatrains from Omar Khayyam, among them the lines beginning "I come like water and like wind I go," and aims to give the reply of science to pessimism, striking a note of courage and common sense in his treatment of "the riddle of life."

HENRY ALTEMUS COMPANY announce a new book by Carolyn Wells, called "Folly in the Forest." This is a fantasia of mythology for children, abounding in humorous touches and at the same time giving acquaintance with some of the most famous characters of myth and legend. Pegasus, the Sphinx, the Geese that saved Rome, Poe's Raven, are some of the creatures that meet and desport themselves with "Folly" in the Forest of the Past.

THE JACOBSEN PUBLISHING COMPANY Chicago, have prepared an important volume devoted to "Modern American Tanning." It is made up of original articles describing modern methods first printed in *Hide and Leather*, and written by well-known tannery experts and chemists, and it is a thorough exposition of the new processes and developments that have so completely revolutionized the leather industry within recent years. The volume contains over two hundred and fifty pages and many illustrations.

THE YOUNG CHURCHMAN Co., Milwaukee, have issued the fourth thousand of "The Truth of Christianity," compiled by Major W. H. Turton, of the Royal Engineers; "Catholic Principles as illustrated in the doctrine, history and organization of the American Catholic Church in the United States commonly called the Protestant Episcopal Church," by Rev. Frank N. Westcott; and "Urbs Beata," a vision of the "Perfect Life," by Herbert Cushing Tolman, with a commendatory by the Bishop of Milwaukee.

E. P. DUTTON & Co. have nearly ready an important contribution to the literature of African exploration. This is Dr. Carl Peters's account of his archæological expedition of 1899-01 to "The Eldorado of the Ancients," the Ophir of ancient days, which he believes he has now proved to be the country between Zambesi and Sabi. The ancient ruins and gold and copper mines discovered there, together with the many adventures of the explorers, are fully described in the volume, which will also contain many illustrations by Tennyson Cole, who accompanied the expedition.

DOUBLEDAY, PAGE & Co. will publish this fall a most entertaining volume in "Memoirs of a Contemporary." This is the narrative of the experiences of a French woman, who donned man's clothes and followed Marshal Ney in the French Army during the Napoleonic wars. It is translated and edited by Lionel Strachey, and is said to abound with vivid and intimate accounts of Napoleon and his generals and of many of the prominent figures of the First Empire. The illustrations will be reproduced from old prints. They have now in preparation "The Wooing of Judith," a romance of early Virginia, by Sara Beaumont Kennedy; and a little volume of poems, by Ellen Glasgow, to be luxuriously printed by De Vinne.

THE MACMILLAN COMPANY will publish in the early autumn two volumes of essays by the late John Fiske, hitherto unpublished, which were completed and made ready for the press before Mr. Fiske's death. Among the subjects dealt with in these essays are Thomas Hutchinson, the last royal governor of Massachusetts; Charles Lee, Alexander Hamilton, Andrew Jackson, Daniel Webster, John Milton and "Reminiscences of Huxley." The next volume to appear in the *English Men of Letters Series* will be Herbert Paul's study of Matthew Arnold. Owen Wister's brilliant story of the West, "The Virginians," is proving among the most popular of this season's books. A second edition was called for within three days of publication.

D. APPLETON & Co. have a most interesting number of books in hand for early fall publication. "The Letters of Charles Darwin," edited by his son, Francis Darwin, will be a notable addition to the biography and to the literature of science. Fiction will include Sir Gilbert Parker's new novel, "Donovan Pasha;" "The Sea Lady," an extravaganza with a matter-of-fact present-day setting, by H. G. Wells; "A Whaleman's Wife," by F. T. Bullen; and John Oliver Hobbes's new volume, "Tales About Temperaments." The latter, by the way, does not consist wholly of tales, but includes two one-act plays, both of which were successfully produced on the stage. They are "A Repentance," brought out at the St. James Theatre, in London, and "Journeys End in Lovers' Meetings," written for and acted by Ellen Terry.

BAKER & TAYLOR will publish this fall a compilation of coffee history, coffee anecdotes and coffee verse, including recipes for the making of coffee from the leading chefs of the country, by Arthur H. Gray, one of the collaborateurs of "Bath Robes and Bachelors" and a contributor to "Tobacco in Song and Story." There will be a trade edition neatly bound and with a striking cover, and a novel gift edition bound in heavy coffee-colored ooze leather, stamped in gold and done up in a coffee sack of rough bagging, tied at the corners and labelled. This firm has also in preparation an attractive edition of the Rolfe Shakespeare, issued through arrangement with the American Book Co. The volumes will be bound in olive green limp leather binding, with decorated title-pages in two colors, and will be suitable for class use or for the private library.

TERMS OF ADVERTISING.

Under the heading "Books Wanted" **book-trade subscribers are given the privilege of a free advertisement for books out of print, of five nonpareil lines exclusive of address, in any issue except special numbers, to an extent not exceeding 100 lines a year. If more than five lines are sent, the excess is at 10 cents a line, and amount should be inclosed.** *Bids for current books and such as may be easily had from the publishers, and repeated matter, as well as all advertisements from non-subscribers, must be paid for at the rate of* 10 *cents a line.*

Under the heading "Books for Sale," the charge to subscribers and non-subscribers is 10 *cents a nonpareil line for each insertion. No deduction for repeated matter.*

All other small, undisplayed, advertisements will be charged at the uniform rate of 10 *cents a nonpareil line. Eight words may be reckoned to the line.*

Parties with whom we have no accounts must pay in advance, otherwise no notice will be taken of their communications.

BOOKS WANTED.

☞ ***In answering, please state edition, condition, and price, including postage or express charges.***

Houses that are willing to deal exclusively on a cash-on-delivery basis will find it to their advantage to put after their firm-name the word (Cash).

☞ ***Write your wants plainly and on one side of the sheet only. Illegibly-written "wants" will be considered as not having been received. The "Publishers' Weekly" does not hold itself responsible for errors.***

It should be understood that the appearance of advertisements in this column, or elsewhere in the "Publishers' Weekly" does not furnish a guarantee of credit. While it is endeavored to safeguard these columns by withdrawing the privilege of their use from advertisers who are not "good pay," booksellers should take the usual precaution, as to advertisers not known to them, that they would take in making sales to any unknown parties.

A. M. Abbott, P. O. Box 24, Montreal, Can.

L'Abbe.
McGeoghegan's Hist. of Ireland.
Robertson's Hist. of America.

Abraham & Straus, Brooklyn, N. Y.

Flowers for Children, by L. M. Child.
History of Suffolk Co., L. I., best one.

Almy, Bigelow & Washburn, Salem, Mass.

Aldrich's Young Folks' Library.
Stoddard Lectures.
Illus. London News, June 21, 1902.

Amer. Bapt. Pub. Soc., 177 Wabash Ave., Chicago.

Hall's Helps to Zion Travellers.
Dissertation on Moral Impotence, by Truman.
Hansell's Reminiscences of New York Baptists.

Amer. Bapt. Pub. Soc., 279 Elm St., Dallas, Tex.

Carson, On Baptism. Pub. by Amer. Bapt. Pub. Soc.

Americus Law Book Co., Americus, Ga.

Life of Marion, by Simms.
State and Federal Government, by Wilson.
Dole, E. P., Talks about Law.
Constitution U. S., E. D. Mead.
American State Cons., Hitchcock.

Antiquarian Book Concern, Omaha, Neb.

Catlin's Indians, col. plates. London, 1841.

Astor Book Shop, 4 Barclay St., N. Y.

Set Bandello Novels.
Bishop's History of Amer. Manufactures, v. 2.
Set Patent Office Reports.

Wm. M. Bains, 1019 Market St., Phila., Pa.

Moore's Modern Don Juan, English ed.
Moore's Drama in Muslin.
E. C. Greville Murray's Works.

C. M. Barnes Co., Chicago, Ill.

19 Hanson's Preparatory Book Latin Poetry, second-hand or new.

N. J. Bartlett & Co., 28 Cornhill, Boston, Mass.

Mather's Magnalia, 2 v. 1853.

Bonnell, Silver & Co., 24 W. 22d St., N. Y.

Dixson's Subject Index Fiction. Dodd.

The Boston Book Co., 83 Francis St., Boston, Mass.

Amer. Biblical Repository, v. 1, Apr., 1846.
Army and Navy Jour., v. 6, 7, 8, 10, 12, 14, 16, 33, 36.
Forum, Sept., 1886. $1.00.
North Amer. Rev., May, 1817; July, Sept., 1818.
Public Opinion, Jan. 15, 1887, or v. 2.
Science, n. s., v. 1, or odd nos.

The Bowen-Merrill Co., Indianapolis, Ind.

Barber, John W., and others, Bible Looking-Glass.

Brentano's, 1015 Pennsylvania Ave., Washington, D. C.

McPherson's History of Rebellion.
Adams' New England Federalism.
Hartman's Geomancy.
Gogol's St. John's Eve.
Brassey's Naval Annual, 1901.
Kipling's Note Book, no. 2.

The Brown, Eager & Hull Co., Toledo, O.

Sill's Poems, Limited ed.

The Burrows Bros. Co., Cleveland, O.

Westropp, Ancient Symbol Worship.
Lord, Notes on Chem. Analysis.
Browning, Bibliography.
Knapp, Lib. of Amer. Hist. 1837.
Hoadley, Boiler Experiments.
Van Buren, Investigation Formulas for Strength of Iron.
Scott, Aesthetics.
Clouston's Neurosis.
Select Statutes of Eliz. and James 1.
Kant, Sensible and Intelligible World, ed. by Eckhoff.
Harrison, History of Sociology.
Howes, Roofs and Trusses in Wood and Steel.
Stratton, Experiments in General Physics.
Kirkman, Railway Disbursements.
China Hunter's Club.
Pennell, Stream of Pleasure.
Green's Eng., 5 v., Pkt. ed., limp olive lambskin.
Gerring, Notes on Eng. Book Plates.
Warnecke, Rare Book Plates of the 15th and 16th Centuries.
2 Proceedings Grand Chap. R. A. Masons, Ohio, '62.
Williams, History of Firelands or Huron and Erie Counties.
Cyclopedia Britannica, Scribner ed.
Wheatley, How to Catalogue a Library.

Case Library, Cleveland, O.

London Weekly Times, no. 841.
Poushkin, Poems from the Russian.
Theuriet's Gerard's Marriage.

Jno. J. Case, 70 Wall St., N. Y.

Job lot Spanish or Italian books, cheap.
Poole's Index to Periodical Literature.
Corporation Accounting.
Set *Congressional Globe*, cheap.
Chapters of Erie or Essays, by C. F. Adams.

A. H. Clapp, 32 Maiden Lane, Albany, N. Y.

In the Quarter.
How to Catalogue a Library, Wheatley. Armstrong
Historic Note Book. J. B. L.

The A. H. Clark Co., Garfield Bldg., Cleveland, O.

Ramsey, A. C., The Other Side, Hist of Mexican War.

The Robert Clarke Co., 31 E. 4th St., Cincinnati, O.

Travels of Alex. Henry. New York, 1804.
Barbe-Marbois, History of Louisiana. Phila., 1830.
History of Albemarle County, Va.
Lawson's History of the American Cup (just issued.)

W. B. Clarke Co., Park and Tremont Sts., Boston, Mass.

Petroleum and its Products, 2 v. Redwood & Holloway.
Royalty of Friendship, A. L. Williams.
Tennyson, 1 v., music in back. Harper, 1872.

BOOKS WANTED.—Continued.

Henry T. Coates & Co., Phila., Pa.

Oscar Wilde's Poems.
Howlett's Four in Hand Driving.

Cohin & Peyran, 405 N. Oregon St., El Paso, Tex.

Old Santa Fé Trail, by Col. Henry Inman.
Life Among the Zuni Indians, by Cushing.
Late copyright books, second-hand.
Any travels on Mexico, Texas or New Mexico.

Wm. G. Colesworthy, 66 Cornhill, Boston, Mass.

From $3 to $5 per copy offered for Townsend ed. of Cooper (Darley plates), as follows: Precaution, Deerslayer, Ways of the Hour, Jack Tier, Miles Wallingford, Afloat and Ashore.
Boston Sunday Herald, March about the 20th (3d Sunday), 1898, will give $1.00 for same.

H. M. Connor, 232 Meridian St., E. Boston, Mass.

Lost Cause, Pollard.
Peregrine Pickle.
Joslyn's Life of St. Patrick.
Fielding, cheap.
Smollet, cheap.

Crusoe & Co., 81 Vermont St., Brooklyn, N. Y.

Gregg's Shorthand.
Ziska Letters.

Cunningham, Curtiss & Welch, 319 Sansome St., San Francisco, Cal.

Blaine's Twenty Years in Congress, v. 2 only, leath.
Personal Memoirs of U. S. Grant, v. 2 only, cl.

Cushing & Co., 34 W. Baltimore St., Baltimore, Md.

The Powers of Europe and Fall of Sebastopol, by a British Officer. Pub. in Boston.

Damrell & Upham, 283 Washington St., Boston, Mass.

Hubbard's Guide to No. Maine.

Davis' Book Store, 35 W. 42d St, N. Y.

Hildreth, History of U. S., 6 v.
Schouler's History of U. S., 5 v., latest ed.
Winsor's Narrative and Critical History, 8 v.
Set Parkman's Works, complete, good ed.

Edwin A. Denham, 28 W. 33d St., N. Y.

Taylor, Bayard, Ximena, 1st ed.

E. F. Dillingham, Bangor, Me.

Prescott Memorial, ed. by Dr. Wm. Prescott.
Modern Eloquence, 10 v., ed. by T. B. Reed.
Novanglus and Massachusettensis. Bost., 1810.
Acts of First Session of Sixth Congress.
Laws of U. S., 3 v. Philadelphia, 1769.
Hist'l Sketch of First Church in Boston. Emerson, 1812.
True Sentiment of America in a Collection of Letters. London, 1768.
Political Register. Philadelphia, 1795.
Discussion of Greek Question in House of Rep. 1824.
Mass. Register, 1808.

Dodd, Mead & Co., 372 Fifth Ave., N. Y.

James, Account of Long's Expedition, 2 v., 4to and Atlas. Phila., 1823.
Eddis's Letters from America. 1792.
Growoll, Adolf, Book-trade Bibliography in the U. S.
More, Hannah, Private Devotion.
Parkman, Count Frontenac. 1877.
Book Lover, no. 2.

Doonan & Lovette, 124 Peachtree St., Atlanta, Ga.

Fisk's Outlines of Cosmic Philosophy.
Whitman's Leaves of Grass.
Freeman's Historical Geog.
Smith's Chronological Church Hist.
M'Call's History of Ga., 2 v.

E. P. Dutton & Co., 31 W. 23d St., N. Y.

Topsys and Turvys, by Peter Newell, 1st ser.
Social and Domestic Religion, 2 v.
Nime's A Presbyterian Clergyman Looking for the Church.
Sarum Missal.

G. Engelke, 225 N. Clark St., Chicago, Ill. [*Cash.*]

Barlow, The Three Voices.
Rise and Fall of Confederate Gov., v. 2, J. Davis, cl.
Norris and Oliver, System of Diseases of the Eye. v. 4.

C. P. Everitt, 219 5th Ave., N. Y.

Mark Twain's Library of Wit and Humor.

C. P. Farrell, 117 E. 21st St., N. Y.

Acts of the Anti-Slavery Apostles, by Parker Pillsbury.
The American Churches the Bulwarks of American Slavery.
A Brotherhood of Thieves, or, a True Picture of the Amer. Church and Clergy, by Jas. D. Birney.
Old Faith and New, by David F. Strauss.
The Self-Destruction of Christianity.
Synodicon of Pappus, by E. Hartmann.

F. A. Fernald, Broadway near 117th St, N. Y. [*Cash.*]

Powell, Cañons of the Colorado. Flood & Vincent.
Grant, U. S., Personal Memoirs.

W. R. Geddis, Brattleboro, Vt.

Six Months in Whitehouse, Carpenter.

Harry E. Gilbert, 301 St. Paul St., Baltimore, Md.

Abbott's Life of Napoleon, 8vo, cl.
Ridpath's Library of Literature, v. 11.
Md. Repts., odd v.

Goodpasture Book Co., Nashville, Tenn.

General Conference Journal, M. E. Church, South. 1866.
Minutes of Annual Conferences, M. E. Church, South, 1845-1857.
Prospectus to John-o-Dreams.

Edwin S. Gorham, 4th Ave. and 22d St., N. Y.

Lange's Commentary on Old Testament.
Complete set of Liddon's Works.
Early Journal of Diocese of Maryland (Episc.)
Christlieb, Modern Doubt and Christian Belief.
Maurice, Commandments as Instruments of National Reform.

All second-hand.

Hyland Bros., Portland, Ore.

Farm Legends, old style, 8vo.
Farm Festivals, old style, 8vo.
Autobiography of Peter Cartwright, 1st ed.
Isis Unveiled, Blavatsky.
Merchind's Theological History.

U. P. James, 127 W. 7th St., Cincinnati, O.

Draper's Civil War in America, 3 v.

Jennings & Pye, 57 Washington St., Chicago, Ill.

Hargrave, Sacred Poems.

E. W. Johnson, 2 E. 42d St., N. Y.

Horace, Text, a good ed.
Documents Colonial Hist. N. Y., after v. 10.
Novels, William H. Peck, pap. covers.

The E. P. Judd Co., New Haven, Conn. [*Cash.*]

Time Machine, by Wells.

Keating, Box 489, N. Y. City.

Plates wanted, good novels, also short dictionary, 16mo, 64 to 128 pages.

Keep's Book Shop, 284 Columbus Ave., Boston, Mass

Any books on English hall marks.
The Buried Temple, Maeterlinck.
Wisdom and Destiny, Maeterlinck.

Geo. Kleinteich, 397 Bedford Ave., Brooklyn, N. Y. [*Cash.*]

Jukes, Names of God in Holy Scripture.
Jukes, Restitution of all Things.

Chas. E. Lauriat Co., 301 Washington St., Boston, Mass.

George Sand's Mauprat; Devil's Pool; any Eng. tr. except Little, Brown & Co. or Roberts Bros. ed.
Balfour's Plea for Philosophical Doubt.
Metternich's Memoirs, v. 5, 8vo, cl. Scribner.
At the Sign of the Sphinx, Carolyn Wells.
Natural Philosophy in Easy Lessons, by Tyndall.

BOOKS WANTED.—Continued.

Chas. E. Lauriat Co.—*Continued.*

Seven Lectures on Electrical Phenomena and Theories, by Tyndall.
Castle of Otranto, by Walpole.
Memoirs of George III., by Walpole.

Leggat Bros., 81 Chambers St., N. Y.

The Divine Human, by a member of the N. Y. Bar, not by Louis.

The Library of Congress, Washington, D. C.

Cranford Enigmas. N. Y., Whittaker, 1895.
Ostwald, Outlines of Chemistry. Macmillan, 1890.
Pierson, Pulpit to Palm Branch. N. Y., Armstrong, 1892.
Tesla, Experiments Alternating Currents. *Electric World*, 1892.

Library of the Univ. of California, Berkeley, Cal.

Hunt's Merchants' Magazine, v. 42-44, 49-63.
Pierce, Trusts and Remedies. 1899.
Pitkin, Statistical View of Commerce. 1816.
Raguet, Principles of Free Trade. 1840.

Little, Brown & Co., 254 Washington St., Boston, Mass.

Fothergill, Borderland.

B. Login, 1328 3d Ave., N. Y.

Scribner's Monthly Magazine, v. 1, nos. 4, 5, 6; v. 3, nos. 1, 4, 5, 6; v. 4, nos. 1, 2, 3, 4, 5, 6; v. 5, nos. 1, 2; v. 16, no. 6; v. 20, no. 3.

Louisville Book Co., 356 4th Ave., Louisville, Ky.

Cy Warman's Poems, Mountain Melodies.

W. H. Lowdermilk & Co., Washington, D. C.

The following school books, new, shelf-worn, or second-hand:

50 Aldrich and Foster, Foundations of French.
50 Adams' Commercial Geography.
10 Allen and Greenough, New Cæsar.
50 Barker, Chemistry.
10 Bergen, Foundations of Botany.
5 Bowser, Calculus. 1897.
5 Bowser, Analy. Geom.
5 Browning, Educational Theories.
25 Collar and Daniel, First Latin Book.
11 Crockett, Trigonometry.
10 Cooke, Laboratory Practice.
50 Chaucer's Prologue and Knight's Tales, etc. Clarendon Press.
20 Cross, Development of English Novel.
100 Crew, Elements of Physics.
30 Gore, Geometry, 2d ed.
15 Genung, Practical Rhetoric.
70 Gibbon's History of Commerce.
5 Garner, Spanish Grammar.
5 Genung, Working Principles of Rhetoric.
25 Henderson and Woodhull, Elements of Physics.
10 James, Psychology, Briefer Course.
3 Johnson, Differential Equations.
40 Jaggeman, German Syntax.
5 Jaggeman, German Composition.
10 Jordan and Kellogg, Animal Life.
25 Knapp, Virgil.
3 Lockwood and Emerson, Composition and Rhetoric.
100 Larned, History of England.
7 Lodge, Elementary Mechanics, blue cl.
10 Loney, Elements of Statics.
10 Loney, Elements of Dynamics.
4 Merriman, Hydraulics.
4 Merriman, Mechanics of Materials.
100 Morey, Outlines Roman History.
50 McLaughlin, History of American Nation.
50 Montgomery, Leading Facts of American History. 1901.
25 Pancoast, Introduction to English Literature.
25 Pattee, History of American Literature.
15 Pattee, Reading Course in American Literature.
50 Poll, German Composition.
10 Parker and Haswell, Zoology, $1.60 ed.
100 Remsen, Introduction to Study of Chemistry. 1901.
40 Remsen, Organic Chemistry. 1901.
5 Richter, Organic Chemistry, v. 1.
5 Richter, Organic Chemistry, v. 2.
20 Seymour, Homer, 6 books and vocabulary, rev. ed.
50 Spanhoofd, Lehrbuch.
75 Scott and Denny, Elementary Composition.
15 Scott, Introduction to Geology.
25 Tracy, Mechanical Drawing.

W. H. Lowdermilk & Co.—*Continued*

50 Thompson, S., Elect. and Magnetism. 1895.
50 Tarr and McMurry, North America.
25 Tunstall, Cicero.
50 Thurston, Tests in Commercial Higher Arithmetic.
10 Taylor, Calculus, rev. ed.
200 Wentworth, New School Algebra.
100 Wentworth, P. & S. Geometry, rev. ed.
50 Wentworth, New P. & S. Trig., Surveying and Tables.
75 Woodhull and Van Arsdale, Physical Experiments.
5 Walker, Political Economy, Briefer Course.
75 White, Business Law.

C. D. Lyon, 20 Monroe St., Grand Rapids, Mich.

Grimm's Fairy Tales, ed. by Lucy Crane.
Whitney, The United States.
Hobhouse, The Labor Movement.
Beyond the Sunrise.

Nathaniel McCarthy, Minneapolis, Minn.

Daudet's Tartarin on the Alps, il., pap. cover. Pub by Routledge.
Hugo's Les Miserables, 5 v., octavo, il. Routledge.
Toilers of the Sea, 2 v. Pub. by Routledge.
Notre Dame, 2 v. Pub. by Routledge.
Hajji Baba.
Price, Across the Continent with the 5th Cavalry. Pub. by Van Nostrand, 1863.

John Jos. McVey, 39 N. 13th St., Phila., Pa.

Oliphant's Literary History of England. Macmillan.
Mrs. Oliphant's History of England in the 18th and 19th Centuries. Macmillan.
Autobiography of Bonaventure Cellini.

H. Malkan, Hanover Sq., N. Y.

Amy's Secret, by Lucy Byerly. London, 1883.
Broadgrins, G. Coleman. Routledge.
Set of Carlyle, ed. de luxe.
Any books on Reconstruction Period, 1865-1876.
Genealogy of Bergen Family. 1876.

The Edw. Malley Co., New Haven, Conn.

Retold Tales of Hills and Shores of Man, by Harriet G. Rowe.

Masonic Book Co., P. O. Box 7, N. Y.

The United States Investor, any vol. or lose numbers previous to 1901.

R. H. Merriam, Hanover Sq., N. Y.

The Columbian Cyclopedia. Funk & W.
Index volume to World's Great Classics.
Records of New Amsterdam, v. 3, shp.
Puritan Age and Rule, Ellis.

Dewitt Miller, P. O. Drawer 1351, Phila., Pa. [*Cash.*]

Compendium of the Life of Lorenzo da Ponte, written by himself; to which is added the first literary conversazione held at his house in New York on the 10th of March, 1807; consisting of several Italian compositions in verse and in prose, translated into English by his scholars. New York, printed by I. Riley & Co., 1807. $15 offered.

Misch & Thron, 68 rue Royale, Brussels.

Complete sets of:

American Journal of Sociology.
Bulletin of the Office of Experimental Stations.
Gunton's Magazine.
John Hopkins University Studies in Historical and Political Science.
Journal of Political Economy.
Political Science Quarterly.
Quarterly Bulletin of Bureau of Economic Research.
Transactions of American Ethnological Soc.
Yale Review.
Quarterly Journal of Economics, v. 1-3; v. 4, no. 1.
American Anthropologist, v. 7 and foll.
Annals of Amer. Academy of Polit. and Social Science, v. 1, fasc. 2.

H. H. Morse, 20 Monroe St., Grand Rapids, Mich.

Leffingwell, Vivisection Question.
Stoddard's Lectures, 11 v.

New England Methodist Book Depository, 38 Bromfield St., Boston, Mass.

White's Warfare of Science with Theology, second-hand.

BOOKS WANTED.—Continued.

E. J. O'Malley, Hanover Sq., N. Y.

The Auctioneer's Guide, J. P. Johnstone.
The Prostrate State (South Car.)
Hell Up to Date.

Martin F. Onnen, 114 5th Ave., N. Y.

Portrait of Henry Earl of Ferrer of Normandy.
View of Ferrer.
Anything relating to the Shirley or Meyner families.
Catalogues of Portraits.

Daniel O'Shea, 1584 Broadway, N. Y.

Harper's Young People, v. 2, nos. 54, 101.
Asiatic Explorations, by Clark.
Samuel Pepys' Diary.
Poems of Cunningham, Hogg, Blacklock.
Rogers' Italy, illus. by Turner.
Anything on Scottish Border minstrelsy.

W. M. Palmer, 20 Monroe St., Grand Rapids, Mich.

Mather, One Summer in Hawaii.
Arvine, Cyclopedia of Anecdotes Religious and Moral.
Compayre's History of Pedagogy, Payne, second-hand.

C. C. Parker, 246 S. Broadway, Los Angeles, Cal. [*Cash.*]

New Hygiene, J. W. Wilson.

The Pilgrim Press, 175 Wabash Ave., Chicago, Ill.

Leibnitz, by Dewey.
Human Understanding, by Locke.
Selections from Des Cartes, Veich.
Text-Book of Kant, Sterling.
Kant and His English Critics, by Svatson.
Hume, by Knight.
Selections from Berkely, by Fraser.
Life of Ven. Padre Junipen Leora, by Very Rev. Francis Palon, tr. by Father Adams, or any other life by Rev. Francis Palon. Pub. by E. D. Dougherty, San Francisco, 1884.

T. Pillot 409 Main St., Houston, Tex.

Records of the Revolutionary War, containing Military Financial Correspondence, etc., by W. T. R. Saffell. Pub. by Pudney & Russell, N. Y., 1858.
Any books on early Texas history.

W. V. Pippin, 805 N. Eutaw St., Baltimore, Md.

Southern Soldier in the Civil War.
American Economist, v. 1 to 28.
Coleridge's Prose Works.
Memoirs of Susana Mason, 16mo.

E. W. Porter, St. Paul, Minn.

Memoirs of the Sanson Family, by H. Sanson, 1 or 2 v., trs.
Set Walpole's Letters, 9 v.

C. S. Pratt, 161 6th Ave., N. Y. [*Cash.*]

Madeline Halley, novel.
Anything on the Irish in the Revolution.
Selden, Last Days of Heine.
Brisbane, Social Destiny of Man (?)
Greenwod, Silas the Conjuror.

Pratt Institute Free Library, Ryerson St., Brooklyn, N. Y.

Theal, G. McC., History of South Africa; the Boers, or Emigrant Farmers. Sonnenschein, 1887.
Reeves, W. P., Australian Democracy. Lond., Marshall & Co., 1901.

Presb. Bd. of Pub. and S. S. Work, 192 Michigan Ave., Chicago, Ill.

Scriptural Doctrine of the Atonement, by Crawford. T. & T. Clark.
Diary of a Minister's Wife.
Development of the Church, by Falconer.
Selections from American Humor, Mark Twain.
A Girl's Money.
Grandma Crosby's Household.

Presb. Bd. of Pub. and S. S. Work, 156 5th Ave., N. Y.

Moffatt's Life of Robert and Mary Moffatt. Armstrong.
Sinker, Ion Keith Falconer. Macmillan.
Moule, New China and Old. Scribner.
Barnes, Behind the Pardah. Crowell.
Bassett's Persia Land of Imans. Scribner.

Presb. Bd. of Pub. and S. S. Work.—*Continued.*

Kellogg's The Jews, or, Prediction and Fulfillment. Randolph.
Kellogg's Light of Asia and Light of the World. Macmillan.
Afflicted Man's Companion. Amer. Tract Society.
Civilizing Mountain Men, E. B. Mason.
In Brightest Asia, H. C. Mabie.
Dr. Grant and Mountain Missionaries, L. Laurin.

Presb. Bd. of Pub. and S. S. Work, 1319 Walnut St., Phila., Pa.

Mrs. Wiggs of the Cabbage Patch, 1st ed.

G. P. Putnam's Sons, 27 W. 23d St., N. Y.

Humboldt Library of Science, nos. 1, 11, 12, 32, 48, 65, 81, 86, 105, 106, 117.
Report of State Botanist, N. Y., 1895, no. 68.
Ireland, Life Jane Welsh Carlyle.
Pragay, Hungarian Struggle. Putnam.
Virgil, trans. by Dryden. Harper.
Oliphant, Son of the Wizard.
Lewis, The Monk.
Stoddard Lectures, 11 v.
Burnham, Limestones and Marbles.
Dawson, Canadian Ice Age.
Goodell, Slavery and Anti-Slavery.
Hodgson, Cradle of the Confederacy.
Houghton, History of Parties.
Jannettez, Determination of Rocks.
Wheeler, Determinative Mineralogy.

Geo. H. Rigby, 1113 Arch St., Phila., Pa.

Broughton, Elements of Astrology.
Coulson Turnbull, Astrology.

A. M. Robertson, 126 Post St., San Francisco, Cal.

Nature's Gems, Embury. Appleton, 1845.

Robson & Adee, Saratoga Springs, N. Y.

Japan and Its Art, by Marcus B. Herish.

E. H. Roller, 419 E. Water St., Milwaukee, Wis.

Hebrew Grammar, Gesenius Davidson.
Calvin Commentaries, Edinb. ed.

Wm. B. Ropes, Mt. Vernon, Skagit Co., Wash.

Cartwright, Eagle's Nest. Scribner.
Sheldon, G., Wedded by Fate.
Southworth, A Noble Lord, pap.
Agnew, D. C. A., Protestant Exiles, 3 v.
Smiles, Huguenots and Amer., sup. 1 v.

J. Francis Ruggles, Bronson, Mich.

Any book, letter or clipping *in re* John Brown or Harper's Ferry, or Underground R.R.
Three Stations in Life, by M. E. Dowling of Detroit.

St. Paul Book and Stationery Co., 5th and St. Peter Sts., St. Paul, Minn.

In God's Country.
Josephine Empress of the French, by Ober.
Warner Library of the World's Best Literature, 30 v., Pop. ed.
Larned's Encyclopedia of History.
Century Dictionary, latest ed., cl. and leath.
Lossing, Encyclopedia of the U. S. History, 2 v. ed.
Appleton's New Universal Encyclopedia, 12 v., cl. and leath.

Schlesinger & Mayer, Chicago, Ill.

Beautiful Mrs. Thorndyke. Lippincott.
Duke and Commoner. Lippincott.

John E. Scopes, 29 Tweddle Bldg., Albany, N. Y.

American Ancestry, v. 9, 10.
Wilkinson, Memoirs, v. 2, and atlas. Phila., 1816.

Scrantom, Wetmore & Co., Rochester, N. Y.

Harper's Magazine for Aug., 1902.

Hobart J. Shanley & Co., Burlington, Vt.

The Genealogy of the Greene Family, by Gen. George S. Greene. Pub. between 1865 and 1871.

John V. Sheehan & Co., 160 Woodward Ave., Detroit, Mich.

Lady Byron Vindicated, by Harriet B. Stowe.

BOOKS WANTED.—Continued.

Shepard Book Co., 272 S. State St., Salt Lake City, U.

The Life and Adventures of Alexander Tardy, the Pirate and Pioneer, or similar title, being a yellow back novel, published in 1862 or earlier perhaps. Will pay a fair price for 1 or more copies.

The Shorthand Institute, 8 Beacon St., Boston, Mass.

Huntington's Penmanship and Stenography. 1819, '21.
Gould's Repertory of Arts and Sc. 1830 and 1832.
Bigelow's Stenographic Guide. Lancaster, 1832.
Stenography. Boston, 1809.
Old shorthand books of all kinds.

Jos. Silk, 147 6th Ave., N. Y.

Lingard's History of England, good ed.
Texas and Pacific Land Trust Agreement. N. Y., about Dec., 1887.
Crafts' History of Wyalusing or Bradford Co., Pa.
Brooks' Guide to Popular Terms Science and Art.

John Skinner, 44 N. Pearl St., Albany, N. Y.

Ruttenber's Indians of the Hudson River.
Holland Land Purchase.
Gazetteer. New York, 1836.

George D. Smith, 50 New St., N. Y.

Catlin's Indians, portfolio, 25 col. plates.
D'Amicis Holland, illus. copy.
Anglo-Saxon Review, 2d and 3d years.
History of the British Plantations in America, 4to. London, 1738.
Jorrock's Jaunts, Surtee's original ed.
Emperor Constance. Kelmscott.
Sketches of Yale College.
Sermons by Henry Ware, 2 v.
Week on the Concord, Thoreau.
Sets of Field, Kipling, Stevenson, Japan paper ed.
Set Balzac, Wormeley trans.

P. A. Smith, Lock Box 915, Fishkill on Hudson, N. Y.

Stolen White Elephant, Twain.
Light and Truth, Dalton and Lewis.
Herb doctor books.
Novel about Jennie Cramner.

Southern Methodist Book Depository, Staunton, Va.

Ency. Britannica, v. 22, 24, Werner Co. 28 v. ed. of 1894, '95, or '96, in hf. mor.

P. Stammer, 123 4th Ave., N. Y.

Essentials of Chemistry, by Withaus.
Outlines of Cosmic Philosophy, v. 2, by John Fiske.

G. E. Stechert, 9 E. 16th St., N. Y.

Depew, 100 Years of Am. Commerce.
French's Hist. Collections of La., 7 v.
Flint, Mississippi Valley, 2 v. Cinn., 1832.
Monette, Hist. Valley of Miss., 2 v. 1846.
Brown, Musical Instruments. 1888.

E. Steiger & Co., 25 Park Place, N. Y. [*Cash.*]

Artistic Homes, new ed.

Strawbridge & Clothier, Market St., Phila., Pa.

Tweedie, A Girl's Ride in Iceland.

T. & Q. Book Shop, Greensburg, Pa.

Marjory, by Katherine Macquoid.
Kate Kennedy.
The Rob of the Bow.
Keeping the Heart, Flavel.

John C. Tredway, 202 Atlantic Ave., Brooklyn, N. Y.

History of the Loco-Foco Party, by Birdsall. 1842.
Puck, nos. 5, 8, 85.

United Presb. Bd. of Pub., Pittsburgh, Pa.

The Psalter Re-adjusted in its Relation to the Temple Service and the Ancient Jewish Faith. Randolph, 1860.
The Historic Doubt Relative to Napoleon, Whately.
The Buddha and His Religion, by Saint Hilaire, tr.

W. H. Walker, 58 Moffatt St., Brooklyn, N. Y.

Naval Portfolio of the Expedition to Mexico under Commodore Perry.
Naval Portfolio, no. 8, Vera Cruz.
Sketches of Mexican War, by Lieut. Walky.
Naval Portfolio, Mouth of Tobasco River, Ascending the Tobasco River, Landing at Tobasco, Capture of Tobasco.

W. H. Walker.—*Continued.*

Oscar Wilde, books by or relating to him.
Catlin's Indians, 2 v., col. plates. London, 1846.

John Wanamaker, N. Y.

Castle of Indolence.

The Washington Book Shop, 509 7th St., N. W., Washington, D. C.

Schoolcraft's History of the Indian Tribes of the U. S., v. 2-4, 5.

David Waters, 494 St. James St., Montreal, Can.

Hochelaga Depicta, by Newton.
Bosworth. Montreal, 1839 or 1846.
Hawkins' Historical Recollections of Quebec. Neilson & Cowan, 1834.
War of 1812, by Major Richardson. 1842.
Eight Years in Canada, by Major Richardson. 1847.
History of Canada, by Wm. Smith. John Neilson Quebec, 1815.
Sir Henry Cavendish's Debates in the House of Commons in 1774.

R. H. White Co., Boston, Mass.

Spartacus, by Kellogg.

Thomas Whittaker, 2 Bible House, N. Y.

Marshall's Life of Washington.
Works of Dr. Thomas Dick, 9 or 11 v., good print.
Genesis in Colos., Prof. Bissell.
Bible Myths Compared, Bouton.

C. Witter, 19 S. Broadway, St. Louis, Mo.

Any of C. D. Gibson's books, must be in fairly good condition.

Wm. H. Ziesenitz, Hudson, N. Y.

Gossips of Rivertown, by Alice B. Neil.

BOOKS FOR SALE.

C. N. Caspar Co., 437 E. Water St., Milwaukee, Wis.

The following second-hand school books in sound condition; at 80 % discount:
225 Harper's Sixth Readers.
60 McGuffey's Rev. 5th Reader.
150 each Harvey's 4th and 5th Readers.
35 each Young Cath. 3d to 6th Readers.
200 Robinson's Beginner's Arith., rev. ed.
250 Appleton-Quackenbos Mental Arith.
183 Swinton's New Lang. Lessons.
100 Swinton's Gram. and Composition.
Send list for other wants.

A. T. Cooper, Cedar Rapids, Ia.

Warner's World's Best Literature, 46 v., Century ed. $125.00.
International Encyclopedia, 15 v., ed. 1890, full set, hf. leath. $37.50.
Character Sketches, 4 v., by Rev. E. C. Brewer, mor. $15.00.
Stanley's Darkest Africa, 2 v. $2.00.
100 Crown (art) Masterpieces, 2 v., mor. $20.00.
All the above in excellent second-hand condition. f. o. b., Cedar Rapids, Iowa, at the above prices.

Goodenough & Woglom Co., 122 Nassau St., N. Y.

American Catalogues, annual vols, 1886 to 1898, inclusive, hf. mor., $1.00 per vol.

Robert L. Jaques' Book Store, Lafayette, Ind.

64 Richter, Inorganic Chemistry, Smith, latest ed., perfectly new. Cash 25 % discount from list.

J. B. Piet, White Plains, N. Y.

History of Maryland, from the Earliest Period to the Present Day, 3 v., J. Thomas Scharf, Original ed. 1879, hf. mor., excellently preserved. Address with offer.

HELP WANTED.

WANTED.—A young man of experience and good address, in a first-class retail book business. Address, stating age, experience, etc., and salary expected, W. S., care of PUBLISHERS' WEEKLY.

BOOKS

Such prices as you may not have heard of; and such service as you will appreciate. Send us an order—that's the way to find out.

A new friend is almost as good as an old one.

H B CLAFLIN COMPANY

Church and Worth Streets New York

PUBLISHERS!

ARE you satisfied with your bookbinder? If so, are you satisfied with his fancy prices? I can satisfy you with both. Investigate my statement in justice to your own interests. Look over my plant and ask those publishing houses who patronize me. Send your dummies and I will show you what I can do.

92–98 CENTRE STREET, NEW YORK. **H. WOLFF,** 143–147 LEONARD STREET, NEW YORK.

WILLIAM R. JENKINS,

851 AND 853 SIXTH AVENUE,
N. W. COR. 48TH STREET, NEW YORK.

FRENCH	**VETERINARY**
and other foreign	(Scientific and Popular,
BOOKS,	**BOOKS,**
School and College Texts,	or Works Treating on
Miscellaneous Literature,	Horses, Cattle, Dogs,
French Plays.	etc. . . . .

Trade List and General Catalogues Supplied.

Periodicals

from

England, Germany,

France and all other countries supplied by

E. Steiger & Co.,
25 Park Place, **New York.**

PRINTING

of all kinds, plain and colored, also engraving and embossing, in any quantity, promptly attended to at the closest possible prices. We can refer to the largest banks, the largest manufacturing concerns, publishers and others in the United States. We shall take pleasure in having you call, or if it suits your convenience better, to call on you. Drop us a line.

ANDREW H. KELLOGG
409 Pearl St., ('Phone 3640 John,) New York

Accuracy. Promptness. Reliability.

KAY PRINTING HOUSE,

66-68 CENTRE STREET,
TELEPHONE 1663 FRANKLIN. NEW YORK.

Estimates Promptly Furnished.

Printers to THE PUBLISHERS' WEEKLY.

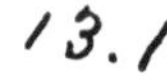

THE
Publishers' Weekly
THE AMERICAN
BOOK TRADE JOURNAL
WITH WHICH IS INCORPORATED
The American Literary Gazette and Publishers' Circular.
[ESTABLISHED 1852.]
PUBLICATION OFFICE, 298 BROADWAY, NEW YORK.
Entered at the Post-Office at New York, N. Y., as second-class matter.

VOL. LXII., No. 9. NEW YORK, August 30, 1902. WHOLE No. 1596

On the Top Wave of Popularit

An interesting compilation of reports from the pro: nent book stores in the United States, of the six l selling books of the month, was printed in *The Bookm Magazine* for August. "The Mississippi Bubble" all others as the best selling novel.

"'The Mississippi Bubble' is one of the truly great romances. It is truth and art combined."—*The Boston Journal.*

MISS GILDER, editor of *The Critic*, says: "It is one of the best novels that has come out of America in many a day."

THE BOWEN-MERRILL COMPANY, *Publis*

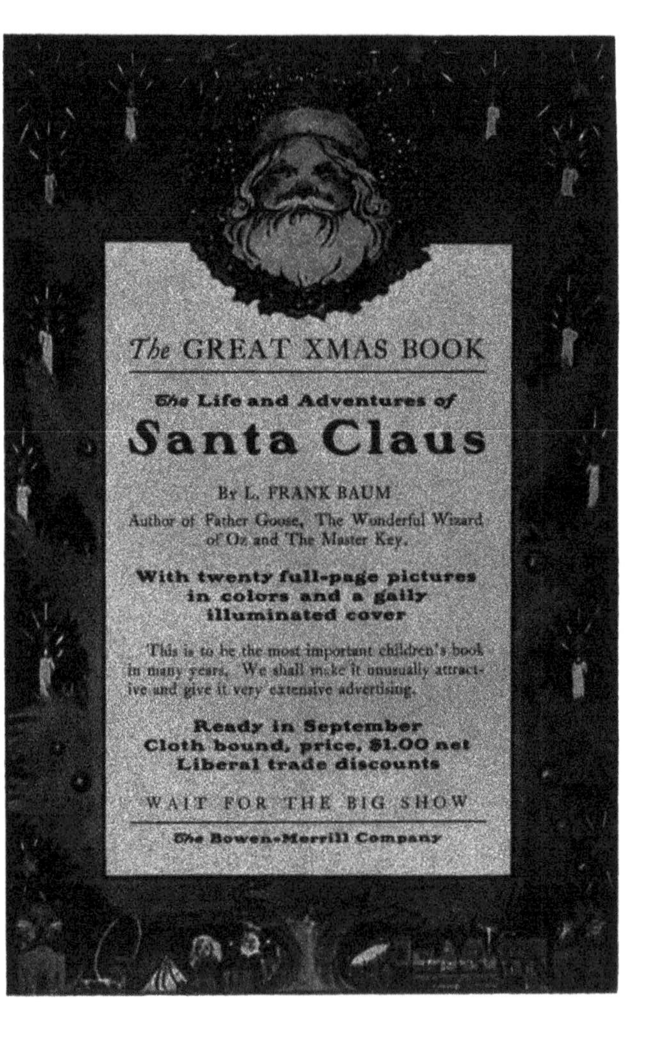
The GREAT XMAS BOOK
The Life and Adventures of
Santa Claus
By L. FRANK BAUM
Author of Father Goose, The Wonderful Wizard of Oz and The Master Key.
With twenty full-page pictures in colors and a gaily illuminated cover
This is to be the most important children's book in many years. We shall make it unusually attractive and give it very extensive advertising.
Ready in September
Cloth bound, price, $1.00 net
Liberal trade discounts
WAIT FOR THE BIG SHOW
The Bowen-Merrill Company

About Book Illustrating

THE half-tone illustrations in the popular fiction of the day cost from $5 to $10 a plate to engrave. The plates for the illustrations in MISS RIVES' novel, "HEARTS COURAGEOUS," were engraved by hand on wood by M Haider, whose price was $125 per plate for engraving them. The exhibit below of the elaborate work put upon the "HEARTS COURAGEOUS" pictures is shown by enlarging a part of the illustration, showing all the lines cut by hand.

FROM "HEARTS COURAGEOUS."

THE BOWEN-MERRILL COMPANY, *Publishers*

The Publishers' Weekly.

AUGUST 30, 1902.

RATES OF ADVERTISING.

One page.. $20 00
Half page.. 12 00
Quarter page.. 6 00
Eighth page.. 4 00
One-sixteenth page.. 2 00

Copyright Notices, Special Notices, and other undisplayed advertisements, 10 cents a line of nonpareil type.

The above prices do not include insertions in the "Annual Summary Number," the "Summer Number," the "Educational Number," or the "Christmas Bookshelf," for which higher rates are charged.

Special positions $5 a page extra. Applications for special pages will be honored in the order of their receipt.

Special rates for yearly or other contracts.

All matter for advertising pages should reach this office not later than Wednesday noon, to insure insertion in the same week's issue.

RATES OF SUBSCRIPTION.

One year, postage prepaid in the United States.... $3 00
One year, postage prepaid to foreign countries.... 4 00
Single copies, 8 cents; postpaid, 10 cents. Special numbers: Educational Number, in leatherette, 50 cents; Christmas Number, 25 cents; the numbers containing the three, six and nine months' Cumulated Lists, 25 cents each. Extra copies of the Annual Summary Number, *to subscribers only*, 50 cents each.

PUBLICATION OFFICE, 298 BROADWAY, P. O. BOX 943, N.Y.

INDEX TO ADVERTISERS — PAGE

NOTES IN SEASON.

LOTHROP PUBLISHING COMPANY have just ready "The Treasure of Shag Rock," telling the adventures of several young men in their search for treasure buried on an island in the South Pacific. The book promises to please wideawake young people.

J. F. LEHMAN, publisher, Heustrasse 20, Munich, Bavaria, will issue in October the German edition of "Memoirs of President Paul Kruger," related by himself. The publication rights for all languages are controlled by J. F. Lehmann, and he announces that the translation rights for all English-speaking countries, (including Great Britain and her colonies,) are for sale. Full information concerning details may be obtained upon application to the publisher.

THE BOWEN-MERRILL COMPANY call special attention to "The Mississippi Bubble," now on the top wave of popularity, and according to August and September *Bookman* first among the six best-selling books of two months. They also show specimens of the fine illustrations in Miss Rives's novel, "Hearts Courageous," which have been engraved on wood by hand by Mr. Harder, who has proved himself proficient in an almost lost art.

FUNK & WAGNALLS will publish September 20 "Love and the Soul Hunters," by John Oliver Hobbes, in which this artistic author claims to have made the effort of her life; "The Needle's Eye," by Florence Morse Kingsley, a story of modern American life; "The Insane Root," by Mrs. Campbell Praed, a story on the order of Dr. Jekyll and Mr. Hyde; "The Searchers," by Margaretta Byrde; and "The Herr Doktor," by Robert McDonald, telling of an American girl's experiences in aiming for a titled husband. The last will be an addition to the *Hour-glass Stories*.

CHARLES SCRIBNER'S SONS published yesterday "The Wings of the Dove," by Henry James, a story in two volumes of a peculiarly insidious temptation which assails the hero and enables the author to show some of his finest work in analysis of character; "The Shadow of the Rope," by E. W. Hornung, the creator of "Raffles," which deals with the solving of the mystery of a murder; and a second series of "Views and Reviews," by W. E. Henley, a volume of comment on the art and artists of the last century, so arranged as to make a valuable handbook of reference. They have also ready a cheaper edition of twenty copyrighted Henty books, printed from the same plates as the original edition and sold in quantities at prices which admit of their being handled in competition with the unauthorized reprints.

HARPER & BROTHERS will issue during September "The Vultures," by Henry Seton Merriman, a novel of love and adventure in Russia, the "vultures" being members of the foreign diplomatic service; "Istar of Babylon," by Margaret Horton Potter, a fascinating novel of the time just before the fall of Babylon, which describes the great feast of Belshazzar, in which the chief character is Istar, the Egyptian Aphrodite; "The Wooing of Wistaria," by Onoto Watanna, a story of Japan and Japanese characters; and three novels with American setting; "The Maid at Arms," by Robert Chambers, treating of Revolutionary times; "The Ship of Dreams," a story of the early settlers of Long Island, by Louise Forsslund; and "Out of the West," by Elizabeth Higgins, giving a vivid picture of a typical little Western town in which an Easterner had quite a dramatic career.

WEEKLY RECORD OF NEW PUBLICATIONS.

☞ Beginning with the issue of July 5, 1902, the titles of *net* books published under the rules of the American Publishers' Association are preceded by a double asterisk **, and the word net follows the price. The titles of *fiction* (not net) published under the rules are preceded by a dagger †. *Net* books not covered by the rules, whether published by members of the American Publishers' Association or not, are preceded by a single asterisk, and the word net follows the price. ☜

The abbreviations are usually self-explanatory. c. after the date indicates that the book is copyrighted; if the copyright date differs from the imprint date, the year of copyright is added. Books of foreign origin of which the edition (annotated, illustrated, etc.) is entered as copyright, are marked c. ed.; translations, c. tr.: n. p., in place of price, indicates that the publisher makes no price, either net or retail, and quotes prices to the trade only upon application.

A colon after initial designates the most usual given name, as: A: Augustus; B: Benjamin; C: Charles; D: David; E: Edward; F: Frederic; G: George; H: Henry; I: Isaac; J: John; L: Louis; N: Nicholas; P: Peter; R: Richard; S: Samuel; T: Thomas; W: William.

Sizes are designated as follows: F. (folio: over 30 centimeters high); Q. (4to: under 30 cm.); O. (8vo: 25 cm.); D. (12mo: 20 cm.); S. (16mo: 17½ cm.); T. (24mo: 15 cm.); Tt. (32mo: 12½ cm.); Fe. 48mo: 10 cm.). Sq., obl., nar., designate square, oblong, narrow books of these heights.

Barker, Wharton, *ed.* The great issues; reprints of some editorials from the American, 1897-1900. Phil., Wharton Barker, 1902. c. 391 p. 12°, cl., $1.

Bechtel, J: Hendricks, *comp.* Proverbs, maxims and phrases, drawn from all lands and times; carefully selected and indexed for convenient reference; furnishing apt illustrations for use in conversation, writing, and public discourse. Phil., Penn Publishing Co., 1902. c. 201 p. 24°, (Popular handbooks.) cl., 50 c.

†Becke, G: L. Breachley—black sheep: novel. Phil., Lippincott, 1902. 300 p. 12°, cl., $1.50.

Beowulf. Beowulf; tr.; out of the old English by Chauncey Brewster Tinker. N. Y., Newson & Co., 1902. c. 158 p. 16°, cl., 80 c.

Bible. The young people's Bible; or, the Scriptures connected, explained and simplified, by Harriet Newell Jones; with introd. by Rev. Malcolm MacGregor. Phil., American Book and Bible House, [1902.] c. 2+480 p. il. 8°, cl., $1.75.

Blount, *Sir* E: C: Memoirs of Sir Edward Blount, K.C.B., etc.; ed. by Stuart J. Reid. N. Y., Longmans, Green & Co., 1902. 6+308 p. pors. O. cl., $4.

Sir E: Blount was director of the London Joint-Stock Bank, and was largely connected with railroads. He was born in the early years of the past century. The titles of his chapters are: Early years; Attaché in Rome and Paris; English banker in Paris; The beginnings of French railways; My railway career in France; My experiences in the Revolution of 1848; Early days of the Second Empire; Franco-German war and the siege of Paris, etc.

Botsford, Amelia Howard. Child life in all nations; or, the Earlingtons' trip around the world. Phil., American Book and Bible House, [1902.] c. 279 p. il. 12°, cl., $1.

Brooks, E: Plane and solid geometry: a complete course in the elements of the science. Rev. ed. Phil., Christopher Sower Co., [1902.] c. '01. 415 p. diagr., 12°, cl., $1.25.

Browne, G: Waldo, ["Victor St. Clair," *pseud.*] From switch to lever; or the young engineer of the mountain express. N. Y., Street & Smith, [1902.] c. 3+5-233 p. D. (Boys' own lib., no. 30.) cl., 75 c.

Browne, G: Waldo, ["Victor St. Clair," *pseud.*] Zip the acrobat; or, the old showman's secret. N. Y., Street & Smith, [1902.] c. 233 p. D. (Boys' own lib., no. 100.) cl., 75 c.

Bryan, W: Jennings. *The Commoner*, condensed. N. Y., Abbey Press, [1902.] c. 12+469 p. por. O. cl., $1.50.

A condensation of matter which has appeared in *The Commoner*, Mr. Bryan's organ, during the first year of its existence. The majority of the editorials are from Mr. Bryan's pen, on topics of permanent interest. There are other editorials from other writers, with poems, fables, etc., that appeared in *The Commoner*.

Burnett, Irwin. The heretic: a story of New Jersey love and Puritanism in 1799. N. Y., Abbey Press, [1902.] c. 6+347 p. D. cl., $1.50.

Chancellor, W: Estabrook. Elementary school mathematics by grades. Seventh book, arithmetic, geometry and algebra. N. Y., Globe School Book Co., [1902.] c. 8+11-176 p. il. 12°, (Globe ser.) cl., 28 c.

Chase, Eliza B. In quest of the quaint; il. by the writer, from water color and pencil sketches. Phil., Ferris & Leach, 1902. c. 6+253 p. D. hf. ooze, $1.50.

Sketches, romances, legends, canoe songs, and gleanings of travel from the pen and pencil of the author of "Over the Border." The scene of this work is the charming region around the lower Saint Lawrence.

Clarkson, Jos. Russell. The A B C of scientific Christianity. Omaha, Neb., Joseph Russell Clarkson, 1901. c. 2+112 p. D. pap., 25 c.

Tells the writer's reasons for ceasing to be a Christian Scientist, and his "conversion to Christianity."

Cline, Alberta. Kindergarten, painting, plays and home entertainments: a book of amusement and instruction for boys and girls. Phil., American Book and Bible House, [1902.] 1+268 p. il. 12°, cl., $1.

****Clodd**, E: Thomas Henry Huxley. N. Y., Dodd, Mead & Co., 1902. 13+252 p. 12°, (Modern English writers.) cl., $1 net.

Cobban, J. M. The green turbans, [a novel.] N. Y., A. L. Burt Co., 1902. c. 326 p. 12°, (Manhattan ser.) pap., 50 c.

Collier's new encyclopedia: an entirely new and original work containing a greater number of titles than any other similar compendium; with articles by over three hundred contributors. N. Y., P: F. Collier & Son, 1902. c. 16 v., il. pl. (partly col.) maps (partly fold.) 8°, cl., per set, $20.

Cyr, Ellen M. Advanced first reader. Bost., Ginn, 1902. 6+104 p. il. S. (Art ser.) cl., 35 c.

Dale, Lucy. The principles of English constitutional history. N. Y., Longmans, Green & Co., 1902. 9+509 p. D. cl., $1.50.
The author calls this "an attempt briefly to set forth the main results of modern historical research, in a form acceptable to the general reader."

Daudet, Alphonse. La Belle-Nivernaise; ed., with notes and vocab., by Ja. Boïelle. Rev. ed. Bost., Heath, 1902. c. 5+117 p. por. il. 16°, (Heath's modern language ser.) cl., 30 c.

†**Devinne**, Paul. The day of prosperity: a vision of the century to come. N. Y., G: W. Dillingham Co., [1902.] [Jl.] c. 3-271 p. D. cl., $1.50.
A story of life in New York City in the year 2000. Offered as a solution of to-day's most mooted problems, differing from Bellamy and kindred thinkers, though following somewhat similar lines. The leading character is a journalist, who is put to sleep for a hundred years by a mysterious little doctor he meets in an east side café in New York. His scheme of life on his awakening is ingenious and most hopeful.

Dhammapada. Hymns of the faith (Dhammapada): being an ancient anthology preserved in the short collection of the sacred scriptures of the Buddhists; tr. from the Pâli by Albert J. Edmunds. Chic., Open Court Publishing Co., 1902. c. 13+109 p. 12°, cl., $1.

Dudley, Emilius Clark, *ed.* Gynecology; ed. by Emilius C. Dudley; with the collaboration of W: Healy. Chic., Year Book Publishers, 1902. c. 212 p. il. 12°, (Practical medicine ser. of year books, v. 4.) cl., $1.50.

Eldridge, E: A California girl: [a novel.] N. Y., Abbey Press, [1902.] c. 247 p. D. cl., $1.50.

Eldridge, E: H. Hypnotism; its uses and abuses; together with full and complete directions showing how any one can learn to hypnotize. Phil., Penn Publishing Co., 1902. c. 4+5-197 p. 16°, (Popular handbooks.) cl., 50 c.

Emerson, Edwin, *jr.* A history of the nineteenth century, year by year; with an introd. by Georg Gottfried Gervinus. N. Y., P: F. Collier & Son, 1902. c. 3 v., il. pl. (partly col.) por. maps, 12°, cl., $3.

Fiske, G: B., *comp.* Poultry architecture: a practical guide for construction of poultry houses, coops and yards. N. Y., Orange Judd Co., 1902. 8+130 p. il. D. cl., 50 c.
These plans have been carefully selected, and only those are given which are in successful use and which are adapted to the needs of practical poultry keepers. The leading chapters treat on location and methods; low cost houses; buildings for colony system; homes for farm poultry; bank and sod structures and extras; incubator and brooder houses; special purpose buildings; coops, yards, fences, etc., etc.

Fowler, G: L. Electricity: a condensed and reliable treatise giving full directions for the construction and operation of any kind of electrical apparatus. Phil., Penn Publishing Co., 1902. c. 205 p. il. diagr., 16°, (Popular handbooks.) cl., 50 c.

Friars (The) must stay; reprint from *The Messenger*, August, 1902. N. Y., [Amer. News Co.,] 1902. 27 p. O. pap., 5 c.
The publishers describe this pamphlet as, "a plea for the friars, giving an account of the influences arrayed against them in the Philippine Islands, with proofs that the Filipino people want them to remain and that some are actually living in their parishes, and that only firm action is needed on the part of our officials to maintain them in rights which Governor Taft testifies to be theirs."

***Garnett**, R:, Vallée, L., *and* Brandl, A., *eds.* The universal anthology. v. 31-33. Westminster ed. N. Y., Merrill & Baker, 1902. c. 3 v., pl., por. 4°, per v., $3.50.

George, Marian M. A little journey to Belgium and Denmark; for home and school, intermediate and upper grades. Chic., A. Flanagan Co., [1902.] c. 108 p. il. 12°, (Plan book ser., v. 5, no. 8.) pap., 15 c.

George, Marian M. A little journey to Switzerland; for intermediate and upper grades. Chic., A. Flanagan Co., [1902.] c. 117 p. il. 12°, (Plan book ser., v. 5, no. 9.) pap., 15 c.

***Gladden**, Washington. The practice of immortality. Bost., Pilgrim Press, [1902.] 24 p. D. (Beacon Hill ser.) bds., 25 c. net.

†**Gunsaulus**, Frank W. Monk and knight: an historical study. 5th ed. Chic., A. C. McClurg & Co., 1902. c. '91. 365+342 p. 12°, cl., $1.50.

Hagerstown town and country almanack for 1903. [no. 106.] Hagerstown, Md., J. Gruber, [1902.] c. 25 p. sq. 8°, pap., 10 c.

Hale, E: Everett, *jr*, *ed.* American essays. N. Y. and Chic., Globe School Book Co., [1902.] c. 12+257 p. 16°, (Hawthorne classics.) cl., 40 c.

Hargis, A. M. Treatise on commercial law and business customs. Grand Island, Neb., A. M. Hargis, 1902. c. 500 p. 12°, cl., $3.

Hennequin, Alfred. New treatise on the French verbs; including an easy and practical method for acquiring the irregular verbs, and rules for the present and past participles. N. Y., American Book Co., [1902.] c. 10+122 p. 12°, cl., 65 c.

Hollinshed, T. E: The new century speaker, writer and etiquette: a standard work on elocution, composition and etiquette; the best selections of the greatest writers of this and other countries. Phil., American Book and Bible House, [1902.] c. 2+454 p. 12°, cl., $1.50.

†**Holmes**, Mary J. The Cromptons. N. Y., G: W. Dillingham Co., [1902.] [Ag.] c. '02: '99. 5-384 p. D. cl., $1.
Aside from its love story, "The Cromptons" illustrates class and family distinctions as they exist in America.

Hutton, T: B. American history outlines; for teachers and high school students in reviewing United States history. Sac City, Ia., Press of *The Sac Sun*, 1902. c. 53 p. 16°, pap., 30 c.

Idaho codes annotated. 4 v. San Francisco, Cal., Bancroft-Whitney Co., 1902. 2771 p. 8°, shp., $17.
Contents: v. 1, Political code of State of Idaho, 1901, 962 p.; Civil code of Idaho, 1901, 420 p.; Code of civil procedure of Idaho, 1901, 788 p.; Penal code of Idaho, 1901, 601 p.

****Lang**, H: Rosemann, *ed.* Cancioneiro gallego-castelhano, the extant Galician poems of the Gallego-Castilian lyric school (1350-1450,) collected and ed. with a literary study, notes and glossary by H: R. Lang. v. 1. N. Y., Scribner, 1902. c. 8°, (Yale bicentennial pubs.) cl., $3 net.

La Ramé, Louise de. The child of Urbino, Raphael: a third reader; ed. by Sara D. Jenkins. Bost. and N. Y., Educational Publishing Co., [1902.] c. 1900. 64 p. pl. por. 12°, cl., 30 c.

****Lavignac**, Albert. Music and musicians; with 94 il. and 510 examples in musical notation; tr. by W: Marchant; ed., with additions on music in America, by H. H. Krehbiel. 3d ed., rev. [Cheaper ed.] N. Y., H: Holt & Co., 1902. 8+504 p. 12°, cl., $1.75 net.

****Lloyd**, Rob. The treasure of Shag Rock: an adventure story; il. by I. B. Hazelton. Bost., Lothrop Pub. Co., [1902.] [Jl.] c. 5-344 p. D. cl., $1 net.
Opens in a preparatory school near Boston, where the hero, George Hurst, makes a record in track athletics. The story then shifts to San Francisco and to a hunt for treasure buried in an island in the South Pacific, the clew to which is a parchment made of human skin. Fights with pirates and other adventures are part of the narrative.

Longfellow, H: Wadsworth. The story of Hiawatha; il. by Rob. Smith; abridged for the use of schools. Bost. and N. Y., Educational Publishing Co., [1902.] c. '99. 5-132 p. il. col. pl. 16°, (Stories of the red children.) cl., 40 c.; bds., 30 c.

Lovejoy, Evelyn Mary Wood. Dandelion; or, out of the shadows. N. Y., Abbey Press, [1902.] c. 294 p. D. cl., $1.
The story of a New England waif, who passes through thrilling experiences, solves the mystery of her birth, and re-unites her parents.

Lungwitz, Anton. The complete guide to blacksmithing, horseshoeing, carriage and wagon building and painting, based on the textbook on horseshoeing; with chapters on carriage-ironing, wagon and buggy painting, varnishing, ornamenting, etc., by C: F. Adams. Chic., M. A. Donohue & Co., [1902.] c. 1+222 p. il. 12°, cl., $1.

***McVickar**, W: Bard. The lays of a lawyer; il. by H. W. McVickar. N. Y., Pelham Press, [for sale by Dodd, Mead & Co.,] 1902. c. 15+1+94 p. 8°, cl., $4 net. [Ed. of 250 copies.]

Municipal year book, 1902; with summaries and editorial discussion; ed. by M. N. Baker. [1st issue.] N. Y., Engineering News Publishing Co., 1902. c. 350 p. 8°, cl., $3.

Murray, Charlotte. Castleton's "prep"; il. by Florence Reason. Phil., Union Press, 1902. 6-292 p. D. cl., $1.25.
After leaving the university Castleton did not feel his education was quite finished. He wished to know more about a poorer class of people than the class in which he had been born. To accomplish this, he chose to keep a stationer's shop in a provincial seaport town. His experience is rich in helpfulness, and his love story interesting.

National standard family and business atlas of the world, specially adapted for commercial and library reference; with all populations according to the 1901 census. Chic., Fort Dearborn Publishing Co., [1902.] c. 2+7-410 p. il. maps, size 12 x 15 in., cl., subs., $4.75.

Neilson, Rob. M. The steam turbine. N. Y., Longmans, Green & Co., 1902. 9+163 p. il. O. cl., $2.50.
"The author has endeavored to describe, not only the principal parts of the leading types of steam turbine, but also the small details which, in the case of this motor, have such a preponderating influence in determining success or failure. The theory of the action of the steam turbine is also treated of, and the subject is likewise dealt with historically."—*Preface.*

Nichberg-Wagner, Mathilde. Im freundeskreisse: dramatische Festspiele und Gelegenheitsscherze für jung und alt. N. Y., G. E. Stechert, [1902.] 166 p. D. cl., $1.

Oman, C: W: Chadwick. Seven Roman statesmen of the later republic: The Gracchi, Sulla, Crassus, Cato, Pompey, Cæsar. N. Y., Longmans, Green & Co., 1902. 6+348 p. il. pors. D. cl., $1.60.
"This little book is not a history, but a series of studies of the leading men of the century, intended to show the importance of the personal element in those miserable days [at the end of the Roman republic] of storm and stress."

†**Oxenham**, J: Bondman free: the remarkable adventures of a gentleman convict; il. by L: F. Grant. N. Y., Federal Book Co., 1902. c. 6+342 p. il. D. cl., 50 c.
John Bellenger steals money to save a dying wife. At her death he delivers himself up to justice. The sympathy his story excites in judge and jury lets him off with a two years sentence of imprisonment. The story deals chiefly with his trouble in getting employment, or keeping it after serving his sentence, where his story is known.

Perdue, Hannah Avis. The new century first reader; revised by H. Avis Perdue and Florence E. La Victoire. Chic., Rand, McNally & Co., [1902.] c. 112 p. il. (New century readers by grades, bk. 1.) cl., 17 c.

****Pierson**, Arthur Tappan. The Gordian knot; or, the problem which baffles infidelity. N. Y., Funk & Wagnalls Co., 1902. c. 3-264 p. nar. S. cl., 60 c. net.
The endeavor is not to belittle difficulties on the one hand, nor deal in unfair evasions on the other, but to ask and answer such questions as these: Is there a God? Is the universe the work of a personal Creator? Whence came the order and perfection of the universe, instinct in animals, intelligence and conscience in man? How can we account for the Bible and Jesus Christ, and is there a life beyond? List of helpful books, 6 p.

Pitman, *Sir* I: Isaac Pitman's shorthand instructor: an exposition of Isaac Pitman's "System of phonography"; designed for class or self-instruction. Twentieth century ed. rev. N. Y., Sir I: Pitman & Sons, 1902. c. '93-1901. 14+276 p. S. cl., $1.50.

Pratt, Mara Louise. Stories of Illinois. Bost. and N. Y., Educational Publishing Co., [1902.] c. 204 p. il. pl. 16°, (Young folk's lib. of choice lit.) cl., 50 c.; bds., 40 c.

Rine, G: W. The essentials of our language: a guide to accuracy in the use of the English language. Oakland, Cal., Pacific Press Publishing Co., [1902.] c. 4-282 p. 12°, cl., 75 c.

Ruskin, J: Mornings in Florence: ed., with introd., notes and il. from the old masters of painting and sculpture; ed. by Margaret Baker. N. Y., Abbey Press, [1902.] 244 p. il. D. cl., $2.

Scott, *Sir* Walter. Waverley novels; abridged by W: Hardcastle Browne. N. Y., P: F. Collier & Son, 1902. c. 25 v., il. 12°, cl., $19.

Shadwell, Arthur. Drink, temperance and legislation. N. Y., Longmans, Green & Co., 1902. 17+304 p. D. cl., $1.75.
Deals mainly with the drink question in Great Britain, but numerous illustrative facts are drawn from other countries. The book is written "from the standpoint of an observer and student who has no interest in the liquor traffic, no connection with any temperance organization, no foregone conclusion to prove and no favorite panacea to advocate." Bibliography (3 p.).

Sheldon, H: I. Notes on the Nicaragua Canal. New ed. Chic., A. C. McClurg & Co., 1902. c. '97, '98, '02. 212 p. 8°, cl., $1.25.

†Sibley, Edwin Day. Stillman Gott, farmer and fisherman. Bost., J: S. Brooks & Co., 1902. c. 9-361 p. D. cl., $1.50.
"The story was written for the purpose of portraying the type of American citizen that can be met, seen, and known on the coast of Maine in any town from Kittery to Eastport, but particularly referring to the half farmer, half fisherman, who lives in the towns along the shores in the neighborhood of Mt. Desert."—*Preface.*

Skiles, May Evelyn. A singular metamorphosis: [a novel.] N. Y., Abbey Press, [1902.] c. 85 p. D. cl., 50 c.

Staedeler, Georg Andreas Karl. A system of qualitative chemical analysis, by Staedeler, Kolbe and Abeljanz; authorized and rev. translation by G: B. Frankforter. 2d American ed. from the 11th German ed. Minneapolis, H. W. Wilson, 1901. c. 5+101 p. D. cl., 60 c.

Sterling, Adaline Wheelock, Holbrook, Florence, *and* Hale, E: E., *jr.* Nature and life: a fourth reader. pt. 1. N. Y., Globe School Book Co., [1902.] c. 432 p. 16°, (Hawthorne readers.) cl., 56 c.; or in 2 pts., ea., 32 c.

Sundara, *Rao,* T. T. Sundara Row's geometric exercises in paper folding; ed. and rev. by Wooster Woodruff Beman and David Eugene Smith. Chic., Open Court Pub. Co., 1902. c. 14+148 p. il. 12°, cl., $1.

†Terhune, Everit Bogert. Michel Gulpe; il. by Sidney Marsh Chase. N. Y., G: W. Dillingham Co., [1902.] [Ag.] c. 3-182 p. D. cl., $1.25.
The scene is a little town in France, not far from Poitiers. Michel Gulpe, the character around whom the story is woven, is a tobacconist. His little shop is avoided by the superstitious folk of the village, to whom he has become a "bogey man." The author wins his confidence, and writes out his story. Michel is a staunch follower of the old Eastern religions, and a devoted worshipper of Brahma. He believes in the transmigration of the soul, and relates the various lives through which he has passed.

Toward the rising sun: sketches of life in Eastern lands. Bost., Ginn, 1902. c. 2+138 p. il. S. (Youth's Companion ser.) cl., 30 c.
Descriptions by well-known authors of life in India, China, Japan, Korea, and the islands of the eastern seas. The volume is designed as a reader for either home or school.

United States. List of observatories. Washington, D. C., Smithsonian Institution, 1902. 48 p. O. (Smithsonian miscellaneous collections, v. 41, no. 1259.) pap., n. p.

†Wells, Carolyn. Folly in the forest; il. by Reginald B. Birch. Phil., H: Altemus Co., 1902. c. 9-282 p. D. cl., $1.
Continues the adventures of "Folly" or "Florinda," who found herself last year in "Fairyland." The present book relates her amusing adventures in the "forest of the past" which is peopled with the creatures of mythology, history and literature, such as Pegasus, the Sphinx, Poe's raven, etc.

****Whitelock,** W: Wallace. When the heart is young: [poems]; il. by Harper Pennington. N. Y., Dutton, 1902. c. 7+83 p. 12°, cl., $1 net.

ORDER LIST.

ABBEY PRESS, 114 Fifth Ave., New York.

Bryan, The *Commoner* condensed..... $1.50
Burnett, The heretic.................. 1.50
Eldridge, A California girl........... 1.50
Lovejoy, Dandelion.................... 1.00
Ruskin, Mornings in Florence......... 2.00
Skiles, A singular metamorphosis..... 50

H. ALTEMUS CO., 507-513 Cherry St., Philadelphia.

†Wells, Folly in the forest........... 1.00

AMERICAN BOOK AND BIBLE HOUSE, 146 N. 10th St., Philadelphia.

Bible, Young people's Bible.......... 1.75
Botsford, Child life in all nations...... 1.00
Cline, Kindergarten, painting, plays, etc...... 1.00
Hollinshed, New century speaker..... 1.50

AMERICAN BOOK CO., 100 Washington Sq., E., New York.

Hennequin, New treatise on the French verbs...... 65

AMERICAN NEWS CO., 39 Chambers St., New York.

Friars (The) must stay............ 5

BANCROFT-WHITNEY CO., 438 Montgomery St., San Francisco.

Idaho codes annotated, 4 v........... 17.00

WHARTON BARKER, Philadelphia.

Barker, Great issues, 1897-1900........ $1.00

A. L. BURT CO., 52-58 Duane St., New York.

Cobban, The green turbans.......... 50

JOHN S. BROOKS & CO., 120 Boylston St., Boston.

†Sibley, Stillman Gott................ 1.50

JOSEPH RUSSELL CLARKSON, Omaha, Neb.

Clarkson, A B C of scientific Christianity...... 25

P. F. COLLIER & SON, 203 Broadway, New York.

Collier's new encyclopædia, 16 v., per set, 20.00
Emerson, History of the nineteenth century, 3 v........ 3.00
Scott, Waverley novels, abridged ed., 25 v........ 19.00

G. W. DILLINGHAM CO., 119 W. 23d St., New York.

†Devinne, The day of prosperity...... 1.50
†Holmes, The Cromptons............ 1.00
†Terhune, Michel Gulpe............ 1.25

DODD, MEAD & CO., 372 Fifth Ave., New York.

**Clodd, Thomas Henry Huxley..net, 1.00
*McVickar, Lays of a lawyer.....net, 4.00

M. A. DONOHUE & Co., 407-429 Dearborn St., Chicago.

Lungwitz, Complete guide to blacksmithing, etc........ .... $1.00

E. P. DUTTON & Co., 31 W. 23d St., New York.

**Whitelock, When the heart is young, net, 1.00

EDUCATIONAL PUBLISHING Co., 63 Fifth Ave., New York; 50 Bromfield St., Boston.

La Ramé, Child of Urbino............ 30
Longfellow, Hiawatha..........30 c.; 40
Pratt, Story of Illinois.........40 c.; 50

ENGINEERING NEWS PUBLISHING Co., 220 Broadway, New York.

Municipal year book, 1902............ 3.00

THE FEDERAL BOOK Co., 52-58 Duane St., New York.

†Oxenham, Bondman free............ 50

FERRIS & LEACH, 29 N. 7th St., Philadelphia.

Chase, In quest of the quaint......... 1.50

A. F. FLANAGAN Co., 267 Wabash Ave., Chicago.

George, Little journey to Belgium.... 15
——, Little journey to Switzerland..... 15

FORT DEARBORN PUBLISHING Co., Chicago.

National standard family and business atlas of the world............subs., 4.75

FUNK & WAGNALLS Co., 30 Lafayette Pl. New York.

**Pierson, The Gordian knot.....net, 60

GINN & Co., 29 Beacon St., Boston.

Cyr, Advanced first reader........... 35
Toward the rising sun................ 30

GLOBE SCHOOL BOOK Co., 103 Fifth Ave., New York.

Chancellor, Elementary school mathematics, 7th bk.................net, 28
Hale, American essays............... 40
Sterling, *and others*, Nature and life, 56 c.; in 2 pts., ea., 32

J. GRUBER, Hagerstown, Md.

Hagerstown and country almanac, 1903. 10

A. M. HARGIS, Grand Island, Neb.

Hargis, On commercial law........... 3.00

D. C. HEATH & Co., 110 Boylston St., Boston.

Daudet, La Belle Nivernaise......... 30

HENRY HOLT & Co., 29 W. 23d St., New York.

**Lavignac, Music and musicians, 3d rev., cheaper ed................net, 1.75

ORANGE JUDD Co., 52 Lafayette Pl., New York.

Fiske, Poultry architecture........... 50

J. B. LIPPINCOTT Co., Washington Sq., Philadelphia.

†Becke, Breachley—black sheep........ 1.50

LONGMANS, GREEN & Co., 91-93 Fifth Ave., New York.

Blount, Memoirs..... .... 4.00
Dale, Principles of English constitutional history....... .... 1.50
Neilson, The steam turbine........... 2.50
Oman, Seven Roman statesmen....... 1.60
Shadwell, Drink, temperance and legislation........ .... 1.75

LOTHROP PUB. Co., 530 Atlantic Ave., Boston.

**Lloyd, Treasure of Shag Rock...net, $1.00

A. C. MCCLURG & Co., 215-221 Wabash Ave., Chicago.

†Gunsaulus, Monk and knight........ 1.50
Sheldon, Notes on the Nicaragua Canal, new ed...................... 1.25

MERRILL & BAKER, 11 E. 16th St., New York.

Garnett *and* Brandl, Universal anthology, v. 31-33.................per v., 3.50

NEWSON & Co., 15 E. 17th St., New York.

Beowulf...... 80

OPEN COURT PUB. Co., 324 Dearborn St., Chicago.

Dhammapada, Hymns of the faith.... 1.00
Sundara *Rao*, Geometric exercises in paper folding...... .... 1.00

PACIFIC PRESS PUB. Co., Oakland, California.

Rine, Essentials of language.......... 75

PENN PUBLISHING Co., 923 Arch St., Philadelphia.

Bechtel, Proverbs, etc................ 50
Eldridge, Hypnotism....... 50
Fowler, Electricity....... 50

PILGRIM PRESS, Congregational House, Boston.

*Gladden, Practice of immortality.net, 25

SIR ISAAC PITMAN & SONS, 33 Union Sq., New York.

Pitman, Shorthand instructor, Twentieth century ed., rev............... 1.50

RAND, MCNALLY & Co., 142 Fifth Ave., New York; 160-174 Adams St., Chicago.

Perdue, New century first reader, rev. 17

PRESS OF THE SAC SUN, Sac City, Iowa.

Hutton, American history outlines.... 30

CHARLES SCRIBNER'S SONS, 153-157 Fifth Ave., New York.

**Lang, Cancioneiro Gallego-Castelhano...... ....net, 3.00

SMITHSONIAN INSTITUTION, Washington, D. C.

United States list of observatories, v. 41...... .... n. p.

CHRISTOPHER SOWER Co., 614 Arch St., Philadelphia.

Brooks, Plane and solid geometry, rev. ed..... .... 1.25

G. E. STECHERT, 9 E. 16th St., New York.

Wagner, Im Freundeskreisse......... 1.00

STREET & SMITH, 238 William St., New York.

Browne, From switch to lever....... 75
——, Zip the acrobat................ 75

UNION PRESS, 1122 Chestnut St., Philadelphia.

Murray, Castleton's "prep"........... 1.25

H. W. WILSON, 315 14th Ave., Minneapolis, Minn.

Staedeler, System of qualitative chemical analysis..... 60

YEAR BOOK PUBLISHERS, 40 Dearborn St., Chicago.

Dudley, Gynecology....... .... 1.50

The Publishers' Weekly.

FOUNDED BY F. LEYPOLDT.

AUGUST 30, 1902.

The editor does not hold himself responsible for the views expressed in contributed articles or communications. All matter, whether for the reading-matter columns or advertising pages, should reach this office not later than Wednesday noon, to insure insertion in the same week's issue.

Books for the "Weekly Record," as well as all information intended for that department, should reach this office by Tuesday morning of each week.

"I hold every man a debtor to his profession, from the which, as men do of course seek to receive countenance and profit, so ought they of duty to endeavor themselves by way of amends to be a help and an ornament thereunto."—LORD BACON.

BOOK REVIEWING.

PERIODICALLY the question is raised whether book reviews, favorable or otherwise, help the sale of books. Much has been written on the subject, and the *con* has been as strongly defended as the *pro*. Nevertheless, the fact remains that the publisher the world over has faith enough in the book review to send out to the press every year a more or less large percentage of his output in the hope that somewhere the printed word of the reviewer may excite either the interest or the curiosity of some reader enough to induce him to buy the book commended or condemned. And, as a rule, his trust is not altogether misplaced. This seems to be confirmed by George S. Goodwin, who contributes to *The Critic* for August the result of inquiries among publishers on the subject of book reviewing. Nine of the more important firms in New York and Boston—D. Appleton & Co., the Century Company, McClure, Phillips & Co., Houghton, Mifflin & Co., Harper & Brothers, Henry Holt & Co., Little, Brown & Co., and Doubleday, Page & Co.—who answered the questions propounded were in favor of having their books reviewed. Only one house, Dodd, Mead & Co., thought it would be a disadvantage to continue the custom of reviewing books, though, strangely enough, in a closing paragraph, they believe "a review in *The Bookman* to be a very desirable asset for a book." A great many other publishers believe this to be true also of other media; hence, the custom of sending books for review to reputable newspapers and periodicals will very likely not be honored in the breach so long as publishing is conducted as it is conducted at present, and as it has been conducted for several hundred years.

We are pleased to note that the predominating views expressed also agree that the critics of to-day are not so degenerate a race as some pessimists describe them, and that, taking into consideration the change in the conditions generally, the criticism of our time is scarcely at all inferior to what it was in those palmy days when Keats reviewed Reynolds and Reynolds Keats, "when Johnson thundered and Dennis swore, and when Hazlitt penned his inimitable critiques of men and books." There is undoubtedly a great deal of perfunctoriness in the writing of reviews; but this is due principally to lack of time during the season when books are rushed upon the tables of the reviewers in a veritable avalanche. To do the work thoroughly and promptly under such pressure it would be necessary for a literary journal to command a staff during five or six months of the year that would make the publishing of such a journal most unprofitable. Under these circumstances it may happen frequently that errors of judgment are committed; but very likely no oftener than they are committed by the literary advisers of the publishing houses. As a rule we believe the more important books receive at the hands of the average reviewer all the consideration that they deserve.

PUBLISHERS ON BOOK REVIEWING.

GEORGE SANDS GOODWIN, in *The Critic* for August, submits the result of an inquiry among a number of publishers in New York and Boston as to the value of book reviewing. The following questions were submitted:

1. Do you think it would be an advantage or disadvantage to discontinue the custom of reviewing books and have them submitted to the public without the intermediary opinions of critics—as most other manufactured commodities are? In other words, would you rather have your publications reviewed or not?

2. Do you observe anywhere a lack of conscientiousness in the reviewing of your books? If so, what remedy have you to suggest?

3. Are the reviews of your books by English critics fairer than those written by American reviewers?

4. Do you think the custom of sending prepared notices with editorial copies of books intended for review a good one?

5. Which do you think is better: that the publisher should be free to send all of his publications, or those he may choose, to the reviewer for criticism, or that the reviewer should himself select the publications he may desire to examine?

6. A recent writer declared that most reviews written nowadays are prepared with a strict eye to the obtaining of advertisements from the publishers. Have you found this to be a fact, and does it appear that the character of the reviews you receive is affected either way by your decision to advertise or not?

Ten publishing houses, eight in New York and two in Boston, answered, nine being in favor of book reviewing and one dissenting. As a fair representative of the views expressed by those in favor of book reviews we quote the letter sent in by W. W. Ellsworth, of the Century Company, who wrote as follows:

1. We prefer to have our publications reviewed. We do not issue any books that we do not believe in, and we feel that public opinion is very considerably helped by critics, especially in publications devoted entirely to book reviews, such as *The Bockman*, *The Critic*, and the *Saturday Review of The New York Times*.

2. We observe no lack of conscientiousness in the reviewing of our books by papers whose reviews are worth while. Of course, papers of a lower grade are not apt to give the attention to books that a strict conscientiousness would lead them to give. They frequently use the prepared notice sent by the publishers.

3. We do not think the reviews of English critics are any fairer than those written in America. In fact, the work of American reviewers seems to us much the better of the two.

4. We can see no objection to sending prepared notices with editorial copies of books intended to be reviewed, especially, if these notices are simply an account of the book and not an expression of opinion containing many compliments. We try to keep exuberant adjectives out of our prepared notices and to make them simply a fair statement of what we believe the book to be.

5. If the reviewer should himself select only the publications he might desire to examine, he would be apt to miss many books that he would find worth his attention. If, however, he made his own selection, he would of course limit his reviews to the important books, and his columns might be the more interesting on this account; nevertheless, he would not be apt to ask for a new book by a new author, and he might miss some of the greatest successes.

6. We do not think that "most reviews written nowadays" are "prepared with an eye to the obtaining of advertisements." We are sure that the reviews of the best class of publications, and the only class in which reviews do the publishers much good, are not prepared for such a purpose. Nevertheless, during the past two or three years, a great number of papers in all parts of the country have started book departments, and it is not unlikely that the publishers of these papers have had in mind the possibility of book advertising to help pay the expenses of such departments and to bring in a fair return. We have never, however, known of a case where the character of reviews of our books was affected by our advertising or not advertising in a paper. Certainly if we knew of such a case we would put the paper on the blacklist and it would have neither books nor advertising.

Dodd, Mead & Co., the one dissenting house, wrote as follows:

We think it would be a disadvantage to continue the custom of reviewing books. This, it seems to us, is self-evident.

Taking your other questions in order: Second. We certainly do find a lack of conscientiousness in the reviewing of books. As the public seems to be satisfied with what they get, however (in many instances where the reviewing is most execrable), we suppose the only remedy is to educate the public.

Third. We do not think English reviews are any fairer than American reviews, though the average as far as scholarship goes is certainly higher abroad than it is with us.

Fourth. We do not think the custom of sending prepared notices with editorial copies of books is a very good one æsthetically, but practically we suppose it brings results.

Fifth. We suppose it would be far better if the reviewer selected his books to review rather than that the publisher did it.

Sixth. There is, of course, in a few mediocre journals always a tendency to over-praise a book if the publisher of the paper thinks he can get advertising by it; but in the long run this over-praise always nullifies itself, and eventually it even drives some advertisers out of the paper.

As a broad proposition, we should say that the book reviews in the *Nation* are the most scholarly; that those in the New York *Sun* are the most interesting, and those in the New York *Times* are probably the most (commercially) valuable, though we believe a review in *The Bookman* to be a very desirable asset for a book. We are rather gloomy about the whole matter of book reviews, and are afraid we shall have to wait for the public to grow a little more discreet, and a little more cultivated; but we also believe that if we give them time, the public in America are going to demand a much higher standard of book reviewing.

SAMUEL WOOD AND WILLIAM WOOD & COMPANY—A CENTURY OF PUBLISHING.

New Yorkers of the present day are usually so deeply engrossed in the occupation of money-getting that they pay but little attention to the past history of their city. Few of the descendants of the old merchants immortalized by "Walter Barrett, Clerk," are actively engaged in business at the present time. In the publishing trade, especially, many of the traditions as well as memories of the past are giving way to what are broadly known as "modern methods," not always, perhaps, to the real advantage of the calling. A very notable example of the continuance of an important establishment through several generations has suggested that a sketch of the life of Samuel Wood, with a brief history of the firm of William Wood & Company, founded by him, might be of interest, as that firm represents the oldest publishing house, with the single exception of the Methodist Book Concern, now doing business in New York.

Samuel Wood was born at Oyster Bay, L. I., on July 17, 1760. He was the only son of Samuel and Freelove Wood, (*née* Wright.) Originally christened William, his name was changed to Samuel on the death of his father in 1762. His father's early death made it necessary for him to rely entirely upon his own resources for the acquirement of an education. He must have had a natural thirst for knowledge and love of books, as his first occupation, school teaching, and his final choice, bookselling and publishing, testify. At the age of twenty-two he married Mary Searing, of Huntington, L. I., and finding the profits of a country school inadequate to his needs, he is known to have tried several occupations, living successively at Hibernia Mills, N. Y., (1794,) New Rochelle (1796,) and, finally, moving to New York City in December, 1803.

In 1804 he opened a bookstore in a small two-story brick building at 362 Pearl Street. At first his business consisted of the sale of miscellaneous books, many of them second-hand. These were largely purchased at the auction sales of Robert McMennomy, held at that time at the corner of Wall and Water Streets, opposite the Tontine Coffee House. He also sold paper, and, for a short time, cotton goods on commission, consigned by Almy & Brown, of Providence, R. I. These two lines were soon discarded, being unprofitable. A small printing plant was added after awhile, and the publication of books was commenced.

Samuel Wood's first publication is said to have been "The Young Child's A B C, or, First Book," a little affair of sixteen pages about three inches square, dated 1806, compiled by himself, and printed by J. C. Totten, 155 Chatham Street. Observing that the limited literature produced for children at that time was uninteresting, if not even in some cases improper, from a strict religious standpoint, he began the preparation and reprinting of juvenile books and leaflets. The earlier ones are very crude, although some are illustrated by copper plates colored by hand. Before long, however, they begin to show wood-

385

SAMUEL WOOD
(1760–1844)
FOUNDER OF THE PUBLISHING HOUSE OF WM. WOOD AND CO.

cuts by Alexander Anderson, the first engraver on wood in America, whose work appeared constantly in the publications of the house until his death in 1870. Many of the little booklets seem to have been made for free distribution, as Mr. Wood is known to have been in the habit of going about with his pocket full of them, and distributing them among the children whom he met. His purpose in this was evidently philanthropic, as the little books are full of moral verses and maxims, although in some cases humor is not wanting.

In 1810 Samuel Wood moved to a larger store at 357 Pearl Street, nearly opposite his original place of business. In 1815 he took into partnership two of his sons, Samuel S. and John, the firm name becoming Samuel Wood & Sons. About this time he published a periodical called *The Friend of Peace*. Among other booksellers then doing business in New York were Thomas A. Ronalds, McDermott & Arden, Wm. B. Gillie, T. & J. Swords, James Oram, Smith & Forman, Richard Scott, Samuel A. Burtis, James Eastburn and Van Winkle & Wiley. These are all unknown at the present day, the last only being represented by an existing house in John Wiley & Sons.

A branch of Samuel Wood & Sons was opened in Baltimore, Md., at 212 Market Street, in charge of Samuel S. Wood, in 1818. It was moderately successful, but was discontinued after a few years, S. S. Wood being required by the business in New York.

Samuel Wood & Sons moved again, in 1817, to 261 Pearl Street, a property owned by Samuel Wood, and another son, William Wood, was admitted to partnership, John Wood retiring. The business had increased considerably, and had become to a large extent wholesale, books of all sorts, as well as stationery, being handled. These quarters soon proved too small, and the business was temporarily removed to a store in Fulton Street, while a substantial five-story brick building was erected at 261 Pearl Street. It was then considered a large building to be devoted entirely to the book business. It is still standing, and is occupied by S. M. Aikman & Co., dealers in lanterns.

The junior partner, William Wood, was from the first especially interested in medical books, and results soon justified his interest in this line of stock, a third of the first floor of the new building being entirely devoted to it. The store became the resort of the noted physicians of that day, such as Drs. Francis, Hosack, Mitchell, Mott and Stevens.

The "New York Readers," a series of primers, spellers and readers, (many of them originally compiled by Samuel Wood himself,) were for many years favorite textbooks; and, as recently as twenty-five years ago, were still published in Philadelphia by Claxton, Remsen & Haffelfinger, to whom the plates had been sold.

In 1836 Samuel S. and William Wood bought out the interest of their father, Samuel Wood, who retired from business and devoted himself almost entirely to public matters. He had been christened in the Church of England, but early in life had joined the Society of Friends, or Quakers, of which body he was an active and influential member until his death. He took part in founding the House of Refuge, the Bank for Savings, and the Society for the Prevention of Pauperism. He was also an active member of the Manumission Society, the Society of the New York Hospital, and other benevolent institutions. For many years he served as a trustee of the public schools, and in this connection observing the extreme prevalence of ophthalmia among the pupils of the school at Bellevue, total blindness resulting in some cases, he addressed the public through the newspapers, urging the inauguration of measures for the relief of these unfortunates. To his efforts, joined with those of Dr. Samuel L. Ackerly, is due the credit for the foundation of the "New York Institution for the Blind." (See 10th Annual Report of the Managers.)

Samuel Wood, as already mentioned, married, on August 8, 1782, Mary, daughter of John and Mary Searing, (*née* Prior,) by whom he had seven sons and six daughters. He died on May 5, 1844, having been partially paralyzed since 1839. In the cyclopædias Samuel Wood figures as a publisher and bookseller, but he was better known in his own times as a philanthropist.

On the retirement of Samuel Wood the business was continued under the name of S. S. & W. Wood. In 1823 were first published Brown's series of English grammars, which, for nearly two generations, held the field as the almost universal textbook. In 1856 the firm removed to 389 Broadway, occupying the entire building. Medical publications continued more and more to form the chief part of the business.

Samuel S. Wood died in 1861. He was unmarried.

For a little over a year William Wood conducted the business under his own name, removing to 61 Walker Street. In 1863 he associated with him his son, Wm. H. S. Wood, the present head of the house, the firm becoming William Wood & Company, the style it has retained ever since. To the energy, sound judgment, and unusual business sagacity of this gentleman is due the development of the business to its present proportions.

In 1866 the publication of the *Medical Record* was commenced. *The American Journal of Obstetrics and Diseases of Women and Children* was begun in 1868. In 1872 the publication of *New Remedies* was commenced. The name of this periodical was changed to *The American Druggist* in 1884. The journal was sold to its present publisher in 1892. Several other medical journals have also been published at various times.

William Wood retired from active business in 1868. He died in April, 1877.

On the retirement of William Wood, William H. S. Wood associated with himself Isaac F. Wood, also a grandson of Samuel Wood, and Alfred S. Griffiths, who had been head clerk for some years. At the end of three years Isaac F. Wood's interest was bought out by his partners, and, until 1884, the firm was composed of William H. S. Wood and A. S. Griffiths. In 1884 Mr. Griffiths' interest was bought out, and the sole member of the firm was William H. S. Wood until 1890, when his oldest son, William C. Wood, was admitted to partnership. In 1892 Gilbert C. Wood, and in 1896 Arnold Wood, respectively second and third sons of William H. S. Wood, were also admitted. The firm is to-day composed of these four. It is unusual in this country to see a business continued uninterruptedly for nearly one hundred years, entirely in the hands of one family.

From about 1861 the publication of general books began to be discontinued, and with but one or two exceptions the house has published medical works only for the past twenty years. Mr. J. H. Vail, who had served in the capacity of chief clerk in the retail department since 1859, purchased in 1881 the good will and stock of this department, and has done business until the present year under the firm style of J. H. Vail & Co. Since that time William Wood & Company have confined themselves almost entirely to the publication, in the usually accepted sense, of medical books and periodicals.

Among the most important publications of the house in recent years may be mentioned Ziemssen's "Cyclopædia of the Practice of Medicine," in twenty royal octavo volumes, begun in 1874. The publication of this great collection of treatises formed the most important advance in the history of medicine at that time, and the American edition was especially remarkable as being the first medical work to be sold by subscription. Through a systematic organization of canvassing, the work was offered to the profession not only in the United States, but as well to the English-speaking physicians throughout the world. But more than any previous enterprise, *Wood's Library of Standard Medical Authors* marked decisively the inauguration of subscription methods of bookselling as applied to medical publications. That series was begun January 1, 1879, and included the monthly issue of important cloth bound octavo medical books, in yearly sets of twelve volumes. The sale of the various series was enormous, and the idea was at once adapted by other publishers to various lines of popular and professional literature with equal success.

The "International Encyclopedia of Surgery," in seven royal octavo volumes, was first published in 1888, and marked the commencement of international co-operation by American writers in the preparation of medical and surgical literature, doing much to place America on a plane with the great European countries in scientific advancement as related to medicine and surgery. The "Twentieth Century Practice of Medicine," in twenty large octavo volumes, was begun in 1895 and completed in 1900. The "Reference Handbook of the Medical Sciences," one of the most widely appreciated medical works ever published, was first issued in nine imperial octavo volumes, in 1885 to 1889, and a revised edition is half completed at the present time.

In 1871 the firm moved to 27 Great Jones Street. In 1882 they removed to 56 and 58 Lafayette Place. In 1892 to 43-47 East Tenth Street, and in 1899 to 51 Fifth Avenue, their present quarters.

OBITUARY NOTES.

PETER S. HOE, the last surviving member of the original firm of R. Hoe & Co., the world-renowned manufacturers of printing presses, died at his home in Montclair, N. J., on Saturday, August 23, of heart failure, brought on by pneumonia. Mr. Hoe was 81 years old. He retired from the firm in 1890.

CHARLES WILDERMANN, the publisher and dealer in Catholic church goods, at 18 Barclay Street, died last week. A meeting of Catholic publishers was held on August 27, at which resolutions of regret and appreciation were unanimously adopted. These resolutions appeared in the *New York Herald* of August 27.

GEORGE M. HOPKINS, associate editor of the *Scientific American*, was stricken by uraemic poisoning while on an electric car between Cheshire and Pittsfield, Mass. He was the author of "Experimental Science," a well-known textbook, was prominent as a patent attorney and conspicuous in scientific research work. He had charge of the electricity department of the *Scientific American*, and also conducted the department of "Questions and Answers."

NOTES ON AUTHORS.

FREDERICK MISTRAL, the greatest living troubadour, is translating Carnegie's "Gospel of Wealth" into Provençal.

DR. W. H. DRUMMOND, of Montreal, the author of "The Habitant," is arranging for a tour next winter through the Northern States. He will recite from his poems. His powers as an entertainer are irresistible.

IT is stated that Jean A. Jusserand, author of several works on English literature, has been selected to succeed Jules Çambon as French ambassador at Washington. M. Jusserand is now French minister at Copenhagen. His wife is an American woman.

GEORGE ILES, author of "Flame, Electricity and the Camera," has edited for Doubleday, Page & Co. a series of six *Little Masterpieces of Science*, to follow the *Little Masterpieces of Literature* issued by that firm. Publication will take place early in September.

JOURNALISTIC NOTES.

THE current *Quarterly Review* contains a remarkable tribute to Dickens by Swinburne, who places Dickens in the direct line of Shakespeare and Fielding, and ranks him not only as the greatest writer, but as the greatest Englishman of his age.

The Century Magazine has secured the first contribution to an American magazine of the author of "Elizabeth and Her German Garden." It is an essay "On the Giving of Books," and delightfully hits off the peculiarities of people who give books to friends and their reasons for choosing them.

The Atlantic for September contains "A Bit of Unpublished Correspondence Between Henry Thoreau and Isaac Hecker;" "What

Public Libraries are Doing for Children;" "William Black," by Edward Fuller; and "A Walk with Mr. Warner," in the Contributor's Club Department.

OLD BOOK NOTES.

THERE is, perhaps, nothing more certain to turn up than a second copy of a book that has been considered "unique." For over four centuries the now famous 1493 edition of the Malermi Bible, (Venice,) was as completely lost as if it had never existed. Within about a month of each other two copies were discovered—one in Italy by Mr. Voynich, the London bookseller, and the other in Vienna, by the Duc de Rivoli. Quite recently a third copy has been unearthed by a continental bookseller, and doubtless other examples will be found in due course. A fine copy is worth at least $1500. The peculiarity of the 1493 issue is that many of the woodcuts are quite different from those in the 1490, 1492 and 1494 editions. Four of these beautiful illustrations are reproduced in facsimile in Mr. Voynich's "Second List of Books."

THERE was recently sold at Sotheby's a copy of the first edition of "Robinson Crusoe" for the record price of $1225. A decade ago it would have been difficult to obtain $200 for the book. The first volume of "Robinson Crusoe" was published April 25, 1719, by William Taylor. The second part was published five months later—August 20, 1719. In 1720 a sequel was published, not by Defoe, however, that was entitled "Serious Reflections During the Life of Robinson Crusoe." The prices for copies of the first edition of "Robinson Crusoe," from 1887 to 1897, have varied from $230 to $395. In April of this year Quaritch bought the Hibbert copy for £206, and last month Pickering & Chatto bought the set referred to above for £245. It was made up of the two volumes of "Robinson Crusoe," the second volume being the second edition, and the sequel.

PERSONAL NOTE.

ERNEST DRESSEL NORTH, of Charles Scribner's Sons, has resigned his position and starts in business for himself on September 1, at 18 East Twentieth Street, New York. Mr. North has been connected with the Scribner house for twenty-five years, and during much of that time has made a specialty of choice and rare books. For the last nineteen years he has made the Scribner catalogues of choice and rare books, and has displayed excellent taste and reliable knowledge in their preparation. He has also been a constant contributor to *The Bookbuyer*, and has conducted its department of "Notes on Rare Books." Mr. North has taken the store formerly occupied by Vail & Co., and he expects to make a specialty of choice, rare and second-hand books. The store has been entirely refitted and decorated, and presents a most attractive appearance. Mr. North's long record in the trade has made for him many friends, as well as customers, and we wish him every possible success in his new enterprise.

LITERARY AND TRADE NOTES.

THE AMERICAN BOOK COMPANY have ready Zschokhe's "Der Zerbrochene Krug," edited for school use by R. O. Berkefeld.

ORANGE JUDD CO. have ready "Poultry Architecture," compiled by George B. Fiske, a practical guide for the construction of poultry houses, coops and yards.

DOUBLEDAY, PAGE & CO. have just issued an illustrated edition of Ellen Glasgow's "The Voice of the People," and a volume of poems by the same author, entitled "The Freeman, and Other Poems."

DODD, MEAD & CO. will publish within a few days "The Blood Tax," by Dorothea Gerard, in which in the form of fiction the author has summed up the arguments for and against compulsory military service.

THE MACMILLAN COMPANY report the great success of Owen Wister's "The Virginian." The story has gone into its seventy-fifth thousand, and at the moment the orders average 1000 a day, one day bringing orders for 4000 copies.

THE chaplain of the Boer prisoners on the Island of St. Helena has written the Vir Publishing Company, Philadelphia, requesting right to translate into Cape Dutch "What a Young Boy Ought to Know" and "What a Young Man Ought to Know."

J. B. LIPPINCOTT COMPANY have taken quarters in the Presbyterian Building, 156 Fifth avenue, New York City, and this autumn will display in Room 420 a full line of their new and standard publications. Their representative will be Mr. Horace S. Ridings.

WM. J. C. DULANY COMPANY take pleasure in announcing that they have engaged Mr. E. R. F. Blogg, (formerly chief clerk for B. G. Eichelberger,) as manager of their retail department. The reputation of Mr. Blogg as a bookman is too well known to the book lovers of Baltimore to need further comment.

A SUPPLEMENT for 1900 and 1901 to "The Literature of American History" will be published toward the close of October by Houghton, Mifflin & Co., for the American Library Association. The parent work has met with so satisfactory a sale that it will soon have a second printing.

DAVID WILLIAMS COMPANY, New York City, have issued "Estimating Frame and Brick Houses," a practicl treatise on estimating the cost of labor and the quantities of materials for the construction of frame, brick and stone houses, stables, barns, etc., by Fred. T. Hodgson, architect.

OPEN COURT PUBLISHING COMPANY, Chicago, have issued "Nirvana," by Paul Carus; "Babel and Bible," by Friedrich Delitzsch; "Creation Story of Genesis," by Hugo Radan; "Biblical Love Ditties," by Paul Haupt; and "Foundations of Geometry," by David Hilbert.

LITTLE, BROWN & CO. have put thirty or more of their best books for the young into a series called the *Boys' and Girls' Bookshelf*, and will issue these books at $1 each. This offers a rare chance to pick up the best-known books of Miss Alcott, Mrs. Ewing, A. G. Plympton, Lily F. Wesselhoeft, etc., in attractive shape to tempt the Christmas buyer.

THE INDUSTRIAL PUBLICATION COMPANY, New York, have in preparation "The Shakespearean Cyclopædia and New Glossary," giving the meaning of all the archaic words found in Shakespeare's works and of the ordinary words used in unusual senses and in unusual forms of construction, which is intended as a supplement to all the ordinary editions of Shakespeare's works, by John Phin, author of "Shakespearean Notes and New Readings," etc.

CHARLES SCRIBNER'S SONS have in press for early issue Henry Norman's long-looked-for work, "All the Russias." This volume was to have been published a year ago, but was held back for further enlargement. As its sub-title indicates, it deals with "travels and studies in contemporary European Russia, Finland, Siberia, the Caucasus and Central Asia," and it is full of Mr. Norman's keen insight into political affairs and graphic literary skill. There is also in preparation a new edition of the Blashfield book on "Italian Cities," first published in the autumn of 1900. It was originally issued without illustrations, but the new edition will contain forty-eight pictures in tint, drawn by Mr. Blashfield.

THE AMERICAN TRACT SOCIETY have among their newest announcements the names of some of the authors for whom the publishers always contend. Louis Albert Banks, Rev. Theodore L. Cuyler, Andrew Murray, Julia McNair Wright, and last, as place of honor, Dr. James Paton, are always names that attract all readers, and the publishers are to be congratulated that they have in their concern a man who could procure for them the latest works of these widely read authors. Dr. Paton has written "The Glory and Joy of the Resurrection;" Julia McNair Wright's book is "Studies in Hearts;" Dr. Cuyler will furnish "Recollections of a Long Life;" and Louis Albert Banks a choice collection of sermons under the head of "The King's Stewards."

A. C. MCCLURG & Co. are preparing a popular edition, in two volumes, of "Lewis and Clark's Travels," edited by Dr. James K. Hosmer; "The Birds of the Rockies," by Dr. Leander S. Keyser, with full-page plates in colors by Fuertes and text illustrations; a new edition of Max Müller's "Memories," illustrated by Blanche Ostertag; "Musical Pastels," by George P. Upton; "Various Views," being further essays by William Morton Payne; and "In Argolis," a personal account of family life in Greece, by George Horton. Fiction will include "On Fortune's Road," a collection of short stories dealing with business and political life in Chicago, by Will Payne; "The Holland Wolves," a novel of the Spanish subjugation of the Netherlands, illustrated by the Kinneys; "A Captive of the Roman Eagles," by Felix Dahn. For younger readers there is Carolyn Wells's "The Pete and Polly Stories;" "Little Mistress Good Hope," by Mary Imlay Taylor; "Mayken," a historical story of Holland, by Jessie A. Chase; "Coquo and the King's Children," by Cornelia Baker; and "Prince Silver Wings," by Edith O. Harrison.

THOMAS WHITTAKER has in preparation for the fall season a volume entitled "Makers of Modern Fiction," by W. J. Dawson, which is the third in the series of studies on the *Makers of Modern English;* "Cameos from Nature," by Mrs. J. T. Gumersall, with numerous illustrations; "The Church and Its Social Mission," by Dr. J. Marshall Lang, the principal of Aberdeen University; "The Book of Psalms," by Professor T. K. Cheyne, an entirely new edition enlarged to three times the bulk of the first edition; "Ourselves and the Universe," by J. Brierly, author of "Studies of the Soul;" an entirely new edition, revised and enlarged, of Professor Beet's well-known commentary on St. Paul's Epistles to the Corinthians; new editions of the late Dr. Dale's work on "The Ten Commandments;" Dr. Dod on the "Parables of Our Lord," and the Rev. G. V. Reichel's "What Shall I Tell the Children?"; a "Robert Browning Birthday Book:" "The Story of Catharine of Sienna," by Florence Witts; and "Up and Down the Pantiles," by Emma Marshall. Mr. Whittaker has just added to his series of anatomical models a "Popular Mannikin," the price of which is $1.50 list, not $1 net, as given in our "Weekly Record" for August 9.

G. P. PUTNAM'S SONS have in preparation "The Writings of James Madison," edited by Gaillard Hunt; also, "The Writings of James Monroe," edited by S. M. Hamilton. Both of these works are to be complete in seven volumes, and will be published uniform with "The Writings of Jefferson," etc., in editions of 750 copies. They also announce "American Constitutional History," by Alexander Johnson, edited by Professor James A. Woodburn; "American Politics," also by Professor Woodburn; "The Administration of Dependencies," a historical study of American and European theory and practice, together with suggestions, based on this study, concerning future American policy, by Alpheus H. Snow; "Government and the State," a consideration of elementary principles and their practical application, by Frederic Wood; "Industrial Conciliation," a report of the proceedings of the conference held under the auspices of the National Civic Federation, at the rooms of the Board of Trade and Transportation in New York, December 16-17, 1901; a King Edward edition of H. D. Traill's and J. S. Mann's "Social England," to be completed in six octavo volumes; "Studies of a Biographer," Parts III. and IV., by Leslie Stephen; "Italian Life in Town and Country," by Luigi Villari, in *Our European Neighbors* series, edited by William Harbutt Dawson; "In City Tents," how to find, furnish and keep a small home on slender means, by Christine Terhune Herrick; also, "Fame for a Woman, or, Splendid Mourning," by Cranstown Metcalfe, with frontispiece by Adolfe Thiede.

TERMS OF ADVERTISING.

Under the heading "Books Wanted" **book-trade subscribers are given the privilege of a free advertisement for books out of print, of five nonpareil lines exclusive of address, in any issue except special numbers, to an extent not exceeding 100 lines a year. If more than five lines are sent, the excess is at 10 cents a line, and amount should be inclosed.** *Bids for current books and such as may be easily had from the publishers, and repeated matter, as well as all advertisements from non-subscribers, must be paid for at the rate of 10 cents a line.*

Under the heading "Books for Sale," the charge to subscribers and non-subscribers is 10 cents a nonpareil line for each insertion. No deduction for repeated matter.

All other small, undisplayed, advertisements will be charged at the uniform rate of 10 cents a nonpareil line. Eight words may be reckoned to the line.

Parties with whom we have no accounts must pay in advance, otherwise no notice will be taken of their communications.

BOOKS WANTED.

☞ ***In answering, please state edition, condition, and price, including postage or express charges.***

Houses that are willing to deal exclusively on a cash-on-delivery basis will find it to their advantage to put after their firm-name the word [Cash].

☞ ***Write your wants plainly and on one side of the sheet only, Illegibly-written "wants" will be considered as not having been received. The "Publishers' Weekly" does not hold itself responsible for errors.***

It should be understood that the appearance of advertisements in this column, or elsewhere in the "Publishers' Weekly" does not furnish a guarantee of credit. While it is endeavored to safeguard these columns by withdrawing the privilege of their use from advertisers who are not "good pay," booksellers should take the usual precaution, as to advertisers not known to them, that they would take in making sales to any unknown parties.

Arthur M. Allen, 508 Fulton St., Troy, N. Y.
De Mille, Cryptogram.
De Mille, American Baron.
De Mille, Lady of the Ice.
Paine, Elements of Railroading.

Amer. Bapt. Pub. Soc., 132 E. 23d St., N. Y.
The Prortrate State, by Pike. Appleton.
Ku-Klux Movement, Books on.
Reconstruction Period, 1865 to 1876, especially from the Southern standpoint, Books on.
Taylor, N. W., Lectures on the Moral Government of God, 2 v. Pub. in New Haven, 1859.

American Tract Soc., 150 Nassau St., N. Y.
Jewish and Heathen Testimonies, by Dr. Nathaniel Lardners.

Wm. Ballantyne & Sons, 428 7th St., Washington, D. C.
Desty, On Taxation, 2 v.
The Young Parson. Pub. by Sheldon.

The Balto. Book Co., 301 St. Paul St., Baltimore, Md.
Sessions Laws, State Journals and Documents, Law Reports Maryland and Delaware

Bartlett's Book Store, 33 E. 22d St., N. Y.
Guernsey, N. Y. City During War of 1812, v. 1, roy. 8vo.
Macaulay's History of England, v. 5, hf. cf., 8vo. Pub. by Harper & Bros., 1856.

W. L. Beekman, 55 E. 5th St., St. Paul, Minn.
International Studio, Nov., Dec., 1899.
Photo Era, July, 1901.
Bart Ridgley, by Riddle.
The Hittites, by Prof. Campbell.
The English Paragraph, by E. H. Lewis.

Bigham & Smith, Agts., Dallas, Tex.
Autobiography of David Crockett. Potter, 1865.
Belden, or, White Chief, by G. P. Belden. 1870.
Commerce of the Prairies, Josiah Gregg. Langley, 1844.

Bigham & Smith, Agts., Nashville, Tenn.
Delitzsch's Commentary on Job, v. 1.

J. W. Bouton, 10 W. 28th St., N. Y.
Furtwangler, Masterpieces of Greek Sculpture.
Lee, Vernon, Phantom Lover, or, Oke of Okehurst.
Linthicum, System of Cutting.
La Fontaine's Tales, 2 v.
Lanman's Adv. in Wilds of America.
Clark, On Organ Construction.
Nicholson, On Organ Tuning.
Temple Shakespeare, 40 v., early issue.
Taine, The Philosophy of Art.
Perrot and Chipiez, Art in Ancient Egypt, 2 v.

The Bowen-Merrill Co., Indianapolis, Ind.
Thompson, Byways and Bird Notes.
Thompson, Sylvan Secrets.
Symonds, Introduction to Study of Browning.

T. L. Bradford, 1862 Frankford Ave., Phila., Pa.
Index Medicus, v. 6; v. 7, no. 6; v. 8, no. 10; v. 11, nos. 8, 9, 10, 11, 12; v. 12, no. 8; v. 13, 14, 15, 16, 20, 21.
Priced auction catalogues of books.
Howard, Physiology Artistic Singing.

Brentano's, Union Sq., N. Y.
Wells, Time Machine. Holt.
Moore, Julia, Sentimental Song Book.
McHenry, Cotton Trade. 1863.
Williams, S. W., Chinese Immigration. Scribner, 1879.
Nordhoff, Cotton States. Appleton.
Robinson Crusoe, with Paget illus., early Cassell impression.
Appleton's Annual Encyclo., any years 1890 to 1902, hf. mor.
Curtiss, Protection and Prosperity. Pan-Amer. Pub.

Brentano's, 1015 Pennsylvania Ave., Washington, D. C.
Huysmann, Cathedral.
Huysmann, En Route.
Dodge, Indians.
Any book, any date, on railroads.
Meinhold, Sidonia the Sorceress.

S. E. Bridgman & Co., 108 Main St., Northampton, Mass.
Child of the Ball, Alarcon.

The Burrows Bros. Co., Cleveland, O.
Prescott, Philip II., v. 3.
Norman, Real Japan.
Schaff, Renaissance.
Birney, Life of Birney.
Field, Stones of Temple.
Dana, Library Problems.
Handbook Library Organization.
Ford, M. H., Balzac's Seraphita.
Ford, M. H., Goethe's Faust to Ethical Symbolism.
Ford, M. H., Holy Grail.
Johnston, Handbook British Constitution.
Headley, Problems of Evolution.
Hazen, New England History.
Hints for Tracing Anglo-American Pedigrees.
Prisoners of the Air.

C. N. Caspar Co., 437 E. Water St., Milwaukee, Wis.
Irish Wit and Humor. Pub. by McGee.
2 copies Lyon, Sherman, Hollow Globe.
Atlas to Du Bois' Graphic Statics. Wiley.
Munsey's Magazine, 1892, '93, odd nos. or v.

Jno. J. Case, 70 Wall St., N. Y.
Club Men of N. Y., 1902.
Report of N. Y. Sanitary Commission. 1865.
Poole's Index, 4 v.
Darley, Cooper, 2d ed.: Precaution; Satanstoe; Wallingford; L. Lincoln.

The Central Print. and Pub. House, 329 Market St., Harrisburg, Pa.
Metallurgical Handbook, by J. H. Cremer and Bicknell, in English. Price $3.00.

The A. H. Clark Co., Garfield Bldg., Cleveland, O.
Tissot, Life of Christ, ordinary ed.
Twain, Mark, Works, 22 v., complete.
Coyner, D. H., The Lost Trappers.

W. B. Clarke Co., Park and Tremont Sts., Boston, Mass.
Dana's Geology of Mass.
Foreign Exchanges, by Goschen.
Sea and Shore. Pub. by Roberts Bros.

BOOKS WANTED.—Continued.

Henry T. Coates & Co., Phila., Pa.

Quest of the Holy Grail, by Abbey. Pub. by Russell.

Geo. H. Colby & Co., 22 Main St., Lancaster, N. H.

Everett's Speeches, v. 4, black cl.
Draper's Civil War, v. 3. brown cl.
Copies in good condition at reasonable prices.
Sheet music, dealers' prices.

Columbian Book Co., 81 Whitehall St., Atlanta, Ga.

Native Races, H. H. Bancroft.

R. W. Crothers, 246 4th Ave., N. Y.

Meditations for Priests, by De Goisbriand.

Crusoe & Co., 81 Vermont St., Brooklyn, N. Y.

Thomas Kyd's Dramatic Works.

P. T. Cunningham, 151 Centre St., N. Y.

Berkeley's Introduction to Cryptogamic Botany.

Cushing & Co., 34 W. Baltimore St., Baltimore, Md.

Carroll, Rhyme and Reason.
Robinson Crusoe, drawings by Harvey, engraved by Adams. Pub. by Derby & Jackson, 1858.
Williams, H. T., Window Gardening.

Damrell & Upham, 283 Washington St., Boston, Mass.

Sermons Preached in the Church of the First Religous Society in Roxbury, by the Rev. George Putnam, D.D., 12mo. Houghton & Osgood Co., 1878.
A New England Tale, Catherine M. Sedgwick.
Redwood, Catherine M. Sedgwick.
Colonial New York Biographical Sketches, by John Austin Stevens.
Historical Tales of Olden Times in New York City, by John F. Watson.
Political and Social Letters of a Lady of the 18th Century, ed. by Miss F. D. Osborne.
Annals of Rajasthan, by Col. Tod.
Travels in Western India.
In a Poppy Garden.
Paola and Francesca, Stephen Phillips, 1st ed.
Herod, Stephen Phillips, 1st ed.
Poems, Stephen Phillips, 1st ed.

E. Darrow & Co., Rochester, N. Y.

Deaver's Surgical Anatomy, v. 2.
Harper's Magazine, Aug., 1902.
Clock Making, Booth or other authors.

DeWolfe, Fiske & Co., 361 Washington St., Boston, Mass.

2 copies A Study of Games, by Johnson.
An Essay on Systematic Training of the Body, by Scharble. Trubner & Co.
The True and the Beautiful, Ruskin.
John A. Symonds, 1st eds.
Walter Mitchell's Poems.
Catherine Sedgwick's books, any.

The H. & W. B. Drew Co., Jacksonville, Fla.

Sprague's Florida, new or second-hand.

Alex. Duncker (H. von Carnap), 178 Fulton St., N. Y.

Elliott, Gas and Petroleum Engines.
Lupton, Chemical Arithmetic.
Transactions Am. Inst. of Mining Eng., set or odd v.
Journal of the Am. Chem. Soc., any v.

Elder & Shepard, 238 Post St, San Francisco, Cal.

Gildersleeve, Essays and Studies.

G. Engelke, 225 N. Clark St., Chicago, Ill. [*Cash.*]

Hallam, Middle Ages, v. 3, cl., W. ed.
Burke's Family Record.
U. Netherland, v. 3, Motley, cl.
Life and Times of Huss, v. 2, Gillett, cl.
Pope, v. 1, shp. S. Andrus, Hartford, 1851.

H. W. Fisher & Co., 1535 Chestnut St., Phila., Pa.

The Lark, v. 1, 2, bound.
House and Garden, Oct., 1901.
Engraved Portraits of Washington, by Baker.

Free Public Library, Jersey City, N. J.

Bancroft, Geo., Plea for the Constitution of the U. S. of America; wounded in the house of its guardians. Harper Bros.

Garrett Books Shoppe, 58 Ann St., Hartford, Conn. [*Cash.*]

McCosh, On the Intuitions.
Taylor, J., Elements of Thought.
Taylor, J., Fanaticism.
Corruption of Christianity, by Vaughan. 1852.
Marion Coffin.

Gimbel Bros., Phila., Pa.

Set Balzac, 53 v., de Tour ed.. Barrie.

Goldsmith Bros., 206 E. Baltimore St., Baltimore, Md.

Fielding's Soul of a People, cl. Pub. by Macmillan.

Goodspeed's Book Shop, 5a Park St., Boston, Mass [*Cash.*]

Gould and Binney. Invertebrata of Massachusetts.
Baker's Engraved Portraits of Washington.

Edwin S. Gorham, 4th Ave. and 22d St., N. Y.

Hawk, Constitutions and Canons.
Gannie, Christian Cemeteries.
Burgon, Lives of Twelve Good Men, cheap.
Vols. of Expositor's Bible, second-hand.
Flint, Theism, second-hand.

Gotham Book Concern, 442 W. 56th St., N. Y.

Galaxy, Feb., 1868.
Overland Monthly, June, 1870; Jan., '83
The Connoisseur, v. 4, nos. 2, 3, 4.

F. E. Grant, 23 W. 42d St., N. Y.

Dramatic and Poetical Works of Lieut.-Gen. J. Burgoyne, 2 v. Lond., 1808.
Book about Old Cemetery at Fairfield Conn. Pub. about 50 years ago.
Brandel's S. T. Coleridge and the English Romantic School.
Crosby's Lexicon to Xenophon's Anabasis.
Marshall's Vocabulary to Xenophon's Anabasis.
Hun's Reports, complete set.
The Last Days of Heinrich Heine, by Camille Selden.
"Confessions," by Heinrich Heine.
Imperial Purple, by Edgar Saltus.
Life in the Old Chateaux, by Savage.
United States Supreme Court Reports, complete to date, also cheaper ed., ed. by Rose.

D M. Henderson, Madison and Howard Sts., Baltimore, Md.

Repertoire du Theatre Francais, 23 or 25 v.
Brewer, French History.

W. S. Houghton, Lynn, Mass.

American Naturalist, Jan., 1885; Sept., Oct., '88. 50 cts. each.
Andover Review, Feb., 1885; Sept., '91.
McClure's Magazine, Aug., Sept., 1893.
Scribner's Monthly, Dec., 1871; July, Sept., '72.

Humphrey's Book Store, 26 Brattle St., Boston, Mass.

Batchelder and Owens, Debate on the Authenticity of the Bible.
Jaeger, No. Amer. Insects, pt. 3. N. Y., 1853.
Frithhof's Saga, tr. by L. A. Sherman.

E. T. Jett Book and News Co., 806 Olive St., St. Louis, Mo.

Goudon's Monsters, in English.

Keating, Box 489, N. Y. City.

Plates wanted, good novels, also short dictionary, 16mo, 64 to 128 pages.

Keep's Book Shop, 284 Columbus Ave., Boston, Mass.

Webster's Unabridged Dictionary, latest, cheap.
Robert the Diable, by Admiral Porter. Appleton.
Fabliore and The Skein of Life.
Books on making toilet perfumes, powders, etc.
Rosedale, by Lester Wallack.

Geo. Kleinteich, 397 Bedford Ave., Brooklyn, N. Y. [*Cash.*]

Ridpath's Hist. of the World, complete.

William H. Lambert, Mutual Life Bldg, Phila., Pa

Anderson, President's Ball. Phila., 1863.
Assassination of Lincoln, Review of Trial of J. H. Surratt. Boston, 1892.
Abbott, Life of Lincoln. N. Y., 1864.
Abram, a military poem. Richmond, 1863.
Bell, The Day and the War. San Francisco, 1864.
Beveridge, Assassination of Lincoln. Troy, 1865.
Baker, Re-eligibility of President Lincoln.
Bionardi. Abramo Lincoln. 1862.
Birch, The Devil's Visit to Old Abe.
Booth, Confession de John Wilkes Booth. Paris, '65.
Botta, Resolutions on Death of Lincoln.
Brooks, Lincoln and the Downfall of Slavery. N. Y., 1894.
Bungener, Lincoln Zijn Leven, Werk en Dood. Utrecht, 1866.
Buntline, The Parricides. N. Y., 1865.
Bush, Death of President Lincoln. Orange, N. J., 1865.

BOOKS WANTED.—Continued.

William H. Lambert—*Continued.*

Campbell, Reminiscence and Documents. Balt., 1887.
Chapin, Sermon, Death of Lincoln. N. Y., 1865.
Dale, Young Men's Republican Vocalist. N. Y., 1860.
Delphine, Solon on the Rebellion of 1861. Chicago 1862.
Drake, Speech, Proclamation of Emancipation. St. Louis, 1863.
Drummond, President Lincoln. London, 1865.
Duganne, The Heroic Succession. N. Y., 1867.
Edge, President Lincoln's Successor. London, 1864.
Edwards, R. S., Life and Character of Lincoln. Peoria, 1865.
Egerton, Letter to Hon. J. J. Crittenden. 1862.
Engleheim, Les Enfants du Travaie Lincoln. Paris, 1865.
Foster, Abraham Lincoln. 1890.
Fowler, Abraham Lincoln. Chicago, 1867.
French, Address, Statue of Lincoln. Wash., 1868.
Frost, Abraham Lincoln. Oberlin, 1891.
Gravert, German version of Howard's Life of Lincoln.
Gregory, Abraham Lincoln, a poem. Bristol, Eng.
Grenier, La Mort du President Lincoln. Paris, 1867.
Gowans, Lincoln as Leader and Martyr.
Haco, J. Wilkes Booth. N. Y., 1865.
Haco, J. H. Surratt. N. Y., 1866.
Hall, Lincoln a Conspirator. New Haven, 1890.
Hasted, Letter to President Lincoln, Dec. 21, 1860.
Helwig, Assassination of Lincoln, a lecture. Springfield, O.
Hicks, Abraham Lincoln. Frederick, Md., 1865.
Hoffmann, Abraham Lincoln. Breslau, 1867.
Howard, Oration, July 4, 1865. Gettysburg, 1865.
Jones, Funeral Sermons. Rockaway, N. J., Dover, N. J., 1882.
Kirkland, Letter to Judge Curtis. N. Y., 1862.
Leslie, Pictorial Life of Lincoln. N. Y., 1865.
Lincoln, *Press* and *Tribune*, Documents no. 1, Cooper Institute Speech.
Lincoln, *N. Y. Demokrat*, Flugblatt no. 4, Cooper Institute Speech.
Lincoln, Facsimile Letter to Gen. Sibley, Dec. 6, 1862.
Lincoln, *Evening Journal*, Doc's no. 1, War Policy of Administration.
Lincoln, *Tribune*, War Tracts no. 5, Vallandingham.
Lincoln, The Murder of Lincoln. Indianapolis, 1895.
Lincoln, Life in Welsh. Utica, N. Y., 1860.
Lincoln, *N. Y. Demokrat* Leben von Lincoln.
Lincoln, To Abraham Lincoln, Considerations on the Slavery Question.
Lincoln, Letter to Lincoln, What Shall be Done with the Confiscated Negroes?
Lincoln, Powers of the President in Time of War. Muscatine, Iowa, 1865.
Lincoln, Letter from the Missouri Delegation to President Lincoln.
Lincoln, Constitution of the Educational Monument Assoc. Washington, 1865.
Lincoln, Lincoln's Assassination. Valparaiso, 1865.
Lincoln, By-Laws Lincoln Association of Jersey City. J. C., 1867.
Lincoln, Portraits and Biographies. Cincinnati, 1865.
Lincoln, Descriptive and Symbolic Key. N. Y., 1868.
Lincoln, Mrs., Behind the Seams. N. Y., 1868.
McCabe, Sermon, Peru, Ind., Apr. 19, 1865. La Fayette, 1865.
McClure, Lincoln's Stories and Speeches. Chicago, 1896.
McClure, Lincoln's Speeches Complete. Chic., 1891.
McGibbon, Our Nation's Sorrow. Berlin, Illinois.
Mackenna, Short Biography of Lincoln. N. Y., 1866
Marshall's Engraving of Lincoln, description. Boston, 16mo, pp. 13.
Moore, Moral Grandeur of the Proclamation of Emancipation. Pittsburgh, 1866.
Naylor, Discourse, Apr. 19, 1865. Salem, Ind., 1865.
Neill, Reminiscences of President Lincoln. St. Paul, 1885.
Newell, Notes on Abraham Lincoln. London, 1864.
Nicolay, Abraham Lincoln. Boston, 1882.
Owen, The Policy of Emancipation. Phila., 1863.
Pascal, Abraham Lincoln. Paris, 1865.
Patton, Lincoln the Man, Magistrate, Martyr.
Pertram, Gen. Pertram's Platform. Boston, 1862.
Phillips, Lincoln, a study of a great man and his work.
Potts, Freeman's Guide to the Polls. N Y., 1864.
Power, Abraham Lincoln, pp. 458. Chicago, 1889.
Proceedings Natl. Republican Convention, June 17, 1856.

William H. Lambert.—*Continued.*

Retcliffe, Abraham Lincoln Historisch Roman. Dresden.
Ruggles, To Abraham Lincoln Prest., June 9, 1862.
Seaman, What Miscegenation is. N. Y.
Sheppard, Abraham Lincoln. Chicago, 1899.
Simonton, Discourse. Rio de Janeiro, 1865.
Smith, Chas. Emory, Address at Galesburg, Oct. 7, 1899.
Smith, The Great American Crisis. Cincinnati, 1882.
Smith, Truman, Considerations on the Slavery Question.
Songs, Connecticut Wide Awake Songster. N. Y., 1860.
President Lincoln Campaign Songster. N. Y.
Lincoln and Hamlin Songster. Phila., Fisher & Bro.
Tremaine Bros., Lincoln and Johnson Campaign Song Book N. Y., 1864.
Speed, Oration Inauguration of Bust of Lincoln. Louisville, 1867.
Springfield, Official Programme Unveiling of Lincoln Statue. Springfield, 1874.
Surratt, Career and Adventures of J. H. Surratt. Phila., C. W. Alexander, 1866.
Swing, Address to the New Generation, Feb. 12, 1888.
Thayer, Greek translation of The Pioneer Boy. Athens, 1865.
Life and Character of Lincoln, pp. 76. Boston, 1864.
Tributes to Memory of Lincoln, facsimile reproduction. Washington, 1881.
Whiting, Military Arrests in Time of War.
Williams, Sermon on Death of Lincoln. Frederick, Md., 1865.
Williams, Eulogy, Abraham Lincoln. London.
Willson, Proclamation of Freedom. Salem, 1863.

Chas. E. Lauriat Co., 301 Washington St., Boston, Mass.

The Giles Memorial; Genealogical Memoirs of the Giles, Gould, and other Families, by John Adams Vinton. Pub. in Boston in 1864.
Knight, Chas., History of England, v. 1.
Fenelon, Lives of Ancient Philosophers, Harper's Family Library.
Executor, Alexander.
Broken Links, by Alexander.
Lucy's Gladstone Parliament. Cassell & Co.
Timbs' Abbeys and Castles, v. 3.
History of Miniature Art, by Propert. Macm., 1887.
Burlington's Fine Art Portraits and Miniatures. 1895.

Leggat Bros., 81 Chambers St., N. Y.

At the Threshold, Picton.
Wells, Every Man His Own Lawyer.
Walpole, Ireland.

Lemcke & Buechner, 812 Broadway, N. Y.

Tuomey and Aolmes, Phiocem Fossils of North Carolina, 4to. 1857.
Adams, Persia by a Persian.
Acta et Decreta Concilii Provincialis Neo-Eboracensis. IV.
Neo-Eboraci typis Societatis pro Libris Catholicis, 8vo, LXVIII.-10 p. g.

Library Clearing House, 140 Wells St., Chicago, Ill.

Any by Calvin or Luther on Epistles, Eng. or Ger.
U. S. Geological Survey, 1st and 14th Annual Repts.
Anything on ostrich farming.
U. S. Dispensatory, 16th or 17th ed., cheap.

Little, Brown & Co., 254 Washington St., Boston, Mass.

Morse, J. T., Jr., Famous Trials. Little, B. & Co.
Blount, Manual of Rifle Practice, latest ed.

George E. Littlefield, 67 Cornhill, Boston, Mass.

Hastings Memorial.
A Daughter of the Druids.
Lincoln's History of Hingham, 4 v.
The Higleys and Their Ancestry.

W. H. Lowdermilk & Co., Washington, D. C.

Hayes, Law of Desolation.
Harrison, Pickett and His Men.
Views of Society and Manners in U. S., by an Englishwoman.
Saxe-Weimar, Travels Thro' N. A.

Macauley Bros., 172 Woodward Ave., Detroit, Mich.

Watson, Theoretical and Spherical Astronomy.

A. C. McClurg & Co., 215 Wabash Ave., Chicago, Ill.

Hamilton, Works, 9 v. Putnam.
Elston Press publications, any.
Lewis and Clark, Coues' ed., 4 v.
McKenney and Hall, Indian Tribes, 4 v., folio.
Pittman, Mississippi.

BOOKS WANTED.—Continued.

S. F. McLean & Co., 44 E. 23d St., N. Y.

Riddle (Judge), Bart Ridgley.
Duval, Early Days in Texas.
League of the Iroquois, old ed.
Brennan, Martin B., Ancient Ireland, Her Milesian Chiefs, Her Kings and Princes, Her Struggles for Liberty, etc. Dublin, 1855.

H. Malkan, Hanover Sq., N. Y.

Any N. Y. daily Mar. 18, 1899.
Badminton's Fallacies of Race Theories.
Records of New Amsterdam, v. 3, shp.
Century Dictionary, 24 pts.

The Edw. Malley Co., New Haven, Conn.

Life and Morals of Jesus of Nazareth, by T. Jefferson.
Royal Little People, by E. S. Tucker.

B. & J. F. Meehan, Bath, Eng.

Dickens, Chas., anything on the author or his works.
Brazil or Portugal, anything.

R. H. Merriam, Hanover Sq., N. Y.

My Lady's Face.
Puritan Age and Rule, Ellis.
Genealogy of Bergen Family. 1876.
Harte and Stockton's 1st eds.
Broadgrins, by Coleman.

John P. Morton Co., Louisville, Ky.

Hammatt, Ipswich Papers.

N. Y. Medical Book Co., 45 E. 42d St., N. Y.

Hamilton, Treatise on Nervous Diseases, latest ed.
Landois and Stirling, Physiology, latest ed.
Yeo, Physiology, latest ed.
Clevenger, Med. Jurisprudence of Insanity, latest ed.

W. W. Nisbet, 12 S. Broadway, St. Louis, Mo.

Hawthorne, Scarlet Letter, 1st ed.
Longstreet, From Bull Run to Appomattox.
Poor Richard's Almanac.
Harris, Adventures of Sut Lovingood.
Colton, Private Correspondence of Clay.

Nusbaum Book and Art Co., 100 Granby St., Norfolk, Va.

No. 147, The Love of Man Under Socialism. Pub. by the Humboldt Library of Science.

R. A. Oakes, Watertown, N. Y. [*Cash.*]

The R. S. Peale Company's additions to the Encyclopædia Britannica, after the 1st 3 vols.

E. J. O'Malley, Hanover Sq., N. Y.

Index Volume of World's Great Classics.
The Virginian, 1st ed.
Columbian Cyclopedia. Funk & W.
The Prostrate State (S. C.) 1865-76.

Martin F. Onnen, 114 5th Ave., N. Y.

Any English ed. and trans. of the Oeuvres de Bernard Palissy.
The American Catalogue, 1876-1900.
The English Catalogue, any v.
Tscherning, Physiologic Optics, second-hand. Phila., 1900.

Daniel O'Shea, 1584 Broadway, N. Y.

Trial of Aaron Burr, v. 2 only. Phila., 1808.
Hist. of the Rod, by Cooper.
The Modern Evil, by Armstrong.
Life of William Cullen Bryant, by Goodwin.
Life of William Cullen Bryant, by Bigelow.
Life of Longfellow.
Life of Holmes.
Life of Shakespeare.
Shakespeare, Stratford ed.
Shakespeare, Duyckinck ed.
Timbs' Abbeys, Castles and Ancient Halls of England and Wales.

W. M. Palmer, 20 Monroe St., Grand Rapids, Mich.

Sachs, Physiology of Plants.
Huish, Samplers and Tapestry Embroideries.
Tyler, Island World of the Pacific Ocean.

C. C. Parker, 246 S. Broadway, Los Angeles, Cal. [*Cash.*]

The Dodge Club.
A Tribute of Flowers to the Memory of Mother.

Geo. B. Peck Dry Goods Co., Kansas City, Mo.

Erasmus, Praise of Folly, Holbein illus.
Dance of Death, Holbein illus.
Thomson, City of Dreadful Night.
Stoddard Lectures, 11 v.
Century Dictionary, last ed.
Prices on job lots, any kind.

H. E. Pendry, Rochester, N. Y.

Harper's Magazine, bound, May, 1870 to 1902, whole or part.
Century, bound, from v. 20, Oct., 1891 to present, whole or part.
Natural History N. Y., complete or odd v.

E. Picken, 33 Beaver Hall Hill, Montreal, Can.

Brown's Spare Hours, 2d ser. only. Ticknor & Fields, 1866.
Dr. Alex. Carlyle's Memoirs. Ticknor, 1868.

T. Pillot 409 Main St., Houston, Tex.

Heart Hungry, Westmoreland.
Problematic Characters, Spielhagen.
Hammer and Anvil, Spielhagen.

C. S. Pratt, 161 6th Ave., N. Y. [*Cash.*]

Pike, The Prostrate State.
Anything on the Reconstruction Period.
Wade, Merchants and Mechanics Com. Arithmetic.
Hammond, Sexual Impotence in the Male.
John Tenier's Works.

Presb. Bd. of Pub. and S. S. Work, 156 5th Ave., N. Y.

Leusden, Greek and Latin Testament.
Encyclopedia Britannica, 9th Edinburgh ed., v. 19 to 25 inclusive, bound in shp.

Presb. Bd. of Pub. and S. S. Work, 1319 Walnut St., Phila., Pa.

Barnes, On Isaiah, 2 v.

Preston & Rounds Co., Providence, R. I.

Lewis' Commercial Organization of Factories.

C. J. Price, 1004 Walnut St, Phila., Pa.

Richardson, Major, Wacousta, or, the Prophecy.
Any books about Jamaica and Martinique, written between 1800 and 1850.

Fleming H. Revell Co., Chicago, Ill.

Morals and Dogmas of Masonry, Albert Pike.

Geo. H. Richmond, 32 W. 33d St., N. Y.

Bryant, White Footed Deer.
Lowell, The President's Policy.
Poe, The Literati. 1850.
Irving, Sketch Book, odd nos. or complete.
Irving, Knickerbocker's New York, odd v. (1809) or complete.
Poe, Raven, 1st ed.
Poe, Works, any 1st eds.
Books on gems.

A. M. Robertson, 126 Post St., San Francisco, Cal.

Napoleon and the Fair Sex. Pub. by Lippincott.

Robson & Adee, Schenectady, N. Y.

Schoharie County. Pub. by Simms.

Wm. B. Ropes, Mt. Vernon, Skagit Co., Wash.

Kinglake, Crimea. Harper.
Bangs, House Boat on the Styx.
The Ladies' Diary, 4 v. London.
Innocents Abroad, 1 v., M. Twain.

J. Francis Ruggles, Bronson, Mich.

Paltock's Peter Wilkin's Adventures.
Thompson's The Doomed Chief, or Gant Gurley.
Beesley's Cataline, Clodius and Tiberius.

The St. Louis News Co., 1008 Locust St., St. Louis, Mo.

U. S. Roster of the United States Soldiers, Civil War: Missouri, Kentucky, Iowa, Kansas, Arkansas, Indiana.

St. Paul Book and Stationery Co., 5th and St. Peter Sts., St. Paul, Minn.

Foundations of 19th Cent., Houston S. Chamberlain.
Young Folks' Library, Aldrich and others.
Our Boys in China.
Our Boys in India.
Our Boys in Ireland.
Celebrated American Indians.
John Gray, Allen.
Count of Monte Cristo, blue cl. ed. Routledge, $1.

BOOKS WANTED.—Continued.

John E. Scopes, 29 Tweddle Bldg., Albany, N. Y.

American Ancestry, v. 10.
Wilkinson, Memoirs, v. 2, and atlas. Phila., 1816.
Engraving, Washington Irving and His Literary Friends at Sunnyside.
The Action Between the "Serapis" and "Bonhomme Richard."

Scrantom, Wetmore & Co., Rochester, N. Y.

Brainerd, The Old Family Doctor, 3 or 4 copies.
Century Book Names.
Century Atlas.

Charles Scribner's Sons, 153 5th Ave., N. Y.

Becke, C. H., The Age of Petronius. Cambridge, Mass.
Noblesse Oblige.

The Shorthand Institute, 8 Beacon St., Boston, Mass.

Sargent's (Gurney) Shorthand. Phila., 1792
Ewington's Stenography. Phila., 1818.
Steed's Grammatical Stenography. Wash., 1828.
Walker's Stenography. Phila., 1821.
Any old shorthand book or pamphlet.

Siegel, Cooper & Co., Chicago, Ill.

Swinburne's Complete Poems and Ballads, Unexpurgated.
Whistler, Gentle Art of Making Enemies

Frank Simmons, Springfield, Ill.

Reynolds, From Belleville to the Crystal Palace.
Collins, Annals of Kentucky.
Epicedium: a Latin poem written on the death of Col. John Daviess at the Battle of Tippecanoe, Nov. 7, 1811.
Swinburne's Poems and Dramas, complete. Pub. by Williams.

George D. Smith, 50 New St., N. Y.

Selden's Table Talk, Pickering ed.
Dorland Genealogy.
Audubon's Quadrupeds, text. 1854.
De Tocqueville, America, 2 v.
American Railway Guide, any nos. N. Y., Curran, Dinsmore & Co.
Washington as an Angler, by Geo. Moore.
Mexico, Books about.
Pitkins, History of U. S., 2 v.
Thackeray, Brookfield Letters.
A Mother's Legacy to Her Unborn Child, Elizabeth Joceline.
Drake, Indians.

P. A. Smith, Lock Box 915, Fishkill on Hudson, N. Y.

Legends of the Shonemunk, P. H. Smith.
Encyclopedia of Biblical Spiritualism.
110 Sermons. Pub. Co., Toronto.
Soldier Monk. Pub. by Blackwood.
Ticket of Leave Man. Pub. by Blackwood.

Wm. H. Smith, Jr., 515 W. 173d St., N. Y.

The Standard, Oct. 12, 1896.

A. H. Smythe, 43 S. High St., Columbus, O.

John Stewart's Narrative of Dumore's War. Pub. in Va.
Forest Rangers, a poetic tale of the western wilderness in 1794, Andrew Coffinberry. Columbus, 1842.

F. S. Stedman, Lewis Bldg., Pittsburgh, Pa.

Reade's Female Poets of America.
Griswold's Female Poets.
The Knickerbocker Gallery, ed. of 1848 or 1849. These must have portraits complete and in good condition.
The Library of G. W. Childs.
Life Edgar Allan Poe, by W. Fearing Gill. Widdleton.

T. & G. Book Shop, Greensburg, Pa.

Reuch's Anthropology.
Two Summer Girls and I, T. B. Sayre.

John C. Tredway, 202 Atlantic Ave., Brooklyn, N. Y.

History of the Loco-Foco Party, by Byrdsall. 1842.
Puck, nos. 5, 8, 85.
Kathie, a Disreputable Story, by Marie Flaacke.
As Some Men Are, by Marie Flaacke, probably in paper covers.

D. H. Tripp & Son, Peoria, Ill.

The Old Flag, first published by Union Prisoners at Camp Ford, Tyler, Texas.

United Presb. Bd. of Pub., Pittsburgh, Pa.

Freeman's Norman Conquest, v. 1, 2, or complete set.
Bruce's Travels in Abyssinia.
Through Abyssinia, F. H. Smith.
Sacred City of the Ethiopians, I. T. Bent.
Jomini's Art of War.
Epistles of the Apostolic Fathers, tr. by William Wake.
The Behemoth, by Thomas Hobbes.

John Wanamaker, N. Y.

H. Heine's Shakespeare's Maidens and Women, tr. by C. G. Leland. N. Y., 1891.
Soldiers Three, by Kipling, blue cl. Macmillan.
Saturday Evening Post (Phila.), June 29th, 1901; Nov. 30th, 1901.
Life of Louis XVII., by Beauschene.
Life of Louis XVII., by Tomes.
Clery's Diary, or, Journal During Captivity of Louis XVI.
Rawlinson's Herodotus, 4 v., cl. $8.

Geo. E. Warner, Minneapolis, Minn.

Bierce, Ambrose, Black Beetles in Amber.
Clowes, Walter F., Record Detroit Light Guard.
Any county atlas or history.

W. H. Wood & Co., 8 E. Main St., Springfield, O.

Anything on Hague Peace Conference.
Coffee from Plantation to Cup, Thurber.
Life and Sermons of Spurgeon.
The Englishman's Bible, by Newberry.
Commentary of New Testament, Henry or Clark.

Jas. C. Young, 1600 2d Ave., S., Minneapolis, Minn.

Forest Buds from the Woods of Maine, by Florence Percy, 1st ed.
If I Were King, Justin H. McCarthy, 1st ed.

BOOKS FOR SALE.

Bartlett's Book Store, 33 E. 22d St., N. Y.

Metaphysical Magazine, any back vols., bound.

Goodenough & Woglom Co., 122 Nassau St., N. Y.

New *Scribner's Magazine*, bound cl., v. 1-13 incl., 6 months to a vol. Each 75 cts.

C. D. Hurd, Clinton, Ia.

Tomes, Robert, The Great Civil War, 3 v., red cl.

Leggat Bros., 81 Chambers St., N. Y.

Harper's Magazine, 99 v., hf. cf., publishers' binding. Each $1.25.
Dumas, 31 v., hf. mor. $28.00.
Reed's Modern Eloquence, 10 v., hf. mor. $25.00.
Family histories and genealogies, 5 v. $50.00.
Loudon's Ladies' Flower Garden, 5 v., hf. mor. $25.00.
Picturesque Europe, 3 v., hf. mor. $7.50.
25 Dream of Self-Consciousness, 16 pp. 3 cts.

Sanford Putnam Co., Worcester, Mass.

Watkins' Yo-Semite Gallery, Photographic Views of the Yo-Semite Falls and Valley, executed by E. L. Watkins, San Francisco, Cal., large folio, full turkey mor., size of vol. 18 x 20 inches, in perfect condition.

Wm. H. Smith, Jr., 515 W. 173d St., N. Y.

Tragedies of Sophocles, 2 v., fine ed.
Josephus' Works, 4 v. 1755.
Dictionary of the Bible, Wm. Smith, hf. mor.
Froude's Hist. of England, 12 v.
Kane's Arctic Explorations, plates perfectly clean.
Early New England pamphlets, 1785 to 1806.
Principles of Natural Religion, J. Wilkins. 1675.
Essays by Marquis D'Argenson. Mass., 1797.

HELP WANTED.

WANTED.—An experienced book and mail-order clerk for retail store. Give references, experience and salary expected. Address A. B. P., care of PUBLISHERS' WEEKLY.

WANTED.—Shipping clerk with experience in book business. Moderate salary. Address X. Y., care of PUBLISHERS' WEEKLY.

HELP WANTED.—Continued.

WANTED.—First-class man to manage stationery department in retail bookstore. Give full particulars as to experience, references, and salary expected, which must be moderate. Address RAWLEY, care of PUBLISHERS' WEEKLY.

SITUATIONS WANTED.

FIRST-CLASS, well posted bookman wishes position as salesman, or head of department. Long experience with largest New York houses. No objection to going out of town or travelling. Address C. L. P., care of PUBLISHERS' WEEKLY.

BOOKKEEPER, accountant and office manager. 20 years' experience, wholesale and manufacturing, desires position. Can adapt to any system or conditions. Excellent references. Salary no object so long as prospects are good. Address WILLSTAN, care of PUBLISHERS' WEEKLY.

WANTED.—Position with Bible publishing house as shipping clerk. Ten years' experience with prominent Bible house in New York City. Thoroughly familiar with manufacturing and a wide experience in management of sheet stock. Can produce good credentials. Address R. L., care of PUBLISHERS' WEEKLY.

GENTLEMAN experienced in practical details of book manufacture and manuscript editing; also author of several well-known technical treatises, would like to make arrangements with publishing house, either to conduct practical manufacture of books or prepare such on consignment. Address AUTHOR, care of PUBLISHERS' WEEKLY.

BUSINESS FOR SALE.

FOR SALE.—Book and Stationery business in Fla. town of 25,000; net profit over 50%; last year's sales, $17,812.00. Good reason for selling. Address W. E. C., 176 Court St., Kankakee, Ill.

COPYRIGHT NOTICES.

LIBRARY OF CONGRESS,
OFFICE OF THE REGISTER OF COPYRIGHTS,
WASHINGTON, D. C.

To wit: *Be it remembered*, That on the 2d day of July, 1902, D. B. Ivison, of United States, hath deposited in this office the title of a book, the title of which is in the following words, to wit: "Robinson's Mathematical Series. The Junior Class Arithmetic. Oral and Written. Designed for Graded Schools. By Daniel W. Fish. A.M. New York, Cincinnati, Chicago, American Book Company," the right whereof he claims as proprietor in conformity with the laws of the United States respecting copyrights.

(Signed) HERBERT PUTNAM, *Librarian of Congress.*
By THORVALD SOLBERG, *Register of Copyrights.*
In renewal for 14 years from December 7, 1902.

LIBRARY OF CONGRESS,
OFFICE OF THE REGISTER OF COPYRIGHTS,
WASHINGTON, D. C.

To wit: *Be it remembered*, That on the 2d day of July, 1902, D. B. Ivison, of United States, hath deposited in this office the title of a book, the title of which is in the following words, to wit: "Robinson's Shorter Course. Complete Arithmetic. Oral and Written. First Part. By Daniel W. Fish, A.M. New York, Cincinnati, Chicago, American Book Company," the right whereof he claims as proprietor in conformity with the laws of the United States respecting copyrights.

(Signed) HERBERT PUTNAM, *Librarian of Congress.*
By THORVALD SOLBERG, *Register of Copyrights.*
In renewal for 14 years from December 7, 1902.

LIBRARY OF CONGRESS,
OFFICE OF THE REGISTER OF COPYRIGHTS,
WASHINGTON, D. C.

To wit: *Be it remembered*, That on the 2d day of July, 1902, D. B. Ivison, of United States, hath deposited in this office the title of a book, the title of which is in the following words, to wit: "Robinson's Shorter Course. The Complete Arithmetic. Oral and Written. Second Part. By Daniel W. Fish, A.M. New York, Cincinnati, Chicago, American Book Company," the right whereof he claims as proprietor in conformity with the laws of the United States respecting copyrights.

(Signed) HERBERT PUTNAM, *Librarian of Congress.*
By THORVALD SOLBERG, *Register of Copyrights.*
In renewal for 14 years from December 7, 1902.

LIBRARY OF CONGRESS,
OFFICE OF THE REGISTER OF COPYRIGHTS,
WASHINGTON, D. C.

To wit: *Be it remembered*, That on the 2d day of July, 1902, D. B. Ivison, of United States, hath deposited in this office the title of a book, the title of which is in the following words, to wit: "Robinson's Shorter Course. Key to the Complete Arithmetic. For Teachers and Private Learners. New York, Cincinnati, Chicago, American Book Company," the right whereof he claims as proprietor in conformity with the laws of the United States respecting copyrights.

(Signed) HERBERT PUTNAM, *Librarian of Congress.*
By THORVALD SOLBERG, *Register of Copyrights.*
In renewal for 14 years from December 7, 1902.

LIBRARY OF CONGRESS,
OFFICE OF THE REGISTER OF COPYRIGHTS,
WASHINGTON, D. C.

To wit: *Be it remembered*, That on the 3d day of July, 1902, Guy D. Peck, of Gallia, N. J., hath deposited in this office the title of a book, the title of which is in the following words, to wit: "First Lessons in Numbers. By William G. Peck, Ph.D., LL.D. New York, Cincinnati, Chicago, American Book Company," the right whereof he claims as proprietor in conformity with the laws of the United States respecting copyrights.

(Signed) HERBERT PUTNAM, *Librarian of Congress.*
By THORVALD SOLBERG, *Register of Copyrights.*
In renewal for 14 years from December 29, 1902.

LIBRARY OF CONGRESS,
OFFICE OF THE REGISTER OF COPYRIGHTS,
WASHINGTON, D. C.

To wit: *Be it remembered*, That on the 28th day of July, 1902, Mrs. Roxana S. Ridpath, of the United States, hath deposited in this office the title of a book, the title of which is in the following words, to wit: "History of the United States. Prepared especially for Schools on a New and Comprehensive Plan, embracing the Features of Lyman's Historical Chart. By John Clark Ridpath, A.M., LL.D.," the right whereof she claims as proprietor in conformity with the laws of the United States respecting copyrights.

(Signed) HERBERT PUTNAM, *Librarian of Congress.*
By THORVALD SOLBERG, *Register of Copyrights.*
In renewal for 14 years from December 5, 1902.

LIBRARY OF CONGRESS,
OFFICE OF THE REGISTER OF COPYRIGHTS,
WASHINGTON, D. C.

To wit: *Be it remembered*, That on the 2d day of July, 1902, Lyman P. Spencer, of United States, hath deposited in this office the title of a book, the title of which is in the following words, to wit: "Theory of Spencerian Penmanship. For schools and private learners, developed by questions and answers, with practical illustrations. Designed to be studied by pupils in connection with the use of the Spencerian Copy-Books. By The 'Spencerian Authors.' New York, Cincinnati, Chicago, American Book Company," the right whereof he claims as author and proprietor in conformity with the laws of the United States respecting copyrights.

(Signed) HERBERT PUTNAM, *Librarian of Congress.*
By THORVALD SOLBERG, *Register of Copyrights.*
In renewal for 14 years from December 29, 1902.

LIBRARY OF CONGRESS,
OFFICE OF THE REGISTER OF COPYRIGHTS,
WASHINGTON, D. C.

To wit: *Be it remembered*, That on the 2d day of August, 1902, Jean Swinton, Executrix, of New York, N. Y., hath deposited in this office the title of a book, the title of which is in the following words, to wit: "Language Primer. Beginner's Lessons in Speaking and Writing English. By William Swinton, A.M., New York, Cincinnati, Chicago,

COPYRIGHT NOTICES.—Continued.

American Book Company," the right whereof she claims as proprietor in conformity with the laws of the United States respecting copyrights.
(Signed) HERBERT PUTNAM, *Librarian of Congress.*
By THORVALD SOLBERG, *Register of Copyrights.*
In renewal for 14 years from August 3, 1902.

LIBRARY OF CONGRESS,
OFFICE OF THE REGISTER OF COPYRIGHTS,
WASHINGTON, D. C.

To wit: *Be it remembered,* That on the 2d day of August, 1902, Jean Swinton, Executrix, of New York, N. Y., hath deposited in this office the title of a book, the title of which is in the following words, to wit: "Outlines of the World's History. Ancient, Mediæval, and Modern. With special relation to the History of Civilization and the Progress of Mankind. For use in the higher classes in Public Schools, Academies, Seminaries, etc. By William Swinton, New York. Cincinnati, Chicago. American Book Company," the right whereof she claims as proprietor in conformity with the laws of the United States respecting copyrights.
(Signed) HERBERT PUTNAM, *Librarian of Congress.*
By THORVALD SOLBERG, *Register of Copyrights.*
In renewal for 14 years from September 14, 1902.

LIBRARY OF CONGRESS,
OFFICE OF THE REGISTER OF COPYRIGHTS,
WASHINGTON, D. C.

To wit: *Be it remembered,* That on the 2d day of July, 1902, Emma H. Watson, of United States, hath deposited in this office the title of a book, the title of which is in the following words, to wit: "Independent Youth's Speller. Printed in imitation of Writing with original classification of words, formations of columns, dictation exercises, orthographical and orthoepical treatise, appendix, etc. By J. Madison Watson. New York, Cincinnati, Chicago, American Book Company," the right whereof she claims as proprietor in conformity with the laws of the United States respecting copyrights.
(Signed) HERBERT PUTNAM, *Librarian of Congress.*
By THORVALD SOLBERG, *Register of Copyrights.*
In renewal for 14 years from October 17, 1902.

LIBRARY OF CONGRESS,
OFFICE OF THE REGISTER OF COPYRIGHTS,
WASHINGTON, D. C.

Class A, XXc, No. 31662.—To wit: *Be it remembered,* That on the 26th day of April, 1902, Laura Abbott Buck, of New York, N. Y., hath deposited in this office the title of a book, the title of which is in the following words, to wit: "Captain William Kidd and others of the Buccaneers. By John S. C. Abbott. New York, Dodd, Mead & Company," the right whereof she claims as proprietor in conformity with the laws of the United States respecting copyrights.
(Signed) HERBERT PUTNAM, *Librarian of Congress.*
By THORVALD SOLBERG, *Register of Copyrights.*
In renewal for 14 years from October 8, 1902.

LIBRARY OF CONGRESS,
OFFICE OF THE REGISTER OF COPYRIGHTS,
WASHINGTON, D. C.

Class A, XXc, No. 35699.—To wit: *Be it remembered,* That on the 18th day of June, 1902, John Foster Kirk, of Philadelphia, Pa., hath deposited in this office the title of a book, the title of which is in the following words, to wit: "The History of the Reign of the Emperor Charles the Fifth. By William Robertson. D.D. With an Account of the Emperor's Life after His Abdication. By William H. Prescott. New Edition. Volume I. Philadelphia, J. B. Lippincott Company," the right whereof he claims as proprietor in conformity with the laws of the United States respecting copyrights.
(Signed) HERBERT PUTNAM, *Librarian of Congress.*
By THORVALD SOLBERG, *Register of Copyrights.*
In renewal for 14 years from December 11, 1902.

LIBRARY OF CONGRESS,
OFFICE OF THE REGISTER OF COPYRIGHTS,
WASHINGTON, D. C.

Class A, XXc, No. 35700.—To wit: *Be it remembered,* That on the 18th day of June, 1902, John Foster Kirk, of Philadelphia, Pa., hath deposited in this office the title of a book, the title of which is in the following words, to wit: "The History of the Reign of the Emperor Charles the Fifth. By William Robertson, D.D. With an Account of the Emperor's Life after His Abdication. By William H. Prescott. New Edition. Volume II. Philadelphia, J. B. Lippincott Company," the right whereof he claims as proprietor in conformity with the laws of the United States respecting copyrights.
(Signed) HERBERT PUTNAM, *Librarian of Congress.*
By THORVALD SOLBERG, *Register of Copyrights.*
In renewal for 14 years from December 11, 1902.

LIBRARY OF CONGRESS,
OFFICE OF THE REGISTER OF COPYRIGHTS,
WASHINGTON, D. C.

Class A, XXc, No. 35701.—To wit: *Be it remembered,* That on the 18th day of June, 1902, John Foster Kirk, of Philadelphia, Pa., hath deposited in this office the title of a book, the title of which is in the following words, to wit: "The History of the Reign of the Emperor Charles the Fifth. By William Robertson, D.D. With an Account of the Emperor's Life after His Abdication. By William H. Prescott. New Edition. Volume III. Philadelphia, J. B. Lippincott Company," the right whereof he claims as proprietor in conformity with the laws of the United States respecting copyrights.
(Signed) HERBERT PUTNAM, *Librarian of Congress.*
By THORVALD SOLBERG, *Register of Copyrights.*
In renewal for 14 years from December 11, 1902.

SPECIAL NOTICES.

Published May, 1902 *Second Edition Now Ready*

RATAPLAN: A ROGUE ELEPHANT

AND OTHER STORIES

By ELLEN VELVIN, F.Z.S.

"Not the slightest apology for the book is needed. It belongs with the classics for young people of whatever age."
—*Boston Transcript.*

"The stories of the adventures of the elephant, giraffe, hippopotamus, jackal, and other beasts are told in a simple way, and with that personation and humanizing of animals which always seem so much to arouse children's imaginations."
—*The Outlook*, New York.

"There is plenty of out-of-door feeling in all the tales and plenty of action, and they should be read with pleasure by the children for whom they are intended."
—*New York Sun.*

"Only a person who knows animals intimately could weave such delightful romances around the inhabitants of the forests."
—*Milwaukee Sentinel.*

"The book is true to life and scientifically accurate. No more beautiful or proper present can be made to a child."
—*Cleveland Recorder.*

"The range of the tales is that of the habitable globe and the navigable seas. One of the best features of these stories is that there is no maudlin sentimentality about them, while, at the same time, the young reader is made to feel how much cruelty is often involved in the treatment of living toys."—*The Churchman*, New York.

Cloth, 12mo, Ornamental, - $1.25 Net; Postage, 13c.

HENRY ALTEMUS COMPANY, Philadelphia

STILLMAN GOTT

FARMER AND FISHERMAN

By EDWIN DAY SIBLEY

THERE'S a good story told in its pages; a story of true folk living on land and on sea, close to nature and unspoiled by contact with convention's artificial laws. The hero is a bright, manly fellow, a scion of the best blood of Maine; he goes out into the world and wins out in splendid course and finish, aided by the love he has for the sweetest girl in all Maine; in fact their love story is the motive of the book. But Stillman Gott is the dominating and pervading element of the story, an element that carries with it the entire sympathy of the reader, who cannot help loving Stillman Gott for his quaint philosophy, business sense, kind heartedness and sturdy independence.

Bound in Red Silk Cloth, Cover Design in Gold
Gilt Top, Uncut Edges, 368 Pages. Price, $1.50

JOHN S. BROOKS & COMPANY
120 BOYLSTON STREET, - - - - BOSTON

NOTHING BUT BOOKS

BUY YOUR BOOKS OF A JOBBER AND YOU WILL SAVE

TIME AND MONEY

WE CARRY COMPLETE LINES OF MISCELLANEOUS AND SCHOOL BOOKS WE CAN FILL YOUR ORDERS WITH

ACCURACY AND DISPATCH

Fifty years of book jobbing, three hundred thousand books in stock, and our location in the leading book market of the country, enable us to offer you everything in the book line at the lowest prices.

THE BAKER & TAYLOR CO., 33-37 East 17th St., Union Sq., North, New York

BOOKS

Such prices as you may not have heard of; and such service as you will appreciate. Send us an order—that's the way to find out.

A new friend is almost as good as an old one.

H B CLAFLIN COMPANY

Church and Worth Streets New York

Books of All Publishers on

MEDICINE, DENTISTRY,

PHARMACY AND ALLIED SCIENCES.

We have the largest miscellaneous stock in the country of American and English Books on these subjects.
Trade and Library Orders Solicited.

P. BLAKISTON'S SON & CO.

1012 Walnut Street, Philadelphia.

MEDICAL BOOKS.

(THE TRADE SUPPLIED.)

A full-priced Catalogue of all Medical and Surgical Books Sent on Application.

E. R. PELTON,

19 East 16th St. (bet. Broadway and 5th Ave.), New York

JOHN J. MURPHY

DEALER IN

Fine Book, Coated and Cover Papers

47 John and 5 Dutch Streets, N. Y.

Refers to "The Publishers' Weekly"

SHORTHAND—ISAAC PITMAN'S

Exclusively adopted in the Commercial Course of New York High Schools.

SHORTHAND INSTRUCTOR (Complete System),	$1.50
ISAAC PITMAN'S MANUAL,	.50
" " TEACHER,	.20
" " SHORTHAND DICTIONARY,	1.50

Liberal Discount to Dealers

ISAAC PITMAN & SONS, 33 Union Sq., N. Y.

FOWLER & WELLS CO.,

Phrenologists and Publishers.

WORKS ON

PHRENOLOGY, PHYSIOGNOMY, MENTAL SCIENCE, AND HYGIENE.

Write for Catalogue.

24 East 22d Street, New York.

THE BEST ILLUSTRATIONS

By half-tone or other photo-engraving processes are made by

COOPER ENGRAVING COMPANY

320 Pearl Street, New York

TELEPHONE "97 JOHN"

Successors to New York Engraving and Printing Co.

BOOKBINDING

Fine Cloth and Leather Edition Work a Specialty. Estimates cheerfully given.

J. F. TAPLEY CO.

33-37 Bleecker Street, New York City

Telephone 824 and 825 Spring

VAN EVEREN'S PAPER ADJUSTABLE BOOK COVERS. Simply made. Easy to apply. Cost little. No better made. Samples on request. Order of your Jobber. P. F. VAN EVEREN, 60 Ann Street, New York.

THE

Publishers' Weekly

THE AMERICAN

BOOK TRADE JOURNAL

WITH WHICH IS INCORPORATED

The American Literary Gazette and Publishers' Circular.

[ESTABLISHED 1852.]

PUBLICATION OFFICE, 298 BROADWAY, NEW YORK.

Entered at the Post-Office at New York, N. Y., as second-class matter.

VOL. LXII., No. 10. NEW YORK, September 6, 1902. WHOLE No. 1597

Little, Brown & Co.'s Popular Fiction

Both Ready Sept. 13th—Second Edition Printed

THE PHARAOH AND THE PRIEST

AN HISTORICAL NOVEL OF ANCIENT EGYPT, FROM THE ORIGINAL POLISH OF **ALEXANDER GLOVATSKI.** Translated by **JEREMIAH CURTIN.** Illustrated. 12mo. $1.50.

No novel of such interest and power as "The Pharaoh and the Priest" has been written about Egypt thus far. The author depicts vividly the desperate conflict between the secular and the ecclesiastical powers in the eleventh century before Christ during the career of Rameses XIII.

THE QUEEN OF QUELPARTE

By ARCHER B. HULBERT. Illustrated. 12mo. $1.50.

A vivid romance of the Far East, with its scene laid near Japan shortly after the war between China and that country.

FICTION IN PREPARATION

The Shadow of the Czar

By JOHN R. CARLING.

An absorbing story of adventure dealing with the claim of Princess Barbara to the throne of Czernova.

The Colonel's Opera Cloak

By CHRISTINE C. BRUSH.

A new edition of a popular story. Profusely illustrated.

Tower or Throne

By HARRIET T. COMSTOCK.

A romance of the girlhood of Elizabeth, told with unusual grace, with picturesque glimpses of the court life.

Miss Belladonna

By CAROLINE TICKNOR

New edition of this social satire with additional chapters.

NEW FICTION OF TESTED POPULARITY

Lafitte of Louisiana

By MARY DEVEREUX. (*3d Edition.*)

The Heroine of the Strait

By MARY C. CROWLEY. (*3d Edition.*)

In the Country God Forgot

By FRANCES CHARLES. (*3d Edition.*)

A Girl of Virginia

By LUCY M. THRUSTON. (*4th Edition.*)

LITTLE, BROWN & COMPANY

BOSTON

The Publishers' Weekly.

SEPTEMBER 6, 1902.

INDEX TO ADVERTISERS

NOTES IN SEASON.

THE CENTURY COMPANY have in preparation a volume on "Title-pages," by Theodore L. De Vinne, which is designed to be an aid to printers and publishers, and also interesting to those who care for the making of good books. They also announce "A Cook's Picture Book," a guide to the preparing of dainty dishes for dainty meals, by May Ronald, the author of "The Century Cook Book."

GODFREY A. S. WIENERS, 662 Sixth Avenue, New York, has purchased from William Doxey the plates of all the titles heretofore published at "The Sign of the Lark." He will shortly bring out new editions of the well-known *Lark Classics,* together with desirable additions; also, a new series, *The Lark Wisdom Series.*

LITTLE, BROWN & Co. will publish on the 13th inst. "The Pharaoh and the Priest," the long-promised historical novel, by Alexander Glovatski, translated by Jeremiah Curtin. The story is said to be one of great interest and power, and depicts vividly the desperate conflict between the secular and ecclesiastical powers in the eleventh century before Christ during the career of Ramesis XIII. The first edition was taken up before day of publication, and a second edition is now ready. They will publish at the same time "The Queen of Quelparte," a romance of the Far East, by Archer B. Hulbert.

CHARLES SCRIBNER'S SONS have just ready Richard Harding Davis's new novel, "Captain Macklin," that deals with a kind of life with which Mr. Davis has become very familiar in the course of his own experiences. Captain Macklin's career carries him through a South American revolution and through various military adventures, and Macklin himself is one of the author's most fascinating heroes. They will publish shortly "Doctor Bryson," by Frank H. Spearman, whose theme is the career of an eminent surgeon, the hero of the modern drama that the warfare of science with death and disease constitutes, with which is interwoven a love story of unusual intensity and charm. They announce the immediate publication of George Meredith's "The Shaving of Shagpat," "The Tragic Comedians," and "Short Stories," completing, with these three volumes, the *Uniform Pocket Edition* of Meredith's fiction, the first twelve volumes of which were published in the spring and early summer.

D. APPLETON & Co. have just ready "The Story of a Strange Career, being the autobiography of a convict; an authentic document," edited by Stanley Waterloo. This work is the authentic life story of a criminal, who was of good birth and education, but he went downward naturally, it seems, from his birth. He gives interesting descriptions of his adventures on a British man-of-war, in the American navy, in Confederate prisons during the Civil War, in the riots in New York, and finally of his life in the Western Penitentiary. They have also just ready in the *Town and Country Library* "Tales About Temperaments," by John Oliver Hobbes," described in a former issue. The following new textbooks have also just been added to their list: "A First Spanish Book and Reader," by William F. Giese, professor of Romance languages in the University of Wisconsin, and Beaumarchais' "Le Barbier de Séville," edited by Antoine Muzzarelli, two new volumes in their *Twentieth Century Textbooks;* also, "Harold's Discussions," by John W. Troeger and Edna Beatrice Troeger, in the *Nature Study Readers.*

WEEKLY RECORD OF NEW PUBLICATIONS.

☞ Beginning with the issue of July 5, 1902, the titles of *net* books published under the rules of the American Publishers' Association are preceded by a double asterisk **, and the word net follows the price. The titles of *fiction* (not net) published under the rules are preceded by a dagger †. *Net* books not covered by the rules, whether published by members of the American Publishers' Association or not, are preceded by a single asterisk, and the word net follows the price. ☜

The abbreviations are usually self-explanatory. c. after the date indicates that the book is copyrighted; if the copyright date differs from the imprint date, the year of copyright is added. Books of foreign origin of which the edition (annotated, illustrated, etc.) is entered as copyright, are marked c. ed.; translations, c. tr.; n. p., in place of price, indicates that the publisher makes no price, either net or retail, and quotes prices to the trade only upon application.

A colon after initial designates the most usual given name, as: A: Augustus; B: Benjamin; C: Charles; D: David; E: Edward; F: Frederic; G: George; H: Henry; I: Isaac; J: John; L: Louis; N: Nicholas; P: Peter; R: Richard; S: Samuel; T: Thomas; W: William.

Sizes are designated as follows: F. (folio: over 30 centimeters high); Q. (4to: under 30 cm.); O. (8vo: 25 cm.); D. (12mo: 20 cm.); S. (16mo: 17½ cm.); T. (24mo: 15 cm.); Tt. (32mo: 12½ cm.); Fe. 48mo: 10 cm.). Sq., obl., nar., designate square, oblong, narrow books of these heights.

Adams, Rob. Chamblet. Good without God. N. Y., P: Eckler, [1902.] c. 3-113 p. D. pap., 25 c.
The author is president of the Montreal Pioneer Freethought Club.

Allen, Monfort B., *M.D.*, *and* McGregor, Amelia C. The ladies' guide to health and beauty; containing full information on all the marvelous and complex matters pertaining to women; together with the diseases peculiar to the female sex; the whole forming a complete medical guide for women. Phil., National Publishing Co., [1902.] c. 14+17-511 p. il. 8°, cl., $1.75.

Aristophanes. The ecclesiazusae; the Greek text rev.; with a tr. into corresponding metres, introd. and commentary, by B: Bickley Rogers. N. Y., Macmillan, 1902. 37+238 p. 8°, cl., $4.

***Atwood**, G: E: Complete graded arithmetic. 8th grade. Bost., Heath, 1902. c. 154 p. 12°, cl., 25 c. net.

***Bates**, Katharine Lee, *and* Coman, Katharine, *comps.* English history told by English poets: a reader for school use. N. Y., Macmillan, 1902. c. 15+542 p. 12°, cl., 80 c. net.

Beaumarchais, Pierre Augustin Caron de. Le barbier de Séville; ed., with explanatory notes and full vocabulary, by Antoine Muzzarelli. N. Y., Appleton, 1902. [Jl.] c. 12+176 p. S. (Twentieth century textbooks.) cl., 35 c.

***Bible.** New Testament. The Gospel according to St. Mark; the Greek text ed., with introd. and notes for the use of schools, by Sir A. F. Hort. N. Y., Macmillan, 1902. 33+202 p. 12°, (Cambridge Univ. Press ser.) cl., 75 c. net.

***Bible.** Old Testament. Cambridge Bible for schools and colleges: The Song of Solomon; with introd. and notes by Rev. Andrew Harper; general ed., A. F. Kirkpatrick, D.D. N. Y., Macmillan, 1902. 51+96 p. 12°, cl., 50 c. net.

****Bible.** Old Testament. The emphasized Bible. v. 1, Genesis to Ruth; v. 2, Samuel to Psalms. N. Y. and Chic., Revell, 1902. 288; 319 p. 8°, cl., per v., $2 net.

***Bible.** Temple ed. In 24 v. vs. 13-14. Phil., Lippincott, 1902. il. sq. T. cl., ea., 40 c. net; flex. leath., 60 c. net.
Contents: v. 13, Luke, ed. by the Rev. Marvin R. Vincent; v. 14, Daniel and the minor prophets, by Rev. R. Sinker.

Blake, Ja. Vila. Songs. Bost., Ja. H. West Co., 1902. c. 109 p. D. cl., $1.
A collection of delicate, fanciful songs, many being love songs. The songs are followed by explanatory notes giving the rhythmical movement in music notes. By the author of "Sonnets," etc.

****Brine**, *Mrs.* Mary Dow Northam. Lassie and Laddie: a story for little lads and lassies. N. Y., Dutton, [1902.] c. 5+241 p. il. 12°, cl., $1 net.

****Brooks**, Amy. Randy and her friends; il. by the author. Bost., Lee & Shepard, 1902. c. 253 p. D. (The Randy books.) cl., 80 c. net.

Browne, George Waldo, ["Victor St. Clair," *pseud.*] For home and honor; or, a brave boy's battles. N. Y., Street & Smith, [1902.] c. 4+5-208 p. 1 il. D. (Boys' own lib., no. 26.) cl., 75 c.

Bruff, Lawrence L. A text book of ordnance and gunnery prepared for the use of cadets of the U. S. M. A. 2d ed. N. Y., J: Wiley & Sons, 1902. c. 5+677 p. 8°, cl., $6.

Byrne, Mary Agnes. The little woman in the spout. Akron, O., Saalfield Pub. Co., 1902. c. 84 p. il. 12°, cl., 60 c.

Byrne, Mary Agnes. Roy and Rosyrocks. Akron, O., Saalfield Pub. Co., 1902. c. 83 p. il. 12°, cl., 60 c.

Chapin, H: D., *M.D.* The theory and practice of infant feeding; with notes on development. N. Y., W: Wood & Co., 1902. 326 p. 8°, cl., $2.25.

Clark, C: S., *and* Bresel, Annie. How to answer a want ad; or, how to apply for a position: a comprehensive, practical work on personal and written applications; with illustrations taken from actual business life. [Rochester, N. Y., New York State Publishing Co.,] 1902. c. 88 p. por. il. maps, Q. pap., $2.

†**Craigie**, *Mrs.* Pearl Maria Teresa, ["John Oliver Hobbes," *pseud.*] Tales about temperaments. N. Y., Appleton, 1902. [Ag.] c. 9+207 p. D. (Appleton's town and country lib., no. 315.) cl., $1; pap., 50 c.
Three stories and two short plays, namely: "The worm that God prepared," "'Tis an ill flight without wings," "A repentance," "Prince Toto," and "Journeys end in lovers meeting."

Dean, Ida M., *and* George, Marian M. A little journey to Holland; for home and school, intermediate and upper grades. Chic., A. Flanagan Co., [1902.] c. 88 p. D. (The plan book, v. 5, no. 7.) pap., 15 c.

Deitch, Guilford A. Digest of insurance cases, embracing all decisions in any manner affecting insurance companies or their contracts, [etc.] v. 13 for the year ending Oct. 31, 1900. v. 14 for the year ending Oct. 31, 1901. Indianapolis, Rough Notes Co., 1902. c. O. hf. shp., ea., $3.

Denison, *Mrs.* Mary Andrews. Barbara's triumphs; or, the fortunes of a young artist. [New issue.] N. Y., Street & Smith, [1902.] c. '91, '02. 2+5-197 p. D. (Girls' popular lib.) cl., 50 c.

Denison, *Mrs.* Mary Andrews. The Frenchman ward. [New issue.] N. Y., Street & Smith, [1902.] c. '92, '02. 2+5-212 p. D. (Girls' popular lib.) cl., 50 c.

Denison, *Mrs.* Mary Andrews. The guardian's trust. [New issue.] N. Y., Street & Smith, [1902.] c. '91, '02. 2+5-283 p. D. (Girls' popular lib.) cl., 50 c.

****Falt**, Clarence Manning. Wharf and fleet: ballads of the fishermen of Gloucester. Bost., Little, Brown & Co., 1902. c. 14+117 p. il. 8°, cl., $1.50 net.

Fielding, H: Works. Temple ed.; ed. by G: Saintsbury. N. Y., Macmillan, 1902. 12 v., 16°, cl., ea., 50 c.; leath., ea., 75 c.

Contents: Tom Jones, 4 v.; Amelia, 3 v.; Joseph Andrews, 2 v.; Jonathan Wild, 1 v.; Miscellanies, 2 v.

****Firth**, C: Harding. Cromwell's army: a history of the English soldier during the Civil wars, the Commonwealth, and the Protectorate: being the Ford lectures, delivered in the University of Oxford in 1900-1901. N. Y., Ja. Pott & Co., 1902. 12-444 p. 12°, cl., $1.75 net.

****Foster**, Edna A. Hortense—a difficult child; il. by Mary Ayer. Bost., Lee & Shepard, 1902. [Ag.] c. 5+290 p. D. cl., 80 c. net.

The interesting experience of the training of an impulsive little girl by a well-meaning young lady relative who attempts to bring her up according to set rules for well-regulated children.

Gautier, Théophile. Works. [Limited ed.] In 24 v. v. 16-18; tr. and ed. by F. C. de Sumichrast. N. Y., G: D. Sproul, 1902. c. pl. por. 8°, per v., buckram, $3.50; hf. mor., $6.

Gavit, Helen E. The essentials of polite correspondence: being a collection of accepted forms of address and salutation, together with other information regarding correct usage in social and official correspondence; with an introduction and chapter on accepted forms of address. N. Y., Marcus Ward Co., [1902.] c. 48 p. il. diagr., 16°, pap., 10 c.

George, Marian M. A little journey to England. pt. 1, London and Liverpool; for intermediate and upper grades. Chic., A. Flanagan Co., [1902.] c. '01. 105 p. D. (The plan book, v. 5, no. 2.) pap., 15 c.

George, Marian M. A little journey to England and Wales; for intermediate and upper grades. Chic., A. Flanagan Co., [1902.] c. '01. 110 p. D. (The plan book, v. 5. no. 3.) pap., 15 c.

George, Marian M., *ed.* A little journey to France; for home and school, intermediate and upper grades. Chic., A. Flanagan Co., [1902.] c. 110 p. D. (The plan book, v. 5, no. 6.) pap., 15 c.

George, Marian M. A little journey to Ireland; for intermediate and upper grades. Chic., A. Flanagan Co., [1902.] c. '01. 98 p. D. (The plan book, v. 5, no. 1.) pap., 15 c.

***Georgian** (The) period: being measured drawings of colonial work. In 3 v. v. 3, pt. 10. Bost., American Architect and Building News Co., 1902. c. il. pl. portfolio, f°, $4.

Each of the three volumes has four parts, making in all 12 parts, numbered consecutively from 1 to 12.

Giese, W: F: A first Spanish book and reader. N. Y., Appleton, 1902. [Jl.] c. 12+362 p. D. (Twentieth century text-books.) cl., $1.20.

A complete first-year book. Material for practice and translation is much more abundant than usual. Disconnected sentences have been eliminated, and connected, usually anecdotal, passages replace them. In pt. 1 a second, and usually a third, passage follows in each lesson, introducing no new words, making sight-reading possible from the start. Pt. 2 is devoted to the irregular verbs, developed according to a new scheme of derivation. Pt. 3 consists of easy reading-matter.

****Glasgow**, Ellen Anderson Gholson. The freeman, and other poems. N. Y., Doubleday, Page & Co., 1902. 5-56 p. D. bds., $1.50 net.

****Glasgow**, Ellen Anderson Gholson. The voice of the people. [New il. ed.;] il. by H: Troth. N. Y., Doubleday, Page & Co., 1902. [S.] c. 1900, '02. 6+444 p. O. cl., $1.50 net.

A new illustrated edition of Miss Glasgow's novel, with twenty-four full-page pictures, taken from photographs that Mr. Troth went to Virginia to secure.

Graydon, W: Murray. The camp in the snow. N. Y., Street & Smith, [1902.] c. 4+5-246 p. 1 il. D. (Boys' own lib., no. 12.) cl., 75 c.

Graydon, W: Murray. Jungles and traitors; or, the wild animal trappers of India. N. Y., Street & Smith, [1902.] c. 262 p. 1 il. D. (Boys' own lib., no. 51.) cl., 75 c.

Henley, W: Ernest. Views and reviews: essays in appreciation: Art. N. Y., Scribner, 1902. 11+174 p. D. cl., $1.

Contents: A note on Romanticism; Profiles romantiques; Five Dutchmen; Some landscape painters; Four portrait painters; Artists and amateurs; Two moderns; A critic of art.

Henry, Walter O. A physician's practical gynecology. Lincoln, Neb., The Review Press, 1902. c. 3+9-229 p. il. D. cl., $2.

****Hillis**, *Rev.* Newell Dwight. The school in the home: a study of the debt parents owe their children; with a list of forty great chapters of the Bible and twenty classic hymns for memorizing. N. Y. and Chic., Revell, 1902. [Je.] 126 p. 16°, cl., 50 c. net.

Hills, *Rev.* Aaron Merritt. A hero of faith and prayer; or, life of Rev. Martin Wells Knapp. Cin., O., Mrs. M. W. Knapp, [Office of "God's Revivalist,"] 1902. c. 3-324 p. por. D. cl., 75 c.; pap., 20 c.

Hills, *Rev.* Aaron Merritt. Life of Charles G. Finney. Cin., O., Mrs. M. W. Knapp, [Office of "God's Revivalist,"] 1902. c. 3-240 p. por. D. cl., 75 c.; pap., 20 c.

Hollingsworth, Ralph. Heliocentric ephemeris; from 1850 to 1904. Minneapolis, Minn., Ralph Hollingsworth, 1902. c. 121 p. D. cl., $1; pap., 75 c.
Tables showing the position of the planets from 1850 to 1904; to be used in astrology or planetary influence, in foretelling coming events.

Hooper, W. W. That minister's boy; or, was he as black as they painted him?; stories for boys; with introd. by Herbert S. Gunnison. Brooklyn, N. Y., The Brooklyn Eagle Press, 1902. c. 260 p. il. D. cl., $1.

†**Hornung,** Ernest W. The shadow of the rope. N. Y., Scribner, 1902. [S.] c. 7+328 p. D. cl., $1.50.
The story of a woman suspected of murdering her husband. She is tried and acquitted, but the world refuses to believe in her innocence. She marries a second time a man who has been present at her trial and who believes her guilty. He also has a history. Why he desires her for a wife is one of the mysteries of the story. Who murdered the woman's first husband is another. They are both ingeniously elucidated, the interest held to the end.

†**James,** H: The wings of the dove. N. Y., Scribner, 1902. [Ag.] c. 2 v., 1+329; 1+439 p. D. cl., $2.50.
Kate Croy, an English girl without fortune, is secretly engaged to Merton Densher, also without any great wealth. She has a dear friend, an American girl, a millionaire, known to be dying. The American girl is fond of Densher, not knowing him to be engaged, and he is urged by Kate to marry the heiress and secure her money before marrying herself. This motive is evolved through many pages of epigrammatic conversation, the *denouement* occupying a few words on the last page.

Jastrow, Morris, *jr., comp.* Dictionary of the Targumin, the Talmud Babli and Yerushalmi and the Midrashic literature. In 12 pts. pts. 8-14. N. Y., Putnam, 1902. 4°, pap., subs., ea., $2.

Jenkins, C: Francis. From Philadelphia to the Poconos: a guide to the Delaware valley, Trenton, Lambertville, Easton, Phillipsburg, Belvidere, Portland, and the Delaware Water Gap. Phil., Ferris & Leach, 1902. c. 47+1 p. il. sq. S. pap., 25 c.

****Johnston,** *Rev.* Howard Agnew. Bible criticism and the average man. N. Y. and Chic., Revell, 1902. [Ag.] 275 p. 12°, cl., $1 net.

***Kingsley,** C: Life and works of Charles Kingsley. Ed. de luxe. In 19 v. v. 13, Two years ago. In 2 v. v. 1. N. Y., Macmillan, 1902. 6+331 p. 8°, cl., $3 net.

Kingsley, Homer Hitchcock. The new era word book. Chic., Eaton & Co., [1902.] c. 126 p. il. 12°, (New era ser.) cl., 20 c.

***Lang,** *Rev.* J: Marshall. The church and its social mission. N. Y., T: Whittaker, 1902. 20+364 p. 12°, (Baird lectures for 1901.) cl., $1.60 net.

Lawyers' reports annot. Book 55. All current cases of general value and importance, with full annots.; Burdett A. Rich and Henry P. Farnham, editors. Rochester, N. Y., Lawyers' Co-op. Pub. Co., 1902. c. 1026 p. O. shp., $5.

Levy, J. H., *ed.* The necessity for criminal appeal as illustrated by the Maybrick case and the jurisprudence of various countries. N. Y., Putnam, 1902. 12+609 p. 8°, cl., $4.20.

Lewis, H: Harrison. Sword and pen; or, a young war correspondent's adventures. N. Y., Street & Smith, [1902.] c. 4+5-259 p. 12°, (Boys' own lib., no. 78.) cl., 75 c.

Lounsberry, Lionel. Randy the pilot; or, perils of the Great Lakes. N. Y., Street & Smith, [1902.] c. 1+7-248 p. D. (Boys' own lib., no. 70.) cl., 75 c.

***McMurry,** C: Alex. A teacher's manual of geography; to accompany Tarr and McMurry's series of geographies. N. Y., Macmillan, 1902. c. 107 p. 12°, cl., 40 c. net.

Martinique, the second Pompeii, by pen and picture: a series of photographs accurately portraying scenes in the island of Martinique both before and after the fatal disaster; with descriptive foot notes. Akron, O., Saalfield Pub. Co., 1902. c. 136 p. il. sq. 8°, cl., $1.50.

***Mason,** Caroline Atwater. Lux Christi: an outline study of India. A twilight land. N. Y., Macmillan, 1902. [Ag15.] c. 12+280 p. 12°, cl., 50 c. net.

****Massachusetts.** *Supreme judicial ct.* Reports 179, May, 1901-Oct., 1901. H: Walton Swift, rep. Bost., Little, Brown & Co., 1902. c. 17+704 p. O. shp., $2 net.

****Miller,** G: A. The problems of the town church: a discussion of needs and methods. N. Y. and Chic., Revell, 1902. [Mr.] 201 p. 12°, cl., 75 c. net.

Missouri. *St. Louis and Kansas City cts. of appeals.* Cases determined from July 3, 1901, to Dec. 17, 1901; rep. by M. R. Smith and Ben Eli Guthrie, off. reps. v. 90. Columbia, E. W. Stephens, 1902. c. 31+749 +11 p. O. shp., $5.

Missouri. *Supreme ct.* Reports of cases, between Nov. 12 and Dec. 17, 1901. Perry S. Rader, rep. v. 165. Columbia, E. W. Stephens, 1902. c. 17+779+7 p. O. shp., $4.

Moran, W: Jos., *and* Brelsford, C. H. The first book of illustrated words and sentences; or, easy lessons in spelling. Phil., Eldredge & Bros., 1902. c. 163 p. il. 12°, (Columbia ser. of graded spelling books.) cl., 20 c.

Moran, W: Jos., *and* Brelsford, C. H. The second book of words and dictation exercises; or, advanced lessons in spelling. Phil., Eldredge & Bros., 1902. c. 191 p. il. 12°, (Columbia ser. of graded spelling books.) cl., 25 c.

****Morgan,** *Rev.* G: Campbell. A first century message to twentieth century Christians: addresses based upon the letters to the seven churches of Asia; the last messages of Christ to men. N. Y. and Chic., Revell, 1902. [Ag.] 217 p. 12°, cl., $1 net.

Morrow, Abbie Clemens. Prayers for public worship, private devotion, personal ministry. N. Y., M. E. Munson, [1902.] c. 195 p. 12°, cl., $1; $1.50; $2.

Mowry, W: A: *and* Arthur May. A history of the United States for schools; including a concise account of the discovery of America, the colonization of the land, and the Revolutionary war. [New ed.] N. Y., Silver, Burdett & Co., [1902.] c. '96-'02. 30+456 p. il. por. maps, 8°, cl., $1.

Naughton, W. W. Kings of the Queensberry realm. Chic., Continental Publishing Co., [1902.] c. 2+315 p. il. D. cl., $1.25.
An account of every heavy-weight champion contest held in America under the Queensberry rules; a sketch of every contestant who has taken part therein, and an account of the invasion of Australian boxers; with a defense of boxing, a comparison of old methods of boxing and training with those in vogue to-day, and the complete ring record of heavy-weight pugilists.

New International encyclopædia; ed. by Daniel Coit Gilman, Harry Thurston Peck and Frank Moore Colby. In 17 v. v. 1. N. Y., Dodd, Mead & Co., 1902. c. il. pl. (partly col.) por. maps, 8°, cl., subs. (Apply to pubs. for prices.)

New York. Code of civil procedure of the state; the 23 chapters in full, the different amendments in their proper sections, as in force on Sept. 1, 1877, [etc.] Alb., Banks & Co., 1902. c. 74+739+220 p. O. shp., $3.50.

New York. *Ct. of appeals.* Reports of cases from and including decisions of Feb. 11 to decisions of Apr. 15, 1902; with notes, references and index; by Edwin A. Bedell, st. rep. v. 170. Alb., J. B. Lyon Co., 1902. c. O. shp., $2.50.

New York. The poor, insanity and state charities law, [as amended to Jan. 1, 1903;] cont. the poor, the insanity law, the state charities law, [etc.;] with forms and annots.; by Robt. C. Cumming and Frank B. Gilbert. Alb., Matthew Bender, 1902. c. 7+546 p. O. shp., $5.

New York (State) municipal court practice: being chapter 580 of the laws of the state of New York, passed 1902. Brooklyn, N. Y., Office of The Brooklyn Daily Eagle, [1902.] 27 p. Q. (Brooklyn Eagle lib., v. 17, no. 11; ser. no. 70.) pap., 10 c.

New York supplement, v. 76. Permanent ed., May 22-July 3, 1902. St. Paul, West Pub. Co., 1902. c. 18+1169 p. O. (National reporter system.) shp., $4.
Contains the decisions of the supreme and lower courts of record of New York state, with tables of N. Y. supplemental cases in vols. 68-70, appel. division reports; 36 misc. reports; 15 N. Y. crim. reports, also add'l tables for vols. 1-70, appel. div. reports; 48-92 Hun's reports; 1-36, miscellaneous reports. A table of statutes construed is given in the index.

***New York.** *Supreme ct.* vs. 68, 69, 70. Reports of cases in the appel. div. Marcus T. Hun, rep., 1902. Off. ed. Alb., J. B. Lyon Co., 1902. c. O. shp., ea., $3 net.

Northeastern reporter, v. 63. Permanent ed., Mar. 28-June 20, 1902. St. Paul, West Pub. Co., 1902. c. 15+1224 p. O. (National reporter system; state ser.) shp., $4.
Contains all the current decisions of the supreme courts of Mass., O., Ill., Ind., appellate court of Ind., and the court of appeals of New York, with tables of northeastern cases published in vols. 193, Illinois reports; 157, Indiana reports; 169, New York reports; 65, Ohio state reports. A table of statutes construed is given in the index.

Official golf guide, 1902, (with which is incorporated Newman's official golf guide:) a directory of all the golf clubs and golf associations in the United States, together with statistical tables, the rules of golf and contributions upon practical subjects connected with the game, by W. J. Travis, A. G. Lockwood, F. G. Beach, W. K. Farrington, Grey Thistle and W. E. Burleck, jr.; ed. by Van Tassel Sutphen. N. Y., Grafton Press, [1902.] c. il. por. 8°, limp leath., $3.

Orton, Ja. K. Beach boy Joe; or, among the life savers. N. Y., Street & Smith, [1902.] c. 4+5-258 p. 1 il. D. (Boys' own lib., no. 4.) cl., 75 c.

Orton, Ja. K. The secret chart; or, treasure hunting in Hayti. N. Y., Street & Smith, [1902.] c. 4+5-257 p. 1 il. D. (Boys' own lib., no. 74.) cl., 75 c.

****Paul**, Herbert W. Matthew Arnold. N. Y., Macmillan, 1902. [Ag13.] c. 8+188 p. 12°, (English men of letters; ed. by J: Morley.) cl., 75 c. net.

Perky, H: D. Wisdom *vs.* foolishness: [papers on hygiene.] Worcester, Mass., Perky Publishing Co., [1902.] c. 100 p. por. 16°, cl., 50 c.

***Philippines** (The). The first civil governor, by Theodore Roosevelt. [*Also*] Civil government in the Philippines, by W: H. Taft. N. Y., The Outlook Co., 1902. c. 2-142 p. por. O. cl., $1 net.
Two articles first published in *The Outlook*. The first is an appreciation of Governor W: H. Taft; the second, by the Governor himself, gives in brief an account of the civil government now existing in "The Philippines."

†**Sangster**, *Mrs.* Marg. Eliz. Munson. Janet Ward: a daughter of the manse. N. Y. and Chic., Revell, 1902. [S.] 301 p. 12°, cl., $1.50.

Scott, *Sir* Walter. Lady of the lake; ed. by Edwin Ginn. Bost., Ginn, 1902. c. '84. 51+219 p. por. D. (Standard English classics.) cl., 35 c.

Shakespeare, W: Macbeth; ed., with an introd. and notes, by Cyrus Lauron Hooper. Chic., Ainsworth & Co., 1902. c. 13+155 p. por. il. 12°, (xxth century Shakespeare.) pap., 30 c.

****Singleton**, Esther, *ed.* London; described bv great writers and travellers. N. Y., Dodd, Mead & Co., 1902. il. 8°, cl., $1.40 net.

†**Slosson**, *Mrs.* Annie Trumbull. Aunt Abby's neighbors. N. Y. and Chic., Revell, 1902. [Je.] 170 p. 16°, cl., $1.

Smith, Albert W. Materials of machines. N. Y., J: Wiley & Sons, 1902. c. 5+142 p. 12°, cl., $1.

†**Smith**, Francis Hopkinson. The novels, short stories, and sketches. Beacon ed. In 12 v. v. 1-4. N. Y., Scribner, 1902. 12°, cl., subs., pr set, $15.

†**Smith**, Francis Hopkinson. The fortunes of Oliver Horn; il. by Walter Appleton Clark. N. Y., Scribner, 1902. [Ag.] c. 7+551 p. D. cl., $1.50.
Oliver Horn is a young Southerner who comes to

New York, just before the Civil War, to seek his fortune. After many vicissitudes, he is able to follow his inclination to study art, and becomes an artist of note. Bohemian and artistic life of thirty years ago, when social New York did not extend far above Union Square, are vividly sketched with both pathos and humor. A Southern gentleman of the old-fashioned type is presented in Oliver's father—a dreamy, impractical inventor, whose fortune is only realized when on his death-bed. Northern and Southern characters are well contrasted.

****Smith,** *Rev.* J: The integrity of scripture: plain reasons for rejecting the critical hypothesis. N. Y. and Chic., Revell, 1902. 283 p. 12°, cl., $1.25 net.

Southwestern reporter, v. 68. Permanent ed., May 26-July 7, 1902. St. Paul, West Pub. Co., 1902. c. 16+1212 p. O. (National reporter system, state ser.) shp., $4.
Contains all the current decisions of the supreme and appellate courts of Ark., Ky., Mo., Tenn., Tex., and O. T. With table of southwestern cases in which rehearings have been denied. Also, table of writs of error denied by the supreme court of Texas in the court of civil appeals. A table of statutes construed is given in the index.

****Speer,** Rob. E. Missionary principles and practice: a discussion of Christian missions and some criticisms upon them. N. Y. and Chic., Revell, 1902. [Ag.] 552 p. 8°, cl., $1.50 net.

Stark, J. Carroll. The King and His kingdom. Hamilton, Ill., J. Carroll Stark, 1902. c. 6+529 p. O. cl., $1.50.
Contents: pt. 1, Theology "theos" God "logos" discourse. Discourse on God; pt. 2, Church organization, what it is, and how it is done. The selection and appointment of its officiary.

Stoddard, J: Lawson. Beautiful scenes of America from Battery Park to the Golden Gate. Akron, O., Saalfield Pub. Co., 1902. c. 128 p. il. with descriptions, sq. 8°, cl., 75 c.

***Stone,** Ja. Kent. The invitation heeded; reasons for a return to Catholic unity. 12th ed. N. Y., Christian Press Assoc. Publishing Co., [1902.] c. 341 p. 16°, cl., 75 c. net.

Story (The) of Lizzie McGuire, by herself. Bost., H: A. Dickerman & Son, [1902.] c. 4-84 p. 1 il. D. cl., 75 c.
A parody of "The story of Mary Maclane."

****Stratemeyer,** E: Marching on Niagara; or, the soldier boys of the old frontier; il. by A. B. Shute. Bost., Lee & Shepard, 1902. [Ag.] c. 8+305 p. D. (Colonial ser., no. 2.) cl., $1 net.
This is a complete story in itself, but forms the second of several volumes to be known by the general title of "Colonial series." The young men of the first volume take part in the taking of Fort Niagara.

Streatfeild, R. A. The opera: a sketch of its development. New rev. ed.; with an introd. by J. A. Fuller-Maitland. Phil., Lippincott, 1902. 8°, cl., $2; hf. levant, $4.50.

Strong, Julia Minor, *ed.* The town and people: a chronological compilation of contributed writings from present and past residents of the town of Woodbury, Ct. N. Woodbury, Ct., Mrs. N. M. Strong, [1902.] c. 364 p. il. 12°, cl., $1.75.

Tennessee. *Supreme ct.* Reports of cases, for the eastern, middle and western divisions 1883, 1884, 1885, 1886. B: J. Lea, rep. vs. 11, 12, 13, 14, 15, 16, [79, 80, 81, 82, 83, 84;] a new ed. with subsequent citations, annots., notes and references, by Rob. T. Shannon. Louisville, Ky., Fetter Law Book Co., 1902. c. O. shp., ea., $3.

****Thompson,** Adele E. Brave Heart Elizabeth: a story of the Ohio frontier; il. by Lilian Crawford True. Bost., Lee & Shepard, 1902. [Ag.] c. 2+286 p. D. (Brave heart ser.) $1 net.
A story of the making of the Ohio frontier, much of it taken from life. The heroine is one of the famous Zane family after which Zanesville, O., takes its name.

Thousand and one nights. Special limited ed.; tr. by E: W. Lane from the Arabic; 21 extra il. by Lalauze, mounted on India paper. Phil., Lippincott, 1902. 6 v., 16°, cl., per set, $10.

****Tomlinson,** Everett Titsworth. Cruising on the St. Lawrence: a summer vacation in historic waters; il. by A. B. Shute. Bost., Lee & Shepard, 1902. [Ag.] c. 9+442 p. D. (St. Lawrence ser., no. 3.) cl., $1.20 net.
Continues the historic story of the St. Lawrence River, begun in "Camping on the St. Lawrence" and "The house-boat on the St. Lawrence." In the present volume our old friends—Bob, Ben, Jock and Bert—have completed their sophomore year. They visit places of interest on the St. Lawrence, in a sloop yacht, devoting much attention to the history of the Indians, their habits, customs, etc.

****Troeger,** J: W. *and* Edna Beatrice. Harold's discussions. N. Y., Appleton, 1902. [Jl.] c. 12+298 p. il. por. S. (Nature study readers, v. 5.) cl., 60 c. net.
The last volume of the popular "Harold" series; completes a graded course of instructive and entertaining reading for the public schools. Book V, "Harold's discussions," deals with some of the more advanced phases of life processes and natural phenomena that are suitable for classes in the higher grammar grades.

Trollope, Anthony. Writings. Collectors' ed. In 30 v. v. 17-27. Phil., Gebbie & Co., 1902. c. il. pl., 8°, crushed levant, subs. (Apply to pubs. for price.)

Vermont. The Vermont prohibitory law, compiled and digested by Russell W. Taft. Burlington, Free Press Assoc., 1902. c. 23 p. D. pap., 10 c.

Virginia. *Supreme ct. of appeals.* Reports. Jefferson-33 Grattan, 1730-1880; annot. under the supervision of Thomas Johnson Michie. vs. 4, 5 and 6, Grattan's reports. Charlottesville, Va., Michie Co., 1902. c. O. shp., ea., $7.50.

Wainwright, Jacob T. Fallacy of the second law of thermodynamics and the feasibility of transmuting terrestrial heat into available energy: an addendum to essay on "Means for transmuting terrestrial heat into available energy." Chic., Jacob T. Wainwright, 1902. 12 p. pap. (for private distribution.)

****Walker,** Patrick. Six saints of the Covenant: Peden, Semple, Wellwood, Cameron, Cargill, Smith; ed., with illustrative documents, introd., notes and a glossary, by D. Hay Fleming. and a foreword by S. R. Crockett. N. Y., Dodd, Mead & Co., 1902. 2 v., O. cl., $7.50 net. (Amer. ed. limited to 100 copies.)

**Waterloo, Stanley, *ed.* The story of a strange career: being the autobiography of a convict; an authentic document. N. Y., Appleton, 1902. [Ag.] c. 12+363 p. D. cl., $1.20 net.

The life story of a criminal, written by him while serving a term in a western penitentiary. Originally of good birth and education, the man seems to have been a born degenerate, swerving naturally into the downward path. He gives many graphic descriptions of his adventures on a whaler in South America; on a British man-of-war; in the American navy; at Fort Fisher; in Confederate prisons during the Civil War; in the New York draft riots; and finally of his life in the penitentiary.

Weyman, Stanley J: The new rector. [New issue.] N. Y., F. M. Buckles & Co., 1901, [1902.] c. 1891. 338 p. D. cl., $1.25.

Whitcomb, Clara E., *and* George, Marian M. Little journeys to Scotland and Ireland. Chic., A. Flanagan Co., 1902. c. '01· 82+81 p. il. map, D. (Library of travel.) cl., 50 c.

*Xenophon. Cyropædia, bk. 1; with introd. and notes founded on those of H. A. Holden, and a complete vocabulary by E. S. Shuckburgh. N. Y., Macmillan, 1902. 20+156 p. 12°, (Pitt Press ser.) cl., 60 c. net.

**Young, *Rev.* Egerton Ryerson. My dogs in the Northland: character studies of great dogs. N. Y. and Chic., Revell, 1902. [S.] 285 p. 8°, cl., $1.25 net.

Young, Ernest A. Boats, bats and bicycles; or, Nimble Jerry's pluck and luck. N. Y., Street & Smith, [1902.] c. 4+5-257 p. 12°, (Boys' own lib., no. 5.) cl., 75 c.

Zschokke, Johann Heinrich Dan. Der zerbrochene Krug; ed. for school use by R. O. Berkefeld. N. Y., Amer. Book Co., [1902.] c. 59 p. S. cl., 25 c.

ORDER LIST.

AINSWORTH & Co., 378-388 Wabash Ave., Chicago.

Shakespeare, Macbeth, 20th century ed. 30

AMERICAN ARCHITECT AND BUILDING NEWS Co., 211 Tremont St., Boston.

Georgian period, pt. 10 .... $4.00

AMERICAN BOOK Co., 100 Washington Sq., E., New York.

Zschokke, Der zerbrochene Krug 25

D. APPLETON & Co., 72 Fifth Ave., New York.

Beaumarchais, Le barbier de Séville... 35
†Craigie, Tales about temperaments (A. T. C. L., 315) .... 50 c.; 1.00
Giese, A first Spanish book and reader. 1.20
**Troeger, Harold's discussions... net, 60
**Waterloo, Story of a strange career, net, 1.20

BANKS & Co., Albany, N. Y.

New York, Code of civil procedure of the state, with amendments in force Sept. 1, 1877 .... 3.50

MATTHEW BENDER, 511-513 Broadway, Albany, N. Y.

New York, The poor, insanity and state charities law, (amended to Jan. 1, 1903) 5.00

OFFICE OF THE BROOKLYN DAILY EAGLE, Eagle Bldg., Brooklyn, N. Y.

New York State, Municipal court practice 10

THE BROOKLYN EAGLE PRESS, Brooklyn, N. Y.

Hooper, That minister's boy 1.00

F. M. BUCKLES & Co., 11 E. 16th St., New York.

Weyman, The new rector, new issue.. 1.25

CHRISTIAN PRESS ASSOCIATION PUBLISHING Co., 23 Barclay St., New York.

*Stone, The invitation heeded...... net, 75

CONTINENTAL PUBLISHING Co., 168 Adams St., Chicago.

Naughton, Kings of the Queensbury realm 1.25

HENRY A. DICKERMAN & SON, 55 Franklin St., Boston.

Story (The) of Lizzie McGuire 75

DODD, MEAD & Co., 372 Fifth Ave., New York.

New International encyclopædia, v. 1, subs .... (Apply to pubs. for price.)
**Singleton, London .... net, $1.40
**Walker, Six saints of the Covenant, net, 7.50

DOUBLEDAY, PAGE & Co., 34 Union Sq., E., New York.

**Glasgow, The freeman .... net, 1.50
**——, The voice of the people, new il. ed .... net, 1.50

E. P. DUTTON & Co., 31 West 23d St., New York.

**Brine, Lassie and Laddie .... net, 1.00

EATON & Co., 203-207 Michigan Ave., Chicago.

Kingsley, The new era word book 20

PETER ECKLER, 35 Fulton St., New York.

Adams, Good without God 25

ELDREDGE & BROS., 17 N. 7th St., Philadelphia.

Moran *and* Brelsford, First book of illustrated words and sentences 20
————, Second book of words and dictation exercises 25

FERRIS & LEACH, 29-31 N. 7th St., Philadelphia.

Jenkins, From Philadelphia to the Poconos 25

FETTER LAW BOOK Co., Louisville, Ky.

Tennessee, *Supreme ct.*, Reports for eastern, middle and western divisions, 1883-1886, new ed., v. 11-16 and 79-84 .... ea., 3.00

A. FLANAGAN Co., 267 Wabash Ave., Chicago.

Dean *and* George, Little journey to Holland 15
George, Litle journey to England. pt. 1. 15
——, Little journey to England and Wales 15
——, Little journey to France 15
——, Little journey to Ireland 15

A. FLANAGAN CO.—*Continued.*

Whitcomb *and* George, Little journeys to Scotland and Ireland............ 50

FREE PRESS ASSOCIATION, Burlington, Vt.

Vermont, Prohibitory law............ 10

GEBBIE & CO., 1710 Market St., Philadelphia.

Trollope, Writings, Collectors' ed., v. 17-27, subs.....(Apply to pubs. for price.)

GINN & CO., 29 Beacon St., Boston.

Scott, Lady of the lake............... 35

GRAFTON PRESS, 70 Fifth Ave., New York.

Official golf guide, 1902............... $3.00

D. C. HEATH & CO., 120 Boylston St., Boston.

*Atwood, Complete graded arithmetic, 8th grade....... ....net, 25

RALPH HOLLINGSWORTH, Minneapolis, Minn.

Hollingsworth, Heliocentric ephemerics..... ....75 c.; 1.00

MRS. M. W. KNAPP, Office of "God's Revivalist," Cincinnati.

Hills, A hero of faith and prayer (Rev. M. W. Knapp)..............20 c.; 75
——, Life of Chas. G. Finney....20 c.; 75

LAWYERS' CO-OPERATIVE PUB. CO., Rochester, N. Y.

Lawyers' reports annot., Bk. 55...... 5.00

LEE & SHEPARD, 202 Devonshire St., Boston.

**Brooks, Randy and her friend..net, 80
**Foster, Hortense....... ....net, 80
**Stratemeyer, Marching on Niagara, net, 1.00
**Thompson, Brave Heart Elizabeth, net, 1.00
**Tomlinson, Cruising on the St. Lawrence...... ....net, 1.20

J. B. LIPPINCOTT CO., Washington Sq., Philadelphia.

*Bible, Temple ed., vs. 13, 14, Luke, Daniel...........ea., net, 40 c.; net, 60
Streatfeild, The opera, new rev. ed.$2; 4.50
Thousand and one nights, Special limited ed., 6 v....................... 10.00

LITTLE, BROWN & CO., 254 Washington St., Boston.

**Falt, Wharf and fleet............net, 1.50
**Massachusetts, *Supreme judicial ct.*, Reports, v. 179 (Swift).........net, 2.00

JAMES B. LYON CO., 36 Beaver St., Albany, N. Y.

New York, *Ct. of appeals*, Reports, v. 170 (Bedell)..... .... 2.50
*New York, *Supreme ct.*, Reports, vs. 68, 69, 70 (Hun)............ea., net, 3.00

MACMILLAN CO., 66 Fifth Ave., New York.

Aristophanes...... .... 4.00
*Bates *and* Coman, English history told by English poets................net, 80
*Bible, New Testament, Gospel according to St. Mark.............net, 75
*——, Old Testament, Cambridge Bible, Solomon..... ....net, 50
Fielding, Works, Temple ed., 12 v., ea., 50 c.; 75

MACMILLAN CO.—*Continued.*

*Kingsley, Life and works, Ed. de luxe, v. 13, Two years ago, v. 1.......net, $3.00
*Mason, Lux Christi..............net, 50
*McMurry, Teacher's manual of geography........ ....net, 40
**Paul, Matthew Arnold..........net, 75
*Xenophon, Cyropædia, bk 1......net, 60

MICHIE CO., Charlottesville, Va.

Virginia, *Supreme ct. of appeals*, Reports, (1730-1880,) vs. 4, 5, and 6, ea., 7.50

M. E. MUNSON, 77 Bible House, New York.

Morrow, Prayers for public worship, etc...... ....$1; $1.50; 2.00

NATIONAL PUBLISHING CO., 241 American St., Philadelphia.

Allen *and* McGregor, Ladies' guide to health and beauty.................. 1.75

NEW YORK STATE PUBLISHING CO., Rochester, N. Y.

Clark *and* Bresel, How to answer a want ad......... .... 2.00

THE OUTLOOK CO., 287 Fourth Ave., New York.

*Philippines (The)...... ....net, 1.00

THE PERKY PUBLISHING CO., Worcester, Mass.

Perky, Wisdom *vs.* foolishness........ 50

JAMES POTT & CO., 119 West 23d St., New York.

**Firth, Cromwell's army..........net, 1.75

G. P. PUTNAM'S SONS, 29 West 23d St., New York.

Jastrow, Dictionary of the Targumin, pts. 8-14..................subs., ea., 2.00
Levy, The necessity for criminal appeal. 4.20

FLEMING H. REVELL CO., 156 Fifth Ave., New York; 63 Washington St., Chicago.

**Bible, Old Testament, The emphasized Bible, v. 1, Genesis to Ruth; v. 2, Samuel to Psalms....net, per v., 2.00
**Hillis, The school in the home...net, 1.00
**Johnston, Bible criticism and the average man....... ....net, 1.00
**Miller, Problems of the town church, net, 75
**Morgan, A first century message to twentieth century Christians.....net, 1.00
†Sangster, Janet Ward................ 1.50
†Slosson, Aunt Abby's neighbors...... 1.00
**Smith, Integrity of scripture.....net, 1.25
**Speer, Missionary principles and practice..... ....net, 1.50
**Young, My dogs in the Northland.net, 1.25

THE REVIEW PRESS, Lincoln, Neb.

Henry, A physician's practical gynecology....... .... 2.00

ROUGH NOTES CO., Indianapolis, Ind.

Deitch, Digest of insurance cases, vs. 13 and 14......................ea., 3.00

SAALFIELD PUBLISHING CO., Akron, O.

Byrne, The little woman in the spout.. 60
——, Roy and Rosyrocks............. 60
Martinique, the second Pompeii....... 1.50
Stoddard, Beautiful scenes of America. 75

CHARLES SCRIBNER'S SONS, 153-157 Fifth Ave., New York.

Henley, Views and reviews........... $1.00
†Hornung, Shadow of the rope....... 1.50
†James, Wings of the dove, 2 v....... 2.50
†Smith, Fortunes of Oliver Horn...... 1.50
†——, Novels, short stories and sketches, 12 v., v. 1-4........subs., per set, 15.00

SILVER, BURDETT & CO., 33 East 19th St., New York.

Mowry, Hist. of United States for schools, new ed..................... 1.00

G. D. SPROUL, 150 Fifth Ave., New York.

Gautier, Works, v. 16-18..per v., $3.50; 6.00

J. CARROLL STARK, Hamilton, Ill.

Stark, The King and His kingdom.... 1.50

E. W. STEPHENS, Columbia, Mo.

Missouri, *St. Louis and Kansas City cts. of appeals*, Cases, v. 90 (Smith and Guthrie).... .... 5.00
——, *Supreme ct.*, Reports, v. 165 (Rader)....... .... 4.00

STREET & SMITH, 238 William St., New York.

Brown, For home and honor.......... 75
Denison, Barbara's triumphs, new issue. 50
——, The Frenchman's ward, new issue. 50
——, The guardian's trust, new issue.. 50
Graydon, The camp in the snow...... 75
——, Jungles and traitors............. 75
Lewis, Sword and pen................ 75
Lounsberry, Randy the pilot.......... 75
Orton, Beach boy Joe................ 75
——, The secret chart................. 75
Young, Boats, bats and bicycles...... 75

MRS. N. M. STRONG, North Woodbury, Ct.

Strong, The town and people........... $1.75

JACOB T. WAINWRIGHT, Chicago.

Wainwright, Fallacy of the second law of thermodynamics. (for private distribution.)

MARCUS WARD CO., 310-318 Sixth Ave., New York.

Gavit, Essentials of polite correspondence..... 10

JAMES H. WEST CO., 79 Milk St., Boston.

Blake, Songs...... .... 1.00

WEST PUB. CO., 52-58 W. 3d St., St. Paul, Minn.

New York supplement, v. 76........... 4.00
Northeastern reporter, v. 63........... 4.00
Southwestern reporter, v. 68.......... 4.00

THOMAS WHITTAKER, 3 Bible House, New York.

*Lang, The church and its social mission...... ....net, 1.60

JOHN WILEY & SONS, 41-45 E. 19th St., New York.

Bruff, Textbook of ordnance, 2d ed... 6.00
Smith, Materials of machines......... 1.00

WILLIAM WOOD & CO., 51 Fifth Ave., New York.

Chapin, Theory and practice of infant feeding...... .... 2.25

RECENT ENGLISH BOOKS.

AMERY, L. S., *ed.* The *Times* history of the war in South Africa, 1899-1902. 6 v., v. 1 and 2. N. Y., Scribner, [imported,] 1902. $30, net. (Sold only in sets.)

BOMPAS, G: C. The problem of the Shakespeare plays. N. Y., Scribner, [imported,] 1902. 7+119 p. 8°, cl., $1.40.

CALLENDAR, H. L. Continuous electrical calorimetry. Dulau. 4°, 4s.

DICTIONARY of artists who have exhibited works in principal London exhibitions from 1760 to 1893. Compiled by Algernon Graves. 3d ed., with additions and corrections. H. Graves. 4°, 12⅛ x 9⅝, 328 p., 42s.

DISTANT, W. L. Fauna of India—Rhynchota. Vol. 1: Heteroptera. Taylor & F. 476 p., 20s.

ENGLISH county songs; words and music coll. and ed. by Lucy E. Broadwood and J. A. Fuller-Maitland; with valuable historical and descriptive notes. N. Y., Scribner, [imported,] 1902. 6+185 p. 8°, cl., $2.40.

FOSTER, J. Some Feudal coats of arms from heraldic rolls, 1298-1418. Illus. with 830 zinco etchings from effigies, brasses, etc. Parker. Sm. ed., roy. 8°, 10 x 6½, 10s. 6d., net.

LONDON in 1902; il. by 20 bird's-eye views of the principal streets, and a large folding map; originally comp. by Herbert Fry, rev. and corr. to date. N. Y., Scribner, [imported,] 1902. 17+256 p. 12°, pap., 40 c.

RAVEN-HILL, L. Our batallion, being some slight impressions of Her Majesty's Auxilary forces in camp and elsewhere. N. Y., Scribner, [imported,] 1902. 112 p. il. 4°, cl., $2.

SOHRAB and Rustem, the epic theme of a combat between father and son, and a study of its genesis and use in literature and popular tradition, by M. A. Potter. N. Y., Scribner, [imported,] 1902. 12+234 p. 8°, (Grimm lib.) cl., $2, net.

RECENT FRENCH AND GERMAN BOOKS.

FRENCH.

DOSTOIEVSKI. Un Adolescent. *Revue Blanche*. 18°, $1.

JUGLAR, L. Le Style dans les arts. *Hachette et Cie*. 16°, $1.

MALAPERT, P. Le Caractère. *O. Doin*. 18°, $1.20.

MOREAU, H. Sir Wilfrid Laurier. *Plon, Nourrit et Cie*. 8°, $1.

VERNE, J. Les Frères Kip. *Hetzel*. 16°, $1.

GERMAN.

BOY-ED, Ida. Die säende Hand. Roman. Stuttgart, *J. G. Cotta Nachf*. 8°, cl., $1.50.

ESCHEN, M. v. (M. v. Eschstruth). Auf dem Wege nach Erkenntnis. Roman. Berlin, *A. Schall*. 8°, cl., $1.65.

EYTH, Max. Hinter Pflug u. Schraubstock. Skizzen aus dem Taschenbuch e. Ingenieurs. Stuttgart, *Deutsche Verlags-Anstalt*. 2 v., cl., $2.70.

FRANZ, *Prof.* W. Die Grundzüge der Sprache Shakespeares. Berlin, *E. Felber*. 8°, $1.

HOFFMANN, Hans. Harzwanderungen. Leipzig, *C. F. Amelang*. 8°, cl., $1.

KUNSTLER-MONOGRAPHIEN. Hrsg. v. H. Knackfuss. Vol. LXI. Ostini, Fritz v. Uhde. Bielefeld, *Velhagen & Klasing*. por. and il., $1.35.

LENZ, Max. Geschichte Bismarcks. Leipzig, *Duncker & Humblot*. 8°, $2.20; cl., $2.70.

OLDBERG, Oda. Das Weib u. der Intellectualismus. Berlin, *Dr. J. Edelheim*. 8°, 70 c.

SCHERR, Johs. Schiller. Kulturgeschichtliche Novelle. Leipzig, *Abel & Müller*. 2 v., 8°, cl., $2.85.

ZABEL, Eug. Zur modernen Dramaturgie. Studien u. Kritiken. Vol. 1. Das deutsche Theater. Vol 2. Ausländische Theater. Oldenburg, *Schulze*. 2 v., 8°, $3.30; cl., $4... ....

IMPORTS AND EXPORTS OF BOOKS AND OTHER PRINTED MATTER.

The summary statement of the values of the imports and exports of books and other printed matter of the United States for the month ending June, 1902, and for the twelve months ending the same, compared with the corresponding periods of 1901, makes the following showing as regards books, music, maps, engravings, etchings, photographs, and other printed matter:

Values of Books and other printed matter, free, imported from other countries.

Imported from:	Month ending June. 1901.	Month ending June. 1902.	Twelve months ending June. 1901.	Twelve months ending June. 1902.
United Kingdom	$107,901	$66,446	$988,602	$1,070,744
France	10,237	8,945	406,651	210,927
Germany	41,793	45,000	576,647	644,788
Other Europe	18,054	15,724	178,828	373,191
British North America	2,882	5,005	40,035	38,562
Other Countries	1,216	1,209	13,883	24,231
Totals	182,083	142,329	2,204,646	2,362,443

Values of Books and other printed matter, dutiable, imported from other countries.

Imported from:	Month ending June. 1901.	Month ending June. 1902.	Twelve months ending June. 1901.	Twelve months ending June. 1902.
United Kingdom	$69,884	$94,706	$1,081,362	$1,214,788
France	6,720	4,841	115,615	100,674
Germany	17,098	20,835	244,767	281,825
Other Europe	4,030	3,706	81,627	89,186
British North America	4,195	4,384	35,201	51,416
China	299	368	6,400	13,542
Japan	1,623	985	14,162	12,953
Other Countries	874	370	8,756	6,388
Totals	104,723	130,295	1,587,890	1,770,772

Values of Books and other printed matter, of Domestic Manufacture, Exported from the United States by Countries.

Countries to which Exported:	Month ending June. 1901.	Month ending June. 1902.	Twelve months ending June. 1901.	Twelve months ending June. 1902.
United Kingdom	$72,994	$84,823	$865,134	$1,108,067
France	5,066	5,200	84,300	74,098
Germany	23,420	14,720	181,260	210,320
Other Europe	5,833	6,430	75,684	97,277
British North America	97,136	101,342	1,209,603	1,306,262
Central American States and British Honduras	892	546	29,337	20,399
Mexico	12,769	9,783	123,039	173,545
Santo Domingo	195	91	5,307	2,079
Cuba	6,777	2,897	111,297	72,350
Puerto Rico	......	......	......	......
Other West Indies and Bermuda	1,600	2,805	25,705	31,894
Argentina	2,077	3,136	50,261	33,391
Brazil	7,992	3,103	61,537	48,120
Colombia	2,804	4,645	75,680	34,912
Other South America	3,553	7,982	74,556	123,290
Chinese Empire	8,378	1,784	34,218	33,077
British East Indies	1,295	1,558	25,408	32,762
Japan	1,990	3,669	43,933	49,343
British Australasia	29,897	24,335	249,488	268,220
Hawaiian Islands	......	......	......	......
Philippine Islands	8,216	14,497	44,160	140,574
Other Asia and Oceanica	1,905	3,447	21,456	22,724
Africa	12,437	4,720	80,976	115,273
Other Countries	......	......	4	120
Totals	307,236	303,453	3,472,343	3,997,977

Values of Exports of Books and other printed matter, of Foreign Manufacture.

	Month ending June. 1901.	Month ending June. 1902.	Twelve months ending June. 1901.	Twelve months ending June. 1902.
Free of Duty. Books and other printed matter	$157	$82	$69,122	$16,733
Dutiable. Books and other printed matter	1,259	1,564	18,871	21,987

Merchandise remaining in warehouse May 31, 1901, $34,295; May 31, 1902, $26,393.

Failures in the Book and Printing Trades, January–June.

Books and Papers.—Liabilities.	1900.	1901.	1902.	*Printing and Engraving.—Liabilities.*	1900.	1901.	1902.
January	$44,340	$25,308	$172,910	January	$20,352	$57,931	$290,034
February	11,114	23,108	48,395	February	48,324	10,700	201,893
March	72,504	80,860	45,430	March	203,444	21,392	549,413
April	28,548	55,607	14,568	April	326,051	86,076	65,214
May	44,711	8,500	9,263	May	147,750	133,153	580,835
June	174,165	70,714	78,400	June	18,119	68,860	70,313

The Publishers' Weekly.

FOUNDED BY F. LEYPOLDT.

SEPTEMBER 6, 1902.

The editor does not hold himself responsible for the views expressed in contributed articles or communications

All matter, whether for the reading-matter columns or advertising pages, should reach this office not later than Wednesday noon, to insure insertion in the same week's issue.

Books for the "Weekly Record," as well as all information intended for that department, should reach this office by Tuesday morning of each week.

Publishers are requested to furnish title-page proofs and advance information of books forthcoming, both for entry in the lists and for descriptive mention. An early copy of each book published should be forwarded, as it is of the utmost importance that the entries of books be made as promptly and as perfectly as possible. In many cases booksellers depend on the PUBLISHERS' WEEKLY solely for their information. The Record of New Publications of the PUBLISHERS' WEEKLY is the material of the "American Catalogue" and so forms the basis of trade bibliography in the United States.

"I hold every man a debtor to his profession, from the which, as men do of course seek to receive countenance and profit, so ought they of duty to endeavor themselves by way of amends to be a help and an ornament thereunto."—LORD BACON.

THE DECLINE OF THE NOVEL.

"I DO not think there will be any novels or romances, at all events in volume form, in fifty or a hundred years from now. . . . They are not necessary, and even now their merit and their interest are fast declining. As historic records, the world will file its newspapers. Newspaper writers have learned to color everyday events so well that to read them will give posterity a truer picture than the historic or descriptive novel could do, and as for the novel psychological, that will soon cease to be and will die of inanition in your own lifetime."—*Jules Verne.*

M. VERNE'S prophecy has on it the musty smell of the silurian age; indeed it became a standing joke in Nineveh, in Shalmaneser's time, and has been resurrected as a new thought once every century since then. M. Verne has been clever enough to foresee much that has come to pass; but in this matter his perspective is blurred as his comments on the psychological novel show:

"The real psychology of life is in its news, and more truth—truth with a big T—can be gathered from the police court story, the railway accident, from the everyday doings of the crowd and from the battles of the future than can be obtained if an attempt is made to clothe the psychological moral in a garb of fiction."

This sounds plausible enough, and is a view that more than one pessimistic professor of English literature has seriously defended. But it is an error nevertheless, because, as the New York *Sun* puts it, "it confounds the raw material employed by the artist with art itself." The artist, to quote the *Sun* further, "is he who makes use of and reduces to order the material supplied by everyday experience, and M. Verne's prediction will hardly be realized until we are all artists or have all lost the taste for art." M. Verne's prophecy is about as reasonable as that of the wiseacres who said that photography would put an end to the art of painting.

Now that the war in South Africa is over some one will probably undertake to arrange its bibliography. Though it looked at one time as if everybody who had ever been in South Africa must write a book about it, the number of books produced on the subject in England during the past three years does not seem to have exceeded 250, including general histories of the campaign, personal narratives of particular operations, fiction, poetry and politics. In Germany, according to a bibliography prepared by S. Perschmann for the *Börsenblatt*, 61 separate books on South Africa and on the Boer question were published before the war began, and 198 since then. In the United States the number of original works by American writers published since 1898 does not seem to have gone beyond the hundred mark—about 96 at a rough estimate. Frederick A. Cleveland, in his monograph, "The South African Conflict—its legal and political aspects," published by the American Academy of Political and Social Science, gives a two-page bibliography, and A. Ireland, in his work on "The Anglo-Boer Conflict," published by Small, Maynard & Co., gives a five-page bibliography. A number of libraries also printed reference lists on the subject from 1898 to the beginning of the present year. These bibliographies, of course, included American as well as foreign publications on the subject.

TO PROTECT CORPORATIONS DOING BUSINESS IN RHODE ISLAND.

THE attention of the trade is called to chapter 980 of the Public Laws of Rhode Island, passed April 3, 1902, providing that no foreign corporation, (except banking or United States corporations,) "shall carry on within this State the business for which it was incorporated, or enforce in the courts of this State any contract made within this State, unless it shall have complied with the following sections of this chapter." These "following sections" provide for the appointment of an agent to accept service and file the power of attorney with the Secretary of State.

The new law does not apply to interstate commerce, but it shuts out a foreign corporation from recovery on all contracts made in Rhode Island, unless it appoints such an agent to accept service. This law would prevent recovery on a contract, if an agent of a foreign corporation went into the State, particularly as book agents do, and secured contracts in Rhode Island, such contracts ordinarily being completed on the spot by the agent.

Book purchases being proverbially hard to enforce, and being often contested, the failure to make the proper appointment of agents would defeat a good many actions.

Of course this recent Rhode Island law cannot properly be held to interfere with subjects of interstate commerce, and in many instances a foreign corporation could get along without appointing an agent. Instances, however, would arise where it would be absolutely necessary, or may be held by the court to be absolutely necessary, and in any event the statute might often be invoked for delay in legal proceedings. It is accordingly preferable to file the power.

The Stationers' Board of Trade of New York has made arrangements to protect its clients by filing a power of attorney and representation in the State at a nominal fee, and we advise all interested to apply for the proper form of document to be executed and other information to Mr. E. H. Loveless, the secretary of the Board.

BOOKTRADE ASSOCIATIONS.

NATIONAL ASSOCIATION OF NEWSDEALERS, BOOKSELLERS AND STATIONERS.

The National Association of Newsdealers, Booksellers and Stationers held its annual meeting in Brooklyn, August 27 and 28. After an eight-hour session the convention in executive session ratified the following resolution:

Resolved, That the National Association of the Newsdealers', Booksellers' and Stationers' Executive Board, in conjunction with the delegates of the following local associations, New York, Brooklyn, Staten Island, Newark, Paterson and Hudson County, shall constitute a committee for the purpose of forming a newsdealers' co-operative news company.

At an adjourned meeting, held on August 27, the committee decided to attempt the organization of a co-operative company to distribute the periodicals which they handle. The new enterprise will be called the Co-operative News Company, and H. Russin, of New York City, is chairman of the committee having the matter in charge. No details respecting the new company have been given out, but it is understood that arrangements will be completed as soon as possible. The company is to have agents in all the large cities, and every effort will be made to limit the stockholdings exclusively to newsdealers.

The following officers were elected to serve during the ensuing year: Thomas F. Martin, president; William H. Skinner, of Newark, N. J., first vice-president; Samuel L. Stratton, of Paterson, N. J., second vice-president; Daniel Brophy, of New York City, treasurer; Morris E. Golde, of New York City, secretary; John Y. Collins, of Brooklyn, custodian. The executive committee was made up as follows: H. Russin, of New York City, chairman; J. H. Nolan, of Providence, R. I.; A. Dixon, of Brooklyn; C. A. Schuldt, of Newark, N. J.; J. O'Rourke, of Bridgeport, Conn.

A NEW WAY TO BUILD MAPS.

Professor William G. Ripley, of the economics department at the Massachusetts Institute of Technology, according to the *Philadelphia Record,* has devised a simple and interesting method of building up statistical maps that is likely to make popular a good deal of curious information which has been neglected in the past because there was no inexpensive way of putting it on paper intelligently and entertainingly.

The old-fashioned method of making graphic maps, as they are called, was to print them in different colors or in different shades of the same color by the lithographic process —which involves a separate printing for each shade and is altogether a costly thing to do. A modification of the principle of the lithographic map was Professor Ripley's idea. Instead of printing this map in outline first and then printing each shade or color upon it separately, he pasted the various tints represented by shadings in black and white upon his outline foundation and then made plates of the resulting patchwork.

The idea is so interesting and is capable of so many applications which are both entertaining and instructive that it is worth describing. The necessary equipment for building the maps is simple—a good map to use as a model, a sheet of tracing paper, a carbon copying sheet and some "stippleboard," which is a kind of paper ruled in fine parallel black lines on a sort of corduroy surface so that it has a grayish tint. Scraping the stippleboard gently with a sharp knife changes the black lines to dots, so that the shade of gray appears lighter, and rubbing it lightly with carbon or crayon brings out cross lines on the whole sheet. By sufficient scraping or carbon rubbing stippleboard can be made pure white or dead black.

Suppose, for example, a student wishes to depict in such a way that the meaning shall be evident at a glance how public health is dependent upon the quality of the water supply, and how important a factor a good system of waterworks is. Having settled on the range of percentages which his shades of color must represent, and having divided the statistical figures—which are so meaningless to many people—in accordance with this plan, he first traces from an atlas the outline of the United States with its various subdivisions on his transparent paper and then by means of a carbon sheet transfers it to a piece of stiff cardboard, which is the basis of his final map. Beginning up in one corner of the country, with the State of Washington, he would transfer the outlines of the State to stippleboard and shade it by erasures or by blacking so as to express his statistics of the Washington water supply in accordance with a scheme of tint gradations, each State having its special tint.

Then he would cut out its northern and western boundaries with the scissors, letting the south and east sides go untrimmed, and paste it down in its proper place on the cardboard backing. Proceeding the same way with Idaho and Oregon—except that they must each be of a different shade, of course, in accordance with their special figures—he would stick them down so that they overlapped the untrimmed edges of Washington, just as shingles overlie one another on a roof, and thus keep on in the same way until he has shingled the entire map down to Florida, which, being the last piece to take its place, must be cut out on all sides. Rivers and the coast line are drawn in with ink, and wherever the "shingles" overlap into the ocean they are scraped white with a penknife.

If the range of figures is very wide it may be necessary to supplement the four or five shades which it is possible to produce by means of the stippleboard with the intermediate tints, and for this purpose paper is specially printed in the required gradations. The interest that can be got out of this simple paste-and-scissors process of graphical statistics by the amateur, the student, the scientist or author is almost without limit, for there is hardly any series of facts that cannot be thus pictured. A great advantage of the process—apart from its simplicity—is its inexpensiveness for reproduction.

GREAT WRITERS.

Few adjectives are so abused in criticism as "great." Writers, booksellers and others who handle books speak of a great book, a great author, forgetting that the word implies a scale of merit—implies it often to destroy it. Professor William P. Trent, of Columbia University, has been endeavoring to make a scale which such persons might keep in mind, and his remarks are not uninteresting. From his article in the *International Monthly* the following table is made up:

GREAT WRITERS.

Homer.	Virgil.	Dante.
Sophocles.	Goethe.	Shakespeare.
Milton.	Molière.	Cervantes, etc.

To this class Professor Trent is inclined to add Balzac and Hugo.

WRITERS OF GREAT POWER, BUT NOT UNIVERSAL IN THEIR GENIUS.

Pindar.	Aristo.	Schiller.
Lucretius.	Montaigne.	Heine.
Petrarch.	Spenser.	Rabelais.
Tasso.	Chaucer.	Gibbon, etc.

WRITERS WHOM ONE CANNOT CALL SUPREME, ALTHOUGH ONE WOULD AS LITTLE THINK OF CALLING THEM MINOR.

Catullus.	Lamb.	Burns.
Horace.	Byron.	Coleridge.
Leopardi.	Browning.	Tennyson.
Marlowe.	Dryden.	Wordsworth.
Ben Jonson.	Pope.	Shelley.
Keats.	Gray.	Landor.
	Hawthorne, etc.	

Professor Trent adds that if his classification has been made on correct lines it needs filling out and requires many qualifications. "And we must always remember that any scheme of classification is bad if it tends to make our judgments hard and fast, if it induces us to think that we can stick a pin through a writer and ticket him as an entomologist does an insect. But if we use such a scheme intelligently it may prove useful, if only by stimulating us to candid objections, for candid objections imply honest thought. and honest thought on such a noble subject as literature cannot but be beneficial."

SIX BEST-SELLING BOOKS FOR JULY-AUGUST.

The six books that have sold best in the order of demand, from July 1 to August 1, according to *The Bookman*, are:

	POINTS.
1. The Virginian. Wister. *Macmillan*	209
2. Mrs. Wiggs of the Cabbage Patch. Hegan. *Century Co*	191
3. The Mississippi Bubble. Hough. *Bowen-Merrill Co*	178
4. Dorothy Vernon. Major. *Macmillan*	149
5. Ranson's Folly. Davis. *Scribner*	106
6. The Hound of the Baskervilles. Doyle. *McClure, Phillips & Co*	80

COMMUNICATIONS.

PERTINENT CRITICISM OF PUBLISHERS' TRADE LISTS.

To the Editor of The Publishers' Weekly.

Dear Sir: On looking over the "Publishers' Trade List Annual" for 1902 I find one thing that has always been troublesome, namely, that some publishers do not have their name at the top of all the pages of their list, making it necessary, sometimes, to look through their entire list to find out whose it is. Of course, in many instances I find the type so familiar that I do not have to do this; but that is not always the case. When one is in a hurry to find what one wants—and who is not in a hurry?—it is very annoying to turn over so much matter to get what he wants. May I also ask, Why cannot publishers confine themselves to their lists and leave out "ads"? To illustrate, I refer you to Albert Brandt's. I have all your lists from the first, and have often thought that as time goes on we can never afford to have so much room taken up with matter not pertaining to the actual title and price of the book. This is more "kicking" than I have ever done, but I think not all without reason, *vide* American Baptist Publication Society.

John Stirling.

COPYRIGHT MATTERS.

CLARENCE F. BIRDSEYE vs. C. W. LITTLE.

Suit has been brought in the United States Circuit Court, before Commissioner Shields, in an action for infringement of copyright by Clarence F. Birdseye against Charles W. Little, publisher of "Cumming and Gilbert's General Laws and Other General Statutes of New York State." The book in question is credited as being compiled by Robert C. Cumming and Frank B. Gilbert, who were for several years on the Statutory Revision Commission.

In his complaint Mr. Birdseye states that in 1879 he began work on the first edition of his "Revised Statutes, Codes and General Laws of the State of New York," a work to which he devoted evenings and holidays for eleven years, and which cost $40,000 to bring out. This book, Mr. Birdseye alleges, was palpably used by Cumming and Gilbert as the basis for their work, and he asks the court to enjoin the publishers from further infringement, and to order the defendants to pay over all profits from the sale of the disputed book.

TO DECIDE THE VALIDITY OF AN ASSIGNMENT OF AMERICAN COPYRIGHT IN CANADA.

THE question whether an assignment of an American copyright would hold good in Canada was brought before Justice Falconbridge in Toronto August 26. McLeod and Allan, who claim to have the copyright for "When Knighthood Was in Flower," brought suit against the Poole Publishing Company and the Musson Book Company for issuing of the book, and to restrain them from further publishing. It seems that the American publishers assigned the copyright to the Canadian houses, and the defendants disputed the legality of the transaction. The judge decided that the case should go to trial, and gave no opinion on it.

OBITUARY NOTES.

PROFESSOR JOSEPH KÜRSCHNER, the author of the "Deutsche Literatur-Kalender," and other handbooks, died suddenly July 29, *en route* to Venice. He was born at Gotha, Saxony, September 20, 1853, and was graduated from the Leipzig University. He compiled a dramatic necrology, (1873;) the "Staats-Hof-und Kommunal-Handbuch," published annually, and the "Literatur-Kalender." He was for a time editor of *Vom Fels zum Meer, Ueber Land und Meer, Deutsche Romanbibliothek,* and *Aus Fremden Zungen.* He also edited the *Collection Speemann* and the *Deutsche National-Literatur,* comprising 220 volumes.

MARCELLUS BETZ, a blind newsdealer of Wiliamsburg, New York, died August 29 in the Eastern District Hospital, Williamsburg, in his seventy-first year, from injuries received two weeks before in a fall. He was born in New York, and at the age of seven began to sell papers. In 1850 he moved to Williamsburg. Ten years later, while a member of the Volunteer Fire Department. he went to a fire and some sparks flew into his eyes. He rubbed the eyelids with his fingers, which caused irritation and subsequently paralysis. He became totally blind. He continued his vocation with the aid of one of his children.

WILLIAM H. ASH, for many years a faithful and trusted employee of G. P. Putnam's Sons, was drowned August 30, at Lake Sunapee, N. H., where he was spending his vacation. His body was found within four feet of the dock. Messrs. Putnam were notified and they arranged for a burial at Newport, N. H. Ash was something of a celebrity among book buyers. He was an unusually bright negro, and spent so many years in the employ of the Putnams that he came to be known for his acquaintance with rare volumes and editions. His mother, with whom he lived at Winfield, L. I., died a few months ago. Ash was twenty-nine years old.

THEODORE FRELINGHUYSEN SEWARD, musical composer and president of the Brotherhood of Christian Unity, died August 30, at Orange, N. J., aged sixty-seven. He began life as a music teacher. Some of his compilations were very successful, the sale of one book, called "The Temple Choir," going beyond 100,000 copies. He introduced the tonic sol-fa system of teaching music, and was for many years editor of various musical periodicals published in New York City. But what he regarded as his most distinctive and interesting musical work was recording and thus preserving many of the religious melodies of the Southern slaves, known as "spirituals," or "slave songs," of which "Swing Low, Sweet Chariot" and "Turn Back, Pharaoh's Army" are types. This work was done in connection with the famous Fisk Jubilee Singers, who raised several hundred thousand dollars by their concerts in America and Europe for their university at Nashville, Tenn.

GEORGE DOUGLAS BROWN, the promising author of "The House With the Green Shutters," died in London, August 28. He was born in 1869 in the west of Scotland in a farming and mining country. He studied at Glasgow University, where he won a scholarship on which he went to Oxford. When he was graduated there he tramped to London with a total capital of £17, with the purpose of becoming a man of letters. His first work was as a reporter on a newspaper. Later he became literary adviser to one of the London publishing houses, and was said to be at work on a new novel at the time of his death. "The House With the Green Shutters" is a story of Scotch country life, written in an uncompromisingly realistic vein. It attracted the attention of critics and the public, and was widely read. It was published under the name of George Douglas. That work enabled him to retire from the daily grind, and he went to live at Haslemere, where Tyndall and Grant Allen lived, and where Dr. Conan Doyle lives now. The young author had been for a year in a jubilant state of mind, and had planned a trip to the Continent, a tramp through Scotland and several pleasure jaunts, when death suddenly struck him down.

DR. EDWARD EGGLESTON, novelist and historian, died September 3, at his home, Owl's Nest, on Dunham Bay, Lake George, N. Y. He would have been sixty-six years old had he lived until December 13, having been born in Vevay, Ind., in 1836. Dr. Eggleston's first work to bring him reputation was "The Hoosier Schoolmaster," published in *Hearth and Home* in 1871. The book had an immediate success, for, in addition to delicate humor, it was marked by a sympathy with the subject which won all who read it. Prior to making this hit Dr. Eggleston had been a Methodist preacher. His father died when he was nine years old, and, handicapped by ill health from boyhood, he was thrown upon his own resources for such education as he got. It was in 1856 that he became a Methodist preacher, riding a four weeks' circuit in Indiana and working always up to the limit of his strength. His health gave way and he went to Minnesota, where he held several pastorates and was general agent for the Bible Society. His first literary work began in 1866 with sketches for the *Little Corporal,* a children's paper published at Evanston, Ill., of which he afterward became associate editor. Subsequently he became editor of the *Sunday School Teacher*, published in Chicago, and he gained a reputation as a speaker at Sunday-school conventions. In 1870 he succeeded Theodore Tilton as editor of the *Independent* and came to New York to live. He afterward was editor of *Hearth and Home*, and from 1874 to 1879 held the pastorate of the Church of Christian Endeaver in Brooklyn, N. Y. Later he retired to his picturesque home, Owl's Nest, on Lake George, and from that time until his death devoted himself exclusively to literary work. In addition to a number of novels, Mr. Eggleston wrote much on American historical topics. Among his books may be mentioned "The Beginners of a Nation," "The Faith Doctor," "Duffels," "The Hoosier Schoolmaster," "Mr. Blake's Walking-Stick," "The Mystery of Metropolisville," "Roxy," "The Circuit Rider; "Book of Queer Stories," "The End of the World," "The Schoolmaster's Stories for Boys and Girls," "Queer Stories for Boys and Girls," "The Graysons," "A History of the United States and Its People, for the Use of Schools," "The Household History of the United States and Its People," "A First Book in American History," four volumes of the *Famous American Indian Series*, and his latest work, "The Transit of Civilization," an admirable study of American colonial conditions, in which his qualities as a careful and sympathetic historian appears at their best.

NOTES ON AUTHORS.

Professor William P. Trent, of Columbia University, is putting the finishing touches to "A History of American Literature."

Sarah Grand, author of "Babs the Impossible," is at work on a play in collaboration with Mr. George R. Sims. The play was begun by Mme. Grand in joint authorship with Robert Buchanan, whose death materially postponed the completion of the work.

According to a corespondent of the New York *Sun*, Owen Wister is a grandson of Fanny. Kemble. The great actress seventy years ago married Mr. Pierce Butler, of Philadelphia. Of their two daughters one married Mr. Wister, of Philadelphia, the father of the distinguished novelist.

Miss Alice MacGowan, whose first novel, "The Last Word," is offered by L. C. Page & Company on their fall list, would seem to be well prepared to write a thoroughly American story without sectional bias. She was born in Ohio, brought up in Tennessee, has lived a good portion of her life in the East, and got her literary impetus in Texas. If such preparation as this does not obliterate provincialism, it would seem that nothing could.

Frederic L. Knowles writes that he had nothing to do with the compiling of the Third Series of "Cap and Gown" which a few weeks ago was credited to him in our "Weekly Record" under the pseudonym of "R. L. Paget," a name under which we understood he produced literary work some time ago. The pseudonym, however, Mr. Knowles claims, is the office property of the publishers, and may cover the work of any one employed by them to compile other issues of this excellent series of college verse.

Kate Douglas Wiggin has recently established a prize at Bowdoin College, to be known as the "Hawthorne Prize," for creative work in English, that will be awarded each year at Commencement to the member of the Junior or Senior class presenting the best poem or short story. Mrs. Wiggin's home, Quillcote-on-Saco, at Hollis, Maine, is not far from Brunswick, where Bowdoin is situated. She has been engaged this summer as for the past two years, on an anthology of verse for children, entitled "Golden Numbers," which will be published by McClure, Phillips & Co., this month.

BUSINESS NOTES.

Alameda, Cal.—Theodore Altona has been succeeded by T. F. Baird.

Alvin, Tex.—Abrams & Ashley, booksellers, were burnt out August 13.

Bath, N. Y.—Spencer F. Lang, bookseller, has filed a voluntary petition in bankruptcy.

Des Moines, Iowa.—A receiver has been appointed for the Shissler-Case Co.

Detroit, Mich.—The Burrows Brothers Company, of Cleveland, have opened a permanent sample room in the Richardson Block, 160 Woodward Avenue. This office, which will be a great convenience to the firm's Michigan friends, will be in charge of B. L. Skadden, who has represented the firm for many years in Michigan. Their full holiday line is now on display here.

Ennis, Tex.—P. B. Rice, of the Ennis Bookstore, has made an assignment.

Esopus, N. Y.—The New Era Publishing Company has been incorporated to do publishing. Capital stock, $250,000. Directors, M. W. Baldwin, Port Ewan, N. Y.; W. H. Bond and H. S. Murphy, of New York City.

Eustis, Fla.—Galen Hutchings has succeeded his father, Dr. Gay Hutchings, for twenty years in the book business.

Fayette, Mo.—E. F. Quinn, of the Fayette Book Company, has been succeeded by H. A. Whiteside.

Fayetteville, N. C.—Matthews & Hinsdale, of the New Book Store Co., have dissolved partnership. P. H. Matthews will continue under old firm name.

Gallipolis, O.—The S. A. Moore Book Company has been incorporated here with a capital of $10,000. The incorporators are Sherwood A. Moore, J. E. Halliday, A. H. Wrig, Max Shober and J. R. McCormick.

Griffin, Ga.—The book store of J. H. Huff & Sons was badly damaged by fire August 18. The loss is covered by insurance.

Kansas City, Mo.—The Kellam book store, at Topeka, Kan., has been sold to the Jones Dry Goods Company, of Kansas City.

The store was one of the best known in Topeka, having been established for twenty-five years. C. C. May is the new manager.

KINGFIELD, ME.—R. F. Cook has purchased the book and stationery business of J. C. French.

MONMOUTH, ORE.—The Normal Book Store, long owned by G. Serfling, has passed into the possession of Harry E. Wagoner, of Independence. Mr. Wagoner is engaged in a similar business at Independence, and for years was publisher of the Independence *Enterprise*.

NASHVILLE, TENN.—The Methodist Publishing House, (Bigham & Smith,) have decided to open an up-to-date retail store in another part of the city. The present retail rooms on the public square will be converted into a wholesale and mailing department.

NEW YORK CITY.—The International Bibliophile Society has been incorporated to do a general publishing business. Capital stock, $5,000. Directors, E. L. McCarthy, A. L. Schwarz and Herbert D. Cohen, all of New York.

NEW YORK CITY.—The Mutual Publishing Company, of 57 Warren Street, has applied to the Supreme Court for the voluntary dissolution of the corporation through Directors Herman A. Groen and John R. Flanery, jr., and James W. Perry has been appointed referee in the matter by Justice Hall, and the order to show cause has been set down for December 1. The company was incorporated in August, 1900, with a capital stock of $20,000, and Mr. Groen is President and Treasurer. The liabilities are $6,979 and assets $3,019.

OSKALOOSA, IA.—The Augustine Company has bought the book and wall paper business of the Hedge, Wilson Co.

PHILADELPHIA, PA.—Owing to the demands of increasing business, H. W. Fisher & Co. have taken larger and more accessible quarters at 127 South 15th Street. Their specialty, as heretofore, will be rare and unusual books, together with the miscellaneous books of the day.

SANTA ROSA, CAL.—The Platt Book and Stationery Company has opened a new store here.

SOUTH PORTLAND, ME.—C. S. & L. Haskell have opened a book and stationery store in the York Block.

JOURNALISTIC NOTES.

The Bookseller, of Chicago, has been acquired by C. A. Huling, who has removed its business and editorial offices to 91 Dearborn Street. R. P. Hayes, the former publisher, will assist Mr. Huling as associate editor, and Chesley R. Perry, secretary of the Chicago Library Club, will conduct a department of Library Affairs. *The Bookseller* is an independent journal that has no axe to grind, and improves steadily in literary quality and typographical apearance.

LITERARY AND TRADE NOTES.

E. P. DUTTON & CO. announce "The Life of Mozart" and "The Life of Brahms," in the *Master Musician Series*.

THE publishing firms of Germany have agreed not to supply books to those retailers who grant discounts to cash customers.

DOUBLEDAY, PAGE & CO. have just brought out the first volume of their *Variorum edition* of Fitzgerald's works. The remaining six volumes are to appear this fall.

CURTIS & CAMERON, Boston, have taken over the book on Edwin A. Abbey's "Quest of the Holy Grail," announced by Noyes, Platt & Co. They will have it ready about October 1.

HENRY HOLT & CO. will publish shortly Bemont and Monod's "Middle Ages in Europe, 395 to 1270," in an English version made under the editorship of Professor George B. Adams of Yale.

J. F. TAYLOR & COMPANY have just ready "The Prophet of the Real," a dramatic story of to-day, by Esther Miller; also, "The Heart of Woman," a romance dealing with the problem of a dual love, by Harry W. Desmond.

ROBERT WATERS, West Hoboken, N. J., will bring out shortly a memorial of John Swinton entitled "The Career and Conversation of John Swinton," with a portrait. Charles H. Kerr & Co., Chicago, will also handle the book.

W. L. MASON, 35 W. Twenty-first Street, New York, has published "How to Become a Law Stenographer," a helpful handbook for stenographers whose ambitions lead them to seek employment as court of law stenographers.

MARCUS WARD & CO., New York, have published in an attractive little pamphlet "The Essentials of Polite Correspondence," giving accepted forms of address and salutation, etc., prepared by Helen E. Gavit, author of "The Etiquette of Correspondence."

A. WESSELS COMPANY have ready a very seasonable book by Edwin L. Sabin, called "The Magic Moshie, and Other Goldfish Stories," in which are collected the author's contributions to *Lippincott's*, *Harper's*, *Outing*, and other periodicals and books.

THE ABBEY PRESS have just ready "Haps and Mishaps of Jack Haselton," by W. H. Morten; "For Bush or Bonnet," by M. E. Hoogstraat; "Sea Breezes and Sand Dunes," by Rebecca Van Duesen; and "Justa Hamlin's Vocation," by Janette Hill Knox.

C. M. CLARK PUBLISHING COMPANY will publish on the 10th inst. "The Climax," by Charles Felton Pidgin, which the publishers tersely characterize as "a capering romance of some things that never happened to Aaron Burr, Alexander Hamilton and others."

THE ALWIL SHOP, Ridgewood, N. J., has just published a special edition of "The Essay on Nature," by Ralph Waldo Emerson. The work is printed in three colors and is bound in birch-wood boards. Fifty copies have been printed on Dutch hand-made paper and colored by hand throughout.

EDWIN S. CRAWLEY, University of Pennsylvania, Philadelphia, will publish on the 10th inst. "A Short Course in Plane and Spherical Trigonometry," by Edwin S. Crawley and Professor Thomas A. Scott. The book is published with and without logarithmic tables (four place.)

JAMES POTT & Co. have in preparation a work on "The Mediterranean," a pictorial survey supplemented by a mine of information; also, a romance of exceptional merit by Virna Sheard, entitled "A Maid of Many Moods," which deals with the Avon district, midway between Stratford and Shottery.

THE BUREAU OF AMERICAN ETHNOLOGY, (Smithsonian Institution,) of which J. W. Powell is director, has published an interesting collection of Chinook stories, entitled "Kathlamet Texts." The originals were told by three natives acquainted with the Kathlamet dialect, and were recorded and translated by Franz Boas.

ELKIN MATTHEW, London, is to publish an interesting "find," which consists of a diary kept by Edward Williams, the friend of Shelley who was drowned with him. Any new and intimate light upon Shelley, such as this diary is likely to supply, cannot fail to be of extreme interest. Dr. Garnett is to write an introduction to the volume.

D. APPLETON & Co. will publish shortly a work on "Social New York Under the First Georges," prepared from authentic records—old wills, inventories, letters, etc.—by Esther Singleton, author of "The Furniture of Our Forefathers," etc.; also, "Sir William Pepperell," the hero of Louisburg in 1745, by Noah Brooks, a volume in the *Life Histories Series:*

GEORGE F. KELLY, (The Kensington Press,) 435 Broadway, New York, will publish this month a volume entitled "American Designers of Book Plates," which will contain articles, by experts, on the ex-libris designs of fifteen of the younger American makers of book plates, and upwards of one hundred plates in the text and a number of extra-inserted plates in colors.

THE LOTHROP PUBLISHING COMPANY announce a volume for early fall publication, entitled "The Whirlwind." It is a story of the Civil War by Rupert Hughes, and the striking title of the book is spoken of as a good description of the sweeping career of the hero who is the centre of a novel which seeks to depict the American life, political and social, in a most impressive way.

THE METHODIST BOOK CONCERN (Eaton & Mains,) will publish on the 15th inst., "The Drillmaster of Methodism," principles and methods for the class leader and pastor, by Charles L. Goodell, D.D. They will publish shortly "William Xavier Ninde," a memorial, by his daughter, and "Minutes of the Annual Conferences of the Methodist Episcopal Church; Spring Conferences, 1902."

WHITE & WARNER, Hartford, Conn., have published a new issue of their useful handbook, "Trolley Trips Through Southern New England." The illustrations are numerous, and there are nine maps, four showing the trolley lines between New York and Boston, the other five showing in detail lines around Bridgeport, New Haven, Hartford, Springfield and Worcester. The tables give the running times, distances and fare.

THE OUTLOOK COMPANY will shortly publish in book form George Kennan's brilliant first hand narrative of "The Tragedy of Pelee," which has been appearing in serial form in the *Outlook*. Mr. Kennan's ascent of Pelee was made in company with Professor Angelo Heilprin, just previous to the greatest volcanic eruption of those that followed the catastrophe of May 8. His story of his experiences and explorations forms a thrilling narrative, and a contribution of importance to the history of the Martinique disaster. The book will be fully illustrated with photographs taken by Mr. Kennan and others.

RICHARD G. BADGER, (Gorham Press,) Boston, has just issued "The Cult of the Purple Rose," by Shirley Everton Johnson, describing a phase of Harvard undergraduate life of 1890; "Maximilian," a play by Edgar Lee Masters, dealing with the ill-fated Emperor of Mexico; "Moses," a drama by Charles Hovey Brown; and four volumes of poetry: "The Great Procession," verses for and about children, by Harriet Prescott Spofford; "The Air Voyage," by William E. Ingersoll; "Thoughts Adrift," poems by Hattie Horner Louthan; and "English Lyrics of a Finnish Harp," by Herman Montague Donner.

HERBERT B. TURNER & Co., 323 Wentworth Building, Summer Street and Atlantic Avenue, Boston, have just ready attractive editions of "A Tale of a Tub," with numerous notes; "Virginibus Puerisque," and "Familiar Studies of Men and Books," both by Robert Louis Stevenson; also, "Commodore Trunnion's Courtship" and "The Cruise of H. M. S. Thunder," from the works of Smollett. Each volume is printed from 12-point Cadmus type, on a high-grade paper, with a photogravure frontispiece and a vignetted photogravure decorative title-page. Mr. H. B. Turner may be remembered by the trade through his connection with the firm of Lothrop Publishing Company.

LITTLE, BROWN & Co. have just published in a separate volume entitled "Glimpses of California and the Missions," Helen Hunt Jackson's delightful California articles, hitherto printed in her European travel sketches, with 37 pictures by Henry Sandham, who illustrated "Romona;" also, a new edition of Fannie Merrit Farmer's "Boston Cooking School Cook Book," with an appendix containing 300 additional recipes. They have in preparation "The Speeches and Other Writings of Daniel Webster, Hitherto Uncollected," in three volumes, which will contain material much of which has until now been inaccessible; also, "American Literature in its Colonial and National Period," by Dr. Lorenzo Sears of Brown University.

W. A. Wilde Co. announce several works for young people which they will have ready shortly. There will be a new volume by Everett T. Tomlinson, entitled "In the Camp of Cornwallis;" "Sweetbrier and Thistle-down," a story by James Newton Baskett; "A Loyal Lass," a story of the Niagara campaign of 1814, by Amy E. Blanchard; "Mr. Pat's Little Girl," by Mary F. Leonard, author of the "Spectacle Man;" "The Baluster Boys," which Blanche M. Channing completed just before her sad and sudden death; "What Gladys Saw," a story of farm and forest, by Francis M. Fox; and "On the Frontier with St. Clair," a story of the opening up of the Ohio country, by Charles M. Wood. All these books are fully illustrated.

The Cathedral Library Association, New York, have in preparation a "Memorial Volume of the Most Rev. Augustine Corrigan, D.D., Archbishop of New York," which will contain a sketch of the life of Mgr. Corrigan, a description of the obsequies and Month's Mind held in the Cathedral, with the sermons preached by the Most Rev. Archbishop of Philadelphia, and the Right Rev. Bishop of Rochester, and a full account of the proceedings at the memorial meeting held by the Catholic societies of New York in Carnegie Hall, June 8, and an extended report of the addresses made on that occasion. There will be photographs of the Archbishop at different periods of his life, and other illustrations. The work will be published by subscription only, and the copies will be numbered.

The Century Company is bringing out a "Bible for Children," printed in two colors, with full page illustrations from the old masters. Rev. Dr. Francis Brown, of the Union Theological Seminary, has arranged the text, and Bishop Potter has furnished the introduction. A book of Bishop Potter's will also shortly appear entitled "The East of Today and Tomorrow," the result of the bishop's recent visit to Japan, China, India and the Hawaiian Islands. The "Essays of Elia," and "The Sentimental Journey" will be added to *The Century Classics;* James H. Stoddart's "Recollections of a Player" will soon appear and this autumn the publication will begin of a new series of books for boys and girls to be called *The St. Nicholas Series,* and to be made up of the long Stories that have appeared in the *St. Nicholas Magazine.*

Harper & Brothers will publish this month "The Ship of Dreams," a story of Long Island life along the Great South Bay, by Louise Forslund, author of "The Story of Sarah;" "The Maid-at-Arms," a romance of life in New York State during 1778, by Robert W. Chambers; also, "The Vultures," Henry Seton Merriman's new story, in which he describes some of the attachès of diplomatic foreign offices who are expected "to be found where the carcass is." They have in preparation "The Christmas Kalends of Provence," by Thomas A. Janvier, which deals with that region of France which the author knows and loves so well; a new volume of poems by Will Carleton; "Poems and Verses," by Edward Sandford Martin; also, a new and revised edition of William Agnew Paton's "Picturesque Sicily."

New Amsterdam Book Co. have ready an excellent reprint of the "History of the Expedition under the Command of Captains Lewis and Clark to the Sources of the Missouri, etc." It is reprinted from the 1814 edition of the "Journals," and is issued in three volumes, well printed and attractively bound, appearing in the *Commonwealth Series.* This house also announces "Three Men on Wheels," a sequel to "Three Men in a Boat," by Jerome K. Jerome; "Joan of the Sword Hand," a novel of stirring adventure, by S. R. Crockett; "The Shadow of Hilton Fernbrook," a tale of love versus hypnotism, by Atha Westbury; "Captain Fanny," by W. Clark Russell; and "With Sword and Crucifix," an historical story of the time of La Salle, by Edward S. Van Zile. The foregoing novels all appear in the *Red Letter Series.*

The Grafton Press, of New York, have just ready "By the Stage Door," a collection of stage stories by Miss Ada Patterson and Miss Victory Bateman; also "The Imperial Republic," an anti-imperialistic drama, by Miss Elizabeth G. Crane, who is already known as the author of "Berquin." They have in preparation a limited edition of Chaucer's "Wife of Bath's Tale," uniform with the *Grafton edition* of the "Cok and Hen;" "The Worth of Words," by Dr. Ralcy Husted Bell, with an introduction by Dr. William Colby Cooper; "Some By-ways of California," by Charles Franklin Carter; "The Senator's Sweetheart," by Rosseter Willard, with an introduction by Mrs. Cushman K. Davis; "The Song of the Wedding Bells: Poems," by William Bonnie Ockhame; also, "Love Songs and Other Poems," by Owen Innsly.

L. C. Page & Co. have just brought out an attractive uniform edition of the novels of Sidney C. Grier, in seven volumes, including "The Warden of the Marches," "Like Another Helen," "Peace with Honor," "His Excellency's English Governess," "Kings of the East," "A Crowned Queen," and "In Furthest Ind;" "Beautiful Joe's Paradise, or, the Island of Brotherly Love," a sequel to "Beautiful Joe," by Marshall Saunders, with illustrations by Charles Livingston Bull; "Councils of Croesus," by May Knight Potter, illustrated by W. H. Dunton; "A Puritan Knight Errant," by Edith Robinson, illustrated by L. J. Bridgman; and two new volumes in the *Cosy Corner Series*—"Jerry's Reward," by Evelyn Snead Barnett, illustrated by Etheldred B. Barry, and "The Flight of Rosy Dawn," by Pauline Bradford Mackie (Mrs. H. Müller Hopkins,) illustrated by Josephine Bruce.

The Bowen-Merrill Company have in preparation "The Loom of Life," a new story by Charles Frederic Goss, author of "The Redemption of David Corson," and "Little Saint Sunshine," a Christmas story, by the same author, with illustrations by Virginia

Keep; "The Long Straight Road," a novel of to-day, by George Horton, author of "Like Another Helen," illustrated by the Kinneys; "The Master of Appleby," a romance of the Carolinas, by Francis Lynde, with illustrations by T. de Thulstrup; "Francezka," a story of youth, splendor and tragedy, by Molly Elliott Seawell, author of "The Sprightly Romance of Marsac," with illustrations by Harrison Fisher; also, "Edges," a story filled with bright talk, with clever bits of philosophy, with fresh and far-seeing observations, by Alice Woods, who also illustrates her work.

Henry T. Coates & Co. have ready "Japan and Her People," by Anna C. Hartshorne, in two volumes and well illustrated; "Vienna and the Viennese," by Maria H. Lansdale; "European and Japanese Gardens," edited by Glenn Brown and illustrated with pictures of representative gardens; "Brevities: Being More Crankisms," by L. de V. Matthewman; "Whimlets," by S. Scott Stinson and C. V. Dwiggins; "Songs and Stories of Tennessee," by John T. Moore; and several works on coffee and tea, their history, culture and blending, by Joseph M. Walsh. The fiction list of this house includes "The Embarrassing Orphan," by W. E. Norris; "Sawdust: a Romance," by Dorothea Gerard; "Kent Fort Manor," by William Henry Babcock; "Last Words," by Stephen Crane; "The Archierey of Samara: a Russian Novel," by Henry Iliowizi; and for younger readers new stories by Alger, Ellis and Castlemon.

The Macmillan Company have just issued "Matthew Arnold," by Herbert W. Paul, in the *English Men of Letters;* "Lux Christi: an outline study of India," by Caroline Atwater Mason; the *Temple edition* of Henry Fielding in twelve volumes, edited by George Saintsbury; and several new text-books, among which are "English History Told by English Poets," a reader compiled by Katherine Lee Bates and Katherine Coman; "A Teacher's Manual of Geography," by Charles McMurry, and several volumes of annotated Latin and Greek classics. They have in preparation Dr. Edward Everett Hale's "Memories of a Hundred Years," which is appearing serially in *The Outlook;* a new book by Jacob A. Riis, entitled "The Battle with the Slum," which includes the material in Mr. Riis's "A Ten Year's War," which he has rewritten and greatly enlarged; also, Marion Crawford's latest novel, "Cecilia, the Last of the Vestals," a story of young women of modern Rome.

Frederick A. Stokes Company have just ready "Tom Moore," an unhistorical romance, founded on certain happenings in the life of Ireland's greatest poet," by Theodore Burt Sayre, author of "Two Summer Girls and I," etc., illustrated; also, "Son! or the Wisdom of 'Uncle Eph,' the Modern Yutzo," by Lord Gilhooly, (Frederick Henri Seymour,) a volume of homely advice and wisdom cleverly conveyed. They will publish shortly "The Mishaps of an Automobilist," by De Witt C. Falls, with colored illustrations; "Wolfville Nights," by Alfred Henry Lewis; "Love, Laurels and Laughter," a volume of verse, by Miss Beatrice Hanscom; "A Woman's Venture," a new story, by David Graham Phillips, author of "The Great God Success," who gives an interesting picture of social life in Washington; "Mary Had a Little Lamb, the true story of the real Mary and the real lamb," with numerous illustrations; "Cats and All About Them," a practical handbook for the cat lover and the cat fancier; also, a new edition of "A Whirl Asunder," by Gertrude Atherton.

Fleming H. Revell Company have just ready "Under Calvin's Spell," by Deborah Alcock, a historical novel of the time of Calvin and the Huguenots, the scene centering in Geneva, but shifting at times into Savoy and France. As a story the plot is vigorous with action, suspense, surprise and critical situations; moreover, its tone is wholesome and its heroism inspiring. They have in press a work entitled "Down in Water Street," a record of sixteen years of labors in what was once the worst section of lower New York, by Samuel H. Hadley, superintendent of the Water Street Mission. In a measure the book is a sequel to "The Life of Jerry McAuley," and naturally enough the latter's name figures prominently in its pages. They will publish shortly "A Maker of the New Orient, Samuel Rollins Brown," by William Elliot Griffis. Brown held an important place in the history of missions and of general progress. He was among the first to instruct the deaf and dumb. He translated the New Testament into Japanese, and brought to America the first Chinese students to be educated abroad.

McClure, Phillips & Co. will publish on the 15th inst. the initial volume of a *First Novel Series*, entitled "The Ragged Edge," by John T. McIntyre. It is a study of ward politics and social life. This will be followed by "The Taskmasters," by George Kibbe Turner, the scene of which is laid in a New England factory town, and the central interest of the plot is the social and political dominance of the great industrial barons. At the same time they will publish "The Hole in the Wall," a story of a public house and its frequenters in Wapping, England, by Arthur Morrison, author of "Tales of Mean Streets;" "Ivan Ilyitch," one of Tolstoi's most powerful short stories, translated by Mrs. Garnett; and a new volume of the Dent edition of the complete works of William Hazlitt. They will publish later in the month "Gabriel Tolliver," by Joel Chandler Harris, a story of Georgia during the "reconstruction" period, in which the author points out the evils and injustice caused by the efforts of the carpet-baggers to organize the negroes and influence them against the Southern whites. In October they will bring out Booth Tarkington's latest novel, "The Two Vanrevels."

Houghton, Mifflin & Co. will have ready on Saturday, September 13, a varied list of books, among which fine editions of standard works take an important place. Among such are the *Riverside edition* of Bret Harte's works, in 16 volumes, sold only in sets; a new one volume *Holiday edition* of Thoreau's "Walden," in dark cloth binding, showing a design in gold of the hut by the Pond; a *Cambridge edition* in five volumes of Lockhart's "Life of Sir Walter Scott"; and new editions of "Robinson Crusoe" and "The Autobiography of Benjamin Franklin." The first volume will also then be ready of "The Argive Heraeum," edited by Charles Waldstein, which will give the results of the excavations made from 1891-95 at the famous shrine of Hera in Argolis in behalf of the Archæological Institute of America and the American School of Classical Studies at Athens. This work will be in two volumes, with 75 full-page plates and 400 other illustrations. "The Champion," by Charles Egbert Craddock, a book for boys of which the hero is a printer's "devil" in Tennessee, and "The Mosque of Judgment," by William Vaughn Moody, a dramatic poem of greater length than he has yet attempted, will also be ready next Saturday.

Manzi, Joyant & Co. successors to Goupil & Co., have in preparation "Goupil's Paris 'Salons,' 1902," which will contain a review of the most remarkable paintings and sculptures exhibited by the Société des Artistes Français and the Société Nationale des Beaux-Arts, by Maurice Hamel, the well-known art critic. The English translation has been made by Paul Villars. The illustrations consist of one hundred full-page plates. The work is issued in a strictly limited edition. They also announce a work, in French, by Pierre de Nolhac, entitled "Louis xv. et Mme. de Pompadour," with fifty photogravures, eight head and tail pieces and two hand-finished water-color facsimiles, limited to 100 copies on Japan paper and 800 copies on handmade paper. The binding for this work is a reproduction of the most magnificent design executed by Padeloup for Louis xv. and will be ornamented on the second cover with the ex-libris of Mme. de Pompadour drawn by Cochin. They have also in preparation a sumptuous work on "Henry viii.," by A. F. Pollard, with forty-three photogravures and one hand-finished water-color frontispiece, the American market for which has been sold to Charles Scribner's Sons. They are preparing a superb work on the Wallace Collection at Hartford House, London, with text by A. G. Temple, director of the Guildhall Gallery, London. This will be in ten parts, each to contain ten full-page plates, including two water-color facsimiles, also a duplicate set of the plates. The edition will be limited to 100 copies on Japan paper at $300 the copy.

Charles Scribner's Sons have in preparation a work of importance by Dr. C. A. Briggs, of Union Seminary, entitled "The Incarnation of the Lord," ten discourses which give the entire New Testament teaching upon the subject of the title; a work entitled "Human Nature and the Social Order," by Professor Charles Horton Cooley, of Ann Arbor, which is considered by Professor Giddings to be "the best treatment of the human nature problem that we have had since the social point of view began to receive attention;" "The Essence of Christianity, a Study in the History of Definition," by Professor William Adams Brown, of Union Theological Seminary, which, as the title indicates, is essentially a discussion, in the light of modern research, of the old question, "What is Christianity?" "The Citizen and the Industrial Situation," a new book by Bishop Potter upon a phase of the capital and labor problem with which he has been so prominently engaged of late as an arbitrator; "The Christian Point of View," containing papers by three professors of Union Theological Seminary—"The Problem for the Church," by Professor George W. Knox, "Theological Reconstruction," by Professor A. C. McGiffert, and "The Religious Value of the Old Testament," by Professor Francis Brown—whose purpose it is to show the effect on Christian doctrine of a consistent belief in Jesus Christ; "The Messages of Israel's Law Givers," a new volume in their series of *The Messages of the Bible*, by Professor Charles Foster Kent, whose basis is the scientific codification and interpretative paraphrase of the laws found in the Old Testament; also, a new volume in their *Historical Series for Bible Students*, on the "History of the Babylonians and Assyrians," by Professor George S. Goodspeed, of the University of Chicago. In the department of Literature they announce a volume of unusual interest in "Shakespeare and Voltaire," by Professor T. R. Lounsbury, of Yale, which is devoted entirely to the part played by Voltaire in Shakespearian controversy, and follows the author's "Shakespeare as a Dramatic Artist." To the series of *Periods of European Literature*, edited by Professor George Saintsbury, they will add a volume entitled "The Mid-Eighteenth Century," by J. H. Millar. They will publish during the fall "John Gayther's Garden and the Stories Told Therein," a posthumous volume of stories by the late Frank R. Stockton; also a new and cheap edition of the historical novels of Bulwer Lytton in six volumes, including "Rienzi," one volume; "The Last Days of Pompeii," one volume; "The Last of the Barons," two volumes; and "Harold, the last of the Saxon Kings," two volumes. Among their books for young people we note a volume of new verse by James Whitcomb Riley with the felicitous title of "The Book of Joyous Children;" "A Captured Santa Claus," by Thomas Nelson Page, with colored illustrations; "In the Wasp's Nest," a story of the war of 1812, by Cyrus Townsend Brady, dealing with stirring times aboard two American warships successively bearing the name of *Wasp;* "King Mombo," a story of the great African forest by Paul Du Chaillu; "What a Girl Can Make and Do, New Ideas for Work and Play," by Lina and Adelia B. Beard, a book that cannot fail to please as well as instruct those for whom it is written; "Sea Fighters, from Drake to Farragut," by Jessie Peabody Frothingham; "Bob and His Gun," by William Alexander Linn, whose aim is to teach boys the difference between mere shooting and true sportsmanship; and three new Henty books, "The Treasure of the Incas," "With Kitchener in the Soudan," and "With the British Legion."

TERMS OF ADVERTISING.

Under the heading "Books Wanted" **book-trade subscribers are given the privilege of a free advertisement for books out of print, of five nonpareil lines exclusive of address, in any issue except special numbers, to an extent not exceeding 100 lines a year. If more than five lines are sent, the excess is at 10 cents a line, and amount should be inclosed.** *Bids for current books and such as may be easily had from the publishers, and repeated matter, as well as all advertisements from non-subscribers, must be paid for at the rate of 10 cents a line.*

Under the heading "Books for Sale," the charge to subscribers and non-subscribers is 10 cents a nonpareil line for each insertion. No deduction for repeated matter.

All other small, undisplayed, advertisements will be charged at the uniform rate of 10 cents a nonpareil line. Eight words may be reckoned to the line.

Parties with whom we have no accounts must pay in advance, otherwise no notice will be taken of their communications.

BOOKS WANTED.

☞ **In answering, please state edition, condition, and price, including postage or express charges.**

Houses that are willing to deal exclusively on a cash-on-delivery basis will find it to their advantage to put after their firm-name the word [*Cash*].

☞ **Write your wants plainly and on one side of the sheet only. Illegibly-written "wants" will be considered as not having been received. The "Publishers' Weekly" does not hold itself responsible for errors.**

It should be understood that the appearance of advertisements in this column, or elsewhere in the "Publishers' Weekly" does not furnish a guarantee of credit. While it is endeavored to safeguard these columns by withdrawing the privilege of their use from advertisers who are not "good pay," booksellers should take the usual precaution, as to advertisers not known to them, that they would take in making sales to any unknown parties.

A. G., P. O. Box 943, N. Y.

The Historical Magazine for 1864, 1865 and 1866.

Arthur M. Allen, 508 Fulton St., Troy, N. Y.

Hutton, Mathematical Tracts.
Cole, Philosophy of Health.
Marshall, Under the Mendips.

Almy, Bigelow & Washburn, Salem, Mass.

Horne, Napoleon. Routledge.

Amer. Bapt. Pub. Soc., 177 Wabash Ave., Chicago.

The Bible Translated (pamphlet), by S. H. Cone and W. H. Wyckoff.
Memoirs of John Stafford with Memoirs of W. R. Williams as an appendix to same vol.

Amer. Bapt. Pub. Soc., 279 Elm St., Dallas, Tex.

Cramp's History of the Baptist. Pub. by A. B. P. S.

Americus Law Book Co., Americus, Ga. [*Cash.*]

White, Statistics Georgia.
O'Neal, Bench and Bar So. Car., 2 v.
Drayton, Views So. Carolina.
Moultrie, Memoirs Revolution in S. C.
History of Sir Wm. Harrington, by a Lady.
Southern Magazine, any.
Southern Bivouac, any.
Southern Literary Messenger, any.
Debow's Review, any.
Cotton is King and Pro-Slavery Arguments.

Astor Book Shop, 4 Barclay St., N. Y.

Appleton's Annuals, 1872-73.
Walmsley's Electric Current.
Combe, Constitution of Man.
Silliman's Journal, 2d and 3d ser., complete.

Bailey & Sackett, Syracuse, N. Y.

Benj. F. Taylor's Poems.

Wm. M. Bains, 1019 Market St., Phila., Pa.

Huxley, Scientific Memoirs, v. 1, 2.

The Baker & Taylor Co., 33 E. 17th St., N. Y.

2 copies Square of Sevens. Harper.
Life of Walter Harriman, by Amos Hadley. H., M. & Co.
Nichols, Search Light, or, Light on Dark Clouds.

The Balto. Book Co., 301 St. Paul St., Baltimore, Md.

Hopkins, Atlas of Baltimore, v. 2.
Memoirs of Bishop Chase.
Scharf, Delaware.
Bromley's Atlas of Baltimore Co.

Bartlett's Book Store, 33 E. 22d St., N. Y.

Saturday Night, story paper from 1870 to 1890, any v., cheap.
Knickerbocker's New York. Grolier Club.
Herbert Spencer, fine binding.
Marco Polo.
Men, Women and Books, v. 2, Leigh Hunt, cl. Harper, 1847.

Bigham & Smith, Agts., Dallas, Tex.

The Course of Time, by Pollock, any ed.
Opera, or, the Works of Virgil, with notes. Sheldon & Co., '83.

Bonnell, Silver & Co., 24 W. 22d St., N. Y.

Mark and Luke, 1 v., Peloubet.

The Book Shop, 63 Spring St., Rochester, N. Y. [*Cash.*]

Lights and Shadows of Spiritualism, by Home.
Phantasms of the Living, 2 v.
Report of the Seybert Commission.
O'Reilly, History of Rochester, N. Y.
Journals of John Lincklaen, an agent of the Holland Land Company.
Donder, On Refraction of the Eye.

The Boston Book Co., 83 Francis St., Boston, Mass.

Brownson's Quar. Rev., Apr., 1862; Jan., Apr., July, '63; Jan., July, Oct., '64; Apr., '75. $1.00 each.
Mag. of Christian Literature, May, June, Oct., '92. 50 cts. each.

The Bowen-Merrill Co., Indianapolis, Ind.

Browning, Men and Women, 2 v., old ed.
A Mute Singer.

Brentano's, 218 Wabash Ave., Chicago, Ill.

Garden of Pleasure, by E. V. Boyle.

Brentano's, Union Sq., N. Y.

Peppergrass, The Spaewife in Holyrood.
Kipling, v. 12, "Outward Bound" de luxe ed.
Lectures on Real Presence. Pub. by O'Shea.
Wister, Lady with the Rubies. Lippincott.
Matter of Honor. Whittaker.
Appleton, W. S., Crane Family of Chilton. 1868.
Downing, Cottage Residences.
Downing, Landscape Gardening and Country Homes.
Gentle Art of Making Enemies, Whistler.
Mlle. de Maupin, in Eng.
Talbot, Royal Lowrie. Lothrop.

Brentano's, 1015 Pennsylvania Ave., Washington, D. C.

A Mummer's Wife.
Belot, Article 47.
Hearn, Gombo Zhebes.
Lebon and Pelot, France as It Is.
Hanson, Memorable London Houses.
Daudet, Tartarin of Tarascon.
Daudet, Tartarin on the Alps.
Routledge ed., green cl. sides, russet leath. back and corners.

S. E. Bridgman & Co., 108 Main St., Northampton, Mass

Judd, History of Hadley, Mass.
Lyman Genealogy.
Southwick Genealogy.

The Burrows Bros. Co., Cleveland, O.

Smith, Lewis Cass.
Choate, Addresses.
Med. of a Parish Priest. Crowell.
Stone, Some Children's Book Plates.
Dircks, Worcesteranae.
The Book of Book Plates. Pub. by Schultze.
Moring, 50 Book Plates.
Moring, 100 Book Plates.
Any books on book plates.
Motley's Netherlands, v. 3, 4, hf. cf. Murray, 1860.
The Courtier. Scribner.
Wisconsin Hist. Society, v. 5.

J. W. Cadby, 131 Eagle St., Albany, N. Y.

Graham's Magazine and *Casket*, 1839, '40, '53, '57.
Democratic Review, 1854-59.
Eclectic Magazine, 1844-46, 1854-56.
Godey's Lady's Book, 1845-46.
Niles' Weekly Register, v. 60-61.

BOOKS WANTED.—*Continued.*

J. W. Cadby.—*Continued.*

Overland Monthly, Mar., 1883; June, '84. 75 cts. each.
Southern Literary Messenger, any v.
Magazine of Western History, Apr., Oct., 1891.
Burton's Gentleman's Magazine, 1837-38.

Callahan's Old Book Store, 74 W. 2d South, Salt Lake City, U.

A History of the Clan-na-Rory, by Rich. F. Cronnelly.
A History of the Clan Eoghan, by Rich. F. Cronnelly.
The American Irish, by Philip H. Bagenal.
Hist. of the Friendly Sons of St. Patrick.

William J. Campbell, Phila., Pa.

Baker's Early American Engravers.

Campion & Horn, 1001 Chestnut St., Phila., Pa.

Callender's Letters to Alexander Hamilton, King of the Feds.
Schliemann's Excavations, with biographical sketch by Dr. C. Schuchardt. London. 1891.

James J. Chapman, Washington, D. C.

McPherson's Handbooks, '74. '84. '88. in any condition if perfect.

The City Library, Springfield, Mass.

Seebohm, Frederic, English Village Community.
Hicks, C. Stansfeld, Yachts, Boats and Canoes. Forest and Stream Pub. Co., or Lond., 1887.

The A. H. Clark Co., Garfield Bldg., Cleveland, O.

Belknap, New Hampshire.
Century Dictionary and Atlas, 10 v.
Kelton, Indian Names of Places.
Morley, Diderot and the Cyclopedists.
Park, M., Life and Travels.
Slade, Vermont State Papers.
Thompson, History of Vermont.
Vermont history, period 1750-1790, any books on.

The Robert Clarke Co., 31 E. 4th St., Cincinnati, O.

Thaxter, Celia, An Island Garden, ed. illus. in colors.

W. B. Clarke Co., Park and Tremont Sts., Boston, Mass.

Bailey, Horticulture, v. 3, 4.
The Eustace Diamonds.
Sea Shore. Pub. by Roberts.
Century Dictionary.
Baldine, etc., trans. Bulwer-Lytton.
Public Men and Events, by Sargent.

Henry T. Coates & Co., Phila., Pa.

Bliss, Labor Strikes and Facts.

Geo. H. Colby & Co., 82 Main St., Lancaster, N. H.

History of Chester, N. H., by Chase. 1869.

Wm. G. Colesworthy, 66 Cornhill, Boston, Mass.

Book-Lover, nos. 1, 2, 3.

Irving S. Colwell, Auburn, N. Y.

Jimombert's Handbook of English.
Versions of Bible. Randolph.
Century Dict., 10 v., 1902 ed.
Life Jerry McAuley, pap.
Memoirs of Rochambeau.

H. M. Conner, 232 Meridian St., E. Boston, Mass.

Musical Composers, Kady May Martin.
Subject of the Will, Haddock.
Peregrine Pickle, cheap.
Mendeleeff, Principles of Chemistry.

A. J. Crawford, 10th and Pine Sts., St. Louis, Mo.

St. Nicholas Magazine, Sept., 1898.

Crusoe & Co., 81 Vermont St., Brooklyn, N. Y.

Crosby, Alpheus, Zenophon's Anabasis, with lexicon.
Crosby, Alpheus, Sentimental Analysis.

Cushing & Co., 34 W. Baltimore St., Baltimore, Md.

Robinson, Bridge of Glass.
Ammen, J. C., The Talking Deaf Man.

Damrell & Upham, 283 Washington St., Boston, Mass.

Mr. Secretary Pepys.
Edward Dowden's Poems.
The Bus Driver.

F. M. DeWitt, 318 Post St., San Francisco, Cal.

Bret Harte, 1st eds.
Madge Morris's Poems.
Poker Chips, all issued.

Daniel Dunn, 677 Fulton St., Brooklyn, N. Y.

Holbrook, Herpetology, 5 v. Phila., 1842.

G. Dunn & Co., St. Paul, Minn.

Philistine, v. 3, nos. 1, 3, 4, 5, 6; v. 4, nos. 1, 2, 4, 5, 6; v. 5, nos. 2, 3, 5.
Anna Lombard.
History of the Spanish Inquisition.

E. P. Dutton & Co., 31 W. 23d St., N. Y.

Princess Amélie, Latimer. L., B. & Co.
World's Great Classics, Sections 5, 6, either cl. or hf. mor.
Two Gentlemen of Old Touraine.
Bailey, Lesson with Plants. Macmillan.

Peter Eckler, 35 Fulton St., N. Y.

The Perfect Way, by Maitland and Kingsford.
Reincarnation, by E. D. Walker.
Magic White and Black.
Pilgrim and Shrine.

Elder & Shepard, 238 Post St., San Francisco, Cal.

Pamela's Prodigy, a comedy, by Clyde Fitch, $3.50. 1893.
Knighting of the Twins, and Ten Other Tales, by Clyde Fitch, $1.25. 1891.
The Delight Makers, Bandelier.

S. W. Fleming, 32 N. 3d St., Room 8, Harrisburg, Pa.

Precious Stones and Gems, by Streeter. Estes.

Forbes & Wallace, Springfield, Mass.

Gutta Percha Willie, by MacDonald.
Hope of the Gospel, by MacDonald.
Poems, by MacDonald.

Fords, Howard & Hulbert, Bible House, 4th Ave., N. Y. [*Cash.*]

The Man Who Outlived Himself, by A. W. Tourgee.

Gotham Book Concern, 442 W. 58th St., N. Y.

Grasshopper. Pub. in Providence, R. I., will pay good price for copies.

Gregory's Book Store, 116 Union St., Providence, R. I.

Riddell, Plato's Apology, Crito, etc.

Martin I. J. Griffin, 2009 N. 12th St., Phila., Pa.

Ives, Colorado River of the West.
Loew, Agricultural Resources of Arizona.
Book of Common Prayer, U. S. eds.

Harvard Co-operative Society, Cambridge, Mass.

Burnham, History and Uses of Limestones and Marbles.

Hyland Bros., Portland, Ore.

Early Recollections of Washington City, Christian Hines.
Bradford's Letter Book (Plymouth Church Records.)
"Mayflower" and Her Log.
Miracle in Stone, Seiss.
Genealogical Notes of Barnstable Families, rev. by C. F. Swift, 2 v. in 1. Pub. by Goss.
Weems, Life of Marion.
Violet, or, the Cross and Crown.
Barbauld's Lessons, Mrs. Barbauld.

L. Indermark, 3211 Barrett St., St. Louis, Mo. [*Cash.*]

Physical Review, N. Y., v. 1-3; v. 10, no. 1.
Astrophysical Journal, Chicago, v. 1, 2, 9, 10.
Jl. Analyt. Chem., v. 1, no. 3; v. 2, nos. 1, 2.
Jl. Amer. Chem. Soc., Jan.-Mar., 1884; '91, all; Feb., Sept., Oct., Dec., '94; Apr., Dec., '95; Jan.-Mar., '96; all except Aug., Dec., '97; Jan.-July, '98; Aug., 1901.

George W. Jacobs & Co., 103 S. 15th St., Phila., Pa.

Hawke, Constitution and Canons of American P. E. Church.
The Wreck of the "Medusa," cheap, cl.

U. P. James, 127 W. 7th St., Cincinnati, O.

Dod's Electrical Psychology.

Jennings & Pye, 57 Washington St., Chicago, Ill.

Complete set of the Methodist Hymnals, beginning with the Asbury Hymnal.

Jennings & Pye, Kansas City, Mo.

Works of Jas. Arminius, D.D., 3 v., tr. by Nichols and Bagnall. 1853.
Life of Jas. Arminius, by Caspar Brandt, tr. by John Guthrie.

BOOKS WANTED.—Continued.

E. T. Jett Book and News Co., 806 Olive St., St. Louis, Mo.

Goodrich, History of all Nations.
The Lost Atlantis.

E. W. Johnson, 2 E. 42d St., N. Y.

History Presbytery of New York City.
Freeman, Norman Conquest.
Raven, Poe, Dore's illus., folio.
Moore, Life of Byron.
Beddoe's Poet. Works.

H. R. Johnson, 313 Main St., Springfield, Mass.

Manual of Botany of California, by Coulter.
History of Bromfield, Mass.
History of Printing, by Isaiah Thomas.
A Relation or Journal of the Plantation at Plymouth, Mourt.
Early History Chas. James Fox, Trevelyan.

Keating, Box 489, N. Y. City.

Plates wanted, good novels, also short dictionary, 16mo, 64 to 128 pages.

Chas. E. Lauriat Co., 301 Washington St., Boston, Mass.

The Diversions of Holly Cot, by Mrs. Johnstone.
Poe's Works, v. 5, Holland pap., ed. issued by Barrie, or complete set.
Wallack's American Trotting Register, 2 copies each of vols. 1 and 2.
Loyd, Chess Strategy.

Leary's Book Store, 9 S. 9th St., Phila., Pa.

Almanac De Gotha, 1854, '55, '56, '57, '58, '59, '69, '98, 1900, must have all the portraits.

Leggat Bros., 81 Chambers St., N. Y.

Inventions, Writings and Researches of Nikola Tesla.
Live Coals, Talmage.
Freytag, Ingraban.
Smith, Dictionary of Greek and Roman Biography and Mythology.

Henry E. Legler, Milwaukee, Wis. [*Cash.*]

Erskine's Speeches, v. 1, 2, 4. Ridgeway, London, 1813.
Beaconsfield's Speeches, v. 1, ed. by Kebbel. London, 1882.
Father Prout's Reliques.
At the Sign of the Sphinx, Carolyn Wells.

Lemcke & Buechner, 812 Broadway, N. Y.

Wilson, W. H., A Brief Review of Railroad History.
Wilson, W. H., Reminiscences of a Railroad Engineer.

Lib. Univ. California, Berkeley, Cal.

Quincy, History of Harvard University.

The Literary Shop, 506 11th St., N. W., Washington, D. C.

Secret Memoirs, 10 v. ed., v. 7, 8, 8vo, gilt top, uncut, green linen, paper labels. Grolier Society.
The Universal Anthology, v. 24, 27, 28, 29, 30, 31, 32, 33, Westminster ed., brown hf. mor.
Ward, English Poets, v. 3. 12mo, sage cl. Macmillan & Co.
Simmons, Men of Mark.

Little, Brown & Co., 254 Washington St., Boston, Mass.

Recollections of a Private, Wilkinson.
Bourne, Apache Campaign.

George E. Littlefield, 67 Cornhill, Boston, Mass.

Cyrus Woodman Family.
Woodman Family, by J. H. Woodman.

Louisville Book Co., 356 4th Ave., Louisville, Ky.

Twain, Mark, Million Dollar Bank Note.

W. H. Lowdermilk & Co., Washington, D. C.

Moultrie, Memoirs of American Revolution.
Emerson, Indian Myths.
Garden, Anecdotes of the Revolution.

T. J. McBride & Son, 71 Broadway, N. Y.

A Serpent Sin, by A. P. Morris.

Alexander McCance, 1247 Washington St., Boston, Mass.

Mr. and Mrs. Spoopendike.

S. F. McLean & Co., 44 E. 23d St., N. Y.

Life of William Curtis.
Webster's Spelling Book, used in schools in 1835-44.
Old English Reader, by Noah Webster.
Sanders, First, Second, Third and Fourth Readers, used in 1845-55.
Townley Cycle Miracle Plays. Pub. Surtees Society.
Chester Miracle Plays.
York Miracle Plays, Miss Toulmin-Smith ed.
Vanity Fair, v. 4. Periodical Pub., N. Y., 1861.
Mitchell, Stellar and Planetary Worlds.
My Uncle the Curate.

John Jos. McVey, 39 N. 13th St., Phila., Pa.

Moore, Redwood and Proctor's Pharmacy. Lea.
Bell and Redwood's Progress of Medicine. London, 1880.
Paracelsus, stating edition and condition.

F. M. Morris, 171 Madison St., Chicago, Ill.

Steel engraving, A Good Old Rebel.

Noah Farnham Morrison, 893 Broad St., Newark, N. J. [*Cash.*]

Official Record of Union and Confederate Navy, odd vols. or sets.
Hollister, Connecticut, v. 1.

H. H. Morse, 20 Monroe St., Grand Rapids, Mich.

Garret, Suggestions for House Decoration in Painting, Woodwork and Furniture.
Pierce, Co-operative Housekeeping.
Carson, Fifteen Cent Dinners for a Family of Six.

New England Methodist Book Depository, 36 Bromfield St., Boston, Mass.

Short Sayings of Great Men, with historical and explanatory notes, Arthur Bent, 2d ed. J. R. Osgood & Co., Boston, 1882.
Great Truths by Great Authors, with Educationary Aids to Reflections. Lippincott, 1860.
St. Patrick and the Western Apostolic Churches. Pub. in 1857 by the American and Irish Christian Union.
Religion of the Ancient Britains and Irish, not Roman Catholic.
Antiquities of the Jesuits and Sufferings of the Albigenses, etc.

W. W. Nisbet, 12 S. Broadway, St. Louis, Mo.

History of the World's Columbian Exposition at Chicago, 4 v.
Works of Alexander Hamilton, ed. by Lodge.
Autograph Letter of Wm. McKinley.
British Poets, v. 5 only. Edinburgh, 1795.

A. J. Ochs & Co., 1781 Washington St., Boston, Mass.

Tommy Atkins of the Ramchunders, by Robt. Blatchford. Pub. Edw'd Arnold, N. Y.
Science and Health, v. 2, Mrs. Eddy, 2d ed.
Science and Health, v. 2, Mrs. Eddy, 3d ed. 1882.
Trench, On Miracles and Parables, cheap.
Negro or Beast?, Henry Wise. Am. Bible and Bk. Co., St. Louis.
Four Months in Libby Prison and Campaigns Against Atlanta, by J. N. Johnston. Meth. Bk. Concern, Cin., O., 1864.

Martin F. Onnen, 114 5th Ave., N. Y.

Uncommon books on the coloring of bronze.
Books on the battle of Waterloo.
Morris, Wm., Letters on Socialism. London, 1894.
Owen, Rob., Opening Speech and His Reply to Al. Campbell on the Recent Public Discussion in Cincinnati. Cincinnati, 1829.
Peace-Republicans' Manual. New York, 1817.

Daniel O'Shea, 1584 Broadway, N. Y.

White Cross Library, v. 1, by Prentice Mulford.

W. M. Palmer, 20 Monroe St., Grand Rapids, Mich.

Twenty-five Cent Dinners for a Family of Six.
Harley, Air and its Relation to Life.

C. C. Parker, 246 S. Broadway, Los Angeles, Cal. [*Cash.*]

Go Forth and Find, Brainerd.
Christian Science Healing, by Frances Lord.
Message and Papers of the Presidents, 1789-1897. v. 9, Richardson, brown cl.

The Pease-Lewis Co, Drawer S, New Haven, Conn.

Century Dictionary, either 6 or 10 v. ed.
Cantatorium Romanum.
Cross, The Monitor.

BOOKS WANTED.—*Continued.*

E. R. Pelton, 19 E. 16th St., N. Y.

Disinfectants and Disinfections, R. A. Smith. Edinburgh, 1869.
Utility and Application of Heat as a Disinfectant, E. Harris, M.D., 1824-84, 2d ed. of a vol. of pamphlets pub. in Boston, 1860.
Some Modern Disinfectants, E. A. De Schweinitz Wash., U. S. Agriculture Dept., 1897; Year Book, 1896.

Phila. Magazine Depot, 117 N. 13th St., Phila., Pa. [*Cash.*]

Am. Journal of Archaeology and Fine Arts, 1886 to 1896, or odd nos.
Anthropologist, v. 1 to 4, or odd nos.
St. Nicholas, v. 1, or odd nos., and v. 20, or odd nos.
Cassier's Magazine, nos. 2, 12.
Forum, v. 1 to 4, or odd nos.
Am. Hist. Register, 1897, or odd nos.
Am. Mag. of Hist., June, July, 1877; Feb., '83; Mar., '93.
Potter's Am. Monthly, v. 15 to 19, or odd nos.
Mag. of Western Hist., odd nos. of v. 9 to 17.
Overland Monthly, 1873 to '75; 1883 to '85, or odd nos.
Franklyn Institute Journal, 1864 to '67; 1876 to '81; '82, '85, '86, '89 to '92, or odd nos.
Job lots of scarce magazines.

Presb. Bd. of Pub. and S. S. Work, 192 Michigan Ave., Chicago, Ill.

Sinlessness of Jesus, by Ullman.
Set Parker's People's Bible, complete, second-hand.
Memorial of a True Life, by Spear.

Presb. Bd. of Pub. and S. S. Work, 156 5th Ave., N. Y.

Stormonth's Dictionary.

Presb. Bd. of Pub. and S. S. Work, 1319 Walnut St., Phila., Pa.

Stumbling Stones Removed, by Arthur T. Pierson.

G. P. Putnam's Sons, 27 W. 23d St., N. Y.

Vogue, Russian Novelists.
Wolkousky, Russian Hist. and Lit. Lamson.
Rousseau, La Nouvelle Heloise, Eng. trans.
Woodbridge, Technique of Drama.
Smith, New York in 1789.
Wegelin, Early American Plays.
History of Hartford Co., Conn.
Woltmann and Worman, Hist. of Painting, v. 2.
Vincent, Hotel de Rambouillet.
Dictes and Sayings. Cranbrook Press.
De Morgan, On a Pincushion.
Pater, Works, 9 v., de luxe.
Wolseley's Expedition to Red River.
Hegeman, Silence. Dodd.
Adams, Chapters of Erie. Holt.

Fleming H. Revell Co., Chicago, Ill.

London Illustrated News, Coronation number.
Restitution of all Things, Juke.

Geo. H. Rigby, 1113 Arch St., Phila., Pa.

Day's Mathematics.
Sue, Eugene, Rival Races.
Jacollet, Among the Fakirs.
Truesdell, Bottom Facts of Modern Spiritualism.

A. M. Robertson, 126 Post St., San Francisco, Cal.

Napoleon, Lover and Husband, by Masson.
Josephine, Ober.
Lady Windermere's Fan.
A Woman of No Importance.
The Importance of Being in Earnest.
Oscar Wilde's Poems.

Philip Roeder, 616 Locust St., St. Louis, Mo.

Cooke, Virginia Comedians.

The St. Louis News Co., 1008 Locust St., St. Louis, Mo.

Comrade, Youth.
2 copies Nord, E., Dr. Naudier's Young Wife, tr. by B. Gillam.

John E. Scopes, 29 Tweddle Bldg., Albany, N. Y.

American Ancestry, v. 10.
Wilkinson, Memoirs, v. 2 and atlas. Phila., 1816.

Rev. E. L. Shettles, Bryan, Tex.

Word Studies, Vincent.
Lost Cause, Pollard.
Richmond During the War, by a Lady.
History of the War, Draper.
Any book on social life in the South before the war.

John Skinner, 44 N. Pearl St., Albany, N. Y.

The Antiquarian and Gen. Rev., v. 2, ed. by Arthur.

George D. Smith, 50 New St., N. Y.

Riedel, Guide to Mexico.
Roger, Mexico.
Romero, Mexico and U. S.
Resources of Mexico. Honduras.
Lummis, Awakening.
Bancroft, Resources and Development of Mexico.
Fielding's Works, v. 7. N. Y., 1813.

Southern Law Book Co., Columbia, S. C.

Any historical works of South Carolina.

Speyer & Peters, Berlin, N. W. 7, Germany.

Annales de Dermatologie.
Annals of Surgery.
Archiv für Mikroskop. Anatomie.
Archives of Laryngology.
Archives of Pediatrics.
Deutsche Chirurgie.
Journal de l'Anatomie. Robin.
Revue de Chirurgie.
Transactions of Amer. Orthop. Assoc.
Offer sets and single vols. or nos.

P. Stammer, 123 4th Ave., N. Y.

Draper, Intellectual Development of Europe, v. 1.
Richardson, American Literature, v. 2.
Fiske, John, Cosmic Philosophy, v. 2.
Pepys' Diary, v. 2. London, 1854.

F. S. Stedman, Lewis Bldg., Pittsburgh, Pa.

Reade's Female Poets of America.
Griswold's Female Poets.
The Knickerbocker Gallery, ed. of 1848 or 1849. These must have portraits complete and in good condition.
The Library of G. W. Childs.
Life Edgar Allan Poe, by W. Fearing Gill. Widdleton.

Strawbridge & Clothier, Market St., Phila., Pa.

Dawson, Canadian Ice Age.
Rockstro, Life of Handel.

H. H. Timby, Conneaut, O.

Wheedon's Commentary.
Si Klegg.
Christian Union, v. 1, 4, 11, 13.
Story of American Coal, Nicolls.
Goodrich's Universal Hist., 2 v.

C. L. Traver, Trenton, N. J. [*Cash.*]

Lodge, Short History of Eng. Colonies in Am.
Gregg, Shorthand.
Wilkinson, Memoirs, v. 1.

D. Van Nostrand Co., 23 Murray St., N. Y.

The Railroad Problem and its Solution, by Albert Fink.
Freight Rates, by Henry Fink.

Henry K. Van Siclen, 413 W. 22d St., N. Y.

Library of the World's Best Literature, vols., quote binding and cash price.

T. B. Ventres, 597 Fulton St., Brooklyn, N. Y.

Life of Buddha, by Miss Albrus.

John Wanamaker, N. Y.

The Problem of Human Life, by Wilford Hall.
Display, by Jane Taylor.
Little Minister, Maude Adams ed. Pub. Russell.
Castle of Indolence.
Decorative Illustration, Walter Crane.

Geo. E. Warner, Minneapolis, Minn.

Parton, Life of Andrew Jackson.
Williamson, Geo., Gleanings of Leisure Hours.
Books of Neighborhood History.

Alfred Warren, 527 Central Ave., Cincinnati, O.

U. S. Dispensatory, late ed.

The Washington Book Shop, 509 7th St., N. W., Washington, D. C.

Mackey, Masonic Jurisprudence.
A Checkered Life, by J. A. Joyce.

E. A. Werner, 35 Chestnut St., Albany, N. Y.

Proceedings of National Political Conventions.
N. Y. State Insurance Dept. Report, 1882.
Whig and *Tribune* Almanacs, 1839, 39, 40, 40, 41, 41, 42, 42, 43, 43, 44, 44, 46, 47, 49, 50, 1, 1, 2, 3, 4, 60, 4, 6, 9, 80, 9, 90, 7, 9, 1900, 01, 01, 02, 02.

BOOKS WANTED.—Continued.

Woodward & Lothrop, Washington, D. C.

Wellby, M. S., Through Unknown Thibet.
Tom the Money King, by W. O. Stoddard, any ed. will answer. Pub. by Price-McGill Co.

Wm. H. Ziesenitz, Hudson, N. Y.

Confession of a French Bride.
Within the Maze.

BOOKS FOR SALE.

King Bros., 3 4th St., San Francisco, Cal.

Any volume of Bancroft's Histories of Pacific States, shp., $2.50; cl., $2 each.

Martin F. Onnen, 114 5th Ave., N. Y.

United States Geological Survey, 4th, 5th and 7th Annual Report. Per vol., $1.50.
Audebert et Vieillet, Oiseaux dores, 2 v., 190 col. plates, full mor. tooled. $72.00.
Heide, J. v. d., Beschryving der slangbrandspuinten, 1 v., with 18 fine plates representing first fire-engines invented by the author. Amsterdam, 1690. $15.00.
Brandt, Gerard, History of the Reformation, 4 v., calf. London, 1720. $8.00.

HELP WANTED.

WANTED.—Assistant in publishing office for inside and outside work. Must have some experience. Address giving particulars S. S., care of PUBLISHERS' WEEKLY.

COPYRIGHT NOTICES.

LIBRARY OF CONGRESS,
OFFICE OF THE REGISTER OF COPYRIGHTS,
WASHINGTON, D. C.

To wit: *Be it remembered,* That on the 28th day of July, 1902, Mrs. Roxana S. Ridpath, of the United States, hath deposited in this office the title of a book, the title of which is in the following words, to wit: "History of the United States. Prepared especially for Schools on a New and Comprehensive Plan, embracing the Features of Lyman's Historical Chart. By John Clark Ridpath, A.M., LL.D.," the right whereof she claims as proprietor in conformity with the laws of the United States respecting copyrights.

(Signed) HERBERT PUTNAM, *Librarian of Congress.*
By THORVALD SOLBERG, *Register of Copyrights.*
In renewal for 14 years from December 5, 1902.

LIBRARY OF CONGRESS,
OFFICE OF THE REGISTER OF COPYRIGHTS,
WASHINGTON, D. C.

To wit: *Be it remembered,* That on the 2d day of August, 1902, Jean Swinton, Executrix, of New York, N. Y., hath deposited in this office the title of a book, the title of which is in the following words, to wit: "Language Primer. Beginner's Lessons in Speaking and Writing English. By William Swinton, A.M., New York, Cincinnati, Chicago, American Book Company," the right whereof she claims as proprietor in conformity with the laws of the United States respecting copyrights.

(Signed) HERBERT PUTNAM, *Librarian of Congress.*
By THORVALD SOLBERG, *Register of Copyrights.*
In renewal for 14 years from August 3, 1902.

LIBRARY OF CONGRESS,
OFFICE OF THE REGISTER OF COPYRIGHTS,
WASHINGTON, D. C.

To wit: *Be it remembered,* That on the 2d day of August, 1902, Jean Swinton, Executrix, of New York, N. Y., hath deposited in this office the title of a book, the title of which is in the following words, to wit: "Outlines of the World's History. Ancient, Mediæval, and Modern. With special relation to the History of Civilization and the Progress of Mankind. For use in the higher classes in Public Schools, Academies, Seminaries, etc. By William Swinton, New York, Cincinnati, Chicago, American Book Company," the right whereot she claims as proprietor in conformity with the laws of the United States respecting copyrights.

(Signed) HERBERT PUTNAM, *Librarian of Congress.*
By THORVALD SOLBERG, *Register of Copyrights.*
In renewal for 14 years from September 14, 1902.

LIBRARY OF CONGRESS,
OFFICE OF THE REGISTER OF COPYRIGHTS,
WASHINGTON, D. C.

Class A, XXc, No. 31662.—To wit: *Be it remembered,* That on the 26th day of April, 1902, Laura Abbott Buck, of New York, N. Y., hath deposited in this office the title of a book, the title of which is in the following words, to wit: "Captain William Kidd and others of the Buccaneers. By John S. C. Abbott. New York, Dodd, Mead & Company," the right whereof she claims as proprietor in conformity with the laws of the United States respecting copyrights.

(Signed) HERBERT PUTNAM, *Librarian of Congress.*
By THORVALD SOLBERG, *Register of Copyrights.*
In renewal for 14 years from October 8, 1902.

SPECIAL NOTICES.

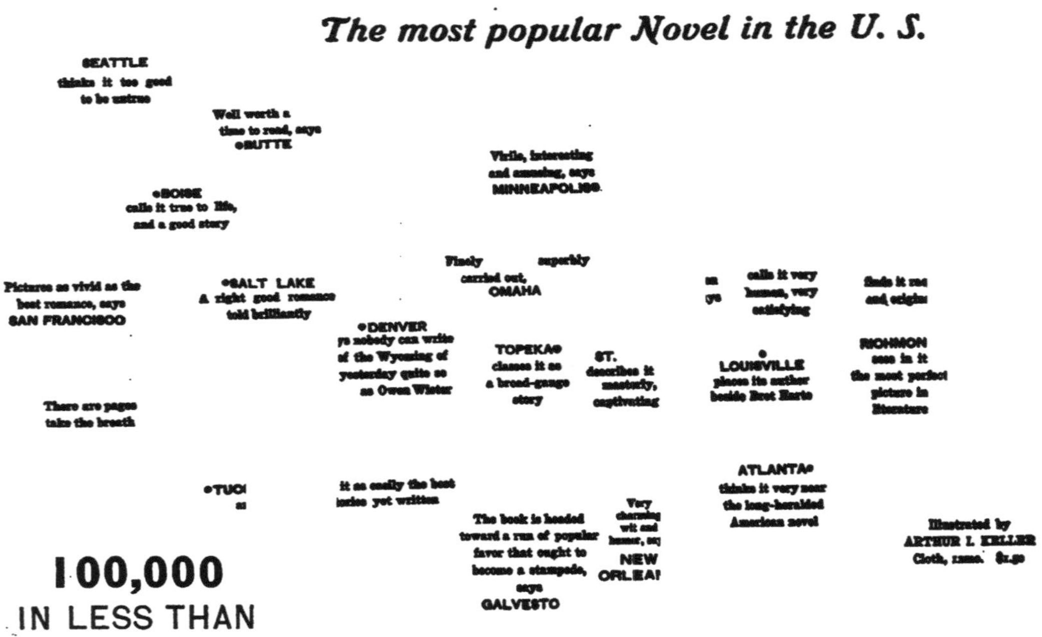
THE VIRGINIAN By Mr. OWEN WISTER
The most popular Novel in the U. S.
SEATTLE thinks it too good to be untrue
Well worth a time to read, says BUTTE
Virile, interesting and amusing, says MINNEAPOLIS
BOISE calls it true to life, and a good story
Finely superbly carried out, OMAHA
Pictures as vivid as the best romance, says SAN FRANCISCO
SALT LAKE A right good romance told brilliantly
DENVER ys nobody can write of the Wyoming of yesterday quite so as Owen Wister
TOPEKA classes it as a broad-gauge story
ST. describes it masterly, captivating
calls it very human, very satisfying
LOUISVILLE places its author beside Bret Harte
finds it rea and origin
RICHMON sees in it the most perfect picture in literature
There are pages take the breath
it as easily the best tories yet written
The book is headed toward a run of popular favor that ought to become a stampede, says GALVESTO
Very charming wit and humor, say NEW ORLEA
ATLANTA thinks it very near the long-heralded American novel
Illustrated by ARTHUR I. KELLER
Cloth, 12mo. $1.50
100,000
IN LESS THAN

Do it Now ! ! !

Anticipate the FALL and HOLIDAY Orders
By laying in an ample stock of

Holman Family and Teachers' Bibles and Testaments at once.

Bountiful Harvests everywhere are sure indications of good business.

Our Reputation is NEARLY A CENTURY OLD and our publications are always in demand. Our latest addition to the popular series of HOLMAN PUBLICATIONS is a new

SELF-PRONOUNCING AGATE TEXT BIBLE

Good clear type, yet small and compact. 32mo. size. Sure to be the most popular and best selling Bible for the little folks.

PUBLISHERS!

ARE you satisfied with your bookbinder? If so, are you satisfied with his fancy prices? I can satisfy you with both. Investigate my statement in justice to your own interests. Look over my plant and ask those publishing houses who patronize me. Send your dummies and I will show you what I can do.

H. WOLFF,

92-98 Centre Street, 143-147 Leonard Street,

NEW YORK

By Sydney George Fisher

The True History of the American Revolution

These are the real facts of the days of 1776. Mr. Fisher has some things to tell about the conduct of the War of the Revolution, its chief figures, and the reasons for its outcome, which will startle every reader of American history.

24 illustrations. Crown 8vo. Cloth, decorated. *Net* . $2.00
Postage, 14 c. extra.

By Clara E. Laughlin

Stories of Authors' Loves

Charlotte Brontë

Nothing in fiction excels the fascination of these romances of real men and women whom we all know by their writings. The volumes are a chronicle of fact, but hold all the charm of a novel. They are superbly illustrated with over 40 photogravures from rare portraits, etc.

Two Volumes. Illustrated. Handsomely bound, in box, *Net* . $3.00
Three-quarters morocco, *Net*. $6.00
Postage, 19 c. extra.

By Jack London

A Daughter of the Snows

A strong and extremely dramatic story. Its plot is unique, its characters boldly drawn, and the love interest intense. The first full length novel from a writer whose tales "The Son of the Wolf," and "The God of His Fathers," etc., have won him much popularity as well as recognition from the first critics. The book is beautifully illustrated in colors from drawings by F. C. Yohn, and is handsomely bound.

Illustrated. 12mo. Decorated cloth . . $1.50

By Cyrus Townsend Brady

Woven with the Ship

Mr. Brady's thousands of readers will derive fresh pleasure from this his new book. It has an intensely interesting plot and something happens on every page. In addition to the novel, which is the most sympathetic love story he has yet written, there are a number of tales in his best manner. The book has stunning drawings by Christy, Leyendecker, Glackens, Parkhurst, and Crawford, and has a striking design in colors.

Illustrated. 12mo. Decorated cloth . $1.50

Publishers—J. B. Lippincott Company—Philadelphia

THE

WITH WHICH IS INCORPORATED

The American Literary Gazette and Publishers' Circular.

[ESTABLISHED 1852.]

PUBLICATION OFFICE, 298 BROADWAY, NEW YORK.

Entered at the Post-Office at New York, N. Y., as second-class matter.

VOL. LXII., No. 11. NEW YORK, September 13, 1902. WHOLE No. 1598

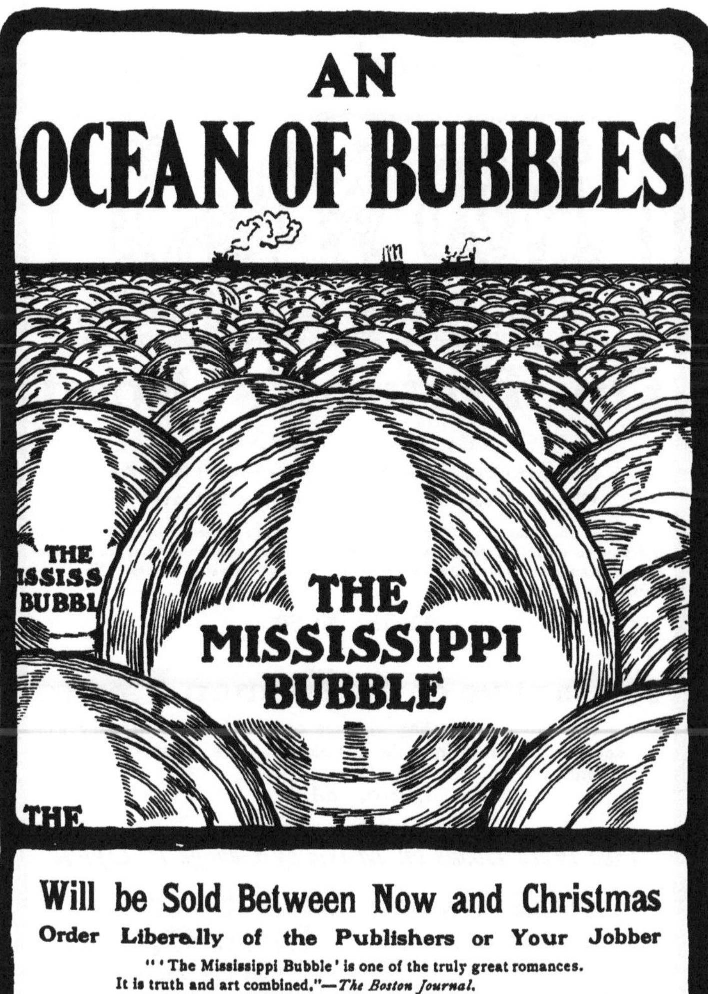

Will be Sold Between Now and Christmas

Order Liberally of the Publishers or Your Jobber

"'The Mississippi Bubble' is one of the truly great romances. It is truth and art combined."—*The Boston Journal.*

Miss Gilder, editor of *The Critic*, says: "It is one of the best novels that has come out of America in many a day."

THE BOWEN-MERRILL COMPANY, *Publishers*

The Publishers' Weekly.

SEPTEMBER 13, 1902.

INDEX TO ADVERTISERS PAGE

NOTES IN SEASON.

THE OFFICE OF THE PUBLISHERS' WEEKLY has just ready the Index volume of "The Publishers' Trade List Annual" for 1902. It is an octavo volume of 1114 double column pages and contains 140,000 references to the catalogues of 247 publishers represented in the main volume.

DODD, MEAD & CO. have just ready "Temporal Power," a study in supremacy, albeit not that of the Pope, by Marie Corelli; "The Blood-Tax," a military romance of the present day, with the scene laid in Germany, by Dorothea Gerard; "Tom Tad," tracing Tom's development as a boy and man in the Middle West, including a dramatic incident of the Ohio River flood of '84, by William Henry Venable; "The Defendant," wherein the author, G. K. Chesterton, has a good word to say for latter-day evils, such as penny dreadfuls, publicity, slang, baby-worship, etc.; and "The Founder of Mormonism," a psychological study of Joseph Smith, Junior, his elusive mental conditions and extraordinary life, by I. Woodbridge Riley.

THE BOWEN-MERRILL COMPANY will publish on the 15th inst. "The Long Straight Road," a story of the lights and shades of life in a great American city, by George Horton, author of "Like Another Helen." They will publish on the 20th inst. "The Loom of Life," a new novel, by Charles Frederic Goss, author of "The Redemption of David Corson," etc. The story is of a young girl, taught to believe in the old Greek myths, who revenges a wrong done to her with life-long persecution. Finally, however, she comes to believe that retribution for wrongdoing belongs to God, and is forced to realize that on earth peace and happiness can be obtained only by forgiving one another's sins. The book shows the same love and sympathy for the many moods of nature which characterizes "The Redemption of David Corson."

HOUGHTON, MIFFLIN & CO. will publish on the 20th inst. a revised and illustrated edition of Alice M. Bacon's "Japanese Girls and Women," with such additions to each chapter as the conditions of this rapidly-changing country have made necessary; "The Right Princess," a story founded on Christian Science, by Clara Louise Burnham; "A Downrenter's Son," by Ruth Hall, the story of an attempt made in New York City sixty years ago to abolish rents; "The Flag on the Hilltop," a story, for boys, of a Southern boy who is placed under the care of a Northern uncle during the Civil War; "Eternalism, a theory of infinite justice," a stimulating argument for the pre-existence of the soul, by Orlando J. Smith; also, "Nathaniel Hawthorne," by Professor George E. Woodberry, a new volume in the *American Men of Letters* series.

CHARLES SCRIBNER'S SONS publish to-day Henry Norman's important work on "All the Russias," with over 100 illustrations; "King Mombo," by Paul du Chaillu, a graphic story for young readers of the author's personal adventures in the romantic region of Equatorial Africa, with illustrations by Victor Perard; "Jeb Hutton," a story for young people of the adventures of a Georgia boy, by James B. Connolly, with illustrations by M. J. Burns; "Shakespeare and Voltaire," by Professor T. R. Lounsberry, who treats of the part played by Voltaire in Shakespearian controversy; "The Incarnation of the Lord," by the Rev. Charles A. Briggs; also, "Human Nature and the Social Order," by Charles Horton Cooley, all of which were fully described by us last week. They have postponed the publication of Richard Harding Davis's new book, "Captain Macklin," until September 20.

WEEKLY RECORD OF NEW PUBLICATIONS.

☞ **Beginning with the issue of July 5, 1902, the titles of *net* books published under the rules of the American Publishers' Association are preceded by a double asterisk **, and the word net follows the price. The titles of *fiction* (not net) published under the rules are preceded by a dagger †. *Net* books not covered by the rules, whether published by members of the American Publishers' Association or not, are preceded by a single asterisk, and the word net follows the price.** ☜

The abbreviations are usually self-explanatory. c. after the date indicates that the book is copyrighted; if the copyright date differs from the imprint date, the year of copyright is added. Books of foreign origin of which the edition (annotated, illustrated, etc.) is entered as copyright, are marked c. ed.; translations, c. tr.; n. p., in place of price, indicates that the publisher makes no price, either net or retail, and quotes prices to the trade only upon application.

A colon after initial designates the most usual given name, as: A: Augustus; B: Benjamin; C: Charles; D: David; E: Edward; F: Frederic; G: George; H: Henry; I: Isaac; J: John; L: Louis; N: Nicholas; P: Peter; R: Richard; S: Samuel; T: Thomas; W: William.

Sizes are designated as follows: F. (folio: over 30 centimeters high); Q. (4to: under 30 cm.); O. (8vo: 25 cm.); D. (12mo: 20 cm.); S. (16mo: 17½ cm.); T. (24mo: 15 cm.); Tt. (32mo: 12½ cm.); Fe. 48mo: 10 cm.). Sq., obl., nar., designate square, oblong, narrow books of these heights.

****Akers**, Elizabeth, [*Mrs.* E. M. Allen.] The sunset song and other verses. [Autograph ed.] Bost., Lee & Shepard, 1902. c. 12+313 p. D. cl., $1.20 net; edition de luxe, $3 net.

A collection of poems by the celebrated author of "Rock me to sleep." Her autograph is on every title-page. Gotten up in holiday style, with cover design, pen and ink head-band and tail-piece by Grace Barton Allen.

Allen, G: Hoyt. Uncle George's letters to the Garcia club. Clinton, N. Y., Cedarine Allen Co., [1902.] c. 2+194 p. il. D. cl., $1.

Familiar letters written to a club of young men, describing a business trip in the United States, in the Orient and in the Philippines.

American digest: a complete digest of all reported Am. cases from the earliest time to 1896. Century ed. v. 34, Manufacturers-miscarriage. St. Paul, West Pub. Co., 1902. c. 8 p. 3254 columns, O. shp., $6.

American state reports, cont. the cases of general value and authority subsequent to those contained in the "Am. decisions" and the "Am. reports," decided in the courts of last resort of the several states; sel., rep. and annot. by A. C. Freeman. v. 85. San Francisco, Bancroft-Whitney Co., 1902. c. 1053 p. O. shp., $4.

Andersen, Hans Christian, *ed.* Hans Andersen's best stories; ed. and adapted for pupils of third reader grade. N. Y., University Publishing Co., [1902.] c. 2-123 p. D. (Standard literature ser., no. 52.) pap., 12½c.

†**Andersen**, Hans Christian. Hans Andersen's fairy tales; tr. from the Danish by Carl Siewers; il. with over eighty text cuts, and twenty-four full-page half-tones by Jos. J. Mora. Bost., Dana Estes & Co., [1902.] c. 4+188 p. il. 4°, cl., $1.50.

Arabian nights' entertainments. History of Sinbad the sailor; from the Arabian nights' entertainments; printed in the easy reporting style of phonography in accordance with the "Manual of phonography," by Benn Pitman and Jerome B. Howard. Cin., O., The Phonographic Institute Co., [1902.] 45 p. S. pap., 25 c.

Atkinson, E: Social bacteria and economic microbes, wholesome and noxious: a study in smalls; reprinted from the *Popular Science Monthly*, August, 1902. Bost., E: Atkinson, 1902. 217-327 p. O. pap., n. p.

†**Ballin**, *Mrs.* Ada S. From cradle to school. N. Y., Dutton, 1902. 12°, cl., $1.25.

Banks, L: Albert, *D.D.* The king's stewards. N. Y., Amer. Tract Society, [1902.] c. 615 p. por. O. cl., $1.25.

Thirty sermons, the book taking its title from the first, "The king's stewards."

Bell, *Mrs.* Euphemia Young. Beautiful Bermuda [from different viewpoints;] just what you want to know. N. Y., E. H. Bell, 1902. c. 145 p. il. pl. maps, plans, 16°, cl., $1; pap., 50 c.; pap., with map of Bermuda, 60 c.

Bellord, Ja., *D.D.* A new catechism of Christian doctrine and practice for school and home use. Notre Dame, Ind., The Ave Maria, 1902. 8+9-115 p. S. pap., 10 c.

****Benton**, C: E. As seen from the ranks: a boy in the Civil war. N. Y., Putnam, 1902. [Jl.] 12+292 p. D. cl., $1.25 net.

A private soldier's account of what he saw of the Civil War, as a member of the 150th New York State Volunteers.

†**Bernstein**, Herman. In the gates of Israel: stories of the Jews. N. Y., J. F. Taylor & Co., 1902. [Je.] c. 3-316 p. D. cl., $1.50.

Contents: Soreh Rivke's vigil; The messenger of the community; The awakening; Alone; The sinners; The straight hunchback; The marriage-broker; The artist; A jealousy cure; The disarmed reformer; A Ghetto romance.

****Brainerd**, Edna S. Millicent in Dreamland; il. by Etheldred B. Barry. Bost., L. C. Page & Co., 1903, [1902.] c. 94 p. il. 12°, (Cosy corner ser.) cl., 40 c. net.

†**Bridgman**, Clara. The bairn's coronation book; written by Clara Bridgman; il. by C: Robinson. N. Y., Dutton, 1902. 120 p. 24°, cl., 60 c.

****Brooks**, Amy. Dorothy Dainty; il. by the author. Bost., Lee & Shepard, 1902. c. 4+203 p. D. cl., 80 c. net.

Brumbaugh, Martin Grove. Brumbaugh's standard readers: First, Second, Third, Fourth, Fifth. Phil., Christopher Sower Co., 1899-1902. c. 5 v., 128; 160; 224; 400; 496 p. il. por. D. hf. leath., 1st., 22 c.; 2d, 33 c.; 3rd, 45 c.; 4th, 67 c.; 5th, 83 c.

****Carpenter**, Kate E. The story of Joan of Arc for boys and girls, as Aunt Kate told it; il. by Amy Brooks and from famous paintings. Bost., Lee & Shepard, 1902. [Ag.] c. 7+184 p. map. D. cl., 80 c. net.

The story of Joan of Arc told in simple language by a young aunt to her nephew aged 11 and her two nieces, aged 10 and 8. They are allowed to ask many questions, to look up places on the map relative to the story, etc.

Chambers, Alfred B., *ed.* Lee's American automobile annual: a handbook for all interested in horseless vehicles. 1902 ed. Chic., Laird & Lee, [1902.] c. 3+7-275 p. il. diagr., 16°, leath., $1.

****Chambers**, Rob. W. Outdoorland: a story for children; il. in col. by Reginald Birch. N. Y., Harper, 1902. [S.] c. 8+106 p. O. cl., $1.50 net.
A number of stories, in which children talk with the plants and animals and insects and gain much information in natural history.

Chesterfield, *Earl of*, [Philip Dormer Stanhope.] Lord Chesterfield's letters to his son; selected and ed., with introd. and notes by Jos. B. Seabury. N. Y., Silver, Burdett & Co., 1902. c. 3-170 p. por. D. (Silver ser. of classics.) cl., 35 c.

****Chesterton**, G. K. The defendant. N. Y., Dodd, Mead & Co., 1902. 2+131 p. D. cl., $1.25 net.
In an introduction, the author humorously offers his reasons for defending the things not generally liked. Following are special defences of "penny dreadfuls," rash vows, skeletons, publicity, nonsense, planets, China shepherdesses, useful information, heraldry, ugly things, farce, humility, slang, baby-worship, detective stories and patriotism.

****Clarke**, Sarah J, ["Penn Shirley," *pseud.*] Boy Donald and his hero; il. by Bertha G. Davidson. Bost., Lee & Shepard, 1902. [Ag.] c. 154 p. S. (Boy Donald ser.) cl., 60 c. net.

***Colorado.** *Ct. of appeals.* Reports, including part of the Ap. term and all of the Sept. term, 1900. J: A. Gordon, rep. v. 15. N. Y., Banks Law Pub. Co., 1902. c. 16+690 p. O. shp., $5 net.

****Comrie**, Margaret S. A loyal Huguenot maid. Phil., G: W. Jacobs & Co., [1902.] [Ag.] c. 5+354 p. il. D. (Pastime and adventure ser.) cl., $1 net.
A romance of the 17th century, with its scene in France. The historical setting affords a graphic picture of the French Huguenots, their persecutions, their wanderings, their sufferings, their loyalty to their faith, etc.

****Comstock**, Harriet T. A boy of a thousand years ago; il. by G: Varian. Bost., Lee & Shepard, 1902. [Ag.] c. 196 p. D. cl., 80 c. net.
The story of Alfred the Great told for young people.

Conant, R. W., *comp.* Theodore Roosevelt. Chic., Orville Brewer Publishing Co., [1902.] 3-30 p. por. O. (Student's ser. of four penny classics.) pap., 4 c.

****Conrad**, Jos. Typhoon; il. by Maurice Greiffenhagen. N. Y., Putnam, 1902. c. 4+205 p. D. cl., $1 net.
A sea story, rich in adventure.

†Corelli, Marie. Temporal power: a study in supremacy. N. Y., Dodd, Mead & Co., 1902. [Ag.] c. 6+559 p. D. cl., $1.50.
It is of the temporal power of kings, and not of Popes, of which Miss Corelli writes. The King of her story, in order to learn the true secret of the discontent of his people, joins a socialistic secret society, falls in love with the queen of the socialists, draws the lot to kill the King, himself, etc.

***Crane**, Eliz. G. The imperial republic: a drama of the day. N. Y., Grafton Press, [1902.] c. 122 p. D. cl., $1 net.
A drama, cast in the form of the history of stirring political events in an imaginary republic; it is the exponent of a belief in the principles of independence, liberty, and democracy, on which our government is founded, and, from the author's point of view, it paints in startling colors the course of the administration of the republic with regard to expansion.

***Cuyler**, Theodore Ledyard, *D.D.* Recollections of a long life: an autobiography. N. Y., Baker & Taylor Co., [1902.] [S.] c. 7+356 p. pors. D. cl., $1.50 net.
Dr. Cuyler is the only one living of the great Brooklyn pastors who, in the last half of the nineteenth century, were famous throughout the world. As a preacher, pastor and author his active life has brought him in contact with the most famous personages at home and abroad. His early life, his travels, his associations with the great writers, statesmen, temperance workers, revivalists and soldiers, his anecdotes of these men, and his account of his home life and church work are told in this fascinating life story.

***Cuyler**, Theodore Ledyard, *D.D.* Help and good cheer. N. Y., Baker & Taylor Co., 1902. [S.] c. 3+170 p. D. cl., $1 net.
A series of brief messages addressed by the venerable Brooklyn pastor to his old friends and all who are in need of help and strengthening.

****Darling**, Mary Greenleaf. A girl of this century: a continuation of "We four girls"; il. by Lilian Crawford True. Bost., Lee & Shepard, 1902. [Ag.] c. 7+264 p. D. cl., $1 net.

De Laurence, Lauron W: The Bible defended; the Holy Scriptures upheld: a reply to Pearson. Chic., F. J. Drake & Co., [1902.] c. 182 p. 1 il. D. cl., $1.
Contents: Introduction; The Bible defended; The miracles of Christ; Cures that have been made by the divine spirit of God acting through true Christians; Sparks of divine wisdom from Christian writers.

†Desmond, Harry W. The heart of woman: the love story of Catrina Rutherford contained in writings of Alexander Adams transmitted to Harry Desmond. N. Y., J. F. Taylor & Co., 1902. [Je] c. 5+311 p. il. D. cl., $1.50.
A story laid in New York during the early days of the Revolution, concerning a man and two women both of whom the man loves in varying degree. Many of the subsidiary figures are historical characters and there are scenes in both armies and on a prison ship. The plot hinges on the effort of a British sympathizer to injure the hero by means of the woman whom both love.

****Dodge**, Mary Abigail, ["Gail Hamilton," *pseud.*] Chips, fragments and vestiges; coll. and arr. by H. Augusta Dodge. Bost., Lee & Shepard, 1902. [Ag.] c. 9+224 p. por. D. cl., $1.20 net.
Short poems and verses written by "Gail Hamilton" from early childhood and through her life; gathered together by her sister.

Donner, Herman Montague. English lyrics of a Finnish harp. Bost., Richard G. Badger, 1902. c. 72 p. D. bds., $1.25.

Dorothy Vernon; or, the beauty of Haddon Hall: [a novel.] Chic., M. A. Donohue & Co., [1902.] c. 311 p. 12°, cl., $1.25; pap., 35 c.

Douglas, Ja. M. The riding master, and other stories. N. Y., F. T. Neely, [1902.] c. 9+135 p. D. cl., $1.

****Emerson**, Edwin, *jr.* A history of the nineteenth century, year by year; with an introd. by Georg Gottfried Gervinus; il. with sixteen colored pls. and thirty-two full-

page half-tone cuts and two maps. N. Y., Dodd, Mead & Co., 1902. c. 3 v., pl. (partly col.,) por. maps, 12°, cl., $3.60 net.
The introduction is G. G. Gervinus' "Einleitung in die geschichte des neunzehnten jahrhunderts" (Leipzig, 1853) tr. by M. Magnus.

Encyclopaedia Britannica. The new volumes of the Encyclopædia Britannica constituting, in combination with the existing volumes of the ninth edition, the tenth edition. In 11 v. v. 1-4. N. Y., The Encyclopædia Britannica Co., 1902. c. il. pl. diagr., 4°, cl., (for 11 v.,) $65; ½ mor., $75; ¾ leath., $90; full mor., $110.

Farmer, Fannie Merritt. The Boston cooking school cook book. New rev ed., with an appendix of three hundred recipes. Bost., Little, Brown & Co., 1902. c. 30+644 p. il. 12°, cl., $2.

†**Farrow**, G: E: The new Panjandrum; il. by Alan Wright. N. Y., Dutton, 1902. 12°, cl., $1.50.

†**Fenn**, G: Manville. Old gold; or, the cruise of the Jason Brig. N. Y., Dutton, 1902. 416 p. il. 8°, cl., $1.50.

****Fernald**, Ja. Champlin, *comp.* Comprehensive standard dictionary of the English language; abridged from "Funk & Wagnalls Standard dictionary" of the English language. N. Y., Funk & Wagnalls Co., 1902. c. 8+534 p. il. D. cl., $1 net.
Gives in concise and convenient form the orthography, pronunciation, meaning, and etymology of over 38,000 words and phrases, with over 800 pictorial illustrations.

Fiske, G: B., *comp.* Poultry appliances and handicraft; how to make and use labor-saving devices; with descriptive plans for food and water supply building and miscellaneous needs; also treats on artificial incubation and brooding. N. Y., Orange Judd Co., [1902.] c. 8+120 p. il. D. cl., 50 c.

French, Anna Warner. His story, their letters; [*Anon.*]: a prologue by F. D. B. Chic., F. J. Drake & Co., [1902.] c. 141 p. 1 il. D. cl., $1.
A story told mostly in letters and dialogues.

Geare, Randolph I. A list of the publications of the United States National Museum, (1875-1900;) including the annual reports, proceedings, bulletins, special bulletins, and circulars; with index to titles. Wash., D. C., Government Print. Office, 1902. 5+168 p. O. cl., 60 c.; pap., 10 c.

†**Gerard**, Dorothea, [*now Mme.* Longard de Longarde.] The blood-tax. N. Y., Dodd, Mead & Co., 1902. [Ag.] c. 2+316 p. D. cl., $1.50.
A military romance of the present day, the scene of which is laid in Germany. The hero is a dragoon officer, a splendid young giant devoted heart and soul to his profession, whose ruin and disgrace, brought about by circumstances utterly beyond his control, appeal strongly to one's sympathies.

†**Green**, Evelyn Everett. Princess Fairston: a history of the days of Charles I.; il. by F. H. Michael. N. Y., Dutton, 1902. 252 p. 12°, cl., $1.25.

†**Grier**, Sydney C., [*pseud.* for Hilda Greig.] A crowned queen: the romance of a minister of state. Bost., L. C. Page & Co., 1902. [Je.] c. 2+590 p. D. cl., $1.25; pap., 50 c.
The name "Sydney C. Grier" is the pseudonym of Miss Hilda Greig, an Englishwoman, who has been writing novels since 1894. Heretofore only one of her books, "The Prince of the captivity," has been reprinted in America. They are all interesting novels of English life, or of English political questions. The works that follow with "A crowned queen" are now issued in a uniform binding, in a box.

†**Grier**, Sydney C., [*pseud.* for Hilda Greig.] His Excellency's English governess. Bost., L. C. Page & Co., 1902. [Je.] c. 6+367 p. D. cl., $1.25; pap., 50 c.

†**Grier**, Sydney C., [*pseud.* for Hilda Greig.] In furthest Ind: the narrative of Mr. Edward Carlyon of Ellswether. Bost., L. C. Page & Co., 1902. [Je.] c. 6+365 p. D. cl., $1.25; pap., 50 c.

†**Grier**, Sydney C., [*pseud.* for Hilda Greig.] The kings of the East: a romance of the near future. Bost., L. C. Page & Co., 1902. 6+363 p. D. cl., $1.25; pap., 50 c.

†**Grier**, Sydney C., [*pseud.* for Hilda Greig.] Like another Helen. Bost., L. C. Page & Co., 1902. [Je.] c. 6+467 p. D. cl., $1.25; pap., 50 c.

†**Grier**, Sydney C., [*pseud.* for Hilda Greig.] Peace with honour. Bost., L. C. Page & Co., 1902. [Je.] c. 5+413 p. D. cl., $1.25; pap., 50 c.

†**Grier**, Sydney C., [*pseud.* for Hilda Greig.] The warden of the Marches. Bost., L. C. Page & Co., 1902. [Je.] c. 4+327 p. il. D. cl., $1.25; pap., 50 c.

****Hall**, *Mrs.* Florence Marion Howe. The correct thing in good society. [New ed.] Bost., Dana Estes & Co., [1902.] c. 361 p. nar. S. cl., 75 c. net.
Fourteen years have elapsed since the first edition of this little book was published. The author has revised it with much care, giving new customs and fashions, while not necessarily condemning the old.

Hancock, Tyre. Church error; or, instrumental music condemned. Dallas, Tex., Tyre Hancock, 1902. c. 72 p. D. pap., 35 c.

Harrington, *Mrs.* Rose Martha, ["Felix St. Xavier," *pseud.*] Conservation of the natural tree-cover. The water systems of the earth. Arid lands. N. Y., Mrs. Rose M. Harrington, [1902.] c. 27 p. D. pap., 50 c.
Papers on forestry.

Harrison, *Mrs.* Mary St. Leger Kingsley, ["Lucas Malet," *pseud.*] The wages of sin; il. by W. E. B. Starkweather. [New ed.] N. Y., R. F. Fenno & Co., 1902. c. 628 p. 1 il. D. cl., $1.50.

Hartfield, T: Walter, *comp.* The world-wide travellers' cipher code for foreign and domestic use. N. Y., G: Watkins, [1902.] 508 p. 16°, cl., per pair, $2.50.

****Hayens**, Herbert. One of the red shirts: a story of Garibaldi's men. Phil., G: W. Jacobs & Co., [1902.] [Ag.] c. 5+368 p. il. O. cl., $1 net.

†**Higgins**, Eliz. Out of the West: a novel. N. Y., Harper, 1902. [S.] c. 4+316 p. D. cl., $1.50.
A novel, embracing the career of a young American in the west. It tells his experiences, the love affair that exerts the one great influence in his life, his rise to power, temptation, struggle, and final victory.

*Hilbert, D: The foundations of geometry; authorized tr. by E. J. Townsend. Chic., Open Court Publishing Co., 1902. c. 7+132 p. diagr., 12°, cl., $1 net.
The original formed the first part of "Festschrift zur feier der enthüllung des Gauss-Weber-denkmals in Göttingen, Grundlagen der geometrie," with the additions made by the author in the French translation, Paris, 1901, incorporated.

Hodgson, Fred T. Modern carpentry: a practical manual. Chic., F: J. Drake & Co., [1902.] c. 2-193 p. il. D. cl., $1.
The sub-title reads: "A new and complete guide containing hundreds of quick methods for performing work in carpentry, joining and general wood work, written in a simple, every-day style that does not bewilder the workingman, illustrated with hundreds of diagrams which are especially made so that anyone can follow them without difficulty."

**Hogan, Louise E. Shimer, ["Mrs. J: L. Hogan."] Children's diet in home and school; with classified recipes and menus: a reference book for parents, nurses, teachers, women's clubs, and physicians. Phil., H: T. Coates & Co., 1902. c. 6+176 p. S. cl., 50 c. net.

Hoogstraat, Moree. E. v. For bush or bonnet? Il. by Rob. L. Stearns. N. Y., Abbey Press, [1902.] c. 2+231 p. D. cl., $1.25.
A story, suggested by a woman's hat adorned by a white bird, which shut off at a musicale, the writer's view of the stage. The book not only teaches a lesson about birds, but shows knowledge of their habits, etc.

Hopkins, G: Irving. Inductive plane geometry; with numerous exercises, theorems, and problems for advance work. New rev. ed. Bost., Heath, 1902. c. 6+208 p. diagr., 12°, hf. leath. 75 c.

Hunt, Violet Brooke. The story of Westminster Abbey: being some account of that ancient foundation, its builders, and those who sleep therein. N. Y., Dutton, 1902. 12+356 p. 12°, cl., $2.

Hunter, S: J: Elementary studies in insect life. Topeka, Kan., Crane & Co., 1902. c. 18+334 p. il. col. pl., 12°, cl., $1.25.

Illinois. *Appellate cts.* Reports of cases, with a directory of the judiciary department of the state, corrected to the 25th of July, 1902, and a table of cases reviewed by the supreme court to the date of the publication of this v. v. 101, 1902; ed. by Martin L. Newell. Chic., Callaghan & Co., 1902. c. 26+689 p. O. shp., $3.75.

Illinois. *Supreme ct.* Reports of cases, v. 195; cont. cases in which opinions were filed in Feb. and Apr., 1902, and cases in which rehearings were denied at the Apr. term, 1902. I: Newton Phillips, rep. Springfield, I: Newton Phillips, 1902. c. 701 p. O. shp., $2.25.

Iowa. The law of taxation; including a comparison of that law with municipal assessments in that state and references to the revenue systems of Minn., No. Dak., So. Dak., and Wis., by Edwin A. Jaggard. St. Paul, Keefe-Davidson Law Bk. Co., 1902. c. 26+1040 p. O. shp., $7.50.

Ireland, Alleyne. China and the powers; chapters in the history of Chinese intercourse with western nations. Bost., Laureus Maynard, 1902. c. 10+140 p. 8°, cl., $2 net. (Limited to 150 copies.)

*Jadassohn, S. A manual of single, double, triple and quadruple counterpoint; from the 3d rev. German ed., by Th. Baker. N. Y., G. Schirmer, 1902. 5+137 p. O. cl., $1.75 net.

**James, Martha. Tom Winstone—"Wide Awake": a story for boys; il. by W. Herbert Dunton. Bost., Lee & Shepard, 1902. [Ag.] c. 234 p. il. D. cl., 80 c. net.

Johnson, Shirley Everton. The cult of the purple rose: a phase of Harvard life. Bost., Richard G. Badger, 1902. c. 170 p. D. cl., $1.25.
Five stories illustrating certain phases of undergraduate life at Harvard, called: Denholm's purple tea; The cult of the purple rose; The cult adopts rules; Literary efforts; The cult's publication.

**Johnston, Alex. History of American politics; rev. and enl. ed. by William M. Sloane; continued by Winthrop More Daniels. N. Y., H: Holt & Co., 1902. c. '90-'02. 13+437 p. 16°, (Handbooks for students and general readers.) cl., 80 c. net.

Knox, Janette Hill. Justa Hamlin's vocation. N. Y., Abbey Press, [1902.] c. 4-238 p. D. cl., $1.25.
The aim of the author is "to entertain, suggest reforms, temper criticism and give to the reader a few incidents in the lives of many with whom the writer has been associated in philanthropic and Christian work."

Lee, Edna Henry. Lee readers: First book. N. Y., Amer. Book Co., [1902.] [Ag29.] c. 128 p. il. sq. D. cl., 25 c.

Lee, Edna Henry. Lee readers: Second book. N. Y., Amer. Book Co., [1902.] [Ag29.] c. 176 p. il. D. cl., 30 c.

Lee, Edna Henry. The Lee readers: Third book. N. Y., Amer. Book Co., [1902.] [S2.] c. 3-240 p. il. D. cl., 40 c.

**Linn, Rob. Alex. Rob and his gun. N. Y., Scribner, 1902. [S.] c. 8+211 p. D. cl., $1 net.
The adventures of a city boy, who visits the farm of his sportsman cousin.

Linthicum, R:, *comp.* Best recitations; readings, declamations and plays for home, school and all public and social entertainments; written, with introd., special selections and lesson talks by Marvin Victor Hinshaw. Chic., W. R. Vansant & Co., [1902.] 2+7-463 p. il. 12°, cl., $1.75; hf. mor., $2.50.

Little, Lucius P. The practice act in force June 16, 1902; with notes on its construction and effect and the practice thereunder; embracing directions to clerks. Louisville, J: P. Morton & Co., 1902. c. 24 p. 8°, cl., 65 c.

Löhre, *Rev.* N. J. Addresses to young men and young women delivered to the St. Paul's congregation, Minneapolis, Minn. Minneapolis, Minn., Rev. N. J. Löhre, 1902. c. 272 p. pors. D. cl., $1.

Louthan, Hattie Horner. Thoughts adrift: [poems.] Bost., Richard G. Badger, 1902. c. 4+13-56 p. D. bds., $1.

Loux, Dubois H. Ongon: a tale of early Chicago. Chic., Dubois H. Loux, 1902. c. 4+182 p. O. cl., $1.50; princess cover, 75 c.
Chicago in the year 1833 is the scene of a weird tale, which introduces Indians as well as white characters. Several romances run through the story.

Mack, W:, *and* Nash, Howard P., *eds.* Cyclopedia of law and procedure. v. 4, (Assignments to baggage.) N. Y., Amer. Law Book Co., 1902. c. 1076 p. O. shp., $6.

†Mackie, Pauline Bradford. The flight of Rosy Dawn; il. by Josephine Bruce. Bost., L. C. Page & Co., 1903, [1902.] [My.] c. 7-98 p. il. D. (Cosy corner ser.) cl., 50 c.

Maryland. *Ct. of appeals.* Reports of cases. J. Shaaff Stockett, state rep. v. 62, 63, 64; cont. cases in Oct. terms, 1883, 1884, 1885, and Apr. terms 1884, 1885; rev. and annot. by W: H. Perkins, jr. Balt., M. Curlander, 1902. c. 21+687; 19+664; 19+679 p. O. shp., subs., ea., $4.

Mason, W: Lesley, *comp.* How to become a law stenographer: a compendium of legal forms; containing a complete set of legal documents, accompanied with full explanations for arranging on the typewriter for stenographers and typewriter operators. N. Y., W: L. Mason, 1902. c. 103 p. 8°, pap., 25 c.

Massey, R: W. Massey's bookkeeping and business practice; with an appendix on commercial law. Columbus, Ga., T. Gilbert, pr., 1902. c. 208 p. por. il. 8°, cl., $2.

Masters, Edgar Lee. Maximilian: a play in five acts. Bost., Richard G. Badger, [1902.] c. 154 p. D. bds., $1.50; full leath., $5.
A drama based upon the events of the life of Maximilian, Emperor of Mexico.

****Matthews,** Ja. Brander. Aspects of fiction, and other ventures in criticism. 3d ed., enl. N. Y., Scribner, 1902. [S.] c. '96 '02. 4+297 p. D. cl., $1.25 net.

****Metcalfe,** Cranstoun. Fame for a woman; or, splendid mourning; with frontispiece by Adolf Thiede. N. Y., Putnam, 1902. [Jl.] c. 4+353 p. D. cl., $1.20 net.
The results of a woman's desire for fame are pictured in this story. Both Edith Glanville and her husband were entirely happy until she became inspired with literary ambition, and wrote a successful book. The argument of the story is, not that a woman should have no interests outside her home, but that she should not pursue a career at the expense of family life. The scene is in London.

****Millar,** J. H. The mid-eighteenth century. N. Y., Scribner, 1902. 12+387 p. D. (Periods of European literature.) cl., $1.50 net.
The period covered extends from the death of Louis XIV. in 1714 to the death, in 1778, of Voltaire, with whose literary career it exactly coincides. As in other volumes of the series, there is a certain amount of overlapping.

†Miller, Esther. A prophet of the real. N. Y., J. F. Taylor & Co., 1902. [My.] c. 2+269 p. il. D. cl., $1.50.
A novel of modern life in London, containing much psychological analysis. Alice Durand was the daughter of a woman who had met a tragic and shameful death. The daughter, thrown upon her own resources, becomes the secretary of Anthony Versehoyle, a literary man, who later marries her in order that he may watch the effect of marriage upon her inherited temperament. The interest of the story lies in the development of these two natures worked upon by love and jealousy, and their subsequent happiness.

Minnesota. Civil procedure in the district and supreme courts of the state; with forms, by B: J. Shipman. In 2 v. v. 2. St. Paul, Keefe-Davidson Co., 1902. c. 22+6+691-1796 p. O. shp., (complete work,) $13.

Molino, Julia Wolff. Mingled sweets and bitters; or, my legacy: [poems.] N. Y., Abbey Press, [1902.] c. 6+265 p. por. obl. O. cl., $1.

Montana. *Supreme ct.* Reports of cases, from Jan. 7, 1901, to Aug. 1, 1901. Off. rep. v. 25. San Francisco, Bancroft-Whitney Co., 1902. c. 26+645 p. O. shp., $4.

Morris, G: Van Derfeer. A man for a' that. Cin., O., Jennings & Pye, [1902.] c. 7-403 p. D. cl., $1.50.
The life of a young man at a college, where the two sexes were educated together, and his after career in the world is the subject of the work.

Morten, W. H. Haps and mishaps of Jack Haselton: a story of adventure. N. Y., Abbey Press, [1902.] c. 264 p. D. cl., $1.50.

Murray, *Rev.* Andrew. The key to the missionary problem: thoughts suggested by the report of the Ecumenical missionary conference held in New York April, 1900. 3d ed. N. Y., Amer. Tract Society, [1902.] 6+204 p. D. cl., 75 c.

***Myers,** Albert Cook. Immigration of the Irish Quakers into Pennsylvania, 1682-1750, with their early history in Ireland. Swarthmore, Pa., Albert Cook Myers, 1902. c. 22+477 p. il. por. facsim., tab. 8°, cl., $3.55 net.
Bibliography: p. 434-444.

National Civic Federation. Industrial conciliation: Report of the proceedings of the conference, held under the auspices of the National Civic Federation at the rooms of the Board of Trade and Transportation in New York, December 16 and 17, 1901. N. Y., Putnam, 1902. [Jl.] c. 12+278 p. D. (Questions of the day, no. 99.) cl., $1.25.

Naylor, Ja. Ball. In the days of St. Clair: a romance of the Muskingum valley; il. by W. H. Fry. Akron, O., The Saalfield Pub. Co., 1902. c. 3-420 p. D. cl., $1.50.

Neville Ja. E., *ed.* Famous sayings of famous Americans: McKinley, Roosevelt, Harrison, Cleveland, Conkling, Seward, Evarts, Blaine, Grant. Syracuse, N. Y., Courier Printing Co., [1902.] 6+11-84 p. 16°, cl., $1.

New York. Civil procedure repts. vs. 31 and 32. N. Y., S. S. Peloubet, 1902. c. 8°, shp., ea., $4.

Norris, Zoe Anderson. The quest of Polly Locke. N. Y., J. S. Ogilvie Pub. Co., [1902.] c. 268 p. por. nar. D. cl., $1.
The quest for the "ideal man" takes Polly Locke, a young and attractive American girl, from Paris to Italy and along the Riviera. She has many amusing experiences, mostly due to her own ignorance and trustfulness.

Northwestern reporter, v. 90. Permanent ed., May 10-July 12, 1902. St. Paul, West Pub. Co., 1902. c. 16+1227 p. O. (Nat. reporter system, state ser.) shp., $4.
Contains all the decisions of the supreme courts of Minn., Wis., Ia., Mich., Neb., No. Dak., So. Dak. With table of northwestern cases in which rehearings have been denied. With tables of northwestern cases published in vs. 84, Minn. reports; 61, Neb. reports. A table of statutes construed is given in the index.

Opportunities in the colonies and Cuba; by Leonard Wood, W: H. Taft, C: H. Allen, Perfecto Lacoste and M. E. Beall. N. Y., Lewis, Scribner & Co., 1902. c. 2+369 p. D. cl., $1.
Articles written by the Governor of the Philippines, the former Governor of Cuba, and the former Governor of Porto Rico, the former Secretary of Agriculture of Cuba, and by Mr. Beall, in charge of the Division of Insular Affairs, Washington, D. C. The articles all aim to give an accurate account of the resources of the islands, and the opportunities they offer to prospective immigrants.

Patterson, Ada, *and* Bateman, Victory. By the stage door. N. Y., Grafton Press, [1902.] [S.] 9+217 p. sq. O. cl., $1.50.
Elev'n short stories of the stage.

Patterson, Howard. Patterson's illustrated nautical encyclopedia. Rev. and enl. ed.: a work of reference for naval revenue, coast survey, transport and lighthouse services; and adapted for the use of the naval reserve. Cleveland, The Marine Review Pub. Co., [1902.] c. 41-514 p. il. por. maps, diagr., 8°, cl., $3.

***Pearse,** Mark Guy. Praise: meditations in the one hundred and third Psalm. Cin., O., Jennings & Pye, [1902.] 4-179 p. T. (Little books on devotion.) cl., 25 c. net.

***Perkins,** Clara Crawford. French cathedrals and chateaux. Bost., Knight & Millet, 1903, [1902.] c. 2 v. 13+299; 5+283 p. il. O. cl., $4 net.
These volumes represent a series of lectures prepared to give, in a simple and condensed form, the development of architectural styles in France, and a history of her great monuments. The subject of French architecture naturally divides itself into two parts; one devoted to the Gothic, and the other to the Renaissance style. Under the first are grouped the great cathedrals, and under the second the palaces and chateaux of France. The later history which associated itself with the great monuments of France is given, and also some account of the peoples whose early migrations founded and moulded the nations. The volumes are profusely illustrated with full-page pictures.

Platt, C: T. Pitmanic shorthand instructor. N. Y., Amer. Book Co., [1902.] [Ag28.] c. 6+286 p. D. cl., $1.20.

Poe, Edgar Allan. Complete works; ed. by Ja. A. Harrison. Virginia ed. N. Y., T: Y. Crowell & Co., [1902.] c. 17 v., handy volume style, S. cl., $17.50; limp leath., $21; hf. cf., $35; de luxe library style, D. cl., $21; hf. cf., $42.
Contents: v. 1, Editor's preface, biography, autobiography, contemporary notices, index. (20+430 p. por.) v. 2-6, Tales, with introd., ["Poe's place in American literature,"] by Hamilton W. Mabie, and textual notes by R. A. Stewart. (40+399; 8+348; 8+324; 8+334; 8+302 p. il.) v. 7, Poems, with introd. by C: W. Kent, and textual notes by R. A. Stewart. (44+288 p. il.) v. 8-13, Literary criticism. (18+340; 8+314; 8+226; 4+281; 10+262; 4+226 p. pors. and il.) v. 14, Essays and miscellanies. (8+292 p. il.) v. 15, The literati, autography. (10+294 p. por.) v. 16, Marginalia, "Eureka," Poe's notes to "Eureka," bibliography, general index to v. 2-16. (8+426 p. por.) v. 18, Poe and his friends, letters relating to Poe, index. (8+452 p. por.)

Post, L: F. Success in life; reprinted by permission from *The Public.* N. Y., Civic Publishing Co., [1902.] 14 p. S. pap., 5 c.

†**Potter,** Mary Knight. Councils of Crœsus; il. by W. H. Dunton. Bost., L. C. Page & Co., 1903, [1902.] [Ag.] c. 7-231 p. S. (Page's commonwealth ser., no. 6.) cl., $1.25.
A novel of modern New York society, in which the contest between love and worldly ambition is portrayed. Mrs. Lorraine, a rich and beautiful widow, and her daughter Laura in their search for happiness unwittingly wound each other.

Powers, Ella M., *and* Balliet, T: M. The Morse readers. First book. N. Y., Morse Co., 1902. c. 3+136 p. il. (partly col.) 12°, (New century ser.) cl., 40 c.

†**Pratt,** *Mrs.* Mary E. Rhoda Thornton's girlhood; il. by C. G. Bush. Bost., Lee & Shepard, [1902.] c. 273 p. 12°, (American girl's ser., v. 13.) cl., $1.

Railroad reports, (v. 25 Am. and Eng. railroad cases, new ser.:) a coll. of all cases affecting railroads of every kind decided by the courts of last resort in the U. S.; ed. by T: J. Michie. v. 2. Charlottesville, Va., Michie Co., 1902. c. 9+1007 p. O. shp., $5.

****Rhoades,** Nina. The little girl next door; il. by Bertha G. Davidson. Bost., Lee & Shepard, 1902. [Ag.] c. 248 p. D. cl., 80 c. net.
The story of a genuine friendship between an impulsive little girl in a fine New York home, and a little blind girl in an apartment next door.

Richardson, *Mrs.* Mary. Physical culture cook book; comp. and written under direction of Bernarr Macfadden, by Mrs. Mary Richardson, assisted by G: Propheter. N. Y., Physical Culture Pub. Co., 1901. c. 249 p. 12°, cl., $1.

****Riley,** I. Woodbridge. The founder of Mormonism: a psychological study of Joseph Smith, jr.; with an introductory preface by G: Trumbull Ladd. N. Y., Dodd, Mead & Co., 1902. [My.] c. 15+446 p. D. cl., $1.50 net.
Investigates the elusive mental conditions of a strangely complex character. From materials gathered at Salt Lake City and elsewhere during eight years, there is now presented both Smith's checkered career and his pedigree for five generations. Here certain suppressed sources disclose the transmission of erratic tendencies, while his environment and bodily conditions account for the young prophet's visions. The Book of Mormon, as a "Record of the American Indians," is traced to the boy's imaginative gifts and his life on the Western Frontier.

****Robins,** E: Romances of early America. Phil., G: W. Jacobs & Co., [1902.] [Jl.] c. 3-268 p. il. por. O. cl., $2.50 net.
Contents: 1, The Meschianza—and love-making, a story of old Philadelphia. 2, Peasant and patrician; in Colonial Boston. 3, War and flirtation; Miss Wister at Penllyn. 4, A belle of Delaware; Miss Vining of Wilmington and Dover. 5, A disappointment in love; legends from Virginia. 6, Conspiracies and Cupid; New York and her royal governors. 7, Born to be a rebel; a pretty Bostonian. 8, Edwin Forrest's first love; New Orleans in the "twenties." 9, An uncompromising Tory; North Carolina and Loyalism. 10, The ghosts of Graeme Park; a Pennsylvania romance. 11, Washington as a wooer; sweethearts in Virginia and New York. 12, A Quaker transformed, the leader of Washington society.

****Robinson,** Edith. A Puritan knight errant; il. by L. J. Bridgman. Bost., L. C. Page & Co., 1903, [1902.] [Ag.] c. 4-280 p. D. cl., $1.20 net.
A story for the young of Boston in Colonial days. Anne Hutchinson, condemned for heresy and driven out into the wilderness, is one of the characters; as are also Sir Harry Vane and Governor Winthrop. The boy and girl friendship of Thomas Savage and Faith Hutchinson develops into love towards the end of the tale.

Sabin, Edwin L. The magic mashie, and other golfish stories. N. Y., A. Wessels Co., 1902. c. 5-210 p. il. D. cl., $1.
Fourteen stories woven around golf incidents.

****Saunders**, Margaret Marshall. Beautiful Joe's paradise; or, the Island of brotherly love: a sequel to "Beautiful Joe"; il. by C: Livingston Bull. Bost., L. C. Page & Co., [1902.] [Ag.] c. 2-365 p. il. D. cl., $1.20 net.
Joe's Paradise is filled with animals of all sorts and kinds. Their conversations relative to those they belonged to on earth, with their present occupations and amusements, form the story.

Savage, R: H: Special orders for Commander Leigh: a story of the lower coast of Louisiana. N. Y., Home Publishing Co., [1902.] c. 235 p. 12°, cl., $1.25; pap., 50 c.

†**Sayre**, Theodore Burt. Tom Moore: an unhistorical romance, founded on certain happenings in the life of Ireland's greatest poet. N. Y., F: A. Stokes Co., [1902.] [S.] c. 12+341 p. il. por. D. cl., $1.50.
This is a romance based on the play of "Tom Moore," by the same author, presented last winter by Andrew Mack. It follows with a certain degree of exactness the incidents in the Irish poet's life, introducing also well-known characters of the day, like Lovelace, Beau Brummell, etc. The poet's love affair with the actress Bessie Dyke forms the plot of the story.

†**Scott, Hugh S.**, ["Henry Seton Merriman," *pseud.*] The vultures: a novel. N. Y., Harper, 1902. c. 5+341 p. D. cl., $1.50.
A story of intrigue, conspiracy, and exciting adventure among the political factions of the great European nations. One of the scenes is in Russia at the time of the assassination of the Czar. The *attachés* of the various Foreign Offices play an important part. It is full of dramatic situations, most of which centre around the love interest of the story—the love of a young English diplomatist for the beautiful Countess Wanda of Warsaw.

****Scripture**, E: Wheeler. The elements of experimental phonetics. N. Y., Scribner, 1902. c. 18+627 p. il. tab. diagr., 8°, (Yale bicentennial pubs.) cl., $7.50 net.

***Seen** by the spectator: being a selection of rambling papers first printed in *The Outlook* under the title "The spectator." N. Y., The Outlook Co., 1902. c. 4+262 p. D. bds., $1 net.
Contents: Seeing a city; At the Virginia Springs; In the Virginia Hills; An East Side political outing; Concerning the sense of humor; Johns Hopkins quarter century; At Berea College; "Be not too tidy;" Uncle Sam's big guns; One kind of mind cure; Heard on the trolley-car; A day in Oxford; A glimpse of New York's China town; The art of shoplifting; Umbrella tales; The woman's page.

Sensenig, D: M., *and* Anderson, Rob. F. Essentials of arithmetic. N. Y., Silver, Burdett & Co., [1902.] c. 8+335 p. D. (Sensenig Anderson ser. of arithmetics.) cl., 60 c.
Intended for grammar grades and the higher grades of ungraded schools. A complete arithmetic, containing all the subjects of arithmetic that are regarded essential by the leading educators of to-day.

****Seymour**, F: H:, ["*Lord* Gilhooley," *pseud.*] Son; or, the wisdom of Uncle Eph, the modern Yutzo. N. Y., F: A. Stokes Co., [1902.] c. unp. il. D. denim, 80 c. net.
The wise sayings on all sorts of subjects of old "Uncle Eph" to his son.

Smith, Emma Stahler. Sweet home stories for the children; il. by Bessie Ford and Julia Smith. [Columbus, O., Mrs. E. S. Smith, 1902.] c. 38 p. sq. O. bds., 25 c.

****Smith**, S. Jennie. Madge, a girl in earnest; il. by Ja. E. McBurney. Bost., Lee & Shepard, 1902. c. 259 p. D. cl., $1 net.
Madge scorns the patronage of an aristocratic relative, and takes upon her strong young shoulders the problem of carrying along the family in an independent manner. Much practical information is presented.

Snider, Denton Jaques. The state: specially the American state psychologically treated. St. Louis, Mo., Sigma Publishing Co., 1902. c. 561 p. O. cl., $1.50.
"This short series of essays has attempted to state the logical basis of our institutions, and to give a cursory view of their historical development."—*The author.*

Southeastern reporter, v. 41. Permanent ed., Apr. 29-July. 15, 1902. St. Paul, West Pub. Co., 1902. c. 13+1116 p. O. (National reporter system, state ser.) shp., $4.
Contains all the decisions of the supreme courts of appeals of Va. and West Va., and supreme courts of N. C., S. C., Ga. With table of southeastern cases in which rehearings have been denied. With tables of southeastern cases published in vs. 114, Ga. reports; 50, West Va. reports. A table of statutes construed is given in the index.

Spofford, *Mrs.* Harriet Eliz. Prescott. The great procession, and other verses for and about children. Bost., Richard G. Badger, 1902. c. 108 p. T. (Arcadian lib., no. 2.) bds., $1.25.

Stevenson, Rob. L: "Virginibus puerisque," and other papers. Bost., Herbert B. Turner & Co., 1902. 9+256 p. por. S. cl., $1.25.

Sunday: reading for the young, 1903; il. by Gordon Browne, C: Sheldon, A. T. Elwes and others. N. Y., E. & J. B. Young & Co., [1902.] 412 p. O. bds., $1.25.

****Tappan**, Eva March. In the days of Queen Elizabeth; il. from famous paintings. Bost., Lee & Shepard, 1902. [Ag.] c. 6+294 p. D. (Makers of England ser., no. 3.) cl., 80 c. net.
The story of the early life of Queen Elizabeth, telling also of her achievements as a monarch and the glories of her age.

Tulley, H: C: Handbook on engineering: the practical care and management of dynamos, motors, boilers, engines, and all branches of steam engineering. New rev., enl. ed. St. Louis, Mo., H. C. Tulley & Co., 1902. c. 7+827 p. por. il. 16°, cl., $3.50.

United States. Supreme court reporter, v. 22. Permanent ed., Dec., 1901-Aug., 1902. St. Paul, West Pub. Co., 1902. c. O. (National reporter system, U. S. ser.) shp., $3.50.
Cases argued and determined in the U. S. supreme court, Oct. term, 1901. With tables of supreme court cases published in vs. 181-184, U. S. reports. A table of statutes construed is given in the index.

United States. *Supreme ct.* Reports, v. 184, Oct. term, 1901. J. C. Bancroft Davis, rep. N. Y., Banks Law Pub. Co., 1902. c. 23+723 p. O. shp., $2.50.

Van Duesen, Rebecca. Sea breezes and sand dunes. N. Y., Abbey Press, [1902.] c. 6+192 p. D. cl., $1.25.
Describes the happy summer the younger members of the Stapleton family spent at Sandpiper Beach.

Vaughan, Watkins Mabry. Vaughan's (complete) Alabama form book; legal forms for use especially in the state of Alabama. Nashville, Tenn., Marshall & Bruce Co., 1902. c. 436 p. 8°, leath., $3.

†**Veblen**, *Mrs.* Ellen Rolfe. The Goosenbury pilgrims: a child's drama: being the adventures of the Mother Goose people on a pilgrimage to St. Ives. [New issue.] Bost., Lothrop Pub. Co., [1902.] c. 5+196 p. O. cl., $1.
Originally published by The University of Chicago Press. *See* notice. "Weekly Record," P. W., December 28, 1901, [1561.]

†**Venable**, W: H: Tom Tad. N. Y., Dodd, Mead & Co., 1902. [Ag.] c. 4+287 p. il. D. cl., $1.50.
A story for boys with the scene laid in the Ohio valley, one of the incidents being a river flood in '84.

****Villari**, Luigi. Italian life in town and country. N. Y., Putnam, 1902. [S.] c. 6+327 p. il. D. (Our European neighbors.) cl., $1.20 net.
Contents: Division of the population; The aristocracy; The middle classes; Questions of wealth and poverty; Social life in town and country; Home life and the position of women; Political life and thought; Religious life and thought; Army and navy; The civil service; The agricultural population; The artisan; Local government and administration of justice; Public education; Amusements of the people; Literature and the press; Art and music of to-day.

Virginia. *Supreme ct. of appeals.* Reports, Jefferson-33 Grattan, 1730-1880; annot. under the supervision of T: Johnson Michie. vs. 1, 2 and 3. Grattan's reports. Charlottesville, Michie Co., 1902. c. 876 p. O. shp., ea., $7.50.

Webster, Noah. Donohue's Webster's school dictionary and American pictorial handy lexicon of the English language. Rev., enl. and corr. to date by C: Walter Brown on the basis of Webster's latest counting-house dictionary. 45th ed. Chic., M. A. Donohue & Co., [1902.] c. 2+371 p. il. T. cl., 50 c.

Williams, W: G: An exposition of the Epistle of Paul to the Romans. Cin., O., Jennings & Pye, [1902.] c. 394 p. O. cl., $2.

****Wilson**, Annie E. Love's leading strings: [a story.] Phil., Amer. Baptist Pub. Soc., [1902.] c. 2-282 p. il. D. cl., $1 net.

†**Winslow**, Helen Maria. Concerning Polly and some others; il. by C: Copeland. Bost., Lee & Shepard, 1902. c. 359 p. D. cl., $1.50.
The story of a life taken in early youth from the squalid tenement district of Boston to be brought to noble womanhood by a typical New England family.

Woolsey, G: Applied surgical anatomy, regionally presented, for the use of students and practitioners of medicine. Phil., Lea Brothers & Co., 1902. c. 7+17-521 p. il. col. pl. 8°, cl., $5; leath., $6.

Wright, *Mrs.* Julia MacNair. Studies in hearts: [stories.] N. Y., Amer. Tract Soc., [1902.] c. 2-190 p. D. cl., 75 c.

Young, Dinsdale T. Neglected people of the Bible. 2d ed. N. Y., Amer. Tract Soc., 1902. 8+277 p. D. cl., $1.
Sermons on: Isaac; Laban the Syrian; Simeon and Levi; Caleb; Saul and the witch of Endor; Barzillai the Gileadite; Obadiah; Gehazi; The Rechabites; Ebed-Melech, the Ethiopian; Mark; Barnabas; Aquila and Priscilla; Apollos and Onesiphorus and the memory of his kindness.

ORDER LIST.

ABBEY PRESS, 114 Fifth Ave., New York.

Hoogstraat, For bush or bonnet....... $1.25
Knox, Justa Hamlin's vocation........ 1.25
Molina, Mingled sweets and bitters... 1.00
Morten, Haps and mishaps of Jack Haselton..... .... 1.50
Van Duesen, Sea breezes and sand dunes..... .... 1.25

AMERICAN BAPTIST PUB. SOC., 1420 Chestnut St., Philadelphia.

**Wilson, Love's leading strings...net, 1.00

AMERICAN BOOK CO., 100 Washington Sq., E., New York.

Lee, Readers: First bk............. 25
——, — Second bk................... 30
——, — Third bk........................ 40
Platt, Pitmanic shorthand instructor... 1.20

AMERICAN LAW BOOK CO., Cor. Liberty and William Sts., New York.

Mack *and* Nash, Cyclopædia of law and procedure, v. 4................. 6.00

AMERICAN TRACT SOC., 150 Nassau St., New York.

Banks, The king's stewards........... 1.25

AMERICAN TRACT SOC.—*Continued.*

Murray, Key to the missionary problem, 3d ed......................... 75
Young, Neglected people of the Bible, 2d ed....... .... $1.00
Wright, Studies in hearts............ 75

EDWARD ATKINSON, P. O. Box 112, Boston.

Atkinson, Social bacteria............. n. p.

THE AVE MARIA, Notre Dame, Ind.

Bellord, New catechism of Christian doctrine...... 10

RICHARD G. BADGER, 194 Boylston St., Boston.

Donner, English lyrics of a Finnish harp...... .... 1.25
Johnson, The ult of the purple rose... 1.25
Louthan, Thoughts adrift............. 1.00
Masters, Maximilian...... ......$1.50; 5.00
Spofford, The great procession........ 1.25

THE BAKER & TAYLOR CO., 33-37 E. 17th St., New York.

*Cuyler, Help and good cheer.....net, 1.00
*——, Recollections of a long life..net, 1.50

BANCROFT-WHITNEY Co., 438 Montgomery St., San Francisco, Cal.

American state reports, v. 85.......... $4.00
Montana, *Supreme ct.*, Repts., v. 25.... 4.00

BANKS LAW PUB. Co., 21 Murray St., New York.

*Colorado, *Court of appeals*, Repts., v. 15........net, 5.00
United States. *Supreme ct.*, Repts., v. 184 (Davis)........ 2.50

E. H. BELL, 200 Greene St. New York.

Bell, Beautiful Bermuda...50 c.; 60 c.; 1.00

ORVILLE BREWER PUBLISHING Co., Auditorium Bldg., Chicago.

Conant, Theodore Roosevelt.......... 4

CALLAGHAN & Co., 114 Monroe St., Chicago.

Illinois, *Appellate cts.*, Repts., v. 101 (Newell)........ 3.75

CEDARINE ALLEN Co., Clinton, N. Y.

Allen, Uncle George's letters to Garcia club........ 1.00

CIVIC PUBLISHING Co., 43 Cedar St., New York.

Post, Success in life.......... 5

HENRY T. COATES & Co., 1222 Chestnut St., Philadelphia.

**Hogan, Children's diet in home and school........net, 50

COURIER PRINTING Co., Syracuse, N. Y.

Neville, Famous sayings of famous Americans........ 1.00

CRANE & Co., Topeka, Kan.

Hunter, Elementary studies in insect life........ 1.25

T: Y. CROWELL & Co., 426 and 428 W. Broadway, New York.

Poe, Complete works, Virginia ed., 17 v...Handy v., per set, $12.50; $21; $35; de luxe lib., $21; 42.00

M. CURLANDER, 208 N. Calvert St., Baltimore, Md.

Maryland, *Ct. of appeals*, Repts., v. 62-64 (Perkins)........subs., ea., 4.00

DODD, MEAD & Co., 372 Fifth Ave., New York.

**Chesterton, The defendant.......net, 1.25
†Corelli, Temporal power.......... 1.50
**Emerson, A history of the nineteenth century, 3 v........net, 3.60
†Gerard, The blood tax.......... 1.50
†Venable, Tom Tad.......... 1.50
**Riley, Founder of Mormonism...net, 1.50

M. A. DONOHUE & Co., 407-429 Dearborn St., Chicago.

Dorothy Vernon........35 c.; 1.25
Webster's (Donohue's Webster's) school dictionary, 45th ed.......... 50

F. J. DRAKE & Co, 356 Dearborn St., Chicago.

De Laurence, The Bible defended..... 1.00
French, His story, their letters....... 1.00
Hodgson, Modern carpentry.......... 1.00

E. P. DUTTON & Co., 31 W. 23d St., New York.

†Ballin, From cradle to school........ $1.25
†Bridgman, Bairn's coronation book... 60
†Farrow, The new Panjandrum...... 1.50
†Fenn, Old gold.......... 1.50
†Green, Princess Fairston.......... 1.25
Hunt, Story of Westminster Abbey... 2.00

ENCYCLOPAEDIA BRITANNICA Co., 225 Fourth Ave., New York.

Encyclopædia Britannica new supplemental volumes, in 11 v., v. 1-4, for set of 11 v..........$65; $75; $90; 110.00

DANA ESTES & Co., 208-218 Summer St., Boston.

Andersen, Fairy tales.......... 1.50
**Hall, The correct thing in good society, [new ed.]........net, 75

R. F. FENNO & Co., 9-11 E. 16th St., New York.

Harrison, Wages of sin, new ed....... 1.50

FUNK & WAGNALLS Co., 30 Lafayette Pl., New York.

**Fernald, Comprehensive standard dictionary........net, 1.00

T. GILBERT, Columbus, Ga.

Massey, Bookkeeping and business practice........ 2.00

GOVERNMENT PRINT. OFFICE, Washington, D. C.

Geare, List of publications of the United States National Museum, (1875-1900)........10 c.; 60

GRAFTON PRESS, 70 Fifth Ave., New York.

*Crane, The imperial republic....net, 1.00
Patterson *and* Bateman, By the stage door........ 1.50

TYRE HANCOCK, Dallas, Tex.

Hancock, Church error.......... 35

HARPER & BROS., Franklin Sq., New York.

**Chambers, Outdoorland........net, 1.50
†Higgins, Out of the West.......... 1.50
†Scott, The vultures.......... 1.50

MRS. ROSE M. HARRINGTON, 521 W. 151st St., New York.

Harrington, Conservation of the natural tree-cover........ 50

D. C. HEATH & Co., 1585 Boylston St., Boston.

Hopkins, Inductive plane geometry, new rev. ed.......... 75

HENRY HOLT & Co., 29 W. 23d St., New York.

**Johnston, History of American politics, new rev., enl. ed..........net, 80

HOME PUBLISHING Co., 3 E. 14th St., New York.

Savage, Special orders for Commander Leigh........50 c.; 1.25

GEORGE W. JACOBS & CO. 103 S. 15th St., Philadelphia.

**Comrie, A loyal Huguenot maid.net, $1.00
**Hayens, One of the red shirts...net, 1.00
**Robins, Romances of early America, net, 2.50

JENNINGS & PYE, 220 W. 4th St., Cincinnati.

Morris, A man for a' that............ 1.50
*Pearse, Praise..... ....net, 25
Williams, Exposition of Paul to the Romans...... .... 2.00

ORANGE JUDD CO., 52 Lafayette Pl., New York.

Fiske, Poultry appliances............ 50

KEEFE-DAVIDSON LAW BOOK CO., St. Paul, Minn.

Iowa, Law of taxation............... 7.50
Minnesota, Civil procedure in the district and supreme cts., v. 2, (Shipman,) (complete work)............ 13.00

KNIGHT & MILLET, Pope Bldg., Columbus Ave., Boston.

*Perkins, French cathedrals and chateaux, 2 v......................net, 4.00

LAIRD & LEE, 263 Wabash Ave., Chicago.

Chambers, Lee's American automobile annual, 1902....... .... 1.00

LEA BROS. & CO., 706-708 Sansom St., Philadelphia.

Woolsey, Applied surgical anatomy.$5; 6.00

LEE & SHEPARD, 202 Devonshire St., Boston.

**Akers, The sunset song.........net, 3.00
**Brooks, Dorothy Dainty........net, 80
**Carpenter, Story of Joan of Arc.net, 80
**Clarke, Boy Donald...........net, 60
**Comstock, A boy of a thousand years ago....... ....net, 80
**Darling, A girl of this century..net, 1.00
**Dodge, Chips, fragments, and vestiges...... ....net, 1.20
**James, Tom Winstone..........net, 80
†Pratt, Rhoda Thornton's girlhood.... 1.00
**Rhoades, The little girl next door.net, 80
**Smith, Madge.......... ....net, 1.00
**Tappan, In the days of Queen Elizabeth.... ....net, 80
†Winslow, Concerning Polly........... 1.50

LEWIS, SCRIBNER & CO., 125 E. 23d St., New York.

Opportunities in the colonies and Cuba. 1.00

LITTLE, BROWN & CO., 254 Washington St., Boston.

Farmer, Boston cooking school cook book, new rev. ed................. 2.00

N. J. LÖHRE, Minneapolis, Minn.

Löhre, Addresses to young men and young women...... .... 1.00

LOTHROP PUB. CO., 530 Atlantic Ave., Boston.

†Veblen, The Goosenbury pilgrims, new issue....... .... 1.00

DU BOIS HENRY LOUX, 4752 Kenwood Ave., Chicago.

Loux, Ongon..... ....75c.; 1.50

MARINE REVIEW PUB. CO., 39-41 Wade Bldg., Cleveland.

Patterson, Illustrated nautical encyclopædia, rev., enl. ed............... $3.00

MARSHALL & BRUCE CO., Nashville, Tenn.

Vaughan, (Complete) Alabama form book....... .... 3.00

WILLIAM L. MASON, 35 W. 21st St., New York.

Mason, How to become a law stenographer...... 25

LAURENS MAYNARD, Boston.

*Ireland, China and the powers, limited ed...... ....net, 2.00

MICHIE CO., Charlottesville, Va.

Railroad reports American and English railroad cases, v. 25........... 5.00
Virginia, *Supreme ct. of appeals*, Repts., 1730-1880, v. 1, 2, 3, Grattan's repts...... ....ea., 7.50

MORSE CO., 96 Fifth Ave., New York.

Powers *and* Balliet, Morse readers, First book........ 40

JOHN P. MORTON & CO., Louisville, Ky.

Little, Practice act in force June 16, 1902...... 65

ALBERT COOK MYERS, Swarthmore, Pa.

*Myers, Immigration of the Irish Quakers into Pennsylvania, 1682-1750..... ....net, 3.55

F. TENNYSON NEELY CO., 114 Fifth Ave., New York.

Douglas, The riding master.......... 1.00

J. S. OGILVIE PUB. CO., 57 Rose St., New York.

Norris, Quest of Polly Locke......... 1.00

OPEN COURT PUB. CO., 324 Dearborn St., Chicago.

*Hilbert, Foundations of geometry.net, 1.00

OUTLOOK CO., 287 Fourth Ave., New York.

*Seen by the spectator...........net, 1.00

L. C. PAGE & CO., 200 Summer St., Boston.

**Brainerd, Millicent in dreamland.net, 40
†Grier, A crowned queen........ 50c.; 1.25
†——, His Excellency's English governess..... ....50c.; 1.25
†——, In furthest Ind...........50c.; 1.25
†——, The kings of the East.....50c.; 1.25
†——, Like another Helen.......50c.; 1.25
†——, Peace with honour.........50c.; 1.25
†——, Warden of the Marches...50c.; 1.25
†Mackie, Flight of Rosy Dawn....... 50
†Potter, Councils of Crœsus.......... 1.25
**Robinson, A Puritan knight....net, 1.20
**Saunders, Beautiful Joe's Paradise, net, 1.20

S. S. PELOUBET, 76 Nassau St., New York.

New York, Civil procedure, repts., vs. 31 and 32.......................ea., 4.00

I. NEWTON PHILLIPS, Springfield, Ill.

Illinois, *Supreme ct.*, Repts., v. 195 (Phillips).... .... 2.25

PHONOGRAPHIC INSTITUTE CO., Cincinnati.

Arabian nights' entertainments, Sinbad the sailor........ 25

PHYSICAL CULTURE PUB. CO., Townsend Bldg., 25th St. and Broadway, New York.

Richardson, Physical culture cook book....... .... $1.00

G. P. PUTNAM'S SONS, 29 W. 23d St., New York.

**Benton, As seen from the ranks.net, 1.25
**Conrad, Typhoon...... ....net, 1.00
**Metcalfe, Fame for a woman.....net, 1.20
National Civic Federation, Industrial conciliation..... .... 1.25
**Villari, Italian life in town and country..... ....net, 1.20

SAALFIELD PUB. CO., Akron, O.

Naylor, In the days of St. Clair....... 1.50

GEORGE SCHIRMER, 35 Union Sq., New York.

*Jadassohn, Manual of single, double, triple and quadruple counterpoint, net, 1.75

CHARLES SCRIBNER'S SONS, 153-157 Fifth Ave., New York.

**Linn, Rob and his gun.........net, 1.00
**Matthews, Aspects of fiction, 3d enl. ed..... ....net, 1.25
**Millar, The mid-eighteenth century, net, 1.50
**Scripture, Elements of experimental phonetics.... ....net, 7.50

SIGMA PUB. CO., 210 Pine St., St. Louis, Mo.

Snider, The state..................... 1.50

SILVER, BURDETT & CO., 29-33 E. 19th St., New York.

Chesterfield, Letters...... 35
Sensenig, Essentials of arithmetic..... 60

MRS. E. S. SMITH, 396 Desler Ave., Columbus, O.

Smith, Sweet home stories............ 25

CHRISTOPHER SOWER CO., 614 Arch St., Philadelphia.

Brumbaugh, Standard readers, 5 books. 1st, 22c.; 2d, 33 c.; 3d, 45 c.; 4th, 67 c.; 5th, 83

F. A. STOKES CO., 5-7 E. 16th St., New York.

†Sayre, Tom Moore.................. $1.50
**Seymour, Son..... ....net, 80

J. F. TAYLOR & CO., 5-7 E. 16th St., New York.

†Bernstein, In the gates of Israel..... 1.50
†Desmond. The heart of woman....... 1.50
†Miller, A prophet of the real........ 1.50

H. C. TULLEY & CO., St. Louis, Mo.

Tulley, Handbook on engineering, new rev., enl. ed.................... 3.50

HERBERT B. TURNER, 323 Wentworth Bldg., Cor. Summer St. and Atlantic Ave., Boston.

Stevenson, Virginibus puerisque....... 1.25

UNIVERSITY PUB. CO., 27-29 W. 23d St., New York.

Andersen, Hans Aandersen's best stories..... .... 12½

W. R. VANSANT & CO., Chicago.

Linthicum, Best recitations......$1.75; 2.50

GEORGE WATKINS, 58 Broad St., New York.

Hartfield, The world wide travellers' cipher code..... ....per pair, 2.50

A. WESSELS CO., 7-9 W. 18th St., New York.

Sabin, The magic mashie............. 1.00

WEST PUB. CO., 52-58 W. 3d St., St. Paul, Minn.

American digest, v. 34................ 6.00
United States supreme ct. reporter, v. 22...... .... 3.50
Northwestern reporter, v. 90.......... 4.00
Southeastern reporter, v. 41.......... 4.00

E. & J. B. YOUNG & CO., 7-9 W. 18th St., New York.

Sunday, 1903...... .... 1.25

RECENT ENGLISH BOOKS.

ANNALS of Carnegie Museum. Vol. 1, No. 3, March, 1902. Plates 16 to 25 and engravings. Wesley. 8°, swd., 10s., net.

AUTOMOBILE: its construction and management. Trans. from Gérard Lavergne's "Manuel Théoretique et Pratique de l'Automobile sur Route," with additions and new illus. Rev. and ed. by Paul N. Hasluck. 536 illus. Cassell. Roy. 8°, 9⅛ x 6½, 624 p., 10s. 6d., net.

BARNES, H. T. On the capacity for heat of water between the freezing and boiling points, together with a determination of the mechanical equivalent of heat in terms of the international electrical units. Dulau. 4°, 6s.

EMPHASIZED Bible. Allenson. Old Testament, vol 3. 8s., net. Ditto, in 1 vol., 22s. 6d., net. Old and New Testament, in 1 vol, 30s., net.

FRENKEL, H. S. Treatment of tabetic ataxia by means of systematic exercise. Redman. 8°, 12s. 6d., net.

HARPER, C. G. Cycle rides round London, ridden, written and il. by C. G. Harper. N. Y., Scribner. [imported.] 1902. 12+288 p. cl., $2.40.

LACORDAIRE, Père. Jesus Christ, God, God and man: conferences delivered at Notre-Dame in Paris. Trans. from French, with author's permission, of a Tertiary of the same order. New ed. Chapman. Cr. 8°, 7½ x 4⅞, 428 p., 3s. 6d., net.

LEWIS, Agnes Smith. Apocrypha: the Prot-evangelium Jacobi and Transitus Mariæ. With texts from the Septuagint, the Corân, the Peshitta, and from a Syriac hymn in a Syro-Arabic Palimpsest of the 5th and other centuries. With an appendix of Palestinian Syriac texts from the Taylor-Schechter collection. Clay. Cr. 4°, 15s., net.

MASSEE, G. European fungus flora: agaricaceæ. Duck-Hutchinson. Imp. 8°, 11⅛ x 8⅜, 300 p., 7s. 6d.

MIDRASH Hag-Gadol: forming a collection of ancient Rabbinic homilies to the Pentateuch. Edited for the first time from various Yemen manuscripts and provided with notes and preface by S. Schechter. Genesis. Clay. 4°, 468 p., swd., 30s., net.

MULLER, E. B. Iwan. Lord Milner and South Africa. N. Y., Scribner, [imported,] 1902. 32+751 p. por. 8°, cl., $6, net.

NIGHTS at the opera; a series of operatic handbooks. V. 1, "Lohengrin," by Richard Wagner; by Wakeling Dry. With accounts of the maker of the music, the character, the story of the drama, etc. N. Y., Scribner, [imported,] 1902. 60 p. 8°, pap., 75 c., net.

PALEY, F. A. Manual of gothic moldings, with directions for copying them and for determining their dates; illustrated by upwards of 600 examples. 6th ed., with additions and improvements, by W. M. Fawcett. N. Y., Scribner, [imported,] 1902. 15+106 p. 31 pl. 8°, cl., $3.

The Publishers' Weekly.

FOUNDED BY F. LEYPOLDT.

SEPTEMBER 13, 1902.

The editor does not hold himself responsible for the views expressed in contributed articles or communications

All matter, whether for the reading-matter columns or advertising pages, should reach this office not later than Wednesday noon, to insure insertion in the same week's issue.

Books for the "Weekly Record," as well as all information intended for that department, should reach this office by Tuesday morning of each week.

Publishers are requested to furnish title-page proofs and advance information of books forthcoming, both for entry in the lists and for descriptive mention. An early copy of each book published should be forwarded, as it is of the utmost importance that the entries of books be made as promptly and as perfectly as possible. In many cases booksellers depend on the PUBLISHERS' WEEKLY solely for their information. The Record of New Publications of the PUBLISHERS' WEEKLY is the material of the "American Catalogue" and so forms the basis of trade bibliography in the United States.

"I hold every man a debtor to his profession, from the which, as men do of course seek to receive countenance and profit, so ought they of duty to endeavor themselves by way of amends to be a help and an ornament thereunto."—LORD BACON.

"AN AMERICAN RAID ON ENGLISH RARE BOOKS."

THERE is much unreasonable talk, it seems to us, in the English press over the so-called "American raid on English rare books." Anent the recent acquisition by John Pierpont Morgan, of the library partly formed by Morris, a writer in the London *Times* querulously cries out, "Can nothing be done to stem the continuous and wholesale exportations of rare, early printed and other books and illuminated manuscripts to the United States?" "The drain," he continues, "has been going on for over half a century; within recent years it has reached huge proportions; and now we have the mournful privilege of chronicling the most important single transaction which has occurred, or, perhaps, is likely to occur in connection with this subject." Other writers, in other English journals, rant in much the same fretful spirit, regarding it as a "national calamity" that Americans are beginning to buy more freely than hitherto what the Englishman has been buying for ages from other nations. In some cases it is ungenerously hinted that the vulgar American gains his advantage over his more modest and erudite European competitor by virtue of money, rather than brains, an assertion that is too preposterous to deserve categorical refutation.

The fact is, the European, particularly the Englishman, seems to have lost interest in a matter that is becoming daily of greater importance to the American—namely, the sources of literature as found in original texts and editions. Time was when the Englishman fought for these in the auction market against all comers. Time is when the American holds his own in the market against the whole world—being favored in all things as no nation in modern times has been known to be favored.

Nor is this a victory of a coarse and blatant plutocracy; it is due, rather, to the desire of an aristocracy of intellect and means combined to acquire their share of the literary treasures of the world for their edification and instruction, and for the profit of their fellow men—a fact to which the munificence of Lenox, Brown, Ticknor, Duyckinck, Astor, Ford, Tilden—but why extend the list—amply testify.

The rivalry between the American and his European competitor in most instances is antagonized rather than favored by the foreign bookseller. The victory must therefore be gained through quick and clear perception of the value of what is offered. In many cases literary treasures go begging among English collectors, sometimes for years, before the American collector is permitted to bid for them. Quaritch, to name but one instance, held the Thorold "Psalter" of 1459 for eighteen years before he sold it to Morgan. Dozens of similar instances might be cited.

We do not think that anything can be done to stem the exportation of rare books and manuscripts to the United States, unless a love for rare books is re-awakened in so-called English bibliophiles. We cannot believe that it is lack of money among the English collectors that permits this exportation, but rather apathy towards things that should evoke enthusiastic interest. When this is overcome there may be another story to tell. But even in that case all the American collector asks for is "a fair field and no favor."

THE RELATION OF THE BOOKSELLER TO THE LIBRARIAN.*

BY CHARLES M. ROE.

IN looking over the announcement of this meeting I noticed that I was put down as a "bookdealer." As that term is not in common use among the members of the trade to which I have the honor of belonging, my curiosity prompted a trip to the dictionary, where I failed to find the word given. The words "deal" and "dealers," however, were there, and from the definitions I received the impression that they referred to transactions and transactors in very ordinary merchandise, and in matters much worse than or-

* A paper read at the Western Library Meeting, Madison, Wis., August 28-30, 1902.

dinary merchandising. I do not wish you to think of the man who sells books as one who fixes up deals or as the ordinary merchant who gives slight heed to the goods which pass through his hands, but rather as one who appreciates with fine discrimination the intrinsic values each volume posseses which he handles with such care and even affection. I desire, therefore, to enter a gentle protest and to ask that you substitute in your minds the word "seller" for "dealer," as it has a much more satisfactory meaning, being defined as one who disposes of his property to another for a valuable consideration. Now, do not misunderstand this as meaning that the bookseller is getting rich by his transactions. Far from it! It will require many years yet under the new net system to reimburse him for his losses of the past ten years. However, more of this later. But I do wish it understood that the property he disposes of is worth a valuable consideration. I maintain that bookselling is one of the most dignified of the trades, and as engaging in such a business the bookseller is entitled to respect and consideration from the book-reading world. But I wish to protest again at being catalogued even as a bookseller without an explanatory clause such as "some sentiment still left" or "books known by their contents as well as by their size, binding, type, etc." In other words, I wish to be known as a bookman rather than only as a bookdealer or bookseller. For as a bookman I am one of you; for surely there are no more enthusiastic bookmen and bookwomen than librarians and those interested in libraries. As such we meet on common ground and grow enthusiastic over topics of common interest, discussing as brothers and sisters our needs and requirements. On this common ground I meet you to-day as one whose interests are broader than a certain branch of trade. I remember with gratitude the influence of the smallest of small town libraries, administered by the editor of the little weekly sheet, who combined with his editorial duties many another vocation, but who took time with all his cares to direct a small boy to the helpful and entertaining books in the pitifully small collection which served as a public library twenty-five years ago. All honor and praise to those pioneer librarians. But what wonderful developments since! What a glorious present is evidenced by this magnificent historical library building, which is a constant delight to the eye, and which is only one of many erected in the United States in the last few years. What an inspiring outlook for the years to come! I fully concur with Mr. Melvil Dewey in his plea for a wider and heartier recognition of the equal necessity of the public library with the public school.

The world of letters, and I suppose librarians and booksellers may claim residence in at least the outskirts of that favored realm, is an interesting place in which to live, for various reasons, among which may be reckoned the various controversies which arise from time to time.

The spice of variety is with us in the tilts between critic and author, author and publisher, publisher and bookseller, and now between bookseller and librarian. As a bookseller for fifteen years and a friend and acquaintance of librarians for over twenty. I stand to-day as a mediator between the belligerents, clasping the hands of both parties and striving to bring them if possible to a better understanding. By these words I do not wish to be understood as admitting that there is a serious breach between these members of the book trade. Oh, no! It is only a small family jar, which, when the heat of the occasion has passed away, will be satisfactorily settled. The cause of the controversy, like that of many another, is a "haggling over prices," to use plain words. The pocketbook is more sensitive than any part of the actual anatomy.

Our great unselfish promoters of public welfare, the daily papers, understand this fully, and so constantly bid for public favor by pointing out periodically some commercial octopus which is plotting to despoil the nation. The "Book Trust" is one of the latest of these dread animals discovered by enterprising Chicago journalism, and, horrible to relate, it is one of the worst of its kind, for it has two heads. Under date of August 6 the *Chicago Tribune* presents six columns of sensational sentences under the heading "The Book Trade has Duplicate Trust." The reading of this article by one acquainted with the conditions which have existed in the publishing and bookselling business for the past twenty years, reveals an utter lack of the knowledge necessary to intelligently present the subject. The reporter who concocted it was, of course, a professional builder of sensational articles, and knew how to meet the wishes of the editor and the desires of his readers. While he raved and ranted about the public having to pay more for its books he gave no inkling of how much more nor why it was necessary to come to some agreement about prices. A full and fair discussion of the subject would not have served the ends of this champion of the people's pocketbook. It may be noted in passing that publishers and booksellers are wondering why the *Tribune* should present only one side of the subject in a way that is apt to do harm to the book trade generally, when its advertising columns are patronized so generously by bookmakers and sellers of books. It may also be asked why it chooses to call the American Publishers' Association and the American Booksellers' Association a "trust." when it is a well-known fact that these associations are not combinations for monopoly, but formed solely for conserving legitimate profits in a business which has been well-nigh ruined by indiscriminate price cutting. The generally accepted definition of a trust is "a combination in restraint of trade." No such purpose has been in the minds of either publisher or bookseller. On the contrary, this form of combination or co-operation is beneficent, inasmuch as it seeks to create and foster bookstores everywhere. It does not purpose to crush out new organizations in its line of business, but only seeks to rectify palpably unfair and unreasonable business methods. Every one must admit that this is altogether different from what is commonly known as a "trust" or monopoly which is organized for the express purpose of crushing all competitors and securing all the business in its line for itself. On the contrary, the booksellers' and publishers' associations exist not for their own corporate aggrandizement, but in order that each individual member, be he never so small, may have an equal chance to secure a reasonable profit. This is a true community of interest, and should be welcomed and encouraged by every fair-minded person. The fact that it is a double combination, as the *Tribune* says, is wholly in its favor, for one body will act as a check upon the other, should either evince a desire to dip into the public pocketbook for more than a suitable profit. If the *Tribune* had discussed the subject fairly something like the following would have appeared: *"A time-honored trade profession more carefully organized."* The public will have to pay somewhat more for its books, but can well afford to do so in consideration of the valuable public service rendered by bookstores and booksellers as well as by book publishers in printing and selling annually thousands of informing and entertaining books. For many years this service has been rendered by the bookseller without sufficient remuneration. Three reasons contributed to this state of affairs:

First: The unfortunate custom of giving discounts to certain classes was gradually extended until it included the entire bookbuying public, and increased from 10 per cent. to 25 per cent., and even 30 per cent., leaving the bookseller scarce enough to pay expenses.

Second: The department store seized upon the popular books for advertising purposes, selling them for a few cents above cost, and often for cost or less, giving the public the impression that the regular bookseller was charging exorbitant prices and making enormous profits, and so alienating the public from him.

Third: Libraries were securing their books at about cost, in some instances at cost, the bookseller losing his expenses.

To save the trade from complete disintegration from these causes the publishers have joined hands with the booksellers in a double organization for the proper protection of their combined interests, in order that the business of selling books may be placed on a profitable basis. This does not mean that books will be published at exorbitant prices, nor that the public will pay much above 10 per cent. more for its books. Books which under the old system sold for $1.12 and $1.18 will now cost $1.20 or $1.25. The bookbuying public, which for the most part is either engaged in varying commercial enterprises that return a good profit or receiving good fees for professional services, will be glad, we are sure, to pay this small extra amount for its literary entertainment with the knowledge that the extra 10 per cent. or so makes it possible for the man who pursues a trade which is acknowledged to be a difficult one to secure a fair profit and have the satisfaction of making something more than a mere living.

Such a statement as this would have caused much more of a sensation than the attack on the book trade to which we have referred, and would have reflected much more credit on the management of a paper to whose prosperity both publishers and booksellers have contributed so generously.

We have gone somewhat afield, however, and must return to a discussion of the effect on librarians and libraries of the new system of net prices. Every one present may not be fully acquainted with the history of this controversy. In a nutshell the situation is this: Until May, 1901, librarians were accustomed to buy books for their libraries, themselves and their friends at one-third off publishers' prices, and very often at even better rates. On the date above named the rule of the American Publishers' Association that booksellers should allow librarians only 10 per cent. from the prices of all new net books went into effect. As soon as librarians saw that under this rule they would pay more for books protests began to be made from all parts of the country. The publishers were urged to increase the discount to 25 per cent. The booksellers protested at this, as it would make the library trade as unprofitable as it was before. To date the Publishers' Association has taken no action in the matter.

In presenting the booksellers' side first, I have not forgotten the librarian's way of looking at the question, and do not blame him for being somewhat disturbed and anxious and inclined to resent the new order of things which cuts down the number of books possible for him to purchase with a given sum of money. He is very naturally thinking of his own beloved library with still some empty shelves and wall space which he longs to see filled, and an ever increasing number of readers whose demands for certain classes of books he cannot meet. He is rightly jealous of the interests of his library, and puts forth every effort to make his appropriation, all too small as it is, buy as many books as it possibly can. I honor him in his fine enthusiasm and in his faithful discharge of a public duty; but I am here to-day to remind him that there are other citizens whose interests should be considered as well as those of his dear library patrons—citizens who have just as much right to the happiness which comes through the securing a reasonable profit as the architect or the contractor of the library building and even the librarian himself with his salary. [I'm sure the librarian would wish to be counted among those who would be glad to know that the bookseller was making a reasonable profit instead of conducting a losing and disheartening business, and knowing the facts as we have presented them he would be the last to continue to petition the publishers to supply him with books at a discount which would allow no profit whatever to the worthy fellow citizen and fellow-bookman who is risking his capital in, and giving his time to, a business which is not greatly profitable at the best, and which, like the library itself, is of a distinct public benefit.] It may very properly be asked why the most necessary part of the entire library outfit should be supplied at no profit to the seller. The architect and contractor of the library building make a profit, and rightly, too. The Library Bureau, or some other supply house, makes a profit on the fittings supplied, and the librarian receives a reasonable salary as he should. Then why not include the bookseller among those who are getting a reasonable profit for the expenditure of public funds. The new system of net prices will make it possible for him to make a small profit—not by any means what it should be, but vastly better than none at all, as formerly; but it would not be possible to increase the 10 per cent. discount to 25 per cent., as the librarians petition, and make anything above bare expenses, if that.

I well remember a conversation of several years ago with a gentleman whom many of you know and esteem highly. He had been a librarian, and had purchased books for an entire state system of libraries. At that time he possessed the idea that much money was made in selling books to libraries. Unfortunately for him this impression led him to embark in the business of retailing books and supplying libraries. My conversation was after his failure in this business. He was telling me his surprise, on receiving his bills from the publisher and deducting their amount from the price he was compelled to allow libraries, at the ridiculously small margin left to pay rent, insurance, losses on dead stock, interest on capital invested, light, clerk hire, incidental expenses, and last but not least, his own profit. He is now engaged in farming, which he finds a much more remunerative employment and much less harrowing to the nerves.

During the past year, even with the help of the net price system, one of the largest houses supplying libraries with books, I am told on good authority, declared a dividend of only 2 per cent. By this it would hardly appear that the public pocketbook had been mulcted very badly. And in startling contrast to this poor showing we again call attention to that watchdog of the people's pocketbook, the *Chicago Tribune*, which has been charging $20 per inch for advertising space in the number celebrating the completion of its magnificent new building. The *Tribune* may say their space is well worth this price to the advertiser, and there is a bare possibility of its being so; but the immense profits that paper has always made would indicate that it was taxing the public pretty heavily. Consistency is a word evidently unknown to its management. Instead of being a true watchdog it would appear to be more of a dog in the manger. Declaring, as it does, each year enormous dividends on its capital stock it could well afford to be generous, and lend its influence for the building up of a business somewhat allied to its own rather than misrepresenting it as a "double-headed monster" stealthily plotting to rob the public purse. I have made the foregoing statements in regard to the unprofitableness of the library business advisedly and with deliberation, not for commercial effect, but from honest conviction and from facts gained by long experience in bookselling, and they would not be changed in any particular if given under oath.

'Tis well said that excessive devotion to the material is the evil of our epoch, and some may be inclined to think that the plea which I have just made for a larger profit for the bookseller is in keeping with the spirit of the times. No one, however, who is acquainted with the history of bookselling for the past decade will think of accusing me of mercenary motives. It is well known that clever merchandisers have been wont to sneer at the sentiment of the bookseller who through sheer love of books has been irresistibly tied to a business which only just pays expenses and allows him a mere pittance upon which to live. I do not, however, ask for a reasonable profit for the profit alone, but largely on account of the principle involved. I believe that it is morally wrong to sell goods without profit. The influence on men in such a business is serious, and no one with the common weal at heart would wish to profit by the disheartenment of another in this way. I wish to know that the various tradesmen with whom I deal are making a reasonable profit on what I buy of them, and it would disturb me seriously to learn that they were losing money or only making expenses on merchandise sold me. The old and bad method of heartless competition must give way to the new and better method of proper combination and co-operation.

I do not agree with Mr. Melvil Dewey in his contention that as the public school has supplanted the private school, so the public library will supplant the circulating library and the small bookstore as well. In the first place, the public school has not supplanted the private school. Changing conditions made it appear to do so; but in the end there was room for both, and to-day the private school thrives as well as ever. So with libraries. The great increase of wealth and of general knowledge assures a steadily increasing body of readers who will make it possible and profitable for the private circulating library and the bookseller to exist along with the greatest possible number of public libraries. No one need be pessimistic. Changes will happen continually, that will jostle us somewhat but not overthrow us. A little readjustment is necessary—a seeking of new methods of cultivating our own special field rather than a loss of temper or a resort to frantic appeals and extreme statements.

The bookseller always has been and always should be the most logical and natural channel through which publishers distribute books to libraries. He has a training and facilities which make it advantageous to both publisher and librarian to have him act as intermediary. He is willing to spend time and money to look up books which he alone knows how to secure, and to advise about the best of the many editions and bindings, and to risk a goodly sum of money in carrying a large stock of books that publishers may be represented and that librarians may have opportunity for selection near at hand; but for all this he very naturally and justly wishes a fair compensation. This the old method would not give, and the new will give only in scant measure. In view of these facts, then, would it not be well for the librarian to desist from presenting further resolutions to the publishers asking for larger disccunts and turn their attention rather to securing larger appropriations for the purchase of books? Of money there is a plenty, and there should be little difficulty in securing enough to give an ample stock of books to every library in the land, unless, indeed, public benefactors are more anxious to be represented by beautiful and striking library buildings which stand all day in the eyes of the people rather than by the more obscure, but in the end more powerful witnesses to their generosity which stand silent on the shelves within. I have faith enough in the good nature and the common sense of librarians and booksellers generally to look forward to the day when both will be working harmoniously, each for the good of the other and for the benefit of the greatest bookreading and bookbuying public the world has ever known—the American people, which they have the extreme good fortune and exalted privilege of serving.

OBITUARY NOTES.

Sir Frederick Augustus Abel, a well-known chemist and writer on scientific subjects, died September 8, in London, where he was born in 1826. His published works are: "The Modern History of Gunpowder," "Gun Cotton," "On Explosive Agents," "Researches in Explosives," and "Electricity Applied to Explosive Purposes." He was joint author, with Colonel Bloxam, of a "Handbook of Chemistry."

Frank Tousey, the publisher, of No. 24 Union Square, East, New York, died at his apartments in the Van Corlear, No. 201 West Fifty-fifth Street. He had been ill from pleurisy for about three weeks. Mr. Tousey, who was a nephew of the late Sinclair Tousey, president of the American News Company, was born in Brooklyn, N. Y., May 24, 1853. He started in business when he was nineteen with the late Norman L. Munro. He left Munro after about ten years, and began a publishing business of his own, with which his brother Sinclair later became associated. He had a varied experience. He founded *Judge*, and was a publisher of many children's periodicals and books. Of late years his company published many popular songs.

Philip James Bailey, chiefly known to fame as the author of "Festus," died at Nottingham, Eng., September 6. He was the son of Thomas Bailey, author of "Annals of Notts," and was born at Nottingham in 1816. He studied at the University of Glasgow, and in 1833 began the study of law, being admitted to the bar in 1840. "Festus" was planned in 1836, and published in 1839. It passed through eleven editions in England and upward of thirty in America. Since the original work was published there have been incorporated with it "The Angel World" (1850), "The Mystic" (1855) and "The Universal Hymn" (1867). He also wrote "The Age," a satire, which was published in 1858, and a prose work on the international policy of the great powers.

William Allen Butler, known to the present generation as the greatest living authority on maritime law and to former generations as the author of "Nothing to Wear," and other poems, died suddenly at his home, Round Oak, Yonkers, N. Y., September 9. He was born in Albany, N. Y., February 20, 1825, and was graduated from the University of New York in 1843. In November, 1857, "Nothing to Wear" appeared anonymously in *Harper's Monthly Magazine*. An impostor claimed it for his work, and Mr. Butler in self-defense revealed himself as its author. It was published in book form by G. W. Carleton and had a wide sale here and in England. He also wrote "The Colonel's Club," "Cities of Art and Early Artists," "The Future," "Barnum's Parnassus," "General Average," "Two Millions," "The Bible by Itself," "Mrs. Limber's Raffle," "Domesticus," "Out of the Way Places in Europe," and a history of the revision of the statutes of New York, with biographical sketches of the revisers.

Professor Rudolf Virchow, the world-renowned pathologist, died in Berlin, September 5. Professor Virchow was born at Schievelbein, in Pomerania, Prussia, October 13, 1821. He obtained his degree as doctor in Berlin. From 1849 to 1856 he held a professorship in the Pathological Academy at Würzburg. In 1856 he returned to Berlin, where he continued to live until the end. Fully half a century ago Professor Virchow started scientific medicine on new courses by his investigations and discoveries in cellular pathology, and the researches and teachings in his laboratory were kept up until two months ago, when he was disabled by an accident that was the indirect cause of his death. Though indefatigable in his scientific and university labors, he devoted forty years of his life to parliamentary labors as a member of the Berlin Municipal Council, and representative in the Prussian Landtag and in the German Reichsrath. In 1852 Virchow founded his "Archives for Pathological Anatomy and Physiology and for Clinical Medicine," and after hesitating five years published in the fourth volume his introduction to or preparation for his "Cellular Pathology," the work which was to make him famous for all time. Three years later in the eighth volume he presented a further contribution to this subject, and the completed work was published in 1858. He wrote a "Handbook of Special Pathology and Therapeutics," instituted "Annual Reports of Advances in Medicine Throughout the World," wrote three volumes on "Morbid Tumors," and published among other things "Collection of Contributions to Scientific Medicine," "The Movement in Favor of Unity in Scientific Medicine," "The Physical and Chemical Properties," "The Metamorphosis," "Origin and the Coagulation of Fibrine," "White Blood Corpuscles," "Inflammation of Blood Vessels," "Contributions to the Pathology of the Skull and Brain," "Granular Appearance of the Walls of Cerebral Ventricles," "Cretinism," "Development of Cretinism," "Cranial Deformities," and "New Formation of Gray Cerebral Substance." Besides these he wrote a number of works on archæological and other subjects.

BOOKTRADE ASSOCIATIONS.

THE AMERICAN PUBLISHERS' ASSOCIATION.

THE membership of the American Publishers' Association is growing steadily. Recently The Jamieson-Higgins Co., of Chicago; Clinton S. Zimmerman, The Baker & Taylor Co., John Wiley & Sons, D. Van Nostrand Co. and Thomas Whittaker, all of New York; also, W. A. Wilde Co. and Herbert B. Turner & Co., of Boston, were admitted. A number of other applications are on file, among the number one from Laird & Lee, of Chicago, and several from Bible publishing houses. Presently it will be unpopular for a publisher to remain outside of the Association—if not unhealthy.

THE BOOKSELLERS' LEAGUE.

THE Booksellers' League will resume its monthly dinners at the rooms of the Aldine Association, New York City, on the evening of October 8. It has not seemed desirable to begin this month, because the vacation terms of quite a number of the members extend into the second and third weeks of September.

The committee has promises of addresses from Francis H. Nichols, author of "Through Hidden Shensi," who will speak on "Shensi, the Hidden Province of China." Robert Pitcher Woodward, author of "On a Donkey's Hurricane Deck," will tell of the experiences gathered on a "Four Thousand Mile Donkey Trip."

The beginning of the fall season would seem a favorable one for intending candidates to apply for membership. As we have often pointed out, the League is doing splendid work, and gives in material and intellectual entertainment full measure for every dollar received in dues.

NOTES ON AUTHORS.

AFTER his retirement Mr. Andrew D. White will settle in Ithaca, N. Y. He is now at work on a book of reminiscences, describing his experiences as Minister at Berlin in 1879-81, as Minister at St. Petersburg in 1892-94, and as Ambassador to Germany from 1897 to his retirement in November next. He is also at work on a volume describing the new Germany of the last decade.

HOWARD PYLE is just finishing work on a book, "The Story of King Arthur," which is a companion volume to the author's popular "Robin Hood." It will appear first as a serial in *St. Nicholas* magazine very fully illustrated by the artist-author. It is said to be no mere recounting of old stories, but an entirely new series of picturesque, romantic tales woven about the old legend of King Arthur.

M. LÉON DAUDET emphatically denies that M. Hugues Le Roux wrote, or even collaborated with his father in the writing of "La Belle Nivernaise." He says that when M. Le Roux first made his claim it brought down upon him "a stern rebuke from my father," whereupon M. Le Roux apologized and promised to be good. M. Le Roux has doubtless told the story so often that he has actually come to believe it.

LITERARY AND TRADE NOTES.

CHARLES R. STENGER, formerly with the Emery Bird Thayer Co., is now in charge of the book department of the Simpson Crawford Co.

JOHN LANE has secured the American rights to Zola's forthcoming novel, "Truth," translated by Ernest Vizetelly. It will not be published, however, until after Christmas.

THE WRIGHT PUBLISHING CO., Akron, O., have brought out a *Beautiful Gem Series*, consisting of biographical and historical cards, each bearing a portrait or picture of the subject, a facsimile autograph, if of a person, and a biographical or historical sketch.

THE INDUSTRIAL PUBLICATION COMPANY, New York City, publish "The Shakespeare Cyclopædia and New Glossary," by John Phinn, intended as a supplement to all the ordinary editions of Shakespeare's works. Edward Dowden furnishes the introduction.

WILLIAM S. LORD, Evanston, Ill., has in press "The Romance of an Old Fool," by Roswell Field, which will continue to the many who have a liking for the work of the genial satirist the happy impression made by his grave drolleries in "The Passing of Mother's Portrait."

THE BLUE SKY PRESS, 4732 Kenwood Avenue, Chicago, announce a special edition of Robert Browning's "In a Balcony," with an introduction by Laura McAdoo Triggs, and a title-page, headings and other designs by W. A. Dwiggins and F. W. Goudy. There will be 400 copies on Van Gelder paper and 15 copies on imperial Japan paper.

A. WESSELS COMPANY will publish shortly in the *"Story of" Series* "The Story of Fish Life," by W. P. Pycraft, and "The Story of Euclid," by W. B. Frankland; also, a life of "Captain John Brown," by John Newton, who describes the stirring scenes of 1855 and 1859, in which the hero of Harper's Ferry so prominently figures in his contest against the pro-slavery party.

THOMAS WHITTAKER has just brought a new book by J. Brierly, entitled "Ourselves and the Universe," studies in life and religion. It may not be generally known that Mr. Brierly is a retired clergyman who frequently contributes to the London *Christian World* over the initials "J. B." Mr. Whittaker has also just published a volume by Dr. John Marshall Lang, entitled "The Church and its Social Mission."

GODFREY A. S. WIENERS, who has succeeded to the publishing business of William Doxey, has in preparation "The Wisdom of à Kempis," "The Wisdom of Schopenhauer," Rossetti's "The House of Life," Lang's "Ballads in Blue China," and a limited edition of the "Rubáiyát," with decorative borders, by Louis B. Coler. The first three books mentioned above contain introductions by Howard V. Sutherland.

J. C. L. CLARK, Lancaster, Mass., has just published a neatly-printed monograph by Mrs. Annie M. L. Clark, entitled "The Alcotts in Harvard." Mrs. Clark gives an interesting account of A. Bronson Alcott's vegetarian community at Harvard, and reminiscences of Louise Alcott and her sisters during the residence of the family at Still River after the collapse of the community. The book contains seven views and four reproductions.

E. P. DUTTON & Co. will publish next week a treatise upon the "Law of Copyright," by E. J. MacGillivray. This work is upon the law of copyright in Great Britain and in the British Possessions and in the United States. It contains a full appendix of all acts of parliament, international conventions, orders in council, treasury minutes and acts of congress in full. They will also bring out with the above "The Roadmender," by Michael Fairless, author of "The Gathering of Brother Hilarious."

FLEMING H. REVELL COMPANY have ready this week a romance of the Northwest, entitled "Two Wilderness Voyagers," a true story of Indian life, by Franklin Welles Calkins. In this book Mr. Calkins writes from his own rich experiences, than which there are none more thrilling, and adding the rare gift of the art of the telling, has produced a realistic, thrilling tale of Indian life. He graphically depicts the exciting adventures of escape and wandering, the drama of the great wilderness.

A. C. McCLURG & Co. publish to-day "On Fortune's Road," a collection of realistic stories of Chicago business life, by Will Payne, with a number of illustrations; "A Captive of the Roman Eagles," a historical novel by Felix Dahn, dealing with the conflicts between Germany and Rome, translated by Mary J. Safford; also, two new books on music by George P. Upton—"Musical Pastels," essays on quaint and curious musical subjects, and "The Standard Light Operas, their plots and their music."

FUNK & WAGNALLS COMPANY will publish on September 20 "Love and the Soul Hunters," by John Oliver Hobbes (Mrs. Craigie), which this artistic author considers the effort of her life; and "The Needle's Eye," by Mrs. Florence Morse Kingsley, a story of modern American life with scenes alternating between vine covered cottages, humble farm-houses, city palaces and the poorest tenements of the slums. The author is always dramatic and humorous, and it is said the latest story will make people laugh, cry and think.

THE Ellwanger family will be represented in Doubleday, Page & Co.'s list this fall by books from George H. and W. D. Ellwanger, both well known in the literary world. George H. Ellwanger's book will be entitled "The Pleasures of the Table," and will deal with the subject chiefly in a historical way. W. D. Ellwanger's volume will be entitled "A Summer Snowflake and Other Poems," which will have illustrations by Wenzell and others. A third brother, H. B. Ellwanger, was the author of an authoritative treatise on the rose.

HENRY HOLT & Co. are about to bring out a new edition of one of their nine volumes devoted to Goethe, being "Egmont," with introduction, notes and bibliography by Professor Robert Waller Deering, of the Western Reserve University, whose editing of "Wilhelm Tell" won such general and hearty approval. They will also issue selected narratives from Wiedemann's "Biblische Geschichten," which most happily combine simplicity with impressiveness. The book will be edited by Professor Lewis A. Rhoades, of the University of Illinois.

THE LOTHROP PUBLISHING COMPANY, of Boston, have just brought out Julian Ralph's brilliant novel of fashionable New York life, entitled "The Millionairess." Mr. Ralph's wide experience with men and things, joined with his picturesque style and skill in narrative has gone to make this one of the notable novels of the early fall. The story gives vivid pictures both of country house and city life, and moves briskly along to a satisfactory end. Mr. Ralph has found a novel motive in depicting a young heiress surrounded by frivolity and fashion, and yet preserving her generous-hearted young womanhood for higher purposes of life.

CHARLES SCRIBNER'S SONS, to meet the very strong demand for a less expensive edition, have just brought out Edith Wharton's successfl story, "The Valley of Decision," in one volume; "Aspects of Fiction and Other Ventures in Criticism," by Brander Matthews; a new edition of "Bob," by Sidney Lanier, with many illustrations in full color, by A. R. Dugmore; "Bob and His Gun," by William Alexander Linn; "The Mid-Eighteenth Century," by J. H. Millar; the concluding volumes of the pocket edition of George Meredith's novels; also, "The Historical Novels of Bulwer Lytton," in six volumes, all fully described by us last week.

D. APPLETON & Co. will publish shortly "The King's Agent," a romance of the days of King William and Queen Mary, by Arthur Patterson. They have in preparation a new novel by J. A. Stewart, entitled "A Son of Gad." The nature of this story is indicated by the passage from the Bible—"a troop shall overcome him, but he shall overcome at last." The characters are British and American, and the development of the story illustrates the process of Americanizing England and Anglicizing America. They will add in the fall to their *Artistic Crafts Series* "Cabinet-making and Designing," by C. Spooner, and "Silverwork and Jewelry," by H. Wilson, both elaborately illustrated.

G. P. PUTNAM'S SONS have just ready "Fame for a Woman, or, Splendid Mourning," the tale of a misguided young wife who leaves domestic happiness because she is persuaded by Cranston Metcalfe that she can "write;" "As Seen from the Ranks, a boy in the Civil War," by Charles E. Benton of the One Hundred and Fiftieth New York State Volunteers; "Italian Life in Town and Country," by Luigi Villari, son of Prof. Villari of Florence; "Industrial Conciliation," the report of the proceedings of the conference held under the auspices of the National Civic Federation, at the rooms of the Board of Trade and Transportation in New York, Dec. 16 and 17, 1901, in *The Questions of the Day Series;* also, "Typhoon," a story of marine life, by Joseph Conrad.

THE BAKER & TAYLOR COMPANY have just ready Dr. Theodore L. Cuyler's autobiography, entitled "Recollections of a Long Life," which is full of material of general interest, owing to the author's intimate acquaintance with many of the noted men of America and Europe. They will publish early in the fall "Reciprocity," by Professor J. Laurence Laughlin, head of the Department of Economics in Chicago University, and Professor H. Parker Willis, of Washington and Lee University; a "Life of Ulrich Zwingli," the Swiss patriot and reformer, by Samuel Simpson; "Help and Good Cheer," a gift book, by Rev. Theodore L. Cuyler, D.D.; "Valid Objections to So-Called Christian Science," by Rev. Andrew F. Underhill; "The Rolfe Shakespeare," in limp leather; and "Over the Black Coffee," compiled by Arthur Gray.

ALBERT BRANDT, Trenton, N. J., announces for the autumn a work dealing with the philosophy of beauty in all forms. The work will be entitled "The Gate Beautiful," being principles and methods in vital art education, and will contain hundreds of charts and reproductions of famous pictures, besides two elaborate color charts. It represents the ripe fruition of a lifetime of trained study, travel and observation by the author, Professor John Ward Stimson, who was long director of art education at the Metropolitan Museum and of the Artist-Artisan Institute, of New York. The work will appear in two editions, one on thick paper, bound in cloth, the other will be printed on thinner paper and bound in paper covers, the purpose being to put it within the possible reach of the many thousands employed in the textile, tile, pottery, jewelry, smithing, and other creative American industries.

LITTLE, BROWN & CO. have in preparation "The Struggle for a Continent," in which Professor Pelham Edgar, of Victoria College, University of Toronto, with the aid of connecting notes gives in Francis Parkman's own language a continuous account of the struggle for the possession of the American continent, beginning with the colonization of Florida by the Huguenots in 1562, and culminating in the fall of Quebec in 1759. The volume includes five hundred pages, with maps, portraits of historical personages, and other illustrations. They will publish during the fall "The Shadow of the Czar," a story of adventure by a new English writer, John R. Carling; "With a Saucepan over the Sea," 600 quaint and delicious recipes used in the kitchens of foreign countries, compiled by Adelaide Keen; also, "Prayers, Ancient and Modern," by Mary W. Tileston, the compiler of "Daily Strength for Daily Needs."

TONNELÉ & CO., 30 East Twenty-first Street, New York, will publish early in October a volume of book-plate essays and pictures, entitled "Book-Plates of To-day," edited by Wilbur Macey Stone. The nucleus of the book will be the matter contained in the first number of the quarterly *Artistic Book-Plates*, the right to use which has been acquired by Messrs. Tonnelé. To this has been added an essay, "The Architect as a Book-plate Designer," by Willis Steell, special reference being made to the work of Mr. Thomas Tryon, of New York. This will be illustrated with ten examples of Mr. Tryon's designs, some of which will be printed in colors. The book will contain seven color plates in all. Lastly, the book will include lists, practically complete to date, of the work of over twenty prominent designers of book-plates. Among them will be found the work of Edwin D. French, Henry Ospovat, Edmund H. New, D. Y. Cameron and Robert Anning Bell.

HARPER & BROTHERS have just published a novel of life in Nebraska, by a new writer, Mrs. Elizabeth Higgins, entitled "Out of the West," which takes into account the conditions that gave rise to the Populist movement, and gives a faithful picture of the life of the small town, stranded on the edge of civilization, of which there were so many in the West some years ago, during that calamitous period. They have also just ready "Outdoorland," a book for children by Robert W. Chambers, the author of "Cardigan," with illustrations by Reginald Birch, seven of which are in color. They will publish shortly "The Reign of Queen Anne," by Justin McCarthy, an introductory volume to the author's histories of England, beginning with his "History of the Four Georges," etc.; "Winslow Plain," by Sarah P. McLean, a new story of New England life, by the author of "Cape Cod Folks," etc.; also, "In the Morning Glow," by Roy Rolfe Gilson, author of "When Love is Young," with illustrations by Alice Barber Stephens.

JAMIESON-HIGGINS CO., Chicago, announce a volume of up-to-date nursery rhymes entitled "Yankee Mother Goose," by Benjamin Cobb and Miss Ella Brison, with a number of colored illustrations; a new issue of "Kids of Many Colors," which was so successful last year; "'2002,' Child Life One Hundred Years from Now," by Laura Dayton Fessenden and R. J. Campbell, fully illustrated; "A Round Robin," a collection of stories and poems for children by well-known authors, edited by Laura Dayton Fessenden, with 16 half-tone engravings; "Old Mother Hubbard," by Harry Kennedy and Charles Jerome Costello; also, "Moon Children," a delightful book for children by Laura Dayton Fessenden and R. J. Campbell. This firm is making an offer of $500 for the most original title, subject and general idea for a child's book. To the person offering the second best they will award $250, and to each of the next five they will award $50, making $1000 in all. The contest will close December 31 and the decision of the judges will be announced January 15, 1903.

LONGMANS, GREEN & CO. will publish shortly a volume of "Historical Essays and Reviews," by Dr. Mandell Creighton, sometime Bishop of London, edited by Louise Creighton; "The Study of the Gospels," by the Rev. J. Armitage Robinson, Canon of Westminster; and "A Christian Apologetic," by the Very Rev. Wilford L. Robbins, Dean of Albany, N. Y., two new volumes of the series of *Handbooks for the Clergy*, edited by Canon Robinson; a new and cheaper edition of "The

Hexateuch According to the Revised Version," edited by J. E. Carpenter and G. Harford-Battersby; "The Great Mountains and Forests of South America," by Paul Fountain; "The Portraitures of Julius Cæsar," a monograph, by Frank J. Scott; "The Characters of Theophrastus," newly translated by Charles E. Bennett and William A. Hammond, professors in Cornell University; "Text-Book of Electro-Chemistry," by Svante Arrhenius, translated by John McCrae; "The Analysis of Steel Works Materials," by Harry Brearley and Fred Ibbotson; also, "A College Manual of Rhetoric," by Charles Sears Baldwin, of Yale. They will bring out this month "In King's By-ways," a collection of stories, by Stanley J. Weyman, and "By the Ramparts of Jezreel," a romance of Jehu, King of Israel, by Arnold Davenport. In October they will publish "The Lord Protector," a story of Cromwell's time, by S. Levett Yeats; Andrew Lang's Christmas book for 1902, entitled "The Book of Romance," with eight colored plates and forty-four other illustrations; also, a new Golliwogg book, in which the clever authors follow the adventures of the Golliwoggs in an air ship.

The Macmillan Company have in preparation the authoritative "Life of William Ewart Gladstone," by John Morley; a new volume by Lafcadio Hearn entitled "Some Japanese Curios, with Sundry Cobwebs;" "The Splendid Idle Forties," a collection of stories of old California, by Gertrude Atherton; "The Four Feathers," a story by A. E. W. Mason, the author of "Miranda of the Balcony;" "The Grey Wig," a collection of short stories, by Zangwill, dealing with the London Ghetto; "A Waif of the Plains," the story of a child kidnapped when very young by Indians, by Frederic Remington, who also illustrates the book; "The Henchman," a novel of love and politics, by Mark Lee Luther; "Bayard's Courier," by B. K. Benson, author of "Who Goes There;" also, "The Children of the Frost," by Jack London, a series of stories dealing with the primitive folk of Alaska, Eskimos and Indians. Among the illustrated books which they have in press are several whose subjects will at once attract attention, and which will be particularly suitable for holiday gifts. Mrs. Alice Morse Earle's "Sun Dials and Roses of Yesterday;" Sir Gilbert Parker's "Quebec: The Place and the People:" Clifton Johnson's "New England and its Neighbors;" each of which is very sumptuously illustrated and handsomely bound. "Ancient Athens" is another finely illustrated work by Ernest Arthur Gardner, formerly director of the British School at Athens; it will be issued in uniform size and style with Mau's handsome work on "Pompeii: Its Life and Art," of which a new and cheaper edition is to appear. Both Mrs. Earle's book and Sir Gilbert Parker's will be issued also in limited large-paper editions. "Furniture of Olden Times," by Miss Frances C. Morse, illustrated with many reproductions of quaint and valuable pieces, will appeal to many readers of taste. It will be published also in a large-paper edition limited to one hundred copies. They also announce "An Illustrated History of English Literature," by Richard Garnett and Edmund Gosse, a feature of which will be the many rare facsimiles and portraits which it will contain.

Thomas Y. Crowell & Co. have just brought out one of the most important literary ventures of the season—the *Virginia edition* of the works of Edgar Allan Poe. The text has been carefully revised by James A. Harrison, professor in the University of Virginia, upon the versions which last came under the author's eye, and the variant readings have been scrupulously recorded. Through the careful searching of the files of periodicals to which Poe contributed, a considerable addition, particularly under the head of criticism, has been made to the collected works of Poe, while these additions are in the main not merely due to editorial instinct—a test which has failed lamentably in the case of Thackeray's anonymous papers—but are attested by letters of Poe or his identifying initials in his own copies. In much of this work of text construction the editor has had access to copies corrected by Poe himself, while he has for the first time collected or printed a complete volume of letters. The works are distributed among seventeen volumes gotten up in two styles—the handy volume style, pocket size, (4 x 6 inches,) in cloth, limp leather and half calf boxed, and in library style, (5½ x 8½ inches,) in cloth and half calf. The first volume contains a new life of Poe, by Professor Harrison, and Poe's autobiography; volumes 2 to 6 contain the tales in their proper chronological order, with an introduction—"Poe's Place in American Literature"—by Hamilton W. Mabie; volume 7 contains the poems, based upon Poe's personal copy of his poems, giving emendations and corrections in the poet's handwriting, with an introduction by Dr. Charles W. Kent and textual notes by R. A. Stewart; volumes 8 to 13 contain Literary Criticism, nearly half of the text being new matter that has not seen the light of print since their original appearance; volumes 14 to 16 contain essays and miscellanies, including Poe's manuscript corrections of "Eureka," and several hitherto unpublished papers; and the 17th volume contains a new collection of letters. The volumes are fully indexed, and accompanied with photogravure frontispieces, including portraits and views. Both editions are printed from new plates on good paper and are attractively bound.

Houghton, Mifflin & Co. will publish late in October or early in November "A Sea Turn, and Other Matters," a collection of new short stories, by Thomas Bailey Aldrich; "The Heart of the Doctor," a love story of the Boston Italian quarter, by Mabel G. Foster; "Uncle Charley," a charming story of a little girl and her whimsical, lovable uncle, by Zephine Humphrey; "The Heritage," a story of Indian fighting in Ohio during the Revolution, by Burton Egbert Stevenson, librarian of the Chillicothe Public Library; an estimate of Longfellow by Thomas Wentworth Higginson, in the *American Men of Letters Series;* "George Rogers Clark," by Frederick J. Turner, in the *Riverside Biographical Series;* a *Cambridge edition* of the complete poems of Pope, edited by Henry W. Boynton; a humorous paraphrase of familiar fairy tales in verse, by Guy Wetmore Carryl, entitled "Grimm Tales Made Gay;" "A Pocketful of Posies," simple verse of child-life, by Abbie Farwell Brown; "The Champion," a present-day Southern story for boys, by Charles Egbert Craddock; "Three Little Marys," stories of little girls of Scotland, England and Ireland, by Nora A. Smith; a holiday edition of Kate Douglas Wiggin's "Penelope's Irish Experiences," with illustrations by Charles E. Brock; a new holiday edition of Thoreau's "Walden," with introduction by Bradford Torrey and twenty photogravures of Concord scenes and persons; a "Handbook of the Birds of the Western United States," by Florence Merriam Bailey, with thirty-three full-page plates by Fuertes; "Aid to the Study of Dante," by Charles A. Dinsmore, which contains considerable quotations from the most important Dante commentators; "Moliere," an attractive literary study of the foremost of French dramatists, by Leon H. Vincent; "The Physiological Aspects of the Liquor Problem," the result of invaluable and painstaking scientific research by famous American specialists, edited by Dr. J. S. Billings; the first part of a work entitled "Trees and Shrubs," a description, by Charles Sprague Sargent, of new or little-known ligneous plants such as would flourish in the gardens of the United States and Europe, with illustrations from drawings by C. E. Faxon; also, "A Study of Prose Fiction," a discussion of the outlines of fiction, the outcome of a course of lectures at Princeton, by Bliss Perry, the editor of the *Atlantic Monthly.*

BUSINESS NOTES.

ATLANTA, GA.—The Southern Book Company has filed a petition for a charter in the Superior Court here. It is to be capitalized at $250,000. The company is said to be the outcome of the movement in the South to secure text-books that deal with the war of 1860-'64 from a Southern point of view.

BATH, N. Y.—Lang's Central Bookstore was sold at auction to Davidson & Harper, of Cooperstown, for $2500. Lang, as reported last week, filed a voluntary petition in bankruptcy, and the stock was sold by Trustee McMaster. The stock and fixtures inventoried at about $3700. The new firm took possession at once.

BOSTON, MASS.—Rockwell & Churchill, the widely-known printing house, has made an assignment.

DENISON, IA.—F. J. Gable has been succeeded by H. A. Carpenter.

GREAT FALLS, MONT.—A. E. Caulfield has bought out the business of Flaherty & Joyce.

IRVINGTON, N. Y—William H. Gledhill has gone into voluntary bankruptcy.

NEW YORK CITY.—M. A. Gropper has purchased the book business of Ludwig Kölner at 78 Fourth Avenue.

SHERMAN, TEX.—Hugh Perry has been succeeded by Richardson & Sanders.

BOOKS WANTED.

☞ In answering, please state edition, condition, and price, including postage or express charges.

Houses that are willing to deal exclusively on a cash-on-delivery basis will find it to their advantage to put after their firm-name the word [Cash].

☞ Write your wants plainly and on one side of the sheet only. Illegibly-written "wants" will be considered as not having been received. The "Publishers' Weekly" does not hold itself responsible for errors.

It should be understood that the appearance of advertisements in this column, or elsewhere in the "Publishers' Weekly" does not furnish a guarantee of credit. While it is endeavored to safeguard these columns by withdrawing the privilege of their use from advertisers who are not "good pay," booksellers should take the usual precaution, as to advertisers not known to them, that they would take in making sales to any unknown parties.

Arthur M. Allen, 508 Fulton St., Troy, N. Y.

Animal Magnetism, Dr. Jno. Ashburne.
Intuition, Mrs. F. Kingman.
Hypnotism, or, Psycho-Therapeutics, by Dr. R. W Elkins.

Almy, Bigelow & Washburn, Salem, Mass.

Harper's Weekly, Apr. 21, 1900.

Amer. Bapt. Pub. Soc., 69 Whitehall St., Atlanta, Ga.

History of Georgia, by Wallace Reid.

Amer. Bapt. Pub. Soc., 177 Wabash Ave., Chicago.

The Holy Spirit in Life and Service, by A. C. Dixon.
Any books on the organization and history of the Jesuits.

Amer. Bapt. Pub. Soc., 279 Elm St., Dallas, Tex.

Cramp's History of the Baptist. Pub. by A. B. P. S.

American Tract Soc., 150 Nassau St., N. Y.

Wreck and the Rescue. Am. Tract Soc.

Americus Law Book Co., Americus, Ga. [*Cash.*]

Southern Bivouac.
Southern Magazine.
Southern Literary Messenger.
Southern Quarterly Review.
Debow's Review.

Jas. I. Anderson & Co., 183 Dundas St., London, Can.

The Authentic Report of the Discussion held at Rome Concerning the Coming of St. Peter to Rome, by Wm. Arthur.

Andrew Carnegie Free Library, Carnegie, Pa.

Davis, Days Afield in Staten Island.

Antiquarian Book Concern, Omaha, Neb.

Johnson, Magna Charta.
Montholon and Gournand, Memoirs of Napoleon.
Phillips, Grattan and Emmet's Speeches.
Myers, Conversations Lexicon, latest ed.
Baldwin Latham, Civil Engineering.
Bengel, Gnomon in English.
Father De Smet's Works.
Edouard von Hartmann's Works.
The Criminal, by Havelock Ellis.
Education and Heredity, by J. M. Guyau.
Evolution of Sex, by Geddes and Thomson.

BOOKS WANTED.—Continued.

Antiquarian Book Concern.—*Continued.*

Man and Woman, by Havelock Ellis.
Primitive Folk, by Elisée Reclus.
Psychology of the Emotions, by Th. Ribot.
Science of Fairy Tales, by Hartland.
Tales from *Blackwood,* both ser.
Walker, Philosophy of Skepticism.
Murphy, On Pentateuch; Psalms.
Tayler Lewis, Six Days of Creation.
Christlieb, Modern Doubt and Christian Belief.
Whately, Historic Doubts Concerning Napoleon.
Alexander (Bp.), The Witness of the Psalms to Christ.
McIntosh, Is Christ Infallible?
Trench, The Fitness of Holy Scriptures for Unfolding Spiritual Life.
Faber, The Difficulties of Infidelity.

D. Appleton & Co., 72 Fifth Ave., N. Y.

Sabine's Deception. Harper.

The Baker & Taylor Co., 33 E. 17th St., N. Y.

Along New England Roads, by W. C. Prime. Harper.

The Balto. Book Co., 301 St. Paul St., Baltimore, Md.

Atlantic Reporter, v. 1 to 23, incl.; v. 44 to 58.
State journals and documents.
Maryland Law Reports, v. 1 to 85.
Thirty-one Orations Upon Alex. Hamilton, Dodge.
The Shallow Hand, Tracy.
Harris and Giel, Md. Report., v. 1.

N. J. Bartlett & Co., 28 Cornhill, Boston, Mass

Owen, Five Great Skeptical Dramas.
Dwight, Travels in New England, 4 v.
Winthrop, New England, 2 v. 1853.

Bellevue College Library, Bellevue, Neb. [*Cash.*]

Arena, Mar., 1902.
Bookman, Dec., 1901.
Current Literature, Oct., 1901; Jan., 1902.
Independent, Sept. 26, 1901.
Review of Reviews, Dec., 1901.

Bigham & Smith, Agts., Dallas, Tex.

Irish Book for Classes in America, 1st and 2d. Lynch, 1878.
Joyce's Grammar of the Irish Language. Lynch.

G. Blatchford, Pittsfield, Mass.

Regimental Losses in Civil War.

Book Exchange, Toledo, O.

Songs from Vagabondia, any v., 1st ed.
Chopin: the Man, Jas. Huneker, 1st ed.
Volumes in Folio; Retrospective Reviews.
Morris, Earthly Paradise, 4 v.; Aeneids; Jason.
2 copies *Harper's Mag.,* July, Aug., 1902.

The Book Supply Co , 266 Wabash Ave., Chicago, Ill.

Set of Carlyle's Life of Oliver Cromwell. Harper.

The Boston Book Co., 83 Francis St., Boston, Mass

Banker's Mag., Feb., 1891.
Eclectic Mag., July, 1848, $1.00, or v. 14, $2.00.
Jour. Military Service Inst., no. 3. $1.00.
Our Day, July, Oct., 1892; Feb.-Aug., Oct., Dec., '96; July, Nov., '97. 25 cts. each.
Political Science Quarterly, Mar., 1899. 75 cts.

The Bowen-Merrill Co., Indianapolis, Ind.

Peacock, History of Arithmetic.

Brentano's, Union Sq., N. Y.

Richardson, The Anti-Nicene Fathers, bibliog., synopsis. Buffalo, 1887.
Singing Mouse, Hough. Forest and Stream.
Beecher's Sermons, v. 1. F., H. & H.
Jonathan Slick.
Dukesboro Tales, R. M. Johnston, pap. D. A. & Co.
Roderick Hudson, Henry James. H., M. & Co.
Captured Cruiser. Scribner.
Problem of Evolution, Headley. Crowell.
Wigwam and War Path, Hope. Scribner.
Affirmations, Ellis.
Liberation of Italy, Cesaresco.
Territorial Acquisitions of U. S., Bicknell. S., M. & Co.
Quebec Past and Present, Sir James Lemoine.
Makers of Florence, v. 3, Min. ser. Macmillan.
A. Trollope's Autobiography. Harper.
Joseph Andrews, Fielding.
A Midsummer Ramble in the Dolomites, Amelia B. Edwards. Routledge.
Davenport Dunne. Warne.
Naval Portfolio of the Expedition to Mexico under Commodore Perry.

Brentano's, N. Y.—*Continued.*

Naval Portfolio, no. 8, Vera Cruz.
Sketches of Mexican War, Lieut. Walke.
Naval Portfolio, Mouth of Tabasco River.
Naval Portfolio, Ascending the Tabasco River.
Naval Portfolio, Landing at Tabasco.
Naval Portfolio, Capture of Tabasco.

Brentano's, 1015 Pennsylvania Ave., Washington, D. C.

Payne, Arabian Nights.
Baker, Secret Service in the Civil War.
Gen. Custer's My Life on the Plains.
Connelly, Irish Family History.
Connelly, The Eugenians.
Gautier, Wanderings in Spain.
Stephens, Hours in a Library.

The Brown, Eager & Hull Co., Toledo, O.

Workshop Reconstruction, by Ashbee.
Laus Veneris, by Swinburne, 1st ed., ed. of 1866.
Bob, Son of Battle, old ed.
Miss Traumerei.

The Burrows Bros. Co., Cleveland, O.

Stendhal, Racine et Shakespeare.
Joy, Ten Englishmen of the 19th Century.
Dawson, Lit. Leaders in Modern Eng.
Hapgood, Survey of Russian Literature.

William J. Campbell, Phila., Pa.

Henry Reed's Lectures on English Literature.

George H. Carr, Newport, R. I.

Evelyn's Diary and Correspondence, any early ed.
Pepys' Diary, and early ed.

Case Library, Cleveland, O.

Allen, Report on American Bison.
Fisk, Cost of Railroad Transportation.
Garland, Private Stables.
Gogol, Dead Souls.
De Mille, The Dodge Club.

A. S. Clark, 174 Fulton St., N. Y.

I will pay $5 per copy for *Eclectic Magazine,* Dec., 1845, and June, 1847.
$3 for *Political Quarterly,* Mar., 1887.

The A. H. Clark Co., Garfield Bldg., Cleveland, O.

O'Callaghan, Docu. Hist. of N. Y., v. 4.
Flint, Socialism.
Hastings, J., Bible Dictionary.
Sabatier, P., St. Francis of Assisi, Life.

The Robert Clarke Co., 31 E. 4th St., Cincinnati, O

Lyall, Edna, Land of the Leal.
Renée and Franz, cl.

W. B. Clarke Co., Park and Tremont Sts., Boston, Mass.

Dictionary of Painters and Engravers, Bryan.
In a Poppy Garden.
Edwin Drood, Lib. ed. London, 1870.
An Island Garden, Thaxter.
Outlines of Irish History, Justin McCarthy.

Henry T. Coates & Co., Phila., Pa.

Habberton, Some Folks.
Adams, Chapters on Erie.
Journal of Elizabeth Drinker.
Gosse, A Naturalist's Sojourn in Jamaica.
Miller, In the Kitchen.

Wm. G. Colesworthy, 66½ Cornhill, Boston, Mass.

From $3 to $6 offered per vol. for Townsend's ed. of Cooper, Darley plates, as follows: Precaution; Afloat and Ashore; Miles Wallingford; Jack Tier; The Ways of the Hour.
A good price paid for Science and Health, by Mary B. Glover. Boston, 1875.

Congdon & Britnell, Toronto, Can.

Pilling's Bibliography of the Athapascan Languages.
Pilling's Bibliography of the Salishan Languages.
Adams' (John Quincy) Memoirs, 12 v., 8vo. Phila., 1874-7.

Coryell & Co., 61 Chambers St., N. Y.

Fifty Years in Both Hemispheres, or, Reminiscences of the Life of a Former Merchant, Vincent Nolte. Redfield, 1854.
Morgan Horses, D. W. Linsley. Pub. in Kansas.

Crusoe & Co., 81 Vermont St., Brooklyn, N. Y.

Facsimiles of English script before 1680, letters, wills, authors' manuscript, journals, legal documents, etc.
Crosby, Sentential Analysis; also Xenophon's Anabasis, with vocab.

BOOKS WANTED.—*Continued.*

Cushing & Co., 34 W. Baltimore St., Baltimore, Md.

Warner's Library, small ed.
Memoir of John Yates, Beall.
Niles' Register, v. 50-75.

Damrell & Upham, 283 Washington St., Boston, Mass.

Fighting Quaker.

A. W. Dellquest & Co., 206 Mesa Ave., El Paso, Tex.

Burke's Peerage.
Any leading paper or magazine pub. in the year 1842 or 1843 containing advertisement for the heirs of Horace Walpole.
U. S. Government Report on the Zuni Expedition.

F. M. DeWitt, 318 Post St., San Francisco, Cal.

Chicago Record Cook Book.
Top or Bottom, Which?
Tales from *Town Topics*, no. 16.

Dixie Book Shop, 35 Nassau St., N. Y.

Knickerbocker's New York. Grolier Club.
Darley's illustrations of Dickens.
Symonds, Cellini, Nimmo ed.
Robt. Louis Stevenson, Edinburgh ed.
Richard Burton, 1st eds.

Dodd, Mead & Co., 372 Fifth Ave., N. Y.

Book-Lover, no. 2.
Franklin Autobiography, L. P. ed. Lippincott.
The World's Orators, v. 1. Putnam.
The Virginian, by Wister, 1st ed. 1902.
Mitchell, Donald G., From Elizabeth to Anne, 1st ed., 1890, in English Lands, Letters and Kings ser.
The Lorgnette, 2 v., 1850.
Paulding, Dutchman's Fireside, any ed.
Cooper, Jas. Fenimore, Precaution, a novel. 2 v., 12mo, Townsend ed., Darley plates. N. Y.
Cable, G. W., The Grandissimes. 1880.
Journal of the Geological Society of London, v. 12. 1856.
Whittier, Poetical Works, 2 v. 1870.
Whittier, A Sabbath Scene. Boston, Ticknor, Reed & Fields, 1853.
Whittier, Tent on the Beach. 1867.
Whittier, Maud Muller. 1867.
Whittier, Child Life. 1872.
Whittier, Tent on the Beach. 1877.
Santayana, Sonnets. H. S. Stone & Co.
Trumbull, Border Lines in the Field of Doubtful Practices. Revell.
Whittier, Hazel Blossoms. 1878.
Whittier, Tent on the Beach. 1868.

Doubleday, Page & Co., 218 5th Ave., N. Y.

Swigo Cornovo's Health, printed in English.

Wm. J. C. Dulany Co., 8 Baltimore St., E., Baltimore, Md.

Greeley, H., What I Know About Farming.
Howlett, Lessons in Driving.
Brown, H., Life of J. A. Symonds.

Daniel Dunn, 677 Fulton St., Brooklyn, N. Y.

Nichols, Business Guide. Naperville, Ills.
Adams, Landlord and Tenant, second-hand.

E. P. Dutton & Co., 31 W. 23d St., N. Y.

Hessians and the Other German Auxiliaries of Great Britain in the Revolutionary War, by E. J. Lowell.
Work on Scriptural Subjects, by Mary Sheffner.

C. P. Everitt, 218 5th Ave., N. Y.

Longfellow, Osgood ed.
Rochefoucauld's Maxims, good ed.
Brann, W. C., Writings of (former editor of the *Iconoclast* of Waco, Texas.)

The Ezekiel & Bernheim Co., 334 Main St., Cincinnati, O.

Cooper's (J. F.) Works: The Deer Slayer; Wing and Wing; The Pioneers; Red Rover; The Pilot; The Prairie, 8vo, cl., original bindings, illus. from drawings by F. O. C. Darley. D. Appleton & Co., 1872-73. State lowest price for one or all.

Harry Falkenau, 167 Madison St., Chicago, Ill.

On Arteries, Frederick Tiedemann.
Veneris Priapus, with illus.
Haward, Hist. of the Mongols, 3 v.

P. K. Foley, 14 Beacon St., Boston, Mass.

Hewlett, Earthwork Out of Tuscany. London, 1895.
Taylor, Bayard, Xinena. Phila., 1844.
Taylor, Translation of Faust, 2 v. Bost., 1870-71.
Taylor, The American Legend. Bost., 1850.
Taylor, Ballad of Abraham Lincoln. 1870.
Thoreau, Early Spring. Bost., 1881 or '94.

P. K. Foley.—*Continued.*

Thoreau, Summer. Bost., 1884.
Thoreau, Winter. Bost., 1888.
Thoreau, Autumn. Bost., 1892.
Thoreau, Thoughts. Bost., 1890.
Thoreau, Familiar Letters. Bost., 1894.
Thoreau, Excursions. Bost., 1894.
King, Thos. Starr, In Memoriam. 1864.
Ward, Artemus, 1st eds.
Harte, Bret, 1st eds.
Twain, Mark, 1st eds.
American periodicals, previous to 1850.
American annuals, gift books, etc.

Fords, Howard & Hulbert, Bible House, N. Y.

Poetry of the Civil War, Richard Grant White. 1866.
Loyal Lyrics, F. Moore. 1864.

W. R. Funk, Agt., Dayton, O.

Brawnville Papers, M. C. Tyler.

Garrett Booke Shoppe, G. W. F. Blanchfield, 58 Ann St., Hartford, Conn. [*Cash.*]

Olmsted, Cotton Kingdom, v. 2.
Black, Guide to Ireland.
Old guide books to Ireland.
Lecture on Public Instruction in Prussia, by G. S. Hillard, 16mo. Phila., 1836.

The J. K. Gill Co., 133 3d St., Portland, Ore.

Grimshaw, On Saws. Pub. by H. C. Baird & Co., price $7.50. If second-hand please state condition.

Edwin S. Gorham, 4th Ave. and 22d St., N. Y.

Watkins, On Holy Matrimony.
All Is Not Gold that Glitters.
Liddon, Divinity and other works, second-hand.
Hawks, Constitutions and Canons.

Gregory's Book Store, 116 Union St., Providence, R. I.

Grenfell, Alexandrian Erotic Fragments.
Butcher, Theory of Fine Arts.

L. Hammel & Co., Mobile, Ala.

Preadamites, by Winchell.
Old Man Gilbert, by Mrs. Bellamy.

Wm. Beverley Harison, 65 E. 59th St., N. Y.

Gouin's Art of Teaching and Studying Languages.

S. F. Harriman, 11 S. High St., Columbus, O.

Life of John Whetsel.
Set Parker's People's Bible.
Life of Winfield Scott, v. 2 only.
Prices on job lots if low.
Success Library, 10 v.

Harvard Co-operative Society, Cambridge, Mass.

Saintsbury's edition of Scott's Dryden.
Conquest of Charlotte.
Cotswold Village.
Barnaby Lee, John Bennett.
Siena, Its Architecture and Art.
Burnham, History and Uses of Limestone.

J. K. Hester, Cozad, Neb.

Campbell and Rice Debate.
Adam Clark's Commentary.
Christian System, by Campbell.

J. A. Hill & Co., 91 5th Ave., N. Y.

Modern Discoveries of the Bible, by John Urquhart.

Walter M. Hill, 31 Washington St., Chicago, Ill.

Vernon Lee's Works, any 1st eds.
Sequin's Idiocy.
Dove Press, Tacitus, Agricola.
Browning (Robert), Paracelsus, 1st ed.
Defoe's Robinson Crusoe, 1st ed.
George Eliot, 1st eds.
Tennyson's Poems. 1833.
Alphabets New and Old, Ex-Libris Ser.
Hunt's Ultra Crepidarius. 1823.
Hunt's Hero and Leander. 1819.
Swinburne, Poems and Ballads, 1st eds. of three ser.
Aldine Poets, Butler, 2 v. 1835.
Aldine Poets, Swift, 3 v. 1833.
Aldine Poets, Churchill, 3 v. 1844.
Aldine Poets, Gray, 1 v. 1836.

The Hub Magazine Co., 67 Broad St., Boston, Mass.

St. Nicholas, v. 1-4, cl., odd nos. in large lots.
Catalogues from second-hand booksellers.

L. Indermark, 3211 Barrett St., St. Louis, Mo. [*Cash.*]

American Chem. Jl., Balto., v. 1-6, any pts. or vols.
Wiley's Agricult. Analysis, v. 3 (Agricult. Products).
Science, vols. and nos. of old series.
Science, vols. and nos. of all series.
Proc. Amer. Assoc. Adv. Sc., 5th, 15th, 21st meet.
Experiment Station Record, from 1897 to date.

BOOKS WANTED.—Continued.

H. N. Jackson, 36 W. 6th St., Cincinnati, O.

McMechen, Legends of Ohio Valley.
Dodge, Redmen of Ohio Valley.
Boyce, Journal Wayne's Campaign. Cinn., 1866.
Abbott, History of Ohio.
Langworthy, Life of R. M. Johnson of Ky.
Good price paid for above.

R. L. Jacques, LaFayette, Ind.

Shakespeare and the Bible, with parallel passages (cash price), by G. Q. Colton.

U. P. James, 127 W. 7th St., Cincinnati, O.

American Statistical Association Publications, v. 1, no. 4.
Great Round World, July 11, 18; Dec. 28, 1901.
Municipal Engineering, Aug., 1901.
Blavatsky, Secret Doctrine, 3 v. and index, good copy.

E. T. Jett Book and News Co., 806 Olive St., St. Louis, Mo.

Robert Tannahill's Poems. Pub. by Cameron & Ferguson, Glasgow, Scotland.
Richard Weaver's Life Story, by Rev. J. Patterson.

E. W. Johnson, 2 E. 42d St., N. Y.

Wilson, Tales of the Border.
Jewett, Ceramics.
Poor's R. R. Manual, 1890, '92, '94, '95, '96, '97, '98.
Hitchcock, Analysis of the Bible.

King's Old Book Store, 15 4th St., San Francisco, Cal.

Blue and Gold, Class of '77, '81, '84, '99, 1900, '01, '02, '03.

Geo. Kleinteich, 397 Bedford Ave., Brooklyn, N. Y. [*Cash.*]

Edwards, The Will.

W. H. Kuhl, 73 Jager-Str., W., Berlin, Germany.

Porter, Cruise to Pacific Ocean. N. Y., '22.
Fanning, Voyage Round the World. N. Y., '33.
Marine Review (xxiv., 23), Dec. 5, 1901.

Chas. E. Lauriat Co., 301 Washington St., Boston, Mass.

Bret Harte's Works, ed. de luxe, hf. mor.
Carver, John, Travels Through the Interior Parts of North America.
Evolution of Woman, Proctor.
The Cryptogram, Ignatius Donnelly.
Aelfric, C. L. White. Lamson, Wolffe Co.
Reading Without Tears, pap. or cl. Harper.
The Banker's Daughter, pap. or cl. Harper.

Leggat Bros., 81 Chambers St., N. Y.

Tit Bits of American Humor. Pub. by White & Allen.
Wild Flowers of America, Buck.
Gulliver's Travels, good ed.
Sach, Text-Book of Botany.

Lemcke & Buechner, 812 Broadway, N. Y.

Ball, Geo. W., Maternal Ancestry of Washington.
Moore, T., Life of Byron.
Bay, Surveyor and President.
Cicero, Philippic Orations, with notes by King, 2d larger ed.
Burnham, New Poultry Book.
Lowell, Hessians and the German Auxiliaries of Great Britain in the Revolutionary War.
Heimburg, Lottie of the Mill.
Chatterbox for 1887.
Reid, Rifle Rangers.

Library Clearing House, 140 Wells St., Chicago, Ill.

Broadus, On Homiletics.
Gardner Genealogy.
Baldwin, Prehistoric Nations.
Semmes, Cruise of the "Alabama," or, Service Afloat.
Prescott, Philip the Second, v. 3.

The Literary Shop, 506 11th St., N. W., Washington, D. C.

U. S. Statutes at Large, v. 7.
Gilmore, Four Years in the Saddle.
Shakespeare's Works, good ed.

S. Login, 1328 3d Ave., N. Y.

Appleton's Popular Science Monthly, v. 54, 55, 56, 57, Aug., 1891; Nov., Dec., 1900.

Lorimer Book Co., 1527 Market St., San Francisco, Cal.

Flynn, On Hydraulics.
Practical Treatise on Hydraulics, by Bowie.

Lyon, Kymer & Palmer Co., Grand Rapids, Mich.

Franklin Square Song Book, nos. 1, 2, pap.

S. F. McLean & Co., 44 E. 23d St., N. Y.

Oliphant, Chronicles of Carlingford, any.
Brandl, S. G. Coleridge and English Romantic Movement, Eng. tr.
De Vere, Essays, Chiefly on Poetry.
Savage, The Falcon Family.
Savage, My Uncle the Curate.

M. N. Maisel, 194 E. Broadway, N. Y. [*Cash.*]

Stubbs, W., Constitutional History of England, v. 1, 3d ed.
Anything by Tourgeneff, Tolstoy, Gogol, Pushkine, Stepniak and Korolenko.

B. & J. F. Meehan, Bath, Eng.

Dickens: books, pamphlets, or magazine articles on Dickens or his works.

F. M. Morris, 171 Madison St., Chicago, Ill

Angel and Devil, Minerva Library.

Noah Farnham Morrison, 893 Broad St., Newark, N. J. [*Cash.*]

Schoolcraft, Indians, v. 6.
Stonehenge, On the Dog, Amer. ed. Pub. by Orange Judd Co.

C. C. Morse & Son, 69 Merrimack St., Haverhill, Mass.

Greeley, American Conflict, v. 1, shp.
Winsor, History of Duxbury, Mass.
Cheney Genealogy.
Winston Genealogy, v. 1, 2.

W. W. Mounts, 802 Penn Ave., Pittsburgh, Pa.

Saudow's Work on Physical Culture, cheap.
The Golden Wreath Song Book. Pub. about 1857.
The Iconoclast.

W. W. Nisbet, 12 S. Broadway, St. Louis, Mo.

Beaumont and Fletcher's Works.
Caroline of Brunswick. Pub. by Peterson.
Histories of Mathematics.
Lee, Shadow of the Christ.
Rolfe's Shakespeare Plays, any.

Daniel O'Shea, 1584 Broadway, N. Y.

Bodley Family (containing The Little Red Hen.)
Index of Conveyances Recorded in the Office of Register of the City and Co. of New York, Grantors, W., pt. 1 only.

H. H. Otis & Sons, 11 W. Swan St., Buffalo, N. Y.

Upham, Interior Life.
Upham, Life of Faith.
Ullmann, Sinlessness of Jesus.

E. T. Pardee, 146 Bowdoin St., Boston, Mass.

Munsey's Magazine, v. 8, no. 1, Oct., 1892; v. 9, no. 4, July, '93.
Book of the Royal Blue, B. & O. R. R., pts. of vols. 1, 2, 3, 4.
Black Diamond Express Monthly, L. V. R. R., pts. of vols. 1, 2, 3.

C. C. Parker, 246 S. Broadway, Los Angeles, Cal. [*Cash.*]

To My Valentine, v. 1, blue cl.

The Pilgrim Press, 175 Wabash Ave., Chicago, Ill.

Fritz Reuter, Old Story of Farming Days.

T. Pillot, 409 Main St., Houston, Tex.

Burke's Dormant and Extinct Peerage.

E. W. Porter, St. Paul, Minn.

Any ed. of the following by Ouida: Afternoon; Frescoes; Pipistrello; Folle Farine; A Leaf in a Storm.

C. S. Pratt, 161 6th Ave., N. Y. [*Cash.*]

Catlin, Shut Your Mouth and Save Your Life.
Rabelais.
Monier-Williams, Buddhism, etc.
Ethnology of the N. W. C. Queensland Aborigines.
Thos. Little's Poems.

Presb. Bd. of Pub. and S. S. Work, 192 Michigan Ave., Chicago, Ill.

Almost a Priest.
Priest and Nun.
Set J. F. and B. Commentary, second-hand.

Preston & Rounds Co., Providence, R. I.

2 copies Phoenixiana, by Derby.

C. J. Price, 1004 Walnut St., Phila., Pa.

Thirlwall, Hist. of Greece.
Matilda de Montgomerie, a sequel to Wacousta, by Major Richardson.

Purdy Book Store, 1009 Congress Ave., Houston, Tex.

Dunglison, Medical Dictionary.

BOOKS WANTED.—Continued.

Peter Reilly, 133 N. 13th St., Phila., Pa.

Hughes, Cyclopedia of Drug Pathogenesis.
Williams, Syllabic Dictionary.

Geo. H. Richmond, 32 W. 33d St., N. Y.

Stevenson, Sub. ed. Scribner.
Kipling, Sub. ed. Scribner.
Gentle Art of Making Enemies, by Whistler.

Geo. H. Rigby, 1113 Arch St., Phila., Pa.

Smithsonian Cont. to Knowledge, odd v.
Michaux and Nuttall, N. A. Sylva.
McKenny and Hall, Indians, folio, old v.
Audubon, Birds and Quadrupeds.
Stoddard, Lectures, 11 v.
Century Dictionary.
Catlin, Indian Portfolio.

A. M. Robertson, 126 Post St., San Francisco, Cal.

The White Blackbird, tr. from the French.

Robson & Adee, Saratoga Springs, N. Y.

Saratoga Chips and Carlsbad Wafers, by Nathan Sheppard.
Campaign of Gen. Burgoyne, by William L. Stone.
State of the Expedition, by Burgoyne.
Dr. Owen, Dr. Buchard or Dr. Church, On the Waters of Saratoga.

Wm. B. Ropes, Mt. Vernon, Skagit Co., Wash.

Hammond, E. P., Conversion of Children.
Ayers, Light Artillery. Wiley.
Powell, Officers' Examiner. Wiley.
Wilkinson, War and Policy.
Ars Vivendi. Pub. by A. Lovell.

J. Francis Ruggles, Bronson, Mich.

Booth, E. G., In War Time. Phila., 1885.
Lewis, Algebra.

St. Paul Book and Stationery Co., 5th and St. Peter Sts., St. Paul, Minn.

Lossing's Civil War, v. 2.

Dr. H. Schliepor, P. O. Box 349, N. Y.

Walt Whitman, Leaves of Grass, 1st ed.
Notes and Fragments, ed. M. Bucke. 1899.

John E. Scopes, 29 Tweddle Bldg., Albany, N. Y.

American Ancestry, v. 10.
Wilkinson, Memoirs, v. 2 and atlas. Phila., 1816.

Scrantom, Wetmore & Co., Rochester, N. Y.

Sense and Sensibility, v. 1, or 2 v., Temple ed., leath. Macmillan.

John V. Sheehan & Co., Detroit, Mich.

Parley, Peter, Universal History.

Sibley, Lindsay & Curr Co., Rochester, N. Y.

Wisdom of the Hindoos, by Williams.

John Skinner, 44 N. Pearl St., Albany, N. Y.

Bergen Family, Descendants of Hans Hansen Bergen.
Chastellux's Travels in N. A.
Holland Purchase.
The Old Merchants of New York, 5th ser., Carleton's ed.
American Ancestry, v. 10.

George D. Smith, 50 New St., N. Y.

Blackstone, Commentaries, 2d ed., 4to. Phila., Bell, 1774.
Farmer, Slang Dictionary.
Lucian. Athenian Society.
Book of Family Crests, 2 v. 1838.
Official Proceedings of Republican National Convention, 1888.
Ananga Ranga, Burton trans.
Perfumed Garden, Burton trans.
Gardiner, History of England, v. 1, 2, 8vo ed.
Memoir of Louis XIV. Pub. by Nichols.
Stowe, Uncle Tom's Cabin, 2 v., 1st ed.

Wm. H. Smith, Jr., 515 W. 173d St., N. Y.

The Independence of the Executive, Cleveland.
Lecture on Shakespeare, Ingersoll.
Culture and Cooking, Cath. Owen.

Smith & Butterfield, 202 Main St., Evansville, Ind.

Edwards, France of To-day.

Smith & McCance, 38 Bromfield St., Boston, Mass.

Garland of Sacred Hymns. Estes & Lauriat, 1887.
American Printer, McKellar.
David Copperfield, v. 1, Household ed.
Christian Science Journal, v. 2, 3.

Speyer & Peters, Berlin, N. W. 7, Germany.

Annales de Dermatologie.

Speyer & Peters.—Continued.

Annals of Surgery.
Archiv für Mikroskop. Anatomie.
Archives of Laryngology.
Archives of Pediatrics.
Deutsche Chirurgie.
Journal de l'Anatomie. Robin.
Revue de Chirurgie.
Transactions of Amer. Orthop. Assoc.
Offer sets and single vols. or nos.

E. Steiger & Co., 25 Park Place, N. Y. [*Cash.*]

Fletcher, Woman Beautiful.
Journal of Geology, v. 1, 2, 5 to 9, complete or odd v.

Strawbridge & Clothier, Market St., Phila., Pa.

Tuflongo, tr. by Holme Lee.
Leigh Hunt's Dante's Inferno.

Syndicate Trading Co., 2 Walker St., N. Y.

White Mountains, Sweetser, latest ed. H., M. & Co.
New England, Sweetser, latest ed. H., M. & Co.
Storming of the Redoubt, by Merimee.

T. B. Ventres, 597 Fulton St., Brooklyn, N. Y.

Story of the Old Willow Pattern.

John D. Walker, 31 De Graaf Bldg., Albany, N. Y.

Philistine, v. 1 to 8, odd nos.
Roycroft books.

John Wanamaker, N. Y.

Sabine, Col., Isodynamic Chart. 1837.
Works of Gauss and Weber on the Magnetism of the Earth. 1836.
Anything on the magnetism of the earth.
Maps showing the magnetic parallels of the earth.
Elements of Christian Science, Wm. Adams, D.D.
Edward Everett's Eulogy on Geo. Washington.
Wendling, Seven Lectures.
The Green Hand, by Cupples. Routledge.
Picturesque North Carolina.

John Wanamaker, Phila., Pa.

Stevenson, Art of Velasquez. Pub. at $18.00.
Truth About Beauty, by Annie Wolf.

Montgomery Ward & Co., Chicago, Ill.

Katy of Catoctin, by Townsend.

Geo. E. Warner, Minneapolis, Minn.

Cobb's Poetical Geography North Carolina.
Sigourney, L. H., Memoir of Mrs. Cook.
Any county atlas or history.

Thomas Whittaker, 2 Bible House, N. Y.

Jenym's Internal Evidences of Christianity.

H. W. Wilson, 315 14th Ave., S. E., Minneapolis, Minn.

James G. Birney, by W. Birney.
Reddaway, Monroe Doctrine.
Fortnightly Review for Mar., 1902.
Harvard Graduates Magazine, no. 37.

W. H. Wood & Co., 8 E. Main St., Springfield, O.

The following Ethnological Reports, state binding, condition and price: 1st Annual Report, 7th Annual Report, 9th, 12th, 15th, 16th.

The Young Churchman Co., Milwaukee, Wis.

2 copies On Both Sides of the Sea, Mrs. Charles.

Wm. H. Ziesenitz, Hudson, N. Y.

Englishmen of Letters, black red title, any v. Harper.

BOOKS FOR SALE.

King Bros., 15 4th St., San Francisco, Cal.

Bret Harte Poem in 14th Anniversary of the Society of Cal. Pioneers (31 p., pamphlet.) S. F., 1864. $4.00.

W. W. Miller, 4432 Indiana Ave., Chicago, Ill.

The Book Mart, complete, 8 v. $6.00.
Genealogical Record of Leland Family. $2.00.
Ralph Waldo Emerson, Oration Dartmouth College, July 24, 1838. Boston, 1838. $3.00.
Poems of W. B. Tappan. Phila., 1822. $2.00.
History of "The Shakers," by Thos. Brown. Troy. 1812. $2.00.
Trumps, by G. Wm. Curtis. N. Y., 1861. $1.50.
Weems, Life Gen. Marion. N. Y., 1835. $1.00.
Deus Homo, God-Man, by Theophilus Parwin. 1868. $2.00.
The Mormons, Lieut. Gunnison. 1856. 75 cts.
Picture of Philadelphia for 1824, Thos. Wilson. Phila., 1823. $1.50.

BOOKS FOR SALE.—Continued.

Martin F. Onnen, 114 5th Ave., N. Y.

Books on industrial art.
Books on architecture.
Illuminated manuscripts and other rare books.
Books illustrative of the history of printing and engraving.
Books on painting and sculpturing.
Special lists and catalogues sent on request.

Wm. H. Smith, Jr., 515 W. 173d St., N. Y.

The Medallic History of Imperial Rome, 2 v.
Encyclopedia Britannica, 30 v. Werner, 1897.
Bohn's Classical Library, any v.
Official Record of Rebellion, 127 v., maps.
Herculaneum et Pompeii, 8 v.
Robert Burns' Works, ed. de luxe, no. 9.
Lee's Life of a Lover, 3 v.
A Good Fellow, De Kock, 1st Am. ed.
Turner Gallery. unbound.

John D. Walker, De Graaf Bldg., Albany, N. Y.

American Catalogue, 1876 to 1890, complete, 4 v., quarto, hf. mor.
The Grave, quarto, bds., illus. by William Blake. London, 1808.

Geo. E. Warner, Minneapolis, Minn.

Atlas of Vernon County, Wisconsin.
Atlas Hocking Co., Ohio.
Atlas Upper Ohio River.
Atlas Marshall Co., Iowa.
Atlas Hennepin and Ramsey Cos., Minnesota.

HELP WANTED.

WANTED.—Young man with good knowledge of the retail book and stationery business. Give references, experience, and salary expected. Address A. F. PENDLETON, 804 Broad St., Augusta, Ga.

SITUATIONS WANTED.

BOOKKEEPER, accountant and office manager. 20 years' experience, wholesale and manufacturing, desires position. Can adapt to any system or conditions. Excellent references. Salary no object so long as prospects are good. Address WILLSTAN, care of PUBLISHERS' WEEKLY.

EDITOR.—Editor of books and literary critic, originator of book series and contributor to the principal literary journals of the country, is open for an engagement. Reader for a publishing house, or literary editor or assistant for a publication. Address A. J., care of PUBLISHERS' WEEKLY.

COPYRIGHT NOTICES.

LIBRARY OF CONGRESS,
OFFICE OF THE REGISTER OF COPYRIGHTS,
WASHINGTON, D. C.

To wit: *Be it remembered*, That on the 28th day of July, 1902, Mrs. Roxana S. Ridpath, of the United States, hath deposited in this office the title of a book, the title of which is in the following words, to wit: "History of the United States. Prepared especially for Schools on a New and Comprehensive Plan, embracing the Features of Lyman's Historical Chart. By John Clark Ridpath, A.M., LL.D.," the right whereof she claims as proprietor in conformity with the laws of the United States respecting copyrights.

(Signed) HERBERT PUTNAM, *Librarian of Congress.*
By THORVALD SOLBERG, *Register of Copyrights.*
In renewal for 14 years from December 5, 1902.

LIBRARY OF CONGRESS,
OFFICE OF THE REGISTER OF COPYRIGHTS,
WASHINGTON, D. C.

To wit: *Be it remembered*, That on the 2d day of August, 1902, Jean Swinton, Executrix, of New York, N. Y., hath deposited in this office the title of a book, the title of which is in the following words, to wit: "Language Primer. Beginner's Lessons in Speaking and Writing English. By William Swinton, A.M., New York, Cincinnati, Chicago, American Book Company," the right whereof she claims as proprietor in conformity with the laws of the United States respecting copyrights.

(Signed) HERBERT PUTNAM, *Librarian of Congress.*
By THORVALD SOLBERG, *Register of Copyrights.*
In renewal for 14 years from August 3, 1902.

LIBRARY OF CONGRESS,
OFFICE OF THE REGISTER OF COPYRIGHTS,
WASHINGTON, D. C.

To wit: *Be it remembered*, That on the 2d day of August, 1902, Jean Swinton, Executrix, of New York, N. Y., hath deposited in this office the title of a book, the title of which is in the following words, to wit: "Outlines of the World's History. Ancient, Mediæval, and Modern. With special relation to the History of Civilization and the Progress of Mankind. For use in the higher classes in Public Schools, Academies, Seminaries, etc. By William Swinton, New York, Cincinnati, Chicago, American Book Company," the right whereof she claims as proprietor in conformity with the laws of the United States respecting copyrights.

(Signed) HERBERT PUTNAM, *Librarian of Congress.*
By THORVALD SOLBERG, *Register of Copyrights.*
In renewal for 14 years from September 14, 1902.

LIBRARY OF CONGRESS,
OFFICE OF THE REGISTER OF COPYRIGHTS,
WASHINGTON, D. C.

Class A, XXc, No. 40358.—To wit: *Be it remembered*, That on the 26th day of August, 1902, Marie Taylor, of New York, N. Y., hath deposited in this office the title of a book, the title of which is in the following words, to wit: "The Prophet. A Tragedy. By Bayard Taylor. Boston and New York, Houghton, Mifflin & Co., The Riverside Press, Cambridge, 1902," the right whereof she claims as proprietor in conformity with the laws of the United States respecting copyrights.

(Signed) HERBERT PUTNAM, *Librarian of Congress.*
By THORVALD SOLBERG, *Register of Copyrights.*
In renewal for 14 years from Aug. 26, 1902.

SPECIAL NOTICES.

A NEW NOVEL.
By MARIE CORELLI.
"TEMPORAL POWER"
A STUDY IN SUPREMACY
DODD, MEAD & CO.
Publishers, New York.

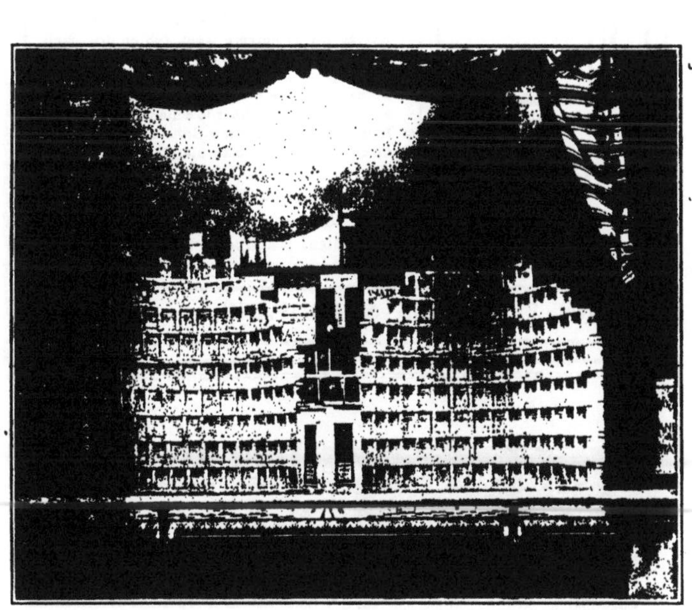

HERE is a book, by a new author and published by a new house, that has achieved instantaneous success. It has been cordially received by critics and reading public alike.

The Louisville *Courier-Journal*, in a review of the book, said :

"Stillman Gott is a 'rural philosopher,' just as his prototypes were, full of dry, droll sayings, witty stories, and quaint expressions. Generous to a fault, lovable and kind beyond words, he is one of those characters we cannot have too much of either in fiction or in real life. It is a pleasure to know Stillman Gott, and the reader will welcome him into American fiction to take his place alongside of David Harum and Eben Holden."

Besides being a good story, the book is well and handsomely bound. The print is clear and the paper is especially fine. Both from the literary and the mechanical standpoint the book is calculated to "wear well."

JOHN S. BROOKS & COMPANY, - BOSTON

Just Ready!!!

New India Paper Holman Bibles

This India Paper is the most opaque thin printing paper made.

Special editions of both Reference and Teachers' Bibles, Minion and Bourgeois Sizes.

Beautiful Bindings. Low Prices.

SEND FOR NEW PRICE LIST.

First Autumn Publications of McClure, Phillips & Co.

141 East 25th Street, New York

FICTION

The Hole in the Wall *By Arthur Morrison*

A vivid story of the London slums by the author of "Tales of Mean Streets."

The latter was pirated by sixteen American publishers in its first year.

Cloth, 12mo, $1.50

The Banner of Blue *By S. R. Crockett*

A new novel of Scotch life by this popular author, with characteristic dash and action. *Cloth, 12mo, $1.50*

The Ragged Edge *By John T. McIntyre*

A stirring story of ward politics and of the ward's social life. Such material is to be found in every newspaper, but Mr. McIntyre takes us into the heart of his world as no man has done before. The initial volume of the "First Novel Series." *Cloth, 12mo, $1.25*

MISCELLANEOUS

Jeanne d'Arc *Edited by T. Douglas Murray*

A remarkable historical document, being the translations from the verbatim reports in Latin, of the ecclesiastical proceedings in the trial of Jeanne d'Arc which have recently come to light. *Illustrated. Cloth, Octavo, net, $5.00*

Indian Boyhood *By Charles A. Eastman*

This book, as a picture of Indian life by one who passed his own boyhood amid the scenes which he describes, is absolutely unique. It is the only instance of literature of aboriginal life in America, treated not from without, but from within. Illustrated by E. L. Blumenschein.

Cloth, Large 12mo, net, $1.60

McClure's Children's Annual *Edited by T. H. W. Carsland*

The amusing pictures and verses, the fascinating stories, the clear, bold type, all go to make up a delightful volume for children. Illustrated with 36 full-page plates in four colors.

Decorated cloth, 9 x 11¼, $1.50

To be Published at Once

HOME LIFE of the BORNEO HEAD-HUNTERS

By WM. H. FURNESS. Illustrated by 81 photogravures and other photographic reproductions. 8vo, gilt top, rough edges, . . $7.50 net. Postage extra.

ALEXANDRE DUMAS, Pere (His Life and Works)

By ARTHUR F. DAVIDSON. Illustrated with many rare photographs and drawings. 8vo, decorated cloth, ... $3.75 net.

THE COMPLEAT ANGLER (Winchester Edition)

Edited by GEORGE A. B. DEWAR. Printed on special paper with wide margins, in large type of clear face, and furnished with illuminated title-page, book-marker, and index. Two volumes, large square 8vo, decorated cloth, gilt top, ... $12.50 net.

Also, large paper edition, limited to one hundred and fifty copies, numbered and signed, of which only twenty-five are for sale in the United States. Two volumes, green vellum, ... $35.00 net.

THE OLD COURT SUBURB

Edited by AUSTIN DOBSON. Illustrated. Two volumes, large square 12mo, cloth, decorated in gold, ... $12.50 net.

Also, large paper edition, limited to one hundred and fifty sets. Two volumes, numbered and signed by the artists, ... $35.00 net.

TWO THOUSAND MILES on an AUTOMOBILE

By "CHAUFFEUR." Illustrated. Crown 8vo, decorated cloth, . $2.00 net. Postage extra.

CONFESSIONS OF A VIOLINIST

By Dr. T. LAMB PHIPSON. 12mo, decorated cloth, ... $1.50 net.

THE SUMMITS OF SUCCESS

By JAMES BURNLEY. The story of the greatest achievements and the careers of notable men. 12mo, decorated cloth, gilt top, ... $1.50 net.

THE HIGHWAY OF FATE

By ROSA NOUCHETTE CAREY. A new novel. 12mo, decorated cloth, $1.50.

THE STORY OF A SCOUT

By JOHN FINNEMORE. An exciting tale of adventure. Illustrated. 12mo, decorated cloth, ... $1.50.

A BLAZE OF 'GLORY

By JOHN STRANGE WINTER. A new novel. 12mo, cloth, . . . $1.25

J. B. Lippincott Company

Publishers PHILADELPHIA

THE PUBLISHERS' WEEKLY

Reference List of New Publications

JANUARY–AUGUST, 1902

MONTHLY CUMULATION, SEPTEMBER, 1902

This Reference List enters the books recorded during the month under (1) author, in **Clarendon** *type; anonymous books having* **Clarendon** *type for the first word; (2) title in* Roman; *(3) subject-heading in* SMALL CAPS; *(4) name of series in Italics. The figures in parentheses are not the imprint date, but refer to the date of "The Publishers' Weekly" in which full title entry will be found and not to the day of publication, for which information should be sought in the full title entry thus indicated. Where not specified, the binding is cloth.*

A apple pie. Greenaway, K. 75 c. Warne.
A B C of banks and banking. Coffin, G: M. $1.25. S: A. Nelson.
A B C of electrical experiments. Clarke, W. J. $1. Excelsior.
A B C of scientific Christianity. Clarkson, J. R. 25 c. J. R. Clarkson
A B C of the telephone. Homans, J. E. $1. Van Nostrand.
A B C of wireless telegraphy. Bubier, E: T. $1. Bubier.
A B C universal commercial electric telegraphic code. 5th ed., enl. '02(Je7) 8°, net, $7. Am. Code.
A la mode cookery. Salis, *Mrs.* H. A. de. $2. Longmans.
Aaron Crane. Tate, H: $1.50. Abbey Press.
Abbatt, W:, *ed. See* Heath, W:
ABBEYS.
See Cathedrals.
Abbott, Alex. C. Manual of bacteriology, 6th ed., rev. and enl. '02(My17) 12°, net, $2.75. Lea.
Abbott, J. H. M. Tommy Cornstalk: features of the So. African war from the point of view of the Australian ranks. '02(Je21) D. $2. Longmans.
Abbott, J: S. C. Christopher Carson, known as Kit Carson. '01· '02(Ap12) 12°, net, 87 c. Dodd.
Abbott, S: W., *ed. See* American yearbook of medicine.
Abbott's cyclopedic digest. *See* New York.
Abegg, R., *and* Herz, W. Practical chemistry; tr. by H. B. Calvert. '01· '02(Ja24) 12°, net, $1.50. Macmillan.
Abernethy, J. W. American literature. '02 (Ap26) 12°, $1.10. Maynard, M. & Co.
Abner Daniel. Harben, W. N. $1.50. Harper.
Abroad with the Jimmies. Bell, L. $1.50. L. C. Page
ABSOLUTION.
See Confession.
ACCIDENTS.
Dickson. First aid in accidents. net, 50 c. Revell.
Doty. Prompt aid to the injured. $1.50. Appleton.
According to season. Parsons, *Mrs.* F. T. net, $1.75. Scribner.
Accountant's guide for executors, etc. Gottsberger, F. $5. Peck.
ACCOUNTS.
See Arithmetic;—Bookkeeping.
Achenbach, H: Two-fold covenant. '02 (Ap12) D. 50 c. Evangelical Press.
Achilles Tatius. Leucippe and Clitophon. '02(Ag2) il. 8°, (Antique gems fr. the Greek and Latin, v. 7.) (App. to pubs. for price.) Barrie.
Achromatic spindle in spore mother-cells of osmunda regalis. Smith, R. W. net, 25 c. Univ. of Chic.
Acorn Club, Ct., pubs. 8°, pap. Case.
—Love. Thomas Short, first printer of Ct. $5. (6.) Case.
ACTIONS AT LAW.
Bradner. New practice in supplementary proceedings. $4. W. C. Little.
Budd. Civil remedies under code system. $6. Palm.
Perley. Practice in personal actions in cts. of Mass. $6.50. G: B. Reed.
Sibley. Right to and cause for action, both civil and criminal. $1.50. W. H. Anderson & Co.
Wait. Law and practice in civil actions and proceedings in justices' cts., [etc.] In 3 v. v. 1, 2. ea., $6.35; per set, $19. M. Bender.
ACTORS AND ACTRESSES.
Clapp. Reminiscences of a dramatic critic. net, $1.75. Houghton, M. & Co.
Hamm. Eminent actors and their homes. $1.25. Pott.
Whitton. Wags of the stage. $2.50. Rigby.
ACTS OF THE APOSTLES.
See Bible.
Adams, C: F. Life and sermons of T. De Witt Talmage. '02(Ag2) il. 12°, $1.25. Donohue.
Adams, Cyrus C., *ed.* Elem. commercial geography. '02(Ag23) il. D. $1.10. Appleton.
Adam, Ja. Texts to il. a course of elem. lectures on Greek philosophy after Aristotle. '02(Mr1) 8°, net, $1.25. Macmillan.
Adams, Braman B. Block system of signalling on Am. railroads. '01· '02(Mr22) 8°, $2. Railroad Gazette.
Adams, C: F. Lee at Appomattox, and other papers. '02(Je7) D. net, $1.50. Houghton, M. & Co.
Adams, C: F. Shall Cromwell have a statue? '02(Jl12) O. pap., 25 c. Lauriat.
ADAMS, Herb. B.
Vincent, *and others.* Herbert B. Adams: tribute of friends. n. p. Johns Hopkins.
Adams, W. T., ["Oliver Optic."] Moneymaker. '01· '02(Je14) 12°, (Yacht club ser., v. 3.) $1.25. Lee & S.

To be Published at Once

HOME LIFE of the BORNEO HEAD-HUNTERS

By **WM. H. FURNESS.** Illustrated by 81 photogravures and other photographic reproductions. 8vo, gilt top, rough edges, . . **$7.50 net.** Postage extra.

ALEXANDRE DUMAS, Pere (His Life and Works)

By **ARTHUR F. DAVIDSON.** Illustrated with many rare photographs and drawings. 8vo, decorated cloth, ... **$3.75 net.**

THE COMPLEAT ANGLER (Winchester Edition)

Edited by **GEORGE A. B. DEWAR.** Printed on special paper with wide margins, in large type of clear face, and furnished with illuminated title-page, book-marker, and index. Two volumes, large square 8vo, decorated cloth, gilt top, ... **$12.50 net.**

Also, large paper edition, limited to one hundred and fifty copies, numbered and signed, of which only twenty-five are for sale in the United States. Two volumes, green vellum, ... **$35.00 net.**

THE OLD COURT SUBURB

Edited by **AUSTIN DOBSON.** Illustrated. Two volumes, large square 12mo, cloth, decorated in gold, ... **$12.50 net.**

Also, large paper edition, limited to one hundred and fifty sets. Two volumes, numbered and signed by the artists, ... **$35.00 net.**

TWO THOUSAND MILES on an AUTOMOBILE

By **"CHAUFFEUR."** Illustrated. Crown 8vo, decorated cloth, . **$2.00 net.** Postage extra.

CONFESSIONS OF A VIOLINIST

By **Dr. T. LAMB PHIPSON.** 12mo, decorated cloth, ... **$1.50 net.**

THE SUMMITS OF SUCCESS

By **JAMES BURNLEY.** The story of the greatest achievements and the careers of notable men. 12mo, decorated cloth, gilt top, ... **$1.50 net.**

THE HIGHWAY OF FATE

By **ROSA NOUCHETTE CAREY.** A new novel. 12mo, decorated cloth, **$1.50.**

THE STORY OF A SCOUT

By **JOHN FINNEMORE.** An exciting tale of adventure. Illustrated. 12mo, decorated cloth, ... **$1.50.**

A BLAZE OF 'GLORY

By **JOHN STRANGE WINTER.** A new novel. 12mo, cloth, . . . **$1.25**

J. B. Lippincott Company

Publishers PHILADELPHIA

THE PUBLISHERS' WEEKLY

Reference List of New Publications

JANUARY–AUGUST, 1902

MONTHLY CUMULATION, SEPTEMBER, 1902

This Reference List enters the books recorded during the month under (1) author, in **Clarendon** *type; anonymous books having* **Clarendon** *type for the first word; (2) title in* Roman; *(3) subject-heading in* SMALL CAPS; *(4) name of series in Italics. The figures in parentheses are not the imprint date, but refer to the date of "The Publishers' Weekly" in which full title entry will be found and not to the day of publication, for which information should be sought in the full title entry thus indicated. Where not specified, the binding is cloth.*

A apple pie. Greenaway, K. 75 c. Warne.
A B C of banks and banking. Coffin, G: M. $1.25. S: A. Nelson.
A B C of electrical experiments. Clarke, W. J. $1. Excelsior.
A B C of scientific Christianity. Clarkson, J. R. 25 c. J. R. Clarkson
A B C of the telephone. Homans, J. E. $1. Van Nostrand.
A B C of wireless telegraphy. Bubier, E: T. $1. Bubier.
A B C universal commercial electric telegraphic code. 5th ed., enl. '02(Je7) 8°, net, $7. Am. Code.
A la mode cookery. Salis, *Mrs.* H. A. de. $2. Longmans.
Aaron Crane. Tate, H: $1.50. Abbey Press.
Abbatt, W:, *ed.* *See* Heath, W:
ABBEYS.
See Cathedrals.
Abbott, Alex. C. Manual of bacteriology, 6th ed., rev. and enl. '02(My17) 12°, net, $2.75. Lea.
Abbott, J. H. M. Tommy Cornstalk: features of the So. African war from the point of view of the Australian ranks. '02(Je21) D. $2. Longmans.
Abbott, J: S. C. Christopher Carson, known as Kit Carson. '01. '02(Ap12) 12°, net, 87 c. Dodd.
Abbott, S: W., *ed.* *See* American yearbook of medicine.
Abbott's cyclopedic digest. *See* New York.
Abegg, R., *and* Herz, W. Practical chemistry; tr. by H. B. Calvert. '01. '02(Ja24) 12°, net, $1.50. Macmillan.
Abernethy, J. W. American literature. '02 (Ap26) 12°, $1.10. Maynard, M. & Co.
Abner Daniel. Harben, W. N. $1.50. Harper.
Abroad with the Jimmies. Bell, L. $1.50. L. C. Page
ABSOLUTION.
See Confession.
ACCIDENTS.
Dickson. First aid in accidents. net, 50 c. Revell.
Doty. Prompt aid to the injured. $1.50. Appleton.
According to season. Parsons, *Mrs.* F. T. net, $1.75. Scribner.
Accountant's guide for executors, etc. Gottsberger, F. $5. Peck.
ACCOUNTS.
See Arithmetic;—Bookkeeping.
Achenbach, H: Two-fold covenant. '02 (Ap12) D. 50 c. Evangelical Press.
Achilles Tatius. Leucippe and Clitophon. '02(Ag2) il. 8°, (Antique gems fr. the Greek and Latin, v. 7.) (App. to pubs. for price.) Barrie.
Achromatic spindle in spore mother-cells of osmunda regalis. Smith, R. W. net, 25 c. Univ. of Chic.
Acorn Club, Ct., pubs. 8°, pap. Case.
—Love. Thomas Short, first printer of Ct. $5. (6.) Case.
ACTIONS AT LAW.
Bradner. New practice in supplementary proceedings. $4. W. C. Little.
Budd. Civil remedies under code system. $6. Palm.
Perley. Practice in personal actions in cts. of Mass. $6.50. G: B. Reed.
Sibley. Right to and cause for action, both civil and criminal. $1.50. W. H. Anderson & Co.
Wait. Law and practice in civil actions and proceedings in justices' cts., [etc.] In 3 v. v. 1, 2. ea., $6.35; per set, $19. M. Bender.
ACTORS AND ACTRESSES.
Clapp. Reminiscences of a dramatic critic. net, $1.75. Houghton, M. & Co.
Hamm. Eminent actors and their homes. $1.25. Pott.
Whitton. Wags of the stage. $2.50. Rigby.
ACTS OF THE APOSTLES.
See Bible.
Adams, C: F. Life and sermons of T. De Witt Talmage. '02(Ag2) il. 12°, $1.25. Donohue.
Adams, Cyrus C., *ed.* Elem. commercial geography. '02(Ag23) il. D. $1.10. Appleton.
Adam, Ja. Texts to il. a course of elem. lectures on Greek philosophy after Aristotle. '02(Mr1) 8°, net, $1.25. Macmillan.
Adams, Braman B. Block system of signalling on Am. railroads. '01. '02(Mr22) 8°, $2. Railroad Gazette.
Adams, C: F. Lee at Appomattox, and other papers. '02(Je7) D. net, $1.50. Houghton, M. & Co.
Adams, C: F. Shall Cromwell have a statue? '02(Jl12) O. pap., 25 c. Lauriat.
ADAMS, Herb. B.
Vincent, *and others.* Herbert B. Adams: tribute of friends. n. p. Johns Hopkins.
Adams, W. T., ["Oliver Optic."] Moneymaker. '01. '02(Je14) 12°, (Yacht club ser., v. 3.) $1.25. Lee & S.

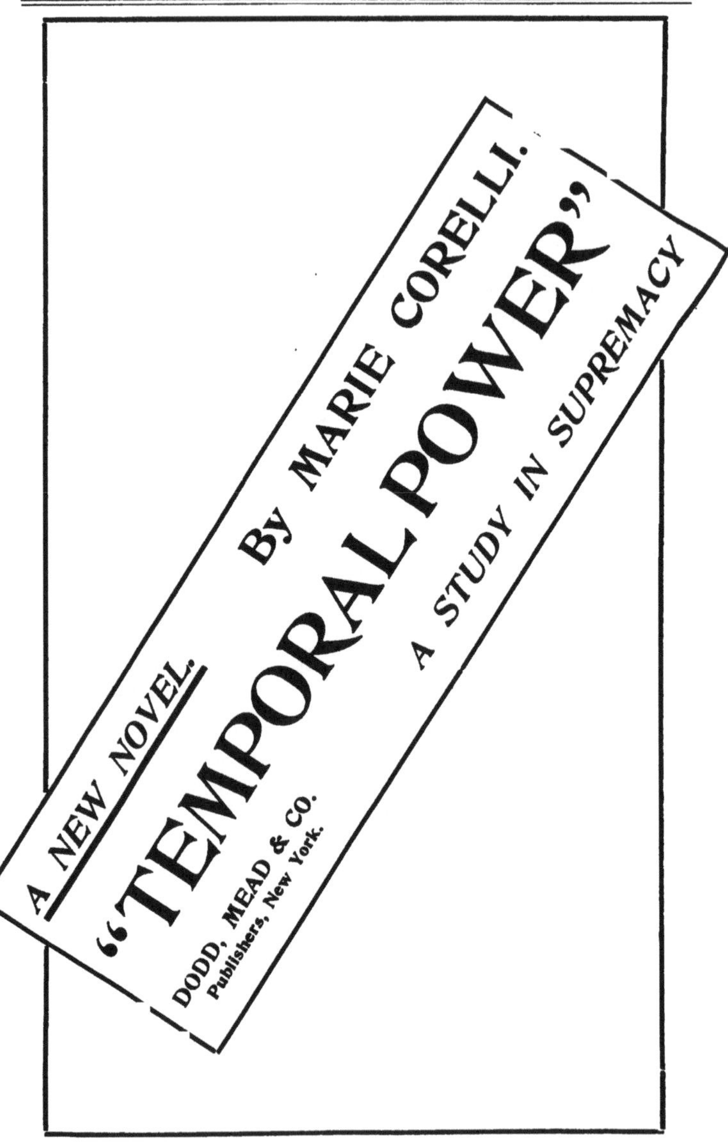
A NEW NOVEL.
By MARIE CORELLI.
"TEMPORAL POWER"
A STUDY IN SUPREMACY
DODD, MEAD & CO.
Publishers, New York.

To be Published at Once

HOME LIFE of the BORNEO HEAD-HUNTERS

By **WM. H. FURNESS.** Illustrated by 81 photogravures and other photographic reproductions. 8vo, gilt top, rough edges, . . **$7.50 net.** Postage extra.

ALEXANDRE DUMAS, Pere (His Life and Works)

By **ARTHUR F. DAVIDSON.** Illustrated with many rare photographs and drawings. 8vo, decorated cloth, ... **$3.75 net.**

THE COMPLEAT ANGLER (Winchester Edition)

Edited by **GEORGE A. B. DEWAR.** Printed on special paper with wide margins, in large type of clear face, and furnished with illuminated title-page, book-marker, and index. Two volumes, large square 8vo, decorated cloth, gilt top, ... **$12.50 net.**

Also, large paper edition, limited to one hundred and fifty copies, numbered and signed, of which only twenty-five are for sale in the United States. Two volumes, green vellum, ... **$35.00 net.**

THE OLD COURT SUBURB

Edited by **AUSTIN DOBSON.** Illustrated. Two volumes, large square 12mo, cloth, decorated in gold, ... **$12.50 net.**

Also, large paper edition, limited to one hundred and fifty sets. Two volumes, numbered and signed by the artists, ... **$35.00 net.**

TWO THOUSAND MILES on an AUTOMOBILE

By **"CHAUFFEUR."** Illustrated. Crown 8vo, decorated cloth, . **$2.00 net.** Postage extra.

CONFESSIONS OF A VIOLINIST

By **Dr. T. LAMB PHIPSON.** 12mo, decorated cloth, ... **$1.50 net.**

THE SUMMITS OF SUCCESS

By **JAMES BURNLEY.** The story of the greatest achievements and the careers of notable men. 12mo, decorated cloth, gilt top, ... **$1.50 net.**

THE HIGHWAY OF FATE

By **ROSA NOUCHETTE CAREY.** A new novel. 12mo, decorated cloth, **$1.50.**

THE STORY OF A SCOUT

By **JOHN FINNEMORE.** An exciting tale of adventure. Illustrated. 12mo, decorated cloth, ... **$1.50.**

A BLAZE OF 'GLORY

By **JOHN STRANGE WINTER.** A new novel. 12mo, cloth, . . . **$1.25**

J. B. Lippincott Company

Publishers PHILADELPHIA

THE PUBLISHERS' WEEKLY

Reference List of New Publications

JANUARY–AUGUST, 1902

MONTHLY CUMULATION, SEPTEMBER, 1902

This Reference List enters the books recorded during the month under (1) author, in **Clarendon** *type; anonymous books having* **Clarendon** *type for the first word; (2) title in* Roman; *(3) subject-heading in* SMALL CAPS; *(4) name of series in Italics. The figures in parentheses are not the imprint date, but refer to the date of "The Publishers' Weekly" in which full title entry will be found and not to the day of publication, for which information should be sought in the full title entry thus indicated. Where not specified, the binding is cloth.*

A apple pie. Greenaway, K. 75 c. Warne.
A B C of banks and banking. Coffin, G: M. $1.25. S: A. Nelson.
A B C of electrical experiments. Clarke, W. J. $1. Excelsior.
A B C of scientific Christianity. Clarkson, J. R. 25 c. J. R. Clarkson
A B C of the telephone. Homans, J. E. $1. Van Nostrand.
A B C of wireless telegraphy. Bubier, E: T. $1. Bubier.
A B C universal commercial electric telegraphic code. 5th ed., enl. '02(Je7) 8°, net, $7. Am. Code.
A la mode cookery. Salis, *Mrs.* H. A. de. $2. Longmans.
Aaron Crane. Tate, H: $1.50. Abbey Press.
Abbatt, W:, *ed.* *See* Heath, W:
ABBEYS.
See Cathedrals.
Abbott, Alex. C. Manual of bacteriology, 6th ed., rev. and enl. '02(My17) 12°, net, $2.75. Lea.
Abbott, J. H. M. Tommy Cornstalk: features of the So. African war from the point of view of the Australian ranks. '02(Je21) D. $2. Longmans.
Abbott, J: S. C. Christopher Carson, known as Kit Carson. '01. '02(Ap12) 12°, net, 87 c. Dodd.
Abbott, S: W., *ed.* *See* American yearbook of medicine.
Abbott's cyclopedic digest. *See* New York.
Abegg, R., *and* Herz, W. Practical chemistry; tr. by H. B. Calvert. '01. '02(Ja24) 12°, net, $1.50. Macmillan.
Abernethy, J. W. American literature. '02 (Ap26) 12°, $1.10. Maynard, M. & Co.
Abner Daniel. Harben, W. N. $1.50. Harper.
Abroad with the Jimmies. Bell, L. $1.50. L. C. Page
ABSOLUTION.
See Confession.
ACCIDENTS.
Dickson. First aid in accidents. net, 50 c. Revell.
Doty. Prompt aid to the injured. $1.50. Appleton.
According to season. Parsons, *Mrs.* F. T. net, $1.75. Scribner.
Accountant's guide for executors, etc. Gottsberger, F. $5. Peck.
ACCOUNTS.
See Arithmetic;—Bookkeeping.
Achenbach, H: Two-fold covenant. '02 (Ap12) D. 50 c. Evangelical Press.
Achilles Tatius. Leucippe and Clitophon. '02(Ag2) il. 8°, (Antique gems fr. the Greek and Latin, v. 7.) (App. to pubs. for price.) Barrie.
Achromatic spindle in spore mother-cells of osmunda regalis. Smith, R. W. net, 25 c. Univ. of Chic.
Acorn Club, Ct., pubs. 8°, pap. Case.
—Love. Thomas Short, first printer of Ct. $5. (6.) Case.
ACTIONS AT LAW.
Bradner. New practice in supplementary proceedings. $4. W. C. Little.
Budd. Civil remedies under code system. $6. Palm.
Perley. Practice in personal actions in cts. of Mass. $6.50. G: B. Reed.
Sibley. Right to and cause for action, both civil and criminal. $1.50. W. H. Anderson & Co.
Wait. Law and practice in civil actions and proceedings in justices' cts., [etc.] In 3 v. v. 1, 2. ea., $6.35; per set, $19. M. Bender.
ACTORS AND ACTRESSES.
Clapp. Reminiscences of a dramatic critic. net, $1.75. Houghton, M. & Co.
Hamm. Eminent actors and their homes. $1.25. Pott.
Whitton. Wags of the stage. $2.50. Rigby.
ACTS OF THE APOSTLES.
See Bible.
Adams, C: F. Life and sermons of T. De Witt Talmage. '02(Ag2) il. 12°, $1.25. Donohue.
Adams, Cyrus C., *ed.* Elem. commercial geography. '02(Ag23) il. D. $1.10. Appleton.
Adam, Ja. Texts to il. a course of elem. lectures on Greek philosophy after Aristotle. '02(Mr1) 8°. net, $1.25. Macmillan.
Adams, Braman B. Block system of signalling on Am. railroads. '01. '02(Mr22) 8°, $2. Railroad Gazette.
Adams, C: F. Lee at Appomattox, and other papers. '02(Je7) D. net, $1.50. Houghton, M. & Co.
Adams, C: F. Shall Cromwell have a statue? '02(Jl12) O. pap., 25 c. Lauriat.
ADAMS, Herb. B.
Vincent, *and others.* Herbert B. Adams: tribute of friends. n. p. Johns Hopkins.
Adams, W. T., ["Oliver Optic."] Moneymaker. '01. '02(Je14) 12°, (Yacht club ser., v. 3.) $1.25. Lee & S.

Addams, Jane. Democracy and social ethics. '02(Je7) D. (Citizen's lib.) $1.25. Macmillan.
Addis, M. E. L. Cathedrals and abbeys of Presbyterian Scotland. '01. '02(F15) il. 12°, net, $2.50. Presb. Bd.
Addison, Jos. Essays; ed. by J: R: Green. '02(Mr29) il. 12°, (Home lib.) $1. Burt.
Adirondack stories. Deming, P. 75 c. Houghton, M. & Co.
Adler, G: J. German and Eng. dictionary. New ed., rev. by F. P. Foster and E: Althaus. '02(Ap26) 4°, $3.50. Appleton.
Admiral's aid. Clark, H. H. **$1 net. Lothrop.
Adoration of the blessed sacrament, Tesnière, A. net, $1.25. Benziger.
Adventure ser. 12°, $1. Yewdale.
—Dee. James Griffin's adventures.
Adventures in Tibet. Carey, W: net, $1.50. Un. Soc. C. E.
Adventures of John McCue, socialist. '02 (My17) D. (Socialist lib., v. 2, no. 1.) pap., 10 c. Socialistic Co-op.
Adventures of Marco Polo. Atherton, E: 65 c. Appleton.
ADVERTISING.
Farrington. Retail advertising. net, $1. Baker & T.
Æneid. *See* Virgil.
AERODYNAMICS.
Langley. Experiments in aerodynamics. $1. Smith. Inst.
Æs triplex. Stevenson, R. L: net, 25 c.-$1. T: B. Mosher.
Aeschylus. The choephori; with crit. notes, etc. '02(Ja18) 8°, (Cambridge Univ. Press ser.) net, $3.25. Macmillan.
AESTHETICS.
B., E. P. God the beautiful. net, 75 c. Beam.
AFRICA.
Graham. Roman Africa. $6. Longmans.
See also Egypt; — Morocco; — South Africa; — Tripoli.
Agnes Cheswick. Haymond, *Mrs.* W. E. net, 60 c. Blanchard.
AGNOSTICISM.
Sloan. Religion, agnosticism and education. net, 80 c. McClurg.
Agricultural almanac, 1903. '02(Jl19) il. 4°, pap., 10 c. Baer.
AGRICULTURE.
See Dairy;—Domestic economy;—Farms and farming; — Forestry; — Fruit; — Gardening; — Insects;—Irrigation;—Land;—Soils;—Vegetables.
Aikins, Herb. A. Principles of logic. '02 '02(My17) D. net, $1.50. Holt.
AIR BRAKES.
Dukesmith. Air brake, its use and abuse. $1. F. H. Dukesmith.
Kirkman. Air brake. $2.50. World R'way.
AIR PASSAGES.
See Breathing.
Airy, Reginald. Westminster. '02(Mr22) 12°. (Handbooks to the great public schools.) $1.50. Macmillan.
Aitken, J. R. Love in its tenderness: idylls. '02(Mr22) D. (Town and country lib., no. 309.) $1; pap., 50 c. Appleton.
Aitkin, W. H. Divine ordinance of prayer. '02(Je7) 12°, $1.25. E. & J. B. Young.
Aiton, G: B., *and* Rankin, A. W. Exercises in syntax for summer schools, etc. '01. '02 (Ap26) 12°, pap., 25 c. Hyde.

Alabama. *Supreme ct.* Repts. v. 122-129. 1900. '02(Jl5) O. shp., ea., $3.75. Brown Pr. Co.
ALABAMA.
Martin. Internal improvement in Ala. 30 c. Johns Hopkins.
Alabama sketches. Peck, S: M. $1. McClurg.
ALASKA.
Balch. Alasko-Canadian frontier. $1. Allen, L. & S.
Albee, Ernest. History of Eng. utilitarianism. '02(Je28) 8°, net, $2.75. Macmillan.
Albert, Eduard. Diagnosis of surgical diseases; fr. the 8th enl. and rev. ed. by R. T. Frank. '02(Je7) il. 8°, $5; $5.50. Appleton.
Alcott, Louisa M. Little button rose. New ed. '01. '02(F15) 16°, (Children's friend ser.) bds., 50 c. Little, B. & Co.
Alden, *Mrs.* Is. M., ["Pansy."] Unto the end. '02(Je7) D. $1.50. Lothrop.
Alden, W: L. Drewitt's dream. '02(Ap12) D. (Town and country lib., no. 310.) $1; pap., 50 c. Appleton.
Aleph the Chaldean. Burr, E. F. $1.25. Whittaker.
Alexander, *Mrs.* *See* Hector, *Mrs.* A. F.
Alexander, Hartley B. Problem of metaphysics and meaning of metaphysical explanation. '02(Jl12) 8°, (Columbia University cont. to philosophy, psychology and education, v. 10, no. 1.) pap., *75 c. net. Macmillan.
Alexander, W: M. Demonic possession in the New Testament. '02(Ap12) 8°, net, $1.50. Scribner.
ALEXANDRA, *Queen of England*.
See Edward VII., *King of England*.
Alford, M., *comp.* Latin passages for translation. '02(Ap12) 12°, net, 80 c. Macmillan.
ALFRED *the Great*.
Bowker. King Alfred millenary. $3. Macmillan.
ALGAE.
Livingston. Nature of the stimulus which causes change in form in polymorphic green algae. net, 25 c. Univ. of Chic.
ALGEBRA.
Bailey. High school algebra. 90 c. Am. Bk.
Beman *and* Smith. Academic algebra. $1.25. Ginn.
Brooks. Normal elem. algebra. pt. 1. 83 c. Sower.
Dickson. College algebra. net, $1.50. Wiley.
Hall. Algebraical examples. net, 50 c. Macmillan.
Kellogg. Elements of algebra. 25 c. Kellogg.
Lippincott's elem. algebra. 80 c. Lippincott.
Milne. Key to Academic algebra. $1.50. Am. Bk.
Wentworth. College algebra. $1.65. Ginn.
White. Grammar school algebra. 35 c. Am. Bk.
See also Mathematics.
Alger, Edith G. Primer of work and play. '02(Mr15) il. sq. D. 30 c. Heath.
Alger, H., *jr.* Tom Turner's legacy and how he secured it. '02(Jl12) il. 12°, (Alger ser.) $1. Burt.
Alger ser. il. 12°, $1. Burt.
—Alger. Tom Turner's legacy.
—Kaler. Treasure of Cocos Island.

Algonkian. *See* Lawson, A. C.
Algonquian series. *See* Tooker, W: W.
Aliens. Wright, M. T. $1.50. Scribner.
Alissas, R. d', [M. *and* K. Roget.] Les histoires de tante. '02(Mr1) 12°, (Primary ser. of Fr. and Germ. reading books.) net, 40 c. Macmillan.
Allen, Alice E. Children of the palm lands. '02(My3) D. 50 c. Educ Pub.
Allen, C: W. Practitioner's manual. '02 (Je7) 8°, $6; mor., $7. Wood.
ALLEN, Ethan.
Brown. Ethan Allen. $1. Donohue.
Allen, F. S. What's what? at home and abroad. '02(Je7) S. net, 50 c. Bradley-W.
Allen, Godfrey. *See* Allen, Phœbe.
Allen, J. H: Diseases and therapeutics of the skin. '02(My24) 12°, $2. Boericke & T.
Allen, J: H. Judah's sceptre and Joseph's birthright. '02(Ag2) il. 12°, $1.50. J: H. Allen.
Allen, May V. Battling with love and fate. '02(Jl19) D. $1. Abbey Press.
Allen, Phœbe *and* Godfrey. Miniature and window gardening. '02(Ap19) D. net, 50 c. Pott.
Allen, T: G. *See* Duff, E: M.
Allen, Willis B. Play away: story of the Boston fire department. '02(Jl19) il. 12°, **75 c. net. Estes.
Allen's (Grant) hist. guide books to the principal cities of Europe. S. net, $1.25. Wessels.
—Cruickshank. The Umbrian towns.
Allgood, G: China war, 1860: letters and journal. '01· '02(F8) il. obl. O. $5. Longmans.
Allibone, S: A. Great authors of all ages. New ed. '01. '02(Mr1) 8°, $2.50. Lippincott.
Allibone, S: A. Poetical quotations. New ed. '01· '02(Mr1) 8°, $2.50. Lippincott.
Allibone, S: A. Prose quotations. New ed. '01· '02(Mr1) 8°, $2.50. Lippincott.
Allin Winfield. Walsh, G: E. $1.50. Buckles.
ALMANACS AND ANNUALS.
Agricultural almanac, 1903. 10 c. Baer.
American Baptist year-book, 1902. 25 c. Am. Bapt.
Annual Am. catalogue, cumulated 1900, 1901. $2. Pub. Weekly.
Arbor and bird day annual for Wis. schools. gratis. Democrat Pr. Co.
Brassey. Naval annual, 1902. net, $7.50. Scribner.
Brooklyn *Daily Eagle* almanac, 1902. 50 c.; 25 c. Brooklyn Eagle.
Catholic yearbook of New England. 25 c. J. K. Waters.
Courier-Journal almanac, 1902. 25 c. Courier-Journ.
Englishwoman's year-book and directory, 1902. $1.50. Macmillan.
Free trade almanac, 1902. 5 c. Am. Free Trade.
Hagerstown town and country almanack, 1903. 10 c. Gruber.
Hawaiian almanac and annual, 1902. 75 c. Thrum.
Hazell's annual for 1902. net, $1.50. Scribner.
Illustrated family Christian almanac, 1902. 10 c. Am. Tr.

ALMANACS AND ANNUALS.—*Continued.*
Indianapolis *Sentinel* year-book and almanac, 1902. 25 c. Indianapolis Sentinel.
International annual of Anthony's photographic bulletin, 1902. $1.25; 75 c. Anthony.
International year-book, 1901. $4. Dodd.
Minneapolis *Journal* almanac and yearbook, 1902. 25 c Journal Pr. Co.
Municipal year book, 1902. $3. Engineering News.
National Temperance almanac and teetotalers year-book, 1902. 10 c. Nat. Temp.
Planets and people: annual yearbook of the heavens. $1. F. E. Ormsby.
Providence *Journal* almanac, 1902. 10 c. Providence Journ.
Public *Ledger* almanac, 1902. gratis. Drexel.
Spalding's official athletic almanac. 10 c. Am. Sports.
Statesmen's year-book, 1902. net, $3. Macmillan.
Telegram almanac and cyclopedia, 1902. 20 c. Providence Telegram.
Tribune almanac and pol. register, 1902. 25 c. Tribune Assoc.
Virginia-Carolina almanac for 1902. gratis. Virginia-Carolina.
Whitaker, *comp.* Almanac for 1902. net, 40 c.; net, $1. Scribner.
World almanac and encyclopedia, 1902. 25 c. Press Pub.
See also under special subjects.
ALPHABETS.
Day. Alphabets old and new. $1.50. Scribner.
ALPHABETS (*ornamental*).
See Lettering.
Alpheus, A., *pseud.* Complete guide to hypnotism. '02(My17) 12°, 50 c.; pap., 25 c. Donohue.
Alpheus, A., *pseud.* *See also* Oxenford, I.
Altdorfer, Albrecht. Albrecht Altdorfer: 71 woodcuts. '02(Ap26) il. O. (Little engravings classical and contemporary, no. 1.) bds., net, $1.50. Longmans.
ALTERNATING CURRENTS.
Houston *and* Kennelly. Alternating electric currents. $1. McGraw.
Oudin. Standard polyphase apparatus and systems. $3. Van Nostrand.
Rhodes. Elem. treatise on alternating currents. $2.60. Longmans.
Sheldon *and* Mason. Dynamo electric machinery. v. 2, Alternating-current machines. net, $2.50. Van Nostrand.
Alton Locke. *See* Kingsley, C:
Altsheler, Jos. A. My captive. '02(Je7) D. $1.25. Appleton.
Ambassador of Christ. Schuyler, W: $1.50. Gorham.
Amber, Miles. Wistons. '02(F15) D. $1.50. Scribner.
AMERICA.
Helmolt, *and others, eds.* Hist. of the world. v. 1, Prehistoric America. $6. Dodd.
See also Huguenots.
AMERICA (*yacht*).
Thompson *and* Lawson. Hist. of the "America's" cup. (for private dist.) W. M. Thompson.

American Acad. of Pol. and Soc. Science pubs. 8°, pap. Am. Acad. Pol. Sci.
—Crowell. Status and prospects of Am. shipbuilding. 15 c. (325.)
—Elwood. Aristotle as a sociologist. 15 c. (332.)
—Farquhar. Manufacturers' need of reciprocity. 15 c. (330.)
—Glasson. Nation's pension system. 25 c. (331.)
—Johnson. Isthmian canal. 25 c. (323.)
—Knapp. Government ownership of railroads. 15 c. (326.)
—Meyer. Advisory councils in railway administration. 15 c. (327.)
—Newcomb. Concentration of railway control. 15 c. (328.)
—Pasco. Isthmian canal question. 25 c. (324.)
—Seager. Patten's theory of prosperity. 15 c. (333.)
—Walker. Taxation of corporations in the U. S. 25 c. (329.)
American and Eng. corporation cases. (T: J. Michie.) v. 15. '02(Je7) O. shp., $4.50. Michie.
American and Eng. encyclopædia of law. (Garland and McGehee.) 2d ed. v. 20. '02(Mr15); v. 21 (Ag2) O. shp., ea., $7.50. E: Thompson.
American and Eng. railroad cases. v. 23. '02(Mr15) O. shp., $5. Michie.
American and Eng. railroad cases. *See also* Railroad repts.
American at Oxford. Corbin, J: net, $1.50. Houghton, M. & Co.
American, Bapt. year-book, 1902; ed. by J. G. Walker. '02(Ap12) O. pap., 25 c. Am. Bapt.
American church dictionary. Miller, W: J. $1. Whittaker.
AMERICAN CATHOLIC CHURCH.
See Protestant Epis. church.
American "commercial invasion" of Europe. Vanderlip, F. A. n. p. Nat. City Bank.
American date book. Simonds, W: E. $1. Kama.
American communities. Hinds, W: A. $1. Kerr.
American corp. legal manual. v. 10. '02 (Jl19) O. shp., $5. Corp. Leg. Co.
American digest, annot.; 1901 B. '02(My10) O. (Am. digest system, 1901.) shp., $6. West Pub.
American digest. Century ed. v. 29. '01-'02(Ja4); v. 30 (Mr15); v. 31 (Ap5); v. 32 (Je14); v. 33 (Jl12) O. shp., subs., ea., $6. West Pub.
American digest system. O. shp., $6. West Pub.
—Am. digest, annot.
American duck shooting. Grinnell, G: B. $3.50. Forest.
American Economic Assoc.: papers and proceedings of the fourteenth annual meeting. '02(My3) 8°, (Am. Econ. Assoc. pubs., v. 3, no. 1.) pap., net, $1.50. Macmillan.
American Economic Assoc. pubs. 8°, pap., net. Macmillan.
—Amer. Economic Assoc. 14th annual meeting. $1.50. (v. 3, 1.)
—Clow. Comparative study of administration of city finances in U. S. $1. (3d ser., v. 2, 4.)
American educational catalogue for 1902. '02 (Ag23) O. leatherette, 50 c. Pub. Weekly.
American electrical cases; ed. by W: W. Morrill. v. 7. '02(My3) O. shp., $6. M. Bender.
American engineering practice in construction of cement plants. Lathbury, B. B. $2. G. M. S. Armstrong.
American federal state. Ashley, R. L. net, $2. Macmillan.
American food and game fishes. Jordan, D: S. net, $4. Doubleday, P.
American fur trade of the far west. Chittenden, H. M. 3 v. net, $10. F. P. Harper.
American gardens. Lowell, G. $7.50. Bates & G.
American horse, cattle and sheep doctor. McClure, R. $1.50. Henneberry.
American immortals. Eggleston, G: C. $10. Putnam.
American law of assemblies. Stevens, E: A. net, $1. E: A. Stevens.
American leaders and heroes. Gordy, W. F. net, 60 c. Scribner.
AMERICAN LITERATURE.
Abernethy. Am. literature. $1.10. Maynard, M. & Co.
Moulton, *and others, eds.* Lib. of literary criticism of Eng. and Am. authors. v. 3, 4. ea., $5; $6.50. Moulton Pub.
Warner. Fashions in literature. net, $1.20. Dodd.
See also Bibliographies;—Essays.
American lumberman telecode. Barry, J. W. net, $5. Am. Lumberman.
American masters of painting. Caffin, C: H. net, $1.25. Doubleday, P.
American negligence digest. Hook, A. J. $6.50. Remick.
American negligence repts. *See* Gardner, J: M.
American newspaper annual, 1902. '02(Ag9) 8°, $5. Ayer.
American newspaper directory. '02(Ag9) 12°, $5. Rowell.
American patriot ser. D. $1. Donohue.
—Brown. John Paul Jones.
American philanthropy of the 19th century. 12°, net. Macmillan.
—Folks. Care of destitute children.
AMERICAN REVOLUTION.
See United States.
American series of popular biographies. Massachusetts ed. '01-'02(Mr1) il. 4°, $17. Graves.
American speaker; for colleges, public and private entertainments. '02(Ap12) il. 4°, pap., 50 c. Conkey.
American sportsman's lib.; ed. by C. Whitney. net, $2; large pap. ed., hf. mor., net, $7.50. Macmillan.
—Sage, *and others.* Salmon and trout.
—Sandys *and* Van Dyke. Upland game birds.
American state repts. (A. C. Freeman.) v. 82. '02(My10); v. 83 (My17); v. 84 (Jl5) O. shp., ea., $4. Bancroft-W.
American street railway investments. [annual.] '02(Je7) F. $5. Street R'way.
American year-book of medicine and surgery; ed. by S: W. Abbott and others. '02 (Mr1) 2 v., il. 8°, ea., net, $3; shp. or hf. mor., ea., net, $3.75. Saunders.
Americanization of the world. Stead, W: T: $1. Markley.
America's story for America's children. Pratt, M. L. v. 5. 40 c. Heath.

Ames, A. F. *See* McLellan, J. A.

Ames, Azel. Elem. hygiene for the tropics. '02(Ag23) il. 16°, 60 c. Heath.

Ames, *Mrs.* Eleanor M. E., ["Eleanor Kirk."] Prevention and cure of old age. '02(Mr8) D. pap., 50 c. Kirk.

Ames, Ja. B. Selection of cases in equity jurisdiction. pt. 2. '01- '02(Ap12) 12°, 75 c. Harvard Law.

Ames, Ja. B., *and* Brewster, L. D. Negotiable instruments law. '02(Ap12) O. 30 c. Harvard Law.

Ames, L: A. Etiquette of yacht colors; cont. yacht codes, storm and weather signals, etc. '02(Jl5) il. sq. S. canvas, 25 c. Annin.

AMIENS CATHEDRAL.
Perkins. Cathedral church of Amiens. $1. Macmillan.

Among the night people. Pierson, C. D. net, $1. Dutton.

Among the water fowl. Job, H. K. net, $1.35. Doubleday, P.

Amor victor. Kenyon, O. $1.50. Stokes.

AMOS.
See Bible.

AMPHIBIA.
Baskett *and* Ditmars.* Story of the amphibians and the reptiles. 60 c. Appleton.

AMUSEMENTS.
See Cards;—Dancing;—Drills; — Entertainments; —Fortune tellers;—Palmistry;—Riddles.

Anacreon. Odes; tr. by Bourne, Fawkes, Moore, and others. '02(Ag2) il. 8°, (Antique gems fr. the Greek and Latin, v. 8.) (Apply to pubs. for price.) Barrie.

ANALYSIS.
See Assaying;—Blowpipe;—Chemistry.

ANARCHY.
See Socialism.

Anarchy. Bauder, E. P. $1; 50 c. Occidental.

ANATOMY.
Cotterell. Pocket Gray; or, Anatomist's vade mecum. net, $1.25. Wood.
Cunningham, *ed.* Text-book of anatomy. *$9 net; $10 net; $11 net. Macmillan.
Gray. Anatomy, descriptive and surgical. net, $5.50-$7.25. Lea.
Kimber, *comp.* Anatomy and physiology. net, $2.50. Macmillan.
Smith. Anatomy, physiology and hygiene. $1. W: R. Jenkins.
Treves. Surgical applied anatomy. net, $2. Lea.
See also Animals;—Autopsy;—Brain;—Dissection; —Eye; — Head; — Intestines; — Mannikin; — Neck;—Nervous system;—Nose; — Physiology; —Surgery;—Teeth;—Vivisection.

ANATOMY FOR ARTISTS.
Fiedler. Studies from the nude human figure in motion. $12. Hessling.

ANCESTRY.
See Genealogy;—Heredity.

ANCIENT AND HON. ARTILLERY CO. OF MASS.
Roberts. Hist. of the Military Co. now called the Ancient and Hon. Artillery Co. of Mass. v. 4. [Sold only to members.] Mudge.

Ancient city. Fustel de Coulanges, N. D. $2. Lee & S.

ANCIENT HISTORY.
See History.

Ancient ruins of Rhodesia. Hall, R. N. net, $6. Dutton.

Andersen, Hans C. Fairy tales; tr. by E. Lucas. '02(Ag16) il. 16°, (Temple classics for young people.) 50 c.; leath., 80 c. Macmillan.

Andersen, Hans C. Selected stories. '01- '02 (Mr1) 12°, pap., 15 c. Lippincott.

Anderson, C: P. The Christian ministry. '02(F22) O. pap., 20 c. Young Churchman.

Anderson, Ja. B. The nameless hero, and other poems. '02(Mr1) D. net, $1. Wessels.

Anderson, J: J., *and* Flick, Alex. C. Short hist. of the state of New York. '01- '02 (Jl12) il. 12°, $1. Maynard, M. & Co.

Anderson, *Sir* Rob. Daniel in the critics' den. '02(Je28) 12°, net, $1.25. Revell.

Andrew, S. O. Greek prose composition. '02 (Je14) 12°, (Greek course.) net, 90 c. Macmillan.

Andrews, Alb. H. *See* Wood, C. A.

Andrews, Alice E. Topics and ref. for the study of Eng. literature. '01- '02(Ap5) D. bds., 15 c. Hyde.

Andrews, H. B. Handbook for street railway engineers. '02(Je21) il. 16°, mor., $1.25. Wiley.

Andrews, W: L. Paul Revere and his engraving. '01. '02(Mr22) $23.50; Japan ed., $40. Scribner.

Angelot. Price, E. C. $1.50. Crowell.

ANGELICO, *Fra.*
Douglas. Fra Angelico. *$6 net. Macmillan.

ANGLICAN CHURCH.
See Church of England.

Anglo-Am. pottery. *See* Barber, E. A.

Animal activities. French, N. S. $1.20. Longmans.

Animal castration. Liautard, A. $2. W: R. Jenkins.

Animal experimentation. Ernst, H. C. net, $1.50; net, $1. Little, B. & Co.

Animal forms. Jordan, D: S. net, $1.10. Appleton.

Animal life in rhymes and jingles. May, E. $1.25. Saalfield.

ANIMAL MAGNETISM.
See Hypnotism.

ANIMALS.
Bourne. Comparative anatomy of animals. v. 2. net, $1.25. Macmillan.
Hulbert. Forest neighbors. net, $1.50. McClure, P.
Ingersoll. Wild life of orchard and field. net, $1.40. Harper.
See also Vivisection;—Zoology.

Animals at home. Bartlett, L. L. 45 c. Am. Bk.

Annandale, C., *ed.* *See* Spofford, A. R.

Annice Wynkoop, artist. Rouse, A. L. $1. Burt.

Annual Am. catalogue. cumulated 1900-1901; with directory of publishers. '02(Ap5) Q. $2. Pub. Weekly.

ANNUALS.
See Almanacs and annuals;—Calendars and yearbooks.

Annunzio, G. d'. The dead city. (G. Mantellini.) '02(Ag9) il. D. $1.25. Laird.

Anstruther, G. E. William Hogarth. '02 (Je28) il. 16°, (Bell's miniature ser. of painters.) leath., $1. Macmillan.

Antarctic queen. Clark, C: $1.75. Warne.

ANTARCTIC REGIONS.
Balch. Antarctica. n. p. Allen, L. & S.

ANTHOLOGIES.
See Oriental religions;—*also* names of literatures.

ANTHONY, *St.*
Lasance. Little manual of St. Anthony of Padua. 25 c. Benziger.
Roulet. Saint Anthony in art. $2. Marlier.

Anthony, C. V. Children's covenant. '02 (F1) D. $1. Jennings.

Anthony, Harold G., *ed.* True romance revealed by a bag of old letters. '02(Je14) D. $1. Abbey Press.

ANTHROPOLOGY.
See Civilization;—Ethnology;—Language;—Woman.

Anticipations. Wells, H. G: net, $1.80. Harper.

Antigone. Sophocles. net, 60 c. Macmillan.

Antique gems from the Gr. and Latin. See Barrie's.

Antoninus, Marcus Aurelius. Helpful thoughts fr. "Meditations." (W. L. Brown.) '02 (Ap12) S. net, 80 c. McClurg.

Anton's **angels**. Trueman, A. 75 c. Alliance.

Antrim, Minna T., ["Titian."] Naked truths and veiled allusions. '02(F22) S. 50 c. Altemus.

ANUS AND RECTUM.
Kelsey. Surgery of the rectum. $3. Wood.

APOSTLES' CREED.
McGiffert. Apostles' creed. net, $1.25. Scribner.

APPLE.
Thomas. Book of the apple; and Preparation of cider. net, $1. Lane.

Appleton's Annual cyclopædia for 1901. '02 (Mr1) 8°, subs., $5; shp., $6; hf. mor., $7; hf. rus., $8. Appleton.

Appleton's Geografia superior ilustrada. '01-'02(F22) 4°, bds., $1.50. Appleton.

Appleton's home-reading books; ed. by W: T. Harris. D. Appleton.
—Atherton, *ed.* Marco Polo. 65 c. (Div. 3, history.)
—Baskett *and* Ditmars. Story of the amphibians and the reptiles. 60 c. (Div. 1, natural history.)

Appleton's international educ. ser. 12°, net. Appleton.
—Compayré. Later infancy of the child. pt. 2. $1.20. (53.)
—Ware. Educational foundations of trade and industry. $1.20. (54.)

Appleton's Latin dictionary; rev. by J. R. V. Marchant and J. F. Charles. '01-'02 (F22) 8°, $1.50. Appleton.

Appleton's lib. of useful stories. il. T. **35 c. net. Appleton.
—Crowest. Story of the art of music.
—Lindsay. Story of animal life.
—Waterhouse. Art of building.

Appleton's life histories. D. net, $1. Appleton.
—Thwaites. Father Marquette.

Appleton's nuevas cartillas cientificas. il. 16°, 40 c. Appleton.
—Hooker. Nociones de botanica.

Appleton's town and country lib. D. $1; pap., 50 c. Appleton.
—Aitken. Love in its tenderness. (309.)
—Alden. Drewitt's dream. (310.)
—Cooper. A fool's year. (308.)
—Norris. Credit of the country. (313.)
—Raine. Welsh witch. (312.)

Appleton's town and country lib.—Continued.
—Roberts. Way of a man. (†314.)
—Smith. Love's itinerary. (307.)
—Wilson. T'bacca queen. (311.)

Appleton's world ser.; ed. by H. J. Mackinder. 8°, $2. Appleton.
—Hogarth. The nearer East. (2.)
—Mackinder. Britain and the British seas. (1.)

AQUARIUM.
Smith. Home aquarium and how to care for it. **$1.20 net. Dutton.

AQUATIC LIFE.
Payne. How to teach aquatic life. 25 c. Kellogg

ARAMAIC LANGUAGE.
See Inscriptions.

Arany, S. A. British-American guide to Carlsbad. 3d Am. ed. '02(Mr8) il. D. pap., 50 c. Abbey Press.

Arbor and bird day annual for Wis. schools. (L. D. Harvey.) '02(Ap26) Q. pap., gratis. Democrat Pr. Co.

ARCHAEOLOGY.
Fowke. Archæological hist. of Ohio: mound builders and later Indians. $5. [Smythe] Ohio Archæolog.
See also Architecture; — Bible; — Civilization; — Cliff-dwellers;—Ethnology; — Folk-lore; — History;—Marriage;—Middle Ages;—Mounds.

ARCHITECTURE.
Coburn. Prize designs for rural school buildings. 25 c. Kellogg.
Complete housebuilder. 50 c.; 25 c. Donohue.
Fletcher. Hist. of architecture. net, $7.50. Scribner.
Georgian period. In 3 v. pt. 8, 9. ea. pt., $4. Am. Architect.
Hodgson. Estimating frame and brick houses. $1. D: Williams.
Kidder. Building construction and superintendence. pt. 2. $4. W: T. Comstock.
Ross. Florentine villas. $25. Dutton.
Ware, *ed.* Topical architecture. 2 v. $7.50. Am. Architect.
Waterhouse. Story of the art of building. net, 35 c. Appleton.
See also Bridges;—Cathedrals;—Church architecture;—Decorations and ornament;—Fine arts;—Roofs;—Sanitary engineering.

Architecture of the brain. Fuller, W: net, $3.50. Fuller.

Archoff, Ludwig. *See* Gaylord, H. R.

ARCTIC REGIONS.
Kersting, *ed.* White world. *$2 net. Lewis.

Ardiane and Barbe Bleue. *See* Maeterlinck, M.

Aretino, Lionardo Bruni. *See* Boccaccio, G.

Argyle, Harvey, *pseud.* *See* McIntire, J: J.

Aristophanes. Comedies; ed. by B: B. Rogers. In 6 v. v. 5. '02(Ap12) 8°, $6. Macmillan.

Aristophanes. The **knights**; ed. by R. A. Neil. '02(Ja18) 8°, (Cambridge Univ. Press ser.) net, $2.50. Macmillan.

ARISTOTLE.
Ellwood. Aristotle as a sociologist. 15 c. Am. Acad. Pol. Sci.

ARITHMETIC.
Atwood. Complete graded arithmetic. v. 3-6. ea., 25 c. Heath.
Baird. Graded work in arithmetic. 25 c. Am. Bk.

ARITHMETIC.—*Continued.*
Browne. Graded mental arithmetic. net, 30 c. Whitaker & R.
Chancellor. Children's arithmetics: Primary, 28 c.—2d bk., 20 c.—3d bk., 24 c.—4th bk., 24 c. Globe School Bk.
Gyim. Chinese-Eng. elem. reader and arithmetic. $1.25. Taylor & M.
Hornbrook. Key to Primary arithmetic and Grammar school arithmetic. 65 c. Am. Bk.
Lippincott's practical arithmetic. 2 v. ea., 40 c. Lippincott.
McLellan, *and others.* Public school arithmetic for grammar grades. net, 60 c. Macmillan.
Milne. Key to Standard arithmetic and Mental arithmetic. 75 c. Am. Bk.
Perkins. Arithmética elemental. 25 c. Appleton.
Pierce. Intermediate arithmetic. 48 c. Silver.
Ruggles. Exercises and problems in arithmetic. 25 c. W: R. Jenkins.
Spangenberg. Practical arith. explained to practical mechanic. 50 c. Zeller.
Vose. Graphic method for solving certain questions in arithmetic or algebra. 50 c. Van Nostrand.
See also Bookkeeping;—Interest.

Arithmetic of electrical measurements. Hobbs, W. R. P. 50 c. Van Nostrand.

ARIZONA.
Bicknell. Guide book of the Grand Canyon of Arizona. 75 c.; 50 c. Harvey.
James. In and around the Grand Canyon. net, $10. Little, B. & Co.

Arkansas. *Supreme ct.* Repts. v. 69. '02 (Ap19) O. shp., $3.50. Thompson Litho.

Arkansaw traveller, *pseud.* *See* Read, O. P.

Arm and hammer ser.; ed. by Lucien Sanial. D. 50 c. N. Y. Labor News.
—Engels. Socialism.
—Marx. Wage-labor and capital; [also] Free trade.

Armature windings of direct current dynamos. Arnold, E. $2. Van Nostrand.

ARMINIUS.
See Hermann der Cherusker.

Armstrong, Annie E. Very odd girl. '02 (Mr29) il. 12°, (Fireside ser.) $1. Burt.

Armstrong, Le Roy. The outlaws. '02(Ap26) D. $1.25. Appleton.

Armstrong, Le Roy. *See also* Banks, C: E.

ARMY.
See Military art and science;—*also* names of countries and states.

Army songster (The): [repr. of 1864.] '02 (Je21) S. pap., 25 c. Bell Bk.

ARNOLD, Benedict.
Codman. Arnold's expedition to Quebec. net, $2.25. Macmillan.
Melvin. Journal of soldier in Arnold's expedition. $2. H. W. Bryant.

Arnold, E. Armature windings of direct current dynamos: fr. orig. Germ. by F. B. De Gress. '02(My3) il. O. $2. Van Nostrand.

Arnold, Edn. L. Lepidus the centurion. '02 (Mr8) D. $1.50. Crowell.

Arnold, Jonathan A., *comp. and ed.* Manual of school laws of Illinois. '01. '02(Mr1) 8°, $1.75. Effingham Democrat.

Arnold, Matt. Dramatic and early poems; ed. by H. B. Forman. '02(My17) 16°, (Temple classics.) 50 c.; flex. leath., 75 c. Macmillan.

Arnold, Matt. Essays in criticism. 1st and 2d ser. '02(Ap19) 12°, (Home lib.) $1. Burt.

Arnold, Matt. Literature and dogma. '02 (My24) 8°, (Commonwealth lib.) net, $1. New Amsterdam.

Arnold, 'Sä. L. Ensellar å leer. '01. '02 (Mr8) il. 12°, 40 c. Silver.

Arnold, *Mrs.* T. B., *ed.* Sabbath school commentary on Internat. lessons, 1902. '02 (Ap12) 8°, 50 c. Revell.

Arnolt, W. M. Theolog. and Semitic literature for 1901. '02(My3) 8°, pap., net, 50 c. Univ. of Chic.

Arnott, S. Books of bulbs. '02(F15) 12°, (Handbooks of practical gardening; ed. by H. Roberts, v. 5.) net, $1. Lane.

Around the "Pan" with Uncle Hank. Fleming, T: $2. Nutshell.

Around the throne. Winchester, P. net, $1. Eichelberger.

Around the world. Carroll, S. W. 60 c. Morse.

Arrabbiata (L'). *See* Heyse, P. J. L.

ARSENIC.
Wanklin. Arsenic. $1. Lippincott.

Art and craft of printing. Morris, W: $5. Elston Press.

Art of folly. Ford, S. **$3 net. Small.

Art of life. Maulde la Clavière, R. de. net, $1.75. Putnam.

Art reader. Cady, M. R. 35 c. Richardson, S.

Art series. *See* Ginn's.

ARTHUR, *King of Britain.*
Malory. King Arthur and his noble knights. $1. Burt.

Arthur, *Mrs.* J. J. Annals of the Fowler family. '02(F22) il. 8°, $3.50. Mrs. J. J. Arthur.

Artificial feeding of infants. Judson, C: F. $2. Lippincott.

ARTILLERY.
See Gunnery.

Artistic crafts ser. of technical handbooks; ed. by W. R. Lethaby. il. D. net. Appleton.
—Cockerell. Bookbinding and the care of books. $1.20. (1.)

ARTISTS.
Wherry. Stories of the Tuscan artists. net, $4. Dutton.
See also Painters.

Artists' lib. *See* Longmans'.

As I saw it. McIntire, J: J. $1.25. Home Pub. Co.

As nature whispers. Davis, S. K. 50 c. Alliance.

As true as gold. Mannix, M. E. 45 c. Benziger.

Asa Holmes. Johnston, A. F. $1. L. C. Page.

Ash, Mark *and* W: Table of federal citations. v. 1. '01. '02(F8); v. 2 (My24) O. shp., (for complete work,) $30. Remick.

Ashley, Roscoe L. American Federal state. '02(Mr1) 12°, net, $2. Macmillan.

ASIA.
See Assyria;—China;—India;—Japan;—Persia;—Siam.

Asiatic Russia. Wright, G: F: 2 v. **$7.50 net. McClure, P.

Askwith, E. H. Introd. to the Thessalonian Epistles. '02(Ap12) 12°, net, $1.25. Macmillan.
Aslauga's knight. *See* La Motte Foque, F. H. K. *Freiherr* de.
Assassins. Meakin, N. M. $1.50. Holt.
ASSAYING.
Miller. Manual of assaying. $1. Wiley.
Rhead *and* Sexton. Assaying and metallurgical analysis. $4.20. Longmans.
See also Blowpipe;—Metals and metallurgy.
ASSYRIA.
Murison. Babylonia and Assyria. net, 20 c. Scribner.
Assyrian and Babylonian contracts. Stevenson, J. H: $2.50. Am. Bk.
ASTROLOGY.
Turnbull. Divine language of celestial correspondence. $2. Alliance.
Valcourt-Vermont. Practical astrology. $1; 50 c. Lee & S.
ASTRONOMY.
Jacoby. Practical talks by an astronomer. net, $1. Scribner.
White. Elements of theoretical and des. astronomy. $2.50. Wiley.
Young. Manual of astronomy. $2.45. Ginn.
See also Almanacs and annuals; — Astrology; — Stars.
At large. Hornung, E. W: $1.50. Scribner.
At Sunwich port. Jacobs, W. W. $1.50. Scribner.
At the back of beyond. Barlow, J. $1.50. Dodd.
Athalie. *See* Racine, J.
Athenæum Press ser. D. Ginn.
—De Quincey. Selections. $1.05.
Atherton, E:, *ed.* Adventures of Marco Polo, the great traveller. '02(Ag16) il. D. (Home reading books; Div. 3, history.) 65 c. Appleton.
Atherton, *Mrs.* Gertrude F. The conqueror. '02(Mr29) D. $1.50. Macmillan.
Athletic lib. *See* Spalding's.
Atkinson, A. A. Electrical and magnetic calculations. '02(Je7) D. net, $1.50. Van Nostrand.
Atkinson, E: Cost of war and warfare from 1898 to 1902, incl; [$700,000,000.] '02 (Ag23) Q. pap., 6 c. E: Atkinson.
Atkinson, Rob. W., *and* Carter, E. Songs of the Eastern colleges. '02(F1) O. $1.25. Hinds.
Atlantic reporter, v. 50. '02(Mr29); v. 51 (Jl19) O. (Nat. reporter system, state ser.) shp., ea., $4. West Pub.
ATLASES.
National standard family and business atlas of the world. subs., $4.75. Fort Dearborn.
See also Encyclopædias;—Geography.
ATTACHMENT.
Rood. On attachments, garnishments, judgments, and executions. $3. Wahr.
ATTIC PROSE.
Flagg. Writer of attic prose: models fr. Xenophon. $1. Am. Bk.
ATTORNEYS.
National list. Directory of bonded attorneys. (App. to pubs. for price.) Nat. Surety.
Atwater, Emily P. How Sammy went to coral-land. '02(Ag2) il. D. **40 c. Jacobs.
Atwater, Fs., *comp.* Atwater history and genealogy. '01. '02(F8) il. 8°, $5; hf. mor., $7.50; full mor., $10. Journal Pub.
Atwood, G: E. Complete graded arithmetic. Grades 3-6. '01. '02(Je7) D. ea., 25 c. Heath.
Audrey. Johnston, M. $1.50. Houghton, M. & Co.
Augsburg, D. R. Drawing. In 3 bks. '02 (My3) sq. O. ea., 75 c. Educ. Pub.
Aulnoy, Marie C. J. de B., *Comtesse d'*, *and* Perrault, C: Once upon a time. New ed. '01. '02(F15) 16°, (Children's friend ser.) bds., 50 c. Little, B. & Co.
Aulnoy, Marie C. J. de B. *Comtesse* de. *See also* Perrault, C:
Aunt Susan, *pseud.* *See* Prentiss, *Mrs.* E.
Austin, A. Tale of true love, and other poems. '02(Ap26) D. net, $1.20. Harper.
Austin, Ma. S. Philip Freneau; the poet of the Revolution. '01. '02(F1) O. net, $2.50. Wessels.
AUSTRIA.
See Prague.
Austrian, Delia. Love songs. '02(Jl5) D. $1. Conkey.
Authorities, deductions and notes in commercial paper. '02(Jl12) interleaved. O. shp., $2.25. Univ. Press.
Author's (The) yearbook for 1902. '02 (Mr29) D. bds., $1. Book-Lover.
AUTHORS.
Allibone. Great authors of all ages. $2.50. Lippincott.
Halsey, *ed.* Authors of our day in their homes. $1.25. Pott.
See also Bibliographies;—Literature;—Musicians.
AUTOGRAPHS.
Joline. Meditations of an autograph collector. net, $3. Harper.
Automatic pen lettering and designs. *See* Faust, C. A.
AUTOMOBILES.
Thompson. The motor-car. $1. Warne.
AUTOPSY.
Schmitt, *ed.* Brief of necroscopy and its medico-legal relation. **$1 net. Funk.
Avare (L'). Molière, J. B. P. de. 50 c. Scott, F. & Co.
Avebury, *Lord*, Barlow, C. A. Montague, Boyle, *Sir* C., *and others.* The King's weigh-house: lectures to business men. '01. '02(Ja4) 12°, 75 c. Macmillan.
Avebury, *Lord.* *See also* Lubbock, *Sir* J:
Avesta. Index verborum, by M. Schuyler, jr. '02(Je14) 8°, (Columbia Univ. Indo-Iranian ser.) net, $2. Macmillan.
Awakening of Anthony Weir. Hocking, S. K. $1.50. Union Press.
Ayer, Jos. C. Rise and development of Christian architecture. '02(My17) il. F. net, $1.50. Young Churchman.
Ayres, Franklin H. Laboratory exercises in elem. physics. '01. '02(F15) il. 12°, net, 50 c. Appleton.
B., E. P. God the beautiful. '02(Ap12) nar. D. net, 75 c. Beam.
Babbitt, Fk. C. Grammar of Attic and Ionic Greek. '02(Jl12) D. $1.50. Am. Bk.
Babcock, M. D. Letters from Egypt and Palestine. '02(Mr22) il. D. net, $1. Scribner.

Babcock, M. D. Three whys and their answer. '01· '02(F15) S. 35 c. Un. Soc. C. E.

Babel and the Bible. Delitzsch, F. *50 c. net. Open Court.

BABYLONIA.
Murison. Babylonia and Assyria. net, 20 c. Scribner.

Bacon, B: W. Sermon on the Mount. '02 (My3) 12°, net, $1. Macmillan.

Bacon, Fs., *Lord.* Works. '02(Je21) 12°, (Caxton ser.) net, $1.25. Scribner.

Bacon, Fs., *Lord.* Essays. '01· '02(Ap5) S. (Little masterpieces.) 50 c. Doubleday, P.

Bacon, Fs., *Lord.* Of gardens. '02(Mr29) 16°, net, 50 c. Lane.

BACON, Fs., *Lord.*
Gallup. Bi-literal cipher of Sir Francis Bacon. $3.75. Howard.
See also Shakespeare-Bacon controversy.

Bacon, Gorham. Manual of otology. 3d ed., rev. and enl. '02(Jl19) il. 12°, *$2.25 net. Lea.

BACTERIA.
Abbott. Manual of bacteriology. net, $2.75. Lea.
Bowhill. Manual of bacteriological technique and spec. bacteriology. $4.50. Wood.
Emery. Bacteriological diagnosis. net, $1.50. Blakiston.
Frost. Lab'y guide in elem. bacteriology. $1.60. W: D. Frost.
Sternberg. Text-book of bacteriology. net, $5: net, $5.75. Wood.
See also Fermentation.

Badminton lib. 8°. Little, B. & Co.
—Harmsworth, *and others.* Motors and motor driving. $3.50; $5.

Baedeker, K. London and its environs. 13th rev. ed. '02(Ag23) 12°, *$1.80 net. Scribner.

Baedeker, K., *ed.* Egypt. 5th rev. ed. '02 (Mr8) il. 12°, (Baedeker's guides.) net, $4.50. Scribner.

Baedeker, K., *ed.* Southern Germany. 9th rev. ed. '02(Mr8) 12°, (Baedeker's guides.) net, $1.80. Scribner.

Bagot, R: Roman mystery. '02(Ap5) 12°, $1.50. Lane.

Bailey, L. H. Nature portraits; studies with pen and camera of our wild birds, animals, fish and insects. '02(Jl12) il. portfolio, 12 x 18 in. App. to pubs. for price. Doubleday, P.

Bailey, Middlesex A. High school algebra. '02(Jl12) sq. S. hf. leath., 90 c. Am. Bk.

Baillie, Alex. F. The Oriental Club and Hanover Square. '01· '02(Ja4) il. 4°, $9. Longmans.

Baillot, Edouard P., *and* Brugnot, Alice G. T. French prose composition. '01· '02(Ja4) S. (Lake French ser.) 50 c. Scott, F. & Co.

BAILMENTS.
Van Zile. Elements of the law and bailments. $5. Callaghan.

Baily, R. C. Mabel Thornley. '02(Mr29) D. $1.25. Abbey Press.

Bain, Ja. *See* Henry, Alex.

Bain, Rob. N. Peter III., Emperor of Russia. '02(Mr29) il. 8°, net, $3.50. Dutton.

Baird, C: W. Hist. of Huguenot emigration to America. New ed. '01· '02(F22) 2 v., 8°, net, $2.50. Dodd.

Baird, S. W. Graded work in arithmetic. 8th year. '02(Ap19) D. 25 c. Am. Bk.

Baker, G: H. Economic locomotive management. 2d lib. ed. '02(Je7) il. D. $1.50. R'way Educ.

Baker, Moses N. Municipal engineering and sanitation. '02(F1) 12°, (Citizen's lib.) hf. leath., net, $1.25. Macmillan.

Balch, F. H. Bridge of the gods. '02(Ag16) il. D. †$1.50. McClurg.

Balch, Edn. S. Antarctica. '02(Jl19) 8°, (for private distribution.) Allen, L. & S.

Balch, Lewis. Manual for boards of health and health officers. '02(Je14) D. $1.50. Banks & Co.

Balch, T: W. Alasko-Canadian frontier. '02(Ap19) 8°, $1. Allen L. & S.

Baldwin, Aaron D. Gospel of Judas Iscariot. '02(My24) D. $1.50. Jamison-H.

Baldwin, Ja. The book lover: guide to best reading. 13th rev. ed. '02(My3) nar. S. net, $1. McClurg.

Baldwin, Ja. F. The scutage and knight service in England. '02(Mr22) 8°, net, $1. Univ. of Chic.

Baldwin, Ja. M.. Development and evolution. '02(Ag2) 8°, **$2.60 net. Macmillan.

Baldwin, Ja. M: Fragments in philosophy and science. '02(Ap19) O. net, $2.50. Scribner.

Baldwin, Ja. M: Social and ethical interpretations in mental development. 3d ed., rev. and enl. '02(Mr29) 8°, net, $2.60. Macmillan.

Baldwin, May. A popular girl. '01· '02 (F15) il. 12°, net, $1.20. Lippincott.

Baldwin, Myra. Nancy's Easter gift [poem.] '02(My24) il. D. 50 c. Abbey Press.

Baldwin, Willis. *See* Michigan. Law of personal injuries.

Baldwin primer. Kirk, M. 35 c. Am. Bk.

Bale marked circle X. Eggleston, G: C. net, $1.20. Lothrop.

Balfour, Arth. J. Foundations of belief. 8th ed., rev. '02(Je7) D. net, $2. Longmans.

Ball Estate Assoc. *See* Gans, E. W:

Ball, Fs. K. Elements of Greek. '02(My3) il. 12°, net, $1. Macmillan.

Ball, *Sir* Rob. S. Earth's beginning. '02 (My24) il. D. net, $1.80. Appleton.

BALL.
See Baseball.

BALLADS.
Book of romantic ballads. net, $1.25. Scribner.
Hale, *ed.* Ballads and ballad poetry. 40 c. Globe Sch. Bk.
Kinard, *ed.* Old English ballads. 40 c. Silver.
Sapte. By the way ballads. *$1.50 net. Dutton.
See also Poetry;—Songs.

Ballagh, Ja. C. Hist. of slavery in Virginia. '02(Ap26) O. (Johns Hopkins Univ. studies, extra v. 24.) $1.50. Johns Hopkins.

Ballance, C: A., *and* Stewart, P. Healing of nerves. '02(F1) 4°, net, $4.50. Macmillan.

Ballard, Eva C. She wanted to vote. '01· '02(Mr8) D. net. $1.40. Brower.

Ballough, C: A. Power that heals and how to use it. '02(Jl19) S. $1. Painter.

Ballough, C: A. Sibylline leaves. '02(Jl19) sq. T. $1. Painter.

BALMANNO, Rob.
Clarke. Letters to an enthusiast. net, $2.50. McClurg.
Balzac, H. de. Best of Balzac; ed. by A. Jessup. '02(Ap26) 16°, (Best writings of great authors.) $1.25; ¾ lev. mor., $3. L. C. Page.

BANDAGES.
Hopkins. Roller bandage. **$1.50 net. Lippincott.
See also Surgery.

Bang, *Mrs.* Marie. Livets alvor. '01· '02 (My17) D. pap., 65 c. M. Bang.
Bangs, J: K. Olympian nights. '02(Je21) D. $1.25. Harper.
Bangs, J: K. Uncle Sam, trustee. '02(My10) il. O. net, $1.75. Riggs.
Banister, H: C. Musical analysis. '02(Ag23) 12°, 75 c. Scribner.

BANKERS.
Sharp & Alleman's Co.'s lawyers' and bankers' directory, 1902. Jan. ed. $5. Sharp & A.

Banks, C: E., *and* Armstrong, L. Theodore Roosevelt, twenty-sixth President of the U. S. '02(Je28) 12°, $1.50; hf. rus., $2.25. Du Mont.
Banks, C: E., *and* Cook, G: C. Authorized and authentic life and works of T. De Witt Talmage, ass. by M. Everett. '02(Ag2) il. 12°, $1.75. Bible House.
Banks, L: A. Great saints of the Bible. '01· '02(Ap12) 8°, $1.50. Eaton & M.
Banks, L: A. Windows for sermons. '02 (Ap12) D. net, $1.20. Funk.
Banks, L: A. *See also* Talmage, F. D.
Banks, Nancy H. Oldfield. '02(Je7) D. $1.50. Macmillan.

BANKS AND BANKING.
Barnett. State banking in the U. S. since passage of Nat. bank act. 50 c. Johns Hopkins.
Coffin. A B C of banks and banking. $1.25. S: A. Nelson.
Handy. Banking systems of the world. $1.50. Jamieson-H.
Michie, *ed.* Banking cases, annot. v. 3. $5. Michie.
Watson. Law of the clearing house. $1.75. Banks.
See also Credit;—Savings-banks.

Bannister, H: M. *See* Brower, D. R.
Banquet book. Reynolds, C. net, $1.75. Putnam.
Banta, Thdr. M. Sayre family. '02(F15) il. 8°, hf. mor., $10. T. M. Banta.

BAPTISM.
Mahon. Token of the covenant; right use of baptism. 50 c. Pub. Ho. of M. E. Ch. So.
Wilson. Great cloud of witnesses. 50 c. Standard Pub.

BAPTIST CHURCH.
Jeter. Baptist principles reset. $1. Rel. Herald.
Merriam. Hist. of Am. Baptist missions. $1.25. Am. Bapt.
Newman, *ed.* Century of Baptist achievements, 1801-1900. net, $1.50. Am. Bapt.

Barbara. Culley, F. C. $1.25. F. C. Culley.
Barbarian invasions of Italy. Villari, P. 2 v. net, $7.50. Scribner.
Barber, Edn. A. Anglo-Am. pottery: old Eng. china; with Am. views. 2d ed., rev. and enl. '02(Ja18) il. 12°, net, $2. [Caspar] E. A. Barber.
Barber, Ed. A. Anglo-Am. pottery. 2d rev., enl. ed. '01· '02(Ap26) il. 8°, $2. Patterson & W.
Barber, F. M. Mechanical triumphs of ancient Egyptians. '01· '02(F22) 16°, net, $1.25. Dodd.
Barbier de Séville. *See* Beaumarchais, P. A. C. de.
Bardeen, C: W. Manual of civics for N. Y. schools. '02(Ja25) D. net. $1. Bardeen.
Barclay, Wilbur F. *See* Methodist Epis. Church.
Barker, Wharton, *ed.* The great issues; repr. of some editorials fr. *The American*, 1897-1900. '02(Ag30) 12°, $1. W. Barker.
Barker, Wharton, *ed.* The great issues: editorials fr. *The American*, 1897-1900. '02 (Je21) 12°, $1; pap., 50 c. Ferris.
Barlow, C. A. Montague. *See* Avebury, *Lord.*
Barlow, Jane. At the back of beyond. '02 My10) D. $1.50. Dodd.
Barnard, C: Farming by inches. '01· '02 (F8) 12°, 40 c. Coates.
Barnard, C: My ten rod farm; or, how I became a florist. '01. '02(F8) 12°, 40 c. Coates.
Barnard, C: A simple flower garden for country homes. '01· '02(F8) 12°, 40 c. Coates.
Barnard, C: The strawberry garden, how planted, what it cost. '01· '02(F8) 12°, 40 c. Coates.
Barnard, C: Two thousand a year on fruits and flowers. '01· '02(F8) 12°, $1. Coates.
Barnes, C: W. Sorrow and solace of Esther, daughter of Ben-Amos. '02(Mr29) S. leatherette, net, 30 c. Jennings.
Barnes, Edn. N. C. Reconciliation of Randall Claymore. '02(Je28) D. $1. Earle.
Barnes, Louisa E., [*Mrs.* Arth. J. Barnes.] Shorthand lessons by the word method. '01· '02(Mr1) 12°, $1.25. A. J. Barnes.
Barnett, Evelyn S. Jerry's reward. '01· '02 (Jl19) il. S. (Cosy corner ser.) 50 c. L. C. Page.
Barnett. G: E. State banking in the U. S. since the passage of the Nat. bank act. '02(My17) O. (Johns Hopkins Univ. studies in hist. and pol. science ser. 20, nos. 2-3.) pap., 50 c. Johns Hopkins.
Barnett, J. M. Mother Goose paint book. '02(Ag9) il. obl. 8°, bds., $1.25. Saalfield.
Barnum, Fs. Grammatical fundamentals of the Innuit language as spoken by the Eskimo of the western coast of Alaska. '01. '02(Jl12) 8°, $5. Ginn.

BARNUM, Phineas T.
Benton. Life of P. T. Barnum. $1. Donohue.

Barr, R., ["Luke Sharp."] Prince of good fellows. '02(Je7) il. D. $1.50. McClure, P.
Barret, F: A. Medical hand book. '02 (Jl12) 16°, $1. Barret Chemical.
Barrett, Jos. H. Life of Abraham Lincoln. '02(Jl19) 12°, (Biographies of famous men.) $1. Donohue.
Barrie, Ja. M. Little minister. '02(Ap5) 12°, (Home lib.) $1. Burt.

Barrie's antique gems from the Greek and Latin. il. 12°. (App. to pub. for price.) Barrie.
—Achilles Tatius. Leucippe and Clitophon. (7.)
—Anacreon. Odes. (8.)
—Horace. Odæ, Epodæ, etc. (3.)
—Longus, Daphnis and Chloe. (4.)
—Lucian. Lucius, the ass. (5.)
—Ovid. Amorum libri tres. (6.)
—Sappho. Odes, bridal songs, epigrams. (9.)
—Theocritus. Idylls. (1.)

Barrow, G. H. S. *See* Waller, A. R.

Barry, H: A. God the Holy Ghost. '02 (Ap12) 12°, $2. Angel Press.

Barry, J: W. American lumberman telecode. '02(Ap26) 8°, flex. leath., net, $5. Am. Lumberman.

Barry Lyndon. *See* Thackeray, W: M.

Bartholomew, J. G. Internat. student's atlas of modern geography. '02(Ap12) 4°, net, $2.25. Scribner.

Bartholomew's physical atlas. v. 1, Meteorology, by A. Buchan. '02(Ag2) f°, hf. mor., **$17.50 net. Lippincott.

Bartlett, Alb. L. A golden way: journey through Ireland, Scotland and England. '02(Mr1) il. D. $1.50. Abbey Press.

Bartlett, Emeline B. *See* Pearson, H: C.

Bartlett, Lillian L. Animals a' home. '02 (My17) il. D. (Eclectic school readings.) 45 c. Am. Bk.

Barton, F:, *comp.* Pulpit power and eloquence. '01. '02(Mr8) 8°, $3.50. F. M. Barton.

Barton, G: A. Roots of Christian teaching as found in the O. T. '02(My24) D. $1.25. Winston.

Barton, G: A. Sketch of Semitic origins, social and religious. '02(F1) 8°, net, $3. Macmillan.

Barton, W: E. I go a fishing: study in progressive discipleship. '02(F8) 16°, 25 c. Revell.

BASEBALL.
Spalding's official baseball guide, 1902. 10 c. Am. Sports.

Basis of social relations. Brinton, D. G. net, $1.50. Putnam.

BASKETRY.
Firth. Cane basket work. 2 v. ea., 60 c. Scribner.

Baskett, Ja. N., *and* Ditmars, R. L. Story of the amphibians and the reptiles. '02(Jl19) D. (Home-reading books; Div. 1, Nat. history.) 60 c. Appleton.

Bass, Edg. W. Elements of differential calculus. 2d ed., rev. '02(Ja11) il. 12°. net, $4. Wiley.

Bassett, Fk. J. *See* Campbell, H. A.

Bassett, Ma. E. S. Judith's garden. '02(Je7) O. $1.50. Lothrop.

Bateson, W. Mendel's principles of heredity: a defence. '02(Ag16) 12°, (Cambridge Univ. Press ser.) *$1.30 net. Macmillan.

Batt, Max. Treatment of nature in German literature from Günther to the appearance of Goethe's Werther. '02(F15) O. pap., net, $1. Univ. of Chic.

Battleground. Glasgow, E. $1.50. Doubleday, P.

Battling with love and fate. Allen, M. V. $1. Abbey Press.

Bauder, Emma P. Anarchy; its cause and cure told in story. '02(Ap12) il. D. $1; pap., 50 c. Occidental Pub.

Baur, T. P., *and* Herbert, H. F. Free thinkers' manual. '02(Je7) il. 8°, $4. Radical.

Bausman, B. Precept and practice. '02(Ap5) D. net, $1. Heidelberg.

BAVARIA.
See **Ludwig** II.

Bayley, Abner. *See* Marden, O. S.

Baylies, Edn. *See* Wait, W:

Bayly, Ada E., ["Edna Lyall."] The hinderers. '02(Je7) D. $1. Longmans.

Beach, Harlan P. Geography and atlas of Protestant missions. v. 1, Geography. '01. '02(F15) 12°, $2.50; pap., per set, $1.75. Student Vol.

Beach, W: H. First New York (Lincoln) cavalry. '02(Jl12) 8°, *$2.50 net. [Caspar] Lincoln Cavalry.

Beacon Hill ser. D. bds., *25 c. net. Pilgrim Press.
—Gladden. Practice of immortality.

Beale, C: C. Book of legal dictation. 2d ed., rev. and enl. '01. '02(F1) D. 50 c. Beale Press.

Beall, St. Clair. Winning of Sarenne. '02 (Ag9) il. 12°, 50 c.; pap., 25 c. Federal.

Beard, Sidney H. Comprehensive guide book to natural, hygienic and humane diet. New ed. '02(Mr22) 16°, $1; pap., 50 c. Alliance.

Beard, Sidney H. Comprehensive guide-book to natural, hygienic and humane diet. [New issue.] '02(My17) D. net, $1. Crowell.

Bears of Blue River. Major, C: $1.50. Macmillan.

Beaumarchais, Pierre A. C. de. Barbier de Seville and Lettres; ed. by G: D. Fairfield. '02(Jl5) 16°, (Lake French classics.) 50 c. Scott, F. & Co.

BEATITUDES.
Lathbury. Code of joy: sermons on the beatitudes. 50 c. Swedenborg.
See also Sermon on the Mount.

Beau's comedy. Dix, B. M. $1.50. Harper.

Beaton, Ja. A. Vest-pocket practical compend of electricity. '02(My17) il. nar. T. 50 c.; leath., 75 c. Laird.

BEAUTIFUL (The).
See Aesthetics.

Bechtel, J: H., *comp.* Proverbs, maxims and phrases, fr. all lands and times. '02 (Ag30) 24°, (Popular handbooks.) 50 c. Penn Pub. Co.

Beck, Carl. Sonnenblicke aus der Amerikanischen praxis. '02(F15) O. pap., net, 30 c. Lemcke.

Becke, G: L: Breachley—black sheep. '02 (Ag30) 12°, †$1.50. Lippincott.

Becker, Fk. S. *See* New York civil and criminal justice.

Beddard, F. E. Mammalia. *See* Harmer, S. F:, *ed.*

Bedell, Edn. A., *rep.* *See* New York. *Ct. of appeals.* Digest.

Bedford, Jessie. *See* Godfrey, E.

Beecher, C: E. Studies in evolution. '01. '02(Mr15) 8°, (Yale bicentennial pub.) net, $5. Scribner.

Beeching, H. C. Inns of court sermons. '01. '02(Ja4) 12°, $1.25. Macmillan.

Beeman, Marion N. Analysis of the Eng. sentence; rev. and enl. '02(Je28) sq. D. (Progredior ser.) 50 c. Flanagan.

Beers, G: E. *See* Stephen, *Sir* J. F.
Behrens, C. Blossom and fruit in decorative arrangement. '02(Jl5) pls. 8°, $12. Hessling.
Behymer, Ida H. Seal of destiny. '01. '02 My10) 12°, $1.50. Neely.
Bek's first corner. Conklin, *Mrs.* J. M. D. $1. Burt.
BELGIUM.
George. Little journey to Belgium and Denmark. 15 c. Flanagan.
Belinda. Egan, M. F. $1. Kilner.
Bell, *Mrs.* Arth. *See* Bell, *Mrs.* N., R. E. M.
Bell, Currer, *pseud. See* Brontë, C.
Bell, Lilian, [*now Mrs.* Arth. Hoyt Bogue.] Abroad with the Jimmies. '02(My10) il. D. $1.50. L. C. Page.
Bell, Malcolm. Rembrandt Van Rijn. '01-'02(Ja4) il. 12°, (Great masters of painting and sculpture.) $1.75. Macmillan.
Bell, *Mrs.* Nancy R. E. M., ["N. D'Anvers."] Thomas Gainsborough. '02(Je28) il. 16°, (Bell's miniature ser. of painters.) leath., $1. Macmillan.
Bell, Roscoe R. *See* Veterinarian's call-book.
Belle-Nivernaise. Daudet, A. 30 c. Heath.
Belles, W: H: Cain's sin. '01- '02(F1) D. $1. W: H: Belles.
Belloc, Bessie R. In a walled garden. 5th ed. '02(Mr8) 8°, net, $1.25. Herder.
Belloc, Bessie R. Passing world. 2d ed. '02(Mr8) 8°, net, $1.25. Herder.
Belloc, Hilaire. The path to Rome. '02(Je21) il. O. net, $2. Longmans.
Belloc, Hilaire. Robespierre: a study. '01. '02(F1) O. net, $2. Scribner.
Bell's cathedral ser. 12°, 60 c. Macmillan.
—Hiatt. Westminster Abbey.
Bell's handbooks to continental churches. il. 12°, $1. Macmillan.
—Perkins. Amiens.
Bell's miniature ser. of painters. il. 16°, 50 c.; limp leath., $1. Macmillan.
—Anstruther. Hogarth.
—Bell. Gainsborough.
—Staley. Watteau.
—Williamson. Holman Hunt.
Belshazzar. Davis, W: S. †$1.50. Doubleday, P.
Beman, W. W., *and* Smith, D: E. Academic algebra. '02(My24) D. hf. leath., $1.25. Ginn.
Ben Hur. Wallace, L. $2.50. Harper.
Bender, Ida C., *ed. See* Judson, H. P.
Bender, Wilbur H. The teacher at work. '02 (Je28) D. 75 c. Flanagan.
Benedictine martyr in England. Camm, B. net, $1.25. Herder.
Benedix, R. J. Der prozess. *See* Fulda, L.
Benjamin, C: H: Notes on machine design. 2d ed. '02(My17) il. 16°, $2. C. H. Holmes.
Benjy in beastland. Ewing, *Mrs.* J. H. 50 c. Little, B. & Co.
Bennett, Arnold. T. Racksole and daughter. '02(My24) il. D. $1.50. New Amsterdam.
Bennie, the Pythian of Syracuse. Fretz, L. B. $1. Scroll Pub.
Benson, E: F. Scarlet and hyssop. '02 (Ap12) D. $1.50. Appleton.
Benson, E: W. Addresses on the Acts of the Apostles. '02(Mr29) il. 8°, net, $7. Macmillan.
Benton, Joel. Life of P. T. Barnum. '02 (My24) 12°, (Biographies of famous men.) $1. Donohue.
Bentzan, Therese. Constances. '02(Ap26) 12°, $1.50. Neely.
Beowulf. Beowulf; tr. out of the old Eng. by C. B. Tinker. '02(Ag30) 16°, 80 c. Newson.
Bergholt, Ernest. *See* Leigh, L.
BERIN, *St.*
Field. Saint Berin, the apostle of Wessex. $1.50. E. & J. B. Young.
Berkeley, W: N. Lab'y work with mosquitoes. '02(My17) O. net, $1. Pediatrics Lab.
BERKELEY HILLS.
Lawson *and* Palache. The Berkeley Hills: coast range geology. 80 c. Univ. of Cal.
Berkleys (The). Wight, E. H. net, 40 c. Benziger.
BERKSHIRE, Mass.
See Lenox.
BERLIOZ, Hector.
Young. Mastersingers; with essay on Hector Berlioz. net, $1.50. Scribner.
Berlitz, M. D. Grammaire partique de la langue française. In 4 v. v. 3. '02(Ap26) 12°, 50 c. Berlitz.
Bernis, François J. de P., *Cardinal* de. Memoirs and letters; fr. orig. mss. by F. Masson. '02(F1) 2 v., il. 8°, (Versailles hist. ser.) subs., per v., $6; ¾ leath., per v. $9. Hardy, P. & Co.
Berrier, Leroy. The new life. '02(Ag2) D. $1. L. Berrier.
Berry, G: R., *ed.* Letters of the Rm. 2 coll. in the British Museum. '02(F15) 8°, pap., net, 50 c. Univ. of Chic.
Besant, *Sir* W. Autobiography. '02(My10) O. net, $2.40. Dodd.
Besant, *Sir* W., *ed.* Fascination of London. [also] Chelsea, by G. E. Mitton. '02(Ag16) 16°, 80 c. Macmillan.
Best, Kenelm D. Victories of Rome and the temporal monarchy of the church. 4th ed., rev. '01- '02(Mr22) S. net, 45 c. Benziger.
Best, Noel R. College man in doubt. '02 (Je21) D. net, 50 c. Westminster.
Best nonsense verses. Daskam, J. D. 50 c. W: S. Lord.
Best stories from the best book. White, J. E. 50 c. Southern Pub.
Best writings of great authors. 16°, $1.25; $3. L. C. Page.
—Balzac. Best of Balzac.
BEVERAGES.
Maloney. 20th century guide for mixing fancy drinks. $1. J. C. Maloney.
Beyond the clouds. Patterson, C: B. $1. Alliance.
Beyond the vail. Nixon, J. H. $1.75. Hudson-K.
Bible. Temple ed. In 24 v. v. 2-4. '01-'02(F1); vs. 5-12 (Je28) il. sq. T. ea., net, 40 c.; flex. leath., ea., net, 60 c. Lippincott.
Bible. The emphasized Bible: new tr. designed to set forth the exact meaning, etc.; expository introd., ref. and app., by Jos. B. Rotherham. v. 1, Genesis-Ruth; v. 2, Samuel-Psalms. '02(Jl12) 8°, ea., $3. Woodward & L.

Bible. Greek Testament; ed. by E. Nestle; app. on irregular verbs by R. F. Weidner. '02(Ap5) 16°, net, $1; leath., net, $1.25. Revell.

Bible. New Testament. Self-pronouncing; tr. out of orig. Gk., with former trans. compared and rev. [Holman ed.] '02 (Ag23) 32°, mor., 50 c. Holman.

Bible. Old and New Testaments; rev. 1881-85; newly ed. by the Am. Revision Com. Standard ed. '02(Ag2) O. leath., $1-$7. Nelson.

Bible. O. T. Cambridge Bible. Psalms. (A. F. Kirkpatrick.) '02(Ap5) 12°, net, $2. Macmillan.

Bible. Old Testament. Cambridge Bible for schools; Psalms; introd. and notes by A. F. Kirkpatrick. v. 9. bks. 4 and 5. '02 (Ja18) 12°, net, 80 c. Macmillan.

Bible. Sunday-school scholars' Bible; ed. by A. F. Schauffler. '02(Je21) 12°, 55 c.; Fr. flex. mor., 75 c.; Fr. mor., $1. Nelson.

Bible. Young people's Bible; Scriptures connected, explained and simplified, by H. N. Jones. '02(Ag30) il. 8°, $1.75. Am. Bk. and Bible.

BIBLE.
- Alexander. Demonic possession in the N. T. net, $1.50. Scribner.
- Askwith. Introd. to the Thessalonian Epistles. net, $1.25. Macmillan.
- Barton. Roots of Christian teaching as found in the O. T. $1.25. Winston.
- Benson. Addresses on the Acts of the Apostles. net, $7. Macmillan.
- Boteler. Side windows; or, lights on Scripture truths. 75 c. Standard Pub.
- Brown, F., *and others, eds.* Hebrew and Eng. lexicon of the Old Testament. pt. 10. net, 50 c. Houghton, M. & Co.
- Brown, W: E. Divine key of the Revelation of Jesus Christ. v. 2. $1.50. Armstrong & B.
- Browne. Help to spiritual interpretation of the penitential Psalms. net, 40 c. Longmans.
- Chase. Credibility of the Acts of the Apostles. $1.75. Macmillan.
- Darby. Analysis of the Acts and Epistles of the N. T. 25 c. J. E. Darby.
- Eadie. Biblical cyclopædia. net, $3.75. Lippincott
- Florer. Biblische geschichten. 40 c. Wahr.
- Goodspeed. Newberry gospels. net, 25 c. Univ. of Chic.
- Grethenbach. Secular view of the Bible. net, $2. Eckler.
- Harper. Constructive studies in the priestly element in the O. T. $1. Univ. of Chic.
- Hoare. Evolution of the Eng. Bible. net, $2.50. Dutton.
- Holborn. The Pentateuch in the light of to-day. *75 c. net. Scribner.
- Knecht. Child's Bible hist. 25 c. Herder.
- Lilley. Pastoral epistles. net, 75 c. Scribner.
- McGarvey. Authorship of the Book of Deuteronomy. $2. Standard Pub.
- Mackail. Biblia innocentium; for children. $1.75. Longmans.

BIBLE.—*Continued.*
- Nash, *ed.* Practical explanation and application of Bible history. net, $1.50. Benziger.
- Oesterley. Studies in the Gr. and Latin versions of Amos. *$1.30 net. Macmillan.
- Patterson. Broader Bible study: Pentateuch. net, 75 c. Jacobs.
- Pattison. The Bible and the 20th century. 10 c. Am. Bapt.
- Prime. Power of God's word. 3 c. Presb. Bd.
- Rice. Our sixty-six sacred books. net, 50 c. Am. S. S.
- Robertson. Lessons on the Gospel of St. Mark. net, 40 c. Revell.
- Robertson. Studies in the Acts of the Apostles. 40 c. Revell.
- Ruble. Wonders of the Revelation of Jesus Christ: expository treatment of [Revelation]. $1. Standard Pub.
- Shepardson. Studies in the Epistles to the Hebrews. $1.50. Revell.
- Strachan. Hebrew ideals fr. story of the patriarchs. pt. 1, Genesis. *60 c. net. Scribner.
- Wade. Old Testament history. $1.50. Dutton.
- White. Best stories from the best book. 50 c. Southern Pub.
- Wilberforce. Com. on the Epistle to the Ephesians. net, $1. Herder.
- Williams. Shall we understand the Bible? net, 50 c. Macmillan.
- Young people's Bible stories. 4 v. ea., $1.25. Saalfield.

See also Catechisms;—Christianity;—God;—Jesus Christ;—Religion and science;—Saints;—Sermon on the Mount;—Theology.

Bible character ser. 16°, 35 c. Pepper.
—Carradine. Gideon.

Bible class handbooks. 12°, net. Scribner.
—Lilley. Pastoral epistles. 75 c.
—Strachan. Hebrew ideals fr. the patriarchs. pt. 1. *60 c.

Bible class primers. 16°, pap., net. 20 c. Scribner.
—Murison. Babylonia and Assyria.

Bible lessons for little beginners. Haven, *Mrs.* M. J. C. net, 75 c. Revell.

Bible stories. *See* Children's.

Bible student's lib. 12°. E. & J. B. Young.
—Girdlestone. Grammar of prophecy. $2.50. (11.)

Biblia innocentium. Mackail, J: W: $1.75. Longmans.

BIBLIOGRAPHIES.
- American educational catalogue for 1902. 50 c. Pub. Weekly.
- Andrews. Paul Revere and his engraving. $23.50; $40. Scribner.
- Annual Am. catalogue, cumulated 1900-01. $2. Pub. Weekly.
- Ballagh. Slavery in Va. $1.50. Johns Hopkins.
- Batt. Treatment of nature in Germ. literature. net, $1. Univ. of Chic.
- Bourne. Teaching of hist. and civics. $1.50. Longmans.
- Brace, *ed.* Laws of radiation and absorption. net, $1. Am. Bk.
- Deems, *comp.* Holy-days and holidays. $5. Funk.

BIBLIOGRAPHIES.—*Continued.*
De Quincey. Selections. $1.05. Ginn.
Dickinson. Music in the hist. of the estern church. net, $2.50. Scribner.
Dyer *and* Hassall. Hist. of modern Europe. v. 6. net, $2. Macmillan.
English catalogue of books for 1901. $1.50. Pub. Weekly.
Fish. Calisthenic dict. $1. Seminar.
Fitzgerald. Writings; incl. complete bibliog. 7 v. subs., ea., $6; $12.50; $35. Doubleday, P.
Fletcher *and* Bowker. Annual literary index, 1901. net, $3.50. Pub. Weekly.
Flint, *and others.* The trust. net, $1.25. Doubleday, P.
Ford, *ed.* Journals of Hugh Gaine, pr. net, $15; net, $25. Dodd.
Fowler. Hist. of ancient Greek literature. net, $1.40. Appleton.
Gauss. Investigations of curved surfaces. *$1.75 net. Princeton Univ.
Green. Facsimile reproductions rel. to Boston and neighborhood. net, $10. Littlefield.
Huddilston. Lessons from Gr. pottery, with bibliog. of Gr. ceramics. net, $1.25. Macmillan.
Jenkins. Guide bk. to historic Germantown. 50 c. Site and Relic.
Kupfer. Greek foreshadowings of mod. metaphysical and epistemological thought. $1. J. S. Cushing.
Larned, *ed.* Literature of Am. history. net, $6; $7.50; $9. Houghton, M. & Co.
Legler. James Gates Percival. net, $1. Mequon Club.
Livingston. Bibliog. of the first ed. in book form of the works of Tennyson. $1. Dodd.
Livingston. Works of Rudyard Kipling: des. of first eds. net, $12; net, $20. Dodd.
Mackinnon. Growth and decline of French monarchy. $7.50. Longmans.
Marks. Outline of Eng. literature. $1. J. A. Marks.
Meyer. Nominating systems. net, $1.50. E. C. Meyer.
Miner. Daniel Boone. $1. Dibdin Club.
Moncrief. Short hist. of the Chr. church. **$1.50 net. Revell.
Nield. Guide to the best historical novels and tales. net, $1.75. Putnam.
Paulsen. Immanuel Kant. net, $2.50. Scribner.
Publishers' trade list annual, 1902. *$1.50 net; in 2 v., with index, $5 net. Pub. Weekly.
Randall, *ed. and tr.* Expansion of gases by heat. $1. Am. Bk.
Richardson, War of 1812. subs., $3. Hist. Pub.
Schmidt. Solomon's temple. net, $1. Univ. of Chic.
Seignobos. Hist. of the Roman people. *$1.25 net. Holt.
Shadwell. Drink, temperance and legislation. $1.75. Longmans.
Smith, E. E. The golden poppy. net, $1.50. E. E. Smith.
Stevenson. Best of Stevenson. †$1.25. L. C. Page.

BIBLIOGRAPHIES.—*Continued.*
Vanderpoel. Color problems. net, $5. Longmans.
Van Dyke. Italian painting. 50 c. Elson.
Vincent, *and others.* H. B. Adams; with bibliog. of the dept. of history, politics and economics of Johns Hopkins Univ. free to subs. Johns Hopkins.
Watkins. Diagnosis by means of the blood. $5. Physicians.
Webb, S. *and* B. P. Trade unionism. net, $2.60. Longmans.
Whitaker & Sons, *comps.* Ref. catalogue of current [Eng.] literature 2 v. *$5 net. Pub. Weekly.
Wilson. Bibliog. of child study. net, 25 c. Stechert.

Biblische geschichten. Florer, W. W. 40 c. Wahr.

Bicknell, P. C. Guide book of the Grand Canyon of Arizona. '02(Je28) sq. S. leath., 75 c.; pap., 50 c. Harvey.

Biglow papers. Lowell, J. R. 75 c. Burt.

Bilingual teaching in Belgian schools. Dawes, T. R. *50 c. net. Macmillan.

Billings, Fk., *and* Stanton, S. C., *eds.* General medicine. '01. '02(Mr8) 8°, (Practical medicine ser. of year-books, no. 1.) $1.50. Year Bk.

Billings, Josh, *pseud.* *See* Shaw, H: W.

Billy Burgundy's letters. '02(Jl12) il. S. †75 c. J. F. Taylor.

Billy Whiskers. Montgomery, F. T. $1. Saalfield.

BIMETALLISM.
See Money.

Bingham, Grace A., *comp.* Two hundred bar examination questions. '02(Je7) S. pap., $1. Commercial Press.

Binkley, Christian. Sonnets and songs for a house of days. '02(Je21) D. bds., net, $1.25. A. M. Robertson.

Biographical ser. S. pap., 10 c. Am. Bapt. Miss. Un.
—Clough. John E. Clough.

Biographies of famous men. 12°, $1. Donohue.
—Barrett. Abraham Lincoln.
—Benton. P. T. Barnum.
—Custis. George Washington.
—Godbey. Henry M. Stanley.
—Johnson. W. T. Sherman.
—Poore *and* Tiffany. U. S. Grant.

BIOGRAPHY.
American ser. of popular biographies. Mass. ed. $17. Graves.
Gans. Pennsylvania pioneer. $6. Kuhl.
Good. Women of the Reformed church. $1. Heidelberg.
Graham. Scottish men of letters in 18th century. net, $4.50. Macmillan.
Lippincott's biog. dict. 2 v. subs., $15; $17.50; $20. Lippincott.
National cyclopædia of Am. biography. v. 11. subs., $10. J. T. White.
Who's who, 1902. $1.75. Macmillan.
See also Authors; — Autographs; — Booksellers; — Diaries; — Genealogy; — Heroes; — History; — Painters; — Popes; — Saints.

Birbeck, Chris. J. Elocution self-taught. '02 (Ag16) il. 12°, $1. Wagner.

Birbeck, Chris. J., *ed.* Select recitations, orations and dramatic scenes. '02(Je7) il. D. $1. Wagner.

Bird play. Spangler, N. Y. 15 c. Kellogg.
BIRDS.
Fowler. More tales of the birds. $1. Macmillan.
Job. Among the water fowl. net, $1.35. Doubleday, P.
Jordan, *comp.* True tales of birds and beasts. 40 c. Heath.
Lord. First book upon birds of Oregon and Washington. 75 c. W: R. Lord.
Maynard. Birds of Washington and vicinity. *$1 net. Woodward & L.
Sandys *and* Van Dyke. Upland game birds. net, $2; net, $7.50. Macmillan.
Wheelock. Nestlings of forest and marsh. net, $1.40. McClurg.
See also Pigeons.
Birrell, A. William Hazlitt. '02(Jl12) 12°, (Eng. men of letters.) **75 c. net. Macmillan.
BIRTHDAY BOOKS.
Tennyson. Birthday book. 75 c.; $1; $1.25. Warne.
Birthright membership of believers' infants. Horton, F. A. 6 c. Presb. Bd.
Bishop, Irving P. Red book of Niagara. '02 (Jl19) il. S. pap., 25 c. Wenborne-S.
Bishop, W: H: Queer people, incl. The brown stone boy. '02(My17) D. $1. Street.
Bishop, W: H: Tons of treasure. New and imp. ed. of The yellow snake. '02(Je7) D. $1. Street.
BISMARCK, *Prince* v.
Lieb. Prince Bismarck and the German people. $1.50; $2.25; $3.25. Dominion.
Bits of broken china. Fales, W: E. S. 75 c. Street.
Bivar, R. D. de. *See* Cid (The).
Bixby, Ja. T. The new world and the new thought. '02(Mr8) D. net, $1. Whittaker.
Bjorling, P. R. Pipes and tubes. '02(Je28) il. 12°, $1. Macmillan.
Black, J: S. *See* Cheyne, T: K.
BLACK, W:
Reid. William Black, novelist. net, $2.25. Harper.
Black cat club. Corrothers, J. D. net, $1. Funk.
Black Evan. Young, J. D. $1. Neely.
Blackie, J: S. On self-culture: (phonography.) '02(F15) S. pap., 35 c. Phonograph.
BLACKSMITHING.
Lungwitz. Guide to blacksmithing, horseshoeing, carriage and wagon building and painting. $1. Donohue.
Blackwood, Alex. L. Diseases of the lungs. '02(Ag2) il. 12°, $2. Halsey.
Blackwood's (*ed.*) philosophical classics. New ed. '01. '02(Mr1) 15 v., 12°, per v., net, 50 c. Lippincott.
Blain, Hugh M. Syntax of the verb in the Anglo-Saxon chronicle from 787 A.D. to 1001 A.D. '01. '02(Mr8) 12°, (University of Virginia monographs, school of Teutonic languages, no. 2.) pap., net, 50 c. Barnes.
Blaisdell, Alb. F. Life and health. '02(Je14) D. $1. Ginn.
Blaisdell, Etta A. *and* Ma. F. Child life fifth reader. '02(Mr29) il. 12°, net, 45 c. Macmillan.
Blake, G: H. Common sense ideas for dairymen. '01. '02(F8) 12°, $1. Coates.
Blake, Ja. V. Sonnets. '02(Ja25) sq. S. $1. J. H. West.
Blake, W: William Blake; ed. by T. S. Moore. '02(Ap26) Q. (Little engravings classical and contemporary, no. 2.) bds., net, $1.50. Longmans.
Blakiston's quiz compend ser. il. 12°, 80 c.; $1. Blakiston.
—Thayer. Compend of general pathology. (15.)
Blanchard, Amy E. Little Miss Oddity. '02 (Ag9) il. D. **80 c. net. Jacobs.
Blanchard, Amy E. Twenty little maidens. '01. '02(F15) il. 12°, $1.25. Lippincott.
Blanden, C: G. Drift of song. '02(Ag2) sq. S. bds, *50 c. net. W: S. Lord.
Blashfield, De Witt C. Treatise on instructions to juries. '02(Ag2) O. shp., $6. Keefe-D.
Blashfield, De Witt C., *ed.* *See* **New York.** Abbott's digest.
Blatchford, Rob., ["Nunquam."] Britain for the British. '02(Ag2) D. 50 c.; pap., 25 c. Kerr.
Blauvelt, Ma. T. Development of cabinet government in England. '02(Mr22) 12°, net, $1.50. Macmillan.
Blazed trail. White, S. E: $1.50. McClure, P.
Bleininger, Alb., *ed.* *See* Seger, H. A:
Blighted rose. Wynne, J. F. $1.50. Angelus.
BLIND (Reading for).
Roosevelt. Message to the two houses of Congress. $1. N. Y. State Lib.
Blind spot. Watkinson, W: L. net, $1. Revell.
Bliss, W: R. September days on Nantucket. '02(Je28) D. net, $1. Houghton, M. & Co.
Blithedale romance. Hawthorne, N. $1. Burt.
Bloch, I. S. Future of war, in its technical, economic and pol. relations. [New issue.] '02(Jl19) D. 60 c. Ginn.
BLOCK ISLAND.
Livermore. Block Island. 25 c. Ball.
Block system of signalling on Am. railroads. Adams, B. B. $2. Railroad Gazette.
Blomfield, Reginald. Formal garden in England. 3d ed. '02(F1) il. 12°, $3. Macmillan.
BLOOD.
Cabot. Clinical examination of the blood. net, $3.25. Wood.
Da Costa. Clinical hematology. net, $5. Blakiston.
Blood will tell. Davenport, B: R. $1.50. Caxton Bk.
Bloomfield, Will. Transplanting an old tree. '02(Mr22) D. $1. Blanchard.
Blossom and fruit in decorative arrangement. Behrens, C. $12. Hessling.
Blouet, Paul, ["Max O'Rell."] English pharisees, French crocodiles. New issue. '01. '02(Ja4) D. $1.25. Abbey Press.
Blouët, Paul. 'Tween you an' I. pt. 1. Concerning men; pt. 2, Concerning women. '02(My24) D. $1.20. Lothrop.
Blount, *Sir* E: C: Memoirs; ed. by S. J. Reid. '02(Ag30) O. $4. Longmans.
BLOWPIPE.
Plattner. Qualitative and quantitative analysis with the blowpipe. net, $4. Van Nostrand
Blue diamond. Keene, R. W. $1.50. Abbey Press

Blum, A. R. Reduction tables for ascertaining with accuracy and rapidity freight charges for any quantity of grain on all standard bases, in Eng. money. '01. '02 (Je14) 4°, leath., net, $3. Am. Code.
Boardman, G: D. Our risen King's forty days. '02(Mr22) D. net, $1.25. Lippincott.
BOATING.
See Canoeing.
BOATS.
Martin. Album of designs for boats, launches and yachts. $1. F. W. Martin.
Mower. How to build a knockabout. $1. Rudder.
See also Yachts and yachting.
Bob o' Link. Waggaman, M. T. 40 c. Benziger
Bobbett, Wa. *See* Neidlinger, D. H.
Boccaccio, G., *and* **Aretino**, L. B. Earliest lives of Dante; fr. the Ital. by Ja. R. Smith. '01. '02(Mr15) O. (Yale studies in Eng., no. 10.) pap., 75 c. Holt.
Bodmer, G. R. Inspection of railway materials. '02(Je7) 12°, $1.50. Macmillan.
BODY AND MIND.
See Mind and body.
Body and soul. Wright, J. C. $1. J. C. Wright.
Body of Christ. Gore, C: $1.75. Scribner.
BOERS.
Davitt. Boer fight for freedom. net, $2. Funk.
Hiley *and* Hassell. Mobile Boer. $1.50. Grafton Press.
See also South Africa.
Boethius, A. M. S. Consolation of philosophy. '02(Mr22) 16°, (Temple classics.) 50 c.; leath., 75 c. Macmillan
Bogue, *Mrs.* A. H. *See* Bell, L.
Bohn's standard lib. 12°, net, $1. Macmillan.
—Prescott. Conquest of Peru. 2 v.—Ferdinand and Isabella. 3 v.
—Swift. Prose works. v. 9.
Boiled-down booklets. Tt. 25 c. Success.
—Hungerford. Success club debater.
BOILERS.
Robertson. Water-tube boilers. $3. Van Nostrand.
Boisot, L: By-laws of private corporations. 2d ed. '02(F8) O. shp., $3. Keefe-D.
BOLINGBROKE, *Lord.*
Sichel. Bolingbroke and his times. pt. 2. $4. Longmans.
Bolza, O. Concerning the geodesic curvature and the isoperimetric problem on a given surface. '02(Jl19) Q. (Univ. of Chic. decennial pub.) pap., *25 c. net. Univ. of Chic.
Bond, Paul S. *See* Hamilton, W: R.
Bondman free. Oxenham, J: †50 c. Federal.
BONDS.
Harris. Law governing the issuing, transfer and coll. of municipal bonds. $4. W. H. Anderson & Co.
Bonehill, Ralph, *pseud.* Boy land boomer. '02(Ag9) il. 12°. $1. Saalfield.
Bonesteel, Ma. Recruit Tommy Collins. '02 (Mr22) S. 45 c. Benziger.
Bonsall, C: Money: its nature and functions. '02(Ag9) 12°, 50 c.; pap., 25 c. M. S. Schwartz.
Book, J. W. Mollie's mistake. '02(Mr8) 16°, pap., 15 c. Herder.
BOOK ILLUSTRATION.
Brothers Dalziel: record of work, 1840-90. net, $6.50. Dutton.
Book lover. Baldwin, J. net, $1. McClurg.
BOOK OF COMMON PRAYER.
Hall. Companion to the prayer book. net, 35 c. E. & J. B. Young.
See also Protestant Epis. church.
Book of forms to be used in connection with the study of criminal procedure in the Univ. of Mich. '02(My24) O. pap., 60 c. Bliss & A.
Book of golden deeds. Yonge, C. M. $1. Burt.
Book of romantic ballads. '02(Je21) il. 16°, (Caxton ser.) net, $1.25. Scribner.
Book of secrets. Dresser, H. W. net, $1. Putnam.
Book of the rifle. Fremantle, T. F. $5. Longmans.
Book of vegetables. Wythes, G: net, $1. Lane.
BOOK-PLATES.
Stone. Women designers of book-plates. net, $1; net, $2. Beam.
BOOKBINDING.
Cockerell. Bookbinding and care of books. net, $1.20. Appleton.
BOOKKEEPING.
Goodyear. Theory of accounts. $1.50. Goodyear-M.
Ingerson. Normal method in double entry bookkeeping. 50 c. Interstate.
Snyder *and* Thurston. Universal system of prac. bookkeeping. $1.25. Am. Bk.
Booklover's lib.; ed. by H: B: Wheatley. S. Armstrong.
—Wheatley. How to make an index. $1.25; $2.50.
BOOKS AND READING.
Baldwin. Book lover: guide to best reading. net, $1. McClurg.
Early Eng. printed books in the Univ. Lib., Cambridge. v. 2. *$5 net. Macmillan.
Hitchcock. Book-builder's handbook of types, scales, etc. net, 50 c. Grafton Press.
Right reading; choice and use of books. net, 80 c. McClurg.
See also Bookbinding; — Fiction; — Literature; — Printing.
Books on Egypt and Chaldea. D. $1.25. Oxford Univ.
—Budge. Hist. of Egypt. v. 1.
BOOKSELLERS.
Marston. Sketches of some booksellers of the time of Dr. Johnson. net, $2. Scribner.
Wilson. Directory of booksellers, stationers, librarians and publishers in the U. S. and Canada. $10. H. W. Wilson.
BOONE, Dan.
Miner. Daniel Boone cont. toward a bibliog. $1. Dibdin Club.
Booth, H: M. Heavenly vision, and other sermons. Memorial ed. [New issue.] '02 (Mr22) D. net, $1. Beam.
Booth, Wa. S. *See* North Dakota. Township manual.
Boothby, Guy. Cabinet secret. '02(Ag23) D. (Select novels.) †$1; pap., 50 c. Lippincott.

Boothby, Guy. Millionaire's love story. '01·'02(Mr29) D. $1.25. Buckles.

Border warfare in Pennsylvania. Shimmell, L. S. 50 c. R. L. Myers.

BORING.
Isler. Well boring for water, brine and oil. $4. Spon.

Borrow, G: The Zincali: acc. of gypsies of Spain. '01· '02(F22) il. D. $2. Putnam.

Bossard, J: Decorative paintings: designs for col. surface decoration. '01· '02(Ja25) col. pls. f°, $8. Hessling.

BOSTON.
Green. Ten facsimile reproductions rel. to old Boston and neighborhood. net, $10. Littlefield.
Historic Boston: sightseeing towns around the Hub. net, 50 c.; net, 30 c. Pilgrim Press.
Pictorial guide to Boston and the country around. 25 c. G. W. Armstrong.
Winslow. Literary Boston of to-day. **$1.20 net. L. C. Page.

Boswell, J. Journal of a tour to the Hebrides. (H. B. Cotterill.) '02(My24) 12°, (Eng. classics.) net, 60 c. Macmillan.

Bosworth, Newton, *ed.* Hochelaga depicta; early hist. and present state of the city and island of Montreal. '01· '02(Mr8) il. D. (Facsimile repr. of early Canadian books, no. 1.) net, $3; Large-pap. ed., net, $4.50. Congdon.

BOTANY.
Bower *and* Vaughan. Practical botany for beginners. net, 90 c. Macmillan.
Caldwell. Lab'y manual of botany. 60 c.; 50 c. Appleton.
Campbell. University text-book of botany. net, $4. Macmillan.
Cowles. Ecological rel. of vegetation on the sand dunes of Lake Michigan. net, 75 c. Univ. of Chic.
Dickson. Linear groups. net, $4. Stechert.
Frye. Development of the pollen in some asclepiadaceæ. net, 25 c. Univ. of Chic.
Ganong. Lab'y course in plant physiology, as a basis for ecology. net, $1. Holt.
Hooker. Nociones de botánica. 40 c. Appleton.
Leavitt. Outlines of botany. 2 v. $1; $1.80. Am. Bk.
Life. Tuber-like rootlets of cycas revoluta net, 25 c. Univ. of Chic.
Lilley *and* Midgley. Studies in plant form. net, $2. Scribner.
Lyon. Study of the sporangia and gametophytes of selaginella apus and selaginella rupestris. net, 25 c. Univ. of Chic.
Macdougal. Elem. plant physiology $1.20. Longmans.
Meier. Herbarium and plant description. 70 c. Ginn.
Nelson. Analytical key to some of the common flowering plants of the Rocky Mt. region. **45 c. net. Appleton.
Overton. Parthenogenesis in thalictrum purpurascens. net, 25 c. Univ. of Chic.
Smith, R. W. Achromatic spindle in spore mother-cells of osmunda regalis. net, 25 c. Univ. of Chic.
Stevens. Gametrogenesis and fertilization in albugo. net, 25 c. Univ. of Chic.

BOTANY.—*Continued.*
Webb. Morphological study of the flower and embryo of spirala. *25 c. net. Univ. of Chic.
See also Algæ;—Bacteria;—Evolution;—Flowers;—Forests and forestry;—Fruit;—Galls;—Gardening;—Microscope;—Orchids;—Trees;—Vegetables.

Boteler, Mattie M. Side windows. '01· '02(Ap12) D. 75 c. Standard Pub.

Botsford, Amelia H. Child life in all nations. '02(Ag30) il. 12°, $1. Am. Bk. and Bible.

BOTTICELLI, Sandro.
Hubbard. Botticelli. 25 c. Roycrofters.

BOUDE FAMILY.
See **Leach, J. G.**

Bourget, P. Monica, and other stories. '02(Ap12) D. $1.50. Scribner.

Bourne, E: G. Essays in hist. criticism. '01· '02(F15) 8°, (Yale bicentennial pub.) net, $2. Scribner.

Bourne, E: G. *See also* New Eng. Hist. Teachers' Assoc.

Bourne, G. C: Introd. to the study of comparative anatomy of animals. v. 2. '02(Ap12) il. 12°, net, $1.25. Macmillan.

Bourne, H: E. Teaching of history and civics in the elem. and secondary school. '02(My10) O. (Am. teachers' ser.) $1.50. Longmans.

Bouton, Eug. Spelling and word building. '02(Jl5) il. sq. D. 29 c. University.

Boutwell, G: S. Reminiscences of sixty years in public affairs. '02(Jl5) 2 v., 8°, **$5 net. McClure, P.

Bowdoin, W. G. James McNeill Whistler, the man and his work. '01· '02(F8) O. bds., net, $1.50. Beam.

Bowen, B. L. First scientific French reader. '02(Je14) D. (Modern lang. ser.) 90 c. Heath.

Bowen, W: A. Why two Episcopal Methodist churches in the U. S.? '01· '02(Mr15) S. 75 c. Pub. Ho. M. E. Ch., So.

Bower, F. O., *and* Vaughan, D. T. G. Practical botany for beginners. '02(My24) 12°, net, 90 c. Macmillan.

Bowhill, T: Manual of bacteriological technique and special bacteriology. 2d ed. '02(Jl12) 8°, $4.50. Wood.

Bowker, Alfr. King Alfred millenary. '02(Jl12) il. 8°, $3. Macmillan.

Bowker, R: R. *See* Fletcher, W: I:

BOX FAMILY.
See Bronsdon family.

Boyden, H: P. Beginnings of the Cincinnati Southern railway, 1869-1878. '01· '02(F8) 8°, pap., 50 c. Clarke.

Boyland boomer. Bonehill, R. $1. Saalfield.

Boyle, *Sir* Courtenay. *See* Avebury, *Lord.*

Boyle, F: Woodland orchids. '02(Ja18) 4°, net, $7. Macmillan.

Boys' own library. D. 75 c. Street.
—Browne. From switch to lever.—Zip the acrobat.

Boys' vacation ser. S. 75 c. Neely.
—Whittier. In the Michigan lumber camps.

Brace, D. B., *ed.* Laws of radiation and absorption. '01· '02(Ja11.) O. (Scientific memoirs, no. 15.) $1. Am Bk.

Bradbury, Ht. B. The new philosophy of health. [New issue.] '02(Mr22) 16°, 75 c. Alliance.

Braddon, Ma. E. *See* Maxwell, *Mrs.* M. E. B.

Braden, Ja. A. Far past the frontier. '02 (Ag9) il. 12°, $1. Saalfield.
Bradish, Sa. P. Stories of country life. '01-'02(Ja4) S. (Eclectic school readings.) 40 c. Am. Bk.
Bradley, C: *See* Bradley, J. P.
Bradley, Jos. P. Miscellaneous writings; with sketch of his life; ed. and comp. by C: Bradley. '02(Ap5) 8°, $3. Hardham.
Bradner, G: W. New practice in supplementary proceedings. 2d ed. '02(Jl5) O. $4. W. C. Little.
Brady, Cyrus T. Hohenzollern. '02(Ap12) il. D. $1.50. Century Co.
Brady, Cyrus T. Quiberon touch. '01-'02 (F22) 12°, $1.50. Appleton.
Brain, Belle M. Fifty missionary programmes. '02(F1) S. 35 c. Un. Soc. C. E.
BRAIN.
Fuller. Architecture of the brain. net, $3.50. Fuller.
See also Insanity;—Mind and body;—Nervous system;—Phrenology;—Psychology.
Bramble brae. Bridges, R. net, $1.25. Scribner.
BRAMSHOTT, ENG.
See Hampshire.
Brand, N. F. Justices' code for the state of Washington. '02(F15) O. shp., $5. Bancroft-W.
Brandes, G: Main currents in nineteenth century literature. v. 2. '02(My17) 8°, net, $2.75. Macmillan.
Brassey, T: A., *Baron, ed.* Naval annual for 1902. '02(Je21) 8°, net, $7.50. Scribner.
Breachley—black sheep. Becke, G: L: †$1.50. Lippincott.
Bread and wine. King, M. E. $1.25. Houghton, M. & Co.
Breaking and riding. Fillis, J. net, $5. Scribner.
BREATHING.
Semon. Principles of local treatment in diseases of the upper air passages. net, $1. Macmillan.
Breaux, Jos. A. *See* Louisiana. *Sup. ct.* Digest.
Brenton, Hilda. Uncle Jed's country letters. '02(Je7) il. D. 30 c. Dickerman.
Breviarium bothanum sive portiforium secundum usum ecclesiæ cujusdam in Scotia; 1900. '02(F8) 4°, $15. Longmans.
Brewer, D: J. American citizenship. '02 (Ap19) D. net, 75 c. Scribner.
Brewster, Lyman D. *See* Ames, J. B.
Bride of Messina. *See* Schiller, J. C. F. v.
Bride's book. Cook, *Mrs.* E. T. net, $1.50. Dutton.
Bridge, Ja. H., *ed.* *See* Flint, C: R.
Bridge, Norman. Rewards of taste, and other essays. '02(Ap5) D. $1.50. H. S. Stone.
BRIDGE.
Dunn. New ideas on bridge. 50 c. Scribner.
Elwell. Bridge; its principles and rules of play. net, $1.25. Scribner.
Smith, C. Bridge condensed. 50 c. Scribner.
Steele. Simple rules for bridge. 50 c. Eichelberger.
Bridge of the gods. Balch, F. H. †$1.50. McClurg.
Bridgeman, T: Flower gardening. '01-'02 (F8) il. 12°, 50 c. Coates.
Bridgeman, T: Fruit gardening. '01-'02 (F8) il. 12°, 50 c. Coates.
Bridgeman, T: Kitchen gardening. '01. '02 (F8) il. 12°, 50 c. Coates.
Bridges, Rob., ["Droch."] Bramble brae. '02(Mr22) D. net, $1.25. Scribner.
BRIDGES.
Merriman *and* Jacoby. Text-book on roofs and bridges. pt. 3, Bridge design. $2.50. Wiley.
Bridgman, L. J. Gulliver's bird book. '02 (Mr29) il. 4°, $1.50. L. C. Page.
Brigham, Alb. P. *See* Gilbert, G. K.
Bright days in merrie England. Honeyman, A. V. net, $1.50. Honeyman.
Brinckley, W: J. Physiology by the laboratory method. '02(Jl5) 8°, $.25. Ainsworth.
BRINGHURST FAMILY.
Leach. Hist. of the Bringhurst family. $5. Lippincott.
Brink, B: M. Early hist. of Saugerties. '02 (Ag2) il. 12°, *$1.50 net. R. W. Anderson.
Brinkley, Fk. Japan; its history, arts and literature. 4 v. '02(Ap5); v. 5 (Je28) 8°, (Oriental ser.) per v., $50. Millet.
Brinton, Dan. G. Basis of social relations. '02(Mr22) 8°, (Science ser., v. 10.) net, $1.50. Putnam.
Brinton Eliot. Farmer, J. E. $1.50. Macmillan.
Britain and the British seas. Mackinder, H. J. $2. Appleton.
Britain for the British. Blatchford, R. 50 c.; 25 c. Kerr.
British-Am. guide to Carlsbad. Arany, S. A. 50 c. Abbey Press.
British vegetable galls. Connold, E: J. net, $4. Dutton.
Britton; Eng. tr. and notes by F. M. Nichols. '01. '02(Mr1) 12°, (Legal classic ser.) shp., $3. Byrne.
Broader Bible study. Patterson, A. net, 75 c. Jacobs.
BRONSDON FAMILY.
Marsh *and* Parker, *comps.* Bronsdon and Box families. 2 pts. $4. Nichols.
Bronson, Wa. H., *ed.* *See* Ritchie, M. G.
Brontë, Ctte., [*Mrs.* Nicholls; "Currer Bell."] Jane Eyre; to which is added The Moores. '02(Ag2) 12°, **$1.60 net. Dodd.
Brooklyn *Daily Eagle* almanac, 1902. '02 (Ja11) 8°, (Eagle lib.) 50 c.; pap., 25 c. Brooklyn Eagle.
Brooklyn Eagle lib. Q. pap. Brooklyn Eagle.
—Lodge, *and others.* The U. S. and the Philippine Islands. 10 c. (v. 17, 9.)
—New York City. Tenement house law. 10 c. (v. 17, 3.)
Brooks, E: Normal elem. algebra: pt. 1. Rev. ed. '01-'02(Jl12) 12°, 83 c. Sower.
Brooks, E: Plane and solid geometry. Rev. ed. '02(Ag30) 12°, $1.25. Sower.
Brooks, H. J. Elements of mind. '02(Je7) O. $4. Longmans.
Brooks, H: *See* Dame, L. L.
Brooks, H: S. Progression to immortality. '02(Je7) D. net, 50 c. Wessels.
Brooks, Hildegard. Master of Caxton. '02 (Ap12) D. $1.50. Scribner.
Brooks, J: A., *rep.* *See* Michigan. *Sup. ct.* Repts.
Brooks, Phillips. Law of growth, and other sermons. '02(Mr29) 12°, net, $1.20. Dutton.

Brooks, S. J., *comp.* *See* Texas. Conflicting civil cases;—Repts.

BROOKS.
Miller. Brook book. net, $1.35. Doubleday, P.

Broome, I: Last days of the Ruskin Co-operative Association. '02(Jl19) 16°, (Standard socialist ser.) 50 c. Kerr.

Brothers (The). Keary, C: F. $1.50. Longmans.

Brothers Dalziel (The). Record of their work in connection with distinguished artists, 1840-1890. '02(Ap5) il. 4°, vellum, net, $6.50. Dutton.

Brounoff, Platon G. *See* Sharp, B. A.

Browder, Jonathan B. Time elements of the Orestean trilogy. '02(Ag16) O. (Bull. of the Univ. of Wis., no. 62; philology and literature ser., v. 2, no. 1.) pap., 35 c. Univ. of Wis.

Brower, Dan. R., *and* Bannister, H: M. Practical manual of insanity. '02(Mr29) 8°, $2. Saunders.

Brown, Abbie F. In the days of giants: Norse tales. '02My3) il. D. net, $1.15. Houghton, M. & Co.

Brown, Allan L. True marriage guide. '01. '02(Ag2) il. 12°, 55 c.; pap., 35 c. Westminster Pub.

Brown, C: C., *ed.* Directory of Am. cement industries. 2d ed., rev. and enl. '02(Ag2) $5. Municipal Eng.

Brown, C: F., *and* Croft, V. E. Outline study of U. S. hist. '01. '02(Je14) 16°, vellum, 50 c. Courier. Pr.

Brown, C: W. American star speaker and model elocutionist. '02(My17) il. 12°, $1.50. Donohue.

Brown, C: W. Ethan Allen. '02(My17) 12°, $1. Donohue.

Brown, C: W. John Paul Jones of naval fame. '02(Je28) D. (Am. patriot ser.) $1. Donohue.

Brown, C: W., *comp.* Comic recitations and readings. '02(My17) 12°, 50 c.; pap., 25 c. Donohue.

Brown, C: W., *comp.* Patriotic recitations and readings. '02(My17) 12°, 50 c.; pap., 25 c. Donohue.

Brown, Christian H:, *comp.* Optician's manual. v. 1 and 2. '02(Je28) il. 12°, ea., $2. Keystone.

Brown, D: W. Science and art of phrase-making; designed to teach stenographic phrasing by principle. '02(Ap5) 12°, $1.50. Shorthand Bu.

BROWN, Ford M.
Rossetti. Ford Madox Brown. net, 35 c. Beam.

Brown, Fs., Driver, S: R., *and* Briggs, C: A., *eds.* Hebrew and Eng. lexicon of the Old Testament. pt. 10. '02(Mr22) 8°, pap., net, 50 c. Houghton, M. & Co.

Brown, Grace M., ["Ione."] Food studies. '02(Ag2) sq. T. pap., 50 c. Reed.

Brown, Grace M., ["Ione."] Studies in spiritual harmony. '02(Mr22) sq. S. $1. Reed.

Brown, J: Rab and his friends, and other dog stories; ed. by C: W. French. '02 (Je14) il. (Canterbury classics.) 25 c. Rand, McN. & Co.

BROWN, J:
Hugo. John Brown: a petition in behalf of the hero of Harper's Ferry. $5; $15. Alwil Shop.

Brown, P. H. History of Scotland. v. 2 '02(Ap26) 12°, (Cambridge hist. ser.) net, $1.50. Macmillan.

Brown, W: B. Gospel of the kingdom and the gospel of the church. '01 (F8) D. $1. Whittaker.

Brown, W: E. Divine key of the Revelation of Jesus Christ. In 2 v. v. 2. '02(Jl12) il. 12°, $1.50. Armstrong & B.

Brown, W: G. Golf. '02(Jl5) S. **50 c. net. Houghton, M. & Co.

Brown, W: G. The lower South in Am. history. '02(My24) 12°, net, $1.50. Macmillan.

Brown, W: G. Stephen Arnold Douglas. '02(Mr29) S. (Riverside biog. ser., no. 13.) net, 65 c.; School ed., net, 50 c. Houghton, M. & Co.

Brown, W: N., *ed.* Workshop wrinkles for decorators, painters and others. '01- '02 (My10) D. net, $1. Van Nostrand.

Brown, W: P. Ralph Granger's fortunes. '02(Ag9) il. 12°, $1. Saalfield.

Browne, *Mrs.* A. B. B. Help to the spiritual interpretation of the penitential Psalms. '02 (Ap19) D. net, 40 c. Longmans.

Browne, D: McM. How to tell the time of night by the stars. '01- '02(Ap12) 8°, 50 c. Lee & S.

Browne, Fk. J. Graded mental arithmetic. '02(Je7) sq. 16°, net, 30 c. Whitaker & R.

Browne, G: W., ["Victor St. Clair."] From switch to lever. '02(Ag30) D. (Boys' own lib., no. 30.) 75 c. Street.

Browne, G: W. Zip the acrobat. '02(Ag30) D. (Boys' own lib., no. 100.) 75 c. Street.

Browne, Gordon. Proverbial sayings. '01- '02(F15) il. 4°, bds., net, $1. Stokes.

Browne, *Sir* T: Religio medici, Urn burial, Christian morals and other essays; ed. by C. J. Holmes. '02(Jl12) 8°, (Vale Press ser.) **$12 net. Lane.

Browne, Wa. S. Rose of the wilderness. '01- '02(Mr1) il. D. $1.25. W. S. Browne.

Browne, W: Hardcastle. *See* Scott, *Sir* W.

Brownies (The) *See* Ewing, *Mrs.* J. H.

Browning, Rob. Sordello; ed. by H. B. Forman. '02(Jl12) 16°, (Temple classics.) 50 c.; flex. leath., 75 c. Macmillan.

Bruce, W. S. Formation of Christian character. '02(My10) 12°, net, $1.75. Scribner.

Brugnot, Alice G. T. *See* Baillot, E. P.

Brühl, Gustav, *and* Politzer, A. Atlas epitome of otology. '02(Ap26) il. 12°. net, $3. Saunders.

Bruno. Dewey, B. S. 50 c. Little, B. & Co.

Brunton, *Sir* Lauder. On disorders of assimilation, digestion, etc. '01- '02(Ja4) il. 8°, net, $4; *Same,* (Ap12) hf. mor., net, $5. Macmillan.

Biyan, W: J. *The Commoner*, condensed. '02(Ag30) O. $1.50. Abbey Press.

Bryce, Alex. Ideal health and how to attain it. '01- '02(Mr1) 12°, pap., 50 c. Treat.

Bubbles. Newberry, F. E. $1. Burt.

Bubier, E: T. A B C of wireless telegraphy. '02(Je21) S. $1. Bubier.

Bubier, E: T. Experimental electricity. New rev. and enl. ed. '02(Je14) il. 16°, $1. Bubier.

Bubier, E: T. How to build dynamo-electric machinery. 2d ed. '02(Je14) il. 8°, $2.50. Bubier.

Buchan, Alex. *See* Bartholomew's physical atlas.

Buck, A. H. A reference handbook of the medical sciences. New ed., rev. and rewritten. v. 4. '02(Ap12) il. 8°, subs., $7; leath., $8; mor., $9. Wood.

Budd, J. L. *and* Hanson, N. E. Am. horticultural manual. '02(My17) 12°, $1.50. Wiley.

Budd, Jos. H. Civil remedies under the code system. '02(Ap12) O. shp., $6. Palm.

BUDDHA AND BUDDHISM.
Dhammapada. Hymns of the faith. $1. Open Court.

Budge, Ernest A. W. Hist. of Egypt. v. 1. '02(Ag23) D. (Books on Egypt and Chaldea.) $1.25. Oxford Univ.

Buell Hampton. Emerson, W. G: $1.50. Forbes.

BUFFALO.
Men of Buffalo. $15. Marquis.

BUILDING.
See Architecture;—Engineering.

BULBS.
Arnott. Book of bulbs. net, $1. Lane.

Bulkley, L. D. *See* Duhring, L: A.

Bullen, Fk. T. Deep-sea plunderings. '02 (My19) il. D. $1.50. Appleton.

Bülow-Wendhausen, *Baroness v.* Life of the Baroness von Marenholtz Bülow. '01. '02 (Ja4) 2 v., O. net, $3.50. W: B. Harison.

BULOW, *Baroness* von Marenholtz.
Bulow-Wendhausen. Life of Baroness von Marenholtz Bülow. 2 v., net, $3.50. W: B. Harison.

Bunge, G. Text-book of physiolog. and patholog. chemistry. 2d Eng. ed.; ed. by E. H. Starling. '02(Jl12) 8°, *$3 net. Blakiston.

BUNKER HILL.
Heath. Memoirs; [also] accounts of the Battle of Bunker Hill, by Gens. Dearborn, Lee and Wilkinson. net, $5. Abbatt.

Bunt and Bill. Mulholland, C. 45 c. Benziger.

Bunyan, J: The holy war. '01(Mr1) 16°, 50 c.; leath., 75 c. Macmillan.

Bunyan, J: Pilgrim's progress. '01. '02 (Ja11) 2 v., il. 16°, (Caxton ser.) flex. lambskin, net, $2.40. Scribner.

Bunzey, Rufus S. Hist. of companies I and E, Sixth regt., Ill. vol. infantry from Whiteside co. '02(Jl12) il. 12°, $2. R. S. Bunzey.

Burdens of local taxation. Purdy, L. 25 c. Public Policy.

Burdick, Alfr. S. Standard medical manual. '01. '02(Mr8) 8°, $4. Engelhard.

Burdick, Fs. M. Essentials of business law. '02(Ag16) D. (Twentieth century textbooks.) $1.25. Appleton.

Burgert, Celia M. *See* Skinner, W. H.

Burgess, J: W. Reconstruction and the constitution, 1866-1876. '02(Mr22) D. (Am. hist. ser.) net, $1. Scribner.

Burghard, F. F. *See* Cheyne, W: W.

Buried temple. Maeterlinck, M. net, $1.40. Dodd.

Burke, Bridget E. McBride literature and art books. bks. 1-3. '01. '02(Mr22) il. 12°, bk. 1, 25 c.; bk. 2, 30 c.; bk. 3, 35 c. McBride.

Burke, Edm. Works. Beaconsfield ed. In 12 v., v. 1-4. '01. '02(F15) 8°, subs., per v., net, $3.50. Little, B. & Co.

Burke, Edm. Thoughts on the cause of the present discontents; ed. by F. G. Selby. '02(Je28) 12°, net, 60 c. Macmillan.

Burks, Martin P. *See* Virginia. *Sup. ct. of appeals.* Repts.

BURMA.
Smith. Ten years in Burma. net, $1. Eaton & M.; Jennings.

Burne, C. With the Naval Brigade in Natal, 1899-1900. '02(Ag2) il. O. $2.50. Longmans.

Burnett, *Mrs.* Fes. H. Methods of Lady Walderhurst. '02(F22) il. D. $1.25. Stokes.

Burnett, J. C. New cure for consumption by its own virus. 4th ed. 1900. '02(Ap5) 12°, $1. Boericke & T.

Burnett, Irwin. The heretic. '02(Ag30) D. $1.50. Abbey Press.

Burnham, Clara L. A great love. '02(Ap5) 16°, (Riverside pap. ser., no. 94.) pap., 50 c. Houghton, M. & Co.

Burns, Harrison. *See* Indiana. Statutes.

Burns, R. Complete poems and songs. (T: Carlyle.) '02(Mr8) 16°, (Caxton ser.) net, $1.20. Scribner.

Burns, R. Complete poetical works. Pocket ed. '02(My17) 12°, (New century lib.) $1.25; limp. leath., $1.75. Nelson.

Burns, R. Poems, epistles, songs, epigrams, and epitaphs; ed. by J. A. Manson. '02 (F1) 12°, net, $1; flex. leath., net, $1.50. Macmillan.

BURR, A.
Jenkinson. Aaron Burr, his rel. with Thos. Jefferson and Alex. Hamilton. $1.25. I: Jenkinson.
Todd. True Aaron Burr. net, 50 c. Barnes.

Burr, Enoch F. Aleph the Chaldean. [New issue.] '02(Ap12) 12°, $1.25. Whittaker.

BURR, Esther.
Rankin. Esther Burr's journal. 75 c. Howard Univ.

Burrow, C: K. Patricia of the hills. '02 (Mr8) D. net, $1.20. Putnam.

Burt, Ma. E., *and* Howells, Mildred. Literary primer. '01. '02(Mr15) 16°, bds., net, 30 c. Scribner.

Burton, E. D., *and* Mathews, S. Constructive studies in the life of Christ. '02(F15) 8°, $1. Univ. of Chic.

Burton, Elias. *See* Holmes, B.

Burton, R: Forces in fiction, and other essays. '02(Ap26) D. net, $1. Bowen-M.

Burton, Thdr. E. Financial crises and period of industrial and commercial depression. '02(Mr1) D. net, $1.40. Appleton.

Burton Holmes lectures. *See* Holmes, B.

Burt's Cornell ser. 12°, 75 c. Burt.
—Lowell. Biglow papers.
—Wilson. Inez.

Burt's fairy lib. il. 12°, $1. Burt.
—Valentine, *comp. and ed.* Old, old fairy tales.

Burt's fairy lib.—Continued.
—Yeats, *comp. and ed.* Irish fairy and folk tales.
Burt's fireside ser. il. 12°, $1. Burt.
—Armstrong. Very odd girl.
—Conklin. Bek's first corner.—Growing up. —Miss Prudence.—Tessa Wadsworth's discipline.
—Le Row. Duxbury doings.
—Newberry. Bubbles.—Joyce's investments. —Sara.
—Robbins. Miss Ashton's new pupil.
—Rouse. Annice Wynkoop, artist.—Deane girls.
—Smith. Daddy's girl.—Very naughty girl.
Burt's home lib. il. 12°, $1. Burt.
—Addison. Essays.
—Arnold. Essays in criticism.
—Barrie. Little minister.
—Chesterfield. Letters, sentences, and maxims.
—Elizabeth and her German garden.
—Emerson. Nature.—Representative men.
—Harris. Rutledge.
—Hawthorne. Blithedale romance.—Marble faun.
—Headley. Napoleon and his marshals.—Washington and his generals.
—Holley. Samantha at Saratoga.
—Holmes, M. J. Cousin Maude and Rosamond.
—Holmes, O. Professor at the breakfast table.
—Ingraham. Throne of David.
—Johnson. Rasselas.
—Kingsley. Alton Locke.—Hereward the Wake.
—Le Sage. Gil Blas.
—Longfellow. Hyperion.—Outre mer.
—Lubbock. Pleasures of life.
—Macaulay. Literary essays.
—Macdonald. David Elginbrod.
—Maggie Miller.
—Malory. King Arthur.
—More. Utopia.
—Parkman. Consniracy of Pontiac.
—Pater. Marius the epicurean.
—Plato. Republic.
—Poe. Murders in the Rue Morgue.
—Rénan. Life of Jesus.
—Saint-Pierre. Paul and Virginia.
—Southworth. Hidden hand.—Ishmael.—Self-raised.
—Stowe. Minister's wooing.
—Taylor. Views afoot.
—Thoreau. Walden.
—Webster. Speeches.
—Yonge. Book of golden deeds.
Burt's little women ser. il. 12°, 75 c. Burt.
—Prentiss. Little Susy stories.
Burt's Manhattan lib. of new copyright fiction. 12°, pap., 50 c. Burt.
—Cobban. Green turbans.
—Hatton. Vision of beauty.
—Sergeant. Master of Beechwood.
Burt's St. Nicholas ser. il. 12°, 75 c. Burt.
—Kaler. Wan Lun and Dandy.
—Molesworth. Grandmother dear.
—Newberry. Comrades.
—Prentiss. Six little princesses.
—Weber. Clock on the stairs.
Bury, J: B. Hist. of Greece to the death of Alex. the Great. '02(My17) 2 v., 8°, net, $8. Macmillan.

BUSINESS.
Avebury, *and others.* King's weigh-house lectures to business men. 75 c. Macmillan.
Burdick. Essentials of business law. $1.25. Appleton.
Carnegie. Empire of business. subs., $3. Doubleday, P.
McMaster. Commercial digest and business forms. $6. Commercial Bk.
Parsons. Hand-bk. of forms: business and social rules. $3; $4. Southern Pub.
Perry. Legal adviser and business guide. $1.50. Pontiac.
Pitman, B. *and* Howard. Business letters. no. 1, 25 c. Phonograph.
Pitman, I: Business corr. in shorthand. no. 2, 30 c. Pitman.
See also Advertising;—Commerce;—Commercial law;—Finance;—Political economy;—Stock-exchange.

BUSINESS EDUCATION.
Stevens. Business education. 15 c. Bardeen.
See also Bookkeeping.

"But Thy love and Thy grace." Finn, F. J. $1. Benziger.
Butler, C: H: Treaty-making power of the U. S. In 2 v. '02(Ap5) O. hf. shp., (complete work,) net, $12. Banks.
BUTLER FAMILY.
Rook. The Butler family. $3. Lakeside Press.
By the gray sea. '02(Mr8) 8°, net, 60 c. Herder.
By the way ballads. Sapte, W., *jr.* *$1.50 net. Dutton.
Bylow Hill. Cable, G: W. $1.25. Scribner.
Byrd, W: Writings of "Col. William Byrd of Westover in Virginia, Esq."; ed. by J. S. Bassett. '02(Mr8) il. f°, net, $10. Doubleday, P.
Byron, G: G. N., *Lord.* Works. Ed. de luxe. v. 13-16. '02(Mr15) 8°. (App. to pubs. for price.) Niccolls.
Byron, G: G. N., *Lord.* Works. New rev., enl. ed. In 12 v. v. 11. '02(Ap12) 12°, $2. Scribner.
Bywater, B. Two thousand years in eternity. '01. '02(Je21) 8°, net, $2.15. Hudson-K.
C., *pseud.* *See* Cox, *Mrs.* J. F.
Caballero, Fernán. La familia de Alvareda. (P. B. Burnet.) '01. '02(Mr15) S. 75 c. Holt.
Cabinet secret. Boothby, G. †$1; 50 c. Lippincott.
Cable, G: W. Bylow Hill. '02(Je7) D. $1.25. Scribner.
Cabot, R: C. Guide to the clinical examination of the blood. 4th rev. ed. '01. '02 (F22) il. 8°, net, $3.25. Wood.
Cadigan, E. S. My ocean trip. '02(Je28) il. 12°, $1. Brentano's.
Cadiot, P. J. Clinical veterinary medicine and surgery. '01. '02(F22) il. 8°, $5.25. W: R. Jenkins.
Cadness, H: Decorative brush-work and elem. design. '02(Ag23) il. 12°, *$1.40 net. Scribner.
Cadwallader, Starr. Story of home gardens. '02(Mr22) O. pap., 25 c. Home Gardening.
Cady, Ma. R., *and* Dewey, Julia M. Art reader no. 1. '02(Jl5) il. 16°, 35 c. Richardson, S.

CAEDMON, *St.*
Gaskin. Caedmon, the first Eng. poet. 40 c. E. & J. B. Young.

Caesar. Commentaries on the Gallic war; vocab. by A. Harkness, assisted by C: H. Forbes. '02(F15) il. D. hf. leath., $1.25. Am. Bk.

CAESARS (The).
Van Santvoord. House of Cæsar and the imperial disease. net, $5.25. Pafraets.

Caffin, C: H. American masters of painting. '02(Ap5) D. net, $1.25. Doubleday, P.

Cain's sin. Belles, W: H: $1. W: H: Belles.

CAIRO.
Poole. Story of Cairo. $2; $2.50. Macmillan.

CALCULUS.
Bass. Elements of differential calculus. net, $4. Wiley.
Durège. Elements of the theory of functions of a complex variable. net, $2. Macmillan
Smith. Elem. calculus. $1.25. Am. Bk.

Caldwell, Otis W: Laboratory manual of botany. '02(Je28) 12°, (Twentieth century text-books.) 60 c.; limp cl., 50 c. Appleton.

CALENDARS AND YEAR-BOOKS.
Daily praise. 15 c.; 20 c.; 25 c. Revell.
Epworth League yearbook, 1902. net, 10 c. Eaton & M.
See also Almanacs and annuals;—Devotional exercises and meditations.

Calhoun, W: P. The Caucasian and the negro in the U. S. '02(Je28) D. pap., 75 c. R. L. Bryan.

California. Code time table; by J. H. Kann. '02(Ap19) D. $1.50; interleaved, $2. Dempster.

California. Constitution; annot. by E: F. Treadwell. '02(F1) S. shp., $4. Bancroft-W.

California. *Superior ct.* Repts. (E. Tauszky.) '02(Ap12) 2 v., O. shp., ea., $5. Dempster.

California. *Supreme ct.* Repts. v. 133, 134. '02(Jl5); v. 135 (Jl19) O. shp., ea., $3. Bancroft-W.

CALIFORNIA.
De Witt. Guide to central Cal. 50 c. F: M. De Witt.
Hershey. Quaternary of So. Cal. 20 c. Univ. of Cal.
Hufford. El camino real: orig. highway connecting the 21 missions. 35 c.; 75 c.; $1; $1.25. D: A. Hufford.
Parsons. Wild flowers of Cal. $2. Payot.
Stoddard. In the footprints of the padres. net, $1.50. A. M. Robertson.
See also Fresno Co.

California girl. Eldridge, E: $1.50. Abbey Press.

CALISTHENICS.
See Gymnastics.

Call to arms. Karr, H: S. $2. Longmans.

Callahan, C. E. Fogg's ferry. '02(Mr15) il. D. 75 c.; pap., 25 c. Laird

Calmerton, Gail, *and* Wheeler, W: H: First reader. '02(Mr22) il. sq. 12°, (Graded readers.) 30 c. W: H: Wheeler.

CALVÉ, Emma.
Wisner. Emma Calvé. $1.50. Russell.

Calvin, Emily R. A Jewish carol and The insuperable barrier. '02(Je7) D. bds., 75 c. Westminster Pub.

Cambridge encyclopædia of esoteric subjects. Demorest, A. F. v. 3, net, $3. Cambridge.

Cambridge historical ser.; ed. by G: W. Prothero. 12°, net. Macmillan.
—Brown. Hist. of Scotland. v. 2. $1.50.

Cambridge natural history. *See* Harmer, S. F:, *ed.*

Cambridge Univ. Press ser. 12°. Macmillan.
—Æschylus. The choephori. $3.25.
—Aristophanes. The knights. net, $2.50.
—Bateson. Mendel's principles of heredity. *$1.30 net.
—Dawes. Bilingual teaching in Belgian schools. *50 c. net.
—De Montmorency. State intervention in Eng. education. $1.50.
—Early Eng. printed books in the Univ. Lib. v. 2. *$5 net.
—Forsyth. Differential equations. v. 4. $3.75.
—Glover. Life and letters in the 4th century. net, $3.25.
—Kenny. Outlines of criminal law. *$2.50 net.
—Laurie. Training of teachers. $1.50.
—Maitland, *and others.* Teaching of history. 75 c.
—Mayor. Chapters on Eng. metre. net, $2.25.
—Oesterley. Studies in the Gr. and Latin versions of the Book of Amos. *$1.30 net.
—Rouse. Greek votive offerings. *$4.50 net.
—Stokes. Mathematical and physical papers. v. 3. $3.75.
—Stokes *and* Strachan. Thesaurus palæohibernicus. v. 1. net, $8.
—Strutt. Scientific papers. v. 3. $5.
—Tennant. Origin and propagation of sin. *$1.10 net.

Cameron, *Mrs.* Emily S. L. A woman's no. '02(Ag9) D. $1.25. Buckles.

Cameron, J. H. Elements of French composition. '01. '02(Ja4) D. 75 c. Holt.

Cameron, V. L. Three sailor boys. '02(My17) 12°, 60 c. Nelson.

Camino (El) real. Hufford, D: A. 35 c.; 75 c.; $1; $1.25. D: A. Hufford.

Camm, Bede. A Benedictine martyr in England: life and times of Dom John Roberts. '02(Mr8) 8°, net, $1.25. Herder.

Campbell, Colin P. *See* Michigan. *Sup. ct.* Index digest.

Campbell, Douglas H. University text-book of botany. '02(My3) 8°, net, $4. Macmillan.

Campbell, Hardy W. Soil culture manual, 1902. '02(My17) il. D. pap., 40 c. H. W. Campbell.

Campbell, Hollis A., Sharpe, W: C., *and* Bassett, Fk. J. Seymour, past and present. '02(Je14) il. 8°, $3. W: C. Sharpe.

Campbell, J. G. D. Siam in the twentieth century. '02(Je7) il. O. net, $5. Longmans.

Campbell, T: Selections; ed. by W. T. Webb. '02(Ag16) 12°, *50 c. net. Macmillan.

Campbell, W: C. A Colorado colonel, and other sketches. '01. '02(F8) il. D. $1.50. Crane.

CANADA.
Henry. Travels in Canada, 1760-1776. $4. Little, B. & Co.
Jesuit relations. v. 72, 73. ea., $3.50. Burrows.

CANADA.—*Continued.*
Morang's annual register of Canadian affairs, 1901. $3; $4. Morang.
See also Indians;—Montreal;—New Brunswick.
Canadian books. *See* Bosworth, N.
CANALS.
Johnson. Isthmian canal. 25 c. Am. Acad. Pol. Sci.
Pasco. Isthmian canal question. 25 c. Am. Acad. Pol. Sci.
See also Nicaragua Canal.
CANDY.
See Confectionery.
Cane basket work. *See* Firth, A.
Canfield, Ja. H. The college student and his problems. '02(F1) 12°, (Personal problem ser.) net, $1. Macmillan.
CANOEING.
Thwaites. Down historic waterways. net, $1.20. McClurg.
Canterbury classics. il. 16°, 25 c. Rand, McN. & Co.
—Brown. Rab and his friends.
—Poe. Gold bug.
Cap and gown. Paget, R. L. †$1.25. L. C. Page.
Cape Cod ballads. Lincoln, J. C. net, $1.25. Brandt.
Capes, W. W. Scenes of rural life in Hampshire among the manors of Bramshott. '02(Ja18) 8°, net, $2.75. Macmillan
CAPITAL AND LABOR.
Kropotkin. Fields, factories and workshops. net, 90 c. Putnam.
Labor and capital. $1.50. Putnam.
Lafarque. Religion of capital. 10 c. Socialistic Co-op.
Marx. Wage-labor and capital. 50 c. N. Y. Labor News.
See also Labor and laboring classes;—Trusts.
Captain Fanny. Russell, W: C. $1.25; 50 c. New Amsterdam.
Captain Jinks, hero. Crosby, E. $1.50. Funk.
Captain Jinks of the Horse marines. Fitch, W: C. $1.25. Doubleday, P.
Captain of the Grayhorse troop. Garland, H. $1.50. Harper.
Card sewing. Maxwell, L. H. 50 c. M. Bradley
CARDS.
Hart. Card language, 20 c. R. M. Hart.
Hart. Card language. 20 c. McEnally.
Roterberg. Card tricks. 25 c. Drake.
See also Bridge;—Fortune-telling;—Whist.
Careless Jane. Pyle, K. net, 75 c.. Dutton.
Carey, W: Adventures in Tibet; incl. diary of Miss A. R. Taylor's journey from Ta-Chien Su through the forbidden land. '02 (Ja25) il. O. net, $1.50. Un. Soc. C. E.
Carey, Wymond. Monsieur Martin. '02 (Mr22) D. net, $1.20. Putnam.
Carhart, H: S., *and* Chute, H. N. Physics for high school students. '02(Ap26) il. 12°, $1.25. Allyn & B.
Carleton, R. W. Will-o'-the-wisp. '01- '02 (Ag23) il. 16°, $1.25. Scroll.
CARLSBAD.
Arany. British-Am. guide to Carlsbad. 50 c. Abbey Press.
Carlyle, T: Past and present; ed. by O. Smeaton. '02(My24) 16°, (Temple classics.) 50 c.; flex. leath., 75 c. Macmillan.

Carman, Bliss. Ode on the coronation of King Edward. '02(Je14) 4°, net, $1. L. C. Page.
Carmichael, M. In Tuscany. New ed. '02. (Ap5) 12°, net, $2. Dutton.
Carmichael, M. Life of John William Walshe, T.S.A. [novel.] '02(Je14) 8°, net, $2. Dutton.
Carnegie, And. Empire of business. '02 (Ap19) O. subs., $3. Doubleday, P.
CAROLINE, *Queen of England.*
Wilkins. Caroline the illustrious Queen-Consort of George II. 2 v. $12. Longmans.
Carpenter, E:, *ed.* Ioläus: anthology of friendship. '02(Je14) sq. D. silk, net, $1.75. Goodspeed.
Carpenter, F. G. Europe. '02(Ap12) il. D. (Geographical readers.) 70 c. Am. Bk.
Carpenter, G. R. *See* Woodley, O. I.
Carpenter, Stephen H. *See* Chaucer, G.
Carpenter prophet. Pearson, C: W. $1.50. H. S. Stone.
Carradine, Beverly. Gideon. '02(My24) 16°, (Bible character ser.) 35 c. Pepper.
Carroll, C: Unpublished letters of Charles Carroll of Carrollton, and of his father, Charles Carroll of Doughoregan; comp. and ed. by T: M. Field. '02(Jl12) O. (United States Cath. Hist. Soc., monograph ser. no. 1.) pap. (not for sale.) U. S. Cath.
Carroll, Stella W. Around the world; third book, home geography. '02(Mr22) il. 12°, (Geographical ser.) 60 c. Morse.
CARS.
Thompson. The motor car. $1. Warne.
CARSON, Kit.
Abbott. Christopher Carson, known as Kit. net, 87 c. Dodd.
Carson, W: H: The fool. '02(Je7) il. D. $1.50. G: W. Dillingham.
Carson, W: H: Hester Blair. '02(Mr1) il. D. $1.50. C. M. Clark.
Carter, Ernest. *See* Atkinson, R. W.
Carter, Eva N. Gleanings from nature. '02 (Ap26) il. D. $1. Abbey Press.
Carter, P: Peter Carter, 1825-1900. '01- '02 (F8) 8°, n. p. Privately pr.
Carter, W: H. Horses, saddles and bridles. 2d ed. '02(Ag23) il. 12°, $2.75. Lord Balto.
CARVING.
See Ivory.
Cary, G: H. How to make and use the telephone. New rev. 2d ed. '02(Je14) il. 16°, $1. Bubier.
CASAS, Bartolomé de las.
Dutto. Life of Bartolomé de las Casas. net, $1.50. Herder.
Case, E. C. Palæontological notes. '02(Jl5) 8°, (Cont. from Walker Museum, v. 1, no. 3.) pap., *25 c. net. Univ. of Chic.
Case, Nelson. European constitutional history. '02(Ag2) O. $1.50. Jennings.
Casgrain, W: T. *See* Noble, A.
Caskoden, Edwin, *pseud.* *See* Major, C:
Cassock of the pines. Daley, J. G. $1. W: H. Young.
Cast iron. Keep, W: J. $2.50. Wiley.
Castle Craneycrow. McCutcheon, G: B. $1.50. H. S. Stone.
Castlemon, Harry, [*pseud.* for C: Austin Fosdick.] Floating treasure. '01- '02(Ja25) il. D. $1. Coates.

Castlemon, Harry. Struggle for a fortune. '02(Ag9) il. 12°, $1. Saalfield.
Castles in Spain. Stoner, W. S. $1. Abbey Press.
Castleton's "prep." Murray, C. $1.25. Union Press.

CAT.
Neel. Cats, how to care for them. 50 c. Boericke & T.
Hill. Diseases of the cat. $1.25. W: R. Jenkins.

CATALOGUING.
Hasse, *comp.* U. S. Government pubs.; handbk. for cataloguer. pt. 1. $1. Lib. Bu.

CATECHISMS.
Deharbe. Catechism of Chr. doctrine. 25 c.—Abr. catechism. 15 c. Pustet.
Färber. Commentar zum (Catholic) katechismus. net, $1.50. Herder.
Macdonald, *ed.* Rev. catechism (Westminster Assembly's "shorter catechism.") $1.25. Macmillan.
Mangasarian. New catechism. 75 c. Open Court.
Nash, *ed.* Explanation and application of Bible history. [Questions and answers.] net, $1.50. Benziger.
Scadding. Direct answers to plain questions for Am. churchmen: expansion of the church catechism. net, 50 c. Whittaker
Staebler. Manual on the Book of books for juniors. 20 c. Mattill & L.

Cathcart, Ja. L. Tripoli; first war with the U. S.; letter book by J. L. Cathcart, first consul to Tripoli. '01- '02(Mr29) 12°, $4. J. B. C. Newkirk.

CATHEDRALS.
Addis. Cathedrals and abbeys of Presb. Scotland. net, $2.50. Presb. Bd.
See also Amiens;—Church architecture;—Westminster Abbey.

Catherine. *See* Thackeray, W: M.

Catherwood, *Mrs.* Ma. H. Craque o' Doom. '02(Je28) 12°, (People's lib., no. 30.) pap., 50 c. Am. News.
Catherwood, *Mrs.* Ma. H. Craque o' Doom. [New issue.] '02(Jl5) il. D. $1.50. Street.
Catherwood, *Mrs.* Ma. H. Story of Tonty. 6th ed. enl. '01- '02(F1) il. D. $1.25. McClurg.
Catholic (The). '02(My10) 12°, $1.50. Lane.
Catholic church from within. '01- '02(Ja4) O. $2.50. Longmans.
Catholic Church. Instructions and prayers for Catholic youth. '01- '02(Ja18) il. Tt. 60 c. Benziger.
Catholic Church. Litanei zum heiligsten Herzen Jesu. '02(Je28) 32°, pap., net, 3 c. Herder.
Catholic Church. Priests' new ritual. [In Latin and Eng.;] by J: Murphy. '02(Ap19) 32°, leath., net, 75 c. Murphy.

CATHOLIC CHURCH.
Best. Victories of Rome and temporal monarchy of the church. net, 45 c. Benziger.
Catholic directory, almanac and clergy list quarterly. $1.25; $1.75. Wiltzius.
De Costa. Whither goest thou? *50 c. net; 25 c. net. Chr. Press.

CATHOLIC CHURCH.—*Continued.*
Galton. Our attitude toward Eng. Roman Catholics. net, $1. Dutton.
Lasance, *comp.* Short visits to the blessed sacrament. 25 c. Benziger.
Novene zu ehren des Heiligen Geistes. net, 3 c. Herder.
Poland. Find the church. net, 5 c. Herder.
Rainy. Ancient Catholic church, A.D. 98-451. net, $2.50. Scribner.
Raycroft. Sermons on the stations of the cross, the Our Father, Hail Mary, etc. net, $1.50. Pustet.
Rosen. The Catholic church and secret societies. net, $1. Caspar.
Tagzeiten zum heiligsten Herzen Jesu. 5 c. Herder.
Tesniere. Adoration of the blessed sacrament. net, $1.25. Benziger.
Vaughan. Holy sacrifice of the mass. 15 c. Herder.
See also Christianity;—Church history;—Church music;—Confession;—Convents;— Indulgences;—Jesus (society of);—Mary, *Virgin*;—Monasticism;—Popes;—Saints.

Catholic directory, almanac and clergy list—quarterly. '02(Ap26) D. pap., $1.25; leatherette, $1.75. Wiltzius.
Catholic principles as il. in the doctrine, hist. and organization of the Am. Cath. church in the U. S. Westcott, F. N. *$1.25 net. Young Churchman.
Catholic yearbook of New England, 1902; ed. and comp. by J. F. Marrin. '02(Ag23) O. pap., 25 c. J. K. Waters.
Cathrein, Victor. Socialism exposed and refuted; fr. the Germ. by J. Conway. 2d ed. '02(Jl12) 12°, *$1.25 net. Benziger.
Cat's paw. Croker, *Mrs.* B. M. $1; 50 c. Lippincott.

CATTLE.
McCallum & Hofer Cattle Co. Stockmen's calculator; cost of any amount from 5 to 32,000 lbs. $1.50. McCallum.
See also Veterinary medicine and surgery.

Caucasian and the negro in the U. S. Calhoun, W: P. 75 c. R. L. Bryan.

CAVALRY.
See Horse.

Caxton ser. 16°, net. Scribner.
—Bacon. Works. $1.25.
—Book of romantic ballads. $1.25.
—Bunyan. Pilgrim's progress. 2 v. $1.20.
—Cervantes Saavedra. Don Quixote. $1.25.
—Hood. Serious poems. $1.25.
—Irving. Sketch book. $1.25.
—La Motte Fouque. Undine [also] Aslauga's knight. $1.20.
—Milton. Complete poems. $1.20.
—Shakespeare. Plays and poems. 3 v. per set, $4.20.
—Shelley. Poetical works. $1.25.
—Tennyson. In memoriam. $1.20.
Celestial message. Gaffield, E. C. n. p. Lee & S.
Cellular toxins. Vaughan, V. C. *$3 net. Lea.

CEMENT.
Brown, *ed.* Directory of Am. cement industries. $5. Municipal Eng.
Lathbury *and* Spackman. Am. engineering practice in construction of rotary Portland cement plants. $2. G. M. S. Armstrong.

CENTRAL AMERICA.
Herbertson, *comp.* Desc. geographies; Central and South Am., with the West Indies. net, 70 c. Macmillan.
See also Nicaragua.
Century dictionary and cyclopedia. New ed. '01. '02(Ap5) 10 v., 4°, subs., $80 to $150. Century Co.
Century of Baptist achievements. Newman, R. H: net, $1.50. Am. Bapt.
CERAMICS.
Barber. Anglo-American pottery. net, $2. [Caspar] E. A. Barber.
Barber. Anglo-Am. pottery. $2. Patterson & W.
Huddilston. Lessons from Greek pottery. net, $1.25. Macmillan.
Monkhouse. Hist. and desc. of Chinese porcelain. net. $10. Wessels
Seger. Collected writings; fr. records of the Royal porcelain factory at Berlin. v. 1. per set, $15. Chemical.
Cervantes Saavedra, M. de. Don Quixote. New ed. '01. '02(F22) 4 v., 12°, per set, $3; limp leath., $5. Dodd.
Cervantes Saavedra, M. de. Don Quixote de la Mancha; ed. by Ma. E. Burt and L. L. Cable. '02(Je7) il. D. (Ser. of school reading.) net, 60 c. Scribner.
Cervantes Saavedra, M. de. Life and achievements of Don Quixote de la Mancha. '02 (Ap12) 16°, (Caxton ser.) flex. lambskin, net, $1.25. Scribner.
Chadwick, H:, *ed.* *See* Spalding's official baseball guide.
Chalmers, Ja. James Chalmers; autobiog. and letters. '02(Je28) 8°, net, $1.50. Revell.
Chalmers, Rob. W: King in yellow. New issue. '02(Je21) il. D. $1.50. Harper.
Chamberlain, Basil H. Things Japanese. Rev., enl. 4th ed. '02(Ag23) 8°, *$4 net. Scribner.
Chamberlain, Leander T. Evolutionary philosophy. '02(My10) D. pap., 50 c. Baker & T.
Chamberlin, T: C. Attempt to frame a working hypothesis of the cause of glacial periods on an atmosphere basis. '01. '02 (Ja11) 8°, pap., net, 25 c. Univ. of Chic.
Chamberlin, T: C. Proposed genetic classification of pleistocence glacial formations. '01. '02(Ja11) 8°, net, 10 c. Univ. of Chic
Chambers of the soul. Woelfkin, C. 35 c. Un. Soc. C. E.
Chambers's concise gazetteer. New ed. '02 (Ag2) 8°, hf. leath., $2. Lippincott.
Chambers's cyclopædia of Eng. literature; ed. by D: Patrick. New ed. 3 v. v. 1. '01. '02(Mr1) il. 8°, per v., net, $5. Lippincott.
Chambers's twentieth century dict. of Eng. language; ed. by T: Davidson. '01. '02 (Mr1) 8°, $1.50; hf. leath., $2. Lippincott.
Champion (The). Murfree, M. N. **$1.20 net. Houghton, M. & Co.
CHAMPLAIN, S: de.
Sedgwick. Samuel de Champlain. net. 65 c.: net, 50 c. Houghton, M & Co
Champney, *Mrs.* Eliz. W. Witch Winnie ser. 9 v. New ed. '01. '02(F22) 12°. per set. $11.25. Dodd.
Chancellor, W: E. Children's arithmetic by grades. Second book. '02(Mr22) D. (Globe ser.) 20 c.; Third book (Mr22) 24 c.; Fourth book (Mr22) 24 c. Globe Sch. Bk.
Chancellor, W: E. Children's arithmetic by series. Primary. '02(Mr22) il. D. (Globe ser., in three books.) 28 c. Globe Sch. Bk.
Chancellor, W: E. Elementary school mathematics by grades; fifth bk., (grade 6,) standard measurements; sixth bk., (grade 7,) commercial affairs. '02(Jl5); seventh bk., (grade 8.) arithmetic, geometry and algebra. (Ag30) il. D. (Globe ser.) ea., 28 c. Globe Sch. Bk.
Chandler, Bessie. Verses. '01. '02(Ap26) 16°, $1.25. Blue Sky Press.
Chanson de Geste. *See* Crabb, W. D.
Chantepie de la Saussaye, P. D. Religion of the Teutons; fr. the Dutch by B. J. Vos. '02(Jl19) 12°, (Handbooks on the history of religions, v. 3.) $2.50. Ginn.
Chanticleer. Hall, V. †$1.50. Lothrop.
Chaplain's experience ashore and afloat. Jones, H. W. $1.25. Sherwood.
Chapman, F: The foraminifera: introd. to study of the protozoa. '02(Ap26) il. O. $3.50. Longmans.
Chapman, G: T. Manual of the pathological treatment of lameness in the horse. '01. '02(F22) 8°, $2. W: R. Jenkins.
CHARACTER.
Bruce. Formation of Christian character. net, $1.75. Scribner.
Macdonald. Guarding the thoughts. 10 c. J. H. West.
Schofield. Springs of character. net, $1.30. Funk.
Washington. Character building. **$1.50 net. Doubleday, P.
Welch. Character photography. $1. Jennings.
See also Christian life;—Conduct of life;—Ethics;—Phrenology;—Physiognomy.
CHARITIES.
Worcester. Works of charity. 25 c. Mass. New-Ch. Un.
Charles, Fes. In the country God forgot. '02 (My3) D. $1.50. Little, B. & Co.
CHARLESTOWN, Mass.
Sawyer. Old Charlestown. *$2 net. J. H. West.
Charlotte. Walford, *Mrs.* L. B. $1.50. Longmans.
CHARTRES.
Headlam. Story of Chartres. $2; $2.50. Macmillan.
Chase, Eliza B. In quest of the quaint. '02 (Ag30) il. D. hf. ooze, $1.50. Ferris.
Chase, F: H: Credibility of the Book of the Acts of the Apostles. '02(Je14) 12°, (Hulsean lectures, 1900-01.) $1.75. Macmillan.
Chase, G: *See* New York. Code of civil procedure.
Chasing an iron horse. Robins, E: **$1 net. Jacobs.
Châteaubriand, F. R. A. *Vicomte de.* Memoirs; tr. by A. Teixera de Maltos. '02(Jl19) 6 v., ea., *$3.75 net. Putnam.
Chatfield-Taylor, Hobart C. *See* Taylor, H. C. Chatfield-.
Chats within the fold. Desmond, H. J. net, 75 c. Murphy.
Chaucer, G. English of the XIVth century; Prologue and Knightes tale. (S. H. Carpenter.) '01. '02(Ap26) 12°, 75 c. Ginn.

Chaucer, G. Nonne's preeste's tale of the cok and hen. '02(Je28) il. 8°, Japan vellum, $6.50; hand painted, $16.50. Grafton Press.

CHAUCER, Geoffrey.
Ten Brink. Language and metre of Chaucer. net, $1.50. Macmillan.

Chaucer's Parlement of foules. *See* Hammond, E. P.

Chelsea. *See* Besant, *Sir* W.

CHEMISTRY.
Abegg *and* Herz. Practical chemistry. net, $1.50. Macmillan.
Bunge. Text-book of physiological and patholog. chemistry. *$3 net. Blakiston.
Chittenden, *ed.* Studies in physiolog. chemistry. net, $4. Scribner.
Clarke *and* Dennis. Elem. chemistry. $1.10. Am. Bk.
Dennis *and* Clarke. Lab'y manual to accompany Elem. chemistry. 50 c. Am. Bk.
Dupre *and* Hake. Inorganic chemistry. $3. Lippincott.
Hessler *and* Smith. Essentials of chemistry. $1.20. Sanborn.
Holleman. Inorganic chemistry. $2.50. Wiley.
Jones. Elements of physical chemistry. net, $4. Macmillan.
Landolt. Optical rotating power of organic substances. *$7.50 net. Chemical.
Morgan. Elements of physical chemistry. $2. Wiley.
Ostwald. Principles of inorganic chemistry. net, $6. Macmillan.
Perkin *and* Lean. Introd. to chemistry and physics. 2 v. ea., net, 50 c. Macmillan.
Prescott *and* Sullivan. Qualitative chemistry for studies of water solution and mass action. net, $1.50. Van Nostrand.
Remsen. Introd. to study of chemistry. $1.12. Holt.
Simon. Physiological chemistry. net, $3.25. Lea
Staedeler. System of qualitative chemical analysis. 60 c. H. W. Wilson.
Thorpe. Essays in historical chemistry. net, $4. Macmillan.
Tilden. Introd. to the study of chemical philosophy: theoretical and systematic. $1.75. Longmans.
Watson. Elem. experimental chemistry, inorganic. net, $1.25. Barnes.
Wells, *ed.* Studies fr. the chemical lab'y of the Sheffield Scientific School. net, $7.50. Scribner.
Young. Elem. principles of chemistry. net, 95 c. Appleton.
See also Blowpipe;—Enzymes;—Fermentation;—Indicators.

Chemistry of the terpenes. Heusler, F. *$4 net. Blakiston.

Cheney, Fk. J. A life of unity, and other stories. '01. '02(F22) 12°, $1.50. Blade.

Cherbuliez, C: V: Le Roi Apépi; notes in Eng. by A. Schinz. '02(Jl12) 12°, (Romans choisis, no. 25.) pap., 60 c. W: R. Jenkins.

Cherished thoughts. Presset, A. L. $1.50; $1.75; $2.25. Skelton.

Chesterfield, *Earl of.* Letters, sentences and maxims. '02(Je14) 12°, (Home lib.) $1. Burt.

Chesterfield, *Earl of.* Letters to his son; ed. by C. Strachey. '01. '02(F22) 2 v., D. (Lib. of standard literature.) ea., $1.75. Putnam.

Cheyne, T: K., *and* Black, J: S., *eds.* Encyclopædia Biblica. v. 3, L-P. '02(My17) 8°, subs., net, $5; hf. mor., net, $7.50. Macmillan.

Cheyne, W: W., *and* **Burghard**, F. F. Manual of surgical treatment. In 7 v. v. 5, '01. '02(Mr1); v. 6 (Jl19) 8°, ea., *$5 net. Lea.

CHICAGO.
Clark. Public schools of Chicago. net, 50 c. Univ. of Chic.

Chiefs of Cambria. Jones, M. P. $1.25. Abbey Press.

Child for Christ. McKinney, A. H. net, 50 c. Revell.

Child life in all nations. Botsford, A. H. $1. Am. Bk. and Bible.

Child of the flood. Leahy, W. T: $1. Kilner.

Child of Urbino. La Ramé, L. de. 30 c. Educ. Pub.

Child stories from the masters. Menefee, M. 75 c. Rand, McN. & Co.

CHILD STUDY.
Wilson. Bibliog. of child study. net. 25 c. Stechert.
See also Kindergarten;—Psychology.

Childe, Cromwell. Water exploring: guide to pleasant steamboat trips everywhere. '02 (Ag2) S. (Eagle lib., v. 17, no. 69.) pap., 10 c. Brooklyn Eagle.

Childe, Cromwell, *comp.* Trolley exploring. '02(My17) S. pap., 10 c. Brooklyn Eagle.

CHILDREN.
Anthony. The children's covenant. $1. Jennings.
Compayré. Later infancy of the child. pt. 2. net, $1.20. Appleton.
Folks. Care of destitute, neglected, and delinquent children. net, $1. Macmillan.
McKinney. The child for Christ. net, 50 c. Revell.
Mundy. Eclectic practice in diseases of children. net, $2.50. Scudder.
Pollak, *ed.* Our success in child-training. $1. Contemporary.
Rotch. Pediatrics, subs., $6; $7. Lippincott.
Worthington. The tocsin—our children in peril. 25 c. Cubery.
See also Education;—Girls;—Kindergarten;—Mothers.

Children of the cold. Schwatka, F. $1.25. Educ. Pub.

Children of the palm lands. Allen, A. E. 50 c. Educ. Pub.

Children's Bible stories told in words of easy reading. '02(F1) 5 v., il. 4°, ea., 75 c. Saalfield.

Children's covenant. Anthony, C. V. $1. Jennings.

Children's friend ser. 16°, 50 c. Little, B. & Co.
—Alcott. Little button rose.
—Aulnoy *and* Perrault. Once upon a time.
—Dewey. Bruno.
—Ewing. Benjy in beastland.
—Gilman. Kingdom of coins.
—Moulton. Her baby brother.
—Perrault *and* Aulnoy. Fairy favorites.

Children's friend ser.—Continued.
—Phelps *and* Ward. Lost hero.
—Sullivan. Ivanhoe and Rob Roy, retold.
—Woolsey. Uncle and aunt.
Children's London. Thorpe, C. net, $4.50. Scribner
Child's Bible hist. Knecht, F. J. 25 c. Herder.
Child's dream of a star. Dickens, C: †50 c. L. C. Page.
Child's garden of verses. Stevenson, R. L: net, 60 c. Scribner.
Child's story. *See* Dickens, C:
Child's story of the life of Christ. Hoyt, H. B. $1.25. W. A. Wilde.
Childs, E: E. Wonders of Mouseland. '01-'02(Ja11) D. $1.25. Abbey Press.
Chimmie Fadden and Mr. Paul. Townsend, E: W. $1.50. Century Co.
CHINA.
Allgood. China war, 1860. $5. Longmans.
Parker. John Chinaman, and a few others. $2.50. Dutton.
Thomson. China and the powers. $4. Longmans.
Van Bergen. Story of China. 60 c. Am. Bk.
See also Manchuria;—Paotingfu.
Chinese-English elem. reader and arithmetic. Gyim, P. L. $1.25. Taylor & M.
CHINESE EXCLUSION.
Quang Chang Ling. Why should the Chinese go? 25 c. Cambridge.
Chipman, C: B. Last cruise of the "Electra." '02(Ag9) il. 12°, $1. Saalfield.
Chiquita. Tileston, M. $1.50. Merrill.
Chittenden, Hiram M. American fur trade of the far west. '02(Mr8) 3 v., il. O. net, $10. F. P. Harper.
Chittenden, Russell H., *ed.* Studies in physiolog. chemistry. '01-'02(Mr15) 8°, (Yale bicentennial pub.) net, $4. Scribner.
Choephori (The). Æschylus. net, $3.25. Macmillan.
Choir and chorus conducting. Wodell, F: W: $1.50. Presser.
Choralia. Powell, J. B. $1.50. Longmans.
Christ and his cross. Rutherford, S: $1. Longmans.
Christ our life. Moberly, R. C. net, $3. Longmans.
Christ the way. Paget, F. 75 c. Longmans.
CHRISTENDOM.
See Christianity;—Church history;—History.
CHRISTIAN LIFE.
Babcock. Three whys and their answer. 35 c. Un. Soc. C. E.
Barton. I go a fishing: progressive discipleship. 25 c. Revell.
Bausman. Precept and practice. net, $1. Heidelberg.
Fradenburgh. Twenty-five stepping stones toward Christ's kingdom. O. P. Fradenburgh.
Gladden. Christian way. 75 c. Dodd.
Keedy. Naturalness of Christian life. net, $1.25. Putnam.
Kyger, *ed.* Hand-book for soul-winners. 50 c. Kyger.
Morozzo. Treatise of spiritual life. *$1 net. Pustet.
Mudge. Life of love. 25 c. Jennings.

CHRISTIAN LIFE.—*Continued.*
Newell. Life worth living. $1. Abbey Press.
Sanders. How are we led? Who is it that leads us? $1.50. Donohue.
Sarles. Man's peerless destiny in Christ. net, 90 c. Funk.
Terry. The new and living way. net, 50 c. Eaton & M.
See also Conduct of life;—Devotional exercises and meditations;—Faith;—Prayer;—Revivals.
Christian ministry. Anderson, C: P. 20 c. Young Churchman.
CHRISTIAN SCIENCE.
Clark. Church of St. Bunco. $1. Abbey Press.
Cushman. The truth in Christian science. 60 c. J. H. West.
Gifford. Christian science against itself. $1. Jennings.
Seward. How to get acquainted with God: meaning of the Christian science movement. net, 50 c. Funk.
Whittaker. Christian science, is it safe? 10 c. Earle.
Christian study manuals; ed. by R. E. Welsh. S. 60 c. Armstrong.
—Gibson. Protestant principles.
—Margoliouth. Religion of Bible lands.
CHRISTIAN UNITY.
Henson. Godly union and concord. $2. Longmans.
Christian way. Gladden, W. 75 c. Dodd.
CHRISTIANITY.
Clarkson. A B C of scientific Christianity. 25 c. J. R. Clarkson.
Fairbairn. Philosophy of the Christian religion. net, $3.50. Macmillan.
Gilbert. Primer of the Christian religion. net, $1. Macmillan.
Grant, *ed.* Christendom Anno Domini 1901. 2 v. $2.50. W: D. Grant.
Islam and Christianity. $1. Am. Tr.
Mason. Christianity, what is it? 80 c. E. & J. B. Young.
Ovenden. To whom shall we go? $1. E. & J. B. Young.
Pierson. The Gordian knot. **60 c. net. Funk.
Selden. Story of the Christian centuries. net, $1. Revell.
Spence. Early Christianity and Paganism. *$4 net. Dutton.
Turton, *comp.* Truth of Christianity. *$1.25 net. Young Churchman.
See also Bible;—Church history;—God;—Missions and missionaries;—Protestantism;—Religion;—Theology.
Christie, R: C. Selected essays and papers; ed., with memoir, by W: A. Shaw. '02 (Mr8) il. O. $5. Longmans.
Christmas rose. Macmillan, H. $1. Macmillan.
Christopher. Lockett, M. F. $1.25. AbbeyPress.
Church, Arth. H. Chemistry of paints and painting. 3d ed., rev. and enl. '02(F15) 8°, $3. Macmillan.
Church, Irving P. Diagrams of mean velocity of uniform motion of water in open channels. '02(Je21) obl. 4°, pap., $1.50. Wiley.
CHURCH ARCHITECTURE.
Ayer. Rise and devel. of Chr. architecture. net, $1.50. Young Churchman.

Church Historical Soc. lectures. 16°. E. & J. B. Young.
—Mason. Christianity, what is it? 80 c.

CHURCH HISTORY.
Guggenberger. General hist. of the Christian era. In 3 v. ea., $1.50. Herder.
Moncrief. Short hist. of the Christian church. **$1.50 net. Revell.
See also Huguenots;—*also* names of churches.

CHURCH MEMBERSHIP.
Clarke. Training the church of the future. net, 75 c. Funk.
Horton. Birthright membership of believers' infants in the N. T. church. 6 c. Presb. Bd.
See also Baptism.

CHURCH MUSIC.
Curwen. Studies in worship music, chiefly congregational singing. $1.75. Scribner.
Dickinson. Music in the hist. of the western church. net, $2.50. Scribner.
Powell. Choralia: for precentors and choirmasters. $1.50. Longmans.
Wodell. Choir and chorus conducting. $1.50. Presser.

Church of Christ. Green, E. T. $1.50. Macmillan.

Church of England. Liber precum publicarum Ecclesiæ Anglicanæ, A. G. Bright et P. G. Medd. '02(Ag9) S. $2. Longmans.

CHURCH OF ENGLAND.
Creighton. The church and the nation. $2. Longmans.
Galton. Our attitude toward Eng. Roman Catholics. net, $1. Dutton.
Gee. Elizabethan prayer-book and ornaments. net, $1.25. Macmillan.
Grafton. Pusey and the church revival. net, 50 c. Young Churchman.
Green. Church of Christ. $1.50. Macmillan.
Henson. Cross-bench views of current church questions. $4. Longmans.
Stephens *and* Hunt, *eds.* Hist. of the Eng. church. v. 3, 4. ea., *$2 net. Macmillan.
See also Confession;—Protestant Epis. church.

Church of St. Bunco. Clark, G. $1. Abbey Press.

CHURCHES.
See Syracuse First Presb. church.

Churchman's lib. 8°. Macmillan.
—Green. Church of Christ. $1.50.
—Mackay. Churchman's introd. to the O. T. $1.50.

Church's one foundation. Nicoll, W: R. $1.25. Armstrong.

Church's outlook for the twentieth century ser. 12°. net, $1. Dutton.
—Cobb. Theology, old and new.

Churton, W: R. William Ralph Churton: theolog. papers and sermons. '02(Ap26) 12°, $1.75. Macmillan.

Chute, H. N. *See* Carhart, H: S.

Cicely. Johnston, A. F. †50 c. L. C. Page.

Cicero. Select orations and letters. Allen and Greenough's ed.; rev. by Greenough and Kittredge. '02(Je14) D. hf. leath., $1.45. Ginn.

Cid, R. D. de Bivar, *called the* Cid. Poem of the Cid; tr. by A. M. Huntington. v. 1, 2. '02(Je28) il. Q. vellum, ea., $25. Putnam.

Cid (Le). Corneille, P. net, 35 c. Holt.

CIDER.
See Apple.

CINCINNATI SOUTHERN RAILWAY.
Boyden. Beginnings of the Cincinnati Southern railway. 50 c. Clarke.

CIPHER.
See Codes.

Citator (The). Iowa. $3. R. Adams.

CITIES.
See Municipal government.

Citizen's lib. of economics, politics and sociology; ed. by R: T. Ely. 12°, net, $1.25. Macmillan.
—Addams. Democracy and social ethics.
—Baker. Municipal engineering and sanitation.
—Reinsch. Colonial government.

CITIZENSHIP.
Brewer. American citizenship. net, 75 c. Scribner.
Smith. Training for citizenship. **90 c. net. Lothrop.
See also Naturalization.

City of Angels. McGrady, T: 10 c. Standard.

City of the seven hills. Harding, C. H. 40 c. Scott, F. & Co.

CIVICS.
See Political science.

CIVIL ACTIONS.
See Actions at law.

CIVIL ENGINEERING.
See Engineering;—Surveying.

Civil government in U. S. Martin, G: H. 90 c. Am. Bk.

CIVIL LAW.
Justinianus. Pandects of Justinian. v. 1. $5. Cambridge.

CIVIL WAR.
See United States.

CIVILIZATION.
Colquhoun. Mastery of the Pacific. net, $4. Macmillan.
Kidd. Principles of western civilization. net, $2. Macmillan.
Stead. Americanization of the world. $1. Markley.
Wells. Anticipations of reaction of mechanical and scientific progress. net, $1.80. Harper.
See also History.

Clapp, H: A. Reminiscences of a dramatic critic. '02(Je7) O. net, $1.75. Houghton, M. & Co.

Clark, A. When bards sing out of tune. '02(My10) D. 50 c. Abbey Press.

Clark, A. Howard, *ed.* *See* Sons of the Am. Revolution.

Clark, C: An Antarctic queen. '01· '02 (My17) il. D. $1.75. Warne.

Clark, Ellery H. *See* Massachusetts. Street railway accident law.

Clark, Fs. E: Training the church of the future; lectures, with special ref. to the Young People's Soc. of Christian Endeavor. '02 (Ap12) il. D. net, 75 c. Funk.

Clark, Gordon. Church of St. Bunco. '01· '02(F15) D. $1. Abbey Press.

Clark, H. H. Admiral's aid. '02(Ag23) il. D. **$1 net. Lothrop.

Clark, Hannah B. Public schools of Chicago. '02(Mr22) 8°, pap., net, 50 c. Univ. of Chic.

Clark, Salter S. The government, what it is, what it does. '02(My10) D. 75 c. Am. Bk.

Clark, Solomon H:, *ed.* Handbook of best readings. '02(Ag2) D. **$1.50 net. Scribner.

Clark, W: *See* Lewis, M.

Clark, W: L., *jr.* Hand-book of criminal law. 2d ed., by F. B. Tiffany. '02(Ag2) O. (Hornbook ser.) shp., $3.75. West Pub.

Clark, W: L., *and* Marshall, W: L. Treatise on the law of private corporations. In 3 v. v. 2. '01. '02(F1); v. 3 (Jl12) O. shp., per v. $6. Keefe-D.

Clarke, F. W., *and* Dennis, L. M. Elementary chemistry. '02(Je21) D. $1.10. Am. Bk.

Clarke, G: K. Descendants of Nathaniel Clarke and his wife Elizabeth Somerby of Newbury, Mass. '02(Jl12) il. 8°, *$5 net. Marvin.

Clarke, Helen A. *See* Porter, C.

Clarke, *Mrs.* Ma. Cowden, [Mary Victoria Novello.] Letters to an enthusiast: add. to Rob. Balmanno; ed. by A. U. Nettleton. '02(My3) O. net, $2.50. McClurg.

Clarke, W. J. A B C of electrical experiments. '02(Ap5) il. D. $1. Excelsior.

CLAKE FAMILY.
Clarke. Descendants of Nathaniel Clarke and Eliz. Somerby. *$5 net. Marvin.

Clarkson, Jos. R. A B C of scientific Christianity. '01· '02(Ag30) D. pap., 25 c. J. R. Clarkson.

CLARKSON FAMILY.
See Leach, J. G.

CLASSICAL PHILOLOGY.
See Dissertationes Americanæ.

CLASSIFICATION.
See Cataloguing.

Clay, *Mrs.* J: M. Frank Logan. '02(F22) il. D. $1. Abbey Press.

Claybornes (The). Sage, W: $1.50. Houghton, M. & Co.

CLAYTON-BULWER TREATY.
Travis. Hist. of the Clayton-Bulwer treaty. $1. Mich. Pol. Sci.

CLEARING HOUSE.
See Banks and banking.

Clemens, G. C. *See* Kansas. Statutes conc. corporations.

Clemens, S: L., ["Mark Twain."] A double-barrelled detective story. '02(Ap19) il. D. $1.50. Harper.

Clement, G: A. Probate repts., annot. v. 6. '02(My24) O. shp., $5.50. Baker, V. & Co.

Clerical capitalist. McGrady, T: 10 c. Socialistic Co-op.

Clewell, J: H: Hist. of Wachovia in N. C.; the Unitas fratrum or Moravian church, 1752-1902. '02(Jl5) il. 8°, **$2 net. Doubleday, P.

CLIFF DWELLERS.
Nordenskiold. The cliff dwellers of the Mesa Verde, southwestern Col. net, $20. Stechert.

Clifford, Chandler R. Period decoration. '01. '02(Ap12) il. 8°, $3. Clifford & L.

Clifford, *Mrs.* Lucy L. A long duel. '01. '02 (Mr22) 12°, pap., net, 25 c. Lane.

Clifford, *Mrs.* Lucy L. Margaret Vincent. '02(Ap26) D. $1.50. Harper.

Climates and baths of Great Britain. 8°, net. Macmillan.

—Ewart, *and others.* Climates of London, central and northen England, Wales and Ireland. $4. (2.)

Cline, Alberta. Kindergarten, painting, plays and home entertainments. '02(Ag30) il. 12°, $1. Am. Bk. and Bible.

CLINIC.
See Pathology.

Clinical psychiatry. Defendorf, A. R. net, $3.50. Macmillan.

Clinton, Major, *pseud.* *See* Culley, F. C.

Clock on the stairs. Weber, A. 75 c. Burt.

Clodd, E: Thomas Henry Huxley. '02 (Ap12) D. (Modern Eng. writers.) net, $1. Dodd.

Cloistering of Ursula. Scollard, C. $1.50. L. C. Page.

Clough, Emma R. John E. Clough, missionary to the Telugus of South India. '02 (Ag2) S. (Biographical ser.) pap., 10 c. Am. Bapt. Miss. Un.

Clow, F: R. Comparative study of the administration of city finances in the U. S. '01· '02(Ja11) O. (Pub. of the Am. Economic Assoc., 3d ser., v. 2, no. 4.) pap., $1. Macmillan.

Clowes, W: L., *and others.* Royal navy. v. 5 and 6. '01. '02(Ja11) 8°, ea., net, $6.50. Little, B. & Co.

COAL.
Hughes. Text-book of coal mining. $7. Lippincott.

Coal oil Johnny. Steele, J: W. $1.50. J: A. Hill.

Coals from the altar. Davis, H: T. 75 c.; 20 c. Knapp.

Coast of freedom. Shaw, A. M. $1.50. Doubleday, P.

Cobb, Sanford H. Rise of relig. liberty in America. '02(My17) 8°, net, $4. Macmillan.

Cobb, W. F. Theology, old and new. '02 (Ap5) 12°. (Church's outlook for the twentieth century ser., no. 1.) net, $1. Dutton.

Cobban, J. M. Green turbans. '02(Ag30) 12°, (Manhattan ser.) pap., 50 c. Burt.

Coburn, F: N. Prize designs for rural school buildings. '01· '02(Ja25) il. 12°, 25 c. Kellogg.

Cochrane, J: M., *rep.* *See* North Dakota. *Sup. ct.* Repts.

Cochrane, Rob. More animal stories. '01· '02(F15) il. 12°, net, $1. Lippincott.

Cockcroft, Ja., *ed.* Encyclopædia of forms and precedents for pleading and practice. (T: E. O'Brien.) v. 15. '02(My17) O. shp.. $6. Cockcroft.

Cockerell, Douglas. Bookbinding and the care of books. '02(F8) il. D. (Artistic crafts ser. of technical handbooks, no. 1.) net, $1.20. Appleton.

Code of joy. Lathbury, C. 50 c. Swedenborg.

CODES.
A B C universal commercial electric telegraphic code. net, $7. Am. Code.
Barry. Am. lumberman telecode. net, $5. Am. Lumberman.
Hartfield. Exchange pocket cipher code. $2. T. W. Hartfield.
Hartmann *and* Needham. Commercial code for the transmission of telegrams and cablegrams. $3. Commercial Code.
International Cable Directory Co., *comp.* Internat. cable directory of the world in conjunction with Western Union telegraphic code system. $15. Int. Cable.

Codman, J:, *2d*. Arnold's expedition to Quebec. 2d ed. '02(Mr1) 8°, net, $2.25. Macmillan.
Cody, S. Selections from the world's greatest short stories. '02(My24) D. net, $1. McClurg.
Coffin, C: E. Gist of whist. 7th ed., rev. '02(Jl5) S. 75 c. Brentano's.
Coffin, G: M. A B C of banks and banking. '01. '02(Ap5) il. S. (Wall street lib., v. 4.) $1.25. S: A. Nelson.
Cohen, Alfr. J., ["Alan Dale."] Girl who wrote. '02(Jl19) il. D. $1.50. Quail & W.

COHERER.
See Electricity.

Cohn, Alfr. I. Indicators and test-papers, their source, preparation, application, and tests for sensitiveness. 2d ed. '02(Je7) 12°, $2. Wiley.
Coit, Stanton, *comp*. The message of man: a book of ethical scriptures. '02(Ag16) 16°, 75 c.; leath., $1. Macmillan.
Colburn, Bertha L. Graded physical exercises. '02(F22) D. $1. Werner.
Colby, Alb. L. Review and text of the Am. standard specifications for steel, adopt. Aug., 1901. 2d ed. '02(Ap5) 12°, net, $1.10. Chemical.
Colcock, Annie T. Margaret Tudor. '02 (Ap19) il. D. $1. Stokes.
Colden, Cadwallader. Hist. of the Five Indian nations of Canada. '02(My24) 2 v., 8°, (Commonwealth lib.) net, per v., $1. New Amsterdam.
Cole, Horace L. The flesh and the devil. '02(Ap26) 12°, $1.50. Neely.
Coleman, Phares, *rep*. *See* Alabama. *Sup. ct.* Repts.
Colemanite from So. California. Eakle, A. S. 15 c. Univ. of Cal.
Coleridge, S: T. Rime of the ancient mariner; ed. by N. H. Pitman. '01· '02(Ap19) S. (Ser. of Eng. classics.) keratol, 30 c.; flex. bds., 25 c. B. F. Johnson.
Coley, W: B., *ed*. *See* Sultan, G:
College chaps. Prune, N. 75 c. Mutual Bk.
College Latin ser. 12°. Allyn & B.
—Plautus. Mostellaria. *$1 net.
College man in doubt. Best, N. R. net, 50 c. Westminster
College student and his problems. Canfield, J. H. net, $1. Macmillan.

COLLEGES AND UNIVERSITIES.
See Oxford Univ.

Collier's new encyclopedia. '02(Ag30) 16 v., il. 8°, per set, $20. Collier.
Collingwood, W: G. Life of John Ruskin. [New rev., abb. ed.] '02(Mr29) O. net, $2. Houghton, M. & Co.
Collins, Cornelius F. Municipal court practice act, annot.: forms and index. '02 (Ag9) O. shp., $5. Banks.
Collins, J: E. Truth about socialism. '02 (Jl12) 16°, pap., 25 c. J. A. Wayland.
Colonel Harold de Lacey. Douglass, F. A. $1.25. Neely.
Colonial days. Welsh, L. D. 50 c. Educ. Pub.

COLONIAL GOVERNMENT.
Reinsch. Colonial government. net, $1.25. Macmillan.

Colonials (The). French, A. $1.50. Doubleday, P.

COLOR.
Vanderpoel. Color problems. net, $5. Longmans.
See also Dyeing;—Light;—Printing.

Color of the soul. Norris, Z. A. net, $1. Funk.
Colorado. Laws passed at an extra session of the 13th general assembly. '02(Je14) O. hf. shp., $2. Smith-B.

COLORADO.
Hatch. Civil government in Col. 60 c. Centennial.
Nordenskiold. Cliff dwellers of the Mesa Verde, southwestern Col. net, $20. Stechert.

Colorado colonel. Campbell, W: C. $1.50. Crane.

COLORADO RIVER.
James. In and around the Grand Canyon. net, $10. Little, B. & Co.

Colquhoun, Arch. R. Mastery of the Pacific. '02(Mr1) 8°, net, $4. Macmillan.
Colton, B. P. Elem. physiology and hygiene. '02(My24) il. D. 60 c. Heath.
Columbia Univ. cont. to philosophy, psychology and education. 8°, pap. Macmillan.
—Alexander. Problem of metaphysics. *75 c. net. (v. 10, 1.)
Columbia Univ. Germanic studies. 8°, pap., net, $1. Macmillan.
—Remy. Influence of India and Persia on the poetry of Germany. (v. 1, 4.)
Columbia Univ. Indo-Iranian ser.; ed. by A. V. Williams Jackson. 8°, net. Macmillan.
—Avesta. Index verborum. $2.
—Gray. Indo-Iranian phonology. $3.
Columbia Univ. Oriental studies. 8°, net, $1.25. Macmillan.
—Gabirol. Improvement of moral qualities. (1.)
Columbia Univ. studies in comparative literature. 12°, net. Macmillan.
—Einstein. Italian Renaissance in England. $1.50.
Columbia Univ. studies in hist., economics and public law. 8°. Macmillan.
—Duggan. Eastern question. *$1.50 net. (v. 14, 3.)
—Hall. Crime in its rel. to social progress. $3 net; $3.50 net. (v. 15.)
—Kinosita. Past and present of Japanese commerce. *$1.50 net. (v. 16, 1.)
Columbia Univ. studies in romance, philol. and literature. Macmillan.
—Segall. Corneille and the Spanish drama. **$1.50 net.
Colville, W. J. Life and power from within. '02(Mr22) D. $1. Alliance.
Colyer, J. F. *See* Smale, M.
Coming King. White, J. E. $1. Southern Pub.
Commander, Lydia K. Marred in the making. '02(Ap12) O. limp chamois, satin-lined, $3; pap., 25 c. Eckler.
Comments of a Countess. '02(My10) 4°, net, $1.50. Lane.

COMMERCE.
Foreign trade requirements (annual). $10. Lewis.
Kinosita. Past and present of Japanese commerce. *$1.50 net. Macmillan.

COMMERCE.—*Continued.*
Marchant. Commercial history. $1. Pitman.
Vanderlip. Amer. "commercial invasion" of Europe. n. p. Nat. City Bank.
Ware. Educational foundations of trade and industry. net, $1.20. Appleton.
See also Commercial law;—Political economy;—Railroads.
COMMERCIAL CORRESPONDENCE.
See Stenography.
Commercial digest and business forms. McMaster, J. S. $6. Commercial Bk.
COMMERCIAL LAW.
Authorities, deductions and notes in commercial paper. $2.25. Univ. Press.
Hargis. Commercial law and business customs. $3. A. M. Hargis.
Hargis. Treatise on commercial law and business customs. 10 c. J. North.
McMaster. Irregular and regular commercial paper. $2.—Commercial cases. $6. Commercial Bk.
See also Attachment;—Contracts;—Conveyancing;—Corporations;—Negotiable instruments;—Sale;—Trusts.
COMMONER (The).
Bryan. *The Commoner,* condensed. $1.50. Abbey Press.
Commonwealth lib. 8°, net, $1. New Amsterdam.
—Arnold. Literature and dogma.
—Colden. Hist. of the Five Indian nations of Canada. 2 v.
—Lewis *and* Clark. Expedition to the sources of the Missouri, etc.
—Mackenzie. Voyages fr. Montreal to the Pacific Ocean.
Commonwealth or empire. Smith, G. net, 60 c. Macmillan.
Commonwealth ser. 16°, $1.25. L. C. Page.
—Wheaton. The Russells in Chicago.
Communion with God. Talling, M. P. $1.25. Revell.
COMMUNISM.
Lockwood. New Harmony communities. $2.50. Chronicle.
Company commander's manual. *See* United States Army.
Compayré, Gabriel. Later infancy of the child; tr. by M. E. Wilson. '02(F22) 12°, (Internat. educ. ser., no. 53.) net, $1.20. Appleton.
Complete housebuilder. '02(My17) 12°, 50 c.; pap., 25 c. Donohue.
Complete pocket guide to Europe. Stedman, E. C. $1.25. W: R. Jenkins.
COMPOSERS.
See Musicians.
COMPOSITION.
See Rhetoric.
COMPOUNCE, Lake.
Norton. Compounce, 1846-1902. 75 c. Tuttle, M. & T.
Comrades. **Newberry**, F. E. 75 c. Burt.
Condict, Alice B. Old glory and the gospel in the Philippines. '02(Ap19) 12°, net, 75 c. Revell.
CONDUCT OF LIFE.
Dresser. Book of secrets, studies in self-control. net, $1. Putnam.
Hillis. Master of science of right-living. net, 50 c. Revell.
Hind. Life's little things. $1.75. Macmillan.
CONDUCT OF LIFE.—*Continued.*
Jordan. Kingship of self-control.—Majesty of calmness. ea., 50 c. Revell.
Mabie. Works and days. net, $1. Dodd.
Marden. Stepping stones. **$1 net. Lothrop.
Slicer. One world at a time. net, $1.35. Putnam.
See also Business;—Character;—Christian life;—Culture;—Ethics;—Knowledge.
Cone, J: A. Man who pleases and the woman who fascinates. '01. '02(Jl12) 12°, $1. Neely.
CONFECTIONERY.
Rigby. Reliable candy teacher and soda and ice cream formulas. $2. W. O. Rigby.
CONFESSION.
Fulham Palace Conference. Confession and absolution. net, $1. Longmans.
Confessions of a matchmaking mother. Davidson, L. C. $1.50 J. F. Taylor.
Confounding of Camelia. Sedgwick, A. D. $1.50. Century Co.
Conger, Arth. B. Religion for the time: six conferences on natural religion. '02(My3) D. net, $1. Jacobs.
CONJURING.
Roterberg. Card tricks; how to do them, and sleight of hand. 25 c. Drake.
Conklin, *Mrs.* Jennie M. D. Bek's first corner. '02(Mr29) il. 12°, (Fireside ser.) $1. Burt.
Conklin, *Mrs.* Jennie M. D. Growing up. '02(Mr29) il. 12°, (Fireside ser.) $1. Burt.
Conklin, *Mrs.* Jennie M. D. Miss Prudence. '02(Mr29) il. 12°, (Fireside ser.) $1. Burt.
Conklin, *Mrs.* Jennie M. D. Tessa Wadsworth's discipline. '02(Mr29) il. 12°, (Fireside ser.) $1. Burt.
Conley, J: W. Evolution and man. '02 (Ap19) 12°, net, 75 c. Revell.
CONNECTICUT.
Jarvis, *ed.* Sketches of church life in colonial Conn. $1. Tuttle, M & T.
Connelley. W: Elsey. *See* Root, F. A.
Connold, E: J. British vegetable galls. '02 (Mr22) f°, net, $4. Dutton.
Conquering corps badge. King, C: $1.25. L. A. Rhodes.
Conqueror (The). Atherton, *Mrs.* G. F. $1.50. Macmillan.
Consolation of philosophy. Boethius, A. M. S. 50 c.; 75 c. Macmillan.
Conspiracy of Pontiac. Parkman, F. $1. Burt.
CONSTABLE, John.
Holmes. Constable. net, $1. Longmans.
CONSTABLES.
Dill. Changes and add. to constables' guide. T. & J. W. Johnson.
See also Justices of the peace.
Constance Hamilton. Wyatt, L. M. L. 50 c. Abbey Press.
Constances. Bentzan, T. $1.50. Neely.
CONSTELLATIONS.
See Astronomy;—Stars.
CONSTITUTIONAL LAW.
See Roman empire.
Constructive Bible studies; ed. by W: R. Harper and E. D. Burton. O. $1. Univ. of Chic.
—Burton *and* Mathews. Life of Christ.
—Harper. Constructive studies in the priestly element in the O. T.

CONSUMPTION.
Burnett. New cure for consumption by its own virus. $1. Boericke & T.
See also Lungs.

CONTAGION.
Poore. The earth in rel. to the preservation and destruction of contagia; with other papers on sanitation. $1.75. Longmans.
See also Bacteria;—Smallpox;—Typhoid fever.

Contemporary science ser. See Scribner's.

CONTRACTS.
Lawson. Making of a contract. 25 c. Stephens.
Shipp. Questions and answers on contracts. 50 c. Byrne.

CONUNDRUMS.
See Riddles.

CONVENTS.
Steele. Convents of Great Britain. net, $2. Herder.

CONVERSION.
Mason. Ministry of conversion. net, 90 c. Longmans.
See also Christian life;—Revivals.

CONVEYANCING.
Pennsylvania. Law of conveyancing. $6. T. & J. W. Johnson.

CONVICTS.
See Crime and criminals;—Prisons.

Conway, Kath. E. Lalor's Maples. 2d ed. '01. '02(Ja11) D. $1.25. Pilot.
Conway, Moncure D., *comp.* The sacred anthology (oriental.) 5th ed. '02(Mr29) 12°, $2. Holt.
Cook, *Mrs.* E. T. The bride's book. '02 (Ap5) 12°, net, $1.50. Dutton.
Cook, E: T. Rights and wrongs of the Transvaal war. New rev. ed. '02(Je7) D. $2. Longmans.
Cook, G: C. *See* Banks, C: E.
Cook, Ja. Three voyages around the world. '02(My17) 12°, (Home lib.) $1. Burt.
Cook, J: T. *See* New York. Code of criminal procedure and penal code.
Cooke, C. J. B. Some recent developments in locomotive practice. '02(Je7) il. 8°, $1. Macmillan.

COOKERY.
Brown. Food studies. 50 c. Reed.
Curtis. Left-overs made palatable. $1. Judd.
Dainty dishes for slender incomes. net, 50 c. New Amsterdam.
Dennis. Cook book. $1.50. Mutual Pub. Co.
H. Grandmother's cook book. 50 c. New Amsterdam.
Keller. Pennsylvania German cook book. 50 c. R. M. Scranton.
Nordhoff guild cook book. 25 c. McGill.
Palmer. Woman's exchange cook book. 70 c. Conkey.
Pierce. Hartley House cook book and household economist. 60 c. Lentilhon.
Rivas. Little French dinners. 50 c. New Amsterdam.
Salis. A la mode cookery. $2. Longmans.
Schaeffer. Metropolitan club cook-book. $1.75. Augsburg.
Seeley. Cook book: Fr. and Amer. cookery. net, $2; net, $3. Macmillan.
Smiley, *ed.* Household cook book. $1.50. Drake.
See also Diet;—Domestic economy;—Hygiene.

Coolidge, Susan, *pseud. See* Woolsey, S. C.

Cooper, E: H. A fool's year. '02(F15) D. (Town and country lib., no. 308.) $1; pap., 50 c. Appleton.

CO-OPERATION.
See Ruskin Co-operative Assoc.;—Socialism;—Trade-unions.

Coppée François. Morceau de pain et autres contes. '02(My3) sq. S. (Contes choises, no. 22.) pap., 25 c. W: R. Jenkins.

COPPER.
Stevens, *comp.* Copper handbook. $2; $3. H. J. Stevens.

Corbin, J: An American at Oxford. '02 (My17) il. D. net, $1.50. Houghton, M. & Co.
Corinne's vow. Waggaman, M. T. $1.25. Benziger.

CORLISS ENGINE.
Lisk. Diagram of the Corliss engine, etc. 25 c. Spon.

Corn of heaven. Macmillan, H. $1.75. Macmillan.
Corneille, P. Le Cid; ed. by E: S. Joynes. New rev. enl. ed. '02(F1) D. (Students' ser. of classic Fr. plays, no. 1.) net, 35 c. Holt.

CORNEILLE, Pierre.
Segall. Corneille and the Spanish drama. **$1.50 net. Macmillan.

Cornell verse. Lyon, H: A. $1. Walton.
Cornwall, E: E. William Cornwall and his descendants. '01. '02(F1) 8°, $5. Tuttle, M. & T.

CORNWALL AND YORK, *Duke and Duchess of.*
Knight. With the royal tour. $2. Longmans.
Wallace. Web of empire: diary of the imperial tour. net, $6.50. Macmillan.

Coronation stone (The) of Great Britain and Israel. '02(Ag9) 12°, (News leaflet, no. 93.) pap., 50 c. Our Race.

CORPORATIONS.
American and Eng. corporation cases. v. 15. $4.50. Michie.
American corp. legal manual, 1902. $5. Corp. Leg. Co.
Boisot. By-laws of private corporations. $3. Keefe-D.
Clark *and* Marshall. Law of private corporations. v. 2. $6. Keefe-D.
Heath. Comparative advantages of the corp. laws of all the states and territories. n. p. Kennebec Journ.
Kansas. Statutes conc. corporations and insurance companies. $1; $1.25. Crane.
Maine. Laws conc. business corporations, annot. gratis. Kennebec Journ.
New York. Laws rel. to general, religious and non-business corporations. $1.50. $2. Banks & Co.
New York. Membership and religious corporations. $2.50; $3. Banks & Co.
New York. Statutory revision of laws affecting misc. corporations. $1.50. Banks & Co.
Smith. Cases on private corporations. net, $6. Harvard Law.
Walker. Taxation of corporations in the U. S. 25 c. Am. Acad. Pol. Sci.
White. On corporations. $5.50. Baker, V. & Co.
Wilgus. Law of private corporations. In 2 v. complete. $9; $10. Bowen-M.
See also Municipal corporations;—Securities.

CORRESPONDENCE.
See Letter-writing;—Letters;—Stenography.
Corrothers, Ja. D. Black cat club. '02(Mr22) D. net, $1. Funk.
Cosmos and the logos. Minton, H: C. net, $1.25. Westminster.
Cost of war, 1898-1902. Atkinson, E: 6 c. E: Atkinson.
Cosy corner ser. il. 50 c. L. C. Page.
—Barnett. Jerry's reward.
—Delano. Susanne.
—Dickens. Child's dream of a star.
—Fox. Little giant's neighbors.
—Johnston. Cicely.
Cotes, *Mrs.* Sara J. D. Those delightful Americans. '02(Je21) D. $1.50. Appleton.
Cotterell, E: The pocket Gray; or, anatomist's vade mecum. 5th rev. ed., ed. by C. H. Fagge. '02(F22) 16°, net, $1.25. Wood.
COTTON.
Whitworth. Cotton calculations. $1. Boardman.
Couch, A. T: Quiller-, ["Q."] The Westcotes. '02(Ap12) il. D. (Griffin ser.) $1. Coates.
Coulevain, Pierre de. Eve triumphant. '02 (My10) 12°, net, $1.20. Putnam.
Counsel of perfection. Harrison, *Mrs.* M. K. †$1. Appleton.
Country life lib. 8°, net, $3.75. Scribner.
—Jekyll, *comp.* Lilies for Eng. gardens.
COURAGE.
Wagner. Courage. $1.25. Dodd.
See also Heroes.
Courage of conviction. Sullivan, T. R. $1.50. Scribner.
Courier-Journal almanac for 1902. '02(Mr22) D. pap., 25 c. Courier-Journ.
Courtship of sweet Anne Page. Talbot, E. V. net, 40 c. Funk.
Cousin Maude and Rosamond. Holmes. *Mrs.* M. J. $1. Burt.
Cowles, H: C. Ecological rel. of the vegetation on the sand dunes of Lake Michigan. '01. '02(Ja11) 8°, (Hull botanical laboratory, no. 13.) pap., net, 75 c. Univ. of Chic.
Cox, *Mrs.* Ja. F., ["C."] Home thoughts. 2d ser. (Je7) D. net, $1.20. Barnes.
Crabb, Wilson D. Culture history in the Chanson de Geste-Aymeri de Narbonne. '02(Mr22) 8°, pap., net, $1.25. Univ. of Chic.
Craddock, C: Egbert, *pseud.* *See* Murfree, M. N.
Crane, Wa. Bases of design. 2d ed. '02 (Ap26) il. 12°, $2.25. Macmillan.
Crane, Wa. Line and form. Cheaper ed. '02 (My3) il. 12°, $2.25. Macmillan.
Craque o' Doom. *See* Catherwood, *Mrs.* M. H.
Craufurd, H. J. Field training of a company of infantry. '02(Ap12) S. $1. Longmans.
Crawford, F. M. Works. New uniform ed. '02(F15) 3 v., 12°, ea., $1.50. Macmillan.
Crawford, F. M. In the palace of the king. Limited pap. ed. '02(Mr8) 12°, (People's lib., no. 27.) pap., 50 c. Am. News.
Crawford, J: J. Negotiable instruments law. 2d ed. '02(Ap12) O. $2.50. Baker, V. & Co.
Crawford, T. D., *rep.* *See* Arkansas. *Sup. ct.* Repts.
Crawley, Ernest. The mystic rose: primitive marriage. '02(Mr22) 8°, net, $4. Macmillan.
Crayon, Jos. P. Rockaway records of Morris county, N. J., families. '02(Jl5) 12°, $3. Rockaway.
Creamer, E: S. The Orphean tragedy. '02 (Mr29) D. $1. Abbey Press.
Creation, re-creation. *See* Lemcke, E. E:
CREDIT.
Laughlin. Credit. *50 c. net. Univ. of Chic.
See also Banks and banking;—Money.
Credit of the county. Norris, W: E: †$1; 50 c. Appleton
CREDIT RATINGS.
See United Merc. Agency.
CREEDS.
See Apostles' creed;—Catechisms.
Creighton, M. The church and the nation; ed. by L. Creighton. '01. '02(Ja11) D. $2. Longmans.
Creighton, M. Thoughts on education. '02(Je7) D. net, $1.60. Longmans.
Cresee, F. A. Practical pointers for patentees. '02(Ag9) 16°, *$1 net. Munn.
Crew, H:, *and* Tatnall, Rob. R. Laboratory manual of physics. '02(F1) 12°, net, 90 c. Macmillan.
Crile, G: W. Research into certain problems rel. to surgical operations. '02(F15) il. 8°, net, $2.50. Lippincott.
CRIME AND CRIMINALS.
Hall. Crime in its relation to social progress. net, $3; $3.50. Macmillan.
See also London police cts.;—Prisons.
CRIMINAL LAW.
Book of forms to be used with the study of criminal procedure in the Univ. of Mich. 60 c. Bliss & A.
Clark. Hand-bk. of criminal law. $3.75. West Pub.
Kenny. Outlines of criminal law. *$2.50. Macmillan.
Pattison. Instructions in criminal cases passed upon by the cts. of Mo. $5. Gilbert Bk.
See also Crime and criminals;—Evidence;—Jury; —*also* names of states.
Crimson wing. Taylor, H. C. C. $1.50. H. S. Stone.
Cripps, Wilfred J. Old English plate: its makers and marks. New il. lib. ed. '01. '02(Ja11) facsimiles, 8°, net, $13.50. Scribner.
CRISES.
See Finance.
Crissey, Forrest. In Thompson's woods: [poems.] '01. '02(Mr1) 16°, bds., $1. Blue Sky Press
CRITICISM.
Arnold. Essays in criticism. $1. Burt.
Bourne. Essays in hist. criticism. net, $2. Scribner.
See also Literature.
Crockett, S: R. The dark o' the moon. '02 (Mr29) il. D. $1.50. Harper.
Croft, Victor E. *See* Brown, C: F.
Croker, *Mrs.* Bertha M. The cat's paw. '02 (F1) D. (Select novels.) $1; pap., 50 c. Lippincott.
Cromptons (The). Holmes, M. J. †$1. G: W. Dillingham.
CROMWELL, Ol.
Adams. Shall Cromwell have a statue? 25 c. Lauriat.
Payn. Cromwell on foreign affairs. net, $1.25. Macmillan.

CROMWELL.—*Continued.*
Quayle. King Cromwell. net, 25 c. Jennings.

CROMWELL, T:
Merriman. Life and letters of Thomas Cromwell. 2 v. $6. Oxford Univ.

Cronholm, Neander N: Hist. of Sweden. '02 (Ap26) 2 v., il. 8°, $5. N. N: Cronholm.

Crosby, Ernest. Captain Jinks, hero. '02 (Mr8) D. $1.50. Funk.

Crosland, T. W. H. The unspeakable Scot. '02(Jl19) D. **$1.25 net. Putnam.

Cross-bench views of current church questions. Henson, H. H. $4. Longmans.

Cross of Christ in Bolo-land. Dean, J: M. net, $1. Revell.

Crothers, T. D. Morphinism and narcomania from opium, cocain, etc. '02(Mr29) 12°, $2. Saunders.

Crowell, J. F. Present status and future prospects of Am. shipbuilding. '02(Mr22) 8°, (Pub. of the soc., no. 325.) pap., 15 c. Am. Acad. Pol. Sci.

Crowest, F: J. Story of the art of music. '02 (Jl19) il. T. (Lib. of useful stories.) **35 c. net. Appleton.

Crowley, Ma. C. Heroine of the strait. '02 (Ap19) il. D. $1.50. Little, B. & Co.

Crowning of flora. Kellogg, A. M. 15 c. Kellogg.

Crozier, Hugh V. Temperance and the Anti-Saloon League. '01. '02(Mr29) 16°, 15 c. Barbee & S.

Cruger, *Mrs.* Julia S., ["Julien Gordon."] World's people. '02(Jl12) D. †$1.50. J. F. Taylor.

Cruger, *Mrs.* Van Rensselaer. *See* Cruger, *Mrs.* J. S.

Cruickshank, J. W. *and* A. M. Umbrian towns. '02(Mr22) S. (Grant Allen's hist. guide books to the principal cities of Europe.) net, $1.25. Wessels.

Cruise of the "Enterprise." Kaler, J. O. $1.50. W. A. Wilde.

Cruising in the West Indies. Stokes, A. P. **$1.25 net. Dodd.

Crumrine, Boyd. Courts of justice, bench and bar of Washington Co., Pa. '02(Ag9) il. 8°, $4; mor., $6. Wash. Bar Assoc.

CRYSTALS.
See Mineralogy.

Cub's career. Wheeler, H. $1. Abbey Press.

Cuentos selectos. S. pap., 35 c. W: R. Jenkins.
—Trueba. El molinerillo. (4.)

Cuffel, C: A. Durrell's Battery in the Civil War. '02(Mr22) il. O. subs., $2. C: A. Cuffel.

Cullen, C. L. More ex-tank tales. '02(Ap5) 12°, $1. Ogilvie.

Cullens, F: B. Where the magnolias bloom. '02(Mr1) D. 50 c. Abbey Press.

Culley, Fk. C., ["Major Clinton."] Barbara. '01. '02(Mr8) il. 12°, $1.25. F. C. Culley.

Culp, H: T. Reuben Green's experience in a large city. '02(Ag2) il. 16°, pap., 25 c. H: T. Culp.

CULTURE.
Blackie. On self-culture. 35 c. Phonograph.

Culture history in the Chanson de Geste-Aymeri de Narbonne. Crabb, W. D. net, $1.25. Univ. of Chic.

CUMBERLAND PRESBYTERIAN CHURCH.
See Presbyterian church.

Cumming, A. N. Public house reform. '01. '02(Ja11) 12°, (Social sci. ser.) $1. Scribner.

Cumming, R. C. *See* New York Laws; Membership and relig. corps.

Cummins, Harle O. Welsh rarebit tales. '02(Je7) il. D. $1.25. Mutual Bk.

CUNEIFORM WRITING.
See Inscriptions.

Cunningham, Dan. J:, *ed.* Text-book of anatomy. '02(Ag16) il. 8°, *$9 net; shp., $10 net; hf. mor., $11 net. Macmillan.

Cuppy, H. A., *ed.* Pictorial natural history. '01. '02(Ap12) il. Q. (Farm and fireside lib., no. 199.) $1. Crowell & K.

Curle, J. H. Gold mines of the world. '02 (Jl12) 4°, $3.50. Engineering.

Curschmann, H. *See* Osler, W:, *ed.*

Curtis, Is. G. Left-overs made palatable. '02 (F15) il. D. oilcloth, $1. Judd.

Curtiss, S: I. Primitive Semitic religion today. '02(Je7) il. 8°, net, $2. Revell.

Curwen, J: S. Studies in worship music, chiefly congregational singing. 1st ser. 3d ed., rev. and enl. '02(Mr8) 12°, $1.75. Scribner.

Cushing, Fk. H. Zuñi folk tales. '01. '02 (Ja25) O. net, $3.50. Putnam.

Cushman, Herb. E. Truth in Christian science. '02(My17) D. 60 c. J. H. West.

Cust, A. M. Ivory workers of the Middle Ages. '02(Mr8) il. 12°, (Handbooks of the great craftsmen.) $2. Macmillan.

Cust, Lionel. Desc. of the sketch-book by Sir Anthony Van Dyck. '02(Mr22) 4°, $17.50. Macmillan.

Cust, Lionel, *ed.* National portrait gallery. Ed. de luxe. In 2 v. v. 1. '02(Mr1) 4°. subs., complete work, net, $30. Cassell.

Custis, G: W. P. Life of George Washington. '02(Je28) 12°, (Biographies of famous men.) $1. Donohue.

Cutter, Sa. J., *comp.* Conundrums, riddles, puzzles and games. Rev., enl. ed. '02 (Ap5) S. 50 c.; pap., 25 c. Otis.

CYANIDE PROCESS.
James. Cyanide practice. $5. Engineering.
See also Gold.

CYCLOPAEDIAS.
See Encyclopædias.

Cyr, Ellen M. Advanced first reader. '02 (Ag30) il. S. (Art ser.) 35 c. Ginn.

Cyr, Ellen M. Cyr readers. bks. 7 and 8. '01. '02(Mr8) il. 12°, ea., 45 c. Ginn.

Cyrano de Bergerac. Rostand, E. 50 c. W: R. Jenkins.

Da Costa, J: C., *jr.* Clinical hematology: guide to the examination of the blood. '01. '02(Ja11) il. col. pls. 8°, net, $5. Blakiston.

Daddy's girl. Smith, *Mrs.* E. T. $1. Burt.

Dadson, A. J. Evolution and its bearing on religion. '02(Ap5) net, $1.25. Dutton.

Dail, C. C. Sunlight and shadows. '02(Je21) il. 8°, $1.50. Hudson-K.

Daily praise: texts and hymns for every day. '02(F8) 32°, 15 c.; 20 c.; 25 c. Revell.

Dainty dishes for slender incomes. New ed. '02(My24) 12°, net, 50 c. New Amsterdam.

Dainty ser. 16°, pap., 50 c. Dutton.
—Smith. Lost Christmas.

DAIRY.
Blake. Common sense ideas for dairymen. $1. Coates.
Russell. Outlines of dairy bacteriology. $1. H. L. Russell.
Dalby, W: E. Balancing of engines. '02 (Mr22) O. $3.75. Longmans.
Dale, Alan, *pseud.* *See* Cohen, A. J.
Dale, Lucy. Principles of Eng. constitutional history. '02(Ag30) D. $1.50. Longmans.
Daley, Jos. G. Cassock of the pines, and other stories. '02(Ap12) il. D. $1. W: H. Young.
Dallin, *Mrs.* Colonna M. Sketches of great painters for young people. '02(Je28) il. D. 90 c. Silver.
Dalman, Gustav. Words of Jesus, considered in the light of post-Biblical Jewish writings and the Aramaic language. '02 (Ag23) 8°, *$2.50 net. Scribner.
Dalton, Test. Role of the unconquered. '02 (F8) D. $1.50. G: W. Dillingham.
Daly, Ida M. Advanced rational speller '02(Je7) S. 25 c. B: H. Sanborn.
DALZIEL BROTHERS.
Brothers Dalziel: record of work, 1840-1890. net, $6.50. Dutton.
DAMAGES.
Mechem. Case on the law of damages. net, $4. West Pub.
Dame, Arthur K. *See* Nebraska. Law of probate.
Dame, Lorin L., *and* Brooks, H: Handbook of the trees of New England. '02(F15) il. D. $1.35. Ginn.
Damsel (A) or two. Moore, F. F. $1.50. Appleton.
Dana, Fs. The decoy. '02(Mr8) 12°, $1.50. Lane.
Danaher, Alb. J. *See* New York. Amendments.
DANCING.
Quick. Guide to ball-room dancing. 50 c.; 25 c. Donohue.
Dandelion. Lovejoy, E. M. W. $1. Abbey Press.
Danger of youth. Jordans, J. 15 c. Herder.
Dangerous trades. Oliver, T. *$8 net. Dutton.
Dangers of spiritualism, by a member of the Soc. of Psychical Research. '02(Je14) il. 8°, net, 75 c. Herder.
DANIEL.
Anderson. Daniel in the critics' den. net, $1.25. Revell.
Daniel Everton, volunteer-regular. Putnam, I. net, $1.20. Funk.
Dante Alighieri. Divine comedy: [prose tr.] by C: E. Norton. New rev. ed. '02(Mr22) O. $4.50; hf. cf. or hf. polished mor., $9.75. Houghton, M. & Co.
DANTE ALIGHIERI.
Boccaccio *and* Aretino. Earliest lives of Dante. 75 c. Holt.
Toynbee. Dante studies and researches. net, $3.50. Dutton.
Wright. Dante and the Divine comedy. net, $1. Lane.
D'Anvers, N., *pseud.* *See* Bell, *Mrs.* N. R. E. M.
Darby, Ja. E. Analysis of the Acts and Epistles of the New Testament. '02(Jl12) D. leatherette, 25 c. J. E. Darby.

Dark Continent. *See* Harding, W:
Dark o' the moon. Crockett, S: R. $1.50. Harper.
Darkie ways in Dixie. Richard, M. A. $1. Abbey Press.
Darkwood (The) tragedy. '02(Je14) 12°, $1.25. Neale.
Darley Dale, *pseud.* *See* Steele, F. M.
Darrow, Clarence S. A Persian pearl, and other essays. '02(My24) O. $1.50. Ricketts.
Daskam, Josephine D. Madness of Philip, and other tales of childhood. '02(Ap26) il. 12°, $1.50. McClure, P.
Daskam, Josephine D., *comp.* Best nonsense verses. '02(My10) 16°, bds., 50 c. W: S. Lord.
Datchet, C: Morchester: story of Am. society. '02(Ap26) D. net, $1.20. Putnam.
Daudet, A. Belle-Nivernaise; ed., with notes and vocab., by J. Boïelle. Rev. ed. '02 (Ag30) il. 16°, (Modern lang. ser.) 30 c. Heath.
Daudet, A. Tartarin de Tarascon. (C. Fontaine.) '02(Mr8) il. D. 45 c. Am. Bk.
Daughters of the Revolution. Thayer, S. H: $1. Abbey Press.
Davenport, B: R. Blood will tell. '02(Je14) 12°, $1.50. Caxton Bk.
Davenport, Fs. H: Diseases of women. 4th ed., rev. and enl. '02(Mr22) il. 12°, net, $1.75. Lea.
Davenport, J: G. The fulfilment. '02(My17) D. net, 40 c. Dutton.
Davey, J: The tree doctor. '02(Jl12) il. O. $1. J: Davey.
David Elginbrod. Macdonald, G: $1. Burt.
Davidson, *Mrs.* H. A. Study of Idylls of the king. '02(Mr8) S. pap., 50 c. Mrs. H. A. Davidson.
Davidson, Lillias C. Confessions of a matchmaking mother. '02(My17) D. $1.50. J. F. Taylor.
Davidson, Marie A. The two Renwicks. '02(Je7) D. $1.50. Neely.
Davies, Gerald S. Franz Hals. '02(Ag16) il. 8°, *$14 net. Macmillan.
Davis, E: P. Mother and child. '02(Ag2) il. 12°, **$1.50 net. Lippincott.
Davis, H: T. Coals from the altar. '02 (Ag23) D. 75 c.; pap., 20 c. Knapp.
Davis, R: H. Ranson's folly. '02(Jl12) il. D. †$1.50. Scribner.
Davis, Stanton K. As nature whispers. '02 (Mr29) 16°, 50 c. Alliance.
Davis, W: M. Elem. physical geography. '02(My24) D. $1.40. Ginn.
Davis, W: S. Belshazzar. '02(Jl5) il. D. †$1.50. Doubleday, P.
Davison, C: S. Selling the bear's hide, and other tales. '02(Jl19) il. S. $1. Nassau Press.
Davitt, Michael. Boer fight for freedom. '02(Je7) il. O. net, $2. Funk.
Dawes, *Mrs.* S. E. Stories of our country. v. 1, 2. '02(Ag2) sq. S. ea., 40 c. Educ. Pub.
Dawes, T. R. Bilingual teaching in Belgian schools. '02(Jl12) 12°, (Cambridge Univ. Press ser.) *50 c. net. Macmillan.
Dawson, J: J. Voice of the boy. '02(Ag2) 12°, pap., 25 c. Kellogg.
Day, Holman F. Pine tree ballads. '02 (Jl19) il. D. **$1 net. Small.

FICTION.
Burton. Forces in fiction. net, $1. Bowen-M.
Cody. Sel. from the world's greatest short stories. net, $1. McClurg.
Nield. Guide to best hist. novels and tales. net, $1.75. Putnam.
Wegelin. Early Am. fiction, 1774-1830. net, $2. O. Wegelin.
See also Fables;—Fairy tales;—Legends.

Fidler, T. C. Calculations in hydraulic engineering. pt. 2, Hydro-kinetics. '02(Ap26) O. (Civil engineering ser.) $3. Longmans.

Fiedler, A. Studies from the nude human figure in motion. '02(Jl5) pls. f°, $12. Hessling.

Field, Eug. Nonsense for old and young. '01· '02(Mr29) il. D. 50 c. Dickerman.

Field, J: E: Saint Berin, the apostle of Wessex. '02(Je7) 12°, $1.50. E. & J. B. Young.

Field book of American wild flowers. Mathews, F. S. net, $1.75. Putnam.

FIELD FAMILY.
Pierce. Field genealogy. 2 v. $10. Conkey.

Field, forest and garden botany. *See* Leavitt, R. G.

Field training of a company of infantry. Craufurd, H. J. $1. Longmans.

Fielde, Adele M. Political primer of New York city and state. [New rev. ed.] '02 (Mr22) S. 75 c.; pap., 50 c. League for Pol. Educ.

Fielding, H: Journal of a voyage to Lisbon. Special ed. '02(Jl19) 8°, bds., **$5 net. Houghton, M. & Co.

Fields, Eliz. Freedom in marriage. '02 (Ag2) D. 50 c. Abbey Press.

Fields, factories, and workshops. Kropotkin, *Prince* P: A. net, 90 c. Putnam.

Fifth string. Sousa, J: P. $1.25. Bowen-M.

Fifty Puritan ancestors. Nash, E. T. $5. Tuttle, M. & T.

Fighting bishop. Hopkins, H. M. $1.50. Bowen-M.

Fillis, Ja. Breaking and riding; with military commentaries. '02(My10) il. 8°, net, $5. Scribner.

FINANCE.
Burton. Financial crises, and periods of industrial and commercial depression. net, $1.40. Appleton.
Norton. Statistical studies in N. Y. money-market. net, $1.50; net, $1. Macmillan.
See also Money.

Finck, H: T. Romantic love and personal beauty. New ed. '02(Mr1) 8°, net, $2. Macmillan.

Find the church. Poland, W: net, 5 c. Herder.

Findlay, J. J. Principles of class teaching. '02(Je28) 12°, (Manual for teachers.) net, $1.25. Macmillan.

FINE ART.
Cust. Desc. of the sketch-book by Sir Anthony Van Dyck. $17.50. Macmillan.
Cust, *ed.* National portrait gallery. v. 1. subs., for complete work, net, $30. Cassell.
Gore. Dutch art as seen by a layman. n. p. Holland-Am.
Van der Kellen. Works of Michel Le Blond. net, $30; net, $35. Dodd.
See also Anatomy for artists;—Architecture;—Artists;—Book illustrations; — Ceramics;—Decoration and ornament;—Drawings;—Engravers and engraving;—Lace; — Music; — Painting;—Photography;—Venus di Milo.

Finegan, T: E. Text-book on New York school law. '02(Ag9) D. $1. H: B. Parsons.

FINLAND.
De Windt. Finland as it is. net, $3. Dutton.
Frederiksen. Finland, its public and private economy. $2. Longmans.

Finn, Fs. J. "But Thy love and Thy grace." $1. Benziger.

FIREARMS.
See Rifle.

FIREMEN.
See Engineering.

Fireside ser. See Burt's.

Fireside university of modern invention, etc., for home circle study. McGovern, J: $2.50; $3.75. Union Pub.

Firey, M. J. **Infant salvation**. '02(F1) D. net, $1.20. Funk.

First aid in accidents. Dickson, C: R. net, 50 c. Revell.

First yearbook of the National Society for the scientific study of education. pts. 1, 2. '02(Ag16) O. pap., ea., *50 c. net. Univ. of Chic.

First years of the life of the redeemed after death. Ulyat, W: C. $1.25. Abbey Press.

Firth, Annie. Cane basket work. 1st and 2d ser. '02(Je21) il. 12°, ea., 60 c. Scribner.

Fisguill, R: Mazel. '02(Ap26) D. $1.50. H. S. Stone.

Fish, A. L. Calisthenic dict.: terms used in Am. gymnasia. '02(My10) D. pap., $1. Seminar.

FISH AND FISHING.
Gregg *and* Gardner. Where, when, and how to catch fish on the east coast of Fla. $4. Matthews-N.
Johnson. Forest, lake and river: fishes of N. E. and eastern Canada. 2 v. per set, $300; $500. F. M. Johnson.
Jordan *and* Evermann. American food and game fishes. net, $4. Doubleday, P.
Turner. Giant fish of Fla. **$3.50 net. Lippincott.
See also Salmon:—Trout.

Fisher, Amos T., *and* Patterson, M. J. Elements of physics. '02(My24) il. D. 60 c. Heath.

Fisher, Herb. How to build a model yacht. '02(Ap26) il. f°, ("How-to" ser.) $1. Rudder.

Fisher, J: I. **Added interest tables.** Rev. ed. '02(Mr29) 8°, $2.50. J: I. Fisher.

Fisher, J: I. **20th century interest tables.** '02(Mr29) 12°, $2.50. J: I. Fisher.

Fisher, Ma. Gertrude Dorrance. '02(Ap12) D. $1.50. McClurg.

Fiske, G: B., *comp.* Poultry appliances. '02 '02(Ag2) 12°, 50 c. Judd.

Fiske, G: B., *comp.* Poultry architecture. (Ag30) il. D. 50 c. Judd.

Fiske, G: B., *comp.* **Prize gardening.** '01-'02(Ja4) il. 12°, $1. Judd.

Fiske, J: Works. Ed. de luxe. '02(Jl19) 24 v., 8°, subs., ea., **$5 net; ¾ levant, ea., $10 net. Houghton, M. & Co.

Fitch, Eug., ["Ironquill."] Some of the rhymes of Ironquill. 11th ed. '02(Jl5) D. $1.50. Putnam.

Fitch, W: C. Captain Jinks of the Horse marines. '02(Ap19) il. O. $1.25. Doubleday, P.

Fitchett, W: H: Tale of the great mutiny. '01. '02(Ja11) 12°, $1.50. Scribner.
Fitzgerald, E: Poetical and prose writings. '02(Mr15) 7 v., large 8°, subs., regular lim. ed., per v., $6; hand-made pap. ed., per v., $12.50; Jap. ed., per v., $35. Doubleday, P.
Fitzpatrick, T: King of Claddagh. '01. '02 (Ja11) 8°, net, $1.25. Herder.
Five little Peppers abroad. Lothrop, *Mrs.* H. M. net, $1.10. Lothrop.
Five Stuart princesses. Rait, R. S. net, $3.50. Dutton.
Flagg, I: Writer of Attic prose: models from Xenophon. '02(Ap19) D. $1. Am. Bk.
FLAGS.
Ames. Etiquette of yacht colors; yacht flags and their use. 25 c. Annin.
Flanagan's educational ser. S. Flanagan.
—Peterson. First steps in Eng. composition. 35 c.
Flanagan's home and school series for young folks. il. S. 50 c. Flanagan.
—Shepard. Life on the farm.
Flanagan's plan book ser. il. sq. D. pap., 15 c. Flanagan
—George. Little journey to Belgium and Denmark. (v. 5, 8.)—Switzerland. (v. 5, 9.)
—Whitcomb. Little journey to Italy. (v. 5, 5.)—Scotland. (v. 5, 4.)
Fleming, G: Operative veterinary surgery. v. 2. '02(Ap26) 8°, net, $3.25. W: R. Jenkins.
Fleming, T: Around the "Pan" with Uncle Hank. '01. '02(Ja4) il. 12°, $2. Nutshell.
Fleming, W: F. *See* Voltaire.
Fleming, W: H. Shakespeare's plots. '02 (Ja25) O. $1.80. Putnam.
Fleming, Wymble. Glimpses of South Africa in peace and in war. '02(Mr22) 12°, $3. Dominion.
Flesh and the devil. Cole, H. L. $1.50. Neely.
Fletcher, Banister. Hist. of architecture on the comparative method. 4th ed., rev. and enl. '01. '02(Ja11) il. 8°, net, $7.50. Scribner.
Fletcher, W: I., *and* Bowker, R: R., *eds.* Annual literary index, 1901. '02(Ap12) Q. net, $3.50. Pub. Weekly.
Flick, Alex. C. *See* Anderson, J: J.
Flight of the *Swallow*. Morgan, E. M. 50 c. Pott.
Flint, C: R., Hill, J. J., [*and others.*] The trust: its book; ed. by J. H. Bridge. '02 (Je7) D. net, $1.25. Doubleday, P.
Floating treasure. Castlemon, H. $1. Coates.
FLORENCE.
Ross. Florentine villas. $25. Dutton.
Ruskin. Mornings in Florence. $2. Abbey Press.
Florer, Warren W. Biblische geschichten und kapitel aus Weizsäcker's und Luther's Bibelübersetzungen. '01. '02(Mr8) S. 40 c. Wahr.
Florida. Index to the laws of a general nature, by T: P. Warlow. '02(Je14) O. pap., $1. W. F. Barnes.
Florilegium Latinum; ed. by F. St. John Thackeray and E. D. Stone. 12°. Lane.
—Pre-Victorian poets. $2.50. (1.)
—Victorian poets. net, $2. (2.)
Flower, Elliott. Policeman Flynn. '02(Mr1) il. D. $1.50. Century Co.
Flower and thorn. Whitby, B. $1.50. Dodd.

FLOWERS.
Bridgeman. Flower gardening. 50 c. Coates.
Mathews. Field book of Amer. wild flowers. net, $1.75. Putnam.
Parsons, F. T. According to season. net, $1.75. Scribner.
Parsons, M. E. Wild flowers of Cal. $2. Payot.
Watson. Flowers and gardens. $1.50. Lane.
See also Botany;—Gardening;—Lilies;—Orchids;—Roses;—Window gardening.
Flowers of Parnassus; ed. by F. B. Money-Coutts. il. 16°, net, 50 c.; leath., net, 75 c. Lane.
—Way, *comp.* Reliques of Stratford-on-Avon. (16.)
Flynt, Josiah, *pseud.* *See* Willard, J. F.
Fogg's ferry. Callahan, C. E. 75 c.; 25 c. Laird.
FOLK-LORE.
Cushing. Zuñi folk tales. net, $3.50. Putnam.
See also Fairy tales.
Folk tales of Napoleon. Kennan, G: *$1 net. Outlook.
Folks, Homer. Care of destitute, neglected, and delinquent children. '02(F15) 12°, (American philanthropy of the nineteenth century.) net, $1. Macmillan.
Folly in the forest. Wells, C. †$1. Altemus.
Folwell, A. P. Sewerage. 5th ed. '02(Ap19) 8°, $3. Wiley.
Folwell, A. P. Water-supply engineering. 2d ed. '02(F1) 8°, $4. Wiley.
FOOD.
Horridge. Dynamic aspects of nutrition. $1.50. Wood.
See also Cookery;—Diet;—Digestion;—Fruit;—Hygiene;—Meat;—Temperance.
Fool (The). Carson, W: H. $1.50. G: W. Dillingham.
Fool's errand. Tourgée, A. W. $1.50. Fords.
Fool's year. Cooper, E: H. $1; 50 c. Appleton.
Foote, *Mrs.* Ma. H. The desert and the sown. '02(Je7) D. $1.50. Houghton, M. & Co.
For a young queen's bright eyes. Savage, R: H. $1.25; 50 c. Home.
For the colours. Hayens, H. $2. Nelson.
Foraminifera (The). Chapman, F: $3.50. Longmans.
FORCE.
See Aerodynamics.
Forces in fiction. Burton, R: net, $1. Bowen-M.
Ford, Ja. T. The dying lamp, the glorious dawn. '02(Ag9) 12°, 75 c. Brown & D.
Ford, P. L., *ed.* Journals of Hugh Gaine, printer. '02(My17) 2 v., il. 8°, net, $15; Jap. pap., net, $25. Dodd.
Ford, Sheridan. Art of folly: [poems.] '02 (Jl12) 8°, **$3 net. Small.
Foreign freemasonry. O'Connor, D. M. 5 c. Kilner.
FOREIGN MISSIONS.
See Missions.
Foreign trade requirements; pub. annually with quarterly supp. '02(Jl5) Q. $10. Lewis.
Foreign view of England. Saussure, C. de. net, $3. Dutton.
Forest, lake and river. Johnson, F. M. $300; $500. F. M. Johnson.

DIPLOMACY.
See Eastern question.
Direct answers to plain questions for Am churchmen. Scadding, C: net, 50 c. Whittaker.
DIRECTORIES.
See names of places and subjects.
DISEASE.
See Pathology.
DISSECTION.
Howes. Atlas of practical elem. zootomy. net, $3.50. Macmillan.
See also Anatomy;—Autopsy;—Vivisection.
Dissertationes Americanæ; classical philology. O. pap. Scott, F. & Co.
—Hellems. Lex de imperio Vespasiani. 50 c. (1.)
Distinctive marks of the Episcopal church. McCormick, J: N. 25 c. Young Churchman.
District of Columbia. *Ct. of appeals.* Repts. (C: C. Tucker.) v. 18. '02(Mr1) O. shp., $5. Lowdermilk.
District of Columbia. Laws rel. to negotiable instruments. '02(Ap26) S. pap., 20 c. Lowdermilk.
Ditmars, Raymond L. *See* Baskett, J. N.
Divine comedy. *See* Dante Alighieri;—*also* Wright, W. J. P.
DIVINE HEALING.
Henley. Divine healing. 75 c.; 10 c. Knapp.
Divine key of the Revelation. Brown, W: E. v. 2. $1.50. Armstrong & R.
Divine language of celestial correspondence. Turnbull, C. $2. Alliance.
Divine religion of humanity. Wilson, C. D. net, 20 c. Presb. Bd.
DIVORCE.
See Marriage.
Dix, Beulah M., *and* Harper, Carrie A. The beau's comedy. '02(Mr29) il. D. $1.50. Harper.
Dix, Dorothy, *pseud.* *See* Gilmer, E. M.
Dixon, T:, *jr.* The leopard's spots. '02 (Mr22) il. D. $1.50. Doubleday, P.
Dmitriev-Mámonóv, A. I., *and* Zdziarski, A. F., *eds.* Guide to the great Siberian railway; Eng. tr. by L. Kúkol-Yasnopólsky. '02(Jl19) il. 8°, *$3.50 net. Putnam.
Doane, W: C. Rhymes from time to time. '01. '02(Mr22) 12°, $1.50. Albany Diocesan Press.
Dobbins, Fk. Story of the world's worship. '02(Mr22) 12°, $2.25; hf. mor., $3.25. Dominion.
Dobson, Austin. Miscellanies. (2d ser.) '01. '02(Mr22) D. net, $1. Dodd.
DOCTRINES.
See Theology.
Dods, M. Parables of our Lord. New issue. '02(Ap12) 12°, $1.50. Whittaker.
Dog-day journal. Drum, B. 50 c. Abbey Press.
Dog of Flanders. La Rame, L. de. 15 c. Houghton, M. & Co.
DOGMA.
See Theology.
Dole, N. H., *ed.* *See* Schiller, J. C. F. v.
Dollar, J: A. W. Operative technique for veterinary surgeons. '02(Jl12) 8°, $3.75. W: R. Jenkins.
Dombey and son. *See* Dickens, C:
DOMESTIC ECONOMY.
Ellsworth. Queen of the household. $2.50. Ellsworth.

DOMESTIC ECONOMY.—*Continued.*
Lush. Domestic economy for scholarship and certificate students. net, 60 c. Macmillan.
Seeley. Cook book; with chap. on domestic servants, etc. net, $2; net, $3. Macmillan.
See also Cookery;—Gardening.
Don Carlos. *See* Schiller, J. C. F. v.
Don Quixote. *See* Cervantes Saavedra.
Donnelly, Fs. P. Imitation and analysis; Eng. exercises. '02(Jl12) S. 60 c. Allyn & B.
Dorothy South. Eggleston, G: C. $1.50. Lothrop.
Dorothy Vernon of Haddon Hall. Major, C: $1.50. Macmillan.
Doty, Alvah H. Manual of instruction in the principles of prompt aid to the injured. 4th ed., rev. and enl. '02(Jl19) il. D. $1.50. Appleton.
Doty, Douglas Z. Pictures of paint-box town. '02(Ag9) il. oblong 16°, bds., $1. Dutton.
Double-barrelled detective story. Clemens, S: L. $1.50. Harper.
DOUBT.
See Faith;—Skepticism.
Douglas, Langton. Fra Angelico. 2d rev., enl. ed. '02(Ag16) il. 8°, *$6 net. Macmillan.
DOUGLAS, Stephen A.
Brown. Stephen Arnold Douglas. net, 65 c.; net, 50 c. Houghton, M. & Co.
Douglass, Fk. A. Colonel Harold de Lacey. '02(Je7) D. $1.25. Neely.
DOUW, G.
Martin. Gerard Douw. $1.75. Macmillan.
Down historic waterways. Thwaites, R. G. net, $1.20. McClurg.
Doyle, A. C. Hound of the Baskervilles. '02(Ap19) il. D. $1.25. McClure, P.
Doyle, A. C. War in South Africa. '02 (Jl5) 12°, 10 c. McClure, P.
Doyle, Sherman. Presbyterian home missions. '02(Je21) il. D. net, $1. Presb. Bd.
Dragons of the air. Seeley, H. G. net, $1.40. Appleton.
DRAMA AND DRAMATISTS.
Schelling. The Eng. chronicle play. net, $2. Macmillan.
See also Actors and actresses; — Opera; — *also* names of dramatists.
DRAWING.
Augsburg. Drawing. 3 bks. ea., 75 c. Educ. Pub.
Crane. Line and form. $2.25. Macmillan.
See also Anatomy for artists;—Decoration and ornament;—Mechanical drawing;—Perspective;—Topographical drawing.
DRAWINGS.
Underwood, *il.* Some pretty girls. $3; $5. Quail & W.
DREAMS.
See Fortune-tellers.
Dresser, Fk. F. Employers' liability, in N. Y., Mass., Ind., Ala., Colo., and Eng. '02 (My24) O. shp., $6. Keefe-D.
Dresser, Horatio W. Book of secrets, with studies in self-control. '02(Mr8) D. net, $1. Putnam.
Dresser, Julius A. True history of mental science; rev., with notes, by H. W. Dresser. [New issue.] '02(Mr22) D. 20 c. Alliance.

Dressler, Flo. Feminology. '02(F15) il. O. $3. Dressler.
Drewitt's dream. Alden, W: L. $1; 50 c. Appleton.
Drift of song. Blanden, C: G. *50 c. net. W: S. Lord.
DRILLS (*fancy*).
Harper. Moral drill for the school-room. $1. Kellogg.
Hatch. Zobo patriotic drill. 15 c. Hints.
Drink, temperance and legislation. Shadwell, A. $1.75. Longmans.
DRINKS.
See Beverages.
Droch, *pseud. See* Bridges, R.
Drude, Paul. Theory of optics; fr. the Germ. '02(My10) O. $4. Longmans.
Drum, Blossom, *pseud.* Dog-day journal. '02(F22) D. 50 c. Abbey Press.
Drummers' yarns. Schofield, R. J. 25 c. Excelsior.
Drummond, Hamilton. The Seigneur de Beaufoy. '02(My17) il. D. $1.50. L. C. Page.
DRUMMOND, H:
Simpson. Henry Drummond. 75 c. Scribner.
Twing. Henry Drummond in spirit life. 10 c. Star.
Drummond, Josiah H., *comp.* Maine masonic text-book. 5th ed. '02(Je7) 12°, $1.40; leath. tuck, $1.50. Berry.
DU BARRY, *Mme.*
Morehead. Madame Du Barry. 50 c. Donohue.
Du Bois, A: J. Mechanics of engineering. v. 1. '01. '02(Ja18) il. 4°, $7.50; v. 2. (Je21) $10. Wiley.
Du Bois, E. F., *comp.* Harvard Univ. songs. '02(Je28) 12°, $1.50. Ditson.
Duchess (The), *pseud. See* Hungerford, *Mrs.* M. H.
DUCK SHOOTING.
See Shooting.
Duckwitz, Louise C. What Thelma found in the attic. [New issue.] '01. '02(Mr22) il. O. $1. Alliance.
Dudeney, *Mrs.* H: Spindle and plough. '02 (Mr22) D. $1.50. Dodd.
Dudevant, *Mme.* A. L. A. *See* Sand, G:
Dudley, E. C., *ed.* Gynecology; with collab. of W: Healy. '02(Ag30) il. 12°, (Practical medicine ser. of year books, v. 4.) $1.50. Year Bk.
Duff, Arch. Theology and ethics of the Hebrews. '02(My10) D. (Semitic ser.) net, $1.25. Scribner.
Duff, E: M., *and* Allen, T: G. Psychic research and gospel miracles. '02(Mr22) D. net, $1.50. Whittaker.
Dugan, M. C., *comp. See* United States naval exam. papers.
Duggan, S. P. H. Eastern question. '02 (Jl12) 8°, (Columbia Univ. studies in history, economics and public law, v. 14, no. 3.) pap., *$1.50 net. Macmillan.
Duguid, C: Story of the Stock Exchange [London.] '02(Mr15) il. 12°, net, $2. Dutton.
Duhring, L: A., Lydston, G. F., *and others.* Syphilis. '02(Ap12) 12°, net, $1. Treat.
Dukesmith, Fk. H. The air brake, its use and abuse. '02(Je21) il. D. $1. F. H. Dukesmith.

Dull Miss Archinard. Sedgwick, A. D. $1.50. Century Co.
Dumas, Alex. Romances. Versailles ed. '02(Mr22) 40 v., il. 8°, subs., net, per v., $1.50. Little, B. & Co.
Dumas, Alex. The King's gallant; tr. by H: L. Williams. '02(Je7) il. D. $1. Street.
Dumas, Alex. Napoleon; adapt. and ed. by W. W. Vaughan. '02(Ap12) 12°, (Siepmann's elem. Fr. ser.) net, 50 c. Macmillan.
Dunbar, Paul L. Sport of the gods. '02(My10) D. $1.50. Dodd.
Dunn, Arch., *jr.* New ideas on bridge. '02 (Mr8) 16°, 50 c. Scribner.
Dunn, F. Veterinary medicines. New rev. ed. '01. '02(F22) 8°, $3.75. W: R. Jenkins.
Dunning, W: A. Hist. of political theories. '02(F22) 8°, net, $2.50. Macmillan.
Dupre, A., *and* Hake, H. W. Manual of inorganic chemistry. '01. '02(F15) 12°, $3. Lippincott.
Durand, W: F: Practical marine engineering. '02(Ap5) il. 8°, $5. Marine Engineering.
Durège, H. Elements of the theory of functions of a complex variable; ed. by G: E. Fisher and I: J. Schwatt. '01. '02(Ja4) 8°, net, $2. Macmillan.
Durham, J: Stevens. *See* Miller, J. M.
Durrell's Battery. *See* Cuffel, C: A.
Dustin, Eddie. The make good book of parodies. '01. '02(Ja11) S. pap., 50 c. E. Dustin.
Dutch art as seen by a layman. Gore, J. H. n. p. Holland-Am.
Dutiful child. Wetzel, F. X. 40 c. Herder.
Dutto, L. A. Life of Bartolomé de las Casas and first leaves of Am. ecclesiastical history. '02(Mr8) 8°, net, $1.50. Herder.
Duxbury doings. Le Row, C. B. $1. Burt.
Dwight, C: A. S. Railroading with Christ. '02(Je21) il. D. $1. Am. Tr.
DYEING.
Rawson, *and others.* Dictionary of dyes, mordants, and other compounds. net, $5. Lippincott.
Dyer, T: H:, *and* Hassall, Arth. History of modern Europe fr. fall of Constantinople. 3d ed., rev. v. 6; with bibliog. and index. '02(Mr8) 12°, net, $2. Macmillan.
Dying lamp, the glorious dawn. Ford, J. T. 75 c. Brown & D.
Dynamic aspects of nutrition. Horridge, F. $1.50. Wood.
DYNAMICS.
See Aerodynamics; — Electricity; — Mechanics; — Physics.
DYNAMOS AND MOTORS.
Arnold. Armature windings of direct current dynamos. $2. Van Nostrand
Bubier. How to build dynamo-electric machinery. $2.50. Bubier.
Harmsworth, *and others.* Motors and motor driving. $3.50; $5. Little, B. & Co.
Sheldon *and* Mason. Dynamo electric machinery. 2 v. ea., net, $2.50. Van Nostrand.
Wiener. Calculation of dynamo-electric machines. $3. Elec. World.
See also Cars.
Eadie, J: Biblical cyclopædia. New ed. '01. '02(Mr1) il. 8°, net, $3.75. Lippincott.
Eagle lib. S. pap. Brooklyn Eagle.
—Childe. Water exploring. 10 c. (v. 17, 10.)

Eagle lib.—Continued.
—Visitor's guide to Paris. 10 c. (v. 17, 7.)
See also Brooklyn Eagle library.
Eakle, Arth. S. Colemanite from So. California. '02(Je14) O. (Univ. of Cal.; bull. of dept. of geology, v. 3, no. 2.) pap., 15 c. Univ. of Cal.
EAR.
Bacon. Manual of otology. *$2.25 net. Lea.
Brühl *and* Politzer. Atlas epitome of otology. net, $3. Saunders.
Gradle. Diseases of the nose, pharynx and ear. net, $3.50. Saunders.
Wood, *and others, eds.* Eye, ear, nose and throat. $1.50. Year Bk.
Earle, Stephen C. Rutland home of Maj. Gen. Rufus Putnam. '01. '02(Mr8) il. O. pap., 30 c., bds., 50 c. S. C. Earle.
Early Am. fiction. Wegelin, O. net, $2. O. Wegelin.
Early Christianity and Paganism. Spence, H: D. M. *$4 net. Dutton.
Early Eng. printed books in the Univ. Lib., Cambridge. '02(Ag2) 8°, (Cambridge Univ. Press ser.) *$5 net. Macmillan.
EARTH.
Ball. Earth's beginning. net, $1.80. Appleton.
See also Geodesy.
Earth in rel. to contagia. Poore, G: V. $1.75. Longmans.
East of the barrier. Graham, J. M. net, $1. Revell.
EASTER.
Swartz. Easter and the resurrection. net, 15 c. Revell.
EASTERN QUESTION.
Duggan. Eastern question. *$1.50 net. Macmillan.
Eastman, Eph. R: Poems. '02(Je7) S. $1. Hadley Pr.
Easy lessons in mechanical drawing. *See* Meyer, J. G. A.
Ebersole, E. C. *See* Iowa. Encyclopedia of law.
Eccles, W. M. Hernia. '02(My10) il. 8°, $2.50. Wood.
Ecclesiazusæ (The). *See* Aristophanes.
Eckley, W: T: *and* Corinne B. Regional anatomy of the head and neck. '02(Mr1) il. 8°, net, $2.50. Lea.
Eclectic manual. See Scudder's.
ECLECTIC MEDICINE.
Mundy. Eclectic practice in diseases of children. net, $2.50. Scudder.
Eclectic school readings. D. Am. Bk.
—Bartlett. Animals at home. 45 c.
—Bradish. Stories of country life. 40 c.
—McCullough. Little stories for little people. 25 c.
ECOLOGY.
See Botany.
Economic interpretation of history. Seligman, E: R. A. **$1.50 net. Macmillan.
Economic tangles. Grenell, J. $1. Purdy.
ECONOMICS.
See Political economy.
Eddy, R:, *ed. See* Universalist register.
Edgerly, Webster. Natural reader. '02(Je28) 12°, $1.50. Ralston.
EDGEWOOD, Pa.
Pennsylvania. Health ordinance of the borough of Edgewood. $1. Nicholson.
Edison, T: A. Telegraphy self-taught. '02 (Je21) il. D. $1. Drake.
Editorial echoes. Payne, W: M. net, $1. McClurg.
Edle blut (Das). Wildenbruch, E. A. v. 30 c. Am. Bk.
Edmunds, Alb. J., *tr. See* Dhammapada.
EDUCATION.
Creighton. Thoughts on education. net, $1.60. Longmans.
De Montmorency. State intervention in Eng. education. net, $1.50. Macmillan.
Dewey. Educational situation. net, 50 c. Univ. of Chic.
Fennell, *and others.* Notes of lessons on Herbartian methods. $1.10. Longmans.
First year book of the Nat. Soc. for the scientific study of education. pts. 1, 2. ea., *50 c. net. Univ. of Chic.
Henderson. Education and the larger life. net, $1.30. Houghton, M. & Co.
Kemp. Hist. of education. net, $1.25. Lippincott.
Lang, *ed.* Educational creeds of the 19th century. 75 c. Kellogg.
Seeley. Foundations of education. $1. Hinds.
Taylor, *ed.* Practical school problems. v. 1, pt. 1. 30 c. [W: B. Harison] Soc. Sch. Problems.
Young. Some types of modern educ. theory. net, 25 c. Univ. of Chic.
See also Business education;—Child study;—Children;—Examinations;—Home study;—Kindergarten;—Knowledge;—Memory;—Psychology;—Schools;—Students;—Teachers and teaching;—*also* National Herbart Soc.
Educational foundations of trade and industry. Ware, F. net, $1.20. Appleton.
EDWARD I., *King of England.*
Jenks. Edward Plantagenet, (Edward I.) net, $1.35; net, $1.60. Putnam.
EDWARD VII., *King of England.*
Carman. Ode on the coronation of King Edward. net, $1. L. C. Page.
Pascoe. Pageant and ceremony of the coronation of their majesties King Edward and Queen Alexandra. net, $1.50. Appleton.
Watson. Ode on day of the coronation of King Edward VII. net, $1; net, $3.50. Lane.
Edwards, Owen M. Wales. '02(Jl19) il. D. (Story of the nations ser., no. 62.) **$1.35 net; hf. leath., $1.60 net. Putnam.
Efird, C. M., *rep. See* South Carolina. *Sup. ct.* Repts.
Effront, Jean. Enzymes and their applications; Eng. tr. by S: C. Prescott. v. 1. '02(F1) 8°, $3. Wiley.
Egan, Maurice F. Belinda. '02(F8) D. $1. Kilner.
Eggleston, G: C. American immortals; record of men whose names are inscribed in the Hall of Fame. '02(Mr22) 8°. $10. Putnam.
Eggleston, G: C. Bale marked circle X. '02 (My24) D. net, $1.20. Lothrop.
Eggleston, G: C. Dorothy South. '02(Mr29) D. $1.50. Lothrop.
EGYPT.
Babcock. Letters from Egypt and Palestine. net, $1. Scribner.
Baedeker, *ed.* Egypt. net, $4.50. Scribner.

EGYPT.—*Continued.*
Barber. Mechanical triumphs of ancient Egyptians. net, $1.25. Dodd.
Budge. Hist. of Egypt. v. 1. $1.25. Oxford Univ.
De Clifford. Egypt, the cradle of ancient masonry. $10; $12. N. F: De Clifford.
Dicey. Story of the Khedivate. net, $4. Scribner.
Guide to Palestine and Egypt. net, $3.25. Macmillan.
See also Cairo.
Ehrlich, *Mrs.* **Bertha.** Light of our spirit. '02(Mr29) S. 25 c. B. Ehrlich.
Einstein, Lewis. Italian Renaissance in England: studies. '02(Ap12) il. 12°, (Columbia University studies in comparative literature.) net, $1.50. Macmillan.
Elbertus, *Fra, pseud. See* **Hubbard, E.**
Eldridge, E: California girl. '02(Ag30) D. $1.50. Abbey Press.
Eldridge, E: H. Hypnotism. '02(Ag30) 16°, (Popular handbooks.) 50 c. Penn Pub. Co.
Eldridge, J. L. What think ye of Christ, etc.: [poems.] '01. '02(Mr1) il. D. $1. Abbey Press.

ELECTIONS.
Jewett, *comp.* Manual for election officers and voters. $2; $1.50. M. Bender.
New York. Jewett's primary election law. 50 c. M. Bender.

ELECTRIC ENGINEERING.
Parr. Electrical engineering testing. net, $3.50. Van Nostrand.

ELECTRIC LIGHT.
Houston *and* Kennelly. Electric arc lighting.—Incandescent lighting. ea., $1. McGraw.

ELECTRIC MEASUREMENT.
Hobbs. Arithmetic of electrical measurements. 50 c. Van Nostrand.
See also Galvanometer.

ELECTRIC MOTORS.
See Dynamos and motors;—Cars.

ELECTRICITY.
American electrical cases. v. 7. $6. M. Bender.
Atkinson. Electrical and magnetic calculations. net, $1.50. Van Nostrand.
Beaton. Vest-pocket compend of electricity. 75 c.; 50 c. Laird.
Bubier. Experimental electricity. $1. Bubier.
Clarke. A B C of electrical experiments. $1. Excelsior.
Fowler. Electricity. 50 c. Penn Pub. Co.
Hadley. Practical exercises in magnetism and electricity. net, 60 c. Macmillan.
Jackson. Elem. text-book on electricity and magnetism, and their applications. net, $1.40. Macmillan.
Munro. Nociones de electricidad. 40 c. Appleton.
Practical electricity. $2. Cleveland Armature.
Swoope. Lessons in practical electricity. net, $2. Van Nostrand.
Webber. Graduated coll. of problems in electricity. $3. Spon.
Wolcott. On the sensitiveness of the coherer. 20 c. Univ. of Wis.
Wordingham. Central electrical stations. $7.50. Lippincott.
See also Alternating currents;—Dynamos and motors;—Electric light;—Roentgen rays;—Telephone.

Elementary electro technical ser. sq. S. $1. McGraw.
—Houston *and* Kennelly. Alternating electric currents.—Electric arc lighting.—Electric incandescent lighting.—Electric telephone.
Elements and notation of music. McLaughlin, J. M. 55 c. Ginn.
Eliot, C: W. Charles Eliot, landscape architect. '02(Ag23) il. 8°, **$3.50 net. Houghton, M. & Co.

ELIOT, George.
Stephen. George Eliot. net, 75 c. Macmillan.
Eliot, H: W., *jr. See* **Hall, F: G.**
Elisabeth, *Madame.* **Memoir and letters of** Madame Elisabeth, sister of Louis XVI. '02(Mr8) il. 8°, (Versailles hist. ser.) subs., per v., $6; ¾ leath., per v., $9. Hardy, P. & Co.
Elizabeth and her German garden. '02(My10) 12°, (Home lib.) $1. Burt.
Elizabethan prayer-book and ornaments. Gee, H: net, $1.25. Macmillan.
Ellacombe, H: N. In my vicarage garden. '02 (My24) 12°, net, $1.50. Lane.
Ellicott, J: M. Life of John Ancrum Winslow, Rear Admiral U. S. N. '02(Ja25) O. $2.50. Putnam.
Elliot, D. G. *See* Roosevelt, T.
Elliot lectures. *See* Orr, J.
Elliott, C: B. Law of insurance. '02(Ap19) O. shp., $4. Bowen-M.
Elliott, Jonathan. Debates on the federal constitution. '01. '02(Mr1) 5 v., 8°, net, $10; shp., net, $12. Lippincott.
Ellis, E: S. Life of William McKinley. '01. '02(F15) 12°, (Undine lib., no. 9.) pap., 25 c. Street.
Ellsworth, Tinnie, [**"*Mrs.* M. W. Ellsworth."**] Queen of the household. New century ed., rev. and enl. '02(Ja18) 12°, $2.50. Ellsworth.
Ellwood, C: A. **Aristotle as a sociologist.** '02(Mr22) 8°, (Pub. of the soc., no. 332.) pap., 15 c. Am. Acad. Pol. Sci.

ELMA, N. Y.
Jackman. Hist. of the town of Elma, Erie Co., N. Y., 1620-1901. $3. Hausauer.
Elmore, Ja. B. A lover in Cuba, and poems. '01. '02(Mr8) il. S. $1. J. B. Elmore.

ELOCUTION.
Birbeck. Elocution self-taught. $1. Wagner.
Ryan. Elocution and dramatic art. 75 c. Angel Press.
See also Orators and oratory;—Preaching;—Readers and speakers;—Voice.

ELOQUENCE.
See Orators and oratory;—Preaching.
Elwell, J. B. Bridge; its principles and rules of play. '02(Ap19) S. net, $1.25. Scribner.
Ely, R. T. *See* Vincent, J: M.

EMBLEMS.
See Tombstones.

EMBRYOLOGY.
Keith. Human embryology and morphology. $4.50. Longmans.
Emerson, E: R. Story of the vine. '02 (Ap12) D. net, $1.25. Putnam.
Emerson, Edn., *jr.* Hist. of the nineteenth century, year by year. '02(Ag30) 3 v., il. 12°, $3. Collier.

Emerson, *Mrs.* Ellen R. Nature and human nature. '02(Mr15) D. net, $1.25. Houghton, M. & Co.
Emerson, R. W. [Essays.] '01. '02(Ap5) S. (Little masterpieces.) 50 c. Doubleday, P.
Emerson, R. W. Nature. '02(Jl12) 12°, (Home lib.) $1. Burt.
Emerson, R. W. Representative men. '02 (My17) 12°, (Home lib.) $1. Burt.
Emerson, Willis G: Buell Hampton. '02 (My10) D. $1.50. Forbes.
Emerton, Ja. H. Common spiders of the U. S. '02(Jl12) il. sq. D. *$1.50 net. Ginn.
Emery, W: D'E. Handbook of bacteriolog. diagnosis, incl. instructions for clinical examination of the blood. '01. '02(F15) 12°, net, $1.50. Blakiston.
Empire of business. Carnegie, A. subs., $3. Doubleday, P.
Employers' liability. Dresser, F. F. $6. Keefe-D.
En son nom. Hale, E: E. $1. W: R. Jenkins.

ENCYCLOPAEDIAS.
Appleton's annual cyclopædia, 1901. subs., $5; $6; $7; $8. Appleton.
Century dict. and cyclopedia. 10 v. subs., $80-$150. Century Co.
Cheyne *and* Black. Encyc. Biblica. v. 3. subs., net, $5; net, $7.50. Macmillan.
Collier's new encyclopedia. 16 v. per set, $20. Collier.
Eadie. Biblical cyclopædia. net, $3.75. Lippincott.
Holst, *ed.* Teachers' and pupils' cyclopædia. v. 1-3. $12.75. Holst.
Morris. 20th century encyclopædia. $3.50; $4.25; $5.50. Winston.
Sellow. Three thousand sample questions. 50 c. Bellows.
Singer, *and others, eds.* Jewish encyclopædia. v. 2. subs., per v., $7; $9. Funk.
Spofford *and* Annandale, *eds.* xxth century cyclopædia and atlas. 8 v. $20; $26. Gebbie.
See also under special subjects.

Engels, F: Socialism; tr. by E: Aveling. '01. '02(F1) D. (Arm and hammer ser.) 50 c. N. Y. Labor News.

ENGINEERING.
Baker. Municipal engineering and sanitation. net, $1.25. Macmillan.
Du Bois. Mechanics of engineering. v. 1. $7.50; v. 2. $10. Wiley.
Harcourt. Civil engineering as app. in construction. $5. Longmans.
Hawkins. Aids to engineers' examinations. $2. Audel.
Hawkins. Handbook of calculations for engineers and firemen. $2. Audel.
Problems in the use and adjustment of engineering instruments. $1.25. Wiley.
See also Architecture;—Bridges;—Electrical engineering;—Hydraulic engineering;—Irrigation;—Marine engineering;—Railroads;—Sanitary engineering;—Steam engine;—Surveying;—Water-supply.

Engineering Magazine. Index, 1896-1900; ed. by H: H. Supplee. '02(Mr1) 8°, $7.50. Engineering Mag.

ENGINES.
Dalby. Balancing of engines. $3.75. Longmans.
See also Corliss engine;—Steam engines.

ENGLAND.
Baldwin. Scutage and knight service in England. net, $1. Univ. of Chic.
Blauvelt. Development of cabinet government in England. net, $1.50. Macmillan.
Blomfield. Formal garden in England. $3. Macmillan.
Dale. Principles of Eng. constitutional history. $1.50. Longmans.
Einstein. Italian Renaissance in England. net, $1.50. Macmillan.
Hall. Society in the Elizabethan age. *$2.50 net. Dutton.
Honeyman. Bright days in merrie England. net, $1.50. Honeyman.
Jesse. Historical memoirs. 30 v. ea., $2.50; or set of 15 v., $37.40; $75. L. C. Page.
Lennox. Life and letters; also pol. sketch of the years 1760-1763. 2 v. net, $9. Scribner.
Lingelbach. Merchant adventurers, their laws and ordinances. $1.25. Univ. of Penn.: Longmans.
Lubbock. Scenery of England and the causes to which it is due. net, $2.50. Macmillan.
Macmillan's summary of Eng. history on the concentric plan; Senior. net, 15 c. Macmillan.
Maitland. Music in England in 19th century. net, $1.75. Dutton.
Medley. Student's manual of Eng. constitutional history. net, $3.50. Macmillan.
Mowry. First steps in the hist. of England. 70 c. Silver.
Rawnsley. Rambler's note-book at the Eng. lakes. $2. Macmillan.
Russell. Onlooker's note-book. net, $2.25. Harper.
Saussure. Foreign view of England in the reign of George I. and George II. net, $3. Dutton.
Traill *and* Mann, *eds.* Social England. v. 1. net, $4.50. Putnam.
Wyckoff. Feudal rel. between the kings of England and Scotland under the early Plantagenets. net, $1. Univ. of Chic.
See also Caroline, *Queen of England*;—Clayton-Bulwer treaty;—Edward I., *King of England*;—Edward VII., *King of England*;—Hampshire;—Henry V., *King of England*;—Hertfordshire;—Jesus (Society of);—London;—H. Malvern;—Peninsular war;—Waterloo;—Wessex.

English catalogue of books, for 1901. '02 (Mr15) O. pap., $1.50. Pub. Weekly.
English chronicle play. Schelling, F. E. net, $2. Macmillan.
English classics, star ser. il. D. Globe Sch. Bk.
—Shakespeare. Julius Cæsar. 32 c.
English composition. Thornton, G. H. 75 c. Crowell.
English essays. Hale, E: E., *jr.* 40 c. Globe Sch. Bk.
English girl in Paris. '02(My24) 12°, $1.50. Lane.

ENGLISH LANGUAGE.
Adler. Germ. and Eng. dictionary. pt. 1. $3.50. Appleton.
Aiton *and* Rankin. Exercises in syntax for summer schools, etc. 25 c. Hyde.
Beeman. Analysis of the Eng. sentence. 50 c. Flanagan.

ENGLISH LANGUAGE—*Continued.*
Blain. Syntax of the verb in Anglo-Saxon chronicle, 787-1001. net, 50 c. Barnes.
Chambers's twentieth century dict. of Eng. language. $1.50; $2. Lippincott.
Donnelly. Imitation and analysis: exercises based on Irving's sketch book. 60 c. Allyn & B.
Fernald, *ed.* Concise standard dict. of the Eng. language. 60 c. Funk.
Krüger *and* Smith. Eng.-Germ. conversation book. 25 c. Heath.
Lewis. Applied Eng. grammar. 2 pts., ea., *35 c. net; complete, *50 c. net. Macmillan.
Murray, *and others, eds.* New Eng. dictionary. v. 3, pts. 30-38. ea., 90 c. Oxford Univ.
Pinney. Spanish and English conversation. 1st, 2d bks. ea., 65 c. Ginn.
Rine. Essentials of our language. 75 c. Pacific Press.
Skinner *and* Burgert. Lessons in Eng. based upon principles of literary interpretation. 50 c. Silver.
Vories. Lab'y method of teaching Eng. and touch typewriting together. $1.25. Inland Pub.
Watrous. First year English. 75 c. Sibley & D.
Woodley *and* Carpenter. Foundation lessons in Eng. lang. and grammar. *65 c. Macmillan.

English law reports, for 1900. '01- '02(F15) 6 v., 8°, shp., $28.50. Little, B. & Co.

ENGLISH LITERATURE.
Andrews. Topics and ref. for the study of Eng. literature. 15 c. Hyde.
Chambers's cyclopædia of Eng. literature. v. 1. net, $5. Lippincott.
Chaucer. English of the XIVth century. 75 c. Ginn.
Marks. Brief hist. outline of Eng. literature. $1. J. A. Marks.
Moody. Hist. of Eng. literature. net, $1.25. Scribner.
Moulton, *and others, eds.* Lib. of literary criticism of Eng. and Am. authors. v. 3, 4. ea., $5; $6.50. Moulton Pub.
Phelps, *comp.* List of general reading, 1580-1902. net, 5 c. Pease-L.

English men of letters ser.; ed. by J: Morley. 12°, **75 c. net. Macmillan.
—Birrell. William Hazlitt.
—Stephen. George Eliot.

English pharisees, French crocodiles. Blouët, P. $1.25. Abbey Press.

English tales in verse. Herford, C: H. $1.50. Scribner.

Englishwoman's year book and directory, 1902; ed. by E. Janes. '02(F1) 12°, $1.50. Macmillan.

Engraved gems. Sommerville, M. net, $1.50. Biddle.

ENGRAVERS AND ENGRAVING.
Altdorfer. Little engravings classical and contemporary. no. 1. net, $1.50. Longmans.
Blake. Little engravings. no. 2. net, $1.50. Longmans.
Whitman. Print-collectors' handbook. net, $5. Macmillan.

Enoch Strone. Oppenheim, E. P. $1.50. G: W. Dillingham.

Enseñar á leer. Arnold, S. L. 40 c. Silver.

ENTERTAINMENTS.
Kellogg. Six musical entertainments. 15 c. Kellogg.
Nies. Deutsche gaben. 25 c.—Rosen im schnee. 50 c. Witter.
See also Drills.

ENTOMOLOGY.
See Insects.

ENZYMES.
Effront. Enzymes and their applications. $3. Wiley.

Eparchæan interval. Lawson, A. C. 10 c. Univ. of Cal.

EPHESIANS.
See Bible.

EPIGRAMS.
Antrim. Naked truths and veiled allusions. 50 c. Altemus.
Sappho. Odes, bridal songs, epigrams. (App. to pubs. for price.) Barrie.
Timby. Lighted lore for gentle folk. $2. Morningside.

EPISTLES (The).
See Bible.

Epstein, A. J. Tarquinius Superbus. '02 (My24) il. D. $1.25. Mutual Pub.

EPWORTH LEAGUE.
Kaufman *and* Nye. Notes on Epworth League prayer meeting topics. 15 c. Eaton & M.
Nicholson *and* Woods. Notes on Epworth League prayer meeting topics. 15 c. Eaton & M.

Epworth League reading course, 1902-1903. '02(Ag16) 3 v., S. $1. Eaton & M.

Epworth League year-book for 1902. '02 (Ja25) S. pap., net, 10 c. Eaton & M.

EQUATIONS.
Forsyth. Theory of differential equations. v. 4. net, $3.75. Macmillan.

EQUITY.
Ames. Equity jurisdiction. pt. 2. 75 c. Harvard Law.
See also Actions at law.

Erasmus, D. Select colloquies; ed. by M. Whitcomb. '02(Je7) D. (Sixteenth century classics.) $1. [Longmans;] Univ. of Penn.

Erdman, C: R. Ruling elder. '02(Je21) S. pap., 3 c. Presb. Bd.

Ernst, Harold C., *ed.* Animal experimentation. '02(Mr8) 8°, net, $1.50; pap., net, $1. Little, B. & Co.

Errand boy of Andrew Jackson. Stoddard, W: O. net, $1. Lothrop.

Ervin, Dayton. The hermitage and random verses. '02(Je7) S. $1. Grafton Press.

Esenwein, J. Berg. How to attract and hold an audience. '02(F1) D. $1. Hinds.

ESKIMOS.
See Innuit language.

ESSAYS.
Hale, *ed.* Amer. essays. 40 c. Globe Sch. Bk.
Hale, *ed.* Eng. essays. 40 c. Globe Sch. Bk.
Miles. How to prepare essays, [etc.] net, $2. Dutton.

Essays of Elia. *See* Lamb, C:

Estados Unidos. Constitucion: (Constitution of the U. S. in Spanish by C. Mexia.) '02 (Je7) 8°, $1. Cambridge.

Esther. Racine, J. 35 c. Holt.
ETHICS.
Gabirol. Improvement of moral qualities. net, $1.25. Macmillan.
Ladd. Philosophy of conduct. net, $3.50. Scribner.
Ritchie. Studies in political and social ethics. $1.50. Macmillan.
Schuyler. Systems of ethics. $1.50. Jennings.
See also Character;—Conduct of life;—Courage;—Crime and criminals;—Culture; — Fiction; — Law;—Utilitarianism.
Ethics in the school. Young, E. F. net, 25 c. Univ. of Chic.
ETHNOLOGY.
Hutchinson, *and others.* Living races of mankind. net, $5. Appleton.
See also Folk-lore;—Language.
ETIQUETTE.
Hollinshed. New century speaker, writer and etiquette. $1.50. Am. Bk. and Bible.
EUGENE, *Prince.*
Sybel. Prinz Eugen von Savoyen. net, 60 c. Macmillan.
EUROPE.
Case. European constitutional history. $1.50. Jennings.
Carpenter. Europe. 70 c. Am. Bk.
Dyer *and* Hassall. Hist. of modern Europe. v. 6. net, $2. Macmillan.
Helmolt, *and others, eds.* Hist. of the world v. 4. The Mediterranean countries $6. Dodd.
Northern Europe: Norway, Russia, the Netherlands, France, Germany and Switzerland. 30 c. Ginn.
Stedman. Complete pocket guide to Europe, 1902. $1.25. W: R. Jenkins.
See also names of countries.
Eustis, Edith. Marion Manning. '02(Je7) D. $1.50. Harper.
Euthyphro. Plato. $1. Am. Bk.
Eve of St. Agnes. *See* Keats, J:
Eve triumphant. Coulevain, P. de. net, $1.20. Putnam.
Evening Post. *See* New York Evening Post.
Evermann, B. W. *See* Jordan, D: S.
Eversley ser. 12°, $1.50. Macmillan.
—Jebb. Modern Greece.
Everybody's opportunity. Rowell, J. H. 10 c. Free Socialist.
EVIDENCE.
Ewbank. Indiana trial evidence. $6. Bowen-M.
Stephen. Digest of the law of evidence; adapt. to New Eng. states; Ohio. ea., $4. Dissell.
Trickett. Law of witnesses in Pa. $6. T. & J. W. Johnson
See also Logic.
EVOLUTION.
Baldwin. Development and evolution. **$2.60 net. Macmillan.
Beecher. Studies in evolution. net, $5. Scribner.
Conley. Evolution and man. net, 75 c. Revell.
Dadson. Evolution and its bearing on religion. net, $1.25. Dutton.
See also Embryology;—Religion and science.
Evolution of the Eng. Bible. Hoare, H. W. net, $2.50. Dutton.
Evolution of the Mason and Dixon line. Robinson, M. P. 25 c. Oracle Pub.

Evolutionary philosophy. Chamberlain, L. T. 50 c. Baker & T.
Ewart, W:, Murrell, W:, *and others.* Climates of London, and of the central and no. portions of England with those of Wales and Ireland. '02(My17) 8°, (Climates and baths of Great Britain, v. 2.) net, $4. Macmillan.
Ewbank, L: B. Indiana trial evidence '02 (My24) O. shp., $6. Bowen-M.
Ewing, *Mrs.* Juliana H. Benjy in beastland. New ed. '01. '02(F15) 16°, (Children's friend ser.) bds., 50 c. Little, B. & Co.
Ewing, *Mrs.* Juliana H. Jackanapes; [also] The brownies; ed. by H: W. Boynton. '02 (My17) S. (Riverside literature ser., no. 151.) pap., net, 15 c. Houghton, M. & Co.
Excelsior lib. O. pap., 25 c. Excelsior.
—Schofield, *comp.* Drummer's yarns and funny jokes. (67.)
EXECUTORS AND ADMINISTRATORS.
Gottsberger. Accountants' guide for executors, administrators, etc. $5. Peck.
Exiled by the world. Imhaus, E. V. $1.50. Mutual Pub.
EXPANSION (political).
Halstead. Pictorial hist. of America's new possessions, the Isthmian canals, and national expansion. $2.50; $3.50; $4.50. Dominion.
Expansion of gases by heat. Randall, W. W. $1. Am. Bk.
EXPERIMENTS.
See Physics.
EXPRESSION.
See Voice.
EYE.
Brown, C. H., *comp.* Optician's manual. 2 v. ea., $2. Keystone.
Greeff. Microscopic examination of the eyes. net, $1.25. Blakiston.
Jennings. Ophthalmoscopy. net, $1.50. Blakiston.
Parsons. Elem. ophthalmic optics. net, $2. Blakiston.
Wood, *and others, eds.* Eye, ear, nose and throat. $1.50. Year Bk.
F., A. M. Tales of my father. '02(Ap19) D. $2. Longmans.
FABLES.
Kleckner. In the misty realm of fable. $1. Flanagan.
Fables of the elite. Gilmer, E. M. $1. Fenno.
Fabre, J. H. Insect life; fr. the Fr.; ed. by F. Merrifield. '02(Ja18) il. 12°, $1.75. Macmillan.
FACE.
See Physiognomy.
Faciology. Stevens, L. B. 25 c. Donohue.
Facsimile reprint of early Canadian books. il. D. net. Congdon.
—Bosworth, *ed.* Hochelaga depicta; Montreal. $3; $4.50.
Facts and comments. Spencer, H. net, $1.20. Appleton.
Fagge, C: H. Text-book of medicine. 4th ed. '02(Ap5) 2 v., 8°, net, $6. Blakiston.
Failure of success. Howard, *Lady* M. $1.50. Longmans.
Failures of vegetarianism. Miles, E. H. net, $1.50. Dutton.
Fairbairn, And. M. Philosophy of the Christian religion. '02(Je7) 8°, net, $3.50. Macmillan.

Fairbanks, Harold W. Home geography for primary grades. '02(My3) il. sq. O. 60 c. Educ. Pub.
Fairchild, Lee. The tippler's vow. '01. '02 (Mr8) il. f°, bds., $10. Croscup.
Fairie, Ja. Notes on lead ores. '01. '02 (My10) D. net, $1. Van Nostrand.
Fairview's mystery. Marquis, G: H. 75 c. Abbey Press.
Fairy favorites. Perrault, C: 50 c. Little, B. & Co.
FAIRY TALES.
  Andersen. Fairy tales. 50 c.; 80 c. Macmillan.
  Andersen. Selected stories. 15 c. Lippincott.
  Brown. In the days of giants: Norse tales. net, $1.10. Houghton, M. & Co.
  O'Shea, *ed.* Old world wonder stories. 25 c. Heath.
  Phillips, *comp.* Indian fairy tales: folk-lore legends and myths. $1.50. Star Pub.
  Valentine, *comp. and ed.* Old, old fairy tales. $1. Burt.
  Yeats, *comp.* Irish fairy and folk tales. $1. Burt.
FAITH.
  Purves. Faith and life. net, $1.25. Presb. Bd.
  Rainsford. Reasonableness of faith. net, $1.25. Doubleday, P.
  See also Religion;—Theology.
Fales, W: E. S. Bits of broken china. '02 (My17) il. S. 75 c. Street.
Falkiner, C. L. Studies in Irish history and biog. mainly of the eighteenth century. '02(Mr8) O. $5. Longmans.
Fallon, Chris. *See* Pennsylvania. Conveyancing.
Fallows, S:, *ed.* Life of William McKinley; with short biog. of Lincoln and Garfield, and life of President Roosevelt. [Internat. memorial ed.] '01. '02(Ap12) 8°, $1.50; hf. mor., $2.25. Regan.
Familia de Alvareda. Caballero, F. 75 c. Holt.
FAMILIES.
  See Genealogy.
Famous children of literature ser.; ed. by F: L. Knowles. 12°, **75 c. net. Estes.
—Dickens. Little Nell.
—Stowe. Little Eva.
Famous Scots ser. 12°, 75 c. Scribner.
—Simpson. Henry Drummond.
Fanning, J: T: Practical treatise on hydraulic and water-supply engineering. 15th rev., enl. ed. '02(Ap5) il. 8°, $5. Van Nostrand.
Far past the frontier. Braden, J. A. $1. Saalfield.
Färber, Wilhelm. Commentar zum katechismus. '02(Je28) 12°, net, $1.50. Herder.
Fargo, Kate M. Songs not set to music. '02 (Mr15) D. $1. Abbey Press.
Farley, Jos. P. West Point in the early sixties, with incidents of the war. '02(Je14) il. O. net, $2. Pafraets.
Farm and fireside lib. il. Q. $1. Crowell & K.
—Cuppy, *ed.* Pictorial natural history. (199.)
—Herbert. Il. hist. of the civil war in America. 25 c. (197.)
Farmer, Ja. E. Brinton Eliot. '02(Je7) 12°. $1.50. Macmillan.
Farmer's school and the visit. Kellogg, A. M. 15 c. Kellogg.
FARMS AND FARMING.
  Barnard. Farming by inches.—My ten rod farm. ea., 40 c. Coates.
  Shepard. Life on the farm. 50 c. Flanagan.
  See also Irrigation.
Farquhar, A. B. Manufacturer's need of reciprocity. '02(Mr22) 8°, (Pub. of the soc., no. 330.) pap., 15 c. Am. Acad. Pol. Sci.
Farrington, Fk. Retail advertising for druggists and stationers. '01. '02(Ja11) D. net, $1. Baker & T.
Farson, C: T. *See* Illinois. Mechanics' lien law.
Fashions in literature. Warner, C: D. net, $1.20. Dodd.
FASTS AND FEASTS.
  See Easter;—Holidays;—Lent;—Sunday.
Father Manners. Young, H. $1. Abbey Press.
FATHERS.
  Swete. Patristic study. net, 90 c. Longmans.
Faust, C. A. Compendium of automatic pen lettering and designs. '01. '02(F1) obl. D. pap., complete bk., $1; alphabet pt., 75 c. Auto Pen.
Favor of princes. Luther, M. L. 50 c. Jamieson-H.
Favorite songs of love. Mason, J. F. $1.50-$5. Dodge.
Feasey, H: J. Monasticism: what is it? '02 (Mr8) 8°, net, $1. Herder.
Federal citations. *See* Ash, M.
Federal reporter. *See* United States.
Felt, Orson B. Parliamentary procedure. '02(Ag9) 12°, flex. leath., 75 c.; pap., 35 c. Hazlitt.
Feminology. Dressler, F. $3. Dressler.
FENELON, François.
  St. Cyres. Life of François Fenelon. net, $2.50. Dutton.
Fennell, M., *and others.* Notes of lessons on the Herbartian methods. '02(Mr22) D. $1.10. Longmans.
FERDINAND, *King of Spain.*
  Prescott. Ferdinand and Isabella, the Catholic. 3 v. net, $3. Macmillan.
FERMENTATION.
  Matthews. Manual of alcoholic fermentation. net, $2.60. Longmans.
  Oppenheimer *and* Mitchell. Ferments and their actions. net, $2.50. Lippincott.
  See also Bacteria.
Fernald, Ja. C., *ed.* Concise standard dict. of the Eng. language. '02(Ag2) S. 60 c. Funk.
FERNS.
  See Botany.
Ferry, I. I. Fonografia española. Rev. por L. Duque. '02(Ag2) 16°, *$1 net. Whitaker & R.
Fersen, *Count* Jean-Axel. Letters and papers; sel. pub. by his great-nephew, Baron R. M. Klinckowström. '02(Mr8) il. 8°, (Versailles hist. ser.) subs., per v., $6; ¾ leath., per v., $9. Hardy, P. & Co.
FEUDALISM.
  Seignobos. Feudal régime. 50 c. Holt.
  Wyckoff. Feudal rel. between the kings of England and Scotland under early Plantagenets. net. $1. Univ. of Chic.
  See also Middle Ages.
FEVER.
  See Malarial fever;—Typhoid fever.
Fickett, M. G., *comp.* *See* Stone, G. L.

FICTION.
Burton. Forces in fiction. net, $1. Bowen-M.
Cody. Sel. from the world's greatest short stories. net, $1. McClurg.
Nield. Guide to best hist. novels and tales. net, $1.75. Putnam.
Wegelin. Early Am. fiction, 1774-1830. net, $2. O. Wegelin.
See also Fables;—Fairy tales;—Legends.
Fidler, T. C. Calculations in hydraulic engineering. pt. 2, Hydro-kinetics. '02(Ap26) O. (Civil engineering ser.) $3. Longmans.
Fiedler, A. Studies from the nude human figure in motion. '02(Jl5) pls. f°, $12. Hessling.
Field, Eug. Nonsense for old and young. '01· '02(Mr29) il. D. 50 c. Dickerman.
Field, J: E: Saint Berin, the apostle of Wessex. '02(Je7) 12°, $1.50. E. & J. B. Young.
Field book of American wild flowers. Mathews, F. S. net, $1.75. Putnam.
FIELD FAMILY.
Pierce. Field genealogy. 2 v. $10. Conkey.
Field, forest and garden botany. *See* Leavitt, R. G.
Field training of a company of infantry. Craufurd, H. J. $1. Longmans.
Fielde, Adele M. Political primer of New York city and state. [New rev. ed.] '02 (Mr22) S. 75 c.; pap., 50 c. League for Pol. Educ.
Fielding, H: Journal of a voyage to Lisbon. Special ed. '02(Jl19) 8°, bds., **$5 net. Houghton, M. & Co.
Fields, Eliz. Freedom in marriage. '02 (Ag2) D. 50 c. Abbey Press.
Fields, factories, and workshops. Kropotkin, *Prince* P: A. net, 90 c. Putnam.
Fifth string. Sousa, J: P. $1.25. Bowen-M.
Fifty Puritan ancestors. Nash, E. T. $5. Tuttle, M. & T.
Fighting bishop. Hopkins, H. M. $1.50. Bowen-M.
Fillis, Ja. Breaking and riding; with military commentaries. '02(My10) il. 8°, net, $5. Scribner.
FINANCE.
Burton. Financial crises, and periods of industrial and commercial depression. net, $1.40. Appleton.
Norton. Statistical studies in N. Y. money-market. net, $1.50; net, $1. Macmillan.
See also Money.
Finck, H: T. Romantic love and personal beauty. New ed. '02(Mr1) 8°, net, $2. Macmillan.
Find the church. Poland, W: net, 5 c. Herder.
Findlay, J. J. Principles of class teaching. '02(Je28) 12°, (Manual for teachers.) net, $1.25. Macmillan.
FINE ART.
Cust. Desc. of the sketch-book by Sir Anthony Van Dyck. $17.50. Macmillan.
Cust, *ed.* National portrait gallery. v. 1. subs., for complete work, net, $30. Cassell.
Gore. Dutch art as seen by a layman. n. p. Holland-Am.
Van der Kellen. Works of Michel Le Blond. net, $30; net, $35. Dodd.
See also Anatomy for artists;—Architecture;—Artists;—Book illustrations;—Ceramics;—Decoration and ornament;—Drawings;—Engravers and engraving;—Lace;—Music;—Painting;—Photography;—Venus di Milo.

Finegan, T: E. Text-book on New York school law. '02(Ag9) D. $1. H: B. Parsons.
FINLAND.
De Windt. Finland as it is. net, $3. Dutton.
Frederiksen. Finland, its public and private economy. $2. Longmans.
Finn, Fs. J. "But Thy love and Thy grace." $1. Benziger.
FIREARMS.
See Rifle.
FIREMEN.
See Engineering.
Fireside ser. See Burt's.
Fireside university of modern invention, etc., for home circle study. McGovern, J: $2.50; $3.75. Union Pub.
Firey, M. J. **Infant salvation.** '02(F1) D. net, $1.20. Funk.
First aid in accidents. Dickson, C: R. net, 50 c. Revell.
First yearbook of the National Society for the scientific study of education. pts. 1, 2. '02(Ag16) O. pap., ea., *50 c. net. Univ. of Chic.
First years of the life of the redeemed after death. Ulyat, W: C. $1.25. Abbey Press.
Firth, Annie. Cane basket work. 1st and 2d ser. '02(Je21) il. 12°, ea., 60 c. Scribner.
Fisguill, R: Mazel. '02(Ap26) D. $1.50. H. S. Stone.
Fish, A. L. Calisthenic dict.: terms used in Am. gymnasia. '02(My10) D. pap., $1. Seminar.
FISH AND FISHING.
Gregg *and* Gardner. Where, when, and how to catch fish on the east coast of Fla. $4. Matthews-N.
Johnson. Forest, lake and river: fishes of N. E. and eastern Canada. 2 v. per set, $300; $500. F. M. Johnson.
Jordan *and* Evermann. American food and game fishes. net, $4. Doubleday, P.
Turner. Giant fish of Fla. **$3.50 net. Lippincott.
See also Salmon;—Trout.
Fisher, Amos T., *and* Patterson, M. J. Elements of physics. '02(My24) il. D. 60 c. Heath.
Fisher, Herb. How to build a model yacht. '02(Ap26) il. f°, ("How-to" ser.) $1. Rudder.
Fisher, J: I. **Added interest tables.** Rev. ed. '02(Mr29) 8°, $2.50. J: I. Fisher.
Fisher, J: I. **20th century interest tables.** '02(Mr29) 12°, $2.50. J: I. Fisher.
Fisher, Ma. Gertrude Dorrance. '02(Ap12) D. $1.50. McClurg.
Fiske, G: B., *comp.* Poultry appliances. '02 '02(Ag2) 12°, 50 c. Judd.
Fiske, G: B., *comp.* Poultry architecture. (Ag30) il. D. 50 c. Judd.
Fiske, G: B., *comp.* Prize gardening. '01· '02(Ja4) il. 12°. $1. Judd.
Fiske, J: Works. Ed. de luxe. '02(Jl19) 24 v., 8°, subs., ea., **$5 net; ¾ levant, ea., $10 net. Houghton, M. & Co.
Fitch, Eug., ["Ironquill."] Some of the rhymes of Ironquill. 11th ed. '02(Jl5) D. $1.50. Putnam.
Fitch, W: C. Captain Jinks of the Horse marines. '02(Ap19) il. O. $1.25. Doubleday, P.

Forest neighbors. Hulbert, W: D. net, $1.50. McClure, P.

FORESTS AND FORESTRY.
Gifford. Practical forestry. net, $1.20. Appleton.
See also Lumber;—Trees.

Forman, S. E. First lessons in civics. Penn. ed. '02(Je14) D. 60 c. Am. Bk.

FORMS (*in law*).
See Criminal law.

Forney, E: J. Inductive lessons, adpt. to Isaac Pitman phonography. '01- '02(Mr8) obl. 24°, pap., 80 c. State Normal Sch.

FORREST, Nathan B.
Mathes. General Forrest. net, $1.50. Appleton.

Forsyth, And. R. Theory of differential equations. v. 4. '02(My17) 8°, (Cambridge Univ. Press ser.) net, $3.75. Macmillan.

FORTUNE-TELLERS.
Mystic fortune teller, dream book and policy player's guide. 50 c.; 25 c. Donohue.
Zanciz. How to tell fortunes by cards. 25 c. Drake.

Fortune's wheel. Gray, M. $1. Abbey Press.

Fosdick, C: Austin. *See* Castlemon, H.

Fosdick, J. W. Honor of the Braxtons. '02 il. D. $1.50. J. F. Taylor.

Foster, Rob. V. The Lord's prayer. '02 (Mr22) S. pap., 10 c. Cumberland Press.

Foundations of belief. Balfour, A. J. net, $2. Longmans.

Foundations of education. Seeley, L. $1. Hinds.

Founders of the Mass. Bay Colony. Smith, S. S. *$5 net. Woodward & L.

Four old Greeks. Hall, J. 35 c. Rand, McN. & Co.

Fourcaut, A. *See* Silva, T.

Fourfold thoughts: four text books. '02(F8) $1. Revell.

Fowke, Gerard. Archæological history of Ohio. '02(Ag2) il. O. $5. [Smythe] Ohio Archæolog.

Fowler, Fk. H. Negatives of the Indo-European languages. '02(Mr22) 8°, pap., net, 50 c. Univ. of Chic.

Fowler, G: L. Electricity. '02(Ag30) il. 16°, (Popular handbooks.) 50 c. Penn Pub. Co.

Fowler, Gilbert J. Sewage works analyses. '02(Jl19) 12°, $2. Wiley.

Fowler, Harold N. Hist. of ancient Greek literature. '02(Mr29) il. D. (Twentieth century text-books.) net, $1.40. Appleton. '02(Ap12) 16°, $1. Benziger.

Fowler, W: W. More tales of the birds. '02 (Ap12) il. 12°, $1. Macmillan.

FOWLER FAMILY.
Arthur. Annals of the Fowler family. $3.50. Mrs. J. J. Arthur.

Fox, Emma A. Parliamentary usage for women's clubs. '02(My3) S. net, 65 c. Baker & T.

Fox, Fes. M. The little giant's neighbors. '02(Je28) il. D. (Cosy corner ser.) 50 c. L. C. Page.

Fox, G: H: Practical treatise on smallpox. '02(Ag2) col. pls., 8°, $3. Lippincott.

Fradenburgh, O. P. Twenty-five stepping stones toward Christ's Kingdom. '02(F8) O. $1. O. P. Fradenburgh.

France, Anatole. Monsieur Bergeret. '02 (Ap19) 12°, (Ser. of modern lang. text-books.) $1. Silver.

FRANCE.
Cæsar. Gallic war. $1.25. Am. Bk.
Mackinnon. Growth and decline of the Fr. monarchy. $7.50. Longmans.
See also Chartres;—Huguenots;—Paris;—Peninsular war;—Waterloo.

Francesca da Rimini. Morehead, G: 25 c. Ogilvie.

FRANCIS *of Assisi, St.*
Lady (The) Poverty: allegory conc. St. Francis of Assisi. net, $1.75. Tennant.
McIlvaine. St. Francis of Assisi. net, 85 c. Dodd.

Francis, *St.*, Third order of. *See* Kaercher, F. O.

Francis, *Mrs.* C. D. Weekly church teaching for the infants. '02(Je7) 32°, 25 c. E. & J. B. Young.

François, Victor E. Advanced Fr. prose composition. '02(My24) D. cl., 80 c. Am. Bk.

Frank Logan. Clay, *Mrs.* J: M. $1. Abbey Press.

FREDERICK *the Great.*
Macaulay. Frederick the Great. net, 40 c. Macmillan.
Schrader. Friedrich der Grosse und der Siebenjährige Krieg. net, 50 c. Macmillan.

Frederiksen, N. C. Finland, its public and private economy. '02(Ap19) O. $2. Longmans.

Frédérique. Prévost, M. $1.50. Crowell.

FREE THOUGHT.
Baur *and* Herbert. Free thinkers' manual. $4. Radical.

FREE TRADE.
See Tariff.

Free trade almanac, 1902. '02(Ja25) S. pap., 5 c. Am. Free Trade.

Freear, Rob. L: Shadow duellers. '02 (Mr22) D. net, 60 c. Blanchard.

Freedom in marriage. Fields, E. 50 c. Abbey Press.

Freeman, A. C. Law of void judicial sales. 4th ed., rev. and enl. '02(Ap12) O. shp., $4. Cen. Law Journ.

Freeman, A. C., *rep.* *See also* American state repts.

Freeman, Flora L. Religious and social work amongst girls. '02((Ap12) 12°, net, $1. Whittaker.

FREEMASONRY.
De Clifford. Egypt, the cradle of ancient masonry; with acct. of the antiquity of masonry. $10; $12. N. F: De Clifford.
Drummond, *comp.* Maine masonic text-book. $1.40; $1.50. Berry.
McGee. Exposition and revelation of ancient free and accepted masonry. $1. J. B. McGee.
O'Connor. Foreign freemasonry. 5 c. Kilner.

Freer, Romeo H., *rep.* *See* West Virginia. *Sup. ct. of appeals.* Repts.

FREIGHT.
See Tables.

Fremantle, T. F. Book of the rifle. '01- '02 (Ja4) il. O. $5. Longmans.

Fremeaux, Paul. With Napoleon at St. Helena; tr. by E. S. Stokoe. '02(Je28) 12°, net, $1.50. Lane.

French, Allen. The colonials. '02(F8) D. $1.50. Doubleday, P.

French, Lillie H. Hezekiah's wives. '02 (Ap5) il. D. net, 85 c. Houghton, M. & Co.

French, N. S. Animal activities. '02(Ap19) il. D. $1.20. Longmans.

French, S: Gibbs. Two wars: autobiog. of Gen. Samuel G. French; Mexican war; war between the states. '01. '02(Ja18) il. 12°, $2. Confederate Veteran.

French classics. See Macmillan's.

FRENCH LANGUAGE.

Alissas. Les histoires de tante. net, 40 c. Macmillan.

Baillot *and* Brugnot. French prose composition. 50 c. Scott, F. & Co.

Beaumarchais. Barbier de Séville and Lettres. 50 c. Scott, F. & Co.

Berlitz. Grammaire partique de la langue française. v. 3. 50 c. Berlitz.

Bowen. First scientific Fr. reader. 90 c. Heath.

Cameron. Elements of Fr. composition. 75 c. Holt.

Coppée. Morceau de pain. 25 c. W: R. Jenkins.

Dumas. Napoleon. net, 50 c. Macmillan.

France. Monsieur Bergeret. $1. Silver.

François. Advanced Fr. prose composition. 80 c. Am. Bk.

Hale. En son nom. $1. W: R. Jenkins.

Hennequin. French verbs. 65 c. Am. Bk.

Ingres. Cours complet de langue Fr. v. 1. net, $1.50. Univ. of Chic.

La Brète. Mon oncle et mon curé. 50 c. Am. Bk.

Renan. Souvenirs d' enfance et de jeunesse. 75 c. Heath.

Ségur. Les malheurs de Sophie. 45 c. Heath.

Voltaire. Zaïre and Epitres. 50 c. Scott, F. & Co.

Yersin. Phonorhythmic method of Fr. pronunciation, accent, diction; Fr. and Eng. $1.25. Lippincott.

FRENCH LITERATURE.

Crabb. Culture hist. in the Chanson de Geste-Aymeri de Narbonne. net, $1.25. Univ. of Chic.

FRENEAU, Philip.

Austin. Philip Freneau: life and times net, $2.50. Wessels.

FRESNO Co., Cal.

Hudson. California vineyards: scenes in Fresno Co. 35 c. H. B. Hudson.

Fretz, Lewis B. Bennie, the Pythian of Syracuse, and other titles. '01. '02(My24) S. $1. Scroll Pub.

Friars (The) must stay; repr. from *The Messenger*. '02(Ag30) O. pap., 5 c. Am. News.

Friedländer, L. Town life in ancient Italy; tr. by W: E. Waters. '02(Mr22) D. 75 c. B: H. Sanborn.

Friend of Nelson. Hutchinson, H. G. *$1.50 net. Longmans.

FRIENDS (Society of).

Myers. Quaker arrivals at Philadelphia, 1682-1750. $1.25. Ferris.

FRIENDSHIP.

Carpenter, *ed.* Ioläus; anthology of friendship. net, $1.75. Goodspeed.

Frisbie, H: S: Prophet of the kingdom. '02(Ap12) 12°, $1.25. Neale.

Frogs (The). *See* Aristophanes.

From switch to lever. Browne, G: W. 75 c. Street.

Frost, T: G. Treatise on guaranty insurance. '02(Ap12) O. shp., $5. Little, B. & Co.

Frost, W: D. Laboratory guide in elem. bacteriology. 2d rev. ed. '02(My24) il. 8°, $1.60. W: D. Frost.

FRUIT.

Goff. Lessons in commercial fruit growing. $1. Univ. Co-op.

Bridgeman. Fruit gardening. 50 c. Coates.

See also Apple;—Gardening;—Strawberry.

Fruit from the tree of life. Kohaus, H. M. 30 c. Alliance.

Frye, Alexis E. Grammar school geography. [New ed.] '02(My3) il. f°. $1.45. Ginn.

Frye, T. C. Development of the pollen in some asclepiadaceæ. '02(F15) 8°, (Cont. from the Hull botanical laboratory, no. 32.) pap., net, 25 c. Univ. of Chic.

FUEL.

See Coal;—Gas and gas-fitting.

Fulda, Ludwig. Der talisman; ed. by C. W: Prettyman. '02(Ap5) S. (Modern lang. ser.) 35 c. Heath.

Fulda, Ludwig. Unter vier Augen; [also,] Der prozess; ed. by W: A. Hervey. '02 (Jl12) S. *35 c. net. Holt.

Fulfilment (The). Davenport, J: G. net, 40 c. Dutton.

Fulham Palace Conference. Confession and absolution; ed. by H: Wace. '02(Ap26) O. net, $1. Longmans.

Fuller, Phœbe W. Shadows cast before. '02 (Ag9) 12°, $1.50. Abbey Press.

Fuller, W: Architecture of the brain. '02 (Mr1) il. 8°, net, $3.50. Fuller.

FUMIGATION.

Johnson. Fumigation methods. $1. Judd.

Funk, I: K., *and* Moses, M. J., *eds.* Standard first reader. '02(My17) sq. O. (Standard reader ser.) 35 c. Funk.

Funk, I: K., *and* Moses, M. J., *eds.* Teachers' manual for first reader. '02(My17) T. (Standard reader ser.) 50 c. Funk.

FUR TRADE.

Chittenden. Am. fur trade of the far west. 3 v. net, $10. F. P. Harper.

Furneaux, W: S. Elem. practical hygiene, (sec. 1.) '01. '02(Mr8) D. (Practical elem. science ser.) 90 c. Longmans.

Furneaux, W: S., *ed.* Popular mannikin. '02 (Ag9) obl. F. bds., *$1.50 net. Whittaker.

Fustel de Coulanges, N. D. The ancient city: study on the religion, laws, and institutions of Greece and Rome. (W. Small.) 10th ed. '01. '02(Je28) 12°, $2. Lee & S.

FUTURE LIFE.

Brooks. Progression to immortality. net, 50 c. Wessels.

Gladden. Practice of immortality. *25 c. net. Pilgrim Press.

Gregg. Dictum of reason on man's immortality. 50 c. Treat.

Hutton. The soul in the unseen world. net, $2. Dutton.

Momerie. Immortality. $1.50. Whittaker.

Ulyat. First years of the life of the redeemed after death. $1.25. Abbey Press.

See also Heaven;—Hell; — Resurrection; — Salvation;—Spiritualism.

Future of war. Bloch, I. S. 60 c. Ginn.
Gabelsberger Shorthand Society, *ed.* Reader to Henry Richter's graphic shorthand. '02 (Jl19) 16°, pap., 50 c. Int. News.
Gabirol, S. I. Improvement of moral qualities; pr. from an unique Arabic ms. '02 (Ap12) 8°, (Columbia Univ. Oriental studies, v. 1.) net, $1.25. Macmillan.
Gabriel, C: H., *comp.* Joyful praise. '02 (Je7) O. 30 c. Jennings.
Gaffield, Erastus C. A celestial message. Private ed. '02(Ap5) 12°, n. p. Lee & S.
Gage, Alfr. P. Introd. to physical science. Rev. ed. '02(Jl5) il. D. $1. Ginn.
Gage, S. H: The microscope. 8th ed., rev. and enl. '01· '02(Mr22) il. O. $1.50. Comstock Pub.

GAINE, Hugh.
Ford, *ed.* Journals of Hugh Gaine, printer. net, $15; net, $25. Dodd.

GAINSBOROUGH, T:
Bell. Thomas Gainsborough. $1. Macmillan.
Hubbard. Gainsborough. 25 c. Roycrofters.

GALLS.
Connold. British vegetable galls. net, $4. Dutton.

GALLSTONE.
Keay. Medical treatment of gall stones. net, $1.25. Blakiston.

Gallup, *Mrs.* Eliz. W. Bi-literal cipher of Sir Francis Bacon. 3d ed. '01· '02(F15) O. $3.75. Howard.
Gallup, *Mrs.* Eliz. W. Tragedy of Anne Boleyn: drama in cipher found in works of Sir Fs. Bacon. '01 '02(F15) O. $1.50. Howard.
Gallus, A., *pseud.* *See* Wisner, A.
Galt, Sterling, *comp.* Lent, the holy season. '02(Ap26) 12°, silk, $1. Neale.
Galton, Arth. Our attitude toward Eng. Roman Catholics and the papal court. '02 (My10) 12°, net, $1. Dutton.

GALVANOMETER.
Nichols. The galvanometer. $1. Spon.

GALVESTON.
Halstead. Galveston. $1.50; $2.25. Dominion.

Game of love. Paterson, W: R. $1.50. Scribner.

GAMES.
See Baseball;—Bridge;—Golf; — Kindergarten; — Ping-pong;—Polo;—Whist.

Gametrogenesis and fertilization in albugo. Stevens, F. L. net, 25 c. Univ. of Chic.
Ganong, W: F. Lab'y course in plant physiology, as a basis for ecology. '01· '02 (F1) il. O. net, $1. Holt.
Gans, E. W: A Pennsylvania pioneer: biog. sketch. '02(F15) 8°, hf. leath., $6. Kuhl.

GARDENING.
Bacon. Of gardens. net, 50 c. Lane.
Barnard. My ten rod farm.—Simple flower garden. ea., 40 c.—Two thousand a year on fruits and flowers. $1. Coates.
Blomfield. Formal garden in England. $3. Macmillan.
Bridgeman. Kitchen gardening. 50 c. Coates.
Budd *and* Hansen. Am. horticultural manual. $1.50. Wiley.
Cadwallader. Story of home gardens. 25 c. Home Gardening.

GARDENING.—*Continued.*
Ellacombe. In my vicarage garden. net, $1.50. Lane.
Fiske, *comp.* Prize gardening. $1. Judd.
Holme. Stray leaves from a border garden. net. $1.50. Lane.
In a Tuscan garden. net, $1.50. Lane.
Lowell, *ed.* American gardens. $7.50. Bates & G.
Sedding. Garden craft, old and new. net, $2.50. Lane.
Triggs. Formal gardens in England and Scotland. 3 pts. net, $25. Scribner.
Williams. Garden in the suburbs. net, $1.50. Lane.
See also Botany;—Flowers;—Fruit;—Window gardening.

Gardiner, Asa B. Discovery of the remains of Maj.-Gen. Nat. Greene; add. del. in Newport, July 4, 1901. '01. '02(Ap5) 8°, pap., n. p. [Blumenberg Press] Soc. R. I. Cincinnati.
Gardner, J: *See* Gregg, W: H.
Gardner, J: M., *ed.* American negligence repts. v. 10. '01. '02(Ja18); v. 11 (Ag2) O. shp., ea., $5.50. Remick.
Gardner, W. M. *See* Rawson, C.

GARFIELD, James A.
See Fallows, S:

Garland, Hamlin. Captain of the Grayhorse troop. '02(Mr29) D. $1.50. Harper.
Garnett, R:, Vallée, L., *and* Brandl, A., *eds.* Universal anthology. v. 31-33. Westminster ed. '02(Ag30) 4°, per v., $3.50. Merrill & B.

GAS AND GAS-FITTING.
Gill. Gas and fuel analysis for engineers. $1.25. Wiley.
Hempel. Methods of gas analysis. net, $2.25. Macmillan.

GASES.
Randall, *ed. and tr.* Expansion of gases by heat. $1. Am. Bk.
Travers. Experimental study of gases. net, $3.25. Macmillan.

Gaskin, Rob. T. Caedmon, the first Eng. poet. '02(Je7) 12°, pap., 40 c. E. & J. B. Young.
Gate of the kiss. Harding, J: W. $1.50. Lothrop.
Gathered sunbeams. Pease, E. S. 75 c. Sun Pr. Co.
Gauss, Karl F. General investigations of curved surfaces of 1827 and 1825; tr. with notes and a bibliog. by J. C. Morehead and A. M. Hiltebeitel. '02(Ag2) Q. *$1.75 net. Princeton Univ.
Gautier, T. Works. Limited ed. v. 13-16. '02(Je28) 8°, per v., $3.50; hf. mor., $6. Sproul.
Gaylord, Harvey R., *and* Archoff, Ludwig. Atlas of patholog. histology. '01. '02(Ja25) col. il. 4°, net, $7.50. Lea.

GAZETTEERS.
Chambers's concise gazetteer. $2. Lippincott.

GEARS AND GEARING.
Grant. Treatise on gear wheels. net, $1. Caspar.

Gee, H: Elizabethan prayer-book and ornaments. '02(Mr22) 12°, net, $1.25. Macmillan.

GEMS.
See Precious stones.

GENEALOGY.

Crayon. Rockaway records of Morris Co., N. J., families. $3. Rockaway.

Haines. Ancestrv of the Haines, Sharp, Collins, Wills, Gardiner, Prickett, Eves, Evans, Moore, Troth, Borton and Engle families. $3. R: Haines.

Nash. Fifty Puritan ancestors. $5. Tuttle, M. & T.

Sellers. Allied families of Delaware. $5. E. J. Sellers.

Van Meter. Genealogies and sketches of some old families. $2.25. Morton.

Watson. Royal lineage. $4.50. Whittet.

Wells. Hist. of Newburg, Vt.; with genealog. records. $2.25; $3; $3.50; $4. Caledonian.

See also Biography.

General digest, Am. and Eng., annot. v. 12, '02(My10) O. shp., $6. Lawyers' Co-op.

GENERATIVE ORGANS.

Ultzmann. Neuroses of the genito-urinary system in the male with sterility and impotence. *$1 net. Davis.

See also Syphilis;—Urine and urinary organs.

Gentleman in literature. Quayle, W: A. net, 25 c. Jennings.

Gentleman Garnet. Vogel, H. B. $1; 50 c. Lippincott.

GEODOSY.

Bolza. Concerning the geodesic curvature and the isoperimetric problem on a given surface. *25 c. net. Univ. of Chic.

Gauss. General investigations of curved surfaces of 1825-27. *$1.75 net. Princeton Univ.

See also Earth;—Surveying.

Geographical readers. il. D. Am. Bk.
—Carpenter. Europe. 70 c.

GEOGRAPHY.

Adams, *ed.* Elem. commercial geog. $1.10. Appleton.

Appleton's geografia superior ilustrada. (Spanish.) $1.50. Appleton.

Bartholomew. Internat. students' atlas of modern geography. net, $2.25. Scribner.

Carroll. Around the world. 60 c. Morse.

Fairbanks. Home geog. for primary grades. 60 c. Educ. Pub.

Frye. Grammar school geography. $1.45. Ginn.

Murché. Teacher's manual of object lessons in geography. net, 80 c. Macmillan.

Roddy. Complete geography. $1; Elem. geography. 50 c. Am. Bk.

Tarr *and* McMurry. 1st bk. Home geog. net, 60 c. 2d bk. Complete geog. *$1 net. Macmillan.

Wagner. New Pacific school geography. net, $1. Whitaker & R.

See also Atlases;—Physical geography;—Voyages and travels.

GEOLOGY.

Hershey. Quaternary of So. California. 20 c. Univ. of Cal.

Lawson. The eparchæan interval. 10 c. Univ. of Cal.

Merriam. Triassic ichthyopterygia fr. Cal. and Nevada. 50 c. Univ. of Cal.

Zittel. Hist. of geology and paleontology to end of 19th century $1.50. Scribner.

See also Berkeley Hills; — Earth; — Evolution;— Glacial period;—Mineralogy;—Paleontology.

GEOMETRY.

Brooks. Plane and solid geometry. $1.25. Sower.

More. Trisection of a given angle geometrically solved. $1. Wickes.

See also Mathematics;—Perspective; — Trigonometry.

George, Marian M. Little journey to Belgium and Denmark. '02(Ag30) il. 12°, (Plan book ser., v. 5, no. 8.) pap., 15 c. Flanagan.

George, Marian M. Little journey to Switzerland. '02(Ag30) il. 12°, (Plan book ser., v. 5, no. 9.) pap., 15 c. Flanagan.

George, Marian M. *See also* Whitcomb, C. E.

Georgia. Supp. to code. v. 4. (H. Van Epps.) '01. '02(Ap5) O. shp., $5. Marshall.

Georgia. *Supreme ct.* Repts. v. 114. '02 (Ag2) O. shp., $5. Georgia Lib.

GEORGIA.

Mitchell. Georgia land and people. $1.25. F. L. Mitchell.

Georgian (The) period. In 3 v. v. 2, pt. 8; v. 3, pt. 9. '02(Mr15) il. portfolio, f°, ea., $4. Am. Architect.

Gerard, Fes. A. A Grand Duchess and her court. '02(Ap5) 2 v., 8°, net, $7.50. Dutton.

Gerard, Fes. A. Romance of King Ludwig II. of Bavaria. New ed. '01. '02(F22) 12°, net, $1.75. Dodd.

GERLACH, *St.*

Houck. Life of St. Gerlach. net, 55 c. Benziger.

GERMAN LANGUAGE.

Adler. German and Eng. dictionary. pt. 1. $3.50. Appleton.

Florer. Biblische geschichten. 40 c. Wahr.

Fulda. Der talisman. 35 c. Heath.

Fulda. Unter vier Augen. *35 c. net. Holt.

Grillparzer. Traum ein leben. 60 c. Heath.

Heyse. Niels mit der offenen hand. 30 c. Heath.

Körner. Zriny ein trauerspiel in fünf aufzügen. 35 c. Heath.

Krüger *and* Smith. English-Germ. conversation book. 25 c. Heath.

Kuttner. German conversation course. 50 c. Abbey Press.

Lange. 20th century system; key to the Germ. language. 50 c. Pamphlet.

Lessing. Minna von Barnhelm. 75 c. Heath.

Lessing. Nathan der Weise. 80 c. Am. Bk.

Moser. Der bibliothekar. 45 c. Am. Bk.

Riehl. Das spielmannskind und stumme ratsherr. 35 c. Am. Bk.

Stern. Geschichten von Deutschen städten. $1.25. Am. Bk.

Wesselhoeft. German composition. 45 c. Heath.

GERMAN LITERATURE.

Batt. Treatment of nature in Germ. literature from Günther to Goethe's Werther. net, $1. Univ. of Chic.

Brandes. Main currents in 19th century lit. v. 2, Romantic school in Germany. net, $2.75. Macmillan.

German opera texts. See Newson's.

GERMAN POETRY.

Remy. Influence of India and Persia on the poetry of Germany. net, $1. Macmillan.

GERMANTOWN, Pa.
Jenkins. Guide book to historic Germantown 50 c. Site and Relic.

GERMANY.
Baedeker, *ed.* Southern Germany. net, $1.80. Scribner.
Henderson. Short hist. of Germany. 2 v. net, $4. Macmillan.
Schiller. Hist. of the thirty years' war. (App. to pubs. for price.) Niccolls.
Veritas. German empire of to-day. $2.25. Longmans.

Gertrude Dorrance. Fisher, M. $1.50. McClurg.

Geyserland and wonderland. Hatfield, W: F: 24 c. Hicks-J.

Giant fish of Florida. Turner, J. T. **$3.50 net. Lippincott.

Giants' gate. Pemberton, M. $1.50. Stokes.

Gibbes, Fes. G. Poems. '02(Ap19) 12°, $1. Neale.

Gibbons, W: F. Those black diamond men. '02(Je14) il. D. $1.50. Revell.

Gibbs, Josiah W. Elem. principles in statistical mechanics. '02(Je28) 8°, (Yale bicentennial pub.) $4. Scribner.

Gibbs, Josiah W. Vector analysis: text-book founded upon the lectures of J. Willard Gibbs by E. B. Wilson. '01. '02(F15) 8°, (Yale bicentennial pub.) net, $4. Scribner.

Gibbs, Mifflin W. Shadow and light: autobiog. '02(Mr29) D. $1.50. M. W. Gibbs.

Gibson, J. M. Protestant principles. '01. '02(F1) S. (Christian study manuals.) 60 c. Armstrong.

Gideon. Carradine, B. 35 c. Pepper.

Gifford, J: Practical forestry for beginners in forestry, agricultural students, and others. '02(My24) il. D. net, $1.20. Appleton.

Gifford, M. W. Christian science against itself. '02(Je14) D. $1. Jennings.

Gifford lectures. *See* James, W:

Gift of power. Tuttle, J: E. net, 25 c. Westminster.

Gil Blas. Le Sage, A. R. $1. Burt.

Gilbert, Fk. One thousand ways to make money. '02(My17) 12°, $1. Donohue.

Gilbert, Fk. B. *See* New York. Laws; Membership and relig. corps.

Gilbert, G: H. Primer of the Christian religion. '02(F15) 12°, net, $1. Macmillan.

Gilbert, Grove K., *and* Brigham, A. P. Introd. to physical geography. '02(Je28) il. D. (Twentieth century text-books.) net, $1.25. Appleton.

Gildersleeve, B. L. Studies in honor of Basil L. Gildersleeve. '02(Je28) 8°, $6. Johns Hopkins.

Gill, A: H. Gas and fuel analysis for engineers. 3d rev., enl. ed. '02(Je7) 12°, $1.25. Wiley.

Gill, Joshua, Kirkpatrick, W: J., *and* Gilmour, H. L. Hymns of grace and glory. '02 (My10) D. bds., 30 c. Mattill & L.

Gilman, B. Kingdom of coins. New ed. '01. '02(F15) 16°, (Children's friend ser.) bds., 50 c. Little, B. & Co.

Gilman, Dan. Coit. *See* Vincent, J: M.

Gilmer, Eliz. M., ["Dorothy Dix."] Fables of the elite. '02(My3) il. S. net, $1. Fenno.

Gilmour, H. L. *See* Gill, J.

Ginn's art ser. il. 16°. Ginn.
—Cyr. Advanced 1st reader. 35 c.

Ginn's handbooks on the history of religions. 12°, $2.50. Ginn.
—Chantepie de la Saussaye. Religion of the Teutons. (3.)

GIOTTO DI BONDONE.
Perkins. Giotto. $1.75. Macmillan.

Girdlestone, R. B. Grammar of prophecy. '01. '02(Ja11) 12°, (Bible students' lib., no. 11.) $2.50. E. & J. B. Young.

Girl from Mexico. Hyde, M. G. $1. Abbey Press.

Girl of Virginia. Thruston, L. M. $1.50. Little, B. & Co.

Girl who wrote. Cohen, A. J. $1.50. Quail & W.

GIRLS.
Freeman. Religious and social work amongst girls. net, $1. Whittaker.
See also Children;—Education;—Woman;—Young women.

Gittings, J. C. *See* Judson, C: F.

GLACIAL PERIOD.
Chamberlin. Proposed genetic classification of pleistocene glacial formations. net, 10 c. Univ. of Chic.
Chamberlin. Working hypothesis of cause of glacial periods on an atmosphere basis. net, 25 c. Univ. of Chic.

Gladden, W. Christian way. New ed. '01. '02(F22) 16°, 75 c. Dodd.

Gladden, W. Practice of immortality. '02 (Ag30) D. (Beacon Hill ser.) bds., *25 c. net. Pilgrim Press.

Gladden, W. Social salvation. '02(My3) D. net, $1. Houghton, M. & Co.

GLADSTONE, W: E.
Handford. William Ewart Gladstone. $1.50; $2.50. Dominion.
Locke. A 19th century crusader. net, 25 c. Jennings.

Glasgow, Ellen. The battleground. '02 (Mr29) il. D. $1.50. Doubleday, P.

Glasson, W: H. Nation's pension system as applied to the civil war and the war with Spain. '02(Mr22) 8°, (Pub. of the soc., no. 331.) pap., 25 c. Am. Acad. Pol. Sci.

Gleanings from nature. Carter, E. N. $1. Abbey Press.

Glenwood. Kensington, C. $1.25. Abbey Press.

Globe series. D. Globe Sch. Bk.
—Chancellor. Arithmetics. Primary. 28 c. —2d bk. 20 c.—3d bk. 24 c.—4th bk. 24 c.
—Chancellor. Mathematics by grades. bks. 5, 6. ea., 28 c.

Glover, Terrot R. Life and letters in the fourth century. '02(F15) 8°, (Cambridge Univ. Press ser.) net, $3.25. Macmillan.

GOD.
Lanier. Kinship of God and man. 2 v. ea., *$1 net. Whittaker.
Leighton. Conceptions of God. net, $1.10. Longmans.
Reed. Idea of God in rel. to theology. net, 75 c. Univ. of Chic.
Thompson. The unknown God. 60 c. Warne.
See also Bible;—Holy Spirit;—Jesus Christ;—Religion;—Theology.

God of things. Whitehouse, F. B. $1.50. Little, B. & Co.

God the beautiful. B., E. P. net, 75 c. Beam.

Godbey, A. M. Life of Henry M. Stanley. '02(Jl19) 12°, (Biographies of famous men.) $1. Donohue.

Godfrey, Eliz., [*pseud.* for Jessie Bedford.] The winding road. '02(Mr22) D. $1.50. Holt.

Godly union and concord. Henson, H. H. $2. Longmans.

Goebel, F. Hermann der Cherusker und die schlacht im Teutoburger walde; ed. by J. Esser. Authorized ed. '02(F22) 12°, net, 50 c. Macmillan.

Goethe, J. W. v. Truth and fiction rel. to my life; ed. by N. H. Dole. Ed. de luxe. v. 1. '02(Je28) 12°, (app. to pubs. for price.) Niccolls.

Goethe, J. W. v. Wilhelm Meister's apprenticeship; ed. by N. H. Dole. Ed. de luxe. '02(Mr15) 2 v., 12°. (App. to pubs for price.) Niccolls.

Goethe, J. W. v. Wilhelm Meister's travels; and Recreations of the German emigrants; ed. by N. H. Dole. Ed. de luxe. '02 (Mr22) 8°. (App. to pubs. for price.) Niccolls.

Goff, E. S. Lessons in commercial fruit growing. '02(My10) il. 12°, (Vellum ser.) $1. Univ. Co-op.

GOLD.
 Curle. Gold mines of the world. $3.50. Engineering.
 Wilson. Cyanide processes. $1.50. Wiley.
 See also Precious metals.

Gold bug. Poe, E. A. 25 c. Rand, McN. & Co.

Gold of Ophir. Gwinn, D. H. $1. Abbey Press.

Golden Fluff. Morris, I. D. 50 c. Abbey Press.

Golden lily. Hinkson, *Mrs.* K. T. 40 c. Benziger.

Golden poppy. Smith, E. E. net, $1.50. E. E. Smith.

Golden way. Bartlett, A. L. $1.50. Abbey Press.

Goldsmith, O. Plays; ed. by A. Dobson. '02 (Mr22) 16°, (Temple classics.) 50 c.; leath., 75 c. Macmillan.

Goldsmith, O. Poems; ed. by A. Dobson. '02(Mr22) 16°, (Temple classics.) 50 c.; leath., 75 c. Macmillan.

Goldsmith, O. Selections. '01· '02(Ap5) S. (Little masterpieces.) 50 c. Doubleday, P.

Goldsmith, P: H. El idioma Inglés: Lib. primero. '02(Ap5) D. 40 c.; *Same*. Lib. segundo. 36 c. Globe Sch. Bk.

GOLF.
 Brown. Golf. **50 c. net. Houghton, M. & Co.
 Harper's official golf guide, 1901. $1. Harper.
 Taylor. On golf. **$1.60 net. Appleton.
 Travis. Practical golf. net, $2. Harper.

Golf lunatic and his cycling wife. Kennard, *Mrs.* M. E. †$1.50. Brentano's.

Good, Ja. I. Historical handbook of the Reformed church in the U. S. 2d ed., rev. '01· '02(Ap5) D. bds., 25 c. Heidelberg.

Good, Ja. I. Women of the Reformed church. '01· '02(Ap5) il. D. $1. Heidelberg.

Good and evil. *See* Lanier, J. J.

Good cheer nuggets. Pennington, J. G. 45 c.; $1. Fords.

Good gravy. Kendall, E. F. 25 c. Helman-T.

Goodell, T: D. Chapters on Greek metric. '01. '02(Mr15) 8°, (Yale bicentennial pub.) net, $2. Scribner.

Goodknight, Alva L. Modern association and railroading. '01· '02(Mr22) D. 50 c. Abbey Press.

Goodspeed, Edg. J. The Newberry gospels. '02(Ap5) il. O. (Hist. and linguistic studies in literature rel. to the N. T., v. 2, Greek texts, pt. 1.) pap., net, 25 c. Univ. of Chic.

Goodwin, J. J. The "sinker" stories of wit and humor. '02(Je28) D. $1. Ogilvie.

Goodyear, S: H. Theory of accounts. '02 (Ap19) Q. $1.50. Goodyear-M.

Gordian knot. Pierson, A. T. **60 c. net. Funk.

Gordon, Granville, *Lord*. Sporting reminiscences. '02(Je7) 8°, net, $4. Dutton.

Gordon, Julien, *pseud.* *See* Cruger, *Mrs.* J. S.

Gordon, S: Strangers at the gate. '02(Je7) D. $1.50. Jewish Pub.

Gordy, J. P. Political hist. of the U. S. v. 2. 2d ed., rev. '02(Ag2) D. **$1.75 net. Holt.

Gordy, Wilbur F. American leaders and heroes: U. S. history. '01· '02(Mr15) il. maps, 12°, net, 60 c. Scribner.

Gore, C: Body of Christ. 2d rev. enl. ed.; with reply to critics of the 1st ed. '01. '02 (Ja11) 12°, $1.75. Scribner.

Gore, Ja. H. Dutch art as seen by a layman. '02(Ag9) il. nar. Q. pap., n. p. Holland-Am.

Gore, Willard C. The imagination in Spinoza and Hume. '02(Je14) 8°, (Univ. of Chic. cont. to philosophy, v. 2, no. 4.) pap., net, 35 c. Univ. of Chic.

Gorky, Maxime, [*pseud.* for Alexei Maximovitch Pyeshkoff.] Tales from Gorky; with a biog. notice of author by R. N. Bain. 3d ed. '02(My3) D. net, $1.20. Funk.

Górky, Máxime. Twenty-six and one, and other stories; fr. the Russian. '02(Mr22) il. D. $1.25. J. F. Taylor.

Gormanius. *See* De Leon, T: C.

Gospel of Judas Iscariot. Baldwin, A. D. $1.50. Jamieson-H.

Gospel of the kingdom and the gospel of the church. Brown, W: B. $1. Whittaker.

Gospel primer (The). 45th ed. '01. '02 (Ag2) D. bds., 25 c. Southern Pub.

Goss, W: F. M. Locomotive sparks. '02 (Ap19) il. 8°, $2. Wiley.

Gothenburg system. *See* National Temp. almanac.

Gottsberger, Fs. Accountant's guide for executors, administrators, etc. '02(Ag2) Q. $5. Peck.

Gould, G: M., *ed.* *See* American year-book of medicine.

Gould, W. R. Greater New York and state lawyer's diary for 1902. '02(Mr1) S. $1. W. R. Gould.

GOVERNMENT.
 See Political science.

Government clerks. Rogers, C: G. $1; 25 c. McQuilkin.

Government ownership of railroads. Knapp, M. A. 15 c. Am. Acad. Pol. Sci.

Gower, Ronald S., *Lord*. Old diaries, 1881-1901. '02(Ap12) il. 8°, net, $4.50. Scribner.

Gower, Ronald S., *Lord*. Sir David Wilkie. '02(Mr8) il. 12°, (Great masters in painting and sculpture.) $1.75. Macmillan.

Gower, Ronald S., *Lord.* Tower of London. v. 2. '02(Mr22) il. 8°, net, $6.50. Macmillan.
Grace of orders. Winston, N. B. $1. Abbey Press.
Graded classics. *See* Haliburton, M. W.
Gradle, H: Diseases of the nose, pharynx and ear. '02(Je28) il. 8°, net, $3.50. Saunders.
Grafton, C: C. Pusey and the church revival. '02(Ap12) il. D. net, 50 c. Young Churchman.
Graham, Alex. Roman Africa. '02(F8) O. $6. Longmans.
Graham, G: E: Schley and Santiago. '02 (F8) D. $1.50. Conkey.
Graham, H: G. Scottish men of letters in the eighteenth century. '02(F1) 8°, net, $4.50. Macmillan.
Graham, J. M. East of the barrier; or, Manchuria in miniature. '02(Je7) 12°, net, $1. Revell.
GRAMMONT, *Count.*
Hamilton. Memoirs of Count Grammont. *$3 net. Scribner.
GRAND CANYON.
See **Arizona;—Colorado river.**
Grand Duchess and her court. Gerard, F. A. 2 v., net, $7.50. Dutton.
Grand Rapids, Mich. Tax list. '02(Ag16) O. $10. Commercial Credit.
Grandmother dear. Molesworth, *Mrs.* M. L. 75 c. Burt.
Grandmother's cook book. H., A. P. 50 c. New Amsterdam.
Grant, *Mrs.* Anne M. Memoirs of an Amer. lady. New ed. '01· '02(F22) 8°, net, $7.50. Dodd.
Grant, G. B. Treatise on gear wheels. 8th ed. '02(Ap26) 8°, net, $1. Caspar.
GRANT, Ulysses S.
Poore *and* Tiffany. U. S. Grant. $1. Donohue.
Grant, W: D., *ed.* Christendom anno domini 1901. '02(Je7) 2 v., O. $2.50. W: D. Grant.
Graphic method for solving questions in arithmetic or algebra. Vose, G: L. 50 c. Van Nostrand.
GRAPHOLOGY.
See **Handwriting.**
Gray, H: Anatomy. 15th ed. '01· '02(Ja25) il. 8°, net, $5.50; shp., net, $6.50; col. il. net, $6.25; shp., net, $7.25. Lea.
Gray, L: H. Indo-Iranian phonology. '02 (Je28) 8°, (Columbia Univ. and Indo-Iranian ser., v. 2.) net, $3. Macmillan.
Gray, Martha. Fortune's wheel. '02(My3) D. $1. Abbey Press.
Gray, W: C. Musings by camp-fire and wayside. '02(F1) O. net, $1.50. Revell.
Graystone. Nicolls, W: J. $1.50. Lippincott.
Great authors of all ages. Allibone, S: A. $2.50. Lippincott.
GREAT BRITAIN.
Bartlett. Golden way: notes on journey through Ireland, Scotland and England. $1.50. Abbey Press.
Karr. Call to arms, 1900-01. $2. Longmans.
Mackinder. Britain and the British seas. $2. Appleton.
Great chancellor. High, J. L. net, $2.50; Callaghan.
Great cloud of witnesses. Wilson, L: A. 50 c. Standard Pub.
Great commanders' ser.; ed. by J. G. Wilson. D. net, $1.50. Appleton.
—Mathes. General Forrest.
Great issues. *See* Barker, W.
Great love. Burnham, C. L. 50 c. Houghton, M. & Co.
Great masters in painting and sculpture. See Macmillan's.
GREECE.
Bury. Hist. of Greece to death of Alexander. 2 v. net, $8. Macmillan.
Fustel de Coulanges. Ancient city: study on the rel., laws, and institutions of Greece and Rome. $2. Lee & S.
Jebb. Modern Greece. $1.75. Macmillan.
Greeff, R. Guide to the microscopic examination of the eyes; fr. the 2d Germ. ed., by H. Walker. '01· '02(Ja11) 12°, net, $1.25. Blakiston.
Greek foreshadowings of mod. metaphysical thought. Kupfer, L. $1. J. S. Cushing.
Greek hero stories. Niebuhr, B. G. $1. Dodd.
GREEK LANGUAGE.
Andrew. Greek prose composition. net, 90 c. Macmillan.
Babbitt. Grammar of Attic and Ionic Greek. $1.50. Am. Bk.
Ball. Elements of Greek. net, $1. Macmillan.
Pearson *and* Bartlett. Key to Pearson's Greek prose composition. 50 c. Am. Bk.
See also **Attic prose.**
GREEK LITERATURE.
Fowler. Hist. of ancient Gr. literature. net, $1.40. Appleton.
GREEK MANUSCRIPTS.
Goodspeed. Newberry gospels: Greek texts. net, 25 c. Univ. of Chic.
Greek myths in Eng. dress. Hale, E: E., *jr.* 40 c. Globe Sch. Bk.
GREEK POETRY.
Goodell Chapters on Greek metric. net, $2. Scribner.
GREEK RELIGION.
Rouse. Greek votive offerings. *$4.50 net. Macmillan.
Greek ser. for colleges and schools. D. $1. Am. Bk.
—Plato. Euthyphro.
Green, B: E. Shakespeare and Goethe on Gresham's law and the single gold standard. '01· '02(F8) D. pap., 25 c. MacGowan.
Green, E. T. Church of Christ. '02(Mr1) 12°. (Churchman's lib.) $1.50. Macmillan.
Green, S: A. Ten facsimile reproductions rel. to old Boston and neighborhood. '01· '02 (Ja11) F. net, $10. Littlefield.
Green fund book. D. net, 50 c. Am. S. S.
—Rice. Our sixty-six sacred books. (10.)
Green turbans Cobban, J. M. 50 c. Burt.
Greenaway, Kate. A apple pie. New ed. '01· '02(Ja25) obl. 8°, bds., 75 c. Warne.
Greene, Ja. G. *See* New York. Analy. decisions and citations.
GREENE, *Gen.* Nat.
Gardiner. Discovery of the remains of Maj.-Gen. Nathaniel Greene. n. p. [Blumenberg Press] Soc. R. I. Cincinnati.

Greene, Ryland W., *ed.* *See* Lippincott's pocket medical dictionary.
Greenleaf, Sue. Liquid from the sun's rays. '02(Ap26) D. $1.50. Abbey Press.
Greenstone, Julius H. Religion of Israel. '02(Mr29) D. 50 c. Bloch.
Gregg, D: Dictum of reason on man's immortality. '02(Je21) D. 50 c. Treat.
Gregg, Hilda, ["Sydney C. Grier."] Prince of the captivity. '02(My17) D. $1.50. L. C. Page.
Gregg, W: H., *and* Gardner, J: Where, when, and how to catch fish on the east coast of Florida. '02(Je7) il. O. $4. Matthews-N.
Gregorovius, F. Hist. of Rome in the Middle Ages. '02(Ap5) 12°, net, $3. Macmillan.
Gregory, J. W. *See* Hutchinson, H. N.
Grenell, Judson. Economic tangles. '02 (Ag23) D. $1. Purdy.
Grenell, Z. The sandals: tale of Palestine. '02(Mr8) il. S. (Hour-glass stories, no. 2.) net, 40 c. Funk.
Grethenbach, Constantine. Secular view of the Bible. '02(Mr22) il. O. net, $2. Eckler.
Grier, Sydney C. *See* Gregg, H.
Griffin, Alb. Why the legal (or force) method of promoting temperance always has done—and always must do—more harm than good. '01· '02(Ja11) S. pap., 15 c. A. Griffin.
Griffin ser. il. D. $1. Coates.
—Couch. The Westcotes.
Griffiths, D: P. Last of the quills: story of Welsh life. '02(Ag9) 12°, $1.50. D: P. Griffiths.
Grillparzer, Franz S. Traum ein leben; ed. by E: S. Meyer. '02(My3) D. (Modern lang. ser.) 60 c. Heath
GRILLPARZER, Franz.
Lessing. Schiller's ein fluss auf Grillparzer. 50 c. Univ. of Wis.
Grinnell, G: B. American duck shooting. '01· '02(F1) il. O. $3.50. Forest
Grove, *Lady* Agnes. Seventy-one days' camping in Morocco. '02(Ap19) il. O. net, $2.50. Longmans.
Growing up. Conklin, *Mrs.* J. M. D. $1. Burt.
Guarding the thoughts. Macdonald. L. B. 10 c. J. H. West
Guggenberger, A. General hist. of the Christian era. In 3 v. v. 2 and 3. '01. '02 (Mr8) 8°, ea., $1.50. Herder.
Guide to best hist. novels and tales. Nield, J. net, $1.75. Putnam.
Guide to Palestine and Egypt. '02(Ja18) 12°, (Macmillan's guides.) net, $3.25. Macmillan.
Guided and guarded. Malone, J. S. $1.25. Abbey Press.
Gulliver's bird book. Bridgman, L. J. $1.50. L. C. Page.
GUN.
See Rifle.
GUNNERY.
Hamilton *and* Bond. Gunner's catechism. $1. Wiley.
Gunsaulus, Fk. W. Monk and knight. 5th ed. '02(Ag30) 12°, †$1.50. McClurg.
Gunter, A. C. Surprises of an empty hotel. '02(Ap5) il. D. $1; pap., 50 c. Home.
Guthe, Karl E. *See* Reed, J: O.
Guthrie, Ben E., *rep.* *See* Missouri. *St. Louis and Kansas City cts. of appeals.* Cases.
Guyse, Eleanor. A movable quartette. '02 (My3) D. $1. Abbey Press.
Gwatkin, H: M. *See* Maitland, F: W:
Gwinn, D. H. Gold of Ophir. '02(Ag2) 12°, $1. Abbey Press.
Gyim, Paul L. Chinese-English elem. reader and arithmetic. '01. '02(Mr22) il. 16°, $1.25. Taylor & M.
GYMNASTICS AND PHYSICAL CULTURE.
Colburn. Graded physical exercises. $1. Werner.
Fish. Calisthenic dict. $1. Seminar.
See also Delsarte system.
GYNECOLOGY.
Davenport. Diseases of women: manual of gynecology. net, $1.75. Lea.
Dudley, *ed.* Gynecology. $1.50. Year Bk.
Herrold. Woman: diseases and remedies. $4; $5. Woman's Pub.
McKay. History of ancient gynæcology. net, $3. Wood.
GYPSIES.
See Zincali.
H., A. P. Grandmother's cook book. '02 (Ap26) sm. 4°, bds., 50 c. New Amsterdam.
Haddon Hall lib. il. 12°, $3. Macmillan.
—Shand. Shooting.
Hadley, H. E. Practical exercises in magnetism and electricity. '02(F22) 12°, net, 60 c. Macmillan.
Hadley, Wilfred J. Nursing—general, medical and surgical; with app. on sick-room cookery. '02(Mr22) 12°, net, $1.25. Blakiston.
Hagen, Hugo v. Reading character from handwriting. '02(Ag23) O. $1. Graphology.
Hagerstown town and country almanack for 1903. '02(Ag30) sq. 8°, pap., 10 c. Gruber.
Haggerty, J: How to treat the trusts and how to win in 1904. '02(Jl5) D. 25 c. Abbey Press.
Hahn, C: C. So fight I. '02(Ap12) 16°, pap., 10 c. Whittaker.
Haines, E. M. *See* Illinois. Laws.
Haines, G: Ancestry of the Haines, Sharp, Collins, Wills, Gardiner, Prickitt, Eves, Evans, Moore, Troth, Borton and Engle families. '02(Ag2) 8°, $3. R: Haines.
HAIR.
Stitson. Human hair. $1.25. Maple.
Hake, H. W. *See* Dupre, A.
Hale, E: E. En son nom, [In his name:] tr. par M. P. Sauveur. '01. '02(Ja4) D. $1. W: R. Jenkins.
Hale, E: E. Man without a country. Birthday ed. '02(Ap12) O. net, $1. Outlook.
Hale, E: E., *jr., ed.* American essays. '02 (Ag30) 16°, (Hawthorne classics, no. 4.) 40 c. Globe Sch. Bk.
Hale, E: E., *jr., ed.* Ballads and ballad poetry. '02(Mr22) D. (Hawthorne classics, no. 2.) 40 c. Globe Sch. Bk
Hale, E: E., *jr., ed.* English essays. '02 (Ag23) 16°, (Hawthorne classics, no. 3.) 40 c. Globe Sch. Bk.
Hale, E: E., *jr., ed.* Greek myths in Eng. dress. '02(Mr22) D. (Hawthorne classics, no. 1.) 40 c. Globe Sch Bk.
Hale, E: E., *jr.* *See also* Sterling, A. W.

Hale, G: E. New star in Perseus. '01. '02 (Ja11) 8°, (Yerkes Observatory bulletin, no. 16.) pap., net, 10 c. Univ. of Chic.

HALE, Nathan.
Partridge. Nathan Hale, the ideal patriot. net, $1. Funk.

Haliburton, Marg. W., *and* Norvell, F. T. Graded classics. Second reader. '02(Ag9) il. sq. D. 35 c. B. F. Johnson.

Haliburton, Marg. W., *and* Norvell, F. T. Graded classics: Third reader. '02(Jl12) il. sq. D. 40 c. B. F. Johnson.

Hall, A. C. A. Companion to the prayer-book. '02(Mr8) S. net, 35 c. E. & J. B. Young.

Hall, A. C. A. Instruction and devotions on the holy communion. '02(F8) S. net, 25 c. Young Churchman.

Hall, Arth. C. Crime in its relation to social progress. '02(Ap12) 8°, (Columbia Univ. studies in history, economics and public law, v. 15.) net, $3; $3.50. Macmillan.

Hall, C: W., *ed.* Regiments and armories of Mass. v. 2. '01. '02(Ja4) il. 8°, per set, $12; hf. cf., $18; seal, $25. W. W. Potter.

Hall, E: H. Jamestown, [1607-1907.] '02 (Ap26) il. 16°, pap., 25 c. Am. Scenic.

Hall, F: G., Little, E: R., *and* Eliot, H: W., *jr., eds.* Harvard celebrities. '02(F22) il. O. bds., $1.25. Univ. Press (Camb.)

Hall, Granville D. Rending of Virginia. '02 (Ap12) il. 8°, $2. Mayer.

Hall, H. S. Algebraical examples. '01. '02 (Ja4) 12°, net, 50 c. Macmillan.

Hall, Hubert. Society in the Elizabethan age. 3d ed. '02(Ag23) 8°, *$2.50 net. Dutton.

Hall, Jennie. Four old Greeks. '02(Mr15) il. 12°, 35 c. Rand, McN. & Co.

HALL, John.
Hall. John Hall, pastor and preacher. net, $1.50. Revell.

Hall, J: L., (*tr.*) Judith, Phœnix, and other Anglo-Saxon poems. '02(Ag23) 12°, 75 c. Silver.

Hall, Jos. Meditations and vows. '02(Mr8) 16°, $1.50. Dutton.

Hall, R. N., *and* Neal, W. G. Ancient ruins of Rhodesia. '02(My10) 8°, net. $6. Dutton.

Hall, Rob. C. Pittsburg securities, a stock exchange handbook, 1902. '02(Jl19) D. pap., gratis. R. C. Hall.

Hall, T: C. John Hall, pastor and preacher. '01. '02(Ja11) 12°, net, $1.50. Revell.

Hall, Violette. Chanticleer. '02(Ag23) il. D. †$1.50. Lothrop.

HALL OF FAME.
Eggleston. American immortals; record of men whose names are inscribed in the Hall of Fame. $10. Putnam.

HALS, Franz.
Davies. Franz Hals. *$14 net. Macmillan.

Halsey, Fs. W. Our literary deluge and some of its deeper waters. '02(Ap5) D. net, $1.25. Doubleday, P.

Halsey, Fs. W., *ed.* Authors of our day in their homes. '02(Mr15) 12°, $1.25. Pott.

Halstead, Murat. Full official hist. of the war with Spain. '02(Mr22) 12°, $3; mor., $4; cf., $6. Dominion.

Halstead, Murat. Galveston. '02(Mr22) 12°, $1.50; hf. mor., $2.25. Dominion.

Halstead, Murat. Life and achievements of Admiral Dewey. '02(Mr22) 12°, $1.50; hf. mor., $2.25; mor., $3.25. Dominion.

Halstead, Murat. Life of Theodore Roosevelt. '02(Je14) 8°, subs., $2.50; hf. mor., $3.75; ed. de luxe, $3.50; ¾ rus., $5. Saalfield.

Halstead, Murat. Pictorial hist. of America's new possessions. '02(Mr22) 12°, $2.50; hf. mor., $3.50; mor., $4.50. Dominion.

Halstead, Murat. Splendors of Paris and the glories of her Exposition. '02(Mr22) 12°, $1.50. Dominion.

Halstead, Murat. Story of the Philippines. '02(Mr22) 12°, $2; mor., $3. Dominion.

Halstead, Murat. Victorious republicanism. '02(Mr22) 12°, $1.50; hf. mor., $2.25. Dominion.

Halstead, Murat. William McKinley: (in Norwegian.) Oversat fra engelsk af P. O. Stromme. '01. '02(F15) il. O. $1.50; hf. mor., $2. J. Anderson Pub.

Halstead, Murat. World on fire. '02(Jl19) il. 12°, $1.50; $2.25; mor., $3. Dominion.

Halstead, Murat, *and* Munson, A. J. Life and reign of Queen Victoria. '02(Mr22) 12°, $1.50; hf. mor., $2.25. Dominion.

Halstead, Murat, *and* Munson, A. J. Life and services of William McKinley. '02 (Mr22) 12°, $1.50; hf. mor., $2.25. Dominion.

Hamersly, Lewis R., *comp.* Records of living officers of the U. S. navy and marine corps. 7th ed., rev., with add. '02(Jl5) 8°, $10. Hamersly.

Hamill, H. M. The Sunday-school teacher. '02(Mr22) D. 50 c. Pub. Ho. M. E. Ch., So.

HAMILTON, Alexander.
See Atherton, *Mrs.* G. F.;—Burr, A.

Hamilton, And. *See* New York. Statutory revision of laws.

Hamilton, *Count* Ant. Memoirs; ed., with notes, by Sir W. Scott. New cheaper ed. '02(Ag23) 8°, *$3 net. Scribner.

Hamilton, *Mrs.* E. J. Lee-. *See* Holdsworth, A. E.

Hamilton, Ja. H: Savings and savings institutions. '02(Je28) 12°, net, $2.25. Macmillan.

Hamilton, W: R., *and* Bond, P. S., *comps.* The gunner's catechism; for artillerymen. '02(Jl19) 18°, $1. Wiley.

Hamm, Margherita A. Eminent actors and their homes. '02(Mr15) 12°, $1.25. Pott.

Hammond, Eleanor P. On the text of Chaucer's Parlement of Foules. '02(Ag2) Q. (Decennial pubs., reprints.) pap., *50 c. net. Univ. of Chic.

HAMPSHIRE, ENG.
Capes. Scenes of rural life in Hampshire. net, $2.75. Macmillan.

Hancock, H. I. Life at West Point. '02 (Je14) il. D. net, $1.40. Putnam.

HAND.
See Palmistry.

Hand of God in Am. history. Thompson, R. E. net, $1. Crowell.

Handbooks for practical workers in church and philanthropy; ed. by S: M. Jackson. S. Lentilhon.
—Pierce. Hartley House cook book. 60 c.

Handbooks for the clergy; ed. by Arth. W. Robinson. D. net, 90 c. Longmans.
—Mason. Ministry of conversion.

Handbooks for the clergy.—Continued.
—Montgomery. Foreign missions.
—Robinson. Personal life of the clergy.
—Swete. Patristic study.

Handbooks of practical gardening. il. 12°, net, $1. Lane.
—Arnott. Book of bulbs. (5.)
—Thomas. Book of the apple. (6.)
—White. Book of orchids.* (8.)
—Wythes. Book of vegetables. (7.)

Handbooks on the history of religions. See Ginn's.

Handford, T: W. William Ewart Gladstone. '02(Mr22) 12°, $1.50; mor., $2.50. Dominion.

HANDWRITING.
Hagen. Reading character from hand writing. $1. Graphology.
See also Autographs;—Penmanship.

Handy, W: M. Banking systems of the world. 3d ed. rev. '02(Jl5) D. $1.50. Jamieson-H.

Handy book of synonyms. New ed. '02 (Ag2) 8°, limp cl., 50 c. Lippincott.

Handy information ser. S. net. Crowell.
—McSpadden. Shakesperian synopses. 45 c.

Hanford, B. Railroading in the U. S. '02 (Ap19) O. (Socialist lib., v. 1, no. 11.) pap., 5 c. Socialistic Co-op.

Hanna, C: A: The Scotch-Irish. '02(Mr29) 2 v., 8°, net, $10. Putnam.

Hannan, W. I. Textile fibres of commerce. '02(Ag2) 8°, $3. Lippincott.

Hannibal, P: M. Thrice a pioneer. '01· '02 (Mr1) 16°, 75 c.; pap., 40 c. Danish Luth.

HANOVER SQUARE.
Baillie. Oriental Club and Hanover Square. $9. Longmans.

Hansen, N. E. *See* Budd, J. L.

Har Lampkins. Patton, A. $1. Abbey Press.

Harben, Will N. Abner Daniel. '02(Je28) D. $1.50. Harper.

Harcourt, L. F. V. Civil engineering as applied in construction. '02(Mr8) il. O. (Civil engineering ser.) $5. Longmans.

Hardcastle, *Mrs.* M. A. Word signs made easy. '02(Mr29) sq. D. $1. M. A. Hardcastle.

Hardesty, Irving. Neurological technique. '01. '02(Ja11) O. net, $1.75. Univ. of Chic.

Hardie, T. Melville. *See* Wood, C. A., *ed.*

Harding, Caro. H. *and* S: B. City of the seven hills. '02(My24) il. S. (Lake history stories.) 40 c. Scott, F. & Co.

Harding, J: W. Gate of the kiss. '02(My17) il. D. $1.50. Lothrop.

Harding, S: B. *See* Harding, C. H.

Harding, W: War in South Africa and the Dark Continent from savagery to civilization. '02(Mr22) 12°, $2; hf. mor., $3; mor., $4. Dominion.

Hardwicke. Rood, H: E: $1.50. Harper.

Hargis, And. M. Treatise on commercial law and business customs. '02(Ag30) 12°, $3. A. M. Hargis.

Hargis, And. M. Treatise on commercial law and business customs. '01. '02(Je28) il. 12°, pap., 10 c. J. North.

Hargrave, W: L. Wallannah. '02(Mr8) il. D. $1.50. B. F. Johnson.

Harland, H:, ["Sidney Luska."] The lady paramount. '02(Ap19) D. $1.50. Lane.

Harmer, S. F:, *and* Shipley, A. E., *eds.* Cambridge natural history. v. 10, Mammalia, by F. E. Beddard. '02(Je28) il. 8°, net, $4. Macmillan.

Harmsworth, Alfr. C., Thompson, *Sir* H:, *and others.* Motors and motor driving. '02 (My17) 8°, (Badminton lib.) $3.50; hf. mor., $5. Little, B. & Co.

HARNESS.
See Horse.

Harper, Carrie A. *See* Dix, B. M.

Harper, J: M. Moral drill for the schoolroom. '01. '02(Ja25) 12°, $1. Kellogg.

Harper, W: R. Constructive studies in the priestly element in the Old Testament. Rev. ed. '02(Ja18) O. (Constructive Bible studies.) $1. Univ. of Chic.

Harper's official golf guide for 1901. '01. '02(Mr1) 12°, $1. Harper.

Harriott, *Mrs.* Clara M. *See* Morris, C.

Harris, C: N. *See* Massachusetts digest.

Harris, Cicero W. Sectional struggle: troubles between the north and the south. '02(Mr29) 8°, net, $2.50. Lippincott.

Harris, H: E. King of Andorra. '01. '02 (F15) D. $1.25. Abbey Press.

Harris, Joel C., ["Uncle Remus."] Making of a statesman, and other stories. '02(My17) D. $1.25. McClure, P.

Harris, *Mrs.* Miriam C. Rutledge. '02(Je14) 12°, (Home lib.) $1. Burt.

Harris, W. H. Law governing the issuing, transfer and coll. of municipal bonds. '02 (Ag2) O. shp., $4. W. H. Anderson & Co.

Harris, W: C. *See* Sage, D.

Harrison, Walter. *See* Ritchie, M. J. G.

Harrison, *Mrs.* Ma. K., ["Lucas Malet."] A counsel of perfection. New ed. '02(Ag23) 12°, $1. Appleton.

Harry, T. E. Infans amoris. '02(My3) D. $1.50. Abbey Press.

Hart, Alb., B., *and* Hazard, Blanche E. Source readers in Am. history. no. 1, Colonial children. '02(Ag2) 12°, *40 c. net. Macmillan.

Hart, Rob. M. Card language. 3d rev., enl. ed. '02(Mr29) nar. O. pap., 20 c. R. M. McEnally.

Hart, Rob. M. Card language. [*also*] Play card cypher. 4th rev. ed. '02(Je28) nar. O. pap., 20 c. R. M. Hart.

Harte, Fs. Bret. Openings in the old trail. '02(My3) D. $1.25. Houghton, M. & Co.

Hartfield, T: W. Exchange pocket cipher code. '02(Jl19) 16°, rus. leath., $2. T: W. Hartfield.

Hartley House cook book. Pierce, E. A. 60 c. Lentilhon.

Hartmann, A., *and* Needham, A. C. Commercial code for the transmission of telegrams and cablegrams. '02(Jl5) 12°, flex. leath., $3. Commercial Code.

Hartpence, W: Ross. *See* Ridgeway, *Major.*

Harvard celebrities. Hall, F: G., *ed.* $1.25. Univ. Press (Camb.)

Harvard union. *See* Higginson, H: L.

HARVARD UNIVERSITY.
Du Bois, *comp.* Harvard Univ. songs. $1.50. Ditson.

Harvey, L. D. Aids for the proper observance of Memorial day by the schools of Wis. '02(Ap26) O. pap., gratis. Democrat Pr.

Harvey, L. D. *See also* Arbor annual.
Hasse, Adelaide R., *comp.* United States Government pubs.: handbook for the cataloguer. pt. 1. '02(My10) O. $1. Lib. Bu.
Hassell, J: A. *See* Hiley, A. R. I.
Hastings, H: Mistress Dorothy of Haddon Hall. '02(Jl5) D. $1. Fenno.
Hatch, Adelaide W. Zobo patriotic drill. '01· '02(Ja11) S. (Hints ed. of novel and successful drills.) pap., 15 c. Hints.
Hatch, Dorus R. Civil government of Col. 7th ed. '01· '02(Ja18) il. 16°, 60 c. Centennial.
Hatcher, W: E. Pastor and the Sunday-school. '02(Jl12) il. 12°, 75 c. Bapt. S. S. Bd.
Hatfield, W: F: Geyserland and wonderland, (Yellowstone national park.) '02(Jl19) il. 24°, 24 c. Hicks-J.
Hatton, Jos. A vision of beauty. '02(Ag2) il. 12°, (Manhattan lib. of new copyright fiction.) pap., 50 c. Burt.
Haultmont, Marie. Marriage of Laurentia. '01· '02(Ja11) 8°, net, $1.60. Herder.
Haven, *Mrs.* Marg. J. C. Bible lessons for little beginners. '02(F8) 12°, net, 75 c. Revell.
Haviland, C. A:, ["Frank Myrtle."] A lawyer's idle hours. '02(Ag2) 12°, $1; pap., 50 c. C. A: Haviland.
Hawaiian almanac and annual for 1902. (T. G. Thrum.) '01. '02(Mr1) 12°, pap., 75 c. Thrum.
Hawkins, C: A. Legal counsellor and form book. '02(Je14) 8°, subs., $3; shp., $4. W. W. Wilson.
Hawkins, *Mrs.* May A. A wee lassie. '02 (Ag2) il. D. $1. Presb. Pub.
Hawkins, N. Aids to engineers' examinations. '01· '02(F8) il. 12°, leath., $2. Audel.
Hawkins, N. Handbook of calculations for engineers and firemen. '01. '02(F8) il. 12°. $2. Audel.
Hawkins, N. Self-help mechanical drawing. '02(Jl19) il. 8°, $2. Audel.
Hawley, Jos. R. New animal cellular therapy. '01. '02(Mr29) il. 12°, $1. Clinic.
Hawthorne, N. The Blithedale romance. '02 (Ap19) 12°, (Home lib.) $1. Burt.
Hawthorne, N. Main Street. '02(Mr1) sq. 12°, bds., $2. Kirgate Press.
Hawthorne, N. Marble faun. '02(Ap19) 12°, (Home lib.) $1. Burt.
Hawthorne classics. D. 40 c. Globe Sch. Bk.
—Hale, *ed.* Am. essays. (4.)—Ballads and ballad poetry. (2.)—Eng. essays. (3.)—Greek myths in Eng. dress. (1.)
Hawthorne readers. 16°. Globe Sch. Bk.
—Sterling, *and others.* Nature and life. pt 1. 32 c.
Hay, J: William McKinley. '02(My17) D. (What is worth while ser.) leatherette, net, 28 c. Crowell.
Hayden, Ja. R. Pocket text-book of venereal diseases. 3d ed. '01· '02(Ja25) 12°, net, $1.75; net, $2.25. Lea.
Hayens, Herb. For the colours. '02(My17) il. 8°, $2. Nelson.
Hayes, H:, *pseud.* *See* Kirk, *Mrs.* E. O.
Haymond, *Mrs.* W. E. Agnes Cheswick. '01. '02(Mr22) D. net, 60 c. Blanchard.
Hazard, Blanche E. *See* Hart, A. B.
Hazell's annual for 1902; ed. by W. Palmer. '02(Mr8) 12°, net, $1.50. Scribner.
Hazen, C: D. *See* New Eng. Hist. Teachers' Assoc.
HAZLITT, W:
Birrell. William Hazlitt. **75 c. net. Macmillan.
Hazlitt, W: Carew. Shakespeare. '02(My10) 8°, net, $2.50. Scribner.
HEAD.
Eckley. Regional anatomy of head and neck. net, $2.50. Lea.
See also Hair;—Phrenology.
Headlam, Cecil. Peter Vischer. '02(My24) 12°, (Handbooks of the great craftsmen.) $2. Macmillan.
Headlam, Cecil. Story of Chartres. '02(Je7) il. 12°, (Mediæval towns ser.) $2; leath., $2.50. Macmillan.
Headley, J. T. Napoleon and his marshals '02(My17) 12°, (Home lib.) $1. Burt.
Headley, J. T. Washington and his generals. '02(My17) 12°, (Home lib.) $1. Burt.
Healing of nerves. Ballance, C: A. net, $4.50. Macmillan.
HEALTH.
See Hygiene.
HEART.
Mackenzie. Study of the pulse, and of the movements of the heart. net, $4.50. Macmillan.
Thorne. Schott methods of treatment of diseases of the heart. *$2 net. Blakiston.
Heart of oak books. *See* Norton, C: E.
Hearth and home essays. Ruskay, E. J. 30 c. Jewish Pub.
Hearts courageous. Rives, H. E. $1.50. Bowen-M.
HEAT.
Dexter. Elem. exercises on sound, light and heat. 90 c. Longmans.
See also Radiation.
Heath, Chris. Clinical lectures on surgical subjects. 2d ser. '02(Ag16) $2. Blakiston.
Heath, Harold. *See* Jordan, D: S.
Heath, Herb. M. Comparative advantages of the corporation laws of all the states and territories. '02(Jl12) O. pap., n. p. Kennebec Journ.
Heath, W: Memoirs of Maj.-Gen. William Heath, by himself. New ed.; ed. by W: Abbatt; [also] acc. of the Battle of Bunker Hill. '01· '02(Ja11) O. net, $5. Abbatt.
Heath's home and school classics. il. D. 20 c.-60 c. Heath.
—Jordan, *comp.* True tales of birds and beasts.
—La Motte Fouqué. Undine. 30 c.
—Lamb. Tales from Shakespeare.
—Melville. Typee. 45 c.
—O'Shea, *ed.* Old world wonder stories.
—Perrault. Tales of Mother Goose.
Heath's modern language ser. S. Heath.
—Bowen. First scientific Fr. reader. 90 c.
—Daudet. Belle-Nivernaise. 30 c.
—Fulda. Talisman. 35 c.
—Grillparzer. Traum ein leben. 60 c.
—Heyse. Niels mit der offenen hand. 30 c.
—Körner. Zriny ein trauerspiel in fünf aufzügen. 35 c.
—Krüger *and* Smith. Eng.-Germ. conversation book. 25 c.
—Lessing. Minna von Barnhelm. 75 c.

Heath's modern language ser.—Continued.
—Renan. Souvenirs d' enfance et de jeunesse. 75 c.
—Ségur. Les malheurs de Sophie. 45 c.
—Verne. Vingt mille lieues sous les mers. 40 c.
—Wesselhoeft. Germ. composition. 45 c.

HEATING.
Lawler. Modern plumbing, steam and hot water heating. $5. Popular.

HEAVEN.
Swedenborg. Heavenly arcana. v. 13. $1.25. Mass. New-Ch. Un.

Heavenly harmonies for earthly living. McLeod, M. J. net, 50 c. Revell.

Heavenly vision. Booth, H: M. net, $1. Beam.

HEBREWS (*Epistles*).
See Bible.

Hebrew ideals from story of the patriarchs. Strachan, J. *60 c. net. Scribner.

HEBRIDES.
Boswell. Journ. of a tour to the Hebrides. net, 60 c. Macmillan.

Hector, *Mrs.* Annie F. Stronger than love. '02(Ag2) D. †$1.50. Brentano's.

Hector, *Mrs.* Annie F., ["*Mrs.* Alexander."] The yellow fiend. '02(Mr22) D. $1.50. Dodd.

Heddle, Ethel F. Mystery of St. Rubes. '02 (Je21) 12°, $1.50. Scribner.

Hedges, S: Statistics concerning education in the Philippine Islands. '02(Jl19) S. pap., 10 c. Benziger.

HELL.
Morton. Thoughts on hell. net, 50 c. Herder.

Hellems, Fred B. R. Lex de imperio Vespasiani. '02(My24) O. (Dissertationes Americanae. Classical philology, no. 1.) pap., 50 c. Scott, F. & Co

Helmolt, Hans F., *and others, eds.* Hist. of the world. In 8 v. v. 1. '02(F22); v. 4 (My24) il. O. ea., $6. Dodd.

Helps, *Sir* A. Spanish conquest in America. New ed. In 4 v. v. 2. '02(Je28) 12°, $1.50. Lane.

HEMATOLOGY.
See Blood.

Hemmeter, J: C. Diseases of the intestines. v. 2. '02(Mr22) il. 8°, net, $5; shp., net, $6. Blakiston.

Hempel, Walther. Methods of gas analysis; fr. 3d Germ. ed.; enl. by L. M. Dennis. '02(My3) 12°, net, $2.25. Macmillan.

Hemstreet, C: When old New York was young. '02(My10) il. O. net, $1.50. Scribner.

Henderson, C. H. Education and the larger life. '02(My3) D. net, $1.30. Houghton, M. & Co.

Henderson, Ernest F. Short hist. of Germany. In 2 v. '02(Mr29) 8°, net, $4. Macmillan.

Henley, M. Divine healing. '02(Ag23) D. (Pentecostal holiness lib., v. 5, no. 8.) 75 c.; pap., 10 c. Knapp.

Hennequin, Alfr. New treatise on the French verbs. '02(Ag30) 12°, 65 c. Am. Bk.

HENRY V., *King of England.*
Kingsford. Henry V. the typical mediæval hero. net, $1.35; net, $1.60. Putnam.

Henry, Alex. Travels and adventures in Canada and the Indian Territories, between the years 1760 and 1776. New ed.; ed., with notes, by J. Bain. '01. '02(F8) il. 8°, net, $4. Little, B. & Co.

Henry, Arth. Island cabin. '02(My24) D. $1.50. McClure, P.

Henry, W. H. F. How to organize and conduct a meeting. 2d ed. '02(Jl12) 12°, 75 c. Hinds.

Henry, W: E., *comp.* State platforms of the two dominant political parties in Ind., 1850-1900. '02(My10) O. $1.50. W: E. Henry.

Henry Esmond. *See* Thackeray, W: M.

Hensman, H. Cecil Rhodes. '02(F8) il. O. leath., net, $5. Harper.

Henson, Herb. H. Cross-bench views of current church questions. '02(Ap26) O. $4. Longmans.

Henson, Herb. H. Godly union and concord. '02(Mr22) O. $2. Longmans.

Her baby brother. Moulton, *Mrs.* L. C. 50 c. Little, B. & Co.

Her Serene Highness. Phillips, D: G. $1.50. Harper.

Heralds of empire. Laut, A. C. $1.50. Appleton.

Herbarium and plant description. Meier, W. H. D. 70 c. Ginn.

Herbartian methods. *See* Fennell, M.

Herbert, G: B. Illustrated hist. of the civil war in America. '01. '02(Ag2) il. 12°, (Farm and fireside lib., no. 197.) pap., 25 c. Crowell & K.

Herbert, H. F. *See* Baur, T. P.

Herbertson, F. D., *comp.* Descriptive geographies fr. original sources, Central and South America with the West Indies. '02 (Ap26) il. 12°, net, 70 c. Macmillan.

Herdman, Lee, *rep.* *See* Nebraska. *Sup. ct.* Repts.

Heredia, J. M. de. Sonnets from Trophies; rendered into Eng. by E. R. Taylor. [3d ed.] '02(Jl12) 12°, bds., *$1.25 net. Elder.

HEREDITY.
Bateson. Mendel's principles of heredity. *$1.30 net. Macmillan.
See also Evolution.

Heretic (The). Burnett, I. $1.50. Abbey Press.

Hereward the Wake. *See* Kingsley, C:

Herford, Brooke. Small end of great problems. '02(My10) D. net, $1.60. Longmans.

Herford, C: H., *ed.* English tales in verse. '02(My10) 12°, (Warwick lib. of Eng. literature.) $1.50. Scribner.

HERMANN *der Cherusker.*
Goebel. Hermann der Cherusker und die schlacht im Teutoburger walde. net, 50 c. Macmillan.

Hermitage. Ervin, D. $1. Grafton Press.

HERNIA.
Sultan. Atlas and epitome of abdominal hernia. *$3 net. Saunders.

Hero ser. il. D. net, 25 c. Jennings.
—Locke. Nineteenth century crusade. (5.)
—Typical American. (2.)
—Quayle. The gentleman in literature. (4.)
—A hero, Jean Valjean. (1.)—King Cromwell. (6.)
—Smith. Abraham Lincoln. (3.)

HEROES.
Gordy. Am. leaders and heroes. net, 60 c. Scribner

HEROES.—*Continued.*
Muzzey. Spiritual heroes. net, $1.25. Doubleday, P.
Price. Wandering heroes. 50 c. Silver.
Heroes of the nations ser.; ed. by E. Abbott. il. D. net, $1.35; net, $1.60. Putnam.
—Jenks. Edward Plantagenet. (35.)
—Kingsford. Henry v. (34.)
Heroine of the strait. Crowley, M. C. $1.50. Little, B. & Co.
Herrold, Maude M. Woman: diseases and remedies. '02(Jl19) il. 8°, $4; hf. mor., $5. Woman's Pub.
Herron, W: Wright. *See* Texas. Supplements.
Hershey, O. H. Quaternary of Southern California. '02(My17) il. Q. (Univ. of Cal. pub., v. 3. no. 1.) pap., 20 c. Univ. of Cal.
Herter, C. A. Lectures on chemical pathology. '02(Ja25) 12°, net, $1.75. Lea.
HERTFORDSHIRE.
Tompkins. Highways and byways in Hertfordshire. $2. Macmillan.
Herz, W. *See* Abegg, R.
He's coming to-morrow. Stowe, H. B. net, 25 c. Revell.
Hesperian tree. Piatt, J: J. $2. J: Scott.
Hessler, J: C., *and* Smith, Alb. L. Essentials of chemistry for secondary schools. '02 (Je7) il. O. $1.20. B: H. Sanborn.
Hester Blair. Carson, W: H: $1.50. C. M. Clark.
Hettinger, Franz. Timothy; tr. and adapt. by V. Stepka. '02(Je14) 12°, net, $1.50. Herder.
Heusler, F. Chemistry of the terpenes; tr. by F. J. Pond. Rev., enl. and corr. ed. '02 (Jl12) 8°, *$4 net. Blakiston.
Hewitt, Emma C. Three little Denvers. '02 (Ag2) il. D. **40 c. net. Jacobs.
Heydecker, E: L., *comp. See* New York. Supp. to general laws.
Heyse, P. J. L. L'arrabbiata; tr. by W. W. Florer. '02(Je28) S. 35 c. Wahr.
Heyse, P. J. L. Niels mit der offenen hand. '02(F1) S. (Modern lang. ser.) 30 c. Heath.
Hezekiah's wives. French, L. H. net. 85 c. Houghton, M. & Co.
Hiatt, C: Westminster Abbey. '02(Ap12) 12°, (Bell's cathedral ser.) 60 c. Macmillan.
Hibbard, Augustine G: Genealogy of the Hibbard family desc. of Rob. Hibbard, of Salem, Mass. '01· '02(F1) 8°, $5. Case.
Hickox, W: E. Correspondent's manual: practical information on letter taking and letter writing. '02(Mr29) S. $1.50. Lee & S.
HICKS, Thos. H.
Radcliffe. Gov. Thomas H. Hicks of Md., and the civil war. 50 c. Johns Hopkins.
Hidden hand. Southworth, *Mrs.* E. D. E. N. $1. Burt.
Higgin, L. Spanish life in town and country; with chaps. on Portuguese life by E. E. Street. '02(My24) il. D. (Our European neighbors.) net. $1.20. Putnam.
Higginson, H: L. Four addresses: The soldier's field: Harvard union I.; Harvard union II.; Robert Gould Shaw. '02(Ag23) D. bds., 75 c.; Japan ed., $5. Updike.
High, Edn. W. Hist. of the Sixty-eighth Reg. Ind. Vol. Inf., 1862-1865. '02(Ag2) il. 8°, $2.25; hf. mor., $3.50. E. W. High.
High, J. L. A great chancellor, and other papers; ed. by E. B. Smith. '01· '02(F15) 8°, net, $2.50. Callaghan.
High-caste Hindu woman. Ramabai Sarasvati. net, 75 c. Revell.
HIGHER CRITICISM.
Holborn. Pentateuch in the light of today. *75 c. net. Scribner.
Margoliouth. Lines of defense of the biblical revelation. net, $1.50. Gorham.
Highways and byways ser. 12°, $2. Macmillan.
—Tompkins. Highways and byways in Hertfordshire.
Hiley, Alan R. I., *and* Hassell, J: A. The mobile Boer. '02(Ap26) il. D. net, $1.50. Grafton Press.
Hill, F: T. The minority: (novel.) '02 (Ap19) D. $1. Stokes.
Hill, G. A. *See* Wentworth, G: A.
Hill, Grace L. An unwilling guest. '02(Je14) il. D. net, $1. Am. Bapt.
Hill, J. W. Diseases of the cat. '01· '02 (Ja4) il. D. $1.25. W: R. Jenkins.
Hill, Ja. J. *See* Flint, C: R.
Hill, Leonard E. Physiology for beginners. '02(Ag2) D. 35 c. Longmans.
Hillis, N. D. Master of the science of right living. '02(Ap12) 12°, bds., net, 50 c. Revell.
Hinchman, Lydia S. Early settlers of Nantucket. 2d rev. enl. ed. '02(F15) 8°, $5. Ferris.
Hind, C. L. Life's little things. '02(F1) 12°, $1.75. Macmillan.
Hinderers (The). Bayly, A. E. $1. Longmans.
Hinds, W: A. American communities; rev. ed., enl. '02(My3) il S. (Murby's sci. ser.) $1. Kerr.
HINDUS.
Ramabai Sarasvati. High-caste Hindu woman. net, 75 c. Revell.
Hines, E. W. *See* Kentucky decisions.
Hinkson, H. A. Point of honour. '02(Mr22) il. D. $1.50. McClurg.
Hinkson, *Mrs.* Kath. T. Golden lily. '02 (Mr22) il. S. 40 c. Benziger.
Hinton, Ma. B. Other notes. '02(Ap12) 16°, $1. Neale.
Hints ed. of novel and successful drills. S. pap., 15 c. Hints.
—Hatch. Zobo patriotic drill.
Hints to small libraries. Plummer, M. W. net, 50 c. M. W. Plummer.
Hiorns, Arth. H. Metallography. '02(Ag2) il. 12°, *$1.40 net. Macmillan.
His mother's letter. Merrill, J. M. $1. Saalfield.
Histoires (Les) de tante. Alissas, R. d'. net, 40 c. Macmillan.
HISTOLOGY.
Gaylord *and* Archoff. Atlas of pathological histology. net, $7.50. Lea.
Schäfer. Essentials in histology. *$3 net. Lea.
See also Microscope.
Historic Boston; sightseeing towns around the Hub. '01. '02(F15) 12°, net, 50 c.; pap., net, 30 c. Pilgrim Press.
Historical and linguistic studies in literature related to the New Testament. il. O. pap., net, 25 c. Univ. of Chic.
—Goodspeed. Newberry gospels. (v. 2, 1.)

Historical sources in schools ser. *See* Macmillan's.

HISTORY.

Bourne. Teaching of history and civics. $1.50. Longmans.

Helmolt, *and others, eds.* History of the world. v. 1, 4. ea., $6. Dodd.

Jesse. Historical memoirs. 30 v. ea., $2.50; complete set of 15 v., $37.40; $75. L. C. Page.

Kidd. Principles of western civilization. net, $2. Macmillan.

Larned, *ed.* Literature of Am. history. net, $6; $7.50; $9. Houghton, M. & Co.

Maitland, *and others.* Essays on the teaching of history. net, 75 c. Macmillan.

New England History Teachers' Assoc.; rept. **60 c. net. Macmillan.

Seligman. Economic interpretation of history. **$1.50 net. Macmillan.

Tout *and* Tait, *eds.* Historical essays. $5. Longmans.

West. Ancient history to death of Charlemagne. $1.50. Allyn & B.

See also Biography;—Church history;—Civilization;—Eastern question;—Ethnology;—Finance;—Middle ages;—Nineteenth century;—Political science;—Slavery;—Social science.

Hitchcock, F: H. Book-builder's handbook of types, scales, etc. [New issue.] '02 (Je28) S. leath., net, 50 c. Grafton Press.

Hoadley, G: A. Teacher's manual to accompany Brief course in physics. '02(Ag23) D. pap., 25 c. Am. Bk.

Hoar, G: F. *See* Lodge, H: C.

Hoare, H. W. Evolution of the Eng. Bible. New cheap ed. '02(My10) 8°, net, $2.50. Dutton.

Hobart, G: V. *See* McHugh, H.

Hobbs, W. R. P. Arithmetic of electrical measurements; rev. by R: Wormell. 9th ed. '02(My3) S. 50 c. Van Nostrand.

Hobhouse, Leonard T. Mind in evolution. '02(F1) 8°, net, $3.25. Macmillan.

Hochelaga depicta. Bosworth, N. net, $3; net, $4.50. Congdon.

Hocking, S. K. Awakening of Anthony Weir. '02(Ag23) D. $1.50. Union Press.

Hodder, Edn. Life of a century, 1800-1900. '01· '02(Ja11) 8°, net, $4. Scribner

Hodge, Clifton F. Nature study and life. '02 (Ap19) il. D. $1.65. Ginn.

Hodgman, F. Home's sweet harmonies: new part songs, quartets, etc. '02(F8) O. pap., 80 c. Home Pub.

Hodgson, Fred T. Estimating frame and brick houses. 2d rev., enl. ed. '02(Je7) il. 12°, $1. D: Williams.

Hoffman, F: L: Windstorm and tornado insurance. 3d ed. '02(Mr22) il. 16°, pap., 25 c. Spectator.

Hoffman, Harry C. Health and strength. '02 (F1) il. sq. D. pap., 25 c. H. C. Hoffman.

Hogan, J: C. Our new heraldry. '02(Ag2) 12°, $1. Lowman.

Hogarth, D: G: The nearer east. '02(Mr29) 8°, (World ser., no. 2.) $2. Appleton.

HOGARTH, W:

Anstruther. William Hogarth. $1. Macmillan.

Hohenzollern. Brady, C. T. $1.50. Century Co.

Holborn, Alfr. The Pentateuch in the light of to-day. '02(Ag23) 12°, *75 c. net. Scribner.

Holbrook, Flo. *See* Sterling, A. W.

Holdsworth, Annie E., [*Mrs.* E. J. Lee-Hamilton.] Michael Ross, minister. '02(Mr22) D. $1.50. Dodd.

HOLIDAYS.

Deems, *comp.* Holy-days and holidays. $5. Funk.

Holiness of the church in the 19th century. Scheeben, M. J. 10 c. Benziger.

Holland, Clive. My Japanese wife. [New rev., enl. ed.] '02(Je7) il. D. $1.50. Stokes.

Holleman, A. F. Text-book of inorganic chemistry; fr. the Dutch by H. C. Cooper. '02(My3) 8°, $2.50. Wiley.

Holley, Marietta, ["Josiah Allen's wife."] Samantha at Saratoga. '02(Ap19) il. 12°, (Home lib.) $1. Burt.

Hollinshed, T. E: New century speaker, writer and etiquette. '02(Ag30) 12°, $1.50. Am. Bk. and Bible.

Hollister, H. J., *and others.* Taxation in Mich. and elsewhere. '01· '02(F15) 8°, pap., 50 c. Mich. Pol. Sci. Assoc.

Holly Tree Inn. Dickens, C: net, $1.50. Lippincott.

Holme, Ma. P. M. Stray leaves from a border garden. '02(My10) il. 12°, net, $1.50. Lane.

Holmes, Burton, [*pseud.* for Elias Burton.] Burton Holmes lectures. In 10 v. v. 1-6. '01. '02(Jl19) il. 8°, subs., per set, $51; ¾ mor., $65. Little-P.

Holmes, C. J. Constable. '01· '02(Ja11) il. O. (Artist's lib., no. 5.) net, $1. Longmans.

Holmes, *Mrs.* Ma. J. Cousin Maude and Rosamond. '02(Ap19) 12°, (Home lib.) $1. Burt.

Holmes, *Mrs.* Ma. J. The Cromptons. '02 (Ag30) D. †$1. G: W. Dillingham.

Holmes, O. W. Professor at the breakfast table. '02(Ag2) 12°, (Home lib.) $1. Burt.

Holmes, T: Pictures and problems from London police courts. Pop. ed. '02(Ag2) D. $1.25. Longmans

Holst, Bernhart P., *ed.* Teachers' and pupils' cyclopædia. v. 1-3. '02(Ap26) 3 v., il. 8°, hf. mor., $12.75. Holst.

Holt's Am. science ser.; briefer course. D. $1.12. Holt.

—Remsen. Introd. to study of chemistry.

Holt's students' ser. of classic Fr. plays. D. net, 35 c. Holt.

—Corneille. Le Cid. (1.)

—Racine. Athalie. (2.)—Esther. (5.)

Holy-days and holidays. Deems, E: M. $5. Funk.

HOLY SPIRIT.

Barry. God the Holy Ghost. $2. Angel Press.

Tuttle. The gift of power. net, 25 c. Westminster.

Holy war. Bunyan, J: 50 c.; 75 c. Macmillan.

Homans, J. E. A B C of the telephone. '02 (F1) il. 12°, $1. Van Nostrand.

Home and school classics. *See* Heath's.

Home and school ser. *See* Flanagan's.

Home coming of autumn queen. Kellogg, A. M. 15 c. Kellogg

Home lib. *See* Burt's.

HOME STUDY.
McGovern. Fireside university of modern invention, discovery, etc., for home circle study and entertainment. $2.50; $3.75. Union Pub.
Powell. 20th century home builder. 25 c. Pub. Ho. of M. E. Ch., So.
Home thoughts. Cox, *Mrs.* J. F. net, $1.20. Barnes.
Homeric society. Keller, A. G. $1.20. Longmans.
Home's sweet harmonies. Hodgman, F. 80 c. Home Pub.
Homing pigeon (The): treatise on training, breeding, [etc.] '02(Mr15) il. T. pap., 25 c. G: E. Howard.
Honeyman, A. Van D. Bright days in merrie England. '02(Ap12) il. 12°, net, $1.50. Honeyman.
Honor of the Braxtons. Fosdick, J. W. $1.50. J. F. Taylor.
Hood, G. D. Dr. Hood's plain talks about the human system. '02(Ag2) il. 8°, $5. Hood.
Hood, G. D. Practical family physician. '01-'02(Ag2) il. 8°, $2.50. Hood.
Hood, T: Serious poems. '02(My10) il. 16°, (Caxton ser.) net, $1.25. Scribner.
Hood, Wharton P. Treatment of injuries by friction and movement. '02(Ap26) 12°, net, $1.25. Macmillan.
Hook, Alfr. J. American negligence digest fr. earliest time to 1902. '02(Jl12) O. shp., $6.50. Remick.
Hooker, *Sir* Jos. D. Nociones de botánica. Nueva ed. (N. León.) '02(Jl12) il. 16°, (Nuevas cartillas cientificas.) 40 c. Appleton.
Hope, Laurence, *comp.* India's love lyrics. '02(Ap19) il. 4°, net, $1.50. Lane.
Hopkins, E: W. India old and new. '01-'02(F15) 8°, (Yale bicentennial pub.) net, $2.50. Scribner.
Hopkins, Herb. M. The fighting bishop. '02 (Mr15) D. $1.50. Bowen-M.
Hopkins, S: A. Care of the teeth. '02(Jl19) D. **75 c. net. Appleton.
Hopkins, W: B. Roller bandage. 5th ed., rev. '02(Jl19) il. 12°, **$1.50 net. Lippincott.
Hopkins, W: J. The sandman: his farm stories. '03- '02(Ag23) il. O. **$1.20 net. L. C. Page.
Horace. Odæ, Epodæ, Carmen sæculare, picturis illustratæ. '01- '02(Mr29) il. 12°, (Antique gems from the Greek and Latin, v. 3.) (App. to pubs. for price.) Barrie.
Horæ Latinæ. Ogilvie, R. $5. Longmans.
Hornbook ser. O. shp. West Pub.
—Clark. Criminal law. $3.75.
Hornbrook, A. R. Key to Primary arithmetic and Grammar school arithmetic. '02(Mr8) D. 65 c. Am. Bk.
Hornung, E. W: At large. '02(F15) D. $1.50. Scribner.
Horridge, Fk. Dynamic aspects of nutrition. '02(Je7) 12°, $1.50. Wood.
Horrocks, W. H. Introd. to the bacteriolog. examination of water. '01- '02(My10) 8°, net, $3.68. Blakiston.
HORSE.
Carter. Horses, saddles and bridles. $2.75. Lord Balto.

HORSE.—*Continued.*
Chapman. Pathological treatment of lameness in the horse. $2. W: R. Jenkins.
Fillis. Breaking and riding; with military commentary. net, $5. Scribner.
Morgan. Twentieth century horse book. $1.50. D: B: Morgan.
Mullen. How to break, educate and handle the horse. $1. W: Mullen.
Russell. Prescriptions and instructions for treating diseases of feet and legs of the horse. $1. Clarke.
See also Veterinary medicine and surgery.
HORSESHOEING.
See Blacksmithing.
HORTICULTURE.
See Flowers;—Fruit;—Gardening.
Horton, Fs. A. Birthright membership of believers' infants in the New Testament church. '02(Je7) S. pap., 6 c. Presb. Bd.
Horton, Wa. F. Land buyer's, settler's and explorer's guide. '02(Jl12) 16°, pap., 25 c. Byron.
Hosmer, Ja. K. Hist. of the Louisiana purchase. '02(My10) il. D. net, $1.20. Appleton.
HOSPITALS.
Smart. Hdbk. for the hospital corps of the U. S. army and state military forces. *$2.50 net. Wood.
Hotchkiss, Chauncey C. Strength of the weak. '02(F1) D. $1.50. Appleton.
Houck, F: A. Life of St. Gerlach. 1900. '02(Mr22) D. net, 55 c. Benziger.
Hough, Emerson. Mississippi bubble. '02 (My3) il. D. $1.50. Bowen-M.
Hound of the Baskervilles. Doyle, A. C. $1.25. McClure, P.
Hour-glass stories. il. S. net, 40 c. Funk.
—Grenell. The sandals.
—Talbot. Courtship of sweet Anne Page.
Hours of the passion. King, H. E. H. net, $1.50. Dutton.
House of Cæsar. Van Santvoord, S. net, $5.25. Pafraets.
HOUSEKEEPING.
See Domestic economy.
Houston, Edn. J., *and* Kennelly, A. E. Alternating electric currents. 3d enl. ed. '02 (Je14) sq. S. (Elem. electro technical ser.) $1. McGraw.
Houston, Edn. J., *and* Kennelly, A. E. Electric arc lighting. 2d enl. ed. '02(Je14) sq. S. (Elem. electro technical ser.) $1. McGraw.
Houston, Edn. J., *and* Kennelly, A. E. Electric incandescent lighting. 2d enl. ed. '02 (Je14) sq. S. (Elem. electro technical ser.) $1. McGraw.
Houston, Edn. J., *and* Kennelly, A. E. Electric telephone. 2d ed., enl. '02(Jl5) sq. S. (Elem. electro-technical ser.) $1. McGraw.
How are we led? Sanders, C: H. $1.50. Donohue.
How Sammy went to coral-land. Atwater, E. P. **40 c. net. Jacobs.
How successful lawyers are educated. Macdonald, G: A. $1.50. Temple Pub.
How to attract an audience. Esenwein, J. B. $1. Hinds.
How to become a competent motorman. Livermore, V. B. $1. W: S. Livermore.
How to become a naturalized citizen. Pritchard, W: A. 10 c. Wehman.

How to break and handle the horse. Mullen, W: $1. W: Mullen.
How to build a knockabout. Mower, C. D. $1. Rudder.
How to build a model yacht. Fisher, H. $1. Rudder.
How to build a racing sloop. Mower, C. D. $1. Rudder.
How to build dynamo-electric machinery. Bubier, E: T. $2.50. Bubier.
How to get acquainted with God. Seward, T. F. net, 50 c. Funk.
How to live. Knapp, A. 36 c. Silver.
How to make an index. Wheatley, H: B: $1.25; $2.50. Armstrong.
How to make the telephone. Cary, G: H. $1. Bubier.
How to organize and conduct a meeting. Henry, W. H. F. 75 c. Hinds.
How to prepare essays, lectures, [etc.] Miles, E. H. net, $2. Dutton.
How to teach about trees. Payne, F. O. 25 c. Kellogg.
How to teach aquatic life. Payne, F. O. 25 c. Kellogg.
How to teach composition writing. Kellogg, A. M. 25 c. Kellogg.
How to tell fortunes. Zancig, *Mme.* 25 c. Drake.
How to tell time by the stars. Browne, D: M. 50 c. Lee & S.
How to treat the trusts. Haggerty, J: 25 c. Abbey Press.
Howard, B: Prisoners of Russia: convict life in Sakhalin and Siberia. '02(Je21) D. net, $1.40. Appleton.
Howard, Eliza B. Two waifs. '02(Jl12) D. 50 c. Abbey Press.
Howard, Hamilton G. Law points to know: treatise, consisting of 8 lectures on elem. law. '02(Jl5) S. pap., $1. H. G. Howard.
Howard, *Lady* Mabel. Failure of success. '01· '02(F8) D. $1.50. Longmans.
Howard, W: L. The perverts. '02(F15) D. $1.50. G: W. Dillingham.
Howe, Edn. D. *See* New York civil and criminal justice.
Howells, Mildred. *See* Burt, M. E.
Howells, W: D. The Kentons. '02(Ap26) D. $1.50. Harper.
Howes, G: B. Atlas of practical elem. zootomy. '02(Mr8) 4°, net, $3.50. Macmillan.
Hoyt, Eleanor. Misdemeanors of Nancy. '02 (Ap19) il. D. $1.50. Doubleday, P.
Hoyt, Helen B. Child's story of the life of Christ. '02(Jl5) il. 12°, $1.25. W. A. Wilde.
Hoyt, L: G. Practice in proceedings in the probate cts. of New Hampshire. '01· '02 (F8) O. shp., $2.50. Rumford Press.
Hoyt, T: A. Theology as a popular science. '02(Je21) S. pap., net, 10 c. Presb. Bd.
Hubbard, Elbert. Botticelli. '02(Ag16) sq. 12°, (Little journeys to the homes of eminent artists, v. 10, no. 3.) pap., 25 c. Roycrofters.
Hubbard, Elbert. Gainsborough. '02(Ag16) sq. D. (Little journeys to the homes of eminent artists, v. 10, no. 5.) pap., 25 c. Roycrofters.
Hubbard, Elbert. Leonardo. '02(Ag16) sq. 12°, (Little journeys to the homes of eminent artists, v. 10, no. 2.) pap., 25 c. Roycrofters.
Hubbard, Elbert. Message to Garcia and thirteen other things. '01. '02(F15) 8° limp leath., $2; $5; ¾ levant, $15. Roycrofters.
Hubbard, Elbert. Raphael. '02(Ag16) sq. 12°, (Little journeys to the homes of eminent artists, v. 10, no. 1.) pap., 25 c. Roycrofters.
Hubbard, Elbert. Thorwaldsen. '02(Ag16) sq. 12°, (Little journeys to the homes of eminent artists, v. 10, no. 4.) pap., 25 c. Roycrofters.
Hubbard, Elbert. Time and chance. '01. '02 (F15) D. $1.50. Putnam.
Hubbard, Elbert. Velasquez. '02(Ag16) sq. 12°, (Little journeys to the homes of eminent artists, v. 10, no. 6.) pap., 25 c. Roycrofters.
Huddilston, J: H. Lessons from Greek pottery, [with] bibliog. of Gr. ceramics. '02 (F1) 8°, net, $1.25. Macmillan.
Hudson, Horace B. California vineyards: scenes in Fresno Co. '02(Ap5) il. obl. D. pap., 35 c. H. B. Hudson.
Hudson, Horace B. Dict. of Minneapolis, 1902. '02(Jl5) il. S. pap., 25 c. H. B. Hudson.
Hufford, D: A. El camino real; highway connecting missions. '01· '02(F15) obl. Tt. pap., 35 c.; burnt yucca or redwood, 75 c.; burnt leath., $1; burnt orangewood, $1.25. D: A. Hufford.
Hufford, D: A. The real Ramona of Helen Hunt Jackson's famous novel. '02(F15) il. D. pap., 35 c.; burnt yucca or redwood, 75 c.; burnt leath., $1; burnt orangewood, $1.25. D: A. Hufford.
Hughes, Erlian. My island. '02(F15) 16°, $1.25. Dutton.
Hughes, H. W. Text-book of coal mining. New enl. ed. '01. '02(F15) il. 8°, $7. Lippincott.
Hughes, R. E. Schools at home and abroad. '02(Ap5) 12°, net, $1.50. Dutton.
Hugo, V. John Brown. '02(Jl12) sq. 12°, bds., $5; hf. leath., $15. Alwil Shop.
Hugo, V. Notre-Dame de Paris; abr. and ed. by J: R. Wightman. '02(Ap5) S. 85 c. Ginn.

HUGUENOTS.
Baird. Hist. of Huguenot emigration to America. 2 v. net, $2.50. Dodd.
Stapleton. Memorials of the Huguenots in America. $1.50. Huguenot.
Hulbert, W: D. Forest neighbors. '02 (My24) il. O. net. $1.50. McClure, P.
Hull, Mattie E. Spirit echoes. '01. '02 (Ap12) 12°, net, 75 c. Sunflower.
Hull Botanical Laboratory contributions. O. pap., net. Univ. of Chic.
—Cowles. Ecological rel. of vegetation on the sand dunes of Lake Mich. 75 c. (13.)
—Life. Tuber-like rootlets of cycas revoluta. 25 c. (26.)
—Livingston. Stimulus which causes change in polymorphic green algae. 25 c. (22.)
—Lyon. Study of the sporangia and gametophytes of selaginella apus and selaginella rupestris. 25 c. (31.)
—Overton. Parthenogenesis in thalictrum purpurascens. 25 c. (35.)
—Smith, R. W. Achromatic spindle in spore mother-cells of osmunda regalis. 25 c. (23.)

Hull Botanical Lib. contributions.—Continued.
—Stevens. Gametrogenesis and fertilization in albugo. 25 c. (29.)
—Webb. Morpholog. study of the flower and embryo of spirala. *25 c. (36.)
Hulsean lectures. *See* Chase, F: H:—Tennant, F. R.
HUMAN FIGURE.
See Anatomy for artists.
Human knowledge. Trask, R. D. *$2 net. R. D. Trask.
Human nature. Robinson, C: H: $2. Longmans.
Humble heroine. Tiddeman, L. E. 15 c. Lippincott.
HUME, D:
Gore. Imagination in Spinoza and Hume. net, 35 c. Univ. of Chic.
Hume, Fergus W. Millionaire mystery. '01-'02(Ja4) D. $1.25. Buckles.
Hume, Fergus W. Pagan's cup. '02(F8) D. $1.25. G: W. Dillingham.
Humphreys, *Mrs.* Eliz. M. J. G., ["Rita."] Sin of Jasper Standish. '02(Mr22) D. $1.25. Fenno.
Hun, Marcus T. *See* New York. *Sup. ct.* Repts.
Huneker, Ja. Melomaniacs. '02(Mr1) D. $1.50. Scribner.
Hungerford, Herb. Success club debater. '01-'02(Mr1) Tt. (Boiled-down booklets.) 25 c. Success.
Hungerford, *Mrs.* Marg. H., ["The Duchess," *formerly Mrs.* Argles.] The three graces. '01- '02(Mr1) 12°, (Popular lib.) $1. Lippincott.
Hunt, A. M. United Mercantile Agency credit ratings for marble, granite and stone dealers. '02(Ag9) 8°, subs., $25. Un. Merc.
HUNT, Holman.
Williamson. Holman Hunt. 50 c. Macmillan.
Hunt, J. N., *and* Gourley, H. I. Modern pronouncing speller. '02(Jl19) 12°, 20 c. Butler.
Hunt, Ma. A. Scientific Bible. Reason—revelation—rapture: [poem.] '02(Ag9) 12°, $1. F. E. Ormsby.
Hunt, W., *ed.* *See* Stephens, W: R. W., *ed.*
Hunter, W: C. Twentieth century wonder book. '02(My17) 12°, 50 c.; pap., 25 c. Donohue.
Huntington, Annie O. Studies of trees in winter: des. of the deciduous trees of Northeastern America. '02(Ja18) il. O. net, $2.25. Knight.
Hurd, Harvey B., *comp. and ed.* *See* Illinois. *Gen. assembly.* Revised statutes.
Hurll, Estelle M., *ed.* Tuscan sculpture. Lib. ed. '02(Ap5) D. (Riverside art ser., no. 11.) net, 75 c.; School ed., net, 50 c.; pap., net, 35 c. Houghton, M. & Co.
Hurll, Estelle M., *ed.* Van Dyck. Lib. ed. '02(Je7) (Riverside art ser., no. 12.) net, 75 c.; School ed., net, 50 c.; pap., net, 35 c. Houghton, M. & Co.
Hurst, C: Hints on steam engine design and construction. '01- '02(F15) 16°, bds., 60 c. Lippincott.
Hurst, J: F. History of rationalism; emb. survey of present state of Protestant theology; rev. '01- '02(F15) 8°, $2.50. Eaton & M.
Hurst, J: F. The new hearthstone: bridal greeting. '02(Mr1) O. $1. Jennings.
Hurst, J: F. Upon the sunroad. '02(My17) 16°, 25 c. Revell.
Hutchinson, H. G. A friend of Nelson. '02(Ag2) D. *$1.50 net. Longmans.
Hutchinson, H. N., Gregory, J. W., *and* Lydekker, R. Living races of mankind. '02(Ap12) il. 8°, net, $5. Appleton.
Hutchinson, Ida W. Gospel story of Jesus Christ. '02(Mr29) 12°, $1.50. Dutton.
Hutchinson, Jos. Primrose diplomacy: [poetry.] '02(Jl19) 12°, $1.25. Abbey Press.
Hutchison, Jos. C. Lessons in physiology and hygiene. 2d bk. for advanced grades. Rev. ed. '02(Jl12) il. 12°, (Physiological ser.) 80 c.; bds., 40 c. Maynard, M. & Co.
Hutchison, Joc. C. Treatise on physiology and hygiene. New ed. '02(Ag23) il. 12° $1. Maynard, M. & Co.
Hutton, E. Studies in the lives of the saints. '02(Ag23) 12°, *$1.25 net. Dutton.
Hutton, R. E. The soul in the unseen world. '02(Ap5) 12°, net, $2. Dutton.
Hutton, T: B. American history outlines. '02(Ag30) 16°, pap., 30 c. Sac Sun.
HUXLEY, T: H:
Clodd. Thomas Henry Huxley. net, $1. Dodd.
Hyde, Miles G. The girl from Mexico, and other stories and sketches. 3d ed. '02(Ap26) D. $1. Abbey Press.
Hyde, W. H., *and* McManman, J. A. Telephone troubles. 8th ed. '01. '02(F15) 16°, pap., 25 c. Caspar.
HYDRAULIC ENGINEERING.
Church. Diagrams of mean velocity of uniform motion of water in open channels. $1.50. Wiley.
Fanning. Hydraulic and water-supply engineering. $5. Van Nostrand.
Fidler. Calculations in hydraulic engineering. pt. 2. $3. Longmans.
HYDRO-KINETICS.
See Hydraulic engineering.
HYDROTHERAPY.
Kellogg. Rational hydrotherapy. subs., $5; $6. Davis.
HYGIENE.
Ames. Elem. hygiene for the tropics. 60 c. Heath.
Balch. Manual for boards of health. $1.50. Banks & Co.
Bryce. Ideal health and how to attain it. 50 c. Treat.
Furneaux. Elem. practical hygiene. 90 c. Longmans.
Hoffman. Health and strength. 25 c. H. C. Hoffman.
Knapp. How to live. 36 c. Silver.
Morris. Right living; or, how a woman can keep well. $1. Bardeen.
Sedgwick. Principles of sanitary science and public health. net, $3. Macmillan.
Smith. Anatomy, physiology and hygiene. $1. W: R. Jenkins.
Van Doren. Students' guide to health. $2. D. T. Van Doren.
Willoughby. Hygiene for students. $1.25. Macmillan.
See also Contagion;—Diet;—Mind and body;—Physiology;—Sanitary engineering.
HYMNS AND HYMNWRITERS.
Gabriel, *comp.* Joyful praise. 30 c. Jennings.

HYMNS AND HYMNWRITERS.—*Continued.*
Gill, *and others.* Hymns of grace and glory. 30 c. Mattill & L.
Nott, *ed.* Seven great hymns of the mediæval church. *$1 net. Gorham.
See also Church music.
Hymns of the faith. Dhammapada. $1. Open Court.
Hypatia. *See* Kingsley, C:
Hyperion. Longfellow, H: W. $1. Burt.
HYPNOTISM.
Alpheus. Guide to hypnotism. 50 c.; 25 c. Donohue.
Ballough. Sibylline leaves. $1. Painter.
De Laurence. Hypnotism and magnetism. $1; 50 c. Drake.
De Laurence. Hypnotism. $1.50. Henneberry.
Eldridge. Hypnotism. 50 c. Penn Pub. Co.
Santanelli. Is man a free agent? Law of suggestion, [etc.] *$1 net. Santanelli.
HYSTERICS.
See Mind and body.
I go a fishing. Barton, W: E. 25 c. Revell.
I promessi sposi. Manzoni, A. $1.20. Silver.
ICE CREAM.
See Confectionery.
Idaho codes annot. 4 v. '02(Ag30) 8°, shp., $17. Bancroft-W.
Idea of God. Reed, E. A. net, 75 c. Univ. of Chic.
Ideal health. Bryce, A. 50 c. Treat.
Ideal messages ser. net, 25 c. Revell.
—Stowe. He's coming to-morrow.
Ideal word book. Smith, E. E. 17 c. Flanagan.
IDEALISM.
Sturt, *ed.* Personal idealism. *$3.25 net. Macmillan.
Idole (L'). Michaud, H. 10 c. W: R. Jenkins.
Idylls. *See* Theocritus.
Idylls of the king. *See* Davidson, *Mrs.* H. A.
If I were king. McCarthy, J. H. $1.50. Russell.
Iliad and Odyssey. *See* Keller, A. G.
Illinois. *Appellate cts.* Repts. v. 97. '02 (Mr1); v. 98 (Mr29); v. 99 (My17); v. 100 (Jl19) O. shp., ea., $3.75. Callaghan.
Illinois. Commentary on the mechanics' lien law, by C: T. Farson. '02(F1) O. net, $4. Callaghan.
Illinois. Compilation of laws rel. to township organization and county affairs, by E. M. Haines. 23d ed., rev., by A. Matteson. '02(Jl12) O. shp., $3; hf. cl., $2.50. Legal Adv.
Illinois. *General assembly.* Revised statutes, 1901. (H. B. Hurd.) '01·'02(Mr8) O. shp., net, $4. Chic. Leg. News.
Illinois. Homestead exemption laws, by A. M. Kales. '02(Jl5) O. *$4 net. Callaghan.
Illinois. Index-digest of repts. In 2 v. v. 1. '02(Ag2); v. 2 (Ag9) O. shp., ea., $9. Flood.
Illinois. *Supreme ct.* Repts. v. 192. '02 (Mr29); v. 193 (My17); v. 194 (Ag9) O. shp., ea., $2.25. Phillips.
ILLINOIS.
Arnold, *comp.* Manual of school laws. $1.75. Effingham Dem.
Bunzey. Hist. of companies I and E, 6th Regt. Ill. Vol. Inf. $2. R. S. Bunzey.
ILLINOIS.—*Continued.*
Pratt. Stories of Ill. 50 c.; 40 c. Educ. Pub.
Illustrated family Christian almanac, 1902. '02(Mr1) sq. 12°, pap., 10 c. Am. Tr.
ILLUSTRATIONS (*religious*).
See Sermons.
ILLUSTRATORS.
See Book illustration.
Im freundes kreise. Nichberg-Wagner, M. $1. Stechert.
Imagination in Spinoza and Hume. Gore, W. C. net, 35 c. Univ. of Chic.
Imhaus, Eliz. V. Exiled by the world. '02 (Mr8) il. D. $1.50. Mutual Pub.
Imitation and analysis. Donnelly, F. P. 60 c. Allyn & B.
Imitator (The): (novel.) '01·'02(Ap5) D. $1.25. W: M. Reedy.
IMMORTALITY.
See Future life.
Improprieties of Noah. Smedberg, H. V. 50 c. Abbey Press.
Improvement of moral qualities. Gabirol, S. I. net, $1.25. Macmillan.
In a Tuscan garden. '02(Je28) il. 12°, net, $1.50. Lane.
In a walled garden. Belloc, B. R. net, $1.25. Herder.
In and around the Grand Canyon. James, G: W. net, $10. Little, B. & Co.
In defense of Judas. Story, W: W. $1. Philosopher Press.
In His name. *See* Hale, E: E.
In memoriam. Tennyson, A. *Lord.* net, $1.20. Scribner.
In my vicarage garden. Ellacombe, H: N. net, $1.50. Lane.
In quest of the quaint. Chase, E. B. $1.50. Ferris.
In Sicily. Sladen, D. 2 v. net, $20. Dutton.
In the country God forgot. Charles, F. $1.50. Little, B. & Co.
In the days of giants. Brown, A. F. net, $1.10. Houghton, M. & Co.
In the eagle's talon. Stevens, *Mrs.* S. $1.50. Little, B. & Co.
In the footprints of the padres. Stoddard, C: W. net, $1.50. A. M. Robertson.
In the Michigan lumber camps. Whittier, C: A. 75 c. Neely.
In the misty realm of fable. Kleckner, E. R. $1. Flanagan.
In the palace of the king. Crawford, F. M. 50 c. Am. News.
In Thompson's woods. Crissey, F. $1. Blue Sky Press.
In Tuscany. Carmichael, M. net, $2. Dutton.
In Viking land. Weborg, J. $1.25. J. C. Weborg.
In white and black. Pinson, W. W. $1.50. Saalfield.
Inauguration of President Watterson. De Leon, T: C. 25 c. Am. Writers.
INDEPENDENT CONG. CHURCH.
See Unitarian church.
INDEXES.
Engineering Magazine. Index, 1896-1900. $7.50. Engineering Mag.
Fletcher *and* Bowker. Annual literary index, 1901. net, $3.50. Pub. Weekly.
INDEXING.
Wheatley. How to make an index. $1.25; $2.50. Armstrong.
See also Cataloguing.

INDIA.
Denning. Mosaics from India. net, $1.50. Revell.
Hopkins. India old and new. net, $2.50. Scribner.
Remy. Influence of India on the poetry of Germany. net, $1. Macmillan.
Russell. Village work in India. net, $1. Revell.

INDIAN MUTINY.
Fitchett. Tale of the great mutiny. $1.50. Scribner.
Norman. Delhi (1857): acc. of the great mutiny. **$8 net. Lippincott.

Indiana. Annot. practice code forms. 2d and rev. ed. in 1 v. '02(Jl5) O. shp., *$6 net. W. H. Anderson & Co.
Indiana. General index of statutes cont. in annot. Ind. statutes; by H. Burns. '01-'02(My24) O. shp. (Sold only with the Ind. statutes.) Bowen-M.

INDIANA.
Ewbank. Ind. trial evidence. $6. Bowen-M.
Henry, *comp.* State platforms of the two dominant pol. parties in Ind. $1.50. W: E. Henry.
High. Hist. of the 68th Regt., Ind. Vol. Infantry, 1862-65. $2.25; $3.50. E. W. High.
McDonald. Treatise on laws of Ind., pertaining to duties of justices of the peace, mayors, etc. net, $7.50. Clarke.
Works. Practice, pleading and forms adapt. to the new rev. code of Ind. v. 1-3. $18. Clarke.

Indiana girl. Lincoln, C: H: $1.50. Neale.
Indianapolis Sentinel year book and almanac, 1902. '01-'02(Ap26) 12°, pap., 25 c. Indianapolis Sentinel.

INDIANS.
Colden. Five Indian nations of Canada. 2 v. net, ea., $1. New Amsterdam.
Parkman. Conspiracy of Pontiac. $1. Burt.
Tooker. Algonquian series. v. 9, 10. ea., *$1.50 net. F. P. Harper.
Trask, *ed.* Letters of Col. Thomas Westbrook and others rel. to Indian affairs in Maine, 1722-26. $5. Littlefield.
See also Iroquois;—Zuñi Indians.

India's love lyrics. Hope, L. net, $1.50. Lane.

INDICATORS.
Cohn. Indicators and test-papers, their source and tests for sensitiveness. $2. Wiley.

INDO-IRANIAN LANGUAGE.
Gray. Indo-Iranian phonology. net, $3. Macmillan.

INDULGENCES.
Kaercher, *comp.* Summary of indulgences, granted to the secular branch of the Third order of St. Francis. 15 c. Herder.
Portiuncula. Indulgence of portiuncula. 5 c. Herder.

Industrial democracy. Webb, S. net, $4. Longmans.
Inez. Wilson, *Mrs.* A. J. E. 75 c. Burt.
Infans amoris. Harry, T. E. $1.50. Abbey Press.
Infant salvation. Firey, M. J. net, $1.20. Funk.

INFANTRY.
Craufurd. Field training of a company of infantry. $1. Longmans.

INFECTIOUS DISEASES.
See Hygiene;—Smallpox.

Ingelow, Jean. Wonder-box tales. '02(Ag2) il. 12°, (Young of heart ser., no. 35.) 50 c. Estes.
Ingersoll, Ernest. Wild life of orchard and field. '02(Mr29) il. D. net, $1.40. Harper.
Ingersoll, Rob. G. Works. In 12 v. v. 1-8. Dresden ed. [New rev., enl. ed.] '02(My10); v. 9-12 (Je28) 8°, per v., $2.50. Dresden.
Ingerson, Carlos I. Normal method in double entry bookkeeping. '01-'02(Je28) 12°, 50 c. Interstate.
Ingraham, Jos. H. Throne of David. '02(My10) 12°, (Home lib.) $1. Burt.
Ingram, Arth. F. M. Under the dome. '02(Je7) 12°, $1.25. E. & J. B. Young.
Ingres, Maxime. Cours complet de langue Française; troisème ed. v. 1. '01-'02(Ja11) O. net, $1.50. Univ. of Chic.

INJURIES.
Hood. Treatment of injuries by friction and movement. net, $1.25. Macmillan.
Michigan. Law of personal injuries. net, $4. Callaghan.
See also Accidents.

Inns of court sermons. Beeching, H. C. $1.25. Macmillan.

INNUIT LANGUAGE.
Barnum. Grammatical fundamentals of the Innuit language as spoken by the Eskimo. $5. Ginn.

INSANITY.
Brower *and* Bannister. Manual of insanity. $2. Saunders.
Defendorf. Clinical psychiatry. net, $3.50. Macmillan.
Mercier. Text-book of insanity. net, $1.75. Macmillan.
Warde. Experiences as a lunatic. $1. J. C. Warde.
See also Brain;—Mind and body;—Nervous system.

INSCRIPTIONS.
Stevenson. Assyrian and Babylonian contracts, with Aramaic ref. notes. $2.50. Am. Bk.
Tolman. Guide to old Persian inscriptions. $1.50. Am. Bk.

INSECTS.
Fabre. Insect life. $1.75. Macmillan.
Sanderson. Insects injurious to staple crops. $1.50. Wiley.
See also Mosquitoes;—Spiders.

Insuperable barrier. *See* Calvin, E. R.

INSURANCE.
Elliott. Law of insurance $4. Bowen-M.
Frost. Treatise on guaranty insurance. $5. Little, B. & Co.
Hoffman. Windstorm and tornado insurance. 25 c. Spectator.
Kerr. Law of insurance. $6. Keefe-D.
New York. Statutory revision of laws affecting insurance companies. $1.50. Banks & Co.
See also Corporations.

INTELLECT.
See Knowledge;—Psychology.

INTEREST.
Fisher. Added interest tables.—20th century interest tables. ea., $2.50. J: I. Fisher.
Van Arsdale. 20th century interest tables. $1.50. Vawter.

Interior decorations and furnishings of London Guild Halls. '02(Mr29) 40 pls., f°, portfolio, net, $12; bound, pls. guarded, net, $15. Helburn.

INTERMEDIATE STATE.
See Future life.

Intermere. Taylor, W: A. $1. XX Century.

Internal improvements in Alabama. Martin, W: E. 30 c. Johns Hopkins.

International annual of Anthony's photographic bulletin and Am. process yearbook. v. 14 for 1902; ed. by W. I. Scandlin. '01-'02(Mr1) il. O. $1.25; pap., 75 c. Anthony.

International Cable Directory Co., *comp.* Internat. cable directory of the world in conjunction with Western Union telegraphic code system. '02(Jl19) O. $15. Int. Cable.

International education ser. *See* Appleton's.

INTERNATIONAL LAW.
Taylor. Treatise on internat. public law. net, $6.50. Callaghan.
See also Citizenship;—Naturalization.

International medical annual, 1902. '02 (Ap12) il. 8°, net, $3. Treat.

International theol. lib.; ed. by S. D. F. Salmond and C: A. Briggs. O. net, $2.50. Scribner.
—Rainy. Ancient Catholic church, A.D 98-451.

International year book, 1901. '02(My24) Q. $4. Dodd.

Interviews with a monocle. Jordon, L. 50 c. Whitaker & R.

INTESTINES.
Hemmeter. Diseases of the intestines. v. 2. net, $5; net, $6. Blakiston.

Into the light. Taylor, E: R. net, 75 c. Elder.

INVENTIONS.
See Patents.

INVERTEBRATES.
Pratt. Course in invertebrate zoölogy. $1.35. Ginn.

INVESTMENTS.
See Railroads.

Ioläus. Carpenter, E: net, $1.75. Goodspeed.

Ione, *pseud.* *See* Brown, G. M.

Iowa. The citator. '02(Jl12) D. limp skiver, $3. R. Adams.

Iowa. Encyclopedia of Iowa law; cont. legal words and phrases, with comments by E. C. Ebersole. '02(Mr8) O. shp., $6. E. C. Ebersole.

IRAN.
See Persia.

Ireland, Ma. E. Timothy and his friends. '02(Ag9) il. 12°, $1. Saalfield.

IRELAND.
Falkiner. Studies in Irish hist. and biog. mainly of 18th century. $5. Longmans.
Martin. Traces of the elder faiths of Ireland. 2 v. $12. Longmans.
O'Byrne. Kings and vikings.—Land of heroes: stories fr. Irish history. ea., $1.25. Scribner.
O'Conor, *comp.* Irish com-all-ye's. 25 c. —Old time songs and ballads of Ireland. $2. Popular.
See also Patrick, St.

IRISH.
See Scots.

Irish fairy and folk tales. Yeats, W: B. $1. Burt.

IRISH LANGUAGE.
O'Growney. Revised simple lessons in Irish. pt. 1. 15 c. Gael.

IRISH LITERATURE.
Stokes *and* Strachan, *eds.* Thesaurus palæohibernicus: coll. of old Irish glosses, scholia, etc. net, $8. Macmillan.

Irish wit and humor. '02(Mr15) S. pap., 25 c. Drake.

IRON.
Keep. Cast iron: record of orig. research. $2.50. Wiley.
West. Metallurgy of cast iron. $3. Cleveland Pr.

Iron Age directory. '02(My24) 16°, flex. linen, 25 c. D: Williams.

Iron hand. Dean, H. $1. Abbey Press.

Ironquill, *pseud.* *See* Fitch, E.

IROQUOIS.
Morgan. League of the Ho-de-no-sau-nee or Iroquois. 2 v. **$15 net; $30 net. Dodd.
Moulthrop. Iroquois. 75 c.; 50 c. Hart.

Irregular and regular commercial paper. McMaster, J. S. $2. McMaster.

IRRIGATION.
Newell. Irrigation in the U. S. net, $2. Crowell.
Wilcox. Irrigation farming. $2. Judd.

Irving, W. Selections from Sketch-book. Regents ed.; ed. by C. T. Benjamin. '02 (F1) D. 50 c. Am. Bk.

Irving, W. Sketch book. '02(Je21) 2 v., il. 16°, (Caxton ser.) net, $1.25. Scribner.

Irving, W. Two selections: Legend of Sleepy Hollow and Rip Van Winkle from Sketch book; notes, etc., by J. W. Graham. '02 (Je7) 12°, leatherette, 25 c. Whitaker & R.

Irwin, Wallace, ["Omar Khayyám, jr."] Love sonnets of a hoodlum. '01. '02(Mr22) 16°, pap., 25 c.; Bandana ed., 50 c. Elder.

Irwin, Wallace. Rubáiyat of Omar Khayyám, jr. '02(My24) il. O. pap., net, 50 c. Elder.

Is man a free agent? Santanelli. *$1 net. Santanelli.

Is the negro a beast? Schell, W: G. 60 c. Gospel Trumpet.

ISABELLA, *Queen of Castile.*
See Ferdinand, *King of Spain.*

Isabella. Keats, J: $1; 60 c. Macmillan.

Isham, F: S. The strollers. '02(Mr22) il. D. $1.50. Bowen-M.

Ishmael. Southworth, *Mrs.* E. D. E. N. $1. Burt.

Islam and Christianity. '01- '02(Mr1) 12°, $1. Am. Tr.

Island cabin. Henry. A. $1.50. McClure, P.

Isler, C. Well boring for water, brine and oil. '02(Ap5) il. 8°, $4. Spon.

Isolation in the school. Young, E. F. net, 50 c. Univ. of Chic.

ISRAEL.
See Jews.

Isthmian canal. Johnson, E. R. 25 c. Am. Acad. Pol. Sci.

Isthmian canal question. Pasco, S: 25 c. Am. Acad. Pol. Sci.

ITALIAN LANGUAGE.
Manzoni. I promessi sposi. $1.20. Silver.

Italian painting. Van Dyke, J: C: 50 c. Elson.

Italian Renaissance in England. Einstein, L. net, $1.50. Macmillan.

ITALY.
Cruickshank. Umbrian towns. net, $1.25. Wessels.
Friedländer. Town life in ancient Italy. 75 c. B: H. Sanborn.
Villari. Barbarian invasions of Italy. 2 v. net, $7.50. Scribner.
Whitcomb. Little journey to Italy. 15 c. Flanagan.
See also Florence;—Medici; — Rome;—Sicily; — Tuscany.

It's up to you. McHugh, H. 75 c. G: W. Dillingham.

Ivanhoe and Rob Roy, retold for children. Sullivan, *Sir* E: 50 c. Little, B. & Co.

IVORY.
Cust. Ivory workers of the Middle Ages. $2. Macmillan.

J., C. J. Otis Grey, bachelor. '02(Je7) S. 75 c. Mutual Bk.

Jack, C: B. Outline of mining law. '02 (Ag9) S. $1; pap., 50 c. Derge.

Jackanapes. Ewing, *Mrs.* J. H. net, 15 c. Houghton, M. & Co.

Jackman, Warren. Hist. of the town of Elma, Erie Co., N. Y. '02(My24) O. $3. Hausauer.

Jackson, Dugald C., *and* Jackson, J: P. Elem text-book on electricity and magnetism. '02 (F22) il. 12°, hf. leath., net, $1.40. Macmillan.

Jackson, J: P. *See* Jackson, D. C.

Jacob, J: T: Christ the indweller. '02 (My3) 12°. $1.50. Macmillan.

Jacobs, W: W. At Sunwich port. '02(My10) il. D. $1.50. Scribner

Jacobson, W. H. A., *and* Steward, F. J Operations of surgery. '02(My17) 2 v., il. 8°, net, $10; shp., or hf. mor. $12. Blakiston.

Jacoby, Harold. Practical talks by an astronomer. '02(Ap12) il. D. net, $1. Scribner.

Jacoby, H: D. *See* Merriman, M.

James, Alfr. Cyanide practice. '01. '02 (Ja25) il. 4°, $5. Engineering.

James, Bushrod W. Political freshman. '02 (Ap19) D. $1.50. Bushrod Lib.

James, *Mrs.* Flor. A. P., ["Florence Warden."] The lovely Mrs. Pemberton. '02 (F8) D. $1.25. Buckles.

James, G: W. In and around the Grand Canyon. Pasadena ed. '01· '02(F22) il. 8°, hf. mor., net, $10. Little, B. & Co.

James, W: Varieties of religious experience. '02(Je21) O. (Gifford lectures, 3d ser.) net, $3.20. Longmans.

James Griffin's adventures on land and sea. Dee, H. $1. Yewdale.

JAMESTOWN, Va.
Hall. Jamestown, 1607-1907. 25 c. Am. Scenic.

Jane Eyre. Brontë, C. **$1.60 net. Dodd.

Janes, Emily, *ed.* *See* Englishwoman's year book.

Janes, L. G. Lewis G. Janes, philosopher, patriot, lover of man. '02(Ap19) il. D. $1. J. H. West.

Janet, Pierre. Mental state of hystericals; tr. by C. R. Corson. '02(Mr1) 12°, $3.50. Putnam.

JAPAN.
Brinkley. Japan. 5 v. ea., $50. Millet.

JAPAN.—*Continued.*
Chamberlain. Things Japanese. *$4 net. Scribner.
Kinosita. Past and present of Japanese commerce. *$1.50 net. Macmillan.
Menpes. Japan. net, $6. Macmillan.
Stead. Japan of to-day. net, $2. Dutton.

Jarvis, Lucy C., *ed.* Sketches of church life in colonial Connecticut. '02(Ag2) 12°, $1. Tuttle, M. & T.

Jastrow, Morris, *jr.* Study of religion. '01· '02(Ja11) 12°, (Contemporary science ser.) $1.50. Scribner.

Jean Mitchell's school. Wray, A. W. $1.25. Public Sch. Pub.

Jean Valjean. *See* Quayle, W: A.

Jebb, *Sir* R: C. Modern Greece: two lectures del. before the philosophical institution of Edinburgh. 2d ed. '02(F1) 12°, (Eversley ser.) $1.75. Macmillan.

JEFFERSON, Thos.
See Burr, A.

Jegi, J: I. Syllabus of human physiology for schools and colleges. '01· '02(Mr8) il. 12°, $1. Gillan.

Jekyll, Gertrude, *comp.* Lilies for English gardens. '01· '02(Ja11) 8°, (Country life lib.) net, $3.75. Scribner.

Jekyll, Gertrude, *and* Mawley, E:, *comps.* Roses for Eng. gardens. '02(Ag23) 8°, *$3.75 net. Scribner.

Jellison, Edn. A: The wounded beast: [poem.] '01· '02(Mr29) D. pap., 25 c. E. A: Jellison.

Jenkins, C: F. Guide book to historic Germantown. '02(Ag2) il. 12°, 50 c. Site and Relic.

Jenkins' contes choisis. sq. S. 40 c.; pap., 25 c. W: R. Jenkins.
—Coppée. Morceau de pain. (22.)

Jenkinson, I: Aaron Burr, his rel. with Thomas Jefferson and Alex. Hamilton. '02 (My3) D. $1.25. I: Jenkinson.

Jenkins's vest-pocket lexicon. New ed. '02 (Ag2) 16°, limp leath., 60 c.; limp leath., with tuck, 75 c. Lippincott.

Jenks, E: Edward Plantagenet, (Edward I.): the Eng. Justinian. '02(Mr8) D. (Heroes of the nations ser., no. 35.) net, $1.35; hf. leath., net, $1.60. Putnam.

Jennings, J: E. Manual of ophthalmoscopy. '02(Mr1) il. 8°. net, $1.50. Blakiston.

Jerry's reward. Barnett, E. S. 50 c. L. C. Page.

Jesse, J: H. Historical memoirs. First ser. (15 v.) and second ser. (15 v.) '02(Ap5) 30 v., 8°, per v., $2.50; complete set of 15 v., (first or second ser.) $37.40; ¾ mor., $75. L. C. Page.

Jessup, Alex., *ed.* *See* Balzac, H. de.—Stevenson, R. L:

Jesuit relations. (Thwaites.) In 73 v. v. 72, 73. Index to entire ser. '01. '02(Mr1) 8°, ea., net, $3.50. Burrows.

JESUITS.
See Jesus (Society of).

JESUS CHRIST.
Boardman. Our risen King's forty days. net, $1.25. Lippincott.
Burton *and* Mathews. Constructive studies in the life of Christ. $1. Univ. of Chic.
Dalman. Words of Jesus. *$2.50 net. Scribner.

JESUS CHRIST.—*Continued.*
Hoyt. Child's story of the life of Christ. $1.25. W. A. Wilde.
Hutchinson. Gospel story of Jesus Christ. $1.50. Dutton.
Jacob. Christ the indweller. $1.50. Macmillan.
Life and works of the Redeemer. net, $2. Dutton.
McClelland. Verba crucis. 50 c. Crowell.
Moberly. Christ our life. net, $3. Longmans.
Nicoll. Church's one foundation, Christ. $1.25. Armstrong.
Paget. Christ the way. 75 c. Longmans.
Pearson. Carpenter prophet. $1.50. H. S. Stone.
Rénan. Life of Jesus. $1. Burt.
Robinson. Human nature: sequel to Studies in the character of Christ. $2. Longmans.
Rutherford. Christ and his cross. $1. Longmans.
Speer. Principles of Jesus app. to some questions of to-day. net, 80 c. Revell
Stretton. New child's life of Christ. $1. Winston.
Taylor, *and others.* Studies in the life of Christ. 75 c. Jennings.
Vincent. What is it to believe on the Lord Jesus Christ? 5 c. Beam.
Weinstock. Jesus the Jew. **$1 net. Funk.
White, J. E. The coming King. $1. Southern Pub.
Wollpert. A man amongst men. 15 c. Eckler.
See also Bible; — Christianity; — Easter; — Lord's supper.

JESUS (Society of).
Jesuit relations v. 72, 73. ea., $3.50. Burrows.
Taunton. Hist of the Jesuits in England, 1580-1773. net, $3.75. Lippincott.

Jeter, J. B. Baptist principles reset. New and enl. ed. '02(Jl19) 16°, $1. Rel. Herald.
Jewett, C: Essentials of obstetrics. 2d ed. '01· '02(Ja25) 12° net, $2.25. Lea.
Jewett, C: Manual of childbed nursing. 5th ed., rev. and enl. '02(Ap5) D. 80 c. Treat.
Jewett, C:, *ed.* Practice of obstetrics, by Am. authors. 2d ed. '01· '02(Ja25) il. 8°, net, $5; shp., net, $6; hf. mor., net, $6.50. Lea.
Jewett, F. G., *comp.* Manual for election officers and voters in N. Y. 10th ed. '02(Jl5) O. shp., $2; pap., $1.50. M. Bender.
Jewett, F. G., *comp. See also* New York. Primary election law.
Jewish carol. Calvin, E. R. 75 c. Westminster.
Jewish Chautauqua Society. Papers presented at the fifth annual session of the summer assembly, July 7-28, 1901. '02(Jl5) S. (Special ser., no. 7.) 30 c. Jewish Pub.
Jewish encyclopædia. *See* Singer, I., *ed.*
Jewish Pub. Soc. special ser. D. 30 c. Jewish Pub.
—Jewish Chautauqua Soc. Papers. (7.)
—Ruskay. Hearth and home essays. (6.)

JEWS.
Allen. Judah's sceptre and Joseph's birthright. $1.50. J: H. Allen.
Duff. Theology and ethics of the Hebrews. net, $1.25. Scribner.
Greenstone. Religion of Israel. 50 c. Bloch.

JEWS.—*Continued.*
Philipson. The Jew in Eng. fiction. net, $1. Clarke.
Peters. The Jew as a patriot. $1. Baker & T.
Robertson. Early religion of Israel. net, $1.60. Whittaker.
See also Semitic peoples.

Jezebel. McLaws, L. †$1.50. Lothrop.
Job, Herb. K. Among the waterfowl. '02 (Je7) il. sq. O. net, $1.35. Doubleday, P.
John Kenadie. Saunders, R. D. $1.50. Houghton, M. & Co.
Johns Hopkins Univ. studies. O. Johns Hopkins.
—Ballagh. Hist. of slavery in Va. $1.50. (extra v. 24.)
Johns Hopkins Univ. studies in hist. and pol. science. O. pap. Johns Hopkins.
—Barnett. State banking in U. S. 50 c. (ser. 20, 2, 3.)
—Martin. Internal improvements in Alabama. 30 c. (ser. 20, 1.)
—Radcliffe. Gov. Thomas H. Hicks of Md., and the civil war. 50 c. (ser. 19, 11, 12.)
—Steiner. Western Maryland in the Revolution. 30 c. (ser. 20, 1.)
—Vincent, *and others.* H. B. Adams; with bibliog. of the dept. of history, etc. (ser. 20, extra no.) free to subs.

JOHNSON, And.
Jones. Life of Andrew Johnson. $1.50. East Tenn.

Johnson, Emory R. Isthmian canal. '02 (Mr22) 8°, (Pub. of the soc., no. 323.) pap., 25 c. Am. Acad. Pol. Sci.
Johnson, Fk. M. Forest, lake and river; fishes of New England and eastern Canada. '02(Jl19) col. il. 2 v. and portfolio, 8°, ed. de luxe, per set, $300; grand ed. de luxe, per set, $500. F. M. Johnson.
Johnson, J. B. Theory and practice of surveying. 16th ed., rev. and enl. '02(Ap5) il. 8°, $4. Wiley.
Johnson, R: B. Popular Eng. ballads. '01· '02(F15) 4 v., il. 12°, $3. Lippincott.
Johnson, Rob. U. Poems. '02(My24) D. net, $1.20. Century Co.
Johnson, S: Essays from The Rambler and The Idler. '01· '02(Ap5) S. (Little masterpieces.) 50 c. Doubleday, P.
Johnson, S: History of Rasselas, Prince of Abyssinia. '02(My10) 12°, (Home lib.) $1. Burt.
Johnson, Virginia W. A world's shrine. '02 (Jl19) il. D. **$1.20 net. Barnes.
Johnson, W. F. Life of W. T. Sherman. '02 (Jl19) 12°, (Biographies of famous men.) $1. Donohue.
Johnson, W: F. Poco a poco. '02(Ag9) il. 12°, $1.50. Saalfield.
Johnson, Willis G. Fumigation methods. '02(Mr22) il. D. $1. Judd.
Johnson ser. of Eng. classics. 16°, 30 c.; 25 c. B. F. Johnson.
—Coleridge. Ancient mariner.
Johnston, Annie F. Asa Holmes. '02 (My17) S. $1. L. C. Page.
Johnston, Annie F. Cicely and other stories. '03· '02(Ag2) D. (Cosy corner ser.) †50 c. L. C. Page.
Johnston, J: W. Riddle of life. '02(F22) D. $1.50. Jennings.

Johnston, Ma. Audrey. '02(Mr1) il. D. $1.50. Houghton, M. & Co.
Jokai, Maurus. Told by the death's head. '02(Jl5) D. $1.50. Saalfield.
Joline, Adrian H. Meditations of an autograph collector. '02(My10) il. O. net, $3. Harper.
Jonathan Fish and his neighbors. Maxwell, H. $1. Acme.
Jones, Ht. Newell. *See* Bible. Young people's Bible.
Jones, Harry C. Elements of physical chemistry. '02(F22) 8°, net, $4. Macmillan.
Jones Harry W. A chaplain's experience ashore and afloat; the *Texas* under fire. '01· '02(Ap12) 12°, $1.25. Sherwood.
Jones, Ja. S. Life of Andrew Johnson, seventeenth president of the U. S. '01· '02 (F8) il. 12°, $1.50. East Tenn.
JONES, J: Paul.
Brown. John Paul Jones. $1. Donohue.
Jones, Marcus E. Utah. '02(Jl12) il. 12°, (Tarr and McMurry's geographies, supp. volumes.) *40 c. net. Macmillan.
Jones, Morgan P. Chiefs of Cambria. '02 (My3) il. D. $1.25. Abbey Press.
Jones, S: I: Mathematical puzzles. '02 (Ag2) il. 16°, pap., 25 c. News Print.
Jones, W: C. Illustrated hist. of the Univ. of California, 1868-1901. Rev. ed. '01. '02 (My24) il. F. $5. Berkeley.
Jordan, D: S., *comp.* True tales of birds and beasts. '02(Je14) il. D. (Home and school classics, young readers' ser.) 40 c. Heath.
Jordan, D: S., *and* Evermann, B. W. American food and game fishes. '02(Je14) Q. net, $4. Doubleday, P.
Jordan, D: S., *and* Heath, H. Animal forms: second book of zoology. '02(Je7) il. D. (Twentieth century text-books.) net, $1.10. Appleton.
Jordan, Eliz. G. Tales of destiny. '02(Je28) il. D. $1.50. Harper.
Jordan, Maggie O. Ways of the world. '02 (Ap26) 12°, $1.50. Neely.
Jordan, W: G: Kingship of self-control. '02 (F8) 12°, bds., 50 c. Revell.
Jordan, W: G: Majesty of calmness. '02 (F8) 12°, bds., 50 c. Revell.
Jordans, Jos Danger of youth and a tried antidote; fr. the Germ. '02(Je28) 16°, 15 c. Herder.
Jordon, Leopold. Interviews with a monocle. '02(Ap12) 12°, pap., 50 c. Whitaker & R.
José. Valdés, A. P. $1.25. Brentano's.
JOSEPH.
Miller. Story of Joseph. net, 35 c. Revell.
Josephine Grahame. Wheeler, J. $1.50. Abbey Press.
Josh Billings' old farmers' allminax. Shaw, H: W. $1.50. G: W. Dillingham.
Josiah Allen's wife, *pseud.* *See* Holley, M.
Josselyn, C: True Napoleon. '02(Je7) O. net, $3.50. Russell.
Journal of a live woman. Van Anderson, H. $1. Alliance.
Journal to Stella. Swift, J. $1.75. Putnam.
Jov in service. Purves, G: T. 50 c. Am. Tr.
Joyce's investments. Newberry, F. E. $1. Burt.
Joyful praise. Gabriel, C: H. 30 c. Jennings.
Judah's lion. Tonna, *Mrs.* C. E. $1. Dodd.
Judah's sceptre and Joseph's birthright. Allen, J: H. $1.50. J: H. Allen.
Judd, D: H. That old kitchen stove: [poem.] '01. '02(Ap5) il. D. 50 c. Abbey Press.
Judith, Phœnix, etc. Hall, J: L., *tr.* 75 c. Silver.
Judith's garden. Bassett, M. E. S. $1.50. Lothrop.
Judson, C: F., *and* Gittings, J. C. Artificial feeding of infants. '02(Jl19) 12°, $2. Lippincott.
Judson, Harry P., *and* Bender, Ida C., *eds.* Graded literature readers. bks. 6-8. '01· '02(Mr1) il. 12°, ea., 50 c. Maynard, M. & Co.
Judson, W. P. City roads and pavements suited to cities of moderate size. 2d ed. '02(Jl19) il. 12°, $2. Engineering News.
Julius Cæsar. *See* Shakespeare, W:
Jungfrau von Orleans. Schiller, J. C. F. v. net, 60 c. Holt.
JURY.
Blashfield. Instructions to juries in civil and criminal cases, incl. province of court on jury. $6. Keefe-D.
JUSTICES OF THE PEACE.
Brand. Justices' code for Wash. $5. Bancroft-W.
Minnesota. Justice's manual. $1.50. Booth.
Justinianus, *Emperor.* Pandects of Justinian; tr. into Eng. by W: Maude. In 4 v., v. 1. '02(Je7) 8°, $5. Cambridge.
Kaercher, F. O., *comp.* Summary of indulgences, privileges and favors granted to the secular branch of the Third order of St. Francis. '02(Je14) 24°, pap., 15 c. Herder.
Kaler, J. O., ["James Otis."] Cruise of the "Enterprise." '02(Jl12) il. 12°, $1.50. W. A. Wilde.
Kaler, J. O. Story of Pemaquid. '02(Mr8) il. D. (Pioneer towns of America, v. 2.) 50 c. Crowell.
Kaler, J. O. Treasure of Cocos Island. '02 (Jl12) 12°, (Alger ser.) $1. Burt.
Kaler, J. O. Wan Lun and Dandy. '02 (Je28) il. 12°, (St. Nicholas ser.) 75 c. Burt.
Kales, Albert Martin. *See* Illinois. Homestead exemption laws.
Kann, Jerome H., *ed.* *See* California. Code time table.
Kansas. *State board of educ.* County examination questions; with answers. No. 9. '02(Mr22) D. pap., 35 c. J. Macdonald.
Kansas. Statutes concerning domestic and foreign corporations for profit, and mutual and fraternal insurance companies; by G. C. Clemens. '02(Je28) O. pap., $1; hf. shp., $1.25. Crane.
Kansas. *Supreme ct.* Repts. (Dewey.) v. 62. '01. '02(Ag2) O. shp., $3.50. W. Y. Morgan.
KANSAS.
Winans. Kansas. *30 c. net. Macmillan.
Kant, Immanuel. Prolegomena to any future metaphysics; ed. in Eng., by P. Carus. '02 (Je28) 12°, net, 75 c.; *Same.* (Mr8) (Religion of sci. lib., no. 53.) pap., 50 c. Open Court.

KANT, Immanuel.
Paulsen. Immanuel Kant, his life and doctrine. net, $2.50. Scribner.
Karr, H: S. Call to arms, 1900-01; review of the imperial yeomanry movement. '02 (Ag2) il. D. $2. Longmans.
Kate Bonnet. Stockton, F. R: $1.50. Appleton.
Kaufman, Matthias S., *and* Nye, C: L. Notes on Epworth League prayer meeting topics. 2d ser. '02(Ag16) S. pap., 15 c. Eaton & M.
Keane, A: H: South America. New rev. ed. '01. '02(F15) il. 8°, (Stanford's compendium of geog. and travel.) $4.50. Lippincott.
Keary, C: F. The brothers: a fairy masque. '02(Ag2) D. $1.50. Longmans.
Keats, J: Eve of St. Agnes, and other poems; ed., with notes, by K. L. Bates. '02 (Ag23) 16°, (Ser. of classics.) 40 c. Silver.
Keats, J: Isabella and the Eve of St. Agnes. '02(Ap12) il. 16°, 60 c.; leath., $1. Macmillan.
Keats, J: Odes. '02(Ap12) il. 16°, 60 c.; leath., $1. Macmillan.
Keay, J. H. Medical treatment of gall stones. '02(My17) 12°, net, $1.25. Blakiston.
Keedy, E: E. Naturalness of Christian life. '02(My3) il. D. 50 c. Abbey Press.
Keeling, Elsa d' E. Sir Joshua Reynolds. '02(Ag23) sq. 8°, (Makers of British art.) *$1.25 net. Scribner.
Keen, Ja. T. *See* Young, O. D.
Keene, Roswell W. The blue diamond. '02 (Jl5) D. $1.50. Abbey Press.
Keep, W: J. Cast iron. '02(Ja18) il. 8°, $2.50. Wiley.
Keese, W: L. Siamese twins and other poems. '02(Je21) 12°, net, $1.25. E. W. Dayton.
Keith, Arth. Human embryology and morphology. '02(Mr8) O. $4.50. Longmans.
Keith, Hannah E. Hist. sketch of internal improvements in Michigan, 1836-46. '02 (F15) 16°, pap., 50 c. Mich. Pol. Sci.
Keller, Alb. G. Homeric society: sociolog. study of the Iliad and Odyssey. '02(F8) D. $1.20. Longmans.
Keller, G. Legenden; ed. by M. Müller and C. Wenckebach. '02(Ap5) S. net, 35 c. Holt.
Keller, Sa. K. Pennsylvania German cook book. Rev. and enl. 02(Jl12) O. pap.. 50 c. R. M. Scranton.
Kellogg, Amos M. Crowning of flora. '01. '02(Ja25) 12°, pap., 15 c. Kellogg.
Kellogg, Amos. M. Elements of algebra. '01. '02(Ja25) 12°, 25 c. Kellogg.
Kellogg, Amos M. Elements of civil government. '01. '02(Ja25) 12°, 25 c. Kellogg.
Kellogg, Amos M. Farmer's school and the visit. '01. '02(Ja25) 12°, pap., 15 c. Kellogg.
Kellogg, Amos M. Home coming of autumn queen. '01. '02(Ja25) 12°, pap., 15 c. Kellogg.
Kellogg, Amos M. How to teach composition writing. '01. '02(Ja25) 12°, 25 c. Kellogg.
Kellogg, Amos M. Our Lysander. '01. '02 (Ja25) 12°, pap., 15 c. Kellogg.
Kellogg, Amos M. Six musical entertainments. '01. '02(Ja25) 12°, pap., 15 c. Kellogg.
Kellogg, Amos M. Uncle Sam's examination. '01. '02(Ja25) 12°, pap., 15 c. Kellogg.
Kellogg, Elijah. A stout heart. '01. '02 (Jl12) il. 12°, (Whispering pine ser.) $1.25. Lee & S.
Kellogg, J. H. Rational hydrotherapy. '01. '02(Mr8) il. 8°, subs., $5; hf. rus., $6. Davis.
Kellor, Fes. A. Experimental sociology. '02 (F1) 8°, net, $2. Macmillan.
Kelsey, C: B. Surgery of the rectum. 6th ed. '02(Ap26) il. 8°, $3. Wood.
Kelsey, W. R. Physical determinations. '01. '02(Ja11) D. $1.50. Longmans.
Keltie, J: S., *ed.* *See* Statesmen's year-book.
Kemp, Ellwood L. Hist. of education. '02 (F1) 12°, (Educ. ser., v. 3.) net, $1.25. Lippincott.
Kendall, Ezra F. Good gravy: wit and humor. '01. '02(Ja18) 12°, pap., 25 c. Helman-T.
Kendall, Reese P. Pacific trail campfires. 02(Jl19) D. $1.50. Scroll Pub.
Kenilworth. Scott, *Sir* W. net, 60 c. Macmillan.
Kennan, G:, *comp and tr.* Folk tales of Napoleon; Napoleonder; fr. the Russian; [also] The Napoleon of the people: fr. the Fr. of Balzac. '02(Jl5) O. bds., *$1 net. Outlook.
Kennard, *Mrs.* Ma. E. The golf lunatic and his cycling wife. '02(Ag2) D. †$1.50. Brentano's.
Kennelly, Arth. E. *See* Houston, E. J.
Kenny, C. S. Outlines of criminal law. '02 (Jl12) 8°, (Cambridge Univ. Press ser.) *$2.50 net. Macmillan.
Kensington, Cathmer. Glenwood. '02(Ap26) D. $1.25. Abbey Press.
Kentons (The). Howells, W: D. $1.50. Harper.
Kentucky decisions as reported by E. W. Hines, in the southwestern reporter, vs. 63-66. '02(Ag16) O. shp., $4. West. Pub.
Kentucky. Practice act in force June 16, 1902; with notes, etc., by L. P. Little. '02 (Ag9) O. 65 c. Morton.
Kenyon, Ja. B. Remembered days. '02 (Ag16) D. $1. Eaton & M.
Kenyon, Orr. Amor victor. '02(Je7) il. D. $1.50. Stokes.
Kern, J: A. Way of the preacher. '02 (Mr22) D. $1.25. Pub. Ho. M. E. Ch., So.
Kern, Marg. Tale of a cat as told by herself. '02(My3) il. D. 50 c. Abbey Press.
Kerr, E. W. Power and power transmission. '02(Ja11) il. 8°, $2. Wiley.
Kerr, W: A. Law of insurance. '02(Ap19) O. shp., $6. Keefe-D.
Kersting, Rudolph, *ed.* The white world; life and adventure within the Arctic circle. '02(Jl12) 12°, *$2 net. Lewis.
Ketler, I: C. The tragedy of Paotingfu: authentic story of the missionaries who suffered martyrdom June 30 and July 1, 1900. '02(Je28) il. 8°, net, $2. Revell.
Kidd, B: Principles of western civilization. '02(F22) D. net, $2. Macmillan.
Kidder, Fk. E. Building construction and superintendence. pt. 2. 4th ed. '02(Je28) il. 8°, shp., $4. W: T. Comstock.

Kilbourne, E: W. Memory and its cultivation. '01. '02(Mr29) D. $1; leatherette, 50 c. Mullin.

Kilpatrick, Van Evrie. Language system of penmanship. In 9 nos. nos. 1-8. '02 (Ap5) il. sq. O. pap., per doz., 66 c. Globe Sch. Bk.

Kimber, Diana C., *comp.* Text-book of anatomy and physiology for nurses. New rev. ed. '02(Mr22) il. 8°, net, $2.50. Macmillan.

Kinard, Ja. P., *ed.* Old English ballads. '02 (Ap26) 12°, (Ser. of classics.) 40 c. Silver.

Kinder, Stephen. The sabertooth. '02(Ap12) il. D. 75 c.; pap., 25 c. Laird.

KINDERGARTEN.
Cline. Kindergarten, painting plays and home entertainments. $1. Am. Bk. and Bible.
Maxwell. Card sewing: for kindergartens. 50 c. M. Bradley.

Kindred of the wild. Roberts, C: G: D. $2. L. C. Page.

King, C: Conquering corps badge, and other stories of the Philippines. '02(Ag2) il. D. $1.25. L. A. Rhodes.

King, C: Way of the West. '02(Je7) il. S. 50 c. Rand, McN. & Co.

King, H. E. H. Hours of the passion. '02 (Ap5) 12°, net, $1.50. Dutton.

King, Maude E. Bread and wine. '02(My17) D. $1.25. Houghton, M. & Co.

King, T: A. Pearls from the Wonderbook. '01. '02(Ap12) 16°, 40 c. Swedenborg.

King, W. W., *comp.* *See* Texas. Conflicting civil cases;—Repts.

King Alfred millenary. Bowker, A. $3. Macmillan.

King and queen of hearts. Lamb, C: **50 c. net. McClure, P.

King Arthur and his noble knights. Malory, *Sir* T: $1. Burt.

King for a summer. Pickering, E. net, $1. Lee & S.

King Henry VI. *See* Shakespeare, W:

King in yellow. Chalmers, R. W: $1.50. Harper.

King Lear. Shakespeare, W: $1.25. Bowen-M.

King of Andorra. Harris, H: E. $1.25. Abbey Press.

King of Claddagh. Fitzpatrick, T: net, $1.25. Herder.

King Richard III. Shakespeare, W: 15 c. Kellogg.

Kingdom of coins. Gilman, B. 50 c. Little, B. & Co.

KINGLAKE, Alex. W:
Tuckwell. A. W. Kinglake. $1.75. Macmillan.

King's gallant. Dumas, A. $1. Street.

King's weigh-house. Avebury, *Lord.* 75 c. Macmillan.

Kings and vikings. O'Byrne, W. L. $1.25. Scribner.

Kingsford, C: L. Henry V. the typical mediæval hero. '01. '02(Ja25) D. (Heroes of the nations ser., no. 34.) net, $1.35; hf. leath., net, $1.60. Putnam.

Kingship of self-control. Jordan, W: G: 50 c. Revell.

Kingsley, C: Life and works. Ed. de luxe. v. 4. '02(F15); v. 5 (Mr8); v. 6 (Ap26); v. 7 (My17); v. 8 (My24); v. 9 (Je28); v. 10 (Ag2); v. 11, 12 (Ag16) 8°, net, ea., $3. Macmillan.

Kingsley, C: Alton Locke. '02(My17) 12°, (Home lib.) $1. Burt.

Kingsley, C: Hereward the Wake. '02 (My17) 12°, (Home lib.) $1. Burt.

Kingsley, C: Westward ho! '02(Je28) 2 v., 16°, (Temple classics.) ea., 50 c.; flex. leath., ea., 75 c. Macmillan.

Kingsley, *Mrs.* Flo. M. Prisoners of the sea. '02(Ap26) 12°, (Red letter ser.) $1.25; pap., 50 c. New Amsterdam.

Kinosita, Yetaro. Past and present of Japanese commerce. '02(Jl12) 8°, (Columbia Univ. studies in history, economics, and public law, v. 16, no. 1.) pap., *$1.50 net. Macmillan.

Kinship of God and man. Lanier, J. J. 2 v. ea., *$1 net. Whittaker.

Kinzie, *Mrs.* Juliette A. M. K. Wau-Bun, the "early day" of the Northwest. New ed., notes and index, by R. G. Thwaites. '01. '02(My3) il. O. ed. lim. to members. Caxton Club.

Kinzie, *Mrs.* Juliette A. M. K. Wau-Bun. New ed., introd. and note by E. K. Gordon. '01. '02(My3) il. D. $1.25. Rand, McN. & Co.

KIPLING, Rudyard.
Livingston. Works of Kipling: des. of first eds. net, $12; net, $20. Dodd.

Kirk, Eleanor, *pseud.* *See* Ames, *Mrs.* E. M. E.

Kirk, *Mrs.* Ellen O., ["Henry Hayes."] A remedy for love. '02(Je7) D. $1.25. Houghton, M. & Co.

Kirk, May. Baldwin primer. Tagalog ed. '02(Jl12) il. sq. D. 35 c. Am. Bk.

Kirkman, M. M. Air brake: supp. to Science of railways. '02(Ap26) il. 8°, $2.50. World R'way.

Kirkpatrick, W: J. *See* Gill, J.

KISSING.
Nyrop. The kiss, and its history. *$2 net. Dutton.

Kitchen gardening. Bridgeman, T: 50 c. Coates.

Kleckner, Emma R. In the misty realm of fable. 2d ed. '02(F15) il. 12°, $1. Flanagan.

Knapp, Adeline. How to live: a manual of hygiene for schools of the Philippine Islands. '02(Jl19) il. 16°, 36 c. Silver.

Knapp, M. A. Government ownership of railroads. '02(Mr22) 8°, (Pub. of the soc., no. 326.) pap., 15 c. Am. Acad. Pol. Sci.

Knecht, F. J. Child's Bible history; tr. from the Germ. 8th Am. ed. '02(Mr8) il. 12°, 25 c. Herder.

Knight, E: F: With the royal tour: recent tour of the Duke and Duchess of Cornwall and York through Greater Britain. '02 (Mr8) il. D. $2. Longmans.

Knightes tale. *See* Chaucer, G.

Knights (The). Aristophanes. net, $2.50. Macmillan.

Knights of St. John. Souvenir of 24th annual convention. '02(Jl12) il. 8°, bds., 13 c. Darrow.

KNOWLEDGE.
Moore. Functional vs. representational theories of knowledge in Locke's essay. *35 c. net. Univ. of Chic.
Pierce. Studies in auditory and visual space perception. net, $2. Longmans.
Trask. Human knowledge and human conduct. *$2 net. R. D. Trask.
See also Education;—Philosophy;—Science.

Kohaus, Hannah M. Fruit from the tree of life. '02(Mr22) 16°, pap., 30 c. Alliance.

Kohaus, Hannah M. Remedies of the Great Physician. '02(Mr22) 32°, pap., 40 c. Alliance.

Kohaus, Hannah M. Soul fragrance. New issue. '02(Mr22) 16°, pap., 50 c. Alliance.

Komensky, J: A. Labyrinth of the world and the paradise of the heart. '02(Mr8) 12°, $1.50. Dutton.

Körner, Karl T. Zriny ein trauerspiel in fünf aufzügen; notes by F. Holzwarth. '02 (F1) S. (Modern lang. ser.) 35 c. Heath.

Kovalevsky, M. Russian political institutions. '02(F15) O. net, $1.50. Univ. of Chic.

Krag and Johnny Bear. Thompson, E. E. S. .60 c. Scribner.

Krehbiel, H. N., *ed.* *See* Lavignac, A.

Kropotkin, *Prince* P: A. Fields, factories and workshops. New popular ed. '01· '02 (F22) il. D. net, 90 c. Putnam.

Krüger, Gustav, *and* Smith, C. A. English-Germ. conversation book. '02(Je21) D. (Modern lang. ser.) 25 c. Heath.

Kuder, Emil. Medical prescription book for everybody. '01. '02(Ap26) $2. Journal Pr.

Kupfer, Lillian. Greek foreshadowings of modern metaphysical and epistemological thought. '01. '02(F15) 8°, $1. J. S. Cushing.

Kuttner, B. German conversation course. (Sec. 1 and 2.) '02(Jl19) D. 50 c. Abbey Press.

Kyger, J: C: F., *ed.* Hand-book for soul-winners. '02(My24) S. 50 c. Kyger.

Laache, N. J. Book of family prayer; Bible lessons with meditations, arr. after the church year; fr. the Norwegian by P. O. Stromme. '02(Ag2) 8°, hf. leath., $1.65; mor., $2.25. Luth. Pub. Ho.

Labor and capital: discussion of rel. of employer and employed; ed. by J: J. Peters. '02(My10) D. (Questions of the day, no. 98.) $1.50. Putnam.

LABOR AND LABORING CLASSES.
See Capital and labor;—Political economy;—Slavery;—Social science;—Woman.

La Brète, Jean de. Mon oncle et mon curé; ed. by E. M. White. '02(My3) D. 50 c. Am. Bk.

Labyrinth of the world and the paradise of the heart. Komensky, J: A. $1.50. Dutton.

LACE.
Palliser. Hist. of lace. net, $12. Scribner.

Lachmi Bai Rani of Jhansi. White, M. $1.50. J. F. Taylor.

Ladd, G: T. Philosophy of conduct. '02 (F22) 12°, net, $3.50. Scribner.

Lady of New Orleans. Thornton, M. E $1.50. Abbey Press

Lady paramount. Harland, H: $1.50. Lane.

Lady (The) Poverty: a XIIIth century allegory (Sacrum commercium Beati Francisci cum Domina Paupertate, A.D. 1227;) tr. and ed. by M. Carmichael. '02(Ap12) 6¾ x 4½ in., net, $1.75. Tennant.

Lafarque, Paul. Religion of capital. [also] Social effect of machinery by F. W. Cotton. '02(My17) O. (Socialist lib., v. 2, no. 2.) pap., 10 c. Socialistic Co-op.

Lafitte of Louisiana. Devereux, M. $1.50. Little, B. & Co.

Laird, Alb. J. Complete manual of syllabic shorthand. '02(Jl12) il. 16°, $2. Neil.

Laird & Lee's diary and time saver, 1902. '02(Ja4) nar. T. leath., 25 c. Laird.

Lake, W: C: Memorials of William Charles Lake, Dean of Durham, 1869-1894. '01. '02(F8) O. $5.50. Longmans.

Lake English classics. S. Scott, F. & Co.
—Poe. Poems and tales. 30 c.

Lake French classics; ed. by E. P. Baillot. S. 50 c. Scott, F. & Co.
—Baillot *and* Brugnot. French prose composition.
—Beaumarchais. Barbier de Séville and Lettres.
—Moliere. Le misanthrope and L'avare.
—Voltaire. Zaïre and Epitres.

Lake history stories. S. il. Scott, F. & Co.
—Harding, C. H. *and* S: B. City of the seven hills. 40 c.

Lalor's Maples. Conway, K. E. $1.25. Pilot.

Lamb, C: Essays; introd. and notes by A. Ainger. In 12 v. v. 1, 2. '02(Ag2) 8°, ea., *$3 net. Pafraets.

Lamb, C: The king and queen of hearts: an 1805 book for children; re-issued in facsim. '02(Jl5) il. 16°, **50 c. net. McClure, P.

Lamb, C: *and* Ma. Tales from Shakespeare. '01. '02(Mr1) il. D. (Home and school classics; young readers' ser.) 40 c. Heath.

Lamb, M. T. The Mormons and their Bible. '01. '02(F1) O. net, 25 c. Am. Bapt.

La Motte Fouque, F. H. K., *Freiherr* de. Undine. [also] Aslauga's knight. '01. '02 (Ja11) il. 16°, (Caxton ser.) flex. lambskin, net, $1.20. Scribner.

La Motte Fouqué. F. H. K., *Freiherr de.* Undine. '02(My17) il. D. (Home and school classics; young reader's ser.) 30 c. Heath.

LANCASTER, Pa.
Law. Lancaster—old and new. n. p. J. D. Law.

LAND.
Horton. Land buyer's, settler's and explorer's guide. 25 c. Byron.
Illinois. Homestead exemption laws. *$4 net. Callaghan.

Land of heroes. O'Byrne, W. L. $1.25. Scribner.

Land of Nome. McKee, L. net, $1.25. Grafton Press.

Landolt, H. H., *and others.* Optical rotating power of organic substances. 2d ed. Authorized Eng. tr. with add. by Dr. J. H. Long. '02(Jl5) il. 8°, *$7.50 net. Chemical.

LANDSEER, *Sir* Edn.
Manson. Sir Edwin Landseer. *$1.25 net. Scribner.

Lane, Michael A. Level of social motion. '02(Mr29) 12°, net, $2. Macmillan.

Lang, H: R., *ed.* Cancioneiro Gallego-Castelhano, extant Galician poems (1350-1450). v. 1. '02(Ag30) 8°, (Yale bicentennial pubs.) **$3 net. Scribner.

Lang, Ossian H., *ed.* Educational creeds of the 19th century. '01. '02(Ja25) 12°, 75 c. Kellogg.

Langbein, G: Electro-deposition of metals; fr. the Germ.; add. by W: T. Brannt. 4th rev. enl. ed. '02(F15) il. 8°, $4. Baird.

Lange, L: Twentieth century system; key to the Germ. language. '02(Ap26) D. pap., 50 c. [San F. News] Pamphlet.

Lange, L: Twentieth century system Spanish course. '02(Ap26) D. pap., 25 c. [San F. News] Pamphlet.

Langley, S: P. Experiments in aerodynamics. 2d ed. '02(Jl19) F. (Smithsonian cont. to knowledge, no. 201.) $1. Smith. Inst.

LANGUAGE.
Fowler. Negatives of the Indo-European languages. net, 50 c. Univ. of Chic.
Oertel. Lectures on study of language. net, $3. Scribner.
See also Rhetoric;—Synonyms;—*also* names of languages.

Lanier, J. J. **Kinship of God and man.** In 2 v. v. 1, Good and evil. '02(F8); v. 2, The master key. (Ag23) D. ea., *$1 net. Whittaker.

Laplace, *Marquis* de. *See* Simon, P.

La Ramé, Louise de, ["Ouida."] Child of Urbino, Raphael: third reader; ed. by S. D. Jenkins. '02(Ag30) 12°, 30 c. Educ. Pub.

La Ramé, Louise de. Dog of Flanders and The Nürnberg stove. '02(Mr22) S. (Riverside lit. ser., no. 150.) pap., 15 c. Houghton, M. & Co.

Larned, J. N., *ed.* Literature of Amer. history: bibliog. guide. '02(Je21) O. net, $6; shp., $7.50; hf. mor., $9. Houghton, M. & Co.

Larry Barlow's ambition. Winfield, A. $1. Saalfield.

Lasance, F. X. Little manual of St. Anthony of Padua. '02(Ap5) Tt. pap., 25 c. Benziger.

Lasance, F. X., *comp.* Short visits to the blessed sacrament. '01. '02(Ja18) Tt. 25 c. Benziger.

La Seer, Elmer J. The hand and its lines. '02(Ag16) nar. O. pap., gratis. Dean & H.

Last century maid. Wharton, A. H. $1.25. Lippincott.

Last cruise of the "Electra." Chipman, C: B. $1. Saalfield.

Last fight of the "Revenge" at sea. Raleigh, *Sir* W. net, $6. Houghton, M. & Co.

Last of the quills. Griffiths, D: P. $1.50. D: P. Griffiths.

Late returning. Williams, M. $1.25. Macmillan.

Later infancy of the child. Compayré, G. pt. 2. net, $1.20. Appleton.

Lathbury, B. B., *and* Spackman, —. Am. engineering practice in the construction of rotary Portland cement plants. '02(My24) il. obl. O. $2. G. M. S. Armstrong.

Lathbury, Clarence. Code of joy: [sermons on the Beatitudes.] '02(Ag2) 12°, 50 c. Swedenborg.

Latimer, *Mrs.* Eliz. W. Prince Incognito. '02 (Ap12) D. $1.50. McClurg.

LATIN LANGUAGE.
Alford, *comp.* Latin passages for translation. net, 80 c. Macmillan.

LATIN LANGUAGE.—*Continued.*
Appleton's Latin dictionary. $1.50. Appleton.
Mellick. Latin composition. 40 c. Am. Bk.
Morris. On principles and methods in Latin syntax. net, $2. Scribner.
Ogilvie. Horæ Latinæ. $5. Longmans.
Reynolds. Rudiments of Latin. $1.25. A. B. Reynolds.
Smith, W: W. Course in first year Latin for Regents' examinations. $1. W: R. Jenkins.
West. Latin grammar. net, 90 c. Appleton.

LATTER-DAY SAINTS.
See Mormonism.

Laughlin, Ja. L. Credit. '02(Ag16) Q. (Decennial pub., fr. v. 4.) pap., *50 c. net. Univ. of Chic.

Laughlin, Ja. L. Elements of political economy. Rev. ed. '02(Mr22) D. $1.20. Am. Bk.

Laurel classics. 16°, 40 c. Birchard.
—Shakespeare. Merchant of Venice.

Laurie, H: Scottish philosophy in its national development. '02(My24) 12°, net, $1.75. Macmillan

Laurie, Simon S. Training of teachers and methods of instruction. '01. '02(Ja4) 12°, (Cambridge Univ. Press ser.) net, $1.50. Macmillan.

Laut, Agnes C. Heralds of empire. '02 (My10) D. $1.50. Appleton.

Lavignac, Alb. Music and musicians; tr. by W: Marchant; ed., with add., by H. H. Krehbiel. 3d ed., rev. [Cheaper ed.] '02 (Ag30) 12°, **$1.75 net. Holt.

Law, Ja. D. Lancaster—old and new. Rev., enl. ed. '02(Ap26) 8°, pap., n. p. J. D. Law.

LAW.
American and Eng. encyclopædia of law. v. 20, 21. ea., $7.50. E: Thompson.
American digest. v. 29-33. subs., ea., $6. West Pub.
American state repts. v. 82-84. ea., $4. Bancroft-W.
Ash. Table of federal citations. 4 v. v. 1, 2. complete work, $30. Remick.
Bingham, *comp.* 200 bar examination questions. $1. Commercial Press.
Britton: Eng. tr. and notes. $3. Byrne.
English law rpts. 6 v. $28.50. Little, B. & Co.
General digest. v. 12. $6. Lawyers' Co-op.
Hawkins. Legal counselor and form book. subs., $3; $4. W. W. Wilson.
Howard. Law points to know. $1. H. G. Howard.
Lawyers' repts. annot. bks. 53, 54. ea., $5. Lawyers' Co-op.
McCall. Clerk's assistant; cont. legal forms and instruments. $6. Banks.
Mack *and* Nash, *eds.* Cyclopedia of law and procedure. v. 3. $6. Am. Law Bk.
Martindale. Am. law directory, 1902. 2 pts. net, $10. Martindale.
Milburn. Curious cases: Am. and Eng. decisions. $3. Michie.
Pollock. Revised repts. v. 46-51. ea., net, $6. Little, B. & Co.
Russell *and* Winslow. Syllabus—digest of decisions of the sup. ct. v. 3. $6.50. Banks.

LAW.—*Continued.*
Seebohm. Tribal custom in Anglo-Saxon law. net, $5. Longmans.
Smith. Studies in juridical law. $3.50. Flood.
Two centuries' growth of Am. law, 1701-1901. net, $4. Scribner.
Warvelle. Essays in legal ethics. $2.50. Callaghan.
See also Actions at law;—Attachment;—Commercial law;—Constables;—Contracts;—Conveyancing;—Corporations;—Damages; — Equity;—Evidence;—Feudalism; —Insurance; — International law;—Jury;—Justices of the peace;—Land;—Lawyers;—Mines and mining;—Negligence;—Negotiable instruments; — Orphans; —Parliamentary law; — Patents; — Pleading and practice;—Prostitution; — Real property; — Saloons;—Star chamber;—Wills.

Law of growth. Brooks, P. net, $1.20. Dutton.
Lawler, Ja. J. Modern plumbing, steam and hot water heating. New ed. '02(F22) 12°, $5. Popular.
Lawrence, F. M. Practical medicine. '02 (Ap5) il. 8°, $3. Boericke & T.
Laws of radiation and absorption. Brace, D. B. $1. Am. Bk.
Lawson, And. C. Eparchæan interval. '02 (Je14) O. (Univ. of Cal. bull. of dept. of geology, v. 3, no. 3.) pap., 10 c. Univ. of Cal.
Lawson, And. C., *and* Palache, C: Berkeley Hills: coast range geology. '02(Ap5) il. O. (Univ. of Cal., bull. of the dept. of geology, v. 2, no. 12.) pap., 80 c. Univ. of Chic.
Lawson, J: D. Making of a contract. '01-'02(F8) O. pap., 25 c. Stephens.
Lawson, T: W. *See* Thompson, W. M.
Lawton, W: H: The singing voice and its practical cultivation. '01- '02(Mr15) il. 8°, $1.50. W: H: Lawton.
Lawyer's idle hours. Haviland, C. A: $1; 50 c. C. A: Haviland.

LAWYERS.
Gould. Greater New York and state lawyers' diary, 1902. $1. W. R. Gould.
Macdonald. How successful lawyers are educated. $1.50. Temple Pub.
Martindale. Am. law directory. net, $10. Martindale.
Perry. Legal adviser and business guide. $1.50. Pontiac.
Sharp & Alleman Co.'s lawyers' and bankers' directory, 1902. 2 v. ea., $5. Sharp & A.
See also Washington Co., Pa.

Lawyers' reports annot.; bks. 53, 54. '02 (Je28) O. shp., ea., $5. Lawyers' Co-op.
Laycock, W. F. *See* Rawson, C.
Lays and lyrics. Smiley, T: E. $1.25. Abbey Press.
Lays of a lawyer. McVickar, W: B. *$4 net. Pelham Press; [Dodd.]
Leach, J. G. History of the Bringhurst family; with notes on the Clarkson, De Peyster and Boude families. '01- '02(Mr8) il. 4°, $5. Lippincott.

LEAD.
Fairie. Notes on lead ore. net, $1. Van Nostrand.

League of Am. Mothers. *See* Proudfoot, A. H.
Leahy, Wa. T: Child of the flood. '02 (Jl19) D. $1. Kilner.
Lean, Bevan. *See* Perkin, W: H:, *jr.*

LEARNING.
See Education;—Knowledge.

LEATHER.
See Tanning.

Leaves from a life-book of to-day. Mills, J. D. 50 c. Swedenborg.
Leavitt, Rob. G. Outlines of botany. '01-'02(Ja4) O. $1. Am. Bk.
Leavitt, Rob. G. Outlines of botany. [also] Field, forest and garden botany. by A. Gray; rev. and enl. by L. H. Bailey. '01-'02(Ja4) il. O. $1.80. Am. Bk.

LE BLOND, Michel.
Van der Kellen. Works of Michel Le Blond: reprod. and accompanied by biog. notice, [etc.] net, $30; net, $35. Dodd.

Lee, Jennette. Son of a fiddler. '02(Ap5) D. $1.50. Houghton, M. & Co.
Lee, J: L. Message of to-morrow. '02(F8) 12°, net, $1.20. Revell.
Lee, Marg. Separation. '02(Jl12) D. $1.25. Buckles.

LEE, Rob. E.
Adams. Lee at Appomattox. net, $1.50. Houghton, M. & Co.

Left-overs made palatable. Curtis, I. G. $1. Judd.
Legal classic ser. 12°. Byrne.
—Britton. $3.
Legal counselor and form book. Hawkins, C: A. subs., $3; $4. W. W. Wilson.
Legend of Sleepy Hollow. *See* Irving, W.
Legenden. Keller, G. net, 35 c. Holt.

LEGENDS.
Zitkala-sa. Old Indian legends. 50 c. Ginn.
See also Fairy tales;—Folk-lore.

Legler, H: E. James Gates Percival; sketch and bibliog. '01. '02(Mr22) S. bds., net, $1. Mequon Club.
Lehfeldt, R. A. Text-book of physics. '02 (Ag2) il. D. $2. Longmans.
Leibnitz, G. W. v. Discourses on metaphysics; Correspondence with Arnauld and Monodology. '02(Je28) 12°, net, 75 c.; *Same* (F22) D. (Religion of sci. lib., no. 52.) pap., 35 c. Open Court.
Leigh, Lennard, *and* Bergholt, Ernest. Principles and practice of whist. '02(Ap5) il. O. net, $1.50. Coates.
Leighton, Jos. A. Typical modern conceptions of God. '01- '02(F8) D. net, $1.10. Longmans.
Lemcke, E. E: Creation, re-creation: [poems.] '01. '02(F8) 16°, n. p. Privately pr.
Lennox, *Lady* Sa. Life and letters, 1745-1826: ed. by the Countess of Ilchester and Lord Stavordale. '01- '02(Ja11) 2 v., il. 8°, net, $9; *Same.* [1-v. ed.] '02(Je7) O. net, $4. Scribner.

LENOX, Mass.
Mallary. Lenox and the Berkshire Highlands. net, $1.75. Putnam.

LENT.
Galt, *comp.* Lent, the holy season. $1. Neale.

Leo XIII., [Gioacchino Pecci,] *Pope.* Poems, charades, inscriptions; tr. and notes by H. T. Henry. '02(Ag23) D. bds., $1.50. Am. Eccles. Review.

LEONARDO DA VINCI.
Hubbard. Leonardo. 25 c. Roycrofters.

Leopard's spots. Dixon, T:, *jr.* $1.50. Doubleday, P.

Lepidus the centurion. Arnold, E. L. $1.50. Crowell.
Le Queux, W: Sign of the seven sins. '02 (Je28) D. (Select novels.) $1; pap., 50 c. Lippincott.
Le Row, Caro. B. Duxberry doings. '02 (Je14) 12°, (Fireside ser.) $1. Burt.
Leroy, W: A silken snare. '02(My3) D. 50 c. Abbey Press.
Le Sage, A. R. Adventures of Gil Blas of Santillane. New ed. '02(Ap19) 12°, (Home lib.) $1. Burt.
Lesley, Susan, *ed.* *See* Tiffany, N. M., *ed.*
Lespinasse, Julie J. E. de. Letters; with notes upon her life and character, and introd. by C. A. Sainte-Beuve. '02(F1) il. 8°, (Versailles hist. ser.) subs., per v., $6; ¾ leath., per v., $9. Hardy, P. & Co.
Lessing, G. E. Minna von Barnhelm; notes by S. Primer. Rev. ed. '02(F1) D. (Modern lang. ser.) 75 c. Heath.
Lessing, G. E. Nathan der Weise; notes and an app. by T. J. C. Dickhoff. '02(Ag2) D. 80 c. Am. Bk.
Lessing, O. E. Schiller's einfluss auf Grillparzer. '02(Ag16) O. (Bull. of the Univ. of Wis., no. 54; philol. and literature ser., v. 2, no. 2.) pap., 50 c. Univ. of Wis.
Lessons from Gr. pottery. Huddilston, J: H. net, $1.25. Macmillan.
Lessons in English. il. D. 50 c. Silver.
—Skinner *and* Burgert. Lessons in Eng. based upon principles of literary interpretation.
Lethaby, W. R., *ed.* *See* Artistic crafts.
LETTER-WRITING.
Hickox. Correspondent's manual. $1.50. Lee & S.
North. Love letters and how to write them. 25 c.; 50 c. Donohue; Drake.
LETTERING.
Faust. Automatic pen lettering and designs. $1; alphabet pt., 75 c. Auto Pen.
LETTERS.
Berry, *ed.* Letters of the Rm. 2 coll. in the British Museum. net, 50 c. Univ. of Chic.
Glover. Life and letters in the 4th century. net, $3.25. Macmillan.
Letters of Mildred's mother to Mildred. Price, E. D. $1. Ogilvie.
Letters to an enthusiast. Clarke, *Mrs.* M. C. net, $2.50. McClurg.
Leucippe and Clitophon. Achilles Tatius. (App. to pubs. for price.) Barrie.
Level of social motion. Lane, M. A. net, $2. Macmillan.
Lewis, Abram H. Sunday legislation. New rev. enl. ed. '02(F8) 12°, net, $1. Appleton.
Lewis, Alfr. H: Wolfville days. '02(F22) il. D. $1.50. Stokes.
Lewis, Alonzo F. Fryeburg Webster centennial. '02(Je28) il. 12°, pap., 50 c. A. F. Lewis.
Lewis, C: B., ["M. Quad."] Life and troubles of Mr. Bowser. '02(My24) il. 8°, $1. Jamieson-H.
Lewis, Edn. H. Text-book of applied Eng. grammar. pt. 1. '02(F15); pt. 2. (Ag16) 12°, ea., *35 c. net; *Same,* complete, *50 c. net. Macmillan.
Lewis, Enrique H. Phil and Dick. '02(Ag9) il. 12°, $1. Saalfield.
Lewis, H: F., *ed.* *See* Peterson, R.
Lewis, Julius A. Sir Walter of Kent. '02 (Ag2) D. $1.50; pap., 50 c. Bonnell.
Lewis, Merriwether, *and* Clarke, W: Hist. of the expedition to the sources of the Missouri: rep. of the ed. of 1814. '02(My24) 3 v., 8°, (Commonwealth lib.) net, per v., $1. New Amsterdam.
Lewis, W: D. *See* Pepper, G: W.
Lex de imperio Vespasiani. Hellems, F. B. R. 50 c. Scott, F. & Co.
LEXINGTON, Mass.
Piper. Lexington, the birthplace of Amer. liberty. 25 c. Lexington.
LIABILITY.
See Negligence.
Liautard, A. Animal castration. 9th ed., rev. and enl. '02(Jl12) il. 12°, $2. W: R. Jenkins.
LIBERTY.
See Democracy;—Religious liberty;—Slavery.
LIBRARIANS AND LIBRARIES.
New York Lib. Club. Libraries of Greater New York. net, 75 c.; net, 50 c. Stechert.
Plummer. Hints to small libraries. net. 50 c. M. W. Plummer.
Wilson. Directory of booksellers, stationers, librarians and pubs. in U. S. and Can. $10. H. W. Wilson.
Wisconsin. List of books for township libraries. 25 c. Wisconsin.
See also Books and reading;—Cataloguing.
Library of literary criticism. *See* Moulton, C: W.
Library of Tribune extras. D. pap., 25 c. Tribune Assoc.
—Tribune almanac, 1902. (v. 14, 1.)
Library of useful stories. *See* Appleton's.
Liddell, Mark H. Introd. to the scientific study of Eng. poetry. '02(My10) D. net, $1.25. Doubleday, P.
Lieb, Hermann. Prince Bismarck and the German people. '02(Mr22) 12°, $1.50; hf. mor., $2.25; mor., $3.25. Dominion.
Life, And. C. Tuber-like rootlets of cycas revoluta. '02(F15) il. 8°, (Cont. to the Hull Botanical lab'y, no. 26.) pap., net, 25 c. Univ. of Chic.
Life and health. Blaisdell, R. F. $1. Ginn.
Life and letters in the 4th century. Glover, T. R. net, $3.25. Macmillan.
Life and power from within. Colville, W. J. $1. Alliance.
Life and troubles of Mr. Bowser. Lewis, C: B. $1. Jamieson-H.
Life and works of the Redeemer. '02(F15) 12°, net, $2. Dutton.
Life at West Point. Hancock, H. I. net, $1.40. Putnam.
Life histories. *See* Appleton's.
Life of a century. Hodder, E. net, $4. Scribner.
Life of John William Walshe, T.S.A. Carmichael, M. net, $2. Dutton.
Life of love. Mudge, J. 25 c. Jennings.
Life of unity. Cheney, F. J. $1.50. Blade.
Life on the farm. Shepard, H. M. 50 c. Flanagan.
Life worth living. Newell, W. C. $1. Abbey Press.
Life's little things. Hind, C. L. $1.75. Macmillan.

LIGHT.
Dexter. Elem. exercises on sound, light and heat. 90 c. Longmans.
Michelsen. Velocity of light. net, 25 c. Univ. of Chic.
See also Radiation;—Roentgen rays.
Light and peace. Quadrupani, R. P. net, 50 c. Herder.
Light of our spirit. Ehrlich, *Mrs.* B. 25 c. B. Ehrlich.
Lighted lore for gentle folk. Timby, T. R. $2. Morningside.
LILIES.
Jekyll, *comp.* Lilies for Eng. gardens. net, $3.75. Scribner.
Liljencrantz, Ottilie A. Thrall of Leif the lucky. '02(Mr29) O. $1.50. McClurg.
Lilley, A: E. V., *and* Midgley, W. Studies in plant form. New enl. ed. '02(Mr8) 8°, net, $2. Scribner.
Lilley, J. P. The pastoral epistles: new tr. with introd., commentary and app. '01-'02(Ja11) 12°, (Bible class handbooks.) net, 75 c. Scribner.
LINCOLN, Abr.
Barrett. Abraham Lincoln. $1. Donohue.
Smith, S. G. Abraham Lincoln. net, 25 c. Jennings.
See also Fallows, S:
Lincoln, Jos. C. Cape Cod ballads. '02(Ap19) il. D. net, $1.25. Brandt.
Lindsay, B. Story of animal life. '02(My24) il. S. (Lib. of useful stories.) net, 35 c. Appleton.
Line and form. Crane, W. $2.25. Macmillan.
Linear groups. Dickson, L. E. net, $4. Stechert.
Line-o'-type lyrics. Taylor, B. L. net, 50 c. W: S. Lord.
Lines of defense of the biblical revelation. Margoliouth, D. S. net, $1.50. Gorham.
Lingelbach, W. E. Merchant adventurers of England, their laws and ordinances, with other documents. '02(Ag2) D. (Translations and reprs. from the orig. sources of European history; 2d ser., v. 2.) $1.25. [Univ. of Penn.] Longmans.
Linn, Ja. W. The second generation: [novel.] '02(F1) 12°, $1.50. Macmillan.
Linn, W: A. Story of the Mormons. '02 (Je21) O. net, $4. Macmillan.
Lippincott's biog. dictionary. New ed. '01-'02(Mr1) 2 v., il. 8°, subs., $15; hf. rus., $17.50; hf. mor., $20. Lippincott.
Lippincott's educ. ser. 12°, net, $1.25. Lippincott.
—Kemp. Hist. of education. (3.)
Lippincott's elem. algebra. (Ja. M. Rawlins.) '01-'02(Mr1) 12°, 80 c. Lippincott.
Lippincott's elem. science readers. 3 pts. '01-'02(F15) pt. 1, 16°, bds., 25 c.; pt. 2, 30 c.; pt. 3, 35 c. Lippincott.
Lippincott's pocket medical dict., incl. the pronunciation and definition of 20,000 of the principal terms used in medicines and the allied sciences; ed. by R. W. Greene. New ed. '02(Ag2) 16°, 50 c. Lippincott.
Lippincott's popular lib. 12°, $1. Lippincott.
—Hungerford. Three graces.
Lippincott's practical arithmetic. '01-'02 (Mr1) 2 pts., 12°, ea., 40 c. Lippincott.
Lippincott's select novels. D. $1; pap., 50 c. Lippincott.
—Boothby. Cabinet secret.
Lippincott's select novels.—Continued.
—Croker. Cat's paw.
—Le Queux. Sign of the seven sins.
—Neilson. Madame Bohemia.
—Vogel. Gentleman Garnet.
Liquid from the sun's rays. Greenleaf, S. $1.50. Abbey Press.
LIQUORS.
See Fermentation.
Lisk, J. P. Diagram of the Corliss engine. '02(Je7) 8°, pap., 25 c. Spon.
Litanei zum heiligsten herzen Jesu. Catholic church. net, 3 c. Herder.
Literary Boston of to-day. Winslow, H. M. **$1.20 net. L. C. Page.
LITERATURE.
Arnold. Literature and dogma. net, $1. New Amsterdam.
Brandes. Main currents in 19th century literature. v. 2. net $2.75. Macmillan.
Halsey. Our literary deluge. net, $1.25. Doubleday, P.
Payne. Editorial echoes.—Little leaders. ea., net. $1. McClurg.
See also Authors;—Bibliographies; — Books;—Essays;—Fiction; — Letters; — Parody;—Quotations;—*also* names of nations and literatures.
Literature of Am. history. Larned, J. N. net, $6; $7.50; $9. Houghton, M. & Co.
Litsey, Edn. C. Love story of Abner Stone. '02(Je21) O. bds., net, $1.20. Barnes.
Little, E: R. *See* Hall, F: G.
Little books on devotion. sq. T. net, 25 c. Jennings.
—Mudge. Life of love.
Little books on doctrine. sq. T. 25 c. Jennings.
—Merrill *and* Warren. Discourses on miracles.
—Methodist Epis. church in America. Doctrines.
—Townsend. Satan and demons.
Little books on practice. T. net, 25 c. Jennings.
—Oliver. Our lay office-bearers.—Soul-winners' secrets.
Little brother. Willard, J. F. $1.50. Century Co.
Little button rose. Alcott, L. M. 50 c. Little, B. & Co.
Little citizen. Waller, M. E. **$1 net. Lothrop.
Little cousin ser. il. D. ea., **50 c. net. L. C. Page.
—Wade. Our little African cousin; Cuban; Eskimo; Hawaiian; Philippine; Porto Rican.
Little engravings. Altdorfer, A. net, $1.50. Longmans.
Little French dinners. Rivas, E. de. 50 c. New Amsterdam.
Little giant's neighbors. Fox, F. M. 50 c. L. C. Page.
Little green god. Mason, C. A. †75 c. Revell.
Little guides ser. S. net, 75 c. Dodd.
—Windle. Malvern country.
Little journeys. *See* George, M. M.—Whitcomb, C. E.
Little journeys to the homes of eminent artists. sq. O. pap., 25 c. Roycrofters.
—Hubbard. Botticelli. — Gainsborough. — Leonardo.—Raphael.—Thorwaldsen. — Velasquez.

Little leaders. Payne, W: M. net, $1. McClurg.

Little masterpieces; ed. by B. Perry. S. 50 c. Doubleday, P.
—Bacon. Essays.
—Emerson. Essays.
—Goldsmith. Selections.
—Johnson. Essays fr. Rambler and Idler.
—Milton. Selections.
—Swift. Selections.

Little memoirs of the 19th century. Paston, G: net, $3. Dutton.

Little minister. Barrie, J. M. $1. Burt.

Little Miss Oddity. Blanchard, A. E. **80 c. net. Jacobs.

Little stories for little people. McCullough, A. W. 25 c. Am. Bk.

Little Susy stories. Prentiss, *Mrs.* E. 75 c. Burt.

Littleton, W: S. Trumpeter's hand book and instructor. '02(Je21) 16°, leath., $1. Hudson-K.

LITURGIES.
See Prayers.

Livermore, S: T. Block Island; ed. by C: E. Perry. '01· '02(Mr22) il. 16°, pap., 25 c. Ball.

Livermore, Virgil B., *and* Williams, Ja. How to become a competent motorman. '02 (Ag2) il. 12°, $1. W: S. Livermore.

Lives of two cats. Viaud, L: M. J. 50 c. Estes.

Livets alvor. Bang, *Mrs.* M. 65 c. M. Bang.

Living races of mankind. Hutchinson, H. N. net, $5. Appleton.

Livingston, Burton E. On the nature of the stimulus which causes the change in form in polymorphic green algae. '02(F1) 8°, (Cont. from Hull botanical laboratory, no. 22.) pap., net, 25 c. Univ. of Chic.

Livingston, Luther S. Bibliog. of the first ed. in book form of the works of Alfred, Lord Tennyson. '01· '02(Ja11) 16°, pap., $1. Dodd.

Livingston, Luther S. Works of Rudyard Kipling: desc. of a set of the first eds. of his books. '01· '02(Ja11) facsimiles, 8°, 65 cop. on hand-made pap., bds., net, $12; 12 cop. on Jap. pap., net, $20. Dodd.

Lloyd, J. W: The natural man. '02(Ag9) S. *$1 net. Prieth.

Lloyd, Rob. Treasure of Shag Rock. '02 (Ag30) il. D. **$1 net. Lothrop.

Locke, C: E: Nineteenth-century crusaders. [Gladstone.] '02(My24) D. (Hero ser., no. 5.) net, 25 c. Jennings.

Locke, C: E: Typical American. [Washington.] '02(My24) il. D. (Hero ser., no. 2.) net, 25 c. Jennings.

Lockett, Ma. F., ["The Princess."] Christopher. '02(My3) il. D. $1.25. Abbey Press.

Lockwood, G: B. New Harmony communities. '02(Jl12) il. O. $2.50. Chronicle.

Lockwood, Sara E. H. Teachers' manual to accompany Composition and rhetoric. '02 (Jl19) 16°, pap., 30 c. Ginn.

LOCOMOTIVES.
Baker. Economic locomotive management. $1.50. R'way Educ.
Cooke. Some recent developments in locomotive practice. $1. Macmillan.
Goss. Locomotive sparks. $2. Wiley.
See also Steam engines.

Lodge, H: C.; Hoar, G: F., *and others.* The United States and the Philippine Islands. '02(Jl5) Q. (Brooklyn Eagle lib., v. 17, no. 9; serial no. 68.) pap., 10 c. Brooklyn Eagle.

Loeb, Jacques. On the production and suppression of muscular twitching and hypersensitiveness of the skin by electrolytes. '02(Ag9) 8°, (Decennial pub., v. 10, repr.) pap., *25 c. net. Univ. of Chic.

LOGARITHMS.
Marshall. Logarithmic tables of measures of length. $2. Van Nostrand.
Smith. Four-place logarithmic tables. net, 50 c. Holt.
See also Trigonometry.

LOGIC.
Aikins. Principles of logic. net, $1.50. Holt.

LONDON.
Baedeker. London and its environs. *$1.80 net. Scribner.
Besant, *ed.* Fascination of London. 80 c. Macmillan.
Ewart, *and others.* Climates of London. net, $4. Macmillan.
Machray. Night side of London. **$2.50 net. Lippincott.
Thorpe. Children's London. net, $4.50. Scribner.
See also Oriental Club;—Stock Exchange.

LONDON GUILD HALLS.
Interior decorations and furnishings of London Guild Halls. net, $12; net, $15. Helburn.

LONDON POLICE COURTS.
Holmes. Pictures and problems from London police cts. $1.25. Longmans.

Long, J: L. Naughty Nan. '02(Mr1) il. D. $1.50. Century Co.

Long duel. Clifford, *Mrs.* L. L. net, $1.25. Lane.

LONG ISLAND.
Ross. Hist. of Long Island. 3 v. $18. Lewis Pub.

Longfellow, H: W. Hyperion. '02(Ap19) 12°, (Home lib.) $1. Burt.

Longfellow, H: W. Outre mer. '02(Jl19) 12°, (Home lib.) $1. Burt.

Longfellow, H: W. Poems; biog. sketch by N. H. Dole. '02(F15) 12°, $1.75. Crowell.

Longfellow, H: W. Story of Hiawatha; abr. for schools. '02(Ag30) il. 16°, (Stories of the red children.) 40 c.; bds., 30 c. Educ. Pub.

Longmans' Am. teachers' ser.; ed. by J. E. Russell. O. $1.50. Longmans.
—Bourne. Teaching of history and civics.

Longmans' artists' lib.; ed. by L. Binyon. il. sq. O. net, $1. Longmans.
—Holmes. Constable. (5.)

Longmans' civil engineering ser. il. O. Longmans.
—Fidler. Calculations in hydraulic engineering. $3.
—Harcourt. Civil engineering as app. to construction. $5.

Longmans' practical elem. science ser. D. 90 c. Longmans.
—Dexter. Sound, light and heat.
—Furneaux. Hygiene.

Longridge, G. Official and lay witness to the value of foreign missions. '02(Je21) 16°, 20 c. E. & J. B. Young.

Longus. Daphnis and Chloe. '02(Mr29) il. 12°, (Antique gems from the Greek and Latin, v. 4.) (App. to pubs. for price.) Barrie.
Lord, W: R. First book upon birds of Oregon and Washington. New rev., enl. ed. '02(Mr29) il. 12°, 75 c. W: R. Lord.
Lord Alingham, bankrupt. Manning, M. $1.50. Dodd.
LORD'S PRAYER.
Foster. The Lord's prayer. 10 c. Cumberland Press.
LORD'S SUPPER.
Gore. Body of Christ. $1.75. Scribner.
Hall. Instructions and devotions on the holy communion. net, 25 c. Young Churchman.
Paret. Reality in holy communion. 10 c. Whittaker.
Preparatio; preparation for holy communion. $2. Longmans.
See also Catholic church;—Token.
Loryea, Ja. Hawthorne. *See* Santanelli.
LOS ANGELES.
Willard. *Herald's* hist. of Los Angeles city. $1.50. Kingsley.
Lost Christmas. Smith, M. R. 50 c. Dutton.
Lost hero. Phelps, E. S. 50 c. Little, B. & Co.
Lost on the Orinoco. Stratemeyer, E: net, $1. Lee & S.
Lothrop, *Mrs.* H. M., ["Margaret Sidney."] Five little Peppers abroad. '02(Je7) il. D. net, $1.10. Lothrop.
Loti, Pierre, *pseud.* *See* Viaud, L: M. J.
LOUISIANA PURCHASE.
Hosmer. Hist. of the Louisiana purchase. net, $1.20. Appleton.
Louisiana repts., v. 106. '02(Jl5) O. (Nat. reporter system ed.) shp., $8. West Pub.
Louisiana. *Supreme ct.* Digest; by J. A. Breaux. '01. '02(F8) O. shp., $20. Hansell.
Louttit, G: W: Maid of the wildwood. '02 (Je21) D. $1.50. Colonial.
Love, W: D. Thomas Short, the first printer of Conn. '01. '02(Ap26) 8°, (Acorn club, Ct., pub. no. 6.) pap., $5. Case.
LOVE.
Finck. Romantic love and personal beauty. net, $2. Macmillan.
Love in its tenderness. Aitken, J. R. $1; 50 c. Appleton.
Love letters and how to write them. *See* North, I.
Love never faileth. Simpson, C. $1.25. Revell.
Love poems. Suckling, *Sir* J: net. 50 c.; 75 c. Lane.
Love songs. Austrian, D. $1. Conkey.
Love sonnets of a hoodlum. Irwin, W. 25 c.; 50 c. Elder.
Love-story masterpieces. Lyon, R. A. net, $1. W: S. Lord.
Love story of Abner Stone. Litsey, E. C. net, $1.20. Barnes.
Lovejoy, Evelyn M. W. Dandelion. '02 (Ag30) D. $1. Abbey Press.
Lovely Mrs. Pemberton. James, *Mrs.* F. A. P. $1.25. Buckles.
Lover, S: Works; introd. by J. J. Roche. Treasure trove ed. 10 v. '02(Mr22) il. 8°, subs., per v., net, $3.50; hf. mor., per v., net, $6.50; de luxe ed., ¾ lev., per v., net, $12. Little, B. & Co.
Lover in Cuba. Elmore, J. B. $1. J. B. Elmore.
Lover's lib. S. net, 50 c.; leath., net, 75 c. Lane.
—Shakespeare. Sonnets.
—Suckling. Love poems.
Lover's progress told by himself. Vizetelly, E. A. $1.50. Brentano's.
Love's itinerary. Snaith, J: C. $1; 50 c. Appleton.
Lovett, Rob. *See* Moody, W: V.
Lowell, Guy, *ed.* American gardens. '02 (Je21) il. 4°, $7.50. Bates & G.
Lowell, Ja. R. The Biglow papers. '02(Ag2) 12°, (Cornell lib.) 75 c. Burt.
Lowell, Ja. R. Democracy. [Limited ed.] '02 (Mr22) 16°, bds., net, $2. Houghton, M. & Co.
Lower South in Am. history. Brown, W: G. net, $1.50. Macmillan.
Lubbock, *Sir* J:, [*Lord* Avebury.] Pleasures of life. '02(My17) 12°, (Home lib.) $1. Burt.
Lubbock, *Sir* J: Scenery of England. '02 (F22) il. 8°, net, $2.50. Macmillan.
Lucian. Lucius, the ass. '02(Je28) il. 12°, (Antique gems from the Gr. and Latin, v. 5.) (apply to pubs. for price.) Barrie.
Lucian. Translations, by A. M. C. Davidson. '02(Ap19) D. $2. Longmans.
Lucius, the ass. Lucian. (app. to pubs. for price.) Barrie.
LUDWIG II. *of Bavaria.*
Gerard. Romance of King Ludwig II. of Bavaria. net, $1.75. Dodd.
LUKE, *St.*
Selwyn. St. Luke the prophet. net, $2.75. Macmillan.
Luke Delmege. Sheehan, P. A. $1.50. Longmans.
LUMBER.
Rosenberger, *comp.* Law for lumbermen. $3.50. Am. Lumberman.
Saley. Realm of the retailer. $1.50. Am. Lumberman.
See also Forests and forestry.
LUNACY.
See Insanity.
LUNGS.
Blackwood. Diseases of the lungs. $2. Halsey.
See also Breathing;—Consumption.
Lungwitz, Anton. Complete guide to blacksmithing, horseshoeing, carriage and wagon building and painting. '02(Ag30) il. 12°, $1. Donohue.
Lunn, C: Philosophy of voice. [New rev., enl. ed.] '02(Ap26) il. O. net, $2. Schirmer.
Lupton, Arnold. Practical treatise on mine surveying. '02(Mr8) il. O. $5. Longmans.
Lush, Ethel R. Domestic economy for scholarship and certificate students. '01. '02 (Ja4) 12°, net, 60 c. Macmillan.
Luska, Sidney, *pseud.* *See* Harland, H:
Luther, Mark L. Favor of princes: [novel.] '01. '02(Ja11) 12°, pap., 50 c. Jamieson-H.
LUTHERAN CHURCH.
Laache. Book of family prayer; Bible lessons with meditations arr. after the church year. $1.65; $2.25. Luth. Pub. Ho.
Lützow, *Count* Fs. Story of Prague. '02 (Ag16) il. 12°, (Mediæval towns ser.) $1.50; leath., $2. Macmillan.

Lyall, Edna, *pseud.* *See* Bayly, A. E.
Lydekker, R. *See* Hutchinson, H. N.
Lydston, G. F. *See* Duhring, L: A.
Lyman, A. J. Preaching in the new age: six lectures del. in Hartford Theol. Sem. upon the Carew foundation. '02(Je28) 12°, net, 75 c. Revell.
Lynch, Laurence L., *pseud.* *See* Van Deventer, E. M.
Lyon, Flo. M. Study of the sporangia and gametophytes of selaginella apus and selaginella rupestris. '02(F15) 8°, (Cont. from the Hull Botanical lab'y, no. 31.) pap., net, 25 c. Univ. of Chic.
Lyon, H: A., *comp.* Cornell verse. 2d ed. '02(Mr8) Tt. $1. Walton.
Lyon, Ralph A., *comp.* Love-story masterpieces. '02(Je21) D. bds., net, $1. W: S. Lord.
Lyrics to the queen. Noble, A. C: n. p. Blue Sky Press.
Mabel Thornley. Baily, R. C. $1.25. Abbey Press.
Mabie, Hamilton W. Parables of life. '02 (Mr29) O. net, $1. Outlook.
Mabie, Hamilton W. Works and days. '02 (My10) S. net, $1. Dodd.
Mabry, W. D. When love is king. '02(Ap26) D. $1.50. Fenno.
McArthur, N. J. *See* Texas. Citations.—Legislature.
Macaulay, T: B., *Lord.* Frederick the Great. '02(F1) 12°, (Eng. classics.) net, 40 c. Macmillan.
Macaulay, T: B., *Lord.* Literary essays. '02 (Ap5) 12°, (Home lib.) $1. Burt.
Macbeth. *See* Porter, C.—Shakespeare, W:
McBride literature and art books. *See* Burke, B. E.
McCall, H: S. The clerk's assistant; rev. and largely rewritten by H. B. Bradbury. 6th ed. '02(Mr.22) O. shp., $6. Banks.
McCall, S: W. Daniel Webster. '02(My17) D. net, 80 c. Houghton, M. & Co.
McCallum & Hofer Cattle Co. Stockmen's calculator. '02(F15) nar. 8°, $1.50. McCallum.
McCarthy, J. H. If I were king. '01· '02 (F8) il. D. $1.50. Russell.
McClelland, T. C. Verba crucis. '02(Mr8) D. 50 c. Crowell.
McClure, Ja. G. K. A mighty means of usefulness: plea for intercessory prayer. '02 (Ap19) 12°, net, 50 c. Revell.
McClure, Rob. American horse, cattle and sheep doctor. '01· '02(Je28) il. 12°, $1.50. Henneberry.
McCormick, J: N. Distinctive marks of the Episcopal church. '02(F22) S. 25 c. Young Churchman.
McCullough, Annie W. Little stories for little people. '02(Ap12) D. (Eclectic school readings.) 25 c. Am. Bk.
McCulloch, S: J. *See* Missouri statute annots.
McCutcheon, G: B. Castle Craneycrow. '02 (Ag23) D. $1.50. H. S. Stone.
McDaniel, *Mrs.* Helen P. War poems, 1861-1865. '02(Ap26) D. $1. Abbey Press.
McDonald, D: Treatise on the laws of Ind. pertaining to the powers and duties of and practice and procedure before justices of the peace. Rev. to date by B: F. Watson. '02 (My24) O. shp., net, $7.50. Clarke.
Macdonald, Duff, *ed.* Revised catechism. (Westminster Assembly's Shorter catechism.) '02(Je28) 12°, $1.25. Macmillan.
Macdonald, G: David Elginbrod. '02(My17) 12°, (Home lib.) $1. Burt.
Macdonald, G: A. How successful lawyers are educated. '02(Jl12) il. 8°, $1.50. Temple Pub
Macdonald, Loren B. Guarding the thoughts. '02(Ja25) S. (Upward ser., no. 1.) pap., 10 c. J. H. West.
Macdonell, Arth. A. Sanskrit grammar for beginners. '01. '02(Ja11) D. $3. Longmans.
Macdonough, Rodney. Macdonough-Hackstaff ancestry. '01. '02(F1) il. sq. 8°, $7.50. R. Macdonough.
Macdougal, Dan. T. Elem. plant physiology. '02(Mr22) il. D. $1.20. Longmans.
MacDowell, Ja. N. Orthodontis: for students in dental colleges. '01. '02(Ja18) il. 8°, net, $4. Colegrove.
McElrath, Fes. The rustler. '02(My3) il. D. net. $1.20. Funk.
McElroy, Lucy C. Silent pioneer. '02(Mr8) il. D. $1.50. Crowell.
Macfadden, B. A. Power and beauty of superb womanhood. '01· '02(Ap12) il. 12°, $1. Physical Culture.
McGarvey, J. W. Authorship of the book of Deuteronomy. '02(Je7) O. $2. Standard.
McGee, Jos. B., *sr.* Complete exposition and revelation of ancient free and accepted masonry. '01· '02(My24) D. $1. J. B. McGee.
McGiffert, A. C. The Apostles' creed. '02 (F1) O. net, $1.25. Scribner.
McGovern, J: Fireside university of modern invention, discovery, industry and art for home circle study and entertainment. [Rev. 18th ed.] '02(My24) 8°. $2.50; mor., $3.75. Union Pub.
McGovern, J: Poems. '02(My24) D. net, $1. W: S. Lord.
McGrady, T: City of Angels. '01. '02 (My10) S. pap., 10 c. Standard.
McGrady, T: Clerical capitalist. '02(Ap19) O. (Socialist lib., v. 1, no. 10.) pap., 10 c. Socialistic Co-op.
McGrady, T: A voice from England. '02 (Ap5) S. (Standard lib.) pap., 10 c. Standard.
Mach, Ernst. Science of mechanics. 2d enl. ed.; tr. by T: J. McCormack. '02(Jl5) 12°, *$2 net. Open Court.
MACHINERY.
Benjamin. Notes on machine design. $2. C. H. Holmes.
Lafarque. Social effect of machinery. 10 c. Socialistic Co-op.
Meyer *and* Peker. Easy lessons in mechanical drawing and machine designs. In 20 pts. subs., ea., 50 c.; or in 2 v., v. 1, $6; v. 2, $4. Indust.
See also Electric engineering;—Locomotives.
Machray, Rob. Night side of London. '02 (Ag2) il. 8°, **$2.50 net. Lippincott.
McHugh, Hugh., [*pseud.* for G: V. Hobart.] It's up to you. '02(Je28) il. nar. S. 75 c. G: W. Dillingham.
McIlvaine, J. H. St. Francis of Assisi. '02 (Ap12) S. net, 85 c. Dodd.
McIntire, J: J., ["Harvey Argyle."] As I saw it. '02(Jl12) il. D. $1.25. Home Pub.

Mack, W:, *and* Nash, H. P., *eds.* Cyclopedia of law and procedure. v. 3. '02(Ap5) O. shp., $6. Am. Law Bk.

Mackail, J: W: Biblia innocentium. pt. 2. '01. '02(Ja4) D. $1.75. Longmans.

Mackay, Angus M. Churchman's introduction to the Old Testament. '01. '02(Ja4) 12°. (Churchman's lib.) $1.50. Macmillan.

McKay, H: J. Poetical works. '02(Ag9) 12°, *$1 net. E. B. Thayer.

McKay, W. J. S. Hist. of ancient gynæcology. '01. '02(F22) 8°, net, $3. Wood.

McKee, Lanier. Land of Nome. '02(Je28) D. net, $1.25. Grafton Press.

Mackenzie, Alex. Voyages from Montreal through the Continent of North America to the Frozen and Pacific Oceans in 1789 and 1793. '02(My24) 2 v., 8°. (Commonwealth lib.) per v., net, $1. New Amsterdam.

Mackenzie, Ja. Study of the pulse, arterial, venous, and hepatic, and of the movements of the heart. '02(My17) il. 8°, net, $4.50. Macmillan.

Mackenzie, J: S. Outlines of metaphysics. '02(Ap26) 12°, net, $1.10. Macmillan.

McKernan, Ja. Forty-five sermons written to meet objections of the present day. '02 (Ag23) D. *$1 net. Pustet.

Mackinder, H. J. Britain and the British seas. '02(F22) 8°, (World ser., no. 1.) $2. Appleton.

McKinley, W: Last speech of President McKinley. '02(Mr1) 12°, bds., $1.50; pap., $1. Kirgate Press.

McKinley, W:

Ellis. Life of William McKinley. 25 c. Street.

Fallows, *ed.* Life of William McKinley. $1.50; $2.25. Regan.

Halstead. William McKinley [in Norwegian.] $1.50; $2. J: Anderson.

Halstead *and* Munson. Life and services of William McKinley. $1.50; $2.25. Dominion.

Hay. William McKinley. net, 28 c. Crowell.

See also Wilson, J. G.

McKinney, A. H. The child for Christ. '02 (Je28) 16°, net, 50 c. Revell.

McKinney, W: M., *ed.* Encyclopædia of pleading and practice. v. 22, 23. '02(My24) O. shp., ea., $6. E: Thompson.

Mackinnon, Ja. Growth and decline of the French monarchy. '02(Je7) O. $7.50. Longmans.

Maclane, Ma. *See* Story of.

McLaughlin, Ja. M. Elements and notation of music. '02(F1) D. 55 c. Ginn.

McLaws, Lafayette. Jezebel. '02(Jl5) il. D. †$1.50. Lothrop.

Maclay, E. S. Hist. of the U. S. Navy. New rev. ed. of v. 3. '02(Mr1) 3 v., il. 8°, per v., net, $3. Appleton.

McLellan, Ja. A., Dewey, J:, *and* Ames, A. F. Public school arithmetic for grammar grades. '02(F1) 12°, net, 60 c. Macmillan.

McLeod, Lorenzo C. A young man's problems. '02(Je7) D. 50 c. Flanagan.

McLeod, Malcolm J. Heavenly harmonies for earthly living. '02(F8) 12°, net, 50 c. Revell.

Macleod, Ma. *See* Malory, *Sir* T:

McManman, J. A. *See* Hyde, W. H.

McManus, L. The wager. '02(My17) D. $1.25. Buckles.

McMaster, J. S. Commercial cases. '01. '02 (Jl19) 8°, leath., $6. Commercial Bk.

McMaster, J. S. Commercial digest and business forms. 1900. '02(Jl19) 8°, leath., $6. Commercial Bk.

McMaster, J. S. Irregular and regular commercial paper. '02(Jl19) 12 x 4 in. $2. McMaster.

Macmillan, Hugh. Christmas rose and other thoughts in verse. '01. '02(Ja4) il. 12°, $1. Macmillan.

Macmillan, Hugh. Corn of Heaven. '02 (Ja18) 12°, $1.75. Macmillan.

Macmillan's classical ser. 12°, net. Macmillan.

—Sophocles. Antigone. 60 c.

Macmillan's Eng. classics. 12°, net, 60 c. Macmillan.

—Boswell. Journal of tour to the Hebrides.

—Scott. Kenilworth.—Quentin Durward.

Macmillan's French classics. 12°, *60 c. net. Macmillan.

—Racine. Athalie.

Macmillan's Greek course. 12°. Macmillan.

—Andrew. Greek prose composition. net, 90 c.

Macmillan's guides. 12°. net. Macmillan.

—Guide to Palestine and Egypt. $3.25.

Macmillan's handbooks of great masters in painting and sculpture. il. 12°, $1.75. Macmillan.

—Bell. Rembrandt.

—Gower. Sir David Wilkie.

—Martin. Gerard Douw.

—Perkins. Giotto.

Macmillan's handbooks of the great craftsmen. il. 12°, $2. Macmillan.

—Cust. Ivory workers of the Middle Ages.

—Headlam. Peter Vischer.

Macmillan's handbooks to the great public schools. 12°, $1.50. Macmillan.

—Airy. Westminster.

Macmillan's historical sources in school ser. 12°. **60 c. net. Macmillan.

—New England History Teachers' Assoc. Report.

Macmillan's manuals for teachers. 12°, net. Macmillan.

—Findlay. Principles of class teaching. $1.25.

Macmillan's mediæval towns ser. il. 12°. Macmillan.

—Headlam. Chartres. $2; $2.50.

—Lützow. Prague.

—Poole. Cairo. $2; $2.50.

Macmillan's new geography readers: Africa and Australasia. '02(My24) 12°, net, 40 c. Macmillan.

Macmillan's new history readers; [bk. 3,] senior. '02(My24) il. 12°, net, 50 c. Macmillan.

Macmillan's personal problem ser. 12°, net, $1. Macmillan.

—Canfield. College student and his problems.

—Oppenheim. Mental growth and control.

Macmillan's Pitt Press ser. 12°, net. Macmillan.

—Sybel. Prinz Eugen von Savoyen. 60 c.

Macmillan's primary ser. of French and Germ. reading books. 12°, net. Macmillan.

—Alissas, d'. Les histoires de tante. 40 c.

Macmillan's summary of Eng. history on the concentric plan; senior. '02(My24) il. 12°, pap., net, 15 c. Macmillan.

Macmillan's Temple classics. 16°, 50 c.; flex. leath., 75 c. Macmillan.
—Arnold. Dramatic and early poems.
—Boethius. Consolation of philosophy.
—Browning. Sordello.
—Carlyle. Past and present.
—Goldsmith. Plays.—Poems.

Macmillan's Temple classics for young people. 16°, net, 50 c.; flex. leath., 80 c. Macmillan.
—Andersen. Fairy tales.
—Perrault. Tales of passed times.

McMurry, C: A., *ed.* Pubs of the National Herbart Society. '02(Jl12) 8°, *$5 net. Univ. of Chic.

Macnab, Fes. Ride in Morocco among believers and fur traders. '02(Ap19) il. O. $5. Longmans.

McSpadden, J. W. Shakesperian synopses. '02(Ap5) S. (Handy information ser.) net, 45 c. Crowell.

McVickar, W: B. Lays of a lawyer. '02 (Ag30) il. 8°, *$4 net. Dodd.

Madame Bohemia. Neilson, F. $1; 50 c. Lippincott.

Mlle. Fouchette. Murray, C: T. $1.50. Lippincott.

Madness of Philip. Daskam, J. D. $1.50. McClure, P.

Maeterlinck, M. The buried temple; tr. by A. Sutro. '02(My10) D. net, $1.40. Dodd.

Maeterlinck, M. Sister Beatrice and Ardiane and Barbe Bleue: two plays; tr. by B. Miall. '02(Ap12) D. net, $1.20. Dodd.

Maggie Miller. '02(Ap19) 12°, (Home lib.) $1. Burt.

Magic key. Tucker, E. S. net, $1. Little, B. & Co.

Magic wheel. Stannard, *Mrs.* H. E. V. $1.25. Lippincott.

MAGNETISM.
See Electricity.

Mahon, R. H. Token of the covenant; or, right use of baptism. 4th ed. '02(My17) D. 50 c. Pub. Ho. M. E. Ch., So.

Mahoney million. Townsend, C: $1.25. New Amsterdam.

Maid of Bar Harbor. Rowe, H. G. $1.50. Little, B. & Co.

Maid of Montauk. Monroe, F. net, $1. W: R. Jenkins.

Maid of Orleans. *See* Schiller, J. C. F. v.

Maid of the wildwood. Louttit, G: W: $1.50. Colonial.

Main currents in 19th century literature. *See* Brandes, G:

Main street. Hawthorne, N. $2. Kirgate Press.

Maine. Laws concerning business corporations, (annot.) (H. M. Heath.) '02(Je7) O. pap., gratis. Kennebec Journ.

Maine. *Supreme judicial ct.* Repts., v. 95. (C: Hamlin.) '01. '02(Mr15) O. shp., $4. W: W. Roberts.

MAINE.
Drummond, *comp.* Maine masonic textbook. $1.40; $1.50. Berry.

Maitland, F: W:, Gwatkin, H: M., Poole, R. L., *and others.* Essays on the teaching of history. '01. '02(Ja4) 12°, (Cambridge Univ. Press ser.) net, 75 c. Macmillan.

Maitland, J: A. F. Music in England in the nineteenth century. '02(Ap5) 12°, net, $1.75. Dutton.

Majesty of calmness. Jordan, W: G: 50 c. Revell.

Major, C:, ["Edwin Caskoden."] Bears of Blue River. [New issue.] '02(Mr8) il. 12°, $1.50. Macmillan.

Major, C: Dorothy Vernon of Haddon Hall. '02(My3) il. D. $1.50. Macmillan.

Make good book of parodies. Dustin, E. 50 c. E. Dustin.

Makers of British art; ed. by J. Manson. sq. 8°, *$1.25 net. Scribner.
—Keeling. Sir Joshua Reynolds.
—Manson. Sir Edwin Landseer.

Making a country newspaper. Munson, A. J. $1. Dominion.

Making of a statesman. Harris, J. C. $1.25. McClure, P.

MALARIAL FEVER.
Ross. Malarial fever. net, 75 c. Longmans.

Malet, Lucas, *pseud.* *See* Harrison, *Mrs.* M. K.

Malheurs de Sophie. Ségur, S. R., *Comtesse* de. 45 c. Heath.

Mallary, R. DeWitt. Lenox and the Berkshire Highlands. '02(Je21) il. O. net, $1.75. Putnam.

Malone, *Mrs.* Eva W. Out among the animals: [stories.] '02(Mr22) S. 75 c. Pub. Ho. M. E. Ch., So.

Malone, Jos. S. Guided and guarded. '02 (Ap26) D. $1.25. Abbey Press.

Maloney, Ja. C. 20th century guide for mixing fancy drinks. 3d ed. enl. '02(Jl19) sq. S. pap., $1. J. C. Maloney.

Malory, *Sir* T: King Arthur and his noble knights: stories from Morte D'Arthur, by M. Macleod. '02(Jl19) il. 12°, (Home lib.) $1. Burt.

MALVERN, Eng.
Windle. Malvern country. net, 75 c. Dodd.

MAMMALIA.
Harmer *and* Shipley, *eds.* Cambridge natural history. v. 10, Mammalia, by F. E. Beddard. net, $4. Macmillan.

MAN.
See Anatomy;—Ethnology;—Evolution;—Heredity;—Physiology;—Sex.

Man amongst men. Wollpert, F: 15 c. Eckler.

Man in the moon. Dendron, B. 50 c. Bonnell.

"**Man** (The) in the street" stories fr. the *New York Times.* '02(Ag2) D. $1. Ogilvie.

Man of no account. Trelawney, D. 10 c. J. H. West.

Man without a country. Hale, E: E. net, $1. Outlook.

Man who pleases and the woman who fascinates. Cone, J: A. $1. Neely.

MANCHURIA.
Graham. East of the barrier; or, Manchuria in miniature. net, $1. Revell.

Mandeville, C. E. Minister's manual and pocket ritual. '02(F8) S. flex. leath., net, 60 c. Jennings.

Mangasarian, M. M. New catechism. 3d ed. '02(My10) D. pap., 75 c. Open Court.

Manhattan lib. of new copyright fiction. *See* Burt's.

Mann, Horace K. Lives of the Popes in the early Middle Ages. v. 1. pt. 1. '02(Je14) 8°, net, $3. Herder.

MANNERS AND CUSTOMS.
See Folk-lore;—Kissing;—Marriage;—Toasts.
MANNIKIN.
Furneaux, *ed.* Whittaker's popular mannikin. *$1.50 net. Whittaker.
Manning, Marie. Lord Alingham, bankrupt. '02(Ap12) D. $1.50. Dodd.
Mannix, Ma. E. As true as gold. '02(Mr22) il. S. 45 c. Benziger.
Man's peerless destiny in Christ. Sarles, J: W. net, 90 c. Funk.
Manson, Ja. A. Sir Edwin Landseer. '02 (Ag23) sq. 8°, (Makers of British art.) *$1.25 net. Scribner.
MANUAL TRAINING.
See Sloyd.
Manufacturers' need of reciprocity. Farquhar, A. B. 15 c. Am. Acad. Pol. Sci.
MANUSCRIPTS.
See Inscriptions;—Irish literature.
Many waters. Shackleton, R. $1.50. Appleton.
Manzoni, A. I promessi sposi; abr. and ed. by M. Levi. '01. '02(Ja25) D. (Silver ser. of modern lang. text-books.) $1.20. Silver.
Marble faun. Hawthorne, N. $1. Burt.
Marchant, J. R. V. Commercial history. '02 (Je7) il. D. (Commercial ser.) $1. Pitman.
Marchmont, Arth. W. Miser Hoadley's secret. '02(Jl12) il. D. (Red letter ser.) $1.25; pap., 50 c. New Amsterdam.
Marchmont, Arth. W. Sarita, the Carlist. '02 (My3) D. $1.50. Stokes.
Marden, Orison S., assisted by Abner Bayley. Stepping stones; essays for every-day living. '02(Ag23) D. **$1 net. Lothrop.
Margaret Bowlby. Vincent, E. L. $1.50. Lothrop.
Margaret Tudor. Colcock, A. T. $1. Stokes.
Margaret Vincent. Clifford, *Mrs.* L. L. $1.50. Harper.
Margoliouth, D: S: Lines of defense of the biblical revelation. '02(Mr8) 12°, net, $1.50. Gorham.
Margoliouth, D: S: Religion of Bible lands. '02(My3) S. (Christian study manuals.) 60 c. Armstrong.
Maria Stuart. Schiller, J. C. F. v. net, 70 c. Holt.
MARINE ENGINEERING.
Durand. Practical marine engineering. $5. Marine Engineering.
MARINE ZOOLOGY.
See Aquatic life:—Protozoa.
Marion Manning. Eustis, E. $1.50. Harper.
Marius the epicurean. Pater, W. $1. Burt.
Marivaux, Pierre C. de C. de. Selection from comedies by E. W. Olmsted. '02 (Mr22) 12°, net, 90 c. Macmillan.
MARK, *St.*
See Bible.
Marks, Jeannette A. Brief hist. outline of Eng. literature. '02(Je28) D. $1. J. A. Marks.
Marlowe, Chris. Passionate shepherd to his love; and The nymph's reply to the shepherd, by Sir. W. Raleigh. '02(My10) sq. 8°, flex. vellum, net, $3.75.) Russell.
MARQUETTE, Jacques.
Thwaites. Father Marquette. net, $1. Appleton.
Marquis, G: H. Fairview's mystery. '01. '02(Mr1) D. 75 c. Abbey Press.
Marred in the making. Commander, L. K. $3; 25 c. Eckler.
MARRIAGE.
Brown. True marriage guide. 55 c.; 35 c. Westminster Pub.
Cook. Bride's book. net, $1.50. Dutton.
Crawley. The mystic rose: study of primitive marriage. net, $4. Macmillan.
Fields. Freedom in marriage. 50 c. Abbey Press.
Hurst. New heartstone: bridal greeting. $1. Jennings.
Westermarck. Hist. of human marriage. net, $4.50. Macmillan.
Wood. Marriage. net, $1.25. Revell.
Marriage of Laurentia. Haultmont, M. net, $1.60. Herder.
Marrin, J: Fs. *See* Cath. year-book.
Marsh, C: L. Not on the chart. '02(Je7) il. D. $1.50. Stokes.
Marsh, G: A singular will. '02(Je7) D. $1.50. Neely.
Marsh, Lucius B., *and* Parker, *Mrs.* Ht. F., *comps.* Bronsdon and Box families. '02 (Ag23) por. 8°, $4. Nichols.
Marshall, Beatrice. Old Blackfriars. '02 (Ap5) il. 12°, $1.50. Dutton.
Marshall, J: S. Principles and practice of operative dentistry. '01. '02(F15) il. 8°, subs., $5; shp., $6. Lippincott.
Marshall, T: W. Logarithmic tables of the measures of length. '02(Jl12) 12°, $2. Van Nostrand.
Marshall, W: L. *See* Clark, W: L.
Marston, E: Sketches of some booksellers of the time of Dr. Samuel Johnson. '02 (My10) 16°, net, $2. Scribner.
Martin, Fred. W. Album of designs for boats, launches and yachts. [2d ed.] '02(My24) il. obl. T. pap., $1. F: W. Martin.
Martin, G: H. Civil government in the U. S. Rev. ed. '02(Ap26) D. 90 c. Am. Bk.
Martin, W. Gerard Douw; fr. the Dutch by Clara Bell. '02(My3) il. 12°, (Great masters in painting and sculpture.) $1.75. Macmillan.
Martin, W. G. W. Traces of the elder faiths of Ireland. '02(F8) 2 v., il. O. $12. Longmans.
Martin, W: E. Internal improvements in Alabama. '02(Jl12) O. (Johns Hopkins Univ. studies in hist. and pol. science, 20th ser., no. 4.) pap., 30 c. Johns Hopkins.
Martindale, J. B. Am. law directory. Jan., 1902. '02(F1) O. shp., net, $10. Martindale.
MARTINIQUE.
Miller *and* Durham. Martinique horror and St. Vincent calamity. $1.50; $2. Nat. Pub. Co.
See also St. Pierre.
Marvelous achievements of the 19th century. Morris, C: $2.50; $3.50. Winston.
Marx, Karl. Wage-labor and capital; also Free-trade. '02(Mr29) D. (Arm and hammer ser.) 50 c. N. Y. Labor News.
MARY, *Virgin.*
Palladino. Mary our mother. net, 15 c. Herder.
Mary Garvin. Pattee, F. L. $1.50. Crowell.
Mary of Bethany. Parks, E. M. 25 c.; 15 c. Pepper.
Mary Starkweather. Williamson, *Mrs.* C. C. $1.50. Abbey Press.

Mary Stuart. *See* Schiller, J. C. F. v.
Mary Tracy's fortune. Sadlier, A. T. 45 c. Benziger.
Maryland. *Ct. of appeals.* Repts. (Brantly.) v. 93. '02(My10) O. shp., $5. Baughman.
Maryland. *Ct. of appeals.* Repts. v. 59. '02(Mr1); v. 60 (My10); v. 61(Je21) O. shp., ea., $4. Curlander.
MARYLAND.
Snowden. Some old historic landmarks of Va. and Md. *25 c. net. Ramey.
Steiner. Western Md. in the Revolution. 30 c. Johns Hopkins.
Mason, Arth. J. Christianity, what is it? '02(Je7) 16°, (Church Hist. Soc. lectures, no. 66.) 80 c. E. & J. B. Young.
Mason, Arth. J. Ministry of conversion. '02 (Mr8) D. (Handbooks for the clergy.) net, 90 c. Longmans.
Mason, Caro. A. Little green god. '02(Ag2) 12°, †75 c. Revell.
Mason, Hobart. *See* Sheldon, S:
Mason, Ja. F:, *comp.* Favorite songs of love. Limited ed. '02(Jl5) 16°, $1.50; ooze cf., $2; Eng. cf., $2.25; Eng. cf. tooled, $5. Dodge.
Mason, W: D. Water-supply (from a sanitary standpoint.) 3d ed., rewritten. '02 (My17) il. 8°, red. to $4. Wiley.
MASON AND DIXON'S LINE.
See United States.
MASONRY.
See Bridges.
MASS.
See Catholic church;—Lord's supper.
Massachusetts digest, supp. [v. 5,] by C: N. Harris. '02(Je28) Q. shp., net, $5. Little, B. & Co.
Massachusetts. *Supreme judicial ct.* Repts. v. 178. (H: W. Swift.) '02(Ap5) O. shp., $2. Little, B. & Co.
Massachusetts. Treatise on the street railway accident law; by E. H. Clark. '02 (Ap19) O. shp., $3.25. Lawyers' Bk.
MASSACHUSETTS.
American ser. of popular biographies. Mass. ed. $17. Graves.
Hall, *ed.* Regiments and armories of Mass. v. 2. per set, $12; $18; $25. W. W. Potter.
Perley. Practice in personal actions in cts. of Mass. $6.50. G: B. Reed.
Smith. Founders of the Mass. Bay Colony. *$5 net. Woodward & L.
Tucker. Preparation of wills: Mass. law. $3.50. G: B. Reed.
See also Ancient and Hon. Artillery Co. of Mass.;—Boston;—Charlestown;—Lenox;— Lexington;—Nantucket Island.
MASSAGE.
Ostrom. Massage and the orig. Swedish movements. $1. Blakiston.
See also Injuries.
Master key. *See* Lanier, J. J.
Master of Beechwood. Sergeant, A. 50 c. Burt.
Master of Caxton. Brooks, H. $1.50. Scribner.
Master of science of right living. Hillis, N. D. net, 50 c. Revell.
Mastery of the Pacific. Colquhoun, A. R. net, $4. Macmillan.
MATABELELAND.
Hall *and* Neal. Ancient ruins of Rhodesia. net, $6. Dutton

Mate of the good ship "York." Russell, W: C. $1.50. L. C. Page.
MATERIA MEDICA.
Murray. Rough notes on remedies. net, $1.25. Blakiston.
See also Pharmacy;—Therapeutics.
MATHEMATICS.
Chancellor. Elem. school mathematics by grades. bks. 5, 6, 7. ea., 28 c. Globe Sch. Bk.
Deel. Practical rapid calculator. 50 c. G: A. Deel.
Gibbs. Vector analysis. net, $4. Scribner.
Jones. Math. puzzles. 25 c. News Pr.
Stokes. Math. and physical papers. v. 3. net, $3.75. Macmillan.
See also Algebra; — Arithmetic; — Astronomy;—Calculus;—Geodesy;—Interest;—Logarithms;—Probabilities;—Surveying;—Trigonometry.
Mathes, J. H. General Forrest. '02(Ap26) D. (Great commanders' ser.) net, $1.50. Appleton.
Matheson, G: Spiritual development of St. Paul. '02(Ap12) 12°, net, 80 c. Whittaker.
Matheson, G: Times of retirement; with biog. sketch of the author by D. MacMillan. '01. '02(Ja11) 12°, net, $1.25. Revell.
Mathews, Ferd. S. Field book of Am. wild flowers. '02(Ap26) il. S. net, $1.75. Putnam.
Mathews, Shailer. *See* Burton, E. D.
Matteson, A., *ed.* *See* Illinois. Laws rel. to township organization.
Matthews, C: G. Manual of alcoholic fermentation and allied industries. '02(Ap19) D. net, $2.60. Longmans.
Matthews, Ja. B. Pen and ink: [essays.] 3d rev., enl. ed. '02(F15) D. net, $1.25. Scribner.
Maulde la Clavière, René de. Art of life; tr. by G: H. Ely. '01. '02(Ja25) D. net, $1.75. Putnam.
Mavor, W: English spelling book; il. by Kate Greenaway. '02(Je28) 16°, bds., 40 c. Warne.
Mawley, E: *See* Jekyll, G.
MAXIMS.
See Proverbs.
Maxwell, Hu. Jonathan Fish and his neighbors. '02(Jl19) O. $1. Acme.
Maxwell, Lucy H. Card sewing: for kindergartens. '02(My3) 16°, pap., 50 c. M. Bradley.
Maxwell, *Mrs.* Ma. E. B. El sacrificio de Elisa. (A. Elias y Pujol.) '01. '02(F22) 12°, pap., 50 c. Appleton.
May, Eliz. Animal life in rhymes and jingles. '02(Ag16) il. 4°, bds., $1.25. Saalfield.
Maynard, *Mrs.* L. W. Birds of Washington and vicinity. '02(Jl12) D. *$1 net. Woodward & L.
Mayor, Jos. B. Chapters on Eng. metre. 2d ed., rev. and enl. '02(Ja18) 8°, (Cambridge Univ. Press ser.) net, $2.25. Macmillan.
Mazel. Fisguill, R: $1.50. H. S. Stone.
Mead, Spencer P. Hist. and genealogy of the Mead family of Fairfield Co., Conn. '01. '02(F8) il. O. $15. Knickerbocker.
Meade, L. T. *See* Smith, *Mrs.* E. T.
Meakin, Budgett. The Moors. '02(Mr29) il. 8°, net, $5. Macmillan.
Meakin, Nevill M. The Assassins. '02 (Mr22) D. $1.50. Holt.

MEAT.
Walley. Guide to meat inspection. $3. W: R. Jenkins.

MECHANICAL DRAWING.
Hawkins. Self-help mechanical drawing. $2. Audel.
Meyer *and* Peker. Easy lessons in mechanical drawing and machine designs. In 20 pts. subs., ea., 50 c.; or in 2 v., v. 1, $6; v. 2, $4. Indust.

Mechanical triumphs of ancient Egyptians. Barber, F. M. net, $1.25. Dodd.

MECHANICS.
Gibbs. Elem. principles in statistical mechanics, with especial ref. to the rational foundation of thermo-dynamics. $4. Scribner.
Mach. Science of mechanics. *$2 net. Open Court.
Reynolds. Papers on mechanical and physical subjects. v. 2. net, $6. Macmillan.
See also Engineering;—Power.

MECHANICS' LIENS.
Illinois. Commentary on mechanics' lien law. net, $4. Callaghan.

Mechanics of engineering. *See* Du Bois, A: J.

Mechem, Floyd R. Case on the law of damages. 3d ed. '02(Mr8) O. net, $4. West Pub.

MEDIAEVAL HISTORY.
See Middle Ages.

Mediæval Rome. Miller, W: **$1.35 net; $1.60 net. Putnam.

Medical directory of the city of New York. '01- '02(F8) 12°, $1.50. Wynkoop.

Medical hand-atlases. See Saunders'.

Medical News pocket formulary for 1902; ed. by E. Q. Thornton. 4th ed. '02(F15) 18°, leath. tuck, net, $1.50. Lea.

Medical News visiting list, 1902. '01- '02 (F22) 16°, leath. tucks, $1.25; thumb-letter index, $1.50. Lea.

MEDICI (The).
Smeaton. The Medici and the Italian Renaissance. $1.25. Scribner.

MEDICINE.
American year-book of medicine and surgery. 2 v. ea., net, $3; net, $3.75. Saunders.
Barret. Medical handbook. $1. Barret Chemical.
Billings *and* Stanton, *eds.* General medicine. $1.50. Year Bk.
Buck. Reference handbook of the medical sciences. v. 4. subs., $7; $8; $9. Wood.
Burdick. Standard medical manual. $4. Engelhard.
Fagge. Text-book of medicine. 2 v. net, $6. Blakiston.
Hood. Practical family physician. $2.50. Hood.
International medical annual, 1902. net, $3. Treat.
Lawrence. Practical medicine. $3. Boericke & T.
Lippincott's pocket medical dict. 50 c. Lippincott.
Medical News pocket formulary, 1902. net, $1.50. Lea.
Paget. Sel. essays and addresses. $5. Longmans.

MEDICINE.—*Continued*
Sajous, *ed.* Analytical encyclopædia of practical medicine. v. 1. subs., ea., $5; $6. Davis.
See also Accidents;—Anatomy; — Autopsy;—Bacteria;—Chemistry;—Contagion; — Diagnosis; — Hygiene;—Mind and body;—Nervous system;—Pathology;—Pharmacy;— Physiology;—Veterinary medicine and surgery.

Meditations and vows. Hall, J. $1.50. Dutton.

Meditations of an autograph collector. Joline, A. H. net, $3. Harper.

Medley, Dudley J. Student's manual of Eng. constitutional history. 3d ed. '02(Je28) 8°, net, $3.50. Macmillan.

Meier, W. H. D. Herbarium and plant description. '01. '02(F1) Q. portfolio, 70 c. Ginn.

Meigs, H: B: Record of the descendants of Vincent Meigs. '02(Jl12) il. 8°, $6; mor., $8. H: B: Meigs.

Melliar, A. F. Book of the rose. 2d ed. '02 (My24) 12°, $1.75. Macmillan.

Mellick, Anna C. Latin composition for classes reading Cæsar. '01. '02(Ja4) S. 40 c. Am. Bk.

Melomaniacs. Huneker, J. $1.50. Scribner.

Melville, Herman. Typee; ed.by W. P. Trent. '02(My17) il. D. (Home and school classics, young reader's ser.) 45 c. Heath.

Melvin, Ja. Journal. [Repr.] '02(Jl12) 12°, $2. H. W. Bryant.

Memoirs of an American lady. Grant, *Mrs.* A. M. net, $7.50. Dodd.

MEMORIAL DAY.
Harvey. Aids for the proper observance of Memorial day by schools of Wis. gratis. Democrat Pr. Co.

MEMORY.
Kilbourne. Memory and its cultivation. $1; 50 c. Mullin.

MEN.
Blouët. 'Tween you an' I; pt. 1, Concerning men. $1.20. Lothrop.

Men and memories. Young, J: R. subs., $5; $3. Neely.

Men of Buffalo. '02(Ag8) 8°, mor., $15. Marquis.

Mendel's principles of heredity. Bateson, W. *$1.30 net. Macmillan.

Menefee, Maud. Child stories from the masters. '02(My10) il. 16°, 75 c. Rand, McN. & Co.

Menpes, Mortimer. Japan. '02(Ja18) il. 8°, net, $6. Macmillan.

MENTAL ARITHMETIC.
See Arithmetic.

Mental growth and control. Oppenheim, N. net, $1. Macmillan.

MENTAL SCIENCE.
Ballough. Power that heals and how to use it. $1. Painter.
Bradbury. New philosophy of health. 75 c. Alliance.
Dresser. True hist. of mental science. 20 c. Alliance.
Patterson. What the new thought stands for. 10 c. Alliance.
Patterson. The will to be well. $1. Alliance.
See also Christian science;—Mind and body.

Mental state of hystericals. Janet, P. $3.50. Putnam.

Merchant adventurers of England. Lingelbach, W. E. $1.25. Univ. of Penn.; Longmans.
Merchant of Venice. *See* Shakespeare, W:
Mercier, C: A. Psychology, normal and morbid. '02(Mr1) 8°, net, $4. Macmillan.
Mercier, C: A. Text-book of insanity. '02 (My17) 12°, net, $1.75. Macmillan.
Merejkowski, Dimitri. Romance of Leonardo da Vinci, the forerunner; authorized tr. of The resurrection of the gods, by H. Trench. '02(Jl19) D. †$1.50. Putnam.
Merriam, Edm. F. Hist. of Am. Bapt. missions. '01. '02(F15) 12°, $1.25. Am. Bapt.
Merriam, J: C. Triassic ichthyopterygia fr. Cal. and Nevada. '02(Ag16) Q. (Univ. of Cal. pub., bull. of the Dept. of geology, v. 3, no. 4.) pap., 50 c. Univ. of Cal.
Merrill, Cath. The man Shakespeare, and other essays. '02(Jl19) 12°, **$1.25 net. Bowen-M.
Merrill, J. M. His mother's letter. '02(Ag9) il. 12°, $1. Saalfield.
Merrill, S. M., *and* Warren, H: W. Discourses on miracles. '02(Mr22) sq. T. (Little books on doctrine.) net, 25 c. Jennings.
Merriman, Mansfield, *and* Jacoby, H: D. Text-book on roofs and bridges. Pt. 3. 4th ed., rewritten. '02(Ap19) 8°, $2.50. Wiley.
Merriman, Roger B. Life and letters of Thomas Cromwell. '02(Ag23) 2 v., pors. O. $6. Oxford Univ.
MESA VERDE.
See Colorado.
Message of man. Coit, S. 75 c.; $1. Macmillan.
Message of to-morrow. Lee, J: L. net, $1.20. Revell.
Message to Garcia and thirteen other things. Hubbard, E. $2; $5; $15. Roycrofters.
METAL-WORK.
See Plate.
Metallurgy of cast iron. West, T: D. $3. Cleveland Pr.
METALS AND METALLURGY.
Hiorns. Metallography. *$1.40 net. Macmillan.
Langbein. Complete treatise on the electro-deposition of metals. $4. Baird.
Phillips, *ed.* Methods for analysis of ores, pig iron and steel. net, $1. Chemical.
See also Assaying;—Blowpipe;—Chemistry;—Copper;—Iron;—Precious metals;—Steel.
METAPHYSICS.
Alexander. Problem of metaphysics and the meaning of metaphysical explanation. *75 c. net. Macmillan.
Kant. Prolegomena to any future metaphysics. 50 c. Open Court.
Leibnitz. Discourse on metaphysics. 35 c.; net, 75 c. Open Court.
Mackenzie. Outlines of metaphysics. net, $1.10. Macmillan.
See also Ethics;—Knowledge;—Logic; — Mind;—Ontology;—Philosophy;—Psychology.
METEOROLOGY.
Bartholomew's physical atlas. v. 1, Meteorlogy. **$17.50 net. Lippincott.
See also Weather.
Methodist Episcopal church. Constitution of churches in America, by W. F. Barclay. '02(My10) D. pap., 40 c. Pub. Ho. M. E. Ch., So.
Methodist Episcopal church in America. Doctrines; comp. and ed. by J: L. Tigert. '02 (Jl19) 2 v., sq. T. (Little books on doctrine.) *50 c. net. Jennings.
Methodist Episcopal church, South. Minutes of the annual conferences for 1901. '01. '02 (My10) O. pap., net, 50 c. Pub. Ho. M. E. Ch., So.
METHODIST EPISCOPAL CHURCH.
Bowen. Why two Episcopal Methodist churches in the U. S.? 75 c. Pub. Ho. of M. E. Ch., So.
Oliver. Our lay office-bearers. net, 25 c. Jennings.
See also Epworth League.
Methods of keeping the public money of the U. S. Phillips, J: B. $1. Mich. Pol. Sci.
Methods of Lady Walderhurst. Burnett, *Mrs.* F. H. $1.25. Stokes.
METRE.
Mayor. Chapters on Eng. metre. net, $2.25. Macmillan.
Metropolitan club cook-book. Schaeffer, *Mrs.* J. $1.75. Augsburg.
Mets, J. A. Naval heroes of Holland. '02 (Je14) il. D. $1.50. Abbey Press.
MEXICO.
Wilkins. Glimpse of old Mexico. 75 c. Whitaker & R.
Meyer, B. H. Advisory councils in railway administration. '02(Mr22) 8°, (Pub. of the soc., no. 327.) pap., 15 c. Am. Acad. Pol. Sci.
Meyer, Ernest C. Nominating systems; with bibliog. and index '02(Ap5) 8°, net, $1.50. E. C. Meyer.
Meyer, J. G. A., *and* Peker, C: G. Easy lessons in mechanical drawing and machine designs. '02(Jl12) in 20 pts., subs., ea., 50 c.; or in 2 v., v. 1, $6; v. 2, $4. Indust.
Meyers, R. C. V. Theodore Roosevelt, patriot and statesman. '02(F22) il. 12°, subs., $1.50; hf. mor., $2. W. W. Wilson.
Meyers, R. C. V. Theodore Roosevelt, patriot and statesman. '02(Mr15) il. 12°, $1.50; hf. rus., $2. Ziegler.
Michael Carmichael. Sandys, M. $1.25. Laird.
Michael Ferrier. Poynter, E. F. $1.50. Macmillan.
Michael Ross, minister. Holdsworth, A. E. $1.50. Dodd.
Michaud, Henri. L'idole. '02(My24) D. (Michaud's ser. of Fr. plays for schools, no. 9.) pap., 10 c. W: R. Jenkins.
Michel Gulpe. Terhune, E. B. †$1.25. G: W. Dillingham.
Michelsen, Alb. A. Velocity of light. '02 (Ap19) O. pap., net, 25 c. Univ. of Chic.
Michie, T: J., *ed.* Banking cases annot. v. 3. '01. '02(Ja18) O. shp., $5. Michie.
Michie, T: J., *ed.* Municipal corporation cases annot. v. 6. '02(Mr1); v. 7 (Ag9) O. shp., ea., $5. Michie.
Michigan. Law of personal injuries, by W. Baldwin. '02(My24) O. shp., net, $4. Callaghan.
Michigan. *Supreme ct.* Index digest, July, 1898-Jan., 1902. (C. P. Campbell.) '02 (Mr22) O. shp., $3.50. Index Digest.
Michigan. *Supreme ct.* Repts. (J: A. Brooks.) v. 125. '01. '02(Ja18); v. 126 (My24) O. shp., ea., $3.50. Callaghan.

MICHIGAN.
Hollister, *and others.* Taxation in Mich. 50 c. Mich. Pol. Sci.
Keith. Historical sketch of internal improvements in Mich., 1836-1846. 50 c. Mich. Pol. Sci.

MICROSCOPE.
Gage. The microscope. $1.50. Comstock Pub.

MIDDLE AGES.
Cust. Ivory workers of the Middle Ages. $2. Macmillan.
Myers. Mediæval and modern history. pt. 1, Middle Ages. $1.20. Ginn.
See also Feudalism;—Monasticism;—Renaissance.

MIDWIFERY.
Jewett. Essentials of obstetrics. net, $2.25. Lea.
Jewett. Practice of obstetrics. net, $5; $6; $6.50. Lea.
Peterson *and* Lewis, *eds.* Obstetrics. $1.25. Year Bk.

Mighty means of usefulness. McClure, J. G. K. net, 50 c. Revell.

Milburn, B. A. Curious cases: a coll. of Am. and Eng. decisions. '02(Ag9) O. shp., $3. Michie.

Miles, Eustace H. Failures of vegetarianism. '02(Ap5) 12°, net, $1.50. Dutton.

Miles, Eustace H. How to prepare essays, lectures, [etc.] '02(F15) 12°, net, $2. Dutton.

MILITARY ART AND SCIENCE.
United States Army. Company commanders' manual of army regulations. $1. Hudson-K.
See also Ancient and Hon. Artillery Co. of Mass.;—Gunnery;—Hospitals;—Infantry;—Tactics;—West Point.

Military topography and sketching. Root, E. A. $2.50. Hudson-K.

Millard, Bailey. Songs of the press, and other adventures in verse. '02(Ag16) D. bds., *75 c. net. Elder.

Miller, Alf. S. Manual of assaying. 2d ed. '02(Je21) il. 16°, $1. Wiley.

Miller, And. J., *comp.* The toastmaster. '02 (Je7) sq. D. pap., n. p. W. M. Rogers.

Miller, E. D. Modern polo; ed. by M. H. Hayes. 2d ed., rev. and enl. '02(Ag23) 8°, *$5 net. Scribner.

Miller, Ja. M., *and* Durham, J: S. Martinique horror and St. Vincent calamity. '02 (Ag2) il. 12°, $1.50; texoderm, $2. Nat. Pub. Co.

Miller, Ja. R. Story of Joseph. '02(F8) 16°, net, 35 c. Revell.

Miller, *Mrs.* Ma. R. The brook book. '02 (My10) O. net, $1.35. Doubleday, P.

Miller, W: Mediæval Rome from Hilderbrand to Clement VIII., 1073-1600. '02(Jl19) D. (Story of the nations ser., no. 63.) **$1.35 net; hf. leath., $1.60 net. Putnam.

Miller, W: J. American church dict. and cyclopedia. '01· '02(Ja4) D. $1. Whittaker.

Millet's Oriental ser. 8°. Millet.
—Brinkley. Japan. 4 v. ea., $50.

Millionaire's love story. Boothby, G. $1.25. Buckles.

Millionaire mystery. Hume, F. W. $1.25. Buckles.

Mills, C: H. *See* New York. Criminal repts.

Mills, Harry E: Select sunflowers: [poems.] '01· '02(F8) 12°, $1. Sunflower Press.

Mills, Jane D., [*Mrs.* Ja. E. Mills.] Leaves from a life-book of to-day. '01· '02(Ja11) S. 50 c. Swedenborg.

Milne, W: J. Key to Academic algebra. '02 (Mr29) O. $1.50. Am. Bk.

Milne, W: J. Key to the Standard arithmetic and the Mental arithmetic. '01. '02 (Ja11) S. 75 c. Am. Bk.

Milroy lectures. *See* Poore, G: V.

Milton, J: Complete poems. '01. '02(Ja11) 16°, (Caxton ser.) flex. lambskin, net, $1.20. Scribner.

Milton, J: Selections. '01. '02(Ap5) S. (Little masterpieces.) 50 c. Doubleday, P.

MIND.
Brooks. Elements of mind. $4. Longmans.
Hobhouse. Mind in evolution. net, $3.25. Macmillan.
Oppenheim. Mental growth and control. net, $1. Macmillan.
See also Intellect:—Mind and body;—Psychology.

MIND AND BODY.
Brown. Studies in spiritual harmony. $1. Reed Pub.
Janet. Mental state of hystericals. $3.50. Putnam.
Wright. Body and soul. $1. J. C. Wright.
See also Hypnotism;—Insanity;—Mental science;—Nervous system;—Psychology.

MIND READING.
See Telepathy.

Mind telegraph. Stay, J. B. 25 c. Alliance.

Miner, W: H. Daniel Boone: cont. toward a bibliog. '01. '02(F15) D. bds., $1. Dibdin Club.

MINERALOGY.
Eakle. Colemanite from So. California. 15 c. Univ. of Cal.
See also Assaying;—Blowpipe;—Geology;—Metals and metallurgy;—Mines and mining.

MINES AND MINING.
Jack. Outline of mining law for miners. $1; 50 c. Derge.
Oregon. Mining laws. 40 c. Or. Mining Journ.
Pratt. Supp. to Mining laws of Colorado. 35 c. Pratt Merc.
See also Cooper;—Engineering;—Gold;—Iron;—Metals and metallurgy.

Minister's wooing. Stowe, *Mrs.* H. B. $1. Burt.

MINISTERS (*of the Gospel*).
Anderson. Christian ministry. 20 c. Young Churchman.
Kern. Way of the preacher. $1.25. Pub. Ho. M. E. Ch., So.
Mandeville. Minister's manual and pocket ritual. net, 60 c. Jennings.
Robinson. Personal life of the clergy. net, 90 c. Longmans.
See also Missions and missionaries;—Ordination;—Preaching;—Priests.

Ministry of conversion. Mason, A. J. net, 90 c. Longmans.

MINNEAPOLIS.
Hudson. Dict. of Minneapolis. 25 c. H. B. Hudson.

Minneapolis Journal almanac and year book, 1902. '02(Ap26) 12°, pap., 25 c. Journal Pr. Co.

Minnesota. Civil procedure in the district and sup. cts. (B: J. Shipman.) In 2 v. v. 1. '02(Jl5) O. shp., (complete work,) $13. Keefe-D.

Minnesota. Justice's manual; by W. S. Booth. 12th ed. '01· '02(Ja18) D. pap., $1.50. Booth.

Minnesota. *Supreme ct.* Repts. v. 83. '02 (Ap5); v. 84 (Jl19) O. shp., ea., $2.75. Dufresne.

MINNESOTA.
See Minneapolis.

Minority (The). Hill, F: T. $1.50. Stokes.

Minton, H: C. The cosmos and the logos. '02(Mr22) O. net, $1.25. Westminster.

MIRACLES.
Merrill *and* Warren. Discourses on miracles. 25 c. Jennings.
See also Psychical research.

Misanthrope (Le). Moliere, J. B. P. de. 50 c. Scott, F. & Co.

Misdemeanors of Nancy. Hoyt, E. $1.50. Doubleday, P.

Miser Hoadley's secret. Marchmont, A. W. $1.25; 50 c. New Amsterdam.

Misérables (Les). *See* Quayle, W: A.

Miss Ashton's new pupil. Robbins, *Mrs.* S. S. $1. Burt.

Miss Petticoats. Tilton, D. $1.50. C. M. Clark.

Miss Prudence. Conklin, *Mrs.* J. M. D. $1. Burt.

MISSIONS AND MISSIONARIES.
Beach. Geography and atlas of Protestant missions. v. 1. $2.50; per set, $1.75. Student Vol.
Brain. Fifty missionary programmes. 35 c. Un. Soc. C. E.
Carey. Adventures in Tibet. net, $1.50. Un. Soc. C. E.
Dean. Cross of Christ in Bololand. net, $1. Revell.
Dennis. Centennial survey of foreign missions. net, $4. Revell.
Jesuit relations: travels and explorations of the Jesuit missionaries in New France, 1610-1791. 73 v. ea.. net, $3.50. Burrows.
Ketler. Tragedy of Paotingfu, China. net, $2. Revell.
Longridge. Official and lay witness to the value of foreign missions. 20 c. E. & J. B. Young.
Montgomery. Foreign missions. net, 90 c. Longmans.
Smith, B. Uncle Boston's spicy breezes. net, $1. Am. Bapt.
Smith, J. Ten years in Burma. net, $1. Jennings.
Warneck. Outline of hist. of Protestant missions. net, $2. Revell.
See also Philippine Islands;—Protestantism;—*also* names of churches.

Mississippi. *Supreme ct.* Repts. v. 78. '01. '02(My10) O. shp., $4. Marshall.

Mississippi bubble. Hough, E. $1.50. Bowen-M.

Missouri. *St. Louis and the Kansas City cts. of appeals.* Cases. v. 89. '01. '02(Mr1) O. shp., $5. Stephens.

Missouri statute annots.; by S: J. McCulloch. 2d ed. '02(My24) O. hf. shp., $3. S: J. McCulloch.

Missouri. *Supreme ct.* Repts. (Rader.) v. 162, 163. '01. '02(Mr1); v. 164 (My10) O. shp., ea., $4. Stephens.

Mr. Whitman. Pullen, *Mrs.* E. $1.50. Lothrop.

Mistress Dorothy of Haddon Hall. Hastings, H: $1. Fenno.

Mrs. Tree. Richards, *Mrs.* L. E. H. †75 c. Estes.

Misunderstood. Montgomery, F. $1. Beam.

Mitchell, C. A. *See* Oppenheimer, C.

Mitchell, Fes. L. Georgia land and people. '02(Ap26) 12°, $1.25. F. L. Mitchell.

Mitton, G. E. The opportunist. '02(Mr8) 12°, $2. Macmillan.

Moberly, R. C. Christ our life. '02(Mr22) O. net, $3. Longmans.

Mobile Boer. Hiley, A. R. I. $1.50. Grafton Press.

Modern Am. tanning; comp. fr. orig. articles printed in *Hide and Leather.* '02(Ag23) 8°, $5. Jacobsen.

Modern association and railroading. Goodknight, A. L. 50 c. Abbey Press.

Modern Eng. writers. 12°, **$1 net. Dodd.
—Clodd. Thomas H: Huxley.

Modern lang ser. *See* Heath's.

Molander, Anna. Scientific sloyd: for teachers and schools. '02(My3) S. 50 c. Bardeen.

Molesworth, *Mrs.* **Ma. L.** Grandmother dear. '02(Je28) il. 12°, (St. Nicholas ser.) 75 c. Burt.

Molesworth, *Mrs.* **Ma. L.** Robin Redbreast. '02(My3) il. 12°, (Fireside ser.) $1. Burt.

Molière, J. B. P. de. Le misanthrope and L'avare; ed. by W: F. Giése. '01. '02 (F15) S. (Lake French classics.) 50 c. Scott, F. & Co.

Molinerillo (El). Trueba, A. de. 35 c. W: R. Jenkins.

Mollie's mistake. Book, J. W. 15 c. Herder.

Momerie, A. W. Immortality, and other sermons. '02(Ap12) 12°, $1.50. Whittaker.

Mon oncle et mon curé. La Brète, J. de. 50 c. Am. Bk.

Monadology. *See* Leibnitz, *Baron* G. W. v.

Monaghan, Ja. *See* Pennsylvania. Digest.

MONASTICISM.
Feasey. Monasticism. net, $1. Herder.

Moncrief, J: W. Short hist. of the Christian church. '02(Ag2) 12°, **$1.50 net. Revell.

Monell, S. H. System of instruction in X-ray methods. '02(My10) il. 8°, subs., hf. mor., $15. Pelton.

MONEY.
Bonsall. Money. 50 c.; 25 c. M. S. Schwartz.
Del Mar. Hist. of money in England. $2.—Netherlands. 50 c.—Germany and other European states. *$2 net. Cambridge.
Green. Shakespeare and Goethe on Gresham's law and the single gold standard. 25 c. MacGowan.
See also Credit;—Finance.

Money-maker. Adams, W: T. $1.25. Lee & S.

Monica. Bourget, P. $1.50. Scribner.

Monk and knight. Gunsaulus, F. W. †$1.50. McClurg.

Monkhouse, Cosmo. History and desc. of Chinese porcelain. '02(Mr15) il. 8°, net, $10. Wessels.

Monroe, Forest, [*pseud.* for Ferdinand G. Wiechmann.] Maid of Montauk. '02 (Ap26) il. D. net, $1. W: R. Jenkins.

Monroe, Ja. Writings. v. 5, 1807-16. '02 8°, hf. leath., subs., $5. Putnam.

Monroe, Lewis B., *ed.* Public and parlor readings. '01. '02(Mr1) 4 v., 12°, ea., $1. Lee & S.

Monroe Rebekah Lodge: semi-centennial of Monroe Rebekah Lodge, no. 1, I. O. O. F., Jan. 23, 1902. '02(Mr8) 8°, pap., 10 c. Darrow.

Monsell, J. R. The pink knight. '01· '02 (Ja18) il. 32°, bds., net, 40 c. Stokes.

Monsieur Bergeret. France, A. $1. Silver.

Monsieur Martin. Carey, W. net, $1.20. Putnam.

Montgomery, Fes. T. Billy Whiskers. '02 (Ag16) il. 4°, bds., $1. Saalfield.

Montgomery, Flo. Misunderstood. [New issue.] '02(Ja4) D. $1. Beam.

Montgomery, H: H. Foreign missions. '02 (Ap26) D. (Handbooks for the clergy.) net, 90 c. Longmans.

MONTREAL.

Bosworth, *ed.* Hochelaga depicta; early hist. of city and island. net, $3; net, $4.50. Congdon.

MONUMENTS.

See Tombstones.

Moody, J:, *ed.* Corporation securities. '02 (Je28) O. $7.50; flex. leath., $10. Moody.

Moody, W: V., *and* Lovett, R. M. Hist. of Eng. literature. '02(My10) O. net, $1.25. Scribner.

Moore, Addison W. Functional versus the representational theories of knowledge in Locke's essay. '02(Ag2) 8°, (Contributions to philosophy, v. 3, no. 1.) pap., *35 c. net. Univ. of Chic.

Moore, Fk. F. A damsel or two. '02(Ap26) D. $1.50. Appleton.

Moore, *Sir* J: W:, *ed.* Variola, vaccination, cholera, erysipelas, etc. '02(Mr22) il. 8°, (Nothnagel's encyclopedia of practical medicine, v. 2.) net, $5; hf. mor., net, $6. Saunders.

Moore, T: E. My Lord Farquhar. '02(My3) D. $1.25. Abbey Press.

Moore's (The). *See* Brontë, C.

MOORS.

Meakin. The Moors. net, $5. Macmillan.

Moral drill. Harper, J: M. $1. Kellogg.

Morang's annual register of Canadian affairs, 1901; ed. and comp. by J. C. Hopkins. '02 (Jl19) O. $3; hf. mor., $4. Morang.

MORAVIAN CHURCH.

Clewell. Hist. of Wachovia, N. C.; Unitas fratum or Moravian church, 1752-1902. **$2 net. Doubleday, P.

Morceau de pain. Coppée, F. 25 c. W: R. Jenkins.

Morchester. Datchet, C: net, $1.20. Putnam.

More, Egbert. Trisection of a given angle geometrically solved and illustrated. '01· '02(F1) il. O. pap., $1. Wickes.

More, *Sir* T: Utopia, and life of More, by W: Roper. '02(My10) 12°, (Home lib.) $1. Burt.

More animal stories. Cochrane, R. net, $1. Lippincott.

More ex-tank tales. Cullen, C. L: $1. Ogilvie.

More tales of the birds. Fowler, W: W. $1. Macmillan.

Morehead, G: Francesca Da Rimini. '02 (Mr22) il. D. (Sunnyside ser., no. 117.) pap., 25 c. Ogilvie.

Morehead, G: Madame Du Barry. '02(My17) 12°, pap., 50 c. Donohue.

Morehead, G: Nell Gwyn. '01. '02(F15) il. 12°, pap., 25 c. Ogilvie.

Morehead, G: Story of François Villon. '01· '02(F15) 12°, (Peerless ser., no. 124.) pap., 25 c. Ogilvie.

Morfill, W. R. Hist. of Russia from Peter the Great to Nicholas II. '02(Mr15) 12°, $1.75. Pott.

Morgan, Alex. Advanced physiography. '01· '02(F8) il. D. $1.50. Longmans.

Morgan, C: Herbert. *See* Taylor, T: E.

Morgan, D: B: Twentieth century horse book; also a short treatise on cattle, swine, dogs and chickens. '02(Jl12) il. 8°, pap., $1.50. D: B: Morgan.

Morgan, Emily M. Flight of the *Swallow*. '02(Mr15) il. 12°, 50 c. Pott.

Morgan, J: L. R. Elements of physical chemistry. 2d ed., rev. and enl. '02(Mr8) 12°, $2. Wiley.

Morley, J:, *ed.* *See* English men of letters.

Morgan, Lewis H: League of the Ho-de-no-sau-nee or Iroquois. New ed.; ed. and annot. by H. M. Lloyd. '02(Jl19) 2 v., il. 8°, hand-made pap., **$15 net; Japan pap., $30 net. Dodd.

MORMONISM.

Lamb. The Mormons and their Bible. net, 25 c. Am. Bapt.

Linn. Story of the Mormons. net, $4. Macmillan.

Mornings in Florence. Ruskin, J: $2. Abbey Press.

MOROCCO.

Grove. Seventy-one days' camping in Morocco. net, $2.50. Longmans.

Macnab. Ride in Morocco. $5. Longmans.

Morozzo, Carlo G. Treatise of spiritual life; fr. the Latin by D. A. Donovan. 2d rev. ed. '02(Ag9) *$1 net. Pustet.

MORPHINISM.

Crothers. Morphinism and narcomania from opium, etc. $2. Saunders.

MORPHOLOGY.

See Anatomy;—Embryology;—Histology.

Morrill, W: W. *See* Am. electrical cases.

Morris, C: Marvelous achievements of the 19th century. 16th ed. '02(Ap5) il. sq. 8°, $2.50; hf. mor., $3.50. Winston.

Morris, C: Twentieth century encyclopædia. '01· '02(Ap5) il. 12°, $3.50; hf. mor., $4.25; mor., $5.50. Winston.

Morris, Clara, [*Mrs.* Harriott.] A pasteboard crown. '02(Je7) il. D. $1.50. Scribner.

Morris, E: P. On principles and methods in Latin syntax. '01· '02(F15) 8°, (Yale bicentennial pubs.) net, $2. Scribner.

Morris, Ella G. Right living; or, how a woman can get well and keep well. '02 (My17) 8°, $1. Bardeen.

Morris, Ida D., [*Mrs.* Ja. E. Morris.] Golden Fluff. '01. '02(Ja18) il. 12°, 50 c. Abbey Press.

Morris, Mowbray. Tales of the Spanish Main. '01· '02(Ja18) il. D. $2. Macmillan.

Morris, W: Art and craft of printing. '02 (Mr15) 8°, bds., $5. Elston Press.

Morrow, Rob. G., *rep.* *See* Oregon. *Sup. ct.* Repts.

Morse's geographical ser. il. 16°. Morse.
—Carroll. Around the world. 60 c.

Morse's new century ser. 12°. Morse.
—Thompson. New century readers. 3d bk: 52 c.

Mortimer, Alfr. G. Catholic faith and practice. 2 pts. 2d ed., rev. '01. '02(Mr8) O. pt. 1, $2; pt. 2, $2.50. Longmans.
Morton, H: H. Genito-urinary disease and syphilis. '02(Mr29) il. 12°, net, $3. Davis.
Morton, Victor. Thoughts on hell. '02(Mr8) 8°, net, 50 c. Herder.
Mosaics from India. Denning, M. net, $1.50. Revell.
Moser, Gustav v. Der bibliothekar; ed. by W: A. Cooper. '02(Mr8) D. 45 c. Am. Bk.
Moses, Montrose J. *See* Funk, I: K.
Mosher's vest-pocket ser. nar. S. T: B. Mosher.
—Stevenson. Æs triplex, and other essays. 25 c.-$1.
MOSQUITOES.
Berkeley. Lab'y work with mosquitoes. net, $1. Pediatrics Lab'y.
Ross. Mosquito brigades and how to organize them. net, 90 c. Longmans.
Mostellaria. Plautus, T. M. *$1 net. Allyn & B.
Mother Goose paint book. Barnett, J. M. $1.25. Saalfield.
Mother Margaret's bunch of flowers. Quinius, A. 5 c. J: G. Quinius.
MOTHER-PLAY.
Proudfoot. A year with the Mother-play. $1. Flanagan.
MOTHERS.
Davis. Mother and child. **$1.50 net. Lippincott.
See also Children.
MOTORMAN.
Livermore *and* Williams. How to become a competent motorman. $1. W: S. Livermore.
MOTORS.
See Cars;—Dynamos and motors.
Moule, H. C. G. Thoughts for the Sundays of the year. '02(Mr8) 12°, net, $1. Revell.
Moulthrop, S: P. Iroquois. '01. '02(Ag23) il. sq. O. 75 c.; pap., 50 c. Hart.
Moulton, C: W., *and others, eds.* Library of literary criticism of Eng. and Am. authors. v. 3. '02(Mr); v. 4 (Ag2) O. ea., $5; hf. mor., $6.50. Moulton Pub.
Moulton, *Mrs.* Louise C. Her baby brother. New ed. '01. '02(F15) 16°, (Children's friend ser.) bds., 50 c. Little, B. & Co.
MOUNDS.
Peterson. The mound building age in N. A. 25 c. Clarke.
Mount of Olives. Saltus, F. S. $1; net, 25 c. Bk. Lover.
Mountaineers. Smith, J: W. $1; $1.50; $2; $2.50. Pub. Ho. of M. E. Ch., So.
Movable quartette. Guyse, E. $1. Abbey Press.
Mower, C: D. How to build a knockabout. '02(Ap26) il. f°, ("How-to" ser.) $1. Rudder.
Mower, C: D. How to build a racing sloop. '02(F15) Q. ("How-to" ser.) $1. Rudder.
Mowry, Arth. M. First steps in the history of England. '02(Je21) il. D. 70 c. Silver.
Moy, Eocha. One: a song of the ages. '02 (Ap26) 12°, $1.50. Neely.
Mudge, G. P. Text-book of zoology. '01. '02(Mr8) D. $2.50. Longmans.
Mudge, Ja. Life of love. '02(F15) sq. T. (Little books on devotion.) 25 c. Jennings.
Muench, Friedrich. Gesammelte lechriften. '02(Je28) 8°, $1.75; mor., $2.50. Witter.
Muirhead, J. H. Philosophy and life, and other essays. '02(My24) 12°, $1.50. Macmillan.
Muirhead, Ja. F. America, the land of contrasts. New ed. '02(F22) 12°, net, $1.20. Lane.
Mulholland, Clara. Bunt and Bill. '02(Mr8) il. S. 45 c. Benziger.
Mullen, W: How to break, educate and handle the horse for the uses of every-day life. '02(F1) il. D. $1. W: Mullen.
Muller, Ma. Wretched Flea; story of a Chinese boy. '01. '02(Ja11) il. S. 35 c. Flanagan.
Mundy, W: N. Eclectic practice in diseases of children. '02(Je21) D. (Eclectic manual, no. 5.) net, $2.50. Scudder.
MUNICIPAL CORPORATIONS.
Michie, *ed.* Municipal corporation cases. v. 6, 7. ea., $5. Michie.
Municipal engineering and sanitation. Baker, M. N. net, $1.25. Macmillan.
MUNICIPAL GOVERNMENT.
Clow. Comparative study of the administration of city finances in the U. S. $1. Macmillan.
Municipal year book, 1902; ed. by M. N. Baker. '02(Ag30) 8°, $3. Engineering News.
Munn, C: C. Rockhaven. '02(Mr29) il. D. $1.50. Lee & S.
Munro, J: Nociones de electricidad. '01. '02 (F22) 18°, 40 c. Appleton.
Munson, A. J. Making a country newspaper. '02(Mr22) 16°, $1. Dominion.
Munson, A. J. *See also* Halstead, M.
Murché, V. T. Rural readers; for senior classes. '02(Ap12) il. 12°, net, 40 c. Macmillan.
Murché, V. T. Teacher's manual of object lessons for rural schools. '02(Ap12) il. 12°, net, 60 c. Macmillan.
Murché, V. T. Teacher's manual of object lessons in geography. '02(Je28) il. 12°, net, 80 c. Macmillan.
Murders in the Rue Morgue. Poe, E. A. $1. Burt.
Murfree, Ma. N., ["Charles Egbert Craddock."] The champion. '02(Ag2) il. 12°, **$1.20 net. Houghton, M. & Co.
Murison, Ross G. Babylonia and Assyria. '01. '02(Ja11) 16°, (Bible class primers.) net. 20 c. Scribner.
Murlin, Edg. L. Illustrated legislative manual; New York red book. '02(My17) 12°, $1. Lyon.
Murphy, J: B., *ed.* General surgery. '01. '02(Mr8) il. D. (Practical medicine ser. of year-books, v. 2.) $1.50. Year Bk.
Murray, C: T. Mlle. Fouchette. '02(Mr15) il. D. $1.50. Lippincott.
Murray, Charlotte. Castleton's "prep." '02 (Ag30) il. D. $1.25. Union Press.
MURRAY, Ja.
Tiffany *and* Lesley, *eds.* Letters of James Murray, loyalist. net, $2.50. W: B. Clarke.
Murray, Ja. A: H:, *and others, eds.* New Eng. dictionary. v. 3. pts. 30-33. '01. '02 (Mr22); pt. 34 (Ap19); pt. 35 (Je7); pt. 36 (Je21); pts. 37, 38 (Ag23) f°. pap., ea., 90 c. Oxford Univ.

Murray, W: Rough notes on remedies. 4th ed. '02(F15) 12°, net, $1.25. Blakiston.
Murrell, W: *See* Ewart, W:
Murrin, F. D. Vocal exercises on the vocal factors of expression. '02(My3) S. bds., net, 50 c. A. M. Allen.
MUSIC.
Banister. Musical analysis. 75 c. Scribner.
Crowest. Story of the art of music. **35 c. net. Appleton.
Lavignac. Music and musicians. **$1.75 net. Holt.
McLaughlin. Elements and notation of music. 55 c. Ginn.
Maitland. Music in England in the 19th century. net, $1.75. Dutton.
Paderewski, *ed.* Century lib. of music. v. 17-20. subs., ea., $2; $4. Century Co.
Wead. Cont. to the history of musical scales. 50 c. Woodward & L.
See also Church music;—Musicians.
MUSICAL INSTRUMENTS.
See Trumpet.
MUSICIANS.
Thomas, *ed.* Famous composers and their music. 16 v. (App. to pubs. for price.) Millet.
Young. Mastersingers. net, $1.50. Scribner.
Musick, W: L. Combination shorthand dictionary and reader. '02(Jl12) 12°, $1.50. W: L. Musick.
Musings by campfire and wayside. Gray, W: C. net, $1.50. Revell.
MUTINY.
See Indian mutiny.
Mussey, D: S. Spiritual heroes. '02(My10) D. net, $1.25. Doubleday, P.
My captive. Altsheler, J. A. $1.25. Appleton.
My island. Hughes, E. $1.25. Dutton.
My Japanese wife. Holland, C. $1.50. Stokes.
My Lord Farquhar. Moore, T: E. $1.25. Abbey Press.
My ocean trip. Cadigan, E. S. $1. Brentano's.
My ten rod farm. Barnard, C: 40 c. Coates.
My trip to the Orient. Simmons, J. C. $1.50. Whitaker & R.
Myer, Edm. J. Renaissance of the vocal art. '02(Ag23) D. $1. Boston Music.
Myers, Alb. C. Quaker arrivals at Philadelphia, 1682-1750. '02(Jl19) 16°, $1.25. Ferris.
Myers, P. V. Mediæval and modern history. pt. 1, Middle Ages. [New rev. ed.] '02 (Jl5) D. $1.20. Ginn.
Myra of the Pines. Vielé, H. K. $1.50. McClure, P.
Myrtle, Fk., *pseud.* *See* Haviland, C. A:
Mystery of St. Rubes. Heddle, E. F. $1.50. Scribner.
Mystery of the sea. Stoker, B. $1.50. Doubleday, P.
Mystic fortune teller, dream book, and policy player's guide. '02(My17) 12°, 50 c.: pap., 25 c. Donohue.
Mystic rose. Crawley, E. net, $4. Macmillan.
MYTHOLOGY.
Hale, *ed.* Greek myths in Eng. dress. 40 c. Globe Sch. Bk.
See also Fairy tales.
Naked truths and veiled allusions. Antrim, M. T. 50 c. Altemus.
Nameless hero. Anderson, J. B. net, $1. Wessels.
Nancy's Easter gift. Baldwin, M. 50 c. Abbey Press.
NANTUCKET ISLAND.
Bliss. September days on Nantucket. net, $1. Houghton, M. & Co.
Hinchman. Early settlers of Nantucket. $5. Ferris.
NAPOLEON I.
Fremeaux. With Napoleon at St. Helena. net, $1.50. Lane.
Headley. Napoleon and his marshals. $1. Burt.
Josselyn. The true Napoleon. net, $3.50. Russell.
Kennan, *comp. and tr.* Folk tales of Napoleon. *$1 net. Outlook.
Rose. Life of Napoleon I. 2 v. net, $4. Macmillan.
Sloane. Napoleon Bonaparte. 4 v. net, $18; net, $32. Century Co.
Watson. Napoleon. $2.25. Macmillan.
See also Waterloo.
Napoleon. Dumas, A. net, 50 c. Macmillan.
Napoleon's letters to Josephine, 1796-1812; notes by H: F. Hall. '02(Mr1) 8°, net, $3. Dutton.
Nash, Eliz. T. Fifty Puritan ancestors, 1628-1660. '02(Ap26) 8°, $5. Tuttle, M. & T.
Nash, J: J., *ed.* Practical explanation and application of Bible history; [for catechism teachers.] '02(Ap19) D. net, $1.50. Benziger.
Nason, Fk. L. To the end of the trail. '02 (My17) D. $1.50. Houghton, M. & Co.
NATAL.
Burne. With the Naval Brigade in Natal, 1899-1900. $2.50. Longmans.
Nathan der Weise. Lessing, G. E. 80 c. Am. Bk.
Nation and the state ser. 16°. Bardeen.
—Roberts. Civil government of Ohio. $1. (2.)
National cyclopædia of Am. biography. v. 11. '01-'02(Je28) il. 8°, subs., $10. White.
NATIONAL HERBART SOC.
McMurry, *ed.* Pubs. of National Herbart Soc. *$5 net. Univ. of Chic.
National (The) list. Directory of bonded attorneys. '02(My24) F.; *Same.* Abr. ed. S. (App. to pubs. for price.) Nat. Surety.
National portrait gallery. *See* Cust, L., *ed.*
National reporter system. O. shp. West Pub.
—Atlantic reporter. v. 50, 51. ea., $4.
—Louisiana repts. v. 106. $8.
—New York supplement, v. 72-74. ea., $4.
—Northeastern reporter. v. 61, 62. ea., $4.
—Northwestern reporter. v. 88. $4.
—Pacific reporter. v. 66-68. ea., $4.
—Pacific reporter. Digest. net, $6.
—Southeastern reporter. v. 39, 40. ea., $4.
—Southern reporter. v. 30, 31. ea., $4.
—Southern reporter. Digest. net, $6.
—Southwestern reporter. v. 64-67. ea., $4.
—United States. Federal reporter. v. 110-114. ea., $3.50.
National standard family and business atlas of the world. '02(Ag30) il. 12 x 15 in. subs., $4.75. Fort Dearborn.
National Temperance almanac and teetotalers year-book, for 1902; also The Gothenburg system. '02(F1) S. pap., 10 c. Nat. Temp.

NATURAL HISTORY.
Cuppy, *ed.* Pictorial natural history. $1. Crowell & K.
Harmer *and* Shipley, *eds.* Cambridge natural history. v. 10. net, $4. Macmillan.
Pierson. Among the night people. net, $1. Dutton.
Roberts. Kindred of the wild. $2. L. C. Page.
See also Aquarium;—Botany;—Chemistry;—Evolution;—Geology; — Microscope; — Nature; — Paleontology;—Physical geography;—Science.

Natural man. Lloyd, J. W. *$1 net. Prieth.

NATURAL RELIGION.
Conger. Religion for the time: six conferences on natural religion. net, $1. Jacobs.
James. Varieties of rel. experience; Gifford lectures on natural religion. net, $3.20. Longmans.

NATURALIZATION.
Pritchard, *comp.* How to become a naturalized citizen. 10 c. Wehman.
See also Citizenship.

Naturalness of Christian life. Keedy, E: E. net, $1.25. Putnam.

NATURE.
Bailey. Nature portraits. (App. to pubs. for price.) Doubleday, P.
Batt. Treatment of nature in Germ. literature. net, $1. Univ. of Chic.
Carter. Gleanings from nature. $1. Abbey Press.
Emerson. Nature. $1. Burt.
Gray. Musings by camp-fire and wayside. net, $1.50. Revell.
Hodge. Nature study and life. $1.65. Ginn.
Kenyon. Remembered days. $1. Eaton & M.
Miller. Brook book. net, $1.35. Doubleday, P.
Smith, C. W: Summer of Saturdays. 65 c. Gillan.
Talmage. Vacation with nature. net, $1. Funk.
Williams. Next to the ground. net, $1.20. McClure, P.

Nature and human nature. Emerson, *Mrs.* E. R. net, $1.25. Houghton, M. & Co.
Nature and life. Sterling, A. W. 56 c.; in 2 pts., ea., 32 c. Globe Sch. Bk.
Nature, myth and story. *See* Thompson, J: G.
Naughty Nan. Long, J: L. $1.50. Century Co.
Nauheim baths. *See* Thorne, W. B.
Nauticus, *pseud.* The truth about the Schley case. '02(F22) D. pap., 25 c. Columbia.

NAVAL ART AND SCIENCE.
Brassey, *ed.* Naval annual, 1902. net, $7.50. Scribner.
Clowes, *and others.* Royal navy. v. 5, 6. ea., net, $6.50. Little, B. & Co.
Hamersly, *comp.* Records of living officers of the U. S. navy and marine corps. $10. Hamersly.
Maclay. Hist. of U. S. Navy. 3 v. ea., net, $3. Appleton.
Mets. Naval heroes of Holland. $1.50. Abbey Press.
United States naval examination papers, 1899-1902. *$1 net. Cushing.

NAVIGATION.
See Astronomy; — Canoeing; — Ship-building; — Voyages and travels.

Neal, W. G. *See* Hall, R. N.
Neale, J. M. Deeds of faith: stories for children. '02(Je7) 12°, 40 c. E. & J. B. Young.
Nearer East. Hogarth, D: G: $2. Appleton.
Nebraska. Law of probate and administration. (A. K. Dame.) '02(Jl5) O. shp., $7.50. Keefe-D.
Nebraska. Page's digest. vs. 1 to 60 of Neb. repts. In 2 v. v. 1. '02(My10); v. 2 (Je21) O. shp., (complete work,) $20. Bancroft-W.
Nebraska. *Supreme ct.* Repts. v. 61. (L. Herdman.) '02(My24) O. shp., $3. State Journ. Co.

NECK.
Eckley. Regional anatomy of head and neck. net, $2.50. Lea.

NECROSCOPY.
See Autopsy.

Needell, *Mrs.* Ma. A., [*Mrs.* J: H. Needell.] Unstable as water. '02(Jl5) D. $1.25. Warne.
Needham, A. C. *See* Hartmann, A.
Neel, Edith K. Cats, how to care for them. '02(My10) 12°, 50 c. Boericke & T.
Neesen, Victor. Rusted spokes. '02(Ag16) 16°, pap., 50 c. New Amsterdam.
Neff, Ma. L. Prescription writing in Latin or Eng. '01. '02(Mr1) 12°, 75 c. Davis.
Negatives of the Indo-European languages. Fowler, F. H. net, 50 c. Univ. of Chic.

NEGLIGENCE.
Dresser. Employers' liability, acts and assumption of risks in N. Y., Mass., Ind., Ala., Col., and England. $6. Keefe-D.
Gardner, *ed.* Am. negligence repts. v. 10. $5.50. Remick.
Hook. Am. neg. digest. $6.50. Remick.
Thompson. Commentaries on the law of negligence. v. 3. $6. Bowen-M.

NEGOTIABLE INSTRUMENTS.
Ames *and* Brewster. Negotiable instruments law. 30 c. Harvard Law.
Crawford. Negotiable instruments law. $2.50. Baker, V. & Co.
District of Columbia. Laws rel. to negotiable instruments. 20 c. Lowdermilk.
Pennsylvania. Negotiable instruments law. $2.50. Baker, V. & Co.
Selover. Law of negotiable instruments for N. Y., Mass., R. I., [etc.] $4. Keefe-D.
See also Commercial law;—Interest.

NEGROES.
Calhoun. The Caucasian and the negro in the U. S. 75 c. R. L. Bryan.
Schell. Is the negro a beast? 60 c. Gospel Trumpet.

Neidlinger, Dan. H., *and* Bobbett, Wa. The squirrel and the crow. '02(Jl12) 16°, hf. cl., 50 c. Rand, McN. & Co.
Neill, Maidie. Tennessee Lee. '02(Ap26) 12°, $1. Neely.
Neilson, Fs. Madame Bohemia. '02(Mr8) D. (Select novels.) $1; pap., 50 c. Lippincott.
Neilson, Rob. M. The steam turbine. '02 (Ag30) il. O. $2.50. Longmans.
Nell Gwyn. Morehead, G: 25 c. Ogilvie.
Nellis, And. J. Law of street surface railroads, as comp. from statutes and decisions in the various states and territories. '02(Ag2) O. shp., $6. M. Bender.

Nelson, Aven. Analytical key to some of the common flowering plants of the Rocky mountain region. '02(Jl12) D. (Twentieth century text-books.) **45 c. net. Appleton.
Nelson's Wall St. lib. il. S. $1.25. S: A. Nelson.
—Coffin. A B C of banks and banking. (v. 4.)
NERVOUS SYSTEM.
Ballance *and* Stewart. Healing of nerves. net, $4.50. Macmillan.
Hardesty. Neurological technique. net, $1.75. Univ. of Chic.
Nestlings of forest and marsh. Wheelock, *Mrs.* I. G. net, $1.40. McClurg.
NETHERLANDS.
Schiller. Hist. of the revolt of the Netherlands. (App. to pubs. for price.) Niccolls.
Nettleship, R: L. Lectures on the Republic of Plato; ed. by G. R. Benson. '01. '02 (Ja4) 8°, net, $2.75. Macmillan.
NEURASTHENIA.
Savill. Clinical lectures on neurasthenia. $1.50. Wood.
Neurological technique. Hardesty, I. net, $1.75. Univ. of Chic.
Neuroses of the genito-urinary system. Ultzmann, R. *$1 net. Davis.
New and living way. Terry, M. S. net, 50 c. Eaton & M.
New animal cellular therapy. Hawley, J. R. $1. Clinic.
NEW BRUNSWICK.
Chase. In quest of the quaint. $1.50. Ferris.
New century lib. 12°, 1.25; $1.75. Nelson.
—Burns. Complete poetical works.
New century readers. See Rand, McNally's.
New century ser. 12°, 24 c. Morse.
—Parlin. Quincy word list.
New child's life of Christ. Stretton, H. $1. Winston.
NEW ENGLAND.
Catholic year book of N. E. for 1902. 25 c. J. K. Waters.
Dame *and* Brooks. Trees of N. E. $1.35. Ginn.
New England History Teachers' Assoc.; rept. by C: D. Hazen, E. G. Bourne and others. '02(Jl12) 12°, (Historical sources in schools ser.) **60 c. net. Macmillan.
New Hampshire. [*Supreme ct.*] Repts. (J. H. Riddell.) v. 70. '01. '02(My24) O. shp., $3.50. J: B. Clarke.
NEW HAMPSHIRE.
Hoyt. Practice in proceedings in probate cts. of N. H. $2.50. Rumford Press.
NEW HARMONY, Ind.
Lockwood. New Harmony communities. $2.50. Chronicle.
New hearthstone. Hurst, J: F. $1. Jennings.
New Jersey. General corporation act. Annots. and forms by J. B. Dill. 4th ed., with the amendments of 1902. '02(My17) O. pap., $1.50. New Jersey.
New Jersey. Laws rel. to corporations; with notes by Ja. B. Dill. '02(Je7) 8°, $3. Baker, V. & Co.
NEW JERSEY.
Parker, *comp.* New Jersey lawyers' diary, 1902. $1.50. Soney.
See also Rockaway.
New Jersey orphans' court practice; with forms by C: F. Kocher. '02(Mr1) O. shp., $6. Soney.

New life. Berrier, L. $1. L. Berrier.
New philosophy of health. Bradbury, H. B. 75 c. Alliance.
New songs for college glee clubs. '02(Mr15) 12°, pap., 50 c. Hinds.
NEW TESTAMENT.
See Bible.
NEW THOUGHT.
See Mental science.
New world and the new thought. Bixby, J. T. net, $1. Whittaker.
New York City standard guide. '01. '02 (Ja4) il. D. (Standard guide ser.) pap., 25 c. Foster & R.
New York City. Tenement house law and the building code. '02(Mr29) 12°, (Brooklyn Eagle lib., no. 62, v. 17, no. 3.) pap., 10 c. Brooklyn Eagle.
NEW YORK CITY.
Denton. Brief desc. of New York. *$1.50 net; $3 net. Burrows.
Fielde. Political primer of New York city and state. 75 c.; 50 c. League Pol. Educ.
Hemstreet. When old New York was young. net, $1.50. Scribner.
Medical directory, 1901. $1.50. Wynkoop.
Norton. Statistical studies in N. Y. money-market. net, $1.50; net, $1. Macmillan.
Social evil, with special ref. to conditions existing in New York. net, $1.25. Putnam.
See also Hall of fame;—Libraries.
New York. [State.] Abbott's cyclopedic digest of decisions of all the courts fr. the earliest time to 1900. (Blashfield.) v. 5. '01. '02(Ja18); v. 6 (Mr1); v. 7 (Ap5); v. 8 (My10); v. 9 (Jl5); v. 10 (Ag16) O. shp., ea., $7.50. N. Y. Law.
New York. Amendments of the code of civil procedure, criminal procedure and penal code, 1902. '02(My24) O. pap., 50 c. Baker, V. & Co.
New York. Amendments of 1902. (A. J. Danaher.) '02(My24) O. pap., 50 c. Banks & Co.
New York. Amendments to Birdseye's revised statutes and general laws. '02(Jl19) pap., $2. Baker, V. & Co.
New York. Analyzed decisions and citations, 1897-1901, by Ja. G. Greene. '02(Je28) O. shp., $8.50. Williamson Law Bk.
New York civil and criminal justice. 3d ed. by F. S. Becker and E. D. Howe. '02 (My24) O. shp., $6.50. Williamson Law Bk.
New York. Code of civil procedure, as amended, 1902. '02(Je21) D. (Chase's pocket code.) flex. skiver, net, $3.50. Banks.
New York. Code of civil procedure. (R. M. Stover.) 6th ed., by A. J. Parker, jr. '02 (Ag2) 2 v., O. shp., $7.50. Banks.
New York. Code of civil procedure, cont. amendments of 1902 by A. J. Parker, jr., rev. by A. J. Danaher. 2d ed. '02(My17) D. flex. skiver, $3.50. Banks & Co.
New York. Code of civil procedure; topical index. (J: C. Thomson.) 27th ed. '02 (Jl5) S. (Complete annot. pocket code.) flex. skiver, $3.50. H: B. Parsons.
New York. Code of criminal procedure. (L. R. Parker.) '02(Je7) D. flex. skiver, $1.50. Banks.

New York. Code of criminal procedure. 21st rev. ed. '02(Jl12). D. canvas, $2. Banks & Co.

New York. Code of criminal procedure and penal code. (Cook.) '02(My17) O. shp., net, $5. H: B. Parsons.

New York. *Ct. of appeals.* Analyzed citations. v. 2; by Ja. G. Greene. '01. '02 (Je28) pr. on one side of leaf, O. $2.50. Williamson Law Bk.

New York. *Ct. of appeals.* Digest of opinions of J: C. Gray. v. 108-164. (E. A. Bedell.) '01. '02(Mr8) Q. limp roan, $5. Lyon.

New York. *Ct. of appeals.* Digest of opinions of [A.] Haight. v. 114-164. '02(Mr8) Q. limp roan, $5. Lyon.

New York. *Ct. of appeals.* Digest of opinions of [D.] O'Brien. v. 119-164. '01. '02 (Mr8) Q. limp roan, $5. Lyon.

New York. *Ct. of appeals.* Digest of opinions of [I. G.] Vann. v. 114-v. 164. '01. '02(Mr8) Q. limp roan, $5. Lyon.

New York. *Ct. of appeals.* Repts. (J: T. Cook.) bk. 33. '02(Mr15) O. shp., $5. H: B. Parsons.

New York. *Cts. of record.* Misc. repts. v. 35. '01. '02(Mr1); v. 36 (Jl12) O. shp., ea., $2. Lyon.

New York. Criminal repts. (C: H. Mills.) v. 15. '02(Jl5) O. shp., $5.50. W. C. Little.

New York. Digest of statutes and repts. '02(Mr1) O. shp., $5. Baker, V. & Co.

New York. Digest of repts. and session laws. for 1901. '02(Mr1) O. shp., $4.50. Lyon.

New York. Highway law. 2d ed., by L. L. Boyce. '02(Jl5) O. shp., $4; Bender ed., pap., $1. M. Bender.

New York. Jewett's primary election law; with forms and complete index. '02(Jl5) O. pap., 50 c. M. Bender.

New York. Laws rel. to general, religious and non-business corporations, etc. 8th ed. '02(Jl12) O. canvas, $1.50; shp., $2. Banks & Co.

New York. Membership and religious corporations. '02(Jl12) O. $2.50; shp., $3. Banks & Co.

New York. Penal code. (L. R. Parker.) '02(Je7) D. flex. skiver, $1.50. Banks.

New York. Penal code. 21st rev. ed. '02 (Jl12) D. canvas, $2. Banks & Co.

New York. Penal code. 16th ed. (C. D. Rust.) '02(Jl5) D. flex. im. alligator, $3.50. M. Bender.

New York. Statutory revision of the laws affecting banks, banking and trust companies 1892. (Hamilton.) '02(My24) O. pap., $1.50. Banks & Co.

New York. Statutory revision of the laws affecting insurance companies. (Hamilton.) '02(Je14) O. pap., $1.50. Banks & Co.

New York. Statutory revision of the laws affecting misc. corporations. (Hamilton.) '02(Je14) O. pap., $1.50. Banks & Co.

New York. Statutory revision of the laws affecting railroads. (Hamilton.) '02(Jl12) O. $2; pap., $1.50. Banks & Co.

New York supplement, v. 72. '02(F1); v. 73 (Ap5); v. 74 (Je14); v. 75 (Jl5) O. (Nat. reporter system.) shp., ea., $4. West Pub.

New York. Supp. to the general laws and revised statutes; comp. by E: L. Heydecker. '02(Jl19) O. pap., $2. M. Bender.

New York. Supp. to the general laws and statutes; comp. by Rob. C. Cumming and F. B. Gilbert. '02(Ag9) O. shp., $3.50. Banks.

New York. *Supreme ct.* **Repts.** (Hun.) v. 62-64. Off. ed. '01. '02(Ja4); v. 65, 66 (Ap5); v. 67 (Ap19) O. shp., ea., net, $3. Lyon.

New York. *Surrogates' cts.* Repts.; with annots., by J: Power. '01. '02(F1) O. shp., $5.50. W. C. Little.

New York. Tax law of 1896, with index and amend. to date. (A. Hamilton.) '02(Je7) O. pap., 50 c. Banks & Co.

New York. Tax law, with amendments of 1897-1902. Bender ed. '02(Je28) O. pap., 50 c. M. Bender.

New York. Village laws, 1902. (Cumming and Gilbert.) '02(Jl5) O. shp., $3. M. Bender.

NEW YORK.
Anderson *and* Flick. Short hist. of state of N. Y. $1. Maynard, M. & Co.
Beach. First N. Y. (Lincoln) cavalry, Ap. 19, 1861-July 7, 1865. *$2.50 net. [Caspar] Lincoln Cavalry.
Finegan. Text-book on N. Y. school law. $1. H: B. Parsons.
Jewett, *comp.* Manual for election officers and voters. $2; $1.50. M. Bender.
Murlin. Il. legislative manual; the N. Y. red book. $1. Lyon.
Purdy. Local option in taxation; with a draft of act to amend tax law. 10 c. N. Y. Tax Reform.
Redfield, *ed.* Repts. Surrogates' cts. v. 1. $6. Banks & Co.
Rumsey. Practice in civil actions in cts. of record in N. Y. v. 1. $6. Banks & Co.
Tarr. Physical geography of N. Y.; with chap. on climate. net, $3.50. Macmillan.
Wait. Law and practice in civil actions, [etc.] in N. Y. v. 1. $6.35; per set, $19. M. Bender.
See also Buffalo;—Elma;—Long Island;—Niagara Falls;—Saugerties.

New York Evening Post: hundredth anniversary number, Nov. 16, 1801-1901. '02 (My17) il. sq. O. $1. N. Y. Eve. Post.

New York Library Club. Libraries of Greater New York. '02(My17) D. net, 75 c.; pap., net, 50 c. Stechert.

Newberry, Fannie E. Bubbles. '02(Mr29) il. 12°, (Fireside ser.) $1. Burt.

Newberry, Fannie E. Comrades. '02(Mr29) il. 12°, (St. Nicholas ser.) 75 c. Burt.

Newberry, Fannie E. Joyce's investments. '02(Mr29) il. 12°, (Fireside ser.) $1. Burt.

Newberry, Fannie E. Sara: a princess. '02 (Mr29) il. 12°, (Fireside ser.) $1. Burt.

Newberry gospels. Goodspeed, E. J. net, 25 c. Univ. of Chic.

NEWBURG, Vt.
Wells. Hist. of Newburg. $2.25; $3; $3.50; $4. Caledonian.

Newcomb, Harry T. Concentration of railway control. '02(Mr22) 8°, (Pub. of the soc., no. 328.) pap., 15 c. Am. Acad. Pol. Sci.

Newcomes. *See* Thackeray, W: M.

Newell, F: H. Irrigation in the U. S. '02 (Mr8) D. net, $2. Crowell.
Newell, Grant. Elements of the law of real property. '02(Mr1) O. shp., $4. Flood.
Newell, Martin L., *rep. See* Illinois. *Appellate cts.* Repts.
Newell, Wilbur C. The life worth living. '02 (My3) il. D. $1. Abbey Press.
Newman, A. H:, *ed.*. Century of Baptist achievements. '01· '02(F15) 12°, net, $1.50. Am. Bapt.
Newman, J: H: Definition of a gentleman; [repr.] '02(Mr1) sq. 12°, bds., $1; pap., 50 c. Kirgate Press.
Newman, J: H: Lives of the Eng. saints. '01· '02(Mr1) 6 v., il. 12°, net, $12. Lippincott.
NEWMAN, J: H:
Waller *and* Barrow. John Henry, Cardinal Newman. 75 c. Small.
Whyte. Newman. net, $1.10. Longmans.
Newson's Germ. opera texts. 16°. Newson.
—Wagner. Rheingold. 75 c. (1.)
NEWSPAPERS.
American newspaper annual. $5. Ayer.
American newspaper directory. $5. Rowell.
Munson. Making a country newspaper. $1. Dominion.
Next great awakening. Strong, J. 75 c. Baker & T.
Next to the ground. Williams, M. M. net, $1.20. McClure, P.
NIAGARA FALLS.
Bishop. Red book of Niagara. 25 c. Wenborne-S.
NICARAGUA.
Walker. Ocean to ocean: acc. of Nicaragua. net, $1.25. McClurg.
NICARAGUA CANAL.
Sheldon. Notes on the Nicaragua canal. $1.25. McClurg.
Nichberg-Wagner, Mathilde. Im freundeskreisse. '02(Ag30) D. $1. Stechert.
Nicholls, *Mrs.* Ctte. B. *See* Brontë, C.
Nichols, E: L. The galvanometer. '02(Mr8) il. 8°, $1. Spon.
Nichols, Fs. M. *See* Britton.
Nicholson, T:, *and* Woods, C: C. Notes on Epworth League prayer meeting topics. 1st ser. '02(Ja25) S. pap., 15 c. Eaton & M.
Nicoll, W: R. The church's one foundation, Christ and recent criticism. '01· '02(F1) D. $1.25. Armstrong.
Nicolls, W: J. Graystone. '02(Mr15) il. D. $1.50. Lippincott.
Niebuhr, B. G. Greek hero stories. New ed. '01· '02(F22) 16°, $1. Dodd.
Nield, J. Guide to the best historical novels and tales. '02(Je21) O. net, $1.75. Putnam.
Nies, Konrad. Deutsche Gaben. '02(Je28) 8°, pap., 25 c. Witter.
Nies, Konrad. Rosen im Schnee. '02(Je28) 8°, pap., 50 c. Witter.
Night side of London. Machray, R. **$2.50 net. Lippincott.
NINETEENTH CENTURY.
Emerson. Hist. of the 19th century, year by year. 3 v., $3. Collier.
Hodder. Life of a century. net, $4. Scribner.
Morris. Marvelous achievements of the 19th century. $2.50; $3.50. Winston.
Nineteenth-century crusader. Locke, C: E: 25 c. Jennings.
Nitzsche, G: E., *comp.* University of Penn.: proceedings at the dedication of the new building of the Dept. of Law, Feb. 21, 22, 1900. '01· '02(Ap26) il. O. $3; hf. mor., $3.50. Univ. of Penn.
Nixon, J. H. Beyond the vail: a comp. of narrations and il. of spirit experiences. '01. '02(Mr22) il. 8°, $1.75. Hudson-K.
Noble, Alden C: Lyrics to the queen. '02 (Je14) sq. S. pap., n. p. Blue Sky Press.
Noble, Alfr., *and* Casgrain, W: T. Tables for obtaining horizontal distances and difference of level, from stadia readings. '02 (Jl12) 12°, $1. Engineering News.
Nociones de botánica. Hooker, *Sir* J. D. 40 c. Appleton.
NOME.
McKee. Land of Nome. net, $1.25. Grafton Press.
Nominating systems. Meyer, E. C. net, $1.50. E. C. Meyer.
None but the brave. Sears, H. $1.50. Dodd.
Nonne's preeste's tale. Chaucer, G. $6.50; $16.50. Grafton Press.
Nonsense for old and young. Field, E. 50 c. Dickerman.
Nordenskiold, G. The cliff dwellers of the Mesa Verde, southwestern Colo. [also] Human remains from the cliff dwellings of the Mesa Verde, by G. Retzius. '01. '02 (Ja25) f°, net, $20. Stechert.
Nordhoff guild, Washington, D. C. Cook book. '02(Jl5) 12°, pap., 25 c. McGill.
Norman, *Sir* H: Delhi (1857): account of the great mutiny. '02(Ag2) il. 8°, **$8 net. Lippincott.
Norris, W: E: Credit of the county. '02 (Jl19) D. (Town and country lib., no. 313.) †$1; pap., 50 c. Appleton.
Norris, Zoe A. Color of the soul. '02(F1) nar. D. bds., net, $1. Funk.
North, Ingolsby. Love letters and how to write them. '02(My17) 12°, 50 c.; pap., 25 c. Donohue.
North, Ingoldsby. Love letters and how to write them. '02(Mr15) S. pap., 25 c. Drake.
NORTH AMERICA.
Rapp. Geographical outline manual of N. A. 35 c. J: M. Rapp.
North Carolina regimental histories, 1861-'65; ed. and written by participants in the war. '02(Jl12) 5 v., 12°, $5; per v., $1. M. O. Sherrell.
North Dakota. *Supreme ct.* Repts. (J: M. Cochrane.) v. 10. '02(Jl19) O. shp., $4.25. Grand Forks Herald.
North Dakota. Township manual; by W. S. Booth. 6th ed. '01· '02(F8) D. pap., 75 c. Booth.
Northcote, Stafford H: *See* St. Cyres, *Viscount.*
Northeastern reporter, v. 61. '02(Mr1); v. 62 (My10) O. (Nat. reporter system, state ser.) shp., ea., $4. West Pub.
Northern Europe. '02(Mr22) il. D. (Youth's Companion ser., no. 2.) 30 c. Ginn.
Northrup, A. J., *ed.* Early records of the First Presbyterian Church of Syracuse, N. Y. '02(Ap5) O. pap., 50 c. [Gill] Genealog. Soc.

Northrup, W: P., *ed.* Diphtheria [*also*] measles, scarlatina, German measles, by T. von Jurgensen. '02(Je28) il. 8°, (Nothnagel's encyc. of practical medicine, Am. ed., v. 3.) net, $5; shp. or hf. mor., $6. Saunders.
Northwestern reporter, v. 88. '02(Ap5); v. 89 (Jl5) O. (Nat. reporter system, state ser.) shp., ea., $4. West Pub.
Norton, Alice J. [Hist. of Lake] Compounce, 1846-1902. '02(Ag23) il. 12°, 75 c. Tuttle, M. & T.
Norton, C: E., *ed.* Heart of oak books. First book. Rhymes, jingles and fables. Rev. ed. '02(Ag23) il. 16°, 25 c. Heath.
Norton, J: P. Statistical studies in New York money-market. '02(My24) net, $1.50; pap., net, $1. Macmillan.
NORWAY.
Spender. Two winters in Norway. $4. Longmans.
Weborg. In Viking land. $1.25. J. C. Weborg.
NOSE.
Gradle. Diseases of the nose, pharynx and ear. net, $3.50. Saunders.
Turner. Accessory sinuses of the nose. $4. Longmans.
Wood, *and others, eds.* Eye, ear, nose and throat. $1.50. Year Bk.
Not on the chart. Marsh, C: L. $1.50. Stokes.
NOTARIES.
Smith. Texas notarial manual and form book. $4. Gammel.
Snyder. Notaries' and commissioners' manual. $1.50. Baker, V. & Co.
Nothnagel's encyclopedia of practical medicine. il. 8°, net, $5; hf. mor., $6. Saunders.
—Moore, *ed.* Variola, vaccination, etc. (2.)
—Northrup, *ed.* Diphtheria, measles, scarlatina, German measles. (3.)
—Osler, *ed.* Typhoid and typhus fevers. (1.)
Notre Dame de Paris. Hugo, V. 85 c. Ginn.
Nott, C: C., *ed.* Seven great hymns of the mediæval church; annot. 2d rev., enl. ed. '02(Ag23) 12°, *$1 net. Gorham.
NOVELS.
See Fiction.
Novene zu Ehren des Heiligen Geistes. New ed. '02(Je28) 32°, pap., net, 3 c. Herder.
Novey, F. G. *See* Vaughan, V. C.
Noyes, C: J. Patriot and Tory. '02(Mr29) il. D. $1.50. Dickerman.
Nugent, Paul C. Plane surveying. '02(Ap5) il. 8°, $3.50. Wiley.
Nuggets ser. T. 45 c.; leath., $1. Fords.
—Pennington, *comp.* Good cheer nuggets
Nunquam, *pseud.* *See* Blatchford, R.
Nürnberg stove. *See* La Rame, L. de.
NURSES AND NURSING.
Hadley. Nursing; app. on sick-room cookery. net, $1.25. Blakiston.
Jewett. Childbed nursing. 80 c. Treat.
See also Accidents;—Diet;—Hospitals.
Nuverbis, [*pseud.* for Dillon Jordan Spotswood.] Out of the beaten track. '02(Mr22) D. $1. Abbey Press.
Nye, C. L. *See* Kaufman, M. S.
Nymph's reply to the shepherd. *See* Marlowe, C.
Nyrop, Chris. The kiss and its history; tr. by W: F: Harvey. '02(Ag23) 12°, *$2 net. Dutton.

O'BRIEN, Jeremiah.
Sherman. Life of Capt. Jeremiah O'Brien of Machias, Me. $2. G: W. Sherman.
OBSERVATORIES.
United States. List of observatories. n. p. Smith. Inst.
OBSTETRICS.
See Midwifery.
O'Byrne, W. L. Kings and vikings. '02 (Ap12) 12°, $1.25. Scribner.
O'Byrne, W. L. Land of heroes: Irish history. '02(Ap12) 12°, $1.25. Scribner.
OCCULTISM.
Demorest, *ed.* Cambridge encyclo. of esoteric subjects. v. 3. net, $3. Cambridge.
OCEAN.
See Seashore.
Ocean to ocean. Walker, J. W. G. net, $1.25. McClurg.
O'Connor, D. M. Foreign freemasonry. '02 (F1) S. pap., 5 c. Kilner.
O'Conor, M. Irish come-all-ye's and old-time songs and ballads of Ireland. '01. '02 (Ja4) 4°, pap., 25 c. Popular.
O'Conor, M., *comp.* Old-time songs and ballads of Ireland. '02(Ja25) O. $2. Popular.
ODD-FELLOWS.
Monroe Rebekah Lodge: semi-centennial, Jan. 23, 1902. 10 c. Darrow.
Odenheimer, Cordelia P. Phantom caravan. '01. '02(F15) D. $1. Abbey Press.
Odes, bridal songs, epigrams. *See* Sappho.
Oertel, Hanns. Lectures on the study of language. '01. '02(Mr15) 8°, (Yale bicentennial pub.) net, $3. Scribner.
Oesterley, W. O. E. Studies in the Greek and Latin versions of the Book of Amos. '02 (Ag16) 8°, (Cambridge Univ. Press ser.) *$1.30 net. Macmillan.
Ogilvie, Rob. Horæ Latinæ: synonyms and syntax; ed. by A. Souter. '01. '02(F8) O. $5. Longmans.
O'Growney, Eug. Revised simple lessons in Irish. pt. 1. '02(Mr15) D. pap., 15 c. Gael.
Ohio. *Cts. of record.* Repts. v. 10, 11. '01-'02(My10) O. shp., ea., $2.50. Laning.
Ohio. *Superior ct. of Cincinnati.* Repts. fr. 1854 to 1857; repr. '02(Jl12) O. (O. decisions ser.) shp., $7.50. Laning.
Ohio. *Supreme ct.* Repts. v. 64. '01. '02 (My10) O. shp., 2.50. Laning.
OHIO.
Fowke. Archæological hist. of Ohio. $5. [Smythe] Ohio Archæolog.
Roberts. Nation and the state: civil govt. of Ohio. $1. Bardeen.
Wilson. Ohio. net, 30 c. Macmillan.
OHIO VALLEY.
Piatt. Hesperian tree. $2. J: Scott.
OLD AGE.
Ames. Prevention and cure of old age. 50 c. Kirk.
Old Blackfriars. Marshall, B. $1.50. Dutton.
Old diaries. Gower, R. S. net, $4.50. Scribner.
Old English ballads. Kinard, J. P. 40 c. Silver.
Old English plate. Cripps, W. J. net, $13.50. Scribner.
Old glory and the gospel in the Philippines. Condict, A. B. net, 75 c. Revell.
Old Indian legends. Zitkala-sa. 50 c. Ginn.

Old, old fairy tales. Valentine, *Mrs.* L. J. $1. Burt.
Old South leaflets. v. 5. nos. 101-125. '02 (My17) D. $1.50. Old South Work.
Old world wonder stories. O'Shea, M. V. 25 c. Heath.
Oldfield. Banks, N. H. $1.50. Macmillan.
Oliver, G. F. Our lay office-bearers. '01. '02(Ja4) sq. D. (Little books on practice.) net, 25 c. Jennings.
Oliver, G. F. Soul-winners' secrets: revival text-book. '02(F8) sq T. (Little books on practice.) 25 c. Jennings.
Oliver, T., *ed.* Dangerous trades; aspects of industrial occupations as affecting public health. '02(Jl19) 8°, *$8 net. Duton.
Olmsted, Everett W., *ed. See* Marivaux, P. C. de C. de.
Olympian nights. Bangs, J: K. $1.25. Harper
Oman, C: W: C. Hist. of the Peninsular war. v. 1. '02(Ag23) O. $4.75. Oxford Univ.
Oman, C: W: C. Seven Roman statesmen of the later republic. '02(Ag30) il. D. $1.60. Longmans.
Omar Khayyám. Rubaiyat. '02(F15) 12°, net, $1.50. Lane.
Omar Khayyám. Rubaiyat. '02(My3) il. 16°, 60 c.; leath., $1. Macmillan.
Omar Khayyám. Rubáiyát. (Fitzgerald.) privately pr. for N. H. Dole. '01. '02(Mr1) 8°, charcoal pap., $10; vellum, $25. Merrymount Press.
Omar Khayyam, *jr., pseud. See* Irwin, W.
On the sensitiveness of the coherer. Wolcott, E. R. 20 c. Univ. of Wis.
Once upon a time. Aulnoy, M. C. J. de B. *Comtesse d'*. 50 c. Little, B. & Co.
One: a song of the ages. Moy, E. $1.50. Neely.
One before (The). Pain, B. †$1.25. Scribner.
One of the craft, *pseud. See* Schofield, R. J.
One thousand ways to make money. Gilbert. F. $1. Donohue.
One world at a time. Slicer, T: R. net, $1.35. Putnam.
Onlooker's note-book. Russell, G: W: E. $2.25. Harper.
ONTOLOGY.
Swedenborg. Ontology. 50 c. Mass. New-Ch. Un.
Openings in the old trail. Harte, F. B. $1.25. Houghton, M. & Co.
OPHTHALMOLOGY.
See Eye.
OPIUM.
See Morphinism.
Oppenheim, E. P. Enoch Strone. '02(Mr29) D. $1.50. G: W. Dillingham.
Oppenheim, N. Mental growth and control. '02(F15) 12°, (Personal problem ser.) net, $1. Macmillan.
Oppenheimer, C., *and* Mitchell, C. A. Ferments and their actions. '01. '02(F15) 12°, net, $2.50. Lippincott.
Opponents (The). Robertson, H. $1.50. Scribner.
Opportunist (The). Mitton, G. E. $2. Macmillan.
Optic, Oliver, *pseud. See* Adams, W: T.
Optical rotating power of organic substances. Landolt, H. H. *$7.50 net. Chemical.
OPTICS.
Drude. Theory of optics. $4. Longmans.
See also Eye;—Light.
ORATIONS.
See Rectitations.
ORATORS AND ORATORY.
Esenwein. How to attract and hold an audience. $1. Hinds.
See also Debates.
ORCHIDS.
Boyle. Woodland orchids. net, $7. Macmillan.
White. Book of orchids. *$1 net. Lane.
ORDINATION.
Stubbs. Ordination addresses. $2.25. Longmans.
Oregon. Mining laws. 2d ed. '01. '02(F1) D. pap., 40 c. Or. Mining Journ.
Oregon. *Supreme ct.* Repts. (R. G. Morrow.) v. 38. '01. '02(Ja4): v. 39 (Je7) O. shp., ea., $5. Leeds.
O'Rell, **Max**, *pseud. See* **Blouët**, P.
ORES.
See Metals and metallurgy;—Mines and mining.
ORESTESIA.
Browder. Time elements of the Orestean trilogy. 35 c. Univ. of Wis.
ORIENT.
Simmons. My trip to the Orient. $1.50. Whitaker & R.
Toward the rising sun. 30 c. Ginn.
ORIENTAL CLUB.
Baillie. Oriental Club and Hanover Square. $9. Longmans.
ORIENTAL RELIGIONS.
Conway, *comp.* Sacred anthology (oriental). $2. Holt.
Oriental ser. See Millet's.
Ormsby, Fk. E., *ed. See* Planets and people.
ORPHANS.
New Jersey orphans' court practice; with forms. $6. Soney.
Orphean tragedy. Creamer, E: S. $1. Abbey Press.
Orr, Ja. Progress of dogma: Elliott lectures. '01. '02(F1) O. $1.75. Armstrong.
Orthodontis. MacDowell, J. N. net, $4. Colegrove.
O'Shea, M. V., *ed.* Old world wonder stories. '02(F8) il. D. (Home and school classics.) 25 c. Heath.
Osler, W:, *ed.* Typhoid and typhus fevers, by H. Curschmann. Am. ed. '02(Mr29) il. 8°, (Nothnagel's encyclopedia of practical medicine, no. 1.) net, $5; hf. mor., $6. Saunders.
Ostrom, Kurre W. Massage and the orig. Swedish movements. 5th ed., rev. and enl. '02(Ag2) il. 12°, $1. Blakiston.
Ostwald, Wilhelm. Principles of inorganic chemistry; tr. by A. Findlay. '02(Je7) 8°, net, $6. Macmillan.
Oswald, Felix. Vaccination a crime. '02 (My17) 8°, pap., 10 c. Physical Culture.
Other notes. Hinton, M. B. $1. Neale.
Otis, James, *pseud. See* Kaler, J. O.
Otis Grey, bachelor. J., C. J. 75 c. Mutual Bk.
OTOLOGY.
See Ear.
Oudin, Maurice A. Standard polyphase apparatus and systems. 3d ed., rev. '02(My3) il. O. $3. Van Nostrand.
Ouida, *pseud. See* **La Rame, L. de.**

Our attitude toward Eng. Roman Catholics. Galton, A. net, $1. Dutton.
Our country's story. Tappan, E. M. 65 c. Houghton, M. & Co.
Our European neighbors ser. il. D. net, $1.20. Putnam.
—Higgin. Spanish life in town and country. (6.)
—Story. Swiss life in town and country. (5.)
Our lay office-bearers. Oliver, G. F. net, 25 c. Jennings.
Our literary deluge. Halsey, F. W. net, $1.25. Doubleday, P.
Our Lysander. Kellogg, A. M. 15 c. Kellogg.
Our new heraldry. Hogan, J: C. $1. Lowman.
Our Race news leaflet. 12°, pap. Our Race.
—Coronation stone of Great Britain and Israel. 50 c. (93.)
Our risen King's forty days. Boardman, G: D. net, $1.25. Lippincott.
Our sixty-six sacred books. Rice, E. W. net, 50 c. Am. S. S.
Our success in child-training. Pollak, G. $1. Contemporary.
Out among the animals. Malone, *Mrs.* E. W. 75 c. Pub. Ho. M. E. Ch., So.
Out of the beaten track. Nuverbis, *pseud.* $1. Abbey Press.
Outlaws. Armstrong, L. $1.25. Appleton.
Outre mer. Longfellow, H: W. $1. Burt.
Ovenden, C. T. To whom shall we go? '02 (Je7) 16°, $1. E. & J. B. Young.
Overland stage to California. Root, F. A. $2.50; $3.50. Root & C.
Overton, Ja. B. Parthenogenesis in thalictrum purpurascens. '02(Je14) 8°, (Cont. from the Hull Botanical Laboratory, no. 35.) pap., net, 25 c. Univ. of Chic.
Ovid. Amorum libri tres. '02(Je28) il. 12°, (Antique gems from the Gr. and Latin, v. 6.) (Apply to pubs. for price.) Barrie.
Owens College. *See* Tout, T: F:
Oxenford, Ina, *and* Alpheus, A., *pseud.* Complete palmist. '02(My17) 12°, 50 c.; pap., 25 c. Donohue.
Oxenham, J: Bondman free. '02(Ag30) il. D. †50 c. Federal Bk.
Oxford lib. of practical theology. D. $1.50. Longmans.
—Worlledge. Prayer.
OXFORD UNIVERSITY.
Corbin. An American at Oxford. net, $1.50. Houghton, M. & Co.
PACIFIC OCEAN.
Colquhoun. Mastery of the Pacific. net, $4. Macmillan.
Helmolt, *and others, eds.* Hist. of the world. v. 1, America and Pacific ocean. $6. Dodd.
Pacific reporter. v. 66. '02(Mr1); v. 67(Je7); v. 68 (Ag9) O. (Nat. reporter system, state ser.) shp., ea., $4. West Pub.
Pacific reporter. Digest of decisions. '02 (Mr8) O. (Nat. reporter system digests, Pacific ser., v. 3.) shp., net, $6. West Pub.
Pacific trail campfires. Kendall, R. P. $1.50. Scroll Pub.
Paderewski, I. J., *ed.* Century lib. of music. v. 17, 18. '02(Mr15); v. 19, 20 (Ap5) il., with music, f°, subs., per v., $2; hf. mor., $4. Century Co.

PAGANISM.
See Christianity.
Pagan's cup. Hume, F. W. $1.25. G: W. Dillingham.
Page, Ernest Clifford. *See* Nebraska digest.
Page, Kate N. Tommy Atkins episode, and other stories. '02(Jl19) D. $1. Abbey Press.
Page, Wa. H. Rebuilding of old commonwealths. '02(Je7) D. net, $1. Doubleday, P.
Pages of socialist history. Tcherkesoff, W. 25 c. C. B. Cooper.
Paget, Fs. Christ the way; four addresses. '02(Ag2) S. 75 c. Longmans.
Paget, *Sir* Ja. Selected essays and addresses; ed. by S. Paget. '02(Ap19) O. $5. Longmans.
Paget, R. L., *pseud.* Cap and gown. 3d ser. '03. '02(Ag16) il. S. †$1.25. L. C. Page.
Pain, Barry. The one before. '02(Jl12) il. D. †$1.25. Scribner.
PAINT.
Church. Chemistry of paints and painting. $3. Macmillan.
Williams. Painter's guide book. $1.50. J: H: Williams.
PAINTERS.
Caffin. American masters of painting. net, $1.25. Doubleday, P.
Dallin. Sketches of great painters for young people. 90 c. Silver.
Roulet. St. Anthony in art, and other sketches. $2. Marlier.
See also Artists.
PAINTING.
Van Dyke. Italian painting. 50 c. Elson.
See also Aesthetics;—Anatomy for artists;—Artists;—Decoration and ornament;—Drawing;—Fine arts;—Paint;—Painters.
PAINTING BOOKS.
Barnett. Mother Goose paint book. $1.25. Saalfield.
Palache, C: *See* Lawson, A. C.
PALEONTOLOGY.
Case. Palæontological notes. *25 c. net. Univ. of Chic.
See also Geology.
PALESTINE.
Babcock. Letters from Egypt and Palestine. net, $1. Scribner.
Guide to Palestine and Egypt. net, $3.25. Macmillan.
Palgrave, Ma. E. Mary Rich, Countess of Warwick, 1625-1678. '02(F15) 12°, net, $1.50. Dutton.
Palladino, L. B. Mary our mother. '02 (Je14) 12°, pap., net, 15 c. Herder.
Pallen, Condé B. Death of Sir Launcelot, and other poems. '02(Ag16) D. *$1 net. Small.
Palliser, *Mrs.* Bury. History of lace. New ed., rev., rewritten and enl., by M. Jourdain and A. Dryden. '02(Mr8) 8°, net, $12. Scribner.
Palmer, B. M. Threefold fellowship and the threefold assurance. '02(Mr29) O. 75 c. Presb. Pub.
Palmer, *Mrs.* Minnie. Woman's exchange cook book. '01. '02(Ap26) il. 8°, 70 c. Conkey.
PALMISTRY.
La Seer. The hand and its lines. gratis. Dean & H.
Oxenford *and* Alpheus. Complete palmist. 50 c.; 25 c. Donohue.

PALMISTRY.—*Continued.*
Perin. Science of palmistry. $1.50. Star Pub.

Pan-American ser. il. D. net, $1. Lee & S
—Stratemeyer. Lost on the Orinoco. (1.)

PANAMA CANAL.
Johnson. Isthmian canal. 25 c. Am. Acad. Pol. Sci.
Pasco. Isthmian canal question as affected by treaties and concessions. 25 c. Am. Acad. Pol. Sci.
Sonderegger. L' achèvement du canal de Panama. $2.50. Stechert.

Pangborn, Georgia W. Roman Biznet. '02 (My3) il. D. $1.50. Houghton, M. & Co.

Pansy, *pseud. See* Alden, *Mrs.* I. M.

Paolo and Francesca. Phillips, S. net, $1.25. Lane.

PAOTINGFU, China.
Ketler. Tragedy of Paotingfu. net, $2. Revell.

PAPER FOLDING.
Sundara. Geometric exercises in paper folding. $1. Open Court.

PARABLES.
Dods. Parables of our Lord. $1.50. Whittaker.

Parables of life. Mabie, H. W. net, $1. Outlook.

Paret, W: Reality in holy communion. '02 (Ap12) 16°, pap., 10 c. Whittaker.

PARIS.
Halstead. Splendors of Paris and glories of her exposition. $1.50. Dominion.
Visitors' guide to Paris. 10 c. Brooklyn Eagle.
Walton. Paris from the earliest period to the present day. v. 6. $3. Barrie.

Parker, Amasa J., *jr. See* New York. Code of civil procedure.

Parker, Arnold. Ping-pong: [table tennis.] '02(Mr15) il. D. net, 75 c. Putnam.

Parker, Arnold. *See also* Ritchie, M. G.

Parker, C: W., *comp.* New Jersey lawyers' diary and bar directory, 1902. '02(Ja18) O. $1.50. Soney.

Parker, E. H. John Chinaman, and a few others. '02(Mr8) 12°, $2.50. Dutton.

Parker, *Mrs.* Ht. F., *comp. See* Marsh, L. B., *comp.*

Parker, Lewis R., *ed. See* New York. Codes.

Parkman, Fs. Writings. La Salle ed., incl. life of Parkman by C: H. Farnham. '02 (Mr22) 20 v., il. 8°, subs., per v., net, $5; ¾ lev. mor., per v., net, $10. Little, B. & Co.

Parkman, Fs. Conspiracy of Pontiac. '02 (Je14) 12°, (Home lib.) $1. Burt.

Parks, Ella M. Mary of Bethany. '02(Jl5) 16°. 25 c.; pap., 15 c. Pepper.

PARLIAMENTARY LAW.
Felt. Parliamentary procedure for deliberative assemblies. 75 c.; 35 c. Hazlitt.
Fox. Parliamentary usage for women's clubs. net, 65 c. Baker & T.
Henry. How to organize and conduct a meeting. 75 c. Hinds.
Sherman. Parliamentary law at a glance. 75 c. H: O. Shepard.
Stevens. Am. law of assemblies. net, $1. E: A. Stevens.
Vancil. School congress. 25 c. Kellogg.

Parlin, Fk. E. Quincy word list, rev. and enl. [4th ed.] '02(Jl12) 12°, (New century ser.) 24 c. Morse.

PARODY.
Dustin. The make good book of parodies. 50 c. E. Dustin.

Parr, G. D. A. Electrical engineering testing. '02(Ap19) il. 8°, net, $3.50. Van Nostrand.

Parson's handbook (The); cont. directions as to the management of the parish church and its services as set forth in the "Book of common prayer." 4th ed., rewritten and enl. '02(My10) 12°, net, $1.50. Young Churchman.

Parsons, *Mrs.* Fes. T. According to season. New enl. ed. '02(Mr22) il. D. net, $1.75. Scribner.

Parsons, J. H. Elementary ophthalmic optics. '01· '02(Ja11) 12°, net, $2. Blakiston.

Parsons, Ma. E. Wild flowers of California. 4th ed., rev. and corr. '02(Ag16) il. O. $2. Payot.

Parsons' [W. F.] hand-book of forms: a comp. of business and social rules. 12th ed., rev. and enl. '02(Ag2) il. O. $3; shp., $4. Southern Pub.

Parthenogenesis in thalictrum purpurascens. Overton, J. B. net, 25 c. Univ. of Chic.

PARTIES (*political*).
See Indiana.

Partridge, W: O. Nathan Hale, the ideal patriot. '02(My17) D. net, $1. Funk.

Pasco, S: Isthmian canal question as affected by treaties and concessions. '02 (Mr22) 8°, (Pub. of the soc., no. 324.) pap., 25 c. Am. Acad. Pol. Sci.

Pascoe, C. E. Pageant and ceremony of the coronation of their majesties King Edward the seventh and Queen Alexandra. '02 (My3) il. D. net, $1.40. Appleton.

Passenger traffic of railways. Weyl, W. E. $1.50; $1. Ginn.

Passing world. Belloc, B. R. net, $1.25. Herder.

Passion flowers. Watson, *Mrs.* A. R. $1.60. Whittet.

Passionate shepherd to his love. Marlowe, C. net, $3.75. Russell.

Past and present. Carlyle, T: 50 c.; 75 c. Macmillan.

Past and present of Japanese commerce. Kinosita, Y. *$1.50 net. Macmillan.

Pasteboard crown. Morris, C. $1.50. Scribner.

Paston, G:, [*pseud. for* E. M. Symonds.] Little memoirs of the nineteenth century. '02(Ap5) il. 8°, net, $3. Dutton.

Pastor Agnorum. Skrine, J: H. net, $1.60. Longmans.

Pastor and the Sunday-school. Hatcher, W: E. 75 c. Bapt. S. S. Bd.

Pastoral epistles. Lilley, J. P. net, 75 c. Scribner.

PATENTS.
Cresee. Pointers for patentees. *$1 net. Munn.

Pater, Wa. H. Marius the epicurean. '02 (Je14) 12°, (Home lib.) $1. Burt.

Paterson, W: R., ["Benjamin Swift."] Game of love. '02(Ap12) D. $1.50. Scribner.

Path to Rome. Belloc, H. net, $2. Longmans.

PATHOLOGY.
Herter. Lectures on chemical pathology. net, $1.75. Lea.
Thayer. Compend of general pathology. 80 c.; $1. Blakiston.
Thayer. Compend of special pathology. 80 c.; $1. Blakiston.
Trudeau. Torture of the clinic. $1; 50 c. Bourguignon.
See also Contagion;—Diphtheria;—Ear; —Eye;—Gallstone; — Hair; — Hernia; — Histology; — Hygiene;—Insanity;—Malarial fever;—Nose;—Skin;—Smallpox;—Throat;—Typhoid fever; —Urine and urinary organs.
Paths to power. Wilson, F. B. $1. Fenno.
Patoma, Fk. The Venus di Milo. '02(Je7) 12°, 50 c. Cambridge.
Patricia of the hills. Burrow, C: K. net, $1.20. Putnam.
PATRICK, *St.*
Sanderson. Story of Saint Patrick; emb. sketch of Ireland. $1.50. Ketcham.
Patrick, J. N. Psychology for teachers. '02 (My3) D. hf. leath., $1. Educ. Pub.
Patriot and Tory. Noyes, C: J. $1.50. Dickerman.
Patristic study. Swete. H: B. net, 90 c. Longmans.
Pattee, F. L. Mary Garvin. '02(Ap5) il. D. $1.50. Crowell.
Pattee, W: S., *comp.* Authorities, reductions, and notes in real property. '02 (My24) O. shp., $2. Univ. Press.
Patten, S. N. Theory of prosperity. '02(F1) 12°, net, $1.25. Macmillan.
Patten, S. N. *See also* Seager, H: R.
Patterson, Alex. Broader Bible study. The Pentateuch. '02(Ap26) D. net, 75 c. Jacobs.
Patterson, C: B. Beyond the clouds. New issue. '02(Mr22) O. $1. Alliance.
Patterson, C: B. What the new thought stands for. '01- '02(Mr22) S. pap., 10 c. Alliance.
Patterson, C: B. The will to be well. '01. '02(Mr22) nar. O. $1. Alliance.
Patterson, Melvin J. *See* Fisher, A. T.
Patterson, Virginia S. Dickey Downy. Phœnix ed. '02(Ap5) S. 25 c. A. J. Rowland.
Pattison, Everett W. Instructions in criminal cases passed upon by the cts. of Missouri. '02(My24) O. shp., $5. Gilbert Bk.
Pattison, T. H. The Bible and the twentieth century. '02(Mr22) D. pap., 10 c. Am. Bapt.
Patton, Abel. "Har Lampkins." '02(Mr1) D. $1. Abbey Press.
PAUL, *St.*
Matheson. Spiritual development of St. Paul. net, 80 c. Whittaker.
Pratt. Life and Epistles of St. Paul. 75 c. Funk.
Wayland. Paul, the herald of the cross. 40 c. Brethren Pub. Ho.
Paul and Virginia. Saint-Pierre, J. H. B. de. $1. Burt.
Paulsen, Friedrich. Immanuel Kant, his life and doctrine; fr. rev. Germ. ed., by J. E. Creighton and A. Lefevre. '02(Mr1) O. net, $2.50. Scribner.
PAVEMENTS.
See Roads.
Payn, F. W. Cromwell on foreign affairs. '02(Mr8) 8°, net, $1.25. Macmillan.
Payne, Fk. O. How to teach about trees. '01- '02(Ja25) 12°, 25 c. Kellogg.
Payne, Fk. O. How to teach aquatic life. '01- '02(Ja25) 12°, 25 c. Kellogg.
Payne, W: M. Editorial echoes. '02(Ap12) D. net, $1. McClurg.
Payne, W: M. Little leaders. [New issue.] '02(Ap12) D. net, $1. McClurg.
Pearls from the Wonderbook. King, T: A. 40 c. Swedenborg.
Pease, Eunice S. Gathered sunbeams: poems. '02(Je7) S. bds., 75 c. Sun Pr. Co.
Pearson, C: W. The carpenter prophet. '02 (Ap26) D. $1.50. H. S. Stone.
Pearson, H: C., *and* Bartlett, Emeline B. Key to Pearson's Greek prose composition. '01- '02(F15) S. pap., 50 c. Am. Bk.
Peck, G: C. Ringing questions. '02(Mr22) D. $1. Eaton & M.
Peck, S: M. Alabama sketches. '02(Mr22) S. $1. McClurg.
PEDIATRICS.
See Children.
Peerless ser. D. pap., 25 c. Ogilvie.
—Morehead. Story of François Villon. (124.)
Peker, C: G. *See* Meyer, J. G. A.
PEMAQUID, Me.
Kaler. Story of Pemaquid. 50 c. Crowell.
Pemberton, Max. The giant's gate. '02(F22) D. $1.50. Stokes.
Pemberton, T. E. Ellen Terry and her sisters. '02(Ap12) O. net, $3.50. Dodd.
Pen and ink. Matthews, J. B. net, $1.25. Scribner.
Pendel, T: F. Thirty-six years in the White House, Lincoln-Roosevelt. '02(Ap26) 12°, $1.50. Neale.
Pendennis. Thackeray, W: M. 3 v. $3. Macmillan.
PENINSULAR WAR.
Oman. Hist. of the Peninsular war. v. 1. $4.75. Oxford Univ.
Penitential Psalms. *See* Browne, *Mrs.* A. B. B.
PENMANSHIP.
Kilpatrick. Language system of penmanship. nos. 1-8. per doz., 66 c. Globe Sch. Bk.
Pennington, Jeanne G., *comp.* Good cheer nuggets. '02(Mr22) T. (Nuggets ser.) 45 c.: leath., $1. Fords.
Pennock, Arth. F. Twenty thousand miles by land and sea. '01. '02(My10) il. D. $1. Mason Pub.
Pennsylvania. *County cts.* Repts. v. 25. '02(Mr1) O. shp., $5. T. & J. W. Johnson.
Pennsylvania. Digest of the general acts of assembly, for the incorporation and government of cities of the 3d class. 2d ed., by L. Richards. '02(Jl5) O. $3. Soney.
Pennsylvania. *District ct.* Repts. v. 10. '01- '02(Ap5) O. shp., $5.25. H. W. Page.
Pennsylvania. Health ordinance of the borough of Edgewood, and health laws of the state; digest index, by M. Pflaum. '02 (Jl5) O. pap., $1. Nicholson.
Pennsylvania. Law of conveyancing, by C. Fallon. '02(F1) O. shp., $6. T. & J. W. Johnson.
Pennsylvania. Monaghan's cumulative annual digest. v. 3. '02(Ap19) O. $6. Soney.

Pennsylvania. Negotiable instruments law; annots. by J: J. Crawford. '02(Ap12) O. $2.50. Baker, V. & Co.

Pennsylvania. *Superior ct.* Repts., v. 17. (Schaffer and Weimer.) '02(Mr15); v. 18 (Je7) O. shp., ea., $2. Banks.

Pennsylvania. *Supreme ct.* Repts., v. 200. '02(Mr29); v. 201 (Jl19) O. shp., ea., $3.50. Banks.

PENNSYLVANIA.
Cuffel. Durrell's Battery in the Civil War. subs., $2. C: A. Cuffel.
Gans. A Pennsylvania pioneer. $6. Kuhl.
Pepper *and* Lewis. Encyclopædia of Pa. law, 1754-1898. v. 13. $7.50. Welsh.
Sharpless. Quaker experiment in government. $1.50. Ferris.
Shimmell. Border warfare in Pa. during Revolution. 50 c. R. L. Myers.
Stapleton. Memorials of the Huguenots in America with special ref. to their emigration to Pa. $1.50. Huguenot.
Trickett. Law of witnesses in Pa. $6. T. & J. W. Johnson.
See also Edgewood;—Germantown;—Lancaster;—Philadelphia.

Pennsylvania German cook book. Keller, S. K. 50 c. R: M. Scranton.

Pennsylvania Society of New York; year book, 1902. '02(My3) O. $1. Penn. Soc. of N. Y.

PENSIONS.
Glasson. Nation's pension system. 25 c. Am. Acad. Pol. Sci.

PENTATEUCH.
See Bible.

Pentecostal holiness lib. D. Knapp.
—Henley. Divine healing. 75 c.; 10 c. (v. 5, 8.)

People's lib. 12°, pap., 50 c. Am. News.
—Crawford. In the palace of the king. (27.)

Pepper, G: W., *and* Lewis, W: D. Digest of decisions. v. 12. '01· '02(Mr15) O. of decisions. v. 12. '01· '02(Mr15); v. 13 (Jl12) O. ea., $7.50. Welsh.

Pepys, S: Diary and correspondence. New ed. '01· '02(F22) 10 v., 12°, $10; limp leath., $15. Dodd.

PERCEPTION.
See Knowledge.

PERCIVAL, Ja. G.
Legler. James Gates Percival. net, $1. Mequon Club.

Percival, Leila. Professor Archie. '02 (My17) 12°, 50 c. Nelson.

Percy, Hugh, *Earl.* Letters of Hugh, Earl Percy, from Boston and New York, 1774-1776; ed. by C. K. Bolton. '02(Jl19) sq. O. bds., *$4 net. Goodspeed.

Perdue, Hannah A. New century first reader; rev. '02(Ag30) il. (New century readers by grades, bk. 1.) 17 c. Rand, McN. & Co.

Perfect woman. Sainte-Foi, C: net, $1. Marlier.

Perin, Carl L. Science of palmistry. '02 (Ag9) il. 12°, $1.50. Star Pub.

Perkin, W: H:, *jr., and* Lean, Bevan. Introd. to chemistry and physics. New ed. '02(Mr1) 2 v., 12°, net, ea., 50 c. Macmillan.

Perkins, F. M. Giotto. '02(Ja14) il. 12°, (Great masters in painting and sculpture.) $1.75. Macmillan.

Perkins, G: R. Arithmética elemental. Neuva ed. '01. '02(F15) 12°, bds., 25 c. Appleton.

Perkins, T: Cathedral church of Amiens. '02(Mr29) 12°, (Bell's handbooks to continental churches.) $1. Macmillan.

Perley, Sidney. Practice in personal actions in the cts. of Mass. '02(Jl12) O. shp., $6.50. G: B. Reed.

Perrault, C: Tales of Mother Goose; new tr. '02(F8) il. D. (Home and school classics.) 25 c. Heath.

Perrault, C: Tales of passed times. '02 (Ja18) il. 16°, (Temple classics for young people.) net, 50 c.; flex. leath., 80 c. Macmillan.

Perrault, C:, *and* Aulnoy, Marie C. J. de B., *Comtesse d'.* Fairy favorites. New ed. '01· '02(F15) 16°, (Children's friend ser.) bds., 50 c. Little, B. & Co.

Perrault, C: *See also* Aulnoy, M. C. J. de B., *Comtesse d'.*

Perry, Stuart H. Legal adviser and business guide. '01. '02(Mr8) O. $1.50. Pontiac.

PERSIA.
Remy. Influence of Persia on the poetry of Germany. net, $1. Macmillan.
Sparroy. Persian children of the Royal family. net, $3.50. Lane.
Sykes. 10,000 miles in Persia. net, $6. Scribner.
See also Inscriptions.

Persian pearl. Darrow, C. S. $1.50. Ricketts.

Personal idealism. Sturt, H: *$3.25 net. Macmillan.

Personal life of the clergy. Robinson, A. W. net, 90 c. Longmans.

Personal problem ser. See Macmillan's.

PERSPECTIVE.
Pratt. Perspective, incl. projection of shadows and reflections. 90 c. Longmans.

PERU.
Prescott. Conquest of Peru. 2 v. net, $2. Macmillan.

Perverts (The). Howard, W: L. $1.50. G: W. Dillingham.

PETER III.
Bain. Peter III., Emperor of Russia. net, $3.50. Dutton.

Peterkin, G: W: Hist. and record of the Protestant Episcopal church in the diocese of West Va. '02(Jl12) 8°, $2.50; hf. leath., $10. Tribune Co.

Peters, J: J. *See* Labor and capital.

Peters, Madison C. The Jew as a patriot. '02(F22) D. $1. Baker & T.

Peterson, C. A. Mound building age in North America. '02(My24) O. pap., 25 c. Clarke.

Peterson, Hans C. First steps in Eng. composition. '02(Mr29) S. (Educational ser.) 35 c. Flanagan.

Peterson, Reuben, *and* Lewis, H: F., *eds.* Obstetrics. '02(Jl12) il. 12°, (Practical medicine ser. of year books, v. 5.) $1.25. Year Bk.

Pflaum, Magnus. *See* Pennsylvania. Health ordinance.

Phantom caravan. Odenheimer, C. P. $1. Abbey Press.

PHARMACY.
Neff. Prescription writing in Latin or Eng. 75 c. Davis.

PHARMACY.—*Continued.*
Ramsay. Pharmacopœia of the Glasgow Royal Infirmary Ophthalmic Institution. *$1.25 net. Macmillan.

PHARYNX.
See Throat.

Phelps, Eliz. S., [*now Mrs.* H. D. Ward,] *and* Ward, H. D. A lost hero. New ed '01. '02(F15) 16°, (Children's friend ser., bds., 50 c. Little, B. & Co.

Phelps, W: L., *comp.* List of general reading in Eng. literature. '02(Ap26) 12°, pap., net, 5 c. Pease-L.

PHI KAPPA PSI.
Van Cleve. Hist. of the Phi Kappa Psi fraternity. $2; $4. Franklin Pr.

Phil and Dick. Lewis, E. H. $1. Saalfield.

PHILADELPHIA.
Myers. Quaker arrivals at Philadelphia, 1682-1750. $1.25. Ferris.

PHILIPPINE ISLANDS.
Condict. Old glory and the gospel in the Philippines. net, 75 c. Revell.
Friars (The) must stay. 5 c. Am. News.
Halstead. Story of the Philippines. $2; $3. Dominion.
Hedges. Statistics conc. education in the Philippine Islands. 10 c. Benziger.
Lodge, *and others.* The U. S. and the Philippine Islands. 10 c. Brooklyn Eagle.

Philip Longstreth. Van Vorst, M. $1.50. Harper.

Philipson, D: Jew in English fiction. New rev., enl. ed. '02(My17) D. net, $1. Clarke.

Phillipps, L. M. With Rimington. '01. '02 (Ja11) O. $2.50. Longmans.

Phillips, D: G. Her Serene Highness. '02 (My10) il. D. $1.50. Harper.

Phillips, Fs. C., *ed.* Methods for the analysis of ores, pig iron and steel in use at the laboratories about Pittsburg, Pa. 2d ed. '01. '02(F1) il. 8°, net, $1. Chemical Pub.

Phillips, H: W. Red Saunders. '02(My24) il. D. $1.25. McClure, P.

Phillips, J: B. Methods of keeping the public money of the U. S. '02(F15) 12°, pap., $1. Mich. Pol. Sci.

Phillips, Stephen. Paolo and Francesca. New ed. '02(Je28) 12°, net, $1.25. Lane.

Phillips, Stephen. Ulysses: a drama. '02 (F15) D. net, $1.25. Macmillan

Phillips, Wa. S., *comp.* Indian fairy tales. '02(Ag2) il. 12°, $1.50. Star Pub.

Philosophical dict. Voltaire, F. M. A. de. 10 v. per set, subs., *$18 net; $24 net. G: Clarke.

PHILOSOPHY.
Adams, *comp.* Texts to il. lectures on Greek philosophy. net, $1.25. Macmillan.
Baldwin. Fragments in philosophy and science. net, $2.50. Scribner.
Blackwood's philosophical classics. 15 v. ea., net, 50 c. Lippincott.
Boethius. Consolation of philosophy. 50 c.; 75 c. Macmillan.
Browne. Religio medici, Urn burial, Christian morals and other essays. **$12 net. Lane.
Chamberlain. Evolutionary philosophy. 50 c. Baker & T.
Kupfer. Greek foreshadowings of modern metaphysical and epistemological thought. $1. J. S. Cushing.

PHILOSOPHY.—*Continued.*
Laurie. Scottish philosophy in its nat. development. net, $1.75. Macmillan.
Muirhead. Philosophy and life. $1.50. Macmillan.
Sidgwick. Philosophy. net, $2.25. Macmillan.
See also Ethics;—Idealism;—Knowledge; — Memory;—Mind and body; — Ontology; — Religion and science; — Skepticism; — Utilitarianism; — *also* Kant, I.

Philosophy of conduct. Ladd, G: T. net, $3.50. Scribner.

Philosophy of the Christian religion. Fairbairn, A. M. net, $3.50. Macmillan.

Philosophy of voice. Lunn, C: net, $2. Schirmer.

Phin, J: Shakespeare cyclopædia and new glossary; introd. by E: Dowden. '02 (Ag23) O. *$1.50 net. Indust.

PHONOGRAPHY.
See Stenography.

Photographic coloring. '02(Ap5) D. pap., 25 c. Acme Water Color.

PHOTOGRAPHY.
International annual of Anthony's photographic bulletin, 1902. $1.25; 75 c. Anthony.
Taylor. Why my photographs are bad. net, $1. Jacobs.

Phrase-making, Science of. *See* Brown, D: W.

PHRENOLOGY.
Windsor. Phrenology. 25 c. Donohue.
See also Physiognomy.

PHYSICAL CULTURE.
See Gymnastics and physical culture.

PHYSICAL GEOGRAPHY.
Davis. Elem. physical geography. $1.40. Ginn.
Gilbert *and* Brigham. Introd. to physical geography. net, $1.25. Appleton.
Morgan. Advanced physiography. $1.50. Longmans.
Warren. Physical geography. $1.25. Butler.
See also Brooks;—Geography;—Geology;—Nature;—Seashore;—Water;—Weather.

PHYSICAL SCIENCE.
See Science.

PHYSICIANS.
Allen. Practitioner's manual. $6; $7. Wood.
Medical directory of the city of N. Y. $1.50. Wynkoop.

PHYSICS.
Ayres. Lab'y exercises in elem. physics. net, 50 c. Appleton.
Carhart *and* Chute. Physics for high school students. $1.25. Allyn & B.
Crew *and* Tatnall. Lab'y manual of physics. net, 90 c. Macmillan.
Fisher *and* Patterson. Elements of physics. 60 c. Heath.
Hoadley. Teachers' manual to accompany Brief course in physics. 25 c. Am. Bk.
Kelsey. Physical determinations. $1.50. Longmans.
Lehfeldt. Text-bk. of physics. $2. Longmans.
Perkin *and* Lean. Introd. to chemistry and physics. 2 v., ea., net, 50 c. Macmillan.
Reed *and* Guthe. Manual of physical measurements. $1.50. Wahr.
Reynolds. Papers on mechanical and physical subjects. v. 2. net, $6. Macmillan.

PHYSICS.—*Continued.*
Sanford. Elements of physics. $1.20. Holt.
Slate. Physics. net, $1.10. Macmillan
Stewart. Nociones de fisica. 20 c. Appleton.
Wentworth *and* Hill. Lab'y exercises in elem. physics. 27 c. Ginn.
See also Chemistry;—Heat;—Light;—Mathematics;—Meteorology;—Radiation;—Sound.

PHYSIOGNOMY.
Stevens. Faciology. 25 c. Donohue.

PHYSIOGRAPHY.
See Geology;—Physical geography.

PHYSIOLOGY.
Blaisdell. Life and health: text-book on physiology. $1. Ginn.
Brinckley. Physiology by the lab'y method. $1.25. Ainsworth.
Colton. Elem. physiology and hygiene. 60 c. Heath.
Hill. Physiology for beginners. 35 c. Longmans.
Hood. Plain talks about the human system. $5. Hood.
Hutchison. Lessons in physiology and hygiene. 2d bk. 80 c.; 40 c. Maynard, M. & Co.
Hutchison. Physiology and hygiene. $1. Maynard, M. & Co.
Jegi. Syllabus of human physiology for schools. $1. Gillan.
Schäfer. Directions for class work in practical physiology. net, $1. Longmans.
Smith. Anatomy, physiology and hygiene $1. W: R. Jenkins.
See also Anatomy;—Heredity;—Hygiene;—Mind and body;—Nervous system.

Piatt, J: J. The Hesperian tree. '02(F22) il. O. $2. J: Scott.

Piccolomini (The). Schiller, J. C. F. v. (App. to pubs. for price.) Niccolls.

Pickering, Edg. King for a summer. '02 (Ap26) il. D. net, $1. Lee & S.

Pickle, G: W., *rep. See* Tennessee. *Sup. ct* Repts.

Pictorial guide to Boston and the country around. '02(Jl12) il. S. pap., 25 c. G. W. Armstrong.

Pictorial natural history. Cuppy, H. A. $1. Crowell & K.

Pictures and problems from London police courts. Holmes, T: $1.25. Longmans.

Pictures of paint-box town. Doty, D. Z. $1. Dutton.

Pidgin, C: F. Stephen Holton. '02(My10) D. $1.50. L. C. Page.

Pierce, Arth. H. Studies in auditory and visual space perception. '01. '02(Ja11) D. net, $2. Longmans

Pierce, Ella A. Hartley House cook book and household economist. '02(F8) S. (Handbooks for practical workers in church and philanthropy.) 60 c. Lentilhon.

Pierce, Ella M. Intermediate arithmetic. '02 (Mr22) il. 12°, (Pierce arithmetics.) 48 c. Silver.

Pierce, F: C. Field genealogy. '01. '02(F8) 2 v., il. 4°. $10. Conkey.

Pierce, Grace A. The silver cord and the golden bowl. '02(Mr1) O. $1. Abbey Press.

Pierson, Arth. T. Gordian knot; or, the problem which baffles infidelity. '02(Ag30) nar. S. **60 c. net. Funk.

Pierson, Clara D. Among the night people. '02(My10) 12°. net. $1. Dutton.

PIGEONS.
Homing pigeon. 25 c. G: E. Howard.
Rice. Robinson method of breeding squabs. 50 c. Plymouth Rock.

Pilgrim's progress. *See* Bunyan, J:

Pine tree ballads. Day, H. F. **$1 net. Small.

PING-PONG.
Parker. Ping-pong: how to play it. net, 75 c. Putnam.
Ritchie *and* Harrison. Table tennis, and how to play it. 50 c. Lippincott.
Ritchie *and* Parker. Ping-pong. 50 c. Street.

Pink knight. Monsell, J. R. net, 40 c. Stokes.

Pinney, Aida E. Spanish and Eng. conversation. First and second books. '02(Jl19) D. ea., 65 c. Ginn.

Pinson, W. W. In white and black. '02 (Mr1) D. $1.50. Saalfield.

Pioneer towns of America. il. D. 50 c. Crowell.
—Kaler. Story of Pemaquid. (2.)

Piper, Fred. S. Lexington, the birthplace of Am. liberty. '02(Ap26) il. sq. S. pap., 25 c. Lexington.

Pipes and tubes. Bjorling, P. R. $1. Macmillan.

Pitman, Benn, *and* Howard, J. B. Business letters: no. 1. '02(My10) S. pap., 25 c. Phonograph.

Pitman, *Sir* I: Business corr. in shorthand: no. 2. Rev. ed. '02(My10) S. pap., 30 c. Pitman.

Pitman, *Sir* I: Phonographic teacher. Twentieth century ed. '02(My10) S. pap., 20 c. Pitman.

Pitman, *Sir* I: Shorthand instructor. Twentieth century ed., rev. '02(Ag30) S. $1.50. Pitman.

Pitman's commercial ser. il. D. Pitman.
—Marchand. Commercial history. $1.

Pitt Press Shakespeare. 12°, net, 40 c. Macmillan.
—Shakespeare. Macbeth.

Plain talks about the human system. *See* Hood, G. D.

Plan book ser. See Flanagan's.

Plane surveying. Nugent, P. C. $3.50. Wiley.

Planets and people; [1902.] annual. F. E. Ormsby, ed. '01. '02(Ja25) O. $1. F. E. Ormsby.

PLANTS
See Botany;—Gardening.

PLATE.
Cripps. Old Eng. plate. net, $13.50. Scribner.

Plato. Euthyphro; notes by W: A. Heidel. '02(Jl12) D. (Greek ser. for coll. and schools.) $1. Am. Bk.

Plato. The republic. (J. L. Davies and D. J. Vaughan.) '02(Ap19) 12°, (Home lib.) $1. Burt.

Plato. The republic. bk. 2. '02(My10) D. pap., 15 c. Kerr.

PLATO.
Nettleship. Lectures on the Republic of Plato. net, $2.75. Macmillan.
Ritchie. Plato. $1.25. Scribner.

Plattner, K. F. Manual of qualitative and quantitative analysis with the blowpipe; tr. by H: B. Cornwall. 8th ed., rev. by F: Kolbeck. '02(My17) il. net, $4. Van Nostrand.

Plautus. Mostellaria; notes by E. W. Fay. '02(Ag2) 12°, (Coll. Latin ser.) *$1 net. Allyn & B.

Play away. Allen, W. B. **75 c. net. Estes.

PLAYS.
Nichberg-Wagner. Im freundes kreise. $1. Stechert.
See also Drama and dramatists.

PLEADING AND PRACTICE.
Cockcroft, *ed.* Encyc. of forms for pleading and practice. v. 15. $6. Cockcroft
Collins. Municipal ct. practice act, annot. $5. Banks.
McKinney. Encyc. of pleading and practice. v. 22, 23. ea., $6. E: Thompson.
Young *and* Keen. Problems in practice and pleading at the common law. 50 c. Mudge.
See also Actions at law.

Pleasures of life. Lubbock, *Sir* J: $1. Burt.

Pleistocene glacial formations. *See* Chamberlin, T: C.

PLUMBING.
Bjorling. Pipes and tubes. $1. Macmillan.
Lawler. Modern plumbing. $5. Popular.

Plummer, Ma. W. Hints to small libraries. 3d ed., rev. and enl. '02(My17) sq. O. net, 50 c. M. W. Plummer.

Pocket Gray. Cotterell, E: net, $1.25. Wood.

Poco a poco. Johnson, W: F. $1.50. Saalfield.

Poe, Edg. A. Works. '02(Ap5) 4 v., 12°, hf. cf., $8. Burt.

Poe, Edg. A. Poems and tales; sel. and ed. by A. G. Newcomer. '02(Ag9) S. (Lake Eng. classics.) 30 c. Scott, F. & Co.

Poe, Edg. A. Gold bug; ed. by T. Gildemeister. '02(Ag2) il. 16°, (Canterbury classics.) 25 c. Rand, McN. & Co.

Poe, Edg. A. Murders in the Rue Morgue, and other tales. '02(Mr29) il. 12°, (Home lib.) $1. Burt.

Poems of life and loving. Shelley, H. S. $1. Neely.

POETRY.
Garnett, Vallée *and* Brandl, *eds.* Universal anthology. v. 31-33. ea., $3.50. Merrill & B.
Lang, *ed.* Cancioneiro Gallego-Castelhano: extant Galician poems. *$3 net. Scribner.
Liddell. Introd. to the scientific study of Eng. poetry. net, $1.25. Doubleday, P.
See also Ballads;—Metre;—Quotations.

POETS.
Thackeray *and* Stone, *eds.* Pre-Victorian poets. $2.50.—Victorian poets. net, $2. Lane.

Point of honour. Hinkson, H. A. $1.50. McClurg.

POISONS.
Vaughan *and* Novey. Cellular toxins. *$3 net. Lea.

Poland, W: Find the church. '02(Mr8) 8°, pap., net, 5 c. Herder.

Poland, W: Socialism; its economic aspect. '02(Je28) 8°, pap., net, 5 c. Herder.

Policeman Flynn. Flower, E. $1.50. Century Co.

POLICY.
See Fortune-tellers.

POLITICAL ECONOMY.
Gladden. Social salvation. net, $1. Houghton, M. & Co.
Grenell. Economic tangles. $1. Purdy.
Laughlin. Elements of political economy. $1.20. Am. Bk.
Patten. Theory of prosperity. net, $1.25. Macmillan.
Phillips. Methods of keeping the public money of the U. S. $1. Mich. Pol. Sci.
Rowell. Pure economy. 10 c. Free Socialist.
Sidgwick. Principles of political economy. net, $4.50. Macmillan.
See also Capital and labor;—Charities;—Credit;—Finance;—Prosperity; — Socialism; — Tariff;—Taxation;—Trusts.

Political freshman. James, B. W. $1.50. Bushrod Lib.

Political primer. Fielde, A. M. 75 c.; 50 c. League Pol. Educ.

POLITICAL SCIENCE.
Ashley. American federal state. net, $2. Macmillan.
Bardeen. Manual of civics for N. Y. schools. net, $1. Bardeen.
Bourne. Teaching of history and civics. $1.50. Longmans.
Dunning. Hist. of political theories, ancient and mediæval. net, $2.50. Macmillan.
Forman. First lessons in civics. 60 c. Am. Bk.
Kellogg. Elements of civil government. 25 c. Kellogg.
Martin. Civil government in U. S. 90 c. Am. Bk.
Meyer. Nominating systems; direct primaries vs. conventions in the U. S. net, $1.50. E. C. Meyer.
See also Citizenship; — Crime and criminals; — Democracy; — Feudalism; — Municipal government;—Reciprocity;—*also* names of states and countries.

Politzer, A. *See* Brühl, G.

Pollak, Gustav, *ed.* Our success in child-training. '02(Ag9) 12°, $1. Contemporary.

Pollock, *Sir* F: Revised reports. v. 46-51. '01- '02(F15) 8°, shp. or hf. cf., ea., net, $6. Little, B. & Co.

POLO.
Miller. Modern polo. *$5 net. Scribner.

Polyphase apparatus. *See* Oudin, M. A.

Pomeroy, C. P., *rep.* *See* California. *Sup. ct.* Repts.

PONTIAC'S WAR.
See Indians.

Poole, R. L. *See* Maitland, F: W:

Poole, Stanley Lane. Story of Cairo. '02 (My24) il. 12°, (Mediæval towns ser.) $2; leath., $2.50. Macmillan.

Poore, B: P., *and* Tiffany, O. H. Life of U. S. Grant. '02(Jl19) 12°, (Biog. of famous men.) $1. Donohue.

Poore, G: V. The earth in rel. to the preservation and destruction of contagia. (Milroy lectures); with other papers on sanitation. '02(Ag2) D. $1.75. Longmans.

Poor's manual of the railroads of the U. S. 1901. '01- '02(F22) 8°, $10. Poor.

POPES.
Mann. Lives of the popes in early Middle Ages. v. 1, pt. 1. net, $3. Herder.

Popular girl. Baldwin, M. net, $1.20. Lippincott.

Popular hand-books. 50 c. Penn Pub. Co.
—Bechtel, *comp.* Proverbs, maxims and phrases.
—Eldridge. Hypnotism.
—Fowler. Electricity.

PORCELAIN.
See Ceramics.

Porter, Ctte., *and* Clarke, Helen A. Shakespeare studies: Macbeth. '01· '02(Ja4) S. 56 c. Am. Bk.

Portiuncula. Indulgence of portiuncula; fr. the German. New ed. '02(Je28) 48°, pap., 5 c. Herder.

PORTLAND CEMENT.
See Cement.

PORTRAITS.
Cust, *ed.* National portrait gallery. v. 1. subs., for complete work, net, $3. Cassell.

PORTUGAL.
Higgin. Spanish life; with chapters on Portuguese life by E. E. Street. net, $1.20. Putnam.

POTTER, Jennie O'Neil.
Diehl. Life of Jennie O'Neill Potter. $1. Blanchard.

POTTERY.
See Ceramics.

POULTRY.
Fiske, *comp.* Poultry appliances.—Poultry architecture. ea., 50 c. Judd.

Powell, Ja. B. Choralia: handy book for parochial precentors and choirmasters. '01· '02(F8) D. $1.50. Longmans.

Powell, Lewis. The twentieth century home builder. '02(Ap5) nar. D. pap., 25 c. Pub. Ho. M. E. Ch., So.

POWER.
Kerr. Power and power transmission. $2. Wiley.

Power of God's word. Prime, R. E. 3 c. Presb. Bd

Power that heals. Ballough, C: A. $1. Painter.

Powers, Harry H. Art of travel. '02(My17) D. pap., 25 c. Bu. Univ. Travel.

Poynter, E. F. Michael Ferrier. '02(Ap26) 12°, $1.50. Macmillan.

Practical electricity, with questions and answers. 3d ed. '01· '02(Mr29) il. 16°, leath., $2. Cleveland Armature.

Practical medicine ser. of year-books; ed. by G. P. Head. il. D. $1.50. Year Bk.
—Billings *and* Stanton, *eds.* General medicine. (1.)
—Dudley, *ed.* Gynecology. (4.)
—Murphy, *ed.* General surgery. (2.)
—Peterson *and* Lewis, *eds.* Obstetrics. (5.)
—Wood, *and others, eds.* Eye, ear, nose and throat. (3.)

Practice of immortality. Gladden, W. *25 c. net. Pilgrim Press.

PRAGUE.
Lützow. Story of Prague. $1.50; $2. Macmillan.

Pratt, H: S. Course in invertebrate zoölogy. '02(F15) il. O. $1.35. Ginn.

Pratt, Mara L. America's story for America's children. In 5 v. v. 5, Foundations of the Republic. '01· '02(Ja4) D. 40 c. Heath.

Pratt, Mara L. Stories of Illinois. '02 (Ag30) il. 16°, (Young folks' lib. of choice lit.) 50 c.; bds., 40 c. Educ. Pub.

Pratt, Rob. Perspective, incl. the projection of shadows and reflections. '01· '02(Mr8) il. F. bds., 90 c. Longmans.

Pratt, S: W. Life and Epistles of St. Paul. '02(F1) map, S. 75 c. Funk.

Pratt, Stephen R. Supp. to Mining laws of Colo., etc. '02(Ap5) O. pap., 35 c. Pratt Merc.

PRAYER.
Aitkin. Divine ordinance of prayer. $1.25. E. & J. B. Young.
McClure. A mighty means of usefulness: intercessory prayer. net, 50 c. Revell.
Talling. Communion with God. $1.25. Revell.
Worlledge. Prayer. $1.50. Longmans.
See also Lord's prayer;—Prayers;—Worship.

PRAYER-BOOK.
See Book of common prayer;—Church of England.

PRAYER-MEETINGS.
See Epworth League.

PRAYERS.
Breviarium bothanum sive portiforium secundum usum ecclesiæ cujusdam in Scotia. $15. Longmans.
Laache. Book of family prayer. $1.65; $2.25. Luth. Pub. Ho.

Pre-Victorian poets. Thackeray, F. St. J: $2.50. Lane.

PREACHING.
Barton, *comp.* Pulpit power and eloquence. $3.50. F. M. Barton.
Lyman. Preaching in the new age. net, 75 c. Revell.
See also Sermons.

Precept and practice. Bausman, B: net, $1. Heidelberg.

PRECIOUS METALS.
Del Mar. Hist. of the precious metals. net, $3. Cambridge.
See also Money.

PRECIOUS STONES.
Sommerville. Engraved gems. net, $1.50. Biddle.

Prentiss, *Mrs.* Eliz. ["Aunt Susan."] Little Susy stories. '02(Mr29) il. 12°, (Little women ser.) 75 c. Burt.

Prentiss, *Mrs.* Eliz. Six little princesses and what they turned into. '02(Je28) il. 12°, (St. Nicholas ser.) 75 c. Burt.

Preparatio; or, notes of preparation for holy communion. '01· '02(Ja11) D. $2. Longmans.

Presbyterian church. General Assembly; twentieth century addresses. '02(Je7) D. net, $1. Presb. Bd.

PRESBYTERIAN CHURCH.
Doyle. Presb. home missions. net, $1. Presb. Bd.
Erdman. The ruling elder. 3 c. Presb. Bd.
Stephens. Evolution of the confession of faith of the Cumberland Presb. church. 10 c. Cumberland.
See also Syracuse, First Presb. church.

Prescott, Alb. B:, *and* Sullivan, Eug. C. First book of qualitative chemistry for studies of water solution and mass action. 11th ed., rewritten. '02(My17) O. net, $1.50. Van Nostrand.

Prescott, W: H. Hist. of the conquest of Peru; ed. by J: F. Kirk. '02(Ap12) 2 v., 12°, (Bohn's standard lib.) net, $2. Macmillan.
Prescott, W: H. Hist. of the reign of Ferdinand and Isabella the Catholic. '02 (Ap12) 3 v., 12°, (Bohn's standard lib.) net, $3. Macmillan.
PRESCRIPTIONS.
Kuder. Medical prescription book. $2. Journal Pr.
See also Pharmacy.
PRESIDENTS.
See United States.
Presset, Anne L. Cherished thoughts in original poems and sketches. '01. '02 (My24) il. D. $1.50; im. mor., $1.75; full mor., $2.25. Skelton.
Prévost, Marcel. Frédérique; tr. by E. Marriage. '02(Mr8) D. $1.50. Crowell.
Price, E. D. Letters of Mildred's mother to Mildred. '01. '02(F15) 12°, $1. Ogilvie.
Price, Eleanor C. Angelot. '02(Ap5) il. D. $1.50. Crowell.
Price, Ja. A. Observations and exercises on the weather. '02(Ap26) O. pap., 30 c. Am. Bk.
Price, Lillian L. Wandering heroes. '02 (Ag23) 8°, (Stories of heroes.) 50 c. Silver.
Price inevitable. Sidner. A. L. $1. Popular.
PRIESTS.
Harper. Constructive studies in the priestly element in the O. T. $1. Univ. of Chic.
See also Catholic church.
Prime, Ralph E. Power of God's word. '02 (Je21) S. pap., 3 c. Presb. Bd.
PRIMERS.
Alger. Primer of work and play. 30 c. Heath.
Burt *and* Howells. Literary primer. net, 30 c. Scribner.
Kirk. Baldwin primer. 35 c. Am. Bk.
Primrose diplomacy. Hutchinson, J. $1.25. Abbey Press.
Prince Incognito. Latimer, *Mrs.* E. W. $1.50. McClurg.
Prince of good fellows. Barr, R. $1.50. McClure, P.
Prince of the captivity. Gregg, H. $1.50. L. C. Page.
Princess (The), *pseud.* *See* Lockett, M. F.
Princess. Tennyson, A. 25 c. Appleton.
Principles of western civilization. Kidd, B: net, $2. Macmillan.
Print-collector's handbook. Whitman, A. net, $5. Macmillan.
PRINTERS.
See Short, T:
PRINTING.
Morris. Art and craft of printing. $5. Elston Press.
Sheldon. Practical colorist. $8. Owl Press.
See also Photography;—Proof-reading.
Prisoners of the sea. Kingsley, *Mrs.* F. M. $1.25; 50 c. New Amsterdam.
PRISONS.
Howard. Prisoners of Russia. net, $1.40. Appleton.
Skinner. Prisons of the nation and their inmates. 10 c. Brooklyn Eagle.
Pritchard, W: A., *comp.* Wehman's how to become a naturalized citizen. '02(Mr8) S. pap., 10 c. Wehman.
Prize designs for rural school buildings. Coburn, F: N. 25 c. Kellogg.
Prize poetical speaker. '01- '02(Ja4) 12°, 75 c. Dickerman.
PROBATE.
See Wills.
PROBABILITIES.
Simon. Philosoph. essay on probabilities. $2. Wiley.
Problems in the use and adjustment of engineering instruments. 4th ed. rev. and enl. '02(Je21) 16°, $1.25. Wiley.
Professor Archie. Percival, L. 50 c. Nelson.
Professor at the breakfast table. Holmes. O. W. $1. Burt.
Progredior ser. sq. D. Flanagan.
—Beeman. Analysis of the Eng. sentence. 50 c.
Progress of dogma. Orr, J. $1.75. Armstrong.
Progression to immortality. Brooks, H: S. net, 50 c. Wessels.
PROJECTION.
See Perspective.
PROOF-READING.
Smith. Proof-reading and punctuation. *90 c. net. Adèle M. Smith.
PROPERTY.
See Real property.
PROPHECY.
Girdlestone. Grammar of prophecy. $2.50. E. & J. B. Young.
Prophet of the kingdom. Frisbie, H: S: $1.25. Neale.
Prose quotations. Allibone, S: A. $2.50. Lippincott.
PROSPERITY.
Seager. Prof. Patten's theory of prosperity. 15 c. Am. Acad. Pol. Sci.
PROSTITUTION.
Social (The) evil. net, $1.25. Putnam.
PROTESTANT EPISCOPAL CHURCH.
Francis. Weekly church teaching for the infants. 25 c. E. & J. B. Young.
Jarvis, *ed.* Sketches of church life in colonial Conn. $1. Tuttle, M. & T.
McCormick. Distinctive marks of the Episcopal church. 25 c. Young Churchman.
Miller. Amer. church dict. and cyclopedia. $1. Whittaker.
Parson's (The) handbook. net, $1.50. Young Churchman.
Peterkin. Hist. and record of Prot. Episc. Ch. in W. Va. $2.50; $10. Tribune Co.
Westcott. Catholic principles as il. in the doctrine, hist. and organ. of the Am. Cath. church. *$1.25 net. Young Churchman.
See also Catechisms;—Church of England;—Lent.
PROTESTANTISM.
Gibson. Protestant principles. 60 c. Armstrong.
PROTOZOA.
Chapman. The foraminifera: introd. to study of the protozoa. $3.50. Longmans.
Proudfoot, A. H. Year with the Mother-play; 2d year's study course of the League of Am. Mothers. '02(Je28) D. $1. Flanagan.
PROVERBS.
Bechtel, *comp.* Proverbs, maxims and phrases. 50 c. Penn Pub. Co.
Browne. Proverbial sayings. net, $1. Stokes.
See also Epigrams;—Quotations.

Providence Journal almanac for 1902. '02 (F8) 12°, pap., 10 c. Providence Journ.
Prozess (Der). *See* Fulda, L.
Prune, Nat. College chaps. '02(Je14) S. 75 c. Mutual Bk.
PSALMS.
See Bible.
PSYCHIATRY.
See Insanity.
PSYCHICAL RESEARCH.
Duff *and* Allen. Psychic research and gospel miracles. net, $1.50. Whittaker.
PSYCHOLOGY.
Baldwin. Social and ethical interpretations in mental development. net, $2.60. Macmillan.
Brinton. Basis of social relations. net, $1.50. Putnam.
Dewey. Psychology and social practice. net, 25 c. Univ. of Chic.
Mercier. Psychology, normal and morbid. net, $4. Macmillan.
Patrick. Psychology for teachers. $1. Educ. Pub.
Sidis. Psychopathological researches. *$3 net. Stechert.
Vance. Rise of a soul. net, $1. Revell.
Witmer. Analytical psychology. $1.60. Ginn.
See also Character; — Heredity; — Hypnotism; — Knowledge;—Mind and body; — Philosophy;— Phrenology;—Telepathy.
Public house reform. Cumming, A. N. $1. Scribner.
Public Ledger almanac, 1902; ed. by G: W. C. Drexel. '01. '02(Ja11) S. pap., gratis to subs. of *Public Ledger*. Drexel.
PUBLISHERS.
See Booksellers.
Publishers' trade list annual, 1902. '02(Ag23) Q, *$1.50 net; in 2 v., with index, $5 net. Pub. Weekly.
Puddicombe, *Mrs.* Beynon. *See* Raine, A.
Pullen, *Mrs.* Elisabeth. Mr. Whitman. '02 (My17) D. $1.50. Lothrop.
Pulpit power and eloquence. Barton, F: $3.50. F. M. Barton.
PULSE.
See Heart.
PUNCTUATION.
See Proof-reading.
Purdy, L. Burdens of local taxation and who bears them. '01. '02(Ja11) D. 25 c. Public Policy.
Purdy, L. Local option in taxation. '02 (F15) D. pap., 10 c. Tax Reform.
Pure economy. Rowell, J. H. 10 c. Free Socialist.
Puron, Juan G. Lector moderno de Appleton, nos. 1-3. '01. '02(F22) 12°, bds., no. 1, 25 c.; no. 2, 35 c.; no. 3, 45 c. Appleton.
Purves, G: T. Faith and life: sermons. '02 (Je7) D. net, $1.25. Presb. Bd.
Purves, G: T. Joy in service. '01. '02(Ja4) D. 50 c. Am. Tr.
PUSEY, Edw. Bouverie.
Grafton. Pusey and the church revival. net, 50 c. Young Churchman.
Putnam, Israel. Daniel Everton, volunteer-regular. '02(My3) il. D. net, $1.20. Funk.
PUTNAM, Rufus.
Earle. Rutland home of Maj. Gen. Rufus Putnam. 30 c.; 50 c. S. C. Earle.
Putnam's lib. of standard literature. D. $1.75. Putnam.
—Chesterfield. Letters to his son.
—Swift. Journal to Stella.
Putnam's science ser. 8°, net. Putnam.
—Brinton. Basis of social relations. $1.50.
PUZZLES.
See Riddles.
Pyeshkoff, Alexéi M. *See* Górky, M.
Pyle, Howard. Some merry adventures of Robin Hood. '02(Je7) il. D. (Ser. of school reading.) net, 60 c. Scribner.
Pyle, Kath. Careless Jane, and other tales. '02(My10) 12°, net, 75 c. Dutton.
Q., *pseud.* *See* Couch, A. T: Quiller-.
Quad, M., *pseud.* *See* Lewis, C: B.
Quadrupani, R. P. Light and peace; from the Fr. 3d ed. '02(Mr8) 12°, net, 50 c. Herder.
Quaker experiment in government. Sharpless, I: $1.50. Ferris.
QUAKERS.
See Friends (Society of).
Quaku. Quinius, H. F. 3 c. J: G. Quinius.
Quang Chang Ling. Why should the Chinese go? '02(Je7) 8°, pap., 25 c. Cambridge.
Quayle, W: A. The gentleman in literature. '02(My24) por. D. (Hero ser., no. 4.) net, 25 c. Jennings.
Quayle. W: A. A hero—Jean Valjean. '02 (Ap26) D. (Hero ser., no. 1.) net, 25 c. Jennings.
Quayle, W: A. King Cromwell. '02(My24) il. D. (Hero ser., no. 6.) net, 25 c. Jennings.
Queen of the household. Ellsworth, T. $2.50. Ellsworth.
Queer people. Bishop, W: H: $1. Street.
Quentin Durward. Scott, *Sir* W. net, 60 c. Macmillan.
Questions of the day. D. Putnam.
—Labor and capital. $1.50. (98.)
Quiberon touch. Brady, C. T. $1.50. Appleton.
Quick, M. I. Complete guide to ball room dancing. '02(My17) 12°, 50 c.; pap., 25 c. Donohue.
Quincy word list. Parlin, F. E. 24 c. Morse.
Quinius, Augusta. Mother Margaret's bunch of flowers. '02(Mr1) T. pap., 5 c. J: G. Quinius.
Quinius, H. F. *and* Augusta. Quaku. '02 (Je28) T. pap., 3 c. J: G. Quinius.
Quiz books. S. pap., 50 c. Byrne.
—Shipp. Questions and answers on contracts.
QUOTATIONS.
Allibone. Poetical quotations.—Prose quotations. ea., $2.50. Lippincott.
Rab and his friends. Brown, J: 25 c. Rand, McN. & Co.
Racine, Jean B. Athalie; ed., with notes, by E: S. Joynes. New enl. ed. '02(F1) D. (Students' ser. of classic Fr. plays, no. 2.) net, 35 c. Holt.
Racine, Jean B. Athalie: ed. by F. C. de Sumichrast. '02(Jl12) 12°, (French classics.) *60 c. net. Macmillan.
Racine, Jean B. Esther: ed., with notes, by E: S. Joynes. [New ed.] '02(F8) D. (Students' ser. of classic Fr. plays, no. 5.) net, 35 c. Holt.
Radcliffe, G: L. P. Governor Thomas H. Hicks of Maryland and the Civil war. '01. '02(Mr8) O. (Johns Hopkins Univ. studies, 19th ser., nos. 11-12.) pap., 50 c. Johns Hopkins.

Rader, Perry S., *rep.* *See* Missouri. *Sup. ct.* Repts.
RADIATION.
Brace, *ed.* Laws of radiation and absorption. $1. Am. Bk.
See also Heat;—Light;—Sound.
Railroad repts. (v. 24, Am. and Eng. railroad cases;) ed. by T: J. Michie. v. 1. '02(Je7) O. shp., $5. Michie.
Railroading with Christ. Dwight, C: A. S. $1. Am. Tr.
RAILROADS.
Adams. Block system of signalling. $2. Railroad Gazette.
American and Eng. railroad cases. v. 23. ea., $5. Michie.
American street railway investments. $5. Street R'way.
Bodmer. Inspection of railway materials. $1.50. Macmillan.
Goodknight. Modern association and railroading. 50 c. Abbey Press.
Hanford. Railroading in the U. S. 5 c. Socialistic Co-op.
Knapp. Government ownership of railroads. 15 c. Am. Acad. Pol. Sci.
Meyer. Advisory councils in railway administration. 15 c. Am. Acad. Pol. Sci.
New York. Statutory revision of the laws affecting railroads. $1.50; $2. Banks & Co.
Newcomb. Concentration of railway control. 15 c. Am. Acad. Pol. Sci.
Poor's manual of railroads of the U. S., 1901. $10. Poor.
Talbot. Railway transition spiral. $1.50. Van Nostrand.
Weyl. Passenger traffic of railways. $1.50; $1. [Univ. of Penn.] Ginn.
See also Air brake;—Cars;—Locomotives;—Street railroads;—*also* Cincinnati Southern railway;—Siberian railway.
Raine, Allen, [*pseud.* for *Mrs.* Beynon Puddicombe.] A Welsh witch. '02(Je7) D. (Town and country lib., no. 312.) $1; pap., 50 c. Appleton.
Rainsford, W: S. Reasonableness of faith, and other addresses. '02(My10) O. net, $1.25. Doubleday, P.
Rainy, Rob. Ancient Catholic church from accession of Trajan to the Fourth General Council, A.D. 98-451. '02(F1) O. (Internat. theol. lib.) net, $2.50. Scribner.
Rait, Rob. S. Five Stuart princesses. '02 (Mr29) il. 8°, net, $3.50. Dutton.
Raleigh, *Sir* Wa. The last fight of the "Revenge" at sea. '02(My10) 4°, net, $6. Houghton, M. & Co.
Ralph Granger's fortunes. Brown, W: P. $1. Saalfield.
Ramabai Sarasvati, *Pundita.* High-caste Hindu woman. '02(Mr22) 12°, net, 75 c. Revell.
Ramal, Wa. Songs of childhood. '02(Ap19) il. S. net, $1.20. Longmans.
Rambler's note-book at the Eng. lakes. Rawnsley, H. D. $2. Macmillan.
RAMONA.
Hufford. The real Ramona of Helen Hunt Jackson's famous novel. 35 c.; 75 c.; $1: $1.25 D: A. Hufford.
Ramsay, A. M. Pharmacopœia of the Glasgow Royal Infirmary Ophthalmic Inst. '02 12°, *$1.25 net. Macmillan.
Ramsey, M. M. Spanish grammar, with exercise. '02(My17) D. net, $1.50. Holt.
Rand, McNally & Co.'s pictorial guide to Washington and environs. '02(Ag9) il. 16°, pap., 25 c. Rand, McN. & Co.
Rand, McNally's new century readers by grades. il. Rand, McN. & Co.
—Perdue. New century 1st reader. 17 c.
Randall, Wyatt W., *ed. and tr.* Expansion of gases by heat. '02(Ap19) O. (Scientific memoirs.) $1. Am. Bk.
Rankin, A. C. Saloon law nullification and its cure. '02(My17) 16°, 50 c. Advance.
Rankin, A. W. *See* Aiton, G:
Rankin, J. E. Esther Burr's journal. 2d ed. '02(Jl12) sq. S. pap., 75 c. Howard Univ.
Ranson's folly. Davis, R: H. †$1.50. Scribner.
RAPHAEL.
Hubbard. Raphael. 25 c. Roycrofters.
Rapp, J: M. Geographical outline manual of North America. '02(Ag2) 8°, pap., 35 c. J: M. Rapp.
Rasselas. *See* Johnson, S:
Rataplan, a rogue elephant. Velvin, E. **$1.25 net. Altemus.
RATIONALISM.
Hurst. Hist. of rationalism. $2.50. Eaton & M.
Rawlins, Ja. M. *See* Lippincott's elem. algebra.
Rawnsley, H. D. A rambler's note-book at the Eng. lakes. '02(Ag2) il. 12°, $2. Macmillan.
Rawson, C., Gardner, W. M., *and* **Laycock**, W. F. Dict. of dyes, mordants, and other compounds. '01- '02(F15) 8°, net, $5. Lippincott.
Raycroft, B: J. Sermons on the stations of the cross, the Our Father, Hail Mary, etc. '02(Je7) 8°, net, $1.50. Pustet.
Read, Opie P., ["Arkansaw traveller."] The Starbucks. '02(Ag2) il. D. $1.50. Laird.
READERS AND SPEAKERS.
Allen. Children of the palm lands. 50 c. Educ. Pub.
American speaker. 50 c. Conkey.
Blaisdell. Child life fifth reader. net, 45 c. Macmillan.
Bradish. Stories of country life. 40 c. Am. Bk.
Brown. Am. star speaker and model elocutionist. $1.50. Donohue.
Burke. Literature and art books. Bks. 1-3. bk. 1, 25 c.; bk. 2, 30 c.; bk. 3, 35 c. McBride.
Cady *and* Dewey. Art reader, no. 1. 35 c. Richardson, S.
Calmerton *and* Wheeler. First reader. 30 c. W: H: Wheeler.
Carpenter. Europe. 70 c. Am. Bk.
Cyr. Advanced 1st reader. 35 c. Ginn.
Cyr. Readers, bks. 7, 8. ea., 45 c. Ginn.
Edgerly. Natural reader. $1.50. Ralston.
Funk *and* Moses, *eds.* Standard first reader. 35 c. Funk.
George. Little journey to Belgium and Denmark:—Switzerland. ea., 15 c. Flanagan.
Gyim. Chinese-Eng. elem. reader and arithmetic. $1.25. Taylor & M.

READERS AND SPEAKERS.—*Continued.*
Haliburton *and* Norvell. Graded classics: 2d reader, 35 c.; 3d reader, 40 c. B. F. Johnson.
Hart *and* Hazard. Source readers in Am. history. no. 1. *40 c. net. Macmillan.
Hollinshed. New century speaker, writer and etiquette. $1.50. Am. Bk. and Bible.
Judson *and* Bender, *eds.* Graded literature readers. bks. 6-8. ea., 50 c. Maynard, M. & Co.
La Rame. Child of Urbino, Raphael: 3d reader. 30 c. Educ. Pub.
McCullough. Little stories for little people. 25 c. Am. Bk.
Macmillan's new geog. readers: Africa and Australasia. net, 40 c. Macmillan.
Macmillan's new hist. readers; Senior. net, 50 c. Macmillan.
Murché. Rural readers. net, 40 c. Macmillan.
Perdue. New century first reader. 17 c. Rand, McN. & Co.
Prize poetical speaker. 75 c. Dickerman.
Shepard. Life on the farm: reading book. 50 c. Flanagan.
Sterling, *and others, eds.* Nature and life. 4th reader, pt. 1. 32 c.; in 2 pts., 56 c. Globe Sch. Bk.
Taylor. School readers: 2d reader. 35 c. Werner Sch. Bk.
Thompson. New century readers. 3d bk. 52 c. Morse
Toward the rising sun. 30 c. Ginn.
Virden. First science reader. 25 c.; 10 c. Flanagan.
Welsh. Colonial days. 50 c. Educ. Pub.
Whitcomb. Little journey to Italy.—Scotland. ea., 15 c. Flanagan.
Wide world. 30 c. Ginn.
See also Primers;—Recitations.

READING.
See Books and reading.

Reading character from handwriting. Hagen, H. v. $1. Graphology.

REAL PROPERTY.
Newell. Elements of law of real property. $4. Flood.
Pattee, *comp.* Authorities, deductions, and notes in real property. $2. Univ. Press.
Warvelle. American law of vendor and purchaser of real property. v. 1, 2. $12. Callaghan.
Washburn. Am. law of real property. 3 v. net, $18. Little, B. & Co.
See also Conveyancing;—Land;—Sale;—Taxation.

Real Ramona. Hufford, D: A. 35 c.; 75 c.; $1; $1.25. D: A. Hufford.
Realm of the retailer. Saley, M. L. $1.50. Am. Lumberman.
Reasonableness of faith. Rainsford, W: S. net, $1.25. Doubleday, P.
Rebuilding of old commonwealths. Page, W. H. net, $1. Doubleday, P.

RECEIPTS.
See Cookery.

RECIPROCITY.
Farquhar. Manufacturers' needs of reciprocity. 15 c. Am. Acad. Pol. Sci.

RECITATIONS.
Birbeck, *ed.* Select recitations, orations, etc. $1. Wagner.

RECITATIONS.—*Continued.*
Brown, *comp.* Comic recitations.—Patriotic recitations. ea., 50 c.; 25 c. Donohue.
Clark, *ed.* Hdbk. of best readings. **$1.50 net. Scribner.
Monroe, *ed.* Public and parlor readings. 4 v. ea., $1. Lee & S.
See also Readers and speakers.

Reconciliation of Randall Claymore. Barnes, E. N. C. $1. Earle.
Reconstruction and the constitution. Burgess, J: W. net, $1. Scribner.
Recreations of the German emigrants. *See* Goethe, J. W. v.
Recruit Tommy Collins. Bonesteel, M. 45 c. Benziger.
Red anvil. Sherlock, C: R. $1.50. Stokes.
Red letter ser. il. 12°, $1.25; pap., 50 c. New Amsterdam.
—Kingsley. Prisoners of the sea.
—Marchmont. Miser Hoadley's secret.
—Russell. Captain Fanny.
Red Saunders. Phillips, H: W. $1.25. McClure, P.
Redfield, Amasa A., *ed.* Repts. of cases Surrogates' cts. of New York. In 5 v., v. 1. '01- '02(My17) 8°. shp., per v., $6. Banks & Co.
Reduction tables. Blum, A. R. net, $3. Am. Code.
Reed, Edn. Bacon and Shake-speare parallelisms. '02(Ap26) O. bds., net, $2.50. Goodspeed.
Reed, Edn. Francis Bacon, our Shakespeare. '02(Ap26) il. O. bds., net, $2. Goodspeed.
Reed, Eliphalet A. Idea of God in relation to theology. '02(F15) 8°, pap., net, 75 c. Univ. of Chic.
Reed, J: O., *and* Guthe, K. E. Manual of physical measurements. '02(Ap12) O. $1.50. Wahr.
Reference catalogue of current literature. Whitaker, J. 2 v. *$5 net. Pub. Weekly.

REFORM.
See Temperance.

REFORMATION (The).
See Church history;—Huguenots.

REFORMED CHURCH.
Good. Historical handbk. of Ref. Ch. in U. S. 50 c.; 25 c. Heidelberg.
Good. Women of the Ref. Ch. $1. Heidelberg.

REGENERATION.
Sloan. Social regeneration the work of Christianity. net, 60 c. Westminster.
See also Salvation.

Regiments and armories of Mass. Hall, C: W. per set, $12; $18; $25. W. W. Potter.
Regional anatomy of head and neck. Eckley, W: T. net, $2.50. Lea.
Reid, *Sir* Wemyss. William Black, novelist. '02(Ap26) D. net, $2.25. Harper.
Reinsch, Paul S. Colonial government. '02 (Je21) D. (Citizen's lib. of economics, politics and sociology.) net, $1.25. Macmillan.
Religio medici. Browne, *Sir* T: **$12 net. Lane.

RELIGION.
Delitzsch. Babel and the Bible. *50 c. net. Open Court.
De Solla. Fallacies of religion. 25 c. Pierce & Z.

RELIGION.—*Continued.*
Jastrow. Study of religion. $1.50. Scribner.
Spalding. Religion, agnosticism and education. net, 80 c. McClurg.
Tolstoï. What is religion? net, 60 c. Crowell.
See also Natural religion;—Revivals;—Skepticism.
RELIGION AND SCIENCE.
Bixby. The new world and the new thought. net, $1. Whittaker.
Smyth. Through science to faith. net, $1.50. Scribner.
See also Evolution;—Natural religion.
Religion for the time. Conger, A. B. net, $1. Jacobs.
Religion of Bible lands. Margoliouth, D: S: 60 c Armstrong.
Religion of capital. Lafarque, P. 10 c. Socialistic Co-op.
Religion of Israel. Greenstone, J. H. 50 c. Bloch.
Religion of science lib. D. pap. Open Court.
—Kant. Prolegomena to any future metaphysics. 50 c. (53.) Open Court.
—Leibniz. Discourse on metaphysics. 35 c. (52.)
RELIGIONS.
Chantepie de la Saussaye. Religion of the Teutons. $2.50. Ginn.
Martin. Traces of the elder faiths of Ireland. 2 v. $12. Longmans.
See also Christianity;—Oriental religions.
Religious and social work amongst girls. Freeman, F. L. net, $1. Whittaker.
RELIGIOUS LIBERTY.
Cobb. Rise of rel. liberty in America. net, $4. Macmillan.
Religious life and influence of Queen Victoria. Walsh, W. net, $2.50. Dutton.
Reliques of Stratford-on-Avon. Way, A. E. net, 50 c.; net, 75 c. Lane.
REMBRANDT, H. van Rijn.
Bell. Rembrandt van Rijn. $1.75. Macmillan.
Remedies of the Great Physician. Kohaus, H. M. 40 c. Alliance.
Remedy for love. Kirk, *Mrs.* E. O. $1.25. Houghton, M. & Co.
Remembered days. Kenyon, J. B. $1. Eaton & M.
Reminiscences of a dramatic critic. Clapp, H: A. net, $1.75. Houghton, M. & Co.
Remsen, Ira. Introd. to the study of chemistry. 6th rev., enl. ed. '01. '02(Mr15) D. (Am. sci. ser.; briefer course.) $1.12. Holt.
Remy, Arth. F. J. Influence of India and Persia on the poetry of Germany. '02(F1) 8°, (Columbia Univ. Germanic studies, v. 1, no. 4.) pap., net, $1. Macmillan.
RENAISSANCE.
Smeaton. The Medici and the Italian Renaissance. $1.25. Scribner.
See also names of countries.
Renaissance of the vocal art. Myer, E. J. $1. Boston Music.
Rénan, J. Ernest. Life of Jesus. '02(Jl12) 12°, (Home lib.) $1. Burt.
Renan, J. Ernest. Souvenirs d' enfance et de jeunesse; ed. by I. Babbitt. '02(Mr8) D. (Modern lang. ser.) 75 c. Heath.
REPENTANCE.
See Confession.

Representative men. Emerson, R: W. $1. Burt.
REPTILES.
Seeley. Dragons of the air: extinct flying reptiles. net, $1.40. Appleton.
See also Amphibia.
Republic of Plato. *See* Nettleship, R: L.—Plato.
REPUBLICAN PARTY.
Halstead. Victorious republicanism. $1.50; $2.25. Dominion.
Rescue (The). Sedgwick, A. D. $1.50. Century Co.
RESURRECTION.
Swartz. Easter and the resurrection. net, 15 c. Revell.
See also Future life;—Jesus Christ.
Retail advertising. Farrington, F. net, $1. Baker & T.
Retzius, G. *See* Nordenskiold, G.
Reuben Green's experience in a large city. Culp, H: T. 25 c. H: T. Culp.
REVELATION (Book of).
See Bible.
Revelations from the eternal world given to one of the mystic brotherhood. no. 1. '02 (Jl19) sq. S. pap., 20 c. Star.
REVERE, Paul.
Andrews. Paul Revere and his engraving. $23.50; $40. Scribner.
Revised repts. *See* Pollock, *Sir* F:
REVIVALS.
Oliver. Soul-winners' secrets: revival textbook. 25 c. Jennings.
Strong. The next great awakening. 75 c. Baker & T.
Rewards of taste. Bridge, N. $1.50. H. S. Stone.
Reynolds, Alphæus. Rudiments of Latin. '02 (Ap26) D. $1.25. A. B. Reynolds.
Reynolds, Cuyler. The banquet book. '02 (Ap12) il. D. net, $1.75. Putnam.
REYNOLDS, *Sir* Joshua.
Keeling. Sir Joshua Reynolds. *$1.25 net. Scribner.
Reynolds, O. Papers on mechanical and physical subjects. v. 2, 1881-1900. '02 (Ap26) 8°, net, $6. Macmillan.
Rhead, E. L., *and* Sexton, A. H. Assaying and metallurgical analysis. '02(Ap19) il. O. $4.20. Longmans.
Rhead, L:, *ed.* Speckled brook trout, by various experts with rod and reel. '02 (Mr29) O. net. $3.50. Russell.
Rheingold. Wagner, R: 75 c. Newson.
RHETORIC.
Kellogg. How to teach composition writing. 25 c. Kellogg.
Lockwood. Teachers' manual to accompany Composition and rhetoric. 30 c. Ginn.
Peterson. First steps in Eng. composition. 35 c. Flanagan.
Scott. Composition literature. $1. Allyn & B.
Thornton. Eng. composition. 75 c. Crowell.
RHODE ISLAND.
Smith, J. J., *comp.* Civil and military list of R. I., 1800-1850. net, $7.50. Preston.
See also Block Island.
RHODES, Cecil.
Hensman. Cecil Rhodes. net, $5. Harper.

Rhodes, J. F. Hist. of the U. S. from compromise of 1850. '02(Ag2) 4 v., 12°, ea., *$2.50 net. Macmillan.
Rhodes, W. G. Elem. treatise on alternating currents. '02(Mr8) il. O. $2.60. Longmans.
RHODESIA.
See Matabeleland.
Rhone, Rosamond D. Days of the Son of man. '02(My24) D. net, $1.20. Putnam.
Rhymes from time to time. Doane, W: C. $1.50. Albany Diocesan Press.
Rhymes, jingles and fables. Norton, C: E. 25 c. Heath.
Rice, Edn. W. Our sixty-six sacred books. 10th ed., enl., with analysis and questions. '02(F1) D. (Green fund book, no. 10.) net, 50 c. Am. S. S.
Rice, Edn. W. Short hist. of the Internat. lesson system, with classified list of lessons for thirty-three years; prep. by C. R. Williams. '02(Jl19) S. leath., *25 c. net. Amer. S. S.
Rice, Elmer C: Robinson method of breeding squabs. '01. '02(Mr15); 2d ed., rev. with supp. (Je28) il. 12°, pap., ea., 50 c. Plymouth Rock
Richard, Marg. A. Darkey ways in Dixie '02(Ap26) il. D. $1. Abbey Press.
Richards, Ellen H., *and* Williams, Louise H. '02(Ap19) 8°, net, $1.50. Wiley.
Richards, *Mrs.* Laura E. H. Mrs. Tree. Handy vol. ed. '02(Jl12) il. S. †75 c. Estes.
Richardson, J: War of 1812; with notes and a life of author, by A. C. Casselman. '02 (Ap26) il. O. subs., $3. Hist. Pub.
Riddell, J: H., *rep.* *See* New Hampshire. *Sup. ct.* Repts.
Riddle of life. Johnston, J. W. $1.50. Jennings.
RIDDLES.
Cutter, *comp.* Conundrums, riddles, puzzles and games. 50 c.; 25 c. Otis.
Ride in Morocco. Macnab, F. $5. Longmans.
Rideal, S: Sewage and the bacterial purification of sewage. 2d ed. '02(Ap5) 8°, $3.50. Wiley.
Ridgeway, *Major*, [*pseud.* for W: Ross Hartpence.] Early recollections of James Whitcomb Riley. '02(Ag23) sq. S. pap., 50 c. W: R. Hartpence.
Ridpath, J: C. Hist. of the U. S. '01. '02 (F15) 4 v. in 2 v., il. 12°, $6. Grosset.
Riehl, W. H. Das spielmannskind und stumme ratsherr; ed. by G: M. Priest. '02(F15) D. 35 c. Am. Bk.
RIFLE.
Fremantle. Book of the rifle. $5. Longmans.
Rigby, Will O. Reliable candy teacher and soda and ice cream formulas. [8th ed., rev. and enl.] '02(Ap12) D. pap., $2. W. O. Rigby.
Riggs, *Mrs.* G: C. *See* Wiggin, *Mrs.* K. D.
Riggs, Sara M. Studies in United States history. '02(Ag9) D. 65 c. Ginn.
Right living. Morris, E. G. $1. Bardeen.
Right reading; counsel on the choice and use of books sel. fr. ten famous authors. '02 (Mr15) S. net, 80 c. McClurg
Rights and wrongs of the Transvaal war Cook, E: T. $2. Longmans.

RILEY, Ja. W.
Ridgeway. Early recollections of James Whitcomb Riley. 50 c. W: R. Hartpence.
Rime of the ancient mariner. Coleridge, S: T. 30 c.; 25 c. B. F. Johnson.
Rine, G: W. Essentials of our language. '02 (Ag30) 12°, 75 c. Pacific Press.
Ringing questions. Peck, G: C. $1. Eaton & M.
Rip Van Winkle. *See* Irving, W.
Rise and development of Chr. architecture. Ayer, J. C. net, $1.50. Young Churchman.
Rise of a soul. Vance, J. J. net, $1. Revell.
Rise of religious liberty in America. Cobb, S. H. net, $4. Macmillan.
Rita, *pseud.* *See* Humphreys, *Mrs.* E. M. J. G.
Ritchie, D: G. Plato. '02(Ap12) D. (World's epoch-makers.) $1.25. Scribner.
Ritchie, D: G. Studies in political and social ethics. '02(Mr29) 12°, $1.50. Macmillan.
Ritchie, M. J. G., *and* Harrison, W. Table tennis, and how to play it. '02(Je7) il. sq. S. 50 c. Lippincott.
Ritchie, M. J. G., *and* Parker, A. Ping-pong; ed. for Am. players by W. H. Bronson. '02 (My3) il. S. 50 c. Street.
RITUAL.
See Ministers (*of the Gospel*).
Rivas, Evelyn de. Little French dinners. '02 (My24) 12°, 50 c. New Amsterdam.
Riverside art ser. D. net, 75 c.; School ed., net, 50 c.; pap., net, 35 c. Houghton, M. & Co.
—Hurll, *ed.* Tuscan sculpture. (11.)—Van Dyck. (12.)
Riverside biog. ser. S. net, 65 c.; School ed., net, 50 c. Houghton, M. & Co.
—Brown. Stephen A. Douglas. (13.)
—Sedgwick. Samuel de Champlain. (14.)
Riverside literature ser. S. pap., net, 15 c. Houghton, M. & Co.
—Ewing. Jackanapes; [also] The brownies.
—La Rame. Dog of Flanders and Nürnberg stove. (150.)
—Shakespeare. Twelfth night. (149.)
Riverside pap. ser. 16°, pap., 50 c. Houghton, M. & Co.
—Burnham. A great love.
Rives, Hallie E. Hearts courageous. '02 (Je7) il. D. $1.50. Bowen-M.
ROADS.
Judson. City roads and pavements. $2. Engineering News.
Spalding. Text-book on roads and pavements. $2. Wiley.
See also Railroads;—Street-railroads.
Rob Roy. *See* Sullivan, *Sir* E:
Robb, Hunter. Aseptic surgical technique. 2d ed., rev. '02(Jl19) il. 12°, $2. Lippincott.
Robbins, *Mrs.* S. S. Miss Ashton's new pupil. '02(Ap5) 12°, (Fireside ser.) $1. Burt
Roberts, C: G: D. Kindred of the wild. '02 (Je7) il. O. $2. L. C. Page.
Roberts, C: G: D. Poems. [New issue.] '02(My10) D. $1.50. L. C. Page.
Roberts, Fk. H. H. The nation and the state: civil government of Ohio. '02(Ag9) il. 16°, (Nation and the state ser., no. 2.) $1. Bardeen.

Roberts, Morley. Way of a man. '02(Ag9) D. (Town and country lib., no. 314.) †$1; pap., 50 c. Appleton.

ROBERTS, John.
Camm Benedictine martyr in England: life and times of Dom John Roberts. net, $1.25. Herder.

Roberts, O. A. Hist. of the Military Company of the Mass., now called the Ancient and Honorable Artillery Co. of Mass., 1637-1888. In 4 v. v. 4. '01. '02(Mr22) 4°. [Sold only to members.] Mudge.

Robertson, A. I. Lessons on the Gospel of St. Mark. '02(Ap12) nar. 16°, net, 40 c. Revell.

Robertson, Harrison. The opponents. '02 (Ap19) D. $1.50. Scribner.

Robertson, Ja. Early religion of Israel. '02 (Ap12) 12°, net, $1.60. Whittaker.

Robertson, Leslie S. Water-tube boilers. '01. '02(Ja4) il. O. $3. Van Nostrand.

Robertson, W: Studies in the Acts of the Apostles. '02(F8) 16°, 40 c. Revell.

ROBESPIERRE, Max. M. I.
Belloc. Robespierre. net, $2. Scribner.

Robin Hood. *See* Pyle, H.

Robins, E: Chasing an iron horse. '02(Ag9) il. O. **$1 net. Jacobs.

Robinson, Arth. W. Personal life of the clergy. '02(F8) D. (Handbooks for the clergy.) net, 90 c. Longmans.

Robinson, C: H: Human nature: sequel to Studies in the character of Christ. '02 (Ag2) D. $2. Longmans.

Robinson, Morgan P. Evolution of the Mason and Dixon line. '02(Ag2) il. facsim., 8°, pap., 25 c. Oracle Pub.

Robinson Crusoe. Defoe, D. 60 c.; 40 c. Educ. Pub.

ROCKAWAY, N. J.
Crayon. Rockaway records of Morris Co., N. J., families. $3. Rockaway.

Rockhaven. Munn, C: C. $1.50. Lee & S.

ROCKY MOUNTAINS.
Nelson. Analytical key to some of the common flowering plants of the Rocky Mt. region. **45 c. net. Appleton.

Roddy, H. J. Complete geography. '02 (Je28) il. F. $1. Am. Bk.

Roddy, H. J. Elem. geography. '02(My24) il. Q. 50 c. Am. Bk.

Roe, Alfr. S. Worcester Young Men's Christian Assoc. '01. '02(Mr22) O. $1. A. S. Roe.

ROENTGEN RAYS.
Monell. Instruction in X-ray methods and medical uses of light, hot air, vibration and high frequency currents. subs., $15. Pelton.
Walsh. Roentgen rays in medical work. net, $2.50. Wood.

Rogers, Alice A. A waiting race. '02(Jl12) D. 50 c. Abbey Press.

Rogers, C: G. Government clerks: (ballads.) '02(Jl19) nar. O. $1; pap., 25 c. McQuilkin.

Roget, M. *and* K. *See* Alissas, R. d'.

Roi Apépi (Le). Cherbuliez, C: V: 60 c. W: R. Jenkins.

Role of the unconquered. Dalton, T. $1.50. G: W. Dillingham

Rollins, Alice W. Story of Azron. '01. '02 (F22) 12°, $1. Holliswood.

Roman Africa. Graham, A. $6. Longmans.

Roman Biznet. Pangborn, G. W. $1.50. Houghton, M. & Co.

ROMAN EMPIRE.
Hellems. Lex de imperio Vespasiani. 50 c. Scott, F. & Co.

ROMAN LAW.
See Civil law.

Roman mystery. Bagot, R: $1.50. Lane.

Romance of a rogue. Sharts, J. W. $1.50. H. S. Stone.

Romance of Leonardo da Vinci, the forerunner. Merejkowski, D. †$1.50. Putnam.

ROMANISM.
See Catholic church.

Romans choisis. 12°, pap. W: R. Jenkins.
—Cherbuliez. Le roi Apépi. 60 c. ·(25.)

Romantic love and personal beauty. Finck, H: T. net, $2. Macmillan.

ROME.
Fustel de Coulanges. Ancient city: study on the rel., laws and institutions of Greece and Rome. $2. Lee & S.
Gregorovius. Rome in the Middle Ages. v. 8. net, $3. Macmillan.
Harding. City of the seven hills. 40 c. Scott, F. & Co.
Miller. Mediæval Rome from Hilderbrand to Clement VIII. **$1.35 net; $1.60 net. Putnam.
Oman. Seven Roman statesmen of the later republic. $1.60. Longmans.
Seignobos. Hist. of the Roman people. *$1.25 net. Holt.
See also Tiberius.

Rood, H: E: Hardwicke. '02(My10) D. $1.50. Harper.

Rood, J: R. Treatise on the law of attachments, garnishments, judgments, and executions. '01. '02(Mr8) O. $3. Wahr.

ROOFS.
Merriman *and* Jacoby. Text-book on roofs and bridges. pt. 3. $2.50. Wiley.

Rook, Alb. W. The Butler family. '01. '02 (Ja11) $3. Lakeside Press.

Roosevelt, T. Message to the two houses at the beginning of the first session of the 57th Congress. '02(Mr29) sq. f°. $1. N. Y. State Lib.

Roosevelt, T. Rough Riders. New permanent lib. ed. '02(Mr1) il. 12°, $1.50. Scribner.

Roosevelt, T., Van Dyke, T. S., Elliot, D. G., *and* Stone, A. J. The deer family. '02 (My17) il. O net, $2. Macmillan.

ROOSEVELT, T.
Banks *and* Armstrong. Theodore Roosevelt. $1.50; $2.25. Du Mont.
Halstead. Life of Theodore Roosevelt. subs., $2.50; $3.75; $3.50; $5. Saalfield.
Meyers. Theodore Roosevelt. subs., $1.50; $2. W. W. Wilson.
Meyers. Theodore Roosevelt. $1.50; $2. Ziegler.
See also Fallows, S.;—Wilson, J. G.

ROOSEVELT FAMILY.
Whittelsey, *comp.* Roosevelt genealogy, 1649-1902. $5. C: B. Whittelsey.

Root, Edn. A. Military topography and sketching. Rev. and enl. [3d] ed. '02 (Jl19) il. 8°, $2.50. Hudson-K.

Root, Fk. A., *and* Connelley, W: E. Overland stage to California. '01. '02(Ap12) il. 12°, $2.50; hf. mor., $3.50. Root & C.

Roots of Christian teaching as found in the O. T. Barton, G: A. $1.25. Winston.
Roper, W: *See* More, *Sir* T:
Rose, J: H. Life of Napoleon I. '02(F22) 2 v., il. 8°, net, $4. Macmillan.
Rose, Wa. M. *See* Texas. Notes on repts.
Rose of the wilderness. Browne, W. S. $1.25. W. S. Browne.
Rosen, P: The Catholic church and secret societies. '02(My10) 12°, net, $1. Caspar.
Rosen im schnee. Nies, K. 50 c. Witter.
Rosenberger, J. L., *comp.* Law for lumbermen. '02(Je28) O. shp., $3.50. Am. Lumberman.
Roses.
Jekyll *and* Mawley, *comps.* Roses for Eng. gardens. *$3.75 net. Scribner.
Melliar. Book of the rose. $1.75. Macmillan.
Ross, Janet. Florentine villas; with reproduction in photogravure from Zocchi's etchings. '02(Mr8) f°, $25. Dutton.
Ross, P: Hist. of Long Island, from its earliest settlement to the present time. '02 (Ag23) 3 v., il. sq. 8°, ½ leath., $18. Lewis Pub.
Ross, Ronald. Malarial fever. New 9th ed., rev. and enl. '02(Ap26) O. net, 75 c. Longmans.
Ross, Ronald. Mosquito brigades and how to organize them. '02(F8) O. net. 90 c. Longmans.
Rossetti, Helen M. M. Ford Madox Brown. '01- '02(F8) il. S. bds., net, 35 c. Beam.
Rostand, E. Cyrano de Bergerac; notes by Reed P. Clark. '02(Mr8) D. pap., 50 c. W: R. Jenkins.
Rostopchine, Sophie de. *See* Segur, S. R., *Comtesse* de.
Rosy cloud. Sand, G: 50 c. Estes.
Rotch, T: M. Pediatrics. New rev. ed. '01- '02(F15) 8°, subs., $6; shp., $7. Lippincott.
Roterberg, A. Card tricks. '02(Mr15) S. pap., 25 c. Drake.
Rotherham, Jos. B. *See* Bible. Emphasized Bible.
Rough notes on remedies. Murray, W: net, $1.25. Blakiston.
Rough Riders.
Roosevelt. The Rough Riders. $1.50. Scribner.
Roulet, Ma. F. N. Saint Anthony in art, and other sketches. '01- '02(Ja11) il. D. $2. Marlier.
Rouse, Adelaide L. Annice Wynkoop, artist. '02(Mr29) il. 12°, (Fireside ser.) $1. Burt.
Rouse, Adelaide L. The Deane girls. '01- '02(Mr29) il. 12°, (Fireside lib.) $1. Burt.
Rouse, Adelaide L. Under my own roof. '02(Mr8) il. D. net, $1.20. Funk.
Rouse, W: H: D. Greek votive offerings. '02(Ag16) 8°, (Cambridge Univ. Press ser.) *$4.50 net. Macmillan.
Row, T. Sundara. *See* Sundara, *Rao* T.
Rowe, Henrietta G. Maid of Bar Harbor. '02(Je21) il. D. $1.50. Little, B. & Co.
Rowell, J. H. Everybody's opportunity; or, quick socialism. '01- '02(Mr8) O. pap., 10 c. Free Socialist.
Rowell, J. H. Pure economy; the rich how, the poor why. '02(Ag9) il. O. pap., 10 c. Free Socialist.
Rowell, J. H. Workingman's opportunity. 2d ed. '01- '02(Mr8) O. pap., 5 c. Free Socialist.
Royal lineage. Watson, *Mrs.* A. R. $4.50. Whittet.
Royal navy. Clowes, W: L. v. 5, 6. ea., net, $6.50. Little, B. & Co.
Rubáiyát. *See* Omar Khayyam.
Rubáiyat of Omar Khayyám, jr. Irwin, W. net, 50 c. Elder.
Ruble, W: Wonders of the Revelation of Jesus Christ. '01- '02(Mr22) D. $1. Standard Pub.
Rudder "how-to" ser. Q. $1. Rudder.
—Fisher. How to build a model yacht.
—Mower. How to build a knockabout.—How to build a racing sloop.
Ruggles, Jean. Exercises and problems in arithmetic. '01- '02(F22) 16°, pap., 25 c. W: R. Jenkins.
Ruling elder. Erdman, C: R. 3 c. Presb. Bd.
Rumsey, W: Practice in civil actions in courts of record of the state of N. Y., under the code of civil procedure. 2d ed. v. 1. '02(Je14) O. shp., $6. Banks & Co.
Ruskay, Esther J. Hearth and home essays. '02(Mr29) D. (Special ser., no. 6.) bds., 30 c. Jewish Pub.
Ruskin, J: Mornings in Florence; ed. by M. Baker. '02(Ag30) il. D. $2. Abbey Press.
Ruskin, J: Pen pictures. Pt. 2. '02(My17) T. $1. Longmans.
Ruskin, John.
Collingwood. Life of John Ruskin. net, $2. Houghton, M. & Co.
Turner. Turner and Ruskin. 2 v. net, $50. Dodd.
Ruskin Co-operative Assoc.
Broome. Last days of the Ruskin Co-operative Assoc. 50 c. Kerr.
Russell, C: E. Such stuff as dreams. '02 (Je28) 8°, net, $2. Bowen-M.
Russell, G: W: E. Onlooker's note-book. '02(Je7) O. net, $2.25. Harper.
Russell, Harry L. Outlines of dairy bacteriology. 5th ed., rev. '02(Mr29) il. 12°, $1. H. L. Russell.
Russell, Norman. Village work in India. '02 (My17) 12°, net, $1. Revell.
Russell, W: Prescriptions and instructions for treating the diseases of the feet and legs of the horse. '02(Jl12) il. 8°, pap., $1. Clarke.
Russell, W: C. Captain Fanny. '02(Ap20) 12°, (Red letter ser.) $1.25; pap., 50 c. New Amsterdam.
Russell, W: C. Mate of the good ship "York." '02(Je7) D. $1.50. L. C. Page.
Russell, W: H., *and* Winslow, W: B. Syllabus-digest of decisions of the sup. ct. of the U. S. v. 3. '02(Ap5) O. shp., $6.50. Banks.
Russells (The) in Chicago. Wheaton, E. $1.25. L. C. Page.
Russia.
Howard. Prisoners of Russia. net, $1.40. Appleton.
Kovalevsky. Russian political institutions. net, $1.50. Univ. of Chic.
Morfill. Hist. of Russia from Peter the Great to Nicholas II. $1.75. Pott.
Wright. Asiatic Russia. 2 v. **$7.50 net. McClure, P.
See also **Finland**;—*also* **Peter III.**

RUSSIAN LITERATURE.
Wiener. Anthology of Russian literature. In 2 pts. pt. 1. net, $3. Putnam.
Rust, C. D. *See* New York. Penal code.
Rusted spokes. Neesen, V. 50 c. New Amsterdam.
Rustler (The). McElrath, F. net, $1.20. Funk.
Rutherford, S: Christ and his cross. '02 (Mr8) S. $1. Longmans.
Ruthless rhymes. *See* Streamer, D.
Rutland home of Rufus Putnam. Earle, S. C. 30 c.; 50 c. S. C. Earle.
Rutledge. Harris, *Mrs.* M. C. $1. Burt.
Ryan, M. B. Elocution and dramatic art. '02(Jl19) 16°, 75 c. Angel Press.
Sabatini, R. Suitors of Yvonne. '02(Je7) D. net, $1.20. Putnam.
Sabertooth (The). Kinder, S. 75 c.; 25 c. Laird.
Sacred anthology. Conway, M. D. $2. Holt.
Sacred beetle. Ward, J: net, $3.50. Scribner.
Sacrificio (El) de Elisa. Maxwell, *Mrs.* M. E. B. 50 c. Appleton.
Sadler, Cora G. Skoot. '02(Ag2) D. 50 c. Jennings.
Sadlier, Anna T. Mary Tracy's fortune. '02 (Mr8) S. 45 c. Benziger.
Sage, Dean, Townsend, C. H., Smith, H. M., *and* Harris, W: C. Salmon and trout. '02 (Je28) il. 12°, (Am. sportsman's lib.) net, $2; large pap. ed., hf. mor., net, $7.50. Macmillan.
Sage, W: The Claybornes. '02(Ap26) il. D $1.50. Houghton, M. & Co.
St. Clair, Victor, *pseud.* *See* Browne, G: W.
St. Cyres, *Viscount*, [Stafford Harry Northcote.] Life of François Fenelon. '02(F15) 8°, net, $2.50. Dutton.
St. Nicholas ser. *See* Burt's.
Saint-Pierre, J. H. B. de. Paul and Virginia. '02(Ap19) il. D. (Home lib.) $1. Burt.
ST. PIERRE.
Welch *and* Taylor. Destruction of St. Pierre, Martinique. 50 c. Fenno.
Sainte-Foi, C: The perfect woman; fr. the Fr., by Z. N. Brown. '01. '02(Ja11) S. net, $1. Marlier.
ST. VINCENT.
See Martinique.
SAINTS.
Banks. Great saints of the Bible. $1.50. Eaton & M.
Hutton. Studies in the lives of the saints. *$1.25 net. Dutton.
Newman. Lives of Eng. saints. 6 v. net, $12. Lippincott.
Scheeben. Holiness of the church in the 19th century. 10 c. Benziger.
See also Fathers.
Sajous, C: E. de M., *ed.* Analytical encyclopædia of practical medicine. Rev. ed. In 6 v. v. 1. '02(Ap26) il. 8°, subs., per v., $5; hf. rus., per v., $6. Davis.
SALE.
Freeman. Law of void judicial sales. $4. Cen. Law Journ.
Saley, Met L. Realm of the retailer; retail lumber trade, its difficulties, successes, etc. '02(Ag2) il. 12°, $1.50. Am. Lumberman.
Salis, *Mrs.* Ht. A. de. A la mode cookery up-to-date recipes. '02(Ap26) il. D. $2. Longmans.

SALMON.
Sage, *and others.* Salmon and trout. net, $2; net, $7.50. Macmillan.
SALOONS.
Rankin. Saloon law nullification and its cure. 50 c. Advance.
See also Temperance.
Saltus, F. S. Mount of Olives: [poem.] '02(Ap12) sq. S. bds., $1; pap., net, 25 c. Bk. Lover.
SALVATION.
Firey. Infant salvation. net, $1.20. Funk.
Gladden. Social salvation. net, $1. Houghton, M. & Co.
Samantha at Saratoga. Holley, M. $1. Burt.
Sand, George, [*pseud.* for A. L. A. Dudevant.] Masterpieces. v. 15. '02(Mr15); v. 16 (Ap5); v. 17, 18 (Je28) 8°, subs. (Apply to pubs. for price.) Barrie.
Sand, George. Rosy cloud. '02(Ag23) il. 12°, (Young of heart ser., no. 33.) 50 c. Estes.
Sandals (The). Grenell, Z. net, 40 c. Funk.
Sanders, C: H. How are we led? and Who is it that leads us? '01. '02(Ja4) 8°, $1.50. Donohue.
Sanderson, E. D. Insects injurious to staple crops. '01. '02(Ja18) il. 12°, $1.50. Wiley.
Sanderson, Jos. Story of Saint Patrick. '02 (Je7) O. $1.50. Ketcham.
Sandman (The). Hopkins, W: J. **$1.20 net. L. C. Page.
Sandys, Edwyn, *and* Van Dyke, T. S. Upland game birds. '02(Je7) il. 8°, (Am. sportsman's lib.) net, $2; large pap. ed., hf. mor., net, $7.50. Macmillan.
Sandys, Miles. Michael Carmichael. '02 (Ag2) D. $1.25. Laird.
Sanford, Fernando. Elements of physics. '02(Ag2) D. $1.20. Holt.
SANITARY ENGINEERING.
Baker. Municipal engineering and sanitation. net, $1.25. Macmillan.
See also Heating;—Plumbing;—Sewage and sewerage;—Water-supply.
SANITARY SCIENCE.
See Contagion;—Hygiene;—Sanitary engineering.
SANSKRIT LANGUAGE.
Macdonell. Sanskrit grammar for beginners. $3. Longmans.
Santanelli, [*pseud.* for Ja. Hawthorne Loryea.] Is man a free agent? The law of suggestion. '02(Jl19) il. O. *$1 net. Santanelli.
SANTIAGO.
See Schley, W. S.
Sappho. Odes, bridal songs, epigrams; trs. by Arnold, Moore, Palgrave, Tennyson and others. '02(Ag9) il. (Antique gems fr. the Gr. and Latin, v. 8.) (App. to pubs. for price.) Barrie.
Sapte, W., *jr.* By the way ballads. '02 (Ag23) il. 12°, *$1.50 net. Dutton.
Sara. Newberry, F. E. $1. Burt.
Sarah the less. Swett, S. net, 75 c. Westminster.
Sarita, the Carlist. Marchmont, A. W. $1.50. Stokes.
Sarles, J: W. Man's peerless destiny in Christ. '01. '02(Mr1) 12°, net, 90 c. Funk.
Satan and demons. Townsend, L. T. net, 25 c. Jennings.

Satchel (A) guide for the vacation tourist in Europe. 1902. '02(Mr15) S. leath., net, $1.50. Houghton, M. & Co.

SATIRE.
See Parody;—Wit and humor.

SAUGERTIES.
Brink. Early hist. of Saugerties. *$1.50 net. R. W. Anderson.

Saunders, Ripley D. John Kenadie. '02 (My17) D. $1.50. Houghton, M. & Co.

Saunders' medical hand-atlases. il. 8°, net. Saunders.
—Sultan. Abdominal hernia. *$3.

Saussure, Cæsar de. Foreign view of England in the reign of George I. and George II. '02(Je7) 8°, net, $3. Dutton.

Savage, R: H. For a young queen's bright eyes. '02(My24) O. $1.25; pap., 50 c. Home.

Savill, T: D. Clinical lectures on neurasthenia. '02(Je28) 8°, $1.50. Wood.

SAVINGS-BANKS.
Hamilton. Savings and savings institutions. net, $2.25. Macmillan.

Savonarola, *Fra* Girolama. Triumph of the cross; ed. by Fa. J: Proctor. '02(Mr8) 8°, net, $1.35. Herder.

Sawyer, Timothy T. Old Charlestown. '02 (Ag9) O. *$2 net. J. H. West.

Sayler, G: W. Skid and I. '02(Ag2) D. $2.50. Sayler.

SAYRE FAMILY.
Banta. Sayre family. $10. T. M. Banta.

Scadding, C: Direct answers to plain questions for Am. churchmen: expansion of the church catechism. '01. '02(Ja4) D. (Grade A handbook.) bds., net, 50 c. Whittaker.

SCARABS.
Ward. Sacred beetle: treatise on Egyptian scarabs. net, $3.50. Scribner.

Scarlet and hyssop. Benson, E: F: $1.50. Appleton.

Scenery of England. Lubbock, *Sir* J: net, $2.50. Macmillan.

Scenes of rural life in Hampshire. Capes, W. W. net, $2.75. Macmillan.

Schaeffer, *Mrs.* Jennie. Metropolitan club cook-book, New York City. '02(Mr15) 16°, oil cl., $1.75. Augsburg.

Schäfer, E. A. Directions for class work in practical physiology. '01. '02(F8) il. O. net, $1. Longmans.

Schäfer, E: A. Essentials in histology. 6th ed. '02(Jl19) il. 8°, *$3 net. Lea.

Schaffer, W: I., *rep. See* Penn. *Superior ct.* Repts.—*Supreme ct.* Repts.

Schauffler, A. F. *See* Bible. Sunday-school scholars' Bible.

Scheeben, M. J. Holiness of the church in the nineteenth century; fr. the Germ.; ed. by J: P. M. Schleuter. '02(My24) S. pap., 10 c. Benziger.

Schell, W: G. Is the negro a beast?: reply to Carroll's book entitled The negro a beast. '01. '02(F15) il. D. 60 c. Gospel Trumpet.

Schelling, Felix E. English chronicle play. '02(F1) 8°, net, $2. Macmillan.

Scherer, Rob. G., *rep. See* New York. *Cts. of record.* Misc. repts.

Schiller, J. C. F. v. Don Carlos, Mary Stuart; ed. by N. H. Dole. Ed. de luxe. '02 (Je28) 12°. (App. to pubs. for price.) Niccolls.

Schiller, J. C. F. v. History of the revolt of the Netherlands; ed. by N. H. Dole. Ed. de luxe. '01. '02(Mr15) 8°. (App. to pubs. for price.) Niccolls.

Schiller, J. C. F. v. History of the thirty years' war in Germany; ed. by N. H. Dole. Ed. de luxe. '02(Mr15) 8°. (App. to pubs. for price.) Niccolls.

Schiller, J. C. F. v. Die jungfrau von Orleans; notes by A. B. Nichols and vocab. by W: A. Hervey. [New ed.] '01. '02 (F1) S. net, 60 c. Holt.

Schiller, J. C. F. v. Maid of Orleans; Bride of Messina; Wilhelm Tell; Demetrius. Ed. de luxe. '02(Jl5) 12°. (App. to pubs. for price.) Niccolls.

Schiller, J. C. F. v. Maria Stuart; ed. by E: S. Joynes; vocab. by W: A. Hervey. [New ed.] '02(F1) S. net, 70 c. Holt.

Schiller, J. C. F. v. The Piccolomini; Death of Wallenstein; Wallenstein's camp; ed. by N. H. Dole. Ed. de luxe. '02(Mr22) 8°. (App. to pubs. for price.) Niccolls.

Schiller, J. C. F. v. Poems; tr. into Eng. by E. P. Arnold-Foster. '02(My24) D. net, $1.60. Holt.

Schiller, J. C. F. v. Wallenstein; notes by W. H. Carruth. 2d ed., rev. '01. '02(F1) S. net, $1. Holt.

SCHILLER, J. C. F. v.
Lessing. Schiller's einfluss auf Grillparzer. 50 c. Univ. of Wis.
Thomas. Life and works of Schiller. **$1.50 net. Holt.

SCHLEY, Winfield Scott.
Graham. Schley and Santiago. $1.50. Conkey.
Nauticus, *pseud.* Truth about the Schley case. 25 c. Columbia.

Schmidt, Emanuel. Solomon's temple in the light of other oriental temples. '02(Je7) il. O. net, $1. Univ. of Chic.

Schmitt, Gustav, *ed.* Brief of necroscopy and its medico-legal relation. '02(Ag9) nar. S. **$1 net. Funk.

Schofield, Alfr. T. Springs of character. '01. '02(Mr1) 8°, net, $1.30. Funk.

Schofield, R. J., *comp.*, ["One of the craft."] Drummer's yarns and funny jokes; 9th crop. '02(Jl12) O. (Excelsior lib., no. 67.) pap., 25 c. Excelsior.

School congress. Vancil, F. M. 25 c. Kellogg.

SCHOOL-HOUSES.
See Architecture.

SCHOOLS.
Clark. Public schools of Chicago. net, 50 c. Univ. of Chic.
Hughes. Schools at home and abroad. net, $1.50. Dutton.
Wray. Jean Mitchell's school. $1.25. Public Sch. Pub.
Young. Ethics in the school. net, 25 c.—Isolation in the school. net, 50 c. Univ. of Chic.
See also Education;—Illinois; — Kindergarten; — Sunday-school;—Westminster;—Wisconsin.

Schrader, Ferd. Friedrich der Grosse und der Siebenjährige Krieg; ed. by R. H. Allpress. Authorized ed. '02(My17) 12°, (Siepmann's elem. Germ. ser.) net, 50 c. Macmillan.

SCHUREMAN FAMILY.
Wynkoop. Schuremans of N. J. $3. R: Wynkoop.
Schuyler, Aaron. Systems of ethics. '02 (My17) O. $1.50. Jennings.
Schuyler, M., *jr., comp. See* Avesta.
Schuyler, W: Ambassador of Christ: biog. of Rev. Montgomery Schuyler. '02 (Mr8) 8°, $1.50. Gorham.
Schwatka, F: Children of the cold. New ed. '02 (Ag2) il. 12°, $1.25. Educ. Pub.
SCIENCE.
Gage. Introd. to physical science. $1. Ginn.
Lippincott's elem. science readers. 3 pts. pt. 1, 25 c.; pt. 2, 30 c.; pt. 3, 35 c. Lippincott.
Strutt. Scientific papers. v. 3, 1887-92. net, $5. Macmillan.
See also Chemistry;—Evolution; — Microscope; — Philosophy;—Religion and science.
Scientific Bible. Hunt, M. A. $1. F. E. Ormsby.
Scientific memoirs; ed. by J. S. Ames. O. $1. Am. Bk.
—Brace, *ed.* Laws of radiation and absorption. (15.)
—Randall, *ed. and tr.* Expansion of gases by heat. (14.)
Scofield, Cora L. Study of the court of star chamber. '02 (Mr22) 8°, pap., net, $1. Univ. of Chic.
Scollard, Clinton. Cloistering of Ursula. '02 (F15) il. D. $1.50. L. C. Page.
SCOTLAND.
Addis. Cathedrals and abbeys of Presb. Scotland. net, $2.50. Presb. Bd.
Brown. Hist. of Scotland. v. 2. net, $1.50. Macmillan.
Whitcomb. Little journey to Scotland. 15 c. Flanagan.
See also England;—Hebrides.
SCOTS.
Crosland. The unspeakable Scot. **$1.25 net. Putnam.
Hanna. The Scotch-Irish. 2 v. net, $10. Putnam.
Scott, Fred N. Composition literature. '02 (Je28) 12°, $1. Allyn & B.
Scott, Temple, *ed. See* Swift, J.
Scott, *Sir* W. Waverley novels; abr. by W: H. Browne. '02 (Ag30) 25 v., il. 12°, $19. Collier.
Scott, *Sir* W. Kenilworth. '02 (Mr22) 12°, (Eng. classics.) net, 60 c. Macmillan.
Scott, *Sir* W. Quentin Durward. '02 (Mr8) 12°, (Eng. classics.) net, 60 c. Macmillan.
Scott, *Sir* W. Stories from Waverley for children. 5th ed. '02 (My3) il. 12°, $1. Macmillan.
Scott, *Sir* W. Waverley; condensed and ed. for school reading by A. L. Bouton. '02 (My10) D. (Standard lit. ser., double no. 50.) 30 c.; pap., 20 c. University.
Scott, *Sir* W. *See also* Sullivan, *Sir* E:
Scottish men of letters in 18th century. Graham, H: G. net, $4.50. Macmillan.
Scottish philosophy in its national development. Laurie, H: net, $1.75. Macmillan.
Scribner's Am. hist. ser. D. net, $1. Scribner.
—Burgess. Reconstruction and the constitution, 1866-1876.
Scribner's contemporary sci. ser.; ed. by H. Ellis. 12°, $1.50. Scribner.
—Jastrow. Study of religion.
—Zittel. Hist. of geology and palæontology to end of 19th century.
Scribner's ser. of school reading. il. D. net, 60 c. Scribner.
—Cervantes Saavedra. Don Quixote.
—Pyle. Some merry adventures of Robin Hood.
—Thompson. Krag and Johnny Bear.
Scribner's social sci. ser. 12°, $1. Scribner.
—Cumming. Public house reform.
Scudder's eclectic manual. D. net, $2.50. Scudder.
—Mundy. Eclectic practice in diseases of children. (5.)
SCULPTURE.
Hurll, *ed.* Tuscan sculpture. net, 75 c.; net, 50 c.; net, 35 c. Houghton, M. & Co.
See also Ivory;—Tombstones.
Scutage and knight service in England. Baldwin, J. F. net, $1. Univ. of Chic.
Seager, H: R. Prof. Patten's theory of prosperity. '02 (Mr22) 8°, (Pub. of the soc., no. 333.) pap., 15 c. Am. Acad. Pol. Sci.
Seal of destiny. Behymer, I. H. $1.50. Neely.
Searching for truth. '02 (My24) O. $1.50. Eckler.
Sears, Hamblen. None but the brave. '02 (Ap12) il. D. $1.50. Dodd.
SEASHORE.
Wheeler. The sea coast. $4.50. Longmans.
SEAWEEDS.
See Algæ.
Second generation. Linn, J. W. $1.50. Macmillan.
SECRET SOCIETIES.
See Catholic church.
Sectional struggle. Harris, C. W. net, $2.50. Lippincott.
SECURITIES.
Hall. Pittsburg securities, 1902. gratis. R. C. Hall.
Moody, *ed.* Manual of corporation securities, 1902. $7.50; $10. Moody.
Sedding, J: D. Garden craft old and new. '02 (Ap26) 8°, net, $2.50. Lane.
Sedgwick, Anne D. Confounding of Camelia. [New issue.] '02 (My17) il. D. $1.50. Century Co.
Sedgwick, Anne D. Dull Miss Archinard. [New issue.] '02 (My17) il. D. $1.50. Century Co.
Sedgwick, Anne D. The rescue. '02 (My10) il. D. $1.50. Century Co.
Sedgwick, H: D., *jr.* Samuel de Champlain. '02 (Ap5) S (Riverside biog. ser., no. 14.) net, 65 c.; School ed., net, 50 c. Houghton, M. & Co.
Sedgwick, J: Correspondence; ed. by C. Stoeckel. v. 1. '02 (Ag9) 12°, 300 cop. for presentation. C. Stoeckel.
Sedgwick, W: T. Principles of sanitary science and the public health. '02 (My17) 8°, net, $3. Macmillan.
Seebohm, F: Tribal custom in Anglo-Saxon law. '02 (Mr8) O. net, $5. Longmans.
Seeley, H. G. Dragons of the air: extinct flying reptiles. '01. '02 (F22) 12°, net, $1.40. Appleton.

Seeley, *Mrs.* L. Cook book; with chapters on domestic servants, and other details of household management. '02(Mr29) il. O. net, $2; hf. leath., net, $3. Macmillan.
Seeley, Levi. Foundations of education. '02 (F1) D. $1. Hinds.
Segall, J. B. Corneille and the Spanish drama. '02(Ag16) 12°, (Columbia Univ. studies in romance, philology and literature.) **$1.50 net. Macmillan.
Seger, Hermann A: Collected writings. In 2 v. v. 1. '02(Ap5) 8°, per set, $15. Chemical.
Segur, Sophie R., *Comtesse* de, [Sophie de Rostopchine.] Les malheurs de Sophie; ed. by E. White. '02(Je14) il. D. (Modern lang. ser.) 45 c. Heath.
Seigneur de Beaufoy. Drummond, H. $1.50. L. C. Page.
Seignobos, C: Feudal régime; tr. ed. by E. W. Dow. '02(Ag16) O. pap., 50 c. Holt.
Seignobos, C: Hist. of the Roman people; ed. by W: Fairley. '02(Jl12) il. D. *$1.25 net. Holt.
SELBORNE.
White. Natural history of Selborne. 2 v. net, $20. Lippincott.
Selden, E: G. Story of the Christian centuries. '02(My3) 12°, net, $1. Revell.
Select sunflowers. Mills, H. E: $1. Sunflower Press.
SELF-CULTURE.
See Culture.
Self-educator ser. D. 75 c. Crowell.
—Thornton. Eng. composition.
Self-raised. Southworth, *Mrs.* E. D. E. N. $1. Burt.
Seligman, E: R. A. Economic interpretation of history. '02(Ag2) 12°, **$1.50 net. Macmillan.
Sellers, Edn. J. Allied families of Delaware. '01- '02(Mr1) 8°, $5. E. J. Sellers.
Selling the bear's hide. Davison, C: S. $1. Nassau Press.
Sellow, Grace E. Three thousand sample questions; [accompanying] Hill's Practical encyclopedia. '02(My10) il. D. pap., 50 c. Bellows.
Selover, A. W. Law of negotiable instruments for N. Y., Mass., Conn., R. I., [etc.] Iowa ed. '02(Je14) D. shp., $4. Keefe-D.
Selwyn, E: C. St. Luke the prophet. '01. '02(Ja4) 12°, net, $2.75. Macmillan.
Sema-Kanda. Turnbull, C. $1.25. Alliance.
SEMITIC LITERATURE.
Arnolt. Theolog. and Semitic literature for 1901. net, 50 c. Univ. of Chic.
SEMITIC PEOPLES.
Barton. Sketch of Semitic origins, social and religious. net, $3. Macmillan.
SEMITIC RELIGION.
Curtiss. Primitive Semitic religion to-day. net, $2. Revell.
Semitic ser. D. net, $1.25. Scribner.
—Duff. Theol. and ethics of the Hebrews. (2.)
Semon, *Sir* Felix. Some thoughts on the principles of local treatment in diseases of the upper air passages. '02(Mr22) 8°, net, $1. Macmillan.
Separation. Lee, M. $1.25. Buckles.
September days on Nantucket. Bliss, W: R. net, $1. Houghton, M. & Co.
Sergeant, Adeline. Master of Beechwood. '02(Jl12) 12°, (Manhattan lib. of new copyright fiction.) pap., 50 c. Burt.
Series of school histories; ed by C: K. Adams. 12°, $1.50. Allyn & B.
—West. Ancient history to death of Charlemagne.
SERMON ON THE MOUNT.
Bacon. Sermon on the Mount. net, $1. Macmillan.
SERMONS.
Banks. Windows for sermons. net, $1.25. Funk.
SERVANTS.
See Domestic economy.
Service (The). Thoreau, H: D: net, $2.50; net, $10. Goodspeed.
Seton-Karr, H: *See* Karr, H: Seton-.
Seton-Thompson, E. E. *See* Thompson, E. E. Seton-.
Seven poor travellers. *See* Dickens, C:
Seven Roman statesmen. Oman, C: W: C. $1.60. Longmans.
Seventy-one days' camping in Morocco. Grove, *Lady* A. net, $2.50. Longmans.
SEWAGE AND SEWERAGE.
Folwell. Sewerage. $3. Wiley.
Fowler. Sewage works analyses. $2. Wiley.
Rideal. Sewage and the bacterial purification of sewage. $3.50. Wiley.
See also Sanitary engineering.
Seward, Thdr. F. How to get acquainted with God: Christian Science movement. '02(Mr29) nar. S. net, 50 c. Funk.
SEX.
Williams. Sex problems. net, $1. Revell.
Sexton, A. H. *See* Rhead, E. L.
SEYMOUR, Ct.
Campbell, *and others.* Seymour, past and present. $3. W: C. Sharpe.
Shackleton, Rob. Many waters. '02(Ap26) D. $1.50. Appleton.
Shadow and light. Gibbs, M. W. $1.50. M. W. Gibbs.
Shadow duellers. Freear, R. L: net, 60 c. Blanchard.
Shadows cast before. Fuller, P. W. $1.50. Abbey Press.
Shadwell, Arth. Drink, temperance and legislation. '02(Ag30) D. $1.75. Longmans.
Shakespeare, W: Works. Dowden ed. (Craig [and] Dowden.) v. 3, King Lear. '02(Je28) 8°, $1.25. Bowen-M.
Shakespeare, W: Complete works. '02 (Ap5) il. 12°, $7; hf. mor., $10.50. Burt.
Shakespeare, W: Works. New century ed. (Is. Gollancz.) Ed. de luxe. In 24 v. v. 19-20. '02(Ap5); v. 21-24 (Jl5) 8°, ea., $3.50. Estes.
Shakespeare, W: [Works.] Chiswick Shakespeare. v. 25, 26. '02(F22); v. 27, 28 (My3); v. 29 (Jl12) 16°, ea., 35 c. Macmillan.
Shakespeare, W: Complete plays and poems. New pocket ed. In 3 v. '02(Mr8) 16°, (Caxton ser.) per set, net, $4.20. Scribner.
Shakespeare, W: Sonnets. '02(My24) 16°, (Lover's lib., v. 11.) net, 50 c.; leath., net, 75 c. Lane.
Shakespeare, W: Julius Cæsar; ed. by A. H. Tolman. '02(Mr22) il. D. (Eng. classics, star ser.) 32 c. Globe Sch. Bk.

Shakespeare, W: King Richard III., adapt. for school use; by A. M. Kellogg. '01. '02 (F8) 16°, pap., 15 c. Kellogg.

Shakespeare, W: Macbeth; ed. by A. W. Verity. '02(Je7) 12°, (Pitt Press Shakespeare.) net, 40 c. Macmillan.

Shakespeare, W: Merchant of Venice; ed. by F: Manley. '02(Mr29) 16°, (Laurel classics.) 40 c. Birchard.

Shakespeare, W: Merchant of Venice; notes by E: E. Hale, jr. '01. '02(F8) 12°, (Standard lit. ser., no. 49.) pap. 20 c. University.

Shakespeare, W: Twelfth night; ed. by R: G. White. '02(Mr22) S. (Riverside lit. ser., no. 149.) pap., 15 c. Houghton, M. & Co.

Shakespeare, W: Twelfth night. '02(Ja11) 8°, (Vale Press Shakespeare, v. 22.) net, $8. Lane.

SHAKESPEARE, W:
Fleming. Shakespeare's plots. $1.80. Putnam.
Hazlitt. Shakespeare. net, $2.50. Scribner.
Lamb. Tales from Shakespeare. 40 c. Heath.
McSpadden. Shakesperian synopses. net. 45 c. Crowell.
Merrill. The man Shakespeare. **$1.25 net. Bowen-M.
Phin. Shakespeare cyclop. and new glossary. *$1.50 net. Indust.
Porter *and* Clarke. Shakespeare studies: Macbeth. 56 c. Am. Bk.
Sherman. What is Shakespeare? net. $1.50; net, $1. Macmillan.
Webb. Mystery of William Shakespeare. $4. Longmans.

Shakespeare and Goethe on Gresham's law. *See* Green, B: E.

SHAKESPEARE-BACON CONTROVERSY.
Gallup. Bi-literal cipher of Sir Francis Bacon. $3.75.—Tragedy of Anne Boleyn. $1.50. Howard.
Reed. Bacon and Shakes-peare parallel. net, $2.50.—Francis Bacon, our Shakespeare. net, $2. Goodspeed.

Shall Cromwell have a statue? Adams, C: F. 25 c. Lauriat.

Shall we understand the Bible? Williams, T. R net, 50 c. Macmillan.

Shand, Alex. I. Shooting. '02(F15) il. 12°, (Haddon Hall lib.) $3. Macmillan.

Shannon, Rob. T. *See* Tennessee. *Sup. ct. Repts.*

Sharp, B. A., [*pseud.* for Platon G. Brounoff.] Stolen correspondence from the "Dead letter" office between musical celebrities. '02 (Mr22) S. 50 c. Gervais.

Sharp, Luke, *pseud.* *See* Barr, R.

Sharp & Alleman Co.'s lawyers' and bankers' directory for 1902. Jan. ed. '02(Ja18): July ed. (Jl19) O. shp., ea., $5. Sharp & A.

Sharpe, W: C. *See* Campbell, H. A.

Sharpless, I: Quaker experiment in government. 4th pop. ed. '02(F15) il. 12°, $1.50. Ferris.

Sharts, Jos. W. Romance of a rogue. '02 (Ap5) D. $1.50. H. S. Stone.

Shaw, Adèle M. Coast of freedom. '02 (Ap19) D. $1.50. Doubleday, P.

Shaw, H: W., ["Josh Billings."] Josh Billings' old farmer's allminax, 1870-79. '02 (Mr8) il. D. $1.50. G: W. Dillingham.

Shaw, Robert Gould. *See* Higginson, H: L.

She wanted to vote. Ballard, E. C. net. $1.40. Brower.

Sheehan, P. A. Luke Delmege. '01. '02 (Ja4) D. $1.50. Longmans.

SHEEP.
See Veterinary medicine and surgery.

Sheldon, F: M. Practical colorist: for the artist printer. '02(F1) il. Q. $8. Owl Press.

Sheldon, H: I. Notes on the Nicaragua Canal. New ed. '02(Ag30) 8°. $1.25. McClurg.

Sheldon, S:, *and* Mason, H. Dynamo electric machinery. v. 1, Direct-current machines. 2d ed. '02(Je14); v. 2, Alternating current machines. '02(Je7) il. D. ea., net, $2.50. Van Nostrand.

Shelley, Ht. S. Poems of life and loving. '02(Ap26) 12°, $1. Neely.

Shelley, P. B. Poetical works. '02(Je21) 16°, (Caxton ser.) net, $1.25. Scribner.

Shepard, Hiram M. Life on the farm: reading book for grammar and high schools. '01. '02(Ja11) il. S. (Home and school ser. for young folks.) 50 c. Flanagan.

Shepardson, Dan. Studies in the Epistles to the Hebrews. '02(F8) 12°, $1.50. Revell.

Sheppard, J: S., *jr.* *See* Rumsey, W:

Sherer, Rob. G., *rep.* *See* New York. *Cts. of record.* Misc. repts.

Sheridan, Philip H: Personal memoirs. New enl. ed.; with acc. of life, by M. V. Sheridan. '02(Mr1) 2 v., il. 8°, net, $4. Appleton.

Sherlock, C: R. Red anvil. '02(Je7) il. D. $1.50. Stokes.

Sherman, And. M. Life of Capt. Jeremiah O'Brien of Machais, Me. '02(Ag9) il. 12°, $2. G: W. Sherman.

Sherman, G: W., *and* And. M., *eds.* Memorials of Lydia Whitney Sherman. '02 (Jl12) il. 12°, $3. G: W. Sherman.

Sherman, L. A. What is Shakespeare? '02 (F1) 12°, net, $1.50; *Same.* School ed. (Mr29) 12°, net, $1. Macmillan.

SHERMAN, Lydia W.
Sherman, *eds.* Memorials of Lydia Whitney Sherman. $3. G: W. Sherman.

Sherman, Ma. B. K. Parliamentary law at a glance. Rev. ed. '01. '02(F8) 16°, 75 c. H. O. Shepard.

SHERMAN, William T.
Johnson. W: T. Sherman. $1. Donohue.

Sherren, Wilkinson. The Wessex of romance. New cheaper il. ed. '02(Ag23) 12°. *$1.50 net. Scribner.

Sherwood, Wa. J. Story of three. '01. '02 (Mr29) il. nar. Q. pap., 25 c. W: S. Lord.

Shiells, Rob. Story of the token as belonging to the sacrament of the Lord's supper. 2d ed. '02(Je21) D. net, $1. Presb. Bd.

Shimmell, Lewis S. Border warfare in Penn. during the Revolution. '01. '02(F22) 16°, pap., 50 c. R. L. Myers.

Ship of silence. Valentine, E: U. net, $1.20. Bowen-M.

Shipley, Arth. E., *ed.* *See* Harmer, S. F:, *ed.*

Shipman, B: J. *See* Minnesota. Civil procedure.

Shipp, E. R: Questions and answers on contracts. '02(Ag9) S. (Quiz books.) pap., 50 c. Byrne.

SHIPS AND SHIPBUILDING.
Crowell. Present status and future prospects of Am. shipbuilding. 15 c. Am. Acad. Pol. Sci.
SHOOTING.
Grinnell. Amer. duck shooting. $3.50. Forest.
Shand. Shooting. $3. Macmillan.
See also Rifle.
SHORE.
See Seashore.
SHORT, T:
Love. Thomas Short, first printer of Conn. $5. Case.
SHORTHAND.
See Stenography.
SIAM.
Campbell. Siam in the 20th century. net, $5. Longmans.
Siamese twins. Keese, W: L. net. $1.25. E. W. Dayton.
SIBERIAN RAILWAY
Dmitriev-Mámonóv *and* Zdziarski, *eds.* Guide to the great Siberian railway. *$3.50 net. Putnam.
Sibley, Edn. D. Stillman Gott, farmer and fisherman. '02(Ag30) D. †$1.50. Brooks.
Sibley, Hiram L. Right to and the cause for action, both civil and criminal. '02(Jl5) D. $1.50. W. H. Anderson & Co.
Siborne, W: Waterloo campaign, 1815. 5th ed. '02(Jl12) 8°, *$1.50 net. Dutton.
Sibylline leaves. Ballough, C: A. $1. Painter.
Sibyl's conquest. Stinchfield, M. I. $1.50. Neely.
Sichel, Wa. Bolingbroke and his times: the sequel. '02(Je7) O. $4. Longmans.
SICILY.
Sladen. In Sicily. 2 v. net, $20. Dutton.
Side windows. Boteler, M. M. 75 c. Standard Pub.
Sidgwick, H: Philosophy. '02(Je7) 8°, net, $2.25. Macmillan.
Sidgwick, H: Principles of political economy. 3d ed. '02(Je7) 8°, net, $4.50. Macmillan.
Sidis, Boris. Psychopathological researches. '02(Ag23) il. Q. *$3 net. Stechert.
Sidner, Aurelia L. Price inevitable. '02 (My17) D. $1. Popular.
Sidney, Marg., *pseud.* *See* Lothrop, *Mrs.* H. M.
Siege of Lady Resolute. Dickson, H. $1.50. Harper.
Siepmann's elem. French ser. 12°, net, 50 c. Macmillan.
—Dumas. Napoleon.
Siepmann's elem. Germ. ser. 12°, net, 50 c. Macmillan.
—Schrader. Friedrich der Grosse.
—Zastrow. Wilhelm der Siegreiche.
Sign of the seven sins. Le Queux, W: $1; 50 c. Lippincott.
SIGNALS.
See Flags.
SIGNS.
See Stenography.
Silent pioneer. McElroy, L. C. $1.50. Crowell.
Silken snare. Leroy, W: 50 c. Abbey Press.
Sill, E: Rowland. Poems. Special ed. '02 (Jl19) 8°, buckram and bds., **$5 net. Houghton, M. & Co.
Silva, T., *and* Fourcaut, A. Lectura y conversación: new Spanish method. '01. '02 (Ja25) D. 60 c. Am. Bk.
SILVER.
See Precious metals.
Silver chord and the golden bowl. Pierce, G. A. $1. Abbey Press.
Silver ser. of classics. 12°. Silver.
—Keats. Eve of St. Agnes. 40 c.
—Kinard, *ed.* Old Eng. ballads. 40 c.
—Wordsworth. Selected poems. 30 c.
Silver ser. of modern lang. text-books; ed. by A. Cohn. D. Silver.
—France. Monsieur Bergeret. $1.
—Manzoni. I promessi sposi. $1.20.
Simmons, J. C. My trip to the Orient. '02 (Je7) il. 8°, $1.50. Whitaker & R.
Simon, C: E. Clinical diagnosis by microscopical and chemical methods. 4th ed. '02(F15) il. 8°, net, $3.75. Lea.
Simon, C: E. Text-book of physiolog. chemistry. '01. '02(Ja25) 8°, net, $3.25. Lea.
Simon, Pierre, *Marquis* de Laplace. Philosophical essay on probabilities; fr. 6th Fr. ed., by F: W. Truscott and F: L. Emory. '02(Jl19) 12°, $2. Wiley.
Simonds, W: E. American date book. '02 (Ag9) 12°, $1. Kama.
Simpson, C. Love never faileth. '02(Je7) D. $1.25. Revell.
Simpson, Ja. Y. Henry Drummond. '01. '02(Ja11) 12°, (Famous Scots.) 75 c. Scribner.
SIN.
Tennant. Origin and propagation of sin. *$1.10 net. Macmillan.
See also Crime and criminals;—Salvation.
Sin of Jasper Standish. Humphreys, *Mrs.* E. M. J. G. $1.25. Fenno.
Sinclair, W. M. Unto you, young women. '01. '02(F15) 12°, net, $1. Lippincott.
Singer, I., *and others, eds.* Jewish encyclopædia. v. 2. '02(Ag2) il. Q. subs., per v., $7; hf. mor., $9. Funk.
SINGING.
Myer. Renaissance of the vocal art. $1. Boston Music.
See also Church music;—Voice.
Singular metamorphosis. Skiles, M. E. 50 c. Abbey Press.
Singular will. Marsh, G: $1.50. Neely.
Sinker stories of wit and humor. Goodwin, J. J. $1. Ogilvie.
Sinnett, Brown. Widow Wiley and some other old folk. '02(F15) 12°, $1.50. Dutton.
Sir Walter of Kent. Lewis, J. A. $1.50; 50 c. Bonnell.
Sister Beatrice. Maeterlinck, M. net, $1.20. Dodd.
Sister in name only. Wall, *Mrs.* D. H. $1. Neely.
Six little princesses. Prentiss, *Mrs.* E. 75 c. Burt.
Sixteenth century classics. D. $1. [Longmans] Univ. of Penn.
—Erasmus. Select colloquies.
SKEPTICISM.
Best. The college man in doubt. net, 50c. Westminster.
Searching for truth. $1.50. Eckler.
See also Agnosticism;—Free thought.
Sketch book. *See* Irving, W.
Skid and I. Sayler, G: W. $2.50. Sayler.

Skiles, May E. A singular metamorphosis. '02(Ag30) D. 50 c. Abbey Press.

SKIN.
Allen. Diseases of the skin. $2. Boericke & T.
Loeb. Production and suppression of muscular twitching of the skin by electrolytes. *25 c. net. Univ. of Chic.
Stelwagon. Disease of the skin. *$6 net; $7 net. Saunders.

Skinner, C: M. Prisons of the nation and their inmates. '02(F8) Q. (Eagle lib., v. 17, no. 2.) pap., 10 c. Brooklyn Eagle.

Skinner, W. H., *and* Burgert, Celia M. Lessons in English based upon principles of literary interpretation. '02(Je21) il. D. (Lessons in English.) 50 c. Silver.

Skoot. Sadler, C. G. 50 c. Jennings.

Skrine, J: H. Pastor Agnorum: a schoolmaster's afterthoughts. '02(Je7) D. net, $1.60. Longmans.

Sladen, Douglas. In Sicily. '02(F1) 2 v., il. 4°. net, $20. Dutton.

Slate, T: Physics: for secondary schools. '02(Je28) 12°, hf. leath., net, $1.10. Macmillan.

SLAVERY.
Ballagh. Hist. of slavery in Va. $1.50. Johns Hopkins.

SLEIGHT OF HAND.
See Conjuring.

Slicer, T: R. One world at a time. '02 (Mr22) O. net, $1.35. Putnam.

Sloan, W. N. Social regeneration the work of Christianity. '02(Je21) S. net, 60 c. Westminster.

Sloane, W: M. Napoleon Bonaparte. New lib. ed. '02(F22) 4 v., il. 4°, net, $18; hf. mor., net, $32. Century.

SLOYD.
Molander. Scientific sloyd. 50 c. Bardeen.

Smale, Morton, *and* Colyer, J. F. Diseases and injuries of the teeth. 2d ed. rev. and enl. '01. '02(F8) O. $7. Longmans.

Small, Albion W. The sociologists' point of view. '02(F1) 8°, pap., net, 10 c. Univ. of Chic.

Small end of great problems. Herford, B. net, $1.60. Longmans.

SMALLPOX.
Fox. Treatise on smallpox. $3. Lippincott.
Moore, *ed.* Variola, vaccination, varicella, etc. net, $5; net, $6. Saunders.

Smart, C: Handbook for the hospital corps of the U. S. army and state military forces. 3d ed. rev. and enl. '02(Jl19) 12°, *$2.50 net. Wood.

Smeaton, O. The Medici and the Italian Renaissance. '01. '02(F1) D. (World's epoch-makers.) $1.25. Scribner.

Smedberg, Harold V. Improprieties of Noah, and other stories. '01. '02(F15) D. 50 c. Abbey Press.

Smiley, Ja. B., *ed.* Household cook book. New century ed. '02(Ag9) il. 12°, oilcl., $1.50. Drake.

Smiley, T: E. Lays and lyrics. '02(Jl19) D. $1.25. Abbey Press.

Smith, Adèle M. Proof-reading and punctuation. '02(Ag9) 16°, *90 c. net. Adèle M. Smith.

Smith, Alb. L. *See* Hessler, J: C.

Smith, Boston. Uncle Boston's spicy breezes. '02(Ja25) il. S. net, $1. Am. Bapt.

Smith, C. Alphonso. *See* Krüger, G.

Smith, C. P. Texas notarial manual and form book. '02(Je7) 8°, shp., $4. Gammel.

Smith, Chester W: A summer of Saturdays. '01. '02(Je7) il. 12°, 65 c. Gillan.

Smith, Colin. Bridge condensed. '02(Mr8) 16°, pap., 50 c. Scribner.

Smith, D: Eug. *See* Beman, W. W.

Smith, E. E. Ideal word book. '02(Je7) S. 17 c. Flanagan.

Smith, E. F. Text-book of anatomy, physiology and hygiene. 2d ed. rev. '01. '02 (F22) il. 12°, $1. W: R. Jenkins.

Smith, *Mrs.* Eliz. T., [*formerly* L. T. Meade.] Daddy's girl. '02(Je14) 12°, (Fireside ser.) $1. Burt.

Smith, *Mrs.* Eliz. T. Very naughty girl. '02(Ap19) il. 12°, (Fireside ser.) $1. Burt.

Smith, Emory E. The golden poppy. '02 (Mr22) il. O. net, $1.50. E. E. Smith.

Smith, Eug. Home aquarium and how to care for it. '02(Jl19) 12°, **$1.20 net. Dutton.

Smith, G. C. Moore, *ed.* *See* Smith, *Sir* H.

Smith, Gipsy. His life and work by himself. '02(Ap19) 8°, net, $1.50. Revell.

Smith, Goldwin. Commonwealth or empire. '02(Ap12) 12°, net, 60 c. Macmillan.

Smith, H. M. *See* Sage, D.

Smith, *Sir* Harry. Autobiography; ed. with supp. chap., by G. C. Moore Smith. '02 (Mr29) 2 v., il. 8°, net, $8. Dutton.

Smith, Horace E. Studies in juridical law. '02(Jl12) O. shp., $3.50. Flood.

Smith, Ja. M. *See* New York. Digest.

Smith, Jeremiah. Selection of cases on private corporations. 2d ed. '02(Je28) 2 v., O. net, $6. Harvard Law.

Smith, J: W., ["Jean Yelsew."] The mountaineers. '02(My24) D. $1; $1.50; hf. mor., $2; mor., $2.50. Pub. Ho. M. E. Ch. So.

Smith, Jos. J., *comp.* Civil and military list of Rhode Island, 1800-1850. '01. '02(Mr1) sq. 4°, net, $7.50. Preston.

Smith, Jos. W. Training for citizenship. '02(Ag2) D. **90 c. net. Lothrop.

Smith, Julius. Ten years in Burma. '02 (Je28) 12°, $1. Eaton & M.

Smith, Julius. Ten years in Burma. '02 (Mr22) D. net, $1. Jennings.

Smith, M. R., *rep.* *See* Missouri. *St. Louis and Kansas City cts. of appeals.* Cases.

Smith, May R. The lost Christmas, and other poems. '01. '02(F15) 16°, (Dainty ser.) pap., 50 c. Dutton.

Smith, Percey F. Elementary calculus. '02 (Mr29) D. $1.25. Am. Bk.

Smith, Percey F. Four-place logarithmic tables. '02(Ap5) O. net, 50 c. Holt.

Smith, Roy W. Achromatic spindle in the spore mother-cells of osmunda regalis. '02 (F1) 8°, (Cont. from Hull botanical lab'y, no. 23.) pap., net, 25 c. Univ. of Chic.

Smith, S: G. Abraham Lincoln. '02(My24) D. (Hero ser., no. 3.) net, 25 c. Jennings.

Smith, Sa. S. Founders of the Mass. Bay Colony. '02(Jl12) il. 12°, *$5 net. Woodward & L.

Smith, *Mrs.* Toulmin. *See* Smith, *Mrs.* E. T.

Smith, W: W. Course in first year Latin for Regents' examinations. '02(F1) D. buckram, $1. W: R. Jenkins.

Smithsonian cont. to knowledge. Smith. Inst.
—Langley. Experiments in aerodynamics. $1.
SMOKE.
See Fumigation.
Smyth, Newman. Through science to faith. '02(F15) O. net, $1.50. Scribner.
Smith, J: C. Love's itinerary. '02. '01 (Ja4) D. (Town and country lib., no. 307.) $1; pap., 50 c. Appleton.
Snowden, W: H. Some old historic landmarks of Virginia and Maryland for the tourist over the Washington, Alexandria and Mount Vernon electric railway. 3d ed. '02(Jl19) il. 12°, pap., *25 c. net. Ramey.
Snyder, C., *and* Thurston, E. L. Universal system of practical bookkeeping. '02(Je7) Q. $1.25. Am. Bk.
Snyder, W: L. Notaries' and commissioners' manual. 7th rev., enl. ed. '02(Je14) O. $1.50. Baker, V. & Co.
So fight I. Hahn, C: C. 10 c. Whittaker.
Social and ethical interpretations in mental development. Baldwin, J. M: net, $2.60. Macmillan.
Social effect of machinery. *See* Lafarque, P.
Social England. Traill, H: D. v. 1. net, $4.50. Putnam.
Social (The) evil, with special ref. to conditions existing in the city of New York. '02(Mr22) 12°, net, $1.25. Putnam.
Social regeneration the work of Christianity. Sloan, W. N. net, 60 c. Westminster.
Social salvation. Gladden, W. net, $1. Houghton, M. & Co.
SOCIAL SCIENCE.
Kellor. Experimental sociology. net, $2. Macmillan.
Lane. Level of social motion. net, $2. Macmillan.
Small. The sociologist's point of view. net, 10 c. Univ. of Chic.
See also Civilization;—Crime and criminals;—Ethics;—Political economy;—Political science;—Socialism;—Temperance.
Social science ser. *See* Scribner's.
SOCIALISM.
Blatchford. Britain for the British. 50 c.; 25 c. Kerr.
Cathrein. Socialism exposed and refuted. *$1.25 net. Benziger.
Collins. Truth about socialism. 25 c. J. A. Wayland.
De Leon. Socialism *vs.* anarchism. 10 c. N. Y. Labor News.
Engels. Socialism. 50 c. N. Y. Labor News.
McGrady. Voice from England. 10 c. Standard.
Poland. Socialism. net, 5 c. Herder.
Rowell. Everybody's opportunity; or, quick socialism. 10 c.—Workingman's opportunity. 5 c. Free Socialist.
Tcherkesoff. Pages of socialist history. 25 c. C. B. Cooper.
See also Communism;—Political economy.
Socialist lib. O. pap. Socialistic Co-op.
—Adventures of John McCue, socialist. 10 c. (v. 2, 1.)
—Hanford. Railroading in the U. S. 5 c. (v. 1, 11.)
—Lafarque. Religion of capital. 10 c. (v. 2, 2.)
—McGrady. Clerical capitalist. 10 c. (v. 1, 10.)
SOCIETIES.
Hinds. Am. communities. $1. Kerr.
Society in the Elizabethan age. Hall, H. *$2.50 net. Dutton.
SOCIOLOGY.
See Social science.
SODA WATER.
See Confectionery.
SOILS.
Campbell. Soil culture manual. 40 c. H. W. Campbell.
Soldiers' field. Higginson, H: L. 75 c.; $5. Updike.
SOLOMON'S TEMPLE.
Schmidt. Solomon's Temple in the light of other oriental temples. net, $1. Univ. of Chic.
SOLUTION.
See Chemistry.
Some letters of Alfred Henry, the third-floorer. '02(Je28) T. 50 c. Informant.
Some merry adventures of Robin Hood. Pyle, H. net, 60 c. Scribner.
Some pretty girls. Underwood, C. F. $3; $5. Quail & W.
Some unpublished letters. Walpole, H. net, $1.50. Longmans.
Sommerville, Maxwell. Engraved gems. '01. '02(F22) O. net, $1.50. Biddle.
Son of a fiddler. Lee, J. $1.50. Houghton, M. & Co.
Sonderegger, C. L' achèvement du canal de Panama. '02(Mr8) O. pap., $2.50. Stechert.
Song of the Sannyasin. Vivekananda, *Swami.* *15 c. net. Van Haagan.
SONG-BOOKS.
Army songster. 25 c. Bell Bk.
Tomlins, *ed.* Laurel song book. $1.50; $1. Birchard.
See also Hymns and hymn writers;—Songs.
SONGS.
Hodgman. Home's sweet harmonies. 80 c. Home Pub.
Johnson. Popular English ballads, ancient and modern. 4 v. $3. Lippincott.
New songs for college glee clubs. 50 c. Hinds.
O'Conor. Irish com-all-ye's. 25 c. Popular.
O'Conor, *comp.* Old time songs and ballads of Ireland. $2. Popular.
See also Ballads;—Church music.
Songs not set to music. Fargo, K. M. $1. Abbey Press.
Songs of childhood. Ramal, W. net, $1.20. Longmans.
Songs of the Eastern colleges. Atkinson, R. W. $1.25. Hinds.
Songs of the press. Millard, B. *75 c. net. Elder.
Songs of the Sahkohnagos. Deveron, H. $1.25. Abbey Press.
Sonnenblicke aus der Amer. praxis. Beck, C. net, 30 c. Lemcke.
Sonnets and songs for a house of days. Binkley, C. net, $1.25. A. M. Robertson.
Sonnets from the Trophies. Heredia, J. M. de. *$1.25 net. Elder.
Sons of the Am. Revolution: national register of the soc.; comp. by L: H. Cornish; register list collated and ed. by A. H. Clark. '02(Ag2) il. 8°, hf. mor., $5. L: H. Cornish.

Sophocles. The Antigone; notes by M. A. Bayfield. '02(Mr22) 12°, (Classical ser.) net, 60 c. Macmillan.
Sordello. Browning, R. 75 c. Macmillan.
Sorrow and solace of Esther. Barnes, C: W. net, 30 c. Jennings.
SOUL.
See Psychology.
Soul fragrance. Kohaus, H. M. 40 c. Alliance.
Soul in the unseen world. Hutton, R. E. net, $2. Dutton.
Soul-winners' secrets. Oliver, G. F. 25 c. Jennings.
SOUND.
Dexter. Elem. exercises on sound, light and heat. 90 c. Longmans.
See also Telephone.
Source readers in Am. history. Hart, A. B. *40 c. net. Macmillan.
Sousa, J: P. The fifth string. '02(F8) il. D. $1.25. Bowen-M.
SOUTH (The).
See United States;—*also* names of Southern states.
SOUTH AFRICA.
Abbott. Tommy Cornstalk. $2. Longmans.
Doyle. War in South Africa. 10 c. McClure, P.
Fleming. Glimpses of South Africa in peace and in war. $3. Dominion.
Harding. War in So. Africa and the Dark Continent from savagery to civilization. $2; $3; $4. Dominion.
Phillipps. With Rimington. $2.50. Longmans.
See also Boers;—Matabeleland;—Natal.
SOUTH AMERICA.
Keane. South America. $4.50. Lippincott.
See also Central America;—Peru.
South Carolina. Code of laws. In 2 v. v. 1, civil code. '02(Ag9) O. shp., $5. State Co.
South Carolina. *Supreme ct.* Repts. v. 60. '01· '02(F1) O. shp., $5.75. Bryan.
South Dakota. *Supreme ct.* Repts. (Horner.) v. 14. '02(Ap5) O. shp., $3. State Pub.
Southeastern reporter, v. 39. Permanent ed. '01. '02(Ja18); v. 40(Je7) O. (Nat. reporter system, state ser.) shp., ea., $4. West Pub.
Southern reporter, v. 30. '02(Mr1); v. 31 (Ag2) O. (Nat. reporter system, state ser.) shp., ea., $4. West Pub.
Southern reporter. Digest of decisions. '02 (My24) O. (Nat. reporter system digests, Southern ser., v. 2.) shp., net, $6. West Pub.
Southwestern reporter, v. 64. Permanent ed. '01. '02(Ja18); v. 65 (Mr29); v. 66 (My17); v. 67 (Jl19) O. (Nat. reporter system, stat ser.) shp., ea., $4. West Pub.
Southworth, *Mrs.* Emma D. E. N. Hidden hand. '02(My3) 12°, (Home lib.) $1. Burt.
Southworth, *Mrs.* Emma D. E. N. Ishmael. '02(Ag2) 12°, (Home lib.) $1. Burt.
Southworth, *Mrs.* Emma D. E. N. Self-raised. '02(Ag9) 12°, (Home lib.) $1. Burt.
Spackman, —. *See* Lathbury, B. B.
SPAIN.
Helps. Spanish conquest of America. v. 2. $1.50. Lane.

SPAIN.—*Continued.*
Higgin. Spanish life in town and country. net, $1.20. Putnam.
See also Ferdinand, *King of Spain*;—Peninsular war;—Spanish-Am. war;—Zincali.
Spalding, F: P. Text-book on roads and pavements. 2d rev., enl. ed. '02(Mr22) il. 12°, $2. Wiley.
Spalding, J: L. Religion, agnosticism and education. '02(Je21) D. net. 80 c. McClurg.
Spalding's athletic lib. 16°, pap., 10 c. Am. Sports.
—Spalding's official athletic almanac. (v. 13, 145.)
—Spalding's official baseball guide. (v. 13, 150.)
Spalding's official athletic almanac; comp. by J. E. Sullivan, 1902. '02(Ap26) il. 16°, (Athletic lib., v. 13, no. 145.) pap., 10 c. Am. Sports.
Spalding's official baseball guide, 1902.; ed. by H: Chadwick. '02(My24) il. S. (Athletic lib., v. 13, no. 150.) pap., 10 c. Am. Sports.
Spangenberg, Eug. Practical arithmetic explained to the practical mechanic. '02(Jl12) T. 50 c. Zeller.
Spangler, Nellie Y. Bird play. '01. '02 (Ja25) 12°, pap., 15 c. Kellogg.
SPANISH-AM. WAR.
Halstead. Full official hist. of the war with Spain. $3; $4; $6. Dominion.
Jones. Chaplain's experience; the "Texas" under fire. $1.25. Sherwood.
See also Rough Riders;—*also* Schley, W. S.
SPANISH LANGUAGE.
Appleton's geografia superior ilustrada. $1.50. Appleton.
Arnold. Enseñar á leer. 40 c. Silver.
Caballero. La familia de Alvareda. 75 c. Holt.
Estados Unidos. Constitucion. $1. Cambridge.
Ferry. Fonografia española. *$1 net. Whitaker & R.
Goldsmith. Idioma Inglés. 1st bk., 40 c.; 2d bk., 36 c. Globe Sch. Bk.
Lange. 20th century system Spanish course. 25 c. [San F. News] Pamphlet.
Maxwell. El sacrificio de Elisa. 50 c. Appleton.
Munro. Nociones de electricidad. 40 c. Appleton.
Pinney. Spanish and Eng. conversation. 1st and 2d bks. ea., 65 c. Ginn.
Puron. El lector moderno de Appleton. nos. 1-3. no. 1, 25 c.; no. 2, 35 c.; no. 3, 45 c. Appleton.
Ramsey. Spanish grammar, with exercise. net, $1.50. Holt.
Silva *and* Fourcaut. Lectura y conversación. 60 c. Am. Bk.
Stewart. Nociones de fisica. 20 c. Appleton.
Velázquez de la Cadena, *comp.* Nuevo diccionario-Inglesa y Española. pt. 2. $3.50. Appleton.
Sparroy, Wilfrid. Persian children of the Royal family. '02(Je28) 8°, net, $3.50. Lane.
SPEAKERS.
See Readers and speakers.

Speer, Rob. E. Principles of Jesus applied to some questions of to-day. '02(My3) 16°, net, 80 c. Revell.
Speckled bird. Wilson, *Mrs.* A. J. E. $1.50. G: W. Dillingham.
SPELLERS.
Bouton. Spelling and word building. 29 c. University.
Daly. Advanced rational speller. 25 c. Sanborn.
Hunt *and* Gourley. Modern pronouncing speller. 20 c. Butler.
Mavor. Eng. spelling book. 40 c. Warne.
Parlin. Quincy word list. 7000 Eng. words. 24 c. Morse.
Smith. Ideal word book. 17 c. Flanagan.
Wheeler's elem. speller. 25 c. W: H: Wheeler.
See also Primers.
Spence, H: D. M. Early Christianity and Paganism, A.D. 64 to the fourth century. '02(Ag23) 8°, *$4 net. Dutton.
Spencer, Herbert. Facts and comments. '02 (My24) O. net, $1.20. Appleton.
Spender, A. Edm. Two winters in Norway. '02(Mr8) il. O. $4. Longmans.
Spenders (The). Wilson, H. L. $1.50. Lothrop
SPIDERS.
Emerton. Common spiders of the U. S. *$1.50 net. Ginn.
Spielmannskind (Das) und stumme ratsherr. Riehl, W. H. 35 c. Am. Bk.
Spindle and plough. Dudeney, *Mrs.* H. $1.50. Dodd.
SPINE.
See Nervous system.
SPINOZA, Benedict de.
Gore. Imagination in Spinoza and Hume. net, 35 c. Univ. of Chic.
Spirit echoes. Hull, M. E. net, 75 c. Sunflower.
Spiritual heroes. Muzzey, D: S. net, $1.25. Doubleday, P.
Spiritual pepper and salt. Stang, W: 30 c. Benziger.
SPIRITUALISM.
Dangers of spiritualism. net, 75 c. Herder.
Gaffield. Celestial message. n. p. Lee & S.
Nixon. Beyond the vail. $1.75. Hudson-K.
Revelations from the eternal world. 20 c. Star.
Twing. Henry Drummond in spirit life. 10 c. Star.
Spofford, A. R., *and* Annandale, C., *eds.* xxth century cyclopædia and at'as. '01. '02(Ap12) 8 v., il. 8°, art v., $20; hf. mis., $26. Gebbie.
Sport of the gods. Dunbar, P. L. $1.50. Dodd.
SPORTS AND SPORTSMEN.
Gordon. Sporting reminiscences. net, $4. Dutton.
See also Baseball;—Canoeing;—Polo;—Yachts and yachting.
Spotswood, Dillon J. *See* Nuverbis, *pseud.*
Springs of character. Schofield, A. T. net, $1.30. Funk.
SQUABS.
See Pigeons.
Squirrel and the crow. Neidlinger, D. H. 50 c. Rand, McN. & Co.

Staebler, C. Manual on the Book of books for juniors: first book in catechetical study. '02(My10) S. (Young people's alliance ser., no. 3.) pap., 20 c. Mattill & L.
Staedeler, Georg A. K. System of qualitative chemical analysis; rev. tr. by G: B. Frankforter. 2d Am. ed. '01. '02(Ag30) D. 60 c. H. W. Wilson.
Staley, Edgcumbe. Watteau, master painter of the Fêtes galantes. '01. '02(Ja4) il. 16°, (Bell's miniature ser. of painters.) 50 c. Macmillan.
Standard guide ser. il. D. pap., 25 c. Foster & R.
—New York City standard guide.
Standard lib. 16°, pap., 10 c. Standard.
—McGrady. Voice from England.
Standard literature ser. 12°, pap., 20 c. University.
—Scott. Waverley. (double no. 50.)
—Shakespeare. Merchant of Venice. (49.)
Standard reader ser. Funk.
—Funk *and* Moses, *eds.* Standard first reader. 35 c.—Teachers' manual for first reader. 50 c.
Standard socialist ser. 16°. Kerr.
—Broome. Last days of the Ruskin Co-operative Assoc. 50 c.
Stanford's compendium of geography and travel. il. 8°. Lippincott.
—Keane. South America. $4.50.
Stang, W: Spiritual pepper and salt for Catholics and non-Catholics. '02(Mr29) S. pap., 30 c. Benziger.
STANLEY, H: M.
Godbey. Henry M. Stanley. $1. Donohue.
Stannard, *Mrs.* Henrietta E. V., ["John Strange Winter."] The magic wheel. '01. '02(Mr8) D. $1.25. Lippincott.
Stanton, S. C., *ed.* *See* Billings, F., *ed.*
Stapleton, Ammon. Memorials of the Huguenots in America. '01. '02(Mr22) il. O. $1.50. Huguenot.
STAR CHAMBER.
Scofield. Study of the court of Star Chamber. net, $1. Univ. of Chic.
Starbucks (The). Read, O. P. $1.50. Laird.
STARS.
Browne. How to tell the time of night by the stars. 50 c. Lee & S.
Hale. New star in Perseus. net, 10 c. Univ. of Chic.
See also Astrology;—Astronomy.
State intervention in Eng. education. De Montmorency, J. E. G. net, $1.50. Macmillan.
Statesmen's (The) year book for 1902. (J. S. Keltie.) '02(Ap26) 12°, net, $3. Macmillan.
STATIONERS AND STATIONERY.
Wilson. Directory of booksellers, stationers, librarians and publishers in the U. S. and Can. $10. H. W. Wilson.
Stay, Jones B. Mind telegraph; tr. fr. the 6th Germ. ed. by Ivry. '01. '02(Mr8) 16°, pap., 25 c. Alliance.
Stead, Alfr. Japan of to-day. '02(My10) 12°, net, $2. Dutton.
Stead, W: T: Americanization of the world. '02(F22) 12°, $1. Markley.
STEAM ENGINE.
Hurst. Hints on steam engine design and construction. 60 c. Lippincott.

STEAM ENGINE.—*Continued.*
Thurston. Stationary steam engines, simple and compound. $2.50. Wiley.
See also Locomotives;—Machinery;—Turbines.
Stebbins, Genevieve. Delsarte system of expression. 6th ed. rev. and enl. '02(F22) D. $2. Werner.
Stechhan, Otto. Unrequited love. '02(Mr1) D. $1. Abbey Press.
Stechhan, Otto. Whither are we drifting? '02(Mr8) D. $1. Abbey Press.
Stedman, E. C. *and* T: L., *eds.* Complete pocket guide to Europe. '02(Je14) T. leath., $1.25. W: R. Jenkins.
STEEL.
Colby. Review and text of the Am. standard specifications for steel. net, $1.10. Chemical.
See also Iron.
Steele, Francisca M., ["Darley Dale."] Convents of Great Britain. '02(Je28) il. 8°, net, $2. Herder.
Steele, J: W. Coal oil Johnny. '02(My17) 12°, $1.50. J: A. Hill.
Steele, K. N. Simple rules for bridge. '02 (Mr22) S. pap., 50 c. Eichelberger.
Steiner, Bernard C. Western Maryland in the Revolution. '02(Mr8) O. (Johns Hopkins Univ. studies, 20th ser., no. 1.) pap., 30 c. Johns Hopkins.
Stelwagon, H: W. Treatise on disease of the skin. '02(Ag2) il. 8°, *$6 net; shp., $7 net. Saunders.
STENOGRAPHY.
Barnes. Shorthand lessons by the word method. $1.25. A. J. Barnes.
Beale. Book of legal dictation. 50 c. Beale Press.
Brown. Science and art of phrase-making. $1.50. Shorthand Bu.
Ferry. Fonografia española. *$1 net. Whitaker & R.
Forney. Inductive lessons. 80 c. State Normal Sch.
Gabelsberger Shorthand Soc., *ed.* Reader to Richter's graphic shorthand. 50 c. Int. News.
Hardcastle. Word signs made easy. $1. M. A. Hardcastle.
Laird. Manual of syllabic shorthand. $2. Neil.
Musick. Combination shorthand dict. and reader: Benn Pitman phonography. $1.50. W: L. Musick.
Pitman, B. *and* Howard. Business letters: no. 1, Misc. corr. 25 c. Phonograph.
Pitman, I: Business corr. in shorthand. no. 2. 30 c.—Phonographic teacher, 20 c. Pitman.
Pitman, I: Shorthand instructor. $1.50. Pitman.
Stephen, *Sir* Ja. F. Digest of the law of evidence; fr. the 5th ed. Am. notes adapt. to N. E. states, by G: E. Beers. '01. '02 (Mr22); adapt. to Ohio (Ag23) D. shp., ea., $4. Dissell.
Stephen, Leslie. George Eliot. '02(Je14) 12°, (English men of letters.) net, 75 c. Macmillan.
Stephen Holton. Pidgin, C: F. $1.50. L. C. Page.
Stephens, J: V. Evolution of the confession of faith of the Cumberland Presb. church. '02(My10) O. pap., 10 c. Cumberland.
Stephens, W: R. W., *and* Hunt, W., *eds.* Hist. of the Eng. church. v. 3, 4. '02 (Ag23) 12°, ea., *$2 net. Macmillan.
Stepping stones. Marden, O. S. **$1 net. Lothrop.
Sterling, Adaline W., Holbrook, Flo., *and* Hale, E: E., *jr.* Nature and life. 4th reader. pt. 1. '02(Ag30) 16°, (Hawthorne readers.) 56 c.; or in 2 pts., ea., 32 c. Globe Sch. Bk.
Stern, Menco. Geschichten von Deutschen städten. '02(Ja25) D. $1.25. Am. Bk.
Sternberg, G: M. Text-book of bacteriology. 2d rev. ed. '01. '02(F22) il. 8°, net, $5; leath., net, $5.75. Wood.
Sterne, L. Sentimental journey through France and Italy. '02(My3) 12°. (Home lib.) $1. Burt.
Stevens, E: A. American law of assemblies applicable to lodges, conventions and public meetings. '01. '02(Mr29) S. net, $1. E: A. Stevens.
Stevens, E: L. Business education. '02 (My3) S. pap., 15 c. Bardeen.
Stevens, Fk. L. Gametrogenesis and fertilization in albugo. '02(F15) 8°, (Cont. from the Hull botanical lab'y, no. 29.) pap., net, 25 c. Univ. of Chic.
Stevens, Horace J., *comp.* Copper handbook; ed. of 1902. '02(Ap26) 8°, $2; full mor., $3. H. J. Stevens.
Stevens, L. B. Faciology. New ed. '02 (My17) 12°, pap., 25 c. Donohue.
Stevens, Sheppard. In the eagle's talon. '02 (Je14) il. D. $1.50. Little, B. & Co.
Stevenson, Ja. H: Assyrian and Babylonian contracts, with Aramaic ref. notes. '02 (Ag2) D. (Vanderbilt Oriental ser.) $2.50. Am. Bk.
Stevenson, R. L: Æs triplex. '02(Mr22) nar. S. (Vest pocket ser.) pap., net, 25 c.; flex. cl., net, 40 c.; flex. leath., net, 75 c.; Jap. vellum ed., $1. T: B. Mosher.
Stevenson, R. L: Best of Stevenson; ed. by A. Jessup. '02(Ag16) D. †$1.25. L. C. Page.
Stevenson, R. L: Child's garden of verses. [New ed.] '01. '02(F1) il. D. net, 60 c. Scribner.
Stevenson, R. L: The pocket R. L. S.: favorite passages. '02(Ag23) 32°, *$1 net. Scribner.
Steward, F. J. *See* Jacobson, W. H. A.
Stewart, Balfour. Nociones de fisica. Neuva ed. Castellana. '01. '02(F22) 18°, 20 c. Appleton.
Stewart, Purves. *See* Ballance, C: A.
Stiles, Ezra. Literary diary of Ezra Stiles, president of Yale College; ed. by F. B. Dexter. '01. '02(Mr15) 3 v., 8°, net, $7.50. Scribner.
Stillman Gott, farmer and fisherman. Sibley, E. D. $1.50. Brooks.
STIMULANTS AND NARCOTICS.
See Morphinism.
Stinchfield, M. Ida. Sibyl's conquest. '02 (Ap26) 12°, $1.50. Neely.
Stitson, J. R. The human hair. '01. '02 (Ap12) 12°, $1.25. Maple.
STOCK BREEDING.
See Cattle.
STOCK EXCHANGE, London.
Duguid. Story of the Stock Exchange. net, $2. Dutton.

Stockett, J. Shaaf, *rep.* *See* Maryland. *Ct. of appeals.* Repts.
Stockmen's calculator. McCallum & Hofer Cattle Co. $1.50. McCallum.
Stockton, F. R: Kate Bonnet. '02(Mr1) D. $1.50. Appleton.
Stoddard, C: W. In the footprints of the padres. '02(F1) D. net, $1.50. Robertson.
Stoddard, W: O. Errand boy of Andrew Jackson. '02(My24) D. net, $1. Lothrop.
Stoeckel, Carl, *ed.* *See* Sedgwick, J:
Stoker, Bram. Mystery of the sea. '02 (Mr29) D. $1.50. Doubleday, P.
Stokes, Anson P. Cruising in the West Indies. '02(Jl19) O. **$1.25 net. Dodd.
Stokes, *Sir* G: G. Mathematical and physical papers: repr. with add. notes. v. 3. '01. '02(Ja4) 8°, (Cambridge Univ. Press ser.) net, $3.75. Macmillan.
Stokes, Whitley, *and* Strachan, J:, *eds.* Thesaurus palæohibernicus: coll. of old Irish glosses, scholia, prose and verse. v. 1. '02(Ja18) 8°, (Cambridge Univ. Press ser.) net, $8. Macmillan.
Stolen correspondence from the Dead Letter Office. Sharp, B. A. 50 c. Gervais.
STOMACH.
Thompson. Acute dilation of the stomach. 75 c. Wood.
See also Digestion.
Stone, A. J. *See* Roosevelt, T.
Stone, E. D. *See* Thackeray, F. St. J.
Stone, Gertrude L., *and* Fickett, M. G., *comps.* Trees in prose and poetry. '02 (Je21) il. sq. D. 50 c. Ginn.
Stone, Wilbur M. Women designers of bookplates. '02(Ap19) il. nar. D. bds., net, $1; Jap. vellum, net, $2. Beam.
STONE DEALERS.
Hunt. United Mercantile Agency credit ratings for the marble, granite and stone dealers of the U. S. and Can. subs., $25. Un. Merc.
Stoner, Winifred S. Castles in Spain, and other sketches in rhyme. '02(Mr1) D. $1. Abbey Press.
STORIES.
See Fairy tales;—Fiction;—Legends.
Stories from Waverley. Scott, *Sir* W. $1. Macmillan
Stories of country life. Bradish, S. P. 40 c. Am. Bk.
Stories of heroes. 8°, 50 c. Silver.
—Price. Wandering heroes.
Stories of Illinois. Pratt, M. L. 50 c.; 40 c. Educ. Pub.
Stories of our country. Dawes, *Mrs.* S. E. v. 1, 2. ea., 40 c. Educ. Pub.
Stories of the red children. il. 16°. 40 c.; bds., 30 c. Educ. Pub.
—Longfellow. Hiawatha.
Stories of the Tuscan artists. Wherry, A. net, $4. Dutton.
Story, Alf. T: Swiss life in town and country. '02(F1) il. D. (Our European neighbors ser., no. 5.) net, $1.20. Putnam.
Story, W: W. In defense of Judas; repr. of A Roman lawyer in Jerusalem. '02(Jl19) sq. 24°, bds., $1. Philosopher Press.
Story of animal life. Lindsay, B. net, 35 c. Appleton.
Story of Azron. Rollins, A. W. $1. Holliswood.
Story of Cairo. Poole, S. L. $2; $2.50. Macmillan.
Story of China. Van Bergen, R. 60 c. Bardeen.
Story of Eden. Wyllarde, D. $1.50. Lane.
Story of François Villon. Morehead, G: 25 c. Ogilvie.
Story of Hiawatha. Longfellow, H: W. 40 c.; 30 c. Educ. Pub.
Story of home gardens. Cadwallader, S. 25 c. Home Gardening.
Story of little Eva. Stowe, *Mrs.* H. E. B. **75 c. net. Estes.
Story of little Nell. Dickens, C: **75 c. net. Estes.
Story (The) of Mary Maclane, by herself. '02(Je14) il. D. $1.50. H. S. Stone.
Story of Paul Dombey. Dickens, C: 15 c. Lippincott.
Story of Pemaquid. Kaler, J. O. 50 c. Crowell.
Story of the amphibians. Baskett, J. N. 60 c. Appleton.
Story of the art of music. Crowest, F: J. **35 c. net. Appleton.
Story of the Christian centuries. Selden, E: G. net, $1. Revell.
Story of the Khedivate. Dicey, E: net, $4. Scribner.
Story of the Mormons. Linn, W: A. net, $4. Macmillan.
Story of the nations ser. il. D. **$1.35 net; hf. leath., $1.60 net. Putnam.
—Edwards. Wales. (62.)
—Miller. Mediæval Rome. (63.)
Story of the Philippines. Halstead, M. $2; $3. Dominion.
Story of the token. Shiells, R. net, $1. Presb. Bd.
Story of the vine. Emerson, E: R. net, $1.25. Putnam.
Story of the world's worship. Dobbins, F. $2.25; $3.25. Dominion.
Story of three. Sherwood, W. J. 25 c. W: S. Lord.
Story of Tonty. Catherwood, *Mrs.* M. H. $1.25. McClurg.
Stout heart. Kellogg, E. $1.25. Lee & S.
Stowe, *Mrs.* Ht. E. B. He's coming to-morrow. '02(Ap12) 12°, (Ideal messages ser.) pap., net, 25 c. Revell.
Stowe, *Mrs.* Ht. E. B. Minister's wooing. '02(My17) 12°, (Home lib.) $1. Burt.
Stowe, *Mrs.* Ht. E. B. Story of little Eva fr. Uncle Tom's Cabin. '02(Ag16) 16°, (Famous children of lit. ser.) **75 c. net. Estes.
Stowe, *Mrs.* Ht. E. B. Uncle Tom's cabin. '02(Mr22) 12°, $2; hf. mor., $3; mor., $4. Dominion.
Strachan, Ja. Hebrew ideals from the story of the patriarchs. pt. 1, Genesis. '02 (Ag23) 12°, (Bible class handbooks.) *60 c. net. Scribner.
Strachan, J:, *ed.* *See* Stokes, W., *ed.*
Strangers at the gate. Gordon, S: $1.50. Jewish Pub.
Stratemeyer, E: Lost on the Orinoco. '02 (Ap26) il. D. (Pan-American ser., no. 1.) net, $1. Lee & S.
STRATFORD-ON-AVON.
Way, *comp.* Reliques of Stratford-on-Avon. 50 c.; 75 c. Lane.

STRAWBERRY.
Barnard. The strawberry garden, how it was planted, etc. 40 c. Coates.
Stray leaves from a border garden. Holme, M. P. M. net, $1.50. Lane.
Streamer, D. Ruthless rhymes for heartless homes. New ed. '01· '02(My3) il. sq. D. $1.25. Russell.
Street, Eug. E. *See* Higgin, L.
STREET-RAILROADS.
Andrews. Handbook for street railway engineers. $1.25. Wiley.
Massachusetts. Street railway accident law. $3.25. Lawyers' Bk.
Nellis. Law of street railroads. $6. M. Bender.
Strength of the weak. Hotchkiss, C. C. $1.50. Appleton.
Stretton, Hesba. New child's life of Christ. '01· '02(Ap26) il. 12°, $1. Winston.
Strollers (The). Isham, F: S. $1.50. Bowen-M.
Strong, J. Next great awakening. '02 (Mr29) D. 75 c. Baker & T.
Stronger than love. Hector, *Mrs.* A. F. †$1.50. Brentano's.
Struggle for a fortune. Castlemon, H. $1. Saalfield.
Strutt, J: W:, [*Baron* Rayleigh.] Scientific papers. v. 3, 1887-1892. '02(Mr8) 8°, (Cambridge Univ. Press ser.) net, $5. Macmillan.
STUARTS.
Rait. Five Stuart princesses. net, $3.50 Dutton.
Stubbs, W: Ordination addresses; ed. by E. E. Holmes. '01· '02(Ja11) D. $2.25. Longmans.
STUDENTS.
Canfield. College student and his problems. net, $1. Macmillan.
Students' guide to health. Van Doren, D. T. $2. D. T. Van Doren.
Studies from the nude human figure in motion. Fiedler, A. $12. Hessling.
Studies in auditory and visual space perception. Pierce, A. H: net, $2. Longmans.
Studies in Gr. and Latin versions of Amos. Oesterley, W. O. E. *$1.30 net. Macmillan.
Studies in Irish hist. and biog. Falkiner, C. L. $5. Longmans.
Studies in spiritual harmony. Brown, G. M. $1. Reed Pub.
Studies of trees in winter. Huntington, A. O. net, $2.25. Knight.
STUDY.
See Home study.
Study of religion. Jastrow, M., *jr.* $1.50. Scribner.
Study of the court of Star Chamber. Scofield, C. L. net, $1. Univ. of Chic.
Sturt, H:, *ed.* Personal idealism: philosoph. essays. '02(Ag16) 8°, *$3.25 net. Macmillan.
Styan, K. E. Short history of sepulchral cross slabs, with ref. to other emblems found thereon. '02(Je28) 8°, net, $3. E. & J. B. Young.
SUCCESS.
Gilbert. 1000 ways to make money. $1. Donohue.
See also Business.
Success club debater. Hungerford, H. 25 c. Success.
Such stuff as dreams. Russell, C: E. net, $2. Bowen-M.
Suckling, *Sir* J: Love poems. '02(Ja11) S. (Lover's lib., no. 8.) net, 50 c.; leath., 75 c. Lane.
SUGGESTION (Mental).
See Hypnotism.
Suitors of Yvonne. Sabatini, R. net. $1.20. Putnam.
Sullivan, *Sir* E: Ivanhoe and Rob Roy, retold for children. New ed. '01· '02(F15) 16°, (Children's friend ser.) bds., 50 c. Little, B. & Co.
Sullivan, Eug. C. *See* Prescott, A. B:
Sullivan, Fk. J: Detective adviser. '02 (My17) S. pap., 60 c. Int. Detective.
Sullivan, Ja. E., *comp.* *See* Spalding's official athletic almanac.
Sullivan, T. R. Courage of conviction. '02 (Je7) D. $1.50. Scribner.
Sultan, G: Atlas and epitome of abdominal hernia; ed., with add., by W: B. Coley. '02(Ag2) il. 8°, (Medical hand atlases.) *$3 net. Saunders.
Summer of Saturdays. Smith, C. W: 65 c. Gillan.
Sundara, *Rao* T. T. Sundara Row's geometric exercises in paper folding: ed. and rev. by W. W. Beman and D. E. Smith. '02(Ag30) il. 12°, $1. Open Court.
SUNDAY.
Lewis. Sunday legislation. net, $1. Appleton.
Moule. Thoughts for the Sundays of the year. net, $1. Revell.
SUNDAY-SCHOOL.
Arnold, *ed.* Internat. S. S. lessons, 1902. 50 c. Revell.
Bible. Sunday-school scholar's Bible. 75 c.; $1. Nelson.
Hamill. Sunday-school teacher. 50 c. Pub. Ho. M. E. Ch., So.
Hatcher. Pastor and the Sunday-school. course no. 1. 75 c. Bapt. S. S. Bd.
Rice. Short hist. of the Internat. lesson system. *25 c. net. Am. S. S.
Sunlight and shadows. Dail, C. C. $1.50. Hudson-K.
Sunnyside ser. il. D. Ogilvie.
—Morehead. Francesca da Rimini. 25 c. (117.)
SUPERSTITION.
See Devil;—Spiritualism.
SURGERY.
American year-book of medicine and surgery. 2 v. ea., net, $3; net, $3.75. Saunders.
Cheyne *and* Burghard. Surgical treatment. v. 5, 6. ea., *$5. Lea.
Crile. Research into problems rel. to surgical operations. net, $2.50. Lippincott.
Heath. Clinical lectures on surgical subjects. $2. Blakiston.
Jacobson *and* Steward. Operations of surgery. 2 v. net, $10; $12. Blakiston.
Murphy, *ed.* General surgery. $1.50. Year Bk.
Robb. Aseptic surgical technique. $2. Lippincott.
Wharton. Minor surgery and bandaging. net, $3. Lea.

SURGERY.—*Continued.*
Zuckerhandl. Atlas and epitome of operative surgery. net, $3.50. Saunders.
See also Accidents;—Anatomy;—Autopsy;—Diagnosis; — Medicine; — Veterinary medicine and surgery.

Surprises of an empty hotel. Gunter, A. C. $1; 50 c. Home.

SURVEYING.
Johnson. Theory and practice of surveying. $4. Wiley.
Lupton. Mine surveying. $5. Longmans.
Noble *and* Casgrain. Tables for obtaining horizontal distances and difference of level, from stadia readings. $1. Engineering News.
Nugent. Plane surveying. $3.50. Wiley.
See also Engineering; — Geodesy; — Railroads;— Topographical drawing;—Trigonometry.

Susanne. Delano, F. J. 50 c. L. C. Page.

Sutherland, Millicent. Wind in the tree: love stories. '02(Ag16) il. 16°, †$1.50. Russell.

Swartz, Joel. Easter and the resurrection. '02(Ap12) 12°, pap., net, 15 c. Revell.

Swartz, Joel. Poems. '01· '02(F15) 12°, $1; $1.25. Coates.

SWEDEN.
Cronholm. Hist. of Sweden. 2 v. $5. N. N: Cronholm.

Swedenborg, E. Heavenly arcana. Rotch ed. v. 13. '02(Mr15) D. $1.25. Mass. New-Ch. Un.

Swedenborg, E. Ontology; or, signification of philosoph. terms; tr. by A. Acton. '01· '02(F1) D. pap., 50 c. Mass. New-Ch. Un.

SWEDISH MOVEMENT.
See Massage.

Sweet danger. Wilcox, *Mrs.* E. W. 50 c. Donohue.

Swete, H: B.. Patristic study. '02(Mr22) D. (Handbooks for the clergy.) net, 90 c. Longmans.

Swett, Sophie. Sarah the less. '02(Je7) il. D. net, 75 c. Westminster.

Swift, B:, *pseud. See* Paterson, W: R.

Swift, H: Walton, *rep. See* Mass. *Sup. judicial ct.* Repts.

Swift, J. Journal to Stella; ed. by G: A. Aitken. '01· '02(F22) D. (Lib. of standard literature.) $1.75. Putnam.

Swift, J. Prose works; ed. by T. Scott. v. 9. Cont. to *The Tatler, Examiner*, etc. '02 (Je7) 12°, (Bohn's standard lib.) net, $1. Macmillan.

Swift, J. Selections. '01· '02(Ap5) S. (Little masterpieces.) 50 c. Doubleday, P.

SWITZERLAND.
George. Little journey to Switzerland. 15 c. Flanagan.
Story. Swiss life in town and country. net, $1.20. Putnam.

Swoope, C. W. Lessons in practical electricity. '02(Je14) il. 8°, net, $2. Van Nostrand.

Sybel, H. v. Prinz Eugen von Savoyen; ed. by E. C. Quiggin. '02(Mr8) 12°, (Pitt Press ser.) net, 60 c. Macmillan.

Sykes, Percy M. Ten thousand miles in Persia; or, eight years in Iran. '02(Je21) il. 12°. net, $6. Scribner.

Symonds, E. M. *See* Paston, G:

Symons, Arth. Poems. '02(F15) 2 v., 8°, net. $3. Lane.

SYNONYMS.
Handy book of synonyms. 50 c. Lippincott.

Syntax of the verb in the Anglo-Saxon chronicle. Blain, H. M. net, 50 c. Barnes.

SYPHILIS.
Duhring, *and others*. Syphilis. net, $1. Treat.
Morton. Genito-urinary disease and syphilis. net, $3. Davis.

SYRACUSE, FIRST PRESB. CHURCH.
Northrup, *ed.* Early records of First Presb. Church of Syracuse, N. Y. 50 c. [Gill] Genealog. Soc.

T. Racksole and daughter. Bennett, A. $1.50. New Amsterdam.

TABLE-TENNIS.
See Ping-pong.

TABLES.
Blum. Reduction tables for ascertaining freight charges, etc. net, $3. Am. Code.

TACTICS.
Wisser. Tactics of coast defense. $2. Hudson-K.
See also Infantry.

Tagzeiten zum heiligsten Herzen Jesu. '02 (Je28) 24°, pap., 5 c. Herder.

Tait, Ja., *ed. See* Tout, T: F:

Talbot, A. N. Railway transition spiral. 3d ed., rev. '02(Ap19) 16°, flex. leath., $1.50. Van Nostrand.

Talbot, Ellen V. Courtship of sweet Anne Page. '02(Mr8) S. (Hour-glass stories.) net, 40 c. Funk.

Tale of a cat. Kern, M. 50 c. Abbey Press.

Tale of the great mutiny. Fitchett, W: H: $1.50. Scribner.

Tale of true love. Austin, A. net, $1.20. Harper.

Tales from Shakespeare. Lamb, C: 40 c. Heath.

Tales from *Town Topics*, no 43. '02(My10); no. 44 (Je7) 12°, pap., ea., 50 c. Town Topics.

Tales of destiny. Jordan, E. G. $1.50. Harper.

Tales of my father. F., A. M. $2. Longmans.

Tales of passed times. Perrault, C: net, 50 c.; 80 c. Macmillan.

Tales of the Spanish Main. Morris, M. $2. Macmillan.

Talisman. Fulda, L. 35 c. Heath.

Talling, Marshall P. Communion with God: extempore prayer. '02(Ag9) 12°, $1.25. Revell.

Talmage, Fk. De W. A vacation with nature. '02(Je21) D. net, $1. Funk.

Talmage, Fk. De W., Banks, L: A., *and others*. Life and work of T. De Witt Talmage. '02(My10) 12°, subs., $2; hf. mor., $2.75; full mor., $3.75. Winston.

TALMAGE, T: De Witt.
Adams. Life and sermons of Rev. T. De Witt Talmage. $1.25. Donohue.
Banks *and* Cook. Life and works of T. De Witt Talmage. $1.75. Bible House.
Talmage, F. D., *and others*. Life and work of T. De Witt Talmage. subs., $2; $2.75; $3.75. Winston.

TANNING.
Modern Am. tanning. $5. Jacobsen

Tappan, Eva M. Our country's story: elem. hist. of the U. S. '02(My24) il. sq. D. 65 c. Houghton, M. & Co.

TARIFF.
Marx. Wage-labor and capital; [also] Free-trade. 50 c. N. Y. Labor News.
See also Taxation.
Tarquinius Superbus. Epstein, A. J. $1.25. Mutual Pub.
Tarr, R. S. Physical geography of New York state. '02(Je14) il. 8°, net, $3.50. Macmillan.
Tarr, R. S., *and* McMurry, Fk. M. Complete geography. '02(Jl12) 12°, (Geographies, two book ser., bk. 2.) hf. leath., *$1 net. Macmillan.
Tarr, R. S., *and* McMurry, F. M. First book: home geography. '02(Je28) il. 12°, (Geographies, two-book ser.) hf. leath., net, 60 c. Macmillan.
Tarr and McMurry's geographies. il. 12°, net. Macmillan.
—Jones. Utah. *40 c.
—Wilson. Ohio. 30 c.
—Winans. Kansas. 30 c.
Tartarin de Tarascon. Daudet, A. 45 c. Am. Bk.
Tarver, J. C. Tiberius the tyrant. '02(Jl12) 8°, *$5 net. Dutton.
Tate, H: Aaron Crane. '02(Ap26) il. D. $1.50. Abbey Press.
Tatnall, Rob. R. *See* Crew, H:
Taunton, Ethelred L. Hist. of the Jesuits in England, 1580-1773. '01. '02(F15) il. 8°, net, $3.75. Lippincott.
Tauszky, Edm., *rep.* *See* California. *Superior ct.* Repts.
TAXATION.
Grand Rapids. Tax list. $10. Commercial Credit.
Hollister, *and others.* Taxation in Michigan and elsewhere. 50 c. Mich. Pol. Sci.
Purdy. Burdens of local taxation and who bears them. 25 c. Public Policy.
Purdy. Local option in taxation. 10 c. N. Y. Tax Reform.
Walker. Taxation of corporations in the U. S. 25 c. Am. Acad. Pol. Sci.
See also Political economy;—Tariff.
Taylor, Bayard. Poetical works. Household ed. '02(Ap5) il. D. $1.50. Houghton, M. & Co.
Taylor, Bayard. Views afoot or Europe seen with knapsack and staff. '02(Ap19) 12°, (Home lib.) $1. Burt.
Taylor, Bret L. Line-o'-type lyrics. '02 (My24) S. bds., net, 50 c. W: S. Lord
Taylor, C: M., *jr.* Why my photographs are bad. '02(Je14) il. O. net, $1. Jacobs.
Taylor, E: R. Into the light. '02(Ap5) 12°, bds., net, 75 c. Elder.
Taylor, Fes. L. School readers: Second reader. '02(Ag16) il. D. 35 c. Werner Sch. Bk.
Taylor, H. E. *See* Welch, J. H.
Taylor, Hannis. Treatise on international public law. '01. '02(F8) O. shp., net, $6.50. Callaghan.
Taylor, Hobart C. C. Crimson wing. '02 (Ap5) D. $1.50. H. S. Stone.
Taylor, J. H. Taylor on golf. '02(Ag9) il. D. **$1.60 net. Appleton.
Taylor, Jos. S., *ed.* Practical school problems. v. 1, pt. 1. '02(Ap5) O. pap., 30 c. [W: B. Harison] Practical Sch. Problems.
Taylor, S. Earl. *See* Taylor, T: E.
Taylor, T: E., Taylor, S. E., *and* Morgan, C: H. Studies in the life of Christ. '02 (Ap12) O. 75 c. Jennings.
Taylor, W: A. Intermere. '02(Ja11) D. $1. XX. Century.
T'bacca queen. Wilson, T. W. $1; 50 c. Appleton.
Tcherkesoff, W. Pages of socialist history. '02(Ag9) O. pap., 25 c. C. B. Cooper.
TEACHERS AND TEACHING.
Bender. The teacher at work. 75 c. Flanagan.
Dawes. Bilingual teaching in Belgian schools. *50 c. net. Macmillan.
Findlay. Principles of class teaching. net, $1.25. Macmillan.
Funk *and* Moses, *eds.* Teachers' manual for first reader. 50 c. Funk.
Laurie. Training of teachers and methods of instruction. net, $1.50. Macmillan.
Murché. Teachers' manual of object lessons for rural schools. net, 60 c. Macmillan.
See also Education;—Kindergarten;—Memory;—Sunday-school.
TEETH.
Hopkins. Care of the teeth. **75 c. net. Appleton.
MacDowell. Orthodontis. net, $4. Colegrove.
Marshall. Principles and practice of operative dentistry. subs., $5; $6. Lippincott.
Smale *and* Colyer. Diseases and injuries of the teeth. $7. Longmans.
Telegram almanac and cyclopedia, 1902. '02 (Mr15) 16°, pap., 20 c. Providence Telegram.
TELEGRAPHY.
Bubier. A B C of wireless telegraphy. $1. Bubier.
Edison. Telegraphy self-taught. $1. Drake.
See also Codes.
TELEPATHY.
Stay. Mind telegraph; telepathic influence of the human will. 25 c. Alliance.
Weltmer. Telepathy and thought transference. $1. Hudson-K.
TELEPHONE.
Cary. How to make and use the telephone. $1. Bubier.
Homans. A B C of the telephone. $1. Van Nostrand.
Houston *and* Kennelly. Electric telephone. $1. McGraw.
Hyde *and* McManman. Telephone troubles and how to find them on the magneto and common battery system. 25 c. Caspar.
TEMPERANCE.
Crozier. Temperance and the Anti-Saloon League. 15 c. Barbee & S.
Cumming. Public house reform. $1. Scribner.
Griffin. Why the legal (or force) method of promoting temperance does more harm than good. 15 c. A. Griffin.
National Temperance almanac, 1902. 10 c. Nat. Temp.
Shadwell. Drink, temperance and legislation. Longmans.
See also Beverages;—Wine.
Temple classics. *See* Macmillan's.
Temple of trusts. *See* De Leon, T: C.

TEMPLES.
See Solomon's temple.

Ten Brink, B. Language and metre of Chaucer. 2d ed., rev. by F. Kluge. '02(F15) 12°, net, $1.50. Macmillan.

Ten years in Burma. Smith, J. net, $1. Eaton & M.; Jennings.

Teniente de los gavilanes. Zayas Enriquez, R. de. †50 c. Appleton.

Tennant, F. R. Origin and propagation of sin: Hulsean lectures del. 1901-2. '02 (Ag16) 12°, (Cambridge Univ. Press ser.) *$1.10 net. Macmillan.

Tennessee. *Supreme ct.* Repts. (G: W. Pickle.) New ed., with annots. by R. T. Shannon. v. 19-21 (103-105.) '02(Ap12) v. 7-18 (92-102.); v. 1-6 (85-90) (Jl12) O. shp., ea., $3. Fetter.

Tennessee. *Supreme ct.* Repts. (G: W. Pickle.) [v. 98-106.] '01- '02(Ap5) O. shp., ea., $3. Marshall.

Tennessee Lee. Neill, M. $1. Neely.

Tennyson, A., *Lord.* In memoriam. '01- '02 (Ja11) 16°, (Caxton ser.) flex. lambskin, net, $1.20. Scribner.

Tennyson, A., *Lord.* The princess ed., by F. T. Baker. '02(Je7) D. (Twentieth century text-books.) 25 c. Appleton.

Tennyson, A., *Lord.* Birthday book; quotations for each day; sel. and arr. by E. J. S. '02(F15) 24°, 75 c.; $1; mor., $1.25. Warne.

TENNYSON, A., *Lord.*
Livingston. Bibliog. of the first ed. in book form of the works of Tennyson. $1. Dodd.

Terhune, Everit B. Michel Gulpe. '02 (Ag30) il. D. †$1.25. G: W. Dillingham.

TERPENES.
Heusler. Chemistry of the terpenes. *4 net. Blakiston.

Terrors of the law. Watt, F. net, $1.25. Lane.

TERRY, Ellen.
Pemberton. Ellen Terry and her sisters. net, $3.50. Dodd.

Terry, Milton S. New and living way. '02 (Je21) D. net, 50 c. Eaton & M.

Tesnière, A. Adoration of the blessed sacrament. '02(F1) D. net, $1.25. Benziger.

Tessa Wadsworth's discipline. Conklin, *Mrs.* J. M. D. $1. Burt.

TEUTONS.
Chantepie de la Saussaye. Religion of the Teutons. $2.50. Ginn.

Texas. Citations to amendments and changes of the revised statutes; ed. by N. J. McArthur. '02(Mr22) D. pap., 50 c. Gammel.

Texas. Conflicting civil cases in repts, from Dallam to v. 93, incl. v. 2, comp., arr. and annot. by W. W. King and S. J. Brooks. '02(Ap5) O. shp., $4. Gilbert Bk.

Texas. *Ct. of criminal appeals.* Repts. (J: P. White.) v. 41. '02(Jl5) O. shp., $4.50. Gammel.

Texas court reporter. v. 3. '02(My24) O. shp., $3. B. C. Jones.

Texas. *Cts. of civil appeals.* Repts. v. 24. '02(Mr29) O. shp., $3. Texas.

Texas. Notes on repts; by W. M. Rose. Bk. 1. '02(Ap26); bk. 2 (Jl12); bk. 3 (Ag9) O. shp., ea., $7.50. Bancroft-W.

Texas. Supp. to Sayles' civil statutes; incl. Texas repts., v. 93, and Southwestern reporter, v. 63. By W. W. Herron. '02 (My24) O. $1. Gilbert Bk.

Texas. Supp. to Willson's statutes; by W. W. Herron. '02(Mr22) O. 50 c. Gilbert Bk.

Texas. *Supreme ct.* Repts. (A. E. Wilkinson.) v. 94. '02(My17) O. shp., $5. Gammel.

Texas. 27th legislature and state administration. (M'Arthur and Wicks.) '01. '02 (F15) O. roan, $5. B. C. Jones.

TEXAS.
Smith. Texas notarial manual and form book. $4. Gammel.
See also Galveston.

Text-books of science. S. $1.75. **Longmans.**
—Tilden. Introd. to the study of chemical philosophy.

TEXTILE FABRICS.
Hannan. The textile fibres of commerce. $3. Lippincott.
See also Cotton;—Dyeing.

Texts to il. lectures on Greek philosophy. Adam, J. net, $1.25. Macmillan.

Thackeray, F. St. J., *and* Stone, E. D., *eds.* Pre-Victorian poets. '02(Je28) 12°, (Florilegium Latinum, v. 1.) $2.50. Lane.

Thackeray, F. St. J., *and* Stone, E. D. *eds.* Victorian poets. '02(Ap26) 12°, (Florilegium Latinum, v. 2.) net, $2. Lane.

Thackeray, W: M. Prose works. Barry Lyndon; ed. by W. Jerrold. '02(Mr22) il. 12°, $1. Macmillan.

Thackeray, W: M. Prose works: Henry Esmond; ed. by W. Jerrold. '02(Ap12) 2 v., il. 12°, $2. Macmillan.

Thackeray, W: M. Prose works. History of Henry Esmond, Esq. New uniform ed. '02(Mr29) 12°, $1. Macmillan.

Thackeray, W: M. Prose works. Memoirs of Barry Lyndon, Esq.; also Catherine. New uniform ed. '02(Je7) il. 12°, $1. Macmillan.

Thackeray, W: M. Prose works. The Newcomes. New uniform ed. '02(Ja18) 12°, $1. Macmillan.

Thackeray, W: M. Prose works. The Newcomes; ed. by W. Jerrold. New uniform ed. '02(Je14) 3 v., il. 12°, $3. Macmillan.

Thackeray, W: M. Prose works. Pendennis; ed. by W. Jerrold. New uniform ed. '02(F1) 3 v., il. 12°, $3. Macmillan.

Thackeray, W: M. Prose works. The Virginians. New uniform ed. '02(F22) il. 12°, $1. Macmillan.

That old kitchen stove. Judd, D: H. 50 c. Abbey Press.

Thayer, A. E: Compend of general pathology. '02(Mr22) il. 12°, (Quiz compend ser., no. 15.) 80 c.; interleaved, $1. Blakiston.

Thayer, A. E: Compend of special pathology. '02(Ag16) il. 12°, (Quiz compend ser.) 80 c.; interleaved, $1. Blakiston.

Thayer, Stephen H: Daughters of the Revolution. '01- '02(F8) D. $1. Abbey Press.

Theocritus. Idylls. '02(Mr15) il. 12°, (Antique gems from the Greek and Latin, v. 1.) (App. to pubs. for price.) Barrie.

Theological and Semitic literature. *See* Arnolt, W. M.

THEOLOGY.
Arnold. Literature and dogma. net, $1. New Amsterdam.
Balfour. Foundations of belief. net, $2. Longmans.
Cobb. Theology, old and new. net, $1. Dutton.
Hoyt. Theology as a popular science. net, 10 c. Presb. Bd.
Minton. The cosmos and the logos. net, $1.25. Westminster.
Mortimer. Catholic faith and practice. pt. 1, $2; pt. 2, $2.50. Longmans.
Orr. Progress of dogma. $1.75. Armstrong.
Reed. Idea of God in relation to theology. net, 75 c. Univ. of Chic.
See also Baptism;—Catechisms;—Christianity;—Devil;—Holy Spirit;—Natural religion;—Religion;—Skepticism.

Theology and ethics of the Hebrews. Duff, A. net, $1.25. Scribner.
Theory of accounts. Goodyear, S: H. $1.50. Goodyear-M.
Theory of prosperity. Patten, S. N. net, $1.25. Macmillan.

THERAPEUTICS.
Hawley. New animal cellular therapy. $1. Clinic.
See also Christian science;—Diet;—Hydrotherapy;—Medicine;—Nurses and nursing;—Pathology;—Roentgen rays.

THERMODYNAMICS.
See Heat;—Mechanics.

Thesaurus palæohibernicus. Stokes, W. net, $8. Macmillan.

THESSALONIANS.
See Bible.

Things Japanese. Chamberlain, B. H. *$4 net. Scribner.
13th district. Whitlock, B. $1.50. Bowen-M.
Thirty-six years in the White House. Pendel. T: F. $1.50. Neale.
Thomas Aquinas, *St.* *See* Wilberforce, B. A.
Thomas, Calvin. Life and works of Friedrich Schiller. Students' ed. '02(Jl5) O. **$1.50 net. Holt.
Thomas, H. H. Book of the apple. '02 (Mr22) il. D. (Handbooks of practical gardening, no. 6.) net, $1. Lane.
Thomas, Thdr., *ed.* Famous composers and their music. Extra il. ed. '01- '02(Mr15) 16 v., il. col. pl. 8°. (App. to pubs. for price.) Millet.
Thompson, E. E. Seton-. Krag and Johnny Bear. '02(Ap26) il. D. (Ser. of school reading.) 60 c. Scribner.
Thompson, H. C. Acute dilation of the stomach. '02(Je7) 8°, 75 c. Wood.
Thompson, *Sir* H: Motor car. '02(My17) 12°, $1. Warne.
Thompson, *Sir* H: The unknown God. '02 (Je21) S. 60 c. Warne.
Thompson, *Sir* H: *See also* Harmsworth, A. C.
Thompson, J: G. *and* T: E. New century readers. 3d bk., Nature, myth and story. '02(My10) 12°, (New century ser.) 52 c. Morse.
Thompson, Rob. E. Hand of God in American history. '02(Mr8) D. net, $1. Crowell.
Thompson, Seymour D. Commentaries on the law of negligence. v. 3. '02(Mr29) O. shp., $6. Bowen-M.
Thompson, Winfield M., *and* Lawson, T: W. Lawson hist. of the "America's" cup. '02 (Ag23) il. 8°, canvas. (for private dist.) W. M. Thompson.
Thomson, H. C. China and the powers. '02 (Ap19) il. O. $4. Longmans.
Thoreau, H: D: The service; ed. by F. B. Sanborn. '02(Je14) O. bds., net, $2.50; 22 cop. on Japan, ea., net, $10. Goodspeed.
Thoreau, H: D: Walden. '02(Ap19) 12°, (Home lib.) $1. Burt.
Thorne, W. B. Schott methods of the treatment of diseases of the heart; with acc. of Nauheim baths. 4th ed. '02(Ag16) il. 8°, *$2 net. Blakiston.
Thornton, E. Quin, *ed.* *See* Medical News.
Thornton, G. H. Eng. composition. '02(Ap12) D. (Self-educator ser.) 75 c. Crowell.
Thornton, Marcellus E. Lady of New Orleans. '02(Mr29) D. $1.50. Abbey Press.
Thorpe, Ctte. The children's London. '01. '02(Ja11) il. 4°, net, $4.50. Scribner.
Thorpe, T: E: Essays in hist. chemistry. 2d ed. '02(Je14) 8°, net, $4. Macmillan.

THORWALDSEN, Alb. Bertel.
Hubbard. Thorwaldsen. 25 c. Roycrofters.

Those black diamond men. Gibbons, W: F. $1.50. Revell.
Those delightful Americans. Cotes, *Mrs.* S. J. $1.50. Appleton.

THOUGHT-TRANSFERENCE.
See Telepathy.

Thoughts for the Sundays of the year. Moule, H. C. G. net, $1. Revell.
Thoughts on education. Creighton, M. net, $1.60. Longmans.
Thrall of Leif the lucky. Liljencrantz, O. A. $1.50. McClurg.
Three graces. Hungerford, *Mrs.* M. H. $1. Lippincott.
Three little Denvers. Hewitt, E. C. **40 c. net. Jacobs.
Three sailor boys. Cameron, V. L. 60 c. Nelson.
Three thousand sample questions. Sellow, G. E. 50 c. Bellows.
Three whys and their answer. Babcock, M. D. 35 c. Un. Soc. C. E.
Three years on the blockade. Vail, I. E. $1.25. Abbey Press.
Threefold fellowship. Palmer, B. M. 75 c. Presb. Pub.
Thrice a pioneer. Hannibal, P: M. 75 c.; 40 c. Danish Luth.

THROAT.
Gradle. Diseases of the nose, pharynx and ear. net, $3.50. Saunders.
Wood, *and others, eds.* Eye, ear, nose and throat. $1.50. Year Bk.
See also Breathing.

Throne of David. Ingraham, J. H. $1. Burt.
Through science to faith. Smyth, N. net, $1.50. Scribner.
Thrum, T: G., *ed.* *See* Hawaiian almanac.
Thruston, Lucy M. A girl of Virginia. '02 (Je14) il. D. $1.50. Little, B. & Co.
Thurber, Alwyn M. Zelma, the mystic. 3d ed. [New issue.] '02(Mr22) il. O. $1.25. Alliance.
Thurston, Ernest L. *See* Snyder, C.
Thurston, Rob. H: Stationary steam engines. simple and compound. 7th ed., rev. and enl. '02(Jl19) il. 8°, $2.50. Wiley.

Thwaites, R. G. Down historic waterways: canoeing upon Ill. and Wis. rivers. 2d ed., rev. '02(Mr15) il. D. net, $1.20. McClurg.
Thwaites, R. G. Father Marquette. '02 (Je21) D. (Life histories.) net, $1. Appleton.
Thwaites, R. G., *ed. See also* Jesuit relations.
TIBERIUS, *Emperor of Rome.*
Tarver. Tiberius the tyrant. *$5 net. Dutton.
TIBET.
Carey. Adventures in Tibet. net, $1.50. Un. Soc. C. E.
Tibio. Wyman, W. E. A. 50 c. W: R. Jenkins.
Tiddeman, Lizzie E. A humble heroine. '01-'02(F15) 12°, pap., 15 c. Lippincott.
Tiffany, Nina M., *and* Lesley, Susan, *eds.* Letters of James Murray, loyalist. '01. '02 (Ja25) 12°, net, $2.50. W: B. Clarke.
Tiffany, O. H. *See* Poore, B: P.
Tigert, J: I., *comp. and ed. See* Methodist Epis. Ch. in America.
Tilden, W: A. Introd. to the study of chemical philosophy. 10th ed., rev. and enl. '01. '02(Ja11) S. (Text-books of science.) $1.75. Longmans.
Tileston, Merrill. Chiquita. '02(Jl12) D. $1.50. Merrill.
Tilton, Dwight. Miss Petticoats. '02 (My24) il. D. $1.50. C. M. Clark.
Timby, Thdr. R. Lighted lore for gentle folk. '02(Ag16) D. $2. Morningside.
TIME.
See Astronomy;—Stars.
Time and chance. Hubbard, E. $1.50. Putnam.
Time elements of the Orestean trilogy. Browder, J. B. 35 c. Univ. of Wis.
Times of retirement. Matheson, G: net, $1.25. Revell.
Timothy. Hettinger, F. net, $1.50. Herder.
Timothy and his friends. Ireland, M. E. $1. Saalfield.
Tinker, Chauncey B., *tr. See* Beowulf.
Tippler's vow. Fairchild, L. $10. Croscup.
Titian, *pseud. See* Antrim, M. T.
To the end of the trail. Nason, F. L. $1.50. Houghton, M. & Co.
To whom shall we go? Ovenden, C. T. $1. E. & J. B. Young.
TOASTS.
Miller, *comp.* The toastmaster. n. p. W. M. Rogers.
Reynolds. Banquet book. net, $1.75. Putnam.
Tocsin (The). Worthington, E. S. 25 c. Cubery.
Todd, C: B. True Aaron Burr. '02(My3) sq. S. net, 50 c. Barnes.
Todd, Marg. G., ["Graham Travers."] Way of escape. '02(Je21) D. $1.50. Appleton.
Todhunter, I:, *and* Leathem, J. G. Spherical trigonometry; rev. by J. G. Leathem. '02 (Mr1) 12°, net, $1.75. Macmillan.
TOKEN.
Shiells. Story of the token as belonging to the sacrament of the Lord's supper. net, $1. Presb. Bd.
Token of the covenant. Mahon, R. H. 50 c. Pub. Ho. of M. E. Ch., So.
Told by the death's head. Jokai, M. $1.50. Saalfield.
Tolman, Herb. C. Guide to old Persian inscriptions. '02(Mr15) il. 12°, $1.50. Am. Bk.
Tolman, Herb. C. Urbs beata: vision of the perfect life. '02(Ag23) D. *75 c. net. Young Churchman.
Tolstoi, *Count* L. N. What is religion? and other new articles and letters. '02(My17) D. net, 60 c. Crowell.
Tom Turner's legacy. Alger, H. $1. Burt.
TOMBSTONES.
Styan. Hist. of sepulchral cross slabs, with ref. to other emblems found thereon. net, $3. E. & J. B. Young.
Tomlins, W: L., *ed.* Laurel song book. '02 (Mr29) 12°, $1.50; bds., $1. Birchard.
Tommy Atkins episode. Page, K. N. $1. Abbey Press.
Tommy Cornstalk. Abbott, J. H. M. $2. Longmans.
Tompkins, Herb. W. Highways and byways in Hertfordshire. '02(Je14) il. 12°, (Highways and byways ser.) $2. Macmillan.
Tonna, *Mrs.* Ctte. E. Judah's lion. New ed. '01. '02(F22) 12°, $1. Dodd.
Tons of treasure. Bishop, W: H: $1. Street.
Tooker, W: W. Algonquian series. In 10 v. v. 9, 10. '02(Jl19) 12°, ea., *$1.50 net. F. P. Harper.
Topical architecture. Ware, W: R. 2 v. $7.50. Am. Architect.
TOPOGRAPHICAL DRAWING.
Root. Military topography and sketching. $2.50. Hudson-K.
Torture of the clinic. Trudeau, L. $1; 50 c. Bourguignon.
Tourgée, A. W. A fool's errand. [New ed.] '02(Je7) il. D. $1.50. Fords.
Tout, T: F., *and* Tait, Ja., *eds.* Historical essays, by members of the Owens College, Manchester. '02(Ap19) O. $5. Longmans.
Toward the rising sun: sketches of life in Eastern lands. '02(Ag30) il. S. (Youth's companion ser.) 30 c. Ginn.
TOWER OF LONDON.
Gower. Tower of London. v. 2. net, $6.50. Macmillan.
Town and country lib. See Appleton's.
Town life in ancient Italy. Friedländer, L. 75 c. B: H. Sanborn.
Townesend, *Mrs.* Stephen. *See* Burnett, *Mrs.* F. H.
TOWNS.
Illinois. Laws of Ill. rel. to township organization. $2.50; $3. Legal Adv.
Townsend, C. H. *See* Sage, D.
Townsend, C: Mahoney million. '02(Ap26) 12°, $1.25. New Amsterdam.
Townsend, E: W. Chimmie Fadden and Mr. Paul. '02(My10) il. D. $1.50. Century Co.
Townsend, Luther T. Satan and demons. '02(My10) sq. T. (Little books on doctrine.) net, 25 c. Jennings.
TOXINS.
See Poisons.
Toynbee, Paget. Dante studies and researches. '02(Je7) 8°, net, $3.50. Dutton.
TRADE.
See Business;—Commerce;—Fur trade;—Tariff.
TRADE-MARKS.
See Plate.

TRADE-UNIONS.
Webb. Hist. of trade unionism. net, $2.60.—Industrial democracy. net, $4. Longmans.

TRADES.
See Useful arts.

Tragedy of Anne Boleyn. Gallup, *Mrs.* E. W. $1.50. Howard.

Traill, H: D., *and* Mann, J. S., *eds.* Social England. [New il. ed.] In 6 v. v. 1. '02 (F1) Q. net, $4.50. Putnam.

Training of teachers. Laurie, S. S. net, $1.50. Macmillan.

Training the church of the future. Clark, F. E: net, 75 c. Funk.

Transplanting an old tree. Bloomfield, W. $1. Blanchard.

TRANSPORTATION.
See Railroads.

TRANSVAAL.
Cook. Rights and wrongs of the Transvaal war. $2. Longmans.
See also Boers;—South Africa.

Trask, Rob. D. Human knowledge and human conduct. '01· '02(Jl19) O. *$2 net. R. D. Trask.

Trask, W. B., *ed.* Letters of Col. Thomas Westbrook and others rel. to Indian affairs in Maine, 1722-1726. '01. '02(Mr8) 8°, $5. Littlefield.

Traum ein leben. Grillparzer, F. S. 60 c. Heath.

TRAVEL.
Powers. Art of travel. 25 c.
See also Voyages and travels.

Travers, Graham, *pseud.* *See* Todd, M. G.

Travers, Morris W. Experimental study of gases; introd. pref. by W: Ramsay. '01-'02(Ja4) il. 8°, net, $3.25. Macmillan.

Travis, Ira D. Hist. of the Clayton-Bulwer treaty. '02(F15) 12°, pap., $1. Mich. Pol. Sci.

Travis, Wa. J. Practical golf. New rev. ed. '02(My10) il. 12°, net, $2. Harper.

Treasure of Cocos Island. Kaler, J. O. $1. Burt.

Treasure of Shag Rock. Lloyd, R. **$1 net. Lothrop.

TREATIES.
See United States.

TREES.
Dame *and* Brooks. Handbook of trees of New England. $1.35. Ginn.
Davey. The tree doctor. $1. J: Davey.
Huntington. Studies of trees in winter. net, $2.25. Knight.
Payne. How to teach about trees. 25 c. Kellogg.
Stone *and* Fickett, *comps.* Trees in prose and poetry. 50 c. Ginn.
See also Botany;—Forests and forestry;—Fruit;—Lumber.

Trelawney, Dayrell. Man of no account. '02 (Ap19) sq. S. (Upward ser., no. 2.) pap., 10 c. J. H. West.

Treves, F: Surgical applied anatomy. New ed. '02(F15) il. 12°, net, $2. Lea.

Triassic ichthyopterygia. Merriam, J: C. 50 c. Univ. of Cal.

Tribal custom in Anglo-Saxon law. Seebohm, F: net, $5. Longmans.

Tribune almanac and political register, 1902. '02(Ja11) D. (Lib. of *Tribune* extras, v. 14, no. 1.) pap., 25 c. Tribune Assoc.

Trickett, W: Law of witnesses in Penn. '02(Mr1) O. shp., $6. T. & J. W. Johnson.

Triggs, H. I. Formal gardens in England and Scotland. In 3 pts. pt. 1. '02(Mr8); pt. 2 (My10) f°, net, complete set, $25. Scribner.

TRIGONOMETRY.
Todhunter *and* Leathem. Spherical trigonometry. net, $1.75. Macmillan.
See also Geodesy; — Geometry; — Logarithms; — Mathematics;—Navigation;—Surveying.

TRIPOLI.
Cathcart. Tripoli. $4. J. B. C. Newkirk.

Triumph of the cross. Savonarola, G. net, $1.35. Herder.

TROLLEY TRIPS.
Childe, *comp.* Trolley exploring. 10 c. Brooklyn Eagle.

Trollope, A. Writings. Collectors' ed. v. 8-16. '02(Mr15) il. 8°, crushed lev., subs. (App. to pubs. for price.) Gebbie.

TROUT.
Rhead. Speckled brook trout. net, $3.50. Russell.
Sage, *and others.* Salmon and trout. net, $2; net, $7.50. Macmillan.

Trudeau, L: Torture of the clinic. '01. '02 (Ja4) O. $1; pap., 50 c. Bourguignon.

True romance revealed by a bag of old letters. Anthony, H. G. $1. Abbey Press.

True tales of birds and beasts. Jordan, D: S. 40 c. Heath.

Trueba, Antonio de. El molinerillo y otros cuetos. (R. D. de la Cortina.) '02(My24) S. (Cuentos selectos, no. 4.) pap., 35 c. W: R. Jenkins.

Trueman, Anita. Anton's angels. '02(Mr22) 16°, 75 c. Alliance.

TRUMPET.
Littleton. Trumpeters' hand book and instructor. $1. Hudson-K.

TRUSTS.
Flint, *and others.* The trust. net, $1.25. Doubleday, P.
Haggerty. How to treat the trusts. 25 c. Abbey Press.
See also Capital and labor.

Truth about socialism. Collins, J: E. 25 c. J. A. Wayland.

Truth about the Schley case. Nauticus, *pseud.* 25 c. Columbia.

Truth of Christianity. Turton, W. H. *$1.25 net. Young Churchman.

Tuber-like rootlets of cycas revoluta. Life, A. C. net, 25 c. Univ. of Chic.

Tucker, C: Cowles, *rep.* *See* District of Columbia. *Ct. of appeals.* Repts.

Tucker, Eliz. S. Magic key. '01. '02(F15) 12°, net, $1. Little, B. & Co.

Tucker, G: F. Manual rel. to the preparation of wills: book of Mass. law. 2d ed. '02 (Mr29) D. shp., $3.50. G: B. Reed.

Tuckwell, W. A. W. Kinglake: biog. and literary study. '02(Ap12) il. 12°, $1.75. Macmillan.

TURBINES.
Neilson. The steam turbine. $2.50. Longmans.

Turnbull, Coulson. Divine language of celestial correspondence. '02(Mr22) 8°, $2. Alliance.

Turnbull, Coulson. Sema-Kanda. '02(Mr22) 12°, $1.25. Alliance.

Turner, A. L. Accessory sinuses of the nose. '02(F8) Q. $4. Longmans.
Turner, J. T. Giant fish of Florida. '02 (Jl5) il. 8°, **$3.50 net. Lippincott.
Turner, Jos. M. W: Turner and Ruskin. '01-'02(F22) 2 v., il. 4°, net, $50 Dodd.
Turton, W. H., *comp.* Truth of Christianity. '02(Ag23) D. *$1.25 net. Young Churchman.
Tuscan sculpture. Hurll, E. M. net, 75 c.; 50 c.; 35 c. Houghton, M. & Co.
TUSCANY.
Carmichael. In Tuscany. net, $2. Dutton.
See also Artists.
Tuttle, J: E. The gift of power: study of the Holy Spirit. '02(Je7) S. net, 25 c. Westminster.
Twain, Mark, *pseud.* *See* Clemens, S: L.
'Tween you an' I. Blouët, P. $1.20. Lothrop.
Twelfth night. *See* Shakespeare, W:
Twentieth century home builder. Powell, L. 25 c Pub. Ho. M. E. Ch., So.
Twentieth century horse book. Morgan, D: B: $1.50. D: B: Morgan.
Twentieth century text-books. il. D. net. Appleton.
—Burdick. Essentials of business law. $1.25.
—Caldwell. Lab'y manual of botany. 50 c.; 60 c.
—Fowler. Hist. of ancient Greek literature. $1.40.
—Gilbert *and* Brigham. Introd. to physical geography. $1.25.
—Jordan *and* Heath. Animal forms. $1.10.
—Nelson. Analyt. key to some of the common flowering plants of Rocky Mt. region. **45 c.
—Tennyson. The princess. 25 c.
—West. Latin grammar. 90 c.
Twentieth century wonder book. Hunter, W: C. 50 c.; 25 c. Donohue.
Twenty-five steppingstones toward Christ's kingdom. Fradenburgh, O. P. $1. O. P. Fradenburgh.
Twenty little maidens. Blanchard, A. E. $1.25. Lippincott.
Twenty-six and one. Górky, M. $1.25. J. F. Taylor.
Twenty thousand miles by land and sea. Pennock, A. F. $1. Mason Pub.
Twing, *Mrs.* Caro. E. S. Henry Drummond in spirit life. '02(Jl19) S. pap., 10 c. Star.
Two centuries' growth of Am. law, 1701-1901. '01. '02(Mr15) 8°, (Yale bicentennial pub.) net, $4. Scribner.
Two-fold covenant. Achenbach, H: 50 c. Evangelical Press.
Two hundred bar exam. questions. Bingham, G. A. $1. Commercial Press.
Two of a trade, by the author of "Val." '02 (My17) 12°, 60 c. Nelson.
Two Renwicks. Davidson, M. A. $1.50. Neely.
Two thousand a year on fruits and flowers. Barnard, C: $1. Coates.
Two thousand years in eternity. Bywater, B. net, $2.15. Hudson-K.
Two waifs. Howard, E. B. 50 c. Abbey Press.
Two wars. French, S: G. $2. Confederate Veteran.
Two winters in Norway. Spender, A. E. $4. Longmans.

Typee. Melville, H. 45 c. Heath.
TYPEWRITING.
Vories. Lab'y method of teaching Eng. and touch typewriting together. $1.25. Inland Pub.
TYPHOID FEVER.
Osler, *ed.* Typhoid and typhus fevers. net, $5; $6. Saunders.
Ultzmann, Rob. Neuroses of the genito-urinary system in the male with sterility and impotence. 2d ed., rev. with notes by the tr., G. W. Allen. '02(Jl12) il. 12°, *$1 net. Davis.
Ulyat, W: C. The first years of the life of the redeemed after death. '01-'02(F15) D. $1.25. Abbey Press.
Ulysses. Phillips, S. net, $1.25. Macmillan.
Umbrian towns. Cruickshank, J. W. net, $1.25. Wessels.
Uncle and aunt. Woolsey, S. C. 50 c. Little, B. & Co.
Uncle Boston's spicy breezes. Smith, B. net, $1. Am. Bapt.
Uncle Jed's country letters. Brenton, H. 30 c. Dickerman.
Uncle Sam, trustee. Bangs, J: K. net, $1.75. Riggs.
Uncle Sam's examination. Kellogg, A. M. 15 c. Kellogg.
Uncle Tom's cabin. Stowe. H. B. $2: $3; $4. Dominion.
Under my own roof. Rouse, A. L. net, $1.20. Funk.
Under sunny skies. '02(Jl12) il. D. (Youth's companion ser., no. 3.) 30 c. Ginn.
Under the dome. Ingram, A. F. M. $1.25. E. & J. B. Young.
Under the red cross. Wright, D: H: 35 c. Biddle.
Underwood, Clarence F., *il.* Some pretty girls. '01. '02(Mr1) 4°, regular ed., $3; de luxe ed., $5. Quail & W.
Undine. *See* La Motte Fouqué, F. H. K. *Freiherr* de.
Undine lib. 12°, pap., 25 c. Street.
—Ellis. Life of Wm. McKinley. (9.)
UNITARIAN CHURCH.
Wilbur. Hist. sketch of the Independent Cong. church, Meadville, Pa., 1825-1900. $1; 50 c. E. G. Huidekoper.
UNITED MERCANTILE AGENCY.
Hunt. United Merc. Agency credit ratings for marble, granite and stone dealers. subs., $25. Un. Merc.
United States Army. Company commanders' manual of army regulations; by W: H. Waldron. '02(Ag2) 12°, $1. Hudson-K.
United States. *Circuit cts. of appeals.* **Repts.,** with annots. v. 47. '01. '02(Ja4): v. 48 (Mr1); v. 49 (Ap19); v. 50 (Jl5) O. shp., ea., $3.35. Lawyers' Co-op.
United States. Federal reporter, v. 110. Permanent ed. '01. '02(Ja18); v. 111 (Mr1); v. 112 (My10); v. 113 (Je7); v. 114 (Ag9) O. (Nat. reporter system, U. S. ser.) shp., ea., $3.50. West Pub.
United States. List of observatories. '02 (Ag30) O. (Smithsonian misc. coll., v. 41, no. 1259.) pap., n. p. Smith. Inst.
United States naval examination papers, 1899-1902; comp. and arr. by M. C. Dugan. '02(Ag16) D. *$1 net. Cushing.

United States. *Supreme ct.* Repts., v. 183. (J. C. B. Davis.) '02(Je7) O. shp., $2.30. Banks.

UNITED STATES.
Brown, C: F., *and* Croft. Outline study of U. S. history. 50 c. Courier Pr.
Brown, W: G. Lower South in Am. history. net, $1.50. Macmillan.
Burgess. Reconstruction and the constitution, 1866-1876. net, $1. Scribner.
Butler. Treaty-making power of the U. S. In 2 v. v. 1. complete work, net, $12. Banks.
Cathcart. Tripoli; first war with the U. S. $4. J. B. C. Newkirk.
Clark. The government, what it is, what it does. 75 c. Am. Bk.
Codman. Arnold's expedition to Quebec. net, $2.25. Macmillan.
Dawes. Stories of our country. v. 1, 2. ea., 40 c. Educ. Pub.
Elliott. Debates of federal constitution. 5 v. net, $10; net, $12. Lippincott.
Farley. West Point in the early sixties, with incidents of the war. net, $2. Pafraets.
French. Two wars: Mexican war; war between the states. $2. Confederate Veteran.
Gordy, J. P. Political hist. of the U. S. v. 2. **$1.75 net. Holt.
Gordy, W. F. Am. leaders and heroes. net, 60 c. Scribner.
Halstead. Hist. of America's new possessions. $2.50; $3.50; $4.50. Dominion.
Harris. Sectional struggle: troubles between the North and South. net, $2.50. Lippincott.
Herbert. Il. history of the Civil war in America. 25 c. Crowell & K.
Hutton. Am. history outlines. 30 c. Sac Sun.
Lodge, *and others.* The United States and the Philippine Islands. 10 c. Brooklyn Eagle.
McDaniel. War poems, 1861-1865. $1. Abbey Press.
Melvin. Journal, in Arnold's expedition against Quebec. $2. H. W. Bryant.
Muirhead. America, the land of contrasts. net, $1.20. Lane.
Page. Rebuilding of old commonwealths. Southern states. net, $1. Doubleday, P.
Pendel. Thirty-six years in the White House. $1.50. Neale.
Phillips. Methods of keeping the public money of the U. S. $1. Mich. Pol. Sci.
Pratt. America's story. v. 5. 40 c. Heath.
Rhodes. Hist. of the U. S. from the compromise of 1850. 4 v. ea., *$2.50 net. Macmillan.
Richardson. War of 1812. subs., $3. Historical.
Ridpath. Hist. of the U. S. from aboriginal times. $6. Grosset.
Riggs. Studies in U. S. history. 65 c. Ginn.
Robinson. Evolution of the Mason and Dixon line. 25 c. Oracle Pub.
Root *and* Connelley. Overland stage to California. $2.50; $3.50. Root & C.
Simonds. American date book. $1. Kama.
Tappan. Our country's story. 65 c. Houghton, M. & Co.

UNITED STATES.—*Continued.*
Thompson. Hand of God in Am. history. net, $1. Crowell.
Wagner. Current history. 25 c. Whitaker & R.
Westbrook. The West-brook drives. $1.25. Eckler.
Wilson, *ed.* Presidents of the U. S. $3.50; $6. Appleton.
See also Clayton-Bulwer treaty; — Lexington; — Louisiana purchase; — Pensions; — Political science;—*also* names of states.

United States Catholic historical soc., monograph ser. pap. (not for sale.) U. S. Cath.
—Carroll. Unpublished letters. (1.)

United States Govt. publications. Hasse, A. R. pt. 1. $1. Lib. Bu.

Universal anthology. *See* Garnett, R:

Universalist register for 1902; ed. by R: Eddy. '02(F8) S. pap., 25 c. Universalist.

UNIVERSITY OF CALIFORNIA.
Jones. Il. hist. of the University of Cal., 1868-1901. $5. Berkeley.

University of Cal. bulletins. il. O. pap. Univ. of Cal.
—Eakle. Colemanite from So. California. 15 c. (v. 3, 2.)
—Hershey. Quaternary of So. Cal. 20 c. (v. 3, 1.)
—Lawson. The eparchæan interval. 10 c. (v. 3, 3.)
—Lawson *and* Palache. Berkeley Hills. 80 c. (v. 2, 12.)
—Merriam. Triassic ichthyopterygia fr. Cal. and Nev. 50 c. (v. 3, 4.)

University of Chicago constructive Bible studies; ed. by W: R. Harper and E. D. Burton. O. Univ. of Chic.
—Harper. Constructive studies in the priestly element in the O. T. $1.

University of Chicago cont. to education. S. pap., net. Univ. of Chic.
—Dewey. Educational situation. 50 c. (3.)
—Dewey. Psychology and social practice. 25 c. (2.)
—Young. Ethics in the school. 25 c. (4.)
—Young. Isolation in the school. 50 c. (1.)
—Young. Some types of modern educ. theory. 25 c. (6.)

Univ. of Chicago cont. to philosophy. 8°, pap., net, 35 c. Univ. of Chic.
—Gore. Imagination in Spinoza and Hume. (v. 2, 4.)
—Moore. Functional vs. representational theories of knowledge in Locke's essay. (v. 3, 1.)

University of Chicago decennial pubs. Q. pap. Univ. of Chic.
—Bolza. Conc. the geodesic curvature. *25c. net
—Hammond. On the text of Chaucer's Parlement of foules. *50 c. net.
—Laughlin. Credit. *50 c. net.
—Loeb. Production and supp. of muscular twitching of the skin byelectrolytes. *25 c. net.

University of Chicago, Walker museum conts. 8°, net. Univ. of Chic.
—Case. Palæontological notes. 25 c. (v. 1, 3.)

University of Chicago. Yerkes Observatory bulletin. 8°, net. Univ. of Chic.
—Hale. New star in Perseus. 10 c. (16.)

UNIVERSITY OF PENNSYLVANIA.
Nitzsche, *comp.* Proceedings at dedication of building of Dept. of law. $3; $3.50. Univ. of Penn.

University of Penn., Dept. of history trs. and reprs. from orig. sources of European hist. D. $1.25. Longmans.
—Lingelbach. Merchant adventurers of England. (2d ser., v. 2.)

University of Penn. pubs., ser. in pol. economy and public law. O. [Univ. of Penn.] Ginn.
—Weyl. Passenger traffic of railways. $1.50; $1. (16.)

University of Va. monographs, school of Teutonic languages. 12°, pap., net, 50 c. Barnes.
—Blain. Syntax of the verb in the Anglo-Saxon chronicle, 787 to 1001. (1.)

University of Wis. bulletins. O. pap. Univ. of Wis.
—Browder. Time elements of the Orestean trilogy. 35 c.
—Lessing. Schiller's einfluss auf Grillparzer. 50 c.
—Wolcott. On the sensitiveness of the coherer. 20 c. (51; science ser., v. 3, 1.)

Unknown God. Thompson, *Sir* H: 60 c. Warne.

Unrequited love. Stechhan, O. $1. Abbey Press.

Unstable as water. Needell, *Mrs.* M. A. $1.25. Warne.

Unter vier augen. Fulda, L. *35 c. net. Holt.

Unto the end. Alden, *Mrs.* I. M. $1.50. Lothrop.

Unto you, young women. Sinclair, W. M. net, $1. Lippincott.

Unwilling guest. Hill, G. L. net, $1. Am. Bapt.

Upland game birds. Sandys, E. net, $2; net, $7.50. Macmillan.

Upward ser. sq. S. pap., 10 c. J. H. West.
—Macdonald. Guarding the thoughts. (1.)
—Trelawney. A man of no account. (2.)

Upon the sun-road. Hurst, J: F. 25 c. Revell.

Urbs beata. Tolman, H. C. *75 c. net. Young Churchman.

URINE AND URINARY ORGANS.
Morton. Genito-urinary disease and syphilis. net, $3. Davis.
See also Generative organs.

Urn burial. *See* Brown, *Sir* T:

USEFUL ARTS.
Brown, *ed.* Workshop wrinkles. net, $1. Van Nostrand.
Oliver. Dangerous trades. *$8 net. Dutton.
See also Blacksmithing; — Bridges; — Cement; — Commerce; — Dyeing; — Electric engineering; — Machinery; — Patents; — Textile fabrics.

UTAH.
Jones. Utah. *40 c. net. Macmillan.

UTILITARIANISM.
Albee. Hist. of Eng. utilitarianism. net, $2.75. Macmillan.

Utopia. More, *Sir* T: $1. Burt.

Vacation with nature. Talmage, F. D. net, $1. Funk.

VACCINATION.
Oswald. Vaccination a crime. 10 c. Physical Culture.
See also Smallpox.

Vail, I. E. Three years on the blockade. '02 (Jl5) D. $1.25. Abbey Press.

Valcourt-Vermont, Edg. de, ["*Comte* C. de Saint-Germain."] Practical astrology; with a hist. of astronomy. '02(Ap26) il. 12°, $1; pap., 50 c. Laird.

Valdés, A. P. José; tr. by Minna C. Smith. '01· '02(Mr8) D. $1.25. Brentano's.

Vale Press ser. 8°. Lane.
—Browne. Religio medici, and other essays. **$12 net.

Vale Press Shakespeare. 8°, net. Lane.
—Shakespeare. Twelfth night. $8. (22.)

Valentine, E: U. Ship of silence and other poems. '02(Je28) 12°, net, $1.20. Bowen-M.

Valentine, *Mrs.* Laura J., *comp. and ed.* Old, old fairy tales. '02(My10) il. 12°, (Fairy lib.) $1. Burt.

VALJEAN, Jean.
Quayle. A hero, Jean Valjean. 30 c. Jennings.

Valley of decision. Wharton, E. 2 v. $2. Scribner.

Van Anderson, Helen. Journal of a live woman. '02(Mr22) D. $1. Alliance.

Van Arsdale, H. Twentieth century interest tables. '02(Jl12) 8°, $1.50. Vawter.

Van Bergen, R. Story of China. '02(My3) il. D. 60 c. Am. Bk.

Vance, Ja. J. Rise of a soul. '02(My17) 12°, net, $1. Revell.

Vancil, Fk. M. The school congress. '02 (Jl19) 12°, 25 c. Kellogg.

Van Cleve, C: L. Hist. of the Phi Kappa Psi Fraternity. '02(Ag23) 8°, $2; levant, $4. Franklin Pr.

Vanderbilt Oriental ser. D. $1. Am. Bk.
—Stevenson. Assyrian and Babylonian contracts with Aramaic ref. notes.

Van Der Kellen, M. J.-Ph. Works of Michel Le Blond. '02(Mr1) portfolio, net, $30; mor. portfolio, net, $35. Dodd.

Vanderlip, Fk. A. American "commercial invasion" of Europe. '02(Ag2) il. O. pap., n. p. Nat. City Bank.

Vanderpoel, Emily N. Color problems. '02 (My10) O. net, $5. Longmans.

Vandersloot, Lewis. History and genealogy of the Von der Sloot family. '01· '02 (Ap5) il. f°, $1. L. Vandersloot.

Van Deventer, E. M., ["Lawrence L. Lynch."] The woman who dared. '02(F22) D. 75 c.; pap., 25 c. Laird.

Van Doren, De W. T. Students' guide to health. '01. '02(F15) 12°, $2. T. Van Doren.

VAN DYCK, Ant.
Cust. Desc. of sketch-book used by Sir Anthony Van Dyck. $17.50. Macmillan.
Hurll, *ed.* Van Dyck. net, 75 c.; net, 50 c.; net, 35 c. Houghton, M. & Co.

Van Dyke, J: C: Italian painting. '02(Jl12) 16°, bds., 50 c. Elson.

Van Dyke, T. S. *See* Roosevelt, T.—Sandys, E.

Van Epps, Howard. *See* Georgia. Supp. to code.

Van Meter, B: F. Genealogies and sketches of some old families of Virginia and Kentucky especially. '01· '02(Ja18) 8°, $2.25. Morton.

Van Nostrand's science ser. T. bds., 50 c. Van Nostrand.
—Vose. Graphic method for solving certain questions in arithmetic or algebra. (16.)
Van Santvoord, S. House of Cæsar and the imperial disease. '02(F22) il. Q. net, $5.25. Pafraets.
Van Vorst, Marie. Philip Longstreth. '02 (Ap19) D. $1.50. Harper.
Van Zile, Philip T. Elements of the law of bailments and carriers. '02(My24) O. shp., $5. Callaghan.
Varieties of religious experience. James, W: net, $3.20. Longmans.
VARIOLA.
See Smallpox.
Vaughan, D. T. G. *See* Bower, F. O.
Vaughan, Herbert. Holy sacrifice of the mass. 4th ed. '02(Je28) 16°, 15 c. Herder.
Vaughan, V. C., *and* Novey, F. G. Cellular toxins. 4th ed. '02(Jl19) 8°, *$3 net. Lea.
Vector analysis. Gibbs, J. W. net, $4. Scribner.
VEGETABLES.
Wythes. Book of vegetables. net, $1. Lane.
See also Gardening.
VEGETARIANS.
Miles. Failures of vegetarianism. net, $1.50. Dutton.
VELASQUEZ, Diego R. de S.
Hubbard. Velasquez. 25 c. Roycrofters.
Velázquez de la Cadena, M. Nuevo diccionario de pronunciacion de las lenguas Inglesa y Espanola. pt. 2. '02(Je14) O. hf. leath., $3.50. Appleton.
Vellum ser. il. 12°, $1. Univ. Co-op.
—Goff. Lessons in commercial fruit growing.
Velocity of light. Michelsen, A. A. net, 25 c. Univ. of Chic.
Velvin, Ellen. Rataplan, a rogue elephant, and other stories. '02(Jl12) il. D. **$1.25 net. Altemus.
VENEREAL DISEASES.
Hayden. Pocket text-book of venereal diseases. net, $2.25. Lea.
See also Syphilis.
VENUS DI MILO.
Patoma. Venus di Milo; its hist. and art. 50 c. Cambridge.
Verba crucis. McClelland, T. C. 50 c. Crowell.
Veritas, *pseud.* The German Empire of to-day. '02(Je7) D. $2.25. Longmans.
VERMONT.
Wilbur. Early hist. of Vt. v. 3. $1.50. L. F. Wilbur.
See also Newburg.
Verne, Jules. Vingt mille lieues sous les mers; abr. and ed. by C. Fontaine. '02 (Je14) S. (Modern lang. ser.) 40 c. Heath.
Versailles hist. ser.; ed. by K. P. Wormeley. il. 8°, subs., $6; leath., $9. Hardy, P. & Co.
—Bernis. Memoirs and letters. 2 v.
—Elisabeth, *Mme.* Memoir and letters.
—Fersen. Letters and papers.
—Lespinasse. Letters.
Very naughty girl. Smith, *Mrs.* E. T. $1. Burt.
Very odd girl. Armstrong, A. E. $1. Burt.
Veterinarian's call book for 1902. (R. R. Bell.) '01- '02(F22) 12°, leath., $1.25. W: R. Jenkins.
VETERINARY MEDICINE AND SURGERY.
Cadiot. Clinical veterinary medicine and surgery. $5.25. W: R. Jenkins.
Dollar. Operative technique for veterinary surgeons. $3.75. W: R. Jenkins.
Dunn. Veterinary medicines. $3.75. W: R. Jenkins.
Fleming. Operative veterinary surgery. v. 2. net, $3.25. W: R. Jenkins.
Liautard. Animal castration. $2. W: R. Jenkins.
McClure. Amer. horse, cattle and sheep doctor. $1.50. Henneberry.
Morgan. Twentieth century horse book; also treatise on cattle, [etc.,] giving diseases and remedies. $1.50. D: B: Morgan.
Wyman. Tibio; neurectomy for relief of spavin. 50 c. W: R. Jenkins.
See also Horse.
Viaud, L: M. J., ["Pierre Loti."] Lives of two cats; fr. the Fr. by M. B. Richards. '02(Ag9) il. 12°, (Young of heart ser., no. 35.) 50 c. Estes.
VICTORIA, *Queen of England.*
Halstead *and* Munson. Life and reign of Queen Victoria. $1.50; $2.25. Dominion.
Walsh. Religious life and influence of Queen Victoria. net, $2.50. Dutton.
Victorian poets. Thackeray, F. St. J. net, $2. Lane.
Victories of Rome. Best, K. D. net, 45 c. Benziger.
Victorious republicanism. Halstead, M. $1.50; $2.25. Dominion.
Vielé, H. K. Myra of the Pines. '02(Je14) D. $1.50. McClure, P.
Viets, Fs. H. Genealogy of the Viets family. '02(Ap26) il. O. $3. Case.
Views afoot. Taylor, B. $1. Burt.
Village work in India. Russell, N. net, $1. Revell.
Villari, P. Barbarian invasions of Italy. '02 (My10) 2 v., il. 8°, net, $7.50. Scribner.
VILLAS.
See Architecture.
VILLON, François.
Morehead. Story of François Villon, the hero of the play "If I were king." 25 c. Ogilvie.
Vincent, Edg. L. Margaret Bowlby. '02 (My17) D. $1.50. Lothrop.
Vincent, J. M., Ely, R: T., Gilman, D. C., *and others.* Herbert B. Adams; with a bibliog. of the Dept. of history, politics and economics. '02(Ap26) O. (Johns Hopkins Univ. studies, v. 20, extra no.) pap. (free to subs.) Johns Hopkins.
Vincent, Marvin R. What is it to believe on the Lord Jesus Christ? '01- '02(F8) S. pap., 5 c. Beam.
VINEYARDS.
See Fresno Co., Cal.
Vingt mille lieues sous les mers. Verne, J. 40 c. Heath.
Virden, *Mrs.* Laura M. N. First science reader. New ed. '01- '02(Mr29) il. 16°, 25 c.; bds., 10 c. Flanagan.
Virgil. Æneid. bks. 1-6; introd., notes and vocab. by H: S. Frieze; rev. by W. Dennison. '02(Ag2) il. D. hf. leath., $1.30. Am. Bk.

Virgil. Æneid. bks. 1-6; tr. by H. H. Ballard. '02(Ap5) D. net, $1.30. Houghton, M. & Co.

Virginia-Carolina almanac, 1902. '02(Mr15) il. 16°, pap., gratis. Virginia-Carolina.

Virginia. Complete annot. digest. v. 8. '02 (Je7) O. shp., $6.50. Hurst & Co.

Virginia. *Supreme ct. of appeals.* Repts. Jefferson—33 Grattan, 1730-1880. (T: J. Michie.) v. 16-18. '01- '02(F8) Grattan's repts. v. 13-15 (Mr15); v. 11, 12 (My10); v. 9, 10 (My24); v. 7, 8 (Jl5) O. shp., ea., $7.50. Michie.

Virginia. *Supreme ct. of appeals.* Repts. (M. P. Burks.) v. 99. '02(My10) O. shp., $3.50. O'Bannon.

VIRGINIA.
Hall. Rending of Va. $2. Mayer.
Snowden. Some old historic landmarks of Va. and Md. *25 c. net. Ramey.
White. Geneal. of descendants of John Walker; also notes pertaining to hist. of Pa., 1600-1902. $6. E. S. White.
See also Jamestown.

Virginian (The). Wister, O. $1.50. Macmillan.

Virginians. Thackeray, W: M. $1. Macmillan.

VISCHER, Peter.
Headlam. Peter Vischer. $2. Macmillan.

Vision of beauty. Hatton, J. 50 c. Burt.

Visitor's (A) guide to Paris. 7th ed. '02 (Jl5) S. (Eagle lib., v. 17, no. 7; ser. no. 66.) pap., 10 c. Brooklyn Eagle.

Vivekananda, *Swami.* Song of the Sannyasin. '02(Ag16) obl. F°, leatherette, *15 c. net. Van Haagen.

VIVISECTION.
Ernst. Animal experimentation. net, $1.50; net, $1. Little, B. & Co.

Vizetelly, Ernest A. Lover's progress told by himself. '01- '02(Mr8) D. $1.50. Brentano's.

Vogel, Harry B. Gentleman Garnet. '02 (Ag23) D. (Select novels.) †$1; pap., 50 c. Lippincott.

VOICE.
Dawson. Voice of the boy. 25 c. Kellogg.
Lawton. The singing voice and its practical cultivation. $1.50. W: H: Lawton.
Lunn. Philosophy of voice. net, $2. Schirmer.
Murrin. Vocal exercises on the vocal factors of expression. net, 50 c. A. M. Allen.
See also Elocution;—Music;—Orators and oratory;—Singing;—Sound;—Throat.

Voice from England. McGrady, T: 10 c. Standard.

Voltaire, F. M. A. de. Philosophical dictionary (in Eng.); introd. by W: F. Fleming. '02(Jl5) 10 v., il. 8°, per set, subs., *$18 net; hf. mor., $24 net. G: Clarke.

Voltaire, F. M. A. de. Zaïre and Epîtres; ed. by C: A. Eggert. '02(Mr22) 16°, (Lake French classics.) 50 c. Scott, F. & Co.

VON DER SLOOT FAMILY.
See Vandersloot, L.

Vorce, C: M. Genealogical and hist. record of the Vorce family in America. '01- '02 (Ja18) 8°, $2. C: M. Vorce.

Vories, Hervey D. Laboratory method of teaching Eng. and touch typewriting together. '01- '02(Ja11) 8°, $1.25. Inland Pub.

Vose, G: L. Graphic method for solving certain questions in arithmetic or algebra. 2d ed. '02(Ag9) il. T. (Science ser., no. 16.) bds., 50 c. Van Nostrand.

VOYAGES AND TRAVELS.
Beck. Sonnenblicke aus der Amer. praxis net, 30 c. Lemcke.
Belloc. Path to Rome. net, $2. Longmans.
Cadigan. My ocean trip. $1. Brentano's.
Fielding. Journal of a voyage to Lisbon. **$5 net. Houghton, M. & Co.
Gray. Musings by camp-fire and wayside. net, $1.50. Revell.
Henry. Travels in Canada and the Indian territories, between 1760-1776. $4. Little, B. & Co.
Honeyman. Bright days in merrie England: four in hand journeys. net, $1.50. Honeyman.
Mackenzie. Voyages from Montreal through the Continent of N. A. to the frozen and Pacific Oceans. 2 v. net, $1. New Amsterdam.
Pennock. Twenty thousand miles by land and sea. $1. Mason Pub.
Satchel guide for vacation tourist in Europe. net, $1.50. Houghton, M. & Co.
Taylor. Views afoot, or, Europe seen with knapsack and staff. $1. Burt.
See also Geography;—Travel.

Wace, H:, *ed. See* Fulham Palace Conference.

WACHOVIA.
Clewell. Hist. of Wachovia, N. C. **$2 net. Doubleday, P.

Wade, G. W. Old Testament history. '02 (Mr8) 12°, $1.50. Dutton.

Wade, Ma. H. Little cousin series. '02 (Ag23) 6 v., il. D. ea., **50 c. net. L. C. Page.

Wage-labor and capital. Marx, K. 50 c. N. Y. Labor News.

Wager (The). McManus, L. $1.25. Buckles.

Waggaman, Ma. T. Bob o' Link. '02(Mr22) il. D. 40 c. Benziger.

Waggaman, Ma. T. Corinne's vow. '02(F15) D. $1.25. Benziger.

Wagner, C: Courage. New ed. '01- '02 (F22) 12°, $1.25. Dodd.

Wagner, Harr. Current history: supp. to California state series history. Rev. ed. '02 (Je7) sq. D. leatherette, 25 c. Whitaker & R.

Wagner, Harr. New Pacific school geography. New ed. '02(Je7) Q. net, $1. Whitaker & R.

Wagner, R: Rheingold; ed. by R. A. von Minckwitz. '02(Je28) 16°, (German opera texts, v. 1.) 75 c. Newson.

WAGONS.
See Blacksmithing.

Wags of the stage. Whitton, J. $2.50. Rigby.

Wait, W: Law and practice in civil actions and proceedings in justices' cts., and in other cts. not of record, and on appeals to county cts. of N. Y. In 3 v. v. 1. 7th ed., by E. Baylies. '02(Mr15); v. 2 (Jl12) O. shp., per v., $6.35; or per set, $19. M. Bender.

Waiting race. Rogers, A. A. 50 c. Abbey Press.

Wakeman, Rob. P. Wakeman genealogy. '02(Ap5) il. 8°, $5; hf. mor., $7.50; full mor., $10. Journal Pub.

Walden. Thoreau, H: D: $1. Burt.

Waldron, W: H. *See* United States Army.

WALES.
Edwards. Wales. **$1.35 net; $1.60 net. Putnam.

Walford, *Mrs.* Lucy B. Charlotte. '02 (Mr22) D. $1.50. Longmans.

Walker, Fs. A. Taxation of corporations in the U. S. '02(Mr22) 8°, (Pub. of the soc., no. 329.) pap., 25 c. Am. Acad. Pol. Sci.

Walker, J. G., *ed.* *See* Am. Bapt. year-book.

Walker, Ja. W. G. Ocean to ocean. '02 (Mr22) il. O. net, $1.25. McClurg.

WALKER, J:
White. Genealogy of the descendants of John Walker of Wigton, Scotland. $6. E. S. White.

Walkey, S. With redskins on the warpath. '01· '02(Ja11) il. D. $1.25. Cassell.

Wall, *Mrs.* D. H. Sister in name only. '02 (Ap26) 12°, $1. Neely.

Wall, W: What great men have said about great men. '02(Ap5) 12°, net, $2.50. Dutton.

Wallace, *Sir* Donald M. Web of empire: diary of the imperial tour of the Duke and Duchess of Cornwall and York, in 1901. '02(Je28) il. 8°, net, $6.50. Macmillan.

Wallace, Lew. Ben Hur. Players' ed. '01· '02(Mr1) il. 12°, $2.50. Harper.

Wallannah. Hargrave, W: L. $1.50. B. F. Johnson.

Wallenstein. Schiller, J. C. F. v. net, $1. Holt

Wallenstein's camp. *See* Schiller, J. C. F. v.

Waller, A. R., *and* Barrow, G. H. S. John Henry, Cardinal Newman. '01· '02(Jl19) 24°, (Westminster biographies.) 75 c. Small.

Waller, M. E. The little citizen. '02(Jl12) il. D. **$1 net. Lothrop.

Walley, T: Practical guide to meat inspection; rewritten and enl. '01· '02(Ja4) il 12°, $3. W: R. Jenkins

Walpole, H. Some unpublished letters; ed. by Sir S. Walpole. '02(Ap26) O. net, $1.50. Longmans.

Walsh, D: Roentgen rays in medical work. 3d ed. '02(Mr29) 8°, net, $2.50. Wood.

Walsh, G: E. Allin Winfield. '02(F8) D. $1.50. Buckles.

Walsh, Wa. Religious life and influence of Queen Victoria. '02(Je14) 8°, net, $2.50. Dutton.

Walton, W: Paris from the earliest period to the present day. v. 6. Lib. ed. '02 (Mr15) il. 8°, per v., $3. Barrie.

Wan Lun and Dandy. Kaler, J. O. 75 c. Burt.

Wandering heroes. Price, L. L. 50 c. Silver.

Wanklin, J. A. Arsenic. '01· '02(F15) 12°, $1. Lippincott.

WAR.
Atkinson. Cost of war from 1898 to 1902. 6 c. E: Atkinson.
Bloch. Future of war. 60 c. Ginn.

WAR OF 1812.
See United States.

War poems, 1861-1865. McDaniel, *Mrs.* H. P. $1. Abbey Press.

Ward, Herb. D. *See* Phelps, E. S.

Ward, *Mrs.* Herb. D. *See* Phelps, E. S.

Ward, J: The sacred beetle: treatise on Egyptian scarabs in art and history. '02 (Mr8) il. 8°, net, $3.50. Scribner.

Warde, Ja. C. Jimmy Warde's experiences as a lunatic. '02(Ag23) 16°, $1. J. C. Warde.

Warden, Florence, *pseud.* *See* James, *Mrs.* F. A. P.

Warden, W: A. Ancestors, kin and descendants of John Warden and Narcissa (Davis), his wife. '01· '02(F1) 8°, $5. W: A. Warden.

Ware, Fabian. Educational foundations of trade and industry. '02(F22) 12°. (Internat. educ. ser., no. 54.) net, $1.20. Appleton.

Ware, W: R., *ed.* Topical architecture. '02 (Jl19) 2 v., pls. 4°, $7.50. Am. Architect.

Warlow, T: P., *comp.* *See* Florida. Index to laws.

Warneck, Gustav. Outline of a history of Protestant missions. '02(F8) 8°, net, $2. Revell.

Warner, Beverley E. Young man in modern life. '02(Ap19) D. net, 85 c. Dodd.

Warner, C: D. Fashions in literature, and other essays. '02(My10) D. net, $1.20. Dodd.

Warren, H: W. *See* Merrill, S. M.

Warren, S: E: Physical geography; rev. '02 (Jl19) il. f°, bds., $1.25. Butler.

Warvelle, G: W. Essays in legal ethics. '02 (Mr29) D. $2.50. Callaghan.

Warvelle, G: W. Treatise on the Am. law of vendor and purchaser of real property. v. 1, 2. 2d ed. '02(Ja18) O. shp., $12. Callaghan.

WARWICK, *Countess of.*
Palgrave. Mary Rich, Countess of Warwick, 1625-1678. net, $1.50. Dutton.

Warwick lib. of Eng. literature. 12°, $1.50. Scribner.
—Herford, *ed.* Eng. tales in verse.

Washburn, Emory. Treatise on the Am. law of real property. 6th ed.; ed. by J: Wurts. '02(Mr29) 3 v., 8°, shp., net, $18. Little, B. & Co.

Washington, Booker T. Character building. '02(Jl5) D. **$1.50 net. Doubleday, P.

WASHINGTON, G:
Custis. George Washington. $1. Donohue.
Headley. Washington and his generals. $1. Burt.
Locke. Typical American. net, 25 c. Jennings

WASHINGTON.
Brand. Justices' code. $5. Bancroft-W.

WASHINGTON, D. C.
Maynard. Birds of Washington and vicinity. *$1 net. Woodward & L.
Rand, McNally & Co.'s pictorial guide to Washington and environs. 25 c. Rand, McN. & Co.
Winchester, *ed.* Aroung the throne. sketches of Wash. society . net. $1. Eichelberger.

WASHINGTON CO., Pa.
Crumrine. Cts. of justice, bench and bar of Washington Co., Pa. $4; $6. Wash. Bar Assoc.

WATER.
Horrocks. Introd. to bacteriolog. examination of water. net, $3.68. Blakiston.
See also Brooks;—Hydraulic engineering;—Physical geography;—Water-supply.

WATER-CURE.
See Hydrotherapy.

Water exploring. Childe, C. 10 c. Brooklyn Eagle.

WATER-FOWL.
See Birds.

WATER-POWER.
See Hydraulic engineering.

WATER-SUPPLY.
Folwell. Water-supply engineering. $4. Wiley.
Mason. Water-supply (fr. a sanitary standpoint). red. to $4. Wiley.
See also Hydraulic engineering.

Water-tube boilers. Robertson, L. S. $3. Van Nostrand.

Waterhouse, Percy L. Story of the art of architecture in America. '01. '02(F8) il. S. (Lib. of useful stories.) net, 35 c. Appleton.

WATERLOO.
Siborne. Waterloo campaign, 1815. *$1.50 net. Dutton.

Watkins, Rob. L. Diagnosis by means of the blood. '02(Jl5) il. O. $5. Physicians.

Watkinson, W: L. The blind spot, and other sermons. '02(Je7) 12°, net, $1. Revell.

Watrous, A. E. Young Howson's wife. '02 (Mr29) D. $1.50. Quail & W.

Watrous, G: A. First year English: syntax and composition. '02(Jl12) 12°, 75 c. Sibley & D.

Watson, *Mrs.* Annah R. Passion flowers. '02(Ap12) 24°, $1.60. Whittet.

Watson, *Mrs.* Annah R. A royal lineage: Alfred the Great, 901-1901. '01. '02 (Ap12) 12°, $4.50. Whittet.

Watson, Arch. R. Law of the clearing house. '02(Ag2) D. $1.75. Banks.

Watson, B: F. *See* McDonald, D:

Watson, Forbes. Flowers and gardens. '02 (My3) 12°, $1.50. Lane.

Watson, T: E. Napoleon. '02(Mr15) O. $2.25. Macmillan.

Watson, W: Ode on the day of the coronation of King Edward VII. '02(Je28) bds., net, $1; 250 cop. Jap. vellum, net, $3.50. Lane.

Watson, W: F. Elementary experimental chemistry, inorganic. '01. '02(F1) 12°, net, $1.25. Barnes.

Watt, Fs. Terrors of the law. '02(My24) 8°, net, $1.25. Lane.

WATTEAU, Jean Antoine.
Staley. Watteau, master painter of the "Fêtes galantes." 50 c. Macmillan.

Wau-Bun. *See* Kinzie, *Mrs.* J. A. M.

Waugh, H. E., *comp.* *See* New York. Laws.

Waverley. *See* Scott, *Sir* W.

Way, A. E., *comp.* Reliques of Stratford-on-Avon. '02(Je14) 16°, (Flowers of Parnassus ser., v. 16.) net, 50 c.; leath., net, 75 c. Lane.

Way of a man. Roberts, M. †$1; 50 c. Appleton.

Way of escape. Todd, M. G. $1.50. Appleton.

Way of the preacher. Kern, J: A. $1.25. Pub. Ho. M. E. Ch., So.

Way of the West. King, C: 50 c. Rand, McN. & Co.

Wayland, J: W. Paul, the herald of the cross. '01. '02(Ja18) 16°, 40 c. Brethren Pub. Ho.

Ways of the world. Jordan, M. O. $1.50. Neely.

Wead, C: K. Cont. to the history of musical scales. '01. '02(Je14) O. pap., 50 c. Woodward & L.

WEATHER.
Price. Observations and exercises on the weather. 30 c. Am. Bk.

Web of empire. Wallace, *Sir* D. M. net, $6.50. Macmillan.

Webb, Jonathan E. Morphological study of the flower and embryo of spirala. '02(Jl12) 8°, (Cont. from the Hull botanical lib., no. 36.) pap., *25 c. net. Univ. of Chic.

Webb, Sidney *and* Beatrice. Hist. of trade unionism. New ed. '02(Ap19) O. net, $2.60. Longmans.

Webb, Sidney *and* Beatrice. Industrial democracy. New ed. 2 v. in 1. '02(Ap19) O. net, $4. Longmans.

Webb, T: E. Mystery of William Shakespeare. '02(Je7) O. $4. Longmans.

Webber, Rob. Graduated coll. of problems in electricity; fr. 3d Fr. ed., by E. A. O'Keeffe. '02(Je7) 12°, $3. Spon.

Weber, Alice. Clock on the stairs and other stories. '02(Je28) il. 12°, (St. Nicholas ser.) 75 c. Burt.

Weborg, Johanna. In Viking land. '02(Mr8) 12°, $1.25. J. C. Weborg.

Webster, Dan. Speeches; sel. by B. F. Tefft. '02(My3) 12°, (Home lib.) $1. Burt.

WEBSTER, Dan.
Lewis. Fryeburg Webster centennial. 50 c. A. F. Lewis.
McCall. Daniel Webster. net, 80 c. Houghton, M. & Co.

WEDDINGS.
See Marriage.

Wee lassie. Hawkins, *Mrs.* M. A. $1. Presb. Pub.

Weekly church teaching for the infants. Francis, *Mrs.* C. D. 25 c. E. & J. B. Young.

Wegelin, Oscar. Early American fiction, 1774-1830. '02(My17) 8°, net, $2. O. Wegelin.

Weimer, Alb. B., *rep.* *See* Pennsylvania. *Superior ct.* Repts.

Weinstock, Harris. Jesus the Jew, and other addresses. '02(Ag16) D. **$1 net. Funk.

Welch, A. C. Character photography. '02 (Ag9) D. $1. Jennings.

Welch, J. H., *and* Taylor, H. E. Destruction of St. Pierre, Martinique. '02(Jl5) D. 50 c. Fenno.

Wells, Carolyn. Folly in the forest. '02 (Ag30) il. D. †$1. Altemus.

Wells, F: P. Hist. of Newbury, Vt.; with genealog. records. '02(Ap26) il. 8°, $2.25; $3; hf. seal, $3.50; Lib. shp., $4. Caledonian.

Wells, Herb. G: Anticipations of the reaction of mechanical and scientific progress upon human life and thought. '02(Mr1) O. net, $1.80. Harper.

Wells, Horace L., *ed.* Studies from the chemical lab'y of the Sheffield Scientific School. '01. '02(Mr15) 2 v., 8°, (Yale bicentennial pub.) net, $7.50. Scribner.

WELLS.
See Boring.
Welsh, Lucie D. Colonial days. '02(My3) il. sq. O. 50 c. Educ. Pub.
Welsh rarebit tales. Cummins, H. O. $1.25. Mutual Bk.
Welsh witch. Raine, A. $1; 50 c. Appleton.
Weltmer, S. A. Telepathy and thought transference. '02(Ag2) 12°, $1. Hudson-K.
Wentworth, G: A. College algebra. Rev. ed. '02(Jl5) D. hf. mor., $1.65. Ginn.
Wentworth, G: A., *and* Hill, G. A. Lab'y exercises in elem. physics. '01. '02(Mr1) 12°, pap., 27 c. Ginn.
Wesselhoeft, E. C. German composition. '02 (Je21) D. (Modern lang. ser.) 45 c. Heath.
WESSEX.
Sherren. The Wessex of romance. *$1.50 net. Scribner.
West, And. F. Latin grammar. '02(Je7) D. (Twentieth century text-books.) net, 90 c. Appleton.
West, T: D. Metallurgy of cast iron. 4th ed. '02(Mr22); 5th ed. (Ag9) il. 8°, ea., $3. Cleveland Pr.
West, Willis M. Ancient history to the death of Charlemagne. '02(Je28) 12°, (Ser. of school histories.) hf. leath., $1.50. Allyn & B.
West-brook drives. Westbrook, H. P. $1.25. Eckler.
WEST INDIES.
Stokes. Cruising in the West Indies. **$1.25 net. Dodd.
See also Central America;—Martinique.
WEST POINT, N. Y.
Farley. West Point in the early sixties. net, $2. Pafraets
Hancock. Life at West Point. net, $1.40. Putnam.
West Virginia. *Supreme ct. of appeals*. Repts. (Freer.) v. 47. '01· '02(Je7); v. 48 (Mr15); v. 49 (My10); v. 50 (Ag2) O. shp., ea., $4.50. Charleston Daily Mail; Tribune Co.
WEST VIRGINIA.
Peterkin. Hist. and record of Prot. Episc. ch. in W. Va. $2.50; $10. Tribune Co.
Westbrook, Henrietta P. West-brook drives. '02(F22) il. D. $1.25. Eckler.
WESTBROOK, T:
Trask, *ed.* Letters of Col. Thomas Westbrook and others rel. to Indian affairs in Me., 1722-26. $5. Littlefield.
Westcotes. Couch, A. T: Q. $1. Coates.
Westcott, Brooke F. Words of faith and hope. '02(Ap26) 12°, $1.25. Macmillan.
Westcott, Fk. N. Catholic principles as il. in the doctrine, hist. and organization of the Am. Catholic church in the U. S. '02 (Ag23) D. *$1.25 net. Young Churchman.
Westermarck, E: History of human marriage. 3d ed. '02(Je28) 8°, net, $4.50. Macmillan.
WESTMINSTER ABBEY.
Hiatt. Westminster Abbey. 60 c. Macmillan.
WESTMINSTER ASSEMBLY.
See Catechisms.
Westminster biographies. T. 75 c. Small.
—Waller *and* Barrow. John Henry Newman.
WESTMINSTER SCHOOL.
Airy. Westminster. $1.50. Macmillan.

Westward ho! *See* Kingsley, C:
Wetzel, Fs. X. The dutiful child; fr. the Germ. 2d ed. '02(Mr8) 16°, 40 c. Herder.
Weyl, Wa. E. Passenger traffic of railways. '01. '02(Ja25) O. (Pub. of the Univ. of Pa., ser. in pol. economy and public law, no. 16.) $1.50; pap., $1. [Univ. of Penn.] Ginn.
Wharton, Anne H. Last century maid. '01. '02(F15) il. 12°, $1.25. Lippincott.
Wharton, Edith. Valley of decision. '02 (Mr1) 2 v., D. $2. Scribner.
Wharton, H: R. Minor surgery and bandaging. 5th ed. '02(Je14) il. 12°, net, $3. Lea
What great men have said about great men. Wall, W: net, $2.50. Dutton.
What is it to believe on the Lord Jesus Christ? Vincent, M. R. 5 c. Beam.
What is religion? Tolstoi, *Count* L. N. net, 60 c. Crowell.
What is Shakespeare? Sherman, L. A. net, $1.50; net. $1. Macmillan.
What is worth while ser. D. leatherette. Crowell.
—Hay. William McKinley. net, 28 c.
What the new thought stands for. Patterson, C: B. 10 c. Alliance.
What Thelma found in the attic. Duckwitz, L. C. $1. Alliance.
What think ye of Christ. Eldridge, J. L. $1. Abbey Press.
What's what. Allen, F. S. net, 50 c. Bradley-W.
Wheatley, H: B: How to make an index. '02(Je14) S. (Booklover's lib.) $1.25; hf. mor., $2.50. Armstrong.
Wheaton, Emily. The Russells in Chicago. '02(Je14) il. 16°, (Commonwealth ser.) $1.25. L. C. Page.
Wheeler, Ht. Cub's career. '02(My3) il. D. $1. Abbey Press.
Wheeler, Jeannette. Josephine Grahame. '02 (Mr15) D. $1.50. Abbey Press.
Wheeler, W. H. The sea-coast. '02(Ap19) il. O. $4.50. Longmans.
Wheeler, W: H: *See* Calmerton, G.
Wheeler's elem. speller. '02(Mr22) il. O. 25 c. W: H: Wheeler.
Wheeler's graded readers. il. sq. D. W: H: Wheeler.
—Calmerton *and* Wheeler. First reader. 30 c.
Wheelock, *Mrs.* Irene G. Nestlings of forest and marsh. '02(Ap12) il. D. net, $1.40. McClurg.
WHEELS.
See Gears and gearing.
When bards sing out of tune. Clark, A. 50 c. Abbey Press.
When love is king. Mabry, W. D. $1.50. Fenno.
When old New York was young. Hemstreet, C: net, $1.50. Scribner.
When the heart is young. Whitelock, W: W. **$1 net. Dutton.
Where the magnolias bloom. Cullens, F: B. 50 c. Abbey Press.
Where, when, and how to catch fish on east coast of Fla. Gregg, W: H. $4. Matthews-N.
Wherry, Abinia. Stories of the Tuscan artists. '02(F15) il. 8°, net, $4. Dutton.
Whispering pine ser. il. 12°, $1.25. Lee & S.
—Kellogg. Stout heart.

WHIST.
Coffin. Gist of whist. 75 c. Brentano's.
Leigh *and* Bergholt. Principles of whist. net, $1.50. Coates.
See also Bridge.

WHISTLER, Ja. McN.
Bowdoin. James McNeill Whistler, the man and his work. net, $1.50. Beam.

Whitaker, Jos. and Sons, *comps.* Whitaker's almanac for 1902. '01. '02(Ja11) 12°, pap., net, 40 c.; *Same*, enl. ed., hf. roan, net, $1. Scribner.

Whitaker, Jos. & Sons, *comps.* Reference catalogue of current literature. '02(Ag16) 2 v., O. hf. leath., *$5 net. Pub. Weekly.

Whitby, Beatrice. Flower and thorn '02 (Mr22) D. $1.50. Dodd.

Whitcomb, Clara E. Little journey to Italy; ed. by M. George. '02(Mr29) il. sq. D. (Plan book, v. 5, no. 5.) pap., 15 c. Flanagan.

Whitcomb, Clara E. Little journey to Scotland. '02(Mr29) il. 12°, (Plan book, v. 5, no. 4.) pap., 15 c. Flanagan.

White, C: J. Elements of theoretical and des. astronomy. 7th ed. rev. '01. '02(F8) il. 12°, $2.50. Wiley.

White, Emerson E. Grammar school algebra. New century ed. '02(Je21) S. 35 c. Am. Bk.

White, Emma S. Genealogy of the descendants of John Walker, of Wigton, Scotland; also, war records and notes pertaining to the hist. of Va., 1600-1902. '02(Ag16) il. O. $6. White.

White, Fk. On corporations. 5th ed. '02 (My17) O. shp., $5.50. Baker, V. & Co.

White, Gilbert. Natural hist. and antiquities of Selborne. '01. '02(F15) 2 v., il. 8°, net, $20. Lippincott.

White, Ja. E. Best stories from the best book. '02(Ag2) sq. O. bds., 50 c. Southern Pub.

White, Ja. E. The coming King. '02(Ag2) il. D. $1. Southern Pub.

White, J: P., *rep.* *See* Texas. *Ct. of criminal appeals.* Repts.

White, Michael. Lachmi Bai Rani of Jhansi, the Jeanne d'Arc of India. '02(Mr8) il. D. $1.50. J. F. Taylor.

White, Stewart E. Blazed trail. '02(My24) il. D. $1.50. McClure, P.

White, W. H. Book of orchids. '02(Jl19) il. D. (Handbooks of practical gardening, no. 8.) *$1 net. Lane.

White world. Kersting, R., *ed.* *$2 net. Lewis.

Whitehouse, Flo. B. God of things. '02 (My3) il. D. $1.50. Little, B. & Co.

Whitelock, W: W. When the heart is young. '02(Ag30) il. 12°, **$1 net. Dutton.

Whither are we drifting? Stechhan, O. $1. Abbey Press.

Whither goest thou? De Costa, B: F. *50 c. net; 25 c. net. Chr. Press.

Whitlock, Brand. The 13th district. '02 (Ap5) D. $1.50. Bowen-M.

Whitman, Alfr. Print-collector's handbook. 2d rev. ed. '02(My24) 8°, net, $5. Macmillan.

Whitney, Caspar, *ed.* *See* Amer. sportsman's lib.

Whittaker, N. T. Christian science, is it safe? '02(Ap5) 12°, pap., 10 c. Earle.

Whittaker's grade A handbook. D. net. Whittaker.
—Scadding. Answers to plain questions for Am. churchmen. 50 c.

Whittelsey, C: B., *comp.* Roosevelt genealogy, 1649-1902. '02(Jl12) 12°, $5. C: B. Whittelsey.

Whittier. C: A. In the Michigan lumber camps. 4th ed. '02(Ap5) S. (Boys' vacation ser., first vacation.) 75 c. Neely.

Whitton, Jos. Wags of the stage. Ed. de luxe. '02(Je7) Q. $2.50. Rigby.

Whitworth, Ernest. Practical cotton calculations. '02(Jl12) 16°, $1. Boardman.

Who's who, 1902. '02(F1) 12°, $1.75. Macmillan.

Why my photographs are bad. Taylor, C: M., *Jr.* net, $1. Jacobs.

Why the legal method of promoting temperance always has done more harm than good. Griffin, A. 15 c. A. Griffin.

Whyte, Alex. Newman: an appreciation in two lectures. '02(Mr8) D. net, $1.10. Longmans.

Wicks, —. *See* Texas. 27th legislature.

Wide world (The). '02(Mr22) il. D. (Youth's (Youth's Companion ser., no. 1.) 30 c. Ginn.

Widow Wiley, and some other old folk. Sinnett, B. $1.50. Dutton.

Wiechmann, Ferdinand Gerhard. *See* Monroe, F.

Wiener, Alfr. E. Practical calculation of dynamo-electric machines. 2d ed., rev. and enl. '02(Ap5) il. 8°, $3. Elec. World.

Wiener, Leo. Anthology of Russian literature from the earliest period to the present time. In 2 pts. pt. 1. '02(Je21) O. net, $3. Putnam.

Wiggin, *Mrs.* Kate D. Diary of a goose girl. '02(My17) il. D. $1. Houghton, M. & Co.

Wight, Emma H. The Berkleys. '02(Mr29) il. S. net, 40 c. Benziger.

Wilberforce, Bertrand A. Devout commentary on the Epistle to the Ephesians; chiefly fr. St. Thomas Aquinas. '02(Je14) 8°, net, $1. Herder.

Wilbur, Earl M. Historical sketch of the Independent Cong. Church, [Unitarian,] Meadville, Pa. 1825-1900. '02(Je28) il. D. $1; pap., 50 c. E. G. Huidekoper.

Wilbur, La Fayette. Early history of Vermont. v. 3. '02(Ap26) 8°, $1.50. L. F. Wilbur.

Wilcox, *Mrs.* Ella W. Sweet danger. New ed. '02(My17) 12°, pap., 50 c. Donohue.

Wilcox, Lucius M. Irrigation farming. Rev. and enl. ed. '02(Je14) D. $2. Judd.

Wild flowers of California. Parsons, M. E. $2. Payot.

Wild life of orchard and field. Ingersoll, E. net, $1.40. Harper.

Wildenbruch, Ernst A. v. Das edle Blut; ed. by C: A. Eggert. '02(Je14) D. 30 c. Am. Bk.

Wilgus, Horace L. Cases on the general principles of the law of private corporations. In 2 v. v. 1. '02(Mr8); v. 2 (Ap5) O. (complete work,) $9; shp., $10. Bowen-M.

Wilhelm Meister's apprenticeship and travels. *See* **Goethe**, J. W. v.

Wilhelm Tell. *See* Schiller, J. C. F. v.

Wilkie, *Sir* David.
Gower. Sir David Wilkie. $1.75. Macmillan.
Wilkins, Ja. H. Glimpse of old Mexico. '02 (Ap5) il. 16°, bds., 75 c. Whitaker & R.
Wilkins, W: H: Caroline the illustrious Queen-Consort of George II. '01. '02(Ja4) 2 v., il. O. $12. Longmans.
Wilkinson, A. E., *rep.* *See* Texas. *Sup. ct.* Repts.
Will-o'-the-wisp. Carleton, R. W. $1.25. Scroll Pub.
Will to be well. Patterson, C: B. $1. Alliance.
Willard, C: D. *Herald's* history of Los Angeles City. '02(Ap5) il. D. $1.50. Kingsley.
Willard, Josiah F., ["Josiah Flynt."] The little brother: story of tramp life. '02 (Mr29) D. $1.50. Century Co.
William I. *of Germany.*
Zastrow. Wilhelm der Siegreiche. net, 50 c. Macmillan.
Williams, Ja. *See* Livermore, V. B.
Williams, J: H: Painter's guide book. '02 (Ag2) 12°, $1.50. J: H: Williams.
Williams, *Mrs.* Leslie. A garden in the suburbs. '02(F15) 12°, net, $1.50. Lane.
Williams, Louise H. *See* Richards, E. H.
Williams, M. B. Sex problems. '02(Ap19) 12°, net, $1. Revell.
Williams, Margery. The late returning. '02 (Je7) 12°, $1.25. Macmillan.
Williams, Martha McC. Next to the ground. '02(My24) D. net, $1.20. McClure, P.
Williams, T. R. Shall we understand the Bible? Rev., enl. ed. '02(Ap26) 12°, pap., net, 50 c. Macmillan.
Williamson, *Mrs.* Corolin C. Mary Starkweather. '02(F22) D. $1.50. Abbey Press.
Williamson, G: C. Holman Hunt. '02(Mr8) il. 16°, (Miniature ser. of painters.) 50 c. Macmillan.
Willoughby, E: F. Hygiene for students. '01. '02(Ja4) 12°, $1.25. Macmillan.
Wills.
Clement. Probate repts., annot. v. 6. $5.50. Baker, V. & Co.
Hoyt. Practice in probate cts. of New Hampshire. $2.50. Rumford Press.
Tucker. Preparation of wills. $3.50. G: B. Reed.
Wilson, *Mrs.* Augusta J. E. Inez. '02(Ag2) 12°, (Cornell ser.) 75 c. Burt.
Wilson, *Mrs.* Augusta J. E. A speckled bird. '02(Ag16) D. $1.50. G: W. Dillingham.
Wilson, Calvin D. Divine religion of humanity. '02(Je21) S. pap., net, 20 c. Presb. Bd.
Wilson, Edn. B. *See* Gibbs, J. W.
Wilson, Eug. B. Cyanide processes. 3d ed. rewritten. '02(Je21) 12°, $1.50. Wiley.
Wilson, Floyd B. Paths to power. '01. '02 (Ja4) D. $1. Fenno.
Wilson, H. W. Directory of booksellers, stationers, librarians and publishers in the U. S. and Canada. '02(Ag23) 8°, pap., $10. H. W. Wilson.
Wilson, Harry L. The spenders. '02(Je14) il. D. $1.50. Lothrop.
Wilson, Ja. G., *ed.* Presidents of the United States. New rev. ed., with life of W: McKinley and sketch of T. Roosevelt. '02 (Mr29) il. 8°, $3.50; hf. mor. or hf. cf., $6. Appleton.
Wilson, L: A. A great cloud of witnesses. '01. '02(Ap26) D. 50 c. Standard Pub.
Wilson, L: N. Bibliography of child study. '02(Mr8) O. pap., net, 25 c. Stechert.
Wilson, Stella S. Ohio. '02(Je7) il. 12°, (Tarr and McMurry's geographies, supp. v.) net, 30 c. Macmillan.
Wilson, Theodora W. T'bacca queen. '02 (My10) D. (Town and country lib., no. 311.) $1; pap., 50 c. Appleton.
Winans, G: M. Kansas. '02(Jl12) il. 12°, (Tarr and McMurry's geographies, supp. v.) *30 c. net. Macmillan.
Winchester, Paul, *ed.* Around the throne: sketches of Washington society. '02(Je14) 12°, net, $1. Eichelberger.
Wind in the tree. Sutherland, M. †$1.50. Russell.
Winding road. Godfrey, E. $1.50. Holt.
Windle, Bertram C. A. The Malvern country. '01. '02(Ap12) il. S. (Little guides ser.) net, 75 c. Dodd.
Window-gardening.
Allen, P. *and* G. Miniature and window gardening. net, 50 c. Pott.
Windows for sermons. Banks, L: A. net, $1.20. Funk.
Windsor, W: Phrenology. '02(My17) 12°, pap., 25 c. Donohue.
Windstorm and tornado insurance. Hoffman, F: L. 25 c. Spectator.
Wine.
Emerson. Story of the vine. net, $1.25. Putnam.
Winfield, A. M., *pseud.* Larry Barlow's ambition. '02(Ag9) il. 12°, $1. Saalfield.
Winning of Sarenne. Beall, St. C. 50 c.; 25 c. Federal.
Winslow, Helen M. Literary Boston of today. '02(Ag23) D. (Little pilgrimages ser.) **$1.20 net. L. C. Page.
Winslow, J: A.
Ellicott. Life of John Ancrum Winslow, Rear Admiral U. S. N. $2.50. Putnam.
Winston, N. B. Grace of orders: [novel.] '02(F22) D. $1. Abbey Press.
Winter, John Strange, *pseud.* *See* Stannard, *Mrs.* H. E. V.
Wisconsin. List of books for township libraries. '02(My24) il. O. pap., 25 c. Wisconsin.
Wisconsin.
Arbor and bird day annual for Wis. schools. gratis. Democrat Pr. Co.
Harvey. Aids for observance of Memorial day by schools of Wis. gratis. Democrat Pr. Co.
Wisner, Arth., ["A. Gallus."] Emma Calvé. '02(Je28) il. 4°, $1.50. Russell.
Wisser, J: P. Tactics of coast defense. '02 (Ag16) O. $2. Hudson-K.
Wister, Owen. The Virginian. '02(Je21) il. D. $1.50. Macmillan.
Wistons. Amber, M. $1.50. Scribner.
Wit and humor.
Bangs. Olympian nights. $1.25. Harper.
Brenton. Unce Jed's country letters. 30 c. Dickerman.
Bridgman. Gulliver's bird book. $1.50. L. C. Page.
Corrothers. Black cat club. net, $1. Funk.
Daskam, *comp.* Best nonsense verses. 50 c. W: S. Lord.

WIT AND HUMOR.—*Continued.*
De Leon. Inauguration of President Watterson. 25 c. Am. Writers.
Field. Nonsense for old and young. 50 c. Dickerman.
Fleming. Around the Pan with Uncle Hank. $2. Nutshell.
Gilmer. Fables of the elite. $1. Fenno.
Goodwin. "Sinker" stories of wit and humor. $1. Ogilvie.
Irish wit and humor. 25 c. Drake.
Irwin. Rubáiyat of Omar Khayyám, jr. net, 50 c. Elder.
Kendall. Good gravy. 25 c. Helman-T.
"Man in the street" stories from the *N. Y. Times.* $1 Ogilvie.
Prune. College chaps. 75 c. Mutual Bk.
Sharp. Stolen correspondence from dead letter office. 50 c. Gervais.
Shaw. Josh Billings' old farmer's allminax. $1.50. G: W. Dillingham.
See also Epigrams;—Parody.

Witch Winnie ser. Champney, *Mrs.* E. W. 9 v. $11.25. Dodd.
With Napoleon at St. Helena. Fremeaux, P. net, $1.50. Lane.
With redskins on the warpath. Walkey, S. $1.25. Cassell.
With Rimington. Phillipps, L. M. $2.50. Longmans.
With the Naval Brigade in Natal. Burne, C. $2.50. Longmans.
With the royal tour. Knight, E: F: $2. Longmans.
Witmer, L. Analytical psychology. '02 (Ap5) O. $1.60. Ginn.
WITNESSES.
See Evidence.
Wodell, F: W: Choir and chorus conducting. '01· '02(F8) il. 12°. $1.50. Presser.
Woelfkin, Cornelius. Chambers of the soul. '02(Mr29) S. 35 c. Un. Soc. C. E.
Wolcott, Edson R. On the sensitiveness of the coherer. '02(My17) O. (Bull. of the Univ. of Wis., no. 51, science ser., v. 3. no. 1.) pap., 20 c. Univ. of Wis.
Wolfville days. Lewis, A. H: $1.50. Stokes.
Wollpert, F: A man amongst men. '02 (Ap5) sq. D. pap., 15 c. Eckler.
WOMAN.
Blouët. 'Tween you an' I. pt. 2, Concerning women. $1.20. Lothrop.
Dressler. Feminology. $3. Dressler.
Macfadden. Power and beauty of superb womanhood. $1. Physical Culture.
Maulde la Clavière. Art of life. net, $1.75. Putnam.
Sainte-Foi. The perfect woman. net, $1. Marlier.
Stone. Women designers of book-plates. net, $1; net, $2. Beam.
Women in the business world. $1.50; 50 c. Alliance.
See also Children; — Domestic economy; — Gynecology;—Home;—Nurses and nursing;—Sex;—Young women.

Woman who dared. Van Deventer, E. M. 25 c. Laird.
Woman's exchange cook book. Palmer, *Mrs.* M. 70 c. Conkey.
Woman's no. Cameron, *Mrs.* E. S. L. $1.25. Buckles.
Women in the business world. [New issue.] '02(Mr22) D. $1.50; pap., 50 c. Alliance.
Women of the Reformed church. Good, J. I. $1. Heidelberg.
Wonder-box tales. Ingelow, J. 50 c. Estes.
Wonders of Mouseland. Childs, E: E. $1.25. Abbey Press.
Wonders of the Revelation of Jesus Christ. Ruble, W: $1. Standard Pub.
Wood, Casey A., Andrews, Alb. H., *and* Hardie, T. M., *eds.* Eye, ear, nose and throat. '02(Mr8) il. D. (Practical medicine ser. of year-books, v. 3.) $1.50. Year Bk.
Wood, *Mrs.* **Ma. A.** Marriage: its duties and privileges. '02(F8) 12°, net, $1.25. Revell.
WOOD-CARVING.
See Sloyd.
Woodland orchids. Boyle, F: net, $7. Macmillan.
Woodley, O. I. *and* M. S., *and* Carpenter, G. R. Foundation lessons in Eng. language and grammar. '02(Ag16) 12°, *65 c. net. Macmillan.
Woods, C: Coke. *See* Nicholson, T:
WOODS.
See Forests and forestry.
Woodworth, Elijah B. Descendants of Walter Woodworth of Scituate, Mass.; Sketch of Samuel Woodworth and his descendants. '02(F22) 8°, $3. G: W. Humphrey.
Woolsey, Sa. C., ["Susan Coolidge."] Uncle and aunt. New ed '01. '02(F15) 16°, (Children's friend ser.) bds., 50 c. Little, B. & Co.
Worcester, J: Works of charity. '01. '02 (F1) sq. S. pap., 25 c. New-Ch. Un.
WORCESTER, Mass.
Roe. Worcester Young Men's Christian Assoc. $1. A. S. Roe.
Word signs made easy. Hardcastle, *Mrs.* M. A. $1. M. A. Hardcastle.
Wordingham, C: H. Central electrical stations. '01. '02(F15) il. 8°, $7.50. Lippincott.
WORDS.
Jenkins. Vest-pocket lexicon. 60 c.; 75 c. Lippincott.
See also Synonyms.
Words of faith and hope. Westcott, B. F. $1.25. Macmillan.
Wordsworth, W: Selected poems; ed. by J. B. Seabury. '02(Ap26) 12°, (Ser. of classics.) 30 c. Silver.
Workingman's opportunity. Rowell, J. H. 5 c. Free Socialist.
Works, J: D. Practice pleading and forms adapt. to new rev. code of Indiana. 3d ed., rev. and enl. v. 1, 2, 3. '02(Je14) O. shp., $18. Clarke.
Works and days. Mabie, H. W. net, $1. Dodd.
Workshop wrinkles. Brown, W: N. net, $1. Van Nostrand.
World almanac and encyclopedia, 1902. '02 (Ja11) il. D. pap., 25 c. Press Pub.
World on fire. Halstead, M. $1.50; $2.25; $3. Dominion.
World ser. See Appleton's.
World's epoch makers; ed. by O. Smeaton. D. $1.25. Scribner.
—Ritchie. Plato.
—Smeaton. The Medici and the Italian Renaissance.
World's people. Cruger, *Mrs.* J. S. †$1.50. J. F. Taylor.

World's shrine. Johnson, V. W. **$1.20 net. Barnes.

Worlledge, Arth. J: Prayer. '02(Mr22) D. (Oxford lib. of practical theology.) $1.50. Longmans.

Wormell, R: *See* Hobbs, W. R. P.

WORSHIP.
Dobbins. Story of the world's worship. $2.25; $3.25. Dominion.
See also Church music;—Devotional exercises and meditations;—Prayer.

Worthington, Eliz. S. The tocsin—our children in peril. '01- '02(Mr22) 12°, pap., 25 c. Cubery.

Wounded beast. Jellison, E. A: 25 c. E. A: Jellison.

Wray, Angelina W. Jean Mitchell's school. '02(F15) il. D. $1.25. Public Sch. Pub.

Wretched Flea. Muller, M. 35 c. Flanagan.

Wright, D: H: Under the red cross: [poems.] '01- '02(F15) 12°, pap., 35 c. Biddle.

Wright, G: F: Asiatic Russia. '02(Jl5) 2 v., il. 8°, leath., **$7.50 net. McClure, P.

Wright, H: W., *comp.* Genealogy of the Wright family from 1639 to 1901. '01- '02 (Mr8) 8°, pap., 25 c. Pelham.

Wright, J. C. Body and soul: lectures del. in trance state. '02(My17) D. $1. J. C. Wright.

Wright, Ma. T. Aliens. '02(Mr22) D. net, $1.50. Scribner.

Wright, W. J. P. Dante and the Divine comedy. '02(My10) 8°, net, $1. Lane.

WRITING.
See Inscriptions;—Letter-writing;—Penmanship;—Typewriting.

Wurtzburg, Caro. A. *See* Ruskin, J:

Wyatt, Lucy M. L. Constance Hamilton. '02(Ap26) D. 50 c. Abbey Press.

Wyckoff, C: T. Feudal relations between the kings of Eng. and Scotland under the early Plantagenets. '02(Mr22) 8°, pap., net, $1. Univ. of Chic.

Wyllarde, Dolf. Story of Eden. '01- '02 (Mr1) 12°, $1.50. Lane.

Wyman, W. E. A. Tibio; peroneal neurectomy for the relief of spavin lameness. '02 (Jl12) 8°, pap., 50 c. W: R. Jenkins.

Wynkoop, R: Schuremans, of New Jersey. 2d ed. '02(Jl19) 8°, $3. R: Wynkoop.

Wynne, Jos. F. A blighted rose. '02(My24) D. $1.50. Angelus.

Wyoming. *Supreme ct.* Repts. (Potter.) v. 9. '02(Jl12) O. shp., $5. Callaghan.

Wythes, G: Book of vegetables. '02(Je7) il. D. (Handbooks of practical gardening, v. 7.) $1. Lane.

X-RAYS.
See Roentgen rays.

XENOPHON.
See Attic prose.

Yacht club ser. 12°, $1.25 Lee & S.
—Adams. Money-maker. (3.)

YACHTS AND YACHTING.
Ames. Etiquette of yacht colors. 25 c. Annin.
Fisher. How to build a model yacht. $1. Rudder.
Mower. How to build a racing sloop. $1. Rudder.

Yale bicentennial pubs. 8°, net. Scribner.
—Beecher. Studies in evolution. $5.

Yale bicentennial pubs.—Continued.
—Bourne. Essays in hist. criticism. $2.
—Chittenden, *ed.* Studies in physiolog. chemistry. $4.
—Gibbs. Elem. principles in statistical mechanics.—Victor analysis. ea., $4.
—Goodell. Chapters on Greek metric. $2.
—Hopkins. India, old and new. $2.50.
—Lang, *ed.* Cancioneiro Gallego-Castelhano. *$3.
—Morris. On principles and methods in Latin syntax. $2.
—Oertel. Study of language. $3.
—Two centuries' growth of Am. law. $4.
—Wells, *ed.* Studies from chemical lab'y of Sheffield Scientific School. 2 v. $7.50.

Yale lectures. *See* Brewer, D. J.

Yale studies in Eng.; ed. by A. S. Cook. O. pap. Holt.
—Boccaccio *and* Aretino. Earliest lives of Dante. 75 c. (10.)

YEAR BOOKS.
See Almanacs and annuals.

Year with the Mother-play. Proudfoot, A. H $1. Flanagan.

Yeats, W: B., *comp. and ed.* Irish fairy and folk tales. '02(My10) il. 12°, (Fairy lib.) $1. Burt.

Yellow fiend. Hector, *Mrs.* A. F. $1.50. Dodd.

Yellow violin. Denison, M. A. $1. Saalfield.

YELLOWSTONE PARK.
Hatfield. Geyserland and wonderland. 24 c. Hicks-J.

Yelsew, Jean, *pseud.* *See* Smith, J: W.

Yerkes observatory bulletin. *See* Univ. of Chicago.

Yersin, Marie *and* Jeanne. Phonorhythmic method of French pronunciation, accent and diction; Fr. and Eng. '02(Ag23) il. 12°, $1.25. Lippincott.

Yonge, Ctte. M., *comp.* Book of golden deeds of all times and all lands. '02(Ap12) 12°, (Home lib.) $1. Burt.

Young, Abram V. E. Elem. principles of chemistry. '01. '02(F22) 12°, net, 95 c. Appleton.

Young, C: A: Manual of astronomy. '02 (Jl5) il. O. hf. leath., $2.45. Ginn.

Young, Ella F. Ethics in the school. '02 (F22) D. (Cont. to educ., no. 4.) pap., net, 25 c. Univ. of Chic.

Young, Ella F. Isolation in the school. '01- '02(Ja11) S. (Univ. of Chic. cont. to education, no. 1.) pap., net, 50 c. Univ. of Chic.

Young, Ella F. Some types of modern educ. theory. '02(My24) D. (Univ. of Chic. cont. to education, no. 6.) pap., net, 25 c. Univ. of Chic.

Young, Filson. Mastersingers; with essay on Hector Berlioz. '02(Ap12) 12°, net, $1.50. Scribner.

Young, Hudson. Father Manners. '02(F22) D. $1. Abbey Press.

Young, J: R. Men and memories. Ed. de luxe. '02(Mr29) 2 v., subs., $5; in 1 v., 12°, subs., $3. Neely.

Young, Julia D. Black Evan. '02(Ap26) 12°, $1. Neely.

Young, Owen D., *and* Keen, Ja. T. Problems in practice and pleading at the common law. '02(Ap12) O. pap., 50 c. Mudge.

Young folks' lib. of choice literature. il. 16°. 50 c.; bds., 40 c. Educ. Pub.
—Pratt. Stories of Ill.
Young Howson's wife. Watrous, A. E.
YOUNG MEN.
McLeod. Young man's problems. 50 c. Flanagan.
Warner. Young man in modern life. net, 85 c. Dodd.
See also Conduct of life;—Culture.
Young of heart ser. il. D. 50 c. Estes
—Ingelow. Wonder-box tales.
—Sand. Rosy cloud.
—Viaud. Lives of two cats.
YOUNG PEOPLE.
Jordans. Danger of youth and a tried antidote. 15 c. Herder.
See also Children;—Girls;—Young men;—Young women.
Young People's Alliance ser. S. pap. Mattill & L.
—Staebler. Manual on the Book of books. 20 c.
Young people's Bible stories. '02(F1) 4 v., il. 4°, ea., $1.25. Saalfield.
YOUNG PEOPLE'S SOC. OF CHR. ENDEAVOR.
Clark. Training the church of the future; lectures, with special ref. to the Young People's Soc. of C. E. net, 75 c. Funk.
YOUNG WOMEN.
Sinclair. Unto you, young women. net, $1. Lippincott.
See also Conduct of life;—Culture;—Girls;—Young people;—Woman.
Youth's companion ser. il. D. 30 c. Ginn.
—Northern Europe. (2.)
—Toward the rising sun. (4.)
—Under sunny skies. (3.)
—Wide world. (1.)
Zaïre and Epitres. Voltaire, F. M. A. de. 50 c. Scott, F. & Co.
Zancis, *Mme.* —. How to tell fortunes by cards. '02(Mr15) S. pap., 25 c. Drake.
Zastrow, Karl. Wilhelm der Siegreiche; ed. by E. P. Ash. Authorized ed. '02(My24) 12°. (Siepmann's elem. Germ. ser.) net, 50 c. Macmillan.
Zayas Enríquez, R. de. El teniente de los gavilanes. '02(Jl5) 12°, pap., †50 c. Appleton.
Zdziarski, A. F., *ed.* *See* Dmitriev-Mámonóv, A. I., *ed.*
Zelma, the mystic. Thurber, A. M. $1.25. Alliance.
ZINCALI.
Borrow. The Zincali. $2. Putnam.
Zip the acrobat. Browne, G: W. 75 c. Street.
Zitkala-sa. Old Indian legends. '01- '02 (Mr8) il. D. 50 c. Ginn.
Zittel, Karl A. v. Hist. of geology and palæontology to the end of the nineteenth century; tr. by M. M. Ogilvie-Gordon. '01-'02(Ap12) D. (Contemporary science ser.) $1.50. Scribner.
Zobo patriotic drill. Hatch, A. W. 15 c. Hints.
ZOOLOGY.
French. Animal activities. $1.20. Longmans.
Jordan *and* Heath. Animal forms. net, $1.10. Appleton.
Lindsay. Story of animal life. net, 35 c. Appleton.
Mudge. Text book of zoology. $2.50. Longmans.
See also Amphibia; — Animals;—Evolution;—Invertebrates;—Protozoa.
ZOOTOMY.
See Dissection.
Zuckerhandl, Otto. Atlas and epitome of operative surgery; fr. 2d rev., enl. Germ. ed.; ed. by J. C. Da Costa. '02(Ap26) il. 12°, net, $3.50. Saunders.
ZUNI INDIANS.
Cushing. Zuñi folk tales. net, $3.50.

RECORD OF SERIES.

A. L. Burt, 58 Duane St., New York.

Alger Series for Boys, 12°, cl., $1 net.

Tom Turner's legacy. Alger, H., jr.
Treasure of Cocos Island. Otis, Ja.

Cornell Series, 12°, cl., 75 c. net.

Minister's wooing. Stowe, H. B.
Murders in the Rue Morgue. Poe, E. A.
Narrative of Arthur Gordon Pym. Poe, E. A.
Nature, addresses and lectures. Emerson, R. W.
Old Curiosity Shop. Dickens, C.
Outre-Mer. Longfellow, H. W.
Paul and Virginia. St. Pierre, B. de.
Pleasures of life. Lubbock, Sir J.
Prince of the House of David. Ingraham, Rev. J. H.
Rasselas. Johnson, S.
Representative men. Emerson, R. W.
Samantha at Saratoga. "Josiah Allen's Wife."
Scottish chiefs. Porter, J.
Self-raised. Southworth, Mrs. E. D. E. N.
Throne of David. Ingraham, Rev. J. H.
Views a-foot. Taylor, Bayard.
Walden. Thoreau, H. D.

Fairy Library, 12°, $1 net.

Irish fairy tales. Yeats, W. B.
Old, old fairy tales. Valentine, Mrs.

Fireside Series for Girls, 12°, cl., $1 net.

Annice Wynkoop, artist. Rouse, A. L.
Bek's first corner. Drinkwater, J. M.
Bubbles. Newberry, F. E.
Daddy's girl. Meade, L. T.
Deane girls, The. Rouse, A. L.
Duxberry doings. Le Row, C. B.
Growing up. Drinkwater, J. M.
Joyce's investments. Newberry, F. E.
Miss Ashton's new pupil. Robbins, Mrs. S. S.
Miss Prudence. Drinkwater, J. M.
Robin redbreast. Molesworth, Mrs.
Sara, a princess. Newberry, F. A.
Tessa Wadsworth's discipline. Drinkwater, J. M.
Very naughty girl, A. Meade, L. T.
Very odd girl, A. Armstrong, A. E.

Little Women Series, 12°, 75 c. net.

Little Susy stories. Prentiss, Mrs. E.

St. Nicholas Series for Boys and Girls, 12°, 75 c. net.

Clock on the stairs. Weber, Alice.
Comrades, a story for boys. Newberry, F. E.
Dog of Flanders. La Rame, L. de.
Rudy and Babette. Andersen, H. C.
Troubles of Tatters. Morris, A. T.

Rugby Series for Boys, 12°, cl., 75 c. net.

Every inch a sailor. Stables, Gordon.
Golden galleon. Leighton, Rob.
Grettir, the outlaw. Baring-Gould, S.
How Jack Mackenzie won his epaulettes. Stables, Gordon.
Log of the "Flying Fish." Collingwood, Harry.
Olaf the glorious. Leighton, Rob.
Story of John G. Paton. Paton, Ja.
To Greenland and the Pole. Stables, Gordon.
Two thousand years ago. Church, A. J.
Wreck of the "Golden Fleece." Leighton, Rob.

Wellesley Series for Girls, 12°, cl., 75 c. net.

The books are the same as given under "Fireside Series for Girls."

Little, Brown & Co., 254 Washington St., Boston.

Boys' and Girls' Bookshelf, 12°, cl., $1.

No
1. My boys. Alcott, Louisa M.
2. Mopsa the fairy. Ingelow, Jean.
3. A Guernsey lily. Coolidge, Susan.
4. Nan at Camp Chicopee. Hamlin, Myra S.
5. Double play. Everett, W.
6. Hester Stanley at St. Mark's. Spofford, Harriet Prescott.
7. A little American girl in India. Cheever, H. A.
8. Jan of the windmill. Ewing, J. H.
9. The resolute Mr. Pansy. Trowbridge, J.
10. A flower of the wilderness. Plympton, A. G.
11. The Island Impossible. Morgan, Harriet.
12. Sparrow the tramp. Wesselhoeft, Lily F.
13. The drifting island. Wentworth, Walter.

Little, Brown & Co.'s *Boys' and Girls' Bookshelf.* —*Continued.*

No.
14. Mice at play. Forest, Neil.
15. Among the lindens. Raymond, Evelyn.
16. The joyous story of Toto. Richards, Laura.
17. Bed-time stories. Moulton, Louise Chandler.
18. With fife and drum at Louisbourg. Oxley, J. M.
19. The boys and girls of Brantham. Raymond, Evelyn.
20. Hope Benham. Perry, Nora.
21. 'Twixt you and me. LeBaron, Grace.
22. Scouting for Washington. True, J. Preston.
23. Jolly good times. Smith, Mary P. Wells.
24. Treasure Island. Stevenson, Rob. L.
25. Their canoe trip. Smith, Mary P. Wells.
26. Six to sixteen. Ewing, Juliana H.
27. Hester Stanley's friends. Spofford, Harriet P.
28. Castle Blair. Shaw, Flora.
29. The secret of the Black Butte. Shattuck, W.
30. Stories told to a child. Ingelow, Jean.

Children's Friend Series, 12°, cl., 50 c.

Pansies and water-lilies. Alcott, Louisa M.
The dolls' journey. Alcott, Louisa M.
A very ill-tempered family. Ewing, Juliana H.
Snap-dragons. Ewing, Juliana H.
The little women play. Adapted from Miss Alcott's story by Elizabeth L. Gould.
The little men play. Adapted from Miss Alcott's story by Elizabeth L. Gould.

Readable Books Series, 12°, cl., $1.

Peter Simple. Marryat, F.
Handy Andy. Lover, S.
Rory O'Moore. Lover, S.

New Amsterdam Book Co., 156 Fifth Ave., New York.

Red Letter Series, 12°, pap., 50 c.

No.
29. Captain Fanny. Russell, W. C.
30. The shadow of Hilton Fernbrook. Westbury, Atha.
31. With sword and crucifix. Van Zile, E. S.

L. C. Page & Co., 200 Summer St., Boston.

The Red Rose Library, 12°, pap., 50 c.

15. The maidens of the rocks. D'Annunzio, Gabriel.

Street & Smith, 238 William St., New York.

Arrow Library, 12°, 10 c.

268. Friendship. Ouida.
269. Viva. Forrester, Mrs.
270. Hearts. Murray, D. C.
271. Heritage of Langdale. Alexander, Mrs.

Bertha Clay Library, 12°, 10 c.

152. A bitter courtship. Clay, B. M.
153. A tragedy of love and hate. Clay, B. M.
154. A stolen heart. Clay, B. M.
155. Every inch a queen. Clay, B. M.

Eagle Library, 12°, 10 c.

274. A romantic girl. Green, E. E.
275. Love's cruel whim. Rowlands, E. A.
276. So nearly lost. Garvice, C.
277. The lady of Darracourt. Garvice, C.

Eden Series, 12°, 10 c.

83. Fenton's quest. Braddon, M. E.
84. Geraldine Hawthorne. Butt, B. M.
85. Joan Wentworth. McQuoid, K. S.
86. My own child. Marryat, F.

Magnet Library, 12°, 10 c.

247. Results of a duel. Du Boisgobey, F.
248. Toss of a coin. Carter, N.
249. Old Stonewall detective. Taylor, J. R.
250. A double handed game. Carter, N.

Medal Library, 12°, 10 c.

165. The secret chart. Orton, J. K.
166. Try and trust. Alger, H., Jr.
167. Frank Merriwell's chums. Standish, B. L.
168. Among Malay pirates. Henty, G. A.

THE

WITH WHICH IS INCORPORATED

The American Literary Gazette and Publishers' Circular.

[ESTABLISHED 1852.]

PUBLICATION OFFICE, 298 BROADWAY, NEW YORK.

Entered at the Post-Office at New York, N. Y., as second-class matter.

VOL. LXII., No. 12. NEW YORK, September 20, 1902. WHOLE No. 15

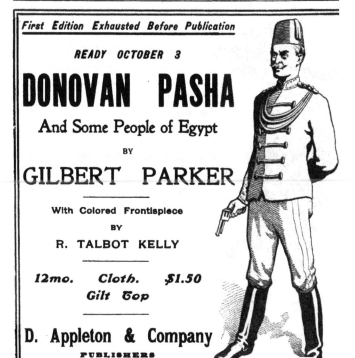

PAGE'S SEPTEMBER PUBLICATIONS

NOW READY

The Leading Juvenile of the Year

BEAUTIFUL JOE'S PARADISE

Or, The Island of Brotherly Love

A Sequel to "Beautiful Joe"

By MARSHALL SAUNDERS

Illustrated by CHARLES LIVINGSTON BULL $1.20 net

A FEW REVIEWS FROM ADVANCE SHEETS

". . . sure to be one of the most popular juvenile books of the fall and winter season . . . is strikingly illustrated by Charles Livingston Bull, the artist who drew the pictures for Prof. Roberts' 'The Kindred o the Wild.' . . . Miss Saunders has put life, humor, action and tenderness into her story."—*Chicago Record Herald.*

"Revives the spirit of 'Beautiful Joe' capitally. Will probably be more successful than its precursor It is fairly riotous with fun, and, as a whole, about as unusual as anything in the animal book line that has seen the light. It is a book for juveniles—old and young."—*Philadelphia Item.*

"Remarkably bright and clever, and will certainly prove a big success with children."—*Louisville Courier-Journal.*

READY SEPTEMBER 30th

Three Notable Novels

$1.50

Barbara Ladd

By CHARLES G. D. ROBERTS

Author of "The Kindred of the Wild," "The Forge in the Forest," etc.

Illustrated in Tints by FRANK VERBECK

A fascinating story of Colonial days.

$1.50

THE LAST WORD

By ALICE MacGOWAN

A story of the heart—of a woman's heart—yet it is such a piquant mixture of humor, practicality and sentiment that the latter never unwelcomely predominates. There is no woman who will read the book without finding in many places her own heart speaking to her from its pages. There are few who will read it without both laughter and tears. It is the greatest autobiography of a woman's love since "Jane Eyre," and it is modern in its essence.

$1.50

Hope Loring

By LILIAN BELL

Author of "Abroad with the Jimmies," "The Love Affairs of an Old Maid," etc.

Illustrated by FRANK T. MERRILL

The story of a wilful, unconventional girl—the most charming heroine ever drawn by Miss Bell.

ORDER THROUGH YOUR JOBBER OR FROM THE PUBLISHERS

L. C. PAGE & COMPANY, - Boston

Harper's October Books

1. **THE INTRUSIONS OF PEGGY. By Anthony Hope.**
A new novel that combines the brightness of the author's "Dolly Dialogues" with the interest of the "Prisoner of Zenda." It is a story of life to-day in London. Illustrated. $1.50.

2. **THE FLIGHT OF PONY BAKER. By W. D. Howells.**
This is a most delightful story of the adventures, experiences, and feelings of a "Real" boy told in a way to interest every one who is interested in boys. Illustrated. $1.25 net.

3. **THE FIRST CHRISTMAS. By Gen. Lew Wallace.**
The great popularity of this beautiful story has necessitated the publication of this new handsome edition. It is printed in two colors, illustrated from reproductions of paintings by Raphael, Murillo, etc. $1 25.

4. **AN OLD COUNTRY HOUSE. By Richard Le Gallienne.**
The story of the plans and ambitions of two young married people in their country home. It is one of the most charming love stories of recent fiction. The volume is handsomely made with illustrations in tint and color by Elizabeth Shippen Green. (In a box) $2.40 net.

5. **THROUGH THE LOOKING GLASS. By Lewis Carroll.**
This delightful story, long since a classic for both old and young, is bound uniformly with the Peter Newell "Alice in Wonderland" published last year. There are forty full-page illustrations by Peter Newell, a frontispiece portrait of the artist, decorative borders in colors. (In a box.) $3.00 net.

6. **IN THE MORNING GLOW. By Roy Rolfe Gilson.**
Stories of home life—the relations of the children with father, mother, grandfather, and so on—written in the vein of tenderness, humor and pathos that will make all readers recognize in them a part of their own experience. The stories, with one exception, appeared in Harper's Magazine. Illustrated by Alice Barber Stephens. $1.25.

7. **AN INTERNATIONAL EPISODE. By Henry James.**
A new edition of what many readers consider the best of Henry James's fiction, daintily bound, uniform with the author's "Daisy Miller." Illustrated by McVickar. $1 25.

8. **THE LOVABLE TALES OF JANEY, JOSEY AND JOE. By Gertrude Smith,** Author of the "Roggie and Reggie Stories."
Delightful stories for children. The subjects are those familiar to all households—tea parties, making cookies, playing circus, stories of the flowers, visits, etc. Fifteen chapters in all, each beautifully illustrated. $1.30 net.

9. **WINSLOW PLAIN. By Sarah P. McLean Greene,** author of "Flood Tide," "Vesty of the Basins," etc.
A story of life in New England, full of the same humor and bright optimism that readers enjoyed in the author's "Flood Tide." No work of the author's will be read with keener interest. $1.50.

10. **THE RED HOUSE. By E. Nesbit.**
A delightful story of the honeymoon and the funny experience of a young married couple who from "love in a cottage" came into an extensive country estate. It is undoubtedly the author's most attractive work of fiction. Illustrated by Keller. $1.50.

11. **THE REIGN OF QUEEN ANNE. By Justin McCarthy,** author of "A History of Our Own Times," etc.
Mr. McCarthy's most recent contribution to his popular histories of England, treating of one of the most brilliant periods in English history—the time of Addison, Swift, Steele, Bolingbroke, and the great Marlborough. The history is in two volumes, uniform with the author's "Reminiscences." 2 vols., cloth (in a box). $4.00 net.

12. **HARPER'S COOK BOOK ENCYCLOPAEDIA.**
This is a book that will come as a boon to every housekeeper. It is arranged like a dictionary so that you can find anything you want simply by opening the book and without hunting through a maze of indexes. Contributions by the most noted authorities on cooking in the world Edited by the editor of Harper's Bazar Bound in washable leather cloth. Illustrated $1.50 net.

13. **THE DESERTED VILLAGE (Abbey Edition). By Oliver Goldsmith.**
The most beautiful edition of this work ever issued. The exquisite illustrations by Edwin A. Abbey, R.A., appeared first in Harper's Magazine. Frontispiece portrait; introductions by Goldsmith, Austin Dobson, and copious annotations by Cunningham. Royal octavo, bound in silk. $3.00.

14. **SONGS OF TWO CENTURIES. By Will Carleton,** author of "Farm Ballads," "City Ballads," etc.
A new book of poems by one of our most popular verse writers. Fully illustrated. $1.50 net.

15. **LITERATURE AND LIFE. By W. D. Howells.**
This volume is another of Mr. Howells's delightful books of reminiscence and criticism of literary things, life, and people. Uniform with the author's "Literary Friends and Acquaintance" and "Heroines of Fiction." 32 full-page illustrations. $2.25 net.

16. **THE CONQUEST OF ROME. By Matilde Serao,** author of "The Land of Cockayne."
The author is without doubt the greatest modern Italian novelist. The main theme of this new novel is the conquest made by Rome over a brilliant young statesman who goes there from the provinces. It is a novel of intense and absorbing interest. $1.50

17. **A DOFFED CORONET. By the author of "Martyrdom of an Empress."**
A most interesting story of the experiences in court life and in America of the titled author of "The Martyrdom of an Empress" and the "Tribulations of a Princess." Illustrated. $2.25 net.

Harper & Brothers, Franklin Square, New York

The Publishers' Weekly.

SEPTEMBER 20, 1902.

INDEX TO ADVERTISERS

NOTES IN SEASON.

L. C. PAGE & Co. will publish on the 30th inst., three notable novels—"Barbara Ladd," a story of Colonial days, by Charles G. D. Roberts, author of "The Forge in the Forest," etc., illustrated in tints by Frank Verbeck; "Hope Loring," a story of a wilful, unconventional girl, by Lilian Bell, author of "The Love Affairs of an Old Maid," etc., with illustrations by Frank T. Merrill; also, "The Last Word," the "autobiography of a woman's love," by Alice MacGowan.

A. C. McCLURG & Co. publish to-day "The Holland Wolves," by J. Breckenridge Ellis, a historical novel of the Spanish invasion of the Netherlands, with illustrations by the Kinneys, who made the fine pictures for "The Thrall of Leif the Lucky;" "In Argolis," a charming description of family life in Greece, by George Horton, with illustrations in tint; also, a holiday edition of Max Müller's story of German love entitled "Memories," with illustrations, embellishments and cover designs by Blanche Ostertag.

HARPER & BROTHERS have just ready "The Wooing of Wistaria," a new novel of Japanese life, by Onoto Watanna, author of "A Japanese Nightingale;" "The Ship of Dreams," by Louise Forsslund, author of "The Story of Sarah," a story of the early settlers of Long Island; "The Maid-at-Arms," a story of American life in 1778, by Robert W. Chambers, author of "Cardigan;" also, a new volume of verse, by E. S. Martin, well-known to the readers of *Harper's Weekly* as the editor of the department "This Busy World."

McCLURE, PHILLIPS & Co. have just ready "The Banner of Blue," S. R. Crockett's new story, described as a "new version of the parable of the prodigal son," in which, against the sombre background of the Disruption Period in Scotland, the author draws two brilliantly colored love stories; "Indian Boyhood," the boyish impressions and experiences up to the age of fifteen of the author, Dr. Charles A. Eastman (Ohiyesa,) a full-blooded Sioux Indian, with illustrations by E. L. Blumenschein; also, "McClure's Children's Annual for 1903, a jolly big book of stories and verse edited by T. W. H. Crosland, with a number of colored full-page pictures and occasional black and white ones in the text.

DOUBLEDAY, PAGE & Co. will publish next week a new book by "J. P. M.," entitled "Tangled Up in Beulah Land," which is a sequel to the author's "A Journey to Nature," in so far as three of its chief characters are "Charlie," his father, and the inimitable "Doctor." They will publish at the same time an illustrated edition of "J. P. M's" delightful story "A Journey to Nature," with sixteen pictures by Henry Troth. Other books to be brought out next week are "The Wooing of Judith," a love story by Sarah Beaumont Kennedy, the author of "Joscelyn Cheshire," the scene of which is laid in Colonial Virginia; "Memoirs of a Contemporary," the memoirs of "Ida Saint-Elme," who went to the Napoleonic wars in men's clothes to follow Marshal Ney, translated from the French and edited by Lionel Strachey, with 48 illustrations from old prints; a limited edition of the text of W. S. Gilbert's famous opera "Patience," printed for the first time without the music, and with a characteristically happy introduction by the author; "Hand in Hand, Poems of Mother and Daughter," a volume of verses by Rudyard Kipling's mother and his sister Alice, that will appeal to all lovers of home life; also a cheaper edition of Frederick A. Cook's intensely interesting work "Through the First Antarctic Night," being a narrative of the voyage of the *Belgica* to the South Pole.

WEEKLY RECORD OF NEW PUBLICATIONS.

☞ Beginning with the issue of July 5, 1902, the titles of *net* books published under the rules of the American Publishers' Association are preceded by a double asterisk **, and the word net follows the price. The titles of *fiction* (not net) published under the rules are preceded by a dagger †. *Net* books not covered by the rules, whether published by members of the American Publishers' Association or not, are preceded by a single asterisk, and the word net follows the price. ☚

The abbreviations are usually self-explanatory. c. after the date indicates that the book is copyrighted; if the copyright date differs from the imprint date, the year of copyright is added. Books of foreign origin of which the edition (annotated, illustrated, etc.) is entered as copyright, are marked c. ed.; translations, c. tr.; n. p., in place of price, indicates that the publisher makes no price, either net or retail, and quotes prices to the trade only upon application.

A colon after initial designates the most usual given name, as: A: Augustus; B: Benjamin; C: Charles; D: David; E: Edward; F: Frederic; G: George; H: Henry; I: Isaac; J: John; L: Louis; N: Nicholas; P: Peter; R: Richard; S: Samuel; T: Thomas; W: William.

Sizes are designated as follows: F. (folio: over 30 centimeters high); Q. (4to: under 30 cm.); O. (8vo: 25 cm.); D. (12mo: 20 cm.); S. (16mo: 17½ cm.); T. (24mo: 15 cm.); Tt. (32mo: 12½ cm.); Fe. 48mo: 10 cm.). Sq., obl., nar., designate square, oblong, narrow books of these heights.

Abady, Jaques. Gas analyst's manual; incorporating F. W. Hartley's "Gas analyst's manual" and "Gas measurements"; il. folding pls. N. Y., Spon & Chamberlain, 1902. 15+561 p. 8°, hf. cl., $6.50.

Abbot, F. L. Faith built on reason: a survey of free and universal religion in the form of question and answer. Bost., Ja. H. West Co., 1902. c. 83 p. D. cl., 50 c.
The book "aims to show that the great ideas of God, freedom, and immortality, which have been from time immemorial the inspiration of the noblest and most beautiful lives, have a solid basis in human intelligence, because they have a solid basis in the known facts of the world."

Adams, Franklin P. In Cupid's court: [poems.] Evanston, Ill., W: S. Lord, 1902. c. 7-60 p. S. bds., 50 c.

Allsop, F: C. Practical electric bell fitting: a treatise on the fitting up and maintenance of electric bells and all the necessary apparatus. 10th ed. N. Y., Spon & Chamberlain, 1902. 15+170 p. il. 12°, cl., $1.25.

Atkinson, W: Walker. The law of the new thought: a study of fundamental principles and their application. Chic., Psychic Research Co., 1902. c. 93 p. O. cl., $1.

Atkinson, W: Walker. Thought-force in business and everyday life: being a series of lessons in personal magnetism, psychic influence, thought-force, concentration, will power and practical mental science. 10th ed. Chic., Psychic Research Co., [1902.] c. 94 p. O. cl., $1.

Barber, F: Walter. The engineer's sketch-book of mechanical movements, devices, appliances, contrivances and details employed in the design and construction of machinery for every purpose. 4th ed. N. Y., Spon & Chamberlain, 1902. 335 p. 8°, cl., $4.

***Bechtel**, E: A. Sanctæ Silviæ peregrinatio. Chic., University of Chicago Press, 1902. c. 3-160 p. O. (University of Chicago studies in classical philology; reprint from v. 4. no. 1.) pap., $1 net.

Boas, Franz, (*comp. and tr.*) Kathlamet texts. Washington, D. C., Government Print. Office, 1901. 3-261 p. il. por. F°, (Smithsonian Institution, Bureau of American ethnology, Bulletin 26.) cl.
Text of myths and tales in the Kathlamet dialect, followed by translations into English. The Kathlamet is the dialect of the Upper Chinook Indians. This collection of texts will, it is expected, be followed by a grammar and dictionary of the language, which will contain a comparison of all the known dialects of the Chinookan stock.

***Bonner**, D: Findley, *D.D.* Saving the world: what it involves and how it is being accomplished. Middletown, N. Y., Hanford & Horton, 1902. c. 4+259 p. D. cl., $1 net.
A little book that "aims simply to describe, comprehensively and yet scripturally, the great work of saving the world as it is being actually accomplished."

****Briggs**, C: A:, *D.D.* The incarnation of the Lord: a series of sermons tracing the unfolding of the doctrine of the incarnation in the New Testament. N. Y., Scribner, 1902. [S.] c. 9+243 p. O. cl., $1.50 net.

Brown, C: Hovey. Moses: a drama. Bost., Richard G. Badger, 1902. c. 69 p. O. bds., $1.25.

Browning, Rob. In a balcony: a drama; with introd. by Laura McAdoo Triggs. Chic., Blue Sky Press, 1902. 8°, bds., 400 copies on pap., ea., $3; 15 copies on Imperial Japan vellum, ea., $5.

****Bunker**, Alonzo, *D.D.* Soo Thah: a tale of the making of the Karen nation. N. Y. and Chic., Revell, 1902. [Ag.] 280 p. il. 12°, cl., $1 net.

***Burgess**, Theodore Chalon. Epideictic literature. Chic., University of Chicago Press, 1902. c. 2+89-261 p. O. (University of Chicago studies in classical philology; reprint from v. 3.) pap., $1 net.

****Burrell**, D: Ja. The wonderful teacher and what he taught. N. Y. and Chic., Revell, 1902. [Ag.] 327 p. 12°, cl., $1.20 net.

***Butler**, G: Frank. A text-book of materia medica, therapeutics and pharmacology. 4th rev. ed. Phil., W. B. Saunders & Co., 1902. 896 p. il. 8°, cl., $4 net; shp. or hf. mor., $5 net.

****Champney**, *Mrs.* Eliz. Williams. Margarita: a legend of the fight for the Great River. N. Y., Dodd, Mead & Co., 1902. [S.] c. 9+341 p. il. D. (Dames and daughters of colonial days.) cl., $1.25.
An historical romance of the 17th century with the scene laid partly in Paris and partly in the French colony of Louisiana. There is a marvellous fire opal, around the appearances and disappearances of which much of the plot circles.

***Chase**, Rob. Howland, *M.D.* General paresis: practical and clinical. Phil., P. Blakiston's Son & Co., 1902. 290 p. il. 12°, cl., $1.75 net.

Clark, Annie M. L. The Alcotts in Harvard. Lancaster, Mass., J. C. L. Clark, 1902. c. 4-43 p. il. sq. D. bds., $1.50.
Reminiscences of Bronson Alcott and his family.

***Clerke**, Agnes Mary. A popular history of astronomy during the nineteenth century. 4th ed., rev. and corr. N. Y., Macmillan, 1902. 15+489 p. il. 8°, cl., $4 net.

Condon, T: The two islands and what came of them. Portland, Ore., J. K. Gill Co., 1902. 211 p. D. cl., $1.50.
A brief account of the geology of Oregon and the northwest, by the professor of Geology, University of Oregon.

****Connolly**, Ja. B. Jeb Hutton: the story of a Georgia boy; il. by M. J. Burns. N. Y., Scribner, 1902. [S.] c. 5+289 p. D. cl., $1.20 net.
A tale of adventure and character-testing episodes along the Savannah River.

***Conway**, *Sir* W. Martin. The domain of art. N. Y., Dutton, 1902. 170 p. 12°, cl., $2.50 net.

****Cooley**, C: Horton. Human nature and the social order. N. Y., Scribner, 1902. [S.] c. 7+413 p. O. cl., $1.50 net.
Author is instructor in Sociology at the University of Michigan. "It is my general aim to set forth," he says, "from various points of view, what the individual is, considered as a member of a social whole." This he does in chapters headed: Society and the individual; Suggestion and choice; Sociability and personal ideas; Sympathy or communion as an aspect of society; The social self—1, the meaning of "I;" The social self—2, various phases of "I;" Hostility; Emulation; Leadership or personal ascendency; The social aspect of conscience; Personal degeneracy; Freedom.

Corneille, Pierre. Le menteur: comedie; ed., with introd. and notes, by J. B. Segall. N. Y., Silver, Burdett & Co., [1902.] c. 35+144 p. D. (Silver ser. of modern language text-books.) cl., 40 c.

Course (A) in personal magnetism, self-control and the development of character. [Ser. A.] Chic., Psychic Research Co., [1902.] c. 1901. no regular paging, il. I. cl., $1.
Gives the practical and religious aspects of mental science, with rules and exercises in character building and Zoism.

Course (A) of instruction in the development of power through clairvoyance. [Ser. C.] Chic., Psychic Research Co., [1902.] [Ja.] c. no regular paging, il. O. cl., $1.
Papers on clairvoyance or crystal gazing, personal magnetism, auto-suggestion, concentration, muscle-reading, mind-reading and "true" telepathy.

Course (A) of instruction in the development of power through psychometry. [Ser. D.] Chic., Psychic Research Co., [1902.] [Ja.] c. no regular paging, il. O. cl., $1.
Consists of papers on psychometry, phrenology, palmistry, astrology, mediumship and somnopathy, the practice of curing disease during natural sleep.

†**Craigie**, *Mrs.* Pearl Maria Teresa, ["John Oliver Hobbes," *pseud.*] Love and the soul hunters. N. Y., Funk & Wagnalls Co., 1902. [S.] c. 3-343 p. D. cl., $1.50.
The chief interest centres around Clementine Gloucester, the daughter of an American woman and an English father. She is desired by two men—Prince Paul of Urseville, Beylestein, a "sentimental libertine" who is "consumed by the desire for beauty—in nature, in art, in souls," and his secretary, Dr. Felshammer, who is "socialistic with a cynical affection for the aristocracy." The struggle ends in the triumph of the woman, who has something to say in the matter.

†**Crawford**, Francis Marion. Works. New uniform ed. N. Y., Macmillan, 1902. 2 v. 12°, cl., ea., $1.50.
Contents: Corleone: a tale of Sicily; Pietro Ghisleri.

†**Crockett**, S: Rutherford. The banner of blue. N. Y., McClure, Phillips & Co., 1902. [O.] c. 5+421 p. D. cl., $1.50.
A story of the Disruption Period in Scotland, with the history of the lives of two brothers, Rupert and John Glendonwyn, sons of the Lord of Gower, furnishing a modern instance of the parable of the Prodigal Son. The tale is brightened by many amusing glimpses of Scotch character and follows the fortunes of two love stories.

****Cross**, Arthur Lyon. The Anglican episcopate and the American colonies. N. Y., Longmans, Green & Co., 1902. c. 9+368 p. O. (Harvard historical studies, no. 9.) cl., $2.50 net.
This monograph, in its original form, was accepted as a dissertation for the degree of Doctor of Philosophy at Harvard University; it also was awarded the Toppan Prize in 1899. Since that time the work has been, to a considerable extent, recast, revised, and enlarged.

Crowell, Melvin E. A manual of experiments in physics for teachers; adapted to the Crowell physical apparatus. Indianapolis, Ind., The Crowell Apparatus Co., [1902.] c. '97, 1901. 231 p. il. D. cl., 75 c.

****Curtis**, Gertrude Benedict. Comforting words for sorrowing mothers. N. Y. and Chic., Revell, 1902. 73 p. 12°, cl., 60 c. net.

†**Dahn**, Felix. Captive of the Roman Eagles; from the German by Mary J. Safford. Chic., A. C. McClurg & Co., 1902. [S13.] c. 5+434 p. D. cl., $1.50.
The "Captive" is a beautiful Teutonic maiden, who is captured by the Romans during one of their invasions, but effects her escape when her masters are defeated by the avenging Germans. The battle which forms the climax is described with great vividness. Published in Germany under the title of "Bissula."

***Davis**, Gwilym G: The principles and practice of bandaging; il. from original drawings by the author. 2d ed., rev. and rewritten. Phil., P. Blakiston's Son & Co., 1902. c. 146 p. il. 8°, cl., $1.50 net.

***Dewey**, J: The child and the curriculum. Chic., University of Chicago Press, 1902. c. 3-40 p. D. (University of Chicago contributions to education, no. 5.) pap., 25 c. net.

***Donaldson**, H: Herbert. On a formula for determining the weight of the central nervous system of the frog from the weight and length of the entire body. Chic., University of Chicago Press, 1902. c. 15 p. 8°, (University of Chicago, Decennial publications; reprinted from v. 10.) pap., 25 c. net.

****Douglas**, Amanda Minnie. A little girl in old Detroit. N. Y., Dodd, Mead & Co., 1902. [S.] c. 4+362 p. D. ("Little girl" ser.) cl., $1.20 net.
A historical story for girls, timed in the last years of the 18th century when Detroit, a flourishing fur-trading station, was eagerly contended for by French and Indians, English and Americans. One of the closing scenes is the total destruction of Detroit by fire.

**Downer, C: Alfred. A first French book. N. Y., Appleton, 1902. 10+348 p. 12°, (Twentieth century text-books.) cl., $1.10 net.

**Du Chaillu, Paul Belloni. King Mombo; il. by Victor Perard. N. Y., Scribner, 1902. [S.] c. 16+225 p. O. cl., $1.50 net.
Further adventures in the great African forest, with the wild men and savage tribes, or in hunting the wild beasts.

**Eastman, C: A. Indian boyhood; il. by E. L. Blumenschein. N. Y., McClure, Phillips & Co., 1902. [O.] c. 7+289 p. O. buckram, $1.60 net.
A record of the author's boyish impressions and experiences up to the age of fifteen years. Dr. Eastman is a full-blooded Sioux Indian, the whole of whose younger days was passed on the plains of the Northwest in the tribal life of his family. Later he left savagery for civilization, but he never lost his love for the old ways of life. E. L. Blumenschein, the illustrator, was sent to Dakota in the summer of 1901 to study and sketch from life Indian scenes and customs.

Esdaile, Ja., *M.D.* Mesmerism in India, and its practical application in surgery and medicine. American ed. Chic., Psychic Research Co., [1902.] c. 165 p. O. cl., $1.

**Eyster, *Mrs.* Nellie Blessing. A Chinese Quaker: an unfictitious novel. N. Y. and Chic., Revell, 1902. [Ag.] 377 p. il. 12°, cl., $1.50.

Ferguson, Manton Marble, *comp.* The contractors' and builders' searchlight: a book specially arranged for contractors' and builders' use. [Pocket ed.] Des Moines, Ia., [F. R. Conaway, 1902.] 176 p. 12°, cl., $1.

**Fernald, Ja. Champlin, *ed.* The grammar-school standard dictionary of the English language; abridged from the Funk & Wagnalls Standard Dictionary of the English language by Ja. C. Fernald. N. Y., Funk & Wagnalls Co., 1902. c. 5-8+533 p. il. D. cl., $1 net.
Designed to give the orthography, pronunciation, meaning, and etymology of about 38,000 words and phrases in the speech and literature of the English-speaking peoples.

Fuller, E: John Malcolm: a novel. Providence, R. I., Snow & Farnham, 1902. c. 6+432 p. il. D. cl., $1.50.
An old-fashioned house in Clinton Place, New York City, is the home of John Malcolm, a very rich retired business man. His son and daughter had long ago left him, the one under suspicion of a crime, the other had fled with a worthless Englishman. When the story opens the daughter, with her daughter, is returning after many years to Clinton Place. The intrigues that are woven around John Malcolm, all aiming at his money, have an unexpected ending.

Gant, S: Goodwin, *M.D.* Diseases of the rectum and anus; designed for students and practitioners of medicine. 2d ed., rewritten and enl. Phil., F. A. Davis Co., 1902. c. 24+687 p. il. pls. 8°, cl., $5; shp. or hf. rus., $6.

Gardiner, J: Hays, Kittredge, G: Lyman, *and* Arnold, Sarah Louise. The mother tongue. bk. 3. Elements of English composition. Bost., Ginn, 1902. c. 20+431 p. D. cl., $1.

*Gleason, E. B. Essentials of diseases of the ear. 3d rev., enl. ed. Phil., W. B. Saunders & Co., 1902. 214 p. il. 12°, (Question compend ser.) cl., $1 net.

†Glovatski, Alex. The pharaoh and the priest: an historical novel of ancient Egypt; from the original Polish, by Jeremiah Curtin; il. from photographs. Bost., Little, Brown & Co., 1902. [S.] c. 8+696 p. por. D. cl., $1.50.
"The ruin of a pharaoh and the fall of his dynasty, with the rise of a self-chosen sovereign and a new line of rulers, are the double consummation in this novel. The book ends with that climax, but the fall of the new priestly rulers is a matter of history, as is the destruction wrought on Egypt by tyrants from Assyria and Persia. The native pharaohs lost power through the priesthood, whose real interest it was to support them; but fate found the priests later on, and pronounced on them also the doom of extinction."—*Preface.* The time is the eleventh century before Christ, when Egypt was already declining.

Gower, Ronald Sutherland. (*Lord.*) Sir Joshua Reynolds; his life and art. N. Y., Macmillan, 1902. 15+144 p. il. 12°, cl., $3.

*Grant, H. Horace, *M.D.* A text-book of surgical pathology and surgical diseases of the face, mouth, and jaws for dental students. Phil., W. B. Saunders & Co., 1902. 215 p. il. 12°, cl., $2.50 net.

Gross, Josiah. Ondell and Dolee: a story of mysticism. N. Y., Abbey Press, [1902.] c. 260 p. D. cl., $1.25.

**Guerber, Helene Marie Adeline. Yourself. N. Y., Dodd, Mead & Co., 1902. [S.] c. 16+283 p. D. cl., $1.20 net.
A handbook in which children are told all they need to know about the laws of physiology and personal hygiene, the lessons being taught in a simple yet graphic way.

**Hadley, S: Hopkins. Down in Water street: a story of sixteen years' life and work in Water street mission: a sequel to the "Life of Jerry McAuley." N. Y. and Chic., Revell, 1902. [Ag.] 242 p. il. 12°, cl., $1 net.

*Hall, Hubert. Court life under the Plantagenets (Reign of Henry II.) N. Y., Dutton, 1902. 6+270 p. il. 8°, cl., $2.50 net.

Hanish, Otoman Zar-Adusht-. Inner studies: a course of twelve lessons. Chic., Sun-Worshiper Publishing Co., 1902. c. 206 p. 12°, cl., $10.

Harte, Francis Bret. Writings of Bret Harte. Riverside ed. Bost., Houghton, Mifflin & Co., 1902. c. '87-'92. 16 v., por. D. cl., $24; hf. cf. or hf. mor., $52.

*Heart of the empire: discussion of problems of modern life in England; with an essay on imperialism. N. Y., Dutton, 1902. 12°, cl., $1.25 net.

**Heath, Lilian M. Eighty good times out of doors. N. Y. and Chic., Revell, 1902. [Jl.] 197 p. 12°, cl., 75 c. net.

*Helferich, Heinrich. Atlas and epitome of traumatic fractures and dislocations; authorized tr. from the German; ed. by Jos. C. Bloodgood. 5th ed., rev. and enl. Phil., W. B. Saunders & Co., 1902. c. 353 p. il. pl. 12°, (Saunders' medical hand-atlas ser.) cl., $3 net.

Henry, Alfred H. By order of the prophet: the story of the occupation of the Great Salt Lake Basin. N. Y. and Chic., Revell, 1902. [Je.] 402 p. il. 12°, cl., $1.50.

***Hewlett**, H. T., *M.D.* Manual of bacteriology. 2d ed., rev. Phil., P. Blakiston's Son & Co., 1902. il. 8°, cl., $4 net.

Hill, Lucy A. Marion's experiences: school days in Germany. N. Y., Educational Publishing Co., [1902.] c. '99, 1902. 251 p. D. cl., 75 c.
A book for a girl of from 12 to 15.

Homans, Ja. E: Self-propelled vehicles: a practical treatise on the theory, construction, operation, care and management of all forms of automobiles. N. Y., Theodore Audel & Co., 1902. c. 6+632 p. il. por. diagr., 12°, cl., $5.

***Hore**, *Rev.* A. H. Student's history of the Greek church. N. Y., E. & J. B. Young & Co., 1902. 532 p. 12°, cl., $2.25 net.

†**Horton**, G: The long straight road; il. by Troy and Margaret West Kinney. Indianapolis, Ind., Bowen-Merrill Co., [1902.] [S.] c. 7+401 p. il. D. cl., $1.50.
Chicago of to-day is the scene of this story, with glimpses of political life and middle-class society.

***Howell**, G: Labor legislation, labor movement, and labor leaders. N. Y., Dutton, 1902. 23+499 p. 8°, cl., $3.50 net.

****Hubbard**, Sara A., *comp.* Catch words of cheer. Chic., A. C. McClurg & Co., 1902. [S6.] c. unp. S. cl., 80 c. net.
For each day in the year, the compiler offers a cheerful, helpful aphorism from a well-known author. Arranged as a birthday book.

†Hulbert, Archer Butler. The Queen of Quelparte; il. by Winfield S. Lukens. Bost., Little, Brown & Co., 1902. [S.] c. 8+328 p. D. cl., $1.50.
A romance, with its scene laid near Japan shortly after the war between China and that country. The chief motive is a Russian intrigue to throw Quelparte, an island province of Korea, into the hands of Japan as a sop for the possession of Port Arthur by the Czar, and the efforts of the Chinese, directed by Prince Tuen, to prevent it.

Ingersoll, W: E. The air voyager: [a narrative poem.] Bost, [Richard G. Badger,] 1902. c. unp. T. bds., 75 c.

****Jacob**, Violet. The sheep-stealers. N. Y., Putnam, 1902. [Ag.] c. 6+462 p. D. cl., $1.20 net.
A romance of Devon in the west of England. "Based upon the old sheep-stealing trade in the earlier half of the nineteenth century, and the riots that spread over South Wales after the passing of a new Highway Act, under which tolls were increased, and the compounding of tolls on easy terms, which had formerly been the custom, was done away with," so says the London *Academy*.

Jane, Fred T., *ed.* All the world's fighting ships. 5th year. [N. Y., Munn & Co., 1902.] 394 p. il. obl. D. cl., $5.
Contents: Pt. 1, The navies of the world. Pt. 2, Articles on naval progress. The 1902 edition has been fully revised and brought up to date.

Jennings, Arthur Seymour. Paint and color mixing: a practical handbook for painters, decorators and all who have to mix colors: with 72 color samples. N. Y., Spon & Chamberlain, 1902. 97 p. 8°, cl., $2.

†**Jerome**, Jerome Klapka. Paul Kelver. N. Y., Dodd, Mead & Co., 1902. [S.] c. 4+424 p. D. cl., $1.50.
Mr. Jerome's first long novel in which he has branched out in an entirely new field. It has been compared to "David Copperfield." While there is plenty of humor, there is also much pathos.

Jervis, W. P., *comp.* The encyclopedia of ceramics; comp. by W. P. Jervis; with much original matter now first published. Tiltonsville, O., published by the author, W. P. Jervis, [1902.] 7-673 p. il. por. O. cl., $6.50.
Originally written for and published in the *Crockery and Glass Journal*, the whole of this work has now been thoroughly revised and much new information added, including the series of "Marks and monograms." A bibliography is included (2 p.) A comprehensive work embracing besides innumerable short articles, many excellent long ones on everything connected with the subject.

Jowett, J. H. Brooks by the traveller's way. N. Y., A. C. Armstrong & Son, 1902. 3-215 p. D. cl., $1.25.
Twenty-six helpful and stimulating addresses.

Joyce, J: A. Brickbats and bouquets. N. Y., F. Tennyson Neely, 1902. c. 6+259 p. por. D. cl., $1.
Philosophical sketches, satires, epigrams, poems, etc. The author says, "My object in writing this book is to throw kiln-dried brickbats of truth at the horrid head of hypocrisy, envy, malice, selfishness and tyranny. . . . The bouquets I throw at the modest few."

†**Kauffman**, Reginald Wright. The things that are Cæsar's: a novel. N. Y., Appleton, 1902. [S.] c. 6+336 p. D. cl., $1.50.
The problem presented in this novel is, whether a man who has broken the laws can, after paying the penalty in punishment, be reinstated in the eyes of the world, and again take his place in business and social life. John Haig had committed forgery in his youth and had served his sentence in prison. When he emerges into the world and begins the struggle to make a living he finds that his debt is not cancelled, that prison, not the crime, cannot be forgotten. By the author of "Jarvis of Harvard"

****Kent**, Eliz. The house opposite: a mystery. N. Y., Putnam, 1902. [Ag.] c. 5+276 p. D. cl., $1 net.
The story is told by a young doctor. Seeking a cool spot, one hot summer night, he ascends to the roof of his house, and thus sees by chance some remarkable occurrences in the house opposite, a fashionable apartment house on Madison Ave. A body of a man is afterwards found in this house, and every effort is made to discover the murderer. An exciting detective story is the result, different persons in turn being suspected, and closely followed up.

King, H: Melville. Why we believe the Bible. N. Y., Amer. Tract Soc., [1902.] c. 2-231 p. il. D. cl., $1.

King, Moses. Philadelphia and notable Philadelphians. N. Y., Moses King, 1902. c. 106 p. il. por. 4°, cl., $5.

Kingsbury, *Rev.* Oliver Addison. The spiritual life. N. Y., Amer. Tract Soc., [1902.] c. 2-117 p. por. D. cl., 50 c.
The subject is considered under the four main elements that the writer considers enter into the spiritual life—namely, worship, morality, service, and communion.

†**Kingsley**, Florence Morse. The needle's eye; il. by W: E. Mears. N. Y., Funk & Wagnalls Co., 1902. [S.] c. 3-386 p. D. cl., $1.50.
The animating principle of the novel is altruism—our duty to those who because of the existing unequal social conditions, have no share in our spiritual and material culture.

***Klenze**, Camillo v. The treatment of nature in the works of Nikolaus Lenau: an essay in interpretation. Chic., University of Chicago Press, 1902. 83 p. O. (University of Chicago Press; printed from v. 7, Decennial publications.) pap., 75 c. net.

**Knox, Edmund Arbuthnott, (*Bp.*) Pastors and teachers: six lectures on pastoral theology delivered in the divinity school, Cambridge, in the year 1902; with an introd. by C: Gore, D.D. N. Y., Longmans, Green & Co., 1902. 300 p. D. cl., $1.60 net.

*Konody, Paul G. The art of Walter Crane. N. Y., Macmillan, 1902. 13+147 p. il. 4°, cl., $20 net.

Leete, C: H. Exercises in geography. 2d ed., rev. and enl. N. Y., Longmans, Green & Co., 1902. [Je.] c. '99, 1902. 21+107 p. D. cl., 60 c.

*Leroy. L:, *M.D.* Essentials of histology. 2d rev., enl. ed. Phil., W. B. Saunders & Co., 1902. 263 p. il. 12°, (Questions compend ser.) cl., $1 net.

*Lilly, W: S: India and its problems. N. Y., Dutton, 1902. 20+324 p. 8°, cl., $3 net.

Lisk, Jos. Phinney. Slide valve instruction chart; showing the various positions of the crank pin, eccentric and piston at the point of admission, lead, and cut-off, etc. N. Y., Spon & Chamberlain, 1902. 11 in. x 14½ in., 25 c.

**Lounsbury, T: Raynesford. Shakespeare and Voltaire. N. Y., Scribner, 1902. [S.] c. 10+463 p. O. cl., $2 net.
The second volume of a series the author calls "Shakespearean wars." The first volume was entitled "Shakespeare as a dramatic critic." The writer is professor of English in Yale University. He says: "It is the story of the relations he [Voltaire] held to Shakespeare, of the influence originally exerted upon him by the English dramatist, of the war he waged against the latter's growing reputation on the Continent, of the hostility evoked in turn towards himself in England, which I have sought to relate."

†McClure's children's annual for 1903; ed. by T. W. H. Crosland. N. Y., McClure, Phillips & Co., [1902.] c. 6-199 p. il. O. cretonne, $1.50.
Colored pictures, short stories and verses in large type.

**McDonald, Rob. The Herr doctor; il. by W. E. Mears. N. Y., Funk & Wagnalls Co., 1902. [S.] c. 3-138 p. il. S. (Hourglass stories, no. 4.) cl., 40 c. net.
A novelette. The plot is simple, the single complication being a modern variation of the old romantic motive, "the prince in disguise."

†McIntyre, J: T. The ragged edge: a tale of ward life and politics. N. Y., McClure, Phillips & Co., 1902. [S.] c. 304 p. D. (First novel ser.) cl., $1.25.
A story of ward politics, portraying the life and characteristics of our Irish-American citizens.

McNeill, I. C. Mental arithmetic. N. Y., Amer. Book Co., [1902.] [S10.] c. 141 p. D. cl., 35 c.
Designed for use in grammar grades.

**Martin, E: Sandford. Poems and verses. N. Y., Harper, 1902. [S.] c. 5+125 p. D. cl., $1.25 net
There are about thirty poems in this volume, some of them written in humorous vein, as, for example, "Eben Pynchot's repentance." There are college poems, poems of more serious turn, as "The sea is his," and lighter verse, as "Blandira," "An urban harbinger," etc. Throughout there is the bright, cheerful optimism.

Mayfield, Eugene O. Fairy tales of the western range, and other tales. Lincoln, J. North & Co., prs., [1902.] c. 165 p. 12°, vellum, $1.25.

†Meldrum, D: Storrar. The conquest of Charlotte. N. Y., Dodd, Mead & Co., 1902. [Ag.] c. 1901, 1902. 4+480 p. D. cl., $1.50.
A love story, the scene of which is laid partly in London and partly in a shipping-town of Fife, from which it derives a particular and varied local color.

Miller, Earl Van Dorn, *ed.* A soldier's honor, with reminiscences of Major-General Earl Van Dorn; by his comrades. N. Y., Abbey Press, [1902.] c. 4-369 p. por. D. cl., $1.50.
A biography of a Confederate officer, who served through the Civil War.

†Morrison, Arthur. The Hole in the Wall. N. Y., McClure, Phillips & Co., 1902. [S.] c. 8+415 p. D. cl., $1.50.
"The Hole in the Wall" is the name of a public-house in Wapping, frequented by sailors, longshoremen, and the loafers of Ratcliffe Highway. A stolen pocket-book containing £800 in bank-notes is entrusted by a thief of the locality to his pal to sell to the landlord of "The Hole in the Wall." This episode sets in motion a plot full of dramatic surprises and exciting incidents.

*Mortimer, Alfred G., *D.D.* Lenten preaching. N. Y., Dutton, 1902. 227 p. 12°, cl., $1.25 net.

**Murfree Mary Noailles, ["Charles Egbert Craddock," *pseud.*] The champion. Bost., Houghton, Mifflin & Co., 1902. [S.] c. 2+257 p. D. cl., $1.20 net.
A story for boys. A printer's "devil," in the office of the local newspaper, who aspires to become a "champion" typesetter, gets entangled in a web of mischances and undergoes a variety of exciting and threatening experiences.

Nansen, Fridtjof, *ed.* The Norwegian North Polar expedition, 1893-1896: scientific results; ed. by Fridtjof Nansen. v. 3; published by the Fridtjof Nansen Fund for the advancement of science. N. Y., Longmans, Green & Co., 1902. c. 11+427+87 p. il. Q. cl., $12.50.
Contents: The oceanography of the North Polar basin; On hydrometers and the surface tension of liquids.

New York City. *Municipal ct.* The law and practice; with the boundaries of boroughs, districts and wards, and also the latest decisions affecting this court; with forms and exhaustive index by G: F. Langbein, J. C. Julius Langbein. 5th ed. N. Y., Baker, Voorhis & Co., 1902. c. 34+628 p. O. shp., $5.

New York. Code of civil procedure as it is Jan. 1, 1903; with notes of the judicial decisions thereon or relating thereto, together with the judiciary article of the constitution, statutory construction law, rules of the court of appeals, general and special rules of practice, and a combined table-index of subject matter of the code of civil procedure and general laws; by G: Bliss. v. 1, embracing chapters 1 to 9, section 1 to section 962. 5th ed., by G: A. Clement. N. Y., Baker, Voorhis & Co., 1902. c. 3 pl. 1618 p. O. shp., $7.50.

Nichols, Wilbur F. Arithmetical problems. Bost., Thompson, Brown & Co., [1902.] c. 1901. 6+167 p. D. cl., 30 c.

*Nicholson, Jos. Shield. Bankers' money: a supplement to "A treatise on money." N.

Y., Macmillan, 1902. 8+84 p. 12°, cl., $1.10 net.

****Norman,** H: All the Russias: travels and studies in contemporary European Russia, Finland, Siberia, the Caucasus and Central Asia; with 129 il. chiefly from the author's photographs. N. Y., Scribner, 1902. [S.] c. 13+476 p. maps, O. cl., $4 net.

"This volume is the outcome of fifteen years' interest in Russian affairs, culminating in four journeys—one of nearly 20,000 miles—in European and Asiatic Russia. In the course of these, besides a residence of some time in St. Petersburg and visits to the principal cities, I travelled in Finland, in Siberia as far as Lake Baikal, in the Causasus, and in Central Asia as far as the frontier of Kashgar. During all these journeys I was afforded opportunities of seeing and investigating every matter that interested me, and of making the acquaintance of the chief Russian administrators in every part."—*Preface.*

***Noyes,** Ella. Saints of Italy: legends retold by Ella Noyes; il. from Fra Angelico and other old masters, by Dora Noyes. N. Y., Dutton, 1902. 14+159 p. obl. 4°, cl., $1.50 net.

Payne, G: H: A great part, and other stories of the stage. N. Y., Continental Publishing Co., [1902.] c. 4-220 p. nar. D. cl., $1.

†**Payne,** Will. On fortune's road: stories of business; drawings by T: Fogarty. Chic., A. C. McClurg & Co., 1902. [S13.] c. 6-290 p. D. cl., $1.50.

Seven short stories by the author of "The story of Eva" and "The money captain."

Peabody, Susie C. Step by step: a primer. Bost., Ginn, 1902. c. 6+98 p. il. (partly col.) sq. D. cl., 35 c.

Pennsylvania. Statutory law of corporations, including annots. and a compete set of forms; by John F. Whitworth and Clarence B. Miller. Phil., T. & J. W. Johnson & Co., 1902. c. 11+930 p. O. shp., $6.

Perfect course (The) of instruction in hypnotism, mesmerism, clairvoyance, suggestive therapeutics and the sleep cure; giving best methods of hypnotizing by masters of the science. [Ser. B.] Chic., Psychic Research Co.,. [1902.] c. 1900, 1901. 54 p. il. O. cl., $1.

Articles dealing with the theory and practice of hypnotism, suggestive therapeutics, magnetic healing, and absent treatment.

Phillips, Walter Shelley. Indian fairy tales; folklore—legends—myths; totem tales as told by the Indians; gathered in the Pacific northwest by W. S. Phillips; with a glossary of words, customs, and history of the Indians; il. by the author. Chic., Star Publishing Co., [1902.] c. 17+19-326 p. sq. O. cl., $1.50.

These thirty-one stories are the result of careful study and research among various tribes of Indians of the northwestern Pacific Coast. The Indian peculiarity of narration is kept as nearly as possible, consistent with an understandable translation from the native tongue into English. The stories constitute the embodiment of the Indian mytho-religious beliefs. The author told the stories to his two little ones, who found them most interesting.

Prelini, C: Tunneling: a practical treatise; with additions by C: S. Hill. 2d ed., rev. N. Y., D. Van Nostrand Co., 1902. c. 6+9-15-311 p. il. diagr., 8°, cl., $3.

***Quilter,** Hugh H., ["Oxon," *pseud.*] Onward and upward: a book for boys and girls. N. Y., Dutton, 1902. 200 p. 12°, cl., $1 net.

†**Ralph,** Julian. The millionairess; il. by C. F. Underwood. Bost., Lothrop Pub. Co., [1902.] [S.] c. 4-422 p. D. cl., $1.50.

A novel dealing with New York society men and women. Most of the scenes are set in a beautiful country home on the Hudson, a mansion over which Miss Lamont, an heiress, pretty and accomplished, presides. The Beaux Arts Club, formed on novel lines, plays a large part in the story.

***Ranske,** Jutta Bell. Health, speech and song: a practical guide to voice production. N. Y., Dutton, 1902. 158 p. 8°, cl., $1.25 net.

***Rossetti,** Gabriele. Gabriele Rossetti: a versified autobiography translated and supplemented by W: Michael Rossetti. N. Y., Dutton. 1902. 13+199 p. 8°, cl., $3 net.

****Rossiter,** F: M. *and* Mary Henry. The story of a living temple: a study of the human body. N. Y. and Chic., Revell, 1902. [Ag.] 348 p. 12°, cl., $1 net.

Scarritt, Eliz. Mariner-. Quid est: [a novel.] N. Y., Abbey Press, [1902.] c. 4+172 p. D. cl., $1.

School (The) question from a Catholic point of view; reprinted from *The Catholic World Magazine.* N. Y., Catholic Book Exchange, [1902.] 16 p. D. pap., 5 c.

Scott, G. H. G., *and* McDowell, G. L. The record of the mounted infantry, City of London Imperial Volunteers, in the late Boer war. Limited ed. N. Y., Spon & Chamberlain, 1902. 200 p. map, D. cl., $2.

***Scudder,** C: L. The treatment of fractures. 3d rev. ed. Phil., W. B. Saunders & Co., 1902. 460 p. il. 8°, buckram, $4.50 net; hf. mor., $5.50 net.

****Singleton,** Esther, *ed. and tr.* Famous paintings, as seen and described by famous writers; ed. and tr. by Esther Singleton. N. Y., Dodd, Mead & Co., 1902. [S.] c. 12+366 p. il. O. cl., $1.60 net.

A continuation, in a measure, of the author's former volume of "Great pictures." It aims to represent several great painters who did not appear in the first volume, such as Crivelli, Luini, Giorgione, Moroni, Landseer, Mantegna and Perugino, who were left out of "Great pictures" for lack of space. The pictures in this series are not only paintings with great reputations, but each one is a painting of the very first rank. The text is from the pens of the most famous writers of all countries.

****Singleton,** Esther, *ed. and tr.* London as seen and described by famous writers; ed. and tr. by Esther Singleton. N. Y., Dodd, Mead & Co., 1902. [S.] c. 12+350 p. il. O. cl., $1.40 net.

In this work, which is a compilation of views and impressions of the British metropolis, the compiler has in some measure followed the plan of her former work on Paris in selecting from a vast number of works descriptions of such external characteristics of the city as are recorded by travellers and famous native and foreign writers. The selections deal largely with general impressions of various sections of the great city—however there will be found descriptions of many of the chief monuments, the streets, the squares, the parks, the old churches and civic buildings with associations, besides much interesting historical matter.

Slosson, *Mrs.* Annie Trumbull. Aunt Abby's neighbors. N. Y. and Chic., Revell, 1902. [Je] c. 4-170 p. D. cl., $1.
Aunt Abby's views on sects, heaven, tithes, friendship, etc.

Smith, Alex., *and* Hall, Edwin H. The teaching of chemistry and physics in the secondary school. N. Y., Longmans, Green & Co., 1902. c. 13+377 p. D. (American teachers' ser.) cl., $1.50.

****Songs** of England's glory. N. Y., Putnam, 1902. 4+233 p. S. leath., $1.25 net.
A collection of poems, from well-known writers, all relating to some famous event in English history.

Soulsby, Lucy H. M. Suggestions on prayer. N. Y., Longmans, Green & Co., 1902. 6+72 p. T. cl., 50 c.

South Carolina. Code of laws, 1902. In 2 v., v. 2, Code of civil procedure and criminal code. Columbia, The State Co., state prs., 1902. c. 481+60+371 p. O. shp., $5.

***Spencer,** J. G. Scalæ primæ: a first Latin reader; with brief notes and vocabulary. N. Y., Macmillan, 1902. 10+132 p. il. 16°, (Bell's illustrated classical ser.) cl., 40 c. net.

***Starr,** F: Physical character of Indians in Southern Mexico. Chic., University of Chicago Press, 1902. c. 59 p. 8°, (University of Chicago Decennial publications; reprinted from v. 4.) pap., 75 c. net.

Stevenson, Rob. Louis. A child's garden of verses; il. by E. Mars and M. H. Squire. Chic., Rand, McNally & Co., [1902.] c. 93 p. il. (partly col.) 12°, cl., 50 c.

***Studies** in classical philology; ed. by a committee representing the departments of Greek, Latin, archæology, and comparative philology. v. 3. Chic., University of Chicago Press, 1902. c. 4+261 p. O. bds., $1.50 net.
Contents: Papyri from Karanis; The use of repetition in Latin to secure emphasis, intensity and distinctness of impression, by Frank Frost Abbott; Epideictic literature, by Theodore Chalon Burgess.

***Taylor,** S. Earl. The price of Africa. Cin., Jennings & Pye, [1902.] c. 225 p. por. maps, D. (The forward mission study courses.) cl., 50 c. net; pap., 35 c. net.
Contents: The price of Africa; David Livingstone; Adolphus C. Good; Alexander C. Mackay; Melville B. Cox; Why this waste?

†**Thackeray,** W: Makepeace. The Paris sketch book of Mr. A. Titmarsh and the Irish sketch book; il. by the author. N. Y., Macmillan, 1902. 15+577 p. 12°, cl., $1.

Thiers, Louis Adolphe. La campagne de Waterloo; abridged and ed., with an introd. and notes, by O. B. Super. N. Y., Silver, Burdett & Co., [1902.] c. 10+102 p. map, D. (Silver ser. of modern language textbooks.) cl., 40 c.

Thoreau, H: D: Walden; with an introd. by Bradford Torrey. [New one-volume holiday ed.] Bost., Houghton, Mifflin & Co., 1902. c. '54-'97. 43+522 p. D. cl., $3; hf. mor., $5.
The present edition is a reissue of the two-volume edition of 1897, with only such changes as were necessary to bring the whole work into a single convenient volume.

****Truscott,** L. Parry. The poet and Penelope. N. Y., Putnam, 1902. 4-254 p. D. cl., $1 net.
A love story of English society life.

***Tschudi,** Clara. Marie Antoinette; authorized tr. from the Norwegian, by E. M. Cope. N. Y., Dutton, 1902. 12+302 p. 8°, cl., $2.50 net.

****Tucker,** *Rev.* H. C. The Bible in Brazil: colporteur experiences. N. Y. and Chic., Revell, 1902. [Ag.] 293 p. 12°, cl., $1.25 net.

***Turner,** Herbert Hall. Modern astronomy: being some account of the revolution of the last quarter of a century. N. Y., Dutton, 1902. 16+286 p. 12°, cl., $2 net.

****Upton,** G: Putnam. Musical pastels; il. from rare prints and facsimiles. Chic., A. C. McClurg & Co., 1902. [S13.] c. 6+213 p. O. cl., $2.
A series of sketches, setting forth certain rare musical events, entitled "Nero, the artist," "The musical small-coals man," "Music and religion," "The first American composer," "The beggar's opera," "The first opera," "A musical royal family," "The man Beethoven," etc.

****Upton,** G: Putnam. The standard light operas, their plots and their music: a handbook. Chic., A. C. McClurg & Co., 1902. [S13.] c. 4-239 p. S. $1.20 net.
Uniform in style and treatment with the author's "Standard operas," "Standard oratorios," etc. Embraces the plots, with lists of characters, of over seventy light operas by Sullivan, Auber, Balfe, Nicolai, Offenbach, Rossini, Gounod, Sousa, Wallace, Thomas, Donizetti, and others.

Wambaugh, Eugene. A selection of cases on insurance. Cambridge, Harvard Law Review Pub. Assoc., 1902. c. 4+1197 p. O. cl., 75 c.
Previously published in six parts.

***Warren,** J. Collins, *and* Pearce, A. Gould, *eds.* The international text-book of surgery, by American and British authors; ed. by J. Collins Warren and A. Pearce Gould. New enl. [2d] ed. In 2 v. v. 1, General surgery; v. 2, Special or regional surgery. Phil., W. B. Saunders & Co., 1902. 947; 1072 p. il. pls. 8°, cl., per v., $5 net; shp. or hf. mor., per v., $6 net.

†**Watanna,** Onoto. The wooing of Wistaria. N. Y., Harper, 1902. [S.] c. 2+388 p. D. cl., $1.50.
A dramatic Japanese love story. The characters are Japanese and the background is one of genuine Japanese history. By the author of "A Japanese nightingale."

Weaver, B: Franklin, *M.D., comp.* Physical atlas; or, practical family doctor book, containing 300 modern and up-to-date recipes for treating both general and special diseases. Bucyrus, O., Dr. B: F. Weaver, 1902. c. 2+7-36 p. il. Q. bds., $1; cl., $1.25.

White, Horace. Money and banking; illustrated by American history. 2d ed., rev. and continued to the year 1902. Bost., Ginn, 1902. c. '95, 1902. 14+474 p. D. cl., $1.65.
The first edition of this work was prepared to meet a popular demand for information on the money question in the presidential campaign of 1896. The

progress of events, of legislation, and of public opinion, however, during the past seven years, suggested revision and addition. While following the general historical plan of the first edition, and adopting its text in part, the author has practically rewritten the book, adding several new chapters, expunging controversial and other matter that has become obsolete, and bringing the whole down to date. It has been his aim to adapt it more particularly to the use of the class room. To this end he has added a brief recapitulation, and a list of authorities, to each chapter.

White, Percy. The new Christians. N. Y., Federal Book Co., 1902. c. 2-468 p. D. cl., 50 c.

A fashionable London religious sect, led by Eustace Fenner, is called the "New Christians." They believe in healing by faith. Fenner is in a large measure a charlatan, troubled by pecuniary difficulties. His troubles with his congregation, and two rich women, either of whom he would marry, have a disastrous conclusion.

***Whiteway**, A. R. Recent object lessons in penal science; with a bibliographical introd. N. Y., Dutton, 1902. 216 p. 12°, cl., $1.25 net.

Whittaker, W. H. Forms of pleading under the codes of civil procedure. v. 2. Cin., W. H. Anderson & Co., 1902. c. 801-1603 p. O. shp., $6.

Wiel, Alethea. The story of Verona; il. by Nelly Erichsen and Helen M. James. N. Y., Macmillan, 1902. 16+314 p. 12°, (Mediæval towns ser.) cl., $2; leath., $2.50.

†**Wodehouse**, P. G. The pothunters: [a novel.] N. Y., Macmillan, 1902. 272 p. il. 12°, cl., $1.50.

***Wundt**, Wilhelm. Outlines of psychology; tr. with the co-operation of the author, by C: Hubbard Judd. 2d rev. English ed. from 4th rev. German ed. N. Y., G. E. Stechert, 1902. 22+390 p. O. cl., $2 net.

More additions and minor revisions have been made in this than in the previous editions. The chief change consists in the addition of brief lists of reading references at the end of each of the sections and chief divisions.

****Zwemer**, A. E. *and* S. M. Topsy turvy land: Arabia pictured for children. N. Y. and Chic., Revell, 1902. [Jl.] 124 p. il. 8°, cl., 75 c. net.

ORDER LIST.

ABBEY PRESS, 114 Fifth Ave, New York.

Gross, Ondell and Dolee.............. $1.25
Miller, A soldier's honor.............. 1.50
Scarritt, Quid est..................... 1.00

AMERICAN BOOK CO., 100 Washington Sq., E., New York.

McNeill, Mental arithmetic........... 35

AMERICAN TRACT SOCIETY, 150 Nassau St., New York.

King, Why we believe................ 1.00
Kingsbury, The spiritual life......... 50

W. H. ANDERSON & CO., 515 Main St., Cincinnati, O.

Whittaker, Forms of pleading under the codes of civil procedure, v. 2..... 6.00

D. APPLETON & CO., 72 Fifth Ave., New York.

**Downer, First French book.....net, 1.10
†Kauffman, The things that are Cæsar's..... .... 1.50

A. C. ARMSTRONG & SON, 3-5 W. 18th St., New York.

Jowett, Brooks by the traveller's way.. 1.25

THEODORE AUDEL & CO., 63 Fifth Ave., New York.

Homans, Self-propelled vehicles....... 5.00

RICHARD G. BADGER, 194 Boylston St., Boston.

Brown, Moses....... .... 1.25
Ingersoll, The air voyager............ 75

BAKER, VOORHIS & CO., 66 Nassau St., New York.

New York City, *Municipal ct.*, Law and practice, 5th ed.................... 5.00
——, Code of civil procedure, 1903, 5th ed.......... .... 7.50

P. BLAKISTON'S SON & CO., 1012 Walnut St., Philadelphia.

*Chase, General paresis............net, 1.75
*Davis, Principles and practice of bandaging, 2d ed., rev. and rewritten.net, 1.50

P. BLAKISTON'S SON & CO.—*Continued.*

*Hewlett, Manual of bacteriology, 2d ed., rev.. ... .net, $4.00

BLUE SKY PRESS, Woodlawn Ave. and 55th St., Chicago.

Browning, In a balcony.$3; Limited ed., 5.00

BOWEN-MERRILL CO., 9-11 W. Washington St., Indianapolis, Ind.

†Horton, The long straight road...... 1.50

CATHOLIC BOOK EXCHANGE, 120 W. 60th St., New York.

School question (The) from a Catholic standpoint...... 5

J. L. C. CLARK, Lancaster, Mass.

Clark, The Alcotts in Harvard........ 1.50

CONTINENTAL PUBLISHING CO., 24 and 26 Murray St., New York.

Payne, A great part.................. 1.00

F. R. CONWAY, Des Moines, Ia.

Ferguson, Contractors' and builders' search light....... .... 1.00

THE CROWELL APPARATUS CO., Indianapolis, Ind.

Crowell, Experiments in physics....... 75

F. A. DAVIS CO., 1914 Cherry St., Philadelphia.

Gant, Diseases of the rectum and anus, 2d ed., rewritten and enl.........$5; 6.00

DODD, MEAD & CO., 372 Fifth Ave., New York.

**Champney, Margarita.........net, 1.25
**Douglas, A little girl in old Detroit, net, 1.20
**Guerber, Yourself...... ....net, 1.20
†Jerome, Paul Kelver................ 1.50
†Meldrum, Conquest of Charlotte..... 1.50
**Singleton, Famous paintings.....net, 1.60
**——, London.... ....net, 1.40

E. P. DUTTON & CO., 31 W. 23d St., New York.

*Conway, The domain of art......net, $2.50
*Hall, Court life under the Plantagenets.....................net, 2.50
*Heart of the empire..............net, 1.25
*Howell, Labor legislation.........net, 3.50
*Lilly, India and its problems.....net, 3.00
*Mortimer, Lenten preaching......net, 1.25
*Noyes, Saints of Italy............net, 1.50
*Quilter, Onward and upward.....net, 1.00
*Ranske, Health, strength, and song, net, 1.25
*Rossetti, Gabriele Rossetti........net, 3.00
*Tschudi, Marie Antoinette........net, 2.50
*Turner, Modern astronomy........net, 2.00
*Whiteway, Recent object lessons in penal science......net, 1.25

EDUCATIONAL PUBLISHING CO., 63 Fifth Ave., New York; 50 Bromfield St., Boston.

Hill, Marion's experiences........... 75

FEDERAL BOOK CO., 52-58 Duane St., New York.

White, The new Christians........... 50

FUNK & WAGNALLS CO., 30 Lafayette Pl., New York.

†Craigie, Love and the soul hunters... 1.50
**Fernald, Grammar school standard dictionary...............net, 1.00
†Kingsley, The needle's eye........... 1.50
**McDonald, The Herr doctor....net, 40

J. K. GILL & CO., Portland, Ore.

Condon, The two islands and what came of them...................... 1.50

GINN & CO., 29 Beacon St., Boston.

Gardiner *and* Arnold, Mother tongue, bk. 3.............................. 1.00
Peabody, Step by step................ 35
White, Money and banking, 2d ed., rev. to 1902....................... 1.65

GOVERNMENT PRINT. OFFICE, Washington, D. C.

Boaz, Kathlamet texts...............

HANFORD & HORTON, Middletown, N. Y.

*Bonner, Saving the world........net, 1.00

HARPER & BROS., Franklin Sq., New York.

**Martin, Poems and verses.......net, 1.25
†Watanna, Wooing of Wistaria...... 1.50

HARVARD LAW REVIEW PUB. ASSOC., Cambridge, Mass.

Wambaugh, Selection of cases on insurance..................... 75

HOUGHTON, MIFFLIN & CO., 4 Park St., Boston.

Harte, Writings of Bret Harte, Riverside ed., 16 v.................$24; 52.00
**Murfree, The champion..........net, 1.20
Thoreau, Walden, new one-v. holiday ed.........................$3; 5.00

JENNINGS & PYE, 220 W. 4th St., Cincinnati.

*Taylor, The price of Africa, net, 36 c.; net, 50

W. P. JERVIS, Tiltonsville, O.

Jervis, Encyclopædia of ceramics...... 6.50

T. & J. W. JOHNSON & CO., 535 Chestnut St., Philadelphia.

Pennsylvania, Statutory law of corporations............................ $6.00

MOSES KING, 225 Fourth Ave., New York.

King, Philadelphia and notable Philadelphians........................ 5.00

LITTLE, BROWN & CO., 254 Washington St., Boston.

†Glovatski, The Pharaoh and the priest. 1.50
†Hulbert, Queen of Quelparte......... 1.50

LONGMANS, GREEN & CO., 91-93 Fifth Ave., New York.

**Cross, The Anglican episcopate..net, 2.50
**Knox, Pastors and teachers.....net, 1.60
Leete, Exercises in geography, 2d ed., rev. and enl....................... 60
Nansen, Norwegian north Polar expedition, 1893-96, v. 3................. 12.50
Smith *and* Hall, Teaching of chemistry. 1.50
Soulsby, Suggestions on prayer....... 50

WILLIAM S. LORD, Evanston, Ill.

Adams, In Cupid's court............. 50

LOTHROP PUB. CO., 530 Atlantic Ave., Boston.

†Ralph, The millionairess............ 1.50

MCCLURE, PHILLIPS & CO., 141-155 E. 25th St., New York.

†Crockett, The banner of blue......... 1.50
**Eastman, Indian boyhood........net, 1.60
†McClure's children's annual for 1903.. 1.50
†McIntyre, The ragged edge.......... 1.25
†Morrison, The Hole in the Wall...... 1.50

A. C. MCCLURG & CO., 215-221 Wabash Ave., Chicago.

†Dahn, Captive of the Roman Eagles.. 1.50
**Hubbard, Catch words of cheer.net, 80
†Payne, On fortune's road............ 1.50
**Upton, Musical pastels..........net, 2.00
**——, Standard light operas......net, 1.20

MACMILLAN CO., 66 Fifth Ave., New York.

*Clerke, Popular history of astronomy, net, 4.00
†Crawford, Works, new uniform ed., 2 v...........................ea., 1.50
Gower, Sir Joshua Reynolds.......... 3.00
*Konody, Art of Walter Crane.....net, 20.00
*Nicholson, Bankers' money........net, 1.10
*Spencer, Scalæ primæ............net, 40
†Thackeray, Paris sketch book........ 1.00
Wiel, Story of Verona.............$2; 2.50
†Wodehouse, The pothunters.......... 1.50

MUNN & CO., 361 Broadway, New York.

Jane, All the world's fighting ships.... 5.00

F. TENNYSON NEELY, 114 Fifth Ave., New York.

Joyce, Brickbats and bouquets........ 1.00

J. NORTH & CO., Lincoln, Neb.

Mayfield, Fairy tales of the western range.............................. 1.25

PSYCHIC RESEARCH CO., The Colonnades, 3835 Vincennes Ave., Chicago.

Atkinson, Law of the new thought.... 1.00
——. Thought force in business........ 1.00

PSYCHIC RESEARCH CO.—*Continued.*

Course in personal magnetism........ $1.00
—— of instruction in development of power through clairvoyance......... 1.00
—— of instruction in development of power through psychometry......... 1.00
Esdaile, Mesmerism in India.......... 1.00
Perfect course of instruction in hypnotism...... .... 1.00

G. P. PUTNAM'S SONS, 29 W. 23d St., New York.

**Jacob, The sheep-stealers........net, 1.20
**Kent, The house opposite........net, 1.00
**Songs of England's glory........net, 1.25
**Truscott, The poet and Penelope.net, 1.00

RAND, MCNALLY & CO., 142 Fifth Ave., New York; 160-174 Adams St., Chicago.

Stevenson, A child's garden of verse.. 50

FLEMING H. REVELL CO., 156 Fifth Ave., New York; 63 Washington St., Chicago.

**Bunker, Soo Thah..............net, 1.00
**Burrell, The wonderful teacher and what he taught..................net, 1.20
**Curtis, Comforting words.......net, 60
**Eyster, A Chinese Quaker.......... 1.50
**Hadley, Down in Water street..net, 1.00
**Heath, Eighty good times out of doors....... ....net, 75
Henry, By order of the prophet....... 1.50
**Rossiter, Story of a living temple, net, 1.00
Slosson, Aunt Abby's neighbors....... 1.00
**Tucker, The Bible in Brazil.....net, 1.25
**Zwemer, Topsy turvy land......net, 75

W. B. SAUNDERS & CO., 925 Walnut St., Philadelphia.

*Butler, Text-book of materia medica, etc.....................net, $4; net, 5.00
*Gleason, Essentials of diseases of the ear, 3d rev., enl. ed............net, 1.00
*Grant, Text-book of surgical pathology...... ....net, 2.50
*Helferich, Atlas and epitome of traumatic fractures and dislocation, 5th rev., enl. ed.....................net, 3.00
*Leroy, Essentials of histology, 2d rev., enl. ed........ ....net, 1.00
*Scudder, Treatment of fractures, 3d ed., rev.............net, $4.50; net, 5.50
Warren *and* Pearce, International text-book of surgery, new enl. 2d ed., 2 v.......net, per v., $5; net, per v., 6.00

CHARLES SCRIBNER'S SONS, 153-157 Fifth Ave., New York.

**Briggs, Incarnation of the Lord..net, 1.50
**Connolly, Jeb Hutton............net, 1.20
**Cooley, Human nature and the social order..... .... .net, 1.50
**Du Chaillu, King Mombo.......net, 1.50
**Lounsbury, Shakespeare and Voltaire...... ....net, 2.00
**Norman, All the Russias........net, 4.00

SILVER, BURDETT & CO., 33 E. 19th St., New York.

Corneille, Le menteur................ 40
Thiers, La campagne de Waterloo..... 40

SNOW & FARNHAM, Providence, R. I.

Fuller, John Malcolm................. $1.50

SPON & CHAMBERLAIN, 123 Liberty St., New York.

Abady, Gas analyst's manual.......... 6.50
Allsop, Practical electric bell fitting, 10th ed......... .... 1.25
Barber, Engineers' sketch book, 4th ed. 4.00
Jennings, Paint and color mixing.... 2.00
Lisk, Slide valve instruction chart.... 25
Scott *and* McDowell, Record of the mounted Infantry, City of London Imperial Vols....... .... 2.00

STAR PUBLISHING CO., 91 Sherman St., Chicago.

Phillips, Indian fairy tales............. 1.50

THE STATE CO., Columbia, S. C.

South Carolina, Code of laws, 1902... 5.00

G. E. STECHERT, 9 E. 16th St., New York.

*Wundt, Outlines of psychology...net, 2.00

SUN-WORSHIPER PUB. CO., Chicago.

Hanish, Inner studies................. 10.00

THOMPSON, BROWN & CO., 76 Summer St., Boston.

Nichols, Arithmetical problems........ 30

UNIVERSITY OF CHICAGO PRESS, Chicago.

*Bechtel, Sanctæ Silviæ peregrinatio, net, 1.00
*Burgess, Epideictic literature.....net, 1.00
*Dewey, The child and the curriculum, net, 25
*Donaldson, On a formula for determining the weight of the central nervous system of the frog.....net, 25
*Klenze, Treatment of nature in the works of Nikolaus Lenau.......net, 75
*Starr, Physical character of Indians in Southern Mexico.............net, 75
*Studies in classical philology.....net, 1.50

D. VAN NOSTRAND CO., 23 Murray St., New York.

Prelini, Tunneling, 2d rev. ed........ 3.00

DR. B. F. WEAVER, 311-313 Sandusky St., Bucyrus, O.

Weaver, Physical atlas.............$1; 1.25

JAMES H. WEST CO., 79 Milk St., Boston.

Abbot, Faith built on reason.......... 50

E. & J. B. YOUNG & CO., 7-9 W. 18th St., New York.

*Hore, Student's history of Greek church...... ....net, 2.25

CORRECTION IN PRICE AND OTHER DATA.

*BATES, Katharine Lee, *and* Coman, Katharine. English history told by English poets; a reader for school use. N. Y., Macmillan, 1902. c. 15+542 p. 12°, cl., 60 c. net. (*Corr. price.*)

DWIGHT, *Rev.* C: A. S. Railroading with Christ. N. Y., Amer. Tract Soc., [1902.] c. '01. 77 p. D. cl., 35 c. (*Corr. price.*)

STEVENSON, Ja. H: Assyrian and Babylonian contracts, with Aramaic reference notes. N. Y., Amer. Book Co., [1902.] c. 206 p. D. (Vanderbilt Oriental ser.; ed. by Herbert Cushing Tolman and Ja. H: Stevenson.) cl. (*Corr. price.*) $2.50.

IMPORTS AND EXPORTS OF BOOKS AND OTHER PRINTED MATTER.

THE summary statement of the values of the imports and exports of books and other printed matter of the United States for the month ending July, 1902, and for the seven months ending the same, compared with the corresponding periods of 1901, makes the following showing as regards books, music, maps, engravings, etchings, photographs, and other printed matter:

Values of Books and other printed matter, free, imported from other countries.

Imported from:	Month ending July. 1901.	Month ending July. 1902.	Seven months ending July. 1901.	Seven months ending July. 1902.
United Kingdom	$ 70,360	$120,618	$510,345	$567,959
France	10,972	11,770	304,706	105,274
Germany	51,543	57,324	328,842	366,239
Other Europe	23,985	27,598	109,235	279,304
British North America	2,806	1,950	24,567	19,644
Other Countries	983	2,009	8,291	11,785
Totals	160,649	221,269	1,285,986	1,350,205

Values of Books and other printed matter, dutiable, imported from other countries.

Imported from:	Month ending July. 1901.	Month ending July. 1902.	Seven months ending July. 1901.	Seven months ending July. 1902.
United Kingdom	$131,966	$106,946	$574,930	$616,315
France	11,915	6,396	70,440	38,971
Germany	19,032	19,518	131,382	154,509
Other Europe	6,766	8,469	36,075	47,126
British North America	4,319	5,476	25,898	31,531
China	700	329	3,119	2,331
Japan	1,680	1,074	6,009	8,071
Other Countries	418	454	17,250	2,885
Totals	177,696	148,662	865,103	901,739

Values of Books and other printed matter, of Domestic Manufacture, Exported from the United States by Countries.

Countries to which Exported:	Month ending July. 1901.	Month ending July. 1902.	Seven months ending July. 1901.	Seven months ending July. 1902.
United Kingdom	$63,779	$73,779	$504,401	$645,494
Belgium *a*	991	1,433	15,271	14,755
France	8,820	4,792	43,341	36,806
Germany	15,230	16,610	118,720	121,969
Italy *a*	2,783	1,378	9,136	9,698
Netherlands *a*	920	1,514	5,661	7,295
Other Europe	3,748	2,500	15,759	22,505
British North America	83,477	113,031	653,968	759,185
Central American States and British Honduras	2,789	1,506	10,451	10,844
Mexico	5,344	19,947	71,167	135,607
Cuba	2,804	4,079	81,534	51,835
Porto Rico	......	......	......	......
Other West Indies and Bermuda	2,391	2,168	16,163	19,977
Argentina	993	3,935	20,146	19,757
Brazil	2,067	2,183	30,139	21,239
Chili *a*	210	3,341	12,461	30,651
Colombia	5,852	868	14,869	17,033
Venezuela *a*	1,423	78	3,638	16,815
Other South America	1,805	9,841	16,502	30,824
Chinese Empire	6,574	2,192	24,606	16,400
British East Indies	2,586	2,765	14,878	15,153
Japan	3,334	5,710	17,529	32,952
British Australasia	28,557	8,328	170,434	145,605
Hawaii	......	......	......	......
Philippine Islands	5,765	8,552	37,368	118,298
Other Asia and Oceanica	3,186	1,020	12,711	9,592
British Africa	5,590	9,400	44,063	71,158
All other Africa	400	922	7,101	4,036
Other countries	......	......	4	......
Totals	261,428	301,872	1,972,021	2,387,383

a Included in "Other Europe" prior to January, 1901.

Values of Exports of Books and other printed matter, of Foreign Manufacture.

	Month ending July. 1901.	Month ending July. 1902.	Seven months ending July. 1901.	Seven months ending July. 1902.
Free of Duty. Books and other printed matter	......	$359	$56,649	$14,370
Dutiable. Books and other printed matter	1,261	1,133	8,880	14,134

Merchandise remaining in warehouse July 31, 1901, $34,814; July 31, 1902, $25,332.

Shipments of Books and other printed matter from the United States to HAWAII, July, 1899, $6,481; July, 1900, 4,367. Shipments of books, etc., from Hawaii to the United States, July, 1901, $500; July, 1902, $702. For the seven months ending July, 1901, the amount was $7,523, and for the same period ending July, 1902, $16,292.

Shipments of Books, etc., from the United States to PORTO RICO, for July, 1901, $5,816; July, 1902, $4,866. For seven months ending July, 1901, $28,038; for the same period ending July, 1902, $33,249.

Shipments of Books, etc., from the United States to the PHILIPPINE ISLANDS, July, 1901, $5,765; July, 1902, $8,552 For seven months ending July, 1901, $37,368; for the same period ending July, 1902, $118,298.

Failures in the Book and Printing Trades, July.

Books and Papers.—Liabilities.	1900.	1901.	1902.	*Printing and Engraving.—Liabilities.*	1900.	1901.	1902.
July	$7,865	$63,712	$16,000	July	$61,325	$199,460	$116,288

The Publishers' Weekly.

FOUNDED BY F. LEYPOLDT.

SEPTEMBER 20, 1902.

The editor does not hold himself responsible for the views expressed in contributed articles or communications

All matter, whether for the reading-matter columns or advertising pages, should reach this office not later than Wednesday noon, to insure insertion in the same week's issue.

Books for the "Weekly Record," as well as all information intended for that department, should reach this office by Tuesday morning of each week.

"I hold every man a debtor to his profession, from the which, as men do of course seek to receive countenance and profit, so ought they of duty to endeavor themselves by way of amends to be a help and an ornament thereunto."—Lord Bacon.

CLEANLINESS IN BOOKMAKING.

In these days of quick, and chiefly machine, work in producing books, it frequently happens that in every batch of books sent out some individual copies do not pass muster—that often a whole batch is open to criticism. This may be inevitable; yet cleanliness is a most important element in the manufacture of books, and its principle should be insisted upon by the maker of books almost from the time that the raw material is worked into paper, until the complete book passes into the hands of its readers. Papermaking processes, properly conducted, should put into the hands of the printer a sheet in every way fit for his best efforts, and the printer, in turn, should hand over to the binder the printed sheets in perfect register, without smear or set-off or any disfigurement which may detract from the beauty of the finished product. The continuing processes should be conducted upon the same lines, and in all subsequent storing and handling the one idea of cleanliness should prevail.

This principle in many cases is lost sight of in details that are too often taken for granted by the one in charge of the manufacturing department. The papermaker is not held rigidly to the grade of product demanded; hence paper of uneven quality is run in and volumes are likely to appear printed on two if not more grades of paper. The printer, in his turn, is permitted to violate the canons of his art, and imperfect spacing, bad letters and other blemishes, not to mention careless proof reading, especially of the last revises, help to multiply the offenses which detract from the neatness of the book. In the press-work objectionable features are to be found in the ink—both in the quality and in the distribution of it—in the matter of register and impression, and in the handling of the printed sheets. It is by no means unusual to find pages in which there is either too little or too much color and too little or too much impression; or there is a blur resulting from set-off in sheets too hurriedly handled; or, if the floor has not actually been wiped up with a part of the edition, many of the sheets are very likely made untidy by the marks of soiled fingers. Rank-smelling ink, strange to say, still turns up in some printing offices, and helps to increase the annoyance of the dainty reader.

In the matter of binding, and especially in finishing, the importance of cleanliness cannot be overestimated. The excellence of design and the good handling of tools will be lost entirely on a volume of sloppy or dirty appearance. In justice to the craft we must admit that the binder, as a rule, commits fewer sins in this direction than his colleague, the printer; however, there are enough exceptions to make out a case also against the binder.

The faults we have pointed out, in no spirit of extreme criticism, let it be said, exist, in many instances, where they ought not to occur, and for this reason are more reprehensible than on work of a lower grade from which little can be expected. Nor are the lapses in good bookmaking to which we have referred so few and far between that they can be ignored; on the contrary, it is because they seem to be increasing that we have ventured to call attention to them, and to point out that in the making of books, no matter of what class, cleanliness should be the ruling principle, whether it be in the thought which the printed page suggests, or in each and every one of the details which belong to the mechanical production of that which is placed in the hands of the reading public.

A WESTERN PAPER MILL TRUST.

The work of forming a combination of all the paper mills in Michigan, Wisconsin, and Minnesota, under the name of the American Consolidated Paper Company, has been undertaken by Dewar & Yerkes, a Chicago firm, which deals in stocks and bonds.

It is proposed to have the trust capitalized at $30,000,000 and to pay full value in cash for all the plants and water power rights, instead of giving stock in the corporation as part payment. If the project goes through the trust will control a daily output of more than 1000 tons of all kinds of paper, from wrapping to finished book.

TRAVELLING CATALOGUES OF THE LIBRARY OF CONGRESS PRINTED CATALOGUE CARDS.

As adjunct to its Card Distribution work, the Library of Congress is now preparing travelling catalogues, especially designed to facilitate the recataloguing of libraries by enabling them to order by serial number. The following paragraphs, in regard to these catalogues, are taken from Bulletin No. 2 of the Card Distribution Section.

The expense of transporting and handling the catalogues will be considerable. Except in the case of the catalogue for American history, the area covered by each is, at present, comparatively small. The time required in the transportation and use of the catalogues is an important item from the point of view of the Library of Congress. A catalogue will not be loaned unless the number of cards ordered from it is likely to be considerable. For the above reasons, libraries are requested to consider carefully, before applying for the use of a travelling catalogue, whether the usual method of ordering cards, on slips by author and title, is not sufficient for their purpose. In this connection the scope of the present stock of L. C. cards, as given in the Handbook, should be carefully noted; also the statements below as to the four catalogues now in preparation.

The following travelling catalogues will be ready by September 20th:

1. *General Catalogue.*

About 85,000 cards, representing all the printed cards now in stock. For details as to the scope of the stock see the Handbook, p. 37-46.

2. *American History.*

About 25,000 cards. This section being now completely recatalogued, the collection of printed cards is representative of the collection of books on this subject at the Library of Congress, with the exception of unfinished serial publications. Besides the general history and description of the United States, this class includes local history and description. In addition to the United States, it covers British, Central, and South America and the outlying islands. It *does not include* the constitutional history of the United States, nor American biography.

3. *Bibliography.*

About 3000 cards, representing works in bibliography and library science which have come by copyright since June, 1898, and by purchase since January 1, 1901; also a selection of the books in most common use, of various dates, from the shelves of the bibliographical section of the Library.

4. *Law.*

About 1200 cards. Covers cards for copyright books received since June, 1898, and books received by purchase since January, 1901. Includes cards for books on common law, constitutional law, and history and theory of law.

In order to economize in the matter of transportation charges as well as in the time required for transportation, circuits will be arranged for the catalogues whenever possible. Libraries making application for either of the catalogues before September 20 will be included in the first circuit, except in case the library applying happens to be far removed from other libraries desiring to use the catalogue in question. Applications received later than September 20 can be included in the first circuit only when the application comes from a library which happens to be in the vicinity of a portion of the circuit not yet covered by the catalogue desired.

A COLUMBIA UNIVERSITY PRINTING PRESS.

A Columbia University printing press, with private printing equipment, according to a writer in the New York *Evening Post*, seems likely to be a development of the next few months. A friend of the university has offered to purchase a house and lot in the neighborhood of the university and endow a printing establishment for the benefit of the university publications. His offer is now awaiting action by the trustees. The history of the affair dates back to last May, when the *Columbia Spectator*, the undergraduate newspaper, decided to extend its sphere and become a daily instead of a semi-weekly publication. It was at once realized that in order to be effective the paper must have its printing office in the vicinity of the college instead of far down town. Accordingly negotiations were begun with several large printers looking to the establishment by some one of them of a branch house near Columbia. Nicholas Muller, one of the managing editors of the *Spectator*, who was fostering the idea, arranged that much of the university printing, as well as that of the *Columbia Literary Monthly*, the *Columbia Jester*, the *Morningside* and other undergraduate publications should be given to the firm locating its branch office near Columbia. To this arrangement a firm of printers agreed, and all plans had been made for the establishment of the plant by October 15, when a friend of the university offered to endow a university printing plant, at a probable cost of $25,000.

It is expected that the university trustees will accept the offer, although several of them are said to be strongly opposed to the university owning a press. Should the university refuse the offer, however, arrangement has been made whereby the *Spectator* and the other college papers will establish their original idea of a private plant by November 1.

A CANADIAN PRAYER-BOOK.

The General Synod of the Church of England in Canada, which is in session at Montreal, has appointed a joint committee to publish an edition of the Book of Common Prayer suitable for Canada. From the tenor of the debate it does not appear that there is any purpose to abbreviate or change in any way the existing service. The purpose, according to the *Toronto Globe*, "appears to be rather to provide additional prayers, which conditions in the Canadian Church seem to require."

COMMUNICATION.

AN EARLY EDITION OF "CRUMBS FROM THE MASTER'S TABLE."

28 Akron St., Roxbury, Mass.
September 14, 1902.

To the Editor of The Publishers' Weekly.

Dear Sir: In your issue of the Publishers' Weekly of July 12, p. 46, is a facsimile of the title-page of the first book published by D. Appleton, "Crumbs from the Master's Table." I have in my collection of rare books a copy identical with one exception, viz., it does not bear the words *Stereotype edition* which is just above the date 1831, therefore is undoubtedly an earlier issue and printed from type, and probably unique.

W. A. Butterfield.

OBITUARY NOTE.

David G. Francis, a member of what was in its day one of the most noteworthy bookselling and publishing firms in this country, died September 14, at New Canaan, Conn. He was born in Boston in 1817 and was a son of David Francis of the well-known firm of Munroe & Francis, in whose employ he learned printing and bookselling. His older brother, Charles S. Francis, established himself in the book business in New York in 1826, taking a store at the corner of Broadway and Dey Street, then practically the centre of the aristocratic residences, which, at that time, had crept up Greenwich Street to Murray Street and to what is now known as Park Place, and on the east side as far up as Beekman Street, where St. George's Church was located. At that time there was no bookstore in that neighborhood, (that of D. Appleton & Co., perhaps, excepted,) that was more frequented than Francis's. As the city moved up town Francis took a store at 252 Broadway, near Murray Street, under the famous Peale's Museum. In 1845 David G. Francis, who a few years before had entered his brother's employ, was taken into partnership. His fellow clerk at this time was James Miller, who subsequently went into the publishing business on his own account, and in time bought the plates of many of the books published by his old employers, among them the popular books of Ware, Mrs. Browning's poems, Bailey's "Festus," and a number of Sunday-school books. In 1855 C. S. Francis & Co. removed to 554 Broadway, between Tiffany's and the Metropolitan Hotel, on the same side of the street. Their store was a large and spacious one, with a marble front, and as much as ever a popular resort of noted people of literary tastes and men-about-town. As the firm published the works of the leading Unitarian clergymen of their day, such as W. E. Channing, Orville Dewey, Henry W. Bellows, O. B. Frothingham and others, their store naturally became what Ralph Waldo Emerson nicknamed it, "Unitarian Headquarters." In 1860 the firm of C. S. Francis & Co. was dissolved when David G. Francis removed to the old Clinton Hall on Astor Place, and devoted himself exclusively to the sale of old and rare books. Charles S. Francis remained in business at the old stand for a few years longer, when he sold out and retired. He died at Tarrytown, N. Y., December 2, 1887. When Clinton Hall was torn down, in April, 1890, to make room for the Mercantile Library building, Mr. Francis removed to No. 12 East Fifteenth Street. In May, 1895, he sold out to George H. Richmond, who a short time before had also absorbed the business of S. B. Luyster and incorporated the firm of D. G. Francis & Co. Since that time Mr. Francis enjoyed his leisure, passing his time at the Union League, the Century and the New England clubs. He was of distinguished appearance, fully six feet tall. With him passes away another of the fast departing booksellers who counted among their patrons and friends the leading American men of the nineteenth century in almost every walk of life.

NOTES ON AUTHORS.

Cyrus Townsend Brady has just returned from Lake Placid, in the Adirondacks, to prepare to move over to Brooklyn.

Mrs. Craigie ("John Oliver Hobbes") thinks that a story of comedy which she now has in hand will run to a full-length novel. Her latest novel, "Love and the Soul Hunters," has just been published by the Funk & Wagnalls Co.

The Pall Mall Gazette says that "Oliver Bath," the author of "Naughty Nancy," in which Kitty Loftus is appearing at the London Savoy Theatre, is the pseudonym of Viscount Tiverton, son of the Earl of Halsbury.

JOURNALISTIC NOTES.

M. Marinoni, the originator of the one-cent papers in Paris, has retired from the management of the *Petit Journal* on account of old age.

Miss Louisa M. Alcott left two unpublished stories, which were written by her for her own little niece. They have been secured by *St. Nicholas* and will appear in that magazine during the coming year.

The *Century* has recently come into possession of an interesting collection of unpublished letters of Sir Walter Scott, written to a very interesting character in the early part of the last century, Mrs. Hughes, the grandmother of the author of "Tom Brown."

The Hoppergrass is the title of a clever little magazine for young people, written, illustrated and printed by young people—"the little Bryces"—at Ashland, Va. It offers lots of fun for fifty cents a year. Those interested may address the general business office at 123 E. Broad Street, Richmond, Va.

Anthony Comstock on the 17th inst. raided the office of *Vanity Fair*, 129 West Forty-second Street, New York, arrested three men and confiscated about a ton of back numbers of the periodical. R. B. Hennessy, managing editor of the publication, says that the raid was made because an offensive advertisement of a Parisian picture seller had appeared in the magazine.

THE first number of *The Hobby* contains articles on "Famous First Editions," "The Curiosities of Collecting," "Books Which Live," "Literary Secrets," "The Book-Lover's Delight," "The Origin of the Star-Spangled Banner," "The Advantage of a 'Pull' in Literature," "Secrets of the Sanctum," and other articles which should interest all book-lovers. *The Hobby* is published quarterly by the American Press Company, Baltimore, Md.

The Reader is the title of a new illustrated monthly magazine to be published in October from No. 10 West Twenty-third Street, New York. It will give illustrated news of writers and books, London and Paris letters, essays, poems, stories and special articles on subjects in all branches of literature, illustrated news of rare books, criticism of the drama, reviews, etc. The subscription price will be $3 the year, and single copies 25 cents.

The Brandur Magazine is the title of a new weekly "periodical of fiction and thought," published by The Brandur Company, 150 Fifth Avenue, New York, of which Orlando J. Smith is president and general manager. The first number, dated September 20, contains contributions by Cyrus Townsend Brady, Ella Wheeler Wilcox, Clara Morris, Julian Hawthorne, Richard Burton, James L. Ford and others equally well known. Subscription price $2 a year, single copies five cents.

BIBLIOGRAPHIC NOTE.

CATALOGUES OF NEW AND SECOND-HAND BOOKS.—*Baker's Great Book Shop,* 14 and 16 John Bright Street, Birmingham, Eng., Miscellaneous. (No. 211, 799 titles.)—*Albert Britnell,* 248 Yonge St., Toronto, Canada, First editions, bibliography, art books, etc. (No. 38, 503 titles;) *also,* American history and geography, Parliamentary, legal and political biography, etc. (No. 127, 781 titles.)—*The Burrows Brothers Company,* Cleveland, O., Americana. No. 30, 368 titles.)—*A. S. Clark,* 174 Fulton St., New York, Literary junk. (No. 54, 32 p. 8°.)—*Davis' Bookstore,* 35 W. 42d St., New York, Scientific catalogue. (No. 9, 12 p. 12°.); *also,* Supplement No. 2 to Catalogue No. 24, Collected works, miscellaneous. (20 p. 12°.)—*William Downing,* 5 Temple Row, Birmingham, Eng., Books from famous collections, Battle Abbey Library, Vale Press, etc. (No. 409, 255 titles.)—*Francis Edwards,* 83 High St., Marylebone, London, W., Miscellaneous. (No. 258, 52 p. 16°.)—*Julia Everson,* 531 Guaranty Loan Building, Minneapolis, Minn., Rare books. (36 p. 16°.)—*Francis Harvey,* 4 St. James St., London, Rare books, autographs, also rare mezzotint portraits. (159 titles.)—*W. Jacobsohn & Co.,* No. 5 Tauentzeinstr., Breslau, Germany, Katholische Theologie. (No. 180, 62 p. 16°); *also,* Art, literature and science. (No. 179, 62 p. 16°.)—*Joseph McDonough,* 39 Columbia St., Albany, N. Y., Americana, angling, poetry, American and English first editions, money, banking, etc. (No. 177, 3233-3882 titles.)—*A. Maurice & Co.,* 23 Bedford St., Strand, London, W. C., (117, 16 p. Fencing, India, Napoleon, miscellaneous, 387 titles; 118 p. 16°, Engravings, etchings, sport.) —*George D. Morse,* 69 Merrimack St., Haverhill, Mass., First editions. (No. 37, 67 titles.) —*Bernard Quaritch,* 15 Piccadilly, London, Manuscripts, books printed on vellum, Americana, English literature, French illustrated books, etc. (No. 217, 475 titles, 1*s.*)—*John E. Scopes,* 29 Tweddle Building, Albany, N. Y., Books relating to America, George Washington, etc. (No. 14, 137 titles.)—*G. E. Stechert,* 9 E. 16th St., New York, Sciences, including library of Dr. Charles Rice. (No. 8, 104 p. 8°;) *also,* Medicine and pharmacy. (No. 9, 69 p. 8°.)—*Herbert A. Thayer,* 15 Moreland Ave., Newton Center, Mass., Theological, etc. (No. 16, 16 p. 8°.)

LITERARY AND TRADE NOTES.

The ISAAC H. BLANCHARD COMPANY will publish next week "Hazel Pierce," a story by an author who signs himself "Ilo."

E. A. WEEKS, representing The Henneberry Company, of Chicago, is in New York City, and will be glad to meet the trade at The Albert.

HINDS & NOBLE have purchased the plates of Dr. Anderson's "Best Methods of Teaching Gymnastics" and will immediately publish a new edition.

FREDERICK WARNE & Co. will publish in October "The Art of Success," by J. T. Knowlton, whose "Art of Thinking" proved so successful and preached such a timely sermon.

FLEMING H. REVELL COMPANY have established branches in London, at 21 Paternoster Square, and in Edinburgh, at 30 St. Mary Street, where such books of theirs as are available for the British market will be on sale.

THE RIGGS PUBLISHING COMPANY will publish October 9 a new book of adventure in cloudland and dreamland, by John Kendrick Bangs, entitled "Bikey, the Skicycle," with eight full-page pictures by Peter Newell, the frontispiece being in colors.

FUNK & WAGNALLS publish to-day "The Herr Doctor," a novelette, by Robert MacDonald, which forms the fourth number of *The Hour-Glass Series.* The plot is simple, the single complication being a modern variation of the old romantic motive, "the prince in disguise."

ALBERT E. TURNER is now representing the lines of Cassell & Co., the Historical Publishing Company, of Philadelphia, and the Bloch Publishing Company, of Cincinnati and New York. He will be pleased to see his old friends in the trade at his headquarters in the office of Cassell & Co., at 7 West Eighteenth Setreet.

THE PAFRAETS BOOK COMPANY, of Troy

N. Y., will publish in December, another book by the Rev. Dr. Frederic R. Marvin, author of "Last Words of Distinguished Men and Women," to be entitled "Flowers of Song from Many Lands." It is a collection of poetical translations from ancient and modern sources.

Of Marie Corelli's new romance, "Temporal Power," upwards of 100,000 copies were taken up in England before the day of publication out of an edition of 120,000. A second edition is in preparation, and before another month it is expected that 150,000 copies will have been sold. The book is also taking well in this country.

Thomas Y. Crowell & Co. will publish shortly Stopford A. Brooke's study of Robert Browning; also "The Coming City," by Dr. Richard T. Ely, a new volume in the *Library of Economics and Politics.* Messrs. Crowell state that, including foreign sales, the ethical and religious books of Dr. J. R. Miller have had an output of more than a million copies.

Sampson Low, Marston & Co. will publish early in October a book entitled "Raliora." It is a volume for collectors by a collector, John Eliot Hodgkin. It contains notes of printed books, manuscripts, historical documents, broadsides, and engravings of coins, medals, pottery, and curios of all kinds collected between 1858 and 1900. The collection thus illustrated contains 22,000 items.

The Writer's Year-Book Co., Granville House, Arundel Street, Strand, London, have just published "The Writer's Year-Book," which is described as a "commercial directory for professional writers, photographers and artists," giving the address, rate and time of payment and conditions of contributorship of 500 English magazines, papers, syndicates and agencies purchasing mss., photos, or drawings.

After much anxious thought Samuel Eberly Gross, author and land dealer, has decided on the disposition of the $1 awarded him as the result of the Gross-Rostand litigation concerning the authorship of "Cyrano de Bergerac." The dollar will form the nucleus of a fund for a new Illinois Women's Soldiers' Home, which will be built in Grossdale on a site donated by Mr. Gross and worth $3000.

T. Fisher Unwin, of London, has secured --for £7000, it is reported—the memoirs of President Krüger, written by himself. He has purchased both the English and American rights. The volume will be 100,000 words in length, and the manuscript contains a number of startling revelations, with many caustic comments on Mr. Chamberlain's policy, and some amusing telegrams from Rhodes, Shaw, Chamberlain, etc. Mr. Unwin will entertain bids for the American rights.

The United States Navy Department has issued a new cook book, entitled "General Mess Manual and Cook Book, United States Navy," prepared by Paymaster General Kenney. It was approved by Secretary Moody, and is law for cooks on every war vessel of the United States. The volume is divided into three parts—general mess, commissary store, and the preparation of food. It also includes recipes for standard articles of food, soups, meats, fish, bread, canned food, and desserts of all kinds. It is explained that these recipes are deduced from a series of experiments made with the articles of the navy rations.

Elder & Shepard, San Francisco, Cal., have in preparation a volume of essays on "The Romance of the Commonplace," by Gelett Burgess, who in this work makes a radical departure from the nonsense work that first brought him into prominence when editor of *The Lark.* They also announce a limited edition of "A Balloon Ascension at Midnight," by George Eli Hall, illustrated with silhouettes in color, by Gordon Ross; a volume of verse by Dailey Millard entitled "Songs of the Press," and a little book of twisted proverbs entitled "The Cynic's Calendar of Revised Wisdom for 1903," by Oliver Herford. Ethel Watts Mumford, and Addison Mizner.

The Macmillan Company will publish shortly "A Joyous Journey Round Rügen," by the author of "Elizabeth and her German Garden," which is full of the liveliest episode centering around the strange adventures of a phaeton. They have in press "David and Bathsheba," Stephen Phillips's new play; three new volumes in *The American Sportsman's Library*—"Wild Fowl," by Leonard C. Sanford and T. S. Van Dyke; "Big Game Fish," by Charles F. Holder; and "Gun and Rifle," by A. W. Money, W. E. Carlin and A. L. A. Himmelwright; also, "How to Sing," a theoretical and practical work of much general interest, by the famous prima donna, Mme. Lilli Lehman-Kalisch.

The Lothrop Publishing Company have just brought out Clara Morris's new volume, "Stage Confidences." The book is in the vein in which Miss Morris is most happy, namely, that of personal reminiscence running off into imaginative treatment of dramatic scenes which have come within her experience during her long stage career. The volume aims to give wholesome advice to stage aspirants of both sexes, especially girls, and is illuminated by humorous and pathetic instances and striking occurrences of theatre life. The volume contains sixteen pictures, all of them for the first time reproduced, the majority showing Miss Morris in her *rôles* from her early days to the present time.

M. F. Tyler, the treasurer of Yale University, New Haven, Conn., announces that on the 25th inst. Yale University will publish its memorial volume containing the official report of the Bicentennial Exercises in October, 1901. The volume will contain the official programme, a list of the guests, the text of all speeches and orations, and the various addresses and letters of congratulations received by the University at that time. It is a volume of six hundred pages, printed at the DeVinne Press and bound in half leather, with a photogravure of the obverse and reverse of the Bicentennial medal as a frontispiece. Its retail price is $5.00 net, the trade price is $4.00 f.o.b. New York.

J. B. LIPPINCOTT COMPANY have just ready a work of lively interest, entitled "Two Thousand Miles on an Automobile," by an enthusiast who hides his identity under the name "Chauffeur," with illustrations by Ver Beck; "The True History of the American Revolution," by Sydney George Fisher, who has some startling things to tell of the conduct of the War of the Revolution, its chief figures and the reasons for its outcome, with 24 illustrations; "Stories of Author's Loves," by Clara E. Laughlin, in two illustrated volumes; "A Daughter of the Snows," a new story by Jack London, with illustrations by Yohn; also, "Woven with the Ship," a story by Cyrus Townsend Brady, with illustrations by Christy, Leyendecker, Glackens, Parkhurst and Crawford.

SCHELTEMA & HOLKEMA'S BOEKHANDEL, Amsterdam, have printed two portfolios of the greatest value to artists and lovers of art, entitled "The Rembrandt Exhibition at Amsterdam, (September-October, 1898,) and London, (January-February, 1899.") The portfolios contain 66 photogravure reproductions of the most representative work of Rembrandt, with letterpress by Dr. Hofstede De Groot. The portfolios were designed and made by C. A. Lion Cachet. The work is published in an ordinary edition at $250, and in an *edition de luxe* at $500, but each section, that is, the one for Amsterdam and the one for London, is sold separately. Martin F. Onnen, 114 Fifth Avenue, New York, the representative of Martin Nijhoff, is the sole agent of the work in the United States and Canada.

R. H. RUSSELL will publish shortly C. D. Gibson's new book, "The Social Ladder," which will contain the latest collection of Mr. Gibson's drawings, marking the full maturity of the artist's power and skill in delineating character and creating types, and his keen gift of social satire; "Abeniki Caldwell," by Carolyn Wells, a humorous burlesque intended as a pleasant antidote to the modern historical novel, illustrated with a series of amusing old wood-cuts; a new Remington book, containing 67 pictures of the wild life of Western America, drawn by Mr. Remington and described by Owen Wister; also, "Her Majesty the King," a captivatingly funny story, by James Jeffrey Roche, with illustrations by Oliver Herford. Mr. Russell has in preparation a number of other books, to which reference will be made later.

HENRY HOLT & CO. have in press "Borrowed Plumes," a volume of burlesques on the Elizabeths of the "Letters" and the "German Garden," "Mr. Dooley," Hall Caine, Henry Harland, Ellen Thorneycroft Fowler, "John Oliver Hobbes" and others, by Owen Seaman, whose "Battle of the Bays" was favorably compared with Calverley's Fly Leaves; a striking novel, "Lord Leonard the Luckless," by W. E. Norris; also a new edition of Anthony Hope's "Dolly Dialogues," including the four additional "Dialogues" and a frontispiece by Christy. They have just sent to press on the same day, Anthony Hope's "Rupert of Hentzau" for the second time this year, (making its 17th impression,) Paul L. Ford's "Honorable Peter Stirling" for the third time this year, (46th impression,) and Jerome K. Jerome's "Idle Thoughts of an Idle Fellow" for its 17th impression. They were also obliged to send Bemont & Monod's "Medieval Europe, 395-1270" to press for a second time only three days after they had received the first impression.

ANTICIPATIONS of a posthumous novel from the pen of George Douglas (Brown), whose novel, "The House With the Green Shutters," won so notable a success this year, will not be realized, so his publishers, McClure, Phillips & Co., announce. It is true, as was widely stated, that up to the time of his death Mr. Brown was at work on a new novel, but the story was so far from completion that he had expected to spend another year at it. It was to have been a story of love and fighting in the time of Oliver Cromwell, and the central figure was one of Cromwell's fighting men. The young author's death, which was almost instantaneous, and is supposed to have been caused by the rupture of a blood vessel, leaves his publishers in a quandary as to what disposition shall be made of the proceeds now on hand and still to come of "The House With the Green Shutters." Mr. Brown, so far as is known, had no living relatives, and it is said that he died intestate. The publishers have written to his fiancee, a young English girl, placing the funds at her disposal.

HOUGHTON, MIFFLIN & CO. will publish next week "New France and New England," by the late John Fiske, which forms the remaining link needed to complete the chain of histories of this country upon which Dr. Fiske had been engaged for so many years; "A Sea Turn and Other Matters," a new collection of short stories, by Thomas Bailey Aldrich, in which the author's fancy sweeps over many lands; "Lois Mallet's Dangerous Gift," by Mary Catherine Lee, who tells with admirable spirit and restraint the story of a Quaker girl of extraordinary beauty—a beauty which the grave Friends considered a "dangerous gift;" "Uncle Charley," by Zephine Humphrey, a charming story of an inventor and a man of genius, a whimsical, dilatory, lovable man, with neither desire nor qualifications for business success; a new *Handy-volume edition* of Holmes's *Breakfast Table Series*, in four volumes, containing the Autocrat, Professor, and Poet at the Breakfast Table, and "Over the Teacups;" also "A Dramatization of Longfellow's 'Song of Hiawatha,'" by Florence Holbrook, which forms an extra number of the *Riverside Literature Series*.

BRENTANO'S fall announcements include, among others, three volumes by Anna, Comtesse de Bremon, which will be known collectively as the *World of Music* and separately as "The Great Composers," "The

Great Singers," and "The Great Virtuosi." Another musical series with the collective title of Nights at the Opera will be formed of Wagner's "Lohengrin," "Tristan and Isolde," "Tannhäuser" and "Meistersinger," each giving the complete plot and critical comments and explanation of the motive representing each character. They will also issue "Annals of Old Manhattan, 1609-1664," by Julia M. Colton; "The Art of Heraldry," by Arthur Charles Fox-Davies; "Siena: its Architecture and Art," by Gilbert Hastings; "The Throne of Individuality," by William George Jordan; and eight Japanese calendars for 1903. Of special interest is a set of *Turner House Classics,* edited by William MacDonald, composed of such standards as "Henry Esmond," Père Goriot," "Cloister and the Hearth," etc.; also, a *Sonnet Series,* of which the first issues will be Keat's "Sonnets" and Mrs. Browning's "Sonnets from the Portuguese."

Alexander Duncker, (H. von Carnap,) 178 Fulton Street, New York, will publish about October 1, an undertaking in Biblical scholarship that is both novel and interesting. It is an attempt to restore the oldest form of the New Testament books with a wider use of apparatus than has yet been attempted, and is under the auspices of Professor Hermann Freiherr von Soden of Berlin. The title of his forthcoming study is announced as "Die Schriften des Neuen Testaments." The first volume will contain an elaborate history of texts, account of manuscript researches and other preliminary matter, a second will give the results of the study, which will be based on no less than 2328 manuscripts, and is said to differ considerably from the text reached by the essentially similar methods of Tischendorf, Weiss, Westcott and Hort. Von Soden has made repeated journeys to the East, and thinks he can prove that the Vatican and Sinaitic and their allied manuscripts represent only one type of text recension, beside which there was another current throughout the middle ages. He thinks he has found traces also of text forms allied to neither.

D. Appleton & Co. have just ready Sir Gilbert Parker's new story, "Donovan Pasha and Some People of Egypt," in which the author of "The Seats of the Mighty" has again brought his genius into play in producing a strong central character. Donovan Pasha, who is supposed to be in the service of the Khedive of Egypt, stands for a type of Englishman who has found his way into Egypt and Arabia, there to emphasize by his own sense of right and wrong the two opposite poles represented by Eastern and Western civilization. They have also just brought out "The Things That Are Cæsar's," a novel by a new writer, Reginald Wright Kauffman, who bases his story upon the question whether or not a man having violated the laws provided for the protection of society and paid the penalty therefor, has cancelled the debt? They will publish this month "The Sea Lady," by H. G. Wells, a fantastic yet wholly amusing story of a modern mermaid, "the incarnation of desire," who is cast up by the sea into the electrified bosom of a respectable British family, and who becomes the embodiment of the unrest, the yearning for the half-known and the unattainable which is inherent in the human soul; also, "The House Under the Sea," by Max Pemberton, a story full of stirring adventures and dramatic situations.

The University of Chicago Press has just published three more reprints from the *University of Chicago Decennial Publications,* viz.: "The Physical Characters of the Indians of Southern Mexico," by Professor Frederick Starr; "The Treatment of Nature in the Works of Nikolaus Lenau," by Professor Camillo von Klenze; and "Concerning the Modern German Relatives, 'Das' and 'Was' in Clauses Dependent upon Substantivized Clauses," by Professor Starr Willard Cutting. This series was planned in connection with the celebration of the completion of the first ten years of the corporate existence of the university, the purpose being to set forth and exemplify the material and intellectual growth of the institution during the first decade. The series, which is in an advanced stage of preparation, will consist of ten regular volumes, issued in quarto form, and about fifteen supplementary volumes in octavo form. The Press will bring out shortly a book entitled "The Place of Industry in Elementary Education," by Katherine Elizabeth Dopp, which is timely, coming in response to a very general demand for some principles by means of which to evaluate the various forms of industry that are being introduced into the elementary school with reference to other factors in education; "The Second Bank of the United States," by Ralph H. C. Catterall, treating at length both the monetary and political questions connected with that institution; also, "The Life and Repentance of Marie Magdalene," a sixteenth century morality play, by Lewis Wager, edited, with an introduction, notes and glossarial index, by Professor Frederick Ives Carpenter, and now for the first time reprinted and provided with editorial apparatus.

Dodd, Mead & Co. have just ready a historical work of considerable importance entitled "The Guardian of Marie Antoinette," being the letters from the Comte de Mercy-Argenteau, Austrian Ambassador to the Court of Versailles, to Marie Therese, Empress of Austria, from 1770 to 1780, translated by Lillian C. Smythe, illustrated with numerous portraits, photographs, facsimile letters, etc. They have also just ready "Famous Paintings as seen and described by famous writers," edited and translated by Esther Singleton, author of "Turrets, Towers and Temples," etc.; "London its life and sights described by great writers," also edited and arranged by Esther Singleton; "Paul Kelver," the first long novel by Jerome K. Jerome, for which great popularity is predicted; "The Conquest of Charlotte," by David S. Meldrum, a love story, the scene of which is laid partly in London and partly in a shipping-town of Fife; "Margarita, a Legend of the Fight for the Great River," a historical romance of the discovery and exploration of the Mississippi River, by Elizabeth W. Champney, a new volume of the *Dames and Daughters of Colonial Days* series; "A Little Girl in Old Detroit," a story for young readers, by Amanda M. Douglas; also, "Yourself," by H. A. Guerber, a handbook which teaches children all they need to know about the laws of physiology and personal hygiene, in a simple yet graphic way. They have in preparation for publication, provided enough interest shall be shown in the subject, a book on organ-building, entitled "The Art of Organ-Building," by George Ashdown Audsley, author of "Ceramic Arts of Japan," etc. It is said to be the largest and most complete treatise on the science and art of organ-building in our language, being the result of thirty years' study of the subject in England. France, Germany, Holland, Belgium, and the United States. The numerous illustrations are accurately drawn by the author, and they will be reproduced by photo-engraving and inserted in the text for easy reference. Each of the two volumes will contain about 500 pages, and there will be two editions, the regular in cloth, and the edition de luxe will probably be limited to 300 copies, each to be numbered and signed by the author.

Charles Scribner's Sons bring out this week Richard Harding Davis's new novel, "Captain Macklin," with illustrations by Walter Appleton Clark; a book entitled "Wayfarers in Italy," by Katherine Hooker, a record of the impression of a discriminating traveller who writes a subtle appreciation of the art, history and scenery of Italy, with a sympathetic comprehension of the spirit and genius of a people whose character she brings out chiefly by illuminating sidelights and suggestive incident; "Shakespeare's Portrayal of the Moral Life," by Frank Chapman Sharp, whose subject is the attitude of the characters in the different dramas to the fundamental principles of moral science; "In the Wasp's Nest," a sea story of the war of 1812, for boys, by Cyrus Townsend Brady; and three new Henty books—"The Treasures of the Incas," a story of Peru; "With Kitchener in the Soudan," a story of Atbara and Omdurman, and "With the British Legation," a story of the Carlist uprising in 1836. They will publish shortly an important volume on the New Testament by well-known authorities, under the title of "Criticism of the New Testament." The volume will contain six lectures delivered under the auspices of Westminster Parish, London, for the purpose of disseminating as widely as possible a sound knowledge of Bible criticism. The lectures are as follows: "The Criticism of the New Testament," by Professor W. Sanday, Canon of Christ Church, Oxford; "Manuscripts," by Dr. F. G. Kenyon, assistant keeper of mss., British Museum; "The Ancient Versions of the New Testament," by F. C. Burkitt, of Trinity College, Cambridge; "The History of the Canon of the New Testament," by Professor F. H. Chase, President of Queen's College, Cambridge; "The Dates of the New Testament Books," by the Rev. A. C. Headlam, Rector of Welwyn; and "The Historical Value of the Acts of the Apostles," by Professor J. H. Bernard, of Trinity College, Dublin. They have made arrangements to bring out in this country a "Library of Art," to be complete in about thirty-six volumes. All schools and periods will be represented in the scheme, but only the greatest masters will be treated in separate biographies. The rest will be treated in relation to their fellows and forerunners as incidents of development. The editor in this way hopes to portray the subject in its true proportions more closely than has hitherto been attempted. The æsthetic side of art criticism will not be neglected, but the chief aim will be to make the volumes a storehouse of positive knowledge. The editor of the entire work will be S. Arthur Strong, librarian of the House of Lords at Westminster, and also librarian of Chatsworth, the mansion of the Duke of Devonshire. They will publish shortly Professor Barrett Wendell's volume of dramatic verse which will contain "Raleigh in Guiana," "A Christmas Masque" and "Rosamond." All three are essays in the Elizabethan manner of dramatic writing; that is, the free translation into dramatic verse of material existing in narrative form.

BUSINESS NOTES.

Charlottesville, Va.—J. T. Hancock and G. F. Spitzer have purchased the book and stationery business of the Old Dominion Printing Company, and will continue it under the same name.

Kansas City, Mo.—The Western Methodist Book Concern will shortly begin the erection of a building for its branch here. For two years past this branch of the publishing house has occupied quarters in the New Nelson building at Missouri Avenue and Main Street. Thirty-eight feet on the east side of McGee Street just north of Twelfth have been secured. On this property a three-story brick building, to be used exclusively by the Kansas City branch of the book concern, will be erected. It is hoped to have the building ready for occupancy by December 1.

Lewiston, Me.—Douglass & Pierce, booksellers, have sold out to Mrs. C. V. Dronne.

Murfreesboro, Tenn. — Huggins & Co., booksellers, have been succeeded by Vickers & Smith.

New York City.—E. R. Miner and Thomas J. Carey have dissolved partnership and Mr. Miner will continue as proprietor of the Popular Publishing Company. He has bought the sole right to publish "Irish Yarns," "Hebrew Yarns," "Travellers' Yarns," etc., and elsewhere in this issue gives notice that he will prosecute any infringement upon his rights in these books.

Tacoma, Wash.—The Central News Company has purchased the book and stationery business of Bloom & Co.

Wabash, Ind.—M. J. Barton, bookseller, has sold out.

TERMS OF ADVERTISING.

Under the heading "Books Wanted" **book-trade subscribers are given the privilege of a free advertisement for books out of print, of five nonpareil lines exclusive of address, in any issue except special numbers, to an extent not exceeding 100 lines a year. If more than five lines are sent, the excess is at 10 cents a line, and amount should be inclosed.** *Bids for current books and such as may be easily had from the publishers, and repeated matter, as well as all advertisements from non-subscribers, must be paid for at the rate of 10 cents a line.*

Under the heading "Books for Sale," the charge to subscribers and non-subscribers is 10 cents a nonpareil line for each insertion. No deduction for repeated matter.

All other small, undisplayed, advertisements will be charged at the uniform rate of 10 cents a nonpareil line. Eight words may be reckoned to the line.

Parties with whom we have no accounts must pay in advance, otherwise no notice will be taken of their communications.

BOOKS WANTED.

☞ ***In answering, please state edition, condition, and price, including postage or express charges.***

Houses that are willing to deal exclusively on a cash-on-delivery basis will find it to their advantage to put after their firm-name the word [Cash].

☞ ***Write your wants plainly and on one side of the sheet only. Illegibly-written "wants" will be considered as not having been received. The "Publishers' Weekly" does not hold itself responsible for errors.***

It should be understood that the appearance of advertisements in this column, or elsewhere in the "Publishers' Weekly" does not furnish a guarantee of credit. While it is endeavored to safeguard these columns by withdrawing the privilege of their use from advertisers who are not "good pay," booksellers should take the usual precaution, as to advertisers not known to them, that they would take in making sales to any unknown parties.

Almy, Bigelow & Washburn, Salem, Mass.

Red Man and White Man, by Ellis.
Catharine, by Nehemiah Adams. Lothrop.

Amer. Bapt. Pub. Soc., 177 Wabash Ave., Chicago.

Book on Mormons, 1st ed.; also Their Doctrine and Covenant.
History of the Mormons, McKay.
Any books on Mormonism.
Wells, Determinants.
Todhunter, Theory of Equations. Macmillan.
Mechanique Celeste.
Select Notes for 1900.
Select Notes for 1901.

Amer. Bapt. Pub. Soc., 279 Elm St., Dallas, Tex.

Cramp's History of the Baptist. Pub. by A. B. P. S.

American Press Co., Baltimore, Md.

Proceedings of the New Jersey Historical Society v. 10.
Aaron Burr, books, pamphlets, magazine articles.
Washington, books and pamphlets.

American Tract Soc., 169 Wabash Ave., Chicago, Ill.

Evidences of Christianity, by Albert Barnes.

Americus Law Book Co., Americus, Ga. [*Cash.*]

Ku Klux Klan and Reconstruction items.
Ramsay, Revolution and Histories.
Garden, Anecdotes of Revolution.
Roger Williams and the Baptist, by D. C. Eddy.

Abe C. Anderson, Henry, Bannock Co., Idaho.

Mormonism: Celestial or Plural Marriage, by Orson Pratt.
Views of the Latter-Day Saints on Marriage, by William Budge. Liverpool, 1879.

Bailey & Sackett, Syracuse, N. Y.

Henry, Dr., History of Masonry.
Preston, W., History of Masonry.

Theo. M. Barber, Box 144, Pittsburgh, Pa. [*Cash.*]

Labouchere, Ladies' Book Plates.
Stone, Children's Book Plates.
Surtees, Ask Mamma. 1858.
Sartain's Magazine.
Graham's Magazine.

Bartlett's Book Store, 33 E. 22d St., N. Y.

The Philistine, v. 6, 8, bound.
Any works by Southwell.

Frank Batterton, Greensburg, Ind.

Entozo, Cobbolt.
American Sportsman, by Dr. Lewis, early ed.

Bellevue College Library, Bellevue, Neb. [*Cash.*]

Annals Amer. Acad., Sept., 1891.
Classical Review, Feb.-July, Oct., 1900.
Library Journal, Jan.-May, 1900; Dec., 1901.
Lit. Digest, Nov. 2, 9, 16, 23, 30; Dec. 7, 14, 21, 28, 1901; Apr. 26, 1902.

Bigham & Smith, Agts., Dallas, Tex.

Dick, John, Essay on Inspiration.
Dick, John, Lectures on Theology.
Descensus Averno, or, the Downward Drift.
The Rice and Campbell Debate.

Bigham & Smith, Agts., Nashville, Tenn.

Night Scenes of the Bible, by Dr. March.

Board of Publication, R. C. A., 25 E. 22d St., N. Y.

Journal of the Am. Oriental Society, containing articles on Arab Music and Medicine, v. 1, by Drs. Van Dyck and Eli Smith.

Book Exchange, Toledo, O.

Warfare of Science, separates, nos. 1, 2, 3.
Morris, John Ball; Guenevere; Odyssey.
Forbes, Mystery of Berwyn Kennedy.
Copeland & Day's Xmas Booklet, 1894.
Any book or pamphlet by Vance Thompson.

The Boston Book Co., 83 Francis St., Boston, Mass.

Book Buyer, Sept., 1884; Feb., '94. 50 cts. each.

J. W. Bouton, 10 W. 28th St., N. Y.

London Notes and Queries, complete set.
Dictionary of National Biography, 66 v. Smith, Elder & Co.
Stone's Life of Red Jacket. 1841.
Marco Polo, Travels, Yule.

The Bowen-Merrill Co., Indianapolis, Ind.

Life of John McLean, Associate Justice of U. S. Supreme Court.

Brentano's, Union Sq., N. Y.

Diplomat's Diary. Lippincott.
Mysteries of Udolpho. Routledge.
Fifty Years in Two Hemispheres.
Common School Speaker, by Noble Butler. John P. Morton & Co., 1856.
Gallia. Lippincott.
McMaster, Commercial Paper.
Forbes of Harvard.
Guide books to all cities of U. S., quote any you have of your own city.
Miller, J., Mother and Baby.
When Charles I. Was King. McClurg.
Ruggles, Germany Seen Without Spectacles. L. & S.
Creeds of all Nations.

Brentano's, 1015 Pennsylvania Ave., Washington, D. C.

Page Family of Virginia, by Page.
Hudson, Naturalist in La Plata.
Hearn, Some Chinese Ghosts.

Bryant & Douglas Book and Stationery Co., 1002 Walnut St., Kansas City, Mo.

Life and Explorations of J. C. Fremont, by C. W. Upham.

Callahan's Old Book Store, 74 W. 2d South, Salt Lake City, U.

History of the Reed Family, by Jacob W. Reed.
History of Switzerland, by MacKenzie.
Almost Persuaded.
Thirlwall, Hist. of Greece (8 v. ed.), v. 1, 2. Longmans, G.

M. E. Carlton, Flint, Mich.

Driftwood, by Celia Thaxter.

Case Library, Cleveland, O.

American Institute of Electrical Engineers Transactions, v. 1 to 9, 13.
De Mille, The Dodge Club.
Matthews, The Indian Fairy Book.
Boyesen, Mammon of Unrighteousness.
Bolton, History of Westchester County.

C. N. Caspar Co., 437 E. Water St., Milwaukee, Wis

Johnson's Universal Encyclopedia, last ed.
Du Bois, Graphic Statics, Atlas thereto.
Lyon, Hollow Globe.

BOOKS WANTED.—*Continued.*

The A. H. Clark Co., Garfield Bldg., Cleveland, O.

Matheson, Searchings in the Silence.
St. Nicholas Mag., complete or odd v.

The Robert Clarke Co., 31 E. 4th St., Cincinnati, O.

Hough, E., Singing Mouse Stories. Forest and Stream.
Brockett, L. P., A Year of Battle. Goodspeed, about 1871.

W. B. Clarke Co., Park and Tremont Sts., Boston, Mass.

Journal of Thomas Raikes, 4 v.
Festival Poems: a collection for Christmas, New Year and Easter.
Dyers' Materials, Heermann.
Downing, Landscape Gardening.
Story Toto Told Me.
Children of the Sea, Conrad.
The Egoist, G. Meredith, 1st ed., brown cl.

Henry T. Coates & Co., Phila., Pa.

Santa Fé Trail, by Inman.
Maritime Enterprise, by R. Cleveland.
The Book of Jade (poems.)
Whistler, Gentle Art of Making Enemies.
Paine, Charles, Elements of Railroading.
Fink, Albert, The Railroad Problem.
Fink, Henry, Freight Rates.
Haupt, Herman, General Theory of Bridge Construction.
Safe Railway Working. Pub. by Crosby, Lockwood & Co.
Hamilton, Alex., Works, 10 v. Putnam.
Whitney, The United States.
Life of Baron von Riedesel, in English.
North, History of Augusta, Maine.

Columbia University Library, N. Y.

School Review, v. 8, complete; v. 9, nos. 1, 2, 3.
Scribner's Magazine, Feb., 1902.
Century, Apr., 1902.

Irving S. Colwell, Auburn, N. Y.

Century Dict., 10 v., hf. mor., 1902 ed.
Stoddard's Travel Lectures, 11 v.
Reed's Modern Eloquence.

Crusoe & Co., 81 Vermont St., Brooklyn, N. Y.

Kempe, A. J., Loseley Manuscripts. Lond., 1835.
Wright, Thomas, Specimens of Lyric Poetry. 1842.

DeWolfe, Fiske & Co., 361 Washington St., Boston, Mass.

Phantasms of the Living, by Edmund Gurney, F. W. H. Meyers and Frank Podmore.

Dixie Book Shop, 35 Nassau St., N. Y.

Appleton's Annuals, 1894 to 1900, shp.
Eastlake, Hist. of Material of colors for Painting.
Symonds, Life of Cellini, Nimmo.

Dodd, Mead & Co., 372 Fifth Ave., N. Y.

Lady of Shallott. Dodd, Mead & Co., 1881.

Wm. J. Douglass, 148 Market St., Chicago, Ill.

Life of A. Lincoln, by J. O. Howard. Cincinnati or Columbus, 1860.
Any Life of Lincoln of 1860.

Daniel Dunn, 677 Fulton St., Brooklyn, N. Y.

Lucius Cary (Viscount Falkland), Poems or Works.
Martin Rattler, by Ballentyne.

E. P. Dutton & Co., 31 W. 23d St., N. Y.

En Route, by Huysmans. New Amsterdam.
Oriental Rugs, Mumford.
Infant Philosopher: Stray Leaves from a Baby's Journal, by T. S. Verdi.
History of Reed Family, by J. W. Reed. Bost., 1861.

Eau Claire Book and Stationery Co., Eau Claire, Wis.

Remarkable Women, Adams.

Elder & Shepard, 238 Post St., San Francisco, Cal.

Dixey, W., Trade of Authorship. 1899.
Dawson, J., Practical Journalism.
Shuman, E. L., Art and Practice of Journalism.

Kenneth B. Elliman, 419 W. 118th St., N. Y.

Documentary History of State of N. Y., v. 1, E. B. O'Callaghan. Albany, 1849.
Science and Health, Mrs. Eddy, 1st, 2d, 3d eds.
Roycroft books.

G. Engelke, 225 N. Clark St., Chicago, Ill. [*Cash.*]

Bancroft, U. S. Hist., v. 10.
Andreas, Hist. of Chicago, v. 3, cheap.
Gen. Cullum, Hist. of the Military Academy West Point.

Fords, Howard & Hulbert, Bible House, N. Y. [*Cash.*]

Beecher, H. W., Lecture Room Talks. J. B. Ford & Co.
Beecher, H. W., Star Papers. J. B. Ford & Co.

W. R. Funk, Agt., Dayton, O.

2 copies Out Door Papers, $1.50 ed.

Wm. J. Gerhard, 2209 Callowhill St., Phila., Pa.

Heilprin, Animal Life of Our Seashore.
Heilprin, Explorations in Florida.
Townsend, Narrative of Journey Across Rocky Mts.
Conrad, Monograph on Unionidæ.

F. L. Goldthwaite, 102 Exchange Pl., New Orleans, La.

Casanova Memoirs, complete set, bound.

Edwin S. Gorham, 4th Ave. and 22d St., N. Y.

Moehler, Symbolism.
Alger, W. R., History of Cross.
Gaume, On Cemeteries.
Gaume, On Confession.
Hawks, Constitutions and Canons.

F. E. Grant, 23 W. 42d St., N. Y.

Stock Brokers and Stock Exchanges, John R. Dos Passos.
Poetical Works of J. and C. Wesley, 13 v., by G. Osborn. London.
Garden, Anecdotes of the American Revolution.
Washington Day by Day. Pub. 1895, Cycle Pub. Co.
Baker, Washington After the Revolution.
2 copies Baker, Itinerary of General Washington, 1775-1783.
Thirlwall, History of Greece.
McMahon, American Gardener.
Cumming, Gordon, Book of Adventures in South Africa.
Thirty Years Among the Players in England and America, by Joe Cowell.
Letters of a Parsee Merchant to Horace Greeley.
The Jesuit's Ring.
Mcmmsen's Digest (text in Latin), stereotype edition in 1 v.
Idle Hours in a Library, by W. H. Hudson. Doxey.
Meditations of a Parish Priest.
Trollope's Autobiography.
Sermons of Lorenzo Dow, Jr.
Sword and Gown, by George Lawrence.
John Wesley's Doctrinal Tracts.
Campbell and Rice Debates.
Xariffa's Poems. Lippincott.
Verses Wise and Otherwise, by Ellen T. Fowler.
History of the Knowlton Family.
Atalanta in the South, by Mrs. Maud Howe Elliott.
Book on the Tabernacle and Solomon's Temple, by T. O. Payne, D.D.
R. H. Stoddard's Poems, complete. Scribner.
The Rossetti Portfolio, a collection of articles which appeared in *The Spectator*.
Nomenclature of Colors for Naturalists, by Ridgeway.
Byways and Bird Notes, by Maurice Thompson.
Birds of Michigan, by A. J. Cook.
Ornithology of Illinois, by Robt. Ridgeway.
Collier's Cyclopedia of Social and Commercial Information, by N. Robinson.
Back vols. of the *Auk*.
Life of John Brown, by Redpath.
Parody on Poe's Raven.

L. Hammel & Co., Mobile, Ala.

Old Man Gilbert, by Kambra Thorpe.
Tom Oaks, by Kambra Thorpe.

F. F. Hansell & Bro., Ltd., 714 Canal St., New Orleans, La.

Monette, Mississippi Valley.

Harvard Co-operative Society, Cambridge, Mass.

Princess of the Gutter.
Lady Betty's Governess.
Lady Rosamond's Book.

D. M. Henderson, Madison and Howard Sts., Baltimore, Md.

Memoirs of Nathan Smith, M.D.
The French Theatre, in French, about 25 v.

Walter M. Hill, 31 Washington St., Chicago, Ill.

Bax, Life of Marat. Small, Maynard.
Tudor Translation, Apuleius.
Tudor Translation, Montaigne, 3 v.
Symonds, Wine, Women and Song. 1884.
Symonds, Benvenuto Cellini, 2 v., 1st ed.
Keats, Works, 4 v., ed. by Buxton Forman. 1883.

BOOKS WANTED.—Continued.

Hinds & Noble, 31 W. 15th St., N. Y.

Shedd's Natural Memory Method.

H. C. Holmes, 1149 Market St., San Francisco, Cal.

Irish Pedigrees, O'Hart.

W. S. Houghton, Lynn, Mass.

St. Nicholas, Nov., Dec., 1873.
Cosmopolitan, Mar., May, 1886; Nov., '88.
Wheelman, Dec., 1882; Aug., '83.
American Naturalist, Jan., 1885.

J. B. Hulst, 936 5th Ave., Grand Rapids, Mich.

Meyer, Commentary on New Testament, complete.
Calvin's Complete Works.

International News Co., 83 Duane St., N. Y.

Broadway Magazine, 1900-1901, complete, bound or pap.
Any books on good manners, illus.

Iowa College Library, Grinnell, Ia.

Mumford, Oriental Rugs.

Wm. Jackson, 7 Ann St., Hartford, Conn.

The House of Douglas. Pub. by Fremantle & Co., London.

Wm. R. Jenkins, 851 6th Ave., N. Y.

Mrs. Cecil Alexander's Poems.

Jennings & Pye, 57 Washington St., Chicago, Ill.

McCosh, Divine Government. Scribner.

E. T. Jett Book and News Co., 806 Olive St., St. Louis, Mo.

Sister Agnes.
Sims, Poems, cl.

Keep's Book Shop, 284 Columbus Ave., Boston, Mass.

Brampton Sketches, by Mrs. Claflin.
Books on checkers.
The Sphinx of the Fireside, by Agnes Repplier.
Letters from Hell.
A True Magdalene.

Kimball Bros., 618 Broadway, Albany, N. Y.

Annals of San Francisco. N. Y., 1865.
A Checkered Life, by J. L. Ver Mehr.
St. Nicholas, v. 1, 2, 1874-5.

King's Old Book Store, 15 4th St., San Francisco, Cal.

Blue and Gold, Class of '77, '81, '84, '99, 1900, '01, '02, '03.

Koelling & Klappenbach, 100 Randolph St., Chicago, Ill.

Stiles, History of Bundling.

Chas. E. Lauriat Co., 301 Washington St., Boston, Mass.

Jane Welsh Carlyle. N Y., circa 1885.
General N. P. Banks, Gordon.
History of Miniature Art, by Propert.
Burlington Fine Art Portraits and Miniatures, 1895.
Story of the Filibusters, Roche. Macmillan.
Songs and Satires, Roche.
Introduction to the Study of Browning, Arthur Symonds.
On Viol and Flute, by Edmund Gosse.
Idle Hours in a Library, by Hudson. Doxey.

Leggat Bros., 81 Chambers St., N. Y.

Marshall, Book of Oratory.

Library Co. of Phila., N. W. cor. Locust and Juniper Sts., Phila., Pa.

Molly Bawn. Phila., 1878.
Fothergill, First Violin. N. Y., 1878.
Publishers' Weekly, Jan. 19, 1901.

The Library of Congress (Periodical Division), Washington, D. C.

The Publishers' Weekly, v. 19, no. 6; v. 34, no. 16.

Little, Brown & Co., 254 Washington St., Boston, Mass.

Brevity and Brilliancy in Chess, by Miron Hazeltine.

B. Login, 1328 3d Ave., N. Y.

Racinet, On Ornament, 2 sets.
U. S. Dispensatory.
The Stage, Its Stars Past and Present, pt. 2.

I. M. Low, Colorado Springs, Colo. [*Cash.*]

Miss Angel.

Lyon, Kymer & Palmer Co., Grand Rapids, Mich.

Todd, Washington, the Universal Capital.
James, Alaska.
Goodell, Slavery and Anti-Slavery.

Nathaniel McCarthy, Minneapolis, Minn.

Strauss, Old Gospel for the New Faith.
The Afterglow of European Travel.
Layard, Nineveh and Babylon.
Stevenson, Travels in Central America, with Catherwood plates.

Joseph McDonough, 39 Columbia St., Albany, N. Y.

Congressional Globe, pts. 1, 2 of appendix to v. 19; pts. 1, 2, 3, of v. 37; pt. 2 of v. 39.
Congressional Record, v. 12; pts. 1, 2, 3, 4, 5 and index of v. 22; pts. 7, 9, 10 and index of v. 26.
Taylor, B. F., Old Time Pictures.
Lippincott's Gazetteer, give date, must be cheap.

John Jos. McVey, 39 N. 13th St., Phila., Pa.

Lilian's Golden Hours. Routledge.

The Edw. Malley Co., New Haven, Conn.

Human Personality and Its Survival of Bodily Death, F. W. H. Myers.

Dewitt Miller, P. O. Drawer 1351, Phila., Pa. [*Cash.*]

The Traitor, or, the Fate of Ambition, a novel dealing with Hamilton and Burr.
4 copies *Lippincott's Magazine*, Feb., 1875. 25 cts. apiece paid.

Edw. Mills, 607 Chestnut St., St. Louis, Mo.

Kirkman, Science of Railway, 12 v.
Mills, Political Economy, v. 1.
Winsor, Narrative and Critical Hist., odd v.

Noah Farnham Morrison, 893 Broad St., Newark, N. J. [*Cash.*]

N. J. Archives, v. 1, 2, 3, 5, 3 copies each.
Van Syckle Genealogy.
Bickley, History of the Settlement and Indian Wars of Tazewell Co., Va.

John P. Morton & Co., Louisville, Ky.

Old Man Gilbert, by E. W. Bellamy.

New England Methodist Book Depository, 38 Bromfield St., Boston, Mass.

Lyons, Colonial Furniture. Houghton, Mifflin.
Wesley's Journal, 2 v., shp., second-hand.

Daniel O'Shea, 1584 Broadway, N. Y.

Old Paris, v. 1 only, by Lady Jackson, cl. Lond., Bentley, 1878.

C. C. Parker, 246 S. Broadway, Los Angeles, Cal. [*Cash.*]

Record of Shelley, Byron and the Author, E. J. Trelawney.

The Pease-Lewis Co, Drawer 8, New Haven, Conn

Bushnell, Works, second-hand.
Comedies of Goldoni. McClurg & Co.
Cross, True Masonic Chart. New Haven.

Geo. B. Peck Dry Goods Co., Kansas City, Mo.

Decoration Flower Studies, J. Foord.
Art of Conversation, J. G. Leland.
Poole's Indexes.
Green, Eng. People, 4 v., Harper's Illus. ed., 8vo.
Venable, Dream of Empire.

Phila. Book Co., 15 S. 9th St., Phila., Pa.

Burnham, Limestone and Marbles.
Cristiani, Perfumery.
Thompson, Electromagnet, 8vo. Spon.

E. Picken, 33 Beaver Hall Hill, Montreal, Can.

Nightingale Valley, by Giraldus. Bell, 1860.
Prayers for Public Worship, John Service.

Pierce & Zahn, 633 17th St., Denver, Colo.

Hasting, Tournament of Chess.
The Lark, v. 2, incl. Epilark.

The Pilgrim Press, 175 Wabash Ave., Chicago, Ill.

Redpath, History of the World, complete.
2 copies They Say.

E. W. Porter, St. Paul, Minn.

Moore, Songs and Ballads of the Amer. Revolution.
La Fontaine, Fables, 2 v., tr. by Wright, 8vo, cl. Boston, 1841.

BOOKS WANTED.—Continued.

Preston & Rounds Co., Providence, R. I.

Owen's Catullus, hand-made pap. ed. Lawrence & Bullen.
Newcomb, Complete Astronomy.

G. P. Putnam's Sons, 27 W. 23d St., N. Y.

Farrell, Art Topics.
Bankside ed. of Shakespeare's Works.
Field, The House, 1st ed. Scribner, 1896.
Drake, History of Boston. 1854.
Adams, Railroads. Putnam.
Wise, Through the Air.
Isaac T. Hopper, by Child.
Leslie, Pencil Sketches, 1st ser.

Fleming H. Revell Co., Chicago, Ill.

Advanced and Backward Races, Brice.

H. M. Reynolds, Box 835, Bisbee, Arizona. [*Cash.*]

The Symmes Memorial.
The Western Avernus, Morley Roberts.
The Donner Party.
The Dead Letter, Seeley Register.

Geo. H. Richmond, 32 W. 33d St., N. Y.

Napoleon, Lover and Husband, any ed.

Geo. H. Rigby, 1113 Arch St., Phila., Pa.

Transactions of the Amer. Institute of Electrical Engineers, any vols. except 6, 10, 11.

Redman & Son, 846 Boulevard, Astoria, L. I. City.

Flint, Philosophy of History—France.
Smith, Simple Introduction to the Study of Philosophy.
Fiske, Discovery of America, v. 1, 2. Houghton, Mifflin, 1896.

Wm. B. Ropes, Mt. Vernon, Skagit Co., Wash.

Wilkinson, Spencer, War and Policy.
Ryan, Father, Poems, latest ed.
Century Cyclopedia, 10 v.
Webster's Collegiate Dict.
Ridpath, Universal History.

J. Francis Ruggles, Bronson, Mich.

Pillsbury, Acts of Anti-Slavery Apostles.
Birney, A Brotherhood of Thieves
Birney, The Churches the Bulwark of Slavery.
Von Holst's John Brown. Cupples & Hurd, 1889.
Richman's John Brown Among the Quakers. Des Moines, 1894.

Sanford-Putnam Co., 310 Main St., Worcester, Mass.

General Average, a satire on sharp practices in mercantile life, by William Allen Butler.

John E. Scopes. 29 Tweddle Bldg., Albany, N. Y.

American Ancestry, v. 10.
Wilkinson, Memoirs, v. 2 and atlas. Phila., 1816.

Charles Scribner's Sons, 153 5th Ave., N. Y.

Tribune Index, 1900, bound.
Gray, Alonzo, and Adams, C. B., Elements of Geology. Harper, 1852.
Whewell, Philosophy of the Inductive Sciences. App.
Seaman, Ezra, American System of Government. Scribner.
Lawson, America's Cup.
Biggs, Four Years at Yale.
Houston, Outlines of Forestry. Lippincott.
Dorr, Flower of England's Face. Macmillan.
Murray, Guide to Russia.
Trollope, Corneille and Racine. Lippincott.
Prentiss, Tanglethread.
Norman, Real Japan. Scribner.
Mitford, Recollections of My Literary Life. Bentley.
Stead, Oberammergau, small ed. without illus.
The following 1st eds. of Hamilton Wright Mabie:
My Study Fire. Dodd, N. Y., 1890.
Our New England, 4to. N. Y., 1890.
My Study Fire, 2d ser. Dodd, 1894.
Essays on Nature and Culture. Dodd, 1896.

Chas. W. Sever & Co., Cambridge, Mass.

Watch and Clock Making, by David Glasgow.

Richard B. Shepard, Salt Lake City, U.

Anything relating to Jas. Bridges, Trapper.
Anything relating to Sublettee Bros., Trappers.
Van Duesen's Bookmaking.
Ann Eliza Young, Wife No. 19.

Sibley, Lindsay & Curr Co., Rochester, N. Y.

Records of the Past. 18 v., A. H. Sayce, good second-hand ed. Pub. in London by Boyle & Son, New York, Jas. Pott & Co.

George D. Smith, 50 New St., N. Y.

The Federalist, v. 1. N. Y., 1788.
Sketches of Yale College. N. Y., 1843.
Our System of Government, Seaman.
Rousseau's Confessions, 2 v., 8vo.
Keys and watches, books about.
Ireland's Napoleon, 4 v.
Galland's Iowa Emigrant. 1840.
Art of Bookbinding, Zaehnsdorf. Lond., 1890.
Audubon's Birds and Quadrupeds.
Stoddard's Lectures, 11 v.
American Museum, odd v., any.
Higgins, Anacalypsis, 2 v.
Inman, Ancient Faiths.
Squiers, Serpent Symbol.
Ouvaroff, Mysteries of Eleusis.

Wm. H. Smith, Jr., 515 W. 173d St., N. Y.

Master Mechanics Proceedings. 1870.
History of Kingsbridge, Edsall.
The Count of Moret. Hilton, publisher, 1860.
Any works with imprint of George, E. P., or H. L. Williams, or Williams Brothers.

Southern Law Book Co., Columbia, S. C.

Galt, On Insanity.
Any historical works of South Carolina.

Speyer & Peters, Berlin, N. W. 7, Germany.

Annales de Dermatologie.
Annals of Surgery.
Archiv für Mikroskop. Anatomie.
Archives of Laryngology.
Archives of Pediatrics.
Deutsche Chirurgie.
Journal de l'Anatomie. Robin.
Revue de Chirurgie.
Transactions of Amer. Orthop. Assoc.
Offer sets and single vols. or nos.

P. Stammer, 123 4th Ave., N. Y.

Lyell, Principles of Geology, latest ed. Appleton.
Rabelais, v. 2, Bohn's extra v. London, 1849.
Ephemeris (Astrological Almanac) for year 1880.
Gibbon, Rome, v. 4, 5, 6, brown cl. Bost., 1860.

G. E. Stechert, 9 E. 16th St., N. Y.

Engineering Record, v. 32, bound or nos.
Burton's Arabian Nights, 16 v. Denver.
Brown, Life of Society. 1885.
Elwell, Nine Jatakas. 1890.
Livingston, E., Life of, by C. H. Hunt. 1864.
Whitney, Hawaiian Guide Book.
Speeches of Josiah Quincy in Congress. '74.
Clevenger, Physiology and Psychology.
Vaughan, Chem. Physiology and Psychology.
Wood, Syphilis of Central Nervous System.
Bell, Climatology of U. S., etc. 1885.
Brown, Labor. Exercises in Materia Medica.
Brush, Instruction of Nurses for Insane.
Buckingham, On Insanity.
Dwight, Anatomy of the Head.
Edmunds, Pathology and Dis. of the Thyroid.
Fothergill, Vasorenal Change, etc.
Friedlander, Microscopic Technology.
Gorton, Neurasthenia.
Kitchin, On Consumption.
McFloaine, 1000 Amer. Drugs.
Peters, Examination of Milk.
Patton, Voice Production. Putnam.
Reid, Ventilation of Am. Dwellings.
Storer, Industrial Organic Chemistry.
Sanitary Care and Treatment of Children.
Saundby, Lectures on Diabetes.
Upshur, Disorders on Menstruation.
Winternitz, Hydrotherapy, etc.

E. Steiger & Co., 25 Park Place, N. Y. [*Cash.*]

Merwin, Patentability of Inventions. Boston, 1883.

Strawbridge & Clothier, Market St., Phila., Pa.

Adams, R. C., History of England in Rhyme. Lothrop Pub. Co, 40 cts.

C. L. Traver, Trenton, N. J. [*Cash.*]

Martineau, Anglers of the Dove.
Voorhees, Family Genealogy.
Nevius, Family Genealogy.
O'Hart, Irish Pedigrees in the U. S., 2 v.

D. H. Tripp & Son, Peoria, Ill.

Munsey, May, July, Aug., 1896; Oct., '97; July, '98.
Cosmopolitan, Jan., 1900.
Century, Jan., Feb., Mar., '99.
Current Literature, July, Dec., 1899.

BOOKS WANTED.—Continued.

C. S. Wake, 5543 Monroe Ave., Chicago, Ill.
Wake, Serpent Worship, and Other Essays.

John Wanamaker, N. Y.
Martyrdom of Man, by Winwood Reade.
Picturesque Mexico.
Principles of Strategy, Bigelow. Lippincott.
Countess Kathleen, by Yeats.
Anglo-Saxon Superiority, by Demolins.
Bigelow, Principles of Strategy. Lippincott

John Wanamaker, Phila., Pa.
Layard, Italian Schools of Painting, 1st ed.
Kugler, German, Flemish, and Dutch Schools of Painting, 1st ed.

Geo. E. Warner, Minneapolis, Minn.
Williamson, Gleanings of Leisure Hours.
Dake, Nebraska Legends and Poems.
Any county atlas or history.

H. W. Wilson, 315 14th Ave., S. E., Minneapolis, Minn.
Hamilton, Lectures in Logic.
Bradley, Principles of Logic.

Chas. L. Woodward, 78 Nassau St., N. Y.
New England Historical and Genealogical Register, v. 18.
Calendar of Wills, by Colonial Dames of State of New York.
Munsell's Collections, v. 4, or reprint containing Genealogies of Albany Families.

Woodward & Lothrop, Washington, D. C.
People of Another World, by H. L. Olcott.
Historic Homes in Washington, by Lockwood.
Everybody's Book of Short Poems.
Housekeeping in Old Virginia.
George Washington Day by Day.
Greenleaf and Law in Federal City.
All in good second-hand.

Leggat Bros., 81 Chambers St., N. Y.
25 Cruise of the "Cachalot, cl. 10 cts.
25 Weaver's Medical Atlas. 10 cts.
10 Diseases of the Horse, U. S. Gov't Report. 50 cts.
25 Stories from the Decameron. 3 cts.
15 Wilks' Solo Whist. 10 cts.
10 Indian Sign Language. $1.00.
5 Buffalo and Senecas. $1.00.
5 Smith's New Jersey. $1.50.
15 Flowers and Gardens. Pub. $1.50. 25 cts.
10 U. S. Fish Commission Reports. Each 50 cts.

Scrantom, Wetmore & Co., Rochester, N. Y.
Harper's Magazine, v. 1, 2, 4, 5, 7, 8, 10, 11, 14.
O'Reilley, History of Rochester.
Make offer for either or all.

BOOKS FOR SALE.

N. J. Bartlett & Co., 28 Cornhill, Boston, Mass
American Book Prices Current, complete set, 7 v., cl., in good condition; also vols. for years 1898, 1899, 1901. Make offer.
One hundred theological books, cl. bound, good condition, almost no duplicates, 12mo and 8vo in size. $5.00.

Dixie Book Shop, 35 Nassau St., N. Y.
Life Henry Clay, by Geo. D. Prentice. $3.00.

F. A. Fernald, Broadway near 117th St., N. Y.
11 Adams, Civilization in Middle Ages. Scribner. 50 % off.
15 Carlyle, Life of Schiller, Popular ed. Scribner. 50 % off.
1 Dana, System of Mineralogy. Wiley. 50 % off.
3 Delitzsch, Assyrian Grammar. Williams & Norgate. @ $3 00.
1 Egleston, Metallurgy of Silver. Wiley. 50 % off
5 Egleston, Tables of Weights, etc. Wiley. 50 % off.
19 Nipher, Electricity and Magnetism. Boland. 25 % off.
10 Fresenius, Qualitative Analysis. Wiley. 50 % off.
1 Fresenius, Quantitative Analysis. Wiley. 50 % off.
7 Gesenius, Kautsch, Hebraische Grammatik, 26th ed. Vogel. @ $1.25.
4 Gore, Geodesy. Wiley. 50 % off.
The above are new and latest editions; have also second-hand copies of some. The following at 50 % off.
30 Shakspere, Coriolanus. Oxford, shelf worn
90 Shakspere, Henry v. Oxford, shelf worn.
6 Airy, Text-book of English History, second-hand. Longmans.
18 Ames, Cases on Pleading, second-hand.
6 Keener, Selections on Contracts, second-hand.
5 Williston's Stephen on Pleading, second-hand.
24 Woodruff, Cases on Domestic Relations, second-hand.

King Bros., 3 4th St., San Francisco, Cal.
Bret Harte Poem in 14th Anniversary of the Society of Cal. Pioneers (31 p., pamphlet.) S. F., 1864. $4.00.

HELP WANTED.

WANTED.—Young man with good knowledge of the retail book and stationery business. Give references, experience, and salary expected. Address A. F. PENDLETON, 804 Broad St., Augusta, Ga.

WANTED.—A traveller who can add to his line, with his principal's permission, a $5 volume not interfering with customary lines of publication. Address G. L. B., P. O Box 943, New York.

WANTED.—In a publisher's office, a lad about 14, of public school education, with good memory and apt at figures. Address, in own handwriting, PUBLISHER, P. O. Box 943, New York.

WANTED.—An energetic, effective young man of good address, for the minor advertising and outside canvassing business of a periodical. Address PERIODICAL, care THE PUBLISHERS' WEEKLY, 298 Broadway, New York.

WANTED.—Young man with a good knowledge of the old book business, having experience in buying and selling old books. Good position to the right party. Address stating experience and last employment. References. HALL N. JACKSON, 36 W. 6th St., Cin., O.

SITUATIONS WANTED.

EMPLOYMENT wanted by artist as literary critic for periodical. Address C. K., care of PUBLISHERS' WEEKLY.

UNIVERSITY GRADUATE, 24 years old; two years' experience desk and editorial work, desires position with publishing house. Small salary expected at start. Address M., care of PUBLISHERS WEEKLY.

BOOKKEEPER, accountant and office manager. 20 years' experience, wholesale and manufacturing, desires position. Can adapt to any system or conditions. Excellent references. Salary no object so long as prospects are good. Address WILLSTAN, care of PUBLISHERS' WEEKLY.

COPYRIGHT NOTICES.

LIBRARY OF CONGRESS,
OFFICE OF THE REGISTER OF COPYRIGHTS,
WASHINGTON, D. C.

Class A, XXc, No. 40358.—To wit: *Be it remembered*, That on the 26th day of August, 1902, Marie Taylor, of New York, N. Y., hath deposited in this office the title of a book, the title of which is in the following words, to wit: "The Prophet. A Tragedy. By Bayard Taylor. Boston and New York, Houghton, Mifflin & Co., The Riverside Press, Cambridge, 1902," the right whereof she claims as proprietor in conformity with the laws of the United States respecting copyrights.
(Signed) HERBERT PUTNAM, *Librarian of Congress*.
By THORVALD SOLBERG, *Register of Copyrights*.
In renewal for 14 years from Aug. 26, 1902.

SPECIAL NOTICES.

OP'S. English, Irish Books, Posters. PRATT, N. Y.

A. S. CLARK, 174 Fulton St. N. Y., will supply any magazine at market value.

BACK NUMBERS, volumes, and sets of magazines and reviews for sale at the AMERICAN AND FOREIGN MAGAZINE DEPOT, 47 Dey St., New York.

Ready Next Week

"There is only one 'J. P. M.,' and we want to hear more from him."—*Los Angeles Herald.*

A NEW BOOK BY "J. P. M."

Time: A Spring Sunrise.
Place: "Tuskaloo."
Present: The narrator of "A Journey to Nature."

[*ENTER POLLY.*]

"I put on my hat and was about to stride aimlessly through the grass, when there—shall I say rose up, or descended, or merely developed like a figure on a film?—a thing in a tucked-up petticoat and tilted chip hat, showing Arcadian ankles in red stockings, dew-stained I swear, and carrying a little basket on her arm, as jauntily as if she had been picking airy pippins in the garden of the Hesperides.

"It was Polly."

Tangled Up in Beulah Land

THE thousands of readers who have found in the author of "A Journey to Nature" the rare touch of real genius this new story will be treasure trove. It is a sequel to that tale in so far as three of its chief characters are "Charlie," his father and the inimitable "Doctor"; but the interest is more personal, despite the fine feeling for nature; and the heroine, Polly, is as new and fresh as the morning dew.

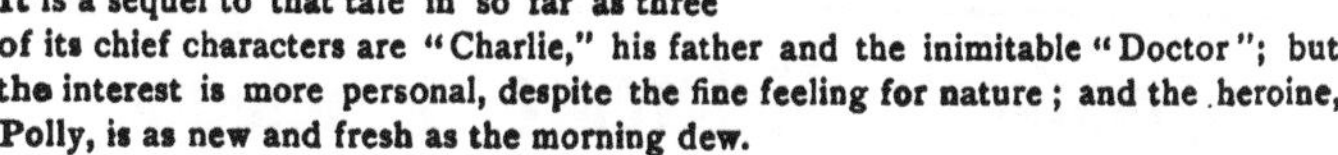

(*Uniform with "A Journey to Nature." Net,* $1.50.)

BY THE SAME AUTHOR:

A Journey to Nature.

"A charming pastoral."—*Life.*

"Very brilliant—chock full of good philosophy and happy description."—*John Burroughs.*

(*Decorated,* $1.50 *net.*)

ILLUSTRATED EDITION. With sixteen beautiful pictures reproduced photographically, by Henry Troth. $3.50 net.

The Making of a Country Home

"Comes like a fresh breath of spring . . . a sweet love story delightfully told."—*Baltimore Sun.*

"All who are home lovers . . . will enter heartily into the spirit of the book."—*Los Angeles Herald.*

(*Decorated,* $1.50 *net.*)

DOUBLEDAY, PAGE & CO., PUBLISHERS

34 Union Square, East, NEW YORK

THE UNIVERSITY OF CHICAGO

Decennial Publications

This series was planned in connection with the celebration of the completion of the first ten years of the educational work of the University of Chicago, the purpose being to set forth and exemplify the material and intellectual growth of the University during its first decade.

The following reprints from the quarto series are ready:

The Velocity of Light, by Albert A. Michelson (25 cents, *net*)

On the Text of Chaucer's Parlement of Foules, by Eleanor Prescott Hammond (50 cents, *net*)

Concerning the Geodesic Curvature and the Isoperimetric Problem on a Given Surface and Proof of the Sufficiency of Jacobi's Condition for a Permanent Sign of the Second Variation in the So-called Isoperimetric Problem, by Oskar Bolza (bound together, 25 cents, *net*)

On the Production and Suppression of Muscular Twitchings and Hypersensitiveness of the Skin by Electrolytes, by Jacques Loeb (25 cents, *net*)

The Treatment of Nature in the Works of Nikolaus Lenau, by Camillo von Klenze (75 cents, *net*)

The Physical Characters of Indians of Southern Mexico, by Frederick Starr (75 cents, *net*)

Credit, by J. Laurence Laughlin (50 cents, *net*)

Formula for Determining the Weight of the Central Nervous System of the Frog from the Weight and Length of the Entire Body, by Henry H. Donaldson (25 cents, *net*)

Concerning the Modern German Relatives, Das and Was, in Clauses Dependent upon Substantivized Adjectives, by Starr Willard Cutting (25 cents, *net*)

Of the Octavo Series there are nearly ready:

The Life and Repentaunce of Marie Magdalene, by Lewis Wager, 1767, edited with an Introduction, Notes, and Glossarial Index, by Frederic Ives Carpenter, $1.50, *net*. (Ready September 15)

The Second Bank of the United States, by Ralph H. C. Catterall. (Ready October 1.)

FOR SALE BY DEALERS OR THE PUBLISHERS

The University of Chicago Press :: Chicago, Illinois

Whitaker's Reference Catalogue.

We are now prepared to supply the "Reference Catalogue of Current English Literature," better known, perhaps, as "Whitaker's Reference List."

The work is arranged on the plan of "The Publishers' Trade List Annual," and contains recent lists of 179 of the more important English publishers. An index is prefixed to the lists containing 35,000 references to the books catalogued. It thus forms one of the most complete records of current English books accessible to the bookseller and librarian.

The work is in two volumes of about 5,000 pages, strongly bound in half leather. The price has been fixed at $5.00 *net*.

As the copies received for the American market are limited, we need hardly remind intending subscribers of the wisdom of placing your order without delay.

THE PUBLISHERS' WEEKLY,

298 BROADWAY, (P. O. BOX 943,) NEW YORK.

A Useful book to the Bookseller, Newsdealer, and Proprietor of Circulating Library.

The Profession of Bookselling:

a handbook of practical hints for the apprentice and bookseller. By A. GROWOLL, managing editor of "The Publishers' Weekly." In 3 Parts. Parts 1 and 2 now ready. Large octavo, interleaved, illustrated, bds., each, *net*, $2.00.

Part 2 contains chapters on "Insurance;" "Moving and Taking Stock;" "How to Keep a Stock of Music;" "Care and Management of Paper-Bound Stock;" "Newspapers, Magazines, and Books issued in parts;" "The Circulating Library," including list of fiction, directions for loaning, etc.; "Bookbinding," including tables of prices, etc., and 15 full-page reproductions of representative bookbindings and a bibliography.

THE PUBLISHERS' WEEKLY,

298 BROADWAY, NEW YORK.

"The Young Bookseller can learn more by a thorough perusal of this book than he could through many years of active experience."—C. N. CASPAR.

By Sydney George Fisher

The True History of the American Revolution

These are the real facts of the days of 1776. Mr. Fisher has some things to tell about the conduct of the War of the Revolution, its chief figures, and the reasons for its outcome, which will startle every reader of American history.

24 illustrations. Crown 8vo. Cloth, decorated. *Net* . $2.00

Postage, 14 c. extra.

By Clara E. Laughlin

Stories *of* Authors' Loves

Charlotte Brontë

Nothing in fiction excels the fascination of these romances of real men and women whom we all know by their writings. The volumes are a chronicle of fact, but hold all the charm of a novel. They are superbly illustrated with over 40 photogravures from rare portraits, etc.

Two Volumes. Illustrated. Handsomely bound, in box, *Net* . $3.00

Three-quarters morocco, *Net*. $6.00

Postage, 19 c. extra.

By Jack London

A Daughter of the Snows

A strong and extremely dramatic story. Its plot is unique, its characters boldly drawn, and the love interest intense. The first full length novel from a writer whose tales "The Son of the Wolf," and "The God of His Fathers," etc., have won him much popularity as well as recognition from the first critics. The book is beautifully illustrated in colors from drawings by F. C. Yohn, and is handsomely bound.

Illustrated. 12mo. Decorated cloth . . $1.50

By Cyrus Townsend Brady

Woven with the Ship

Mr. Brady's thousands of readers will derive fresh pleasure from this his new book. It has an intensely interesting plot and something happens on every page. In addition to the novel, which is the most sympathetic love story he has yet written, there are a number of tales in his best manner. The book has stunning drawings by Christy, Leyendecker, Glackens, Parkhurst, and Crawford, and has a striking design in colors.

Illustrated. 12mo. Decorated cloth . $1.50

Publishers—J. B. Lippincott Company—Philadelphia

FALL ANNOUNCEMENT NUMBER.

WITH WHICH IS INCORPORATED

The American Literary Gazette and Publishers' Circular.

[ESTABLISHED 1852.]

PUBLICATION OFFICE, 298 BROADWAY, NEW YORK.

Entered at the Post-Office at New York, N. Y., as second-class matter.

VOL. LXII., No. 13. NEW YORK, September 27, 1902. WHOLE No. 16

CHARLES SCRIBNER'S SONS' FALL PUBLICATIONS

WAYFARERS IN ITALY. By KATHARINE HOOKER. *With* 50 *full page illustrations and many decorations.* 8*vo*, (Postage 22 cents,) $3.00 *net*

A record of the impressions of a discriminating traveller who writes with a subtle appreciation of the art, poetry and scenery of Italy and with sympathetic comprehension of the spirit and genius of the Italian people.

CONTENTS—On the Lombard Plain. Sojourning in Florence. Driving through Tuscany. April in the Marches. In the Abruzzi. Monte Cassino and Ravello. The heart of Umbria. Across the Apenines. The Shore of the Adriatic. Siena and the Palio. Towered Cities. Venice. Roman Excursions.

ALL THE RUSSIAS. By HENRY NORMAN, M.P., *Author of "The Peoples and Politics of the Far East." Travels and studies in contemporary European Russia, Finland, Siberia, the Caucasus and Central Asia. With over* 100 *striking and timely illustrations.* 8*vo*, (Postage 26 cents,) $4.00 *net*

The best contemporary picture of the great Empire and its affairs which is accessible to the English reading public, and above all an entertaining study of an observer thoroughly up to-date in his knowledge of all political questions and their bearings, deeply interested in a country and race whose future he regards as superlatively important, and well able to communicate his enthusiasm. Mr. Norman is unfailingly graphic, suggestive and vivid, and whether or not the reader agrees with all the conclusions, he will find an entirely new comprehension of and interest in Russian problems dating from his reading of it.

LIBRARY OF ART. Edited by S. ARTHUR STRONG, *Librarian of the House of Lords at Westminster, and also Librarian of Chatsworth, the Mansion of the Duke of Devonshire.* (*In Press*)

Representing all schools and periods, only the greatest masters to be included as separate biographies. There will be about 38 volumes, each by the recognized authority on its particular subject. The special aim of the series is to set forth the art of all times in true proportion and perspective. Special announcements later.

NEW YORK SKETCHES. By JESSE LYNCH WILLIAMS. *With many illustrations by* R. M. MCCARTER, JULES GUERIN, EVERETT SHINN, W. L. LEIGH, *and others.* *Sq.* 8*vo*, (Postage 20 cents)

HENRY VIII. By A. F. POLLARD, M.A., F.R. HIST. SOC., *late Assistant-Editor of the "Dictionary of National Biography."*

Will be produced in style similar to "Prince Charles Edward," by Andrew Lang, and "Charles II.," by Osmund Airy, M.A., LL.D., and will be issued in two forms, as follows:

Edition de Luxe, on Japanese Paper, with facsimile frontispiece in colors, about thirty other full-page illustrations, and twelve smaller ones. Duplicate set of portraits. Limited to 250 copies. Royal Quarto, $50.00 *net*.

Fine Paper Edition, as above, excepting duplicate portraits. Limited to 1150 copies. Half Red Morocco, $25.00 *net*.

BOOKBINDERS AND THEIR CRAFT. By S. T. PRIDEAUX. *Edition limited to* 500 *numbered copies, post* 8*vo, rough edges, gilt top. Copiously illustrated from the author's and others' designs, and with a cover design by* MISS PRIDEAUX. (*In Press*)

This beautifully illustrated book is an authoritative discussion of its subject by a practical designer who, more than any other woman, has wrought in her field with originality and power.

ITALIAN CITIES. By E. H. and E. W. BLASHFIELD. *A New and Sumptuous Edition. With* 48 *full-page illustrations in tint.* *In* 2 *vols.*, $5.00 *net*

A new edition of this stimulating and authoritative work sumptuously illustrated.

LITERARY LANDMARKS OF OXFORD. By LAURENCE HUTTON. *Drawings by* HERBERT RAILTON. (*In Press*)

A worthy companion to the well-known "Literary Landmarks" volumes by Mr. Hutton.

AN INLAND VOYAGE. By ROBERT LOUIS STEVENSON. *With* 12 *full-page illustrations.* 12*mo*, $1.25

Illustrated from photographs, taken especially for the purpose by James B. Carrington, of scenes mentioned in Stevenson's text.

CHARLES SCRIBNER'S SONS' FALL PUBLICATIONS

POETRY

A NONSENSE ANTHOLOGY. Edited by CAROLYN WELLS, *Author of "The Jingle Book," etc.* *12mo*, (Postage 11 cents,) $1.25 *net*

This is the first anthology of nonsense in English, and should prove an extremely popular collection. It is preceded by an amusing and appreciative analysis of nonsense.

RALEGH IN GUIANA. By BARRETT WENDELL, *Professor in Harvard University. Author of "A Literary History of America,' etc.* *12mo*, (Postage 7 cents.) $1.50 *net*

Contains three essays in dramatic verse, made in the Elizabethan manner:—"Ralegh in Guiana," "Rosamond," and "The Christmas Masque."

PHILOSOPHY, SOCIOLOGY, ETC.

THE CITIZEN IN HIS RELATION TO THE INDUSTRIAL SITUATION. By THE RT. REV. HENRY C. POTTER, D.D., LL.D. *A new volume of the Yale Lectures on the Responsibilities of Citizenship.* *12mo*, (Postage 10 cents.) $1.00 *net*

Considers the Citizen in relation to the industrial situation, the workingman, the capitalist, the consumer, the corporation and the State.

HUMAN NATURE AND THE SOCIAL ORDER. By CHARLES HORTON COOLEY, *of the University of Michigan.* *12mo*, (Postage 13 cents,) $1.50 *net*

"The best treatment of the human nature problem we have had," says Professor Giddings.

HEGEL'S LOGIC. *An Essay in Interpretation.* By JOHN GRIER HIBBEN, PH.D., *Stuart Professor of Logic in Princeton University.* (Postage 12 cents.) $1.25 *net*

THE GREEK THINKERS, a History of Ancient Philosophy. By PROFESSOR THEODOR GOMPERZ, *of Vienna University, Hon. LL. D., Dublin, Ph. D., Konigsberg, etc. Vol. II. Plato and Aristotle—Translated by* G. G. BERRY, M.A., *Balliol College, Oxford.* 8vo, $4.00 *net*

FICTION

THE FORTUNES OF OLIVER HORN. By F. HOPKINSON SMITH, *Author of "Tom Grogan," "Caleb West," etc., with full-page illustrations by* WALTER APPLETON CLARK. *12mo*, $1.50

This should be close to the top of the "best selling" list.

CAPTAIN MACKLIN. *His Memoirs.* By RICHARD HARDING DAVIS *Author of "Soldiers of Fortune," etc., with full-page illustrations by* WALTER APPLETON CLARK. *12mo*, $1.50

The longest, most ambitious and most important of Mr. Davis's books.

RANSON'S FOLLY. By RICHARD HARDING DAVIS. 40*th* 1000. *Elaborately illustrated by five artists.* 16 *full-page illustrations.* $1.50

"The best collection of his best work."

THE BLUE FLOWER. *Stories of Search for Happiness.* By HENRY VAN DYKE, *Author of the "Ruling Passion," etc., with illustrations in color.* $1.50

After the manner of the "Ruling Passion," a volume of stories of the real holiday flavor.

THE LITTLE WHITE BIRD, or Adventures in Kensington Garden. By J. M. BARRIE, *Author of "The Little Minister," "Sentimental Tommy," etc.* *12mo*, $1.50

A tender, fanciful and poetic story told by a whimsical Charles-Lamb-like character.

JOHN GAYTHER'S GARDEN and the Stories Told Therein. By FRANK R. STOCKTON. *12mo*, $1.50

A volume of eleven new stories in Mr. Stockton's most amusing manner.

CHARLES SCRIBNER'S SONS' FALL PUBLICATIONS

DOCTOR BRYSON. *A Novel.* By FRANK H. SPEARMAN. *12mo,* $1.50
A very strong novel involving a realistic picture of Chicago life.

WHOM THE GODS DESTROYED. By JOSEPHINE DODGE DASKAM, *Author of "Fables for the Fair," "Smith College Stories,' etc.* *12mo,* $1.50
A group of dramatic stories of the artistic temperament.

THE SHADOW OF THE ROPE. By E. W. HORNUNG, *Author of "The Amateur Cracksman," "Raffles," etc.* *12mo,* $1.50
An absorbing tale of mystery with an unexpected ending.

THE WINGS OF THE DOVE. By HENRY JAMES, *Author of "The Sacred Fount," etc.* *2 vols., 12mo,* $2.50
"The most important book Henry James has put forth in recent years."—*Springfield Republican.*

OUT OF GLOUCESTER. By JAMES B. CONNOLLY. *With illustrations by* M. J. BURNS *and* FRANK BRANGWYN. *12mo,* $1.50
Stories of the sea by a new writer who knows it and the men who sail upon it.

VIVE L'EMPEREUR. By MARY RAYMOND SHIPMAN ANDREWS. *Illustrated by* F. C. YOHN. *12mo,* (*In Press*)
A bold and romantic story of fascinating interest, dealing with certain events, half fact, half rumor, in the life of Napoleon I.

THE WHITE WOLF, and Other Fireside Tales. By A. T. QUILLER-COUCH ("Q,"), *Author of "The Ship of Stars," etc.* *12mo,* $1.50
A volume of twenty-two characteristic new tales—in the author's best style.

JETHRO BACON and THE WEAKER SEX. By F. J. STIMSON (J. S., of Dale), *Author of "King Noanett," etc.* *12mo,* $1.00
Two stories, the first involving an extremely dramatic situation touched with humor, the second showing the author in a wholly new vein.

THE VALLEY OF DECISION. By EDITH WHARTON. 25*th* 1000. *In one volume.* $1.50
A new one volume edition of this distinguished novel.

THEOLOGICAL AND RELIGIOUS

THE INCARNATION OF THE LORD. By CHARLES AUGUSTUS BRIGGS, D.D., D.LITT., *of Union Theological Seminary.*
8vo, (Postage 16 cents,) $1.50 *net*

HISTORY OF THE BABYLONIANS AND ASSYRIANS. By GEORGE S. GOODSPEED, PH.D., *Professor of Ancient History and Comparative Religion in the University of Chicago. Historical Series for Bible Students.* (Postage 12 cents,) $1.25 *net*

THE MESSAGES OF ISRAEL'S LAWGIVERS. By CHARLES FOSTER KENT, PH.D., *Woolsey Professor of Biblical Literature in Yale University. Messages of the Bible.* *16mo,* (Postage 11 cents,) $1.25

THE CHRISTIAN POINT OF VIEW. *Three Addresses by Professors in Union Theological Seminary.* *12mo,* (Postage 8 cents,) 60 cents *net*
CONTENTS—"The Problem for the Church," by GEORGE WILLIAM KNOX. "Theological Reconstruction," by ARTHUR CUSHMAN MCGIFFERT. "The Religious Value of the Old Testament," by FRANCIS BROWN.

CHARLES SCRIBNER'S SONS' FALL PUBLICATIONS

THE LATER CATHOLIC CHURCH. By Rev. Robert Rainy, D.D., LL.D. *Principal of the New College, Edinburgh. International Theological Library.* (Postage 18 cents,) $2.50 *net*

International Critical Commentary.

CRITICAL AND EXEGETICAL COMMENTARY ON NUMBERS. By Rev. G. Buchanan Gray, M.A. *Lecturer in Hebrew, Mansfield College, Oxford.* (*In Press*)

THE ESSENCE OF CHRISTIANITY. *A Study in the History of Definition.* By William Adams Brown, *of Union Theological Seminary.* 8*vo*, (Postage 16 cents,) $1 50 *net*

THE GROUNDS OF THEISTIC AND CHRISTIAN BELIEF. By George P. Fisher, D.D., LL.D., *Professor of Ecclesiastical History in Yale University. A New Edition Printed from New Plates.* $2.50

THE SPIRIT IN MAN. *Sermons and Fragments that Remain.* By Horace Bushnell, D.D. 12*mo*, (Postage 12 cents,) $1.25 *net*

LIFE AND LETTERS OF HORACE BUSHNELL. Edited by Mary Bushnell Cheney. *With Portraits. A New Edition.* 8*vo*, $3.00

THE CRITICISM OF THE NEW TESTAMENT. *An Important Volume on the New Testament by Famous Authorities.* Edited by H. Hensley Henson, *of Westminster Parish, London.* (*In Press*)

The Criticism of the New Testament, by Professor W. Sanday, D.D., Canon of Christ Church, Oxford.
Manuscripts, by F. G. Kenyon, D.Litt., Ph.D., Assistant Keeper of Mss., British Museum.
The Ancient Versions of the New Testament, by F. C. Burkitt, M.A., Trinity College, Cambridge.
The History of the Canon of the New Testament, by Professor F. H. Chase, D.D., President of Queen's College, Cambridge.
The Dates of The New Testament Books, by Rev. A. C. Headlam, B.D., Rector of Welwyn.
The Historical Value of the Acts of the Apostles, by Professor J. H. Bernard, D.D.

EDUCATIONAL

HAND-BOOK OF BEST READINGS. Selected and Arranged by S. H. Clark, *Professor of Public Speaking in the University of Chicago.* 12*mo*, $1.50 *net*

ELEMENTARY PHYSICS. By Frank W. Miller and Aug. F. Foerste, *Instructors in Science in the Steele High School, Dayton, Ohio.* (*In Press*)

PLANE AND SPHERICAL TRIGONOMETRY. *A Text-Book for High Schools and Colleges.* By C. H. Ashton, *Instructor in Mathematics in Harvard University*, and W. R. Marsh, *Head Master, Pingry School.*
85 cents *net*; the same with logarithmic tables $1.20 *net*; tables, separate, 60 cents *net*.

FIRST LESSONS IN ENGLISH. By Wilbur Fiske Gordy, *Principal of North Grammar School, Hartford, Conn.*, and William Edward Mead, *Professor of the English Language in Wesleyan University. Illustrated.* (*In Press*)

A HISTORY OF ENGLISH LITERATURE. By William Vaughn Moody, *Assistant Professor of English Literature in the University of Chicago*, and Robert Morss Lovett, *Assistant Professor of English in the University of Chicago.* 12*mo, about* 480 *pages.* $1.25 *net*

CHARLES SCRIBNER'S SONS

Publishers, - 153-157 Fifth Avenue, New York

N E W I M P O R T A T I O N S

NOVA SOLYMA: The Ideal City of Zion; or, Jerusalem Regained. Translated from the Latin by the Rev. WALTER BEGLEY, and by him attributed to JOHN MILTON. *2 volumes, 8vo,* $5.00 *net*

An anonymous romance, in Prose and Verse, of 1628-1648.

TEN THOUSAND MILES IN PERSIA; or, Eight Years in Iran. By MAJOR P. M. SYKES. *With maps and many illustrations, Med. 8vo, $6.00 net*

With special reference to the Geography and History of the Country, as well as to its commercial resources, the opening up of Trade routes, and the journeys of Alexander the Great and Marco Polo.

MODERN MURAL DECORATIONS. By ALFRED L. BALDRY. *Cr. 4to, $5.00 net.*

With 70 full-page illustrations in black and white, and colors, and many others in the text. Consisting of reproductions of works by Michael Angelo, Raphael, Baudry, Burne-Jones, Lord Leighton, William Morris, etc., etc.

HISTORY OF LACE. By MRS. BURY PALLISER. *Royal 8vo, $12.00 net*

Profusely illustrated and the great authority on the subject.

PLANT FORM. By A. E. LILLEY and W. MIDGLEY. *8vo, $2.00 net*

With some suggestions for their application to design. New Edition, much enlarged. Profusely illustrated.

DECORATIVE BRUSH WORK AND ELEMENTARY DESIGN.—A Manual for the use of teachers and students in elementary, secondary and technical schools. By HENRY CADNESS, *Second Master of the Municipal School of Art, and Lecturer on Textile Design at the Municipal School of Technology, Manchester England. Cr. 8vo, $1.40 net*

With 38 plates drawn by the Author, and from Photogravures, showing 400 examples of design.

FORMAL GARDENS IN ENGLAND AND SCOTLAND—Their planning and arrangements, architectural and ornamental features. A Series of Illustrations, mainly from old example, with an Introduction and Descriptive Accounts. By H. INIGO TRIGGS. *3 parts, Folio. $25.00 net* (*Sold only in sets*).

THE CAXTON SERIES. *Illustrated reprints of famous classics. Printed in large clear type, on antique wove paper, with Photogravure Frontispiece. Each volume illustrated. Bound in limp lambskin, gilt top. Per vol. $1.25 net*

Shakespeare's Complete Works. 3 Vol. (Sold only in sets.)
Burns Poems.
Milton's Poems.
Hood's Serious Poems.
Tennyson's "In Memoriam."
Don Quixote.
The Story of Rosalind.
Herrick's Hesperides and Noble Numbers.
Bunyan's "Pilgrim's Progress" 2 vols. (Sold only in sets.)
Undine and Aslauga's Knight.
Don Quixote translated by Motteux.
Bacon's Works, comprising the Essays New Atlantis, etc.
Shelley's Poems.
A Book of Romantic Ballads.
Irving's "Sketch Book" 2 vols. (Sold only in sets.)

CHARLES SCRIBNER'S SONS' NEW IMPORTATIONS

STORY OF THE KHEDIVATE. By EDWARD DICEY, C.B., *8vo, $4.00 net*

A consecutive narrative of the events which under the Khedivate have rendered England a Paramount Power in Egypt.

THE BARBARIAN INVASION OF ITALY. By PASQUALE VILLARI. Translated by LINDA VILLARI. *With Frontispiece and Maps. 2 Vols. 8vo, $7.50 net.*

MEMOIRS OF COUNT GRAMMONT. By A. HAMILTON. With Notes by SIR WALTER SCOTT. *New and cheaper edition.* *8vo, $3.00 net*

With Portrait of the Author and 11 other etchings by L. Boisson, after original designs by C. Delort.

OLD DIARIES. By LORD RONALD GOWER. *With Plates and Illustrations. 8vo, $4.50 net.*

Selections and passages containing many entertaining reminiscences of the most distinguished men and women of the time, taken from his Diaries. 1881-1901.

SHAKESPEARE—A Study of His Life and Character. By W. CAREW HAZLITT. *8vo, $2.50 net*

THE MAKERS OF BRITISH ART—A Series of Illustrated Monographs. Edited by JAMES A. MANSON. *Sq. Cr. 8vo, $1.25 net*

Illustrated with Photogravure Portraits, half-tone and line reproductions of the best pictures.

"Sir Edward Landseer," by the Editor. *Now Ready.*
"John Constable," by the Rt. Hon. Lord Windsor.
"Sir J. E. Millais," by J. Eadie Reid.
"Sir Joshua Reynolds," by Elsa D'Esterre Keeling. *Now Ready.*
"George Romney," by Sir Herbert Maxwell.
"J. M. W. Turner," by Robert Chignell.
"Sir David Wilkie," by Prof. Bayne.
Others in preparation.

THINGS JAPANESE—Being Notes on various subjects connected with Japan, for the use of Travelers and others. By BASIL HALL CHAMBERLAIN, *Professor Imperial University at Tokyo. 4th Edition, much enlarged and revised. 12mo, $4.00 net.*

MODERN POLO. By CAPT. E. D. MILLER. Edited by CAPT. M. H. HAYES. *With numerous illustrations from photogravures and drawings. 1 Vol. Demy 8vo, $5.00 net.*

BREAKING AND RIDING—With Military Commentaries. By JAMES FILLIS, *Ecuyer en Chef to the Central Cavalry Schools at St. Petersburg. Translated by M. H. Hayes. With 70 illustrations, drawings and photographs.* *1 Vol. Med. 8vo, $5.00 net*

INTERNATIONAL STUDENT'S ATLAS OF MODERN GEOGRAPHY. By J. G. BARTHOLOMEW. *4to, $2.25 net*

105 Physical, Political and Statistical Maps, compiled from British and Foreign Surveys, and the latest results of International research.

ROSES FOR ENGLISH GARDENS. By MISS GERTRUDE JEKYLL and MR. E. MAWLEY. *12mo, $3.75 net*

Profusely illustrated, including, The Old Roses of English Gardens; New Roses for Free Pictorial Use; including Bowers, Arches, and Pergolas, Roses in Gardens Formal and Free, on Houses, Walls, etc., etc.

SCRIBNER'S NEW BOOKS *for* YOUNG PEOPLE

The Book of Joyous Children
By JAMES WHITCOMB RILEY

A Captured Santa Claus
By THOMAS NELSON PAGE

See page opposite first index page.

In the Wasp's Nest. The Story of a Sea-Waif in the War of 1812

By CYRUS TOWNSEND BRADY. Illustrated by RUFUS F. ZOGBAUM. $1.50 *net* (postage 15 cents).

An absorbing story of battle and adventure.

King Mombo

By PAUL DU CHAILLU, author of "The World of the Great Forest," etc. With 24 illustrations by VICTOR PERARD. $1.50 *net* (postage 15 cents).

A graphic account of the great explorer's perilous and exciting adventures in the African forest.

Jeb Hutton. The Story of a Georgia Boy

By JAMES B. CONNOLLY. Illustrations by M. J. BURNS. $1.20 *net* (postage 11 cents).

A tale of adventure and character-testing episodes along the Savannah River.

Sea Fighters from Drake to Farragut

By JESSIE PEABODY FROTHINGHAM. Illustrated by REUTERDAHL. $1.20 *net* (postage 11 cents).

Characteristic exploits in the careers of Drake, Tromp, De Reuter, Tourville, Suffren, Paul Jones, Nelson and Farragut.

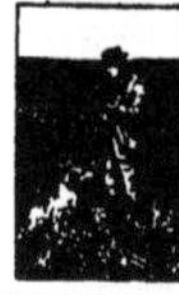

Rob and His Gun

By WILLIAM ALEXANDER LINN. With 8 illustrations. $1.00 *net* (postage 9 cents).

Detailing the adventures of a city boy with his new gun on the farm of his sportsman cousin.

This Season's HENTY BOOKS

Each fully illustrated. $1.20 *net* each (postage 16 cents).

The Treasure of the Incas. A Tale of Adventure in Peru.

With Kitchener in the Soudan. A Story of Atbara and Omdurman.

With the British Legion. A Story of the Carlist Uprising of 1836.

What a Girl can Make and Do.

New Ideas for Work and Play

By LINA BEARD and ADELIA B. BEARD, authors of "The American Girl's Handy Book." Profusely illustrated. $1.60 *net* (postage 16 cents).

A large and admirable collection of entirely new and original indoor and outdoor pastimes for American girls, fully and interestingly described.

CHARLES SCRIBNER'S SONS
153-157 FIFTH AVENUE, NEW YORK

FALL ANNOUNCEMENTS
AND
RECENT PUBLICATIONS

KNIGHT & MILLET

French Cathedrals and Chateaux

By CLARA CRAWFORD PERKINS

Illustrated with photogravure frontispieces and sixty-two half-tone engravings

2 vols. Crown octavo (size 5¾ x 8⅜ inches), ornamental cloth, gilt tops.
For the set, *net*, $4.00
THE SAME, three-quarters levant morocco......... " " " " 7.50

A work of genuine artistic value, as well as a compact and comprehensive treatment of the subject. It embodies the essential artistic and historical facts, effectively and copiously illustrated. The work is notable for its excellent arrangement, setting forth very clearly the artistic basis of the themes in outlining the architectural development of the most typical monumental structures of France, ecclesiastical and secular, describing sufficiently the most characteristic qualities and distinctive features of each, and illuminating the record with an account of the part in history borne by each particular edifice. Volume I. is devoted to the cathedrals and Volume II. to the palaces and chateaux, thus covering the two great fields, the Gothic and the Renaissance, into which French architecture naturally divides itself.

Reminiscences, Musical and Other

By FANNY REED

12mo (Size 5¼ x 7¾ inches), cloth, gilt top..................... $1.50

The author, well known in London and Paris, and long a resident abroad, has gathered into this volume her personal recollections of many distinguished musicians, artists and actors.

The Life of John Howard

By EDGAR C. S. GIBSON. With twelve half-tone illustrations. 16mo (size 4½ x 7 in.), cloth, gilt top, each, $1.00; full flexible leather, gilt edges, each, $1.75.

In College Days

Recent 'Varsity Verse. Chosen by JOSEPH LEROY HARRISON, editor of "Cap and Gown," "With Pipe and Book," etc. 16mo (size about 5 x 7 in.), cloth, gilt top, ornamental cover design, $1.25.

Studies of Trees in Winter

A description of the deciduous trees of North-eastern America. By ANNIE OAKES HUNTINGTON, with an introduction by Charles S. Sargent, professor of arboriculture in Harvard University. Illustrated with twelve colored plates by Mary S. Morse, and 66 half-tones from photographs by the author. Crown 8vo (size 6 x 8 in.), cloth, gilt top, net, $2.25.

A Wanderer

From the papers of the late H. Ogram Matuce. By C. F. KEARY, author of "The Journalist," etc. A volume of travel pictures. 16mo (size 4¼ x 6⅜ in.), cloth, gilt top, $1.00.

Memoirs and Correspondence of Madame Recamier

Translated from the French of Madame Lenormant, by ISAPHENE M. LUYSTER.

Madame Recamier and Her Friends

Translated from the French of Madame Lenormant, by ISAPHENE M. LUYSTER. New illustrated edition, with twenty-four half-tones, printed in tint. Two volumes. Crown 8vo (size 5⅜ x 8 in.), ornamental cloth binding, for the set, $3.00; three-quarters levant binding, for the set, $7.50.

KNIGHT & MILLET, 221 Columbus Avenue, Boston, Mass.

CONTINUED ON NEXT PAGE

CONTINUED ON NEXT PAGE

CONTINUED ON NEXT PAGE

Dodd, Mead & Co.'s Fall Books

HAMILTON WRIGHT MABIE

WORKS. Library Edition. In 11 volumes. Each volume with frontispiece and photogravure on Japan paper. Printed on Mittineague paper, and in paper, type and binding a thoroughly handsome and standard edition. Each, 1 vol., 12mo, *special net*, ... $2.00
Set, 11 volumes, *special net*, ... $22.00

MY STUDY FIRE

UNDER THE TREES AND ELSEWHERE

SHORT STUDIES IN LITERATURE

ESSAYS IN LITERARY INTERPRETATION

MY STUDY FIRE. Second Series

ESSAYS ON NATURE AND CULTURE

ESSAYS ON BOOKS AND CULTURE

ESSAYS ON WORK AND CULTURE

THE LIFE OF THE SPIRIT

NORSE STORIES

WORKS AND DAYS

HAMILTON WRIGHT MABIE

PARABLES OF LIFE. By Hamilton Wright Mabie, author of "My Study Fire," "Under the Trees and Elsewhere," "Essays on Books and Culture," etc. 8vo, cloth, *net*, ... $1.00

M. A. DEWOLFE HOWE

AMERICAN BOOKMEN. By M. A. DeWolfe Howe. (New Edition.) With over 60 illustrations. 8vo, cloth, *net* $1.75

EDWIN EMERSON, JR.

A HISTORY OF THE NINETEENTH CENTURY YEAR BY YEAR. By Edwin Emerson, Jr. With an introduction by Georg Gottfried Gervinus. Illustrated with 16 colored plates and 32 full-page half-tone cuts and 2 maps. In 3 vols. 12mo, cloth, *net*, ... $3.60

ALFREDO UNTERSTEINER

A SHORT HISTORY OF MUSIC. Translated by Miss C. S. Very. 12mo, cloth, illustrated, *net*, ... $1.20

GILBERT CHESTERTON

THE DEFENDANT. By Gilbert Chesterton. 12mo, cloth, *net*, . . . $1.25

CONTINUED ON NEXT PAGE

NEW NOVEL.
By MARIE CORELLI.
"TEMPORAL POWER"
A STUDY IN SUPREMACY
DODD, MEAD & CO.
Publishers, New York.

A. C. McClurg & Co.'s Fall Books

THE CONQUEST.

Being the true story of Lewis and Clark. The marvelous tale of the most romantic event in American history. By Eva Emery Dye. With frontispiece. 12mo, $1.50.

ON FORTUNE'S ROAD.

Six capital short stories of business life in which realism, excitement, and romance are cleverly blended. By Will Payne. Illustrated by Thomas Fogarty. 12mo, $1.50.

THE HOLLAND WOLVES.

An absorbing story dealing with the Spanish invasion of the Netherlands. By J. Breckenridge Ellis. With six illustrations by the Kinneys. 12mo, $1.50.

THE BRIDGE OF THE GODS.

A romance of Indian Oregon two centuries ago. By F. H. Balch. New (*seventh*) edition. With eight striking illustrations by L. Maynard Dixon. 12mo, $1.50.

A CAPTIVE OF THE ROMAN EAGLES.

A powerful romantic novel of the conflicts between Germany and Rome. Translated from the German of Felix Dahn by Mary J. Safford. 12mo, $1.50.

THE EXPEDITION OF LEWIS AND CLARK.

A reprint of the edition of 1814. With introduction and notes by James K. Hosmer. With maps and photogravure portraits. Two square 8vo volumes, $5.00 net.

BIRDS OF THE ROCKIES.

A most entertaining account of Colorado birds. By Leander S. Keyser, author of "In Bird Land." With many illustrations in color and black-and-white by Louis Agassiz Fuertes and Bruce Horsfall. Square 8vo, $3.00 net.

MEMORIES.

A story of German love. By Max Muller. Holiday edition (forty-fifth thousand) from new plates. With illustrations and decorations by Blanche Ostertag. Square 8vo, $2.00 net.

IN ARGOLIS.

An account of a summer in Greece. By George Horton. A sumptuous gift book, illustrated from photographs and printed at the Merrymount Press. Square 8vo, $1.75 net.

A. C. McClurg & Co., *Publishers, Chicago*

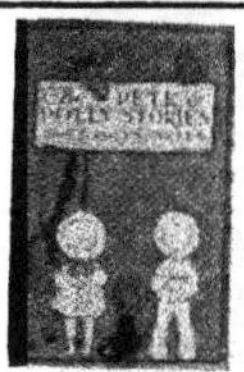

A. C. McClurg & Co.'s Fall Books

THE PETE AND POLLY STORIES.

A book of nonsense prose and verse. By Carolyn Wells. Illustrated by Fanny Young Cory. Large 8vo, $1.50 net.

PRINCE SILVER WINGS.

Seven fairy stories. By Edith Ogden Harrison (Mrs. Carter H. Harrison). Illustrated in color by Lucy F Perkins. 4to, $1.75 net.

LITTLE MISTRESS GOOD HOPE.

And other fairy tales. By Mary Imlay Taylor. Illustrated in color by Jessie Wilcox Smith. Square 12mo, $1.50 net.

COQUO AND THE KING'S CHILDREN.

A fairy tale. By Cornelia Baker. Illustrated in color by Lucy F. Perkins. Small 4to, $1.50 net.

MAYKEN.

A historical story of Holland for children. By Jessie Anderson Chase. Illustrated by the Kinneys. Uniform with "Margot." Small 4to, $1.20 net.

MUSICAL PASTELS.

Essays on quaint and curious musical subjects. By George P. Upton. Illustrated from rare wood engravings. Square 8vo, $2.00 net.

THE STANDARD LIGHT OPERAS.

Their plots and their music. A Handbook. By George P. Upton. 16mo, $1.20 net.

SOCIALISM AND LABOR,

And Other Arguments. A book of essays along the lines indicated by the title. By Rt. Rev. J. L. Spalding, Bishop of Peoria. 16mo, 80 cents net.

VARIOUS VIEWS.

Essays on literature and education. By William Morton Payne. Uniform with the same author's "Little Leaders" and "Editorial Echoes." 18mo, $1.00 net.

CATCH WORDS OF CHEER.

Helpful thoughts for each day in the year. A Compilation. By Sara A. Hubbard. 18mo, 80 cents net.

A. C. McClurg & Co. Publishers, Chicago

THE
WHIRLWIND

By RUPERT HUGHES Price, $1.50

This is a story of a striking personality from his humble, country childhood through a brilliant political and war record, up to a Presidential candidacy,—all of it graphic, typical, and of compelling interest.

JUDITH'S GARDEN

By MARY E. STONE BASSETT Price, $1.50

Illustrations in Four Colors by GEORGE WRIGHT

BROOKLYN DAILY EAGLE SAYS:

"It is a beautiful, idyllic story, this romance of 'Judith's Garden,' fascinating to one who finds Mother Nature the most satisfying of friends."

CHANTICLEER

By VIOLETTE HALL Price, $1.50

Eight Three-color Illustrations
Three by W. GRANVILLE SMITH

This is an idyl of modern life in which a love story of charming sweetness develops. A book that will appeal to all lovers of nature.

MR. WHITMAN

By ELISABETH PULLEN. Price, $1.50

A brilliant romance of comedy and adventure.

CLEVELAND DAILY WORLD SAYS:

"Altogether the story is bright, engaging, novel, and delightful."

MARGARET BOWLBY

By EDGAR L. VINCENT Price, $1.50

BOSTON TRANSCRIPT SAYS:

"A 'political' novel and a strenuous one,—one, withal, that appears to be well worth the while both of the author and of the reader."

RICHARD GORDON

By ALEXANDER BLACK

Six Illustrations by ERNEST FUHR Price, $1.50

This is one of the strongest novels of the day. The scenes are laid in upper New York society, with a dash into Bohemia that is refreshing and vivid.

STAGE CONFIDENCES

By CLARA MORRIS Sixteen Illustrations
Price, net, $1.20; postpaid, $1.25

In this fascinating book Miss Morris talks with humor, point, and charm of the mysterious, alluring, exacting life behind the foot-lights.

THE GATE OF THE KISS

By JOHN W. HARDING. Illustrated. Price, $1.50

BOSTON JOURNAL SAYS:

"It can readily be seen that this is no mere conventional romance of Bible times, but a story of notable strength and boldness."

JEZEBEL

By LAFAYETTE McLAWS, Author of "WHEN THE LAND WAS YOUNG." Four Illustrations by CORWIN K. LINSON Price, $1.50

DETROIT FREE PRESS SAYS:

"'Jezebel' may be named as a vivid and picturesque story. A very real and human character is the proud and strong-willed heroine."

'TWEEN YOU AND I

By MAX O'RELL. $1.20 net; postpaid, $1.35

ST. LOUIS GLOBE-DEMOCRAT SAYS:

"The volume throughout sparkles with bright comment and pertinent anecdote, and is delightful reading."

THE NEW HAMLET

BY

WM. HAWLEY SMITH and THE SMITH FAMILY, FARMERS

"Bound in Boards" *Retail, 50 Cents*

THIS PLAY WAS COMPOSED BY SHAKESPEARE AND THE SMITH FAMILY. THEN IT WAS DONE INTO A BOOK AND BOUND IN BOARDS. (No. 2, FENCING.) BY HAND, AT THE BARN, ON THE FARM, BY FARMERS. - - - - - -

THE most unique, original, up-to date and out-of-the-ordinary book of the season. This new version of Shakespeare is a very clever satire on the two plays "Hamlet" and "Romeo and Juliet." Nobody gets killed, or even hurt, Hamlet marries Juliet, Romeo is wedded to Ophelia, and they all live long and prosper. The make-up of the book is in keeping with its contents. It is printed on manila paper, and is literally "bound in boards," the covers being No. 2 fencing, the whole tied together with binding twine.

JUVENILE BOOKS

The Squirrel and the Crow

By W. W. NEIDLINGER and WALTER BOBBETT, authors of "The Owl and the Woodchuck," etc. Illustrated. Boards, cloth back. Retail, 50 cents.

Puggery Wee

By W. A. FRISBIE and BART, authors of "The Pirate Frog," "The Bandit Mouse," etc. Illustrated. Boards, cloth back. Retail, $1.00.

The Owl and the Woodchuck

By WILLIAM HAROLD NEIDLINGER and WALTER BOBBETT. Illustrated. Boards, cloth back, size 8¼ x 9¾ inches. Retail, 50 cents.

The Pirate Frog and Other Tales

By W. A. FRISBIE and BART. Illustrated. Boards, cloth back, size 9 x 11½ inches. Retail, $1.00.

The Nidding Nod of Once-Upon-a-Time

By H. ESCOTT-INMAN. Illustrated. Cloth, 12mo. Retail, $1.00.

Illustrated Catalogue of Our Publications Sent on Application

RAND, McNALLY & COMPANY, Publishers, Chicago and New York

READY NOVEMBER 1

ESHEK—THE OPPRESSOR

By GERTRUDE POTTER DANIELS

Author of "The Warners," "Halamar," etc.

Cloth, 12mo. ***Retail, $1.50***

But few authors possess the faculty of writing a novel wherein the characters are realistic—clothed in everyday habiliments, saying and doing things that are natural for them to say and do. In her latest work Mrs. Daniels has demonstrated the fact that she is a past-master in the art of creating a human story, one teeming with alluring scenes and incidents and characters of absorbing interest that hold the reader spell-bound during perusal.

"Eshek—The Oppressor" is a strong story. The style is simple and direct, the language forcible, and the plot one that is well conceived and carried to a logical conclusion The struggle for an existence, the temptation, fall and subsequent career of Jarvis Kennedy, the virile pen-pictures of city life, with its varying lights and shades, the oil excitement in Texas, the evil of trusts, the labor question, romance and tragedy—these form the basis of one of the most thrilling stories written in recent years.

READY NOVEMBER 1

FATHER TOM OF CONNEMARA

By ELIZABETH O'REILLY NEVILLE

Illustrated. ***Cloth, 12mo.*** ***Retail, $1.50***

Rarely has Irish life been depicted with such strength and truthfulness as is done in "Father Tom of Connemara." The author, being a native of that part of the Emerald Isle so forcefully described, brings into her stories all those elements of realism and of local color that stamp them as genuine, and without which no tale can be successfully told.

These stories are not fiction. They are founded on fact, and many of the characters are still performing their parts in the drama of life. Into these sketches are wrought, with infinite skill, various phases of the Irish people—wit, humor, pathos and tragedy, and all set forth with such consummate art as to cause the reader to take the characters to his heart and treat them as personal friends.

Father Tom, himself, is a typical Irish priest, full of quaint humor and keen wit, and with a heart large enough to encompass all the trials and tribulations of the members of his extensive parish. To him the people took their woes and their joys; he officiated at their wakes, their christenings and their weddings, participated in all their celebrations, settled all disputes, and wound himself about their heart-strings, shedding his beneficence upon all who sought his aid.

RAND, McNALLY & COMPANY, Publishers, Chicago and New York

LEE & SHEPARD'S NEW BOOKS

Two Beautiful Volumes of Poems.

Sunset Song and Other Verses

By ELIZABETH AKERS, author of "Rock Me to Sleep." *Autograph Edition.* Illuminated title-page. Cover design, pen and ink head-band and tail-piece by Grace Barton Allen. Fine laid paper, deckel-edge, gilt top, cloth with gold, $1.20 *net* (postage, 13 cents.)

EDITION DE LUXE. Ooze leather, Roycroft style, boxed, $3.00 *net* (postage, 15 cents.)

One of the finest literary treasures of the year, and a beautiful gift.

Chips, Fragments and Vestiges

By "GAIL HAMILTON." Collected and arranged by H. Augusta Dodge, editor of "Gail Hamilton's Life in Letters." Illustrated from photographs. Fine laid paper, deckel edge, gilt top, $1.20 *net* (postage, 12 cents.)

Of great interest to every admirer of this brilliant and famous writer.

A New England Novel of Uncommon Excellence.

Concerning Polly and Some Others

By HELEN M. WINSLOW, editor of "The Club Woman." Author of "Concerning Cats," etc. Illustrated by Charles Copeland. 12mo, cloth, $1.50.

The character-drawing ability of Mary E. Wilkins, the descriptive grace of Sarah Orne Jewett, and the rich humor and strong common sense of "Josiah Allen's Wife," are combined in this splendid story.

FOURTEEN FINE BOOKS FOR BOYS AND GIRLS

The Largest Number of Equally Worthy and Well-Made Books for Young Readers ever Published at One Time by Any One House.

MARCHING ON NIAGARA

Or, The Soldier Boy of the Old Frontier.

Second volume of the "Colonial Series." By EDWARD STRATEMEYER. Illustrated by A. Burnham Shute. 12mo, cloth, 300 pages, $1.00 *net* (postage, 13 cents.)

CRUISING ON THE ST. LAWRENCE

Or, A Summer Vacation in Historic Waters.

Third volume of the "St. Lawrence Series." By E. T. TOMLINSON. Illustrated by A. Burnham Shute. 12mo, cloth, $1.20 *net* (postage, 15 cents.)

TOM WINSTONE "WIDE AWAKE"

By "MARTHA JAMES," author of "My Friend Jim." Illustrated by W. Herbert Dunton. Large 12mo, cloth, 80 cents *net* (postage, 12 cents.)

A BOY OF A THOUSAND YEARS AGO

By HARRIET T. COMSTOCK. Profusely illustrated with full-page drawings and chapter headings by George Varian. Large 12mo, cloth, 80 cents *net* (postage, 12 cents.)

IN THE DAYS OF QUEEN ELIZABETH

Third volume of "The Makers of England" Series. By EVA MARCH TAPPAN, Ph.D. Illustrated from famous paintings. 12mo, cloth, 80 cents *net* (postage, 12 cents.)

BOY DONALD AND HIS HERO

Third volume of the "Boy Donald Series." By PENN SHIRLEY." Illustrated by Bertha G. Davidson. 16mo, cloth, 60 cents *net* (postage, 8 cents.)

A GIRL OF THIS CENTURY

By MARY G. DARLING. Illustrated by Lilian Crawford True. Cloth, $1.00 *net* (postage, 12 cents.)

BRAVE HEART ELIZABETH

A Story of the Ohio Frontier.

Second volume of the "Brave Heart Series." By ADELE E. THOMPSON. Illustrated by Lilian Crawford True. 12mo, cloth, $1.00 *net* (postage, 12 cents.)

THE STORY OF JOAN OF ARC

For Boys and Girls—Told by Aunt Kate.

By KATE E. CARPENTER. Illustrated by Amy Brooks, also from paintings, and with map. Large 12mo, cloth, 80 cents *net* (postage, 10 cents.)

RANDY AND HER FRIENDS

Third volume of the "Randy Books." By AMY BROOKS. Finely illustrated by the author. 12mo, cloth, 80 cents *net* (postage, 12 cents.)

DOROTHY DAINTY

First volume of the "Dorothy Dainty Series." By AMY BROOKS. Finely illustrated by the author. Large 12mo, cloth, 80 cents *net* (postage, 10 cents.)

MADGE

A Girl in Earnest.

By S. JENNIE SMITH. Illustrated by James E. McBurney. 12mo, cloth, $1.00 *net* (postage, 12 cents.)

THE LITTLE GIRL NEXT DOOR

By NINA RHOADES, author of "Only Dollie." Illustrated by Bertha G. Davidson. Large 12mo, cloth, 80 cents *net* (postage, 10 cents.)

HORTENSE, A DIFFICULT CHILD

By EDNA A. FOSTER, editor Children's Page *Youth's Companion.* Illustrated by Mary Ayer. 12mo, cloth, 80 cents *net* (postage, 10 cents.)

Ask any Bookseller or Jobber for Them.

LEE & SHEPARD, Publishers, BOSTON

Fleming H. Revell Company

Representative Fall Issues

Faith and Character. By Newell Dwight Hillis, D.D.

UNIFORM WITH "A MAN'S VALUE TO SOCIETY" AND "THE INVESTMENT OF INFLUENCE." 12MO, CLOTH, 75 CENTS NET.

The simple announcement of studies in character building by Dr. Hillis argues one of his best efforts, for his chosen line of study is distinctly in the direction of the development of character.

A First Century Message to Twentieth Century Christians. By G. Campbell Morgan. 12MO, CLOTH, $1.00 NET.

It is only necessary to name this author to say that the addresses are at once profound, scholarly, and immediately applied to our life of to-day. They will stir up the Church as well as inspire the individual.

The Religion of a Mature Mind. By Professor George A. Coe.

STUDIES IN MODERN PROBLEMS BY AUTHOR OF "THE SPIRITUAL LIFE." CLO., GILT TOP, $1.50 NET.

Some of the contents are: Modern Manhood; Authority in Religion; The Right to be Called a Child of God; The Breadth of Religious Experience; Are Conversions Going Out of Date; The Life of Prayer; The Consciousness of Sin; The Christ of Personal Experience, etc.

The Evolution of a Girl's Ideal. By Clara E. Laughlin.

A LITTLE RECORD OF THE RIPENING OF THE AFFECTIONS TO THE TIME OF LOVE'S COMING. 16MO, DECORATED BOARDS, 50 CENTS NET.

This delightful essay cannot but charm the reader, the more especially if that reader be of womankind To the young woman it will be a tonic in these days of hers contemporary with Miss Laughlin's picture. To the older reader there will come a sweet flood of sweet reminiscence and tender memories.

This Is for You. Edited by William Sinclair Lord.

LOVE POEMS OF THE SANER SORT. 12MO, VELLUM, BOARDS, $1.00 NET.

An exquisite gift book for everyone. The verse selected is of sweetest sentiment and highest literary value. In its makeup it is as dainty and inviting as such a gift book should be.

Missionary Principles and Practice. By Robert E. Speer.

A DISCUSSION OF CHRISTIAN MISSIONS AND SOME CRITICISMS UPON THEM. 8VO, CLOTH, $1.50 NET.

No living man is more competent for this than Mr. Speer. He may be said to have created a science of missions. He has here explained the general principles and applied them illustratively; he has shown both the need and the results of the work, and he has pressed the duty and privilege of a serious and systematic evangelization of the world.

A Maker of the New Orient.

SAMUEL ROBBINS BROWN, PIONEER EDUCATOR IN CHINA, AMERICA AND JAPAN. THE STORY OF HIS LIFE AND WORK. ILLUSTRATED. 12MO, CLOTH, $1.25 NET.

Dr. Griffis' latest work records the life of a man only too little known by the rising generation. As *The Interior* said of his previous work, "Verbeck of Japan," "We owe Dr. Griffis, too, who spent years in Japan as a teacher in the Imperial University, a debt of gratitude for the able and sympathetic way in which he has treated his theme."

The Gift of the Magic Staff. By Fannie E. Ostrander.

12MO, FULLY ILLUSTRATED. $1.00 NET.

The demand for a high order of books for children is meeting response from many sources, yet it is doubtful if a more ideal combination has been made or can be made than this blending of the healthfully fanciful, fascinating fairy element with the helpful teaching of elementary morals.

Rollicking Rhymes for Youngsters. By Amos R. Wells.

ILLUSTRATED BY L. J. BRIDGMAN. 12MO, CLOTH, $1.00 NET.

Mr. Wells is well known already as a versatile author. Now he comes to the front as a brilliant verse maker for young folk. Mr. Bridgman has already won fame as the illustrator of "Guess."

My Dogs in the Northland. By Egerton R. Young.

PROFUSELY ILLUSTRATED. 8VO, CLOTH, $1.25 NET.

Experiences with Eskimo and St. Bernard dogs, covering years of sledge travel in the frozen wilds of British America. An exciting story in which the marvels of dog instinct, intelligence and strength play the chief part.

NEW YORK: 158 Fifth Avenue | **CHICAGO:** 63 Washington Street | **TORONTO:** 27 Richmond Street, W.

NEW PUBLICATIONS OF

GOUPIL & CO., of Paris

Goupil's Paris "Salons," 1902

A review of the most remarkable Paintings and Sculptures exhibited by the "Société des Artistes Français" and the "Société Nationale des Beaux-Arts." Text by Maurice Hamel. English translation by Paul Villars. This year's edition has been considerably embellished and is now only issued in a strictly limited edition with French or English Text, which cannot fail to enhance its value to all Bibliophiles and Art Collectors as well as to regular subscribers.

The illustrations consist of ONE HUNDRED FULL-PAGE PLATES and include:

Two Hand-Finished Water-Color Facsimiles, viz.:

"**THE CHILDREN'S DANCE.**" By J. A. Muenier. An exquisite out-door picture, full of life, color and atmosphere.

"**AN ENGLISH DRUMMER BOY** (1798.)" By G. W. Joy. A most striking military subject.

Three Remarque Artist Proof Etchings, viz.:

"**AN ALDER TREE.**" By H. Harpignies, the greatest living French Landscapist. Etched by G. Garen, a medallist in this year's Salon. The Remarque is a portrait of M. Harpignies, who is now in his 84th year.

"**Tizianella.**" By Mlle. Juana Romani, a pupil of Roybet, etched by R. Spinelli. The Remarque is a portrait of Mlle. Romani.

"**LOBSTER FISHERS.**" By Le Gout-Gérard, a rising marine painter. Etched by Garen. The remarque is the head of a typical old fisherman.

Also an Original Etching by J. Patricot, the celebrated engraver:

"**PORTRAIT OF M. GEORGE PERROT, MEMBER OF THE INSTITUTE OF FRANCE.**"

All the above make handsome framed pictures, and as such are worth more than the price of the entire book.

Intending subscribers should secure their copies at once, as both of this year's very limited De Luxe Editions will soon be out of print.

PRICES

French Text Edition, limited to 500 numbered and registered copies (of which only 100 are reserved for America), printed on Dutch hand-made paper and bound in red silk cloth with "Palette" design in gold and colors.......... $25 00

The Same, in three-quarter morocco binding.......... 30 00

English Text Edition, limited to 200 copies, printed on Dutch hand-made paper and bound in red silk cloth with "Palette" design in gold and colors.......... 30 00

The Same, in three-quarter morocco.......... 35 00

TO BE READY IN NOVEMBER

LOUIS XV ET MADAME DE POMPADOUR

By PIERRE DE NOLHAC (*French Text*)

Same size and style as "La Reine Marie Antoinette," "La Dauphine Marie Antoinette" and "Louis XV et Marie Leczinska," by the same author, in "Goupil's French Historical Series."

The illustrations will consist of fifty photogravures, including forty full-page plates (of which three are double pages), eight head and tail pieces and two hand finished water-color facsimiles.

The entire edition is limited to

One hundred copies on Imperial Japanese paper, numbered I to C, with an extra set of all the illustrations in various tints on Japan.

Price per Copy, in Paper Binding.......... $62 50
In Full Polished Levant Morocco Binding.......... 87 50

(*The above edition is all subscribed.*)

Eight hundred copies, numbered 1 to 800 on Rives hand-made paper, specially manufactured for this work.

Price per Copy, in Paper Binding.......... $25 00
In Full Blue French Morocco Binding.......... 37 50
In Full Polished Blue Levant Morocco Binding.......... 50 00

The binding for these editions is a reproduction of the most magnificent design that was executed by Padeloup for Louis XV, and will be ornamented on the inside with the "ex libris" of Mme. de Pompadour, drawn by Cochin.

N.B.—As a very few copies only of this magnificent work are unsubscribed, orders should be booked immediately, and preference will be given to our regular subscribers for the preceding volumes in the same series.

MANZI, JOYANT & CO., 170 Fifth Avenue, New York City.

THE FALL ANNOUNCEMENT NUMBER.

Table of Contents.

INDEX TO ADVERTISERS.

WEEKLY RECORD OF NEW PUBLICATIONS.

☞ Beginning with the issue of July 5, 1902, the titles of *net* books published under the rules of the American Publishers' Association are preceded by a double asterisk **, and the word net follows the price. The titles of *fiction* (not net) published under the rules are preceded by a dagger †. *Net* books not covered by the rules, whether published by members of the American Publishers' Association or not, are preceded by a single asterisk, and the word net follows the price. ☜

The abbreviations are usually self-explanatory. c. after the date indicates that the book is copyrighted; if the copyright date differs from the imprint date, the year of copyright is added. Books of foreign origin of which the edition (annotated, illustrated, etc. is entered as copyright, are marked c. ed.; translations, c. tr.; n. p., in place of price, indicates that the publisher makes no price, either net or retail, and quotes prices to the trade only upon application.

A colon after initial designates the most usual given name, as: A: Augustus; B: Benjamin; C: Charles; D: David; E: Edward; F: Frederic; G: George; H: Henry; I: Isaac; J: John; L: Louis; N: Nicholas; P: Peter; R: Richard; S: Samuel; T: Thomas; W: William.

Sizes are designated as follows: F. (folio: over 30 centimeters high); Q. (4to: under 30 cm.); O. (8vo: 25 cm.); D. (12mo: 20 cm.); S. (16mo: 17½ cm.); T. (24mo: 15 cm.); Tt. (32mo: 12½ cm.); Fe. 48mo: 10 cm.). Sq., obl., nar., designate square, oblong, narrow books of these heights.

Ball, Timothy Horton. Francis Ball's descendants; or, the West Springfield Ball family, from 1640 to 1902. Crown Point, Ind., T. H. Ball, 1902. c. 81 p. pl. por. map, 12°, cl., $1.50.

Ballou, Clara E. Played on hearts: [a novel.] N. Y., J. S. Ogilvie Pub. Co., 1902. c. 235 p. 12°, cl., $1; pap., 50 c.

Bingham, Guillermo Marcial, *comp.* Bingham's numerical system commercial cable and telegraph code of 1,660,000 words. San Francisco, Cal., G. M. Bingham, 1902. [Ag7.] c. 1901. 36+536 p. F. hf. leath., $25.

A most elaborate combination of figures to be used with the cable or telegraph in the commercial and financial world. It is the result of over twenty-five years' experience in the use and compilation of codes for all branches of business.

Bronson, Walter H. How to play ping-pong; with diagrams and laws and hints on how to conduct tournaments, clubs, etc. N. Y., Street & Smith, [1902.] c. 52 p. il. 18°, cl., 15 c.

****Brown**, Glenn, *ed.* European and Japanese gardens; papers read before the American Institute of Architects; ed. for the American Institute of Architects by Glenn Brown, secretary. Phil., H: T. Coates & Co., 1902. c. 2+162 p. il. sq. 8°, cl., $2 net.

Contents: The Italian formal garden, by A. D. F. Hamlin; English gardens, by R. C. Sturgis; French gardening and its masters, by J. G. Howard; Japanese gardens, by K. Honda; Notes on a Japanese garden in California, by C. H. Townsend.

Burton, F: R. Her wedding interlude: [a novel.] N. Y., Street & Smith, [1902.] c. 4+7-239 p. 12°, cl., $1.

Catholic home annual, 1903. 20th year. N. Y., Benziger Bros., 1902. c. 80 p. il. sq. O. pap., 25 c.

Chaney, Ja. M. Mae and Mary, the young scientists; or, science for young people. Kansas City, Mo., J. M. Chaney, jr., 1902. c. 173 p. diagr., 16°, cl., 60 c.

Chapman, J. Wilbur, *D.D.* The man who said he would. Bost. and Chic., United Society of Christian Endeavor, [1902.] c. 7+9-87 p. 16°, cl., 35 c.

****Compayré**, Jules Gabriel. Development of the child in later infancy: being pt. 2 of The intellectual and moral development of the child; tr. from the French by Mary E. Wilson. N. Y., Appleton, 1902. c. 31+300 p. 12°, (International education ser., v. 53.) cl., $1.20 net.

Conwell, Russell Herman. Present successful opportunities: an original presentation from the standpoint of to-day of the master-motives and methods that determine success in life, in connection with the author's great lecture, "Acres of diamonds." Phil., The Temple Press, [1902.] c. 492 p. pors. il. 8°, subs., $2; hf. mor., $2.75; full mor., $4.

***Cutting**, Starr Willard. Concerning the modern German relatives, "das" and "was," in clauses dependent upon substantivized adjectives. Chic., University of Chicago Press, 1902. c. 2+113 p. O. (University of Chicago Decennial publications; reprinted from v. 7.) pap., 25 c. net.

****Ellis**, E: Sylvester. Jim and Joe, two brave boys Phil., H: T. Coates & Co., 1902. c. 4+450 p. il. 12°, (True grit ser.) cl., 80 c. net.

Emerson, W: Ralph. The architecture and furniture of the Spanish colonies during the seventeenth and eighteenth centuries, including Mexico, Cuba, Porto Rico and the Philippines. Bost., G. H. Polley & Co., [1902.] c. 3+70 p. pl. 13½ x 18 in., portfolio, $30.

Evans, H: Ridgely. The spirit world unmasked; illustrated investigations into the phenomena of spiritualism and theosophy. Chic., Laird & Lee, [1902.] c. '97. 302 p. il. por. facsimile, D. cl.; 75 c.

Formerly entitled "Hours with the ghosts."

Fire insurance laws, taxes and fees; cont. a digest of the statutory requirements in the U. S. and Canada relating to fire insurance companies and agents, with many quotations from the statutes; also, a compilation of county and municipal taxes and fees; rev. to July 15, 1902. N. Y., The Spectator Co., 1902. c. 352 p. O. shp., $5.

Forbes, Arthur Holland. Architectural gardens of Italy: a series of photogravure plates from photographs made and selected by A. Holland Forbes. N. Y., Forbes & Co., Ltd., 1902. c. f°, $50.

Foster, Horatio A. Electrical engineer's pocket-book: a handbook of useful data for electricians and electrical engineers; by Horatio A. Foster; with the collaboration of eminent specialists. 2d ed., corr. N. Y., D. Van Nostrand Co., 1902. c. 5+987 p. il. diagr., 12°, cl., $5.

Goethe, Johann Wolfgang v. The sorrows of young Werther; Elective affinities; tr. by R. D. Boylan; ed. by Nathan Haskell Dole. Ed. de luxe. Bost., F. A. Niccolls

& Co., [1902.] c. 5+515 p. pl. 8°, cl. (Apply to pubs. for price.)

Gould, A. C., *comp.* American rifleman's encyclopedia: being a collection of words and terms used by riflemen of the United States, with definitions and explanations and general suggestions for rifle shooting. Cin., Peters Cartridge Co., [1902.] c. 137 p. il. T. pap., 10 c.

***Grayson,** C: Prevost. Diseases of the nose, throat and ear; illustrated with 129 engravings and 8 plates in colors and monochrome. Phil., Lea Brothers & Co., 1902. c. 7+17-540 p. 8°, cl., $3.50 net.

Green, Evelyn Everett. Alwyn Ravendale. N. Y., Amer. Tract Soc., [1902.] 6+375 p. il. D. cl., $1.25.
A good story for boys; pictures the full development of a noble character under exceptional conditions.

Hadley, H: Harrison. The blue badge of courage. Akron, O., The Saalfield Publishing Co., 1902. c. 468 p. por. D. cl., $1.25.
A life of "Col." Hadley (written by himself), whose work in the cause of temperance has made him well known in New York and other cities. He is General of the Blue Button Army, and Director of the National Christian Abstainers' Union.

Heston, Alfred Miller. Heston's handbook, 1902: being an account of the settlement of Eyre Haven, and a succinct history of Atlantic City and county during the 17th, 18th and 19th centuries. [Twentieth century souvenir ed.] Atlantic City, N. J., Alfred Miller Heston, 1902. c. 130 p. il. por. fold. map, D. bds., 25 c.

King, C: The iron brigade: a story of the Army of the Potomac; il. by R. F. Zogbaum. N. Y., G: W. Dillingham Co., [1902.] c. 3+9-379 p. D. cl., $1.50.

Lansing, *Mrs.* Jennie H. Stickney. Earth and sky, number 2. Bost., Ginn, 1902. c. 8+118 p. il. 12°, (Study and story nature readers.) cl., 30 c.

McGregory, Jos. Frank. Lecture notes on general chemistry. Hamilton, N. Y., Republican Press, 1902. c. 2+374 p. 12°, cl., $1.50.

****Malot,** Hector Henri. Sans famille; abridged, with introd., notes, and vocabulary, by Hugo Paul Thieme. N. Y., H: Holt & Co., 1902. c. 9+219 p. S. cl., 40 c. net.

Maryland. The public school law, as contained in the Md. code, public general laws, ed. of 1888, and subsequent amendments to Jan. session, 1902. Balt., W: J. C. Dulany Co., 1902. c. 54 p. O. pap., 15 c.

****Mérimée,** Prosper. Quatre contes; ed., with introd., notes, and vocabulary, by F. C. L. van Steenderen. N. Y., H: Holt & Co., 1902. c. 13+122 p. S. cl., 35 c. net.

New York. Mason on highways; cont. the New York highway law and all constitutional and general statutory provisions relating to highways; highway officers, their powers and duties, including the good roads law of 1898 and 1901; all as amended to the session of 1903, with annots. and forms; by Herbert Delavan Mason. Alb., Banks & Co., 1902. c. 31+322 p. O. buckram, $2; shp., $2.50.

Payne, Eli Lawrence. Payne's natural methods in arithmetic for business men, advanced students and teachers. Emporia, Kan., Eli Lawrence Payne, 1902. c. 152 p. D. pap., 40 c.

Pierce, B: Washington. Foregleams in nature of redemption in Christ; or, the spiritual remedial system foreshadowed in the physical. Rev., enl. ed. Kansas City, Mo., Hudson-Kimberly Pub. Co., 1902. c. 212+1 p. por. 12°, cl., $1.

***Puterbaugh,** Sabin D. Puterbaugh's chancery pleading and practice: a practical treatise on the forms of chancery suits, pleading and practice now in use in the state of Ill., and wherever the same system prevails, with forms of bills, answers, pleas, demurrers, exceptions, petitions, orders, decrees, etc., and practice in the supreme and appellate courts; rev. by Leslie D. Puterbaugh. 5th ed. Chic., Callaghan & Co., 1902. c. 106+1019 p. O. shp., $6 net.

Rogers, H. Edson. The Rogers compendium of the Graham system of shorthand: a practical, synthetic method; being a concise presentation of reporting-style principles, and an epitome of the principles of phrasing and abbreviation exemplified throughout the entire series of publications and literature devoted to standard phonography. Battle Creek, Mich., The Fireside Accounting Publishing Co., Ltd., 1902. c. 270 p. 12°, cl., $2.

Scherer, Paul. The business of farming in Virginia: a study of some of our agricultural resources. Roanoke, Press of the Stone Printing and Manufacturing Co., [1902.] c. 32 p. O. pap., for free distribution.

Schiller, Johann Christoph Friedrich v. The robbers, Fiesco, Love and intrigue; ed. by Nathan Haskell Dole. Ed. de luxe. Bost., F. A. Niccolls & Co., [1902.] c. 14+423 p. 12°, cl. (Apply to pubs. for price.)

***Seabury,** W: Jones. Notes on the constitution of 1901. N. Y., T: Whittaker, [1902.] c. 143 p. 8°, cl., $1 net; pap., 75 c. net.
Appendix: Constitution [of the Protestant Episcopal church in the U. S.] as in 1898, and 1901.

Sever, Franklin Pierce. Elements of agriculture; with industrial lessons. Bost., Heath, 1902. c. 9+141 p. il. 16°, cl., 50 c.

Texas. The law of corporations, as contained in the latest statutes and session laws and as interpreted by the highest courts; by R. L. Batts. St. Louis, Mo., Gilbert Book Co., 1902. c. 57+614 p. O. shp., $6.

Todd, C: Burr. A general history of the Burr family; with a genealogical record from 1193 to 1902. 4th ed. N. Y., printed for the author, [C: Burr Todd,] by the Knickerbocker Press, 1902. c. 29+10+600 p. facsim., pl. (partly col.) por. 12°, cl., $5.

Vilas, C: Atwood. The law of special verdicts in Wisconsin: a digest of cases in vs. 1-3 Pinney and vs. 1-112 Wis. reports. Chic., Callaghan & Co., 1902. c. 84 p. O. buckram, $1.50.

Wilson, *Rev.* H: Bible lamps for little feet. Nyack, N. Y., Christian Alliance Pub. Co., [1902.] c. 184 p. por. il. 12°, cl., $1.

ORDER LIST.

AMERICAN TRACT SOC., 150 Nassau St., New York.

Green, Alwyn Ravendale............. $1.25

D. APPLETON & Co., 72 Fifth Ave., New York.

**Compayré, Development of the child in later infancy.................net, 1.20

T. H. BALL, Crown Point, Ind.

Ball. Francis Ball's descendants....... 1.50

BANKS LAW PUB. CO., 21 Murray St., New York.

New York, Mason on highways....$2; 2.50

BENZIGER BROS., 36 Barclay St., New York.

Catholic Home Annual, 1903, 20th year. 25

G. M. BINGHAM, San Francisco, Cal.

Bingham, Numerical system commercial cable and telegraphic code...... 25.00

CALLAGHAN & Co., 114 Monroe St., Chicago.

*Puterbaugh, Chancery pleading and practice...... ....net, 6.00

Vilas, Law of special verdicts in Wisconsin....... .... 1.50

J. M. CHANEY, JR., Kansas City, Mo.

Chaney, Mae and Mary, the young scientists...... 60

CHRISTIAN ALLIANCE PUB. CO., Nyack, N. Y.

Wilson, Bible lamps for little feet.... 1.00

HENRY T. COATES & Co., 1222 Chestnut St., Philadelphia.

**Brown, European and Japanese gardens..... ....net, 2.00

**Ellis, Jim and Joe.............net, 80

G. W. DILLINGHAM CO., 119 W. 23d St., New York.

King, The iron brigade.............. 1.50

WILLIAM J. C. DULANY CO., 8 Baltimore St., East Baltimore, Md.

Maryland, The public school law..... 15

FIRESIDE ACCOUNTING CO., Battle Creek, Mich.

Rogers, Compendium of the Graham system of shorthand............... 2.00

FORBES & Co., 160 Fifth Ave., New York.

Forbes, Architectural gardens of Italy. 50.00

GILBERT BOOK CO., 205 N. 4th St., St. Louis, Mo.

Texas, Law of corporations.......... 6.00

GINN & Co., 29 Beacon St., Boston.

Lansing, Earth and sky, no. 2........ 30

D. C. HEATH & Co., 120 Boylston St., Boston.

Sever, Elements of agriculture....... 50

ALFRED MILLER HESTON, Atlantic City, N. J.

Heston, Handbook [of Atlantic City], 20th century souvenir ed.......... 25

HENRY HOLT & Co., 29 W. 23d St., New York.

**Malot, Sans famille............net, 40

**Mérimée, Quatre contes.........net, 35

HUDSON-KIMBERLY PUB. CO., 1014 Wyandotte St., Kansas City, Mo.

Pierce, Foregleams in nature of redemption in Christ, rev., enl. ed..... $1.00

LAIRD & LEE, 263 Wabash Ave., Chicago.

Evans, The spirit world unmasked... 75

LEA BROS. & Co., 706-708 Sansom St., Philadelphia.

*Grayson, Diseases of the nose, throat and ear......... ....net, 3.50

F. A. NICCOLLS & Co., 212 Summer St., Boston.

Goethe, Sorrows of young Werther. (Apply to pubs. for price.)

Schiller, The robbers, etc. (Apply to pubs. for price.)

J. S. OGILVIE PUB. CO., 57 Rose St., New York.

Ballou, Played on hearts........50 c.; 1.00

ELI LAWRENCE PAYNE, Emporia, Kan.

Payne, Natural methods in arithmetic. 40

PETERS CARTRIDGE CO., Cincinnati.

Gould, American rifleman's encyclopædia..... 10

G. H. POLLEY & Co., Boston.

Emerson, Architecture and furniture of the Spanish colonies............ 30.00

REPUBLICAN PRESS, Hamilton, N. Y.

McGregory, Lecture notes on general chemistry... .... 1.50

SAALFIELD PUB. CO., Akron, O.

Hadley, Blue badge of courage....... 1.25

SPECTATOR CO., 95 William St., New York.

Fire insurance laws, etc.............. 5.00

PRESS OF THE STONE PRINT. AND MANUFACTURING CO., Roanoke, Va.

Scherer, Business of farming in Virginia..... .... gratis.

STREET & SMITH, 238 William St., New York.

Bronson, How to play ping-pong..... 15

Burton, Her wedding interlude........ 1.00

TEMPLE PRESS, 1232 Arch St., Philadelphia.

Conwell, Present successful opportunities...............subs., $2; $2.75; 4.00

C. BURR TODD, New York.

Todd, General history of the Burr family....... .... 5.00

UNITED SOCIETY OF CHRISTIAN ENDEAVOR, Boston.

Chapman, The man who said he would. 35

UNIVERSITY OF CHICAGO PRESS, Chicago.

*Cutting, Concerning the modern German relatives "das" and "was"..net, 25

D. VAN NOSTRAND CO., 23 Murray St., New York.

Foster, Electrical engineer's pocket-book, 2d corr. ed.................. 5.00

THOMAS WHITTAKER, 3 Bible House, New York.

*Seabury, Notes on the constitution of 1901............net, 75 c.; net, 1.00

INDEX TO FALL ANNOUNCEMENTS.

In this list publishers' announcements are indexed by author, title or subject and series. Titles already recorded in The Publishers' Weekly *have been generally excluded. The cumulation "Reference List of New Publications, January-August," published September 13, and the present index of announcements of books to be published during the fall and winter, include a record of all books of which we have received information since January 1. We shall be pleased to have word of omissions of published works at once, in order that they may be included in the "Reference List of New Publications, January-September," which will be issued October 11.*

Where binding is not stated the books are generally understood to be in cloth binding; "bds.," particularly in the department of Juvenile fiction, generally means illuminated or fancy board covers.

Fuller information of the books announced will be found in the publishers' advertising pages, index to which is given on page 485.

Algebra, Academic. *See* Milne's. Am. Bk.

Algebra, Beginner's. Wells, W., *and* Gerrish, C. Heath.

Algebra. *See* Bailey's high school.—White's grammar school. Am. Bk.

Algebraic equations, Introduction to the theory of. Dickson, L. E. Wiley.

**Alger, Horatio, *jr.* Andy Grant's pluck. il. 12°. 80 c. net. Coates.

Alger, Horatio, *jr.* Erie train boy. (New Kalon ser.) il. 12°. 50 c. Caldwell.

**Alger, J. G. Paris, 1789-1794. 8°. $3 net; ¼ mor., $5 net. Pott.

†Alice in wonderland.—Through the looking-glass. Carroll, Lewis. $2. Wessels.

†Alice in wonderland. Carroll, Lewis. $1. Wessels.

Alick's adventures. W. R. Longmans.

**"Alien" [*pseud.* for *Mrs.* L. "Alien" Baker.] Maid of mettle. (Pastime and adventure ser.) il. 12°. $1 net. Jacobs.

Allchin, W. H. *ed.* Manual of medicine. 5 v. Macmillan.

New volumes: v. 4, Diseases of respiratory and circulatory systems.—v. 5, Diseases of the digestive system and kidneys.

Allegories. Farrar, F: W. $1. Longmans.

Allen. Tables for earthwork curves. Spon & C.

Allen, Grant. Anglo-Saxon Britain. (Early Britain ser.) 12°. $1. Young.

Allen, Grant. Venice. 2 v. il. Large 16°. $3; ¼ mor., $7. L. C. Page.

*Allen, Grant: a memoir. Clodd, E: $1.25 net. Wessels.

Allen, J. B. Elementary Greek grammar. Oxford Univ.

Allen, P. S., *and* Hatfield, J. T., *eds.* Diary and correspondence of Wilhelm Müller. Univ. of Chic.

Allen, Phœbe. Pick of the basket. 12°. $1. Young.

Allen, T. W. *See* Monro, D. B. Oxford Univ.

Allen, Willis B. Pine tree flag. $1.25. Pilgrim Press.

**Allen, Willis B. Play away. 12°. 75 c. net. Estes.

*Allen's, Grant, historical guides. 12°. ea., $1.25 net. Wessels.

New volume: Cruickshank, Umbrian towns.

Allsop, F. C. Practical electric bell fitting. 10th ed. 180 il. 12°. $1.25. Spon & C.

Almanac, Family Christian, 1903. 10 c. Am. Tr.

**Alphabet book. Mayer, H: 40 c. net. Stokes.

*Alsop, G. Character of the province of Maryland. (London, 1666.) *Repr.* 250 copies, bds., about $2; 15 copies Jap. pap., $3 net Burrows.

Alwyn Ravendale. Green, E. E. $1.25. Am. Tr.

America, Historic highways of. Hulbert, A. B. vols. 1, 2, ea., $2; vols. 3-16, ea., $3.50. A. H. Clark.

America, how found and settled. *See* Dickson, M. S. Macmillan.

**America in its relations to the great epochs of history. Mann, W: J. $1 net. Little, B. & Co.

**America, Romances of early. Robins, E: $2.50 net: $5 net. Jacobs.

America. Spanish conquest in. Helps, Sir A. New ed., in 4 v. v. 3. il. 12°. $1.50. Lane.

American Academy of Political and Social Science. *See* Social legislation. McClure.

**American animals. Stone, Witmer. $3 special net. Doubleday, P.

American artist's portfolio. Colored pictures. 12x18. $1.50. Russell.

*American designers of book-plates. il. Edition de luxe. Lim. ed. vellum, $4 net. Kelly.

American (An) with Lord Roberts. Ralph, J. 50 c. Stokes.

**American book prices current. Livingstone, L. W. $6; $15 special net. Dodd, Mead & Co.

**American bookmen. Howe, M. A. De Wolfe. New ed. il. $1.75 net. Dodd, Mead & Co.

**American church calendar for 1903. 25 c. net. Jacobs.

American citizen ser.; ed. by A. B. Hart. Longmans.

New volumes: Dewey, Financial history of the U. S.—Hart, Actual government as applied under American conditions.

**American diary of a Japanese girl. Glory, Miss Morning. $1.60 net. Stokes.

American government, *See* Handbook of. Macmillan.

**American idea as expounded by American statesmen. Gilder, J. B., *ed.* $1.20 net. Dodd, Mead & Co.

**American literature. Sears, L. S. $1.50 net. Little, B. & Co.

**American literature, History of. Trent, W: P. $1.20 net. Appleton

**American men of letters ser. 16°. ea., $1.10 net. Houghton, M. & Co.

New volumes: Nathaniel Hawthorne, by G. F. Woodberry; Henry Wadsworth Longfellow, by T: W. Higginson.

**American merchant marine. Marvin, W. L. $2 net. Scribner.

**American merchant ships and sailors. Abbot, W. J. $2 net. Dodd, Mead & Co.

American municipal progress. Zueblin, C: Macmillan.

American navigation. Bates, W: W. 8°. Houghton, M. & Co.

**American orations, Early. (Macmillan's pocket classics.) 18°. 25 c. net. Macmillan.

**American people, History of. Wilson, W. 5 v. $17.50 net; $30 net. Harper.

American philanthropy of the XIXth century ser. 12°. Macmillan.

New volume: Lee, Constructive and preventive philanthropy.

[American] revolution, Heroes and patriots of. Hart, A. B. Macmillan.

American revolution, Loyalists in. Van Tyne, C. H. Macmillan.

**American revolution, True history of. Fisher, S. G: $2 net. Lippincott.

American sportsman's library; ed. by C. Whitney. 12 v. il. 8°. Macmillan.

New volumes: Sanford and others, Wild fowl.—Holder, Big game fish.—Money and others, Gun and rifle.

**American statesmen, Wit and humour of. Reddale, F:, *comp.* 50 c. net; 80 c. net. Jacobs.
American teachers ser. Longmans.
New volumes: Smith and Hall, Teaching of chemistry and physics in the secondary school.—Bourne, Teaching of history and civics in the elementary and secondary school.
Americans in process. Woods, Robt. A. 12°. Houghton, M. & Co.
Amherst, Alicia, *pseud.* for *Mrs.* E. Cecil.
**Among the greatest masters of warfare. Rowlands, W., *ed.* $1.20; $2.40 net. Estes.
Analysis of steel works materials. Brearley, H. Longmans.
Analysis, Qualitative, Manual of. Dennis, L. M. Ginn.
Anatomy. *See also* Mann, Gustav. Oxford Univ.
Anatomy and histology of the mouth and teeth. Broomell, I. N. $4.50. Blakiston.
Anatomy, Text-book of. Cunningham, D. G., *ed.* $9: sheep, $10; hf. mor., $11. Macmillan.
Anatomy, Text-book of. Morris, H. $6-$8. Blakiston.
**Ancestor (The). Barron, O., *ed.* per part, $1.50 net. Lippincott.
Ancient history. Rollin, C: 4 v. $4-$8. Wessels.
Ancient history for beginners. Botsford, G: W. Macmillan.
Ancient languages, Introduction to the teaching of. Sauveur, L. 25 c. W: R. Jenkins.
**Ancient Peruvian art. Bohessler, A. per pt., $7.50 special net. Dodd, Mead & Co.
†Andersen, Hans Christian. Fairy tales; ed. by J. J. Mora. 4°. $1.50. Estes.
†Andersen, Hans Christian. Fairy tales. (Temple classics for young people.) il. 16°. 50 c.; leather, 80 c. Macmillan.
**Andersen, Hans Christian. Fairy tales. New ed. il. 8°. $1.60 net. Stokes.
Anderson. Best methods of teaching gymnastics. New ed. Hinds.
*Anderson, Ja. B. Nameless hero, and other poems. 12°. $1 net. Wessels.
**Anderson, Rob. Jack Champney. (Pastime and adventure ser.) il. 12°. $1 net. Jacobs.
Andrews, Ernest J., *and* Howland, H. N. Physics. 12°. Macmillan.
†Andrews, Mary R. S. Vive l'empereur. il. 12°. Scribner.
Andromaque. Racine, J. Holt.
†Andy and the ignoramus. Brill, G: R. Biddle.
**Andy Grant's pluck. Alger, H., *jr.* 80 c. net. Coates.
Anecdota Oxoniensis ser. Oxford Univ.
New volumes: Collations from the Codex Cluniacensis s. Holkhamicus (9th century ms. of Cicero), ed. by W. Peterson; Firdausi's Yusuf and Zalikha, ed. by H. Ethé; Kanva Satapatha Brahmana, ed. by J. Eggeling; Bale's Index Britanniæ scriptorum, ed. by R. L. Poole and Mary Bateson.
**Anglican episcopate and the American colonies. Cross, A. L. $2.50 net. Longmans.
Anglo-Saxon Britain. Allen, Grant. $1. Young.
Animal classification, Synopsis of. Wilder, H. H. Holt.
Animal life in rhymes and jingles. May, Eliz. il. 4°. bds., $1.25. Saalfield.
Animal nutrition, Principles of. Armsby, H: P. Wiley.
Animal picture book, Baby's. Large type. il. $1. Warne.
**Animals, American. Stone, Witmer. $3 special net. Doubleday, P.
Animals at home, Bartlett's. 45 c. Am. Bk.
**Animals at the fair. Blaisdell, W. $1.40 net. Russell
Animals before man in North America. Lucas, F. A. Appleton
**Ann Arbor tales. Harriman, K. E. $1.20 net. Jacobs.
†Anne of Argyle. Eyre-Todd, G: 50 c. Stokes.
**Anne (Queen) Reign of. McCarthy, J. 2 v. $4 net. Harper.
Annealing of steel. *See* Woodworth, J. V. Henley.
Annunzio, Gabriele d'. The dead city. il. $1.25. Laird.
**Annunzio, Gabriele d'. Paolo and Francesca Tr. New ed. 16°. $1 net. Stokes.
Anstey, F. A Bayard of Bengal. il. 12°. Appleton.
Antarctic queen (An). Clark, C: $1.75. Warne.
Anthology of humorous verse. Cook, T. A., *ed.* 75 c. Brentano's.
Antiquarian companion to English history. Barnard, F. P., *ed.* Oxford Univ.
**Anti-slavery papers. Lowell, J. R. 2 v. (Special ed. of 400 numbered copies.) Houghton, M. & Co.
Antrim, Minna T. Book of toasts. 16°. 50 c.; ooze cf., $1. Altemus.
Antrim, Minna T. Don'ts for girls. 16°. 50 c.; ooze cf., $1. Altemus.
Anus and rectum. *See* Tuttle, J. P. Appleton.
Anxious inquirer (The). James, J: A. 75 c. Caldwell.
†Aphrodite. Gifford, F. K. 50 c. Small, M.
**Appleton, *Miss* —. Mrs. Ginger. (Dumpy books for children.) il. bds., 40 c. net. Stokes.
Appleton's business series. 12°. Appleton.
New volumes: Cleveland, F. A., Funds and their uses.—Pratt, S. S., The work of Wall street.
**Appleton's supplementary readers. 12°. 60 c. net. Appleton.
New volume: Book 5, Nature study readers. Harold's discussions, by J. W. Troeger.
Appointing power, History of the. Salmon, L. M. Macmillan.
Apollo and Keats on Browning. Lanier, C. $1.50. Badger.
**Apostles' creed. Hopkins, Arch. 60 c. net. Am. Unitarian.
Aquarium. *See* Smith, Eugene. Dutton.
Arabia, Kinship and marriage in early. Smith, W. R. Macmillan.
Arabia. *See* Zwemer, S: M. *and* Amy E. Revell.
Arbitration. *See also* Industrial conciliation. Putnam.
Arc, Jeanne d'. *See* Carpenter, K. E. Lee & Shepard.
**Arc, Jeanne d'. Murray, T. D. $5 net. McClure.

*Archer, W: Study and stage. 8°. $1.50 net. Wessels.
†Archierey (The) of Samara. Iliowizi, H. $1. Coates.
Ariel booklets. Photogrv. frontis. 32°. Flex. red leath., ea., 75 c. Putnam.
New volumes: 31, Calverley's Verses and Flyleaves.—32, Thackeray's Novels by eminent hands.—33, Cranford.—34, Vicar of Wakefield.—35, Tales by H: Zschokke.—36, Rasselas.—37, Shakespeare's Sonnets.—38, Wit and wisdom of C: Lamb.—39, Baron Munchausen.—40, Aesop's Fables.—41, Franklin's autobiography.—42, Sayings of Poor Richard.—43, Christmas carol—44, Cricket on the hearth.—45, Blessed damozel.—46, Carové's Story without an end.—47, Rubáiyát of Omar Khayyám.—48, Father Tom and the Pope.—49, Winthrop's Love and skates.—50, Tennyson's Princess.—51, Pater's Child in the house.—52, Poe's Poems.—53, Buonarotti's Sonnets. 54, Cicero and Emerson on Friendship.—55, Sketch book, pt. 1.—56 Sketch book, pt. 2.—57, Leslie Stephen on R. L. Stevenson.
Argenteau, *Comte* de. *See* Secret correspondence. Dodd, Mead & Co.
**Argive Heræum. Waldstein, C: il. 2 v. 4°. $30 net. Full morocco, $60 net. Houghton, M. & Co.
*Aristotle. Ethics. (A. L. Humphrey's large type books.) 8°. pap., $7.50 net. Wessels.
Aristotle. Politics. Newman, W. L., *ed.* Final v. 3, 4, with index. Oxford Univ.
Aristotle. Psychology; tr. and ed. by W: Hammond. 8°. Macmillan.
Arithmetic. *See* Baird's.—Winslow's. Am. Bk.
Arithmetic, Principles of. Siefert, H. O. R. (For teachers and normal students.) 75 c. Heath.
Arithmetic without a pencil. Joy, Edith M. (For grammar grades.) Heath.
Arlent-Edwards, S. Ethel Barrymore in "Captain Jinks." Colored print. 125 signed prints. 12½ x 14. $30. Russell.
**Arms and armour. Lacombe, M. P. $1.75 net. Lippincott.
Armsby, H: P. Principles of animal nutrition. 8°. Wiley.
Armstrong, Margaret. Ad Astra. Selections from the Divine comedy. il. 9 x 12. bds., $5. Russell.
Arnold, *Sir* Edwin. Light of Asia. (Chateau ser.) il. 6 x 4. boxed, 75 c. Caldwell.
**Arnold, Matthew. Paul, H. W. 75 c. net. Macmillan.
*Arnott, S. Book of climbing plants. (Handbooks of practical gardening, 10.) il. $1 net. Lane.
Around the world through Japan. Del Mar, W. Macmillan.
Arrhenius, Svante. Text-book of electrochemistry Tr. il. 8°. Longmans.
**Art, British, Makers of. *See* Manson, J. A., *ed.*
**Art. Delight; the soul of. Eddy, A. J. $1.50 net. Lippincott.
**Art, History of. Lübke, W: $10 net. Dodd, Mead & Co.
Art, Library of. Strong, S. A., *ed.* Scribner.
Art, Nineteenth century, and Scottish historical antiquities. 2 v. il. 4°. Macmillan.
**Art of the Vatican. Potter, Mary K. il. Large 12°. $2 net; ¾ mor., $4 net. L. C. Page.
Art of Walter Crane. Konody, P. G. Macmillan.
Art, World's great pictures. $10. Young.
**Artificial feeding of infants. Judson, C: F. $2 net. Lippincott.
**Artistic crafts ser. il. 12°. $1.20 net. Appleton.
New volumes: Spooner, C., Cabinet-making and designing.—Wilson, H., Silver work and jewelry.
**As seen from the ranks: a boy in the Civil War. Benton, C: E. 12°. $1.25 net. Putnam.
**As you like it. Shakespeare, W: 25 c. net. Macmillan.
*Ascent of man. (Baby Roland booklets.) il. Flexible. 50 c. net. Elder.
†Ashes of empire. Chambers, R. W. 50 c. Stokes.
Ashton, C. H., *and* Marsh, W. R. Plane and spherical trigonometry. Scribner.
Asoka: Buddhist emperor of India. Smith, Vincent A. (Supp. vol. to "Rulers of India.") Oxford Univ.
**Aspects of fiction. Matthews, B. $1.25 net. Scribner.
Asser. *See* Stevenson, W. H., *ed.* Oxford Univ.
Assyrian and Babylonian letters. Harper, R. F. 8°. Univ. of Chic.
**Assyrians, History of. *See* Goodspeed, G: S.
Astor lib. of poetry. ea., 60 c. Crowell.
New volumes: Bates, Cambridge book of poetry.—Tennyson's In memoriam.—Persian poets; ed. by N. H. Dole. Walt Whitman; introd. by J: Burroughs.
Astor library of prose. 222 v. 8°. ea., 60 c. Crowell.
New volumes: Bulfinch, Age of chivalry; Age of fable; Legends of Charlemagne.—Dumas, The black tulip.—Hawthorne, Marble faun.—Holmes, Professor at the breakfast table.—Raspe, Baron Munchausen.—Spyri, Heidi.—Thackeray, English humorists.
Astrology, Practical. St. Germain, *Comte* C. de. $1. Laird.
**Astronomers, The great. Ball, R. S. $1.50 net. Lippincott.
Astronomy for engineers, Field. Comstock, G: C. Wiley.
**[Astronomy] In the higher heavens. Ball, R. S. $1.50 net. Lippincott.
Astronomy in 19th century, History of. Clerke, A. M. Macmillan.
Astronomy, New, Todd's. $1.30. Am. Bk.
Astrophysics, Problems in. Clerke, A. M. Macmillan.
†At the court of Catherine the great. Whishaw, F: 50 c. Stokes.
Athalie. Racine, J. Holt.
Atharva-Veda-Samhita; tr. by W. D. Whitney. (Harvard Oriental ser., vs. 5 and 6.) 2 v. Ginn.

**Atwater, Emily P. How Sammy went to Coral-land. (Lad and lassie ser.) il. 12°. 40 c. net. Jacobs.
Athens, Ancient. Gardner, E. A. Macmillan.
**Athens, Story of. Butler, Howard C. il. $2.40 net. Century.
Atherton, Gertrude F. Splendid idle forties. il. 12°. Macmillan.
†Atherton, Gertrude F. A whirl asunder. New ed. il. 12°. $1. Stokes.
Atlas of modern Europe, Historical. *See* Poole, R. P. Oxford Univ.
**Atlas of modern geography, International student's. Bartholomew, J. G. $2.25 net. [Imp.] Scribner.
Attic prose. *See* Flagg's A writer of. Am. Bk
**Audubon, J: J. Burroughs, J: 75 c. net; $1 net. Small, M.
**Audsley, G: A. Art of organ building. 2 v. il. 4°. $15 special net; ed. de luxe, $25 special net. Dodd, Mead & Co.
†Aunt Abby's neighbors. Slosson, Annie T. $1. Revell.
Aunt Diana. Carey, R. N. $1. Caldwell.
†Austen, Jane. Works. (Hampshire ed.) 5 v. 16°. per v., $1; per set, $5. Putnam.
**Austen, Jane. Beeching, H. C. 75 c. net. Macmillan.
Austen, Jane. *See* Bonnell, H: H. Longmans.
Austin, Alf. Haunts of ancient peace. il. 8°. Macmillan.
*Austin, Alfred. Victoria the wise. 4°. vellum. $2.50 net. Young.
Authors. *See* Halsey, F. W. Pott.
**Authors at home. Gilder, Jeannette, L., *ed.* $1 net. Wessels.
**Authors' loves, Stories of. Laughlin, C. E. 2 v. $3 net; $6 net. Lippincott.
**Autobiography of a "newspaper girl." Banks, E. L. $1.20 net. Dodd, Mead & Co.
Autocrat of the breakfast table. Holmes, O. W. $1.25. Caldwell.
**Automobile, 2000 miles on an. "Chauffeur." $2 net. Lippincott.
**Automobilist. Mishaps of an; col. il. by De W. C. Falls. 4°. 80 c. net. Stokes.
Ave Roma immortalis. Crawford, F. M. Macmillan.
Averil. Carey, R. N. $1. Caldwell.
Avery, Harold. Sale's sharpshooters. il. $1.25. Nelson.
†Avery. Phelps, *Mrs.* E. S. $1. Houghton, M. & Co.
Avignon. Marriage, E. Macmillan.
Awakening (The) of Anthony Weir. Hocking, S. K. $1.50. Am. S. S.
Babbitt's Grammar of Attic and Ionic Greek. $1.50. Am. Bk.
**Babcock, Bernie. An uncrowned queen. (Frances E. Willard.) 12°. 75 c. net. Revell.
Babcock, R. H. Diseases of the heart and lungs. Appleton.
†Babcock, W.: H: Kent Fort manor. (Griffin ser.) 12°. $1. Coates.
Babel and Bible. Delitzsch, F. 50 c. Open Court.
*Baby Roland booklets. Hansen, G:, *ed.* ea., 50 c. net. Elder.
Babylonian letters. *See* Harper, R. F. Univ. of Chic.
**Babylonians and Assyrians, History of. Goodspeed, G: S. $1.25 net. Scribner.
Baby's animal picture book. Large type. il. $1. Warne.
**Baby's Baedeker. Streamer, D. $1.20 net. Russell.
Bach. *See* Oxford musical ser. Oxford Univ.
Bacon, Alice M. Japanese girls and women. Rev. ed. col. il. 12°. $4. Houghton, M. & Co.
**Bacon, Edgar M. Hudson river from ocean to source. il. 8°. $3.50 net. Putnam.
Bacon, Edwin M. Literary pilgrimages in New England. il. Silver.
Bacon, F. Essays. Chateau ser., 75 c.—Sesame classics, $1.25. Caldwell.
**Bacon, Fes. [Selections.] (Little masterpieces, 2d ser.) 4 x 6. flex. silk clo. ea., 40 c. net. Doubleday, P.
Bacteriologic technique. Eyre, J. W. H. Saunders.
Bacteriology, Manual of. Hewlett, H. T. 2d ed., rev. $4 net. Blakiston.
Bacteriology, Manual of. Muir, R. Macmillan.
**Baedeker K., *ed.* London. (Baedeker's guides.) New ed. 12°. $1.80 net. [Imp.] Scribner.
**Baedeker K. Northern Italy. (Baedeker's guides.) New ed. 12°. $2.10 net. [Imp.] Scribner.
**Baedeker, K. South Germany. (Baedeker's guides.) New ed. 12°. $1.50 net. [Imp.] Scribner.
**Baedeker, K. Southern France. (Baedeker's guides.) New ed. 12°. $2.70 net [Imp.] Scribner.
**Baedeker's guides. [Imp.] Scribner.
New editions: London.—South Germany.—Southern France.—Northern Italy.
**Baessler, A. Ancient Peruvian art. In 15 pts. col. pl. 50 cop. for America. per pt., $7.50 special net. Dodd, Mead & Co.
†Bagot, R: The just and the unjust. 12°. $1.50. Lane.
†Bagot, R: A Roman mystery. 12°. $1.50. Lane.
**Bailey, Florence Merriam. Handbook of miscellaneous birds of the western United States. 12°. Houghton, M. & Co.
Bailey, L. H. First lessons in agriculture. 16°. Macmillan.
Bailey's High school algebra. 90 c. Am. Bk.
Bain, J: Tobacco in song and story; [also] Gray, A. Bathrobes and bachelors. Holiday ed. 2 v. ooze cf., padded and boxed, $3.50. Caldwell.
Baird lectures, 1901. *See* Lang, J: M. Whittaker.
Baird's Graded work in arithmetic. 8 bks. for 8 years. Am. Bk.
**Baker, Cornelia. Coquo and the king's children. il. sm. 4°. $1.50 net. McClurg.
Baker, E. A. Guide to fiction. 8°. Macmillan.
Baker, G: P. Public exposition and argumentation. Holt.
Baker, Ira O. Treatise on roads and pavements. 8°. $5. Wiley.
Baker, *Mrs.* L. "Alien." *See* "Alien," *pseud.*
Baker, Ray S. Boy's book of inventions. New ed. il. 12°. $2. McClure.

Balaster boys (The). Channing, B. M. $1.25. Wilde.
Balch, F. H. Bridge of the gods. 7th ed. il. 12°. $1.50. McClurg.
**Baldry, Alf. L. Modern mural decorations. il. 4°. $5 net. Scribner.
Baldwin, C: S. College manual of rhetoric. 8°. Longmans.
**Baldwin, Ja. M. Development and evolution. 8°. $2.60 net. Macmillan.
Baldwin, Ja. M. Nociones de psicología. Appleton.
Baldwin, Ja. M., *ed.* Dictionary of philosophy and psychology. vols. II. and III. 8°. Macmillan.
†Baldwin, May. Plucky Nell. il. 12°, $1.50. Lippincott.
Baldwin's school readers. 8 bk. ser., or 5 bk. ser. Am. Bk.
Bale's Index. Britanniæ scriptorum. Poole, R. L., *and* Bateson, Mary, *eds.* Oxford Univ.
Ball, Allan P. Satire of Seneca on the Apotheosis of Claudius. (Columbia Univ. studies in classical philology.) Macmillan.
**Ball, Rob. S. The great astronomers. il. 8°. $1.50 net. Lippincott.
**Ball, Rob. S. In the high heavens. il. 8°. $1.50 net. Lippincott.
Ballads in blue china. Lang, A. Wieners.
**Ballads, Old English. (Macmillan's pocket classics.) 18°. 25 c. net. Macmillan.
*Balloon ascension at midnight. Hall, G: E. $1 net; $5 net. Elder.
Ballou, Clara E. Played on hearts. 12°. $1; pap., 50 c. J. S. Ogilvie.
Balzac, Honoré de. Complete works. New issue. il. 16 v., $16; ½ leath., $24. Wessels.
Balzac, Honoré de. A passion in the desert. (Remarque ser.) 3⅞ x 5⅝. 40 c.; limp leath., boxed, 75 c.; limp chamois, $1.25. Caldwell.
†Balzac, Honoré de. Père Goriot. il. 12°. Turner house classics.) 75 c. Brentano's.
**Bandage, Roller. Hopkins, W: B. $1.50 net. Lippincott.
*Bandaging, Princ. and pract. of. Davis, G. G. $1.50 net. Blakiston.
**Bane and the antidote. Watkinson, W. L. $1 net. Revell.
Bangs, J: Kendrick. Bikey the skicycle; il. by Peter Newell. $1.50. Riggs Pub. Co.
**Bangs, J: K. Mollie and the unwiseman. il. 12°. $1 net. Coates.
**Banks, Eliz. L. Autobiography of a "newspaper girl." 12°. $1.20 uet. Dodd, Mead & Co.
Banks, L: A. Healing of souls. 8°. $1.50. Eaton & M.
Banks, L: A. The king's stewards. 12°. $1.25. Am. Tr.
Banks, Martha B. Dame Dimple's Christmas celebration. il. 50 c. Am. Tr.
**Bannerman, Helen. Little black Mingo. (Dumpy books for children.) il. bds., 40 c. net. Stokes.
†Barbara Ladd. Roberts, C: G. D. $1.50. L. C. Page.
Barber, T. W. Engineer's sketch-book of mechanical movements, devices, appliances, etc., employed in the design and construction of machinery. 4th ed. 8°. $4. Spon & C.
**Barbizon days. Smith, C: S. $2 net. Wessels.
**Barbour, R. H. Behind the line: story of school and football; il. by C. M. Relyea. 12°. $1.20 net. Appleton.
*Barham, R: H., ["Thomas Ingoldsby."] Ingoldsby legends. New ed.; il. by H. Cole. 8°. $1.50 net. Lane.
Barham, R: H., ["Thomas Ingoldsby."] Jackdaw of Rheims. New ed. col. il. $2. Young.
**Barine, Arvède. Youth of La Grande Mademoiselle. Meyer, L. G., *tr.* il. 8°. net. Putnam.
**Baring, Maurice. Black prince, and other poems. 12°. $1.25 net. Lane.
†Baring-Gould, S. The broom squire. (Copyright ser.) 12°. 50 c. Stokes.
†Baring-Gould, S. Domitia. (Copyright ser.) 12°. 50 c. Stokes.
†Baring-Gould, S. Pabo, the priest. (Copyright ser.) 12°. 50 c. Stokes.
†Barlow, Jane. The founding of fortunes. 12°. $1.50. Dodd, Mead & Co.
†Barnaby Lee. Bennett, J: $1.50. Century.
Barnaby Rudge. Dickens, C: 75 c. Caldwell.
Barnard, F. P., *ed.* Antiquarian companion to English history. Oxford Univ.
Barnard, P. M. Homily of Clement of Alexandria entitled Who is the rich man who is being saved? (Early church classics.) 16°. 40 c. Young.
**Barnes, Ja. With the flag in the channel; or, the adventures of Capt. Gustavus Conyngham. il. 12°. (Heroes of the navy ser.) 80 c. net. Appleton.
Barnes's Natural slant penmanship. bks., per doz., 75 c.; charts, per set, $1.50. Am. Bk.
Barnett, J. M. Mother Goose paint book. il. bds., $1.25. Saalfield.
Barr, Amelia E. Preacher's daughter. $1.25. Pilgrim Press.
†Barr, Amelia E. A song of a single note. il. 12°, $1.50. Dodd, Mead & Co.
†Barr, Rob., ["Luke Sharp."] Jennie Baxter, journalist. (Library of successes.) 12°. pap., 50 c. Stokes.
†Barr, Rob. The mutable many. (Copyright ser.) 12°. 50 c. Stokes.
†Barr, Rob. Revenge. (Copyright ser.) 12°. 50 c. Stokes.
†Barr, Rob. A woman intervenes. (Copyright ser.) 12°. 50 c. Stokes.
Barrie, Ja. M. The little minister. Il. lib. of famous bks., 75 c.—New Kalon ser., 2 v., ea., 50 c. Caldwell.
†Barrie, Ja. M. Little white bird. 12°. $1.50. Scribner.
Barrie, Ja. M. Window in Thrums. (Chateau ser.) 75 c. Caldwell.
**Barron, Oswald, *ed.* The ancestor: quarterly. il. Large pap. bds., per pt., $1.50 net. Lippincott.
†Barrow-North, H. Jerry Dodds, millionaire. il. 12°. $1.25. Lippincott.

**Barry, W: Papal monarchy. il. 12°. (Story of the nations, no. 65.) $1.35 net; hf. leath., $1.60 net. Putnam.
Barrymore, Ethel, in "Captain Jinks." Ar-lent-Edwards, S. colored print, 125 signed prints. 12½ x 14. $30. Russell.
Bart. *See* Frisbie, W. A. Rand, McN. & Co.
**Bartholomew, J. G. International student's atlas of modern geography. 4°. $2.25 net. [Imp.] Scribner.
Bartlett, J: Familiar quotations. Laureate ser., 75 c.—New Kalon ser., 50 c.—Sesame classics, $1.25. Caldwell.
Bartlett, *Mrs.* N. G. Mother Goose of modern days. New ed. 4°. $1.50. L. C. Page.
Bartlett, *Mrs.* N. G. Old friends with new faces. New ed. 4°. $1.50. L. C. Page.
Bartlett's Animals at home. 45 c. Am. Bk.
*Bartrum, E. Book of pears and plums. il. (Handbooks of practical gardening, no. 11.) $1 net. Lane.
Baskett, Ja. N. Sweetbrier and thistledown. $1.50. Wilde.
*Bassett, Austen B. The country church. 18°. 65 c. net. Lentilhon.
Bateman, Victory. *See* Patterson, Ada. Grafton Press.
†Bates, Arlo. Diary of a saint. Cr. 8°. $1.50. Houghton, M. & Co.
Bates, Katharine L., *and* Coman, Katharine, *comps.* English history as told by English poets. 12°. Macmillan.
Bates, W: W. American navigation. 8°. Houghton, M. & Co.
Bateson, Mary, *ed.* *See* Poole, R. L. Oxford Univ.
Bathrobes and bachelors. Gray, A. [also] Tobacco in song and story. Bain, J:, *jr.* 2 v. $3.50. Caldwell.
Battle with the slum. Riis, J. A. Macmillan.
**Baum, L. F. The life and adventures of Santa Claus. col. il. 8°. $1 net. Bowen-M.
Bayard of Bengal. Anstey, F. Appleton.
Bayard's courier. Benson, B. K. Macmillan.
Bayley, A. E. *See* Lyall, Edna, *pseud.*
**Bayliss, *Sir* Wyke. Five great painters of the Victorian era. il. 8°. $3 net. Pott.
**Bayne, *Prof.* Sir David Wilkie. il. 8°. (Makers of British art.) $1.25 net. [Imp.] Scribner.
†Bayou Triste: a story of Louisiana. Nicholls, J. H. $1.50. Barnes.
Bazán, Emilia P. Pascual López. (International modern language ser.) Ginn.
**Beacon biographies. 5⅝ x 3¾. 75 c. net; lambskin, $1 net. Small, M.
New volume: Burroughs, J: J. Audubon.
Beacon library. pap., ea., 50 c. Small, M.
Contents: Rayner, Free to serve; Visiting the sin.—Gifford, Aphrodite.—Norris, Grapes of wrath.—Plympton, In the shadow of the black pine.—Harris, Road to Ridgeby's.
Beall, St. Clair. The winning of Sarenne. 50 c. Federal Bk. Co.
Beams, Flexure of. *See Guy,* A. E. Van Nostrand.
**Beard, Lina B. *and* Adelia B. What a girl can make and do. il. 8°. $1.60 net. Scribner.
**Beautiful Joe's Paradise. Saunders, M. $1.20 net. L. C. Page.
**Beautiful Mrs. Moulton. Stephenson, N. $1.20 net. Lane.
Beautiful scenes of America. Stoddard, J: L. 75 c. Saalfield.
Beautiful thoughts ser. 75 c.; Persian cf., $1. Pott.
New volume: Whittier and Holmes. Selections.
Beauty and nature. Ruskin, J: 50 c.; $1.25. Caldwell.
Beauty of a life of service. Brooks, P. 30 c. Caldwell.
†Becke, L: Breachley—black sheep. 12°. $1.50. Lippincott.
**Beecher, H: W. Norwood. New ed. $1 net. Pilgrim Press.
Beecher, H: W. Selections. (Street and Smith little classics.) 18°. 50 c. Street.
**Beeching, H. C. Jane Austen. (English men of letters ser.) 75 c. net. Macmillan.
*Bees, Book of. Harrison, C: $1 net. Lane.
Beet, J. A. Commentary on St. Paul's Epistle to the Romans. 9th ed., rev. 8°. $2.50. Whittaker.
**Beggars garden. Lawrence, R. $1 net. Brentano.
Beggars of the sea. Pickering, E. $1.50. Warne.
**Beginner's course. (Bible lessons.) il. 30 c. net; quarterly pts., ea., 5 c. Pilgrim Press.
Begtrup, Julius. Slide valve and its functions. Diagrams. Van Nostrand.
**Behind the line. Barbour, R. H. $1.20 net. Appleton.
Bell, *Mrs.* A. J. Saints in Christian art. v. 2. il. 4°. Macmillan.
Bell, Lilian. Birthday book; ed. by A. H. Bogue. 12°. $1.50; ¾ mor., $3.50. L. C. Page.
†Bell, Lilian. Hope Loring. il. 12°. $1.50. L. C. Page.
*Bell, Ralcy H. Worth of words. 12°. $1.50 net. Grafton Press.
Bell fitting, Practical electric. Allsop, F. C. $1.25. Spon & C.
Bello, Andrés. Nuevo compendio de la gramática castellana. Appleton.
**Bellot, H. H. L. The Inner and Middle Temple (old London.) il. 12°. $2 net. Pott.
Bemont, C., *and* Monod, G. Mediæval Europe; ed by G. B. Adams. 12°. Holt.
**Bending of the twig. Russell, W. $2 net. Dodd, Mead & Co.
Benner, A. R. Homer's Iliad. 12°. (20th century text-books.) Appleton.
†Bennett, J: Barnaby Lee. il. 12°. $1.50. Century.
†Bennie Ben Cree. Colton, A. 50 c. McClure.
Benson, B. K. Bayard's courier. il. 12°. Macmillan.
**Benton, C: E. As seen from the ranks: a boy in the Civil War. 12°. $1.25 net. Putnam.
†Benton, Kate A. Geber. (Copyright ser.) 12°. 50 c. Stokes.
Beranger, P. J. de. Les chansons de; notes by L. Sauveur. 12°. $1.25. W: R. Jenkins.

Berenson, Bernhard. Study and criticism of Italian art. 2d ser. 8°. Macmillan.
Berkeley *and* Walker. Practical receipts. $3. Spon & C.
Bernhardt, Sarah. Gallus, A. 50 c. Russell.
Bernhardt, W:, *ed.* *See* Storm, T., *and* Lilliencron. Heath.
**Besant, *Sir* Walter. Art of fiction. 12°. 50 c. net. Brentano.
†Besant, *Sir* Walter. The changeling. (Copyright ser.) 12°. 50 c. Stokes.
Besant, *Sir* Walter. London in the 18th century. il. 8°. Macmillan.
†Besant, *Sir* Walter. The master craftsman. (Copyright ser.) 12°. 50 c. Stokes.
†Besant, *Sir* Walter. No other way. il. 12°. $1.50. Dod, Mead & Co.
Besant, *Sir* Walter. Westminster and South London. New ed. 2 v. il. $3. Stokes.
Best methods of teaching gymnastics. Anderson. Hinds.
Betchel, E: A. Sanctæ silviæ peregrinatio. 6¾ x 9½. (Studies in classical philology. v. 4, no. 1.) pap., $1 net. Univ. of Chic.
**Betts, Lillian W. Leaven in a great city. il. 12°. $1.50 net. Dodd, Mead & Co.
†Bewitched fiddle. MacManus, S. 75 c. McClure.
*Bibelot (The. v. 8. 4°. bds., $1.50 net. Mosher.
Bibelots ser.; ed. by J. Potter Briscoe. por. leath., $1. Lane.
New volume: Chaucer's Canterbury tales.
Bible. Addresses on the Revised Version. Ellicott, C. J. 80 c. Young.
Bible. Am. standard ed. of revised Bible. $1-$12. Nelson.
Bible. Book of Job. *See* Blake, W: Putnam.
Bible. Books of Kings. *See* Burney, C. F. Oxford Univ.
**Bible criticism and the average man. Johnston, H. A. 12°. $1 net. Revell.
Bible, Dictionary of. Hasting, J., *and others, eds.* 4 v. subs. only, per. v., $6; hf. mor., $8. Scribner.
Bible dictionaries. Smith's revised ed. 5000 subjects.—Self pronouncing. Holman.
*Bible, Emphasized. Bryant, J. B. 3 v. ea., $2 net. Revell.
**Bible encyclopedia. Cheyne, T. K., *ed.* v. 4. $5 net; $7.50 net. Macmillan.
Bible for children. Brown, F., *and* Gilder, *Mrs.* J. B., *eds.* $3. Century.
Bible. Fourth Gospel. *See* Pusey, P: E: Oxford Univ.
**Bible in Brazil. Tucker, H. C. $1.25 net. Revell.
Bible, Landscapes of the. Tristram, H. B. $1. Young.
Bible lessons. *See* Beginner's course. Pilgrim Press.
Bible, Messages of. Scribner.
New volume: Kent, Messages of Israel's lawgivers.
Bible, Neglected people of. Young, D. T. $1. Am. Tr.
Bible. Old Testament. *See* Pinches, T. G. Young.
**Bible. Old Testament for the young. Weed, G: L. 60 c. net. Jacobs.
**Bible students, Historical series for. Scribner.
New volume: Goodspeed, History of Babylonians and Assyrians.
Bible students' library. 12°. $2.50. Young.
New volumes: 9. Handbook to the Psalms, by J. Sharpe.—10. Samuel and his age, by G: C. M. Douglas.—11. Grammar of prophecy, by R. B. Girdlestone.
**Bible studies in the life of Christ. 12°. 50 c. net; paper, 25 c. net. Revell.
**Bible study, Broader. Patterson, A. 75 c. net. Jacobs.
Bible, S. S. scholars'. Schauffler, A. F., *ed.* 55 c.-$1.40. Nelson.
**Bible. Temple. 24 v. il. 16°. ea., 40 c. net; limp leath., 60 c. net. Lippincott.
Bible, Why we believe the. King, H: M. $1. Am. Tr.
Bible. *See also* New Testament.
Bibles, Interleaved. $5.50-$10. Nelson.
Bibles. *See* advertisements. American Tract; Holman; Nelson; G. W. Ogilvie; Oxford; Pott; Presbyterian Pub.; Revell; Whittaker; Young.
Bibles, Teachers'. *See* advertisement. G. W. Ogilvie.
Bibles, Teachers'. *See* advertisements. Oxford.
Biblical love ditties. Haupt, P. 5 c. Open Court.
**Biblical quotations in old English prose writers. Cook, A. S. net. Scribner.
Biblische geschichten. Wiedemann, F. Holt.
†Biddle, A. J. D. Froggy fairy book. (Froggy fairy ser. of juveniles.) New ed. il. 50 c. Biddle.
†Biddle, A. J. D. Second froggy fairy book. (Froggy fairy ser. of juveniles.) New ed. il. 50 c. Biddle.
Biedermann, K. Deutsche bildungszustaende im 18. jahrhundert; ed. by J: A. Walz. Holt.
Bikey the skicycle and other tales of Jimmie boy. Bangs, J: K. il. by Peter Newell. 12°. $1.50. Riggs.
Billings, E: E. Redman of quality. il. 12°. $1.25. Saalfield.
Billings, J: S., *ed.* Physiological aspects of the liquor problem. (Committee of Fifty.) 2 v. 8°. Houghton, M. & Co.
Billows and bergs. Metcalf, W. C. $1.75. Warne.
†Billy Burgundy's letters. il. 16°. 75 c. J. F. Taylor.
Billy Burgundy's opinions. 16°. 50 c.; 25 c. J. S. Ogilvie.
Billy Whiskers: autobiography of a goat. Montgomery, F. T. $1. Saalfield.
†Biography of a prairie girl. Tully, E. G. $1.50. Century.
Biological laboratory methods. Mell, P. H. Macmillan.
Birds, Little folks' book of. Large type. il. $1. Warne.
Birds of God. Radcliffe-Whitehead, J. B. $3. Russell.
**Birds' nests. Dixon, C: $1.20 net. Stokes.
**Birds of the Rockies. Keyser, L. S. il. sq. 8°. $3 net. McClurg.

**Birds of the western United States, Handbook of. Bailey, F. M. Houghton, M. & Co.
**Birdsall, Kath. L. Jack of all trades. col. il. by W. Russell. $1.20 net. Appleton.
**Birrell, Augustine. Browning. 12°. (Modern Eng. writers.) $1 net. Dodd, Mead & Co.
Birthday book. Bell, Lilian. $1.50; $3.50. L. C. Page.
Birthday book. Browning, R. 50 c. Whittaker.
Birthday garland. (Birthday book); il. by K. Greenaway. Warne.
**Bismarck, *Prince* von. Personal reminiscences of. Whitman, S. Appleton.
**Bismarck, *Prince* von and Kaiser Wilhelm I., Letters between. 2 v. 8°. $4 net; ¾ levant, $8 net. Stokes.
Bitter Sweet. Holland, J. G. 50 c.-$1.50. Caldwell.
Bivouac of the dead. O'Hara, T. Clarke.
†Black, Alex. Richard Gordon. il. 5¼x7¾. $1.50. Lothrop.
Black, Ja. M., *ed.* Gospel chorus. 8°. per copy, 20 c.; per 100, $15. Eaton & M.
**Black prince. Baring, M. $1.25 net. Lane.
Black rock. Connor, R. 50 c.; 75 c. Caldwell.
Blaisdell, Etta A., *and* Ma. F. Child life sixth reader. il. 4°. Macmillan.
**Blaisdell, Warde. Animals at the fair. col. il. bds., 9x12. $1.40 net. Russell.
**Blake, S. L. Separates of New England. $1.25 net. Pilgrim Press.
*Blake, W: Illustrations to the Book of Job. Photogrv. f°. $4 net. Putnam.
**Blanchan, Neltje. How to attract the birds. il. 6½x8¼. $1.35 net. Doubleday P.
**Blanchard, Amy E. Little Miss Oddity. il. 12°. (Little maid ser.) 80 c. net. Jacobs.
Blanchard, Amy E. A loyal lass. il. $1.50. Wilde.
**Blashfield, E. H., *and* E. W. Italian cities. new ed. 2 v. $5 net. Scribner.
†Blaze of glory. Winter, J: S. $1.25. Lippincott.
Bleak House. Dickens, C: 75 c. Caldwell.
†Blood-tax (The). Gerard, D. $1.50. Dodd, Mead & Co.
Blount, *Sir* E: Memoirs 1815-1902; ed. by S. J. Reid. il 8°. $4. Longmans.
Blue badge of courage. Hadley, H. H. $1.50. Saalfield.
†Blue flower (The). Van Dyke, H: $1.50. Scribner.
Blundell, *Mrs.* Francis. *See* Francis, M. E.
Blunt, Ellen M. Jim's temptation. 16°. 30 c. Young.
Blunt, R. F. L. Notes of confirmation lectures on the church catechism. New rev. ed. 12°. 60 c. Young.
Boas, F. S., *ed. See* Kyd, T: Oxford Univ.
Boat club. Optic, O. 75 c. Caldwell.
Bob. Lanier, S. $1 net. Scribner.
**Bob Knight's diary camping out. Smith, C. C. $1.20 net. Dutton.
†Bob, the photographer. Winfield, A. M. $1.25. Wessels.
†Bobby Bumpkin. Brill, G: R. Biddle.
Bodleian MSS. *See* Ethé, H., *and* Madan, F. Oxford Univ.
Boer war. *See* Scott, G. H. G. Spon & C.
Bogey book; written by E. S. 18 full-p. col. il. by R. J. S. $2.50. Young.
Bogue, A. H., *ed. See* Bell, Lilian. L. C. Page.
Boileau. —. Les héros de Roman. (International modern language ser.) Ginn.
Bolen, G: L. Plain facts about the trusts, and tariff. 12°. Macmillan.
Bolland, W. E. St. Paul and his churches. 16°. Young.
**Bolton, C: K. Private soldier under Washington. il. $1.25 net. Scribner.
Bolton, *Mrs.* S. K. Famous artists. Holiday ed. il. 8°. $2.50. Crowell.
Bolga, O. Calculus of variations. 8°. Univ. of Chic.
Bond, R. W., *ed. See* Lyly, J: Oxford Univ.
Bondman free. Oxenham, J: 50 c. Federal Bk. Co.
Bonehill, Ralph, (*pseud.*) Boy land boomer. il. 12°. $1. Saalfield.
†Bonehill, Ralph. Lost in the land of ice. il. 12°. $1.25. Wessels.
Bonehill, Ralph. Three young ranchmen. il. 12°. $1. Saalfield.
Bonehill, Ralph. Tour of the Zero club. 12°. $1.25.................Street.
**Bonehill, Ralph. Under Scott in Mexico. 12°. $1 net. Estes.
Bonnell, H: H. Charlotte Brontë, Jane Austen, George Eliot, Studies in their works. 8°. Longmans.
Bonney, J. T. Mediterranean: its storied cities and venerable ruins. il. map. 8°. $3; ¾ mor., $6.................Pott.
**Book of beauty. Williamson, F. H., *ed.* $35 net. Lippincott.
Book of bugs. Sutherland, H. $1.25. Street.
Book of Common Prayer. *See* Esdaile, E. Young.
Book of Common Prayer. *See* Hall, A. C. A. Young.
**Book of joyous children. Riley, J. W. $1.50 net. Scribner.
**Book of mystery and vision. Waite, A. E: $2 net. Brentano's.
**Book of romance. Lang, A. $1.60 net. Longmans.
**Book of weddings. Kingsland, *Mrs.* B. $1.20 net. Doubleday, P.
Book prices. *See* Livingston, L. S. Dodd, Mead & Co.
**Bookbinding, Phases of the art of. Prideaux, S. T. net. Scribner.
Bookkeeping, Modern illustrative. Am. Bk.
*Book-plates, American designers of. Edition de luxe. il. Lim. ed. vellum, $4 net. Kelly.
*Book-plates of to-day. Stone, W. M. $1.50 net. Tonnelé.
**Boone, Daniel. Thwaites, R. G. $1 net. Appleton.
Booth, Arthur J: Discovery and decipherment of the triangular cuneiform inscriptions. 8°. Longmans.
**Border fights and fighters. Brady, C. T. $1.30 net. McClure.
**Borneo head-hunters, Home life of the. Furness, W: H. $7.50 net. Lippincott.
Borrowed plumes. Seaman, O. Holt.

Bosanquet, *Mrs.* Bernard. Strength of the people. 8°. Macmillan.
Bose, J. C. Response in the living and non-living. il Longmans.
Bossuet's oraison funèbre de Louis de Conde and sermon sur les devoirs des rois. (Macmillan's French classics.) Macmillan.
Boston. *See* Winslow, H. M. L. C. Page.
Boston cooking school cook book. Farmer, F. M. $2. Little, B. & Co.
**Boston days. Whiting, L. $1.50 net. Little, B. & Co.
Botany. *See* Jepson, W. L.
Botany. *See* Leavitt's outlines. Am. Bk.
Botsford, G. W. Ancient history for beginners. Macmillan.
†Bottome, Phyllis. Life the interpreter. 8°. Longmans.
Bottone, S. R. Galvanic batteries. il. 12°. Macmillan.
**Boult, M. Romance of Cinderella. il. bds., 6¼x9½. $2.40 net. Russell.
Bourdillon, F. W. The night has a thousand eyes. (Impression leaflets.) 10 c. Elder.
*Bourne, Eugene. Book of the daffodil. il. (Handbooks of practical gardening, no. 14.) $1 net. Lane.
Bourne, H: E. Teaching of history and civics in the elementary and secondary school. (American teachers ser.) 8°. $1.50. Longmans.
**Boutell, C: English heraldry. il. 8°. $1.75 net. Lippincott.
Boutell, C: *See* Lacombe, M. P. Lippincott.
Bowditch, H: I. Life and correspondence of. Bowditch, V. Y. 2 v. Houghton, M. & Co
Bowditch, V. Y. Life and correspondence of Henry Ingersoll Bowditch. 2 v. Houghton, M. & Co.
**Boy and the baron. Knapp, A. $1 net. Century.
**Boy Donald and his hero. Shirley, P. 60 c. Lee & Shepard.
Boy land boomer. Bonehill, R. $1. Saalfield.
**Boy of a thousand years ago. Comstock, H. T. 80 c. net. Lee & Shepard.
Boy squatter (The). Jarrold, E. 60 c. Jamieson-H.
Boylan, Grace D. Young folks' Uncle Tom's cabin. il. 12°. 60 c. Jamieson-H.
Boynton, H: W., *ed.* Complete poems of Alexander Pope. Cambridge ed. Cr. 8°, $2. Houghton, M. & Co.
Boys' and girls' bookshelf. 30 v. il. 12°, $1. Little, B. & Co.
Boys' book of inventions. Baker, R. S. $2. McClure.
Boys' Iliad. Perry, W. C. Macmillan
**Boys of Bunker Academy. Stoddard, W. O. $1 net. Jacobs.
Boys of Spartan House School. $1.50. Young.
Boys of the Central. Thurston, *Mrs.* I. T. $1. Pilgrim Press.
**Boys of the Rincon ranch. Canfield, H. S. $1. Century.
**Boys of Waveney College. Leighton, R. net. Putnam.
Boys' self governing clubs. Buck, W. Macmillan.
Braden, Ja. A. Far past the frontier. il. 12°. $1. Saalfield.
**Bradford, Amory H. Messages of the masters. $2 net. Crowell.
Bradford ser. Wessels.
Contents: Savile, The lady's New Year's gift.—Practical wisdom.—Friendship.
**Brady, Cyrus T. Border fights and fighters. il. 12°. $1.30 net. McClure.
**Brady, Cyrus T. In the wasp's nest. il. 8°. $1.50 net. Scribner.
†Brady, Cyrus T. Woven with the ship. il. 12°. $1.50. Lippincott.
Braeme, C. M., ["Bertha M. Clay."] Dolores; traducida al castellano por Don Vicente Becerra. Appleton.
**Brain, Belle M. Stories of sunrise land (Japan). 12°. 75 c. net. Revell.
**Brainerd, Edna S. Millicent in dreamland. (Cosy corner ser.) 40 c. net. L. C. Page.
**Bramble brae. Bridges, R. $1.25 net. Scribner.
**Brave heart Elizabeth. Thompson, A. M. $1 net. Lee & Shepard.
Brave little cousin. Marchant, B. $1. Young.
**Brazil. *See* Tucker, H. C. Revell.
†Breachley—black sheep. Becke, L: $1.50. Lippincott.
Breakfast table series. *See* Holmes, O. W. Houghton, M. & Co.
**Breaking and riding. Fillis, J. $5 net. [Imp.] Scribner.
Breakneck farm. Raymond, E. $1.25. Street.
Brearley, Harry, *and* Ibbotson, F: Analysis of steel works materials. Diagrams. 8°. Longmans.
†Breckenridge, Alice J. Holland wolves. il. 12°. $1.50. McClure.
Breckenridge, S. P. Legal tender. 8°. Univ. of Chic.
Breeding, Stock. *See* Brewer, W. H. Macmillan.
**Brenda's cousin at Radcliffe. $1.20 net. Little, B. & Co.
*Bretherton, R. H. The child mind. 12°. $1.20 net. Lane.
**Brevities. Matthewman, L. de V. 80 c. net. Coates.
Brewer, W. H. Principles of stock breeding. (Rural science ser.) 16°. Macmillan.
Bridge of the gods. Balch, F. H. $1.50. McClurg.
Bridges, R. (England.) Milton's prosody. Oxford Univ.
**Bridges, Rob., ["Droch."] Bramble brae. $1.25 net. Scribner.
Bridgman, L. J. Kewts. (Caldwell's instructive juveniles.) col. il. 8¼ x 10⅝. $1. Caldwell.
Bridgman, L. J. Guess again. (Caldwell's 20th century juveniles.) col. il. $1.25. Caldwell.
Brierly, J. Ourselves and the universe. 12° Whittaker
**Briggs, C: A: Incarnation of the Lord. 8°. $1.50 net. Scribner.
†Brill, G: R. Andy and the ignoramus. il Biddle.
†Brill, G: R. Bobby Bumpkin. il. Biddle.
Brilliants series. il. 6⅞ x 4¼. 35 c. Caldwell.
New volumes: Brilliants from Talmage. —Brilliants from Spurgeon.

**Brine, Mary D. Lassie and laddie. il 12°. net, $1. Dutton.
Britanniæ scriptorum, Index. *See* Poole, R. L. Oxford Univ.
Britannicus. Racine, J. Holt.
British America. *See* Young, E. R. Revell.
**British art, Makers of. *See* Manson, J. A., *ed.*
British colonies and protectorates. Jenkyns, *Sir* H: Oxford Univ.
Brocade series. *See* Mosher's.
*Bronchi, Diseases of the. *See* Nothnagel's encyclopedia of practical medicine. Saunders.
Brontë, Charlotte. *See* Bonnell, H: H. Longmans.
Brontë, Charlotte, Emily *and* Anne. Poems. Limited ed. Dodd, Mead & Co.
**Brooke, S. A. Robert Browning. 12°. $1.50 net. Crowell.
**Brooks, Amy. Dorothy Dainty. il. 12°. 80 c. net. Lee & Shepard.
**Brooks, Amy. Randy and her friends. il. 12°. 80 c. net. Lee & Shepard.
Brooks, Edith H. Rain blossoms. 16°. 80 c. Young.
*Brooks, H. S. Progression to immortality. 12°. 50 c. net. Wessels.
**Brooks, Noah. Sir William Pepperell. 12°. (Life histories ser.) $1 net. Appleton.
Brooks, Phillips. Addresses. (Sesame classics.) il. 7 x 4¼. limp ooze cf., boxed, $1.25. Caldwell.
Brooks, Phillips. The beauty of a life of service. (Words of help ser.) 30 c. Caldwell.
Brooks, Phillips. The Christ in whom Christians believe. (Words of help ser.) 30 c. Caldwell.
Brooks, Phillips. The duty of the Christian business man. (Words of help ser.) 30 c. Caldwell.
**Brooks, Phillips. Law of growth, and other sermons. 12°. $1.20 net. Dutton.
Brooks by the traveller's way. Jowett, J. H. Armstrong.
Broom squire (The). Baring-Gould, S. 50 c. Stokes.
Broomell, I. N. Anatomy and histology of the mouth and teeth. il. 2d ed. rev. 8°. $4.50. Blakiston.
Brown, Abbie F. Pocketful of posies. il. 12°. Houghton, M. & Co.
Brown, J: Rab and his friends. (Chateau ser.) il. 6 x 4. boxed, 75 c. Caldwell.
**Brown, *Capt.* John, of Harper's Ferry. Newton, J: $1.25 net. Wessels.
Brown, Elmer E. Making of middle schools. 8°. Longmans.
Brown, F., *and* Gilder, *Mrs.* J. B., *eds.* The Bible for children. col. il. 4°. $3. Century.
Brown, Francis. *See* Knox, G: W:
Brown, Glenn, *ed.* European and Japanese gardens. il. sm. 4°. $2. Coates.
**Brown, S: Pollins: a missionary biography. Griffis, W: E. il. $1.25 net. Revell.
**Brown, T. A. History of the New York stage. Limited ed. 2 v. $25 special net; Japan cop., $50 special net. Dodd, Mead & Co.
**Brown, W: A. Essence of Christianity. 8°. $1.50 net. Scribner.
Brown, W: P. Ralph Granger's fortunes. il. 12°. $1. Saalfield.
Browne, E: G. Literary history of Persia. (Library of literary history.) $4. Scribner.
Brownies (The). Ewing, J. H. 50 c. Caldwell.
**Browning, Eliz. B. Poems. (Macmillan's pocket classics.) 18°. 25 c. net. Macmillan.
**Browning, Eliz. B. Sonnets from the Portuguese. (Sonnet ser.) 4°. vellum, $4 net. Brentano.
*Browning, Eliz. B. Sonnets from the Portuguese. (Mosher's vest pocket ser.) 25 c.-$1 net. Mosher.
Browning, Eliz. B. Sonnets from the Portuguese. Dec. and col. il. by Marg. Armstrong. 12°. $2.50. Putnam.
Browning, Eliz. B. Sonnets from the Portuguese. 12°. (Kelmscott books.) $1. Pott.
Browning, Rob. In a balcony. Introd. by Laura McAdoo Triggs. il. 12°. $3. 15 copies on Japan vellum, $5. Blue Sky Press.
Browning, Rob. Men and women. (Remarque ser.) 3⅞ x 5⅜. 40 c.; limp leath., boxed, 75 c.; limp chamois, $1.25. Caldwell.
Browning, Rob. Pippa passes. Il. holiday ed. 12°. $1.50. Estes.
Browning, Rob. Pippa passes. 8°. (Mosher's old world ser.) $1 net; Jap. vellum, $2.50 net. Mosher.
Browning, Rob. Selections. Laureate ser. 75 c.; $1.50.—New Kalon, 50 c.—Sesame classics, $1.25. Caldwell.
**Browning, Rob. Birrell, A. $1 net. Dodd, Mead & Co.
**Browning, Rob. Brooke, S. A. $1.50 net. Crowell.
**Browning, Rob. Chesterton, G. K. 75 c. net. Macmillan.
Browning, Rob. Birthday book. 24°. 50 c. Whittaker.
Browning, Robert, poet and man. Cary, E. L. $2.50; $3.50 net. Putnam.
Bruce, W. H Some properties of the triangle and its circles. (Mathematical monograph ser., no. 8.) Heath.
**Bruce, W. S. Formation of Christian character. 12°. $1.75 net. [Imp.] Scribner.
†Brush, Christine C. Colonel's opera cloak. New ed. il. 12°. $1.50. Little, B. & Co.
Bryant, Anna F B. Christmas cat. Pilgrim Press.
**Bryant, W: C. Selected poems. 18°. (Macmillan's pocket classics.) 25 c. net. Macmillan
Bryce, Ja. Studies in history and jurisprudence. 2 v. 8°. Oxford Univ.
Buchheim, C. A., *ed.* *See* Goethe. Oxford Univ.
Buck, Carl D. *See* Hale, W: G.
Buck, Winifred. Boy's self governing clubs. 12°. Macmillan.
Buckland, A. R., *and* Mullins, J. D. Missionary speaker's manual. $1.25. Am. Tr.
Buckley, Arabella B. Nature articles for children. (Title not yet selected.) Holt.

*Budd, T. Good order established in Pennsylvania and New Jersey (1678). Reprint. 250 copies, bds., about $2; 15 copies, Jap. pap., $3 net. Burrows.
**Buell, A: C. Sir William Johnson. il. 12°. (Historic lives ser.) $1 net. Appleton.
**Builders of the republic. Hamm, M. A. $2 net. Pott.
Building construction and superintendence. 3 v. il. 8°. ea., $4. W: T. Comstock. *New volumes:* pt. 1, Mason's work, 5th ed.—pt. 3, Trussed roofs and roof trusses.
Bullen, Fk. T. Cruise of the "Cachalot." (Il. lib. of fam. bks.) il. 12°. 75 c. Caldwell.
†Bullen, Fk. T. A whaleman's wife. il. 12°. $1.50. Appleton.
Bulwer-Lytton, *Earl.* Complete works. Author's ed. New issue. 15 v. buckram, $15; hf. leath., $22; hf. cf., $30. Wessels.
+Bulwer-Lytton, *Earl.* Historical novels. il. 6 v. ea., $1.25. Scribner.
†Bulwer-Lytton, *Earl.* Last days of Pompeii. (Turner house classics.) il. 12°. 75 c. Brentano.
Bunch of buckskins. Remington, F: $6; single prints, $1. Russell.
Bunch of rope yarns. King, S. H. $1.25. Badger.
*Bunyan, J: (New century.) Complete in 1 v. $1 net; $1.50 net. Nelson.
†Bunyan, J: Pilgrim's progress; il. by Bennett. New ed. 8°. $1.50; ¾ mor., $3.50. Lippincott.
**Burdick, Francis M Essentials of business law. 12°. $1.25 net. Appleton.
Burgert, Celia M. *See* Skinner, W. H. Silver.
Burges letters (The). Lyall, Edna. Longmans.
*Burgess, Gelett. Romance of the commonplace. 8°. $1.50 net; Autograph ed., 90 copies, ½ parch., $5 net; 10 copies, levant, $15 net. Elder.
Burgess, Theodore C. Epideictic literature. 6¾ x 9½. (Studies in classical philology, v. 3, no. 5.) pap., $1 net. Univ. of Chic.
Burglar's (The) daughter. Penrose, Marg. 50 c. Caldwell.
**Burker, Alonzo. Soo Thah. il. 12°. $1 net. Revell.
Burlesques. Thackeray, W: M. 75 c. Caldwell
Burn, J. H. Our reasonable service: thoughts from the writings of W. J. Knox-Little. 16°. $1. Young.
**Burne-Jones, *Sir* E: Pictures of romance and wonder. Pictures. buckram, 11 x 14. $5 net. Russell.
Burnet, *Bishop.* Memoirs of. Foxcroft, *Miss* H. F., *ed.* Oxford Univ.
Burnett, Frances Hodgson. Editha's burglar. (New Kalon ser.) il. 12°. 50 c. Caldwell.
Burney, C. F. Notes on the Hebrew text of the Books of Kings. Oxford Univ.
Burney, Frances. *See* D'Arblay, *Mme.*
†Burnham, Clara L. Right princess. 12°. $1.50. Houghton, M. & Co.
**Burnley, Ja. Summits of success. 12°. $1.50 net. Lippincott.
**Burns, Rob. Poems. il. (Caxton ser.) lambskin, $1.25 net. Scribner.
*Burns, Rob. Poems and songs. (New century.) $1 net; $1.50 net. Nelson.
**Burns, Rob. Scottish songs. (Sonnet ser.) 4°. vellum, $4 net. Brentano.
Burr, W: H. Ancient and modern civil engineering and the Isthmian canal. 8°. Wiley.
**Burrell, D: J. A quiver of arrows. [Sermons.] Sel. by T: Douglas. 8°. $1.20 net. Funk.
**Burrell, D: J. Wonderful Teacher and what He taught. 12°. $1.20 net. Revell.
**Burroughs, J: John James Audubon. (Beacon biographies.) 5⅝ x 3¾. 75 c. net; lambskin, $1 net. Small, M.
Burton, F: R. The song and the singer. il. 12°. $1.50 net. Street.
Bury, F. B. *See* Foreign statesmen series. Macmillan.
Bushnell, Horace. Life and letters of. Cheney, M. B., *ed.* $3. Scribner.
Bushnell, Horace. Spirit in man. 12°. $1.25. Scribner.
Business. *See* Appleton's business series.
**Business law, Essentials of. Burdick, F. M. $1.25 net. Appleton.
Butler, Clementina. Life of William Butler. il. 8°. Eaton & M.
**Butler, Howard C. Story of Athens. il. $2.40 net. Century.
Butler, N: M. Meaning of education New ed. 12°. Macmillan.
Butler, William, Life of. Butler, C. Eaton & M.
**Butterworth, Hezekiah. Traveler tales of the Pan-American countries. 8°. $1.20 net. Estes.
†By order of the prophet. Henry, A. H. il. 12°. $1.50. Revell.
*By sundown shores. Macleod, F. 75 c. net. Mosher.
†By the ramparts of Jezreel. Davenport, A. $1.50. Longmans.
By the stage door. Patterson, A. $1.50. Grafton Press.
Byford, H: T. Manual of gynecology. 3d ed. rev. il. $3. Blakiston.
†Bylow Hill. Cable, G: W. $1.25. Scribner.
†Byrde, Margaretta. The searchers. 12°. $1.50. Funk.
Byrne, Mary A. Little woman in the spout. il. 12°. 60 c. Saalfield.
Byrne, Mary A. Roy and Rosyrocks. il. 12°. 60 c. Saalfield.
Byron, *Lord.* Works; ed. by R. E. Prothero and E. H. Coleridge. New ed. 12 v. 8°. per v., $2; set, $24. [Imp.] Scribner.
**Cabinet-making and designing. Spooner, C. $1.20 net. Appleton.
†Cable, G: W. Bylow Hill. col. il. $1.25. Scribner
**Cadness, H: Decorative brush work and elementary design. il. 8°. $1.40 net. Scribner.
Caedmon, the first English poet. Gaskin, R. T. 40 c. Young.
**Cæsar, Augustus. Firth, J. B. $1.35 net; $1.60 net. Putnam.
Cæsar, Julius. Gallic war. Bk. I. A word for word rendering into English. Sauveur, L. 25 c. W: R. Jenkins.

Cæsar, Julius, Portraitures of. Scott, F. J. Longmans.
Cæsar, Julius, Talks with, de Bello Gallico. Sauveur, L. $1.25. W: R. Jenkins.
Cæsar's commentaries. Westcott, J: H. 12°. (20th century text-books.) Appleton.
Cæsar's Gallic war. Harkness *and* Forbes. $1.25. Am. Bk.
†Caffyn, *Mrs.* K. Mannington, ["Iota."] Comedy in spasms. (Copyright ser.) 12°. 50 c. Stokes.
Cagliostro and company. Funck-Brentano, F. $1.50. Pott.
Calculus, Introduction to the. Echols, W. H. Holt.
Calculus of variations. Bolza, O. 8°. Univ. of Chic.
Caldwell's illustrated lib. of famous books. il. 12°. ea., 75 c. Caldwell.
New volumes: Thackeray, Adventures of Philip; Burlesques; Christmas books; Paris sketch book; Roundabout papers.—Dickens, Barnaby Rudge; Bleak House; Christmas stories; Dombey and son; Great expectations; Little Dorrit; Martin Chuzzlewit; Nicholas Nickleby.—Bullen, Cruise of the "Cachalot."—Eliot, G:, Poems; Essays.—Gaboriau, Gilded clique; In peril of his life; The Lerouge case; File no. 113.—Gulliver's travels.—Barrie, The little minister.—Sterne, Sentimental journey.
Caldwell's instructive juveniles. Caldwell.
New volume: Bridgman, Kewts.
Caldwell's new Berkeley library. il. 12°. ea., $1. Caldwell.
New volumes: Carey, Aunt Diana; Averil; Merle's crusade; Our Bessie.—Lever, Charles O'Malley.—Lamb, Essays of Elia.—Clement, Constantinople.—Doyle, Firm of Girdlestone.—Dumas, The forty-five; The last vendee; La dame de Monsoreau; Taking the Bastile; Louise de La Vallière; Two Dianas; Man with the iron mask.—Lyall, Knight errant.—"Duchess," Molly Bawn.—Dickens, Our mutual friend.—Thackeray, Pendennis.—Carlyle, Past and present.—Dana, Two years before the mast.
Caldwell's 20th century juveniles. Caldwell.
New volume: Bridgman, Guess again.
**Calendar for 1903, Christy. Christy, H. C. $3 net. Scribner.
*Calendar for shavers. *See* Franklin, J. D. E. W. Dayton.
Calendars. *See* advertisements: E. P. Dutton & Co.—Elder & Shepard.—W: R. Jenkins.—F. H. Revell.—R. H. Russell.—F. A. Stokes Co.—A. Wessels Co.
California. *See* Tarr *and* McMurry geographies. Macmillan.
California, Glimpses of. Jackson, H. $1.50. Little, B. & Co.
*California, Some byways of. Carter, C: F. $1.25 net. Grafton Press.
California, Stories of. Sexton, E. M. Macmillan.
†Calkins, F. W. Two wilderness voyagers. 12°. $1.50. Revell.
Calkins, N. A. Nuevo manual de enseñanzo objectiva. Appleton.
Callahan, C. E. Fogg's ferry. il. 75 c.; pap., 25 c. Laird.
Called to fight. Hallett, C. M. 75 c. Young.
Calvé, Emma. Gallus, A. $1.50. Russell.
Cambridge historical series; ed. by G. W. Prothero. Macmillan.
New volumes: Pollard, Germany, 1500-1792.—Headlam, Germany, 1815-1889.
Cambridge modern history. *See* Ward, A. W., *ed.* Macmillan.
Cambridge Platonists, Selections from. Campagnac, E. T., *ed.* Oxford Univ.
Cameos from nature. Gumersall, *Mrs.* J. T. $1.80. Whittaker.
Campagnac, E. T., *ed.* Selections from the Cambridge Platonists. Oxford Univ.
Campbell, A. M. G. Sarah's first start in life. 16°. 20 c. Young.
**Campbell, Alex. C. Insurance and crime. 8°. net. Putnam.
**Canfield, H. S. Boys of the Rincon ranch. (St. Nicholas ser.) il. 12°. $1. Century.
**Canfield, W. W. Legends of the Iroquois. Lim. ed. il. 8°. pap. bds., $2.50 net. Wessels.
Canterbury tales. Chaucer, G. $1. Lane.
*Canton, W:, *and* Robinson, H. P., *comps.* Songs of England's glory. lamb., $1.25 net. Putnam.
Cap and gown. Paget, R. L., *ed.* 3d ser. $1.25; $2.50. L. C. Page.
†Capes, Bernard. From door to door. (Copyright ser.) 12°. 50 c. Stokes.
†Captain (The). Williams, F. C. $1.50. Lothrop.
**Captain Craig: a book of poems. Robinson, E. A. $1 net; $1.25 net. Houghton, M. & Co.
†Captain Fanny. Russell, W. C. 50 c New Amsterdam.
†Captain Macklin. Davis, R: H. $1.50. Scribner.
†Cap'n Titus. Mayo, C. $1. Doubleday, P.
Captive of the Roman eagles. Dahn, F. $1.50. McClurg.
†Captured Santa Claus. Page, T: N. 75 c. Scribner.
**Careless Jane. Pyle, K. 75 c. net. Dutton.
Carey, Rosa N. Aunt Diana. (New Berkeley lib.) il. 12°. $1. Caldwell.
Carey, Rosa N. Averil. (New Berkeley lib.) il. 12°. $1. Caldwell.
†Carey, Rosa N. Highway of fate. il. 12°. $1.50. Lippincott.
Carey, Rosa N. Merle's crusade. (New Berkeley lib.) il. 12°. $1. Caldwell.
Carey, Rosa N. Our Bessie. (New Berkeley lib.) il. 12°. $1. Caldwell.
Carita. Pendleton, L: 75 c. Badger.
**Carleton, Will. Songs of two centuries. il. sq. 8°. $1.50 net. Harper.
Carlin, W. E. *See* Money, A. W.
†Carling, J: R. Shadow of the czar. 12°. $1.50. Little, B. & Co.
**Carlyle, Jane Welch. New letters and memorials; ed. with introd. il. pors. facsims. 2 v. 8°. Lane.
Carlyle, T: Complete works. 10 v. il. 8°. per set, $10; $12.50; hf. leath., $15; hf. cf., $25. Crowell.
Carlyle, T: Complete works. Author's ed. New issue. 10 v. buckram, $10; hf. leath., $15; hf. cf., $20. Wessels.
*Carlyle, T: French revolution. (New century.) $1 net; $1.50 net. Nelson.

Carlyle, T: French revolution. (Putnam's lib. of standard lit., no. 8.) 8°. $1.75. Putnam.

Carlyle, T: Past and present. (New Berkeley lib.) il. 12°. $1. Caldwell.

**Carman, Bliss. Pipes of Pan. ea., $1 net. L. C. Page.

Contents: 1, From the Book of myths.—2, From the Green book of the bards.

**Carnegie, Andrew. Alderson, B. $1.40 net. Doubleday, P.

Carpenter, F: I., *ed.* Life and repentance of Marie Magdalene. 8°. Univ. of Chic.

Carpenter, H. W. Church of England. 16°. Young.

**Carpenter, Kate E. Story of Joan of Arc for boys and girls. il. 12°. 80 c. net. Lee & Shepard.

Carpenter, R. C. Heating and ventilation of buildings. 4th ed. rev. 8°. $4. Wiley.

Carrington, Fitz Roy. *See* Song of songs. Russell.

†Carroll, Lewis [*pseud.* for C: L. Dodgson.] Alice in Wonderland. New ed. col. il. 4°. $1. Wessels.

†Carroll, Lewis. Alice in Wonderland.—Through the looking-glass. New ed. col. il. 4°. $2. Wessels.

**Carroll, Lewis. Through the looking-glass. il. 8°. vellum, $3 net. Harper.

**Carruth, Frances W. Fictional rambles in and about Boston. il. 12°. $1.50 net. McClure.

**Carryl, G. W. Grimm tales made gay. il. 12°. $1.50 net. Houghton, M. & Co.

*Carter, C: F. Some by-ways of California. 12°. $1.25 net. Grafton Press.

**Carter, *Mrs.* Leslie, as Madame Du Barry. il. 12°. bds., 50 c. net. Stokes.

**Cartoons in colors. Christy, H. C. 6 in box. $5 net. Scribner.

Cartwright, Julia, [*Mrs.* H: Ady.] J. F. Millet. 2d ed. il. 8°. Macmillan.

*Carus, Paul. Nirvana. 8 x 5½. 60 c. net. Open Court.

*Cary, Eliz. L. Browning, poet and man. 8°. hf.-tone il. $2.50; photogrv., $3.50 net. Putnam.

*Cary, Eliz L. The Rossettis, Dante, Gabriel and Christina. 8°. hf.-tone il. $2.50; photogrv., $3.50 net. Putnam.

*Cary, Eliz. L. Tennyson: his homes, his friends, and his work. 8°. hf.-tone il., $2.50; photogrv., $3.50 net. Putnam.

**Cary, Eliz. L. William Morris: poet, craftsman, socialist. il. 8°. $3.50 net. Putnam.

Cast away in the jungle. St. Clair, V. Street.

†Castle, Egerton Light of Scarthey. (Copyright ser.) 12°. 50 c. Stokes.

†Castle, Egerton. Light of Scarthey. (Library of successes.) 12°. pap., 50 c. Stokes.

Castle Blair. Shaw, F. L. Heath.

†Castle Craneycrow. McCutcheon, G: B. $1.50. Stone.

†Castle Omeragh. Moore, F. F. $1.50. Appleton.

**Castlemon, Harry, [*pseud.* for C: A. Fosdick.] The haunted mine. il. 12°. 80 c. net. Coates.

Castlemon, Harry. Struggle for a fortune. il. 12°. $1. Saalfield.

Castles of England and Wales. *See* Timbs, J: Warne.

Castleton's "Prep." Murray, C. $1.25. Am. S. S.

Catalogue of the Turkish, Hindustani, and Pushtu MSS. in the Bodleian Library. Pt. 2. Oxford Univ.

**Catch words of cheer. Hubbard, S. H. 80 c. net. McClurg.

**Caterpillars and their moths. Eliot, I. M. $2 net. Century.

**Catharine's proxy. Hamlin, M. S. $1.20 net. Little, B. & Co.

Cathcart, W: L. Machine elements. Tables, diagrams. Van Nostrand.

Cathcart, W: L. Marine engine design. Van Nostrand.

Cathcart, W: L. Stationary engine design. Van Nostrand.

Cathedral churches of England; notes by P. Home. il. 4°. $3. Young.

**Cathedrals, English. Litchfield, P. A. $2 net; $2.50 net. Lippincott.

Catherine of Sienna, Story of. Witts, F. 50 c. Whittaker.

**Catholic church, Later. Rainy, R. $2 net. Scribner.

**Cats and all about them. Simpson, F. $1 net. Stokes.

Catterall, R. C. H. History of the United States Bank. 8°. Univ. of Chic.

Causeries avec les enfants. Sauveur, L. $1. W: R. Jenkins.

Causeries avec mes élèves. Sauveur, L. $1.25. W: R. Jenkins.

Causeries avec mes élèves, Corrigé des traductions des. Sauveur, L. 25 c. W: R. Jenkins.

**Caxton ser. Scribner.

New volumes: Burns, Poems.—Story of Rosalind.—Herrick's Hesperides and Noble numbers.—Don Quixote, tr. by Motteux.

Cecil, *Mrs.* Evelyn, [Alicia Amherst.] Children's gardens. il. 8°. Macmillan.

Cecilia, the last of the vestals. Crawford, F. M. Macmillan.

Celestial mechanics, Introdution to. Moulton, F. R. Macmillan.

*Censorinus, Golden book of. Tr. 8°. $1.50 net. Cambridge.

Centennial of home missions, 1802-1902. 12°. Presb. Bd.

**Century classics. 12°. ea., $1.25 net. Century.

New volumes: Lamb's Essays of Elia.—Sterne's Sentimental journey.

**Century of sonnets. Herrick, *Mrs.* S. B. $2.60 net. Russell.

*Cervantes, Miguel de. Don Quixote. (New Century.) $1 net; $1.50 net. Nelson.

**Cervantes, Miguel de. Don Quixote. (Motteux, tr.) (Caxton ser.) il. lambskin, $1.25 net. Scribner.

Chadwick, J: W. *and* Anne H. Out of the heart. New ed. il. 12°. $1.25; ¾ mor., $3. L. C. Page.

Challacombe, Jessie. How the fire spread. 16°. 40 c. Young.

Challacombe, Jessie. Poor man's palace. 16°. 20 c. Young.

**Chalmers, Ja.. Autobiography and letters. Lovett. R:, *ed.* $1.50 net. *Revell.*
**Chamberlain, Basil H. Things Japanese. 4th ed. 12°. $4 net. [Imp.] Scribner.
**Chambers, Arthur. Our life after death. 12°. 80 c. net. Jacobs.
†Chambers. Rob. W. Ashes of empire. (Copyright ser.) 12°. 50 c. Stokes.
†Chambers. Rob. W. Maid-at-arms. il. post 8°. $1.50. Harper.
**Chambers, Rob. W. Outdoorland. $1.50 net. Harper.
**Chambers' cyclopædia of English literature; ed. by D. Patrick. New ed. il. 3 v. v. 3. 8°. per v., $5 net. Lippincott.
**Champion (The). Murfree, M. N. $1.20 net. Houghton, M. & Co.
**Champney, Eliz. W. Margarita: legend of the fight for the great river. il. 12°. (Dames and daughters of colonial days.) $1.25 net. Dodd, Mead & Co.
Chandler, J. A. C. Virginia supplement. (Tarr and McMurry geographies.) Macmillan.
†Changeling (The). Besant, *Sir* W. 50 c. Stokes.
Channing, Blanche M. The Balaster boys. il. $1.25. Wilde.
Channing, E: First lessons in U. S. history. il. 12°. Macmillan.
Channing, E: *See* Higginson, T: W. Longmans.
**Channing, W: Ellery. Note-book. (Grace E. Channing.) 50 c. net. Am. Unitarian.
Chanson (La) de Roland; ed. by J. Geddes, jr. (Macmillan's French classics.) Macmillan.
Chansons (Les) de Beranger. $1.25. W: R. Jenkins.
**Character building, Four studies in. Hillis, N. D. 75 c. net. Revell.
*Character of the province of Maryland. Alsop, G. (London, 1666.) Repr. $2; $3 net. Burrows.
Character of Theophrastus; tr. by C: E. Bennett and W: A. Hammond. 16°. Longmans.
**Character, Pursuit of. Willett, H. L. 35 c. net. Revell.
Charlemagne and twelve peers of France, Stories of. Church, A. J. Macmillan.
Charles O'Malley. Lever, C: $1. Caldwell.
Chase, G: D. Cornelius Nepos. 12°. (20th century text-books.) Appleton.
**Chase, Jessie Anderson. Mayken. il. sm. 4°. $1.20 net. McClurg.
Chase, Rob. H. General paresis. il. $1.75 net. Blakiston.
**Chasing an iron horse. Robins, E: $1 net. Jacobs.
Chateau ser. 6 x 4. boxed. ea., 75 c. Caldwell. *New volumes:* Doyle, Study in scarlet.—Bacon's essays.—Optic, The boat club.—Connor, Black Rock.—Holland, Bitter Sweet.—Stevenson, Child's garden of verses.—Fowler, Concerning Isabel Carnaby.—Franklin, Autobiography.—Mitchell, Dream life.—Lamb, Essays of Elia.—Shelley, Frankenstein.—Gold dust.—Thomas à Kempis, Imitation of Christ.—Hamerton, Intellectual life.—Weyman, King's stratagem.—Murray, Like Christ.—Mill, Liberty.—Arnold, Light of Asia.—Clifford, Love letters of a worldly woman.—Sienkiewicz, Let us follow Him.—Kipling, Letters of marque; Mine own people; Phantom 'rickshaw; Under the deodars.—Drummond, Natural law in the spiritual world.—Hall, Come to Jesus.—Brown, Rab and his friends.—Ruskin, Sesame and lilies.—Glyn, Visits of Elizabeth.—Barrie, Window in Thrums.
**Chatterbox for 1902. il. 4°. $1.40 net; bds., 90 c. net. Estes.
Chatterton, Eyre. Story of fifty years' mission work in Chhota Nagpur. map. il. 8°. $2. Young.
Chaucer, G. Canterbury tales. (Bibelots ser.) leath., $1. Lane.
Chaucer, G. Nonnes preestes tale of the cok and hen. Jap. vellum, $7.50; hand illum., over $16.50. Grafton Press.
**Chaucer, G. Prologue and knight's tale. (Macmillan's pocket classics.) 18°. 25 c. net. Macmillan.
Chaucer, G. Wife of Bath's tale. 150 copies, decor., ea., $10; 50 copies, hand illum., ea., $35. Grafton Press.
Chaucer's, Indebtedness of. Troilus and Criseyde to Guido delle Colonne's Historia Trojana. Hamilton, G: L. Macmillan.
**"Chauffeur." 2000 miles on an automobile. il. 8°. $2 net. Lippincott.
Chaytor, H. J. Troubadours of Dante. Oxford Univ.
**Cheever, *Mrs.* Harriet A. Doctor Robin. 12°. 40 c. net. Estes.
Cheever, *Mrs.* Harriet A. Elmcove. il. 12°. $1.25. Am. Tr.
**Cheever, *Mrs.* Harriet A. Maid Sally. 12°. $1 net. Estes.
Chemistry, Analytical, Short text book of. 2 v. v. 1. Treadwell, F. P. Wiley.
*Chemistry by induction. Hinds, J. I. D. 75 c. net. Wiley.
Chemistry, Inorganic. Hinds, J. I. D. $3. Wiley.
Chemistry, Lessons in elementary. Roscoe, *Sir* H: E. Macmillan
Chemistry, Organic. Holleman, A. F. Wiley.
Chemistry, Organic. Noyes, W: A. Holt.
Chemistry, Teaching of. *See* Smith, Alex. Longmans.
Chemistry. *See* Clarke *and* Dennis's. Am. Bk.
Chemistry. *See* Garvin, J: B. Heath.
Chemistry, Laboratory manual. *See* Clarke and Dennis's. Am. Bk.
Cheney, Ma. B., *ed.* Life and letters of Horace Bushnell. New ed. il. 8°. $3. Scribner.
Chesterfield, *Lord.* Letters. (Silver ser. of classics.) 35 c. Silver.
**Chesterton, G. K. Browning. (English men of letters.) 75 c. net. Macmillan.
**Chesterton, Gilbert. The defendant. 12°. $1.25 net. Dodd, Mead & Co.
†Chevalier d'Auriac (The). Yeats, S. L. $1.25. Longmans.
Cheyne, T: K. Book of Psalms. New ed. 2 v. 8°. $9.60. Whittaker.
**Cheyne, T: K., *and* Black, J. S., *eds.* Encyclopædia Biblica. 4 v. v. 4. 8°. subs. only. ea., $5 net; hf. mor., $7.50 net. Macmillan.

**Chignell, Rob. J. M. W. Turner. il. 8°. (Makers of British art.) $1.25 net. [Imp.] Scribner.
Child (The) and the curriculum. Dewey, J: 25 c. net. Univ. of Chic.
Child life sixth reader. Blaisdell, E. A. Macmillan.
*Child mind. Bretherton, R. H. $1.20 net. Lane.
**Children, Book of joyous. Riley, J. W. $1.50 net. Scribner.
Children, Diseases of. Hatfield, M. P. 80 c.; $1. Blakiston.
Children, Diseases of. Holt, L. E. $6. Appleton.
Children, How to bring up your. Locke, J: 50 c. Wessels.
**Children of our town. Wells, C. $4.20 net. Russell.
Children of the frost. London, J. Macmillan.
*Children of the thorn wreath. La Page, G. $1.50 net. Elder.
**Children of the west. Deming, T. O. $1 net. Stokes.
**Children's diet in home and school. Hagan, Louise E. 50 c. net.
Children's favorite classics. 36 v. il. ea., 60 c. Crowell.
New volumes: Butterworth, History of Rome.—Calcott, History of England; History of France.—Raspe, Baron Munchausen.—Spyri, Heidi.—Walpole, History of Greece.
Children's friend ser. il. 50 c. Little, B. & Co.
New volumes: Alcott, Doll's journey; Pansies and water lilies.—Ewing, Snapdragons; Very ill-tempered family.—Hyde, Holly-berry and mistletoe.—Little men play.—Little women play.
Children's gardens. Cecil, *Mrs.* E. Macmillan.
**Children's London. Thorpe, C: $2.50 net. [Imp.] Scribner.
**Child's dream of a star, and Child's story. Dickens, C: 40 c. net. L. C. Page.
Child's garden of verses. Stevenson, R. L: 75 c.; $1.50. Caldwell.
*Child's guide to the Book of Common Brayer. Esdaile, E. 50 c. net. Young.
Child's story of the life of Christ. Hoyt, H. B. $1.25. Wilde.
China and the Chinese. Giles, H. A. Macmillan.
**China, Glimpses of. Morse, E. S. $1.50 net. Little, B. & Co.
China, Story of, Van Bergen's. 60 c. Am. Bk.
**China. Through hidden Shensi. Nichols, F. H. $3.50 net. Scribner.
†Chinese Quaker. Eyster, *Mrs.* N. B. $1.50. Revell.
Chipman, C: P. Last cruise of the "Electra." il. 12°. $1. Saalfield.
**Chips, fragments, and vestiges. Hamilton, G. $1.20 net. Lee & Shepard.
†Cholmondeley, Mary. Love in extremes, and other stories. 12°. $1.50. Dodd, Mead & Co.
**Christ, A canonical life of. Pick, B. $1.20 net. Funk.
**Christ, Bible studies in the life of. 12°. 50 c. net; pap., 25 c. net. Revell.
*Christ in Hades. Phillips, S. 50 c. net.; 75 c. net. Lane.
Christ (The) in whom Christians believe. Brooks, P. 30 c. Caldwell.
Christ (Life of) Child's story of the. Hoyt, H. B. $1.25. Wilde.
Christian apologetic (A). Robbins, W. L. Longmans.
Christian belief, Grounds of. *See* Fisher, G: P.
**Christian character, Formation of. Bruce, W. S. $1.75 net. [Imp.] Scribner.
**Christian church, Short history of. Moncrief, J. W. $1.50 net. Revell.
Christian literature, Early. Platner, J. W. Macmillan.
Christian of to-day. Coe, G: A. $1.50 net. Revell.
**Christian point of view. Knox, G: W: $1 net. Scribner.
*Christian science, Valid objections to so-called. Underhill, A. F. 50 c. net; 25 c. net. Baker & T.
Christian teaching. Tolstoi, *Count* L. 50 c. Stokes.
Christian tradition (The). Pullan, L. Longmans.
Christians. *See* Morgan, G. C. Revell.
Christianity. Mason, A. J. 80 c. Young.
**Christianity, Essence of. Brown, W: A. $1.50 net. Scribner.
Christmas books. Thackeray, W: M. 50 c. Caldwell.
*Christmas carol ser. Sickal, H. M., *ed.* ea., 35 c. net. Elder.
Christmas carols, ancient and modern. Sylveste, J., *ed.* $1. Wessels.
Christmas cat. Bryant, A. F. B. Pilgrim Press.
Christmas, The first. Wallace, L. $1.25. Harper.
**Christmas greeting (A). Corelli, M. $1.50 net. Dodd, Mead & Co.
**Christmas kalends of Provence. Janvier, T: A. $1.25 net. Harper.
Christmas stories. Dickens, C: 75 c. Caldwell.
Christmas stories for children. Dickens, C: 60 c. Jamieson-H.
Christopher, E. E. The invisibles. il. 12°. $1.50. Saalfield.
**Christy, Howard C. Cartoons in colors. 6 in box. $5 net. Scribner.
**Christy, Howard C. Christy calendar for 1903. col. il. $3 net. Scribner.
**Christy calendar for 1903. Christy, H. C. $3 net. Scribner.
Chubb, Percival. Teaching of English. 12°. (Teachers' professional lib.) Macmillan.
Chubby: a nuisance. Penrose, *Mrs.* Longmans.
Church, A. J. Stories of Charlemagne and twelve peers of France. il. 12°. Macmillan.
Church, S: H. Penruddock of the White Lambs. 12°. $1.50. Stokes.
Church and its social mission. Lang, J: M. $1.60. Whittaker.
Church and the ministry in the early centuries. Lindsay, T. H. Armstrong.

**Church calendar for 1903, American. 25 c. net. Jacobs.
Church fasts and festivals. Osborne, E., *and others.* 80 c. Young.
Church Historical Society. *See* Mason, A. J. Young.
Church of England. Carpenter, H. W. Young.
Church of England. History from the abolition of the Roman jurisdiction. Dixon, R. W. v. 5, 6. Oxford Univ.
Church of England, Penny history of. Jessopp, A. 5 c. Young.
Church, Town. *See* Miller, G: A. Revell.
**Churchill, Winston. The crisis. (Jas. K. Hackett ed.) il. 12°. $1.50 net. Macmillan.
**Cicely. Johnston, *Mrs.* A. F. 40 c. net. L. C. Page.
*Cicero. De Officiis. (Arthur L. Humphreys' large type books.) 8°. pap., $7.50 net. Wessels.
Cicero. Friendship. *See* Emerson *and* Cicero. Wessels.
Cicero. Orations and letters. (Macmillan Latin ser.) Macmillan.
Cicero. Tusculan disputations, bk. I., and the Somnium Scipionis; ed. by F. E. Rockwood. (College ser. of Latin authors.) Ginn.
Cicero. *See* Harper and Gallup's. Am. Bk.
Cicero. *See also* Peterson, W. Oxford Univ.
Ciceronis opera rhetorica. Wilkins, A. S., *ed.* Oxford Univ.
Cicero's orations. Forbes, C: H. Appleton.
Circulatory system, Diseases of. Allchin, W. H. Macmillan.
**Citizen and the industrial situation. Potter, H: C. $1 net. Scribner.
Citizen's lib. of economics, politics and sociology; ed. by R: T. Ely. 12°. Macmillan.
New volumes: Ely, Custom and competition.—Zueblin, American municipal progress.—Salmon, History of the appointing power.
*City evangelization. North, F. M. 65 c. net. Lentilhon.
City of mystery. Gunter, A. C. $1.50; 50 c. Home Pub.
City youth. Davidson, J. T. 60 c. net. Am. Tr.
Civics, Teaching of. *See* Bourne, H: E. Longmans.
Civil government, New. *See* Martin's. Am. Bk.
Civil War. *See* Benton, C: E. Putnam.
†Clark, Alf. Finding of Lot's wife. (Copyright ser.) 12°. 50 c. Stokes.
Clark, C: An antarctic queen. $1.75. Warne.
Clark, C: H., ["Max Adeler."] Out of the hurly burly. New ed. il. 12°. $1.25. Coates.
**Clark, S. H. Handbook of best readings. 12°. $1.50 net. Scribner.
Clark, W: *See* Lewis, M., *and* Clark, W:
Clarke and Dennis's Elementary chemistry. $1.10. Am. Bk.
Clarke and Dennis's Laboratory manual. 50 c. Am. Bk.
Clarke's The government. 75 c. Am. Bk.
Classical metres in English verse. Stone, W: J. Oxford Univ.
*Cleaveland, *Mrs.* E. H. J. No sects in heaven: [poem.] flexible, 50 c. net; Lim. ed., flex. suede, $1.50 net. Elder.
Clement *of Alexandria.* *See* Barnard, P. M. Young.
Clement, C. E. Constantinople. (New Berkeley lib.) il. 12°. $1. Caldwell.
Clerke, Agnes M. History of astronomy in 19th century. New ed. il. Macmillan.
Clerke, Agnes M. Problems in astrophysics. il. Macmillan.
Cleveland, F. A. Funds and their uses. il. 12°. (Appletons' business ser.) Appleton.
Clifford, *Mrs.* W. K. Love letters of a worldly woman. (Chateau ser.) il. 6 x 4. boxed, 75 c. Caldwell.
Climatology. Hann, J. Macmillan.
Climax (The). Pidgin, C: F. $1.50. C. M. Clark.
*Climbing plants, Book of. Arnott, S. $1 net. Lane.
Clinical methods. Hutchinson, R. $2.50 net. Keener.
**Clive, *Lord.* Macaulay, T: B. 25 c. net. Macmillan.
*Clodd, E: Grant Allen: a memoir. 12°. $1.25 net. [Imp.] Wessels.
Cloister and the hearth. *See* Reade, C:
Cloud, Virginia W. A wayside harp: [poetry.] 12°. $1. Badger.
Clubs, Boys' self-governing. Buck, W. Macmillan.
**Coal mining, Elementary. Kerr, G: L. $1.25 net. Lippincott.
**Coates, Ella M. Four little Indians. il. 12°. 80 c. net. Coates.
Cobb, B: F. Yankee Mother Goose. col. il. 9 x 11. bds., $1.25. Jamieson-H.
Codrington, T. Roman roads in Britain. map. Young.
**Coe, G: A. Christian of to-day. 12°. $1.50 net. Revell.
**Coffee: its history, classification and description. Walsh, J. M. $2 net. Coates.
Coit, Stanton. Message of man. 16°. 75 c.; leath., $1. Macmillan.
Cok and hen. *See* Chaucer, G. Grafton Press.
Cole, Timothy, *engraver.* *See* Van Dyke, J: C. Century.
Coleridge, Christabel R. Life of Charlotte M. Yonge. il. 8°. Macmillan.
Coleridge, S: T., Select poems of. George, A. J., *ed.* Heath.
Collations from the codex Cluniacensis s. Holkhamicus. (9th century ms. of Cicero.) Peterson, W. Oxford Univ.
College entrance examination board. Questions at examinations held June 16-21, 1902. Ginn.
College ser. of Latin authors. Ginn.
New volume: Cicero, Tusculan disputations, bk. I., and Somnium Scipionis.
Collins, J. C., *ed.* *See* Greene, R. Oxford Univ.
Colomba. Mérimée, P. Ginn.
†Colonel's opera cloak. Brush, C. C. $1.50. Little, B. & Co.
Colonial systems. *See* Snow, A. H. Putnam.
Color mixing. Jennings, A. S. $2. Spon & C.
**Colorado river, Romance of. Dellenbaugh, F: S. net. Putnam.

†Colton, Arthur. Bennie Ben Cree. 16°. 50 c. McClure.
**Columbia Univ. Indo-Iranian ser.; ed. by A. V. W. Jackson. 8°. net. Macmillan.
New volumes: Jackson, Sanskrit grammar.—Schuyler, Bibliography of Sanskrit drama.
Columbia Univ. studies in classical philology; ed. by H. T. Peck *and* E: D. Perry. Macmillan.
Contents: Ball, Satire of Seneca on Apotheosis of Claudius.
Columbia Univ. studies in romance, literature and philology; ed. by A. Cohn *and* H: A. Todd. Macmillan.
New volumes: Hamilton, Indebtedness of Chaucer.—Segall, Corneille and the Spanish drama.—Holbrook, Dante and the animal kingdom.
**Columbus, Chris. Thacher, J: B. 3 v. Putnam.
Coman, Katharine. *See* Bates, Katharine. Macmillan.
Come to Jesus, and follow Jesus. Hall, N. 50 c.; 75 c. Caldwell.
†Come with me into Babylon. Ward, J. M. $1.50. Stokes.
Comedies, Representative English. Gayley, C: M., *ed.* 5 v. 8°. Macmillan.
†Comedy in spasms. Caffyn, *Mrs.* M. 50 c. Stokes.
Comfort, Will L. Lady of Fallen Star island. il. 12°. $1.25. Street.
**Comforting words for sorrowing mothers. il. 60 c. net. Revell.
**Commentary on numbers. Gray, G. B. $2.50 net-$3 net. Scribner.
Commentary on St. Paul's Epistle to the Romans. Beet, J. A. 8°. $2.50. Whittaker.
**Comments of a countess. (Anonymous.) 12°. $1 net. Lane.
Commerce and industries, History of. Ford, W. C. Appleton.
Commerce, Economics of. Scott, W: A. Macmillan.
Commerce, General history of. Webster, W. C. Ginn.
Commerce, Geography of. Trotter, S. Macmillan.
Commerce, History of. Herrick, C. K. Macmillan.
Commerce, Raw material of. Dolley, C: S. Macmillan.
Committee of Fifty on the liquor problem. *See* Billings, J: S. Houghton, M. & Co.
Commonwealth ser. *See* Page's. L. C. Page.
**Compleat angler. Walton, I: 2 v. $12.50 net; $35 net. Lippincott.
**Comrie, Marg. S. Loyal Huguenot maid. (Pastime and adventure ser.) il. 12°. $1 net. Jacobs.
Comstock, G: C. Field astronomy for engineers. 8°. Wiley.
**Comstock, Harriet T. A boy of a thousand years ago. il. 12°. 80 c. net. Lee & Shepard.
†Comstock, Harriet T. Tower or throne: romance of the girlhood of Elizabeth. il. 12°. $1.50. Little, B. & Co.
Concerning children. Stetson, C. P. 50 c. Small, M.
Concerning Isabel Carnaby. Fowler, Ellen T. 50 c.; 75 c. Caldwell.
†Concerning Polly. Winslow, H. M. $1.50. Lee & Shepard.
Conductors for electrical distribution. Perrine, F. A. C. Van Nostrand.
Cone, Orello. Rich and poor in the New Testament. 12°. Macmillan.
**Confessions of a violinist. Phipson, T. L. $1.50 net. Lippincott.
†Confessions of a wife. Adams, Mary, *pseud.* $1.50. Century.
Confirmation lectures on the church catechism. Blunt, R. F. L. 60 c. Young.
**Conger, Arthur B. Religion for the time. 12°. $1 net. Jacobs.
**Conjurer, Modern. Neil, C. L. $2 net. Lippincott.
Conklin, G: W. Civil and business law.—Familiar quotations.—500 ways to make money.—Synonyms and antonyms. (Vest pocket ser.) ea., 25 c.; 50 c. G. W. Ogilvie.
Conklin, G: W. Why? 25 c.-$5. G. W. Ogilvie.
**Connolly, Ja. B. Jeb Hutton. il. 12°. $1.20 net. Scribner.
†Connolly, Ja. B. Out of Gloucester. il. 12°. $1.50. Scribner.
Connor, Ralph. Black Rock. (Chateau ser.) il. 6 x 4. boxed, 75 c. Caldwell.
Conquest (The). Dye, Eya E. $1.50. McClurg.
†Conquest of Charlotte. Meldrum, D. S. $1.50. Dodd, Mead & Co.
†Conquest of Rome. Serao, M. $1.50. Harper.
Conquest of the air. Alexander, J: 75 c. Wessels.
**Conrad, Jos. Typhoon. il. 12°. $1 net. Putnam.
**Constable, J: Windsor, *Lord.* $1.25 net. [Imp.] Scribner.
Constantinople. Clement, C. E. $1. Caldwell.
Contes merveilleux. Sauveur, L. $1.50. W: R. Jenkins.
**Cook, Alb. S. Biblical quotations in old English prose writers. (Yale bicentennial publications.) 8°. net. Scribner.
Cook, Alb. S., *and* Tinker, Chauncey B., *eds.* Select translations from old English poetry. Ginn.
Cook, *Mrs.* E. T. London highways and byways. (Highways and byways ser.) il. 8°. Macmillan.
**Cook, F. A. Through the first Antarctic night. New cheaper ed. 100 il. $2 net. Doubleday, P.
Cook, Theo. A., *ed.* Anthology of humorous verse. (Turner house classics.) il. 12°. 75 c. Brentano.
Cook, Webster. Government of Michigan. (Handbooks of American government.) 12°. Macmillan.
**Cook-book encyclopedia, Harper's. il. $1.50 net. Harper.
Cookery book for little girls. *See* Aggie's cooking party. E. W. Dayton.
**Cooking, Practical, and serving. Hill, J. M. $2 net. Doubleday, P.
**Cooley, C: H. Human nature and the social order. $1.50 net. Scribner.

Cooper, Ja. Fenimore. Selections. (Street and Smith little classics.) 18°. 50 c. Street.
Coptic version of the New Testament, in the Northern dialect; with transl. Final vols., 3 and 4. Oxford Univ.
†Copyright series of famous authors. 12°. ea., 50 c. Stokes.
**Coquo and the king's children. Baker, C. $1.50 net. McClurg.
**Corbin, J: New portrait of Shakespeare; with ref. to the so-called Droeshout original and the Ely Palace portrait. il. 12°. $1.25 net. Lane.
**Corelli, Marie. A Christmas greeting. il. 12°. $1.50 net. Dodd, Mead & Co.
Corelli, Marie. Sol de media noche; trad. por Alfredo Elías y Pujol. Appleton.
†Corelli, Marie. Temporal power: a study in supremacy. 12°. $1.50. Dodd, Mead & Co.
Corelli, Marie. Thelma. il. 12°. $1.50. Fenno.
Corneille, P. Le menteur. (Silver ser. of modern language text-books.) Silver.
**Corneille and the Spanish drama. Segall, J. B. $1.50 net. Macmillan.
Cornelius Nepos. Chase, G: D. Appleton.
Cornet Strong of Ireton's Horse. McChesney, Dora G. Lane.
†Cornford, L. Cope. The last buccaneer. il. 8°. $1.50. Lippincott.
Cornman, Oliver P. Spelling in the elementary school. (Experimental studies in psychology and pedagogy.) Ginn.
**Corpus juris civilis. Latin and English; tr. by V. B. Denslow and others. 4 v. 8°. $6 net. Cambridge.
**Correct thing. Hall, F. H. 75 c. net. Estes.
Couchman, Mary. The noes have it. 16°. 20 c. Young.
†Councils of Crœsus. Potter, Mary K. $1.25. L. C. Page.
Counsels to inquirers. (New Kalon ser.) il. 12°. 50 c. Caldwell.
Count of Monte Cristo. *See* Dumas, A. Heath.
*Country church (The). Bassett, A. B. 65 c. net. Lentilhon.
**Country life in America. L. H. Bailey, *ed.* il. 10¼ x 14. Bound v. v. 1, 2. ea., $2.50 special net. Doubleday, P.
Courtship of Commodore Trunnion. *See* Smollett, T. G: Turner.
Courtship of Miles Standish. Longfellow, H: W. $1.25. Caldwell.
Cowham, Hilda. Fiddlesticks: nursery rhymes. col. il. 4°. bds., $1. Young.
Cowley, A., *ed.* Samaritan liturgies. Oxford Univ.
**Crabbe, Ainger, A. 75 c. net. Macmillan.
Craddock, C: E., *pseud.* *See* Murfree, Ma. N.
Craigie, *Mrs.* P. M. T. *See* Hobbes, J: Oliver.
Cram, W: Everitt. *See* Stone, W. Doubleday, P.
*Crane, Eliz. G. Imperial republic: a drama. 12°. $1 net. Grafton Press.
†Crane, Stephen. Active service. (Copyright ser.) 12°. 50 c. Stokes.
†Crane, Stephen. Last words. (Griffin ser.) 12°. $1. Coates.
Crane, Walter, Art of. Konody, P. G. Macmillan.
Cranford. Gaskell, *Mrs.* $1.25. Caldwell.
Crawford, F. Marion. Works. New uniform ed. ea., $1.50. Macmillan.
Crawford, F. Marion. Ave Roma immortalis. New ed. in 1 v. il. 8°. Macmillan.
Crawford, F. Marion. Cecilia, the last of the vestals. il. 12°. Macmillan.
**Crawford, Ma. C. Romance of old New England rooftrees. il. large 16°. $1.20 net; ¾ lev., $2.50 net. L. C. Page.
Crawley, Edwin S. Short course in plane and spherical trigonometry. With tables, $1; without tables, 90 c. Crawley.
*Creation story of Genesis. Radau, H. 75 c. net. Open Court.
Creeds (The). Mortimer, A. G. Longmans.
†Creelman, Ja. Eagle blood. il. 12°. silk cl., $1.50. Lothrop.
Creighton, Mandell, *Bp.* Historical essays and reviews; ed. by L. Creighton. 8°. $2. Longmans.
**Crime, Insurance and. Campbell, A. C. net. Putnam.
**Crisis (The). Churchill, W. (Jas. K. Hackett ed.) $1.50 net. Macmillan.
**Criticism, History of. Saintsbury, G: v. 2. $3.50 special net. Dodd, Mead & Co.
Crocker, H. R. Diseases of the skin. 3d ed. il. $5. Blakiston.
†Crockett, S. R. Joan of the sword hand. (Red letter ser.) il. pap., 50 c. New Amsterdam.
†Crockett, S: R. Surprising adventures of Sir Toady Lion. New ed. il. 12°. $1. Stokes.
†Crockett, S: R. Sweetheart travellers. New ed. il. 12°. $1. Stokes.
Crockett, W: S. Scott country. il. 8°. Macmillan.
Cromwell, T:, *Earl of Essex.* Life and correspondence. Merriman, R. B. Oxford Univ.
**Cromwell's army. Firth, C. A. $1.75 net. Pott.
**Crosby, Ernest. Swords and plowshares. 12°. $1 net. Funk.
Crosland, T. W. H., *ed.* McClure's children's annual. col. il. $1.50. McClure.
**Cross, Arthur L. Anglican episcopate and the American colonies. (Harvard historical studies, v. 9.) 8°. $2.50 net. Longmans.
**Cross country with horse and hound. Peer, F. S. $3 net. Scribner.
Crossman, R. M. *See* Weed, C. M. Heath.
Crowell's poets: Astor ed., 90 v. ea., 60 c.; Gladstone ed., 57 v. ea., 75 c.; hf. cf., $1.75; Limp leather ed., 30 v., ea., $1.75; Circuit ed., 25 v., ea., $2; Favorite ed., 15 v., ea., $4.50; $6. Crowell.
†Crown of life. Gissing, G: 50 c. Stokes.
**Crowninshield, F: A painter's moods. il. 12°. $2 net. Dodd, Mead & Co.
Crowther, Alice. Golden thoughts from great authors. New ed. (Miniature volumes.) marble enamel, 50 c. Stokes.
Crucifixion of Philip Strong. Sheldon, C: M. 50 c.; 75 c. Caldwell.
Cruger, *Mrs.* Van Rensselaer. *See* Gordon, Julien.

*Cruikshank, J. W. *and* A. M. The Umbrian towns. (Grant Allen's historical guides.) 12°. $1.25 net. Wessels.
Cruise of H. M. S. "Thunder." *See* Smollett, T. G: Turner.
Cruise of the "Cachalot." Bullen, F. T. 75 c. Caldwell.
**Cruise of the "Dazzler." London, J. $1. Century.
Cruise of the "Enterprise." Otis, J. $1.50. Wilde.
**Cruising in the West Indies. Stokes, A. P. $1.25 net. Dodd, Mead & Co.
**Cruising on the St. Lawrence. Tomlinson, E. T. $1.20 net. Lee & Shepard.
Cubberley, Elwood P. Lectures on the history of education; with selected bibliographies. 8°. Macmillan.
Cullen, Clarence L. More ex-tank tales. $1. J. S. Ogilvie.
Cult of the purple rose. Johnson, S. E. $1.25. Badger.
†Cummins, Maria S. Lamplighter. New ed. cr. 8°. $1.50. Houghton, M. & Co.
Cuneiform inscriptions, Discovery and decipherment of the tri-lingual. Booth, A. J. Longmans.
Cunningham, D. J., *ed.* Text-book of anatomy. il. 8°. $9; $10; hf. mor., $11. Macmillan.
Cunningham, R. Two little travellers. il. $1. Nelson.
Cupid is king. Greene, R. F. $1.25. Badger.
**Curtis, Gertrude B. Comforting words for sorrowing mothers. il. 60 c. net. Revell.
Cushing, H. H. Compend of histology. il. 12°. (Quiz-compend, no. 17.) 80 c.; interleaved, $1. Blakiston.
Custance, Olive. Rainbows. 16°. $1.25. Lane.
Custom and competition. Ely, R: T. Macmillan.
†Cutting, Mary Stewart. Little stories of married life. il. 12°. $1.25. McClure.
*Cuyler, Theodore L. Help and good cheer. 12°. $1 net. Baker & T.
*Cuyler, Theo. L. Recollections of a long life. il. 12°. $1.50 net. Am. Tr.
*Cuyler, Theo. L. Recollections of a long life. il. 8°. $1.50 net. Baker & T.
*Cynics' calendar of revised wisdom. Herford. V. 75 c. net. Elder.
*Doffodil, Book of the. Bourne, E. $1 net. Lane.
Dahlia, Peploe's reaping. Finnemore, E. P. 80 c. Young.
**Dahlinger, C: W. German evolution of 1849. 8°. Putnam.
†Dahn, Felix. A captive of the Roman eagles; tr. by Mary J. Safford. 12°. $1.50. McClurg.
Daily helps. Spurgeon, C: H. 50 c. Caldwell.
**Dainty dames of society. ea., $1 net. Brentano.
Dale, Lucy. Principles of English constitutional history. 8°. $1.50. Longmans.
Dale, R. W. Ten commandments. New ed. 12°. Whittier.
Dallin, Colonna M. Sketches of great painters. il. 90 c. Silver.
**Dalman, Gustaf. Words of Jesus; tr. by D. M. Kay. 8°. $2.50 net. [Imp.] Scribner.
Dame de Monsoreau (La). Dumas, A. $1. Caldwell.
Dame Dimple's Christmas celebration. Banks, M. B. 50 c. Am. Tr.
**Dames and daughters of Colonial days ser. il. $1.25 net. Dodd, Mead & Co.
New volume: Margarita, by E. W. Champney.
†Dana, Fs. The decoy. 12°. $1.50. Lane.
Dana, R. H., *jr.* Two years before the mast. il. 12°. (New Berkeley lib.) $1. Caldwell.
Dancers (The). Thomas, E. M. $1.50. Badger.
Dances, *See* Old English. Longmans.
Daniels, Gertrude P. Eshek—the oppressor. $1.50. Rand, McN. & Co.
†Danny. Ollivant, D. $1.50. Doubleday, P.
**Dante and his times. Federn, C. $1.75 net. McClure.
Dante and the animal kingdom. Holbrook, R: T. Macmillan.
Dante society, Cambridge, Mass. Twentieth annual report. Ginn.
Dante, Troubadours of. Chaytor, H. J. Oxford Univ.
**D'Arblay, *Mme.* Diary and letters of Frances Burney, Madame D'Arblay. Windsor ed.; ed. by Sarah C. Woolsey. 2 v. pors. 8°. $6 net. Little, B. & Co.
**Darling, Mary G. Girl of this century. il. $1 net. Lee & Shepard.
Darwin, C: Letters; ed. by Francis Darwin. 2 v. 500 p. ea. Appleton.
Darwin, C: Selections. (Street and Smith little classics) 50 c. Street.
†Daskam, Josephine D. Whom the gods destroyed. 12°. $1.50. Scribner.
†Daughter of an Egyptian king. Ebers, G: $1.25. Lippincott.
†Daughter of the sea. Le Feuvre, A. $1.50. Crowell.
†Daughter of the snows. London, J. $1.50. Lippincott.
Dauntless three. Radford, B. 40 c. Young.
†Davenport, Arnold. By the ramparts of Jezreel. 8°. $1.50. Longmans.
David and Bathsheba. [Play.] Phillips, S. Macmillan.
Davidson, J. Thain. The city youth. New ed. 60 c. net. Am. Tr.
Davidson. J. Thain. Forewarned—forearmed. New ed. 60 c. net. Am. Tr.
Davidson, J. Thain. A good start. New ed. 60 c. net. Am. Tr.
Davidson, J. Thain. Sure to succeed. New ed. 60 c. net. Am. Tr.
Davidson, J. Thain. Sure to succeed. New New ed. 60 c. net. Am. Tr.
Davidson, Ja. W. Island of Formosa. il. 8°. Macmillan.
**Davies, G. S. Franz Hals. il. cap folio. $14 net. Macmillan.
**Davis, A. McF., *ed.* Tracts relating to the currency of Massachusetts Bay, 1682-1721. net. Houghton, M. & Co.
**Davis, E: P. Mother and child. il. 12°. $1.50 net. Lippincott.
*Davis, G. G. Principles and practice of bandaging. $1.50 net. Blakiston.
†Davis, R: Harding. Captain Macklin. il. 12°. $1.50. Scribner.
†Davis, R: H. In the fog. col. il. 6x9. $1.50. Russell.

†Davis, R: H. Ranson's folly. il. $1.50. Scribner.

Dawson, E. C. In the days of the dragons. 16°. 60 c. Young.

Dawson, Ethel. A happy failure. il. 60 c. Nelson.

**Dawson, W: Harbutt, *ed.* *See* Our European neighbors ser. Putnam.

Dawson, W: J. Makers of modern fiction. 8°. $2. Whittaker.

**Day, Holman F. Pine tree ballads. 7½ x 4⅞. $1 net. Small, M.

Dayton's book of gifts. flex. leath., $3. E. W. Dayton.

*Dayton's steamer letters. $1.50 net. E. W. Dayton.

*De officiis. Cicero. $7.50 net. Wessels.

Dead city (The). Annunzio, G. d'. $1.25. Laird.

Death of Christ. Denney, *Prof.* Ja. Armstrong.

**Death (The) of Sir Launcelot, and other poems. Pallen, C. B. $1 net. Small, M.

Deaver, J: B. Surgical anatomy. il. 3 v. v. 3. 8°. subs., sets only, $21; hf. mor. or shp., $24; hf. russia, $27. Blakiston.

**Decorative brush work and elementary design. Cadness, H: $1.40 net. Scribner.

†Decoy (The). Dana, Fs. $1.50. Lane.

Deecke, W. Italy; tr. by H. A. Nesbitt. il. 8°. Macmillan.

Deeds of faith. Neale, J. M. 40 c. Young.

**Defendant (The). Chesterton, G. $1.25 net. Dodd, Mead & Co.

Defoe, Dan. Robinson Crusoe. 70 eng. by Keeley Halswelle. $1.25. Nelson.

Delano, Frances J. One of thirteen. $1. Pilgrim Press.

De Leon, Fr. L. Perfecta Casada; ed. by Eliz. Wallace. 8°. Univ. of Chic.

**Delhi (1857). Young, K. $8 net. Lippincott.

**Delight; the soul of art. Eddy, A. J. $1.50 net. Lippincott.

Delitzsch, Friedrich. Babel and Bible. 9 x 6. 50 c. Open Court.

**Dellenbaugh, F: S. Romance of the Colorado river. il. 8°. net. Putnam.

*Del Mar, Alex. History of monetary crimes. 8°. 75 c. net. Cambridge.

*Del Mar, Alex. Science of money. 3d ed. 8°. $2 net. Cambridge.

Del Mar, Walter. Around the world through Japan. 8°. Macmillan.

**Deming, Therese O. Children of the west. col. il. by E. W. Deming. 4°. $1 net. Stokes.

**Deming, Therese O. Little brothers of the west. col. il. by E. W. Deming. 4°. $1 net. Stokes.

**Deming, Therese O. Red folk and wild folk. col. il. by E. W. Deming. 4°. $1.60 net. Stokes.

Democracy. Ostrogorski, M. Macmillan.

**Demon horse (The). (Toy books.) col. pictures. 4°. bds., $1.20 net.

Denison, Mary A. Yellow violin. il. 12°. $1. Saalfield.

Denney, *Prof.* Ja. The death of Christ. Armstrong.

**Denning, Marg. B. Mosaics from India. il. 12°. $1.25 net. Revell.

Dennis, L. M. Manual of qualitative analysis. Ginn.

*Denslow, V. B. Principles of political economy. 2d ed. 8°. $3 net. Cambridge.

Denton, Dan. Brief description of New York; ed. by Felix Neumann. por. $2; $3. Burrows.

Description of the province and city of New York. *See* Miller, J. Burrows.

Deserted village. Goldsmith, O. $3. Harper.

**Design, Elementary. *See* Cadness, H:

*Designers, American, of book-plates. il. edition de luxe. Lim. ed. vellum, $4 net. Kelly.

Deutsche bildungzustaende im 18. jahrhundert. Biedermann, K. Holt.

**Development and evolution. Baldwin, J. M. $2.60 net. Macmillan.

**De Vinne, Theo. L. Title-pages. $2 net. Century.

Dewey, Davis R. Financial history of the U. S. (American citizen ser.) 8°. Longmans.

Dewey, J: The child and the curriculum. 5⅛ x 7¾. pap., 25 c. net. Univ. of Chic.

Dewey, J:, *ed.* Studies in logical theory. 8°. Univ. of Chic.

Dewey, J:, *and* Tufts, J. M. Outlines of ethics. Holt.

Diamond mines of South Africa. Williams, G. F. Macmillan.

Diary of a journey to England, 1761-62. Kielmansegg, *Count* F: Longmans.

†Diary of a saint. Bates, A. $1.50. Houghton, M. & Co.

**Dicey, E: Story of the Khedivate. 8°. $4 net. [Imp.] Scribner.

Dickens, C: Complete works. Author's ed. New issue. 15 v. buckram, $15; ½ leath., $22.50; ½ calf, $30. Wessels.

Dickens, C: Barnaby Rudge. 12°. (Il. lib. of fam. bks.) 75 c. Caldwell.

Dickens, C: Bleak house. 12°. (Il. lib. of fam. bks.) 75 c. Caldwell.

**Dickens, C: Child's dream of a star, and Child's story. il. 12°. (Cosy corner ser.) 40 c. net. L. C. Page.

Dickens, C: Christmas stories. (Il. lib. of fam. bks.) 12°. 75 c. Caldwell.

Dickens, C: Christmas stories for children; ed. by M. K. Bellew. il. 12°. 60 c. Jamieson-H.

Dickens, C: Dombey and son. 12°. (Il. lib. of fam. bks.) 75 c. Caldwell.

Dickens, C: Great expectations. 12°. (Il. lib. of fam. bks.) 75 c. Caldwell.

Dickens, C: Little Dorrit. 12°. (Il. lib. of fam. bks.) 75 c. Caldwell.

Dickens, C: Martin Chuzzlewit. 12°. (Il. lib. of fam. bks.) 75 c. Caldwell.

Dickens, C: Nicholas Nickleby. 12°. (Il. lib. of fam. bks.) 75 c. Caldwell.

Dickens, C: Our mutual friend. (New Berkeley lib.) il. 12°. $1. Caldwell.

**Dickens, C:, Life of. Henley, W. E. $1 net. Dodd, Mead & Co.

Dickens, Chips from. Mason, T. 50 c. Stokes.

**Dickerson, Fannie M. Mary had a little lamb. il. 4°. $1 net. Stokes.

Dickson, Leonard E. Introduction to the theory of algebraic equations 8°. Wiley.

Dickson, Marguerite S. From the old world to the new. il. 12°. Macmillan.

Dictionary, New English. Murray, *ed.* v. 5 (H-K). Oxford Univ.

Dictionary of foreign phrases. Jones, H. P., *ed.* $3. Lippincott.
Dictionary, Worcester's primary. 12°. 50 c. Lippincott.
Dies, their construction and use. Woodworth. J. V. Henley.
Dietetics, Practical. Thompson, W. G. $5; $5.50. Appleton.
Digestive system, Diseases of. Allchin, W. H. Macmillan.
Dilke, *Lady* E. F. S. French engravers and draughtsmen in 18th century. il. 8°. Macmillan.
Dillon, E. J. Maxime Gorky, his life and writings. McClure.
Diplomat's (A) diary. Gordon, J. $1. J. F. Taylor.
Diseases of children. Hatfield, M. P. 80 c.; $1. Blakiston.
Diseases of the digestive system and the kidneys. Allchin, W. H. Macmillan.
Diseases of the heart and lungs. Babcock, R. H. Appleton.
Diseases of the respiratory and circulatory systems. Allchin, W. H. Macmillan.
Diseases of the skin. Crocker, H. R. $5. Blakiston.
†Disentanglers (The). Lang, A. Longmans.
Disinfection and disinfectants. Rosenau, M. J. $2. Blakiston.
Divine ordinance of prayer. Aitkin, W. H. $1.25. Young.
Dix, Beulah M. Little captive lad. il. 12°. Macmillan.
Dix, Dorothy. Fables of the elite. il. 12°. $1. Fenno.
**Dixon, C: Birds' nests. il. 12°. $1.20 net. Stokes.
Dixon, R. W. History of the Church of England from the abolition of the Roman jurisdiction; ed. by H: Gee. v. 5, 6. Oxford Univ.
**Djurklou, *Baron* G. Fairy tales. Tr. by H. L. Braekstad. il. 8°. $1.20 net. Stokes.
**Dobson, Austin. Hogarth; with introd. by Sir Walter Armstrong. il. with 70 pl. 4°. $25 net. Ed. with portfolio of pl. on India pap., $60 net. Ed. with portfolio of pl. on India pap. and Jap. vellum, $120 net. McClure.
**Dobson, Austin. Richardson. (Eng. men of letters) 75 c. net. Macmillan.
†Doctor Bryson. Spearman, F. H. $1.50. Scribner.
**Doctor Robin. Cheever, H. A. 40 c. net. Estes.
Doctor's recreation ser. Moulton, C: W., *ed.* il. 8°. ea., $2.50; hf. mor., ea., $4. Saalfield.

Contents: 1, Doctor's leisure hour, ed. by P. Davies.—2, Doctor's red lamp, ed. by C: W. Moulton.—3, Dr. Jonathan Brush, by S: W. Kelley.—4, Book about doctors, by J: C. Jeaffreson.—5, Doctor's window, ed. by Ina R. Warren.—6, Doctor's Who's who, ed. by C: W. Moulton.—7, Passages from the diary of a late physician, by S: Warren.—8, Inn of rest (hospital life), ed. by S. E. Ames.—9, Doctors of the old school, ed. by P. Davies.—10, Shrine of Aesculapius, ed. by Oswald Sothene.—11, Doctor's domicile, ed. by I. A. King.—12, Cyclopaedia of medical history, ed. by C: W. Moulton.

**Dodd, Anna B. In the palaces of the Sultan. il. 8°. $4 net. Dodd, Mead & Co.
Dodge and Tuttle's Latin prose composition. 75 c. Am. Bk.
Dodgson, C: L. *See* Carroll, Lewis.
**Doffed coronet. il. Cr. 8°. $2.25 net. Harper.
Dog fiend. Marryat, F: 79 c. Caldwell.
Dogtown. Wright, M. O. Macmillan.
Dole, N. H. Famous composers. Holiday ed. il. 2 v. 12°. per set, $3. Crowell.
Dolley, C: S. Raw material of commerce. (Macmillan's commercial ser.) 12°. Macmillan.
Dolly dialogues. Hawkins, A. H. $1.50. Holt.
Dolores. Braeme, C. M. Appleton.
Dombey & Son. *See* Dickens, C:
Domestic economy. *See* Herrick, Christine T. Putnam.
†Domitia. Baring-Gould, S. 50 c. Stokes.
Don Luis' wife. Shuey, L. H. 75 c. Badger.
Don Malcolm. Thurston, *Mrs.* I. T. $1.25. Pilgrim Press.
Don Quixote. *See* Cervantes, M.
Donner, Herman M. English lyrics of a Finnish harp. [Poems] 12°. bds., $1.25. Badger.
†Donovan pasha. Parker, *Sir* G. $1.50. Appleton.
Don'ts for boys. 16°. 50 c.; ooze cf., $1. Altemus.
Don'ts for girls. Antrim, M. T. 50 c.; $1. Altemus.
**Doom of King Acrisius. Morris, W: $2.75 net. Russell.
Dopp, Kath. E. Place of industry in elementary education. Univ. of Chic.
**Dörnfield summer. Haley, M. M. $1.20 net. Little, B. & Co.
Dorothea, *Princess Lieven*, Letters of, during residence in London, 1812-34; ed. by L. G. Robinson. $5. Longmans.
**Dorothy Dainty. Brooks, A. 80 c. net. Lee & Shepard.
†Dorr, Julia C. R. In kings' houses. New ed. il. large 12°. $1.50. L. C. Page.
Dorsey, *Mrs.* Sabel. Stories in stone from the Roman forum. il. 12°. Macmillan.
**Dorsey, the young inventor. Ellis, E: S. 80 c. net. Coates.
Dotey, Douglas Z. Pictures of Paintbox Town. il. obl. bds., $1. Dutton.
**Doucet, Jerome. Tales of the spinner. Tr. il. decor. vellum, 6 x 9. $5 net. Russell.
†Doughnuts and diplomas. Jackson, G. E. $1. Altemus.
**Douglas, Amanda M. A little girl in old Detroit. 12°. $1.20 net. Dodd, Mead & Co.
**Douglas, Amanda M. Sherburne quest. 12°. 90 c. net. Dodd, Mead & Co.
Douglas, G: C. M. Samuel and his age. (Bible students' handbks.) 12°. $2.50. Young.
**Douglas, Langton. Fra Angelico. 2d ed. rev. il. 8°. $6 net. Macmillan.

**Down in Water Street. Hadley, S. H. il. $1 net. Revell.
**Downer, C: A. First book in French. 12°. (20th century text bks.) $1.10 net. Appleton.
†Downrenter's son. Hall, Ruth. Cr. 8°. $1.50. Houghton, M. & Co.
*Dowson, Ernest. Poems. 4°. (Mosher's miscellaneous ser.) $2.50 net; Jap. vellum, $5 net. Mosher.
Doyle, A. C. Firm of Girdlestone. (New Berkeley lib.) il. 12°. $1. Caldwell.
Doyle, A. C. Study in scarlet. (Chateau ser.) il. 6 x 4. boxed, 75 c. Caldwell.
Drainage, Land, Engineering for. Elliott, C: G. Wiley.
Drama. *See* Brown, T. A. Dodd, Mead & Co.
**Dramatic verse, Volume of. Wendell, B. net. Scribner.
**Dream days. Grahame, K. $2.50 net. Lane.
Dream Life. Mitchell, D. 75 c. Caldwell.
*Dream of John Ball. Morris, W: $1; $2.50 net. Mosher.
Dreams. *See* Schreiner, O. Caldwell.
Drei freier (Die). Schucking. Ginn.
Dreissigjährige Krieg. *See* Schiller, F. v. Heath.
Drillmaster of Methodism. Goodell, C: L. $1.25. Eaton & M.
Droch, *pseud.* *See* Bridges, Rob.
Drummond, H: Natural law in the spiritual world (Chateau ser.) il. 6 x 4. boxed. 75 c. Caldwell.
**Drummond, Jas. Life of James Martineau. 2v. 8°. $10 net. Dodd, Mead & Co.
Dryer's Physical geography. $1.20. Am. Bk.
Du Barri, *Mme.*, Memoirs of; tr. by H. T. Riley. Vancouleur ed. il. Lim. ed. 2v. 6 x 9½. Silk clo., $7.50; ¾ crushed levant, $18. Caldwell.
Du Barry, *Mme.*, Mrs. Leslie Carter as. il. 12°. bds., 50 c. net. Stokes.
**Du Barry, Story of. Ford, J. L. $2 net; $25 net. Stokes.
Dublin castle and Dublin society, Recollections of. 12°. $1.25. Brentano.
**Du Chaillu, Paul. King Mombo. il. 8°. $1.50 net. Scribner.
"Duchess." Molly Bawn. (New Berkeley lib.) il. 12°. $1. Caldwell.
Duchess of Sutherland. The wind in the tree. 5¼ x 7⅝. buckram, $1.50. Russell.
**Ducks, Natural history of British surface-feeding. Millais, J: G. $40 net. Longmans.
**Duff Gordon, *Lady.* Letters from Egypt; introd. by G: Meredith. $2.50 net. McClure.
**Dugmore, A. Radclyffe. Nature and the camera. il. 6½ x 8¾. $1.35 net. Doubleday P.
Dumas, Alex., *père.* Complete works. Author's ed. New issue. 15 v. buckram, $15; ½ leath., $22.50; ½ cf., $30. Wessels.
Dumas, Alex. Count of Monte Cristo; ed. by Spier. Heath.
Dumas, Alex. La dame de Monsoreau. (New Berkeley lib.) il. 12°. $1. Caldwell.
Dumas, Alex. Louise de Vallière. (New Berkeley lib.) il. 12°. $1. Caldwell.
Dumas, Alex. Man with the iron mask. (New Berkeley lib.) il. 12°. $1. Caldwell.
Dumas, Alex. Master Adam the Calabrian. 12°. $1. Fenn.
Dumas, Alex. The forty-five. (New Berkeley lib.) il. 12°. $1. Caldwell.
Dumas, Alex. The last vendée. (New Berkeley lib.) il. 12°. $1. Caldwell.
Dumas, Alex. The Speronara; tr. by Kath. P. Wormeley. 16°. $1.25. Little, B. & Co.
Dumas, Alex. Taking the Bastile. (New Berkeley lib.) il. 12°. $1. Caldwell.
Dumas, Alex. Three musketeers. Popular il. ed. 2 v. 8°. $2.50. Little, B. & Co.
Dumas, Alex. Two Dianas. (New Berkeley lib.) il. 12°. $1. Caldwell.
**Dumas, Alex., *père*, Life of. Spurr, H: A. $2 net. Stokes.
**Dumpy books for children. il. bds., ea., 40 c. net. Stokes.
New Volumes: Appleton, Mrs. Ginger. —Bannerman. Little Black Mingo.—Mayer, Alphabet book.
†Duncan. Sara J. Hilda. (Copyright ser.) 12°. 50 c. Stokes.
Dunn, "Farmer." The weather and practical methods of forecasting. 12°. $2. Dodd, Mead & Co.
Durley, R. J. Elementary text book of the kinematics of machines. 8°. Wiley.
Duty (The) of the Christian business man. Brooks, P. 30 c. Caldwell.
Dwight, C: A. S. Railroading with Christ. il. 12°. 35 c. Am. Tr.
Dye, Eva Emery. The conquest. (True story of Lewis and Clark.) $1.50. McClurg.
Dye. Lighting by acetylene. 12°. $2.50. Spon & C.
*Eagle blood. Creelman, J. $1.50. Lothrop.
Earle, Alice M. Sun-dials and roses of yesterday. il. 8°. Large paper. Macmillan.
**Earle, Ma. T. Flag on the hilltop. il. 12°. 90 c. net. Houghton, M. & Co.
Early Britain ser. 12°. $1. Young.
New volume: Anglo-Saxon Britain, by Grant Allen.
Early Christian literature. Platner, J. W. Macmillan.
Early church classics ser. 16°. 60 c. Young.
New volumes: A homily of Clement of Alexandria, entitled Who is the rich man who is being saved, by P. M. Barnard.—The shepherd of Hermas, by C. Taylor.
**Early prose writings of James Russell Lowell. port. 12°. $1.20 net. Lane.
Earncliffe of Errington. Forrester, F. B. $1.50. Young.
**Earth and the fulness thereof. Rosegger, P: $1.50 net. Putnam.
Earthwork curves. Allen. Spon & C.
**East of to-day and to-morrow. Potter, H: C. $1 net. Century.
**Eastman, C: A. Indian boyhood. il. 12°. $1.60 net. McClure.
†Ebers, G: Daughter of an Egyptian king. Tr. 12°. $1.25. Lippincott.
Ecclesiastical polity, Hooker's. bk. 5. Macmillan.

Echols, W. H. Introduction to the calculus. Holt.
Eclectic Eng. classics, Annotated. 44 v. Am. Bk.
Economics of commerce. Scott, W: A. Macmillan.
Economics, Principles of. Ely, R: T. Macmillan.
**Eddy, Arthur J. Delight; the soul of art. 12°. $1.50 net. Lippincott.
Edgar, J. Clifton. Text-book of obstetrics. il. 8°. Blakiston.
**Edgar, Pelham, *ed.* The struggle for a continent: ed. from the writings of Francis Parkman. il. pors. 12°. $1.50 net. Little, B. & Co.
**Edgar, W: C. Story of a grain of wheat. il. 16°. (Lib. of useful stories) 35 c. net. Appleton.
Edgecombe, Kenelm, *ed.* Whittaker's electrical engineer's pocket book. Macmillan.
†Edges. Woods. A. $1.50. Bowen-M.
Edgren, Hjalmar. Italian and English dictionary. Holt.
Editha series. il. 7½ x 5¼. 50 c. Caldwell.
New volumes: Mulock, The little lame prince; The sleeping beauty; Adventures of a brownie.—Hawthorne, The pigmies.—Ewing, The brownies.
Editha's burglar. Burnett, F. H. 50 c. Caldwell.
Education, Elementary methods in. 2 ser. 12°. Macmillan.
Education, Lectures on the history of. Cubberley, E. P. Macmillan.
Education, Meaning of. Butler, N: M. Macmillan.
Education, Place of industry in elem. Dopp, Kath E. Univ. of Chic.
[Education.] Principles of general method based on Herbart. McMurry, C: A. Macmillan.
Education readers, New. bks. 1, 2, ea., 35 c.; bk. 3, 40 c.; bk. 4, 45 c. Am. Bk.
Education. *See* Dewey, J: The child and the curriculum. 25 c. net. Univ. of Chic.
Edward I., Welsh wars of. Morris, J. E. Oxford Univ.
**Edward VII., Era of. *See* Williamson, F. H. Book of beauty. Lippincott.
Edwards, G: W. *See* Old English ballads. Macmillan.
Eggeling, J., *ed.* Kanva Satapatha Brahmana. (Anecdota Oxoniensis ser.) Oxford Univ.
Eggert, C. A., *ed.* *See* Schiller, F. v. Heath.
**Eglée, a girl of the people. Trowbridge, W. R. N. $1 net. Wessels.
Egmont. Goethe, J. W. v. Holt.
Egypt. Kelly, R. T. Macmillan.
*Egypt, Industrial resources of. Waage, R. G. $2 net. Cambridge.
Egypt. *See* Duff Gordon, *Lady.* McClure.
Ehrke, E. Helps to German prose composition. Oxford Univ.
**Eight girls and a dog. Wells, Carolyn. $1. Century.
**Eight sermons. Park, E. A. $1.50 net. Pilgrim Press.
**Eighty good times out of doors. Heath, Lillian. 75 c. net. Revell.
Electric bell fitting, Practical. Allsop, F. C. $1.25. Spon & C.
Electric lighting and power distribution, v. 2. Maycock, W. P. Macmillan.
Electric traction. Rider, J. H. Macmillan.
Electric waves. Macdonald, H. M. Macmillan.
Electrical distribution, Conductors for. Perrine, F. A. C. Van Nostrand.
Electrical engineer's pocket book, Whittaker's. Macmillan.
Electrical problems. Hooper, W: L. Ginn.
Electrical properties of gases. Thomson, J. J. Macmillan.
**Electricity and its similitudes. Tyndall, C. H. $1 net. Revell.
Electricity, Problems in. Weber. $3. Spon & C.
Electro-chemistry, Text-book of. Arrhenius, S. Longmans.
**Elegy of faith. Rader, W: 50 c. net. Crowell.
Elementary methods in education. 2 ser. 12°. Macmillan.
Eliot, George. Complete works. Warwick ed. 12 v. ea., $1; leath., $1.25. Dodd, Mead & Co.
Eliot, George. Complete works. Author's ed. New issue. 8 v. buckram, $8; ½ leath., $12; ¼ cf., $16. Wessels.
Eliot, George. Essays. (Il. lib. of fam. bks.) 12°. 75 c. Caldwell.
Eliot, George. Mill on the Floss. (New pocket lib., no. 6.) 24°. 50 c. net; leath., 75 c. net. Lane.
Eliot, George. Poems. (Il. lib. of fam. bks.) 12°. 75 c. Caldwell.
Eliot, George. *See* Bonnell, H: H. Longmans.
**Eliot, Ida M., *and* Soule, Caroline G. Caterpillars and their moths. il. $2 net. Century.
†Elivas, Knarf. John Ship, mariner. (Copyright ser.) 12°. 50 c. Stokes.
Elizabeth and her German garden. (New Kalon ser.) il. 12°. 50 c. Caldwell.
Elizabethan critical essays (1570-1603). Smith, G. G., *ed.* Oxford Univ.
Elizabethan Shakespeare; ed. by Mark H. Liddell. lim. ed. Doubleday, P.
Ellicott, C. J. Addresses on the Revised Version of Holy Scripture. 16°. 80 c. Young.
Elliott, C: G. Engineering for land drainage. 12°. Wiley.
**Elliott, J. Wilkinson. Plea for hardy plants. il. $1.60 net. Doubleday, P.
**Ellis, E: S. Dorsey, the young inventor. il. 12°. 80 c. net. Coates.
**Ellis, E: S. Jim and Joe. il. 12°. 80 c. net. Coates.
**Ellis, E: S. Lucky Ned. 12°. $1 net. Estes.
†Ellis, J. Breckenridge. Holland wolves. il. 12°. $1.50. McClurg.
†Ellis, J. Breckenridge. Red box clew. 12°. 50 c. Revell.
**Ellis, J. Breckenridge. Revenge of Adnah. 12°. $1 net. Jacobs.
Ellis, Robinson. Aetna: a critical recension of the text, [etc.] Oxford Univ.

**Ellwanger, G: H. The pleasures of the table. il. 6 x 9. $2.50 net. Doubleday, P.
**Ellwanger, W. D. A summer snowflake. il. 6 x 9. $2 net. Doubleday, P.
Elmcove. Cheever, *Mrs.* H. A. $1.25. Am. Tr.
Elrington, H. Ralph Wynward. $1. Nelson.
**Elsie's winter trip. Finley, M. 85 c. net. Dodd, Mead & Co.
**Elson, Arthur. Orchestral instruments and their use. (Music lovers' ser.) il. 12°. $1.60 net; ¾ mor., $4 net. L. C. Page.
Elson, H: W. Star gazer's hand-book. 30 c. net; seal grain, 40 c. net. Biddle.
Ely, R: T. Custom and competition. (Citizens' lib. of economics, politics and sociology.) 12°. Macmillan.
Ely, R: T., *ed.* *See* Citizens' lib. of economics. Macmillan.
Ely, R: T., *and* Wicker, G: R. Principles of economics. 12°. Macmillan.
†Embarrassing orphan. Norris, W. E. $1. Coates.
Embryology, Laboratory text-book of. Minot, C: S. Blakiston.
Embryology, Manual of. McMurrich, J. P. Blakiston.
**Emerson, Edwin, *jr.* History of the 19th century year by year; introd. by G. G. Gervinus. il. col. pl. 3 v. 12°. $3.60 net. Dodd, Mead & Co.
Emerson, Oliver F. Middle English reader. 12°. Macmillan.
**Emerson, Ralph Waldo. Essay on nature; Birch-wood woods. $1 net; Lim. ed., hand col., $5. Alwil.
**Emerson, Ralph Waldo. Essays. (Macmillan's pocket classics.) 18°. 25 c. net. Macmillan.
**Emerson, Ralph Waldo. [Selections.] (Little masterpieces, 2d ser.) 4 x 6. flex. silk cl., ea., 40 c. net. Doubleday, P.
Emerson, Ralph Waldo, *and* Cicero. Friendship. (Bradford ser.) 16°. $1; limp crushed leath., $1.25. Wessels.
**Emerson, Ralph Waldoo. Woodberry, G: E: 75 c. net. Macmillan.
†Emmy Lou. Martin, G: M. $1.50. McClure.
*Emphasized Bible. Bryant, J. B. 3 v. ea., $2 net. Revell.
**Encyclopædia Biblica. Cheyne, T. K., *ed.* v. 4. $5 net; $7.50 net. Macmillan.
Engels, F: Origin of the family. (Standard soc. ser.) Kerr.
Engels, F: Private property and the state. (Standard soc. ser.) Kerr.
Engine. *See* Marine; Stationary.
Engineering, Civil, Ancient and modern, and the Isthmian canal. Burr, W: H. Wiley.
Engineering for land drainage. Elliott, C: G. Wiley.
Engineering, Steam, Elements of. Spangler, H. W. Wiley.
Engineer's sketchbook of mechanical movements, devices, etc. Barber, T. W. $4. Spon & C.
Engineers, Field astronomy for. Comstock, G: C. Wiley.
England, Abbeys, castles and ancient halls of. *See* Trinbs, J: Warne.
England, First steps in the hist. of. Mowry, A. M. 70 c. Silver.
England, History of. Macaulay, T: B. $5-$10. Estes.
England, Hist. of. Macaulay, T: B. $5-$10. Wessels.
England, Rural. Haggard, H. R. Longmans.
**England, Social; ed. by H. D. Traill and J. S. Mann. 6 v. il. sets only. Putnam.
New volumes: 2, Edward I.-Henry VII., $5 net.—3, Henry VIII.-Elizabeth.
England. *See also* British.
England. *See also* Malan, A. H. Putnam.
*England's glory, Songs of. Canton, W: $1.25 net. Putnam.
**English book collectors. Fletcher, W: Y. $4 special net. Dodd, Mead & Co.
**English bookman's library ser. 4 v. $4 special net. Dodd, Mead & Co.
New volumes: English book collectors, by W: Younger Fletcher; ed. by A. Pollard.
**English cathedrals. Litchfield, P. A. $2 net; $2.50 net. Lippincott.
English constitutional hist., Principles of. Dale, L. $1.50. Longmans.
English, First lessons in. Gordy, W. F. Scribner.
English government, Theory and practice of the. Moran, T: F. Longmans.
English grammar, Applied. Lewis, E. H. Macmillan.
**English heraldry. Boutell, C: $1.75 net. Lippincott.
English hist. as told by English poets. Bates, K. L. Macmillan.
English hist. for Americans. Higginson, T: W. Longmans.
English hist. *See also* Barnard, F. P. Oxford Univ.
English language. *See* Maxwell's Eng. course. Am. Bk.
English, Lessons in. Skinner, W. H. 50 c. Silver.
**English literature, Hist. of. Moody, W: V. $1.25 net. Scribner.
**English literature, Hist. of. Simonds, W: E. $1.25 net. Houghton, M. & Co.
English literature, Illustrated hist. of. Garnett, R: Macmillan.
English literature. *See* Halleck's hist. $1.25. Am. Bk.
English lyrics of a Finnish harp. Donner, H. M. $1.25. Badger.
**English men of letters ser. ea., 75 c. net. Macmillan.
New volumes: Lyall, Tennyson.—Harrison, Ruskin.—Beeching, Jane Austen.—Ainger, Crabbe.—Stephen, Hobbes.—Chesterton, Browning.—Dobson, Richardson.—Van Dyke, Lowell.—Woodberry, Emerson.—Wister, Benj. Franklin.—Paul, Matthew Arnold.—Higginson, Whittier.
English orphans. Holmes, *Mrs.* Ma. J. $1. Saalfield.
English people, Hist. of the. Green, J: R. 4 v. $4-$8. Wessels.
English pleasure gardens. Nichols, R. S. Macmillan.

English poems, from Chaucer to Kipling. Parrott, T: M., *ed.* Ginn.
English prose, Standard. Pancoast, H: S. Holt.
English, Teaching of. Chubb, P. Macmillan.
English theological lib. 12°. Macmillan. *New volume:* Hooker's Ecclesiastical polity. bk. 5.
*English thought in the 18th century. 3d rev. ed. 2 v. 8°. $8 net. Putnam
English verse, Classical metres in. Stone, W: J. Oxford Univ.
English verse, Specimens of. Alden, R. M., *ed.* Holt
Englishwoman's (An) love letters. (New Kalon ser.) il. 12°. 50 c. Caldwell.
Engravers, French, in 18th century. *See* Dilke, *Lady.* Macmillan.
Epagogé: an essay. Wilson, J. C. Oxford Univ.
Epictetus, Golden sayings of; tr. and ed. by H. Crossley. (Golden treasury ser.) Macmillan.
Epideictic literature. Burgess, T. C. $1 net Univ. of Chic.
Epistles. *See* Moorehead, W. G. Revell.
Erie train boy. Alger, H., *jr.* 50 c. Caldwell.
Erromonga, the martyr isle. Robertson of Erromonga. Armstrong.
Escott-Inman, H. Nidding-Nod of Once-upon-a-time. il. 12°. $1. Rand, McN. & Co.
*Esdaile, Ernest. Child's guide to the Book of Common Prayer; ed. by C. M. Yonge. 32°. 50 c. net. Young.
Eshek, the oppressor. Daniels, G. P. $1.50. Rand, McN. & Co.
Essays of Elia. *See* Lamb, C:
Essex, *Earl of.* *See* Cromwell, T: Oxford Univ.
**Etching and etchers. Hamerton, P. G. $5 net. Little, B. & Co.
*Etching, Masters of. Paloma, F. $40 net. Cambridge.
**Eternalism: a theory of infinite justice. Smith, O. J. $1.25 net. Houghton, M. & Co.
Ethé, H. Catalogue of the Turkish, Hindustani, and Pushtu mss. in the Bodleian Library. pt. 2. Oxford Univ.
Ethé, H., *ed.* Firdausi's Yusuf and Zalikha. (Anecdota Oxoniensis ser.) Oxford Univ.
*Ethics. Aristotle. $7.50 net. Wessels.
Ethics of Green, Spencer and Martineau. Sidgwick, H: Macmillan.
Ethics, Outlines of. Dewey, J: Holt.
Ethics. *See also* Larned, J. N.
Ethics. *See also* Spinoza. Oxford Univ.
Euclid, Story of. Frankland, W. B. 75 c. Wessels
Euripidis tragoediae. Tom. I.; ed. by G. G. A. Murray. (Oxford class. ser.) Oxford Univ.
Europe, History of. Whitcomb, M. Appleton.
Europe, Mediæval. Bemont, C: Holt.
Europe, Modern. Historical atlas from decline of Roman empire. pts. 28-30. Poole, R. P., *ed.* Oxford Univ.
Europe, Modern, Hist. atlas of. *See* Poole, R. P. Oxford Univ.
Europe, Western, Introduction to hist. of. Robinson, Ja. H. Ginn.
European and Japanese gardens; ed. by Glenn Brown. il. sm. 4°. $2. Coates.
Eusebii chronicorum liber. Fotheringham, J. K., *ed.* facsims. Oxford Univ.
Eusebius. Praeparatio evangelica; ed. by E. H. Gifford. Oxford Univ.
Evangeline. Longfellow, H: W. $1.25. Caldwell.
Evans, Lawrence B., *ed.* *See* Handbooks of American govt. Macmillan.
Eve of St. Agnes. Keats, J: 40 c. Silver
Everett, C: C. Psychological basis of religious faith. Macmillan.
**Every day in the year. Lord, J. L. *and* M. K. $2 net. Dodd, Mead & Co.
**Evolution, Next step in. Funk, I: K. 50 c. net. Funk
**Evolution of a girl's ideal. Laughlin, Clara E. 50 c. net. Revell.
Ewing, Juliana H. The brownies. il. (Editha ser., 50 c.—New Kalon ser., 50 c.) Caldwell.
Ewing, Juliana H. Jackanapes. (New Kalon ser.) il. 12°. 50 c. Caldwell.
Experimental studies in psychology and pedagogy. Witmer, L., *ed.* Ginn. *Contents:* Cornman's Spelling in the elementary school.—McKeag, Sensation of pain.
Experiments on the flexure of beams. Guy, A. E. Van Nostrand.
**Extempore prayer. Talling, M. P. $1.25 net. Revell.
Eye, Diseases of the. Fox, L. W. Appleton.
†Eye of a god. Fraser, W. A. $1.25. McClure.
Eyre, J. W. H. Bacteriologic technique. il. 8°. Saunders.
†Eyre-Todd, G: Anne of Argyle. (Copyright ser.) 12°. 50 c. Stokes.
†Eyster, *Mrs.* Nellie B. Chinese quaker. il. 12°. $1.50. Revell.
Fables. La Fontaine, J. de. $1.50. W: R. Jenkins.
Fables of the elite. Dix, Dorothy. $1. Fenno.
Face, Surgical pathology and diseases of. *See* Grant, H. H. Saunders.
Factory accounts. Garcke *and* Fells. Van Nostrand.
*Fagge, C. H. Text-bk. of medicine. 4th ed.; rev. and ed. by P. H. Pye-Smith. 2 v. ea., $6 net. Blakiston.
Fairbanks, Harold W. California supplement. (Tarr and McMurry geographies.) Macmillan.
**Fairchild family (The). Sherwood, *Mrs.* $1.60 net. Stokes.
†Fairy tales. *See* Andersen, H. C.
**Fairy tales. Djurklou, *Baron* G. $1.20 net. Stokes.
†Fairy tales from afar. Grundtvig, S. $1.50. Wessels.
Faith, fellowship and fealty. *See* McAfee, C. B. 3 pts. Revell.
†Faithful; by the author of Miss Toosey's mission. 16°. $1. Little, B. & Co.
Fallen fortunes. Green, E. E. $1.25. Nelson.
**Fame for a woman. Metcalfe, C. $1.20. Putnam.

Familiar studies of men and books. Stevenson, R. L: 2 v. $2.50. Turner.
Family Christian almanac, 1903. 10 c. Am. Tr.
Famous American actors of to-day. Wingate, C: E. L. $2.75. Crowell.
Famous artists. Bolton, *Mrs.* S. K. $2.50. Crowell.
Famous books for boys. il. 12°. 79 c. Caldwell.
New volumes: Hawthorne, Twice-told tales; Tanglewood tales.—Marryatt. The phantom ship; The dog fiend; Japhet in search of a father; Jacob Faithful; Peter Simple.
**Famous children of literature ser.; ed. by F: L. Knowles. 12°. 75 c. net. Estes.
New volumes: Little Eva, adapted from Uncle Tom's cabin.—Little Nell, adapted from Old curiosity shop.
Famous composers. Dole, N. H. $3. Crowell.
**Famous families of New York. Hamm, M. A. net. Putnam.
*Famous homes; ed. by A. H. Malan. Library ed. 2 v. 8°. $7.50 net. Putnam.
Contents: Famous homes of Great Britain and their stories; More famous homes of Great Britain.
**Famous paintings. Singleton, E. $1.60 net. Dodd, Mead & Co.
Fanshawe, F. C. That doll. 16°. 30 c. Young.
Far past the frontier. Braden, J. A. $1. Saalfield.
Farm of Aptonga. Neale, J. M. 80 c. Young.
Farmer, Fanny M. Boston cooking school cook book. New ed., with additional recipes. il. 12°. $2. Little, B. & Co.
Farmiloe, Edith. Mr. and Mrs. Tiddliwinks. il. 4°. bds. Young.
Farrar, F: W: Allegories. il. New ed. 8°. $1. Longmans.
Father Tom of Connemara. Neville, Eliz. O'R. $1.50. Rand, McN.
Favorite edition of poets. oriental seal, ea., $4.50; full cr. lev., ea., $6. Crowell.
New volumes: Mrs. Browning.—Rob. Browning. — Burns. — Byron.—Cambridge book.—Jean Ingelow.—Keats.—Longfellow. — Milton. — Moore. — Scott. — Shelley. — Tennyson.—Whittier.—Wordsworth.
**Federn. Carl. Dante and his times. il. $1.75 net. McClure.
**Feeding of infants, Artificial. *See* Judson, C: F. Lippincott
Fells (author). *See* Garcke. Van Nostrand.
Fenn, G: Manville. Peril finders. 12°. $2. Young.
Fernow, B. E. Economics of forestry. 12°. Crowell.
Fessenden, Laura D. Moon children. col. il. bds., $1.25. Jamieson-H.
Fessenden, Laura D. "2002:" child life 100 years from now. il. 4°. bds., $1.25. Jamieson-H.
Fessenden, Laura D., *ed.* A round robin. il. 4°. $1.25. Jamieson-H.
**Fiction, Art of. Besant, *Sir* W. 50 c. net. Brentano.
**Fiction, Aspects of. Matthews, B. $1.25 net. Scribner.
Fiction, Guide to. Baker, E. A. Macmillan.
Fiction, Prose. Perry, B. Houghton, M. & Co.
**Fictional rambles in and about Boston. Carruth, F. W. $1.50 net. McClure.
Fiddlesticks. Cowham, H. $1. Young.
Field, J: E: Saint Berin, the apostle of Wessex. 16°. $1.50. Young.
Field, Roswell. Romance of an old fool. $2. W: S. Lord.
Field astronomy for engineers. Comstock, G: C. Wiley.
**Field book of American wild flowers. Mathews, F. S. $1.75 net; $2.25 net. Putnam.
†Fielding, H. Works; ed. by G: Saintsbury. (Temple classics.) 12 v. 8°. ea., 50 c.; leath., 75 c. Macmillan.
Fifty years' mission work in Chhota Nagpur. Chatterton, E. $2. Young.
**Fighting frigate, and other essays. Lodge, H: C. $1.50 net. Scribner.
File 113. Gaboriau, E. 75 c. Caldwell.
†Filibusters (The). Hyne, C. 50 c. Stokes.
**Fillis, Ja. Breaking and riding; tr. by M. H. Hayes. il. 8°. $5 net. [Imp.] Scribner.
Financial history of the U. S. Dewey, D. R. Longmans.
†Finding of Lot's wife. Clark, A. 50 c. Stokes.
**Finley, Martha. Elsie's winter trip. 12°. 85 c. net. Dodd, Mead & Co.
Finnemore, Emily P Dahlia Peploe's reaping. 16°. 80 c. Young.
†Finnemore, J: Story of a scout. il. 12°. $1.50. Lippincott.
Firdausi's Yusuf and Zalikha. Ethé, H., *ed.* Oxford Univ.
Firm of Girdlestone. Doyle, A. C. $1. Caldwell.
**First century message to twentieth century Christians. $1 net. Revell.
First Christmas (The). Wallace, L. $1.25. Harper.
†First novel ser. 12°. $1.25. McClure.
New volumes: McIntyre, J: T., The ragged edge.—Turner, G: K., The task-masters.
First steps in the history of England. Mowry, A. M. 70 c. Silver.
†First violin. Fothergill, Jessie. 2 v. $3. Brentano.
**Firth, C. A. Cromwell's army: hist. of the English soldier during the Civil War, the Commonwealth, and the Protectorate. 12°. $1.75 net. Pott.
**Firth, J. B. Augustus Cæsar. (Heroes of the nations ser., no. 35.) il. 12°. $1.35 net.; hf. leath., $1.60 net. Putnam.
Fish, Big game. Holder, C: F. Macmillan.
Fish life, Story of. Pycraft, W. P. 75 c. Wessels.
Fisher G: P. Grounds of theistic and Christian belief. New ed. Scribner.
**Fisher, Sidney G: True hist. of the American Revolution. il. 8°. $2 net. Lippincott.
Fiske, J: Essays. 2 v. 12°. Macmillan.

**Fiske, J: New France and New Enkland. cr. 8°. $1.65 net. Houghton, M. & Co.
Fitch, Anne. Poems; ed. by Myra Reynolds. 8°. Univ. of Chic.
Fitz, R. H. *See* Packard, F. A. Saunders.
Fitz Gerald, E: *See* Groome, F. H.
**Fitzsimmons, Rob. Physical culture and self-defense. il. 12°. $1.50 net. Biddle.
**Five great painters. Bayliss, *Sir* W. $3 net. Pott.
**Flag on the hilltop. Earle, Ma. T. 90 c. net. Houghton, M. & Co.
Flagg's A writer of Attic prose. $1. Am. Bk.
†Flandrau, C: M. Harvard episodes. (Harvard lib.) pap., 50 c. Small, M.
Fleming, J. A. Waves and ripples in water, air, and ether. il. 12°. $2. Young.
Fletcher, C. R. L., *ed.* *See* Carlyle, T: Putnam.
**Fletcher, W: Y. English book collectors; ed. by Alfred Pollard. 4°. $4 special set. Dodd, Mead & Co.
**Flight of Pony Baker. Howells, W: D. $1.25 net. Harper.
**Flight of Rosy Dawn. Mackie, Pauline B. 40 c. net. L. C. Page.
Flood tide. Morrison, G. H. Armstrong.
Flora of the Pacific coast, Key to. Jepson, W. L. Appleton.
Florence. Gardner, E. G. Macmillan.
Flowers from Persian gardens. Holden, E: S. $1.25; $10. Russell.
*Flowers of Parnassus ser.; ed. by F. B. Money-Coutts. il. 16°. 50 c. net; leath., 75 c. net. Lane.
New volumes: 13, The sensitive plant, by P. B. Shelley.—14, Christ in Hades, by Stephen Phillips.—15, Wordsworth's grave, by W: Watson.—16, Reliques of Stratford-on-Avon, comp. by A. E. Way.—17, Lycidas, by J: Milton.
†Flowers of the dust. Oxenham, J: $1.50. Wessels.
Flowers, Wild, Field bk. of American. *See* Mathews, Ferd. S. Putnam.
**Flowers, Wild, Guide to the. *See* Lounsberry, Alice. Stokes.
Fluch der Schonheit. *See* Riehl, W: H. v. Heath.
*Fluctuations of gold. Humboldt, *Baron* A. v. $1.50 net. Cambridge.
Foerster, A: F. *See* Miller, F. W.
Fogg's ferry. Callahan, C. E. 75 c.; 25 c. Laird.
†Folly in the forest. Wells, Carolyn. $1. Altemus.
*Food in health and disease. Yeo, I. B. $2.50 net. Keener.
†Fool's gold. Stillman, Annie R. $1.50. Revell.
For a lady brave. Hotchkiss, C. C. $1.50. Street.
For a young queen's bright eyes. Savage, R: H: $1.25; 50 c. Home Pub.
For crown and covenant. Grey, C. $1. Am. Tr.
†For prey and spoils. Ober, F: $1. Altemus.
For whom Christ died. Richards, W: R. Presb. Bd.
†Foray of the "Hendrik Hudson." Saville, F. M. $1. Stokes.
Forbes, C: H. Cicero's orations. 12°. Appleton.
†Forbes, *Mrs.* W. R. D. Unofficial. 12°. (Town and country lib.) $1; pap., 50 c. Appleton.
Force of mind. Schofield, A. T. $2. Blakiston.
**Ford, Ja. L. The story of Du Barry. il. 8°. $2 net; Lim. ed., col. il., levant. $25 net. Stokes.
**Ford, Ja. L. *and* Mary K. Every day in the year: poetical year book. 8°. $2 net. Dodd, Mead & Co.
†Ford, Paul L. Wanted: a chaperon; col. il. by H. C. Christy. 8°. $2. Dodd, Mead & Co.
Ford, W. C. History of commerce and industries. 12°. (20th century text-books) Appleton.
Foreign statesmen ser.; ed. by F. B. Bury. ea., 75 c. Macmillan.
New volume: Hassall, Mazarin.
Forestry, Economics of. Fernow, B. E. Appleton.
Forewarned—forearmed. Davidson, J. T. 60 c. net. Am. Tr.
†Forman, Justus M. Garden of lies. 12°. $1.50. Stokes.
**Formation of Christian character. Bruce, W. S. $1.75 net. [Imp.] Scribner.
Formosa, Island of. Davidson, J. W. Macmillan.
Forrester, F. B. Earncliffe of Errington. 12°. $1.50. Young.
†Forsslund, Louise. Ship of dreams. post 8°. $1.50. Harper.
Fortune from the sky. Kuppord, S. il. 80 c. Nelson.
†Fortunes of Oliver Horn. Smith, F. Hopkinson. $1.50. Scribner.
Fortunes of the Vanderbergs. Weber, A. $1. J. S. Ogilvie.
Forty-five (The). Dumas, A. $1. Caldwell.
Forum, Stories in stone from the. Dorsey, *Mrs.* S. Macmillan.
**Foster, Edith F. Jimmy Crow. 4°. 60 c. net. Estes.
**Foster, Edna A. Hortense, a difficult child. il. 12°. 80 c. net. Lee & Shepard.
**Foster, H: Life's secrets, gathered from the study of a Christian physician. 12°. $1 net. Revell.
†Foster, Mabel G. Heart of the doctor. 12°. $1.50. Houghton, M. & Co.
†Fothergill, Jessie. The first violin. New ed. il. 2 v. $3. Brentano.
Fotheringham, J. K., *ed.* Eusebii chronicorum liber. facsims. Oxford Univ.
**Founder of Mormonism. Riley, I. W. $1.50 net. Dodd, Mead & Co.
†Founding of fortunes. Barlow, J. $1.50. Dodd, Mead & Co.
Fountain, Paul. Great mountains and forests of So. America. 8°. Longmans.
Four feathers. Mason, A. E. W. Macmillan.
**Four little Indians. Coates, Ella M. 80 c. net. Coates.
**Four studies in character building. Hillis, N. D. 75 c. net. Revell.
Fournier, A. Napoleon I.; tr.; ed. by E: G. Bourne. Holt.

Fowler, Ellen T. Concerning Isabel Carnaby. (Chateau ser., 75 c.—New Kalon, 50 c.) Caldwell.
†Fowler, Ellen T. Fuel of fire. il. 12°. $1.50. Dodd, Mead & Co.
Fowler's new [phrenological] chart for the use of examiners, giving a delineation of the character. Fowler.
Fox, Frances M. What Gladys saw. il. $1.25. Wilde.
Fox, G: H: Smallpox. col. il. subs., $3. Lippincott.
Fox, L. Webster. Text-book of diseases of the eye. Appleton.
**Fox-Davies, Arthur C: Art of heraldry. col. il. folio, buckram, $45 net. Brentano.
Foxcroft, *Miss* H. F., *ed.* Memoirs of Bishop Burnet. Oxford Univ.
**Foxy the faithful. Wesselhoeft, L. F. $1.20 net. Little, B. & Co.
**Fra Angelico. Douglas, L. $6 net. Macmillan.
*Fractures and luxations, Atlas and epitome of. Helferich, H. $3 net. Saunders.
*Fractures, Treatment of. Scudder, C: L. $4.50 net; $5.50 net. Saunders.
*Fragilia labilia. Symonds, J: A. $1; $2 net. Mosher.
Française, La parole. Sauveur, L. $1. W: R. Jenkins.
France, Hist. of. Guizot, F. P. G. $8-$16. Wessels.
*France, Industrial resources of. Waage, R. G. $3 net. Cambridge.
**France, Southern. Baedeker, K. $2.70 net. [Imp.] Scribner.
†Francezka. Seawell, M. E. $1.50. Bowen-M.
†Francis, M. E., [*Mrs.* Francis Blundell.] The manor farm. 8°. $1.50. Longmans.
François, V. E., *and* Girond, F. P. First French reader. Holt.
François's Advanced Fr. prose composition. 80 c. Am. Bk.
François's Introd. Fr. prose composition. 25 c. Am. Bk.
Frank Denham, foreman. 16°. 60 c. Young.
Frankenstein. Shelley, M. W. 75 c. Caldwell.
Frankland, W. B. Story of Euclid. 16°. 75 c. Wessels.
Franklin, B: Autobiography. (Chateau ser.) il. 6x4. boxed, 75 c. Caldwell.
**Franklin, Benjamin. Wister, O. 75 c. net. Macmillan.
*Franklin, Jeannie D. Just shavings. [Calendar for shavers.] 75 c. net. E. W. Dayton.
**Franz Hals. Davies, G. S. $14 net. Macmillan.
**Fraser, J: F. The real Siberia. il. 12°. $2 net. Appleton.
†Fraser, W. A. The eye of a god. il. 16°. $1.25. McClure.
†Fraser, W. A. Thoroughbreds. il. 12°. $1.50. McClure.
†Free to serve. Rayner, E. 50 c. Small, M.
**Freeman (The). Glasgow, E. $1.50 net. Doubleday, P.
**French, A. Sir Marrok. (St. Nicholas ser.) il. 12°. $1 net. Century.
French, Arthur W., *and* Ives, Howard C. Stereotomy. 8°. Wiley.
**French. Lillie Hamilton. Homes and their decoration. 100 il. 8°. $3.50 net. Dodd, Mead & Co.
*French cathedrals and chateaux. Perkins, Clara C. $4 net; $7.50 net. Knight.
French course, Muzzarelli's brief. $1.25. Am. Bk.
French-English dictionary, Comprehensive. W: R. Jenkins.
French engravers and draughtsmen in 18th century. Dilke, *Lady.* Macmillan.
[French grammar.] Petite grammaire Française. W: R. Jenkins.
[French grammar.] Premières leçons de grammaire Française. Sauveur, M. L. 75 c. W: R. Jenkins.
French grammar. *See* Downer, C: A. Appleton.
French grammar. *See* Sauveur, L. W: R. Jenkins.
French language. *See* Sauveur, L. W: R. Jenkins.
French poetry. *See* Jenkins, T. A. Appleton.
French prose composition. *See* François's. Am. Bk.
French reader, First. François, V. E. Holt.
French readings. 22 v. Am. Bk.
French Revolution. Carlyle, T: $1.75. Putnam.
**French wit and humour. 16°. 50 c. net; leath., 80 c. net. Jacobs.
†Friend of the people. Rowsell, Ma. C. 50 c. Stokes.
Friendship. Emerson *and* Cicero. $1; $1.25. Wessels.
*Friendship: booklet of quotations. flex. Japan vellum, 75 c. net. Elder.
Frieze's Virgil's Æneid. complete, $1.50; 6 bks., $1.30. Am. Bk.
Frisbie, W. A. *and* Bart. Pirate frog, and other tales. il. 9x11½. bds., $1. Rand, McN. & Co.
Frisbie, W. A. *and* Bart. Puggery Wee. il. bds., $1. Rand, McN. & Co.
†Froggy fairy ser. of juveniles. New ed. il. ea., 50 c. Biddle.
Contents: Biddle, Froggy fairy book.—Second froggy fairy book.
†From door to door. Capes, B. 50 c. Stokes.
From the old world to the new. Dickson, M. S. Macmillan.
**Frothingham, Jessie P. Sea-fighters from Drake to Farragut. il. 12°. $1.20 net. Scribner.
**Froude, J. A. Hobbes, J: Oliver. $1 net. Dodd, Mead & Co.
Frozen treasure. Lampen, C. D. $1. Young.
**Fry, Horace B. Little Italy. Tragedy. por. 5¼x7¾. $1 net. Russell.
Fuchs, Otto. Linear perspective shadows and reflections. il. Ginn.
†Fuel of fire. Fowler, E. T. $1.50. Dodd, Mead & Co.
Fulda, L. Der talisman; ed. by E: Meyer. 16°. Holt.

†Fuller, Anna. Peak and prairie; and Pratt portraits. New ed. 2 v. in box. il. 16°. ea., $1.25. Putnam.
Fuller, E: John Malcolm. Snow & Farnham.
Fulleylove, J:, *and* Kelman, J: Holy land. col. il. 8°. Macmillan.
Funck-Brentano, F. Cagliostro and company; tr. by G: Maidmont. 12°. $1.50. Pott.
Funds and their uses. Cleveland, F. A. Appleton.
**Funk, I: K. Next step in evolution. 16°. 50 c. net. Funk.
**Furness, W: H. Home life of the Borneo head-hunters. il. 8°. $7.50 net. Lippincott.
Furniture of olden times. Morse, F. C. Macmillan.
Fussy four-feeted folks Krecker, A. M. 60 c. Jamieson-H.
Fyffe, C. A. Nociones de historia de Roma. Appleton.
**Gabe, Julius. Yachting. il. 12°. $2.50 net. Lippincott.
Gaboriau, Emile. File 113. (Il. lib. of fam. bks.) il. 12°. 75 c. Caldwell.
Gaboriau, Emile. The gilded clique. (Il. lib. of fam. bks.) il. 12°. 75 c. Caldwell.
Gaboriau, Emile. In peril of his life. (Il. lib. of fam. bks.) il. 12°. 75 c. Caldwell.
Gaboriau, Emile. The Lerouge case. (Il. lib. of fam. bks.) 12°. 75 c. Caldwell.
†Gabriel Tolliver. Harris, J. C. $1.50. McClure.
Galdos, B. P. Marianela. [Spanish.] W: R. Jenkins.
**Gallego-Castilian court of 14th and 15th centuries. Lang, H: R. $3 net. Scribner.
Gallus, A. Emma Calvé. il. bds. 8½ x 11. $1.50. Russell.
Gallus, A. Sarah Bernhardt. il. 8½ x 11. pap., 50 c. Russell.
Galvanic batteries. Bottone, S. R. Macmillan.
†Game of life (The). Hall, B. $1. Wessels.
Garcke *and* Fells. Factory accounts. New ed. Van Nostrand.
**Garden of girls. Nosworthy, Florence E. $1 net. Russell.
†Garden of lies. Forman, J. M. $1.50. Stokes.
*Gardening, Handbooks of practical; ed. by H. Roberts. il. ea., $1 net. Lane.
New volumes: 10, Book of climbing plants, by S. Arnott.—11, Book of pears and plums, by E. Bartrum.—12, Book of herbs, by *Lady* Rosalind Northcote.—13, Book of bees, by C: Harrison.—14, Book of the daffodil, by Eugene Bourne.
Gardens, Children's. Cecil, *Mrs.* E. Macmillan.
Gardens, English pleasure. Nichols, R. S. Macmillan.
**Gardens. Formal, in England and Scotland. Triggs, H. I. 3 pts. $25 net. Scribner.
Gardner, E. G. Florence. (Mediæval towns ser.) il. large-pap. ed. Macmillan.
Gardner, E. G. Siena. (Mediæval towns ser.) il. large-pap. ed. Macmillan.
Gardner, Ernest A. Ancient Athens. il. 8°. Macmillan.
Gargantua. Rabelais. Macmillan.
Garis, Howard R. With force and arms. il. 12°. $1. J. S. Ogilvie.
*Garland of Rachel. (Mosher's reprints of privately printed books.) 8°. $2 net; Jap. vellum, $5 net. Mosher.
Garnett, R:, *and* Gosse, Edm. Illustrated hist. of English literature. il. 8°. Macmillan.
Garrett, E. H. Pilgrim shore. New ed. il. 12°. $1.50; bds., $1. Little, B. & Co.
Garrett, E. H. Romance and reality of the Puritan coast. New ed. il. 12°. $1.50; bds., $1. Little, B. & Co.
Garrigues, H: J. Obstetrics. il. subs., $5; shp., $6. Lippincott.
Garvin, J: B. Brief qualitative chemical analysis. Heath.
Gas analyst's manual. Abady, J. $6.50. Spon & C.
Gas engineers' laboratory hand-bk. Hornby. $2.50. Spon & C.
Gas, gasoline and oil engines. Hiscox, G. D. $2.50. Henley.
Gases, Electrical properties of. Thomson, J. J. Macmillan.
Gaskell, *Mrs.* Cranford. (Sesame classics.) il. 7 x 4¼. limp ooze cf., boxed, $1.25. Caldwell.
Gaskin, R. T. Caedmon, the first English poet. 12°. pap., 40 c. Young.
**Gate beautiful. Stimson, J: W. $3.50 net; $7.50 net. Brandt.
Gatty, *Mrs.* A. Parables from nature. 18°. 50 c. Appleton.
Gatty, *Mrs.* A. Parables from nature. New ed. il. 12°. $1.50. Pott.
†Gautier, Theophile. Romance of a mummy; tr. 12°. $1.25. Lippincott.
Gayley, C: M., *ed.* Representative English comedies. 5 v. 8°. Macmillan.
**Gazetteer of the world, Longman's. $6.40 net. Longmans.
Gearing. *See* Halsey, F. A. Van Nostrand.
†Geber. Benton, K. A. 50 c. Stokes.
Geddes *and* Josselyn, *eds.* *See* Goldoni, C: Heath.
Gee, Annie L. Won—not by might. 12°. $1.50. Young.
Gee, H:, *ed.* *See* Dixon, R. W. Oxford Univ.
Geikie, Archibald. Nociones de geologia. Appleton.
Gems of thought from classical authors. Wilson, A. 50 c. Stokes.
Genito-urinary *organs.* *See* Keyes, E. L. Appleton.
*Genius loci, and other essays. Lee, V. $1.25 net. Wessels.
†Gentleman Garnet. Vogel, H. B. $1; 50 c. Lippincott.
Geografiá fisica superior ilustrada de Appleton. Puron, J. G. Appleton.
Geographies. *See* Carpenter's geographical reader.—Roddy's geographies. Am. Bk.
Geography. Exercises in. Leete, C. H. Longmans.
Geography of commerce. Trotter, S. Macmillan.

**Geography, Modern, Atlas of. Bartholomew, J. G. $2.25 net. [Imp.] Scribner.
Geography, Teachers' manual of. McMurry, C: A. Macmillan.
Geometry, Descriptive. Hall, W: S. 2 v. Van Nostrand.
*Geometry, Foundations of. Hilbert, D: $1 net. Open Court.
Geometry. *See* Milne's Elements. Am. Bk.
George, A. J., *ed.* Select poems of Coleridge. Heath.
+Gerard, Dorothea. The blood-tax. 12°. $1.50. Dodd, Mead & Co.
†Gerard, Dorothea. Sawdust. (Griffin ser.) 12°. $1. Coates.
German grammar. Learned, M. D. Appleton.
German language. *See* Keller's. Am. Bk.
*German literature, Hist. of. Robertson, J: G. Putnam.
German prose composition, Helps to. Ehrke, E. Oxford Univ.
German readings. 39 v. Am. Bk.
**German Revolution of 1849. Dahlinger, C: W. Putnam.
German social democracy. Kampffmeyer, P. Kerr.
Germany and the empire, 1500-1792. Pollard, A. F. Macmillan.
Germany, 1815-1889. Headlam, J. W. 2 v. Macmillan.
*Germany, Industrial resources of. Waage, R. G. $3 net. Cambridge.
**Germany of to-day. Schierbrand, W. v. $2.40 net. Doubleday, P.
**Germany, South. Baedeker, K. $1.50 net. [Imp.] Scribner.
Gerrare, Wirt. Greater Russia. il. 8°. Macmillan.
Gerrish, Claribel. *See* Wells, W. Heath.
*Gertha's lovers. Morris, W: 75 c. net. Mosher.
Gesenius. Lexicon. *See* Robinson, E. Oxford Univ.
Gesture, How to. Ott. Hinds.
**Ghetto silhouettes. Warfield, D. $1.25 net. Pott.
**Ghetto, Spirit of the. Hapgood, H. $1.20 net. Funk.
Gibbon, E: History of decline and fall of Roman Empire. Author's ed. New issue. 5 v. buckram, $5; ½ leath., $7.50; ½ cf., $10. Wessels.
**Gibson, C: D. The social ladder. Drawings. Large folio. Japan vellum, boxed, $5 net; lim. ed. de luxe, $10 net. Russell.
Gibson, G. A. Physical diagnosis. il. 12°. $3. Appleton.
**Giese, W: F. First book in Spanish. 12°. (20th century text-books.) $1.20 net. Appleton.
Gifford, E. H., *ed.* *See* Eusebius. Oxford Univ.
†Gifford, Franklin K. Aphrodite. (Beacon lib.) 7½ x 5. pap., 50 c. Small, M.
**Gift of the magic staff. Ostrander, Fannie E. $1 net. Revell.
Gifts, Dayton's book of. flex. leath., $3. E. W. Dayton.
Gilbert, C: B. *See* Price, L. L. Silver.
Gilbert, C: B., *ed.* *See* Stories of heroes. Silver.
Gilbert, G: In the shadow of the purple. 12°. $1.50. Fenno.
**Gilbert, W. S. Patience, or Bunthorne's bride. $1 net; lim. ed., $2.50 net. Doubleday, P.
Gilded clique. Gaboriau, E. 75 c. Caldwell.
**Gilder, Jeannette L. *and* J. B., *eds.* Authors at home. il. 12°. $1 net. Wessels.
†*Gilder, Jos. B., *ed.* American idea as expounded by American statesmen; introd. by Andrew Carnegie. 12°. $1.20 net. Dodd, Mead & Co.
Gilder, Jos. B. *See also* Gilder, Jeannette L. Wessels.
Gilder, *Mrs.* Jos. B. *See* Brown, F. Century.
Giles, Herb. A. China and the Chinese. 8°. Macmillan.
**Gilhooley, *Lord* F: S. Son! or, the Wisdom of Uncle Eph. 12°. 80 c. net. Stokes.
Gilman, *Mrs.* *See* Stetson, C. P.
†Gilson, Roy R. In the morning glow. il. post 8°. $1.25. Harper.
Girdlestone, R. B. Grammar of prophecy. (Bible students' handbooks.) 12°. $2.50. Young.
**Girl of this century. Darling, M. G. $1 net. Lee & Shepard.
**Girl. What a girl can make and do. Beard, L. $1.60 net. Scribner.
Girls of the Bible. Handy, S. C. $1.25. Jamieson-H.
Girls. *See* Laughlin, Clara E. Revell.
Girond, F. P. *See* François, V. E.
†Gissing, G: Crown of life. (Copyright ser.) 12°. 50 c. Stokes.
†Gissing, G: The town traveller. (Copyright ser.) 12°. 50 c. Stokes.
+Gissing, G: The whirlpool. (Copyright ser.) 12°. 50 c. Stokes.
Gittings, J. Claxton. *See* Judson, C: F.
**Gladden, Washington. Practice of immortality. (Beacon Hill ser.) 25 c. net. Pilgrim Press.
Gladstone, W: E., Life of. Morley, J: 3 v. Macmillan.
**Glasgow, Ellen. The freeman and other poems. $1.50 net. Doubleday, P.
**Glasgow, Ellen A. G. Poems. 5 x 8. bds., $1.50 net. Doubleday, P.
**Glasgow, Ellen A. G. The voice of the people. Il. ed. 5½ x 8¼. $1.50 net. Doubleday, P.
Gleason *and* Atherton's First Greek book. $1. Am. Bk.
Gleason's Xenophon's Cyropædia. $1.25. Am. Bk.
†Glentworth, Marguerite L. The tenth commandment. il. 12°. $1.50. Lee & Shepard.
**Glory, *Miss* Morning, *pseud.* Am. diary of a Japanese girl. 8°. $1.60 net. Stokes.
Glory and joy of the resurrection. Paton, J. $1. Am. Tr.
†Glovatski, Alex. The Pharaoh and the priest; from the Polish by Jeremiah Curtin. il. 12°. $1.50. Little, B. & Co.
Glyn, Elinor. Visits of Elizabeth. (Chateau ser., 75 c.—New Kalon, 50 c.) Caldwell.

Goddard, J: C. Leave of absence, and other leaves. New ed. il. $1.25. Pilgrim Press.
*Godolphin, E. C. Rape of the earth. 8°. $3 net. Cambridge.
*Gods, Story of. Abbott, A. A. $2 net. Cambridge.
**Goepp, Philip H. Symphonies and their meanings. 2d ser. 12°. $2 net; 1st and 2d ser., boxed, $4 net. Lippincott.
Goethe, J. W. v. Egmont; ed. by R. W. Deering. Holt.
Goethe, J. W. v. Hermann and Dorothea; ed. by C. A. Buchheim. Oxford Univ.
Gold dust. (Chateau ser., 75 c.—Sesame classics, $1.25.) Caldwell.
*Gold, Fluctuations of. Humboldt, *Baron* A. v. $1.50 net. Cambridge.
Gold mining, Rand. Stuart, J: $1.50. Warne.
*Golden book of Censorinus; tr. 8°. $1.50 net. Cambridge.
Golden counsel ser. il. 16°. boxed, 75 c. Caldwell.
New volumes: Sheldon, In His steps; The crucifixion of Philip Strong.—James, The anxious inquirer.
**Golden hour ser. 11 v. il. 8°. ea., 50 c. net. Crowell.
New volumes: Barry, E. B. Miss De Peyster's boy.—Comstock, H. T. A little dusky hero.—Greene, H. Whispering tongues.—Hawkes, C. W. Master Frisky.—Madden, E. A. The I can school.—Otis, J. How the twins captured a Hessian.—Raymond, E. Daisies and Diggleses.—Swett, S. The wonder ship.—Ulrich, B. K. The child and the tree.—Wells, A. R. The Caxton Club.
**Golden numbers. Wiggin, K. D., *and* Smith, N. A., *eds.* $2 net. McClure.
Golden text book. *See* international S. S. lessons Eaton & M.
Golden thoughts from great authors. Crowther, A., *comp.* 50 c. Stokes.
Golden treasury ser. Macmillan.
New volumes: Epictetus.—Selections from Steele.
*Golden wings. Morris, W: 75 c. net. Mosher.
Goldoni, C: Il vero amico; ed. by Geddes and Josselyn. Heath.
Goldsmith, Oliver. Deserted village. il. Royal 8°. silk, $3. Harper.
Goldsmith, Oliver. Essays. (Temple classics.) 16°. 50 c.; leath., 75 c. Macmillan.
**Goldsmith, Oliver. [Selections.] (Little masterpieces, 2d ser.) 4 x 6. flex. silk cl., ea., 40 c. net. Doubleday, P.
Goldsmith, Oliver. She stoops to conquer. New ed. (Miniature volumes.) marble enamel. 50 c. Stokes.
Goldsmith, Oliver, Life of. Irving, W. Longmans.
Goldziher, Ignaz. *See* Hadith. Young.
†Golf lunatic (The). Kennard, *Mrs.* E. $1.50. Brentano.
**Golliwogg's air-ship. Upton, B. $1.50 net. Longmans.
Gomme, G: L., *ed.* King's story-book. New ed. il. 8°. Longmans.
Gomperz, Theo. Greek thinkers; tr. by G. G. Berry. v. 2. 8°. $4. Scribner.
*Good order established in Penn. and N. J. (1678.) Budd, T. Repr. about $2: $3 net. Burrows.
Good start. Davidson, J. T. 60 c. net. Am. Tr.
Goodell, C: L. Drillmaster of Methodism. 12°. $1.25. Eaton & M.
Goodell, T: D. School grammar of Attic Greek. 12°. (20th century text-bks.) Appleton.
Goodell, T: D., *and* Morrison, F: S. First Greek book. 12°. (20th century text-bks.) Appleton.
**Goodspeed, G: S. Hist. of Babylonians and Assyrians. (Historical series for Bible students.) 8°. $1.25 net. Scribner.
Gordon, *Lady* Duff. *See* Duff-Gordon, *Lady.*
Gordon, Emma K. Comprehensive method of teaching reading. bks. 1, 2. Heath.
**Gordon, H. R. Logan, the Mingo. il. 12°. $1.20 net. Dutton.
Gordon, Julien, [*Mrs.* Van Rensselaer Cruger.] A diplomat's diary. 12°. $1. J. F. Taylor.
**Gordy, J. P. Political history of the U. S. 4 v. v. 3, 4. 12°. ea., $1.75 net. Holt.
Gordy, Wilbur F., *and* Mead, W: E: First lessons in English. Scribner.
Gorky, Maxime. Dillon, E. J. McClure.
Gospel chorus. Black, J. M., *ed.* 20 c.; per 100, $15. Eaton & M.
Gospel, Fourth. *See* Pusey, P: E: Oxford Univ.
Gospel in the Christian year. McKim, R. H. Longmans.
Gospel, Recovery and statement of. Osborn, L. D. Univ. of Chic.
Gospels. Four, Manual of. *See* Stokoe, T. H. Oxford Univ.
Gospels, Study of the. Robinson, J. A. Longmans.
†Goss, C: F: Little Saint Sunshine. il. 12°. $1.25. Bowen-M.
†Goss, C: F: The loom of life. 12°. $1.50. Bowen-M.
Gosse, Edm. *See* Garnett, R:
Goupil's Paris Salons, 1902. French and English text. 100 illustrations. Ed. de luxe. Lim. ed. Manzi & J.
Government, American, *See* Handbooks of. Macmillan.
Government, American. *See* Hart, A. B. Longmans.
**Government and the state. Wood, F: $2.25 net. Putnam.
Government: its origin, growth and form in the U. S. Lansing, R. Silver.
Government of Maine. MacDonald, W: Macmillan.
Government of Michigan. Cook, W. Macmillan.
Government of N. Y. Morey, W: C. Macmillan.
Government of Ohio. Siebert, W. H. Macmillan.
Government (The). *See* Clark's. Am. Bk.
Gower, J: Complete works; ed. by G. C. Macaulay. v. 4. Latin works, etc. Oxford Univ.

Gower, *Lord* Ronald S. Sir Joshua Reynolds. il. 4°. Macmillan.
**Graham, Douglas. Massage. 3d rev. ed. il. 8°. $4 net. Lippincott.
†Graham, Ja. M. Son of the czar. (Copyright ser., 50 c.—Lib. of successes, 50 c.) Stokes.
**Grahame, K. Dream days. New ed. photogrv. 8°. $2.50 net. Lane.
Grammar, English, Applied. Lewis, E. H. Macmillan.
**Grammont, *Count* de, Memoirs of. Hamilton, A. Notes by *Sir* W. Scott. New il. ed. 8°. $3 net. [Imp.] Scribner.
**Grande Mademoiselle (La), Youth of. Barine, A. net. Putnam.
Grant, H. H. Text-book of surgical pathology and surgical diseases of face, mouth and jaws for dental students. il. 8°. Saunders.
†Grapes of wrath. Norris, Ma. H. 50 c. Small, M.
Graves, C. L. Life of Sir George Grove. 8°. Macmillan.
Gray, A. Bathrobes and bachelors; [also] Bain, J: Tobacco in song and story. Holiday ed. 2 v. ooze cf., padded and boxed, $3.50. Caldwell.
*Gray, A., *comp.* Over the black coffee. il. 16°. 75 c. net; Gift ed., ooze leath., $1.50 net. Baker & T.
**Gray, G: Buchanan. Commentary on Numbers. (Internat. critical com.) 8°. $2.50 net; $3 net. Scribner.
Gray, P. L. In a car of gold. il. 12°. $1. Saalfield.
Great Britain, Homes of. *See* Malan, A. H. Putnam.
Great Britain. *See also* British.
**Great commanders ser.; ed. by James Grant Wilson. por. 12°. $1.50 net. Appleton.
New volume: Admiral Porter, by J. R. Soley.
Great expectations. Dickens, C: 75 c. Caldwell.
Great mountains and forests of South America. Fountain, P. Longmans.
Great procession (The). Spofford, Harriet P. 50 c. Badger.
Great white way. Paine, A. B. $1.50. J. F. Taylor.
Greek, Attic and Ionic. *See* Babbitt's Grammar. $1.50. Am. Bk.
*Greek church, Students' history. Hore, A. H. $2.25 net. Young.
Greek councils of 4th and 5th centuries. *See* Turner, C. H. Oxford Univ.
Greek grammar, Elementary. Allen, J. B. Oxford Univ.
Greek grammar. *See* Goodell, T: D. Appleton.
Greek grammar. *See* Hadley *and* Allen's. Am. Bk.
Greek heroes. Kingsley, C: 50 c. Caldwell.
Greek historical inscriptions. Hicks, E. L. Oxford Univ.
Greek language. *See* Gleason *and* Atherton's First bk. Am. Bk.
**Greek literature, Masterpieces of. Wright, J: H., *ed.* $1 net. Houghton, M. & Co.
Greek prose composition. *See* Pearson's. 90 c. Am. Bk.
Greek thinkers. Gomperz, T. v. 2. $4. Scribner.
Greeks, Life of the ancient. Gulick, C: B. Appleton.
Green, E. Everett. Fallen fortunes. $1.25. Nelson.
Green, E. M. Left to themselves. 12°. 80 c. Young.
Green, Evelyn E. Alwyn Ravendale. il. 12°. $1.25. Am. Tr.
Green, J: R: History of English people. Author's ed. New issue. 4 v. buckram, $4; ½ leath., $6; ½ cf., $8. Wessels.
Green, T: H., Ethics of. *See* Sidgwick, H: Macmillan.
Green room editions. il. Caldwell.
New volume: Ouida, Under two flags.
Greenaway, Kate. Reissues of works. Warne.
Greenbacks, History of. Mitchell, W. C. Univ. of Chic.
Greene, A. M., *jr.* *See* Spangler, H. W. Wiley.
Greene, Homer. Pickett's gap. 12°. Macmillan.
Greene, Ma. A. Woman's manual of law. Silver.
Greene, Rob., Plays and poems of; ed. by J. C. Collins. Oxford Univ.
Greene, Roy F. Cupid is king. [Poetry.] il. 12°. $1.25. Badger.
†Greene, Sa. P. McLean. Winslow plain. post 8°. $1.50. Harper.
**Greenough, Jeanie A. B., *comp.* Year of beautiful thoughts. 12°. $1.20 net. Jacobs.
Grey, Cyril. For crown and covenant. il. 12°. $1. Am. Tr.
Grey wig. Zangwill, I. Macmillan.
†Griffin ser. 12°. ea., $1. Coates.
New volumes: Norris, The embarrassing orphan.—Gerard, Sawdust.—Babcock, Kent Fort Manor.—Crane, Last words.—Iliowizi, The archierey of Samara.
**Griffis, W: Eliot. Samuel Pollins Brown; a missionary biog. il. $1.25 net. Revell.
*Grimaudet, François. Law of payment; tr. 8°. $1.50 net. Cambridge.
**Grimm tales made gay. Carryl, G. W. $1.50 net. Houghton, M. & Co.
Gripped. Hocking, S. K. $1.25. Warne.
Groff, J: E. Materia medica for nurses. 2d ed. rev. 12°. $1.25. Blakiston.
*Groome, Francis Hinde. Edward Fitz Gerald. 4°. (Mosher's miscellaneous ser.) $2.50 net; Jap. vellum, $5 net. Mosher.
Grove, Sir G:, Life of. Graves, C. L. Macmillan.
†Grundtvig, Svend. Fairy tales from afar; tr. by J. Muller. New ed. il. 12°. $1.50. Wessels.
Gudeman, Alf. Sources of Plutarch's life of Cicero. (Publications of the Univ. of Pa.) Ginn.
**Guerber, H. A. Yourself. il. 12°. $1.20 net. Dodd, Mead & Co.
Guess again. Bridgman, L. J. $1.25. Caldwell.

**Guest book (A). Sahler, Flo. L. 80 c. net. Stokes.
Guizot, F. P. G. Hist. of France; tr. by R. Black. 8 v. il. 8°. $8; $10; hf. leath., $12; hf. cf., $20. Crowell.
Guizot, F. P. G. Hist. of France. Author's ed. New issue. 8 v. buckram, $8; ½ leath., $12; ½ cf., $16. Wessels.
Gulick, C: B. Life of the ancient Greeks. 12°. (20th century text-bks.) Appleton.
Gulliver's travels. Swift, J. 75 c. Caldwell.
Gumersall, *Mrs.* J. T. Cameos from nature. il. 12°. $1.80. Whittaker.
Gun and rifle. Money, A. W. Macmillan.
Gunby, A. A. Colonel John Gunby of the Maryland line. il. Clarke.
Gunby, Colonel John, of the Maryland line. Gunby, A. A. Clarke.
Gunn, Alex. *See* Timbs, J: Warne.
Gunnison, W. B., *and* Harley, Wa. S. First year of Latin. Silver.
Gunter, Arch. C. City of mystery. $1.50; pap., 50 c. Home Pub.
Gunter, Arch. C. Surprises of an empty hotel. $1.50; pap., 50 c. Home Pub.
Guy, Albert E. Experiments on the flexure of beams. Van Nostrand.
Gwilliam, G: H:, *ed.* *See* Pusey, P: E: Oxford Univ.
Gymnastics, Best methods of teaching. Anderson. Hinds.
Gynecology, Manual of. Byford, H: T. $3. Blakiston.
Gynecology, Text-book of. Appleton.
†Gypsy, the talking dog. Jenks, T. $1. Altemus.
"H. H.," *pseud.* *See* Jackson, Helen.
**Habberton, J: The tiger and the insect. il. bds. 5⅛ x 7⅝. $1.20 net. Russell.
Hadith and the New Testament; tr. by Lady Young from Muhammadanische Studien, vol. 2, by Ignaz Goldziher. 8°. Young.
Hadley, H. H. Blue badge of courage. 12°. $1.50. Saalfield.
**Hadley, S. H. Down in Water street. il. $1 net. Revell.
Hadley *and* Allen's Greek grammar. $1.50. Am. Bk.
*Hadrian, Emperor, Life of. Spartianus, Aelianus. $1.50 net. Cambridge.
Haggard, H. Rider. Rural England. il. 2 v. 8°. Longmans.
Hale, E: Everett. How to live. New ed. 12°. $1. Little, B. & Co.
Hale, E: Everett. Man without a country. (New Kalon ser.) il. 12°. 50 c. Caldwell.
Hale, E: Everett. Memories of a hundred years. il. 8°. Macmillan.
Hale, *Sir* Matthew. *See* Raleigh, *Sir* W. Wessels.
Hale, W: G., *and* Buck, Carl D. Latin grammar. Ginn.
Halévy, Ludovic. Abbé Constantin. (Sesame classics.) il. 7 x 4¼. limp ooze cf., boxed, $1.25. Caldwell.
**Haley, Mary M. Dornfield summer. il. $1.20 net. Little, B. & Co.
Half hours with best authors. Knight, C: $4-$8. Wessels.
*Hall, A. C. A. Companion to the Prayer-book. 16°. 35 c. net. Young.
†Hall, Bolton. The game of life. 16°. $1. Wessels.
Hall, C: W. The lost brigade. 12°. bds., $1.25. Badger.
Hall, Edwin H. *See* Smith, Alex. Longmans.
**Hall, Flo. Howe. The correct thing. New rev. ed. 16°. 75 c. net. Estes.
*Hall, G: E. Balloon ascension at midnight. il. 12°. bds., $1 net. Autograph ed. 30 copies. suede, $5 net. Elder.
Hall, Jos., *ed.* King Horn. 8°. Oxford Univ.
Hall, Newman. Come to Jesus. (Chateau ser., 75 c.—New Kalon, 50 c.) Caldwell.
†Hall, Ruth. Downrenter's son. cr. 8°. $1.50. Houghton, M. & Co.
†Hall, Tom, Tales by. (Copyright ser.) 12°. 50 c. Stokes.
Hall, W: S. Descriptive geometry. 2 v. pl. Van Nostrand.
Halleck's hist. of English literature. $1.25. Am. Bk.
Hallett, Caroline M. Called to fight: book for boys. 16°. 75 c. Young.
Halsey, F. A. Worm and spiral gearing. (Science ser., no. 116.) Van Nostrand.
**Halsey, F. W. Authors of our day in their homes; American authors and their homes. 2 v. 12°. per set, boxed, $2.50 net; ¾ levant, $5 net. Pott.
Halstead, Murat. Life of Theodore Roosevelt. il. 8°. $2.50; hf. mor., $3.50; ed. de luxe, $3.50; ¾ rus., $5. Saalfield.
Hamblen, Herb. E. The red shirts. il. 12°. $1.50. Street.
**Hamerton, P. G. Etching and etchers. New ed. il. 8°. $5 net. Little, B. & Co.
Hamerton, P. G. Intellectual life. (Chateau ser.) il. 6 x 4. boxed, 75 c. Caldwell.
**Hamerton, P. G. Intellectual life. Laneside ed. pors. 8°. $1.50 net; hf. mor., $3 net. Little, B. & Co.
Hamilton, *Count* Anthony. *See* Grammont, *Count.*
**Hamilton, Gail. Chips, fragments, and vestiges; coll. and arr. by H. A. Dodge. il. $1.20 net. Lee & Shepard.
Hamilton, G: L. Indebtedness of Chaucer's Troilus and Crisseyde to Guido delle Colonne's historia Trojana. (Columbia Univ. studies in romance, literature and philology.) 12°. Macmillan.
**Hamilton, Stanislaus Murray, *ed.* Letters to Washington. vol. V., 1774-1775. 8°. $5 net. Houghton, M. & Co.
Hamilton, S. M., *ed.* *See* Monroe, Ja. Putnam.
**Hamlet. Shakespeare, W: 25 c. net. Macmillan.
Hamlet, The new. Smith, W: H. 25 c.; 50 c. Rand, McN.
**Hamlin, Myra S. Catharine's proxy: story for girls. il. 12°. $1.20 net. Little, B. & Co.
**Hamm, Margherita A. Builders of the republic. il. 12°. $2 net. Pott.
**Hamm, Margherita A. Eminent actors in their homes. il. 12°. $1.25 net; ¾ levant, $2.50 net. Pott.
**Hamm, Margherita A. Famous families of New York. 2 v. il. 8°. net. Putnam.

**Hand in hand: poems of mother and daughter. $1.20 net. Doubleday, P.
Handbooks for the clergy; ed. by A. W. Robinson. Longmans.
New volumes: Robinson, Study of the gospels.—Robbins, A Christian apologetic.
Handbooks of American government; ed. by L. B. Evans. 12°. Macmillan.
New volume: Siebert, Govt. of Ohio.
Handel. *See* Oxford musical ser. Oxford Univ.
Handy, Susan C. Girls of the Bible. il. 4°. $1.25. Jamieson-H.
**Handy information ser. 18°. 45 c. net. Crowell.
New volume: Mead, L. Word coinage.
Handy volume classics. Limp lizard ed. 25 v. ea., $1.50. Crowell.
New volumes: See advertisement.
Handy volume classics. 110 v. ea., 75 c. Crowell.
New volumes: Bulfinch, Age of chivalry; Age of fable: Legends of Charlemagne.—Dumas, Black tulip.—Hawthorne, Fanshawe; Grandfather's chair; Marble faun, 2 v.; Tanglewood tales; Wonder book.—Holmes, Professor at the breakfast table.—Poetical quotations.—Prose quotations.—Tennyson, Poems by two brothers. —Thackeray. English humorists.
Handy volume sets. Crowell.
New volumes: Hawthorne's Romances. Lenox ed. 14 v. in box, $10.50 and upwards.—Poe's Complete works. Virginia ed. 17 v. in box, $7.50.—Tennyson's Poetical works. Farringford ed. 10 v. in box. $7.50.
Hanks, Nancy. Hitchcock, C. H. 50 c. McClure.
Hann, Julius. Climatology; tr. by R. DeC. Ward. Macmillan.
**Hannan, W: I. Textile fibres of commerce. il. 8°. $3 net. Lippincott.
**Hanscom, Beatrice. Love, laurels and laughter. 12°. $1.20 net. Stokes.
*Hansen, G:, *ed.* Baby Roland booklets. il. flexible. ea., 50 c. net. Elder.
Contents: Vespers.—Ascent of man.—Lima beans
**Hapgood, Hutchins. The spirit of the Ghetto. il. 12°. $1.20 net. Funk.
Happiness, Quest of. Hillis, N. D. Macmillan.
Happy failure. Dawson, E. 60 c. Nelson.
**Harker, *Mrs.* A. Romance of the nursery. il. 12°. $1.25. Lane.
Harkness *and* Forbe's Cæsar's Gallic war. $1.25. Am. Bk.
Harkness's Complete Latin grammar. $1.25. Am. Bk.
*Harley. Robt., *Earl of Oxford,* Life and times of. pl. 8°. net. Putnam.
Harley, Wa. S. *See* Gunnison, W. B. Silver.
Harmless revolution. White, Grace M. 50 c.; pap., 25 c. J. S. Ogilvie.
**Harold's discussions. Troeger, J. W. 60 c. net. Appleton.
Harper. Olive. The show girl. il. 12°. pap., 25 c. J. S. Ogilvie.
Harper, Robt. F. Assyrian and Babylonian letters. 8°. Univ. of Chic.
Harper *and* Gallup's Cicero. $1.30. Am. Bk.
Harper *and* Wallace's Xenophon's Anabasis. $1.50. Am. Bk.
**Harper's cook-book encyclopædia. il. $1.50 net. Harper.
**Harriman, Karl Edwin. Ann Arbor tales. 12°. $1.20 net. Jacobs.
**Harrington, J: W. Adventures of Admiral Frog. col. il. 7 x 9. bds., $1.40 net. Russell.
†Harris, Frank B. The road to Ridgeby's. Popular ed. (Beacon lib.) pap., 50 c. Small, M.
†Harris, Joel Chandler. Gabriel Tolliver. 12°. $1.50. McClure.
Harris, N. M. *See* Muir, R. Macmillan.
Harris, Wa. *See* Ritchie, M. J. G. Lippincott.
*Harrison, C: Book of bees. (Handbooks of practical gardening, no. 13.) il. $1 net. Lane.
**Harrison, Edith Ogden. Prince Silver Wings. il. 4°. $1.75 net. McClurg.
Harrison, F: Boys of Spartan House School. 12°. $1.50. Young.
**Harrison, F: Ruskin. (English men of letters ser.) 75 c. net. Macmillan.
Hart, Alb. B. Actual government: as applied under American conditions. (American citizen ser.) il. 8°. Longmans.
Hart, Alb. B. Source readers of American history. il. 4 v. 12°. Macmillan.
New volume: v. 2, Heroes and patriots of the Revolution.
Harte, Bret. Works. (Riverside ed.) 16 v. 12°. $24. (sold only in sets.) Houghton, M. & Co.
**Harte, Bret, Biography of. Pemberton, T. E. $3.50 net. Dodd, Mead & Co.
**Hartshorne. Anna C. Japan and her people. il. 8°. 2 v. boxed, $4 net; ¾ cr. mor., $8 net; ed. de luxe, lim., $10 net. Coates.
†Harvard episodes. Flandrau, C: M. 50 c. Small, M.
Harvard historical studies. Longmans.
New volumes: Cross, Anglican episcopate and the American colonies.—Moran, Theory and practice of English government.
Harvard lib. pap., ea., 50 c. Small, M.
Contents: Flandrau, Harvard episodes. —Pier, The pedagogues.
Harvard Oriental ser.; ed. by C: R. Lanman. Ginn.
New volumes: Atharva-Veda-Samhita, 2 v.
Harzreise (Die). Heine, H. Ginn.
**Haskins, C: W. How to keep household accounts. 16°. $1 net. Harper.
Hassall, Arthur H. Mazarin. (Foreign statesmen ser.) 75 c. Macmillan.
**Hastings, Gilbert. Siena, its architecture and art. il. 8°. $2 net. Brentano.
Hastings, Ja., Selbie, J: A., *and others, eds.* Dict. of the Bible. il. 4 v. 8°. Subs. only. per vol., $6; hf. mor., per vol., $8. Scribner.
Hatfield. Marcus P. Diseases of children. (No. 14 Quiz-Compend.) 3d ed. 12°. 80 c.; interleaved, $1. Blakiston.
Hatfield, J. T., *ed. See* Allen, P. S. Univ. of Chic.

**Haunted (The) mine. Castlemon, H. 80 c. net. Coates.
Haunts of ancient peace. Austin, A. Macmillan.
Haupt, Paul. Biblical love ditties. Pamphlet. 5 c. Open Court.
Haverfield, E. L. Stanhope. il. 8°. $1.25. Nelson.
Havergal, F. R. My king, and Royal invitation. (New Kalon ser.) il. 12°. 50 c. Caldwell.
Hawkins, Anthony H. Dolly dialogues; cont. the 4 additional dialogues. 12°. $1.50. Holt.
Hawthorne, Nathaniel. Works. (New Wayside ed.) 12 v. 16°. $12. Houghton, M. & Co.
Hawthorne, Nath. Romances. Lenox ed.; with introd. to each v. by Kath. Lee Bates. il. 14 v. 18°. per set, $10.50; $17.50; $29. Crowell.
Hawthorne, Nath. Romances. 7 v. il. 8°. $7; $8.75; hf. leath., $10.50; hf. cf., $17.50. Crowell.
Hawthorne, Nath. The marble faun. il. 8°. $1.50. Appleton.
Hawthorne, Nat. The pigmies. (Editha ser.) il. 7½ x 5¼. 50 c. Caldwell.
Hawthorne, Nat. Tanglewood tales. (Famous books for boys.) il. 12°. 79 c. Caldwell.
Hawthorne, Nat. Twice-told tales. (Famous books for boys.) il. 12°. 79 c. Caldwell.
**Hawthorne, Nathaniel, Life of. Woodberry, G: E. (Amer. men of letters ser.) 16°. $1.10 net. 8° ed., 350 copies, $3.50 net. Houghton, M. & Co.
**Hayens, Herb. One of the red shirts. (Pastime and adventure ser.) il. 12°. $1 net. Jacobs.
Hayes, M. H. *See* Fillmore, J. Miller, E. D.
**Haynie, H: Paris, past and present. il. 2 v. 8°. boxed. $4 net; ¾ levant, $8 net. Stokes.
Hazlitt, W: Complete works; ed. by A. R. Waller and A. Glover, with introd. by W. E. Henley. (Lib. ed.) 12 v. 8°. sets only, $36. McClure.
**Hazlitt, W: Shakespeare. A study. 8°. $2.50 net. [Imp.] Scribner.
Headlam, J. W. Germany, 1815-1889. 2 v. 12°. Macmillan.
Healing of souls. Banks, L: A. 8°. $1.50. Eaton & M.
Hearn, Lafcadio. Kotto. il. 12°. Macmillan.
†Heart of Denise and other tales. Yeats, S. L. $1.25. Longmans.
†Heart of the doctor. Foster, Mabel G. 12°. $1.50. Houghton, M. & Co.
**Heath, Lillian M. Eighty good times out of doors il. 12°. 75 c. net. Revell.
†Heath, Robinson W. Adventures of Uncle Lubin. 4°. $1.50. Brentano.
Heath's English classics. Heath.
New volume: Scott's Lady of the Lake; ed. by L. DuP. Syle.
Heath's home and school classics. Heath.
New volumes: Castle Blair, by F. L. Shaw; Story without an end.
Heath's mathematical monograph ser. Heath.
New volume: 8, Some properties of the triangle and its circles, by W. H. Bruce.
Heating and ventilation of buildings. Carpenter, R. C. $4. Wiley.
Hebrew and English lexicon of the Old Testament, based on lexicon of Gesenius. Robinson, E., *tr.* Brown, F., Driver, S. R., Briggs, C. A., *eds.* pt. 10. Oxford Univ.
**Hedge, *Rev.* F: H: Sermons. 5¼ x 7. $1 net. Am. Unitarian.
**Hedge, F: H: Hours with German classics. New ed. 8°. $2 net. Little, B. & Co.
**Hegel's logic. Hibben, J: G. net. Scribner.
Heine, H. Die Harzreise, with selections. (Internat. modern language ser.) Ginn.
*Helferich, H. Atlas and epitome of fractures and luxations; ed. by J. C. Bloodgood. col. il. $3 net. Saunders.
*Help and good cheer. Cuyler, T. L. $1 net. Baker & T.
**Helpful thoughts ser. 18°. 80 c. net. McClurg.
New volume: Catch words of cheer, by S. H. Hubbard.
Helps, *Sir* A. Spanish conquest in America. New ed., in 4 v. v. 3. il. 12°. $1.50. Lane.
Helps to German prose composition. Ehrke, E. Oxford Univ.
Henchman (The) Luther, M. L. Macmillan.
**Henley, W: E. Dickens. 12°. (Modern Eng. writers.) $1 net. Dodd, Mead & Co.
Henley, W: E. I am the captain of my soul. (Impression leaflets.) 10 c. Elder.
Henley, W: E. Views and reviews. 2d ser. $1. Scribner.
Henry. New normal U. S. history. New ed. Hinds.
†Henry, Alfred H. By order of the prophet. A tale of Utah. il. 12°. $1.50. Revell.
Henry, Ma. *See* Rossiter, F: M. Revell.
**Henry VIII. Pollard, A. F. $50 net; $25 net. Scribner.
†Henry, Esmond. Thackeray, W: M. 75 c. Brentano.
Henslow, G. Poisonous plants in field and garden. il. 12°. $1. Young.
Henty, G: A. Copyright volumes. price on application. Scribner.
**Henty, G: A. Treasure of the Incas. il. 12°. $1.20 net. Scribner.
**Henty, G: A. With the British legion. il. 12°. $1.20 net. Scribner.
**Henty, G: A. With Kitchener in the Soudan. il. 12°. $1.20 net. Scribner.
†Her lord and master. Morton, M. $1.50. Biddle.
†Her majesty the king. Roche, J. J. $1.50. Russell.
**Heraldry, Art of. Fox-Davies, A. C: $45 net. Brentano.
**Heraldry, English. Boutell, C: $1.75 net. Lippincott.
*Herbs, Book of. Northcote, *Lady* Rosalind. $1 net. Lane.
Heredity. Essays in. Pearson, K. Macmillan.
*Herford, Vincent, Mumford, Edith W., *and* Mizner, Addison. Cynics calendar of revised wisdom. il. 16°. gingham, 75 c. net. Elder.

†Heritage (The). Stevenson, B. E. cr. 8°. $1.50. Houghton, M. & Co.
Hermann und Dorothea. Goethe, J. W. v. Buchheim, C. A., *ed.* Oxford Univ.
Heroes and patriots of the Revolution. Hart, A. B. Macmillan.
Heroes of chivalry. Maitland, Louise. Silver.
Heroes of myth. Price, L. L. Silver.
Heroes of the nations ser. il. 12°. $1.35 net; hf. leath., $1.60 net. Putnam.
New volume: 35, Augustus Cæsar, by J. B. Firth.
**Heroes of the navy ser. il. 12°. 80 c. net. Appleton.
New volume: Barnes, J. With the flag in the channel.
**Heroines of poetry. Maud, Constance. il. 12°. $1.50 net. Lane.
Héros de Roman (Les). Boileau. Ginn.
**Herr doctor (The). Macdonald, R. 40 c. net. Funk.
Herrick, Cheesman K. History of commerce. (Macmillan's commercial ser.) 12°. Macmillan.
Herrick, Cheesman K., *ed. See* Macmillan's commercial series. Macmillan.
**Herrick, Christine T. In city tents. 16°. net. Putnam.
Herrick, H. M. Kingdom of God in the writings of the fathers. Univ. of Chic.
**Herrick, Rob. Hesperides and Noble numbers. (Caxton ser.) il. lambskin, $1.25 net. Scribner.
**Herrick, *Mrs.* S. B. Century of sonnets. decor. vellum. 5¾ x 7¾. $2.60 net. Russell.
Hertwig, R. Text-book of zoology; tr. from 5th German ed. by J. S. Kingsley. il. Holt.
**Hesperides and Noble numbers. Herrick, Rob. $1.25 net. Scribner.
Hewett, G. M. A. Open air boy. il. $1.25. Fenno.
**Hewitt, Emma C. Three little Denvers. (Lad and lassie ser.) il. 12°. 40 c. net. Jacobs.
*Hewlett, R. T. Manual of bacteriology. il. 2d ed. rev. $4 net. Blakiston.
Hexateuch according to the revised version arranged in its constituent documents. New rev. ed.; ed. by J. E. Carpenter and G. Harford-Battersby. 2 v. 8°. Longmans.
Heydrick. How to study literature. Hinds.
Hiawatha. Longfellow, H: W. $1.25. Caldwell.
**Hibben, J: G. Hegel's logic. net. Scribner.
Hicks, E. L., *and* Hill, G. F. Greek historical inscriptions. 2d ed. Oxford Univ.
†Higgins, Eliz. Out of the west. post 8°. $1.50. Harper.
**Higginson, T: W. Henry Wadsworth Longfellow. (Amer. men of letters ser.) 16°. $1.10 net; uncut ed., 300 copies, $1.50 net. Houghton, M. & Co.
**Higginson, T: W. Whittier. (English men of letters.) 75 c. net. Macmillan.
Higginson, T: W., *and* Channing, E: English history for Americans. New ed. rev. il. 8°. Longmans.
†Highway of fate. Carey, R. N. $1.50. Lippincott.
Highways and byways ser. il. 8°. Macmillan.
New volume: Cook, London highways and byways.
*Hilbert, D: Foundations of geometry. 8 x 5½. $1 net. Open Court.
†Hilda. Duncan, S. J. 50 c. Stokes.
Hill, G. F. Illustrations to school classics. col. il. 8°. Macmillan.
Hill, G. F. *See* Hicks, E. L. Oxford Univ.
**Hill, Janet M. Practical cooking and serving. 5½ x 8½. $2 net. Doubleday, P.
Hill, W. E., *and* Sons. Antonio Stradivari: his life and work. Dodd, Mead & Co.
†Hillern, Wilhelmine v., *and* Safford, Ma. J. On the cross. il. 12°. $1.50. Biddle.
**Hillis, Newell D. Four studies in character-building. 12°. 75 c. net. Revell.
**Hillis, Newell D. The home school. A study of the debt parents owe their children. 50 c. net. Revell.
Hillis, Newell D. Quest of happiness. 12°. Macmillan.
Himmelweight, A. L. A. *See* Money, A. W.
*Hinds, J. I. D. Chemistry by induction. 12°. 75 c. net. Wiley.
Hinds, J. I. D. Inorganic chemistry. 8°. $3. Wiley.
Hindustani mss. in Bodleian library. *See* Ethé, H. Oxford Univ.
**Hippodrome (The). (Toy books.) 12 col. pictures. 4°. bds., $2 net. Stokes.
His mother's letter. Merrill, J. M. il. 12°. $1. Saalfield.
Hiscox, Gardner D. Gas, gasoline and oil engines. 10th ed. rev. $2.50. Henley.
Histology, Compend of. Cushing, H. H. 80 c.; $1. Blakiston.
Historic highways of America. Hulbert, A. B. vs. 1, 2. ea., $2. vs. 3-16. ea., $2.50. A. H. Clark.
**Historic houses of New Jersey. Mills, W. J. $5 net. Lippincott.
**Historic lives ser. il. 12°. $1 net. Appleton.
New volumes: Daniel Boone, by R. G. Thwaites.—Sir William Johnson, by A: C. Buell.
Historical essays and reviews. Creighton, M. $2. Longmans.
Historical essays. Stubbs, W: Longmans.
Historical lectures. Acton, *Lord.* 2 v. Macmillan.
**Historical series for Bible students. Scribner.
New volume: Goodspeed, History of Babylonians and Assyrians.
History, Ancient. Rollin, C: 4 v. $4-$8. Wessels.
History, Ancient, for beginners. Botsford, G: W. Macmillan.
History, Cambridge modern. *See* Ward, A. W. Macmillan.
**History of English literature. Simonds, W: E. il. 8°. $1.25 net. Houghton, M. & Co.
History of our times. McCarthy, J. 2 v. $2-$4. Wessels.
**History of over sea. Morris, W:, *tr.* $1.50 net Russell.
History: suggestions as to its study and teachings. Salmon, L. M. Macmillan.

History, Teaching of. *See* Bourne, H: E. Longmans.
Hitchcock, Caroline H. Nancy Hanks: the story of Abraham Lincoln's mother. il. 16°. 50 c. McClure.
Hoadley's Brief course in physics. $1.20. Am. Bk.
Hoare, G. W. Life in St. John's Gospel. 16°. 40 c. Young.
**Hobbes, J: Oliver, [*pseud.* for *Mrs.* P. M. T. Craigie.] Froude. 12°. (Modern Eng. writers.) $1 net. Dodd, Mead & Co.
†Hobbes, J: O., [*pseud.* for *Mrs.* Craigie.] Love and the soul hunters. 12°. $1.50. Funk.
†Hobbes, J: Oliver. Robert Orange. (Library of successes.) 12°. pap., 50 c. Stokes.
†Hobbes, J: Oliver. Tales about temperaments 12°. (Town and country lib.) $1; pap., 50 c. Appleton.
†Hobbes, J: Oliver, Tales of. (Copyright ser.) 12°. 50 c. Stokes.
**Hobbes, T: Stephen, *Sir* L. 75 c. net. Macmillan.
Hocking, Silas K. The awakening of Anthony Weir. il. 12°. $1.50. Am. S. S.
Hocking, Silas K. Gripped. $1.25. Warne.
**Hogan, Louise E. Children's diet in home and school. 16°. 50 c. net. Coates.
**Hogarth, W: Dobson, A. $25; $60; $120 net. McClure.
**Holborn, Alf. Pentateuch in light of today. 12°. 75 c. net. [Imp.] Scribner.
**Holbrook, Florence. Book of nature myths. il. 12°. 45 c. net. Houghton, M. & Co.
Holbrook, R: T. Dante and the animal kingdom. (Columbia Univ. studies in romance, literature and philology.) Macmillan.
Holbrook, Theo. S. *See* Otto, A. F.
Holden, E: S., *comp.* Flowers from Persian gardens. decor. 6 x 9½. $1.25; Lim. ed., $10. Russell.
**Holder, C: F. Adventures of Torqua. il. $1.20 net. Little, B. & Co.
Holder, C: F. Big game fish. (American sportsman's lib.) il. 8°. Macmillan.
†Hole in the wall. Morrison, A. $1.50. McClure.
Holiday ser. il. $1.25. Dodd, Mead & Co.
New volumes: Barr, A. E., Bow of orange ribbon; Maid of Maiden Lane.—Eliot, G:, Silas Marner.—Shakespeare, W:, As you like it.
Holland, J. G. Bitter Sweet. (Chateau ser., 75 c.—Laureate ser., $1.50.—New Kalon, 50 c.—Sesame classics, $1.25.) Caldwell.
†Holland wolves. Ellis, J. B. $1.50. McClurg.
Holleman, A. F. Organic chemistry; tr. by A. J. Walker *and* O. E. Mott. 8°. Wiley.
Holley, Marietta, [Josiah Allen's wife, *pseud.*] Samantha at Saratoga. (New Kalon ser.) il. 12°. 50 c. Caldwell.
Hollis, Gertrude. Scholar of Lindisfarne: tale of the time of S. Aidan. 12°. $1. Young.
**Holmes, Edmond. Triumph of love. 12° $1.25. Lane.
Holmes, *Mrs.* Ma. J. English orphans. il. 12°. $1. Saalfield.
Holmes, *Mrs.* Ma. J. Homestead on the hillside. il. 12°. $1. Saalfield.
Holmes, Oliver W. Autocrat of the breakfast-table. (Sesame classics.) il. 7 x 4¼. limp ooze cf., boxed, $1.25. Caldwell.
Holmes, Oliver W. Breakfast-table series. (New handy volume ed.) 4 v. 16°. $4 (sold separately or in sets.)
Contents: Autocrat, Professor, and Poet at the breakfast-table, and Over the teacups.
Holmes, Oliver W. The professor at the breakfast-table. (New Kalon ser.) il. 12°. 50 c. Caldwell.
Holt, L. Emmett. Diseases of children. New rev. ed., 1902. $6. Appleton.
Holtzmann, *Prof.* Life of Jesus. Macmillan.
Holy land. Fulleylove, J: Macmillan.
Holy Week, Addresses in. Ingram, A. F. W. 75 c. Young.
†Home, Andrew. Jack and Black. il. 12°. $1.25. Lippincott.
**Home decoration, Principles of. Wheeler, C. $2.40 net. Doubleday, P.
**Home life of the Borneo head-hunters. Furness, W: H. $7.50 net. Lippincott.
**Home school: a study of the debt parents owe their children. 50 c. net. Revell.
**Homely virtues. Watson, J: $1.20 net. Dodd, Mead & Co.
Homer. Iliad. Benner, A. R., *ed.* Appleton.
Homer. Iliad. Monro, D. B., *and* Allen, T. W., *eds.* (Oxford class. ser.) Oxford Univ.
Homer. Odyssey xiii.-xxiv. Monro, D. B., *ed.* 8°. Oxford Univ.
**Homes and their decoration. French, L. H. $3.50 net. Dodd, Mead & Co.
Homestead on the hillside. Holmes, *Mrs.* Ma. J. il. 12°. $1. Saalfield.
**Hooker, Katharine. Wayfarers in Italy. il. 8°. $3 net. Scribner.
Hooker's ecclesiastical polity. bk. 5; ed. by R. Bayne. (English theological lib.) 8°. Macmillan.
Hooper, W: L., *and* Wells, Roy T. Electrical problems. Ginn.
†Hope, Anthony. Intrusions of Peggy. il. post 8°. $1.50. Harper.
†Hope Loring. Bell, Lilian. il. 12°. $1.50. L. C. Page.
**Hopkins, Arch. The apostles' creed. 5¼ x 7¾. 60 c. net. Am. Unitarian.
**Hopkins, W: B. Roller bandage. New 5th ed. il. 12°. $1.50 net. Lippincott.
**Hopkins, W: J. Sand man: his farm stories. il. large 12°. $1.20 net. L. C. Page.
*Hore, A. H. Student's history of the Greek church. $2.25 net. Young.
Hornby. Gas engineers' laboratory handbk. 2d ed. 12°. $2.50. Spon & C.
†Hornung, E. W. Shadow of the rope. 12°. $1.50. Scribner.
**[Horse] Breaking and riding. Fillis, J. $5 net. [Imp.] Scribner.
Horseless road locomotion. Sennett, A. R. Macmillan.
**Hortense. Foster, E. A. 80 c. net. Lee & Shepard.
**Horton, G: In Argolis: family life in Greece. il. 8°. $1.75 net. McClurg.
†Horton, G: The long straight road. il. 12°. $1.50. Bowen-M.

Hotchkiss, Chauncey C. For a lady brave. il. $1.50. Street.
Hotchkiss, Chauncey C. Mistress Hetty. $1. Street.
**Hour glass stories. il. 12°. 40 c. net. Funk.
New volume: Macdonald, The herr doctor.
**Hours with German classics. Hedge, F: H: $2 net. Little, B. & Co.
House at Brambling Minster. Marchant, B. 80 c. Young.
House of life. Rossetti, D. G. Wieners.
†House of the Combrays. Le Notre, G. $1.50. Dodd, Mead & Co.
**House opposite: a mystery. Kent, Eliz. net. Putnam.
†House under the sea. Pemberton, M. $1.50. Appleton.
**Household accounts. How to keep. Haskins, C: W. $1 net. Harper.
Housewives of Edenrise. 12°. Appleton.
Housekeeping. *See* Herrick, Christine T. Putnam.
**How Sammy went to Coral-land. Atwater, E. P. 40 c. net. Jacobs.
How the fire spread. Challacombe, J. 40 c. Young.
How the story ended. MacSorley, C. M. 40 c. Young.
**How to attract the birds. Blanchan, N. $1.35 net. Doubleday, P.
How to bring up your children. Locke, J: 50 c. Wessels.
How to gesture. Ott. New ed. il. Hinds.
How to live. Hale, E: E. $1. Little, B. & Co.
How to sing. Lehmann-Kalisch, L. Macmillan.
How to study literature. Heydrick. Hinds.
Howard, Sydney. Wayside inn. Quail & W.
Howe, Malverd A. Design of simple roof trusses in wood and steel, with an introduction to the elements of graphic statics. 8°. $2. Wiley.
**Howells, W: D. Flight of Pony Baker. il. post 8°. $1.25 net. Harper.
**Howells, W: D. Literature and life. il. cr. 8°. $2.25 net. Harper.
Howland, H. N. *See* Andrews, E. J. Macmillan.
Hoyt, Helen B. Child's story of the life of Christ. il. $1.25. Wilde.
**Hubbard, Sarah H., *comp.* Catch words of cheer. 18°. (Helpful thoughts ser.) 80 c. net. McClurg.
**Hudson river from ocean to source. Bacon, E. M. il. 8°. $3.50 net. Putnam.
Hughes. Lessons on practical subjects. Hinds.
†Hughes, Rupert. The whirlwind. 12°. silk cl., $1.50. Lothrop.
Hugo, Victor. Complete works. Author's ed. New issue. 10 v. buckram, $10; hf. leath., $12; hf. calf, $16. Wessels.
Hugo, Victor. Notre Dame de Paris. Anniversary ed.; tr. by A. L. Alger. il. 2 v. [Also] all photographs of the play as presented at Daly's theatre. $6; ¾ crushed levant, $15. Caldwell.
†Hugo, Victor. Notre Dame de Paris. Bertha Galland ed. il. 2 v. 8°. boxed, $3. Wessels.
Hugo, Victor. Sur les bords du Rhin; ed. by T. B. Bronson. Holt.
†Hulbert, A. R. Queen of Quelparte. il. 12°. $1.50. Little, B. & Co.
Hulbert, Arth. H. Historic highways of Am. vs. 1, 2. ea., $2. vs. 3-16. ea., $2.50. A. H. Clark.
**Human nature and the social order. Cooley, C: H. $1.50 net. Scribner.
*Humboldt, *Baron* Alex. v. Fluctuations of gold; tr. 8°. $1.50 net. Cambridge.
Humorous plays. Sheridan, R: B. 75 c. Brentano.
Humorous verse, Anthology of. Cook, T. A., *ed.* 75 c. Brentano.
†Humphrey, Zephine. Uncle Charley. 12°. $1.25. Houghton, M. & Co.
*Humphreys, Arth. L. Large type books. 8°. pap., net, ea., $7.50. Wessels.
New volumes: Cicero, De Officiis.—Aristotle's Ethics.
*Humphreys, Arth. L. Large type books. New ser. 16°. pap., net. Wessels.
Contents: Raleigh and others, Practical wisdom.—La Rochefoucauld, Maximes.—Thomas à Kempis, Imitation of Christ.—Marcus Aurelius, Meditations.
Humpty Dumpty nursery rhymes. col. il. Warne.
Hundred most famous pictures in the world; notes by A: Van Cleef. 20 parts. pts I. and II. antique paper, folio. ea., 25 c. Stokes.
**Hunt, Gaillard. Life of Ja. Madison. il. 6 x 9¼. $2.50 net. Doubleday, P.
Hunt, Gaillard, *ed.* *See* Madison, Ja. Putnam.
**Hunt, Leigh. Old court suburb. New ed.; ed. by A. Dobson. il. 2 v. 12°. $12.50 net; large-pap. lim. ed., $35 net. Lippincott.
Huntington, Helen. The solitary path and other poems. Doubleday, P.
**Hurdy-gurdy (The). Richards, L. E. 75 c. net. Estes.
*Hutchinson, R., *and* Rainy, R. Clinical methods. il. 5th ed. 4½ x 6½. $2.50 net. Keener.
†Hutten, *Baroness* von. Our lady of the beeches. 12°. $1.25. Houghton, M. & Co.
**Hutton, Laurence. Literary landmarks of Oxford. il. net. Scribner.
Hyde, W: DeW. Jesus' way. 16°. Houghton, M. & Co.
Hygiene, Personal. *See* McFarland, Jos. Blakiston.
†Hyne, Cutcliffe. The filibusters. (Copyright ser.) 12°. 50 c. Stokes.
I am the captain of my soul. Henley, W: E. 10 c. Elder.
Ibbotson, F: *See* Brearley, H.
Iddesleigh, *Earl of.* Luck o' Lanendale. $1.50. Lane.
Idle thoughts. Jerome, J. K. $1.25. Caldwell.
†If I were king. McCarthy, J. H. $1.50. Russell.
Iles, Malvern W. Lead smelting. 12°. $2.50. Wiley.
Iliad. *See* Homer.
Iliad, Boy's. Perry, W. C. Macmillan.
†Iliowizi, H: The archierey of Samara. (Griffin ser.) 12°. $1. Coates.
Illingworth, J. R. Reason and revelation. 8°. Macmillan.

Illustrations to school classics. Hill, G. F. Macmillan.
Illustrative lesson notes. *See* International S. S. lessons. Eaton & M.
Imitation, Laws of. Tarde, G. Holt.
Imitation of Christ. *See* Thomas à Kempis.
Imitation of Christ, Golden thoughts from. *See* Lindsay, T. M. Stokes.
Immensee. *See* Storm, Theo.
*Imperial republic: a drama. Crane, Eliz. G. $1 net. Grafton Press.
Impression leaflets. illum. cards. ea., 10 c. Elder.
New numbers: Stevenson, Requiem.—Henley, I am the captain of my soul.—Bourdillon, The night has a thousand eyes.
*Impressions calendar for 1903. 13 leaves. col. il. boxed, $1 net. Elder.
In a balcony. *See* Browning, R. Blue Sky Press.
In a car of gold. Gray, P. L. il. 12°. $1. Saalfield.
**In Argolis. Horton, G: $1.75 net. McClurg.
**In chimney corners. MacManus, S. $1.50 net. McClure.
**In city tents. Herrick, Christine T. 16°. net. Putnam.
In His steps. Sheldon, C: 75 c. Caldwell.
†In kings' byways. Weyman, S. J. Longmans.
†In kings' houses. Dorr, Julia C. R. $1.50. L. C. Page.
In memoriam. *See* Tennyson, A.
In peril of his life. Gaboriau, E. 75 c. Caldwell.
In spite of all. Lyall, E. 50 c. Am. News.
In the camp of Cornwallis. Tomlinson, E. T. $1.50. Wilde.
In the day of trouble. Ovenden, C: T. 80 c. Young.
**In the days of Queen Elizabeth. Tappan, E. M. 80 c. net. Lee & Shepard.
In the days of St. Clair. Naylor, Ja. B. $1.50. Saalfield.
In the days of the dragons. Dawson, E. C. 60 c. Young.
†In the fog. Davis, R: H. $1.50. Russell.
**In the green forest. Pyle, K. $1.50 net. Little, B. & Co.
**In the high heavens. Ball, R. S. $1.50 net. Lippincott.
**In the hour of silence. McFayden, J: E. (Companion to "The divine pursuit.") $1 net. Revell.
**In the land of the lamas. Rijnhart, Susie C. 75 c. net. Revell.
†In the morning glow. Gilson, R. R. $1.25. Harper.
**In the palaces of the sultan. Dodd, A. B. $4 net. Dodd, Mead & Co.
†In the shadow of the black pine. Plympton, A. G. 50 c. Small, M.
In the shadow of the purple. Gilbert, G: $1.50. Fenno.
**In the wasp's nest. Brady, C. T. $1.50 net. Scribner.
Incaland. Wetmore, C. H. $1.50. Wilde.
**Incarnation of the Lord. Briggs, C: A: $1.50 net. Scribner.
**India, Mediæval, under Mohammedan rule. Poole, Stanley L. $1.35 net; $1.60 net. Putnam.
India, Outline study of. *See* Mason, *Mrs.* C. A. Lux Christi. Macmillan.
India, Rulers of. *See* Smith, Vincent A. Oxford Univ.
India. *See also* Denning, Marg. B. Revell.
**Indian boyhood. Eastman, C: A. $1.60 net. McClure.
Indians of So. Mexico, Physical characters of. Starr, F: 75 c. net. Univ. of Chic.
**Industrial conciliation. Proceedings National Civic Federation Conference, Dec. 16-17, 1901. (Questions of the day ser., no. 99.) 8°. Putnam.
*Industrial resources of Germany, France, Russia, Spain and Egypt. *See* Waage, R. G. Cambridge.
†Inevitable (The). Mighel, P. V. $1.50. Lippincott.
Infancy of our Lord. col. il. 48°. bds., 15 c. Young.
**Infants, Artificial feeding of. *See* Judson, C: F. Lippincott.
Infelicia. Menken, A. I. $1.50. Lippincott.
Ingoldsby, T:, *pseud.* *See* Barham, R:
Ingoldsby legends. *See* Barham, R:
Ingram, A. F. W. Addresses in Holy Week. 12°. 75 c. Young.
Ingram, A. F. W. Men who crucify Christ: six Lenten sermons. 16°. 50 c. Young.
Ingram, A. F. W. Under the dome. $1.25. Young.
Inhalation methods. *See* Tissier, P. Blakiston.
Inland voyage, An. Stevenson, R. L: $1.25. Scribner.
**Inner and Middle Temple. Bellot, H. H. L. $2 net. Pott.
**Innes, J. H. New Amsterdam and its people. il. 8°. $2.50 net. Scribner.
*Innsly, O., *ed.* Love songs and other poems. 16°. $1 net. Grafton Press.
†Insane root (The). Praed, *Mrs.* C. $1.50. Funk.
**Instruction concerning erecting of a library. Naudé, Gabriel. price on application. Houghton, M. & Co.
**Insurance and crime. Campbell, Alex. C. 8°. net. Putnam.
**Integrity of Scripture. Smith, J: 12°. $1.25 net. Revell.
Intellectual life. *See* Hamerton, P. G.
**International critical commentary. Scribner.
New volume: Gray, Commentary on Numbers.
International encyclopædia, The new; ed. by D. C. Gilman, Harry Thurston Peck, Frank Moore Colby, *and others.* 17 v. apply to publishers. Dodd, Mead & Co.
†International episode. James, H: $1.25. Harper.
International modern language ser. New ed. 12°. Ginn.
New volumes: Heine's Die Harzreise.—Schücking's Die drei freier.—Mérimée's Colomba.
**International student's atlas of modern geography. Bartholomew, J. G. $2.25 net. [Imp.] Scribner.

*International S. S. lessons, 1903. Neely, T: B:, *ed.* Eaton & M.
Contents: First lesson book. (Beginner's.) 16°. 15 c. net.—Young people's lesson book. (Intermediate.) 16°. 15 c. net—Lesson hand-book. (Senior.) 18°. 20 c. net: flex. leath., 25 c. net.

International S. S. lessons. Illustrative lesson notes, 1903. Neely, T: B:, *and* Doherty, Robt. R., *eds.* il. maps. 8°. $1.25. Eaton & M.

*International S. S. lessons. Golden Text Book for 1903. Neely, T: B:, *ed.* 24°. Per doz., 30 c. net; per 100, $2 net. Eaton & M.

**International theological library. Scribner.
New volume: Rainy, Later Catholic Church.

Interpretative reading. Marsland, Cora. Longmans.

Introduccion à la lengua castellana. Marion *and* des Garennes, *eds.* Heath.

†Intrusions of Peggy. Hope, A. $1.50. Harper.

**Invention, Romance of modern. Williams, A. $1.50 net. Lippincott.

Invisibles (The). Christopher, E. E. $1.50. Saalfield.

Iota, *pseud.* *See* Caffyn, *Mrs.* K. Mannington.

Ireland, Mary E. Timothy and his friends. il. 12°. $1. Saalfield.

**Iroquois legends. Canfield, W. W. $2.50 net. Wessels.

Irving, Washington. Complete works. Author's ed. New issue. 8 v. buckram, $8; ½ leath., $12; ½ cf., $16. Wessels.

Irving, Washington. Life of Goldsmith. (Longman's English classics.) Longmans.

**Irving, Washington. Sketch book. (Caxton ser.) il. 2 v. lambskin. ea., $1.25 net. Scribner.

Irving's (Wash.) Sketch book. (Regents' ed.) 50 c. Am. Bk.

*Irwin, Wallace. Love sonnets of a hoodlum. Autograph ed. 100 copies, ½ parch. $2 net. Elder.

*Irwin, Wallace. Rubaiyat of Omar Khayyam, *jr.* il. Tobaconalian ed. 12°. $1 net; autograph ed., 100 copies, ½ parch., $3 net. Elder.

Isherwood, Bradford. Me, Nos, and the others. 16°. 20 c. Young.

Isthmian canal. *See* Burr, W: H. Wiley.

Islam and Christianity. 12°. $1. Am. Tr.

†Istar of Babylon. Potter, M. H. $1.50. Harper.

Italian and English dictionary. Edgren, H. Holt.

Italian art, Study and criticism of. Berenson, B. Macmillan.

**Italian cities. Blashfield, E. H. 2 v. $5 net. Scribner.

Italian grammar. Young, Ma. V. Holt.

**Italian life in town and country. Villari, Luigi. $1.20 net. Putnam.

Italy. Deecke, W. Macmillan.

**Italy. Vermilye, D. B., *tr.* $3 net. Brentano.

[Italy] Land of the Latins. Willard, A. R. Longmans.

**Italy, Northern. Baedeker, K. $2.10 net. [Imp.] Scribner.

**Italy, Wayfarers in. Hooker, K. $3 net. Scribner.

**Ivan Ilyitch. Tolstoy, *Count* L. N. $2 net. McClure.

**Ives, G: B., *ed.* *See* Montaigne. Houghton, M. & Co.

Ives, Howard C. *See* French, A. W. Wiley.

"J. P. M." *pseud.* *See* Mowbray, J. P.

J. S. of Dale. *pseud.* for Stimson, F. J.

Jacberns, Raymond. New pupil. il. 8°. Macmillan.

Jacberns, Raymond. Peggy Morton. 16°. 40 c. Young.

†Jack and Black. Home, A. $1.25. Lippincott.

**Jack and his island. Thruston, L. M. $1.20 net. Little, B. & Co.

**Jack Champney. Anderson, R. $1 net. Jacobs.

Jackanapes. Ewing, J. H. 50 c. Caldwell.

Jackdaw of Rheims. Barham, R: $2. Young.

**Jacks of all trades. Birdsall, K. L. $1.20 net. Appleton.

Jackson, *Dr.* Last squire of Inglewood. 8°. il. 80 c. Nelson.

**Jackson, A. V. W: Sanskrit grammar for beginners. (v. 1., Columbia Univ. Indo-Iranian ser.) 8°. net. Macmillan.

†Jackson, Gabrielle E. Doughnuts and diplomas. il. 12°. $1. Altemus.

Jackson, Helen, ["H. H.," *pseud.*] Glimpses of California and the missions. New ed. il. 12°. $1.50. Little, B. & Co.

Jacob Faithful. Marryat, F: 79 c. Caldwell.

**Jacobs, *Mrs.* Violet. The sheep-stealers. 12°. Putnam.

†Jacobs, W. W. The lady of the barge. il. 12°. $1.50. Dodd, Mead & Co.

†James, H: International episode. il. $1.25. Harper.

†James, H: Wings of the dove. 2 v. 12°. $2.50. Scribner.

James, J: A. The anxious inquirer. (Golden counsel ser.) 1 il. boxed. 16°. 75 c. Caldwell.

James, J: A. Line upon line. (New Kalon ser.) il. 12°. 50 c. Caldwell.

**James, Martha. Tom Winstone, Wide awake. il. 12°. 80 c. net. Lee & Shepard.

James the Sixth and the Gowrie mystery. Lang, A. Longmans.

Janet *and* Seailles. History of philosophy; tr. 8°. Macmillan.

†Janet Ward. Sangster, Marg. E. 12°. $1.50. Revell.

**Janvier, T: A. Christmas kalends of Provence. il. post 8°. $1.25 net. Harper.

**Japan and her people. Hartshorne, A. C. $4 net-$10 net. Coates.

Japan, Around the world through. Del Mar, W. Macmillan.

**Japan, Mythological. Otto, A. F. $7.50 net. Biddle.

Japan. *See also* Brain, Belle M. Revell.

**Japanese girl, American diary of a. Glory, *Miss* Morning. $1.40 net. Stokes.

Japanese girls and women. Bacon, Alice M. $4. Houghton, M. & Co.

**Japanese, Things. Chamberlain, B. H. $4 net. [Imp.] Scribner.

Japhet in search of a father. Marryat, F: 79 c. Caldwell.

Jarrold, Ernest. The boy squatter. il. 12°. 60 c. Jamieson-H.
†Javan Ben Seir. Kennedy, W. 50 c. Stokes.
Jaws, Surgical pathology and diseases of. *See* Grant, H. H. Saunders.
**Jeb Hutton. Connolly, J. B. $1.20 net. Scribner.
*Jeffries, R: Nature and eternity. 16°. (Mosher's brocade ser.) 75 c. net. Mosher.
**Jekyll, Gertrude, *and* Mawley, E. Roses for English gardens. il. 12°. $3.75 net. [Imp.] Scribner.
Jenkins, T. A. Longer French poems. 12°. (20th century text-books.) Appleton.
†Jenks, Tudor. Gypsy, the talking dog. il. 12°. $1. Altemus.
Jenkyns, *Sir* H: British colonies and protectorates. Oxford Univ.
†Jennie Baxter, journalist. Barr, R. 50 c. Stokes
Jennings, Arthur S. Paint and color mixing: practical handbook for painters, decorators and all who mix colors. 9 il. 72 col. samples. 8°. $2. Spon & C.
Jennings, A. S. Wallpapers and wall coverings. 8°. $2. W: T. Comstock.
Jepson, Willis L. Key to the flora of the Pacific slope. 12°. (20th century text-books.) Appleton.
Jerome, J. K. Idle thoughts. (Sesame classics.) il. 7 x 4¾. limp ooze cf., boxed, $1.25. Caldwell.
†Jerome, J. K. Paul Kelver. 12°. $1.50. Dodd, Mead & Co.
Jerome, J. K. Three men in a boat (New Kalon ser.) il. 12°. 50 c. Caldwell.
†Jerome, J. K. Three men on wheels. (Red letter ser.) il. pap., 50 c. New Amsterdam.
**Jerrold, Wa. Nonsense nonsense; col. il. by C: Robinson. 4°. bds., $1.60 net. Stokes.
Jerrold, Wa. Reign of King Oberon and Queen Titania; il. by C: Robinson. 12°. Macmillan.
†Jerry Dodds—millionaire. Barrow-North, H. $1.25. Lippincott.
Jessopp, Augustus. Penny history of the Church of England. 16°. pap., 5 c. Young.
Jesus Christ, Infancy of our Lord. 15 c. Young.
Jesus Christ, Life of. Holtzmann, *Prof.* Macmillan.
Jesus' way. Hyde, W: DeW. 16°. Houghton, M. & Co.
**Jesus, Words of. Dalman, G. $2.50 net. [Imp.] Scribner.
Jesus. *See also* Burrell, D: J. Revell.
†Jethro Bacon and the weaker sex. Stimson, F. J. $1. Scribner.
Jewish encyclopedia. il. 12 v. v. 3. 4°. subs., $72; hf. mor., $96; mor., $120. Funk.
Jews, Hist. of the. Josephus. 3 v. $3-$6. Wessels.
**Jim and Joe. Ellis, E. S. 80 c. net. Coates.
**Jimmy Crow. Foster, E. F. 60 c. net. Estes.
Jim's temptation. Blunt, E. M. 30 c. Young

Joachim, H. H. Study of the ethics of Spinoza. Oxford Univ.
†Joan of the sword hand. Crockett, S. R. 50 c. New Amsterdam.
*Job, Book of; il. by W: Blake. photogrv. f°. $4 net. Putnam.
John Malcolm. Fuller, E: Snow & Farnham.
John Mytton, Memoirs of the life of. Nimrod. $15 net. Brentano.
†John Ship, mariner. Elivas, K. 50 c. Stokes.
Johnson, Clifton. New England and its neighbors. il. 8°. Macmillan.
**Johnson, S: Prayers; introd. and critical notes by W. A. Bradley. por. 12°. $1 net; 250 cop. on Eng. handmade pap., $2.50 net; 50 cop. on parchment, $5 net. McClure.
Johnson, S: Prologue, spoken at opening of Drury Lane Theatre in 1747; introd. by Austin Dobson. facsimile reprint. Dodd, Mead & Co.
**Johnson, S: [Selections.] (Little masterpieces, 2d ser.) 4 x 6. flex. silk cl., ea., 40 c. net. Doubleday, P.
Johnson, Shirley E. Cult of the purple rose. 12°. $1.25. Badger.
**Johnson, *Sir* W: Buell, A: C. $1 net. Appleton.
Johnson, W: F. Poco à poco. il. 12°. $1.50. Saalfield.
**Johnston, *Mrs.* Annie F. Cicely. (Cosy corner ser.) il. 12°. 40 c. net. L. C. Page.
**Johnston, *Mrs.* Annie F. Little colonel's hero. il. 12°. $1.20 net. L. C. Page.
**Johnston, Howard A. Bible criticism and the average man. 12°. $1 net. Revell.
**Johnston, *Sir* Harry. The Uganda protectorate. 2 v. 500 il. 9 maps. col. pl. 4°. $12.50 net. Dodd, Mead & Co.
Joke and dream books. *See* advertisement. J. S. Ogilvie.
**Jolly aunt (The). (Toy books.) col. pictures. 4°. bds., 80 c. net. Stokes.
**Jolly uncle (The). (Toy books.) col. pictures. 4°. bds., 80 c. net. Stokes.
Jones, Gary M. *See* Lansing, R. Silver.
Jones, H. P., *ed.* Dictionary of foreign phrases. ½ mor., $3. Lippincott.
*Jordan, D: S. Philosophy of despair. 12°. bds., 75 c. net; suede, $1.50 net. Elder.
**Jordan, W: G. Power of truth, individual problems and possibilities. 12°. 75 c. net. Brentano.
**Jordan, W: G: Throne of individuality. 12°. 75 c. net. Brentano.
**Jorrocks' jaunts and jollities. Surtees, R. S. $15 net. Brentano.
Josephus. History of the Jews. Author's ed. New issue. 3 v. buckram, $3; ½ leath., $4.50; ¼ cf., $6. Wessels.
"Josiah Allen's wife," *pseud.* *See* Holley, Marietta.
**Josselyn, C: The true Napoleon. il. 6 x 8. $3.50 net. Russell.
Josselyn, *ed.* *See* Goldoni, C: Heath.
Jowett, J. H. Brooks by the traveller's way. Armstrong.
Joy, Edith M. Arithmetic without a pencil. (for grammar grades.) Heath.

Joyous journey round Rügen; by the author of "Elizabeth and her German garden." il. 12°. Macmillan.
**Judson, C: F., *and* Gittings, J. Claxton. Artificial feeding of infants. 12°. $2 net. Lippincott.
†Just and the unjust. Bagot, R: 12°. $1.50. Lane.
*Just shavings. Franklin, J. D. 75 c. net. E. W. Dayton.
**Just so stories. Kipling, R. $1.20 net. Doubleday, P.
Kampffmeyer, Paul. Hist of the German social democracy. Kerr.
Kanva Satapatha Brahmana. Eggeling, J., *ed.* (Anecdota Oxoniensis ser.) Oxford Univ.
†Kauffman, R. W. The things that are Cæsar's. 12°. $1.50. Appleton.
Keats, J: Eve of St. Agnes. (Silver ser. of classics.) 40 c. Silver.
Keats, J: Poetical works; ed. by H. B. Forman. 3d ed. il. 3 v. 12°. $4.50; ¾ mor., $10. Lippincott.
**Keats, J: Sonnets. (Sonnet ser.) 4°. vellum, $4 net. Brentano.
**Keats and his circle. Shelley, H: C. net. Putnam.
Keble's Christian year, Leading ideas of. Price, C. 20 c. Young.
**Keeling, Elsa D'E. Sir J. Reynolds. (Makers of British art.) il. 8°. $1.25 net. [Imp.] Scribner.
**Keen, Adelaide. With a saucepan over the sea: recipes from the kitchens of foreign countries. il. 12°. $1.50 net. Little, B. & Co.
Keller's First year in German. $1; 2d year, $1.20. Am. Bk.
Kelman, J: *See* Fulleylove, J:
Kelmscott books ser. il. 12°. $1. Pott. *New volume:* 7, Sonnets from the Portuguese.
Kelly, R. Talbot. Egypt. col. il. 8°. Macmillan.
†Kennard, *Mrs.* E: The golf lunatic. 8°. $1.50. Brentano.
*Kennard, Jos. S. Some early printers. parchment, $3 net. Jacobs.
†Kennedy, Sara B. The wooing of Judith. 5 x 8. $1.50. Doubleday, P.
†Kennedy, Walker. Javan Ben Seir. (Copyright ser.) 12°. 50 c. Stokes.
Kent, C: F. Messages of Israel's lawgivers. (Messages of the Bible.) 16°. $1.25. Scribner.
**Kent, Eliz. House opposite: a mystery. net. Putnam.
Kent Fielding's ventures. Thurston, *Mrs.* I. T. $1.25. Pilgrim Press.
†Kent Fort manor. Babcock, W: H. $1. Coates.
Kern, Marg. Vesper sparrow. 12°. $1. J. S. Ogilvie.
**Kerr, G: L. Elementary coal mining. il. 12°. $1.25 net. Lippincott.
Kewts. Bridgman, L. J. $1. Caldwell.
Key to the missionary problem. Murray, And. 75 c. Am. Tr.
Keyes, E. L. Surgical diseases of the genito-urinary organs. Appleton.
**Keyser, Leander S. Birds of the Rockies. $3 net.
**Khedivate, Story of the. Dicey, E: $4 net. [Imp.] Scribner.
Kidder, F. E. Building construction and superintendence. pt. 1, Mason's work. 5th ed. il. 8°. $4. W: T. Comstock.
Kidder, F. E. Building construction and superintendence. pt 3, Trussed roofs and roof trusses. 8°. $4. W: T. Comstock.
Kielmansegg, *Count* F: Diary of a journey to England, 1761-62. il. 8°. Longmans.
Kidneys, Diseases of. Allchin, W. H. Macmillan.
Kinard, Ja. P., *ed.* Old English ballads. (Silver ser. of classics.) 40 c. Silver.
Kinder, Stephen. The Sabertooth. il. 12°. 75 c. Laird.
Kinematics of machinery. *See* Le Conte, J. N. Macmillan.
Kinematics of machines, Elementary textbook of the. Durley, R. J. Wiley.
King, Anna E., (*Mrs.* J: Lane.) Kitwyk stories. il. 12°. $1.50. Lane.
King, Clarence. Mountaineering in the Sierra Nevada. New ed. $1.50. Scribner.
King, H: Churchill. Theology and the social consciousness. 12°. Macmillan.
King, H: M. Why we believe the Bible. 12°. $1. Am. Tr.
King, Stanton H. Bunch of rope yarns. 12°. $1.25. Badger.
King Horn. Hall, Jos., *ed.* 8°. Oxford Univ.
**King Mombo. Du Chaillu, P. $1.50 net. Scribner.
Kingdom of God in the writings of the fathers. Herrick, H. M. Univ. of Chic.
King's agent. Paterson, A. $1.50. Appleton.
**King's (The) race-horses. Spencer, E: $30 net. Brentano.
King's story-book. Gomme, G: L., *ed.* Longmans.
King's (The) stewards. Banks, L: A. $1.25. Am. Tr.
King's stratagem. Weyman, S. 75 c. Caldwell.
Kings, Books of. Notes on the Hebrew text. Burney, C. F. Oxford Univ.
Kingsbury, Oliver A. The spiritual life. 12°. 50 c. Am. Tr.
**Kingsland, *Mrs.* Burton. The book of weddings. il. 5 x 7½. $1.20 net. Doubleday, P.
Kingsley, C: Greek heroes. (New Kalon ser.) il. 12°. 50 c. Caldwell.
†Kingsley, C: The water-babies. col. il. New ed. 8°. $2. Wessels.
Kingsley, C: Water of life. (New Kalon ser.) il. 12°. 50 c. Caldwell.
Kingsley, C: Water of life and Out of the deep. (Lotus ser., 2 v. sets.) il. 2 v. 12°. $1. Caldwell.
†Kingsley, C: Westward ho! (Temple classics for young people.) il. 2 v. 16°. ea., 50 c.; leather, 80 c. Macmillan.
†Kingsley, Florence M. The needle's eye. il. 12°. $1.50. Funk.
†Kingsley, Flo. M. Wings and fetters. il. 12°. $1. Altemus.
†Kinross, Alb. An opera and Lady Grasmere. (Copyright ser.) 12°. 50 c. Stokes.
†Kinross, Alb. Philbrick Howell. (Copyright ser.) 12°. 50 c. Stokes.

Kinship and marriage in early Arabia. Smith, W. R. Macmillan.
Kinship of God and man. Lanier, J. J. v. 2, The master-key. 12°. $1. Whittaker.
**Kipling, R. Just so stories. il. 5 x 8. $1 20 net. Doubleday, P.
Kipling, R. Letters of marque. (Chateau ser., 75 c.—New Kalon, 50 c.) Caldwell.
Kipling, R. Mine own people. (Chateau ser.) il. 6 x 4. boxed, 75 c. Caldwell.
Kipling, R. Phantom rickshaw. (Chateau ser.) il. 6 x 4. boxed, 75 c. Caldwell.
Kipling, R. Under the deodars (Chateau ser.) il. 6 x 4. boxed, 75 c. Caldwell.
Kirtland, J. C., *jr.*, *and* Rogers, G. B. Introduction to Latin. Macmillan.
Kitwyk stories. King, Anna E. $1.50. Lane.
Kleist, H. v. Michael Kohlhaas; ed. by W: Kurrelmeyer. 16°. Holt.
Klenze, Camillo v. Treatment of nature in the works of Nikolaus Lenau. 8¾ x 11¼. (Decennial pubs., v 7.) 75 c. net. Univ. of Chic.
**Knapp, Adeline. Boy and the baron. (St. Nicholas ser.) il. 12°. $1 net. Century.
Knight, C: Half hours with best authors. Author's ed. New issue. 4 v. buckram, $4; ½ leath., $6; ½ cf., $8. Wessels.
Knight errant (The). Lyall, E. $1. Caldwell.
**Knox, Edm. A. Pastors and preachers. 8°. $1.60 net. Longmans.
**Knox, G: W: McGiffert, A. C., *and* Brown, Francis. Christian point of view. 12°. $1 net. Scribner.
Knox Little, W. J., Thoughts from. *See* Burn, J. H. Young.
**Knowles, F: L., *ed.* Treasury of humorous poetry. 12°. $1.20 net; hf. mor., $2.40 net. Estes.
Kocher, Theodore. Text-book of operative surgery; tr. by H J. Stiles. il. Author's ed. rev. Macmillan.
Konody, P. G. Art of. Walter Crane. il. 4°. Macmillan.
Kotto. Hearn, L. Macmillan.
Krecker, Ada M. Fussy four-footed folks. il. 12°. 60 c. Jamieson-H.
**Kropotkin, *Prince* P. A. Mutual aid, a factor in evolution. $2.50 net. McClure.
**Kuloskap, the master, with other poems. Leland, C: G. $2 net. Funk.
Kuppord, S. A fortune from the sky. 80 c. Nelson.
Kyd, T:, Works. Boas, F. S., *ed.* Oxford Univ.
Laboratory text-book of embryology. Minot, C: S. Blakiston.
**Lace, History of. Palliser, *Mrs.* B. $12 net. Scribner.
**Lacombe, M. P. Arms and armour; tr. by C: Boutell. New ed. il. 8°. $1.75 net. Lippincott.
**Lad and lassie series. Jacobs.
New volumes: Atwater, How Sammy went to Coral-land.—Hewitt, Three little Denvers.
Lady of Fallen Star Island. Comfort, W. L. $1.25. Street.
†Lady of the barge. Jacobs, W. W. $1.50. Dodd, Mead & Co.
Lady of the lake. *See* Scott, *Sir* W.
Lady's New Year's gift. Savile, *Sir* G: $1: $1.25. Wessels.
La Fontaine, Jean de. Fables. Notes by L. Sauveur. 12°. $1.50. W. R. Jenkins.
**Laing, Gordon J., *ed.* Masterpieces of Latin literature. 8°. $1 net. Houghton, M. & Co.
Laird and Lee's diary and time saver for 1903. 12 maps. leather, 25 c. Laird.
Lake, K. Texts from Mt. Athos. (Studia Biblica, 2.) Oxford Univ.
**Lahee, H: C. Organ and its masters. (Music lovers' ser.) il. 12°. $1.60 net; ¾ mor., $4 net. L. C. Page.
†Lakewood. Norris, M. H. 50 c. Stokes.
Lamb, C: Adventures of Ulysses. il. 7¼ x 9½. $2.50. Russell.
Lamb, C: Essays of Elia. (Chateau ser., 75 c.—New Berkeley, $1.) Caldwell.
**Lamb, C: Essays of Elia. (Century classics.) 12°. $1.25 net. Century.
**Lamb, C: Essays of Elia. New ed. Ed. by E. B. Lucas. il. 8°. $3.50 net; ½ levant, $6 net. Lippincott.
Lamb, C: *and* Ma. Tales from Shakespeare. (Sesame classics.) il. 7 x 4¼. limp ooze cf., boxed, $1.25. Caldwell.
Lamb, Ma. *See* Lamb, C:
Lampen, C. Dudley. Frozen treasure: tale of arctic Russia. 12°. $1. Young.
†Lamplighter (The). Cummins, Maria S. $1.50. Houghton, M. & Co.
Land defence, Principles of. Thuillier, H. F. Longmans.
Land drainage. *See* Elliott, C: G. Wiley.
Land of the Latins. Willard, A. R. Longmans.
Landnama-boc (The). Vigfusson, G., *and* Powell, F. Y., *eds.* Oxford Univ.
Landscapes of the Bible. Tristram, H. B. $1. Young.
**Landseer. *Sir* E: Manson, J. A. $1.25 net. [Imp.] Scribner.
Lane, *Mrs.* J: *See* King, Anna E. Lane.
†Lane (The) that had no turning. Parker, G. $1.50. Doubleday, P.
Lane's new pocket library. 24°. 50 c. net; leath., 75 c. net. Lane.
New volume: 6, Mill on the Floss, by George Eliot.
Lang, Andrew. Ballads in blue china. Wieners.
†Lang, Andrew. The disentanglers. il. 8°. Longmans.
**Lang, Andrew. History of Scotland. v. 2. 8°. $3.50 special net. Dodd, Mead & Co.
Lang, Andrew. James the Sixth and the Gowrie mystery. il. 8°. Longmans.
**Lang, Andrew, *ed.* Book of romance. il. 8°. $1.60 net. Longmans.
**Lang, H: R. Gallego-Castilian court of 14th and 15th centuries. (Yale bicentennial publications.) 8°. $3 net. Scribner.
Lang, J: M. Church and its social mission. (Baird lectures, 1901.) 12°. $1.60. Whittaker.
[Language.] De l'enseignement des langues vivantes. Sauveur, L. 25 c. W: R. Jenkins.
Languages, Ancient, Introduction to the teaching of. Sauveur, L. 25 c. W: R. Jenkins.
Languages, Introduction to the teaching of living. Sauveur, L. 25 c. W: R. Jenkins.

Lanier, Clifford. Apollo and Keats on Browning. [Poems.] 12°. bds., $1.50. Badger.
Lanier, J. J. Kinship of God and man. v. 2, The master-key. 12°. $1. Whittaker.
**Lanier, Sidney. Bob. col. il. New ed. $1 net. Scribner.
**Lanier, Sidney. Shakspere and his forerunners. il. 7 x 10. $10 net; Holiday ed., ¾mor., $20 net; ed. de luxe, large-pap., $25 net. Doubleday, P.
**Lankester, E. Ray, ed. Treatise in zoology. il. 10 pts. pts. I.-IV. Macmillan.
**Lansdale, Maria H. Vienna and the Viennese. il. 8°. boxed, $2.40 net; crushed levant mor., $5.60 net. Coates.
Lansing, Rob., and Jones, Gary M. Government: its origin, growth and form in the U. S. Silver.
*La Page, Gertrude. The children of the thorn wreath. il. 4°. $1.50 net. Elder.
La Ramé, L. D. See Ouida, pseud.
*Large type books. See Humphreys, A. L. Wessels.
Larned, J. N. Primer of right and wrong. Houghton, M. & Co.
*La Rochefoucauld. Maximes. (A. L. Humphreys' large type books.) English and French. 16°. pap., $3 net. Wessels.
Larry Barlow's ambition. Winfield, A. M. $1. Saalfield.
**Lassie and laddie. Brine, M. D. $1 net. Dutton.
†Last (The) American. Mitchell, J: A. $1.50. Stokes.
†Last (The) buccaneer. Cornford, L. C. $1.50. Lippincott.
Last cruise of the "Electra." Chipman, C: P. $1. Saalfield.
†Last days of Pompeii. Bulwer-Lytton, Sir E: G. 75 c. Brentano.
Last of the Nappingtons. Norris, Jos. Quail & W.
Last vendée. Dumas, A. $1. Caldwell.
†Last word. MacGowan, Alice. $1.50. L. C. Page.
†Last words. Crane, Stephen. $1. Coates.
Latin. See Smiley and Storke's Beginner's. Am. Bk.
Latin, First year of. Gunnison, W. B. Silver.
Latin grammar. Hale, W: G. Ginn.
Latin grammar. See Harkness's. Am. Bk.
Latin grammar. See Moore, C. H. Appleton.
Latin, Introduction to. Kirtland, J. C., jr. Macmillan.
**Latin literature, Masterpieces of. Laing, G. J., ed. $1 net. Houghton, M. & Co.
Latin prose composition. See Dodge and Tuttle's. 75 c. Am. Bk.
Latin versions of the canons of the Greek councils of the 4th and 5th centuries. pt. 2. Oxford Univ.
**Laughlin, Clara E. Evolution of a girl's ideal. 16°. 50 c. net. Revell.
**Laughlin, Clara E. Stories of authors' loves. il. 2 v. boxed, $3 net; ¼ mor., $6 net. Lippincott.
Laughlin, J. Laurence, and Willis, H. Parker. Reciprocity. 12°. Baker & T.
Laughlin's Elements of pol. econ.; revised. $1.20. Am. Bk.
Laureate ser. of the poets. il. 12°. wood, 75 c.; leather, $1.50. Caldwell.
New volumes: Browning, Selections.—Rubaiyat of Omar Khayyam.—Bartlett, Familiar quotations.—Stevenson, Child's garden of verses.—Holland, Bitter sweet.
Laurel series Ooze calf ed. 30 v. ea., 60 c. Crowell.
Laurel series. ea., 60 c. Crowell.
New volumes: See advertisement.
Laurence, C. E., ed. Scenes from Sophocles' Antigone. Oxford Univ.
*Laus veneris. Swinburne, A. C: 25 c.-$1 net. Mosher.
Laut, A. C. Story of the trapper. il. 12°. (Story of the west ser.) Appleton.
**Lavender and old lace. Reed, Myrtle. $1.50 net-$3.50 net. Putnam.
**Lavignac, Alb. Music and musicians; tr.; ed. by H. E. Krehbiel. il. 3d ed. rev. 12°. $1.75 net. Holt.
**Law of growth. Brooks, P. $1.20 net. Dutton.
*Law of payment. Grimaudet, F. $1.50 net. Cambridge.
Law, Woman's manual of. Greene, M. A. Silver.
**Lawrence, Ruth. Beggar's garden. 16°. $1 net. Brentano.
Lay of Havelok the Dane. Skeat, W. W., ed. Oxford Univ.
Layard, Sir H: Autobiography; with additional chapters by Sir A. Otway; ed. by W: Bruce. il. 8°. [Imp.] Scribner.
Lays of ancient Rome. Macaulay, T: B. 50 c.; 75 c. Macmillan.
Lead smelting. Iles, M. W. $2.50. Wiley.
Learned, Marion D. German grammar. 12°. (20th century text-books.) Appleton.
Leathes, Stanley. See Ward, A. W.
Leave of absence and other leaves. Goddard, J: C. $1.25. Pilgrim Press.
**Leaven in a great city. Betts, L. W. $1.50 net. Dodd, Mead & Co.
Leavitt's Outlines of botany; with flora. $1.80. Am. Bk.
Le Conte, Joseph N. Kinematics of machinery and mechanics of the steam engine. il. 12°. Macmillan.
**Lee, Gerald S. Lost art of reading. 12°. net. Putnam.
Lee, Joseph. Constructive and preventive philanthropy. (American philanthropy of the XIXth century ser.) 12°. Macmillan.
**Lee, Mary C. Lois Mallet's dangerous gift. 12°. 85 c. net. Houghton, M. & Co.
*Lee, Vernon, [pseud. for Violet Paget.] Genius Loci and other essays. 12°. $1.25 net. [Imp.] Wessels.
*Lee, Vernon. Limbo and other essays. 12°. $1.25 net. [Imp.] Wessels.
Leete, C. H. Exercises in geography. 2d ed. rev. 12°. Longmans.
†Le Feuvre, Amy. A daughter of the sea. il. 12°. $1.50. Crowell.
Leffmann, H: See McFarland, Jos. Blakiston.
Left to themselves. Green, E. M. 80 c. Young.
Legal tender. Breckenridge, S. P. 8°. Univ. of Chic.

**Le Gallienne, R: Mr. Sun and Mrs. Moon. il. 8½ x 11. pap. bds., $1.60 net. Russell.

**Le Gallienne, R: An old country house. $2.40 net. Harper.

Le Gallienne, R: Old love-stories retold. il. large 12°. $2. L. C. Page.

**Le Gallienne, R: Perseus and Andromeda. il. 5½ x 8½. $1.40 net. Russell.

**Legends of the Iroquois. Canfield, W. W. $2.50 net. Wessels.

**Leighton, Robt. Boys of Waveney College. net. Putnam.

Lehmann-Kalisch, Lilli. How to sing. il. 12°. Macmillan.

**Leland, C: G., *and* Prince, D. Kuloskap. the master. with other poems. il. $2 net. Funk.

Lenau, Nikolaus, Treatment of nature in works of. Klenze, C. v. 75 c. net. Univ. of Chic.

†Le Notre, G. House of the Combrays; tr. by *Mrs.* J. B. Gilder. 12°. $1.50. Dodd, Mead & Co.

Leonard, Ma. F. Mr. Pat's little girl. il. $1.50. Wilde.

†Le Queux, W: Stolen souls. (Copyright ser.) 12°. 50 c. Stokes.

†Le Queux, W: Zoraida. (Copyright ser.) 12°. 50 c. Stokes.

Lerouge (The) case. Gaboriau, E. 75 c. Caldwell.

Lesson in the school of prayer. Pierson, A. T. 50 c. Caldwell.

Lessons on practical subjects. Hughes. Hinds.

Let us follow him. Sienkiewicz, H. 75 c. Caldwell.

†Letters from a self-made merchant to his son. Lorimer, G: H. $1.50. Small, M.

**Letters from Egypt. Duff Gordon, *Lady.* $2.50 net. McClure.

Letters of marque. Kipling, R. 50 c.; 75 c. Caldwell.

**Letters to Washington, vol. v., 1774-1775. Hamilton, S. M., *ed.* $5 net. Houghton, M. & Co.

Lever, C: Writings. Barrington ed. 32 v. il. 8°. ea., $1.50. Little, B. & Co.

Lever, C: Charles O'Malley. (Caldwell's new Berkeley lib.) il. 12°. $1. Caldwell.

**Lewis, Alex. Manhood making. $1 net. Pilgrim Press.

†Lewis, Alfred H: Wolfville nights. 12°. $1.50. Stokes.

Lewis, Edwin H. Applied English grammar. complete ed. Macmillan.

Lewis, Enrique H. Phil and Dick. il. 12°. $1. Saalfield.

**Lewis, M., *and* Clark, W: Travels; introd. by J. K. Hosmer. 2 v. 8°. $5 net. McClurg.

**Lewis and Clark expedition; reprint of ed. of 1814. 2 v. 8°. $5 net. McClurg.

Liberty. Mill, J: S. 75 c. Caldwell.

**Library, Instruction concerning erecting of a. Naudé, Gabriel. price on application. Houghton, M. & Co.

Library of art. Strong, S. A., *ed.* Scribner.

Library of literary history. Scribner.
New volume: Browne, Literary history of Persia.

Library of standard literature. *See* Putnam's.

†Library of successes. 12°. pap., ea., 50 c. Stokes.
Contents: Barr, Jennie Baxter.—Benton, Geber.—Castle, Light of Scarthey.—Graham, Son of the czar.—Hobbes, Robert Orange.—Shiel, Lord of the sea.

**Library of useful stories ser. il. 16°. 35 c. net. Appleton.
New volume: Edgar, W: C., Story of a grain of wheat.

†Liddell, E. Louise. Polly Perkins' adventures. il. 12°. $1. Altemus.

Lieven, *Princess.* *See* Dorothea, *Princess* Lieven. Longmans.

**Life and adventures of Santa Claus. Baum, L. F. $1 net. Bowen-M.

**Life and how to live it. Aldrich, A. R. $1 net. Biddle.

***Life,* Books from: rhymes and roundelays. il. 4½ x 7. bds., 60 c. net; leath., $1.20 net. Doubleday, P.

**Life histories ser. 12°. $1 net. Appleton.
New volume: Sir William Pepperell, by Noah Brooks.

Life in mind and conduct. Maudsley, H: Macmillan.

***Life,* Rhymes and roundelays from. 60 c net; $1.20 net. Doubleday, P.

Life in St. John's Gospel. Hoare, J. G. 40 c. Young.

**Life of a sportsman. Nimrod. $20 net. Brentano.

†Life of a woman. Risley, R. V. $1.50. Stone.

†Life the interpreter. Bottome, P. Longmans.

**Life's secrets, gathered from the study of a Christian physician. 12°. $1 net. Revell.

Light behind. Ward, *Mrs.* W. $1.50. Lane.

Light of Asia. Arnold, *Sir* E. 75 c. Caldwell.

†Light of Scarthey. Castle, E. 50 c. Stokes.

Light waves and their uses. Michelson, A. A. 8°. Univ. of Chic.

Lighted taper (The). Patton, M. O. $1.50. Botolph.

Lighting by acetylene. Dye. $2.50. Spon & C.

Lights and shadows of a long episcopate. Whipple, H: B: Macmillan.

Like Christ. Murray, A. 75 c. Caldwell.

**Lilley, A. E., *and* Midgley, W. Plant form. New ed. il. 8°. $2 net. Scribner.

Lilliencron, Anno 1870. Bernhardt, W:, *ed.* Heath.

*Lima beans. (Baby Roland booklets.) il. flexible, 50 c. net. Elder.

*Limbo, and other essays. Lee, V. $1.25 net. Wessels.

**Lincoln, Abraham. Nicolay, J: G. $2.40 net. Century.

Lindsay, *Prof.* T. H. Church and the ministry in the early centuries. Armstrong.

Lindsay, *Prof.* T. H. Church and the ... Kempis's Imitation of Christ. (Miniature volumes.) New ed. marble enamel, 50 c. Stokes.

Line upon line. James, J: A. 50 c. Caldwell.
**Linn, W: A. Rob and his gun. il. 12° $1 net. Scribner.
†Lippincott's series of select novels. 8°. $1; pap., 50 c. Lippincott.
New volume: Vogel, Gentleman Garnet.
Liquor problem, Physiological aspects of. (Committee of Fifty.) Billings, J: S., *ed.* 2 v. 8°. Houghton, M. & Co.
Lisk. A B C of the steam engine. 6 pl. 50 c. Spon & C.
Lisk, J. P. Slide valve instruction chart, showing the various positions of the crank pin, eccentric and piston at the point of admission, etc. 11 x 14½. 25 c. Spon & C.
**Litchfield, P. A. English cathedrals. il 12°. India pap., $2 net; limp leath., $2.50 net. Lippincott.
**Literary Boston of to-day. Winslow, Helen M. $1.20 net; $2.50 net L. C. Page.
Literary history, Library of. Scribner.
New volume: Browne, Literary history of Persia.
**Literary landmarks of Oxford. Hutton. L. net. Scribner.
Literary pilgrimages in New England. Bacon, E. M. Silver.
**Literature and life. Howells, W: D. $2.25 net. Harper.
Literature, How to study. Heydrick. Hinds.
**Literatures of the world ser.; ed. by E. Gosse. 12°. $1.20 net. Appleton.
New volumes: Trent. W: P., History of American literature.
**Little black Mingo. Bannerman, Helen. 40 c. net Stokes.
**Little book of ping-pong verse. 16°. 75 c. net. Estes.
**Little brothers of the west. Deming, T. O. $1 net. Stokes.
Little captive lad. Dix, B. M. Macmillan.
**Little colonel's hero. Johnston, *Mrs.* Annie F. $1.20 net. L. C. Page.
**Little cousin ser., 1902. Wade, Mary H. *See* Page's. L. C. Page.
Little Dorrit. Dickens, C: 75 c. Caldwell.
Little folks' book of birds. large type. il. $1. Warne.
"Little folks" for 1902. il. 8°. bds., $1.25; cl., $1.75. Caldwell.
Little folks' picture natural history. Step, E: $1.50. Warne.
**Little girl in old Detroit. Douglas, A. M. $1.20 net. Dodd, Mead & Co.
**Little girl next door. Rhoades, N. 80 c. net. Lee & Shepard.
†Little green god. Mason, *Mrs.* C. A. 16°. 75 c. net. Revell.
**Little guides: no. 2, The lake country. 8°. net, 75 c. Dodd, Mead & Co.
**Little Italy. Fry, H. B. $1 net. Russell.
Little (The) lame prince. Mulock, D. M. 50 c. Caldwell.
**Little library. 14 v. 16°. 50 c.; 75 c. net. Dodd, Mead & Co.
Little maid Marigold. Stooke, E. H. 75 c. Am. Tr.
**Little maid series. Jacobs.
New volume: Blanchard, Little Miss Oddity.

**Little masterpieces, Second ser.; ed. by Bliss Perry. 6 v. ea., 40 c. net. Doubleday, P.
Little (The) minister. Barrie, J. M. 75 c.; 2 v., ea., 50 c. Caldwell.
**Little Miss Oddity. Blanchard, A. E. 80 c. net. Jacobs.
Little Mistress Good Hope. Taylor, Ma. I. $1.50 net. McClurg.
†Little Saint Sunshine. Goss, C: F: $1.25. Bowen-M.
Little stories for little people, McCullough's 25 c. Am. Bk.
†Little stories of married life. Cutting, Mary S. $1.25. McClure.
†Little white bird. Barrie, J. M. $1.50. Scribner.
Little woman in the spout. Byrne, Mary A. 60 c. Saalfield.
Little women. Alcott, L. M. $2. Little, B. & Co.
*Liver, Diseases of the. *See* Nothnagel's encyclopedia of practical medicine. Saunders.
Livingston, B. E. Rôle of diffusion and osmotic pressure in plants. 8°. Univ. of Chic.
**Livingston, L. S. American book prices current, Sept. 1, 1901, to Sept. 1, 1902. 8°. buckram, $6 special net; large pap. ed. 4°. $15 special net. Dodd, Mead & Co.
**Lloyd, J: U. Red-head. il. 12°. $1.60 net. Dodd, Mead & Co.
Locke, J: How to bring up your children. 16°. pap. bds., 50 c. Wessels.
Lockhart, J: G. Memoirs of the life of Sir Walter Scott, Bart. Cambridge ed., in 5 v. il. 8°. $10. Houghton, M. & Co.
Lockwood, Laura A. Lexicon to poetical works of J: Milton. 8°. Macmillan.
Locomotives: simple, compound and electric. Reagan, H. C. $2. Wiley.
**Lodge, H: C. Fighting frigate, and other essays. 12°. $1.50 net. Scribner.
Loeb, Jacques. Studies in general physiology. 8°. Univ. of Chic.
**Logan, the Mingo. Gordon, H. R. $1.20 net. Dutton.
**Logic, Hegel's. Hibben, J: G. net. Scribner.
**Lois Mallet's dangerous gift. Lee, Mary C. 85 c. net. Houghton, M. & Co.
**Lollipops (The). Long, O. M. 50 c. net. Russell.
London, Jack. Children of the frost. il. 12°. Macmillan.
**London, Jack. Cruise of the "Dazzler." (St. Nicholas ser.) il. 12°. $1 net. Century.
†London, Jack. Daughter of the snows. il. 12°. $1.50. Lippincott.
**London. Baedeker, K., *ed.* $1.80 net. [Imp.] Scribner.
**London. Singleton, E. $1.40 net. Dodd, Mead & Co.
**London, Children's. Thorpe, C. $2.50 net. [Imp.] Scribner.
London highways and byways. Cook, *Mrs.* E. T. Macmillan.
London in the 18th century. Besant, *Sir* W. Macmillan.
London, Mediæval. Wheatley, H. B. Macmillan.
**London, Night side of. Machray, R. $2.50 net. Lippincott.

London, South, and Westminster. Besant, *Sir* W. 2 v. $3. Stokes.
London. *See* Bellot, H. H. L. Pott.
Long, A: W. *See* Parrott, T: M. Ginn.
**Long, Olive M. The lollipops. il. 6 x 9. bds., 50 c. net. Russell.
Long lectures, 1891-92. *See* Tisdall, W. St. C. Young.
†Long (The) straight road. Horton, G: $1.50. Bowen-M.
Longee, Susan C. *See* Sauveur, M. L. W: R. Jenkins.
Longfellow, H: W. Poems. (Sesame classics.) il. 7 x 4¼. limp ooze cf., boxed, $1.25. Caldwell.
Longfellow, H: W. Courtship of Miles Standish. (Sesame classics). il. 7 x 4½. limp ooze cf., boxed. $1.25. Caldwell.
Longfellow, H: W. Evangeline. (Sesame classics. il. 7 x 4¼. limp ooze cf., boxed, $1.25. Caldwell.
Longfellow, H: W. Hiawatha. (Sesame classics.) il. 7 x 4¼. limp ooze cf., boxed, $1.25. Caldwell.
Longfellow, H: W., Tales from; ed. by M. K. Bellew. il. 12°. 60 c. Jamieson-H.
**Longfellow, H: W., Life of. Higginson, T: W. $1.10 net; $1.50 net. Houghton, M. & Co.
Longmans' English classics. Longmans.
New volumes: Irving's Life of Goldsmith.—Tennyson's Gareth and Lynette, Passing of Arthur, and Launcelot and Elaine.—Macaulay's Essays.
**Longmans' gazetteer of the world; ed. by G: G. Chisholm. New ed. 8°. $6.40 net. Longmans.
Longridge, G. Official and lay witness to the value of foreign missions. 16°. 20 c. Young.
†Loom (The) of life. Goss, C: F: $1.50. Bowen-M.
**Lord, W: S., *ed.* This is for you: love poems of the saner sort. 12°. vellum bds., $1 net. Revell.
†Lord of the sea. Shiel, M. P. 50 c. Stokes.
†Lord (The) protector. Yeats, S. L. $1.25. Longmans.
†Lorimer, G: H. Letters from a self-made merchant to his son. il. 7½ x 4⅞. $1.50. Small, M.
Loss of heat from covered steam pipes. Paulding, C: P. Van Nostrand.
**Lost art of reading. Lee, Gerald S. net. Putnam.
Lost brigade (The). Hall, C: W. $1.25. Badger.
†Lost in the land of ice. Bonehill, R. $1.25. Wessels.
Lost leader. Townsend, D. 80 c. Young.
**Lost wedding ring (The). Myers, C. 75 c. net. Funk.
Lost squire of Inglewood. Jackson, *Dr.* 80 c. Nelson.
Loti, P. Pêcheur d'Islande. Super, O. B., *ed.* Heath.
Lotus ser. 2 v. sets. il. 12°. boxed, per set, $1. Caldwell.
New volumes: Schreiner, Dreams; Story of an African farm.—Kingsley, Water of life; Out of the deep.
Louis de Condé. *See* Bossuet. Macmillan.
Louis XIV. and the court of France. Pardoe, J. $4.50; $9. Pott.
Louis XV. et Mme. de Pompadour. Nolhac, P. de. Manzi & J.
Louise de Vallière. Dumas, A. $1. Caldwell.
**Lounsberry, Alice. Guide to the trees; il. by *Mrs.* E. Rowan. New ed. $1.75 net; $2; leath., $3.50 net. Stokes.
** Lounsberry, Alice. Guide to the wild flowers; il. by *Mrs.* E. Rowan. New ed. $1.75 net; $2.50 net; leather, $3.50 net. Stokes.
**Lounsbury T. R. Shakespeare and Voltaire. 8°. $2 net. Scribner.
Louthan, Hattie H. Thoughts adrift: [poems.] 12°. bds., $1. Badger.
†Lovable tales of Janey and Josey and Joe. Smith, G. $1.50.
**Lovable tales of Janey and Josey and Joe. Smith, G. $1.30 net. Harper.
†Love and the soul hunters. Hobbes, J: O. $1.50. Funk.
†Love in extremes. Cholmondeley, M. $1.50. Dodd, Mead & Co.
**Love, laurels and laughter. Hanscom, B. $1.20 net. Stokes.
Love letters of a worldly woman. Clifford, *Mrs.* W. K. 75 c. Caldwell.
Love poems. (New Kalon ser.) il. 12°. 50 c.; $1.25. Caldwell.
Love poems. *See* Lord, W: S., *ed.* Revell.
*Love songs and other poems. Innsly, O., *ed.* $1 net. Grafton Press.
*Love-songs from the Greek. Sedgwick, Jane M., *ed.* (Lovers' library, no. 12.) decor. 5¼ x 3. ea., 50 c. net; leath., 75 c. net. Lane.
*Love sonnets of a hoodlum. Irwin, W. $2 net. Elder.
†Love with honor. Marriott, C: $1.50. Lane.
Lovelace, R: Songs and sonnets. col. il. 5¼ x 7¾. $1. Russell.
Lover, S: Novels, Irish legends, plays and poems; introd. by James Jeffrey Roche. New lib. ed. 6 v. il. 12°. ea., $1.50; per set, hf. mor., $19.50. Little, B. & Co.
*Lovers' library. Chapman, F:, *ed.* decor. 5¼ x 3 in. ea., 50 c. net; leath., 75 c. net. Lane.
New volumes: (11) Sonnets of Shakespeare; (12) Love-songs from the Greek; ed. by Jane M. Sedgwick.
**Loves, Authors', Stories of. Laughlin, C. E. 2 v. $3 net; $6 net. Lippincott.
Lovett, R:, *ed.* *See* Chalmers, James. Revell.
Lovett, Rob. M. *See* Moody, W: V.
**Lowell, Ja. Russell. Anti-slavery papers. 2 v. (special ed. of 400 numbered copies.) Houghton, M. & Co.
**Lowell, Ja. Russell. Early prose writings. port. 12°. $1.20 net. Lane.
**Lowell, Ja. Russell. Van Dyke, H: 75 c. net. Macmillan.
**Loyal Huguenot maid. Comrie, M. S. $1 net. Jacobs.
Loyal (A) lass. Blanchard, A. E. $1.50. Wilde.
Loyalists in the American Revolution. Van Tyne, C. H. Macmillan.
**Lübke, W: Outlines of the history of art; ed., rev. and enl. by Russell Sturgis. 2 v. $10 net. Dodd, Mead & Co.
Lucas, E: V. The visit to London: [rhyme.] col. il. 4°. $1.50. Brentano.
Lucas, F. A. Animals before man in North America. il. 12°. Appleton.

Lucile. Meredith, O. $1.25. Caldwell.
†Luck o' Lassendale. Iddesleigh, *Earl of.* $1.50. Lane.
**Lucky Ned. Ellis, E: S. $1 net. Estes.
**Lull, Raymond. Zwemer, S. M. 75 c. net. Funk.
**Lumholtz, Carl. Unknown Mexico. il. large 8°. 2 v. $12 net. Scribner.
**Luncheon dishes, 365. 16°. 40 c. net. Jacobs.
**Luncheons. Ronald, Mary. $1.40 net. Century.
Lupton, N. T. Nociones de agricultura cientifica; trad. por Ignacio Alvarado. Appleton.
Luther, Mark L. The henchman. 12°. Macmillan.
Lutzow, *Count.* Prague. (Mediæval towns ser.) il. Macmillan.
Lux Christi. Mason, *Mrs.* C. A. Macmillan.
**Lyall, *Sir* Alf. Tennyson. (English men of letters ser.) 75 c. net. Macmillan.
Lyall, Edna, [*pseud.* for A. E. Bayly.] The Burges letters. il. 8°. Longmans.
Lyall, Edna. In spite of all. (People's lib.) 50 c. Am. News.
Lyall, Edna. The knight errant. (New Berkeley lib.) il. 12°. $1. Caldwell.
*Lycidas. Milton, J: 50 c. net; 75 c. net. Lane.
Lyly, J: Works. Bond, R. W., *ed.* Oxford Univ.
Lynch, Lawrence L. The woman who dared. il. 12°. 75 c.; pap., 25 c. Laird.
†Lynde, Francis. The master of Appleby. il. 12°. $1.50. Bowen-M.
Lyster, Annette. Worth while. 16°. 80 c. Young.
†Lyttle Salem maide. Mackie, Pauline B. $1.50. L. C. Page.
**Mabie, Hamilton W. Works. Library ed. 11 v. 12°. ea., $2 special net; per set, $22 special net. Dodd, Mead & Co.
**Mabie, Hamilton W. Parables of life. 8°. $1 net. Dodd, Mead & Co.
**Mabie, Hamilton W. Under the trees. il. by C: L. Hinton. 12°. $2 net. Dodd, Mead & Co.
Mabie, Hamilton W. *See* Old English ballads. Macmillan.
Mabinogion; tr. by *Lady* Ctte. Guest; ed. by Prof. Williams. (Temple classics.) 16°. 50 c.; leath., 75 c. Macmillan.
McAfee, Cleland B. Faith, fellowship and fealty. (Quiet hour ser.) 3 pts. 25 c. (ea. pt. sep. for the use of pastors. 5 c.) Revell.
Macaulay, G. C., *ed.* *See* Gower, J: Oxford Univ.
Macaulay, *Lord* T: B. Complete essays. 3 v. 12°. $3; hf. cf., $6. Estes.
Macaulay, *Lord* T: B. Essays. (Longmans' English classics.) Longmans.
Macaulay, *Lord* T: B. Essays on Milton and Addison; ed. by J. A. Tufts. Holt.
Macaulay, *Lord* T: B. History of England. New Sterling ed. 5 v. 12°. $5; hf. cf., $10. Estes.
Macaulay, *Lord* T: B. Hist. of England. Author's ed. New issue. 5 v. buckram, $5; ½ leath., $7.50; ½ cf., $10. Wessels.
Macaulay, *Lord* T: B. Lays of ancient Rome. (Temple classics.) 16°. 50 c.; leath., 75 c. Macmillan.
**Macaulay, *Lord* T: B. Lord Clive. (Macmillan's pocket classics.) 18°. 25 c. net. Macmillan.
Macaulay, *Lord* T: B. Miscellaneous essays and poems. Author's ed. New issue. 3 v. buckram, $3; ½ leath., $4.50; ½ cf., $6. Wessels.
Macbeth. *See* Porter *and* Clarke's Shakespeare studies. 56 c. Am. Bk.
**McCabe, Joseph. St. Augustine and his age. port. 8°. $2 net. Putnam.
McCarthy, Justin H. François Villon. 4 x 6¼. white vellum, 50 c. Russell.
McCarthy, Justin H. Hist. of our times. Author's ed. New issue. 2 v. buckram, $2; ½ leath., $3; ½ cf., $4. Wessels.
†McCarthy, Justin H. If I were king. col. il. 6 x 9. $1.50. Russell.
**McCarthy, Justin H. Reign of Queen Anne. 2 v. cr. 8°. $4 net. Harper.
McCullough's Little stories for little people. 25 c. Am. Bk.
**Macdonald, Rob. The herr doctor. (v. 4, Hour-glass stories.) il. 12°. 40 c. net. Funk.
Macdonald, H. M. Electric waves. Macmillan.
MacDonald, W: Government of Maine. (Handbooks of American government.) 12°. Macmillan.
McDonell, G. L. *See* Scott, G. H. G. Spon & C.
*MacDonnell, A. Sons of St. Francis. il. 8°. $3.50 net. Putnam.
McFarland, Jos., Leffmann, H:, *and others.* Prophylaxis—Personal hygiene—Care of the sick. (v. 5 System of physiologic therapeutics.) il. 8°. Blakiston.
**McFayden, J: E. In the hour of silence. (Companion to "The divine pursuit.") 12°. $1 net. Revell.
McGiffert, Arthur C. *See* Knox, G: W.
†MacGowan, Alice. Last word. il. 12°. $1.50. L. C. Page.
McChesney, Dora G. Cornet Strong of Ireton's horse. Lane.
McGuffey readers, New. 5 bk. ser. Am. Bk.
Machine elements. Cathcart, W: L. tables, diagrams. Van Nostrand.
Machine shop tools, Modern. Vandervoort, W. H. Henley.
Machinery, Kinematics of. *See* Le Conte, J. N. Macmillan.
Machinery. *See* Barber, T. W. Spon & C.
Machines, Kinematics of. Elementary textbook of the. Durley, R. J. Wiley.
**Machray, Rob. Night side of London. il. 8°. $2.50 net. Lippincott.
†McIntyre, J: T. The ragged edge. 12°. $1.25. McClure.
McKay, F. E. *See* Wingate, C: E. L., *and* McKay, F. E.
McKeag, Anna J. Sensation of pain. (Experimental studies in psychology and pedagogy.) Ginn.
**Mackie, Pauline B. Flight of Rosy Dawn. (Cosy corner ser.) il. 12°. 40 c. net. L. C. Page.
**Mackie, Pauline B. Story of Kate. il. 12°. $1.20 net. L. C. Page.

†Mackie, Pauline B. Ye lyttle Salem maide. New ed. il. large 12°. $1.50. L. C. Page.
McKim, Randolph H. Gospel in the Christian year. Longmans.
Maclaren, Ian, *pseud.* *See* Watson, J:
*Macleod, Fiona. By sundown shores. 16°. (Mosher's brocade ser.) 75 c. net. Mosher.
*Macleod, Fiona. Silence of amor: prose poems. 4°. (Mosher's miscellaneous ser.) Mosher.
McClure's children's annual. Crosland, T. W. H., *ed.* $1.50. McClure.
McCorkle, *Mrs.* L. North Carolina stories. il. Heath.
McCrady, E: History of So. Carolina. vol. 4. 12°. Macmillan.
†M'Cutcheon, G: B. Castle Craney crow. 12°. $1.50. Stone.
†MacManus, Seumas. The bewitched fiddle, and other stories. 16°. 75 c. McClure.
**MacManus, Seumas. In chimney corners: tales of Irish folk lore. $1.50 net. McClure.
†MacManus, Seumas. Through the turf smoke. 16°. 75 c. McClure.
**McMaster, J: B. Daniel Webster. il. $2 net. Century.
McMaster's United States hist. Primary, 60 c.; School, $1. Am. Bk.
Macmillan's commercial series; ed. by C. K. Herrick. 12°. Macmillan.
Contents: Trotter, Geography of commerce.—Herrick, History of commerce.—Scott, Economics of commerce.—Dolley, Raw material of commerce.
Macmillan's French classics for college use: ed. by F: de Sumichrast. Macmillan.
New volumes: Le chanson de Roland.—Rabelais, Gargantua.
Macmillan's Latin series; ed. by J. C. Kirtland, *jr.* Macmillan.
New volumes: Ovid, Selections.—Cicero's orations and letters.
**Macmillans' pocket classics. 18°. levanteen, ea., 25 c. net. Macmillan.
New volumes: Mrs. Browning, Poems.—Chaucer's Prologue and knight's tale.—Macaulay, Clive.—Shakespeare, Hamlet.—Old English ballads.—Early American orations.—Woolman, Journals.—Bryant, Selected poems.—Shakespeare, As you like it.—Emerson, Essays.
McMurrich, J. Playfair. Manual of embryology. il. Blakiston.
McMurry, C: A. Method of the recitation. (Elementary methods in education.) New ed. 12°. Macmillan.
McMurry, C: A. Principles of general method based on Herbart. (Elementary methods in education.) rev. 12°. Macmillan.
McMurry, C: A. School management. (Elementary methods in education.) 12°. Macmillan.
McMurry, C: A. Special method in primary reading. (Elementary methods in education.) 12°. Macmillan.
McMurry, C: A. Special method in reading. (Elementary methods in education.) New ed. 12°. Macmillan.
McMurry, C: A. Teacher's manual of geography. (Tarr and McMurry geographies.) Macmillan.
MacSorley, C. M. How the story ended. 16°. 40 c. Young.
Madan, F. Summary catalogue of Bodleian mss. v. 5, 6. Oxford Univ.
*Madison, Ja., Writings of. Hunt, Gaillard, *ed.* 6 or 7 v. Limited ed. of 750 copies. sets only. 8°. hf. leath., subs., $5 net. Putnam.
New volumes: 3, 4, Madison's journal of the Constitutional Convention.
**Madison, Ja., Life of. Hunt, G. $2.50 net. Doubleday, P.
†Magic (The) mashie. Sabin, Edwin L. $1. Wessels.
†Magnetic north (The). Robins, E. $1.50. Stokes.
Magnificat, Pre-Christian antiphons. 25 c. Young.
**Mahan, A. T. Retrospect and prospect. 8°. $1.60 net. Little, B. & Co.
†Maid at arms. Chambers, R. W. $1.50. Harper.
**Maid of many moods. Sheard, V. $1.25 net. Pott.
**Maid of mettle. "Alien." $1 net. Jacobs.
**Maid Sally. Cheever, H. A. $1 net. Estes.
Maine, Government of. MacDonald, W: Macmillan.
Maitland, J. A. F. Age of Bach and Handel. (Oxford musical ser.) Oxford Univ.
Maitland, Louise. Heroes of chivalry. (Stories of heroes.) il. Silver.
**Makers of British art. *See* Manson, J. A., *ed.*
Makers of modern fiction. Dawson, W: J. 8°. $2. Whittaker.
Making of our middle schools. Brown, E. E. Longmans.
*Malan, A. H., *ed.* Famous homes. Library ed. 2 v. 8°. $7.50. Putnam.
Contents: Famous homes of Great Britain and their stories; More famous homes of Great Britain.
Mallandaine, Catharine E. Against the grain. 12°. $1.50. Young.
Mallandaine, Catharine E. The will and the way. 16°. 60 c. Young.
Malet, Lucas. Wages of sin. 12°. $1.50. Fenno.
Mallet, Bernard. Mallet du Pan and the French Revolution. 8°. Longmans.
Mallet du Pan and the French Revolution. Mallet, B. Longmans.
Man in the street stories; from N. Y. *Times.* 12°. $1. J. S. Ogilvie.
Man with the iron mask. Dumas, A. $1. Caldwell.
Man without a country. Hale, E: E. 50 c. Caldwell.
**Manhood making. Lewis, Alex. $1 net. Pilgrim Press.
Mann, Gustav. Micro-anatomy. Oxford Univ.
Mann, J. S., *ed.* *See* Traill, H. D. Putnam.
**Mann, W: J. America in its relations to the great epochs of history. 16°. $1 net. Little, B. & Co.
†Manor farm (The). Francis, M. E. $1.50. Longmans.
Man's place in the cosmos, and other essays. Pattison, A. S. P. [Imp.] Scribner.
**Manson, Ja. A., *ed.* Makers of British art. il. 8°. ea., $1.25 net. [Imp.] Scribner.

Contents: Manson, Landseer.—Windsor, Constable.—Reid, Millais.—Keeling, Reynolds.—Maxwell, Romney.—Chignell, Turner.—Bayne, Wilkie.
**Manson, Ja. A. *Sir* E: Landseer. (Makers of British art.) il. 8°. $1.25 net. [Imp.] Scribner.
*Manual (A) of treatment. Yeo, I. B. 2 v. $5 net. Keener.
**Marble, Annie R. Thoreau: his home, friends, and books. il. 8°. $2 net. Crowell.
Marble faun. Hawthorne, N. $1.50. Appleton.
March of the White Guard. Parker, G. $1.25. Fenno.
Marchant, Bessie. Brave little cousin. 12°. $1. Young.
Marchant, Bessie. House at Brambling Minister. 12°. 80 c. Young.
*Marcus Aurelius. Meditations. (A. L. Humphreys' large type books.) 16°. pap., $3 net. Wessels.
**Margarita. Champney, E. W. $1.25 net. Dodd, Mead & Co.
Margoliouth, *Mrs.* Compendious Syriac dictionary. pt. 4. Oxford Univ.
Maria Theresa. *See* Secret correspondence. Dodd, Mead & Co.
Marianela. Galdos, B. P. W: R. Jenkins.
Marine engine design. Cathcart, W: L. Van Nostrand.
Marion *and* des Garennes, *eds.* Introduccion à la lengua castellana. Heath.
*Marked New Testament. *See* New Testament. Revell.
Marlborough series. 2 v. sets. ea., $2. Crowell.
New volumes: See advertisement.
Marlowe, Christopher. Passionate shepherd to his love, and The nymph's reply, by *Sir* Wa. Raleigh. decor. Lim. ed. de luxe. 8 x 11. $2.75. Russell.
Marriage, Ellen. Avignon. (Mediæval towns ser.) il. Macmillan.
†Marriott, C: Love with honor. 12°. $1.50. Lane.
Marryatt, F: The dog fiend. (Famous books for boys.) il. 12°. 79 c. Caldwell.
Marryatt, F: Jacob Faithful. (Famous books for boys.) il. 12°. 79 c. Caldwell.
Marryatt, F: Japhet in search of a father. (Famous books for boys.) il. 12°. 79 c. Caldwell.
Marryatt, F: Peter Simple. (Famous books for boys.) il. 12°. 79 c. Caldwell.
Marryatt, F: The phantom ship. (Famous books for boys.) il. 12°. 79 c. Caldwell.
Marsh, W. R. *See* Ashton, C. H.
Marshall, Emma. Up and down the Pantiles. il. 16°. $1. Whittaker.
Marshall, Frances. The trivial round. 16°. 60 c. Young.
Marshall, S. M. *See* Spangler, H. W. Wiley.
Marshland, Cora. Interpretative reading. diag. Longmans.
**Martin, E: S. Poems and verses. post 8°. $1.25 net. Harper.
†Martin, G: M. Emmy Lou: her book and heart. il. $1.50. McClure.
Martin Chuzzlewit. Dickens, C: 75 c. Caldwell.
**Martineau, James. Drummond, J. $10 net. Dodd, Mead & Co.
Martineau, James, Ethics of. *See* Sidgwick, H: Macmillan.
Martinique: the second Pompeii. By pen and picture. il. 11 x 14. $1.50. Saalfield.
Martin's New civil government. 90 c. Am. Bk.
Marvel, I. K., *pseud. See* Mitchell, D.
**Marvin, Winthrop L. American merchant marine. 8°. $2 net. Scribner.
**Mary had a little lamb. Dickerson, F. M. $1 net. Stokes.
Mary Magdalene, Life and repentance of. Wager, L: Univ. of Chic.
†Mary Neville. 12°. $1.50. Brentano.
**Mary, Queen of Scots, Palaces, prisons and resting places of. Shoemaker, M. M. $12 net. Brentano.
Maryland, 1666. *See* Alsop, G. Burrows.
Mason, A. E. W. Four feathers. 12°. Macmillan.
†Mason, A. E. W. The watchers. (Copyright ser.) 12°. 50 c. Stokes.
Mason, A. J. Church Historical Society lecture: no. 66, Christianity, what is it? 16°. 80 c. Young.
†Mason, *Mrs.* Caroline A. The little green god. 16°. 75 c. net. Revell.
Mason, *Mrs.* Caroline A. Lux Christi. (United study of missions ser.) 12°. Macmillan.
Mason, T. Chips from Dickens. (Miniature volumes.) New ed. marble enamel, 50 c. Stokes.
Mason, T., *comp.* Witty, humorous and merry thoughts. (Miniature volumes.) New ed. marble enamel, 50 c. Stokes.
Mason's work. Kidder, F. E. $4. W: T. Comstock.
**Masque of judgment. Moody, W: V. $1.50 net. Houghton, M. & Co.
**Massachusetts Bay, 1682-1721, Tracts relating to the currency of. Davis, A. McF., *ed.* net. Houghton, M. & Co.
**Massage. Graham, D. $4 net. Lippincott.
Master Adam the Calabrian. Dumas, A. $1. Fenno.
†Master craftsman. Besant, *Sir* W. 50 c. Stokes.
†Master of Appleby. Lynde, F. $1.50. Bowen-M.
Master Herbert. Picton, E. A. 25 c. Young.
Master-key (The). Lanier, J. J. $1. Whittaker.
**Masterpieces of Greek and Latin literature. Wright, J: H. 2 v. ea., $1 net. Houghton, M. & Co.
Masterpieces of prose and verse. il. 19 v. 32°. cf., per v., $1. Stokes.
Masters, Edgar L. Maximilian: play in 5 acts. 12°. bds., $1.50; leath., $5. Badger.
*Masters of etching. Paloma, F. $40 net. Cambridge.
Materia medica for nurses. Groff, J: E. $1.25. Blakiston.

Mathematics, Higher, for students of chemistry and physics. Mellor, J. W. $4. Longmans.
Matheson, G: Representative men of the Bible. Armstrong.
**Mathews, Ferd. S. Field book of American wild flowers. il. col. pl. 16°. $1.75 net; leath., $2.25 net. Putnam.
Matthay, Tobias. Pianoforte tone production. diagrams. 8°. Longmans.
**Matthewman. L. de V. Brevities. il. 16°. 80 c. net. Coates.
**Matthews, Ja. Brander. Aspects of fiction. New ed. $1.25 net. Scribner.
Mau, August. Pompeii; tr. by F. W. Kelsey. New ed. il. 8°. Macmillan.
**Maud, Constance. Heroines of poetry. il. 12°. $1.50 net. Lane.
Maudsley, H: Life in mind and conduct. 8°. Macmillan.
Mawley, E. *See* Jekyll, G.
*Maximes. La Rochefoucauld. $3 net. Wessels.
Maximilian. Masters, E. L. $1.50; $5. Badger.
**Maxwell, *Sir* . Herbert. G: Rommey. (Makers of British art.) il. 8°. $1.25 net. [Imp.] Scribner.
Maxwell's Eng. course. First bk. in Eng., 40 c.; Introd. lessons in Eng. grammar, 60 c. Am. Bk.
Maxwell *and* Smith's Writing in English. 75 c. Am. Bk.
May, Eliz. Animal life in rhymes and jingles. il. 4°. bds., $1.25. Saalfield.
Maycock, W. Perren. Electric lighting and power distribution. il. v. 2. 12°. Macmillan.
**Mayer. H: Alphabet book. (Dumpy books for children.) il. bds., 40 c. net. Stokes.
**Mayken. Chase, J. A. $1.20 net. McClurg.
†Mayo, Clayton. Cap'n Titus. $1. Doubleday, P.
Mayo, N. S. Care of stock. (Rural science ser.) 16°. Macmillan.
Mayo-Robinson, A. W., *and* Moynihan, B. G. A. Diseases of the pancreas. il. 8°. Saunders.
Mazarin. Hassall, A. H. 75 c. Macmillan.
Me, Nos, and the others. Isherwood, B. 20 c. Young.
**Mead. Leon. Word coinage. 18°. (Handy information ser.) 45 c. net. Crowell.
**Mead, Lucia A. Milton's England. il. 12°. $1.60 net. L. C. Page.
Mead, W: E: *See* Gordy, W. F.
Meade, E. S. Trust finance. 12°. Appleton.
†Meade, *Mrs.* L. T. Rebel of the school. il. 12°. $1.50. Lippincott.
Meade, *Mrs.* L. T. Sister of the Red Cross. il. 8°. $1.25. Nelson.
Mechanics and heat. Nichols, E: L. Macmillan.
Mechanics, Celestial, Introduction to. Moulton, F. R. Macmillan.
Mechanics of the steam engine. *See* Le Conte, J. N. Macmillan.
Mediæval Europe. Bemont, C. Holt.
Mediæval towns series. Macmillan.
New volumes: Wheatley, Mediæval London. — Marriage, Avignon.—Lutzow, Prague.—Wiel, Verona.—Gardner, Florence [large pap.]—Gardner, Siena (large pap.]
**Mediæval India. *See* India. Putnam.
*Medicine, Nothnagel's encyclopedia of practical. ea., $5 net; $6 net. Saunders.
*Medicine, Text book of. Fagge, C. H. 2 v. ea., $6. Blakiston.
Medicis, Marie de. Life of. Pardoe, J. $4.50; $9. Pott.
*Meditations. Marcus Aurelius. $3 net. Wessels.
Mediterranean (The). Bonney, J. T. $3; $6. Pott.
†Meekins, Lynn R. Adam Rush. 12°. $1.50. Lippincott.
†Meldrum, D. S. Conquest of Charlotte. 12°. $1.50. Dodd, Mead & Co.
Mellor, J. W. Higher mathematics for students of chemistry and physics. 8°. $4. Longmans.
**Memoirs of a contemporary; tr. and ed. by L. Strachey. il. 6 x 7¼. $2.75 net. Doubleday, P.
**Memoirs of the life of the late John Mytton. Nimrod. $15 net. Brentano.
**Memorable places among the holy hills. Stewart, Robt. L. $1 net. Revell.
Memories of a hundred years. Hale, E: E. Macmillan.
Men and women. Browning, R. 40 c.; $1.25. Caldwell.
Men who crucify Christ. Ingram, A. F. W. 50 c. Young.
Menken, Adah I. Infelicia. [Poems.] 12°. $1.50. Lippincott.
Menpes, Dorothy. *See* Menpes, Mortimer.
**Menpes, Mortimer. World pictures. colored pictures; letter press by Dorothy Menpes. $5 net; lim. ed. de luxe, large pap., $15 net. Russell.
Menteur (Le). Corneille, P. Silver.
**Menus, Nursery and school. *See* Hogan, L. E. Coates.
**Merchant marine, American. Marvin, W. L. $2 net. Scribner.
**Meredith, G: Novels. 15 v. ea., 75 c. net. Scribner.
Meredith, Owen. Lucile. (Sesame classics.) il. 7 x 4¾. limp ooze cf., boxed, $1.25. Caldwell.
**Merejkowski, D. Tolstoi as man and artist. Authorized trans. Putnam.
Mérimée, Prosper. Colomba. (International modern language ser.) Ginn.
Merle's crusade. Carey, R. N. $1. Caldwell.
Merriam, Florence. *See* Bailey, Florence M.
Merrill, J. M. His mother's letter. il. 12°. $1. Saalfield.
†Merriman, H: S. The vultures. il. post 8°. $1.50. Harper.
Merriman, R. B. Life and correspondence of T: Cromwell, Earl of Essex. Oxford Univ.
Message of man. Coit, S. 75 c.; $1. Macmillan.
Message to the Magians. Talmage, F. DeW. 75 c. Revell.

Messages of Israel's lawgivers. Kent, C: F. $1.25. Scribner.
Messages of the Bible. Scribner.
New volume: Kent, Messages of Israel's lawgivers.
**Messages of the masters. Bradford, A. H. $2 net. Crowell.
Metal plate work. Millis. $3. Spon & C.
Metcalf, W. C. Billows and bergs. $1.75. Warne.
**Metcalfe, Cranstoun. Fame for a woman. 12°. $1.20 net. Putnam.
Method of the recitation. McMurry, C: A. Macmillan.
Methodism, Drillmaster of. Goodell, C: L. $1.25. Eaton & M.
*Methodist Episcopal church. Minutes of the annual conferences. Spring conferences, 1902. 8°. $1 net. Eaton & M.
Mexico, Southern. *See* Starr, F: Univ. of Chic.
**Mexico, Unknown. Lumholtz, C. 2 v. $12 net. Scribner.
*Meyer, Annie N. My park book. 16°. 75 c. net. E. W. Dayton.
Meyer, F. B. Samuel and Saul. (Old Testament heroes.) 12°. $1. Revell.
Meyer, L. G., *tr.* *See* Barine, Arvède. Putnam.
Michael Carmichael. Sandys, M. $1.25. Laird.
Michael Kohlhaas. Kleist, H. von. Holt.
Michelson, A. A. Light waves and their uses. 8°. Univ. of Chic.
Michigan, Government of. Cook, W. Macmillan.
Micro-anatomy. Mann, Gustav. Oxford Univ.
Middle ages. *See* Robinson, J. H. Introduction to the history of Western Europe. Ginn.
Middle ages, History of. Munro, D. C. Appleton.
**Mid-eighteenth century. Millar, J. H. $1.50 net. Scribner.
Midgley, W. *See* Lilley, A. E.
†Mighel, Philip V. The inevitable. 12°. $1.50. Lippincott.
Miles, Eustace H. Tennis, racquets and squash. il. 12°. Appleton.
Mill, J: S. Liberty. (Chateau ser.) il. 6 x 4. boxed, 75 c. Caldwell.
Mill on the Floss. Eliot, G: 50 c. net; 75 c. net. Lane.
Millais, *Sir* J: E., Life and letters of. Millais, J: G. 2 v. $6-$20. Stokes.
**Millais, *Sir* J: E. Reid, J. E. $1.25 net. [Imp.] Scribner.
Millais, J: G. Life and letters of Sir J: E. Millais. New ed. il. 2 v. 8°. $6; ed. de luxe, lim., $15; ¾ levant, $20. Stokes.
**Millais, J: G. Natural history of British surface-feeding ducks. col. il. Lim. ed. 4°. $40 net. Longmans.
**Millar, J. H. Mid-eighteenth century. (Periods of European literature.) $1.50 net. Scribner.
*Millard, Bailey. Songs of the press and Others adventure. (Verse.) 12°. bds., 75 c. net. Elder.
**Miller, E. D. Modern polo; ed. by M. H. Hayes. il. 8°. $5 net. [Imp.] Scribner.
**Miller, G: A. Problems of the town church. 12°. 75 c. Revell.
Miller, Frank W., *and* Foerste, A: F. Elementary physics. Scribner.
*Miller, J. Description of the province and city of New York. (Written 1695; pub. 1843.) Repr. 250 copies, bds., about $2; 15 copies, Jap. pap., $3 net. Burrows.
**Miller, J. R. To-day and to-morrow. il. 12°. 50 c. net. Crowell.
**Miller, J. R. The upper currents. 16°. 65 c.; 85 c. net. Crowell.
Millet. Jean F. Cartwright, J. Macmillan.
**Millicent in dreamland. Brainerd, Edna S. 40 c. net. L. C. Page.
†Millionaires (The). Ralph, J. $1.50. Lothrop.
Millis. Metal plate work. 4th ed. $3. Spon & C.
**Mills, W. Jay. Historic houses of New Jersey. il. 8°. boxed, $5 net. Lippincott.
Milne's Academic algebra. $1.25. Am. Bk.
Milne's Elements of plane and solid geometry. $1.25. Am. Bk.
*Milton, J: Lycidas. (Flowers of Parnassus ser., no. 17.) il. 16°. 50 c. net; leath., 75 c. net. Lane.
**Milton, J: [Selections.] (Little masterpieces, 2d ser.) 4 x 6. flex. silk cl., 40 c. net. Doubleday, P.
Milton, J:, Lexicon to poetical works. Lockwood, L. A. Macmillan.
**Milton's England. Mead, Lucia A. $1.60 net. L. C. Page.
Milton's prosody. Bridges, R. Oxford Univ.
Mind, The force of. Schofield, A. T. $2. Blakiston.
**Mind power and privileges. Olston, A. B. $1.50 net. Crowell.
Mine own people Kipling, R. 75 c. Caldwell.
Miner, G: W. Accounting and business practice. Ginn.
Miniature volumes. New ed. marble enamel, 10 v., ea., 50 c. Stokes.
Contents: Chips from Dickens.—Chips from Thackeray.—Gems from classical writers.—Gleanings from Wordsworth.—Crowther, Golden thoughts from great authors.—Lindsay, Golden thoughts from T: à Kempis.—Goldsmith, She stoops to conquer.—Scott, Lady of the lake.—Philpot, Pickings from a "Pocket of pebbles."—Witty, humorous and merry thoughts.
Mining, Coal. *See* Kerr, G: L. Lippincott.
Minot, C: S. Laboratory text-book of embryology. Blakiston.
**Minstrelsy of the Scottish border. Scott, *Sir* W. 4 v. $10 net. [Imp.] Scribner.
**Mishaps of an automobilist; col. il. by De W. C. Falls. 4°. 80 c. net. Stokes.
†Miss Belladonna. Ticknor, C. $1. Little, B. & Co.
**Miss Lochinvar. Taggart, M. A. $1.20 net. Appleton.
Miss Petticoats. Tilton, D. C. M. Clark.
Missionaries, Memories of. *See* Trumbull, H: C. Revell.
**Missionary principles and practice. Speer, Robt. E. 8°. $1.50 net. Revell.
Missionary problem, Key to the. Murray, A. 75 c. Am. Tr.

Missionary speakers' manual. Buckland, A. R. $1.25. Am. Tr.
Missions. *See* Chatterton, E. Young.
Missions, Centennial of home: 1802-1902. 12°. Presb. Bd.
Missions, Witness to the value of. Longridge, G. 20 c. Young.
Mr. and Mrs. Tiddlewinks. Farmiloe, E. Young.
Mr. Pat's little girl. Leonard, Ma. F. $1.50. Wilde.
**Mr. Sun and Mrs. Moon. Le Gallienne, R: $1.60 net. Russell.
**Mrs. Ginger. Appleton, *Miss.* 40 c. net. Stokes.
Mistress Hetty. Hotchkiss, C. C. $1. Street.
Mrs. Moffat's brownie. Wood, F. H. 80 c. Young.
†Mrs. Tree. Richards, L. E. 75 c. Estes.
Mitchell, Donald, ["Ik Marvel."] Dream life. (Chateau ser.) il. 6x4 Boxed. 75 c. Caldwell.
†Mitchell, J: A. The last American. Edition de luxe. (Special holiday edition.) col. il. by F. W. Read. 12°. $1.50. Stokes.
Mitchell, W. C. History of the greenbacks. 8°. Univ. of Chic.
†Mitford, Bertram. The white shield. (Copyright ser.) 12°. 50 c. Stokes.
Mitford, Ma. R. Our village. (New Kalon ser.) il. 12°. 50 c. Caldwell.
Mizner, Addison. *See* Herford, V.
Model engineer. v. 6. 4°. $2. Spon & C.
Modern Amer. tanning. Jacobsen Pub. Co.
**Modern conjurer. Neil, C. L. $2 net. Lippincott.
**Modern English writers ser. 12°. $1 net. Dodd, Mead & Co.
New volumes: Browning, by Augustine Birrell.—Dickens, by W. E. Henley.—Froude, by J: Oliver Hobbes.
**Modern etching and engraving. 4°. $2 net. Lane.
Modern illustrative bookkeeping. Introd. course; Complete course. Am. Bk.
Modern machine shop tools. Vandervoort, W. H. Henley.
Modern painters. Ruskin, J: $1.25. Caldwell.
Mohammedanism. *See* Tisdall, W. St. C. Young.
Molesworth. Planometer areas. 50 c. Spon & C.
Molesworth, *Mrs.* M. L. Peterkin. il. 12°. Macmillan.
**Mollie and the unwiseman. Bangs, J: K. $1 net. Coates.
Molly Bawn. "Duchess." $1. Caldwell.
Molly Hesketh; by E. C. M. 60 c. Young.
**Moncrief, J. W. Short history of the Christian church. 12°. $1.50 net. Revell.
*Monetary crimes, History of. Del Mar, A. 75 c. net. Cambridge.
Money, A. W., Carlin, W. E., *and* Himmelweight, A. L. A. Gun and rifle. (American sportsman's lib.) il. 8°. Macmillan.
Money. Walford, L. B. 20 c. Young.
Money, Lectures on. Nicholson, J. S. Macmillan.
*Money, Science of. Del Mar, Alex. $2 net. Cambridge.
Monod, G. *See* Bemont, C:
Monroe, D. B., *ed.* *See* Homer. Oxford Univ.
*Monroe, Ja., Writings. Hamilton, S. M., *ed.* 7 v. Limited ed. of 750 copies. Sets only. 8°. hf. leath., subs., $5 net. *New volume,* 6. Putnam.
**Montaigne, Michel de. Essays and letters. B., *ed.* 3 v. (Special decorated ed. of 250 copies.) Houghton, M. & Co.
**Montaigne, Michel de. Essays and letters. 4 v. 8°. $12 net. Scribner.
Montgomery, Frances T. Billy Whiskers: autobiography of a goat. il. 4°. bds., $1. Saalfield.
**Moody, D. L. Notes from my Bible. (Nonpareil ser.) 25 c. net. Revell.
**Moody, W: V. Masque of judgment. 12°. $1.50; uncut ed.. 150 copies, bds., $1.50 net. Houghton, M. & Co.
**Moody, W: V., *and* Lovett, Rob. M. History of English literature. 12°. $1.25 net. Scribner.
**Moon (The). Pickering, W: H. $10 special net. Doubleday, P.
Moon children. Fessenden, L. D. $1.25. Jamieson-H.
Moore, C. H. First Latin book. 12°. (20th century text-books.) Appleton.
†Moore, F. Frankfort. Castle Omeragh. 12°. $1.50. Appleton.
†Moore, J: T. Songs and stories of Tennessee. il. 12°. $1.25. Coates.
**Moorehead, W. G. Outline studies in the Acts and Epistles. 12°. $1.20 net.
Moral (La) in ejemplos históricos. Puron, J. G. Appleton.
**Moral life, Shakespeare's portrayal of. Sharp, F. C. $1.25 net. Scribner.
Moran, T: F. Theory and practice of the English government. (Harvard historical studies.) 8°. Longmans.
More ex-tank tales. Cullen, C. L. $1. J. S. Ogilvie.
Morey, W: C. Government of N. Y. (Har l-books of American government.) 12 M nillan.
Morey's Roman history. $1. n. Bk.
**Morgan, G. C. First century message to twentieth century Christians. $1 net. Revell.
Morley, J: Life of W: E. Gladstone. il. 8°. 3 v. Macmillan.
Mormon church. *See* Henry, A. H. Revell.
Mormonism. *See* Riley, I. W. Dodd, Mead & Co.
**Morning Glory, *Miss. pseud.* American diary of a Japanese girl. il. 8°. $1.60 net. Stokes.
†Morris, Clara. Pasteboard crown. $1.50. Scribner.
**Morris, Clara. Stage confidences. il. 5x7¾. $1.20 net. Lothrop.
†Morris, Gouverneur. Aladdin O'Brien. 12°. $1.25. Century.
Morris, H:, Sutton, J. B., *and others, eds.* Text-book of anatomy. col. il. 3d ed. 8°. $6; leather., $7; hf. Russia, $8. Blakiston.
Morris, J. E. Welsh wars of Edward I. Oxford Univ.
**Morris, W: The doom of King Aerisius; il. by Burne-Jones. White buckram. 6¼ x 8½. $2.75 net. Russell.
*Morris, W: Dream of John Ball. 8°. (Mosher's old world ser.) net, $1; Japan vellum, $2.50 net. Mosher.

*Morris, W: Gertha's lovers. 16°. (Mosher's brocade ser.) 75 c. net. Mosher.

*Morris, W: Golden wings. 16°. (Mosher's brocade ser.) 75 c. net. Mosher.

*Morris, W: Story of the unknown church: three tales. 16°. (Mosher's brocade ser.) 75 c. net. Mosher.

**Morris, W:, *tr.* The history of over sea. il. decor. Japan pap. bds., 8 x 10. $1.50 net. Russell.

**Morris, W:, poet, craftsman, socialist. Cary, Eliz. L. $3.50 net. Putnam.

†Morrison, Arthur. The hole in the wall. 12°. $1.50. McClure.

Morrison, F: S. *See* Goodell, T: D.

Morrison, G. H. Flood tide. Armstrong.

**Morse, E. S. Glimpses of China and Chinese homes. il. 12°. $1.50 net. Little, B. & Co.

Morse, Fes. C. Furniture of olden times. il. 8°. [Also.] Large paper ed. Macmillan.

Mortimer, A. G. The creeds. (Oxford lib. of practical theology.) Longmans.

Mortimer, *Mrs.* M. Peep of day. (New Kalon ser.) il. 12°. 50 c. Caldwell.

Mortimer, *Mrs.* M. Peep of day. col. il. New ed. 16°. $1.25. Longmans.

Mortimer, *Mrs.* M. Precept upon precept. (New Kalon ser.) il. 12°. 50 c. Caldwell

Morton, *Mrs.* Talks to children about Jesus. (New Kalon ser.) il. 12°. 50 c. Caldwell.

†Morton, Martha. Her lord and master. il. 12°. $1.50. Biddle.

**Mosaics from India. Denning, Marg. B. $1.25 net. Revell.

Moser, G. V. Das stiftungsfest. W. R. Jenkins.

*Mosher's Brocade series. 16°. ea. in brocade slide case. 75 c. net. Mosher.
New volumes: XXXI., Immensee, by T. Storm.—XXXII., Gertha's lovers, by W: Morris.—XXXIII., Golden wing, by W: Morris.—XXXIV., Story of the unknown church; three tales by W: Morris.—XXXV., Nature and eternity, by R: Jeffries.—XXXVI., By sundown shores, by Fiona Macleod.

*Mosher's miscellaneous ser. 4°. $2.50 net; Jap. vellum, $5 net. Mosher.
New volumes: XVII., Poems of Ernest Dowson.—XVIII., Edward Fitzgerald, by Francis Hindes Groome.—XIX., The silence of amor, by Fiona Macleod.

*Mosher's Old world ser. nar. 8°. $1 net; Japan vellum, $2.50 net. Mosher.
New volumes: XXVI., In memoriam.—XXVII., Pippa passes.—XXVIII., Dream of John Ball, by W: Morris.

*Mosher's Quarto ser. 4°. Mosher.
New volumes: IV., Poems and ballads, 3d ser., by A. C. Swinburne. bds., $5 net; Jap. vellum, $20 net.—V., Poems, MDCCCLXX., by D. G. Rossetti. bds., $5 net; Jap. vellum, $20 net.—VI., The Renaissance, by W. Pater. bds., $4 net; Jap. vellum, $15 net.

*Mosher's Reprints of privately printed books. Mosher.
New volumes: X., Fragilia labilia, by J: A. Symonds. 8°. $1 net; Jap. vellum, $2 net.—XI., Garland of Rachel. 8°. $2 net; Jap. vellum, $5 net.—XII., Rubaiyat of Omar Khayyam. 4°. $5 net; Jap. vellum, $10 net.

*Mosher's Vest pocket ser. 40 c. net; pap. 25 c. net; leath., 75 c. net; Jap. vellum, $1 net. Mosher.
New volumes: I., Rubaiyat of Omar Khayyam.—II., Sonnets from the Portuguese.—III., Laus veneris, by A. C. Swinburne.—IV., Aes triplex and other essays, by R. L. Stevenson.

**Mother and child. Davis, E: P. $1.50 net. Lippincott.

Mother Goose of modern days. Bartlett, *Mrs.* N. G. $1.50. L. C. Page.

Mother Goose paint book. Barnett, J. M. $1.25. Saalfield.

Moths. *See* Caterpillars.

Motley, J: L. Selections. (Street and Smith little classics.) 18°. 50 c. Street.

**Motor cars, or the application of mechanical power to road vehicles. il. 8°. $5 net. Pott.

**Moule, H. C. G. Thoughts for the Sundays of the year. 8°. $1 net. Revell.

Moulton, C: W., *ed.* *See* Doctor's Recreation ser. Saalfield.

Moulton, Forest R. Introduction to celestial mechanics. il. 8°. Macmillan.

Moulton, R: C. Shakespeare's moral system. 12°. Macmillan.

Mountaineering in the Sierra Nevada. King, C. $1.50. Scribner.

Mounted infantry city of London Imperial Volunteers, Record of. Scott, G. H. G. $2. Spon & C.

Mouth and teeth. *See* Broomell, I. N. Blakiston.

Mouth, Surgical pathology and diseases of. *See* Grant, H. H. Saunders.

**Mowbray, J. P. ["J. P. M." *pseud.*] Tangled up in Beulah land. 5 x 8. $1.50 net. Doubleday, P.

Mowry, Arthur M. First steps in the history of England. il. 70 c. Silver.

Mowry, W: A. Territorial growth of the U. S. Silver.

Moynihan, B. G. A. *See* Mayo-Robinson, A. W. Saunders.

Muir, Rob., *and* Ritchie, Ja. Manual of bacteriology; ed. by N. M. Harris. Am. ed. il. 12°. Macmillan.

Müller, F. Max. Life of. Müller, *Mrs.* Max. Longmans.

**Müller, F. Max. Memories. hol. ed. 45th thousand. il. sq. 8°. $2 net. McClurg.

Müller, *Mrs.* Max. Life of Max Müller. il. 2 v. Longmans.

Müller, W: Diary and correspondence of. Allen, P. S., *and* Hatfield, J. T., *eds.* Univ. of Chic.

Mullins, J. D. *See* Buckland, A. R. Am. Tr.

Mulock, D. M. Adventures of a brownie. (Editha ser.) il. 7½ x 5¼. 50 c. Caldwell.

Mulock, D. M. The little lame prince. (Editha ser.) il. 7½ x 5¼. 50 c. Caldwell.

Mulock, D. M. The sleeping beauty. (Editha ser.) il. 7½ x 5¼. 50 c. Caldwell.
Mumford, Edith W. *See* Herford, V.
**Mumford, J: K. Oriental rugs. col. il. 8°. New ed. $7.50 net. Scribner.
Municipal progress, American. Zueblin, C: Macmillan.
Munro, D. C. History of the Middle Ages. 12°. Appleton.
**Mural decorations, Modern. Baldry, A. L. $5 net. Scribner.
**Murfree, Mary N. [Craddock, C: E. *pseud.*] The champion. 12°. $1.20 net. Houghton, M. & Co.
Murray, And. Key to the missionary problem. 75 c. Am. Tr.
Murray, And. Like Christ. (Chateau ser.) il. 6 x 4. Boxed. 75 c. Caldwell.
Murray, And. The new life. (New Kalon ser.) il. 12°. 50 c. Caldwell.
Murray, Charlotte. Castleton's "Prep." il. 12°. $1.25. Am. S. S.
Murray, G. G. A., *ed. See* Euripides. Oxford Univ.
Murray, Ja. A: H: *and others, eds.* New English dictionary. v. 5. (H-K.) Oxford Univ.
**Murray, T. Douglas. Jeanne d'Arc. il. 8°. $5 net. McClure.
Museum editions. il. 16°. ea., $1. Brentano.
New volume: Rabelais, Works.
**Music and musicians. Lavignac, A. $1.75 net. Holt.
**Music, Short history of. Untersteiner, A. $1.20 net. Dodd, Mead & Co.
Music. *See* Natural course. Am. Bk.
Music. *See* Oxford musical ser. Oxford Univ.
**Music-lovers' series. *See* Page's. L. C. Page.
**Musical pastels. Upton, G: P. $2 net. McClurg.
**Musser, J: H., *ed.* Diseases of the bronchii: Diseases of the pleura: Pneumonia. (Nothnagel's encyclopaedia of practical medicine, v. 7.) col. il. 8°. $5 net; $6 net. Saunders.
†Mutable many (The). Barr, R. 50 c. Stokes.
**Mutual aid a factor in evolution. Kropotkin, *Prince.* $2.50 net. McClure.
Muzzarelli's Brief French course. $1.25. Am. Bk.
**My dogs in the northland. Young, Egerton R. $1.25 net. Revell.
My King, and Royal invitation. Havergal, F. R. 50 c. Caldwell.
*My park book. Meyer, A. N. 75 c. net. E. W. Dayton.
**Myers, Cortland. The lost wedding ring. 16°. 75 c. net. Funk.
**Mythological Japan. Otto, A. F. $7.50 net. Biddle.
*Nameless hero *and other poems.* Anderson, Ja. B. $1 net. Wessels.
**Nansen, Fridtjof, *ed.* Norwegian north polar expedition, 1893-96. il. v. 3. 4°. $12.50 net. Longmans.
Napoleon I. Fournier, A. Holt.
†Napoleon Jackson. Stuart, Ruth McE. il. in tint. 16°. $1. Century.
Napoleon's addresses and anecdotes. (Remarque ser.) 3⅞ x 5⅝. 40 c.; limp leath., boxed, 75 c.; limp chamois, $1.25. Caldwell.
**Nash, Harriet A. Polly's secret: story of the Kennebec. il. 12°. $1.20 net. Little, B. & Co.
**Nathalie's chum. Ray, A. R. $1.20 net. Little, B. & Co.
**National Civic Federation. Proceedings of conference, Dec. 16-17, 1901. *See* Industrial conciliation. Putnam.
Natural course in music. Full course, 7 bks. and 7 charts.—Short course, 2 bks. Am. Bk.
Natural history, Child's pictorial. Park, C. M. 50 c. Young.
Natural history, Little folks' picture. Step, E: $1.50. Warne.
**Natural history of British surface-feeding ducks. Millais, J: G. $40 net. Longmans.
Natural law in the spiritual world. Drummond, H: 75 c. Caldwell.
*Nature and eternity. Jeffries, R: 75 c. net. Mosher.
**Nature and the camera. Dugmore, A. R. $1.35 net. Doubleday, P.
**Nature, Essay on. Emerson, R. W. $1 net; $5. Alwil.
**Nature myths, Book of. Holbrook, Florence. 45 c. net. Houghton, M. & Co.
Nature study readers. *See* Troeger, J. W. Appleton.
**Naudé, Gabriel. Instruction concerning erecting of a library. 16°. hf. leath. (special decorated ed. of 400 numbered copies.) price on application. Houghton, M. & Co.
Navigation, American. Bates, W: W. 8°. Houghton, M. & Co.
Navigation. *See* Wentworth, G: A. Ginn.
Naylor, Ja. B. In the days of St. Clair. il. 12°. $1.50. Saalfield.
**Naylor, W. Trades waste. il. 8°. $6.50 net. Lippincott.
Neale, J. M. Deeds of faith. 16°. 40 c. Young.
Neale, J. M. Farm of Aptonga: story of the times of S. Cyprian. 12°. 80 c. Young.
Neale, J. M. Tales of Christian heroism. New ed. 60 c. Young.
Needell, *Mrs.* J. H. Unstable as water. $1.25. Warne.
†Needle's eye (The). Kingsley, F. M. $1.50. Funk.
Neely, T: B:, *ed. See* International S. S. lessons. Eaton & M.
Neglected people of the Bible. Young, D. T. $1. Am. Tr.
Negro, The future of the American. Washington, B. T. 50 c. Small, M.
**Neil, C. Lang. Modern conjurer. il. 12°. $2 net. Lippincott.
Neilson, Rob. M. Steam turbine. il. 8°. $2.50. Longmans.
Neither bound nor free. Pryor, G. L. $1. J. S. Ogilvie.
†Nesbit, E. The red house. il. post 8°. $1.50. Harper.
†Nesbit, E. Treasure seekers. New ed. il. 12°. $1.50. Stokes.

**Netherlands, Journal of a tour in the. Southey, Robt. price on application. Houghton, M & Co.
Neville, Eliz. O'Reilly. Father Tom of Connemara. il. $1.50. Rand, McN.
**New Amsterdam and its people. Innes, J. H. $2.50 net. Scribner.
New century physiologies. Elementary, 75 c. —Intermediate, 40 c.—Primary, 30 c.—Oral lesson bk., $1. Am. Bk.
New Christians. White, P. 50 c. Federal Bk. Co.
New empire. Adams, B. Macmillan.
New England and its neighbours. Johnson, C. Macmillan.
**New England rooftrees, Romance of. Crawford, Mary C. $1.20 net; $2.50 net. L. C. Page.
**New England, Separates of. Blake, S. L. $1.25 net. Pilgrim Press.
New England. *See also* Fiske, J:
New England dictionary. Murray, *ed.* v. 5 (H-K.) Oxford Univ.
**New France and New England. Fiske, J: $1.65 net. Houghton, M. & Co.
New Hamlet. Smith, W: H. 50 c. Rand, McN.
**New Jersey, Historic houses of. Mills, W. J. $5 net. Lippincott.
New Jersey. *See* Budd, T. Burrows.
New Jersey. *See* Tarr and McMurry geographies. Macmillan.
New Kalon ser. il. 12°. ea., 50 c. Caldwell.
New volumes: An Englishwoman's love-letters. — Æsop's fables. — Connor, Black rock.—Holland, Bitter Sweet.—Ruskin, Beauty and nature.—Browning's Selections. —Penrose, The burglar's daughter.—Ewing, The brownies.—Fowler, Concerning Isabel Carnaby. — Sheldon, Crucifixion of Philip Strong. — Counsels to inquirers. — Hall, Come to Jesus.—Spurgeon, Daily help. — Burnett, Editha's burglar. — Alger, Erie train boy.—Elizabeth and her German garden. — Bartlett, Familiar quotations. — Kingsley, Greek heroes. — Ewing, Jackanapes.—Pierson, Lessons in the school of prayer.—James, Line upon line.—Love poems. — Barrie, Little minister. — Kipling, Letters of marque.—Havergal, My king, and Royal invitation.—Hale, Man without a country. — Murray, New life. — Mitford, Our village.—Mortimer, Peep of day; Precept upon precept. — Ruskin, Precious thoughts; Pearls for young ladies; Stones of Venice; True and beautiful.—St. Pierre, Paul and Virginia.—Holmes, Professor at the breakfast table. — Rubaiyat of Omar Khayyam.—Shadow of the rock.—Holley, Samantha at Saratoga.—Morton, Talks to children about Jesus.—Jerome, Three men in a boat.—Stowe, Uncle Tom's cabin.—Glyn, Visits of Elizabeth.—Kingsley, Water of life.
New life (The). Murray, A. 50 c. Caldwell.
New pupil (The). Jacberns, R. Macmillan.
New Testament. Coptic version, in the Northern dialect; with trans. Final vols., 3 and 4. Oxford Univ.
New Testament handbooks; ed. by S. Mathews. 12°. Macmillan.
New volume: Platner, Early Christian literature.
*New Testament, The marked. New eds. russia, 50 c. net; mor., 75 c. net; calf, 75 c. net. Revell.
New Testament. *See* Sanday, W., *ed.* Oxford Univ.
New York, Families of. *See* Hamm, Margherita A. Putnam.
New York, Government of. Morey, W: C. Macmillan.
**New York old and new. Wilson, R. R. 2 v. $3.50 net. Lippincott.
**New York, Picturesque. Williams, J. L. net. Scribner.
New York. *See* Denton, D: Burrows.
New York, 1695. *See* Miller, J., Description of the province and city of New York. Burrows.
New York, 1678-1701. *See* Wolley, C: Burrows.
**New York stage, History of. Brown, T. A. $25; $50 special net. Dodd, Mead & Co.
New York state. *See* Southworth, G. V. D. Appleton.
New York under the first Georges. Singleton, E. Appleton.
Newbolt, W. C. E. Priestly blemishes. 8°. Longmans.
Newell, Peter, *il.* Bikey the skicycle. $1.50. Riggs Pub. Co.
**Newell, P: Topsys and turvys. New ed. $1 net. Century.
Newman, W. L., *ed.* *See* Aristotle. Oxford Univ.
**Newton, J: Capt. J: Brown of Harper's Ferry. il. 12°. $1.25 net. Wessels.
**Next step in evolution. Funk, I: K. 50 c. net. Funk.
Nicholas Nickleby. Dickens, C: 75 c. Caldwell.
†Nicholls, Josephine H. Bayou Triste: a story of Louisiana. il. 12°. $1.50. Barnes.
Nichols, E: L., *and* Franklin, W: S. Elements of physics. Macmillan.
New volume: 3, Mechanics and heat. New ed.
**Nichols, Francis H. Through hidden Shensi. il. 8°. $3.50 net. Scribner.
Nichols, Rose S. English pleasure gardens. il. 8°. Macmillan.
Nicholson, J. Shield. Lectures on money. 8°. Macmillan.
**Nicolay, J: G. Abraham Lincoln; condensed from Nicolay and Hay's "Abraham Lincoln: a history." $2.40 net. Century.
Nidding-Nod of Once-upon-a-time. Escott-Inman, H. $1. Rand, McN. & Co.
Niell, P. H. Biological laboratory methods. il. 12°. Macmillan.
Night (The) has a thousand eyes. Bourdillon, F. W. 10 c. Elder.
**Night side of London. Machray, R. $2.50 net. Lippincott.
**Nimrod. Life of a sportsman. col. il. Large pap., $20 net. Brentano.
**Nimrod. Memoirs of the life of the late John Mytton: cont. a mem. of Nimrod by R. S. Surtees. col. il. 8°. $15 net. Brentano.
Ninde, W: X. A memorial; by his daughter. 8°. Eaton & M.
Nineteenth century art and Scottish historical antiquities. 2 v. il. 4°. Macmillan.
**Nineteenth century, History of the. Emerson, E., *jr.* $3.60 net. Dodd, Mead & Co.

*Nirvana. Carus, Paul. 60 c. net. Open Court.
†No other way. Besant, *Sir* W. $1.50. Dodd, Mead & Co.
*No sects in heaven. Cleaveland, *Mrs.* E. H. J. 50 c. net; $1.50 net. Elder.
Nociones de agricultura cientifica. Lupton, N. T. Appleton.
Nociones de geologia. Geikie, A. Appleton.
Nociones de historia des Roma. Fyffe, C. A. Appleton.
Nociones de psicologia. Baldwin, J. M. Appleton.
Noes have it. Couchman, M. 20 c. Young.
Nolhac, Pierre de. Louis XV. et Mme. de Pompadour. [French text.] il. 4°. Lim. ed. Manzi & J.
†Noll and the fairies. White, H. $1.50. Stone.
Nonnes preestes tale of the cok and hen. Chaucer, G. $7.50; over $16.50. Grafton Press.
**Nonsense anthology. Wells, C., *ed.* $1.25 net. Scribner.
**Nonsense nonsense. Jerrold, W. $1.60 net. Stokes.
Norman, *Sir* H: All the Russias. il. 8°. $4 net. Scribner.
**Norman, *Sir* H: *See* Young, K. Lippincott.
Normandie series. 20 v. inlaid binding, ea., $1; limp walrus, ea., $2. Crowell.
New volumes: See advertisement.
†Norris, Frank. The pit. 5½ x 8¾. $1.50. Doubleday, P.
Norris, Jos. Last of the Nappingtons. Quail & W.
†Norris, Ma. H. The grapes of wrath. (Beacon lib.) il. 7⅛ x 5¼. pap., 50 c. Small, M.
†Norris, Ma. H. Lakewood. (Copyright ser.) 12°. 50 c. Stokes.
†Norris, W. E. The embarrassing orphan. (Griffin ser.) 12°. $1. Coates.
Norris, Zoe A. Quest of Polly Locke. 12°. $1. J. S. Ogilvie.
*North, F. Mason. City evangelization. 18°. 65 c. net. Lentilhon.
North Carolina stories. McCorkle, *Mrs.* L. il. Heath.
*Northcote, *Lady* Rosalind. Book of herbs. (Handbooks of practical gardening, no. 12.) il. $1 net. Lane.
**Northward over the great ice. Peary, R. E. $5 net-$17.50 net. Stokes.
**Norwegian north polar expedition. Nansen, F., *ed.* v. 3. $12.50 net. Longmans.
**Norwood. Beecher, H: W. $1 net. Pilgrim Press.
**Nosworthy, Florence E. A garden of girls. pictures. 12 x 18. $1 net. Russell.
**Notes from my Bible. Moody, D. L. 25 c. net. Revell.
Notes on the Hebrew text of the Books of Kings. Burney, C. F. Oxford Univ.
*Nothnagel's encyclopedia of practical medicine. Amer. ed. il. 8°. ea., $5 net; hf. mor., $6 net. Saunders.
New volumes: (7) Musser, *ed.*, Diseases of the bronchi, Diseases of the pleura, etc. —(9) Packard, *ed.*, Diseases of the liver, Diseases of the pancreas, etc.
Notre Dame. *See* Hugo, V.

Nova legenda Angliae. 2 v. New ed. 8°. Oxford Univ.
Noyes, W: A. Organic chemistry. Holt.
Nuevo compendio de la gramatica castellana. Bello, A. Appleton.
Nuevo manual de enseñanza objetiva. Appleton.
**Numbers, Commentary on. Gray, G. B. $2.50 net-$3 net. Scribner.
Nurseries of nobility; or, the day of small things; by E. M. P. 40 c. Young.
**Nursery and school menus and recipes. Hogan, Louise E. 50 c. net. Coates.
Nursery rhymes, Humpty Dumpty. col. il. Warne.
Nursery rhymes, Old Mother Goose. col. il. Warne.
Nursery story wonder books. col. il. 3 vols. ea., 50 c. Warne.
Nurse's (A) guide for the operating room. Senn, N. $1.50. Keener.
Nurses, Materia medica for. Groff, J: E. $1.25. Blakiston.
Nursing, Text-book of. Weeks-Shaw, C. S. $1.75. Appleton.
Nymph's reply (The). *See* Raleigh, *Sir* Wa. Russell.
†Ober, F: A. For prey and spoils. il. 12°. $1. Altemus.
Obstetrics. Garrigues, H: J. subs., $5; $6. Lippincott.
Obstetrics, Text-book of. Edgar, J. C. Blakiston.
Obstetrics, Text-book of. Williams, J. W. Appleton.
*Ockhame, W: B. Song of the wedding bells. 16°. $1 net. Grafton Press.
Odyssey, XIII.-XXIV. Homer, *ed.* Oxford Univ.
O'Hara, Theodore. Bivouac of the dead; argument by S. B. Dixon. il. Clarke.
Ohio, Government of. Siebert, W. H. Macmillan.
**Olcott, Mary. Poems. 12°. $1 net. Lane.
**Old court suburb. Hunt, L. 2 v. $12.50 net; $35 net. Lippincott.
**Old country house. Le Gallienne, R: $2.40 net. Harper.
**Old English ballads. (Macmillan's pocket classics.) 18°. 25 c. net. Macmillan.
Old English ballads; ed. by H. W. Mabie; il. by G: W. Edwards. New ed. 8°. Macmillan.
Old English ballads. Kinard, J. P. 40 c. Silver.
**Old English masters. Van Dyke, J: C. $8 net; $150 net. Century.
Old English poetry, Select translations from. Cook, A. S., *ed.* Ginn.
Old English songs and dances; col. il. by G. Robertson. folio. Longmans.
Old-fashioned girl. Alcott, L. M. $2. Little, B. & Co.
Old friends with new faces. Bartlett, *Mrs.* N. G. $1.50. L. C. Page.
Old love-stories retold. Le Gallienne, R: $2. L. C. Page.
Old Mother Goose nursery rhymes. col. il. Warne.
Old Mother Hubbard. il. 11½ x 9¾. bds., $1.25. Jamieson-H.
**Old Testament for the young. Weed, G: L. 60 c. net. Jacobs.

Old Testament heroes. Meyer, F. B. 12°. ea., $1. Revell.
New volume: Samuel and Saul.
Old Testament lessons. Rule, U. Z. Oxford Univ.
**Old time student volunteers. Trumbull, H: C. $1 net. Revell.
Old world series. *See* Mosher's.
Oliver Langton. Powles, G: A. $1.50. Fenno.
†Ollivant, Alf. Danny. il. 5½ x 8¼. $1.50. Doubleday, P.
**Olston, A. B. Mind power and privileges. 12°. $1.50 net. Crowell.
Oman, C: Seven Roman statesmen of the later republic. il. 8°. $1.60. Longmans.
Omar Khayyám. Rubáiyát; tr. by E. Fitzgerald. (New Kalon ser., 50 c.—Laureate ser., 75 c.; $1.50.—Sesame classics, $1.25.) Caldwell.
**Omar Khayyám. Rubáiyát; tr. from the French of J. B. Nicolas, with reprint of French text; introd. by N. H. Dole. 12°. $2.50 net. Lane.
*Omar Khayyám. Rubáiyát; tr. by E: Fitzgerald. Facsimile of *ed. princeps.* 4°. (Mosher's reprints of privately printed books.) $2 net; Jap. vellum, $10 net. Mosher.
*Omar Khayyám. Rubáiyát; tr. by E: Fitzgerald; preface and vocab. by N. H. Dole. (Mosher's vest pocket ser.) 25 c.-$1 net. Mosher.
Omar Khayyám. Rubaiyat; decorative borders by Louis B. Coley. Wieners.
†On fortune's road. Payne, W: $1.50. McClurg.
**On guard. True, J: P. $1.20 net. Little, B. & Co.
On Satan's mount. Tilton, D. C. M. Clark.
†On the cross. Hillern, W. v. $1.50. Biddle.
On the frontier with St. Clair. Wood, C: S. $1.50. Wilde.
†One (The) before. Pain, B. $1.25. Scribner.
One of the red shirts. Hayens, H. $1 net. Jacobs.
One of thirteen. Delano, F. J. $1. Pilgrim Press.
Open air boy. Hewitt, G. M. A. $1.25. Fenno.
Opera (The). Streatfield, R. A. $2, $4.50. Lippincott.
†Opera (An) and Lady Grasmere. Kinross, A. 50 c. Stokes.
Operas. *See* Upton, G: B. McClurg.
Opportunities. Penrose, V. F. Presb. Bd
Optic, Oliver. The boat club. (Chateau ser.) il. 6 x 4. boxed, 75 c. Caldwell.
Oraison funèbre de Louis de Condé, Bossuet. Macmillan.
**Orations, Early American. (Macmillan's pocket classics.) 18°. 25 c. net. Macmillan.
**Orchestral instruments and their use. Elson, Arthur. $1.60 net; $4 net. L. C. Page.
**Orcutt, W: D. Princess Kallisto and other tales. col. il. $2 net. Little, B. & Co.
Ordeal (The) of Elizabeth. $1.50. J. F. Taylor.
Orderly book of Valley Forge. Limited ed. Facsimile reprint. Dodd, Mead & Co.
**Organ and its masters. Lahee, H: C. $1.60 net: $4 net. L. C. Page.
**Organ building, Art of. Audsley, G: A. $15; $25 special net. Dodd, Mead & Co.
**Oriental rugs. Mumford, J: K. $7.50 net. Scribner.
Osborn, L. D. Recovery and statement of the Gospel. Univ. of Chic.
Osborne, E., *and others.* Church fasts and festivals: short papers for young children. il. 4°. 80 c. Young.
Osborne, E., *and others.* Pictorial church teaching: short papers for young children. il. 4°. 80 c. Young.
**Ostrander, Fannie E. Gift of the magic staff. il. 12°. $1 net. Revell.
Ostrogorski, M. Democracy and the organization of political parties; tr. by F: Clarke. 2 v. 8°. Macmillan.
Other boy (The). Sharp, E. Macmillan.
Otis, Ja. The cruise of the "Enterprise." il. $1.50. Wilde.
Ott. How to gesture. New ed. il. Hinds.
**Otto, Alex. F., *and* Holbrook, Theo. S. Mythological Japan. col. il. Lim. ed. 8 x 10½ in. silk, boxed, $7.50 net. Biddle.
Ouida. [*pseud. for* Louise de La Ramé.] Under two flags. Blanche Bates ed. (Green room ed.) il. boxed. 8°. $2.50. Caldwell.
Ourselves and the universe. Brierly, J. Whittaker.
Otway, *Sir* A. *See* Layard, *Sir* H:
Our Bessie. Carey, R. N. $1. Caldwell.
**Our European neighbors ser. Dawson, W: H., *ed.* il. 12°. ea., $1.20 net. Putnam.
New volume: 7, Italian life in town and country, by Luigi Villari.
Our Josephine *and other tales.* Read, O. 75 c. Street.
†Our lady of the beeches. Hutten, *Baroness* von. $1.25. Houghton, M. & Co.
**Our life after death. Chambers, A. 80 c. net. Jacobs.
**Our little African cousin. Wade, M. H. 50 c. net. L. C. Page.
**Our little Cuban cousin. Wade, M. H. 50 c. net. L. C. Page.
**Our little Eskimo cousin. Wade, M. H. 50 c. net. L. C. Page.
**Our little Hawaiian cousin. Wade, M. H. 50 c. net. L. C. Page.
Our little pet's library. 12 v., 6 titles. il. 16°. bds. Per set, $1.80. Whittaker.
**Our little Philippine cousin. Wade, M. H. 50 c. net. L. C. Page.
**Our little Porto Rican cousin. Wade, M. H. 50 c. net. L. C. Page.
Our mutual friend. *See* Dickens, C: Caldwell.
**Our noblest friend, the horse. Ware, F. M. $1.20 net. L. C. Page.
Our reasonable service. Burn, J. H. $1. Young.
Our village. Mitford, M. R. 50 c. Caldwell.
Ourselves and the universe. Brierly, J. 12°. Whittaker.
†Out of Gloucester. Connolly, Ja. B. $1.50. Scribner.

Out of the deep. *See* Kingsley, C: Caldwell.
Out of the heart. Chadwick, J: W. $1.25; $3. L. C. Page.
Out of the hurly burly. Clark, C: H. $1.25. Coates.
†Out of the west. Higgins, E. $1.50. Harper.
**Outdoorland. Chambers, R. W. $1.50 net. Harper.
**Outline studies in the Acts and Epistles. Moorehead, W. G. $1.20 net. Revell.
Ovenden, C: T. In the day of trouble. 12°. 80 c. Young.
Ovenden, C: T. To whom shall we go? 16°. $1. Young.
*Over the black coffee. Gray, A., *comp.* 75 c. net; $1.50 net. Baker & T.
Ovid. Selections. (Macmillan Latin ser.) Macmillan.
Owen, W. C. Telephone lines. Macmillan.
Oxenham, J: Bondman free. 50 c. Federal Bk. Co.
†Oxenham, J: Flowers of the dust. 12°. $1.50. Wessels.
Oxford, *Earl of.* *See* Harley, Robt. Putnam.
Oxford classical texts. Oxford Univ.
New volumes: Homeri Ilias, by D. B. Monro and T. W. Allen.—Euripidis tragoediae, v. 1., ed. by G. G. A. Murray.—Propertii carmina, ed. by J. S. Phillimore.—Ciceronis opera rhetorica, ed. by A. S. Wilkins.
Oxford library of practical theology; ed. by W. C. E. Newbolt *and* D. Stone. Longmans.
New volumes: Mortimer, The creeds.—Pullan, Christian tradition.—Trevelyan, Sunday.
**Oxford, Literary landmarks of. Hutton, L. net. Scribner.
Oxford musical ser. Oxford Univ.
New volumes: The polyphonic period, pt. 1, by H. E. Wooldridge; The 17th century, by *Sir* C. H. H. Parry; Age of Bach and Handel, by J. A. F. Maitland.
†Oxley, J. Macdonald. With Rogers on the frontier. il. 12°. $1.25. Wessels.
Oxoniensis anecdota. *See* Anecdota. Oxford Univ.
†Pabo, the priest. Baring-Gould, S. 50 c. Stokes.
*Packard, F: A., *and* Fitz, R. H., *eds.* Diseases of the liver; Diseases of the pancreas; Diseases of the supra-renals. (Nothnagel's encyclopedia of practical medicine, v. 9.) il. 8°. $5 net; hf. mor., $6 net. Saunders.
Padovan, Adolfo. The sons of glory; tr. by Duchess Litta Visconti Arese. 12°. $1.50. Funk.
†Page, T: N. Captured Santa Claus. col. il. 75 c. Scribner.
†Page's Commonwealth ser. il. 16°. ea., $1.25. L. C. Page.
New volume: No. 6, (New York,) Councils of Crœsus, by Mary K. Potter.
**Page's Cosy corner ser., 1902. il. 12°. ea., 40 c. net. L. C. Page.
Contents: Child's dream of a star and Child's story, by C: Dickens; Cicely, by Annie F. Johnston; Flight of Rosy Dawn, by B. Mackie; Jerry's reward, by E. S. Bartlett; Little giant's neighbors, by F. M. Fox; Millicent in dreamland, by E. S. Brainerd.
**Page's Little cousin ser., 1902; by Wade, Mary H. 6 v. il. in tint. ea., 50 c. net; per set, $3 net. L. C. Page.
Contents: Our little Cuban cousin; Our little Hawaiian cousin; Our little Eskimo cousin; Our little Philippine cousin; Our little Porto Rican cousin; Our little African cousin.
**Page's Music lovers' ser. il. 12°. $1.60 net; ¾ mor., $4 net. L. C. Page.
New volumes: Organ and its masters, by H: C. Lahee; Orchestral instruments and their use, by Arthur Elson.
**Page's Stage lovers' ser. il. 12°. L. C. Page.
New volume: Plays and players of the last quarter century, by Lewis C. Strang. 2 v. $3.20 net; ¾ mor., $8 net.
Page's Travel lovers' library. il. large 16°. L. C. Page.
New volume: Venice, by Grant Allen. 2 v. $3; ¾ mor., $7.
Paget, R. L., *ed.* Cap and gown. Third ser. large 16°. $1.25; hf. mor., $2.50. L. C. Page.
Paget, Violet. *See* Vernon Lee, *pseud.*
†Pain, Barry. The one before. il. 12°. $1.25. Scribner.
Paine, Albert B. The great white way. il. $1.50. J. F. Taylor.
Paint and color mixing. Jennings, A. S. $2. Spon & C.
Paint book, Mother Goose. Barnett, J. M. $1.25. Saalfield.
**Painter's moods (A). Crowninshield, F: $2 net. Dodd, Mead & Co.
Painters, Modern. Ruskin, J: $1.25. Caldwell.
Painters, Sketches of great. Dallin, C. M. 90 c. Silver.
Painters. *See* Bayliss, *Sir* W.
**Palaces, prisons and resting-places of Mary, Queen of Scots. Shoemaker, M. M. $12 net. Brentano.
Palestine. *See* Stewart, Rob. L. Revell.
**Pallen, Condé B. The death of Sir Launcelot, and other poems. 16°. bds., $1 net. Small, M.
**Palliser, *Mrs.* Bury. History of lace. il. 8°. $12 net. Scribner.
*Paloma, Frank. Masters of etching. etchings. folio. $40 net. Cambridge.
*Paloma, Frank. Venus di Milo. 8°. 50 c. net. Cambridge.
Pan-American ser.; by E: Stratemeyer. il. 12°. $1. Lee & Shepard.
New volume: Young volcano explorers.
Pancoast, H: S. Standard English prose. 8°. Holt.
Pancreas, Diseases of the. Mayo-Robinson, A. W. Saunders.
*Pancreas, Diseases of the. *See* Nothnagel's encyclopedia of practical medicine. Saunders.
**Paolo and Francesca; tr. Annunzio, G. d'. $1 net. Stokes.
**Papal monarchy. Barry, W: $1.35 net; $1.60 net. Putnam.
Parables from nature. *See* Gatty, *Mrs.* A.

**Parables of life. Mabie, H. W. $1 net. Dodd, Mead & Co.

Pardoe, Julia. Complete historical works. Lib. ed. 9 v. il. $13.50; ¾ mor., $27. Pott.

Pardoe, Julia. Life of Marie de Medicis. 3 v. il. 12°. $4.50; ¾ mor., $9. Pott.

Pardoe, Julia. Louis XIV. and the court of France in the 17th century. 3 v. il. 12°. $4.50; ¾ mor., $9. Pott.

*Paresis, General. Chase, R. H. $1.75 net. Blakiston.

**Paris, past and present. Haynie, H: 2 v. $4 net; $8 net. Stokes.

Paris "Salons," 1902. *See* Goupil's. Manzi & J.

**Paris, 1789-1794. Alger, J. G. $3; $5 net. Pott.

Paris sketch book. Thackeray, W: M. 75 c. Caldwell.

Park, C. M. Child's pictorial natural history. il. 4°. bds., 50 c. Young.

**Park, Edwards A. Eight sermons. $1.50 net. Pilgrim Press.

†Parker, *Sir* Gilbert. Donovan Pasha. il. 12°. $1.50. Appleton.

†Parker, Gilbert. The lane that had no turning, and other stories. 5½ x 8¼. $1.50. Doubleday, P.

Parker, Gilbert. March of the White Guard. $1.25. Fenno.

Parker, *Sir* Gilbert. Quebec. il. 2 v. 8°. [also] large pap. Macmillan.

Parkinson, R: M. Light railway construction. diagrams. 8°. Longmans.

Parkman, Francis. Struggle for a continent. *See* Edgar, P., *ed.* Little, B. & Co.

Parole (La) française. Sauveur, L. W: R. Jenkins.

Parrott, T: M., *and* Long, A: W., *eds.* English poems: from Chaucer to Kipling. Ginn.

Parry, *Sir* C. H. H. The seventeenth century. (Oxford musical ser.) Oxford Univ.

Pascal, Thoughts of. Smith, B: E., *tr. and ed.* (Thumb-nail ser.) $1. Century.

Pascual López. Bazan, E. P. Ginn.

Passion (A) in the desert. Balzac, H. de. 40 c.-$1.25. Caldwell.

Passionate shepherd to his love. *See* Marlowe, Christopher. Russell.

Past and present. Carlyle, T: $1. Caldwell.

†Pasteboard crown. Morris, C. $1.50. Scribner.

**Pastime and adventure series. Jacobs.
New volumes: Comrie, Loyal Huguenot maid.—"Alien," Maid of mettle.—Robins, Chasing an iron horse.—Hayens, One of the red shirts.—Stoddard, Boys of Bunker academy.—Anderson, Jack Champney.

**Pastors and preachers. Knox, Edm. A. $1.60 net. Longmans.

*Pater, Walter. The Renaissance. 4°. (Mosher's quarto ser.) bds., $4 net; Jap. vellum, $15 net. Mosher.

†Paterson, Arthur. The king's agent. 12°. $1.50. Appleton.

**Patience; or, Bunthorne's bride. Gilbert, W. S. $1 net; $2.50 net. Doubleday, P.

Paton, Ja. Glory and joy of the resurrection. 12°. $1. Am. Tr.

Paton, W: A. Picturesque Sicily. il. cr. 8°. $2.50. Harper.

Patterson, Ada, *and* Bateman, V. By the stage door. 8°. $1.50. Grafton Press.

**Patterson, Alex. Broader Bible study. il. 12°. 75 c. net. Jacobs.

Pattison, A. S. P. Man's place in the cosmos, and other essays. 2d ed. 8°. [Imp.] Scribner.

Patton, Myron O. The lighted taper. 12°. $1.50. Botolph.

**Paul, Herb. W. Matthew Arnold. (English men of letters.) 75 c. net. Macmillan.

Paul and Virginia. St. Pierre, J. H. B. de. 50 c. Caldwell.

†Paul Kelver. Jerome, J. K. $1.50. Dodd, Mead & Co.

Paulding, C: P. Loss of heat from covered steam pipes. Van Nostrand.

Payne, Will. On fortune's road. il. 12°. $1.50. McClurg.

**Payne, W: Morton. Various views. $1 net. McClurg.

†Peak and prairie and Pratt portraits. Fuller, Anna. 2 v. ea., $1.25. Putnam.

Pearls for young ladies. Ruskin, J: 50 c. Caldwell.

*Pears and plums, Book of. Bartrum, E. $1 net. Lane.

Pearson, Karl. Essays in heredity. 8°. Macmillan.

Pearson's Greek prose composition. 90 c. Am. Bk.

**Peary, Rob. E. Northward over the great ice. New ed. il. 2 v. 8°. $5 net; hf. mor., $10 net; mor., $15 net; ¾ levant, $17.50 net. Stokes.

Pêcheur d'Islande. Loti, P. Heath.

Peck, H. T., *ed.* *See* Columbia univ. studies in classical philology. Macmillan.

†Pedagogues (The). Pier, A. S. 50 c. Small, M.

Pedagogy. *See* Dewey, J: The child and the curriculum. 25 c. net. Univ. of Chic.

Peep of day. *See* Mortimer, *Mrs.* M.

**Peer, Frank S. Cross country with horse and hound. il. 8°. $3 net. Scribner.

Peggy Morton. Jacberns, R. 40 c. Young.

Peking, Siege of. *See* Ransome, J. Young.

†Pemberton, Max. House under the sea. il. 12°. $1.50. Appleton.

**Pemberton, T. E. Authorized biography of Bret Harte. il. 8°. $3.50 net. Dodd, Mead & Co.

Pendennis. Thackeray, W: M. $1. Caldwell.

Pendleton, L: Carita. 12°. bds., 75 c. Badger.

†Penelope's Irish experiences. Wiggin, Kate D. $2. Houghton, M. & Co.

Penmanship. *See* Barnes's Natural slant. Am. Bk.

Pennsylvania. *See* Budd, T. Burrows.

Pennsylvania. *See* Tarr and McMurry geographies. Macmillan.

Penrose, *Mrs.* Chubby: a nuisance. il. 8°. Longmans.

Penrose, Margaret. The burglar's daughter. (New Kalon ser.) il. 12°. 50 c. Caldwell.

Penrose, V. F. Opportunities. il. 12°. Presb. Bd.

†Penruddock of the White lambs. Church, S: H. $1.50. Stokes.
**Pentateuch in light of to-day. Holborn, A. 75 c. net. [Imp.] Scribner.
**Pepperell, *Sir* W: Brooks, N. $1 net. Appleton.
†Père Goriot. Balzac, H. de. 75 c. Brentano.
Perfecta Casada (La). Wallace, Eliz., *ed.* 8°. Univ. of Chic.
Peril finders. Fenn, G: M. $2. Young.
**Periods of European literature. Scribner.
New volume: Millar, Mid-eighteenth century.
*Perkins, Clara C. French cathedrals and chateaux. il. 2 v. 8°. $4 net; ¾ levant, $7.50 net. Knight.
Perrine, F. A. C. Conductors for electrical distribution. hf. tones, diagrams. Van Nostrand.
Perry, Bliss. Study of prose fiction. 12°. Houghton, M. & Co.
**Perry, Bliss, *ed.* Second ser. Little masterpieces. 6 v. 4x6. flexible silk cl. and leath. ea., 40 c. net. Doubleday, P.
Contents: Emerson.—Goldsmith.—Milton.—Swift.—Bacon.—Johnson.
Perry, E: D., *ed.* *See* Columbia Univ. studies in classical philology. Macmillan.
Perry, Walter C. Boy's Iliad. il. 8°. Macmillan.
**Perseus and Andromeda. Le Gallienne, R: $1.40 net. Russell.
Persia, Literary history of. Browne, E: G. $4. Scribner.
**Persia, 10,000 miles in. Sykes, P. M. $6 net. Scribner.
Perspective, Linear, shadows and reflections. Fuchs, O. Ginn.
*Pertwee, Ernest. Use of the voice in reading and in speaking. Putnam.
Peru. *See* Baessler, A.
**Peruvian art, Ancient. Baessler, A. per pt., $7.50 special net. Dodd, Mead & Co.
**Pete and Polly stories. Wells, Carolyn. $1.50 net. McClurg.
Peter Simple. Marryatt, F: 79 c. Caldwell.
Peterkin. Molesworth, *Mrs.* Macmillan.
Peterson, W., *ed.* Collations from the codex Cluniacensis s. Holkhamicus (9th century ms. of Cicero.) (Anecdota Oxoniensis ser.) Oxford Univ.
Petites causeries. Sauveur, L. $1. W: R. Jenkins.
Petites causeries, Corrigé des exercises et traductions des. Sauveur, L. 15 c. W: R. Jenkins.
Phantom 'rickshaw. Kipling, R. 75 c. Caldwell.
Phantom ship. Marryatt, F: 79 c. Caldwell.
†Pharaoh and the priest. Glovatski, A. $1.50. Little, B. & Co.
†Phelps, *Mrs.* Eliz. Stuart. Avery. 12°. $1. Houghton, M. & Co.
**Phenomenal fauna (A). Wells, C. A. $1.20 net. Russell.
Phil and Dick. Lewis, E. H. il. $1. Saalfield.

Philanthropy, Constructive and preventive. Lee, Jos. Macmillan.
†Philbrick Howell. Kinross, A. 50 c. Stokes.
Phillimore, J. S., *ed.* *See* Properti. Oxford Univ.
*Phillips, Stephen. Christ in Hades. (Flowers of Parnassus ser., no. 14.) il. 16°. 50 c. net; leath., 75 c. net. Lane.
Phillips, Stephen. David and Bathsheba. [Play.] 16°. [also] large paper ed. Macmillan.
Phillips, Wendell. Selections. (Street and Smith little classics.) 18°. 50 c. Street.
Phillips *and* Strong's Plane and spherical trigonometry. (Tables.) $1.40. Am. Bk.
†Phillpotts, Eden. The river. 12°. $1.50. Stokes.
Philology, Studies in classical. v. 3. Univ. of Chic.
Philosophy, Dictionary of. *See* Baldwin, J. M., *ed.* Macmillan.
Philosophy, History of. Janet, *Prof.* Macmillan.
*Philosophy of despair. Gordon, D: S. 75 c. net; $1.50 net. Elder.
Philpot, W: Pickings from a "Pocket of pebbles." (Miniature volumes.) New ed. marble enamel, 50 c. Stokes.
**Phipson, T. Lamb. Confessions of a violinist. 12°. $1.50 net. Lippincott.
**Phonetics, Elements of experimental. Scripture, E: W. net. Scribner.
**Photographs. Why my photographs are bad. Taylor, C: M., *jr.* $1 net. Jacobs.
Photography. Vogel, E. Macmillan.
Phrenology. Fowler's new chart for the use of examiners, giving a delineation of the character. Fowler.
Physical characters of Indians of Southern Mexico. Starr, F: 75 c. net. Univ. of Chic.
**Physical culture and self-defense. Fitzsimmons, R. $1.50 net. Biddle.
Physical diagnosis. Gibson, G. A. $3. Appleton.
Physical geography. *See* Dryer's. Am. Bk.
Physicians. *See* Foster, H: Revell.
Physics. Andrews, E. J. Macmillan.
Physics, Brief course in, Hoadley's. $1.20. Am. Bk.
Physics, Elementary. Miller, F. W. Scribner.
Physics, Laboratory exercises in. Twiss, G: R. Macmillan.
Physics, Teaching of. *See* Smith, Alex. Longmans.
Physiological aspects of the liquor problem. Committee of Fifty. 2 v. Houghton, M. & Co.
**Physiology, fear and faith. Sperry, L. B. 25 c net. Revell.
Physiology, Studies in general. Loeb, Jacques. Univ. of Chic.
Physiology. *See* New century. Am. Bk.
Physiology. *See* Rossiter, F: M. Revell.
Physiology. *See also* Whittaker's.
Pianoforte tone production. Matthay, T. Longmans.
Picciola. Saintine, J. X. B. Super, O. B., *ed.* Heath.
**Pick, Bernhard. A canonical life of Christ. 12°. $1.20 net. Funk.

Pick of the basket. Allen, P. $1. Young.
Pickering, Edgar. Beggars of the sea. $1.50. Warne.
Pickering, Edgar. True to the watchword. il. $1.50. Warne.
**Pickering, W: H. The moon. il. 8 x 11. $10 special net. Doubleday, P.
Pickett's gap. Greene, H. Macmillan.
Pickings from a "Pocket of pebbles." Philpot, W: 50 c. Stokes.
Picton, Esther A. Master Herbert: a reminiscence. pap., 25 c. Young.
Pictorial church teaching. Osborne, E. 80 c. Young.
Picture book, Sunbeam. 75 c. Warne.
Pictures, Famous. *See* Hundred most famous pictures. Stokes.
Pictures of Paintbox Town. Dotey, D. Z. $1. Dutton.
**Pictures of romance and wonder. Burne-Jones, *Sir* E: $5 net. Russell.
Pidgin, C: F. The climax. $1.50. C. M. Clark.
†Pier, Arthur S. The pedagogues. (Harvard lib.) pap., 50 c. Small, M.
Pierce, G: J. Plant physiology. Holt.
Pierson, Arthur T. Lesson in the school of prayer. (New Kalon ser.) il. 12°. 50 c. Caldwell.
**Pierson, Clara D. Among the night people. il. 12°. $1.20 net. Dutton.
Pigmies (The). Hawthorne, N. 50 c. Caldwell.
Pilgrim shore. Garrett, E. H. $1.50; $1. Little, B. & Co.
**Pilgrim songs, No. 2. Per 100, $35 net; bds., $25 net. Pilgrim Press.
†Pilgrim's progress. Bunyan, J: $1.50; $3.50. Lippincott.
Pinches, T. G. The Old Testament, in the light of historical records and legends of Assyria and Babylonia. 12°. $3. Young.
**Pine tree ballads. Day, H. F. $1 net. Small, M.
Pine tree flag. Allen, W. B. $1.25. Pilgrim Press.
Ping-pong. Ritchie, M. J. G. 50 c. Lippincott.
**Ping-pong verse, Little book of. 75 c. net. Estes.
Pinturicchio. Ricci, Corraido. Lippincott.
**Pipes of Pan. Carman, Bliss. ea., $1 net. L. C. Page.
Contents: No. 1, From the Book of Myths; No. 2, From the Green Book of the Bards.
Pippa passes. *See* Browning, R.
Pirate frog, and other tales. Frisbie, W. A. $1. Rand, McN. & Co.
†Pit (The). Norris, Frank. $1.50. Doubleday, P.
Pitmanic shorthand instructor. *See* Platt's. Am. Bk.
Place of industry in elementary education. Dopp, Kath. E. Univ. of Chic.
Plainsmen (The). Remington, F: (Pictures.) 4 in box. $3. Scribner.
Planometer areas. Molesworth. 50 c. Spon & C.
**Plant form. Lilley, A. E. $2 net. Scribner.
Plant life, Introduction to the study of. Stevens, W. C. Heath.
Plant physiology. Pierce, G: J. Holt.
**Plantation bird legends. Sheppard, E. $1.60 net. Russell.
**Plants, Plea for hardy. Elliott, J. W. $1.60 net. Doubleday, P.
Plants, Rôle of diffusion and osmotic pressure in. Livingston, B. E. Univ. of Chic.
Plants. *See* Henslow, G. Young.
Platner, J. W. Early Christian literature from Paul to Eusebius. (New Testament handbooks.) 12°. Macmillan.
Platt's Pitmanic shorthand instructor. $1.20. Am. Bk.
Plautus. Rudens. Sonnenschein, E. A., *ed.* 8°. Oxford Univ.
**Play away. Allen, W. B. 75 c. net. Estes.
Played on hearts. Ballou, C. E. $1; 50 c. J. S. Ogilvie.
**Plays and players of the last quarter-century. Strang, Lewis C. 2 v. $3.20 net; $8 net. L. C. Page.
**Pleasures (The) of the table. Ellwanger, G: H. $2.50 net. Doubleday, P.
*Pleura, Diseases of the. *See* Nothnagle's encyclopedia of practical medicine. Saunders.
Pliny the younger, Selected letters; ed. by E. T. Merrill. Macmillan.
†Plucky Nell. Baldwin, M. $1.50. Lippincott.
*Plums, Book of. *See* Pears. Lane.
Plutarch. Lives. New Sterling ed. 3 v. 12°. $3; hf. cf., $6. Estes.
Plutarch. Lives. Oxford ed. Dryden's tr. 5 v. 8°. $7.50; hf. mor., $17.50. Little, B. & Co.
Plutarch. Lives. Author's ed. New issue. 3 v. buckram, $3; hf. leath., $4.50; hf. calf, $6. Wessels.
Plutarch's life of Cicero, Sources of. Gudeman, A. Ginn.
†Plympton, A. G. In the shadow of the black pine. (Beacon lib.) pap., 50 c. Small, M.
Pneumatotherapy and inhalation methods. Tissier, P. Blakiston.
*Pneumonia. *See* Nothnagel's encyclopedia of practical medicine. Saunders.
Pocket library. *See* Lane's. Lane.
Pocket of pebbles, Picking from. Philpot, W: 50 c. Stokes.
Pocketful of posies. Brown. Abbie F. Houghton, M. & Co.
Poco à poco. Johnson, W: F. $1.50. Saalfield.
Poe, Edgar Allan. Complete works. De luxe lib. ed. 17 v. il. $21; hf. cf., $42. Crowell.
Poe, Edgar Allan. Complete works. Virginia ed. il. 17 v. 18°. per set, $12.50; $21; $35. Crowell.
Poems, English, from Chaucer to Kipling. Parrott, T: M., *ed.* Ginn.
**Poems of mother and daughter. 5 x 7. $1.20 net. Doubleday, P.
**Poet and Penelope. Truscott, L. P. Putnam.
Poetry, Old English. Select translations from. Cook, A. S., *ed.* Ginn.
Poisonous plants in field and garden. Henslow, G. $1. Young.
**Polar expedition, Norwegian. *See* Nansen, F. Longmans.

*Political economy, Principles of. Denslow, V. B. $3 net. Cambridge.
Political economy. *See* Laughlin's. Am. Bk.
Political history of slavery. *See* Slavery. Putnam.
**Political history of the U. S. Gordy, J. P. v. 3 and 4. ea., $1.75 net. Holt.
Political parties, Organization of. Ostrogorski, M. Macmillan.
Pollard, A. F. Germany and the empire, 1500-1792. (Cambridge historical ser.) 12°. Macmillan.
**Pollard, A. F. Henry VIII. il. Edition de luxe. 4°. $50 net; hf. mor., $25 net. Scribner.
†Polly Perkins' adventures. Liddell, E. L. $1. Altemus.
**Polly's secret. Nash, H. A. $1.20 net. Little, B. & Co.
**Polo, Modern. Miller. E. D. $5 net. [Imp.] Scribner.
Polyphonic period. Wooldridge, H. E. Oxford Univ.
Pompeii. Mau, A. Macmillan.
Poole, R. L., *ed.* Historical atlas of modern Europe from the decline of the Roman empire. pts. 28-30. Oxford Univ.
Poole, R. L., *and* Bateson, Mary, *eds.* Bale's Index Britanniæ scriptorum. (Anecdota Oxoniensis ser.) Oxford Univ.
**Poole, Stanley L. Mediæval India under Mohammedan rule. (Story of the nations ser., 64.) il. 12°. $1.35 net; hf. leath., $1.60 net. Putnam.
Poor man's palace. Challacombe, J. 20 c. Young.
Pope, Alex. Complete poems. Boynton, H: W., *ed.* Cambridge ed. cr. 8°. $2. Houghton, M. & Co.
Popular library. 10 v. ea., $1.25. Crowell. *New volumes:* Motley, Rise of the Dutch Republic.—Prescott. Conquest of Mexico; Conquest of Peru.
**Porter, *Admiral.* Soley, J. R. $1.50 net. Appleton.
Porter *and* Clarke's Shakespeare studies: Macbeth. 56 c. Am. Bk.
Potter, Beatrix. Tale of Peter Rabbit. col. il. 50 c. Warne.
**Potter, H: C. Citizen and the industrial situation. 12°. $1 net. Scribner.
**Potter, H: C. The east of to-day and to-morrow. 12°. $1 net. Century.
†Potter, Marg. H. Istar of Babylon. post 8°. $1.50. Harper.
**Potter, Mary K. Art of the Vatican. il. large 12°. $2 net; ¼ mor., $4 net. L. C. Page.
†Potter, Mary K. Councils of Croesus. (Commonwealth ser.) il. large 16°. $1.25. L. C. Page.
Powell, F. Y., *ed.* *See* Vigfusson, G. Oxford Univ.
**Power of truth, individual problems, and possibilities. Jordan, W: G: 75 c. net. Brentano.
Powles. G: A. Oliver Langton. $1.50. Fenno.
Praag, Fs. W. van. Weaving of webs. 12°. $1.50. Fenno.
*Practical wisdom. Raleigh, *Sir* Wa. $3 net. Wessels.
Practical wisdom, letters to young men. Raleigh, *Sir* Wa. $1; $1.25. Wessels.
**Practice of immortality. Gladden, W. 25 c. net. Pilgrim Press.
Praed, *Mrs.* Campbell. The insane root. 12°. $1.50. Funk.
Praeparatio evangelica. Eusebius. Oxford Univ.
Prague. Lutzow, *Count.* Macmillan.
Pratt, Sereno S. The work of Wall Street. 12°. (Appleton's business ser.) Appleton.
†Pratt portraits. *See* Fuller, Anna. Putnam.
*Prayer book, Companion to the. Hall, A. C. A. 35 c. net. Young.
Prayer, Divine ordinance of. Aitkin, W. H. $1.25. Young.
**Prayer, Extempore. Talling, M. P. $1.25 net. Revell.
Prayer, Suggestions on. Soulsby, L. H. M. 50 c. Longmans.
Prayers ancient and modern; sel. and arr. for daily reading. New ed. 18°. $1.50. Little, B. & Co.
**Prayers of Dr. Johnson. $1; $2.50; $5 net. McClure.
Preacher's daughter. Barr, A. E. $1.25. Pilgrim Press.
Precept upon precept. Mortimer, *Mrs.* M. 50 c. Caldwell.
Pre-Christian antiphons: antiphons to the Magnificat; printed in gold and colors. 25 c. Young.
Precious thoughts. Ruskin, J: 50 c. Caldwell.
Presbyterian pulpit. v. 1 and 2. 12°. Presb. Bd.
Contents: v. 1., Purves, Sermons.—v. 11., Richards, For whom Christ died.
Prescott. W: H. Selections. (Street and Smith little classics.) 18°. 50 c. Street.
[President of U. S.] History of the appointing power. Salmon, L. M. Macmillan.
Prettiman, C. W., *ed.* *See* Schiller, F. v. Heath.
Price, C. Leading ideas of Keble's Christian year. 32°. 20 c. Young.
Price, Lillian L. Wandering heroes. (Stories of heroes.) il. 50 c. Silver.
Price, Lillian L., *and* Gilbert, C: B. Heroes of myth. (Stories of heroes.) il. Silver.
Price's Observations, etc., on the weather. 30 c. Am. Bk.
Prices, History of. *See* Rogers, J. E. Thorold. Oxford Univ.
**Prideaux, S. T. Phases of the art of bookbinding. il. 8°. net. Scribner.
Priestly blemishes. Newbolt, W. C. E. Longmans.
Primer of right and wrong. Larned, J. N. Houghton, M. & Co.
Prince, Dyneley. *See* Leland, C: G. Funk.
†Prince, Helen C. Strongest master. 12°. $1.50. Houghton, M. & Co.
**Prince Silver Wings. Harrison, E. O. $1.75 net. McClurg.
**Princess Kallisto and other tales. Orcutt, W: D. $2 net. Little, B. & Co.
Principles of general method based on Herbart. McMurray, C: A. Macmillan.
**Printers, Some early. Kennard, Jos. S. $3 net. Jacobs.

**Private soldier under Washington. Bolton, C: K. $1.25 net. Scribner.
**Problems of the town church. Miller, G: A. 75 c. Revell.
Professor at the breakfast table. Holmes, O. W. 50 c. Caldwell.
*Progression to immortality. Brooks, H. S. 50 c. net. Wessels.
**Prologue and Knight's tale. Chaucer, G. 25 c. net. Macmillan.
Propertii carmina. Phillimore, J. S., *ed.* (Oxford class. ser.) Oxford Univ.
Prophecy, Grammar of. Girdlestone, R. B. $2.50. Young.
Prophylaxis. *See* McFarland, Jos. Blakiston.
**Prothalamion and Epithalamion. Spenser, E. Price on application. Houghton, M. & Co.
Prothero, G. W. *See* Cambridge historical series. Macmillan.
Prothero, G. W. *See* Ward, A. W.
Pryor, G. L. Neither bound nor free. 12°. $1. J. S. Ogilvie.
Pryor, W: R. Text-book of gynecology. Appleton.
Psalms, Book of. Cheyne, T. K. New ed. 2 v. 8°. $9.60. Whittaker.
Psalms, Student's handbook to. Sharpe, J. $2.50. Young.
Psychological basis of religious faith. Everett, C: C. Macmillan.
Psychological norms in men and women. Thompson, Helen B. Univ. of Chic.
Psychology. Aristotle. Macmillan.
Psychology, Dictionary of. *See* Baldwin, J. M., *ed.* Macmillan.
Psychology, Outlines of. Royce, J. Macmillan.
Public exposition and argumentation. Baker, G: P. Holt.
Publications of the Univ. of Pa. ser. in philology, literature and archæology. Ginn.
New volume. Gudeman, Sources of Plutarch's life of Cicero.
Puggery Wee. Frisbie, W. A. $1. Rand, McN. & Co.
Pullan, Leighton. The Christian tradition. (Oxford lib. of practical theology.) Longmans.
**Puritan knight errant. Robinson, Edith. $1.20 net. L. C. Page.
Purón, Juan G. Geografía física superior ilustrada des Appleton. Nueva ed. Appleton.
Purón, Juan G. La moral en ejemplos históricos. Nueva ed. Appleton.
**Pursuit of character. Willett, H. L. 35 c. net. Revell.
Purves, G: T. Sermons. (Presbyterian pulpit.) 12°. Presb. Bd.
Pusey, P: E: Tetraeuangelium sanctum. Gwilliam, G: H:, *ed.* Oxford Univ.
Pushtu mss. in Bodleian library. *See* Ethé, H. Oxford Univ.
Putnam's Library of standard literature. 8°. ea., $1.75. Putnam.
New volume: (8) Carlyle's French Revolution; ed. by C. R. L. Fletcher.
Pycraft, W. P. Story of fish life. (Story of ser.) 16°. 75 c. Wessels.
**Pyle, Katharine. Careless Jane, and other tales. il. 12°. 75 c. net. Dutton.
**Pyle, Katharine. In the green forest. il. 8°. $1.50 net. Little, B. & Co.
**Pyle, Katharine. Where the wind blows. il. 6¾ x 10½. $2.50 net. Russell.
"Q," *pseud.* for Quiller-Couch, A. T.
Quail, Jos. N. Adventures of Dick Lee. Quail & W.
Quain's dictionary of medicine. New rev., enl. ed. for 1902. pl. hf. mor., $10. Appleton.
Qualitative chemical analysis. Garvin, J: B. Heath.
Quantitative experiments. Titchener, E: B. 2 pts. Macmillan.
Quarto series. *See* Mosher's.
Quebec. Parker, *Sir* G. 2 v. Macmillan.
†Queen of Quelparte. Hulbert, A. R. $1.50. Little, B. & Co.
**Queen's rosary (The). Van Cleve, A. D. $1.20 net. Russell.
Quest of happiness. Hillis, N. D. Macmillan.
Quest of Polly Locke. Norris, Zoe A. $1. Ogilvie.
**Quest of the Holy Grail. Abbey, E. A. $5 net. Curtis & C.
**Questions of the day ser. Putnam.
New volume: (99) Industrial conciliation: Proceedings of conference of National Civic Federation, Dec. 16-17, 1901.
Quiet hour ser. *See* Revell's. Revell.
†Quiller-Couch, A. T., ["Q," *pseud.*] Collection of stories. 12°. $1.50. Scribner.
**Quiver of arrows (A). [Sermons.] Burrell, D: J. $1.20 net. Funk.
Quiz compends. Blakiston.
New volumes: Cushing, Compend of histology.—Hatfield, Diseases of children.
Quotations, Familiar. Bartlett, J: 50 c.-$1.50. Caldwell.
Quran (The) and the Bible. 12°. $1. Am. Tr.
Rab and his friends. Brown, J: 75 c. Caldwell.
**Rabbi Ben Ezra. Slade, W: 50 c. net. Crowell.
Rabelais, François. Works. (Museum editions.) il. 4 v. leath., $4. Brentano.
Rabelais, François. Gargantua. (Macmillan's French classics.) Macmillan.
†Racer of Illinois. Somerville, H: $1.50. McClure.
Racine, J. Andromaque, Britannicus and Athalie; ed. by F. M. Warren. Holt.
*Radan, Hugo. Creation story of Genesis. 9 x 6. 75 c. net. Open Court.
Radcliffe-Whitehead, Jeannette B. Birds of God. Pictures. Text by R. Radcliffe-Whitehead. 11¼ x 14. $3. Russell.
*Rader, W: Elegy of faith. 50 c. net. Crowell.
Radford, B. Dauntless three. 16°. 40 c. Young.
†Ragged edge. McIntyre, J: T. $1.25. McClure.
Railroading with Christ. Dwight, C: A. S. 35 c. Am. Tr.
Railway construction, Light. Parkinson, R: M. Longmans.
Rain blossoms. Brooks, E. H. 80 c. Young.
Rainbows. Custance, *Lady.* 16°. $1.25. Lane.

**Rainsford, W. S. The reasonableness of faith, and other addresses. 5 x 8. $1.25 net. Doubleday, P.
Rainy, R. *See* Hutchinson, R. Keener.
**Rainy, Rob. Later Catholic church. (International theological lib.) $2 net. Scribner.
Raleigh, *Sir* Wa. The nymph's reply; cont. in Marlowe's Passionate shepherd to his love. Russell.
Raleigh, *Sir* Wa., Hale, *Sir* M., *and others.* Practical wisdom: letters to young men. (Bradford ser.) 16°. $1; limp crushed leath., $1.25. Wessels.
*Raleigh, *Sir* Wa., Saville, *Sir* G:, *and others.* Practical wisdom. (A. L. Humphreys' large type books.) 16°. pap., $3 net. Wessels.
Ralph, Julian. An American with Lord Roberts. (Copyright ser.) 12°. 50 c. Stokes.
†Ralph, Julian. The millionaires. il. 5¼ x 7¾. $1.50. Lothrop.
Ralph, Julian. Towards Pretoria. (Copyright ser.) 12°. 50 c. Stokes.
Ralph Granger's fortunes. Brown, W: P. $1. Saalfield.
Ralph Wayward. Elrington, H. $1. Nelson.
Ramanuga's Sribhashya. Thibaut, G., *tr.* (Sacred books of the East, no. 48.) Oxford Univ.
Rand gold mining. Stuart, J: $1.50. Warne.
Randall, O. E. Shades, shadows and perspective. Ginn.
Ransome, Jessie. Story of the siege hospital in Peking, and diary of events from May to August. 12°. 60 c. Young.
Ranson's folly. Davis, R: H. $1.50. Scribner.
*Rape of the earth. Godolphin, E. C. $3 net. Cambridge.
**Rataplan. Velvin, Ellen. $1.25 net. Altemus.
Rawlinson, G: Seven great monarchies. Author's ed. New issue. 3 v. buckram, $3; hf. leath., $4.50; hf. calf, $6. Wessels.
**Ray, Anna C. Nathalie's chum. il. 12°. $1.20 net. Little, B. & Co.
Raymond, Evelyn. Breakneck farm. il. 12°. $1.25. Street.
†Rayner, Emma. Free to serve. (Beacon lib.) 7⅛ x 5¼. pap., 50 c. Small, M.
†Rayner, Emma. Visiting the sin. (Beacon lib.) pap., 50 c. Small, M.
Read, Opie. Our Josephine, and other tales. 75 c. Street.
Read, Opie. The Starbucks. il. 12°. $1.50. Laird.
†Reade, C: Cloister and the hearth. (Turner house classics.) il. 12°. 75 c. Brentano.
†Reade, C: Cloister and the hearth. Edition de luxe. il. New ed. 4°. $3.50. Stokes.
Reade, C: Selections. (Street and Smith little classics.) 18°. 50 c. Street.
Reade, F. E. Triumph of love. 16°. 40 c. Young.
Reader, Middle English. Emerson, O. F. Macmillan.
Readers. *See* Baldwin's.—New education readers.—New McGuffey readers. Am. Bk.
Reading, Comprehensive method of teaching. Gordon, Emma K. Heath.
Reading, Interpretative. Marsland, C. Longmans.
**Reading, Lost art of. Lee, Gerald S. net. Putnam.
Reading (Primary) Special method in. McMurry, C: A. Macmillan.
Reading, Special method in. McMurry, C: A. Macmillan.
**Readings, Handbook of best. Clark, S. H. $1.50 net. Scribner.
Reagan, H. C. Locomotives: simple, compound and electric. 4th ed. 12°. $2. Wiley.
Reason and revelation. Illingworth, J. R. Macmillan.
**Reasonableness of faith. Rainsford, W. S. $1.25 net. Doubleday, P.
†Rebel of the school. Meade, L. T. $1.50. Lippincott.
Reciprocity. Laughlin, J. L. Baker & T.
Recollections of a long life. *See* Cuyler, T. L.
**Recollections of a player. Stoddart, J. H. $1.80 net. Century.
Recollections of Dublin castle and Dublin society. 12°. $1.25. Brentano.
Recovery and statement of the Gospel. Osborn, L. D. Univ. of Chic.
†Red box clew. Ellis, J. B. 50 c. Revell.
**Red folk and wild folk. Deming, T. O. $1.60 net. Stokes.
**Red-head. Lloyd, J: U. $1.60 net. Dodd, Mead & Co.
†Red house (The). Nesbit, E. $1.50. Harper.
†Red letter ser. pap., ea., 50 c. New Amsterdam.
Red shirts (The). Hamblen, H. E. $1.50. Street.
**Reddale, F:, *comp.* Wit and humour of American statesmen. 16°. 50 c. net; leath., 80 c. net. Jacobs.
Redman of quality. Billings, E: E. $1.25. Saalfield.
Reed, Fanny. Reminiscences: musical and other. 12°. $1.50. Knight.
**Reed, Helen L. Brenda's cousin at Radcliffe. il. 12°. $1.20 net. Little, B. & Co.
**Reed, Myrtle. Lavender and old lace. 12°. $1.50 net; red leath., $2 net; gray ooze leath., $2.50 net; lavender silk, $3.50 net. Putnam.
Refrigeration, Mechanical. Williams, H. Macmillan.
Reichel, G: V. What shall I tell the children? 12°. $1. Whittaker.
**Reid, J. Eadie. *Sir* J: E. Millais. (Makers of British art.) il. 8°. $1.25 net. [Imp.] Scribner.
Reign of King Oberon and Queen Titania. Jerrold, W. Macmillan.
**Religion for the time. Conger, A. B. $1 net. Jacobs.
Religion of the crescent. Tisdall, W. St. C. $1. Young.
Religious classics. 18 v. ea., $1. Crowell.
New volumes: See advertisement.
Religious faith, Psychological basis of. Everett, C: C. Macmillan.
*Reliques of Stratford-on-Avon. Way, A. E., *comp.* 50 c. net; 75 c. net. Lane.

Remarque ser. 3⅞ x 5⅝. 40 c.; limp leath., boxed, 75 c.; limp chamois, $1.25. Caldwell.
New volumes: Stevenson, Will o' the mill.—Browning, Men and women.—Napoleon's addresses and anecdotes.—Balzac. Passion in the desert.

Remington, F: A bunch of buckskins. 8 pastel drawings. 20 x 26. In portfolio. $6; single prints, $1. Russell.

**Remington, F: New Remington book. Pictures. Text by O. Wister. Japan vellum. 12 x 18. boxed, $5 net; lim. ed. de luxe, $10 net. Russell.

Remington, F: The plainsmen. col. pictures. 4 in box, $3. Scribner.

Remington, F: Waif of the plains. il. 12°. Macmillan.

Renaissance (The). (Cambridge modern history.) Macmillan.

Renaissance (The). *See* Pater, W. Mosher.

Representative English comedies. Gayley, C: M., *ed.* 5 v. 8°. Macmillan.

Representative men of the Bible. Matheson, G: Armstrong.

Requiem. Stevenson, R. L: 10 c. Elder.

Respiratory system, Diseases of. Allchin, W. H. Macmillan.

Response in the living and non-living. Bose, J. C. Longmans.

**Retrospect and prospect. Mahan, A. T. $1.60 net. Little, B. & Co.

Revell's Quiet hour ser. Revell.
New volume: Faith, fellowship and fealty, by C. B. McAfee.

†Revenge. Barr, R. 50 c. Stokes.

**Revenge of Adnah. Ellis, J. B. $1 net. Jacobs.

Reynolds, *Sir* Joshua. Gower, *Lord* R. S. Macmillan.

**Reynolds, *Sir* Joshua. Keeling, E. D'E. $1.25 net. [Imp.] Scribner.

Reynolds, Myra, *ed.* *See* Fitch, Anne. Univ. of Chic.

**Rhead, L:, *ed.* Speckled brook trout. il. Imitation birch bark. 6 x 8. $3.50 net; lim. ed. de luxe, $16 net. Russell.

Rhetoric, College manual of. Baldwin, C: S. Longmans.

**Rhodes, Nina. The little girl next door. il. 12°. 80 c. net. Lee & Shepard.

**Rhode Island: its making and its meaning. Richman, Irving B. $5 net. Putnam.

**Rhymes and roundelays from *Life.* 60 c. net; leath., $1.20 net. Doubleday, P.

Ricci, Corrado. Pinturicchio. il. 4°. Lippincott.

*Rice, Edwin W. Short history of the international lesson system. 25 c. net. Am. S. S.

Rice's Rational spelling bk. pt. 1, 17 c.; pt. 2, 22 c. Am. Bk.

Rich and poor in the New Testament. Cone, O. Macmillan.

†Richard Gordon. Black, A. $1.50. Lothrop.

Richard Hume. Warnock, T. D. $1.25. Fenno.

**Richards, Laura E. The hurdy-gurdy. 4°. 75 c. net. Estes.

†Richards, Laura E. Mrs. Tree. 16°. 75 c. Estes.

Richards, W: R. For whom Christ died. (Presbyterian pulpit.) 12°. Presb. Bd.

**Richardson. Dobson, A. 75 c. net. Macmillan.

**Richman, Irving B. Rhode Island: its making and its meaning. 2 v. maps. 8°. $5 net. Putnam.

**Ricketson, Anna *and* Walton. Daniel Ricketson and his friends. il. $4 net. Houghton, M. & Co.

**Ricketson, Daniel, and his friends. Ricketson, Anna. $4 net. Houghton, M. & Co.

Rider, J. H. Electric traction. 12°. Macmillan.

Riehl, W: H. v. Fluch der Schönheit. Thomas, Calvin, *ed.* Heath.

†Right princess. Burnham, Clara L. $1.50. Houghton, M. & Co.

Riis, Jacob A. Battle with the slum. il. Macmillan.

**Rijnhart, Susie C. In the land of the llamas. (Tibet.) 12°. 75 c. net. Revell.

**Riley, I. W. The founder of Mormonism: a psychological study of Joseph Smith, *jr.* 12°. $1.50 net. Dodd, Mead & Co.

**Riley, Ja. W. Book of joyous children. il. 12°. $1.50 net. Scribner.

†Risley, R. V. The life of a woman. 12°. $1.50. Stone.

Ritchie, Ja. *See* Muir, R. Macmillan.

Ritchie, M. J. G., *and* Harris, Wa. Ping-pong. il. 16°. 50 c. Lippincott.

Rivals (The). *See* Sheridan, R: B.

†River (The). Phillpotts, E. $1.50. Stokes.

Rivers, Improvement of. Thomas, B. F. Wiley.

†Road (The) to Ridgeby's. Harris, F. B. 50 c. Small, M.

Roads and pavements, Treatise on. Baker, I. O. $5 net. Wiley.

**Rob and his gun. Linn, W: A. $1 net. Scribner.

Robbins, Wilford L. A Christian apologetic. (Handbooks for the clergy.) Longmans.

†Robert Orange. Hobbes, J: O. 50 c. Stokes.

†Roberts, C: G. D. Barbara Ladd. il. in tint. 12°. $1.50. L. C. Page.

**Roberts, E. P. Adventures of Capt. J: Smith. maps and il. 8°. $1.50 net. Longmans.

*Robertson, J: G. History of German literature. Putnam.

Robertson of Erromonga, *Rev.* H. A. Erromonga, the martyr isle. Armstrong.

Robinhood. (New Kalon ser., 50 c.—Sesame classics, $1.25.) Caldwell.

**Robins, E: Chasing an iron horse. (Pastime and adventure ser.) il. 12°. $1 net. Jacobs.

**Robbins, E: Romances of early America. il. cr. 8°. $2.50 net; levant, $5 net. Jacobs.

†Robins, Eliz. The magnetic north. 12°. $1.50. Stokes.

Robinson, E., *tr.* Hebrew and English lexicon of the Old Testament based on lexicon of Gesenius. Brown, F., Driver, S. R., Briggs, C. A., *eds.* pt. 10. Oxford Univ.

**Robinson, Edith. Puritan knight errant. il. 12°. $1.20 net. L. C. Page.

**Robinson, Edwin A. Captain Craig: a book of poems. 12°. $1 net; uncut ed., 125 copies, bds., $1.25 net. Houghton, M. & Co.
Robinson, H. P., *comp.* *See* Canton, W. Putnam.
Robinson, J. Armitage. Study of the gospels. (Handbooks for the clergy.) Longmans.
Robinson, Ja. H. Introduction to the history of western Europe. il. pt. 1, Middle ages. Ginn.
Robinson Crusoe. *See* Defoe, Dan.
†Roche, Ja. Jeffrey. Her majesty the king. il. 5¼ x 7¾. $1.50. Russell.
Rochester, and other literary rakes of the court of Charles II. il. 8°. Longmans.
Roddy's geographies. Elementary, 50 c.—Complete. $1. Am. Bk.
Roger Drake. Webster, H. K. Macmillan.
Rogers, G: B. *See* Kirtland, J. C., *jr.* Macmillan.
Rogers, J. E. Thorold. History of agriculture and prices. v. 7. Oxford Univ.
†Rogue's daughter (A). Sargeant, A. 50 c. Stokes.
Roland, Le chanson de; ed. by J. Geddes, jr. (Macmillan's French classics.) Macmillan.
Roll-call of Westminster Abbey. Smith, *Mrs.* E. T. M. Macmillan.
**Roller bandage. Hopkins, W: B. $1.50. net. Lippincott.
**Rollicking rhymes for youngsters. Wells, Amos R. $1 net. Revell.
Rollin, C: Ancient history. Authors' ed. New issue. 4 v. buckram, $4; hf. leath., $6; hf. calf, $8. Wessels.
Rollins, Clara S. Threads of life. 16°. bds., 50 c. Badger.
Roman empire. Hist. of the decline and fall of the. Gibbon, E: $5-$10. Wessels.
Roman history. *See* Morey's. Am. Bk.
†Roman mystery (A). Bagot, R: $1.50. Lane.
Roman roads in Britain. Codrington, T. map. Young.
Roman statesmen of the later republic, Seven. Oman, C: $1.60. Longmans.
Romance and reality of the Puritan coast. Garrett, E. H. $1.50; $1. Little, B. & Co.
**Romance, Book of. Lang, A. $1.60 net. Longmans.
†Romance of a mummy. Gautier, T. $1.25. Lippincott.
Romance of an old fool. Field, R. $2. W. S. Lord.
**Romance of Cinderella. Boult, M. $2.40 net. Russell.
**Romance of modern invention. Williams, A. $1.50 net. Lippincott.
**Romance of old New England rooftrees. Crawford, Mary C. $1.20 net; $2.50 net. L. C. Page.
**Romance of the Colorado River. Dellenbaugh, F: S. net. Putnam.
*Romance of the commonplace. Burgess, G. $1.50 net-$15 net. Elder.
**Romance of the nursery. Harker, *Mrs.* A. $1.25. Lane.
Romance of Wolf hollow. Wolfrom, A. $1 Badger.
**Romances of early America. Robins, E: $2.50 net; $5 net. Jacobs.
Romans. Epistle to the, Commentary on. Beet, J. A. $2.50. Whittaker.
Rome. Ave Roma immortalis. Crawford, F. M. Macmillan.
**Romney, G: Maxwell, *Sir* H. $1.25 net. [Imp.] Scribner.
**Ronald, Mary. Luncheons. il. $1.40 net. Century.
Roof trusses in wood and steel, Design of: with an introduction to the elements of graphic statics. Howe, M. A. $2. Wiley.
Roosevelt, Theo., Life of. Halstead, M. $2.50-$5. Saalfield.
**Rosalind, Story of. (Caxton ser.) il. lambskin, $1.25 net. Scribner.
Roscoe, *Sir* H: E. Lessons in elementary chemistry. New ed. Macmillan.
**Rosegger, P: The earth and the fullness thereof; tr. by Frances E. Skinner. 12°. $1.50 net. Putnam.
Roseneau, M. J. Disinfection and disinfections. il. 12°. $2. Blakiston.
**Roses for English gardens. Jekyll, G. $3.75 net. [Imp.] Scribner.
*Rosseter, Willard. Senator's sweetheart. il. 12°. $1.50 net. Grafton Press.
Rossetti, Dan. G. House of life; introd. by H. V. Sutherland. Wieners.
*Rossetti, Dan. G. Poems: MDCCCLXX. 4°. (Mosher's quarto ser. bds., $5 net; Jap. vellum, $20 net. Mosher.
Rossettis (The), Dante Gabriel and Christina. Cary, Eliz. L. $2.50; $3.50 net. Putnam.
**Rossiter, F: M., *and* Henry, Ma. Story of a living temple. 12°. $1 net. Revell.
*Rotherham, J. B. Emphasized Bible. 3 v. 8°. ea., $2 net. Revell.
Round robin. Fessenden, L. D., *ed.* $1.25. Jamieson-H.
Roundabout papers. Thackeray, W: M. 75 c. Caldwell.
**Rowlands, Walter, *ed.* Among the greatest masters of warfare. 12°. $1.20 net; hf. mor., $2.40 net. Estes.
†Rowsell, Ma. C. Friend of the people. (Copyright ser.) 12°. 50 c. Stokes.
Roy and Rosyrocks. Byrne, Mary A. 60 c. Saalfield.
Royalty of friendship. Williams, Alice L. $1.50-$4. Caldwell.
Royce, Josiah. Outlines of psychology. 12°. Macmillan.
Rubaiyat. *See* Omar Khayyam.
*Rubaiyat of Omar Khayyam, jr. Irwin, W. $1 net; $3 net. Elder.
Rufe and Ruth: a partnership. Sweet, F. E. $1. Pilgrim Press.
Rugs, How to make. Wheeler, Candace. $1 net. Doubleday, P.
**Rugs, Oriental. Mumford, J: K. $7.50 net. Scribner.
Rule, U. Z. Old Testament lessons. Oxford Univ.
Runaway Robinson. Snyder, C: M. Biddle.
Rupert, W. W. Pennsylvania and N. J. supplement. (Tarr and McMurry geographies.) Macmillan.
Rural England. Haggard, H. R. Longmans.
Rural science ser.; ed. by L. H. Bailey. 16°. Macmillan.
New volumes: Brewer, Principles of stock breeding.—Mayo, Care of stock.

Ruskin, J: Beauty and nature. (New Kalon ser., 50 c.—Sesame classics, $1.25.) Caldwell.
Ruskin, J: Modern painters. (Sesame classics.) il. limp ooze calf, boxed, 7 x 4¼. $1.25. Caldwell.
Ruskin, J: Pearls for young ladies. (New Kalon ser.) il. 12°. 50 c. Caldwell.
Ruskin, J: Precious thoughts. (New Kalon ser.) il. 12°. 50 c. Caldwell.
Ruskin, J: Sesame and lilies. (Chateau ser., 75 c.—Sesame classics, $1.25.) Caldwell.
Ruskin, J: Stones of Venice. (New Kalon ser., 50 c.—Sesame classics, $1.25.) Caldwell.
Ruskin, J: True and beautiful. (New Kalon ser., 50 c.—Sesame classics, $1.25.) Caldwel
**Ruskin, J: Harrison, F: 75 c. net. Macmillan.
†Russell, W. Clark. Captain Fanny. (Red letter ser.) il. pap., 50 c. New Amsterdam.
**Russell, Walter. Bending of the twig. over 100 il. 8°. $2 net. Dodd, Mead & Co.
Russia, Greater. Gerrare, W. Macmillan.
*Russia, Industrial resources of. Waage, R. G. $3 net. Cambridge.
**Russias, All the. Norman, H: $4 net. Scribner.
Rustic life in France. Theuriet, A. $2.50. Crowell.
Sabertooth (The). Kinder, S. 75 c. Laird.
†Sabin, Edwin L. The magic mashie. il. 12°. $1. Wessels.
Sacred books of the East. Oxford Univ.
New volume: 48 (completing 2d ser.), Ramanuga's Sribhashya; tr. by G. Thibaut.
Safford, Ma. J. *See* Hillern, W. v.
**Sahler, Florence L. A guest book. 4°. 80 c. net. Stokes.
**St. Augustine and his age. McCabe, Jos. port. 8°. $2 net. Putnam.
St. Berin. Field, J: E: $1.50. Young.
St. Clair, Victor. Cast away in the jungle. il. $1.25. Street.
*St. Francis, Sons of. MacDonnell, A. il. 8°. $2 net. Putnam.
**St. George and the dragon; il. by Burne-Jones. scroll decor. 10 x 40. $1.60 net. Russell.
St. Germain, *Comte* C. de. Practical astrology. il. $1. Laird.
St. John's Gospel. *See* Hoare, J. G. Young.
Saint Neots. *See* Stevenson, W. H. Oxford Univ.
**St. Nicholas ser. il. 12°. ea., $1 net. Century.
Contents: Sir Marrok; French, A.—Cruise of the "Dazzler"; London, J.—Boy and the baron; Knapp, Adeline.—Boys of the Rincon ranch; Canfield, H. S.—Tommy Remington's battle; Stevenson, B. E.—Eight girls and a dog; Carolyn Wells.
St. Paul and his churches. Bolland, W. E. Young.
St. Pierre, J. H. B. de. Paul and Virginia. (New Kalon ser.) il. 12°. 50 c. Caldwell.
St. Pierre. *See* Martinique. Saalfield.
Saintine, J. X. B. Picciola. Super, O. B., *ed.* Heath.
Saints in Christian art. Bell, *Mrs.* A. J. Macmillan.
**Saintsbury, G: History of criticism. v. 2. 8°. $3.50 special net. Dodd, Mead & Co.
Sale's sharpshooters. Avery, H. $1.25. Nelson.
Salmon, Lucy M. History of the appointing power. (Citizen's lib. of economics, politics and sociology.) 12°. Macmillan.
Salmon, Lucy M. History: suggestions as to its study and teaching. 12°. Macmillan.
Samantha at Saratoga. Holley, M. 50 c. Caldwell.
Samaritan liturgies. Cowley, A., *ed.* Oxford Univ.
Samuel and his age. Douglas, G: C. M. $2.50. Young.
Samuel and Saul. Meyer, F. B. 12°. $1. Revell.
Sanctae silviae peregrinatio. Betchel, E. A. $1 net. Univ. of Chic.
Sancti Irenaei Novum Testamentum. Sanday, W., *ed.* Oxford Univ.
**Sand man: his farm stories. Hopkins, W: J. $1.20 net. L. C. Page.
Sanday, W., *ed.* Sancti Irenaei Novum Testamentum. Oxford Univ.
Sandys, Miles. Michael Carmichael. il. $1.25. Laird.
Sanford, Leonard C., *and* Van Dyke, T. S. Wild fowl. (American sportsman's library.) il. 8°. Macmillan.
†Sangster, Marg. E. Janet Ward. 12°. $1.50. Revell.
**Sanskrit grammar, Bibliography of. Schuyler, M. net. Macmillan.
**Sanskrit grammar for beginners. Jackson, A. V. W: net. Macmillan.
**Santa Claus, The life and adventures of. Baum, L. F. $1 net. Bowen-M.
Sarah's first start in life. Campbell, A. M. G. 20 c. Young.
**Sargent, C: S. Silva of North America, vols. XIII. and XIV. il. 4°. $25 per vol. (sold only in sets, $350 net.) Houghton, M. & Co.
**Sargent, C: S. Little known trees and shrubs. v. 1., pt. 1. il. 4°. $5 net. Houghton, M. & Co.
**Saunders, M. Beautiful Joe's Paradise. il. $1.20 net. L. C. Page.
*Saunder's medical hand atlas ser. Saunders.
New volume: Helferich, Atlas and epitome of fractures and luxations.
Sauveur, L. Causeries avec les enfants. 12°. $1. W: R. Jenkins.
Sauveur, L. Causeries avec mes élèves. il. 12°. $1.25. W: R. Jenkins.
Sauveur, L. Contes merveilleux. 12°. $1.50. W: R. Jenkins.
Sauveur, L. Corrigé des exercises de la petite grammaire française. pap. 12°. 50 c. W: R. Jenkins.
Sauveur, L. Corrigé des exercises et traductions des petites causeries. pap. 12°. 15 c. W: R. Jenkins.
Sauveur, L. Corrigé des traductions des causeries avec mes élèves. pap. 12°. 25 c. W: R. Jenkins.
Sauveur, L. De l'enseignement des langues vivantes. pap. 12°. 25 c. W: R. Jenkins.
Sauveur, L. Entretiens sur la grammaire. 12°. $1.50. W: R. Jenkins.

Sauveur, L. Introduction to the teaching of ancient languages. pap. 12°. 25 c. W: R. Jenkins.
Sauveur, L. Introduction to the teaching of living languages. pap. 12°. 25 c. W: R. Jenkins.
Sauveur, L. La parole française. 12°. $1 W: R. Jenkins.
Sauveur. L. Petite grammaire française pour les Anglais. 12°. $1.25. W: R. Jenkins.
Sauveur, L. Petites causeries. 12°. $1. W: R. Jenkins.
Sauveur, L. Talks with Caesar de Bello Gallico. 12°. $1.25. W: R. Jenkins.
Sauveur, L. Vade mecum of the Latinist. pap. 12°. 25 c. W: R. Jenkins.
Sauveur, L. A word for word rendering into English of Caesar's Gallic war. Book 1. pap. 12°. 25 c. W: R. Jenkins.
Sauveur, Marie Louise, *and* Longee, Susan C. Premières lecons de grammaire Française. 12°. 75 c. W: R. Jenkins.
**Savage, Minot J. Spiritism or telepathy? 12°. net. Putnam.
Savage, R: H: For a young queen's bright eyes. $1.25; 50 c. Home Pub.
Savage, R: H: Special orders for Commander Leigh. $1.25; pap., 50 c. Home Pub.
Savile, *Sir* G: Lady's New Year's gift. (Bradford ser.) 16°. $1. limp crushed leath., $1.25. Wessels.
Savile, *Sir* G: *See* Raleigh, *Sir* W.
†Saville, Frank M. Foray of the Hendrik Hudson. il. 12°. $1. Stokes.
†Sawdust. Gerard, D. $1. Coates.
†Sayre, Theodore B. Tom Moore. il. 12°. $1.50. Stokes.
Scenes from Sophocles' Antigone. Laurence, C. E., *ed.* Oxford Univ.
**Schenck, Ferd. S. Ten commandments and the Lord's prayer. 12°. $1 net. Funk.
**Schierbrand, Wolf v. Germany of to-day. 6x9¼. $2.40 net. Doubleday, P.
Schiller, F. v. Dreissigjähriger Krieg, Bk. 3. Prettiman, C. W., *ed.* Heath.
Schiller, F. v. Wallensteins Tod. Eggert, C. A., *ed.* Heath.
Schmidt, Nathaniel. Son of man and son of God in modern theology. (Works on modern theology.) 12°. Macmillan.
Schofield, A. T. The force of mind. $2. Blakiston.
Scholar of Lindisfarne. Hollis, G. $1. Young.
School management. McMurry, C: A. Macmillan.
Schools, Making of our middle. Brown, E. E. Longmans.
Schopenhauer, Arthur. The wisdom of Schopenhauer: introd. by H. V. Sutherland. Wieners.
Schreiner, Olive. Story of an African farm and Dreams. (Lotus ser. 2 v. sets.) il. 2 v. 12°. $1. Caldwell.
Schücking, Die drei freier. (International modern language ser.) Ginn.
**Schuyler, Montgomery, *jr.* Bibliography of Sanskrit grammar. (v. III. Columbia Univ. Indo-Iranian ser.) 8°. net. Macmillan.
**Scientific side-lights, Cyclopedia. il. 8°. $5 net. Funk.
**Scotland, History of. Lang, A. $3.50 special net. Dodd, Mead & Co.
Scott, Frank J. Portraitures of Julius Cæsar. il. 4°. Longmans.
Scott, G. H. G., *and* McDonell, G. L. Record of the Mounted Infantry, City of London Imperial Volunteers in the late Boer war. Lim. ed. map. $2. Spon & C.
Scott, *Sir* Wa. Complete works. Author's ed. New issue. 12 v. buckram, $12; hf. leath., $18; hf. cf., $24. Wessels.
†Scott, *Sir* Wa. Waverley novels. Victoria ed. Notes by D: Laing. il. 25 v. 8°. ea., 60 c. Macmillan.
Scott, *Sir* Wa. Waverley novels. (Sir Walter Scott edition.) New issue. il. 12°. 24 v. ¾ leath., boxed, $36. Wessels.
Scott, *Sir* Walter. Lady of the lake. (English classics.) il. Heath.
Scott, *Sir* Walter. Lady of the lake. (Miniature volumes.) New ed. Marble enamel. 50 c. Stokes.
**Scott, *Sir* Walter. Minstrelsy of the Scottish border; ed. by I. F. Henderson. New ed. 4 v. 8°. $10 net. [Imp.] Scribner.
Scott, *Sir* Walter. Poems. New cabinet ed. 6 v. 12°. $9; hf. cf., $18. Estes.
Scott, *Sir* Walter. Selections. (Street & Smith's little classics.) 18°. 50 c. Street.
Scott, *Sir* Walter. Memoirs of the life of. Lockhart, J: G. 5 v. $10. Houghton, M. & Co.
Scott, W: A. Economics of commerce. (Macmillan's commercial ser.) 12°. Macmillan.
Scott country. Crockett, W: S. Macmillan.
Scottish historical antiquities. *See* Nineteenth century art. Macmillan.
**Scottish songs. Burns, R. $4. net. Brentano
†Scout, Story of a. Finnemore, J: $1.50. Lippincott.
**Scripture, E: W. Elements of experimental phonetics. (Yale bicentennial publications.) net. Scribner.
Scripture books for children. col. il. 16°. bds., 25 c. Young.
New volumes: Pictured miracles of our Lord.—Pictured parables of our Lord.
**Scripture, Integrity of. Smith, J: $1.25 net. Revell.
*Scudder, C: L. The treatment of fractures, il. 3d ed., rev. 8°. $4.50 net; hf. mor., $5.50 net. Saunders.
**Sea-fighters from Drake to Farragut. Frothingham, J. P. $1.20 net. Scribner.
†Sea lady. Wells, H. G. $1.50. Appleton.
†Sea turn and other matters. Aldrich, T: B. $1.25. Houghton, M. & Co.
Seailles, *Prof.* *See* Janet, *Prof.* Macmillan.
Seaman, Owen. Borrowed plumes. 16°. Holt.
†Searchers (The). Byrde, Margaretta. $1.50. Funk.
**Sears, L. S. American literature in its colonial and national periods. 12°. $1.50 net. Little, B. & Co.
†Seawell, Molly E. Franceзka. il. 12°. $1.50. Bowen-M.

**Secret correspondence of Maria Theresa and the Comte d'Argenteau. 2 v. il. 8°. $6.50 net. Dodd, Mead & Co.
Seeds of April's sowing. Sutton, Adah L. $1.25. Saalfield.
**Segall, J. B. Corneille and the Spanish drama. (Columbia Univ. studies in romance, literature and philology.) $1.50 net. Macmillan.
Selbie, J: A. *See* Hasting, J.
Selections from the Cambridge Platonists. Campagnac, E. T., *ed.* Oxford Univ.
**Sell, H. T. Bible studies in the life of Christ. 12°. 50 c. net; pap., 25 c. net. Revell.
**Selleck, W. C. Spiritual outlook: survey of the religious life of our time as related to progress. 12°. $1 net. Little, B. & Co.
Selwyn, G: A.; *Bp.* Memoir of Tucker, H. W. $3. Young.
*Senator's sweetheart. Rosseter, W. $1.50 net. Grafton Press.
Seneca, Satire on the Apotheosis of Claudius. Ball, A. P. Macmillan.
Senn, N. A nurse's guide for the operating room. il. 6 x 9½. $1.50. Keener.
Sennett, A. R. Horseless road locomotion. il. 2 v. 8°. Macmillan.
Sensation of pain. McKeag, A. J. Ginn.
*Sensitive plant. Shelley, P. B. 50 c. net; 75 c. net. Lane.
**Sentimental journey. *See* Sterne, Laurence.
**Separates of New England. Blake, S. L. $1.25 net. Pilgrim Press.
*Sepulchral cross-slabs. Styan, K. E. $3 net. Young.
†Serao, Matilde. Conquest of Rome. Post 8°. $1.50. Harper.
†Serao, Matilde. Sister Joan of the cross. Post 8°. $1.50. Harper.
†Sergeant, Adeline. A rogue's daughter. (Copyright ser.) 12°. 50 c. Stokes.
Sermon sur les devoirs des rois. *See* Bossuet. Macmillan.
Sesame and lilies. Ruskin, J: 75 c.; $1.25. Caldwell.
Sesame classics. il. Limp ooze calf. 27 v. 7 x 4¼. boxed, ea., $1.25. Caldwell.
Seven great monarchies. Rawlinson, G: 3 v. buckram, $3; hf. leath., $4.50; hf. cf., $6. Wessels.
Seven Roman statesmen of the later republic. Oman, C: $1.60. Longmans.
Sever, F. P. Elements of agriculture. il. 50 c. Heath.
Sewell, C. H. Wireless telegraphy. Van Nostrand.
Sexton, Ella M. Stories of California.
Shades, shadows and perspective. Randall, O. E. Ginn.
†Shadow (The) of Hilton Fernbrook. Westbury, A. 50 c. New Amsterdam.
†Shadow of the Czar. Carling, J: R. $1.50. Little, B. & Co.
Shadow of the rock. (New Kalon ser.) il. 12°. 50 c. Caldwell.
†Shadow of the rope. Hornung, E. W. $1.50. Scribner.
Shakespeare. Elizabethan Shakespeare; ed. by M. H. Liddell. lim. ed. Doubleday, P.
*Shakespeare, W: Works. (Rolfe ed.) il. 40 v. leather, ea., 90 c. net; set, boxed, $36 net. Baker & T.
**Shakespeare, W: Works. (Variorum ed.) Ed. by H. H. Furness. 8°. per v., $4 net; set, hf. mor., $65 net. Lippincott.
New volume: Twelfth night.
**Shakespeare, W: Works. (Edinburgh edition.) Ed. by W. E. Henley. 40 parts. ea., $2 net. Stokes.
Shakespeare, W: Works. (Bedford ed.) 12 v. Boxed. Limp lambskin. Warne.
**Shakespeare, W: As you like it. (Macmillan's pocket classics.) 18°. 25 c. net. Macmillan.
**Shakespeare, W: Hamlet. (Macmillan's pocket classics.) 18°. 25 c. net. Macmillan.
*Shakespeare, W: Sonnets. (Lover's lib., 11.) decor. 5¼ x 3 in. 50 c. net; leath., 75 c. net. Lane.
Shakespeare, W: *See also* Corbin, J: Lane.
**Shakespeare: a study. Hazlitt, W. C. $2.50 net. [Imp.] Scribner.
**Shakespeare and his forerunners. Lanier, S. $10 net-$25 net. Doubleday, P.
**Shakespeare and Voltaire. Lounsbury, T. R. $2 net. Scribner.
Shakespeare studies: Porter *and* Clarke's Macbeth. 56 c. Am. Bk.
Shakespeare. Tales from. Lamb, C: $1.25. Caldwell.
Shakespeare's moral system. Moulton, R: G. Macmillan.
**Shakespeare's portrayal of moral life. Sharp, F. C. $1.25 net. Scribner.
Sharp, Evelyn. The other boy. il. 12°. Macmillan.
**Sharp, Frank C. Shakespeare's portrayal of moral life. 12°. $1.25 net. Scribner.
Sharp, Luke. *pseud. for* Barr, Rob.
Sharpe, J. Students' handbook to the Psalms. (Bible students' lib.) 12°. $2.50. Young.
Shaw, F. L. Castle Blair. (Home and school classics.) Heath.
She stoops to conquer. Goldsmith, O. 50 c. Stokes.
**Sheard, Virna. Maid of many moods. il. $1.25 net. Pott.
**Sheep-stealers (The). Jacobs, *Mrs.* Violet. Putnam.
Sheldon, C: Crucifixion of Philip Strong. (Golden counsel ser., 75 c.—New Kalon ser., 50 c.) Caldwell.
Sheldon, C: In his steps. (Golden counsel ser.) il. boxed, 16°, 75 c. Caldwell.
**Shelley, H: C. Keats and his circle. il. 12°. net. Putnam.
Shelley, Ma. W. Frankenstein. (Chateau ser.) il. 6 x 4; boxed, 75 c. Caldwell.
Shelley, P. B. Adonais and Alastor. (Silver ser. of classics.) 35 c. Silver.
*Shelley, P. B. Sensitive plant. (Flowers of Parnassus ser., 13.) il. 16°. 50 c. net; leath., 75 c. net. Lane.
**Shensi, Through hidden. Nichols, F. H. $3.50 net. Scribner.
Shepherd of Hermas. Taylor, C. Young.
**Sheppard, Eli. Plantation bird legends. il. 6 x 9. $1.60 net. Russell.

**Sherburne quest. Douglas, A. M. 90 c. net. Dodd, Mead & Co.
Sheridan, R: B. Humorous plays. (Turner house classics.) il. 12°. 75 c. Brentano.
Sheridan, R: B. Life and works. 2 v. il. 12°. $3; ¼ mor., $6. Pott.
Sheridan, R: B. Selections. (Street and Smith little classics.) 18°. 50 c. Street.
Sheridan, R: B. The rivals. (Thumb nail ser.) $1. Century.
**Sherwood, *Mrs.* The Fairchild family. il. 8°. $1.60 net. Stokes.
†Shiel, M. P. Lord of the sea. (Copyright ser.) 12°. 50 c. Stokes.
†Shiel, M. P. Lord of the sea. (Library of successes.) 12°. pap., 50 c. Stokes.
†Ship of dreams. Forsslund, L. $1.50. Harper.
**Shirley, Penn. Boy Donald and his hero. il. 16°. 60 c. net. Lee & Shepard.
**Shoemaker, Michael M. Palaces, prisons and resting-places of Mary, Queen of Scots; rev. by T: A. Croal. il. 4°. $12 net. Brentano.
**Short history of the Christian church. Moncrief, J. W. $1.50 net. Revell.
Short story, Writing of the. Smith, L. W. Heath.
Shorthand. *See* Platt's Pitmanic shorthand. Am. Bk.
Shorter, *Mrs.* Clement K. *See* Sigerson, D.
Show girl (The). Harper, Olive. 12°. 25 c. J. S. Ogilvie.
Shuey, Lillian H. Don Luis' wife. 12°. bds., 75 c. Badger.
**Siberia, The real. Fraser, J. F. $2 net. Appleton.
Sibley, Edwin D. Stillman Gott. 12°. $1.50. John S. Brooks.
Sicily, Picturesque. Paton, W: A. $2.50. Harper.
Sick, Care of the. *See* McFarland, Jos. Blakiston.
*Sickal, H. M., *ed.* Christmas carol ser. il. ea., 35 c. net. Elder.
Contents: I saw three ships.—Good King Wenceslas.—The first Nowell.—Coventry carol.—The wassail song.—God rest you, merry gentlemen.
Sidgwick, H: Ethics of Green, Spencer and Martineau. 8°. Macmillan.
Siebert, Wilbur H. Government of Ohio. (Handbooks of Amer. government.) 12°. Macmillan.
Siefert, H. O. R. Principles of arithmetic (for teachers and normal students.) 75 c. Heath.
Siena. Gardner, E. G. Macmillan.
**Siena, its architecture and art. Hastings, G. $2 net. Brentano.
Sienkiewicz, Henryk. Let us follow him. (Chateau ser.) il. 6 x 4. boxed, 75 c. Caldwell.
Sierra Nevada. Mountaineering in the. King, C. $1.50. Scribner.
Sigerson, Dora, [*Mrs.* Clement Shorter.] The woman who went to hell. 75 c. Brentano.
†Silberrad, Una L. The story of a success. 5½ x 8. $1.50. Doubleday, P.
*Silence of amor. Macleod, F. Mosher.

**Silva of North America. vols. XIII. and XIV. Sargent, C: S. $25 per vol. (sold only in sets, $350 net.) Houghton, M. & Co.
Silver ser. of classics. Silver.
New volumes: Kinard, Old English ballads.—Shelley, Adonais and Alastor.—Chesterfield, Letters.—Keats, Eve of St. Agnes.
Silver ser. of modern language text-books. Silver.
New volume: Corneille, Le menteur.
**Silver work and jewelry. Wilson, H. $1.20 net. Appleton.
**Simonds, W: E. History of English literature. il. 8°. $1.25 net. Houghton, M. & Co.
**Simpson, Frances. Cats and all about them. il. 16°. bds., $1 net. Stokes.
*Simpson, S: Life of Ulrich Zwingli. il. 12°. $1.25 net. Baker & T.
Sing, How to. Lehmann-Kalisch, L. Macmillan.
**Singleton, Esther. Famous paintings; described by great writers. il. 8° $1.60 net. Dodd, Mead & Co.
**Singleton, Esther. London; described by great writers. il. 8°. $1.40 net. Dodd, Mead & Co.
Singleton, Esther. Social New York under the first Georges. 100 half-tone il. 8°. Appleton.
**Sir Marrok. French, A. $1 net. Century.
†Sister Joan of the cross. Serao, M. $1.50. Harper.
Sister of the Red Cross. Meade, *Mrs.* L. T. $1.25. Nelson.
Skeat, W. W., *ed.* Lay of Havelok the Dane. Oxford Univ.
Sketch-book, Irving's. (Regent ed.) 50 c. Am. Bk.
**Sketch book. Irving, W. $1.25 net. Scribner.
Sketches of great painters. Dallin, C. M. 90 c. Silver.
Skin, Diseases of the. Crocker, H. R. $5. Blakiston.
Skinner, Frances E., *tr.* *See* Rosegger, P: Putnam.
Skinner, W. H., *and* Burgert, Cecila M. Lessons in English. il. 50 c. Silver.
**Slade, W: A. Rabbi Ben Ezra. 50 c. net. Crowell.
**Slavery, Political history of. Smith, W: H: 2 v. $4.50 net. Putnam.
Sleeping (The) beauty. Mulock, D. M. 50 c. Caldwell.
Slide valve and its functions. Begtrup, J. Van Nostrand.
Slide valve instruction chart. Lisk, J. P. 25 c. Spon & C.
†Slosson, Annie T. Aunt Abby's neighbors. il. $1. Revell.
Smallpox. Fox, G: H: subs., $3. Lippincott.
Smelting, Lead. Iles, M. W. $2.50. Wiley.
Smiley *and* Storke's Beginner's Latin book. $1. Am. Bk.
Smith, Alex., *and* Hall, Edwin H. Teaching of chemistry and physics in the secondary school. (American teachers ser.) diag. 8°. $1.50. Longmans.

Smith, B: E., *tr. and ed.* Thoughts of Pascal. $1. Century.
**Smith, C: S. Barbizon days. il. 8°. $2 net. Wessels.
**Smith, Charlotte C. Bob Knight's diary camping out. il. 12°. $1.20 net. Dutton.
Smith, *Mrs.* E. T. Murray. Roll-call of Westminster Abbey. il. 8°. Macmillan.
**Smith, Eugene. Home aquarium and how to care for it. il. 12°. $1.20 net. Dutton.
†Smith, F. Hopkinson. Fortunes of Oliver Horn. il. 12°. $1.50. Scribner.
Smith, G. G., *ed. See* Elizabethan. Oxford Univ.
**Smith, Gertrude. Lovable tales of Janey and Josey and Joe. $1.30 net. Harper.
**Smith, Captain J:, Adventures of. Roberts, E. P. $1.50 net. Longmans
**Smith, J: Integrity of Scripture. 12°. $1.25 net. Revell.
**Smith, Joseph, the founder of Mormonism. Riley, I. W. $1.50 net. Dodd, Mead & Co.
Smith, L. W. Writing of the short story. Heath.
**Smith, Nora A. Three little Marys. il. 12°. 85 c. net. Houghton, M. & Co.
Smith, Nora A. *See* Wiggin, Kate D.
**Smith, Orlando J. Eternalism: a theory of infinite justice. 8°. $1.25 net. Houghton, M. & Co.
Smith, Vincent A. Asoka, Buddhist emperor of India. (supp. vol. to "Rulers of India.") Oxford Univ.
Smith, W. Robertson. Kinship and marriage in early Arabia. New ed. 12°. Macmillan.
Smith, W: H., *and* the Smith family, farmers. The new Hamlet. bds., 25 c. Rand, McN.
**Smith, W: H: Political history of slavery. 2 v. 8°. $4.50 net. Putnam.
Smith, W: Hawley *and* the Smith family, farmers. The new Hamlet. (No. 2, Fencing.) bds., 50 c. Rand, McN.
Smollett, Tobias. Selections. (Street and Smith little classics.) 18°. 50 c. Street.
Smollett, Tobias G: Courtship of Commodore Trunnion (excerpt from Peregrine Pickle) and the Cruise of H. M. S. "Thunder" (selection from Roderick Random.) 4¼ x 6¼. $1.25. Turner.
**Snow, Alpheus H. Administration of dependencies. 8°. $3.50 net. Putnam.
Snow, C: H. Principal species of wood. 8°. Wiley.
Snyder, C: M. Runaway Robinson. il. Biddle.
**Social England. Traill *and* Mann, *eds. See* England. Putnam.
**Social ladder (The). Gibson, C: D. $5 net; $10 net. Russell.
**Social legislation and social activity: papers read at sixth annual meeting of the American Academy of Political and Social Science. $1.50 net. McClure.
**Social life in the early republic. Wharton, A. H. $3 net; $6 net. Lippincott.
**Socialism and labor. Spalding, J. L. 80 c. net. McClurg.
Socialist movement. Vail, C: H. 10 c. Kerr.
Sol de media noche. Corelli, M. Appleton.
**Soley, James R. Admiral Porter. por. 12°. (Great commanders ser.) $1.50 net. Appleton.

Solitary path. Huntington, H. Doubleday, P.
*Some by-ways of California. Carter, C: F. $1.25 net. Grafton Press.
Some properties of the triangle and its circles. Bruce, W. H. Heath.
†Somerville, H: Racer of Illinois. 12°. $1.50. McClure.
Sommerville, Maxwell. A wanderer's legend. il. 12°. $1. Biddle.
**Son! Gilhooley, *Lord.* 80 c. net. Stokes.
†Son of God. Steuart, J. A. $1.50. Appleton.
Son of man and son of God in modern theology. Schmidt, N. Macmillan.
†Son of the czar. Graham, J. M. 50 c. Stokes.
Song and the singer (The). Burton, F: R. $1.50. Street.
Song at midnight. Adams, Ma. M. $1.50. Badger.
†Song of a single note. Barr, A. E. $1.50. Dodd, Mead & Co.
**Song of songs; arr. by Fitz Roy Carrington; il. by Burne Jones. 11 x 14. $1 net; $1.75 net; ed. de luxe, white buckram, $2.50 net. Russell.
*Song of the wedding bells. Ockhame, W: B. $1 net. Grafton Press.
†Songs and stories of Tennessee. Moore, J: T. $1.25. Coates.
*Songs of England's glory. Canton, W:, *comp.* $1.25 net. Putnam.
*Songs of the press and Others adventure. Millard, B. 75 c. net. Elder.
**Songs of two centuries. Carleton, Will. $1.50 net. Harper.
Songs. *See* Old English. Longmans.
Sonnenschein, E. A, *ed. See* Plautus. Oxford Univ.
**Sonnet ser. 4°. vellum, ea., $4 net. Brentano.
Contents: Burns, Scottish songs.—Browning, Sonnets from the Portuguese.—Keats, Sonnets.
Sonnets from the Portuguese. *See* Browning, E. B.
Sons of glory (The). Padovan, A. $1.50. Funk.
*Sons of St. Francis. MacDonnell, A. $2 net. Putnam.
**Soo Thah. Burker, A. $1 net. Revell.
Sophocles' Antigone, Scenes from. Laurence, C. E., *ed.* Oxford Univ.
Soul of honour. Winter, J: S. $1. Fenno.
Soule, Caroline G. *See* Eliot, Ida M. Century.
Soulsby, Lucy H. M. Suggestions on prayer. 18°. 50 c. Longmans.
South America, Great mountains and forests of. Fountain, P. Longmans.
South Carolina, History of. McCrady, E: v. 4. Macmillan.
**Southey, Robt. Journal of a tour in the Netherlands. 8°. (Special limited ed.) price on application. Houghton, M. & Co.
Southworth, Gertrude Van Duyn. Story of the empire state. il. 12°. Appleton.
*Spain, Industrial resources of. Waage, R. G. $3 net. Cambridge.
**Spain, Travels through. Zimmerman, J. $2 net. Jacobs.

**Spalding, *Bp.* J. L. Socialism and labor. 16°. 80 c. net. McClurg.
Spangler, H. W., Greene, A. M., *jr., and* Marshall, S. M. Elements of steam engineering. 8°. Wiley.
Spanish conquest in America. Helps, *Sir* A. v. 3. $1.50. Lane.
**Spanish, First book in. Giese, W: F. $1.20 net. Appleton.
Spanish grammar. *See* Bello, A. Appleton.
Spanish language. *See* Marion. Heath.
*Spartianus, Ælianus. Life of the Emperor Hadrian; tr. 8°. $1.50 net. Cambridge.
†Spearman, Frank H. Doctor Bryson. 12°. $1.50. Scribner.
Special orders for Commander Leigh. Savage, R: H: $1.25; 50 c. Home Pub.
**Speckled brook trout. Rhead, L:, *ed.* $3.50 net: $15 net. Russell.
**Speer, Robt. E. Missionary principles and practice. 8°. $1.50 net. Revell.
Spelling book. *See* Rice's Rational. Am. Bk.
Spelling in the elementary school. Cornman, O. P. Ginn.
**Spencer, E: The king's race-horses. il. lim. ed. 4°. $30 net. Brentano.
Spencer, Herb., Ethics of. *See* Sidgwick, H: Macmillan.
Spencer, Herb. Selections. (Street and Smith little classics.) 18°. 50 c. Street.
**Spenser, E. Prothalamion and Epithalamion; photogravures from drawings by Blashfield. 4°. (Special limited ed.) price on application. Houghton, M. & Co.
Speronâra (The). Dumas, A. $1.25. Little, B. & Co.
**Sperry, L. B. Physiology, fear and faith. 12°. pap., 25 c. net. Revell.
Spiers, *ed.* *See* Dumas, Alex. Heath.
Spinoza, Study of the ethics of. Joachim, H. H. Oxford Univ.
Spirit in man. Bushnell, H. $1.25. Scribner.
**Spirit of the Ghetto. Hapgood, H. $1.20 net. Funk.
**Spiritism or telepathy? Savage, Minot J. net. Putnam.
Spiritual (The) life. Kingsbury, O. A. 50 c. Am. Tr.
**Spiritual outlook. Selleck, W. C. $1 net. Little, B. & Co.
Splendid idle forties. Atherton, G. F. Macmillan.
Spofford, Harriet P. The great procession. [Poetry.] New ed. 16°. bds., 50 c. Badger.
**Spooner, C. Cabinet-making and designing. il. 12°. (Artistic crafts ser.) $1.20 net. Appleton.
*Sport, Book of. il. J. F. Taylor.
**Sportsman, The life of a. Nimrod. $20 net. Brentano.
Sportsman's library, American. *See* American.
Spurgeon, C: H., Brilliants from. (Brilliants ser.) il. 6⅞ x 5¼. 35 c. Caldwell.
Spurgeon, C: H. Daily help. (New Kalon ser.) il. 12°. 50 c. Caldwell.
Spurgeon, C: H. Popular ser. of sermons. 8°. ea., 50 c. Revell.
New volumes: On vital questions, Christian work, Conversion, Hope, Repentance, Heaven, Holiness, Joy, Peace: To young men. (10 v., twelve sermons each.)
**Spurr, H: A. Life of Alex. Dumas, père. il. 8°. $2 net. Stokes.
**Stable-lore, First-hand bits of. Ware, F. M. $2 net. Little, B. & Co.
**Stage confidences. Morris, C. $1.20 net. Lothrop.
**Stage lovers' ser. *See* Page's. L. C. Page.
Standard English prose. Pancoast, H: S. Holt.
**Standard light operas. Upton, G: P. $1.20 net. McClurg.
Standard sets. Crowell.
New volumes: Carlyle's Complete works. 10 v. $10.—Guizot's Hist. of France. 8 v. $8.—Hawthorne's Romances. 7 v. $7.—Poe's Complete works. 17 v. $21; hf. cf., $42.
Stanhope. Haverfield, E. L. $1.25. Nelson.
**Stanton, Frank L. Up from Georgia. 16°. $1.20 net. Appleton.
**Star gazer's hand-book Elson, H: W. 30 c. net; 40 c. net. Biddle.
Starbucks (The). Read, O. $1.50. Laird.
Starr, F: Physical characters of Indians of Southern Mexico. 8⅝ x 11⅛. pap., 75 c. net. Univ. of Chic.
Statics, Graphic, Introduction to the elements of. *See* Howe, M. A. Wiley.
Stationary engine design. Cathcart, W: L. Van Nostrand.
Steam engine, A B C of. Lisk. 50 c. Spon & C.
Steam engine, Mechanics of. *See* Le Conte, J. N. Macmillan.
Steam engineering, Elements of. Spangler, H. W. Wiley.
Steam pipes, Loss of heat from. *See* Paulding, C: P. Van Nostrand.
Steam turbine. Neilson, R. M. $2.50. Longmans.
*Steamer letters, Dayton's. $1.50 net. E. W. Dayton.
Steel, Annealing, hardening and tempering of. Woodworth, J. V. Henley.
Steel works materials. Brearley, H. Longmans.
Steel works materials, Analysis of. Brearley, H. Longmans.
Steele. R: Selections from works of. (Golden treasury ser.) Macmillan.
Step, E: Little folks picture natural history. col. il. 4°. bds., $1.50. Warne.
*Stephen, *Sir* Leslie. English thought in the eighteenth century. 3d rev. ed. 2 v. 8°. $8 net. Putnam.
**Stephen, *Sir* Leslie. Hobbes. (English men of letters.) 75 c. net. Macmillan.
*Stephen, *Sir* Leslie. Studies of a biographer. New ser. 2 v. ea., $2 net. Putnam.
**Stephenson, Nath. Beautiful Mrs. Moulton. 12°. $1.20 net. Lane.
Stereotomy. French, Arthur W. Wiley.
Sterne, Laurence. A sentimental journey. (Caldwell's illustrated lib. of famous books.) il. 12°. 75 c. Caldwell.
**Sterne, Laurence. A sentimental journey. (Century classics.) 12°. $1.25 net. Century.
Stetson, Charlotte P., [*Mrs.* Gilman.] Concerning children. Popular ed. pap., 7¼ x 5½. 50 c. Small, M.

Stetson, Charlotte P. Women and economics. Popular ed. pap., 50 c. Small. M.
†Steuart, J. A. A son of God. 12°. $1.50. Appleton.
Stevens, A. A. Text-book of modern therapeutics. 3d ed. 8°. Saunders.
Stevens, W. C. Introduction to the study of plant life. il. analyt. key. Heath.
†Stevenson, B. E. The heritage. cr. 8°. $1.50. Houghton, M. & Co.
**Stevenson, B. E. Tommy Remington's battle. (St. Nicholas ser.) il. 12°. $1. Century.
*Stevenson, Rob. L: Aes triplex, and other essays. (Mosher's vest pocket ser.) 25 c.-$1 net. Mosher.
Stevenson, Rob. L: An inland voyage. il. $1.25. Scribner.
Stevenson, Rob. L: Child's garden of verses. (Chateau ser., 75 c.—Laureate ser., 75 c.: $1.50.—Sesame classics, $1.25.) Caldwell
Stevenson, Rob. L: Familiar studies of men and books. il. 2 v. 4¼ x 6¼. boxed, $2.50. Turner.
Stevenson, Rob. L: Requiem. (Impression leaflets.) 10 c. Elder.
Stevenson, Rob. L: Virginibus Puerisque. 4¼ x 6¼. $1.25. Turner.
Stevenson, Rob. L: Will o' the mill, and a biog. sketch. (Remarque ser.) 3⅞ x 5⅝. 40 c.; limp leath., boxed, 75 c.; limp chamois, $1.25. Caldwell.
Stevenson, W. H., *ed.* Asser's Life of King Alfred, *with the* Annals of Saint Neots. Oxford Univ.
**Stewart, Robt. L: Memorable places among the holy hills. il. 12°. $1 net. Revell.
Stiftungsfest (Das). Moser, G. v. W: R. Jenkins.
†Stillman, Annie R. Fool's gold. 12°. $1.50. Revell.
Stillman Gott. Sibley, Edwin D. $1.50. John S. Brooks.
†Stimson, F. J. [J. S. of Dale, *pseud.*[Jethro Bacon and the weaker sex. 12°. $1. Scribner.
**Stimson, J: Ward. The gate beautiful: principles and methods in vital art education. $7.50 net; $3.50 net. Brandt.
**Stinson, S. Scott, *and* Dwiggins, C. W. Whimlets. il. 16°. 80 c. net. Coates.
Stock, Care of. Mayo, U. S. Macmillan.
Stockbreeding, Principles of. Brewer, W. H. Macmillan.
†Stockton, Frank R. Volume of stories. 12°. $1.50. Scribner.
Stoddard, J: L. Beautiful scenes of America. il. 11 x 14 in. 75 c. Saalfield.
**Stoddard, W: O. Boys of Bunker Academy. (Pastime and adventure ser.) 12°. $1 net. Jacobs.
**Stoddard, W: O. Voyage of the *Charlemagne.* 12°. $1 net. Estes.
**Stoddart, J. H. Recollections of a player. il. tall 12°. $1.80 net. Century.
**Stokes, Ansen Phelps. Cruising in the West Indies. 12°. $1.25 net. Dodd, Mead & Co.
Stokoe, J: With Napoleon at St. Helena. (Diary.) $1.50 net. Lane.
Stokoe, T. H. Manual of the four Gospels: pt. 1, Gospel narrative; pt. 2, Gospel teaching. Oxford Univ.
†Stolen souls. Le Queux, W: 50 c. Stokes.
Stone, Wilbur Macey. Book-plates of today. 90 il.; 7 col. pl. 1 full p. copper pl. eng. by E. D. French. $1.50; Special ed., $2.50. Tonnelé & Co.
Stone, W: J. Classical metres in English verse. Oxford Univ.
**Stone, Witmer, *and* Cram. W: Everitt. American animals. il. 7¾ x 10⅜. $3 special net. Doubleday, P.
Stones of Venice. Ruskin, J: 50 c.; $1.25. Caldwell.
Stooke, Eleanor H. Little Marigold. il. 12°. 75 c. Am. Tr.
Stories in stone from the Roman forum. Dorsey, *Mrs.* S. Macmillan.
Stories of heroes; ed. by C: B. Gilbert.
Contents: Price and Gilbert, Heroes of myth.—Price, Wandering heroes.—Maitland. Heroes of chivalry.
**Stories of sunrise land. Brain, Belle M. 75 c. net. Reveil.
Storm, Theo. Immensee. Bernhardt, W:, *ed.* Heath.
*Storm, Theo. Immensee. 16°. (Mosher's brocade ser.) 75 c. net. Mosher.
**Story of a grain of wheat. Edgar, W: C. 35 c. net. Appleton.
**Story of a living temple. Rossiter, F: M. $1 net. Revell.
†Story of a scout. Finnemore, J: $1.50. Lippincott.
**Story of a strange career. Waterloo, S., *ed.* $1.20 net. Appleton.
†Story of a success. Silberrad, U. L. $1.50. Doubleday, P.
Story of an African farm. *See* Schreiner, O. Caldwell.
Story of Euclid. Frankland, W. B. 75 c. Wessels.
Story of fish life. Pycraft, W. P. 75 c. Wessels.
**Story of Joan of Arc for boys and girls. 80 c. net. Lee & Shepard.
**Story of Kate. Mackie, Pauline B. $1.20 net. L. C. Page.
**Story of Rosalind. (Caxton ser.) il. lambskin, $1.25 net. Scribner.
Story of ser. 16°. ea., 75 c. Wessels.
New volumes: Frankland, Story of Euclid.—Pycraft, Story of fish life.
Story of the empire state. Southworth, G. V. D. Appleton.
*Story of the gods. Abbott, A. A. $2 net. Cambridge.
**Story of the nations ser. il. 12°. ea., $1.35 net; hf. leath., $1.60 net. Putnam.
New volumes: 64, Mediaeval India under Mohammedan rule, by Stanley L. Poole.—65, Papal monarchy, by W: Barry.
Story of the trapper. Laut, A. C. Appleton.
*Story of the unknown church. Morris, W: 75 c. net. Mosher.
Story of the west ser.; ed. by Ripley Hitchcock. il. 12°. Appleton.
New volume: Laut, A. C., Story of the trapper.

Story without an end. (Home and school classics.) Heath.
Stowe, Harriet B. Uncle Tom's cabin. (New Kalon ser.) il. 12°. 50 c. Caldwell.
**Strachey, Lionel, *ed.* *See* Memoirs of a contemporary. Doubleday, P.
Stradivari, Antonio. Prep. by Hill & Sons. Dodd, Mead & Co.
**Strang, Lewis C. Plays and players of the last quarter-century. (Stage lovers' ser.) 2 v. il. 12°. $3.20 net; ¾ mor., $8 net. L. C. Page.
†Stratemeyer, E: With Washington in the west; or, a soldier boy's battle in the wilderness. il. 12°. $1.25. Lee & Shepard.
**Stratemeyer, E: Young volcano explorers. il. 12°. (Pan-American ser.) $1 net. Lee & Shepard.
Stratemeyer, E: *See also* Bonehill, Ralph and Winfield, Arthur M., *pseud.*
*Stratford-on-Avon, Reliques of. Way, A. E., *comp.* 50 c. net; 75 c. net. Lane.
**Streamer, D. Baby's Baedeker. il. bds., 5¼ x 7¾. $1.20 net. Russell.
Streatfield, R. A. The opera. New ed. 8°. $2; hf. levant, $4.50. Lippincott.
Street and Smith little classics. 12 v. 18°. ea., 50 c. Street.
Contents: Read, C:—Darwin, C:—Spencer, H.—Scott, *Sir* W.—Sheridan, R: B.—Smollett, T.—Motley, J: L.—Prescott, W: H.—Beecher, H: W.—Phillips, W.—Taylor, B.—Cooper, J. F.
Strength of the people. Bosanquet, *Mrs.* B. Macmillan.
Strong, S. Arth., *ed.* Library of art. Scribner.
Strong, T. B. Manual of theology. Macmillan.
†Strongest master. Prince, Helen C. $1.50. Houghton, M. & Co.
**Struggle for a continent. Edgar, P., *ed.* $1.50 net. Little, B. & Co.
Struggle for a fortune. Castlemon, H. $1. Saalfield.
Stuart, J: Rand gold mining. il. $1.50. Warne.
†Stuart, Ruth McE. Napoleon Jackson. il. in tint. 16°. $1. Century.
Stubbs, W: Historical essays; ed. by A. Hassall. Longmans.
**Student volunteers, Old-time. Trumbull, H: C. $1 net. Revell.
Studia Biblica. Oxford Univ.
New volume: 2, Texts from Mt. Athos, by K. Lake.
Studies in classical philology. v. 3. 6⅝ x 9⅛. bds., $1.50 net. Univ. of Chic.
Studies in general physiology. Loeb, Jacques. Univ. of Chic.
Studies in hearts. Wright, J. M. 75 c. Am. Tr.
Studies in history and jurisprudence. 2 v. 8°. Oxford Univ.
Studies in logical theory. Dewey, J:, *ed.* Univ. of Chic.
*Studies of a biographer. Stephen, Leslie. 2 v. ea., $2 net. Putnam.
*Study and stage. Archer, W: $1.50 net. Wessels.
Study (A) in scarlet. Doyle, A. C. 75 c. Caldwell.
Study of prose fiction. Perry. Bliss. Houghton, M. & Co.
Study of the ethics of Spinoza. Joachim, H. H. Oxford Univ.
*Styan, K. E. Short history of sepulchral cross-slabs, with reference to other emblems found thereon; with notes and il. 8°. $3 net. Young.
Su caro enemigo. Alexander, *Mrs.* Appleton.
Summary catalogue of Bodleian mss. v. 5, 6. Madan, F. Oxford Univ.
**Summer (A) snowflake. Ellwanger, W. D. $2 net. Doubleday, P.
**Summits of success. Burnley, Ja. $1.50 net. Lippincott.
Sun-dials and roses of yesterday. Earle, A. M. Macmillan.
Sunbeam picture book. 75 c. Warne.
Sunday. Trevelyan, W. B. Longmans.
Sunday, for 1903. il. $1.25; $2. Young.
*[Sunday school.] Short history of the international lesson system. Rice, E. W. 25 c. net. Am. S. S.
**Sunset song. Akers, E. $1.20: $3 net. Lee & S.
Super, O. B., *ed.* *See* Loti, P., *and* Saintine, J. X. B. Heath.
*Supra-renals, Diseases of the. *See* Nothnagel's encyclopedia of practical medicine. Saunders.
Sur les bords du Rhin. Hugo, V. Holt.
Sure to succeed. Davidson, J. T. 60 c. net. Am. Tr.
Surgery, Operative, Text-book of. Kocher, T. Macmillan.
Surgical anatomy. v. 3. Deaver, J: B. Blakiston.
Surgical diseases. Diagnosis of. Albert, E. $5. Appleton.
Surgical diseases of the face, mouth, etc. *See* Grant, H. H. Saunders.
Surgical pathology of the face, mouth, etc. *See* Grant, H. H. Saunders.
Surprises of an empty hotel. Gunter, A. C. $1.50; 50 c. Home Pub.
†Surprising adventures of Sir Toady Lion. Crockett, S. R. $1. Stokes.
**Surtees, R. S. Jorrock's jaunts and jollities. il. 8°. $15 net. Brentano.
Surtees, R. S. Memoir of Nimrod. *See* Nimrod, John Mytton. Brentano.
Surveying. *See* Wentworth, G: A. Ginn.
Sutherland, Harvey. Book of bugs. il. $1.25. Street.
Sutton, Adah L. Seeds of April's sowing. $1.25. Saalfield.
Sutton, J. B. *See* Morris, H: Blakiston.
**Swedish fairy tales. *See* Djurklou, *Baron* G. Stokes.
Sweet, F. E. Rufe and Ruth: a partnership. $1. Pilgrim Press.
Sweetbrier and thistledown. Baskett, J. N. $1.50. Wilde.
†Sweetheart travellers. Crockett, S. R. $1. Stokes.
Swift, Jonathan. Gulliver's travels. (Caldwell's illustrated lib. of famous books.) il. 12°. 75 c. Caldwell.
Swift, Jonathan. Tale of a tub. 4¼ x 6¼. $1.25. Turner.
**Swift, Jonathan. [Selections.] (Little masterpieces, 2d ser.) 4 x 6. Flex. silk clo., ea., 40 c. net. Doubleday, P.

*Swinburne, A. C: Laus veneris. (Mosher's vest pocket series.) 25 c.; $1 net. Mosher.
*Swinburne, A. C. Poems and ballads: 3d ser. 4°. (Mosher's quarto ser.) bds., $5 net; Jap. vellum, $20 net. Mosher.
Swinton, J:. Life of. Waters, R. 25 c. Kerr.
**Swords and plowshares. Crosby, E. $1 net. Funk.
**Sykes, P. M. 10,000 miles in Persia. il. 8°. $6 net. Scribner.
Sylveste, Joshua, *ed.* Christmas carols, ancient and modern. il. 12°. $1. Wessels.
*Symonds, J: A. Fragilia labilia. 8°. (Mosher's reprints of privately printed books.) $1 net; Jap. vellum, $2 net. Mosher.
**Symphonies and their meanings. 2d ser. Goepp, P. H. $2 net. 1st and 2d ser. boxed, $4 net. Lippincott.
Syriac dictionary, Compendious. Margoliouth, *Mrs.* pt. 4. Oxford Univ.
System (A) of physiologic therapeutics. *See* Therapeutics. Blakiston.
Table-tennis. *See* Ping-pong. Lippincott.
**Taggart, Marion Ames. Miss Lochinvar: story for girls. il. 12°. $1.20 net. Appleton.
**Taggart, Marion Ames. Wyndham girls. il. 12°. $1.20 net. Century.
Taking the Bastile. Dumas, A. $1. Caldwell.
Tale of a tub. Swift, J. $1.25. Turner.
Tale of Peter Rabbit. Potter, B. 50 c. Warne.
†Tales about temperaments. Hobbes, J: O. $1; 50 c. Appleton.
Tales from Shakespeare. Lamb, C: $1.25. Caldwell.
Tales of Christian heroism. Neale, J. M. 60 c. Young.
**Tales of the spinner. Doucet, J. $5 net. Russell.
Talisman (Der). Fulda, L. Holt.
Talks to children about Jesus. Morton, *Mrs.* 50 c. Caldwell.
Talks with Cæsar de Bello Gallico. Sauveur, L. $1.25. W: R. Jenkins.
Talks with young men. Davidson, J. T. 60 c. net. Am. Tr.
**Talling, M. P. Extempore prayer. 12°. $1.25 net. Revell.
Talmage, F. DeW. Message to the Magians. 12°. 75 c. Revell.
Talmage, T: DeW., Brilliants from. (Brilliants ser.) il. 6⅞ x 5¼. 35 c. Caldwell.
Tangled in the stars. Wetherald, E. $1. Badger.
**Tangled up in Beulah land. Mowbray, J. P. $1.50 net. Doubleday, P.
Tanglewood tales. Hawthorne, N. 79 c. Caldwell.
Tanning, Modern Amer. 8°. Jacobsen Pub. Co.
**Tappan, Eva M. In the days of Queen Elizabeth. il. 12°. 80 c. net. Lee & Shepard.
Tarde, G. Laws of imitation; tr. Holt.
Tariff, Plain facts about. *See* Bolen, G: L. Macmillan.

**Tarkington, Booth. The two Van Revels. col. il. 12°. $1.50 net; 250 cop. of 1st ed. in imp. Japan pap. with author's autograph, $3 net. McClure.
Tarr *and* McMurry geographies. Macmillan.
New volumes: Rupert, Pennsylvania and N. J. supplement.—Chandler, Virginia supplement.—Fairbanks, California supplement.—McMurry, Teacher's manual.
†Task masters (The). Turner, G: K. $1.25. McClure.
Tasty dishes. 50 c. Fenno.
Taylor, Bayard. Selections. (Street and Smith little classics.) 18°. 50 c. Street.
Taylor, C. The shepherd of Hermas. (Early church classics.) 16°. Young.
**Taylor, C: M., *jr.* Why my photographs are bad. il. 12°. $1 net. Jacobs.
**Taylor, Ma. Imlay. Little Mistress Good Hope. il. sq. 12°. $1.50 net. McClurg.
Taylor, T. U. Plane and spherical trigonometry. Ginn.
**Tea blending as a fine-art. Walsh, Jos. M. $2 net. Coates.
**Tea: its history and mystery. Walsh, Jos. M. $2 net. Coates.
Teachers' professional library; ed. by N: M. Butler. Macmillan.
New volume: Chubb, Teaching of English.
Teaching of chemistry and physics in the secondary school. Smith, Alex. $1.50. Longmans.
Teaching of English. Chubb, P. Macmillan.
Teaching of history and civics in the elementary and secondary school. Bourne, H: E. $1.50. Longmans.
Teeth, Anatomy and histology of. Broomell, I. N. Blakiston.
Teeth. *See* Grant, H. H. Saunders.
Telegraphy, Wireless. Sewell, C. H. Van Nostrand.
Telepathy. *See* Savage, Minot J. Putnam.
Telephone lines. Owen, W. C. Macmillan.
Tempering of steel. *See* Woodworth, J. V. Henley.
Temple, A. G. The Wallace collection at Hartford house, London. il. 10 pts. lim. ed. subs., $300. Manzi & J.
**Temple Bible. 24 v. il. 16°. ea., 40 c. net; limp leath., 60 c. net. Lippincott.
Temple classics; ed. by I. Gollancz. 16°. ea., 50 c.; leath., ea., 75 c. Macmillan.
New volumes: Mabinogion.—Macaulay, Lays of ancient Rome.—Goldsmith, Essays.—Fielding, Works.
Temple classics for young people. 16°. ea., 50 c.; leather, 80 c. Macmillan.
New volumes: Andersen, Fairy tales.—Kingsley, Westward ho!
†Temporal power. Corelli, M. $1.50. Dodd, Mead & Co.
Ten commandments. Dale, R. W. Whittaker.
**Ten commandments and the Lord's prayer. Schenck, F. S. $1 net. Funk.
†Tennessee, Songs and stories of. Moore, J: T. $1.25. Coates.
Tennis, racquets and squash. Miles, Eustace H. Appleton.
Tennyson, *Lord* Alfred. Poems. New cabinet ed. 12 v. 12°. $18; hf. cf., $36. Estes.

Tennyson, *Lord* Alfred. Poetical works. Farringford ed. il. 10 v. per set, $7.50; leath., $12.50; hf. cf., $21. Crowell.
*Tennyson, *Lord* Alfred. Poetical works. (1830-1859.) (New century.) $1 net; $1.50 net. Nelson.
Tennyson, *Lord* Alfred. Gareth and Lynette, Passing of Arthur, Launcelot and Elaine. (Longmans' English classics.) Longmans.
*Tennyson, *Lord* Alfred: his homes, his friends, and his work. Cary, Eliz. L. $2.50; $3.50 net. Putnam.
Tennyson, *Lord* Alfred. Idylls of the king; photogrv. from Dore. 2 v. 8°. Putnam.
Tennyson, *Lord* Alfred. In memoriam. (Thumb-nail ser.) $1. Century.
*Tennyson. *Lord* Alfred. In memoriam. 8°. (Mosher's old world ser.) $1 net; Jap. vellum, $2.50 net. Mosher.
Tennyson, *Lord* Alfred, Tales from; ed. by M. K. Bellew. il. 12°. 60 c. Jamieson-H.
**Tennyson, *Lord* Alfred. Lyall, *Sir* A. 75 c. net. Macmillan.
†Tenth commandment. Glentworth, M. L. $1.50. Lee & Shepard.
Territorial growth of the U. S. Mowry, W: A. Silver.
Tetraeuangelium sanctum. Pusey, P. E: Oxford Univ.
**Textile fibres of commerce. Hannan, W: I. $3 net. Lippincott.
Texts from Mt. Athos. Lake, K. (Studia Biblica, no. 2.) Oxford Univ.
**Thacher, J: Boyd. Christopher Columbus. 3 v. il. ports. facsims. 8°. vellum back. Putnam.
Thackeray, W: M. Complete works. Author's ed. New issue. 10 v. buckram, $10; hf. leath., $15; hf. calf, $20. Wessels.
†Thackeray, W: M. Works; ed. by W. Jerrold. 30 v. il. 12°. ea., $1. Macmillan.
New volumes: Virginians, 3 v.—English humourists and four Georges.—Paris sketch book.—Irish sketch book.—Philip, 2 v.—Yellowplush papers.—Book of snobs.
Thackeray, W: M. Adventures of Philip. (Il. lib. of fam. bks.) 12°. 75 c. Caldwell.
Thackeray, W: M. Burlesques. (Il. lib. of fam. bks.) 12°. 75 c. Caldwell.
Thackeray, W: M. Christmas books. (Il. lib. of fam. bks.) 12°. 75 c. Caldwell.
†Thackeray, W: M. Henry Esmond. (Turner house classics.) il. 12°. 75 c. Brentano.
Thackeray, W: M. Paris sketch book. (Il. lib. of fam. bks.) 12°. 75 c. Caldwell.
Thackeray, W: M. Pendennis. (New Berkeley lib.) il. 12°. $1. Caldwell.
Thackeray, W: M. Roundabout papers. (Il. lib. of fam. bks.) il. 12°. 75 c. Caldwell.
Thackeray, Chips from. Mason, T. 50 c. Stokes.
That doll. Fanshawe, F. C. 30 c. Young.
Theater. *See* Patterson, Ada. Grafton Press.
Theistic and Christian belief, Grounds of. Fisher, G: P. Scribner.
Thelma, Corelli, M. $1.50. Fenno.
**Theologia; or, the doctrine of God. Weidner, R. F. 75 c. net. Revell.
Theology and the social consciousness. King, H: C. Macmillan.
Theology, Manual of. Strong, T. B. Macmillan.
Theology, Works on modern; ed. by Ja. W. Whiton. 12°. Macmillan.
New volume: Schmidt, Son of man and son of God in modern theology.
Theophrastus, Chracter of: tr. by C: E. Bennett and W: A. Hammond. 16°. Longmans.
Therapeutics, A system of physiologic; ed. by S. S. Cohen. il. 8°. Complete set, $27.50; ½ mor., $38.50. Blakiston.
New volumes: v. 5, McFarland. Leffmann and others. Prophylaxis.—v. 10, Tissier, Pneumatotherapy.
*Therapeutics, Clinical. *See* Yeo, I. B. Manual of treatment. Keener.
Therapeutics, Text-book of modern. Stevens, A. A. Saunders.
Theuriet, André. Rustic life in France. il. by Léon Lhermitte. 2 v. $2.50. Crowell.
Thibaut, G., *tr.* Ramanuga's Sribhashya. (Sacred books of the East, 48.) Oxford Univ.
†Things that are Cæsar's. Kauffman, R. W. $1.50. Appleton.
**This is for you. Love poems of the saner sort. Lord, W: S., *ed.* $1 net. Revell.
**Thistles of Mount Cedar. Tilghman, Emily. 80 c. net. Coates.
Thomas à Kempis, Golden thoughts from. *See* Lindsay, T. M. Stokes.
*Thomas à Kempis. Imitation of Christ. (A. L. Humphrey's large type books.) 16°. pap., $3 net. Wessels.
Thomas à Kempis. Imitation of Christ. (Chateau ser.) il. 6 x 4. boxed. 75 c. Caldwell.
Thomas à Kempis. Imitation of Christ. (Sesame classics.) il. 7 x 4¼. limp ooze cf., boxed, $1.25. Caldwell.
Thomas à Kempis. The wisdom of à Kempis; introd. by H. V. Sutherland. Wieners.
Thomas, B. F., *and* Watt, D. A. The improvement of rivers. 4°. Wiley.
Thomas, Calvin, *ed.* *See* Riehl, W: H. v. Heath.
Thomas, Edith M. The dancers. [Poems.] 12°. $1.50. Badger.
**Thompson, Adele M. Brave heart Elizabeth. il. 12°. $1 net. Lee & Shepard.
Thompson, Helen B. Psychological norms in men and women. Univ. of Chic.
Thompson, W. G. Practical dietetics. New rev. ed. 8°. $5: $5.50. Appleton.
Thomson, J. J. Electrical properties of gases. Macmillan.
Thoreau, H: D. Walden. *Holiday ed.* il. 12°. $3. Houghton, M. & Co.
**Thoreau: his home, friends, and books. $2 net. Crowell.
**Thormanby, *pseud.* Dainty dames of society. il. 16°. leath., ea., $1 net. Brentano.
†Thoroughbreds. Fraser, W. A. $1.50. McClure.
**Thorpe, Ctte. Children's London. il. 4°. $2.50 net. [Imp.] Scribner.
Thoughts adrift. Louthan, H. H. $1. Badger.
Thoughts by the way. Woodhouse, H. $1.50. Young.

**Thoughts for the Sundays of the year. Moule, H. C. G. $1 net. Revell.
†Thousand and one nights. New ed. Tr. by E: W. Lane. (Special lim. ed.) il. 6 v. per set, $10. Lippincott.
Threads of life. Rollins, C. S. $50. Badger.
**Three little Denvers. Hewitt, E. C. 40 c. net. Jacobs.
**Three little Marys. Smith, Nora A. 85 c. net. Houghton, M. & Co.
Three men in a boat. Jerome, J. K. 50 c. Caldwell.
Three men on wheels. Jerome, J. K. 50 c. New Amsterdam.
Three musketeers. Dumas, A: $2.50. Little, B. & Co.
Three young ranchmen. Bonehill, R. $1. Saalfield.
**Throne of individuality. Jordan, W: G: 75 c. net. Brentano.
**Through hidden Shensi. Nichols, F. H. $3.50 net. Scribner.
Through the first Antarctic night. Cook, F. A. $2 net. Doubleday, P.
Through the looking-glass. *See* Carroll, L:
†Through the turf smoke. MacManus, S. 75 c. McClure.
**Thruston, Lucy M. Jack and his island. il. 12°. $1.20 net. Little, B. & Co.
Thuillier, H. F. Principles of land defence. il. 8°. Longmans.
Thumb-nail ser. 2¾ x 5½. ea., $1. Century.
New volumes: Tennyson's In memoriam.—Thoughts of Pascal.—Sheridan's Rivals.
Thurston, *Mrs.* I. T. Boys of the Central. $1. Pilgrim Press.
Thurston, *Mrs.* I. T. Don Malcolm. $1.25. Pilgrim Press.
Thurston, *Mrs.* I. T. Kent Fielding's ventures. $1.25. Pilgrim Press.
Thurston, *Mrs.* I. T. Village contest. $1.25. Pilgrim Press.
**Thwaites, R. G. Daniel Boone. il. 12°. (Historic lives ser.) $1 net. Appleton.
Thy kingdom come. Williams, T. L. $1.25. Young.
Tibet. *See* Rijnhart, Susie C. Revell.
†Ticknor, Caroline. Miss Belladonna. New ed., with additional chapters. il. 16°. $1. Little, B. & Co.
**Tiger and the insect (The). Habberton, J: $1.20 net. Russell.
**Tilghman, Emily. Thistles of Mount Cedar. il. 12°. 80 c. net. Coates.
Tilton, Dwight. Miss Petticoats. C. M. Clark.
Tilton, Dwight. On Satan's mount. C. M. Clark.
Timbs, J:, *and* Gunn, Alex. Abbeys, castles and ancient halls of England and Wales. New ed. il. 3 v. $5; ¾ mor., $12. Warne.
Timothy and his friends. Ireland, Mary E. $1. Saalfield.
Tinker, Chauncey B. *See* Cook, A. S., *ed.* Ginn.
Tisdall, W. St. Clair. The religion of the Crescent, or Islam: its strength, its weakness, its origin, its influence. James Long lectures on Mohammedanism, 1891-92. 16° $1. Young.
Tissier, Paul. Pneumatotherapy and inhalation methods. (v. 10, System of physiologic therapeutics.) il. 8°. Blakiston.
Titchener, E: B. Experimental psychology. il. 2 v. 12°. Macmillan.
New volume: vol. II., Quantitative experiments, 2 pts.
**Title-pages. DeVinne, Theo. L. $2 net. Century.
Toasts, Book of. Antrim, M. T. 50 c.; $1. Altemus.
Tobacco in song and story. Bain, J: [also] Bathrobes and bachelors. Gray, A. 2 v. $3.50. Caldwell.
**To-day and to-morrow. Miller, J. R. 50 c. net. Crowell.
Todd's New astronomy. $1.30. Am. Bk.
Tolstoi, *Count* L. N. Christian teaching. (Copyright ser.) 12°. 50 c. Stokes.
**Tolstoi, *Count* L. N. Ivan Ilyitch; tr. by Mrs. Garnett. $2 net. McClure.
†Tolstoi, *Count* L. N. More tales from; tr. 12°. $1.50 Brentano.
**Tolstoi as man and artist. Merejkowski, D. Putnam.
†Tom Moore. Sayre, T. B. $1.50. Stokes.
†Tom Tad. Venable, W: H: $1.50. Dodd, Mead & Co.
**Tom Winstone, wide awake. James, M. 80 c. net. Lee & Shepard.
**Tomlinson, Everett T. Cruising on the St. Lawrence. il. 12°. $1.20 net. Lee & Shepard.
Tomlinson, Everett T. In the camp of Cornwallis. il. $1.50. Wilde.
**Tomlinson, Everett T. Under colonial colors. il. 8°. $1.20 net. Houghton, M. & Co.
**Tommy Remington's battle. Stevenson, B. E. $1. Century.
Tools, Modern machine shop. Vandervoort, W. H. Henley
**Topsy-turvy land. (Arabia.) Zwemer, S: M. 75 c. net. Revell.
**Topsys and turvys. Newell, P: $1. Century.
Tour of the Zero club. Bonehill, R. $1.25. Street
Towards Pretoria. Ralph, J. 50 c. Stokes.
†Tower or throne. Comstock, H. T. $1.50. Little, B. & Co.
†Town and country lib. 12°. $1; pap.. 50 c. Appleton.
New volumes: Forbes, *Mrs.* W. R. D., Unofficial.—Hobbes, J: O., Tales about temperaments.
†Town traveller (The). Gissing, G: 50 c. Stokes.
Townsend, Dorothea. A lost leader: tale of Restoration days. 12°. 80 c. Young.
**Tracts relating to the currency of Massachusetts Bay, 1682-1721. Davis, A. McF., *ed.* net. Houghton, M. & Co.
**Trades waste. Naylor, W. $6.50 net. Lippincott.
**Traill, H. D., *and* Mann, J. S., *eds.* Social England. 6 v. il. sets only. Putnam.
New volumes: 2, Edward I.-Henry VII. $5 net.—3, Henry VIII.-Elizabeth.
Train, G: Francis. My life in many states and in foreign lands. il. 12°. Appleton.
Travel-lovers' library. *See* Page's. L. C. Page.
**Traveler tales of the Pan-American countries. Butterworth, H. $1.20 net. Estes.
**Travels through Spain. Zimmerman, J. $2 net. Jacobs.

Traverse tables. Repr. from Scribner's Pocket table book. (Science ser., no. 115.) 16°. bds. Van Nostrand.
Treadwell, F. P. Short text-book of analytical chemistry. 2 v. v. 1, Qualitative analysis; tr. fr. 2d ed. by W: T. Hall. 8°. Wiley.
**Treasure of the Incas. Henty, G: A. $1.20 net. Scribner.
†Treasure seekers. Nesbit, E. $1.50. Stokes.
**Treasury of humorous poetry. Knowles, F: L., *ed.* $1.20; $2.40 net. Estes.
Treatment of nature in works of Nikolaus Lenau. Klenze, C. v. 75 c. net. Univ. of Chic.
**Trees and shrubs. Sargent, C: S. vol. 1., pt. 1. $5 net. Houghton, M. & Co.
**Trees, Guide to the. Lounsberry, Alice. $1.75 net-$3.50 net. Stokes.
**Trent, W: P. History of American literature. 12°. (Literatures of the world ser.) $1.20 net. Appleton.
Trevelyan, W. B. Sunday. (Oxford lib. of practical theology.) Longmans.
Triangle. *See* Bruce, W. H. Heath.
**Triggs, H. Inigo. Formal gardens in England and Scotland. il. 3 pts. sold only in sets. $25 net. Scribner.
Trigonometry, Plane and spherical. Ashton, C. H. Scribner.
Trigonometry, Plane and spherical. Taylor, T. U. Ginn.
Trigonometry, Plane and spherical. *See* Wentworth, G: A. Ginn.
Trigonometry. *See* Crawley, Edwin S. Crawley.
Trigonometry. *See* Phillips *and* Strong's. Am. Bk.
Tristram, H. B. Landscapes of the Bible and their story. col. il. 16°. $1. Young.
**Triumph of love. Holmes, Edmond. $1.25. Lane.
Triumph of love. Reade, F. E. 40 c. Young.
Trivial round. Marshall, F. 60 c. Young.
**Troeger, J. W. Harold's discussions: book 5, Nature study readers. 12°. (Appleton's supplementary readers.) 60 c. net. Appleton.
Trotter, Spencer. Geography of commerce. (Macmillan's commercial ser.) 12°. Macmillan.
†Trotty's trip. Wells, C. Biddle.
Troubadours of Dante. Chaytor, H. J. Oxford Univ.
**Trowbridge, W. R. N. Eglée—a girl of the people. 12°. $1 net. Wessels.
**True, J: P. On guard! against Tarleton and tory. il. 12°. $1.20 net. Little, B. & Co.
True and beautiful. Ruskin, J: 50 c.; $1.25. Caldwell.
**True Napoleon (The). Josselyn, C: $3.50 net. Russell.
True to the watchword. Pickering, E. $1.50. Warne.
**Trumbull, H: C. Old time student volunteers. 12°. $1 net. Revell.
**Truscott, L. Parry. Poet and Penelope. 12°. Putnam.
Trussed roofs and roof trusses. Kidder, F. E. $4. W: F. Comstock.
Trust finance. Meade, E. S. Appleton.
Trusts, Plain facts about the. Bolen, G: L. Macmillan.
**Tucker, H. C. Bible in Brazil. il. 12°. $1.25 net. Revell.
Tucker, H. W. Memoir of life and episcopate of G: A: Selwyn, D.D. [New ed.] pors. 8°. $3. Young.
Tufts, J. M. *See* Dewey, J:
†Tully, Eleanor G. Biography of a prairie girl. 12°. $1.50. Century.
Turkish mss. in Bodleian library. *See* Ethé, H. Oxford Univ.
Turner, C. H. Latin versions of the canons of the Greek councils of the 4th and 5th centuries. pt. 2. Oxford Univ.
†Turner, G: K. The taskmasters. 12°. $1.25. McClure.
**Turner, J. M. W. Chignell, R. $1.25 net. [Imp.] Scribner.
Turner house classics; ed. by W: MacDonald. il. 12°. ea., 75 c. Brentano.
Contents: Cook, Anthology of humorous verse.—Reade, Cloister and the hearth.—Thackeray, Henry Esmond.—Sheridan's humorous plays.—Bulwer-Lytton, Last days of Pompeii.—Balzac, Père Goriot.
Tuttle, James P. Diseases of the anus, rectum and pelvic colon. il. 8°. Appleton.
**Twentieth century text books. 12°. Appleton.
New volumes: Benner, A. R. Homer's Iliad.—Burdick, F. M. Essentials of business law.—Chase, G: D. Cornelius Nepos.—Downer, C: A. First book in French.—Ford, W. C. History of commerce and industries.—Giese, W: F. First book in Spanish.—Goodell, T: D. School grammar of Attic Greek.—Goodell, T: D. *and* Morrison, F: S. First Greek book.—Gulick, C: B. Life of the ancient Greeks.—Jenkins, T. A. Longer French poems.—Jepson, W. L. Key to the flora of the Pacific slope.—Learned, M. D. German grammar.—Moore, C. H. First Latin book.—Westcott, J: H. Cæsar's commentaries.—Whitcomb, M. History of modern Europe.
Twice told tales. Hawthorne, N. 79 c. Caldwell.
Twiss, G: R. Laboratory exercises in physics. Macmillan.
Two Dianas. Dumas, A. $1. Caldwell.
Two little travellers. Cunningham, R. $1. Nelson.
"2002:" child life 100 years from now. Fessenden, L. D. $1.25. Jamieson-H.
**2000 miles on an automobile. "Chauffeur." $2 net. Lippincott.
**Two Van Revels (The). Tarkington, B. $1.50; $3 net. McClure.
†Two wilderness voyagers. Calkins, F. W. $1.50. Revell.
Two years before the mast. Dana, R. H., *jr.* $1. Caldwell.
Two years' journal in New York and part of its territories in America. (1701.) Wolley, C: $2; $3 net. Burrows.
**Tyndall, C. H. Electricity and its similitudes. il. 12°. $1 net. Revell.
**Typhoon. Conrad, Jos. $1 net. Putnam.

**Typography, Practice of, ser. DeVinne, Theo. L. 12°. ea., $2 net. Century.
New volume: Title-pages.

Tyson, Ja. Guide to the examination of urine. 10th ed. rev. il. 12°. $1.50. Blakiston.

**Uganda protectorate. Johnston, *Sir* H. $12.50 net. Dodd, Mead & Co.

Ulysses, Adventures of. Lamb, C: $2.50. Russell.

*Umbrian towns (The). Cruickshank, J. W. $1.25 net. Wessels.

†Uncle Charley. Humphrey, Zephine. $1.25. Houghton, M. & Co.

*Uncle Sam, trustee. 8°. $1.75 net. Riggs Pub. Co.

Uncle Tom's cabin. Stowe, H. B. 50 c. Caldwell.

Uncle Tom's cabin, Young folks'. Boylan, G. D. 60 c. Jamieson-H.

**Uncrowned queen. Babcock, B. 75 c. net. Revell.

†Under Calvin's spell. Alcock, Deborah. $1.50. Revell.

**Under colonial colors. Tomlinson, E. T. $1.20 net. Houghton, M. & Co.

**Under Scott in Mexico. Bonehill, R. $1 net. Estes.

Under the deodars. Kipling, R. 75 c. Caldwell.

Under the dome. Ingram, A. F. W. $1.25. Young.

*Under the nursery lamp. New ed. il. 16°. pap., $1 net. Lentilhon.

**Under the trees. Mabie, H. W. $2 net. Dodd, Mead & Co.

Under two flags. La Rame, L. de. $2.50. Caldwell.

*Underhill, And. F. Valid objections to so-called Christian science. 3d ed. 12°. 50 c. net; pap., 25 c. net. Baker & T.

United States Bank, History of. Catterall, R. C. H. Univ. of Chic.

United States. Financial history of. Dewey, D. R. Longmans.

United States histories. *See* McMaster's. Am. Bk.

United States history, First lessons in. Channing, E: Macmillan.

United States history, New normal. Henry. Hinds.

**United States, Political history of the. Gordy, J. P. v. 3 and 4. ea., $1.75 net. Holt.

United States, Territorial growth of the U. S. Mowry, W. A. Silver.

United study of missions ser. 12°. Macmillan.
New volume: Mason, Lux Christi.

University of Chicago. Decennial publications. First ser. 10 v. 4°. Univ. of Chic.
Contents: v. 1, 2, Reports of the President of the Univ. to the Board of Trustees; v. 3-10, Scientific articles.

University of Chicago. Decennial publications; second ser. 8°. Univ. of Chic.
Contents: Carpenter, F: I., *ed.*, Wager's Life and Repentance of Marie Magdalene. Dewey, J:, *ed.*, Studies in logical theory. Mitchell, W. C., History of the greenbacks. Breckinridge, S. P., Legal tender. Bolza, O., Calculus of variations. Michelson, A. A., Light waves and their uses. Reynolds, Myra, *ed.*, Poems of Anne Fitch. Livingston, B. E., Role of diffusion and osmotic pressure in plants; Loeb, J., Studies in general physiology. Catterall, R. C. H., History of the U. S. Bank. Harper, R. F., Assyrian and Babylonian letters. Wallace, Eliz., *ed.*, De Leon's Perfecta Casada.

†Unofficial. Forbes, *Mrs.* W. R. D. $1; 50 c. Appleton.

Unstable as water. Needell, *Mrs.* J. H. $1.25. Warne.

**Untersteiner, Alfredo. Short history of music; tr. by S. C. Very. il. 12°. $1.20 net. Dodd, Mead & Co.

Up and down the Pantiles. Marshall, Emma. Whittaker.

**Up from Georgia. Stanton, F. L. $1.20 net. Appleton.

**Upper currents. Miller, J. R. 65 c.; 85 c. net. Crowell.

**Upton, Bertha. Golliwogg's air-ship. col. il. by F. K. Upton. bds., 4°. $1.50 net. Longmans.

**Upton, G: P. Musical pastels. il. sq. 8°. $2 net. McClurg.

**Upton, G: P. Standard light operas. (v. 5, Upton's standard handbooks on music.) 12°. $1.20 net. McClurg.

Urine, Guide to the examination of. Tyson, Ja. $1.50. Blakiston.

*Use of the voice in reading and in speaking. Pertwee, E. Putnam.

Vade mecum of the Latinist. Sauveur, L. 25 c. W: R. Jenkins.

Vail, C: H. Socialist movement. 10 c. Kerr.

†Valley of decision. Wharton, E. $1.50. Scribner.

Valve, Slide. *See* Begtrup, Julius. Van Nostrand.

Van Bergen's Story of China. 60 c. Am. Bk.

Van Cleef, A: *See* Hundred most famous pictures. Stokes.

**Van Cleve, Alice D. The queen's rosary. decor. vellum bds. 5¾ x 7¾. $1.20 net. Russell.

Vandervoort, W. H. Modern machine shop tools. il. Henley.

**Van Dyke, H: Ja. R. Lowell. (English men of letters.) 75 c. net. Macmillan.

**Van Dyke, J: C. Old English masters. Wood engravings and critical notes by Timothy Cole. super-royal 8°. $8 net; ed. de luxe, limited, $150 net. Century.

†Van Dyke, H: The blue flower. il. $1.50. Scribner.

Van Dyke, T. S. *See* Sanford, L. C.

Van Nostrand's Science ser. Van Nostrand.
New volumes: 115, Traverse tables.—116, Worm and spiral gearing, by F. A. Halsey.

Van Tyne, Claude H. Loyalists in the American revolution. 12°. Macmillan.

**Van Tyne, Claude H., *ed.* Letters of Daniel Webster. por. 8°. $5 net. McClure.

**Van Vorst, Marie. Poems. il. 8°. $2 net. Dodd, Mead & Co.

†Van Zile, E: S. With sword and crucifix. (Red letter ser.) il. pap., 50 c. New Amsterdam.

Variations in animals and plants. Vernon, H. M. Holt.
**Various views. Payne, W: M. $1 net. McClurg.
**Vatican, Art of the. Potter, Mary K. $2 net; $4 net. L. C. Page.
**Velvin, Ellen. Rataplan and other stories. il. 12°. $1.25 net. Altemus.
†Venable, W: H: Tom Tad. il. 12°. $1.50. Dodd, Mead & Co.
Venice. Allen, G. 2 v. $3; $7. L. C. Page.
*Venus di Milo. Paloma, F. 50 c. net. Cambridge.
**Vermilye, D. B., *tr.* Italy. il. 8°. $3 net. Brentano.
Vernon, H. M. Variations in animals and plants. 12°. Holt.
Verona. Wiel, *Mme.* Macmillan.
Vesper Sparrow. Kern, M. $1. J. S. Ogilvie.
†Vespers. (Baby Roland booklets.) il. flexible. 50 c. net. Elder.
Vest-pocket series. *See* advertisement. G. W. Ogilvie.
Vest pocket series. *See* Mosher's.
*Victoria, the wise. Austin, A. $2.50 net. Young.
**Vienna and the Viennese. Lansdale, M. H. $2.40 net; $5.60 net. Coates.
Views and reviews. Henley, W. E. 2d ser. $1. Scribner.
Vigfusson, G., *and* Powell, F. Y., *eds.* The Landnama-boc. 2 v. 8°. Oxford Univ.
†Vignette-series. il. 25 vols. 12°. cf. per vol, $2. Stokes.
Village contest. Thurston, *Mrs.* I. T. $1.25. Pilgrim Press.
**Villari, Luigi. Italian life in town and country. (Our European neighbors ser., 7.) il. 12°. $1.20 net. Putnam.
Villon, François. McCarthy, F. 50 c. Russell.
**Violinist, Confessions of a. Phipson, T. L. $1.50 net. Lippincott.
Virgil. Æneid. *See* Frieze's. Am. Bk.
Virginia. *See* Tarr *and* McMurry geographies. Macmillan.
Virginibus Puerisque. Stevenson, R. L: $1.25. Turner.
Visit (The) to London. Lucas, E: V. $1.50. Brentano.
†Visiting the sin. Raynor, Emma. 50 c. Small, M.
Visits of Elizabeth. Glyn, E. 50 c.; 75 c. Caldwell.
†Vive l'empereur. Andrews, Ma. R. S. Scribner.
Vogel, E. Photography; revised by E. C. Conrad. 3d ed. il. 8°. Macmillan.
†Vogel, Harry B. Gentleman Garnet. (Lippincott's ser. of select novels.) 8°. $1; pap., 50 c. Lippincott.
Voice (The) of the people. Glasgow, Ellen. $1.50. Doubleday, P.
**Voice (The) of the people. Glasgow, Ellen. $1.50 net. Doubleday, P.
*Voice. Use of the voice in reading and in speaking. Pertwee, E. Putnam.
**Voyage of the "Charlemagne." Stoddard, W: O. $1 net. Estes.
†Vultures (The). Merriman, H: S. $1.50. Harper.
W. R. Alick's adventures. il. 8°. Longmans.
*Waage, R. G. Industrial resources of Egypt. 8°. $2 net. Cambridge.
*Waage, R. G. Industrial resources of France. 8°. $3 net. Cambridge.
*Waage, R. G. Industrial resources of Germany. 8°. $3 net. Cambridge.
*Waage, R. G. Industrial resources of Russia. 8°. $3 net. Cambridge.
*Waage, R. G. Industrial resources of Spain. 8°. $3 net. Cambridge.
**Wade, Mary H. Little cousin ser., 1902. *See* Page's. L. C. Page.
Wager, L: Life and repentance of Marie Magdalene. Carpenter, F: I., *ed.* 8°. Univ. of Chic.
Wages of sin. Malet, Lucas. $1.50. Fenno.
Waif of the plains. Remington, F: Macmillan.
**Waite, Arthur E: A book of mystery and vision. [Poems.] 4°. $2 net. Brentano.
Walden. Thoreau, H: D. $3. Houghton, M. & Co.
Waldorf library. 222 v. ea., 75 c. Crowell.
**Waldstein, C: Argive Heraeum. il. 2 v. 4°. $30 net; full morocco, $60 net.
Wales, Abbeys, castles and ancient halls of. *See* Timbs, J: Warne.
Walford, L. B. Money: the boy and the man. 16°. 20 c. Young.
**Walker, Ja. Sermons. $1 net. Am. Unitarian.
Wall street, Work of. Pratt, S. S. Appleton.
Wallace, Eliz., *ed.* De Leon's Perfecta Casada. Univ. of Chic.
Wallace, Lew. The first Christmas. il. cr. 8°. $1.25. Harper.
Wallace (The) collection at Hartford house, London. Temple, A. G. $300. Manzi & J.
Wallenstein's Tod. Schiller, F. v. Heath.
Wallpapers and wall coverings. Jennings, A. S. $2. W: T. Comstock.
**Walsh, Joseph M. Coffee: its history, classification and description. il. 12°. $2 net. Coates.
**Walsh, Joseph M. Tea blending as a fine art. il. 12°. $2 net. Coates.
**Walsh, Joseph M. Tea: its history and mystery. il. 12°. $2 net. Coates.
**Walton, I. Compleat angler. (Winchester ed.) New ed.; ed. by G: A. B. Dewar. il. 2 v. 8°. $12.50 net; large pap. lim. ed., vellum, $35 net. Lippincott.
Wanderer's legend (A). Sommerville, M. $1. Biddle.
Wandering heroes. Price, L. L. 50 c. Silver.
†Wanted, a chaperon. Ford, P. L. $2. Dodd, Mead & Co.
Ward, A. W., Prothero, G. W., *and* Leathes, Stanley, *eds.* Cambridge modern history. 12 v. 8°. Macmillan.
Vol. 1, The Renaissance.
†Ward, Josiah M. Come with me into Babylon. il. 12°. $1.50. Stokes.
Ward, *Mrs.* Wilfrid. The light behind. $1.50. Lane.
**Ware, F. M. First-hand bits of stable lore il. 8°. $2 net. Little, B. & Co.
**Ware, F. M. Our noblest friend, the horse. 12°. $1.20 net. L. C. Page.

**Warfield, D: Ghetto silhouettes. il. 12°. $1.25 net. Pott.
**Warner classics. New ed. il. 5 x 7. 4 v. ea., $1 net; 2 v., boxed, $1.75 net; set, 4 v. boxed, $3.50 net. Doubleday, P.
Warnock, T. D. Richard Hume. 12°. $1.25. Fenno.
Washington, Booker T. The future of the American negro. Popular ed. 7⅝ x 5. pap., 50 c. Small, M.
**Washington, G:, Letters to. vol. v., 1774-1775. Hamilton, S. M., *ed.* $5 net. Houghton, M. & Co.
**Waste, Trades. Naylor, W. $6.50 net. Lippincott
Watanna, Onoto. Wooing of Wistaria. post 8°. $1.50. Harper.
†Watchers (The). Mason, A. E. W. 50 c. Stokes.
†Water-babies (The). Kingsley, C: $2. Wessels
Water of life. *See* Kingsley, C: Caldwell.
**Waterloo, Stanley, *ed.* Story of a strange career: autobiography of a convict. 12°. $1.20 net. Appleton.
Waters, Robt. The career and conversation of John Swinton. 25 c. Kerr.
**Watkinson, W. L. Bane and the antidote. 12°. $1 net. Revell.
**Watson, J:, [Ian Maclaren, *pseud.*] The homely virtues. 12°. $1.20 net. Dodd, Mead & Co.
*Watson, W: Wordsworth's grave. (Flowers of Parnassus ser., no. 15.) il. 16°. 50 c. net; leath., 75 c. net. Lane
Watt, D. A. *See* Thomas, B. F. Wiley.
**Watts-Dunton, Theo. New poems. 12°. $1.50 net. Lane.
Waverley novels. *See* Scott, *Sir* W.
Waves and ripples in water, air, and ether. Fleming, J. A. $2. Young.
*Way, A. E., *comp.* Reliques of Stratford-on-Avon. (Flowers of Parnassus ser., no. 16.) il. 16°. 50 c. net; leath., 75 c. net. Lane.
**Wayfarers in Italy. Hooker, K. $3 net. Scribner.
Wayside harp (A). Cloud, V. W. $1. Badger.
Wayside inn. Howard, Sydney. Quail & W.
Weather (The), and forecasting. Dunn, "Farmer." $2. Dodd, Mead & Co.
Weather (The). *See* Price's Observations. Am. Bk.
Weaving of webs. Praag, Fs. W. $1.50. Fenno.
Weber. Problems in electricity. 3d ed. 12°. $3. Spon & C.
Weber, Adele. Fortunes of the Vanderbergs. il. 12°. $1. Ogilvie.
**Webster, Daniel, Letters; ed. by C. H. Van Tyne. por. 8°. $5 net. McClure.
**Webster, Daniel. McMaster, J: B. $2 net. Century.
**Webster, Daniel, Speeches and other writings of, hitherto uncollected. 3 v. por. 8°. $9 net. Little, B. & Co.
Webster, H. K. Roger Drake. il. 12°. Macmillan.
Webster, W. C. General history of commerce. Ginn.
**Wedding bells, Song of the. Ockhame, W: B. $1 net. Grafton Press.
**Weddings, Book of. Kingsland, *Mrs.* B. $1.20 net. Doubleday, P.
Weed, C. M., *and* Crossman, R. M. Guide to laboratory study of zoology. il. Heath.
**Weed, G: L. Old Testament for the young. il. 12°. 60 c. net. Jacobs.
Weeks-Shaw, Clara S. Text-book of nursing. 3d ed., rev. and enl. $1.75. Appleton.
**Weidner, R. F. Theologia; or, the doctrine of God. 12°. 75 c. net. Revell.
**Wells, Amos R. Rollicking rhymes for youngsters; il. by L. J. Bridgman. 12°. $1 net. Revell.
**Wells, Carolyn. A phenomenal fauna. col. il. 8 x 8½. bds., $1.20 net. Russell.
†Wells, Carolyn. Abeniki Caldwell. il. 5⅛ x 7⅝. $1.50. Russell.
**Wells, Carolyn. Children of our town. col. il. 11 x 14. bds., $4.20 net. Russell.
**Wells, Carolyn. Eight girls and a dog. (St. Nicholas ser.) il. 12°. $1. Century.
†Wells, Carolyn. Folly in the forest. il. 12°. $1. Altemus.
**Wells, Carolyn. Pete and Polly stories. il. large 8°. $1.50 net. McClurg.
†Wells, Carolyn. Trotty's trip. il. Biddle.
**Wells, Carolyn, *ed.* Nonsense anthology. 12°. $1.25 net. Scribner.
†Wells, H. G. The sea lady. il. 12°. $1.50. Appleton.
Wells, Roy T. *See* Hooper, W: L. Ginn.
Wells, W., *and* Gerrish, Claribel. Beginner's algebra. Heath.
Welsh wars of Edward I. Morris, J. E. Oxford Univ.
**Wendell, Barrett. Volume of dramatic verse. 12°. net. Scribner.
Wentworth, G: A. Plane and spherical trigonometry, surveying and navigation. rev. ed. Ginn.
**Wesselhoeft, Lily F. Foxy the faithful. il. 12°. $1.20 net. Little, B. & Co.
Wessex. *See* Field, J: E: Young.
†Westbury, Atha. The shadow of Hilton Fernbrook. (Red letter ser.) il. pap., 50 c. New Amsterdam.
Westcott, Arthur. Life of Bishop Brooke F. Westcott. 2 v. 8°. Macmillan.
Westcott, *Bp.* Brooke F., Life of. Westcott, A. Macmillan.
Westcott, J: H., *ed.* Caesar's commentaries. Appleton.
Westminster abbey, Roll-call of. Smith, *Mrs.* E. T. M. Macmillan.
Westminster and South London. Besant, *Sir* W. 2 v. $3. Stokes.
†Westward Ho! Kingsley, C: 2 v. ea., 50 c.: 80 c. Macmillan.
Wetherald, Ethelwyn. Tangled in the stars. [Poetry.] 12°. bds., $1. Badger.
Wetmore, Claude H. Incaland. il. $1.50. Wilde.
†Weyman, Stanley J. In King's byways. 8°. Longmans.
Weyman, Stanley. King's stratagem. (Chateau ser.) il. 6 x 4. boxed, 75 c. Caldwell.
†Whaleman's wife (A). Bullen, F. T. $1.50. Appleton.

**Wharton, Anne H. Social life in the early republic. il. 8°. $3 net; ½ levant, $6 net. Lippincott.
†Wharton, Edith. Valley of decision. $1.50. Scribner.
**What a girl can make and do. Beard, L. $1.60 net. Scribner.
What Gladys saw. Fox, F. M. $1.25. Wilde.
**What is worth while ser. 140 v. ea., 28 c. net. Crowell.
New volumes: Bullen, F. T. Light Ho, Sir!—Clark, Kate U. Move upward.—Desmond, H. J. Ways of well doing.—Gates, O., *ed.* Daily maxims from Amiel's journal.—Hay, J: William McKinley.—Hyde, W: DeW. Cardinal virtues.—Miller, J. R. In perfect peace.—Storm, T. Immensee.—Thwing, C: F. If I were a college student.
What shall I tell the children? Reichel, G: V. $1. Whittaker.
Wheat. *See* Edgar, W: C. Appleton.
Wheatley, H. B. Mediaeval London. (Mediaeval towns ser.) il. Macmillan.
**Wheeler, Candace. How to make rugs. il. $1 net. Doubleday, P.
**Wheeler, Candace. Principles of home decoration. il. 5 x 7½. $2.40 net. Doubleday, P.
When the heart is young. Whitelock, W: W. $1. Dutton.
Where American independence began. Wilson, D. M. Houghton, M. & Co.
**Where the wind blows. Pyle, Katharine. $2.50 net. Russell.
**Whimlets. Stinson, S. S. 80 c. net. Coates.
Whipple, H: B: Lights and shadows of a long episcopate. il. 8°. New ed. Macmillan.
†Whirl, A, asunder. Atherton, Gertrude. $1. Stokes.
†Whirlpool, The. Gissing, G: 50 c. Stokes.
†Whirlwind (The). Hughes, R. $1.50. Lothrop.
†Whishaw, F: At the court of Catherine the Great. (Copyright ser.) 12°. 50 c. Stokes.
Whitcomb, Merrick. History of modern Europe. 12°. (20th century text-books.) Appleton.
White, Grace M. Harmless revolution. il. 12°. 50 c.; pap., 25 c. J. S. Ogilvie.
†White, Hervey. Noll and the fairies. il. 12°. $1.50. Stone.
White, Percy. The new Christians. 50 c. Federal Bk. Co.
†White shield (The). Mitford, B. 50 c. Stokes.
White's Grammar school algebra. 35 c. Am. Bk.
Whitelock, W: W. When the heart is young. il. 12°. $1. Dutton.
**Whiting, Lilian. Boston days. pors. il. 12°. $1.50 net. Little, B. & Co.
Whitman, Sidney. Personal reminiscences of Bismarck. pors. 12°. Appleton.
Whitman, Walt. Complete prose works. Popular ed. 7⅛ x 4¾. $1.25. Small, M.
Whitney, C., *ed.* *See* American sportsman's library. Macmillan.
Whittaker's electrical engineer's pocket book; ed. by K. Edgecombe. Macmillan.
Whittaker's popular manikin. (Superimposed plates.) bds., $1.50. Whittaker.
Whittier, J: G. Poems. (Sesame classics.) il. 7 x 4½. limp ooze calf, boxed, $1.25 Caldwell.
**Whittier, J: G. Higginson, T: W. 75 c net. Macmillan.
†Whom the gods destroyed. Daskam, J. D. $1.50. Scribner.
Why? Conklin, G: W. 25 c.-$1. G. W. Ogilvie.
**Why my photographs are bad. Taylor, C: M., jr. $1 net. Jacobs.
Why we believe the Bible. King, H: M. $1. Am. Tr.
Wicker, G: R. *See* Ely, R: T.
Wiedemann, F. Biblische Geschichten; ed. by L. A. Rhoades. Holt.
Wiel, *Mme.* Verona. (Mediæval towns ser.) il. Macmillan.
Wife of Bath's tale. Chaucer, G. $10; $35. Grafton Press.
†Wiggin, Kate D. Penelope's Irish experiences. Holiday ed. il. 12°. $2. Houghton, M. & Co.
**Wiggin, Kate D., *and* Smith, Nora A., *eds.* Golden numbers. 12°. $2 net. McClure.
**Wild flowers, Guide to the. Lounsberry, Alice. $1.75 net-$3.50 net. Stokes.
Wild flowers. *See also* Mathews, Ferd. S. Putnam.
Wild fowl. Sanford, L. C. Macmillan.
Wilder, H. H. Synopsis of animal classification. Holt.
**Wilhelm I., *Kaiser, and* Bismarck, Letters between. 2 v. 8°. $4 net; ¾ levant, $8 net. Stokes.
**Wilkie, *Sir* D: Bayne, *Prof.* $1.25 net. [Imp.] Scribner.
Wilkins, A. S., *ed.* *See* Ciceronis. Oxford Univ.
†Wilkins, Ma. E. The wind in the rose bush, and other stories. il. 5 x 8. $1.50 net. Doubleday, P.
Will and the way. Mallandaine, C. E. 60 c. Young.
Will o' the mill. Stevenson, R. L: 40 c.-$1.25. Caldwell.
Willard, Ashton, R. Land of the Latins. il. 8°. Longmans.
Willard, Frances E. *See* Babcock, Bernie. Revell.
Willard, Rosseter. The senator's sweetheart. Grafton Press.
**Willett, Herbert L. Pursuit of character. 12°. bds., 35 c. net. Revell.
Williams, Alice L. Royalty of friendship. New ed. 12°. $1.50; chamois, $2.50; ed. de luxe, lim. suede, $4. Caldwell.
**Williams, Archibald. Romance of modern invention. il. 12°. $1.50 net. Lippincott.
†Williams, Francis C. The captain. il. 12°. silk cl., $1.50. Lothrop.
Williams, Gardner F. Diamond mines of South Africa. il. 8°. [also] large pap. ed. Macmillan.
Williams, Hal. Mechanical refrigeration. 12°. Macmillan.
Williams, J. W. Text-book of obstetrics. Appleton

**Williams, Jesse L. Picturesque New York. il. 8°. net. Scribner.
Williams, T. L. Thy kingdom come. 12°. $1.25. Young.
**Williamson, F. H., *ed.* Book of beauty. il. folio $35 net. Lippincott.
Willis, H. Parker. *See* Laughlin, J. L.
Wilson, Aimee. Gems of thoughts from classical authors. (Miniature volumes.) New ed. marble enamel, 50 c. Stokes.
Wilson, Daniel M. Where American independence began. Houghton, M. & Co.
**Wilson, H. Silver work and jewelry. il. 12°. (Artistic crafts ser.) $1.20 net. Appleton.
Wilson, J. Cook. Epagogé: an essay. Oxford Univ.
**Wilson, Rufus R. New York old and new. il. 2 v. extra buckram, $3.50 net. Lippincott.
**Wilson, Woodrow. History of American people. 5 v. 8°. $17.50 net; cf. or levant, $30 net. Harper.
†Wind (The) in the rose bush. Wilkins, Ma. E. $1.50 net. Doubleday, P.
†Wind in the tree. Duchess of Sutherland. $1.50. Russell.
Window in Thrums. Barrie, J. M. 75 c. Caldwell.
**Windsor, *Lord* J: Constable. (Makers of British art.) il. 8°. $1.25 net. [Imp.] Scribner.
†Winfield, Arth. M. Bob, the photographer. il. $1.25. Wessels.
Winfield, Arth. M. Larry Barlow's ambition. il. 12°. $1. Saalfield.
Winfield, Arth. M. Young bridge tender. il. 12°. $1.25. Street.
Wingate, C: E. L., *and* McKay, F. E., *eds.* Famous American actors of to-day. il. 12°. 2 v. $2.75. Crowell.
†Wings and fetters. Kingsley, F. M. $1. Altemus.
†Wings of the dove. James, H: 2 v. $2.50. Scribner.
Winning of Sarenne. Beall, St. Clair. 50 c. Federal Bk. Co.
†Winslow, Helen M. Concerning Polly, and some others. il. 12°. $1.50. Lee & Shepard.
**Winslow, Helen M. Literary Boston of to-day. il. large 16°. $1.20 net; ¾ lev., $2.50 net. L. C. Page.
†Winslow plain. Greene, S. P. M. $1.50. Harper.
Winslow's Natural arithmetic. bk. 1, 30 c.; bk. 2, 40 c.; bk. 3, 50 c. Am. Bk.
†Winter, J: S. Blaze of glory. 12°. $1.25. Lippincott.
Winter, J: Strange. Soul of honor. 12°. $1. Fenno.
Wireless telegraphy. Sewell, C. H. Van Nostrand.
Wisdom of à Kempis. Thomas à Kempis. Wieners.
**Wister, Owen. Benjamin Franklin. (English men of letters.) 75 c. net. Macmillan.
**Wit and humour, French. 16°. 50 c. net: leath., 80 c. net. Jacobs.
**Wit and humour of American statesmen. Reddale, F:, *comp.* 50 c. net; 80 c. net. Jacobs.
**Wit and humour ser. Jacobs.
New volume: French wit and humour.
**With a saucepan over the sea. Keen, A. $1.50 net. Little, B. & Co.
With force and arms. Garis, H. R. $1. J. S. Ogilvie.
**With Kitchener in the Soudan. Henty, G: A. $1.20 net. Scribner.
*With Napoleon at St. Helena. Stokoe, *Dr.* J: $1.50 net. Lane.
†With Rogers on the frontier. Oxley, J. M. $1.25. Wessels.
†With sword and crucifix. Van Zile, E: S. 50 c. New Amsterdam.
**With the British legion. Henty, G: A. $1.20 net. Scribner.
**With the flag in the channel. Barnes, J. 80 c. net. Appleton.
†With Washington in the west. Stratemeyer, E: $1.25. Lee & Shepard.
Without counting the cost. 16°. 40 c. Young.
Witts, Florence. Story of Catherine of Sienna. 50 c. Whittaker.
Witty, humorous and merry thoughts, selected by T. Mason. 50 c. Stokes.
†Wolfville nights. Lewis, A. H: $1.50. Stokes.
Wolfrom, Anna. Romance of Wolf hollow. il. 12°. bds., $1. Badger.
*Wolley, C: Two years' journal in New York and part of its territories in America. (1701.) Repr. bds., about $2; Jap. pap., $3 net. Burrows.
†Woman (A) intervenes. Barr, R. 50 c. Stokes.
Woman who dared. Lynch, L. L. 75 c.; 25 c. Laird.
Woman who went to hell. Sigerson, D. 75 c. Brentano.
Woman's manual of law. Greene, M. A. Silver.
Woman and economics. Stetson, C. P. 50 c. Small, M.
Won—not by might. Gee, A. L. $1.50. Young.
Wonder books. (Nursery stories.) col. il. 3 v. ea., 50 c. Warne.
**Wonderful Teacher and what He taught. Burrell, D: J. $1.20 net. Revell.
Wood, C: S. On the frontier with St. Clair. il. $1.50. Wilde.
Wood, Frances H. Mrs. Moffat's brownie. 16°. 80 c. Young.
**Wood, F: Government and the state. 12°. $2.25 net. Putnam.
Wood, Principal species of. Snow, C: H. Wiley.
**Woodberry, G: E: Nathaniel Hawthorne. (Amer. men of letters ser.) 16°. $1.10 net; 8° ed., 350 copies, $3.50 net. Houghton, M. & Co.
**Woodberry, G: E: R. W. Emerson. (English men of letters.) 75 c. net. Macmillan.
Woodhouse, H. Thoughts by the way. 12°. $1.50. Young.
†Woods, Alice. Edges. il. 12°. $1.50. Bowen-M.

Woods, Robt. A. Americans in process. 12°. Houghton, M. & Co.
Woodworth, Joseph V. Annealing, hardening and tempering of steel. Henley.
Woodworth, Joseph V. Dies, their construction and use. il. Henley.
Wooing of Judith. Kennedy, Sa. B. $1.50. Doubleday, P.
Wooing of Wistaria. Watanna, O. $1.50. Harper.
**World pictures. Menpes, Mortimer. $5 net; $15 net. Russell.
Wooldridge, H. E. Polyphonic period. Oxford Univ.
Wooley, C: *See* Wolley, C: Burrows.
**Woolman, J: Journal. (Macmillan's pocket classics.) 18°. 25 c. net. Macmillan.
Worcester's primary dictionary. 12°. 50 c. Lippincott.
**Word coinage. Mead, L. 45 c. net. Crowell.
Words of help ser. ea., 30 c. Caldwell.
New volumes: Brooks, Beauty of a life of service; Duty of the Christian business man; Christ in whom Christians believe.
**Words of Jesus. Dalman, G. $2.50 net. [Imp.] Scribner.
Wordsworth, Gleanings from. (Miniature volumes.) New ed. marble enamel, 50 c. Stokes.
*Wordsworth's grave. Watson, W: 50 c. net; 75 c. net. Lane.
World's greatest pictures: *Daily Mail* art gallery of 100 masterpieces suitable for framing. fol. $10. Young.
**World's work (The). il. bound volumes. 7⅛ x 10. 3 v. ea., $2.10; leath., $3.50 net. Doubleday, P.
Worm and spiral gearing. Halsey, F. A. Van Nostrand.
*Worth of words. Bell, Raley H. $1.50 net. Grafton Press.
Worth while. Lyster, A. 80 c. Young.
†Woven with the ship. Brady, C. T. $1.50. Lippincott.
**Wright, J: H., *ed.* Masterpieces of Greek literature. 8°. $1 net. Houghton, M. & Co.
Wright, Julia MacN. Studies in hearts. il. 12°. 75 c. Am. Tr.
Wright, Mabel O. Dogtown. il. 12°. Macmillan.
Writing in English. *See* Maxwell *and* Smith's. Am. Bk.
Writing of the short story. Smith, L. W. Heath.
**Wyndham girls. Taggart, Marion A. $1.20 net. Century.
Xenophon's Anabasis. *See* Harper *and* Wallace's. Am. Bk.
Xenophon's Cyropædia. *See* Gleason's. Am. Bk.
**Yachting. Gabe, Julius. $2.50 net. Lippincott.
**Yale bicentennial publications. Scribner.
New volumes: Cook, Biblical quotations.—Scripture, Experimental phonetics.—Lang, Gallego.—Castilian court.

Yankee mother goose. Cobb, B: F. $1.25. Jamieson-H.
**Year of beautiful thoughts. Greenough, J. A. B., *comp.* $1.20 net. Jacobs.
†Yeats, S. Levett. The chevalier d'Auriac. 8°. $1.25. Longmans.
†Yeats, S. Levett. Heart of Denise *and other tales.* 8°. $1.25. Longmans.
†Yeats, S. Levett. The lord protector. 8°. $1.25. Longmans.
Yellow violin. Denison, Mary A. $1. Saalfield.
*Yeo, I. B. A manual of treatment. 10th ed. 2 v. 5¼ x 8½. $5 net. Keener.
*Yeo, I. B. Food in health and disease. 2d ed. 5¼ x 8½. $2.50 net. Keener.
Yonge, Ctte. M., Life of. Coleridge, C. R. Macmillan.
Young, Dinsdale T. Neglected people of the Bible. 12°. $1. Am. Tr.
**Young, Egerton R. My dogs in the Northland. il. 8°. $1.25 net. Revell.
**Young, Keith. Delhi (1857); ed. by Sir H: Norman. il. 8°. $8 net. Lippincott.
Young, Mary V. Italian grammar. Holt.
Young, W: Ah, what riddles these women be! bds., 6½ x 8. $1. Russell.
Young bridge tender. Winfield, A. M. $1.25. Street.
Young folks' Uncle Tom's cabin. Boylan, G. D. 60 c. Jamieson-H.
**Young George. il. by E. Farmiloe. 4°. $1.20 net. Stokes.
†Young of heart series. 12°. 50 c. Estes.
New volumes: Dickens, C: Christmas carol.—Ewing, J. H. Jackanapes.—Ingelow, Jean. Wonderbox tales.—Loti, Pierre. Lives of two cats.—Sand, G: Grandmother's story.
Young people's missionary library. 12°. ea., 75 c. Revell.
Contents: 1. Stories of sunrise land, by Belle M. Brain.—2. In the land of the lamas, by Susie C. Rijnhart.
**Young volcano explorers. Stratemeyer, E: $1 net. Lee & Shepard.
**Yourself. Guerber, H. A. $1.20 net. Dodd, Mead & Co.
**Youth of La Grande Mademoiselle. Barine Arvède. net. Putnam.
Yusuf and Zalikha. *See* Ethé, H., *ed.* Oxford Univ.
Zangwill, I. Grey wig. il. 12°. Macmillan.
**Zimmerman, Jeremiah. Travels through Spain. il. cr. 8°. $2 net. Jacobs.
Zoology, Guide to laboratory study of. Weed, C. M. Heath.
Zoology, Text book of. Hertwig, R. Holt.
**Zoology, Treatise in. Lankester, E. R., *ed.* 10 pts. pts. 1.-iv. Macmillan.
†Zoraida. LeQueux, W: 50 c. Stokes.
Zueblin, C: American municipal progress. (Citizen's lib. of economics, politics and sociology.) 12°. Macmillan.
**Zwemer, S. M. Raymond Lull. il. 12°. 75 c. net. Funk.
**Zwemer, S: M., *and* Amy E. Topsy-turvy land. (Arabia.) il. 75 c. net. Revell.
*Zwingli, Ulrich, Life of. Simpson, S: $1.25 net. Baker & T.

The Publishers' Weekly.

FOUNDED BY F. LEYPOLDT.

SEPTEMBER 27, 1902.

The editor does not hold himself responsible for the views expressed in contributed articles or communications. All matter, whether for the reading-matter columns or advertising pages, should reach this office not later than Wednesday noon, to insure insertion in the same week's issue.

***"I hold every man a debtor to his profession, from the which, as men do of course seek to receive countenance and profit, so ought they of duty to endeavor themselves by way of amends to be a help and an ornament thereunto."*—LORD BACON.**

THE FALL OUTLOOK.

THE prosperity of the past few years continues buoyant, and, apparently, irrepressible. From all parts of the country reports of business done so far and in prospect are uniformly good and encouraging. While certain sections, unfortunately, have suffered from abnormal weather conditions, a greater area has been fortunate in this respect, and business has been phenomenally good in New York and in other eastern cities, where unusually cool weather has prevailed during the summer.

Encouraged by these conditions, the publishers are announcing a larger number of books than ever before, and the average of quality is also quite up to the standard which for the past two or three years has been steadily advancing.

For a year or two wars and the general unrest attending a change of government, and a postponed coronation, have made the newspaper so all-absorbing that English publishers feared the public would not need books of lasting worth, and therefore the works of both American and English authors of note, always published simultaneously here and in England, were kept back. But now confidence seems restored, and the books we are to have this fall are goodly in number and promising in matter. The department of history and biography promises to be especially strong, and almost every publisher has on his list an original work by some noted authority, or a new edition brought down to date of some well-known standard work on the subject.

The death roll of the year among the writers is a long one on both sides of the ocean, and the last work and the posthumous and collected works, and the biographical studies of these authors furnish a notable share of the coming books. Among such authors are John Fiske, Paul L. Ford, F. Bret Harte, E. L. Godkin, Frank Stockton, H. E. Scudder, Mrs. Stoddard, Edward Eggleston, E. S. Brooks and J. G. Nicolay in America, and Kate Greenaway, Charlotte M. Yonge, and the scientists Virchow, Pasteur and Schenk in Europe. Autobiographies strongly appealing to the general buyer will also be furnished in the recollections of many noted persons.

Books on trade questions, finance and business, strikes, trusts and the many problems now before the industrial world are to be numerous, and the names of their authors vouch for their importance. Many natural phenomena, volcanic irruptions, inundations, storms of unusual fury of wind and fatality of lightning have been features of the year, and many of the causes of these phenomena are to be treated in the forthcoming books.

Fiction is always the best source of income to the bookseller, and it is to be lavishly provided by old and new writers.

On the whole, the booktrade may look into the future with greater hope than for many years past. The associations created for their protection are growing stronger day by day and are doing increasingly effective work. The opposition is practically narrowed down to one house of any importance whatever, the half dozen or more small fry elsewhere being simply feeders to the underseller in New York. If all concerned will be steadfast and loyal to the cause during another busy season, willing to make a sacrifice as well as to reap a reward, victory will at no far distant day perch upon the banner of the united booktrade.

THE "Index to Fall Announcements" in this issue of THE PUBLISHERS' WEEKLY will be found to be more inclusive than usual, because it has been our purpose to make this list in a measure supplementary to the Index to "The Publishers' Trade List Annual." That index includes the announcements publishers were ready to make up to August 1 of the present year; the index in this issue covers, also, all announcements made up to September 20, including those of all the books that are likely to be published during the fall and holiday season. With the Index to "The Publishers' Trade List Annual," the subscriber to THE PUBLISHERS' WEEKLY is now enabled to trace easily the current books through that work, the index in the present issue, and the monthly cumulated lists, until the issue in January next of the cumulated annual catalogue.

SALES OF "STOCK IN BULK."

THE following bill has been signed by the Governor and is now the law of the State of New York regulating the sales of stocks of goods in bulk by retailers:

An act to regulate the sale of merchandise in bulk.

The People of the State of New York, represented in Senate and Assembly, do enact as follows:

SECTION 1. A sale of any portion of a stock of merchandise other than in the ordinary course of trade in the regular and usual prosecution of the sellers business, or the sale of an entire stock of merchandise in bulk, shall be fraudulent and void as against the creditors of the seller, unless the seller and purchaser shall at least five days before the sale make a full and detailed inventory showing the quantity, and, so far as possible with the exercise of reasonable diligence, the cost price to the seller of each article to be included in the sale, and unless such purchaser shall at least five days before the sale in good faith make full explicit inquiry of the seller as to the name and place of residence or place of business of each and every creditor of the seller, and the amount owing each creditor, and unless the purchaser shall at least five days before the sale in good faith notify or cause to be notified personally or by registered mail each of the seller's creditors of whom the purchaser has knowledge, or can with the exercise of reasonable diligence acquire knowledge, of such proposed sale and of the stated cost price of merchandise to be sold and of the price proposed to be paid therefor by the purchaser.

SEC. 2. That, except as provided in the preceding section, nothing therein contained, nor any act thereunder, shall change or affect the present rules of evidence or the present presumptions of law.

SEC. 3. This act shall take effect immediately.

BOOK THEFTS AT BRENTANO'S.

BRENTANO'S at New York, owing to a deep-laid conspiracy, have been losing books in small quantities since last February, and in consequence Frederick Evans, the assistant order clerk, has been arrested. The specific charge is the theft of books to the value of $15.77, on August 18. Evans occupied a position of trust, and was employed only after a personal examination by one of the firm of a list of twelve references, all of which were found unimpeachable.

Mr. Simon Brentano became convinced that books were being stolen from the store, and he engaged a detective September 10th to find out the culprit. It was discovered that the books were being taken out of the shop by three of the boys under direction of Evans. The stolen books were taken to the Manhattan Delivery Company, where they were re-addressed to the bookstore of Charles P. Cox, No. 257 West 125th Street, and to other small book dealers. A visit of the detective to Cox's store revealed a number of volumes readily identified as having come from Brentano's. These were mostly books listed at $1.50, and readily salable.

Mr. Cox said that he had bought the books of Evans, who had represented himself as one of a large jobbing firm that could let him have popular novels at less than market prices. The chance seemed too good to be let slip, so, he said, he had been buying books from Evans right along.

An examination of the boys who had been carrying the books showed that they had been delivering books for Evans at the rate of 15 cents a volume. One of the boys had made some trouble for Evans, and so he received from one to three volumes a day to dispose of himself. Evans had told the boys if they were ever questioned about what they were doing to make a stout denial, and he would stand by them. Judicious cross questioning, however, proved too much for them, and they confessed all.

On the 20th inst., Evans was arrested and the next day was brought before Justice Flammer at the Jefferson Market Police Court, who held him in default of $1,000 bail. The hearing will very likely come off early in October, and some startling developments are expected.

OBITUARY NOTES.

DR. ALBRECHT KIRCHHOFF, for some time chairman of the Library Committee of the German Börsenverein and member of the Historical Committee of that association, died in Leipzig, August 20. He was acting librarian of the library of the Börsenverein from March till November, 1869, and presented to that institution his exceedingly valuable collection of material relating to the history of the German booktrade.

THE REV. DR. HENRY AUGUSTUS PIERSON TORREY, oldest professor in term of service in the University of Vermont, died at Beverly, Mass., September 20. He was born in Beverly, January 8, 1837. He graduated from the University of Vermont in 1858, and from the Union Theological Seminary, New York, in 1865. He edited Professor Joseph Torrey's book, "Theory of Fine Art," and in 1892 published "The Philosophy of Descartes."

JOHN STEBBINS LEE, D.D., Professor of Church History, and the first president of St. Lawrence University, died on the 10th inst., at Canton, N. Y., aged eighty-two years. He was graduated from Amherst College in the class of 1845. He was the oldest educator in the Universalist denomination, having been connected with denominational schools and colleges for fifty-seven years. He was a frequent contributor to denominational papers, and the author of "Nature and Art in the Old World" and "Sacred Critics."

MAJOR JOHN WESLEY POWELL, the eminent naturalist and director of the Bureau of Ethnology at the Smithsonian Institution in Washington, died at Haven, Me., on the 23d inst. Major Powell was born in Mount Morris, Livingston Co., N. Y., March 24, 1834, and was the son of a Methodist clergyman. When about seven years old the family removed to Jackson, Ohio, where the boy became interested in scientific matters. He attended school in Illinois, Wisconsin and

Ohio. He was graduated from Illinois Wesleyan with the degrees of A.M. and Ph.D. Later he received the degree of LL.D. from Columbia University, of Washington, in 1882, the same from Harvard in 1886 and a Ph.D. from Heidelberg the same year. Enlisting in the Second Illinois Artillery, at Shiloh he lost his right arm. He was mustered out with the rank of major. After the war he again devoted his attention to scientific pursuits. He explored the then little known Grand Canyon of the Colorado in 1869. He was appointed director of the United States Bureau of Ethnology in 1879, and of the United States Geological Survey a year later, when he also was elected to membership in the American Academy of Science. In 1884 Professor Powell resigned the post of director of the Geological Survey, but remained at the head of the Bureau of Ethnology. Major Powell was the author of "The Exploration of the Colorado River of the West and Its Tributaries," "Report on the Geology of the Uintah Mountains," "Introduction to the Study of Indian Languages," "Studies in Sociology," "Canyons of the Colorado" and "Truth and Error."

NOTES ON AUTHORS.

Miss Alice Caldwell Hegan, the author of that successful little story, "Mrs. Wiggs of the Cabbage Patch," has written her second book, and it is to appear serially in *The Century*. She calls it "Lovey Mary," and the many admirers of Mrs. Wiggs will be glad to know that this optimistic character reappears in the new story.

The Rev. Dr. Henry C. McCook, a prominent clergyman of the Presbyterian church, resigned as pastor of the Tabernacle Presbyterian Church, Philadelphia, on the 21st inst., after a service of thirty-three years, to devote himself entirely to literary work. Dr. McCook is the author of a work on "American spiders," "The Martial Graves of Our Fallen Heroes," "Gospel in Nature," "The Latimers," "Old Farm Fairies," etc.

Pearl Mary Teresa Craigie, who writes under the pen-name of John Oliver Hobbes, is an American by birth and parentage, being the daughter of John Morgan Richards, a wealthy manufacturer of Boston. At an early age she married Reginald Walpole Craigie, a young Englishman, from whom she was separated a few years later. Her first published book was "Some Emotions and a Moral," (1891.) This was followed by "The Sinner's Comedy," (1892;) "A Study in Temptations," (1893;) "A Bundle of Life," (1894;) "Journeys End in Lovers Meeting," being a one-act play written for Ellen Terry, (1894;) "The Gods. Some Mortals, and Lord Wickenham," (1895;) "The Herb-Moon," (1896;) "School for Saints," (1897;) two plays produced at the St. James' Theatre: "The Ambassador," (1898,) and "A Repentance," (1899;) "Osberne and Useyne," (1899,) a three-act tragedy; "Robert Orange," (1900;) and "A Word to the Wise," (1901.) She will shortly produce a play in collaboration with Murray Carson, one of the authors of "Rosemary."

JOURNALISTIC NOTES.

Collier's Weekly formally opened its new publishing house on West Thirteenth Street, New York, on September 23.

The John L. Whitman Moral Improvement Association Journal is the title of a semi-monthly just begun at the Cook County Jail, Chicago. Subscription price $1 a year, five cents the copy.

The Spirit of the Times and New York Sportsman, successor of *Wilkes's Spirit of the Times*, which for many years from 1858 on was the *Bell's Life* of America, and a prosperous sporting newspaper, has gone bankrupt. William T. Porter established the original *Spirit of the Times* in 1831. George Wilkes came in in 1853 or 1854 and became sole proprietor in 1858. In 1875 Col. Elisha A. Buck bought from Mr. Wilkes a half interest in the paper, and in 1879 the other half. Twenty years later a stock company, of which Mr. Buck was president, took the paper. Mr. Buck was killed in a railroad accident in August, 1893, and Horace Russell has since been president. He is the principal petitioning creditor in bankruptcy, his claim being $10,000 for money lent in the past five years. F. W. Leslie has been appointed temporary receiver and will very likely purchase the paper if he is permitted to continue its publication uninterruptedly.

LITERARY AND TRADE NOTES.

Harper & Brothers will bring out next month Serao's "The Conquest of Rome."

William Heinemann, one of the most enterprising English publishers, intends to pay this country a visit in the fall.

John Saint Loe Strachey, the editor and proprietor of *The Spectator*, will make a visit to this country some time in November.

A. C. McClurg & Co. will publish in November a novel dealing with the Northwest, by Mrs. Eva Emery Dye, entitled "The Conquest—the true story of Lewis and Clark."

Hurst & Co. have made a number of additions to their many series and libraries. They have about 2500 titles put up in various styles, printed on good paper and bound in cloth or leather, as may be desired.

The book for collectors by a collector that Sampson Low, Marston & Co. will publish next month, and that was referred to in our last week's issue, is "Rariora," and not the thing that the linotype made us say.

G. & C. Merriam & Co. call attention to their new edition of "Webster's International Dictionary," with 25,000 additional words, phrases and definitions, printed from new plates. The Merriams have again proven that they are not content to leave well enough alone, and that they are determined, whenever the opportunity presents itself, to make better the best.

John Lane will bring out shortly a library edition of "Lowell's Early Prose Writings," compiled and edited by Walter Littlefield. Dr. Edward Everett Hale has written a brief preface for the book, in which he presents his recollections of Lowell as he knew him at Harvard and as a contributor to his brother's magazine, *The Boston Miscellany,* from which all but two of the articles and stories are taken.

THE AMERICAN BAPTIST PUBLICATION SOCIETY will publish this fall an *edition de luxe* of Mrs. Caroline Atwater Mason's popular novel, "A Lily of France." This edition will contain 14 superb photogravures, with a beautiful frontispiece from an original painting. The binding will be dark blue cloth, with the combined coats of arms of William of Orange and Charlotte de Bourbon in gold.

FROM the Sign of the Hop-Pole, Crockham Hill, Eden Bridge, Kent, England, is to appear at Michaelmas a reprint of an essay written in 1865 by Henry David Thoreau, entitled "Life Without Principle," with a short biographical account of the author by Ralph Waldo Emerson The edition is to be limited to 1000 copies. This volume is to be the first of a series intended to be issued from this address at Michaelmas, Christmas, Candlemas and Easter of each year.

THE dramatization of "Dorothy Vernon of Haddon Hall" is now having the finishing touch put to it by the author, Charles Major, and the dramatist, James McArthur. Mr. McArthur, it will be remembered, was the dramatist of "The Bonny Brier Bush." He was for many years one of the editors of the *Bookman* and is at present one of Harper & Brothers' literary advisers. Charles Frohmann is arranging for the production of the play, and the announcement of the leading rôles may be made at any moment.

E. P. DUTTON & Co. have just ready a work entitled "Vital Religion, or, the Personal Knowledge of Christ," by G. H. Walpole, D.D., principal of Bede College, Durham, England, which is the third volume published of a series of handbooks on current ecclesiastical problems. The problems, which are discussed in this series of handbooks, are all of primary importance to such as take an intelligent interest in the Anglican Communion. The object aimed at is to treat these problems in a sympathetic and broad-minded spirit.

PRESIDENT ROOSEVELT in his Bangor speech referred to Charles Wagner's book, "The Simple Life," as one so wholesome and containing such sound doctrine that he wished it could be used "as a tract throughout our country" Almost immediately orders began to come into the publishers, McClure, Phillips & Co., and the book, which had before had a quiet though steady sale, leaped from a second edition into a third, and is now about going into a fourth.

McCLURE, PHILLIPS & Co. will publish within the next fortnight "The Two Vanrevels," a novel of Indiana life in the 40's, by Booth Tarkington; "Racer of Illinois," by Henry Somerville, author of "Jack Racer," to which the present novel is a sequel; "Gabriel Tolliver," the first long novel by Joel Chandler Harris, the creator of "Uncle Remus;" "Border Fights and Fighters," by the Rev. Cyrus Townsend Brady; "Letters from Egypt," by Lady Duff Gordon, with introduction by George Meredith; also, "Dante and His Times," by Dr. Karl Federn, a profound student of Italian literature.

A. C. ARMSTRONG & SON announce "Erromonga, the Martyr Isle," by the Rev. H. A. Robertson, of Erromonga, a missionary biography expected to rival that of John G. Paton, already in its 22d thousand; "The Death of Christ," by Professor James Denney; "Flood-Tide: Sunday Evenings in a City Pulpit," by the Rev. G. H. Morrison, of Glasgow; and "The Church and the Ministry in the Early Centuries," by Professor T. H Lindsay. This house will also bring out a new edition of Dr. George Matheson's "Representative Men of the Bible;" and the fifth thousand of "Brooks by the Traveller's Way," by the Rev. J. H. Jowett..

BRENTANO'S are preparing for fall publication a dainty edition of Walter Besant's "Art of Fiction;" and an illustrated library edition of Jessie Fothergill's "The First Violin," in two volumes, with upwards of 60 illustrations after wash drawings by George W. Brenneman, of the Salmagundi Club. They have nearly ready "Italy," by Theophile Gautier; "Avon of Shakespeare," by James Thorne; "A Visit to London," by Edward V. Lucas; "Palaces, Prisons and Resting Places of Mary, Queen of Scots," by M. M. Shoemaker; and *Museum editions* of the most notable books of all ages and all countries, beginning with "The Odes of Anacreon" and taking in the best-known works of Emerson, De Quincey, Rabelais and Montaigne. For children they have in preparation "The Adventures of Uncle Lubin," by W. Heath Robinson.

CHARLES SCRIBNER'S SONS announce a volume compiled from the literary remains of Horace Bushnell, the hundredth anniversary of whose birth has again directed attention to his writings. The title will be "The Spirit in Man: Sermons and Fragments That Remain." During October will appear "New Amsterdam and Its People: studies social and topographical of the town under Dutch rule," by J. H. Innes, with maps, plans, views and portraits; "The Private Soldier Under Washington," by Charles Knowles Bolton, librarian of the Boston Athenæum; "Sea Fighters from Drake to Farragut," by Jessie Peabody Farragut; "The Blue Flower," a new book of stories by Henry Van Dyke; and "Whom the Gods Destroyed," by Josephine Dodge Daskam, a group of stories giving studies of the artistic temperament. Kipling's "Kim" has just been added to the *Outward Bound edition* of his works.

BOWEN-MERRILL COMPANY will publish at once "Edges," by Miss Alice Woods, a new Indiana author, a story of American and Parisian painters' life; "The Loom of Life," a new story, by Charles Frederic Goss, in which he follows lines laid down in his "Redemption of David Corson," dealing as the story does with the struggles of a strong soul against temptation; also, "The Long Straight Road," by George Horton, who takes his title from a phrase of Robert Louis Stevenson: "Times are changed with him who marries; there are no more by-path meadows where you may innocently linger, but the road lies long and straight and dusty to the grave." This rather sombre view of the married man's lot is lightened, it is said, with plenty of American humor and cheerful tenderness. This is Mr. Horton's first story of American life, his previous novels being romances of modern Greece, where Mr. Horton spent five years as consul at Athens.

Small, Maynard & Co. will publish at once "Letters from a Self-Made Merchant to His Son," by George Horace Lorimer, which achieved such notable success during their serial publication in the Philadelphia *Saturday Evening Post;* also, a popular edition of Walt Whitman's "Complete Prose Works," in one volume, uniform with their popular edition of "Leaves of Grass." With the exception of the sumptuous edition of his works in eight volumes, which G. P. Putnam's Sons are about to issue, by special arrangement with Small, Maynard & Company, in a limited edition for subscribers, these are the only authorized and complete editions of Whitman's writings. It is amusing to note that in an unauthorized and incomplete volume of Whitman's poems made up of material on which copyright has expired, the editor naively refers to the restraint of the copyright law in the following words: "For the errors of omission, conditions which I could not control are alone responsible, a fact which time will yet correct."

Houghton, Mifflin & Co. will publish on October 4 Thomas Wentworth Higginson's "Life of Henry Wadsworth Longfellow" in the *American Men of Letters Series;* and Robert Southey's "Journal of a Tour in the Netherlands," of which the manuscript has only just been obtained for publication. A posthumous volume of Bret Harte's will also appear, containing a second series of "Condensed Novels—New Burlesques," which parody "Rupert of Hentzau," "The Christian," "Sherlock Holmes" and "David Harum;" also two new novels: "The Strongest Master," by Helen Choate Prince, a story dealing with labor problems; and "The Heart of the Doctor," by Mabel G. Foster, a story of the old North End of Boston, now given over to the Italians. For younger readers there will be issued "Under Colonial Colors," by Everett T. Tomlinson; and "Three Little Marys," by Nora Archibald Smith, who tells a story of an English, an Irish and a Scotch little Mary. "Captain Craig," a book of poems, by Edwin A. Robinson, completes the list for October 4.

The Arthur H. Clark Company, Garfield Building, Cleveland, O., announce a series of monographs to be published under the general title of "The Historic Highways of America," by Archer Butler Hulbert, dealing with the history of America, as portrayed in the evolution of its highways of war, commerce and social expansion. The series will be divided as follows: (1) Paths of the Mound-Building Indians and Great Game Animals; (2) Indian Thoroughfares; (3) Washington's Road: the First Chapter of the Old French War; (4) Braddock's Road; (5) The Old Glade (Forbes's) Road; (6) Boone's Wilderness Road; (7) Portage Paths: the Keys of the Continent; (8) Military Roads of the Mississippi Basin; (9) Historic Waterways; (10) The Cumberland Road; (11 and 12) Pioneer Roads of America; (13 and 14) The Great American Canals; (15) The Future of Road-Making in America. The sixteenth volume will contain a comprehensive index. The first volume is about ready. The other volumes will be published at the rate of a volume every two months.

James Pott & Co. have an interesting fall list, upon which "The Life and Works of Richard Brinsley Sheridan," in two volumes, stands out prominently. The volumes give a vivid picture of the times of Sheridan and of all the noted people of his day, and throw light upon the inspiration Sheridan received for his celebrated comedies, dramas, farces and poems. A new addition to the *Photogravure Series* will be "The Mediterranean: its storied cities and venerable ruins," by J. T. Bonney; and other books in preparation include "Ghetto Silhouettes," by the playwright and actor, David Warfield; "A Maid of Many Moods," by Vivian Sheard, in which the merry days of Shakespeare are made alive and real; "Builders of the Republic," by the author of "Famous Families of New York," a book telling of the twenty-five great men who made the United States; "Paris, 1789-1794," by J. G. Alger; "Five Great Painters of the Victorian Era," by Sir Wyke Bayliss; "Cromwell's Army," by C. H. Firth; "Louis XIV. and the Court of France in the 17th Century," in three volumes, and "Marie de Medicis, Queen of France," in three volumes, both by Julia Pardoe.

Funk & Wagnalls Company have just ready Mrs. Craigie's ("John Oliver Hobbes") new novel, "Love and the Soul Hunters;" "The Needle's Eye," a novel, by Florence Morse Kingsley, which deals with the difficulties that beset a young man in his efforts to administer for the good of the people the trust of great riches which it has imposed upon him; "The Insane Root," an exciting novel, by Mrs. Campbell Praed, the basis of which is the legend of the mysterious virtue of the mandrake root; an American edition of "The Searchers," a novel by Mrs. Margaretta Byrde, which has been very successful in England; a dissertation on "The Ten Commandments and the Lord's Prayer," by Dr. F. S. Schenck, which is a revised edition of the author's previous work, "The Ten Commandments in the Nineteenth Century," with the addition of "The Lord's Prayer" portion; "The Lost Wedding Ring," a series of essays upon marriage, by the Rev. Cortland Myers, D.D., who treats the subject from a religious standpoint and illuminates it by numerous illustrations in prose and verse; also, "Sons of Glory," a book of "studies in genius," by a talented young psychologist of

Italy, by name Adolfo Padovan, who combats the theory of Lombroso that genius is a form of insanity.

G. P. PUTNAM'S SONS have in press the following fiction: "Typhoon," a new story by Joseph Conrad, author of "Tales of Unrest," etc.; "The Earth and the Fullness Thereof," a tale of modern Styria, by Peter Rosegger, translated by Frances E. Skinner; "The Sheep-Stealers," a romance of the west of England, by Violet Jacob; "The House Opposite: a Mystery," by Elizabeth Kent; "Lavender and Old Lace," a story of a quaint corner of New England, by Myrtle Reed, author of "Love Letters of a Musician;" "The Poet and Penelope," a delightful story by L. Parry Truscott; "Peak and Prairie" and "Pratt Portraits," thirteen stories from "A Colorado Sketch Book," and thirteen stories of New England life, by Anna Fuller, author of "A Literary Courtship," etc., old favorites in a new and more worthy dress; also, "The Boys of Waveney," a story of school-boy life in England, by Robert Leighton. They also announce the *Hampshire edition* of the works of Jane Austen, and a library edition of the earlier works of Miss Cary, including "Browning, Poet and Man: a Survey," "Tennyson, His Homes, His Friends, His Work," and "The Rossettis, Dante Gabriel and Christina." Of the limited edition of William Blake's illustrations to the Book of Job, Messrs. Putnam have secured a portion for the American market. This series of designs represent the most noteworthy productions of the famous artist. The designs have never before been reproduced in the size of the originals, or in any such manner as would give an adequate impression of the force and power of the artist's work.

LITTLE, BROWN & CO. have just ready "The Shadow of the Czar," the romantic story of Princess Barbara of the old Polish principality of Szernova, by John R. Carling, an author who, as the publishers assert, is as unknown to them as to the reading public at large, but whose fanciful story of love and adventure they predict will prove a popular one. They have also just ready the following juveniles: "Nathalie's Chum," by Anna Chapin Ray; "Foxy, the Faithful," by Lily F. Wesselhoeft; "On Guard! Against Tarleton and Tory," by John Preston True; and "Grandma's Girls," by Helen Morris. Their publications for the autumn include "American Literature in its Colonial and National Periods," by Professor Lorenzo Sears, of Brown University; "Glimpses of China and Chinese Homes," by Professor Edward S Morse, author of "Japanese Homes and Their Surroundings;" "The Speeches and Other Writings of Daniel Webster, Hitherto Uncollected," (in three volumes;) "Retrospect and Prospect," eight critical essays by Captain Alfred Mahan; "The Struggle for a Continent," a one-volume Parkman, edited by Professor Pelham Edgar, of the University of Toronto; Katharine Prescott Wormeley's translation of Dumas's "The Speronara;" "The Spiritual Outlook," a survey of the religious life of our time as related to progress, by Willard Chamberlain Selleck; "Boston Days," a literary record by Lilian Whiting; "America in its Relations to the Great Epochs of History," by Wm. J. Mann; "First Hand Bits of Stable Lore," by Francis M. Ware, the director of horse shows; and "With a Saucepan Over the Sea," quaint recipes from foreign kitchens, by Adelaide Keen.

THOMAS NELSON & SONS have just published the smaller size of the "American Standard Edition of the Revised Bible" in bourgeois type, which has met with general approbation in the press and among Bible scholars. The *Popular Series of Nelson's Teachers' Bibles* now contain the "Helps" arranged in alphabetical order, which is a decided advantage. The new edition of their Long Primer Self-Pronouncing Teachers' Bible, printed on Nelson's India paper, shows the highest perfection in Bible manufacture. Nelson's Sunday-School Scholars' Bible, with practical "Helps," and a new Bible catechism is specially designed for young people, and the "Helps" are written by prominent Sunday-school workers, and are edited by the Rev. Dr. Schauffler, a member of the International Sunday-School Lesson Committee. Their prayer and hymnal line is as large and varied as ever, and they have recently added some new and exquisite styles in the finest bindings. The *New Century Library*, printed on Nelson's India paper, now contains the complete works of Dickens and Thackeray, and the complete novels of Scott. The size of these volumes is only 4¼ x 6¼ inches, some of them contain 950 pages, while the paper is so thin that a volume is no thicker than an ordinary monthly magazine. There are also special sets beautifully bound in morocco and ooze calf, with cases to match. Uniform with the above they issue: Burns's "Poetical Works," Carlyle's "French Revolution," Tennyson's "Poems, 1830-1859," and Bunyan's "Pilgrim's Progress." Other volumes are in preparation. Their new giftbooks include "A Fortune from the Sky," by Skelton Kuppord, author of "The Uncharted Island," etc.; "Sale's Sharpshooters, the Historical Records of a Very Irregular Corps," by Harold Avery; "Ralph Wynward," by H. Elrington; "Fallen Fortunes: being the adventures of a gentleman of quality in the days of Queen Anne," by E. Everett-Green; "Stanhope: a romance of the days of Cromwell," by E. L. Haverfield; "Two Little Travellers," by Ray Cunningham; "The Lost Squire of Inglewood, or, adventures in the caves of Robin Hood," by Dr. Johnson; "A Happy Failure," by Edith Dawson; also, a very choice line of "Toy Books" from 20 cents upward.

AUCTION SALES.

SEPTEMBER 30, 7:30 P.M.—*Americana.* (361 lots.)—*Anderson.*

OCTOBER 6, 7, 3 P.M.—Library of Professor Samuel Lockwood, including works on natural history, etc., and historical and topographical works. (712 lots.)—*Bangs.*

OCTOBER 8-10, 3 P.M.—English, classical, French and German books and periodicals. (849 lots.)—*Bangs.*

PICK-UPS.

MR. DOOLEY ON READING.—"Readin', me friend," says Mr. Dooley in the *Century,* "is talked about be all readin' people as though it was th' on'y thing that makes a man betther thin his neighbors. But th' thruth is that readin' is th' nex' thing this side iv goin' to bed f'r restin' th' mind. With mos' people it takes th' place iv wurruk. A man does n't think whin he's readin', or if he has to, th' book is no fun.

"Did ye iver have something to do that ye ought to do, but did n't want to, an' while ye was wishin' ye was dead, did ye happen to pick up a newspaper? Ye know what occurred. Ye did n't jus' skim through th' spoortin' intillygince an' th' crime news.

"Whin ye got through with thim, ye read th' other quarther iv th' pa-aper. Ye read about people ye niver heerd iv, an' happenin's ye did n't undhersthand—th' fashion notes, th' theatrical gossip, th' s'ciety news from Peoria, th' quotations on oats, th' curb market, th' rale-estate transfers, th' marredge licenses, th' death notices, th' wants ads, th' dhry-goods bargains, an' even th' iditoryals. Thin ye r-read thim over again, with a faint idee ye'd read thim befure. Thin ye yawned, studied th' design iv th' carpet, an' settled down to wurruk. Was ye exercisin' ye-er joynt intelleck while ye was readin'? No more thin if ye'd been whistlin' or writin' ye-er name on a pa-aper.

"If anny wan else but me come along they might say: 'What a mind Hinnissy has! He's always readin'.' But I wu'd kick th' book or pa-aper out iv ye'er hand, an' grab ye be th' collar an' cry, 'Up, Hinnissy, an' to wurruk!' f'r I'd know ye were loafin'. It seems like it, an' whin it comes out in talk sometimes, it sounds like it. It's a kind iv nearthought that looks ginooyne to the thoughtless, but ye can't get annything on it. Manny a man I've knowed has so doped himself with books that he'd stumble over a carpet-tack.

"Am I again' all books, says ye? I'm not. If I had money, I'd have all th' good lithrachoor iv th' wurruld on me table at this minyit. I might n't read it, but there it'd be so that anny iv me fri'nds c'u'd dhrop in an' help thimsilves if they did n't care f'r stimylants.

"I have no taste f'r readin', but I won't deny it's a good thing f'r thim that's addicted to it. In modheration, mind ye. In modheration, an' after th' chores is done. F'r as a fri'nd of Hogan says, 'Much readin' makes a full man,' an' he knew what he was talkin' about. An' do I object to th' pursuit iv lithrachoor? Oh, faith, no. As a pursuit 'tis fine, but it may be bad f'r anny wan that catches it."

MCCLURE, PHILLIPS & CO. recently received an order for "The Hound of Basker Bill." The same firm recently received from a magazine devoted to poultry interests a request for a review copy of Denslow's "Mother Goose," the editor writing that he thought the book would be "specially interesting to our constituency!"

BOOKS WANTED.

☞ **In answering, please state edition, condition, and price, including postage or express charges.**

Amer. Bapt. Pub. Soc., 69 Whitehall St., Atlanta, Ga.
Bhagavad Gita, by Wm. Judge.

Amer. Bapt. Pub. Soc., 177 Wabash Ave., Chicago.
History of Massachusetts from the First Settlement Thereof in 1628 to 1750, by Thos. Hutchinson, v. 2 only.
Stewart's Criticism of Goodspeed's Messiah's Second Coming.
Four Years in Rebel Capitals, by T. C. Leon.
Isis Unveiled, Madam Blavatsky.
Century Dictionary; Century Atlas; Century Book of Names.
The Genius of Christianity, by Chateaubriand.
11th Government Census Report of the United States Indians, Taxed and Untaxed.

Amer. Bapt. Pub. Soc., 132 E. 23d St., N. Y.
15 copies Butler's Analogy. with Emory's notes.

John R. Anderson, 114 5th Ave., N. Y.
Appleton's Cyclo. Biography, v. 1.

Antiquarian Book Concern, Omaha, Neb.
Cornelius Agrippa.
The Christian Book of Concord.
Books relating to early western travels.

Wm. M. Bains, 1019 Market St., Phila., Pa.
Richardson, Pamela.
Richardson, Sir Charles Grandison.
Richardson, Clarissa Harlowe.
John Decastro and His Brother Bat.

The Baker & Taylor Co., 33 E. 17th St., N. Y.
Besant, Life of Richard Jefferies. L., G. & Co.

Wm. Ballantyne & Sons, 428 7th St., Washington, D. C.
Pidgin, Practical Statistics. Boston.

The Balto. Book Co., 301 St. Paul St., Balto., Md.
Ladies' Repository, v. 34 to 50.
Neill, Founders of Maryland.
Neill, Terra Mariæ.
Bound vols. of newspapers.
Odd vols. of Md. Repts.

Banks & Co., Albany, N. Y.
Abbott's Practice Reports, New Series, v. 14, 15, 16.
Abbott's New Cases, v. 30, 31, 32.
Abbott's New Practice and Forms, 2 v. 1871.
Jones and Spencer's Reports, any late vols.
Howard's U. S. Reports, v. 17.
Angell, On Watercourses, 7th ed. 1877.

Beecher & Kymer, Kalamazoo, Mich.
Lossing, Cyclopedia of American History, next to last ed.

Retail Store of Bigham & Smith, Agts., Nashville, Tenn.
Christ the Spirit.

Harry Bishop, care of German Bank, Louisville, Ky.
S. R. Gardiner, any 8vo vols., Lib. ed.
Tennyson, Ed. de luxe, cl.
Shelley, Forman ed., cl.

BOOKS WANTED.—Continued.

Book Exchange, Toledo, O.

Field, Michael, Long Ago. Mosher.
Procter, E. D., Prose and Poems, best eds.
Anything by Arthur Symons.
2 copies *National Mag.*, Dec., 1899.

The Bowen-Merrill Co., Indianapolis, Ind.

Complete set of *World* Almanac to date.
Oliphant, Zaidee.

Brentano's, 218 Wabash Ave., Chicago, Ill.

Conference on Manual Training, ed. by Mrs. L. C. Barrows. Pub. by New England Educational Workers in 1891 at Boston, Mass.

S. E. Bridgman & Co., 108 Main St., Northampton, Mass.

Curse of Education, Gorst.
Coligny and the Failure of the French Revolution, Besant.
Analysis of Air and Water, Lavoisier, reprint.
Hours with German Classics, Hedge.
Jonathan Edwards' Works, v. 5, 1st Amer. ed., 8 v., 12mo, leath. Worcester, 1808.
Peele's Plays and Poems, Morley Library.
Richard Simpson's School of Shakespeare, 2 v. London, Chatto & Windus, 1878.
Lyly's Dramatic Works, 2 v. London, John Russell Smith, 1858.
The Old Dramatists, Green and Peele. Routledge.
Hazlitt's Dodsley's Old Plays, 14 v. Reeves & Turner, 1874.

Brown, Eager & Hull Co., Toledo, O.

Palæographia Sacra Pictoria, by J. O. Westwood, il. with 50 plates, quarto. London, 1843 to 1850.

The Burrows Bros. Co., Cleveland, O.

Gunther, Study of Fishes.
Wilson, Mem. Hist. of N. Y.
Schaff, Renaissance.
Roberts, In and Out of Book and Journal.
Torrey, Portraiture of Slavery.
Field, Stones of the Temple.
Freeman, Historical Geography.
Rapp, Memoirs of Napoleon in Eng.
Lawrence, Breakspeare.
Bartram, Travels, Rpt. of 1751.
Washington, Rules of Civility.
Birney, Life of Birney.
Brookes, Theol. of the Eng. Poets.
Lippard, The Nazarene.
Lippard, The Entranced.
Lippard, Legends of Mexico.
Lippard, The Bank Director's Son.
Bourrienne, Memoirs of Napoleon, 4 v., 8vo, red cl. Phipps, Merrill & Baker.
Stubbs, Kirk Genealogy. 1872.
Pulliam, Constitutional Conventions of Va.

William J. Campbell, Phila., Pa.

Egle's Penna. Genealogies.
Du Bois Family Reunion.
Thompson Family, anything genealogical.
Stiles, Ancient Windsor.
Gracian's Complete Gentlemen, tr. from the Spanish.

Campion & Hern, 1001 Chestnut St., Phila., Pa.

Guizot, History of France, 6 v., 8vo. Boston.

Casino Book Co., 1374 Broadway, N. Y. [*Cash.*]

The Great Rebellion, by J. M. Botts. Harper, 1867.
Linton, Golden Apples of Hesperus.

A. H. Clapp, 32 Maiden Lane, Albany, N. Y.

How to Catalogue a Library, Wheatley. Armstrong.
Tale of Two Cities, brown cl., Excelsior ed. Am. News Co.
Great Expectations, brown cl., Excelsior ed. Am. News Co.
Our Mutual Friend, brown cl., Excelsior ed. Am. News Co.
Bleak House, brown cl., Excelsior ed. Am. News Co.
Martin Chuzzlewit, brown cl., Excelsior ed. Am. News Co.
Barnaby Rudge, brown cl., Excelsior ed. Am. News Co.

The Robert Clarke Co., 31 E. 4th St., Cincinnati, O.

Bandelier, Delight Makers.
Bandelier, Mexico.
Bandelier, Historical Introduction to Study Among Indians of New Mexico.
Bandelier, History of Southwest Portion of U. S.
Bandelier, Report of Archæological Tour in Mexico.
Bandelier, Report of Invest. Among the Indians, 2 v.
Lyall, Land of the Leal.
Prisoners of 1776. Boston, 1854.

W. B. Clarke Co., Park and Tremont Sts., Boston, Mass.

Sanford, New Book of Charades.

Henry T. Coates & Co., Phila., Pa.

1st editions of Bret Harte: On the Frontier; By Shore and Sedge; Maruja; Snowbound at Eagle's; Phyllis of the Sierras; Crusade of the "Excelsior"; Ward of the Golden Gate; Sappho of Green Springs; Colonel Starbottle's Client; Susy; Story of a Mine; Drift from Two Shores; Thankful Blossom; Twins of Table Mountain; Carquinez Wood; Two Men of Sandy Bar.
Complete set of London *Punch*, original issue.
Besant, The Chaplain of the Fleet.
Doubleday, Gettysburg Made Plain.
Cruise of the "Walnut Shell."

Geo. H. Colby & Co., 22 Main St., Lancaster, N. H.

Catalogues and discount sheets of old American and English publishing houses whose lists are not in Trade List Annual, 1902.

H. M. Conner, 232 Meridian St., E. Boston, Mass.

Lever's Works, cheap.
May Martin.
Don Quixote, 2 v., with Johannot illus.
Rabelais, Unexpurgated ed.

Crusoe & Co., 81 Vermont St., Brooklyn, N. Y.

Patent Sermons, by Lorenzo Dow, Jr.

Cushing & Co., 34 W. Baltimore St., Baltimore, Md.

Kennedy, Rob of the Bowl.

John F. Davies, Silver Bow Block, Butte, Mont.

Grady, Henry W., Life, Letters and Speeches.
Century Cyclopædia of Names.
O'Reilly, John Boyle, Poems.

Edwin W. Dayton, 763 5th Ave., N. Y.

With Friend and Book, Roger Rees.
Pleasures of a Book Worm, Roger Rees.

F. R. DeWitt, 318 Post St., San Francisco, Cal.

Irving's Washington, National ed., black cl., complete or odd vols.
Rovings in the Pacific, 2 v.

DeWolfe, Fiske & Co., 361 Washington St., Boston, Mass.

Stoddard's Lectures, v. 1, best ed.
Ilian, or, the Curse of the Old South Church. Pub. by J. B. L.
Appleton's Annuals, 1883 to 1901, hf. mor.

Dixie Book Shop, 35 Nassau St., N. Y.

1st eds. George Meredith.
Boccaccio's Life of Dante. Grolier Club.
English Writers, Langland to Withers. Grolier Club.
Hugo, any odd vols., hf. calf. Little, Brown & Co., 1887.

Dodd, Mead & Co., 372 Fifth Ave., N. Y.

Large paper Holmes.
Large paper Lowell.
The Dilemma, a novel of the Indian Mutiny.
Tales of Mean Streets, by Arthur Morrison.
Nigger of the "Narcissus," or Children of the Sea.
Longfellow, Kavanagh. 1849.
Lowell, Among My Books. 1876.
Lowell, Conversations on Old Poets, 1845, or any earlier ed.
Arnold's First Report of a Book Collector.

Chas. H. Dressel, 561 Broad St., Newark, N. J.

Proceedings Republican National Conventions, 1856, '60, '64, '68, '72, '76, '80, '84, '88, '92, must be clean, good copies, bound in cloth.
Brooks, On the Oyster.

Eau Claire Book and Stationery Co., Eau Claire, Wis.

Adventures of Early Discoverers, Humphrey.
Little Pilgrims at Plymouth, Humphrey.
Wonder Stories of Science, Beach.
Rocky Fort, Catherwood.

B. G. Eichelberger, 308 N. Charles St., Baltimore, Md.

Norman, The Real Japan. Scribner.
Saltus, Mr. Incoul's Misadventure, cl. or pap. Benjamin.
Knights of the Golden Horseshoe.
Hare, Florence. Macmillan.
Hare, Venice. Macmillan.

Elder & Shepard, 238 Post St., San Francisco, Cal.

Colton, Three Years in California. New York, 1850.
Willey, S. H., Thirty Years in California. San Francisco, 1879.

BOOKS WANTED.—Continued.

Elder & Shepard.—*Continued.*

Whistler, The Gentle Art of Making Enemies.
Bulkley, Dr. L. D., Eczema and Its Management. New York, 1881-84.
Carmen Sylva, Bard of Dimbovitza.

C. P. Everitt, 219 5th Ave., N. Y.

Susan Aked, Paris, English tr.
Squibob Papers, by J. P. Squibob.
Longfellow's Poems. Osgood.

C. P. Farrell, 117 E. 21st St., N. Y.

Voltaire's Philosophical Dictionary.
The Septuagint, Greek and English, complete, with Apocrypha, in good order and cheap.

H. W. Fisher & Co., 127 S. 15th St., Phila., Pa.

Battles and Leaders of the Civil War, cheap.
Thaxter, Island Garden, color illus. Houghton, Mifflin & Co.
Mme. de Stael's Memoirs.
Modern American Eloquence, ed. by Thos. B. Reed.
Harper's Weekly, war nos.
Baker's Portraits of Washington.
Schoolcraft, American Indians, v. 6.
Audubon, Birds and Quadrupeds, 8vo ed., uniform.
Robt. Browning's Poems, v. 9. Smith, Elder & Co.
Lewis and Clark's Expedition, 4 v., large pap. Harper.
Thackeray, Contributions to *Punch*, Popular ed.

FitzGerald & Co., 196 High St., Holyoke, Mass.

Set Rawlinson's Works, octavo ed., complete.

P. K. Foley, 14 Beacon St., Boston, Mass.

Emerson, Works, large pap. Cambridge, 1883-4.
Hawthorne, Works, large pap. 1883.
Holmes, Works, large pap. 1891.
Longfellow, Works, large pap. 1886-87.
Lowell, Works, large pap. 1890.
Whittier, Works, large pap. 1888-9.
Montaigne's Essays, Tudor ed.
Harte, Lost Galleon. 1867.
Harte, Condensed Novels. 1867.
Harte, Heathen Chinee, any separate ed.
Harte, Pliocene Skull. Washington, 1871.
Harte, Poetical Works. 1883.
Harte, Works. 1882.
Harte, M'liss. 1873.
Harte, all 1st eds. previous to 1890.
Fields, Osgood & Co.'s Vest-pocket Series, 1875-70. Quote only reprints of American authors.
Hearn, Chinese Ghosts. 1887.
Prime, Pottery and Porcelain. 1878.
Hope Leslie, by Miss Sedgwick, state date.
West Point Tic Tacs. 1878.
Sill, Poems, Limited ed. 1902.
The Collegian, Cambridge, 1830, any nos.
The Amateur, Boston, 1830-31, any nos.

Jos. J. Foster, 414 Washington Ave., St. Louis, Mo.

Brick Pomeroy's Nonsense.

Free Public Library, New Haven, Conn.

Jesse, George Selwyn.

W. R. Funk, Agt., Dayton, O.

Ridpath, Universal History.

Goldsmith Bros., 206 E. Baltimore St., Baltimore, Md.

Ibsen, Ghosts.

F. E. Grant, 23 W. 42d St., N. Y.

Lady Anne Hamilton's Secret History of the Court of England.
Notes from Plymouth Pulpit, by Augusta Moore. Pub. by Derby & Jackson, 1859.
Walter Besant's Life of Richard Jefferies.
Guicciardini's History of Florence.
A Book of Strange Sins, by Coulson Kernahan.
The Story of American Codes, by Wm. Jasper Nicolls.
The Captain's Bargain, by J. M. Wright (?)
For Better or Worse, by M. Leslie (?)
Ballyshan Castle.
Rip Van Winkle, pap. cover, designed and etched by Felix O. C. Darley, 1848, for the members of American Art Union.
Legend Sleepy Hollow, designed and etched by F. O. C. Darley, for members of American Art Union.
Nott's Translation of Odes from the Persian Poet Hafiz, with notes both critical and explanatory. Pub. 1787.

Gregory's Book Store, 116 Union St., Providence, R. I. [*Cash.*]

Tooke's Lucian, 2 v.
Thaxter, An Island Garden.
3 copies Mitchell, O. M., The Orbs of Heaven.

Martin I. J. Griffin, 2009 N. 12th St., Phila., Pa.

Madden, Lives of United Irishmen.

Isaac Hammond, Charleston, S. C.

Prostrate State, Pike.
Our Women in the War. Charleston, 1885 (?)
Sketch of Marion, James.
O. P. Historical Books on S. C.
Landscape in Poetry, Palgrave. Macmillan.

Wm. Helburn, 10 E. 16th St., N. Y. [*Cash.*]

American Architect and Building News, from 1893 to 1901, incl.

Herr & Herr, South Bend, Ind.

City Ballads, Carleton, 8vo, red binding.

The Herrick B. & S. Co., Denver, Colo.

The Standard Dictionary, 2 v., full leath., latest. state price.

John Highlands, 16 N. 11th St., Phila., Pa.

Brinley Catalogue, pt. 1, with or without prices.
Parton, Life of Andrew Jackson, v. 1, 8vo, cl. Mason & Co., New York, 1860.
Cameron Hall, a story of the Civil War, by Miss M. A. Cruse.
Flush Times in Alabama and Mississippi, by Joseph S. Baldwin.
My Life is Like a Summer Rose.

Walter M. Hill, 31 Washington St., Chicago, Ill.

Sequin's Idiocy.
Hewlett, Earthwork Out of Tuscany, 1st ed., or any 1st eds. of Maurice Hewlett.
Propert, Miniatures.
Addison, Damascus and Palmyra, 2 v., col. plates.
Bax, Life of Marat.
Dictionary of National Biography, 63 v. and supp.
Dove Press books, any.
Browning, Paracelsus, 1st ed.
Gardiner, England, v. 1, 2, Library ed.
Browning, E. B., Sonnets from the Portuguese; 1st ed. Reading, 1847.
Goupil's Biographical Series in English, any vols.

Howard Memorial Library, New Orleans, La.

Davis and Lee: a Vindication of the Southern States, by P. C. Centz.

U. P. James, 127 W. 7th St., Cincinnati, O.

Textile Record, Sept., 1901.
Wilson Photo. Mag., Feb., 1901.
Power, April, 1901.
Moore's Life of Byron.

Jennings & Pye, 220 W. 4th St., Cincinnati, O.

Grindrod, R. B., Bacchus, an essay.
Burns, Dawson, Temperance History, 2 v. Nat. Temp. League.
Kerr, Dr. Norman, Inebriety. Pub. H. K. Lewis.
Winshill, P. T., Temperance Movement and Its Workers. Blackie.
Couder, Tent Work in Palestine. Appleton, 1878.

E. T. Jett Book and News Co., 806 Olive St., St. Louis, Mo.

Boys of Beechwood.
Gates of Temptation, A. Bradshaw, pap.
The Awakening.
Birth of a Soul, Mrs. Alfred Phillips, pap.

E. W. Johnson, 2 E. 42d St., N. Y.

Beddoes, Poetical Works, 2 v. Will party who offered this for $1.00 or $1.25 please write again.
Poor's R. R. Manual, 1901, 1902.
Toxl. Harper & Bros.
Dutch Dominie of the Catskills.
Rhyme and Reason, Carroll.
Guizot, Hist. of Civilization.
Common Council Manual, 1845, imperfect copy will do.

F. H. Johnson, 15 Flatbush Ave., Brooklyn, N. Y.

Martin, Indian Empire, 3 v., octavo, illus. Lond.

The E. P. Judd Co., New Haven, Conn. [*Cash.*]

Index vol. Encyclo. Britannica, 9th ed., black or brown mor. backs and corners.
Larned, History for Ready Reference, v. 6, shp.
Last Fight of the "Revenge," Limited ed. H., M. & Co.

BOOKS WANTED.—*Continued.*

N. M. Ladd, 123 E. 23d St., N. Y.

Agassiz, Contributions to the Natural History of U. S., v. 1, 2.
Ferguson's Ill. Handbook of Architecture, v. 1.
Kendall's Travels to Northern Part of U. S., v. 3. N. Y., 1809.

Chas. E. Lauriat Co., 301 Washington St., Boston, Mass.

All works of Theodore Winthrop:
Canoe and the Saddle.
Cecil Dreeme.
Edwin Brothertoff.
John Brent.
Life in the Open Air.
Audubon, Birds, v. 2, 7.
Lecky, England, 8vo, London ed.
Records of Girlhood, 3 v., Kemble.
Records of Later Life, 3 v.
Doran, Habits of Men. London.
Doran, Queen Adelaide. London.
Some Emotions and a Moral, Cassell & Co. ed.
Read, Buchanan, Drifting, illus.
Memoirs of Sir Matthew Hale. London, 1835.
Mrs. Rowson's Charlotte Temple, state edition, etc.

Thomas Laurie, 13 Paternoster Row, London, E. C., Eng.

Paulsen, Introduction to Philosophy.
Barnard, English Pedagogy, 2 v.

Leary Book Store, 9 S. 9th St., Phila., Pa.

Hutton, On Bone Setting.

Leggat Bros., 81 Chambers St., N. Y.

Through the Air, John Wise.
Astor Castor.
Bandelier, Delight Makers.
Wheeler, North Carolina.
Prince and Pauper, 1st ed.

Henry E. Legler, Milwaukee, Wis. [*Cash.*]

Century Guild Hobby Horse.
Catalogue John Carter Brown Library.
Hamilton's Parodies, v. 1.

Lemcke & Buechner, 812 Broadway, N. Y.

Fischer's Latin Grammar, 2 v. N. Y., 1876.

Paul Lemperly, Cleveland, O.

Rossetti's Works, 2 v. London, 1886.
The Old Swimmin' Hole, Riley. Indianapolis, 1883.
Any 1st eds. of Thos. Hardy's books.

Edward E. Levi, 820 Liberty St., Pittsburgh, Pa.

McHenry, The Wilderness.
12 v. of Rebellion Record.
Smith, Old Redstone.
Botta, Universal Literature.
Ainsworth, Old London Bridge.

Library Clearing House, 140 Wells St., Chicago, Ill.

Parton, Life of Andrew Jackson, v. 2, cl. preferred.
Eaton, Ferns of North America, 2 v.
Williamson, Ferns of Kentucky.
Lexicon Pseudonymorum.
Oliphant, Sympneumata.

W. H. Lowdermilk & Co., Washington, D. C.

Whiting, Memoir of Rev. Samuel Whiting.
Hurd, Theory of National Existence.
Spon, Engineers' Price Book.
Powel and Macmillan, Trees for Street and Shade.
Kendall, Life of Jackson, complete or nos. 5, 6, 7.
Drone, On Copyright.
Fink, The Railroad Problem and its Solution.
Subaltern in America.
Willis, Outdoors at Idlewild.
Adams, J. Q., Report on Weights and Measures.

C. J. Lundstroem, Upsala, Sweden.

Zoega, Georg, Catalogus Codicorum Copticorum Manuscriptorum qui in Museo Borgiano Velitris Adservantur. Romae, 1810.

Lyon, Kymer & Palmer Co., Grand Rapids, Mich.

Richardson, National Banks.

Macauley Bros., 172 Woodward Ave., Detroit, Mich.

Seala. Pub. by Lee & Shepard.

Joseph McDonough, 39 Columbia St., Albany, N. Y.

Chemicals and Colors.
Field, Home Sketches in France. Putnam, 1875.
Anderson, Life of Thorwaldsen.
Puck, v. 1-7.
St. Charles Borromeo's Instructions on Eccl. Building, tr. by Wagley. Lond., 1857.

McLaren's Old Book Shop, 81 4th Ave., N. Y.

Any book on water marks in paper.

S. F. McLean & Co., 44 E. 23d St., N. Y.

McCausland, Builders of Babel. London, 1875.
Clark, Libraries in the Mediæval and Renaissance Periods.

The Edw. Malley Co., New Haven, Conn.

Illustrated Guide to the Hudson and Catskills, by E. Ingersoll.

Megeath Stationery Co., Omaha, Neb. [*Cash.*]

Life of Dr. Caldwell, by Robt. Carruthers.

Isaac Mendoza, 17 Ann St., N. Y. [*Cash.*]

History of the British Turf, v. 1, Rice. Lond., 1879.
Jonathan Slick.
British Photographic Almanac, any year.
Numa Roumestan, Rand-McNally ed.

R. H. Merriam, Hanover Sq., N. Y.

Leland's Heine's Pictures of Travel.
Morgan's Ancient Society.
Set of Eugene Field, Sabine ed.
Johnson, C. S., Arith. Raleigh, N. C., 1864.
Columbian Encyclopedia. F. & W.

F. M. Morris, 171 Madison St., Chicago, Ill.

Timbs, Curiosities of Science Past and Present, 2 v.
Harper's Weekly, 1861-1865, bound or unbound.

N. Y. Medical Book Co., 45 E. 42d St., N. Y.

Howard, Physiology of the Voice.

John P. Nicholson, 139 S. 7th St., Phila., Pa.

The Story of a Cannoneer, Buell.

W. W. Nisbet, 12 S. Broadway, St. Louis, Mo.

Investigation of Texas or Southern Cattle Fever, Drs. Smith and Kilborne. Dept. of Agrl., Wash., 1893.
Main, Ancient Law; Village Communities; and Early Institutions.

Ernest Dressel North, 18 E. 20th St., N. Y.

Palgrave's Golden Treasury, L. P., after 1884.
Green's England, illus., v. 3, 4 only.
Bullen's England's Helicon, London ed.
Grolier Club, Boccaccio's Dante.
Grolier Club, Franklin Etching.
Bergh's Anthologie (Greek.)
Lowell's Life, by Scudder, 2 v., L. P.

A. J. Ochs & Co., 1781 Washington St., Boston, Mass.

Meditations of a Parish Priest. Crowell.
Hist. N. Y. 6th Regt. Cavalry, Alonzo Foster.
Hist. N. Y. 1st Regt. Dragoons.
Brief Narrative of the War in Missouri, Henry M. Painter.
Idle Hours in a Library, Hudson. Doxey.
Story of Tunnel Escape from Libby Prison. Chicago, J. L. Ransom, 1895.
Confederate Mail Carriers, James Bradley. Mexico, Mo., 1894.
Patriots and Guerillas of Tennessee and Ky., John A. Brents.
Hist. Minnesota 2d Regt., Judson W. Bishop. St. Paul, 1890.
Detroit Light Guard, Hist., etc., by Fred. S. Isham, etc. Detroit, '96.

E. J. O'Malley, Hanover Sq., N. Y.

Index vol. to World's Great Classics.
1st eds. of Harte and Stockton.
The Virginian, O. Wister, 1st ed.
Memoirs of Casanova.
Euphrosyne. H. S. Stone & Co.

Daniel O'Shea, 1584 Broadway, N. Y.

Punchinello.
History of the Rebellion and Civil Wars in England, Clarendon, v. 3, pt. 2. Oxford, 1706.

The Pease-Lewis Co., Drawer S, New Haven, Conn. [*Cash.*]

Sunday World, July 6, 1902.
2 copies Old Harbor Town, Watson, pap. Dillingham.

Phila. Mag. Depot, 117 N. 13th St., Phila., Pa. [*Cash.*]

Writings of Washington, v. 1, by J. Sparks, 8vo, Boston, 1833 or '34.
Life and Works of John Adams, v. 1, 5, 7, 9, 10, by Chas. F. Adams, 8vo, cl. Boston.
Works of Benjamin Franklin, v. 1, 10, by J. Sparks, 8vo, cl. Boston.
Works of Daniel Webster, v. 3, 8vo, cl., 8th ed. Boston, 1854.
Writings of Washington, v. 1, 2, 3, 4, by J. Sparks, 8vo, cl. Boston, 1855.

BOOKS WANTED.—*Continued.*

Phila. Mag. Depot.—*Continued.*

History of Kentucky, v. 2, by H. Marshall, 8vo, calf. Frankford, 1824.
History of N. Carolina, v. 2, by F. L. Hawks, 8vo, cl. Fayetteville, N. C., 1857.
History of the State of Rhode Island, v. 2, by S. G. Arnold, 8vo, cl. N. Y., 1859 or '60.
History of Georgia, v. 2, by W. B. Stevens, 8vo, cl. N. Y., 1847.
Memoirs of Hist. Soc. of Pennsylvania, v. 1. 1828.
Niles' Weekly Register, vols. after 50.
St. Nicholas, v. 1 to 4, or odd nos.
Cassier's Mag., v. 1, no. 2; v. 2, no. 12.
Forum, v. 1 to 4, or odd nos.
Am. Hist. Register, nos. for 1897.
Am. Monthly Mag., v. 1, nos. 1, 4, 5; v. 2, no. 3; v. 6, no. 3; v. 7, no. 2; v. 14, no. 2; 1892 to 1899.
N. A. Rev., 1815 to 1819; 1851 to '76, or odd nos.
Monist, v. 9 to 12, or odd nos.
Mag. of Western Hist., odd nos. of vols. 9 to 17.
Chautauquan, v. 1, 1881.
Catholic Quar. Rev., Jan., 1879; Apr., '80; July, Oct., '83; July, '86.

The Pilgrim Press, 175 Wabash Ave., Chicago, Ill.

Yeats, Countess Kathleen.
Yeats, Secret Rose.

T. Pillot, 409 Main St., Houston, Tex.

Travels and Explorations in Central America, Chiapas and Yucatan, by Jno. L. Stephens.

C. S. Pratt, 161 6th Ave., N. Y. [*Cash.*]

Pike, The Prostrate State.
Romance of Maurice Buckler, a novel.

C. J. Price, 1004 Walnut St., Phila., Pa.

1 each examples in 8vo size of the work of the following Amer. engravers: E. S. Best; T. D. Booth; J. G. Chapman; R. Field; Wm. Hoagland; H. Houston; C. W. Peale; Jacob Perkins; Paul Revere (a book plate would do); Jas. K. Rice; P. C. Verger; St. Memin, Port. of Washington.

Peter Reilly, 133 N. 13th St., Phila., Pa.

Dental Jurisprudence, by Rehfuss.

A. M. Robertson, 126 Post St., San Francisco, Cal.

Genealogy of the Wooster Family.

Philip Roeder, 616 Locust St., St. Louis, Mo.

Winship, Cabot Bibliography.

Wm. B. Ropes, Mt. Vernon, Skagit Co., Wash.

Thompson, Maurice, A Winter Garden.
Mr. Stranger's Sealed Packet, 12mo. About 1890.
Churchill, The Crisis; Richard Carvel.
Hough, The Mississippi Bubble.
Lloyd, Stringtown on the Pike.

J. Francis Ruggles, Bronson, Mich.

Channing, John Brown and Heroes of Harper's Ferry.
Pollard, Lost Cause.
Derry's Story of the Confed. States.
De Leon's Four Years in Rebel Capitals.

The St. Louis News Co., 1008 Locust St., St. Louis, Mo.

National Municipal League, Proceedings of the 10th and Subsequent Meetings.
Congress of Religion, Proceedings of 1, 2, 3, 4. Unity Pub. Co.
Socialist Labor Party, Proceedings 1 to 5, also 7 to 8. New York Labor News Co.
Roster Soldiers Civil War, Kansas, Kentucky, Iowa, Missouri and Illinois.
Eastman, Mrs., Legends of the Sioux.

St. Paul Book and Stationery Co., 5th and St. Peter Sts., St. Paul, Minn.

Rambles in Old Boston, by Rev. E. G. Porter.
Lora, the Major's Daughter.
Boy Slaves in Bokahai, by Kerr.
Fortune's Darling.
Pulpit Power and Eloquence.
Ossian's Poems, complete.
Story of Liberty.
Poetical Works of George Crabbe.
Genealogy of the Descendants of Richard Bailey, an early settler of Rowley, Mass., by Alfred Poor. Pub. in Salem, Mass., in 1858.

John E. Scopes, 29 Tweddle Bldg., Albany, N. Y.

American Ancestry, v. 10.
Wilkinson, Memoirs, v. 2 and atlas. Phila., 1816.

Scrantom, Wetmore & Co., Rochester, N. Y.

Ben Perley Poore, Reminiscences.

John Skinner, 44 N. Pearl St., Albany, N. Y.

The Chess Magazine for 1850-7, v. 1.

George D. Smith, 50 New St., N. Y.

Notes on New England, Henry Adams.
Book Plate Collections.
Rousseau's Confessions, 2 v., Nichols ed.
Rossetti's Sonnets. Kelmscott.
La Fontaine's Tales, 2 v., Eisen plates.
Mountain Climbing in the High Andes, Whymper.
Worship of Priapus. Knight, 1865.
Last Years of Louis xv., St. Amand.
Club of Odd Volumes.
Catalogue of an Exhibition of Nineteenth Century Bindings. Caxton Club, 1898.
Liveing, On Megrim and Sick Headache.
Lingard, History of England.

Smith & McCance, 38 Bromfield St., Boston, Mass.

Voices from the Press. N. Y., 1850.
New World, Extra Series. N. Y., 1842.
Phœnixiana. N. Y., 1856.
Squibob Papers. N. Y., 1865.
Christian Science Journal, v. 1-3, incl.

Southern Book Exchange, 104 Whitehall St., Atlanta, Ga. [*Cash.*]

5000 school books, all kinds used anywhere in the South, send list.
Stephens, War Between the States.
Standard Dictionary, in 1 or 2 v.
Burton, Anatomy of Melancholy.
Law and medical books, send list.
Gilmer, Georgians.
Encyclopedia Britannica.

Speyer & Peters, Berlin, N. W. 7, Germany.

Annales de l'Institut Pasteur.
Annals of Surgery.
Brain.
Centralblatt fuer Chirurgie.
Engineering, v. 1.
Journal of Anatomy a. Physiol.
Zeitschrift fuer Biologie.
Zeitschrift fuer Psychiatrie.
Please offer sets or single vols. or nos.

F. S. Stedman, Lewis Bldg., Pittsburgh, Pa.

The Raven, with illus. by Doré, quarto, cl.

E. Steiger & Co., 25 Park Place, N. Y. [*Cash.*]

Correspondence of Carlyle and Emerson, Supplement. Boston, 1886.
Hilprecht, Babylonian Expedition, v. 1, pt. 1.
Aeronautical Annual for 1895, '96, '97.

John Sterling, 5 Washington Hall Block, Watertown, N. Y.

English Hymns, Their Authors and History, by S. Willoughby Duffield. Funk.
Age of Pericles, by W. W. Lloyds.

Stout's Book Exchange, 612 5th St., San Diego, Cal.

6 copies Coming Slavery, Spencer, pap.
Ed. Wortley Montagu, Auto.
Hints to Horsekeepers, Herbert.
Old Forest Ranger, Herbert.
Robt. M. Bird's Novels, any.

Tower Mfg. and Novelty Co., 306 Broadway, N. Y.

Pauline Clarendon, Court of London Series.

C. L. Traver, Trenton, N. J. [*Cash.*]

Napier, Florentine History.
Lubbock, Ants, Bees and Wasps.
Proceedings of N. J. Hist. Soc., odd v.
Through the Dark Continent, v. 1.

D. H. Tripp & Son, Peoria, Ill.

Ford, Illinois.
Reynolds, Life and Times.
Reynolds, History of Illinois.
Herndon, Lincoln.

Henry K. Van Siclen, 413 W. 22d St., N. Y. [*Cash.*]

Proceedings of the American Academy of Sciences, v. 4, must be in good condition.

John D. Walker, 31 De Graaf Bldg., Albany, N. Y.

Philistine, v. 1, no. 6; v. 2, no. 4; v. 3, nos. 4, 5.
Book of Job. Roycroft Press.
Burns' Poems, Nimmo edition.

John Wanamaker, N. Y.

Countess Kathleen, by W. B. Yeats. L., B. & Co.
Palestine in the Time of Christ, by Stapfer. Armstrong.
Philip van Artevelde, by Taylor.
Picturesque North Carolina.
Essays in Free Thinking, Stephens. Longmans.

BOOKS WANTED.—Continued.

John Wanamaker, Phila., Pa.

Wacousta, by J. Richardson.

The Washington Book Shop, 509 7th St., N. W., Washington, D. C.

Bryant's Library of Poetry and Song, Memorial ed. N. Y., 1880.
The Dial, no. 6. Boston, 1840-41.

L. S. Wells, Columbus, O. [*Cash.*]

Da Vinci, Treatise on Painting.
Amicis, Studies of Paris.
Havard, Heart of Holland.
Jarvis, Glimpses of Art of Japan.
Lockhart, Life Sir Walter Scott, 4 v.

Thomas Whittaker, Bible House, N. Y.

Man, Whence and Whither?, by Westbrook.
Treasury of Bible Knowledge, by John Eyre.
Creighton, Thoughts on Education.
Moberly, Reason and Religion.
Webb's Fifth Normal Reader.
Garland of Praise, by Asa Hull.

W. H. Wood & Co., 8 E. Main St., Springfield, O.

Blaine, Twenty Years in Congress.
The Wandering Soul.
Mommsen, Universal History.
Bryant, Library of Poetry and Song.
Finney, On Masonry.

Woodward & Lothrop, Washington, D. C.

'Annie Grayson, or, Life in Washington, by Lazelle.
Maclay's History of the U. S. Navy, v. 1 only.

The Young Churchman Co., Milwaukee, Wis.

Church's Broken Unity, v. 3, Bennett.

Wm. H. Ziesenitz, Hudson, N. Y.

Dogs in Health and Disease, by Stonehenge.
Art of Cookery, Willard.
Kitchen and Dining Room, Willard.

BOOKS FOR SALE.

John R. Anderson, 114 5th Ave. N. Y.

Appleton's Library Atlas, hf. mor., second-hand. $2.00.
Johnson's Cyclo., last 8 v. ed., hf. mor. $20.00.
Biography John Sullivan Dwight. 75 cts.
A Woman's Paris. 40 cts.
The Spanish Revolution, Strobel. 55 cts.
School Architecture, Wheelwright. $2.75.
History of Sport, Bradlee Whidden. Pub. at $50.00 net; $5.00.
Even as You and I, Bolton Hall. 25 cts.
Differences, by Hervey White. 35 cts.
Grant's Memoirs, v. 1. 60 cts.
Personal Recollections, Sutherland Edwards. 50 cts.
Memoir, Wm. Landels, D.D. 50 cts.
Cassell's Guide to Paris. 15 cts.
Napier's Peninsular War, 5 v., unbound. $3.00.

Samuel Austen, 324 York St., Jersey City, N. J.

Genealogical Dictionary, by James Savage, 4 v., 8vo, cl. Boston, 1860. Clean, uncut set, $75.00.

F. M. DeWitt, 318 Post St., San Francisco, Cal.

Religion of a Bookseller. Pub. in London, 1720, clean copy.
Works of Fielding, 10 v., illus. Pub. Smith, Elder & Co., 1882. Limited ed., $93.00.

Farquhar & Albrecht, 378 Wabash Ave., Chicago, Ill.

Standard Dictionary, 2 v., late ed., from original plates, full mor., with stand. $15.00.

King Bros., 15 4th St., San Francisco, Cal.

Bret Harte Poem in 14th Anniversary of the Society of Cal. Pioneers (31 p., pamphlet.) S. F., 1864. $4.00.

C. L. Traver, Trenton, N. J.

Transactions of Soc. of Mechanical Engineers, complete 22 v. and index. Make offer.
N. J. history, genealogy, state reports a specialty.

H. Williams, 114 5th Ave., N. Y.

Popular Science Monthly, 1st 9 v., hf. mor. $4.50.
The Bookman (Dodd, Mead & Co.), 1st 12 v., cl. $12.00.
The Chap Book, complete, 9 v., buckram. $12.00.

HELP WANTED.

WANTED.—Young man with good knowledge of the retail book and stationery business. Give references, experience, and salary expected. Address A. P. PENDLETON, 804 Broad St., Augusta, Ga.

WANTED.—Young man with experience in retail book business. Permanent position to the right man. Salary first year $10.00 per week. Address with references, etc., GREGORY'S BOOKSTORE, Providence, R. I.

SITUATIONS WANTED.

A YOUNG MAN with ten years' experience in the book business and a thorough knowledge of stenography and typewriting, seeks a new position. Best references. Address SEEKER, care of PUBLISHERS' WEEKLY.

BOOKKEEPER, accountant and office manager. 20 years' experience, wholesale and manufacturing, desires position. Can adapt to any system or conditions. Excellent references. Salary no object so long as prospects are good. Address WILLSTAR, care of PUBLISHERS' WEEKLY.

COPYRIGHT NOTICES.

LIBRARY OF CONGRESS,
OFFICE OF THE REGISTER OF COPYRIGHTS,
WASHINGTON, D. C.

Class A, XXc, No. 39808.—To wit: *Be it remembered*, That on the 6th day of August, 1902, Mrs. Eva A. Ingersoll, of New York, N. Y., hath deposited in this office the title of a book, the title of which is in the following words, to wit: "The Gods and Other Lectures." Contents: "The Gods," "Humboldt," "Thomas Paine," "Individuality," "Heretics and Heresies." By Robert G. Ingersoll. New York: C. P. Farrell, 1902, the right whereof she claims as proprietor in conformity with the laws of the United States respecting copyrights.

(Signed) HERBERT PUTNAM, *Librarian of Congress.*
By THORVALD SOLBERG, *Register of Copyrights.*
In renewal for 14 years from September 8, 1902.

LIBRARY OF CONGRESS,
OFFICE OF THE REGISTER OF COPYRIGHTS,
WASHINGTON, D. C.

Class A, XXc, No. 39602.—To wit: *Be it remembered*, That on the 14th day of August, 1902, Lucy Abbott Martin, of East Orange, N. J., hath deposited in this office the title of a book, the title of which is in the following words, to wit: "A Digest of New York Statutes and Reports, from the Earliest Period. By Benjamin Vaughan Abbott and Austin Abbott. Comprising the Adjudications of all the Courts of the State, [etc.] Preceded by a table of cases criticized. New Edition, complete to the year 1873. Vol. VI. New York: Baker, Voorhis & Co., 1874," the right whereof she claims as proprietor in conformity with the laws of the United States respecting copyrights.

(Signed) HERBERT PUTNAM, *Librarian of Congress.*
By THORVALD SOLBERG, *Register of Copyrights.*
In renewal for 14 years from October 21, 1902.

LIBRARY OF CONGRESS,
OFFICE OF THE REGISTER OF COPYRIGHTS,
WASHINGTON, D. C.

Class A, XXc, No. 40358.—To wit: *Be it remembered*, That on the 26th day of August, 1902, Marie Taylor, of New York, N. Y., hath deposited in this office the title of a book, the title of which is in the following words, to wit: "The Prophet. A Tragedy. By Bayard Taylor. Boston and New York, Houghton, Mifflin & Co., The Riverside Press, Cambridge, 1902," the right whereof she claims as proprietor in conformity with the laws of the United States respecting copyrights.

(Signed) HERBERT PUTNAM, *Librarian of Congress.*
By THORVALD SOLBERG, *Register of Copyrights.*
In renewal for 14 years from Aug. 26, 1902.

SPECIAL NOTICES.

OP'S. English, Irish Books, Posters. PRATT, N. Y.

A. S. CLARK, 174 Fulton St. N. Y., will supply any magazine at market value.

BACK NUMBERS, volumes, and sets of magazines and reviews for sale at the AMERICAN AND FOREIGN MAGAZINE DEPOT, 47 Dey St., New York.

Have Just Published

A VOLUME OF MASTERLY PARODIES

Borrowed Plumes

By OWEN SEAMAN, author of "The Battle of the Bays." 16mo, $1.25.

Mr. Seaman, whose "Battle of the Bays" is already in its fourth edition, has been favorably compared with Calverley by critics on both sides of the Atlantic. It is doubtful whether he has a superior among living parodists. **Borrowed Plumes** opens with the droll idea of having the Elizabeth of the *Letters* visit the Elizabeth of the *German Garden*. The parodies that follow cover *Mr. Dooley*, Hall Caine's *Eternal City*, Harland's *Cardinal's Snuff Box*, Ellen Thorneycroft Fowler's *Double Thread*, John Oliver Hobbes' *Robert Orange*, Mrs. Ward's *Robert Elsmere*, and works by Hewlett, Henry James, Sir John Lubbock, Maeterlinck, Mrs. Meynell, etc.

Medieval Europe

By CH. BEMONT and G. MONOD. Translated by MARY SLOAN. Edited by Prof. G. B. ADAMS. *With Ten Maps in Color.* 12mo, $1.60 *net.*

A second edition of this history was sent to press three days after the first was in the publisher's hands. This work is generally considered the best on the period.

A New Edition, uniform with the Author's Prisoner of Zenda, Rupert of Hentzau, and Father Stafford, of

The Dolly Dialogues

By ANTHONY HOPE. Containing the four additional "Dialogues." With a frontispiece by CHRISTY. 12mo, $1.50.

Recently Published

A Political History of the United States

By Prof. J. P. GORDY. *To be Completed in Four Volumes. Each,* $1.75 *net.* (Postage 14c.)

Ready. VOL. I. **The Federal Period, 1783-1809.** VOL. II. **1809-28.**
In Preparation. VOL. III. **1829-60.** VOL. IV. **1860 to Hayes's Inauguration.**

The Roman People

By Prof. CH. SEIGNOBOS. Edited and brought down to Charlemagne by Dr. WM. M. FAIRLEY. *With Maps and Illustrations.* 12mo, $1.25 *net.*

*** BY THE SAME AUTHOR. *A Political History of Europe since 1814.* $3 *net.*—*The Feudal Régime.* Paper, 50c. *net.*

CHEAPER EDITIONS OF THREE STANDARD WORKS

Lavignac's Music and Musicians.; $1.75 *net.* (Postage 18c.) Practically a Cyclopædia of its subject, with numerous illustrations.

Thomas's Life and Works of Schiller. *Student's Edition.* $1.50 *net.*

Taine's English Literature. *With 28 Portraits.* 4 vols. in box. $6.

Henry Holt & Co., 29 West 23d St., New York

Fall Announcements, 1902

THE NEW PHOTOGRAVURE BOOKS

JAPAN AND HER PEOPLE

By ANNA C. HARTSHORNE

Illustrated with 50 photogravures. 2 vols. Crown 8vo. Cloth extra, gilt tops; in cloth box.................................Net, $4 00
Three-quarters crushed morocco, gilt top......................Net, 8 00
Edition De Luxe, limited to 150 copies.............. ....Net, 10 00

Miss Hartshorne writes of Japan and the Japanese people from an intimate knowledge of her subject at first hands, having been a resident of the country and brought closely into touch with native life. The book will take rank as a thorough exposition of the Island Kingdom and is written in a charming style. No more attractive holiday book will be issued this season.

VIENNA AND THE VIENNESE

By MARIA HORNOR LANSDALE

Illustrated with 25 photogravures and a map. Crown 8vo. Cloth extra, gilt top; in cloth box........ ....Net, $2 40
Full crushed Levant morocco, gilt edges.......... ... .Net, 5 60

Vienna is in many respects the most fascinating and brilliant city in Europe. Miss Lansdale has handled the theme with her accustomed skill, making one of the most readable books of the year. The fine photogravures are quite equal to the others that have made the whole series so noteworthy and popular.

A COMPANION VOLUME TO "CRANKISMS"

WHIMLETS

By S. SCOTT STINSON, pictured by Clare Victor Dwiggins. Square 16mo. With 100 full-page illustrations........ ....Net, $0 80

Mr. Stinson has contributed 100 rhymed conceits, which Mr. Dwiggins illustrates in the very clever style which has made him a name in connection with Mr. Matthewman's "Crankisms." This little volume will be one of the books of the year.

SONGS AND STORIES FROM TENNESSEE

By JOHN TROTWOOD MOORE, author of "A Summer Hymnal." 12mo. Illustrated.................... .... $1 25

This volume contains Mr. Moore's famous story, "Ole Mistis," and many others of equal merit, with some of the poems which in fugitive form have found so many admirers.

"A Summer Hymnal" is selling with gathering popularity, and the many readers who have been charmed by it will want this book also.

EUROPEAN AND JAPANESE GARDENS

Edited by GLENN BROWN, Secy. American Institute of Architects. 145 illustrations of the representative gardens of Italy, England, France, and Japan, accompanying scholarly papers upon

Italian Gardens, by Prof. A. D. F. HAMLIN, School of Architecture, Columbia University.

French Gardens, by JOHN GALEN HOWARD, Architect of the University of California.

English Gardens, by R. CLIPSTON STURGIS, Architect, Boston.

Japanese Gardens, by K. HONDA, of the Japanese Horticultural Society.

180 pages, text and illustrations, small quarto. Cloth................ $2 00

The edition of this book is limited to 2000, more than half of which have already been disposed of.

COFFEE: Its History, Classification and Description

By JOSEPH M. WALSH. 12mo. Cloth extra. Illustrated........Net, $2 00

TEA: Its History and Mystery

By JOSEPH M. WALSH. 12mo. Cloth extra. Illustrated........Net, $2 00

TEA BLENDING AS A FINE ART

By JOSEPH M. WALSH. 12mo. Cloth extra. Illustrated........Net, $2 00

These three handbooks, by an expert upon tea and coffee, are the only works of the kind to be had and are authoritative upon the subjects. To the dealer in these commodities they are invaluable.

HENRY T. COATES & CO., Publishers, Philadelphia

LONGMANS, GREEN & CO.'S Announcements

BIOGRAPHY AND HISTORY

JAMES THE SIXTH AND THE GOWRIE MYSTERY. By ANDREW LANG. With 2 Photogravures and other Illustrations and Plans. 8vo. [*In the press*

*** This book tries to throw new light, from contemporary manuscripts, hitherto unpublished, on the unsolved problem of the "Gowrie Conspiracy" (1600) and on its sequel in the affair of Logan of Restalrig in 1608-1609. One factor in the problem is definitely settled, and the author trusts that he has demonstrated the innocence of the king.

Reproductions of handwriting in the matter of the disputed plot-letters, portraits and pictures of Falkland Palace, Restalrig, Dirleton, and Fastcastle are given.

THE ADVENTURES OF CAPTAIN JOHN SMITH: Captain of Two Hundred and Fifty Horse, and sometime President of Virginia. By E. P. ROBERTS. With 3 Maps and 17 Illustrations. Crown 8vo, pp. xiv.-307, $1.50 *net.* By mail $1.65. [*Nearly ready*

LETTERS OF DOROTHEA, PRINCESS LIEVEN, during her residence in London, 1812-1834. Edited by LIONEL G. ROBINSON. With 2 Photogravure Portraits. 8vo, pp. xxii.-406, $5.00. [*Nearly ready*

*** These letters were, with one or two exceptions, addressed to Princess Lieven's brother, General Alexander Benckendorff, who, after a brilliant military career, was, on the accession of Nicholas I. to the throne, appointed to a post of confidence which, until his death, kept him in close relations with the Emperor. In his position as Chief of the Third Division he was also practically in charge of the political police system of the Russian Empire.

DIARY OF A JOURNEY TO ENGLAND IN THE YEARS 1761-1762. By Count FREDERICK KIELMANSEGG. With 4 Illustrations. Crown 8vo. [*In the press*

THE LIFE OF THE RIGHT HON. PROFESSOR F. MAX MULLER, K.M., late Foreign Member of the French Institute. By MRS. MAX MULLER. With 6 Portraits. 2 vols. [*In the press*

MEMOIRS OF SIR EDWARD BLOUNT, K.C.B., Etc., 1815-1902. Edited by STUART J. REID, Author of "The Life and Times of Sydney Smith," etc. With 3 Photogravure Plates. 8vo, pp. viii.-308, $4.00. [*Just ready*

*** Sir Edward Blount's reminiscences open with the return of Lord Anglesey, after the Battle of Waterloo, and practically end with the death of Queen Victoria. He describes his life as a schoolboy at St. Mary's College, Oscott, under Dr. Walsh and Monsignor Weedall, his life as a Foreign Office clerk, and as an attaché in Rome and Paris in the reigns of George IV. and William IV. and his subsequent career in the French capital as an English banker and as a pioneer of railways in France. The book throws vivid side-lights on the reign of Louis Philippe and the Revolution of 1848, the early days of the Second Empire, the Mexican War, and the Siege of Paris. Sir Edward Blount was Her Majesty's Consul during the closing dramatic weeks of the investment of Paris, and the letters which he despatched by balloon to his wife are freely quoted, and give a realistic picture of the privations of the beleaguered city when the advance of the German Army cut off all communication with the outer world. The book also contains many interesting details about political and social celebrities, railway progress in France, club life, etc.

HISTORICAL ESSAYS AND REVIEWS. By MANDELL CREIGHTON, D.D., D.C.L., LL.D., etc., sometime Bishop of London. Edited by LOUISE CREIGHTON. Crown 8vo, pp. viii.-356, $2.00. [*Immediately*

CONTENTS. Dante—Æneas Sylvius—A Schoolmaster of the Renaissance—A Man of Culture—A Learned Lady of the Sixteenth Century—Wiclif—The Italian Bishops of Worcester—The Harvard Commemoration—The Moscow Coronation. *Reviews.* The Renaissance in Italy, by J. A. SYMONDS—Il Principe-Machiavelli, edited by L. A. BURD—Caterina Sforza, COUNT PASOLINI—State Papers of the Reign of Henry VIII., edited by JAMES GAIRDNER.

SEVEN ROMAN STATESMEN OF THE LATER REPUBLIC: The Gracchi, Sulla, Crassus, Cato, Pompey, Cæsar. By CHARLES OMAN, M.A., Deputy Professor of Modern History at University of Oxford, Author of "A History of Greece," etc. With Portraits and Illustrations. Crown 8vo, pp. iv.-348, $1.60.* [*Just ready*

*** There are several general histories of the decline and fall of the Roman Republic, dealing with its political and constitutional aspects. This is not a history, but a series of studies of the leading men of the century intending to show the importance of the personal element in those days of storm and stress.

AMERICAN CITIZEN SERIES

(*New Volume*)

FINANCIAL HISTORY OF THE UNITED STATES. By DAVIS R. DEWEY, Professor of Economics and Statistics in the Massachusetts Institute of Technology; Member of State Commissions on Public Charitable Institutions; Author of "Study of Statistics," etc., etc. With Diagrams. Crown 8vo. [*In the press*

NEW FICTION

IN KINGS' BYWAYS. By STANLEY J. WEYMAN, Author of "A Gentleman of France," "Under the Red Robe," "Count Hannibal," etc., etc. With a Frontispiece by GEORGE VARIAN. Crown 8vo, cloth, ornamental. $1.50. [*In September*

*** The volume consists of three parts: (1) MISCELLANEOUS STORIES OF THE OLD REGIME; (2) THE DIARY OF A STATESMAN: Episode of the Fowl in the Pot—Episode of the Boxwood Fire—Episode of the Snowball; (3) KING TERROR: A Daughter of the Gironde—In the Name of the Law.

THE LORD PROTECTOR. A Story. By S. LEVETT YEATS, Author of "The Chevalier D'Auriac," "The Heart of Denise," etc., etc. With Frontispiece. Crown 8vo, cloth, ornamental, $1.50. [*In October*

LONGMANS, GREEN & CO., 91 and 93 FIFTH AVE., NEW YORK

LONGMANS, GREEN & CO.'S Announcements

THE DISENTANGLERS. By ANDREW LANG. With 7 Full-page Illustrations by H. J. FORD. Crown 8vo. [*In the press*

CONTENTS: I. The Great Idea—II. From the Highways and Hedges—III. Adventure of the First Clients—IV. Adventure of the Rich Uncle—V. Adventure of the Office Screen—VI. A Lover in Cocky—VII. Adventure of the Exemplary Earl—VIII. Adventure of the Lady Patroness—IX. Adventure of the Lady Novelist and the Vaccinationist—X. Adventure of the Fair American—XI. Adventure of the Miserly Marquis—XII. Adventure of the Canadian Heiress.

BY THE RAMPARTS OF JEZREEL. A Romance of Jehu, King of Israel. By ARNOLD DAVENPORT. Crown 8vo, cloth, ornamental, $1.50. [*Shortly*

LIFE THE INTERPRETER. A Story Based Upon Life and Work in the East End of London. By PHYLLIS BOTTOME. Crown 8vo. [*In the press*

THE MANOR FARM. A Novel. By M. E. FRANCIS (Mrs. Francis Blundell). Author of "Pastorals of Dorset," "Fiander's Widow," "Yeoman Fleetwood," etc., etc. With Frontispiece by CLAUD C. DU PRE COOPER. Crown 8vo, cloth, ornamental, $1.50. [*Just ready*

BOOKS FOR YOUNG PEOPLE

MR. LANG'S CHRISTMAS BOOK FOR 1902

THE BOOK OF ROMANCE. Edited by ANDREW LANG. With 8 Colored Plates and 44 other Illustrations by H. J. FORD. Crown 8vo, gilt edges, $1.60 *net*, postage extra. [*In October*

THE NEW GOLLIWOGG BOOK

THE GOLLIWOGG'S AIR-SHIP. With Colored Pictures by FLORENCE K. UPTON and Verses by BERTHA UPTON. Oblong 4to, boards, $1.50 *net*, postage extra. [*In October*

THE BURGES LETTERS: A Record of Child Life in the Sixties. By EDNA LYALL. With Colored Plate and 8 other Full-page Illustrations by WALTER S. STACEY. Crown 8vo. [*In the press*

MISCELLANEOUS

THE LAND OF THE LATINS. By ASHTON R. WILLARD. Author of "Modern Italian Art." With 11 Illustrations from Photographs. Crown 8vo, $1.40 *net* [*In the press*

This book presents various interesting aspects of Italian life. The author draws a picture of modern social life at Rome, which is coming to be recognized as one of the most attractive social centres of Europe. He takes the reader into the studios and the theatres; the Italian country-house is described and life at one of the principal seaside resorts. Besides the more general views of Italian society the author gives some personal impressions of the more interesting figures in modern Italian life—such as Leo XIII., Queen Margherita, the Duchess of Genoa, Eleonora Duse, Salvini, and other persons of prominence.

HIGHER MATHEMATICS FOR STUDENTS OF CHEMISTRY AND PHYSICS. With Special Reference to Practical Work. By J. W. MELLOR, D.Sc., late Senior Scholar, and 1851 Exhibition Scholar, New Zealand University; Honorary Research Fellow, the Owens College, Manchester. With 142 diagrams. 8vo, pp. xxiv.-543, $4.00.* [*Just ready*

LONGMAN'S GAZETTEER OF THE WORLD. Edited by GEORGE G. CHISHOLM, M.A., B.Sc., Fellow of the Royal Geographical and Statistical Societies. *Cheaper re-issue.* Imperial 8vo, $6.40 *net*, postage extra. [*Just ready*

THE STEAM TURBINE. By ROBERT M. NEILSON, Associate Member of the Institute of Mechanical Engineers, Lecturer on Steam and the Steam Engine at the Heginbottom Technical School, Ashton-under-Lyne. With Plates and 145 Illustrations in the text. 8vo, pp. xii.-163, $2.50.* [*Just ready*

**The author has endeavored in this book to describe, not only the principal parts of the leading types of steam turbine, but also the small details which, in the case of this motor, have such a preponderating influence in determining success or failure. The theory of the action of the steam turbine is also treated of, and the subject is likewise dealt with historically.

EDUCATION AND TEXT-BOOKS

American Teachers Series

THE TEACHING OF CHEMISTRY AND PHYSICS IN THE SECONDARY SCHOOL. By ALEXANDER SMITH, B.Sc., Ph.D., Associate Professor of Chemistry in the University of Chicago, and EDWIN H. HALL, Ph.D., Professor of Physics in Harvard University. With 21 Diagrams, References and Bibliographies and Index. Crown 8vo, pp. xiii.-377, $1.50. [*Just ready*

THE TEACHING OF HISTORY AND CIVICS IN THE ELEMENTARY AND THE SECONDARY SCHOOL. By HENRY E. BOURNE, B.A., B.D., Professor in the College for Women, Western Reserve University. With Bibliographies and Index. Crown 8vo, pp. x.-385, $1.50. [*Just ready*

A COLLEGE MANUAL OF RHETORIC. By CHARLES SEARS BALDWIN, Ph.D., Assistant Professor of Rhetoric in Yale University. Crown 8vo, pp. xvi.-451, $1.35.* [*In September*

THE PRINCIPLES OF ENGLISH CONSTITUTIONAL HISTORY. By LUCY DALE, late Scholar of Somerville College, Oxford. Crown 8vo, pp. xii.-509, $1.50.* [*Just ready*

LONGMANS, GREEN & CO., 91 and 93 FIFTH AVE., NEW YORK

A. Wessels Company Announce

The Bertha Galland Edition.

NOTRE DAME DE PARIS. Victor Hugo.

2 vols., 8vo, in box, illustrated, cloth gilt $3.00

A beautifully illustrated edition of Hugo's masterpiece with EXTRA illustrations from scenes in the play, by permission of Mr. D. Frohman and Miss Galland, and two portraits in color of Miss Galland as Esmeralda, as frontispieces taken especially for this edition.

****BARBIZON DAYS,** Millet, Corot, Rousseau, Barye. Charles Sprague Smith.

Square 8vo, cloth, decorative, gilt top, 46 illustrations . . . . . $2.00 *net*

These studies, written in the Forest of Fontainebleau, show the close relation between the life and surroundings of each artist and his creative work—a book of permanent value, which will appeal to all interested in art and answers all requirements of an attractive gift-book.

****THE LEGENDS OF THE IROQUOIS.** W. W. Canfield.

Small 8vo, paper boards, 2 illustrations (edition limited to 500 numbered copies), $2.50 *net*

BIOGRAPHY

****AUTHORS AT HOME,** Personal and Biographical Sketches of Well-known American Writers, edited by J. L. & J. B. Gilder.

12mo, cloth, decorative, with 5 portraits . . . . $1.00 *net*

****CAPTAIN JOHN BROWN OF HARPER'S FERRY,** a Preliminary Incident of the Great Civil War. John Newton.

12mo, cloth, illustrated . . . . $1.25 *net*

****EGLÉE—A GIRL OF THE PEOPLE.** W. R. H. Trowbridge.

12mo, cloth . . . . $1.00 *net*

FICTION

†FLOWERS OF THE DUST. John Oxenham.

12mo, cloth, decorative (Ready in Oct.) $1.50

†THE MAGIC MASHIE. Edwin L. Sabin.

12mo, cloth, illustrated $1.00

†THE GAME OF LIFE Bolton Hall.

16mo, cloth $1.00

THE CONQUEST OF THE AIR, with an Introduction by Sir Hiram Maxim. John Alexander.

12mo, cloth, illustrated 75

An interesting and timely volume which gives in compact form the history of ballooning, and the construction of air ships, with portrait of M. Santos-Dumont as frontispiece.

HOW TO BRING UP YOUR CHILDREN. John Locke.

16mo, paper boards 50

From the "*Essay on Education*."—'A book for every parent.'

SEND FOR COMPLETE FALL ANNOUNCEMENT, CATALOGUE AND TERMS.

7 and 9 WEST 18th STREET, NEW YORK

J. B. LIPPINCOTT COMPANY'S

Autumn Announcement

Postage extra is charged on all books marked with an asterisk (*).

Ͳhe True History of the American Revolution

These are the real facts of the days ‹f 1776. Mr. Fisher ‹as some things to tell ‹bout the conduct of ‹he War of the Revo‹ution, its chief fig‹res, and the reasons ‹or its outcome, which will startle every reader of ‹merican history. The great struggle is treated ‹n the same candid fashion as are the characters ‹nd lives of the Americans who are included in ‹he widely-known "True Biog‹aphies."

‹y Sydney George Fisher

24 illustrations. Crown 8vo. Cloth, decorated, *Net* . . $2.00*

Social Life in *the* Early Republic

Miss Wharton's wide knowledge of the practically untouched period following on Colonial and Revolutionary years, and her ability to make us see the men and women of past times as they really were, are here ‹iven the most interesting expression. The vol‹me promises to rival in popu‹rity her "Salons Colonial and ‹epublican," and "Through ‹olonial Doorways."

‹y Anne H. Wharton

Colored frontispiece. Profusely illustrated. Crown 8vo. Decorated cloth, gilt top, *Net* . . . $3.00*
Half levant, *Net* . . . $6.00*

¶ Few books of a biographical character have had the popularity of those known as the **True Biographies.** Besides Mr. Fisher's volume here noted he has also written **The True Benjamin Franklin** and **The True William Penn.** The late Paul Leicester Ford was the author of the initial volume of the series, **The True George Washington,** which earned much attention. William E. Curtis is the author of **The True Thomas Jefferson,** published last year.

¶ Miss Wharton's books are notable for the vividness of their portraiture. In her **Salons Colonial and Republican, Through Colonial Doorways,** and **Colonial Days and Dames** she began this review of social history, and in **Heirlooms in Miniatures** revived other graceful figures of the past.

¶ Of kindred interest is the finely illustrated **Famous American Belles of the Nineteenth Century,** in which Miss Virginia Tatnall Peacock sketches the characters and lives of distinguished women.

J. B. Lippincott Company: Autumn Books *and other Good books*

The Ancestor

A quarterly review of County and Family History, Heraldry, Heirlooms, Ancestral Seats, Treasures, Arms, Armor, and Antiquity, which will be a recognized guide for all those who are interested in these subjects. Its distinctive note is its accuracy and authority. Genealogy receives particular attention. All modern means of reproduction have been employed in its illustration.

Illustrated. Large superroyal, paper boards, per part, *Net* . . . $1.50

Edited by Oswald Barron, F.S.A.

The Kissing Walk.

New York Old and New

Its story as told by its landmarks. The writer is the author of "Rambles in Colonial Byways," and "Washington: The Capital City," etc., and this is the first authoritative, comprehensive and at the same time readable book yet put out on New York City itself. The volume is handsomely illustrated with many reproductions from photographs, old prints, etc., and contains a wealth of new material.

Two Volumes. Illustrated. Extra buckram, *Net* . $3.50*

By Rufus Rockwell Wilson

Confessions of a Violinist

The romance and realities of a musical life as related by a former President of the Bohemian Orchestral Society, and the author of several well-received books. A volume with personal charm, which will delight every reader of refined tastes.

12mo. Decorated cloth, *Net* . $1.50

By Dr. T. Lamb Phipson

¶ History books are more entertaining to-day than they used to be. It has been shown that accuracy does not always depend upon formality. Rufus Rockwell Wilson is one of the writers who has demonstrated this. Beginning with his **Rambles in Colonial Byways**, in which he gave many glimpses of famous men, he took up in **Washington: The Capital City** the story of the most beautiful as well as one of the most picturesque of American communities. Indeed that volume was the first of its kind on the subject and has been received with general critical approval.

¶ **Confessions of a Violinist** reminds us of **Famous Violinists and Fine Violins** and **Voice and Violin**, titles which speak for the contents of the books; also of a third book by Dr. Phipson of speculative interest, **Researches of the Past and Present into the History of the Earth's Atmosphere.**

J. B. Lippincott Company : Autumn Books *and other Good Books*

Home Life of the Borneo Head-Hunters

Mr. Furness writes from many months of life among the people he describes. He penetrated parts of the island which had never before been explored by a white man, and his experiences are as valuable for the light they throw upon the customs and surroundings, relations and lore of the savages, as they are interesting for their novelty and excitement and the fresh enthusiasm and simplicity with which they are narrated. The book is illustrated by eighty-one photogravures and other photographic reproductions, and is handsomely bound.

By Wm. H. Furness, 3d

Illustrated. 8vo. Gilt top, rough edges, *Net* $7.50*

Stories of Authors' Loves

Charlotte Brontë.

Two fascinating volumes of the romances of the most widely-known American, English, and European authors. There is nothing in fiction to compare with the fascination of the romances of the real men and women who we all know by their writings. The volumes have the value of being a chronicle of fact, but hold all the charm of a novel. Their author is the literary editor of the *Chicago Interior*. The books have photogravure frontispieces and forty duogravure portraits and views.

By Clara E. Laughlin

Two Volumes. Illustrated. Handsomely bound, in box, *Net* . $3.00*
Three-quarters morocco, *Net* $6.00*.

¶ Books of travel are always in demand. Here are some recently published which have enjoyed large popularity : **Through Persia on a Side-Saddle,** by Ella C. Sykes, one of the very first women to go to this part of the East ; **To the Pacific and Mexico,** a personal account in the most entertaining manner of that veteran journalist Col. A. K. McClure.

¶ Also may be mentioned here **A Sportswoman in India,** being travels, adventures, and experiences in known and unknown India by Isabel Savory ; **Intimate China,** an account of the Chinese as seen on their own ground, by Mrs. Archibald Little ; **Sands of Sahara,** by the well-known authority Prof. Maxwell Sommerville ; and **Sketches and Studies in South Africa,** by W. J. Knox Little.

¶ All of these books are handsomely bound, most of them are profusely illustrated.

J. B. Lippincott Company: Autumn Books *and other Good Books*

Symphonies and Their Meanings

(Second Series)

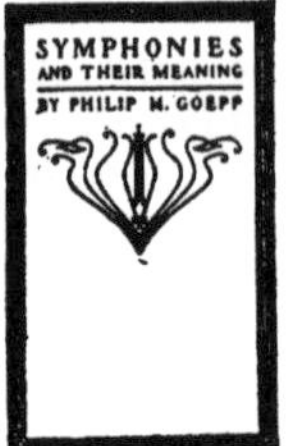

A review of the symphonic compositions of the great composers, completing the modern repertory. Illustrated by remarks and excerpts from the scores. Mr. Goepp shows the individuality and special intention of the great masters and, like the first volume of this series, the book is an unrivalled aid to the study of the symphony.

12mo. Decorated cloth, *Net* . $2.00*
First and second volumes, in box, *Net* . $4.00*

By Philip H. Goepp

Delight; the Soul of Art

Five thoughtful lectures upon the inspiration, principles, and substance of art in all its expressions, which separately bear title,—The Soul of Art, Certainty and Conviction, Inspiration, Delight in the Symbol, and Delight in Labor.

12mo. Decorated cloth, *Net* . $1.50*

By Arthur Jerome Eddy

The English Cathedrals

A sympathetic and informing book upon the great monuments of religious life in England, their place in history, their traditions, appearance, and surroundings, and the men in whose lives they have figured. Charmingly illustrated with many sketches and drawings by Railton, Symington, Critkmore, James, and Fletcher, and printed on thin India paper.

Illustrated. Small 12mo. Decorated cloth, *Net* . $2.00
Limp leather, gilt top, *Net* . . $2.50

By the Rev. P. A. Litchfield

¶ The literature of Musical Art offers such a rich field that we can do no more than mention a few recent and well-liked publications. Besides the first volume of Mr. Goepp's **Symphonies**, there is **Music and Its Masters**, by O. B. Boise, formerly of Berlin, and now a Musical Director in the Peabody Institute at Baltimore.

¶ **The Life of Wagner** is an authoritative book which has been widely quoted, by Alfred Stewart Chamberlain; **Stories of Famous Songs**, a book of more than the interest of curiosity, by S. J. A. Fitzgerald; and **Famous Violinists and Fine Violins**, and **Voice in Violin**, by Dr. Phipson, mentioned on another page as the author of **Confessions of a Violinist**. Also **The Philosophy of the Human Voice**, an able work by Dr. James Rush; and **The Opera**, which in the form of a new edition furnishes a sketch of every work of importance in the modern repertory. The author of this last book is R. A. Streatfeild.

J. B. Lippincott Company: Autumn Books and other Good Books

Historic Houses of New Jersey

The story of the old dwellings which have played important parts in the history of a State peculiarly rich in colonial and revolutionary souvenirs. Especially notable for its illustions, nineteen in number; photogravures reproduced from original drawings by John Rae, and from old pictures and photographs. Printed in old-face type on fine paper, with specially designed initials.

By W. Jay Mills

Illustrated. 8vo. Decorated cloth, in box, *Net* . $5.00*

Chambers's Cyclopaedia of English Literature

A history, critical and biographical, of authors in the English tongue, from the earliest times till the present day, with specimens of their writings. American literature is treated by competent pens, and the work, which has been pronounced by cholars the best in its field, in its present form is ery largely improved, both in its arrangement and ts comprehensive and exact character. The illusrations are carefully selected facsimiles and over hree hundred portraits executed expressly for the rork. The editors include: Dr. Stopford Brooke, Mr. Austin Dobson, Mr. Edmund Gosse, Mr. Andrew Lang, Mr. Sidney Lee and Professor Saintsbury.

Edited by David Patrick

Illustrated. Volumes I. and II. ready; Volume III. shortly. Three Volumes. Imperial octavo. 800 pages. Cloth, per volume, *Net* $5.00*

¶ Mr. Mills's book brings to mind the charming volumes of Miss Wharton upon Revolutionary and Colonial biography and history touched upon on another page, also Mr. Wilson's **Rambles in Colonial Byways,** and besides these **A Literary Pilgrimage, Literary Shrines, Literary Haunts and Homes of American Authors,** and **Literary Rambles at Home and Abroad,** all by Dr. Theodoıe F. Wolfe.

¶ Chambers's Cyclopædia of English Literature suggests the standard and widely known **Lippincott's Biographical Dictionary** and **Chambers's Encyclopædia** (new edition), both of which books are to-day at the very head of literature in their separate fields. It might also be proper to mention in this relation **Allibone's Dictionary of Authors,** the reputation of which for comprehensiveness and accuracy is everywhere known; likewise **Great Authors of All Ages,** by the same Dr. Allibone; and **Allibone's Poetical Quotations** and **Prose Quotations.**

J. B. Lippincott Company: Autumn Books *and other Good Books*

Pinturicchio

(His Life, Work, and Time)

This is the first adequate life of Pinturicchio, and it has been done with energy, thoroughness, and intelligence. The book will appeal to every earnest student of art in his higher aspects. It has fifteen full page plates in color, besides other full-page photogravures and smaller illustrations. Illustrated. Large Imperial quarto. Decorated cloth. *In press. Net* $20.00

By Corrado Ricci

The Tragedy of Martinique

A comprehensive account of the eruption of Mt. Pelée and the destruction of St. Pierre, from observations and personal investigation made by this renowned scientist. A close and authoritative study of the conditions anticipating, attending, and following volcanic disturbances and of the phenomena of like convulsions. Illustrated. Crown 8vo. *In Press.*

By Professor Angelo Heilprin

The Summits of Success

The story of the greatest achievements and the careers of notable men. An anecdotal history of what has been accomplished in science, industry, and commerce, by the skill and energy of individual men. A record of the advancement and enlightenment of the world. 12mo. Decorated cloth, gilt top, *Net* . . $1.50

By James Burnley

Worcester's New Primary Dictionary

This is not a revision of any former edition of Worcester's Primary Dictionary, but is an entirely new book. The vocabulary is very full and great care has been exercised in the selection of words. The definitions are clear and concise. The varied spelling of words is given, as also are irregular and foreign plurals. Correct pronunciation is indicated by syllabification and by diacritical marks. When the pronunciation cannot thus be clearly indicated the words are spelled phonetically. Bound in half leather $0.50

¶ Among volumes dealing with art an important contribution is **The Works of William Hogarth**, containing the life of the artist, with anecdotal descriptions of his pictures by John Ireland and John Nichols, in three volumes, handsomely bound.

¶ **Elements of Art Criticism**, by G. W. Samson, is a treatise on the principles of art, together with an historic survey of the methods of art execution and its various manifestations. It is a useful handbook for amateurs and for artists.

¶ Among the most successful reproductions of a great painter's canvases are the half-hundred photogravures in **Fifty Masterpieces of Anthony Van Dyck**. The work is a large quarto.

¶ Besides **Summits of Success**, James Burnley has written a book which is full of contemporary interest and stimulus to ambition. Its title is **Millionaires and Kings of Enterprise**, and its subjects are almost all Americans—engineers, merchants, shipbuilders, financiers, and lawyers.

J. B. Lippincott Company: Autumn Books *and other Good Books*

Two Thousand Miles on an Automobile

An extremely interesting account of a journey on American roads, of its delights, adventures, and mishaps. The book tells all about running and caring for an automobile and makes plain and unprejudiced comparison of the advantages and disadvantages of different models and makes. By an enthusiastic automobile driver. VerBeck's illustrations, eighteen in number, are fully in the spirit of the narrative.

Illustrated. Crown 8vo. Decorated cloth, *Net* $2.00*

By "Chauffeur"

The Night Side of London

On Piccadilly at Night.

What happens on London streets, in her theatres, dance halls, and her hundreds of fashionable and Bohemian places of amusement during gaslight hours. A near view of the greatest city on earth, by a man who knows his London from an acquaintance of many years. Profusely illustrated with full-page and text drawings, by Tom Browne.

Illustrated. 8vo. Decorated cloth, *Net* $2.50*

By Robert Machray

Alexandre Dumas (père)

(His Life and Works)

A close range and modern view of the great French romancer by a long-time student, formerly scholar of Keble College, Oxford. Especially timely in view of the celebration of the centenary of Dumas's birth. Illustrated with many rare photographs and drawings. Handsomely printed and bound.

Illustrated. 8vo. Decorated cloth. *Net* $3.75

By Arthur F. Davidson

¶ The automobile is never likely to displace the coach of the amateur driver. Four-in-hand driving to-day is as fashionable as ever. One of its masters among gentlemen was the late Fairman Rogers. His superb volume of over five hundred pages, **A Manual of Coaching,** with its profusion of full-page plates and engravings, will probably long remain the most authoritative and interesting review and reference-work upon the subject.

¶ Of equal authority in its field is **Cricket in Many Climes,** by the famous Englishman, P. F. Warner. There are seventy-two illustrations from photographs in this book, which is appropriately bound.

¶ **The Night Side of London** naturally suggests the gay city across the channel, and there is a book on this which is absolutely unique of its kind, **Bohemian Paris.** W. C. Morrow wrote it from notes by Edouard Cucuel. Over a hundred spirited drawings by Cucuel illuminate every phase of modern French life, and are one of the chief attractions of the volume.

J. B. Lippincott Company: Autumn Books *and other Good Books*

The Book of Beauty

(The Era of King Edward VII.)

A superb work of art, containing over fifty exquisite full-page and many smaller photogravure portraits, including a hitherto unpublished picture of Queen Alexandra, and a series of pictures of the beauties of King Edward's Court, including several American women. The pictures are reproduced from celebrated paintings. The letter-press, which tells the story of fashionable life and gives views of the court from the inside, is contributed by Rudyard Kipling, Sir Edwin Arnold, Max Pemberton, and others equally well known, and the volume is one of the richest and most distinguished works of the kind ever issued.

Edited by F. H. Williamson

Illustrated. Folio. Bound in cloth, gold decorations and gilt top, *Net* . $35.00

Arms and Armour

(In Antiquity and Middle Ages)

English Heraldry

The first of these books is a new edition of the translation from the French of M. P. Lacombe, and contains also a description of modern weapons, a preface, notes, and an additional chapter on arms and armor in England. There are many different illustrations of specimens from notable collections of arms.

The second book is especially intended for the use of heraldic students. It reviews heraldry from its earliest days, touching upon its history, vocabulary, insignia, supporters, orders, colleges, and the development of its study. There are four hundred and sixty wood cuts in the text engraved especially for the work.

By Chas. Boutell

Illustrated. Crown 8vo. Decorated cloth, each, *Net* . . . $1.75

¶ There are many beautiful women also in Miss Wharton's **Heirlooms in Miniatures**, of which we have spoken, and which is lavishly illustrated with fine reproductions and portraits.

¶ Miss Peacock's **Famous American Belles of the Nineteenth Century**, with its frontispiece in colors and twenty full-page illustrations, may also be mentioned again in this connection. Perhaps, too, **The Diamond Necklace**, by Franz Funck-Brentano, an astonishing narrative of the famous necklace which played so large a part in one of the most romantic chapters of French history has a place here because of the notable men and women who figure in its pages.

¶ **Men and Women of the French Renaissance**, by Edith Sichel, which enjoyed one of the largest sales among recent history books, is another volume which will well repay the reader who would know more of notable personalities.

J. B. Lippincott Company: Autumn Books and other Good Books

The Modern Conjurer

Trewey as a Chinaman.

An elaborately illustrated volume upon the new magic, explaining both by text and drawings the most entertaining tricks of such masters of conjuring as Maskelyne, Trewey, Bertram, Patrice, Kennard, and others. The four hundred illustrations are from photographs of actual tricks, and the book is intensely interesting and is absolutely unique in its field.

By C. Lang Neil

Illustrated. 12mo. Decorated cloth, *Net* . $2.00

Ping-Pong

(And How to Play It)

A hand-book of table-tennis up-to-date, containing its history and a short treatise upon the scientific development and rules of the game succinctly stated; also, a description of the notable strokes, a chapter on tournament play, another on inter-club matches, and one on equipment. The book for the beginner.

By M. J. G. Ritchie, and Walter Harris

Illustrated. Square 16mo. Decorated cloth . 50c.

Yachting

A history of the sport from its earliest days to the present time, by one whose familiarity with the subject makes him an authority. The book gives especial attention to international yacht racing. The contests for the America Cup are reviewed fairly and accurately. The seventy-five pictures are a feature.

By Julius Gabe

Illustrated. 12mo. Cloth, *Net* . $2.50

¶ Out-of-doors sports have laid under contribution a large number of enthusiastic writers.

¶ Besides Mr. Warner's book, **Cricket in Many Climes,** previously mentioned, there is Paul E. Stevenson's **A Deep-Water Voyage** and **By Way of Cape Horn,** two of the most entertaining narratives of experience on American ships on long voyages that have ever been written. Indeed, Mr. Stevenson's books are well worthy of a place beside Dana's classic.

¶ There, too, is Turner-Turner's volume **The Giant Fish of Florida,** with its extraordinary photographs of fish in action. Also Isabel Savoy's **A Sportswoman in India,** and Sir William Conway's **The Alps from End to End,** and Hugh L. Willoughby's **Across the Everglades.**

¶ To speak of more technical work we may refer with confidence to Griffin's **Nautical Series,** with its volumes on seamanship, sailing, and like subjects.

J. B. Lippincott Company : Autumn Books *and other Good Books*

Novels

A Daughter of the Snows

A strong and extremely dramatic story. Its plot is unique, its characters boldly drawn, and the love interest intense. The first full length novel from a writer whose tales, "The Son of the Wolf," and "The God of His Fathers," etc., have won him much popularity as well as recognition from the first critics. The book is beautifully illustrated in colors from drawings by F. C. Yohn, and is handsomely bound.

Illustrated. 12mo. Decorated cloth . . . $1.50

By Jack London

Woven with the Ship

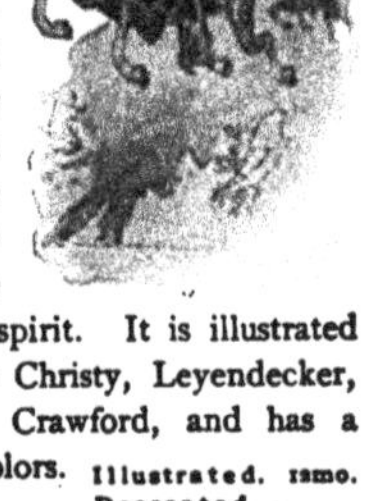

Mr. Brady's thousands of readers will derive fresh pleasure from this his new book. It has an intensely interesting plot and something happens on every page. The novel from which it takes title is the most sympathetic love story he has yet written, and the other tales are in the same spirit. It is illustrated with stunning drawings by Christy, Leyendecker, Glackens, Parkhurst, and Crawford, and has a striking cover design in colors.

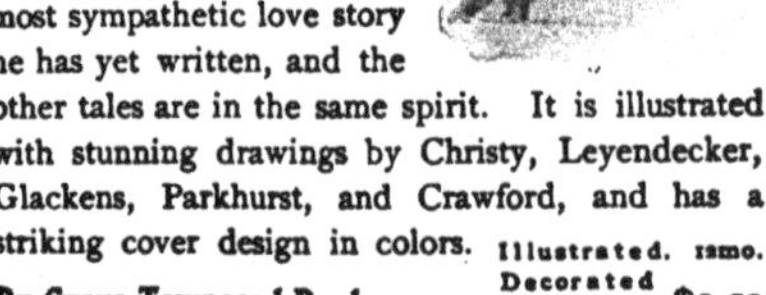

Illustrated. 12mo. Decorated cloth . . . $1.50

By Cyrus Townsend Brady

¶ Here is an armful of fiction, every volume of which will well repay the reader who wants to be entertained with a story out of the common. Mrs. Voynich contributes **Jack Raymond,** the most startling as well as the latest book by the author of **The Gadfly.** This book has sold by the thousands. George Moore, perhaps the most conspicuous figure in serious English fiction to-day, is the author of **Sister Teresa.** Of **That Mainwaring Affair,** by A. Maynard Barbour, we need scarcely do more than mention the title. It is liberally illustrated and has sold into eight editions already.

¶ A lively French story, with some astonishing chapters on French manners and life in the Quartier, is **Mlle. Fouchette.** It also is illustrated with capital drawings. Another good novel is **Graystone,** a quiet story of to-day, by William Jasper Nicolls, which will please all those who want an old-fashioned love-tale.

J. B. Lippincott Company: Autumn Books *and other Good Books*

The Highway of Fate

Miss Carey's new book is the best thing she has done. The love story is fascinating. Here is the charm of sentiment and character which mark the large number of novels that have won for her high place.

12mo. Decorated cloth. $1.50

By Rosa Nouchette Carey

Adam Rush

A new and interesting figure in a love story with the charm of country and village life in every chapter. The character of the new Adam Rush is an absorbing piece of work. By an author well-known to many thousands of readers by his shorter writings.

By Lynn Roby Meekins

12mo. Frontispiece by Francis Day. Decorated cloth . . . $1.50

The Inevitable

The hero of Mr. Mighels's book is an exceedingly interesting and good-looking young fellow of twenty-four years, whose parentage is shrouded in mystery. His love story has the fascination of uncertainty from the very beginning.

With frontispiece in colors by John Wolcott Adams.

12mo. Decorated cloth . . . $1.50

By Philip Verrill Mighels

The Last Buccaneer

A rattling novel by the author of "The Master Beggars." Mr. Cornford has steadily advanced. This new novel of adventure shows fine imagination.

By L. Cope Cornford 12mo. Cloth $1.50

¶ An old favorite, **Dorothy Fox,** by Louisa Parr, is very much the same sort of story, though entirely different in scene; **The Herb of Grace,** by the always popular Rosa N. Carey; **Glass and Gold,** a psychological study of power, by J. O. G. Duffy, and **The Lifting of a Finger,** a dainty conceit and a curious complication by Ina Brevoort Roberts.

¶ **Marr'd In Making** and **Miss Carmichael's Conscience** are two clever stories by the author of **Our Lady of the Beeches.**

¶ Now, too, Marie Corelli's famous **Barabbas** is to be had in Christmas covers and with illustrations in colors and photogravure by Marchetti, the famous French artist. Captain King's stirring novel **The Deserter**; a spirited story of adventure by John Finnemore, **The Lover Fugitives,** illustrated; and **Chevrons,** a sparkling love-story of West Point, by B. H. L., are also to be commended.

J. B. Lippincott Company: Autumn Books *and other Good Books*

The Story of a Scout

An exciting tale of adventure and intrigue on the French and Spanish border during the days of Wellington's campaign. By the author of "The Red Men of the Dusk," "The Lover Fugitives," and other novels of adventure. There are eight pictures. Illustrated. 12mo. Decorated cloth . . . $1.50

By John Finnemore

Breachley—Black Sheep

Another stirring story of the South Seas by the author of "By Reef and Palm," "The Tapu of Banderah," and other tales. Stamped by an intensely dramatic imagination. 12mo. Decorated cloth, gilt top $1.50

By Louis Becke

Love and Louisa

The latest novel of a writer whose books, "The Fault of One," "A Faithful Traitor," "My Pretty Jane," and "The Spell of Ursula" will be recalled immediately. 12mo. Decorated cloth, *Net* . $1.50

By Effie Adelaide Rowlands

A Blaze of Glory

A new novel by an author whose thousands of readers attest to her continued popularity. This is one of her strongest and brightest stories.

By John Strange Winter 12mo. Cloth $1.25

Gentleman Garnet

A tale of old Tasmania by a popular novelist. The vivid descriptions of life in penal settlements are not the least interesting portion of Mr. Vogel's powerful story of life in its unusual ways. 12mo. Decorated Cloth. . . $1.00 Paper . 50 cents

By Harry B. Vogel

¶ The best novel by B. M. Croker, a story of India, is a new one, **The Cat's-Paw.** Katharine Tynan's latest Irish love-story is **That Sweet Enemy.**

¶ The title of a collection of really good tales of life at our big universities, by authors who are well known, is **Stories of the Colleges.** A piece of imaginative work in Guy Boothby's best style, **Farewell, Nikola,** illustrated, should likewise be called to attention.

¶ Louis Becke is the author of a number of other capital books of adventure. Any of the following tales may be relied on to give entertainment: **By Reef and Palm and His Native Wife, The Ebbing of the Tide, The Tapu of Banderah,** and **Yorke, the Adventurer.**

¶ John Strange Winter's novels make a long list. Here are a few of the most popular: **A Name to Conjure With, A Magnificent Young Man, Into An Unknown World, Heart and Sword,** and **Aunt Johnnie.**

J. B. Lippincott Company: Autumn Books *and other Good Books*

New Editions

The Compleat Angler

(Winchester Edition)

The most beautiful and sympathetic issue of Izaak Walton's masterpiece yet seen. The work also contains Charles Cotton's "How to Angle for a Trout and Grayling in a Clear Stream." It holds likewise an essay by Sir Edward Gray, Bart. There are numerous etchings by William Strang and E. Y. Cameron. Printed on special paper with wide margins, in large type of clear face, and furnished with illuminated title-page, book-marker, and index.

Izaak Walton.

Edited by George A. B. Dewar

Two volumes. Large square 8vo. Decorated cloth, gilt top, *Net* $12.50

Also, large paper edition, limited to one hundred and fifty copies, numbered and signed, of which only twenty-five are for sale in the United States. **Two volumes. Green vellum, *Net* $35.00**

The Old Court Suburb

The introduction and notes by Austin Dobson add to this exquisitely quaint work just the information required to know Kensington in its historical perspective,—to bridge over the time between the old court suburb of Leigh Hunt's day and that part of London in the present century. The illustrations are by Railton, Sullivan, and Shepperson.

Edited by Austin Dobson

Illustrated. Two volumes. Large square 12mo. Cloth. Decorated in gold, *Net* . $12.50

Also, large paper edition, limited to one hundred and fifty sets. Two volumes, numbered and signed by the artists. ***Net* . . . $35.00**

¶ Walton's classic brings to mind other books on angling, and of these we can heartily recommend the newest, **The Giant Fish of Florida,** to which we have already alluded. Mr. Turner's text is capital, but the astonishing pictures of fish under water and in action will first attract attention. "Rarely," says the *Chicago Post,* "has there been placed in the hands of the sportsmen such a sumptuous volume."

¶ Akin to **The Compleat Angler** in its enthusiasm for out-door life and its beautiful dress is Gilbert White's **Natural History and Antiquities of Selborne,** edited by R. Bowdler Sharp, LL.D., of the British Museum, to which is joined a Garden Kalendar, with introduction by the Very Rev. Dean Hole.

¶ This edition of the **Compleat Angler,** which is limited to two hundred and eight numbered copies, is superbly illustrated and appropriately bound.

J. B. Lippincott Company: Autumn Books and other Good Books

The Thousand and One Nights

(**Special Edition**)

A beautiful edition of this wonderful collection of the best tales of three Eastern continents of the world. Mr. Lane's version is full and adequate in its interpretation of the original Arabic. There is an introduction by Joseph Jacobs, and the illustrations are by Brangwyn, together with twenty-one extra illustrations mounted on India paper by A. Lalawze.

Six volumes. Illustrated. 16mo. Bound in white and gold, limited to 350 sets, per set . . $10.00

Translated by Edward W. Lane

Charles Lamb.

The Essays of Elia

In one sumptuous volume are brought together the most widely known of Lamb's writings. They are introduced by a biographical note, and an appreciation of Lamb by one of his most attentive students. The illustrations are drawings in broad line—many of them full-page—by A. Garth Jones.

Illustrated. Crown 8vo. Decorated cloth, gilt top, *Net* $3.50
Half levant, *Net* . . . $6.00

Edited with introduction by E. B. Lucas

Re-Issues

The Opera

A sketch of its development from the earliest times, with a full description of every work of importance in the modern repertory. A comprehensive book of special value. The present volume is an entirely new and revised edition, made from new plates, and contains an introduction by J. A. Fuller-Maitland.

8vo. Cloth, gilt top . . $2.00
Half levant . $4.50

By R. A. Streatfeild

¶ We have most of the English novelists in editions of uniform binding, and printed in a style which makes them especially suitable for the libraries of those who will have only books which satisfy the artistic sense.

¶ A new library edition of **George Eliot's Complete Works** is in 10 volumes, illustrated with photogravures; the **Novels of Thackeray**, in handsome bindings, are also to be had in 24 volumes, bound in cloth, half calf, or three-quarters calf, and fully illustrated.

¶ **Edgar Allan Poe's Complete Works** in 8 volumes, illustrated with twenty-four photogravures, have been very well received, and the volumes are truly delightful. The Victoria edition of **Sir Walter Scott's Novels**, in 25 volumes, has been not less popular.

¶ In this connection we also call attention to the fine English editions alluded to on the opposite page. We will be glad to furnish a full descriptive pamphlet of these and other fine editions.

J. B. Lippincott Company: Autumn Books *and other Good Books*

The Pilgrim's Progress

A new issue of Bennett's Bunyan, widely known to scholars. Printed on laid paper in the most finished style. This is the first special edition of a presentation of Bunyan which is unequalled. Bennett's illustrations are powerful and yet subtle. The preface is Charles Kingsley's.

Illustrated. Crown 8vo. Decorated cloth, gilt top . . $1.50
Three-quarters morocco . . . $3.50

Mother and Child

A book for the use of the mother. It does not supplant the doctor, but assists him. It supplies common sense advise upon the care of the mother before the baby comes. It tells her what to eat and wear and the exercise she should take. It gives plain directions for the dress and feeding of the child during infancy and childhood, and treatment of common ailments and accidents. Written in simple language.

By Edward P. Davis, M.D.

12mo. 21 full-page illustrations, Cloth, *Net* . $1.50

Juveniles

Romance of Modern Invention

An interesting and up-to-date account of air ships, sub-marines, sun motors, dirigible torpedoes, mono railways, telautographs, and other examples of invention and scientific achievement. With many anecdotes.

By Archibald Williams

Illustrated. 12mo. Pictorial cover design, *Net* . $1.50

¶ People like their copies of standard works in bindings which are better than those of the usual library books. To these we offer a series of fine English Editions at a moderate price. The books in cover, paper, printing, and arrangement will satisfy both the eye and hand. We mention some of them:

¶ **Boccaccio,** in 4 volumes; **Cervantes,** in 6 volumes; **Lamb,** in 6 volumes; **Poe,** in 8 volumes; **Rousseau,** in 4 volumes; **Smollett,** in 12 volumes; **Richardson,** in 20 volumes; **Ainsworth,** in 20 volumes; **Arabian Nights,** in 6 volumes; **The Heptameron,** in 5 volumes; **Sainte-Beuve,** in 3 volumes.

¶ All of these in cloth and half morocco, many of them illustrated, and all from authoritative texts.

¶ On the next page are noted some boys' and girls' books. The stories are told by authors whose names you will immediately recognize, and we heartily recommend each and every one of them.

J. B. Lippincott Company: Autumn Books *and other Good Books*

Jerry Dodds—Millionaire

A capital yarn of schoolboys and of the fun and mystery surrounding the experiences of a certain lad. We heartily recommend this story. It is illustrated by Harold Coffing.

By H. Barrow-North Illustrated. 12mo. Decorated cloth $1.25

"The Professor gripped him by the collar."

Jack and Black

A story of boy life by the author of those popular books, "The Spy in School," "Through Thick and Thin," "Out of Bounds," etc., etc. Part of this story is laid in scenes that will be new to Mr. Home's readers and which will make him many new friends.

By Andrew Home Illustrated. 12mo. Decorated cloth . . . $1.25

The Rebel of the School

A charming story for girls by one of the most liked writers for young people, the author of "Daddy's Girl."

By L. T. Meade Illustrated. 12mo. Decorated cloth . . . $1.50

A Plucky Girl

Another clever and entertaining story by the author of "A Popular Girl." Relating the interesting adventures of Miss Nell. Six capital drawings are by Jessie Macgregor.

By May Baldwin Illustrated. 12mo. Decorated cloth . . . $1.50

¶ **The Lost Gold of the Montezumas,** by W. O. Stoddard: **Trooper Ross,** and **Signal Butte,** and **From School to Battle-field,** by General Charles King: **Captain Chap,** and **The Young Master of Hyson Hall,** by Frank P. Stockton; **Brahmin's Treasure,** by G. A. Henty; **The Belt of Seven Totems,** by Kirk Munroe; **The Cruise of the Pretty Polly,** by W. Clark Russell.

¶ For girls we suggest Amy Blanchard's **Girls Together, Two Girls,** and **Betty of Wye;** Mrs. Molesworth's stories; and Elizabeth Wetherill's volumes, **Queechy,** and **Wide, Wide World.**

¶ By Mrs. Laura T. Meade, **The Rebel of the School** and **A Very Naughty Girl,** etc., are entertaining reading.

¶ Ouida's stories for children are also good, and may safely be offered. Besides these there are a hundred others, any one of which is sure to be liked.

FALL FICTION LIST OF
McClure, Phillips & Co.

Gabriel Tolliver

By

JOEL CHANDLER HARRIS

The First Complete Novel by the Famous Creator of "Uncle Remus"

THE scene of Mr. Harris's charming romance is laid in Georgia, at the troublous period of reconstruction. Not only is the masterly style and kindly humor of the author's short stories here reproduced, but many of the characters make their re-entry on a larger stage. $1.50

Thoroughbreds

A Romance of Men Women, and Horses

By W. A. FRASER

IN this novel, the author, himself a turfman of long experience, shows us the race-course and those whose lives centre about it as they really are. There is no glossing over the evils of "the sport of kings." Nevertheless Mr. Fraser shows us that there are high principles and noble ideals, as well as meanness and treachery, in the racing game. The story has a swing that carries you with it like the rush of a hard-fought race.

Illustrated by F. Lowenheim $1.50

The Hole in the Wall

By Arthur Morrison

Author of "Tales of Mean Streets," "A Child of the Jago," etc.

This is a story of the London slums that is neither revolting nor pessimistic. Grim enough it is, but its grimness is relieved by the central characters, Captain Nat, the old, fighting ex-riverman and his little grandson, Stephen, as quaint and lovable a pair of partners as ever warmed the heart of a reader.

Price $1.50

The Banner of Blue

By S. R. Crockett

Author of "The Firebrand," "The Stickit Minister," etc.

This is a new version of the parable of the prodigal son. Against the sombre background of the Disruption Period in Scotland Mr. Crockett draws with a master-hand two brilliantly colored love-stories, the one intense to its tragic end, the other delightful in its quaint Scotch humor.

Price $1.50

THE FIRST NOVEL SERIES

The Taskmasters

By George K. Turner

"The Taskmasters" pictures a New England that has never appeared in literature before, and which is, after all, the typical and dominating New England of modern times. In the great manufacturer, ruling like a feudal baron his town-full of employees, Mr. Turner finds a figure significant, picturesque and singularly unknown to art.

Price $1.25

The Ragged Edge

By John T. McIntyre

"The Ragged Edge" is a stirring story of ward politics and of the ward's social life; bosses and heelers and pugilists are the shining lights of the balls as of the primaries; withal the life of the ward centres in much-loved homes and is moulded by universal human passions. Such material is to be found in every newspaper, but Mr. McIntyre takes us into the heart of his world as no one has done before.

Price $1.25

A New Novel By

Booth Tarkington

Author of "The Gentleman from Indiana" and "Monsieur Beaucaire"

The rescue of the "two Vanrevels." Illustration by Henry Hutt

The Two Vanrevels

Illustrated in Colors by Henry Hutt *Price $1.50*

This story of Indiana life in the late 40's combines the virility of "The Gentleman from Indiana" with the charm of "Monsieur Beaucaire"

FOR SALE EVERYWHERE

Note—Special Edition of 500 copies in Full Imperial Japan Vellum with extra illustration drawn by Mr. Tarkington *$3.00 net*
Extra Edition of 500 copies uncut; bound in boards *$1.50 net*

ANNOUNCEMENT OF AUTUMN FICTION

"The most winsome little heroine in contemporary fiction."
Toledo Times.

Emmy Lou
Her Book & Heart
By George Madden Martin
Illustrated by C. L. Hinton

The Record of Emmy Lou's School Days from the First Reader up through the High School

In these stories Mrs. Martin has done two very notable things. First she has created the most lovable little girl in contemporary fiction. Secondly, she has drawn the first faithful and sympathetic picture of American public-school life. The skill with which she has sketched the teachers by whom Emmy Lou passes in her ascent of the "Readers" would alone make the reputation of the book. But Emmy Lou is more real than they; and finest of all, perhaps, is the wonderful insight into the growth of the child's mind that gives these stories, though written to stand separately, all the dramatic coherence and development of a great novel.

In his illustrations, Charles L. Hinton has shown the same ability and sympathy with children that Mrs. Martin displays in the narrative.

Price $1.50

Racer of Illinois
By Henry Somerville
Author of "Jack Racer"

Plot and action mark this book, as delightful character-drawing did its predecessor. This story transfers the activities of Jack Racer to a larger and more important field than the little prairies town of the earlier work. Here we find Jack, with the courage of ignorance and the buoyance of youth, ranging himself against a big railroad corporation, choosing the State Senate as a suitable arena.

Price $1.50

Little Stories of Married Life
By Mary Stewart Cutting

Mrs. Cutting begins where other story-tellers leave off. Marriage is a very general experience, and the married in actual life seem as much alive as other people; but in literature they generally pass out of any existence worth the name when the ceremony is performed. In the very heart of domesticity Mrs. Cutting finds moving crises and climaxes, perils and triumphs.

Frontispiece *Price $1.25*

McClure, Phillips & Co. New York

IMPORTANT AUTUMN PUBLICATIONS OF

McCLURE PHILLIPS AND COMPANY

Indian Boyhood

By Charles A. Eastman [Ohiyesa] and with pictures by E. L. Blumenschein.

More than thirty years ago a little Indian boy, Ohiyesa, a Santee Sioux, was roaming the prairies of the Northwest with his tribe. His father having been taken captive years before and his mother having died, he was in charge of an aged grandmother who taught him all kinds of useful Indian wisdom and legendary lore. One day, to the surprise of all, the father returned, no longer as a savage warrior, however, but as a missionary to his own people. Little Ohiyesa was sent to the East to be schooled in the ways of the white men. He is now government physician on the Crow Creek Agency, South Dakota. His book, the record of the memories of his early experiences, is absolutely unique as a picture of Indian life, not from without but intimately from within, and is a narrative full of beauty, poetry and information.

Price, net, $1.60.

The Letters of Daniel Webster

Edited by C. H. Van Tyne, Ph.D.

This is the definitive edition of the correspondence of the great American orator and statesman. So much of the correspondence is of a highly confidential and private nature that it would have been manifestly indiscreet to make public the bulk of the letters until the field should have been completely cleared of contemporary witnesses. Everything concerning the age in which Webster lived and worked is now legitimate matter for history, and the present volume will be of more assistance in completely reconstructing that age for the student of historical research and for the general reader than any other document in existence.

Price, net, $5.00

Golden Numbers: A Book of Verse for Youth

Edited by Kate Douglas Wiggin & Nora Archibald Smith

The names of the editors of this book are a sufficient guarantee of its high character. The publishers are confident that it is the best collection of its kind ever issued, and that it is destined to supersede all others not only for private use but for employment in schools and academies. Kate Douglas Wiggin has contributed an Introduction and a series of Interleaves to the scheme of the book.

Price, net, $2.00.

KATE DOUGLAS WIGGIN

The Complete Works of William Hazlitt

With an introduction by W. E. Henley

WILLIAM HAZLITT

This is the first complete edition of the works of the greatest literary critic that the English-speaking world has known. That the entire writings of such a master should never have been collected in a uniform edition similar to those of DeQuincey and Lamb, has always been a matter of regret to lovers of English letters. The Dent edition supplies this deficiency in a manner that cannot but delight every admirer of Hazlitt. The set, which is in twelve volumes, includes all of Hazlitt's literary, political, dramatic, and miscellaneous writings. The edition is limited to three hundred and fifty sets. A special circular will be sent on application.

Price per set, net, $36.00.

Mutual Aid, a Factor in Evolution

By Prince Kropotkin

It has been too much taken for granted that evolution of the race takes place only by the weakest going to the wall and by the stronger surviving, and that any means of preventing this natural process will lead to the degeneration of the race. Prince Kropotkin shows that among animals, savages, barbarians, and modern races there is another side to the question, suggested by Darwin but not so fully worked out by him. He explains by many examples the large extent to which mutual aid replaces competition.

Price, net, $2.50.

The Prayers of Dr. Johnson

For the first time the many prayers composed by Dr. Johnson have been taken from their original setting in his journal, and presented not merely on the strength of their autobiographic interest, but as a body of divine exhortations unsurpassed in the English language. Notes and introduction have been furnished by Mr. William Aspenwall Bradley. The book has for a frontispiece a reproduction, in photogravure, of a portrait by Sir Joshua Reynolds. Published in three editions. A special circular will be sent on application.

Price about, net, $1.00.

Border Fights and Fighters

By Cyrus Townsend Brady

Daniel Boone, Sam Houston, David Crockett, William Henry Harrison, and Andrew Jackson—these are some of the men of whom Cyrus Townsend Brady writes in his "Border Fights and Fighters." Their exploits form the most romantic chapters in American history; they themselves stand as the hardiest and most picturesque group among the makers of the nation. From Tohopeka in the south to Vincennes and Fort Stephenson in the north; from King's Mountain to the Alamo and San Jacinto, their battles in the wilderness and on the plains mark the decisive steps by which the boundaries of the nation were pushed westward.

C. T. BRADY

Price, net, $1.30.

Jeanne d'Arc

With introduction and critical notes by T. Douglas Murray

Translations from the verbatim reports in Latin, of the ecclesiastical proceedings in the trial of Jeanne d'Arc. These documents have recently come to light. It is probably the only instance of a complete biographical record of the greatest historical importance being taken down by evidence on oath. The trial is one of the most enthralling dramas in all history. The depositions cover the whole pathetic story of the childhood of the Maid, her military career as commander-in-chief of the French armies, her capture, imprisonment, and death at the stake, as described by eye-witnesses.

Price, net, $5.00.

LADY DUFF GORDON

Fictional Rambles in and About Boston

By Frances Weston Carruth

The list of the novelists who have written stories with Boston for a background is a long and imposing one. Hawthorne, Holmes, Howells, James, Cooper—these are some of the names that are included in it. Naturally this body of fiction has given Boston a set of associations second in interest to its historical associations only, if indeed we may not consider, as we may well do, these imaginative plots and characters as part of the real history of the city to which they belong. Miss Carruth has made a thorough study of her subject and the book is fully illustrated.

Price, net, $1.50.

Letters from Egypt

By Lady Duff Gordon, with an introduction by George Meredith and frontispiece portrait after portrait by G. F. Watts

The reprint of a famous series of letters by one of the most brilliant Englishwomen of her time. They are of permanent literary and historical value, and the fascinating personality of the woman, whose greatness of heart and of mind will make them live, is drawn by Mr. Meredith in a sympathetic manner. Like Diana and Aminta, though in a different sense, she is one of his heroines.

Price, net, $2.50.

Hogarth

By Austin Dobson and Sir Walter Armstrong

This book, which contains seventy plates, is a magnificent monument to the memory of Hogarth. In a way it presents a new treatment of the great English artist. For while not neglecting his unquestioned gifts as a social censor and humorist, it is part of the aim of the present publication to accentuate the legacy he has left as a painter. Published in three limited editions. Special circular will be sent on application.

Illustrated with 70 plates. Large Imperial Quarto. Net $25.00.
With additional portfolio of plates on India paper, net $60.00.
With additional portfolio of plates on India paper and Japanese vellum, net $120.00.

SIMON, LORD LOVAT
By HOGARTH

COUNT TOLSTOY

Astronomy for Everybody

By Prof. Simon Newcomb

Foremost astronomer of America, and one of the acknowledged authorities of the world on his subject, no man is better qualified than Professor Newcomb to write a handbook on astronomy that shall be at once popular and scientific, not too compendious for a handbook yet not too brief to cover the field without slighting a single important aspect of the subject—in short, that shall be the ideal book of the kind that is needed for the wide dissemination of sound knowledge of every sort in this country.

Price, net, $2.00.

Dante and His Time

By Karl Federn

A distinguished work by a prominent Dante scholar. The aim of the work is to give a picture of Dante in his proper historical *milieu*—to show him in the Florence of the fourteenth century as a figure in the political, literary and social life of his times. *Price, net, $2.00.*

Ivan Ilyitch

By Count Léof Tolstoy

The second of a new series of translations, direct from the Russian, of the early novels of Tolstoy, by Mrs. Garnett. *Anna Karenin* appeared last season and *War and Peace* is announced for next year. *Price, net, $1.00.*

TWO BOOKS OF THE DAY

The Simple Life

By Charles Wagner

President Roosevelt said in a recent speech: "The other day I picked up a little book called 'The Simple Life,' written by an Alsatian, Charles Wagner, and he preached such wholesome, sound doctrine that I wish it could be used as a tract throughout our country." *Price $1.25.*

The Trust Problem

By J. W. Jenks, Ph.D.

Just the book for the man who is thinking about this question. The author gives all the facts and presents both sides of the question with equal fairness. Prof. Jenks drew up the "Trust Bill" framed to carry out the suggestions in Governor Roosevelt's annual message in January, 1900, and is thoroughly qualified to deal with the subject. *Price, net, $1.00.*

DANTE

McClure, Phillips & Co.'s complete catalogue, including a description of all autumn publications, will be sent to any address on application to their office at 141 East 25th Street, New York City.

FREDERICK A. STOKES, *President.* MAYNARD A. DOMINICK, *Secretary.* GEORGE F. FOSTER, *Treasurer.*

"For hym was levere have at his beddes heed
Twenty bookes, clad in blak or reed,
Than robes riche or fithele or gay sautrie."

Frederick A. Stokes Company's

FALL ANNOUNCEMENT OF NEW - - PUBLICATIONS AND NEW EDITIONS

An edition of Shakespeare that will satisfy the most fastidious bibliophile.

THE EDINBURGH EDITION.

A series of Folios was initiated recently with an edition of Shakespeare, which the publishers hope will prove a type and exemplar of modern book-making.

It was their desire to produce a series as beautiful and as dignified as paper and print could make it. Sixteen parts of this first series have now been issued as follows:

THE MERCHANT OF VENICE,
THE TEMPEST,
THE MERRY WIVES OF WINDSOR,
THE COMEDY OF ERRORS,
MEASURE FOR MEASURE,
MUCH ADO ABOUT NOTHING,
LOVE'S LABOUR LOST,
TWO GENTLEMEN OF VERONA,
A MIDSUMMER NIGHT'S DREAM,
AS YOU LIKE IT,
THE TAMING OF THE SHREW,
THE WINTER'S TALE,
ALL'S WELL THAT ENDS WELL,
TWELFTH NIGHT,
KING JOHN,
KING RICHARD II.

These beautiful books have been printed by Messrs. Constable & Company, of Edinburgh, who have given them the benefit of their best skill.

The typographical interest notwithstanding, this series is, above all, a Shakespeare to be read. The editor is Mr. W. E. Henley, whose notes are neither explanatory nor critical, and who has kept the text as close to the first Folio as he could.

The parts, though tall and stately, are neither heavy nor cumbersome; the type is black, bold, and eminently easy to the eye; the paper is hand-made, sunny-white, durable, yet light.

There will be forty parts, and all will be so paged as to be bound in eight volumes, yet each part is complete in itself, and so cased in temporary binding as to be handled with convenience and to stand uninjured in the library.

There will be ten authentic portraits in the series, several of Shakespeare himself, and others of Jonson, Fletcher, Burbage, Southampton and Pembroke.

The edition will consist of 1000 copies, *of which only 360 are for sale in America.*

Each volume will be numbered.

The cost of each part is $2.00 net, but the work is sold in complete sets only.

Two parts are issued each month.

The most complete history published of the most beautiful capital in the world.

PARIS, PAST AND PRESENT.

By HENRY HAYNIE.

Chevalier de la Legion d'Honneur, etc.

This history of the capital of Europe, as Paris is often called, is a work wherein every page is full of thought and is admirably written by an American who lived in France for twenty years. It is a work which gives a complete and graphic account of Paris from its earliest moments to the present time.

Readers, when they have finished with this work, will know more of the religious, political, social, moral, economical, intellectual and artistic life of Paris than they ever knew before, or can possibly learn from any other similar publication.

The English-reading public generally will be interested in this full account of the famous place from its baptism until it has come to be the most magnificent capital in existence.

Cloth, gilt top, profusely illustrated with photogravures and half-tone engravings.

Two volumes, 8vo, gilt tops, boxed, . net, $4.00
Postpaid, ... $4.32

Same, three-quarters crushed levant, boxed, net, $8 00. Postpaid, ... $8.32

FREDERICK A. STOKES COMPANY'S ANNOUNCEMENTS.

A remarkable biography of France's most famous novelist.

THE LIFE AND WRITINGS OF ALEXANDER DUMAS.

By HARRY A. SPURR.

With the exception of this work no adequate life of Dumas is in existence. No impartial and complete biography exists even in French.

Part I. of the work is devoted to the career of Dumas from his birth to his manhood and fame. Part II. deals with the character of the man. Part III. deals briefly with the plays and gives much attention to the romances—their origin, merit and authenticity, with illustrative anecdotes concerning the more notable books. Part IV. comprises a defense of Dumas against the charges generally brought against him, with an attempt at an appreciation of his genius.

A list of authorities, a full chronology of the events of his life, the publication of his works, etc., and an index round out this notable biography.

One volume, octavo, with numerous portraits, etc., gilt top, net, $2.00; postpaid, ... $2.15

New light on the characters of Kaiser Wilhelm I. and Bismarck.

BISMARCK AND KAISER WILHELM I., LETTERS BETWEEN.

Edited by HORST KOHL.

These letters extend from 1852, when Wilhelm I. was still a prince, to 1887. They cover a wide variety of subjects, but, of course, the greater portion of them has to do with the political questions of the day.

With a steel engraving of the Emperor, and a considerable number of letters in *facsimile* from the Emperor to Bismarck, and *vice versa.*

Two volumes, 8vo, cloth, well printed and bound, gilt tops, ... net, $4.00
Postpaid, ... $4.30

Same, three-quarters crushed levant, gilt tops, boxed, ... net, $8.00
Postpaid, ... $8.30

American customs as they appear from the Japanese standpoint.

THE AMERICAN DIARY OF A JAPANESE GIRL.

By MISS MORNING GLORY.

A modern Japanese girl gives her impressions of America. Miss Morning Glory is quaint, romantic, simple, and clever at once. She writes with a sprightly grace and distinction of style that show her to be an artist, true to the traditions of Japan.

Beautifully illustrated by the well-known Japanese artist, Genjiro Yeto. With one full-page in color, a number of full-page half-tone engravings and Japanese borders in tints. Bound with grass-cloth back and white and gold sides.

Octavo, 6½ x 9½ inches, ... net, $1.60
Postpaid, ... $1.75

A De Luxe edition of a satire that has become almost a classic.

THE LAST AMERICAN.

By JOHN A. MITCHELL.

Author of "Amos Judd," "The Pines of Lory," etc.

"A fragment from the Journal of Khan-li, Prince of Dimph-yoo-chur, an Admiral in the Persian Navy."

An amusing and satirical account of the adventures of a party of Persian explorers among the ruins of America in the year 2951 A.D.

Fifteen editions of this popular book have been issued, and in consequence of the increased demand for it, the publishers have decided to make a special *HOLIDAY EDITION.*

The special features of this *Edition de Luxe* will be *eight full-page illustrations in COLORS* by *F. W. READ,* made under the supervision of Mr. Mitchell. In addition there will be decorations by Alfred D. Blashfield, and all of Mr. Mitchell's own illustrations, with few exceptions, will be shown. The typographical part of the work will be done anew in the best manner, and the printing and binding will be especially attractive.

It will be one of the most beautiful presentation books published during the year.

12mo, cloth, ... $1.50

A popular work that treats a scientific subject in an interesting way.

BIRDS' NESTS.

By CHARLES DIXON.

An Introduction to the science of caliology. Mr. Dixon is a well-known authority on bird-life, and is the author of ten or more books on this subject.

The present volume has been written with the object of guiding the student to an acquisition of a scientific knowledge of Birds' Nests. Many lines of original research have been indicated, and a plan promulgated upon which the science of caliology may at all events provisionally be based.

With sixteen full-page, half-tone illustrations by A. T. Elwes.

12mo, cloth, ... net, $1.20
Postpaid, ... $1.32

An interesting work on Mme. Du Barry and David Belasco's famous play.

THE STORY OF DU BARRY.

By JAMES L. FORD.

Author of "Dolly Dillenbeck," "The Literary Shop," etc

A long and interesting account of the story of Mme. Du Barry and of the production of David Belasco's great play, by James L. Ford, who has made an exhaustive study of the period of Louis XV.

A great deal of valuable information is given in Mr. Ford's text, and the illustrations are the finest ever made for any such book. There are nearly sixty half-tone engravings and six photogravures. These are all taken from photographs of Mr. Belasco's company and give a complete series of pictures of the play. Some of these also reproduce the unique stage properties which were used in the play. For example, the gold cup and saucer belonging to Madame Du Barry, used on the stage during the performance, are shown here.

8vo, cloth, gilt top, boxed, ... net, $2.00
Postpaid, ... $2.20

FREDERICK A. STOKES COMPANY'S ANNOUNCEMENTS.

A collection of light lyrical verse written to please every mood.

LOVE, LAURELS AND LAUGHTER.

By BEATRICE HANSCOM.

The seventy or more graceful poems gathered together under this decidedly original title have mostly appeared in the "Century," in "Life," in "Puck" and in other American periodicals. As shown by what has been printed in these periodicals, Miss Hanscom has a light touch and a good ear; her metre is smooth and her poems are musical and contain original ideas very neatly expressed.

Printed on good paper, and daintily bound, with a frontispiece in two colors by William J. Hurlbut.

12mo, cloth, ... net, $1.00
Postpaid, ... $1.20

Valuable hints for all lovers of Tabby.

CATS AND ALL ABOUT THEM.

By FRANCES SIMPSON.

Miss Simpson is one of the greatest authorities in England on cats. As she says in her preface, she has had many years' experience with cats and kittens, and has a real love for them, without which she does not believe anyone can be a successful breeder or exhibitor of cats.

The object of this book is to assist cat-lovers to become cat-fanciers. The book has twenty-four illustrations, the frontispiece being a picture of the author and her famous cat "Cambyses." The other pictures give specimens of the different breeds of cats.

12mo, cloth, with cover in colors, . . . net, $1.00
Postpaid, ... $1.10

A worthy companion to the successful volume, "Yutzo."

SON! or The Wisdom of "Uncle Eph," the Modern Yutzo.

By LORD GILHOOLEY (Frederic Seymour)

Printed on tobacco paper and with a binding of blue denim with roughened edges.

Each of the aphorisms in the book is introduced by the word "Son!" as coming from the lips of Uncle Eph.

With frontispiece, decorative borders, etc.
12mo, ... net, 80 cts.
Postpaid, ... 88 cts.

Plenty of fun by the author of a "Golf Alphabet."

THE MISHAPS OF AN AUTOMOBILIST.

By DE WITT CLINTON FALLS.

With twelve full-page plates in colors showing the comical accidents that often happen to the automobilist and laughable incidents connected with them. They are accompanied and explained by humorous verses. There are also twelve little pictures, sequels to the larger ones, showing the amusing results of the accidents.

Oblong, 4to, boxed, ... net, $1.00
Postpaid, ... $1.12

Examples of classic art at a price within the reach of all.

THE HUNDRED MOST FAMOUS PICTURES IN THE WORLD.

Comprising the most renowned examples of the art of all periods and nations, with brief explanatory and critical notes by Augustus Van Cleef.

This is a most important work, showing the famous paintings of the world reproduced in a suitable manner and published at a price which brings them within the reach of all. It will consist of twenty parts; each part contains five reproductions of paintings that have been accepted by the critics and art-lovers as masterpieces.

The first of these parts was issued early in September and two will follow each month until the series is completed. The average size of the plates will be 6½ x 9¼ inches. The twenty paintings reproduced in the first four parts are as follows:

Part I. Mrs. Siddons, Gainsborough; The Wasps' Nest, Bouguereau; The Virgin of the Chair, Raphael; The Angelus, Millet; The Return from Moscow, Meissonier.

Part II. Children of Charles I. of England, Van Dyke; Paris and Helen, David; Une Matinée, Corot; La Cruche Cassée, Greuze; The Holy Family, Murillo.

Part III. The Horse Fair, Marie Rosalie Bonheur; His Own Portrait, Rembrandt Van Ryn; Portrait of Lavinia, Titian; Descent from the Cross, Peter Paul Rubens; The Gleaner, Jules Breton.

Part IV. The Fighting Téméraire, Joseph M. W. Turner; Beatrice Cenci, Guido Reni; The Last Supper, Leonardo da Vinci; Shoeing the Bay Mare, Sir Edwin Landseer; The Artist and Her Daughter, Wm. Le Brun.

Each part, large folio, antique paper covers, well printed, ... 25 cts.

An edition de luxe of an English classic.

THE CLOISTER AND THE HEARTH.

By CHARLES READE.

This is an entirely new edition, set from new type, and illustrated by sixteen photogravures and eighty-four half-tone illustrations after designs by Matt. B. Hewerdine.

Small 4to, cloth, gilt top, boxed, ... $3.50

A new version of a well known tragedy by a famous Italian author.

FRANCESCA DA RIMINI.

By GABRIEL D'ANNUNZIO.

A new play by the author of "The Triumph of Death," "The Flame of Life," etc.

It is a magnificently spectacular play, and will without doubt make a great success when presented by Duse on her tour of this country.

It is translated by Arthur Symons.

16mo, ½ cloth, net, $1.00; postpaid. . . $1.10

FICTION.

A number of copyrighted novels by the most popular authors of the day are offered.

The River.

By EDEN PHILLPOTTS.

This is the first long novel by the author of "Chil-

FREDERICK A. STOKES COMPANY'S ANNOUNCEMENTS.

dren of the Mist," for about two years, and the author regards it as the strongest work he has ever done.

In length, scene, incident and solid literary merit, "The River" has every qualification for repeating or surpassing the notable success of "Children of the Mist," which has gone into fifteen editions.

The scenes are laid in Devonshire, as were those of his former greatest novel.

12mo, cloth, with frontispiece, ... $1.50

Wolfville Nights.

By **ALFRED HENRY LEWIS.**

This is the third of Mr. Lewis's delightful series of works on Wolfville life.

This deals with the same characters that appeared in his two preceding books, and the scene is laid in the same locality.

12mo, cloth, with frontispiece, ... $1.50

A Woman Ventures.

By **DAVID GRAHAM PHILLIPS (John Graham).**

This is a romance woven with materials that make up the life of American men and women of to-day in town and country. The heroine is a young American girl, beautiful and full of charm, but contemptuous of conventionalities, though always high minded. The style is simple and direct, and the story is fascinating in the extreme.

12mo, cloth, with frontispiece, ... $1.50

Come With Me Into Babylon.

By **JOSIAH M. WARD.**

Mr. Ward has taken his readers back to the time of Nebuchadnezzar and the last days of Nineveh He gives us not a glimpse, but a picture of the lives of the Babylonians, whose name has come to be a synonym for luxury and wantonness.

Those were heroic days really, when the greatest nations of that remote antiquity, the Babylonians, Medes, Lydians and Egyptians, met over the carcass of Assyria and engaged in a fierce struggle for the mastery of the world.

There is a romantic love story of uninterrupted interest running through the book.

With eight illustrations. Well printed and bound.

12mo, cloth, ... $1.50

A Daughter of Raasay.

By **WILLIAM MacLEOD RAINE.**

This is a romance of the mad days when the Stuarts made their last desperate attempt to regain the throne of England. The story rushes along from one episode to another, unraveling a capital plot by daring adventures, sparkling dialogues and situations of surprising dramatic intensity, while Aileen, the heroine, is at once the despair of her lover and the delight of the reader.

12mo, cloth, illustrated, ... $1.50

Tom Moore.

By **THEODORE BURT SAYRE.**

This is a romance by the author of "Two Summer Girls and I."

It is founded on the play which was produced with so much success throughout the country, with Andrew Mack in the title role.

Mr. Sayre makes his hero a rollicking, charming Irishman who wins the hearts of all of his readers by his humor and genial qualities.

One special feature of the hook is the excellent illustrations. They are half-tone engravings made from photographs of the play. They are graceful and without the usual theatrical effect.

12mo, cloth, ... $1.50

The Garden of Lies.

By **JUSTUS MILES FORMAN.**

"The Garden of Lies" is a romantic story of love and adventure in modern Paris with a very beautiful young American girl as the heroine. There is a medley of plot and intrigue, jealousy and idyllic love, and some clash of swords. A most striking and original story.

12mo, cloth, with frontispiece, ... $1.50

Penruddock of the White Lambs.

By **SAMUEL H. CHURCH.**

An exciting romance by the author of "John Marmaduke." The hero is Colonel Penruddock, a Royalist, formerly Colonel of the "White Lambs," the Duke of Newcastle's famous regiment which Cromwell cut to pieces at Marston Moor.

When their uniforms were made there was no dye at hand to color them red, and they told the Duke if he would let them wear the white woolen clothes they would dye them with blood—and they did, only forty of them surviving, out of one thousand, when Cromwell had finished his charge down the moor.

The author is one of the greatest living authorities on the history of Cromwell's time.

12mo, cloth, with frontispiece, ... $1.50

A Whirl Asunder.

By **GERTRUDE ATHERTON.**

This is a new edition of one of Mrs. Atherton's earlier works and one of her strongest.

It is an exciting story of California life. The opening scene is in the red-wood forests of that state, with a striking description of the Midsummer Jinks of the Bohemian Club of San Francisco.

12mo, cloth, illustrated, ... $1.00

The Foray of the Hendrik Hudson.

By **FRANK MACKENZIE SAVILE.**

A story of adventure as fascinating as "The Prisoner of Zenda." *With four attractive illustrations.*

12mo, cloth, ... $1.00

COPYRIGHT SERIES OF FAMOUS AUTHORS.

A new series of books by popular authors. It is intended to give in this series cloth bound books at the same price as those formerly issued in paper.

1. **The Light of Scarthey.** Egerton Castle.
2. **The Son of the Czar.** James M. Graham.
3. **Gober.** Kate A. Benton.

FREDERICK A. STOKES COMPANY'S ANNOUNCEMENTS.

4. **The Lord of the Sea.** M. P. Shiel.
5. **A Woman Intervenes.** Robert Barr.
6. **The Master Craftsman.** Sir Walter Besant.
7. **Zoraida.** William Le Queux.
8. **Ashes of Empire.** Robert W. Chambers.
9. **Active Service.** Stephen Crane.
10. **The Crown of Life.** George Gissing.
11. **The Changeling.** Sir Walter Besant.
12. **At the Court of Catherine the Great.** Fred Whishaw.
13. **Pabo, the Priest.** S. Baring-Gould.
14. **Tales by Tom Hall.**
15. **The White Shield.** Bertram Mitford.
16. **Comedy of Spasms.** Mrs. Mannington Caffyn.
17. **Philbrick Howell.** Albert Kinross.
18. **Hilda.** Sara Jeannette Duncan.
19. **The Town Traveller.** George Gissing.
20. **The Watchers.** A. E. W. Mason.
21. **The Filibusters.** Cutcliffe Hyne.
22. **From Door to Door.** Bernard Capes.
23. **John Ship, Mariner.** Knarf Elivas.
24. **The Christian Teaching.** Tolstoi.
25. **A Rogue's Daughter.** Adeline Sargeant.
26. **Friend of the People.** Mary C. Rowsell.
27. **The Broom Squire.** S. Baring-Gould.
28. **The Whirlpool.** George Gissing.
29. **Anne of Argyle.** George Eyre-Todd.
30. **Lakewood.** Mary H. Norris.
31. **Javan Ben Seir.** Walker Kennedy.
32. **Domitia.** S. Baring-Gould.
33. **An Opera and Lady Grasmere.** Albert Kinross.
34. **Tales of John Oliver Hobbes.**
35. **Stolen Souls.** William Le Queux.
36. **The Finding of Lot's Wife.** Alfred Clark.
37. **Revenge.** Robert Barr.
38. **Towards Pretoria.** Julian Ralph.
39. **An American with Lord Roberts.** Julian Ralph.
40. **The Mutable Many.** Robert Barr

Each, 12mo, cloth, ... 50 cts.

Three interesting books by the greatest painter of Indian life.

RED FOLK AND WILD FOLK.

Illustrated by Edwin W. Deming. Text by Therese O. Deming.

Edwin W. Deming's pictures show the little Indian people in their happy forest homes, with their animal playfellows.

The stories are taken from the old Indian folk-lore, most of them received directly from the Indians by the author, Therese O. Deming.

They tell of the long ago, when the animal people and the Red people lived happily together and were rewarded for their good deeds or punished for their evil ones.

These tales are the lessons taught to Indian children by the old men and women, and are very real to them.

With 12 pictures in colors by Mr. Deming.

4to, cloth, cover in colors, ... net, $1.60
Postpaid, ... $1.76

Children of the Wild.
Little Brothers of the West.

Each of these books contains just half the pictures and text contained in the volume "Red Folk and Wild Folk."

Each, 4to, cloth, cover in colors, . . net, $1.00
Postpaid, ... $1.12

A new edition of a juvenile long accepted as a classic.

THE FAIRCHILD FAMILY.

By **MRS. SHERWOOD.**

Mrs. Sherwood was a popular writer for children in the early part of the 19th century, whose works are regarded in England as almost classics.

The history of the Fairchild family, which is the best of these, was begun in 1818, when George I. was on the throne, and when the Battle of Waterloo was still quite a recent event; but the children then had just the same traits as the children of to-day, and the book will be found charming as a story, and delightful as a picture of the times.

Mary E. Palgrave has edited the work, and has written an interesting introduction to it, giving a sketch of Mrs. Sherwood's life and writings.

With seventy-five illustrations in pen and ink by Florence Rudland, many of them full-page.

Large 8vo, with cover stamped in colors. net, $1.60
Postpaid, ... $1.77

Fairy stories as they are told to the children of Sweden.

FAIRY TALES.

From the Swedish of Baron G. Djurklou.

By **H. L. BRAEKSTAD.**

With illustrations by Th. Kittelsen and Eric Werenskiold.

These Swedish Folk and Fairy Tales, hitherto quite unknown to lovers of folk-lore outside Sweden, are by Baron Gabriel Djurklou, who has devoted much time and study to the life, the folk-lore and the various dialects of the peasantry of his native country, where his work has been met with great recognition both at the hands of the public and of learned societies.

The many illustrations are by Mr. T. Kittelsen and Mr. E. Werenskiold, two well-known Norwegian artists, who have admirably caught the spirit of each story.

There will also be a frontispiece by Mr. Carl Larsson, the prince of Swedish illustrators.

8vo, cloth, ... net, $1.20
Postpaid, ... $1.36

The real facts about one of the most popular of nursery ballads.

MARY HAD A LITTLE LAMB.
The True Story of the Real Mary and the Real Lamb.

By **FANNIE M. DICKERSON.**

The story of this poem is most delightfully told by Mary herself and by Miss Fannie M. Dickerson, an instructor in the South Lancaster Academy, which is located near the scene of the story. The book is very pleasingly illustrated by original pen drawings of the scenes of the story by Herbert A. Owen. It is an entertaining book not only for the children but for those older.

4to, cloth, net, $1.00; postpaid, ... $1.10

FREDERICK A. STOKES COMPANY'S ANNOUNCEMENTS.

Amusing pictures and rhymes that combine to make an ideal gift for children of any age.

NONSENSE! NONSENSE!

With 28 pages in full color, 36 pages in two colors, cover design and end papers, by Charles Robinson. There are appropriate verses for all the pictures by Walter Jerrold.

Mr. Charles Robinson has excelled himself in this irresistibly droll series of nonsense pictures. No verbal description can do justice to the humorous exaggeration, the quaint distortions, the extraordinary play of imagination that distinguish these drawings.

Mr. Robinson has had a fruitful source of inspiration in the verses of Mr. Walter Jerrold, who shows himself a master of the difficult art of writing nonsense jingles for children.

Large quarto, cover in colors, . . . net, $1.60
Postpaid, ... $1.75

A popular series of toy books for young children

MOVING PICTURE BOOKS.

The Hippodrome.

An interesting toy book which gives a number of scenes from a circus. First, there is a programme of the different scenes to be enacted, and then they come one after the other.

The pictures are all in color, and the figures are arranged so that they stand out from the book, making a very life-like scene, which will amuse and interest the children. There are twelve pictures in all.

Large quarto in shape, and with the different pictures attached to each other like scenes, so that they all can be spread out and seen at once.

Large quarto, with cover in colors, . net, $2.00
Postpaid. $2.18

The Demon Horse.

A very amusing book with horses as the central figures, and with numerous riders. The pages are so arranged that many humorous combinations of the different pictures can be made.

Large quarto, with covers in colors, . net, $1.20
Postpaid, ... $1.35

The Jolly Uncle.

The Jolly Aunt.

Two funny toy books, with pictures in colors.

The pages are so arranged that many humorous combinations of the different pictures can be made.

Quarto, with covers in colors, . . . net, 80 cts.
Postpaid, ... 88 cts.

THE TREASURE SEEKERS.

By **E. NESBIT.**

A new edition of the charming book for children by the author of "The Wouldbegoods," etc.

It concerns the history of the Bastable children, the same characters that appeared in "The Wouldbe goods."

With numerous illustrations by Gordon Browne.

12mo, cloth, ... $1.50

FAIRY TALES FROM HANS ANDERSEN.

A new edition of this popular classic illustrated by Gordon Browne, R. I., and an introduction by Edward Clodd.

This is a beautiful gift book, profusely illustrated by this popular artist.

Gilt top, fancy cloth sides, large crown 8vo, net, $1.60
Postpaid, ... $1.75

YOUNG GEORGE.

A very interesting book for children, with numerous pictures in half-tones and in colors by Miss Edith Farmiloe.

Quarto, cloth, with cover in colors, . net, $1.20
Postpaid, ... $1.35

New volumes in a series of established popularity.

DUMPY BOOKS FOR CHILDREN.

The Story of Little Black Mingo. By Helen Bannerman.

The Bad Mrs. Ginger. By Miss Appleton.

Little People: an Alphabet. By Henry Mayer.

Each 32mo, illustrated, ... *net*, 40 cents.
Postpaid, ... 45 cents.

A unique novelty for the amusement of guests at lunch and dinner parties.

A GUEST BOOK.

Arranged by **FLORENCE L. SAHLER.**

This unique little guest book consists of a number of blank pages with a distorted proverb at the head of each, such as, "Spare the Pen and spoil the Pig," etc. Underneath each proverb is a space, and the guest is expected to shut his eyes and draw a complete picture of a pig, and sign his name underneath.

The purpose of the book is explained by the author as follows:

"When visits, dinners, luncheons end
This book is brought to every friend.
One is not asked to write fine prose,
Nor to assume the poet's pose.
One only need his eyes to close
And draw a pig from tail to nose."

Oblong quarto, cloth, ... net, 80 cts.

MRS. LESLIE CARTER AS MADAME DU BARRY.

A souvenir of the greatest theatrical success ever made in this country. Mr. David Belasco, the author of this play, produced it with a lavishness never equalled in this or any other country. Over $80,000 was spent by him before the first night.

This souvenir is not simply a collection of a few pictures, but contains a careful sketch of Mr. Belasco's work and a brief biography of Madame Du Barry, and it brings out all the interesting facts regarding the valuable properties used in the play. Numerous half-tone illustrations show these properties, and there are three engravings of Mrs. Carter in different scenes of the play and a portrait of Mr. Belasco.

With a cover specially designed by Wilfred Buckland.

12mo, boards, ... net, 50 cts.
Postpaid, ... 58 cts.

MINIATURE VOLUMES.

A new edition of these beautiful little volumes, well printed, so that they can be easily read in spite of their small size.

Ten volumes come in an unusually attractive new binding.

Chips from Dickens. By T. Mason.

FREDERICK A. STOKES COMPANY'S ANNOUNCEMENTS.

Chips from Thackeray. By T. Mason.

Gems of Thought from Classical Authors. By Aimee Wilson.

Gleanings from Wordsworth.

Golden Thoughts from Great Authors. Selected by Alice Crowther.

Golden Thoughts from Thomas a Kempis's Imitation of Christ. Selected by T. M. Lindsay, D.D.

Goldsmith's "She Stoops to Conquer."

Lady of The Lake, The. By Sir Walter Scott.

Pickings from a "Pocket of Pebbles." By William Philpot. Preface by A. B. Grosart, LL.D, F.S.A.

Witty, Humorous, and Merry Thoughts. Selected by T. Mason.

Each, "marble enameled" binding, ornamental sides, gilt edges, boxed, ... 50 cents

New Edition.

NORTHWARD OVER THE GREAT ICE.

By **ROBERT E. PEARY, U. S. N.**

Peary's narrative abounds in infinite variety. It is in two volumes of about 600 pages each, and contains over 800 half-tone engravings, made from Peary's wonderful photographs, together with valuable maps, diagrams, etc.

2 vols., 8vo, cloth, boxed, ... net, $5.00

Half morocco, gilt top, boxed, . . . net, 10.00

Full morocco, gilt top, boxed, . . . net, 15.00

Three-quarter crushed levant, gilt top, boxed, net, 17.50

New Edition.

THE LIFE AND LETTERS OF SIR JOHN EVERETT MILLAIS, PRESIDENT OF THE ROYAL ACADEMY.

By **JOHN G. MILLAIS.**

These two magnificent volumes contain the authoritative biography by his son of the most distinguished and popular painter of the last century.

Not the least attractive and remarkable feature of this work is the magnificent illustrations. There are over two hundred pictures and sketches in half-tone which have never been reproduced before, and also seven of Millais' finest pictures are reproduced in photogravure.

2 vols., royal 8vo, 300 illustrations, cloth, gilt top, boxed, ... $6.00

Same, de Luxe edition, limited, boxed, . $15.00

Same, three-quarters crushed levant, boxed, $20.00

A new and popular edition of two standard works.

WESTMINSTER.

Fully illustrated by William Patten and others, and giving *facsimiles* of many quaint old documents and missals, memorial windows, and wonderful buildings of this "city which has no citizens."

South London.

This work includes descriptions of Southwark, Lambeth, Greenwich, Woolwich, and other famous historic towns. Profusely illustrated by Percy Wadham and other artists.

Two volumes as a set, gilt tops, boxed, cloth, $3.00

VIGNETTE SERIES.

This beautiful series of English classics is now offered in a new leather binding—mottled calf, full gilt, boxed, at $2.00 per volume.

Each volume is a remarkably beautiful 12mo, illustrated profusely by half-tone engravings. 25 titles. Send for catalogue.

MASTERPIECES OF PROSE AND VERSE.

This delightful series of little volumes is now offered in a new and attractive leather binding—mottled calf, full gilt, boxed, at $1.00 per volume.

Each volume is 32mo, and contains twenty or more vignette illustrations, chiefly full-page but occasionally set into the type. Printed on coated paper with wide margins, and with a cut on each title page. 19 titles.

CALENDARS.

One hundred and seventy-five varieties, of all prices, styles, and shapes, both domestic and foreign.

This is unquestionably the finest line of calendars ever offered.

There are a number of important new calendars made up of imported French pictures; there are also many photogravure reproductions of some of the best works of modern and ancient painters.

Among the calendars by American artists are "The Calendar of Fair Americans," by W. J. Hurlbut; "The Girl of To-day Calendar," by C. F. Underwood; a "Calendar of Notable Actresses," containing reproductions in half-tone of six of the most popular actresses on the American stage.

Other popular subjects are:

"The Fencer's Calendar;" "The Automobile Calendar;" "The Calendar of the Wild;" "Calendar of Society Belles;" "The Maude Adams Calendar;" "The Cat Calendar;" New Photogravure Calendars, etc., etc.

SEND FOR CATALOGUE OR CALL,

Frederick A. Stokes Company,

5 and 7 East 16th Street, - - NEW YORK.

An International Episode. By Henry James.

A new edition of what many readers consider the best of Henry James' fiction, attractively bound, uniform with the author's "Daisy Miller." Illustrated by McVickar. $1.25.

The Vultures. By Henry Seton Merriman, author of "The Sowers."

The announcement of a new novel by Henry Seton Merriman will be welcome to every reader of fiction. This is an exciting novel of love, adventure, and international intrigue in Russia, etc. The attachés of the diplomatic foreign offices play an important part. It is a story of absorbing interest from start to finish. Illustrated. $1.50.

The Red House. By E. Nesbit.

This is a delightful story of the honeymoon and the funny experiences of a young married couple who from " love in a cottage" come into an extensive country estate. Their difficulties and adventures in settling their new home, the love affair after marriage of the two young people are told with rare charm and humor. So far it is the author's most attractive work of fiction. Illustrated by Keller. $1.50.

Istar of Babylon. By Margaret Horton Potter, author of "The House of de Mailly," etc.

This is a most interesting novel of the time just before the fall of Babylon, up to and including the great feast of Belshazzar. Istar is the Babylonian Aphrodite. Around her as the central figure the author has written a story of wonderful power. It is original. It will be widely read and talked of. Illustrated. $1.50.

The Conquest of Rome. By Matilde Serao, author of "The Land of Cockayne."

The author is without doubt the greatest modern Italian novelist. The main theme of this new novel is the conquest made by Rome over a brilliant young statesman who goes there from the provinces. It is a novel of intense and absorbing interest. $1.50.

Sister Joan of the Cross. By Matilde Serao.

This is another powerful novel by Serao, whom Edmund Gosse, the famous English critic, describes as "the most prominent imaginative writer of the latest generation in Italy." Serao was born in Patras, Greece, of an Italian father and a Greek mother of noble blood. Her early years were spent in journalistic work; and in order to study life in places not frequented by women, she occasionally wore man's attire. This zeal resulted in a wonderful knowedge of life, which is evident in her work. $1.50.

Out of the West. By Elizabeth Higgins.

This is the story of the career of a young man who goes from the East to the West—his rise to power, temptation, struggle, success. Every phase of the life of the young American, as the author describes it, is true. It is, besides, a story of life—the home life, society, the actual every-day experiences of the people of a typical little Western town. A remarkably strong and interesting work of fiction. $1.50.

The Wooing of Wistaria. By Onoto Watanna, author of "A Japanese Nightingale," etc,

This is a new novel by the well-known Japanese author, Onoto Watanna. The scene is in Japan, and the characters are Japanese. It is a love story, with all the poetic charm and feeling that made "A Japanese Nightingale" one of the most delightful and popular novels of recent fiction. Frontispiece portrait of author in tint. $1.50.

History

The Reign of Queen Anne. By Justin McCarthy. (Uniform with McCarthy's "Reminiscences.")

This history of the life and times of Queen Anne is a very fitting introductory volume to the series of Mr. McCarthy's popular histories of England, her men, manners, and events. The age of Queen Anne is one of the most brilliant periods of English history—the time of Addison, Swift, Steele, Bolingbroke, and the great Marlborough. Anne was the second daughter of James II. She came to the throne in 1702, on the death of William III., and died in 1714. The McCarthy histories begin, in point of time, with this Life of Anne; then follow "A History of the Four Georges and of William IV.," and "A History of Our Own Times," which ends with Queen Victoria's Golden Jubilee. Two volumes. Crown 8vo, uncut edges, gilt top, cloth. In a box. $4.00 net.

A History of the American People. By Woodrow Wilson, Ph.D., Litt.D., LL.D., President of Princeton University,

President Woodrow Wilson has devoted the best years of his life to the preparation of his great work, "A History of the American People," from the earliest times to the accession of President Theodore Roosevelt. The work, which is just completed, is monumental in character and scope, represents the genius of the greatest historical thinker of modern times, and is written in that delightfully flowing style which makes it read like a romance. It is printed from new type especially cast in 1902. In the matter of illustration, every field of human activity has been searched, and hundreds upon hundreds of new portraits, prints, maps, plans, and pictures make the pictorial features alone tell their wonderful story of the finding of the continent and the birth and growth of what is the United States of America. There is a photogravure frontispiece to each volume, and portraits in India tint and black. It is a curious fact that there is not a single complete history of the United States in existence to-day. Dr. Woodrow Wilson's is the first. In five volumes. 8vo, Library Binding, Uncut Edges, Gilt Tops. In a box. Per set, $17.50 net; ¾ Calf or ¾ Levant, in a box, per set, $30 net.

Biography

A Doffed Coronet. By the author of "Martyrdom of an Empress."

This is the story of the actual experiences of the titled author of "The Martyrdom of an Empress" and the "Tribulations of a Princess." It tells of the intrigues and adventures of the secret diplomatic agents at the European courts, where the princess was brought up, and shows from actual observation the ins and outs of life among the titled nobility. Her experiences in America, where she lived for a time incognito, make most interesting reading. Illustrated Ornamented Cloth. $2.25 net.

Poetry

Songs of Two Centuries. By Will Carleton.

A new book of poems by one of the most popular poets of our times. It was written, as its name indicates in the last years of the nineteenth and the first years of the twentieth century. The book is divided into different sections, and shows in the fullest degree the versatility of its author's style. There are "Songs of the Nation," "Songs of the Rivers," "Songs of the Mountains," "Songs of Pleasure and Pain," "Songs of Months and Days," etc., etc., ranging from grave to gay, and from the most dignified English to the quaintest dialect. The work is published in the large, square 8vo edition which has been so popular, so much in demand for holiday and other presents, and is profusely illustrated. Illustrated. Square Ornamented Cloth. $1.50 net.

Poems and Verses. By E. S. Martin, author of "Lucid Intervals," etc.

This is an attractive volume of verse written in the genial, humorous vein that all readers look for and enjoy in Mr. Martin's work. There are about thirty poems in the volume—all of them of rare charm and beauty. Frontispiece, title-page in two colors. $1.25 net.

Belles-Lettres

Literature and Life. By W. D. Howells.

This volume is another of Mr. Howells' delightful books of reminiscence and criticism of literary things, life and people. It is written in the same style and is bound uniformly with the author's "Literary Friends and Acquaintance" and "Heroines of Fiction." Thirty-two full-page illustrations. $2.25 net.

The Christmas Kalends of Provence.

By Thomas A. Janvier, author of "The Passing of Thomas," "In Great Waters," etc.

Nowhere is Christmas celebrated with more genuine jollity, and at the same time true reverence, than in the French province of Provence. Mr. Janvier knows the country in all its phases—the people, their quaint customs, their naïve manners, their ceremonies, hospitality. A chapter in this genuine and charming volume is the story of "A Feast-day on the Rhône," and another tells of the remarkable performances of the finest dramatic company of Europe, the Comédie Française, on the noble stage of the restored Roman theatre at Orange, in southeastern France, where classic dramas were given. The volume is artistic, delightful in tone, and written with Mr. Janvier's accustomed grace of style. Illustrated. Post 8vo, Ornamented Cloth. $1.25 net.

Travel

Picturesque Sicily. By William Agnew Paton.

This is one of the most thoroughly attractive books of travel in print. The new and revised edition is now published in answer to a continuous demand. The island of Sicily is one of the gems of the Eastern Mediterranean, rich in magnificent remains of early Grecian architecture, and is visited and admired by thousands annually. Mr. Paton's book fulfils more than any other the requirements of a volume on Sicily. The author has so successfully described the island, its floral, architectural, and racial features, that it has also been translated into Italian and published in Italy. New Revised Edition. Beautifully Illustrated from Photographs. Crown 8vo, Ornamented Cloth, $2.50.

Special Books for Women

Harper's Cook-Book Encyclopædia.

This is *the* cook-book of the 20th century. There is no other cook-book which is made like a dictionary, so that you can turn instantly to what you want without going through a maze of indexes and tables of contents. It contains a comprehensive number of approved recipes by which the most famous cooking authorities of the world are represented. The book is indispensable to every household, experienced or otherwise. Some of the contributors are: Brillat-Savarin, Marion Harland, Juliet Corson, Christine Terhune Herrick, Mary Stuart Smith, Mrs. Henderson, Mrs. Blay, Mrs. Margaret Hamilton Welch, Ysaguirre, La Marca Francatelli, Margaret Sangster, Eliza R. Parker, and numerous others. Bound in Washable Leather Cloth. Contributions by every Cooking Expert. Edited by the Editor of *Harper's Bazar.* Illustrated. $1.50 net.

How to Keep Household Accounts. By

Charles Waldo Haskins, C.P.A., L.H.M., Dean and Professor of Auditing and of the History of Accountancy in the School of Commerce, Accounts and Finance of New York University.

This little book will do more for womankind than any other book published in years. It will save housekeepers time, money, and worry, by showing them the practical, easy way of keeping simple accounts. It requires no previous knowledge of bookkeeping or anything of the kind. Its style is conversational, and the classification of receipts and expenses is simple and clear. The method may be put in practice immediately, beginning at any period of the year, by any one. Dean Haskins is well known as the head of the firm of Haskins & Sells, certified public accountants, of New York, London, Chicago, St. Louis, and Cleveland. He is the founder and head of the only university college of accounts in the world; was the first president of the board of examiners appointed by the Regents under the accountants act of the New York Legislature; is president of the New York State Society of Certified Public Accountants, and is active as a lecturer and writer on the science of accounts. No father, husband, or brother could give a present that would cause more satisfaction to the whole household than this valuable little book. 16mo, cloth, $1.00 net.

Gift Books

Through the Looking-Glass. By Lewis Carroll.

The Peter Newell edition of "Alice's Adventures in Wonderland" was one of the most successful books published last year. It therefore seemed advisable to bring out "Through the Looking-Glass" in a similar handsome edition. The great favor with which Mr. Newell's clever pictures have been received has thoroughly justified the selection of him as the one artist best fitted to make the illustrations for these unique and immortal stories of a little girl's adventures in a land of wonders. This edition is not intended for young people more than for their elders. It is a standard book for every reader, and no library can be deemed complete without it. Forty Full-page Illustrations by Peter Newell. (Uniform with "Alice's Adventures in Wonderland.") Frontispiece Portrait of Peter Newell. Decorative Borders in Color by Robert Murray Wright. 8vo, Ornamented Vellum, Deckel Edges and Gilt Top. In a box. $3.00 net.

The Deserted Village. By Oliver Goldsmith.

This is the finest edition extant of Goldsmith's immortal poem. Mr. Abbey, famous throughout the world as an artist of consummate skill, has been at work for many years on the illustrations, which appeared first in *Harper's Magazine.* The edition has introductions by Goldsmith and by Austin Dobson, and there are copious annotations by Cunningham. Exquisitely Illustrated by Edwin A. Abbey, R.A. Frontispiece Portrait of E. A. Abbey. Royal 8vo, Red Silk Cloth, Full Gilt, $3.00.

An Old Country House. By Richard Le Gallienne.

The story of the plans and ambitions of two young people who are happily married and who finally acquire and fit up a little country house according to their own ideas. It is not only a most delightfully written story of country life, but one of the most charming love stories of recent fiction. Illustrated by Elizabeth Shippen Green. Printed in two colors. Leather back, decorated sides and gilt top (in a box). $2.40 net.

The First Christmas. By Gen. Lew Wallace, author of "Ben Hur."

The great popularity of this beautiful story has necessitated the publication of this handsome new edition. It is designed especially for a Christmas gift. It is printed in two colors, illustrated from reproductions of paintings by Raphael, Murillo, etc. and with artistic marginal drawings by William Martin Johnson. Gilt top, uncut edges. $1.25.

Juveniles

Outdoorland. By Robert W. Chambers, author of "Cardigan," "The Conspirators," "Lorraine," etc.

This is Mr. Chambers' first book for children. It contains stories of outdoor nature life; stories told to two charming little children by the butterfly, the robin, the trout, and others of their outdoor friends. It is all simply and interestingly told, and the volume is beautifully illustrated with paintings in color by Reginald Birch, the illustrator of "Little Lord Fauntleroy," etc. Cover, type, and paintings in tint and color. $1.50 net.

The Flight of Pony Baker. By W. D. Howells.

This is a most delightful story of the adventures, experiences and feelings of a "real" boy. It is a book for grown people as well as for boys, for it portrays in a vein of rare insight and humor the actual life of boy-town as all know it. It is an inimitable story told in a way to interest every one who is interested in boys. Illustrated. $1.25 net.

The Lovable Tales of Janey and Josey and Joe. By Gertrude Smith, author of "The Roggie and Reggie Stories."

These are the nicest little stories imaginable about Janey, a sweet, unselfish child, her sister Josey, and her brother Joe. The subjects are those familiar to all households—tea-parties, making cookies, playing circus on the lawn, flowers, visits—but they are dealt with in a charming manner peculiar to Miss Smith's original method. There are fifteen chapters, each one beautifully illustrated. Illustrated with 16 Full-page Colored Pictures by E. Mars and M. H. Squire, with striking Pictorial Cover in six colors and gold. Square 8vo, Cloth, $1.30 net.

HARPER & BROTHERS

Franklin Square, New York City

PUBLICATIONS FOR THE AUTUMN OF 1902
G. P. PUTNAM'S SONS

NEW YORK, 27 AND 29 WEST 23d STREET
LONDON, 24 BEDFORD STREET, STRAND

Sonnets from the Portuguese

By Elizabeth Barrett Browning. Decorated and illustrated in color by Margaret Armstrong. 12mo. With 50 designs in color. $2.00; Half vellum, $2.50; Red leather, $3.00; Full vellum, $3.50; Satin, $4.00.

Idylls of the King

Enid, Vivien, Elaine, Guinevere. By Alfred Tennyson. With 31 photogravure plates after designs by Gustav Doré. Two volumes, 8vo, uniform with Irving's "Rip Van Winkle" and "Sleepy Hollow." Each, $1.75.

This is a reprint of the famous Moxon edition.

William Morris; Poet, Craftsman, Socialist

By Elisabeth Luther Cary, author of "The Rossettis," "Robert Browning," "Tennyson," etc. 8vo. Fully illustrated, uniform with "The Rossettis," "Browning," etc. Net, $3.50. By mail, $3.75.

MISS CARY'S EARLIER WORKS: Library Edition.

Browning, Poet and Man.

A Survey. 8vo. With photogravure frontispiece and 16 illustrations in half-tone, $2.50. Photogravure edition, net, $3.50.

Tennyson

His Homes, his Friends, and his Work. 8vo. With photogravure frontispiece and 16 illustrations in half-tone, $2.50.. Photogravure edition, net, $3.50.

The Rossettis

Dante Gabriel and Christina. 8vo. With photogravure frontispiece and 16 illustrations in half-tone, $2.50. Photogravure edition, net, $3.50.

FAMOUS HOMES SERIES: Library Edition.

Two volumes. Elaborately illustrated. Royal octavo, in a box, net, $7.50.

Famous Homes of Great Britain and Their Stories

Edited by A. H. Malan. Among the writers are the Duke of Marlborough, the Duchess of Cleveland, Lady De L'Isle Dudley, Lady Newton, Lady Warwick, Lord Emlyn, and A. H. Malan. With nearly 200 illustrations.

More Famous Homes of Great Britain

Edited by A. H. Malan. Among the writers are: Lord Sackville, Lady Glamis, Lady Ernestine Edgcumbe, Countess of Pembroke, Lord Savile and A. H. Malan. With about 200 illustrations.

(2) AUTUMN PUBLICATIONS, 1902

Famous Families of New York

Historical and Biographical Sketches of Families which in Successive Generations have been Identified with the Development of the Nation. By MARGHERITA ARLINA HAMM. Two volumes. Half vellum. Royal octavo. Fully illustrated.

The Hudson River From Ocean to Source

Historical—Legendary—Picturesque. By EDGAR MAYHEW BACON, author of "Chronicles of Tarrytown," etc. 8vo. With over 100 illustrations.

The Romance of the Colorado River

A Complete Account of the First Discovery of the Explorations from 1540 to the Present Time, with Particular Reference to the two Voyages of Powell through the Line of the Great Canyons. By FREDERICK S. DELLENBAUGH, Member of the U. S. Colorado River Expedition of 1871 and 1872, author of "North Americans of Yesterday," etc. 8vo. Fully illustrated.

The American Immortals

The Record of Men who by their Achievements in Statecraft, War, Science, Literature, Art, Law, and Commerce have created the American Republic, and whose names are inscribed in the Hall of Fame. By GEORGE CARY EGGLESTON. The volume is in all its mechanical aspects a model of sumptuous elegance and excellence in bookmaking. Royal 8vo. Illustrated, net, $10 00. By express paid, $10.50.

Illustrations to the Book of Job

By WILLIAM BLAKE. Reproduced in photogravure from the original etchings and in the same size as the originals. Folio boards. Net, $4.00.

Anthology of Russian Literature

From the Earliest Times to the Present Day. By LEO WIENER, Assistant Professor of Slavic Languages, Harvard University, author of "History of Yiddish Literature," "Songs from the Ghetto," etc. In two parts. Each complete in itself and indexed.

Part I. From Earliest Times to the Close of the Eighteenth Century.
Part II. From the Close of the Eighteenth Century to the Present Day. (In press.)

Each, 8vo, net, $3.00. By mail, $3.25.

The Unspeakable Scot

By T. W. H. CROSLAND. 12mo. Net, $1.25. By mail, $1.35.

The Lost Art of Reading

By GERALD STANLEY LEE. 12mo. Net, $.

OUR EUROPEAN NEIGHBOURS

No. 7. Italian Life in Town and Country

By LUIGI VILLARI. 12mo. Fully illustrated. Net, $1.20. By mail, $1.30.

A History of German Literature

By JOHN G. ROBERTSON, Ph.D., Lecturer in the University of Strasburg. A complete summary of the evolution of German literature from the earliest times to the close of the 20th century. 8vo. Net, $3.50.

Some of the Rhymes of Ironquill

(A Book of Moods.) 12mo. Eleventh edition. $1.50.

(4) AUTUMN PUBLICATIONS, 1902

Twenty-six Historic Ships of the United States and Confederate States Navies (1775-1902)

By F. STANHOPE HILL, late U. S. N., author of "Twenty Years at Sea," etc. Fully illustrated. With introduction by Rear-Admiral Belknap.

St. Augustine and His Age

By JOSEPH MCCABE, author of "Peter Abélard," etc. With Portrait. 8vo. Uniform with "Peter Abélard." Net, $2.00. By mail, $2.20.

The Sons of St. Francis

By A. MACDONELL. With eight full-page illustrations, octavo cloth, net, $3.50.

Tolstoi as Man and Artist

With an Essay on Dostoievski. By DMITRI MEREJKOWSKI. Authorized translation.

Studies of a Biographer

By LESLIE STEPHEN, author of "Hours in a Library," etc. New Series. Two volumes in a box, each, net, $2.00.

HEROES OF THE NATIONS

No. 36. Augustus Caesar

And the Organization of the Empire of Rome. By J. B. FIRTH, M.A. 12mo. Fully illustrated. Net, $1.35. Half leather, gilt top, net, $1.60. Postage, 15 cents.

The Administration of Dependencies

A Study of the Evolution of the Federal Empire, with Special Reference to American Colonial Problems. By ALPHEUS H. SNOW. 8vo. Net, $3.50. By mail, $3.75.

Government and the State

A Consideration of Elementary Principles and Their Practical Application. By FREDERIC WOOD. 12vo. Net, $2.25. By mail, $2.40.

In City Tents

How to Find, Furnish, and Keep a Small Home on Slender Means. By CHRISTINE TERHUNE HERRICK, author of "First Aid to the Young Housekeeper," "The Chafing-Dish Supper," etc. 16mo. Net, $. By mail, $.

The Use of the Voice in Reading and in Speaking

By ERNEST PERTWEE.

Industrial Conciliation

Report of the Proceedings of the Conference held under the Auspices of the National Civic Federation, at the rooms of the Board of Trade and Transportation in New York, December 16-17, 1901. Questions of the Day Series, No. 99. 8vo.

Spiritism or Telepathy?

Results of Psychical Research. By MINOT J. SAVAGE, author of "Life Beyond Death," etc. 12mo.

DANA ESTES & CO. of Boston.

AUTUMN ANNOUNCEMENT of New Books and New Editions for A.D. MCMII. * * * * * *

Mrs. Tree.

By LAURA E. RICHARDS. Illustrated by Frank T. Merrill. Tall 16mo, uniform with "Geoffrey Strong, unique binding, gilt top $0 75

JUVENILES.

Chatterbox for 1902.

The only genuine *Chatterbox*, containing a great variety of original stories, sketches, and poems for the young. All the illustrations were expressly designed for it by the most eminent English artists. More than 200 full-page illustrations, including six handsomely colored plates. Small 4to, illuminated board covers .... *net*, 0 90

Same. Cloth, full gilt edges .... *net*, 1 40

Traveller Tales of the Pan-American Countries.

By HEZEKIAH BUTTERWORTH, author of the "Zigzag" Series. Folk-lore, legends and historical tales of South America, Central America, Panama, etc. Illustrated by over 40 full-page reproductions of new photographs and sketches. Uniform with "Traveller Tales of China." Cloth, octavo .... *net*, 1 20

Hans Andersen's Fairy Tales.

A new edition embodying many original features. With more than 100 illustrations, from drawings made especially for this edition by J. J. Mora, illustrator of "The Animals of Æsop," etc. Cloth, quarto 1 50

Voyage of the *Charlemagne.*

By WILLIAM O. STODDARD, author of "Ned, Son of Webb," etc. A story for boys, relating to electrical discovery and invention. The "Charlemagne" is a wonderful electrical ship, and among the chief passengers are a very live boy, his sister, and a brilliant inventor. Cloth, 12mo, illustrated .... *net*, 1 00

Jimmy Crow.

By EDITH FRANCIS FOSTER. A companion volume to "Where Was the Little White Dog." The story is told by means of rebus illustrations. Cloth, oblong quarto .... *net*, 0 60

Play Away!

By WILLIS BOYD ALLEN, author of "The Pineboro Quartette," etc. A story of the Boston Fire Department. Illustrated by six full-page half-tones. Cloth, 12mo .... *net*, 0 75

Under Scott in Mexico.

By Captain RALPH BONEHILL. The third and concluding volume in the "Mexican War Series." Uniform with "For the Liberty of Texas," and "With Taylor on the Rio Grande." Cloth, 12mo, illustrated.. *net*, 1 00

Lucky Ned.

By EDWARD S. ELLIS, author of "Our Jim," etc. One of the best books for boys written by this ever-popular author. Cloth, 12mo, illustrated .... *net*, 1 00

DANA ESTES & CO.'S NEW BOOKS AND NEW EDITIONS.—Continued.

The Hurdy-Gurdy.

By LAURA E. RICHARDS. A book of original and diverting nonsense rhymes. Every poem has an illustration by J. J. Mora. Square quarto........*net,* 0 75

Doctor Robin.

By HARRIET A. CHEEVER, author of "Madame Angora," etc. A bird story told with great humor and sympathy. Cloth, 12mo, illustrated........*net,* 0 40

Maid Sally.

By HARRIET A. CHEEVER. A charming story for girls, the scene of which is laid in old colonial days just before the American Revolution. Cloth, 12mo, illustrated........*net,* 1 00

THE "YOUNG OF HEART" SERIES.

Five New Titles. Each volume thin 12mo, illustrated, special cover design, 50 cents.

A Christmas Carol.

By CHARLES DICKENS. Illustrated by Bertha G. Davidson.

Lives of Two Cats.

By PIERRE LOTI. Translated by M. B. Richards. Illustrated by C. E. Allen.

The Rosy Cloud.

By GEORGE SAND. A new translation. Illustrated by Diantha W. Horne.

Jackanapes.

By JULIANA HORATIA EWING. Illustrated by Josephine Bruce.

Wonder-Box Tales.

By JEAN INGELOW. Illustrated by Diantha W. Horne.

THE FAMOUS CHILDREN OF LITERATURE SERIES.

Edited by FREDERIC LAWRENCE KNOWLES. Each, cloth, 12mo, *net,* 75 cents.

1. Little Eva.

Adapted from "Uncle Tom's Cabin" by Mrs. STOWE. Fully illustrated from new designs by Miss Etheldred B. Barry.

2. Little Nell.

Adapted from "Old Curiosity Shop," by CHARLES DICKENS. Fully illustrated from new designs by Etheldred B. Barry.

GIFT BOOKS.

Among the Great Masters of Warfare.

Edited by WALTER ROWLANDS, compiler of "Among the Great Masters of Oratory," etc. Scenes from the lives of Great Military Commanders. Illustrated by 32 full-page half-tones. Printed on all-rag laid deckle edge paper. Cloth, Small 12mo, gilt top, boxed........*net,* 1 20
Same. Half-calf or morocco, gilt top........*net,* 2 40

A Treasury of Humorous Poetry.

Edited by FREDERIC LAWRENCE KNOWLES, compiler of "A Year-Book of Famous Lyrics," etc. The selections are drawn from British and American sources, and comprise examples of current as well as classic humor. There are full notes and indexes. More than 250 poems are included. Cloth, 12mo, fully illustrated, gilt top........*net,* 1 20
Same. Half-calf or morocco........*net,* 2 40

DANA ESTES & CO.'S NEW BOOKS AND NEW EDITIONS.—Continued.

Pippa Passes.

By ROBERT BROWNING. Illustrated Holiday Edition. No more beautiful edition of Browning's popular play has ever been placed on the market. The text followed is that of the London edition of 1876. There are full notes, a critical introduction, and a bibliography. The six full-page photogravures from original designs by Louis Meynell, catch the spirit of the original with unusual fidelity. Cloth, 12mo, gilt top........ 1 50

MISCELLANEOUS.

The Correct Thing.

By FLORENCE HOWE HALL, author of "Social Customs." An entirely new and revised edition, brought carefully down to date. Much new material has been added. Practical, trustworthy, and authoritative. Entirely reset from new type. Cloth, tall 16mo, beautiful binding, gilt top........*net*, 0 75

A Little Book of Ping-Pong Verse.

A gay little compilation devoted to the most popular of indoor games. Nearly 100 selections from current periodicals, and in addition, the complete and authorized rules for playing table-tennis. An ideal prize for the winners of parlor tournaments. Cloth, unique cover design, 16mo........*net*, 0 75

STANDARD SETS.—New Sterling Editions.

Macaulay's History of England.

By THOMAS BABINGTON MACAULAY. Five volumes, cloth, 12mo, gilt top, 25 illustrations in photogravure and half-tone........ 5 00

Same. Half-calf, gilt backs and tops........ 10 00

Macaulay's Complete Essays.

By THOMAS BABINGTON MACAULAY. Critical, historical and miscellaneous essays and poems, three volumes, 12mo, cloth, gilt tops, 51 illustrations in photogravure and half-tone........ 3 00

Same. Half-calf, gilt backs and tops........ 6 00

Plutarch's Lives.

Illustrated by 19 photogravures and half-tones. Three volumes, 12mo, gilt tops........ 3 00

Same. Half-calf, gilt backs and tops........ 6 00

NEW CABINET EDITIONS.

Scott's Poems.

The complete poetical works of Sir Walter Scott, uniform with the Cabinet Edition of "Scott's Waverley Novels." With introductions, glossaries, and notes for each volume by Andrew Lang. Illustrated with more than 30 photogravures, besides numerous etchings by W. H. W. Bicknell. Six volumes, sold in complete sets or as separate works, as follows: Vol. I. Lay of the Last Minstrel; Ballads. Vol. II. Marmion. Vol. III. Lady of the Lake; Miscellaneous. Vol. IV. Rokeby; Vision of Don Roderick. Vol. V. Lord of the Isles; Occasional Pieces. Vol. VI. Bridal of Triermain; Minor Poems.

Complete sets, 6 vols., cloth, gilt........ 9 00

Single volumes........ 1 50

Same. Half-calf or morocco........ 18 00

Tennyson's Poems.

The complete poetical works of Alfred, Lord Tennyson, edited and annotated by Prof. WILLIAM J. ROLFE. In twelve volumes, with about five illustrations to each, including photogravures and etchings from paintings by Edward Lear, one of the poet's lifelong friends, and also from landscapes and figure paintings by Doré, Edwin A. Abbey, Frederick Dielman, and others. The text of the edition has been collated and edited by Dr. Rolfe with scrupulous accuracy, and the variorum readings and other critical memoranda are invaluable to the reader. In the prosecution of his work the editor obtained the cordial approval and co-operation of Lord Tennyson and his family. This edition is in the most literal sense definitive. Sold only in sets. Complete sets, 12 vols., cloth, gilt tops........ 18 00

Same. Half-calf or morocco........ 36 00

A Notable Novel

MRS. TREE

BY

LAURA E. RICHARDS

Author of "Captain January," "Melody," Etc.

A Companion Story to "Geoffrey Strong."

The Romance of a Maine Seacoast Village

Quotations From the Press

"Quite equal in interest to 'Captain January.'"—*Norwich Bulletin.*

"The jolliest, merriest, drollest book Mrs. Richards ever wrote."—*Detroit Free Press.*

"Mrs. Tree is easily one of the most delightful old ladies in fiction."—*Louisville Courier-Journal.*

"Mrs. Richards' latest venture into fiction must be accepted as a masterpiece of its kind."—*Milwaukee Sentinel.*

Nearly 600,000 of Mrs. Richards' previous books have been sold

Tall 16mo, bound in original style, gilt top, illustrated by FRANK T. MERRILL - - - - - - - - - Seventy-five Cents

DANA ESTES & COMPANY

Publishers **Boston**

SELECTIONS FROM

T. Y. CROWELL & COMPANY'S

New Books and New Editions

FICTION.

Each book $1.50.

Lepidus the Centurion. By EDWIN LESTER ARNOLD.

A Daughter of the Sea. By AMY LE FEUVRE.

The Silent Pioneer. By LUCY CLEAVER MCELROY.

Mary Garvin. By FRED LEWIS PATTEE.

Frederique. By MARCEL PREVOST. Tr. by ELLEN MARRIAGE.

Angelot. By ELEANOR C. PRICE.

MISCELLANEOUS.

Guide Book to Hygienic Diet. (A Vegetarian Cook Book.) By SIDNEY H. BEARD. $1.00 net. Postage, 10 cents.

Famous Artists. By SARAH K. BOLTON. Holiday Edition, with 40 illustrations. $2.50.

Famous Composers. By NATHAN HASKELL DOLE. Holiday Edition, with 40 illustrations. 2 vols. Per set, $3.00.

Famous American Actors of To-day. Edited by CHARLES E. L. WINGATE and F. E. MCKAY. Holiday Edition, with 40 illustrations. 2 vols. Per set, $2.75.

The Marble Faun. By NATHANIEL HAWTHORNE. Luxembourg Illustrated Edition, $1.50.

Thoreau. By ANNIE RUSSELL MARBLE. $2.00 net. Postage, 20 cents.

Mind Power and Privileges. By ALBERT B. OLSTON. $1.50 net. Postage, 15 cents.

The Story of Pemaquid. By JAMES OTIS. 50 cents.

Rustic Life in France. By ANDRE THEURIET. Tr. by HELEN B. DOLE. 2 vols. Per set, $2.50.

The Hand of God in American History. By ROBERT ELLIS THOMPSON, S. T. D. $1.00 net. Postage, 10 cents.

Self-Educator in English Composition. By G. H. THORNTON, M. A. 75 cents.

Robert Browning. By STOPFORD A. BROOKE. $1.50 net. Postage, 15 cents.

HANDY INFORMATION SERIES.

Shaksperian Synopses. By J. WALKER MCSPADDEN. 45 cents net. Postage, 5 cents.

Word Coinage. By LEON MEAD. 45 cents net. Postage, 5 cents.

ETHICAL AND RELIGIOUS.

Messages of the Masters. By AMORY H. BRADFORD, D. D. $2.00 net. Postage, 20 cents.

Parables from Nature. By MRS. ALFRED GATTY. 50 cents.

Verba Crucis. By the REV. T. CALVIN MCCLELLAND. 50 cents net. Postage, 6 cents.

The Upper Currents. By the REV. J. R. MILLER, D.D. 65 cents net; cloth, 85 cents net. Postage, 8 cents.

Today and Tomorrow. By the REV. J. R. MILLER, D.D. 50 cents net. Postage, 6 cents.

The Elegy of Faith. A study of "In Memoriam." By WILLIAM RADER. 50 cents net. Postage, 6 cents.

Rabbi Ben Ezra. A study of Browning's poem. By WILLIAM ADAMS SLADE. 50 cents net. Postage, 6 cents.

What Is Religion? By LYOF N. TOLSTOI. 60 cents net. Postage, 8 cents.

ECONOMICS.

Economics of Forestry. By BERNHARD E. FERNOW. $1.50 net. Postage, 15 cents.

Irrigation in the United States. By FREDERICK H. NEWELL. $2.00 net. Postage, 20 cents.

The Coming City. By RICHARD T. ELY. 60 cents net. Postage, 8 cents.

"WHAT IS WORTH WHILE" SERIES.

Each book 28 cents net. By mail 35 cents.

The Cardinal Virtues. By WILLIAM DEWITT HYDE.

Daily Maxims from Amiel's Journal. Edited by ORLINE GATES.

If I Were a College Student. By CHARLES F. THWING.

Immensee. By THEODOR STORM.

In Perfect Peace. By J. R. MILLER, D.D.

Light Ho, Sir! By FRANK T. BULLEN.

Move Upward. By KATE UPSON CLARK.

Ways of Well Doing. By HUMPHREY J. DESMOND.

William McKinley. By JOHN HAY.

T. Y. CROWELL & CO.'S NEW BOOKS—Continued.

HANDY VOLUME SETS.

Hawthorne's Romances. "Lenox" Edition, edited by Prof. Katharine Lee Bates. 14 vols., in box. $10.50 and upwards.

Poe's Complete Works. "Virginia" Edition, edited by Prof. James A. Harrison. 17 vols., in box. $12.50 and upwards.

Tennyson's Poetical Works. "Farringford" Edition, edited by Prof. Eugene Parsons. 10 vols., in box. $7.50 and upwards.

STANDARD SETS.

Carlyle's Complete Works. 10 vols. $10.00 and upwards.

Guizot's History of France. Tr. by Robert Black. 8 vols. $8.00 and upwards.

Hawthorne's Romances. 7 vols. $7.00 and upwards.

Poe's Complete Works. De Luxe Edition. 17 vols. Cloth, $21.00; half calf, $42.00.

CHILDREN'S FAVORITE CLASSICS.

Each book 60 cents

Baron Munchausen. Raspe.
Heidi. Spyri.
History of England. Calcott.
History of France. Calcott.
History of Greece. Walpole.
History of Rome. Butterworth.

THE GOLDEN HOUR SERIES.

Eleven new books for young people. Each book, net, 50 cents. Postage, 8 cents.

The Caxton Club. Amos R. Wells.
The Child and the Tree. Bessie Kenyon Ulrich.
Daisies and Diggleses. Evelyn Raymond.
How the Twins Captured a Hessian. James Otis.
The I Can School. Eva A. Madden.
A Little Dusky Hero. Harriet T. Comstock.
Master Frisky. Clarence W. Hawkes.
Miss De Peyster's Boy. Etheldred B. Barry.
Molly. Barbara Yechton.
Whispering Tongues. Homer Greene.
The Wonder Ship. Sophie Swett.

RELIGIOUS CLASSICS.

Padded White Binding. 18 vols. Each $1.00.

A Good Start. Meyer.
Bright Threads. Johnston.
Bringing up Boys. Clark.
Chat-wood. Du Bois.
Daily Food.
Daily Light and Strength.
Glimpses through Life's Windows. Miller.
Gold Dust.
Heaven Every Day. Seward.
Imitation of Christ. à Kempis.
Parables from Nature. Gatty.
Pilgrim's Progress. Bunyan.
Soul's Inquiries.
Sunshine for Shut Ins.
Thoughts for Mother. Paull.
Through My Spectacles. Perkins.
Toward the Light. Lloyd.
Young People's Problems. Miller.

ASTOR LIBRARY OF PROSE.

Cloth Binding. Each 60 cents.

Age of Chivalry. Bulfinch.
Age of Fable. Bulfinch.
Baron Munchausen. Raspe.
The Black Tulip. Dumas.
English Humorists. Thackeray.
Fanshawe. Hawthorne.
Heidi. Spyri.
Legends of Charlemagne. Bulfinch.
The Marble Faun. Hawthorne.
The Professor at the Breakfast Table. Holmes. (Introduction by Richard Burton.)

ASTOR LIBRARY OF POETRY.

Cloth Binding. Each 60 cents.

Cambridge Book of Poetry. Bates.
In Memoriam. Tennyson. Edited by Parsons.
The Persian Poets. Edited by N. H. Dole.
Walt Whitman. (Introduction by John Burroughs.)

HANDY VOLUME CLASSICS.

Limp Leather Edition. Each volume 75 cents.

Age of Chivalry. Bulfinch.
Age of Fable. Bulfinch.
The Black Tulip. Dumas.
English Humorists. Thackeray.
Fanshawe. Hawthorne.
Grandfather's Chair. Hawthorne.
Legends of Charlemagne. Bulfinch.
Marble Faun. 2 vols. Hawthorne.
Poems by Two Brothers. Tennyson.
Poetical Quotations.
Professor at the Breakfast Table. Holmes.
Prose Quotations.
Tanglewood Tales. Hawthorne.
Wonder Book. Hawthorne.

T. Y. CROWELL & CO.'S NEW BOOKS—Continued.

THE LAUREL SERIES.

Ooze Calf Edition. Each volume 60 cents.

Ancient Mariner. COLERIDGE.
The Choice of Books. CARLYLE.
Deserted Village. GOLDSMITH.
Enthusiasm. GEORGE JACKSON.
The Future Life. CHANNING.
The Gold Bug. POE.
Gray's Elegy.
Heaven in Earthly Homes. FARRAR.
Immortality of the Soul. PLATO.
J. Cole. GELLIBRAND.
Jessica's First Prayer. STRETTON.
John Ploughman's Talk. SPURGEON.
King of the Golden River. RUSKIN.
Kingdom of the Truth. ROBERTSON.
Laddie.
Legend of Sleepy Hollow. IRVING.
Literary Ethics. EMERSON.
Little Cares of Every Day. GEORGE DAWSON.
Love and Friendship. EMERSON.
Miss Toosey's Mission.
Pleasures of Learning. RUSKIN
Power of Purpose. W. J. DAWSON.
Recessional. KIPLING.
Rip Van Winkle. IRVING.
Rubaiyat of Omar Khayyam.
Saul. BROWNING.
Sweetness and Light. ARNOLD.
True Rest and Hope of Man. MAURICE.
Vision of Sir Launfal. LOWELL.
Where Love is there God is. TOLSTOI.

HANDY VOLUME CLASSICS.

Limp Lizard Edition. Each volume $1.50.

Mrs. Browning.
Burns.
Byron (Selections).
Courtship of Miles Standish. LONGFELLOW.
Cranford. MRS. GASKELL.
Dream Life. MITCHELL.
Evangeline. LONGFELLOW.
Favorite Poems.
Hiawatha. LONGFELLOW.
Idylls of the King. TENNYSON.
Imitation of Christ. A KEMPIS.
Keats.
Lady of the Lake. SCOTT.
Lalla Rookh. MOORE.
Lucile. MEREDITH.
Princess. TENNYSON.
Prose Quotations. WARD.
Poetical Quotations. WARD.
Reveries of a Bachelor. MITCHELL.
Rubaiyat of Omar Khayyam.
Shelley.
Tales from Shakespeare. LAMB.
Whittier.
Voices of the Night. LONGFELLOW.
Wordsworth.

THE MARLBOROUGH SERIES.

Dainty Two-Volume Sets. Per set, $2.00.

The Autocrat, and The Professor at the Breakfast Table. HOLMES.
Beauties of Shakespeare. 2 vols.
Cranford, by GASKELL, and **Vicar of Wakefield,** by GOLDSMITH.
Courtship of Miles Standish, and Hiawatha. LONGFELLOW.
Dream Life, and Reveries of a Bachelor. MITCHELL
Ekkehard. SCHEFFEL. 2 vols.
Longfellow and Whittier.
Marble Faun. HAWTHORNE. 2 vols.
Tartarin, and Tartarin on the Alps. DAUDET.
Walden, and Week on the Concord. THOREAU.

THE NORMANDIE SERIES.

Inlaid Binding; each book $1.00. Limp Walrus; each book $2.00.

Abbe Constantin. HALÉVY.
Autocrat of the Breakfast Table. HOLMES.
Barrack Room Ballads. KIPLING.
Courtship of Miles Standish. LONGFELLOW.
Cranford. GASKELL.
Dream Life. MITCHELL.
Evangeline. LONGFELLOW.
Favorite Poems.
Hiawatha. LONGFELLOW.
House of Seven Gables. HAWTHORNE.
Idylls of the King. TENNYSON.
Lady of the Lake. SCOTT.
Lucile. MEREDITH.
Prue and I. CURTIS.
Reveries of a Bachelor. MITCHELL.
Rubaiyat of Omar Khayyam.
Stevenson's Poems.
Tales from Shakespeare. LAMB.
Vicar of Wakefield. GOLDSMITH.
Walden. THOREAU.

THE POPULAR LIBRARY.

Three Notable Histories. Each $1.25.

Conquest of Mexico. PRESCOTT.
Conquest of Peru. PRESCOTT.
Rise of the Dutch Republic. MOTLEY.

COMPLETE ILLUSTRATED CATALOGUE SENT ON REQUEST.

THOMAS Y. CROWELL & COMPANY, - 426-8 West Broadway, New York.

OXFORD UNIVERSITY PRESS

FALL ANNOUNCEMENTS

JUST PUBLISHED!

THE ONLY ILLUSTRATED EDITION ON INDIA PAPER

OXFORD INDIA PAPER EDITION

OF

Charles Dickens' Works

Complete Edition in Seventeen Volumes, Containing Over 600 Illustrations. Beautifully Printed on Oxford India Paper. Published by Arrangement with Messrs. CHAPMAN & HALL, Owners of the Copyright. . . . .

FROM $1.25 UPWARD

In addition to some Portraits of CHARLES DICKENS, upwards of SIX HUNDRED ILLUSTRATIONS will be given, being reproductions from the originals by Seymour, "Phiz," George Cruikshank, F. Walker, Sir Edwin Landseer, R.A., D. Maclise, R.A., John Leech, Marcus Stone, and by Harry Furniss and others.

Life and Letters of Thomas Cromwell

By ROGER BIGELOW MERRIMAN. With a Portrait and Facsimile. 2 vols. 8vo, $6.00.

A History of the Peninsular War

By CHARLES OMAN, M.A. Vol. I., 1807-1809, from the Treaty of Fontainebleau to the Battle of Corunna. With Maps, Plans and Portraits. 8vo, $4.75.

Companion to English History (Middle Ages)

Edited by FRANCES PIERREPONT BARNARD, M.A., F.S.A. Cr. 8vo, cloth, with 97 full-page plates, $2.90.

Although this volume is designed primarily for higher educational purposes, it is believed that it will also prove of interest to the reading public at large.

A Supplement to Burnet's History of My Own Time

Derived from his Original Memoirs, his Autobiography, his Letters to Admiral Herbert, and his Private Meditations. All hitherto unpublished. Edited by Miss H. C. FOXCROFT. Demy 8vo, cloth, $5.35.

Studies in History and Jurisprudence

By JAMES BRYCE, D.C.L. 8vo, cloth, $3.50 *net*; half morocco, $6.00 *net*; postage 27 cts.

"Taken as a whole, these essays constitute an incomparable treatise on the legal aspects of history."—*N. Y. Nation*, February 20, 1902.

For Sale by all Booksellers. Send for Catalogue.

OXFORD UNIVERSITY PRESS

AMERICAN BRANCH

91 and 93 Fifth Avenue, - - - - New York

OXFORD UNIVERSITY PRESS

American Branch

FALL ANNOUNCEMENTS

Oxford Teachers' Bibles

NEW STYLES

NEW BINDINGS

REFERENCES

CONCORDANCE

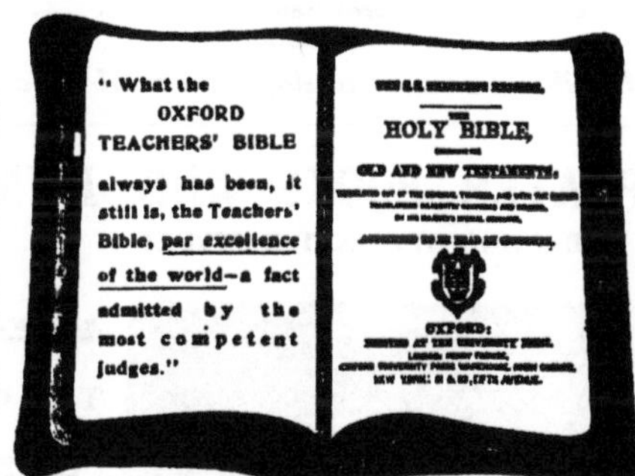

LIGHT, THIN, COMPACT, BEAUTIFULLY PRINTED ON OXFORD INDIA PAPER . .

JUST ISSUED

OXFORD MINION 8vo SELF-PRONOUNCING BIBLES.

THE THINNEST REFERENCE BIBLES IN THE WORLD

REFERENCE—CONCORDANCE—TEACHERS. **Beautifully printed on Fine White and the Famous Oxford India Papers**

An Entirely New Series on an Improved Plan. The Model Line of Self-Pronouncing Editions.

PRACTICAL SCHOLARLY SIMPLE

NOTE ON THE MARKINGS—It is claimed for this book that it goes further in this direction than any previous book, and that it also indicates the pronunciation of certain other words, such as "leviathan," "homer," "cherub," etc., which cannot be called proper names, but which might present difficulties to an unskilled reader.

RECENTLY PUBLISHED

THE OXFORD LONG PRIMER

SELF-PRONOUNCING BIBLES

Large Clear Type. Beautifully Printed on Fine White and the Famous Oxford India Papers

THE OXFORD TWO-VERSION BIBLES

WITH REFERENCES

Being the Authorized Version with the differences of the Revised Version printed in the margins, so that both texts can be read from the same page. Size, 8¼ x 5¾ x ⅞. Printed on fine white and the famous Oxford India Papers.

NEW STYLES

OXFORD INTERLEAVED BIBLES

Interleaved with a blank ruled leaf between every *two* leaves, and also with a blank ruled leaf between *every* leaf. The handiest and most useful Bibles for Ministers and Teachers ever published.

Also—New Styles in OXFORD GIFT, REFERENCE, CONCORDANCE, TEACHERS' BIBLES, TESTAMENTS, Etc., Etc.

Oxford University Press, American Branch, Fall Publications—Continued

JUST ISSUED

OXFORD SUNDAY SCHOOL BIBLE—Illustrated

Clearly Printed on Oxford White Paper. Contains Sixteen Illustrations on Calendered Paper. Also Fifty-two Pages of Helps to Bible Study. Chronologies, Harmony of the Gospels, Miracles, Parables, Prophecies, etc., etc., and Six Beautifully Colored Maps. . . . .

An Ideal Bible for a Sunday School Scholar

OXFORD PRAYER BOOKS AND HYMNALS

NEW AND ATTRACTIVE STYLES

TEN EDITIONS ON FINE WHITE AND OXFORD INDIA PAPERS

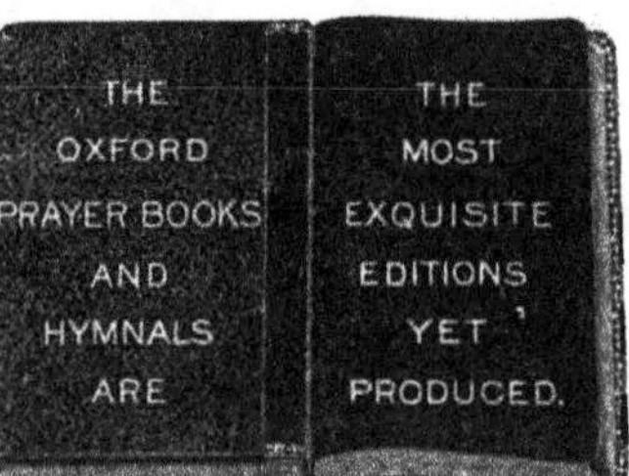

RECENTLY ISSUED

THE OXFORD ELONGATED RED RUBRIC EDITIONS

RECENTLY PUBLISHED!

THE NEW CENTURY BIBLE (Annotated)

Each book of the Bible in a handy and beautiful volume edited with introduction and notes in both authorised and revised versions.

General Editor, WALTER F. ADENEY, M.A.

Each volume of the NEW CENTURY BIBLE is complete in itself with Maps, and can be purchased separately. Price, in limp cloth, 75 cents.

NEW EDITION NOW READY!

MARKED NEW TESTAMENT

From 15 Cents Upwards

For Sale by all Booksellers. Send for Catalogue.

OXFORD UNIVERSITY PRESS

AMERICAN BRANCH

91 and 93 Fifth Avenue, - - - New York City

D. VAN NOSTRAND COMPANY'S

ANNOUNCEMENT OF

Recent and Forthcoming Publications

RECENT PUBLICATIONS

FOSTER, H. A. Electrical Engineer's Pocket Book. With the collaboration of Eminent Specialists. A handbook of useful data for Electricians and Electrical Engineers. With innumerable tables, diagrams, and figures. Pocket size, full leather, 1,000 pages. Second edition, revised....$5.00

WALKER, FREDERICK, C. E. Aerial Navigation; a Practical Handbook on the Construction of Dirigible Balloons, Aërostats, Aëroplanes, and Aëromotors. With diagrams and engravings. 8vo, cloth. Illustrated, 151 pp....net, $3.00

EISSLER, M., M.E. The Hydro-metallurgy of Copper; being an account of processes adopted in the Hydro-metallurgical treatment of Cupriferous Ores, including the manufacture of Copper Vitriol. With a chapter on the sources of supply of copper, and the roasting of copper ores. 8vo, cloth. Illustrated. 228 pp....net, $4.50

KNIGHT, AUSTIN M., Lieutenant-Commander U. S. N. Modern Seamanship. Illustrated with 136 full page plates and diagrams. 8vo, cloth, illustrated. Third edition, revised.......net, $6.00
Half morocco....$7.50

OUIDIN, M. A. Standard Polyphase Apparatus and Systems. With many photo-reproductions and diagrams. Third edition revised. Illustrated. 8vo, cloth....$3.00

SHELDON, SAMUEL, Ph.D., and HOBART MASON, Alternating Current Machines. Being the second volume of the authors' "Dynamo Electric Machinery." Second edition, revised 8vo, cloth. Illustrated....net, $2.50

PRESCOTT, A. B. First Book in Qualitative Chemistry. Thoroughly revised edition. 12mo, cloth....net, $1.50

PLATTNER'S Manual of Qualitative and Quantitative Analysis with the Blow-Pipe. Translated by H. B. Cornwall, Ph.D., assisted by John H. Caswell, A. M. Eighth edition, revised after the sixth German edition, by Prof. Friederich Kolbeck. With numerous engravings and figures. Illustrated. 8vo, cloth....net, $4.00

CHRISTIE, WM. WALLACE. Chimney Design and Theory. A book for Engineers and Architects With numerous half-tone illustrations and plates of famous chimneys. Second edition, revised. Illustrated. 8vo, cloth....$3.00

FANNING, J. T. A Practical Treatise on Hydraulic and Water-Supply Engineering. Relating to the Hydrology, Hydrodynamics, and practical construction of water-works in North America. With numerous tables and illustrations. Fifteenth edition, revised, enlarged, and new tables and illustrations added. Illustrated. 8vo, cloth....$5.00

MACKROW, CLEMENT. The Naval Architect's and Ship Builder's Pocketbook of Formulae, Rules, and Tables, and Marine Engineer's and Surveyor's Handy-Book of Reference. Eighth edition, revised and enlarged. 12mo. Leather, illustrated . $5.00

SWOOPE, C. WALTON. Lessons in Practical Electricity; Principles, Experiments, and Arithmetical Problems. An Elementary Text-Book, with numerous Tables and Formulae, and two large Instruction Plates. 8vo, cloth, 385 pages....net, $2.00

ARNOLD, E. Armature Windings of Direct Current Dynamos. Extension and Application of a General Winding Rule. Translated from the original German by Francis B. DeGress. M.E. With many diagrams. Illustrated. 8vo, cloth....$2.00

ATKINSON, A. A. (Ohio University). Electrical and Magnetic Calculations. For the use of Electrical Engineers and Artisans, Teachers, Students, and all others interested in the theory and application of Electricity and Magnetism. With figures and illustrations. 8vo, cloth....net, $1.50

ANDERSON, CAPT. GEO. L., U. S. A. Handbook for the Use of Electricians in the Operation and Care of Electrical Machinery and Apparatus of the U. S. Seacoast Defenses. Prepared under the direction of the Lieut.-General Commanding the Army. 8vo, cloth. Illustrated....$3.00

BEGTRUP, JULIUS. Slide Valve and its Functions. With special reference to modern practice in the United States. With many diagrams. 8vo, cloth....$2.00

WALLIS-TAYLER, A. J. Refrigeration, Cold Storage and Ice Making. A practical treatise on the Art and Science of Refrigeration. 8vo, cloth. Illustrated....net, $4.50

CAIN, WM. Theory of Steel Concrete Arches and of Vaulted Structures. Being a thoroughly revised edition of the author's work on "Voussoir Arches Applied to Stone Bridges, Tunnels, Culverts, and Domes." *Van Nostrand's Science Series, No. 42*....50 cents

HALSEY, F. A. ("American Machinist.") Worm and Spiral Gearing. With illustrations and diagrams. *Van Nostrand's Science Series, No. 116*....50 cents

IN PRESS.

HALL, PROF. WM. S. Descriptive Geometry. Text and plates. Two vols.

PAULDING, CHAS. P. Practical Laws and Data on the Condensation of Steam, in Covered and Bare Pipes: To which is added a translation of Peclet's Theory and Experiments on the Transmission of Heat through insulating materials.

GUY, ALBERT E. Experiments on the Flexure of Beams.

GARCKE AND FELLS. Factory Accounts. New edition.

PHILIP, ARNOLD. The Electro-plating and Electro-refining of Metals: being a new edition of Alexander Watt's Electro-Deposition revised and largely rewritten. 8vo, cloth, illustrated.

PERRINE, F. A. C. Conductors for Electrical Distribution; their Manufacture and Materials, the Calculation of Circuits, Pole Line Construction, Underground Working, and other uses. With half-tone engravings and diagrams.

CATHCART, PROF. WM. L. (Columbia University). Machine Elements; Machine Design; Fastenings. With tables and diagrams.

——Marine Engine Design.

——Stationary Engine Design.

SEWALL, C. H. Wireless Telegraphy.

TRAVERSE TABLES, showing the difference of Latitude and Departure for distances between 1 and 100, and for angles to quarter degrees between 1 degree and 90 degrees. Reprinted from *Scribner's Pocket Table Book*. 16mo, boards. *Van Nostrand's Science Series, No. 115.*

D. VAN NOSTRAND COMPANY

Publishers and Booksellers. **23 Murray and 27 Warren Sts., N. Y.**

HOUGHTON, MIFFLIN & COMPANY'S NEW FICTION

OUR LADY OF THE BEECHES

By the BARONESS VON HUTTEN, author of "Miss Carmichael's Conscience," "Marr'd in Making," etc. 12mo. $1.25.

This is the story of a romantic attachment growing out of a group of letters. The situation is handled with such skill, humor, and delicacy, and in so charming a manner as to make the tale exceptionally attractive.

THE RIGHT PRINCESS

By CLARA LOUISE BURNHAM, author of "Miss Pritchard's Wedding Trip," "A West Point Wooing," etc. 12mo. $1.50.

An account of an English family who have come to America in search of health for the heir of the house. A young New England girl proves "the right princess" and restores the sought for health through the medium of Christian Science. The story is one of much interest and charm.

THE DIARY OF A SAINT

By ARLO BATES, author of "Love in a Cloud," "The Puritans," etc. Crown 8vo. $1.50.

The story of this novel is told by the heroine, Ruth Privet, in her diary for an eventful year. The central thought is that saintship is a matter rather of conduct than theory. The development of events and character is unusually clear.

AVERY

By ELIZABETH STUART PHELPS, author of "A Singular Life," "Gates Ajar," etc. Illustrated by Albert E. Sterner. 12mo. $1.00.

Miss Phelps' power of narration is here present in full measure. It is the story of man and wife, of a beautiful love, of a passing act of neglect and its tremendous consequences. The unexpected outcome of it all is stimulating and satisfying.

A DOWNRENTER'S SON

By RUTH HALL, author of "The Golden Arrow," "The Black Gown," etc. Crown 8vo. $1.50.

Like Miss Hall's earlier books, this novel contains abundant adventure, incident, and color. It deals with the strange attempt to abolish rents in New York about sixty years ago. The story is of equal interest both to older and younger readers.

A SEA TURN AND OTHER MATTERS

By THOMAS BAILEY ALDRICH, author of "Marjorie Daw," "The Story of a Bad Boy," etc. 12mo. $1.25.

A new collection of short stories in which the author's fancy sweeps over many lands with the scenes as far apart as Budapest and Virginia. Each story shows Mr. Aldrich's characteristic cheerful mood.

THE STRONGEST MASTER

By HELEN CHOATE PRINCE, author of "The Story of Christine Rochefort," "A Transatlantic Chatelaine," etc. 12mo. $1.50.

This is the most striking piece of work we have had from Mrs. Prince's hand. The hero, a young Harvard man of good family, begins his life under a cloud, having been expelled from college. His strongest desire is to reform his own character and the working out of his theories forms much of the interest of the story.

THE HERITAGE

By BURTON EGBERT STEVENSON, author of "A Soldier of Virginia." Crown 8vo. $1.50.

The scene of this novel is laid in Ohio toward the end of the Revolution and it is a thoroughly good tale of adventure and love. The hero takes part in St. Clair's ill-starred expedition against the Indians, is taken prisoner and held captive for three years but escapes and takes part in the victorious attack at Fallen Timbers.

THE HEART OF THE DOCTOR

By MABEL G. FOSTER. With a frontispiece. 12mo. $1.50.

A love story that has its setting in the old North End of Boston, now taken possession of by the Italians, with a young doctor as hero, and as heroine the daughter of an old Boston family. It is one of the best stories of modern Boston and a delightful romance.

UNCLE CHARLEY

By ZEPHINE HUMPHREY. 12mo. $1.25.

This is a charming story of a man of genius, whimsical but lovable, and his niece, to whom he is a hero and the chief figure in her world. The tale is told with delicacy and discrimination.

Houghton, Mifflin & Company

BOSTON AND NEW YORK

HOUGHTON, MIFFLIN & COMPANY'S NEW JUVENILE BOOKS

UNDER COLONIAL COLORS

By Everett T. Tomlinson, author of "In the Hands of the Redcoats," "A Jersey Boy in the Revolution," etc. Illustrated by Clyde O. Deland. Crown 8vo. $1.20 net. (Postage extra.)

Mr. Tomlinson has chosen for the foundation of this story the heroic enterprise of Arnold's expedition to Quebec. It is told with much spirit and with such mastery of historic detail that it carries the reader along completely convinced.

LOIS MALLET'S DANGEROUS GIFT

By Mary Catherine Lee, author of "A Quaker Girl of Nantucket," "A Soulless Singer," etc. With a frontispiece by W. L. Taylor. 12mo. 85 cents net. (Postage 7 cents.)

The tale of a Quaker girl of great beauty, of the maiden's discovery of this and of its temptation. The book is entirely wholesome and charming.

THREE LITTLE MARYS

By Nora Archibald Smith, author of "Under the Cactus Flag," "The Children of the Future," etc. Illustrated by A. F. Schmitt. Sq. 12mo. 85 cents net. (Postage extra.)

Three stories of three little girls who all had names which in different tongues stand for Mary. One lived in Scotland, another in England and the third in Ireland. There is a touch of excitement as well as sympathy and humor in these stories which make an attractive book for girls.

A POCKETFUL OF POSIES

By Abbie Farwell Brown, author of "In the Days of Giants," "The Lonesomest Doll," etc. Illustrated by Fanny Y. Cory. 12mo. $1.00 net. (Postage extra.)

Miss Brown has a rare faculty for entering into the mind of a child in a joyous spirit. These verses are full of sprightliness, humor, and grace and present in variety of simple verse-forms a little panorama of child life. The book is attractively illustrated and printed with marginal comments in red.

THE CHAMPION

By Charles Egbert Craddock, author of "The Prophet of the Great Smoky Mountain," etc. With a frontispiece by Alice Barber Stephens. 12mo. $1.20 net. (Postage 10 cents.)

This book for boys has swift play of action and abundance of interest. The hero is a printer's "devil" in the office of a Southern newspaper. He goes through experiences exciting enough to delight the heart of any boy.

MISS MUFFET'S CHRISTMAS PARTY

By Samuel M. Crothers. With delightful illustrations by Olive M. Long. sq. 12mo.

A gathering of all the favorite heroes and heroines of juvenile literature into a story of irresistible attractions. It shows a quick sympathy with children's minds, and a rare capacity for sharing their fancies. Miss Muffet's party was one after a little girl's own heart.

THE FLAG ON THE HILLTOP

By Mary Tracy Earle, author of "Through Old-Rose Glasses," etc. Illustrated by W. S. Lukens. 12mo. 90 cents net. (Postage 7 cents.)

The story of a Southern boy who is placed under the care of a Northern uncle during the Civil War. This uncle lives in a Copperhead community in southern Illinois, a region dominated by Confederate sympathizers. The boy's loyalty to his uncle and his loyalty to the South bring about exciting events.

Houghton, Mifflin & Company

BOSTON AND NEW YORK

THOMAS NELSON & SONS' FALL ANNOUNCEMENTS.

Nelson's Sunday-School Scholars' Bible

With Practical Helps and a new Bible Catechism especially designed for the young. The Helps are written by JOHN POTTS, D.D., Chairman International Sunday-School Lesson Committee; Prof. H. M. HAMILL, D.D., JESSE LYMAN HURLBUT, D.D., and other prominent Sunday-School workers. Edited by A. F. SCHAUFFLER, D.D., Secretary of the International Sunday-School Lesson Committee.

NEW EDITIONS OF

Prayer Books and Hymnals

In numerous sizes of type and latest designs in fine bindings, making an excellent variety printed on fine white and Nelson's India paper.

NEW STORY BOOKS

FALLEN FORTUNES. By E. EVERETT-GREEN, author of "French and English," "In the Days of Chivalry," etc. Illustrated by W. H. Margetson. 8vo. Cloth extra. **$1 25.**

SALE'S SHARPSHOOTERS. The Historical Records of a very Irregular Corps. By HAROLD AVERY, author of "Heads or Tails," etc. 8vo. Cloth. Illustrated. **$1.25.**

STANHOPE. A Romance of the Days of Cromwell. By E. L. HAVERFIELD, author of "Rhoda," "Our Vow," etc. 8vo. Cloth. Illustrated. **$1.25.**

RALPH WYNWARD. A New Story for Boys. By H. ELRINGTON. 8vo. Cloth. Illustrated. **$1.00.**

TWO LITTLE TRAVELLERS. A Story for Girls. By RAY CUNNINGHAM. 8vo. Cloth extra. Illustrated. **$1.00.**

A FORTUNE FROM THE SKY. By SKELTON KUPPORD, author of "The Uncharted Island," etc. 8vo. Cloth. Illustrated. **80c.**

THE LOST SQUIRE OF INGLEWOOD; or, Adventures in the Caves of Robin Hood. A Boy's Story of Adventure. By DR. JACKSON. 8vo. Cloth. Illustrated. **80c.**

A HAPPY FAILURE. A Story for Girls. By ETHEL DAWSON. 8vo. Cloth extra. Illustrated. **60c.**

New choice line of colored Toy Books, including Bible Stories, Fairy Tales, Mother Goose Verses, Scenes in the Country, Wild Animals, etc., beautifully printed on paper and linen. List Prices, 20c. and upwards.

THOMAS NELSON & SONS, Publishers, 37-41 EAST 18th ST., NEW YORK

THOMAS NELSON & SONS' FALL ANNOUNCEMENTS.

New Century Library

NEW SIZE, One Volume.

OLD SIZE, Two Volumes.

Type same size in both.

Dickens
Thackeray
Scott

The use of Nelson's India paper, the thinnest printing paper in the world, makes it possible to condense 950 pages into a single volume no thicker than a magazine. The size is only 4¼ x 6¼ inches, and fits the pocket. Each novel is complete in a single volume. The New Century Library editions of these great works are the neatest, most convenient and readable ever published and make choice library sets.

DICKENS' WORKS, complete in 17 vols.
THACKERAY'S WORKS, complete in 14 vols.
SCOTT'S NOVELS, complete in 25 vols.

Handsomely bound in the following styles: Cloth, gilt top, **$1.00** a volume; Leather Limp, gilt top, **$1.25** a volume; Leather Boards, gilt edges, **$1.50** a volume.

Exquisite Sets of Dickens and Thackeray
In Cases.

Size, 9¼ x 6¾ x 5 inches.

DICKENS. 17 vols. Size of case, 12½ x 7 x 5¼ inches.
Persian Morocco, in maroon, dark green or dark blue. Limp, gold roll, red under gold edges; frontispiece. In case to match. **$50.00.**
Maroon Ooze Calf, limp, gold roll, red under gold edges; frontispiece. In case to match. **$65.00.**

THACKERAY. 14 vols.
No. 1. Cloth, gilt top, silk marker, frontispiece, in cloth case. **$17.50.**
No. 4. Persian, semi-flexible, gilt top, silk marker, frontispiece, in cloth case. **$21.00.**
No. 6. Venetian Morocco, semi-flexible, gilt edges, silk marker, frontispiece, in Venetian Morocco case. **$27.50.**
No. 10. German Calf, limp, red under gold edges, gold roll, gilt back, silk marker, frontispiece, in calf case. **$42.00.**
No. 15. German Morocco, boards, red under gold edges, gold roll, gilt back, silk marker, frontispiece, in Morocco case. **$50.00.**

Persian Morocco, in maroon, dark green, or dark blue, limp, gold roll, red under gold edges, frontispiece, in case to match. **$**

Maroon Ooze Calf, limp, gold roll, red under gold edges, frontispiece, in case to match. **$**

Selected Works of the Best Authors
In Single Volumes.

BUNYAN. The Pilgrim's Progress, The Holy War and Grace Abounding. Complete in 1 volume. Cloth, gilt top, **$1.00**; Venetian Morocco Limp, gilt edges, **$1.50.**

TENNYSON. The Poetical Works (1830-1859) of Alfred Lord Tennyson. Complete in 1 volume. Cloth, gilt top, **$1.00**; Leather Limp, gilt edges, **$1.50.**

CARLYLE. The French Revolution. Complete in 1 volume. Cloth, gilt top, **$1.00**; Leather Limp, gilt edges, **$1.50.**

BURNS. The Poems and Songs of Robert Burns. Complete in 1 volume. Cloth, gilt top, **$1.25**; Leather Limp, gilt edges, **$1.75.**

DON QUIXOTE; The Life and Adventures of. Translated from the Spanish. Complete in 1 volume.

OTHER VOLUMES WILL FOLLOW

THOMAS NELSON & SONS, Publishers, 37-41 EAST 18th ST., NEW YORK

R. H. Russell's Books

Drawn by C. D. Gibson

THE SOCIAL LADDER. By CHARLES DANA GIBSON. His latest collection of drawings, showing his art in its full maturity. Decorated Japan vellum cover. Enclosed in decorated box. [*Edition de luxe*, $10.00 *net*.] 12x18 in........$5.00 *net.*

OBSERVATIONS BY MR. DOOLEY. By F. P. DUNNE. A new treasury of Ar-rchey Road philosophy. 7½x5¼ in., $1.50

THE GIRL PROPOSITION. A Cluster of He-and-She Fables. By GEORGE ADE. Illustrated by JOHN T. MCCUTCHEON. 7x4½ in........$1.00

ABENIKI CALDWELL. By CAROLYN WELLS. A burlesque historical novel, illustrated with old wood cuts. 5½x7⅝ in........$1.50

DONE IN THE OPEN. By FREDERIC REMINGTON. The strongest and most recent work of this great artist of Western life. Text by OWEN WISTER. [*Edition de luxe*, $10.00 *net*.] 12x18 in........$5.00 *net.*

HER MAJESTY THE KING. By JAMES JEFFREY ROCHE. A masterpiece of humor. Illustrated by OLIVER HERFORD. 5¼x7¾ in........$1.50

PICTURES OF ROMANCE AND WONDER. By SIR EDWARD BURNE-JONES. Handsome reproductions, with the poems that inspired the pictures. 11x14 in........$5.00 *net.*

A PHENOMENAL FAUNA. By CAROLYN WELLS. Comic verses, illustrated in color by OLIVER HERFORD. 8x8½ in........$1.20 *net.*

BIRDS OF GOD. Eighteen photogravures of angels, etc., from the Old Masters. Text by R. RADCLIFFE-WHITEHEAD. Portfolio. 11¼x14 in........$8.00

THE TIGER AND THE INSECT. By JOHN HABBERTON, author of "Helen's Babies." A story of two children. Illustrated by WALTER RUSSELL. 5½x7⅝ in........$1.20 *net*

TALES OF THE SPINNER. By JEROME DOUCET. Quaint French fairy tales translated. Illustrated by ALFRED GARTH JONES. Bound in vellum. 6x9 in........$5.00 *net.*

A CENTURY OF SONNETS. A fine selection made by MRS. S. B. HERRICK. Bound in vellum. 5¾x7¾........$2.60 *net*

THE HISTORY OF OVER SEA. By WILLIAM MORRIS. Old romance illustrated by LOUIS RHEAD. 8x10 in........$1.50 *net.*

THE ROMANCE OF CINDERELLA. By ELLA M. BOULT. A charming new version of the old story. Pictures in colors. 6¼x9¼ in........$2.40 *net.*

ST. GEORGE AND THE DRAGON. The old ballad in the form of a scroll, 10x40 in., with pictures by BURNE-JONES........$1.60 *net.*

AD ASTRA. Selections from DANTE'S "Divine Comedy," richly illustrated by MARGARET ARMSTRONG. 9x12 in........$5.00

THE WIND IN THE TREE. By the DUCHESS OF SUTHERLAND. Seven strong love stories. Frontispiece by WALTER CRANE. 5¼x7⅝ in........$1.50

THE QUEEN'S ROSARY. By ALICE D. VAN CLEVE. Sixty sonnets in honor of Victoria. 5¾x7¾ in........$1.20 *net.*

MR. SUN AND MRS. MOON. By RICHARD LE GALLIENNE. Child verses, illustrated by BEATRICE BAXTER RUYL. 8½x11 in........$1.60 *net.*

THE BABY'S BAEDEKER. By COL. D. STREAMER. Nonsense verses. Illustrated. 5¼x7¾ in........$1.20 *net.*

WHERE THE WIND BLOWS. By KATHARINE PYLE. Strange fairy tales, illustrated in colors by BERTHA CORSON DAY. 6¾x10½ in........$2.50 *net.*

THE ADVENTURES OF ADMIRAL FROG. By JOHN W. HARRINGTON. Juvenile. Illustrated by WILLARD BERTRAM PRICE. 7x9 in........$1.40 *net*

THE ANIMALS AT THE FAIR. By E. WARDE BLAISDELL. Verses for young folk, with pictures in colors. 9x12 in........$1.40 *net.*

A GARDEN OF GIRLS. By FLORENCE ENGLAND NOSWORTHY. Twelve ideal heads. Portfolio. 12x18 in........$1.00 *net.*

THE DOOM OF KING ACRISIUS. By WILLIAM MORRIS. The Perseus legend, with 12 pictures in photogravure by BURNE-JONES. 6¾x8½ in........$2.75 *net.*

THE TRUE NAPOLEON. By CHARLES JOSSELYN. An extremely useful epitome of Napoleon's life, richly illustrated. 6x8 in........$3.50 *net.*

PLANTATION BIRD LEGENDS. By ELI SHEPPARD. Illustrated by J. M. CONDÉ. 6x9 in........$1.60 *net.*

PERSEUS AND ANDROMEDA. By RICHARD LE GALLIENNE. New prose version. Illustrated with old prints. 5½x8½ in........$1.40 *net.*

THE SONG OF SONGS. Solomon's Song with pictures by BURNE-JONES. [*Editions de luxe*, $1.75 *net* and $2.50 *net*.] Japan vellum cover. 7x11 in. Popular edition........$1.00 *net.*

CHILDREN OF OUR TOWN. By CAROLYN WELLS. Verses, with beautifully colored pictures by M. H. SQUIRE and E. MARS. 11x14 in........$4.20 *net.*

THE ADVENTURES OF ULYSSES. By CHARLES LAMB. The story of the Odyssey, illustrated in color by M. H. SQUIRE and E. MARS. Printed in large type. 7½x9½ in........$2.50

THE AMERICAN ARTISTS' PORTFOLIO. Examples of color work by 12 artists, including KEMBLE, FROST, REMINGTON, STERNER, etc. 14x21 in........$1.50

WORLD PICTURES. By MORTIMER MENPES. Text by DOROTHY MENPES; 50 exquisite color pictures, 50 in tint, and 400 in black and white. [*Edition de luxe*, $15.00 *net*.] 6¼x9 in..$5.00 *net.*

SIGNORA, A CHILD OF THE OPERA HOUSE. By GUSTAV KOBBÉ. Illustrated with photographs, etc. 7½x5¼ in........$1.50

R. H. RUSSELL ❧ PUBLISHER ❧ NEW YORK

D. APPLETON & COMPANY'S

Admiral Porter

By JAMES RUSSELL SOLEY. (*Great Commanders series*, edited by General James Grant Wilson.) Portrait. 12mo ,cloth, $1.50 *net*; postage, 11 cents additional.

The Story of the Trapper

By A. C. LAUT. (*Story of the West series.*) Illustrated. 12mo, cloth.

The Real Siberia

Together with an Account of a Dash Through Manchuria. By J. FOSTER FRASER. Illustrated. 12mo, cloth, $2.00 *net*.

The Romance of My Childhood and Youth

By MADAME ADAM. Portrait and ornamental title. 12mo, cloth.

APPLETONS' SERIES OF HISTORIC LIVES

Daniel Boone

By REUBEN G. THWAITES. 12mo, cloth, $1.00 *net*; postage, 10 cents additional.

Sir William Johnson

By AUGUSTUS C. BUELL, author of "Paul Jones," founder of the American Navy. Illustrated. 12mo, cloth, $1.00 *net*; postage, 10 cents additional.

Sir William Pepperell

By NOAH BROOKS. 12mo, cloth, $1.00 *net*; postage, 10 cents additional.

Animals Before Man in North America

By Dr. F. A. LUCAS. Illustrated. 12mo, cloth.

American Literature

By Prof. W. P. TRENT. (*Literatures of the World series*, edited by Edmund Gosse.) 12mo, cloth, $1.20 *net*; postage, 12 cents additional.

Scandinavian Literature

By Dr. GEORG BRANDES. (*Literatures of the World series.*) 12mo, cloth, $1.20 *net*; postage, 12 cents additional.

Letters of Charles Darwin

Edited by FRANCIS DARWIN. Two volumes, 500 pages each. Cloth.

The Work of Wall Street

By SERENO S. PRATT. (*Appletons' Business series.*) 12mo, cloth.

Funds and Their Uses

By Dr. F. A. CLEVELAND of the University of Pennsylvania. (*Appletons' Business series.*) 12mo, cloth, *net*.

Social New York Under the First Georges

By ESTHER SINGLETON. 100 illustrations. 8vo, cloth.

Trust Finance

By Dr. E. S. MEADE of the University of Pennsylvania. 12mo, cloth.

Musical Education

By A. LAVIGNAC. (*Appletons' Musical Library.*) 12mo, cloth.

Taylor on Golf

By J. H. TAYLOR. Illustrated. 12mo, $1.60 *net*; postage, 16 cents additional.

Cabinet-Making and Designing

By C. SPOONER. (*Artistic Crafts series.*) Illustrated. 12mo, half-bound, $1.20 *net*; postage, 12 cents additional.

Silver Work and Jewelry

By H. WILSON. (*Artistic Crafts series.*) Illustrated. 12mo, half-bound, $1.20 *net*; postage, 12 cents additional.

The Story of a Grain of Wheat

By WM. C. EDGAR. (*Library of Useful Stories.*) 16mo, 35 cents *net*; postage, 4 cents additional.

D. APPLETON & COMPANY, PUBLISHERS, New York

E. & J. B. YOUNG & CO.'S
Novelties for 1902

CHRISTMAS BOOKLETS.

Handsome Cover Designs. Beautiful Full Color Illustrations.

Upward of 20 New Issues.

Retailing at 5c, 10c., 15c., 20c. and 25c. Each.

CALENDARS FOR 1903.

Lithographed in full color and gold. Consisting of "Turn Overs" and "Fancy Shaped Folders." Thirty-seven novel designs.

Retailing at 5c., 8c., 12c., 15c. and 30c.

AUTOGRAPHIC CHRISTMAS CARDS.

Lithographed in color; gold and monotint; embossed and shaped. Landscapes, Figure Pieces, Floral and Combination Designs in handsome boxes containing 6, 8, 10 and 15 Cards.

Retailing at 35c., 75c., $1.00 and $1.25 per Box.

THE "C. B." PACKETS AND BOXES.

Embracing a large range of Christmas and New Year's Cards.

Containing Cards to Retail at 1c., 2c., and 3c. Each.

"THE EMPIRE SERIES OF" CHRISTMAS CARDS.

Dainty Productions in Photogravure, Letter Stamping, Hand Coloring and Engraving. Embracing upwards of 200 varieties. Distinctively English, Scotch, Irish and Religious Christmas Cards.

Retailing at 5c., 10c., 15c., 20c. and 25c. Each.

Illustrated Catalogue and Quotations, Mailed on Application.

E. & J. B. YOUNG & CO., 9 West 18th St., New York.

LONDON BIBLE WAREHOUSE

THE EYRE & SPOTTISWOODE

TEACHERS' BIBLES.

New "Universal" Editions.

Up-to-Date! Illustrated! Concise!

Improved Non-Tearable Binding!

Superior English presswork, paper and binding. Not cheap reprints, but genuine books at popular prices.

Our Prices Are as Low as the Cheapest.

BIBLES.

From the Press of the King's Printers, London. The Oldest Bible Press in the World.

Pocket Bibles,
Landscape Bibles,
Text Bibles,
Reference Bibles,
Family Bibles.

We offer the most comprehensive line in the market; everything in current demand, from a small inexpensive Pocket Edition to the most exquisite Family, Pulpit or Lodge Bible.

Testaments

in all sizes, from miniature Vest Pocket Editions to Large Type Books for old people.

Episcopal Prayer Books and Hymnals.

Most Complete Line and Largest Variety in the Market. Everything in demand, from the cheap mission books to the superior India-paper editions in costly binding.

The New-Shaped Prayer Book and Hymnal. A pronounced success. Dainty, unique, salable.

The Children's Popular Annual.

SUNDAY.

NEW VOLUME FOR 1903.

A book of delightful stories and poetry for old and young. All new matter, with 250 original illustrations.

Illuminated board covers, $1.25; cl., illuminated sides, gilt edges, $2.00.

The World's Greatest Pictures.

The Daily Mail Art Gallery of 100 masterpieces suitable for framing. A Portfolio containing 100 Reproductions of the World's Most Famous Pictures. Printed by the Woodbury Process. The collection embraces subjects suitable for the Drawing Room, the Smoking Room, the Study, or the Nursery. Imperial folio, $10.00.

The Cathedral Churches of England.

Containing 32 Woodbury Collotype illustrations, with brief explanatory notes by Percy Home, oblong 4to, cloth, gilt edges, $3.00.

Illustrated Catalogue Mailed on Application

E. & J. B. YOUNG & CO., 9 West 18th St., New York.

LITTLE, BROWN & CO.'S FALL ANNOUNCEMENTS

THE SPEECHES AND OTHER WRITINGS OF DANIEL WEBSTER, HITHERTO UNCOLLECTED

More than 1300 octavo pages of new material. With portraits. 3 vols., $9.00 *net.*

A ONE VOLUME PARKMAN

The Struggle for a Continent

Edited from the Writings of FRANCIS PARKMAN by Prof. Pelham Edgar of Victoria College, University of Toronto. With fifty portraits, full-page plates, maps, etc. 12mo, cloth, $1.50 *net.*

CAPT. MAHAN'S NEW BOOK

Retrospect and Prospect

By CAPT. A. T. MAHAN, LL.D., author of "Types of Naval Officers," etc. Crown 8vo, $1.60 *net.*

A LITERARY HISTORY

American Literature in Its Colonial and National Periods

By LORENZO SEARS, L.H.D., Professor of American Literature in Brown University. 12mo, $1.50 *net.*

JOURNEYS WITH DUMAS

The Speronara

Translated from the French of ALEXANDRE DUMAS by Katharine Prescott Wormeley. 16mo, $1.25.

GLIMPSES OF CHINA AND CHINESE HOMES

By Prof. E. S. MORSE, author of "Japanese Homes and Their Surroundings," etc. With more than fifty sketches from the author's journal. 12mo, $1.50 *net.*

The Spiritual Outlook

A Survey of the Religious Life of Our Time as Related to Progress. By WILLARD CHAMBERLAIN SELLECK. 16mo, cloth, $1.00 *net.*

America in Its Relation to Great Epochs of History

By WILLIAM J. MANN. 16mo, $1.00 *net.*

With a Saucepan Over the Sea

Quaint and Delicious Recipes from the Kitchens of Foreign Countries. By ADELAIDE KEEN. With illustrations. 12mo, cloth, $1.50 *net.*

First-Hand Bits of Stable-Lore

By FRANCIS M. WARE. A practical work for horse owners. Illustrated. Crown 8vo, $2.00 *net.*

LILIAN WHITING'S NEW BOOK: BOSTON DAYS

A Literary Record. By LILIAN WHITING, author of "The World Beautiful" "The World Beautiful in Books," etc. With portraits and other illustrations. 12mo, $1.50 *net.*

SOME NEW EDITIONS

Plutarch's Lives (Oxford Edition)

The translation called Dryden's. Corrected from the Greek and revised by A. H. Clough, late Professor at University College. In five volumes. Photogravure frontispieces. Crown 8vo, gilt top, $7.50; half morocco, gilt top, $17.50.

Glimpses of California and the Missions

By HELEN JACKSON, author of "Ramona," etc. With 37 pictures by Henry Sandham, including numerous full-page plates. 12mo, decorated cloth, $1.50.

The Diary and Letters of Frances Burney, Madame D'Arblay (Windsor Edition)

Edited by Sarah Chauncey Woolsey. With portraits. Edition limited to 500 copies. 2 vols., 8vo, gilt top, $6.00 *net.*

Prayers, Ancient and Modern

Selected and Arranged for Daily Reading by Mary W. Tileston, Editor of "Daily Strength for Daily Needs." 18mo, $1.00. *Red Line Edition.* 16mo, $1.50.

THE WRITINGS OF CHARLES LEVER (Barrington Edition).

Comprising his Military Novels, Novels of Adventure, Novels of Irish Life, and Novels of Foreign Life. Illustrated. Complete in 32 volumes. Crown 8vo, $1.50 per volume.

The Boston Cooking School Cook Book

By FANNIE MERRITT FARMER. With an appendix containing three hundred additional recipes. Illustrated. 12mo, cloth, $2.00.

The Intellectual Life

By PHILIP GILBERT HAMERTON. Laneside Edition. With portraits. Crown 8vo, gilt top, $1.50 *net;* half crushed morocco, gilt top, $3.00 *net.*

LITTLE, BROWN & CO., *Publishers,* BOSTON, MASS.

LITTLE, BROWN & CO.'S FALL ANNOUNCEMENTS

A Powerful Novel of Ancient Egypt by a New Polish Writer

THE PHARAOH AND THE PRIEST

From the original Polish of Alexander Glovatski. By Jeremiah Curtin, translator of "Quo Vadis," etc. Illustrated. 12mo, $1.50.

A ROMANCE OF THE FAR EAST

The Queen of Quelparte

By Archer B. Hulbert. Illustrated. 12mo, $1.50.

Tower or Throne

A Romance of the Girlhood of Elizabeth. By Harriet T. Comstock. Illustrated. 12mo, $1.50.

Faithful (To which is added) Ward's Cross

By the author of "Miss Toosey's Mission," "Laddie," etc. 16mo, $1.00.

ABSORBING STORY OF ADVENTURE

The Shadow of the Czar

By John R. Carling. Illustrated. 12mo, $1.50.

The Colonel's Opera Cloak

By Christine C. Brush. *New Edition*, with full-page pictures and decorative chapter. 12mo, $1.50.

Miss Belladonna. A Social Satire

By Caroline Ticknor. *New Edition.* With additional chapters. Illustrated. 16mo, $1.00.

NOVELS, IRISH LEGENDS, PLAYS AND POEMS OF SAMUEL LOVER

With an introduction by James Jeffrey Roche. First Collected Edition. Illustrated. 6 vols., 12mo, extra gilt top, $1.50 per vol.; the set, 6 vols., half crushed morocco, gilt top, $19.50.

ILLUSTRATED JUVENILES

Little Women

Or, Meg, Jo, Beth, and Amy. By Louisa M. Alcott. With 15 full-page illustrations by Alice Barber Stephens. Crown 8vo, $2.00.

An Old-Fashioned Girl

By Louisa M. Alcott. With 12 full-page pictures by Jessie Willcox Smith. Crown 8vo, $2.00.

IN THE GREEN FOREST

By Katharine Pyle, author of "The Christmas Angel," "As the Goose Flies," etc. With full-page pictures and illustrations in the text from drawings by the author. Crown 8vo, $1.50 *net.*

Nathalie's Chum

By Anna Chapin Ray, author of "Teddy: Her Book," etc. Illustrated by Ellen Bernard Thompson. 12mo, $1.20 *net.*

Brenda's Cousin at Radcliffe

By Helen Leah Reed, author of "Brenda, Her School and Her Club." Illustrated by Alice Barber Stephens. 12mo, $1.20 *net.*

On Guard! Against Tory and Tarleton

By John Preston True, author of "Scouting for Washington," etc. Illustrated by Lilian Crawford True. 12mo, $1.20 *net.*

The Adventures of Torqua

By Charles F. Holder, author of "The History and Antiquity of Catalina," etc. Illustrated. 12mo, $1.20 *net.*

THE PRINCESS KALLISTO AND OTHER TALES OF THE FAIRIES

By William Dana Orcutt. With several full-page plates and decorative drawings by Harriette Amsden, in color. 4to, $2.00 *net.*

Catharine's Proxy

Story of Schoolgirl Life. By Myra Sawyer Hamlin, author of "Nan at Camp Chicopee." With pictures by Florence E. Plaisted. 12mo, decorated cloth, $1.20 *net.*

Foxy the Faithful

By Lily F. Wesselhoeft, author of "Sparrow the Tramp," etc. Illustrated by H. C. Ireland. 12mo, decorated cloth, $1.20 *net.*

Polly's Secret

A Story of the Kennebec. By Harriet A. Nash. Illustrated by Harry C. Edwards. 12mo, $1.20 *net.*

Jack and His Island

By Lucy M. Thruston, author of "A Girl of Virginia," etc. Illustrated by Clyde O. De Land. 12mo, decorated cloth, $1.20 *net.*

Grandma's Girls

By Helen Morris. Illustrated by P. L. Hoyt. 12mo, $1.20 *net.*

A Dornfield Summer

By Mary M. Haley. Illustrated by Harriet Roosevelt Richards. 12mo, $1.20 *net.*

THE BOYS' AND GIRLS' BOOKSHELF

A series of 30 illustrated twelvemo volumes by Popular Juvenile Authors, attractively bound in cloth, extra. Formerly published at $1.50 or $1.25. Each, $1.00.

LITTLE, BROWN & CO., *Publishers*, BOSTON, MASS.

Send for Richly Illustrated Catalogue.

The Century Co.'s

The Serial Hit of the Year. *Ready in book form October 15*

Confessions of a Wife

By Mary Adams

No serial published in *The Century* for many years has attracted as much attention as this remarkable book by an unknown and pseudonymous author. It is a story dealing with courtship and marriage, and it is considered one of the most unusual and striking pieces of writing that have appeared for many years. The book is enriched with six illustrations by Granville Smith. 12mo, 400 pages, $1.50.

Luncheons

By the Author of "The Century Cook Book."

This is a guide to the preparation of dainty dishes for dainty meals, elaborately illustrated by photographs. It is a book of illustrated receipts, thoroughly indexed, which will prove a most helpful assistant to the housekeeper. 8vo, 200 pages, 208 photographs, price $1.40 net (postage 15 cents).

Caterpillars and Their Moths

By IDA MITCHELL ELIOT and CAROLINE GRAY SOULE. The result of more than twenty years spent in studying and rearing moths. The illustrations are very striking. They are made from photographs and show actual size. 8vo, 300 pages of text and 80 insets, with index, price $2.00 net (postage 18 cents).

New Books in the "Thumb-Nail" Series

Exquisite Little Books in Embossed Leather Bindings. Size, 2 3-4 by 5 1-8. $1.00 each

In Memoriam. By ALFRED, Lord TENNYSON, with an introduction by Edmund Clarence Stedman, and a portrait of Lord Tennyson taken about the time "In Memoriam" was written.

The Rivals. By RICHARD BRINSLEY SHERIDAN. With a portrait of the author and an introduction from "The Autobiography of Joseph Jefferson." A charming setting for Sheridan's masterpiece.

Thoughts of Pascal. Translated from the French and with an introduction by Benjamin E. Smith. With a portrait of the author.

Biography of a Prairie Girl

By ELEANOR GATES. Describing in a most charming manner the life of a little girl in the Northwest twenty-five years ago. Full of color and adventure, with touches of delightful humor. 12mo, 350 pages, price $1.50.

Barnaby Lee

By John Bennett

A book for older readers and for boys and girls as well. The scene and time are New Amsterdam under Peter Stuyvesant, the hero a boy who has run away from a piratical ship captain. Illustrations by Clyde O. DeLand. 12mo, 454 pages, price $1.50.

A New Story by the Author of "Tom Beauling"

Aladdin O'Brien

By GOUVERNEUR MORRIS, whose "Tom Beauling" is one of the recent successes in fiction. Humor and pathos play hide-and-seek through the pages of Mr. Morris's latest romance. It is the story of two men in love with the same girl, told in the delightfully original style that is distinctive of this promising young author. The three brothers of the heroine are real creations. 12mo, 300 pages, $1.25.

The East of To-Day and To-Morrow

By Right Rev. Henry C. Potter, D.D.

Dealing with the religion, politics, etc., of China, the Philippines, Japan, India, and the Hawaiian Islands. $1.00 net (postage 9 cents).

The Call of the Sea

Poems by L. Frank Tooker.

A collection of poems which have attracted wide attention as they have appeared in various periodicals. 12mo, 175 pages. Price $1.25 net (postage 6 cents).

THE CENTURY CO · UNION SQUARE · NEW YORK

MOON
By
LAURA
DAYTON
FESSENDEN
Childre
GIRLS
of the
BIBLE
YANKEE
MOTHER
GOOSE
AN
ALPHABET
of
BIRDS
By
A
ALPHABET
WILD
FLOWERS
KIDS OF MANY
COLORS
"2002"
CHILDLIFE
HELEN'S BABIES
A
ROUND
ROBIN
STORIES
for
CHILDREN
By
Mary Hartwell Catherwood
Alfred Henry Lewis-Kate Upson Clark-
Garrett Newkirk-Peter Dunne, Etc. Etc.
CHICAGO-JAMIESON-HIGGINS CO.
Old Mother Hubbard . $1.25
40 Colors. A Revelation in Printing.
Moon Children 1.25
20 Colors. An exquisite.
Kids of Many Colors 1.25
The Original.
Yankee Mother Goose . . . 1.00
Nothing Like it.
"2002" 1.25
Child Life 100 Years from Now.
A Round Robin 1.25
The Enjoyable.
An Alphabet of Birds } Each .75
An Alphabet of Flowers
Nature Studies in Colors.
Girls of the Bible 1.00
The Uplifting.
Helen's Babies 1.00
The Classic of Child Life.
The Jamieson-Higgins Co. Juveniles
are...
Famous
for Originality
for Artistic Finish
for Literary Excellence
for Color Printing
.....Complete Catalogue Sent on Application.....
JAMIESON-HIGGINS
CO. Publishers Chicago

Popular 60c. Books

"Helen's Babies."

"Fun with Magic."

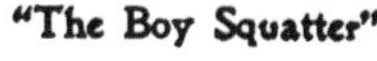

"The Boy Squatter"

"Tales from Tennyson."

"The Princess of Hearts."

"When the Band Played."

"Adventures in Toyland"

"Tales from Longfellow"

"Fuzzy Four-Footed Folks"

"Young Folks' Uncle Tom's Cabin"

"Dicken's Christmas Stories for Children"

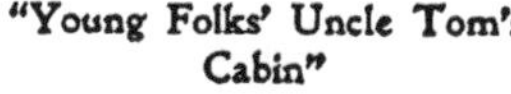

.....Complete Catalogue Sent on Application.....

JAMIESON-HIGGINS CO. Publishers Chicago

Forthcoming Fall Publications of the Funk & Wagnalls Company

FICTION

THE NEEDLE'S EYE

By FLORENCE MORSE KINGSLEY

Author of "Titus," "The Transfiguration of Miss Philura," "Prisoners of the Sea," "Stephen," etc.

"The Needle's Eye" is a remarkable story of modern American life—not of one phase but of many phases, widely different and in startling contrast. 12mo, Cloth. Illustrated Price, $1.50, Post-paid. (*Ready Sept. 20th.*)

LOVE AND THE SOUL HUNTERS

By JOHN OLIVER HOBBES

Author of "The Gods, Some Mortals, and Lord Wickenham," "The Herb Moon," "Schools for Saints," "Robert Orange," etc.

In this new novel Mrs. Craigie (John Oliver Hobbes) has made, according to her own statement, the great effort of her life. It is the most brilliant creation of an author whose talent and versatility have surprised readers and critics in both Europe and America for several years. 12mo, Cloth. Price, $1.50, Post-paid. (*Ready Sept. 20th.*)

THE SEARCHERS

By MARGARETTA BYRDE

A delightful novel bearing the impress of a fervent belief that the secret of life is a noble one, and of a fervent desire to pursue it. 12mo, Cloth, 452 pages. Price, $1.50, Post-paid. (*Ready Sept. 20th.*)

THE INSANE ROOT

By Mrs. CAMPBELL PRAED

Author of "Nadine"; "The Scourge Stick"; "As a Watch in the Night," etc.

This story has a similar *motif* to that of Stevenson's Dr. Jekyl and Mr. Hyde, and a weird treatment resembling that of Bulwer's "Strange Story." 12mo, Cloth, 380 Pages. Price, $1.50, Post-paid. (*Ready Sept. 20th.*)

THE HERR DOCTOR

Volume IV. of the Hour-Glass Stories

By ROBERT MACDONALD

A bright, vivacious story telling of the remarkable experiences of two American women traveling in Germany. Small 12mo, Cloth, Illustrated. Price, 40 cents, *net*; by Mail, 45 cents. (*Ready Sept. 20th.*)

POETRY

KULOSKAP, THE MASTER

By Hon. CHARLES GODFREY LELAND, F.R.S.L., M.A., and JOHN DYNELEY PRINCE, Ph.D.

WITH OTHER ALGONKIN LEGENDS AND POEMS. 12mo, Cloth, birch-bark tracings after Indian designs, by MR. LELAND, and text illustrations by F. BERKELEY SMITH. Frontispiece in colors by EDWIN WILLARD DEMING. Price, $2.00, *net*. (*Ready in October.*)

SWORDS AND PLOWSHARES

By ERNEST CROSBY

Author of "Plain Talk in Psalm and Parable," "Captain Jinks, Hero," etc.

A collection of poems by the leading disciple of Tolstoy in America. They are filled with the hatred of war and the love of nature which are characteristic of the author. 12mo, Cloth. Price, $1.00, *net*. (*Ready in November.*)

FUNK & WAGNALLS COMPANY,

Forthcoming Fall Publications of the Funk & Wagnalls Company

MISCELLANEOUS

THE LOST WEDDING RING

By CORTLAND MYERS, D.D.

A series of essays discussing the subject of marriage. The topic is treated from a religious standpoint, and illuminated by numerous illustrations in prose and verse. 16mo, Cloth. Price, 75 cents, *net*; by Mail, 80 cents. (*Ready Sept. 27th.*)

THE SONS OF GLORY

Studies in Genius by ADOLFO PADOVAN

Translated and adapted from the Italian by the Duchess Litta Visconti Arese. 12mo, Cloth, 306 Pages. Price, $1.50, Post-paid. (*Ready Sept. 27th.*)

THE TEN COMMANDMENTS AND THE LORD'S PRAYER

By FERDINAND S. SCHENCK, D.D.

Professor of Practical Theology, Theological Seminary of the Reformed (Dutch) Church in America, New Brunswick, N. J.

This volume is a revised edition of Prof. Schenck's previous work, "The Ten Commandments in the Nineteenth Century," with the addition of "The Lord's Prayer" portion. 12mo, Cloth. Price, $1.00, *net*; by Mail, $1.10. (*Ready Sept. 27th.*)

THE SPIRIT OF THE GHETTO

By HUTCHINS HAPGOOD

Studies and sketches of the life, customs, institutions, types of character, and prominent personages of the celebrated East Side Jewish quarter of New York. Profusely illustrated with drawings from life by Jacob Epstein, one of the most prominent of the younger Ghetto artists. 12mo, Cloth. Price, $1.20, *net*. (*Ready in October.*)

VOL. III. OF THE JEWISH ENCYCLOPEDIA

Comprising the history, literature and customs of the Jewish people, from the earliest times down to the present day, prepared by about 400 scholars and specialists. Sold by subscription. Twelve volumes, quarto, with about 2,000 illustrations. Special Advance of Publication Prices: Cloth, $72.00; Half Morocco, $96.00; Full Morocco, $120.00. (Volumes I. and II. Ready.) *Vol. III. Ready in October.*

SCIENTIFIC SIDE-LIGHTS

A new cyclopedia, containing in 4,000 paragraphs over 15,000 illustrations from science, besides about 40,000 indexed topics. Several hundred standard works have been drawn from, representing writings of two hundred specialists in all the various branches of science. 8vo, Cloth. Price, $5.00, *net*; by Mail, $5.42. (*Ready in November.*)

RAYMOND LULL

First Missionary to the Moslems. A biographical sketch of his life by Rev. S. M. Zwemer, D.D., F.R.G.S., author of "Arabia," "The Cradle of Islam," "Topsey Turvey Land," etc. Illustrated. 12mo, Cloth. Price, 75 cents, *net*. (*Ready in November.*)

A QUIVER OF ARROWS

Sermons of David J. Burrell, D.D., LL.D., delivered in the Marble Collegiate Church of New York City, selected and epitomized by Thomas Douglas, Ph.D. 8vo, Cloth, 350 Pages. Price, $1.20, *net*. (*Ready in November.*)

PUBLISHERS, 30 LAFAYETTE PLACE, NEW YORK.

SOME OF THE MACMILLAN COMPANY'S FALL BOOKS

New Novels, Etc.

LAFCADIO HEARN'S NEW BOOK

KOTTO: Some Japanese Curios, with Sundry Cobwebs

By LAFCADIO HEARN, Author of "Shadowings," "Kokoro," "Some Chinese Ghosts," "Stray Leaves from Stray Literature," etc. Rich in the indescribable charm of his delicate picturing of the exotic East. Illustrated. *Cloth, probably* $1.50 net.

GERTRUDE ATHERTON'S NEW BOOK

THE SPLENDID IDLE FORTIES: Stories of Old California

By GERTRUDE ATHERTON, Author of "The Conqueror," "Senator North," etc. A picture of old Spanish life in California. With illustrations by HARRISON FISHER. *Cloth*, $1.50

A. E. W. MASON'S NEW MILITARY NOVEL

THE FOUR FEATHERS

By A. E. W. MASON, Author of "The Courtship of Morris Buckler," etc. A story of a young officer in the Soudan War, tense with interest most skillfully maintained. *Cloth, 12mo*, $1.50

MARK LEE LUTHER'S NEW POLITICAL STORY

THE HENCHMAN

By MARK LEE LUTHER, Author of "The Favor of Princes," etc. A rarely strong and successful political story as well as a charming and inspiring love story. *Cloth, 12mo*, $1.50

JACK LONDON'S NEW ALASKAN BOOK

CHILDREN OF THE FROST

By JACK LONDON, Author of "The Son of the Wolf," "The God of His Father." Illustrated by R. MARTINE REAY. *Cloth, 12mo*, $1.50

HENRY K. WEBSTER'S NEW STORY OF A TRUST

ROGER DRAKE: Captain of Industry

By HENRY K. WEBSTER, Author of "The Banker and the Bear," Co-author of "Calumet K," etc. Copiously illustrated by HOWARD GILES. *Cloth, 12mo*, $1.50

B. K. BENSON'S NEW WAR STORY

BAYARD'S COURIER: A Story of Love and Adventure in the Cavalry

By B. K. BENSON, Author of "A Friend with the Countersign," "Who Goes There?" Illustrated by LOUIS BETTS. *Cloth, 12mo*, $1.50

FOR THE YOUNGER FOLKS

A LITTLE CAPTIVE LAD

By BEULAH MARIE DIX, Author of "The Making of Christopher Ferringham," "Soldier Rigdale," "Hugh Gwyeth." Illustrated by WILL H. GREFÉ. *Cloth, 12mo*, $1.50

PICKETT'S GAP

By HOMER GREENE, Author of "The Blind Brother," "Coal and the Coal Mines," etc. A story of a railroad war for the right of way and of the part a boy played in it. Illustrated. *Cloth, 12mo*, $1.50

Mrs. WRIGHT'S NEW BOOK

DOGTOWN: Being Some Chapters from the Annals of the Waddles Family

By MABEL OSGOOD WRIGHT, Author of "Tommy Anne and the Three Hearts," "Citizen Bird," "Wabeno," etc. Profusely illustrated. *Cloth, 12mo*, $1.50 net.

Poetry

Mr. STEPHEN PHILLIPS' NEW PLAY

DAVID AND BATHSHEBA

By STEPHEN PHILLIPS, Author of "Ulysses," "Paola and Francesca," etc. *Cloth, 16mo*, $1.25 net.

Also an edition on large paper, limited to one hundred copies.

A list of this Autumn's new books will be sent free on application by

THE MACMILLAN COMPANY, 66 Fifth Ave., New York

JOHN WILEY & SONS'

SCIENTIFIC PUBLICATIONS

Lead-Smelting

The Construction, Equipment, and Operation of Lead Blast-furnaces, and Observations on the Influence of Metallic Elements on Slags and the Scientific Handling of Smoke. With Numerous Plates and Diagrams. By MALVERN WELLS ILES, Ph.D., 12mo, cloth, $2.50 net, postage added.

Materials of Machines

By ALBERT W. SMITH, Professor of Mechanical Engineering in Leland Stanford Junior University, California. 12mo, v+142 pages, 17 figures, cloth, $1.00.

CONTENTS.—Outline of the metallurgy of Iron and Steel—Testing; Stress-strain Diagrams; Cast Iron; Wrought Iron and Steel; Alloys.

Inorganic Chemistry

With the Elements of Physical and Theoretical Chemistry. By J. I. D. HINDS, Ph.D., Professor of Chemistry in the University of Nashville. 8vo, viii+566 pages, 69 figures, cloth, $3.00.

CONTENTS.—Part I. Introduction.—Part II. Physical chemistry.—Part III. Theoretical Chemistry.—Part IV. Descriptive Chemistry.

Chemistry

By Observation, Experiment, and Induction. A Laboratory Manual for Students. By Prof. J. I. D. HINDS. 12mo, 46 figures, cloth, 75 cents net.

CONTENTS.—Part I. Introduction.—Part II. Physical Chemistry.—Part III. Theoretical Chemistry.—Part IV. Chemistry of Elements and Compounds.

The Design of Simple Roof-Trusses in Wood and Steel

With an Introduction to the Elements of Graphic Statics. By MALVERD A. HOWE, C.E., Professor of Civil Engineering, Rose Polytechnic Institute. 8vo, 67 figures, and 3 folding plates, cloth, $2.00.

CONTENTS.—General Principles of Methods. Beams and Trusses. Strength of materials. Roof-trusses and their Design. Design of a Wooden Roof-truss. Design of a Steel Roof-truss. Tables.

Stereotomy: A Practical Treatise

By ARTHUR W. FRENCH, Professor of Civil Engineering in Worcester Polytechnic Institute, Worcester, Mass., and HOWARD C. IVES, Instructor in Civil Engineering, Worcester Polytechnic Institute. 8vo, cloth, $2.50. *October.*

A Short Course in Statics by Graphic and Algebraic Methods

By Professor L. J. JOHNSON, Lawrence Scientific School, Harvard University. 8vo, cloth. *October.*

The Principles of Animal Nutrition

By HENRY PRENTICE ARMSBY, Director of the State College of Pennsylvania, State College, Pa. 8vo, cloth. *October.*

A Manual of Assaying

The Fire Assay of Gold, Silver, and Lead, including Amalgamation and Chlorination Tests. By ALFRED STANLEY MILLER, A.M., E.M., Ph.D., Professor of Mining and Metallurgy, University of Idaho. Second edition, revised and enlarged. First thousand. 16mo, viii+142 pages, 47 figures, cloth, $1.00.

An Elementary Text-Book of the Kinematics of Machines

By R. J. DURLEY, Professor of Mechanical Engineering in McGill University, Montreal, Canada. 8vo, cloth. *October.*

Cyanide Processes

By E. B. WILSON, E.M. Third edition, rewritten. Increased from 122 to 214 pages. 12mo, cloth, $1.50.

Organic Chemistry

By A. F. HOLLEMAN, Professor Ordinarius in the University of Groningen, Netherlands. Translated by A. Jamieson Walker, Ph.D., Head of the Department of Chemistry, Municipal Technical College, Derby, England; assisted by Owen E. Mott, Ph.D., Demonstrator in Chemistry in Municipal Technical College. 8vo, cloth, 550 pages. *November.*

Heating and Ventilation of Buildings

By R. C. CARPENTER. Fourth edition, mostly rewritten and enlarged. xvi+562 pages, 8vo, cloth, $4.00.

A Text-Book of Ordnance and Gunnery

Prepared for the Use of Cadets of the U. S. Military Academy by Captain LAWRENCE L. BRUFF, Ordnance Dept., U.S.A., formerly Instructor of Ordnance and Gunnery, U. S. Military Academy. 2d edition. 8vo, v+677 pages, 401 figures, cloth, $6.00 net.

Revised by Captain F. E. Hobbs, Captain C. C. Jamieson and Captain G. G. Heiner.

Lectures on Explosives

A Course of Lectures Prepared Especially as a Manual and Guide in the Laboratory of the U. S. Artillery School. By Capt. WILLOUGHBY WALKE, U. S. A. Instructor. 3d edition revised. 8vo, cloth, $4.00. *October.*

An Introduction to the Theory of Algebraic Equations

By LEONARD EUGENE DICKSON, Associate Professor of Mathematics in the University of Chicago. 12mo, cloth. *November.*

A Short Text-Book of Analytical Chemistry.

By Doctor F. P. TREADWELL, Professor of Analytical Chemistry in the Polytechnic Institute at Zurich, Switzerland. In two volumes. Volume I., Qualitative Analysis. Authorized translation from second enlarged and revised German edition by William T. Hall, Instructor in Chemistry in the Massachusetts Institute of Technology, Boston. 8vo, cloth. *December.*

The Elements of Steam Engineering

By H. W. SPANGLER, Professor of Mechanical Engineering in the University of Pennsylvania; A. M. GREENE, Jr., Professor of Mechanical Engineering in the University of Missouri, and S. M. MARSHALL, Instructor in Mechanical Engineering, University of Pennsylvania. 8vo, cloth. *December.*

A Treatise on Roads and Pavements

By Ira O. Baker, Professor of Civil Engineering in the University of Illinois. 8vo, cloth, about 650 pages, $5.00. *December.*

Ancient and Modern Civil Engineering and the Isthmian Canal

By Wm. H. Burr, Professor of Civil Engineering in Columbia University in the City of New York. 8vo, cloth. *December.*

The Improvement of Rivers

By B. F. Thomas, Engineer, U. S. Army, and D. A. Watt, Engineer, U. S. Army. 4to, cloth. *December.*

Field Astronomy for Engineers

By George C. Comstock, Director of Washburn Observatory University of Wisconsin, Madison, Wis. 8vo, cloth. *November.*

Engineering for Land Drainage

By Charles G. Elliott, Editor of the *Drainage Journal*, Indianapolis, Ind. 12mo, cloth.

A Manual of Drawing

By Prof. C. E. Coolidge, Sibley College, Cornell University.

The Principles of American Forestry

By Samuel B. Green, Professor of Horticulture and Forestry, the University of Minnesota.

Manual for Resident Engineers

By F. A. Molitor and E. J. Beard.

Principal Species of Wood: Their Characteristic Properties

By Charles H. Snow, Dean of the School of Applied Science, University of the City of New York. 8vo, cloth.

Locomotives: Simple, Compound, and Electric

Being the 4th Edition of Locomotive Mechanism and Engineering. By H. C. Reagan. 12mo, cloth, illustrated.

Systematic Pomology

Being Part II. of American Horticultural Manual. By J. L. Budd, Professor Emeritus of Horticulture in the Iowa State College of Agriculture and the Mechanic Arts, Assisted by N. E. Hansen, Professor in the South Dakota Agricultural College.

Free Hand Lettering

By Victor T. Wilson, Sibley College, Cornell University.

Laboratory Notes for Physiological Chemistry

By John A. Mandel, Professor of Physiological Chemistry in New York University and Bellevue Medical College. 12mo, cloth.

43 and 45 East 19th St., New York City

JOHN KENDRICK BANGS'S

Bikey the Skicycle

A New Book of Adventure in Cloudland and Dreamland by this Charming and Popular Writer

Illustrated with Eight Full-Page Pictures by PETER NEWELL

FRONTISPIECE IN FOUR COLORS

Published October 9, 1902 **Price, $1.50**

RIGGS PUBLISHING COMPANY

1123 BROADWAY NEW YORK

LAIRD AND LEE'S POPULAR BOOKS

THE STARBUCKS. By OPIE READ. 8 illustrations in colors. Cloth, special ornamental cover $1.50
None of the many stories from Mr. Read's prolific pen surpasses this latest work in delightful and quaint humor, eloquent pathos and dramatic interest. It is one of the best sellers among recent current literature.
"Opie Read's splendid gifts of imaginative sympathy and literary invention entitle him to rank as one of the truest story writers of this country."—*Chicago Record-Herald.*

MICHAEL CARMICHAEL. By MILES SANDYS. A thrilling romance of exceptional dramatic power. 8 full-page illustrations; frontispiece in colors. Cloth, ornamental cover $1.25

THE DEAD CITY. By GABRIELE D'ANNUNZIO. Eleonora Duse, the great Italian actress, will produce this celebrated tragedy on her American tour this fall. 7 full-page illustrations; frontispiece in colors, ornamental cover $1.25

BABY GOOSE: His Adventures. By FANNIE E. OSTRANDER. Royal quarto, boards; done in colors throughout $1.00

FROLICS OF THE A B C. By FANNIE E. OSTRANDER. Royal quarto, boards; printed in colors . . . . 75c.

OPIE READ'S BEST BOOKS. The new edition. Bound in vellum de luxe cloth, 12mo, stamped covers, printed on superfine paper. Ten titles, sold singly, **75c.** each, or in set (two boxes) at $7.50

THE CARPETBAGGER	A KENTUCKY COLONEL*
THE JUCKLINS*	MY YOUNG MASTER*
OLD EBENEZER*	A TENNESSEE JUDGE*
WIVES OF THE PROPHET	ON THE SUWANEE RIVER*
EMMETT BONLORE	LEN GANSETT

OPIE READ'S SELECT WORKS. 6 vols. (marked with * in above list), uncut edges, gold top, **$1.00** each. Set, in a box $6.00

PRACTICAL ASTROLOGY. By COMTE C. DE SAINT-GERMAIN. 100 engravings. Cloth, special cover in colors $1.00

PRACTICAL PALMISTRY. By COMTE C. DE SAINT-GERMAIN. Cloth, 71 illustrations. 16 hands of celebrities, unique cover . . . . 75c.

PRACTICAL HYPNOTISM. By COMTE C. DE SAINT-GERMAIN. Cloth, cover in gold and ink. 47 illustrations . . . . 75c.

HERRMANN THE GREAT: The Famous Magician's Tricks. By H. J. BURLINGAME. Illus. Cloth, special cover design in colors . . . . . . 75c.

THE SPIRIT WORLD UNMASKED. By H. R. EVANS. Tricks and frauds of clairvoyants, mind readers, slate writers, etc., fearlessly exposed. Illustrated. 12mo, extra cloth . . . . 75c.

TWENTIETH CENTURY FORTUNE TELLER. By MADAME CARLOTTA DE BARSY. Cloth, extra half-tones, unique cover . . . . 75c.

THE GREAT DREAM BOOK. By MADAME CARLOTTA DE BARSY. With a New List of Lucky Numbers. Cloth, unique cover . . . . 75c.

THE HEART OF A BOY. By EDMONDO DE AMICIS. *Edition de luxe.* 8vo. 59 Illustrations. Cloth, cover in colors $1.25

FIRESIDE BATTLES. By ANNIE G. BROWN. *Edition de luxe.* 8vo. Illustrated by J. C. LEYENDECKER. Cloth, cover in colors $1.25

AIR CASTLE DON. By B. FREEMAN ASHLEY, 12mo. Cloth, illus. . . . 75c.

TAN PILE JIM. " " " " " " . . . 75c.

DICK AND JACK'S ADVENTURES. " " " " " " . . . 75c.

REX WAYLAND'S FORTUNE. By H. A. STANLEY. 12mo. Cloth, illus., 75c.

TWO CHUMS. By MINERVA THORPE. 12mo, Cloth, illustrated . . 75c.

COMPLETE DRAMATIC WORKS OF HONORE DE BALZAC. First and only English version. 2 vols., 12mo. Silk cloth, illustrated $2.50

FAMOUS ADVENTURES OF THE BROWNIES. 150 illustrations by PALMER COX. Cloth, inlaid cover panel . . . . 75c.

CONVENTIONAL LIES OF OUR CIVILIZATION. By MAX NORDAU. 12mo. Cloth $1.00

NEW CENTURY STANDARD LETTER-WRITER. A complete compendium of correspondence. Board, **50c.** Cloth . . . . 75c.

LAIRD & LEE'S DIARY AND TIME SAVER, 1903. Fifth year. The Standard. Besides diary proper has 12 pages of colored maps, U. S. and possessions, etc., Census tables, etc. Full leather. Full gilt . . . . 25c.

Annual Catalogue, 1902-1903, Now Ready.

LAIRD AND LEE, Publishers
263-265 Wabash Ave., Chicago, U.S.A.

Liberal Discount to the Trade.

NEW PUBLICATIONS.

The Open Court Publishing Co.

BABEL AND BIBLE.

A Lecture on the Significance of Assyriological Research for Religion Twice Delivered Before the German Emperor. By Dr. Friedrich Delitzsch, Professor of Assyriology in the University of Berlin. Profusely illustrated. Pp. 66. Price, boards, 50 cents net (2s. 6d. net).

This lecture is by one of the foremost Assyriologists and theologians of the world. It gives in brief compass the history of Babylon and its civilization and portrays the immense influence it exerted on all early antiquity, and especially on the religious conceptions of the Jews and hence on us their spiritual descendants. This lecture aroused much discussion in Germany.

NIRVANA.

A Story of Buddhist Psychology. By Paul Carus. Illustrated by Kwasong Suzuki. Printed on India tint paper. Boards, gilt top, 60 cents net.

"Karma" and "Amitâba," companion stories to "Nirvana," in preparation.

HYMNS OF THE FAITH.
(DHAMMAPADA)

Being an Ancient Anthology Preserved in the Short Collection of the Sacred Scriptures of the Buddhists. Translated from the Pâli by Albert J. Edmunds. Cloth binding, gilt top. Printed on India tint paper. Pages, xiv, 110. Price, $1.00.

FOUNDATIONS OF GEOMETRY.

A systematic discussion of the axioms upon which the Euclidean Geometry is based. By David Hilbert, Professor of Mathematics, University of Göttingen. Translated from the German by E. J. Townsend, University of Illinois. Pages, 140. Price, Cloth, $1.00 net (4s. 6d. net).

SEND FOR CATALOGUE AND TRADE PRICES.

THE OPEN COURT PUBLISHING CO., CHICAGO, 324 Dearborn Street.

London: Kegan Paul, Trench, Trübner & Co., Ltd.

Our Latest Books

Incaland.

A Story of Adventure in the Interior of Peru. By Claude H. Wetmore. 309 pp. 12mo. Illustrated. Cloth, $1.50.

The Cruise of the Enterprise.

Being a Story of the Struggle and Defeat of the French Privateering Expeditions against the United States in 1799. By James Otis. 359 pp. 12mo. Illustrated. Cloth, $1 50.

In the Camp of Cornwallis.

A Story of Reuben Denton and His Experiences during the New Jersey Campaign in 1777. By Everett T. Tomlinson. 353 pp. 12mo. Illustrated. Cloth, $1.50.

A Loyal Lass.

A Story of the Niagara Campaign of 1814. By Amy E. Blanchard. 319 pp. 12mo. Illustrated. Cloth, $1.50.

Sweetbrier and Thistledown.

A Story. By James Newton Baskett. Three-color frontispiece. 340 pp. 12mo. Cloth, $1.50.

Peloubet's Select Notes.

A Commentary on the Sunday School Lessons for 1903. By Rev. F. N. Peloubet. 362 pp. Cloth, $1.25.

What Gladys Saw.

A Nature Story of Farm and Forest. By Frances Margaret Fox. 318 pp. 12mo. Illustrated. Cloth, $1.25.

On the Frontier with St Clair.

A Story of the Early Settlement of the Ohio Country. By Charles S. Wood. 343 pp. 12mo. Illustrated. Cloth, $1.50.

The Balaster Boys.

A Story. By Blanche M. Channing. 294 pp. 16mo. Illustrated. Cloth, $1.25.

Mr. Pat's Little Girl.

A Story of the Arden Foresters. 322 pp. 12mo. Illustrated. Cloth, $1.50.

A Child's Story of the Life of Christ.

By Helen B. Hoyt. 233 pp. 137 half-tone Illustrations. Cloth, $1.25.

W. A. WILDE COMPANY, Boston and Chicago.

NEW BOOKS

By LOUIS ALBERT BANKS, D.D. The King's Stewards. Large 12mo, 315 pages, cloth, $1.25. A choice collection of sermons by one of America's most famous preachers. Bound in an unusually tasteful style.

By Rev. THEODORE L. CUYLER, D.D. Recollections of a Long Life. An autobiography. 12mo, cloth, 5 illustrations, about 370 pages, $1.50 *net.*

By HENRY M. KING, D.D. Why We Believe the Bible. 12mo, 222 pages, $1.00. The writer shows his personal acquaintance with the recent literature bearing on his subject. He has marshalled together in a very strong way the facts which lead the Christian to believe the Bible.

By ANDREW MURRAY. Key to the Missionary Problem. 204 pages, 75 cents.

By JAMES PATON, D.D. The Glory and Joy of the Resurrection. 12mo, cloth, 227 pages, $1.00. The author writes: "The height of my ambition is that, to devout readers of this book, and to thoughtful students of this great New Testament theme, there may come some portion of the glory and joy which manifestly thrilled the heart and fired the brain of the followers of Jesus in those early Apostolic days."

By JULIA MacNAIR WRIGHT. Studies in Hearts. 12mo, 192 pages, 10 illustrations, 75 cents. Here is a series of charming sketches, portraying varied types of life, and revealing on the part of the distinguished author a deep knowledge of the human heart and its workings.

By EVELYN EVERETT GREEN. Alwyn Ravendale. 12mo, 375 pages, illustrated, $1.25. This is a fascinating story, showing the growth and development of an attractive boy into a noble young man.

By DINSDALE T. YOUNG. Neglected People of the Bible. 12mo, 280 pages, cloth, $1.00.

By Mrs. HARRIET A. CHEEVER. Elmcove. 12mo, about 330 pages, illustrated, $1.25. A delightful story by a favorite author.

By Rev. OLIVER A. KINGSBURY. The Spiritual Life. Large 12mo, 117 pages, cloth, 50 cents. A book with which to refresh the inner springs of the spiritual life of every reader.

By Revs. A. R. BUCKLAND, M. A., and J. D. MULLINS, M. A. Missionary Speakers' Manual. 12mo, 368 pages, $1.25. A most useful compendium of help to, and information concerning missionary work.

By ELEANOR H. STOOKE. Little Maid Marigold. 12mo, 223 pages, illustrated, 75 cents. The story of a sweet young girl, who won the hearts of all with whom she became associated.

By CYRIL GREY. For Crown and Covenant. 12mo, 320 pages, illustrated, $1.00. A stirring story of the Covenanters of Scotland with their oppressors.

ISLAM AND CHRISTIANITY; or, The Quran and the Bible. 12mo, cloth, 225 pages, $1.00.

By CHARLES A. S. DWIGHT. Railroading with Christ. 12mo, 80 pages, 22 illustrations, cloth, 35 cents.

FAMILY CHRISTIAN ALMANAC, 1903. 10 cents.

NEW CHEAP EDITIONS

By J. THAIN DAVIDSON. Talks with Young Men, 286 pages. **The City Youth,** 291 pages. **Forewarned—Forearmed,** 286 pages **A Good Start,** 283 pages. **Sure to Succeed,** 289 pages. In new attractive cloth binding, price 60 cents each, *net;* or the set of 5 volumes in a box, $2.50 *net.*

By MARTHA BURR BANKS. Dame Dimple's Christmas Celebration. 85 pages, illustrated, 50 cents. A charming story suitable for the old as well as the young; setting forth the true Christmas spirit.

AMERICAN TRACT SOCIETY

New York. Boston. Chicago.

SPON & CHAMBERLAIN'S

NEW BOOKS

ABADY. Gas Analysts' Manual. 575 pp. Illus. 8vo, half-mor. . . . . $6.50‡

BARBER. Mechanical Movements. 4th ed. $4.00

BERKELEY and WALKER. Practical Receipts. 8vo, cloth. $3.00

DYE. Lighting by Acetylene. 12mo, cloth $2.50

HORNBY. Gas Engineers' Laboratory Handbook. 2d ed. 12mo, cloth. $2.50

JENNINGS. Paint and Color Mixing. With 72 sample colors. . . . . $2.00‡

LISK. A B C of the Steam Engine. With 6 large plates. $0 50

MILLIS. Metal Plate Work. 4th ed. $3.50

MOLESWORTH. Planometer Areas. In case. $0.50

WEBER. Problems in Electricity. 3d ed. 12mo, cloth. $3.00

IN THE PRESS

ALLEN. Tables for Earthwork Curves.

New Catalogue Now Ready.

123 Liberty Street, New York

SOUND SENSE IN CONCENTRATED LOZENGES

DON'TS FOR GIRLS

By MINNA THOMAS ANTRIM

A MANUAL OF MISTAKES

Like Gautier, the author "does not write for little girls whose bread is cut to squares," but without preachment, and in a

WITTILY PHILOSOPHICAL

way, tells young misses how to avoid the

Pleasant Paths That Entice to Nowhere

Seeming to know the individual needs of her readers, she does not treat them as so many manikins—to be jerked into positions, but as rational beings, to be led, not driven, toward

GRACIOUS WOMANHOOD

Mrs. Antrim's objectivity and plain speech cannot fail to make a lasting impression also upon

THE WOMAN HIDDEN IN THE CHILD

The book is full of wisdom, but not of the stereotyped kind, and has walked straight into popularity.

Cloth, Ornamental, 50c Ooze Calf, gilt top, $1.00

HENRY ALTEMUS COMPANY
PHILADELPHIA

BUSY BOOKSELLERS

Buying their FALL STOCK will find it a Saving of Time to call on Us

ALL BOOKS ON ONE FLOOR

It is CONVENIENT AND ECONOMICAL to Buy Books of Us at All Times

THE BAKER & TAYLOR CO.
33 E. 17TH ST. BOOKS FOR THE TRADE NEW YORK

BOOK-PLATES OF TO-DAY

A Volume of Essays and Pictures
Edited by WILBUR MACEY STONE

With 7 Color Plates and 1 from the Copper. Price, $1.50 net

Special Edition of 50 Copies, $2.50 net

READY FOR DELIVERY EARLY IN OCTOBER. SEND FOR DESCRIPTIVE ANNOUNCEMENT

TONNELÉ & CO., 30-32 East 21st Street, New York

A Useful book to the Bookseller, Newsdealer, and Proprietor of Circulating Library.

The Profession of Bookselling:

a handbook of practical hints for the apprentice and bookseller. By A. Growoll, managing editor of "The Publishers' Weekly." In 3 Parts. Parts 1 and 2 now ready. Large octavo, interleaved, illustrated, bds., each, *net*, $2.00.

Part 2 contains chapters on "Insurance;" "Moving and Taking Stock;" "How to Keep a Stock of Music;" "Care and Management of Paper-Bound Stock;" "Newspapers, Magazines, and Books issued in parts;" "The Circulating Library," including list of fiction, directions for loaning, etc.; "Bookbinding," including tables of prices, etc., and 15 full-page reproductions of representative bookbindings and a bibliography.

THE PUBLISHERS' WEEKLY,
298 Broadway, New York.

"The Young Bookseller can learn more by a thorough perusal of this book than he could through many years of active experience."—C. N. CASPAR.

WILLIAM R. JENKINS,

851 AND 853 SIXTH AVENUE,
N. W. COR. 48TH STREET, NEW YORK.

FRENCH	**VETERINARY**
and other foreign	(Scientific and Popular
BOOKS,	**BOOKS,**
School and College Texts,	or Works Treating on
Miscellaneous Literature,	Horses, Cattle, Dogs,
French Plays.	etc. . . . .

Trade List and General Catalogues Supplied.

Accuracy. Promptness. Reliability

KAY PRINTING HOUSE,

66-68 CENTRE STREET,
TELEPHONE 1568 FRANKLIN. NEW YORK.

Estimates Promptly Furnished.

Printers to THE PUBLISHERS' WEEKLY.

A Key to Books in Print

The users of THE PUBLISHERS' TRADE LIST ANNUAL for 1902 will be interested to learn that the

Index Volume

is now in course of delivery to advance subscribers who will probably receive their copies before this advertisement appears in print. On the opposite page we present a sample page of the Index volume as an illustration of its scope. The books of the 246 publishers who this year have contributed the lists bound up in alphabetical order in the Catalogues volume, are indexed, it will be noticed, by author, title and subject catchword, furnishing, by means of 140,000 entries, ready reference to the books of the leading publishers in print on July 1, 1902, and to forthcoming books of which they could furnish information in August. The Index volume and the Catalogues volume of

The Publishers' Trade List Annual, 1902

will be found the most useful, as well as the least expensive, single book trade reference work yet issued, especially for the booksellers and small libraries who cannot afford to buy many trade tools. In order to give every possible opportunity to those who desire the work at the original subscription rate, on cash orders received before October 1, the price therefor will be $5 for the two volumes together; after that date the price will be $2 for the Catalogues volume and $5 for the Index volume, or $7 together, absolutely net.

The Catalogues volume is a huge octavo, probably the largest volume now issued, reaching, with 1902, 5700 pages, being 8¼ inches in thickness and weighing 20 pounds. Directions for enclosure delivery in New York should accompany the order, unless shipment is to be by express at the charge of the subscriber.

The Index volume, an octavo of 1114 pages, will be sent on approval to any bookseller or library enclosing 10 cents for partial postage. Of the Catalogues volume only 300 remain unsubscribed, and the edition of the Index volume is also limited. Address,

The Office of THE PUBLISHERS' WEEKLY
298 Broadway, New York

SCRUPLES 879 SEA

Scruples. Cobb, T: $1.50 .... *Lane*

SCRUTTA.

—(P. E.) Elec. in town and country houses. $1. *Macmillan*

SCRYMGEOUR.

—(W:) Lessons on life of Christ. (Bible class handbook.) net, 75 c. .... *Scribner*

SCUDAMORE.

—(W. E.) Steps to the altar. (Devotional ser.) $1. *Longmans*

—*Same.* 50 c.-$1.50 .... *Young*

SCUDDER.

—(*Mrs.* A. M.) *and* Clark (F. E.) Attractive truths. $1.25 .... *Revell*

—(C: D.) Personal purity. 25 c.; 50 c. *Y. M. C. A.*

—(C: L.) Treatment of fractures. $4.50; $5.50. *Saunders*

—(E.) Hymns and sonnets. $1 .... *Houghton*

—(H. E.) Bodley books. 8 v. ea., $1.50; set, $12. *Houghton*

Boston town. $1.50 .... *Houghton*

Childhood in lit. and art. $1.25 .... *Houghton*

Children's book. $2.50 .... *Houghton*

Columbus. (Riverside biog.) net, 50 c. *Houghton*

Dream children. $1 .... *Houghton*

Dwellers in five-sisters court. $1.25 .. *Houghton*

Fables. 50 c. .... *Houghton*

Folk stories. 40 c.; 60 c. .... *Houghton*

G: Washington. 40 c.; 60 c. .... *Houghton*

Histories. 3 v. ea., 60 c.-$1 .... *Butler, S.*

Ja. R. Lowell. net, $3.50 .... *Houghton*

Legends. (Riverside lib.) net, 15 c.-50 c. *Houghton*

Literature in school. (Riverside lit.) net, 15 c. *Houghton*

Men and letters. $1.25 .... *Houghton*

Men and manners a hundred years ago. $1.25. *Scribner*

N. Webster. (Am. men of letters.) $1.25-$2.50. *Houghton*

Recollect. of S: Breck. $2 .... *Coates*

Seven little people. $1 .... *Houghton*

Stories and romances. $1.25 .... *Houghton*

Stories from my attic. $1 .... *Houghton*

—*ed.* Am. commonwealths ser. ea., $1.25. *Houghton*

Am. poems. net, $1 .... *Houghton*

Am. prose. net, $1 .... *Houghton*

—*See also* Scudder, E.—Shakespeare.—Taylor, B., *and* Taylor, M. H. .... *Houghton*

—(*Mrs.* J.) Captain Waltham. 75 c. .... *Presb. Pub.*

—(J. W.) First Latin reader. 90 c. .. *Allyn & B.*

Gradatim, Stories for beginners. 50 c. *Allyn & B.*

Sallust's Catiline, with parallel passages from Cicero. $1 .... *Allyn & B.*

—(J:) Provision for passing over Jordan. 15 c.; 20 c. .... *Am. Tr.*

—(J: K.), *ed.* Eclectic medical journal. per yr., net, $2 .... *Scudder*

—(J: M.) Am. eclectic mat. medica, etc. net, $4; $4.50 .... *Scudder*

Diseases of women. net, $2.75; $3.50 .. *Scudder*

Eclectic medicine for families. net, $3; $5. *Scudder*

Eclectic pract. in dis. of children. net, $2.50; $3 .... *Scudder*

Eclectic practice of medicine. net, $4.50; $5. *Scudder*

Prin. of medicine. net, $1.50; $2 ...... *Scudder*

Specific diagnosis. net, $1.50 .... *Scudder*

Specific medication and medicines. net, $2. *Scudder*

—*and* (W: B.) Medicated inhalations. net, 75 c. *Scudder*

—(M. T.) N. Y.: its state and local govt. 40 c. *Maynard, M.*

—(S. H.) Butterflies. net, $1.50 .... *Holt*

Butterflies of east. U. S. and Canada 3 v. net, $75 .... *Houghton*

Every-day butterflies. $2 .... *Houghton*

Fossil insects of N. Am. $20 .... *Macmillan*

Frail children of the air. 75 c.; $1.50. *Houghton*

Guide to the common butterflies. $1.50 .... *Holt*

Life of a butterfly. $1 .... *Holt*

—(V. D.) Eng. lit. net, $1.20 .... *Globe*

Introd. to Ruskin. (Stud. ser. Eng. class.) (Lib. ed.) 50 c. .... *Sibley & D.*

Life of the Spirit in mod. Eng. poets. $1.75. *Houghton*

Social ideals in Eng. letters. $1.75 .. *Houghton*

Witness of denial. 50 c.; $1 .... *Dutton*

—*See also* Shelley, P. B. .... *Heath*

—(W: B.) *See* Scudder, J: M. .... *Scudder*

—(*Mrs.* W: W.) Nineteen centuries of missions. (Clark.) $1 .... *Revell*

—*Same.* (Cong. mis.) .... *Un. Soc. C. E.*

SCULLY.

—(W: C:) Kafir stories. (Buckram ser.) 75 c. *Holt*

White hecatomb. (Buckram ser.) 75 c. .. *Holt*

Sculptor caught napping. $1 .... *Dutton*

Sculptors and artists, Painters. *See* Vasari .. *Macmillan*

Sculptors and sculpture, Famous. Shedd, J. A. $2. *Houghton*

Sculptors (French) of 18th century. *See* Dilke, *Lady.* *Macmillan*

SCULPTURE.

—Clement, C. E. $2 .... *Stokes*

—Flaxman, J. net, $1.75 .... *Macmillan*

—and painting. Doremus, S. D. $1 .... *Appleton*

—as represent. art. Raymond, G. L. $2.50. *Putnam*

—Egyptian, Assyrian, Greek and Roman. Redford, G: $2 .... *Scribner*

—Greek. (Riverside art.) net, 75 c. .. *Houghton*

— —Murray, A. S. net, $14.40 .... *Scribner*

— —Wherry, A. $2.50 .... *Scribner*

— —Introd. to. Upcott, L. E. net, $1.10. *Oxford*

— —Masterpieces of. *See* Furtwangler, H. *Scribner*

—Hist. of. Marquand, A. $1.50 ...... *Longmans*

—Hist. of anc. Mitchell, L. M. $7.50; $15. *Dodd*

—in Belgium. Destree, O. G. net, 75 c. *Macmillan*

—(Italian), Histor. handbk. Perkins, C: C. $4. *Scribner*

—Italian, of the Renaissance. Freeman, L. J. net, $3 .... *Macmillan*

—Primer of. Mullins, E. R. 75 c. ...... *Cassell*

—Renaissance and mod. Scott, L. $2 .. *Scribner*

—Roman. *See* Young, W:, *ed* .... *Spon*

—Schools, etc., of. Radcliffe, A. G. $3; $5. *Appleton*

—Technique of. Partridge, W. O. $1 ..... *Ginn*

—Tuscan. Hurll, E. M. net, 35 c.-75 c. *Houghton*

—Wonders of. *See* Viardot, L: .... *Scribner*

—work, Decor. Zeyer .... *Hessling*

— —Germ. Schulz .... *Hessling*

— —Stone and wood. Niedling ...... *Hessling*

Sculptured tombs of Hellas. Gardner, P. net, $8. *Macmillan*

Sculptures of Copàn and Quiriguà, Stone. Meye, H: $20 .... *Dodd*

Sculp., Specimens of. *See* Modern art ..... *Appleton*

SCUPOLI.

—(L.) Spiritual combat. (Lib. spiritual works.) $1; $1.75 .... *Longmans*

—*Same.* 40 c. .... *Murphy*

Spiritual conflict. (Aids to inner life.) 25 c.; 50 c. .... *Longmans*

Scutage and knight service. Baldwin, Ja. F. net, $1. *Univ. Chic.*

Scylla or Charybdis. Broughton, Rhoda. 50 c.; $1. *Appleton*

SEA.

—air; sea bathing. Packard, J: H. 40 c. *Blakiston*

—and its wonders. Kirby, M. *and* E. $1.75. *Nelson*

—and land. Shaler, N. S. $2.50 ...... *Scribner*

—and living wonders. Hartwig, G. $3. *Longmans*

—Avoidance of collision at. Hoff, W: B. 75 c. *Van N.*

—beach at ebb tide. Arnold, A. F. net, $2.40. *Century*

—Bottom of the. Sourel, N. .... *Scribner*

—coast. Wheeler, W. H. $4.50 .... *Longmans*

—coast: destruction, littoral, drift, protection. *Longmans*

—Depths of the. Thompson, *Sir* W. $7.50. *Macmillan*

—fights, Am. (Drawings.) *See* Gibbs, G: . *Russell*

— —and adventures. Laughton, J: K. $2. *Longmans*

—fisherman. Wilcocks, J. C. $2 ...... *Longmans*

—fishing. Bickerdyke, J: .... *Longmans*

— —Hudson, F. 40 c. .... *Scribner*

—going engineers, Hints to. Reed. $1.40. *Van N.*

—kings and naval heroes. Edgar, J: G: $1. *Harper*

— —James, H. 50 c. .... *Altemus*

— —and sea fights, Britain's. $2.50 ...... *Cassell*

—mosses. Hervey, A. B. net, $2 .... *Knight*

— —*See also* Algæ.—Sea weed.

—power, Influence of. *See* Mahan, A. T. *Little, B.*

—Products of the. Simmonds, P. L. $1.75. *Appleton*

—Resources of. McIntosh, W: C. $4.25. *Macmillan*

—sickness. Beard, G. M. $1 .... *Treat*

— —Dutton, T: net, 75 c. .... *Pelton*

— —Barker, F. 75 c. .... *Appleton*

—Story of the. Quiller-Couch. 2 v. ea., $1.75. *Cassell*

Sample page of the Index Volume of "The Publishers' Trade List Annual."

Beg To Announce To The Book Trade

That their new Fall and Holiday Catalogue is ready and a postal card request will bring it to you, showing all the special inducements in the way of prices and values. Our Catalogue contains three lines of Poets, each embracing 52 titles and bound as follows: "Padded Leather," "Gilt Top Cloth," Plain Cloth. — Our popular "Aetna Series" of 12-mos of 250 titles. — Our "Aurora Series of Illustrated Masterpieces." Our "New Alpine" Gilt Top 12mos. — Our "Fireside Henty Series," olivene edged embracing 87 titles. — Our new "Snug Corner" Series for Girls embracing 50 titles. — Our complete and the only edition of "Harkaway Series" of 15 titles. — Celebrated "Vassar Series" for Girls, containing 50 titles, and numerous other 12mo cloth bound books uniquely and attractively stamped. Handy Volume Classic 16mos as follows: "Cloth Bound," "Dresden Edition," "Embossed Leather," "Watered Silk" and "Devotional."—Popular and Gilt Top Standard Books in Sets. — A large variety of Holiday Gift Books in 12mo and Quarto size. — Birthday Books. — Biographies. — New and Popular Romances. — Humorous Books. — Liberal Thought Books. — Dictionaries, in a great variety of sizes. — Cook Books. — Games. — Hand Books. — Guides, etc. — Speakers, both in cloth and paper. — Works on Poultry, Horses, Cattle and Sheep. — Family Bibles. — An entirely new line of quarto Juvenile board books in illuminated and lithographed covers, containing over 100 varieties. — Our Modern Authors' Library bound in paper with a special cover on each book, containing over 350 titles of the World's best Fiction.

Our stocks are now complete and orders can be given prompt attention and the Trade will find it much more satisfactory to order early and get a complete shipment and arrange their displays in time.

Thanking the Trade for past courtesies and soliciting a continuance of your esteemed patronage, we remain

Yours very truly,
M. A. DONOHUE & CO.

Book Publishers and Manufacturers

407-429 Dearborn Street, Chicago, Illinois

THE CLIMAX

Or WHAT MIGHT HAVE BEEN

BY CHARLES FELTON PIDGIN

Author of "QUINCY ADAMS SAWYER" and "BLENNERHASSETT"

NEW YORK JOURNAL, Sept. 13, said: "No more interesting book has been written for a long time than 'The Climax.' It founds a new school in historical novel writing, and whether one agrees with the author in his hero worship and theories or not, it is well worth reading."

Price $1.50

"DEFEND YOURSELF"

A Capering Romance of What Never Happened to Aaron Burr, Alexander Hamilton, Thomas Jefferson, and Others in Utopian America about 1820

ARE YOU SELLING IT? **MISS PETTICOATS** A LEADING FALL BOOK

By DWIGHT TILTON

In Preparation **ON SATAN'S MOUNT** Also by Dwight Tilton

C. M. CLARK PUBLISHING COMPANY, - 211 Tremont Street, BOSTON

Lightning Source UK Ltd.
Milton Keynes UK
UKHW012122180219
337529UK00012B/1477/P